HARRAP'S
Paperback

DICTIONARY · DICIONÁRIO
Português–Inglês · English–Portuguese

D1341204

HARRAP

HARRAP'S
Paperback

DICTIONARY · DICIONÁRIO

Português–Inglês · English–Portuguese

HARRAP

This edition published in Great Britain 2007
by Chambers Harrap Publishers Ltd
7 Hopetoun Crescent, Edinburgh EH7 4AY

© Larousse 2007

ISBN: 978 0245 60789 9

www.harrap.co.uk

Colaboradores/Contributors

LAURA BOCCO ELIANE B. FREIRE USHIJIMA
JOSÉ A. GÁLVEZ DANIEL GRASSI
JANICE MCNEILLIE SORAIA LUANA REIS
CAMILA WERNER

Colaboradores da edição anterior/Contributors to the previous edition

ALISON AIKEN MARIA INÊS ALVES
LUZIA ARAÚJO SHIRLEY BROTHERTON-PINNIGER
LAURA BOCCO KAROLL FERREIRA
SALETE CECHIN DANIEL GRASSI
JOSÉ A. GÁLVEZ VALERIE GRUNDY
MIKE HARLAND BILL MARTIN
JANICE MCNEILLIE VIVIANE POSSAMAI
CHRISTINE ROBINSON JULIA RICE
SERGIO TELLAROLI

Printed and bound in France by Maury

ABREVIATURAS		ABBREVIATIONS
pejorativo	*pej*	pejorative
plural	*pl*	plural
política	POL	politics
particípio passado	*pp*	past participle
preposição	*prep*	preposition
pronome	*pron*	pronoun
passado	*pt*	past tense
marca registrada	®	registered trademark
religião	*RELIG*	religion
substantivo	*s*	noun
alguém	*sb*	somebody
educação, escola	SCH	school, education
separável	*sep*	separable
singular	*sg*	singular
algo	*sthg*	something
sujeito	*suj/subj*	subject
superlativo	*sup(erl)*	superlative
termos técnicos	*TEC(H)*	technology
inglês britânico	UK	British English
inglês americano	US	American English
televisão	TV	television
verbo	*v/vb*	verb
verbo intransitivo	*vi*	intransitive verb
verbo impessoal	*v impess/v impers*	impersonal verb
verbo pronominal	*vp*	pronominal verb
verbo transitivo	*vt*	transitive verb
vulgar	*vulg*	vulgar
equivalente cultural	≃	cultural equivalent

OS COMPOSTOS EM INGLÊS

Em inglês, os compostos são expressões formadas por mais de uma palavra, mas contendo um único significado: **point of view**, **kiss of life** ou **virtual reality**, por exemplo. Uma das características deste dicionário é o fato de os compostos terem uma entrada própria e seguirem rigorosamente a ordem alfabética. Assim, **blood poisoning** figura depois de **blood group**, que, por sua vez, sucede a **blood**.

MARCAS REGISTRADAS

O símbolo ® indica que a palavra em questão é uma marca registrada. Este símbolo, ou a sua eventual ausência, não afeta, no entanto, a situação legal da marca.

ENGLISH COMPOUNDS

A compound is a word or expression which has a single meaning but is made up of more than one word, e.g. **point of view**, **kiss of life** and **virtual reality**. It is a feature of this dictionary that English compounds appear in the AZ list in strict alphabetical order. The compound **blood poisoning** will therefore come after **blood group** which itself follows **blood**.

TRADEMARKS

Words considered to be trademarks have been designated in this dictionary by the symbol ®. However, neither the presence nor the absence of such designation should be regarded as affecting the legal status of any trademark.

TRANSCRIÇÃO FONÉTICA

Vogais portuguesas

[a]	pá, amar
[ɛ]	sé, seta, hera
[e]	ler, mês
[i]	ir, sino, nave
[ɔ]	nota, pó
[o]	corvo, avô
[u]	azul, tribo

Ditongos portugueses

[aj]	faixa, mais
[ej]	leite, rei
[ɛj]	hotéis, pastéis
[ɔj]	herói, bóia
[oj]	coisa, noite
[uj]	azuis, fui
[aw]	nau, jaula
[ɛw]	céu, véu
[ew]	deus, seu
[iw]	riu, viu

Vogais nasais

[ã]	maçã, santo
[ẽ]	lençol, sempre
[ĩ]	fim, patim
[õ]	onde, com, honra
[ũ]	jejum, nunca

Ditongos nasais

[ãj]	cãibra, mãe
[ãw]	camarão, cão
[ẽj]	bem, quem
[õj]	cordões, leões

Semivogais

eleito, maio	[j]
luar, quadro	[w]

PHONETIC TRANSCRIPTION

English vowels

[ɪ]	pit, big, rid
[e]	pet, tend
[æ]	pat, bag, mad
[ʌ]	run, cut
[ɒ]	pot, log
[ʊ]	put, full
[ə]	mother, suppose
[iː]	bean, weed
[aː]	barn, car
[ɔː]	born, lawn
[uː]	loop, loose
[ɜː]	burn, learn, bird

English diphthongs

[eɪ]	bay, late, great
[aɪ]	buy, light, aisle
[ɔɪ]	boy, foil
[əʊ]	no, road, blow
[aʊ]	now, shout, town
[ɪə]	peer, fierce, idea
[eə]	pair, bear, share
[ʊə]	sure, tour

Semi-vowels

you, yellow

wet, why, twin

Consoantes		Consonants
beijo, abrir	[b]	bottle, bib
casa, dique	[k]	come, kitchen
dama, prenda	[d]	dog, did
dia, bonde	[dʒ]	jet, fridge
faca, afinal	[f]	fib, physical
grande, agora	[g]	gag, great
gelo, cisne, anjo	[ʒ]	usual, measure
	[h]	how, perhaps
lata, feliz, cola	[l]	little, help
folha, ilha	[ʎ]	
mel, amigo	[m]	metal, comb
novo, mina	[n]	night, dinner
linha, sonho	[ɲ]	
anca, inglês	[ŋ]	sung, parking
pão, gripe	[p]	pop, people
cura, era	[r]	right, carry
rádio, terra	[x]	
cima, desse, caça	[s]	seal, peace
noz, bis, caixa, chá	[ʃ]	sheep, machine
tema, lata, porta	[t]	train, tip
tio, infantil	[tʃ]	chain, wretched
	[θ]	think, fifth
	[ð]	this, with
vela, ave	[v]	vine, love
zelo, brisa	[z]	zip, his

[ʳ] só se pronuncia quando é seguido de uma palavra que começa por vogal.

O símbolo fonético [(x)] em português indica que o 'r' no final da palavra é apenas levemente pronunciado, exceto quando seguido de palavra iniciada por vogal: nesse caso, pronuncia-se [r].

O símbolo ['] indica que a sílaba subseqüente é a tônica, sobre a qual recai o acento principal; [ˌ] indica que a sílaba subseqüente é a subtônica, sobre a qual recai o acento secundário.

As regras de pronúncia aplicadas ao português refletem a língua falada no Rio de Janeiro.

[ʳ] is pronounced only when followed by a word beginning with a vowel.

The symbol [(x)] in Portuguese phonetics indicates that the final 'r' is often barely sounded unless it is followed by a word beginning with a vowel, in which case it is pronounced [r].

The symbol ['] indicates that the following syllable carries primary stress and [ˌ] that the following syllable carries secondary stress.

Portuguese phonetics reflect the language as spoken in Rio de Janeiro.

VERBOS PORTUGUESES/PORTUGUESE VERBS

Chave: A = presente do indicativo, **B** = pretérito imperfeito do indicativo, **C** = pretérito perfeito do indicativo, **D** = pretérito mais-que-perfeito do indicativo, **E** = futuro do indicativo, **F** = futuro do pretérito, **G** = presente do subjuntivo, **H** = futuro do subjuntivo, **I** = pretérito imperfeito do subjuntivo, **J** = imperativo, **K** = gerúndio, **L** = infinitivo pessoal, **M** = particípio passado.

ANDAR: A ando, andas, anda, andamos, andais, andam, **B** andava, andavas, andava, andávamos, andáveis, andavam, **C** andei, andaste, andou, andamos, andastes, andaram, **D** andara, andaras, andara, andáramos, andáreis, andaram, **E** andarei, andarás, andará, andaremos, andareis, andarão, **F** andaria, andarias, andaria, andaríamos, andaríeis, andariam, **G** ande, andes, ande, andemos, andeis, andem, **H** andar, andares, andar, andarmos, andardes, andarem, **I** andasse, andasses, andasse, andássemos, andásseis, andassem, **J** anda, ande, andemos, andai, andem, **K** andando, **L** andar, andares, andar, andarmos, andardes, andarem, **M** andado.

chover: **A** chove, **B** chovia, **C** choveu, **G** chova, **H** chover, **I** chovesse, **M** chovido.

COMER: A como, comes, come, comemos, comeis, comem, **B** comia, comías, comia, comíamos, comíeis, comiam, **C** comi, comeste, comeu, comemos, comestes, comeram, **D** comera, comeras, comera, comêramos, comêreis, comeram, **E** comerei, comerás, comerá, comeremos, comereis, comerão, **F** comeria, comerias, comeria, comeríamos, comeríeis, comeriam, **G** coma, comas, coma, comamos, comais, comam, **H** comer, comeres, comer, comermos, comerdes, comerem, **I** comesse, comesses, comesse, comêssemos, comêsseis, comessem, **J** come, coma, comamos, comei, comam, **K** comendo, **L** comer, comeres, comer, comermos, comerdes, comerem, **M** comido.

conduzir: **A** conduzo, conduzes, conduz, etc., **B** conduzia, etc., **C** conduzi, conduziste, etc., **G** conduza, etc., **I** conduzisse, etc., **J** conduz, conduza, etc., **M** conduzido.

conhecer: **A** conheço, conheces, etc., **B** conhecia, etc., **C** conheci, conheceste, etc., **D** conhecera, etc., **I** conhecesse, conhecesses, etc., **J** conhece, conheça, etc., **M** conhecido.

conseguir: **A** consigo, consegues, consegue, etc., **C** consegui, conseguiste, etc., **D** conseguira, conseguiras, etc., **E** conseguirei, conseguirás, etc., **J** consegue, consiga, consigamos, consegui, consigam.

dar: **A** dou, dás, dá, damos, dais, dão, **B** dava, etc., **C** dei, deste, deu, demos, destes, deram, **D** dera, deras, etc., **E** darei, darás, etc., **F** daria, etc., **G** dê, dês, dê, demos, deis, dêem, **H** der, deres, etc., **I** desse, desses, etc., **J** dá, dê, demos, dai, dêem, **K** dando, **L** dar, dares, dar, darmos, dardes, darem, **M** dado.

dizer: **A** digo, dizes, diz, dizemos, dizeis, dizem, **B** dizia, dizias, etc., **C** disse, disseste, disse, dissemos, dissestes, disseram, **D** dissera, disseras, etc., **E** direi, dirás, dirá, etc., **F** diria, dirias, etc., **G** diga, digas, etc., **H** disser, disseres, disser, dissermos, disserdes, disserem, **I** dissesse, dissesses, etc., **J** diz, diga, etc., **K** dizendo, **L** dizer, dizeres, dizer, dizermos, dizerdes, dizerem, **M** dito.

dormir: A durmo, dormes, dorme, dormimos, dormis, dormem, B dormia, dormias, etc., C dormi, dormiste, etc., H dormir, dormires, etc., J dorme, durma, durmamos, dormi, durmam, M dormido.

escrever: A escrevo, escreves, etc., B escrevia, escrevias, etc., C escrevi, escreveste, escreveu, etc., D escrevera, escreveras, etc., I escrevesse, escrevesses, etc., J escreve, escreva, etc., M escrito.

ESTAR: A estou, estás, está, estamos, estais, estão, B estava, estavas, estava, estávamos, estáveis, estavam, C estive, estiveste, esteve, estivemos, estivestes, estiveram, D estivera, estiveras, estivera, estivéramos, estivéreis, estiveram, E estarei, estarás, estará, estaremos, estareis, estarão, F estaria, estarias, estaria, estaríamos, estaríeis, estariam, G esteja, estejas, esteja, estejamos, estejais, estejam, H estiver, estiveres, estiver, estivermos, estiverdes, estiverem, I estivesse, estivesses, estivesse, estivéssemos, estivésseis, estivessem, J está, esteja, estejamos, estai, estejam, K estando, L estar, estares, estar, estarmos, estardes, estarem, M estado.

fazer: A faço, fazes, faz, etc., B fazia, fazias, etc., C fiz, fizeste, fez, fizemos, fizestes, fizeram, D fizera, fizeras, etc., E farei, farás, etc., F faria, farias, etc., G faça, faças, etc., H fizer, fizeres, etc., I fizesse, fizesses, etc., J faz, faça, façamos, fazei, façam, M feito.

ir: A vou, vais, vai, vamos, ides, vão, B ia, ias, íamos, etc., C fui, foste, foi, fomos, fostes, foram, D fora, foras, fora, fôramos, fôreis, foram, E irei, irás, irá, iremos, ireis, irão, F iria, irias, iríamos, etc., G vá, vás, vá, vamos, vades, vão, H for, fores, for, formos, fordes, forem, I fosse, fosses, fosse, fôssemos, fôsseis, fossem, J vai, vá, vamos, ide, vão, K indo, L ir, ires, ir, irmos, irdes, irem, M ido.

ler: A leio, lês, lê, lemos, ledes, lêem, B lia, lias, etc., C li, leste, leu, etc., G leia, leias, etc., M lido.

nascer: A nasço, nasces, etc., B nascia, etc., C nasci, nasceste, nasceu, etc., D nascera, etc., G nasça, nasças, etc., H nascer, nasceres, etc., I nascesse, etc., M nascido.

negociar: A negoc(e)io, negoc(e)ias, negoc(e)ia, negociamos, negociais, negoc(e)iam, B negociava, etc., C negociei, negociaste, etc., G negoc(e)ie, negoc(e)ies, negoc(e)ie, negociemos, negocieis, negoc(e)iem, J negoc(e)ia, negoc(e)ie, negociemos, negociai, negoc(e)iem, M negociado.

oferecer: A ofereço, ofereces, etc., B oferecia, etc., C ofereci, ofereceste, ofereceu, etc., D oferecera, etc., G ofereça, ofereças, etc., I oferecesse, etc., J oferece, ofereça, ofereçamos, oferecei, ofereçam, M oferecido.

ouvir: A ouço, ouves, ouve, etc., B ouvia, etc., C ouvi, ouviste, ouviu, etc., D ouvira, etc., G ouça, ouças, etc., H ouvir, ouvires, etc., I ouvisse, ouvisses, etc., J ouve, ouça, ouçamos, ouvi, ouçam, M ouvido.

parecer: A pareço, pareces, parece, etc., B parecia, etc., C pareci, pareceste, etc., D parecera, etc., G pareça, pareças, etc., H parecer, pareceres, etc., I parecesse, parecesses, etc., M parecido.

PARTIR: A parto, partes, parte, partimos, partis, partem, B partia, partias, partia, partíamos, partíeis, partiam, C parti, partiste, partiu, partimos, partistes, partiram, D partira, partiras, partira, partíramos, partíreis, partiram, G parta, partas, parta, partamos, partais, partam, H partir, partires, partir, partirmos, partirdes, partirem, I partisse, partisses, partisse, partíssemos, partísseis, partíssem, **J** parte, parta, partamos, parti, partam, **K** partindo, **L** partir, partires, partir, partirmos, partirdes, partirem, **M** partido.

passear: **A** passeio, passeias, passeia, passeamos, passeais, passeiam, **B** passeava, passeavas, etc., **C** passeei, passeaste, etc., **E** passearei, passearás, etc., **G** passeie, passeies, etc., **J** passeia, passeie, passeemos, passeai, passeiem, **M** passeado.

pedir: **A** peço, pedes, pede, etc., **C** pedi, pediste, pediu, etc., **G** peça, peças, etc., **J** pede, peça, peçamos, pedi, peçam, **M** pedido.

perder: **A** perco, perdes, perde, perdemos, perdeis, perdem, **C** perdi, perdeste, perdeu, etc., **F** perderia, perderias, etc., **G** perca, percas, perca, etc., **H** perder, perderes, etc., **I** perdesse, perdesses, etc., **J** perde, perca, percamos, perdei, percam, **M** perdido.

poder: **A** posso, podes, pode, podemos, podeis, podem, **B** podia, podias, etc., **C** pude, pudeste, pôde, pudemos, pudestes, puderam, **G** possa, possamos, etc., **H** puder, puderes, puder, etc., **I** pudesse, pudéssemos, etc.

pôr: **A** ponho, pões, põe, pomos, pondes, põem, **B** punha, púnhamos, etc., **C** pus, puseste, pôs, pusemos, pusestes, puseram, **D** pusera, puséramos, etc., **E** porei, porás, etc., **F** poria, porias, etc., **G** ponha, ponhas, etc., **H** puser, pusermos, etc., **I** pusesse, puséssemos, etc., **J** põe, ponha, ponhamos, ponde, ponham, **K** pondo, **L** pôr, pores, pôr, pormos, pordes, porem, **M** posto.

querer: **A** quero, queres, quer, queremos, quereis, querem, **C** quis, quiseste, quis, quisemos, quisestes, quiseram, **D** quisera, quiséramos, etc., **G** queira, queiramos, etc., **H** quiser, quisermos, etc., **I** quisesse, quiséssemos, etc., **J** quer, queira, queiramos, querei, queiram, **K** querendo, **L** querer, quereres, querer, querermos, quererdes, quererem, **M** querido.

rir: **A** rio, ris, ri, rimos, rides, riem, **B** ria, ríamos, etc., **C** ri, riste, riu, rimos, ristes, riram, **D** rira, ríramos, etc., **G** ria, rias, etc., **H** rir, rires, etc., **I** risse, ríssemos, etc., **J** ri, ria, riamos, ride, riam, **K** rindo, **M** rido.

saber: **A** sei, sabes, sabe, sabemos, sabeis, sabem, **B** sabia, sabíamos, etc., **C** soube, soubeste, soube, soubemos, soubestes, souberam, **D** soubera, soubéramos, etc., **G** saiba, saibas, saiba, saibamos, saibais, saibam, **H** souber, souberes, etc., **I** soubesse, soubesses, etc., **J** sabe, saiba, saibamos, sabei, saibam, **M** sabido.

sair: **A** saio, sais, sai, saímos, saís, saem, **B** saía, saías, etc., **C** saí, saíste, saiu, etc., **D** saíra, saíras, etc., **G** saia, saias, saia, saiamos, saiais, saiam, **H** sair, saíres, sair, etc., **I** saísse, saísses, etc., **J** sai, saia, saiamos, saí, saiam, **M** saído.

sentar-se: **A** sento-me, sentas-te, senta-se, sentamo-nos, sentais-vos, sentam-se, **B** sentava-me, sentavas-te, sentava-se, sentávamo-nos, sentáveis-vos, sentavam-se, **C** sentei-me, sentaste-te, sentou-se, sentamo-nos, sentastes-vos, sentaram-se, **D** sentara-me, sentaras-te, sentara-se, sentáramo-nos, sentáreis-vos, sentaram-se, **E** sentar-me-ei, sentar-te-ás, sentar-se-á, sentar-nos-emos, sentar-vos-eis, sentar-se-ão, **F** sentar-me-ia, sentar-te-ias, sentar-se-ia, sentar-nos-íamos, sentar-vos-íeis, sentar-se-iam, **G** me sente, te sentes, se sente, nos sentemos, vos senteis, se sentem, **H** me sentar, te sentares, se sentar, nos sentarmos, vos sentardes, se sentarem, **I** me sentasse, te sentasses, se sentasse, nos sentássemos, vos sentásseis, se sentassem, J senta-te, sente-se, sentemo-nos, sentai-vos, sentem-se, K sentando-se, L sentar-me, sentares-te, sentar-se, sentarmo-nos, sentardes-vos, sentarem-se, M sentado.

sentir: A sinto, sentes, sente, sentimos, sentis, sentem, B sentia, sentias, etc., C senti, sentiste, sentiu, etc., D sentira, etc., G sinta, sintas, etc., H sentir, sentires, etc., I sentisse, sentisses, etc., J sente, sinta, sintamos, senti, sintam, M sentido.

SER: A sou, és, é, somos, sois, são, B era, eras, era, éramos, éreis, eram, C fui, foste, foi, fomos, fostes, foram, D fora, foras, fora, fôramos, fôreis, foram, F seria, serias, seria, seríamos, seríeis, seriam, G seja, sejas, seja, sejamos, sejais, sejam, H for, fores, for, formos, fordes, forem, I fosse, fosses, fosse, fôssemos, fôsseis, fossem, J sê, seja, sejamos, sede, sejam, K sendo, L ser, seres, ser, sermos, serdes, serem, M sido.

TER: A tenho, tens, tem, temos, tendes, têm, B tinha, tinhas, tinha, tínhamos, tínheis, tinham, C tive, tiveste, teve, tivemos, tivestes, tiveram, D tivera, tiveras, tivera, tivéramos, tivéreis, tiveram, E terei, terás, terá, teremos, tereis, terão, F teria, terias, teria, teríamos, teríeis, teriam, G tenha, tenhas, tenha, tenhamos, tenhais, tenham, H tiver, tiveres, tiver, tivermos, tiverdes, tiverem, I tivesse, tivesses, tivesse, tivéssemos, tivésseis, tivessem, J tem, tenha, tenhamos, tende, tenham, K tendo, L ter, teres, ter, termos, terdes, terem, M tido.

trazer: A trago, trazes, traz, trazemos, trazeis, trazem, B trazia, trazias, etc., C trouxe, trouxeste, trouxe, trouxemos, trouxestes, trouxeram, D trouxera, trouxeras, etc., E trarei, trarás, trará, traremos, trareis, trarão, F traria, trarias, etc., G traga, tragas, etc., H trouxer, trouxeres, etc., I trouxesse, trouxesses, etc., J traz, traga, tragamos, trazei, tragam, K trazendo, L trazer, trazeres, trazer, trazermos, trazerdes, trazerem, M trazido.

ver: A vejo, vês, vê, vemos, vedes, vêem, B via, vias, etc., C vi, viste, viu, vimos, vistes, viram, D vira, viras, etc., E verei, verás, etc., G veja, vejas, veja, etc., H vir, vires, vir, virmos, virdes, virem, I visse, visses, visse, etc., J vê, veja, vejamos, vede, vejam, K vendo, L ver, veres, ver, vermos, verdes, verem, M visto.

vir: A venho, vens, vem, vimos, vindes, vêm, B vinha, vinhas, etc., C vim, vieste, veio, viemos, viestes, vieram, D viera, vieras, etc., E virei, virás, etc., G venha, venhas, etc., H vier, vieres, vier, etc., I viesse, viesses, etc., J vem, venha, venhamos, vinde, venham, K vindo, L vir, vires, vir, virmos, virdes, virem, M vindo.

English Irregular Verbs/Verbos Irregulares Ingleses

Infinitive	Past Tense	Past Participle
arise	arose	arisen
awake	awoke	awoken
be	was/were	been
bear	bore	born(e)
beat	beat	beaten
begin	began	begun
bend	bent	bent
bet	bet/betted	bet/betted
bid	bid	bid
bind	bound	bound
bite	bit	bitten
bleed	bled	bled
blow	blew	blown
break	broke	broken
breed	bred	bred
bring	brought	brought
build	built	built
burn	burnt/burned	burnt/burned
burst	burst	burst
buy	bought	bought
can	could	-
cast	cast	cast
catch	caught	caught
choose	chose	chosen
come	came	come
cost	cost	cost
creep	crept	crept
cut	cut	cut
deal	dealt	dealt
dig	dug	dug
do	did	done
draw	drew	drawn
dream	dreamed/dreamt	dreamed/dreamt
drink	drank	drunk
drive	drove	driven
eat	ate	eaten
fall	fell	fallen
feed	fed	fed
feel	felt	felt
fight	fought	fought
find	found	found
fling	flung	flung
fly	flew	flown
forget	forgot	forgotten
freeze	froze	frozen
get	got	got (US gotten)
give	gave	given
go	went	gone

Infinitive	Past Tense	Past Participle
grind	ground	ground
grow	grew	grown
hang	hung/hanged	hung/hanged
have	had	had
hear	heard	heard
hide	hid	hidden
hit	hit	hit
hold	held	held
hurt	hurt	hurt
keep	kept	kept
kneel	knelt/kneeled	knelt/kneeled
know	knew	known
lay	laid	laid
lead	led	led
lean	leant/leaned	leant/leaned
leap	leapt/leaped	leapt/leaped
learn	learnt/learned	learnt/learned
leave	left	left
lend	lent	lent
let	let	let
lie	lay	lain
light	lit/lighted	lit/lighted
lose	lost	lost
make	made	made
may	might	-
mean	meant	meant
meet	met	met
mow	mowed	mown/mowed
pay	paid	paid
put	put	put
quit	quit/quitted	quit/quitted
read	read	read
rid	rid	rid
ride	rode	ridden
ring	rang	rung
rise	rose	risen
run	ran	run
saw	sawed	sawn
say	said	said
see	saw	seen
seek	sought	sought
sell	sold	sold
send	sent	sent
set	set	set
shake	shook	shaken
shall	should	-
shed	shed	shed
shine	shone	shone
shoot	shot	shot

Infinitive	Past Tense	Past Participle
show	showed	shown
shrink	shrank	shrunk
shut	shut	shut
sing	sang	sung
sink	sank	sunk
sit	sat	sat
sleep	slept	slept
slide	slid	slid
sling	slung	slung
smell	smelt/smelled	smelt/smelled
sow	sowed	sown/sowed
speak	spoke	spoken
speed	sped/speeded	sped/speeded
spell	spelt/spelled	spelt/spelled
spend	spent	spent
spill	spilt/spilled	spilt/spilled
spin	spun	spun
spit	spat	spat
split	split	split
spoil	spoiled/spoilt	spoiled/spoilt
spread	spread	spread
spring	sprang	sprung
stand	stood	stood
steal	stole	stolen
stick	stuck	stuck
sting	stung	stung
stink	stank	stunk
strike	struck	struck/stricken
swear	swore	sworn
sweep	swept	swept
swell	swelled	swollen/swelled
swim	swam	swum
swing	swung	swung
take	took	taken
teach	taught	taught
tear	tore	torn
tell	told	told
think	thought	thought
throw	threw	thrown
tread	trod	trodden
wake	woke/waked	woken/waked
wear	wore	worn
weave	wove/weaved	woven/weaved
weep	wept	wept
win	won	won
wind	wound	wound
wring	wrung	wrung
write	wrote	written

a¹, A [a] *m* [letra] a, A.

a² [a] ⟨> *artigo definido* ▷ **o**. ⟨>
prep **-1.** [introduz um complemento indireto]
to; **mostrar algo a alguém** to show sthg
to sb, to show sb sthg; **diga ao Zé para
vir** tell Zé to come; **peça o chapéu ao
Paulo** ask Paulo for the hat. **-2.** [relativo à direção] to; **fomos à praia** we went to
the beach; **vamos ao cinema** we're
going to the movies; **cheguei a Salvador ontem** I arrived in Salvador yesterday; **ele percorreu o país de norte a sul**
he travelled the country from north to
south. **-3.** [relativo a posição, lugar, distância]: **é à esquerda/direita** it's on the left/
right; **fica na saída do teatro** it's on the
way out of the theatre. **-4.** [introduz um
complemento direto]: **amar a Deus** to love
God; **ele criou o menino como a um filho**
he raised the boy like his own son. **-5.**
[relativo à quantidade, medida, preço]: **aos
centos/às dezenas** by the hundred/
dozen; **a quanto estão as peras?** how
much are the pears?; **a quilo/metro** by
the kilo/metre. **-6.** [indica modo, maneira]: **feito à mão** handmade; **bater à máquina** to type; **ir a pé/cavalo** to go on
foot/horseback; **viajar a trabalho/passeio** to go on a business/pleasure trip;
à moda da casa house style; **sal a gosto**
salt to taste; **pagar à vista/a prazo** to
pay cash/on time; **a olho nu** with the
naked eye. **-7.** [relativo à velocidade]: **dirigir a 60 km/h** to drive at 60 kph; **ela ia a
100 km/h** she was doing 100 kph. **-8.**
[indica freqüência]: **três vezes ao dia** three
times a day; **estou lá às terças e quintas**
I'm there on Tuesdays and Thursdays.
-9. [introduz complemento de tempo]: **as lojas abrem às nove horas** the shops open
at nine (o'clock); **eles chegam daqui a 2
horas** they're arriving in two hours'
time; **fica a dez minutos daqui** it's ten
minutes from here; **à noite** at night. **-10.** [indica série]: **de ... a** from ... to; **façam
os exercícios de um a dez** do exercises
one to ten. **-11.** [seguido de infinitivo para
exprimir momento]: **ele começou a falar**
he started speaking; **ele tropeçou ao
subir no ônibus** he tripped as he was
getting on the bus. **-12.** [seguido de infinitivo indicando duas ações]: **ela saiu a cantar**
she went out singing; **ele nunca aprendeu a assobiar** he never learned to
whistle; **começou a chover** it started to
rain. **-13.** [em locuções]: **a não ser que**
unless; **à exceção de** except for; **a partir
de** from; **a respeito de** regarding.

à [a] = **a + a**.

AA (*abrev de* **Alcoólicos Anônimos**) *m*
AA.

AACC (*abrev de* **Associação de Assistência à Criança com Câncer**) *f Brazilian
association for assistance to children
with cancer*.

AACD (*abrev de* **Associação de Assistência à Criança Defeituosa**) *f Brazilian
association for assistance to disabled children*.

aba ['aba] *f* **-1.** [de chapéu] brim. **-2.** [de
casaca] tail.

abacate [aba'katʃi] *m* avocado.

abacaxi [abaka'ʃi] *m* **-1.** [fruta] pineapple. **-2.** *fam* [problema, dificuldade] difficulty; **ter ~s para resolver** to have
some difficulties to sort out; **descascar
um ~** to get out of a fix.

abade, dessa [a'badʒi, desa] *m, f* abbot
(*f* abbess).

abadia [aba'dʒia] *f* abbey.

abafado, da [aba'fadu, da] *adj* **-1.** [ar, sala] stuffy. **-2.** [pessoa - sem ar] suffocated.
-3. [som] muffled.

abafamento [abafa'mẽntu] *m* **-1.** [sufoco]
suffocation. **-2.** [de som] muffling.

abafar [aba'fa(x)] ⟨> *vt* **-1.** [sufocar] to
suffocate. **-2.** [cobrir] to cover. **-3.** [apagar] to smother. **-4.** [amortecer] to muffle. **-5.** [ocultar] to cover up. ⟨> *vi* **-1.**
[sufocar] to suffocate. **-2.** *fam* [fazer sucesso] to steal the show.

abagunçado, da [abagũn'sadu, da] *adj*
messed-up.

abagunçar [abagũn'sa(x)] *vt* to mess sthg up.

abaixado, da [abaj'ʃadu, da] ⟨⟩ *pp* ⟩ **abaixar.** ⟨⟩ *adj* -**1.** [pessoa] stooped. -**2.** [persiana] lowered.

abaixar [abaj'ʃa(x)] *vt* to lower; ~ o volume to turn down the volume.

➡ **abaixar-se** *vp* [curvar-se] to crouch down.

abaixo [a'bajʃu] ⟨⟩ *adv* -**1.** [posição] down; **mais** ~ lower down. -**2.** [direção] further down; **escada** ~ downstairs; **ladeira** ~ downhill; **rio** ~ downstream. -**3.** [em texto] below. ⟨⟩ *interj* down with; ~ **a opressão!** down with oppression!

➡ **abaixo de** *loc prep* -**1.** [em posição inferior] below. -**2.** [em número inferior etc.] under.

abaixo-assinado [a,bajʃuasi'nadu] (*pl* **abaixo-assinados**) *m* petition.

abajur [aba'ʒu(x)] (*pl* -**es**) *m* -**1.** [pantalha] shade. -**2.** [lâmpada] table lamp.

abalado, da [aba'ladu, da] *adj* -**1.** [pessoa] shaken. -**2.** [saúde] impaired.

abalar [aba'la(x)] *vt* -**1.** [prédio, fundações] to rock. -**2.** [pessoa] to shake. -**3.** [saúde] to impair.

➡ **abalar-se** *vp* [comover-se] to be moved.

abalizado, da [abali'zadu, da] *adj* -**1.** [profissional] skilled. -**2.** [opinião] expert.

abalo [a'balu] *m* -**1.** [tremor] tremor; ~ **sísmico** earth tremor. -**2.** [efeito ruim] setback. -**3.** *fig* [comoção] uproar.

abanar [aba'na(x)] *vt* -**1.** [com leque, jornal] to fan. -**2.** [com mão, lenço] to wave. -**3.** [rabo] to wag. -**4.** [cabeça] to shake.

➡ **abanar-se** *vp* [ventilar-se] to fan o.s.

abandonado, da [labãndo'nadu, da] *adj* -**1.** [desamparado] abandoned. -**2.** [descuidado] neglected.

abandonar [abãndo'na(x)] *vt* -**1.** [desamparar] to abandon. -**2.** [negligenciar] to neglect. -**3.** [deixar - estudos, profissão] to give up; [- cônjuge] to leave. -**4.** [renegar] to reject.

➡ **abandonar-se** *vp* -**1.** [desleixar-se] to let o.s. go. -**2.** [entregar-se]: ~-**se a algo** to surrender o.s. to sthg.

abandono [abãn'donu] *m* -**1.** [ato] abandonment. -**2.** [estado] neglect. -**3.** [relaxamento] shabbiness. -**4.** [entrega] surrender.

abarcar [abax'ka(x)] *vt* -**1.** [abranger] to comprise. -**2.** [alcançar] to cover. -**3.** [monopolizar] to monopolize.

abarrotado, da [abaxo'tadu, da] *adj*: ~ **(de)** packed (with).

abarrotar [abaxo'ta(x)] *vt*: ~ **algo (de)** to pack sthg (with).

abastado, da [abaʃ'tadu, da] *adj* well-off.

abastecer [abaʃte'se(x)] *vt*: ~ **algo (de)** to supply sthg (with).

➡ **abastecer-se** *vp*: ~-**se (de algo)** to stock up (with sthg).

abastecimento [abaʃtesi'mẽntu] *m* supply.

abatedouro [abate'doru] *m* [matadouro] slaughterhouse.

abater [aba'te(x)] *vt* -**1.** [matar - animais] to slaughter; [- pessoa] to kill. -**2.** [diminuir] to reduce. -**3.** [enfraquecer] to weaken. -**4.** [desanimar] to shatter.

abatido, da [aba'tʃidu, da] *adj* -**1.** [pálido] drawn. -**2.** [enfraquecido] weakened. -**3.** [desanimado] downcast.

abatimento [abatʃi'mẽntu] *m* -**1.** [palidez] paleness. -**2.** [fraqueza] weakness. -**3.** [desânimo] dejection. -**4.** [redução] reduction; **fazer um** ~ to give a discount.

abaulado, da [abaw'ladu, da] *adj* convex.

abdicação [abdʒika'sãw] (*pl* -**ões**) *f* abdication.

abdicar [abdʒi'ka(x)] *vi* to abdicate; ~ **de algo** *fig* to forgo sthg.

abecê [abe'se] *m* -**1.** [alfabeto] ABC. -**2.** *fig* [rudimentos] fundamentals (*pl*).

abecedário [abese'darju] *m* alphabet.

abeirar [abej'ra(x)] *vt* to bring near.

➡ **abeirar-se** *vp*: ~-**se de** to draw near to.

abelha [a'beʎa] *f* bee.

abelha-mestra [a,eʎa'meʃtra] (*pl* **abelhas-mestras**) *f* queen bee.

abelhudo, da [abe'ʎudu, da] *adj* nosy.

abençoar [abẽn'swa(x)] *vt* to bless; **(que) Deus te abençoe!** God bless you!

aberração [abexa'sãw] (*pl* -**ões**) *f* aberration.

aberto, ta [a'bɛxtu, ta] ⟨⟩ *pp* ⟩ **abrir.** ⟨⟩ *adj* -**1.** [ger] open. -**2.** [registro, torneira] turned on. -**3.** [sem cobertura - terraço] open-air; [- carro] convertible. -**4.** [céu] clear. -**5.** [embrulho, pacote etc.] unwrapped. -**6.** [camisa etc.] undone. -**7.** [sincero] frank. -**8.** [liberal] open-minded.

abertura [abex'tural] *f* -**1.** [ger] opening; **cerimônia de** ~ opening ceremony. -**2.** [orifício] gap. -**3.** [início] start. -**4.** [de golfo, enseada] width. -**5.** [em roupa] neckline. -**6.** [em idéias] openness. -**7.** *FOT* aperture. -**8.** *MÚS* overture. -**9.** [*POL* - democrática] liberalization; [- de aeroporto, porto] deregulation.

abestalhado, da [abeʃta'ʎadu, da] *adj* moronic.

ABF (abrev de **Associação Brasileira de Franchising**) f Brazilian franchising association.

ABI (abrev de **Associação Brasileira de Imprensa**) f Brazilian press association.

abismado, da [abiʒ'madu, da] adj dismayed.

abismo [a'biʒmu] m -1. [precipício] abyss. -2. fig [grande diferença] chasm. -3. fig [situação difícil]: **estar à beira de um ~** to be on the brink.

abjeto, ta [ab'ʒεtu, ta] adj abject.

ABL (abrev de **Academia Brasileira de Letras**) f Brazilian academy of arts.

abnegado, da [abne'gadu, da] adj self-sacrificing.

abnegar [abne'ga(x)] vi [renunciar]: **~ de algo** to renounce sthg.

➡ **abnegar-se** vp [sacrificar-se] to sacrifice o.s.

ABNT (abrev de **Associação Brasileira de Normas Técnicas**) f Brazilian body overseeing technical standards, ≃ BSI UK, ≃ ANSI US.

abóbada [a'bɔbada] f vault.

abóbora [a'bɔbora] f pumpkin.

abolição [abolisãw] f abolition.

abolir [abo'li(x)] vt to abolish.

abominação [abomina'sãw] (pl -ões) f abomination.

abominar [abomi'na(x)] vt to loathe.

abonado, da [abo'nadu, da] ◇ adj [rico] well-off. ◇ m, f [rico] well-off person; **os ~s** the well-off.

abonar [abo'na(x)] vt -1. [gen] to back up. -2. [afiançar] to guarantee. -3. [aprovar] to approve. -4. [dar] to grant. -5. [adiantar] to advance. -6. [relevar] to excuse.

abono [a'bonu] m -1. [aprovação] approval. -2. [fiança] collateral. -3. [pagamento extra] bonus- 4. [relevação] pardon.

abordagem [abox'daʒẽ] (pl -ns) f approach.

abordar [abox'da(x)] vt -1. [ir a bordo de] to board. -2. [pessoa] to approach. -3. [assunto] to broach.

aborígine [abo'riʒeni] adj -1. [indígena] native. -2. [da Austrália] aboriginal.

aborrecer [aboxe'se(x)] vt -1. [amolar] to annoy. -2. [entediar] to bore.

➡ **aborrecer-se** vp [amolar-se]: **~-se com alguém** to get annoyed with sb.

aborrecido, da [aboxe'sidu, da] adj -1. [amolado] annoyed. -2. [enfadonho] boring.

aborrecimento [aboxesi'mẽntu] m [amolação] annoyance.

abortar [abox'ta(x)] ◇ vi [MED - espon-

taneamente] to have a miscarriage; [- intencionalmente] to have an abortion. ◇ vt [plano, greve etc.] to abort.

aborto [a'boxtu] m [MED - espontâneo] miscarriage; [- intencional] abortion.

abotoadura [abotwa'dura] f cuff-link.

abotoar [abo'twa(x)] vt [roupa] to button.

abr. (abrev de **abril**) Apr.

abraçar [abra'sa(x)] vt -1. [com os braços] to hug. -2. fig [seguir] to embrace.

➡ **abraçar-se** vp to hug each other.

abraço [a'brasu] m hug; **dar um ~ em alguém** to give sb a hug.

abrandar [abrãn'da(x)] ◇ vt -1. [dor] to ease. -2. [lei, palavreado] to moderate. ◇ vi -1. [ger] to soften. -2. [dor, ira, calor, vento] to die down.

abranger [abrãn'ʒe(x)] vt -1. [incluir] to include. -2. [entender] to grasp. -3. [conter em sua área] to comprise.

abrasar [abra'za(x)] vt -1. [incendiar] to set alight. -2. [esquentar muito] to scorch.

abreviar [abre'vja(x)] vt -1. [pôr em abreviatura] to abbreviate. -2. [resumir] to abridge. -3. [tornar breve] to shorten.

abreviatura [abrevja'tura] f abbreviation.

abridor [abri'do(x)] (pl -es) m: **~ de garrafa** bottle opener; **~ de lata** can opener.

abrigar [abri'ga(x)] vt [albergar] to shelter.

➡ **abrigar-se** vp [albergar-se] to take shelter.

abrigo [a'brigu] m -1. [refúgio] shelter; **~ anti-aéreo** bomb shelter. -2. [cobertura] cover. -3. [asilo] home.

abril [a'briw] m April; veja também **setembro**.

abrir [a'bri(x)] ◇ vt -1. [ger] to open. -2. [pernas, braços] to stretch out. -3. [camisa etc.] to undo. -4. [mapa] to open out. -5. [registro, torneira, água] to turn on. -6. [túnel] to bore. -7. [estrada] to make. -8. [exceção, precedente] to create. -9. [apetite] to whet. ◇ vi -1. [ger] to open. -2. [sinal de tráfego] to turn green. -3. [tempo] to clear up.

➡ **abrir-se** vp [confidenciar]: **~-se com alguém** to confide in sb.

abrolho [a'broʎu] m thorn.

abrupto, ta [a'bruptu, ta] adj -1. [súbito] sudden. -2. [áspero] abrupt.

ABS (abrev de **antilock braking system**) m ABS; **freios ~** ABS brakes.

absolutamente [abso,luta'mẽntʃi] adv -1. [completamente] absolutely. -2. [de modo nenhum] absolutely not.

absoluto, ta [abso'lutu, ta] adj absolute; **em ~** not at all.

absolver [absow've(x)] vt: ~ **alguém (de algo)** JUR to acquit sb (of sthg); RELIG to absolve sb (of sthg); [inocentar] to clear sb (of sthg).

absolvição [absowvi'sãw] f -1. JUR acquittal. -2. RELIG absolution.

absorção [absox'sãw] f -1. [de água, vapores, gases] absorption. -2. [de valores, cultura] absorption.

absorto, ta [ab'soxtu, ta] adj [concentrado] absorbed.

absorvente [absox'vẽntʃi] adj -1. [substância] absorbent. -2. [pessoa, leitura, trabalho] absorbing.
◆ **absorvente** m: ~ **higiênico** sanitary towel.

absorver [absoxve(x)] vt to absorb; ~ **energia** to use up energy; ~ **tempo** to take up time.

abstêmio, mia [abʃ'temju, mja] <> adj abstemious. <> m, f teetotaller.

abstenção [abʃtẽn'sãw] (pl -ões) f -1. [de prazeres, de fumo] abstinence. -2. [do voto] abstention.

abster-se [abʃ'texsil] vp: ~ **(de algo/de fazer algo)** to abstain (from sthg/from doing sthg).

abstrair [abʃtra'i(x)] vt -1. [afastar] to keep away from. -2. [isolar] to separate out.
◆ **abstrair-se** vp -1. [alhear-se]: ~-se de to distance o.s. from. -2. [concentrar-se]: ~-se em to absorb o.s. in.

abstrato, ta [abʃ'tratu, ta] adj abstract.

absurdo, da [ab'suxdu, da] adj absurd.
◆ **absurdo** m absurdity.

abulia [abu'lia] f apathy.

abundância [abūn'dãnsja] f -1. [grande quantidade] abundance; **em** ~ in abundance. -2. [riqueza]: **ele vive com** ~ he is a man of means.

abundante [abūn'dãntʃi] adj: ~ **(em/de)** abundant (in/with).

abundar [abūn'da(x)] vi to abound.

abusado, da [abu'zadu, da] adj forward.

abusar [abu'za(x)] vi -1. [aproveitar-se, exceder-se] to go too far. -2. [praticar excessos]: ~ **de algo** to abuse sthg. -3. [aproveitar-se]: ~ **de alguém/algo** to take advantage of sb/sthg. -4. [sexualmente]: ~ **de alguém** to abuse sb.

abuso [a'buzul] m: ~ **(de)** abuse (of); ~ **sexual** sexual abuse.

abutre [a'butril] m vulture.

AC (abrev de **Estado do Acre**) m State of Acre.

a.C. (abrev de **antes de Cristo**) adj BC.

acabamento [akaba'mẽntul] m finish.

acabar [aka'ba(x)] <> vt -1. [terminar] to finish. -2. [rematar] to finish off. <> vi -1. [terminar] to finish, to end; ~ **de fazer algo** to finish doing sthg; [há pouco] to have just done sthg. -2. [ter como consequência]: ~ **em algo** to end up in sthg. -3. [abolir]: ~ **com algo** to put an end to sthg. -4. [destruir]: ~ **com algo** to destroy sthg. -5. [tornar-se] to end up.
◆ **acabar-se** vp -1. [terminar] to finish, to end. -2. [desgastar-se] to wear o.s. out.

acabrunhar [akabru'ɲa(x)] vt -1. [desanimar] to dishearten. -2. [envergonhar] to embarrass.

academia [akade'mial] f -1. [escola] school. -2. [sociedade] academy. -3. ESP school.

acadêmico, ca [aka'demiku, ka] <> adj academic. <> m, f academic.

açafrão [asa'frãw] m saffron.

acalentar [akalẽn'ta(x)] vt -1. [ninar] to lull. -2. fig [nutrir] to cherish. -3. [aconchegar] to cuddle.

acalmar [akaw'ma(x)] <> vt [pessoa, ânimos] to calm. <> vi -1. [pessoa] to calm down. -2. [ventania] to abate. -3. [mar] to become calm.
◆ **acalmar-se** vp [pessoa, ânimos] to calm down.

acalorado, da [akalo'radu, da] adj [discussão etc.] heated.

acamado, da [aka'madu, da] adj bedridden.

açambarcar [asãnbax'ka(x)] vt -1. [apropriar-se de] to appropriate. -2. [monopolizar] to corner.

acampamento [akãnpa'mẽntul] m -1. [atividade] camping; [lugar] campsite. -2. MIL encampment.

acanhado, da [aka'ɲadu, da] adj shy.

acanhar-se [aka'ɲaxsil] vp: ~ **(de fazer algo)** to be shy (about doing sthg).

ação [a'sãw] (pl -ões) f -1. [atuação] action. -2. [feito] act; ~ **de graças** thanksgiving. -3. [capacidade de agir]: **sem** ~ helpless. -4. [efeito] effect. -5. [enredo] plot. -6. JUR legal action; **mover uma** ~ **contra alguém** to bring a legal action against sb. -7. FIN share; ~ **ordinária** ordinary share; ~ **preferencial** preference share. -8. MIL action.

acarajé [akara'ʒɛ] m bean fritter.

acarear [aka'rja(x)] vt to confront.

acariciar [akari'sja(x)] vt to caress.

acarretar [akaxe'ta(x)] vt to cause.

acaso [a'kazul] m chance; **essa descoberta foi um** ~ it was a chance discovery.
◆ **ao acaso** loc adv at random.
◆ **por acaso** loc adv by chance.

acatamento [akata'mẽntul] m -1. [respeito]: ~ **(a)** respect (for). -2. [cumprimento]: ~ **(a ou de)** deference (to).

acatar [aka'ta(x)] *vt* **-1.** [respeitar] to respect. **-2.** [cumprir] to obey.

acautelar [akawte'la(x)] *vt* to caution.
➡ **acautelar-se** *vp*: ∼**-se (contra)** to guard (against).

acebolado, da [asebo'ladu, da] *adj* cooked with onions.

aceder [ase'de(x)] *vi*: ∼ **a algo** to accede to sthg.

aceitação [asejta'sãw] *f* **-1.** [anuência] acceptance. **-2.** [admissão, aprovação] approval. **-3.** [receptividade] acceptability.

aceitar [asej'ta(x)] *vt* **-1.** [anuir a] to accept. **-2.** [admitir, aprovar] to approve.

aceito, ta [a'sejtu, ta] ◇ *pp* ▷ **aceitar.** ◇ *adj* **-1.** [pessoa, produto] well-received. **-2.** [proposta, solução] accepted.

aceleração [aselera'sãw] *f* **-1.** *FÍS* acceleration. **-2.** [de processo etc.] progress.

acelerador [aselera'do(x)] (*pl* **-es**) *m* accelerator.

acelerar [asele'ra(x)] ◇ *vt* **-1.** *AUTO* to accelerate. **-2.** [apressar] to hurry. ◇ *vi* *AUTO* to accelerate.

acenar [ase'na(x)] ◇ *vt* **-1.** [sinalizar] to indicate. **-2.** [fazer movimento com - cabeça] to nod; [- mãos] to wave. ◇ *vi* **-1.** [sinalizar - com cabeça] to nod; [- com mãos, lenço] to wave. **-2.** [prometer]: ∼ **algo (a alguém)** to offer (sb) sthg.

acendedor [asẽnde'do(x)] *m* [de bico de gás] lighter.

acender [asẽn'de(x)] ◇ *vt* **-1.** [cigarro, fósforo] to light. **-2.** [lâmpada, luz] to switch on. **-3.** *fig* [ânimo] to excite. ◇ *vp* [lâmpada, luz] to be turned on.

aceno [a'senu] *m* **-1.** [gesto] gesture. **-2.** [com a cabeça] nod. **-3.** [com a mão] wave.

acento [a'sẽntu] *m* **-1.** [gráfico] accent. **-2.** [intensidade] stress.

acentuação [asẽntwa'sãw] *f* accentuation.

acentuar [asẽn'twa(x)] *vt* **-1.** [palavra, vogal] to stress. **-2.** [enfatizar] to emphasize. **-3.** [realçar] to accentuate.

acepção [asep'sãw] (*pl* **-ões**) *f* sense.

acerca [a'sexka] ➡ **acerca de** *loc adv* about, concerning.

acerola [ase'rɔla] *f* fruit similar to Barbados Cherry, commonly drunk as a fruit juice, rich in vitamins and minerals.

acertado, da [asex'tadu, da] *adj* **-1.** [relógio] correct. **-2.** [medida, decisão] sensible. **-3.** [combinado] arranged.

acertar [asex'ta(x)] ◇ *vt* **-1.** [relógio] to set. **-2.** [combinar] to arrange. **-3.** [contas] to settle. **-4.** [igualar] to even up. **-5.** [en-

direitar] to put right. **-6.** [encontrar] to find. **-7.** [fazer atingir]: ∼ **algo em algo** to land sthg on sthg. **-8.** [aplicar] to strike. ◇ *vi* **-1.** [em adivinhação, jogo] to guess correctly. **-2.** [atingir]: ∼ **em algo/alguém** to hit sthg/sb.

acerto [a'sextu] *m* **-1.** [em decisão, escolha] right decision. **-2.** [acordo] agreement. **-3.** [de contas] settling.

acervo [a'sexvu] *m* [patrimônio] collection.

aceso, sa [a'sezu, za] ◇ *pp* ▷ **acender.** ◇ *adj* **-1.** [cigarro, fósforo] lit. **-2.** [lâmpada, luz] on. **-3.** *fig* [pessoa] excited.

acessar [ase'sa(x)] *vt* *COMPUT* to access.

acessível [ase'sivɛw] (*pl* **-eis**) *adj* **-1.** [de acesso fácil] accessible. **-2.** [que se pode obter] available. **-3.** [tratável] approachable. **-4.** [inteligível] comprehensible. **-5.** [módico] affordable.

acesso [a'sesu] *m* **-1.** [ger] access. **-2.** [aproximação] approach. **-3.** [ímpeto] fit. **-4.** *MED* attack. **-5.** *COMPUT* access; ∼ **discado** dial-up access.

acessório, ria [ase'sɔrju] *adj* accessory.
➡ **acessório** *m* accessory.

achado [a'ʃadu] *m* **-1.** [coisa encontrada] find. **-2.** [descoberta] discovery. **-3.** [pechincha] bargain. **-4.** [coisa providencial] godsend.

achaque [a'ʃaki] *m* ailment.

achar [a'ʃa(x)] *vt* **-1.** [encontrar - procurando] to find; [- por acaso] to come across. **-2.** [descobrir, encontrar] to find. **-3.:** ∼ **graça em algo** to find sthg amusing. **-4.** [supor, opinar] to think; ∼ **que ...** to think that ...; **acho que sim** I think so.
➡ **achar-se** *vp* **-1.** [estar] to be. **-2.** [considerar-se] to consider o.s.

achatar [aʃa'ta(x)] *vt* **-1.** [aplanar] to flatten. **-2.** [rebaixar] to lower.

achegar-se [aʃe'gaxsi] *vp*: ∼ **(a/de)** to get closer (to).

acidentado, da [asidẽn'tadu, da] ◇ *adj* **-1.** [terreno] rough. **-2.** [viagem, vida] turbulent. **-3.** [pessoa] injured. ◇ *m, f* [pessoa] injured person.

acidental [asidẽn'taw] (*pl* **-ais**) *adj* **-1.** [fortuito] accidental. **-2.** [secundário] incidental.

acidente [asi'dẽntʃi] *m* **-1.** [desastre] accident; ∼ **de carro** car accident. **-2.** [eventualidade] circumstance; **por** ∼ by chance. ∼ **geográfico** geographic accident. ∼ **de trabalho** accident at work, industrial accident. ∼ **vascular cerebral** *MED* stroke.

acidez [asi'deʒ] *f* acidity.

ácido, da [ˈasidu, da] *adj* **-1.** *QUÍM* acid. **-2.** [bebida, fruta, sabor] acidic.

ácido *m* **-1.** QUÍM acid. **-2.** *fam* [droga] acid.

acima [a'sima] *adj* **-1.** [ger] above; **mais ~ higher** up. **-2.** [em direção à parte superior]: **morro** OU **ladeira ~** uphill.

➥ acima de *loc prep* **-1.** [em posição superior] above. **-2.** [quantia, quantidade] more than.

acinte [a'sĩtʃi] *m* provocation.

acintosamente [asĩtoza'mẽtʃil] *adv* deliberately.

acionar [asjo'na(x)] *vt* **-1.** [mecanismo, medidas] to set in motion. **-2.** JUR to sue.

acionista [asjo'niʃta] *mf* shareholder.

acirrado, da [asi'xadu, da] *adj* **-1.** [luta, discussão, ânimo] tough. **-2.** [ódio] bitter.

aclamação [aklama'sãw] *f* **-1.** [ovação] ovation. **-2.** [proclamação] proclamation.

aclamar [akla'ma(x)] *vt* **-1.** [ovacionar] to applaud. **-2.** [proclamar] to proclaim.

aclive [a'klivi] *m* slope; **um caminho em ~** an uphill slope.

ACM (*abrev de* **Associação Cristã de Moços**) *f* ≃ YMCA.

aço [a'asul] *m* steel; **~ inoxidável** stainless steel.

ações [a'sõjʃ] *pl* ▷ **ação**.

açoitar [asoj'ta(x)] *vt* **-1.** [com açoite] to whip. **-2.** [suj: vento, temporal] to lash.

açoite [a'sojtʃi] *m* whip.

acolá [ako'la] *adv* over there.

acolchoado, da [akow'ʃwadu, da] *adj* [forrado] quilted.

➥ acolchoado *m* quilt.

acolchoar [akow'ʃwa(x)] *vt* [forrar] to quilt.

acolhedor, ra [akoʎe'do(x), ra] *adj* welcoming.

acolher [ako'ʎe(x)] *vt* **-1.** [ger] to welcome. **-2.** [hospedar] to put sb up. **-3.** [admitir] to receive.

acolhida [ako'ʎida] *f* **-1.** [hospedagem] hospitality. **-2.** [recepção] welcome.

acometer [akome'te(x)] *vt* **-1.** [atacar] to attack. **-2.** [suj: doença, desejo, sentimento] to strike.

acomodação [akomoda'sãw] (*pl* -**ões**) *f* **-1.** [alojamento] accommodation. **-2.** [aposento, instalação] room. **-3.** [arranjo, arrumação] layout. **-4.** [adaptação] adaptation.

acomodado, da [akomo'dadu, da] *adj* **-1.** [alojado, instalado] settled. **-2.** [conformado] reconciled.

acomodar [akomo'da(x)] *vt* [alojar, instalar] to accommodate.

➥ acomodar-se *vp* **-1.** [alojar-se, instalar-se] to settle o.s. **-2.** [conformar-se] to reconcile o.s.

acompanhado, da [akõnpa'ɲadu, da] *adj* accompanied.

acompanhamento [akõnpaɲa'mẽtul] *m* **-1.** [de processo, doença] monitoring. **-2.** MÚS accompaniment. **-3.** CULIN side order, side dish.

acompanhante [akõnpa'ɲãtʃil] *mf* companion.

acompanhar [akõnpa'ɲa(x)] ◇ *vt* **-1.** [ger] to accompany. **-2.** [processo, doença] to monitor. **-3.** [suj: problema, preocupações] to stay with. **-4.** [margear] to run parallel to. **-5.** [compreender] to keep up with. **-6.** CULIN to go with. ◇ *vi* MÚS to accompany.

aconchegante [akõnʃe'gãtʃil] *adj* cosy.

aconchegar [akõnʃe'ga(x)] *vt* **-1.** [nos braços] to cuddle. **-2.** [na cama, nas cobertas] to tuck up OU in.

➥ aconchegar-se *vp* **-1.** [nos braços] to snuggle. **-2.** [na cama, nas cobertas] to tuck o.s. up OU in.

aconchego [akõn'ʃegul] *m* warmth.

acondicionamento [akõndʒisjona'mẽtul] *m* packaging.

acondicionar [akõndʒisjo'na(x)] *vt* **-1.** [embrulhar] to wrap. **-2.** [embalar] to package.

aconselhar [akõnse'ʎa(x)] *vt* **-1.** [dar conselho a]: **~ alguém (a fazer algo** OU **a que faça algo)** to advise sb (to do sthg). **-2.** [recomendar] to recommend.

➥ aconselhar-se *vp* to seek advice; **~-se com alguém** to seek the advice of sb.

aconselhável [akõnse'ʎavɛw] (*pl* -**eis**) *adj* advisable.

acontecer [akõnte'se(x)] *vi* to happen.

acontecimento [akõntesi'mẽtul] *m* event.

acoplado, da [ako'pladu, da] *adj* [conectado - peças] connected; [- naves espaciais] docked.

acordado, da [akox'dadu, da] *adj* **-1.** [desperto] awake; **sonhar ~** to daydream. **-2.** [combinado] agreed.

acordar [akox'da(x)] ◇ *vt* [despertar] to wake. ◇ *vi* [despertar] to wake.

acordeão [akox'dʒjãw] (*pl* -**ões**) *m* accordion.

acordo [a'koxdul] *m* agreement; **chegar a um ~** to arrive at an agreement; **de ~** agreed; **de ~ com** [conforme] according to; **estar de ~ (com alguém/em fazer algo)** to be in agreement (with sb/to do sthg); **de comum ~** by common accord.

acorrentar [akoxẽn'ta(x)] *vt* to chain.

acossado, da [ako'sadu, da] ◇ *adj* [perseguido] persecuted, hounded. ◇ *m, f* victim.

acossar [ako'sa(x)] *vt* **-1.** [perseguir] to pursue. **-2.** [acuar] to corner.

acostamento [akoʃta'mẽntu] *m* hard shoulder.

acostumado, da [akoʃtu'madu, da] *adj* **-1.** [habitual] usual. **-2.** [habituado]: **estar ~ a** *ou* **com algo** to be used to sthg; **estar ~ a fazer algo** to be in the habit of doing sthg.

acostumar [akoʃtu'ma(x)] *vt*: **~ alguém/algo a algo** to accustom sb/sthg to sthg; **~ alguém a fazer algo** to accustom sb to doing sthg.
　acostumar-se *vp* to accustom o.s.; **~-se a algo/a fazer algo** to accustom o.s. to/to doing sthg.

acotovelar [akotove'la(x)] *vt* **-1.** [para chamar a atenção] to nudge. **-2.** [empurrar] to elbow.
　acotovelar-se *vp* [empurrar-se] to elbow one's way.

açougue [a'sogi] *m* butcher's.

açougueiro, ra [aso'gejru, ra] *m* butcher.

acre ['akri] *adj* **-1.** [ácido, amargo] acrid. **-2.** *fig* [áspero] harsh.

acreditar [akredʒi'ta(x)] *⟨⟩ vt* **-1.** [crer] to believe. **-2.** [abonar] to confirm. *⟨⟩ vi* **-1.** [crer]: **~ em algo/alguém** to believe in sthg/sb. **-2.** [confiar]: **~ em algo/ alguém** to have confidence in sthg/ sb.

acrescentar [akresẽn'ta(x)] *vt* to add.

acréscimo [a'kresimu] *m* **-1.** [adição] addition. **-2.** [aumento] increase.

acrílico [a'kriliku] *m* acrylic.

acrobacia [akroba'sia] *f* acrobatics *(pl)*.

acrobata [akro'bata] *mf* acrobat.

acuado, da [a'kuadu, da] *adj* [acossado] cornered.

açúcar [a'suka(x)] *m* sugar; **~ mascavo** brown sugar.

açucareiro [asuka'rejru] *m* sugar bowl.

açude [a'sudʒi] *m* dam.

acudir [aku'dʒi(x)] *⟨⟩ vt* to run to help. *⟨⟩ vi* to rush to sb's aid.

acumular [akumu'la(x)] *vt* **-1.** [ajuntar] to accrue. **-2.** [amontoar] to accumulate. **-3.** [reunir] to collate. **-4.** [cargos] to combine.

acúmulo [a'kumulu] *m* accumulation.

acupuntura [akupũn'tural] *f* acupuncture.

acusação [akuza'sãw] *(pl*-ões) *f* **-1.** [incriminação] accusation. **-2.** [promotoria]: **a ~** the prosecution.

acusado, da [aku'zadu, da] *m, f* [réu] defendant.

acusar [aku'za(x)] *vt* **-1.** [gen]: **~ alguém (de algo)** to accuse sb (of sthg). **-2.** *JUR*:

~ alguém de algo to charge sb with sthg. **-3.** [mostrar] to reveal.

acústico, ca [a'kuʃtʃiku, ka] *adj* acoustic.
　acústica *f* *FÍS* acoustics.

AD (*abrev de* **Anno Domini**) AD.

adaptação [adapta'sãw] *(pl*-ões) *f* adaptation.

adaptar [adap'ta(x)] *vt* **-1.** [fixar] to fit. **-2.** [peça teatral, música, linguagem] to adapt.
　adaptar-se *vp* [ambientar-se] to adapt o.s.

adega [a'dɛga] *f* cellar.

ademais [adʒi'majʃ] *adv* [além disso] moreover.

adentro [a'dẽntru] *adv*: **casa/noite ~** into the house/night; **mar ~** out to sea.

adepto, ta [a'dɛptu, ta] *m, f*: **~ (de)** follower (of).

adequado, da [ade'kwadu, da] *adj* appropriate.

adequar [ade'kwa(x)] *vt*: **~ algo a algo** to adapt sthg to sthg.

aderente [ade'rẽntʃi] *⟨⟩ adj* [substância] adhesive. *⟨⟩ mf* [adepto] adherent.

aderir [ade'ri(x)] *vi* **-1.** [colar-se] to stick. **-2.** [a partido, campanha] to adhere. **-3.** [a moda, estilo de vida] to follow.

adesão [ade'zãw] *(pl*-ões) *f* [a partido, campanha] adhesion; **documento de ~** petition.

adesivo, va [ade'zivu, va] *adj* adhesive.
　adesivo *m* Sellotape® *UK*, Scotch tape® *US*.

adestramento [adeʃtra'mẽntu] *m* training.

adestrar [adeʃ'tra(x)] *vt* to train.

adeus [a'dewʃ] *⟨⟩ m* farewell. *⟨⟩ interj* goodbye!

adiamento [adʒia'mẽntu] *m* [prorrogação] postponement.

adiantado, da [adʒiãn'tadu, da] *adj* **-1.** [trabalho] ahead of schedule. **-2.** [relógio] fast. **-3.** [pagamento] advance *(antes de subst)*. **-4.** [aluno, povo] advanced.
　adiantado *adv*: **pagar ~** to pay in advance; **cheguei ~ ao encontro** I arrived early for the meeting.

adiantamento [adʒiãnta'mẽntu] *m* **-1.** [progresso] progress. **-2.** [de quantia, salário] advance.

adiantar [adʒiãn'ta(x)] *⟨⟩ vt* **-1.** [trabalho] to get ahead with. **-2.** [relógio] to put forward. **-3.** [quantia, salário] to advance. **-4.** [dizer antecipadamente] to anticipate. *⟨⟩ vi* **-1.** [relógio] to be fast. **-2.** [trazer benefício]: **~ fazer algo** to be worth doing sthg.
　adiantar-se *vp* [em trabalho, estudos] to get ahead.

adiante [a'dʒjãntʃi] adv -1. [na frente] ahead; mais ~ [no espaço] further on; [no tempo] later on. -2. levar algo ~ [obra, plano] to go ahead with sthg.

adiar [a'dʒja(x)] vt to postpone.

adição [adʒi'sãw] (pl -ões) f -1. [acréscimo] addition. -2. MAT sum.

adicionar [adʒisjo'na(x)] vt -1. [acrescentar] to add. -2. MAT to add up.

adido, da [a'dʒidu, da] m,f [em embaixada] attaché.

adivinhar [adʒivi'ɲa(x)] vt -1. [presente, futuro] to predict. -2. [resposta, causa, intenção] to guess. -3. [enigma, mistério] to solve.

adivinho, nha [adʒi'viɲu, ɲa] m,f fortune-teller.

adjacências [adʒa'sẽsjaʃ] fpl neighbourhood.

adjacente [adʒa'sẽtʃi] adj adjacent.

adjetivo [adʒe'tʃivu] m adjective.

adjudicação [adʒudʒika'sãw] (pl -ões) f JUR adjudication.

adjudicar [adʒudʒi'ka(x)] vt JUR : ~ algo a alguém to adjudicate sthg for sb.

adjunto, ta [ad'ʒũntu, ta] <> adj [assistente] assistant. <> m, f -1. [assistente] assistant. -2. GRAM adjunct.

administração [adʒiminiʃtra'sãw] (pl -ões) f -1. [ger] administration; ~ de empresas [curso] business studies. -2. [pessoal] management.

administrador, ra [adʒiminiʃtra'do(x), ra] (mpl -es, fpl -s) m, f administrator.

administrar [adʒiminiʃ'tra(x)] vt -1. [gerir] to manage. -2. [dar] to administer.

administrativo, va [adʒiminiʃtra'tʃivu, va] adj administrative.

admiração [adʒimira'sãw] f -1. [respeito] admiration. -2. [surpresa] surprise.

admirado, da [adʒimi'radu, da] adj [respeitado] admired.

admirador, ra [adʒimira'do(x), ra] m, f admirer.

admirar [adʒimi'ra(x)] <> vt -1. [respeitar, contemplar] to admire. -2. [surpreender] to surprise. <> vi [surpreender] to be astounding; não é de ~ (que ...) it's no wonder (that ...).
➝ **admirar-se** vp -1. [mutuamente] to admire each other. -2. [surpreender-se]: ~-se (de algo) to be surprised (at sthg).

admirável [adʒimi'ravɛw] (pl -eis) adj -1. [excelente] admirable. -2. [assombroso] amazing.

admissão [adʒimi'sãw] (pl -ões) f -1. [ger] admission. -2. [contratação] employment.

admitir [adʒimi'tʃi(x)] vt -1. [ger] to admit. -2. [aceitar] to tolerate. -3. [consentir em] to permit. -4. [contratar] to take on. -5. [comportar] to allow.

admoestação [adʒmweʃta'sãw] (pl -ões) f -1. [advertência] warning. -2. [reprimenda] reprimand.

ADN (abrev de ácido desoxirribonucleico) m DNA.

adoçante [ado'sãntʃi] m sweetener.

adoção [ado'sãw] (pl -ões) [-õjʃ] f adoption.

adoçar [ado'sa(x)] vt -1. [café, chá] to sweeten. -2. fig [velhice, vida] to ease.

adoecer [adwe'se(x)] <> vi: ~ (de) to fall ill (with). <> vt to make ill.

adoidado, da [adoj'dadu, da] <> adj [amalucado] mad. <> adv fam [muito] madly.

adolescência [adole'sẽsja] f adolescence.

adolescente [adole'sẽtʃi] <> adj adolescent. <> mf adolescent.

adorar [ado'ra(x)] vt -1. [divindade] to adore. -2. [gostar muito de] to love.

adorável [ado'ravɛw] (pl -eis) adj lovely.

adormecer [adoxme'se(x)] <> vi -1. [dormir] to fall asleep. -2. [ficar dormente] to go numb. <> vt [causar sono a] to make sleepy.

adornar [adox'na(x)] vt to adorn.

adorno [a'doxnu] m adornment.

adotar [ado'ta(x)] vt to adopt.

adotivo, va [ado'tʃivu, va] adj adoptive.

adquirir [adʒiki'ri(x)] vt -1. [comprar] to buy. -2. [conseguir] to acquire.

adro ['adrul] m churchyard.

aduana [a'dwana] f customs (pl).

aduaneiro, ra [adwa'nejru, ra] adj customs (pl).

adubar [adu'ba(x)] vt to fertilize.

adubo [a'dubu] m [fertilizante] fertilizer; ~ orgânico/químico organic/chemical fertilizer.

adulação [adula'sãw] f flattery.

adular [adu'la(x)] vt to flatter.

adulterar [aduwte'ra(x)] vt -1. [texto] to falsify. -2. [alimento, medicamento] to adulterate.

adultério [aduw'tɛrju] m adultery.

adúltero, ra [a'duwteru, ra] <> adj adulterous. <> m, f adulterer (f adulteress).

adulto, ta [a'duwtu, ta] <> adj adult. <> m, f adult.

advento [adʒ'vẽntu] m advent.

advérbio [adʒ'vɛxbjul] m adverb.

adversário, ria [adʒivex'sarju, rja] m, f adversary.

adversidade [adʒivexsi'dadʒi] f adversity.

adverso, sa [adʒi'vɛxsu, sa] *adj* [difícil] adverse.

advertência [adʒivex'tẽnsja] *f* -1. [aviso] warning. -2. [repreensão] reprimand.

advertir [adʒivex'tʃi(x)] *vt* -1. [prevenir, avisar] to warn. -2. [repreender] to reprimand.

advir [adʒi'vi(x)] *vi* [resultar]: ~ **de** to result from.

advocacia [adʒivoka'sia] *f* advocacy.

advogado, da [adʒivo'gadu, da] *m, f* lawyer.

advogar [adʒivo'ga(x)] ⬦ *vt* -1. JUR to advocate. -2. *fig* [defender] to defend. ⬦ *vi* [exercer a profissão de advogado] to practise law.

aéreo, rea [a'ɛrju, rja] *adj* -1. AERON air *(antes de subst)*. -2. [pessoa] absent-minded.

aerobarco [aɛro'baxku] *m* hovercraft.

aeróbico, ca [ae'rɔbiku, ka] *adj* aerobic.
  ⬥ **aeróbica** *f* aerobics *(sg)*.

aeroclube [aɛro'klubi] *m* flying club.

aerodinâmico, ca [aɛrodʒi'nãmiku, ka] *adj* aerodynamic.
  ⬥ **aerodinâmica** *f* aerodynamics *(pl)*.

aeródromo [aɛ'rɔdromul] *m* airfield.

aerograma [aɛro'grama] *m* aerogramme UK, aerogram US.

aeromoça [aɛro'mosa] *f* air stewardess, flight attendant.

aeronáutica [aɛro'nawtʃika] *f* -1. [ciência] aeronautics *(sg)*. -2. MIL air force.

aeronave [aɛro'navi] *f* aircraft.

aeroporto [aɛro'poxtu] *m* airport.

afã [a'fã] *m* -1. [ânsia - por sucesso] longing; [- de agradar] eagerness; [- para fazer algo] urge. -2. [entusiasmo, vontade] enthusiasm.

afabilidade [afabili'dadʒi] *f* affability.

afagar [afa'ga(x)] *vt* -1. [person] to caress. -2. [animal, hair] to stroke.

afamado, da [afa'madu, da] *adj* famous.

afanar [afa'na(x)] *vt fam* [roubar] to nick, to steal.

afastado, da [afaʃ'tadu, da] *adj* -1. [praia, terras] remote. -2. [casa] isolated. -3. [parente] distant. -4. [pernas] apart.

afastamento [afaʃta'mẽntul] *m* -1. [distanciamento] withdrawal. -2. [de cargo] removal.

afastar [afaʃ'ta(x)] *vt* -1. [tirar do caminho] to push out of the way. -2. [apartar] to put aside. -3. [pôr de lado] to part. -4. [distanciar] to keep away *(sep)*. -5. [de cargo] to remove. -6. [frustrar] to thwart.
  ⬥ **afastar-se** *vp* -1. [distanciar-se - no espaço] to move aside *(sep)*; [- de amigos etc.] to part. -2. [sair] to leave. -3. [de cargo] to take leave from.

afável [a'favɛwl] *(pl* -eis*)* *adj* affable.

afazeres [afa'zeriʃ] *mpl* affairs; ~ **domésticos** housework *(sg)*.

afeição [afej'sãwl] *f* affection; **sentir** ~ **por alguém/algo** to feel affection for sb/sthg.

afeiçoado, da [afej'swadu, da] *adj* attached.

afeiçoar-se [afej'swaxsi] *vp*: ~ **a alguém/algo** to become attached to sb/sthg.

afeito, ta [a'fejtu, ta] *adj*: ~ **a** accustomed to.

aferir [afe'ri(x)] *vt* -1. [conferir] to check. -2. [avaliar] to estimate. -3. [cotejar]: ~ **algo/alguém por algo** to judge sthg/sb by sthg.

aferrado, da [afe'xadu, da] *adj* [apegado] attached.

aferrar-se [afe'xaxsi] *vp* [apegar-se]: ~ **a algo** to cling to sthg.

afetado, da [afe'tadu, da] *adj* affected.

afetar [afe'ta(x)] *vt* to affect.

afetividade [afetʃivi'dadʒi] *f* -1. affection. -2. PSIC affectivity.

afetivo, va [afe'tʃivu, va] *adj* -1. affectionate, kind. -2. PSIC affective.

afeto [a'fɛtul] *m* -1. affection. -2. PSIC affect.

afetuoso, osa [afe'tuozu, ɔza] *adj* affectionate.

afiado, da [a'fjadu, da] *adj* sharp.

afiançar [afjãn'sa(x)] *vt* -1. [réu] to bail out. -2. [dívida, empréstimo] to guarantee.

afiar [a'fja(x)] *vt* [faca, tesoura] to sharpen.

aficionado, da [afisjo'nadu, da] *m, f* enthusiast.

afilhado, da [afi'ʎadu, da] *m, f* godchild.

afiliar [afi'lja(x)] *vt* to affiliate.
  ⬥ **afiliar-se** *vp*: ~-**se a algo** to join sthg.

afim [a'fĩ] *(pl* -ns*)* *adj* -1. [objetivos] similar. -2. [almas] kindred.

afinado, da [afi'nadu, da] *adj* -1. [instrumento] tuned. -2. [pessoa]: ~ **com** attuned to.

afinal [afi'nawl] *adv* -1. [por fim] finally, in the end; ~ , **ele vem ou não vem?** so is he coming or not?; ~ **(de contas)** in the end. -2. [pensando bem] all things considered.

afinar [afi'na(x)] ⬦ *vt* [voz, instrumento] to tune. ⬦ *vi* -1. [emagrecer] to slim down. -2. [concordar]: ~ **com alguém em algo** to see eye to eye with sb over sthg.

afinco [a'fĩŋkul] *m* perseverance; **com** ~ assiduously.

afinidade [afini'dadʒi] f [semelhança] affinity.

afins [a'fĩʃ] pl ▷ **afim**.

afirmação [afixma'sãw] (pl -ões) f -1. [declaração] assertion. -2. [auto-afirmação] self-assertion.

afirmar [afix'ma(x)] vt -1. [declarar] to declare. -2. [confirmar] to assert.

➡ **afirmar-se** vp -1. [estabelecer-se] to establish o.s. -2. [sentir-se seguro] to assert o.s.

afirmativo, va [afixma'tʃivu, va] adj affirmative.

➡ **afirmativa** f assertion.

afivelar [afive'la(x)] vt to buckle.

afixar [afik'sa(x)] vt [aviso, cartaz] to affix.

aflição [afli'sãw] (pl -ões) f -1. [sofrimento] distress (U). -2. [ansiedade] anxiety. -3. [desconforto] : **dar** ~ **a alguém** to unsettle sb.

afligir [afli'ʒi(x)] vt -1. [fazer sofrer] to distress. -2. [causar ansiedade a] to trouble. -3. [suj: mal] to torment.

➡ **afligir-se** vp: ~ -**se (com)** to worry (about).

aflito, ta [a'flitu, ta] adj distressed; **estar** ~ **com algo/para fazer algo** to be desperate about sthg/to do sthg.

aflorar [aflo'ra(x)] vi -1. [vir à tona] to come to the surface. -2. [surgir] to surface.

afluência [aflu'ẽnsja] f -1. [de líquido] flow. -2. [de pessoas] flood. -3. [riqueza] affluence.

afluente [aflu'ẽntʃi] ◇ adj [rico] affluent. ◇ m [curso de rio] tributary.

afluir [a'flwi(x)] vt: ~ **a** ou **para/de** to flow into ou towards/from; [pessoas] to flock into ou towards/from.

afobação [afoba'sãw] f -1. [agitação, atrapalhação] turmoil. -2. [pressa] haste. -3. [ansiedade] anxiety.

afobado, da [afo'badu, da] adj -1. [ger] flustered. -2. [ansioso] upset.

afobamento [afoba'mẽntu] m = **afobação**.

afobar [afo'ba(x)] vt -1. [ger] to fluster. -2. [deixar ansioso] to perturb.

➡ **afobar-se** vp -1. [ficar agitado] to get flustered. -2. [apressar-se] to fret. -3. [ficar ansioso] to worry.

afogado, da [afo'gadu, da] adj -1. [pessoa] drowned. -2. [motor] flooded. -3. [em dívidas] weighed down. -4. [em trabalho] swamped.

afogador [afoga'do(x)] (pl -es) m AUTO choke.

afogamento [afoga'mẽntu] m drowning.

afogar [afo'ga(x)] ◇ vt -1. [pessoa] to drown. -2. [motor] to flood. -3. [pensamentos, sentimento] to quell. ◇ vi -1. [pessoa] to drown. -2. [motor] to flood.

➡ **afogar-se** vp [pessoa] to drown o.s.

afoito, ta [a'fojtu, ta] adj in a hurry (depois de subst/de verbo).

afônico, ca [a'foniku, ka] adj silent.

afora [a'fɔra] ◇ adv: **pelo mundo** ~ throughout the world; **mar** ~ across the sea; **pela vida** ~ throughout life; **sair** ou **ir por aí** ~ to go off; **porta** ~ out the door. ◇ prep apart from.

afortunado, da [afoxtu'nadu, da] adj fortunate.

Afoxés [a'foʃɛʃ] mpl traditional groups who parade through the streets during Carnival.

afresco [a'freʃku] m fresco.

África ['afrikal] n Africa.

africano, na [afri'kãnu, na] ◇ adj African. ◇ m, f African.

afro-americano, na [afrwameri'kãnu, na] ◇ adj Afro-American. ◇ m, f Afro-American.

afro-brasileiro, ra [afrobrazi'lejru, ra] adj Afro-Brazilian.

afronta [a'frõnta] f affront.

afrontar [afrõn'ta(x)] vt -1. [ultrajar] to outrage. -2. [atacar] to confront.

afrouxar [afro'ʃa(x)] ◇ vt -1. [soltar] to loosen. -2. [relaxar] to relax. ◇ vi -1. [soltar-se] to come undone. -2. [pessoa] to give up.

afta ['afta] f mouth ulcer.

afugentar [afuʒẽn'ta(x)] vt to chase away.

afundar [afũn'da(x)] ◇ vt -1. [fazer ir ao fundo - pessoa] to force to the ground; [- âncora] to drop. -2. [aprofundar] to deepen. ◇ vi to sink.

➡ **afundar-se** vp -1. fam [em exame] to fail. -2. [embrenhar-se - em afazeres] to become engulfed; [- no matagal] to go deep. -3. [imergir] to sink. -4. [perder-se] to lose o.s.

agá [a'gal] m aitch.

agachar-se [aga'ʃaxsi] vp -1. [acocorar-se] to squat. -2. fig [aviltar-se] to grovel.

agarrado, da [aga'xadu, da] adj -1. [preso com força]: ~ **a** ou **em algo** clinging to ou sthg. -2. [apegado]: ~ **a** ou **com alguém** clinging to ou sb.

agarrar [aga'xa(x)] ◇ vt -1. [segurar com força] to grasp. -2. [capturar] to catch. ◇ vi -1. [segurar com força]: ~ **em** to hold on to. -2. [goleiro] to defend.

➡ **agarrar-se** vp -1. [segurar com força]: ~ -**se a** ou **em** to hold on to. -2. [abraçar fortemente] to cling to each other.

agasalhar [agaza'ʎa(x)] *vt* to wrap up warmly.
◆ **agasalhar-se** *vp* to wrap o.s. up warmly.

agasalho [aga'zaʎul] *m* **-1.** [casaco, manta] warm clothing. **-2.** [suéter] jumper.

ágeis ['aʒejʃ] *pl* ▷ **ágil**.

agência [a'ʒẽsja] *f* **-1.** [empresa] agency; ~ **de viagens** travel agency. **-2.** [sucursal] branch; ~ **de correios** post-office branch.

agenciamento [a'ʒẽsjamẽntul] *m* **-1.** [negociação] negotiation. **-2.** [representação] representation. **-3.** [obtenção, busca] recruitment.

agenciar [a'ʒẽsja(x)] *vt* **-1.** [ger] to manage. **-2.** [servir de agente a] to act as agent for.

agenda [a'ʒẽnda] *f* **-1.** [de compromissos] diary. **-2.** [programação - de semana] schedule.

agente [a'ʒẽntʃi] ◇ *m, f* [pessoa] agent; ~ **secreto** secret agent. ◇ *m* **-1.** [ger] agent. **-2.** *GRAM* subject.

ágil ['aʒiw] (*pl* **ágeis**) *adj* agile.

agilidade [aʒili'dadʒi] *f* agility.

ágio ['aʒju] *m* interest.

agiota [a'ʒjɔta] *m, f* [usurário] usurer.

agir [a'ʒi(x)] *vi* to act; ~ **bem/mal** to act properly/wrongly.

agitação [aʒita'sãw] (*pl* **-ões**) *f* **-1.** [movimento - de garrafa] shaking; [- de líquido] stirring; [- de braços] waving. **-2.** *PSIC* [excitação] agitation. **-3.** [inquietação] restlessness. **-4.** [rebuliço] agitation. **-5.** [política, social] unrest.

agitado, da [aʒi'tadu, da] *adj* **-1.** [excitado] agitated. **-2.** [inquieto] disturbed. **-3.** [tumultuado] unsettled. **-4.** [mar] rough.

agitar [aʒi'ta(x)] ◇ *vt* **-1.** [movimentar - garrafa etc.] to shake; [- líquido] to stir; [- braços] to wave. **-2.** [excitar] to unnerve. **-3.** [inquietar] to worry. **-4.** [sublevar] to agitate. **-5.** *fam* [fazer, organizar] to organize. ◇ *vi* [movimentar]: **'agite antes de usar'** 'shake before use'.
◆ **agitar-se** *vp* **-1.** [inquietar-se] to become agitated. **-2.** [movimentar-se - na cama] to be restless; [- na rua, no trabalho etc.] to run around.

aglomeração [aglomera'sãw] (*pl* **-ões**) *f* **-1.** [de coisas] stack. **-2.** [de pessoas] mass.

aglomerado [aglome'radul] *m* **-1.** [de coisas] pile. **-2.** [de pessoas] mass.

aglomerar [aglome'ra(x)] *vt* to mass.
◆ **aglomerar-se** *vp* [pessoas] to swarm.

aglutinação [aglutʃina'sãw] *f* **-1.** [fusão] agglutination. **-2.** [combinação] almagamation.

ago. (*abrev de* **agosto**) Aug.

agonia [ago'nia] *f* **-1.** [ger] agony. **-2.** [de moribundo] death throes (*pl*). **-3.** *fig* [declínio] decline.

agonizante [agoni'zãntʃi] *adj* dying.

agonizar [agoni'za(x)] *vi* to be dying.

agora [a'gɔra] ◇ *adv* **-1.** [neste momento] now; ~ **mesmo** right now; [há pouco] just now; **até** ~ until now; **de** ~ **em diante** from now on. **-2.** [atualmente] nowadays. **-3.** [doravante] from now on. ◇ *conj* [mas] now.

agosto [a'goʃtul] *m* August; *veja também* **setembro**.

agourar [ago'ra(x)] ◇ *vt* [pressagiar] to portend. ◇ *vi* [fazer mau agouro] to bode ill.

agouro [a'gorul] *m* omen; **mau** ~ bad omen.

agradar [agra'da(x)] ◇ *vt* [causar prazer a] to please. ◇ *vi* **-1.** [satisfazer]: ~ **(a) alguém** to please sb. **-2.** [aprazer]: ~ **a** to delight. **-3.** [ser agradável] to please, to be pleasing.

agradável [agra'davew] (*pl* **-eis**) *adj* pleasant.

agradecer [agrade'se(x)] ◇ *vt*: ~ **algo** to say thank you for sthg. ◇ *vi* **-1.** [dizer obrigado] to say thank you; ~ **a alguém por algo** to thank sb for sthg. **-2.** [ficar grato] to be grateful.

agradecido, da [agrade'sidu, da] *adj* grateful.

agradecimento [agradesi'mẽntul] *m* [gratidão] thanks (*pl*), thank you; **carta de** ~ thank-you letter.
◆ **agradecimentos** *mpl* thanks.

agrado [a'gradul] *m*: **fazer um** ~ **a alguém** [presentear] to give sb a present; [acariciar] to be affectionate with sb.

agrário, ria [a'grarju, rja] *adj* agrarian.

agravamento [agrava'mẽntul] *m* worsening.

agravante [agra'vãntʃi] ◇ *adj* aggravating. ◇ *m* [o que piora a situação]: **o agravante é que ...** the annoying thing is that ...

agravar [agra'va(x)] *vt* [piorar] to worsen.
◆ **agravar-se** *vp* [piorar] to worsen.

agravo [a'gravul] *m* *JUR* appeal.

agredir [agre'dʒi(x)] *vt* **-1.** [atacar] to attack. **-2.** [insultar] to insult. **-3.** *fig* [afetar] to offend.

agregado, da [agre'gadu, da] ◇ *adj* attached. ◇ *m, f* [hóspede] guest.

agregar [agre'ga(x)] *vt* to add.

agressão [agre'sãw] (*pl* **-ões**) *f* aggression.

agressivo, va [agre'sivu, va] *adj* aggressive.

agressor, ra [agre'so(x), ra] *m, f* aggressor.

agreste [a'grɛʃtʃi] ◇ *adj* rural. ◇ *m*

stony, unfertile area of north-eastern Brazil.

agrião [agri'ãw] (pl **-ões**) m watercress.

agrícola [a'grikola] adj agricultural.

agricultor, ra [agrikuw'to(x), ra] m, f farmer.

agricultura [agrikuw'tura] f agriculture; ~ **orgânica** organic farming.

agridoce [agri'dosi] adj **-1.** [comida] sweet and sour. **-2.** [emoções] bittersweet.

agronomia [agrono'mia] f agronomy.

agropecuário, ria [agrope'kwarju, rja] adj mixed-farming (antes de subst).
➡ **agropecuária** f mixed farming.

agrupar [agru'pa(x)] vt to collect.
➡ **agrupar-se** vp to be grouped together.

água ['agwa] f **-1.** water; ~ **corrente** running water; ~ **doce/salgada** fresh/salt water; **peixe de** ~ **doce** freshwater fish; ~ **mineral/gasosa/sem gás** mineral/sparkling/still water; ~ **oxigenada** hydrogen peroxide; ~ **sanitária** chemically purified water; **com** ~ **na boca** watering at the mouth. **-2.** fig [plano]: **ir por** ~ **abaixo** to go down the drain.

aguaceiro [agwa'sejru] m downpour.

água-de-coco [,agwadʒi'koku] f coconut milk.

água-de-colônia [,agwadʒiko'lonja] (pl **águas-de-colônia**) f eau de cologne.

aguado, da [a'gwadu, da] adj watereddown.

água-furtada [,agwafux'tada] (pl **águas-furtadas**) f garret.

aguar [a'gwa(x)] vt **-1.** [diluir] to water down. **-2.** [regar] to water.

aguardar [agwax'da(x)] ⋄ vt to await. ⋄ vi to wait.

aguardente [agwax'dẽntʃi] f brandy; ~ **de cana** cachaça.

aguarrás [agwa'xaʃ] f turpentine.

água-viva [,agwa'viva] (pl **águas-vivas**) f jellyfish.

aguçado, da [agu'sadu, da] adj **-1.** [ger] sharp. **-2.** [apetite] keen; [interesse] lively.

agudo, da [a'gudu, da] adj **-1.** [ger] acute. **-2.** [penetrante] sharp. **-3.** [nota, voz] shrill.

agüentar [agwẽn'ta(x)] ⋄ vt **-1.** [ger] to bear; ~ **fazer algo** to be able to bear to do sthg. **-2.** [tolerar] to put up with. ⋄ vi [resistir] to support; **não** ~ **de algo** to be unable to bear sthg.

águia ['agja] f **-1.** [ave] eagle. **-2.** fig [pessoa] talented person.

agulha [a'guʎa] f needle.

ai [,aj] ⋄ interj **-1.** [de dor] ouch! **-2.** [de cócegas] eek! **-3.** [suspiro] oh! **-4.** [lamento] oh dear! **-5.** [gemido] oh no! ⋄ m [de dor] groan.
➡ **ai de** loc adj damn.

aí [a'i] ⋄ adv **-1.** [ger] there; **espera** ~! wait there! **-2.** [em lugar indeterminado] **por** ~ around. **-3.** [junto, em anexo] herewith. **-4.** [nesse caso, então] then.
➡ **aí agora** loc adv just now.
➡ **aí ainda bem** loc adv just as well.
➡ **ainda por cima** loc adv still; **ele não ajuda, e** ~ **por cima reclama** he's not helping, and on top of that he's complaining.
➡ **ainda que** loc conj even if.

AIDS (abrev de **Acquired Immunodeficiency Syndrome**) f AIDS.

ainda [a'ĩnda] adv **-1.** [ger] still; ~ **não** not yet; ~ **(assim)** still. **-2.** [um dia] one day.
➡ **ainda agora** loc adv just now.
➡ **ainda bem** loc adv just as well.
➡ **ainda por cima** loc adv still; **ele não ajuda, e** ~ **por cima reclama** he's not helping, and on top of that he's complaining.
➡ **ainda que** loc conj even if.

aipim [aj'pĩ] (pl **-ns**) m cassava.

aipo ['ajpu] m celery.

ajeitar [aʒej'ta(x)] vt **-1.** [endireitar] to straighten. **-2.** [arrumar] to tidy up. **-3.** [acomodar] to tuck up.
➡ **ajeitar-se** vp **-1.** [arrumar-se] to tidy o.s. up. **-2.** [a emprego] to adapt. **-3.** [acomodar-se] to settle down.

ajoelhado, da [aʒwe'ʎadu, da] adj kneeling.

ajoelhar [aʒwe'ʎa(x)] vi to kneel.
➡ **ajoelhar-se** vp to kneel down.

ajuda [a'ʒuda] f **-1.** [auxílio] help; **dar** ~ **a alguém (em algo)** to help sb (with sthg). **-2.** ECON & POL aid; ~ **de custo** financial assistance.

ajudante [aʒu'dãntʃi] mf assistant.

ajudar [aʒu'da(x)] ⋄ vt **-1.** [auxiliar]: **alguém (em algo)** to help sb (with sthg); ~ **alguém a fazer algo** to help sb do sthg. **-2.** [facilitar] to help. ⋄ vi **-1.** [auxiliar] to help; ~ **a alguém** to help sb; ~ **em algo** to help with sthg. **-2.** [facilitar] to help.
➡ **ajudar-se** vp to help each other.

ajuizado, da [aʒwi'zadu, da] adj sensible.

ajuntamento [aʒũnta'mẽntu] m **-1.** [de pessoas] gathering. **-2.** [de objetos] pile.

ajuntar [aʒũn'ta(x)] vt **-1.** [reunir] to assemble. **-2.** [acrescentar] to add.

ajustável [aʒuʃ'tavew] (pl **-eis**) adj adjustable.

ajuste [a'ʒuʃtʃi] m **-1.** [acordo] agreement. **-2.** [de peça - encaixe] fitting; [- aperto] tightening. **-3.** [regulagem] adjustment. **-4.** [acerto]: ~ **de contas** settlement of accounts; fig settling of scores.

alérgico

AL (*abrev de* **Estado de Alagoas**) *n State of Alagoas*.

ala ['alal *f* -**1.** [ger] wing. -**2.** [de escola de samba] group; **a ~ das baianas** *the section of the carnival parade made up of women wearing typical Bahia costumes*.

Alá [a'lal *m* Allah.

alagar [ala'ga(x)] *vt* to flood.

ALALC (*abrev de* **Associação Latino-Americana de Livre Comércio**) *f Latin-American free trade association*.

alambique [alān'bikil *m* still (*for making alcohol*).

alameda [ala'medal *f* avenue.

alarde [a'laxdʒil *m* -**1.** [ostentação] ostentation. -**2.** [bazófia] boastfulness; **fazer ~ de algo** to brag about sthg.

alardear [alax'dʒja(x)] *vt* -**1.** [ostentar] to parade. -**2.** [gabar-se de] to brag about.

alargar [alax'ga(x)] *vt* -**1.** [estrada] to widen. -**2.** [roupa] to let out.

alarido [ala'ridul *m* [gritaria, algazarra] uproar.

alarmante [alax'mãntʃil *adj* alarming.

alarmar [alax'ma(x)] *vt* to alarm.
 ◆ **alarmar-se** *vp* to become alarmed.

alarme [a'laxmil *m* alarm; **dar o ~** to sound the alarm.

alastrar [alaʃ'tra(x)] *vt* [propagar, espalhar] to spread.
 ◆ **alastrar-se** *vp* to spread.

alavanca [ala'vãŋka] *f* -**1.** [peça] lever; **~ de mudanças** *AUTO* gear lever. -**2.** *fig* [meio de ação] lever.

Albânia [aw'bãnja] *n* Albania.

albergue [aw'bɛxgil *m* -**1.** [hospedaria] hostel; [para jovens] youth hostel. -**2.** [asilo] refuge.

álbum ['awbũl (*pl* -**ns**) *m* album.

ALCA (*abrev de* **Área de Livre Comércio das Américas**) *f* FTAA.

alça ['awsal *f* [de mala, vestido] strap.

alcachofra [awka'ʃofral *f* artichoke.

alçada [aw'sadal *f* -**1.** [competência] competence; **ser da ~ de alguém** to be sb's responsibility. -**2.** *JUR* jurisdiction.

alcançar [awkãn'sa(x)] *vt* -**1.** [ger] to reach. -**2.** [pegar] to catch. -**3.** [entender] to grasp. -**4.** [conseguir] to attain.

alcance [aw'kãnsil *m* -**1.** [de arma, míssil] range. -**2.** [de pessoa]: **ao meu/ao teu ~** within my/your reach; **ao ~ da vista** within sight; **fora do ~ de** [objeto, pessoa] out of reach of; [entendimento] beyond the grasp of.

alçapão [awsa'pãw] (*pl* -**ões**) *m* -**1.** [portinhola] trapdoor. -**2.** [armadilha] trap.

alcaparra [awka'paxal *f* caper.

alçar [aw'sa(x)] *vt* -**1.** [levantar - carga, viga]

to lift; [- braço] to raise. -**2.** [voz] to raise. -**3.** [vôo] to rise.

alcatéia [awka'tɛjal *f* [de lobos] pack.

alcatrão [awka'trãw] *m* tar.

álcool ['awkowl (*pl* -**óis**) *m* alcohol.

alcoólatra [aw'kɔlatral ◇ *adj* alcoholic. ◇ *mf* alcoholic.

alcoólico, ca [aw'kwɔliku, kal *adj* alcoholic.

Alcorão [awko'rãwl *m* Koran.

alcova [aw'koval *f* dressing room.

alcunha [aw'kuɲal *f* nickname.

aldeão, deã [aw'dʒjãw, djal (*mpl* -**ões**, -**ãos**, *fpl* -**s**) *m*, *f* villager.

aldeia [aw'dejal *f* village.

aldraba [aw'drabal *f* [de bater] door-knocker.

aleatório, ria [alea'tɔrju, rjal *adj* random.

alecrim [ale'krĩl *m* rosemary.

alegação [alega'sãwl (*pl* -**ões**) *f* allegation.

alegar [ale'ga(x)] *vt* to allege; **~ que** to allege that; *JUR* to allege that.

alegoria [alego'rial *f* allegory.

alegórico, ca [ale'gɔrikul *adj* allegorical;
 ▷ **carro**.

alegrar [ale'gra(x)] *vt* to cheer up.
 ◆ **alegrar-se** *vp* to be happy; **alegre-se!** cheer up!

alegre [a'lɛgril *adj* -**1.** [pessoa] cheerful. -**2.** [festa, bar, voz] lively. -**3.** [cor] bright. -**4.** [embriagado] merry.

alegria [ale'grial *f* -**1.** [qualidade] cheerfulness. -**2.** [satisfação] contentment. -**3.** [júbilo] joy.

aleijado, da [alej'ʒadu, dal ◇ *adj* crippled. ◇ *m*, *f* cripple.

além [a'lẽjl ◇ *m* [o outro mundo]: **o ~** the beyond. ◇ *adv* -**1.** [em lugar afastado] over there. -**2.** [mais adiante] further on; **mais ~** further.
 ◆ **além de** *loc prep* -**1.** [mais adiante de] beyond. -**2.** [do outro lado de, acima de] beyond. -**3.** [afora] apart from.
 ◆ **além disso** *loc conj* besides.
 ◆ **além do mais** *loc conj* furthermore.

Alemanha [ale'mãɲal *n* Germany.

alemão, mã [ale'mãw, mãl ◇ *adj* German. ◇ *m*, *f* German.
 ◆ **alemão** *m* [língua] German.

alentado, da [alẽn'tadu, dal *adj* -**1.** [animoso] brave. -**2.** [volumoso] bulky. -**3.** [corpulento] stout.

alento [a'lẽntul *m* -**1.** [ânimo] courage. -**2.** [fôlego] breath.

alergia [alex'ʒial *f* *MED* allergy; **ter ~ a algo** to be allergic to sthg.

alérgico, ca [a'lɛxʒiku, kal *adj* *MED* : **~ (a)** allergic (to).

alerta [aˈlɛxta] ◇ *adj* alert. ◇ *adv* alert. ◇ *m* warning.

alertar [alexˈta(x)] *vt*: ~ alguém (de/sobre algo) to alert sb (to sthg).

alfabético, ca [awfaˈbɛtʃiku, ka] *adj* alphabetical.

alfabetização [awfabetʃizaˈsãw] *f* -1. [ato] teaching to read and write. -2. [estado] literacy.

alfabetizado, da [awfabetʃiˈzadu, da] *adj* literate.

alfabeto [awfaˈbɛtu] *m* alphabet.

alface [awˈfasi] *f* lettuce.

alfaiate [awfaˈjatʃi] *m* tailor.

alfândega [awˈfãdega] *f* -1. [administração] customs *(pl)*. -2. [local] customs house.

alfandegário, ria [awfãdeˈgarju, rja] *adj* customs *(antes de subst)*.

alfazema [awfaˈzemal] *f* lavender.

alfinetada [awfineˈtada] *f* -1. [picada de alfinete] pin-prick. -2. [dor] sharp pain. -3. *fig* [dito] stinging remark; **dar uma ~ em alguém** to make a stinging remark to sb.

alfinete [awfiˈnetʃil] *m* -1. *COST* pin. -2. [prendedor]: ~ **de fralda** nappy pin; ~ **de segurança** safety pin. -3. [jóia] pin.

alga [ˈawga] *f* seaweed.

algarismo [awgaˈriʒmu] *m* number.

algazarra [awgaˈzaxa] *f* shouting; **fazer ~** to make a racket.

álgebra [ˈawʒebra] *f* algebra.

algébrico, ca [awˈʒɛbriku, ka] *adj* MAT algebraic.

algemas [awˈʒemaʃ] *fpl* handcuffs.

algo [ˈawgu] ◇ *pron* -1. *(em frases afirmativas)* something. -2. *(em frases interrogativas)* anything. ◇ *adv* somewhat.

algodão [awgoˈdãw] *m* cotton; ~ **(hidrófilo)** cotton wool; **uma camisa de ~** a cotton shirt.

algodoeiro [awgoˈdwejru] *m* cotton plant.

algoz [awˈgoʒ] *m* -1. [carrasco] executioner. -2. [pessoa cruel] cruel person.

alguém [awˈgẽj] ◇ *pron indef* -1. [alguma pessoa] someone; ~ **quebrou este vaso** someone broke this vase; **tem ~ lá embaixo** there's someone downstairs -2. [em frases interrogativas] anybody, anyone; ~ **me telefonou?** did anybody phone me?; ~ **quer mais café?** does anybody want more coffee?; **tem ~ aí?** is anybody there?; ~ **mais** anybody else. -3. [determinada pessoa] somebody; **ele sabia que haveria ~ à sua espera** he knew there would be somebody waiting for him; **você é ~**

que admiro muito you are somebody I admire greatly. -4. *fig* [pessoa importante] somebody; **se um dia eu me tornar ~, lembrarei dos velhos amigos** if one day I become somebody, I'll remember my old friends; **ele é ~ na empresa?** is he somebody in the company?; **ser ~ (na vida)** to be somebody in life. ◇ *m* [uma pessoa]: **esse ~** that person; **um ~** a person.

algum, ma [awˈgũ, mal] *(mpl -ns, fpl -s)* ◇ *adj* -1. [indeterminado] some; **ela morou ~ tempo em Londres** she lived for some time in London; **me dê ~ dinheiro** give me some money; ~ **dia vamos te visitar** some day we'll come and see you -2. [em interrogativas, negativas] any; ~ **problema?** any problems?; **de jeito ou modo ~** in no way; **não há problema ~** there's no problem, there aren't any problems; **em parte alguma do país** nowhere in the country; **coisa alguma** nothing; **não há melhora alguma** there is no improvement, there isn't any improvement. ◇ *pron* -1. [indicando pessoa] somebody; **alguns preferem cinema, outros, teatro** some people prefer the cinema, others the theatre -2. [indicando coisa] one; **abra a caixa de bombons e prove alguns** open the box of sweets and try some -3. [em interrogativas: pessoa] anybody -4. [em interrogativas: coisa] any; ~ **dia** one *ou* some day; **alguma coisa** something, anything; **alguma vez** sometime.

➠ **alguns** *pron pl* some.

➠ **alguma** *f* [evento, feito]: **deve ter lhe acontecido alguma** something must have happened to him; **esse menino aprontou alguma** that boy has been up to something.

alheamento [aʎeaˈmẽtul] *m* [indiferença] indifference.

alheio, alheia [aˈʎeju, aˈʎeja] *adj* -1. [de outra pessoa]: **um problema ~** somebody else's problem. -2. [afastado, abstraído]: ~ **(a)** unaware (of).

alho [ˈaʎu] *m* garlic.

alho-poró [aʎupoˈrɔ] *(pl alhos-porós) m* leek.

alhures [aˈʎuriʃ] *adv* elsewhere.

ali [aˈlil] *adv* -1. [naquele lugar] there; ~ **dentro/fora** in/out there; **logo ~** right there; **por ~** around there. -2. [naquele momento] then.

aliado, da [aˈljadu, dal] ◇ *adj* allied. ◇ *m, f* ally.

➠ **Aliados** *mpl*: **os Aliados** the Allies.

aliança [aˈljãnsal] *f* -1. [pacto] alliance. -2. [anel] wedding ring.

aliar [a'lja(x)] *vt* [qualidades] to combine.
➤ **aliar-se** *vp* [nações] to become allied.

aliás [a'ljajʃ] *adv* **-1.** [a propósito] as a matter of fact. **-2.** [diga-se de passagem] incidentally. **-3.** [ou por outra] or rather.

álibi ['alibi] *m* alibi.

alicate [ali'katʃi] *m* pliers *(pl)*; ~ **de unhas** nail clippers *(pl)*.

alicerce [ali'sexsi] *m* CONSTR foundation.

aliciamento [alisia'mẽtu] *m* [sedução] seduction.

aliciar [ali'sja(x)] *vt* **-1.** [atrair, seduzir] to entice. **-2.** [convocar] to recruit. **-3.** [subornar] to bribe.

alienação [aljena'sãw] *f* **-1.** [falta de consciência, participação] lack of awareness. **-2.** PSIC : ~ **mental** mental illness. **-3.** [de bens] assignment.

alienado, da [alje'nadu, da] *adj* **-1.** [não participante] alienated. **-2.** [louco] insane. **-3.** [bens] assigned.

alienígena [alje'niʒena] *mf* alien.

alijar [ali'ʒa(x)] *vt* **-1.** [carga] to jettison. **-2.** [isentar]: ~ **alguém de algo** to free sb of sthg.

alimentação [alimẽta'sãw] *f* **-1.** [ato] feeding. **-2.** [dieta] diet. **-3.** [de máquina, impressora] feeding. **-4.** ELETR supply.

alimentador [alimẽta'do(x)] *m*: ~ **de papel** paper feed.

alimentar [alimẽ'ta(x)] *(pl* **-es)** <> *adj* alimentary. <> *vt* **-1.** [ger] to feed. **-2.** [nutrir] to feed. **-3.** [esperança] to feed. <> *vi* [nutrir] to provide nourishment.
➤ **alimentar-se** *vp* to feed o.s.; ~ **-se de algo** to live on sthg.

alimentício, cia [alimẽ'tʃisju, sja] *adj* **-1.** [qualidades] nutritious. **-2.** [pensão] maintenance.

alimento [ali'mẽtu] *m* **-1.** [comida] food. **-2.** [nutrição] nourishment.

alinhado, da [ali'ɲadu, da] *adj* **-1.** [posto em linha reta] in a row. **-2.** [elegante] elegant. **-3.** [correto] correct.

alinhar [ali'ɲa(x)] *vt* **-1.** [enfileirar] to line up. **-2.** [estrada] to straighten. **-3.** TIP to justify.

alinhavar [aliɲa'va(x)] *vt* COST to tack UK, to baste.

alíquota [a'likwota] *f* tax rate.

alisar [ali'za(x)] *vt* **-1.** [tornar liso - cama, cabelo] to smooth; [- tábua] to plane. **-2.** [acariciar] to caress.

alistamento [aliʃta'mẽtu] *m* **-1.** [em partido] enrolment. **-2.** MIL enlistment.

alistar [aliʃ'ta(x)] *vt* **-1.** [em partido] to enrol. **-2.** MIL to enlist.
➤ **alistar-se** *vp* **-1.** [em partido] to enrol. **-2.** MIL to enlist.

aliviado, da [ali'vjadu, da] *adj* **-1.** [pessoa - tranqüilizado] relieved; [- folgado] slackened. **-2.** [consciência] relieved. **-3.** [embarcação] lightened.

aliviar [ali'vja(x)] <> *vt* **-1.** [gen] to relieve. **-2.** [folgar] to slacken. **-3.** [desafogar]: ~ **alguém de algo** to unburden sb of sthg. **-4.** [embarcação] to lighten. <> *vi* **-1.** [diminuir] to ease. **-2.** [confortar] to comfort.
➤ **aliviar-se** *vp* to be relieved; ~ **-se de algo** to be relieved of sthg.

alívio [a'livju] *m* relief; **que** ~! what a relief!

alma ['awma] *f* **-1.** [essência humana] soul. **-2.** [espírito desencarnado] spirit. **-3.** [pessoa]: **não ver viva** ~ not to see a living soul. **-4.** [caráter] heart. **-5.** *fig* [de negócio, empresa, partido] essence.

almanaque [awma'naki] *m* almanac.

almejar [awme'ʒa(x)] *vt* to long for; ~ **fazer algo** to long to do sthg.

almirante [awmi'rãtʃi] *m* admiral.

almoçar [awmo'sa(x)] <> *vt* to have for lunch. <> *vi* to have lunch.

almoço [aw'mosu] *m* lunch; **na hora do** ~ at lunchtime; ~ **de negócios** business lunch.

almofada [awmo'fada] *f* cushion.

almôndega [aw'mõdega] *f* meatball.

almoxarifado [awmoʃari'fadu] *m* warehouse.

alô [a'lo] <> *interj* [ao telefone] hello! <> *m* hello.

alocar [alo'ka(x)] *vt* to allocate.

aloirado, da [aloj'radu, da] *adj* fair-haired.

alojamento [aloʒa'mẽtu] *m* **-1.** [ger] accommodation. **-2.** MIL billet.

alojar [alo'ʒa(x)] *vt* **-1.** [hospedar] to accommodate. **-2.** MIL to billet. **-3.** [armazenar] to store.
➤ **alojar-se** *vp* **-1.** [hospedar-se] to stay. **-2.** [acampar] to camp.

alongar [alõ'ga(x)] *vt* **-1.** [ger] to lengthen. **-2.** [perna, braço] to stretch. **-3.** [conversa] to prolong.
➤ **alongar-se** *vp* **-1.** [corpo] to stretch. **-2.** [conversa] to prolong. **-3.** [sobre assunto] to expand.

aloprado, da [alo'pradu, da] *adj fam* crazy.

alourado, da [alow'radu, da], **aloirado, da** [aloj'radu, da] *adj* fair-haired.

alpendre [aw'pẽdril] *m* [telheiro] porch.

Alpes ['awpiʃ] *npl*: **os** ~ the Alps.

alpinismo [awpi'niʒmu] *m* mountaineering.

alpinista [awpi'niʃta] *mf* mountaineer.

alpino, na [aw'pinu, na] *adj* Alpine.

alqueire [aw'kejri] *m measure for land area* = 4.84 *hectares in Rio de Janeiro, Minas Gerais e Goiás and* 2.42 *hectares in São Paulo.*

alquimia [awki'mia] *f* alchemy.

alta ['awta] *f* ▷ **alto**.

altar [aw'ta(x)] *(pl -es) m* altar.

alta-roda [,awta'xɔda] *(pl altas-rodas) f* high society.

alta-tensão [,awtatẽsãw] *(pl altas-tensões) f* high voltage.

altear [awte'a(x)] *vt* -1. [construção] to build. -2. [preço, voz] to raise. -3. [posição]: ~ **sua posição numa firma** to move up within a company.

alteração [awtera'sãw] *(pl -ões) f*-1. [modificação - em gosto, clima, programação] change; [- de texto, roupa] alteration. -2. [perturbação] worry. -3. [tumulto] commotion.

alterar [awte'ra(x)] *vt* -1. [modificar] to change. -2. [perturbar] to worry.
◆ **alterar-se** *vp* [perturbar-se] to be worried.

altercar [awtex'ka(x)] *vi*: ~ **(com)** to quarrel (with).

alternar [awtex'na(x)] ⬥ *vt*: ~ **algo (com)** to alternate sthg (with). ⬥ *vi*: ~ **com** to alternate with.
◆ **alternar-se** *vp* [revezar-se] to alternate; [pessoas] to take turns.

alternativo, va [awtexna'tʃivu, va] *adj* alternative.
◆ **alternativa** *f* alternative.

alteza [aw'teza] *f*: **Sua Alteza** Your Highness.

altissonante [awtʃiso'nãntʃi] *adj* -1. [voz] booming. -2. [orquestra] majestic.

altitude [awtʃi'tudʒi] *f* altitude.

altivez [awtʃi'veʒ] *f* -1. [arrogância] presumption. -2. [dignidade] dignity.

altivo, va [aw'tʃivu, va] *adj* -1. [arrogante] presumptuous. -2. [digno] dignified.

alto, ta ['awtu, ta] *adj* -1. [ger] high; [forte] loud; **ler em voz** ~ to read aloud. -2. [em estatura] tall. -3. *(antes de subst)* [superior] high. -4. *(antes de subst)* [importante - cargo] top; [- negócio] big. -5. *(antes de subst)* [grave - risco] high; [- perigo] grave. -6. *GEOGR* upper. -7. [*MÚS* - tom, nota] high; [- voz, saxofone] alto. -8. *fam* [embriagado] high.
◆ **alto** ⬥ *m* -1. [topo] top. -2. *MÚS* [saxofone] alto. -3. [mando, poder]: **do** ~ from above. ⬥ *adv* -1. [falar] aloud. -2. [voar] high. ⬥ *interj*: **alto!** stop!
◆ **alta** *f*-1. *MED* discharge; **dar/receber** ~ to discharge/to be discharged. -2. [de preços] rise. -3. [de cotação] rise; **estar em** ~ [cotação] to be rising; *fam* [repu-

tação] to be in favour; *fam* [moda] to be highly fashionable.
◆ **por alto** *loc adv* roughly.

alto-falante [,awtufa'lãntʃi] *(pl -s) m* loudspeaker.

alto-mar [,awtu'ma(x)] *(pl altos-mares) m* open sea.

altura [aw'tura] *f* -1. [ger] height; **a dez mil metros de** ~ at an altitude of ten thousand metres. -2. [de som, volume] level. -3. [momento] time. -4. [localização]: **na** ~ **de** close to; **a loja fica na avenida principal, mas em que** ~ **?** the shop is on the main road, but how far up? -5. [nível]: **à** ~ **de** equal to.

alucinação [alusina'sãw] *(pl -ões) f* hallucination.

alucinado, da [alusi'nadu, da] ⬥ *adj* -1. *PSIC* hallucinated. -2. *fig* [apaixonado]: ~ **por** crazy about. -3. *fig* [desvairado] frantic. ⬥ *m, f PSIC* lunatic.

alucinante [alusi'nãntʃi] *adj fam* -1. [enlouquecedor] maddening. -2. [ótimo, incrível] amazing.

aludir [alu'dʒi(x)] *vi*: ~ **a** to allude to.

alugar [alu'ga(x)] *vt* -1. [tomar de aluguel - carro, traje] to hire; [- apartamento] to rent. -2. [dar em aluguel - carro, traje] to hire out; [- apartamento] to rent out. -3. *fam* [incomodar] to annoy.

aluguel [alu'gewl] *(pl -eis) m* -1. [ato - carro] rental; [- apartamento] renting. -2. [pagamento] rent.

alumínio [alu'minju] *m* aluminium *UK*, aluminum *US*.

alunissar [aluni'sa(x)] *vi* to land on the moon.

aluno, na [a'lunu, na] *m, f* pupil.

alusão [alu'zãw] *(pl -ões) f* allusion.

alvejante [awve'ʒãntʃi] ⬥ *adj* bleaching. ⬥ *m* bleach.

alvejar [awve'ʒa(x)] *vt* -1. [mirar em] to aim at. -2. [branquear] to bleach, to whiten.

alvenaria [awvena'ria] *f* masonry; **de** ~ stonework.

alvéolo [al'vewlu] *f* -1. [cavidade] cavity. -2. [*ANAT* - do pulmão]: ~ **pulmonar** alveolus; [- de dente] cavity.

alvo, va ['awvu, 'va] *adj* white.
◆ **alvo** *m* -1. [mira] target; **acertar no** ~ to hit the target. -2. *fig* [objeto]: **ser** ~ **de** to be the target of.

alvorada [awvo'rada] *f* dawn.

alvorecer [awvore'se(x)] ⬥ *m* [alvorada] daybreak. ⬥ *vi* [amanhecer] to dawn.

alvoroçar [awvoro'sa(x)] *vt* -1. [agitar] to stir up. -2. [entusiasmar] to excite.
◆ **alvoroçar-se** *vp* -1. [agitar-se] to be startled. -2. [entusiasmar-se] to get excited.

alvoroço [awvo'rosul *m* [agitação] commotion.

alvura [aw'vura] *f* **-1.** [branqueza] whiteness. **-2.** [pureza] innocence.

AM <> *f* (*abrev de* **Amplitude Modulation**) AM. <> *m* (*abrev de* **Estado do Amazonas**) *State of Amazon.*

amabilidade [amabili'dadʒi] *f* **-1.** [delicadeza, cortesia] courtesy. **-2.** [de gesto, palavra] kindness.

amaciante [ama'sjãntʃi] *m*: ~ **de roupas** fabric conditioner.

amaciar [ama'sja(x)] <> *vt* **-1.** [tornar macio] to soften. **-2.** [bife] to tenderize. **-3.** [motor] to run in. <> *vi* [motor] to run in.

ama-de-leite [ˌãmadʒi'lejtʃi] (*pl* **amas-de-leite**) *f* wet nurse.

amado, da [a'madu, da] <> *adj* **-1.** [ger] favourite. **-2.** [person] beloved. <> *m, f* beloved, love.

amador, ra [ama'do(x)] (*mpl* **-es,** *fpl* **-s**) <> *adj* amateur. <> *m, f* amateur.

amadurecer [amadure'se(x)] <> *vt* **-1.** [fruta] to ripen. **-2.** *fig* [pessoa] to mature. <> *vi* **-1.** [fruta] to ripen. **-2.** *fig* [pessoa] to mature. **-3.** *fig* [idéia, projeto] to come to fruition.

âmago [l'ãmagul *m* **-1.** [cerne - de madeira] heart; [- de questão] heart. **-2.** [essência] essence. **-3.** [alma, interior] heart.

amaldiçoar [amawdi'swa(x)] *vt* to curse.

amálgama [a'mawgamal *m* amalgam.

amalgamar [amawga'ma(x)] *vt* to amalgamate.

amalucado, da [amalu'kadu, da] *adj* crazy.

amamentar [amamẽn'ta(x)] *vt* & *vi* to breastfeed.

amanhã [ama'ɲã] <> *adv* tomorrow; ~ **de manhã** tomorrow morning; ~ **à noite** tomorrow night; ~ **de tarde** tomorrow afternoon/evening; **depois de** ~ the day after tomorrow. <> *m* tomorrow.

amanhecer [amaɲe'se(x)] <> *m* dawn; **ao** ~ at dawn. <> *vi* **-1.** [dia] to dawn. **-2.** [pessoa]: **hoje amanheci com dor de cabeça** today I woke up with a headache.

amansar [amãn'sa(x)] <> *vt* **-1.** [animal] to break in. **-2.** *fig* [pessoa etc.] to calm down. <> *vi* **-1.** [animal] to become tame. **-2.** *fig* [pessoa etc.] to relent.

amante [a'mãntʃi] *mf* lover.

Amapá [ama'pal *n* Amapá.

amar [a'ma(x)] <> *vt* **-1.** [sentir amor por] to love. **-2.** [fazer amor com] to make love to. <> *vi* [sentir amor] to be in love.

➡ **amar-se** *vp* **-1.** [mutuamente] to love

each other. **-2.** [fazer amor] to make love.

amarelado, da [amare'ladu, da] *adj* yellowish.

amarelo, la [ama'rɛlu, la] *adj* yellow.

➡ **amarelo** *m* yellow.

amarfanhar [amaxfa'ɲa(x)] *vt* to crumple.

amargar [amax'ga(x)] <> *vt* **-1.** [tornar amargo] to make bitter. **-2.** *fig* [fazer sofrer] to embitter. <> *vi* [tornar-se amargo] to go bitter.

amargo, ga [a'maxgu, ga] *adj* bitter.

amargor [amax'go(x)] *m* **-1.** [sabor amargo] bitter taste. **-2.** [sensação de desgosto] bitterness.

amargura [amax'gura] *f* **-1.** [ger] bitterness. **-2.** *fig* [sofrimento] bitterness.

amarrado, da [ama'xadu, da] *adj* **-1.** [atado] tied up. **-2.** *fig* [cara] glowering. **-3.** *fam fig* [comprometido] committed.

amarrar [ama'xa(x)] *vt* **-1.** [atar] to tie. **-2.** NÁUT to moor. **-3.** *fig*: ~ **a cara** to glower.

amarrotar [amaxo'ta(x)] <> *vt* to crumple. <> *vi* to be crumpled.

amassado, da [ama'sadu, da] *adj* [tecido, roupa, papel] crumpled; [carro] smashed up.

amassar [ama'sa(x)] *vt* **-1.** [massa] to knead; [bolo, pão] to mix. **-2.** [roupa] to crease. **-3.** [papel] to crumple. **-4.** [carro] to smash up.

amável [a'mavɛw] (*pl* **-eis**) *adj* friendly.

amazona [ama'zonal *f* **-1.** [mulher que anda a cavalo] horsewoman. **-2.** [mulher guerreira] Amazon.

Amazonas [ama'zonaʃ] *n* **-1.** [rio]: **o** ~ the Amazon. **-2.** [estado] Amazonas.

AmBev (*abrev de* **American Beverage Company**) *f* ≃ AmBev, *Brazilian drinks manufacturer.*

ambição [ãnbi'sãw] (*pl* **-ões**) *f* ambition.

ambicionar [ãnbisjo'na(x)] *vt* to set one's sights on.

ambicioso, osa [ãnbi'sjozu, ɔza] <> *adj* ambitious. <> *m, f* go-getter.

ambidestro, tra [ãnbi'deʃtru, tra] *adj* ambidextrous.

ambiental [ãnbjẽn'taw] (*pl* **-ais**) *adj* environmental.

ambientalista [ãnbjẽnta'liʃta] <> *adj* environmental. <> *mf* environmentalist.

ambientar [ãnbjẽn'tar] *vt* **-1.** [filme, enredo] to set. **-2.** [adaptar] to acclimatize.

➡ **ambientar-se** *vp* [adaptar-se] to mingle.

ambiente [ãn'bjẽntʃi] <> *adj* ambient. <> *m* **-1.** [gen & COMPUT] environment.

-2. [em sala, boate] area. **-3.** *fig* [atmosfera] atmosphere.

ambigüidade [ãnbigwi'dadʒi] *f* ambiguity.

ambíguo, gua [ãn'bigwu, gwa] *adj* ambiguous.

âmbito ['ãnbitu] *m* [campo de ação] field.

ambivalente [ãnbiva'lẽntʃi] *adj* ambivalent.

ambos, bas ['ãnbuʃ, baʃ] ◇ *adj* both. ◇ *pron* both.

ambrosia [ãnbro'zia] *f a sweet dish of eggs and milk.*

ambulância [ãnbu'lãnsja] *f* ambulance.

ambulante [ãnbu'lãntʃi] ◇ *adj* **-1.** [vendedor, pipoqueiro - na calçada] street *(antes de subst)*; [- de porta em porta] door-to-door *(antes de subst)*. **-2.** [biblioteca, posto médico] mobile. **-3.** *fam fig*: ele é uma enciclopédia ~ he's a walking encyclopedia. ◇ *mf* [vendedor ambulante] street vendor.

ambulatório [ãnbula'tɔrju] *m* outpatient department.

ameaça [a'mjasa] *f* threat.

ameaçar [amja'sa(x)] *vt* to threaten; ~ fazer algo to threaten to do sthg.

ameba [a'mɛba] *f* amoeba UK, ameba US.

amedrontar [amedrõn'ta(x)] *vt* to frighten.
◆ **amedrontar-se** *vp* to feel afraid.

ameixa [a'mejʃa] *f* **-1.** [fresca] plum. **-2.** [seca] prune.

amém [a'mẽ] *interj* amen!

amêndoa [a'mẽndwa] *f* almond.

amendoeira [amẽn'dwejra] *f* almond tree.

amendoim [amẽn'dwĩ] *(pl* -ns) *m* peanut; ~ torrado roasted peanut.

amenidade [ameni'dadʒi] *f* **-1.** [suavidade] mildness. **-2.** [delicadeza] gentleness.
◆ **amenidades** *fpl* [futilidades] trivialities.

amenizar [ameni'za(x)] *vt* **-1.** [abrandar] to reduce. **-2.** [tornar agradável] to make pleasant. **-3.** [briga, conflito] to settle. **-4.** [facilitar] to lighten.

ameno, na [a'menu, na] *adj* **-1.** [brando - sabor] mild; [- repreensão] quiet; [- pena] light. **-2.** [agradável] pleasant.

América [a'mɛrika] América; ~ Central Central America; ~ do Norte North America; ~ do Sul! South America; ~ Hispânica Spanish America; ~ Latina Latin America.

americanizar [amerikãni'za(x)] *vt* to Americanize.

americano, na [ameri'kãnu, na] ◇ *adj* American. ◇ *m, f* American.

amesquinhar [ameʃki'na(x)] *vt* [tornar mesquinho] to demean.
◆ **amesquinhar-se** *vp* **-1.** [tornar-se avaro] to become mean. **-2.** [humilhar-se] to demean o.s.

ametista [ame'tʃiʃta] *f* amethyst.

amianto [a'mjãntu] *m* asbestos.

amido [a'midu] *m* starch.

amigável [ami'gavɛw] *(pl* -eis) *adj* friendly.

amígdala [a'migdala] *f* tonsil.

amigdalite [amigda'litʃi] *f* tonsillitis.

amigo, ga [a'migu, ga] ◇ *adj* friendly. ◇ *m, f* friend.

amistoso, osa [amiʃ'tozu, ɔza] *adj* friendly.
◆ **amistoso** *m* ESP friendly.

amizade [ami'zadʒi] *f* **-1.** [relação] friendship; fazer ~ (com alguém) to make friends (with sb); ~ colorida *fam* casual relationship. **-2.** [estima] friendliness; ela o tratou com ~ she treated him in a friendly manner.

amnésia [am'nɛzja] *f* amnesia.

amolação [amola'sãw] *(pl* -ões) *f* [incômodo, aborrecimento] hassle.

amolar [amo'la(x)] ◇ *vt* **-1.** [faca] to sharpen. **-2.** [incomodar, aborrecer] to annoy. ◇ *vi* [causar incômodo] to be annoying.
◆ **amolar-se** *vp* [aborrecer-se] to get annoyed.

amoldar [amow'da(x)] *vt* [adaptar, ajustar]: ~ algo (a) to adapt sthg (to).
◆ **amoldar-se** *vp* [adaptar-se, ajustar-se]: ~-se (a) to adapt o.s. (to).

amolecer [amole'se(x)] ◇ *vt* **-1.** [tornar mole] to soften. **-2.** *fig* [abrandar] to mollify. ◇ *vi* **-1.** [tornar-se mole] to soften. **-2.** *fig* [tornar-se brando] to relent.

amônia [a'monja] *f* ammonia.

amoníaco [amo'niaku] *m* ammonia.

amontoar [amõn'twa(x)] *vt* to pile up.

amor [a'mo(x)] *(pl* -es) *m* love; fazer ~ to make love; pelo ~ de Deus! for God's sake!; ser um ~ (de pessoa) to be a gem (of a person).

amora [a'mɔra] *f* mulberry.

amoral [amo'raw] *(pl* -ais) ◇ *adj* amoral. ◇ *mf* unscrupulous person.

amora-preta [a,mɔra'preta] *(pl* amoras-pretas) *f* mulberry.

amordaçar [amoxda'sa(x)] *vt* to gag.

amornar [amox'na(x)] ◇ *vt* to warm up. ◇ *vi* to cool down.

amoroso, osa [amo'rozu, ɔza] *adj* [pessoa] loving; um caso ~ a love affair.

amor-perfeito [a,moxpex'fejtu] *(pl* amores-perfeitos) *m* heartsease.

amor-próprio [a͜mox'prɔprjul (*pl* **amo-res-próprios**) *m* -**1.** [auto-estima] self-esteem. -**2.** [orgulho] conceitedness.

amortecedor [amoxtese'do(x)l (*pl* -**es**) *m* shock absorber.

amortização [amoxtiza'sãw] (*pl* -**ões**) *f* -**1.** [pagamento parcial] part payment. -**2.** *FIN* [de ações] amortization.

amortizar [amoxti'za(x)] *vt* -**1.** [pagar parte] to repay (in part). -**2.** *FIN* [ações] to amortize.

amostra [a'mɔʃtra] *f* sample.

amotinar [amoʧi'na(x)] *vt* to lead into mutiny.
  ◆ **amotinar-se** *vp* to mutiny.

amparar [ãnpa'ra(x)] *vt* -**1.** [escorar, segurar] to hold. -**2.** [ajudar] to support.
  ◆ **amparar-se** *vp* [escorar-se, segurar-se]: ∼-**se** (**contra/em**) to lean (against/on).

amparo [ãn'parul *m* -**1.** [apoio] hold. -**2.** [ajuda] support.

amperagem [ãnpe'raʒẽ] *f* [eletr] amperage.

ampère [ãn'pɛril *m* amp, ampere.

ampliação [ãnplia'sãw] (*pl* -**ões**) *f* -**1.** [aumento - de forma, imagem] enlargement; [- de ângulo] widening. -**2.** [extensão] extension. -**3.** [desenvolvimento - de estudos] broadening; [- de negócio] expansion. -**4.** [*FOT* - processo] blow-up; [- exemplar] enlargement.

ampliar [ãnpli'a(x)] *vt* -**1.** [aumentar - forma, imagem] to enlarge; [- ângulo] to widen. -**2.** [estender] to extend. -**3.** [desenvolver - estudos] to broaden; [- negócio] to expand.

amplificação [ãnplifika'sãw] (*pl* -**ões**) *f* -**1.** [aumento - de forma, imagem] enlargement; [- de ângulo] widening. -**2.** [de som] amplification.

amplificador [ãnplifika'do(x)] (*pl* -**es**) *m* [de som] amplifier.

amplificar [ãnplifi'ka(x)] *vt* -**1.** [aumentar - forma, imagem] to enlarge; [- ângulo] to widen. -**2.** [som] to amplify.

amplitude [ãnpli'tudʒil *f* -**1.** [espaço] spaciousness. -**2.** *fig* [abrangência] scope. -**3.** *TEC* amplitude.

amplo, pla ['ãnplu, 'plal *adj* -**1.** [espaçoso] spacious. -**2.** [abrangente] broad. -**3.** [lato]: **no sentido mais** ∼ **da palavra** in the broadest sense of the word. -**4.** (*antes de subst*) [ilimitado] ample.

ampulheta [ãnpu'ʎetal *f* hour-glass.

amputar [ãnpu'ta(x)] *vt* to amputate.

Amsterdã [amiʃtex'dã] *n* Amsterdam.

amuado, da [a'mwadu, dal *adj* [aborrecido] sulking.

amuar [a'mwa(x)] *vt* [aborrecer] to annoy.

◆ **amuar-se** *vp* [aborrecer-se]: ∼-**se** (**com** *ou* **contra**) to get annoyed (with).

anã [a'nã] *f* ▷ **anão**.

anacronismo [anakro'niʒmul *m* anachronism.

anafilático, ca [anafi'latiku, kal *adj* ▷ choque.

anagrama [ana'grãmal *m* anagram.

anágua [a'nagwal *f* petticoat.

anais [a'najʃ] *mpl* annals.

anal [a'naw] (*pl* -**ais**) *adj* anal.

analfabetismo [anawfabe'ʧiʒmul *m* illiteracy.

analfabeto, ta [anawfa'bɛtu, tal ⟨▷ *adj* illiterate. ⟨▷ *m*, *f* illiterate.

analgésico, ca [anaw'ʒɛziku, kal *adj* analgesic.
  ◆ **analgésico** *m* [remédio] painkiller, analgesic.

analisar [anali'za(x)] *vt* -**1.** [examinar, avaliar] to analyse. -**2.** *PSIC* to put through analysis.

análise [a'nalizil *f* [ger & *PSIC*] analysis.

analista [ana'liʃtal *mf* -**1.** [ger & *PSIC*] analyst; ∼ **de sistemas** systems analyst.

analogia [analo'ʒial *f* analogy.

análogo, ga [a'nalogu, gal *adj* analogous.

ananás [ana'naʃ] (*pl* -**ases**) *m* pineapple.

anão, ã [a'nãw, ãl (*mpl* -**ões**, *fpl* -**s**) *m*, *f* dwarf.

anarquia [anax'kial *f* -**1.** [ausência de governo] anarchy. -**2.** *fig* [bagunça] shambles.

anarquista [anax'kiʃtal ⟨▷ *adj* [partido, sociedade] anarchist. ⟨▷ *mf* -**1.** [militante] anarchist. -**2.** *fig* [bagunceiro, agitador] agitator.

ANATEL (*abrev de* **Agência Nacional de Telecomunicações**) *f Brazilian state telecommunications regulator*, ≃ Oftel *UK*, ≃ ODTR *US*.

anatomia [anato'mial *f* anatomy.

anatômico, ca [ana'tomiku, kal *adj* anatomical.

anca ['ãŋkal *f* -**1.** [de pessoa] hip. -**2.** [de animal] haunch.

ancestral [ãn'seʃtrawl (*pl* -**ais**) ⟨▷ *adj* ancestral, age-old. ⟨▷ *mf* ancestor.
  ◆ **ancestrais** *mpl* ancestors.

anchova [ãn'ʃoval *f* anchovy.

ancião, ciã [ã'sjãw, sjãl (*mpl* -**ões**, *fpl* -**s**) ⟨▷ *adj* aged. ⟨▷ *m*, *f* venerable person.

ancinho [ãn'sinul *m* rake.

anciões [ã'sjõjʃl *pl* ▷ **ancião**.

ancoradouro [ãŋkora'dorul *m* anchorage.

ancorar [ãŋko'ra(x)] ⟨▷ *vt* -**1.** [fundear]

to anchor. - **2.** *fig* [basear] to base. ◇ *vi* [fundear] to base.

andaime [ãn'dãjmi] *m* scaffolding.

andamento [ãnda'mẽntul *m* - **1.** [prosseguimento] progress; **estar em ~** to be under way. - **2.** [direção] direction. - **3.** *MÚS* tempo.

andança [ãn'dãnsaʃl *f* [viagem] travel.

andar [ãn'da(x)] *(pl* -**es**) ◇ *m* - **1.** [jeito de caminhar] walk. - **2.** [pavimento] storey *UK*, story *US*. ◇ *vi* - **1.** [caminhar] to walk. - **2.** [usar como transporte]: **~ de bicicleta/a cavalo** to ride a bicycle/horse; **~ de avião/carro/trem** to go by plane/car/train. - **3.** [movimentar-se] to go. - **4.** [errar] to wander. - **5.** [progredir, funcionar] to go. - **6.** [passar] to go, to pass. - **7.** [conviver]: **~ com alguém** to get along with sb. - **8.** [estar] to be; **~ em** *OU* **por** to be travelling in; **~** fazendo algo to be doing sthg. - **9.** [ir-se]: **ir andando** to be on one's way. - **10.** [apressar-se]: **anda (com isso)!** get a move on! ◇ *vt* [percorrer] to do; **andamos 50 quilômetros em um dia** we did 50 kms in one day.

Andes ['ãndiʃ] *npl*: **os ~** the Andes.

andino, na [ãn'dinu, nal ◇ *adj* Andean. ◇ *m, f* Andean.

andorinha [ãndo'riɲal *f* swallow.

Andorra [ãn'doxal *n*: (o principado de) **~** (the principality of) Andorra.

anedota [ane'dɔtal *f* joke.

anel [a'nɛwl *(pl* -**éis**) *m* - **1.** [ger] ring. - **2.** [de corrente] circuit. - **3.** [de cabelo] lock.

anelado, da [ane'ladu, dal *adj* curly.

anemia [ane'mial *f* anaemia *UK*, anemia *US*.

anestesia [aneʃte'zial *f* - **1.** [efeito] anaesthesia *UK*, anesthesia *US*. - **2.** [anestésico] anaesthetic *UK*, anesthetic *US*; **~ geral/local** general/local anaesthetic.

anestesiado, da [aneʃte'zjadu, dal *adj* [paciente] anaesthetized.

anestésico, ca [aneʃ'teziku, kal *adj* anaesthetizing *UK*, anesthetizing *US*.
◆ **anestésico** *m* anaesthetic *UK*, anesthetic *US*.

anexado, da [ane'ksadu, dal *adj* COMPUT attached.

anexar [anek'sa(x)] *vt* COMPUT : **~ um arquivo** to attach a file.

anexo [a'nɛksul *m* COMPUT attachment.

ANFAVEA (*abrev de* **Associação Nacional dos Fabricantes de Veículos Automotores**) *f Brazilian association of automobile manufacturers.*

anfíbio, bia [ãn'fibju, bjal *adj* amphibious.
◆ **anfíbio** *m* amphibian.

anfiteatro [ãnfi'tʃjatrul *m* amphitheatre *UK*, amphitheater *US*.

anfitrião, triã [ãnfi'trjãw, trjãl *(mpl* -**ões**, *fpl* -**s**) *m, f* host (*f* hostess).

angariar [ãnga'rja(x)] *vt* to attract.

angina [ãn'ʒinal *f*: **~ (do peito)** angina (pectoris).

anglicano, na [ãngli'kanu, nal ◇ *adj* Anglican. ◇ *m, f* Anglican.

anglo-saxão, xã [ãnglosak'sãw, sãl *(mpl* -**ões**, *fpl* -**ãs**) ◇ *adj* Anglo-Saxon. ◇ *m, f* Anglo-Saxon.

Angola [ãn'gɔlal *n* Angola.

angorá [ãngo'ral ◇ *adj* angora. ◇ *m* [tecido] angora. ◇ *mf* [gato] angora.

angra ['ãngral *f* bay.

angu [ãn'gul *m* - **1.** [ger] ≃ porridge. - **2.** *fam fig* [confusão, problema]: **um ~-de-caroço** a tough nut to crack.

ângulo ['ãngulul *m* - **1.** [ger] angle. - **2.** [canto] corner. - **3.** [de mira] angle (of vision).

anguloso, sa [ãngu'lozu, lɔzal *adj* angled.

angústia [ãn'guʃtʃjal *f* anguish.

angustiante [ãnguʃ'tʃjãntʃil *adj* harrowing.

angustiar [ãnguʃ'tʃja(x)] *vt* to cause anguish to.
◆ **angustiar-se** *vp* to become distressed; **~-se com algo** to be distressed by sthg.

anil [a'niwl *m* [cor] blue.

animação [anima'sãwl *f* - **1.** [entusiasmo] enthusiasm. - **2.** [alegria] jollity. - **3.** [movimento] hustle and bustle. - **4.** *CINE* animation.

animado, da [ani'madu, dal *adj* - **1.** [entusiasmado] spirited. - **2.** [alegre, movimentado] lively.

animador, ra [anima'do(x), ral *(mpl* -**es**, *fpl* -**s**) ◇ *adj* encouraging. ◇ *m, f* animator.

animal [ani'mawl *(pl* -**ais**) ◇ *adj* - **1.** [ger] animal. - **2.** *fam pej* [pessoa] brutal. ◇ *mf fam pej* [pessoa - bruto] brute; [- ignorante] ass. ◇ *m ZOOL* animal; **~ doméstico** [de estimação] domestic animal; [de criação] livestock.

animalesco, ca [anima'leʃku, kal *adj* animal.

animar [ani'ma(x)] *vt* - **1.** [ger] to liven up. - **2.** [encorajar]: **~ alguém (a fazer algo)** to encourage sb (to do sthg). - **3.** [entusiasmar] to enthuse. - **4.** [fomentar, estimular] to stimulate. - **5.** [dar animação] to animate. - **6.** *RELIG* [dar vida a] to bring to life.
◆ **animar-se** *vp* - **1.** [tomar coragem]: **~-se (a fazer algo)** to resolve (to do sthg).

-2. [entusiasmar-se] to become enthusiastic. **-3.** [debate, conversa, festa] to liven up. **-4.** [alegrar-se] to cheer up. **-5.** *RELIG* [ganhar vida] to come to life.

ânimo [ˈãnimu] ⟨⟩ *m* **-1.** [coragem] courage. **-2.** [entusiasmo] enthusiasm; **perder o ~** to lose courage. **-3.** [estímulo] life; **representar um novo ~ para** to give a new lease of life to. ⟨⟩ *interj*: **~!** come on!

animosidade [animozi'dadʒi] *f* animosity.

aniquilar [aniki'la(x)] *vt* **-1.** [anular] to rescind. **-2.** [esgotar] to exhaust. **-3.** [destruir] to annihilate. **-4.** *fig* [arruinar] to ruin.

➡ **aniquilar-se** *vp* **-1.** [esgotar-se] to be exhausted. **-2.** *fig* [moralmente] to destroy o.s.

anis [aˈniʃ] *(pl* **-es)** *m* aniseed; **licor de ~** anisette.

anistia [aniʃˈtʃia] *f* amnesty.

anistiado, da [aniʃˈtʃiadu, da] ⟨⟩ *adj* amnestied. ⟨⟩ *m, f person granted amnesty.*

aniversariar [anivexsaˈrja(x)] *vi* **-1.** [pessoa] *to celebrate one's birthday/anniversary.* **-2.** [cidade] *to celebrate its anniversary.*

aniversário [anivexˈsarju] *m* **-1.** [de acontecimento] anniversary. **-2.** [de nascimento] birthday. **-3.** [festa] birthday party.

anjo [ˈãʒu] *m* angel; **~ da guarda** guardian angel.

ano [ˈãnu] *m* [período] year; **no ~ de 1969, o homem foi à Lua** in 1969, man went to the moon; **os ~s 70** the 1970s; **~ bissexto** leap year; **~ fiscal** tax year; **~ letivo** academic year; **há ~s ou faz ~s que** it's years since; **faz ~s que não o vejo** it's years since I saw him, I haven't seen him for years; **(no) ~ passado** last year; **(no) ~ que vem** next year.

➡ **anos** *mpl* [idade]: **tenho vinte ~ (de idade)** I'm twenty (years old); **quantos ~s você tem?** how old are you?; **ela faz nove ~s em outubro** she'll be nine in October.

anões [aˈnõjʃ] *pl* ➢ **anão**.

anoitecer [anojteˈse(x)] ⟨⟩ *m* nightfall; **ao ~** at nightfall. ⟨⟩ *vi* **-1.** [cair a noite]: **quando anoiteceu, acendemos as luzes** when it got dark we turned on the lights. **-2.** [estar em algum lugar ao anoitecer] to be somewhere when night falls; **anoitecemos na estrada** night fell while we were on the road.

ano-luz [ˌãnuˈluʃ] *(pl* **anos-luz)** *m* light year.

anomalia [anomaˈlia] *f* abnormality.

anônimo, ma [aˈnonimu, ma] *adj* anonymous.

ano-novo [ˌãnuˈnovu] *(pl* **anos-novos)** *m* **-1.** [período] new year. **-2.** [festa] New Year.

anoréxico, ca [anoˈreksiku, ka] ⟨⟩ *adj* anorexic. ⟨⟩ *m, f* anorexic.

anormal [anoxˈmaw] *(pl* **-ais)** ⟨⟩ *adj* **-1.** [ger] abnormal. **-2.** [incomum] unusual. **-3.** [extraordinário] extraordinary. **-4.** [deficiente] retarded. ⟨⟩ *m* **-1.** [pessoa excepcional] abnormal person. **-2.** *fam pej* [idiota] cretin.

anormalidade [anoxmaliˈdadʒi] *f* **-1.** [anomalia] abnormality. **-2.** [situação] abnormal situation.

anotação [anotaˈsãw] *(pl* **-ões)** *f* note.

anotar [anoˈta(x)] *vt* **-1.** [tomar nota de] to note down. **-2.** [apor observações a] to annotate.

anseio [ãˈsejul] *m* desire; **no ~ de fazer algo** in one's eagerness to do sthg.

ânsia [ˈãsja] *f* **-1.** [desejo]: **ter ~ (por algo/de fazer algo)** to be longing for sthg/to do sthg; **~s de vômito** nausea. **-2.** [ansiedade] anxiety.

ansiar [ãˈsja(x)] *vi*: **~ por algo/por fazer algo** to long for sthg/to do sth.

ansiedade [ãsjeˈdadʒi] *f* **-1.** [ger] anxiety; **com ~** anxiously. **-2.** [desejo] longing.

ansioso, osa [ãˈsjozu, ɔza] *adj* [angustiado, desejoso] anxious; **o presidente aguarda ~ o resultado das eleições** the president is anxiously awaiting the election results.

antagonista [ãtagoˈniʃta] ⟨⟩ *adj* **-1.** [candidato, partido] opposing. **-2.** [opinião, idéia] conflicting. ⟨⟩ *mf* [rival] opponent.

antártico, ca [ãnˈtaxtʃiku, ka] *adj* Antarctic.

➡ **Antártico** *n*: **o (oceano) ~** the Antarctic (Ocean).

Antártida [ãnˈtaxtʃida] *n*: **a ~** Antarctica.

ante [ˈãntʃi] *prep* **-1.** [diante de] before; **jurar ~ a Bíblia** to swear on the Bible; **jurar ~ o juiz** to swear before the judge. **-2.** [em consequência de] as a result of.

ante- [ˈãntʃi-] *prefixo* ante-.

antebraço [ãntʃiˈbrasul] *m* forearm.

antecedência [ãnteseˈdẽsja] *f*: **com ~** in advance; **com uma semana de ~** a week in advance.

antecedente [ãnteseˈdẽntʃi] ⟨⟩ *adj* [precedente] preceding. ⟨⟩ *m* **-1.** [precedente] predecessor. **-2.** *GRAM, MAT* antecedent.

➡ **antecedentes** *mpl* [pessoais] track

record *(sg)*; **ter bons** ~**s** to have a clean record; ~**s criminais** criminal record *(sg)*.

anteceder [ãntese'de(x)] *vt* [preceder, chegar antes de] to precede.

antecessor, ra [ãntese'so(x), ra] ◇ *adj* preceding. ◇ *m, f* predecessor.

antecipação [ãntesipa'sãw] *(pl* -ões) *f* -**1.** [adiantamento]: **a** ~ **de metas** the early achievement of goals; **a** ~ **do comunicado provocou uma crise** the bringing forward of the announcement caused a crisis. -**2.** [salarial] advance. -**3.** [antecedência]: **com** ~ in advance; **com uma semana/um mês de** ~ a week/month in advance.

antecipadamente [ãntesi,pada'mẽntʃi] *adv* in advance.

antecipado, da [ãntesi'padu, da] *adj* -**1.** [pagamento] advance *(antes de subst)*. -**2.** [eleições] early.

antecipar [ãntesi'pa(x)] *vt* -**1.** [fazer ocorrer mais cedo] to bring forward. -**2.** [adiantar-se a] to anticipate.

antemão [ãnte'mãw] ◆ **de antemão** *loc adv* beforehand.

antena [ãn'tena] *f* -**1.** [ger] antenna. -**2.** *RÁDIO, TV* aerial; ~ **parabólica** satellite dish.

anteontem [ãntʃi'õntẽ] *adv* the day before yesterday.

antepassado, da [,ãntepa'sadu, da] *m, f* ancestor.

antepor [ãnteêpo(x)] *vt* [contrapor]: ~ **algo a algo** to respond to sthg with sthg.

anterior [ãnte'rjo(x)] *(pl* -es) *adj* -**1.** [prévio]: ~ **(a)** before. -**2.** [antigo]: ~ **(a)** previous (to). -**3.** [em posição] front; **membro** ~ forelimb; **músculo** ~ anterior muscle.

antes ['ãnʃiʃ] *adv* -**1.** [previamente] beforehand; **o quanto** ~ as soon as possible; **pouco** ~ a little before. -**2.** [antigamente] in the past. -**3.** [de preferência] rather. -**4.** [ao contrário] on the contrary.
◆ **antes de** *loc prep* before; ~ **de fazer algo** before doing sthg; ~ **da hora/do tempo** early; ~ **de tudo** above all.
◆ **antes que** *loc conj* before; **fui embora** ~ **que chovesse** I left before it rained.

antever [ãnte've(x)] *vt* to foresee.

antevisão [,ãnte'vizãw] *f* -**1.** [visão antecipada]: **ter uma** ~ **de** to foresee. -**2.** [pressentimento] premonition.

anti- [ãntʃi-] *prefixo* anti-, non-.

antiácido, da [ãn'tʃjasidu, da] *adj* antacid.
◆ **antiácido** *m* antacid.

antiaéreo, rea [ãntʃja'ɛrju, rja] *adj* anti-aircraft; **abrigo** ~ bomb shelter.

antialérgico, ca [ãntʃja'lɛxʒiku, ka] *adj* hypo-allergenic.
◆ **antialérgico** *m* antihistamine.

antibiótico, ca [ãntʃi'bjɔtʃiku, ka] *adj* antibiotic.
◆ **antibiótico** *m* antibiotic.

anticlímax [ãntʃi'klimãks] *m inv* anticlimax.

anticoncepcional [ãntʃikõnsepsjo'naw] *(pl* -ais) ◇ *adj* contraceptive. ◇ *m* [pílula, dispositivo] contraceptive.

anticorpo [ãntʃi'koxpu] *m* antibody.

antídoto [ãn'tʃidotu] *m* antidote.

antiético, ca [ãn'tʃjɛtʃiku, ka] *adj* unethical.

antigamente [ãntʃiga'mẽntʃi] *adv* in the past; **de** ~ old-fashioned.

antigo, ga [ãn'tʃigu, ga] *adj* -**1.** [ger] old. -**2.** [antiquado, remoto] old-fashioned. -**3.** *(antes de subst)* [anterior] former, previous. -**4.** *(antes de subst)* [veterano] longstanding; **ser** ~ **no clube** to be a longstanding member of the club; **ser** ~ **na empresa** to be a longstanding member of staff; **ser** ~ **no cargo** to be an old hand at the job. -**5.** *HIST* [da Antigüidade] ancient.
◆ **antigos** *mpl HIST* [homens] ancients.

antigüidade [ãntʃigwi'dadʒi] *f* -**1.** [idade] age. -**2.** [em cargo, função] seniority. -**3.** [peça, monumento] antique.
◆ **Antigüidade** *f* [época] antiquity.
◆ **antigüidades** *fpl* -**1.** [peças] antiques; **loja de** ~**s** antique shop. -**2.** [monumentos] ancient monuments.

anti-higiênico, ca [ãntʃi'ʒeniku, ka] *(mpl* -s, *fpl* -s) *adj* unhygienic.

anti-histamínico, ca [ãntʃi'iʃta'miniku, ka] *adj* antihistamine.
◆ **anti-histamínico** *m* antihistamine.

anti-horário [ãntʃjo'rarju] *adj*: **sentido/movimento** ~ anticlockwise direction/movement.

antiinflamatório, ria [ãntʃiĩnflama'tɔriu, rja] ◇ *adj* anti-inflammatory. ◇ *m* anti-inflammatory.

antílope [ãn'tʃilopi] *m* antelope.

antinuclear [ãntʃinukle'a(x)] *adj* antinuclear.

antipático, ca [ãntʃi'patʃiku, ka] *adj* unpleasant.

antipatizar [ãntʃipatʃi'za(x)] *vi*: ~ **com alguém** to dislike sb.

antiperspirante [ãntʃipexʃpi'rãntʃi] ◇ *adj* antiperspirant. ◇ *mf* antiperspirant.

antiquado, da [ãntʃi'kwadu, da] *adj* antiquated.

antiquário, ria [ăntʃi'kwarju, rjal *m, f* [comerciante] antique dealer.

➥ **antiquário** *m* [loja] antique shop.

antiquíssimo, ma [ăntʃi'kisimu, mal *superl* ➩ **antigo**.

anti-semita [ăntʃise'mita] (*pl* -s) ◇ *adj* anti-Semitic. ◇ *mf* [pessoa] anti-Semite.

anti-séptico, ca [antʃi'sɛptʃiku, kal *adj* antiseptic.

➥ **anti-séptico, antisséptico** *m* [desinfetante] antiseptic.

anti-social [ăntʃiso'sjaw] (*pl* -ais) *adj* antisocial.

antisséptico [ˌăntʃi'sɛptʃikul = **anti-séptico**.

antitabagista [ăntʃitaba'ʒistal ◇ *adj* anti-smoking. ◇ *mf* anti-smoker.

antitérmico, ca [ăntʃi'tɛxmiku, kal *adj* antipyretic.

➥ **antitérmico** *m* [comprimido] antipyretic.

antiterrorista [ăntʃitexo'riʃtal ◇ *adj* anti-terrorist. ◇ *mf* anti-terrorist.

antítese [ăn'tʃitezil *f* antithesis.

antivírus [ăntʃi'viruʃ] *m inv* INFORM anti-virus software.

antologia [ăntolo'ʒial *f* anthology.

antológico, ca [ănto'lɔʒiko, kal *adj* outstanding.

antro ['ăntrul *m* - **1.** [caverna] cave. - **2.** [de animal] lair. - **3.** [de bandidos etc.] den.

antropófago, ga [ăntro'pɔfagu, gal ◇ *adj* cannibalistic. ◇ *m, f* cannibal.

antropologia [ăntropolo'ʒial *f* anthropology.

anual [a'nwawl (*pl* -ais) *adj* annual, yearly.

anuário [a'nwarjul *m* yearbook.

anuidade [anwi'dadʒil *f* annuity.

anulação [anula'sãwl (*pl* -ões) *f* - **1.** [cancelamento, invalidação] cancellation. - **2.** [casamento] annulment. - **3.** [pena] revocation. - **4.** [gol] disallowance.

anular [anu'la(x)l ◇ *vt* - **1.** [cancelar, invalidar] to cancel. - **2.** [casamento] to annull. - **3.** [pena] to revoke. - **4.** [gol] to disallow. - **5.** [sobrepujar] to cancel out. ◇ *adj* - **1.** [forma] circular. - **2.** [dedo] ring. ◇ *m* [dedo] ring finger.

anunciante [anũn'sjăntʃil *m* COM advertiser.

anunciar [anũn'sja(x)l *vt* - **1.** [ger] to announce. - **2.** COM [produto] to advertise.

anúncio [a'nũnsjul *m* - **1.** [comunicado] announcement. - **2.** [cartaz, aviso] notice. - **3.** [publicitário] advertisement; ~ **s** classificados classifieds.

ânus ['ănuʃl *m inv* anus.

anzol [ăn'zɔwl (*pl* -óis) *m* hook.

ao [awl = a + o.

aonde [a'õndʒil *adv* where; ~ **quer que** ... wherever ...

aos [awʃl = a + os.

AP (*abrev de* **Estado do Amapá**) *n State of Amapá*.

APAE (*abrev de* **Associação de Pais e Amigos dos Excepcionais**) *f Brazilian association of parents and friends of the disabled*.

apagado, da [apa'gadu, dal *adj* - **1.** [fogo] extinguished. - **2.** [desligado] out *(depois de verbo)*. - **3.** [com borracha] rubbed out *UK*, erased *US*. - **4.** [desvanecido] faded. - **5.** *fig* [sem brilho] lacklustre. - **6.** *fig* [pessoa] dull.

apagão [apa'gãwl (*pl* -ões) *m* [blecaute] power cut.

apagar [apa'ga(x)l ◇ *vt* - **1.** [fogo] to put out. - **2.** [vela] to blow out. - **3.** [luz, lanterna] to turn out. - **4.** [lustre] to dim. - **5.** [com borracha, apagador] to rub out. - **6.** [fazer desvanecer-se] to fade. - **7.** [abrandar] to dull. - **8.** COMPUT [eliminar] to delete. - **9.** *fam fig* [matar] to wipe out. ◇ *vi fam fig* [adormecer] to crash out.

➥ **apagar-se** *vp* - **1.** [extingüir-se] to die out. - **2.** [desligar-se] to go out. - **3.** [desvanecer-se] to fade. - **4.** [abrandar-se] to dull.

apaixonado, da [apajʃo'nadu, dal *adj* - **1.** [enamorado] in love; **estar** ~ **(por alguém)** to be in love (with sb). - **2.** [exaltado] impassioned. - **3.** [aficcionado]: **ser** ~ **(por algo)** to be passionate about sthg.

apaixonar-se [apajʃo'naxsil *vp* - **1.** [enamorar-se]: ~ **(por alguém)** to fall in love (with sb). - **2.** [aficcionar-se]: ~ **(por algo)** to become passionate (about sthg).

apalermado, da [apalex'madu, dal *adj* idiotic.

apalpar [apaw'pa(x)l *vt* to feel.

➥ **apalpar-se** *vp* [examinar-se] to examine o.s.

apanhado [apã'nadul *m* - **1.** [resumo] summary. - **2.** [de flores] bunch.

apanhar [apã'na(x)l ◇ *vt* - **1.** [ger] to catch. - **2.** [pegar] to pick out. - **3.** [alcançar] to get. - **4.** [pegar do chão] to pick up. - **5.** [agarrar] to grab. - **6.** [colher] to pick. - **7.** [ir buscar] to fetch. - **8.** [tomar condução] to take. ◇ *vi* - **1.** [ser espancado] to be beaten; ~ **de alguém** to take a beating from sb; ~ **de algo** to be beaten with sthg. - **2.** ESP [perder] to lose. - **3.** *fig* [ter dificuldades] to go through a lot.

apara [a'paral *f* - **1.** [madeira] shaving. - **2.** [papel] shred.

aparador [apara'do(x)] (pl -es) m [móvel] sideboard.

aparafusar [aparafu'za(x)] vt -1. [parafuso] to screw in. -2. [prender] to screw.

aparar [apa'ra(x)] vt -1. [cabelo, barba, unhas] to trim. -2. [unhas] to clip. -3. [golpe] to fend off. -4. [tábua, folhas] to smooth out.

aparato [apa'ratu] m -1. [pompa] ceremony. -2. [conjunto - de ferramentas] collection; [- de armas] apparatus. -3. fig [de conceitos, análises] structure.

aparecer [apare'se(x)] vt -1. [ger] to appear. -2. [ser perceptível] to be apparent. -3. [comparecer] to turn up; fam [fazer visita] to drop in. -4. fam pej [exibir-se] to show off.

aparecimento [aparesi'mēntu] m appearance.

aparelhado, da [apare'ʎadu, da] adj -1. [preparado] prepared. -2. [madeira] planed.

aparelhagem [apare'ʎaʒēl] (pl -ns) f -1. [equipamento] equipment; [de som] sound system. -2. [da madeira] planing. -3. NÁUT rigging.

aparelhar [apare'ʎa(x)] vt -1. [preparar] to equip. -2. NÁUT to rig.
➔ **aparelhar-se** vp [preparar-se] to equip o.s.

aparelho [apa'reʎu] m -1. [conjunto] set; ~ de chá tea set. -2. [equipamento] equipment; ~ de som sound system. -3. [máquina] machine; ~ de barbear shaving equipment; ~ de rádio/TV radio/television set. -4. PESCA tackle. -5. POL hideout. -6. ANAT system; ~ digestivo digestive system.

aparência [apa'rēnsja] f -1. [aspecto] appearance; sob a ~ de in the guise of; na ~ by all appearances. -2. [ilusão] show.
➔ **aparências** fpl [exterioridades] appearances; as ~s enganam prov one shouldn't judge us by appearances; manter as ~s to keep up appearances.

aparentar [aparēn'ta(x)] vt -1. [parecer] to seem. -2. [fingir] to pretend.

aparente [apa'rēntʃi] adj -1. [falso] feigned. -2. [visível] visible.

aparição [apari'sāw] (pl -ões) f apparition.

apartamento [apaxta'mēntu] m -1. [residência] apartment, flat UK. -2. [de hotel] hotel suite.

apartar [apax'ta(x)] vt -1. [separar] to split. -2. [briga] to break up.
➔ **apartar-se** vp [afastar-se] to split from.

aparte [a'paxtʃi] m [observação] aside; fazer um ~ to make an aside.

apartheid [apax'tajdʒi] m apartheid.

apartidário, ria [apartʃi'darju, rja] adj non-partisan.

apatetado, da [apate'tadu, da] adj [trapalhão] foolish.

apatia [apa'tʃia] f indifference.

apático, ca [a'patʃiku, ka] adj indifferent.

apavorado, da [apavo'radu, da] adj terrified.

apavorante [apavo'rāntʃi] adj terrifying.

apavorar [apavo'ra(x)] <> vt to terrify.
<> vi to be terrifying.
➔ **apavorar-se** vp to become terrified.

apaziguar [apazi'gwa(x)] vt to calm.
➔ **apaziguar-se** vp -1. to calm down. -2. [inimigos] to make peace.

apear [a'pja(x)] vi to dismount.

apedrejar [apedre'ʒa(x)] vt to stone.

apegado, da [ape'gadu, da] adj [afeiçoado]: ~ (a) attached (to).

apegar-se [ape'gaxsi] vp [afeiçoar-se]: ~ a algo/alguém to become attached to sthg/sb.

apego [a'pegu] m [afeição] attachment; ter ~ por to be attached to.

apelação [apela'sāw] (pl -ões) f -1. [apelo] appeal. -2. JUR appeal. -3. fam [vulgarização] solicitation.

apelar [ape'la(x)] vi -1. [recorrer]: ~ a to appeal to; ~ (para a violência) to turn nasty. -2. [invocar]: ~ a [compreensão, amizade] to call upon. -3. JUR : ~ (de) to appeal (against). -4. [vulgarmente] to turn nasty.

apelidar [apeli'da(x)] vt: ~ alguém de algo to nickname sb sthg.

apelido [ape'lidu] m [alcunha] nickname.

apelo [a'pelu] m appeal; ~ a alguém/ algo appeal to sb/sthg.

apenas [a'penaʃ] adv [só] only.

apêndice [a'pēndʒisi] m appendix.

apendicite [apēndʒi'sitʃi] f appendicitis.

aperceber-se [apexse'bexsi] vp: ~ de to realize.

aperfeiçoamento [apexfejswa'mēntu] m [aprimoramento] improvement.

aperfeiçoar [apexfej'swa(x)] vt to improve.
➔ **aperfeiçoar-se** vp [aprimorar-se] to improve; ~-se em algo to improve in ou at sthg.

aperitivo, va [aperi'tʃivu, va] adj appetizing.
➔ **aperitivo** m -1. [bebida] aperitif. -2. [petisco] appetizer.

aperreado, da [ape'xjadu, da] adj -1. [aborrecido] vexed. -2. [em situação difícil] troubled.

apertado, da [apex'tadu, da] <> adj -1. [ger] tight. -2. [passagem] narrow. -3. [poltrona, sala, teatro] cramped. -4. [difícil] hard. -5. [sem tempo] pressed. -6. [sem dinheiro] strapped for cash; **orçamento ~** tight budget. -7. *fam* [para ir ao banheiro]: **estar ~** to be desperate to go to the bathroom. -8. [coração]: **estar com o coração ~** to be anguished. <> adv [com dificuldade] only just.

apertar [apex'ta(x)] <> vt -1. [cingir]: **~ algo (contra/entre)** to clasp sthg (against/between); **~ alguém (contra/entre)** to clasp sb (against/between); **~ a mão de alguém** [cumprimentar] to shake sb's hand. -2. [espremer] to squeeze. -3. [incomodar por ser justo] to constrict. -4. [tornar mais justo] to tighten. -5. [pressionar - botão] to do up; [- gatilho] to squeeze. -6. *fig* [intensificar] to tighten up on. -7. [passo, ritmo] to speed up. -8. [cortar] to cut. -9. [coração] to wring. -10. *fig* [pessoa] to put pressure on. <> vi -1. [roupa, sapato] to be tight. -2. [chuva, frio, fome] to intensify. -3. [prazo] to run out. -4. [estrada, rio] to narrow.

aperto [a'pextu] m -1. [em cumprimento]: **~ de mãos** handshake. -2. *fig* [apuro] problem; **passar um ~** to have a rough time. -3. *fig* [financeiro] hardship.

apesar [ape'za(x)] prep: **~ de** in spite of; **~ de que** even though; **~ disso** in spite of this.

apetecer [apete'se(x)] vi to be appetizing; **~ a alguém** to appeal to sb.

apetecível [apete'sivew] (pl -eis) adj -1. [prato, receita] appetizing. -2. *fig* [idéia proposta] attractive.

apetite [ape'tʃitʃi] m appetite; **bom ~!** enjoy your meal!; **ter um ~ de sucesso/riqueza/poder** to have an appetite for success/wealth/power.

apetitoso, osa [apetʃi'tozu, ɔza] adj tasty.

apetrechos [ape'treʃuʃ] mpl -1. [de guerra] equipment (U). -2. [de pesca] tackle (U).

ápice ['apisi] m -1. [cimo] top, summit. -2. *fig* [apogeu] peak.

apiedar-se [apje'daxsi] vp: **~ (de alguém/algo)** to feel sorry (for sb/sthg).

apimentado, da [apimẽn'tadu, da] adj -1. [com muita pimenta] peppery. -2. *fig* [sensual] spicy.

apimentar [apimẽn'ta(x)] vt to pepper.

apinhado, da [api'ɲadu, da] adj crowded.

apinhar [api'ɲa(x)] vt [lotar] to crowd.
➠ **apinhar-se** vp -1. [aglomerar-se] to crowd. -2. [lotar]: **~-se (de gente)** to be crowded (with people).

apitar [api'ta(x)] <> vi -1. [com apito] to whistle. -2. *fam* *fig* [ter autoridade] to know a lot; **ele apita muito em medicina** he knows a lot about medicine; **ele não apita nada em casa** he's not the one who wears the trousers. <> vt [ESP - arbitrar] to referee; [- falta, pênalti] to whistle.

apito [a'pitu] m [instrumento, silvo] whistle.

aplacar [apla'ka(x)] <> vt -1. [serenar] to subdue. -2. [abrandar] to assuage. <> vi -1. [serenar-se] to die down. -2. [abrandar-se] to calm down.
➠ **aplacar-se** vp to calm down.

aplainar [aplaj'na(x)] vt -1. [madeira] to plane. -2. [nivelar] to level out.

aplanar [apla'na(x)] vt -1. [nivelar] to level out. -2. [alisar] to smooth. -3. *fig* [obstáculos] to smooth out.

aplaudir [aplaw'di(x)] <> vt to applaud. <> vi to clap, to applaud.

aplauso [a'plawzuI] m -1. [ger] applause; **o filme recebeu o ~ da crítica** the film received critical acclaim. -2. *fig* [aprovação] approval; **as medidas contra o crime contam com meu ~** I applaud the measures against crime.

aplicação [aplika'sãw] (pl -ões) f -1. [ger] application. -2. [ornato] adornment.

aplicado, da [apli'kadu, da] adj -1. [esforçado] hard-working. -2. [prático] applied.

aplicar [apli'ka(x)] <> vt -1. [ger] to apply. -2. [injeção] to give. -3. *FIN* to invest. <> vi *FIN* to invest.
➠ **aplicar-se** vp -1. [esforçar-se]: **~-se em/para algo** to work hard at/for sthg. -2. [adequar-se]: **~-se a algo** to apply to sthg.

aplicativo, va [aplika'tʃivu, va] adj *COMPUT*: **programa ~** application.
➠ **aplicativo** m *COMPUT* application.

APM (abrev de **Associação de Pais e Mestres**) f ≃ PTA.

apocalipse [apoka'lipsi] m apocalypse.

apoderar-se [apode'raxsi] vp: **~ de algo** to take over sthg.

apodrecer [apodre'se(x)] vi -1. [comida] to go off. -2. [dente] to rot. -3. *fam* [pessoa] **~ em** to rot in.

apodrecimento [apodresi'mẽntu] m rot.

apogeu [apo'ʒew] m -1. [de império, carreira, romance] crowning point. -2. *ASTRON* apogee.

apoiar [apo'ja(x)] vt -1. [ger] to support. -2. [firmar]: **~ algo em** *ou* **sobre algo** to rest sthg on sthg. -**3.** [fundamentar]: ~ **algo em** *ou* **sobre algo** to base sthg on sthg.

◆ **apoiar-se** *vp* -**1.** [amparar-se mutuamente] to support one another. -**2.** [firmar-se] to lean. -**3.** [fundamentar-se] to be based on.

apoio [a'poju] *m* -**1.** [ger] support. -**2.** [patrocínio] sponsorship. -**3.** [alicerce] foundations *(pl)*. -**4.** *fig* [fundamento] basis.

apólice [a'polisil] *f* policy; ~ **de seguro** insurance policy.

apologia [apolo'ʒial] *f* defence.

apontador [apõnta'do(x)] *(pl -es) m* -**1.** [de lápis] pencil sharpener. -**2.** [de jogo] marker.

apontamento [apõnta'mẽntu] *m* [anotação] notes *(pl)*.

apontar [apõn'ta(x)] ◇ *vt* -**1.** [ger] to point out. -**2.** [arma] to aim. -**3.** [citar] to name. -**4.** [notas] to make notes. -**5.** [jogo] to mark. -**6.** [lápis] to sharpen. ◇ *vi* -**1.** [com arma]: ~ **para** to aim at; **apontar! aim!** -**2.** [com o dedo]: ~ **para** to point at. -**3.** [aparecer] to appear.

apoquentar [apokẽnta(x)] *vt* to annoy.

◆ **apoquentar-se** *vp* to get annoyed.

após [a'pɔjʃ] *prep* after.

aposentado, da [apozẽn'tadu, da] ◇ *adj* -**1.** [pessoa] retired. -**2.** [sapato] discarded. -**3.** [carro, máquina] disused. ◇ *m, f* retired person.

aposentadoria [apozẽntado'rial] *f* -**1.** [condição] retirement. -**2.** [vencimentos] pension.

aposentar [apozẽn'ta(x)] *vt* -**1.** [pessoa] to pension off. -**2.** [máquina] to discard.

◆ **aposentar-se** *vp* to retire.

aposento [apo'zẽntul] *m* bedroom.

apossar-se [apo'saxsil] *vp*: ~ **de algo** to take possession of sthg.

aposta [a'pɔʃtal] *f* bet.

apostar [apoʃ'ta(x)] ◇ *vt* to bet; ~ **que** to bet that. ◇ *vi*: ~ **em** to bet on.

apostila [apoʃ'tʃilal] *f* -**1.** [nota marginal] marginal note. -**2.** [matéria de aula] handout.

apóstolo [a'pɔʃtulul] *m* apostle.

apóstrofo [a'pɔʃtroful] *m* apostrophe.

apoteose [apote'ɔzil] *f* apotheosis.

aprazível [apra'zivɛwl] *(pl -eis) adj* pleasant.

apreciação [apresja'sãwl] *(pl -ões) f* -**1.** [análise] consideration. -**2.** [julgamento] assessment.

apreciar [apre'sja(x)] *vt* -**1.** [ger] to appreciate. -**2.** [gostar de] to enjoy.

apreciativo, va [apresja'tʃivu, val *adj* appreciative.

apreço [a'presul *m* [estima, consideração] consideration.

apreender [aprjẽn'de(x)] *vt* -**1.** [tomar] to seize. -**2.** [compreender] to understand, to comprehend.

apreensão [aprjẽn'sãwl *(pl -ões) f* -**1.** [tomada] seizure. -**2.** [percepção] understanding, comprehension. -**3.** [preocupação] apprehension.

apreensivo, va [aprjẽn'sivu, val *adj* apprehensive.

apregoar [apre'gwa(x)] *vt* to proclaim.

aprender [aprẽn'de(x)] ◇ *vt* to learn. ◇ *vi* to learn; ~ **a fazer algo** to learn to do sthg; ~ **de cor** to learn by heart.

aprendiz [aprẽn'dʒiʒl *(pl -es) mf* learner.

aprendizado [aprẽndʒi'zadul *m*, **aprendizagem** *f* [aprẽndʒi'zaʒẽl *(pl -ns)* learning.

apresentação [aprezẽnta'sãwl *(pl -ões) f* [ger] presentation.

apresentador, ra [aprezẽnta'do(x), ral *m, f* -**1.** [de seminário, painel] speaker. -**2.** *RÁDIO,TV* presenter.

apresentar [aprezẽn'ta(x)] *vt* -**1.** [ger] to present; ~ **uma comunicação** to give a talk. -**2.** [fazer] to make. -**3.** [moção, recurso] to introduce.

◆ **apresentar-se** *vp* -**1.** [dar-se a conhecer] to introduce o.s. -**2.** [comparecer] to present o.s. -**3.** [manifestar-se] to arise. -**4.** [candidatar-se] to put o.s. forward.

apressado, da [apre'sadu, da] *adj* hurried; **estar** ~ to be in a hurry.

apressar [apre'sa(x)] *vt* to hurry.

◆ **apressar-se** *vp* to hurry.

aprimorar [aprimo'ra(x)] *vt* to improve.

◆ **aprimorar-se** *vp*: ~-**se (em algo)** to try hard (at sthg).

aprisionamento [aprizjona'mẽntul *m* -**1.** [de pessoa] imprisonment. -**2.** [de passarinho] captivity.

aprisionar [aprizjo'na(x)] *vt* -**1.** [prender] to imprison. -**2.** [meter em prisão] to put in prison. -**3.** [capturar] to keep in captivity.

aprofundamento [aprofũnda'mẽntul *m* in-depth examination.

aprofundar [aprofũn'da(x)] *vt* -**1.** [ger] to deepen. -**2.** [investigação] to intensify. -**3.** [conhecimentos] to improve. -**4.** [divergências] to increase.

◆ **aprofundar-se** *vp* -**1.** [no solo, no mar] to go down. -**2.** [em investigações, análise] to intensify. -**3.** [em área de conhecimento] to immerse o.s. -**4.** [em selva, mato] to penetrate deeper.

aprontar [aprõnta(x)] ◇ *vt* -**1.** [preparar] to prepare. -**2.** [terminar] to complete. -**3.** *fam* [briga, confusão] to cause.

◇ *vi fam* [criar confusão] to play up.

◆ **aprontar-se** *vp* -**1.** [vestir-se, arrumar-se] to get ready. -**2.** [preparar-se] to prepare o.s.

apropriação [aproprja'sãw] (*pl* -ões) *f* -**1.** [assenhoramento] takeover. -**2.** [tomada] seizure.

apropriado, da [apro'prjadu, da] *adj* -**1.** [adequado] appropriate. -**2.** [tomado] seized.

apropriar [apro'prja(x)] *vt* [adequar] to adapt.

◆ **apropriar-se** *vp*: ~-se de algo to take possession of sthg.

aprovação [aprova'sãw] (*pl* -ões) *f* -**1.** [ger] approval. -**2.** [em exame] pass.

aprovar [apro'va(x)] *vt* -**1.** [apoiar] to approve. -**2.** [sancionar] to approve. -**3.** [em exame] to pass.

aproveitador, ra [aprovejta'do(x), ra] (*mpl* -es, *fpl* -s) ◇ *adj* opportunistic. ◇ *m,f* opportunist.

aproveitamento [aprovejta'mẽntul] *m* -**1.** [uso] good use. -**2.** [nos estudos] improvement; **ter um bom** ~ to do well.

aproveitar [aprovej'ta(x)] ◇ *vt* -**1.** [não desperdiçar] to make the most of, to put to good use. -**2.** [usar] to use. ◇ *vi* [tirar proveito]: ~ **para fazer algo** to take opportunity to do sthg; **aproveite enquanto é tempo!** make the most of it while you can!, make hay while the sun shines!

◆ **aproveitar-se** *vp*: ~-se de algo/alguém to take advantage of sthg/sb.

aprovisionar [aprovizjo'na(x)] *vt* [abastecer] to supply.

aprox. (*abrev de* aproximadamente) *adv* approx.

aproximação [aprosima'sãw] (*pl* -ões) *f* -**1.** [chegada] approach. -**2.** [estimativa] approximation. -**3.** [de países] coming together. -**4.** [de pontos de vista] similarity.

aproximado, da [aprosi'madu, da] *adj* approximate.

aproximar [aprosi'ma(x)] *vt* -**1.** [precipitar] to bring forward. -**2.** [cálculo] to approximate. -**3.** [pessoas, países] to bring together. -**4.** [levar para perto] to draw up. -**5.** [fazer parecer perto] to bring closer.

◆ **aproximar-se** *vp* -**1.** [achegar-se] to approach. -**2.** [pessoas, países] to draw closer. -**3.** [assemelhar-se] to be similar.

aptidão [aptʃi'dãw] (*pl* -ões) *f* -**1.** [ger] aptitude. -**2.** [jeito]: **ter** ~ **para** to have an aptitude for.

apto, ta ['aptu, ta] *adj* suitable.

Apto. (*abrev de* apartamento) *m* Flat *no. UK*, Apt. *US*.

apunhalar [apuɲa'la(x)] *vt* -**1.** [esfaquear] to stab. -**2.** *fig* [trair] to stab in the back.

apuração [apura'sãw] (*pl* -ões) *f* -**1.** [de votos] counting. -**2.** [de fatos, informações] examination. -**3.** [de conta] checking.

apurado, da [apu'radu, da] *adj* -**1.** [ger] refined. -**2.** [aguçado] sharp.

apurar [apu'ra(x)] *vt* -**1.** [tornar puro] to purify. -**2.** [refinar] to refine. -**3.** [aprimorar] to perfect. -**4.** [aguçar] to sharpen. -**5.** [averiguar] to verify. -**6.** [votos] to count. -**7.** [conta] to check.

◆ **apurar-se** *vp* -**1.** [tornar-se puro] to become pure. -**2.** [no trajar] to smarten o.s. up. -**3.** [aprimorar-se] to become perfect.

apuro [a'purul *m* -**1.** [esmero] care. -**2.** [dificuldade] fix; **estar em** ~**s** to be in a fix. -**3.** [aperto financeiro] hardship.

aquarela [akwa'rɛla] *f* water colour.

aquário [a'kwarju] *m* [para peixes] aquarium.

◆ **Aquário** *m* [zodíaco] Aquarius; *veja também* **Virgem**.

aquático, ca [a'kwatʃiku, ka] *adj* aquatic; **pólo/massagem** ~ water polo/massage; **ginástica** ~ aquarobics; **esportes** ~**s** aquatics.

aquecedor [akese'do(x)] (*pl* -es) *adj* heating.

◆ **aquecedor** *m* heater.

aquecer [ake'se(x)] ◇ *vt* -**1.** [ger] to warm up. -**2.** [esquentar] to heat. ◇ *vi* -**1.** [esquentar] to become hot. -**2.** [dar calor] to give warmth.

◆ **aquecer-se** *vp* -**1.** [ger] to warm up. -**2.** [esquentar-se] to warm o.s. -**3.** *fig* [debate] to become heated.

aquecimento [akesi'mẽntul *m* -**1.** [ger] heating; ~ **central** central heating. -**2.** [econômico] warming. -**3.** *ESP* [muscular] warm up.

àquela [a'kɛla] = a + aquela.

aquele, aquela [a'keli, a'kɛla] ◇ *adj* that, those *pl*. ◇ *pron* that one; ~ **ali** that one there; ~ **que** [relativo a pessoa] the one who, those who *pl*; [relativo a objeto] the one which; **peça àquele homem/àquela mulher** ask that man/woman.

àquele [a'keli] = a + aquele.

aquém [a'kẽj] *adv* -**1.** [deste lado] this side; ~ **de** on this side of. -**2.** [abaixo]: ~ **de** below.

aqui [a'ki] *adv* -**1.** [neste lugar] here; ~ **mesmo** right here; **eis** ~ here is; **por** ~ round here; **estar por** ~ **(com algo/alguém)** to be up to here (with sthg/

aquietar

sb). **-2.** [neste momento] at that point; **até ~** up to now. **-3.** [nisto] on this point.

aquietar [akje'ta(x)] *vt* to quieten.
➡ aquietar-se *vp* to quieten down.

aquilo [a'kilu] *pron* that; **você chama aquilo de carro!** you call that a car!

àquilo [a'kilu] = **a + aquilo**.

aquisição [akizi'sãw] (*pl* **-ões**) *f* acquisition.

aquisitivo, va [akizi'tʃivu, va] *adj* [poder] acquisitive.

ar [a(x)] (*pl* **-ares**) *m* **-1.** [ger] air; **o avião está no ~** the plane is in the sky; **ao ~ livre** in the open air; **~ condicionado** [atmosfera] air conditioning; **ir pelos ares** to be blown sky-high. **-2.** RÁDIO, TV : **no ~** on the air; **ir ao ~** to be broadcast, to go on the air. **-3.** *fig* [aspecto] appearance. **-4.** *loc*: **apanhar as coisas no ~** to pick things up quickly; **estar no ~** to be up in the air.

árabe ['arabi] *adj* Arab. *m, f* Arab. *m* [língua] Arabic.

arabesco [ara'beʃku] *m* arabesque.

Arábia Saudita [a,rabjasaw'dʒita] *n* Saudi Arabia.

arábico, ca [a'rabiku, ka] *adj* **-1.** [da Arábia] Arabian. **-2.** [algarismo] Arabic. **-3.** [goma]: **goma arábica** gum arabic.

Aracaju [araka'ʒu] *n* Aracaju.

arado [a'radu] *m* plough.

aragem [a'raʒẽ] (*pl* **-ns** [a'raʒẽʃ]) *f* breeze.

arame [a'rãmi] *m* [cabo] wire; **~ farpado** barbed wire.

aranha [a'rãɲa] *f* spider.

aranha-caranguejeira [a,rãɲakarãge'ʒejra] (*pl* **aranhas-caranguejeiras**) *f* bird-eating spider.

arar [a'ra(x)] *vt* to plough.

arara [a'raral] *f* macaw.

arbitragem [axbi'traʒẽ] (*pl* **-ns**) *f* **-1.** [julgamento] arbitration. **-2.** ESP [- ato] adjudication; [- decisão] decision; [- os juízes] referees (*pl*).

arbitrar [axbi'tra(x)] *vt* **-1.** [questão, litígio] to arbitrate. **-2.** ESP [partida, campeonato] to referee.

arbitrariedade [axbitrarje'dadʒi] *f* arbitrariness.

arbitrário, ria [axbi'trarju, rja] *adj* arbitrary.

arbítrio [ax'bitrju] *m* **-1.** [resolução] judgment. **-2.** [faculdade] free will.

árbitro ['axbitru] *m* **-1.** [de questão, litígio] mediator. **-2.** [juiz] judge. **-3.** [ESP - em futebol, box] referee; [- em tênis] umpire.

arborizado, da [axbori'zadu, da] *adj* **-1.** [bairro, terreno] wooded. **-2.** [rua] tree-lined.

arbusto [ax'buʃtu] *m* bush.

arca ['axka] *f* **-1.** [caixa] chest. **-2.** [barca]: **Arca de Noé** Noah's Ark.

arcada [ax'kada] *f* **-1.** [de arcos] arcade; **~ dentária** dental arch. **-2.** [arco] arch.

arcaico, ca [ax'kajku, ka] *adj* **-1.** [antigo] archaic. **-2.** [antiquado] antiquated.

arcaizante [axkaj'zãntʃi] *adj* archaic.

arcar [ax'ka(x)] *vi*: **~ com algo** to take responsibility for sthg.

arcebispo [axse'biʃpu] *m* archbishop.

arco ['axku] *m* **-1.** [ger] arch. **-2.** [arma, instrumento musical] bow; **~-e-flecha** ESP archery. **-3.** GEOM , ELETR & MAT arc. **-4.** [de barril] hoop.

arco-íris [ax'kwiriʃ] (*pl* **arcos-íris**) *m inv* rainbow.

ar-condicionado [,a(x)kõndʒisjo'nadul (*pl* **ares-condicionados**) *m* [aparelho] air-conditioning.

ardência [ax'dẽnsja] *f* burning.

ardente [ax'dẽntʃi] *adj* burning.

arder [ax'de(x)] *vi* **-1.** [ger] to burn. **-2.** [ferimento] to sting.

ardido, da [ax'dʒidu, da] *adj* **-1.** [costas, olhos] stinging. **-2.** [pimenta, comida] hot.

ardil [ax'dʒiw] (*pl* **-is**) *m* cunning.

ardiloso, losa [axdʒi'lozu, lɔza] *adj* [pessoa] cunning.

ardor [ax'do(x)] (*pl* **-es**) *m* [paixão] ardour.

ardoroso, rosa [axdo'rozu, rɔza] *adj* amorous.

ardósia [ax'dɔzja] *f* slate.

árduo, dua ['axdwu, dwa] *adj* **-1.** [escarpado] arduous. **-2.** [difícil] hard. **-3.** [sofrimento] painful.

área ['arja] *f* **-1.** [ger] area; **~ de serviço** service point. **-2.** [de conhecimento etc.] field.

areia [a'reja] *f* sand; **~ movediça** quicksand.

arejado, da [are'ʒadu, da] *adj* **-1.** [ventilado] airy. **-2.** [fig] [pessoa, cabeça] open-minded.

arena [a'renal] *f* **-1.** [ger] arena. **-2.** [de circo] ring. **-3.** [de teatro] amphitheatre.

arenito [are'nitul] *m* sandstone.

arenoso, osa [are'nozu, ɔza] *adj* sandy.

arenque [a'rẽŋki] *m* herring.

ares ['ariʃ] **➪ ar.**

argamassa [axga'masa] *f* mortar.

Argel [ax'ʒɛw] Algiers.

Argélia [ax'ʒɛlja] Algeria.

argelino, na [axʒe'linu, na] *adj* Algerian. *m, f* Algerian.

Argentina [axʒẽn'tʃina] *n*: **(a) ~** Argentina.

argentino, na [axʒẽn'tʃinu, na] *adj* Argentinian. *m, f* Argentinian.

argila [ax'ʒila] f clay.

argola [ax'gola] f -1. [aro] ring. -2. [de porta] knocker.

argumentação [axgumẽnta'sãw] (pl -ões) f argument, reasoning.

argumentar [axgumẽn'ta(x)] ⟨⟩ vt [alegar] to argue. ⟨⟩ vi [expor argumentos] to argue one's case.

argumento [axgu'mẽntu] m -1. [em teoria, debate] argument. -2. [de filme, TV, romance] theme, plot.

arguto, ta [ax'gutu, ta] adj -1. [agudo] shrewd. -2. [sutil] subtle.

ária ['arja] f MÚS aria.

aridez [ari'deʒ] f -1. [de clima, estação] dryness. -2. [de terra, região] aridity. -3. fig [de teoria, pensamento] barrenness.

árido, da ['aridu, da] adj -1. [clima, estação] dry. -2. [terra, região] arid. -3. fig [teoria, pensamento] barren.

Áries ['arjʃ] m Aries; veja também **Virgem**.

aristocrata [arifto'krata] mf aristocrat.

aristocrático, ca [arifto'kratfiku, ka] adj aristocratic.

aritmético, ca [aritf'mɛtfiku, ka] adj arithmetic.
    ⬦ **aritmética** f arithmetic.

arma ['axma] f -1. [ger] weapon; ~ **de fogo** firearm; ~ **nuclear** nuclear weapon; ~ **química** chemical weapon. -2. MIL [do Exército] force.
    ⬦ **armas** fpl -1. [forças armadas] forces. -2. [brasão] arms.

armação [axma'sãw] (pl -ões) f -1. [de barraca, estrutura, peças] framework. -2. [estrutura] frame. -3. [de óculos] frames (pl). -4. [de onda] point near a shoreline where the waves start to break. -5. [de tempestade] gathering. -6. fam [golpe] con. -7. fam [programa, aventura] move.

armada [ax'mada] ⬦ **Armada** f navy.

armadilha [axma'diʎa] f trap.

armador, ra [axma'do(x), ra] m, f [NÁUT - dono] shipowner; [- firma] ship chandler's.

armadura [axma'dura] f -1. [de cavaleiro] armour. -2. [de ouriço, besouro] shell. -3. ELETR armature. -4. CONSTR framework.

armamentista [axmamẽn'tfifta] adj ⬦ corrida.

armamento [axma'mẽntu] m -1. [armas] armament. -2. NÁUT fitting out.

armar [ax'ma(x)] vt -1. [com arma] to arm. -2. [carregar] to load. -3. [gatilho] to cock. -4. [montar] to assemble. -5. [preparar] to set up. -6. [saia etc.] to give body to. -7. fam [planejar - golpe] to plot; [- programa, aventura] to plan. -8. fam [provocar] to cause. -9. NÁUT to fit out.

armar-se vp [com armas] to arm o.s.

armarinho [axma'riɲu] m haberdasher's UK, notions store US.

armário [ax'marju] m -1. [de roupa] wardrobe; ~ **embutido** fitted wardrobe. -2. [de cozinha etc.] cupboard.

armazém [axma'zẽl] (pl -ns) m -1. [depósito] warehouse. -2. [loja] store.

armazenar [axmaze'na(x)] vt to store.

arminho [ax'miɲu] m ermine.

aro ['aru] m -1. [ger] rim. -2. [argola] ring. -3. [de porta] frame.

aroma [a'roma] m -1. [de perfume] scent. -2. [de café, comida] aroma.

aromático, ca [aro'matfiku, ka] adj -1. [essência, erva] aromatic. -2. [tempero, comida] spicy.

arpão [ax'pãw] (pl -ões) m harpoon.

arpões [ax'põjʃ] pl ⬦ arpão.

arqueado, da [ax'kjadu, da] adj -1. [pernas] bandy. -2. [sobrancelhas] arched.

arquear [ax'kja(x)] vt to arch.
    ⬦ **arquear-se** vp to bend.

arqueiro, ra [ax'kejru, ra] m, f -1. [atirador] archer. -2. [goleiro] goalkeeper.

arqueologia [axkjolo'ʒia] f archaeology.

arqueólogo, ga [ax'kjɔlogu, ga] m, f archaeologist.

arquibancada [axkibãŋ'kada] f -1. [local] terrace; **ir de** ~ to sit on the terraces. -2. [público] terraces (pl).

arquipélago [axki'pɛlagu] m archipelago.

arquiteto, ta [axki'tɛtu, ta] m, f architect.

arquitetônico, ca [axkite'toniku, ka] adj architectural.

arquitetura [axkite'tura] f architecture.

arquivar [axki'va(x)] vt -1. [ger] to file. -2. [projeto, processo] to shelve.

arquivista [axki'vifta] mf archivist.

arquivo [ax'kivu] m -1. [ger] file; **abrir/ fechar um** ~ to open/close a file. -2. [local] archive. -3. [móvel] filing cabinet. -4. [de instituição] file.

arraia [a'xaja] f [peixe] ray.

arraial [axa'jaw] (pl -ais) m [povoado] village.

arraigado, da [axaj'gadu, da] adj -1. [costume, idéia, mentalidade] deep-rooted. -2. fig [defensor, admirador] staunch.

arraigar [axaj'ga(x)] vi [criar raízes] to put down roots.
    ⬦ **arraigar-se** vp -1. [ger] to take root. -2. [pessoa] to settle down.

arrancada [axãŋ'kada] f -1. [puxão] tug. -2. [partida] start. -3. [em competição, disputa] spurt; **dar uma** ~ to jump ahead.

arrancar [axãŋ'ka(x)] <> vt -1. [tirar]: ~ algo de alguém to pull sthg off sb; ~ algo (de algo) [pétala, botão] to pull sthg (off sthg); [folha] to tear sthg (out of sthg); [raiz] to pull sthg up (out of sthg). -2. [conseguir]: ~ algo de alguém to draw sthg from sb. -3. [fazer sair]: ~ alguém de algum lugar to turf sb out of somewhere. <> vi -1. [dar partida] to start off. -2. [em competição] to put on a spurt.

➤ **arrancar-se** vt fam [fugir]: ~-se (de) to scarper (from).

arranha-céu [a͜xãɲa'sɛw] (pl arranha-céus) m skyscraper.

arranhão [axã'ɲãw] (pl -ões) m scratch.

arranhar [axa'ɲa(x)] <> vt -1. [ger] to scratch. -2. fig [tocar mal] to bash away at. -3. fig [idioma] to scratch by. <> vi [provocar arranhão] to scratch.

➤ **arranhar-se** vp to scratch o.s.

arranjar [axã'ʒa(x)] vt -1. [ger] to arrange. -2. [resolver] to sort out. -3. [conseguir] to obtain. -4. [contrair] to catch. -5. [encontrar] to find.

➤ **arranjar-se** vp [virar-se] to get by.

arranjo [a'xãʒu] m -1. [ger] arrangement. -2. [acordo] deal. -3. [mamata] scam.

arranque [a'xãŋki] m ➢ motor.

arrasado, da [axa'zadu, da] adj -1. [devastado] razed, devastated. -2. [arruinado] ruined. -3. [deprimido] devastated. -4. [muito cansado] worn out.

arrasador, ra [axaza'do(x), ra] adj -1. [devastador] crippling. -2. [notícia, crítica] devastating. -3. [vitória] overwhelming.

arrasar [axa'za(x)] vt -1. [devastar] to raze. -2. [arruinar] to destroy. -3. [com críticas] to demolish.

➤ **arrasar-se** vp -1. [ser devastado] to be devastated. -2. [destruir-se] to be destroyed. -3. [arruinar-se] to collapse in ruins. -4. [em exame, competição] to flop.

arrastão [axaʃ'tãw] (pl -tões) m -1. [PESCA - rede] dragnet; [- ato] haul. -2. [puxão] tug. -3. fig [assalto] mobbing.

arrastar [axaʃ'ta(x)] <> vt [ger] to drag. <> vi [roçar] to drag.

➤ **arrastar-se** vp -1. [rastejar] to crawl. -2. [andar com dificuldade] to drag o.s. -3. [decorrer lentamente] to drag on.

arrear [a'xja(x)] vt [montaria] to harness.

arrebatado, da [axeba'tadu, da] adj -1. [impetuoso] impetuous. -2. [exaltado] fiery.

arrebatar [axeba'ta(x)] vt -1. [arrancar]: ~ algo de algo/alguém to grab sthg from sthg/sb. -2. [carregar] to drag off. -3. fig [aplausos] to draw. -4. fig [coração] to break.

➤ **arrebatar-se** vp -1. [exaltar-se] to get carried away. -2. [maravilhar-se] to be entranced.

arrebentação [axebẽnta'sãw] f [local] point close to a shoreline at which the waves break.

arrebentado, da [axebẽn'tadu, da] adj -1. [em mau estado] broken. -2. [ferido] battered. -3. [muito cansado] worn out.

arrebentar [axebẽn'ta(x)] <> vt -1. [quebrar, romper] to break. -2. [estragar] to wreck. -3. [ferir] to smash. <> vi -1. [quebrar, romper-se] to snap. -2. [bomba] to explode. -3. fig [guerra, revolução] to break out.

➤ **arrebentar-se** vp [ferir-se] to smash o.s.up.

arrebitado, da [axebi'tadu, da] adj -1. [para cima] turned up. -2. [bumbum, nariz] pert.

arrecadação [axekada'sãw] (pl -ões) f -1. [coleta] collection. -2. [receita] revenue.

arrecadar [axeka'da(x)] vt to collect.

arrecife [axe'sifi] m reef.

arredar [axe'da(x)] vt [retirar] to remove; ~ (o) pé (de) [de lugar] to budge from; [de intenção, princípios] to budge (from).

arredio, dia [axe'dʒiu, dʒia] adj [pessoa] withdrawn.

arredondado, da [axedõn'dadu, da] adj round.

arredondar [axedõn'da(x)] vt -1. [formato] to round off. -2. [conta] to round up.

arredores [axe'dɔriʃ] mpl -1. [cercanias] neighbourhood. -2. [periferia] outskirts.

arrefecer [axefe'se(x)] <> vt -1. [tornar frio] to cool. -2. [febre] to lower. -3. fig [desanimar] to cool. <> vi -1. [tornar-se frio] to cool down. -2. [ger] to subside.

ar-refrigerado [͜a(x)xefriʒe'radu] (pl ares-refrigerados) m -1. [aparelho] air-conditioner. -2. [sistema] air-conditioning.

arregaçar [axega'sa(x)] vt to roll up.

arregalado, da [axega'ladu, da] adj staring.

arregalar [axega'la(x)] vt to open wide.

arreganhado, da [axega'ɲadu, da] adj gaping.

arregimentar [axeʒimẽn'ta(x)] vt to drum up.

arreio [a'xeju] m [cavalo] harness.

arrematar [axema'ta(x)] vt -1. [ger] to finish off. -2. [dizer concluindo] to conclude. -3. [em leilão - comprar] to bid successfully for; [- vender] to auction off.

arremessar [axeme'sa(x)] vt to throw.

arremesso [axe'mesu] m [lançamento] throw; ~ de peso ESP shot-put.

arremeter [axeme'te(x)] *vi* to charge; ~ **contra** to attack.

arrendamento [axẽnda'mẽntul] *m* leasing, hiring, rental.

arrendar [axẽn'da(x)] *vt* -**1.** [dar] to let, to lease. -**2.** [tomar] to rent, to take a lease on.

arrepender-se [axepẽn'dexsil] *vp* to repent; ~ **de algo/de fazer algo** to regret sthg/doing sthg.

arrependido, da [axepẽn'dʒidu, dal] *adj* repentant, sorry.

arrependimento [axepẽndʒi'mẽntul] *m* -**1.** [remorso] regret. -**2.** [de crime] remorse. -**3.** *RELIG* repentance.

arrepiado, da [axe'pjadu, dal] *adj* -**1.** [eriçado - cabelo] standing on end *(depois de subst/verbo)*; [- pele] goose-pimpled. -**2.** *fig* [assustado] terrified.

arrepiar [axe'pja(x)] *vt* -**1.** [eriçar - cabelo] to cause to stand on end; [- pele] to give goose pimples. -**2.** [fig] [assustar] to terrify; **(ser) de** ~ **os cabelos** to be enough to make your hair stand on end.

  ➤ **arrepiar-se** *vp* [ficar eriçado - cabelo] to stand on end; [- pessoa] to shiver.

arrepio [axe'piwl] *m* shiver; **dar** ~ **s (a alguém)** *fig* to send shivers up sb's spine.

arresto [a'xɛʃtul] *m* JUR confiscation.

arriar [a'xja(x)] ⬦ *vt* -**1.** [abaixar - cortina, calça] to lower; [- pneu] to let down. -**2.** [cansar muito] to exhaust. -**3.** [pôr de cama] to lay up. ⬦ *vi* -**1.** [pneu, bateria] to go flat. -**2.** [vergar] to sag. -**3.** [desanimar] to lose heart.

arriscado, da [axiʃ'kadu, dal] *adj* -**1.** [perigoso] hazardous, risky. -**2.** [audacioso] daring.

arriscar [axiʃ'ka(x)] ⬦ *vt* -**1.** [pôr em perigo] to put at risk. -**2.** [palpite] to risk. ⬦ *vi* [tentar] to take the risk.

  ➤ **arriscar-se** *vp* [pôr-se em perigo] to take a risk; ~**-se a fazer algo** to risk doing sthg.

arrivista [axi'viʃtal] ⬦ *adj* opportunistic. ⬦ *mf* opportunist.

arroba [a'xobal] *f* COMPUT at.

arrocho [a'xoʃul] *m* -**1.** [diminuição] lessening; ~ **salarial** wage squeeze. -**2.** [dificuldade financeira] hardship. -**3.** *fam fig* [pressão] grilling.

arrogância [axo'gãnsjal] *f* arrogance.

arrogante [axo'gãntʃil] *adj* arrogant.

arroio [a'xojul] *m* stream.

arrojado, da [axo'ʒadu, dal] *adj* -**1.** [ger] bold. -**2.** [ousado] daring. -**3.** [temerário] rash.

arrolamento [axola'mẽntul] *m* -**1.** [levantamento] register. -**2.** [lista] list.

arrolar [axo'la(x)] *vt* [listar] to list.

arrombamento [axõnba'mẽntul] *m* [abertura forçada]: **foi necessário o** ~ **da porta** it was necessary to break down the door.

arrombar [axõn'ba(x)] *vt* -**1.** [ger] to break into. -**2.** [porta] to break down.

arrotar [axo'ta(x)] ⬦ *vi* [dar arroto] to belch. ⬦ *vt* -**1.** [cheiro] to burp. -**2.** *fam fig* [alardear] to boast about.

arroto [a'xotul] *m* burp.

arroubo [a'xobul] *m* [enlevo] moment of ecstasy.

arroz [a'xoʒ] *m* rice.

arroz-doce [axoʒ'dosil] *m* CULIN *rice pudding sprinkled with cinnamon and cloves.*

arruaça [a'xwasal] *f* riot.

arruaceiro, ra [axwa'sejru, ral] ⬦ *adj* rowdy. ⬦ *m, f* rioter.

arruela [a'xwɛlal] *f* washer.

arruinado, da [axwi'nadu, dal] *adj* ruined.

arruinar [axwi'na(x)] *vt* -**1.** [arrasar] to demolish. -**2.** [destruir] to destroy. -**3.** [causar falência] to ruin.

  ➤ **arruinar-se** *vp* [ruir] to be ruined.

arrulhar [axu'ʎa(x)] *vi* -**1.** [pombo] to coo. -**2.** *fig* [namorados] to bill and coo.

arrumação [axuma'sãw] *f* -**1.** [arranjo] arrangement. -**2.** [de quarto, armário] tidying. -**3.** [de malas, bagagem] packing.

arrumadeira [axuma'dejral] *f* [criada] maid.

arrumar [axu'ma(x)] *vt* -**1.** [pôr em ordem] to arrange. -**2.** [quarto, armário] to tidy. -**3.** [malas, bagagem] to pack. -**4.** [vestir, aprontar] to straighten up. -**5.** [conseguir] to get.

  ➤ **arrumar-se** *vp* -**1.** [vestir-se, aprontar-se] to get ready. -**2.** [na vida] to set o.s. up. -**3.** [virar-se] to fend for o.s.

arsenal [axse'naw] *(pl* -**ais***)* *m* arsenal.

arsênio [ax'senjul] *m* arsenic.

arte ['axtʃil *f* -**1.** [ger] art; ~ **dramática** theatre. -**2.** [arte-final] artwork. -**3.** [ofício] art. -**4.** [técnica] art; ~ **culinária** cuisine; ~ **marcial** martial art. -**5.** [primor]: **com** ~ skilfully. -**6.** [astúcia] cunning. -**7.** *fam* [travessura] mischief; **fazer** ~ to get up to mischief.

  ➤ **artes** *fpl* -**1.** [visuais] arts; ~**s plásticas** plastic arts. -**2.** [curso]: **(belas-)**~**s** fine arts. -**3.** [artifício]: **por** ~**s de** through the artful wiles of.

artefato [axte'fatul] *m* -**1.** [instrumento] artefact. -**2.** [produto] goods *(pl)*.

artéria [ax'tɛrjal] *f* artery.

arterial [axte'rjawl] *(pl* -**ais***)* *adj* arterial.

artesã [axte'zã] f ▷ **artesão**.

artesanal [axteza'naw] (pl **-ais**) adj craftwork.

artesanato [axteza'natu] m craftwork.

artesão, sã [axte'zãw, zã] (mpl **-ãos**, fpl **-s**) m, f craftsman (f craftswoman).

ártico, ca l'axtʃiku] adj Arctic.
    ➡ **Ártico** n: o **Ártico** the Arctic; o **Oceano Glacial Ártico** the Arctic Ocean.

articulação [axtʃikula'sãw] (pl **-ões**) f **-1.** [ligação] connection. **-2.** ANAT joint. **-3.** POL link.

articulista [axtʃiku'liʃta] mf JORN article writer.

artífice [ax'tʃifisil] mf **-1.** [artesão] craftsman (f craftswoman). **-2.** [criador, mentor] author.

artificial [axtʃifi'sjaw] (pl **-ais**) adj **-1.** [ger] artificial. **-2.** [dissimulado] false.

artifício [axtʃi'fisju] m **-1.** [processo] artifice. **-2.** [subterfúgio] trick. **-3.** [dissimulação] pretence.

artigo [ax'tʃigu] m article; ~ **de luxo** luxury item; ~**s esportivos** sports goods.

artilharia [axtʃiʎa'ria] f artillery.

artista [ax'tʃiʃta] mf **-1.** [ger] artist. **-2.** [ator] actor (f actress). **-3.** [pessoa manhosa] crafty person.

artístico, ca [ax'tʃiʃtʃiku, ka] adj artistic.

artrite [ax'tritʃi] f arthritis.

árvore ['axvoril] f **-1.** [vegetal] tree; ~ **de Natal** Christmas tree. **-2.** TEC shaft.

arvoredo [axvo'redu] m grove.

as [aʃ] ▷ **a**.

ás, ases l'ajʃ, 'azeʃ] ◇ mf [pessoa exímia]: ~ **de algo** ace at sthg. ◇ m [carta] ace.

às [ajʃ] = a + as.

asa l'aza] f **-1.** [de pássaro, avião, inseto] wing. **-2.** [de xícara] handle.

asa-delta [,aza'ʒ'dɛwta] (pl **asas-delta**) f **-1.** [veículo] hang-glider. **-2.** [esporte] hang gliding.

ascendência [asēn'dēnsja] f **-1.** [antepassados] descent. **-2.** [influência, domínio] influence; **ter** ~ **sobre** to hold sway over.

ascendente [asēn'dēntʃil] ◇ adj rising. ◇ m, f [antepassado] ancestor.

ascender [asēn'de(x)] vi to rise.

ascensão [asēn'sãw] (pl **-ões**) f **-1.** [ger] rise. **-2.** [subida] climb.

ascensorista [asēnso'riʃta] mf lift operator.

ASCII (abrev de **American Standard Code for Information Interchange**) m ASCII.

asco l'aʃku] m disgust; **dar** ~ **a alguém** to make sb sick.

asfaltado, da [aʃfaw'tadu, da] adj asphalted.

asfalto [aʃ'fawtul m asphalt.

asfixia [aʃfik'sia] f asphyxia.

asfixiar [aʃfik'sja(x)] vt **-1.** [matar por asfixia] to asphyxiate. **-2.** [sufocar] to be suffocating. **-3.** fig [oprimir] to suppress.
    ➡ **asfixiar-se** vp **-1.** [morrer por asfixia] to be asphyxiated. **-2.** [sufocar-se] to gasp for breath.

Ásia l'azjal n Asia.

asiático, ca [a'zjatʃiku, ka] ◇ adj Asian. ◇ m, f Asian.

asilo [a'zilu] m **-1.** [para órfãos, anciãos] home. **-2.** [refúgio] refuge. **-3.** POL asylum; ~ **político** political asylum.

asma l'aʒma] f asthma.

asneira [aʒ'nejra] f [ação] blunder.

asno l'aʒnul m **-1.** [animal] ass, donkey. **-2.** fam fig & pej [idiota] silly ass.

aspargo [aʃ'paxgu] m asparagus.

aspas l'aʃpaʃ] fpl quotation marks.

aspecto [aʃ'pɛktu] m **-1.** [aparência] look. **-2.** [faceta] aspect. **-3.** [ângulo] angle. **-4.** [visão, detalhe] view.

aspereza [aʃpe'reza] f **-1.** [no tato] roughness. **-2.** fig [severidade, rispidez] harshness.

aspergir [aʃpex'ʒi(x)] vt to sprinkle.

áspero, ra l'aʃperu, ral adj **-1.** [ao tato] rough. **-2.** fig [severo, ríspido] harsh.

asperso, sa [aʃ'pexsu, sa] pp ▷ **aspergir**.

aspiração [aʃpira'sãw] (pl **-ões**) f **-1.** [de ar - por pessoa] inhalation; [- por máquina] suction. **-2.** LING aspiration.

aspirador [aʃpira'do(x)] (pl **-es**) m: ~ **(de pó)** vacuum cleaner; **passar o** ~ **(em)** to vacuum, to hoover.

aspirante [aʃpi'rãntʃi] mf **-1.** [candidato]: **ser** ~ **(a algo)** to be a candidate (for sthg). **-2.** MIL & NÁUT cadet.

aspirar [aʃpi'ra(x)] ◇ vt **-1.** [sugar] to aspirate, to suck in. **-2.** [ar - pessoa] to inhale; [- máquina] to suction. **-3.** LING to aspirate. ◇ vi **-1.** [desejar]: ~ **a algo** to aspire to sthg. **-2.** [respirar] to breathe. **-3.** [soprar brisa] to blow.

aspirina [aʃpi'rina] f aspirin®.

asqueroso, osa [aʃke'rozu, ɔza] adj disgusting.

assado, da [a'sadu, da] adj roast.
    ➡ **assado** m roast.

assadura [asa'dura] f **-1.** [em bebê] nappy rash. **-2.** [em adulto] rash.

assaltante [asaw'tãntʃi] mf **-1.** [na rua] mugger. **-2.** [de banco] robber. **-3.** [de casa] burglar.

assaltar [asaw'ta(x)] vt **-1.** [atacar] to attack. **-2.** [roubar - na rua] to mug; [-

banco] to rob; [- casa] to break into. **-3.**
fig [acometer] to assail.

assalto [a'sawtul] *m* **-1.** [ataque] attack.
-2. [na rua] mugging. **-3.** [a banco] robbery. **-4.** [a casa] burglary.

assar [a'sa(x)] ⇔ *vt* **-1.** [no forno] to
roast. **-2.** [na grelha] to grill. ⇔ *vi* to
roast.

assassinar [asasi'na(x)] *vt* **-1.** [matar] to
murder. **-2.** *POL* to assassinate.

assassinato [asasi'natul, **assassínio**
[asa'sinjul *m* **-1.** [de pessoa comum] murder. **-2.** *POL* assassination.

assassino, na [asa'sinu, nal ⇔ *adj*
deadly. ⇔ *m, f* **-1.** [de pessoa comum]
killer, murderer. **-2.** *POL* assassin.

asseado, da [a'sjadu, dal *adj* clean, neat.

assediar [ase'dʒja(x)] *vt* **-1.** [sitiar] to
besiege. **-2.** [perseguir] to hound. **-3.** [se-
xualmente] to harass.

assédio [a'sɛdʒjul *m* **-1.** [cerco] siege. **-2.**
[insistência] hounding; **ele se acostumou
com o ~ dos repórteres** he became
used to being hounded by reporters;
~ sexual sexual harassment.

assegurar [asegu'ra(x)] *vt* **-1.** [garantir] to
ensure; **~ algo a alguém** to assure sb
sthg. **-2.** [afirmar] to give an assurance.
➡ **assegurar-se** *vp*: **~-se de fazer algo**
to make sure of doing sthg.

asseio [a'sejul *m* cleanliness, neatness.

assembléia [asẽn'blɛjal *f* **-1.** [reunião]
meeting; **~ geral** annual general
meeting. **-2.** [órgão] assembly.

assemelhar [aseme'ʎa(x)] *vt* [tornar se-
melhante] to liken.
➡ **assemelhar-se** *vp* [ser parecido] to
look alike; **~-se a algo/alguém** to look
like sthg/sb.

assentado, da [asẽn'tadu, dal *adj* **-1.** [fir-
me] secure. **-2.** [combinado] arranged.
-3. [ajuizado] sound. **-4.** [em terras]
landed.

assentar [asẽn'ta(x)] ⇔ *vt* **-1.** [firmar] to
set. **-2.** [colocar] to place. **-3.** [tijolos] to
lay. **-4.** [em terras] to settle. **-5.** *fig* [ba-
sear] to base. **-6.** [anotar, registrar] to note
down. **-7.** [estabelecer] to establish. **-8.**
[determinar] to agree. **-9.** [decidir] to
resolve. ⇔ *vi* [ger] to settle.
➡ **assentar-se** *vp* **-1.** [firmar-se] to be
founded. **-2.** *fig* [basear-se] to be based.
-3. *fig* [ajuizar-se] to settle down.

assente [a'sẽntʃil ⇔ *pp* ▷ **assentar**.
⇔ *adj* [combinado, fixo] agreed.

assentir [asẽn'tʃi(x)] *vi* **-1.** [concordar]: **~
(em)** to agree (to). **-2.** [aceder]: **~ (a)** to
accede (to).

assento [a'sẽntul *m* **-1.** [para sentar] seat.
-2. *fig* [base]: **ter ~** to be based on.

assessor, ra [ase'so(x), ral *m, f* **-1.** [consul-
tor] consultant. **-2.** [assistente] adviser.
-3. *POL* aide.

assessoria [aseso'rial *f* **-1.** [consultoria]
consultancy. **-2.** [assistência] assistance.
-3. [setor, órgão, conselho] advisors *(pl)*.

assiduidade [asidwi'dadʒil *f* **-1.** [a aulas,
trabalho] regular attendance. **-2.** [dili-
gência] diligence; **com ~** diligently.

assíduo, dua [a'sidwu, dwal *adj* **-1.** [a aulas, trabalho] regularly attending. **-2.** [di-
ligente] diligent.

assim [a'sĩl ⇔ *adv* **-1.** [deste modo] just
like that; **como ~?** how do you mean?
-2. [igualmente] the same; **e ~ por diante** and so on; **~ como** [tal como] just
like; [também] as well as. **-3.** [deste tama-
nho]: **ser grande ~** to be this big. ⇔
conj [então] so; **~ mesmo, mesmo ~**
even so.
➡ **assim que** *loc conj* as soon as.

assimilar [asimi'la(x)] *vt* **-1.** [ger] to
assimilate. **-2.** [apropriar-se de] to absorb.

assinalar [asina'la(x)] *vt* **-1.** [marcar] to
mark. **-2.** [distinguir] to indicate. **-3.**
[especificar] to specify. **-4.** [observar] to
point out. **-5.** [celebrizar] to distinguish.

assinante [asi'nãntʃil *mf* subscriber.

assinar [asi'na(x)] ⇔ *vt* **-1.** [firmar] to
sign. **-2.** [ser assinante de] to subscribe to.
⇔ *vi* [firmar] to sign.

assinatura [asina'tural *f* **-1.** [firma] signature. **-2.** [subscrição] subscription.

assistência [asiʃ'tẽnsjal *f* **-1.** [ger] assistance, aid; **~ técnica** technical
assistance. **-2.** [presença] attendance.
-3. [espectadores] audience. **-4.** [ambulân-
cia] emergency assistance.

assistente [asiʃ'tẽntʃil ⇔ *adj* [auxiliar]
assistant. ⇔ *mf* **-1.** [auxiliar] assistant;
~ social social worker. **-2.** [espectador -
em jogo] spectator; [- em teatro, cinema]
member of the audience.

assistir [asiʃ'tʃi(x)] ⇔ *vt* **-1.** [socorrer] to
assist. **-2.** [auxiliar] to assist. **-3.** [fazer
companhia a] to attend. ⇔ *vi* **-1.** [estar
presente]: **~ a** [ver] to watch; [testemu-
nhar] to witness; [comparecer a] to attend.
-2. [caber]: **~ a alguém** to pertain to sb.

assoalho [a'swaʎul *m* floor.

assoar [a'swa(x)] *vt* to blow *(one's
nose)*.

assobiar [aso'bja(x)] *m* = **assoviar**.

assobio [aso'biwl *m* = **assovio**.

associação [asosja'sãwl *(pl* **-ões)** *f* **-1.**
[ger] association; **~ de moradores**
residents' association. **-2.** [parceria, ali-
ança] partnership.

associado, da [aso'sjadu, dal ⇔ *adj* **-1.**

[relacionado] associated. **-2.** [sócio] associate. **-3.** [médico, advogado etc.] associate. ◇ *m, f* [sócio] associate, partner.

associar [aso'sja(x)] *vt* relacionar; ~ **algo a algo** to associate sthg with sthg.
➡ **associar-se** *vp* **-1.** COM [formar associação] to form a partnership. **-2.** [entrar de sócio]: ~**-se a** to become a member of.

assolar [aso'la(x)] *vt* to devastate.

assombração [asõnbra'sãw] *(pl* **-ões)** *f* ghost.

assombrar [asõn'bra(x)] *vt* **-1.** [assustar] to frighten. **-2.** [rondar] to haunt. **-3.** [impressionar] to amaze.

assombro [a'sõnbru] *m* **-1.** [admiração] astonishment. **-2.** [espanto, maravilha]: **ser um** ~ to be amazing.

assoviar [aso'vja(x)], **assobiar** [aso'bja(x)] *vi & vt* to whistle.

assovio [aso'viw], **assobio** [aso'bju] *m* whistling, whistle.

assumir [asu'mi(x)] ◇ *vt* **-1.** [chamar a si] to assume. **-2.** [reconhecer - filho] to recognize; [- erro] to admit. **-3.** [tomar posse de] to take up. **-4.** [adotar, adquirir] to take on. **-5.** [homossexualidade] to come out. ◇ *vi* [tomar posse] to take office.

Assunção [asũn'sãw] *n* [cidade] Asunción.

assunto [a'sũntu] *m* [tema] subject.

assustador, ra [asuʃta'do(x), ra] *(mpl* **-es,** *fpl* **-s)** *adj* **-1.** [amedrontador] terrifying. **-2.** [alarmante] alarming.

assustar [asuʃ'ta(x)] ◇ *vt* **-1.** [amedrontar] to frighten. **-2.** [alarmar] to alarm. ◇ *vi* **-1.** [amedrontar] to be terrifying. **-2.** [alarmar] to be alarming.
➡ **assustar-se** *vp*: ~**-se (com)** [amedrontar-se] to be terrified (by); [alarmar-se] to be alarmed (by).

asteca [aʃ'tɛka] ◇ *adj* Aztec. ◇ *mf* Aztec.

asterisco [aʃte'riʃku] *m* asterisk.

astral [aʃ'traw] *(pl* **-ais)** ◇ *adj* ASTRO astrological. ◇ *m* [humor, ambiente] mood.

astrologia [aʃtrolo'ʒia] *f* astrology.

astrólogo, ga [aʃ'trɔlogu, ga] *m, f* astrologist.

astronauta [aʃtro'nawta] *mf* astronaut.

astronomia [aʃtrono'mia] *f* astronomy.

astronômico, ca [aʃtro'nomiku, ka] *adj* astronomical.

astúcia [aʃ'tusja] *f* **-1.** [esperteza] shrewdness. **-2.** [ardil] ruse.

astuto, ta [aʃ'tutu, ta] *adj* **-1.** [esperto] shrewd. **-2.** [ardiloso] cunning.

at. *(abrev de* **atenção** *a)* attn.

ata [ata] *f* [de reunião] minutes *(pl).*

atacadista [ataka'dʒiʃta] ◇ *adj* COM [comércio, mercado, vendedor] wholesale. ◇ *mf* [vendedor] wholesaler.

atacado, da [ata'kadu, da] *adj fam* [pessoa]: **estar** OU **andar** ~ to be in a foul mood.
➡ **atacado** *m* COM : **no/por** ~ wholesale.

atacante [ata'kãntʃi] ◇ *adj* attacking. ◇ *mf* attacker.

atacar [ata'ka(x)] ◇ *vt* **-1.** [lançar ataque contra] to attack. **-2.** [acometer] to strike at. **-3.** *fig* [combater] to tackle. **-4.** *fig* [criticar] to hit out at. ◇ *vi* **-1.** [lançar ataque] to attack. **-2.** [vírus] to strike. **-3.** ESP [time, jogador] to go on the attack. ◇ *interj*: **atacar!** charge!

atado, da [a'tadu, da] *adj* **-1.** [desajeitado] clumsy. **-2.** [confuso, perplexo] bewildered.

atadura [ata'dura] *f* bandage.

atalho [a'taʎu] *m* COMPUT shortcut.

atapetar [atape'ta(x)] *vt* to carpet.

ataque [a'taki] *m* [ger] attack; ~ **aéreo** air strike; ~ **cardíaco** heart attack; **ter um** ~ **(de raiva)** *fam* to have a fit (of rage).

atar [a'ta(x)] *vt* to tie; **não** ~ **nem desatar** [pessoa] to shilly-shally; [negócio, namoro] to be getting nowhere.

atarefado, da [ˌatare'fadu, da] *adj* busy.

atarracado, da [ataxa'kadu, da] *adj* **-1.** [pessoa] thickset. **-2.** [pescoço, perna] thick.

até [a'tɛ] ◇ *prep* **-1.** [no espaço] as far as, up to; **de ...** ~ **...** from ... to ... **-2.** [no tempo] until, till; ~ **que enfim!** at long last!; ~ **agora** so far, up until now. **-3.** [prazo - antes de] before; [- extensão] until. **-4.** [despedida]: **até!** see you!; ~ **amanhã** until tomorrow; ~ **já** see you soon. **-5.** [com quantidades] up to. ◇ *adv* [mesmo, inclusive] even.
➡ **até que** *loc conj* [até quando) until.

atear [ate'a(x)] *vt* **-1.** [fogo]: ~ **fogo a algo** to set fire to sthg. **-2.** *fig* [espalhar] to inflame.

atéia [a'tɛja] *f* ▷ ateu.

ateliê [ate'ljel] *m* studio.

atemorizador, ra [atemoriza'do(x), ra] *adj* alarming.

atemorizar [atemori'za(x)] *vt* **-1.** [assustar] to frighten. **-2.** [intimidar] to alarm.

Atenas [a'tenaʃ] *n* Athens.

atenção [atẽn'sãw] *(pl* **-ões)** ◇ *f* **-1.** [interesse] attention; **chamar a** ~ **(de)** [atrair] to catch the eye (of); **chamar a** ~ **de alguém** [advertir] to warn sb. **-2.** [cuidado] care. **-3.** [cortesia] consideration

(U). <> *interj:* ~ ! [cuidado] beware!; [exigindo concentração] pay attention!; [em aeroporto, conferência] your attention please!

atencioso, osa [atẽn'sjozu, ɔsa] *adj* **-1.** [que presta atenção] attentive. **-2.** [polido, cortês] considerate.

atender [atẽn'de(x)] <> *vt* **-1.** [satisfazer] to attend to. **-2.** [deferir] to grant. **-3.** [receber] to receive. **-4.** [responder] to answer. **-5.** [em loja] to serve. **-6.** [cuidar de - convidado, hóspede] to look after; [- paciente, ferido] to tend. <> *vi* **-1.** [satisfazer]: ~ a to attend to. **-2.** [responder]: ~ (a) to answer. **-3.** [loja, vendedor] to serve.

atendimento [atẽndʒi'mẽntu] *m* **-1.** [serviço] service; **horário de ~** opening times. **-2.** [recepção]: **tivemos pronto ~ no ministério** we were dealt with swiftly at the ministry.

atentado [atẽn'tadu] *m* **-1.** [ataque] attack; **~ terrorista** terrorist attack. **-2.** [contra pessoa] attempt on one's life. **-3.** [contra edifício, monumento]: ~ (a/contra) attack (on/against). **-4.** [crime, ofensa]: ~ (a algo) attack (on sthg).

atentar [atẽn'ta(x)] *vi* **-1.** [prestar atenção]: ~ **para** *ou* **a** to pay attention to. **-2.** [cometer atentado]: ~ **contra (a vida de) alguém** to make an attempt on sb's life; ~ **contra algo** [violar, ofender] to offend against sthg.

atento, ta [a'tẽntu, ta] *adj* **-1.** [interessado, concentrado] attentive. **-2.** [cuidadoso] painstaking.

atenuante [ate'nwãntʃi] <> *adj* extenuating. <> *m JUR* extenuating circumstance.

atenuar [ate'nwa(x)] *vt* **-1.** [pressão, pena] to reduce. **-2.** [combate] to die down. **-3.** [dor] to ease.

aterragem [ate'xaʒej] *(pl* **-ns)** *f* = aterrissagem.

aterrar [ate'xar] *vt* [cobrir com terra] to level.

aterrissagem [atexi'saʒej] *(pl* **-ns)** *f* landing.

aterrissar [atexi'sa(x)], **aterrizar** [atexi'za(x)] *vi* to land.

aterro [a'texu] *m* [área aterrada] levelling.

aterrorizante [atexori'zãntʃi] *adj* terrifying.

aterrorizar [atexori'za(x)] *vt* to terrorize.

ater-se [a'texsi] *vp* **-1.** [limitar-se]: ~ a to keep to. **-2.** [fiar-se por] to rely on.

atestado, da [ateʃ'tadu, da] *adj* certified.
→ **atestado** *m* **-1.** [certificado] certificate; ~ **médico** medical certificate.

-2. *fig* [prova] confirmation. **-3.** *JUR* testimony.

atestar [ateʃ'ta(x)] *vt* **-1.** [certificar] to certify. **-2.** [provar] to confirm. **-3.** [testemunhar] to vouch for.

ateu, atéia [a'tew, a'tɛja] <> *adj* atheist. <> *m, f* atheist.

atinar [atʃi'na(x)] <> *vt* **-1.** [descobrir, acertar] to work out. **-2.** [perceber] to realize. <> *vi* **-1.** [encontrar]: ~ **com** to come up with. **-2.** [ter consciência de]: ~ **em** to be aware of.

atingir [atʃĩ'ʒi(x)] *vt* **-1.** [ger] to reach. **-2.** [acertar] to hit. **-3.** [objetivo] to achieve. **-4.** *fig* [ferir] to wound. **-5.** [afetar] to affect. **-6.** [compreender] to grasp.

atirador, ra [atʃira'do(x), ra] *m, f* shot, shooter.

atirar [atʃi'ra(x)] <> *vt* **-1.** [lançar]: ~ **algo (em)** to throw sthg (into); ~ **algo (por)** to throw sthg (through). **-2.** [fig] [olhares, beijos] to cast. <> *vi* [dar disparo]: ~ **(em)** to fire (at).
→ **atirar-se** *vp* **-1.** [lançar-se]: ~ -se **(a/em)** to throw o.s. (at); **fig** [dedicar-se] to throw o.s. into. **-2.** *fam* [insinuar-se amorosamente] to come on to.

atitude [atʃi'tudʒi] *f* **-1.** [modo de agir] response. **-2.** [postura] attitude.

ativa [a'tʃiva] *f* ➤ ativo.

atividade [atʃivi'dadʒi] *f* **-1.** [ger] activity. **-2.** [ocupação] pursuit. **-3.** [movimento intenso] bustle.

ativo, va [a'tʃivu, va] *adj* **-1.** [ger] active. **-2.** [que trabalha] working. **-3.** [ágil, movimentado] lively.
→ **ativo** *m COM* assets *(pl).*

atlântico, ca [at'lãntʃiku, ka] *adj* Atlantic.
➤ **Atlântico** *n:* **o (oceano) Atlântico** the Atlantic Ocean.

atlas ['atlaʃ] *m inv* atlas.

atleta [a'tlɛta] *mf* athlete.

atlético, ca [a'tlɛtʃiku, ka] *adj* athletic.

atmosfera [atmoʃ'fɛra] *f* **-1.** *GEOGR* atmosphere. **-2.** *fig* [ambiente] mood.

ato ['atu] *m* **-1.** [ger] act; **no ~** [imediatamente] on the spot. **-2.** [cerimônia] action; ~ **público** public ceremony.

à-toa [a'toa] *adj* **-1.** [sem importância] insignificant. **-2.** [simples] simple.

atoalhado, da [atwa'ʎadu, da] *adj* towelling.

atolar [ato'la(x)] *vt* to get bogged down.
➤ **atolar-se** *vp fig* [pessoa] to be snowed under.

atoleiro [ato'lejru] *m* **-1.** [de lama] quagmire. **-2.** *fig* [situação] morass.

atômico, ca [a'tomiku, ka] *adj* atomic.

átomo ['atomu] *m* atom.

atônito, ta [a'tonitu, ta] *adj* astonished.

ator, atriz [a'to(x), a'triʒ] (*mpl* **-res**, *fpl* **-zes**) *m*, *f* actor, actress.

atordoado, da [atox'dwadu, da] *adj* dazed.

atordoamento [atoxdwa'mẽntul *m* bewilderment.

atordoante [atox'dwãntʃi] *adj* deafening.

atordoar [atox'dwa(x)] *vt* to daze.

atormentado, da [atoxmẽn'tadu, da] *adj* tormented.

atormentar [atoxmẽn'ta(x)] *vt* to torment.

ATP (*abrev de* **Associação dos Tenistas Profissionais**) *f* ATP.

atração [atra'sãw] (*pl* **-ões**) *f* **-1.** *FÍS* attraction. **-2.** [de cinema, teatro] main attraction. **-3.** [propensão] pull. **-4.** [sexual] attraction.

atracar [atra'ka(x)] *vt & vi NÁUT* to moor.
 atracar-se *vp* **-1.** *fig* [em briga] to come to blows. **-2.** *fam fig* [amorosamente] to clinch.

atraente [atra'ẽntʃi] *adj* **-1.** [objeto, efeito] eye-catching. **-2.** [proposta, vantagem] appealing. **-3.** [pessoa] attractive.

atrair [atra'i(x)] *vt* **-1.** [fascinar] to attract. **-2.** [chamar a si] to bring. **-3.** [aliciar] to entice.

atrapalhar [atrapa'ʎa(x)] ⬥ *vt* **-1.** [confundir] to muddle. **-2.** [perturbar] to upset. **-3.** [dificultar] to confound. ⬥ *vi* [perturbar] to be disturbing.
 atrapalhar-se *vp* [confundir-se] to get into a muddle.

atrás [a'trajʃ] *adv* **-1.** [posição] behind; **lá ~** back there. **-2.** [no tempo] ago. **-3.** [em classificação]: **estar/ficar ~ (de)** to be ranked behind.
 atrás de *loc prep* **-1.** [posição] behind. **-2.** [em seguimento a] after; **logo ~ de** right behind. **-3.** [em busca de - pessoa] after; [- objeto, explicação] looking for.

atrasado, da [atra'zadu, da] *adj* **-1.** [ger] slow. **-2.** [tardio] late. **-3.** [país, povo, costume] backward. **-4.** [pagamento, conta] overdue. **-5.** [número, edição] back.
 atrasados *mpl* arrears.

atrasar [atra'za(x)] ⬥ *vt* **-1.** [fazer demorar] to delay. **-2.** [retardar] to hold back. **-3.** [relógio] to put back. **-4.** [pagamento] to be late with. ⬥ *vi* **-1.** [demorar] to be delayed. **-2.** [publicação] to be late. **-3.** [relógio] to be slow. **-4.** [pagamento] to arrive late. **-5.** [em trabalho, encomenda] to fail to keep up.
 atrasar-se *vp* [pessoa]: **~-se (para)** to be late (for).

atraso [a'trazu] *m* **-1.** [demora] delay. **-2.** [de pagamento] late payment. **-3.** [de país, povo, costumes] backwardness.

atrativo, va [atra'tʃivu, va] *adj* attractive.
 atrativo *m* attraction.

atravancar [atravãŋ'ka(x)] *vt* **-1.** [bloquear] to block. **-2.** [lotar] to clutter.

através [atra'vɛʃ] *adv* [de lado a lado] through.
 através de *loc adv* **-1.** [por entre] amongst. **-2.** [pelo centro de] through. **-3.** [no decorrer de] through. **-4.** [por meio de] by means of. **-5.** [por via de] through.

atravessar [atrave'sa(x)] *vt* **-1.** [ger] to cross. **-2.** [pôr de través] to place across. **-3.** [transpassar] to pierce. **-4.** *fig* [passar por] to go through.

atrever-se [atre'vexsi] *vp*: **~ (a fazer algo)** to dare (to do sthg).

atrevido, da [atre'vidu, da] *adj* **-1.** [petulante] impertinent. **-2.** [ousado] bold.

atrevimento [atrevi'mẽntul *m* **-1.** [petulância] insolence. **-2.** [ousadia - condição] boldness; [- ato] effrontery.

atribuir [atri'bwi(x)] *vt* [imputar]: **~ algo a alguém/algo** to attribute sthg to sb/sthg.

atributo [atri'butul *m* attribute.

átrio [a'triul *m* **-1.** [vestíbulo] hallway. **-2.** [pátio] courtyard.

atritar [atri'ta(x)] *vt* to rub.

atrito [a'tritul *m* **-1.** [fricção] friction. **-2.** *fig* [conflito] conflict; **entrar em ~** to have a misunderstanding.

atriz [a'triʒ] *f* ▷ **ator**.

atrocidade [atrosi'dadʒi] *f* atrocity.

atropelamento [atropela'mẽntul *m* [de pedestre] running over.

atropelar [atrope'la(x)] *vt* **-1.** [pedestre] to run over. **-2.** [esbarrar em, empurrar] to crash into.

atroz [a'trɔʒ] *adj* **-1.** [cruel] atrocious. **-2.** [terrível] terrible.

atuação [atwa'sãw] (*pl* **-ões**) [-õjʃ] *f* **-1.** [ger] performance. **-2.** [participação] role.

atual [a'twaw] (*pl* **-ais**) *adj* **-1.** [corrente] present. **-2.** [moderno] current.

atualidade [atwali'dadʒi] *f* **-1.** [período atual] present time. **-2.** [modernidade] modernity.
 atualidades *fpl JORN* news *(sg)*.

atualização [aktualiza'sãw] *f COMPUT* update.

atualizar [atwali'za(x)] *vt* to update.
 atualizar-se *vp* [pessoa] to bring o.s. up to date.

atualmente [atwaw'mẽntʃi] *adv* **-1.** [no momento] currently. **-2.** [hoje em dia] nowadays.

atuante [a'twãntʃi] *adj* active.

atuar [a'twa(x)] *vi* -**1.** [ger] to act. -**2.** [participar de]: ~ **em** to act on/in. -**3.** [influenciar]: ~ **sobre** to influence.

atum [a'tũ] (*pl* -**ns**) *m* tuna.

aturar [atu'ra(x)] *vt* to endure, to put up with.

aturdido, da [atur'dʒidu, da] *adj* stunned.

aturdir [atux'dʒi(x)] <> *vt* to stun. <> *vi* to deafen.

audácia [aw'dasja] *f* -**1.** [intrepidez] boldness. -**2.** [insolência] audacity.

audacioso, sa [awda'sjozu, ɔza] *adj* -**1.** [pessoa] intrepid. -**2.** [ato] gallant. -**3.** [decisão] bold.

audaz [aw'daʒ] (*pl* -**es**) *adj* [intrépido] audacious.

audição [awdʒi'sãw] (*pl* -**ões**) *f* -**1.** [ger] hearing. -**2.** [concerto] audition.

audiência [aw'dʒjẽnsja] *f* -**1.** [ger] audience. -**2.** [mídia - RÁDIO] listeners (*pl*); [- TV] viewers (*pl*); **índices de** ~ ratings (*pl*). -**3.** JUR hearing.

audiovisual [ˌawdʒuvi'zwaw] (*pl* -**ais**) <> *adj* audiovisual. <> *m* projector.

auditor, ra [awdʒi'to(x), ra] *m, f* -**1.** FIN auditor. -**2.** [juiz] judge, magistrate. -**3.** [ouvinte] listener.

auditoria [awdʒito'ria] *f* -**1.** [serviço] audit; **fazer a** ~ **de** to carry out an audit of. -**2.** [empresa] firm of accountants.

auditório [awdʒi'tɔrju] *m* -**1.** [recinto] courtroom. -**2.** [plateia] auditorium.

auê [aw'e] *m fam* [confusão] uproar; **fazer um** ~ to create an uproar.

auge ['awʒi] *m* height.

augúrio [aw'gurju] *m* -**1.** [prognóstico] prophecy. -**2.** [sinal] indication.

aula ['awla] *f* [escola] -**1.** lesson; **dar** ~ to teach. -**2.** [universidade] lecture.

aumentar [awmẽn'ta(x)] <> *vt* [ger] to increase. <> *vi* to increase.

aumento [aw'mẽntu] *m* -**1.** [ger] price increase. -**2.** [de salário] rise *UK*, raise *US*. -**3.** [crescimento] increase. -**4.** [ampliação] magnification.

auréola [aw'rɛwla] *f* halo.

aurora [aw'rɔra] *f* dawn.

ausência [aw'zẽnsja] *f* -**1.** [falta de presença] absence. -**2.** *fig* [inexistência] lack.

ausentar-se [awzẽn'taxsi] *vp* to absent o.s.

ausente [aw'zẽntʃi] <> *adj* -**1.** [não-presente] absent. -**2.** [omisso] neglectful. <> *mf* [não-presente] absent.

auspício [awʃ'pisju] *m* -**1.** [prenúncio] sign. -**2.** [patrocínio]: **sob os** ~ **s de** under the auspices of.

austeridade [awʃteri'dadʒi] *f* -**1.** [severi-

dade, seriedade] severity. -**2.** [em gastos] austerity.

austero, ra [awʃ'tɛru, ra] *adj* -**1.** [severo] strict. -**2.** [em gastos] austere.

austral [awʃ'trawl] (*pl* -**ais**) *adj* southern.

Austrália [awʃ'tralja] *n* Australia.

australiano, na [awʃtra'ljãnu, na] <> *adj* Australian. <> *m, f* Australian.

Áustria ['awʃtria] *n* Austria.

austríaco, ca [awʃ'triaku, ka] <> *adj* Austrian. <> *m, f* Austrian.

autenticidade [awtẽntʃisi'dadʒi] *f* [genuinidade] authenticity.

autêntico, ca [aw'tẽntʃiku, ka] *adj* -**1.** [genuíno] authentic. -**2.** [original] original. -**3.** *(antes de subst) pej* [verdadeiro] real.

auto ['awtu] *m* -**1.** JUR (legal) brief. -**2.** TEATRO medieval allegorical play.
 ➤ **autos** *mpl* JUR legal papers.

auto-adesivo, va [ˌawtwade'zivu, va] (*pl* -**s**) <> *adj* self-adhesive. <> *m* sticker.

autobiografia [awtobjogra'fia] *f* autobiography.

autocrítica [awto'kritika] *f* self-criticism; **fazer uma** ~ to admit to one's faults.

autodefesa [awtude'feza] *f* self-defence.

autodeterminação [awtudetexmina'sãw] *f* self-determination.

autodidata [awtodʒi'data] <> *adj* self-taught. <> *mf* self-taught person.

autódromo [aw'tɔdromul] *m* racetrack.

auto-escola [ˌawtwiʃ'kɔla] (*pl* **auto-escolas**) *f* driving school.

auto-estima [ˌawtwiʃ'tʃimal] *f* self-esteem.

auto-estrada [ˌawtwiʃ'trada] (*pl* **auto-estradas**) *f* motorway *UK*, freeway *US*.

autógrafo [aw'tɔgraful] *m* autograph.

automação [awtoma'sãw] *f* = **automatização**.

automático, ca [awto'matʃiku, ka] *adj* automatic.

automatização [awtomatʃiza'sãw] (*pl* -**ões**) *f* automation.

automobilismo [awtomobi'liʒmul] *m* motor racing.

automóvel [awto'mɔvɛw] (*pl* -**eis**) *m* car.

autonomia [awtono'mia] *f* -**1.** [independência] autonomy. -**2.** [de veículo] range.

autônomo, ma [aw'tonomu, ma] <> *adj* -**1.** [independente] autonomous. -**2.** [trabalhador] autonomist. <> *m, f* [trabalhador] autonomist.

autópsia [aw'tɔpsja] *f* autopsy.

autor, ra [aw'to(x), ra] (*mpl* -**es**, *fpl* -**s**) *m, f* author.

autoral [awto'raw] (*pl* -**ais**) *adj* authorial.

auto-retrato [ˌawtoxeˈtratu] (pl **auto-re-tratos**) m self-portrait.

autoria [awtoˈrial f -1. LITER authorship; **ser de ~ de alguém** to be written by sb. -2. [de crime] perpetration.

autoridade [awtoriˈdadʒi] f [ger] authority.

autoritário, ria [awtoriˈtarju, ja] adj authoritarian.

autorização [awtorizaˈsãw] (pl -ões) f permission; **dar ~ a alguém (para algo/para fazer algo)** to give sb permission (for sthg/to do sthg).

autorizar [awtoriˈza(x)] vt -1. [permitir] to authorize. -2. [capacitar] to enable.

auto-suficiente [ˌawtusufiˈsjẽntʃi] (pl -s) adj self-sufficient; **ser ~ em algo** to be self-sufficient in sthg.

auxiliar [awsiˈlja(x)] (pl -es) ◇ adj -1. [ger] assistant. -2. [enfermeiro] auxiliary. ◇ mf assistant. ◇ vt to assist.

auxílio [awˈsilju] m assistance.

av. (abrev de avenida) f Av.

avacalhar [avakaˈʎa(x)] vt -1. [pôr em ridículo] fam to make a travesty of. -2. [executar com desleixo] fam to make a mess of.

aval [aˈvaw] (pl -ais) m -1. [ger] backing. -2. [garantia] warranty.

avalanche [avaˈlãnʃi], **avalancha** [avaˈlãnʃa] f avalanche.

avaliação [avaljaˈsãw] (pl -ões) f -1. [de preço, prejuízos] estimate. -2. [de qualidade, vantagens] appraisal. -3. [opinião] opinion. -4. EDUC assessment.

avaliar [avaˈlja(x)] vt -1. [preço, prejuízo] to estimate. -2. [imóvel] to value. -3. [qualidade, vantagens, idéia] to evaluate. -4. EDUC to assess.

avançado, da [avãnˈsadu, da] adj -1. [adiantado] jutting out. -2. [hora] late. -3. [nível] advanced. -4. [idéia, pessoa] progressive.

avançar [avãˈsa(x)] ◇ vi -1. [adiantar-se] to move forward. -2. [estender-se] to spread. -3. [atacar, investir] to advance. -4. [atirar-se]: **~ em algo** to throw o.s. upon sthg. ◇ vt [adiantar] to advance.

avanço [aˈvãsu] m -1. [de tropa] advance. -2. [adiantamento] headway. -3. [melhora] step in the right direction. -4. [progresso] progress.

avante [aˈvãntʃi] ◇ adv -1. [adiante] ahead. -2. [para diante] onward. ◇ interj forward!

avarento, ta [avaˈrẽntu, ta] ◇ adj miserly. ◇ m, f miser.

avareza [avaˈreza] f avarice.

avaria [avaˈria] f -1. [de veículo, máquina] breakdown. -2. [de carga, casco] damage.

avariado, da [avaˈrjadu, da] adj -1. [veículo, máquina] broken down. -2. [carga, casco] damaged.

avaro, ra [aˈvaru, ra] ◇ adj avaricious. ◇ m, f miser.

ave [ˈavi] f bird.

aveia [aˈveja] f oat.

avelã [aveˈlã] f hazelnut.

avenida [aveˈnida] f avenue.

avental [avẽnˈtaw] (pl -ais) m -1. [proteção] apron. -2. [vestido] pinafore dress.

aventura [avẽnˈtura] f -1. [experiência] adventure. -2. [amorosa] love affair.

aventureiro, ra [avẽntuˈrejru, ra] ◇ adj adventurous. ◇ m, f adventurer (f adventuress).

averiguação [averigwaˈsãw] (pl -ões) f -1. [investigação] investigation. -2. [verificação] check.

averiguar [averiˈgwa(x)] vt -1. [investigar] to investigate. -2. [verificar] to check.

avermelhado, da [avexmeˈʎadu, da] adj reddish.

aversão [avexˈsãw] (pl -ões) f aversion; **ter ~ a algo** to have an aversion to sthg.

avesso, ssa [aˈvesu] adj [lado] wrong.
➡ **avesso** m [lado] underside; **virar pelo ~** [blusa etc.] to turn inside out; fig [revirar] to turn upside down.
➡ **às avessas** loc adj [oposto]: **ser um santo às avessas** to be anything but a saint.

avestruz [aveʃˈtruʃ] (pl -es) f ostrich.

aviação [avjaˈsãw] f -1. [sistema] aviation. -2. [força aérea] air force.

aviador, ra [avjaˈdo(x), ra] m, f pilot, aviator.

aviamento [avjaˈmẽntul] m -1. COST trimmings (pl). -2. [de receita médica] preparation.

avião [aˈvjãw] (pl -ões) m [veículo] aeroplane; **~ a jato** jet plane; **ir de ~** to fly.

avicultura [avikuwˈtura] f poultry breeding.

avidez [aviˈdeʒ] f -1. [desejo] eagerness; **com ~** eagerly. -2. [cobiça] greed.

ávido, da [ˈavidu, da] adj -1. [desejoso] eager. -2. [cobiçoso] greedy.

aviltar [aviwˈta(x)] vt [degradar] to weaken.
➡ **aviltar-se** vp [degradar-se] to degenerate.

avisar [aviˈza(x)] ◇ vt [informar] to warn; **~ alguém de algo** to inform sb of sthg. ◇ vi [informar] to give warning.

aviso [aˈvizul m -1. [placa] notice. -2. [notificação] notification. -3. [informação] sign. - **4.** [advertência] warning sign; ~ **prévio** [notificação, período] notice.

avistar [avi∫'ta(x)] *vt* to catch sight of.

avizinhar-se [avizi'naxsi] *vp* [aproximar-se] to draw near.

avo ['avu] *m* [fração] fractional part.

avô [a'vol, **avó** [a'vɔl *m, f* grandfather (*f* grandmother).

 ➡ **avós** *pl* grandparents.

avoado, da [avo'adu, da] *adj* scatty.

avós [a'vɔ∫] *pl* ⊳ **avô**.

avulso, sa [a'vuwsu, sa] *adj* loose.

axila [ak'sila] *f* armpit.

axiomático, ca [aksio'mat∫iku, ka] *adj* axiomatic.

azaléia [aza'lɛja] *f* azalea.

azar [a'za(x)] (*pl* **-es**) *m* bad luck; ~ **!** tough!; **que** ~ **!** damn!; **dar** ~ to bring bad luck.

azedar [aze'da(x)] ⟨⟩ *vt* -**1.** [comida, leite] to cause to go sour. -**2.** *fig* [pessoa] to irritate. ⟨⟩ *vi* [leite, vinho] to go sour.

azedo, da [a'zedu, da] *adj* -**1.** [sabor] sour. - **2.** *fig* [pessoa] bitter.

azeite [a'zejt∫i] *m*: ~ **(de oliva)** (olive) oil.

azeitona [azej'tona] *f* olive.

azeviche [aze'vi∫i] *m* [cor] jet black.

azia [a'zia] *f* heartburn.

aziago, ga [azi'agu, ga] *adj* ill-omened.

azucrinar [azukri'na(x)] *vt* to annoy.

azul [a'zuw] (*pl* **azuis**) ⟨⟩ *adj* blue; **está tudo** ~ *fig* everything is rosy. ⟨⟩ *m* blue.

azulado, da [azu'ladu, da] *adj* bluish.

azul-claro, ra [a'zuwklaru, ra] ⟨⟩ *adj* light blue. ⟨⟩ *m* light blue.

azulejo [azu'leʒu] *m* (ornamental) tile.

azul-escuro, ra [a'zuwi∫kuru, ra] ⟨⟩ *adj* dark blue. ⟨⟩ *m* dark blue.

azul-marinho [a,zuwma'riɲul ⟨⟩ *adj inv* ultramarine. ⟨⟩ *m* ultramarine.

azul-turquesa [a,zuwtux'keza] ⟨⟩ *adj inv* turquoise. ⟨⟩ *m* turquoise.

B

b, B [be] *m* [letra] b, B.

BA (*abrev de* **Estado da Bahia**) *n* State of Bahia.

B2B (*abrev de* **business-to-business**) *m* B2B.

baba ['baba] *f* dribble.

babá [ba'ba] *f* nursemaid.

babaca [ba'baka] *m fam adj* stupid.

baba-de-moça [,babaʒi'mosa] (*pl* babas-de-moça) *m, f* CULIN egg and coconut pudding.

babado, da [ba'badu, da] *adj* [molhado de baba] dribbly.

 ➡ **babado** *m* -**1.** [em roupa etc.] frill. - **2.** *fam* [caso] gossip.

babador [baba'do(x)] *m* bib.

babar [ba'ba(x)] ⟨⟩ *vt* to dribble on. ⟨⟩ *vi* -**1.** [deitar baba] to dribble. - **2.** *fam* [ficar impressionado] to drool.

 ➡ **babar-se** *vp* [deitar baba em si] to dribble.

baby-sitter [,bejbi'site(x)] (*pl* **baby-sitters**) *mf* baby-sitter.

bacalhau [baka'ʎaw] *m* cod.

bacalhoada [bakaʎo'ada] *f a dish made with salt cod boiled with potatoes, cabbage, whole onions and other vegetables, mixed with hard-boiled eggs and olives and seasoned with vinegar and olive oil.*

bacana [ba'kãna] ⟨⟩ *adj* cool. ⟨⟩ *mf fam* [pessoa] toff.

BACEN (*abrev de* **Banco Central do Brasil**) *m central bank of Brazil.*

bacharel [ba∫a'rɛw] (*pl* **-éis**) *mf*: ~ **em Artes/Direito/Economia** Arts/Law/Economics graduate.

bacharelar-se [ba∫are'laxsil *vp*: ~ **(em algo)** to obtain a degree (in sthg).

bacia [ba'sia] *f* -**1.** [ger] basin. - **2.** [sanitária] lavatory. - **3.** ANAT pelvis.

backbone [bak'bonil (*pl* **backbones**) *m* backbone.

baço, ça ['basu, 'sa] ⟨⟩ *adj* -**1.** [pele] dull. - **2.** [metal] tarnished. ⟨⟩ *m* ANAT spleen.

bacon ['bejkõ] *m* bacon.

bactéria [bak'tɛrja] *f* bacterium.

 ➡ **bactérias** *fpl* bacteria.

badalado, da [bada'ladu, da] *fam adj* -**1.** [movimentado, divertido] swinging. - **2.** [famoso, falado] much talked about.

 ➡ **badalada** *f* [de sino] peal.

badalar [bada'la(x)] ⟨⟩ *vt* [tocar] to ring. ⟨⟩ *vi* -**1.** [tocar] to peal. - **2.** *fam* [sair, divertir-se] to go out and enjoy o.s.

badalo [ba'dalul *m* -**1.** [de sino] peal. - **2.** *fam* [diversão] fun.

badejo [ba'deʒul *m* serran.

baderna [ba'dɛxnal *f* -**1.** [bagunça] mess. - **2.** [tumulto] revelry.

badulaque [badu'lakil *m* trinket.

 ➡ **badulaques** *mpl* odds and ends.

bafo ['baful *m* breath; ~ **-de-onça** *fam* bad breath.

bafômetro [baˈfometru] *m* breathaly-zer.

baforada [bafoˈrada] *f* [fumaça] blast.

bagaço [baˈgasu] *m* [de fruta] remains of fruit *(once juice has been ex-tracted)*; **estar/ficar um ~** *fig* to be drained, to be exhausted.

bagageiro [bagaˈʒejru] *m AUTO* luggage rack.

bagagem [baˈgaʒẽ] *(pl* **-ns)** *f* **-1.** [equipa-gem] luggage. **-2.** *fig* [conhecimentos, ex-periência] experience.

bagatela [bagaˈtɛla] *f fig* [ninharia] next to nothing.

bago [ˈbagu] *m* **-1.** [fruto] berry. **-2.** [uva] grape. **-3.** [de chumbo] shot. **-4.** *vulg* [tes-tículo] ball.

baguete [baˈgɛtʃi] *f* baguette.

bagulho [baˈguʎu] *m* [objeto] trinket.

bagunça [baˈgũsa] *f* mess.

bagunçado, da [bagũˈsadu, da] *adj* cluttered.

bagunçar [bagũˈsa(x)], *vt* **-1.** [fazer con-fusão em] to clutter. **-2.** *fig* [atrapalhar, tu-multuar] to upset.

bagunceiro, ra [bagũˈsejru, ra] *adj* [pes-soa - desordeiro] disorderly; [- relaxado] untidy.

baía [baˈia] *f* bay.

baião [bajˈãw] *(pl* **-ões)** *m* [ritmo, dança] baião, *popular music from north-eastern Brazil.*

bailado [bajˈladu] *m* dance.

bailar [bajˈla(x)] *vt & vi* to dance.

bailarino, na [bajlaˈrinu, na] *m, f* dan-cer.

baile [ˈbajli] *m* ball; **~ de carnaval** carnival ball; **dar um ~ em** *fig* [superar] to crush.

bainha [baˈiɲa] *f* **-1.** [de arma] sheath. **-2.** *COST* hem.

bairrista [bajˈxiʃta] *<> adj* **-1.** [que de-fende interesse do bairro] community-based. **-2.** [muito patriota] regionalistic. *<> mf* **-1.** [do local] local. **-2.** [patriota] regionalist.

bairro [ˈbajxu] *m* neighbourhood.

baixa [ˈbajʃa] *adj* ⊳ **baixo**.

baixada [bajˈʃada] *f GEOGR* valley.

baixar [bajˈʃa(x)] *vt COMPUT* [fazer down-load]: **~ um arquivo** to download a file.

baixaria [bajʃaˈria] *f* **-1.** [ger] depravity. **-2.** [escândalo] disgrace.

baixista [bajˈʃiʃta] *mf* bass player.

baixo, xa [ˈbajʃu, ʃa] *adj* **-1.** [ger] low. **-2.** [pessoa] short. **-3.** [cabeça, olhar] lowered. **-4.** [bairro, cidade] lower. **-5.** [metal] base. **-6.** *(antes de subst)* [rio] downriver. **-7.** *(antes de subst)* [época] late. **-8.** *(antes*

de subst) [vil, grosseiro] base; **palavrão de ~** swear word.

➡ baixo *<> m* **-1.** [MÚS - instrumento] bass; [- cantor] bass player. **-2.** *fam* [bair-ro] lower town. *<> adv* **-1.** [a pouca altura] low. **-2.** [falar] softly.

➡ baixa *f* **-1.** [ger] drop; **em baixa** fall-ing. **-2.** [de serviço] sick-leave. **-3.** *MIL* loss.

➡ para baixo *loc adv* downwards.

➡ por baixo (de) *loc adv* underneath.

baixo-astral [ˌbajʃwaʃˈtraw] *m fam* glumness.

bajulador, ra [baʒulaˈdo(x), ra] *<> adj* adulatory. *<> m, f* adulator.

bajular [baʒuˈla(x)] *vt* to adulate.

bala [ˈbala] *f* **-1.** [munição] bullet; **~ de festim** blank cartridge. **-2.** [doce] boiled sweet.

balada [baˈlada] *f* ballad.

balaio [baˈlaju] *m* basket.

balança [baˈlãsa] *f* scales *(pl)*; **~ co-mercial** balance of trade.

➡ Balança *f* [zodíaco] Libra; *veja tam-bém* **Virgem**.

balançar [balãˈsa(x)] *<> vt* **-1.** [fazer os-cilar - bebê, navio] to rock; [- quadril] to wiggle; [- galho, carro, avião] to shake. **-2.** [compensar] to counterbalance. *<> vi* **-1.** [oscilar] to shake. **-2.** [em balanço, ca-deira] to rock.

➡ balançar-se *vp* [sacudir-se] to sway.

balanço [baˈlãsu] *m* **-1.** [de criança] swing. **-2.** [ação] swinging. **-3.** *ECON:* **~ de pagamentos** balance of payments.

balão [baˈlãw] *(pl* **-ões)** *m* **-1.** [dirigível] airship. **-2.** [de brinquedo] balloon. **-3.** [sonda] probe. **-4.** [tanque]: **~ de oxigê-nio** oxygen cylinder. **-5.** [em estrada etc.] *place for doing U-turns.* **-6.** [em história em quadrinhos] bubble.

balaústre [balaˈuʃtri] *m* baluster.

balbuciar [bawbuˈsja(x)] *<> vt* to stam-mer. *<> vi* to babble.

balbúrdia [bawˈbuxdʒja] *f* hustle and bustle.

balcão [bawˈkãw] *(pl* **-ões)** *m* **-1.** [sacada] balcony. **-2.** [de loja] counter. **-3.** *DE TEATRO* dress circle; **~ nobre** balcony; **~ simples** upper circle.

Bálcãs [ˈbawkãʃ] *npl:* **os ~** the Balkans.

balconista [bawkoˈniʃta] *mf* shop assis-tant.

balde [ˈbawdʒi] *m* bucket.

baldeação [bawdʒjaˈsãw] *(pl* **-ões)** *f* transfer; **fazer ~** to change.

baldio, dia [bawˈdʒiu, dʒja] *adj* gone to wasteland.

balé [baˈlɛ] *m* ballet.

baleia [baˈleja] *f ZOOL* whale.

baleiro, ra [ba'lejru, ra] ⟨⟩ *m, f* [vendedor] sweet seller. ⟨⟩ *m* [pote] sweet jar.

balística [ba'liʃtʃika] *f* ballistics *(sg)*.

baliza [ba'liza] *f* - **1.** [estaca] goalpost. - **2.** [bóia] buoy. - **3.** [luminosa] beacon. - **4.** *ESP* goal.

balizamento [baliza'mẽntu] *m* beaconing, signposting.

balneário [baw'njarju] *m* baths *(pl)*.

balões [ba'lõjʃ] *pl* ⊳ **balão**.

balofo, fa [ba'lofu, fal] ⟨⟩ *adj* puffy. ⟨⟩ *m, f* puffed-up person.

balsa ['bawsa] *f* - **1.** [jangada] raft. - **2.** [barca] catamaran. - **3.** [salva-vidas] lifeboat.

bálsamo ['bawsamu] *m* balsam.

Báltico ['bawtʃiku] *n*: **o (mar)** ~ the Baltic (Sea).

baluarte [ba'lwaxtʃil] *m* stronghold.

bamba ['bãnba] *fam* ⟨⟩ *adj* [perito] expert. ⟨⟩ *mf* [perito] expert.

bambo, ba ['bãnbu, bal] *adj* - **1.** [corda, laço, parafuso] loose. - **2.** [perna] faltering.

bambolear [bãnbo'lja(x)] ⟨⟩ *vt* [balançar] to sway. ⟨⟩ *vi* to sway.

bambu [bãn'bul] *m* - **1.** [planta] bamboo. - **2.** [vara] bamboo-stick.

banal [ba'naw] *(pl* -**ais***)* *adj* mundane.

banalidade [banali'dadʒil] *f* simplicity.

banana [ba'nãnal] ⟨⟩ *f* [fruta] banana; **dar uma** ~ **(para alguém)** *vulg fig* to say 'up yours!' (to sb). ⟨⟩ *mf fam fig & pej* [bobo, idiota] fool.

bananada [bana'nadal] *f* banana sweetmeat.

banca ['bãŋkal] *f* - **1.** [de jogo] game of chance. - **2.** [estande]: ~ **(de jornal)** newspaper stand. - **3.** [comissão]: ~ **(examinadora)** (examination) board. - **4.** [escritório] desk. - **5.** [mesa de trabalho] worktop; **botar** ~ to boss about.

bancada [bãŋ'kadal] *f* - **1.** [banco] bench. - **2.** [*POL* - de partido] bench; [- de estado] representatives *(pl)*. - **3.** [mesa de trabalho] workbench.

bancar [bãŋ'ka(x)] *vt* - **1.** [financiar] to back. - **2.** [comportar-se como] to play.

bancário, ria [bãŋ'karju, rjal] ⟨⟩ *adj* bank. ⟨⟩ *m, f* [empregado] bank employee.

bancarrota [bãŋka'xotal] *f* bankruptcy; **ir à** ~ to go bankrupt.

banco ['bãŋkul *m* - **1.** [ger] bank; ~ **24 horas** 24-hour bank; ~ **de sangue** blood bank. - **2.** [assento] bench. - **3.** *COMPUT*: ~ **de dados** databank. - **4.** *GEOL*: ~ **de areia** sandbank.

banda ['bãndal *f* - **1.** side; - **2.** [filarmónica] brass band; [de rock] band; - **3.**: **de** ~ **(de lado)** sideways - **4.**: ~ **larga** *COMPUT* broadband.

Band-aid® [bãn'dejdʒl *m* Band-Aid®.

bandalheira [bãnda'ʎejral *f* roguery.

bandeira [bãn'dejra, ral *f* - **1.** [ger] flag; ~ ~ **a meio pau** flag at half-mast; ~ **dois** taxi night-rate. - **2.** [estandarte] standard. - **3.** [de porta] fanlight. - **4.** *loc*: **dar** ~ **de que** to let it be known that.

bandeirante [bãndej'rãntʃil ⟨⟩ *m* [explorador] expedition member. ⟨⟩ *f* [moça] Girl Guide.

bandeirinha [bãndej'riɲal *m ESP* linesman.

bandeja [bãn'deʒal *f* tray.

bandejão [bãnde'ʒãwl *(pl* -**ões***)* *m* [*UNIV* - refeição] meal on a tray; [- refeitório] canteen.

bandido, da [bãn'dʒidu, dal ⟨⟩ *m, f* - **1.** [marginal] bandit. - **2.** [mau-caráter] rogue. ⟨⟩ *adj fam fig* [malvado, ruim] cruel.

banditismo [bãndʒi'tʃiʒmul *m* banditry.

bando ['bãndul *m* - **1.** [de pessoas, animais] flock; **em** ~ in flocks. - **2.** [quadrilha] gang. - **3.** [facção] group. - **4.** [monte] stack.

bandô [bãn'dol *m* pelmet.

bandoleiro, ra [bãndo'lejru, ral *m, f* bandit.

bandolim [bãndo'lĩl *(pl* -**ns***)* *m* mandolin.

bandolinista [bãndoli'niʃtal *mf* mandolin player.

bangalô [bãŋga'lol *m* bungalow.

banha ['bãɲal *f* - **1.** [no homem] fat. - **2.** [de porco] lard.

banhar [bã'ɲa(x)] *vt* - **1.** [dar banho em] to bathe. - **2.** [mergulhar]: ~ **algo (em)** to dip sthg (into). - **3.** [rio, mar] to wash. ⬦ **banhar-se** *vp* [tomar banho] to bathe.

banheira [bã'ɲejral *f* - **1.** [para banho] bathtub. - **2.** *fam fig* [carro] charabanc.

banheiro [bã'ɲejrul *m* toilet.

banhista [bã'ɲiʃtal *mf* bather.

banho ['bãɲul *m* - **1.** [ger] immersion. - **2.** [de entusiasmo] wave. - **3.** [para asseio]: ~ **(de chuveiro)** shower; **tomar** ~ to have a shower; **tomar** ~ **(de banheira)** to take a bath. - **4.** [na praia]: **tomar um** ~ **de sol** to sunbathe. - **5.** *fam fig* [surra]: **dar um** ~ **em alguém** to wipe sb out. - **6.** *loc*: **vai tomar** ~! *fam* get away!

banho-maria [ˌbãɲuma'rial *(pl* **banhos-marias, banhos-maria***)* *m CULIN* double boiler, bain-marie.

banir [ba'ni(x)] *vt* to banish.

banqueiro, ra [bãŋ'kejru, ral *m, f* banker.

banqueta [bãŋ'ketal *f* banquette.

banquete [bãŋ'ketʃil *m* banquet.

baque ['bakil *m* - **1.** [choque] shock; **levar um** ~ to be given a shock; **ele levou um**

baque com a notícia the news gave him a shock. - **2.** [ruído] thud. - **3.** [queda] fall.

bar ['ba(x)] (pl -es) m bar.

baralho [ba'raʎu] m pack.

barão, ronesa [ba'rãw, 'neza] m, f baron (f baroness).

barata [ba'rata] f cockroach.

barateiro, ra [bara'tejru, ra] adj cut-price.

baratinado, da [baratʃi'nadu, da] adj - **1.** [sobrecarregado, apressado] stressed. - **2.** [transtornado - pessoa] upset; [- idéia, atitude] disturbed.

baratinar [baratʃi'na(x)] vt - **1.** [atrapalhar, assoberbar] to stress. - **2.** [transtornar] to upset.

barato, ta [ba'ratu, ta] <> adj - **1.** [produto, serviço, preço] cheap. - **2.** [barateiro] cut-price. - **3.** fam [ordinário] common or garden. <> adv [cobrar etc.] cheaply. <> m - **1.** gír droga high. - **2.** fam [legal]: que ~! how cool!; ser um ~ to be cool.

barba ['baxba] f - **1.** [de homem] beard; fazer a ~ to shave; pôr as ~ s de molho fig to lie low. - **2.** [de animal] whiskers.

barbado, da [bax'badu, da] adj bearded.

Barbados [bax'baduʃ] n Barbados.

barbante [bax'bãntʃi] m string.

barbaramente [baxbara'mẽntʃi] adv - **1.** [cruelmente] brutally. - **2.** [demasiadamente] atrociously.

barbaridade [baxbari'dadʒi] f - **1.** [crueldade] barbarity. - **2.** [expressando espanto]: que ~! great!

barbárie [bax'barje] f barbarity.

bárbaro, ra ['baxbaru, ra] adj - **1.** [terrível] barbaric. - **2.** [ótimo] great.

barbatana [baxba'tãna] f fin.

barbeador [barbja'do(x)] (pl -es) m razor.

barbear [bax'bja(x)] vt to shave.

  ➡ **barbear-se** vp to shave.

barbearia [baxbja'ria] f barbershop.

barbeiragem [baxbej'raʒẽ] f fam [no trânsito] bad driving.

barbeiro, ra [bax'bejru, ra] <> adj fam [motorista] careless. <> m - **1.** [quem corta cabelos, barba] barber. - **2.** [barbearia] barbershop. - **3.** [inseto] kissing bug.

barbudo, da [bax'budu, da] <> adj bearded. <> m bearded man.

barca ['baxka] f ship.

barcaça [bax'kasa] f barge.

barco ['baxku] m boat; ~ a motor motor boat; ~ a remo rowing boat; ~ a vela sailing boat; estar no mesmo ~ fig to be in the same boat; tocar o ~ para frente fig to carry on with one's life.

barganha [bax'gãɲa] f bargain.

barganhar [baxgã'ɲa(x)] vt & vi to bargain.

barítono, na [ba'ritonu, na] <> adj baritone. <> m baritone.

barman ['baxmẽ] (pl -s) m barman.

barões [ba'rõjʃ] pl ⊳ **barão**.

barômetro [ba'rometru] m barometer.

baronesa [baro'neza] f ⊳ **barão**.

barqueiro, ra [bax'kejru, ra] m, f boatman.

barra ['baxa] f - **1.** [ger] bar; ~ de chocolate chocolate bar; ~ s paralelas parallel bars. - **2.** [de metal] ingot. - **3.** [de madeira] pole. - **4.** [de balé] barre. - **5.** [traço] score. - **6.** [acabamento] trimming. - **7.** [faixa] strip. - **8.** GEOGR sandbar. - **9.** loc: agüentar a ~ fam to stick it out; forçar a ~ to make things difficult.

barraca [ba'xaka] f - **1.** [ger] tent. - **2.** [em feira] stall. - **3.** [de madeira] hut.

barracão [baxa'kãw] (pl -ões) m - **1.** [telheiro] shed. - **2.** [habitação] big house.

barraco [ba'xaku] m shack.

barragem [ba'xaʒẽ] (pl -ns) f - **1.** [represa] dam. - **2.** [barreira] barrage.

barranco [ba'xãŋku] m - **1.** [ribanceira] ravine. - **2.** [escarpa] escarpment. - **3.** [precipício] precipice.

barra-pesada [ˌbaxape'zada] (pl barras-pesadas) fam adj - **1.** [violento] threatening. - **2.** [difícil] tough.

barrar [ba'xa(x)] vt - **1.** [obstruir] to block. - **2.** [excluir] to bar.

barreira [ba'xejra] f - **1.** [escarpa] embankment. - **2.** fig [dificuldade] barrier. - **3.** [fronteira] roadblock. - **4.** ESP hurdle.

barrento, ta [ba'xẽntu, ta] adj clayey.

barricada [baxi'kada] f barricade.

barriga [ba'xiga] f - **1.** ANAT belly. - **2.** [saliência] bulge.

barrigudo, da [baxi'gudu, da] adj potbellied.

barril [ba'xiw] (pl -is) m cask.

barro ['baxu] m clay.

barroco, ca [ba'xoku, ka] adj baroque.

barulhento, ta [baru'ʎẽntu, ta] adj noisy.

barulho [ba'ruʎu] m - **1.** [ruído] noise. - **2.** fig [confusão] fuss.

basco, ca ['baʃku, ka] <> adj Basque. <> m, f Basque.

  ➡ **basco** m [língua] Basque.

basculante [baʃku'lãntʃi] m swivel window.

base ['bazi] f - **1.** [ger] base; ~ monetária monetary base. - **2.** [camada] base coat. - **3.** fig [fundamento] basis; com ~ em based on; na ~ de with the support of.

baseado, da [ba'zjadu, da] adj [fundamentado] based.

  ➡ **baseado** m fam [droga] spliff.

basear [ba'zja(x)] *vt*: ~ algo em algo to base sthg on sthg.

➤ **basear-se** *vp*: ~-se em algo to base o.s. on sthg.

básico, ca ['baziku, ka] *adj* basic.

basílica [ba'zilika] *f* basilica.

basquete [baʃ'kɛtʃi], **basquetebol** [baʃ'kɛtʃi'bɔw] *m* basketball.

basta ['baʃta] <> *m*: dar um ~ em to stop. <> *interj* that's enough!

bastante [baʃ'tãntʃi] <> *adj* -1. [suficiente] enough. -2. [numeroso] many. <> *adv* enough.

bastão [baʃ'tãw] (*pl* -ões) *m* stick.

bastar [baʃ'ta(x)] *vi* [ser suficiente] to be enough.

bastardo, da [baʃ'taxdu, da] *adj* bastard.

bastidor [baʃtʃi'do(x)] *m* [moldura] frame.

➤ **bastidores** *mpl* -1. TEATRO wings. -2. [lado secreto] shadowy side.

bastões [baʃ'tõjʃ] *pl* ⊳ **bastão**.

bata ['bata] *f* -1. [blusa] blouse. -2. [jaleco] white coat, overall.

batalha [ba'taʎa] *f* -1. [ger] battle. -2. *fig* [esforço] struggle.

batalhador, ra [bataʎa'do(x), ra] *adj* hardworking.

batalhão [bata'ʎãw] (*pl* -ões) *m* -1. MIL battalion. -2. [multidão] crowd.

batata [ba'tata] *f* potato; ~ frita chips *UK*, fries *US*; ~ da perna calf *(of the leg)*.

batata-doce [ba,tata'dosi] (*pl* batatas-doces) *f* sweet potato.

bate-boca [,batʃi'boka] (*pl* bate-bocas) *m* quarrel.

batedor [bate'do(x)] *m* -1. [polícia] escort. -2.: ~ de carteiras [ladrão] bag-snatcher.

batente [ba'tẽntʃi] *m* -1. [ombreira] doorpost. -2. *fam* [trabalho] work; pegar firme no ~ to toil away.

bate-papo [,batʃi'papu] (*pl* bate-papos) *m* *fam* chat.

bater [ba'te(x)] <> *vt* -1. [ger] to beat; ~ o pé to stamp one's foot. -2. [datilografar]: ~ algo (à máquina) to type sthg out. -3. [fechar com força] to slam. -4. [foto] to take. -5. [usar todo dia] to wear every day. -6. *fam* [furtar]: ~ carteira to pickpocket. <> *vi* -1. [dar pancadas]: ~ em alguém/algo to hit sb/sthg. -2. [colidir]: ~ em algo to collide with sthg. -3. [horas, sino] to strike. -4. [coração] to beat. -5. *loc*: não ~ bem *fam* [ser meio doido] to be off one's rocker.

➤ **bater-se** *vp*: ~-se por to fight for.

bateria [bate'ria] *f* -1. [de cozinha] set of kitchen utensils. -2. [MÚS - instrumentos de percussão] percussion; [- conjunto de pratos, caixa e bombo] drum kit. -3. ELETR battery.

baterista [bate'riʃta] *mf* [MÚS - percussionista] percussionist; [- que toca bateria] drummer.

batido, da [ba'tʃidu, da] <> *adj* -1. [ger] beaten. -2. [comum demais] worn out. <> *adv* [às pressas] in a hurry.

➤ **batida** *f* -1. [ger] beat. -2. [de relógio, sino] strike. -3. [à porta] knock. -4. AUTO collision. -5. [bebida] crush.

batina [ba'tʃina] *f* RELIG cassock.

batismo [ba'tʃiʒmu] *m* baptism.

batistério [batʃiʃ'tɛrju] *m* baptistery.

batizar [batʃi'za(x)] *vt* -1. [ger] to baptize. -2. [apelidar] to nickname.

batom [ba'tõ] (*pl* -ns) *m* lipstick.

batucada [batu'kada] *f* street gathering for samba music and expression.

batucar [batu'ka(x)] *vi* -1. MÚS to dance and sing the batuque. -2. [martelar] to hammer.

batuque [ba'tuki] *m* Afro-Brazilian dance.

batuta [ba'tuta] *f* [de maestro] baton.

baú [ba'u] *m* trunk.

baunilha [baw'niʎa] *f* vanilla.

bazar [ba'za(x)] (*pl* -es) *m* -1. [ger] bazaar. -2. [loja] bazaar.

BB (*abrev de* Banco do Brasil) *m* Brazilian state-owned bank.

BC (*abrev de* Banco Central do Brasil) *m* central bank of Brazil.

beato, ta [be'atu, ta] <> *adj* -1. [beatificado] blessed. -2. [fanático religioso] churchy. <> *m* -1. [quem foi beatificado] beatified person. -2. [devoto] worshipper.

bêbado, da ['bebadu, da] <> *adj* drunk. <> *m, f* -1. [que bebe regularmente] drunkard. -2. [que bebeu demais] drunk.

bebê [be'be] *m* baby.

bebedeira [bebe'dejra] *f* -1. [estado do bêbado] drunkenness; tomar uma ~ to get drunk. -2. [ato de se embebedar] drinking bout.

bêbedo, da ['bebedu] *adj* ⊳ **bêbado**.

bebedouro [bebe'doru] *m* -1. [aparelho] drinking fountain. -2. [para animais] drinking trough.

beber [be'be(x)] <> *vt* -1. [tomar líquido] to drink. -2. [absorver] to soak up. <> *vi* -1. [tomar bebida alcoólica] to have a drink. -2. [embriagar-se] to get drunk.

bebida [be'bida] *f* -1. [líquido potável] drink. -2. [alcoólica] (alcoholic) drink.

beça ['bɛsa] *f*: à ~ [em grande quantidade] in large numbers; [ao extremo] gostei à ~ da nova revista I enjoyed the new magazine very much.

beco ['bekul *m* alley; **estar num ~ sem saída** to be in a catch-22 situation.

beduíno, na [be'dwinu, na] <> *adj* Bedouin. <> *m, f* Bedouin.

bege ['bɛʒi] <> *adj inv* beige. <> *m* beige.

begônia [be'gonja] *f* begonia.

beiço ['bejsu] *m* lip.

beija-flor [,bejʒa'flo(x)] (*pl* beija-flores) *m* hummingbird.

beijar [bej'ʒa(x)] *vt* to kiss.
- **beijar-se** *vp* to kiss.

beijo ['bejʒu] *m* kiss; **dar um ~ em alguém** to give sb a kiss.

beira ['bejra] *f* edge; **à ~ de** [na borda] on the edge of; *fig* on the brink of.

beira-mar [,bejra'ma(x)] *f*: **à ~** by the sea.

beirar [bej'ra(x)] *vt* **-1.** [caminhar à beira de] to walk alongside. **-2.** [estar à beira de] to be on the edge of. **-3.** [estar próximo de] to be close to.

beisebol [bejze'bɔw] *m* baseball.

belas-artes [,bɛla'zaxtʃiʃ] *fpl* fine arts.

beldade [bew'dadʒi] *f* **-1.** [beleza] beauty. **-2.** [mulher bonita] beautiful woman.

Belém [be'lẽj] *n* **-1.** [no Brasil] Belém. **-2.** [na Palestina] Bethlehem.

beleza [be'leza] *f* **-1.** [de lugar etc.] beauty. **-2.** [mulher bela] beautiful woman.

belga ['bɛwga] <> *adj* Belgian. <> *m, f* Belgian.

Bélgica ['bɛwʒika] *n* Belgium.

Belgrado [bew'gradu] *n* Belgrade.

beliche [be'liʃi] *m* bunk bed.

bélico, ca ['bɛliku, ka] *adj* war (*antes de subst*).

beliscão [beliʃ'kãw] (*pl* -ões) *m* pinch.

beliscar [beliʃ'ka(x)] *vt* **-1.** [pessoa] to pinch. **-2.** *fig* [comida] to pick at (*food*).

belo, la ['bɛlu, la] <> *adj* **-1.** [perfeito] lovely. **-2.** [sublime] wonderful. **-3.** (*antes de subst*) [considerável] fine. **-4.** (*antes de subst*) [gratificante] excellent. **-5.** [indefinido]: **um ~ dia** ... one fine day ... <> *m* [estética] beauty.

bem ['bẽj] <> *adv* **-1.** [ger] well. **-2.** [muito, bastante] very. **-3.** [exatamente] exactly; **~ ali** right there. **-4.** [de bom grado]: **~ que eu gostaria de ajudar, mas não posso** I'd very much like to help, but I can't. **-5.** [expressando opinião]: **estar ~** [de saúde] to be well; [de aspecto] to look good; [financeiramente] to be well-off; **fazer ~ a alguém** [suj: exercício etc.] to be good for sb; **ficar** *ou* **cair ~** [atitude] to be suitable. **-6.** [saudando]: **tudo ~?** *fam* how are you?; **tudo ~** [em resposta] fine. **-7.** [concordando]: **tá ~** all right. **-8.** [em conclusão, introdu-

ção] well now. **-9.** [em congratulação]: **muito ~!** well done! <> *m* **-1.** [ger] good. **-2.** [pessoa amada] loved one. **-3.** *fam* [forma de tratamento]: **meu ~** my darling. **-4.** [patrimônio] assets (*pl*).
- **bens** *mpl* **-1.** [patrimônio] assets. **-2.** [produtos]: **~ de consumo** consumer goods.
- **bem como** *loc adv* as well as.
- **se bem que** *loc conj* even though.

bem-acabado, da [bẽjaka'badu, da] (*mpl* -s, *fpl* -s) *adj* well-finished.

bem-apessoado, da [bẽjape'swadu, da] (*mpl* -s, *fpl* -s) *adj* presentable.

bem-arrumado, da [bẽjaxu'madu, da] (*mpl* -s, *fpl* -s) *adj* **-1.** [pessoa] well dressed. **-2.** [casa] well appointed.

bem-casado, da [bẽjka'zadu, da] (*mpl* -s, *fpl* -s) *adj* happily married.

bem-conceituado, da [bẽjkõnsej'twadu, da] (*mpl* -s [-ʃ], *fpl* -s [-ʃ]) *adj* well respected.

bem-disposto, ta [bẽjdʒiʃ'poʃtu, ta] *adj* good-humoured.

bem-educado, da [bẽjedu'kadu, da] (*mpl* -s, *fpl* -s) *adj* well bred.

bem-estar [bẽjʃ'ta(x)] *m* well-being.

bem-feito, ta [bẽj'fejtu, ta] (*mpl* -s, *fpl* -s) *adj* **-1.** [bem-acabado] well made. **-2.** [de belas formas] elegant. **-3.** [quando algo ruim ocorre]: **~** serves you right!

bem-humorado, da [bẽjumo'radu, da] (*mpl* -s, *fpl* -s) *adj* good-humoured.

bem-intencionado, da [bẽjĩntẽnsjo'nadu, da] (*mpl* -s, *fpl* -s) *adj* well meaning.

bem-me-quer [bẽjmi'kɛ(x)] *m* daisy.

bem-passado, da [bẽjpa'sadu, da] (*mpl* -s, *fpl* -s) *adj* [carne] well cooked.

bem-sucedido, da [bẽjsuse'dʒidu, da] (*mpl* -s, *fpl* -s) *adj* successful.

bem-vindo, da [bẽj'vĩndu, da] *adj* welcome.

benchmarking [bɛnʃmarkiŋ] *m* ECON benchmarking.

bênção [bẽnsãw] (*pl* -çãos) *f* blessing.

bendito, ta [bẽn'dʒitu, ta] *adj* [abençoado] blessed.

bendizer [bẽndʒi'ze(x)] *vt* **-1.** [falar bem de] to praise. **-2.** [abençoar] to bless.

beneficência [benefi'sẽnsja] *f* **-1.** [bondade] kindness. **-2.** [caridade] charity.

beneficiado, da [benefi'sjadu, da] <> *adj* [que se beneficiou] benefitting. <> *m* [beneficiário] beneficiary.

beneficiar [benefi'sja(x)] *vt* **-1.** [favorecer] to benefit. **-2.** [processar] to process. **-3.** [melhorar] to improve.
- **beneficiar-se** *vp* [favorecer-se] to profit.

benefício [bene'fisju] *m* benefit.

benéfico, ca [be'nɛfiku, ka] *adj* -**1.** [ger] beneficial. -**2.** [favorável] favourable.

benemérito, ta [bene'mɛritu, ta] ◇ *adj* -**1.** [que merece o bem] deserving. -**2.** [digno de honras] praiseworthy. -**3.** [ilustre] renowned. ◇ *m* worthy person.

benevolente [benevo'lẽntʃi] *adj* -**1.** [bondoso] kindly. -**2.** [complacente] friendly.

benfeitor, ra [bẽnfej'to(x), ra] ◇ *adj* [benévolo] benevolent. ◇ *m* [aquele que faz benfeitoria] benefactor.

bengala [bẽŋ'gala] *f* walking stick.

benigno, na [be'nignu, na] *adj* -**1.** [benévelo] gentle. -**2.** [complacente] friendly. -**3.** *MED* benign.

benjamim [bẽnʒa'mĩ] (*pl* -**ns**) *m ELETR* adaptor.

bens [bẽjʃ] *pl* ⊳ **bem**.

bento, ta ['bẽntu, ta] ◇ *pp* ⊳ **benzer**. ◇ *adj* holy.

benzer [bẽn'ze(x)] *vt* [abençoar] to bless.
⬧ **benzer-se** *vp* [fazer o sinal-da-cruz] to make the sign of the cross.

berço ['bexsul] *m* cradle.

Berlim [bex'lĩ] *n* Berlin.

berimbau [berĩ'baw] *m MÚS* berimbau, *small Brazilian percussion instrument.*

berinjela [berĩ'ʒɛla] *f* aubergine *UK*, eggplant *US*.

bermuda [bex'muda] *f* Bermuda shorts (*pl*).

berreiro [be'xejru] *m* -**1.** [gritaria] shouting. -**2.** [choradeira] wailing.

berro ['bɛxu] *m* bellow.

besouro [be'zorul] *m* beetle.

besta ['beʃta] *fam* ◇ *adj* -**1.** [pedante] pedantic. -**2.** [idiota] idiotic. -**3.** [surpreso]: **ficar** ~ to be dumbfounded. -**4.** [insignificante] insignificant. ◇ *f* -**1.** [animal] beast. -**2.** *fam* [pessoa pedante] pedant. -**3.** *fam* [pessoa idiota] fool.

bestial [beʃ'tjaw] (*pl* -**ais**) *adj* -**1.** [brutal] bestial. -**2.** [repugnante] depraved.

best-seller [ˌbɛʃt'sɛlɛ(x)] (*pl* -**s**) *m* bestseller.

besuntar [bezũn'ta(x)] *vt* [untar]: ~ **de** *ou* **com** to grease with.

beterraba [bete'xaba] *f* beetroot.

betume [be'tumi] *m* bitumen.

bexiga [be'ʃiga] *f ANAT* bladder.

bezerro, rra [be'zexu, xa] *m, f* calf.

bibelô [bibe'lo] *m* [objeto decorativo] knick-knack.

bíblia ['biblja] *f* bible.
⬧ **Bíblia** *f* Bible.

bíblico, ca ['bibliku, ka] *adj* biblical.

bibliografia [bibljogra'fia] *f* bibliography.

biblioteca [bibljo'tɛka] *f* library.

bibliotecário, ria [bibljote'karju, rja] *m, f* librarian.

bica ['bika] *f* water outlet.

bicampeão, peã [bikãnpjãw, pja] (*mpl* -**peões**, *fpl* -**s**) ◇ *adj* twice champion. ◇ *m* twice champion.

bicar [bi'ka(x)] *vt* -**1.** [dar bicadas] to peck. -**2.** [bebericar] to sip.

bicentenário, ria [bisẽnte'narju, rja] ◇ *adj* bicentennial. ◇ *m* bicentenary.

bicha ['biʃa] *f* -**1.** [lombriga] earthworm. -**2.** *fam pej* [efeminado] fairy.

bicheiro [bi'ʃejru] *m* [em jogo do bicho] bookie (*collecting money for illegal lottery bets*).

bicho ['biʃul] *m* -**1.** [animal] animal. -**2.** [inseto, piolho] insect. -**3.** *fam* [sujeito] mate.

bicicleta [besi'klɛta] *f* bicycle; **andar de** ~ to ride a bike.

bico ['biku] *m* -**1.** [de ave] beak. -**2.** [ponta] tip. -**3.** *fam* [boca] mouth; **calar o** ~ to pipe down. -**4.** [chupeta] teat. -**5.** *fam* [biscate] odd job. -**6.** *ANAT* : ~ **do peito** nipple. -**7.** [de gás] burner.

bicombustível [bikõnbuʃ'tʃivew] *adj* dual-fuel.

BID (*abrev de* **Banco Interamericano de Desenvolvimento**) *m* IDB.

bidê [bi'de] *m* bidet.

Bielo-Rússia [bjɛlo'xusja] *n* Belarus.

bienal [bje'naw] (*pl* -**ais**) ◇ *adj* biennial. ◇ *f* biennial.

bife ['bifi] *m CULIN* steak; ~ **a cavalo** steak with a fried egg; ~ **à milanesa** steak milanese.

bifocal [bifo'kaw] (*pl* -**ais**) *adj* bifocal.

bifurcar [bifux'ka(x)] *vi* to fork.
⬧ **bifurcar-se** *vp* to fork.

bígamo, ma ['bigamu, mal] ◇ *adj* bigamous. ◇ *m, f* bigamist.

bigode [bi'gɔdʒi] *m* moustache.

bigorna [bi'gɔxna] *f* anvil.

bijuteria [biʒute'ria] *f* piece of jewellery.

bilhão [bi'ʎãw] (*pl* -**ões**) *num* billion.

bilhar [bi'ʎa(x)] (*pl* -**es**) *m* -**1.** [jogo] billiards (*sg*). -**2.** [estabelecimento] billiard hall.

bilhete [bi'ʎetʃi] *m* -**1.** [ger] ticket; ~ **de ida** one-way ticket; ~ **de ida e volta** return ticket. -**2.** [mensagem] note.

bilheteria [biʎete'ria] *f* ticket office.

bilhões [bi'ʎõjʃ] *pl* ⊳ **bilhão**.

bilíngüe [bi'lĩgwi] *adj* bilingual.

bilionário, ria [biljo'narju, rja] ◇ *adj* billionaire. ◇ *m, f* billionaire.

bílis ['biliʃ] *f (inv)* bile.

bimestral [bimeʃ'traw] (*pl* -**ais**) *adj* two-monthly.

bimotor [bimo'to(x)] <> *adj* twin-engined. <> *m* twin-engined plane.

bingo ['bĩŋgu] *m* bingo.

binóculo [bi'nɔkulu] *m* binoculars (*pl*).

binômio [bi'nomju] *m* MAT binomial.

biodegradável [bjodegra'davew] (*pl* -eis) *adj* biodegradable.

biodiversidade [bjodʒivexsi'dadʒi] *f* biodiversity.

bioengenharia [biowẽnʒeɲa'ria] *f* bioengineering.

biografia [bjogra'fia] *f* biography.

biográfico, ca [bjo'grafiku, ka] *adj* biographical.

biologia [bjolo'ʒia] *f* biology.

biológico, ca [bjo'lɔʒiku, ka] *adj* biological.

biólogo, ga ['bjɔlogu, ga] *m, f* biologist.

biomassa [bio'masa] *f* biomass.

biombo ['bjõnbu] *m* screen.

biopirataria [biopirata'ria] *f* biopiracy.

BIOS (*abrev de* Basic Input/Output System) *m* BIOS.

bipartidarismo [bipaxtʃida'riʒmu] *m* bipartisanship.

biquíni [bi'kini] *m* bikini.

BIRD (*abrev de* Banco Internacional de Reconstrução e Desenvolvimento) *m* IBRD.

birita [bi'rita] *f fam* (alcoholic) drink.

birosca [bi'rɔʃka] *f* - **1.** [pequena mercearia] small shop. - **2.** [botequim] snack bar.

birra ['bixa] *f* - **1.** [teimosia] temper. - **2.** [irritação, zanga]: **ficar de ~ com alguém** to be at loggerheads with sb.

biruta [bi'ruta] <> *adj* [pessoa] mad. <> *m* [pessoa] madman. <> *f* [dispositivo] windsock.

bis ['biʃ] <> *m* encore; **pedir um ~** to demand an encore; **fazer** *ou* **dar um ~** to give an encore. <> *interj* encore!

bisavô, vó [biza'vo, vɔ] *m, f* great-grandfather (*f* great-grandmother).

➡ **bisavós** *mpl* great-grandparents.

bisbilhotar [biʒbiʎo'ta(x)] <> *vt* [examinar] to pry. <> *vi fam* [fazer mexericos] to gossip.

bisbilhoteiro, ra [biʒbiʎo'tejru, ra] <> *adj* - **1.** [curioso] nosy. - **2.** [mexeriqueiro] gossipy. <> *m, f* - **1.** [pessoa curiosa] nosy parker. - **2.** [pessoa mexeriqueira] gossip.

biscate [biʃ'katʃi] *m fam* odd job.

biscoito [biʃ'kojtu] *m* biscuit.

bisnaga [biʒ'naga] *f* - **1.** [pão] baguette. - **2.** [tubo] tube.

bisneto, ta [biʒ'nɛtu, ta] *m, f* great-grandchild.

bispo ['biʃpu] *m* bishop.

bissexto, ta [bi'sejʃtu, ta] *adj*: **ano ~** leap year.

➡ **bissexto** *m* 29 February.

bissexual [bisek'swaw] (*pl* -ais) <> *adj* bisexual. <> *m* bisexual.

bisturi [biʃtu'ri] *m* scalpel.

bit ['bitʃi] *m* COMPUT bit.

bitmap ['bitimapi] *m* COMPUT bitmap.

bitola [bi'tɔla] *f* gauge.

bizarro, a [bi'zaxu, xa] *adj* bizarre.

black-tie [blɛk'taj] *m* black tie, dinner jacket.

blasé [bla'ze] *adj* blasé.

blasfemar [blaʃfe'ma(x)] <> *vt* RELIG to take in vain. <> *vi* RELIG to swear.

blasfêmia [blaʃ'femja] *f* - **1.** RELIG blasphemy. - **2.** [ultraje] defamation.

blazer ['blejzɛ(x)] (*pl* -es) *m* blazer.

blecaute [ble'kawtʃi] *m* blackout.

blefar [ble'fa(x)] *vi* - **1.** [em jogo] to bluff. - **2.** [tapear] to deceive.

blefe ['blɛfi] *m* - **1.** [truque] trick. - **2.** [no jogo] bluff.

blindado, da [blĩn'dadu, da] *adj* armoured.

blindagem [blĩn'daʒe] *f* armour.

blitz ['blitiʃ] (*pl* **blitze**) *f* blitz.

bloco ['blɔku] *m* - **1.** [ger] block. - **2.** [papel] pad. - **3.** [grupo]: **~ de Carnaval** group of carnival revellers.

➡ **em bloco** *loc adv* en bloc.

blog ['blɔgi] *m* COMPUT blog.

bloquear [blo'kja(x)] *vt* - **1.** [cercar] to surround. - **2.** [impedir] to block off. - **3.** PSIC to block.

bloqueio [blo'keju] *m* - **1.** [cerco] blockade. - **2.** [obstrução] obstacle; MED, PSIC blockage.

blusa ['bluza] *f* blouse.

BM (*abrev de* Banco Mundial) *m* World Bank.

BM & F (*abrev de* Bolsa de Mercadorias e Futuros) *f Brazilian commodities and futures market.*

BNDES (*abrev de* Banco Nacional de Desenvolvimento Econômico e Social) *m Brazilian bank for financing economic and social development.*

BNH (*abrev de* Banco Nacional da Habitação) *m national bank for financing low-paid workers to buy their own homes.*

BO (*abrev de* Boletim de Ocorrência) *m Brazilian crime report.*

boa ['boa] *f* ➤ **bom**.

boate ['bwatʃi] *f* nightclub.

boato ['bwatu] *m* rumour.

boa-vida [,boa'vida] (*pl* **boas-vidas**) *m* bon vivant.

Boa Vista [,boa'viʃta] *n* Boa Vista.

bobagem [bo'baʒɛ] (pl -ns) <> f -1. [coisa supérflua] frippery. -2. [dito] rubbish. -3. [fato sem importância] trifle. <> adj [desaconselhável]: **ser ~ fazer algo** to be foolish to do sthg.

bobeada [bo'bjada] f fam foolishness; **dar uma ~** to be a fool.

bobear [bo'bja(x)] vi -1. [fazer besteira] to make a mistake. -2. [deixar-se enganar] to be tricked. -3. [descuidar-se] to be careless. -4. [perder uma chance] to blow it.

bobeira [bo'bejra] f mistake; **marcar ~** fam [ser enganado] to be a fool; [perder uma chance] to blow it.

bobina [bo'bina] f bobbin.

bobo, ba ['bobu, ba] <> adj foolish. <> m, f fool.
    ◆ **bobo** m: **~ da corte** court jester.

bobó [bo'bɔ] m CULIN : **~ (de camarão)** shrimp bobó.

boca ['boka] f -1. [ger] mouth; **~ do estômago** MED cardia; **cala a ~!** fam shut up! -2. [de calça] top. -3. fam [emprego] opening. -4. fam [pessoa para alimentar] mouth to feed. -5. loc: **bater ~** to argue; **falar da ~ para fora** not to mean what one is saying.

boca-a-boca [ˌboka'boka] <> m MED mouth-to-mouth resuscitation. <> adj: **respiração ~** kiss of life.

boca-de-fumo [ˌbokadʒi'fumu] (pl bocas-de-fumo) f fam drug-dealing patch.

bocadinho [boka'dʒiɲu] m -1. [pequena quantidade]: **um ~ (de)** a little bit (of). -2. [tempo curto]: **um ~** a little bit.

bocado [bo'kadu] m -1. [grande quantidade]: **um ~ de** quite a lot of. -2. [pedaço, porção]: **um ~ (de)** a bit (of). -3. [mordida] mouthful.
    ◆ **um bocado** loc adv [bastante] quite.

bocal [bo'kaw] (pl -ais) m -1. [ger] mouth. -2. MÚS mouthpiece.

boçal [bo'saw] (pl -ais) adj -1. [ignorante] stupid. -2. [grosseiro] rude.

bocejar [bose'ʒa(x)] vi to yawn.

bocejo [bo'seʒu] m yawn.

bochecha [bu'ʃeʃa] f cheek.

bochecho [bo'ʃeʃu] m mouthwash.

bodas ['bodaʃ] fpl wedding anniversary (sg); **~ de ouro** golden wedding (sg); **~ de prata** silver wedding (sg).

bode ['bɔdʒi] m ZOOL billy goat; **~ expiatório** fig scapegoat.

boêmio, mia [bo'emju, mja] <> adj -1. [vida etc.] bohemian. -2. [da Boêmia] Bohemian. <> m, f -1. [pessoa boêmia] bohemian. -2. [da Boêmia] Bohemian.

bofe ['bɔfi] m fam -1. [pulmão] lungs (pl). -2. fam [pessoa feia] monster.

bofetada [bofe'tada] f slap in the face.

bofetão [bofe'tãw] (pl -ões) m hard slap on the face.

Bogotá [bogo'ta] n Bogotá.

boi ['boj] m ox.

bóia ['bɔja] f -1. NÁUT buoy; **~ salva-vidas** lifebuoy. -2. fam [comida] grub.

boiada [bo'jada] f drove of oxen.

boiar [bo'ja(x)] vi -1. [flutuar] to float. -2. fam [não entender]: **estar/ficar boiando** to be thrown by.

boicotar [bojko'ta(x)] vt to boycott.

boicote [boj'kɔtʃi] m boycott.

boiler ['bɔjle(x)] (pl -s) m boiler.

boina ['bɔjna] f cap.

bojo ['boʒu] m -1. [saliência] bulge. -2. [de navio] belly.

bola ['bɔla] f -1. [objeto] ball; **ser bom de ~** to play football very well; **~ de futebol** football. -2. ESP [jogada] shot. -3. loc: **dar ~ para alguém** [flertar] to flirt with sb; **não dar ~ (para)** [ignorar] to ignore; **não dar ~ para algo** [não dar importância a] to ignore sthg; **pisar na ~** fig to make a mistake.

bolacha [bo'laʃa] f -1. [biscoito] biscuit; **~ d'água** water biscuit. -2. fam [bofetada]: **dar uma ~ em alguém** to slap sb. -3. [em bares, restaurantes] coaster.

bolada [bo'lada] f -1. [pancada] hit (with a ball). -2. [de dinheiro] jackpot.

bolar [bo'la(x)] <> vt to devise. <> vi to be successful.

boléia [bo'lɛja] f lorry driver's seat.

boletim [bole'tʃĩ] (pl -ns) m -1. [publicação] bulletin. -2. EDUC school report. -3. [nota] memo; **~ médico** medical report.

bolha ['boʎa] <> f -1. [em líquido, material] bubble. -2. [na pele] blister. <> mf fam [pessoa] bore.

boliche [bo'liʃi] m -1. [jogo] pool. -2. [estabelecimento] pool room.

bolinagem [bolina'ʒɛ̃] (pl -ns) f fam touching up.

bolinar [boli'na(x)] vt fam to touch up.

bolinho [bo'liɲu] m croquette; **~ de bacalhau** salt cod croquette.

Bolívia [bo'livja] n Bolivia.

boliviano, na [boli'vjãnu, na] <> adj Bolivian. <> m, f Bolivian.

bolo ['bolu] m -1. CULIN cake. -2. [quantidade]: **um ~ de** a load of. -3. fam [confusão] commotion; **dar o maior ~** to cause a commotion; **deu o maior ~ quando ...** there was a great to-do when ... -4. [em jogo etc.] stake. -5. loc: **dar o ~ em alguém** to stand sb up.

bolor [bo'lo(x)] *m* mould.

bolsa ['bowsa] *f* -1. [acessório] purse. -2. *EDUC*: ~ (de estudos) bursary. -3. *FIN*: ~ (de valores) stock market.

bolso ['bowsu] *m* pocket; de ~ pocket *(antes de subst)*.

bom, boa ['bõ, 'boa] *(mpl* bons, *fpl* boas) *adj* -1. [ger] good; ser ~ em algo to be good at sthg; ficar ~ to be well made/done. -2. [curado] well. -3. [seguro] safe. -4. [amplo, confortável] spacious. -5. [pedindo opinião, permissão]: está ~? all right?
● bom *interj*: que ~! how great!
● às boas *loc adv*: voltar às boas (com alguém) to make up (with sb).

bomba ['bõba] *f* -1. [explosivo] bomb; ~ atômica atomic bomb. -2. [fogo de artifício] rocket. -3. [máquina, aparelho] pump; ~ d'água water pump; ~ de gasolina petrol pump. -4. *fig* [acontecimento] shock. -5. *fig* [coisa ruim]: ser uma ~ to be a flop. -6. *EDUC*: levar ~ (em algo) to fail at sthg. -7. [doce] bombe.

bombardear [bõbax'dʒja(x)] *vt* to bombard.

bombardeio [bõbax'deju] *m* bombardment.

bomba-relógio [ˌbõbaxe'lɔʒju] *(pl* bombas-relógios, bombas-relógio) *f* time bomb.

bombear [bõ'bja(x)] *vt* & *vi* to pump.

bombeiro [bõ'bejru] *m* -1. [de incêndios] fire fighter. -2. [encanador] plumber.

bombom [bõ'bõ] *(pl* -ns) *m* sweetie.

bom-tom [bõ'tõ] *m* good manners; ser de ~ to be socially acceptable.

bonança [bo'nãsa] *f* -1. *NÁUT* calm. -2. *fig* [tranqüilidade] calm.

bondade [bõ'dadʒi] *f* -1. [qualidade] kindness. -2. [benevolência] goodness; ter a ~ de fazer algo to be kind enough to do sthg.

bonde ['bõdʒi] *m* -1. [veículo] tram; pegar o ~ andando *fig* to come in (a conversation) half way. -2. *fam* [mulher feia] ugly woman.

bondoso, sa [bõ'dozu, ɔza] *adj* kind.

boné [bo'nɛ] *m* cap.

boneca [bo'nɛka] *f* -1. [ger] doll. -2. *fam* [homosexual] queen.

boneco [bo'nɛku] *m* -1. [ger] stencil. -2. [brinquedo] doll. -3. *fig* [fantoche] puppet.

boníssimo, ma [bo'nisimu, mal *superl* ⊳ bom.

bonito, ta [bo'nitu, tal *adj* -1. [ger] beautiful. -2. *iron* [lamentável] lovely.
● bonito *adv* [bem] well.

bons ['bõjʃ] *pl* ⊳ bom.

bônus ['bonuʃ] *m (inv)* -1. [prêmio] prize. -2. [debênture] share.

boot ['butil *(pl* boots) *m* *COMPUT* [inicialização] boot-up; dar ~ to reboot.

boquiaberto, ta [bokja'bɛxtu, tal *adj* gaping.

boquinha [bo'kiɲa] *f* *fig* [refeição]: fazer uma ~ snack.

borboleta [boxbo'leta] *f* -1. *ZOOL* butterfly. -2. [roleta] turnstile.

borbotão [boxbo'tãw] *(pl* -ões) *m*: aos borbotões in spurts.

borbulhante [boxbu'ʎãntʃi] *adj* fizzy.

borbulhar [boxbu'ʎa(x)] *vi* to bubble.

borda ['boxda] *f* -1. edge. -2. [lençol] hem. -3. [jardim] border. -4. [rio] bank. -5. [piscina] side.

bordadeira [boxda'dejra] *f* embroiderer.

bordado, da [box'dadu, dal *adj* embroidered.
● bordado *m* embroidery.

bordão [box'dãw] *(pl* -ões) *m* -1. [cajado] crook. -2. *fig* [arrimo] prop. -3. [*MÚS* - corda] bass string; [- nota] lowest note. -4. [frase] slogan.

bordar [box'da(x)] *vt* & *vi* to embroider.

bordejar [boxde'ʒa(x)] *vi* *NÁUT* to tack.

bordel [box'dɛw] *(pl* -eis) *m* brothel.

bordo ['bɔxdu] *m* -1. [de navio] board; a ~ on board. -2. [ao bordejar] tack.

bordões [box'dõjʃ] *pl* ⊳ bordão.

borla ['boxla] *f* -1. [pendão] tassel. -2. [pompom] pompom.

borra ['boxa] *f* -1. [de café] grounds *(pl)*. -2. [de vinho] dregs *(pl)*.

borracha [bo'xaʃa] *f* -1. [ger] rubber. -2. [para apagar] rubber, eraser.

borrachudo [boxa'ʃudul *m* black fly.

borracheiro [boxa'ʃejru] *m* -1. [pessoa] tyre fitter. -2. [oficina] tyre-fitting workshop.

borrão [bo'xãw] *(pl* -ões) *m* stain.

borrar [bo'xa(x)] *vt* -1. [manchar] to stain. -2. [riscar] to cross out. -3. [pintar] to smear. -4. *fam* [de fezes] to foul.

borrasca [bo'xaʃka] *f* -1. [tempestade] thunderstorm. -2. [em alto-mar] squall.

borrifar [boxi'fa(x)] *vt* to spray.

borrifo [bo'xiful *m* spray.

borrões [bo'xõjʃ] *pl* ⊳ borrão.

Bósnia-Herzegovina [ˌbɔʒnjexzego'vinal Bosnia-Herzegovina.

bósnio, nia ['bɔʒnju, nja], **bosniano, na** [boʒni'ãnu, nal ◇ *adj* Bosnian. ◇ *m, f* Bosnian.

bosque ['bɔʃkil *m* wood.

bossa ['bɔsal *f* -1. [ger] bump. -2. *fam* [charme] appeal; ter ~ to be appealing.

bosta ['bɔʃtal *f* -1. [de animal] dung. -2. [de ser humano] excrement.

bota ['bɔtal *f* boot; ~s de borracha wellington boots, rubber boots.

botânico, ca [bo'taniku, ka] <> *adj* botanic. <> *m, f* botanist.
➡ **botânica** *f* botany.

botão [bo'tãw] (*pl* -ões) *m* -1. [ger] button. - 2. [de jogo] counter. - 3. [de flor] bud.

botar [bo'ta(x)] <> *vt* -1. [ger] to put; ~ algo em dia to bring sthg up to date. - 2. [roupa, sapatos] to put on. - 3. [defeito] to point out. <> *vi loc*: ~ para quebrar [empreender mudanças] to make sweeping changes; [fazer sucesso] to be a huge hit.

bote ['bɔtʃil *m* -1. [barco] boat; ~ salva-vidas lifeboat. - 2. [golpe - com arma] thrust; [- salto] leap; [- de cobra] lunge; dar o ~ to lunge.

boteco [bo'tɛkul (*pl* -s), **botequim** [bote'kĩl (*pl* -ns) *m* tavern.

boticário, ria [botʃi'karju, rja] *m, f* dispensing chemist.

botijão [botʃi'ʒãw] (*pl* -ões) *m* cylinder.

botões [bo'tõʃl *pl* ➣ botão.

Bovespa (*abrev de* **Bolsa de Valores do Estado de São Paulo**) *f São Paulo stock exchange*.

bovino, na [bo'vinu, nal *adj* bovine.

boxe ['bɔksil *m* -1. *ESP* boxing. - 2. [em banheiro] shower cubicle.

boxeador [boksja'do(x)] *m* boxer.

boy ['bɔjl *m* = bói.

bps [bepe'esil (*abrev de* **bit por segundo**) *COMPUT* bps.

BR *abrev de* Brasil.

braça ['brasal *f NÁUT* fathom.

braçada [bra'sadal *f* -1. [de flores] armful. - 2. [em natação] stroke.

braçadeira [brasa'dejral *f* -1. [para o braço] armband. - 2. [de cortina] tie-back. - 3. [metálica] clasp. - 4. *ESP* [correia] wristband.

braçal [bra'sawl (*pl* -ais) *adj* physical; trabalho ~ physical work.

bracelete [brase'letʃil *m* bracelet.

braço ['brasul *m* -1. [ger] arm; de ~s cruzados with arms folded; *fig* [impassível] impassively; dar o ~ a alguém to give one's arm to sb; de ~ dado arm in arm; ~ direito *fig* right arm. - 2. [de toca-discos] arm. - 3. [de balança] pointer. - 4. [trabalhador] hand. - 5. [ramo] limb. - 6. *loc*: não dar o ~ a torcer to stick to one's guns; receber (alguém) de ~s abertos to welcome (sb) with open arms.

bradar [bra'da(x)] <> *vt* to proclaim. <> *vi* to shout.

Bradesco (*abrev de* **Banco Brasileiro de Descontos**) *m largest private Brazilian bank*.

brado ['bradul *m* shout.

braguilha [bra'giʎal *f* flies *UK* (*pl*), fly *US*.

bramido [bra'midul *m* -1. [ger] roar. - 2. [grito] scream.

bramir [bra'mi(x)] *vi* -1. [ger] to roar. - 2. [gritar] to scream.

branco, ca ['brãŋku, kal <> *adj* -1. [ger] white; arma ~ weapon with a blade. - 2. [versos] blank. <> *m, f* [pessoa] White.
➡ **branco** *m* -1. [cor] white; ~ do olho white of the eye. - 2. [espaço] blank space.
➡ **em branco** <> *loc adj* [espaço] blank. <> *loc adv* [sem dormir]: passar a noite em ~ to have a sleepless night.

brancura [brãŋ'kural *f* whiteness.

brandir [brãn'dʒi(x)] *vt* to brandish.

brando, da ['brãndu, dal *adj* -1. [ger] mild. - 2. [fraco - ação] weak; [- febre] mild. - 3. [fogo, forno] warm.

brandura [brãn'dural *f* mildness.

brasa ['brazal *f* -1. [de carvão] embers (*pl*); na ~ in the embers. - 2. [incandescência] heat; em ~ red-hot. - 3. *loc*: mandar ~ *fam* to get cracking.

brasão [bra'zãw] (*pl* -ões) *m* coat of arms.

braseiro [bra'zejrul *m* brazier.

Brasil [bra'ziwl *n*: (o) ~ Brazil.

brasileiro, ra [brazi'lejru, ral <> *adj* Brazilian. <> *m, f* Brazilian.

brasões [bra'zõʃl *pl* ➣ brasão.

bravata [bra'vatal *f* bravado.

bravio, via [bra'viw, vial *adj* -1. [selvagem] wild. - 2. [feroz] fierce.

bravo, va ['bravu, val <> *adj* -1. [corajoso] brave. - 2. [animal] wild. - 3. [mar] rough. <> *m, f* [pessoa] intrepid person.
➡ **bravo** *interj* bravo!

bravura [bra'vural *f* -1. [coragem] courage. - 2. [de animal] wildness.

brecha ['brɛʃal *f* -1. [ger] gap. - 2. [fenda, abertura] opening. - 3. [prejuízo] hole. - 4. *fam* [oportunidade] break.

brechó [bre'ʃɔl *m* second-hand shop.

brejo ['brɛʒul *m* swamp.

breu ['brewl *m* -1. pitch. - 2. [escuridão] darkness.

breve ['brɛvil <> *adj* -1. [ger] short. - 2. [rápido] fleeting. - 3. [conciso] brief. - 4. *MÚS* [nota] short. <> *adv*: até ~ see you soon; (dentro) em ~ soon. <> *f MÚS* breve.

brevidade [brevi'dadʒil *f* -1. [curteza]

shortness. -**2.** [rapidez] brevity. -**3.** CULIN cassava flour cake.

bridge ['bridʒi] m bridge.

briga ['briga] f -**1.** [luta] brawl. -**2.** [desavença] dispute. -**3.** [rixa] fight.

brigadeiro [briga'dejru] m -**1.** MIL brigadier. -**2.** CULIN confectionery made with condensed milk and chocolate, very common at birthday parties.

brigão, gona [bri'gãw, gɔna] (mpl -ões, fpl -s) <> adj brawling. <> m, f brawler.

brigar [bri'ga(x)] vi -**1.** [ger] to fight; ~ por algo to fight for sthg. -**2.** [desavir-se] to fall out.

brilhante [bri'ʎãntʃi] <> adj -**1.** [que reluz] sparkling. -**2.** fig [notável] brilliant. <> m [diamante] sparkler.

brilhar [bri'ʎa(x)] vi -**1.** [reluzir] to shine. -**2.** fig [distinguir-se] to excel.

brilho ['briʎu] m -**1.** [luz] shine. -**2.** [de cor] brightness. -**3.** [de metal etc.] gleam. -**4.** fig [distinção] excellence. -**5.** fig [esplendor] splendour. -**6.** gír droga [cocaína] coke.

brincadeira [brĩŋka'dejra] f -**1.** [divertimento] play. -**2.** [jogo] game. -**3.** [gracejo] joke; de ~ as a joke; deixe de ~! stop kidding! -**4.** fam [coisa fácil] child's play; não ser ~ to be no joke.

brincalhão, ona [brĩŋka'ʎãw, ɔna] (mpl -ões, fpl -s) adj playful.

brincar [brĩŋ'ka(x)] vi -**1.** [divertir-se] to play; ~ de algo/de fazer algo to play with/at doing sthg. -**2.** [gracejar]: ~ com alguém to joke with sb; está brincando? are you kidding?; estar (só) brincando to be (only) joking. -**3.** [no Carnaval] to party. <> vt [Carnaval] to celebrate.

brinco ['brĩŋku] m [adorno] earring.

brindar [brĩn'da(x)] <> vt [no ato de beber] to toast. <> vi [no ato de beber]: ~ a algo to drink a toast to sthg.

brinde ['brĩndʒi] m -**1.** [no ato de beber] toast. -**2.** [presente] free gift.

brinquedo [brĩŋ'kedu] m toy.

brio ['briw] m -**1.** [honra, dignidade] honour. -**2.** [galhardia] dignity.

brioche [bri'ɔʃi] m brioche.

brisa ['briza] f breeze.

brita ['brita] f CONSTR gravel.

britânico, ca [bri'tãniku, ka] <> adj British. <> m, f British person, Briton.

broa ['broa] f cornflour bread; ~ de milho maize flour bread.

broca ['brɔka] f drill.

broche ['brɔʃi] m brooch.

brochura [bro'ʃura] f -**1.** [livro] binding. -**2.** [folheto] brochure.

brócolis ['brɔkoliʃ] mpl broccoli (sg).

bronco, ca ['brõŋku, ka] adj -**1.** [rude] ill-mannered. -**2.** [burro] slow-witted.

➡ **bronca** f fam [repreensão] telling-off.

bronquear [brõŋ'kja(x)] vi fam to get furious.

bronquite [brõŋ'kitʃi] f bronchitis.

bronze ['brõzi] m bronze.

bronzeado, da [brõ'zeadu, da] adj tanned.

➡ **bronzeado** m tan.

bronzeador [brõzea'do(x)] (pl -es) adj suntan (antes de subst).

➡ **bronzeador** m suntan lotion.

bronzear [brõ'zja(x)] vt to tan.

➡ **bronzear-se** vp to sunbathe.

brotar [bro'ta(x)] vi -**1.** [germinar, desabrochar - planta] to sprout; [- muda] to begin; [- flor] to blossom. -**2.** [manar] to flow. -**3.** fig [esperança, suspeita, paixão] to grow.

broto ['brotu] m -**1.** [de vegetal] sprout; ~ de bambu bamboo shoot; ~ de feijão bean sprout. -**2.** [de flor] shoot. -**3.** [jovem] sapling.

bruços ['brusuʃ] mpl: de ~ lying face down.

bruma ['bruma] f mist.

brumoso, osa [bru'mozu, ɔza] adj misty.

brusco, ca ['bruʃku, ka] adj -**1.** [repentino] sudden. -**2.** [tosco, grosseiro] coarse.

brutal [bru'taw] (pl -ais) adj -**1.** [violento, bárbaro] brutal. -**2.** [tremendo, grande] tremendous.

brutalidade [brutali'dadʒi] f brutality.

bruto, ta ['brutu, ta] adj -**1.** [rude, grosseiro] brutish. -**2.** [tosco] coarse. -**3.** (antes de subst) [tremendo, grande] tremendous. -**4.** [violento] brutal. -**5.** [produto] raw; em ~ raw. -**6.** [sem decréscimo] gross.

bruxa ['bruʃa] f -**1.** [feiticeira] witch. -**2.** [mariposa] moth. -**3.** fam pej [mulher má] bad woman. -**4.** fam pej [mulher feia] hag.

bruxaria [bruʃa'ria] f witchcraft.

Bruxelas [bru'ʃɛlaʃ] n Brussels.

bruxo ['bruʃu] m sorcerer.

Bucareste [buka'rɛʃtʃi] n Bucharest.

buço ['busu] m down.

Budapeste [buda'peʃtʃi] n Budapest.

budismo [bu'dʒizmu] m Buddhism.

bueiro [bu'ejru] m gutter.

Buenos Aires [bwenu'zajriʃ] n Buenos Aires.

búfalo ['bufalu] m buffalo.

bufar [bu'fa(x)] vi -**1.** [ofegar] to pant. -**2.** [de raiva] to fume.

bufê, buffet [bu'fe] m buffet.

bug ['bugi] (pl bugs) m COMPUT bug.

bugiganga [buʒĩŋ'gãŋga] f piece of junk.

bujão [bu'ʒãw] (*pl* -**ões**) *m* cylinder; ~ **de gás** gas cylinder.

bula ['bula] *f MED* information leaflet.

bulbo ['buwbu] *m* bulb.

buldôzer [buw'doze(x)] (*pl* -**es**) *m* bulldozer.

bule ['buli] *m* pot.

Bulgária [buw'garja] *n* Bulgaria.

búlgaro, ra ['buwgaru, ra] <> *adj* Bulgarian. <> *m, f* Bulgarian.

➡ **búlgaro** *m* [língua] Bulgarian.

bumbum [bũn'bũ] (*pl* -**ns**) *m fam* bottom, bum.

bunda ['bũnda] (*pl* -**ns**) *f fam* bottom, bum.

buquê [bu'ke] *m* bouquet; ~ **de flores** bouquet of flowers.

buraco [bu'raku] *m* -**1.** [ger] hole; ~ **da fechadura** keyhole. -**2.** [de agulha] eye. -**3.** [jogo] rummy.

burguês, guesa [bux'geʃ, geza] <> *adj* bourgeois. <> *m, f* [pessoa] bourgeois.

burguesia [buxge'zia] *f* bourgeoisie.

burla ['buxla] *f* -**1.** [fraude] double-dealing. -**2.** [zombaria] jeering.

burlar [bux'la(x)] *vt* -**1.** [fraudar, lesar] to cheat. -**2.** [enganar] to deceive. -**3.** [lei] to defraud.

burocracia [burokra'sia] *f* bureaucracy.

burocrata [buro'krata] *m f* bureaucrat.

burrice [bu'xisi] *f* -**1.** [estupidez] stupidity. -**2.** [ato, dito] something stupid; **foi** ~ **minha ter aceitado a proposta** it was silly of me to accept that offer.

burro, a ['buxu, xa] <> *adj* stupid. <> *m, f* [pessoa imbecil] ass.

➡ **burro** *m ZOOL* donkey.

➡ **pra burro** *fam loc adv*: **ele pinta mal pra** ~ he paints terribly; **a mulher do hotel era feia pra** ~ the woman in the hotel was terribly ugly.

busca ['buʃka] *f* search; **em** ~ **de** in search of; **dar** ~ **a** to search for.

buscador [buʃka'do(x)] *m COMPUT* search engine.

buscar [buʃ'ka(x)] *vt* -**1.** [procurar] to search for. -**2.** [tratar de obter] to seek. -**3.** [pegar, trazer] to fetch; **ir** ~ to go and fetch; **mandar** ~ to send for. -**4.** [esforçar-se por]: ~ **fazer algo** to try to do sthg. -**5.** *COMPUT* to search.

bússola ['busola] *f* compass.

bustiê [buʃ'tʃje] *m* bustier.

busto ['buʃtu] *m* -**1.** [ger] bust; **ela tem 85 cm de** ~ her bust size is 85 cm. -**2.** [torso] torso.

butique [bu'tʃiki] *f* boutique.

buzina [bu'zina] *f* horn, hooter.

buzinar [buzi'na(x)] <> *vt* -**1.** *AUTO* to honk. -**2.** *fig* [dizer com insistência] to harp on. <> *vi AUTO* to honk.

búzio ['buzju] *m* [concha] conch.

byte ['bajtʃi] *m COMPUT* byte.

C

c, C ['se] *m* [letra] c, C.

➡ **C** *abrev de* **celsius**.

cá ['ka] *adv* -**1.** [lugar] here; **vem** ~ ! come here!; **de** ~ **para lá** from here to there; **do lado de** ~ this side. -**2.** [tempo]: **de uma semana para** ~ for the past week. -**3.** [na intimidade]: ~ **entre nós** just between ourselves.

CA (*abrev de* **Centro Acadêmico**) *m centre in a Brazilian university where students meet to discuss problems concerning their course etc.*

caatinga [ka'tʃĩga] *f* caatinga.

cabal [ka'baw] (*pl* -**ais**) *adj* -**1.** [pleno, completo] utter. -**2.** [exato] complete. -**3.** [prova] ultimate.

cabalístico, ca [kaba'liʃtʃiku, ka] *adj* cabalistic.

cabana [ka'bãna] *f* hut.

cabaré [kaba're] *m* cabaret.

cabeça [ka'besa] <> *f* -**1.** [ger] head; **de** ~ [calcular] in one's head; **de** ~ head first; **por** ~ per head; **passar pela** ~ to cross one's mind; **subir à** ~ [suj: sucesso, dinheiro] to go to one's head; ~ **fria** *fig* cool-headed; ~ **a** ~ neck and neck. -**2.** [inteligência] mind; **usar a** ~ to use one's head. -**3.** [pessoa inteligente] brains. -**4.** [topo, parte de cima]: **de** ~ **para baixo** upside down. -**5.** [de lista] top. - **6.** *fam* [de glande] glans. -**7.** [loc]: **fazer a** ~ **de alguém** to influence sb's thinking; **não esquentar a** ~ *fam* not to get hot and bothered; **perder a** ~ to lose one's head. <> *mf* head.

cabeçada [kabe'sada] *f* -**1.** [pancada] headbutt. -**2.** *FUT* header.

cabeçalho [kabe'saʎu] *m* -**1.** [de livro] title. -**2.** [de página, capítulo] heading.

cabecear [kabe'sja(x)] *FUT vt* [bola] to head.

cabeceira [kabe'sejra] *f* head; **livro de** ~ bedside book.

cabeçudo, da [kabe'sudu, da] *adj* -**1.** [de cabeça grande] big-headed. -**2.** *fam* [teimoso] pig-headed.

cabeleira [kabe'lejra] *f* **-1.** [natural] head of hair. **-2.** [peruca] wig.

cabeleireiro, ra [kabelej'rejru, ra] *m, f* [profissional] hairdresser.

➔ **cabeleireiro** *m* [salão] hairdressing salon.

cabelo [ka'belu] *m* [ger] hair; ~ **liso/crespo/pixaim** straight/curly/woolly hair.

cabeludo, da [kabe'ludu, da] *adj* **-1.** hairy. **-2.** *fam fig* [complicado, obsceno] hairy.

➔ **cabeludo** *m fam* [homem] hairy man.

caber [ka'be(x)] *vi* **-1.** [ger] to fit; ~ **(em)** to fit (in); ~ **fazer algo** to have to do sthg. **-2.** [ser oportuno] to be time to. **-3.** [competir]: ~ **a alguém fazer algo** to be the responsibility of sb to so sthg. **-4.** [partilha]: ~ **a alguém** to be allocated to sb.

cabide [ka'bidʒi] *m* [de armário] clothes hanger; [de pé] coat hanger; [de parede] coat hook; ~ **de empregos** *fig* [pessoa] Jack-of-all-trades (but master of none); *fig* [empresa estatal] jobs-for-the-boys organisation.

cabimento [kabi'mẽntu] *m* [adequação] sense; **ter/não ter** ~ to make/not to make sense.

cabine [ka'bini] *f* **-1.** [ger] cabin. **-2.** [telefônica] phone box *UK*, phone booth *US*. **-3.** [guarita] sentry box. **-4.** *FERRO* [compartimento] carriage, compartment. **-5.** *AERON* [de comando] cockpit. **-6.** [vestuário] changing room.

cabisbaixo, xa [kabiʒ'bajʃu, ʃa] *adj* crestfallen.

cabo ['kabu] *m* **-1.** [de panela, faca, vassoura] handle. **-2.** [fim] end. **-3.** *CORDA* ~ **de aço** iron cable. **-4.** *ELETR* cable. **-5.** *GEOGR* cape. **-6.** *MIL* corporal. **-7.** [fim]: **dar** ~ **de** [pessoa] to kill; [problema] to put an end to; [tarefa] to finish; **levar algo a** ~ [tarefa, projeto] to see sthg through; **ao** ~ **de** by the end of.

caboclo, cla [ka'boklu, kla] <> *adj* **-1.** [pele] copper-coloured. **-2.** [pessoa] bumpkinish. <> *m, f* **-1.** [mestiço de branco com índio] caboclo. **-2.** [pessoa da roça] bumpkin.

cabra ['kabra] <> *f* [animal] goat. <> *m fam* [homem] guy.

cabra-cega [ˌkabra'sɛga] (*pl* **cabras-cegas**) *f* blind man's buff.

cabreiro, ra [ka'brejru, ra] *adj fam* [desconfiado] suspicious.

cabresto [ka'breʃtu] *m* [para cavalos] halter.

cabrito [ka'britu] *m* kid.

caça ['kasa] <> *f* **-1.** [ato] hunt. **-2.** [animal

- caçado por homem] game; [- caçado por outro animal] prey; game. **-3.** [passatempo] hunting. <> *m AERON* fighter.

caçada [ka'sada] *f* [jornada] hunting trip.

caçador, ra [kasa'do(x), ra] (*mpl* **-es**, *fpl* **-s**) *m, f* hunter.

caça-níqueis [ˌkasa'nikejʃ] *m inv* **-1.** [máquina] slot-machine. **-2.** *fam* [empresa, loja] cowboy outfit.

cação [ka'sãw] (*pl* **-ões**) *m* dogfish.

caçar [ka'sa(x)] <> *vt* **-1.** [animais] to hunt. **-2.** [a tiro] to shoot. **-3.** [buscar - documentos, prova, tesouro] to search for; [- recompensa] to seek. **-4.** [perseguir] to hunt down. **-5.** *fam* [marido] to hunt for. <> *vi* [andar à caça] to hunt.

cacarejar [kakare'ʒa(x)] *vi* to cluck.

caçarola [kasa'rɔla] *f* casserole.

cacau [ka'kaw] *m* **-1.** [fruto] cacao. **-2.** [semente] cocoa bean. **-3.** [pó] cocoa.

cacetada [kase'tada] *f* whack (*with stick*).

cacete [ka'setʃi] <> *adj* [tedioso] tedious. <> *m* **-1.** [porrete] truncheon. **-2.** *vulg* [pênis] rod.

➔ **pra cacete** *mfam* <> *loc pron*: **gente pra** ~ shitloads of people. <> *loc adv*: **chato/bom/forte pra cacete** bloody boring/good/strong.

cachaça [ka'ʃasa] *f* sugar-cane brandy.

cachaceiro, ra [kaʃa'sejru, ra] <> *adj* drunken. <> *m, f* drunkard.

cachê [ka'ʃe] *m* fee (*for performance*).

cacheado, da [ka'ʃjadu, da] *adj* curly.

cachecol [kaʃe'kɔw] (*pl* **-óis**) *m* scarf.

cachimbo [ka'ʃĩbu] *m* pipe.

cacho ['kaʃu] *m* **-1.** [ger] bunch. **-2.** [de cabelos - anel] lock; [- mecha] strand.

cachoeira [ka'ʃwejra] *f* waterfall.

cachorra [ka'ʃoxa] *f* ⊳ **cachorro**.

cachorrada [kaʃo'xada] *f* **-1.** [matilha] pack of dogs. **-2.** *fam fig* [canalhice] scam; **fazer uma** ~ **com alguém** to scam sb.

cachorro, rra [ka'ʃoxu, ra] *m, f* **-1.** [cão] dog; **soltar os** ~**s (em cima de alguém)** *fig* to lash out (at sb). **-2.** *fam pej* [patife] bastard.

cachorro-quente [kaˌʃoxu'kẽntʃi] (*pl* **cachorros-quentes**) *m* hot dog.

cacique [ka'siki] *m* **-1.** [indígena] cacique, tribal chief. **-2.** *fig* [chefão] boss.

caco ['kaku] *m* **-1.** [de vidro etc.] shard. **-2.** *fam* [pessoa]: **estar um** ~ [estar velho] to be a wreck; [estar desgastado] to be a wreck; [estar exausto] to be wiped out.

caçoar [ka'swa(x)] *vi* to mock; ~ **de algo/alguém** to make fun of sthg/sb.

cações [ka'sõjʃ] *pl* ⊳ **cação**.

cacoete [ka'kwetʃi] *m* tic.

cacto ['kaktu] *m* cactus.

caçula [ka'sulaʃ] <> *adj* youngest. <> *mf* youngest child.

CAD (*abrev de* **Computer Aided Design**) *m* CAD.

cada ['kada] *adj (inv)* **-1.** [valor de unidade] each; **uma coisa de** ~ **vez** one thing at a time; ~ (**um**) [em preço] each; ~ **qual**, ~ **um** each one. **-2.** [todo] every; **a** ~ **every**; **aumentar a** ~ **dia** to increase from day to day. **-3.** [valor intensivo] such.

cadafalso [kada'fawsu] *m* gallows (pl).

cadarço [ka'daxsu] *m* shoelace.

cadastramento [kadaʃtra'mẽntu] *m* registration.

cadastro [ka'daʃtru] *m* **-1.** [registro] register. **-2.** [ato] registration. **-3.** [ficha de criminoso] criminal record. **-4.** [de banco, clientes] records (pl). **-5.** [de imóveis] land registry. **-6.** *COMPUT* [de dados] data record.

cadáver [ka'davɛ(x)] (*pl* **-es**) *m* corpse.

cadê [ka'de] *adv fam* where is/are.

cadeado [ka'dʒjadu] *m* padlock.

cadeia [ka'deja] *f* **-1.** [ger] chain. **-2.** [prisão] prison. **-3.** [série, seqüência] series *(inv)*; ~ **de montanhas** mountain range. **-4.** [de emissoras de TV] network.

cadeira [ka'dejra] *f* **-1.** [ger] chair; ~ **de balanço** rocking chair; ~ **de rodas** wheelchair. **-2.** [disciplina] subject. **-3.** [em teatro] seat.

➡ **cadeiras** *fpl* ANAT hips.

cadela [ka'dɛla] *f* [cão] bitch ⊳ **cão**.

cadência [ka'dẽnsja] *f* **-1.** [ritmo] rhythm. **-2.** [de estilo, fala] cadence.

caderneta [kadex'neta] *f* **-1.** [livrete] note pad. **-2.** [escolar] mark sheet. **-3.** *FIN:* ~ **de poupança** savings account.

caderno [ka'dɛxnu] *m* **-1.** [de notas] notebook. **-2.** [de jornal] section.

cadete [ka'detʃi] *m* cadet.

caducar [kadu'ka(x)] *vi* **-1.** [prazo, documento, lei] to expire. **-2.** [pessoa] to become senile.

caduco, ca [ka'duku, ka] *adj* **-1.** [prazo, documento, lei] expired. **-2.** [pessoa] senile. **-3.** *BOT* deciduous.

cães ['kãjʃ] *pl* ⊳ **cão**.

cafajeste [kafa'ʒeʃtʃi] *fam* <> *adj* **-1.** [canalha] crooked. **-2.** [vulgar] vulgar. <> *mf* [pessoa canalha] con man.

café [ka'fɛ] *m* **-1.** [ger] coffee; ~ (**preto**) black coffee; ~ **com leite** white coffee *UK*, coffee with cream *US*; ~ **expresso** espresso. **-2.** [desjejum]: ~ (**da manhã**) breakfast. **-3.** [estabelecimento] café.

cafeeiro, ra [kafe'ejru, ra] <> *adj* [setor, indústria] coffee (*antes de subst*). <> *m* coffee bush.

cafeína [kafe'ina] *f* caffeine.

cafetão, tina [kafe'tãw, tʃina] (*mpl* **-ões**, *fpl* **-s**) *m, f* pimp.

cafeteira [kafe'tejra] *f* coffee pot.

cafetina [kafe'tʃina] *f* ⊳ **cafetão**.

cafezal [kafe'zaw] (*pl* **-ais**) *m* coffee plantation.

cafezinho [kafe'ziɲu] *m fam* small black coffee.

cafona [ka'fona] <> *adj* [pessoa, roupa, música] tacky. <> *mf* [pessoa] tacky person.

cafuné [kafu'nɛ] *m*: **fazer** ~ **em alguém** to scratch sb's head gently.

cagada [ka'gada] *f vulg* crap.

cágado ['kagadu] *m* terrapin.

cagar [ka'ga(x)] *vulg vi* **-1.** [defecar] to have a crap. **-2.** *fig* [menosprezar]: ~ **para alguém/algo** not to give a shit about sb/sthg.

caiado, da [ka'jadu, da] *adj* ≃ whitewashed.

caiaque [ka'jaki] *m* kayak.

caiar [ka'ja(x)] *vt* to whitewash.

caído, da [ka'idu, da] *adj* **-1.** [derrubado] fallen. **-2.** [pendente] droopy. **-3.** *fig* [abatido] depressed. **-4.** *fig* [desanimado] subdued. **-5.** *fig* [feio] saggy.

➡ **caída** *f* [queda] fall.

caipira [kaj'pira] *fam* <> *adj* provincial. <> *mf* [pessoa - do interior] country bumpkin; [- sem traquejo social] boor.

caipirinha [kajpi'riɲa] *f* caipirinha, *cocktail made with sugar-cane brandy and lime juice.*

cair [ka'i(x)] *vi* **-1.** [ger] to fall; ~ **em** to fall into. **-2.** [desabar] to collapse. **-3.** [desprender-se - dente, cabelo, folha] to fall out; [- botão] to fall off. **-4.** [deixar-se enganar] to fall for. **-5.** *euf* [ser morto] to fall. **-6.** *EDUC* [em prova] to crop up. **-7.** *loc*: ~ **bem/mal** [penteado, roupa, cor] to suit/not to suit; [frase, atitude] to go down well/badly; [comida, bebida] to agree/not to agree with; ~ **em si** [reconhecer o erro] to accept one's mistake; [voltar à realidade] to come down to earth; **não ter onde** ~ **morto** to have nothing to one's name.

cais ['kajʃ] *m inv* quay.

caixa ['kajʃa] <> *f* **-1.** [ger] box; ~ **acústica** loudspeaker. **-2.** [para correspondência]: ~ **de correio** postbox *UK*, mailbox *US*; ~ **postal** *ou* **de coleta** postal box. **-3.** [mecanismo]: ~ **de marchas** *ou* **de mudanças** gearbox. **-4.** [máquina]: ~ **registradora** cash till. **-5.** [seção] till. **-6.** [banco] savings bank; ~ **dois** undeclared assets; ~ **econômica** national savings bank. **-7.** *TIP* : ~ **alta/baixa**

upper/lower case. <> *m* -1. [máquina]: ~ eletrônico cashpoint. -2. [livro] ledger; ~ dois fraudulent books *(pl)*. <> *mf* [funcionário] cashier.

caixa-d'água [ˈkajʃaˈdagwa] *(pl* caixas-d'água*)* f water tank.

caixa-de-fósforos [ˈkajʃadʒiˈʃɔʃforuʃ] *f fam* [habitação, carro] matchbox.

caixa-forte [ˈkajʃaˈfɔxtʃi] *(pl* caixas-fortes*) f* safe.

caixão [kajˈʃãw] *(pl* -ões) *m* [ataúde] coffin.

caixa-preta [ˈkajʃaˈpreta] *(pl* caixas-pretas*) f AERON* black box.

caixeiro-viajante, caixeira-viajante [kajˌʃejruvjaˈʒãntʃi, kajˌʃejravjaˈʒãntʃi] *m, f* commercial traveller.

caixilho [kajˈʃiʎu] *m* [moldura] frame.

caixões [kajˈʃõjʃ] *pl* ⊳ **caixão**.

caixote [kajˈʃɔtʃi] *m* crate.

caju [kaˈʒu] *m* cashew.

cajueiro [kaˈʒwejru] *m* cashew tree.

cal [ˈkaw] *f* -1. [substância] lime, quick-lime. -2. [extinta] slaked lime. -3. [para caiar] whitewash.

calabouço [kalaˈbosu] *m* dungeon.

calado, da [kaˈladu, da] *adj* quiet.

calafetagem [kalafeˈtaʒẽl] *(pl* -ns) *f* caulking.

calafrio [kalaˈfriw] *m* shiver; ter ~s to have the shivers.

calamar [kalaˈma(x)] *m* squid.

calamidade [kalamiˈdadʒi] *f* calamity.

calamitoso, tosa [kalamiˈtozu, tɔza] *adj* calamitous.

calar [kaˈla(x)] <> *vt* -1. [ocultar] to keep quiet about. -2. [silenciar] to silence; **cala a boca!** shut up! -3. [conter] to ignore. -4. *euf* [armas, canhões] to silence. <> *vi* [manter-se em silêncio] to keep quiet. ➠ **calar-se** *vp* [parar de falar] to go quiet, to stop talking.

calça [ˈkawsa] *f* trousers *UK (pl)*, pants *US (pl)*.

calçada [kawˈsada] *f* pavement *UK*, sidewalk *US*.

calçadão [kawsaˈdãw] *(pl* -ões) *m* pavement.

calçadeira [kawsaˈdejra] *f* shoehorn.

calçado, da [kawˈsadu, da] *adj* -1. [caminho, rua] paved. -2. [pessoa, pé] with shoes on *(depois de subst)*. ➠ **calçado** *m* [sapato, tênis] footwear.

calçamento [kawsaˈmẽntu] *m* paving.

calcanhar [kawkaˈɲa(x)] *(pl* -es) *m* heel.

calção [kawˈsãw] *(pl* -ões) *m* shorts *(pl)*; ~ de banho swim shorts *(pl)*.

calcar [kawˈka(x)] *vt* -1. [pisar] to tread on. -2. *fig* [basear]: ~ algo em to base sthg on.

calçar [kawˈsa(x)] *vt* -1. [sapatos, luvas] to

put on; [tamanho] to take a size. -2. [pavimentar] to pave. -3. [pôr calço em] to wedge. ➠ **calçar-se** *vp* [pôr sapatos] to put one's shoes on.

calcário, ria [kawˈkarju, rja] *adj* -1. [substância, pedra] chalky, calcareous. -2. [água] hard. ➠ **calcário** *m* [rocha] limestone.

calcinha [kawˈsiɲa] *f* panties *(pl)*.

cálcio [ˈkawsju] *m* calcium.

calço [ˈkawsu] *m* [cunha] wedge.

calções [kawˈsõjʃ] *pl* ⊳ **calção**.

calculadora [kawkulaˈdora] *f* calculator.

calcular [kawkuˈla(x)] <> *vt* -1. [fazer conta de] to calculate. -2. [avaliar, estimar] to estimate. -3. [imaginar] to imagine. -4. [supor, prever]: ~ que to guess that. <> *vi* [fazer contas] to calculate.

calculista [kawkuˈliʃta] <> *adj* calculating. <> *mf* opportunist.

cálculo [ˈkawkulu] *m* -1. [conta] calculation. -2. [estimativa] estimate. -3. *MAT* calculus. -4. *MED* stone; ~ renal kidney stone.

calda [ˈkawda] *f* syrup.

caldeira [kawˈdejra] *f TEC* boiler.

caldeirão [kawdejˈrãw] *(pl* -ões) *m* cauldron.

caldo [ˈkawdu] *m* -1. [sopa] broth; ~ verde green vegetable and potato soup. -2. [sumo] juice; ~ de cana sugar-cane juice. -3. [tempero]: ~ de carne/galinha beef/chicken stock.

calefação [kalefaˈsãw] *f* heating.

calendário [kalẽnˈdarju] *m* calendar.

calha [ˈkaʎa] *f* -1. [sulco] channel. -2. [para a chuva] gutter.

calhamaço [kaʎaˈmasu] *m* tome.

calhar [kaˈʎa(x)] *vi* -1. [concidir] to happen that; **calhou de elas usarem vestidos iguais** they happened to be wearing the same dress. -2. [convir]: vir a ~ to come at just the right time.

calibragem [kaliˈbraʒẽl] *(pl* -ns) *f* calibration.

calibre [kaˈlibri] *m* [de cano] calibre.

cálice [ˈkalisi] *m* -1. [taça] liqueur glass. -2. *RELIG* chalice.

cálido, da [ˈkalidu, da] *adj* warm.

caligrafia [kaligraˈfia] *f* -1. [arte] calligraphy. -2. [letra] handwriting.

calista [kaˈliʃta] *m f* chiropodist *UK*, podiatrist *US*.

calma [ˈkawma] *f* ⊳ **calmo**.

calmante [kawˈmãntʃi] <> *adj* calming. <> *m* tranquillizer.

calmaria [kawmaˈria] *f* lull.

calmo, ma [ˈkawmu, ma] *adj* [ger] calm. ➠ **calma** *f* -1. [quietude] tranquillity. -2.

[serenidade] serenity; **calma!** just a moment!

calo ['kalu] *m* [endurecimento da pele] callus; [no pé] corn.

calor [ka'lo(x)] *m* -1. [ger] heat; **estar com ~, sentir ~** to be/feel hot; **fazer ~** to be hot. -2. [quentura] warmth.

calorento, ta [kalo'rẽntu, ta] *adj* -1. [pessoa] sensitive to heat. -2. [local] hot.

caloria [kalo'rial] *f* calorie.

caloroso, osa [kalo'rozu, ɔza] *adj* -1. [ger] warm. -2. [manifestação, protesto] fervent.

calota [ka'lɔta] *f* AUTO hubcap.

calouro, ra [ka'loru, ra] *m, f* -1. EDUC fresher *UK*, freshman *US*. -2. [novato] novice.

calúnia [ka'lunja] *f* calumny.

calunioso, niosa [kalu'njozu, njɔza] *adj* slanderous.

calvo, va ['kawvu, va] *adj* bald.

cama ['kãma] *f* bed; **~ de casal** double bed; **~ de solteiro** single bed; **estar de ~** [estar doente] to be bedridden.

camada [ka'mada] *f* -1. [ger] layer. -2. [de tinta] coat.

camafeu [kama'few] *m* cameo.

câmara ['kãmara] *f* -1. [ger] chamber; **Câmara dos Deputados** House of Representatives. -2. CINE & FOTO camera; **~ escura** darkroom. -3. TV television camera; **em ~ lenta** in slow motion. -4. [de pneu]: **~ (de ar)** inner tube.

camarada [kama'rada] *adj* -1. [amigável] friendly. -2. [preço] good.

camarão [kama'rãw] (*pl* -ões) *m* -1. [comum] shrimp. -2. [graúdo] prawn.

camareiro, ra [kama'rejru, ra] *m, f* -1. [in hotel] chambermaid, room cleaner. -2. [on boat] cabin cleaner.

camarim [kama'rĩ] (*pl* -ns) *m* dressing room.

camarote [kama'rɔtʃi] *m* -1. NÁUT cabin. -2. TEATRO box.

cambaleante [kãnba'ljãntʃi] *adj* unsteady.

cambalear [kãnba'lja(x)] *vi* to stagger.

cambalhota [kãnba'ʎɔta] *f* somersault.

câmbio ['kãnbju] *m* -1. [ger] exchange; **~ livre** free trade; **~ negro** black economy; **~ oficial/paralelo** official/parallel exchange; [taxa] exchange rate. -2. AUTO [mudança] gear stick.

cambista [kãn'biʃta] *mf* -1. [de moeda] money changer. -2. [de ingressos] (ticket) tout.

camburão [kãnbu'rãw] (*pl* -ões) *m* police van.

camelo [ka'melu] *m* -1. [animal] camel. -2. *fig* [pessoa burra] idiot.

camelô [kame'lo] *m* pedlar.

câmera ['kãmera] <> *f* camera. <> *mf* [operador] camera operator.

caminhada [kami'nada] *f* -1. [passeio] walk. -2. [extensão] trek.

caminhão [kami'nãw] (*pl* -ões) *m* lorry *UK*, truck *US*.

caminhar [kami'na(x)] *vi* -1. [andar] to walk. -2. [progredir] *fig* to progress; **~ para** to lead to.

caminho [ka'miɲu] *m* -1. [via, estrada] road. -2. [extensão, direção] way. -3. *fig* [meio] way. -4. *fig* [rumo] route.

caminhoneiro, ra [kamiɲo'nejru, ra] *m, f* lorry driver *UK*, truck driver *US*.

caminhonete [kamjo'nɛtʃi], **camione- ta** [kamio'nɛta] *f* van.

camisa [ka'miza] *f* shirt; **~ esporte** sports shirt; **~ pólo** polo shirt; **~ social** dress shirt.

camisa-de-força [ka,mizadʒi'foxsa] (*pl* **camisas-de-força**) *f* straitjacket.

camisa-de-vênus [ka,mizadʒi'venuʃ] = **camisinha**.

camiseta [kami'zeta] *f* T-shirt.

camisinha [kami'ziɲa] *f* condom.

camisola [kami'zɔla] *f* nightdress.

camomila [kamo'mila] *f* camomile.

campainha [kãmpa'iɲa] *f* bell.

campanha [kãn'pãɲa] *f* -1. [ger] campaign; **fazer ~ (de/contra)** to campaign for/against. -2. [planície] plain.

campeão, ã [kãn'pjãw, ã] (*mpl* -ões, *fpl* -s) <> *adj* [time etc.] champion. <> *m, f* champion.

campeonato [kãnpjo'natu] *m* championship.

campestre [kãn'pɛʃtri] *adj* rural.

camping [kãn'pĩ] *m* -1. [atividade] camping. -2. [lugar] campsite.

campismo [kãn'piʒmu] *m* camping.

campista [kãn'piʃta] *mf* camper.

campo ['kãnpul] *m* -1. [ger] field. -2. [zona rural] countryside; **casa de ~** country house. -3. [área] camp; **~ de concentração** concentration camp. -4. ESP: **~ de golfe** golf course; **~ de tênis** tennis court. -5. *fig* [âmbito] field. -6. *fig* [ocasião] scope. -7. *loc*: **embolar o meio de ~** to mess it all up.

Campo Grande [,kãnpu'grãndʒi] *n* Campo Grande.

camponês, esa ['kãnpo'neʃ, eza] (*mpl* -eses, *fpl* -s) <> *adj* rural. <> *m, f* countryman (*f* countrywoman).

campus ['kãnpuʃ] *m inv* campus.

camuflado, da [kamu'fladu, da] *adj* camouflaged.

camuflagem [kamu'flaʒẽ] (*pl* ns) *f* camouflage.

camundongo [kamũn'dõŋgu] *m* mouse.

camurça [ka'muxsa] *f* suede.

cana [ka'nal *f* -1. [ger] cane. -2. *fam* [cachaça] gut-rot, cachaça, *sugar-cane brandy*. -3. *fam* [cadeia] jail; **ir em ~** to be locked up.

Canadá [kana'da] *n*: (o) ~ Canada.

cana-de-açúcar [ˌkãnadʒja'suka(x)] (*pl* **canas-de-açúcar**) *f* sugar cane.

canadense [kana'dẽnsi] <> *adj* Canadian. <> *mf* Canadian.

canal [ka'naw] (*pl* -ais) *m* -1. [ger] canal. -2. *GEOGR, TV* channel. -3. [conduto] pipe. -4. *fig* [meio, via] channel.

canalha [ka'naʎa] <> *adj* despicable. <> *mf* rotter.

canalizar [kanali'za(x)] *vt* -1. [rios] to channel. -2. [pôr canos de esgotos] to lay with pipes. -3. [abrir canais] to canalize. -4. *fig* [dirigir] to channel.

Canárias [ka'narjaʃ] *npl*: **as (Ilhas)** ~ the Canary Islands, the Canaries.

canário [ka'narju] *m* canary.

canastrão, trona [kanaʃ'trãw, trona] (*mpl* -ões, *fpl* -s) *m*, *f* *TEATRO* ham actor.

canavial [kana'vjaw] (*pl* -ais) *m* cane field.

canção [kãn'sãw] (*pl* -ões) *f* song.

cancela [kãn'sɛla] *f* gate.

cancelamento [kãnsela'mẽntu] *m* -1. [passagem] cancellation. -2. [processo] overruling.

cancelar [kãnse'la(x)] *vt* -1. [anular] to cancel. -2. [riscar] to cross out. -3. [desistir de] to call off. -4. [suprimir - atividade, pagamento] to cancel; [- regalia] to revoke.

câncer [ˈkãse(x)] (*pl* -es) *m* *MED* cancer.

➤ **Câncer** *m* [zodíaco] Cancer; *veja também* **Virgem**; **Trópico de** ~ Tropic of Cancer.

canceriano, na [kãnse'rjãnu, na] <> *adj* *ASTRO* Cancerian. <> *m*, *f* Cancerian.

canções [kãn'sõjʃ] *pl* ➤ **canção**.

candelabro [kãnde'labru] *m* -1. [castiçal] candlestick. -2. [lustre] chandelier.

candidatar-se [kãndʒida'taxsi] *vp* -1. [à presidência da república] to stand for. -2. [à vaga] to apply for.

candidato, ta [kãndʒi'datu, ta] *m* -1. *POL* candidate. -2. [pretendente - a vaga] applicant; [- a exame] candidate.

candidatura [kãndʒida'tura] *f* -1. [ger] candidature. -2. [proposta] application.

cândido, da [ˈkãndʒidu, da] *adj* -1. [imaculado] candid. -2. *fig* [inocente] naive.

candomblé [kãndõn'blɛ] *m* -1. [religião] *Yoruba religious tradition in Bahia and its ceremony*. -2. [local] Candomblé shrine.

caneca [ka'nɛka] *f* mug.

canela [ka'nɛla] *f* -1. [especiaria] cinnamon. -2. *ANAT* shin.

caneta [ka'neta] *f* pen; ~ **esferográfica** ballpoint pen.

caneta-tinteiro [kaˌnetatʃĩn'tejru] (*pl* **canetas-tinteiros**) *f* fountain pen.

cangote [kãn'gotʃi] *m* (back of the) neck.

canguru [kãŋgu'ru] *m* kangaroo.

cânhamo [ˈkãɲamu] *m* hemp.

canhão [ka'ɲãw] (*pl* -ões) *m* *MIL* cannon.

canhões [ka'ɲõjʃ] *pl* ➤ **canhão**.

canhoto, ta [ka'ɲotu, ta] <> *adj* left-handed. <> *m*, *f* left-handed person.

➤ **canhoto** *m* [em talão] stub.

canibal [kani'baw] (*pl* -ais) <> *adj* cannibalistic. <> *m*, *f* cannibal.

caniço [ka'nisu] *m* -1. *PESCA* rod. -2. *fam* [perna fina] pin.

canil [ka'niw] (*pl* -is) *m* kennel.

caninha [ka'niɲa] *f* sugar-cane alcohol.

canino, na [ka'ninu, na] *adj* -1. [ger] canine. -2. [fome] ravenous.

➤ **canino** *m* [dente] canine.

canivete [kani'vetʃi] *m* penknife.

canja [ˈkãnʒa] *f* -1. *CULIN* broth of rice and chicken. -2. *MÚS*: **dar uma** ~ to do a turn.

canjica [kãn'ʒika] *f* a sweet dish of maize, coconut milk and cinnamon.

cano [ˈkãnu] *m* -1. [tubo] pipe; ~ **de esgoto** sewer pipe. -2. [de arma] barrel. -3. [de bota] leg. -4. [trambique] swindle. -5. *loc*: **entrar pelo** ~ to come a cropper.

canoa [ka'noa] *f* canoe.

canonização [kanoniza'sãw] (*pl* -ões) *f* canonization.

cansaço [kãn'sasu] *m* weariness.

cansado, da [kãn'sadu, da] *adj* -1. [fatigado] tired. -2. [enfastiado] weary.

cansar [kãn'sa(x)] <> *vt* -1. [fatigar] to tire. -2. [entediar] to bore. <> *vi* -1. [ficar cansado] to get tired; ~ **de algo/alguém** to get tired of sthg/sb; ~ **de fazer algo** to be tired of doing sthg. -2. [fazer ficar cansado] to be tiring. -3. [aborrecer] to be boring. -4. [desistir]: ~ **de fazer algo** to weary of doing sthg.

➤ **cansar-se** *vp* -1. [fatigar-se] to get tired. -2. [entediar-se]: ~**-se de algo** to get bored with sthg. -3. [aborrecer-se]: ~**-se de algo** to become weary of sthg.

cansativo, va [kãnsa'tʃivu, va] *adj* -1. [fatigante] tiring. -2. [enfadonho] boring.

canseira [kãn'sejra] *f* -1. [cansaço] weariness. -2. *fam* [esforço] hassle.

cantar [kãn'ta(x)] <> *vt* -1. [ger] to sing. -2. [dizer em voz alta] to sing out. <> *vi* *MÚS* to sing.

cantarolar [kãntaro'la(x)] *vt* & *vi* to hum.
canteiro [kãn'tejru] *m* -**1.** [jardim]: ~ de
flores flower bed. -**2.** [construção]: ~ de
obras work site. -**3.** [operário] stone
mason.
cantiga [kãn'tʃiga] *f* ballad.
cantil [kãn'tʃiw] (*pl* -is) *m* -**1.** [frasco]
flask. -**2.** [ferramenta] plane.
cantina [kãn'tʃina] *f* canteen.
canto [ˈkãntu] *m* -**1.** [ger] corner. -**2.** [de
triângulo] angle. -**3.** [lugar retirado] quiet
corner. -**4.** [*MÚS* - som musical] song; ~
gregoriano Gregorian chant; [- arte]
singing.
cantor, ra [kãn'to(x), ra] (*mpl* -es, *fpl* -s)
m, f singer.
canudo [ka'nudu] *m* -**1.** [tubo] tube. -**2.**
[para beber] straw. -**3.** *fam* [diploma] certificate.
cão [ˈkãw] (*pl* cães) *mf* -**1.** *ZOOL* dog. -**2.**
loc: quem não tem ~ caça com gato
there is more than one way to skin a
cat.
➡ de cão *loc adj* [dia, férias etc.] dreadful.
caolho, lha [ka'oʎu, ʎa] <> *adj* -**1.** [za-
rolho] one-eyed. -**2.** [estrábico] cross-
eyed. <> *m, f* -**1.** [pessoa zarolha] one-
eyed person; ele é um ~ he only has
one eye. -**2.** [pessoa estrábica] cross-eyed
person.
caos [ˈkawʃ] *m inv* chaos.
caótico, ca [ka'ɔtʃiku, ka] *adj* chaotic.
capa [ˈkapa] *f* -**1.** [ger] cover; ~ dura
hard cover; de ~ dura hardback; ~
frontal [para celular] fascia. -**2.** [roupa]
cape; ~ (de chuva) rain cape. -**3.** *fig*
[aparência] cloak.
capacete [kapa'setʃil] *m* helmet.
capacho [ka'paʃu] *m* -**1.** [tapete] door
mat. -**2.** *fig* [pessoa servil] toady.
capacidade [kapasi'dadʒi] *f* -**1.** [ger] capacity. -**2.** [habilidade] ability. -**3.** *fig* [su-
midade] genius.
capacitar [kapasi'ta(x)] *vt* [habilitar]: ~
alguém a fazer algo to prepare sb to do
sthg.
capado, da [ka'padu, da] <> *adj* [castra-
do] castrated. <> *m* gelded pig.
capataz [kapa'taʒ] *m* foreman.
capaz [ka'paʃ] (*pl* -es) *adj* -**1.** [competente]
competent. -**2.** [apropriado] capable. -**3.**
[provável]: é ~ de nevar it might snow.
-**4.:** ser ~ de fazer algo [dispor-se a, ter
coragem de] to be capable of doing sthg.
capcioso, osa [kap'sjozu, ɔza] *adj* [per-
gunta] trick.
capela [ka'pɛla] *f* chapel.
capenga [ka'pẽŋga] <> *adj* lame. <>
mf cripple.

CAPES (*abrev de* Coordenação de Aperfeiçoamento de Pessoal de Nível Superior) *f Brazilian educational body
that finances postgraduate studies.*
capeta [ka'peta] *m* -**1.** [diabo] devil. -**2.**
fam [traquinas] troublemaker.
capim [ka'pĩ] *m* grass.
capinar [kapi'na(x)] *vt* [limpar] to weed.
capita [ˈkapita] ➡ per capita *loc adj*
per capita.
capital [kapi'taw] (*pl* -ais) <> *adj* -**1.** [es-
sencial] major. -**2.** [pena] capital. <> *m*
ECON capital. <> *f* [cidade] capital.
capitalismo [kapita'liʒmul] *m* capitalism.
capitalista [kapita'liʃta] <> *adj* capitalist. <> *mf* capitalist.
capitalização [kapitaliza'sãw] *f ECON*
capitalization.
capitão, ã [kapi'tãw, ãl] (*mpl* -ães, *fpl* -s)
m, f -**1.** [ger] captain. -**2.** [chefe] leader.
capitular [kapitu'la(x)] <> *vi* to capitulate. <> *adj* capitular. <> *f* [letra]
capital.
capítulo [ka'pitulu] *m* chapter.
capô [ka'po] *m AUTO* bonnet *UK*, hood *US*.
capoeira [ka'pwejra] *f* [dança] capoeira,
*acrobatic game in dance form that is
very popular in north-eastern Brazil.*
capoeirista [kapwej'riʃta] *mf person
who does capoeira dancing.*
capota [ka'pɔta] *f AUTO* hood.
capotar [kapo'ta(x)] *vi* to overturn.
capricho [ka'priʃu] *m* -**1.** [esmero] care.
-**2.** [vontade] whim. -**3.** [teimosia] obstinacy.
caprichoso, osa [kapri'ʃozu, ɔza] *adj* -**1.**
[cuidadoso] meticulous. -**2.** [voluntarioso]
capricious. -**3.** [teimoso] obstinate.
capricorniano, na [kaprikox'njãnu, na]
<> *adj* Capricorn. <> *m, f* Capricorn.
Capricórnio [kapri'kɔxnju] *m* [zodíaco]
Capricorn; *veja também* Virgem; Trópico
de ~ Tropic of Capricorn.
cápsula [ˈkapsula] *f* capsule.
captar [kap'ta(x)] *vt* -**1.** [atrair] to win. -**2.**
[sintonizar] to pick up. -**3.** [água] to
collect. -**4.** [compreender] to catch.
captura [kap'tura] *f* capture.
capuz [ka'puʃ] (*pl* -es) *m* hood.
caqui [ka'kil] *m inv* kaki fruit.
cáqui [ˈkakil] <> *adj inv* khaki. <> *m*
drill.
cara [ˈkara] <> *f* -**1.** [rosto] face; ~ a ~
face to face; ser a ~ de alguém to be
the image of sb. -**2.** [aspecto] look. -**3.**
[de moeda] side. -**4.** *fam* [coragem] nerve.
<> *m* -**1.** *fam* [sujeito] guy. -**2.** *loc:* dar de
~ com alguém to bump into sb; encher
a ~ *fam* to have a skinful; estar com ~

de que [parecer que] to look like; **estar na** ~ to be staring one in the face; **não ir com a** ~ **de alguém** not to be keen on sb.

carabina [kara'bina] f rifle.

Caracas [ka'rakaʃ] n Caracas.

caracol [kara'kɔw] (pl **-óis**) m -1. [molusco] snail. -2. [de cabelo] curl.

➤ **de caracol** loc adj [escada] spiral.

caractere [karak'tɛril] m character.

caractere-curinga [karak'tɛ(e)-ku'rīŋgal] m COMPUT wildcard.

caracteres [karak'tɛriʃ] pl ▷ **caráter**.

➤ **caracteres** mpl -1. [características individuais] characteristics. -2. [legendas, créditos] credits.

característico, ca [karakte'riʃtʃiku, kal] adj characteristic.

➤ **característica** f characteristic.

caracterizar [karakteri'za(x)] vt -1. [descrever] characterize. -2. [TEATRO - maquilagem] to make up; [- indumentária] to dress.

➤ **caracterizar-se** vp [distinguir-se]: ~ **-se por** to be characterized by.

cara-de-pau [ˌkaradʒi'paw] fam <> adj shameless. <> mf shameless person.

carambola [karãm'bɔla] f star fruit.

caramelado, da [karame'ladu, dal] adj caramelized.

caramelo [kara'mɛlul] m -1. [calda] caramel. -2. [bala] toffee.

caramujo [kara'muʒul] m shellfish.

caranguejo [karãŋ'geʒul] m crab.

caraquenho, nha [kara'kẽɲu, ɲãl] <> adj Caracas (antes de subst). <> m, f person from Caracas.

caratê [kara'tel] m karate.

caráter [ka'rate(x)] (pl **-es**) m [índole, natureza, cunho] character; **uma pessoa de** ~ /sem ~ a person of good moral fibre/with no moral fibre.

➤ **a caráter** loc adv [vestir-se] in character.

caravana [kara'vãnal] f caravan.

carboidrato [kaxbwi'dratul] m carbohydrate.

carbônico, ca [kax'boniku, kal] adj carbonic.

carbono [kax'bonul] m QUÍM carbon.

carburador [kaxbura'do(x)l] (pl **-es**) m carburettor UK, carburator US.

carcaça [kax'kasal] f -1. [esqueleto] carcass. -2. [armação] frame. -3. [de navio] hull.

cárcere ['kaxseril] m jail.

carcereiro, ra [kaxse'rejru, ral] m jailer.

carcomer [kaxko'me(x)] vt [roer] to eat into.

carcomido, da [kaxko'midu, dal] adj -1. [roído] worm-eaten. -2. [gasto] frayed. -3. fig [rosto] pockmarked.

cardápio [kax'dapjul] m menu.

cardeal [kax'dʒjaw] (pl **-ais**) <> m RELIG cardinal. <> adj [ponto] cardinal.

cardíaco, ca [kax'dʒiaku, kal] <> adj cardiac, heart; **ataque** ~ heart attack. <> m, f heart patient, person with heart problems.

cardigã [kaxdʒi'gãl] m cardigan.

cardinal [kaxdʒi'naw] (pl **-ais**) adj cardinal.

cardiovascular [ˌkaxdʒjovaʃku'la(x)l] (pl **-es**) adj cardiovascular.

cardume [kax'dumil m shoal.

careca [ka'rɛkal] <> adj bald; **estar** ~ **de saber algo** to know sthg full well. <> m bald man. <> f bald patch.

carecer [kare'se(x)] vt -1. [não ter]: ~ **de** to lack. -2. [precisar]: ~ **de** to need.

careiro, ra [ka'rejru, ral] adj pricey.

carência [ka'rēnsjal] f -1. [falta]: ~ **de** lack of. -2. [falta de afeto]: ~ **afetiva** lack of care. -3. [em seguro, financiamento]: **período de** ~ moratorium.

carente [ka'rēntʃil] adj -1. [desprovido] lacking. -2. [pobre] needy.

carestia [kareʃ'tʃial] f -1. [custo alto] high cost. -2. [escassez] scarcity.

careta [ka'retal] <> adj -1. fam [conservador - pessoa] fuddy-duddy; [- roupa, festa] dated. -2. fam [que não usa drogas] clean. <> f [com o rosto] grimace; **fazer** ~ to pull faces.

caretice [kare'tʃisil] f fam [convencionalismo]: **meu pai é a** ~ **em pessoa** my father is as old-fashioned as they come.

carga ['kaxgal] f -1. [ato] loading. -2. [carregamento] cargo. -3. [fardo] load. -4. [de arma de fogo] charge. -5. [de caneta] cartridge. -6. ELETR: ~ **elétrica** electric charge. -7. fig [peso] burden. -8. fig [responsabilidade] load.

cargo ['kaxgul] m -1. [função] post. -2. [responsabilidade] responsibility.

cargueiro, ra [kax'gejru, ral] adj cargo.

➤ **cargueiro** m cargo ship.

cariado, da [ka'riadu, dal] adj [dente] decayed.

Caribe [ka'ribil] n: **o (mar do)** ~ the Caribbean (Sea).

caricatura [karika'tural] f -1. [desenho] caricature. -2. fig [reprodução malfeita] distortion.

carícia [ka'risjal] f caress.

caridade [kari'dadʒil] f -1. [benevolência] charity. -2. [esmola] alms (pl).

caridoso, osa [kari'dozu, ɔzal] adj charitable.

cartão

cárie ['kari] f caries.

carimbar [karĩ'ba(x)] vt to stamp.

carimbo [ka'rĩbu] m stamp.

carinho [ka'riɲu] m -1. [afago] caress. -2. [cuidado] care.

carinhoso, osa [kari'ɲozu, ɔza] adj affectionate.

carisma [ka'riʒma] m charisma.

caritativo, va [karita'tʃivu, va] adj charitable.

carnal [kax'naw] (pl -ais) adj -1. [da carne, do corpo] carnal. -2. [consangüíneo] blood- (antes de subst).

carnaval [kaxna'vaw] (pl -ais) m -1. [festa popular] carnival. -2. fig [desordem] mess. -3. fig [estardalhaço] racket.

carnavalesco, ca [kaxnava'leʃku, ka] adj -1. [relativo ao carnaval] carnival. -2. [extravagante] over the top.
◆ **carnavalesco** m -1. [folião] reveller. -2. [organizador] carnival planner.

carne ['kaxni] f -1. [ger] flesh; **em ~ e osso** in the flesh; **em ~ viva** raw; **ser de ~ e osso** fig to be only human, after all. -2. CULIN meat; **~ assada** roast meat. -3. [parentesco] flesh and blood.

carnê [kax'ne] m [de pagamento] slate.

carne-de-sol [ˌkaxnidʒi'sɔw] (pl carnes-de-sol) f CULIN lightly dried meat.

carneiro [kax'nejru] m lamb.

carne-seca [ˌkaxni'seka] (pl carnes-secas) f CULIN dried meat.

carniça [kax'nisa] f carrion; **pular ~** to play leapfrog.

carnificina [kaxnifi'sina] f carnage.

carnívoro, ra [kax'nivoru, ra] adj carnivorous.
◆ **carnívoro** m carnivore.

carnudo, da [kax'nudu, da] adj -1. [lábios] full. -2. [fruta, perna] plump.

caro, ra ['karu, ra] adj -1. [ger] expensive. -2. [querido, custoso] dear.
◆ **caro** adv -1. [por alto preço] for a high price. -2. fig [com alto custo] dear.

carochinha [karo'ʃina] f ▷ história.

caroço [ka'rosu] m stone.

carona [ka'rona] f lift; **dar/pegar ~** to give/hitch a lift.

carpete [kax'pɛtʃi] m fitted carpet.

carpintaria [kaxpĩta'ria] f -1. [ofício] carpentry. -2. [oficina] carpenter's shop.

carpinteiro, ra [kaxpĩ'tejru, ra] m, f carpenter.

carranca [ka'xãŋka] f -1. fam [cara fechada] sour face. -2. [em embarcação] figurehead.

carrapato [kaxa'patu] m -1. [inseto] tick. -2. fam [pessoa dependente] hanger-on.

carrasco [ka'xaʃku] m -1. [algoz] executioner. -2. fig [tirano] tyrant.

carregado, da [kaxe'gadu, da] adj -1. [caminhão etc.]: **~ (de)** laden with. -2. [fisionomia] sullen. -3. [ambiente] dismal. -4. [estilo] dark. -5. [céu] threatening.

carregador [kaxega'do(x)] (pl -es) m, f -1. [de bagagem] porter. -2. [transportador] carrier.

carregamento [kaxega'mẽntu] m -1. [ato] loading. -2. [carga] load.

carregar [kaxe'ga(x)] ⬦ vt -1. [ger] to load. -2. [levar] to transport. -3. fig [sentimento etc.] to carry. -4. [bateria] to charge. -5. [impregnar] to fill. ⬦ vi [pôr em demasia]: **~ em** to overdo.

carreira [ka'xejra] f -1. [correria] run. -2. [profissão] career. -3. NÁUT slipway. -4. [turfe] racecourse. -5. [trilha] track.

carreta [ka'xeta] f -1. [caminhão] truck. -2. [carroça] cart.

carretel [kaxe'tɛw] (pl -éis) m -1. [cilindro] reel. -2. [molinete] fishing reel.

carretilha [kaxe'tʃiʎa] f -1. [roldana] pulley. -2. [cortadeira] pastry cutter.

carrilhão [kaxi'ʎãw] (pl -ões) m -1. [sinos] carillon. -2. [relógio] chime.

carrinho [ka'xiɲu] m -1. [para transportar criança] pushchair UK, stroller US. -2. [para transportar comida etc.] trolley; **~ de chá** tea trolley UK, tea cart US; **~ de mão** handcart.

carro ['kaxu] m -1. [veículo] car; **~ alegórico** float; **~ de bombeiro** fire engine; **~ de praça** taxi. -2. [vagão] waggon. -3. [de bois] cart. -4. [de máquina de escrever] carriage.

carro-bomba [ˌkaxu'bõnba] (pl carros-bombas, carros-bomba) m car bomb.

carroça [ka'xɔsa] f -1. [de tração animal] cart. -2. [calhambeque] trap.

carroceria [kaxose'ria] f car body.

carro-chefe [ˌkaxu'ʃefi] (pl carros-chefes) m leading float.

carrocinha [kaxo'sina] f dog wagon.

carrossel [kaxo'sɛw] (pl -éis) m roundabout UK, merry-go-round US.

carruagem [ka'xwaʒẽ] (pl -ns) f carriage.

carta ['kaxta] f -1. [missiva] letter; **~ registrada** registered letter. -2. [de baralho] playing card; **dar as ~s** to deal the cards. -3. [mapa] map. -4. [constituição]: **~ magna** charter.

cartão [kax'tãw] (pl -ões) m card; **~ de crédito** credit card; **~ de telefone** phone card; **~ de embarque** boarding card; **~ pré-pago** [para celular] prepaid card.

cartão-postal [kaxˌtãwpoʃtaw] (*pl* **cartões-postais**) *m* postcard.

cartaz [kax'taʃ] (*pl* **-es**) *m* **-1.** [anúncio] poster. **-2.** *CINE & TEATRO* : **estar em** ~ to be showing.

carteira [kax'tejra] *f* **-1.** [para dinheiro]: ~ **(de notas)** wallet. **-2.** [mesa] desk. **-3.** [documento]: ~ **de identidade** identity card; ~ **de estudante** student card; ~ **de investimentos** *ECON* investment portfolio; ~ **de sócio** membership card; ~ **de motorista** driving licence *UK*, driver's license *US*. **-4.** [de cigarros] pack. **-5.** [de títulos, ações] portfolio.

carteiro, ra [kax'tejru, ral] *m, f* postman (*f* postwoman).

cartola [kax'tɔla] <> *f* [chapéu] top hat. <> *m* **-1.** *fam* [pessoa importante] snob. **-2.** *pej* & *FUT club manager who abuses his position.*

cartolina [kaxto'lina] *f* card.

cartomante [kaxto'mãntʃi] *mf* card reader.

cartório [kax'tɔrju] *m* **-1.** [arquivo] archive. **-2.** [de registro civil] registry office. **-3.** [de registro de imóveis] Land Registry.

cartucho [kax'tuʃu] *m* **-1.** [de arma] cartridge. **-2.** [invólucro] tube. **-3.**: ~ **de tinta** ink cartridge.

cartum [kax'tũ] (*pl* **-ns**) *m* cartoon.

cartunista [kaxtu'niʃta] *mf* cartoonist.

carvalho [kax'vaʎu] *m* oak.

carvão [kax'vãw] (*pl* **-ões**) *m* **-1.** [combustível] coal; ~ **vegetal** charcoal. **-2.** [tição] cinder.

casa ['kaza] *f* **-1.** [ger] house. **-2.** [lar] home; **em** ~ at home; **ir para** ~ to go home. **-3.** [estabelecimento] building; ~ **de câmbio** bureau de change; **Casa da Moeda** Mint; ~ **de saúde** hospital. **-4.** [de botões] buttonhole. **-5.** *MAT* place.

casacão [kaza'kãw] (*pl* **-ões**) *m* overcoat.

casaco [ka'zaku] *m* coat; ~ **de pele** fur coat.

casa-grande [ˌkaza'grãndʒi] (*pl* **casas-grandes**) *f* main house.

casal [ka'zaw] (*pl* **-ais**) *m* **-1.** [homem e mulher] couple. **-2.** [de filhos] pair.

casamento [kaza'mẽntu] *m* **-1.** [ger] marriage. **-2.** [cerimônia] wedding.

casar [ka'za(x)] <> *vt* **-1.** [ger] to marry. **-2.** [emparelhar] to pair. <> *vi* [em matrimônio]: ~ **(com alguém)** to marry (sb); ~ **no civil/no religioso** to have a civil/religious wedding.
➤ casar-se *vp* **-1.** [em matrimônio] to marry. **-2.** [combinar-se] to go.

casarão [kaza'rãw] (*pl* **-ões**) *m* large house.

casca ['kaʃka] *f* **-1.** [de pão] crust. **-2.** [de

ferida] scab. **-3.** [de ovo] shell. **-4.** [de fruta] peel. **-5.** *fig* [aparência] sullenness.

cascalho [kaʃ'kaʎu] *m* gravel.

cascão [kaʃ'kãw] (*pl* **-ões**) *m* **-1.** [crosta] hard crust. **-2.** [de sujeira] grime.

cascata [kaʃ'kata] *f* **-1.** [queda d'água] waterfall. **-2.** *fam* [mentira] fib. **-3.** *fam* [bazófia] bragging.

cascavel [kaʃka'vɛw] (*pl* **-éis**) <> *m ZOOL* rattlesnake. <> *f fig* [mulher] cow.

casco ['kaʃku] *m* **-1.** [de navio] hull. **-2.** [de tartaruga] shell. **-3.** [garrafa] cask. **-4.** [crânio] scalp.

casebre [ka'zɛbri] *m* hovel.

caseiro, ra [ka'zejru, ral] <> *adj* **-1.** [produto] home-made. **-2.** [trabalho] home-*(antes de subst)*. **-3.** [roupa] homespun. **-4.** [pessoa] family man. <> *m, f* [empregado] çaretaker.

caserna [ka'zɛxna] *f MIL* barracks (*pl*).

caso ['kazu] <> *m* **-1.** [fato] matter. **-2.** [circunstância]: **em todo** ~ anyway; **neste** ~ in that case; **no** ~ de should there be; ~ **de emergência** emergency. **-3.** [história] story. **-4.** [amoroso] affair. **-5.** [problema]: **criar** ~ to cause a problem. **-6.** *MED, GRAM* case. <> *conj* if.

caspa ['kaʃpa] *f* dandruff.

casquinha [kaʃ'kiɲa] *f* [de pele] scab.

cassado, da [ka'sadu, da] *m, f person deprived of his/her civil rights.*

cassete [ka'sɛtʃi] <> *adj inv* [fita, gravador] tape- *(antes de subst)*. <> *m* [gravador] tape.

cassetete [kase'tɛtʃi] *m* truncheon.

cassino [ka'sinu] *m* casino.

casta ['kaʃta] *f* **-1.** [camada social] caste. **-2.** *fig* [raça] race.

castanha [kaʃ'tãɲa] *f* ▷ **castanho**.

castanha-do-pará [kaʃˌtãɲadupa'ral] (*pl* **castanhas-do-pará**) *m* Brazil nut.

castanheiro [kaʃtã'ɲejru] *m* chestnut tree.

castanho, nha [kaʃ'tãɲu, ɲa] *adj* [olhos etc.] brown. ➤ **castanha** *f* [fruto] chestnut; ~ **-de-caju** cashew.

castanholas [kaʃtã'ɲɔlaʃ] *fpl* castanets.

castelo [kaʃ'tɛlu] *m* castle.

castiçal [kaʃtʃi'saw] (*pl* **-ais**) *m* candlestick.

castiço, ça [kaʃ'tʃisu, sal] *adj* **-1.** [puro] top-breed. **-2.** [de boa casta] well-bred. **-3.** *fig* [vernáculo] vernacular.

castidade [kaʃtʃi'dadʒil] *f* chastity.

castigar [kaʃtʃi'ga(x)] *vt* **-1.** [punir] to punish. **-2.** [fam] [tocar] to bash out.

castigo [kaʃ'tʃigul] *m* **-1.** [punição] punishment. **-2.** *fig* [mortificação] torture; **ser um** ~ to be torture.

casto, ta ['kaʃtu, tal] *adj* chaste.

casual [ka'zwaw] (pl -ais) adj chance (antes de subst).

casualidade [kazwali'dadʒil] f chance; por ~ by chance.

casulo [ka'zulul] m -1. [de insetos] cocoon. -2. [de sementes] boll.

cata [ˈkata] f: à ~ de algo/alguém in search of sthg/sb.

catalão, lã [kata'lãw, lã] <> adj Catalan. <> m, f Catalan.
➡ **catalão** m [língua] Catalan.

catalogar [katalo'ga(x)] vt to catalogue.

catálogo [ka'talogu] m catalogue; ~ (de telefones) telephone directory.

Catalunha [kata'luɲal] n Catalonia.

catapora [kata'pɔral] f chickenpox.

catar [ka'ta(x)] vt -1. [procurar] to search for. -2. [pegar, recolher] to pick up. -3. [tirar, limpar de] to pick out; ~ piolhos to delouse. -4. [escolher] to pick over; ~ feijão/arroz to pick over beans/rice.

catarata [kata'ratal] f -1. [queda-d'água] waterfall. -2. MED cataract.

catarro [ka'taxul] m catarrh.

catástrofe [ka'taʃtrofil] f catastrophe.

cata-vento [kata'vẽtul] (pl cata-ventos) m weathervane.

catecismo [kate'siʒmul] m catechism.

cátedra [ˈkatedral] f -1. UNIV chair. -2. RELIG throne.

catedral [kate'drawl] (pl -ais) f cathedral.

catedrático, ca [kate'dratʃiku, kal] <> m, f chair. <> adj chair.

categoria [katego'rial] f -1. [grupo] category. -2. [qualidade] quality; de (alta) ~ high quality. -3. [social] standing. -4. [cargo] position.

categorização [kategoriza'sãwl] (pl -ões) f categorization.

catequese [kate'kɛzil] f religious instruction.

cateterismo [katete'riʒmul] m MED catheterization.

cativar [katʃi'va(x)] vt -1. [escravizar] to capture. -2. [seduzir] to captivate.

cativeiro [katʃi'vejrul m -1. [escravidão] slavery. -2. [prisão] captivity.

cativo, va [ka'tʃivu, val] <> adj -1. [preso] captive. -2. [cadeira] exclusive. <> m, f [escravo] slave. -2. [prisioneiro] prisoner.

catolicismo [katoli'siʒmul] m Catholicism.

católico, ca [ka'tɔliku, kal] adj RELIG Catholic.

catorze [ka'toxzil] num fourteen; veja também seis.

catucar [katu'ka(x)] vt = cutucar.

caução [kaw'sãwl] (pl -ões) f -1. [cautela] care. -2. [garantia] pledge. -3. JUR bail.

cauções [kaw'sõjʃ] fpl ▷ caução.

cauda [ˈkawdal] f -1. [de animal] tail. -2. [de vestido] train.

caudaloso, osa [kawda'lozu, ɔzal] adj torrential.

caudilho [kaw'dʒiʎul] m military commander.

caule [ˈkawlil] m stem.

causa [ˈkawzal] f -1. [ger] cause. -2. [motivo] reason; por ~ de because of.

causador, ra [kawza'do(x), ral] <> adj causal. <> m, f cause.

causar [kaw'za(x)] vt to cause.

cautela [kaw'tɛlal] f -1. [precaução] precaution. -2. [título] share certificate. -3. [de penhor] pawn ticket.

cauteloso, osa [kawte'lozu, ɔzal] adj cautious.

cava [ˈkaval] f ▷ cavo.

cavala [ka'valal] f [peixe] mackerel.

cavalaria [kavala'rial] f -1. MIL cavalry. -2. [cavalos] herd of horses. -3. [ordem] chivalry.

cavalariça [kavala'risal] f [estrebaria] stable.

cavalariço [kavala'risul] m [estribeiro] groom UK, stableman US.

cavaleiro, ra [kava'lejrul m, f [quem monta] horseman (f horsewoman).
➡ **cavaleiro** m [medieval] knight.

cavalete [kava'letʃil] m -1. [de pintor] easel. -2. [de mesa] trestle. -3. [para instrumento] bridge.

cavalgar [kavaw'ga(x)] vt & vi to ride.

cavalheiro [kava'ʎejrul] <> m gentleman. <> adj [educado] well-bred.

cavalo [ka'valul] m -1. ZOOL horse; a ~ on horseback. -2. [em xadrez] knight. -3. fig [pessoa agressiva] pig; ele agiu como um ~ he behaved like a pig. -4. [cavalo-vapor] horsepower. -5. loc: pode tirar o ~ da chuva que ela não vai aceitar sua proposta you can forget that, as she's not going to accept your proposal.

cavalo-de-pau [kavaludʒi'pawl] (pl cavalos-de-pau) m wheel spin.

cavalo-de-tróia [ka'valudʒitrɔjal] (pl cavalos-de-Tróia) m COMPUT Trojan horse.

cavanhaque [kava'ɲakil m goatee.

cavaquinho [kava'kiɲul m small guitar.

cavar [ka'va(x)] <> vt -1. [ger] to dig. -2. [emprego] to search long and hard. <> vi [escavar] to dig.

cave [ˈkavil] f cellar.

caveira [ka'vejral] f -1. [crânio] skull. -2. fig [rosto macilento] cavernous face.

caverna [ka'vɛxnal] f cavern.

caviar [ka'vja(x)] m caviar.

cavidade [kavi'dadʒil] f cavity.

cavilha [ka'viʎal] f peg.

cavo, va ['kavu, va] adj [côncavo] hollow.
◆ **cava** f [de manga] armhole.

caxumba [ka'ʃũba] f mumps (sg).

CBF (abrev de Confederação Brasileira de Futebol) f Brazilian football federation.

c/c (abrev de conta corrente) f c/a.

CD [se'de] (abrev de Compact Disc) m CD.

CDB (abrev de Certificado de Depósito Bancário) m type of investment offered by Brazilian banks.

CDC (abrev de Código de Defesa do Consumidor) m Brazilian consumer protection legislation.

CD-i (abrev de Compact Disc-Interativo) m CD-I.

CD-ROM (abrev de Compact Disc-Read Only Memory) m CD-ROM.

CE ◇ f (abrev de Comunidade Européia) EC. ◇ m (abrev de Estado do Ceará) State of Ceará.

cear ['sja(x)] ◇ vt to have for supper. ◇ vi to have supper.

CEASA (abrev de Companhia de Entrepostos e Armazéns S.A) m Brazilian company of fruit and vegetable wholesalers.

cebola [se'bola] f onion.

cebolinha [sebo'liɲa] f chive.

CEBRAP (abrev de Centro Brasileiro de Análise e Planejamento) m independent research centre for the study of Brazilian society.

cê-cedilha [ˌsese'dʒiʎa] (pl cês-cedilhas) m c-cedilha.

ceder [se'de(x)] ◇ vt -1. [dar] to hand over. -2. [emprestar] to loan. ◇ vi -1. [aquiescer]: ~ a algo to give in to sthg. -2. [diminuir] to fall. -3. [afrouxar-se] to loosen. -4. [curvar-se ao peso] to give way. -5. [sucumbir]: ~ a algo to give way to sthg. -6. [transigir] to give in.

cedilha [se'diʎa] f cedilha.

cedo ['sedu] adv [de manhãzinha] early; **mais ~ ou mais tarde** sooner or later; **quanto mais ~ melhor** the sooner the better.

cedro ['sedru] m cedar.

cédula ['sedula] f -1. [dinheiro] banknote. -2. [em votação]: ~ eleitoral ballot paper.

CEF (abrev de Caixa Econômica Federal) f Brazilian state-owned bank financing loans for house purchase.

cegar [se'ga(x)] vt -1. [ger] to blind. -2. [suj: paixão, raiva] to make blind. -3. [tesoura etc.] to blunt.

cego, ga ['segu, ga] ◇ adj -1. [ger] blind. -2. [tesoura] blunt. ◇ m, f blind person.

◆ **às cegas** loc adv -1. [sem ver] blindly. -2. [sem saber] in the dark.

cegonha [se'goɲa] f [ave] stork; **esperar a chegada da ~** fam to be pregnant.

cegueira [se'gejra] f blindness.

ceia ['seja] f supper; ~ **de Natal** Christmas Eve midnight supper.

ceifa ['sejfa] f -1. [ato] harvest. -2. [época] harvest-time. -3. fig [destruição, mortandade] death-toll.

cela ['sɛla] f cell.

celebração [selebra'sãw] (pl -ões) f -1. [realização] celebration. -2. [comemoração] commemoration.

celebrar [sele'bra(x)] vt -1. [ger] to celebrate. -2. [exaltar] to glorify.

célebre ['sɛlebri] adj famous.

celebridade [selebri'dadʒi] mf celebrity.

celeiro [se'lejru] m -1. [para cereais] granary. -2. [depósito] store.

celeste [se'lɛʃtʃi] adj heavenly.

celibato [seli'batu] m celibacy.

celofane [selo'fãni] ◇ adj [papel] cellophane. ◇ m cellophane.

celsius [sew'siuʃ] adj Celsius.

celta ['sɛwta] ◇ adj Celtic. ◇ mf [pessoa] Celt. ◇ m [língua] Celtic.

célula ['sɛlula] f cell; ~ **fotoelétrica** photo-electric cell.

celular [selu'la(x)] ◇ adj cellular. ◇ m TELEC cellular phone.

célula-tronco ['sɛlula-trõŋkul f stem cell.

celulite [selu'litʃi] f cellulite.

cem ['sẽ] num -1. [cardinal] one/a hundred; ~ **por cento** one/a hundred per cent; **veja também seis**. -2. [muitos]: ~ **vezes** hundreds of times.

◆ **cem por cento** ◇ loc adj: **ser ~ por cento** to be one hundred per cent. ◇ loc adv [totalmente] completely.

cemitério [semi'tɛrju] m cemetery.

cena ['sena] f -1. [de peça, filme, novela] scene. -2. [palco] stage; **em ~** on stage. -3. [acontecimento] spectacle.

cenário [se'narju] m -1. [ger] scene. -2. [em teatro, cinema, TV] scenery. -3. [panorama] sight.

cenografia [senogra'fia] f scenography.

cenógrafo, fa [se'nɔgrafu, fa] m, f scenographer.

cenoura [se'nora] f carrot.

censo ['sẽsul m census.

censura [sẽ'sura] f -1. [crítica] criticism. -2. [repreensão] reprimand. -3. [condenação] condemnation. -4. [prática] censure. -5. [organismo] board of censors. -6. [proibição] censorship. -7. [corte] cut.

censurado, da [sẽsu'radu, da] adj [proibido] censored.

censurar [sẽnsu'ra(x)] vt **-1.** [criticar] to criticise. **-2.** [repreender] to reprove. **-3.** [condenar] to condemn. **-4.** [examinar] to censor. **-5.** [proibir] to ban. **-6.** [cortar] to cut.

centavo [sẽn'tavul] m cent; **estar sem um ~** to be penniless.

centeio [sẽn'teju] m rye.

centelha [sẽn'teʎa] f spark.

centena [sẽn'tenal] f hundred; **às ~s** in their hundreds; **uma ~ de vezes** a hundred times.

centenário, ria [sẽnte'narju, rjal] <> adj: **um homem ~** a hundred-year-old man; **ele é ~** he is a hundred years old. <> m, f [pessoa] centenarian.

   ➡ **centenário** m [comemoração] centenary.

centésimo, ma [sẽn'tɛzimu, mal <> num hundredth. <> m, f [pessoa] hundredth.

   ➡ **centésimo** m hundredth.

centígrado, da [sẽn'tʃigradul adj centigrade (depois de subst).

   ➡ **centígrado** m centigrade.

centilitro [sẽntʃi'litrul m centilitre.

centímetro [sẽn'tʃimetrul m centimetre.

cento ['sẽntul num: **~ e dez** one/a hundred and ten; **por ~** per cent; veja também **seis**.

centopéia [sẽnto'pɛjal f centipede.

central [sẽn'trawl (pl **-ais**) <> adj **-1.** [ger] central. **-2.** fig [problema, ponto, argumento] central. <> f **-1.** [agência, delegacia]: **~ de polícia** police station; **~ de atendimento** call centre; **~ de correios** post office; **~ telefônica** telephone exchange. **-2.** [usina]: **~ elétrica** power station.

centralizar [sẽntrali'za(x)] vt to centralize.

centrar [sẽn'tra(x)] <> vt **-1.** [ger] to centre. **-2.** FUT [bola, passe]: **~** to kick into the centre. <> vi FUT to shoot.

centrífuga [sẽntri'fugal, **centrifugadora** [sẽntri'fuga'doral f centrifuge.

centro ['sẽntrul m **-1.** [ger] centre; **ser o ~ das atenções** to be the centre of attention; **~ comercial** shopping centre UK, shopping mall US; **~ cultural** cultural centre; **~ espírita** spiritualist centre; **~ de processamento de dados** data processing centre. **-2.** [de cidade] (city) centre; **ir ao ~** to go downtown. **-3.** [metrópole] metropolis.

centroavante [ˌsẽntrw'vãntʃil m centre forward.

CEP (abrev de **Código de Endereçamento Postal**) m ≃ post code UK, ≃ zip code US.

CEPAL (abrev de **Comissão Econômica para a América Latina**) f ECLAC.

cera ['seral f **-1.** [ger] wax. **-2.** [para polir] wax polish.

cerâmica [se'rãmikal f **-1.** [ger] ceramics. **-2.** [fábrica] pottery. **-3.** [argila cozida] ceramic.

ceramista [sera'miʃtal mf potter, ceramicist.

cerca ['sexkal f [de arame, madeira, ferro] fence; **~ viva** hedge.

   ➡ **cerca de** loc prep around.

cercanias [sexka'niaʃl fpl **-1.** [arredores] outskirts. **-2.** [vizinhança] neighbourhood.

cercar [sex'ka(x)] vt **-1.** [ger] to surround. **-2.** [pôr cerca em] to fence.

   ➡ **cercar-se** vp [rodear-se]: **~-se de** to surround o.s. with.

cerco ['sexkul m [assédio] siege; **pôr ~ a** to lay siege to.

cereal [se'rjal] (pl **-ais**) m cereal.

cérebro ['sɛrebrul m **-1.** ANAT brain. **-2.** fig [líder, mentor]: **o ~** the brains (sg).

cereja [se'reʒal f cherry.

cerimônia [seri'monjal f **-1.** [solenidade] ceremony. **-2.** [formalidade] formality; **fazer ~** to stand on ceremony.

cerne ['sexnil m **-1.** [de madeira] heartwood. **-2.** fig [de questão] heart.

ceroulas [se'rolaʃl fpl long johns.

cerração [sexa'sãwl f [neblina] fog.

cerrado, da [se'xadu, dal adj **-1.** [fechado - porta, olhos] closed; [- punhos, dentes] clenched. **-2.** [intenso] [bombardeio] heavy. **-3.** [denso, espesso] thick.

   ➡ **cerrado** m [vegetação] dense, low vegetation found in northern and central Brazil.

cerrar [se'xa(x)] vt [fechar - porta, olhos] to close; [-punhos, centes] to clench.

certa ['sɛxtal f ▷ **certo**.

certeiro, ra [sex'tejru, ral adj accurate.

certeza [sex'tezal f certainty; **ter ~ de algo** to be sure about sthg; **ter ~ de que** to be sure that; **com ~** definitely.

certidão [sextʃi'dãwl (pl **-ões**) f certificate; **~ de casamento** marriage certificate; **~ de nascimento** birth certificate.

certificação [sextʃifika'sãwl (pl **-ões**) f certification.

certificado [sextʃifi'kadul m certificate.

certificar [sextʃifi'ka(x)] vt **-1.** [assegurar]: **~ alguém de algo/de que** to assure sb of sthg/that. **-2.** [atestar] to affirm.

   ➡ **certificar-se** vp: **~-se de que/de algo** to make sure that/of sthg.

certo, ta ['sɛxtu, tal <> adj **-1.** [ger] right. **-2.** [correto, certeiro] correct. **-3.**

[sensato, acertado] sensible. **- 4.** [infalível, seguro] certain. **- 5.** [com razão]: **estar** ~ to be right. **- 6.** [com certeza]: **estar** ~ **de que/de algo** to be sure that/of sthg. <> *pron* **-1.** *(antes de subst)* [um, algum] right; **certa vez** once. **- 2.** *loc*: **dar** ~ to work; **está** ~ [está bem] all right. ◆ **certo** <> *m* **-1.** [correto] (what is) right; **ele não sabe distinguir entre o** ~ **e o errado** he doesn't know the difference between right and wrong. **-2.** [verdade] truth. <> *adv* **-1.** [certamente] certainly. **- 2.** [corretamente] correctly. <> **certa** *f*: **na certa** definitely. ◆ **ao certo** *loc adv* for sure.

cerveja [sex'veʒa] *f* [bebida] beer.

cervejaria [sexveʒa'ria] *f* **-1.** [fábrica] brewery. **- 2.** [estabelecimento] *beer bar, usually serving food if wanted.*

cessação [sesa'sãw] *f* ending.

cessão [se'sãw] (*pl* **-ões**) *f* **-1.** [cedência] assignment. **- 2.** [transferência] transfer.

cessar [se'sa(x)] <> *vi* to come to an end; **sem** ~ non-stop. <> *vt* **-1.** [fogo] to cease. **- 2.** [trabalho] to stop.

cessar-fogo [se,sax'fogu] *m (inv)* cease-fire.

cessões [se'sõjʃ] *pl* ⊳ **cessão**.

cesta ['seʃta] *f* **-1.** [ger] basket; ~ **básica** *basic monthly supplies that the average lower-middle-class family needs in order to survive.* **- 2.** [conteúdo] basketful. **- 3.** [ESP - aro] basket; [- ponto] stitch.

cesto ['seʃtu] *m* basket.

CETESB (*abrev de* **Companhia Estadual de Tecnologia de Saneamento Básico e Defesa do Meio Ambiente**) *f São Paulo environment agency.*

cético, ca ['sɛtʃiku, ka] <> *adj* sceptical. <> *m, f* sceptic.

cetim [se'tʃĩ] *m* satin.

cetro ['sɛtru] *m* sceptre.

céu ['sɛw] *m* **-1.** [firmamento] sky; **cair do** ~ *fig* to be heaven-sent. **- 2.** RELIG heaven. **- 3.** ANAT : ~ **da boca** roof of the mouth.

cevada [se'vada] *f* barley.

cevar [se'va(x)] *vt* **- 1.** [alimentar] to feed. **- 2.** [fazer engordar] to fatten.

CFC (*abrev de* **clorofluorocarboneto**) *m* CFC.

chá ['ʃa] *m* [ger] tea; ~ **completo** afternoon tea; ~ **de camomila/menta** camomile/mint tea; ~ **preto** black tea.

chã ['ʃã] *f* plain.

chacal [ʃa'kaw] (*pl* **-ais**) *m* jackal.

chácara ['ʃakara] *f* **-1.** [no campo] smallholding. **- 2.** [na cidade] large town house. **- 3.** [casa de campo] country house.

chacina [ʃa'sina] *f* slaughter.

chacota [ʃa'kɔta] *f* **-1.** [deboche] ridicule. **- 2.** [objeto de deboche] butt of ridicule.

chafariz [ʃafa'riʃ] (*pl* **-es**) *m* fountain.

chafurdar [ʃafux'da(x)] *vi*: ~ **em** [lama etc.] to wallow in; *fig* [vícios etc.] to become involved in.

chaga ['ʃaga] *f* **-1.** [ferida] wound. **- 2.** *fig* [mal] scourge.

chalé [ʃa'lɛ] *m* cottage.

chaleira [ʃa'lejra] *f* kettle.

chama ['ʃama] *f* flame; **em** ~**s** in flames.

chamada [ʃa'mada] *f* **-1.** [telefônica] call; **fazer uma** ~ **a cobrar** to make a reverse charge call *UK*, to call collect *US*. **- 2.** [verificação de presença] roll call. **- 3.** JORN headline.

chamar [ʃa'ma(x)] <> *vt* **-1.** [ger] to call; **ela decidiu chamá-la de Júlia** she decided to call her 'Júlia'. **- 2.** [com gesto] to hail. **- 3.** [convocar] to summon; [para função]: ~ **alguém para algo** to call sb for sthg. **- 4.** [convidar] to invite; ~ **a atenção** [suj: pessoa, roupa] to attract attention; [para aspecto etc.] to draw attention. **- 5.** [acordar] to wake. **- 6.** [qualificar]: ~ **algo/alguém de algo** to call sthg/sb sthg. <> *vi* **-1.** [dar sinal para vir] to call over; **chamei, mas ela não quis vir** I called her over but she didn't want to come. **- 2.** [para acudir]: ~ **por alguém** to call out for sb. **- 3.** [telefone] to ring. ◆ **chamar-se** *vp* [ter por nome] to be called; **como você se chama?** what's your name?

chamariz [ʃama'riʃ] *m* **-1.** [isca] bait. **- 2.** [seta, anúncio] advert. **- 3.** *fig* [engodo] illusion.

chamativo, va [ʃama'tʃivu, va] *adj* flashy.

chaminé [ʃami'nɛ] *f* chimney.

champanha [ʃãm'paɲa], **champanhe** [ʃãm'paɲi] *m ou f* champagne.

chamuscar [ʃamuʃ'ka(x)] *vt* **-1.** [roupa] to scorch. **- 2.** [cabelo] to singe. **- 3.** [pessoa, braço] to burn.

chance ['ʃãnsi] *f* chance; **dar uma** ~ **a** *ou* **para alguém/algo** to give sb/sthg a chance; **ele tem boas** ~**s de ganhar** he has a good chance of winning.

chanceler [ʃãnse'lɛ(x)] *mf* **-1.** [ministro] minister. **- 2.** [chefe de governo] head of government.

chantagear [ʃãnta'ʒja(x)] *vt* to blackmail.

chantagem [ʃãn'taʒẽ] (*pl* **-ns**) *f* blackmail.

chantagista [ʃãnta'ʒiʃta] *mf* blackmailer.

chão [ˈʃãw] *m* -1. [piso] floor. -2. [solo] ground.

chapa [ˈʃapa] ⟨⟩ *f* -1. [folha] sheet; ~ **de metal/aço** metal/steel sheet. -2. [para grelhar] hotplate; **bife na** ~ steak on the griddle. -3. *AUTO* [placa] number plate *UK*, license plate *US*. -4. [de impressão] plate. -5. *FOT* shot. -6. [radiografia] X-ray. -7. *POL* [eleitoral] roll.

chapéu [ʃaˈpɛw] *m* hat; **de tirar o** ~ fantastic.

chapinha [ʃaˈpiɲa] *f* [de garrafa] stopper.

charada [ʃaˈrada] *f* [enigma] puzzle.

charco [ˈʃaxku] *m* puddle.

charge [ˈʃaxʒi] *f* cartoon.

chargista [ʃaxˈʒiʃta] *mf* cartoonist.

charlatão, tã [ʃaxlaˈtãw, tã] (*mpl* -ães, *fpl* -s) ⟨⟩ *adj* charlatan. ⟨⟩ *m, f* impostor.

charme [ˈʃaxmi] *m* charm.

charmoso, osa [ʃaxˈmozu, ɔza] *adj* charming.

charrete [ʃaˈxɛtʃi] *f* chariot.

charter [ˈʃarte(x)] ⟨⟩ *adj inv* charter. ⟨⟩ *m* charter plane.

charuto [ʃaˈrutu] *m* cigar.

chassi [ʃaˈsi] *m* -1. [ger] chassis. -2. *ARTE* [de tela] stretcher.

chateação [ʃatʃjaˈsãw] (*pl* -ões) *f* -1. [aborrecimento] boredom. -2. [maçada] bore.

chatear [ʃaˈtʃja(x)] ⟨⟩ *vt* -1. [aborrecer] to annoy. -2. [incomodar] to bother. -3. [enfadar] to irritate. -4. [implicar com] to tease. ⟨⟩ *vi* -1. [aborrecer] to be boring. -2. [incomodar] to be annoying.
➡ **chatear-se** *vp* [aborrecer-se] to become bored.

chatice [ʃaˈtʃisi] *f* boredom.

chato, ta [ˈʃatu, ta] ⟨⟩ *adj* -1. [superfície, forma] flat; **ele tem pés** ~**s** he's got flat feet. -2. [filme, música] boring. -3. [desagradável] unwelcome. -4. [embaraçoso] tricky. ⟨⟩ *m, f* bore; **um** ~ **de galochas** a drag.

chauvinista [ʃoviˈniʃta] *mf* chauvinist.

chavão [ʃaˈvãw] (*pl* -ões) *m* hackneyed phrase.

chave [ˈʃavi] *f* -1. [de fechadura] key. -2. [ferramenta] spanner; ~ **de fenda** *OU* **parafusos** screwdriver; ~ **inglesa** adjustable spanner *UK*, monkey wrench *US*. -3. *ELETR* switch. -4. [golpe] blow. -5. [sinal gráfico] curly bracket. -6. *fig* [de problema] key.

chaveiro [ʃaˈvejru] *m* -1. [utensílio] key-rack. -2. [profissional] locksmith.

chavões [ʃaˈvõjʃ] *pl* ⊳ **chavão**.

checar [ʃeˈka(x)] *vt* to check.

check-up [ʃeˈkapi] (*pl* **check-ups**) *m* check-up.

chefe [ˈʃɛfi] *mf* -1. [superior] head; ~ **de estado** head of state. -2. *fam* [garçom] waiter. -3. *fam* [freguês] mate.

chefia [ʃeˈfia] *f* -1. [direção] management. -2. [repartição, sala] management office.

chefiar [ʃeˈfja(x)] *vt* to lead.

chega [ˈʃega] *m fam* [repreensão]: **dar um** ~ **(para lá) em alguém** to tear a strip off sb.

chegada [ʃeˈgada] *f* -1. [vinda, regresso] arrival. -2. [aproximação] approach. -3. *ESP* finishing line.

chegar [ʃeˈga(x)] ⟨⟩ *vi* -1. [a um lugar]: ~ **em** to arrive at; ~ **em casa** to arrive home; ~ **de** to arrive from. -2. [aproximar-se] to approach. -3. [afastar-se]: **chega para lá** [ir embora] go away; [deslocar-se] move over. -4. [verão, noite, hora] to arrive. -5. [bastar] to be enough; **chegar!** that's enough! -6. [alcançar] to reach; **não** ~ **aos pés de** [não ser comparável a] to come nowhere near. -7. [conseguir]: ~ **a (ser) algo** to succeed in becoming sthg; ~ **a fazer algo** to manage to do sthg. -8. [ir ao extremo]: ~ **a fazer algo** to reach the point of doing sthg. ⟨⟩ *vt* -1. [aproximar]: ~ **algo para cá** to bring sthg over here. -2. [afastar]: ~ **algo para lá/para o lado** to move sthg over there/to one side.
➡ **chegar-se** *vp* [aproximar-se] to come closer.

cheio, cheia [ˈʃeju, ˈʃeja] *adj* -1. [ger] full; ~ **de si** [orgulhoso] proud; [arrogante] full of o.s. -2. [gordo] plump. -3. *fam* [farto]: **estar** ~ **(de alguém/algo)** to be fed up with sb/sthg.
➡ **cheia** *f* -1. [de rio] flood. -2. [época] flood season.
➡ **em cheio** *loc adv*: **acertar em** ~ to hit the mark.

cheirar [ʃejˈra(x)] ⟨⟩ *vt* -1. [flor, perfume, comida] to smell. -2. [cocaína] to snort. ⟨⟩ *vi* -1. [flor, perfume, comida] to smell; ~ **a** [ter cheiro de] to smell of; *fig* [parecer] to smack (of); ~ **bem/mal** to smell nice/bad. -2. [cocaína]: **passou a noite cheirando** he spent the whole night snorting cocaine.

cheiroso, osa [ʃejˈrozu, ɔza] *adj* scented.

cheiro-verde [ˌʃeju'vexdʒi] (*pl* **cheiros-verdes**) *m* parsley and spring onion.

cheque [ˈʃɛki] *m* cheque; ~ **especial** guaranteed cheque; ~ **nominal** nominative cheque; ~ **pré-datado** pre-dated cheque; ~ **voador** *OU* **sem fundos** bounced cheque.

chiado [ˈʃjadu] *m* -1. [de roda, porta] squeak. -2. [de passarinho] chirp.

chiar [ˈʃja(x)] *vi* -1. [emitir chio - pessoa, respiração] to wheeze; [- vento] whistle. -2. *fam* [reclamar] to kick up a stink.

chiclete [ʃiˈklɛtʃi] *m* chewing gum; ~ de bola bubble gum.

chicória [ʃiˈkɔrja] *f* chicory.

chicote [ʃiˈkɔtʃi] *m* whip.

chicotear [ʃikoˈtʃja(x)] *vt* to whip.

chifrada [ʃiˈfradal] *f* horn thrust.

chifrar [ʃiˈfra(x)] *vt* -1. [toureiro, tronco] to gore. -2. *fam fig* [marido, namorada] to two-time.

chifre [ˈʃifri] *m* [de animal] horn; pôr ~ s em *fam fig* [em marido, namorada] to two-time.

Chile [ˈʃili] *n* Chile.

chileno, na [ʃiˈlenu, na] <> *adj* Chilean. <> *m, f* Chilean.

chimarrão [ʃimaˈxãw] *(pl* -ões) *m herbal tea.*

chimpanzé [ʃĩpãˈzɛ] *m* chimpanzee.

China [ˈʃina] *n*: (a) ~ China.

chinelo [ʃiˈnɛlul *m* slipper.

chinês, esa [ʃiˈneʃ, ezal *(pl* -eses, *fpl* -s) <> *adj* Chinese. <> *m, f* [da China] Chinese.

chip [ˈʃipi] *m COMPUT* microchip.

Chipre [ˈʃipril *n* Cyprus.

chique [ˈʃiki] *adj* chic.

chiqueiro [ʃiˈkejru] *m* -1. [de porcos] pigsty. -2. *fam fig* [bagunça] pigsty.

chispa [ˈʃiʃpa] *f* [faísca] spark.

chispar [ʃiʃˈpa(x)] *vi* [correr] to race.

chocalhar [ʃokaˈʎa(x)] <> *vt* to rattle. <> *vi* [soar] to rattle.

chocalho [ʃoˈkaʎul *m* -1. *MÚS* maraca. -2. [brinquedo] rattle. -3. [de gado, cavalo] bell.

chocante [ʃoˈkãtʃil *adj* -1. [assustador, ofensivo] shocking. -2. *fam* [ótimo] wicked.

chocar [ʃoˈka(x)] <> *vt* -1. [assustar, ofender] to shock. -2. *ZOOL* to hatch. <> *vi* -1. [causar espanto, ofensa] to shock. -2. *ZOOL* to brood.

→ **chocar-se** *vp* -1. [colidir]: ~-se (contra) to collide (with). -2. [assustar-se]: ~-se (com) to be shocked (by). -3. [discordar]: ~-se em relação a to clash over.

chocho, cha [ˈʃoʃu, ʃal *adj* -1. [sem graça] dull. -2. [fruta, ovo] rotten.

chocolate [ʃokoˈlatʃil *m* chocolate.

chofer [ʃoˈfɛ(x)] *(pl* -es) *mf* driver.

chope [ˈʃopil *m* beer.

choque [ˈʃɔki] *m* -1. [ger] shock. -2. [colisão] crash. -3. [conflito, confronto] clash.

choramingar [ʃoramĩˈga(x)] *vi* to whine.

choramingo [ʃoraˈmĩŋgul *m* whine.

chorão, ona [ʃoˈrãw, onal *(mpl* -ões, *fpl* -onas) <> *adj* moaning. <> *m, f* [pessoa] crybaby.

→ **chorão** *m BOT* weeping willow.

chorar [ʃoˈra(x)] <> *vi* -1. [verter lágrimas] to cry. -2. *fig* [barganhar] to haggle. <> *vt* -1. [lágrima] to cry. -2. *fig* [barganhar] to haggle.

chorinho [ʃoˈriɲu] *m MÚS* = choro.

choro [ˈʃorul *m* -1. [pranto] crying. -2. *MÚS* a type of traditional Brazilian music started at the end of the nineteenth century.

chorona [ʃoˈronal *f* ➭ chorão.

choroso, osa [ʃoˈrozu, ɔzal *adj* tearful.

chouriço [ʃoˈrisul *m* chorizo.

chover [ʃoˈve(x)] *v impess* -1. *METEOR* to rain. -2. *fig* [cair do alto] to shower. -3. *fig* [sobrevir em demasia] to pour in.

chuchu [ʃuˈʃul *m fruit-bearing climbing plant;* está frio pra ~ *fam* it's bloody cold; tinha comida pra ~ *fam* there was loads of food at the party.

chucrute [ʃuˈkrutʃil *m* choucroute, sauerkraut.

chulé [ʃuˈlɛl *m* smell of feet.

chulo, lo [ˈʃulu, lal *adj* vulgar.

chumaço [ʃuˈmasul *m* -1. [enchimento] padding. -2. [de algodão, gaze] wadding.

chumbar [ʃũˈba(x)] *vt* -1. [soldar] to solder. -2. [grade, portão] to secure. -3. [rede, anzol] to drop.

chumbo [ˈʃũbul *m* lead.

chupar [ʃuˈpa(x)] *vt* to suck.

chupeta [ʃuˈpetal *f* -1. [de criança] dummy *UK*, comforter *US*. -2. *fam AUTO* : fazer uma ~ to use jump-leads.

churrascaria [ʃuxaʃkaˈrial *f restaurant specializing in grilled and spit-roasted meat;* ~ rodízio *restaurant where diners may pick and choose from food offered.*

churrasco [ʃuˈxaʃkul *m* -1. [carne] barbecued meat. -2. [refeição] barbecue.

churrasqueira [ʃuxaʃˈkejral *f* rotisserie.

churrasquinho [ʃuxaʃˈkiɲul *m* kebab.

chutar [ʃuˈta(x)] <> *vt* -1. [objeto, pessoa] to kick. -2. *fam* [resposta] to take a stab at. -3. *fam* [funcionário, namorado]: ~ alguém to give sb the push. <> *vi* -1. [dar chute] to kick. -2. *fam* [em prova] to take a pot shot.

chute [ˈʃutʃil *m* -1. [pontapé] kick. -2. *fam* [mentira] bullshit. -3. *fam* [dispensa] push; dar um ~ em alguém to give sb the push.

chuteira [ʃuˈtejral *f* football boot; pendurar as ~ s [aposentar-se] to hang up one's boots.

chuva [ˈʃuval] f -**1.** METEOR rain; ~ **de granizo** OU **pedra** hail. -**2.** fig [de papel picado etc.] shower.

chuveirada [ʃuvejˈrada] f shower.

chuveiro [ʃuˈvejru] m shower.

chuviscar [ʃuviʃˈka(x)] vi to drizzle.

chuvisco [ʃuˈviʃku] m -**1.** [chuva] drizzle. -**2.** CULIN confection made of egg-yolk and sugar.

chuvoso, osa [ʃuˈvozu, ɔza] adj rainy.

Cia. (abrev de **Companhia**) f Co.

cibercafé [sibexˈkafe] m cybercafé.

ciberespaço [sibeˈreʃˈpasu] m cyberspace.

cibernética [sibexˈnɛtʃika] f cybernetics (sg).

cibernético, ca [sibexˈnetʃiku, ka] adj cybernetic.

‣ **cibernética** f cybernetics.

ciberpunk [sibexˈpũŋki] mf net hacker.

CIC (abrev de **Cartão de Identificação do Contribuinte**) m Brazilian tax-payer's identity card for individual contributions.

cicatriz [sikaˈtriʃ] (pl -**es**) f scar.

cicatrizar [sikatriˈza(x)] <> vt -**1.** [fechar] to heal. -**2.** [cobrir de cicatrizes] to scar. <> vi [fechar-se] to heal.

cicerone [siseˈroni] mf guide.

ciclismo [siˈkliʒmu] m cycling.

ciclista [siˈkliʃta] mf cyclist.

ciclo [ˈsiklu] m cycle.

ciclone [siˈkloni] m cyclone.

ciclotimia [siklotʃiˈmia] f PSIC cyclothymia.

ciclotímico, ca [sikloˈtʃimiku, ka] <> adj cyclothymic. <> m, f cyclothymic.

ciclovia [sikloˈvia] f bicycle lane.

cidadã [sidaˈdã] f ⊳ **cidadão**.

cidadania [sidadaˈnia] f citizenship.

cidadão, dã [sidaˈdãw, dã] (pl -**ãos**, fpl -**s**) m, f citizen.

cidade [siˈdadʒi] f -**1.** [centro urbano] city; [pequena] small town; ~ **satélite** satellite town. -**2.** [bairro central] town. -**3.** fig [população] city.

Cidade do México [si,dadʒiduˈmɛʃikul] n Mexico City.

cidra [ˈsidra] f citron.

ciência [ˈsjẽsja] f -**1.** [saber] science. -**2.** [da vida, do amor] art. -**3.** [conhecimento] knowledge.

ciente [ˈsjẽtʃi] adj learned.

cientificismo [sjẽtʃifiˈsiʒmul] m scientific spirit.

científico, ca [sjẽˈtʃifiku, ka] adj scientific.

cientista [sjẽˈtʃiʃta] mf scientist.

cifrão [siˈfrãw] (pl -**ões**) m dollar sign.

cifrar [siˈfra(x)] vt to write in code.

cigano, na [siˈgãnu, na] <> adj gipsy. <> m, f gipsy.

cigarra [siˈgaxa] f -**1.** ZOOL cicada. -**2.** [campainha] buzzer.

cigarrilha [sigaˈxiʎa] f cheroot.

cigarro [siˈgaxul] m cigarette.

cilada [siˈladal] f -**1.** [ger] trap. -**2.** [emboscada] ambush.

cilindro [siˈlĩdrul] m GEOM, AUTO cylinder.

cílio [ˈsiljul] m eyelash.

cima [ˈsimal] f: **lá em** ~ [no topo, no alto] up there; [em andar superior] upstairs; **andar de** ~ upstairs; **ainda por** ~ on top of that; **de** ~ from the top; **de** ~ **para baixo** from top to bottom; **em** ~ **de** on top of; **em** ~ **da mesa** on the table; **para** ~ upwards; **por** ~ **de** over; **dar em** ~ **de alguém** to chat sb up.

cimentado, da [simẽˈtadu, dal] adj -**1.** CONSTR cemented. -**2.** [consolidado] sealed.

cimentar [simẽˈta(x)] vt to cement.

cimento [siˈmẽtul] m cement.

cimo [ˈsimul] m top.

cinco [ˈsĩŋkul] num five; veja também seis.

cineasta [siˈnjaʃta] mf cinematographer.

cinegrafista [sinegraˈfiʃta] mf cameraman (f camerawoman).

cinema [siˈnema] m cinema.

cinematografia [sinematograˈfia] f cinematography.

Cingapura [sĩŋgaˈpural] n Singapore.

cínico, ca [ˈsiniku, ka] <> adj shameless. <> m, f immoral person.

cinismo [siˈniʒmul] m impudence.

cinqüenta [sĩŋˈkwẽta] num fifty; veja também seis.

cinqüentão, tona [sĩŋkwẽˈtãw, tɔnal] (mpl -**ões**, fpl -**s**) <> adj quinquagenarian. <> m, f quinquagenarian.

cinta [ˈsĩta] f -**1.** [faixa] belt. -**2.** [feminina] girdle.

cinta-liga [ˌsĩtaˈliga] (pl **cintas-ligas**) f suspender belt.

cintilar [sĩtʃiˈla(x)] vi to scintillate.

cinto [ˈsĩtul] m belt; ~ **de segurança** safety belt.

cintura [sĩˈtural] f waist.

cinturão [sĩtuˈrãw] (pl -**ões**) m belt; ~ **verde** green belt.

cinza [ˈsĩzal] <> adj inv [cor] grey. <> m [cor] grey.

‣ **cinzas** fpl ashes.

cinzeiro [sĩˈzejrul] m ashtray.

cinzento, ta [sĩˈzẽtu, tal] adj grey.

cio [ˈsiw] m rut.

CIPA (abrev de **Comissão Interna de Prevenção de Acidentes**) f Brazilian *commission for prevention of accidents at work,* ≃ HSE *UK,* ≃ OHSA *US.*

cipreste [si'prɛʃtʃi] *m* cypress.

circo ['sixku] *m* circus.

circuito [six'kujtu] *m* circuit.

circulação [sixkula'sãw] *f* circulation.

circulante [sirku'lãntʃi] *adj* -1. [itinerante] itinerant. - 2. *ECON* : **capital** ~ **ready capital.**

circular [sixku'la(x)] *(pl* -es) *<>* *adj* [formato] circular. *<> m* [ônibus] shuttle. *<> f* [carta, ofício] circular. *<> vt*-1. [rodear] to circle. - 2. [dar voltas por] to surround. *<> vi* -1. [ger] to circulate. - 2. [percorrer] to wander.

círculo ['sixkulu] *m* -1. *GEOM* circle. - 2. *fig* [meio, grupo] circle.

circuncisão [sixkũnsi'zãw] *f* circumcision.

circundar [sixkũn'da(x)] *vt* to surround.

circunferência [sixkũnfe'rẽnsja] *f* circumference.

circunflexo [sixkũn'flɛksu] *GRAM <> adj* circumflex. *<> m* circumflex.

circunscrição [sixkũnʃkri'sãw] *(pl* -ões) *f* [repartição] division.

circunspe(c)ção [sixkũnʃpe(k)sãw] *(pl* -ões) *f* circumspection.

circunspecto, ta [sixkũnʃ'pɛktu, ta] *adj* circumspect.

circunstância [sixkũnʃ'tãnsja] *f* -1. [ger] circumstance. - 2. *JUR* : ~ s atenuantes/agravantes attenuating/aggravating circumstances. - 3. [caso] event.

circunstanciado, da [sixkũnʃtãn'sjadu, da] *adj* detailed.

cirurgia [sirux'ʒia] *f* surgery; ~ plástica plastic surgery; ~ estética aesthetic surgery *UK,* esthetic surgery *US;* ~ reconstrutora *ou* reparadora reconstructive surgery.

cirurgião, ã [sirux'ʒjãw͂ʒjã, a] *(pl* -ões, *fpl* -s) *m, f* surgeon.

cirurgião-dentista, cirurgiã-dentista [sirux͵ʒjãwdẽn'tʃiʃta, sirux͵ʒjãdẽntʃiʃtal *(mpl* **cirurgiões-dentistas,** *fpl* **cirurgiãs-dentistas)** *m, f* dental surgeon.

cirúrgico, ca [si'ruxʒiku, ka] *adj* surgical.

cisco ['siʃku] *m* dust.

cisma ['siʒma] *<> m* schism. *<> f* [mania] crazy idea.

cismado, da [siʒ'madu, da] *adj* wary.

cismar [siʒ'ma(x)] *<> vt* [convencer-se de]: ~ **que** to be convinced that. *<> vi* -1. [decidir]: ~ **de** *ou* **em fazer algo** to determine upon doing sthg. - 2. [implicar]: ~ **com** to clash with. - 3. [insistir]: ~ **em** to insist on.

cisne ['siʒnil *m* swan.

cisões [si'zõjʃ] *pl* ▷ **cisão.**

cisterna [siʃ'tɛxna] *f* cistern.

citação [sita'sãw] *(pl* -ões) *f* -1. [de trecho, autor] quotation. - 2. *JUR* citation.

citar [si'ta(x)] *vt* -1. [trecho, autor] to quote. - 2. *JUR* to summons.

cítrico, ca ['sitriku, ka] *adj* -1. [fruta] citrus. - 2. [ácido] citric.

ciúme ['sjumil *m* jealousy.

ciumento, ta [sju'mẽntu, ta] *adj* jealous.

cívico, ca ['siviku, ka] *adj* civic.

civil [si'viw] *(pl* -is) *<> adj* -1. [direito, tribunal] civil. - 2. [vida, traje] civilian. *<> mf* [pessoa] civilian.

civilidade [sivili'dadʒi] *f* courtesy.

civilização [siviliza'sãw] *(pl* -ões) *f* civilization.

civismo [si'viʒmul *m* public spirit.

cl *(abrev de* **centilitro)** *m* cl.

clã ['klã] *(pl* clãs) *m* clan.

clamar [kla'ma(x)] *<> vt* to clamour. *<> vi:* ~ **por/contra algo** to clamour for/to protest against sthg.

clamor [kla'mo(x)] *(pl* -es) *m* clamour *UK,* clamor *US.*

clamoroso, osa [klamo'rozu, ɔza] *adj* clamorous.

clandestino, na [klãndeʃ'tʃinu, na] *adj* clandestine.

clara ['klara] *f* ▷ **claro.**

clarabóia [klara'bɔja] *f* skylight.

clarão [kla'rãw] *(pl* -ões) *m* -1. [de raio, flash] flash. - 2. [claridade] brightness.

clarear [kla'rja(x)] *<> vt* -1. [iluminar] to light up. - 2. [dia, céu] to brighten. *<> vi* -1. [amanhecer] to get light. - 2. [dia, céu] to brighten.

clareira [kla'rejra] *f* [em floresta] glade, clearing.

clareza [kla'reza] *f* clarity.

claridade [klari'dadʒi] *f* [luz] clarity.

clarim [kla'rĩ] *(pl* -ns) *m* bugle.

clarinete [klari'netʃi] *m* clarinet.

clarividente [klarivi'dẽntʃi] *<> adj* -1. [sagaz] wise. - 2. [prudente] cautious. - 3. [vidente] clairvoyant. *<> mf* [vidente] clairvoyant.

claro, ra ['klaru, ra] *adj* -1. [ger] bright. - 2. [límpido, nítido, explícito] clear; **ser** ~ **(que)** to be obvious (that).
→ **claro** *adv* [evidentemente]: **claro!** of course!; ~ **que sim!/que não!** of course!/of course not! *<> m* -1. [em escrita] space. - 2. [em pintura] highlight.
→ **clara f:** ~ **(de ovo)** egg white.
→ **às claras** *loc adv* in broad daylight.
→ **em claro** *loc adv:* **passar a noite em** ~ to have a sleepless night.

clarões [kla'rõjʃ] ▷ **clarão.**

classe ['klasi] *f* -**1**. [ger] class; ~ **média** middle class; ~ **executiva** business class; ~ **turística** tourist class; **primeira** ~ first class. -**2**. [categoria]: **de primeira** ~ first class; **de** ~ classy.

clássico, ca ['klasiku, ka] *adj* -**1**. [ger] classic; **música** ~ classical music. -**2**. [da Antigüidade] classical.
➡ **clássico** *m* [obra-prima] classic.

classificação [klasifika'sãw] (*pl* -ões) *f* -**1**. [ger] classification. -**2**. [qualificação] label. -**3**. [para cinema e TV] rating.

classificado, da [klasifi'kadu, da] <> *adj* classified. <> *m, f* [em concurso, competição] classified entrant.
➡ **classificados** *mpl* JORN [seção] classifieds.

classificar [klasifi'ka(x)] *vt* to classify.
➡ **classificar-se** *vp* -**1**. [ser aprovado] to pass. -**2**. [obter posição de]: ~-**se em primeiro lugar** to be first.

claudicante [klawdʒi'kãntʃi] *adj* [capengante] hobbling.

claustro ['klawʃtru] *m* cloister.

claustrofobia [klawʃtrofo'bia] *f* claustrophobia.

cláusula ['klawzula] *f* clause.

clausura [klaw'zura] *f* -**1**. [recinto] enclosure. -**2**. [vida] seclusion.

clave ['klavi] *f* MÚS clef.

clavícula [kla'vikula] *f* clavicle, collarbone.

clemência [kle'mēnsja] *f* -**1**. [qualidade] leniency. -**2**. [perdão] clemency.

clero ['klɛru] *m* clergy.

clicar [kli'ka(x)] *vi* to click.

clichê [kli'ʃe] *m* -**1**. FOT proof. -**2**. [chavão] cliché. -**3**. [tipográfico] type.

cliente [kli'ẽntʃi] *m* COMPUT client.

clientela [kliẽn'tɛla] *f* -**1**. clientele. -**2**. [de médico] patients (*pl*).

clima ['klima] *m* -**1**. METEOR climate. -**2**. *fam fig* [atmosfera] atmosphere.

clímax ['klimaks] *m inv* -**1**. [ger] climax. -**2**. [auge] peak.

clínico, ca ['kliniku, ka] <> *adj* clinical. <> *m, f* [médico] doctor; ~ **geral** general practitioner, GP.
➡ **clínica** *f* -**1**. [local] clinic. -**2**. [prática] medicine.

clipe ['klipi] *m* -**1**. [videoclipe] clip. -**2**. [para papéis] paper clip.

clitóris [kli'tɔriʃ] *m inv* clitoris.

clonagem [klo'naʒē] (*pl* -ns) *f* BIOL cloning.

clonar [klo'na(x)] *vt* BIOL to clone.

cloro ['klɔru] *m* chlorine.

clorofila [kloro'fila] *f* chlorophyll.

clorofórmio [kloro'fɔxmju] *m* chloroform.

close ['klɔzi] *m* close-up.

CLT (*abrev de* **Consolidação das Leis do Trabalho**) *f* Brazilian legislation regulating the rights and responsibilities of workers.

clube ['klubi] *m* club.

cm (*abrev de* **centímetro**) *m* cm.

CNH (*abrev de* **Carteira Nacional de Habilitação**) *f* driving licence UK, driver's license US.

coação [koa'sãw] *f* force.

coadjuvante [kwadʒu'vãntʃi] <> *adj* back-up; **ator** ~ supporting actor; **criminoso** ~ accomplice. <> *mf* -**1**. CINE, TEATRO, TV supporting role. -**2**. [cúmplice] accomplice.

coador [kwa'do(x)] (*pl* -es) *m* -**1**. [crivo] sieve. -**2**. [de café] filter. -**3**. [para legumes] colander.

coagir [kwa'ʒi(x)] *vt*: ~ **alguém (a fazer algo)** to coerce sb (into doing sthg).

coagulação [kwagula'sãw] (*pl* -ões) *f* [do sangue] clotting.

coagular [kwagu'la(x)] <> *vt* [solidificar] to clot. <> *vi* -**1**. [sangue] to clot. -**2**. [leite] to curdle.
➡ **coagular-se** *vp* -**1**. [sangue] to clot. -**2**. [leite] to curdle.

coágulo ['kwagulu] *m* [de sangue] clot.

coalhado, da [kwa'ʎadu, da] *adj* [leite] curdled.
➡ **coalhada** *f* clabber.

coalhar [kwa'ʎa(x)] <> *vt* to curdle. <> *vi* to curdle.

coalizão [kwali'zãw] (*pl* -ões) *f* coalition.

coar ['kwa(x)] *vt* -**1**. [líquido] to filter. -**2**. [café] to percolate.

cobaia [ko'baja] *f* guinea pig.

cobalto [ko'bawtu] *m* cobalt.

coberto, ta [ko'bɛxtu, ta] <> *pp* ⊳ **cobrir**. <> *adj* covered.
➡ **coberta** *f* -**1**. [colcha, cobertor] bed cover. -**2**. [cobertura] covering. -**3**. [telhado] roofing.

cobertura [kobex'tura] *f* -**1**. [ger] cover; **dar** ~ **a** to cover up. -**2**. [apartamento] penthouse. -**3**. [calda] topping. -**4**. JORN coverage.

cobiça [ko'bisa] *f* greed.

cobiçar [kobi'sa(x)] *vt* to covet.

cobra ['kɔbra] <> *adj fam* [perito] ace. <> *f* -**1**. ZOOL snake. -**2**. *pej* [mau-caráter] snake. <> *mf fam* [perito] ace.

cobrador, ra [kobra'do(x), ra] (*mpl* -es, *fpl* -s) *m, f* -**1**. [recebedor, caixa] debt collector. -**2**. [de ônibus] conductor.

cobrança [ko'brãnsa] *f* -**1**. [de taxa, passagem, ingresso] fee. -**2**. *fig* [exigência] demands (*pl*). -**3**. ESP penalty; ~ **de pênalti** FUT penalty kick.

cobrar [ko'bra(x)] *vt* -**1**. [taxa, passagem, ingresso] to collect. -**2**. [preço] to charge. -**3**. *fig* [promessa, favor] to exact. -**4**. *ESP* to take a penalty; ~ **um pênalti** *FUT* to take a penalty.

cobre ['kɔbri] *m* -**1**. [metal] copper. -**2**. [dinheiro, moeda] coin.

cobrir [ko'bri(x)] *vt* -**1**. [ger] to cover. -**2**. [ocultar] to conceal. -**3**. [envolver] to wrap up. -**4**. [exceder] to exceed. -**5**. *ZOOL* [fêmea] to breed.

⇌ **cobrir-se** *vp* -**1**. [ocultar-se, resguardar-se] to hide o.s. -**2**. [com cobertor] to cover o.s.

cocada [ko'kada] *f* coconut ice *UK*, coconut candy *US*.

cocaína [koka'ina] *f* cocaine.

coçar [ko'sa(x)] <> *vt* to scratch. <> *vi* to itch.

⇌ **coçar-se** *vp* to scratch o.s.

cocar [ko'ka(x)] *m* crest.

cócegas ['kɔsigaʃ] *fpl*: **fazer** ~ **em alguém** to tickle sb; **sentir** ~ to feel itchy.

coceira [ko'sejra] *f* [sensação] itch.

cochichar [koʃi'ʃa(x)] *vi* to whisper.

cochilar [koʃi'la(x)] *vi* -**1**. [dormir um pouco] to take a nap. -**2**. [dormitar] to doze off.

cochilo [ko'ʃilu] *m* nap; **tirar um** ~ to take a nap.

coco ['koku] *m* -**1**. [fruta] coconut. -**2**. *fam fig* [cabeça] nut.

cocô [ko'ko] *m fam* poo.

cócoras ['kɔkoraʃ] ⇌ **de cócoras** *loc adv* squatting.

codificação [kodʒiʃika'sãw] (*pl* -ões) *f COMPUT* coding.

código ['kɔdʒigu] *m* [ger] code; ~ **de barras** bar code; ~ **civil** civil code.

codorna [ko'dɔxna] *f* quail.

co-editor, ra [koedʒi'to(x), ra] (*mpl* -res, *fpl* -ras) *m, f* co-editor.

coeficiente [koefi'sjẽntʃi] *m* -**1**. *MAT* coefficient. -**2**. *fig* [fator] factor.

coelho ['kweʎu] *m* rabbit.

coentro ['kwẽntru] *m* coriander.

coerção [koex'sãw] *f* coercion.

coercivo, va [koex'sivu, va], **coercitivo, va** [koexsi'tʃivu, va] *adj* coercive.

coerência [koe'rẽnsja] *f* coherence.

coerente [koe'rẽntʃi] *adj* coherent.

coesão [koe'zãw] *f* cohesion.

COFINS (*abrev de* **Contribuição para o Financiamento da Seguridade Social**) *m Brazilian employer's social security contributions, based on profits.*

cofre ['kɔfri] *m* safe.

cofre-forte [ˌkɔfri'fɔxtʃi] (*pl* **cofres-fortes**) *m* strongroom.

cogitar [koʒi'ta(x)] <> *vt* -**1**. [considerar] to consider. -**2**. [planejar]: ~ **fazer algo** to consider doing sthg. <> *vi* [refletir] to deliberate.

cogumelo [kogu'mɛlu] *m* [comestível] mushroom.

COI (*abrev de* **Comitê Olímpico Internacional**) *m* IOC.

coibir [koj'bi(x)] *vt* to restrain; ~ **alguém de fazer algo** to restrain sb from doing sthg.

coice ['kojsil *m* -**1**. [de animal] backward kick; **dar um** ~ **em** *fig* to give sb a kick in the teeth. -**2**. [de arma] butt.

coincidência [koĩnsi'dẽnsja] *f* coincidence.

coincidente [koĩnsi'dẽntʃi] *adj* coincidental.

coincidentemente [koĩnsidẽntʃi'mẽntʃi] *adv* coincidentally.

coincidir [koĩnsi'di(x)] *vi* -**1**. [eventos, datas] to coincide. -**2**. [concordar]: ~ **(em)** to agree (upon).

coisa ['kojza] *f* -**1**. [ger] thing. -**2**. [assunto] topic. -**3**. *loc*: **ele não diz** ~ **com** ~ he talks absolute rubbish; **que** ~! goodness me!; **ser uma** ~ [ser terrível] to be dreadful.

⇌ **coisa de** *loc adv* roughly.

coitado, da [koj'tadu, da] <> *adj* [pessoa] wretched; **coitado!** poor thing! <> *m, f* poor wretch.

coito ['kojtu] *m* sex; ~ **anal** anal sex.

cola ['kɔla] *f* -**1**. [adesivo] glue. -**2**. *fam EDUC* [ato] cribbing. -**3**. *fam EDUC* [objeto] crib.

colaboração [kolabora'sãw] (*pl* -ões) *f* -**1**. [ajuda] cooperation. -**2**. [em jornal etc.] freelance work.

colaborador, ra [kolabora'do(x), ra] *m, f* -**1**. [ajudante] collaborator. -**2**. [de jornal etc.] freelance.

colaborar [kolabo'ra(x)] *vi* -**1**. [ajudar] to cooperate; ~ **em algo/com alguém** to cooperate on sthg with sb. -**2**. [em jornal etc.]: ~ **em algo** to freelance on sthg.

colagem [ko'laʒẽ] (*pl* -ns) *f* -**1**. [ato] glueing. -**2**. *ARTE* collage.

colante [ko'lãntʃi] *adj* [roupa] clinging.

colapso [ko'lapsu] *m* collapse; ~ **cardíaco** heart failure; ~ **nervoso** nervous breakdown.

colar [ko'la(x)] (*pl* -res [-riʃ]) <> *vt* to glue, to stick. <> *vi* to stick. <> *m* necklace.

⇌ **colar de** *v* + *prep* to crib from.

colarinho [kola'riɲu] *m* -**1**. [de camisa] collar. -**2**. *fam* [de cerveja] head; **com/ sem** ~ with/without a head.

colateral [kolate'raw] (*pl* -ais) *adj* collateral.

colcha ['kowʃa] *f* bedspread.

colchão [kow'ʃãw] (*pl* -ões) *m* mattress.

colcheia [kow'ʃeja] *f* MÚS quaver UK, eighth note US.

colchete [kow'ʃetʃi] *m* -1. [de roupa] hook; ~ **de gancho** hook and eye; ~ **de pressão** press stud. -2. [sinal] bracket.

colchões [kow'ʃõjʃ] *pl* ▷ **colchão**.

colchonete [kowʃo'nɛtʃi] *m* bolster.

coleção [kole'sãw] (*pl* -ões) *f* collection.

colecionador, ra [kolesjona'do(x), ral (*mpl* -res, *fpl* -s) *m, f* collector.

colecionar [kolesjo'na(x)] *vt* to collect.

colega [ko'lɛga] *mf* -1. [amigo] friend. -2. [de escola] schoolfriend. -3. [de trabalho] colleague.

colegial [kole'ʒjaw] (*pl* -ais) ◇ *adj* school (*antes de subst*). ◇ *mf* schoolboy (*f* schoolgirl).

colégio [ko'lɛʒju] *m* [escola] school.

coleira [ko'lejra] *f* dog collar.

cólera ['kɔlera] ◇ *f* [ira] anger. ◇ *m* MED cholera.

colérico, ca [ko'lɛriku, ka] ◇ *adj* [irado] angry. ◇ *m, f* MED cholera victim.

colesterol [kolɛʃte'rɔw] *m* cholesterol.

coleta [ko'lɛta] *f* collection; ~ **de dados** fact-gathering; ~ **seletiva** waste segregation.

coletar [kole'ta(x)] *vt* to collect.

colete [ko'letʃi] *m* waistcoat UK, vest US; ~ **salva-vidas** life jacket.

coletivo, va [kole'tʃivu, va] *adj* -1. [de muitos] collective. -2. [transporte, banheiro] public.
◆ **coletivo** *m* -1. [ônibus] public transport. -2. [futebol] trials. -3. [ling] collective noun.

coletor, ra [kole'to(x), ra] *m, f* [de impostos] collector.

colheita [ko'ʎejta] *f* -1. [ger] harvest. -2. [produto] crop.

colher [ko'ʎe(x)] (*pl* -es [ko'ʎeriʃ]) ◇ *f* -1. [talher] spoon; ~ **de chá** teaspoon; ~ **de sobremesa** dessertspoon; ~ **de sopa** tablespoon. -2. [ferramenta]: ~ **de pedreiro** trowel. ◇ *vt* -1. [fruta, verdura, safra] to pick. -2. [dados] to gather.

colherada [koʎe'rada] *f* spoonful.

colibri [koli'bri] *m* hummingbird.

cólica ['kɔlika] *f* colic.

colidir [koli'dʒi(x)] *vi* [chocar-se] to collide; ~ **com/contra** to collide with/against.

coligação [koliga'sãw] (*pl* -ões) *f* coalition.

coligir [koli'ʒi(x)] *vt* to compile.

colina [ko'lina] *f* hill.

colírio [ko'lirju] *m* eyewash.

colisão [koli'zãw] (*pl* -ões) *f* collision.

collant [ko'lã] *m* tights (*pl*).

colméia [kow'mɛja] *f* beehive.

colo ['kɔlu] *m* -1. [ger] neck. -2. [regaço] lap.

colocação [koloka'sãw] (*pl* -ões) *f* -1. [ato] fitting. -2. [posição, emprego] position. -3. [em concurso, competição] place. -4. [observação] observation.

colocar [kolo'ka(x)] *vt* -1. [ger] to place. -2. [dar emprego a] to employ. -3. [situar-no espaço] to site. -4. [instalar - ar-condicionado] to install; [- pneu] to fit; [- carpete] to lay; [- cortina] to hang. -5. [levantar] to raise.
◆ **colocar-se** *vp* -1. [pôr-se] to position o.s. -2. [em concurso, competição] to be placed. -3. [imaginar-se]: **coloque-se no meu lugar** put yourself in my place.

Colômbia [ko'lõbja] *n* Colombia.

colombiano, na [kolõn'bjãnu, na] ◇ *adj* Colombian. ◇ *m, f* Colombian.

cólon ['kɔlõ] *m* ANAT colon.

colônia [ko'lonja] *f* -1. [ger] colony. -2. [para crianças]: ~ **de férias** summer camp. -3. [perfume] cologne; **água de** ~ eau de cologne.

colonial [kolo'njaw] (*pl* -ais) *adj* colonial.

colonização [koloniza'sãw] *f* colonization.

colonizador, ra [koloniza'do(x), ra] ◇ *adj* [nação, esforço] colonizing. ◇ *m, f* [pessoa] settler.

colono, na [ko'lɔnu, na] *m, f* -1. [povoador] colonist. -2. [cultivador] smallholder.

coloquial [kolo'kjaw] (*pl* -ais) *adj* colloquial.

coloquialismo [kolokja'liʒmul *m* familiar tone.

colóquio [ko'lɔkju] *m* -1. [congresso] symposium. -2. *ant* [conversa] conversation.

colorido, da [kolo'ridu, da] *adj* multicoloured UK, multicolored US.
◆ **colorido** *m* colour UK, color US.

colorir [kolo'ri(x)] *vt* -1. [dar cor a] to colour UK, to color US. -2. *fig* [avivar] to brighten.

coluna [ko'luna] *f* -1. [ger] column; ~ **social** society column. -2. [pilar] pillar. -3. ANAT : ~ **vertebral** spinal column.

colunável [kolu'navew] (*pl* -eis) ◇ *adj* [pessoa, festa] glamorous. ◇ *mf* [celebridade] celebrity.

colunista [kolu'niʃta] *mf* columnist.

com [kõ] *prep* -1. with; **ela mora** ~ **um amigo** she lives with a friend; ~ **quem você vai?** who are you going with? -2.

[relativo a modo] with; ~ **cuidado** with care; [relativo a instrumento] with; **ela escreve** ~ **a mão direita** she writes with her right hand; ~ **o tempo, a mulher conseguiu superar o trauma** with time, the woman managed to overcome the trauma **- 3.** [indica causa] with, because of; **só** ~ **muito esforço é que ele conseguiu** only with a lot of effort did he manage to do it; **estar** ~ **dor de cabeça** to have a headache; **estar** ~ **fome** to be hungry; **estar** ~ **pressa** to be in a hurry. **- 4.** [apesar de] in spite of; ~ **todo esse trabalho ele ainda encontra tempo para estudar** in spite of all that work, he still finds time to study; **você vai jogar bola** ~ **chuva?** are you going to play football in the rain?; ~ **86 anos, ele continua cheio de energia** at 86, he is still full of energy. **- 5.** *(em loc prep)* with; ~ **relação a** in relation to; ~ **vistas a** with an aim to; **de acordo** ~ in accordance with; **em parceria** ~ in partnership with.

coma ['koma] *m* MED coma.

comadre [ko'madri] *f* **- 1.** [madrinha] *a godmother in relation to her godchild's parents; a child's mother in relation to its godparents.* **- 2.** [amiga] friend. **- 3.** [urinol] bedpan.

comandante [komãn'dãntʃi] *mf* **- 1.** MIL, NÁUT commander. **- 2.** [dirigente] leader.

comandar [komãn'da(x)] *vt* **- 1.** MIL, NÁUT to command. **- 2.** [dirigir] to head.

comando [ko'mãndu] *m* [ger] command.

combate [kõn'batʃi] *m* **- 1.** [luta, oposição] fight. **- 2.** [bélico] skirmish; **fora de** ~ *fig* flat on one's back.

combater [kõnba'te(x)] <> *vt* [lutar contra, opor-se a] to struggle. <> *vi* [belicamente] to fight.

combinação [kõnbina'sãw] *(pl* -ões) *f* **- 1.** [ger] combination. **- 2.** QUÍM compound. **- 3.** [acordo, plano] agreement. **- 4.** [peça de roupa] slip.

combinar [kõnbi'na(x)] <> *vt* **- 1.** [associar, reunir] to combine. **- 2.** [encontro, jantar] to fix; **combinado!** agreed! **- 3.** [plano, fuga] to plan. <> *vi* **- 1.** [planejar]: **combinamos de ir ao cinema** we fixed up to go to the cinema. **- 2.** [cores, roupas] to match; ~ **com algo** to go with sthg.

comboio [kõn'boju] *m* **- 1.** [ger] convoy. **- 2.** FERRO train.

combustível [kõnbuʃ'tʃivɛw] *(pl* -eis) <> *adj* combustible. <> *m* fuel.

começar [kome'sa(x)] <> *vt* to start. <> *vi* to begin, to start; ~ **a fazer algo** to start doing sthg, to start to do sthg; ~ **por** to begin with.

começo [ko'mesu] *m* beginning.

comédia [ko'mɛdʒja] *f* comedy.

comedido, da [kome'dʒidu, da] *adj* **- 1.** [moderado] moderate. **- 2.** [prudente] prudent.

comemoração [komemora'sãw] *(pl* -ões) *f* celebration.

comemorar [komemo'ra(x)] *vt* to celebrate.

comentar [komẽn'ta(x)] *vt* **- 1.** [fato, festa, incidente] to comment on. **- 2.** [observar]: ~ **que** to remark that. **- 3.** ESP [partida] to commentate.

comentário [komẽn'tarju] *m* commentary; **fazer um** ~ to do a commentary.

comentarista [komẽnta'riʃta] *mf* commentator; ~ **esportivo** sports commentator; ~ **político** political commentator.

comer [ko'me(x)] *(pl* -es) <> *vt* **- 1.** [alimentar-se de] to eat. **- 2.** *fig* [suprimir] to swallow. **- 3.** *fig* [corroer] to corrode. **- 4.** *fig* [consumir] to devour. **- 5.** [em damas, xadrez] to take. **- 6.** *vulg fig* [sexualmente] to fuck. <> *vi* [alimentar-se] to eat; **dar de** ~ **a alguém** to feed sb.

comercial [komex'sjaw] *(pl* -ais) <> *adj* commercial. <> *m* [anúncio] advertisement, commercial.

comercialização [komexsjaliza'sãw] *(pl* -ões) *f* commercialization.

comercializar [komexsjali'za(x)] *vt* to market.

comerciante [komex'sjãntʃi] *mf* businessman (*f* businesswoman).

comerciar [komex'sja(x)] *vi* to trade.

comércio [ko'mɛxsju] *m* **- 1.** [compra e venda] trade; ~ **eletrônico** e-commerce. **- 2.** [tráfico] trafficking. **- 3.** [estabelecimento] premises. **- 4.** [mercado comercial] business. **- 5.** *fig* [troca de idéias, influências] exchange.

comes ['kɔmiʃ] *mpl fam*: ~ **e bebes** food and drink.

comestíveis [komeʃ'tʃiveiʃ] *mpl* comestibles.

comestível [komeʃ'tʃivɛw] *(pl* -eis) *adj* edible.

cometa [ko'meta] *m* comet.

cometer [kome'te(x)] *vt* to commit.

comichão [komi'ʃãw] *(pl* -ões) *f* itch.

comício [ko'misju] *m* rally.

cômico, co ['komiku, ka] <> *adj* comical. <> *m, f* [comediante] comedian.

comida [ko'mida] *f* **- 1.** [alimento] food. **- 2.** [refeição] meal; ~ **caseira** home cooking.

comigo [ko'migu] *pron*: **ela não fala** ~ she won't speak to me; **o livro dele está** ~ I've got his book; **matemática é** ~

compelir

mesmo maths is my thing; **ela acenou, mas pensei que não era** ~ she nodded, but I thought that she didn't agree with me; **isto não é justo, pensei** ~ that isn't fair, I thought to myself; **deixa** ~ **!** leave it with me!

comilão, lona [komi'lãw, lona] (*mpl* -ões, *fpl* -s) <> *adj* gluttonous. <> *m, f* glutton.

cominho [ko'miɲu] *m* cumin.

comiserar-se [komize'raxsi] *vp* to feel pity; ~ **(de)** to feel pity for.

comissão [komi'sãw] (*pl* -ões) *f* -1. [comitê] committee. -2. [gratificação] commission.

comissário, ria [komi'sarju, rja] *m, f* agent; ~ **de bordo** air steward (*f* air stewardess).

comissionar [komisjo'na(x)] *vt* -1. [encarregar] to commission. -2. [confiar] to entrust.

comitê [komi'te] *m* committee.

comitiva [komi'tʃiva] *f* retinue.

como ['komu] <> *adj* as. -2. [de que modo] how; ~ **?** [o que você disse?] I'm sorry?; ~ **assim?** how do you mean? -3. [comparativo]: **ser** ~ **algo/alguém** to be like sthg/sb. -4. [exclamativo]: **como!** what!; **e** ~ **!** *fam* and how!; ~ **não!** [pois não] of course! <> *conj* -1. [porque] because. ~ **2.** [conforme] as.

➤ **como que** *loc adv*: ~ **que por um golpe de mágica, tudo desapareceu** as if by magic, everything disappeared.

➤ **como quer que** *loc conj* however.

➤ **como se** *loc conj* as if.

comoção [komo'sãw] (*pl* -ões) *f* -1. [abalo] shock. -2. [revolta] unrest.

cômoda ['komoda] *f* chest of drawers.

comodidade [komod3i'dad3i] *f* -1. [conforto] comfort. -2. [conveniência] convenience.

comodismo [komo'd3i3mu] *m* indolence.

comodista [komo'd3iʃta] <> *adj* passive. <> *mf* passive person.

cômodo, da ['komodu, da] *adj* -1. [confortável] comfortable. -2. [conveniente] appropriate.

➤ **cômodo** *m* [aposento] room.

comovente [komo'vẽntʃi], **comovedor, ra** [komove'do(x), ra] *adj* moving.

comover [komo've(x)] <> *vt* to move. <> *vi* to be moving.

➤ **comover-se** *vp* to be moved.

comovido, da [komo'vidu, da] *adj* moved.

compactador [kõmpak'tado(x)] *m* COMPUT [file] compressor.

compactar [kõmpzk'ta(x)] *vt* COMPUT: ~ **arquivos** to compress files.

compacto, ta [kõm'paktu, ta] *adj* -1. [pequeno] compact. -2. [denso, comprimido] dense.

➤ **compacto** *m* [disco] compact disc, CD.

compadecer-se [kõnpade'sexsi] *vp*: ~ **de** to take pity on.

compadecido, da [kõnpade'sidu, da] *adj* compassionate.

compadre [kõn'padri] *m* -1. [padrinho do filho] *a godfather in relation to his godchild's parents* ou *a child's father in relation to its godparents*. -2. *fam* [companheiro] companion.

compaixão [kõnpaj'ʃãw] *f* -1. [piedade] compassion. -2. [misericórdia] mercy.

companheirismo [kõnpaɲej'ri3mu] *m* companionship.

companheiro, ra [kõnpa'ɲejru, ra] *m, f* -1. [que acompanha] companion. -2. [colega] colleague. -3. [marido, namorado] partner. -4. *fam* [amigo] mate.

companhia [kõnpa'ɲia] *f* [ger] company; **em** ~ **de** in the company of; **fazer** ~ **a alguém** to keep sb company.

comparação [kõnpara'sãw] (*pl* -ões) *f* comparison.

comparar [kõnpa'ra(x)] *vt*: ~ **algo/ alguém (com)** to compare sthg/sb (with).

comparável [kõnpa'ravew] (*pl* -eis) *adj* comparable.

comparecer [kõnpare'se(x)] *vi*: ~ **(a)** to appear (at).

comparecimento [kõnparesi'mẽntu] *m* presence.

comparsa [kõn'paxsa] *mf* -1. [cúmplice] accomplice. -2. TEATRO extra.

compartilhar [kõmpaxtʃi'ʎa(x)] <> *vt* [partilhar] to share. <> *vi* [participar]: ~ **de** to share in.

compartimento [kõnpaxtʃi'mẽntu] *m* -1. [divisão] compartment. -2. [aposento] room.

compartir [kõnpax'tʃi(x)] *vt & vi* = **compartilhar.**

compassado, da [kõnpa'sadu, da] *adj* -1. [pausado] measured. -2. [cadenciado] rhythmic. -3. [comedido] moderate.

compassivo, va [kõnpa'sivu, va] *adj* compassionate.

compasso [kõn'pasu] *m* -1. [instrumento] pair of compasses. -2. MÚS beat. -3. [ritmo] time.

compatível [kõnpa'tʃivew] (*pl* -eis) *adj* compatible.

compatriota [kõnpatri'ɔta] *mf* compatriot.

compelir [kõnpe'li(x)] *vt*: ~ **alguém a fazer algo** to force sb to do sthg.

compêndio [kõn'pẽndʒiu] *m* **-1.** [livro] textbook. **-2.** [síntese] summary.

compensação [kõnpẽnsa'sãw] (*pl* **-ões**) *f* **-1.** [reparação] compensation; **em ~** to make up for it. **-2.** [equilíbrio] balance. **-3.** [de cheque] clearance.

compensado [kõnpẽn'sadu] *m* [madeira] plywood.

compensar [kõnpẽn'sa(x)] <> *vt* **-1.** [dar reparo a] to make up for. **-2.** [equilibrar] to compensate for. **-3.** [cheque] to clear. <> *vi* [valer a pena] to pay.

competência [kõnpe'tẽnsja] *f* **-1.** [habilidade] competence. **-2.** [responsabilidade] responsibility.

competente [kõnpe'tẽntʃi] *adj* **-1.** [hábil] competent. **-2.** [responsável] responsible.

competição [kõnpetʃi'sãw] (*pl* **-ões**) *f* **-1.** [disputa, concorrência] competition. **-2.** *ESP* [prova] contest.

competidor, ra [kõnpetʃi'do(x), ra] *m, f ESP* competitor.

competir [kõnpe'tʃi(x)] *vi* to compete.

compilação [kõnpila'sãw] *f* compilation.

compilar [kõnpi'la(x)] *vt* to compile.

complacente [kõnpla'sẽntʃi] *adj* complacent.

complementar [kõnplemẽn'ta(x)] (*pl* **-es**) <> *adj* additional. <> *vt* to complement.

complemento [kõnple'mẽntu] *m* **-1.** [acréscimo] addition. **-2.** *GRAM* object.

completamente [kõm,pleta'mẽntʃi] *adv* completely.

completar [kõnple'ta(x)] *vt* **-1.** [terminar] to complete. **-2.** [idade] to reach. **-3.** [com gasolina *etc.*] to fill up.

completo, ta [kõn'plɛtu, ta] *adj* **-1.** [trabalho] finished. **-2.** [tanque] full.
◆ **por completo** *loc adv* [inteiramente] completely.

complexo, xa [kõm'plɛksu, sa] *adj* complex.
◆ **complexo** *m* complex.

complicado, da [kõnpli'kadu, da] *adj* complicated.

complicar [kõnpli'ka(x)] *vt* [tornar complexo] to complicate.

complô [kõn'plo] *m* conspiracy.

componente [kõnpo'nẽntʃi] *m* component.

compor [kõn'po(x)] <> *vt* **-1.** [formar, integrar] to comprise. **-2.** [música, versos] to compose. **-3.** [discurso, livro] to write. **-4.** [enfeitar] to arrange. **-5.** *POL* [aliança, acordo] to constitute. **-6.** *TIP* to typeset. <> *vi* **-1.** [música] to compose. **-2.** *TIP* to typeset.

◆ **compor-se** *vp* **-1.** [ser integrado por]: **~-se de** to consist of. **-2.** [controlar-se] to compose o.s.

comporta [kõn'pɔxta] *f* floodgate.

comportamento [kõnpoxta'mẽntu] *m* **-1.** [de pessoa] behaviour. **-2.** [reação] reaction.

comportar [kõnpox'ta(x)] *vt* **-1.** [suportar] to hold. **-2.** [conter] to contain.
◆ **comportar-se** *vp* **-1.** [pessoa] to behave. **-2.** [reagir] to behave.

composição [kõnpozi'sãw] (*pl* **-ões**) *f* **-1.** [ger] composition. **-2.** [de trem, metrô] formation. **-3.** *TIP* typesetting.

compositor, ra [kõnpozi'to(x), ra] (*mpl* **-es**, *fpl* **-s**) *m, f MÚS* composer.

composto, ta [kõn'poʃtu, ta] <> *pp* ▷ **compor.** <> *adj* composed.
◆ **composto** *m QUÍM* compound.

compostura [kõnpoʃ'tura] *f* composure.

compota [kõn'pɔta] *f* stewed fruit, fruit compote.

compra ['kõnpra] *f* **-1.** [ato] purchase; **fazer ~s** to shop. **-2.** [coisa comprada] shopping.

comprar [kõn'pra(x)] *vt* **-1.** [adquirir] to buy. **-2.** *fig* [subornar] to bribe.

compreender [kõnprjẽn'de(x)] *vt* **-1.** [entender] to understand. **-2.** [abranger] to comprise.

compreensão [kõnprjẽ'sãw] *f* **-1.** [entendimento intelectual] comprehension. **-2.** [aceitação] understanding. **-3.** [percepção] realization.

compreensivo, va [kõnprjẽ'sivu, va] *adj* **-1.** [pessoa, atitude] understanding. **-2.** [medida] comprehensive.

compressor, ra [kõnpre'so(x), ra] *adj* ▷ **rolo.**

comprido, da [kõn'pridu, da] *adj* **-1.** [longo] long. **-2.** [alto] tall.

comprimento [kõnpri'mẽntu] *m* length; **três metros de ~** three metres in length, three metres long.

comprimido, da [kõnpri'midu, da] *adj* compressed.
◆ **comprimido** *m* tablet.

comprimir [kõnpri'mi(x)] *vt* **-1.** [reduzir sob pressão - ar, volume] to compress; [- barriga] to pull in. **-2.** [apertar] to squeeze.

comprometer [kõnprome'te(x)] *vt* **-1.** [ger] to compromise. **-2.** [empenhar] to commit.
◆ **comprometer-se** *vp* [assumir compromisso]: **~-se (com)** to make a commitment (to).

comprometido, da [kõnprome'tʃidu, da] *adj* **-1.** [ocupado] busy. **-2.** [amorosamente] engaged.

compromisso [kõnpro'misu] m -1. [encontro etc.] appointment. -2. [promessa] promise. -3. [obrigação] obligation; **sem ~** under no obligation. -4. [acordo] agreement. -5. [namoro, noivado] engagement.

comprovante [kõnpro'vantʃi] <> adj confirming. <> m receipt.

comprovar [kõnpro'va(x)] vt to confirm.

compulsão [kõnpuw'sãw] (pl -ões) f compulsion.

compulsivo, va [kõnpuw'sivu, va] adj compulsive.

compulsório, ria [kõnpuw'sɔrju, rja] adj compulsory.

computação [kõnputa'sãw] f -1. [ato] computation. -2. [ciência, curso] computing.

computador [kõnputa'do(x)] (pl -es) m computer.

computadorizar [kõnputadori'za(x)] vt to computerize.

computar [kõnpu'ta(x)] vt -1. [contar] to count. -2. [calcular] to compute, to calculate. -3. [incluir] to include.

comum [ko'mũ] (pl -ns) <> adj -1. [ordinário] ordinary. -2. [mútuo] mutual; **ter algo em ~** to have sthg in common. -3. [usual] common. <> m [usual] usual thing; **o ~ é ficarmos em casa aos domingos** we usually stay at home on Sundays; **fora do ~** [extraordinário] out of the ordinary.

comungar [komũ'ga(x)] vi -1. RELIG to receive Communion. -2. fig [partilhar]: **~ de algo** to share sthg.

comunhão [komu'ɲãw] (pl -ões) f -1. [união] unity; **~ de bens** [em matrimônio] joint ownership of property. -2. RELIG Communion.

comunicação [komunika'sãw] (pl -ões) f -1. [ato] communication. -2. [ciência] communications (sg). -3. [mensagem] message. -4. [em congresso, simpósio] speech. -5. [ligação] link.

comunicar [komuni'ka(x)] vt -1. [informar sobre]: **~ algo a alguém** to inform sb of sthg. -2. [ligar] to link.

  comunicar-se vp -1. [dialogar, entender-se] to communicate. -2. [entrar em contato]: **~-se com** to contact.

comunicativo, va [komunika'tʃivu, va] adj communicative.

comunidade [komuni'dadʒi] f community; **Comunidade Européia** European Community.

comunismo [komu'niʒmu] m communism.

comunista [komu'niʃta] <> adj communist. <> mf communist.

comunitário, ria [komuni'tarju, rja] adj community.

concatenação [kõnkatena'sãw] (pl -ões) f [encadeamento] (close) linkage.

côncavo, va ['kõnkavu, va] adj concave.

conceber [kõnse'be(x)] <> vt [gerar] to conceive. <> vi [engravidar] to conceive.

conceder [kõnse'de(x)] vt [dar, outorgar] to concede.

conceito [kõn'sejtu] m -1. [idéia] concept. -2. [opinião] opinion. -3. [reputação] reputation. -4. EDUC [nota] grade.

conceituação [kõnsejtua'sãw] (pl -ões) f -1. [definição] conceptualization. -2. [avaliação] rating.

conceituado, da [kõsej'twadu, da] adj respected.

concentração [kõnsẽntra'sãw] (pl -ões) f -1. [ger] concentration. -2. ESP athletic briefing and training usually the day before an important event.

concentrado, da [kõsẽn'tradu, da] adj -1. [ger] concentrated. -2. [centralizado] centralized. -3. [aglomerado] gathered together.

  concentrado m [substância] concentrate.

concentrar [kõnsẽn'tra(x)] vt -1. [ger] to concentrate. -2. [centralizar] to centralize. -3. [aglomerar] to bring together, to mass.

  concentrar-se vp -1. [aglomerar-se] to mass. -2. [pessoa, atenção, esforço]: **~-se (em algo)** to concentrate (on sthg).

concepção [kõnsep'sãw] (pl -ões) f -1. [geração] conception. -2. [conceito] concept. -3. [opinião] opinion.

concernente [kõnsex'nẽntʃi] adj: **~ a** concerning.

concernir [kõnsex'ni(x)] vi: **~ a** to concern; **no que me concerne, ...** as far as I'm concerned, ...

concerto [kõn'sextu] m MÚS concert.

concessão [kõnse'sãw] (pl -ões) f -1. [ger] concession. -2. [entrega - de empréstimo, licença etc.] granting; [- de prêmio] awarding. -3. [permissão] permission.

concessionário, ria [kõnsesjo'narju, rja] m, f concessionaire.

  concessionária f [empresa] agency.

concha ['kõnʃa] f -1. [de molusco] shell. -2. [para líquidos] ladle.

conchavo [kõn'ʃavu] m conspiracy.

conciliação [kõnsilja'sãw] (pl -ões) f reconciliation.

conciliador, ra [kõnsilja'do(x), ra] <> adj conciliatory. <> m, f [pessoa] conciliator.

conciliar [kõnsi'lja(x)] vt to reconcile.

concílio [kõn'silju] m RELIG council.

concisão [kõnsi'sãw] f concision.

conciso, sa [kõn'sizu, za] adj concise.

conclamar [kõnkla'ma(x)] vt -1. [bradar] to shout. -2. [aclamar] to acclaim. -3. [convocar]: ~ alguém a fazer algo to incite sb to do sthg.

concluir [kõŋklu'i(x)] vt -1. [terminar] to conclude. -2. [deduzir] to deduce.

conclusão [kõŋklu'zãw] (pl -ões) f [ger] conclusion; **chegar a uma** ~ [chegar a uma dedução] to reach a conclusion; [chegar a um acordo] to come to an agreement; ~: fam [resultado] upshot.

conclusivo, va [kõŋklu'zivu, va] adj conclusive.

concordância [kõŋkox'dãnsja] f agreement.

concordar [kõŋkox'da(x)] <> vt: ~ que to agree that. <> vi to agree; ~ com algo/alguém to agree with sthg/sb; ~ em fazer algo to agree to do sthg; não concordo! I disagree!

concorrência [kõŋko'xẽnsja] f -1. [ger] competition. -2. fig [licitação] tender.

concorrente [kõŋko'xẽntʃi] adj -1. [competidor] competitor. -2. [candidato] candidate.

concorrer [kõŋko'xe(x)] vi [ger] to compete; ~ com alguém to compete with sb; ~ a algo [ger] to apply for sthg; POL to be running for sthg.

concretizar [kõŋkreti'za(x)] vt to realize.
◆ **concretizar-se** vp [sonho, projeto, anseio] to be realized.

concreto, ta [kõŋ'krɛtu, ta] adj [sólido] concrete.
◆ **concreto** m concrete.

concretude [kõŋkre'tudʒi] f concrete nature.

concupiscente [kõŋkupis'sẽntʃi] adj materialistic.

concursado, da [kõŋkux'sadu, da] <> adj referring to a person who has been successful in a competitive examination giving access to a position, particularly in public office.

concurso [kõŋ'kuxsu] m -1. [exame] competitive examination. -2. [sorteio] lottery.

condado [kõn'dadu] m county.

condão [kõn'dãw] m ⊳ **varinha.**

conde, dessa ['kõndʒi, dʒesa] m, f count (f countess).

condecorar [kõndeko'ra(x)] vt to decorate.

condenação [kõndena'sãw] (pl -ões) f -1. JUR conviction. -2. [reprovação] condemnation.

condenar [kõnde'na(x)] vt -1. [ger] to condemn; ~ alguém a algo to sentence sb to sthg. -2. JUR [declarar culpado] to find guilty. -3. fig [interditar] to condemn. -4. fig [desenganar] to disillusion; ~ um paciente to give up hope of saving a patient.

condensação [kõndẽnsa'sãw] (pl -ões) f condensation.

condensar [kõndẽn'sa(x)] vt to condense.
◆ **condensar-se** vp to condense.

condescendente [kõndesẽn'dẽntʃi] adj condescending.

condescender [kõndesẽn'de(x)] vi to acquiesce; ~ a ou em to agree to.

condessa [kõn'desa] f ⊳ **conde.**

condição [kõndʒi'sãw] (pl -ões) f -1. [ger] position. -2. [exigência] condition; **com a** ~ **de que** on condition that. -3. [natureza] nature.
◆ **condições** fpl -1. [ger] conditions; **condições próprias/impróprias de banho** [praia] suitable/unsuitable conditions for swimming; **condições de trabalho** working conditions. -2. [estado] condition (sg); **em boas condições (de uso)** in good (working) order. -3. [capacidade] requirement; **estar em condições de fazer algo** to be able do sthg. -4. [meios] means.

condimento [kõndʒi'mẽntul] m condiment.

condizer [kõndʒi'ze(x)] vi: ~ com to match.

condomínio [kõndo'minju] m -1. [conjunto de casas, apartamentos] condominium. -2. [pagamento] service charge.

condução [kõndu'sãw] (pl -ões) f -1. [ato] transportation. -2. [transporte] transport. -3. [ônibus] bus. -4. FÍSICA conduction.

conduta [kõn'duta] f conduct, behaviour.

conduto [kõn'dutul] m -1. [tubo] tube. -2. [cano] pipe. -3. [canal] channel.

condutor, ra [kõndu'to(x), ra] (mpl -es, fpl -s) <> adj [de eletricidade] conductor. <> m, f [de veículo] driver.
◆ **condutor** m ELETR conductor.

conduzir [kõndu'zi(x)] <> vt -1. [levar]: ~ algo/alguém (a) to transport sthg/sb (to). -2. [empresa, equipe] to lead. -3. ELETR to conduct. <> vi [levar]: ~ a to lead to.

cone ['koni] m cone.

conectar [konek'ta(x)] vt to connect.
◆ **conectar-se** vp to connect; ~ à internet to connect to the Internet.

conectividade [konektʃivi'dadʒi] f connectivity.

cônego ['konegu] *m* canon.

conexão [konek'sãw] (*pl* -ões) *f* -1. [ger & COMPUT] connection; ~ **discada** OU dial-up dial-up connection; ~ **a cabo** cable connection. -2. [nexo] link. -3. [relação] relationship.

confecção [kõnfek'sãw] (*pl* -ões) *f* -1. [ger] making. -2. [fábrica de roupas] clothing factory.

confeccionar [kõnfeksjo'na(x)] *vt* [fabricar, fazer] to make.

confederação [kõnfedera'sãw] (*pl*-ões) *f* confederation.

confeitar [kõnfej'ta(x)] *vt* [bolo] to sugarcoat.

confeitaria [kõnfejta'ria] *f* cake shop.

confeiteiro, ra [kõnfej'tejru, ra] *m, f* confectioner.

conferência [kõnfe'rẽsja] *f* -1. [verificação] check. -2. [palestra] lecture.

conferir [kõnfe'ri(x)] <> *vt* -1. [verificar] to check. -2. [cotejar, comparar] to compare. -3. [dar]: ~ **algo a alguém/algo** to invest sb/sthg with sthg. -4. [título, encargo] to confer. <> *vi* -1. [estar correto]: ~ **(com)** to agree (with). -2. [garantir] to make sure.

confessar [kõnfe'sa(x)] <> *vt* -1. [fazer confissão de] to confess. -2. RELIG [ouvir confissão de] to hear confession. <> *vi* -1. [fazer confissão] to make a confession. -2. RELIG to confess.

◆ **confessar-se** *vp* -1. RELIG to confess. -2. [admitir ser] to confess to being; ~-se **culpado** JUR to plead guilty.

confesso, sa [kõn'fesu, sa] *adj* confessed.

confete [kõn'fɛtʃi] *m* confetti.

confiabilidade [kõnfjabili'dadʒi] *f* [credibilidade] reliability.

confiado, da [kõn'fjadu, da] *adj* [atrevido] cheeky.

confiança [kõn'fjãsa] *f* -1. [segurança] confidence. -2. [fé] trust; **ter** ~ **em alguém** to have confidence in sb; **de** ~ trustworthy.

confiante [kõn'fjãntʃi] *adj* -1. [seguro] confident. -2. [esperançoso]: ~ **(em)** trusting (in).

confiar [kõn'fja(x)] <> *vi*: ~ **em** to trust in. <> *vt* [entregar]: ~ **algo a alguém** to entrust sthg to sb.

confiável [kõn'fjavew] (*pl* -eis) *adj* reliable.

confidência [kõnfi'dẽsja] *f* confidence; **em** ~ in confidence.

confidencial [kõnfidẽn'sjaw] (*pl* -ais) *adj* confidential.

confinamento [kõnfina'mẽntu] *m* confinement.

confinar [kõnfi'na(x)] <> *vt* [isolar, en-clausurar]: ~ **alguém/algo em** to confine sb/sthg to/in. <> *vi* ◆ **confinar-se** *vp* [isolar-se, enclausurar-se] to isolate o.s.

confins [kõn'fĩʃ] *mpl* [limite extremo] ends.

confirmação [kõnfixma'sãw] (*pl* -ões) *f* confirmation.

confirmar [kõnfix'ma(x)] *vt* [comprovar] to confirm.

◆ **confirmar-se** *vp* -1. [cumprir-se] to be confirmed. -2. [justificar-se] to be justified.

confiscar [kõnfiʃ'ka(x)] *vt* to confiscate.

confisco [kõn'fiʃku] *m* confiscation.

confissão [kõnfi'sãw] (*pl* -ões) *f* [de falta, crime] confession.

conflito [kõn'flitu] *m* [ger] conflict; **entrar em** ~ **(com)** to clash (with).

conformação [kõnfoxma'sãw] (*pl* -ões) *f* -1. [resignação] resignation. -2. [forma] shape.

conformado, da [kõnfox'madu, da] *adj* [resignado] resigned.

conformar [kõnfox'ma(x)] *vt* [formar] to shape.

◆ **conformar-se** *vp* [resignar-se]: ~-se **com** to resign o.s. to.

conforme [kõn'fɔxmi] <> *prep* [de acordo com, segundo] in accordance with. <> *conj* -1. [ger] as. -2. [de acordo com] according to. -3. [dependendo de] depending on.

conformidade [kõnfoxmi'dadʒi] *f* [acordo] agreement; **em** ~ **com** in accordance with.

conformista [kõnfox'miʃta] *mf* conformist.

confortar [kõnfox'ta(x)] *vt* [consolar] to comfort.

confortável [kõnfox'tavew] (*pl* -eis) *adj* comfortable.

conforto [kõn'foxtu] *m* comfort.

confraria [kõnfra'ria] *f* fraternity.

confraternização [kõnfratexniza'sãw] (*pl* -ões) *f* fraternization.

confrontar [kõnfrõn'ta(x)] *vt* -1. [comparar] to compare. -2. [acarear] to confront.

◆ **confrontar-se** *vp* [defrontar-se] to face each other.

confronto [kõn'frõntu] *m* -1. [comparação] comparison. -2. [choque] confrontation.

confundir [kõnfũn'di(x)] *vt* -1. [ger] to confuse; ~ **algo com** to confuse sthg with. -2. [misturar] to muddle. -3. [trocar] to mix up.

◆ **confundir-se** *vp* to become confused; ~-se **com** to become confused with.

confusão [kõfu'zãw] (pl -ões) f -1. [mistura] muddle. -2. [troca] mixing up. -3. [indistinção] confusion. -4. [caos] mess. -5. [problema] hassle; **dar ~** to cause a hassle. -6. [tumulto] melee.

confuso, sa [kõ'fuzu, za] adj -1. [obscuro] obscure. -2. [misturado] muddled. -3. [indistinto] hazy. -4. [atrapalhado] confused.

congelado, da [kõʒe'ladu, da] adj frozen.
◆ **congelado** m frozen food (inv).

congelador [kõʒela'do(x)] (pl -es) m freezer.

congelamento [kõʒela'mẽntul] m -1. [de água, alimento etc.] freezing. -2. ECON [de preços, salários] freeze.

congelar [kõʒe'la(x)] <> vt [água, rio, alimento] to freeze. <> vi -1. [ficar congelado] to freeze. -2. [sentir frio] to be freezing.

congênito, ta [kõʒenitu, ta] adj congenital.

congestionado, da [kõʒeʃtjo'nadu, da] adj -1. [trânsito] congested. -2. [nariz, artéria] blocked.

congestionamento [kõʒeʃtjona'mẽntul] m -1. [engarrafamento] congestion. -2. [de nariz, artéria] blockage.

congestionar [kõʒeʃtjo'na(x)] vt -1. [trânsito]: **~ o trânsito** to cause traffic congestion. -2. [nariz, artéria] to block.

conglomerado [kõŋglome'radul] m conglomerate.

congregação [kõŋgrega'sãw] (pl -ões) f -1. RELIG congregation. -2. [reunião] coming together.

congregar [kõŋgre'ga(x)] vt [reunir] to bring together.

congressista [kõŋgre'siʃta] m f -1. [participante] delegate (at a conference). -2. POL congressman (f congresswoman).

congresso [kõŋ'grɛsu] m -1. [conferência] conference. -2. POL: **o Congresso** Congress.

conhaque [ko'ɲaki] m cognac.

conhecedor, ra [koɲese'do(x), ra] (mpl -es, fpl -s) <> adj [ciente]: **~ (de)** aware (of). <> m, f [especialista]: **~ (de)** specialist (in).

conhecer [koɲe'se(x)] vt -1. [ger] to know. -2. [entender de] to understand. -3. [pessoa pela primeira vez] to meet. -4. [loja, casa etc.] to see. -5. [país] to visit. -6. [reconhecer]: **~ algo/alguém (por)** to recognize sthg/sb (by).
◆ **conhecer-se** vp -1. [a si próprio] to know o.s. -2. [pessoas] to know one another; [pela primeira vez] to meet.

conhecido, da [koɲe'sidu, da] <> adj -1. [famoso] well-known; **~ por** known for. -2. [sabido] wise. -3. [notório] notorious. <> m, f [pessoa] acquaintance.

conhecimento [koɲesi'mẽntul] m -1. [saber] knowledge; **levar algo ao ~ de alguém** to bring sthg to the attention of sb; **ter ~ de** to be aware of. -2. [conhecido] acquaintance.
◆ **conhecimentos** mpl -1. [noções] knowledge (sg.). -2. [relações, conhecidos] friends.

conivência [koni'vẽnsja] f connivance.

conivente [koni'vẽntʃi] adj conniving; **ser ~ com** to connive in.

conjugação [kõʒuga'sãw] (pl -ões) f -1. [união] union. -2. GRAM conjugation.

conjugado, da [kõʒu'gadu, da] adj -1. [apartamento, sala] adjoining. -2. GRAM conjugated.
◆ **conjugado** m [apartamento] adjoining apartment.

conjugal [kõʒu'gaw] (pl -ais) adj marital.

cônjuge ['kõʒuʒi] m spouse.

conjunção [kõʒũn'sãw] (pl -ões) f -1. [união] combination. -2. GRAM conjunction.

conjuntivite [kõʒũntʃi'vitʃi] f conjunctivitis.

conjunto, ta [kõ'ʒũntu, ta] adj combined, joint.
◆ **conjunto** m -1. [grupo] combination. -2. [totalidade]: **o ~ de** the whole of; **em ~ together**. -3. MÚS group. -4. [residencial] complex; **~ habitacional** housing complex. -5. [traje] suit. -6. MAT set.

conjuntura [kõʒũn'tura] f conjuncture.

conosco [ko'noʃku] pron pess with us.

conquanto [kõ'kwãntu] conj although.

conquista [kõ'kiʃta] f conquest.

conquistador, ra [kõŋkiʃta'do(x), ra] <> adj -1. [exército, país] conquering. -2. [sedutor] seductive. <> m, f -1. [de terras, país] conqueror. -2. [sedutor - homem] lady-killer; [- mulher] femme fatale.

conquistar [kõŋkiʃ'ta(x)] vt -1. [subjugar] to conquer. -2. [alcançar] to achieve. -3. [ganhar] to win. -4. [seduzir] to seduce.

consagração [kõsagra'sãw] (pl -ões) f -1. [aclamação] acclaim. -2. [exaltação] acclamation; **fazer a ~ de** to be an acclamation of. -3. [dedicação] dedication. -4. [aceitação] acceptance. -5. RELIG consecration.

consagrar [kõsa'gra(x)] vt -1. [levar à aclamação] to lead to the acclamation of. -2. [exaltar] to glorify. -3. [dedicar] to dedicate. - **4.** [tornar aceito] to become accepted. - **5.** RELIG to consecrate.

➤ **consagrar-se** *vi* [atingir a aclamação] to achieve acclaim.

consangüíneo, nea [kõnsãn'gwinju, nja] <> *adj* related by blood. <> *m, f* [parente] blood relation.

consciência [kõn'sjẽnsja] *f* - **1.** [conhecimento] awareness; **ter/tomar ~ de** to be/become aware of. - **2.** [sentidos]: **perder a ~** to lose consciousness. - **3.** [moral] conscience; **estar com a ~ limpa/pesada** to have a clear/guilty conscience. - **4.** [cuidado, responsabilidade] care.

consciencioso, osa [kõnsjẽn'sjozu, oza] *adj* conscientious.

consciente [kõn'sjẽntʃi] <> *adj* conscious. <> *m* PSIC consciousness.

consecutivo, va [kõnseku'tʃivu, va] *adj* consecutive.

conseguinte [kõnse'gĩntʃi] ➤ **por conseguinte** *loc conj* consequently.

conseguir [kõnse'gi(x)] *vt* - **1.** [obter] to obtain. - **2.** [alcançar] to achieve; **~ fazer algo** to manage to do sthg.

conselheiro, ra [kõnse'ʎejru, ral] *m, f* - **1.** [ger] adviser. - **2.** [membro de conselho] councillor.

conselho [kõ'seʎu] *m* - **1.** [advertência] advice. - **2.** [órgão] council; **~ de ministros** Cabinet; **~ de guerra** council of war.

consenso [kõn'sẽnsul] *m* consensus.

consentimento [kõnsẽntʃi'mẽntul] *m* consent.

consentir [kõnsẽn'tʃi(x)] <> *vt* - **1.** [permitir] to grant. - **2.** [aprovar] to approve. <> *vi* [concordar, anuir]: **~ em algo** to consent to sthg.

conseqüência [kõnse'kwẽnsja] *f* [resultado] consequence; **em ~ de** because of, owing to; **por ~** consequently.

conseqüente [kõnse'kwẽntʃi] *adj* - **1.** [resultante] consequent. - **2.** [coerente] coherent.

consertar [kõnsex'ta(x)] *vt* - **1.** [reparar] to repair. - **2.** [remediar] to rectify.

conserto [kõn'sextul] *m* repair.

conserva [kõn'sɛrval] *f* preserve; **em ~** preserved.

conservação [kõnsexva'sãw] *f* - **1.** [ger] conservation. - **2.** [preservação] preservation.

conservador, ra [kõnsexva'do(x), ral] <> *adj* conservative. <> *m, f* conservative.

conservante [kõnser'vãntʃi] *m* preservative.

conservar [kõnsex'va(x)] *vt* - **1.** [preservar] to preserve. - **2.** [sabor, qualidade *etc.*] to conserve. - **3.** [manter] to maintain.

➤ **conservar-se** *vp* - **1.** [pessoa] to be well preserved. - **2.** [permanecer] to remain.

conservatório [kõnsexva'tɔrjul] *m* conservatoire.

consideração [kõnsidera'sãw] (*pl* -ões) *f* - **1.** [ger] consideration; **levar em ~** to take into consideration; **falta de ~ (com alguém)** lack of consideration (towards sb). - **2.** [pensamento] thought.

considerar [kõnside'ra(x)] *vt* - **1.** [ger] to consider. - **2.** [respeitar, estimar]: **~ muito alguém/algo** to have a high regard for sb/sthg.

➤ **considerar-se** *vp* [julgar-se] to consider o.s.

considerável [kõnside'ravɛw] (*pl* -eis) *adj* considerable.

consignação [kõnsigna'sãw] (*pl* -ões) *f* - **1.** [registro] report. - **2.** COM consignment; **em ~** on consignment. - **3.** [de verbas] allocation.

consignar [kõnsig'na(x)] *vt* - **1.** [produtos] to consign. - **2.** [registrar] to record. - **3.** [verbas] to allocate.

consigo [kõn'sigul] *pron pess* with him/her/you/it.

consistência [kõnsiʃ'tẽnsja] *f* consistency; **ganhar ~** to thicken.

consistente [kõnsiʃ'tẽntʃi] *adj* - **1.** [sólido] solid. - **2.** [espesso] thick. - **3.** [coerente, sólido] consistent.

consistir [kõnsiʃ'tʃi(x)] *vi* [constituir-se]: **~ em** to consist of; **~ em fazer algo** to consist in doing sthg.

consoante [kõn'swãntʃi] <> *adj* LING consonant. <> *f* LING consonant. <> *prep* [de acordo com] according to.

consolação [kõnsola'sãw] (*pl* -ões) *f* comfort.

consolar [kõnso'la(x)] *vt* to comfort.

➤ **consolar-se** *vp*: **~-se (com)** to console o.s. (with).

console [kõn'soli] *m* console.

consolidação [kõnsolida'sãw] (*pl* -ões) *f* [estabilização] consolidation.

consolidar [kõnsoli'da(x)] <> *vt* - **1.** [estabilizar, ratificar] to consolidate. - **2.** [fratura] to calcify. <> *vi* [tornar-se sólido] to solidify.

consolo [kõn'solul] *m* - **1.** [consolação] comfort. - **2.** *vulg* [consolo-de-viúva] dildo.

consomê [kõnso'me] *m* consommé.

consórcio [kõn'sɔxsjul] *m* - **1.** [união] partnership. - **2.** [de interesses, necessidades] uniting. - **3.** COM consortium.

conspícuo, cua [kõnʃ'pikwu, kwal] *adj* - **1.** [evidente] conspicuous. - **2.** [ilustre] remarkable.

conspiração [kõnʃpira'sãw] (pl -ões) f
conspiracy.

conspirador, ra [kõnʃpira'do(x), ra] m, f
conspirator.

conspirar [kõnʃpi'ra(x)] ⋄ vi: ~ (contra) to conspire (against). ⋄ vt to
plot.

conspiratório, ria [kõʃpira'tɔrju, rja] adj
conspiratorial.

constante [kõnʃ'tãntʃi] adj -1. [ger]
constant. -2. [pessoa, amor] faithful.
-3. [que consta]: ~ de pertaining to.

constar [kõnʃ'ta(x)] vi -1. [informação]: ~
(em ou de) to appear (in). -2. [constituir-se]: ~ de to consist of.

constatação [kõnʃtata'sãw] (pl -ões) f -1.
[observação] observation. -2. [comprovação] confirmation.

constatar [kõnʃta'ta(x)] vt -1. [observar]
to notice. -2. [comprovar] to prove.

constelação [kõnʃtela'sãw] (pl -ões) f
constellation.

consternado, da [kõnʃter'nadu, da] adj
dismayed.

consternar [kõnʃtex'na(x)] vt to discourage.

constipação [kõnʃtʃipa'sãw] (pl -ões) f
-1. [prisão de ventre] constipation. -2.
[resfriado] cold.

constipado, da [kõnʃtʃi'padu, da] adj -1.
[resfriado]: **estar** ~ to have a cold. -2.
[com prisão de ventre] constipated.

constitucional [kõnʃtʃitusjo'naw] (pl
-ais) adj constitutional.

constituição [kõnʃtʃitwi'sãw] (pl -ões) f
-1. [formação] make-up. -2. [consistência]
composition. -3. POL [carta] constitution.

constituinte [kõnʃtʃi'twĩntʃi] ⋄ adj
-1. [componente] constituent. -2. POL
representative. ⋄ mf POL [deputado]
deputy.

➡ **Constituinte** f POL [assembléia]: **a
Constituinte** the Constituent Assembly.

constituir [kõnʃtʃi'twi(x)] vt -1. [compor,
ser] to constitute. -2. [criar, estabelecer]
to establish.

➡ **constituir-se** vp -1. [estabelecer-se como]: ~-se em algo to establish o.s. as
sthg. -2. [ser]: ~-se em algo to be sthg,
to constitute sthg.

constrangedor, ra [kõnʃtrãnʒe'do(x), ra]
adj -1. [embaraçador] embarrassing. -2.
[repressivo] repressive.

constranger [kõnʃtrãn'ʒe(x)] vt -1. [embaraçar] to embarrass. -2. [reprimir, refrear] to curb.

➡ **constranger-se** vp [ficar embaraçado]
to be embarrassed.

constrangimento [kõnʃtrãnʒi'mẽntu] m
-1. [embaraço] embarrassment. -2. [repressão] restriction.

construção [kõnʃtru'sãw] (pl -ões) f -1.
[edifício] building; **em** ~ under construction (depois de verbo). -2. [intelectual, imaginária] feat.

construir [kõnʃtru'i(x)] vt to build.

construtivo, va [kõnʃtru'tʃivu, va] adj
constructive.

construtor, ra [kõnʃtru'to(x), ra] (mpl -es,
fpl -s) ⋄ adj building (antes de subst).
⋄ m, f builder.

➡ **construtora** f [empresa] building
company.

cônsul ['kõnsuw] (pl -es) m consul.

consulado [kõnsu'ladu] m consulate.

cônsules ['kõnsuliʃ] pl ⟼ cônsul.

consulesa [kõnsu'leza] f -1. [diplomata]
consul. -2. [esposa] consul's wife.

consulta [kõn'suwta] f -1. [sobre problema, dúvida] query. -2. MED consultation;
horário de ~ surgery hours; **ter uma**
~ (com) to have an appointment
(with).

consultar [kõnsuw'ta(x)] vt to consult.

consultor, ra [kõnsuw'to(x), ra] m, f consultant.

consultório [kõnsuw'tɔrju] m MED consulting room.

consumação [kõnsuma'sãw] (pl -ões) f
-1. [realização] realization, carrying
out. -2. [completude] completion. -3.
[de casamento] consummation. -4. [em
restaurante, bar]: ~ **mínima** minimum
order.

consumar [kõnsu'ma(x)] vt -1. [realizar] to
realize, to carry out. -2. [completar] to
complete. -3. [casamento] to consummate.

➡ **consumar-se** vp -1. [realizar-se] to be
realized, to be carried out. -2. [completar-se] to be completed. -3. [casamento] to be consummated. -4.
[profecia] to come true.

consumidor, ra [kõsumi'do(x), ra] (mpl
-es, fpl -s) ⋄ adj consumer. ⋄ m, f
consumer.

consumir [kõnsu'mi(x)] ⋄ vt -1. [ger] to
consume. -2. [comprar] to purchase.
-3. [corroer, devorar] to corrode. -4. fig
[desgastar] to consume. ⋄ vi [comprar]
to consume.

➡ **consumir-se** vp -1. [combustível, fogo]
to burn itself out. -2. fig [pessoa] to
wear o.s. out.

consumo [kõn'sumu] m -1. [ger]
consumption. -2. [compra] sale; **bens
de** ~ consumer goods. -3. [de drogas]
use.

conta ['kõnta] f-**1.** [ger] account; **pôr na ~** to charge to one's account; **abrir uma ~** to open an account; **~ conjunta** joint account; **~ corrente** current account. -**2.** [cálculo] counting; **acertar** OU **ajustar contas com alguém** fig to settle a score with sb; **pedir as ~s** fig [demitir-se] to resign; **afinal de ~s** after all. -**3.** [em restaurante] bill; **a ~, por favor!** the bill, please!; **pedir a ~** to ask for the bill. -**4.** [fatura] invoice; **~ de gás/luz/telefone** gas/electricity/telephone bill. -**5.** [consideração]: **levar algo em ~** to take sthg into account; **dar (-se) ~ de** to realize. -**6.** [justificação, razão]: **por ~ de** because of. -**7.** [informação, satisfação] account; **dar ~ de** to give an account of; **prestar ~s de** to account for. -**8.** [responsabilidade, capacidade]: **dar ~ de** to manage; **não ser da ~ de alguém** to be nobody's business; **tomar ~ de alguém/algo** [cuidar, encarregar-se de] to look after sb/sthg; **tomar ~ de** [difundir-se por] to take over. -**9.** [de colar] bead. -**10.** loc: **fazer de ~ que** [imaginar] to pretend; [fingir] to pretend; **ficar por ~** to get angry.
◆ **por conta própria** loc adv on one's own account.

contabilidade [kõtabili'dadʒil f-**1.** [ofício] accountancy. -**2.** [setor] accounts department.

contabilista [kõtabi'liʃta] m f accountant.

contabilizar [kõtabili'za(x)] vt-**1.** [registrar] to keep accounts. -**2.** [calcular] to count.

contador [kõta'do(x)] (pl -es) m, f COM accountant.
◆ **contador** m TEC meter.

contagem [kõ'taʒẽl (pl -ns) f-**1.** [ato] counting. -**2.** [escore] score.

contagiar [kõta'ʒja(x)] vt-**1.** [infectar] to infect. -**2.** fig [influenciar] to affect.

contágio [kõ'taʒjul m contagion.

contagioso, osa [kõta'ʒjozu, za] adj contagious.

contaminação [kõtamina'sãw] (pl -ões) f contamination.

contaminar [kõtami'na(x)] ◇ vt [contagiar] to contaminate. ◇ vi fig [corromper] to corrupt.

contanto [kõ'tãntul ◆ **contanto que** loc adv provided that.

contar [kõ'ta(x)] ◇ vt-**1.** [enumerar] to count. -**2.** [narrar] to tell. -**3.** [supor]: **~ que** to expect. ◇ vi-**1.** [fazer contas] to count. -**2.** [importar] to matter. -**3.**: **~ com** [ger] to count on; [dispor] to have.

contatar [kõta'ta(x)] vt to contact.

contato [kõ'tatul m contact.

contemplar [kõtẽn'pla(x)] vt-**1.** [olhar] to contemplate. -**2.** [premiar] to reward.
◆ **contemplar-se** vp [olhar-se] to look at o.s.

contemplativo, va [kõtẽnpla'tʃivu, val adj contemplative.

contemporaneidade [kõtẽnporanej'dadʒil f contemporary nature.

contemporâneo, nea [kõtẽmpo'ranju, njal ◇ adj contemporary. ◇ m, f contemporary.

contenção [kõtẽn'sãw] f-**1.** [diminuição - de despesas] cutback; [- de gestos, palavras] restraint. -**2.** [interrupção de fluxo] containment.

contenda [kõ'tẽnda] f dispute.

contentamento [kõtẽnta'mẽntul m -**1.** [alegria] happiness. -**2.** [satisfação] contentment.

contentar [kõtẽn'ta(x)] vt-**1.** [satisfazer] to content. -**2.** [agradar] to please.
◆ **contentar-se** vp [satisfazer-se]: **~-se com** to be satisfied with.

contente [kõ'tẽntʃil adj happy.

contento [kõ'tẽntul ◆ **a contento** loc adv satisfactorily.

conter [kõ'te(x)] vt-**1.** [controlar] to control. -**2.** [ter] to contain.
◆ **conter-se** vp [controlar-se] to restrain o.s.

conterrâneo, nea [kõte'xãnju, njal ◇ adj fellow (antes de subst); **é um amigo ~** he is a friend who comes from the same place as me. ◇ m, f compatriot.

contestação [kõteʃta'sãw] (pl -ões) f-**1.** [negação] dispute. -**2.** [impugnação] challenge. -**3.** [oposição] opposition. -**4.** [réplica] reply.

contestar [kõteʃ'ta(x)] ◇ vt-**1.** [negar] to dispute. -**2.** [impugnar] to challenge. ◇ vi [opor-se] to oppose.

contestatório, ria [kõteʃta'tɔrju, rjal adj contentious; **movimento ~** protest movement.

conteúdo [kõ'tjudul m contents (pl).

contexto [kõ'teʃtul m context.

contextualização [kõteʃtwaliza'sãw] (pl -ões) f contextualization.

contextualizar [kõteʃtwali'za(x)] vt to put into context.

contigo [kõ'tʃigul pron pess with you.

contíguo, gua [kõ'tʃigwu, gwal adj adjacent; **~ a** next to.

continental [kõntʃinẽn'taw] (pl -ais) adj continental.

continente [kõntʃi'nẽntʃil m continent.

contingência [kõntʃĩn'ʒẽnsjal f contingency.

contingente [kõntʃĩn'ʒẽntʃi] <> *adj* contingent. <> *m* contingent.

continuação [kõntʃinwa'sãw] (*pl* -ões) *f* continuation.

continuar [kõntʃi'nwa(x)] <> *vt* [prosseguir] to continue. <> *vi* -**1.** [perdurar] to continue. -**2.** [prolongar-se] to go on. -**3.** [prosseguir]: ~ **em algo** to continue with sthg; ~ **fazendo algo** *ou* **a fazer algo** to continue doing sthg/to do sthg. <> *v de ligação (antes de adjetivo)* [expressa qualidade, estado]: **a cidade continua bonita** the city is still beautiful.

continuidade [kõntʃinwi'dadʒi] *f* continuity.

contínuo, nua [kõn'tʃinwu, nwa] <> *adj* -**1.** [sem interrupção] continuous. -**2.** [constante] constant. <> *m* [pessoa] office junior.

conto ['kõntu] *m* story.

contorção [kõntox'sãw] (*pl* -ões) *f* contortion.

contorcer [kõntox'se(x)] *vt* to warp.
➤ **contorcer-se** *vp* to writhe.

contornar [kõntox'na(x)] *vt* -**1.** [rodear] to go around. -**2.** *fig* [resolver] to get around.

contorno [kõn'toxnu] *m* outline.

contra ['kõntra] <> *prep* [ger] against. <> *adv* against. <> *m* -**1.** [dificuldade] hard knock. -**2.** [contestação] objection; **pesar os prós e os** ~**s** to weigh up the pros and the cons; **ser do** ~ to object on principle.

contra-ataque [ˌkõntra'taki] (*pl* **contra-ataques**) *m* counter-attack.

contrabaixo [ˌkõntra'bajʃu] *m* -**1.** [instrumento] double bass. -**2.** [músico] bassist.

contrabandear [ˌkõntrabãn'dʒja(x)] *vt* to smuggle.

contrabandista [ˌkõntrabãn'dʒiʃta] *mf* smuggler.

contrabando [ˌkõntra'bãndu] *m* -**1.** [ato] smuggling. -**2.** [mercadoria] contraband; **fazer** ~ to smuggle.

contração [kõntra'sãw] (*pl* -ões) *f* contraction.

contracapa [ˌkõntra'kapa] *f* inside cover.

contracepção [ˌkõntrasep'sãw] (*pl* -ões) *f* contraception.

contraceptivo, va [ˌkõntrasep'tʃivu, va] *m* contraceptive.

contracheque [ˌkõntra'ʃɛki] *m* payslip.

contradição [ˌkõntradʒi'sãw] (*pl* -ões) *f* contradiction.

contraditório, ria [ˌkõntradʒi'tɔrju, rja] *adj* contradictory.

contradizer [ˌkõntradʒi'ze(x)] *vt* to contradict.
➤ **contradizer-se** *vp* to contradict o.s.

contrafilé [ˌkõntrafi'lɛ] *m* rump steak.

contragosto [kõntra'goʃtu] ➤ **a contragosto** *loc adv* unwillingly.

contrair [kõntra'i(x)] *vt* -**1.** [ger] to contract. -**2.** [assumir]: ~ **matrimônio** to get married; ~ **dívidas** to run up debts; ~ **compromisso** to take on responsibilities. -**3.** [adquirir - doenças] to catch; [- hábitos] to acquire.
➤ **contrair-se** *vp* [encolher-se] to contract.

contramão [ˌkõntra'mãw] <> *adj* [em sentido contrário] one-way. <> *f*: **na** ~ on the wrong side of the road.

contramestre [ˌkõntra'mɛʃtri] *m* -**1.** [em fábrica *etc.*] foreman. -**2.** [náut] first mate.

contrapartida [ˌkõntrapar'tʃida] *f* -**1.** [oposto] opposite. -**2.** [compensação]: **em** ~ in compensation.

contrapeso [ˌkõntra'pezu] *m* counterbalance.

contrapor [ˌkõntra'po(x)] *vt* [confrontar] to confront; ~ **algo a algo** to set sthg against sthg.

contraproducente [ˌkõntraprodu'sẽntʃi] *adj* counterproductive.

contra-regra [ˌkõntra'xɛgra] (*pl* **contra-regras**) *mf* stage manager.

contrariado, da [kõntra'rjadu, da] *adj* annoyed.

contrariar [kõntra'rja(x)] *vt* -**1.** [vontade, interesse] to thwart. -**2.** [declaração, informação] to contradict. -**3.** [desobedecer - ordem, instrução] to disobey; [- lei] to break. -**4.** [descontentar] to annoy.

contrário, ria [kõn'trarju, rja] *adj* -**1.** [lado] opposite. -**2.** [ponto de vista, decisão] opposing; **ser** ~ **a algo** to be against sthg; **caso** ~ otherwise.
➤ **contrário** *m* opposite; **do** ~ otherwise; **pelo** *ou* **ao** ~ on the contrary; **ao** ~ [de outra maneira] the other way round; [roupa] back to front.

contra-senso [ˌkõntra'sẽnsu] (*pl* **contra-sensos**) *m* nonsense (*inv*).

contrastante [kõntraʃ'tãntʃi] *adj* contrasting.

contrastar [kõntraʃ'ta(x)] <> *vt*: ~ **algo com algo** to contrast sthg with sthg. <> *vi* to contrast.

contraste [kõn'traʃtʃi] *m* contrast.

contratação [kõntrata'sãw] (*pl* -ões) *f* recruitment.

contratante [kõntra'tãntʃi] <> *adj* contracting. <> *mf* contractor.

contratar [kõntra'ta(x)] *vt* to recruit.

contratempo [ˌkõntra'tẽnpu] *m* -**1.** [imprevisto] setback. -**2.** [dificuldade] hurdle. -**3.** [aborrecimento] upset.

contrato [kõn'tratu] *m* -**1.** [documento] contract. -**2.** [acordo] agreement.

contribuição [kõntribwi'sãw] (*pl* -**ões**) *f* -**1.** [ger] contribution. -**2.** [tributo - sindical] dues (*pl*); [- fiscal] tax.

contribuinte [kõntri'bwĩntʃi] *m f* -**1.** [colaborador] contributor. -**2.** [aquele que paga imposto] taxpayer.

contribuir [kõntri'bwi(x)] *vi* -**1.** [ger] to contribute; ~ **com algo (para algo)** [fornecer, colaborar] to contribute sthg (for/ to sthg). -**2.** [ter parte em um resultado]: ~ **para algo** to contribute to sthg.

controlar [kõntro'la(x)] *vt* to control.
◆ **controlar-se** *vp* [dominar-se] to control o.s.

controle [kõn'trɔli] *m* control; ~ **remoto** remote control.

controvérsia [kõntro'vɛrsja] *f* controversy.

controverso, sa [kõntro'vɛrsu, sa] *adj* controversial.

contudo [kõn'tudu] *conj* however.

contumaz [kõntu'majʒ] *adj* obstinate.

contundir [kõntũn'dʒi(x)] *vt* to bruise.
◆ **contundir-se** *vp* to bruise o.s.

contusão [kõntu'zãw] (*pl* -**ões**) *f* bruise.

convalescença [kõnvaleʃ'sẽsa] *f* convalescence.

convalescer [kõnvale'se(x)] *vi* to convalesce.

convenção [kõnvẽn'sãw] (*pl* -**ões**) *f* convention.

convencer [kõnvẽn'se(x)] ⬦ *vt* [persuadir]: ~ **alguém (de algo)** to convince sb (of sthg); ~ **alguém a fazer algo** to persuade sb to do sthg. ⬦ *vi fig* [agradar] to impress.
◆ **convencer-se** *vp* [persuadir-se]: ~ **-se de algo** to convince o.s. of sthg.

convencido, da [kõnvẽn'sidu, da] *adj* -**1.** [convicto] convinced. -**2.** *fig* [presunçoso] conceited.

convencional [kõnvẽnsjo'naw] (*pl* -**ais**) *adj* -**1.** [ger] conventional. -**2.** *pej* [comum] commonplace.

conveniência [kõnve'njẽsja] *f* convenience.

conveniente [kõnve'njẽntʃi] *adj* -**1.** [ger] convenient. -**2.** [oportuno] opportune.

convênio [kõn'venju] *m* -**1.** [acordo] agreement. -**2.** [entre instituições] accord.

convento [kõn'vẽntu] *m* convent.

convergência [kõnver'gẽsja] *f* convergence.

convergir [kõnvex'ʒi(x)] *vi* -**1.** [mesma direção]: ~ **para** to converge on. -**2.** [afluir]: ~ **(de/para)** to converge (from/towards).

conversa [kõn'vɛxsa] *f* -**1.** [diálogo] chat; ~ **fiada** *ou* **mole** chit-chat. -**2.** *loc*: **passar uma** ~ **em alguém** to soft-soap sb.

conversação [kõnvexsa'sãw] (*pl* -**ões**) *f* conversation.

conversão [kõnvex'sãw] (*pl* -**ões**) *f* conversion.

conversar [kõnvex'sa(x)] *vi* to talk, to hold a conversation.

conversível [kõnvex'sivew] (*pl* -**eis**) ⬦ *adj* convertible. ⬦ *m AUTO* convertible.

conversor [kõnvex'so(x)] *m* -**1.** [dispositivo] transformer. -**2.** *COMPUT* converter.

converter [kõnvex'te(x)] *vt* -**1.** [transformar]: ~ **algo/alguém em algo** to convert sthg/sb into sthg. -**2.** *POL & RELIG*: ~ **alguém a** to convert sb to.
◆ **converter-se** *vp POL & RELIG*: ~ **-se (a)** to convert (to).

convertido, da [kõnvex'tʃidu, da] ⬦ *adj* converted. ⬦ *m, f POL & RELIG* convert.

convés [kõn'vɛʃ] (*pl* -**veses**) *m* deck.

convexo, xa [kõn'vɛksu, sa] *adj* convex.

convicção [kõnvik'sãw] (*pl* -**ões**) *f* conviction.

convicto, ta [kõn'viktu, ta] ⬦ *adj* -**1.** [convencido] convinced. -**2.** [réu] convicted. ⬦ *m, f* [presidiário] convict.

convidado, da [kõnvi'dadu, da] *m, f* guest.

convidar [kõnvi'da(x)] *vt* [ger] to invite.

convidativo, va [kõnvida'tʃivu, va] *adj* inviting.

convincente [kõnvĩn'sẽntʃi] *m* convincing.

convir [kõn'vi(x)] *vi* -**1.** [concordar]: ~ **(com alguém) em algo** to agree (with sb) about sthg. -**2.** [ser conveniente, proveitoso]: ~ **a alguém** to be convenient for sb. -**3.** [condizer]: ~ **a alguém** to be appropriate for sb.

convite [kõn'vitʃi] *m* invitation.

convivência [kõnvi'vẽsja] *f* -**1.** [convívio] closeness. -**2.** [familiaridade] familiarity.

conviver [kõnvi've(x)] *vi* -**1.** [coexistir] to coexist. -**2.** [lidar]: ~ **com** to cope with.

convívio [kõn'vivju] *m* [convivência] closeness.

convocar [kõnvo'ka(x)] *vt* -**1.** [chamar] to summon. -**2.** [reunir] to convene. -**3.** *MIL* to call up.

convosco [kõn'voʃku] *pron pess* with you.

convulsão [kõnvuw'sãw] (*pl* -**ões**) *f* -**1.** *MED* convulsion. -**2.** *fig* upheaval.

convulsionar [kõnvuwsjo'na(x)] *vt* -**1.** [pôr em convulsão] to convulse. -**2.** *fig* [povo, país] to agitate.

cookie [ˈkokil] (*pl* **cookies**) *m COMPUT* cookie.

cooper ['kupe(x)] *m* jogging; **fazer** ~ **to go jogging.**

cooperação [kwopera'sãw] (*pl* -**ões**) *f* cooperation.

cooperar [kwope'ra(x)] *vi*: ~ **(com) to** cooperate (with).

◆ **cooperativa** *f* cooperative.

cooperativo, va [kwopera't∫ivu, va] *adj* cooperative.

◆ **cooperativa** *f* cooperative.

coordenação [kooxdena'sãw] *f* [ato] co-ordination.

coordenada [kooxde'nada] *f* -**1.** *fam* [orientação] instructions. -**2.** *GEOM* coordinate.

coordenar [koorde'na(x)] *m* to coordinate.

copa ['kɔpa] *f* -**1.** [cômodo] pantry. -**2.** [parte superior] crown. -**3.** *ESP* cup.

◆ **copas** *fpl* [naipe] hearts.

Copenhague [kõpe'nagi] *n* Copenhagen.

cópia ['kɔpja] *f* -**1.** [ger] copy. -**2.** [fotocópia] photocopy.

copiadora [kopja'dora] *f* -**1.** [loja] print shop. -**2.** [máquina] photocopier.

copiar [ko'pja(x)] *vt* to copy.

copioso, piosa [ko'pjozu, pjɔzal *adj* -**1.** [ger] copious. -**2.** [refeição] copious.

copo ['kɔpu] *m* -**1.** [recipiente] glass. -**2.** [conteúdo] glassful.

COPOM (*abrev de* **Comitê de Política Monetária**) [ko'põ] *m* [econ] Monetary Policy Committee.

copular [ko'pula(x)] *vi* to copulate.

coqueiro [ko'kejru] *m* coconut palm.

coqueluche [koke'luʃi] *f* -**1.** [doença] whooping cough. -**2.** *fig* [moda]: **o bambolê foi** ~ **nos anos setenta the** hula hoop was all the rage in the seventies.

coquetel [koke'tɛw] (*pl* -**éis**) *m* -**1.** [drinque] cocktail. -**2.** [festa] cocktail party.

cor ['ko(x)] (*pl* -**es**) *f* -**1.** [tom] colour. -**2.** [de pele] complexion; **ficar sem** ~ **to go** pale. -**3.** *fig* [feição] tone.

◆ **de cor** *loc adv* by heart.

coração [kora'sãw] (*pl* -**ões**) *m* [ger] heart.

corado, da [ko'radu, da] *adj* -**1.** [na face] ruddy. -**2.** [avermelhado] reddish. -**3.** *fig* [envergonhado] shamefaced. -**4.** *CULIN* sautéed.

coragem [ko'raʒẽ] *f* courage.

corajoso, osa [kora'ʒozu, ɔza] *adj* courageous.

coral [ko'raw] (*pl* -**ais**) ◇ *m* -**1.** [ger] coral. -**2.** *MÚS* choir. ◇ *f* [cobra] coral snake. ◇ *adj* coral.

corante [ko'rãntʃi] ◇ *adj* colouring. ◇ *m* dye.

corcova [kox'kɔva] *f* hump.

corcunda [kox'kũnda] ◇ *adj* hunchbacked. ◇ *mf* hunchback.

corda ['kɔrda] *f* -**1.** [ger] spring; **dar** ~ **em** to wind up. -**2.** [fio] rope. -**3.** [varal] clothesline.

◆ **cordas** *fpl* -**1.** *ANAT:* ~ **s vocais** vocal cords. -**2.** *MÚS:* **quarteto de** ~ **s string** quartet.

cordão [kor'dãw] (*pl* -**ões**) *m* -**1.** [corda fina] twine. -**2.** [jóia] chain. -**3.** [cadarço] shoelace. -**4.** [bloco carnavalesco] carnival block. -**5.** *ANAT:* ~ **umbilical** umbilical cord.

cordeiro [kor'dejru] *m* lamb.

cordel [kor'dɛw] (*pl* -**éis**) *m* -**1.** [barbante] string. -**2.** *LITER:* **(literatura de)** ~ popular Brazilian literature.

cor-de-rosa [,kordʒi'xɔza] ◇ *adj* -**1.** [cor] pink. -**2.** *fig* [feliz] rose-tinted. ◇ *m* [cor] pink.

cordial [kor'dʒjaw] (*pl* -**ais**) *adj* -**1.** [gentil] cordial. -**2.** [afetuoso] warm.

cordilheira [kordʒi'ʎejra] *f* mountain range.

cordões *pl* ⊳ **cordão**.

Coréia [ko'rɛja] *n* Korea; ~ **do Norte** North Korea; ~ **do Sul** South Korea.

coreografia [korjogra'fia] *f* choreography.

coreto [ko'retu] *m* bandstand.

coriza [ko'riza] *f* runny nose.

corja ['kɔxʒa] *f* gang.

córnea ['kɔxnja] *f* cornea.

córner ['kɔxne(x)] *m* corner (kick).

corneta [kox'neta] *f* cornet.

coro ['koru] *m* -**1.** [cantores] choir. -**2.** [balcão] organ loft.

coroa [ko'roa] ◇ *f* -**1.** [ger] crown. -**2.** [de flores] garland. -**3.** [calvície] bald spot. ◇ *mf* [pessoa] *fam* old fogey.

coroação [korwa'sãw] (*pl* -**ões**) *f* coronation.

coroar [koro'a(x)] *vt* -**1.** [ger] to crown. -**2.** [premiar] to reward.

coronel [koro'nɛw] (*pl* -**éis**) *m* -**1.** *MIL* colonel. -**2.** *POL* political baron.

coronha [ko'roɲa] *f* butt.

coronhada [koro'nada] *f* blow with a rifle butt.

corpete [kox'petʃi] *m* bodice.

corpo ['koxpu] *m* -**1.** [ger] body; ~ **de bombeiros** fire department; ~ **diplomático** diplomatic corps. -**2.** [cadáver] corpse, body. -**3.** [consistência]: **tomar** ~ **to thicken.**

corporação [koxpora'sãw] (*pl* -**ões**) *f* corporation.

corporal [koxpo'raw] (*pl* -**ais**) *adj* corporal.

corporativismo [koxporatʃi'viʒmul *m* corporatism.

corporativo, va [koxpo'ratʃivu, va] *adj* corporative.

corpulento, ta [koxpu'lẽntu, ta] *adj* corpulent.

correção [koxe'sãw] (*pl* **-ões**) *f* **-1.** [ato] marking. **-2.** [qualidade] exactness.

corre-corre [kɔxi'kɔxi] *m* mad rush.

corredor, ra [koxe'do(x), ra] (*mpl* **-es**, *fpl* **-s**) *m, f* [atleta] runner.
 ➡ **corredor** *m* [passagem - em casa] corridor; [- em avião, etc.] aisle.

córrego ['kɔxegu] *m* brook.

correia [ko'xeja] *f* **-1.** [tira] strap. **-2.** [em máquina] belt. **-3.** [em carro] fan belt.

correio [ko'xeju] *m* **-1.** [serviço] mail; ~ **de voz** voice mail. **-2.** [correspondência] post; **agência dos** ~**s** post office. **-3.** *fig* [carteiro] postman *UK*, mailman *US*.

corrente [ko'xẽntʃi] ◇ *adj* **-1.** [atual] current. **-2.** [comum] common. **-3.** [fluente - língua] fluent; [- estilo] flowing. **-4.** [água] running. ◇ *f* **-1.** [ger] current; **remar contra a** ~ *fig* to swim against the tide. **-2.** [corrente] chain. **-3.** [vento]: ~ **de ar** draught.

correnteza [koxẽn'teza] *f* current.

correr [ko'xe(x)] ◇ *vi* **-1.** [ger] to run. **-2.** [passar] to fly past. **-3.** [circular] to circulate. **-4.** [espalhar-se] to spread. ◇ *vt* **-1.** [percorrer]: ~ **a fazenda** to go all over sthg. **-2.** [passar de leve] to run. **-3.** [olhar rapidamente]: **corri os olhos pela revista** I ran my eyes over the magazine. **-4.** [estar exposto a]: ~ **o risco de algo** to run the risk of sthg.

correria [koxe'ria] *f* rushing about.

correspondência [koxeʃpõn'dẽnsja] *f* correspondence.

correspondente [koxeʃpõn'dẽntʃi] ◇ *adj* corresponding. ◇ *mf* correspondent.

corresponder [koxeʃpõn'de(x)] *vi* [ger]: ~ **a** to correspond to.
 ➡ **corresponder-se** *vp* to correspond with.

correto, ta [ko'xɛtu, ta] *adj* **-1.** [ger] correct. **-2.** [íntegro] honest.

corretor, ra [koxe'to(x), ra] (*mpl* **-es**, *fpl* **-s**) *m, f* [agente] broker; ~ **de imóveis** estate agent *UK*, realtor *US*; ~ **de Bolsa** stockbroker.

corrida [ko'xida] *f* **-1.** [ato] running. **-2.** *ESP* racing. **-3.** [de táxi] fare.

corrido, da [ko'xidu, da] *adj* [rápido] rushed.

corrigir [koxi'ʒi(x)] *vt* **-1.** [retificar] to correct. **-2.** [eliminar] to repair. **-3.** [repreender] to tell off. **-4.** [atenuar] to attenuate.
 ➡ **corrigir-se** *vp* [emendar-se] to correct o.s.

corrimão [koxi'mãw] (*pl* **-ãos**, **-ões**) *m* handrail.

corriqueiro, ra [koxi'kejru, ra] *adj* everyday.

corroborar [koxobo'ra(x)] *vt* to corroborate.

corroer [koxo'e(x)] *vt* **-1.** [carcomer] to eat away. **-2.** [danificar] to corrode. **-3.** *fig* [depravar] to undermine.

corromper [koxõn'pe(x)] *vt* **-1.** [perverter] to pervert. **-2.** [subornar] to corrupt. **-3.** [adulterar] to tamper with.
 ➡ **corromper-se** *vp* [perverter-se] to become corrupt.

corrosão [koxo'sãw] (*pl* **-ões**) *f* **-1.** [de metais] corrosion. **-2.** *GEOL* erosion.

corrosivo, va [koxo'zivu, va] *adj* corrosive.

corrupção [koxup'sãw] (*pl* **-ões**) *f* **-1.** [perversão] perversion. **-2.** [suborno] corruption.

corrupto, ta [ko'xuptu, ta] *adj* corrupt.

Córsega ['kɔxsega] *n* Corsica.

cortada [kox'tada] *f ESP* smash; **dar uma** ~ **em alguém** *fig* to cut sb short.

cortado, da [kox'tadu, da] *adj* **-1.** [ger] cut. **-2.** [relações] severed. **-3.** *fig* [coração] broken.

cortador [koxta'do(x)] *m* cutter.

cortante [kox'tãntʃi] *adj* **-1.** [ger] cutting. **-2.** [que corta] sharp.

cortar [kox'ta(x)] ◇ *vt* **-1.** [ger] to cut. **-2.** [árvore] to cut down. **-3.** [suprimir] to cut out. **-4.** *AUTO* to stall. **-5.** [interromper] to interrupt. **-6.** [pôr fim a] to end. **-7.** [encurtar]: ~ **caminho** to take a short cut. ◇ *vi* **-1.** [ter bom gume] to cut. **-2.** *ESP* to smash the ball.
 ➡ **cortar-se** *vp* [ferir-se] to cut o.s.

corte¹ ['kɔxtʃi] *m* **-1.** [ger] cut. **-2.** [gume] cutting edge. **-3.** [porção de tecido]: ~ **de algo** length of sthg. **-4.** [trecho censurado] edited material.

corte² ['kɔxtʃi] *f* **-1.** [ger] court. **-2.** *fig* [de admiradores *etc*.] entourage.

cortejar [koxte'ʒa(x)] *vt* to court.

cortejo [kox'teʒul] *m* **-1.** [séquito] cortege. **-2.** [procissão] procession.

cortês [kox'teʃ] *adj* polite.

cortesão, sã [koxte'zãw, zã] (*mpl* **-ãos**, **-ões**, *fpl* **-s**) ◇ *adj* courtly. ◇ *m, f* courtier. ◇ *f* courtesan.

cortesia [koxte'zia] *f* **-1.** [delicadeza] courtesy. **-2.** [presente] complimentary gift. **-3.** [mesura] bow.

cortiça [kox'tʃisa] *f* cork.

cortiço [kox'tʃisul] *m* **-1.** [para abelhas] beehive. **-2.** [habitação] slum dwelling.

cortina [kox'tʃinal] *f* **-1.** [peça] curtain. **-2.** *fig* [nuvem] screen.

coruja [ko'ruʒa] <> f ZOOL owl. <> adj [pai, mãe] doting.

corvo ['koxvu] m crow.

cós ['kɔʃ] m inv **-1.** [tira de pano] waistband. **-2.** [cintura] waist.

coser [ko'ze(x)] <> vt to stitch. <> vi to sew.

cosmético, ca [koʒ'mɛtʃiku, ka] adj cosmetic.
  ◆ **cosmético** m cosmetic.

cosmopolita [koʒmopo'lita] <> adj cosmopolitan. <> mf [pessoa] cosmopolitan person.

costa ['kɔʃta] f [litoral] coast.

costado [koʃ'tadu] m NÁUT [forro] hull cladding.

Costa Rica [,kɔʃta'xika] n Costa Rica.

costa-riquense [,kɔʃtaxi'kẽnsi], **costar-riquenho, nha** [,kɔʃtaxi'kẽnju, ja] <> adj Costa Rican. <> m, f Costa Rican.

costas ['kɔʃtaʃ] fpl **-1.** [ger] back. **-2.** [encosto] backrest. **-3.** loc: carregar nas ~ fig to shoulder the burden; **ter** ~ **quentes** fig to be under sb's wing.

costela [koʃ'tɛla] f rib.

costeleta [koʃte'leta] f **-1.** CULIN chop. **-2.** [suíças] sideburns.

costumar [koʃtu'ma(x)] vt **-1.** [ter o hábito de]: ~ **fazer algo** to be in the habit of doing sthg; **costumo correr todas as manhãs** I usually go running every morning. **-2.** [habituar] to accustom.

costume [koʃ'tumi] m [hábito] habit; **como de** ~ as usual.
  ◆ **costumes** mpl [de um povo] customs.

costumeiro, ra [koʃtu'mejru, ra] adj usual, customary.

costura [koʃ'tura] f **-1.** [ger] sewing; **alta** ~ haute couture. **-2.** [linha de junção] seam.

costurar [koʃtu'ra(x)] <> vt **-1.** COST to stitch. **-2.** fig [texto] to tidy up. <> vi **-1.** COST to sew. **-2.** fam AUTO to weave in and out.

costureira [koʃtu'rejra] f seamstress.

cota ['kɔta] f **-1.** [quinhão] quota. **-2.** [prestação, parcela] instalment.

cotação [kota'sãw] (pl -ões) f **-1.** [ato] quoting. **-2.** [preço] quote. **-3.** fig [possibilidade de êxito] chance. **-4.** fig [conceito] reputation.

cotado, da [ko'tadu, da] adj **-1.** [com bom preço] well priced. **-2.** fig [favorito] favourite. **-3.** fig [conceituado] respected. **-4.** [avaliado] valued.

cotar [ko'ta(x)] vt **-1.** [ger] to quote. **-2.** [avaliar]: ~ **algo/alguém em** to value sthg/sb at.

cotejar [kote'ʒa(x)] vt to compare.

cotejo [ko'teʒu] m comparison.

cotidiano, na [kotʃi'dʒjanu, na] adj everyday.
  ◆ **cotidiano** m routine.

coto m **-1.** [mus] koto. **-2.** [zool] feather follicle.

cotonete [koto'nɛʃil] m cotton bud.

cotovelada [kotove'lada] f **-1.** [batida] hefty nudge. **-2.** [cutucada] nudge.

cotovelo [koto'velu] m **-1.** ANAT elbow; **falar pelos** ~ **s** fig to talk non-stop. **-2.** [de estrada etc.] bend.

couraça [ko'rasa] f **-1.** [armadura] breastplate. **-2.** [de animal] plating. **-3.** NÁUT armour plate.

couraçado, da [kora'sadu, da] adj [que tem couraça] armoured.
  ◆ **couraçado** m NÁUT battleship.

couro ['koru] m [de animal] hide; [curtido] leather; ~ **cru** rawhide.

couve ['kovi] f spring greens.

couve-de-bruxelas [,kovidʒibru'ʃɛlaʃ] (pl **couves-de-bruxelas**) f Brussels sprout.

couve-flor [,kovi'flo(x)] (pl **couves-flores**) f cauliflower.

couvert [ko've(x)] m cover charge.

cova ['kɔva] f **-1.** [sepultura] grave. **-2.** [caverna] cavern. **-3.** [buraco] hole.

covarde [ko'vaxdʒi] <> adj cowardly. <> mf coward.

covardia [kovax'dʒia] f cowardice.

covil [ko'viw] (pl -is) m **-1.** [ger] den. **-2.** fig [casebre] hovel.

coxa ['koʃa] f ANAT thigh.

coxear [ko'ʃja(x)] vi to limp.

coxia [ko'ʃia] f aisle.

coxo, xa ['koʃu, ʃa] adj **-1.** [ger] lame. **-2.** [móvel] wobbly (on account of having one leg shorter than the others).

cozer [ko'ze(x)] vt to cook.

cozido, da [ko'zidu, da] adj cooked.
  ◆ **cozido** m stew.

cozinha [ko'ziɲa] f **-1.** [cômodo] kitchen. **-2.** [arte] cookery.

cozinhar [kozi'ɲa(x)] <> vt **-1.** [cozer] to cook. **-2.** fig [adiar] to put off. <> vi to cook.

cozinheiro, ra [kozi'ɲejru, ra] m, f cook.

CPD (abrev de **Centro de Processamento de Dados**) m data-processing department.

CPF (abrev de **Cadastro de Pessoa Física**) m Brazilian tax-payer's identity card for individual contributions, ≃ NI number UK, ≃ social security number US.

CPMF (abrev de **Contribuição Provisória sobre Movimentação Financeira**) f Brazilian tax on bank transactions.

crachá [kra'ʃa] m badge.

crack ['kraki] m crack (cocaine).

crânio ['krãnju] m ANAT skull.

craque ['kraki] <> mf [pessoa exímia]: **ser um ~ em algo** to be an expert in sthg. <> m FUT football star UK, soccer star US.

crasso, ssa ['krasu, sa] adj -1. [grosseiro] crass. -2. [espesso] viscous.

cratera [kra'tɛra] f crater.

cravar [kra'va(x)] vt -1. [fazer penetrar] to drive in. -2. [engastar] to set. -3. fig [fixar]: **~ os olhos em alguém** to stare at sb.

cravejar [krave'ʒa(x)] vt -1. [com cravos] to nail. -2. [com pedras preciosas] to set.

cravo ['kravu] m -1. [flor] carnation. -2. [prego] nail. -3. MÚS harpsichord. -4. [especiaria] clove. -5. [na pele] blackhead.

creche ['krɛʃi] f crèche.

credenciais [kredẽnsi'ajʃ] fpl [qualificações] credentials.

credenciamento [kredẽnsia'mẽntu] m accreditation.

crediário [kre'dʒjarju] m hire purchase.

creditar [kredʒi'ta(x)] vt [depositar] to deposit.

crédito ['krɛdʒitu] m -1. [ger] credit; **digno de ~** creditworthy. -2. FIN credit. -3. [boa reputação] credibility.

credo ['krɛdu] m -1. [crença] belief. -2. [reza]: **o Credo** the Creed.

credor, ra [kre'do(x), ra] (mpl -es, fpl -s) <> adj -1. FIN credit (antes de subst). -2. [merecedor] deserving. <> m, f FIN creditor.

cremar [kre'ma(x)] vt to cremate.

crematório [krema'tɔrju] m crematorium.

creme ['krɛmi] <> adj inv [cor] cream. <> m -1. [ger] cream; **~ de leite** dairy cream. -2. [cosmético] face cream. -3. [pasta]: **~ dental** toothpaste.

cremoso, osa [kre'mozu, ɔza] adj creamy.

crença ['krẽnsa] f -1. RELIG belief. -2. [convicção] conviction.

crendice [krẽn'dʒiʃi] f superstition.

crente ['krẽntʃi] <> adj -1. [que tem fé] believing. -2. [protestante] Protestant. <> mf -1. [quem tem fé] believer. -2. [protestante] Protestant.

crepúsculo [kre'puʃkulu] m -1. [ao amanhecer] dawn. -2. [ao anoitecer] dusk. -3. fig [declínio] twilight.

crer ['kre(x)] <> vt [ger] to believe. <> vi [acreditar]: **~ em** to believe in.

crescente [kre'sẽntʃi] <> adj -1. [tamanho] growing. -2. [formato] crescent. <> m [fase da lua] crescent moon.

crescer [kre'se(x)] vi -1. [aumentar] to grow. -2. CULIN to rise.

crescimento [kresi'mẽntu] m growth.

crespo, pa ['krɛʃpu, pa] adj -1. [anelado] curly. -2. [áspero] rough.

cretinice [kretʃi'nisil f stupidity.

cretino, na [kre'tʃinu, na] <> adj cretinous. <> m, f cretin.

cria ['krial f offspring (inv).

criação [krja'sãw] (pl -ões) f -1. [ger] creation. -2. [de animais] raising. -3. [de filhos] upbringing. **de criação** loc adj adopted.

criado-mudo [ˌkrjadu'mudu] (pl criados-mudos) m bedside table.

criador, ra [krja'do(x), ra] (mpl -es, fpl -s) <> adj creative. <> m, f -1. [autor] creator. -2. [de animais] breeder.

criança [kri'ãnsa] f -1. [infante] child. -2. [pessoa infantil] child.

criançada [krjãn'sada] f: **a ~** the kids (pl).

criar [kri'a(x)] vt -1. [produzir] to create. -2. [fundar] to found. -3. [educar] to bring up. -4. [animais] to raise. -5. [plantas] to cultivate. **criar-se** vp [educar-se] to grow up.

criatividade [kriatʃivi'dadʒi] f creativity.

criativo, va [kria'tʃivu, va] adj creative.

criatura [kria'tura] f creature.

crime ['krimi] m crime.

criminal [krimi'naw] (pl -ais) adj criminal.

criminalidade [kriminali'dadʒi] f criminality.

criminoso, osa [krimi'nozu, ɔza] <> adj criminal. <> m, f criminal.

crina ['krina] f mane.

crioulo, la ['krjolu, la] <> adj -1. [comida, dialeto] Creole. -2. [negro] black. <> m, f [pessoa negra] black person.

criptografar [kriptogra'fa(x)] vt COMPUT to encrypt.

crisântemo [kri'zãntemu] m chrysanthemum.

crise ['krizi] f -1. MED attack. -2. [escassez] shortage. -3. [fase difícil] crisis. -4. fig [acesso] fit.

crisma ['kriʒma] f confirmation.

crismar [kriʒ'ma(x)] vt REL to confirm.

crista ['kriʃta] f -1. [de galo] comb. -2. [cume] crest.

cristal [kriʃ'taw] (pl -ais) m crystal.

cristaleira [kriʃta'lejra] f display cabinet.

cristalino, na [kriʃta'linu, na] adj crystalline.

cristalização [kriʃtaliza'sãw] (pl -ões) f crystallization.

cristandade [kriʃtãn'dadʒi] f Christianity.

cristão, ã [kriʃ'tãw, ã] <> adj Christian. <> mf Christian.

cristianismo [kriʃtʃjã'niʒmul m Christianity.

cristo [ˈkriʃtul m fig [vítima] victim.

Cristo [ˈkriʃtul m Christ.

critério [kri'tɛrjul m criterion.

criterioso, osa [krite'rjozu, ɔzal adj selective.

criticar [kritʃi'ka(x)] vt -1. [censurar] to criticize. -2. [analisar] to review.

crítico, ca [ˈkritʃiku, kal <> adj critical. <> m, f [pessoa] critic.
 ➡ **crítica** f -1. [censura] criticism (inv). -2. [análise] review. -3. [os críticos]: **a** ~ critics (pl).

crivar [kri'va(x)] vt -1. [com balas, facadas] to riddle. -2. [fig] [com perguntas] to bombard.

crível [ˈkrivewl (pl -eis) adj believable.

crivo [ˈkrivul m -1. [peneira] sieve. -2. fig [escrutínio] scrutiny.

Croácia [kro'asjal n Croatia.

croata [kro'atal <> adj Croat. <> mf Croat.

crocante [kro'kãntʃil adj crunchy.

crochê [kro'ʃel m crochet.

crocodilo [kroko'dʒilul m crocodile.

cromo [ˈkromul m chrome.

cromossomo [kromo'somul m [genética] chromosome.

crônica [ˈkronikal f -1. HIST & LITER chronicle. -2. JORN column.

crônico, ca [ˈkroniku, kal adj -1. [ger] chronic. -2. [inveterado] inveterate.

cronista [kro'niʃtal m f -1. HIST & LITER chronicler. -2. JORN columnist.

cronológico, ca [krono'lɔʒiku, kal adj chronological.

cronometrar [kronome'tra(x)] vt to time.

cronômetro [kro'nometrul m stopwatch.

croquete [kro'kɛtʃil m croquette.

croqui [kro'kil m sketch.

crosta [ˈkroʃtal f -1. [de pão, terra] crust. -2. [de ferida] scab.

cru, crua [ˈkru, ˈkrual adj -1. [não cozido] raw. -2. [não refinado] crude. -3. fig [duro] harsh.

crucial [kru'sjawl (pl -ais) adj -1. [ger] crucial. -2. [difícil] important.

crucificação [krusifika'sãwl (pl -ões) f RELIG: a ~ the Crucifixion.

crucificar [krusifi'ka(x)] vt to crucify.

crucifixo [krusi'fiksul m crucifix.

cruel [kru'ɛwl (pl -éis) adj -1. [perverso]

cruel. -2. [doloroso] cruel. -3. [violento] violent.

crueldade [kruew'dadʒil f cruelty.

cruz [ˈkruʃl (pl -es) f [kruziʃl) f cross.
 ➡ **Cruz Vermelha** f Red Cross.

cruzada [kru'zadal f crusade.

cruzado, da [kru'zadu, dal adj crossed.
 ➡ **cruzado** m [moeda] cruzado (former Brazilian currency).

cruzador [kruza'do(x)] m NÁUT cruiser.

cruzamento [kruza'mẽntul m -1. [de estradas] junction. -2. [de raças] crossbreeding.

cruzar [kru'za(x)] <> vt -1. [ger] to cross. -2. [animais] to crossbreed. <> vi -1. [rua]: ~ **com** to intersect. -2. [navio] to cruise. -3. fig [encontrar]: ~ **com alguém** to bump into sb.

cruzeiro [kru'zejrul m -1. NÁUT cruise. -2. [moeda] cruzeiro (former Brazilian currency).

CTI (abrev de Centro de Terapia Intensiva) m ICU.

cu [ˈkul m vulg arse; **fazer** ~-**doce** to act cool; ~-**do-mundo** arsehole.

Cuba [ˈkubal n Cuba.

cubano, na [ˈkubãnu, nal <> adj Cuban. <> m, f Cuban.

cubículo [ku'bikulul m cubicle.

cubista [ku'biʃtal <> adj cubist. <> mf cubist.

cubo [ˈkubul m -1. [ger] cube. -2. GEOM hexahedron.

cuca [ˈkukal fam f -1. [cabeça] head. -2. [mente] intellect; **fundir a** ~ [baratinar] to do one's head in; [confundir] to addle one's brain. -3. CULIN sponge cake.

cuco [ˈkukul m -1. [ave] cuckoo. -2. [relógio] cuckoo clock.

cueca [ˈkwɛkal f underpants (pl).

Cuiabá [kuja'bal n Cuiabá.

cuíca [ˈkwikal f cuíca, an instrument resembling a drum whose sound is produced by vibrating a cord on the inside.

cuidado, da [kwi'dadu, dal adj [tratado]: **bem/mal** ~ well/badly cared for.
 ➡ **cuidado** m [ger] care; ~**!** careful!

cuidadoso, osa [kwida'dozu, ɔzal adj careful.

cuidar [kwi'da(x)] vi [tratar]: ~ **de alguém/algo** to take care of sb/sthg.
 ➡ **cuidar-se** vp -1. [tratar-se] to take care of o.s. -2. [prevenir-se] to be careful.

cujo, ja [ˈkuʒu, ʒal pron rel -1. [de quem] whose. -2. [de que] whose.

culinário, ria [kuli'narju, rjal adj culinary.
 ➡ **culinária** f cookery.

culminar [kuwmi'na(x)] *vi*: ~ com algo to culminate with sthg.

culote [ku'lɔtʃil *m* -1. [calça] jodphurs *(pl)*. -2. [nas coxas] big thighs *(pl)*.

culpa ['kuwpa] *f* -1. [falta] fault; pôr a ~ em to blame. -2. *JUR* guilt.

culpabilidade [kuwpabili'dadʒi] *f* guilt.

culpado, da [kuw'padu, dal ⟨⟩ *adj* guilty. ⟨⟩ *m, f* criminal.

culpar [kuw'pa(x)] *vt*: ~ alguém (de) [atribuir a culpa] to blame sb (for); [acusar] to accuse sb (of).

cultivar [kuwtʃi'va(x)] *vt* to cultivate.

cultivo [kuw'tʃivul *m* cultivation.

culto, ta ['kuwtu, tal *adj* -1. [instruído] well educated. -2. [civilizado] civilized.
➡ **culto** *m* -1. *RELIG* ritual. -2. [veneração] worship.

cultura [kuw'tura] *f* -1. [conhecimento] culture. -2. [civilização] civilization. -3. [cultivo] culture. -4. [criação - de animais] breeding; [- de germes, bactérias] culture.

cultural [kuwtu'raw] *(pl* -ais) *adj* cultural.

cume ['kumi] *m* -1. [topo] summit. -2. *fig* [apogeu] apex.

cúmplice ['kũplisil *mf* -1. [co-autor] accomplice. -2. *fig* [parceiro] partner.

cumplicidade [kũplisi'dadʒi] *f* complicity.

cumprimentar [kũprimẽ'ta(x)] *vt* -1. [saudar] to greet. -2. [elogiar] to compliment.

cumprimento [kũpri'mẽtul *m* -1. [saudação] congratulation. -2. [elogio] compliment. -3. [realização] fulfilment.

cumprir [kũ'pri(x)] ⟨⟩ *vt* -1. [dever, obrigação] to fulfill. -2. [lei] to obey. -3. [promessa] to keep. -4. [caber] to be sb's responsibility. ⟨⟩ *vi* [convir] to be necessary, to be convenient.

cúmulo ['kumulul *m* height.

cunhado, da [ku'nadu, dal *m, f* brother-in-law, sister-in-law.

cunhar [ku'na(x)] *vt* -1. [moedas] to mint. -2. [palavras] to create.

cunho ['kunul *m* -1. [marca] mark. -2. *fig* [selo] stamp. -3. *fig* [caráter] nature.

cupim [ku'pĩ] *(pl* -ns) *m* termite.

cupom [ku'põl *(pl* -ns) *m* coupon.

cúpula ['kupula] *f* -1. [abóbada] dome. -2. [chefia] leadership.

cura ['kural ⟨⟩ *f* -1. [ger] cure; **não ter** ~ *fig* to be incurable. -2. [recuperação] recovery. ⟨⟩ *m* [pároco] curate.

curador, ra [kura'do(x), ral *m, f* -1. *JUR* [de menores] guardian. -2. [de instituições] caretaker. -3. [de arte] curator.

curandeiro, ra [kurãn'dejru, ral *m* healer.

curar [ku'ra(x)] *vt* [pessoa, doença] to cure.

curativo [kura'tʃivul *m* dressing.

curdo, da ['kurdu, dal ⟨⟩ *adj* Kurdish. ⟨⟩ *m, f* [pessoa] Kurd.
➡ **curdo** *m* [língua] Kurdish.

curiosidade [kurjozi'dadʒi] *f* curiosity.

curioso, osa [ku'rjozu, ozal ⟨⟩ *adj* -1. [ger] curious. -2. [bisbilhoteiro] nosy. -3. [interessante] interesting. ⟨⟩ *m, f* -1. [pessoa interessada] bystander. -2. [amador] amateur.
➡ **curioso** *m* [coisa singular]: **o** ~ **é** ... the strange thing is ...
➡ **curiosos** *mpl* [espectadores] onlookers.

curral [ku'xaw] *(pl* -ais) *m* corral.

currar [ku'xa(x)] *vt fam* to rape.

currículo [ku'xikulul *m* -1. [histórico] curriculum vitae *UK*, resume *US*. -2. [matérias] curriculum.

cursar [kux'sa(x)] *vt* -1. [curso] to study. -2. [escola] to attend.

cursinho [kur'sinul *m* [pré-vestibular] *preparatory course for university entry*.

curso ['kursul *m* -1. [ger] flow. -2. [rumo] course. -3. [andamento]: **em** ~ current. -4. [*EDUC* - nível] key stage *UK*, grade *US*; [- estabelecimento] school; ~ **superior** degree course; ~ **supletivo** supplementary course.

cursor [kux'so(x)] *(pl* -es) *m COMPUT* cursor.

curtição [kuxtʃi'sãw] *f* -1. [de couro] tanning. -2. *fam* [prazer] fun.

curtido, da [kux'tʃidu, dal *adj* -1. [couro] tanned. -2. *fig* [sofrido] fed up. -3. *fig* [endurecido] hard-boiled.

curtir [kux'tʃi(x)] *vt* -1. [couro] to tan. -2. [sofrer] to suffer. -3. *fam* [desfrutar de] to enjoy.
➡ **curtir-se** *vp fam*: **eles se curtem muito** they really hit it off.

curto, ta ['kuxtu, tal ⟨⟩ *adj* -1. [com pouco comprimento] short. -2. [breve] brief. -3. [limitado] intellectually limited. ⟨⟩ *m ELETR* = **curto-circuito**.

curto-circuito [ˌkuxtusix'kujtul *(pl* curtos-circuitos) *m ELETR* short circuit.

curva ['kuxval *f* -1. [de rua *etc.*] bend; ~ **fechada** sharp bend, hairpin bend. -2. [arqueamento] curve. -3. *GEOM* arc. -4. [em gráfico] curve.

curvar [kux'va(x)] ⟨⟩ *vt* -1. [arquear] to arch. -2. *fig* [dominar] to subdue. ⟨⟩ *vi* [envergar] to stoop.
➡ **curvar-se** *vp* -1. [envergar-se] to bend down. -2. [prostrar-se] to bow. -3. *fig* [submeter-se]: ~-**se a** to give in to.

curvo, va ['kuxvu, val *adj* -1. [arqueado]

cuscuz 90

curved. **-2.** [sinuoso - estrada, caminho] bendy; [- rio] meandering.

cuscuz [kuʃˈkuʃ] *m* couscous.

cusparada [kuʃpaˈrada] *f* gob of spittle.

cuspe [ˈkuʃpi] *m* spittle.

cuspida [kuʃˈpida] *f fam*: dar ~ s em to spit on *ou* at.

cuspido, da [kuʃˈpidu, da] *adj* **-1.** [telefone] crackling. **-2.** [pessoa] affronted.

cuspir [kuʃˈpi(x)] <> *vt* to spit. <> *vi* to spit.

custa [ˈkuʃta] *f*: à ~ de at the expense of.
◆ **custas** *fpl JUR* costs.

custar [kuʃˈta(x)] <> *vt* **-1.** [preço] to cost; *fig* ~ os olhos da cara to cost an arm and a leg. **-2.** *fig* [acarretar] to cause; não ~ nada fazer algo not to cost anything to do sthg. <> *vi* **-1.** [produto, serviço]: ~ barato/caro to be cheap/expensive. **-2.** [ser difícil, penoso]: não custava você ter ajudado ... it wouldn't have hurt you to help me ...; ~ caro to cost a great deal. **-3.** [demorar] to be late; ~ a fazer algo to take a lot of doing.

custo [ˈkuʃtu] *m* **-1.** [preço] cost; ~ de vida cost of living. **-2.** *fig* [dificuldade]: a todo ~ at all costs.

custódia [kuʃˈtɔdʒja] *f* custody.

CUT (*abrev de* **Central Única dos Trabalhadores**) *f central trade union body*, ≃ TUC *UK*.

cutelo [kuˈtɛlu] *m* cutlass.

cutia [kuˈtʃia] *f* agouti.

cutícula [kuˈtʃikula] *f* cuticle.

cútis [ˈkutʃiʃ] *f (inv)* cutis.

cutucar [kutuˈka(x)], **catucar** [katuˈka(x)] *vt* **-1.** [com o cotovelo] to nudge. **-2.** [com o dedo] to poke.

C.V. (*abrev de* **curriculum vitae**) *m* CV.

CVM (*abrev de* **Comissão de Valores Mobiliários**) *f regulatory body overseeing the sale of shares*, ≃ FSA *UK*.

czar, ina [ˈkza(x), ina] *m, f* czar (*f* czarina).

D

d, D [de] *m* [letra] d, D.

da [da] = de + a.

DAC (**Departamento de Aviação Civil**) *m civil aviation department*, ≃ CAA.

dadaísta [dadaˈiʃta] <> *adj* Dadaist. <> *mf* Dadaist.

dádiva [ˈdadiva] *f* **-1.** [donativo] donation. **-2.** [dom] gift.

dado, da [ˈdadu, da] *adj* **-1.** [ger] given. **-2.** [presenteado] presented. **-3.** [afável] friendly.
◆ **dado** *m* **-1.** [em jogo] dice. **-2.** [informação] data.
◆ **dados** *mpl COMPUT* data.
◆ **dado que** *loc conj* given that.

daí [daˈi] = de + aí.

dali [daˈli] = de + ali.

daltônico, ca [dawˈtoniku, ka] <> *adj* colour-blind. <> *m, f* colour-blind person.

dama [ˈdama] *f* **-1.** [mulher] lady; ~ de honra bridesmaid. **-2.** [em uma área específica] grande dame. **-3.** [em xadrez, baralho] queen.
◆ **damas** *fpl* [jogo] checkers.

damasco [daˈmaʃku] *m* **-1.** [fruta] apricot. **-2.** [tecido] damask.

danado, da [daˈnadu, da] <> *adj* **-1.** [amaldiçoado] damned. **-2.** [zangado] annoyed. **-3.** [travesso] mischievous. **-4.** [incrível] unbelievable. <> *m* **-1.** [pessoa amaldiçoada] cursed person. **-2.** *fam* [esperto] joker.

dança [ˈdãsa] *f* dance.

dançar [dãˈsa(x)] <> *vi* **-1.** [bailar] to dance. **-2.** *fam* [sair-se mal] to flop. **-3.** *fam* [deixar de acontecer] to fall through. <> *vt* [bailar] to dance.

dançarino, na [dãsaˈrinu, na] *m, f* ballet dancer.

danceteria [dãseteˈria] *f* dancehall.

danificar [danifiˈka(x)] *vt* to damage.
◆ **danificar-se** *vp* to get damaged.

dano [ˈdãnu] *m* damage.

Danúbio [daˈnubju] *n*: o ~ the Danube.

daquela [daˈkɛla] = de + aquela ⊳ aquele.

daquele [daˈkeli] = de + aquele ⊳ aquele.

daqui [daˈki] = de + aqui ⊳ aqui.

daquilo [daˈkilu] = de + aquilo ⊳ aquilo.

dardo [ˈdaxdu] *m* **-1.** [seta] dart. **-2.** *ESP* javelin.

dar [ˈda(x)] <> *vt* **-1.** [entregar, presentear] to give; ~ algo a alguém to give sb sthg, to give sthg to sb. **-2.** [produzir] to yield. **-3.** [causar, provocar] to give; isto me dá sono/pena this makes me sleepy/sad; isto vai ~ muito que fazer this is going to be a lot of work; o amor só dá problemas love is nothing but trouble. **-4.** [filme, programa]: deu no noticiário hoje it was on the news today.

- 5. [exprime ação] to give; ~ **um berro** to cry out; ~ **um pontapé em alguém** to kick sb; ~ **um passeio** to go for a walk. **- 6.** [festa, concerto] to have, to hold; **vão** ~ **uma festa** they're going to have ou throw a party. **-7.** [dizer] to say; **ele me deu boa-noite** he said good night to me. **- 8.** [ensinar] to teach; **o que é que você está dando nas suas aulas?** what do you teach in your class?; **ela dá aula numa escola** she teaches at a school; **eu gostaria de** ~ **aulas de inglês** I would like to teach English. **- 9.** [aprender, estudar] to do; **o que é que estão dando em Inglês?** what are you doing in English at the moment?; **estamos dando o verbo "to be"** we're doing the verb "to be". <> vi **-1.** [horas]: **já deram cinco horas** it's just gone five o'clock. **- 2.** [condizer]: ~ **com** to go with; **as cores não dão umas com as outras** the colours clash. **- 3.** [proporcionar]: ~ **de beber a alguém** to give sb sthg to drink; ~ **de comer a alguém** to feed sb. **- 4.** [em locuções]: **dá igual/no mesmo** it doesn't matter; ~ **ares de** to look like; ~ **à luz** to give birth; ~ **de si** to give of o.s.

<> **dar com** v + prep [encontrar, descobrir] to meet; **dei com ele no cinema** I met him at the movies.

<> **dar em** v + prep [resultar]: **a discussão não vai** ~ **em nada** the discussion will come to nothing.

<> **dar para** v + prep [servir para, ser útil para] to be good for; [suj: varanda, janela] to look onto; [suj: porta] to lead to; [ser suficiente para] to be enough for; [ser possível] to be possible; **dá para você fazer isso hoje?** could you do it today?; **dá para ir a pé?** is it within walking distance?; **não vai** ~ **para eu chegar na hora** I won't be able to get there on time.

<> **dar por** v + prep [aperceber-se de] to notice.

<> **dar-se** vp: ~-**se bem/mal com alguém** to get on well/badly with sb; **o professor deu-se mal com a brincadeira** the teacher did not appreciate the joke; ~-**se por vencido** to give up.

das [daʃ] = **de** + **as**.

DAT (abrev de **digital audio tape**) f DAT.

data ['data] f [em carta etc.] date.

datar [da'ta(x)] <> vt **- 1.** [pôr data em] to date. **- 2.** [considerar que existe]: ~ **algo de** to date sthg at. <> vi [existir]: ~ **de** to date from.

datilógrafo, fa [datʃi'lɔgrafu, fa] m, f typist.

DC (abrev de **Depois de Cristo**) AD.

DDT (abrev de **Dicloro-Difenil-Tricloretana**) m DDT.

de [dʒi] prep **-1.** [indica posse] of; **o lápis do Mário** Mário's pencil; **o carro daquele homem** that man's car; **a recepção do hotel** the hotel reception; **a casa é dela** it's her house, the house is hers; **as fases da lua** the phases of the moon. **- 2.** [indica matéria] (made) of; **um bolo** ~ **chocolate** a chocolate cake; **um relógio** ~ **ouro** a gold watch. **- 3.** [indica conteúdo] of; **um copo d'água** a glass of water. **- 4.** [usado em descrições, determinações]: **uma camiseta** ~ **manga curta** a short-sleeved T-shirt; **uma nota** ~ **50 reais** a 50-real note; **o senhor** ~ **preto** the man in black. **- 5.** [indica assunto] about; **fale da viagem** tell me about the trip; **um livro** ~ **informática** a book about ou on computers; **um livro** ~ **geografia** a geography book. **- 6.** [indica origem] from; **sou** ~ **Salvador** I'm from Salvador; **os habitantes do bairro** the locals; **um produto do Brasil** a Brazilian product. **-7.** [indica tempo]: **o jornal das nove** the nine o'clock news; **partimos às três da tarde** we left at three in the afternoon; **trabalho das nove às cinco** I work from nine to five. **- 8.** [indica uso]: **a sala** ~ **espera** the waiting room; **uma máquina** ~ **calcular** a calculator; **a porta** ~ **entrada** the front door. **- 9.** [usado em denominações, nomes] of. **-10.** [indica causa, modo]: **chorar** ~ **alegria** to cry with joy; **está tudo** ~ **pernas para o ar** everything is upside down; **morrer** ~ **frio** to freeze to death; **ele viajou** ~ **carro** he travelled by car. **-11.** [indica autor] by; **um filme** ~ **Glauber Rocha** a film by Glauber Rocha; **o último livro** ~ **Ferreira Gullar** Ferreira Gullar's latest book. **-12.** [introduz um complemento]: **cheio** ~ **gente** full of people, crowded; **desconfiar** ~ **alguém** to distrust sb; **difícil** ~ **esquecer** hard to forget; **gostar** ~ **algo/alguém** to like sthg/sb. **-13.** [em comparações]: **do que** than; **teu carro é mais rápido do que este** your car is faster than this one. **-14.** [em superlativos] of; **o melhor** ~ **todos** the best of all. **-15.** [dentre] of; **uma daquelas cadeiras** one of those chairs; **um dia destes** one of these days; **um desses hotéis serve** one of those hotels will do. **-16.** [indica série]: ~ **dois em dois dias** every two days; ~ **quinze em quinze minutos** every fifteen minutes; ~ **três em três metros** every three metres.

debaixo [de'bajʃu] adv underneath.

<> **debaixo de** loc prep under.

debate [deˈbatʃi] *m* **-1.** [discussão] debate. **-2.** [disputa] discussion.

debatedor, ra [debateˈdo(x)], ral *m,f* debater.

debater [debaˈte(x)] <> *vt* **-1.** [discutir] to debate. **-2.** [questionar] to dispute. <> *vi* [discutir] to discuss.

➡ **debater-se** *vp* [agitar-se] to struggle.

débeis [ˈdɛbejʃ] *pl* ▷ **débil**.

debelar [debeˈla(x)] *vt* **-1.** [ger] to overcome. **-2.** [dominar] to defeat.

débil [ˈdɛbiw] (*pl* **-eis**) <> *adj* **-1.** [fraco] weak. **-2.** *PSIC* retarded. <> *mf PSIC*: ~ **mental** mentally retarded person; *fam* [idiota] fool.

debilidade [debiliˈdaʒi] *f* **-1.** [fraqueza] weakness. **-2.** *PSIC*: ~ **mental** mental retardation.

debilitar [debiliˈta(x)] *vt* to debilitate.

➡ **debilitar-se** *vp* to weaken.

debilóide [debiˈlɔjdʒi] *fam* <> *adj* stupid. <> *mf* dunderhead.

debitar [debiˈta(x)] *vt* to debit.

débito [ˈdɛbitu] *m* debit.

debochado, da [deboˈʃadu, dal *adj* scornful.

debochar [deboˈʃa(x)] *vi*: ~ **de algo/alguém** to scorn sb/sthg.

deboche [deˈbɔʃil *m* scorn.

debruçar [debruˈsa(x)] *vt* to lean.

➡ **debruçar-se** *vp* to lean over.

década [ˈdɛkadal *f* decade.

decadência [dekaˈdẽsjal *f* decadence.

decadente [dekaˈdẽtʃil *adj* decadent.

decair [dekaˈi(x)] *vi* **-1.** [deteriorar] to deteriorate. **-2.** [pender] to wither. **-3.** [diminuir] to diminish.

decapitar [dekapiˈta(x)] *vt* to decapitate.

decatleta [dekaˈtlɛtal *mf ESP* decathlete.

decatlo [deˈkatlul *m* decathlon.

decência [deˈsẽsjal *f* decency.

decente [deˈsẽtʃil *adj* **-1.** [digno] decent. **-2.** [decoroso] demure. **-3.** [apropriado, asseado - roupa] decent; [- restaurante, casa] clean. **-4.** [bem-feito] well done.

decentemente [desẽtʃiˈmẽtʃil *adv* **-1.** [dignamente, com decoro] decently. **-2.** [adequadamente] satisfactorily.

decepar [deseˈpa(x)] *vt* to cut off.

decepção [desepˈsãw] (*pl* **-ões**) *f* **-1.** [desapontamento] disappointment. **-2.** [desilusão] disillusion.

decepcionado, da [desepsjoˈnadu, dal *adj* **-1.** [desapontado] disappointed. **-2.** [desiludido] disillusioned.

decepcionar [desepsjoˈna(x)] *vt* **-1.** [desapontar] to disappoint. **-2.** [desiludir] to disillusion.

➡ **decepcionar-se** *vp* [desapontar-se]:

~ **-se com algo/alguém** to be disappointed with sthg/sb.

decerto [dʒiˈsextul *adv* surely.

decididamente [desidʒidaˈmẽtʃil *adv* **-1.** [com certeza] certainly. **-2.** [resolutamente] decidedly.

decidido, da [desiˈdʒidu, dal *adj* **-1.** [resolvido] resolved. **-2.** [resoluto] resolute.

decidir [desiˈdʒi(x)] <> *vt* **-1.** [resolver] to resolve. **-2.** [deliberar] to decide. **-3.** [concluir] to decide. <> *vi* **-1.** [tomar decisão]: ~ **(sobre algo)** to make a decision (about sthg). **-2.** [optar]: ~ **entre** to decide between.

➡ **decidir-se** *vp* **-1.** [tomar decisão] to make a decision. **-2.** [optar]: ~ **-se por** to opt for.

decifrar [desiˈfra(x)] *vt* **-1.** [ler, interpretar] to decipher. **-2.** [entender] to unravel.

décima [ˈdɛsimal ▷ **décimo**.

decimal [desiˈmaw] (*pl* **-ais** [dɛsiˈmajʃl) <> *adj* decimal. <> *m* decimal.

décimo, ma [ˈdɛsimu, mal *num* tenth.

➡ **décimo** *m* tenth part; *veja também* **sexto**.

decisão [desiˈzãw] (*pl* **-ões**) *f* **-1.** [deliberação] decision; **tomar uma** ~ to make a decision. **-2.** [qualidade] decisiveness.

decisivo, va [desiˈzivu, val *adj* **-1.** [deliberativo, crítico] decisive. **-2.** [terminante] deciding.

declaração [deklaraˈsãw] (*pl* **-ões**) *f* **-1.** [documento] written declaration. **-2.** [depoimento] testimony; **fazer uma** ~ to make a declaration.

declarado, da [deklaˈradu, dal *adj* **-1.** [patenteado] declared. **-2.** [confessado] self-declared.

declarante [deklaˈrãtʃil *mf JUR* declarant.

declarar [deklaˈra(x)] *vt* **-1.** [ger] to declare. **-2.** [confessar] to confess.

➡ **declarar-se** *vp* **-1.** [manifestar-se]: ~ **-se a favor de/contra** to declare o.s for/against. **-2.** [confessar-se] to confess o.s. to be. **-3.** [designar-se] to declare o.s.

declinar [dekliˈna(x)] <> *vt* **-1.** [ger] to decline. **-2.** [revelar] to disclose. <> *vi* **-1.** [astro] to set. **-2.** [mesa, terreno] to slope. **-3.** [dia, tarde] to draw to a close.

declínio [deˈklinjul *m* decline.

declive [deˈklivil *m* [de terreno] slope.

decodificador [dekodʒifikaˈdo(x)] *m COMPUT & TV* decoder.

decodificar [dekodʒifiˈka(x)] *vt COMPUT & TV* to decode.

decolagem [dekoˈlaʒẽl (*pl* **-ns**) *f* take-off.

decolar [dekoˈla(x)] *vi* to take off.

decompor [dekõn'po(x)] *vt* **-1.** [separar elementos de] to break down. **-2.** [dividir em partes] to dissect. **-3.** [estragar] to rot. **-4.** [alterar] to change.
◆ **decompor-se** *vp* **-1.** [estragar-se] to rot. **-2.** [alterar-se] to change o.s.

decomposição [dekõnpozi'sãw] (*pl* **-ões**) *f* **-1.** [apodrecimento] rotting. **-2.** [divisão em partes] dissection. **-3.** [separação de elementos] breakdown. **-4.** [alteração] change. **-5.** [desorganização] break-up.

decoração [dekora'sãw] (*pl* **-ões**) *f* decoration.

decorador, ra [dekora'do(x), ra] *m, f* [profissional] decorator.

decorar [deko'ra(x)] *vt* **-1.** [memorizar] to learn by heart. **-2.** [ornamentar] to decorate.

decorativo, va [dekora'tʃivu, va] *adj* decorative.

decoro [de'koru] *m* **-1.** [decência] decency. **-2.** [dignidade] dignity.

decoroso, osa [deko'rozu, ɔza] *adj* decent.

decorrência [deko'xẽnsja] *f* consequence; **em ~ de** as a consequence of.

decorrente [deko'xẽntʃi] *adj:* **~ de** resulting from.

decorrer [deko'xe(x)] ⬦ *m* [decurso]: **no ~ de** in the course of, during. ⬦ *vi* **-1.** [derivar]: **~ de** to stem from. **-2.** [passar] to pass.

decorrido, da [deko'xidu, da] *adj* [terminado]: **decorrida a votação, ...** once the voting was over, ...

decote [de'kɔtʃi] *m* décolletage.

decrepitude [dekrepi'tudʒi] *f* [caducidade] decrepitude.

decrescer [dekre'se(x)] *vi* to decrease.

decréscimo [de'krɛsimu] *m* decrease.

decretar [dekre'ta(x)] ⬦ *vt* **-1.** [ordenar] to decree. **-2.** [determinar] to determine. ⬦ *vi* [ordenar] to decree.

decreto [de'krɛtu] *m* [ordem] decree; [judicial] fiat.

decreto-lei [de,krɛtu'lej] (*pl* **decretos-lei**) *m* law by decree.

decurso [de'kuxsu] *m* course; **no ~ de** in the course of.

dedal [de'daw] (*pl* **-ais**) *m* thimble.

dedão [de'dãw] (*pl* **-ões**) *m* **-1.** [polegar] thumb. **-2.** [do pé] big toe.

dedetização [dedetʃiza'sãw] (*pl* **-ões**) *f* fumigation.

dedicação [dedʒika'sãw] (*pl* **-ões**) *f* **-1.** [devotamento] dedication. **-2.** [amor] devotion.

dedicado, da [dedʒi'kadu, da] *adj* dedicated.

dedicar [dedʒi'ka(x)] *vt* [devotar]: **~ algo a alguém** to devote sthg to sb; [oferecer] to dedicate.
◆ **dedicar-se** *vp* [devotar-se]: **~-se a fazer algo** to devote o.s to doing sthg.

dedicatória [dedʒika'tɔrja] *f* dedication.

dedo ['dedu] *m* **-1.** [da mão] finger; **~ anular** ring finger; **~ indicador** forefinger; **~ mindinho** *ou* **mínimo** little finger; **~ polegar** thumb. **-2.** [do pé] toe. **-3.** *loc:* **cheio de ~s** finicky; **não levantar um ~** not to lift a finger.

dedões [de'dõjʃ] *pl* ⬦ **dedão**.

dedução [dedu'sãw] (*pl* **-ões**) *f* deduction.

dedutível [dedu'tʃivew] (*pl* **-eis**) *adj* deductible.

deduzir [dedu'zi(x)] ⬦ *vt* **-1.** [subtrair] to subtract. **-2.** [concluir] to deduce. ⬦ *vi* [tirar dedução] to deduce.

defasado, da [defa'zadu, da] *adj* out of phase.

defasagem [defa'zaʒẽ] (*pl* **-ns**) *f* [discrepância] gap.

defecar [defe'ka(x)] *vi* to defecate.

defeito [de'fejtu] *m* **-1.** [físico] defect. **-2.** [moral] flaw. **-3.** [falha] fault; **com ~** out of order.

defeituoso, osa [defej'twozu, ɔza] *adj* **-1.** [com falha] faulty. **-2.** [físico] defective.

defender [defẽn'de(x)] *vt* **-1.** [proteger]: **~ algo/alguém (contra *ou* de)** to defend sthg/sb (against). **-2.** [sustentar] to stand up for.
◆ **defender-se** *vp* [proteger-se]: **~-se (contra *ou* de)** to defend o.s (against).

defensivo, va [defẽn'sivu, va] *adj* defensive.
◆ **defensiva** *f* **-1.** [meios de defesa] defences *UK*, defenses *US*. **-2.** [atitude]: **estar/ficar na ~** to be/stay on the defensive.

defensor, ra [defẽn'so(x), ra] (*mpl* **-es**, *fpl* **-s**) *m, f* **-1.** [de causa *etc.*] defender. **-2.** *JUR* defendant.

deferir [defe'ri(x)] ⬦ *vt* **-1.** [atender] to grant. **-2.** [conceder]: **~ algo a alguém** to award sthg to sb. ⬦ *vi* [acatar]: **~ a algo** to respect sthg.

defesa [de'feza] *f* **-1.** [proteção] defence. **-2.** *JUR* defence lawyer. **-3.** *FUT* defence.

deficiente [defi'sjẽntʃi] ⬦ *adj* deficient. ⬦ *mf* *MED*: **~ (físico/mental)** physically/mentally disabled.

déficit ['dɛfisitʃ] *m* *ECON*: **~ público** public deficit.

definhamento [defiɲa'mẽntu] *m* [debilitação] debilitation, wasting away.

definhar [defiˈɲa(x)] ⬦ *vt* to drain. ⬦ *vi* to waste away.

definição [definiˈsãw] (*pl* -ões) *f* -**1**. [explicação] explanation. -**2**. [decisão] decision. -**3**. [de imagem] definition.

definir [defiˈni(x)] *vt* -**1**. [fixar, explicar] to define. -**2**. [decidir] to determine.

➡ **definir-se** *vp* -**1**. [pronunciar-se]: ~ -se sobre/contra/a favor de to come out for/against/in favour of. -**2**. [decidir-se] to make up one's mind. -**3**. [descrever-se]: ~ -se como to describe o.s. as.

definitivamente [definiˌtʃivaˈmẽtʃi] *adv* -**1**. [para sempre] definitively. -**2**. [decididamente] definitely.

definitivo, va [definiˈtʃivu, va] *adj* -**1**. [final] definitive. -**2**. [permanente] permanent.

deformação [defoxmaˈsãw] (*pl* -ões) *f* distortion.

deformar [defoxˈma(x)] *vt* -**1**. [tornar disforme] to deform. -**2**. [deturpar] to distort.

➡ **deformar-se** *vp* [tornar-se disforme] to become deformed.

defraudar [defrawˈda(x)] *vt* to defraud.

defrontar [defrõˈta(x)] ⬦ *vi* [estar]: ~ com to face onto. ⬦ *vt* -**1**. [encarar] to face. -**2**. [confrontar] to compare.

➡ **defrontar-se** *vp* [deparar-se]: ~ -se com to come face to face with.

defronte [deˈfrõtʃi] ⬦ *adv* [em frente] opposite. ⬦ *prep*: ~ a/de in front of.

defumador [defumaˈdo(x)] *m* -**1**. [recipiente] burner. -**2**. [substância] *substance used in burners for its smell.*

defumar [defuˈma(x)] *vt* -**1**. [curar] to cure. -**2**. [perfumar] to perfume.

defunto, ta [deˈfũtu, ta] ⬦ *adj* [morto] dead. ⬦ *m, f* [cadáver] corpse.

degelar [deʒeˈla(x)] ⬦ *vt* [descongelar] to defrost. ⬦ *vi* [derreter-se] to melt.

degelo [deˈʒelu] *m* thaw.

degenerar [deʒeneˈra(x)] *vi* -**1**. [ger] to degenerate. -**2**. [depravar-se] to become depraved.

➡ **degenerar-se** *vp* [depravar-se] to be led astray.

degenerativo, va [deʒeneraˈtʃivu, va] *adj* degenerative.

deglutição [deglutʃiˈsãw] (*pl* -ões) *f* swallowing.

deglutir [degluˈtʃi(x)] ⬦ *vt* & *vi* to swallow.

degola [deˈgɔla] *f* -**1**. [decapitação] decapitation. -**2**. [demissão] large-scale redundancy. -**3**. *ESP* sacking.

degolar [degoˈla(x)] *vt* to behead.

degradante [degraˈdãtʃi] *adj* [aviltante] demeaning.

degradar [degraˈda(x)] *vt* -**1**. [privar] to strip. -**2**. [aviltar] to demean.

➡ **degradar-se** *vp* [aviltar-se] to demean o.s.

degrau [deˈgraw] *m* -**1**. [de escada] step. -**2**. *fig* [meio] means.

degredo [deˈgredu] *m* -**1**. [pena] exile. -**2**. [lugar] place of exile.

degringolar [degrĩgoˈla(x)] *vi* -**1**. [cair] to fall down. -**2**. *fig* [deteriorar-se] to go off the rails. -**3**. *fig* [desordenar-se - esquema] to get in a mess; [- fila, jogo] to become disorderly. -**4**. [arruinar-se] to go bankrupt.

degustação [deguʃtaˈsãw] (*pl* -ões) *f* tasting.

degustar [deguʃˈta(x)] *vt* -**1**. [provar] to taste. -**2**. [saborear] to savour.

deitada [dejˈtada] *f fam*: dar uma ~ to have a lie-down.

deitado, da [dejˈtadu, da] *adj* -**1**. [pessoa] lying down (*depois de verbo*). -**2**. [objeto] set down (*depois de verbo*).

deitar [dejˈta(x)] ⬦ *vt* -**1**. [pessoa] to lay down. -**2**. [objeto] to set down. ⬦ *vi* [pessoa] to lie down; ~ e rolar *fig* to call the shots.

➡ **deitar-se** *vp* [pessoa] to go to bed.

deixa [ˈdejʃa] *f* -**1**. [dica] hint. -**2**. *TEATRO* cue. -**3**. [chance] opportunity.

deixar [dejˈʃa(x)] ⬦ *vt* -**1**. [ger] to leave. -**2**. [abandonar] to abandon. -**3**. [demitir-se de] to resign. -**4**. [consentir]: ~ alguém fazer/que alguém faça algo to allow sb to do sthg; ~ passar algo to overlook sthg. -**5**. [tornar possível]: não ~ alguém fazer algo not to allow sb to do sthg. -**6**. [esperar] to let. -**7**. [ignorar]: ~ algo/alguém pra lá to let sthg/sb be. -**8**. [não considerar, esquecer] to forget; me deixa (em paz)! leave me alone! ⬦ *vi* -**1**. [parar]: ~ de fazer algo to stop doing sthg. -**2**. [não se preocupar]: pode ~ it's fine; deixa pra lá! forget it! -**3**. [expressando pedido]: não deixe de ir no concerto! make sure you go to the concert! -**4**. *loc*: ~ (muito) a desejar to leave much to be desired.

➡ **deixar-se** *vp* [permitir-se]: ~ -se fazer algo to allow o.s. to do sthg.

dela [ˈdela] = de + ella.

delação [delaˈsãw] (*pl* -ões) *f* -**1**. [denúncia] accusation. -**2**. [acusação] charge.

delas [ˈdelaʃ] = de + ellas.

delatar [delaˈta(x)] *vt* -**1**. [denunciar] to denounce. -**2**. [acusar] to accuse. -**3**. [informar] to inform.

delator, ra [delaˈto(x), ra] *m, f* informer.

dele [ˈdeli] = de + ele.

delegação [delega'sãw] (*pl* -ões) *f* delegation; ~ **de poderes** transfer of powers.

delegacia [delega'sial] *f* police station; ~ **de polícia** police station.

delegado, da [dele'gadu, da] *m, f* delegate; ~ **de polícia** chief of police.

delegar [dele'ga(x)] *vt* -1. [dar]: ~ **algo a alguém** to delegate sthg to sb. -2. [enviar] to send sb as a delegate.

deleitar [delej'ta(x)] *vt* to delight.
➡ **deleitar-se** *vp*: ~-**se com** to rejoice in.

deleite [de'lejtʃi] *m* delight.

deleitoso, osa [delej'tozu, ɔza] *adj* delightful.

deles ['delif] = **de** + **eles**.

deletar [dele'ta(x)] *vt* COMPUT to delete.

delgado, da [dew'gadu, da] *adj* -1. [fino] slim. -2. [esbelto] slender.

deliberação [delibera'sãw] (*pl* -ões) *f* -1. [discussão] discussion; **em** ~ under discussion. -2. [decisão] decision.

deliberar [delibe'ra(x)] ⬦ *vt* [decidir] to decide. ⬦ *vi* [refletir sobre]: ~ **sobre** to ponder upon.

delicadeza [delika'deza] *f* -1. [ger] delicacy. -2. [leveza] fineness. -3. [fragilidade] fragility. -4. [apuro]: ~ **de detalhes** attentiveness to detail. -5. [cortesia] politeness.

delicado, da [deli'kadu, da] *adj* -1. [ger] delicate. -2. [sensível] urbane. -3. [cortês] polite.

delícia [de'lisja] *f* -1. [deleite] delight. -2. [coisa saborosa]: **ser/estar uma** ~ to be delicious.

deliciar [deli'sja(x)] *vt* to delight.
➡ **deliciar-se** *vp*: ~-**se com algo** to be delighted with sthg.

delicioso, osa [deli'sjozu, ɔza] *adj* -1. [vinho, doce] delicious. -2. [passeio] delightful.

delineador [delinja'do(x)] *m* eyeliner.

delinear [deli'nja(x)] *vt* to outline.

delinqüência [deliŋ'kwẽsja] *f* delinquency.

delinqüente [deliŋ'kwẽtʃi] ⬦ *adj* delinquent. ⬦ *mf* delinquent.

delirante [deli'rãtʃil] *adj* -1. PSIC delirious. -2. [extravagante, aloucado] wild. -3. [maravilhoso] wonderful.

delirar [deli'ra(x)] *vi* -1. PSIC to be delirious. -2. [sentir intensamente]: ~ **de algo** to be overcome with sthg.

delírio [de'lirju] *m* -1. PSIC delirium. -2. [excitação] excitement. -3. [êxtase] ecstasy.

delito [de'litu] *m* -1. [falta] sin. -2. [crime] crime.

delonga [de'lõŋga] *f* delay; **sem mais** ~ without further delay.

delongar [de'lõŋ'ga(x)] *vt* [retardar] to postpone.
➡ **delongar-se** *vp* -1. [demorar-se] to delay. -2. [prolongar-se] to prolong.

demagogia [demago'ʒia] *f* demagogy.

demais [de'majʃ] *adv* -1. [em demasia, muitíssimo] too much. -2. *fam* [ótimo]: **estar/ser** ~ to be amazing.

demanda [de'mãnda] *f* -1. ECON demand. -2. JUR lawsuit. -3. [disputa] dispute. -4. [pedido] request.

demão [de'mãw] (*pl* -s) *f* coat.

demarcação [demaxka'sãw] (*pl* -ões) *f* -1. [delimitação] demarcation. -2. [separação] boundary.

demasia [dema'zia] *f* excess; **em** ~ in excess.

demasiadamente [demazjada'mẽtʃil] *adv* -1. [demais] excessively. -2. [muito] too.

demasiado, da [dema'zjadu, da] ⬦ *adj* excessive. ⬦ *adv* too much.

demente [de'mẽtʃil] *adj* -1. MED demented. -2. [louco] insane.

demissão [demi'sãw] (*pl* -ões) *f* -1. [solicitado pelo empregador] dismissal. -2. [solicitado pelo empregado] resignation; **pedir** ~ to tender one's resignation.

demitir [demi'tʃi(x)] *vt* to dismiss.
➡ **demitir-se** *vp* to resign.

democracia [demokra'sial] *f* democracy.

democrata [demo'krata] *mf* democrat.

democrático, ca [demo'kratʃiku, kal] *adj* -1. [relativo a democracia] democratic. -2. [indiferente às classes sociais] egalitarian.

demolição [demoli'sãw] (*pl* -ões) *f* -1. demolition. -2. *fig* [ger] de reputação] destruction; [- de obstáculo] elimination.

demolidor, ra [demo'lido(x), ral] ⬦ *adj* demolition (*antes de subst*). ⬦ *m,f* demolition expert.

demolir [demo'li(x)] *vt* -1. [destruir] to demolish. -2. *fig* [- reputação] to destroy; [- obstáculo] to overcome.

demônio [de'monju] *m* demon.

demonstração [demõnʃtra'sãw] (*pl* -ões) *f* -1. [ger] demonstration. -2. [apresentação] display.

demonstrar [demõnʃ'tra(x)] *vt* -1. [ger] to demonstrate. -2. [afeto, antipatia *etc*.] to show. -3. [habilidades, talentos] to display.

demora [de'mɔral] *f* [atraso] delay; **sem** ~ without delay.

demorado, da [demo'radu, da] *adj* delayed.

demorar [demo'ra(x)] <> *vt* [retardar] to delay. <> *vi* **-1.** [tardar] to be late; **~ a fazer algo** to take a long time to do sthg. **-2.** [permanecer] to stay.
➤ **demorar-se** *vp* **-1.** [tardar] to be late. **-2.** [permanecer] to remain.

demover [demo've(x)] *vt* **-1.** [dissuadir]: **~ alguém de algo/fazer algo** to dissuade sb from sthg/doing sthg. **-2.** [remover] to move.

DENARC (*abrev de* **Departamento de Investigações sobre Narcóticos**) *m Brazilian police narcotics department.*

DENATRAN (*abrev de* **Departamento Nacional de Trânsito**) *m Brazilian national department responsible for transport law.*

dendê [dēn'de] *m* **-1.** *BOT* palm. **-2.** [azeite] palm oil.

denegrir [dene'gri(x)] *vt* [escurecer] to blacken.

dengoso, osa [dēn'gozu, ɔza] *adj* whining.

dengue ['dēŋgi] *f MED* dengue.

denominação [denomina'sāw] (*pl* **-ões**) *f* **-1.** [nomeação] name. **-2.** [designação] designation. **-3.** *REL* denomination.

denominar [denomi'na(x)] *vt* **-1.** [nomear] to name. **-2.** [designar] to designate.
➤ **denominar-se** *vp* to be called.

denotar [deno'ta(x)] *vt* **-1.** [indicar] to indicate. **-2.** [significar] to denote.

densidade [dēnsi'dadʒi] *f* density; **de alta/dupla ~** high/double density.

denso, sa ['dēnsu, sa] *adj* **-1.** [ger] dense. **-2.** [espesso] thick.

dentada [dēn'tada] *f* bite.

dentadura [dēnta'dura] *f* **-1.** [natural] set of teeth. **-2.** [postiça] denture.

dental [dēn'taw] (*pl* **-ais**) *adj* dental; **pasta ~** toothpaste.

dente ['dēntʃi] *m* **-1.** [ger] tooth; **~ de leite** milk tooth; **~ de siso** wisdom tooth. **-2.** [de elefante] tusk. **-3.** [alho] clove.

dentifrício, cia [dēntʃi'frisju, sja] *adj* dental.
➤ **dentifrício** *m* toothpaste.

dentista [dēn'tʃifta] *mf* dentist.

dentre ['dēntri] *prep* among.

dentro ['dēntru] <> *adv* in; **aí/lá ~** in there. <> *prep* **-1.:** **~ de** [no interior de] inside; [no tempo] within; **por ~** [na parte interna] inside. **-2.** *loc*: **estar por ~ (de algo)** *fam* to be in touch (with sthg).

dentuço, ça [dēn'tusu, sa] <> *adj* buck-toothed. <> *m, f* [pessoa] buck-toothed person.

denúncia [de'nũnsja] *f* **-1.** [acusação] accusation. **-2.** [à polícia] report. **-3.**

[*JUR* - de pessoa, crime] condemnation; [- de contrato] termination.

denunciar [denũn'sja(x)] *vt* **-1.** [acusar] to denounce. **-2.** [divulgar] to expose. **-3.** [*JUR* - pessoa, crime] to condemn; [- contrato] to terminate. **-4.** [evidenciar] to reveal.

deparar [depa'ra(x)] *vi*: **~ com** to come across.

departamento [departa'mēntu] *m* department.

depauperado, da [depawpe'radu, da] *adj* **-1.** [empobrecido] impoverished. **-2.** [enfraquecido] exhausted.

dependência [depēn'dēnsja] *f* **-1.** [ger] dependency. **-2.** [cômodo] room.

dependente [depēn'dēntʃil] <> *adj* [subordinado] dependent. <> *mf* dependant.

depender [depēn'de(x)] *vi* [financeiramente]: **~ de** to be dependent upon.

depilador, ra [depila'do(x), ra] *m, f* beautician who does hair-removal.

depilar [depi'la(x)] *vt* to remove hair from.
➤ **depilar-se** *vp* **-1.** [com cera - na estética] to have a wax; [- em casa] to wax. **-2.** [com lâmina] to shave.

deplorar [deplo'ra(x)] *vt* to lament.

deplorável [deplo'ravew] (*pl* **-eis**) *adj* **-1.** [lamentável] lamentable. **-2.** [detestável] deplorable.

depoimento [depoj'mēntu] *m* **-1.** [ger] statement. **-2.** [ato] testimony.

depois [de'pojʃ] <> *adv* **-1.** [posteriormente] after. **-2.** [além disso] besides. <> *prep*: **~ de fazer algo** after doing sthg.
➤ **depois que** *loc conj* after.

depor [de'po(x)] <> *vt* **-1.** [colocar] to put down. **-2.** [destituir] to depose.

deportar [depox'ta(x)] *vt* to deport.

depositar [depozi'ta(x)] *vt* to deposit.
➤ **depositar-se** *vp* [assentar] to settle.

depósito [de'pozitu] *m* **-1.** [ger] deposit. **-2.** [reservatório] depository.

depravado, da [depra'vadu, da] <> *adj* depraved. <> *m, f* depraved person.

depravar [depra'va(x)] *vt* **-1.** [corromper] to corrupt. **-2.** [estragar] to ruin.
➤ **depravar-se** *vp* [corromper-se] to become corrupted.

depreciação [depresja'sāw] (*pl* **-ões**) *f* [desvalorização] depreciation.

depreciar [depre'sja(x)] *vt* **-1.** [desvalorizar] to devalue. **-2.** [subestimar] to undervalue.
➤ **depreciar-se** *vp* **-1.** [desvalorizar-se] to fall in value. **-2.** [subestimar-se] to underestimate o.s.

depredar [depre'da(x)] *vt* **-1.** [destruir] to destroy. **-2.** [saquear] to loot.

depressa [de'prɛsal *adv* quickly.

depressão [depre'sãw] (*pl* **-ões**) *f* **-1.** PSIC depression. **-2.** [en terreno, superfície] dip. **-3.** *fig* [abatimento] despondency.

deprimente [depri'mẽtʃil *adj* depressing.

deprimido, da [depri'midu, dal *adj* depressed.

deprimir [depri'mi(x)] *vt* to depress.

➡ **deprimir-se** *vp* to become depressed.

depto. (*abrev de* **departamento**) *m* dept.

depurar [depu'ra(x)] *vt* to purify.

deputado, da [depu'tadu, dal *m, f* **-1.** POL deputy. **-2.** [delegado] representative.

deque [ˈdɛki] *m* decking.

DER (*abrev de* **Departamento de Estradas de Rodagem**) *m* Brazilian highways department.

deriva [de'rival *f* drift; à ~ drifting.

derivado, da [deri'vadu, dal *adj* [proveniente]: ~ **de** derived from.

➡ **derivado** *m* derivative.

derivar [deri'va(x)] *vi* **-1.** [resultar]: ~ **de** to derive from. **-2.** [ficar à deriva] to drift.

dermatológico, ca [dexmato'lɔʒiku, kal *adj* dermatological.

dermatologista [dexmatolo'ʒiʃtal *mf* dermatologist.

derradeiro, ra [dexa'dejru, ral *adj* final.

derramamento [dexama'mẽtul *m* **-1.** [de água, leite] spillage. **-2.** [de lágrimas] flow; ~ **de sangue** bloodshed.

derramar [dexa'ma(x)] *vt* **-1.** [ger] to spill **-2.** [espalhar] to strew

➡ **derramar-se** *vp* [verter] to spill.

derrame [de'xãmil *m* **-1.** [de líquido] spillage. **-2.** [de lágrimas, sangue] flow. **-3.** MED haemorrhage; ~ **cerebral** brain haemorrhage.

derrapagem [dexa'paʒẽl (*pl* **-ns**) *f* skid.

derrapar [dexa'pa(x)] *vi* to skid.

derredor [dexe'do(x)] *adv fml*: em ~ (**de**) around.

derreter [dexe'te(x)] ⟨> *vt* to melt. ⟨> *vi* [liquefazer-se] to melt.

➡ **derreter-se** *vp* **-1.** *fig* [comover-se]: ~ (**com algo**) to be moved (by sthg). **-2.** *fig* [apaixonar-se]: ~-**se todo** (**por alguém**) to fall completely (for sb).

derretido, da [dexe'tʃidu, dal *adj* **-1.** [liquefeito] melted. **-2.** *fig* [comovido] moved. **-3.** *fig* [apaixonado] besotted.

derrota [de'xɔtal *f* **-1.** [fracasso] defeat. **-2.** NÁUT course.

derrotado, da [dexo'tadu, dal *adj* defeated.

derrotar [dexo'ta(x)] *vt* to defeat.

derrubar [dexu'ba(x)] *vt* **-1.** [fazer cair] to knock down. **-2.** [vencer] to overcome. **-3.** [destituir] to overthrow. **-4.** [destruir] to defame. **-5.** [prostrar] to lay low. **-6.** *fam* [prejudicar] to knock.

desabafar [dʒizaba'fa(x)] ⟨> *vt*: ~ **algo** (**com alguém**) to share sthg (with sb). ⟨> *vi*: ~ (**com alguém**) to open up (to sb).

➡ **desabafar-se** *vp*: ~-**se** (**com alguém**) to open up (to sb).

desabafo [dʒiza'baful *m* outpouring.

desabalado, da [dʒizaba'ladu, dal *adj* [excessivo] enormous.

desabamento [dʒizaba'mẽtul *m* collapse.

desabar [dʒiza'ba(x)] *vi* **-1.** [ruir] to tumble down. **-2.** [cair com força] to fall heavily.

desabitado, da [dʒizabi'tadu, dal *adj* unoccupied.

desabotoar [dʒizabo'twa(x)] *vt* to unbutton.

desabrigado, da [dʒizabri'gadu, dal ⟨> *adj* **-1.** [sem casa] homeless. **-2.** [exposto] unsheltered. ⟨> *m, f* [pessoa] homeless person; os ~s the homeless.

desabrigar [dʒiza'briga(x)] *vt* [tirar do abrigo] to leave without shelter.

desabrochar [dʒizabro'ʃa(x)] *vi* **-1.** [flor] to bloom. **-2.** *fig* [pessoa] to blossom.

desacatar [dʒizaka'ta(x)] ⟨> *vt* **-1.** [afrontar] to disrespect. **-2.** [desprezar] to disregard. ⟨> *vi fam* [causar espanto] to stun.

desacato [dʒiza'katul *m* **-1.** [afronta] disrespect. **-2.** [desprezo] disregard.

desacerto [dʒiza'sextul *m* **-1.** [erro] mistake. **-2.** [tolice] blunder.

desacompanhado, da [dʒizakõnpa'nadu, dal *adj* unaccompanied.

desaconselhar [dʒizakõnse'ʎa(x)] *vt*: ~ **algo** (**a alguém**) to warn (sb) against sthg.

desaconselhável [dʒizakõnse'ʎavewl (*pl* **-eis**) *adj* not recommended (*depois de verbo*).

desacordado, da [dʒizakox'dadu, dal *adj* senseless.

desacordo [dʒiza'koxdul *m* **-1.** [falta de acordo] disagreement. **-2.** [desarmonia] disharmony.

desacostumado, da [dʒizakoʃtu'madu, dal *adj*: ~ (**a**) unaccustomed (to).

desacostumar [dʒizakoʃtu'ma(x)] *vt*: ~ **alguém de algo** to wean sb off sthg.

➡ **desacostumar-se** *vp* [desabituar-se]: ~-**se de algo/de fazer algo** to wean o.s. off sthg/doing sthg.

desacreditar [dʒizakredi'ta(x)] *vt* to discredit. ◆ **desacreditar-se** *vp* [perder o crédito] to become discredited.

desafeto [dʒiza'fɛtu] *m* opponent.

desafiador, ra [dʒizafja'do(x), ra] <> *adj* challenging. <> *m, f* challenger.

desafiar [dʒiza'fja(x)] *vt* -1. [propor luta] to challenge. -2. [afrontar] to defy.

desafinado, da [dʒizafi'nadu, da] *adj* out of tune.

desafinar [dʒizafi'na(x)] <> *vt*: ~ um instrumento to put an instrument out of tune. <> *vi* to be out of tune.

desafio [dʒiza'fiw] *m* -1. [provocação] challenge. -2. LITER & MÚS *literary/musical competition between two people*.

desafogado, da [dʒizafo'gadu, da] *adj* -1. [pessoa - de preocupações, de opressão] relieved; [- de trabalho] unencumbered. -2. [trânsito] clear.

desafogar [dʒizafo'ga(x)] <> *vt* -1. [desoprimir - garganta] to clear; [- espírito] to free. -2. [desabafar] to relieve. <> *vi* [desabafar-se]: ~ (com alguém) to open up (to sb). ◆ **desafogar-se** *vp* [desabafar-se] to unburden o.s.

desafogo [dʒiza'fogu] *m* -1. [alívio] relief. -2. [de trabalho] break.

desaforado, da [dʒizafo'radu, da] *adj* insulting.

desaforo [dʒiza'foru] *m* insult; **eu não levo ~ para casa** I'm not going to take it lying down.

desafortunado, da [dʒizafoxtu'nadu, da] *adj* unfortunate.

desagasalhado, da [dʒizagaza'ʎadu, da] *adj* unsheltered.

desagradar [dʒizagra'da(x)] <> *vt* to displease. <> *vi*: ~ a alguém to displease sb.

desagradável [dʒizagra'davew] (*pl* -eis) *adj* unpleasant.

desagrado [dʒiza'gradu] *m* displeasure.

desagravo [dʒiza'gravu] *m* -1. [reparação de agravo] recompense. -2. JUR reparation.

desaguar [dʒiza'gwa(x)] <> *vi* [vazar-se]: ~ em to flow into. <> *vt* [drenar] to drain.

desajeitado, da [dʒizaʒej'tadu, da] *adj* clumsy.

desajuste [dʒiza'ʒuʃtʃil] *m* -1. PSIC maladjustment. -2. [de peças, máquina] loosening.

desalentado, da [dʒizalẽn'tadu, da] *adj* discouraged.

desalentar [dʒizalẽn'ta(x)] <> *vt* to discourage. <> *vi* to lose heart.

desalento [dʒiza'lẽntu] *m* discouragement.

desalinhado, da [dʒizali'ɲadu, dal] *adj* dishevelled.

desalinhar [dʒiza'liɲa(x)] *vt* -1. [tirar do alinhamento] to break up. -2. [desarrumar] to mess up.

desalinho [dʒiza'liɲu] *m* dishevelment.

desalmado, da [dʒizaw'madu, da] *adj* soulless.

desalojar [dʒizalo'ʒa(x)] *vt*: ~ alguém de to remove sb from

desamarrar [dʒizama'xa(x)] <> *vt* [desfazer] to untie. <> *vi* NÁUT to lift anchor.

desamassar [dʒizama'sa(x)] *vt* to straighten out.

desambientado, da [dʒizãnbjẽn'tadu, da] *adj* disorientated.

desamor [dʒiza'mo(x)] *m* antipathy.

desamparado, da [dʒizãnpa'radu, da] *adj* -1. [pessoa - abandonado] abandoned; [- sem ajuda] unassisted. -2. [lugar] abandoned.

desamparar [dʒizãnpa'ra(x)] *vt* [abandonar] to abandon.

desandar [dʒizãn'da(x)] *vi fam* [clara, maionese] to separate.

desanimador, ra [dʒizanima'do(x), ra] *adj* disheartening.

desanimar [dʒizani'ma(x)] <> *vt* -1. [fazer perder o ânimo]: ~ alguém to dishearten sb. -2. [desencorajar]: ~ alguém de fazer algo to discourage sb from doing sthg. <> *vi* -1. [perder o ânimo] to become disheartened; ~ de fazer algo to become disheartened about doing sthg. -2. [ser desencorajador] to be discouraging.

desânimo [dʒi'zãnimul] *m* despondency.

desanuviar [dʒizanu'vja(x)] *vt* -1. [céu] to clear. -2. fig [pessoa, mente] to calm. ◆ **desanuviar-se** *vp* -1. [céu] to clear. -2. fig [pessoa, mente] to become calm.

desaparafusar [dʒizaparafu'za(x)] *vt* to unscrew.

desaparecer [dʒizapare'se(x)] *vi* to disappear.

desaparecido, da [dʒizapare'sidu, da] <> *adj* missing. <> *m, f* [pessoa] missing person.

desaparecimento [dʒizaparesi'mẽntul] *m* -1. [sumiço] disappearance. -2. [falecimento] loss.

desapegado, da [dʒizape'gadu, da] *adj* detached.

desapego [dʒiza'pegul] *m* -1. [desamor] lack of love. -2. [indiferença] indifference.

desapertar [dʒizapex'ta(x)] *vt* to loosen.

desapiedado, da [dʒizapje'dadu, da] *adj* ruthless.

desapontador, ra [dʒizapõnta'do(x), ral
  adj disappointing.

desapontamento [dʒizapõnta'mẽntul
  m disappointment.

desapontar [dʒizapõn'ta(x)] *vt* to disappoint.

  ➡ **desapontar-se** *vp* to be disappointed.

desapropriação [dʒizaproprja'sãw] (*pl*
  -ões) *f* dispossession.

desapropriar [dʒizapro'prja(x)] *vt* -1.
  [desapossar]: ~ **alguém de algo** to deprive sb of sthg. -2. [expropriar]: ~ **algo
(de alguém)** to expropriate sthg (from
sb).

desaprovação [dʒizaprova'sãw] (*pl* -ões)
  f disapproval.

desaprovar [dʒizapro'va(x)] *vt* -1. [repro-
var] to disapprove. -2. [censurar] to
censure.

desarmado, da [dʒizax'madu, dal *adj* -1.
  [ger] disarmed. -2. [sem arma] unarmed.

desarmamento [dʒizaxma'mẽntul *m*
disarmament.

desarmar [dʒizax'ma(x)] *vt* -1. [ger] to
disarm. -2. [barraca, brinquedo] to take
down. -3. [arma] to disable.

desarmonia [dʒizaxmo'nial *f* -1. [falta de
harmonia] disharmony. -2. *fig* [divergên-
cia] discord.

desarranjado, da [dʒizaxãn'ʒadu, dal
  adj -1. [desarrumado] untidy. -2. *MED*: **estar** ~ to be queasy.

desarranjar [dʒizaxãn'ʒa(x)] *vt* [desarru-
mar] to make untidy.

desarranjo [dʒiza'xãnʒul *m* disorder.

desarrumado, da [dʒizaxu'madu, dal
  adj untidy.

desarrumar [dʒizaxu'ma(x)] *vt* -1. [ger]
to make untidy. -2. [mala] to unpack.

desarticulado, da [dʒizaxtʃiku'ladu, dal
  adj -1. [deslocado] dislocated. -2. [des-
feito] broken up.

desarticular [dʒizaxtʃiku'la(x)] *vt* to dislocate.

desassossego [dʒizaso'segul *m* uneasiness.

desastrado, da [dʒiza'ʃtradu, dal *adj*
clumsy.

desastre [dʒi'zaʃtril *m* -1. [acidente]
accident. -2. *fig* [fracasso]: **ser um** ~ to
be a disaster.

desastroso, osa [dʒizaʃ'trozu, ɔzal *adj*
disastrous.

desatar [dʒiza'ta(x)] ◇ *vt* -1. [desfazer]
to undo. -2. [desprender] to loosen. ◇
vi [começar]: ~ **a fazer algo** to start to do
sthg suddenly.

desatento, ta [dʒiza'tẽntu, tal *adj* inattentive.

desatinado, da [dʒizatʃi'nadu, dal ◇
  adj mad. ◇ *m, f* mad person.

desatino [dʒiza'tʃinul *m* idiocy.

desativar [dʒizatʃi'va(x)] *vt* -1. [tornar ina-
tivo] to close down. -2. [desmontar] to
deactivate.

desatualizado, da [dʒizatwali'zadu, dal
  adj out-of-date.

desavença [dʒiza'vẽnsal *f* -1. [briga]
enmity. -2. [dissensão] dissent.

desavergonhado, da [dʒizavexgo'nadu,
  dal *adj* unashamed.

desavisado, da [dʒizavi'zadu, dal *adj* not
made aware.

desbancar [dʒiʒbãŋ'ka(x)] *vt*: ~ **alguém
(em algo)** to outdo sb (at sthg).

desbaratar [dʒiʒbara'ta(x)] *vt* -1. [dissi-
par]: ~ **algo (em algo)** to squander sthg
(on sthg). -2. [arruinar] to destroy. -3.
[vencer] to defeat.

desbastar [dʒiʒbaʃ'ta(x)] *vt* to thin (out).

desbocado, da [dʒiʒbo'kadu, dal *adj fig*
lewd.

desbotado, da [dʒiʒbo'tadu, dal *adj*
faded.

desbotar [dʒiʒbo'ta(x)] *vt* to fade.

desbragadamente [dʒiʒbragada'mẽntʃil *adv* shamelessly.

desbravador, ra [dʒiʒbrava'do(x), ral *m,
f* -1. [de terra, mata] explorer. -2. [de ani-
mais] tamer.

desbravar [dʒiʒbra'va(x)] *vt* -1. [terras,
matas] to explore. -2. [animais selvagens]
to tame. -3. [cavalo] to break in.

descabelar [dʒiʃkabe'la(x)] *vt fam* to
ruffle the hair of.

  ➡ **descabelar-se** *vp fam* to ruffle one's
hair.

descabido, da [dʒiʃka'bidu, dal *adj* -1.
  [absurdo] ridiculous. -2. [impróprio] inappropriate.

descalabro dʒiʃka'labrul *m* disaster,
ruin.

descalçar [dʒiʃkaw'sa(x)] *vt* to take off.

  ➡ **descalçar-se** *vp* to take off one's
shoes/gloves.

descalço, ça [dʒiʃ'kawsu, sal *adj* barefoot.

descampado, da [dʒiʃkãn'padu, dal *adj*
uninhabited.

  ➡ **descampado** *m* open country.

descansado, da [dʒiʃkãn'sadu, dal *adj*
-1. [tranqüilo] calm. -2. [lento] slow.

descansar [dʒiʃkãn'sa(x)] ◇ *vt* -1. [ger]
to rest. -2. *fig* [tranqüilizar] to calm. ◇
vi -1. [repousar] to rest. -2. *fig* [tranqüili-
zar-se] to calm down. -3. *ant* & *fig* [mor-
rer] to be at rest.

descanso [dʒiʃ'kãnsul *m* -1. [repouso]
rest. -2. [folga] break. -3. [para travessa
etc.] trivet.

descarado, da [dʒiʃka'radu, da] <> *adj*
shameless. <> *m, f* shameless person.

descaramento [dʒiʃkara'mẽntul] *m* shamelessness.

descarga [dʒiʃ'kaxga] *f* -1. [ato]
unloading. -2. [vaso sanitário] flush; **dar
a** ~ to flush. -3. [de arma] fire. -4. *ELETR* :
~ **elétrica** electrical discharge.

descarregar [dʒiʃkaxe'ga(x)] <> *vt* -1.
[carga] to unload. -2. [arma] to fire. -3.
ELETR to discharge. -4. [desabafar] to give
vent to. -5. *COMPUT* to download. <> *vi*
[bateria] to go flat.

descarrilamento [dʒiʃkaxila'mẽntul] *m*
derailment.

descarrilar [dʒiʃkaxi'la(x)] *vt & vi* to
derail.

descartar [dʒiʃkax'ta(x)] *vt* to discard.
➡ **descartar-se** *vp*: ~-**se de** [de carta,
pessoa] to get rid of; [de compromisso] to
free o.s. of.

descartável [dʒiʃkax'tavɛw] (*pl* -eis) *adj*
disposable.

descascador [dʒiʃkaʃka'do(x)] *m* peeler.

descascar [dʒiʃkaʃ'ka(x)] <> *vt* to peel.
<> *vi* -1. [perder a casca] to lose its shell.
-2. [perder a pele] to peel; **com tanto sol,
estou descascando todo** with all this
sun, I'm peeling all over.

descaso [dʒiʃ'kasu] *m* negligence.

descendência [desẽn'dẽnsja] *f* descen-
dancy.

descendente [desẽn'dẽntʃi] <> *adj* des-
cendent; **ser** ~ **de** to be a descendant
of. <> *mf* [pessoa] descendant.

descender [desẽn'de(x)] *vi* [pessoa]: ~ **de**
to be descended from.

descer [de'se(x)] <> *vt* -1. [escada] to go
down. -2. [carga] to take down. <> *vi*
-1. [ger] to go down. -2. [de ônibus] to
get off.

descida [de'sida] *f* [declive] descent.

desclassificar [dʒiʃklasifi'ka(x)] *vt* -1.
[eliminar] to disqualify. -2. [desmoralizar]
to disgrace.

descoberto, ta [dʒiʃko'bɛxtu, ta] <> *pp*
➣ **descobrir**. <> *adj* -1. [ger]
discovered. -2. [exposto] uncovered.
-3. *BANCO* [conta] overdrawn. ➡ **descoberta** *f* discovery.

descobridor, ra [dʒiʃkobri'do(x), ra] *m, f*
discoverer.

descobrimento [dʒiʃkobri'mẽntul] *m* [de
continentes] discovery.

descobrir [dʒiʃko'bri(x)] *vt* -1. [ger] to
discover. -2. [tirar a proteção de] to
uncover o.s. -3. [estátua] to unveil.
➡ **descobrir-se** *vp* [tirar a coberta] to
appear.

descolar [deʃko'lar] *vt* -1. [desgrudar]: ~
algo (de) to detach sthg (from). -2. *fam*
[conseguir] to fix up.

descolorir [dʒiʃkolo'ri(x)] <> *vt* [tirar a
cor] to discolour. <> *vi* [perder a cor] to
fade.

descompor [dʒiʃkõn'po(x)] *vt* [desorde-
nar] to muddle.

descomposto, osta [dʒiʃkõn'poʃtu,
ɔʃta] <> *pp* ➣ **descompor**. <> *adj*
-1. [desalinhado] confused. -2. [desfeito]
disordered. -3. [desfigurado] upset.

descompostura [dʒiʃkõnpoʃ'tural *f* -1.
[repreensão] reprimand; **passar uma** ~
em alguém to reprimand sb. -2. [insul-
to] affront.

descomunal [dʒiʃkomu'naw] (*pl* -ais) *adj*
-1. [gigantesco] huge. -2. [fora do comum]
unusual.

desconcentrar [dʒiʃkõnsẽn'tra(x)] *vt* to
distract.
➡ **desconcentrar-se** *vp* to lose concentration.

desconcertante [dʒiʃkõnsex'tãntʃi] *adj*
-1. [desorientador] confusing. -2. [frus-
trante] upsetting.

desconcertar [dʒiʃkõnsex'ta(x)] *vt* -1.
[desorientar] to confuse. -2. [frustrar] to
upset.
➡ **desconcertar-se** *vp* -1. [desarranjar-
se] to break down. -2. [perturbar-se] to
become bewildered. -3. [frustrar-se] to
be upset.

desconectar [dʒiʃkonek'ta(x)] *vt* to disconnect.
➡ **desconectar-se** *vp* [comput] to be
disconnected.

desconexo, xa [dʒiʃko'nɛksu, ksa] *adj* -1.
[incoerente] incoherent. -2. [desunido]
disconnected.

desconfiado, da [dʒiʃkõn'fjadu, da] *adj*
distrustful.

desconfiança [dʒiʃkõn'fjãnsa] *f* distrust.

desconfiar [dʒiʃkõn'fja(x)] <> *vt* [conje-
turar]: ~ **que** to fear that. <> *vi* -1. [ficar
suspeitoso] to suspect. -2. [não confiar
em]: ~ **de** to be distrustful of. -3. [sus-
peitar de]: ~ **de** to be suspicious of.

desconfortável [dʒiʃkõnfor'tavɛw] (*pl*
-eis) *adj* uncomfortable.

desconforto [dʒiʃkõn'foxtul *m* discomfort.

descongelar [dʒiʃkõnʒe'la(x)] *vt* to defrost.

descongestionante [dʒiʃkõnʒeʃtʃjo'-
nãntʃil <> *adj* decongestant. <> *m*
decongestant.

descongestionar [dʒiʃkõnʒeʃtʃjo'na(x)]
vt -1. to decongest. -2. *fig* [trânsito,
rua] to clear.

desconhecer [dʒiʃkoɲe'se(x)] vt -1. [ignorar] not to know. -2. [estranhar] not to recognize. -3. [ser ingrato a] to be ungrateful for.

desconhecido, da [dʒiʃkoɲe'sidu, da] ◇ adj [incógnito] unknown. ◇ m, f [pessoa] unknown person.

desconhecimento [dʒiʃkoɲesi'mẽntul m ignorance.

desconsolado, da [dʒiʃkõnso'ladu, da] adj disconsolate.

desconsolar [dʒiʃkõnso'la(x)] ◇ vt to sadden. ◇ vi to become saddened.
◆ **desconsolar-se** vp to become dispirited.

descontar [dʒiʃkõn'ta(x)] vt -1. [deduzir]: ~ algo (de) to deduct sthg (from). -2. [título de crédito - pagar] to pay off; [- receber] to receive. -3. fam [revidar]: ~ algo (em alguém) to pay sthg back (to sb). -4. fig [não fazer caso de] to take no notice of.

descontentamento [dʒiʃkõntẽnta'mẽntul m -1. [desprazer] displeasure. -2. [insatisfação] dissatisfaction.

descontentar [dʒiʃkõntẽn'ta(x)] vt to displease.
◆ **descontentar-se** vp to be displeased.

descontente [dʒiʃkõn'tẽntʃi] adj displeased.

descontínuo, nua [dʒiʃkõn'tʃinwu, nwa] adj discontinued.

desconto [dʒiʃ'kõntul m discount.

descontraído, da [dʒiʃkõntra'idu, da] adj relaxed.

descontrair [dʒiʃkõntra'i(x)] vt to relax.
◆ **descontrair-se** vp to relax.

descontrolar [dʒiʃkõntro'la(x)] vt to lose control of.
◆ **descontrolar-se** vp -1. [pessoa] to lose control of o.s. -2. [situação] to get out of control.

desconversar [dʒiʃkõnvex'sa(x)] vi to change the subject.

descorar [dʒiko'ra(x)] ◇ vt [desbotar] to discolour. ◇ vi [empalidecer] to turn pale.

descortês, tesa [dʒiʃkox'teʃ, tezal adj discourteous.

descortesia [dʒiʃkoxte'zial f discourtesy.

descortinar [dʒiʃkoxtʃi'na(x)] vt -1. [avistar] to reveal. -2. [correndo a cortina] to unveil. -3. [revelar]: ~ algo a alguém to reveal sthg to sb.

descoser [dʒiʃko'ze(x)], **descosturar** [dʒiʃkoʃtu'ra(x)] ◇ vt to unstitch. ◇ vi to come unstiched.

descrédito [dʒiʃ'krɛdʒitul m discredit.

descrença [dʒiʃ'krẽnsal f disbelief.

descrente [dʒiʃ'krẽntʃi] adj disbelieving.

descrever [dʒiʃkre've(x)] vt -1. [expor] to describe. -2. [traçar] to trace.

descrição [dʒiʃkri'sãw] (pl -ões) f description.

descuidado, da [dʒiʃkuj'dadu, da] adj -1. [desleixado] uncared-for. -2. [irrefletido] careless.

descuidar [dʒiʃkuj'da(x)] vi: ~ de algo to neglect sthg.
◆ **descuidar-se** vp: ~-se de algo to become careless about sthg.

descuido [dʒiʃ'kujdu] m -1. [ger] carelessness. -2. [erro] error.

desculpa [dʒiʃ'kuwpal f -1. [ger] excuse. -2. [perdão] forgiveness; **pedir ~ s a alguém por algo** to ask sb forgiveness for sthg.

desculpar [dʒiʃkuw'pa(x)] vt -1. [perdoar]: ~ alguém (por algo) to forgive sb (for sthg). -2. [justificar] to give as an excuse.
◆ **desculpar-se** vp [justificar-se]: ~-se (com alguém) por algo to apologize (to sb) for sthg.

desculpável [dʒiʃkuw'pavew] (pl -eis) adj forgiveable.

desde ['deʒdʒi] prep -1. [tempo] since; ~ então from then on; ~ já straight away. -2. [espaço] from.
◆ **desde que** loc conj -1. [tempo] since. -2. [visto que] as. -3. [contanto que] as long as.

desdém [deʒ'dẽl m disdain.

desdenhar [deʒde'ɲa(x)] vt -1. [desprezar] to despise. -2. [escarnecer] to scorn.

desdenhoso, osa [deʒde'ɲozu, ɔzal adj disdainful.

desdita [dʒiʒ'dʒital f bad luck.

desdizer [dʒiʒdʒi'ze(x)] vt -1. [negar] to deny. -2. [desmentir] to contradict.
◆ **desdizer-se** vp [negar o que havia dito] to retract.

desdobrar [dʒiʒdo'bra(x)] vt -1. [abrir] to unfold. -2. [dividir]: ~ algo em algo to divide sthg into sthg. -3. [aumentar] to develop.
◆ **desdobrar-se** vp -1. to unfold. -2. [empenhar-se]: ~-se (em algo) fig to make an effort (at sthg).

desejar [deze'ʒa(x)] ◇ vt -1. [querer] to wish. -2. [ambicionar]: ~ algo to wish for sthg; ~ fazer algo to wish to do sthg. -3. [formulando votos]: ~ algo a alguém to wish sb sthg. -4. [sexualmente] to desire. ◇ vi: deixar a ~ to leave sthg to be desired.

desejável [dese'ʒavew] (pl -eis) adj desirable.

desejo [de'zeʒu] *m* -1. [ger] desire. -2. [ambição] wish. -3. [de grávida] craving.

desejoso, osa [dese'ʒosu, ɔsa] *adj*: ~ **de algo/de fazer algo** keen for sthg/to do sthg.

desembaraçar [dʒizĩbara'sa(x)] *vt* -1. [livrar] to free. -2. [desemaranhar] to loosen. -3. [liberar] to unencumber.

◆ **desembaraçar-se** *vp* -1. [desinibir-se] to open up. -2. [livrar-se]: ~**-se de algo/ alguém** to free o.s. of sthg/sb.

desembaraço [dʒizĩba'rasu] *m* -1. [desinibição] ease. -2. [agilidade] agility.

desembarcar [dʒizĩbax'ka(x)] ◇ *vt* -1. [carga] to unload. -2. [passageiros] to disembark. ◇ *vi* [descer de transporte] to disembark.

desembarque [dʒizĩ'baxki] *m* disembarkation.

desembocar [dʒizĩbo'ka(x)] *vi* [rio, rua]: ~ **em** to discharge into.

desembolsar [dʒizĩbow'sa(x)] *vt* [gastar] to spend.

desembolso [dʒizĩ'bowsu] *m* [gasto] expenditure.

desembrulhar [dʒizĩbru'ʎa(x)] *vt* to unwrap.

desempacotar [dʒizĩpako'ta(x)] *vt* to unpack.

desempatar [dezĩpa'ta(x)] ◇ *vt ESP*: ~ **a partida** to score a deciding point or goal in a match. ◇ *vi* to decide; **a eleição só desempatou no final** the election was only decided at the finish.

desempate [dʒizĩ'patʃi] *m ESP* decision.

desempenhar [dʒizĩpe'ɲa(x)] *vt* -1. [ger] to perform. -2. [cumprir] to carry out.

desempenho [dʒizĩ'peɲu] *m* performance.

desempregado, da [dʒizĩpre'gadu, da] ◇ *adj* unemployed. ◇ *m, f* unemployed person.

desemprego [dʒizĩ'pregu] *m* unemployment.

desencadear [dʒizĩŋka'dʒja(x)] *vt* [provocar] to unleash.

◆ **desencadear-se** *vp* [irromper] to break out.

desencaixar [dʒizĩŋkaj'ʃa(x)] *vt* to dislocate.

◆ **desencaixar-se** *vp* to become dislocated.

desencaixotar [dʒizĩŋkajʃo'ta(x)] *vt* to take out of a box.

desencanto [dʒizĩŋ'kãntu] *m* [desilusão] disenchantment.

desencargo [dʒizĩŋ'kaxgu] *m* [cumprimento] carrying out; **por** ~ **de consciência** to clear one's conscience.

desencarregar-se [dʒizĩŋkaxe'gaxsi] *vp* [desobrigar-se]: ~ **de algo** to unburden o.s. of sthg.

desencontrar [dʒizĩŋkõn'tra(x)] *vt* [fazer que não se encontrem] to send in different directions.

◆ **desencontrar-se** *vp* -1. [não se encontrar]: ~**-se (de)** to diverge (from). -2. [perder-se um do outro] to fail to meet one another.

desencontro [dʒizĩŋ'kõntru] *m* -1. [falta de encontro] failure to meet. -2. [divergência] difference.

desencorajar [dʒizĩŋkora'ʒa(x)] *vt* to discourage.

desencostar [dʒizĩŋkoʃ'ta(x)] *vt*: ~ **algo/alguém (de)** to move sthg/sb away (from).

◆ **desencostar-se** *vp*: ~**-se de algo** to stop leaning against sthg.

desenfreado, da [dʒizẽnfre'adu, da] *adj* wild.

desenganado, da [dʒizẽŋga'nadu, da] *adj* [sem cura] incurable; [desiludido] disenchanted.

desenganar [dʒizẽŋga'na(x)] *vt* -1. [doente] to give up hope for. -2. [desiludir] to disillusion.

desengano [dʒizĩ'gãnu] *m* [desilusão] disillusionment.

desengonçado, da [dʒizẽŋgõ'sadu, da] *adj* -1. [desconjuntado] disjointed. -2. [desajeitado] clumsy.

desenhar [deze'ɲa(x)] ◇ *vt* -1. [traçar] to outline. -2. *TEC* to design. -3. *ARTE* to draw. ◇ *vi* [traçar desenhos] to draw up.

desenhista [deze'niʃta] *m, f* designer.

desenho [de'zeɲu] *m* -1. [expressão de formas] drawing. -2. *ARTE* & *TEC* design. -3. *CINE*: ~ **animado** (animated) cartoon.

desenlace [dʒizẽn'lasi] *m* unfolding, development.

desenrolar [dʒizẽnxo'la(x)] ◇ *m* to progress. ◇ *vt* -1. [estender] to unroll. -2. [expor] to unfold.

◆ **desenrolar-se** *vp* -1. [desenroscar-se] to uncurl o.s. -2. [mostrar-se] to open out.

desentender-se [dʒizẽntẽn'dexsi] *vp*: ~ **(com)** to disagree (with).

desentendido, da [dʒizẽntẽn'dʒidu, da] *adj*: **fazer-se de** ~ to pretend not to understand.

desentendimento [dʒizĩntẽndʒi'mẽntu] *m* misunderstanding.

desenterrar [dʒizẽnte'xa(x)] *vt* -1. [ger] to dig up. -2. [exumar] to exhume. -3. [descobrir] to unearth.

desentupir [dʒizẽntu'pi(x)] *vt* to un-block.

desenvoltura [dʒizĩnvow'tura] *f* lack of inhibition.

desenvolver [dʒizĩnvow've(x)] *vt* -1. [ger] to develop. -2. [melhorar] to improve. -3. [teorizar sobre] to expand on. -4. [correr] to run.
  ➡ **desenvolver-se** *vp* -1. [crescer] to develop. -2. [progredir] to progress.

desenvolvido, da [dʒizẽvow'vidu, da] ◇ *pp* ▷ **desenvolver**. ◇ *adj* -1. [concebido] conceived. -2. [adiantado] advanced. -3. [crescido] developed.

desenvolvimento [dʒizĩnvowvi'mẽntu] *m* -1. [crescimento] development; ~ **sustentável** sustainable development. -2. [concepção] conception.

desequilibrado, da [dʒizekili'bradu, da] ◇ *adj* -1. [sem equilíbrio] unbalanced. -2. PSIC unstable. ◇ *m, f* PSIC unstable person.

desequilibrar [dʒizekili'bra(x)] *vt* -1. [fazer perder o equilíbrio] to unbalance.
  ➡ **desequilibrar-se** *vp* -1. PSIC to become unstable. -2. *fig* [descontrolar] to get out of control.

desequilíbrio [dʒizeki'librju] *m* -1. [falta de equilíbrio] lack of balance. -2. PSIC instability.

desertar [dezex'ta(x)] ◇ *vt* [abandonar] to abandon. ◇ *vi* MIL to desert.

deserto, ta [de'zɛxtu, ta] *adj* deserted.
  ➡ **deserto** *m* desert.

desertor, ra [dezex'to(x), ra] *m, f* deserter.

desesperado, da [dʒiziʃpe'radu, da] *adj* -1. [sem esperança] desperate. -2. [irritado] irritated. -3. [intenso - briga, competição] fierce; [- amor] intense.

desesperador, ra [dʒiziʃpera'do(x), ra] *adj* -1. [sem esperança] hopeless. -2. [irritante] irritating.

desesperança [dʒiziʃpe'rãnsa] *f* despair.

desesperar [dʒizeʃpe'ra(x)] ◇ *vt* -1. [arrasar] to dishearten. -2. [irritar] to drive mad. ◇ *vi* [perder a esperança] to give up hope.
  ➡ **desesperar-se** *vp* -1. [perder a esperança] to give up hope. -2. [afligir-se] to get upset.

desespero [dʒiziʃ'perul] *m* -1. [desesperança] despair. -2. [aflição] despondency; **levar alguém ao** ~ to lead sb to despair.

desestimular [dʒiziʃtʃimu'la(x)] *vt* to discourage.

desfalcar [dʒiʃfaw'ka(x)] *vt* -1. [reduzir] to reduce. -2. [privar] to deprive. -3. [defraudar] to defraud.

desfalecer [dʒiʃfale'se(x)] *vi* [desmaiar] to faint.

desfalque [dʒiʃ'fawki] *m* -1. [redução] reduction. -2. [privação] loss. -3. [fraude] fraud.

desfavorável [dʒiʃfavo'ravɛw] (*pl* -eis) *adj* -1. [desvantajoso] unfavourable. -2. [oposto] adverse.

desfazer [dʒiʃfa'ze(x)] *vt* -1. [desmanchar] to undo. -2. [dispersar] to disperse. -3. [acabar com] to put an end to. -4. [anular] to annul.
  ➡ **desfazer-se** *vp* -1. [desmanchar-se] to come undone. -2. [dispersar-se] to disperse. -3. [acabar-se] to end. -4. [despojar-se]: ~-**se de algo** to be stripped of sthg. -6. *fig* [desmanchar-se]: ~-**se em lágrimas** to burst into tears; ~-**se em sorrisos** to break into smiles; ~-**se em gentilezas** to be desperate to please.

desfechar [dʒiʃfe'ʃa(x)] *vt* -1. [disparar] to fire. -2. [insultos] to loose off.

desfecho [dʒiʃ'feʃu] *m* ending.

desfeita [dʒiʃ'fejta] *f* insult.

desfeito, ta [dʒiʃ'fejtu, tal] ◇ *pp* ▷ **desfazer**. ◇ *adj* -1. [desmanchado] undone. -2. [acabado] ended. -3. [desarrumada] untidy. -4. [anulado] annulled.

desferir [dʒiʃfe'ri(x)] *vt* [aplicar] to direct.

desfiar [dʒiʃ'fja(x)] ◇ *vt* -1. [tecido *etc.*] to unravel. -2. [terço] to unthread. -3. [galinha] to cut up. ◇ *vi* [tecido *etc.*] to unravel.

desfigurar [dʒiʃfigu'ra(x)] *vt* -1. [transformar] to disfigure. -2. *fig* [adulterar] to adulterate.
  ➡ **desfigurar-se** *vp* [transformar-se] to alter.

desfiladeiro [dʒiʃfila'dejru] *m* ravine.

desfilar [dʒiʃfi'la(x)] ◇ *vt* [exibir] to parade. ◇ *vi* [passar em desfile - soldado] to march past; [- manequim, escola de samba] to parade.

desfile [dʒiʃ'fili] *m* [passar em desfile - soldado] march past; [- manequim, escola de samba] parade.

desforra [dʒiʃ'fɔxa] *f* revenge.

desfrutar [dʒiʃfru'ta(x)] ◇ *vt* to enjoy. ◇ *vi*: ~ **de algo** to enjoy sthg.

desgarrado, da [dʒiʒga'xadu, da] *adj* [perdido] lost.

desgarrar-se [dʒiʒga'xaxsi] *vp* [perder-se]: ~ **de algo** to lose sight of sthg; ~ (**do caminho**) to lose one's way.

desgastante [dʒiʒgaʃ'tãntʃi] *adj* -1. [estressante] stressful. -2. [cansativo] tiring. -3. [desprestigiante] damaging.

desgastar [dʒiʒgaʃ'ta(x)] *vt* -1. [ger] to wear out. -2. [gastar] to wear away. -3. [desprestigiar] to damage.

desgaste [dʒiʒ'gaʃtʃi] m -1. [deterioração] deterioration. -2. [dano] harm.

desgostar [dʒiʒgoʃ'ta(x)] <> vt [contrariar] to displease. <> vi [não gostar]: ~ de algo to dislike sthg.

➤ **desgostar-se** vp [deixar de gostar]: ~-se de algo/de fazer algo to no longer enjoy sthg/doing sthg.

desgosto [dʒiʒ'goʃtu] m -1. [desprazer] displeasure. -2. [pesar] regret.

desgostoso, osa [dʒiʒgoʃ'tozu, ɔza] adj -1. [triste] sad. -2. [contrariado] displeased.

desgraça [dʒiʒ'grasa] f -1. [infortúnio] misfortune. -2. [miséria] penury. -3. fig [pessoa inábil]: ser uma ~ to be a disgrace.

desgraçado, da [dʒiʒgra'sadu, da] <> adj -1. [desafortunado] unfortunate. -2. [miserável] wretched. -3. [vil] vile. -4. m fam [grande] hellish. <> m, f -1. [desafortunado] unfortunate. -2. [pessoa vil] beggar.

desgraçar [dʒiʒgra'sa(x)] vt to disgrace.

desgrenhado, da [dʒiʒgre'ɲadu, da] adj -1. [despenteado] tousled. -2. [desarrumado] untidy.

desgrudar [dʒiʒgru'da(x)] vt -1. [descolar]: ~ algo de algo to unstick sthg from sthg. -2. [afastar]: ~ alguém de alguém/algo fig to drag sb away from sb/sthg.

➤ **desgrudar-se** vp [afastar-se] to break away.

desidratar [dʒizidra'ta(x)] vt to dehydrate.

➤ **desidratar-se** vp to become dehydrated.

design [dʒi'zajni] (pl -s) m design.

designar [dezig'na(x)] vt -1. [denominar] to designate. -2. [simbolizar] to symbolize. -3. [determinar] to award. -4. [escolher]: ~ alguém para algo to appoint sb as sthg.

designer [dʒi'zajnɛ(x)] (pl -s) mf designer.

desigual [dezi'gwaw] (pl -ais) adj -1. [diferente] different. -2. [irregular] irregular. -3. [injusto] unfair.

desiludir [dʒizilu'dʒi(x)] vt: ~ alguém (de algo/de fazer algo) to dissuade sb (from sthg/from doing sthg).

➤ **desiludir-se** vp: ~-se (com algo) to be disappointed (by sthg).

desilusão [dʒizilu'zãw] (pl -ões) f disappointment.

desimpedir [dʒizĩnpe'dʒi(x)] vt to clear.

desinfetante [dʒizĩnfe'tãntʃi] <> adj disinfectant. <> m disinfectant.

desinfetar [dʒizĩnfe'ta(x)] vt MED to disinfect.

desinibido, da [dʒizini'bidu, da] adj uninhibited.

desintegração [dʒizĩntegra'sãw] f disintegration.

desinteressado, da [dʒizĩntere'sadu, da] adj -1. [sem interesse] disinterested. -2. [despreendido] detached.

desinteressar [dʒizĩntere'sa(x)] vt: ~ alguém de algo to destroy sb's interest in sthg.

➤ **desinteressar-se** vp: ~-se de algo to lose interest in sthg.

desinteresse [dʒizĩnte'resi] m -1. [falta de interesse] lack of interest. -2. [despreendimento] detachment.

desistência [deziʃ'tẽnsja] f withdrawal.

desistir [deziʃ'tʃi(x)] vi to give up; ~ de algo/de fazer algo to give up sthg/doing sthg.

desjejum [dʒiʒe'ʒũl] (pl -ns) m breakfast.

deslavado, da [dʒiʒla'vadu, da] adj brazen.

desleal [dʒiʒ'ljaw] (pl -ais) adj disloyal.

desleixado, da [dʒiʒlej'ʃadu, da] adj messy.

desligado, da [dʒiʒli'gadu, da] adj -1. ELETR switched off. -2. [desconectado] disconnected. -3. [afastado]: ~ de detached from. -4. fig [despreendido] indifferent. -5. fig [distraído] absentminded.

desligar [dʒiʒli'ga(x)] <> vt ELETR to switch off; ~ o carro to switch off the engine. <> vi fam [despreocupar-se] to switch off.

➤ **desligar-se** vp -1. [afastar-se]: ~-se de to switch off from. -2. fig [despreender-se]: ~-se de to abandon. -3. fig [distrair-se] to switch off.

deslizamento [dʒiʒliza'mẽntu] m slip; ~ de terra landslide.

deslizar [dʒiʒli'za(x)] vi -1. [movimentar-se - cisnes, dançarino] to glide; [- terra, encosta] to slide. -2. [escorregar] to slip. -3. fig [falhar] to make a slip.

deslize [dʒiʒ'lizil] m -1. [escorregão] slip. -2. fig [falha] blunder. -3. fig [engano] slip.

deslocado, da [dʒiʒlo'kadu, da] adj -1. MED dislocated. -2. [transferido] transferred. -3. fig [desambientado] out of place.

deslocar [dʒiʒlo'ka(x)] vt -1. MED to dislocate. -2. [transferir] to transfer. -3. [mover] to move.

➤ **deslocar-se** vp [mover-se] to move around.

deslumbramento [dʒiʒlũnbra'mẽntul] m dazzle.

desorganizar

deslumbrante [dʒiʒlũn'brãntʃi] *adj* dazzling.

deslumbrar [dʒiʒlũn'bra(x)] ⟨⟩ *vt* to dazzle. ⟨⟩ *vi* to be dazzling.

➡ **deslumbrar-se** *vp* to be dazzled.

desmaiado, da [dʒiʒma'jadu, da] *adj* -1. MED unconscious. -2. [pálido] pale.

desmaiar [dʒiʒmaj'a(x)] *vi* to faint.

desmaio [dʒiʒ'maju] *m* faint.

desmamar [dʒiʒma'ma(x)] ⟨⟩ *vt* to wean. ⟨⟩ *vi* to be weaned.

desmancha-prazeres [dʒiʒ,mãnʃapra'-zeriʃ] *mf inv* killjoy.

desmanchar [dʒiʒmãn'ʃa(x)] *vt* -1. [desfazer] to undo. -2. [acabar com] to break off.

➡ **desmanchar-se** *vp* -1. [dissolver-se] to come undone. -2. *fig* [expandir-se]: ∼-se em algo to be lavish with sthg.

desmarcar [dʒiʒmax'ka(x)] *vt* -1. [tirar as marcas de] to remove markings from. -2. [adiar] to postpone.

desmascarar [dʒiʒmaʃka'ra(x)] *vt* -1. [revelar] to reveal. -2. [desmoralizar] to demoralize.

desmatamento [dʒiʒmata'mẽntu] *m* deforestation.

desmatar [dʒiʒma'ta(x)] *vt* to deforest.

desmedido, da [dʒiʒme'dʒidu, da] *adj* immense.

desmentir [dʒiʒmẽn'tʃi(x)] *vt* -1. [negar] to deny. -2. [discrepar de] to disagree with. -3. [contradizer] to contradict.

➡ **desmentir-se** *vp* [contradizer-se] to contradict o.s.

desmerecer [dʒiʒmere'se(x)] *vt* -1. [menosprezar] to despise. -2. [não merecer] not to deserve.

desmesurado, da [dʒiʒmezu'radu, da] *adj* excessive.

desmiolado, da [dʒiʒmjo'ladu, da] *adj* -1. [sem juízo] brainless. -2. [esquecido] forgetful.

desmontar [dʒiʒmõn'ta(x)] ⟨⟩ *vt* -1. [separar as partes de] to dismantle. -2. *fig* [destruir] to destroy. ⟨⟩ *vi* [apear]: ∼ (de algo) to dismount (from sthg).

desmoralizar [dʒiʒmorali'za(x)] *vt* to demoralize.

➡ **desmoralizar-se** *vp* to be demoralized.

desmoronamento [dʒiʒmorona'mẽntu] *m* landslide.

desmoronar [dʒiʒmoro'na(x)] ⟨⟩ *vt* to knock down. ⟨⟩ *vi* to collapse.

desmotivado, da [dʒiʒmotʃi'vadu, da] *adj* demotivated.

desnatado, da [dʒiʒna'tadu, da] *adj* skimmed.

desnecessário, ria [dʒiʒnese'sarju, rja] *adj* unnecessary.

desnível [dʒiʒ'nivɛw] (*pl* -eis) *m* unevenness.

desnorteado, da [dʒiʒnox'tʃjadu, da] *adj* [perturbado] bewildered.

desnortear [dʒiʒnox'tʃja(x)] *vt* -1. [desorientar] to disorientate. -2. *fig* [perturbar] to confuse.

➡ **desnortear-se** *vp* -1. [perder-se] to get lost. -2. *fig* [perturbar-se] to become confused.

desnudar [dʒiʒnu'da(x)] *vt* -1. [despir] to undress. -2. *fig* [revelar] to reveal.

➡ **desnudar-se** *vp* [despir-se] to undress.

desnutrição [dʒiʒnutri'sãw] (*pl* -ões) *f* malnutrition.

desobedecer [dʒizobede'se(x)] *vi*: ∼ (a) to disobey.

desobediência [dʒizobe'dʒjẽnsja] *f* disobedience.

desobediente [dʒizobe'dʒjẽntʃi] *adj* disobedient.

desobrigar [dʒizobri'ga(x)] *vt*: ∼ alguém de algo/de fazer algo to release sb from sthg/doing sthg.

desobstruir [dʒizobʃtru'i(x)] *vt* to clear.

desocupado, da [dʒizoku'padu, da] ⟨⟩ *adj* -1. [ocioso] idle. -2. [disponível] available. -3. [vazio] empty. ⟨⟩ *m, f* -1. [desempregado] unemployed person. -2. [vagabundo] layabout.

desocupar [dʒizoku'pa(x)] *vt* -1. [deixar livre] to leave free. -2. [esvaziar] to empty.

desodorante [dʒizodo'rãntʃi] *m* deodorant.

desolação [dezola'sãw] (*pl* -ões) *f* -1. [tristeza] sadness. -2. [devastação] devastation.

desolado, da [dezo'ladu, da] *adj* -1. [triste] sad. -2. [devastado] devastated.

desolar [dezo'la(x)] *vt* to devastate.

desonesto, ta [dʒizo'nɛʃtu, ta] ⟨⟩ *adj* -1. [indigno] contemptible. -2. [mentiroso] dishonest. ⟨⟩ *m, f* [pessoa indigna] despicable person.

desonra [dʒi'zõnxa] *f* dishonour.

desonrar [dʒizõn'xa(x)] *vt* to dishonour.

➡ **desonrar-se** *vp* to disgrace o.s.

desordeiro, ra [dʒizox'dejru, ra] ⟨⟩ *adj* rowdy. ⟨⟩ *m, f* rowdy person.

desordem [dʒi'zoxdẽ] (*pl* -ns) *f* -1. [bagunça] mess. -2. [tumulto] commotion.

desorganização [dʒizoxganiza'sãw] (*pl* -ões) *f* confusion.

desorganizar [dʒizoxgani'za(x)] *vt* to throw into confusion.

➡ **desorganizar-se** *vp* to be disorganized.

desorientação [deʒizorjẽntaˈsãw] (pl -ões) f disorientation.

desorientar [deʒizorjẽnˈta(x)] vt -1. [desnortear] to disorientate. -2. [perturbar] to bewilder. -3. PSIC to disturb.

➡ **desorientar-se** vp -1. [desnortear-se] to become disorientated. -2. [perturbar-se] to become disconcerted.

desossar [deʒizoˈsa(x)] vt to bone.

desovar [deʒizoˈva(x)] <> vi [pôr ovos] to lay eggs. <> vt fig [livrar-se de] to get rid of.

despachado, da [deʒiʃpaˈʃadu, da] adj -1. [enviado] dispatched. -2. [eficiente] efficient.

despachar [deʒiʃpaˈʃa(x)] vt -1. [enviar] to send. -2. [resolver] to dispatch. -3. [atender] to attend to. -4. [mandar embora] to get rid of.

despacho [deʒiʃˈpaʃul m -1. [resolução] determination. -2. ESPIRIT religious offering.

despedaçar [deʒiʃpedaˈsa(x)] vt [quebrar em pedaços] to smash.

➡ **despedaçar-se** vp [quebrar-se em pedaços] to smash.

despedida [deʒiʃpeˈdʒidal f [ato] farewell.

despedir [deʒiʃpeˈdʒi(x)] vt [demitir] to dismiss.

➡ **despedir-se** vp [dizer adeus]: ~-se (de alguém) to say goodbye (to sb).

despeitado, da [deʒiʃpejˈtadu, da] adj -1. [invejoso] envious. -2. fam [que tem o peito magro] flat.

despeito [deʒiʃˈpejtul m [inveja] spite.

➡ **a despeito de** loc conj [apesar de] despite.

despejar [deʒiʃpeˈʒa(x)] vt -1. [inquilino] to evict. -2. [entornar] to pour.

despejo [deʒiʃˈpeʒul m [de inquilino] eviction.

despencar [deʒiʃpẽnˈka(x)] vi [cair]: ~ de algo to fall from sthg.

despensa [deʒiʃˈpẽnsal f pantry.

despentear [deʒiʃpẽnˈtʒja(x)] vt to tousle.

➡ **despentear-se** vp fig to let one's hair down.

despercebido, da [deʒiʃpexseˈbidu, da] adj unnoticed.

desperdiçar [deʒiʃpexdʒiˈsa(x)] vt to waste.

desperdício [deʒiʃpexˈdʒisjul m waste.

despertador [deʒiʃpextaˈdo(x)] (pl -es) m alarm clock.

despertar [deʒiʃpexˈta(x)] <> m awakening. <> vt -1. [acordar] to wake. -2. [provocar] to awaken. -3. fig [tirar]: ~ alguém de algo to rouse sb from sthg. <> vi -1. [ger] to wake up. -2. fig [sair]: ~ de algo to rouse o.s. from sthg.

desperto, ta [deʒiʃˈpextu, tal adj awake.

despesa [deʒiʃˈpezal f expense.

despido, da [deʒiʃˈpidu, dal adj -1. [nu] naked. -2. fig [desprovido]: ~ de algo lacking sthg.

despir [deʒiʃˈpi(x)] vt [roupa, pessoa] to undress.

➡ **despir-se** vp -1. [tirar a roupa] to get undressed. -2. fig [despojar-se]: ~-se de algo to abandon sthg.

despojado, da [deʒiʃpoˈʒadu, dal adj -1. [privado] de algo stripped of sthg. -2. [desprendido] generous. -3. [sem enfeite] unadorned.

despojar [deʒiʃpoˈʒa(x)] vt -1. [roubar] to rob. -2. [espoliar] to clean out.

➡ **despojar-se** vp [privar-se]: ~-se de algo to renounce sthg.

despojos [deʒiʃˈpoʒoʃl mpl remains; ~ mortais mortal remains.

despoluir [deʒiʃpoˈlwi(x)] vt to clean up.

despontar [deʒiʃpõnˈta(x)] vi to rise.

déspota [ˈdɛʃpotal <> adj despotic. <> mf despot.

despovoado, da [deʒiʃpoˈvwadu, dal adj uninhabited.

desprazer [deʒiʃpraˈze(x)] m displeasure.

despregar [deʒiʃpreˈga(x)] <> vt: ~ algo (de) to unfasten sthg (from); não despregou os olhos de mim fig he didn't take his eyes off me. <> vi to come undone.

➡ **despregar-se** vp [soltar-se] to come loose.

desprender [deʒiʃprẽnˈde(x)] vt -1. [soltar]: ~ alguém/algo (de algo) to untie sthg (from sthg). -2. [escalar] to release.

➡ **desprender-se** vp -1. [soltar-se]: ~-se (de algo) to get free (from sthg). -2. [exalar]: ~-se de algo to extricate o.s. from sthg.

despreocupado, da [deʒiʃpreokuˈpadu, dal adj carefree.

despreparado, da [deʒiʃprepaˈradu, dal adj unprepared.

desprestigiar [deʒiʃpreʃtʃiˈʒja(x)] vt to discredit.

despretensioso, osa [deʒiʃpretẽnˈsjozu, ɔzal adj unpretentious.

desprevenido, da [deʒiʃpreveˈnidu, dal adj [distraído] unaware; ser pego ~ to be taken by surprise.

desprezar [deʒiʃpreˈza(x)] vt -1. [menosprezar] to despise. -2. [não dar importância] to scorn. -3. [não considerar] to disregard.

desprezível [deʒiʃpreˈzivewl (pl -eis) adj -1. [vil] despicable. -2. [ínfimo] least.

desprezo [deʒiʃˈprezul m -1. [desdém] disdain. -2. [repulsa] revulsion.

desproporcional [dʒiʃpropoxsjo'naw] (pl -ais) adj: ~ (a) disproportionate (to).

despropositado, da [dʒiʃpropozi'tadu, da] adj unreasonable.

despropósito [dʒiʃpro'pɔzitul] m -1. [disparate] absurdity. -2. fig [excesso]: un ~ more than enough.

desprover [dʒiʃpro've(x)] vt: ~ alguém (de algo) to deprive sb (of sthg).

desprovido, da [dʒiʃpro'vidu, da] adj: ~ de algo lacking sthg.

desqualificar [dʒiʃkwalifi'ka(x)] vt -1. [tornar indigno] to render unfit. -2. [inabilitar] to disqualify; ~ alguém (para) to disqualify sb (from).

desregrado, da [dʒiʒxe'gradu, da] <> adj -1. [desordenado] disorderly. -2. [devasso] dissolute. <> m, f [devasso] debauched person.

desrespeitar [dʒiʒxeʃpej'ta(x)] vt -1. [desacatar] to disregard. -2. [desobedecer] to disobey.

desrespeito [dʒiʒxeʃ'pejtul] m: ~ (a) disrespect (for).

dessa ['dɛsa] = de + essa.

desse ['desi] = de + esse.

destacado, da [dʒiʃta'kadu, da] adj -1. [separado] detached. -2. [proeminente] eminent.

destacar [dʒiʃta'ka(x)] vt -1. [ger] to detach. -2. [fazer sobressair] to highlight.
◆ **destacar-se** vp [fazer-se notar] to be outstanding.

destampar [dʒiʃtãn'pa(x)] vt to remove the lid from.

destapar [dʒiʃta'pa(x)] vt to uncover.

destaque [dʒiʃ'taki] m -1. [realce] prominence. -2. [pessoa ou assunto relevante] highlight.

desta ['dɛʃta] = de + esta.

deste ['deʃʃi] = de + este.

destemido, da [dʒiʃte'midu, da] adj fearless.

desterrar [dʒiʃte'xa(x)] vt to exile.

desterro [dʒiʃ'texul] m exile.

destilar [deʃtʃi'la(x)] vt to distil.

destilaria [deʃtʃila'ria] f distillery.

destinação [deʃtʃina'sãw] (pl -ões) f destination.

destinar [deʃtʃi'na(x)] vt -1. [reservar] to put aside. -2. [aplicar] to allocate.
◆ **destinar-se** vp -1. [ser designado]: ~ -se a to be intended for. -2. [dedicar-se] to dedicate oneslf.

destinatário, ria [deʃtʃina'tarju, rja] m, f addressee.

destino [deʃ'tʃinul] m -1. [direção] destination. -2. [aplicação] purpose. -3. [futuro] destiny.

destituição [deʃtʃitwi'sãw] (pl -ões) f destitution.

destituir [deʃtʃi'twi(x)] vt -1. [privar]: ~ alguém de algo to deprive sb of sthg. -2. [demitir]: ~ alguém (de algo) to deprive sb (of sthg).

destorcer [dʒiʃtox'se(x)] vt [endireitar] to straighten.

destorcido, da [dʒiʃtox'sidu, da] adj untwisted.

destrancar [dʒiʃtrãŋ'ka(x)] vt to unlock.

destratar [dʒiʃtra'ta(x)] vt to offend.

destreza [deʃ'treza] f skill.

destro, tra ['dɛʃtru, tra] adj dexterous.

destroçar [dʒiʃtro'sa(x)] vt -1. [ger] to destroy. -2. [despedaçar] to pull to pieces.

destroços [dʒiʃ'trɔsuʃ] mpl wreckage (sg).

destroncar [dʒiʃtrõŋ'ka(x)] vt -1. [deslocar] to dislocate. -2. [decepar] to cut off.

destruição [dʒiʃtruj'sãw] (pl -ões) f destruction.

destruidor, ra [dʒiʃtruj'do(x), ral] <> adj destructive. <> m, f destroyer.

destruir [dʒiʃtru'i(x)] <> vt -1. [ger] to destroy. -2. [aniquilar] to annihilate. <> vi [ter efeito negativo] to be destroying.
◆ **destruir-se** vp -1. [a si próprio] to destroy o.s. -2. [um ao outro] to destroy one another.

desumano, na [dʒizu'mãnu, na] adj inhuman.

desunião [dʒizun'jãw] (pl -ões) f -1. [separação] separation. -2. [discórdia] discord.

desvairado, da [dʒiʒvaj'radu, da] <> adj -1. [louco] crazy. -2. [descontrolado] uncontrolled. <> m, f -1. [pessoa louca] crazy person. -2. [pessoa descontrolada] person who is quite out of control.

desvalorizar [dʒiʒvalori'za(x)] vt & vi to devalue.

desvantagem [dʒiʒvãn'taʒẽ] (pl -ns) f disadvantage; em ~ at a disadvantage.

desvão [dʒiʒ'vãw] (pl desvãos) m loft.

desvario [dʒiʒva'riw] m madness.

desvelo [dʒiʒ'velul] m [zelo] zeal.

desvencilhar [dʒiʒvẽnsi'ʎa(x)] vt [soltar]: ~ algo/alguém (de algo) to save sthg/ sb (from sthg).
◆ **desvencilhar-se** vp -1. [soltar-se]: ~ -se (de algo) to free o.s. (from sthg). -2. fig [livrar-se]: ~ de alguém/algo to get rid of sb/sthg.

desvendar [dʒiʒvẽn'da(x)] vt -1. [tirar a venda de] to remove the blindfold from. -2. [revelar] to reveal.

desventura [dʒiʒvẽn'tural] f misfortune.

desviar [dʒiʒ'vja(x)] *vt* **-1.** [mudar a direção de] to deviate. **-2.** *fig* [roubar] to misappropriate.

◆ **desviar-se** *vp* [mudar a direção] to deviate.

desvio [dʒiʒ'viw] *m* **-1.** [mudança de direção] diversion. **-2.** [da coluna vertebral] curvature. **-3.** *fig* deviation. **-4.** [roubo] misappropriation.

desvirar [dʒiʒvi'ra(x)] *vt* to turn back to the normal position.

detalhadamente [detaʎada'mẽntʃil] *adv* in detail.

detalhado, da [deta'ʎadu, da] *adj* detailed.

detalhar [deta'ʎa(x)] *vt* to detail.

detalhe [de'taʎil *m* detail.

detalhista [deta'ʎiʃta] *adj* meticulous.

detectar [detek'ta(x)] *vt* to detect.

detector [detek'to(x)] (*pl* -es) *m* detector.

detenção [detẽn'sãw] (*pl* -ões) *f* detention.

détente [de'tãntʃil *f POL* détente.

deter [de'te(x)] *vt* **-1.** [parar] to stop. **-2.** [prender] to detain. **-3.** [manter, reter] to keep. **-4.** [reprimir] to hold back. **-5.** [ter em seu poder] to retain.

◆ **deter-se** *vp* **-1.** [parar] to stop. **-2.** [ficar] to remain. **-3.** [reprimir-se] to hold back. **-4.** [ocupar-se]: ~-se em algo to dwell on sthg.

detergente [detex'ʒẽntʃil ◇ *adj* cleansing. ◇ *m* detergent.

deterioração [deterjora'sãw] (*pl* -ões) *f* deterioration.

deteriorar [deterjo'ra(x)] ◇ *vt* **-1.** [estragar] to spoil. **-2.** [piorar] to damage. ◇ *vi* [piorar] to worsen.

◆ **deteriorar-se** *vp* **-1.** [estragar] to become spoiled. **-2.** *fig* [piorar] to deteriorate.

determinação [detexmina'sãw] (*pl* -ões) *f* **-1.** [empenho] determination. **-2.** [ordem] order.

determinado, da [detexmi'nadu, da] *adj* **-1.** [resoluto] determined. **-2.** [estabelecido] fixed. **-3.** *(antes de subst)* [certo] certain; em ~ momento ... at a certain moment.

determinar [detexmi'na(x)] *vt* **-1.** [ger] to determine. **-2.** [precisar] to state.

detestar [deteʃ'ta(x)] *vt* to detest.

◆ **detestar-se** *vp* to detest o.s.

detestável [deteʃ'tavew] (*pl* -eis) *adj* detestable.

detetive [dete'tʃivil *mf* detective.

detido, da [de'tʃidu, da] *adj* **-1.** [retido] retained. **-2.** [preso] detained.

detonação [detona'sãw] (*pl* -ões) *f* detonation.

detonar [deto'na(x)] ◇ *vt* [arma, bomba] to detonate. ◇ *vi* **-1.** [arma, bomba] to detonate. **-2.** [trovão] to thunder.

DETRAN (*abrev de* Departamento Estadual de Trânsito) *m Brazilian state department responsible for licensing of drivers and vehicles,* ≃ DVLA.

detrás [de'trajʃl *adv* behind.

◆ **detrás de** *loc prep* behind.

◆ **por detrás** *loc adv* from behind.

detrimento [detri'mẽntul *m*: em ~ de to the detriment of.

detrito [de'tritul *m* detritus.

deturpação [detuxpa'sãw] (*pl* -ões) *f* corruption.

deturpar [detux'pa(x)] *vt* **-1.** [adulterar] to distort. **-2.** [corromper] to corrupt.

deus, sa l'dewʃ, sal (*mpl* -ses, *fpl* -sas) *m,* *f* god.

◆ **Deus** *m* God; graças a Deus! thank God!; meu Deus do céu! my goodness!

deus-nos-acuda [ˌdewʃnuʃa'kudal *m* commotion.

devagar [dʒiva'ga(x)] ◇ *adv* slowly. ◇ *adj inv fam* **-1.** [lento] slow. **-2.** [sem graça] boring; ser ~ quase parando to go at a snail's pace.

devaneio [deva'nejul *m* reverie.

devassado, da [deva'sadu, da] *adj* open.

devassidão [devasi'dãw] *f* licentiousness.

devasso, ssa [de'vasu, sal ◇ *adj* debauched. ◇ *m, f* debauched person.

devastar [devaʃ'ta(x)] *vt* **-1.** [assolar] to devastate. **-2.** [despovoar] to drive people out of.

deve l'dɛvil *m COM* debit.

devedor, ra [deve'do(x), ral ◇ *adj* [firma, pessoa] in debt. ◇ *m, f* debtor.

dever [de've(x)] (*pl* -es) ◇ *m* **-1.** [obrigação] duty. **-2.** *EDUC*: ~ (de casa) homework. ◇ *vt* **-1.** [dinheiro, favores]: ~ algo (a alguém) to owe sthg (to sb). **-2.** [expressando probabilidade]: deve fazer sol amanhã it ought to be sunny tomorrow; deve ser meia-noite it must be midnight; ela deve chegar à noite she should arrive in the evening; deve ter acontecido alguma coisa something must have happened. **-3.** [expressando sugestão]: você deve sair cedo you ought to go out early. **-4.** [expressando obrigação]: você deve ser pontual sempre you must always be on time. ◇ *vi* [ter dívida]: ele deve muito na praça she owes a lot at the market; ela deve a todos os amigos she owes a lot to all her friends, she's in debt to all her friends.

◆ **dever-se** *a vp* [ser consequência de] to be due to.

diferenciar

deveras [de'vɛɾaʃ] adv really.

devidamente [de,vida'mẽntʃi] adv duly.

devido, da [de'vidu, da] adj due; **no ~ tempo** in due course.
➡ **devido a** loc adv due to.

devoção [devo'sãw] (pl -**ões**) f -**1.** RELIG devotion. -**2.** [dedicação] dedication.

devolução [devolu'sãw] (pl -**ões**) f return.

devolver [devow've(x)] vt -**1.** [restituir] to return. -**2.** [replicar] to respond to. -**3.** [vomitar] to throw up.

devorar [devo'ra(x)] vt -**1.** [ger] to consume. -**2.** [comida] to devour. -**3.** fig [livro] to read voraciously.

devotar [devo'ta(x)] vt: **~ algo a algo/ alguém** to devote sthg to sthg/sb.
➡ **devotar-se** vp: **~-se a algo/alguém** to devote o.s. to sthg/sb.

devoto, ta [de'votu, ta] <> adj devout. <> m, f devotee.

dez [ˈdɛʒ] num ten; veja também **seis**.

dez. (abrev de **dezembro**) Dec.

dezembro [de'zẽnbru] m December; veja também **setembro**.

dezena [de'zena] f -**1.** [ger] ten. -**2.** [em jogo]: **ganhei na ~** I got ten numbers right.

dezenove [deze'nɔvi] num nineteen; veja também **seis**.

dezesseis [deze'sejʃ] num sixteen; veja também **seis**.

dezessete [deze'sɛtʃi] num seventeen; veja também **seis**.

dezoito [de'zojtu] num eighteen; veja também **seis**.

DF (abrev de **Distrito Federal**) m Federal District.

dia [ˈdʒia] m -**1.** [gen] day; **bom ~!** good morning!; **de um ~ para outro** from one day to the next; **no ~ anterior/seguinte** the previous/next day; **mais ~, menos dia** sooner or later; **o ~ todo** all day long; **todo ~, todos os ~s** all day, every day; **~ cheio** busy day; **um ~ daqueles** one of those days. -**2.** [data] date; **no ~ dez** on the tenth. -**3.** [luz do sol]: **de ~** in the daytime. -**4.** [atualidade]: **em ~** up-to-date; **hoje em ~** nowadays. -**5.** [horário de trabalho]: **~ de folga** day off; **~ útil** working day.

dia-a-dia m daily routine.

diabetes [dʒia'bɛtʃiʃ] m ou f diabetes.

diabético, ca [dʒia'bɛtʃiku, ka] <> adj diabetic. <> m, f diabetic.

diabo [ˈdʒiabu] <> m devil; **aconteceu o ~** it all happened; **comer o pão que o ~ amassou** to go through hell; **fazer o ~** to run riot. <> interj damn!
➡ **como o diabo** loc adv fam: **é feia como o ~!** she's as ugly as sin!

diabrura [dʒia'brura] f devilish trick.

diafragma [dʒia'fragma] m diaphragm.

diagnóstico [dʒiag'nɔʃtʃikul] m diagnosis.

diagonal [dʒiago'naw] (pl -**ais**) <> adj diagonal. <> f diagonal.

diagrama [dʒia'grãma] m diagram.

diagramador, ra [dʒiagrama'do(x), ra] m, f typesetter.

dialeto [dʒia'lɛtu] m dialect.

dialogar [dʒialo'ga(x)] vi -**1.** [conversar]: **~ (com)** to talk (to). -**2.** [negociar]: **~ (com)** to negotiate (with).

diálogo [ˈdʒialogul] m dialogue.

diamante [dʒia'mãntʃi] m diamond.

diâmetro [dʒia'mãmetru] m diameter.

diante ➡ **por diante** loc adv: **e assim ~** and so on.
➡ **diante de** loc adv in the face of; **~ de algo/alguém** in front of sthg/sb.

dianteira [dʒiãn'tejra] f lead; **na ~** ahead.

dianteiro, ra [dʒiãn'tejru, ra] adj front.

diapositivo [dʒiapozi'tʃivul] m slide.

diário, ria [ˈdʒiarju, rja] adj daily.
➡ **diário** m -**1.** [caderno] diary. -**2.** [para viagem] journal. -**3.** [jornal] daily paper. -**4.** COM ledger.
➡ **diária** f [de hotel] daily rate.

dica [ˈdʒika] f fam hint.

dicção [dʒik'sãw] f diction.

dicionário [dʒisjo'narju] m dictionary.

dicionarista [dʒisjona'riʃta] mf lexicographer.

dicotomia [dʒikoto'mia] f dichotomy.

didático, ca [dʒi'datʃiku, ka] adj -**1.** [pessoa] didactic. -**2.** [explicação] instructive.

DIEESE (abrev de **Departamento Intersindical de Estatísticas e Estudos Sócio-Econômicos**) m trade union body for the support of workers in São Paulo.

diesel [ˈdʒizɛw] m diesel; **motor (a) ~** diesel engine.

dieta [ˈdʒiɛta] f diet; **fazer ~** to diet.

dietético, ca [dʒie'tɛtʃiku, ka] adj dietary; **chocolate ~** diet chocolate; **bebida ~** diet drink.

difamar [dʒifa'ma(x)] vt to slander.

diferença [dʒife'rẽnsa] f -**1.** [desigualdade] difference. -**2.** [distinção]: **fazer ~ entre** to distinguish between; **fazer ~** to make a difference. -**3.** [discordância]: **ter ~(s) com alguém** to have one's differences with sb. -**4.** MAT remainder.

diferenciar [dʒiferẽn'sja(x)] vt: **~ algo/ alguém (de)** to distinguish sthg/sb (from).
➡ **diferenciar-se** vp to differ.

diferente [dʒife'rẽntʃi] <> adj different; ~ **de** different from UK, different than US. <> adv differently.

diferir [dʒife'ri(x)] vi: ~ **(em algo)** to differ (on sthg); ~ **de algo/alguém** to differ from sthg/sb.

difícil [dʒi'fisiw] (pl -eis) <> adj -1. [ger] difficult, hard. -2. [delicado] tricky. -3. [improvável]: **acho muito** ~ **ele vir hoje** I think it is very unlikely he will come today. <> adv: **falar/escrever** ~ to use fancy words. <> m: **o** ~ **é** the trouble is.

dificilmente [dʒifisiw'mẽntʃi] adv: ~ **voltarei a falar com ele** it will be hard for me ever to speak to him again.

dificuldade [dʒifikuw'dadʒi] f -1. [ger] problem; **ter** ~ **em fazer algo** to have difficulty in doing sthg. -2. [qualidade de difícil] difficulty. -3. [impedimento] snag. -4. [situação crítica] trouble; **em** ~ **(s)** in trouble.

dificultar [dʒifikuw'ta(x)] vt to complicate.

difundir [dʒifũn'di(x)] vt to spread.

difuso, sa [dʒi'fuzu, za] adj diffuse.

digerir [dʒiʒe'ri(x)] vt to digest.

digestão [dʒiʒeʃ'tãw] (pl -ões) f digestion.

digitação [dʒiʒita'sãw] (pl -ões) f COMPUT keying-in.

digital [dʒiʒi'taw] (pl -ais) adj -1. [ger] digital. -2. [dos dedos] finger.

digitalizar [dʒiʒitali'za(x)] vt COMPUT to digitize.

digitar [dʒiʒi'ta(x)] vt COMPUT to key in.

dígito ['dʒiʒitu] m digit.

dignidade [dʒigni'dadʒi] f -1. [cargo] office. -2. [decência, honra] dignity; **com** ~ with dignity.

digno, na ['dʒignu, na] adj worthy; **ser** ~ **de algo/de fazer algo** to be worthy of sthg/doing sthg.

dilacerante [dʒilase'rãntʃi] adj agonizing.

dilacerar [dʒilase'ra(x)] vt [despedaçar] to tear to pieces.

➤ **dilacerar-se** vp [afligir-se] to be torn apart.

dilapidar [dʒilapi'da(x)] vt -1. [derrubar] to reduce to rubble. -2. [esbanjar] to squander.

dilatar [dʒila'ta(x)] vt -1. [ampliar] to dilate. -2. [adiar] to delay.

dilema [dʒi'lema] m dilemma.

diletante [dʒile'tãntʃi] <> adj dilettantish. <> mf dilettante.

diligência [dʒili'ʒẽnsja] f -1. [cuidado] diligence. -2. [presteza] promptness.

-3. [pesquisa] enquiry. -4. [veículo] stagecoach. -5. JUR formality.

diligente [dʒili'ʒẽntʃi] adj diligent.

diluição [dʒilwi'sãw] f dilution.

diluir [dʒi'lwi(x)] vt: ~ **algo (em algo)** to dilute sthg (in sthg).

dilúvio [dʒi'luviw] m flood.

dimensão [dʒimẽn'sãw] (pl -ões) f -1. [ger] dimension. -2. [tamanho] size.

diminuição [dʒiminwi'sãw] (pl -ões) f reduction.

diminuir [dʒimi'nwi(x)] <> vt -1. [reduzir] to reduce. -2. [subtrair]: ~ **algo de ou em algo** to deduct sthg from sthg. <> vi [reduzir-se] to lessen; ~ **de peso/largura** to decrease in weight/width.

diminutivo [dʒiminu'tʃivul] m GRAM diminutive.

diminuto, ta [dʒimi'nutu, ta] adj minute.

dinâmico, ca [dʒi'nãmiku, ka] adj dynamic.

➤ **dinâmica** f -1. MEC dynamics (pl). -2. fig [atividade] dynamic; ~ **de grupo** teamwork.

dinamismo [dʒina'miʒmu] m dynamism.

dinamite [dʒina'mitʃi] f dynamite.

Dinamarca [dʒina'marka] n Denmark.

dinamarquês, esa [dʒinamax'keʃ, ezal] <> adj Danish. <> m, f Dane.

➤ **dinamarquês** m [língua] Danish.

dínamo ['dʒinamul] m dynamo.

dinastia [dʒinaʃ'tʃial] f dynasty.

dinheirão [dʒiɲej'rãw] m fam: **um** ~ a mint.

dinheiro [dʒi'ɲejrul] m money; ~ **vivo** hard cash.

dinossauro [dʒino'sawrul] m dinosaur.

diocese [dʒjo'sezil] f diocese.

dióxido ['dʒjɔksidul] m QUÍM dioxide; ~ **de carbono** carbon dioxide.

diploma [dʒi'ploma] m diploma.

diplomacia [dʒiploma'sia] f -1. [ciência] diplomacy. -2. [representantes] diplomatic corps. -3. fig [tato] tact; **com** ~ tactfully.

diplomado, da [dʒiploma'du, da] <> adj [formado] graduated. <> m, f graduate.

diplomar [dʒiplo'ma(x)] vt to graduate.

➤ **diplomar-se** vp: ~-**se (em algo)** to get a diploma/degree (in sthg).

diplomata [dʒiplo'mata] mf -1. [representante] diplomat. -2. fig [negociador hábil] mediator.

diplomático, ca [dʒiplo'matʃiku, ka] adj diplomatic.

dique ['dʒikil] m dyke.

direção [dʒire'sãw] (pl -ões) f -1. [rumo, sentido] direction; **em** ~ **a** towards, headed for. **-2.** [de empresa] management. **-3.** [de partido] leadership. **-4.** [de filme, peça de teatro] direction. **-5.** [de jornal] editors. **-6.** [diretores] board of directors. **-7.** AUTO steering.

direcionamento [dʒiresiona'mẽntuʃ] *m* COMPUT forwarding.

direita [dʒi'rejta] *f* ➪ **direito**.

direito, ta [dʒi'rejtu, ta] *adj* **-1.** [lado] right-hand. **-2.** [destro] right. **-3.** [digno] honest. **-4.** [arrumado] straight.

➡ **direito** ◇ *m* **-1.** JUR law; ~ civil civil law. **-2.** [prerrogativa] right. **-3.** [lado] right side. ◇ *adv* properly.

➡ **direita** *f* **-1.** [lado direito] right-hand side; à ~ on OU to the right. **-2.** POL right.

➡ **direitos** *mpl*: ~ autorais copyright *(sg)*; ~ humanos human rights.

direto, ta [dʒi'rɛtu, ta] *adj* **-1.** [ger] direct. **-2.** TV [transmissão] live.

➡ **direto** *adv* straight.

diretor, ra [dʒire'to(x), ra] *(mpl* **-res**, *fpl* **-ras)** *m, f* **-1.** [de escola] head. **-2.** [de empresa, teatro, cinema] director. **-3.** [de jornal] editor.

diretoria [dʒireto'ria] *f* **-1.** [de escola] headship. **-2.** [de empresa] directorship.

DIRF *(abrev de* **Declaração de Imposto de Renda na Fonte)** *f Brazilian declaration of income tax at source.*

dirigente [dʒiri'ʒẽntʃi] *mf* leader.

dirigir [dʒiri'ʒi(x)] ◇ *vt* **-1.** [administrar - empresa, hotel] to manage; [- filme, peça de teatro] to direct. **-2.** AUTO to drive. **-3.** [bicicleta] to ride. **-4.** [atenção, esforços]: ~ esforços para algo to direct one's energy towards sthg. **-5.** [enviar] to address. ◇ *vi* AUTO to drive.

➡ **dirigir-se** *vp* **-1.** [encaminhar-se]: ~-se a to go to. **-2.** [falar com]: ~-se a alguém to speak to sb.

discagem [dʒiʃ'kaʒẽ] *f* dialling; ~ direta direct dialling.

discar [dʒiʃ'ka(x)] *vt* to dial.

discernimento [dʒisexni'mẽntu] *m* discernment.

disciplina [dʒisi'plina] *f* discipline.

discípulo, la [dʒi'sipulu, la] *m, f* disciple.

disc-jóquei [dʒisk'ʒɔkej] *(pl* disc-**jóqueis)** *mf* disc jockey.

disco ['dʒiʃku] *m* **-1.** [ger] disc; ~ voador flying saucer. **-2.** MÚS record; ~ laser compact disc; não mudar o ~ to keep banging on. **-3.** [de telefone] dial. **-4.** COMPUT disk; ~ **flexível/rígido** floppy/hard disk; ~ **de sistema** system disk.

discordar [dʒiʃkox'da(x)] *vi*: ~ **(de algo/alguém)** to disagree (with sthg/sb).

discórdia [dʒiʃ'kɔrdʒia] *f* discord.

discoteca [dʒiʃko'tɛka] *f* **-1.** [boate] discotheque. **-2.** [coleção de discos] record collection.

discotecário, ria [dʒiʃkote'kariw, ria] *m, f* disc jockey.

discrepância [dʒiʃkre'pãnsia] *f* discrepancy.

discreto, ta [dʒiʃ'krɛtu, ta] *adj* **-1.** [roupa] modest. **-2.** [pessoa] discreet.

discrição [dʒiʃkri'sãw] *f* discretion.

discriminação [dʒiʃkrimina'sãw] *(pl* **-ões)** *f* **-1.** [diferenciação] differentiation. **-2.** [segregação] discrimination.

discriminador, ra [dʒiʃkrimina'do(x), ra] *adj* biased.

discriminar [dʒiʃkrimi'na(x)] *vt* **-1.** [listar] to itemize. **-2.** [segregar] to isolate.

discursar [dʒiʃkux'sa(x)] *vi*: ~ **(sobre)** to make a speech (about).

discurso [dʒiʃ'kuxsu] *m* speech.

discussão [dʒiʃku'sãw] *(pl* **-ões)** *f* **-1.** [debate] discussion. **-2.** [briga] argument.

discutir [dʒiʃku'tʃi(x)] ◇ *vt* [debater]: ~ **algo (com alguém)** to discuss sthg (with sb). ◇ *vi* [brigar]: ~ **com alguém** to argue (with sb).

discutível [dʒiʃku'tʃivew] *(pl* **-eis)** *adj* arguable.

disenteria [dʒizẽnte'ria] *f* dysentery.

disfarçar [dʒiʃfax'sa(x)] *vt* [dissimular] to disguise.

➡ **disfarçar-se** *vp* [fantasiando-se]: ~-se de algo to disguise o.s. as sthg.

disfarce [dʒiʃ'faxsi] *m* disguise.

díspar ['dʒiʃpa(x)] *adj* disparate.

disparado, da [dʒiʃpa'radu, da] *adj* [lançado - tiro, flecha] fired; [- pedra] hurled.

➡ **disparado** *adv* **-1.** [a toda velocidade] at full speed. **-2.** [com grande superioridade] by far.

➡ **disparada** *f*: em ~ like a shot.

disparar [dʒiʃpa'ra(x)] ◇ *vt* [desfechar, lançar - tiro, flecha] to fire; [- pedra] to hurl. ◇ *vi* **-1.** [descarregar-se] to fire. **-2.** [correr] to shoot off.

disparatado, da [dʒiʃpara'tadu, da] *adj* absurd.

disparate [dʒiʃpa'ratʃi] *m* nonsense.

disparidade [dʒiʃpari'dadʒi] *f* disparity.

dispensa [dʒiʃ'pẽnsa] *f* dispensation.

dispensar [dʒiʃpẽn'sa(x)] *vt* **-1.** [prescindir] to do without. **-2.** [conceder]: ~ **algo a alguém** to grant sthg to sb. **-3.** [eximir]: ~ **alguém (de algo)** to excuse sb (from sthg).

dispensável [dʒiʃpẽn'savew] *(pl* **-eis)** *adj* expendable.

dispersar [dʒiʃpex'sa(x)] vt to disperse.
➡ **dispersar-se** vp to disperse.

displicência [dʒiʃpli'sẽnsja] f carelessness.

displicente [dʒiʃpli'sẽntʃi] adj careless.

disponível [dʒiʃpo'nivɛw] (pl -eis) adj
available.

dispor [dʒiʃ'po(x)] <> m: ao ~ de alguém at sb's disposal. <> vt -1. [arru-
mar] to arrange. -2. [determinar] to
decide. <> vi -1. [usar]: ~ de to have
at one's disposal; **disponha!** go ahead!
-2. [ter]: ~ de to have available.
➡ **dispor-se** vp -1. [decidir-se] to
decide. -2. [propor-se] to be prepared.

disposição [dʒiʃpozi'sãw] (pl -ões) m -1.
[arrumação] arrangement. -2. [ânimo,
vontade]: **minha ~ para trabalhar hoje é
pouca** I don't feel much like working
today. -3. [subordinação]: à ~ de available to.

dispositivo [dʒiʃpozi'tʃivu] m -1. [meca-
nismo] mechanism, device; ~ intra-
uterino intrauterine device. -2. JUR
provision. -3. fig [meio] measures (pl).

disposto, ta [dʒiʃ'poʃtu, ta] adj -1. [arru-
mado] arranged. -2. [animado] in a good
mood.

disputa [dʒiʃ'puta] f -1. [briga] dispute.
-2. [competição] contest.

disputar [dʒiʃpu'ta(x)] <> vt -1. [concor-
rer a] to enter. -2. [competir por] to
compete for. <> vi [rivalizar]: ~ com al-
go/alguém to rival sthg/sb.

disquete [dʒiʃ'kɛtʃi] m COMPUT floppy
disk.

dissabor [dʒisa'bo(x)] m annoyance.

dissecar [dʒise'ka(x)] vt -1. [corpo] to
dissect. -2. fig [analisar] to examine in
detail.

disseminar [dʒisemi'na(x)] vt to spread.
➡ **disseminar-se** vp to spread.

dissertação [dʒisexta'sõw] (pl -ões) f -1.
[tratado] dissertation. -2. [discurso] lecture.

dissidência [dʒisi'dẽnsja] f -1. [divergên-
cia] difference of opinion. -2. [cisão]
breakaway. -3. [dissidentes] dissidents
(pl).

dissidente [dʒisi'dẽntʃi] <> adj dissident. <> mf dissident.

dissimular [dʒisimu'la(x)] <> vt -1. [dis-
farçar] to disguise. -2. [fingir] to feign.
<> vi [disfarçar] to dissimulate.

dissipar [dʒisi'pa(x)] vt -1. [dispersar] to
disperse. -2. [esbanjar] to squander.
➡ **dissipar-se** vp to vanish.

disso ['dʒisu] = de + isso.

dissociar [dʒiso'sja(x)] vt: ~ algo de algo to dissociate sthg from sthg.

dissolução [dʒisolu'sãw] (pl -ões) f dis-
solution.

dissoluto, ta [dʒiso'lutu, ta] adj dissolute.

dissolver [dʒisow've(x)] vt to dissolve.
➡ **dissolver-se** vp -1. [extinguir-se] to
break up. -2. [desmanchar-se] to dissolve.

dissuadir [dʒiswa'di(x)] vt: ~ alguém
(de algo/de fazer algo) to dissuade sb
(from sthg/doing sthg).

dissuasão [dʒiswa'zãw] f dissuasion.

distância [dʒiʃ'tãnsja] f -1. [espaço] distance; **manter-se à ~ de** to keep at a
distance from. -2. fig [intervalo] gap. -3.
[diferença] difference.

distanciar [dʒiʃtãn'sja(x)] vt to separate.
➡ **distanciar-se** vp to move away.

distante [dʒiʃ'tãntʃi] adj -1. [longe]
distant. -2. fig [alheado] aloof.

distender [dʒiʃtẽn'de(x)] vt [ger] to
stretch; [músculo] to pull.

distensão [dʒiʃtẽn'sãw] f -1. MED
relaxation. -2. POL calm.

distinção [dʒiʃtʃĩn'sãw] (pl -ões) f [ger]
distinction; [honraria] honour.

distinguir [dʒiʃtʃĩŋ'gi(x)] vt -1. [caracteri-
zar] to typify. -2. [discernir] to
distinguish. -3. [separar] to
differentiate. -4. [perceber] to make
out. -5. [premiar] to decorate.
➡ **distinguir-se** vp [sobressair-se] to
stand out.

distintivo, va [dʒiʃtʃĩn'tʃivu, va] adj distinctive. ➡ **distintivo** m badge.

distinto, ta [dʒiʃ'tʃĩntu, ta] adj -1. [dife-
rente] different. -2. [perceptível]
distinct. -3. [ilustre] distinguished. -4.
[elegante - pessoa] refined; [- roupa]
elegant; [- postura] distinguished.

disto ['dʒiʃtu] = de + isto.

distorcer [dʒiʃtox'se(x)] vt to distort.

distração [dʒiʃtra'sãw] (pl -ões) f -1.
[descuido] carelessness. -2. [diversão]
distraction.

distraído, da [dʒiʃtra'idu, da] adj -1. [de-
satento] inattentive. -2. [alheio] absent-
minded.

distrair [dʒiʃtra'i(x)] vt -1. [divertir] to
amuse. -2. [entreter] to entertain. -3.
[desviar a atenção]: ~ alguém (de) to
distract sb (from).
➡ **distrair-se** vp -1. [divertir-se] to
amuse o.s. -2. [alhear-se] to lose concentration.

distribuição [dʒiʃtribwi'sãw] (pl -ões) f
distribution.

distribuidor, ra [dʒiʃtribwi'do(x), ra]
(mpl -es, fpl -s) m, f [pessoa] distributor.
➡ **distribuidor** m AUTO distributor.

distribuir [dʒiʃtri'bwi(x)] vt -1. [repartir] to distribute. -2. [atribuir] to allocate. -3. [entregar] to deliver. -4. [dispor] to arrange. -5. [levar] to supply. -6. [dirigir] to bestow.

distrito [dʒiʃ'tritu] m -1. [divisão administrativa] district; ~ **eleitoral** electoral constituency. -2. [policial] *administrative area of a town or city in which there is at least one police station*, police district US.

➡ **Distrito Federal** m [no Brasil] Brasilia.

distúrbio [dʒiʃ'tuxbjul m -1. [agitação] disturbance. -2. [sublevação] riot. -3. MED & PSIC problem.

ditado, ra [dʒi'tadul m -1. [exercício escolar] dictation. -2. [provérbio] saying.

ditador, ra [dʒita'do(x), ral (mpl -es, fpl -s) m, f -1. POL dictator. -2. fig [pessoa autoritária] despot.

ditadura [dʒita'dural f dictatorship.

ditar [dʒi'ta(x)] vt -1. [texto] to dictate. -2. [impor] to impose.

dito, ta ['dʒitu, tal ◇ pp ▷ **dizer**. ◇ adj aforementioned.

ditongo [dʒi'tõŋgul m diphthong.

DIU (abrev de Dispositivo Intra-Uterino) m IUD.

diurno, na ['dʒjuxnu, nal adj daytime.

divã [dʒi'vãl m couch.

divagar [dʒiva'ga(x)] vi -1. [vaguear]: ~ **por** to wander about. -2. [devanear] to daydream. -3. [desviar-se do assunto] to digress.

divergir [dʒivex'ʒi(x)] vi -1. [afastar-se] to branch off. -2. [discordar]: ~ **(de alguém)** to disagree (with sb).

diversão [dʒivex'sãw] (pl -ões) f -1. [entretenimento] entertainment, amusement. -2. [passatempo] pastime.

diversidade [dʒivexsi'dadʒi] f -1. [variedade] diversity. -2. [divergência] difference.

diverso, sa [dʒi'vexsu, sal adj [diferente] different.

➡ **diversos** adj pl [vários] various.

divertido, da [dʒivex'tʃidu, dal adj entertaining, amusing.

divertimento [dʒivextʃi'mẽntul m entertainment, amusement.

divertir [dʒivex'tʃi(x)] vt to entertain, to amuse.

➡ **divertir-se** vp to have a good time.

dívida ['dʒividal f debt.

dividendo [dʒivi'dẽndul m dividend.

dividir [dʒivi'dʒi(x)] ◇ vt -1. [ger] to divide. -2. [repartir] to share. -3. [separar] to split. -4. [demarcar] to mark out. ◇ vi MAT to divide.

➡ **dividir-se** vp -1. [separar-se] to split up. -2. [divergir] to be divided.

divindade [dʒivĩn'dadʒil f divinity.

divisa [dʒi'vizal f -1. [fronteira] border. -2. [insígnia] emblem. -3. [slogan] slogan.

➡ **divisas** fpl FIN foreign exchange (sg).

divisão [dʒivi'zãwl (pl -ões) f -1. [partilha] sharing. -2. MAT division. -3. [discórdia] disagreement. -4. [compartimento] compartment.

divisório, ria [dʒivi'zɔrju, rjal adj dividing.

➡ **divisória** f partition.

divorciado, da [dʒivox'sjadu, dal ◇ adj divorced. ◇ m, f divorcé (f divorcée).

divorciar [dʒivox'sja(x)] vt -1. [cônjuge] to divorce. -2. [separar] to separate.

➡ **divorciar-se** vp -1. [cônjuges]: ~-se **(de)** to get divorced (from). -2. fig [afastar-se] to cut o.s. off.

divórcio [dʒi'vɔxsjul m divorce.

divulgar [dʒivuw'ga(x)] vt -1. [notícias] to publicize. -2. [doutrina, conhecimento, cultura] to spread. -3. [segredo] to disclose. -4. [produto] to market.

dizer [dʒi'ze(x)] ◇ vt -1. [ger] to tell. -2. [falar] to say; ~ **que** to say that; ~ **que sim/não** to say yes/no; ~ **algo (a alguém)** to tell (sb) sthg; ~ **uma prece** to say a prayer. -3. [aconselhar, pensar, opinar] to say. -4. [significar] to mean; **esse título não me diz nada** the title means nothing to me; **querer** ~ to mean; **quer** ~, ... that is to say, ... -5. [atrair] to appeal. ◇ vi [falar]: **tive uma idéia! - diga!** I've had an idea! - tell me!; **dito e feito** no sooner said than done. ◇ v impess [afirmar]: **dizem que** it is said that; **a bem** ~ [na verdade] in fact; **que dirá** [quanto mais] let alone; [muito menos] even less.

➡ **dizer-se** vp [afirmar de si mesmo] to claim to be.

➡ **até dizer chega** loc adv beyond belief.

➡ **por assim dizer** loc adv so to speak.

dizimar [dʒizi'ma(x)] vt -1. [destruir em parte] to decimate. -2. fig [dissipar] to squander.

DJ [di'ʒej] (abrev de Disc jockey) m DJ.

dl (abrev de decilitro) m dl.

DLL (abrev de Dynamic Link Library) f DLL.

dm (abrev de decímetro) m dm.

DNA (abrev de ácido desoxirribonucléico) m DNA.

do [dul = de + o.

doação [dwa'sãwl (pl -ões) f donation.

doador, ra [dwa'do(x), ra] *m, f* donor.

doar ['dwa(x)] *vt*: ~ algo (a alguém/algo) to donate sthg (to sb/sthg).

dobra ['dɔbra] *f* -1. [parte voltada] fold. -2. [prega] pleat. -3. [vinco] crease.

dobradiça [dobra'disa] *f* hinge.

dobrado, da [do'bradu, da] *adj* -1. [com dobras] folded. -2. [flexionado] bent. -3. [duplicado] doubled.

dobrar [do'bra(x)] <> *vt* -1. [fazer dobras em] to fold. -2. [flexionar] to bend. -3. [duplicar] to double. -4. [circundar] to turn. -5. *fig* [fazer ceder] to win sb over. <> *vi* -1. [duplicar-se] to double. -2. [sino] to toll. -3. [envergar] to bend.
➡ **dobrar-se** *vp* -1. [curvar-se] to stoop. -2. *fig* [ceder] to give in.

dobro ['dobru] *m* double.

DOC (*abrev de* Documento de Operação de Crédito) *m Brazilian certificate of credit transfer between accounts*.

doca ['dɔka] *f* dock.

doce ['dosi] <> *adj* -1. [no sabor] sweet. -2. [terno] gentle. -3. [água] fresh. <> *m* -1. *CULIN* dessert, pudding. -2. [loc]: fazer ~ *fam* to play hard to get; ser um ~ (de pessoa) to be a sweetie.

docente [do'sẽntʃi] <> *adj* teaching. <> *mf* teacher.

dócil ['dɔsiw] (*pl* -eis) *adj* docile.

documentação [dokumẽnta'sãw] *f* -1. [em arquivos] documentation. -2. [pessoal] papers.

documental [dokumẽn'taw] (*pl* -ais) *adj* documentary.

documentário [dokumẽn'tarju] *m* documentary.

documento [doku'mẽntu] *m* document.

doçura [do'sura] *f* -1. [gosto doce] sweetness. -2. [suavidade] gentleness.

doença ['dwẽnsa] *f* -1. *MED* illness. -2. *fig* [mania] obsession.

doente ['dwẽntʃi] <> *adj* -1. *MED* sick, ill. -2. *fam* [fanático] obsessed. <> *mf* [pessoa] patient.

doentio, tia [dwẽn'tʃiw, tʃia] *adj* -1. [débil] sickly. -2. [mórbido] unhealthy.

doer ['dwe(x)] *vi* -1. [fisicamente] to hurt. -2. [causar pena, dó]: ~ (a alguém) to distress (sb).

doido, da ['dojda, da] <> *adj* -1. [maluco] mad. -2. [imprudente, insensato] foolish. -3. [excêntrico] crazy. -4. [exagerado] insane. -5. [apaixonado]: ser ~ por to be mad about. -6. [encantado] thrilled. <> *m, f* [pessoa] madman (*f* madwoman).

doído, da [do'idu, da] *adj* -1. [dolorido] sore. -2. [doloroso] painful. -3. [magoado] pained.

dois, duas ['dojʃ, 'duaʃ] *num* two; *veja também* seis.

dois-pontos [,dojʃ'põntuʃ] *m inv* colon (*punctuation mark*).

dólar ['dɔla(x)] (*pl* -es) *m* dollar.

dolo ['dɔlu] *m* fraud.

dolorido, da [dolo'ridu, da] *adj* sore.

doloroso, osa [dolo'rozu, ɔza] *adj* painful.
➡ **dolorosa** *f fam* [conta] tab.

dom ['dõ] (*pl* -ns) *m* -1. [dádiva] gift. -2. [aptidão] knack. -3. [virtude] talent.

dom. (*abrev de* domingo) *f* Sun.

domar [do'ma(x)] *vt* -1. [animal] to tame. -2. [subjugar] to subdue. -3. [reprimir] to repress.

doméstica [do'mɛʃtʃika] *f* ▷ doméstico.

domesticado, da [domeʃtʃi'kadu, da] *adj* domesticated.

domesticar [domeʃtʃi'ka(x)] *vt* to domesticate.

doméstico, ca [do'mɛʃtʃiku, ka] *adj* domestic.
➡ **doméstica** *f* maid.

domiciliar [domisi'lja(x)] *adj* home.

domicílio [domi'silju] *m* residence; entrega a ~ home delivery.

dominador, ra [domina'do(x), ra] <> *adj* domineering. <> *m, f* [pessoa] ruler.

dominante [domi'nãntʃi] *adj* dominant.

dominar [domi'na(x)] <> *vt* -1. [controlar] to dominate. -2. [conhecer] to master. -3. [abranger] to overlook. <> *vi* [ter influência]: ~ em to hold sway over.
➡ **dominar-se** *vp* [controlar-se] to control o.s.

domingo [do'mĩngu] *m* Sunday; *veja também* sábado.

domínio [do'minju] *m* -1. [dominação]: ~ (sobre) control (over). -2. [posse] power. -3. [território] domain. -4. [controle] command. -5. [conhecimento] mastery. -6. *COMPUT* domain.

domo ['domu] *m* dome.

dona ['dona] *f* ▷ dono.

donde ['dõndɛ] = de + onde.

dondoca [dõn'dɔka] *f fam* socialite.

dono, na ['donu, na] *m, f* [proprietário, senhor] owner; ser ~ de seu nariz to lead one's own life.
➡ **dona** *f* -1. [título - de casada] Mrs, Ms; [- de solteira] Miss, Ms. -2. *fam* [mulher] madam.
➡ **dona de casa** *f* housewife.

dons *pl* ▷ dom.

donzela [dõn'zɛla] *f* virgin.

dor ['do(x)ʃ] (pl -es) f -1. [física] pain. -2. [pesar] grief.

dor-d'olhos ['do(x)dɔʎuʃ] (pl dores-d'olhos) f fam eye infection.

dormente [dor'mẽtʃi] adj numb.
◆ **dormente** m [ferro] sleeper.

dormir [dor'mi(x)] <> vi [cair no sono] to sleep. <> vt [sesta, noite]: **dormi uma deliciosa noite** I had a wonderful night's sleep; **dormimos uma sesta ótima esta tarde** we had a really good nap this afternoon.

dormitório [dormi'tɔrju] m -1. [coletivo] dormitory. -2. [quarto] bedroom.

dorso ['doxsu] m back.

dos [duʃ] = de + os.

DOS (abrev de Disc Operating System) m DOS.

dosagem [do'zaʒẽ] (pl -ns) f dosage.

dosar [do'za(x)] vt -1. [regular - medicamento, drinque] to measure out; [- palavras] to measure. -2. [misturar] to mix.

dose ['dɔzi] f -1. [remédio] dose. -2. [bebida] measure.

dossiê [do'sje] m dossier.

dotado, da [do'tadu, da] adj -1. [que tem dote] gifted. -2. [possuidor]: ~ **de** endowed with.

dotar [do'ta(x)] vt -1. [em casamento]: ~ **alguém de algo** to give sthg to sb as a dowry. -2. [favorecer]: ~ **alguém/algo de algo** to endow sb/sthg with sthg. -3. [prover]: ~ **algo de algo** to provide sthg with sthg.

dote ['dɔtʃi] m -1. [bens] dowry. -2. fig [dom natural] gift.

DOU (abrev de Diário Oficial da União) m official Brazilian government publication, ≈ Weekly Information Bulletin UK, ≈ Federal Register US.

dourado, da [do'radu, da] adj golden; **peixinho** ~ goldfish.
◆ **dourado** m -1. [cor] golden colour. -2. [peixe] gilthead.

douto, ta ['dotu, ta] adj: ~ **(em)** learned (in).

doutor, ra [do'to(x), ra] (mpl -es, fpl -s) m, f -1. MED doctor. -2. UNIV: ~ **(em)** doctor (of). -3. [conhecedor]: ~ **em** expert on.

doutorado [doto'radu] m doctorate.

doutrina [do'trina] f doctrine.

doutrinar [dotri'na(x)] <> vt -1. [ensinar] to teach. -2. [convencer] to indoctrinate. <> vi to give instruction.

download [dawn'lowdʒi] m COMPUT download; **fazer um** ~ **de um arquivo** to download a file.

doze ['dozi] num twelve; veja também **seis**.

DP (abrev de Distrito Policial) m police district.

Dr. (abrev de Doutor) m Dr.

Dra. (abrev de Doutora) f Dr.

dragão [dra'gãw] (pl -ões) m dragon.

drama ['drãma] m -1. TEATRO play. -2. fig [catástrofe] tragedy. -3. loc: **fazer** ~ to make a scene; **ser um** ~ to be a nightmare.

dramático, ca [dra'matʃiku, ka] adj dramatic.

dramatizar [dramatʃi'za(x)] <> vt to dramatize. <> vi fig [ser dramático] to exaggerate.

dramaturgo, ga [drama'turgu, ga] m, f dramatist, playwright.

drástico, ca ['draʃtʃiku, ka] adj drastic.

drenagem [dre'naʒẽ] (pl -ns) f drainage.

drenar [dre'na(x)] vt to drain.

driblar [dri'bla(x)] vt -1. FUT to dribble. -2. fig [enganar] to dodge.

drinque ['drĩki] m drink.

drive ['drajvi] (pl drives) m COMPUT disk drive.

droga ['drɔga] <> f -1. [medicamento, entorpecente] drug. -2. fam fig [coisa ruim]: **ser uma** ~ to be a disaster. <> interj fam damn!

drogado, da [dro'gadu, da] <> adj drugged. <> m, f [pessoa] drug addict.

drogaria [droga'ria] f chemist's (shop) UK, drugstore US.

dromedário [drome'darju] m dromedary.

duas ['duaʃ] num ▷ **dois**.

dubiedade [dubje'dadʒi] f [ambigüidade] dubiousness.

dúbio, bia ['dubju, bja] adj dubious.

dublado, da [du'bladu, da] adj CINE dubbed.

dublagem [du'blaʒẽ] (pl -ns) f CINE dubbing.

dublar [du'bla(x)] vt CINE to dub.

dublê [du'ble] mf double.

Dublin n Dublin.

dublinense [dubli'nẽsi] <> adj Dublin (antes de subst.). <> mf Dubliner.

ducha ['duʃa] f -1. [jorro de água] shower. -2. [boxe] shower (cubicle).

duelar [dwe'la(x)] vi -1. [combater] to fight a duel. -2. fig [confrontar] to confront each other.

duelo ['dwɛlu] m duel.

dueto ['dwetu] m duet.

dupla ['dupla] f ▷ **duplo**.

duplex m duplex.

duplicar [dupli'ka(x)] <> vt -1. [dobrar] to double. -2. [aumentar] to redouble. <> vi [dobrar] to double.

duplicata [dupli'kata] f -1. [título] trade note. -2. [cópia] duplicate.

duplo, pla ['duplu, plal *adj* double; **du-pla cidadania** dual nationality.

duque, duquesa ['duki, du'kezal *m, f* duke (*f* duchess).

duração [dura'sãwl (*pl* -ões) *f* duration.

duradouro, ra [dura'doru, ral *adj* lasting.

durante [du'rãntʃil *prep* during.

durar [du'ra(x)] *vi* to last.

durável [du'ravew] (*pl* -eis) *adj* lasting, durable.

durex® [du'rɛkiʃ] *m* [fita adesiva] Sellotape® *UK*, Scotch tape® *US*.

dureza [du'reza] *f* -1. [rijeza] hardness. - 2. [rigor] harshness. - 3. [crueldade] callousness. - 4. *fam* [dificuldade]: **ser uma ~** to be a hardship. - 5. *fam* [falta de dinheiro]: **estar na maior ~** to be hard up.

duro, ra ['duru, ral *adj* -1. [ger] harsh. - 2. [carne, material, água] hard. - 3. [vida, trabalho, tarefa] tough. - 4. *fam* [sem dinheiro]: **estar ~** to be hard up. - 5. *loc*: **dar ~ (para algo/ fazer algo)** to work flat out (for sthg/to do sthg).

dúvida l'duvidal *f* doubt; **sem ~** without a doubt.

duvidar [duvi'da(x)] <> *vt*: **~ que** to doubt that. <> *vi*: **~ de alguém/algo** to doubt sb/sthg.

duvidoso, osa [duvi'dozu, ɔzal *adj* -1. [incerto] doubtful. - 2. [suspeito] dubious.

duzentos, tas [du'zẽntuʃ, taʃl *num* two hundred; *veja também* **seis**.

dúzia l'duzjal *f* dozen; **meia ~** half a dozen.

DVD (*abrev de* **Digital Video Disk**) *m* DVD.

E

e, E [ɛl *m* [letra] e, E.

ébano ['ɛbanul *m* ebony.

ébrio, ébria ['ɛbrju, 'ɛbrjal <> *adj* drunk. <> *m, f* drunkard.

EBTU (*abrev de* **Empresa Brasileira de Transportes Urbanos**) *f Brazilian company for urban transport planning*.

ebulição [ibuli'sãwl *f* -1. [de líquido] boiling. - 2. *fig* [agitação] excitement.

e-business [ɛbusi'nɛesil *m ECON* e-business.

eclesiástico, ca [ekle'zjastʃiku, kal *adj* ecclesiastical.

◆ **eclesiástico** *m* [membro do clero] clergyman.

eclético, ca [e'klɛtʃiku, kal *adj* eclectic.

eclipse [e'klipsil *m* eclipse.

eclosão [eklo'zãwl (*pl* -ões) *f* -1. [aparecimento] emergence. - 2. [desenvolvimento] development. - 3. [de flor] blooming.

eclusa [e'kluzal *f* lock (*on waterway*).

eco ['ɛkul *m* echo.

ecoar [e'kwa(x)] *vt & vi* to echo.

ecologia [ekolo'ʒial *f* ecology.

ecológico, ca [eko'lɔʒiku, kal *adj* ecological.

ecólogo, ga [e'kɔlogu, gal *m, f* ecologist.

e-commerce [ɛko'mɛxsil *m ECON* e-commerce.

economia [ekono'mial *f* -1. [ger] economy; **~ de mercado** market economy; **fazer ~** to economize. - 2. [estudo] economics.

◆ **economias** *fpl* [poupança] savings.

econômico, ca [eko'nomiku, kal *adj* -1. [ger] economical. - 2. [relativo à economia] economic.

economista [ekono'miʃtal *mf* economist.

economizar [ekonomi'za(x)] <> *vt* -1. [gastar, usar com moderação] to economize on. - 2. [acumular] to save. <> *vi* [fazer economia] to economize.

ecossistema [ˌɛkosiʃ'temal *m* ecosystem.

ecoturismo [ɛkotu'riʃmul *m* ecotourism.

ecoturista [ɛkotu'riʃtal *mf* ecotourist.

ECT (*abrev de* **Empresa Brasileira de Correios e Telégrafos**) *f Brazilian postal service*, ≃ The Post Office *UK*, ≃ USPS *US*.

ecumênico, ca [eku'meniku, kal *adj* ecumenical.

ed. (*abrev de* **edifício**) *m* building.

edição [edʒi'sãwl (*pl* -ões) *f* -1. [ger] edition; **~ atualizada** revised edition; **~ pirata** pirate copy. - 2. [publicação] publication; - 3. [seleção] editing.

edificante [edʒifi'kãntʃil *adj* -1. [moralizante] edifying. - 2. [instrutivo] instructive.

edifício [edʒi'fisjul *m* building.

edital [edʒi'tawl (*pl* -ais) *m* proclamation.

editar [edʒi'ta(x)] *vt* -1. [ger] to produce. - 2. [livro, revista] to publish. - 3. [preparar texto] to edit.

edito le'dʒitul *m* edict.

editor, ra [edʒi'to(x), ral <> *adj* [casa] publishing. <> *m, f* -1. [ger] editor. - 2.

[dono de editora] publisher. **- 3.** RÁDIO & TV producer. **- 4.** COMPUT: ~ **de texto** text editor.

➡ **editora** f [estabelecimento] publisher.

editoração [edʒitora'sãw] f editing; ~ **eletrônica** electronic publishing.

editorial [edʒitor'jaw] (pl **-ais**) ◇ adj editorial. ◇ m editorial.

edredom [edre'dõ] (pl **-ns**) m eiderdown.

educação [eduka'sãw] f **- 1.** [ensino] education. **- 2.** [criação] upbringing. **- 3.** [polidez] manners; **falta de** ~ bad manners.

educacional [edukasjo'naw] (pl **-ais**) adj educational.

educar [edu'ka(x)] vt **- 1.** [instruir] to educate. **- 2.** [criar] to bring up. **- 3.** [adestrar] to instruct.

➡ **educar-se** vp [instruir-se] to teach o.s.

EEUU (abrev de **Estados Unidos da América do Norte**) mpl USA.

efeito [e'fejtu] m effect; **fazer** ~ to have an effect; **levar a** ~ to put into effect; ~ **colateral** side effect; ~ **s especiais** CINE special effects; ~ **estufa** greenhouse effect.

efervescente [eferve'sẽntʃi] adj **- 1.** [líquido, comprimido] effervescent. **- 2.** fig [agitado] excited.

efetivo, va [efe'tʃivu, va] adj **- 1.** [positivo] effective. **- 2.** [permanente] permanent. **- 3.** [seguro] certain.

➡ **efetivo** m **- 1.** MIL military strength. **- 2.** COM liquid assets.

efetuar [efe'twa(x)] vt to carry out.

eficácia [efi'kasja] f **- 1.** [de pessoa] efficiency. **- 2.** [de medida, tratamento] effectiveness.

eficaz [efi'kaʃ] (pl **-es**) adj **- 1.** [pessoa] efficient. **- 2.** [medida, tratamento] effective.

eficiência [efi'sjẽnsja] f efficiency.

eficiente [efi'sjẽntʃi] adj efficient.

efusivo, va [efu'zivu, va] adj fig [expansivo] effusive.

e.g. (abrev de **exempli gratia**) e.g.

egípcio, cia [e'ʒipsju, ja] ◇ adj Egyptian. ◇ m, f Egyptian.

Egito [e'ʒitu] n Egypt.

egocêntrico, ca [ego'sẽntriku, ka] ◇ adj egocentric. ◇ m, f egocentric person.

egoísmo [e'gwiʒmu] m egoism.

egoísta [e'gwiʃta] ◇ adj egotistic. ◇ mf [pessoa] egotist.

égua ['ɛgwa] f mare.

ei [ej] interj hey!

ei-lo ['ejlu] = **eis** + **o**.

eis ['ejʃ] adv here is/are.

eixo ['ejʃu] m **- 1.** [de rodas] axle. **- 2.** [de máquina] shaft. **- 3.** MAT axis. **- 4.** [trecho] area (between two points).

ejacular [eʒaku'la(x)] vt & vi to ejaculate.

ela ['ɛla] ➡ **ele**.

elaboração [elabora'sãw] (pl **-ões**) f preparation.

elaborar [elabo'ra(x)] vt to prepare.

elástico, ca [e'laʃtʃiku, ka] adj **- 1.** [tecido etc.] elastic. **- 2.** fig [flexível] adaptable.

➡ **elástico** m **- 1.** [para prender notas etc.] rubber band. **- 2.** [para roupa] elastic. **- 3.** [para cabelo] elastic band.

ele, ela ['eli, 'ɛla] (mpl **eles**, fpl **elas**) pron pess (de + ele = **dele**; de + ela = **dela**; em + ele = **nele**; em + ela = **nela**) **- 1.** [pessoa] he (f she); ~ **é médico** he is a doctor; **ela foi embora** she has gone away; **elas viajaram** they travelled; **eles têm uma filha** they have one daughter; **que só** ~ as only he can be/do; ~ **mesmo** ou **próprio** him himself. **- 2.** [animal, coisa] it; **o cachorro?** ~ **uivou a noite inteira** the dog? it howled all night long; **ela dá flor em novembro** it flowers in November; **o relatório? aqui está** ~ the report? here it is; **eles já foram vendidos** they have already been sold; ~ **mesmo** itself. **- 3.** [depois de prep] [pessoa] him, her, it; **este livro pertence a** ~ this book belongs to him; **jantei com** ~ I had dinner with them; **todos olharam para eles** ~ everybody looked at them; **sou mais velho que** ~ I am older than him; **decidimos ir sem ela** we decided to go without her; **deram um tiro nele** they shot him; **aquele é o carro dele** that's his car; **os jornais só falam dela** the newspapers talk about nothing but her. **- 4.** loc: **agora é que são elas** there's the rub; **ser elas por elas** to be tit for tat.

elefante [ele'fãntʃi] m elephant.

elegância [ele'gãnsja] f elegance; **com** ~ elegantly.

elegante [ele'gãntʃi] adj elegant.

eleger [ele'ʒe(x)] vt **- 1.** [por meio de votos] to elect. **- 2.** [escolher] to select.

elegível [ele'ʒivew] (pl **-eis**) adj eligible.

eleição [elej'sãw] (pl **-ões**) f **- 1.** [por meio de votos] election. **- 2.** [escolha] selection.

eleito, ta [e'lejtu, ta] ◇ pp ➡ **eleger**. ◇ adj **- 1.** [por votos] elected. **- 2.** [escolhido] selected.

eleitor, ra [elej'to(x), ra] (mpl **-es**, fpl **-s**) m, f voter.

eleitorado [elejto'radu] m electorate;

conhecer o seu ~ *fam fig* to know who one is dealing with.

eleitoreiro, ra [elejto'rejru, ra] *adj pej* vote-catching.

elementar [elemẽn'ta(x)] (*pl* -es) *adj* -1. [rudimentar] elementary. -2. [fundamental] fundamental.

elemento [elemẽntul] *m* element.
◆ **elementos** *mpl* -1. [ger] elements. -2. [dados] facts.

elencar [elẽn'ka(x)] *vt* [listar] to list.

elenco [e'lẽŋkul] *m* -1. *TEATRO* cast list. -2. [rol] list.

eletricidade [eletrisi'dadʒi] *f* electricity.

eletricista [eletri'siʃta] *mf* electrician.

elétrico, ca [e'lɛtriku, ka] *adj* -1. *ELETR* electric. -2. *fig* [agitado] excited.

eletrificar [eletrifi'ka(x)] *vt* to electrify.

eletrizar [eletri'za(x)] *vt* -1. *ELETR* to electrify. -2. *fig* [arrebatar] to thrill.

Eletrobras (*abrev de* **Centrais Elétricas Brasileiras S/A**) *f* Brazilian electricity company.

eletrocardiograma [e͵lɛtrokaxdʒo'grãmal] *m* *MED* electrocardiogram.

eletrocutar [eletroku'ta(x)] *vt* to electrocute.

eletrodinâmica [eletrodʒi'nãmika] *f* *FÍS* electrodynamics (*sg*).

eletrodo [ele'trodul] *m* electrode.

eletrodomésticos [eletrodo'mɛʃtʃikuʃ] *mpl* domestic appliances.

eletroeletrônico, ra [elɛktro'eletronico, ka] ◇ *adj* electronics. ◇ *m, f* electronic device.

eletrônica [ele'tronika] *f* electronics (*sg*).

eletrônico, ca [ele'troniku, ka] *adj* electronic.

elevação [eleva'sãw] (*pl* -ões) *f* -1. [ger] elevation. -2. [aumento] rise.

elevado, da [ele'vadu, da] *adj* -1. [alto] high. -2. [nobre] noble.
◆ **elevado** *m* [via] flyover.

elevador [eleva'do(x)] (*pl* -es) *m* lift *UK*, elevator *US*.

elevar [ele'va(x)] *vt* -1. [erguer] to lift up. -2. [aumentar] to raise. -3. [exaltar] to acclaim.
◆ **elevar-se** *vp* to rise.

eliminar [elimi'na(x)] *vt* -1. [ger] to eliminate. -2. [descartar] to exclude.

eliminatório, ria [elimina'tɔrju, rja] *adj* eliminatory.
◆ **eliminatória** *f* -1. *ESP* heat. -2. *EDUC* test.

elite [e'litʃil] *f* elite.

elo ['ɛlul] *m* link.

elocução [eloku'sãw] *f* elocution.

elogiar [elo'ʒjar] *vt* to praise.

elogio [elo'ʒiul] *m* praise.

El Salvador *n* El Salvador.

elucidar [elusi'da(x)] *vt* to explain.

em [ẽ] *prep* (*em* + *o* = *no*; *em* + *a* = *na*) -1. [lugar - dentro de] in; **no bolso/estojo/quarto** in the pocket/case/bedroom; **na bolsa/caixa/sala** in the purse/box/living room; [- num certo ponto de] at; ~ **casa** at home; **no trabalho** at work; **nas ruas** on the streets; **moramos na capital** we live in the capital; **depositei o dinheiro no banco** I deposited the money in the bank; [- sobre] on; **o bife mal cabia no prato** the steak hardly fitted on the plate; **havia um vaso de flores na mesa** there was a vase of flowers on the table; [- cidade, país] in; ~ **Londres/São Paulo** in London/São Paulo; **no Porto/Rio de Janeiro** in Oporto/Rio de Janeiro; ~ **Portugal** in Portugal; **no Brasil** in Brazil; **na França** in France; **nos Estados Unidos** in the United States. -2. [tempo] in; **inaugurado** ~ **1967** officially opened in 1967; **ele tirou férias** ~ **maio** he took his holidays in May; ~ **7 de setembro de 1622** on 7th September 1622; **comemoram a liberdade no 25 de abril** freedom is celebrated on 25th April; **no Natal** at Christmas; **na Semana Santa** during Holy Week; **ela fez tudo** ~ **uma semana** she did everything in one week; **o serviço ficará pronto** ~ **dois dias** the work will be ready in two days' time; **naquela época** ~ **breve** at that time in those days; ~ **breve** soon. -3. [introduzindo o objeto indireto] in; **enfiar/esquecer/guardar algo** ~ to slip/forget/keep sthg in; **acreditar** ~ to believe in; **pensar** ~ to think of; **ele caiu num buraco** he fell in a hole; **ela caiu/no chão** she fell on the floor; **ela entrou na sala** she entered the room; **vou no jornaleiro e já volto** I am going to the newsagent's and I'll be right back. -4. [assunto] in; **doutorado** ~ **sociologia** graduated in sociology; **ele é perito** ~ **balística** he is an expert in ballistics. -5. [modo] in; **ele falou** ~ **voz baixa** he spoke in a low voice; **ela falou** ~ **português** she spoke in Portuguese; **ele dirige** ~ **alta velocidade** he drives fast; **ela pagou** ~ **libras/reais** she paid in pounds sterling/reals; **o preço aumentou** ~ **10%** the price has gone up by 10%; **ele gasta tudo o que ganha** ~ **livros** he spends all he earns on books; **bife na chapa** grilled steak. -6. [estado]: **a multidão** ~ **euforia** the rejoicing crowd; **ela ainda está** ~ **convalescença** she is still convalescing; **um**

carro usado ~ boas condições a well-kept second-hand car; **países ~ guerra** countries at war. **- 7.** [material]: **estátua ~ bronze** bronze statue; **camisa ~ viscose** rayon shirt. **- 8.** (em loc adv, loc prep) on; **com base ~** based on/in; **de tempos ~ tempos** from time to time; **~ busca de** in search of; **~ caso de** in case of; **~ geral** in general; **~ meio a** in the middle of; **na verdade ~** in truth; **no mínimo/máximo** at least/the most.

emagrecer [emagre'se(x)] <> vt [causar perda de peso] to cause to lose weight. <> vi **-1.** [perder peso] to lose weight. **-2.** [definhar] to slim down.

emagrecimento [emagresi'mẽntul] m slimming.

e-mail m e-mail.

emanar [ema'na(x)] vi **-1.** [exalar-se]: **~ de** to emanate from. **- 2.** [originar-se]: **~ de** to stem from.

emancipado, da [emãnsi'padu, da] adj liberated.

emancipar [emãnsi'pa(x)] vt **-1.** [ger] to emancipate. **-2.** [país] to liberate.
    ◆ **emancipar-se** vp **-1.** [mulheres] to become emancipated. **-2.** [menor] to come of age. **-3.** [país] to become free.

emaranhado, da [emarã'ɲadu, da] adj [embaraçado] tangled.
    ◆ **emaranhado** m [confusão] confusion.

emaranhar [emarã'ɲa(x)] vt **-1.** [enredar] to tangle. **-2.** fig [complicar] to confuse.
    ◆ **emaranhar-se** vp [enredar-se] to become entangled.

embaçado, da [ẽnba'sadu, da] adj **-1.** [vidro] misted up. **-2.** [olhos] misty.

embaixada [ẽnbaj'ʃada] f **-1.** [local] embassy. **-2.** [cargo] ambassadorial duties. **-3.** [funcionários] embassy staff.

embaixador, ra [ẽnbajʃa'do(x), ra] (mpl -es, fpl -s) m, f ambassador.

embaixatriz [ẽnbajʃa'triʃ] f [esposa do embaixador] ambassadress.

embaixo [ẽn'bajʃul] adv: **~ de** underneath; **aí ~** down there; **lá ~** downstairs.
    ◆ **embaixo de** loc prep under.

embalado, da [ẽnba'ladu, da] <> adj **-1.** [empacotado] wrapped, packed. **-2.** [acelerado] fast. **-3.** [drogado] high. <> adv [aceleradamente] more quickly.

embalagem [ẽnba'laʒẽ] (pl -ns) f **-1.** [ato] wrapping, packing. **-2.** [invólucro] package.

embalar [ẽnba'la(x)] vt **-1.** [acondicionar] to wrap. **-2.** [berço] to rock. **-3.** [balanço] to swing.

embalsamado, da [ẽnbawsa'madu, da] adj **-1.** [cadáver] embalmed. **-2.** [perfumado] scented.

embaraçar [ẽnbara'sa(x)] vt **-1.** [obstruir] to block. **-2.** [acanhar] to embarrass. **-3.** [cabelos] to tangle. **-4.** [dificultar] to complicate.
    ◆ **embaraçar-se** vp [embaralhar-se] to become embroiled.

embaraço [ẽnba'rasu] m **-1.** [obstáculo] obstacle. **-2.** [acanhamento] embarrassment. **-3.** [dificuldade] difficult situation.

embaraçoso, osa [ẽnbara'sozu, ɔza] adj embarrassing.

embaralhar [ẽnbara'ʎa(x)] vt **-1.** [cartas] to shuffle. **-2.** [confundir] to jumble.
    ◆ **embaralhar-se** vp [confundir-se] to become confused.

embarcação [ẽnbaxka'sãw] (pl -ões) f vessel.

embarcadouro [ẽnbaxka'doru] m quay.

embarcar [ẽnbax'ka(x)] <> vt **-1.** [pessoa] to board. **-2.** [carga] to load. <> vi **~ (em)** [subir a bordo] to board; [viajar] to travel.

embargar [ẽnbax'ga(x)] vt **-1.** [JUR - apreender] to seize; [- impedir] to block. **-2.** [conter] to control.

embargo [ẽn'baxgul] m **-1.** JUR seizure. **-2.** [obstáculo] impediment.

embarque [ẽn'baxkil] m **-1.** [de pessoa] boarding. **-2.** [de carga] loading.

embasamento [ẽnbaza'mẽntul] m **-1.** [base] foundation. **-2.** fig [fundamento] basis.

embebedar [ẽnbebe'da(x)] vt & vi to intoxicate.
    ◆ **embebedar-se** vp to become intoxicated.

embelezar [ẽnbele'za(x)] vt [tornar belo] to beautify.
    ◆ **embelezar-se** vp [enfeitar-se] to make o.s. beautiful.

embicar [ẽnbi'ka(x)] <> vt [tornar bicudo] to sharpen. <> vi **-1.** [esbarrar] to meet. **-2.** [implicar]: **~ com algo/alguém** to become entangled with sthg/sb.

embocadura [ẽnboka'dura] f **-1.** [de rio] mouth. **-2.** [de instrumento] mouthpiece.

êmbolo [ˈẽnbolul] m **-1.** [bomba] piston. **-2.** [seringa] plunger. **-3.** MED embolism.

embolsar [ẽnbow'sa(x)] vt **-1.** [receber] to pocket. **-2.** [pagar] to pay.

embora [ẽn'bɔral] <> conj although. <> adv: **ir ~** to go; **vá-se ~** I go away!

emboscada [ẽnboʃ'kada] f ambush.

Embraer (abrev de Empresa Brasileira de Aeronáutica) f Brazilian aeronautical company.

Embratel (abrev de Empresa Brasileira de Telecomunicações S/A) f Brazilian telecommunications company.

embreagem [ẽnbre'aʒẽl (pl **-ns**) f clutch.
embrear [ẽm'brja(x)] <> vt to engage (the clutch). <> vi to engage the clutch.
embrenhar-se [ẽnbre'naxsil vp: ~-se **em/por** to conceal o.s. in.
embriagar [ẽnbrja'ga(x)] <> vt to intoxicate. <> vi [embebedar] to intoxicate.
◆ **embriagar-se** vp [enlevar-se] to become intoxicated.
embriaguez [ẽnbrja'geʒ] f **-1.** [ebriedade] drunkenness. **-2.** fig [enlevo] intoxication.
embrião [ẽn'brjãw] (pl **-ões**) m embryo.
embromar [ẽnbro'ma(x)] <> vt **-1.** [enrolar] to fool. **-2.** [enganar] to bamboozle. <> vi **-1.** [protelar] to procrastinate. **-2.** [fazer rodeios] to beat about the bush.
embrulhada [ẽnbru'ʎadal f fam [confusão] muddle.
embrulhar [ẽnbru'ʎa(x)] vt **-1.** [empacotar] to wrap. **-2.** fig [estômago] to upset. **-3.** [confundir] to screw up. **-4.** [enganar] to trick.
embrulho [ẽn'bruʎul m **-1.** [pacote] package. **-2.** [confusão] confusion.
embrutecer [ẽnbrute'se(x)] <> vt to make brutal. <> vi to brutalize.
◆ **embrutecer-se** vp to become brutalized.
emburrado, da [ẽnbu'xadu, dal adj [aborrecido] sulky.
embuste [ẽn'buʃtʃil m **-1.** [mentira] deception. **-2.** [armadilha] trick.
embusteiro, ra [ẽnbuʃ'tejru, ral <> adj deceitful. <> m, f [pessoa] trickster.
embutido, da [ẽnbu'tʃidu, dal adj [armário, estante] built-in.
emenda [e'mẽndal f **-1.** [correção] correction. **-2.** JUR amendment. **-3.** COST repair. **-4.** [ligação] join.
emendar [emẽn'da(x)] vt **-1.** [corrigir] to correct. **-2.** JUR to amend. **-3.** [reparar] to redress. **-4.** [ligar] to join.
◆ **emendar-se** vp [corrigir-se] to mend one's ways.
emergência [emex'ʒẽnsjal f **-1.** [ger] emergency. **-2.** [surgimento] emergence.
emergir [emex'ʒi(x)] vi to emerge.
emigração [emigra'sãw] (pl **-ões**) f **-1.** [de pessoas] emigration. **-2.** [de aves] migration.
emigrado, da [emi'gradu, dal <> adj emigrant. <> m, f émigré.
emigrante [emi'grãntʃil <> adj emigrant. <> mf émigré.
emigrar [emi'gra(x)] vi **-1.** [pessoa] to emigrate. **-2.** [ave] to migrate.

eminência [emi'nẽnsjal f **-1.** [ger] eminence. **-2.** [título, tratamento] Eminence. **-3.** [pessoa importante] important person.
eminente [emi'nẽntʃil adj **-1.** [ilustre] eminent. **-2.** [elevado] high.
Emirados Árabes Unidos n: os ~ the United Arab Emirates.
emissão [emi'sãw] (pl **-ões**) f **-1.** [ger] emission. **-2.** [de moeda, títulos, passagens aéreas] issue. **-3.** RÁDIO & TV transmission.
emissário, ria [emi'sarju, rjal m, f [mensageiro] emissary.
◆ **emissário** m [esgoto] outlet.
emissor, ra [emi'so(x), ral (mpl **-es**, fpl **-s**) adj FIN issuing.
◆ **emissor** m [transmissor] transmitter.
◆ **emissora** f transmitter.
emitir [emi'tʃi(x)] <> vt **-1.** [ger] to issue. **-2.** [sons, raios] to emit. **-3.** [opinião, idéias] to transmit. <> vi FIN to issue money.
emoção [emo'sãw] (pl **-ões**) f emotion.
emocional [emosjo'naw] (pl **-ais**) adj emotional.
emocionante [emosjo'nãntʃil adj **-1.** [comovente] moving. **-2.** [empolgante] gripping.
emocionar [emosjo'na(x)] <> vt **-1.** [comover] to move. **-2.** [excitar] to thrill. <> vi [provocar emoção] to thrill.
◆ **emocionar-se** vp [comover-se]: ~-se **com algo/alguém** to get emotional about sthg/sb.
emoldurar [emowdu'ra(x)] vt to frame.
emoticon [emo'tʃikõl (pl **-ns**) m COMPUT emoticom.
emotivo, va [emo'tʃivu, val adj emotional.
empacotar [ẽnpako'ta(x)] <> vt [embalar] to wrap up. <> vi fam [morrer] to snuff it.
empada [ẽn'padal f CULIN pie.
empadão [ẽnpa'dãwl (pl **-ões**) m pie.
empalhar [ẽnpa'ʎa(x)] vt **-1.** [animal] to stuff. **-2.** [cadeira, garrafa] to cover in wickerwork.
empalidecer [ẽnpalide'se(x)] <> vt [tornar pálido] to cause to turn pale. <> vi [perder a cor] to turn pale.
empanada [ẽnpa'nadal f CULIN large pie.
empanturrado, da [ẽnpãntu'xadu, dal adj stuffed full.
empanturrar [ẽnpãntu'xa(x)] vt: ~ **alguém de algo** to stuff sb with sthg.
◆ **empanturrar-se** vp: ~-se **de algo** to stuff o.s. with sthg.
empapuçar [ẽnpapu'sa(x)] vt [inchar] to stuff.

emparelhado, da [ēmpare'ʎadu, da] *adj* [lado a lado] paired.

emparelhar [ēnpare'ʎa(x)] ⬦ *vt* [por em pares] to pair up. ⬦ *vi* -1. [equivaler]: ~ **(em algo)** to be equal (in sthg). -2. [equiparar-se]: ~ **com** to be equal to. -3. [correr parelhas]: ~ **(com alguém)** to draw alongside.

empatar [ēnpa'ta(x)] ⬦ *vi* [em jogo]: ~ **com** to draw with. ⬦ *vt* -1. [impedir] to hinder. -2. [ocupar] to take up. -3. [aplicar] to tie up.

empate [ēn'patʃi] *m* [jogo, votação] tie; **dar** ~ to end in a draw.

empecilho [ēnpe'siʎu] *m* obstacle.

empedernido, da [ēnpedex'nidu, da] *adj* harsh.

empedrar [ēnpe'dra(x)] *vt* [cobrir com pedras] to pave.

empenar [ēnpe'na(x)] ⬦ *vt* [entortar] to warp. ⬦ *vi* [entortar-se] to warp.

empenhado, da [ēnpe'ɲadu, da] *adj* -1. [disposto] determined. -2. [penhorado] pawned.

empenhar [ēnpe'ɲa(x)] *vt* -1. [dar em penhor] to pawn. -2. [aplicar] to apply. -3. [comprometer] to pledge.

➡ **empenhar-se** *vp* [aplicar-se]: ~-**se (para fazer algo)** to commit o.s. (to do sthg). ~-**se em algo** to get into debt over sthg.

empenho [ēn'peɲu] *m* -1. [diligência] commitment; **pôr todo o** ~ **em algo** to put all one's effort into sthg. -2. [compromisso] commitment. -3. [penhor] pledge.

emperrado, da [ēmpe'xadu, da] *adj* -1. [entravado] jammed. -2. [teimoso] stubborn.

emperrar [ēnpe'xa(x)] ⬦ *vi* [tornar-se imóvel] to stick. ⬦ *vt* -1. [entravar] to cause to stick. -2. [dificultar] to bog down.

empestar [ēmpeʃ'ta(x)] *vt* -1. [contaminar] to infest. -2. [infectar com mau cheiro]: ~ **algo (com algo)** to stink out sthg (with sthg).

empilhar [ēnpi'ʎa(x)] *vt* [amontoar] to stack.

empinado, da [ēnpi'nadu, da] *adj* straight.

empinar [ēnpi'na(x)] ⬦ *vt* -1. [peito, corpo, nariz] to thrust out. -2. [pipa] to empty. ⬦ *vi* [cavalo] to rear.

emplastro [ēn'plaʃtru] *m* [medicamento] plaster.

empobrecer [ēnpobre'se(x)] ⬦ *vt* -1. [tornar pobre] to impoverish. -2. [o solo] to deplete. ⬦ *vi* [tornar-se pobre] to become poor.

empobrecimento [ēnpobresi'mēntu] *m* -1. [ger] impoverishment. -2. [do solo] depletion.

empoeirado, da [ēnpoej'radu, da] *adj* dusty.

empolado, da [ēnpo'ladu, da] *adj* -1. [pele] blistered. -2. *fig* [linguagem, estilo] pompous.

empolgação [ēnpowga'sãw] *f* enthusiasm.

empolgante [ēnpow'gãntʃi] *adj* thrilling.

empolgar [ēnpow'ga(x)] *vt* to fill with enthusiasm.

➡ **empolgar-se** *vp* [entusiasmar-se] to become enthusiastic.

empório [ēn'pɔrju] *m* -1. [mercado] market. -2. [armazém] department store.

empossar [ēnpo'sa(x)] *vt* [dar posse a] to install in office.

empreendedor, ra [ēnprjēnde'do(x), ra] ⬦ *adj* [ativo] enterprising. ⬦ *m, f* [pessoa] entrepreneur.

empreender [ēnprjēn'de(x)] *vt* to undertake.

empreendimento [ēnprjēndʒi'mēntu] *m* undertaking.

empregado, da [ēnpre'gadu, da] *m, f* [funcionário] employee.

➡ **empregada** *f* [em casa de família]: **empregada (doméstica)** maid.

empregador, ra [ēnprega'do(x), ra] *m, f* employer.

empregar [ēnpre'ga(x)] *vt* -1. [ger] to use. -2. [dar emprego a] to employ. -3. [ocupar] to put to use.

➡ **empregar-se** *vp* [obter trabalho] to get a job.

emprego [ēn'pregu] *m* -1. [trabalho] job. -2. [local de trabalho] work. -3. [uso] use.

empreiteira [ēnprej'tejra] *f* contracting company.

empreiteiro [ēnprej'tejru] *m* contractor.

empresa [ēn'preza] *f* -1. [firma] company; ~ **estatal/privada** state-owned/privately-owned company. -2. [empreendimento] enterprise.

empresário, ria [ēnpre'zarju, rja] *m, f* -1. [dono de empresa] employer. -2. [de artista, jogador] agent.

emprestado, da [ēnpreʃ'tadu, da] *adj* loaned; **pedir algo** ~ to borrow sthg.

emprestar [ēnpreʃ'ta(x)] *vt* to lend.

empréstimo [ēn'prɛʃtʃimul] *m* [de dinheiro] loan.

empurrão [ēnpu'xãw] (*pl* -ões) *m* shove.

empurrar [ēnpu'xa(x)] *vt* -1. [impelir com força] to shove; **'empurre'** [aviso] 'push' -2. [impingir] to palm off.

emudecer [emude'se(x)] <> *vt* [fazer calar] to silence. <> *vi* [calar-se] to go quiet.

enamorado, da [enamo'radu, da] *adj* in love.

encabeçar [eŋkabe'sa(x)] *vt* -1. [vir à frente de] to head. -2. [chefiar] to lead.

encabulado, da [eŋkabu'ladu, da] *adj* -1. [acanhado] embarrassed. -2. [envergonhado] ashamed.

encabular [eŋkabu'la(x)] <> *vt* [envergonhar] to embarrass. <> *vi* [acanhar-se] to be embarrassed.
➔ **encabular-se** *vp* -1. [acanhar-se] to be embarrassed. -2. [envergonhar-se] to be ashamed.

encadernação [eŋkadexna'sãw] (*pl* -ões) *f* bookbinding.

encadernado, da [eŋkadex'nadu, da] *adj* bound.

encadernar [eŋkadex'na(x)] *vt* to bind.

encaixar [eŋkaj'ʃa(x)] <> *vt* -1. [inserir]: ~ algo (em algo) to fit sthg (into sthg). -2. [encaixotar] to box. <> *vi* [entrar no encaixe] to fit.
➔ **encaixar-se** *vp* to fit.

encaixe [eŋ'kajʃi] *m* -1. [ato] entrance. -2. [cavidade] groove. -3. [junção] joint.

encalço [eŋ'kawsu] *m*: estar no ~ de algo/alguém to be in pursuit of sthg/sb.

encalhado, da [eŋka'ʎadu, da] *adj* -1. [embarcação] aground. -2. [mercadoria] unsaleable. -3. *fam* [pessoa solteira] on the shelf.

encalhar [eŋka'ʎa(x)] *vi* -1. [embarcação] to run aground. -2. [mercadoria] to remain unsold. -3. [processo] to grind to a halt. -4. *fam* [pessoa solteira] to be left on the shelf.

encaminhar [eŋkami'ɲa(x)] *vt* -1. [dirigir] to direct. -2. [orientar] to guide. -3. [dar andamento] to get going.
➔ **encaminhar-se** *vp* [dirigir-se]: ~-se para/a to set out for/to.

encanador, ra [eŋkana'dox, ra] (*mpl* -es, *fpl* -s) *m, f* plumber.

encanamento [eŋkana'mẽntu] *m* [sistema] plumbing.

encanar [eŋka'na(x)] *vt* -1. [canalizar] to channel. -2. *fam* [prender] to lock up.

encantado, da [eŋkãn'tadu, da] (*mpl* -es, *fpl* -s) *adj* [ger] enchanted.

encantador, ra [eŋkãnta'do(x), ra] (*mpl* -es, *fpl* -s) *adj* -1. [fascinante] charming. -2. [deslumbrante] fantastic.

encantamento [eŋkãnta'mẽntu] *m* -1. [magia] enchantment. -2. [deslumbramento] fascination.

encantar [eŋkãn'ta(x)] *vt* -1. [enfeitiçar] to bewitch. -2. [fascinar] to charm. -3. [deslumbrar] to fascinate.
➔ **encantar-se** *vp*: ~-se com algo to be enchanted by sthg.

encanto [eŋ'kãntu] *m* -1. [ger] charm. -2. *fam* [pessoa]: ser um ~ to be a charming person.

encapado, da [eŋka'padu, da] *adj* covered.

encapar [eŋka'pa(x)] *vt* to cover.

encapetar-se [eŋkape'ta(x)si] *vp* [endiabrar-se] to go into a tantrum.

encapotar [eŋkapo'ta(x)] *vt* [cobrir] to wrap.
➔ **encapotar-se** *vp* [cobrir-se] to wrap o.s. up.

encarar [eŋka'ra(x)] *vt* -1. [fitar] to stare at. -2. [enfrentar] to face up to. -3. [considerar] to consider.

encarcerar [eŋkaxse'ra(x)] *vt* [prender] to incarcerate.

encardido, da [eŋkar'dʒidu, da] *adj* -1. [roupa] soiled. -2. [pele] grimy.

encardir [eŋkax'dʒi(x)] <> *vt* -1. [roupa] to soil. -2. [pele] to make grimy. <> *vi* [ficar mal lavado] to be badly washed.

encarecer [eŋkare'se(x)] <> *vt* -1. [tornar mais caro] to make more expensive. -2. [elogiar] to praise. <> *vi* [ficar mais caro] to go up in price.

encarecidamente [eŋkaresida'mẽntʃil] *adv* [insistentemente]: pedir ~ to ask insistently.

encargo [eŋ'kaxgu] *m* -1. [ger] duty. -2. [responsabilidade] responsibility.

encarnação [eŋkaxna'sãw] (*pl* -ões) *f* -1. [ger] incarnation. -2. [personificação]: ser a ~ de algo to be the embodiment of sthg. -3. *fam* [implicância] teasing.

encarnado, da [eŋkax'nadu, da] *adj* [vermelho] red.

encarnar [eŋkax'na(x)] <> *vi* -1. [alma, espírito] to represent. -2. [implicar] *fam*: ~ em alguém to tease sb. <> *vt* -1. [personificar] to personify. -2. *TEATRO* to play.

encarregado, da [eŋkaxe'gadu, da] <> *adj*: ~ de algo/fazer algo in charge of sthg/with doing sthg. <> *m, f* person in charge.

encarregar [eŋkaxe'ga(x)] *vt*: ~ alguém de algo to put sb in charge of sthg.
➔ **encarregar-se** *vp*: ~-se de algo/fazer algo to take charge of sthg/doing sthg.

encarte [eŋ'kaxtʃi] *m* -1. [em publicação] insertion. -2. [de disco, CD] insert.

encenação [ẽnsena'sãw] *f* -1. *TEATRO* staging. -2. [produção] production. -3. *fig* [fingimento] play-acting.

encenar [ẽnse'na(x)] *vt* **-1.** *TEATRO* to stage. **-2.** [produzir] to produce. **-3.** *fig* [fingir] to play-act.

encerado, da [ẽnse'radu, da] *adj* waxed.
◆ **encerado** *m* [oleado] tarpaulin.

encerar [ẽnse'ra(x)] *vt* to polish.

encerramento [ẽnsexa'mẽntu] *m* closure.

encerrar [ẽnse'xa(x)] *vt* **-1.** [acabar]: ~ algo (com algo) to close sthg (with sthg). **-2.** [confinar] to shut. **-3.** [conter] to contain.
◆ **encerrar-se** *vp* [enclausurar-se]: ~-se (em) to shut o.s. up (in).

encharcado, da [ẽnʃar'kadu, da] *adj* **-1.** [alagado] flooded. **-2.** [ensopado] soaking wet.

encharcar [ẽnʃar'ka(x)] *vt* **-1.** [alagar] to flood. **-2.** [ensopar] to drench.
◆ **encharcar-se** *vp* [ensopar-se] to become soaked.

enchente [ẽn'ʃẽntʃi] *f* flood.

encher [ẽn'ʃe(x)] *vt* **-1.** [ger] to fill; ~ o saco (de alguém) *m fam* to piss sb off. **-2.** [fartar]: ~ algo (de) to saturate sthg (with). **-3.** [balão, bola, pneu] to inflate. ◇ *vi* [tornar-se cheio] to become full.
◆ **encher-se** *vp* **-1.** [tornar-se cheio] to become full. **-2.** [fartar-se]: ~-se de to have too much of. **-3.** [aborrecer-se] to become fed up.

enchimento [ẽnʃi'mẽntu] *m* **-1.** [ato] filling. **-2.** [coisa com que se enche] stuffing.

enchova [ẽn'ʃova] *f* anchovy.

enciclopédia [ẽnsiklo'pedʒja] *f* **-1.** [obra] encyclopedia. **-2.** *fam* [pessoa sábia] walking encyclopedia.

enciumar-se [ẽnsju'maxsi] *vp* to be jealous.

encoberto, ta [ẽnko'bextu, ta] ◇ *pp* ▷ **encobrir**. ◇ *adj* **-1.** [céu, tempo] overcast. **-2.** [escondido] hidden. **-3.** [disfarçado] concealed.

encobrir [ẽnko'bri(x)] *vt* **-1.** [ger] to conceal. **-2.** [esconder] to hide.
◆ **encobrir-se** *vp* **-1.** [esconder-se] to hide. **-2.** [disfarçar-se] to disguise o.s. **-3.** [céu, sol] to become overcast.

encolher [ẽnko'ʎe(x)] ◇ *vt* **-1.** [contrair] to tuck in; ~ os ombros to shrug one's shoulders. **-2.** [diminuir o tamanho de] to shrink. ◇ *vi* [roupa] to shrink.
◆ **encolher-se** *vp* **-1.** [espremer-se] to squeeze up. **-2.** [de frio] to shrivel.

encomenda [ẽnko'mẽnda] *f* **-1.** [mercadoria] order; fazer uma ~ to order; feito sob ~ made to order. **-2.** [pacote] parcel.

encomendar [ẽnkomẽn'da(x)] *vt* **-1.** [obra, compra]: ~ algo a alguém to order sthg from sb. **-2.** *RELIG* to commend.

encontrão [ẽnkõn'trãw] (*pl* -ões) *m* **-1.** [esbarrão] bump; dar um ~ to shove. **-2.** [empurrão] shove.

encontrar [ẽnkõn'tra(x)] ◇ *vt* **-1.** [pessoa - por acaso] to meet; [- em certa condição] to find. **-2.** [coisa perdida, procurada] to find. **-3.** [dificuldades] to come up against. **-4.** [solução, erro] to discover. ◇ *vi*: ~ com alguém [por acerto] to meet up with sb; [por acaso] to meet sb.
◆ **encontrar-se** *vp* **-1.**: ~-se (com alguém) [por acerto] to have a meeting (with sb); [por acaso] to meet sb). **-2.** [estar] to be. **-3.** [colidir] to collide. **-4.** *PSIC* to find o.s.

encontro [ẽn'kõntru] *m* meeting; ir ao ~ de to go to meet; de ~ a [contra] against; o carro foi de ~ ao muro the car crashed into the wall; [em contradição a] in contrast with.

encorajar [ẽnkora'ʒa(x)] *vt* to encourage.

encorpar [ẽnkox'pa(x)] *vt* **-1.** [fazer crescer] to make grow. **-2.** [engrossar] to thicken.

encosta [ẽn'kɔʃta] *f* hillside.

encostar [ẽnkoʃ'ta(x)] ◇ *vt* **-1.** [aproximar] to put against. **-2.** [quase fechar] to leave ajar. **-3.** [estacionar] to pull up. **-4.** [deitar] to rest. **-5.** *fig* [pôr de lado] to put aside. ◇ *vi* [tocar]: ~ em algo/alguém to lean against sthg/sb.
◆ **encostar-se** *vp* **-1.** [deitar-se] to recline. **-2.** [apoiar-se] to lean. **-3.** *fig* [fugir de trabalho] to lie back.

encosto [ẽn'kɔʃtu] *m* [espaldar] back.

encrenca [ẽ'ŋkrẽnka] *f* **-1.** [problema] tight spot. **-2.** [briga] fight; meter-se numa ~ to get caught up in a fight.

encrencar [ẽŋkrẽn'ka(x)] ◇ *vt* [meter em complicação] to embarrass. ◇ *vi* **-1.** [quebrar - carro] to break down; [- computador] to go down. **-2.** [complicar-se] to become complicated. **-3.** *fam* [implicar]: ~ com alguém/algo to take issue with sb/sthg.

encrespar [ẽŋkreʃ'pa(x)] *vt* **-1.** [cabelo] to curl. **-2.** [mar] to ripple.
◆ **encrespar-se** *vp* **-1.** [mar] to become choppy, to get choppy. **-2.** *fig* [irritar-se] to become angry, to get angry.

encruzilhada [ẽŋkruzi'ʎada] *f* crossroads (*sg*).

encurralado, da [ẽŋkuxa'ladu, da] *adj* [cercado] cornered.

encurralar [ẽŋkuxa'la(x)] *vt* to herd.

encurtar [ẽŋkux'ta(x)] *vt* to shorten.

end. (*abrev de* **endereço**) *m* add.

endêmico, ca [ĕn'demiku, ka] *adj* endemic.

endereçamento [ĕnderesa'mĕntul *m* -**1.** [ger] address. -**2.** COMPUT addressing.

endereçar [ĕndere'sa(x)] *vt* -**1.** [sobrescrever] to address. -**2.** [enviar] to send.

endereço [ĕnde'resul *m* address; ~ eletrônico e-mail address.

endiabrado, da [ĕndʒia'bradu, dal *adj* mischievous.

endinheirado, da [ĕndʒiɲej'radu, dal *adj* well-off.

endireitar [ĕndʒirej'ta(x)] *vt* -**1.** [descurvar] to straighten. -**2.** [arrumar] to tidy.
 endireitar-se *vp* [corrigir-se] to go straight.

endividado, da [ĕndʒivi'dadu, dal *adj* in debt.

endividar-se [ĕndʒivi'daxsil *vp* to fall into debt.

endocrinologia [ĕn,dokrinolo'ʒial *f* endocrinology.

endoidecer [ĕndojde'se(x)] <> *vt* to drive mad. <> *vi* to go mad.

endossar [ĕndo'sa(x)] *vt* to endorse.

endosso [ĕn'dosul *m* endorsement.

endurecer [ĕndure'se(x)] <> *vt* to harden. <> *vi* -**1.** [ficar duro] to go hard. -**2.** [ficar difícil] to be hard. -**3.** *fig* [tornar-se frio]: ~ (com alguém) to harden (towards sb).

endurecimento [ĕnduresi'mĕntul *m* hardening.

ENEM (*abrev de* Exame Nacional do Ensino Médio) *m exam taken at the end of middle education in Brazil.*

energia [enex'ʒial *f* energy; ~ atômica/nuclear/solar atomic/nuclear/solar energy.

enérgico, ca [e'nɛxʒiku, ka] *adj* energetic.

enervante [enex'vãntʃil *adj* annoying.

enevoado, da [ene'vwadu, dal *adj* misty.

enfado [ĕn'fadul *m* boredom.

enfadonho, nha [ĕnfa'doɲu, ɲal *adj* boring.

enfaixar [ĕnfaj'ʃa(x)] *vt* to bandage.

enfarte [ĕn'faxtʃil *m* MED clot.

ênfase [ˈĕnfazil *f* emphasis.

enfastiado, da [ĕnfaʃ'tʃjadu, dal *adj* bored.

enfastiar [ĕnfaʃ'tʃja(x)] *vt* to bore.
 enfastiar-se *vp* to get bored.

enfático, ca [ĕn'fatʃiku, ka] *adj* emphatic.

enfatizar [ĕnfatʃi'za(x)] *vt* to emphasize.

enfeitar [ĕnfej'ta(x)] *vt* to decorate.
 enfeitar-se *vp* to dress up.

enfeite [ĕn'fejtʃil *m* decoration.

enfeitiçar [ĕnfejtʃi'sa(x)] *vt* -**1.** [lançar feitiço] to bewitch. -**2.** *fig* [fascinar] to charm.

enfermagem [ĕnfex'maʒɛl *f* nursing.

enfermaria [ĕnfexma'rial *f* sickroom.

enfermeiro, ra [ĕnfex'mejru, ral *m, f* nurse.

enfermidade [ĕnfexmi'dadʒil *f* illness.

enfermo, ma [ĕn'fexmu, mal <> *adj* sick. <> *m, f* sick person.

enferrujado, da [ĕnfexu'ʒadu, dal *adj* [oxidado] rusty.

enferrujar [ĕnfexu'ʒa(x)] <> *vt* to rust. <> *vi* to go rusty.

enfezar [ĕnfe'za(x)] *vt* to annoy.
 enfezar-se *vp* to get annoyed.

enfiar [ĕn'fja(x)] *vt* -**1.** [introduzir]: ~ algo (em algo) to thread sthg (onto sthg). -**2.** [vestir] to slip on. -**3.** [pôr] to put.
 enfiar-se *vp* [meter-se]: ~-se em algo to slip into sthg.

enfim [ĕn'fĩl *adv* finally; até que ~ finally.

enfocar [ĕnfo'ka(x)] *vt* to focus.

enfoque [ĕn'fɔkl *m* focus.

enforcar [ĕfox'ka(x)] *vt* -**1.** [pessoa] to hang. -**2.** *fam fig* [dia de trabalho, aula] to skip.
 enforcar-se *vp* [pessoa] to hang o.s.

enfraquecer [ĕnfrake'se(x)] <> *vt* to weaken. <> *vi* to grow weak.
 enfraquecer-se *vp* to weaken o.s.

enfrentamento [ĕnfrĕnta'mĕntul *m* clash, confrontation.

enfrentar [ĕnfrĕn'ta(x)] *vt* to face.

enfurecer [ĕnfure'se(x)] *vt* to infuriate.
 enfurecer-se *vp* to get infuriated.

enfurecido, da [ĕnfure'sidu, dal *adj* infuriated.

engajado, da [ĕnga'ʒadu, dal *adj* engaged.

engajar [ĕnga'ʒa(x)] *vt* [trabalhadores] to take on.
 engajar-se *vp* -**1.** POL: ~-se (em) to engage o.s. (in). -**2.** MIL: ~-se (em) to become engaged (in). -**3.** [em campanha, luta]: ~-se em to get involved (in). -**4.** [trabalhador]: ~-se (em) to be engaged (in).

enganador, ra [ĕngana'do(x), ral *adj* deceptive.

enganar [ĕnga'na(x)] *vt* -**1.** [iludir] to deceive. -**2.** [trair] to cheat.
 enganar-se *vp* -**1.** [iludir-se] to fool o.s. -**2.** [cometer um erro] to make a mistake.

enganchar [ĕngãn'ʃa(x)] <> *vt*: ~ algo (em algo) to hook sthg up (to sthg). <> *vi*: ~ (em algo) to catch (in sthg).

engano [ĕn'gãnul *m* [equívoco] error; [em

telefonema]: **ser** ~ to be a wrong number.

engarrafado, da [ēŋaxa'fadu, dal] *adj* -**1**. [bebida] bottled. -**2**. [rua, trânsito] blocked.

engarrafamento [ēŋaxafa'mēntul] *m* -**1**. [de bebida] bottling. -**2**. [no trânsito] traffic jam.

engarrafar [ēŋaxa'fa(x)] *vt* -**1**. [bebida] to bottle. -**2**. [rua, trânsito] to block.

engasgar [ēŋaʒ'ga(x)] <> *vt* [na garganta] to choke. <> *vi* to choke.

◆ **engasgar-se** *vp* [na garganta] to choke o.s.

engasgo [ēŋ'gaʒgul] *m* [na garganta] choking.

engastar [ēŋaʃ'ta(x)] *vt* to set.

engatar [ēŋa'ta(x)] *vt* -**1**. [atrelar]: ~ algo (em algo) to couple sthg (with sthg). -**2**. [engrenar] to get into gear. -**3**. [iniciar] to start.

engate [ēŋ'gatʃil] *m* connection.

engatinhar [ēŋgatʃi'na(x)] *vi* -**1**. [bebê] to crawl. -**2**. *fig* [ser principiante]: ~ em algo to feel one's way in sthg.

engendrar [ēŋʒēn'dra(x)] *vt* to create.

engenharia [ēŋʒeŋa'rial] *f* engineering; ~ genética genetic engineering.

engenheiro, ra [ēŋʒe'ŋejru, ral] *m, f* engineer.

engenho [ēŋ'ʒeŋul] *m* -**1**. [habilidade] inventiveness. -**2**. [máquina] engine. -**3**. [moenda] mill. -**4**. [fazenda de cana-de-açúcar] sugar plant.

engenhoso, osa [ēŋʒe'ŋozu, ɔzal] *adj* ingenious.

engessado, da [ēŋe'sadu, dal] *adj* plastered.

engessar [ēŋʒe'sa(x)] *vt* to put in plaster.

englobar [ēŋglo'ba(x)] *vt* to encompass.

engodo [ēŋ'godul] *m* -**1**. [isca] bait. -**2**. [farsa] flattery.

engolir [ēŋgo'li(x)] *vt fig* [sobrepujar]: ~ alguém to eclipse sb.

engomar [ēŋgo'ma(x)] *vt* to starch.

engordar [ēŋgox'da(x)] <> *vt* to fatten. <> *vi* to put on weight; **açúcar engorda** sugar is fattening.

engordurado, da [ēŋgoxdu'radu, dal] *adj* greasy.

engraçado, da [ēŋgra'sadu, dal] *adj* amusing.

engradado [ēŋgra'dadul] *m* crate.

engrandecer [ēŋgrãnde'se(x)] *vt* to elevate.

◆ **engrandecer-se** *vp* to elevate o.s.

engravidar [ēŋgravi'da(x)] <> *vt* to make pregnant. <> *vi* to become pregnant.

engraxar [ēŋgra'ʃa(x)] *vt* to polish.

engraxate [ēŋgra'ʃatʃil] *mf* shoe shiner.

engrenagem [ēŋgre'naʒēl] (*pl* -**ns**) *f* -**1**. *AUTO* gear. -**2**. *fig* [política, social] mechanism.

engrenar [ēŋgre'na(x)] *vt* -**1**. *AUTO* to put in gear. -**2**. [iniciar] to start.

engrossar [ēŋgro'sa(x)] <> *vt* -**1**. [aumentar] to enlarge. -**2**. [encorpar] to thicken. -**3**. [tornar grave] to deepen. <> *vi fig* [ser grosseiro]: ~ (com alguém) to be rough (with sb).

enguia [ēŋ'gial] *f* eel.

enguiçar [ēŋgi'sa(x)] *vi* -**1**. [carro] to break down. -**2**. [relógio] to stop.

enguiço [ēŋ'gisul] *m* breakdown.

enigma [e'nigma] *m* enigma.

enjaular [ēnʒaw'la(x)] *vt* to put in a cage.

enjeitado, da [ēnʒej'tadu, dal] *adj* rejected.

enjeitar [ēnʒej'ta(x)] *vt* -**1**. [rejeitar] to reject. -**2**. [abandonar] to abandon.

enjoado, da [ēn'ʒwadu, dal] *adj* -**1**. [nauseado] nauseous. -**2**. *fig* [cansado]: ~ de algo/de fazer algo fed up with sthg/with doing sthg. -**3**. *fig* [chato] boring.

enjoar [ēn'ʒwa(x)] <> *vt* -**1**. [nausear] to make nauseous. -**2**. *fig* [cansar] to bore. <> *vi* -**1**. [nausear-se] to feel sick. -**2**. *fig* [cansar-se]: ~ de algo/de fazer algo to become bored with sthg/with doing sthg.

enjôo [ēn'ʒoul] *m* [náusea] sickness; ~ de gravidez morning sickness.

enlaçar [ēnla'sa(x)] *vt* -**1**. [prender com laço] to tie up. -**2**. [envolver] to bog down.

enlace [ēn'lasil] *m* -**1**. [união] union. -**2**. [casamento] marriage.

enlatado, da [ēnla'tadu, dal] *adj* canned.

◆ **enlatado** *m* -**1**. [comida em lata] canned food. -**2**. *pej* [série de TV] trash TV.

enlatar [ēnla'ta(x)] *vt* to can.

enlouquecer [ēnloke'se(x)] <> *vt* to drive mad. <> *vi* to go mad.

enlouquecido, da [ēnloke'sidu, dal] *adj* crazed.

enlouquecimento [ēnlokesi'mēntul] *m* (growing) insanity.

enojado, da [eno'ʒadu, dal] *adj* disgusted.

enorme [e'nɔxmil] *adj* enormous.

enormidade [enoxmi'dadʒil] *f* enormity; **uma** ~ **de** a vast quantity of.

enquadramento [ēŋkwadra'mēntul] *m* CINE & FOTO frame.

enquadrar [ēŋkwa'dra(x)] <> *vt* -**1**. [ajustar]: ~ algo em algo to frame sthg in sthg. -**2**. [autuar] to charge. <> *vi* [combinar]: ~ com to fit in with.

➤ **enquadrar-se** *vp* [ajustar-se]: ~**-se (em algo)** to fit in (with sthg).

enquanto [ẽŋ'kwãntul] *conj* -**1.** [ger] while. -**2.** [considerado como]: **isso é interessante ~ experiência** it's interesting as an experience; ~ **isso** meanwhile.

➤ **por enquanto** *loc adv* for the time being.

enquete [ẽn'kɛtʃi] *f* survey.

enraivecer [ẽnxajve'se(x)] *vt* to anger.

➤ **enraivecer-se** *vp* to become angry.

enrascada [ẽnxaʃ'kadal] *f* tight spot; **meter-se numa ~** to get into a tight spot.

enredo [ẽn'xedul] *m* plot.

enriquecer [ẽnxike'se(x)] <> *vt* to enrich. <> *vi* to become rich.

➤ **enriquecer-se** *vp*: ~**-se com algo** to become rich in sthg.

enriquecimento [ẽnxikesi'mẽntul] *m* -**1.** [financeiro] increase in wealth. -**2.** [cultural] enrichment.

enrolado, da [ẽnxo'ladu, dal *adj* -**1.** [embrulhado]: ~ **em algo** rolled up in sthg. -**2.** [cabelo] coiled. -**3.** *fam* [confuso] screwed up.

enrolar [ẽnxo'la(x)] <> *vt* -**1.** [dar forma de rolo] to roll. -**2.** [embrulhar]: ~ **algo/ alguém em algo** to wrap sthg/sb up in sthg. -**3.** *fam* [complicar] to screw up. -**4.** *fam* [enganar] to take in. <> *vi fam* [protelar] to put things off.

➤ **enrolar-se** *vp* -**1.** [agasalhar-se]: ~**-se em algo** to wrap o.s. up in sthg. -**2.** *fam* [confundir-se] to screw things up.

enroscar [ẽnxoʃ'ka(x)] *vt*: ~ **algo em** to entwine sthg in.

➤ **enroscar-se** *vp* -**1.** [encolher-se de frio] to curl up. -**2.** [embolar-se] to become entangled.

enrubescer [ẽnxube'se(x)] <> *vt* to redden. <> *vi* to blush, go red.

enrugado, da [ẽnxu'gadu, dal *adj* wrinkled.

enrugar [ẽnxu'ga(x)] *vt & vi* to wrinkle.

ensaiar [ẽnsaj'ja(x)] *vt* to practise *UK*, to practice *US*.

ensaio [ẽn'saju] *m* -**1.** [experiência] trial. -**2.** *TEATRO* rehearsal. -**3.** *LITER* essay.

ensangüentado, da [ẽnsãŋgwẽn'tadu, dal *adj* blood-stained.

enseada [ẽn'sjadal *f* inlet.

ensejo [ẽn'seʒul *m* opportunity.

ensinamento [ẽnsina'mẽntul *m* instruction.

ensinar [ẽnsi'na(x)] *vt*: ~ **alguém a fazer algo** to teach sb how to do sthg; ~ **algo a alguém** to teach sthg to sb.

ensino [ẽn'sinul *m* -**1.** [transmissão de conhecimento] teaching. -**2.** [educação]

education; ~ **fundamental/medio** primary/secondary education; ~ **suple-tivo** speeded-up education programme for adults who missed out on a full schooling.

ensolarado, da [ẽnsola'radu, dal *adj* sunny.

ensopado, da [ẽnso'padu, dal *adj* -**1.** *CULIN* stewed. -**2.** *fig* [encharcado] soaking. ➤ **ensopado** *m CULIN* stew.

ensopar [ẽnso'pa(x)] *vt* to soak.

ensurdecer [ẽnsuxde'se(x)] *vt* to deafen.

entalar [ẽnta'la(x)] <> *vt* [apertar] to squeeze. <> *vi* [encravar] to stick.

entalhar [ẽnta'ʎa(x)] *vt* to carve.

entalhe [ẽn'taʎil *m* groove.

entanto [ẽn'tãntul ➤ **no entanto** *loc adv* however.

então [ẽn'tãw] *adv* then; **até ~** up until then; **desde ~** since then; **para ~** so that; **pois ~** then.

entardecer [ẽntaxde'se(x)] <> *vi* to get late. <> *m* sunset.

ente l'ẽntʃil *m* -**1.** [ser] being. -**2.** [corporação, órgão] entity.

enteado, da [ẽn'tʒjadu, dal *m, f* stepchild, stepson (*f* stepdaughter).

entediar [ẽnte'dʒa(x)] *vt* to bore.

➤ **entediar-se** *vp* to get bored.

entender [ẽntẽn'de(x)] <> *vt* -**1.** [compreender] to understand; **dar a ~** to give the impression. -**2.** [ouvir] to hear. -**3.** [interpretar] to perceive. -**4.** [deduzir]: ~ **que** to see (that). <> *vi* [conhecer]: ~ **de** to know about. <> *m*: **no ~ de alguém** in the opinion of sb.

➤ **entender-se** *vp* -**1.** [comunicar-se] to get along. -**2.** [chegar a um acordo]: ~**-se (com alguém)** to see eye to eye (with sb).

entendido, da [ẽntẽn'dʒidu, dal <> *adj* -**1.** [perito] expert; ~ **em algo** expert in sthg. -**2.** *fam* [homossexual] gay. <> *m, f* -**1.** [perito] expert. -**2.** *fam* [homossexual] gay.

➤ **bem entendido** *loc adv* understood.

entendimento [ẽntẽndʒi'mẽntul *m* -**1.** [compreensão] understanding. -**2.** [juízo] perception. -**3.** [acordo] agreement.

enternecer [ẽntexne'se(x)] *vt* to touch.

➤ **enternecer-se** *vp* to be touched.

enterrar [ẽnte'xa(x)] *vt* -**1.** to bury. -**2.** *fig* [encerrar] to close. -**3.** *fig* [arruinar] to ruin. -**4.** [enfiar]: **enterrou a estaca no coração do vampiro** he rammed the stake into the vampire's heart; **enter-rou o chapéu na cabeça** he rammed his hat on his head.

enterro [ẽn'texul *m* -**1.** [sepultamento] burial. -**2.** [funeral] funeral.

entidade [ẽntʃi'dadʒi] f entity.

entoar [ẽn'twa(x)] vt to chant.

entonação [ẽntona'sãw] f intonation.

entornar [ẽntox'na(x)] ⬦ vt -1. [derramar] to spill. -2. [despejar] to pour. ⬦ vi fig [embriagar-se] to drink heavily.

entorpecente [ẽntoxpe'sẽntʃi] m narcotic.

entorpecer [ẽntoxpe'se(x)] vt -1. [causar torpor] to stupefy. -2. fig [insensibilizar] to numb.

entortar [ẽntox'ta(x)] ⬦ vt -1. [curvar] to bend. -2. [empenar] to jam. ⬦ vi [empenar - porta] to warp; [- roda] to buckle.

entrada [ẽn'trada] f -1. [ger] entry; 'proibida a ~' 'no entry'. -2. [lugar] entrance. -3. [admissão] admission. -4. [porta] doorway. -5. [corredor] hallway. -6. CULIN starter. -7. [calvície] receding hairline. -8. [pagamento inicial] down payment. -9. [ingresso] ticket; ~ gratuita ou franca free admission; meia ~ half price. -10. [abertura] opening. -11. TEC inlet. -12. COMPUT input.

entra-e-sai [ˌẽntri'saj] m inv coming and going.

entranhado, da [ẽntra'ɲadu, da] adj deep-seated.

entranhas [ẽn'traɲaʃ] fpl -1. [vísceras] bowels. -2. fig [profundeza] depths.

entrar [ẽn'tra(x)] vi -1. [adentrar] ~ **(em)** to go/come (into). -2. [penetrar] to enter. -3. [começar a trabalhar] to begin. -4. [contribuir]: ~ **com algo** to contribute sthg. -5. [envolver-se]: ~ **em algo** to become involved in sthg. -6. [caber]: ~ **em algo** to fit into sthg. -7. [ser componente]: ~ **em algo** to be part of sthg. -8. [ingressar]: ~ **para algo** [universidade] to go to sthg; [clube] to join sthg. -9. COMPUT: ~ **com algo** to enter sthg.

entre ['ẽntri] prep between; **os dois dividiram o bolo ~ eles** the two shared the cake between them; **os alunos sempre conversavam ~ si** the schoolchildren always talked among themselves.

entreaberto, ta [ˌẽntrja'bextu, ta] adj -1. [porta] ajar. -2. [olho] half-open.

entreabrir [ẽntrja'bri(x)] vt to half-open.

➤ **entreabrir-se** vp to open up.

entrecortar [ẽntre'koxta(x)] vt -1. [cortar] to cut off. -2. [interromper] to interrupt.

entrega [ẽn'trega] f -1. [de carta, prêmio] delivery; ~ **em domicílio** home delivery. -2. [dedicação]: ~ **a algo/alguém** dedication to sthg/sb. -3. [rendição] surrender.

entregador, ra [ẽntrega'do(x), ra] m, f [funcionário] delivery person.

entregar [ẽntre'ga(x)] vt -1. [passar às mãos de - mercadoria, carta] to deliver; [- presente] to give; [- prêmio] to award. -2. [delatar] to inform on. -3. [devolver] to return.

➤ **entregar-se** vp -1. [render-se - inimigo] to surrender; [- à dor etc.]: ~**-se a algo** to surrender to sthg. -2. [dedicar-se]: ~**-se a algo** to dedicate o.s. to sthg. -3. [deixar-se seduzir]: ~**-se a alguém** to give o.s. to sb.

entregue [ẽn'tregi] pp ▷ entregar.

entreguismo [ẽntre'giʒmu] m selling-out, policy of allowing exploitation of the country's natural resources by foreign entities.

entreguista [ẽntre'giʃta] adj supportive or typical of selling-out.

entrelaçamento [ẽntrelasa'mẽntu] m [união] interlinking.

entrelaçar [ẽntrela'sa(x)] vt to entwine.

entrelinha [ẽntre'liɲa] f [espaço] line space.

➤ **entrelinhas** fpl: nas ~s fig [subentendido] between the lines.

entremear [ẽntre'mja(x)] vt: ~ **algo com** algo to mix sthg with sthg.

entreolhar-se [ẽntrjo'ʎaxsi] vp to exchange glances.

entretanto [ẽntri'tãntu] conj however.

entretenimento [ẽntriteni'mẽntu] m -1. [passatempo] pastime. -2. [diversão] entertainment.

entreter [ẽntre'te(x)] vt -1. [ger] to entertain. -2. [ocupar] to occupy.

➤ **entreter-se** vp -1. [divertir-se] to amuse o.s. -2. [ocupar-se] to occupy o.s.

entrevista [ẽntre'viʃta] f interview; ~ **coletiva** press conference.

entrevistado, da [ẽntre'viʃtadu, da] m, f interviewee.

entrevistar [ẽntre'viʃ'ta(x)] vt to interview.

entristecer [ẽntriʃte'se(x)] ⬦ vt to sadden. ⬦ vi to become sad.

entroncamento [ẽntrõŋka'mẽntu] m junction.

entulhar [ẽntu'ʎa(x)] vt: ~ **algo (de** ou **com)** to cram sthg with.

entulho [ẽn'tuʎu] m debris.

entupido, da [ẽntu'pidu, da] adj -1. [pia, nariz, ouvido] blocked. -2. [de comida] stuffed. -3. [de gente] packed.

entupimento [ẽntupi'mẽntu] m blockage.

entupir [ẽntu'pi(x)] vt to block.

➤ **entupir-se** vp: ~**-se de comida** to stuff o.s. with food; ~**-se de bebida** to pump o.s. full of drink.

entusiasmar [ẽntuzjaʒ'ma(x)] *vt* to fill with enthusiasm.

➡ **entusiasmar-se** *vp* to get enthusiastic.

entusiasmo [ẽntu'zjaʒmul *m* enthusiasm.

entusiasta [ẽntu'zjaʃtal ◇ *adj* enthusiastic. ◇ *mf* enthusiast.

enumerar [enume'ra(x)l *vt* to enumerate.

enunciado, da [enũ'sjadu, dal ◇ *adj* stated. ◇ *m* statement.

enunciar [enũ'sja(x)l *vt* to state.

envelhecer [ẽnveʎe'se(x)l ◇ *vt* -1. [tornar velho] to age. -2. [fazer parecer velho]: ~ **alguém** to make sb look older. ◇ *vi* -1. [ficar velho] to grow old. -2. [fazer parecer velho] to age.

envelhecimento [ẽnveʎesi'mẽntul *m* ageing.

envelopar [ẽnve'lopa(x)l *vt* to put in an envelope.

envelope [ẽnve'lɔpil *m* envelope.

envenenamento [ẽnvenena'mẽntul *m* poisoning.

envenenar [ẽnvene'na(x)l *vt* -1. [intoxicar] to poison. -2. [corromper] to corrupt. -3. *AUTO* to soup up.

➡ **envenenar-se** *vp* [intoxicar-se] to poison o.s.

enveredar [ẽnvere'da(x)l *vi* to make one's way; ~ **por/para** to head for.

envergadura [ẽnvexga'dural *f* -1. [dimensão] wingspan. -2. *fig* [importância] scope. -3. *fig* [capacidade]: **é um poeta de pouca** ~ he's a poet of little talent.

envergonhado, da [ẽnvexgo'ɲadu, dal *adj* -1. [tímido] shy. -2. [por má ação] ashamed.

envergonhar [ẽnvexgo'ɲa(x)l *vt* -1. [acanhar] to embarrass. -2. [com má ação] to disgrace.

➡ **envergonhar-se** *vp* -1. [acanhar-se] to be embarrassed. -2. [por má ação] to be ashamed.

envernizado, da [ẽnvexni'zadu, dal *adj* [com verniz] varnished.

envernizar [ẽnvexni'za(x)l *vt* to varnish.

enviado, da [ẽn'vjadu, dal *m, f* envoy.

enviar [ẽn'vja(x)l *vt*: ~ **algo a** *ou* **para alguém** to send sthg to sb.

envidraçar [ẽnvidra'sa(x)l *vt* to glaze.

enviesar [ẽnvje'za(x)l *vt* -1. [pôr obliquamente] to put at an angle. -2. [envesgar] to cross.

envio [ẽn'viul *m* dispatch.

enviuvar [ẽnvju'va(x)l *vi* to be widowed.

envolto, ta [ẽn'vowtu, tal ◇ *pp* ▷ **envolver**. ◇ *adj* wrapped.

envoltório [ẽnvow'tɔrjul *m* wrapping.

envolvente [ẽnvow'vẽntʃil *adj* compelling.

envolver [ẽnvow've(x)l *vt* -1. [cobrir]: ~ **algo/alguém (em)** to wrap sthg/sb (in). -2. [comprometer]: ~ **alguém (em)** to involve sb (in). -3. [acarretar] to involve. -4. [abraçar] to embrace.

➡ **envolver-se** *vp* -1. [comprometer-se]: ~-**se em** *ou* **com** to get involved in *ou* with. -2. [intrometer-se]: ~-**se em** to get involved in.

envolvimento [ẽnvowvi'mẽntul *m* involvement.

enxada [ẽn'ʃadal *f* hoe.

enxaguar [ẽnʃa'gwa(x)l *vt* to rinse.

enxame [ẽn'ʃamil *m* swarm.

enxaqueca [ẽnʃa'kekal *f* migraine.

enxergar [ẽnʃex'ga(x)l ◇ *vt* -1. [ver] to catch sight of. -2. *fig* [perceber] to make out. ◇ *vi* [ver] to see.

enxofre [ẽn'ʃofril *m* sulphur *UK*, sulfur *US*.

enxotar [ẽnʃo'ta(x)l *vt* to drive away.

enxoval [ẽnʃo'vawl (*pl* -ais) *m* [de noiva] trousseau.

enxugador [ẽnʃuga'do(x)l *m* clothes dryer.

enxugar [ẽnʃu'ga(x)l *vt* -1. [secar] to dry. -2. *fig* [diminuir] to rationalize.

enxurrada [ẽnʃu'xadal *f* -1. [torrente] torrent. -2. *fig* [amontoado] flood.

enxuto, ta [ẽn'ʃutu, tal *adj* -1. [seco] dry. -2. *fig* [bonito] good-looking.

épico, ca ['ɛpiku, kal *adj* epic.

➡ **épico** *m LITER* epic.

epidemia [epide'mial *f* -1. *MED* epidemic. -2. *fig* [modismo] mania.

epigrama [epi'gramal *f* epigram.

epilepsia [epilep'sial *f* epilepsy.

epiléptico, ca [epi'lɛptʃiku, kal ◇ *adj* epileptic. ◇ *m, f* epileptic.

epílogo [e'pilugul *m* epilogue.

episódico, ca [epi'zɔdiku, kal *adj* episodic.

episódio [epi'zɔdjul *m* episode.

epístola [e'piʃtolal *f* -1. [bíblia] Epistle. -2. [carta] letter.

epistolar [epiʃto'la(x)l *adj* epistolary.

epitáfio [epi'tafjul *m* epitaph.

época ['ɛpokal *f* -1. [período] age; **naquela** ~ at that time; **fazer** ~ to be epoch-making. -2. [estação] season.

epopéia [epo'pɛjal *f* epic.

equação [ekwa'sãwl (*pl* -ões) *f* equation.

equacionamento [ekwasiona'mẽntul *m* rationalizing.

equador [ekwa'do(x)l *m* equator.

Equador [ekwa'do(x)l *n* Ecuador.

equânime [e'kwãnimil *adj* unbiased.

equatorial [ekwato'rjawl (*pl* -ais) *adj* equatorial.

equatoriano, na ◇ *adj* Ecuadorean. ◇ *m*, *f* Ecuadorean.

eqüestre [e'kwɛʃtri] *adj* equestrian.

equilibrado, da [ekili'bradu, da] *adj* balanced.

equilibrar [ekili'bra(x)] *vt* to balance.
➡ **equilibrar-se** *vp* to balance.

equilíbrio [eki'libriw] *m* equilibrium.

equipamento [ekipa'mẽntu] *m* equipment.

equipar [eki'pa(x)] *vt*: ~ algo/alguém (de) to equip sthg/sb (with).
➡ **equipar-se** *vp*: ~-se (de) to equip o.s. (with).

equiparar [ekipa'ra(x)] *vt*: ~ algo (a ou com algo) to compare sthg (against sthg).
➡ **equiparar-se** *vp* -1. [igualar-se]: ~-se (a ou com algo) to compare o.s. (with sthg). -2. [comparar-se]: ~-se (a ou com alguém) to compare o.s. (with sb).

equipe [e'kipi] *f* team.

equitação [ekita'sãw] *f* horse-riding.

eqüitativo, va [ekwita'tʃivu, va] *adj* equitable.

equivalente [ekiva'lẽntʃi] *adj* equivalent.

equivocado, da [ekivo'kadu, da] *adj* mistaken.

equivocar-se [ekivo'kaxsi] *vp* to make a mistake.

equívoco [e'kivoku] *m* mistake.

era ['ɛra] *f* era.

erário [e'rarju] *m* exchequer.

ereção [ere'sãw] (*pl* -ões) *f* erection.

eremita [ere'mita] *mf* hermit.

ereto, ta [e'rɛtu, ta] *adj* erect.

erguer [ex'ge(x)] *vt* -1. [levantar] to raise. -2. [construir] to erect.
➡ **erguer-se** *vp* [levantar-se] to get up.

eriçado, da [ɛri'sadu, da] *adj* standing on end.

eriçar [eri'sa(x)] *vt* to make stand on end.

erigir [eri'ʒi(x)] *vt* to erect.

ermo, ma ['exmu, ma] *adj* deserted.

erosão [ero'zãw] *f* erosion.

erótico, ca [e'rɔtʃiku, ka] *adj* erotic.

erotismo [ero'tʃiʒmu] *m* eroticism.

erradicar [exadʒi'ka(x)] *vt* to eradicate.

errado, da [e'xadu, da] *adj* -1. [incorreto] wrong. -2. [inadequado] inappropriate. -3. *loc*: dar ~ to go wrong.

errar [e'xa(x)] ◇ *vt* [não acertar - alvo] to miss; [- conta, resposta] to get wrong. ◇ *vi* -1. [enganar-se]: ~ (em algo) to be wrong (in sthg). -2. [proceder mal] to go wrong. -3. [vagar] to wander.

erro ['exul] *m* [ger] error; ~ de impressão printing error.

errôneo, nea [e'xonju, nja] *adj* erroneous.

erudição [erudʒi'sãw] *f* erudition.

erudito, ta [eru'dʒitu, ital] ◇ *adj* erudite. ◇ *m*, *f* scholar.

erupção [erup'sãw] (*pl* -ões) *f* eruption.

erva ['ɛxval] *f* -1. *BOT* herb; ~ daninha weed. -2. *fam* [maconha] grass.

erva-cidreira [,ɛxva'sidrejra] (*pl* ervas-cidreiras) *f* lemon verbena.

erva-doce [,ɛxva'dosil] (*pl* ervas-doces) *f* fennel.

erva-mate [,ɛxva'matʃil] (*pl* ervas-mates) *f* matte.

ervilha [ex'viʎa] *f* pea.

ES (*abrev de* Estado do Espírito Santo) *m* state of Espírito Santo.

esbaforido, da [iʒbafo'ridu, da] *adj* breathless.

esbanjador, ra [iʒbãnʒa'do(x), ra] *adj* spendthrift.

esbanjar [iʒbãn'ʒa(x)] *vt* -1. [dinheiro] to squander. -2. [saúde] to be bursting with.

esbarrão [iʒba'xãw] *m* bump.

esbarrar [iʒba'xa(x)] *vi*: ~ em algo/alguém to bump into sthg/sb.

esbelto, ta [iʒ'bɛwtu, tal] *adj* svelte.

esboçar [iʒbo'sa(x)] *vt* -1. [ger] to sketch. -2. [sorriso] to trace.

esboço [iʒ'bosul] *m* -1. [desenho] sketch. -2. [primeira versão] draft. -3. [tentativa] hint. -4. [resumo] outline.

esbofetear [iʒbofe'tʃja(x)] *vt* to slap.

esborrachar-se [iʒboxa'ʃaxsil] *vp* -1. [arrebentar-se] to burst. -2. [cair] to fall sprawling.

esbranquiçado, da [iʒbrãnki'sadu, da] *adj* whitish.

esbugalhado, da [iʒbuga'ʎadu, da] *adj* bulging.

esburacado, da [iʒbura'kadu, da] *adj* -1. [rua, jardim] potholed. -2. [rosto] pitted.

esburacar [iʒbura'ka(x)] *vt* to make holes in.

escabeche [iʃka'bɛʃil] *m* marinade.

escada [iʃ'kadal] *f* -1. [interna] stairs (*pl*), staircase. -2. [externa] steps (*pl*); ~ de armar ladder; ~ de caracol spiral staircase; ~ de incêndio fire escape; ~ rolante escalator. -3. *fig* [meio] ladder.

escadaria [iʃkada'rial] *f* staircase.

escala [iʃ'kalal] *f* -1. [ger] scale. -2. [parada] stopover; sem ~ non-stop. -3. [turno] turn.

escalada [iʃka'ladal] *f* climbing.

escalão [iʃka'lãw] (*pl* -ões) *m* level; o alto ~ do governo the upper echelon of government.

escalar [iʃka'la(x)] *vt* -1. [subir] to climb. -2. [designar] to select.

escaldar [iʃkaw'da(x)] *vt* to scald.

escaler [iʃka'lɛ(x)] *m* launch.

escalonar [iʃkalo'na(x)] *vt* to schedule.

escalope [iʃka'lɔpi] *m* escalope.

escalpelar [iʃkawpe'la(x)] *vt* [escalpar] to scalp.

escama [iʃ'kãma] *f* scale.

escamar [iʃka'ma(x)] ⟨⟩ *vt* [peixe] to scale. ⟨⟩ *vi* [pele] to flake.

escamotear [iʃkamo'tʃja(x)] *vt* to filch.

escancarado, da [iʃkãŋka'radu, da] *adj* -**1.** [aberto] wide open. -**2.** [evidente] brazen. -**3.** [franco] open.

escancarar [iʃkãŋka'ra(x)] *vt* -**1.** [abrir] to open wide. -**2.** [exibir] to display openly.

escandalizar [iʃkãndali'za(x)] *vt* to scandalize.
➡ **escandalizar-se** *vp* to be shocked.

escândalo [iʃ'kãndalu] *m* -**1.** [fato] scandal. -**2.** [indignação] outrage. -**3.** [alvoroço]: **fazer** *ou* **dar um** ~ to make a scene.

escandaloso, sa [iʃkãnda'lozu, ɔza] *adj* -**1.** [chocante] shocking. -**2.** [chamativo] outrageous.

escanear [iʃkã'nea(x)] *vt* COMPUT to scan.

escangalhar [iʃkãŋga'ʎa(x)] *vt* -**1.** [ger] to break. -**2.** [sapatos] to fall apart.

escaninho [iʃka'niɲu] *m* pigeon-hole.

escanteio [iʃkãn'teju] *m* corner.

escapar [iʃka'pa(x)] *vi* -**1.** [sobreviver]: ~ (de algo) to escape (from sthg). -**2.**: ~ a alguém to escape (from) sb. -**3.** [fugir] to escape from. -**4.** [esquivar-se] to avoid. -**5.** *loc*: ~ **de boa** to have a close shave; **deixar** ~ [não aproveitar] to miss; [revelar por descuido] to let drop.

escapatória [iʃkapa'tɔrja] *f* -**1.** [saída] way out. -**2.** [desculpa] excuse.

escapulir [iʃkapu'li(x)] *vi*: ~ (de algo) to escape (from sthg).

escaramuça [iʃkara'musa] *f* skirmish.

escaravelho [iʃkara'veʎu] *m* beetle.

escarcéu [iʃkax'sɛw] *m*: **fazer um** ~ to throw a fit.

escarlate [iʃkax'latʃi] *adj* scarlet.

escarlatina [iʃkaxla'tʃinal] *f* scarlet fever.

escárnio [iʃ'karnju] *m* -**1.** [desdém] scorn. -**2.** [zombaria] mockery.

escarpado, da [iʃkar'padu, da] *adj* steep.

escarrar [iʃka'xa(x)] ⟨⟩ *vt* to spit. ⟨⟩ *vi* to hawk.

escarro [iʃ'kaxul] *m* phlegm.

escassear [iʃka'sja(x)] *vi* to become scarce.

escassez [iʃka'seʒ] *f* shortage.

escasso, a [iʃ'kasu, sa] *adj* scarce.

escavação [iʃkava'sãw] (*pl* -**ões**) *f* excavation.

escavar [iʃka'va(x)] *vt* to dig.

esclarecer [iʃklare'se(x)] *vt*-**1.** [explicar] to clarify. -**2.** [elucidar] to explain. -**3.** [informar] to inform.
➡ **esclarecer-se** *vp* [informar-se] to find out.

esclarecimento [iʃklaresi'mẽntul] *m* -**1.** [explicação] explanation. -**2.** [informação] (piece of) information.

esclerose [iʃkle'rɔzi] *f* sclerosis; ~ **múltipla** multiple sclerosis.

escoadouro [iʃkoa'dorul] *m* drain.

escoar [iʃ'kwa(x)] *vi*: ~ (por) to drain (through).

escocês, esa [iʃko'seʒ, ezal] ⟨⟩ *adj* Scottish. ⟨⟩ *m*, *f* Scot.
➡ **escocês** *m* [língua] Gaelic.

Escócia [iʃ'kɔsjal] *n* Scotland.

escola [iʃ'kɔlal] *f* [ger] school; ~ **particular/pública** private/public school *US*, private/state school *UK*; ~ **naval** naval college; ~ **de samba** group of musicians and samba dancers who perform in street parades during carnival celebrations in Brazil.

escolar [iʃko'la(x)] (*pl* -**es**) *adj* school (antes de subst).

escolaridade [iʃkolari'dadʒil] *f* schooling.

escolha [iʃ'koʎal] *f* choice.

escolher [iʃko'ʎe(x)] *vt* to choose.

escolhido, da [iʃko'ʎidu, dal] *adj* selected, chosen.

escoliose [iʃkoli'ɔzil] *f* MED curvature of the spine.

escolta [iʃ'kɔwtal] *f* escort.

escombros [iʃ'kõnbruʃl] *mpl* ruins.

esconder [iʃkõn'de(x)l] *vt* to hide.
➡ **esconder-se** *vp* to hide.

esconderijo [iʃkõnde'riʒul] *m* hiding place.

escondidas [iʃkõn'dʒidaʃl] ➡ **às escondidas** *loc adv* secretly.

escopeta [iʃko'petal] *f* shotgun.

escopo [iʃ'kopul] *m* purpose.

escora [iʃ'kɔral] *f* prop.

escorar [iʃko'ra(x)] *vt* [pôr escoras] to support, to prop up.
➡ **escorar-se** *vp* -**1.** [encostar-se]: ~ **-se (em)** to lean (on). -**2.** [fundamentar-se]: ~ **-se em** to go by.

escoriação [iʃkorja'sãw] (*pl* -**ões**) *f* abrasion.

escorpiano, na [iʃkox'pãjanu, nal] ⟨⟩ *adj* Scorpio. ⟨⟩ *m*, *f* Scorpio.

escorpião [iʃkox'pjãw] (*pl* -**ões**) *m* ZOOL scorpion.
➡ **Escorpião** *m* [zodíaco] Scorpio; *veja também* **Virgem**.

escorredor [iʃkoxe'do(x)] *m* [para alimentos] colander; ~ **de pratos** dish drainer, draining board.

escorregadiço, dia [iʃkoxega'dʒisu, dʒial, **escorregadio, dia** [iʃkoxega'dʒiu, dʒia] *adj* slippery.

escorregador [iʃkoxega'do(x)] *m* slide.

escorregão [iʃkoxe'gãw] (*pl* -**ões**) *m* -**1.** [queda] slip. -**2.** *fig* [deslize] slip-up.

escorregar [iʃkoxe'ga(x)] *vi* -**1.** [deslizar] to slip. -**2.** *fig* [errar]: ~ **em algo** to slip up on sthg.

escorrer [iʃko'xe(x)] ⟨> *vt* [tirar líquido de] to drain. ⟨> *vi* [verter] to drip.

escoteiro, ra [iʃko'tejru, ra] *m* scout.

escotilha [iʃko'tiʎa] *f* hatch, hatchway.

escova [iʃ'kova] *f* [utensílio] brush; ~ **de dentes** toothbrush; ~ **de cabelo** hair brush.

escovar [iʃko'va(x)] *vt* to brush.

escrachar [iʃkra'ʃa(x)] *vt* *fam* -**1.** [desmascarar] to unmask. -**2.** [repreender] to tick off.

escravidão [iʃkravi'dãw] *f* slavery.

escravizar [iʃkravi'za(x)] *vt* -**1.** [tornar escravo] to enslave. -**2.** *fig* [subjugar] to dominate.

escravo, va [iʃ'kravu, va] ⟨> *adj* -**1.** [ger] slave. -**2.** *fig* [dominado]: **ser** ~ **de alguém/algo** to be sb/sthg's slave. ⟨> *m, f* slave.

escravocrata [iʃkravo'krata] ⟨> *adj* slave-owning. ⟨> *mf* slave-owner.

escrevente [iʃkre'vẽntʃi] *mf* clerk.

escrever [iʃkre've(x)] *vt & vi* to write.
➤ **escrever-se** *vp* -**1.** [pessoas] to correspond. -**2.** [palavras] to spell; **esta palavra se escreve com x** this word is spelt with an 'x'.

escrita [iʃ'krita] *f* -**1.** [letra] handwriting. -**2.** [tradição] tradition.

escrito, ta [iʃ'kritu, ta] ⟨> *pp* ▷ **escrever.** ⟨> *adj* written; **por** ~ in writing.
➤ **escrito** *m* text.
➤ **escritos** *mpl* [obra literária] manuscripts.

escritor, ra [iʃkri'to(x), ra] (*mpl* -**es**, *fpl* -**s**) *m, f* writer.

escritório [iʃkri'tɔrjul] *m* -**1.** COM office. -**2.** [em casa] study.

escritura [iʃkri'tural] *f* -**1.** JUR deed. -**2.** [na compra de imóvel] exchange of contracts.
➤ **Escrituras** *fpl*: **as** ~ the Scriptures.

escriturar [iʃkritu'ra(x)] *vt* to draw up.

escrivã [iʃkri'vã] *f* ▷ **escrivão.**

escrivaninha [iʃkriva'niɲa] *f* desk.

escrivão, vã [iʃkri'vãw, vã] (*mpl* -**ões**, *fpl* -**s**) *m, f* registrar.

escrúpulo [iʃ'krupulu] *m* -**1.** [ger] scruple; **sem** ~**s** unscrupulous. -**2.** [cuidado] care.

escrupuloso, osa [iʃkrupu'lozu, ɔza] *adj* scrupulous.

escrutínio [iʃkru'tʃinju] *m* scrutiny.

escudo [iʃkudu] *m* -**1.** [proteção] shield. -**2.** [moeda] escudo.

esculhambado, da [iʃkuʎãn'badu, da] *adj* messed up.

esculhambar [iʃkuʎãn'ba(x)] *fam* *vt* -**1.** [repreender] to tell off. -**2.** [avacalhar] to trash. -**3.** [desarrumar] to mess up. -**4.** [quebrar] to screw up.

esculpir [iʃkuw'pi(x)] *vt* to sculpt.

escultor, ra [iʃkuw'to(x), ra] (*mpl* -**es**, *fpl* -**s**) *m, f* sculptor.

escultura [iʃkuw'tural] *f* sculpture.

escuna [iʃ'kunal] *f* schooner.

escuras [iʃ'kuraʃ] *fpl* ▷ **escuro.**

escurecer [iʃkure'se(x)] ⟨> *vt* [tornar escuro] to darken. ⟨> *vi* -**1.** [anoitecer] to go dark. -**2.** [ficar escuro] to get dark.

escuridão [iʃkuri'dãw] *f* darkness.

escuro, ra [iʃ'kuru, ra] *adj* -**1.** [ger] dark. -**2.** [pessoa] dark-skinned.
➤ **escuro** *m* [escuridão] darkness.
➤ **às escuras** *loc adv* -**1.** [sem luz] in the dark. -**2.** *fig* [às escondidas] on the quiet.

escusa [iʃ'kuzal] *f* excuse.

escusar [iʃku'za(x)] *vt* [desculpar]: ~ **alguém (de)** to excuse sb (for).
➤ **escusar-se** *vp* -**1.** [desculpar-se]: ~**-se (de)** to excuse o.s. (for). -**2.** [dispensar-se]: ~**-se de** to be excused from.

escuta [iʃ'kutal] *f* listening; ~ **telefônica** phone tap.
➤ **à escuta** *loc adv* listening.

escutar [iʃku'ta(x)] ⟨> *vt* -**1.** [ouvir] to hear; [prestar atenção] to listen to. -**2.** [dar ouvidos a] to hear out. -**3.** [atender a] to heed. ⟨> *vi* [ouvir] to hear; [prestar atenção] to listen.

esfacelar [iʃfase'la(x)] *vt* to destroy.
➤ **esfacelar-se** *vp* to destroy o.s.

esfaquear [iʃfa'kja(x)] *vt* to stab.

esfarelar [iʃfare'la(x)] *vt* to crumble.
➤ **esfarelar-se** *vp* to crumble.

esfarrapado, da [iʃfaxa'padu, da] *adj* -**1.** [roto] scruffy. -**2.** [não-convincente] unconvincing.

esfarrapar [iʃfaxa'pa(x)] *vt* to tear up.

esfera [iʃ'fɛral] *f* -**1.** [ger] sphere. -**2.** [globo] globe.

esférico, ca [iʃ'fɛriku, ka] *adj* spherical.

esferográfica [iʃfero'grafikal] *f* ballpoint pen.

esfomeado, da [iʃfɔ'mjadu, da] *adj* starving.

esforçado, da [iʃfox'sadu, da] *adj* committed.

esforçar-se [iʃfox'saxsi] *vp* to make an effort.

esforço [iʃ'foxsul] *m* effort.

esfregar [iʃfre'ga(x)] *vt* -**1.** [friccionar] to scrub. -**2.** [lavar] to scrub.

➡ **esfregar-se** *vp* -**1.** [friccionar-se] to rub o.s. -**2.** [lavar-se] to scrub o.s. -**3.** *fam* [bolinar-se] to fondle each other.

esfriar [iʃfri'a(x)] ◇ *vt* to cool. ◇ *vi* -**1.** [perder o calor] to get cold. -**2.** *fig* [arrefecer] to cool.

esfuziante [iʃfu'zjãntʃi] *adj* [alegre] effusive.

esganar [iʒga'na(x)] *vt* to strangle.

esganiçado, da [iʒgani'sadu, da] *adj* shrill.

esgarçar [iʒgax'sa(x)] ◇ *vt* to tear. ◇ *vi* to wear thin.

esgotado, da [iʒgo'tadu, da] *adj* -**1.** [exausto] exhausted. -**2.** [acabado - paciência, crédito] exhausted; [- reservas naturais] depleted; [- prazo] finished. -**3.** *fig* [esquadrinhado] scrutinized. -**4.** [totalmente vendido] sold out.

esgotamento [iʒgota'mẽntul] *m* [exaustão] exhaustion.

esgotar [iʒgo'ta(x)] *vt* -**1.** [ger] to exhaust. -**2.** [esquadrinhar] to scrutinize. -**3.** [esvaziar, secar] to drain.

➡ **esgotar-se** *vp* -**1.** [ger] to be exhausted. -**2.** [ser vendido totalmente] to be sold out.

esgoto [iʒ'gotul] *m* drain.

esgrima [iʒ'grimal] *f* fencing.

esguelha [iʒ'geʎal] *f* slant.

➡ **de esguelha** *loc adv* obliquely; **olhar de esguelha** to cast a sidelong glance.

esguichar [iʒgi'ʃa(x)] ◇ *vt* to squirt. ◇ *vi* to gush.

esguicho [iʒ'giʃul] *m* squirt.

esguio, guia [iʒ'giu, guia] *adj* willowy.

esmagador, ra [iʒmaga'do(x), ral (*mpl* -es, *fpl* -s) *adj fig* overwhelming.

esmagar [iʒma'ga(x)] *vt* -**1.** [esmigalhar] to crush. -**2.** *fig* [vencer] to overpower.

esmalte [iʒ'mawtʃil] *m* enamel; ~ de unha nail polish *UK*, nail enamel *US*.

esmerado, da [iʒme'radu, da] *adj* -**1.** [cuidadoso] meticulous. -**2.** [bem acabado - produção] accomplished; [- trabalho] well finished.

esmeralda [iʒme'rawdal] *f* emerald.

esmerar-se [iʒme'raxsil] *vp*: ~ **se em algo/em fazer algo** to be meticulous about sthg/about doing sthg.

esmero [i'ʒmerul] *m* meticulousness.

esmigalhar [iʒmiga'ʎa(x)] *vt* -**1.** [fazer em migalhas] to crumble. -**2.** [despedaçar] to shatter. -**3.** [esmagar] to crush.

➡ **esmigalhar-se** *vp* -**1.** [fazer-se em migalhas] to crumble. -**2.** [despedaçar-se] to shatter.

esmiuçar [iʒmju'sa(x)] *vt* -**1.** [explicar] to explain in great detail. -**2.** [investigar] to scrutinize.

esmo [l'eʒmul] ➡ **a esmo** *loc adv* at random.

esmola [iʒ'mɔlal] *f* alms (*pl*).

esmorecer [iʒmore'se(x)] ◇ *vt* [pessoa] to discourage. ◇ *vi* -**1.** [pessoa] to lose heart. -**2.** [luz] to diminish.

esmurrar [iʒmu'xa(x)] *vt* to punch.

esnobe [iʒ'nɔbil] ◇ *adj* snobbish. ◇ *mf* snob.

esnobismo [iʒno'biʒmul] *m* snobbishness.

esotérico, ca [ezo'tɛriku, kal *adj* esoteric.

esoterismo [ezote'riʒmul] *m* esotericism.

espaçado, da [iʃpa'sadu, da] *adj* -**1.** [com intervalos] spaced out. -**2.** [esparso] scattered.

espacial [iʃpa'sjawl] (*pl* -ais) *adj* space (*antes do subst*).

espaço [iʃ'pasul] *m* -**1.** [ger] space; ~ aéreo air space. -**2.** [o universo] outer space. -**3.** [de tempo] space.

espaçoso, osa [iʃpa'sozu, ɔzal *adj* spacious.

espada [iʃ'padal] *f* [arma] sword.

➡ **espadas** *fpl* [naipe] spades.

espádua [iʃ'padwal] *f* shoulder blade.

espaguete [iʃpa'getʃil] *m* spaghetti.

espairecer [iʃpajre'se(x)] *vt & vi* to relax.

espaldar [iʃpaw'da(x)] *m* [de cadeira, sofá] back.

espalhafato [iʃpaʎa'fatul *m* commotion.

espalhar [iʃpa'ʎa(x)] *vt* -**1.** [ger] to spread. -**2.** [dispersar - semente] to scatter; [- fumaça, odor] to spread. -**3.** [difundir] to diffuse.

➡ **espalhar-se** *vp* -**1.** [dissipar-se] to dissipate. -**2.** [propagar-se] to be spread.

espanador [iʃpana'do(x)] (*pl* -es) *m* duster.

espancamento [iʃpãŋka'mẽntul *m* beating.

espancar [iʃpãŋ'ka(x)] *vt* to beat.

Espanha [iʃ'pãɲal] *n* Spain.

espanhol, la [iʃpã'ɲɔw, lal (*mpl* -óis, *fpl* -s) ◇ *adj* Spanish. ◇ *m, f* Spaniard.

➡ **espanhol** *m* [língua] Spanish.

espantado, da [iʃpãn'tadu, da] *adj* -**1.** [assustado] startled. -**2.** [surpreso] astonished.

espantalho [iʃpãn'taʎu] *m* [boneco] scarecrow.

espantar [iʃpãn'ta(x)] <> *vt* **-1.** [assustar] to frighten. **-2.** [afugentar] to frighten (away). **-3.** [surpreender] to amaze. <> *vi* [surpreender] to be amazing.

◆ **espantar-se** *vp* **-1.** [assustar-se] to be frightened. **-2.** [surpreender-se] to be amazed.

espanto [iʃ'pãntu] *m* **-1.** [susto] fright. **-2.** [assombro] amazement.

espantoso, osa [iʃpãn'tozu, ɔza] *adj* **-1.** [surpreendente] startling. **-2.** [admirável] astounding.

esparadrapo [iʃpara'drapu] *m* sticking plaster *UK*, Band-Aid® *US*.

esparramar [iʃpaxa'ma(x)] *vt* **-1.** [espalhar] to scatter. **-2.** [derramar] to splash.

◆ **esparramar-se** *vp* [refestelar-se] to sprawl.

esparso, sa [iʃ'paxsu, sa] *adj* **-1.** [espalhado] sparse. **-2.** [raro] scarce.

espartilho [iʃpax'tiʎu] *m* corset.

espasmo [iʃ'paʒmu] *m* spasm.

espatifar [iʃpatʃi'fa(x)] *vt* & *vi* to smash.

◆ **espatifar-se** *vp* to shatter.

espátula [iʃ'patula] *f* spatula.

especial [iʃpe'sjaw] (*pl* **-ais**) *adj* special; **em** ~ in particular.

especialidade [iʃpesjali'dadʒi] *f* speciality.

especialista [iʃpesja'liʃta] <> *adj* [perito]: ~ **em** expert in. <> *mf* **-1.** [profissional] expert. **-2.** [perito]: ~ **em** specialist in.

especializar-se [iʃpesjali'zaxsi] *vp*: ~ **(em)** to specialize (in).

especiaria [iʃpesja'ria] *f* spice.

espécie [iʃ'pɛsji] *f* **-1.** *BIOL* species. **-2.** [tipo] kind.

◆ **em espécie** *loc adv* *FIN* (in) cash.

especificar [iʃpesifi'ka(x)] *vt* to specify.

específico, ca [iʃpe'sifiku, ka] *adj* specific.

espécime [iʃ'pɛsimil] (*pl* **-es**), **espécimen** [iʃ'pɛsimẽl] (*pl* **-ns**) *m* specimen.

espectador, ra [iʃpekta'do(x), ra] (*mpl* **-res**, *fpl* **-ras**) *m, f* **-1.** [testemunha] witness. **-2.** [de espetáculo *etc*.] spectator.

◆ **espectadores** *mpl* viewers.

espectro [iʃ'pɛktru] *m* **-1.** [fantasma] ghost. **-2.** *FÍSICA* spectrum. **-3.** *fig* [pessoa esquálida] wretch.

especulação [iʃpekula'sãw] (*pl* **-ões**) *f* speculation.

especular [iʃpeku'la(x)] *vt* [averiguar] to speculate upon.

espelho [iʃ'peʎu] *m* mirror; ~ **retrovisor** rearview mirror.

espera [iʃ'pɛra] *f* **-1.** [ato] wait; **à** ~ **de** waiting for. **-2.** [tempo] delay. **-3.** [tocaia] ambush.

esperança [iʃpe'rãnsa] *f* **-1.** [expectativa] expectation. **-2.** [confiança] hope.

esperançoso, osa [iʃperãn'sozu, ɔza] *adj* hopeful.

esperar [iʃpe'ra(x)] <> *vt* **-1.** [aguardar] to wait for. **-2.** [bebê] to expect. **-3.** [desejar]: ~ **que** to hope that; ~ **fazer algo** to hope to do sthg. **-4.** [supor] to expect. **-5.** [estar destinado a] to await. **-6.** [contar obter] to expect. <> *vi* [aguardar]: to hope; **espera (aí)!** wait (a moment)!

◆ **esperar-se** *vp*: **como era de se** ~ as was to be expected.

esperma [iʃ'pexma] *m* sperm.

espermicida [iʃpexmi'sida] <> *adj* spermicidal. <> *m* spermicide.

espernear [iʃpex'nja(x)] *vi* **-1.** [sacudir as pernas] to kick one's legs. **-2.** *fig* [protestar] to (put up a) protest.

espertalhão, ona [iʃpexta'ʎãw, ona] (*mpl* **-ões**, *fpl* **-s**) <> *adj* crafty. <> *m, f* smart operator.

esperteza [iʃpex'teza] *f* **-1.** [inteligência] intelligence. **-2.** [astúcia] shrewdness; **foi muita** ~ **dele fazer isso** it was very shrewd of him to do that.

esperto, ta [iʃ'pextu, ta] *adj* **-1.** [inteligente] smart. **-2.** [ativo] lively. **-3.** [espertalhão] clever. **-4.** *fam* [bacana] groovy.

espesso, a [iʃ'pesu, a] *adj* thick.

espessura [iʃpe'sura] *f* thickness.

espetacular [iʃpetaku'la(x)] (*pl* **-es**) *adj* amazing.

espetáculo [iʃpe'takulu] *m* **-1.** [show] show. **-2.** [maravilha]: **ser um** ~ to be amazing. **-3.** [cena ridícula] spectacle; **ele deu o maior** ~ **aqui por causa da bebedeira** he made a spectacle of himself here being so drunk.

espetar [iʃpe'ta(x)] *vt* to impale.

◆ **espetar-se** *vp* to prick o.s.

espeto [iʃ'petu] *m* **-1.** [utensílio de churrasco] (roasting) spit. **-2.** *fig* [pessoa magra] beanpole. **-3.** *fig* [situação difícil]: **ser um** ~ to be difficult.

espevitado, da [iʃpevi'tadu, da] *adj* lively.

espevitar [iʃpevi'ta(x)] ◆ **espevitar-se** *vp* **-1.** [mostrar-se afetado] to show off. **-2.** [irritar-se] to fly off the handle.

espezinhar [iʃpɛzi'ɲa(x)] *vt* **-1.** [implicar com] to put down. **-2.** [humilhar] to trample (on).

espiada [iʃ'pjada] *f* peep; **dar uma** ~ to have a peep, to have a look-see.

espião, piã [iʃ'pjãw, pjã] (*mpl* -ões, *fpl* -s) *m, f* spy.

espiar [iʃ'pja(x)] ⟨⟩ *vt* -1. [olhar] to watch. -2. [espionar] to spy on. ⟨⟩ *vi* -1. [olhar]: ~ **(por)** [pela fechadura] to look (through); [pelo canto do olho] to glance. -2. [espionar] to spy.

espichado, da [iʃpi'ʃadu, da] *adj* -1. [pessoa] stretched out. -2. [corda] tight.

espichar [iʃpi'ʃa(x)] ⟨⟩ *vt* [esticar] to stretch out. ⟨⟩ *vi* [crescer] to shoot up.
◆ **espichar-se** *vp* [espreguiçar-se] to stretch (out).

espiga [iʃ'piga] *f* ear.

espinafrar [iʃpina'fra(x)] *vt* -1. [repreender] to reprimand. -2. [criticar] to lambaste.

espinafre [iʃpi'nafri] *m* spinach.

espingarda [iʃpĩŋ'gaxda] *f* shotgun.

espinha [iʃ'piɲa] *f* -1. [na pele] pimple. -2. [de peixe] bone. -3. ANAT spine.

espinho [iʃ'piɲu] *m* -1. [de planta] thorn. -2. [de porco-espinho] quill. -3. [de ouriço] spine. -4. *fig* [dificuldade] snag.

espinhoso, osa [iʃpi'nozu, ɔza] *adj* thorny.

espionagem [iʃpio'naʒẽ] *f* espionage.

espionar [iʃpio'na(x)] ⟨⟩ *vt* to spy on. ⟨⟩ *vi* to snoop.

espiral [iʃpi'raw] (*pl* -ais) ⟨⟩ *adj* spiral. ⟨⟩ *f* spiral; em ~ in a spiral; **escada em** ~ spiral staircase.

espiritismo [iʃpiri'tʃiʒmu] *m* spiritualism.

espírito [iʃ'piritu] *m* -1. [ger] spirit. -2. [temperamento]: ~ **esportivo** competitive spirit.
◆ **Espírito Santo** *m* Holy Spirit.

espiritual [iʃpiri'twaw] (*pl* -ais) *adj* spiritual.

espirituoso, osa [iʃpiri'twozu, ɔza] *adj* witty.

espirrar [iʃpi'xa(x)] ⟨⟩ *vi* -1. [dar espirro] to sneeze. -2. [jorrar] to squirt out. ⟨⟩ *vt* [jorrar] to squirt.

espirro [iʃ'pixu] *m* sneeze.

esplanada [iʃpla'nada] *f* esplanade.

esplêndido, da [iʃ'plẽdʒidu, da] *adj* splendid.

esplendor [iʃplẽ'do(x)] *m* splendour UK, splendor US.

espólio [iʃ'pɔlju] *m* -1. [herança] inheritance. -2. [restos] remains (*pl*).

esponja [iʃ'põʒa] *f* -1. [ger] sponge. -2. *fig* [beberrão] soak.

espontâneo, nea [iʃpõ'tãnju, nja] *adj* spontaneous.

espora [iʃ'pɔra] *f* spur.

esporádico, ca [iʃpo'radʒiku, ka] *adj* sporadic.

esporte [iʃ'pɔxtʃi] *m* sport.

esportista [iʃpox'tʃiʃta] ⟨⟩ *adj* sporty. ⟨⟩ *mf* sportsman (*f* sportswoman).

esportivo, va [iʃpox'tʃivu, va] *adj* sports (*antes de subst*).
◆ **esportiva** *f* (sense of) fair play.

esposa [iʃpo'za] *f* wife.

esposo [iʃ'pozu] *m* husband.

espreguiçadeira [iʃpregiza'dejra] *f* deckchair.

espreguiçar-se [iʃpregi'saxsi] *vp* to stretch.

espreita [iʃ'prejta] *loc*: à ~ **(de)** on the lookout (for).

espremedor [iʃpreme'do(x)] (*pl* -es) *m* masher; ~ **de laranja** orange squeezer.

espremer [iʃpre'me(x)] *vt* -1. [apertar] to squeeze. -2. [comprimir - fruta] to squeeze; [- toalha molhada] to wring out.

espuma [iʃ'puma] *f* foam.

espumante [iʃpu'mãtʃi] *adj* sparkling.

espumar [iʃpu'ma(x)] *vi* to foam.

espúrio, ria [iʃ'purju, rja] *adj* spurious.

esquadra [iʃ'kwadra] *f* -1. NAÚT fleet. -2. MIL squadron.

esquadrão [iʃkwa'drãw] (*pl* -ões) *m* squadron.

esquadrilha [iʃkwa'driʎa] *f* flotilla.

esquartejar [iʃkwaxte'ʒa(x)] *vt* to quarter.

esquecer [iʃke'se(x)] ⟨⟩ *vt* to forget; ~ **que** to forget that. ⟨⟩ *vi*: ~ **(de algo/alguém)** to forget (sth/sb); ~ **de fazer algo** to forget to do sth.
◆ **esquecer-se** *vp*: ~-se **(de algo)** to forget (about sth); ~-se **de fazer algo** to forget to do sth.

esquecido, da [iʃke'sidu, da] *adj* -1. [não lembrado] forgotten. -2. [distraído] forgetful.

esqueleto [iʃke'letu] *m* -1. [ossatura] skeleton. -2. [estrutura] skeleton. -3. [esboço] rough draft. -4. *fig* [pessoa magra] bag of bones, skeleton.

esquema [iʃ'kema] *m* -1. [gráfico] diagram. -2. [plano] plan. -3. [resumo] schema.

esquentar [iʃkẽ'ta(x)] ⟨⟩ *vt* [aquecer] to heat up. ⟨⟩ *vi* -1. [aquecer] to get hot. -2. *fig* [exaltar-se] to become irritable.
◆ **esquentar-se** *vp* -1. [aquecer-se] to warm o.s. up. -2. *fig* [exaltar-se] to get annoyed.

esquerdo, da [iʃ'kexdu, da] *adj* left.
◆ **esquerda** *f* -1. [lado] left; à ~ on the left. -2. POL left wing.

esquete [iʃ'kɛtʃi] *m* sketch.

esqui [iʃ'ki] *m* -1. [patim] ski. -2. [esporte] skiing; ~ **aquático** water-skiing.

esquiador, ra [iʃkja'do(x), ral *m*, *f* skier.

esquiar [iʃ'kja(x)] *vi* to ski.

esquilo [iʃ'kilul *m* squirrel.

esquimó [iʃki'mɔl] ◇ *adj* Eskimo. ◇ *mf* Eskimo.

➡ **esquimó** *m* [língua] Eskimo.

esquina [iʃ'kinal *f* corner; **dobrar a** ~ to turn the corner.

esquisito, ta [iʃki'zitu, tal *adj* **-1.** [incomum] strange. **- 2.** [pessoa] strange.

esquivar-se [iʃki'vaxsil *vp*: ~-**se de algo** to dodge sthg.

esquivo, va [iʃ'kivu, val *adj* aloof.

➡ **esquiva** *f* dodge.

esse, essa ['esi, 'ɛsal ◇ *adj* that, those *(pl)*. ◇ *pron* that (one), those (ones) *(pl)*.

essência [e'sēnsjal *f* essence.

essencial [esēn'sjawl (*pl* -**ais**) ◇ *adj* **-1.** [ger] essential. **- 2.** [preocupação, benefício, trecho] main. ◇ *m*: **o** ~ [o mais importante] the main thing.

esta ['ɛʃtal ▷ **este**.

estabelecer [iʃtabele'se(x)] *vt* **-1.** [ger] to establish. **- 2.** [instalar] to set up.

➡ **estabelecer-se** *vp* **-1.** [firmar-se] to establish o.s. **- 2.** [instalar-se] to be established. **- 3.** [em negócio] to become established. **- 4.** [determinar-se]: ~-**se (que)** to be established (that).

estabelecimento [iʃtabelesi'mēntul *m* establishment.

estabilidade [iʃtabili'dadʒil *f* stability.

estabilizador [iʃtabiliza'do(x)] (*pl* -**es**) *m* COMPUT transformer.

estabilizar [iʃtabili'za(x)] *vt* to stabilize.

➡ **estabilizar-se** *vp* to become stable.

estábulo [iʃ'tabulul *m* stable.

estaca [iʃ'takal *f* **-1.** [para cravar] stake. **- 2.** [de construção] support. **- 3.** [de barraca] post.

estação [iʃta'sāwl (*pl* -**ões**) *f* **-1.** [de trem, metrô, ônibus] station. **- 2.** [período]: ~ (**do ano**) season (of the year); ~ **de chuvas** rainy season; [de colheita]: **frutas da** ~ fruits of the season. **-3.** [estância]: ~ **de águas** spa. **- 4.** [para fins científicos] station. **- 5.** RÁDIO & TV station.

estacionamento [iʃtasjona'mēntul *m* **-1.** [ato] parking. **- 2.** [lugar] car park.

estacionar [iʃtasjo'na(x)] ◇ *vt* AUTO to park. ◇ *vi* **-1.** AUTO to park. **- 2.** [não evoluir] to remain stationary.

estacionário, ria [iʃtasjo'narju, rjal *adj* **-1.** [parado] stationary. **- 2.** ECON [estagnado] stagnant.

estada [iʃ'tadal, **estadia** [iʃ'tadʒial *f* stay.

estádio [iʃ'tadʒiul *m* stadium.

estadista [iʃta'dʒiʃtal *mf* statesman.

estado [iʃ'tadul *m* **-1.** [ger] state; **em**

bom/mau ~ in good/bad condition; ~ **civil** marital status; ~ **de espírito** state of mind; ~ **de saúde** (state of) health; ~ **de sítio** state of siege; ~ **gasoso/líquido/sólido** gaseous/liquid/solid state. **- 2.** POL state.

➡ **Estado** *m* [país] state.

estado-maior [iʃ,taduma'jɔ(x)] (*pl* **estados-maiores**) *m* MIL general staff *UK*, army/air staff *US*.

Estados Unidos da América *n*: **os** ~ the United States of America.

estadual [iʃta'dwawl (*pl* -**ais**) *adj* [receita, constituição] state (*antes de subst*).

estadunidense [iʃtaduni'dēnsil ◇ *adj* American. ◇ *mf* American.

estafa [iʃ'tafal *f* **-1.** [esgotamento] exhaustion; **ter uma** ~ to be exhausted. **-2.** [fadiga] exhaustion.

estafado, da [iʃta'fadu, dal *adj* exhausted.

estagflação [iʃtag'flasãwl *f* ECON stagflation.

estagiário, ria [iʃta'ʒjarju, rjal *m*, *f* trainee.

estágio [iʃ'taʒul *m* **-1.** [fase] stage. **- 2.** [treinamento] training period.

estagnação [iʃtagna'sãwl *f* stagnation.

estagnado, da [iʃtag'nadu, dal *adj* stagnant.

estagnar [iʃtag'na(x)] ◇ *vt* to make stagnant. ◇ *vi* to stagnate.

➡ **estagnar-se** *vp* to be stagnant.

estalagem [iʃta'laʒēl (*pl* -**ns**) *f* inn.

estalar [iʃta'la(x)] ◇ *vt* **-1.** [dedos] to snap. **- 2.** [nozes, ovos] to crack. ◇ *vi* **-1.** [rachar] to crack. **- 2.** [crepitar] to crackle.

estaleiro [iʃta'lejrul *m* shipyard.

estalido [iʃta'lidul *m* **-1.** [de dedos] snapping. **- 2.** [de chicote, fogos] cracking.

estalo [iʃ'talul *m* [de dedos] snap; [de chicote] crack; [de trovão] crash; [de foguete] bang; **de** ~ [de repente] suddenly.

estampa [iʃ'tānpal *f* **-1.** [ger] print. **- 2.** [aparência] appearance.

estampado, da [iʃtān'padu, dal *adj* **-1.** [tecido] printed. **- 2.** *fig* [evidente] etched.

➡ **estampado** *m* **-1.** [tecido] printed cloth. **- 2.** [padrão impresso] print.

estampar [iʃtān'pa(x)] *vt* **-1.** [imprimir] to print. **- 2.** [marcar] to imprint. **- 3.** *fig* [mostrar]: **a mulher estampava no rosto seu desespero** the woman's despair was etched on her face.

estampido [iʃtān'pidul *m* bang.

estancar [iʃtān'ka(x)] *vt & vi* to stem *UK*, to staunch *US*.

estância [iʃ'tānsjal *f* **-1.** [fazenda] estate.

- 2. [estação]: ~ hidromineral spa. **- 3.** [estrofe] strophe, stanza.

estandarte [iʃtãn'daxtʃi] *m* standard.

estanho [iʃ'tãɲu] *m* tin.

estante [iʃ'tãntʃi] *f* **- 1.** [móvel] bookcase. **- 2.** [suporte] stand.

estapafúrdio, dia [iʃtapa'furdʒju, dʒja] *adj* outlandish.

estar [iʃ'ta(x)] *vi* **- 1.** [com lugar] to be; [em casa] to be at home, to be in; **ela estará lá à hora certa** she'll be there on time; **estarei no emprego às dez** I'll be at work at ten. **- 2.** [exprime estado] to be; **está quebrado** it's out of order; ~ **bem/ mal de saúde** to be well/unwell; **está muito calor/frio** it's very hot/cold. **- 3.** [manter-se] to be; **estive em casa toda a tarde** I was at home all afternoon; **estive esperando** I was waiting; **estive fora três anos** I lived abroad for three years; **deixe** ~ ... let it be ... **- 4.** [em locuções]: **está bem** *ou* **certo!** OK!, all right!

➡ **estar a** *v + prep* [relativo a preço] to cost, to be; **o camarão está a 25 reais o quilo** shrimp cost *ou* are 25 reals a kilo.

➡ **estar de** *v + prep*: ~ **de baixa/férias** to be on sick leave/vacation; ~ **de saia** to be wearing a skirt; ~ **de vigia** to keep watch.

➡ **estar para** *v + prep*: ~ **para fazer algo** to be about to do sthg; **estou para sair** I'm about to go out, I'm on my way out; **ele está para chegar** he'll be here any minute now; **não estou para brincadeiras** I'm not in the mood for silly games.

➡ **estar perante** *v + prep* [frente a] to be facing; **você está perante um gênio** you're in the presence of a genius.

➡ **estar por** *v + prep* [apoiar] to support; [por realizar]: **a cama está por fazer** the bed hasn't been made yet; **a limpeza está por fazer** the cleaning hasn't been done yet.

➡ **estar sem** *v + prep*: **estou sem tempo** I don't have time; **estou sem dinheiro** I don't have any cash; **ele está sem comer há dois dias** he hasn't eaten for two days.

estardalhaço [iʃtaxda'ʎasu] *m* **- 1.** [bulha] racket. **- 2.** [ostentação] flamboyance.

estarrecer [iʃtaxe'se(x)] *vt* to appal *UK*, to appall *US*. ◇ *vi* to be appalled.

estarrecido, da [iʃtaxe'sidu, da] *adj* shaken.

estatal [iʃta'taw] (*pl* **-ais**) ◇ *adj* state (antes de subst). ◇ *f* [empresa] state-owned company.

estatelado, da [iʃtate'ladu, da] *adj* [no chão] sprawled.

estático, ca [iʃ'tatʃiku, ka] *adj* **-1.** [imóvel] still. ◇ *FÍS* static.

estatístico, ca [iʃta'tʃiʃtʃiku, ka] ◇ *adj* statistical. ◇ *m, f* [profissional] statistician.
➡ **estatística** *f* statistics.

estátua [iʃ'tatwal] *f* statue.

estatura [iʃta'tural] *f* **- 1.** [física] stature; ~ **alta/baixa/mediana** tall/short/medium stature. **- 2.** [intelectual, moral] standing.

estatuto [iʃta'tutul] *m* statute.

estável [iʃ'tavewl] (*pl* **-eis**) *adj* **-1.** [ger] stable. **-2.** [cotação] fixed.

este¹ [ˈeʃtʃil] *m* east

este², esta [ˈeʃtʃil] ◇ *adj* this, these (*pl*). ◇ *pron* this (one), these ones (*pl*).

esteio [iʃ'tejul] *m* **-1.** [escora] prop. **- 2.** *NÁUT* chock. **- 3.** *fig* [amparo] breadwinner.

esteira [iʃ'tejral] *f* **- 1.** [tecido] woven mat. **- 2.** [usada na praia] reed mat. **- 3.** [rolante] moving carpet. **- 4.** [em academia] treadmill. **- 5.** *fig* [caminho] path; **na** ~ **de** in the course of.

estelionato [iʃteljo'natul] *m* swindle.

estender [iʃtẽn'de(x)] *vt* **-1.** [ger] to spread. **- 2.** [roupa] to hang out. **- 3.** [corda, fio] to stretch out. **- 4.** [massa] to roll out. **- 5.** [pernas, braços, mãos] to stretch out. **- 6.** [limites] to extend. **- 7.** [oferecer]: ~ **algo para alguém** to give sthg to sb. **- 8.** [prolongar] to prolong.
➡ **estender-se** *vp* **-1.** [ocupar]: ~**-se por** to spread out over. **- 2.** [durar]: ~**-se (por)** to last (for). **- 3.** [deitar-se]: ~**-se (em)** to lie down (on).

estenodatilógrafo, fa [iʃtenodatʃi'lɔgrafu, fal] *m, f* shorthand typist *UK*, stenographer *US*.

estenografia [iʃtenogra'fial] *f* shorthand *UK*, stenography *US*.

estepe [iʃ'tɛpil] ◇ *m* [pneu] spare wheel. ◇ *f* [vegetação] steppe.

esterco [iʃ'texkul] *m* manure.

estéreo [iʃ'tɛrjul] *adj* stereo.

estereofônico, ca [iʃterjo'foniku, ka] *adj* stereophonic.

estereótipo [iʃte'rjotʃipul] *m* stereotype.

estéril [iʃ'tɛriwl] (*pl* **-eis**) *adj* **-1.** [ger] sterile. **- 2.** [terreno] barren. **- 3.** *fig* [inútil, infrutífero] pointless.

esterilização [iʃteriliza'sãwl] (*pl* **-ões**) *f* sterilization.

esterilizado, da [iʃterili'zadu, dal] *adj* sterilized.

esterilizar [iʃterili'za(x)] *vt* to sterilize.

esterlino, na [iʃtɛr'linu, na] <> adj: libra ~ pound sterling. <> m sterling.

estético, ca [iʃ'tɛtiku, ka] adj -1. [artístico] aesthetic UK, esthetic US. -2. [harmonioso] tasteful.
➤ **estética** f -1. FILOSOFIA aestheticism UK, estheticism US. -2. [beleza] beauty; [do corpo] physical beauty.

estetoscópio [iʃtetoʃ'kɔpju] m stethoscope.

estiagem [iʃ'tʃiaʒē] (pl -ns) f -1. [período seco] dry spell. -2. [de rio, fonte] drying out.

estiar [iʃ'tʃja(x)] vi -1. [parar de chover] to stop raining. -2. [faltar chuva] to be dry.

estibordo [iʃtʃi'bɔxdu] m starboard; a ~ to starboard.

esticar [iʃtʃi'ka(x)] <> vt to stretch. <> vi -1. [distender-se] to stretch. -2. fam [prolongar saída]: ~ (em) to go on (to).
➤ **esticar-se** vp [pessoa] to stretch.

estigma [iʃ'tʃigma] m -1. [ger] stigma. -2. [ferrete] mark; a **Inquisição o condenou a usar o ~ de cristão-novo** the Inquisition branded him a neo-Christian.

estigmatizar [iʃtʃigmatʃi'za(x)] vt -1. [com infâmia] to stigmatize. -2. [com preconceito] to revile.

estilhaçar [iʃtʃiʎa'sa(x)] vt to shatter.
➤ **estilhaçar-se** vp to be shattered.

estilhaço [iʃtʃi'ʎasu] m -1. [de plástico, granada] splinter. -2. [de vidro] shard.

estilista [iʃtʃi'liʃta] mf -1. [escritor] stylist. -2. [de moda] fashion designer.

estilo [iʃ'tʃilu] m style; ~ **de vida** way of life; **em grande** ~ [com pompa] in grande style.

estima [iʃ'tʃima] f -1. [apreço] esteem. -2. [afeição] affection.

estimação [iʃtʃima'sāw] f: **de** ~ prized; **minha caneta de** ~ my favourite pen; **animal de** ~ (family) pet.

estimado, da [iʃtʃi'madu, da] adj -1. [avaliado] estimated. -2. [querido] esteemed.

estimar [iʃtʃi'ma(x)] vt -1. [ger] to prize. -2. [avaliar]: ~ **algo (em)** to estimate sthg (at). -3. [desejar]: ~ **as melhoras de alguém** to hope sb gets better; ~ **que** to hope that.

estimativa [iʃtʃima'tʃiva] f estimation.

estimulante [iʃtʃimu'lãntʃi] <> adj stimulating. <> m stimulant.

estimular [iʃtʃimu'la(x)] vt -1. [excitar, ativar] to stimulate. -2. [instigar] to incite. -3. [incentivar]: ~ **alguém (a fazer algo)** to encourage sb (to do sthg).

estímulo [iʃ'tʃimulu] m -1. [ger]

stimulus. -2. [excitação] stimulant. -3. [incentivo] motivation.

estipular [iʃtipu'la(x)] vt to stipulate.

estirar [iʃtʃi'ra(x)] vt -1. [alongar] to stretch. -2. [estender ao comprido] to stretch out.
➤ **estirar-se** vp [deitar-se] to stretch o.s out.

estivador, ra [iʃtʃiva'do(x), ra] (mpl -es, fpl -s) m, f stevedore.

estocada [iʃto'kada] f stab.

estocar [iʃto'ka(x)] vt -1. [armazenar] to stock. -2. [dar estocada em] to stab.

Estocolmo [iʃto'kowmul n Stockholm.

estofar [iʃto'fa(x)] vt -1. [revestir] to upholster. -2. [acolchoar] to stuff.

estofo [iʃ'tofu] m -1. [revestimento] reupholstery. -2. [acolchoamento] stuffing.

estoicismo [iʃtoj'siʒmul m stoicism.

estóico, ca [iʃ'tɔjku, ka] <> adj -1. FILOSOFIA stoical, stoic. -2. fig [austero] stoical. <> m, f fig [pessoa austera] stoic.
➤ **estóica** f FILOSOFIA stoicism.

estojo [iʃ'toʒu] m case; ~ **de unhas** manicure set.

estola [iʃ'tɔla] f stole.

estômago [iʃ'tomagu] m -1. ANAT stomach. -2. fig [paciência]: **ter** ~ **para (fazer) algo** to have the stomach for (doing) sthg.

Estônia [iʃ'tonja] n Estonia.

estoque [iʃ'tɔki] m -1. [provisão] stock. -2. [local] store.

estória [iʃ'tɔrja] f story.

estorricar [iʃtoxi'ka(x)] vt & vi to scorch.

estorvo [iʃ'tɔxvu] m -1. [obstáculo] obstacle; [pessoa] hindrance. -2. [incômodo] disturbance.

estourado, da [iʃto'radu, da] adj -1. [temperamental] boisterous. -2. fam [fatigado] knackered.

estourar [iʃto'ra(x)] <> vi -1. [bomba] to explode. -2. [pneu] to blow up. -3. [guerra, revolução] to break out. -4. [escândalo] to become public. -5. fig [rebentar] to burst; **estar estourando de raiva/alegria** to be bursting with rage/joy. -6. [no mais tardar]: **estourando cinco e meia** no later than five-thirty. <> vt -1. [bomba] to explode. -2. [boca-de-fumo] to bust up.

estouro [iʃ'torul m -1. [ger] explosion. -2. fam: **ser um** ~ [filme, pessoa] to be a hit; [notícia, carro] to be a sensation.

estrábico, ca [iʃ'trabiku, ka] adj crosseyed.

estrabismo [iʃtra'biʒmul m squint, strabismus.

estraçalhar [iʃtrasa'ʎa(x)] vt -1. [livro,

objeto] to tear to shreds. **-2.** [pessoa] to kill.

➡ estraçalhar-se *vp* **-1.** [objeto] to smash. **-2.** [pessoa] to smash one another.

estrada [iʃ'tradal *m* **-1.** road; ~ **de ferro** railway track *UK*, railroad *US*. **-2.** *fig* [carreira] work; **estar na** ~ to be in the field.

estrado [iʃ'tradul *m* **-1.** [de cama] frame. **-2.** [tablado] platform.

estragado, da [iʃtra'gadu, dal *adj* **-1.** [podre] rotten. **-2.** [danificado] damaged. **-3.** [mimado] spoilt.

estragão [iʃtra'gãw] *m* tarragon.

estraga-prazeres [iʃ,tragapra'zeriʃ] *mf inv* killjoy, spoilsport.

estragar [iʃtra'ga(x)] ⟨⟩ *vt* **-1.** [ger] to spoil. **-2.** [danificar] to damage. ⟨⟩ *vi* [apodrecer] to go off.

➡ estragar-se *vp* **-1.** [deteriorar-se] to be ruined. **-2.** [avariar-se] to go wrong. **-3.** [apodrecer] to go rotten.

estrago [iʃ'tragul *m* **-1.** [dano] damage. **-2.** [desperdício] disaster.

estrangeiro, ra [iʃtrãn'ʒejru, ral ⟨⟩ *adj* foreign. ⟨⟩ *m, f* [pessoa] foreigner.

➡ estrangeiro *m*: no ~ abroad.

estrangular [iʃtrãŋgu'la(x)] *vt* to strangle.

estranhamento [iʃtrãɲa'mentul *m* [espanto] surprise.

estranhar [iʃtrã'ɲa(x)] ⟨⟩ *vt* **-1.** [achar fora do comum] to find strange. **-2.** [surpreender-se com] to be surprised by. **-3.** [não se habituar a] to be unaccustomed to. **-4.** [retrair-se diante de] to feel ill at ease with. **-5.** [hostilizar] to harass. ⟨⟩ *vi* [causar estranheza] to be strange.

➡ estranhar-se *vp* [hostilizar-se] to fall out with each other.

estranho, nha [iʃ'trãɲu, ɲal *adj* **-1.** [diferente, estrangeiro] foreign. **-2.** [incomum, desconhecido] strange.

estratagema [iʃtrata'ʒemal *m* stratagem.

estratégia [iʃtra'tɛʒjal *f* strategy.

estratégico, ca [iʃtra'tɛʒiku, kal *adj* strategic.

estrategista [iʃtrate'ʒiʃtal *mf* strategist.

estrato [iʃ'tratul *m* stratum.

estrear [iʃtre'a(x)] ⟨⟩ *vt* **-1.** [roupa, carro] to try out for the first time. **-2.** [filme, show] to premiere. **-3.** [carreira] to start. ⟨⟩ *vi* **-1.** [filme, show] to premiere. **-2.** [artista, jogador] to debut.

estrebaria [iʃtreba'rial *f* stable.

estréia [iʃ'trɛjal *f* **-1.** [de filme, show] premiere. **-2.** [de artista, jogador] debut. **-3.** [de roupa, carro] first time out.

estreitar [iʃtrej'ta(x)] ⟨⟩ *vt* **-1.** [diminuir] to shrink. **-2.** [apertar] to narrow. **-3.** [roupa] to constrict. **-4.** [relações, laços] to strengthen. **-5.** [tornar mais rigoroso] to tighten up. ⟨⟩ *vi* [estrada] to narrow.

➡ estreitar-se *vp* **-1.** [largura] to narrow. **-2.** [amizade, união] to strengthen.

estreito, ta [iʃ'trejtu, tal *adj* **-1.** [apertado] narrow. **-2.** [vestido, saia] straight. **-3.** [relação, amizade] strong.

➡ estreito *m GEOGR* strait.

estrela [iʃ'trelal *f* [ger] star; ~ **cadente** shooting star.

estrela-de-davi [iʃ'treladzidavil *(pl* **estrelas-de-davi)** *f* Star of David.

estrelado, da [iʃtre'ladu, dal *adj* **-1.** [céu, noite] starry. **-2.** [ovo] fried.

estrela-do-mar [iʃtreladu'ma(x)] *(pl* **estrelas-do-mar)** *f* starfish.

estremecer [iʃtreme'se(x)] ⟨⟩ *vt* to shake. ⟨⟩ *vi* **-1.** [tremer de espanto] to shiver. **-2.** [sacudir] to shudder. **-3.** [sofrer abalo] to be shaken.

estremecimento [iʃtremesi'mentul *m* shaking.

estrépito [iʃ'trɛpitul *m* racket.

estressado, da [iʃtre'sadu, dal *adj* stressed (out).

estressante [iʃtre'sãntʃil *adj* stressful.

estresse [iʃ'tresil *m* stress.

estria [iʃ'trial *f* **-1.** [sulco] groove. **-2.** [na pele] stretch mark.

estribeira [iʃtri'bejral *f*: **perder as** ~ **s** *fam* to lose one's head.

estribo [iʃ'tribul *m* **-1.** [de cavalo] stirrup. **-2.** [degrau] step.

estridente [iʃtri'dẽntʃil *adj* strident.

estripulia [iʃtripu'lial *f* mischief.

estritamente [iʃtrita'mẽntʃil *adv* [à risca] to the letter.

estrito, ta [iʃ'tritu, tal *adj* **-1.** [rigoroso] strict. **-2.** [exato] precise; **no sentido** ~ **da palavra** in the strict sense of the word.

estrofe [iʃ'trɔfil *f* stanza.

estrogonofe [iʃtrogo'nɔfil *m CULIN* stroganoff.

estrondo [iʃ'trõndul *m* rumble.

estrondoso, osa [iʃtrõn'dozu, ɔzal *adj* **-1.** [ruidoso] roaring. **-2.** [espetacular] spectacular.

estropiado, da [iʃtro'pjadu, dal *adj* **-1.** [aleijado] crippled. **-2.** [exausto] worn out.

estropiar [iʃtro'pja(x)] *vt* **-1.** [aleijar] to cripple. **-2.** [cansar] to tire out. **-3.** *fig* [mutilar] to mutilate. **-4.** *fig* [pronunciar mal] to mispronounce.

estrume [iʃ'trumil *m* manure.

estrutura [iʃtru'tura] f **-1.** CONST structure. **-2.** [armação] frame.

estruturação [iʃtrutura'sãw] (pl -ões) f structuring.

estrutural [iʃtrutu'raw] (pl -ais) adj structural.

estruturalista [iʃtrutura'liʃta] adj structuralist.

estuário [iʃ'twarju] m estuary.

estudante [iʃtu'dãntʃi] mf student.

estudantil [iʃtudãn'tʃiw] (pl -is) adj student (antes de subst).

estudar [iʃtu'da(x)] vt & vi to study.

estúdio [iʃ'tudʒju] m studio.

estudioso, osa [iʃtu'dʒjozu, ɔza] <> adj studious. <> m, f expert.

estudo [iʃ'tudu] m study.

  ➡ **estudos** mpl [formação escolar] studies.

estufa [iʃ'tufa] f **-1.** [para plantas] greenhouse. **-2.** [aquecedor] stove.

estupefação [iʃtupefa'sãw] f [espanto] amazement.

estupefato, ta [iʃtupe'fatu, ta] adj [espantado] amazed.

estupendo, da [iʃtu'pẽndu, da] adj **-1.** [maravilhoso] wonderful. **-2.** [espantoso] amazing.

estupidez [iʃtupi'deʃ] f **-1.** [condição] stupidity. **-2.** [ato] stupid thing.

estúpido, da [iʃ'tupidu, da] <> adj **-1.** [burro] stupid. **-2.** [grosseiro] rude; um calor ~ fig an unbearable heat. <> m, f **-1.** [pessoa burra] stupid person. **-2.** [pessoa grosseira] rude person.

estuprar [iʃtu'pra(x)] vt to rape.

estupro [iʃ'tupru] m rape.

estuque [iʃ'tuki] m stucco.

esvair-se [iʒva'ixsi] vp **-1.** [desaparecer] to disappear. **-2.** [desmaiar] to faint. **-3.** loc: ~ em sangue to bleed copiously; ~ em lágrimas to dissolve into tears.

esvaziar [iʒva'zja(x)] vt **-1.** [desocupar] to empty. **-2.** [beber de uma só vez] to drain. **-3.** [tirar a importância de] to nullify.

esvoaçante [iʒvwa'sãntʃi] adj fluttering.

esvoaçar [iʒvwa'sa(x)] vi to flutter.

ET (abrev de **Extraterrestre**) m ET.

ETA (abrev de **Euskadi Ta Askatasuna**) m ETA.

etapa [e'tapa] f stage.

etc. (abrev de **et cetera**) etc.

eternidade [etexni'dadʒi] f eternity.

eternizar [etexni'za(x)] vt **-1.** [tornar eterno] to eternalize. **-2.** [imortalizar] to immortalize. **-3.** fam [prolongar] to drag out.

  ➡ **eternizar-se** vp **-1.** [tornar-se eterno] to become eternal. **-2.** [imortalizar-se] to

become immortal. **-3.** fam [prolongar-se] to drag on.

eterno, na [e'texnu, na] adj eternal.

ético, ca [ˈɛtʃiku, ka] adj ethical.

  ➡ **ética** f ethics (pl).

Etiópia [e'tʃjɔpja] n Ethiopia.

etiqueta [etʃi'keta] f **-1.** [ger] label; ~ adesiva sticky label. **-2.** [boas maneiras] etiquette. **-3.** [de preço] ticket; [de roupa] label.

etnia [etʃ'nia] f ethnic group.

étnico, ca [ˈɛtʃniku, ka] adj ethnic.

etnocentrismo [etʃnosẽn'triʒmu] m ethnocentrism.

eu [ˈew] pron I; **e** ~ ? what about me?; **sou** ~ it's me; ~ **mesmo** OU **próprio** (I) myself.

EUA (abrev de **Estados Unidos da América**) n USA.

eucalipto [ewka'liptul m eucalyptus.

eucaristia [ewkariʃ'tʃia] f Eucharist.

eufemismo [ewfe'miʒmul m euphemism.

euforia [ewfo'ria] f euphoria.

euro [ˈewro] m euro.

eurodólar [ewro'dɔla(x)] m Eurodollar.

Europa [ew'rɔpa] n Europe.

europeu, péia [ewro'pew, pɛja] <> adj European. <> m, f European.

evacuação [evakwa'sãw] (pl -ões) f evacuation.

evacuar [eva'kwa(x)] <> vt [desocupar] to evacuate. <> vi [defecar] to evacuate.

evadir [eva'dʒi(x)] vt **-1.** [evitar] to avoid. **-2.** [eludir] to evade.

  ➡ **evadir-se** vp [escapar] to escape.

evangelho [evãn'ʒɛʎu] m Gospel.

evangélico, ca [evãn'ʒɛliku, ka] <> adj evangelical. <> m, f [pessoa] evangelist.

evangelização [evãnʒeliza'sãw] (pl -ões) f conversion (to Christianity).

evangelizar [evãnʒeli'za(x)] vt to convert (to Christianity).

evaporar [evapo'ra(x)] <> vt [vaporizar] to evaporate. <> vi to evaporate.

evasão [eva'zãw] (pl -ões) f **-1.** [fuga] escape. **-2.** fig [evasiva] evasion.

evasivo, va [eva'zivu, va] adj evasive.

  ➡ **evasiva** f evasion.

evento [e'vẽntu] m event.

eventual [evẽn'twaw] (pl -ais) adj chance (antes de subst).

eventualmente [evẽntwal'mẽntʃi] adv [às vezes] sometimes.

Everest [eve'rɛʃtʃi] n: **o** ~ (Mount) Everest.

evidência [evi'dẽnsja] f evidence; **em** ~ [destacado] obvious.

evidenciar [eviden'sja(x)] vt -1. [comprovar] to prove. -2. [mostrar] to be evidence of. -3. [destacar] to show clearly.
➡ **evidenciar-se** vp -1. [comprovar-se] to be proven. -2. [destacar-se] to be shown clearly.

evidente [evi'dentʃi] adj obvious.

evidentemente [evidentʃi'mentʃi] adv clearly.

evitar [evi'ta(x)] vt -1. [fugir a] to avoid; ~ **fazer algo** to avoid doing sthg. -2. [impedir] to prevent.

evocar [evo'ka(x)] vt [trazer à lembrança] to bring to mind.

evolução [evolu'sãw] (pl -ões) f -1. BIOL evolution. -2. [desenrolar] development. -3. [movimento] expansion. -4. MIL exercise.

evoluir [evo'lwi(x)] vi -1. [espécie] to evolve. -2. [adiantar-se] to progress.

ex. (abrev de exemplo) e.g.

exacerbar [ezasex'ba(x)] vt -1. [intensificar] to exacerbate. -2. [irritar] to provoke.
➡ **exacerbar-se** vp -1. [intensificar-se] to be exacerbated. -2. [irritar-se] to be provoked.

exagerado, da [ezaʒe'radu, da] <> adj exaggerated. <> m, f: **o que ele diz é típico de um** ~ what he says is typical of an exaggerator.

exagerar [ezaʒe'ra(x)] vt & vi to exaggerate.

exagero [eza'ʒerul] m exaggeration.

exalação [ezala'sãw] (pl -ões) f exhalation.

exalar [eza'la(x)] vt to exhale.

exaltado, da [ezaw'tadu, da] adj -1. [facilmente irritável] irritable. -2. [fanático] fanatical. -3. [exacerbado] irritated.

exaltar [exaw'ta(x)] vt -1. [engrandecer] to exalt. -2. [irritar] to irritate. -3. [excitar] to excite.
➡ **exaltar-se** vp [irritar-se] to become irritated.

exame [e'zãmi] m -1. [ger] examination. -2. EDUC [teste] examination, exam; **fazer um** ~ to sit an examination. -3. [inspeção] inspection.

examinar [ezami'na(x)] vt -1. [ger] to examine. -2. [inspecionar] to inspect.

exasperado, da [ezaʃpe'radu, da] adj exasperated.

exasperar [ezaʃpe'ra(x)] vt to exasperate.
➡ **exasperar-se** vp to become exasperated.

exatidão [ezatʃi'dãw] f -1. [precisão] accuracy. -2. [perfeição] perfection.

exato, ta [e'zatu, tal adj -1. [preciso] exact. -2. [correto] correct, right.

exaurir [ezaw'ri(x)] vt [esgotar] to exhaust.
➡ **exaurir-se** vp to be exhausted.

exaustão [ezawʃ'tãw] f exhaustion.

exausto, ta [e'zawʃtu, tal <> pp ▷ **exaurir**. <> adj exhausted.

exaustor [ezawʃ'to(x)] (pl -es) m extractor fan.

excedente [ese'dentʃi] <> adj excess (antes de subst). <> m -1. COM surplus. -2. [aluno] student on waiting list.

exceder [ese'de(x)] vt exceed.
➡ **exceder-se** vp [cometer excessos] to go too far.

excelência [ese'lẽnsja] f -1. [primazia] excellence. -2. [tratamento]: **(Vossa) Excelência** Your Excellency.

excelente [ese'lentʃi] adj excellent.

excentricidade [esẽntrisi'dadʒi] f eccentricity.

excêntrico, ca [e'sẽntriku, kal <> adj eccentric. <> m, f eccentric.

excepcional [esepsjo'naw] (pl -ais) <> adj -1. [extraordinário, excelente] exceptional. -2. MED disabled. <> mf MED [pessoa] person with special needs.

excerto [e'sextul m excerpt.

excessivamente [esesiva'mentʃi] adv excessively.

excessivo, va [ese'sivu, val adj excessive.

excesso [e'sɛsul m -1. [ger] excess; ~ **de velocidade** excessive speed. -2. COM surplus. -3. [desmando]: **cometer** ~s to go too far.

exceto [e'sɛtul prep except.

excetuar [ese'twa(x)] vt to except.

excitação [esita'sãw] f -1. [agitação] excitement. -2. [sexual] arousal.

excitado, da [esi'tadu, dal adj -1. [agitado] excited. -2. [sexualmente] aroused.

excitante [esi'tãntʃil adj -1. [ger] stimulating; **uma droga** ~ a stimulant. -2. [filme] exciting.

excitar [esi'ta(x)] vt -1. [agitar] to excite. -2. [sexualmente] to arouse. -3. [incitar] to incite.
➡ **excitar-se** vp -1. [agitar-se] to become excited. -2. [sexualmente] to become aroused.

exclamação [iʃklama'sãw] (pl -ões) f exclamation.

exclamar [iʃkla'ma(x)] vi to exclaim.

excluir [iʃklu'i(x)] vt -1. [eliminar] to exclude. -2. [omitir]: ~ **algo/alguém de** to exclude sthg/sb from. -3. [privar]: ~ **algo/alguém de** to leave sthg/sb out of. -4. [por incompatibilidade] to preclude.

exclusão [iʃklu'zãw] (pl -ões) f exclusion.

141

exclusivista [iʃkluzi'viʃta] <> *adj* [individualista] self-centred. <> *mf* self-centred person.

exclusivo, va [iʃklu'zivu, va] *adj* exclusive.

excomungar [iʃkomũ'ga(x)] *vt* to excommunicate.

excremento [iʃkre'mẽntu] *m* excrement.

excretar [iʃkre'ta(x)] *vt* [expelir] to excrete.

excursão [iʃkux'sãw] (*pl* -ões) *f* -1. [ger] excursion. -2. [em caminhada] walk, ramble.

excursionista [iʃkuxsjo'niʃta] *mf* [turista] tourist; [por um dia] day-tripper; [em caminhada] walker, rambler.

execução [ezeku'sãw] (*pl* -ões) *f* -1. [ger] execution. -2. [de peça musical] performance.

executar [ezeku'ta(x)] *vt* -1. [ger] to execute. -2. [peça musical] to perform. -3. [cumprir] to carry out.

executivo, va [ezeku'tʃivu, va] <> *adj* executive. <> *m, f* executive.

executor, ra [ezeku'to(x), ra] *m, f* executor.

exemplar [ezẽn'pla(x)] (*pl* -es) <> *adj* [modelar] exemplary. <> *m* -1. [de livro, jornal] copy. -2. [peça] example. -3. [modelo] model. -4. *BIOL* [espécie] specimen.

exemplo [e'zẽnplu] *m* [ger] example; **por** ~ for example; **bom/mau** ~ good/bad example; **a** ~ **de** just like.

exéquias [eˈɛzɛkjaʃ] *fpl* funeral rites.

exercer [ezex'se(x)] *vt* -1. [desempenhar] to carry out; [profissão] to practise *UK*, to practice *US*. -2. [fazer sentir]: ~ **algo (sobre)** to exert sthg (on).

exercício [ezex'sisju] *m* -1. [ger] exercise; **fazer** ~ to exercise; **em** ~ [presidente, diretor] in office; [professor] in service; [de profissão] practising; [de direitos] exercising. -2. *EDUC* exercise. -3. *COM*: ~ **anterior/corrente** previous/current financial year.

exército [e'zɛxsitu] *m* army.

exibição [ezibi'sãw] (*pl* -ões) *f* -1. [demonstração] exhibition. -2. [do corpo] exhibition. -3. [de filme, obra de arte] exhibition.

exibido, da [ezi'bidu, da] *fam* <> *adj* [exibicionista] flamboyant. <> *m, f* [pessoa] exhibitionist.

exibir [ezi'bi(x)] *vt* -1. [ger] to show. -2. [ostentar] to exhibit. -3. [expor] [obra de arte] to exhibit.

◆ **exibir-se** *vp* -1. [mostrar-se] to show off. -2. [indecentemente] to expose o.s.

exigência [ezi'ʒẽnsja] *f* -1. [imposição] demand. -2. [requisito] requirement. -3. [rigor] urgent request.

exigente [ezi'ʒẽntʃi] *adj* [rigoroso] demanding.

exigir [ezi'ʒi(x)] *vt* -1. [reclamar] to demand; ~ **que alguém faça algo** to demand that sb do sthg. -2. [requerer] to require.

exíguo, gua [e'zigwu, gwa] *adj* -1. [diminuto] tiny. -2. [minguado] meagre.

exilado, da [ezi'ladu, da] <> *adj* [pessoa] exiled. <> *m, f* [pessoa] exile.

exilar [ezi'la(x)] *vt* to exile.

◆ **exilar-se** *vp* to be exiled.

exílio [e'zilju] *m* -1. [ger] exile. -2. [expatriação] deportation.

exímio, mia [e'zimju, mja] *adj* [excelente] excellent.

eximir [ezi'mi(x)] *vt*: ~ **alguém de algo** to exempt sb from sthg.

◆ **eximir-se** *vp*: ~-se **de algo** to excuse o.s. from sthg.

existência [eziʃ'tẽnsja] *f* existence.

existente [eziʃ'tẽntʃi] *adj* -1. [que existe] existing. -2. [vivente] living.

existir [eziʃ'tʃi(x)] *vi* -1. [haver] to be. -2. [viver] to exist. -3. *loc* [ser fantástico]: **não** ~ *fam* to be incredible; **este sorvete não existe!** this ice cream is incredible!

êxito [ˈezitu] *m* [sucesso] success; **ter/não ter** ~ **(em)** to be successful/unsuccessful (in).

êxodo [ˈezodu] *m* exodus; ~ **rural** rural exodus.

exonerar [ezone'ra(x)] *vt* -1. [demitir]: ~ **alguém de algo** to exonerate sb from sthg. -2. [desobrigar]: ~ **alguém de algo** to exonerate sb from sthg.

◆ **exonerar-se** *vp* -1. [demitir-se]: ~-se **de algo** to exonerate o.s. from sthg. -2. [desobrigar-se]: ~-se **de algo** to release o.s. from sthg.

exorbitância [ezoxbi'tãnsja] *f* -1. [excesso] excess. -2. *fam* [preço excessivo] extortionate price.

exortar [ezox'ta(x)] *vt*: ~ **alguém a fazer algo** to exhort sb to do sthg.

exótico, ca [e'zɔtʃiku, ka] *f* exotic.

expandir [iʃpãn'dʒi(x)] *vt* [ger] to spread.

◆ **expandir-se** *vp* -1. [dilatar-se] to spread, to be spread. -2. [ser expansivo] to be expansive.

expansão [iʃpãn'sãw] (*pl* -ões) *f* -1. [ato] expansion. -2. [efusão] outpouring.

expansivo, va [iʃpã'sivu, va] *adj* expansive.

expatriação [iʃpatrja'sãw] (*pl* -ões) *f* expatriation.

expatriar [iʃpa'trja(x)] *vt* to expatriate.

expectativa [iʃpekta'tʃival *f* expectation; **na ~ de** in the expectation of; **~ de vida** life expectancy.

expedição [iʃpedʒi'sãw] (*pl* -ões) *f* - 1. [de mercadorias] dispatch. - 2. [por navio] shipment. - 3. [por correio] dispatch. - 4. [viagem] expedition. - 5. [de documento] issue.

expediente [iʃpe'dʒjentʃi] <> *adj* [desembaraçado, diligente] efficient; **ser ~** to be efficient. <> *m* - 1. [horário] office hours; **meio ~** part-time. - 2. [pessoal] resourceful. - 3. [desembaraço, diligência]: **ter ~** to be resourceful. - 4. [meios, recursos] expedient. - 5. [correspondência] correspondence.

expedir [iʃpe'dʒi(x)] *vt* - 1. [carta, mercadoria] to send. - 2. [documento etc.] to issue.

expedito, ta [iʃpe'dʒitu, ta] *adj* - 1. [pessoa] efficient. - 2. [trabalho, solução] expeditious.

expelir [iʃpe'li(x)] *vt* to expel.

experiência [iʃpe'rjēnsja] *f* experience.

experiente [iʃpe'rjēntʃi] *adj* experienced.

experimentar [iʃperimēn'ta(x)] *vt* - 1. [testar] to test. - 2. [provar - comida, bebida] to try; [- roupa] to try on. - 3. [sofrer] to go through. - 4. [sentir] to experience.

experimento [iʃperi'mēntu] *m* experiment.

expiar [iʃ'pja(x)] *vt* to atone for.

expiatório, ria [iʃpja'tɔrju, rja] *adj* ▷ bode.

expirar [iʃpi'ra(x)] <> *vt* [ar] to exhale. <> *vi* - 1. [encerrar] to expire. - 2. [morrer] to die.

explicação [iʃplika'sãw] (*pl* -ões) *f* explanation.

explicar [iʃpli'ka(x)] *vt* & *vi* to explain.
➤ **explicar-se** *vp* [justificar-se] to explain o.s.

explicativo, va [iʃplika'tʃivu, va] *adj* explanatory.

explícito, ta [iʃ'plisitu, ta] *adj* explicit.

explodir [iʃplo'di(x)] <> *vi* - 1. [bomba, avião, carro] to explode. - 2. *fig* [não se conter] to burst; **~ de** to be bursting with; **~ em** to burst into. <> *vt* - 1. [bomba] to detonate. - 2. [edifício, avião] to blow up.

exploração [iʃplora'sãw] (*pl* -ões) *f* - 1. [ger] exploration. - 2. [emprego] use. - 3. [de negócio] running. - 4. [agrícola] cultivation, growing. - 5. [abuso] exploitation. - 6. [exorbitância]: **ser uma ~** to be exorbitant. ·

explorador, ra [iʃplora'do(x), ra] <> *adj* - 1. [pessoa, companhia] exploring, exploratory. - 2. [aproveitador] exploitative. <> *m, f* - 1. [desbravador] explorer. - 2. [aproveitador] exploiter.

explorar [iʃplo'ra(x)] *vt* - 1. [ger] to exploit. - 2. [empregar] to use. - 3. [negócio] to run. - 4. [desbravar] to explore.

exploratório, ria [iʃplora'tɔriu, rja] *adj* exploratory.

explosão [iʃplo'zãw] (*pl* -ões) *f* explosion.

explosivo, va [iʃplo'zivu, va] *adj* explosive.
➤ **explosivo** *m* [material] explosive.

EXPO (*abrev de* **Exposição**) *f* exhibition.

expor [iʃ'po(x)] *vt* - 1. [mostrar] to display. - 2. [explicar] to explain. - 3. [exibir] to exhibit. - 4. [revelar] to reveal. - 5. [submeter]: **~ algo (a algo)** to expose sthg (to sthg).
➤ **expor-se** *vp* - 1. [submeter-se]: **~-se a algo** to expose o.s. to sthg. - 2. [exibir-se] to expose o.s.

exportação [iʃpoxta'sãw] (*pl* -ões) *f* - 1. [ato] export. - 2. [produtos] exports (*pl*).

exportador, ra [iʃpoxta'do(x), ra] <> *adj* - 1. [país, companhia] exporting. - 2. [política] export (*antes de subst*). <> *m, f* exporter.

exportar [iʃpox'ta(x)] *vt* to export.

exposição [iʃpozi'sãw] (*pl* -ões) *f* - 1. [mostra] display. - 2. [explicação] explanation. - 3. [narração] narrative. - 4. *FOTO* exposure.

exposto, osta [iʃ'poʃtu, oʃta] <> *pp* ▷ **expor**. <> *adj* [à vista - mercadoria] on show; [- corpo] exposed; [- fratura] compound.

expressão [iʃpre'sãw] (*pl* -ões) *f* - 1. [ger] expression; **~ artística** artistic expression. - 2. [manifestação]: **~ (de algo)** expression (of sthg). - 3. [vivacidade] expressiveness.

expressar [iʃpre'sa(x)] *vt* to express.
➤ **expressar-se** *vp* to express o.s.

expressivo, va [iʃpre'sivu, va] *adj* expressive.

expresso, sa [iʃ'prɛsu, sa] <> *pp* ▷ **expressar**. <> *adj* express.
➤ **expresso** *m* express.

exprimir [iʃpri'mi(x)] *vt* to express.
➤ **exprimir-se** *vp* to express o.s.

expulsão [iʃpuw'sãw] (*pl* -ões) *f* - 1. [saída forçada] expulsion. - 2. *ESP* sending-off.

expulsar [iʃpuw'sa(x)] *vt* - 1. [ger] to expel. - 2. [inimigo] to drive out. - 3. [deportar] to deport. - 4. *ESP* to send off.

expulso, sa [iʃ'puwsu, sa] <> *pp* ▷ **expulsar**. <> *adj* expelled.

expurgar [iʃpux'ga(x)] *vt* **-1.** [limpar] to clean. **-2.** [corrigir] to expurgate. **-3.** [livrar]: ~ **algo (de)** to purge sthg (of).

êxtase ['eʃtazi] *m* **-1.** [enlevo] ecstasy. **-2.** [transe]: **estar em** ~ to be in ecstasy.

extasiar [iʃta'zja(x)] *vt* to enrapture.
➡ **extasiar-se** *vp* to be entranced.

extensão [iʃtẽn'sãw] (*pl* **-ões**) *f* **-1.** [ger] extent. **-2.** [dimensão, área] area. **-3.** [comprimento] length; **a vegetação cobria toda a** ~ **da praia** the vegetation covered the whole length and breadth of the beach. **-4.** [duração] duration. **-5.** [ampliação] scope. **-6.** [ramal telefônico, fio elétrico] extension.

extensivo, va [iʃtẽn'sivu, va] *adj* **-1.** [extensível] extending. **-2.** [amplo] extensive.

extenso, sa [iʃ'tẽnsu, sa] *adj* **-1.** [ger] long. **-2.** [amplo, abrangente] extensive. **-3.** *loc:* **por** ~ in full.

extenuado, da [iʃte'nwadu, da] *adj* worn out.

extenuante [iʃte'nwãntʃi] *adj* **-1.** [cansativo] exhausting. **-2.** [debilitante] debilitating.

extenuar [iʃtẽ'nwa(x)] *vt* **-1.** [cansar] to wear out. **-2.** [debilitar] to debilitate.
➡ **extenuar-se** *vp* **-1.** [cansar-se] to wear o.s. out. **-2.** [debilitar-se] to be debilitated.

exterior [iʃte'rjo(x)] (*pl* **-es**) ◇ *adj* **-1.** [externo] outer. **-2.** [com outros países] external. **-3.** [aparência] external. **-4.** [o estrangeiro]: **o** ~ abroad. ◇ *m* [aparência] appearance.

exterioridade [iʃterjori'dadʒi] *f* external nature; [aparências] (outward) appearances.

exterminar [iʃtexmi'na(x)] *vt* **-1.** [aniquilar] to exterminate. **-2.** [erradicar] to eradicate.

extermínio [iʃtex'minju] *m* extermination.

externa [iʃ'tɛxna] *f* ▷ **externo**.

externato [iʃtɛx'natu] *m* day school.

externo, na [iʃ'tɛxnu, na] *adj* **-1.** [exterior - parede] external; [- lado] external. **-2.** [aparente] exterior. **-3.** [medicamento]: **uso** ~ external use.

extinção [iʃtʃĩn'sãw] *f* extinction; **em** ~ endangered.

extinguir [iʃtĩŋ'gi(x)] *vt* **-1.** [fogo] to extinguish. **-2.** [exterminar] to exterminate. **-3.** [dissolver] to dissolve. **-4.** *ECOL* to endanger. ➡ **extinguir-se** *vp* **-1.** [fogo] to go out. **-2.** [desaparecer] to disappear. **-3.** *ECOL* to become extinct.

extinto, ta [iʃ'tʃĩntu, ta] *adj* **-1.** [ger] extinct. **-2.** [fogo] extinguished. **-3.** [associação] defunct.

extintor [iʃtʃĩn'to(x)] (*pl* **-res**) *m*: ~ **(de incêndio)** (fire) extinguisher.

extirpar [iʃtix'pa(x)] *vt* **-1.** [arrancar] to pull out. **-2.** [extrair - dente] to extract; [- tumor] to remove. **-3.** [erradicar] to eradicate.

extorquir [iʃtox'ki(x)] *vt*: ~ **algo (de alguém)** to extort sthg (from sb).

extorsão [iʃtox'sãw] (*pl* **-ões**) *f* extortion.

extra ['ɛʃtra] ◇ *adj* [extraordinário] extra. ◇ *mf* extra.

extração [iʃtra'sãw] (*pl* **-ões**) *f* **-1.** [ger] extraction. **-2.** [sorteio] draw.

extraditar [iʃtradʒi'ta(x)] *vt* to extradite.

extrair [iʃtra'i(x)] *vt* [tirar]: ~ **algo (de)** to extract sthg (from).

extraordinário, ria [iʃtraordʒi'narju, rja] *adj* extraordinary.

extrapolação [eʃtrapola'sãw] (*pl* **-ões**) *f* extrapolation.

extrapolar [iʃtrapo'la(x)] *vt* to go beyond.

extraterrestre [eʃtrate'xɛʃtri] ◇ *adj* extraterrestrial. ◇ *mf* extraterrestrial.

extrato [iʃ'tratu] *m* **-1.** [ger] extract; ~ **de tomate** tomato puree. **-2.** [resumo] excerpt; ~ **bancário** bank statement.

extravagância [iʃtrava'gãnsja] *f* extravagance; **fazer uma** ~ to be extravagant.

extravagante [iʃtrava'gãntʃi] ◇ *adj* [excêntrico] eccentric.

extravasar [iʃtrava'sa(x)] ◇ *vt* [exteriorizar - sentimento, alegria] to show; [- raiva] to give vent to. ◇ *vi* **-1.** [expandir-se] to burst out. **-2.** [transbordar] to spill over.

extraviado, da [iʃtra'vjadu, da] *adj* missing.

extraviar [iʃtra'vja(x)] *vt* **-1.** [perder] to lose. **-2.** [dinheiro] to embezzle. **-3.** *fig* [perverter] to lead astray.
➡ **extraviar-se** *vp* **-1.** [carta] to go astray; [processo] to get lost. **-2.** [pessoa - perder-se] to get lost; *fig* [perverter-se] to be led astray.

extravio [iʃtra'vju] *m* **-1.** [perda]: ~ **(de algo)** loss (of sthg). **-2.** [roubo] embezzlement.

extremidade [iʃtremi'dadʒi] *f* **-1.** [fim, limite] end. **-2.** [ponta] tip. **-3.** [beira] edge.
➡ **extremidades** *fpl* *ANAT* extremities.

extremo, ma [iʃ'tremu, ma] *adj* (*antes de subst*) **-1.** [ger] extreme; **o Extremo Oriente** the Far East. **-2.** [derradeiro, exagerado] extreme.

extremo *m* **-1.** [limite, ponta] extreme. **-2.** [máximo] utmost; **ao ~** to the utmost.

extroversão [iʃtrovex'sãw] *f* extroversion.

extrovertido, da [iʃtrovex'tʃidu, da] <> *adj* extrovert. <> *m, f* extrovert.

exuberante [ezube'rãntʃil] *adj* exuberant.

exultante [ezuw'tãntʃil] *adj* exultant.

exultar [ezuw'ta(x)] *vi*: **~ (de)** to exult (in).

exumação [ezu'masãw] (*pl* **-ões**) *f* exhumation.

exumar [ezu'ma(x)] *vt* **-1.** [corpo] to exhume. **-2.** *fig* [lembranças] to dig up.

F

f, F ['ɛfi] *m* [letra] f, F.

fá [fa] *m* MÚS F, fa(h).

fã [fã] (*pl* **fãs**) *mf* fan.

FAB (*abrev de* **Força Aérea Brasileira**) *m* Brazilian Air Force.

fábrica ['fabrika] *f* factory.

fabricação [fabrika'sãw] (*pl* **-ões**) *f* manufacture; **de ~ caseira** home-made.

fabricar [fabri'ka(x)] *vt* **-1.** [manufaturar] to manufacture. **-2.** [inventar] to fabricate.

fábula ['fabula] *f* **-1.** [conto] fable. **-2.** *fam* [fortuna] fortune.

fabuloso, osa [fabu'lozu, ɔza] *adj* [ger] fabulous.

faca ['faka] *f* knife; **ser uma ~ de dois gumes** *fam* to be a double-edged sword.

facada [fa'kada] *f* **-1.** [golpe] stab. **-2.** *fam* cut; **dar uma ~ em alguém** [pedir dinheiro a alguém] to cadge money off sb.

façanha [fa'sãɲa] *f* exploit.

facão [fa'kãw] (*pl* **-ões**) *m* carving knife.

facção [fak'sãw] (*pl* **-ões**) *f* faction.

face ['fasi] *f* **-1.** [ger] face; **fazer ~ a** *fig* [enfrentar] to face up to; [custear] to take on board; **~ a ~** face to face. **-2.** [lado] side. **-3.** [aspecto] facet.

~ em face de *loc prep* [diante de] faced with.

fáceis ['fasejʃ] *pl* ⊳ **fácil**.

faceta [fa'seta] *f* [aspecto] facet.

fachada [fa'ʃada] *f* **-1.** [de prédio] façade. **-2.** *fig fam* [aparência] mug.

fácil ['fasiw] (*pl* **-eis**) *adj* **-1.** [simples] easy. **-2.** [dócil] easy(-going). **-3.** *pej* [mulher] easy.

~ fácil *adv* easily.

facilidade [fasili'dadʒi] *f* **-1.** [ausência de dificuldade] ease. **-2.** [aptidão]: **ter ~ (para algo)** to have an aptitude (for sthg).

~ facilidades *fpl* [meios] facilities.

facílimo, ma [fa'silimu, ma] *adj superl* ⊳ **fácil**.

facilitar [fasili'ta(x)] <> *vt* **-1.** [tornar fácil] to make easy. **-2.** [facultar] to facilitate. <> *vi* [descuidar-se] to be careless.

facões [fa'kõjʃ] *pl* ⊳ **facão**.

fac-símile [fak'simili] (*pl* **fac-símiles**) *m* **-1.** [cópia] facsimile. **-2.** [máquina] fax machine.

faculdade [fakuw'dadʒi] *f* **-1.** [capacidade] faculty. **-2.** [propriedade] property. **-3.** [escola superior] faculty.

facultativo, va [fakuwta'tʃivu, va] <> *adj* optional. <> *m, f* (medical) doctor.

fada ['fada] *f* fairy.

fadado, da [fa'dadu, da] *adj*: **estar ~ a algo** to be fated to sthg.

fadiga [fa'dʒiga] *f* fatigue.

fado ['fadu] *m* **-1.** [destino] fate. **-2.** MÚS fado, *type of Portuguese folk song*.

fagulha [fa'guʎa] *f* spark.

fahrenheit [fare'najtʃi] *adj* Fahrenheit.

faia ['faja] *f* beech tree.

faisão [faj'zãw] (*pl* **-ões**) *m* pheasant.

faísca [fa'iʃka] *f* spark.

faiscar [fajʃ'ka(x)] *vi* **-1.** [fogo] to flicker. **-2.** [olhos] to flash.

faixa ['fajʃa] *f* **-1.** [tira] strip. **-2.** [para a cintura] belt. **-3.** [para o peito] sash; **~ presidencial** presidential sash. **-4.** [para pedestres]: **~ (de pedestres)** (pedestrian) crossing. **-5.** [pista] lane. **-6.** [atadura] bandage. **-7.** [de terra] strip. **-8.** [para mensagem] banner. **-9.** [intervalo] interval; **~ etária** age group. **-10.** [de disco] track.

fala ['fala] *f* **-1.** [ger] speech. **-2.** [parte de diálogo] words (*pl*).

falácia [fa'lasja] *f* fallacy.

falante [fa'lãntʃi] *adj* talking.

falar [fa'la(x)] <> *vi* **-1.** [verbalmente] to speak; **~ de** *ou* **em algo** to talk about sthg; **~ com alguém** to speak to sb; **~ alto/baixo** to speak loudly/softly; **~ da boca para fora** *fam* not to mean a word one is saying; **~ mais alto** *fig* to win the day; **~ pelos cotovelos** [falar muito] to talk one's head off; **~ por alguém** to speak on behalf of sb; ~ **por** ~ to talk for the sake of talking; ~ **sozinho/dormindo** to talk to o.s./in one's sleep; **por** ~ **em ...** speaking ou talking of ...; **sem** ~ **de** ou **em ...** not to mention ...; **falou, está falado!** fam [OK] OK! -**2.** [discursar] to make a speech. -**3.** [tratar]: ~ **de** ou **sobre algo** to talk about sthg. -**4.** [confessar] to talk. ◇ vt -**1.** [idioma]: ~ **inglês/espanhol** to speak English/Spanish. -**2.** [dizer] to say; ~ **que** to say that; ~ **bem/mal de** to speak well/ill of; ~ **bobagem** to talk nonsense. -**3.** [contar]: ~ **algo (a alguém)** to tell (sb) sthg.

➡ **falar-se** vp -**1.** [dialogar] to talk. -**2.** [estar em boas relações] to be talking to one another; **não se** ~ to not be talking to one another.

falatório [fala'tɔrju] m -**1.** [ruído] voices (pl). -**2.** [discurso] diatribe. -**3.** [maledicência] slander.

falecer [fale'se(x)] vi to pass away.

falecido, da [fale'sidu, da] ◇ adj [pessoa] deceased. ◇ m, f [pessoa] deceased.

falência [fa'lēnsja] f bankruptcy; **abrir** ~ to declare o.s. bankrupt; **ir à** ~ to go bankrupt; **levar à** ~ to bankrupt.

falésia [fa'lɛzja] f cliff.

falha [ˈfaʎa] f -**1.** [fenda] fault. -**2.** [defeito] defect. -**3.** [omissão] omission.

falhar [fa'ʎa(x)] ◇ vt -**1.** [errar] to fail. -**2.** [faltar com - promessa] to break; [- obrigação] to fail. ◇ vi -**1.** [não funcionar, fracassar] to fail. -**2.** [não acertar] to miss.

falho, lha [ˈfaʎu, ʎa] adj -**1.** [defeituoso] faulty. -**2.** [deficiente] flawed.

falido, da [fa'lidu, da] ◇ adj bankrupt. ◇ m, f bankrupt.

falir [fa'li(x)] vi -**1.** [abrir falência] to go bankrupt. -**2.** [fracassar] to fail.

falo [ˈfalu] m phallus.

falsário, ria [faw'sarju, rja] m -**1.** [falsificador] forger. -**2.** [perjuro] perjurer.

falsidade [fawsi'dadʒi] f -**1.** [fingimento] hypocrisy. -**2.** [mentira] lie; ~ **ideológica** false declaration.

falsificação [fawsifika'sãw] (pl -ões) f forgery.

falsificar [fawsifi'ka(x)] vt -**1.** [ger] to forge. -**2.** [adulterar - alimento, remédio] to adulterate; [- documento] to falsify. -**3.** [desvirtuar] to misrepresent.

falso, sa [ˈfawsu, sa] adj -**1.** [ger] false. -**2.** [falsificado] forged. -**3.** [fingido] deceitful. -**4.** [errôneo] erroneous. -**5.** loc: **pisar em** ~ to miss one's step.

falta [ˈfawta] f -**1.** [carência] lack; **ter** ~ **de** to be in need of; ~ **de ar** airlessness;

~ **de respeito** lack of respect. -**2.** [ausência] absence; **sentir** ~ **de algo/alguém** to miss sthg/sb; **na** ~ **de** for lack of; **sem** ~ without fail. -**3.** [erro, pecado] fault. -**4.** ESP foul.

faltar [faw'ta(x)] vi -**1.** [não haver]: **falta água/luz/comida** there's no water/electricity/food; **falta honestidade** there's a lack of honesty; ~ **sal/tempero** to need salt/seasoning. -**2.** [estar ausente] to be absent; **ontem faltaram cinco alunos** yesterday five students were absent; **falta o Hélio** Hélio's not here, Hélio's missing. -**3.** [ser escasso]: **falta-lhe dinheiro** he hasn't got enough money; **falta-lhe saúde** he's not too healthy; **faltou-lhe força de vontade** he lacked the willpower; **nada nos falta** we have everything we need, we want for nothing. -**4.** [restar - por fazer]: **só falta fazermos o bolo** all that's left for us to do is make the cake; **falta pintarmos a casa** we've still got to paint the house; **só me faltava essa!** fam that's all I needed!; [- por decorrer]: **faltam dois meses para o festival** there are two months to go before the festival; **falta uma semana para irmos embora** it's a week until we go. -**5.** [omitir-se]: **nunca faltou quando a família precisava** he was always there when the family needed him. -**6.** [morrer] to die.

fama [ˈfãma] f -**1.** [celebridade] fame. -**2.** [reputação] reputation.

família [fa'milja] f family; **ser de** ~ to run in the family.

familiar [fami'lja(x)] (pl -es) ◇ adj -**1.** [relativo à família] family (antes de subst). -**2.** [conhecido] familiar. ◇ mf [pessoa da família]: **um** ~ a family member; **os** ~ **es** the family (sg).

familiaridade [familjari'dadʒi] f -**1.** [intimidade] familiarity. -**2.** [informalidade] informality.

familiarizar [familjari'za(x)] vt to familiarize.

➡ **familiarizar-se** vp: ~ -**se com algo/alguém** to familiarize o.s. with sthg/sb.

faminto, ta [fa'mĩntu, ta] adj famished.

famoso, osa [fa'mozu, ɔza] adj famous.

fanático, ca [fa'natʃiku, ka] ◇ adj -**1.** POL & RELIG fanatical. -**2.** [apaixonado]: ~ **(por)** crazy (about). ◇ m, f [pessoa] fanatic.

fanfarronice [fãnwfaxo'nisi] f [gabarolice] boasting.

fanho, nha [ˈfaɲu, ɲal, **fanhoso, sa** [fã'nozu, za] adj -**1.** [voz] nasal. -**2.** [pessoa] with a nasal-sounding voice.

fantasia [fãnta'zia] f -**1.** [coisa imaginada]

fantasy; **jóia de** ~ [bijuteria] costume jewellery. **- 2.** [imaginação] fancy. **- 3.** [capricho] whim. **- 4.** [traje] fancy dress; ~ **de árabe/pirata** Arab/pirate costume. **- 5.** MÚS fantasia.

fantasiar [fãnta'zja(x)] vt **- 1.** [imaginar] to imagine. **- 2.** [devanear] to daydream.
➡ **fantasiar-se** vp: ~-**se (de)** to dress up (as).

fantasioso, osa [fãta'zjozu, ɔza] adj fanciful.

fantasma [fãn'taʒma] m **- 1.** [espectro] ghost. **- 2.** [alucinação] phantom. **- 3.** fig [coisa terrível] spectre.

fantástico, ca [fãn'taʃtʃiku, ka] adj **- 1.** [ger] fantastic. **- 2.** fam [ótimo] fantastic.

fantoche [fãn'tɔʃi] m puppet.

FAQs (abrev de **Frequently Asked Questions**) fpl FAQs.

FARC (abrev de **Forças Armadas Revolucionárias da Colômbia**) f FARC.

farda ['faxda] f [uniforme] uniform.

fardo ['faxdu] m **- 1.** [carga] load. **- 2.** fig [peso] burden.

farejar [fare'ʒa(x)] <> vt to sniff. <> vi [tomar o faro] to pick up the scent.

farelo [fa'rɛlu] m **- 1.** [de pão] crumb. **- 2.** [de cereal] husk; ~ **de trigo** wheat bran.

farfalhar [faxfa'ʎa(x)] vi to rustle.

farinha [fa'riɲa] f: ~ (**de mesa** OU **de mandioca**) cassava flour; ~ **de rosca** toasted breadcrumbs; ~ **de trigo** wheat flour.

farmacêutico, ca [farma'sewtʃiku, ka] <> adj pharmaceutical. <> m, f pharmacist.

farmácia [fax'masja] f **- 1.** [ger] pharmacy. **- 2.** [coleção de medicamentos] first-aid box OU cabinet.

faro ['faru] m **- 1.** [olfato] sense of smell. **- 2.** fig [intuição] nose.

farofa [fa'rɔfa] f CULIN fried manioc flour.

farol [fa'rɔw] (pl **-óis**) m **- 1.** [para navegantes] lighthouse. **- 2.** AUTO headlight; ~ **alto/baixo** full/low beam.

farolete [farɔ'letʃi] m AUTO indicator; ~ **dianteiro** sidelight; ~ **traseiro** rear light.

farpa ['faxpa] f **- 1.** [de madeira] splinter. **- 2.** [metálica] shard. **- 3.** fam [crítica] barb.

farpado, da [fax'padu, da] adj ▷ **arame**.

farra ['faxa] f binge.

farrapo [fa'xapu] m [trapo] rag; **estar um** ~ fig [coisa] to be ragged; [pessoa] to be in rags.

farsa ['faxsa] f **- 1.** TEATRO farce. **- 2.** fig [fraude] sham.

farsante [fax'sãntʃi] mf **- 1.** [pessoa sem palavra] fraud. **- 2.** [pessoa brincalhona] buffoon.

fartar [fax'ta(x)] vt [saciar] to satiate.
➡ **fartar-se** vp **- 1.** [saciar-se]: ~-**se (de algo)** to gorge (on sthg). **- 2.** [cansar-se]: ~-**se (de algo/alguém)** to have had enough of sthg/sb.

farto, ta ['faxtu, ta] adj **- 1.** [saciado] replete. **- 2.** [abundante] lavish. **- 3.** [cansado]: **estar** ~ (**de algo/alguém**) to be fed up (with sthg/sb).

fartura [fax'tura] f [abundância] abundance; ~ **de algo** abundance of sthg.

fascículo [fa'sikulu] m [de publicação] fascicle.

fascinante [fasi'nãntʃi] adj **- 1.** [cativante] fascinating. **- 2.** [deslumbrante] amazing.

fascinar [fasi'na(x)] <> vt [cativar] to fascinate. <> vi [deslumbrar] to delight.

fascínio [fa'sinju] m [atração] fascination.

fascismo [fa'siʒmu] m fascism.

fase ['fazi] f **- 1.** [ger] phase. **- 2.** ASTRON: **as** ~**s da Lua** the phases of the moon.

fastidioso, osa [faʃtʃi'dʒjozu, ɔza] adj fastidious.

FAT (abrev de **Fundo de Amparo ao Trabalhador**) m Brazilian fund for the support of workers.

fatal [fa'taw] (pl **-ais**) adj **- 1.** [mortal] fatal. **- 2.** [inevitável] inevitable.

fatalidade [fatali'dadʒi] f **- 1.** [destino] fate. **- 2.** [desgraça] misfortune.

fatia [fa'tʃia] f slice.

fatiado, da [fa'tʃiadu, da] adj sliced.

fatigante [fatʃi'gãntʃi] adj **- 1.** [cansativo] tiresome. **- 2.** [enfadonho] tedious.

fatigar [fatʃi'ga(x)] vt **- 1.** [cansar] to tire. **- 2.** [enfadar] to bore.
➡ **fatigar-se** vp **- 1.** [cansar-se] to tire. **- 2.** [enfadar-se] to become bored.

fato ['fatu] m [ger] fact.
➡ **de fato** loc adv in fact.

fator [fa'to(x)] (mpl **-res**) m factor; ~ **Rh** rhesus factor.

fatura [fa'tura] f invoice.

faturamento [fatura'mẽntu] m **- 1.** COM turnover. **- 2.** [fatura] invoicing.

faturar [fatu'ra(x)] <> vt **- 1.** [mercadorias]: ~ **algo a alguém** to invoice sb for sthg. **- 2.** [dinheiro]: **faturou um bom dinheiro** he got a good price. **- 3.** fam [obter] to land. <> vi fam [ganhar dinheiro] to rake it in.

fauna ['fawna] f fauna.

faustoso, sa [fawʃ'tozu, ɔza] adj [luxuoso] sumptuous.

fava ['fava] f: **ser** ~**s contadas** to be a sure thing; **mandar alguém às** ~**s** to send sb on their way.

favela [fa'vɛla] f slum.

favelado, da [fave'ladu, da] m, f slum dweller.

favo ['favu] m honeycomb.

favor [fa'vo(x)] (pl -es) m -1. [ger] favour UK, favor US; fazer um ~ para alguém to do sb a favour UK, to do sb a favor US; pedir um ~ a alguém to ask a favour of sb UK, to ask a favor of sb US; por ~ please; por ~, que horas são? excuse me, what time is it?; fam [em repriminda] do me a favour!; quer fazer o ~ de se calar? would you kindly shut up! -2. [benefício]: a ~ de in favour of UK, in favor of US.

favorável [favo'ravew] (pl -eis) adj: ~ (a algo/a fazer algo) favourable (to sthg/to doing sthg).

favorecer [favore'se(x)] vt -1. [ger] to favour UK, to favor US. -2. [melhorar] to improve.

favorito, ta [favo'ritu, ta] <> adj favourite UK, favorite US. <> m, f favourite UK, favorite US.

faxina [fa'ʃina] f bundle of twigs; fazer uma ~ to have a spring clean.

faxineiro, ra [faʃi'nejru, ra] m, f cleaner.

fax-modem (pl -dens) m fax-modem.

fazenda [fa'zẽnda] f -1. [propriedade rural] fazenda. -2. [de gado] cattle ranch. -3. [de café, cacau] plantation. -4. [tecido] cloth. -5. ECON revenue.

fazendeiro, ra [fazẽn'dejru, ra] m, f -1. [dono de fazenda] rancher. -2. [de café, cacau] planter. -3. [de gado] cattle rancher.

fazer [fa'ze(x)] <> vt -1. [produzir] to make; ~ muito barulho to make a lot of noise; ~ planos/um vestido to make plans/a dress; ~ uma pergunta to ask a question. -2. [comida] to cook. -3. [gerar] to produce. -4. [realizar]: estou fazendo um curso de computadores I'm taking a computer course; vamos ~ uma festa let's have a party. -5. [praticar] to do; você devia ~ mais exercício you should exercise more; faço jogging todas as manhãs I go jogging every morning. -6. [cama] to make; ~ a cama to make the bed. -7. [transformar] to make; ~ alguém feliz to make sb happy. -8. [anos]: faço anos amanhã it's my birthday tomorrow; fazemos cinco anos de casados we've been married (for) five years. -9. [obrigar] to make; ~ alguém fazer algo to make sb do sthg; ~ alguém rir/chorar to make sb laugh/cry. -10. [cálculo, conta] to do; faz a conta para ver quanto é work out the check to see what it comes to. <> vi -1. [causar]: ~ bem/mal a algo to be good/bad for sthg; ~ bem/mal a alguém [coisa] to be good/bad for sb; ~ mal a alguém [pessoa] to hurt sb. -2. [obrigar]: faça (com) que ele venha make him come; [imaginar]: ~ de conta que ... to pretend that ... <> v impess -1.: faz frio/calor it's cold/hot. -2. [tempo]: faz um ano que não o vejo it's been a year since I last saw him; faz tempo que estou à espera I've been waiting for a while; o Sérgio partiu faz três meses Sérgio left three months ago. -3. [importar]: não faz mal se está quebrado it doesn't matter if it's broken; tanto faz it doesn't matter.

➤ **fazer-se** vp [preparar-se] to be made; [ser correto]: é assim que se faz that's the way to do it; ~-se com [ser preparado com] to be made with.

➤ **fazer-se de** vp + prep [pretender ser]: ele gosta de ~-se de importante he likes to act important; ~-se de tolo to act stupid; ~-se de desentendido to feign ignorance.

FBI (abrev de Federal Bureau of Investigation) m FBI.

fé ['fɛ] f [ger] faith; de boa ~ in good faith; de má ~ dishonestly.

FEBEM (abrev de Fundação Estadual do Bem-Estar do Menor) f organization set up by individual states in Brazil for the rehabilitation of young offenders.

Febraban (abrev de Federação Brasileira de Associações de Bancos) f Brazilian banking representative body.

febre ['fɛbri] f -1. MED fever; ~ amarela yellow fever; ~ do feno hayfever. -2. fig [mania] mania.

febril [fe'briw] (pl -is) adj feverish.

fechado, da [fe'ʃadu, da] adj -1. [ger] closed. -2. [pessoa] reticent. -3. AUTO [sinal] red light. -4. [tempo, céu] overcast. -5. [mato] dense. -6. [expressão] blank.

fechadura [feʃa'dura] f lock.

fechar [fe'fa(x)] <> vt -1. [ger] to close. -2. AUTO to cut in front of. <> vi -1. [cicatrizar-se] to close. -2. [tempo] to turn close. -3. [sinal de trânsito] to turn red. -4. [parar de funcionar] to close down.

➤ **fechar-se** vp -1. [encerrar-se] to close o.s. off. -2. [retrair-se] to shut o.s. off.

fecho ['feʃu] m -1. [de roupa] fastening; ~ ecler zip. -2. [de porta, bolsa] catch. -3. [término] end.

fécula ['fɛkula] f starch.

fecundar [fekũn'da(x)] vt to fertilize.

feder [fe'de(x)] vi to stink; não ~ nem cheirar to be wishy-washy.

federação [federaˈsãw] (*pl* -ões) *f* federation.

federal [fedeˈraw] (*pl* -ais) *adj* -1. [da Federação] federal. -2. *fam* [enorme] huge.

federativo, va [federaˈtʃivu, va] *adj* federalist.

fedor [feˈdo(x)] *m* stench.

fedorento, ta [fedoˈrẽntu, ta] *adj* stinking.

feijão [fejˈʒãw] (*pl* -ões) *m* bean.

feijão-fradinho [fejʒãwfraˈdʒiɲul] (*pl* feijões-fradinhos) *m* black-eyed bean.

feijão-preto [fejʒãwˈpretul] (*pl* feijões-pretos) *m* black bean.

feijão-tropeiro [fejʒãwtroˈpejrul] (*pl* feijões-tropeiros) *m* bean casserole.

feijoada [fejˈʒwada] *f typical Brazilian dish made with black beans, pork, sausage and vegetables.*

feio, feia [ˈfejo, ˈfeja] *adj* -1. [ger] ugly. -2. [tempo] nasty.
➡ **feio** *adv*: **fazer** ~ [dar vexame] to behave badly; **ficar** ~ [dar má impressão] to be rude.

feira [ˈfejra] *f* [ger] fair; ~ **livre** vegetable market.

feiticeiro, ra [fejtʃiˈsejru, ral] <> *adj* [encantador] bewitching. <> *m, f* [pessoa] sorcerer (*f* witch).

feitiço [fejˈtʃisu] *m* spell; **voltar-se o** ~ **contra o feiticeiro** to be hoist by one's own petard.

feitio [fejˈtʃiw] *m* -1. [forma] shape. -2. [natureza] make-up. -3. [de roupa] cut.

feito, ta [ˈfejtu, tal] <> *pp* ➡ **fazer**. <> *adj* -1. [concluído, pronto] finished. -2. [adulto]: **homem** ~ /**mulher feita** grown man/woman.
➡ **feito** <> *m* [façanha] deed. <> *conj* [tal qual] just like.

feixe [ˈfejʃil] *m* -1. [molho] bunch. -2. [de luz] beam.

fel [ˈfew] *m* -1. [ger] bitterness. -2. [bílis] bile.

felicidade [felisiˈdadʒil] *f* -1. [ventura] happiness. -2. [êxito] success. -3. [boa sorte] good luck.
➡ **felicidades** *fpl* congratulations.

felicíssimo, ma [feliˈsisimu, mal] *superl* ➡ **feliz**.

felicitação [felisitaˈsãw] (*pl* -ões) *f* praise.
➡ **felicitações** *fpl* congratulations.

felino, na [feˈlinu, nal] <> *adj* -1. [ger] feline. -2. *fig* [traiçoeiro] sly. <> *m* [animal] feline.

feliz [feˈliʒ] (*pl* -es) *adj* -1. [ger] happy; **ser** ~ (**em algo**) to be lucky (in sthg); ~ **aniversário** happy birthday; **Feliz**

Natal happy Christmas *UK*, merry Christmas *US*. -2. [oportuno] good. -3. [bem-sucedido] successful.

felizmente [feliʒˈmẽntʃil] *adv* -1. [por felicidade] luckily. -2. [de modo feliz] happily.

feltro [ˈfewtrul] *m* felt.

fêmea [ˈfemja] *f* female.

feminilidade [feminiliˈdadʒil] *f* femininity.

feminino, na [femiˈninu, nal] *adj* feminine.
➡ **feminino** *m* GRAM feminine.

feminismo [femiˈniʒmul] *m* feminism.

feminista [femiˈniʃta] <> *adj* feminist. <> *mf* feminist.

fêmur [ˈfemu(x)] *m* femur.

fenda [ˈfẽnda] *f* -1. [rachadura] crack. -2. GEOL crevice.

fender [fẽnˈde(x)] *vt* to split.
➡ **fender-se** *vp* to split.

fenecer [feneˈse(x)] *vi* -1. [extinguir-se] to die out. -2. [morrer] to die. -3. [murchar] to wilt.

feno [ˈfenul] *m* hay.

fenomenal [fenomeˈnaw] (*pl* -ais) *adj* -1. [maravilhoso] wonderful. -2. [surpreendente] phenomenal.

fenômeno [feˈnomenul] *m* phenomenon.

fera [ˈfera] *f* -1. *fig* [animal] wild animal. -3. *fam fig* [pessoa perita] ace; **ser (uma)** ~ **em algo** *fam fig* to be an ace at sthg.

féretro [ˈfɛretrul] *m* coffin.

feriado [feˈrjadul] *m* (public) holiday.

férias [ˈfɛrjaʃ] *fpl* holidays *UK*, vacation (*sg*) *US*; **de** ~ on holiday *UK*, on vacation *US*; **entrar/sair de** ~ to go on holiday *UK*, to go on vacation *US*.

ferida [feˈrida] *f* wound.

ferido, da [feˈridu, dal] <> *adj* -1. [machucado] wounded. -2. [magoado] wounded. <> *m, f* [pessoa] injured person; **os** ~ **s** the injured.

ferimento [feriˈmẽntul] *m* injury.

ferir [feˈri(x)] *vt* -1. [machucar] to wound. -2. *fig* [magoar] to wound.
➡ **ferir-se** *vp* -1. [machucar-se] to hurt o.s. -2. *fig* [magoar-se]: ~**-se com** to be wounded by.

fermentar [fexmẽnˈta(x)] <> *vt* to ferment. <> *vi* to ferment.

fermento [fexˈmẽntul] *m* yeast; ~ **em pó** powdered yeast.

Fernando de Noronha *m National Marine Park situated off the coast of Rio Grande do Norte in Brazil.*

ferocidade [ferosiˈdadʒil] *f* ferocity.

ferocíssimo, ma [feroˈsisimu, mal] *superl* ➡ **feroz**.

feroz [fe'rɔʃl] (*pl* **-es**) *adj* fierce.

ferradura [fexa'dura] *f* horseshoe.

ferragem [fe'xaʒẽ] (*pl* **-ns**) *f* **-1.** [peças] hardware. **-2.** [guarnição] ironwork.

ferramenta [fexa'mẽ̃ta] *f* tool.

ferramental [fexa'mẽ̃taw] (*pl* **-ais**) *m* tool kit.

ferrão [fe'xãw] (*pl* **-ões**) *m* **-1.** [de inseto] sting. **-2.** [aguilhão] barb.

ferreiro [fe'xejru] *m* blacksmith.

ferrenho, nha [fe'xeɲu, ɲa] *adj* **-1.** [inflexível] iron. **-2.** [obstinado] passionate.

férreo, rrea ['fexju, xja] *adj* iron.

ferro ['fexul *m* **-1.** [material] iron; **de ~** *fig* [vontade, punhos] of iron; **~ batido** wrought iron; **~ fundido** cast iron; **~ ondulado** corrugated iron; **~ velho** [sucata] scrap metal. **-2.** [aparelho]: **~ (de passar)** iron; **passar a ~** to iron.

ferroar [fe'xwa(x)] <> *vt* **-1.** [picar] to sting. **-2.** [criticar] to criticize. <> *vi* **-1.** [picar] to sting. **-2.** [latejar, doer] to really hurt.

ferrões [fe'xõjʃl *pl* ▷ **ferrão**.

ferrolho [fe'xoʎu] *m* bolt.

ferro-velho [,fexu'vɛʎu] (*pl* **ferros-velhos**) *m* **-1.** [estabelecimento] scrapyard. **-2.** [sucata] scrap metal.

ferrovia [fexo'via] *f* railway *UK*, railroad *US*.

ferroviário, ria [fexo'vjarju, ja] <> *adj* railway *UK*, railroad *US*. <> *m, f* railway employee *UK*, railroad employee *US*.

ferrugem [fe'xuʒẽ] *f* rust.

fértil ['fɛxtiw] (*pl* **-eis**) *adj* **-1.** [terreno, período] fertile. **-2.** [pessoa] productive.

fertilidade [,fextʃili'dadʒi] *f* **-1.** [de terra, pessoa] fertility. **-2.** [abundância] abundance.

fertilizante [fextʃili'zãntʃi] <> *adj* fertilizing; **método ~** method of fertilization. <> *m* fertilizer.

fertilizar [fextʃili'za(x)] *vt* to fertilize.

fervente [fex'vẽntʃi] *adj* boiling.

ferver [fex've(x)] <> *vt* to boil; **~ algo em fogo baixo** to simmer on a low heat. <> *vi* to become excited; **~ de raiva** *fig* to be steaming with anger.

fervilhar [fexvi'ʎa(x)] *vi* **-1.** [ferver] to boil. **-2.** *fig* [pulular]: **~ (de)** to swarm (with). **-3.** *fig* [de excitação] to bubble.

fervor [fex'vo(x)] *m* fervour *UK*, fervor *US*.

fervoroso, osa [fexvo'rozu, ɔza] *adj* **-1.** [ardoroso] fervent. **-2.** [dedicado] devoted.

festa ['fɛʃta] *f* **-1.** [reunião] party. **-2.** [comemoração]: **~ da Independência** Independence Day party. **-3.** [alegria] thrill. **-4.** [carinho]: **fazer ~ (s) (em)** to cuddle up to.

➡ **festas** *fpl* [Natal e Ano-Novo] festive season (*sg*).

festejar [feʃte'ʒa(x)] *vt* to celebrate.

festejo [feʃ'teʒu] *m* celebration.

festim [feʃ'tʃĩl (*pl* **-ns**) *m* **-1.** [festa] feast. **-2.** [cartucho sem bala]: **tiro de ~** blank shot.

festival [feʃtʃi'vawl (*pl* **-ais**) *m* **-1.** [festa] festival. **-2.** *fig* [grande quantidade] load.

festividade [feʃtʃivi'dadʒi] *f* festivity.

festivo, va [feʃ'tʃivu, va] *adj* festive.

fetiche [fe'tʃiʃil *m* fetish.

fétido, da ['fɛtʃidu, da] *adj* fetid.

feto ['fɛtul *m* foetus *UK*, fetus *US*.

fev. (*abrev de* **fevereiro**) Feb.

fevereiro [feve'rejrul *m* February; *veja também* **setembro**.

fezes ['fɛzif] *fpl* faeces *UK*, feces *US*.

FGTS (*abrev de* **Fundo de Garantia por Tempo de Serviço**) *m monthly contribution towards the support of sacked and unemployed workers in Brazil.*

FGV (*abrev de* **Fundação Getúlio Vargas**) *f Brazilian private educational organization for improvement in public administration.*

FIA (*abrev de* **Federação Internacional de Automobilismo**) *f* FIA.

fiação [fja'sãw] (*pl* **-ões**) *f* **-1.** ELETR wiring. **-2.** [fábrica] spinning mill.

fiado, da ['fjadu, da] *adj* **-1.** [vendido a crédito] sold on credit (*depois do subst*). **-2.** [conversa]: **isso é conversa fiada** that's far-fetched.

➡ **fiado** *adv* [a crédito] on credit.

fiador, ra [fja'do(x), ra] *m, f* guarantor.

fiambre ['fjãnbril *m* ham.

fiança ['fjãnsa] *f* **-1.** [garantia] guarantee. **-2.** *JUR* bail; **sob ~** on bail; **pagar ~** to post bail.

fiapo ['fjapul *m* thread.

fiar l'fja(x)] *vt* [reduzir a fio] to spin.

➡ **fiar-se** *vp* [confiar em]: **~-se em alguém/algo** to trust sb/sthg.

fiasco ['fjaʃkul *m* fiasco.

fibra ['fibral *f* [ger] fibre *UK*, fiber *US*; **~ óptica** fibre optics (*pl*) *UK*, fiber optics (*pl*) *US*; **~ de vidro** fibreglass *UK*, fiberglass *US*.

fibroso, sa [fi'brozu, ɔza] *adj* fibrous.

ficar [fi'ka(x)] *vi* **-1.** [ger] to remain; **só ficaram duas garrafas de refrigerante** there are only two bottles of soda left. **-2.** [permanecer] to stay; **~ sentado/de pé** to remain seated/standing; **~ por isso mesmo** to remain the same. **-3.** [estar situado] to be. **-4.** [tornar-se] to become; ~ **com frio** to be cold; ~ **feliz com algo** to be happy about sthg; ~ **bom** [de doença] to recover; [pintura etc.] to be good. **- 5.** [ser adiado]: ~ **para** to leave until. **- 6.** [combinar]: ~ **de fazer algo** to agree to do sthg. **- 7.** [persistir]: ~ **fazendo algo** to go on doing sthg. **- 8.** [prometer]: ~ **de fazer algo** to promise to do sthg. **- 9.** [custar]: ~ **em** to come to. **-10.** [ser]: **não fica bem** it's not right. **-11.** [assentar a]: ~ **bem em** ou **para alguém** to look good on sb; ~ **bem de algo** to look good in sthg. **-12.** [vir a]: ~ **sabendo de algo** to get to know sthg. **-13.** *loc*: ~ **atrás** [ser inferior] to be behind.

ficção [fik'sãw] (*pl* -ões) *f* fiction.

ficcional [fik'sionawl] (*pl* -ais) *adj LITER* fictional.

ficha ['fiʃa] *f* **-1.** [ger] file. **-2.** [de telefone] plug. **-3.** [de jogo] token.

fichar [fi'ʃa(x)] *vt* to file.

fichário [fi'ʃarju] *m* **-1.** [ger] file. **-2.** [móvel] filing cabinet.

fictício, cia [fik'tʃisju, sja] *adj* fictitious.

fidalgo, ga [fi'dawgu, ga] *m, f* noble.

fidalguia [fidaw'gia] *f* nobility.

fidelidade [fideli'dadʒi] *f* **-1.** [lealdade] faithfulness. **-2.** [conjugal] fidelity. **-3.** [precisão] precision; **com** ~ faithfully.

fiel ['fjɛw] (*pl* -éis) *adj* **-1.** [ger] faithful. **-2.** [constante] loyal.

◆ **fiéis** *mpl RELIG*: **os fiéis** the faithful (*pl inv*).

FIFA (*abrev de* **Féderation Internationale de Football Association**) *f* FIFA.

figa ['figaʃ] *f* charm.

fígado ['figadu] *m* liver.

figo ['figu] *m* fig.

figura [fi'gura] *f* **-1.** [ger] figure; **ser uma** ~ *fam* to be a character; **mudar de** ~ to change. **-2.** [em carta] picture card, court card. **-3.** *GRAM*: ~ **de linguagem** figure of speech.

figurante [figu'rãntʃi] *mf* extra.

figurão [figu'rãw] (*pl* -ões) *m* bigwig.

figurar [figu'ra(x)] ◇ *vt* **-1.** [representar] to represent. **-2.** [ter a forma de] to look like. **-3.** [aparentar] to look. ◇ *vi* [fazer parte]: ~ **em/entre** to appear on/among.

figurino [figu'rinu] *m* **-1.** [molde] pattern. **-2.** [revista] fashion magazine. **-3.** *CINE , TEATRO & TV* [exemplo] model. **-4.** *fig*: **como manda o** ~ as it should be.

fila ['fila] *f* [fileira - de pessoas] queue *UK*, line *US*; [- de cadeiras] row; **em** ~ in line; **fazer** ~ to queue *UK*, to form a line *US*; ~ **indiana** single file.

filamento [fila'mẽntul] *m* filament.

filantropia [filãntro'pia] *f* philanthropy.

filantrópico, ca [filãn'tropiku, ka] *adj* philanthropic.

filarmônico, ca [filax'moniku, ka] *adj* philharmonic.

◆ **filarmônica** *f* philharmonic.

filatelia [filate'lia] *f* philately, stamp collecting.

filé [fi'lɛ] *m* fillet; ~ **mignon** filet mignon.

fileira [fi'lejra] *f* row.

◆ **fileiras** *fpl MIL* ranks.

filha ['fiʎa] *f* ▷ **filho**.

filho, lha ['fiʎu, 'fiʎa] *m, f* **-1.** [descendente] son; ~ **adotivo** adopted son; ~ **da mãe** *vulg* bastard; ~ **da puta** *vulg* son of a bitch. **-2.** *loc*: **ter um** ~ *fig* to have a turn, to have a fainting fit; **ser** ~ **único de mãe solteira** *fig* to be unique.

filhote [fi'ʎotʃi] *m* **-1.** [de animal - de leão, urso] cub; [- de cachorro] puppy. **-2.** [filho] young son.

filial [fi'ljaw] (*pl* -ais) ◇ *adj* [amor] filial. ◇ *f* [sucursal] branch.

filiar [fi'ʎa(x)] *vt*: ~ **alguém a algo** to sign sb up to sthg.

◆ **filiar-se** *vp*: ~-**se a algo** to sign o.s. up to sthg.

Filipinas [fili'pinaʃ] *npl*: **(as)** ~ the Philippines.

filipino, na [fili'pinu, na] ◇ *adj* Filipino. ◇ *m, f* Filipino.

◆ **filipino** *m* [língua] Filipino.

filmadora [fiwma'dora] *f* movie camera.

filmagem [fiw'maʒẽ] (*pl* -ns) *f* filming.

filmar [fiw'ma(x)] ◇ *vt* to film. ◇ *vi* to film.

filme ['fiwmi] *m* **-1.** [obra cinematográfica] film *UK*, movie *US*. **-2.** *loc*: **queimar o** ~ to ruin one's image.

filmografia [fiwmogra'fia] *f* filmography.

filões [fi'lõjʃ] *mpl* ▷ **filão**.

filologia [filolo'ʒia] *f* philology.

filosofia [filozo'fia] *f* philosophy.

filósofo, fa [fi'lozofu, fi'lozofaʃ] *m, f* philosopher.

filtragem [fiwtra'ʒẽ] (*pl* -ns) *f* [filtração] filtration.

filtrar [fiw'tra(x)] *vt* **-1.** [purificar] to filter. **-2.** [selecionar] to select.

filtro ['fiwtru] *m* filter; ~ **de ar** air filter.

fim [fi] (*pl* -ns) *m* [ger] end; ~ **de semana** weekend; **no** ~ **das contas** after all; **ser o** ~ **(da picada)** to be the last straw; **por** ~ finally.

◆ **a fim de** *loc prep* in order to; **estar a** ~ **de fazer algo** to be planning on doing sthg.

final [fi'naw] (*pl* -ais) ⬦ *adj* final; **minuto** ~ last minute; **ponto** ~ full stop. ⬦ *m* end. ⬦ *f ESP* final.

finalidade [finali'dadʒi] *f* end.

finalista [fina'liʃta] *mf* finalist.

finalizar [finali'za(x)] ⬦ *vt* [concluir] to conclude. ⬦ *vi FUT* [fazer gol] to score.

finanças [fi'nãnsaʃ] *fpl* [situação financeira] finances.

financeiro, ra [finãn'sejru, ra] *adj* financial.
　◆ **financeira** *f* [firma] finance company.

financiamento [finãnsja'mẽntu] *m* financing.

financiar [finãn'sja(x)] *vt* to finance.

fineza [fi'neza] *f* -1. [espessura] fineness. -2. [gentileza] politeness.

fingimento [fĩʒi'mẽntu] *m* pretence *UK*, pretense *US*.

fingir [fĩ'ʒi(x)] ⬦ *vt* to fake. ⬦ *vi* to pretend.
　◆ **fingir-se** *vp*: ~-se de algo to pretend to be sthg.

finito, ta [fi'nitu, ta] *adj* finite.

finitude [fini'tudʒi] *f* [limitação] finite nature.

finlandês, esa [fĩlãn'dejʃ, eza] ⬦ *adj* Finnish. ⬦ *m, f* Finnish person, Finn.
　◆ **finlandês** *m* [língua] Finnish.

Finlândia [fĩ'lãndʒja] *n* Finland.

fino, na ['finu, na] *adj* -1. [ger] fine. -2. [agudo] shrill. -3. [refinado] elegant. -4. *loc*: tirar uma ~ de to come within a hair's breadth of.

fins [fĩʃ] *mpl* ▷ fim.

finura [fi'nura] *f* -1. [espessura] fineness. -2. [refinamento] refinement.

fio ['fiw] *m* -1. [ger] thread. -2. *ELETR* wire. -3. [gume] blade. -4. [filete] trickle.
　◆ **a fio** *loc adj*: dias/horas a ~ days/hours on end.
　◆ **sem fio** *loc adj* wireless.

fiorde ['fjoxdʒi] *m* fjord.

firewall ['fajex'uɔw] *m COMPUT* firewall.

firma ['fixma] *f* -1. *COM* firm. -2. [assinatura] signature.

firmar [fix'ma(x)] ⬦ *vt* -1. [fixar] to steady. -2. [assinar] to sign. -3. [estabelecer] to establish. -4. [basear]: ~ algo em algo to base sthg on sthg. ⬦ *vi* [estabilizar-se] to settle.
　◆ **firmar-se** *vp* to settle.

firme ['fixmi] *adj* -1. [ger] firm. -2. [fixo] steady, stable. -3. [constante] settled. -4. [estável] stable.

firmeza [fix'meza] *f* -1. [ger] firmness. -2. [estabilidade] steadiness, stability. -3. [segurança] soundness.

fiscal [fiʃ'kaw] (*pl* -ais) ⬦ *adj* [relativo ao fisco] fiscal. ⬦ *mf* -1. [aduaneiro] customs officer. -2. [supervisor - de impostos] inspector; [- de prova] invigilator.

fiscalizar [fiʃkali'za(x)] *vt* -1. [estabelecimento, obras] to oversee. -2. [prova] to invigilate.

fisco ['fiʃku] *m*: o ~ the public purse.

fisgar [fiʒ'ga(x)] *vt* -1. [peixe] to harpoon. -2. [pessoa] to understand.

físico, ca ['fiziku, ka] ⬦ *adj* [ger] physical. ⬦ *m, f FÍSICA* physicist.
　◆ **físico** *m* [corpo] physique.
　◆ **física** *f* [ciência] physics *(sg)*.

fisionomia [fizjono'mia] *f* features (*pl*), appearance; ela está com boa ~ she's looking well.

fisioterapia [fizjotera'pia] *f* physiotherapy.

fissura [fi'sura] *f* -1. *GEOL* fissure. -2. *fam* [gana] hankering.

fissurado, da [fisu'radu, da] *adj* -1. [rachado] cracked. -2. *fam* [maluco por]: ~ em mad about.

fita ['fita] *f* -1. [tira] ribbon; ~ durex® *ou* colante Sellotape® *UK*; Scotch tape® *US*; ~ de impressora typewriter ribbon; ~ isolante insulating tape; ~ métrica tape measure, measuring tape. -2. [filme] tape. -3. [cassete]: ~ de vídeo videotape; ~ virgem blank tape. -4. [manha] play-acting.

fivela [fi'vɛla] *f* -1. [fecho] buckle. -2. [de cabelo] hair clip.

fixador [fiksa'do(x)] (*pl* -es) *m* -1. [de cabelo] hairspray. -2. [de essência] fixing agent.

fixar [fik'sa(x)] *vt* -1. [prender] to fix. -2. [apreender] to make stick. -3. [estabelecer] to set.
　◆ **fixar-se** *vp* -1. [estabilizar-se] to be fixed. -2. [estabelecer residência] to settle. -3. [fitar]: ~ em to stare at.

fixo, xa ['fiksu, ksa] *adj* fixed.

flácido, da ['flasidu, da] *adj* flaccid.

flagelado, da [flaʒe'ladu, da] *adj* flogged.

flagelante [flaʒe'lãntʃi] *adj* -1. [chicote] searing. -2. [isolamento] punishing.

flagrante [fla'grãntʃi] ⬦ *adj* flagrant. ⬦ *m*: pegar em ~ (de algo) to catch in the act (of sthg); em ~ red-handed, in flagrante.

flagrar [fla'gra(x)] *vt* to catch in the act.

flambar [flã'ba(x)] *vt* to flambé.

flamejante [flame'ʒãntʃi] *adj* flaming.

flamenco, ca [fla'mẽŋku, ka] ⬦ *adj* flamenco.
　◆ **flamenco** *m* flamenco.

flâmula ['flãmula] *f* pennant.

flanco [ˈflãŋku] *m* flank.

flanela [flaˈnɛla] *f* flannel.

flanelinha [flaneˈliɲa] *mf fam unofficial car-park attendant.

flash [ˈflɛʃi] *(pl -es) m* flash.

flauta [ˈflawta] *f* flute; ~ **doce** tin whistle; ~ **transversa** transverse flute.

flecha [ˈflɛʃa] *f* arrow.

flechada [fleˈʃada] *f* -**1.** [arremesso] arrow shot. -**2.** [ferimento] arrow wound.

flertar [flexˈta(x)] *vi:* ~ **(com alguém)** to flirt (with sb).

fleuma [ˈflewma] *f* phlegm.

flexão [flekˈsãw] *(pl -ões) f* -**1.** [movimento] flexing. -**2.** *GRAM* inflexion.

flexibilidade [fleksibiliˈdadʒi] *f* flexibility.

flexibilização [fleksibilizaˈsãw] *(pl -ões) f* relaxation.

flexionado, da [fleksioˈnadu, da] *adj LING* inflected.

flexível [flekˈsivew] *(pl -eis) adj* flexible.

flexões [flekˈsõjʃ] *fpl* ⊳ **flexão**.

fliperama [flipeˈrãma] *m* -**1.** [máquina] pinball machine. -**2.** [estabelecimento] amusement arcade.

floco [ˈflɔku] *m* flake; ~ **de milho** cornflake; ~ **de neve** snowflake.

➡ **flocos** *mpl*: **sorvete de** ~ **s** chocolate chip ice-cream.

flor [ˈflo(x)] *(pl -es) f* -**1.** [pessoa boa]: **ser uma** ~ to be a gem. -**3.** *loc*: **a fina** ~ **de** the flower of.

floreado, da [floˈrjadu, da] *adj* flowery.

florescente [floreˈsẽtʃi] *adj* -**1.** [BOT - árvore] blossoming; [- planta] flowering. -**2.** *fig* [próspero] flowering.

florescer [floreˈse(x)] *vi* -**1.** [BOT - árvore] to blossom; [- planta] to flower. -**2.** *fig* [prosperar] to flower.

floresta [floˈrɛʃta] *f* forest.

florido, da [floˈridu, da] *adj* flower-filled.

florista [floˈriʃta] *mf* florist.

fluente [fluˈẽtʃi] *adj* fluent.

fluido, da [ˈflu'idu, ida] *adj* -**1.** [substância] fluid. -**2.** *fig* [fácil] flowing; **tráfego** ~ smooth-flowing traffic.

➡ **fluido** *m* fluid.

fluir [flwi(x)] *vi* to flow.

flúor [ˈfluo(x)] *m* fluoride.

flutuar [flu'twa(x)] *vi* -**1.** [ger] to float. -**2.** [variar] to fluctuate.

fluvial [fluˈvjaw] *(pl -ais) adj* river *(antes de subst).

fluxo [ˈfluksu] *m* -**1.** [ger] flow. -**2.** *COM*: ~ **de caixa** cash flow. -**3.** *MED*: ~ **menstrual** menstrual flow.

fluxograma [flukso'grama] *m* flow chart.

FM *(abrev de* **freqüência modulada***) m* FM.

FMI *(abrev de* **Fundo Monetário Internacional***) m* IMF.

fobia [foˈbia] *f* phobia.

foca [ˈfɔka] ⇔ *f ZOOL* seal. ⇔ *mf* [jornalista] cub reporter.

focalizar [fokaliˈza(x)], **focar** [foˈka(x)] *vt* to focus.

focinho [foˈsiɲu] *m* -**1.** [de suíno] snout. -**2.** [de cão] muzzle.

foco [ˈfɔku] *m* focus.

foder [ˈfode(x)] *vulg* ~ ⇔ *vt* [copular com] to fuck. ⇔ *vi* [copular] to fuck.

➡ **foder-se** *vp vulg* [dar-se mal] to fuck up.

fofo, fa [ˈfofu, fa] *adj* -**1.** [macio] soft. -**2.** [gracioso] cute.

fofoca [foˈfɔka] *f* gossip.

fofocar [fofoˈka(x)] *vi* to gossip.

fogão [foˈgãw] *(pl -ões) m* stove, cooker.

fogareiro [fogaˈrejru] *m* (paraffin) cooker, coal pot.

fogo [ˈfogu] *(pl fogos) m* -**1.** [ger] fire; **pegar** ~ to catch fire; **ser** ~ **(na roupa)** to mean trouble. -**2.** [excitação] flame. -**3.** [desejo sexual] sex drive. -**4.** [disparo]: **abrir** ~ to open fire; **fogo!** fire! -**5.** [pirotecnia]: ~**(s) de artifício** fireworks.

fogões [foˈgõjʃ] *mpl* ⊳ **fogão**.

fogoso, osa [foˈgozu, ɔza] *adj* -**1.** [arrebatado] fiery. -**2.** [sexualmente] aroused.

fogueira [foˈgejra] *f* bonfire.

foguete [foˈgetʃi] *m* rocket.

foguetório [fogeˈtɔrju] *m* noise of fireworks.

foice [ˈfojsi] *f* scythe.

folclore [fowˈklɔri] *m* folklore.

folclórico, ca [fowˈklɔriku, ka] *adj* folk.

fole [ˈfɔli] *m* bellows *(pl).*

fôlego [ˈfolegu] *m* -**1.** [respiração] breath; **perder o** ~ to lose one's breath. -**2.** *fig* [ânimo]: **recuperar o** ~ to recover one's breath.

folga [ˈfowga] *f* -**1.** [descanso] break; **dia de** ~ day off. -**2.** [abuso]: **que** ~**!** what a cheek! -**3.** [sobra de espaço] space. -**4.** [sobra de tempo] gap.

folha [ˈfoʎa] *f* -**1.** *BOT* leaf. -**2.** [página] page; ~ **de pagamento** pay sheet. -**3.** [chapa] plate. -**4.** [jornal] newspaper. -**5.** [lâmina] blade. -**6.** [pedaço de papel] sheet.

➡ **em folha** *loc adv*: **novo em** ~ brand new.

folhagem [foˈʎaʒẽ] *(pl -ns) f* foliage.

folheado, da [foˈʎadu, da] *adj* -**1.** [revestido]: ~ **a ouro/prata** gold-/silverplated. -**2.** *CULIN*: **massa folheada** puff pastry.

folhear [fo'ʎja(x)] vt to leaf through.

folheto [fo'ʎetu] m pamphlet.

folhinha [fo'ʎiɲa] f [calendário] calendar.

folia [fo'lia] f revelry.

folião, ona [fo'ljãw, ɔna] (mpl -ões, fpl -s) m, f reveller.

foliona [fo'ljona] f ⊳ folião.

fome ['fɔmi] f [ger] hunger; **estar com ~** to be hungry; **passar ~** to go hungry.

fomentar [fomēn'ta(x)] vt to foment.

fomento [fo'mēntu] m **-1.** MED poultice. **-2.** [estímulo] fomentation.

fone ['fɔni] (abrev de **telefone**) m phone.

fonético, ca [fo'nɛtʃiku, ka] adj phonetic.

➡ **fonética** f phonetics (sg).

fonoaudiologia [fonawdʒiolo'gia] f speech therapy.

fonte ['fõntʃi] ◇ f **-1.** [ger] source. **-2.** [chafariz] fountain. ◇ m COMPUT source code.

fora [fɔra] ◇ m **-1.** [gafe] gaffe; **dar um ~** to commit a gaffe. **-2.** fig [dispensa]: **dar um ~ em alguém** to rebuff sb; **fora!** get out! **-3.** loc: **dar o ~** [partir] to skedaddle. ◇ adv **-1.** [na parte exterior]: **do lado de ~** on the outside; **por ~** outside. **-2.** [ao ar livre]: **lá ~** outside. **-3.** [em outro lugar] away, out; **fui para ~ a semana passada** I went away last week; **jantei ~ ontem** I went out to dinner yesterday; **a família está ~ no momento** the family is out OU away at the moment; [no estrangeiro] abroad. **- 4.** fig [distanciado]: **~ de** out of; **estar ~ de si** to be beside o.s. ◇ prep [exceto] except for, apart from.

➡ **para fora** loc adv: **ela costura para ~** she takes sewing in.

➡ **por fora** loc adv **-1.** [cobrar, pagar]: **cobrar por ~** to receive on the side; **pagar por ~** to pay on the side. **-2.** [ignorante]: **estar por ~ (de)** to be unaware (of).

➡ **fora de série** loc adj [excepcional] exceptional.

foragido, da [fora'ʒidu, da] ◇ adj fugitive. ◇ m, f fugitive.

forasteiro, ra [foraʃ'tejru, ra] m, f foreigner.

forca ['foxka] f gallows (sg).

força ['foxsa] f **-1.** [ger] power. **-2.** [energia física, moral] strength; **ter ~ para fazer algo** to have (the) strength to do sthg; **~ de vontade** will power. **-3.** [violência] force; **à ~** by force. **-4.** [esforço]: **fazer ~** to try hard. **-5.** MIL force; **~ s armadas** armed forces. **-6.** [ânimo, apoio]: **dar ~ a alguém** to give support to sb.

forçado, da [fox'sadu, da] adj **-1.** [ger] forced. **-2.** [interpretação] far-fetched.

forçar [fur'sar] vt **-1.** [obrigar]: **~ alguém (a algo/a fazer algo)** to force sb (to sthg/to do sthg). **-2.** [arrombar] to force. **-3.** [obter por força] to (obtain by) force. **-4.** [vista, voz] to strain. **-5.** [desvirtuar] to misinterpret. **-6.** loc: **~ a barra** [insistir, pressionar] to force sb's hand.

➡ **forçar-se** vp: **~ -se a fazer algo** to force o.s. to do sthg, to make o.s. do sthg.

forçoso, osa [fox'sozu, ɔza] adj necessary.

forjado, da [fox'ʃadu, da] adj **-1.** [utensílio, metal] forged. **-2.** [notícia] fabricated.

forjar [fox'sa(x)] vt to forge.

forma ['fɔxma] f **-1.** [ger] form; **desta ~** in this way, thus. **-2.** [estado físico, feitio] shape; **em ~ de** in the shape of; **estar em ~** to be in shape.

➡ **de forma que** loc conj so that.

➡ **da mesma forma** loc adv similarly.

➡ **de forma alguma** loc adv in no way.

➡ **de tal forma** loc adv in such a way.

fôrma ['foxma] f **-1.** [ger] mould. **-2.** [molde] mould, cast. **-3.** [de sapato] last.

formação [foxma'sãw] (pl -ões) f **-1.** [ger] formation. **-2.** [educação] upbringing.

formado, da [fox'madu, da] adj **-1.** [constituído]: **~ por** made up of. **-2.** [graduado]: **ser ~ por** to be educated by.

formal [fox'maw] (pl -ais) adj formal.

formalidade [foxmali'dadʒi] f formality; **com ~** formally.

formão [fox'mãw] (pl -ões) m chisel.

formar [fox'ma(x)] ◇ vt **-1.** [ger] to form. **-2.** [educar] to educate. ◇ vi MIL [entrar em fila] to fall in.

➡ **formar-se** vp **-1.** [constituir-se] to form. **-2.** [graduar-se] to graduate.

formatar [foxma'ta(x)] vt COMPUT to format.

formato [fox'matu] m **-1.** [forma] shape. **-2.** [modelo] format.

fórmica ['fɔxmika] f formica®.

formidável [foxmi'davɛw] (pl -eis) adj **-1.** [fantástico] fantastic. **-2.** [imenso] formidable.

formiga [fox'miga] f ant.

formigar [foxmi'ga(x)] vi [coçar] to have pins and needles.

formigueiro [foxmi'gejru] m **-1.** [de formigas] anthill. **-2.** fig [multidão] swarm.

formoso, osa [fox'mozu, ɔza] adj beautiful.

fórmula ['fɔxmula] f **-1.** [ger] formula. **-2.** [modo] (polite) phrase, (politeness) formula. **-3.** AUTO: **~ um** Formula One.

formulário [foxmu'larju] *m* form; ~ **contínuo** COMPUT continuous stationery.

fornecedor, ra [foxnese'do(x), ra] (*mpl* **-es**, *fpl* **-s**) <> *adj* supplying. <> *m, f* supplier.

fornecer [foxne'se(x)] *vt* to supply.

fornecimento [foxnesi'mẽntu] *m* supply.

forno ['foxnu] *m* **-1.** CULIN oven; ~ **de microondas** microwave (oven). **-2.** [fornalha] kiln.

foro ['foru] *m* forum.

forra ['foxa] *f*: **ir à** ~ to take one's revenge.

forrar [fo'xa(x)] *vt* **-1.** [ger] to line. **-2.** [sofá, chão] to cover. **-3.** [parede] to paper.

forro ['foxu] *m* **-1.** [interno] lining. **-2.** [externo] cover.

forró [fo'xɔ] *m typical Brazilian dance of the north-east.*

fortalecer [foxtale'se(x)] *vt* to strengthen.

fortaleza [foxta'leza] *f* **-1.** [forte] fortress. **-2.** *fig* [bastião] fortress.

forte ['fɔxtʃi] <> *adj* **-1.** [ger] strong. **-2.** [piada, palavra, filme] crude. **-3.** [poderoso] powerful. **-4.** [versado]: **ser** ~ **em algo** to be strong at sthg. **-5.** [intenso - emoção, calor, dor] intense; [- chuva] heavy. **-6.** [violento] violent. <> *m* **-1.** [fortaleza] stronghold. **-2.** *fig* [ponto forte] strength. <> *adv* heavily.

fortuito, ta [fox'twitu, ta] *adj* fortuitous.

fortuna [fox'tuna] *f* fortune.

fosco, ca ['foʃku, ka] *adj* tarnished.

fósforo ['fɔʃfuru] *m* **-1.** QUÍM phosphor. **-2.** [palito] matchstick.

fossa ['fɔsa] *f* **-1.** [buraco] hole; ~ **nasal** nostril; ~ **das Marianas** Mariana Trench. **-2.** [esgoto] ditch. **-3.** *fig* [depressão] slump; **estar/entrar na** ~ to be down in the dumps.

fóssil ['fɔsiw] (*pl* **-eis**) *m* fossil.

fosso ['fosu] *m* ditch.

foto ['fɔtu] *f* photo.

fotocópia [foto'kɔpja] *f* photocopy.

fotocopiar [fotoko'pja(x)] *vt* to photocopy.

fotografia [fotogra'fia] *f* **-1.** [técnica] photography. **-2.** [foto] photograph.

fotógrafo, fa [fo'tɔgrafu, fa] *m, f* photographer.

fóton ['fɔtõ] (*pl* **-tons**, **-nes**) *m* [fís] photon.

fotonovela [fotono'vɛla] *f* photo-strip story.

foz ['fɔʃ] *f* estuary.

fração [fra'sãw] (*pl* **-ões**) *f* **-1.** [pedaço] bit. **-2.** MAT fraction.

fracassar [fraka'sa(x)] *vi* to fail.

fracasso [fra'kasu] *m* failure.

fracionário, ria [frasiona'riu, ria] *adj* MAT fractional.

fraco, ca ['fraku, ka] *adj* **-1.** [ger] weak. **-2.** [medíocre]: ~ **(em)** weak (at). **-3.** [não ativo - bebida] weak; [- cigarro] mild; [- perfume] delicate. <> **fraco** <> *adv* weakly. <> *m* **-1.** [ponto fraco] weak point. **-2.** [inclinação] weakness.

frade ['fradʒi] *m* friar.

fragata [fra'gata] *f* frigate.

frágil ['fraʒiw] (*pl* **-eis**) *adj* fragile.

fragilidade [fraʒili'dadʒi] *f* fragility.

fragmentação [fragmẽnta'sãw] (*pl* **-ões**) *f* fragmentation.

fragmento [frag'mẽntu] *m* fragment.

fragrância [fra'grãnsja] *f* fragrance.

fralda ['frawda] *f* **-1.** [cueiro] nappy UK, diaper US. **-2.** [de camisa] shirt tail.

framboesa [frãn'bweza] *f* raspberry.

frame ['frejmi] *m* COMPUT frame.

França ['frãnsa] *n* France.

francamente [,frãŋka'mẽntʃi] *adv* frankly.

francês, esa [frã'seʃ, eza] (*mpl* **-eses**, *fpl* **-s**) <> *adj* French. <> *m, f* Frenchman (*f* Frenchwoman). <> **francês** *m* [língua] French.

franco, ca ['frãŋku, ka] *adj* **-1.** [ger] free. **-2.** [sincero] frank. **-3.** [clara] candid. <> **franco** *m* [moeda] franc.

franco-atirador, ra ['frãŋkuatʃiɾado(x), ra] *m, f* sniper.

francófono, na [frãn'kɔfonu, na] <> *adj* French-speaking. <> *m,f* French speaker.

frango ['frãŋgu] <> *m* ZOOL chicken. <> *m* FUT easy goal.

franja ['frãnʒa] *f* fringe.

franjado, da [frãn'ʒadu, da] *adj* **-1.** [cabelo, xale] fringed. **-2.** [rebuscado] recherché.

franquear [frãŋ'kja(x)] *vt* **-1.** [liberar]: **a entrada foi franqueada, vamos à festa!** they've opened the doors, let's party! **-2.** [isentar de imposto] to exempt (from). **-3.** [pagar o transporte] to pay transport costs (for). **-4.** [ceder franquia] to franchise.

franqueza [frãn'keza] *f* frankness.

franquia [frãn'kia] *f* **-1.** COM franchise. **-2.** [isenção] exemption.

franzido, da [frãn'zidu, da] *adj* **-1.** [saia] gathered, pleated. **-2.** [pele] wrinkled.

franzino, na [frã'zinu, na] *adj* delicate.

franzir [frãn'zi(x)] *vt* **-1.** [pregueaɾ] to pleat. **-2.** [enrugar] to wrinkle; ~ **a sobrancelha** to frown.

fraque [ˈfraki] *m* frock coat.

fraqueza [fraˈkeza] *f* weakness.

frasco [ˈfraʃku] *m* flask.

frase [ˈfrazi] *f* -**1.** [oração] sentence; ~ **feita** aphorism. -**2.** *MÚS* phrase.

frasqueira [fraʃˈkejra] *f* bottle rack.

fraternidade [fratɛxniˈdadʒi] *f* fraternity.

fraterno, na [fraˈtɛxnu, na] *adj* fraternal, brotherly.

fratura [fraˈtura] *f* fracture.

fraturar [fratuˈra(x)] *vt* to fracture.

fraudar [frawˈda(x)] *vt* to defraud.

fraude [ˈfrawdʒi] *f* fraud.

freada [freˈada] *f* braking; **dar uma** ~ **to brake**.

frear [freˈa(x)] ⬦ *vt* -**1.** *AUTO* to brake. -**2.** *fig* [controlar] to curb. ⬦ *vi AUTO* to brake.

freeware [friˈwaril (*pl* **freewares**) *m* *COMPUT* freeware.

freezer [ˈfrizɛx] (*pl* -**res**) *m* freezer.

freguês, esa [freˈgeʃ, eza] (*mpl* -**eses**, *fpl* -**s**) *m, f* -**1.** [cliente] customer. -**2.** [paroquiano] parishioner.

freguesia [fregeˈzia] *f* -**1.** [clientela] clientele. -**2.** [paroquia] parish.

frei [frej] *m* friar.

freio [ˈfreju] *m* -**1.** [cavalo] rein. -**2.** [carro] brake; ~ **de mão** handbrake.

freira [ˈfrejra] *f* nun.

fremir [freˈmi(x)] *vi* -**1.** [rugir] to roar. -**2.** [tremer] to tremble.

frêmito [ˈfremitul] *m* shiver.

frenesi [freneˈzi] *m* frenzy.

frente [ˈfrẽtʃi] *f* -**1.** [lado dianteiro]: **na** ~ **(de)** in front (of); **estar à** ~ **de** *fig* to be ahead of. -**2.** [avante]: **em** ~ ahead; **ir para a** ~ to move on. -**3.** [resistência] front; ~ **de combate** frontline. -**4.** [presença] in front of; ~ **a** ~ face to face.

frentista [frẽtʃiʃta] *mf* forecourt attendant.

freqüentar [frekwẽtˈa(x)] *vt* -**1.** [visitar] to frequent. -**2.** [cursar] to attend.

freqüente [freˈkwẽtʃi] *adj* recurrent.

frescão [freʃˈkãw] (*pl* -**ões**) *m* de luxe coach.

fresco, ca [ˈfreʃku, ka] *adj* -**1.** [ger] fresh. -**2.** [ameno] cool. -**3.** *fam* [luxento] posh. -**4.** *fam* [homossexual] camp.
   ➤ **fresca** *f* [aragem] breeze.

frescobol [freʃkoˈbɔwl] (*pl* -**óis**) *m* beach tennis.

frescões [freʃˈkõjʃl] *mpl* ▷ **frescão**.

frescura [freʃˈkura] *f* -**1.** [frescor] freshness. -**2.** [afetação] affectation. -**3.** [formalidade] convention.

fretar [freˈta(x)] *vt* to hire *UK*, to rent *US*.

frete [ˈfrɛtʃil] *m* freight.

frevo [ˈfrevul] *m* *Brazilian carnival street-dance, where dancers improvise their own dances.*

fria [ˈfria] *f* *fam* [apuros] fix; **entrar numa** ~ to be in a fix.

fricção [frikˈsãw] *f* friction.

fricoteiro, ra [frikoˈtejru, ral] ⬦ *adj* vain. ⬦ *m, f* show-off.

frieza [ˈfrjezal] *f* -**1.** [insensibilidade] cold-heartedness. -**2.** [desinteresse] offhandedness.

frigideira [friʒiˈdejral] *f* frying pan.

frígido, da [ˈfriʒidu, dal] *adj* frigid.

frigir [friˈʒi(x)] *vt* to fry.

frigorífico [frigoˈrifikul] *m* -**1.** [loja] cold store. -**2.** [aparelho] fridge, refrigerator.

frio, fria [ˈfriu, ˈfria] *adj* -**1.** [sem calor] cold. -**2.** [insensível] cold. -**3.** [falso] fake. -**4.** [cor] cold. -**5.** [luz] cold.
   ➤ **frio** *m* [baixa temperatura] cold; **estar com** ~ to be cold; **fazer** ~ to be cold.
   ➤ **frios** *mpl* [carne] cold meats.

frisa [ˈfrizal] *f TEATRO* box.

frisar [friˈza(x)] *vt* -**1.** [salientar] to highlight. -**2.** [enrolar] to curl.

fritar [friˈta(x)] *vt* to fry.

frito, ta [ˈfritu, tal] *adj* -**1.** *CULIN* fried. -**2.** *fam* [em apuros]: **estar** ~ to be in hot water.
   ➤ **fritas** *fpl* chips *UK*, (French) fries *US*.

frívolo, la [ˈfrivolu, lal] *adj* frivolous.

fronha [ˈfroɲal] *f* pillowcase.

fronte [ˈfrõtʃil] *f* forehead.

fronteira [frõˈtejral] *f* ▷ **fronteiro**.

fronteiro, ra [frõˈtejru, ral] *adj* facing.
   ➤ **fronteira** *f* -**1.** [extremidade] border. -**2.** *fig* [limite] border.

frota [ˈfrɔtal] *f* fleet.

frouxo, xa [ˈfroʃu, ʃal] *adj* -**1.** [folgado] loose. -**2.** [fraco, ineficiente] weak. -**3.** [condescendente]: **ser** ~ **com alguém** to be weak with sb. -**4.** [covarde] feeble.

frustração [fruʃtraˈsãw] (*pl* -**ões**) *f* -**1.** [malogro] frustration. -**2.** [decepção] frustration.

frustrante [fruʃˈtrãtʃil] *adj* frustrating.

frustrar [fruʃˈtra(x)] *vt* -**1.** [malograr] to frustrate. -**2.** [decepcionar] to cheat.
   ➤ **frustrar-se** *vp* -**1.** [malograr-se] to be frustrated. -**2.** [decepcionar-se] to be disappointed.

fruta [ˈfrutal] *f* fruit.

fruta-de-conde [ˌfrutadʒiˈkõdʒil] (*pl* **frutas-de-conde**) *f* custard apple.

fruteiro, ra [fru'tejru, ra] *adj* fruit-loving.
➡ **fruteira** *f* fruit tree.

frutífero, ra [fru'tʃiferu, ra] *adj* **-1.** [árvore] fruit-bearing. **-2.** [proveitoso] fruitful.

fruto ['frutu] *m* **-1.** [fruta] fruit. **-2.** *fig* [resultado] fruit.

FTP (*abrev de* **File Transfer Protocol**) *m* FTP.

fubá [fu'bal *m* **-1.** [de milho] maize flour. **-2.** [de arroz] rice flour.

fuga ['fuga] *f* **-1.** [escapada] escape. **-2.** *fig* [alívio] escape. **-3.** *MÚS* fugue.

fugaz [fu'gaʒ] *adj* fleeting.

fugir [fu'ʒi(x)] *vi* **-1.** [escapar]: ~ **(de)** to escape (from). **-2.** [evitar]: ~ **de algo/ alguém** to avoid sthg/sb.

fugitivo, va [fuʒi'tʃivu, va] <> *adj* fugitive. <> *m, f* fugitive.

fulano, na [fu'lanu, na] *m, f* so-and-so; ~ **de tal** some so-and-so.

fulgor [fuw'go(x)] *m* brilliance.

fulgurante [fuwgu'rãntʃi] *adj* shining.

fuligem [fu'liʒẽl *f* soot.

fulminante [fuwmi'nãntʃi] *adj* **-1.** [mortal] deadly. **-2.** *fig* [irado] vicious.

fulminar [fuwmi'na(x)] *vt* **-1.** [matar] to kill. **-2.** [aniquilar] to annihilate.

fumaça [fu'masa] *f* smoke.

fumante [fu'mãntʃi] *mf* smoker; **não** ~ non-smoker.

fumar [fu'ma(x)] <> *vt* to smoke. <> *vi* to smoke.

fumê [fu'mel *adj inv* smoky.

fumo ['fumu] *m* **-1.** [tabaco] tobacco. **-2.** [maconha] dope. **-3.** [vício] smoking.

fumódromo [fu'mɔdromu] *m fam* smoking area.

FUNAI (*abrev de* **Fundação Nacional do Índio**) *f Brazilian government organization for the protection of the indigenous population.*

FUNARTE (*abrev de* **Fundação Nacional de Arte**) *f Brazilian government organization for the promotion of artistic activities.*

FUNASA (*abrev de* **Fundação Nacional de Saúde**) *f Brazilian government organization for health education and prevention of disease among indigenous peoples.*

função [fũn'sãw] (*pl* **-ões**) *f* **-1.** [cargo] function. **-2.** [responsabilidade] function. **-3.** [utilidade] role. **-4.** [espetáculo] performance. **-5.** [papel] function. **-6.** [atribuição] function. **-7.** *GRAM* function. **-8.** *MAT* function.
➡ **em função de** *loc prep* due to.

funcionalidade [fũnsjonali'dadʒi] *f* functionality.

funcionalismo [fũnsjona'liʒmul *m* [servidores]: ~ **público** civil service.

funcionamento [fũnsjona'mẽntul *m* functioning; **horário de** ~ opening hours, working hours.

funcionar [fũsjo'na(x)] *vi* **-1.** [máquina *etc.*] to work; **pôr algo para** ~ to switch sthg on. **-2.** [loja *etc.*] to be open. **-3.** [exercer função]: ~ **como algo** to work as sthg. **-4.** [dar certo] to work.

funcionário, ria [fũsjo'narju, rja] *m, f* employee; ~ **público** civil servant.

funções [fũn'sõjʃ] *fpl* ▷ **função**.

fundação [fũnda'sãw] (*pl* **-ões**) *f* **-1.** [alicerce] foundation. **-2.** [instituição] foundation. **-3.** [criação] founding.

fundamental [fũndamẽn'taw] (*pl* **-ais**) *adj* fundamental.

fundamento [fũnda'mẽntul *m* fundament.

FUNDAP (*abrev de* **Fundação do Desenvolvimento Administrativo**) *f Brazilian organization for the coordination of training and educational programmes.*

fundar [fũn'da(x)] *vt* **-1.** [instituir] to found. **-2.** [criar] to establish.

fundir [fũn'dʒi(x)] *vt* **-1.** [derreter] to melt. **-2.** [moldar] to cast. **-3.** [incorporar] to merge.
➡ **fundir-se** *vp* **-1.** [derreter-se] to melt. **-2.** [incorporar-se] to merge.

fundo, da ['fũndu, da] *adj* **-1.** [profundo] deep. **-2.** [reentrante] sunken. **-3.** *fam* [despreparado]: ~ **(em algo)** weak (at sthg).
➡ **fundo** <> *m* **-1.** [base] bottom. **-2.** [de local] rear. **-3.** [segundo plano] background. **-4.** [de tecido, papel] background. **-5.** *MÚS*: ~ **musical** background music. **-6.** [íntimo]: **eu o perdoei do** ~ **da alma** I forgave him from the bottom of my heart. **-7.** *fig* [teor] element. **-8.** *FIN* fund; ~ **de garantia** security; ~ **de investimento** investment fund. <> *adv* [profundamente] deeply; **a** ~ in depth.
➡ **fundos** *mpl* **-1.** [de casa] funds. **-2.** [capital] capital; **cheque sem** ~ unsecured cheque.
➡ **no fundo** *loc adv* [intrinsecamente] basically.

fúnebre ['funebri] *adj* funereal.

funeral [fune'rawl (*pl* **-ais**) *m* funeral.

funesto, ta [fu'neʃtu, ta] *adj* dire.

fungo ['fũngul *m* fungus.

funil [fu'niwl (*pl* **-is**) *m* funnel.

FUNRURAL (*de abrev* **Fundo de Assistência e Previdência ao Trabalhador Rural**) *m Brazilian fund for the*

galho

assistance and support of rural workers.

furacão [fura'kãw] (*pl* **-ões**) *m* [ciclone] cyclone.

furado, da [fu'radu, da] *adj* **-1.** [pneu] punctured. **-2.** [orelha] pierced. **-3.** [sapato] holey. **-4.** *fam* [infrutífero] unsuccessful.

furão, rona [fu'rãw, rɔna] (*mpl* **-ões**, *fpl* **-s**) *adj* [cavador] unreliable.

furar [fu'ra(x)] ⬦ *vt* **-1.** [pneu] to puncture. **-2.** [orelha] to pierce. **-3.** [sapato] to make a hole in. **-4.** [frustrar] to fail. **-5.** [não aderir a] to leave. ⬦ *vi* **-1.** [perfurar] to puncture. **-2.** [sapato] to get a hole. **-3.** [malograr] to fail.

furgão [fux'gãw] (*pl* **-ões**) *m* van.

fúria ['furja] *f* fury.

furioso, osa [fu'rjozu, ɔza] *adj* **-1.** [raivoso] furious. **-2.** [violento] furious.

furo ['furu] *m* **-1.** [buraco] puncture. **-2.** [orelha] hole. **-3.** [sapato] hole. **-4.** *fig* [falha] mistake; **dar um ~** to put one's foot in it.

furões [fu'rõjʃ] *mpl* ⊳ **furão**.

furona [fu'rona] *f* ⊳ **furão**.

furor [fu'ro(x)] *m* **-1.** [fúria] fury. **-2.** *loc*: **causar ~** to cause fury.

furtar [fux'ta(x)] ⬦ *vt* [roubar] to steal. ⬦ *vi* [roubar] to steal.

◆ **furtar-se** *vp* [esquivar-se]: **~-se a algo** to dodge sthg.

furtivo, va [fux'tʃivu, va] *adj* **-1.** [às ocultas] furtive. **-2.** [dissimulado] furtive.

furto ['fuxtu] *m* theft.

fusão [fu'zãw] (*pl* **-ões**) *f* **-1.** [ger] fusion. **-2.** *com* amalgamation. **-3.** [liga] amalgam.

fusível [fu'zivew] (*pl* **-eis**) *m* fuse.

fuso ['fuzu] *m* [peça] screw.

◆ **fuso horário** *m* time zone.

fusões [fu'zõjʃ] *fpl* ⊳ **fusão**.

fustigar [fuʃtʃi'ga(x)] *vt* to whip.

futebol [futʃi'bɔw] *m* football; **~ de salão** (indoor) five-a-side football.

fútil ['futʃiw] (*pl* **-eis**) *adj* **-1.** [leviano] frivolous. **-2.** [insignificante] trivial.

futilidade [futʃili'dadʒi] *f* **-1.** [leviandade] frivolity. **-2.** [insignificância] triviality. **-3.** [coisa fútil] triviality.

futuro, ra [fu'turu, ra] *adj* future.

◆ **futuro** *m* **-1.** [tempo] future. **-2.** [destino] future. **-3.** *GRAM* future.

FUVEST (*abrev de* **Fundação do Vestibular do Estado de São Paulo**) *f* organization regulating entrance examinations at some universities in São Paulo.

fuzil [fu'ziw] (*pl* **-is**) *m* rifle.

fuzilar [fuzi'la(x)] *vt* **-1.** [atirar] to shoot. **-2.** *fig* [ameaçar]: **~ alguém com os olhos** to look daggers at sb.

fuzileiro [fuzi'lejru] *m* rifleman; **~ naval** marine.

G

g¹, G [ʒe] *m* [letra] g, G.

g² (*abrev de* **grama**) *m* g.

gabar-se [gabax'si] *vp*: **~-se (de)** to boast (about).

gabinete [gabi'netʃi] *m* **-1.** [escritório] study. **-2.** *POL* cabinet.

gado ['gadu] *m* cattle.

gafanhoto [gafã'ɲotu] *m* grasshopper.

gafe ['gafi] *f* gaffe.

gafieira [ga'fjejra] *f* **-1.** [baile] ball. **-2.** [dança] dance.

gago, ga ['gagu, ga] ⬦ *adj* stammering. ⬦ *m, f* stammerer.

gaguejar [gage'ʒa(x)] *vt & vi* to stammer.

gaiato, ta [ga'jatu, ta] *adj* mischievous.

gaiola [ga'jɔla] ⬦ *f* **-1.** [clausura] cage. **-2.** *fam* [prisão] jail. ⬦ *m* [vapor] steamboat.

gaita ['gajta] *f* **-1.** *MÚS* mouth organ; **~ de foles** bagpipe. **-2.** *fam fig* [dinheiro] dosh.

gaivota [gaj'vɔta] *f* seagull.

gala ['gala] *f*: **de ~** gala; **uniforme de ~** dress uniform.

galante [ga'lãntʃi] *adj* gallant.

galanteio [galã'teju] *m* gallantry.

galão [ga'lãw] (*pl* **-ões**) *m* **-1.** *MIL* stripe. **-2.** [enfeite] braid. **-3.** [medida] gallon.

galáxia [ga'laksja] *f* galaxy.

galera [ga'lɛra] *f* **-1.** *NÁUT* galley. **-2.** *fam* [grupo] crowd.

galeria [gale'ria] *f* **-1.** *TEATRO* circle. **-2.** [coleção] collection. **-3.** [canalização] drainage. **-4.** [loja de arte] gallery. **-5.** [centro comercial] shopping centre.

Gales ['galiʃ] *n*: **País de ~** Wales.

galês, esa [ga'leʃ, ezal] ⬦ *adj* Welsh. ⬦ *m, f* Welshman (*f* Welshwoman).

◆ **galês** *m* [língua] Welsh.

galeto [ga'letu] *m* roast poussin.

galheteiro [gaʎe'tejru] *m* cruet-stand.

galho [ga'ʎu] *m* **-1.** *BOT* branch. **-2.** *fam* [problema] pickle; **quebrar um ~** to get out of a pickle.

Galícia [ga'lisja] n Galicia.

galinha [ga'liɲa] ◇ f -1. [ave] hen. -2. CULIN chicken. -3. fam [namorador] easy lay.

galinheiro [gali'ɲejru] m poulterer.

galo ['galu] m -1. [ave] cockerel, rooster. -2. [inchaço] bump.

galocha [ga'lɔʃa] f galosh.

galopar [galo'pa(x)] vi to gallop.

galope [ga'lɔpi] m gallop.

galpão [gaw'pãw] (pl -ões) m hangar.

gama ['gãma] f -1. MÚS scale. -2. fig [série] range.

gamão [ga'mãw] m backgammon.

gamar [ga'ma(x)] vi to be hooked; ~ por algo/alguém to fall for sthg/sb.

gambá [gãn'ba] m ZOOL opossum.

game ['gejmi] m COMPUT game.

gana ['gãna] f -1. [desejo]: ~ de algo/de fazer algo desire for sthg/to do sthg. -2. [raiva]: ter ~ de alguém to be furious with sb.

ganância [ga'nãnsja] f greed.

ganancioso, osa [ganã'sjozu, ɔza] adj greedy.

gancho ['gãnʃu] m -1. [peça] hook. -2. COST hook. -3. fig [recurso] bait.

gangorra [gãŋ'goxa] f seesaw.

gângster ['gãŋgiʃte(x)] m gangster.

gangue ['gãŋgi] f gang.

ganhador, ra [gaɲa'do(x), ra] ◇ adj winning. ◇ m, f winner.

ganha-pão [ˌgãɲa'pãw] (pl ganha-pães) m -1. [trabalho] living, livelihood. -2. [objeto de trabalho] livelihood.

ganhar [ga'ɲa(x)] ◇ vt -1. [ger] to win. -2. [receber] to get. -3. [salário] to earn. -4. [lucrar] to gain. -5. [atingir] to reach. ◇ vi -1. [vencer]: ~ de alguém to beat sb; ~ de alguém em algo to outdo sb at sthg. -2. [como remuneração] to earn. -3. [lucrar]: ~ (com) to profit (from); sair ganhando to come out on top.

ganho ['gãɲu] ◇ pp ⟼ ganhar. ◇ m -1. [salário] earnings (pl). -2. [lucro] profit. -3. JUR: ~ de causa successful lawsuit.

ganir [ga'ni(x)] vi to whine.

ganso ['gãnsu] m goose.

GAPA (abrev de Grupo de Apoio à Prevenção à Aids) m Brazilian non-governmental organization working in AIDS prevention.

garagem [ga'raʒẽ] (pl -ns) f garage.

garanhão [gara'ɲãw] (pl -ões) m -1. [cavalo] stallion. -2. fig [homem] stud.

garantia [garãn'tʃia] f -1. [ger] guarantee. -2. [de dívida] collateral.

garantir [garãn'tʃi(x)] vt -1. [assegurar]: ~ algo a alguém to assure sb of sthg;

~ que to guarantee that. -2. [prometer]: ~ algo a alguém to promise sb sthg. -3. [asseverar] to guarantee.
 ◆ **garantir-se** vp [defender-se]: ~-se contra algo to protect o.s. against sthg.

garça ['gaxsa] f heron.

garçom [gax'sõ] (pl -ns) m waiter.

garçonete [garso'nɛtʃi] f waitress.

garfo ['gaxfu] m fork.

gargalhada [gaxga'ʎada] f burst of laughter; cair na ~ to fall about laughing.

gargalo [gax'galu] m -1. [de garrafa] neck. -2. [obstáculo] fig bottleneck.

garganta [gax'gãnta] f -1. ANAT throat. -2. [desfiladeiro] mountain pass.

gargarejar [gaxgare'ʒa(x)] vi to gargle.

gargarejo [gaxga'reʒu] m -1. [ato] gargling. -2. [líquido] gargle.

gari [ga'ri] mf roadsweeper.

garimpeiro, ra [garĩn'pejru, ra] m, f prospector.

garimpo [ga'rĩnpu] m [mina] mining deposit.

garoa [ga'roa] f drizzle.

garota [ga'rota] f ⟼ **garoto**.

garotada [garo'tada] f: a ~ the kids (pl).

garoto, ta [ga'rotu, ta] m, f [menino] boy, kid.
 ◆ **garota** f [namorada] girlfriend.

garoupa [ga'ropa] f grouper.

garra ['gaxa] f -1. [de animal] claw. -2. fig [entusiasmo] enthusiasm; ter ~ to be enthusiastic.

garrafa [ga'xafa] f bottle; ~ térmica Thermos flask® UK, Thermos bottle® US.

garrote [ga'xɔtʃi] m -1. [de tortura] garrotte UK, garrote US. -2. [torniquete] tourniquet.

garupa [ga'rupa] f -1. [de cavalo] hindquarters, rump. -2. [de bicicleta, moto] pillion.

gás ['gajʃ] (pl gases) m -1. [fluido] gas; ~ natural natural gas; ~ lacrimogêneo tear gas. -2. [do intestino] wind, flatulence. -3. fam fig [entusiasmo] go.

gasoduto [gazo'dutu] m gas pipeline.

gasolina [gazo'lina] f petrol UK, gasoline US.

gasoso, osa [ga'zozu, ɔza] adj fizzy.
 ◆ **gasosa** f fizzy drink UK, soda US.

gastador, ra [gaʃta'do(x), ra] ◇ adj wasteful. ◇ m, f wasteful person.

gastar [gaʃ'ta(x)] ◇ vt -1. [despender] to spend. -2. [consumir - energia, gasolina] to consume; [- tempo] to take up. -3. [usar - roupa, sapato] to wear; [- cosmético, produto] to use. -4. [desperdiçar] to waste. -5. [desgastar] to wear out.

vi **-1.** [despender dinheiro] to spend money. **-2.** [desgastar-se] to wear out.

➤ **gastar-se** *vp* [desgastar-se] to wear out.

gasto, ta [ˈgaʃtu, ta] ⬦ *pp* ⊳ **gastar**.
⬦ *adj* **-1.** [ger] worn out. **-2.** [produto, cosmético] used up. **-5.** [desperdiçado] wasted. **-6.** [envelhecido] worn.

➤ **gasto** *m* [despesa] expense.

➤ **gastos** *mpl* [despesas] expenses.

gástrico, ca [ˈgaʃtriku, ka] *adj* gastric.

gastronomia [gaʃtronoˈmia] *f* gastronomy.

gata [ˈgata] *f* ⊳ **gato**.

gateway [gejtʃiˈwej] (*pl* **gateways**) *m* COMPUT gateway.

gatilho [gaˈtʃiʎu] *m* trigger.

gato, ta [ˈgatu, ta] *m, f* **-1.** [animal] cat; ~ **montês** wild cat; **vender** ~ **por lebre** to sell a pig in a poke. **-2.** *fam* [pessoa] sexy person.

➤ **gato** *m* ELETR illegal electrical connection; **fazer um** ~ to make an illegal electrical connection.

gatuno, na [gaˈtunu, na] ⬦ *adj* thieving. ⬦ *m, f* thief.

gaveta [gaˈveta] *f* drawer.

gavião [gaˈvjãw] (*pl* **-ões**) *m* hawk.

gaze [ˈgazi] *f* **-1.** [tecido] gauze. **-2.** [para curativo] antiseptic gauze.

gazela [gaˈzɛla] *f* gazelle.

gazeta [gaˈzeta] *f* [jornal] gazette.

GB (*abrev de* **Great Britain**) *n* GB.

geada [ˈʒjada] *f* frost.

gel [ʒɛl] *f* gel.

geladeira [ʒelaˈdejra] *f* refrigerator, fridge.

gelado, da [ʒeˈladu, da] *adj* **-1.** [comida] frozen. **-2.** [bebida] chilled. **-3.** [mar, vento] icy.

gelar [ʒeˈla(x)] ⬦ *vt* **-1.** [comida] to freeze. **-2.** [bebida] to chill. ⬦ *vi* to be freezing.

gelatina [ʒelaˈtʃina] *f* **-1.** [gel] gelatine. **-2.** [sobremesa] jelly *UK*, Jell-O® *US*.

gelatinoso, osa [ʒelatʃiˈnozu, ɔza] *adj* gelatinous.

geléia [ʒeˈlɛja] *f* jam *UK*, jelly *US*.

geleira [ʒeˈlejra] *f* glacier.

gélido, da [ˈʒɛlidu, da] *adj* **-1.** [gelado] icy. **-2.** *fig* [imóvel] frozen.

gelo [ˈʒelu] ⬦ *adj inv* light grey *UK*, light gray *US*. ⬦ *m* **-1.** [água solidificada] ice. **-2.** [cor] light grey *UK*, light gray *US*. **-3.** *fig* [indiferença] **dar um** ~ **em alguém** to give sb the cold shoulder; **quebrar o** ~ to break the ice. **-4.** *loc*: **estar um** ~ to be freezing cold.

gema [ˈʒema] *f* **-1.** [do ovo] yolk. **-2.** [pedra preciosa] gem.

gemada [ʒeˈmada] *f* eggnog.

gêmeo, mea [ˈʒemju, mja] ⬦ *adj* twin. ⬦ *m, f* twin.

➤ **Gêmeos** *mpl* [zodíaco] Gemini; **ser Gêmeos** to be Gemini.

gemer [ʒeˈme(x)] *vi* **-1.** [de dor] to groan. **-2.** [lastimar-se] to moan. **-3.** [ranger] to wail. **-4.** *fig* [vento] to howl.

gemido [ʒeˈmidu] *m* **-1.** [de dor] groan. **-2.** [de animal] howl. **-3.** [lamento] wail.

geminiano, na [ʒemiˈnanu, na] ⬦ *adj* Gemini (*antes de subst*). ⬦ *m, f* Gemini.

gene [ˈʒeni] *m* gene.

genealógico, ca [ʒenjaˈlɔʒiku, ka] *adj* genealogical; **árvore genelógica** family tree.

Genebra [ʒeˈnɛbra] *n* Geneva.

general [geneˈraw] (*pl* **-ais**) *m* general.

generalizar [generaliˈza(x)] ⬦ *vi* [fazer generalizações] to generalize. ⬦ *vt* [difundir] to spread.

➤ **generalizar-se** *vp* [difundir-se] to spread.

genérico [ʒeˈnɛriku] *m* generic drug.

gênero [ˈʒeneru] *m* **-1.** [ger] gender. **-2.** [tipo] kind. **-3.** [estilo] style. **-4.** BIO genus.

➤ **gêneros** *mpl* [mercadorias] goods; ~**s alimentícios** foodstuffs.

generosidade [ʒeneroziˈdadʒi] *f* generosity.

generoso, osa [ʒeneˈrozu, ɔza] *adj* generous.

genética [ʒeˈnɛtʃika] *f* genetics (*sg*).

genético, ca [ʒeˈnɛtʃiku, ka] *adj* genetic.

gengibre [ʒẽˈʒibri] *m* ginger.

gengiva [ʒẽˈʒival] *f* gum.

gengivite [ʒẽʒiˈvitʃil] *f* gingivitis.

genial [ʒeˈnjaw] (*pl* **-ais**) *adj* **-1.** [extraordinário] inspired. **-2.** *fam* [formidável] terrific.

genialidade [ʒenjaliˈdadʒi] *f* genius.

gênio [ˈʒenju] *m* **-1.** [ger] genius. **-2.** [temperamento] nature; ~ **bom/ruim** good-/bad-tempered. **-3.** MITOL genie.

genital [ʒeniˈtaw] (*pl* **-ais**) *adj* genital.

genitor, ra [ʒeniˈto(x), ra] *m, f* progenitor.

genocídio [ʒenoˈsidʒju] *m* genocide.

genoma [ʒeˈnoma] *m* genome.

genro [ˈʒẽxu] *m* son-in-law.

gente [ˈʒẽtʃi] ⬦ *f* **-1.** [pessoas] people; ~ **bem** upper classes; **toda a** ~ everybody; *fam* [amigos, colegas] folks; **oi/ tchau,** ~ hi/bye, folks. **-2.** [alguém] somebody, someone. **-3.** *fam* [nós]: **a** ~ **vai viajar** we're going travelling; **você quer ir com a** ~**?** do you want to come with us?; **o carro da** ~ **está**

enguiçado our car has broken down. <> *interj* [exprimindo espanto] gosh!

gentil [ʒẽn'tʃiw] (*pl* -**is**) *adj* kind.

gentileza [ʒẽntʃi'lezal] *f* kindness; **por ~ poderia me ajudar?** would you be so kind as to help me?

genuíno, na [ʒe'nwinu, nal] *adj* genuine.

geografia [ʒjogra'fial] *f* geography.

geográfico, ca [ʒeo'grafiku, kal] *adj* geographical.

geologia [ʒjolo'ʒial] *f* geology.

geometria [ʒjome'trial] *f* geometry.

geométrico, ca [ʒeo'mɛtriku, kal] *adj* geometric.

geração [ʒera'sãwl] (*pl* -**ões**) *f* generation; **de última ~** COMPUT & TEC latest generation.

gerador [ʒera'do(x)] (*pl* -**res**) *adj*: **empresa ~ a de empregos** job-creating company; **grupo ~ de problemas** problem-causing group.

▸ **gerador** *m* TEC generator.

geral [ʒe'raw] (*pl* -**ais**) <> *adj* [genérico] general; **de um modo ~** on the whole. <> *m* [o normal] normal thing. <> *f* -**1.** FUT & TEATRO gallery. -**2.** [revisão, arrumação] spring clean; **dar uma ~ em algo** to have a blitz on sthg.

▸ **em geral** *loc adv* in general.

geralmente [ʒeraw'mẽntʃi] *adv* generally.

gerânio [ʒe'rãnju] *m* geranium.

gerar [ʒe'ra(x)] *vt* -**1.** [ger] to generate. -**2.** [ter filhos] to beget. -**3.** [causar] to breed.

gerência [ʒe'rẽnsja] *f* management.

gerenciamento [ʒerẽnsja'mẽntu] *m* management.

gerenciar [ʒerẽn'sja(x)] <> *vt* to manage. <> *vi* to manage.

gerente [ʒe'rẽntʃi] *mf* manager.

gergelim [ʒexʒe'lĩ] *m* sesame.

gerir [ʒe'ri(x)] *vt* to manage.

germanófono, na [ʒexma'nɔfonu, nal] <> *adj* German-speaking. <> *m,f* German speaker.

germe [ʒ'ɛxmi] *m* germ.

germinar [ʒexmi'na(x)] *vi* to germinate.

gesso ['ʒesu] *m* -**1.** [nas artes plásticas] plaster of Paris. -**2.** [em parede] cast.

gestante [ʒeʃ'tãntʃi] *f* pregnant woman.

gestão [ʒeʃ'tãw] (*pl* -**ões**) *f* -**1.** [administração] administration. -**2.** [gerência] management.

gesticular [ʒeʃtʃiku'la(x)] *vi* to gesticulate.

gesto ['ʒɛʃtul] *m* gesture; **fazer um ~** to make a gesture.

gestual [ʒeʃ'tuaw] (*pl* -**ais**) *adj* gestural.

Gibraltar [ʒibraw'ta(x)] *n* Gibraltar.

GIF (*abrev de* Graphics Interchange Format) *m* GIF.

gigabyte [giga'baijtʃil] (*pl* **gigabytes**) *m* COMPUT gigabyte.

gigante [ʒi'gãntʃil] <> *adj* gigantic. <> *m* giant.

gigantesco, ca [ʒigãn'teʃku, kal] *adj* gigantic.

gilete [ʒi'lɛtʃi] <> *f* [lâmina] razor blade. <> *m vulg* [bissexual] AC/DC.

gim ['ʒĩ] (*pl* -**ns**) *m* gin.

ginasial [ʒina'ziawl] (*pl* -**ais**) <> *adj* [relativo a ginásio] secondary school *UK*, high school *US*. <> *m* [curso] *dated* primary education.

ginásio [ʒi'nazjul] *m* -**1.** EDUC secondary school. -**2.** [para esportes] gymnasium.

ginástica [ʒi'naʃtʃika] *f* -**1.** [esporte] gymnastics *(sg).* -**2.** [aeróbica, corretiva] exercises *(pl).*

ginecologia [ˌʒinekolo'ʒial] *f* gynaecology.

ginecologista [ˌʒinekolo'ʒiʃtal] *mf* gynaecologist.

girafa [ʒi'rafal] *f* giraffe.

girar [ʒi'ra(x)] <> *vi* -**1.** [rodar] to rotate. -**2.** *fig* [funcionar]: **~ em torno de** to revolve around. <> *vt* [fazer rodar] to turn.

girassol [ˌʒira'sɔwl] (*pl* -**óis**) *m* sunflower.

giratório, ria [ʒira'tɔrju, rjal] *adj* revolving; **cadeira giratória** swivel chair; **ponte giratória** swing bridge.

gíria ['ʒirjal] *f* -**1.** [calão] slang. -**2.** [jargão] jargon.

giro, ra ['ʒiru, ral] *m* -**1.** [volta] rotation. -**2.** *fam* [passeio] stroll; **dar um ~** to take a stroll.

giz ['ʒiʒ] *m* chalk.

glaciação [glasia'sãw] (*pl* -**ões**) *f* [período geológico] glaciation.

glacial [gla'sjaw] (*pl* -**ais**) *adj* glacial.

glamouroso, osa [glamu'rozu, ɔzal] *adj* glamorous.

glândula ['glãndula] *f* gland.

glicerina [glise'rinal] *f* glycerine.

glicose [gli'kɔzil] *f* glucose.

global [glo'baw] (*pl* -**ais**) *adj* -**1.** [total] total. -**2.** [relativo ao globo] global.

globalização [globaliza'sãwl] (*pl* -**ões**) *f* globalization.

globalizado, da [globali'zadu, dal] *adj* globalized.

globalizante [globali'zãntʃil] *adj* globalizing.

globalizar [globa'liza(x)] *vt* to globalize.

▸ **globalizar-se** *vp* to become globalized.

globo ['globul] *m* globe; **~ ocular** eyeball.

glória [ˈglɔrjal f glory.

glorificação [glorifikaˈsãw] (pl -ões) f glorification.

glorificar [glorifiˈka(x)] vt -1. [honrar] to glorify. -2. [canonizar] to canonize.

glorioso, osa [gloˈrjozu, ɔza] adj glorious.

glossário [gloˈsarju] m glossary.

GLP (abrev de Gás Liquefeito de Petróleo) m LPG.

glúten [ˈglutẽ] (pl -s) m gluten.

glúteo, tea [ˈglutew, tʃia] <> adj ANAT gluteal. <> m gluteus.

GO (abrev de Estado de Goiás) n State of Goiás.

godê [goˈde] adj flared.

goela [ˈgwɛla] f throat.

goiaba [goˈjaba] f guava.

goiabada [gojaˈbada] f guava jelly.

gol [ˈgow] (pl -es) m goal; marcar um ~ to score a goal.

gola [ˈgɔla] f collar.

gole [ˈgɔli] m gulp; de um ~ só in one gulp.

goleada [goˈljada] f FUT hammering.

goleiro [goˈlejru] m goalkeeper.

golfe [ˈgowfi] m golf.

golfinho [gowˈfiɲu] m dolphin.

golfista [gowˈfiʃta] mf golfer.

golfo [ˈgowfu] m gulf.

Golfo Pérsico [ˌgowfuˈpɛxsiku] n Persian Gulf.

golpe [ˈgowpi] m -1. [ger] stroke; ~ de sorte stroke of luck; ~ de mestre master stroke. -2. [pancada, abalo moral] blow; [soco] punch; [de faca] slash; [de chicote] lash; ~ baixo fam fig dirty trick; ~ mortal mortal blow. -3. POL coup; ~ de Estado coup d'état.

golpear [gowˈpja(x)] vt -1. [dar pancada em] to hit; [com soco] to punch; [com chicote] to lash; [com faca] to slash. -2. [moralmente] to wound.

goma [ˈgoma] f gum, glue; ~ de mascar chewing gum.

gomo [ˈgomu] m slice.

gongo [ˈgõgu] m -1. MÚS gong. -2. [sino] bell.

gorar [goˈra(x)] <> vt [fracassar] to thwart. <> vi [fracassar] to fail.

gordo, da [ˈgordu, da] <> adj -1. [pessoa] fat; nunca ter visto alguém mais ~ [não conhecer] not have seen sb before. -2. [carne] fatty. -3. fig [quantia] considerable. <> m, f fat person.

gordura [goxˈdura] f -1. [banha] fat. -2. [líquida] grease. -3. [obesidade] fatness.

gorduroso, osa [goxduˈrozu, ɔza] adj -1. [ger] greasy. -2. [comida] fatty.

gorila [goˈrila] m gorilla.

gorjeta [goxˈʒeta] f tip.

gorro [ˈgoxu] m cap.

gosma [ˈgɔʒma] f spittle.

gosmento, ta [gɔʒˈmẽtu, ta] adj slimy.

gostar [goʃˈta(x)] vi -1. [ter prazer, gosto]: ~ de to enjoy; ~ de fazer algo to enjoy doing sthg; eu ~ ia de ir I would like to go; gostei de vê-lo feliz it was good to see him happy; ~ mais de algo do que de to prefer sthg to; ~ de alguém [simpatizar com] to like sb; [sentir afeição por] to be fond of sb. -2. [aproveitar]: ~ de to enjoy. -3. [ter costume]: ~ de fazer algo to like doing sthg. -4. [aprovar]: ~ de to like.

◆ **gostar-se** vp [mutuamente] to be fond of each other ou one another.

gosto [ˈgoʃtu] m -1. [ger] taste; ter ~ de to taste of; de bom/mau ~ in good/bad taste; falta de ~ lack of taste. -2. [prazer] pleasure.

gostoso, osa [goʃˈtozu, ɔza] adj -1. [comida, bebida] tasty. -2. [cheiro] lovely. -3. [ambiente, música] pleasant. -4. [cama, cadeira] comfortable. -5. [risada] hearty. -6. fam [sensual, bonito] gorgeous.

gota [ˈgɔta] f -1. [ger] drop. -2. [de suor] bead. -3. MED gout.

goteira [goˈtejra] f [buraco no telhado] leak.

gotejar [goteˈʒa(x)] vt & vi to drip.

gourmet [guxˈmel] (pl -s) mf gourmet.

governabilidade [govexnabiliˈdadʒi] f governability.

governador, ra [govexnaˈdo(x), ra] m, f governor.

governamental [govexnamẽˈtaw] (pl -ais) adj government (antes de subst), governmental.

governanta [govexˈnãta] f -1. [de criança] governess. -2. [de casa] housekeeper.

governante [govexˈnãtʃi] <> adj [que governa] governing. <> mf [quem governa] governor.

governar [govexˈna(x)] <> vt -1. POL to govern. -2. [embarcação] to steer. -3. [dominar] to dominate. <> vi POL to govern.

governo [goˈvexnu] m -1. POL government. -2. [controle]: o carro estava sem ~ the car was out of control. -3. NÁUT steering.

gozação [gozaˈsãw] (pl -ões) f teasing.

gozar [goˈza(x)] <> vt -1. [desfrutar] to enjoy. -2. fam [troçar de] to make fun of. <> vi -1. [desfrutar]: ~ de to enjoy. -2. fam [troçar] to mock; ~ da cara de alguém to mock sb. -3. fam [ter orgasmo] to come.

gozo ['gozu] *m* -1. [prazer] pleasure. -2. [uso]: ~ de algo use of sthg; **estar em pleno ~ das faculdades mentais** to be in full possession of one's mental faculties. - 4. [orgasmo] orgasm.

GP (*abrev de* **Grande Prêmio**) *m* grand prix.

GPS (*abrev de* **Global Positioning System**) *m* GPS.

Grã-Bretanha [ˌgrãbre'tãɲa] *n*: (a) ~ Great Britain.

graça ['grasa] *f* -1. [ger] grace. -2. [humor] wit; **achar ~ de** *ou* **em algo** to find sthg funny; **ter ~** to be funny. -3. [encanto] charm; **cheio de ~** full of charm; **sem ~** dull; **não sei que ~ ela vê nele** I don't know what she sees in him. - 4. [favor, proteção] favour. -5. [nome] name.
 ◆ **graças a** *loc prep* -1. [devido a] due to, thanks to. -2. [agradecimento]: **dar ~s a** to give thanks to; **~s a Deus!** thank goodness!
 ◆ **de graça** *loc adj* -1. [grátis] free. -2. [muito barato] given away.

gracejar [grase'ʒa(x)] *vi* to joke.

gracejo [gra'seʒu] *m* joke.

gracinha [gra'siɲa] *f*: **ser uma ~** [criança, rosto] to be sweet; [cidade, desenho] to be attractive; **que ~!** how sweet!

gracioso, osa [gra'sjozu, ɔza] *adj* gracious.

gradativo, va [grada'tʃivu, va] *adj* gradual.

grade ['gradʒi] *f* -1. [em janela] grille. -2. [no chão] grating. -3. *loc*: **atrás das ~s** *fam* [na cadeia] behind bars.

gradeado, da [gra'dʒiadu, da] *adj* [com grades - jardim] fenced; [- janela] with a grating (*antes de subst*).
 ◆ **gradeado** *m* [gradeamento] fencing.

gradear [gra'dʒia(x)] *vt* -1. [janela] to put bars on. -2. [área] to fence off.

gradual [gra'dwaw] (*pl* -ais) *adj* gradual.

graduar [gra'dwa(x)] *vt* -1. [regular] to regulate. -2. [classificar]: ~ **em** to classify according to. -3. [marcar os graus] to graduate. -4. *EDUC*: ~ **alguém em algo** to confer a degree on sb in sthg. -5. *MIL*: ~ **alguém em general/coronel** to promote sb to general/colonel.
 ◆ **graduar-se** *vp EDUC*: ~-**se em algo** to graduate in sthg.

grafia [gra'fia] *f* -1. [escrita] writing. -2. [ortografia] spelling.

gráfico, ca ['grafiku, ka] ◇ *adj* -1. [visual] graphic. -2. [tipográfico] typographic. ◇ *m, f* [profissional] typesetter.
 ◆ **gráfico** *m* -1. [diagrama] diagram; ~ **de barras** bar chart. -2. *MAT* graph.

gráfica *f* [estabelecimento] graphics studio.

grã-fino, na [grã'finu, na] (*mpl* **grã-finos**, *fpl* **grã-finas**) ◇ *adj* posh. ◇ *m, f* toff.

grafite [gra'fitʃi] *f* -1. [material] graphite. -2. [de lápis] lead. -3. [pichação] graffiti.

grama ['grãma] ◇ *f* [relva] grass. ◇ *m* [medida] gramme.

gramado [gra'madu] *m* -1. [de parque, jardim] lawn. -2. *FUT* pitch.

gramar [gra'ma(x)] *vt* to sow with grass.

gramática [gra'matʃika] *f* ⊳ **gramático.**

gramatical [gramatʃi'kaw] (*pl* -ais) *adj* grammatical.

gramático, ca [gra'matʃiku, ka] ◇ *adj* grammatical. ◇ *m, f* grammarian.
 ◆ **gramática** *f* -1. [disciplina] grammar. -2. [livro] grammar book.

gramofone [gramo'fɔni] *m* gramophone.

grampeador [grãpja'do(x)] (*pl* -es) *m* stapler.

grampear [grãm'pja(x)] *vt* -1. [prender com grampos] to staple. -2. [telefone] to tap.

grampo ['grãpu] *m* -1. [para papel] staple. -2. [para cabelos] hairgrip. -3. [de chapéu] hatpin. -4. [de carpinteiro] clamp. -5. [de telefone] tap.

granada [gra'nada] *f* -1. [arma] projectile; ~ **de mão** hand grenade. -2. [pedra] garnet.

grande ['grãdʒi] *adj* -1. [em tamanho] large. -2. [em altura] tall. -3. [crescido] grown-up. - 4. (*antes de subst*) [intenso] great. -5. (*antes de subst*) [excessivo] grand. -6. (*antes de subst*) [notável] great. -7. (*antes de subst*) [excepcional] great. -8. (*antes de subst*) [generoso] generous.
 ◆ **grandes** *mpl*: **os ~s** [os poderosos] the great.

grandeza [grã'deza] *f* -1. [ger] greatness. -2. [ostentação] grandeur.

grandiloquência [grãdʒilo'kwẽsja] *f* grandiloquence.

grandioso, osa [grã'dʒozu, ɔza] *adj* grandiose.

granel [gra'nɛw] *m*: **a ~** in bulk.

granito [gra'nitu] *m* granite.

granizo [gra'nizu] *m* hailstone; **chover ~** to hail; **chuva de ~** hail.

granja ['grãʒa] *f* farm.

granulado, da [granu'ladu, da] *adj* granulated.

grão ['grãw] (*pl* **grãos**) *m* -1. [semente] seed; [de café] bean. -2. [de areia] grain.
 ◆ **grãos** *mpl* [cereais] cereal.

grão-de-bico [ˌgrãwdʒiˈbikul (*pl* grãos--de-bico) *m* chick pea *UK*, garbanzo bean *US*.

grasnar [graʒˈna(x)] *vi* -**1.** [corvo] to caw. -**2.** [pato] to quack. -**3.** *fig* [gritar] to shout.

gratidão [gratʃiˈdãw] *f* gratitude.

gratificação [gratʃifikaˈsãw] (*pl* -ões) *f* -**1.** [bônus] bonus. -**2.** [recompensa] reward. -**3.** [gorjeta] tip.

gratificante [gratʃifiˈkãntʃi] *adj* gratifying.

gratificar [gratʃifiˈka(x)] *vt* -**1.** [dar bônus] to give a bonus. -**2.** [dar gorjeta a] to tip. -**3.** [recompensar] to reward; *esse trabalho gratifica muito* this work is very rewarding.

gratinado, da [gratʃiˈnadu, da] *adj* au gratin, gratiné.

grátis [ˈgratʃiʃ] *adj* free.

grato, ta [ˈgratu, ta] *adj* -**1.** [agradecido]: *ficar* ~ *a alguém por algo/por fazer algo* to be grateful to sb for sthg/doing sthg. -**2.** (*antes de subst*) [agradável] pleasant.

gratuito, ta [graˈtwitu, ta] *adj* -**1.** [grátis] free. -**2.** [sem fundamento] gratuitous.

grau [ˈgraw] *m* -**1.** [ger] degree. -**2.** [nível, gradação] level.

gravação [gravaˈsãw] (*pl* -ões) *f* -**1.** [em fita, disco, telefone] recording. -**2.** [em madeira] carving.

gravador, ra [gravaˈdo(x), ra] (*pl* -es) *m, f* [quem faz gravuras] engraver.
➤ **gravador** *m* [aparelho] tape recorder.
➤ **gravadora** *f* [empresa] record company.

gravar [graˈva(x)] *vt* -**1.** [ger] to record. -**2.** [em pedra, metal, madeira] to carve. -**3.** [na memória] to memorize.

gravata [graˈvata] *f* [adereço] tie.

gravata-borboleta [graˌvataboxboˈleta] (*pl* **gravatas-borboletas, gravatas-borboleta**) *f* bow tie.

grave [ˈgravi] *adj* -**1.** [profundo] serious. -**2.** [sério] grave. -**3.** [rígido] grave. -**4.** *MÚS* deep. -**5.** *LING* [acento] grave.

gravemente [graveˈmẽntʃi] *adv* seriously.

grávida [ˈgravida] *adj* pregnant.

gravidade [graviˈdadʒi] *f* gravity.

gravidez [graviˈdeʒ] *f* pregnancy.

graviola [graˈvjɔla] *f* sweetsop.

gravura [graˈvura] *f* -**1.** [estampa] print. -**2.** [em madeira, metal] engraving.

graxa [ˈgraʃa] *f* -**1.** [para couro] polish; ~ *de sapatos* shoe polish. -**2.** [lubrificante] grease.

Grécia [ˈgrɛsja] *f* Greece.

grego, ga [ˈgregu, ga] <> *adj* -**1.** [relativo à grécia] Greek. -**2.** *fig* [obscuro]: *isso para mim é* ~ that's Greek to me. <> *m, f* [pessoa] Greek.
➤ **grego** *m* *LING* Greek; *falar* ~ *fam* to speak a foreign language.

grelha [ˈgreʎa] *f* grill; *na* ~ cooked on the grill.

grelhado, da [greˈʎadu, da] *adj* grilled.
➤ **grelhado** *m* grilled food.

grelhar [greˈʎa(x)] *vt* to grill.

grêmio [ˈgremjul] *m* -**1.** [associação] guild. -**2.** [clube] club.

grená [greˈna] <> *adj* dark red. <> *m* dark red.

greta [ˈgreta] *f* crack.

greve [ˈgrɛvi] *f* strike; *fazer* ~ to strike.

grevista [greˈviʃta] *mf* striker.

grifar [griˈfa(x)] *vt* -**1.** [compor em grifo] to italicize. -**2.** [sublinhar] to underline. -**3.** *fig* [enfatizar] to emphasize.

grife [ˈgrifi] *f* label.

grifo [ˈgrifu] *m* italics.

grilagem [griˈlaʒẽ] (*pl* -ns) *f* falsification of property deeds.

grileiro, ra [griˈlejru, ra] *m, f* forger of property deeds.

grilhão [griˈʎãw] (*pl* -ões) *m* chain.

grilo [ˈgrilu] *m* -**1.** [inseto] cricket. -**2.** *fam* [problema] hiccup; *dar* ~ to cause a hiccup.

grinalda [griˈnawda] *f* garland.

gringo, ga [ˈgrĩŋgu, ga] *m, f* *fam pej* foreigner.

gripado, da [griˈpadu, da] *adj*: *estar/ficar* ~ to have/get flu.

gripe [ˈgripi] *f* flu.

grisalho, lha [griˈzaʎu, ʎa] *adj* greying *UK*, graying *US*.

gritante [griˈtãntʃi] *adj* -**1.** [evidente] glaring. -**2.** [de cor viva] dazzling.

gritar [griˈta(x)] *vt & vi* to shout; ~ *com alguém* to shout at sb.

gritaria [gritaˈria] *f* shouting.

grito [ˈgritu] *m* -**1.** [brado] shout; *falar aos* ~*s* to shout; *protestar aos* ~*s* to shout protests; *chegar aos* ~*s* to reach screaming point; *dar um* ~ to give a shout. -**2.** [de animal] scream. -**3.** [de dor] scream. -**4.** [de pavor] scream.

Groenlândia [groẽˈlãndʒja] *n* Greenland.

grosar [groˈza(x)] *vt* [limar, debastar] to file.

groselha [groˈzɛʎa] *f* redcurrant.

grosseiro, ra [groˈsejru, ra] *adj* -**1.** [rude] rude. -**2.** [chulo] vulgar. -**3.** [ordinário] coarse.

grosseria [groseˈria] *f* rudeness; *dizer/fazer uma* ~ to say/do something rude.

grosso, ssa ['grosu, sa] adj -1. [ger] thick. -2. [áspero] rough. -3. [rude] rude. -4. fam [abundante]: **dinheiro ~** a considerable sum of money.

➨ **grosso** adv: **falar ~ com alguém** to get tough with sb.

➨ **grosso modo** loc adv roughly.

grossura [gro'sura] f -1. [espessura] thickness. -2. fam [grosseria] rudeness.

grotesco, ca [gro'teʃku, ka] adj grotesque.

grudar [gru'da(x)] ⇔ vt: **~ algo em algo** to stick sthg on sthg. ⇔ vi to stick.

grude ['grudʒi] m -1. [cola] glue. -2. fam [comida ruim] muck.

grunhido [gru'ɲidu] m grunt.

grunhir [gru'ɲi(x)] vi -1. [porco] to grunt. -2. fig [resmungar] to grumble.

grupo ['grupu] m group; **~ sanguíneo** blood group; **~ de discussão** COMPUT newsgroup.

gruta ['gruta] f cave, grotto.

guache [gwaʃi] m gouache.

guaraná [gwara'na] m guarana; **~ em pó** powdered guarana; **~ natural** natural guarana.

guarda ['gwaxda] ⇔ f -1. [proteção] care; **ficar de ~** to stand guard. -2. MIL guard. ⇔ mf [policial] police officer.

guarda-chuva [ˌgwaxda'ʃuval] (pl guarda-chuvas) m umbrella.

guarda-costas [ˌgwaxda'kɔʃtaʃ] mf inv -1. NÁUT coastguard. -2. fig [para defesa] bodyguard.

guardados [gwax'daduʃ] mpl bits and pieces.

guarda-florestal [ˌgwaxdafloreʃ'taw] (pl guardas-florestais) mf forest ranger.

guarda-louça [ˌgwaxda'losa] (pl guarda-louças) m dresser.

guardanapo [ˌgwaxda'napu] m (table) napkin.

guarda-noturno [ˌgwaxdano'tuxnul] (pl guardas-noturnos) mf nightwatchman.

guardar [gwax'da(x)] vt -1. [ger] to keep; **~ segredo sobre algo** to keep quiet about sthg. -2. [pôr no lugar]: **~ algo (em)** to put sthg away (in). -3. [reservar]: **~ algo (para)** to keep sthg (for). -4. [gravar na memória] to remember. -5. [vigiar] to guard. -6. [cuidar de] to look after. -7. [observar] to keep; **guardadas as (devidas) proporções** to a certain extent.

➨ **guardar-se** vp -1. [proteger-se]: **~-se de** to steer clear of. -2. [prevenir-se]: **~-se de** to watch out for.

guarda-roupa [ˌgwaxda'xopa] (pl guarda-roupas) m wardrobe.

guarda-sol [ˌgwaxda'sɔwl] (pl guarda-sóis) m parasol.

guarda-volumes [ˌgwaxdavo'lumiʃ] m (inv) left-luggage office.

guardião, diã [gwax'dʒjãw, dʒjã] (mpl -ães, -ões, fpl -s) m, f guardian.

guarnecer [gwaxne'se(x)] vt -1. [abastecer] to supply; **~ alguém de algo** to supply sb with sthg. -2. MIL to occupy. -3. NÁUT to crew.

guarnição [gwaxni'sãw] (pl -ões) f -1. [ger] garnish. -2. MIL garrison. -3. NÁUT crew.

Guatemala [gwate'mala] n Guatemala.

guatemalteco, ca [gwatemaw'tɛku, ka] ⇔ adj Guatemalan. ⇔ m, f Guatemalan.

gude ['gudʒi] m ▷ **bola.**

guelra ['gɛwxa] f gill.

guerra ['gɛxa] f -1. [ger] war; **em ~** at war; **~ civil** civil war; **~ fria** cold war; **~ mundial** world war; **fazer ~ a** to do battle with. -2. fig [disputa] battle.

guerra-relâmpago [gɛxa'xelãmpaɡul] (pl guerras-relâmpago) f blitzkrieg.

guerreiro, ra [ge'xejru, ra] ⇔ adj -1. [belicoso] warlike. -2. [espírito, índole] fighting. ⇔ m, f [pessoa] warrior.

guerrilha [ge'xiʎa] f guerrilla warfare.

guerrilheiro, ra [gexi'ʎejru, ra] ⇔ adj guerrilla (antes de subst). ⇔ m, f guerrilla.

gueto ['getu] m ghetto.

guia ['gia] ⇔ f guide. ⇔ m [manual - turístico, cultural] guide; [- de instruções] manual. ⇔ mf [pessoa] guide; **~ turístico** tourist guide.

Guiana [gwi'jãna] n Guyana.

guianense [gwija'nẽnsil] ⇔ adj Guyanese. ⇔ mf Guyanese.

guiar ['gja(x)] ⇔ vt -1. [orientar] to guide. -2. [proteger] to watch over. -3. AUTO [dirigir] to drive. ⇔ vi AUTO to drive.

➨ **guiar-se** vp [orientar-se] to orientate o.s.

guichê [gi'ʃe] m -1. [no cinema, teatro] ticket office. -2. [em banco] counter.

guidom [gi'dõ] (pl -ns) m handlebars (pl).

guilhotina [giʎo'tʃina] f guillotine.

guinada [gi'nada] f -1. NÁUT yaw. -2. AUTO veer; **dar uma ~** to veer.

guincho ['gĩʃul] m -1. [reboque] tow. -2. [chiado] squeal.

guindaste [gĩ'daʃtʃil] m crane.

guisado, da [gi'zadu, da] m CULIN stew.

guisar [gi'za(x)] vt to stew.

guitarra [gi'taxa] f: **~ (elétrica)** electric guitar.

guitarrista [gita'xiʃta] mf guitarist.

gula [ˈgula] *f* gluttony.
gulodice [guloˈdʒisi] *f* greediness.
guloseima [guloˈzejma] *f* titbit.
guloso, osa [guˈlozu, ɔza] *adj* greedy.
gume [ˈgumi] *m* blade.
guri, ria [guˈri, ria] *m* kid.
gurizada [guriˈzada] *f* [criançada] kids
(pl).
guru [guˈru] *m* guru.

h¹, H [aˈga] *m* [letra] h, H.
h² *(abrev de hora) f* hr., h.
ha *(abrev de hectare) m* ha.
hábil [ˈabiw] *(pl* -eis) *adj* - **1.** [ger] skilful.
- **2.** [sutil] subtle. - **3.** *loc*: em tempo ~ in
due course.
habilidade [abiliˈdaʒi] *f* - **1.** [aptidão]
ability. - **2.** [competência] talent. - **3.** [as-
túcia] skill. - **4.** [sutileza] subtlety.
habilidoso, osa [abiliˈdozu, ɔza] *adj* skilful *UK*, skillful *US*.
habilitação [abilitaˈsãw] *(pl* -ões) *f* - **1.**
[aptidão] aptitude. - **2.** [conhecimento for-
mal] qualification. - **3.** *JUR* [documento]
validation.
   habilitações *fpl* [qualificações] qualifications.
habilitado, da [abiliˈtadu, da] *adj* - **1.**
[profissional liberal] qualified. - **2.** [operá-
rio] skilled.
habilitar [abiliˈta(x)] *vt* - **1.** [capacitar] to
enable. - **2.** [preparar] to prepare. - **3.**
[dar direito a] to entitle to.
   habilitar-se *vp* [capacitar-se] to prepare o.s.
habitação [abitaˈsãw] *(pl* -ões) *f* - **1.** [ca-
sa] house. - **2.** *POL* [moradia] housing.
habitante [abiˈtãntʃi] *mf* inhabitant.
habitar [abiˈta(x)] ⟨⟩ *vt* - **1.** [morar em]
to live in. - **2.** [povoar] to inhabit. ⟨⟩ *vi*
[viver] to live.
hábitat [ˈabitatʃ] *m* habitat.
hábito [ˈabitu] *m* habit.
habituado, da [abiˈtwadu, da] *adj*: ~ **(a**
algo) used (to sthg); ~ **a fazer algo**
used to doing sthg.
habitual [abiˈtwaw] *(pl* -ais) *adj* habitual.
habituar [abiˈtwa(x)] *vt* to accustom to;
~ **alguém a algo/a fazer algo** to get sb
used to sthg/to doing sthg.

   habituar-se *vp*: ~ **-se a (fazer)** algo
to get used to (doing) sthg.
hacker [xake(x)ʃ] *(pl* **hackers)** *m* COMPUT
hacker.
hadoque [aˈdɔki] *m* haddock.
Haia [ˈaja] *n* The Hague.
hálito [ˈalitu] *m* breath; **mau** ~ bad
breath.
hall [ˈɔw] *m* hall; ~ **de entrada** entrance
hall.
halterofilista [awterofiˈliʃta] *mf* weight
lifter.
hambúrguer [ãnˈbuxge(x)] *(pl* -es) *m*
hamburger.
handicap [ãndʒiˈkapi] *m* handicap.
hangar [ãnˈga(x)] *(pl* -es) *m* hangar.
haras [ˈaraʃ] *m inv* stud *(for race-
horses)*.
hardware [axˈdwɛ(x)] *m* COMPUT hardware.
harmonia [axmoˈnia] *f* harmony.
harmônico, ca [axˈmoniku, ka] *adj* har-
monic.
   harmônica *f* harmonica, mouth
organ.
harmonioso, osa [axmoˈnjozu, jɔza] *adj*
harmonious.
harmonizar [axmoniˈza(x)] *vt* - **1.** *MÚS* to
harmonize. - **2.** [conciliar]: ~ **algo com**
algo to reconcile sthg with sthg.
   harmonizar-se *vp*: ~ **-se (com algo)**
to be in harmony (with sthg).
harpa [ˈaxpa] *f* harp.
haste [ˈaʃtʃi] *f* - **1.** [de bandeira] pole. - **2.**
[caule] stalk.
hasteamento [aʃtʃjaˈmẽntu] *m* hoisting.
havana [aˈvãna] ⟨⟩ *adj* [cor] beige. ⟨⟩
m [charuto] Havana cigar.
haver [aˈve(x)] *v impess* - **1.** [existir, estar,
ter lugar]: **há** there is, there are *pl*; **havia**
there was, there were *pl*; **há um café**
muito bom ao fim da rua there's a very
good café at the end of the street; **não**
há nada aqui there's nothing here; **não**
há correio amanhã there's no mail
tomorrow. - **2.** [exprime tempo]: **estou**
esperando há dez minutos I've been
waiting for ten minutes; **há séculos**
que não vou lá I haven't been there
for ages; **há três dias que não o vejo** I
haven't seen him for three days. - **3.**
[exprime obrigação]: **há que esperar três**
dias you'll have to wait three days.
- **4.** [em locuções]: **haja o que houver**
come what may; **não há de quê!** don't
mention it! ⟨⟩ *v aux* [em tempos
compostos] to have; **ele havia chegado**
há pouco he had just arrived; **como**
não havia comido estava com fome I
was hungry because I hadn't eaten;

havíamos reservado com antecedência we'd reserved in advance.

➤ **haver de** *v + prep* [dever] to have; [exprime intenção]: **hei de ir** I'll go.

➤ **haver-se com** *vp + prep*: ~**-se com alguém** [prestar contas a] to answer to sb.

➤ **haveres** *mpl* [pertences] belongings; [bens] assets.

haxixe [a'ʃiʃi] *m* hashish.

HC (*abrev de* **Hospital das Clínicas**) *m famous teaching hospital in São Paulo.*

HD (*abrev de* **Hard Disk**) *m* HD.

hectare [εk'tari] *m* hectare.

hedge [εdʒi] *m ECON* [proteção cambial] hedge.

hediondo, da [e'dʒõndu, da] *adj* hideous.

hegemonia [eʒemo'nia] *f* hegemony.

hegemônico, ca [ege'moniku, ka] *adj* hegemonic.

hélice [ˈεlisi] *f* propeller.

helicóptero [eli'kɔpterul] *m* helicopter.

hematoma [ema'toma] *f* bruise, haematoma *UK*, hematoma *US*.

hemisfério [emiʃ'fεrjul] *m* hemisphere.

hemodiálise [emo'dʒjalizil] *f* dialysis.

hemofílico, ca [εmo'filiku, ka] ◇ *adj* haemophilic *UK*, hemophilic *US*. ◇ *m*, *f* haemophiliac *UK*, hemophiliac *US*.

hemorragia [emoxa'ʒia] *f* haemorrhage *UK*, hemorrhage *US*.

hemorrágico, ca [emo'xagiku, ka] *adj* haemorrhagic.

hemorróidas [emo'xɔjdaʃ] *fpl* haemorrhoid *UK*, hemorrhoid *US*.

hepatite [epa'tʃitʃil] *f* hepatitis.

hera [ˈεral] *f* ivy.

heráldica [e'rawdʒikal] *f* heraldry.

herança [e'rãnsal] *f* inheritance.

herdar [εx'da(x)] *vt* [ger]: ~ **algo de alguém** to inherit sthg from sb.

herdeiro, ra [εx'dejru, ral] *m*, *f* heir.

herege [e'rεʒil] *mf* heretic.

heresia [ere'zial] *f* heresy.

hermético, ca [εx'mεtʃiku, ka] *adj* **-1.** [bem fechado] hermetic, airtight. **-2.** *fig* [obscuro] hermetic.

hérnia [ˈεxnjal] *f* hernia; ~ **de disco** slipped disc.

herói [e'rɔjl] *m* hero.

heróico, ca [e'rɔjku, ka] *adj* heroic.

heroína [e'rwinal] *f* heroine.

herpes [ˈεxpiʃ] *m* herpes.

hesitação [ezita'sãwl] (*pl* **-ões**) *f* hesitation.

hesitante [ezi'tãntʃil] *adj* hesitant.

hesitar [ezi'ta(x)] *vi*: ~ **em fazer algo** to hesitate to do sthg.

heterogêneo, nea [etero'ʒenju, njal] *adj* heterogeneous.

heterossexual [eterosek'swawl] (*pl* **-ais**) ◇ *adj* heterosexual. ◇ *mf* heterosexual.

hibernar [ibex'na(x)l] *vi* to hibernate.

hibisco [i'biʃkul] *m* hibiscus.

híbrido, da [ˈibridu, dal] *adj* [mesclado] hybrid.

➤ **híbrido** *m* [animal ou vegetal]: **ser um ~ (de)** to be a hybrid (of).

hidramático, ca [idra'matʃiku, kal] *adj* Hydra-Matic®.

hidratante [idra'tãntʃil] ◇ *adj* moisturizing. ◇ *m* moisturizer.

hidratar [idra'ta(x)l] *vt* **-1.** [pele] to moisturize. **-2.** *MED* to hydrate.

hidráulico, ca [i'drawliku, kal] *adj* hydraulic.

hidrelétrica [idre'lεtrikal] *f* **-1.** [usina] hydroelectric power station. **-2.** [empresa] hydroelectric company.

hidrófobo, ba [i'drɔfobu, bal] ◇ *adj* hydrophobic. ◇ *m*, *f* hydrophobic person.

hidrogênio [idro'ʒenjul *m* hydrogen.

hidromassagem [idruma'saʒēl (*pl* **-ns**) *f* hydromassage.

hiena [ˈjenal] *f* hyena.

hierarquia [ljerar'kial] *f* hierarchy.

hierárquico, ca [lje'raxkiku, kal] *adj* hierarchical.

hieróglifo [lje'rɔglifull *m* hieroglyph.

hífen [ˈifēl] (*pl* **-es**) *m* hyphen.

hifenizar [ifeni'za(x)] *vt* hyphenate.

Hi-Fi (*abrev de* **High Fidelity**) *m* hi-fi.

higiene [i'ʒjenil] *f* hygiene.

higiênico, ca [i'ʒjeniku, kal] *adj* hygienic; **papel ~** toilet paper.

higienizar [ʒjeni'za(x)l] *vt* to sterilize.

hilariante [ila'rjãntʃil] *adj* hilarious.

hilário, ria [i'larju, rjal] *adj* [hilariante] hilarious.

Himalaia [ima'lajal] *n*: **o ~** the Himalayas (*pl*).

hindi [ˈĩndʒi] *m* Hindi.

hindu [ĩn'dul] (*pl* **hindus**) ◇ *adj* **-1.** [da Índia] Indian. **-2.** *RELIG* Hindu. ◇ *m*, *f* **-1.** [da Índia] Indian. **-2.** *RELIG* Hindu.

hino [ˈinul] *m* hymn; ~ **nacional** national anthem.

hiper [ˈipe(x)l] *prefixo* **-1.** [extremo, grande] hyper-. **-2.** *fam* [super] hyper-.

hipermercado [ipexmex'kadul] *m* hypermarket.

hipertensão [ipextēn'sãwl] (*pl* **-ões**) *f* high blood pressure, hypertension.

hipertenso, sa [ipex'tẽsu, sal] *adj* with high blood-pressure; **ser ~** to have high blood pressure.

hipertexto [ipex'tejʃtul] *m COMPUT* hypertext.

hipertrofia [ipextroˈfia] f -1. MED hypertrophy. -2. [fig] excessive increase.

hipertrofiar [ipextroˈfja(x)] vt to overstretch.
➡ **hipertrofiar-se** vp to become overdeveloped.

hípico, ca [ˈipiku, ka] adj -1. [clube, competição] riding. -2. [sociedade] equestrian.

hipismo [iˈpiʒmu] m horse riding, equestrianism.

hipnose [ipˈnɔzi] f hypnosis.

hipnótico, ca [ipˈnɔtʃiku, ka] adj hypnotic.
➡ **hipnótico** m [substância] hypnotic.

hipnotizado, da [ipnotʃiˈzadu, da] adj hypnotized.

hipnotizar [ipnotʃiˈza(x)] vt to hypnotize.

hipocondria [ipokõˈdria] f hypochondria.

hipocondríaco, ca [ˌipokõˈdriaku, ka] ◇ adj hypochondriac. ◇ m, f hypochondriac.

hipocrisia [ipokriˈzia] f hypocrisy.

hipócrita [iˈpɔkrita] ◇ adj hypocritical. ◇ mf hypocrite.

hipódromo [iˈpɔdrumu] m racecourse.

hipopótamo [ipoˈpɔtamu] m hippopotamus.

hipoteca [ipoˈtɛka] f mortgage.

hipótese [iˈpɔtezi] f -1. [conjectura] hypothesis. -2. [possibilidade] eventuality; **não abandonaria meus filhos em ~ alguma** I wouldn't abandon my children under any circumstances, under no circumstance would I abandon my children; **na melhor/pior das ~s** at best/worst.

hispânico, ca [iʃˈpaniku, ka] ◇ adj Hispanic. ◇ m, f Hispanic.

hispano, na [iʃˈpãnu, na] ◇ adj Hispanic. ◇ m, f Hispanic.

hispano-americano, na [iʃˌpãnwameriˈkãnu, na] ◇ adj Spanish-American. ◇ m, f Spanish American.

histeria [iʃteˈrial] f hysteria.

histérico, ca [iʃˈtɛriku, ka] adj hysterical.

história [iʃˈtɔrja] f -1. [ger] history. -2. [narração] story; **~ em quadrinhos** comic strip. -3. [lorota] nonsense. -4. [explicação] excuse. -5. [idéia, proposta] suggestion. -6. [acontecimento] event; [caso amoroso] love affair. -7. [enredo] storyline. -8. [boato] rumour. -9. [tradição] tradition. -10. [problema] problem. -11. fam [abuso]: **que ~ é essa de ...?** what's the idea of ...?

historiador, ra [iʃtorjaˈdo(x), ra] m, f historian.

historicidade [iʃtorisiˈdadʒi] f historicity, historical authenticity.

histórico, ca [iʃˈtɔriku, ka] adj -1. [ger] historical. -2. [importante] historic.
➡ **histórico** m history.

histrião [iʃtriˈãw] (pl -ões) m [comediante] comic.

histriônico, ca [iʃtriˈoniku, ka] adj histrionic.

hit [ˈiti] m COMPUT hit.

HIV (abrev de **Human Immunodeficiency Virus**) m HIV.

hobby [ˈɔbi] m hobby.

hoje [ˈoʒi] adv today; **de ~ em diante** from today onwards, from this day forth; **~ noite** tonight; **~ em dia** nowadays.

Holanda [oˈlãnda] f Holland, The Netherlands.

holandês, esa [olãnˈdeʃ, eza] (mpl -eses fpl -s) ◇ adj Dutch. ◇ m, f Dutchman (f Dutchwoman).
➡ **holandês** m [língua] Dutch.

holofote [oloˈfɔtʃi] m searchlight.

home banking [ˈxomibãŋkĩn] m COMPUT home banking.

homem [ˈɔmẽl] (pl -ns) m -1. [ger] man; **~ de negócios** businessman. -2. [humanidade]: **o ~** mankind.

homem-rã [ˌomẽnˈxã] (pl **homens-rãs**) m frogman.

homenagear [omenaˈʒja(x)] vt to pay homage to.

homenagem [omeˈnaʒẽ] (pl -ns) f homage; **em ~ a algo/alguém** in homage to sthg/sb.

homeopatia [omjopaˈtʃia] f homeopathy.

homeopático, ca [omjoˈpatʃiku, ka] adj homeopathic.

homicida [omiˈsida] ◇ adj homicidal. ◇ mf murderer.

homicídio [omiˈsidʒju] m homicide; **~ culposo** manslaughter.

homogêneo, nea [omoˈʒenju, nja] adj homogeneous.

homologação [omologaˈsãw] (pl -ões) f ratification.

homologar [omoloˈga(x)] vt -1. [lei, casamento] to ratify. -2. [sociedade] to grant official recognition to.

homossexual [omosekˈswawl] (pl -ais) ◇ adj homosexual. ◇ m, f homosexual.

homossexualidade [omosekswaliˈdadʒil] f homosexuality.

Honduras [õnˈduraʃ] n Honduras.

hondurenho, nha [õnduˈreɲu, ɲal] ◇ adj Honduran. ◇ m, f Honduran.

honestidade loneʃtʃi'dadʒil f honesty; **com ~** honestly.

honesto, ta lo'nɛʃtu, tal adj honest.

honorário, ria lono'rarju, rjal adj honorary.

honorários lono'rarjuʃl mpl fee (sg).

honra ['ɔ̃nxal f -1. [ger] honour UK, honor US; **em ~ de alguém** in honour of sb UK, in honor of sb US. -2. [motivo de orgulho] credit.

◆ **honras** fpl honours UK, honors US; **~ militares** military honours UK, military honors US.

honradez lõnxa'deʒl f honesty.

honrado, da lõ'xadu, dal adj -1. [digno] worthy. -2. [respeitado] respectable.

honrar lõ'xa(x)l vt [respeitar] to honour UK, to honor US.

honroso, osa lõ'xozu, ɔzal adj honourable UK, honorable US.

hóquei ['ɔkejl m hockey; **~ sobre gelo** ice hockey.

hora ['ɔral f -1. [do dia] hour; **de ~ em ~** every hour. -2. [ger] time; **altas ~s** very late at night; **que ~s são?** what time is it?; **~ extra** extra time; **fazer algo fora de ~** to do sthg at the wrong time; **estar na ~ de fazer algo** to be time to do sthg; **na ~ H** on the dot; **de última ~** last minute (antes de subst); **não vejo a ~ de ir embora** I can't wait for the time to leave; **na ~** on time; **perder a ~** to be late. -3. [compromisso]: **marcar ~ com alguém** to make an appointment with sb. -4. loc: **fazer ~** to waste time.

horário, ria lo'rarju, rjal adj hourly.

◆ **horário** m -1. [tabela] timetable. -2. [hora prefixada] time; **~ nobre** prime time; **~ de verão** summer time.

horda ['ɔxdal f horde.

horizontal lorizõn'tawl (pl -ais) <> adj horizontal. <> f [linha] horizontal.

horizonte lori'zõntʃil m horizon.

hormônio lox'monjul m hormone.

horóscopo lo'rɔʃkopul m horoscope.

horrendo, da lo'xẽndu, dal adj -1. [atemorizante] frightful. -2. [feio] horrendous.

horrível lo'xivɛwl (pl -eis) adj -1. [ger] terrible. -2. [feio] horrible.

horror lo'xo(x)l (pl -es) m -1. [medo]: **ter ~ (de ou a algo)** to have a horror (of sthg). -2. [repulsa]: **ter ~ a algo/fazer algo** to have a horror of sthg/doing sthg. -3. [coisa feia]: **fiquei um ~ com essa roupa** I looked a fright in those clothes. -4. [atrocidade]: **que ~!** how awful! -5. [ruim]: **ser um ~** to be terrible.

◆ **horrores** mpl -1. [palavras injuriosas]:

dizer ~ de algo/alguém to say horrible things about sthg/sb. -2. [ações terríveis]: **fazer ~** to do horrible things. -3. [quantia vultuosa]: **ele está faturando ~ es** he is raking it in.

horrorizar loxori'za(x)l vt to terrify.

◆ **horrorizar-se** vp to be terrified.

horroroso, osa loxo'rozu, ɔzal adj -1. [ger] terrible. -2. [feio] frightful.

horta ['ɔxtal f vegetable garden.

hortaliças loxta'lisaʃl fpl vegetables.

hortelã loxte'lãl f mint.

hortelã-pimenta loxte,lãpi'mẽntal (pl hortelãs-pimenta) f peppermint.

hortênsia lox'tẽnsjal f hydrangea.

horticultor, ra loxtʃikuw'to(x), ral (mpl -es, fpl -s) m, f horticulturist.

hortifrutigranjeiro, ra loxtʃiʃrutʃigrãn'ʒejru, ral adj relating to fruit, vegetable and small farm production.

◆ **hortifrutigranjeiro** m smallholder (producing fruit and vegetables).

hortigranjeiros loxtʃigrãn'ʒeiruʃl mpl farm produce.

horto ['ɔxtul m allotment.

hospedagem loʃpe'daʒẽl (pl -ns) f -1. [acomodação] accommodation. -2. [diária] board and lodging. -3. [pensão] inn.

hospedar loʃpe'da(x)l vt to lodge.

◆ **hospedar-se** vp to lodge.

hospedaria loʃpeda'rial f guest house.

hóspede ['ɔʃpedʒil mf guest.

hospício loʃ'pisjul m hospice.

hospital loʃpi'tawl (pl -ais) m hospital.

hospitaleiro, ra loʃpita'lejru, ral adj hospitable.

hospitalidade loʃpitali'dadʒil f hospitality.

host ['xoʃtʃil m COMPUT host.

hostess ['ɔʃtesl f hostess.

hostil loʃ'tiwl (pl -is) adj -1. [contrário]: **~ a algo/alguém** hostile to sthg/sb. -2. [agressivo] hostile.

hostilidade loʃtʃili'dadʒil f [sentimento] hostility.

hostilizar loʃtili'za(x)l vt to be hostile towards.

hotel lo'tɛwl (pl -éis) m hotel.

hp (abrev de horsepower) m hp.

HTML (abrev de Hypertext Markup Language) m HTML.

HTTP (abrev de Hypertext Transfer Protocol) m HTTP.

humanidade lumani'dadʒil f humanity.

humanitário, ria lumani'tarju, rjal adj humanitarian.

humano, na lu'manu, nal adj -1. [da humanidade] human; **ser ~** human being. -2. [bondoso] human, understanding.

humanóide [uma'nɔjdʒil] ◇ adj humanoid. ◇ mf humanoid.

humildade [umiw'dadʒil] f - **1.** [pobreza] humbleness. - **2.** [modéstia] humility. - **3.** [submissão] humility; **com ~** humbly.

humilde [u'miwdʒil] adj humble; **os ~ s** the poor (pl).

humildemente [umiwdʒi'mēntʃil] adv humbly.

humilhação [umiʎa'sãw] (pl -ões) f humiliation.

humilhar [umi'ʎa(x)] vt to humiliate.

humor [u'mo(x)] m - **1.** [ger] humour UK, humor US. - **2.** [ânimo] mood; **estar de bom/mau ~** to be good-/bad-tempered. - **3.** [senso de humor] sense of humour UK, sense of humor US.

humorista [umo'riʃta] mf comedian.

humorístico, ca [umo'riʃtʃiku, ka] adj comedy (antes de subst).

húngaro, ra ['ũŋgaru, ra] ◇ adj Hungarian. ◇ m, f Hungarian.
➡ **húngaro** m [língua] Hungarian.

Hungria [ũŋ'gria] n Hungary.

Hz (abrev de **hertz**) m Hz.

i, I [il m [letra] i, I.

ianque ['jãŋkil] ◇ adj Yankee. ◇ m, f Yank.

iate ['jatʃil m yacht.

iatismo [ja'tʃiʒmul m yachting, sailing.

iatista [ja'tʃiʃta] mf yachtsman (f yachtswoman).

IBAMA (abrev de **Instituto Brasileiro do Meio Ambiente e dos Recursos Naturais Renováveis**) m Brazilian organization responsible for preserving the country's natural environment.

Ibase (abrev de **Instituto Brasileiro de Análises Sociais e Econômicas**) m Brazilian institute for social and economic analysis.

IBDF (abrev de **Instituto Brasileiro de Desenvolvimento Florestal**) m Brazilian institute for forestry development.

IBGE (abrev de **Instituto Brasileiro de Geografia e Estatística**) m Brazilian institute of geography and statistics.

Ibope (abrev de **Instituto Brasileiro de Opinião Pública e Estatística**) m Brazilian opinion poll institute.

IBP (abrev de **Instituto Brasileiro de Petróleo**) m Brazilian petroleum institute.

içar [i'sa(x)] vt to hoist.

iceberg [ajs'bɛxgil m iceberg.

ICMS (abrev de **Imposto sobre a Circulação de Mercadorias e Serviços**) m government tax on goods and services, ≃ VAT UK.

ícone ['ikonil m icon.

iconoclasta [ikono'klaʃta] ◇ adj iconoclastic. ◇ mf iconoclast.

ida ['idal f - **1.** [ato de ir] going. - **2.** [partida] departure. - **3.** [viagem] journey; **na ~** on the outward journet; **(bilhete de) ~ e volta** return ticket. - **4.** [bilhete]: **só comprei a ~** I only bought a single (ticket).

idade [i'dadʒil f [ger] age; **de ~** [idoso] elderly; **ser menor/maior de ~** to be under/of age; **pessoa da terceira ~** senior citizen; **Idade Média** Middle Ages (pl); **~ da pedra** Stone Age.

ideal [i'deawl (pl -ais) ◇ adj ideal. ◇ m - **1.** [valores] ideal. - **2.** [perfeição] ideal thing.

idealista [idea'liʃta] ◇ adj idealistic. ◇ mf idealist.

idealizador [idealiza'do(x)] m, f planner.

idealizar [ideali'za(x)] vt - **1.** [endeusar] to idealize. - **2.** [planejar] to plan.

idear ['idea(x)] vt [planejar] to plan.

idéia [i'dɛjal f - **1.** [ger] idea; **estar com ~ de** to be thinking of; **ter uma ~ errada de algo** to have the wrong idea about sthg; **fazer ou ter ~ de algo** to have an idea of sthg. - **2.** [mente, opinião] mind; **mudar de ~** to change one's mind.

idem ['idɛl pron idem.

idêntico, ca [i'dʒēntʃiku, ka] adj identical.

identidade [idēntʃi'dadʒil f identity; **(carteira de) ~** identity card.

identificação [idēntʃifika'sãw] (pl -ões) f identification.

identificar [idʒēntʃifi'ka(x)] vt to identify.
➡ **identificar-se** vp - **1.** [revelar-se] to identify o.s. - **2.** [espelhar-se]: **~-se com algo/alguém** to identify o.s. with sthg/sb.

ideologia [ideolo'ʒial f ideology.

ídiche ['idiʃil m = **iídiche**.

idílico, ca [i'dʒiliku, ka] adj idyllic.

idioma [i'dʒjomal m language.

idiomático, ca [idʒo'matʃiku, ka] adj idiomatic; **expressão idiomática** idiomatic expression.

idiota [iˈdʒɔtal] ⬦ *adj* idiotic. ⬦ *mf* idiot.

idiotia [idʒjoˈtʃial] *f* idiocy.

ido, ida [ˈidu, ˈidal] *adj* past.

idólatra [iˈdɔlatral] ⬦ *adj* idolatrous. ⬦ *mf* [de ídolos] idol worshipper.

idolatrar [idolaˈtra(x)] *vt* to idolize.

ídolo [ˈidulul] *m* idol.

idôneo, nea [iˈdonju, njal] *adj* -1. [pessoa, julgamento] fitting. -2. [empresa] suitable.

idoso, osa [iˈdozu, ɔzal] *adj* aged.

Iemanjá [jemãˈʒal] *f* goddess of the sea and water, in Afro-Brazilian lore.

Ierevan [jereˈval] *n* Yerevan.

ignição [igniˈsãwl] *f* ignition.

ignomínia [ignoˈminjal] *f* ignominy.

ignorado, da [ignoˈradu, dal] *adj* unknown.

ignorância [ignoˈrãnsjal] *f* -1. [desconhecimento] ignorance. -2. [grosseria] rudeness; **com ~** rudely. -3. [violência]: **apelar para a ~** to resort to violence.

ignorante [ignoˈrãntʃil] ⬦ *adj* -1. [leigo]: **~ (em)** ignorant (of). -2. [grosseiro] rude. ⬦ *mf* -1. [leigo] lay person. -2. [grosseiro] rude person.

ignorar [ignoˈra(x)] *vt* -1. [desconhecer] not to know. -2. [desprezar] to ignore.

IGP (*abrev de* Índice Geral de Preços) *m* general price index.

IGP-M (*abrev de* Índice Geral de Preços de Mercado) *m* general index of market prices.

igreja [iˈgreʒal] *f* church.

Iguaçu [igwaˈsul] *n*: **as cataratas do ~** the Iguaçu Falls.

igual [iˈgwawl] (*pl* -ais) ⬦ *adj* -1. [idêntico] equal. -2. [uniforme] the same. ⬦ *mf* que all the same as.

igualar [igwaˈla(x)] *vt* -1. [tornar igual] to make equal. -2. [nivelar] to level.
◆ **igualar-se** *vp* -1. [tornar-se igual]: **~-se a algo/alguém** to equal sthg/sb. -2. [comparar-se]: **~-se a algo/alguém** to bear comparison with sthg/sb.

igualdade [igwawˈdadʒil] *f* -1. [ger] equality. -2. [constância] regularity.

igualmente [igwawˈmẽntʃil] *adv* equally.

iguaria [igwaˈrial] *f* delicacy.

iídiche [ˈjidiʃil], **ídiche** [ˈidiʃil] *m* Yiddish.

ilegal [ileˈgawl] (*pl* -ais) *adj* illegal.

ilegítimo, ma [ileˈʒitʃimu, mal] *adj* illegitimate.

ilegível [ileˈʒivɛwl] (*pl* -eis) *adj* illegible.

ileso, sa [iˈlezu, zal] *adj* unharmed.

iletrado, da [ileˈtradu, dal] *adj* -1. [inculto] unlettered. -2. [analfabeto] illiterate.

ilha [ˈiʎal] *f* island.

ilhéu, ilhoa [iˈʎɛw, iˈʎoal] *m, f* islander.

ilhota [iˈʎɔtal] *f* islet.

ilícito, ta [iˈlisitu, tal] *adj* illicit.

ilimitado, da [ilemiˈtadu, dal] *adj* unlimited.

ilógico, ca [iˈlɔʒiku, kal] *adj* illogical.

iludir [iluˈdi(x)] *vt* to delude.
◆ **iludir-se** *vp* to delude o.s.

iluminação [iluminaˈsãw] (*pl* -ões) *f* -1. [luzes] lighting. -2. *fig* [insight] inspiration.

iluminar [ilumiˈna(x)] *vt* -1. [alumiar] to light up. -2. *fig* [esclarecer] to enlighten.

Iluminismo [ilumiˈniʒmul] *m* Enlightenment.

iluminista [ilumiˈniʃtal] ⬦ *adj* Enlightenment (*antes de subst*). ⬦ *mf* member or follower of the Enlightenment.

ilusão [iluˈzãwl] (*pl* -ões) *f* illusion; **~ de ótica** optical illusion; **viver de ilusões** to delude o.s.

ilusionista [iluzjoˈniʃtal] *mf* illusionist.

ilusório, ria [iluˈzɔrju, rjal] *adj* illusory.

ilustração [iluʃtraˈsãwl] (*pl* -ões) *f* illustration.

ilustrado, da [iluʃˈtradu, dal] *adj* -1. [com figuras] illustrated. -2. [instruído] learned.

ilustrar [iluʃˈtra(x)] *vt* -1. [ger] to illustrate. -2. [instruir] to enlighten.

ilustre [iˈluʃtril] *adj* illustrious, distinguished; **um ~ desconhecido** a complete unknown.

ilustríssimo, ma [iluʃˈtrisimu, mal] *superl* ⬦ ilustre; **~ senhor** honourable gentleman *UK*, honorable gentleman *US*.

ímã [ˈimãl] *m* magnet.

imaculado, da [imakuˈladu, dal] *adj* immaculate.

imagem [iˈmaʒẽl] (*pl* -ns) *f* -1. [gen] image. -2. [TV] picture.

imaginação [imaʒinaˈsãwl] *f* imagination.

imaginar [imaʒiˈna(x)] ⬦ *vt* -1. [fantasiar] to imagine. -2. [supor]: **~ que** to imagine that. ⬦ *vi* to daydream; **imagina!** just imagine!
◆ **imaginar-se** *vp* [supor-se] to imagine o.s.

imaginário, ria [imaʒiˈnarju, rjal] *adj* imaginary.

imaginativo, va [imaʒinaˈtʃivu, val] *adj* imaginative.

imaturo, ra [imaˈturu, ral] *adj* immature.

imbatível [ĩnbaˈtʃivɛwl] (*pl* -eis) *adj* unbeatable.

imbecil [ĩnbeˈsiwl] (*pl* -is) ⬦ *adj* stupid, idiotic. ⬦ *mf* imbecile.

imbecilidade [ĩnbesiliˈdadʒil] *f* stupidity.

imediações [imedʒja'sõiʃ] *fpl* vicinity *(sg)*; **nas ~ de** near, in the vicinity of.

imediatamente [ime,dʒjata'mẽntʃi] *adv* immediately.

imediatismo [imedʒja'tʃiʒmu] *m* immediacy.

imensidão [imẽsi'dãw], **imensidade** [imẽsi'dadʒi] *f* immensity.

imenso, sa li'mẽsu, sa] *adj* immense; **sinto uma saudade imensa dele** I miss him immensely.

imerecido, da [imere'sidu, da] *adj* undeserved.

imergir [imex'ʒi(x)] <> *vt* to immerse. <> *vi* -1. [afundar] to sink. -2. *fig* [entrar]: **~ em algo** to sink into sthg.

imerso, sa li'mexsu, sa] *adj* immersed.

imigração [imigra'sãw] *(pl -ões)* *f* immigration.

imigrante [imi'grãntʃi] <> *adj* immigrant. <> *mf* immigrant.

iminente [imi'nẽntʃi] *adj* imminent.

imitação [imita'sãw] *(pl -ões)* *f* imitation.

imitar [imi'ta(x)] *vt* -1. [arremedar] to imitate. -2. [falsificar] to forge.

IML *(abrev de* **Instituto Médico Legal)** *m* Brazilian institute of forensic medicine.

imobiliário, ria [imobi'larju, rja] *adj* property *(antes de subst)*.
➔ **imobiliária** *f* estate agency.

imobilizar [imobili'za(x)] *vt* to immobilize.

imodesto, ta [imo'dɛʃtu, ta] *adj* immodest.

imoral [imo'raw] *(pl -ais)* *adj* immoral.

imoralidade [imorali'dadʒi] *f* immorality.

imortal [imox'taw] *(pl -ais)* <> *adj* immortal. <> *mf* member of the Academia Brasileira de Letras.

imortalidade [imoxtali'dadʒi] *f* immortality.

imóvel [i'mɔvɛw] *(pl -eis)* <> *adj* -1. [pessoa] immobile. -2. [olho, bem] fixed; **bens imóveis** real estate *(U)*. <> *m* property.

impaciência [ĩpa'sjẽsja] *f* impatience.

impacientar [ĩmpasjẽ'ta(x)] *vt* to be impatient.
➔ **impacientar-se** *vp* to become impatient.

impaciente [ĩpa'sjẽntʃi] *adj* -1. [sem paciência] impatient. -2. [ansioso] anxious.

impactar [ĩpak'ta(x)] <> *vt* -1. [impressionar, abalar] to shatter. -2. [colidir contra] to crash into. <> *vi* to have an impact.

impacto [ĩ'paktu] *m* impact.

impagável [ĩmpa'gavɛw] *(pl -eis)* *adj* priceless.

ímpar ['ĩpa(x)] *(pl -es)* *adj* -1. [número] odd. -2. [único] peerless; **ele é um amigo ~** he's a friend in a million.

imparcial [ĩpax'sjaw] *(pl -ais)* *adj* impartial.

impasse [ĩ'pasi] *m* deadlock, impasse.

impassível [ĩpa'sivɛw] *(pl -eis)* *adj* impassive.

impecável [ĩpe'kavɛw] *(pl -eis)* *adj* impeccable.

impedido, da [ĩmpe'dʒidu, da] *adj* -1. [bloqueado] blocked. -2. *FUT* off-side. -3. [impossibilitado]: **~ de fazer algo** prevented from doing sthg.

impedimento [ĩpedʒi'mẽntu] *m* -1. *FUT* off-side. -2. *fig* [obstáculo] impediment. -3. *POL* impeachment.

impedir [ĩmpe'dʒi(x)] *v* -1. [obstruir] to obstruct. -2. [coibir] to prevent; **~ alguém de fazer algo** to prevent sb from doing sthg.

impelir [ĩmpe'li(x)] *vt* -1. [empurrar] to thrust. -2. [instigar]: **~ alguém a algo** to drive sb to sthg; **~ alguém a fazer algo** to impel sb to do sthg.

impenetrável [ĩpene'travɛw] *(pl -eis)* *adj* impenetrable.

impensado, da [ĩpẽ'sadu, da] *adj* -1. [não-pensado] thoughtless. -2. [imprevisto] unthought of.

impensável [ĩpẽ'savɛw] *(pl -eis)* *adj* unthinkable.

imperador [ĩpera'do(x)] *(mpl -es)* *m* emperor *(f* empress).

imperativo, va [ĩpera'tʃivu, va] *adj* -1. [urgente] imperative. -2. [autoritário] imperious.
➔ **imperativo** *m* imperative.

imperatriz [ĩpera'triʃ] *(mpl -zes)* *f* ▷ **imperador**.

imperdível [ĩpex'dʒivɛw] *(pl -eis)* *adj* -1. [show, filme, aula] unmissable. -2. [jogo, eleição, questão] impossible to lose *(depois de verbo)*.

imperdoável [ĩpex'dwavɛw] *(pl -eis)* *adj* unforgivable.

imperfeição [ĩpexfej'sãw] *(pl -ões)* *f* [defeito] imperfection.

imperfeito, ta [ĩpex'fejtu, ta] *adj* imperfect.
➔ **imperfeito** *m* *GRAM* imperfect.

imperial [ĩpe'rjaw] *(pl -ais)* *adj* imperial.

imperialismo [ĩperja'liʒmu] *m* imperialism.

imperícia [ĩpe'risja] *f* -1. [inabilidade] incompetence. -2. [inexperiência] inexperience.

império [ĩn'pεrju] *m* empire.

impermeável [ĩnpex'mjavεw] *(pl* -eis)
<> *adj* impermeable, waterproof.
<> *m* [capa de chuva] raincoat.

impertinência [ĩnpextʃi'nẽnsja] *f* imper-
tinence.

impertinente [ĩnpextʃi'nẽntʃi] *adj* impertinent.

imperturbável [ĩnpextux'bavεw] *(pl* -eis)
adj imperturbable.

impessoal [ĩnpe'swaw] *(pl* -ais) *adj* -1.
[objetivo] objective. -2. GRAM impersonal.

ímpeto ['ĩnpetu] *m* -1. [movimento brus-
co] sudden movement; **ele se levantou
num ~** he stood up with a start. -2.
[impulso] urge, impulse; **sentir um ~
de fazer algo** to feel an urge to do sthg.

impetuoso, osa [ĩmpe'twozu, ɔza] *adj* -1.
[pessoa] impetuous. -2. [chuva] driving.
-3. [rio] fast-flowing.

impiedade [ĩnpje'dadʒi] *f* [crueldade]
cruelty.

impiedoso, osa [ĩmpje'dozu, ɔza] *adj*
merciless.

ímpio, pia [ˈĩmpiu, pia] <> *adj* pitiless.
<> *m,f* pitiless person.

implacável [ĩnpla'kavεw] *(pl* -eis) *adj* -1.
[impiedoso] implacable. -2. [inexorável]
unrelenting.

implantação [ĩnplãnta'sãw] *f* -1. [intro-
dução] establishing. -2. [implementação]
implementation. -3. MED implant.

implementar [ĩmplemẽn'ta(x)] *vt* to implement.

implemento [ĩnple'mẽntu] *m* implement.

implicância [ĩnpli'kãnsja] *f* -1. [provoca-
ção] provoking; **meus filhos passam o
dia inteiro de ~ um com o outro** my
children spend the whole day provoking each other. -2. [antipatia]: **ter uma
~ com alguém** to dislike sb.

implicar [ĩmpli'ka(x)] <> *vt* [envolver]:
~ alguém em algo to involve sb in
sthg. <> *vi* -1. [pressupor]: **~ em algo**
to involve sthg. -2. [acarretar]: **~ em algo**
to result in sthg. -3. [provocar]: **~ com
alguém** to torment sb.

implícito, ta [ĩn'plisitu, ta] *adj* implicit.

implorar [ĩmplo'ra(x)] *vt*: **~ algo (a alguém)** to beg (sb) for sthg.

imponderável [ĩnpõnde'ravεw] *(pl* -eis)
adj imponderable.

imponente [ĩnpo'nẽntʃi] *adj* impressive, imposing.

impontual [ĩnpõn'twaw] *(pl* -ais) *adj*
unpunctual.

impopular [ĩnpopu'la(x)] *(pl* -es) *adj*
unpopular.

impopularidade [ĩnpopulari'dadʒi] *f*
unpopularity.

impor [ĩm'po(x)] *vt* to impose; **~ algo a
alguém** to impose sthg on sb.

➤ impor-se *vp* [afirmar-se] to establish
o.s.

importação [ĩnpoxta'sãw] *(pl* -ões) *f* -1.
[ato] importation. -2. [produtos] imports *(pl)*.

importador, ra [ĩnpoxta'do(x), ra] <>
adj importing *(antes de subst)*. <> *m, f*
importer.

➤ importadora *f* -1. [companhia]
importer. -2. [loja] *shop selling
imported goods*.

importância [ĩnpox'tãnsja] *f* -1. [mérito]
importance; **não dar ~ a alguém/algo**
to not care about sb/sthg; **ela não
dá ~ ao que ele disse** she doesn't
care about what he said; **isso não tem
~** that doesn't matter. -2. [quantia]
sum.

importante [ĩnpox'tãntʃi] *adj* important.

importar [ĩmpox'ta(x)] <> *vt* COM to
import. <> *vi* -1. [ser importante] to
matter. -2. [resultar]: **~ em** to result in.
-3. [atingir]: **~ em** to add up to.

➤ importar-se *vp* [fazer caso]: **não ~
-se (com algo/de fazer algo)** not to mind
sthg/about doing sthg.

importunar [ĩmpoxtu'na(x)] *vt* to annoy.

importuno, na [ĩnpox'tunu, na] *adj* annoying.

imposição [ĩnpozi'sãw] *(pl* -ões) *f* imposition.

impossibilidade [ĩnposibili'dadʒi] *f* im-
possibility.

impossibilitado, da [ĩnposibili'tadu,
da] *adj*: **~ de fazer algo** unable to do
sthg.

impossibilitar [ĩmposi'bili'ta(x)] *vt*: **~
algo** to make sthg impossible; **~ alguém de fazer algo** to prevent sb from
doing sthg.

impossível [ĩnpo'sivεw] *(pl* -eis) *adj* impossible.

imposto, osta [ĩm'poʃtu, ɔsta] *pp* ⊳
impor.

➤ imposto *m* tax; **~ sobre Circulação
de Mercadorias e Serviços** ≃ value
added tax *UK*, ≃ sales tax *US*; **~ predial** ≃ council tax *UK*; **~ de renda**
income tax.

impostor, ra [ĩnpoʃ'to(x), ra] *(mpl* -es, *fpl*
-s) *m* impostor.

impotente [ĩnpo'tẽntʃi] *adj* impotent.

impraticável [ĩnpratʃi'kavεw] *(pl* -eis) *adj*
-1. [impossível] impossible. -2. [inexeqüível]

unworkable. **-3.** [intransitável] impassable.

impreciso, sa [ĩnpre'sizu, za] *adj* imprecise.

impregnar [ĩmpreg'na(x)] ⟨> *vt* to impregnate; ~ **algo de algo** to impregnate sthg with sthg. ⟨> *vi*: ~ **en** to pervade.

imprensa [ĩn'prẽnsal *f* **-1.** [ger] press. **-2.** [tipografia] printing press.

imprescindível [ĩnpresĩn'dʒivɛw] (*pl* **-eis**) *adj* indispensable.

impressão [ĩnpre'sãw] (*pl* **-ões**) *f* **-1.** [marca] imprint. **-2.** [reprodução] printing. **-3.** [sensação] feeling; **ter boa/má impressão de alguém/algo** to have a good/bad impression of sb/sthg.

impressionante [ĩnpresjo'nãntʃil *adj* impressive.

impressionar [ĩnpresju'na(x)] ⟨> *vt* to impress. ⟨> *vi* to impress.

➡ **impressionar-se** *vp*: **-se com alguém/algo** [comover-se] to be moved by sb/sthg.

impresso, a [ĩn'presu, sal ⟨> *pp* ⟩ **imprimir**. ⟨> *adj* printed.

➡ **impresso** *m* printed matter *(sg)*.

impressora [ĩnpre'soral *f* printer; ~ **laser** laser printer; ~ **a jato de tinta** inkjet printer; ~ **matricial** dot matrix printer.

imprestável [ĩnpreʃ'tavɛw] (*pl* **-eis**) *adj* **-1.** [inútil] unhelpful. **-2.** [estragado] useless.

imprevidente [ĩnprevi'dẽntʃil *adj* **-1.** [imprudente] imprudent. **-2.** [que não soube prever] improvident.

imprevisível [ĩnprevi'zivɛw] (*pl* **-eis**) *adj* unforeseeable.

imprevisto, ta [ĩmpre'viʃtu, tal *adj* unexpected.

➡ **imprevisto** *m*: surgiu um ~ **nos nossos planos** something unforeseen cropped up in our plans.

imprimir [ĩmpri'mi(x)] ⟨> *vt* to print. ⟨> *vi* COMPUT to print.

improcedente [ĩnprose'dẽntʃil *adj* unjustified.

improdutivo, va [ĩnprodu'tʃivu, val *adj* unproductive.

impróprio, pria [ĩn'proprju, prjal *adj* inappropriate.

improvável [ĩnpro'vavɛw] (*pl* **-eis**) *adj* improbable.

improvisado, da [ĩnprovi'zadu, dal *adj* improvised.

improvisar [ĩmprovi'za(x)] ⟨> *vt* to improvise. ⟨> *vi* **-1.** to improvise. **-2.** *TEATRO* to ad-lib.

improviso [ĩnpro'vizul *m* **-1.** [repente]: **de** ~ [de repente] suddenly; [sem preparação] off the cuff; **falar de** ~ to speak off the cuff. **-2.** *TEATRO* improvisation.

imprudente [ĩnpru'dẽntʃil *adj* careless.

impugnação [ĩnpugna'sãw] (*pl* **-ões**) *f* [contestação] challenge.

impulsionar [ĩmpuwsju'na(x)] *vt* **-1.** [impelir] to propel. **-2.** [estimular] to speed up.

impulsivo, va [ĩnpuw'sivu, val *adj* impulsive.

impulso [ĩn'puwsul *m* **-1.** [ger] impulse, urge. **-2.** [força] thrust; **tomar** ~ to take a run.

impune [ĩn'punil *adj* unpunished.

impunidade [ĩnpuni'dadʒil *f* impunity.

impureza [ĩnpu'rezal *f* impurity.

impuro, ra [ĩm'puru, ral *adj* impure.

imputação [ĩnputa'sãw] (*pl* **-ões**) *f* [acusação] accusation.

imundície [ĩmũn̪'dʒisjil, **imundícia** [ĩmũn'dʒisjal *f* [falta de asseio] filthiness.

imundo, da [i'mũndo, dal *adj* filthy.

imune [i'munil *adj*: ~ **(a)** immune to.

imunidade [imuni'dadʒil *f* immunity.

imunizar [imuni'za(x)] *vt* to immunize.

imutável [imu'tavɛw] (*pl* **-eis**) *adj* immutable.

inábil [i'nabiwl (*pl* **-eis**) *adj* **-1.** [desajeitado] clumsy. **-2.** [incapaz] incapable.

inabilidade [inabili'dadʒil *f* inability.

inabitado, da [inabi'tadu, dal *adj* uninhabited.

inabitável [inabi'tavɛwl (*pl* **-eis**) *adj* uninhabitable.

inacabado, da [inaka'badu, dal *adj* unfinished.

inacabável [inaka'bavɛwl (*pl* **-eis**) *adj* unending.

inaceitável [inasej'tavɛwl (*pl* **-eis**) *adj* unacceptable.

inacessível [inase'sivɛwl (*pl* **-eis**) *adj* inaccessible.

inacreditável [inakredʒi'tavɛwl (*pl* **-eis**) *adj* unbelievable.

inadiável [ina'djavɛwl (*pl* **-eis**) *adj* pressing.

inadimplência [inadʒĩn'plẽnsjal *f* JUR non-compliance.

inadvertidamente [inadʒivertʃida'mẽntʃil *adv* inadvertently.

inadvertido, da [inadver'tʃidu, dal *adj* inadvertent.

inalação [inala'sãw] (*pl* **-ões**) *f* inhalation.

inalar [ina'la(x)l *vt* to inhale.

inalterado, da [inawte'radu, dal *adj* **-1.** [imutado] unaltered. **-2.** [calmo] composed.

inanimado, da [inani'madu, da] *adj* in-animate.

inaptidão [inaptʃi'dãw] *f* inabilty.

inapto, ta [i'naptu, ta] *adj* unsuitable.

inatingível [inatʃĩn'ʒivɛw] (*pl* -eis) *adj* unattainable.

inatividade [inatʃivi'dadʒi] *f* **-1.** [ger] retirement. **-2.** [inércia] inactivity. **-3.** [desemprego] inactivity.

inativo, va [ina'tʃivu, va] *adj* **-1.** [ger] retired. **-2.** [parado] idle.

inato, ta [i'natu, ta] *adj* innate.

inaudito, ta [inaw'dʒitu, ta] *adj* unheard of.

inaudível [inaw'dʒivew] (*pl* -eis) *adj* in-audible.

inauguração [inawgura'sãw] (*pl* -ões) *f* inauguration.

inaugural [inawgu'raw] (*pl* -ais) *adj* in-augural.

inaugurar [inawgu'ra(x)] *vt* to open.

inca ['ĩŋka] <> *adj* Inca. <> *mf* Inca.

incalculável [ĩŋkawku'lavew] (*pl* -eis) *adj* incalculable.

incandescente [ĩŋkãnde'sẽntʃi] *adj* in-candescent.

incansável [ĩŋkãn'savɛw] (*pl* -eis) *adj* tireless.

incapacidade [ĩŋkapasi'dadʒi] *f* **-1.** [deficiência] incapacity. **-2.** [incompetência] incompetence.

incapacitado, da [ĩŋkapasi'tadu, da] <> *adj* **-1.** [inválido] disabled. **-2.** [impedido] unable; **estar ~ de fazer algo** to be unable to do sthg. <> *m, f* disabled person.

incapaz [ĩŋka'paʃ] (*pl* -es) *adj* **-1.** [incompetente]: **~ (para)** incompetent (for). **-2.** *JUR* incompetent. **-3.** [preguiçoso]: **ser ~ de fazer algo** [não se dignar a] to be incapable of doing sthg.

incauto, ta [ĩŋ'kawtu, ta] *adj* **-1.** [imprudente] reckless. **-2.** [ingênuo] naive.

incendiar [ĩsẽn'dʒja(x)] *vt* to set fire to.
➤ **incendiar-se** *vp* to catch fire.

incendiário, ria [ĩsẽn'dʒjarju, rja] <> *adj* [bomba etc.] incendiary. <> *m, f* arsonist.

incêndio [ĩn'sẽndʒiul *m* fire; **~ provocado** *OU* **criminoso** arson.

incenso [ĩn'sẽnsu] *m* incense.

incentivar [ĩsẽntʒi'va(x)] *vt* to stimulate.

incentivo [ĩsẽn'tʃivu] *m* incentive.

incerteza [ĩnsex'teza] *f* uncertainty.

incerto, ta [ĩ'sɛxtu, ta] *adj* uncertain.

incessante [ĩnse'sãntʃi] *adj* incessant.

incesto [ĩn'sɛʃtu] *m* incest.

inchação [ĩnʃa'sãw] *f* swelling.

inchaço [ĩn'ʃasu] *m fam* swelling.

inchado, da [ĩ'ʃadu, da] *adj* swollen.

inchar [ĩ'sa(x)] <> *vt* to swell. <> *vi* to swell.

incidência [ĩnsi'dẽnsja] *f* incidence.

incidente [ĩnsi'dẽntʃi] *m* incident.

incinerador, ra [ĩnsine'rado(x), ra] <> *adj* incineration (*antes de subst*). <> *m* incinerator.

incipiente [ĩnsi'pjẽntʃi] *adj* incipient.

incisivo, va [ĩsi'zivu, va] *adj* **-1.** [cortante] cutting. **-2.** [direto] incisive.

incitar [ĩsi'ta(x)] *vt* **-1.** [instigar]: **~ alguém a algo** to incite sb to sthg; **~ alguém a fazer algo** to incite sb to do sthg. **-2.** [suj: ambição etc.]: **~ alguém (a algo/a fazer algo)** to drive sb to sthg/to do sthg. **-3.** [animal] to urge on.

incivilidade [ĩsivili'dadʒi] *f* discourtesy.

inclemente [ĩŋkle'mẽntʃi] *adj* **-1.** [impiedoso] ruthless. **-2.** *fig* [rigoroso] merciless.

inclinado, da [ĩŋkli'nadu, da] *adj* **-1.** [oblíquo] inclined. **-2.** *fig* [propenso]: **estar ~ a algo/a fazer algo** to be inclined towards sthg/to do sthg.

inclinar [ĩŋkli'na(x)] *vt* **-1.** [fazer pender] to tilt. **-2.** [curvar] to bend.
➤ **inclinar-se** *vp* **-1.** [curvar-se] to bow. **-2.** [tender a]: **~-se a** to tend towards.

incluir [ĩŋklu'i(x)] *vt* **-1.** [abranger] to include. **-2.** [inserir]: **~ algo em algo** to insert sthg in sthg.
➤ **incluir-se** *vp* to include o.s.

inclusão [ĩŋklu'zãw] (*pl* -oes) *f* inclusion.

inclusive [ĩŋklu'zivil *adv* **-1.** [com inclusão de] including; **de segunda a sábado ~** from Monday to Saturday inclusive. **-2.** [até mesmo] even.

incluso, sa [ĩŋ'kluzo, za] *adj* included.

incoerente [ĩŋkwe'rẽntʃi] *adj* **-1.** [ilógico] illogical. **-2.** [discordante] conflicting. **-3.** [incompreensível] incoherent.

incógnito, ta [ĩŋ'kɔgnitu, ta] *adj* incognito *(depois de verbo)*.
➤ **incógnita** *f* **-1.** *MAT* unknown quantity. **-2.** [mistério]: **ser uma ~** to be a mystery.
➤ **incógnito** *adv* incognito.

incolor [ĩŋko'lo(x)] (*pl* -es) *adj* colourless.

incólume [ĩŋ'kɔlumi] *adj* safe and sound.

incomodar [ĩŋkomo'da(x)] <> *vt* to annoy. <> *vi* [irritar]: **~ a** to annoy.
➤ **incomodar-se** *vp* **-1.** [irritar-se] to become annoyed. **-2.** [importar-se] to mind; **você se incomoda se eu fechar a porta?** would you mind if I closed the door?

incômodo, da [ĩŋ'komodu, da] *adj* **-1.**

[ger] uncomfortable. **-2.** [enfadonho] boring.

➡ **incômodo** m **-1.** [embaraço] problem. **-2.** [menstruação] period, time of the month.

incomparável [ĩŋkõnpaˈravɛw] (pl -eis) adj incomparable.

incompatível [ĩŋkõnpaˈtʃivɛw] (pl -eis) adj incompatible.

incompetente [ĩŋkõnpeˈtẽntʃi] ⬦ adj incompetent. ⬦ mf incompetent.

incompleto, ta [ĩŋkõnˈplɛtu, ta] adj incomplete, unfinished.

incompreendido, da [ĩŋkõnprjẽnˈdʒidu, da] adj misunderstood.

incompreensível [ĩŋkõnprjẽnˈsivɛw] (pl -eis) adj incomprehensible.

incomum [ĩŋkoˈmũl] (pl -ns) adj uncommon.

incomunicável [ĩŋkomuniˈkavɛw] (pl -eis) adj **-1.** [sem comunicação] cut off. **-2.** [que não deve se comunicar] incommunicado. **-3.** fig [insociável] uncommunicative.

inconcebível [ĩŋkõnseˈbivɛw] (pl -eis) adj inconceivable.

inconciliável [ĩŋkõnsiˈljavɛw] (pl -eis) adj irreconcilable.

incondicional [ĩŋkõndʒisjoˈnaw] (pl -ais) adj **-1.** [total] unconditional. **-2.** [fiel] loyal.

inconfidente [ĩŋkõnfiˈdẽntʃi] ⬦ adj disloyal. ⬦ mf untrustworthy person.

inconformado, da [ĩŋkõnfoxˈmadu, da] adj: ela está ~ she has not come to terms with it.

inconfundível [ĩŋkõnfũnˈdʒivɛw] (pl -eis) adj unmistakable.

inconsciência [ĩŋkõnˈsjẽnsja] f **-1.** MED unconsciousness. **-2.** [leviandade] lack of awareness.

inconsciente [ĩŋkõnˈsjẽntʃi] ⬦ adj **-1.** [ger] unconscious. **-2.** [leviano] thoughtless. ⬦ m PSIC: o ~ the unconscious.

inconseqüente [ĩŋkõnseˈkwẽntʃi] ⬦ adj **-1.** [incoerente] inconsistent. **-2.** [irresponsável] irresponsible. ⬦ mf irresponsible person.

inconsistente [ĩŋkõnsiʃˈtẽntʃi] adj **-1.** [fraco] inconsistent. **-2.** [fluido] runny.

inconstante [ĩŋkõnʃˈtãntʃi] adj **-1.** [instável] unstable. **-2.** [volúvel] inconstant.

inconstitucionalidade [ĩŋkõnʃtʃitusjonaliˈdadʒi] f unconstitutionality.

incontável [ĩŋkõnˈtavɛw] (pl -eis) adj countless.

incontestável [ĩŋkõnteʃˈtavɛw] (pl -eis) adj incontestable.

inconteste [ĩŋkõnˈtɛʃtʃi] adj undisputed.

incontinência [ĩŋkõntʃiˈnẽnsja] f MED incontinence.

incontrolável [ĩŋkõntroˈlavɛw] (pl -eis) adj uncontrollable.

inconveniência [ĩŋkõnveˈnjẽnsja] f **-1.** [falta de conveniência] inconvenience. **-2.** [grosseria] rudeness.

inconveniente [ĩŋkõnveˈnjẽntʃi] ⬦ adj **-1.** [inoportuno] inconvenient. **-2.** [inadequado] unsuitable. **-3.** [incômodo] annoying. ⬦ m **-1.** [desvantagem] disadvantage. **-2.** [obstáculo] obstacle.

INCOR (abrev de Instituto do Coração do Hospital das Clínicas) m institute of coronary diseases at the Hospital das Clínicas in São Paulo.

incorporar [ĩŋkoxpoˈra(x)] vt **-1.** COM to incorporate. **-2.** [espírit] to become possessed by. **-3.** [juntar]: ~ algo a algo to include sthg in sthg.

➡ **incorporar-se** vp [juntar-se] to join.

incorrer [ĩŋkoˈxe(x)] vi: ~ em algo to fall into sthg.

incorreto, ta [ĩŋkoˈxɛtu, ta] adj incorrect.

incorrigível [ĩŋkoxiˈʒivɛw] (pl -eis) adj incorrigible.

incorruptível [ĩŋkoxupˈtʃivɛw] (pl -eis) adj incorruptible.

INCRA (abrev de Instituto Nacional de Colonização e Reforma Agrária) m Brazilian land reform institute.

incrédulo, la [ĩŋˈkrɛdulu, la] adj incredulous.

incremento [ĩŋkreˈmẽntu] m **-1.** [aumento] increment. **-2.** [desenvolvimento] development.

incriminar [ĩŋkrimiˈna(x)] vt to incriminate.

incrível [ĩŋˈkrivɛw] (pl -eis) adj **-1.** [inacreditável] incredible. **-2.** fam [maravilhoso] incredible.

incrustação [ĩŋkruʃtaˈsãw] (pl -ões) f inlay.

incubação [ĩŋkubaˈsãw] f incubation.

incubadora [ĩŋkubaˈdora] f incubator.

incumbência [ĩŋkũnˈbẽnsja] f incumbency.

incumbir [ĩŋkũmˈbi(x)] ⬦ vt: ~ alguém de algo to put sb in charge of sthg. ⬦ vi: ~ a alguém fazer algo to be sb's responsibility to do sthg.

➡ **incumbir-se** vp: ~-se de algo to take charge of sthg.

incurável [ĩŋkuˈravɛw] (pl -eis) adj incurable.

incursão [ĩŋkuxˈsãw] (pl -ões) f incursion.

incutir [ĩŋkuˈtʃi(x)] vt: ~ algo (a ou em alguém) to inspire sthg (in sb).

indagação [ĩndaga'sãw] f inquiry.

indagar [ĩnda'ga(x)] ⟨⟩ vt to ask for. ⟨⟩ vi to make inquiries.

indecente [ĩnde'sẽntʃil] adj -1. [obsceno] indecent. -2. [imoral] unscrupulous.

indecifrável [ĩndesi'fravew] (pl -eis) adj indecipherable.

indecisão [ĩndesi'zãw] (pl -ões) f indecision.

indeciso, sa [ĩnde'sizu, za] adj indecisive.

indecoroso, osa [ĩndeko'rozo, ɔza] adj indecent.

indeferir [ĩndefe'ri(x)] vt to reject.

indefeso, sa [ĩnde'fezu, za] adj defenceless.

indefinido, da [ĩndefi'nidu, da] adj -1. [ger] indefinite. -2. [vago] vague.

indelével [ĩnde'lɛvew] (pl -eis) adj indelible.

indelicado, da [ĩndeli'kadu, da] adj indelicate.

indenização [ĩndeniza'sãw] (pl -ões) f indemnity, compensation.

indenizar [ĩndeni'za(x)] vt: ~ alguém (por algo) to indemnify sb (for sthg), to compensate sb (for sthg).

independência [ĩndepẽn'dẽnsja] f independence.

independente [ĩndepẽn'dẽntʃil] adj -1. [ger] independent. -2. [separado, de livre acesso] separate. -3. [auto-suficiente] independent. -4. [financeiramente] of independent means, financially independent.

indescritível [ĩndeʃkri'tʃivɛw] (pl -eis) adj indescribable.

indesculpável [ĩndʒiʃkuw'pavew] (pl -eis) adj unforgivable.

indesejável [ĩndeze'ʒavew] (pl -eis) adj undesirable.

indestrutível [ĩndeʃtru'tʃivɛw] (pl -eis) adj -1. [não destrutível] indestructible. -2. fig [inabalável] enduring.

indeterminado, da [ĩndetexmi'nadu, da] adj -1. [não fixado] indeterminate; por tempo ~ for an indefinite length of time. -2. [impreciso] imprecise.

indevassável [ĩndeva'savew] (pl -eis) adj impenetrable.

indevido, da [ĩnde'vidu, da] adj -1. [imerecido] undeserved. -2. [impróprio] inappropriate.

Índia ['ĩndʒja] n India.

indiano, na [ĩn'dʒjanu, na] ⟨⟩ adj [da Índia] Indian. ⟨⟩ m, f [habitante da Índia] Indian.

indicação [ĩndʒika'sãw] (pl -ões) f -1. [denotação] sign. -2. [de caminho etc.] sign. -3. [recomendação] recommendation;

~ de uso instructions for use. -4. [menção] indication.

indicado, da [ĩndʒi'kadu, da] adj -1. [recomendado] recommended. -2. [apropriado] appropriate.

indicador, ra [ĩndʒika'do(x), ra] (pl -es, fpl -s) adj [que indica]: ~ de indicator of. ◆ **indicador** m -1. [ger] indicator. -2. [dedo] index finger.

indicar [ĩndʒi'ka(x)] vt -1. [ger] to indicate. -2. [apontar]: ~ algo com o dedo to point to sthg. -3. [recomendar] to recommend. -4. [mencionar] to indicate. -5. [designar] to name.

indicativo, va [ĩndʒika'tʃivu, va] adj -1. [que indica] indicative. -2. GRAM indicative. ◆ **indicativo** m GRAM indicative.

índice ['ĩndʒisi] m -1. [lista] index; ~ onomástico name index. -2. [medida] level. -3. [dedo] index finger.

indício [ĩn'dʒisju] m -1. [vestígio] sign. -2. JUR [prova] evidence (inv).

Índico n: o (Oceano) ~ the Indian Ocean.

indiferença [ĩndʒife'rẽnsa] f indifference.

indiferente [ĩndʒife'rẽntʃil] adj: ~ (a algo) indifferent (to sthg).

indígena [ĩn'dʒiʒena] ⟨⟩ adj indigenous. ⟨⟩ mf native.

indigência [ĩndʒi'ʒẽnsja] f -1. [miséria] poverty. -2. [indigentes]: a ~ do país the indigence of the country. -3. [falta] lack.

indigestão [ĩndʒiʒeʃ'tãw] (pl -ões) f indigestion.

indigesto, ta [ĩndʒi'ʒɛʃtu, ta] adj indigestible.

indignação [ĩndʒigna'sãw] (pl -ões) f indignation.

indignado, da [ĩndʒig'nadu, da] adj indignant; ficar ~ (com) to be indignant (at).

indignidade [ĩndʒigni'dadʒi] f -1. [falta de dignidade] indignity. -2. [ultraje] outrage.

indigno, gna [ĩn'dʒignu, gna] adj -1. [não merecedor]: ~ de algo unworthy of sthg. -2. [vil] despicable.

índio, dia ['ĩndʒju, dʒja] ⟨⟩ adj Indian. ⟨⟩ m, f Indian.

indireto, ta [ĩndʒi'rɛtu, ta] adj indirect. ◆ **indireta** f hint.

indisciplina [ĩndʒisi'plina] f indiscipline.

indiscreto, ta [ĩndʒiʃ'krɛtu, ta] adj indiscreet.

indiscriminado, da [ĩndʒiʃkrimi'nadu, da] adj indiscriminate.

indiscutível [ĩndʒiʃku'tʃivɛw] (*pl* -eis) *adj* incontestable.

indispensável [ĩndʒiʃpẽ'savɛw] (*pl* -eis) <> *adj* indispensable, essential. <> *m*: o ~ the essentials.

indispor [ĩndʒiʃ'po(x)] *vt* -1. [adoecer] to make ill, to upset. -2. [inimizar] to set at odds.

➡ indispor-se *vp* [inimizar-se]: ~-se com alguém to fall out with sb.

indisposto, osta [ĩndʒiʃ'poʃtu, ɔʃta] <> *pp* ⊳ **indispor**. <> *adj* unwell.

indistinto, ta [ĩndʒiʃ'tʃĩntu, ta] *adj* indistinct.

individual [ĩndʒivi'dwaw] (*pl* -ais) *adj* individual.

indivíduo [ĩndʒi'vidwu] *m* -1. [pessoa] individual. -2. *fam* [cara] person.

indócil [ĩn'dɔsiw] (*pl* -eis) *adj* -1. [rebelde] wayward. -2. [impaciente] restless.

indo-europeu, éia [ĩndwewro'pew, pɛja] *adj* Indo-European.

➡ indo-europeu *m* [língua] Indo-European.

índole ['ĩndoli] *f* -1. [temperamento] temperament. -2. [tipo] character.

indolência [ĩndo'lẽsja] *f* indolence.

indolente [ĩndo'lẽtʃi] *adj* indolent.

indolor [ĩndo'lo(x)] (*pl* -es) *adj* painless.

indomável [ĩndo'mavew] (*pl* -eis) *adj* indomitable.

Indonésia [ĩndo'nɛʒja] *n* Indonesia.

indulgência [ĩnduw'ʒẽsja] *f* -1. [tolerância] leniency. -2. [perdão] indulgence. -3. *JUR* clemency.

indulgente [ĩnduw'ʒẽtʃi] *adj* lenient.

indulto [ĩn'duwtu] *m JUR* reprieve.

indumentária [ĩndumẽn'tarja] *f* attire.

indústria [ĩn'duʃtrial] *f* industry; ~ leve *ou* de consumo light industry; ~ pesada heavy industry; '~ brasileira' 'made in Brazil'.

industrial [ĩnduʃ'trjaw] (*pl* -ais) <> *adj* industrial. <> *mf* industrialist.

industrialização [ĩnduʃtrjaliza'sãw] *f* industrialization.

industrializar [ĩnduʃtrjali'za(x)] *vt* -1. [ger] to industrialize. -2. [produto] to manufacture. -3. [usar na indústria] to put to industrial use.

➡ industrializar-se *vp* to become industrialized.

industrioso, osa [ĩnduʃ'trjozu, -ɔza] *adj* -1. [habilidoso] clever. -2. [diligente] industrious.

induzir [ĩndu'zi(x)] *vt* [levar]: ~ alguém a algo to lead sb to sthg; ~ alguém a fazer algo to persuade sb to do sthg.

inebriante [ine'brjãtʃi] *adj* intoxicating.

inebriado, da [inebri'adu, da] *adj* [extasiado] intoxicated.

ineditismo [inedʒi'tʃiʒmu] *m*: o ~ dos contos the fact that the stories are unpublished.

inédito, ta [i'nɛdʒitu, ta] *adj* -1. [não publicado] unpublished. -2. [novo] novel.

ineficaz [inefi'kaʃ] (*pl* -es) *adj* -1. [ger] ineffective. -2. [pessoa] inefficient.

ineficiente [inefi'sjẽtʃi] *adj* inefficient.

inegável [ine'gavɛw] (*pl* -eis) *adj* undeniable.

inelegível [inele'givɛw] (*pl* -eis) *adj* unelectable.

inépcia [i'nɛpsja] *f* ineptitude.

inepto, ta [i'nɛptu, ta] *adj* inept.

inequívoco, ca [ine'kivoku, ka] *adj* unmistakable.

inércia [i'nɛxsja] *f* inertia.

inerente [ine'rẽtʃi] *adj* inherent.

inerte [i'nɛxtʃi] *adj* inert.

inescrupuloso, osa [ineʃkrupu'lozu, ɔza] *adj* unscrupulous.

inescrutável [ineʃkru'tavew] (*pl* -eis) *adj* inscrutable.

inesgotável [ineʒgo'tavɛw] (*pl* -eis) *adj* -1. [inacabável] inexhaustible. -2. [copioso] profuse.

inesperado, da [ineʃpe'radu, da] *adj* unexpected.

➡ inesperado *m* surprise.

inesquecível [ineʃke'sivɛw] (*pl* -eis) *adj* unforgettable.

inestimável [ineʃtʃi'mavɛw] (*pl* -eis) *adj* -1. [ger] priceless. -2. [prejuízo] incalculable.

inevitável [inevi'tavɛw] (*pl* -eis) <> *adj* inevitable. <> *m*: o ~ the inevitable.

inexato, ta [ine'zatu, ta] *adj* inaccurate.

inexequível [ineze'kwivɛw] (*pl* -eis) *adj* unfeasible.

inexistência [ineziʃ'tẽsja] *f* -1. [não existência] absence. -2. [carência] lack.

inexistente [inezʃ'tẽtʃi] *adj* non-existent.

inexorável [inezo'ravɛw] (*pl* -eis) *adj* inexorable.

inexperiência [ineʃpe'rjẽsja] *f* inexperience.

inexperiente [ineʃpe'rjẽtʃi] *adj* inexperienced.

inexplorado, da [ineʃplo'radu, da] *adj* unexplored.

inexpressivo, va [ineʃpre'sivu, va] *adj* -1. [rosto] expressionless. -2. [diferença] inexpressible.

infalível [ĩnfa'livɛw] (*pl* -eis) *adj* infallible.

infame [ĩn'fãmi] *adj* -1. [vil] shameful. -2. [péssimo] dreadful.

infâmia [ĩn'fãmja] *f*-1. [calúnia] slander.
-2. [desonra] discredit. -3. [vilania] infamy.

infância [ĩn'fãnsja] *f* childhood.

infantaria [ĩnfãnta'ria] *f* infantry.

infantil [ĩnfãn'tiw] (*pl* -is) *adj* -1. [próprio da infância] childhood (*antes de subst*). -2. [para criança] children's (*antes de subst*). -3. *fig* [imaturo] childish.

infarto [ĩn'faxtu] *m* = enfarte.

infatigável [ĩnfatʃi'gavew] (*pl* -eis) *adj* -1. [incansável] tireless. -2. [zeloso] untiring.

infecção [ĩnfek'sãw] (*pl* -ões) *f* infection.

infeccionar [ĩfeksjo'na(x)] ⟨⟩ *vt* to infect. ⟨⟩ *vi* to become infected.

infeccioso, osa [ĩnfek'sjozu, ɔza] *adj* infectious.

infelicidade [ĩnfelisi'dadʒi] *f*-1. [tristeza] unhappiness. -2. [desgraça] misfortune. -3. [azar] bad luck; **por ~** unfortunately.

infeliz [ĩnfe'liʒ] (*pl* -es) ⟨⟩ *adj* -1. [ger] unfortunate. -2. [triste] unhappy. -3. [desafortunado] wretched. ⟨⟩ *mf* -1. [triste] unfortunate person. -2. [desgraçado] wretch.

infelizmente [ĩnfeliʒ'mẽntʃi] *adv* unfortunately.

inferior [ĩnfe'rjo(x)] (*pl* -es) ⟨⟩ *adj* -1. [que está mais baixo] lower. -2. [em valor]: **~ (a)** lower (than). -3. [em quantidade]: **~ (a)** fewer (than). -4. [em altura]: **~ a** shorter (than). -5. [em qualidade]: **~ (a)** inferior (to). ⟨⟩ *mf* [subalterno] inferior.

inferioridade [ĩnferjori'dadʒi] *f*-1. [condição, posição] inferiority. -2. *PSIC*: **complexo de ~** inferiority complex.

inferir [ĩfe'ri(x)] *vt*: **~ algo (de)** to infer sthg (from).

infernal [ĩnfex'naw] (*pl* -ais) *adj fig* infernal.

inferninho [ĩnfex'niɲu] *m* dive.

inferno [ĩn'fɛxnu] *m* hell; **vá para o ~ !** go to hell!

infértil [ĩ'fɛxtiw] *adj* infertile.

infertilidade [ĩnfextʃili'dadʒi] *f* infertility.

infestado, da [ĩnfeʃ'tadu, da] *adj* infested.

infestar [ĩnfeʃ'ta(x)] *vt* to infest.

infidelidade [ĩnfideli'dadʒi] *f* infidelity.

infiel [ĩn'fjɛw] (*pl* -éis) ⟨⟩ *adj* -1. [desleal] unfaithful. -2. [inexato] inaccurate. ⟨⟩ *mf RELIG* non-believer.

infiltrar [ĩfiw'tra(x)] *vt* [parede] to penetrate.
➡ **infiltrar-se** *vp* to infiltrate; **~-se em algo** to filter (into) sthg.

ínfimo, ma ['ĩfimu, ma] *adj* insignificant; **preço ~** rock-bottom price.

infindável [ĩnfĩn'davew] (*pl* -eis) *adj* -1. [inacabável] interminable. -2. [permanente] unending. -3. [energia] boundless.

infinidade [ĩnfini'dadʒi] *f*: **uma ~ de vezes/roupas** countless times/clothes.

infinitivo, va [ĩnfini'tʃivu, va] *GRAM adj* infinitive.
➡ **infinitivo** *m* infinitive.

infinito, ta [ĩnfi'nitu, ta] *adj* -1. [ger] infinite. -2. [inumerável] countless.
➡ **infinito** *m LING* infinitive.

inflação [ĩnfla'sãw] *f ECON* inflation.

inflacionário, ria [ĩnflasjo'narju, rja] *adj ECON* inflationary.

inflamação [ĩnflama'sãw] (*pl* -ões) *f MED* inflammation.

inflamado, da [ĩnfla'madu, da] *adj* -1. *MED* inflamed. -2. *fig* [exaltado] heated.

inflamar [ĩfla'ma(x)] ⟨⟩ *vt* to inflame. ⟨⟩ *vi MED* to become inflamed.

inflamável [ĩnfla'mavew] (*pl* -eis) *adj* inflammable.

inflar [ĩ'fla(x)] *vt* -1. [balão, bóia] to inflate. -2. [vela] to fill. -3. [peito] to puff out.

inflexível [ĩnflek'sivew] (*pl* -eis) *adj* -1. [invergável] stiff. -2. *fig* [implacável] inflexible.

infligir [ĩfli'ʒi(x)] *vt*: **~ algo (a alguém)** to inflict sthg (on sb).

influência [ĩnflu'ẽnsja] *f* influence.

influenciar [ĩflwẽn'sja(x)] ⟨⟩ *vt* to influence. ⟨⟩ *vi*: **~ em algo** to influence sthg.
➡ **influenciar-se** *vp*: **~-se (por alguém/algo)** to be influenced (by sb/sthg).

influente [ĩnflu'ẽntʃi] *adj* influential.

influir [ĩnflu'i(x)] *vi* -1. [importar] to matter, to be important. -2. [atuar]: **~ em algo** to interfere in sthg. -3. [influenciar]: **~ para algo** to play a role in sthg.

influxo [ĩn'fluksu] *m* -1. [convergência] influx. -2. [maré alta] high tide.

infográfico, ca [ĩnfo'grafiku, ka] *adj* computer graphic (*antes de subst*).
➡ **infográfico** *m* computer graphics designer.

informação [ĩnfoxma'sãw] (*pl* -ões) *f*-1. [ger] information. -2. [notícia] news. -3. *MIL* intelligence. -4. *COMPUT* data (*inv*).

informal [ĩnfox'maw] (*pl* -ais) *adj* informal.

informalidade [ĩnfoxmali'dadʒi] *f* informality.

informante [ĩnfox'mãntʃi] *mf* informant.

informar [ĩfox'ma(x)] ◇ vt -1. [esclarecer] to inform. -2. [notificar]: ~ **alguém de algo** to notify sb of sthg. ◇ vi [ser informativo] to inform.

◆ **informar-se** vp -1. [atualizar-se] to keep o.s. up to date. -2. [esclarecer-se]: ~**-se sobre algo** to make inquiries about sthg, to inquire about sthg.

informático, ca [ĩfox'matʃiku, ka] ◇ adj computer (antes de subst). ◇ m, f [pessoa] IT specialist.

◆ **informática** f -1. [ciência] computer science. -2. [atividade] computing.

informativo, va [ĩfoxma'tʃivu, va] adj informative.

informatizar [ĩfurmati'za(x)] vt to computerize.

informe [ĩ'fɔxmi] ◇ adj shapeless. ◇ m -1. [informações] information. -2. MIL (piece of) intelligence.

infortúnio [ĩfox'tunju] m misfortune.

infração [ĩfra'sãw] (pl -ões) f -1. [de lei etc.] infringement; ~ **de trânsito** driving offence UK, driving offense US. -2. ESP foul.

Infraero (abrev de **Empresa Brasileira de Infra-Estrutura Aeroportuária**) f Brazilian company responsible for airport insfrastructure, ≃ BAA UK.

infra-estrutura [ĩfraʃtru'tura] (pl infra-estruturas) f infrastructure.

infrator, ra [ĩfra'to(x), ra] (mpl -es, fpl -s) ◇ adj law-breaking, ≃ BAA UK, f infringer.

infravermelho, lha [ĩfravex'meʎu, ʎa] adj infrared.

infringir [ĩfrĩ'ʒi(x)] vt to infringe.

infrutífero, ra [ĩfru'tʃiferu, ra] adj fruitless.

infundado, da [ĩfũ'dadu, da] adj unfounded, groundless.

infusão [ĩfu'zãw] (pl -ões) f infusion.

ingênuo, nua [ĩ'ʒenwu, nwa] ◇ adj ingenuous, naive. ◇ m, f ingenuous person, naive person.

ingerência [ĩʒe'rẽnsja] f intervention.

ingerir [ĩʒe'ri(x)] vt to ingest.

ingestão [ĩʒeʃ'tãw] f ingestion.

Inglaterra [ĩgla'texa] n England.

inglês, esa [ĩ'gleʃ, eza] (mpl -eses, fpl -s) ◇ adj English. ◇ mf Englishman (f Englishwoman).

◆ **inglês** m [língua] English.

inglório, ria [ĩ'glɔrju, rja] adj inglorious.

ingovernabilidade [ĩgovexnabili'dadʒi] f ungovernability.

ingratidão [ĩgratʃi'dãw] f ingratitude.

ingrato, ta [ĩ'gratu, ta] adj -1. [sem gratidão] ungrateful. -2. [ruim] disagreeable.

ingrediente [ĩgre'djẽtʃi] m ingredient.

íngreme [ĩ'gremi] adj steep.

ingressar [ĩgre'sa(x)] vi: ~ **em algo** to enter sthg.

ingresso [ĩ'gresu] m -1. [bilhete] (entrance) ticket. -2. [entrada] entry. -3. [admissão] entrance.

inhame [i'ɲami] m yam.

inibição [inibi'sãw] (pl -ões) f inhibition.

inibido, da [ini'bidu, da] adj inhibited.

inibir [ini'bi(x)] vt -1. [embaraçar] to embarrass. -2. [dificultar] to inhibit.

◆ **inibir-se** vp [ficar inibido] to become inhibited.

iniciação [inisja'sãw] (pl -ões) f initiation.

inicial [ini'sjaw] (pl -ais) ◇ adj initial. ◇ f [letra] initial.

◆ **iniciais** fpl initials.

iniciante [ini'sjãtʃi] ◇ adj [pessoa] beginning. ◇ mf [pessoa] beginner.

iniciar [ini'sja(x)] vt -1. [começar] to initiate, to begin. -2. [introduzir]: ~ **alguém em algo** to introduce sb to sthg.

◆ **iniciar-se** vp [introduzir-se]: ~**-se em algo** to get into sthg.

iniciativa [inisja'tʃiva] f initiative; ~ **privada** private initiative.

início i'nisju] m beginning; **no** ~ in the beginning.

inimigo, ga [ini'migu, ga] ◇ adj enemy (antes de subst). ◇ m, f enemy.

inimizade [inimi'zadʒi] f enmity.

ininterrupto, ta [inĩte'xuptu, ta] adj uninterrupted.

injeção [ĩʒe'sãw] (pl -ões) f injection.

injetar [ĩʒe'ta(x)] vt to inject.

injúria [ĩ'ʒurja] f insult.

injuriar [ĩʒu'rja(x)] vt [insultar] to insult.

◆ **injuriar-se** vp fam [zangar-se] to get angry.

injustiça [ĩʒuʃ'tʃisa] f injustice.

injustificável [ĩʒuʃtʃifi'kavew] (pl -eis) adj unjustifiable.

injusto, ta [ĩ'ʒuʃtu, ta] adj unfair.

INL (abrev de **Instituto Nacional do Livro**) m Brazilian national book institute.

INMETRO (abrev de **Instituto Nacional de Metrologia, Normalização e Qualidade Industrial**) m Brazilian national institute of industrial standards, ≃ TSI UK, ≃ NIST US.

inocência [ino'sẽnsja] f innocence.

inocentar [inosẽn'ta(x)] vt: ~ **alguém de algo** to clear sb of sthg.

◆ **inocentar-se** vp: inocentou-se por sua sinceridade his sincerity showed that he was innocent.

inocente [ino'sẽntʃi] <> *adj* innocent. <> *mf* innocent person.

inocular [inoku'la(x)] *vt* to innoculate.

inócuo, cua [i'nɔkwu, kwa] *adj* innocuous.

inodoro, ra [ino'dɔru, ra] *adj* odourless.

inofensivo, va [inofẽ'sivu, va] *adj* inoffensive.

inoportuno, na [inopox'tunu, na] *adj* inopportune.

inóspito, ta [i'nɔʃpitu, ta] *adj* inhospitable.

inovação [inova'sãw] (*pl* -ões) *f* innovation.

inovador, ra [inova'do(x), ra] <> *adj* innovative. <> *m, f* innovator.

inovar [ino'va(x)] *vt* to innovate.

inoxidável [inoksi'davεw] (*pl* -eis) *adj* ⊳ aço.

INPC (*abrev de* Índice Nacional de Preços ao Consumidor) *m* national index of retail prices, ≃ RPI *UK*.

inquérito [ĩŋ'kεritu] *m* enquiry.

inquietação [ĩŋkjeta'sãw] (*pl* -ões) *f* anxiety.

inquietante [ĩŋkje'tãntʃi], **inquietador, ra** [ĩŋkjeta'do(x), ra] *adj* worrying.

inquietar [ĩŋkje'ta(x)] *vt* to worry.

➡ **inquietar-se** *vp* to worry.

inquieto, ta [ĩŋ'kjεtu, ta] *adj* -1. [apreensivo] worried. -2. [agitado] restless.

inquilino, na [ĩŋki'linu, na] *m, f* tenant.

Inquisição [ĩŋkizi'sãw] *f*: a ~ the Inquisition.

insaciável [ĩnsa'sjavεw] (*pl* -eis) *adj* insatiable.

insalubre [ĩnsa'lubri] *adj* -1. [local, clima] unhealthy. -2. [trabalho] damaging to the health. -3. [água] unfit for drinking.

insanidade [ĩnsani'dadʒi] *f* insanity.

insano, na [ĩ'sanu, na] *adj* -1. [demente] insane. -2. *fig* [incansável] relentless. <> *m, f* madman (*f* madwoman).

insaciabilidade [ĩnsasjabili'dadʒi] *f* insatiable appetite.

insatisfação [ĩnsatʃiʃfa'sãw] (*pl* -ões) *f* dissatisfaction.

insatisfatório, ria [ĩnsatʃiʃfa'tɔrju, rja] *adj* unsatisfactory.

insatisfeito, ta [ĩnsatʃiʃ'fejtu, ta] *adj* dissatisfied.

inscrever [ĩʃkre've(x)] *vt* -1. [gravar] to inscribe. -2. [pessoa]: ~ alguém (em algo) to register sb (for sthg).

➡ **inscrever-se** *vp* [pessoa]: ~-se (em algo) to register (for sthg).

inscrito, ta [ĩ'ʃkritu, ta] <> *pp* ⊳ inscrever. <> *adj* -1. [mensagem] inscribed. -2. [pessoa] registered.

insegurança [ĩnsegu'rãnsa] *f* -1. [falta de segurança] lack of safety. -2. [de pessoa] insecurity.

inseguro, ra [ĩnse'guru, ra] *adj* -1. [perigoso] unsafe. -2. [pessoa] insecure.

inseminação [ĩnsemina'sãw] (*pl* -ões) *f* insemination; ~ artificial artificial insemination.

insensatez [ĩnsẽnsa'teʒ] *f* foolishness.

insensato, na [ĩnsẽn'satu, na] *adj* foolish.

insensível [ĩnsẽn'sivεw] (*pl* -eis) *adj* -1. [sem sensibilidade] numb. -2. [impassível] insensitive.

inseparável [ĩnsepa'ravεw] (*pl* -eis) *adj* inseparable.

inserção [ĩnsex'sãw] (*pl* -ões) *f* -1. [introdução]: ~ (de algo em algo) insertion (of sthg into sthg). -2. *COMPUT* insertion.

inserir [ĩse'ri(x)] *vt* -1.: ~ algo em algo to insert sthg into sthg. -2. *COMPUT* to insert.

➡ **inserir-se** *vp*: ~ -em algo to fit into sthg.

inseticida [ĩnsetʃi'sida] *m* insecticide.

inseto [ĩn'sεtu] *m* insect.

insígnia [ĩn'signja] *f* insignia.

insignificante [ĩnsignifi'kãntʃi] *adj* insignificant.

insincero, ra [ĩnsĩ'sεru, ra] *adj* insincere.

insinuação [ĩnsinwa'sãw] (*pl* -ões) *f* -1. [indireta, sugestão] insinuation. -2. [amorosa] advance.

insinuante [ĩnsi'nwãntʃi] *adj* [que se insinua] insinuating.

insinuar [ĩnsi'nwa(x)] *vt* -1. [afirmar indiretamente] to hint at. -2. [sugerir]: ~ que to suggest that.

➡ **insinuar-se** *vp* -1. [passar]: ~-se por *ou* entre to insinuate o.s. in *ou* among. -2. [amorosamente]: ~-se (para alguém) to make advances (to sb).

insípido, da [ĩn'sipidu, da] *adj* -1. [sem sabor] insipid. -2. *fig* [sem graça] insipid.

insistente [ĩnsiʃ'tẽntʃi] *adj* insistent.

insistir [ĩnsiʃ'ti(x)] *vi* [perseverar]: ~ em (fazer algo) to insist on (doing sthg); ~ para alguém fazer algo to insist that sb do sthg.

insociável [ĩnso'sjavεw] (*pl* -eis) *adj* antisocial.

insolação [ĩnsola'sãw] (*pl* -ões) *f* sunstroke.

insolente [ĩnso'lẽntʃi] <> *adj* insolent. <> *mf* insolent person.

insólito, ta [ĩn'sɔlitu, ta] *adj* unusual.

insolúvel [ĩnso'luvεw] (*pl* -eis) *adj* insoluble.

insone [ĩn'soni] *adj* -1. [pessoa] insomniac. -2. [noite] sleepless.

insônia [ĩn'sonja] f insomnia.

insosso, ssa [ĩn'sosu, sal adj -1. [sem sal] unsalted. -2. [sem sabor] tasteless. -3. fig [sem graça] dull.

inspeção [ĩnʃpe'sãw] (pl -ões) f inspection.

inspetor, ra [ĩnʃpe'to(x), ra] (mpl -es, fpl -s) m, f inspector; ~ da alfândega customs officer.

inspiração [ĩnʃpira'sãw] (pl -ões) f -1. [estímulo] inspiration. -2. [na respiração] breathing in.

inspirador, ra [ĩnʃpira'do(x), ra] (mpl -es, fpl -s) adj inspiring.

inspirar [ĩʃpi'ra(x)] vt -1. [estimular] to inspire. -2. [ar] to breathe in.
→ **inspirar-se** vp [obter estímulo] to be inspired.

instabilidade [ĩnʃtabili'dadʒi] f instability.

instalação [ĩnʃtala'sãw] (pl -ões) f -1. [ger] installation. -2. [sistema]: ~ elétrica/hidráulica electric/hydraulic plant.
→ **instalações** fpl -1. [para esporte, lazer] facilities. -2. [de indústria] plant.

instalar [ĩʃta'la(x)] vt -1. [ger] to install. -2. [estabelecer] to establish. -3. [num cargo]: ~ alguém em to install sb in.
→ **instalar-se** vp -1. [alojar-se] to install o.s. -2. [em um cargo] to install o.s.

instância [ĩnʃ'tãnsja] f -1. [solicitação] demand; em última ~ as a last resort. -2. [jurisdição] jurisdiction. -3. JUR stages of a law suit.

instantâneo, nea [ĩnʃtãn'tãnju, nja] adj instant.
→ **instantâneo** m FOT snap, snapshot.

instante [ĩnʃ'tãntʃi] <> m moment; nesse ~ at that moment; num ~ in a moment. <> adj -1. [iminente] imminent. -2. [urgente] urgent.

instar [ĩ'ta(x)] <> vt [pedir]: ~ que alguém faça algo to request that sb do sthg. <> vi [insistir]: ~ com alguém para que faça algo to urge sb to do sthg.

instauração [ĩnʃtawra'sãw] (pl -ões) f establishment.

instaurar [ĩʃtaw'ra(x)] vt -1. [estabelecer] to establish. -2. [criar] to set up.

instável [ĩnʃ'tavew] (pl -eis) adj -1. [ger] unstable. -2. [sem equilíbrio] wobbly.

instigar [ĩʃtʃi'ga(x)] vt -1. [incitar]: ~ alguém a fazer algo to encourage sb to do sthg. -2. [provocar]: ~ alguém contra alguém to rouse sb against sb.

instintivo, va [ĩnʃtʃĩn'tʃivu, va] adj instinctive.

instinto [ĩnʃ'tʃĩntu] m instinct.

instituição [ĩnʃtʃitwi'sãw] (pl -ões) f institution.

instituir [ĩʃtʃitwi(x)] vt -1. [estabelecer] to institute. -2. [marcar] to set. -3. [nomear] to name.

instituto [ĩnʃtʃi'tutu] m institute; ~ de beleza beauty parlour.

instrução [ĩnʃtru'sãw] (pl -ões) f -1. [educação] education. -2. [ordem] instruction.
→ **instruções** fpl instructions.

instruído, da [ĩʃ'trwidu, da] adj educated.

instruir [ĩʃtru'i(x)] vt -1. [ger] to instruct. -2. [educar] to educate. -3. [informar]: ~ alguém sobre algo to instruct sb on sthg. -4. [adestrar] to train.
→ **instruir-se** vp [educar-se] to become educated.

instrumental [ĩnʃtrumẽn'taw] (pl -ais) adj MÚS instrumental.

instrumento [ĩnʃtru'mẽntu] m -1. [ger] instrument; ~ de sopro wind instrument. -2. [ferramenta] tool; ~ de trabalho work tool.

instrutivo, va [ĩnʃtru'tʃivu, va] adj educational.

instrutor, ra [ĩnʃtru'to(x), ra] (mpl -es, fpl -s) m, f instructor.

insubordinação [ĩnsuboxdʒina'sãw] (pl -ões) f insubordination.

insubordinado, da [ĩnsuboxdʒi'nadu, da] adj insubordinate.

insubstituível [ĩnsubʃtʃi'twivɛw] (pl -eis) adj irreplaceable.

insucesso [ĩnsu'sɛsu] m failure.

insuficiência [ĩnsufi'sjẽnsja] f -1. [carência] lack. -2. MED insufficiency.

insuficiente [ĩnsufi'sjẽntʃi] <> adj -1. [não-suficiente] insufficient. -2. [incompetente] inadequate. <> m [nota escolar] fail.

insuflar [ĩsu'fla(x)] vt -1. [soprar] to blow into. -2. fig [incutir]: ~ algo em alguém to provoke sthg in sb.

insular [ĩsu'la(x)] adj insular.

insulina [ĩnsu'lina] f insulin.

insultar [ĩsuw'ta(x)] vt to insult.

insulto [ĩn'suwtu] m insult.

insuperável [ĩnsupe'ravɛw] (pl -eis) adj -1. [invencível] insuperable. -2. [imbatível] unsurpassable.

insuportável [ĩnsupox'tavɛw] (pl -eis) adj unbearable.

insurgir-se [ĩsux'ʒixsi] vp to revolt.

insurreição [ĩnsuxej'sãw] (pl -ões) f insurrection.

insuspeito, ta [ĩnsuʃ'pejtu, ta] adj -1. [inocente] beyond suspicion. -2. [imparcial] impartial.

insustentável [ĩnsuʃtẽn'tavɛw] (pl -eis) adj untenable.

intacto, ta [ĩn'ta(k)tu, ta] *adj* = intato.

intangibilidade [ĩntãnʒibili'dadʒi] *f* intangibility.

intato, ta [ĩn'tatu, ta] *adj* -1. [ileso] intact. -2. *fig* [puro] inviolate.

íntegra ['ĩntegra] *f* entirety; **na** ~ in entirety.

integração [ĩntegra'sãw] (*pl* -ões) *f* integration.

integral [ĩnte'grawl] (*pl* -ais) *adj* [total] whole; **leite** ~ full-cream milk; **cereal** ~ wholegrain cereal; **arroz** ~ brown rice; **pão** ~ wholemeal bread.

integrante [ĩnte'grãntʃi] ⟨⟩ *adj* component. ⟨⟩ *mf* -1. [membro] constituent. -2. [parte] component. -3. *GRAM* conjunction.

integrar [ĩnte'gra(x)] *vt* -1. [unir] to integrate. -2. [formar] to comprise. -3. [fazer parte] to be a member.
➡ **integrar-se** *vp* -1. [inteirar-se] to combine. -2. [juntar-se]: ~-se em *ou* a algo to join sthg.

integridade [ĩntegri'dadʒi] *f* integrity.

íntegro, gra ['ĩntegru, gra] *adj* -1. [inteiro] entire. -2. [honesto] honest.

inteiramente [ĩn,tejra'mẽntʃi] *adv* entirely.

inteirar [ĩntej'ra(x)] *vt* -1. [completar] to make up. -2. [informar]: ~ alguém de algo to inform sb of sthg.
➡ **inteirar-se** *vp* [informar-se]: ~-se de algo to find out about sthg.

inteiro, ra [ĩn'tejru, ra] *adj* -1. [todo] whole. -2. [intacto] intact. -3. [completo] entire. -4. [ileso] in one piece (*depois de verbo*). -5. [inteiriço] all-in-one (*antes de subst*); [total] complete. -6. *fam* [conservado] in good shape.

intelecto [ĩnte'lɛktu] *m* intellect.

intelectual [ĩntelɛ'twaw] (*pl* -ais) ⟨⟩ *adj* intellectual. ⟨⟩ *mf* intellectual.

inteligência [ĩnteli'ʒẽnsja] *f* -1. [destreza mental] intelligence. -2. [entendimento] comprehension. -3. [pessoa] brain. -4. *COMP*: ~ artificial artificial intelligence.

inteligente [ĩnteli'ʒẽntʃi] *adj* intelligent.

inteligível [ĩnteli'ʒivew] (*pl* -eis) *adj* intelligible.

intempestivo, va [ĩntẽmpeʃ'tʃivu, va] *adj* untimely.

intenção [ĩntẽn'sãw] (*pl* -ões) *f* intention; **com boa** ~ with good intentions, well meaning; **segundas intenções** ulterior motives; **ter a** ~ **de fazer algo** to intend to do sthg, to have the intention of doing sthg.

intencional [ĩntẽnsjo'naw] (*pl* -ais) *adj* intentional.

intencionar [ĩntẽnsjo'na(x)] *vt* to intend.

intensidade [ĩntẽnsi'dadʒi] *f* intensity.

intensificar [ĩntẽnsifi'ka(x)] *vt* to intensify.
➡ **intensificar-se** *vp* to intensify.

intensivo, va [ĩntẽ'sivu, va] *adj* intensive.

intenso, sa [ĩn'tẽsu, sa] *adj* intense.

interação [ĩntera'sãw] (*pl* -ões) *f* interaction.

interatividade [ĩnteratʃivi'dadʒi] *f COMPUT* interactivity.

interativo, va [ĩntera'tʃivu, va] *adj* interactive.

intercâmbio [,ĩnter'kãnbju] *m* exchange.

interceder [ĩntexse'de(x)] *vi*: ~ **por alguém** to intercede on behalf of sb.

interceptar [ĩntexsep'ta(x)] *vt* -1. [ger] to cut off. -2. [fazer parar] to stop. -3. [apoderar-se de] to intercept.

intercontinental [ĩntexkõntʃinẽn'taw] (*pl* -ais) *adj* intercontinental.

interdição [ĩntexdʒi'sãw] (*pl* -ões) *f* -1. [proibição] ban. -2. [bloqueio] closure. -3. *JUR* injunction.

interdisciplinaridade [ĩntexdʒisiplinari'dadʒi] *f* interdisciplinary nature.

interditado, da [ĩntexdʒi'tadu, da] *adj* -1. [proibido] banned. -2. [bloqueado] closed.

interditar [ĩntexdʒi'ta(x)] *vt* -1. [proibir] to ban. -2. [bloquear] to close. -3. *JUR* to interdict.

interessado, da [ĩntere'sadu, da] ⟨⟩ *adj* interested. ⟨⟩ *m, f* interested party.

interessante [ĩntere'sãntʃi] *adj* interesting.

interessar [ĩntere'sa(x)] ⟨⟩ *vt* to interest. ⟨⟩ *vi* [despertar interesse] to be of interest; **a quem possa** ~ *fml* to whom it may concern.
➡ **interessar-se** *vp* [ter interesse]: ~-se em *ou* por to take an interest in.

interesse [ĩnte'resi] *m* -1. [ger] interest. -2. [vantagem] benefit; **no** ~ **de** in the interest of; **por** ~ **próprio** out of self-interest.

interesseiro, ra [ĩntere'sejru, ra] ⟨⟩ *adj* self-seeking. ⟨⟩ *m, f* egotist.

interface [,ĩntex'fasi] *f COMPUT* interface.

interferência [ĩntexfe'rẽnsja] *f* interference.

interferir [ĩntexfe'ri(x)] *vi* -1. [intervir]: ~ **em algo** to interfere in sthg. -2. [em rádio, televisão] to cause interference.

interfonar [ĩntexfo'na(x)] *vi*: ~ **a alguém** to call sb on the internal phone.

interfone [,ĩntex'foni] *m* intercom.

ínterim ['ĩnterĩ] *m* interim; **nesse** ~ meanwhile.

interior [ĩnte'rjo(x)] (*pl* -es) ◇ *adj* inner. ◇ *m* interior.

interiorano, na [ĩnterjo'rãnu, na] ◇ *adj* country *(antes de subst)*. ◇ *m,f* country dweller.

interjeição [ĩntexʒej'sãw] (*pl* -ões) f exclamation.

interlocutor, ra [ĩntexloku'to(x), ra] (*pl* -es, *fpl* -s) *m,* f interlocutor.

interlúdio [ĩntex'ludʒul *m* interlude.

intermediar [ĩntexme'dʒja(x)] *vt* -1. [servir como mediador] to mediate; ~ um debate entre to chair a debate between. -2. [entremear, intercalar] to mix.

intermediário, ria [ĩntexme'dʒjarju, rja] ◇ *adj* intermediate. ◇ *m,* f -1. [mediador] mediator. -2. COM intermediary.

intermédio [ĩnter'mɛdʒul *m*: por ~ de through.

interminável [ĩntexmi'navɛw] (*pl* -eis) *adj* endless.

intermitente [ĩntexmi'tẽntʃi] *adj* intermittent.

internação [ĩntexna'sãw] (*pl* -ões) f -1. [de doente] admission. -2. [de aluno] boarding.

internacional [ĩntexnasjo'naw] (*pl* -ais) *adj* international.

internamento [ĩntexna'mẽntul *m* admission.

internar [ĩntex'na(x)] *vt* -1. MED to admit. -2. [aluno] to board. -3. POL to intern.

internato [ĩntex'natul *m* EDUC boarding school.

internauta [ĩntex'nawta] *mf* COMPUT Internet user ou surfer.

Internet [ĩntex'nɛtʃil f: a ~ the Internet.

interno, na [ĩn'tɛxnu, na] ◇ *adj* -1. [interior] inside; de uso ~ for internal use. -2. POL internal. -3. [aluno] boarding. ◇ *m,* f -1. MED houseman UK, intern US. -2. [aluno] boarder.

Interpol (*abrev de* **International Criminal Police Organization**) f Interpol.

interpretação [ĩntexpreta'sãw] (*pl* -ões) f -1. [ger] interpretation. -2. [tradução] interpreting.

interpretar [ĩntexpre'ta(x)] *vt* -1. [ger] to interpret. -2. [traduzir] to interpret.

interpretativo, va [ĩntexpreta'tʃivu, va] *adj* interpretative.

intérprete [ĩn'tɛxpretʃi] *mf* -1. LING interpreter. -2. CINE, TEATRO & TV performer.

inter-relacionar [ĩntexelasjo'na(x)] *vt* to interrelate.

interrogação [ĩntexoga'sãw] (*pl* -ões) f interrogation; ponto de ~ question mark.

interrogar [ĩntexu'ga(x)] *vt* -1. [indagar]: ~ alguém (sobre algo) to interrogate sb (about sthg). -2. JUR to put questions to.

interrogativo, va [ĩntexoga'tʃivu, va] *adj* -1. [indagativo] questioning. -2. GRAM interrogative.

interrogatório [ĩntexoga'tɔrju] *m* interrogation.

interromper [ĩntexõm'pe(x)] *vt* to interrupt.

interrupção [ĩntexup'sãw] (*pl* -ões) f interruption.

interruptor [ĩntexup'to(x)] (*pl* -es) *m* switch.

interseção [ĩntexse'sãw] (*pl* -ões) f intersection.

interurbano, na [ˌĩnterux'bãnu, na] *adj* -1. intercity UK, inter-urban US. -2. [telefonema] long distance.
➡ **interurbano** *m* [telefonema] long distance call.

intervalo [ĩntex'valul *m* -1. [ger] interval; a ~s at intervals; ~ comercial commercial break. -2. [no espaço] distance.

intervenção [ĩntexvẽn'sãw] (*pl* -ões) f -1. [interferência] intervention; ~ cirúrgica operation, surgical intervention. -2. JUR mediation.

intervencionismo [ĩntexvẽnsjo'niʒmul *m* interventionism.

intervencionista [ĩntervẽnsjo'niʃtal ◇ *adj* interventionist. ◇ *mf* interventionist.

interventor, ra [ĩntexvẽn'to(x), ral *m,* f interim governor.

intervir [ĩntex'vi(x)] *vi* to intervene.

intestino [ĩnteʃ'tʃinul *m* intestine.

intimação [ĩntʃima'sãw] (*pl* -ões) f -1. [ordem] order. -2. JUR summons *(sg)*.

intimar [ĩntʃi'ma(x)] *vt* -1. [ordenar]: ~ alguém (a fazer algo) to order sb (to do sthg). -2. JUR to summons.

intimidade [ĩntʃimi'dadʒil f -1. [vida íntima] privacy. -2. [familiaridade] intimacy; ter ~ com alguém to be close to sb.

intimidar [ĩntʃimi'da(x)] *vt* to intimidate.
➡ **intimidar-se** *vp* to be intimidated.

íntimo, ma ['ĩntʃimu, mal ◇ *adj* -1. [interior e profundo] intimate. -2. [privado] private. ◇ *m* -1. [âmago] no ~, ela sabia que estava errada deep down, she knew that she was wrong. -2. [amigo] close friend.

intolerância [ĩntole'rãnsjaɫ] f intolerance.

intolerante [ĩntole'rãntʃi] adj intolerant.

intolerável [ĩntole'ravɛwɫ] (pl -eis) adj intolerable.

intoxicação [ĩntoksika'sãwɫ] (pl -ões) f poisoning; ~ **alimentar** food poisoning.

intoxicar [ĩntoksi'ka(x)] vt to poison.
◆ **intoxicar-se** vp to poison o.s.

intragável [ĩntra'gavɛwɫ] (pl -eis) adj unpalatable.

intranet ['ĩtranetʃi] f COMPUT intranet.

intranqüilidade [ĩntrãŋkwili'dadʒi] f disquiet.

intranqüilo [ĩntrãn'kwilu] adj restless.

intransferível [ĩntrãnʃfe'rivɛwɫ] (pl -eis) adj **-1.** [bilhete, documento] nontransferable. **-2.** [inadiável] nonpostponable.

intransigente [ĩntrãnzi'ʒẽntʃi] adj **-1.** [intolerante] intransigent. **-2.** fig [austero] uncompromising.

intransitável [ĩntrãnzi'tavɛwɫ] (pl-eis) adj impassable.

intransitivo, va [ĩntrãnzi'tʃivu, va] adj intransitive.

intransponível [ĩntrãnʃpo'nivɛwɫ] (pl -eis) adj **-1.** [rio, barreira] impassable. **-2.** [problema, obstáculo] insurmountable.

intratável [ĩntra'tavɛwɫ] (pl -eis) adj [insociável] intractable.

intravenoso, osa [ĩntrave'nozu, ɔza] adj intravenous.

intrépido, da [ĩn'trɛpidu, da] adj intrepid.

intricado, da [ĩntri'kadu, da] adj **-1.** [emaranhado] tangled. **-2.** [confuso] intricate.

intriga [ĩn'triga] f **-1.** [trama] intrigue. **-2.** [cilada] conspiracy. **-3.** [enredo] plot.
◆ **intrigas** fpl [fofoca] gossip (sg).

intrigante [ĩntri'gãntʃi] adj intriguing.

intrigar [ĩntri'ga(x)] <> vt [despertar curiosidade de] to intrigue. <> vi [excitar a curiosidade] to intrigue.

introdução [ĩntrodu'sãwɫ] (pl -ões) f introduction.

introduzir [ĩntrodu'zi(x)] vt **-1.** [inserir]: ~ **algo (em)** to introduce sthg (into). **-2.** [fazer adotar] to introduce.
◆ **introduzir-se** vp: ~ **(em)** to find one's way (into).

intrometer-se [ĩntrome'texsi] vp: ~-**se em algo** to meddle in sthg.

intrometido, da [ĩntrome'tʃidu, da] <> adj meddlesome, interfering. <> m, f meddler.

introvertido, da [ĩntrovex'tʃidu, da] <> adj introverted. <> m, f introvert.

intruso, sa [ĩn'truzu, za] m, f intruder.

intuição [ĩntwi'sãwɫ] (pl -ões) f intuition.

intuir [ĩn'twi(x)] <> vt to intuit. <> vi to be intuitive.

intuitivo, va [ĩntwi'tʃivu, va] adj intuitive.

intuito [ĩn'twitu] m **-1.** [objetivo] purpose. **-2.** [intento] intention.

inumano, na [inu'manu, na] adj inhuman.

inúmeros, ras [i'numeruʃ, raʃ] adj pl [antes de subst] innumerable.

inundação [inũnda'sãwɫ] (pl-ões) f flood.

inundado, da [inũn'dadu, da] adj **-1.** [de água] flooded. **-2.** fig covered.

inundar [inũn'da(x)] <> vt [alagar] to flood; fig [encher] to swamp. <> vi [transbordar] to flood.

inusitado, da [inuzi'tadu, da] adj unusual.

inútil [i'nutʃiwɫ] (pl -eis) adj **-1.** [imprestável] useless. **-2.** [desnecessário] needless. **-3.** [vão] pointless.

inutilizar [inutʃili'za(x)] vt **-1.** [tornar inútil] to render useless. **-2.** [danificar] to ruin. **-3.** [frustrar] to thwart.

inutilmente [i,nutʃiwmẽntʃi] adv uselessly.

invadir [ĩnva'di(x)] vt **-1.** [ger] to invade. **-2.** fig [dominar] to overwhelm.

invalidez [ĩnvali'deʒ] f disability.

inválido, da [ĩnvalidu, da] <> adj **-1.** [nulo] invalid. **-2.** [pessoa] invalid, disabled. <> m, f [pessoa] invalid.

invariável [ĩnva'rjavɛwɫ] (pl -eis) adj invariable.

invasão [ĩnva'zãwɫ] (pl -ões) f invasion.

invasivo, va [ĩnva'zivu, va] adj **-1.** [agressivo] invasion (antes de subst). **-2.** MED invasive.

invasor, ra [ĩva'zo(x), ra] <> adj invading. <> m, f invader.

inveja [ĩn'veʒa] f envy.

invejar [ĩnve'ʒa(x)] <> vt **-1.** [ter inveja de] to envy. **-2.** [cobiçar] to covet. <> vi [ter inveja] to be envious.

invejoso, osa [ĩnve'ʒozu, ɔza] <> adj [pessoa] envious. <> m, f [pessoa] envious person.

invenção [ĩnvẽn'sãwɫ] (pl -ões) f **-1.** [ger] invention. **-2.** fig [mentira] fabrication.

invencível [ĩnvẽn'sivɛwɫ] (pl -eis) adj invincible.

inventar [ĩnvẽn'ta(x)] vt to invent.

inventário [ĩnvẽn'tarjuɫ] m inventory.

inventivo, va [ĩnvẽn'tʃivu, va] adj inventive.

inventor, ra [ĩnvẽn'to(x), ra] (mpl -es, fpl -s) m, f inventor.

inverdade [ĩnvex'dadʒi] f untruth.

inverno [ĩn'vɛxnu] m winter.

inverossímil [ĩnvero'simiw] (pl -eis) adj implausible.

inverso, sa [ĩn'vɛxsu, sa] adj -1. [invertido] inverse. -2. [oposto] opposite.
➡ **inverso** m [contrário] opposite.

invertebrado, da [ĩnvexte'bradu, da] ◇ adj [animal] invertebrate. ◇ m [animal] invertebrate.

inverter [ĩnvex'te(x)] vt -1. [virar ao contrário] to reverse. -2. [trocar a ordem de] to invert. -3. [mudar] to alter.

invés [ĩn'vɛʃ] m inside out.
➡ **ao invés de** loc prep instead of.

investida [ĩnveʃ'tʃida] f -1. [ataque] attack. -2. fig [tentativa] attempt.

investidor, ra [ĩnveʃtʃi'do(x), ra] m, f investor.

investigação [ĩnveʃtʃiga'sãw] (pl -ões) f -1. [inquérito] investigation. -2. [pesquisa] inquiry.

investigador, ra [ĩnveʃtʃiga'do(x), ra] m, f [agente policial] detective.

investigar [ĩnveʃtʃi'ga(x)] vt -1. [inquirir] to investigate. -2. [pesquisar] to research.

investimento [ĩnveʃtʃi'mẽntu] m investment.

investir [ĩveʃ'tʃi(x)] ◇ vt [dinheiro, verba] to invest. ◇ vi -1. [aplicar dinheiro, verba]: ~ **(em algo)** to invest (in sthg). -2. [atacar]: ~ **contra algo** to storm sthg. -3. [atirar-se]: ~ **para algo** to rush to sthg.

inveterado, da [ĩnvete'radu, da] adj [muito antigo] inveterate.

inviabilizar [ĩvjabili'za(x)] vt to make unviable.
➡ **inviabilizar-se** vp to become unviable.

inviável [ĩn'vjavɛw] (pl -eis) adj unviable.

invicto, ta [ĩn'viktu, ta] adj unbeaten.

inviolabilidade [ĩnviolabili'dadʒi] f inviolability.

invisível [ĩnvi'zivɛw] (pl -eis) adj invisible.

invocar [ĩvo'ka(x)] ◇ vt -1. [chamar] to invoke. -2. fam [irritar] to wind up, to annoy. ◇ vi fam [antipatizar]: ~ **com alguém** to dislike sb.

invólucro [ĩn'vɔlukru] m -1. [envoltório] envelope. -2. [membrana] membrane. -3. [caixa] casing.

involuntário, ria [ĩnvolũn'tarju, rja] adj involuntary.

iodo [ʹjodu] m iodine.

IOF (abrev de Imposto sobre Operações Financeiras) m Brazilian tax on financial transactions.

ioga [ʹjɔga] f yoga.

iogue [ʹjɔgi] ◇ adj yoga (antes de subst). ◇ mf yogi.

iogurte [ju'guxtʃi] m yoghurt.

íon [ʹjõ] (pl íons) m ion.

IPC (abrev de Índice de Preços ao Consumidor) m consumer price index.

IPEM (abrev de Instituto de Pesos e Medidas) m Brazilian institute of weights and measures.

IPTU (abrev de Imposto Predial e Territorial Urbano) m annual tax based on the value of a house.

IPVA (abrev de Imposto sobre Propriedade de Veículos Automotores) m tax paid annually on the value of a car, ≈ road tax UK.

ir [ʹi(x)] vi -1. [deslocar-se] to go; **fomos de ônibus** we went by bus; **iremos a pé** we'll go on foot, we'll walk; **vamos?** shall we go? -2. [assistir, freqüentar] to go; **ele nunca vai às reuniões** he never goes to the meetings; **você não vai à aula?** aren't you going to your class?; **vou ao cinema muitas vezes** I often go to the cinema. -3. [estender-se] to go; **o caminho vai até ao lago** the path leads to the lake. -4. [desenrolar-se] to go; **isto não vai nada bem** this isn't going at all well; **como vai você?** how are you?; **como vão as coisas?** how are things?; **os negócios vão mal** business is bad. -5. [exprime duração gradual]: ~ **fazendo algo** to continue doing sthg; **vá tentando!** keep trying! -6. [seguido de infinitivo]: **vou falar com ele** I'll speak to him; **você vai gostar** you'll like it; **não vou fazer nada** I'm not going to do anything. -7. [seguido de gerúndio]: **eu ia caindo** I almost fell. -8. [em locuções]: ~ **dar em** [desembocar] to lead to; ~ **ter com** [encontrar] to go and meet up with.
➡ **ir de** v + prep [ir disfarçado] to go as; [escolher]: **eu vou de filé com fritas, e você?** I'll have the steak and fries, what about you?
➡ **ir por** v + prep [auto-estrada, escadas] to take; ~ **pela esquerda/direita** to go (on the) left/right; ~ **pelo jardim** to go through the garden.
➡ **ir-se** vp [partir] to go; **ele já se foi** he's already left; ~-**se embora** to leave; **vai-te embora!** go away!

IR (abrev de Imposto de Renda) m income tax.

ira [ʹira] f anger.

Irã [i'rã] m: (o) ~ Iran.

irado, da [i'radu, da] adj angry.

iraniano, na [ira'njãnu, na] ◇ adj Iranian. ◇ m, f Iranian.

Iraque [i'raki] *n*: **(o)** ~ Iraq.

iraquiano, na [ira'kjanu, na] <> *adj* Iraqi. <> *m, f* Iraqi.

irascível [ira'sivɛw] (*pl* -eis) *adj* irascible.

ir-e-vir [iri'vi(x)] (*pl* ires-e-vires) *m* coming and going.

íris ['irisʃ] *f inv* iris.

Irlanda [ix'lãnda] *n* Ireland; ~ **do Norte** Northern Ireland.

irlandês, esa [ixlãn'desʃ, ezal] (*mpl* -eses, *fpl* -s) <> *adj* Irish. <> *m, f* Irishman (*f* Irishwoman).
→ **irlandês** *m* [língua] Irish.

irmã [ix'mã] *f* ⊳ **irmão**.

irmandade [ixmãn'dadʒil] *f* -**1**. [RELIG - de irmãos] brotherhood; [- de irmãs] sisterhood. -**2**. [confraternidade] fraternity.

irmão, mã [ix'mãw, mã] *m, f* -**1**. [parente] brother (*f* sister); ~ **de criação** stepbrother; ~ **gêmeo** twin brother. -**2**. [afim] twin.

ironia [iro'nia] *f* irony.

irônico, ca [i'roniku, ka] *adj* ironic.

IRPF (*abrev de* **Imposto de Renda de Pessoa Física**) *m income tax paid by individuals.*

IRPJ (*abrev de* **Imposto de Renda de Pessoa Jurídica**) *m corporation tax.*

irracional [ixasjo'naw] (*pl* -ais) *adj* irrational.

irradiação [ixadʒia'sãw] (*pl* -ões) *f* -**1**. [transmissão] broadcast. -**2**. [propagação] diffusion. -**3**. *MED* irradiation.

irradiar [ixa'dʒia(x)] *vt* -**1**. [transmitir] to broadcast. -**2**. [propagar] to spread. -**3**. *fig* [externar] to radiate.

irreal [i'xjaw] (*pl* -ais) *adj* unreal.

irreconciliável [ixekõnsi'ljavɛw] (*pl* -eis) *adj* irreconcilable.

irreconhecível [ixekoɲe'sivɛw] (*pl* -eis) *adj* unrecognizable.

irrecuperável [ixekupe'ravɛw] (*pl* -eis) *adj* irrecoverable.

irrecusável [ixeku'zavɛw] (*pl* -eis) *adj which cannot be refused.*

irredutível [ixedu'tʃivɛw] (*pl* -eis) *adj* indomitable.

irregular [ixegu'la(x)] (*pl* -es) *adj* -**1**. [desigual] irregular. -**2**. [pouco convencional] unorthodox. -**3**. [irrecuperável] incurable.

irrelevante [ixele'vãntʃil] *adj* irrelevant.

irremediável [ixeme'dʒiavɛw] (*pl* -eis) *adj* irreparable.

irrepreensível [ixeprjɛ̃n'sivɛw] (*pl* -eis) *adj* irreproachable.

irreprimível [ixepri'mivɛw] (*pl* -eis) *adj* irrepressible.

irrequieto, ta [ixe'kjɛtu, ta] *adj* [desassossegado] restless.

irresistível [ixeziʃ'tʃivɛw] (*pl* -eis) *adj* irresistible.

irresoluto, ta [ixezo'lutu, ta] *adj* irresolute.

irresponsável [ixeʃpõn'savɛw] (*pl* -eis) <> *adj* irresponsible. <> *mf* irresponsible person.

irrestrito, ta [ixeʃ'tritu, ta] *adj* unlimited, limitless.

irreverente [ixeve'rẽntʃil] *adj* irreverent.

irreversível [ixevex'sivɛw] (*pl* -eis) *adj* irreversible.

irrigação [ixiga'sãw] (*pl* -ões) *f* irrigation.

irrigar [ixi'ga(x)] *vt* to irrigate.

irrisório, ria [ixi'zɔrju, rja] *adj* -**1**. [de zombaria] derisory. -**2**. *fig* [ínfimo] derisory.

irritação [ixita'sãw] (*pl* -ões) *f* irritation.

irritadiço, ça [ixita'dʒisu, sa] *adj* irritable.

irritante [ixi'tãntʃil] *adj* irritating.

irritar [ixi'ta(x)] *vt* to irritate.
→ **irritar-se** *vp* [exasperar-se] to become irritated.

irritável [ixi'tavɛw] (*pl* -eis) *adj* irritable.

irromper [ixõm'pe(x)] *vi* -**1**. [entrar]: ~ **em** to burst into. -**2**. [surgir]: ~ **de** to surge from.

isca ['iʃka] *f* -**1**. [ger] bait. -**2**. *CULIN* morsel.

isenção [izẽn'sãw] (*pl* -ões) *f* -**1**. [dispensa] exemption. -**2**. [livramento] release. -**3**. [imparcialidade] impartiality.

isentar [izẽn'ta(x)] *vt* -**1**. [dispensar]: ~ **alguém de algo/de fazer algo** to exempt sb from sthg/from doing sthg. -**2**. [livrar]: ~ **alguém de algo/fazer algo** to let sb off from sthg/from doing sthg.
→ **isentar-se** *vp* to free o.s.

isento, ta [i'zẽntu, ta] *adj* -**1**. [dispensado] exempt. -**2**. [livre] free. -**3**. [imparcial] unbiased.

Islã [iʒ'lã] *m* Islam.

islâmico, ca [iʒ'lamiku, ka] *adj* Islamic.

islamismo [iʒla'miʒmu] *m* Islam.

islandês, esa [iʒlãn'deʃ, ezal] <> *adj* Icelandic. <> *m, f* Icelander.
→ **islandês** *m* [língua] Icelandic.

Islândia [iʒ'lãndʒja] *f* Iceland.

ISO (*abrev de* **International Standards Organization**) *f* ISO.

isolado, da [izo'ladu, da] *adj* -**1**. [separado] isolated. -**2**. [só] lone. -**3**. [afastado] remote. -**4**. *ELETR* insulated.

isolamento [izola'mẽntu] *m* -**1**. [ger] isolation. -**2**. *ELETR* insulation.

isolar [izo'la(x)] *vt* -**1**. [ger] to isolate; ~ **algo de algo** to isolate sthg from sthg. -**2**. *ELETR* to insulate.

jeans

◆ **isolar-se** vp [afastar-se]: ~-se de alguém/algo to isolate o.s from sb/sthg.

isonomia [izono'mia] f equality.

isopor [izo'pox] m polystyrene.

isqueiro [iʃ'kejru] m lighter.

Israel [iʒxa'ɛwl] n Israel.

israelense [iʒxe'lẽsil], **israelita** [iʒxae'lita] ◇ adj Israeli. ◇ mf Israeli.

isso ['isul] ◇ pron that; **é isso aí!** that's right!; **foi por isso que ele não veio** that's why he didn't come; **é por isso mesmo que en não vou!** that is exactly why I'm not going!; **isso não!** no way!; **não gosto disso** I don't like that; **não mexa nisso!** leave that alone!

◆ **por isso** loc adv therefore; **nem por ~** not really.

Istambul [iʃtãn'buwl] n Istambul.

istmo ['iʃtʃimul] m isthmus.

isto ['iʃtul] pron this; **disto eu não quero** I don't want any of this; **escreva nisto** write on this; **isto é** [quer dizer] that is (to say); **isto é que é vida!** this is the life!

Itália [i'talja] n Italy.

italiano, na [ita'ljanu, na] ◇ adj Italian. ◇ m, f Italian.

◆ **italiano** m [língua] Italian.

itálico, ca [i'taliku, ka] adj TIPO italic.

◆ **itálico** m TIPO italic.

Itamarati [itamara'tʃil] m Brazilian foreign ministry.

item ['itɛl] (pl itens) m -1. [ger] item. -2. JUR [artigo] point.

itinerário [itʃine'rarjul m -1. [roteiro] route. -2. [caminho] itinerary.

Iugoslávia [iwgo'ʒlavjal f Yugoslavia; **a ex-~** the ex-Yugoslavia.

iugoslavo, va [iwgoʒ'lavu, va] ◇ adj Yugoslav. ◇ m, f Yugoslav.

J

j, J ['ʒɔta] m [letra] j, J.

já ['ʒa] ◇ adv -1. [ger] already. -2. [agora] now. -3. [sem demora] just; **~ vou** just coming. -4. [até mesmo] even. -5. [daqui a pouco] soon; **até ~** see you soon. -6. [alguma vez] ever. ◇ conj however. ◇ loc: **~ era!** fam that's history!

◆ **desde já** loc prep from now on.

◆ **já que** loc conj since.

jabuti [ʒabu'tʃil m jabuti, indigenous Brazilian tortoise.

jabuticaba [ʒabutʃi'kabal f jaboticaba, Brazilian evergreen tree or the fruit of this tree.

jaca ['ʒakal f jack fruit.

jacarandá [ʒakarãn'dal f jacaranda.

Jacarta [ʒa'kaxta] n Djakarta, Jakarta.

jacinto [ʒa'sĩntul m hyacinth.

jade ['ʒadʒil m jade.

jaguar [ʒa'gwa(x)l (pl -es) m jaguar.

jaguatirica [ʒagwatʃi'rikal f leopard.

Jamaica [ʒa'majkal f Jamaica.

jamais [ʒa'majʃl adv never; (com palavra negativa) ever.

jamanta [ʒa'mãntal f [caminhão] articulated truck.

jan. (abrev de janeiro) Jan.

janeiro [ʒa'nejrul m January; veja também setembro.

janela [ʒa'nɛlal f window.

jangada [ʒãŋ'gadal f raft.

jantar [ʒãn'ta(x)l (pl -es) ◇ vt to have for dinner. ◇ vi to have dinner. ◇ m dinner.

Japão [ʒa'pãwl n: (o) ~ Japan.

japonês, esa [ʒapo'neʃ, ezal (mpl -eses, fpl -s) ◇ adj Japanese. ◇ m, f Japanese person.

◆ **japonês** m [língua] Japanese.

jaqueta [ʒa'ketal f jacket.

jararaca [ʒara'rakal f -1. [cobra] viper. -2. fig [pessoa] harridan.

jardim [ʒax'dʒil (pl -ns) m garden; **~ botânico** botanical garden; **~ zoológico** zoo.

jardim-de-infância [ʒaxdʒĩndʒĩfãnsjal (pl jardins-de-infância) m kindergarten.

jardinagem [ʒaxdʒi'naʒẽl f gardening.

jardineiro, ra [ʒaxdʒi'nejru, ral m, f [pessoa] gardener.

◆ **jardineira** f -1. [móvel] jardinière. -2. [em parapeito] window box. -3. [roupa] overalls (pl).

jargão [ʒax'gãwl (pl -ões) m jargon.

jarra ['ʒaxal f [pote] carafe; [vaso] vase.

jarro ['ʒaxul m jug.

jasmim [ʒaʒ'mĩl (pl -ns) m jasmine.

jato ['ʒatul m -1. [raio] beam. -2. [avião] jet. -3. [propulsão]: **a ~** jet propelled. -4. [jorro] stream.

jaula ['ʒawlal f cage.

Java ['ʒaval n Java.

javali [ʒava'lil m wild boar.

jazida [ʒa'zidal f seam.

jazigo [ʒa'zigul m grave.

jazz ['ʒajʃl m jazz.

JC (abrev de Jesus Cristo) m JC.

jeans ['ʒĩnʃl m inv jeans (pl).

jeca-tatu [ˈʒɛkatatu] (*pl* **-tus**) *m charac- ter from children's literature repre- senting the village people of the Brazilian interior.*

jegue [ˈʒɛgi] *m* ass.

jeito [ˈʒejtu] *m* **-1.** [modo] way; **ao ~ de** in the manner of; **de ~ algum!** no way!; **de qualquer ~** anyway; [sem cui- dado] any old how. **-2.** [aspecto] air. **-3.** [índole] disposition. **-4.** [torção]: **dar um mau ~ em** to sprain. **-5.** [propen- são]: **ter** *ou* **levar ~ para (fazer) algo** to be good at (doing) sthg. **-6.** [habilidade] aptitude; **ter falta de ~ para (fazer) al- go** to be bad at (doing) sthg. **-7.** [graça]: **ficar sem ~** to feel embarrassed. **-8.** [arrumação] clean up; **dar um ~ em algo** to tidy up. **-9.** [solução] solution; **dar um ~ em algo** to do something about sthg. **-11.** [juízo]: **tomar ~** to grow up.

jeitoso, osa [ʒejˈtozu, ɔza] *adj* **-1.** [habili- doso] dexterous. **-2.** [funcional] practical. **-3.** [diplomático] tactful.

jejuar [ʒeˈʒwa(x)] *vi* to fast.

jejum [ʒeˈʒũ] (*pl* **-ns**) *m* fast; **em ~** fasting.

jérsei [ˈʒɛxsej] *m* jersey.

Jerusalém [ʒeruzaˈlẽ] *n* Jerusalem.

jesuíta [ʒeˈzwital] <> *adj* Jesuit. <> *m* Jesuit.

jesuítico, ca [ʒezuˈitʃiku, ka] *adj* [período, missão] Jesuitical.

jesus [ʒeˈzuʃ] *interj* (good) heavens!

jet set [ʒetˈsetʃil] *m* jet set.

jibóia [ʒiˈbɔja] *f* [cobra] boa.

jiló [ʒiˈlɔ] *m type of Brazilian vegetable.*

jingle [ˈʒĩgow] *m* jingle.

jipe [ˈʒipi] *m* jeep.

joalheiro, ra [ʒwaˈʎejru, ra] *m, f* jeweller *UK*, jeweler *US*.

joalheria [ʒwaʎeˈria] *f* jewellers *UK*, jewelers *US*.

joaninha [ʒwaˈniɲa] *f* **-1.** [inseto] ladybird. **-2.** [carro de polícia] patrol car.

jocoso, sa [ʒokoˈzu, za] *adj* [divertido, cô- mico] jocular.

joelho [ʒweˈʎu] *m* knee; **de ~s** knee- ling, on one's knees; **ficar de ~s** to kneel down.

jogada [ʒoˈgada] *f* **-1.** [ESP - tática] strategy; [- lance] shot. **-2.** *fam* [esque- ma] scam. **-3.** *fam* [intenção] intention.

jogador, ra [ʒogaˈdo(x), ra] *m, f* **-1.** [atle- ta] player. **-2.** [apostador] gambler.

jogar [ʒoˈga(x)] <> *vt* **-1.** [tomar parte em jogo de] to play. **-2.** [atirar] to throw. **-3.** [apostar]: **~ algo em algo** to gamble sthg on sthg. **-4.** [desfazer-se de]: **~ algo fora** to throw sthg out. <> *vi* **-1.** [divertir-se

num jogo] to play. **-2.** [apostar]: **~ em algo** to bet on sthg. **-3.** [manipular]: **~ com algo** to play around with sthg. **-4.** [balançar] to toss.

jogar-se *vp* [lançar-se] to throw o.s.

jogging [ˈʒɔgĩ] *m* **-1.** [corrida] jogging; **fazer ~** to go jogging. **-2.** [roupa] tracksuit.

jogo [ˈʒogu] (*pl* **jogos**) *m* **-1.** [ger] game; **~ de azar** game of chance. **-2.** [partida] match. **-3.** [vício de jogar] gambling. **-4.** [conjunto] collection. **-5.** [aposta] bet. **-6.** *MEC* set. **-7.** *fig* [ardil] ruse. **-8.** [ma- nipulação] play. **-9.** [movimentação] mo- vement. **-10.** [balanço] tossing. **-11.** *AUTO* running. **-12.** *fam* [intenção] game. **-13.** *loc*: **abrir o ~** to lay one's cards on the table; **ter ~ de cintura para algo** to be quite capable of getting out of sthg.

jóia [ˈʒɔja] <> *adj fam* delightful. <> *f* **-1.** [enfeite] jewel. **-2.** [taxa] fee.

joio [ˈʒoju] *m* darnel; **separar o ~ do tri- go** to separate the wheat from the chaff.

jóquei [ˈʒɔkej] *m* Jockey Club.

jornada [ʒoxˈnada] *f* **-1.** [ger] journey. **-2.** [período] duration; **~ de trabalho** working day.

jornal [ʒoxˈnaw] (*pl* **-ais**) *m* **-1.** [gazeta] newspaper. **-2.** [noticiário] news.

jornaleiro, ra [ʒoxnaˈlejru, ra] *m, f* [pes- soa] newspaper vendor.

jornaleiro *m* [banca] news-stand.

jornalista [ʒoxnaˈliʃta] *mf* journalist.

jorrar [ʒoˈxa(x)] <> *vt* to spurt. <> *vi* to gush.

jovem [ˈʒɔvẽl] (*pl* **-ns**) <> *adj* **-1.** [juvenil] youthful. **-2.** [para jovens] young. <> *mf* young person.

jovial [ʒoˈvjaw] (*pl* **-ais**) *adj* jovial.

joystick [ʒɔjˈʃtʃik] (*pl* **joysticks**) *m COMPUT* joystick.

juba [ˈʒuba] *f* mane.

jubileu [ʒubiˈlew] *m* jubilee; **~ de prata** silver jubilee.

júbilo [ˈʒubilu] *m* elation.

judaico, ca [ʒuˈdajku, ka] *adj* Jewish.

judaísmo [ʒudaˈiʒmul] *m* Judaism.

judeu, dia [ʒuˈdew, dʒia] <> *adj* Jewish. <> *m, f* Jewish person, Jew.

judicial [ʒudʒiˈsjaw] (*pl* **-ais**) *adj* judicial.

judiciário, ria [ʒudʒiˈsjarju, rja] *adj* judi- cial.

Judiciário *m*: **o ~** the judiciary.

judicioso, osa [ʒudʒiˈsjozu, ɔza] *adj* judi- cious.

judô [ʒuˈdo] *m* judo.

jugo [ˈʒugu] *m*: **sob o ~ de** under the yoke of.

juiz, íza [ˈʒwiʃ, izal] (*mpl* -**ízes**, *fpl* -**s**) *m, f*
-**1.** *JUR* judge; ~ **de paz** justice of the
peace. -**2.** *ESP* referee.

juizado [ʒujˈzadu, dal] *m* court; ~ **de me-
nores** juvenile court.

juízo [ˈʒwizul] *m* -**1.** [julgamento]
judgement. -**2.** [conceito] opinion. -**3.**
[sensatez] prudence; **perder o** ~ to lose
one's mind. -**4.** *JUR* [foro] tribunal.

jujuba [ʒuˈʒubal] *f* -**1.** *BOT* jujube. -**2.**
[bala] *jujube-flavoured boiled sweet.*

jul. (*abrev de* julho) Jul.

julgamento [ʒuwgaˈmẽntul] *m* -**1.** [juízo]
judgement. -**2.** [audiência] hearing.
-**3.** [sentença] sentence.

julgar [ʒuwˈga(x)] *vt* -**1.** [sentenciar sobre]
to judge. -**2.** [avaliar]: ~ **algo/alguém
por algo** to judge sthg/sb by sthg. -**3.**
[supor] to think.

➤ **julgar-se** *vp* [supor-se] to consider
o.s.

julho [ˈʒuʎul] *m* July; *veja também* setembro.

jumento [ʒuˈmẽntul] *m* donkey.

jun. (*abrev de* junho) Jun.

junção [ʒũnˈsãwl] (*pl* -**ões**) *f* -**1.** [união]
union. -**2.** [ponto] junction.

junco [ˈʒũŋkul] *m* reed.

junho [ˈʒunul] *m* June; *veja também* setembro.

júnior [ˈʒunjo(x)] (*pl* **juniores**) <> *adj*
junior. <> *mf* *ESP* junior.

junta [ˈʒũntal] *f* -**1.** [comissão] council.
-**2.** *POL* junta. -**3.** [articulação] joint. -**4.**
[órgão]: ~ **comercial** chamber of com-
merce.

juntar [ʒũnˈta(x)] <> *vt* -**1.** [unir]: ~ **algo (a algo)** to mix sthg (with sthg). -**2.**
[aproximar]: ~ **alguém (a alguém)** to
unite sb (with sb). -**3.** [colocar junto] to
mix (together). -**4.** [aglomerar] to
assemble. -**5.** [recolher] to collect. <>
vi [aglomerar-se] to cluster. <> *vi* [econo-
mizar]: ~ (**para**) to save (for).

➤ **juntar-se** *vp* [associar-se]: ~-**se a** to
mix with; ~-**se com** to unite o.s with.

junto, ta [ˈʒũntu, tal] <> *adj* together.
<> *adv* at the same time; ~ **de** next to.

➤ **junto a, junto de** *loc prep* next to.

jura [ˈʒural] *f* vow.

jurado, da [ʒuˈradu, dal] <> *adj* sworn.
<> *m, f* juror.

juramento [ʒuraˈmẽntul] *m* oath.

jurar [ʒuˈra(x)] <> *vt* -**1.** [prometer] to
swear; ~ **fazer algo** to swear to do
sthg; ~ **que** to swear that. -**2.** [sob
juramento]: ~ **fazer algo** to take an oath
to do sthg. <> *vi* [prestar juramento]: ~
(**por/sobre**) to swear (by/on).

júri [ˈʒuril] *m* jury.

jurídico, ca [ʒuˈridʒiku, kal] *adj* legal.

jurisdição [ʒurizdʒiˈsãwl] *f* jurisdiction.

juros [ˈʒuruʃ] *mpl* interest (*sg*); ~ **fixos/
variáveis** fixed/variable interest.

justamente [ʒuʃtaˈmẽntʃil] *adv* -**1.** [com
justiça] rightly. -**2.** [precisamente] precisely.

justapor [ʒuʃtaˈpo(x)] *vt*: ~ **algo (a algo)** to juxtapose sthg (with sthg).

➤ **justapor-se** *vp* to be juxtaposed.

justaposto, osta [ʒuʃtaˈpoʃtu, ɔʃtal] *pp*
➥ **justapor.**

justiça [ʒuʃˈtʃisal] *f* -**1.** [virtude] fairness;
com ~ justly; **fazer** ~ **a alguém/algo** to
do justice to sb/sthg. -**2.** [eqüidade]
equality; ~ **social** social justice. -**3.**
[tribunal] justice; **ir á** ~ to go to court.
-**4.** [poder judiciário]: **a Justiça** the judiciary.

justiceiro, ra [ʒuʃtʃiˈsejru, ral] *adj* just.

justificação [ʒuʃtʃifikaˈsãwl] (*pl* -**ões**) *f*
justification.

justificar [ʒuʃtʃifiˈka(x)] *vt* to justify.

➤ **justificar-se** *vp* [explicar-se]: ~-**se
por algo** to excuse o.s for sthg.

justo, ta [ˈʒuʃtu, tal] <> *adj* -**1.** [ger] fair.
-**2.** [apertado] tight. -**3.** [exato] precise.
-**4.** [merecido] just. <> *adv* just.

juvenil [ʒuveˈniwl] (*pl* -**is**) <> *adj* -**1.** [de
jovens] youth, teenage. -**2.** *ESP* junior.
<> *m* *ESP* [campeonato] junior.

juventude [ʒuvẽnˈtudʒil] *f* youth.

k, K [kal] *m* [letra] k, K.

kafkiano, na [kafˈkianu, nal] *adj* Kaf-
kaesque.

karaokê [karawˈkel] *m* -**1.** [atividade]
karaoke. -**2.** [casa noturna] karaoke
bar.

kardecismo [kaxdeˈsiʒmul] *m* *religious
doctrine of the Frenchman Allan
Kardec.*

kart [ˈkaxtʃil] *m* go-cart.

kartódromo [kaxˈtɔdromul] *m* go-kart
track.

Kb (*abrev de* **quilobyte**) *m* Kb.

kg (*abrev de* **quilograma**) *m* kg.

ketchup [kɛˈtʃupil] *m* (tomato) ketchup.

kit [ˈkitʃil] *m* kit.

kitsch [kitʃil] *adj inv* kitsch.

kiwi [ˈkiwi] *m* [fruta] kiwi fruit.

kl (*abrev de* quilolitro) *m* kl.

km (*abrev de* quilômetro) *m* km.

km/h (*abrev de* quilômetro por hora) *m* km/h.

know-how [now'haw] *m* know-how.

Kuwait [ku'ajtʃi] *n* Kuwait.

kW (*abrev de* kilowatt) *m* kW.

L

l, L [ˈɛli] *m* [letra] l, L.

-la [la] *pron* -**1.** [pessoa] her; -**2.** [coisa] it; -**3.** [você] you.

lá [ˈla] *adv* there; **quero lá saber!** what do I care!; **sei lá!** how should I know; **para lá de** beyond.

lã [ˈlã] *f* wool; **de pura ~** pure wool.

labareda [laba'reda] *f* flame.

lábia [ˈlabja] *f* [conversa] smooth talk; **ter ~** to have the gift of the gab.

labial [la'bjaw] (*pl* -ais) *adj* labial.

lábio [ˈlabju] *m* [ANAT - beiço] lip; [- genital] labium.

labirinto [labi'rĩtu] *m* labyrinth.

laboratorial [laborato'rjaw] (*pl* -ais) *adj* laboratory (*antes de subst*).

laboratório [labora'tɔrju] *m* laboratory.

labuta [la'buta] *f* toil.

laca [ˈlaka] *f* lacquer.

laçar [la'sa(x)] *vt* [animal] to lasso.

laço [ˈlasu] *m* -**1.** [nó] bow; **dar um ~ em algo** to tie a bow in sthg. -**2.** [para laçar animais] lasso. -**3.** *fig* [vínculo] tie; **~s de família** family ties.

lacônico, ca [la'koniku, ka] *adj* laconic.

lacrar [la'kra(x)] *vt* to seal.

lacre [ˈlakri] *m* sealing wax.

lacrimejar [lakrime'ʒa(x)] *vi* -**1.** [olhos] to water. -**2.** [pessoa] to weep.

lacrimogêneo, nea [lakrimo'ʒenju, nja] *adj* ⊳ **gás.**

lactação [lakta'sãw] (*pl* -ões) *f* [amamentação] lactation.

lácteo, tea [ˈlaktju, tja] *adj* -**1.** [produto] milky. -**2.** ⊳ **via.**

lactose [lak'tɔzi] *f* lactose.

lacuna [la'kuna] *f* -**1.** [vão] gap. -**2.** [espaço em branco] blank. -**3.** [omissão] omission.

ladeira [la'dejra] *f* -**1.** [rampa] slope. -**2.** [rua íngreme] steep road.

lado [ˈladu] *m* -**1.** [ger] side; **do ~ avesso** inside out; **estar do ~ de alguém** to be on sb's side; **por um ~ ... por outro ~** on the one hand ... on the other hand. -**2.** [direção, local] direction; **de todos os ~s** everywhere; **de um ~ para outro** from one side to the other; **do ~ de fora** outside.

➡ **ao lado** *loc adv* -**1.** [na casa adjacente] next door. -**2.** [próximo] close by.

➡ **ao lado de** *loc prep* next to.

➡ **de lado** *loc adv* [sentar, andar] on the side; **deixar algo de ~** [pôr de reserva] to put sthg aside; [desconsiderar] to drop sthg.

ladrão, ladra [la'drãw, 'ladra] (*mpl* -ões, *fpl* -s) ⬦ *adj* thieving. ⬦ *m, f* thief; **~ de loja** shoplifter.

➡ **ladrão** *m* [tubo] overflow pipe.

ladrar [la'dra(x)] *vi* to bark.

ladrilho [la'driʎu] *m* tile.

ladrões [la'drõjʃ] *pl* ⊳ **ladrão.**

lagarta [la'gaxta] *f* ZOOL caterpillar.

lagartixa [lagax'tʃiʃa] *f* (small) lizard.

lagarto [la'gaxtu] *m* ZOOL lizard.

lago [ˈlagu] *m* -**1.** GEOGR lake. -**2.** [de jardim] pond. -**3.** *fig* [poça] puddle; **a cozinha está um ~** the kitchen is flooded.

lagoa [la'goa] *f* flake.

lagosta [la'goʃta] *f* lobster.

lagostim [lagoʃ'tʃĩ] (*pl* -ns) *m* crayfish.

lágrima [ˈlagrima] *f* tear.

laguna [la'guna] *f* lagoon.

laje [ˈlaʒi] *f* -**1.** [pedra] flagstone. -**2.** CONSTR concrete flooring.

lajota [la'ʒota] *f* small flagstone.

lama [ˈlama] *f* -**1.** [ger] mud. -**2.** *fig* [má situação]: **tirar alguém da ~** to help sb out of trouble.

lamaçal [lama'saw] (*pl* -ais), **lamaceiro** [lama'sejru] *m* muddy place.

lamacento, ta [lama'sẽtu, ta] *adj* muddy.

lambada [lãn'bada] *f* -**1.** [golpe] blow. -**2.** *fig* [descompostura] telling-off. -**3.** [dança] lambada.

lamber [lãm'be(x)] *vt* to lick.

lambida [lãn'bida] *f* lick; **dar uma ~ em algo** to have a lick of sthg, to lick sthg.

lambido, da [lãm'bidu, da] *adj* -**1.** [cara] clean. -**2.** [cabelo] straight.

lambiscar [lãmbiʃ'ka(x)] ⬦ *vt* to nibble. ⬦ *vi* to pick.

lambri [lãn'bri] (*pl* -bris) *m* panelling.

lambuja [lãn'buʒa] *f* [vantagem] advantage.

lambuzar [lãmbu'za(x)] *vt*: **~ alguém/algo (de com algo)** to cover sb/sthg (in sthg).

lamentar [lamẽn'ta(x)] *vt* to regret; **la-mento muito, mas ...** I am very sorry, but ...
➡ **lamentar-se** *vp*: ~ **-se (de algo)** [lastimar-se] to feel sorry (about sthg).

lamentável [lamẽn'tavɛw] (*pl* **-eis**) *adj* **-1.** [lastimável] regrettable. **-2.** [deplorável] deplorable.

lamento [la'mẽntul] *m* lament.

lâmina ['lãmina] *f* **-1.** [ger] blade. **-2.** [de vidro] slide.

lâmpada ['lãnpada] *f* **-1.** [bulbo] light; ~ **(elétrica)** (light) bulb; ~ **fluorescente** fluorescent light bulb. **-2.** [aparelho] lamp; ~ **de mesa** table lamp.

lamparina [lãnpa'rina] *f* [aparelho] blow-lamp.

lampião [lãn'pjãw] (*pl* **-ões**) *m* street light.

lamuriar-se [lamu'rjaxsi] *vp*: ~ **(de algo)** to moan (about sthg).

LAN (*abrev de* **Local Area Network**) *f* LAN.

lança ['lãsa] *f* spear.

lançamento [lãsa'mẽntu] *m* **-1.** [arremesso] throw. **-2.** ESP: ~ **de dardos** to play darts; ~ **de disco** discus throwing. **-3.** [ger] launch; **novo** ~ [livro] new title. **-4.** [escrituração] entry. **-5.** [de impostos] rate.

lançar [lã'sa(x)] *vt* **-1.** [ger] to launch. **-2.** [atirar] to throw. **-3.** [pôr em voga] to start. **-4.** [escriturar] to enter. **-5.** [impostos] to set. **-6.** [dirigir] to cast.
➡ **lançar-se** *vp* **-1.** [atirar-se] to throw o.s. **-2.** [iniciar-se]: ~**-se em algo** to take up sthg; ~**-se como algo** to set o.s.up as sthg.

lance ['lãsi] *m* **-1.** [episódio, passagem] moment. **-2.** [fato] incident. **-3.** [em leilão] bid. **-4.** [no jogo - aposta] bet; [- jogada] play. **-5.** [de escada] staircase. **-6.** [de casas] terrace. **-7.** [rasgo] surge.

lancha ['lãʃa] *f* **-1.** NÁUT launch. **-2.** *fam* [pé] large foot. **-3.** *fam* [calçado] large shoe; **este sapato está uma** ~ this shoe is like a boat.

lanchar [lã'ʃa(x)] <> *vt* to snack on. <> *vi* to have tea.

lanche ['lãʃi] *m* [refeição ligeira] snack (*in the afternoon*).

lanchonete [lãnʃo'nɛtʃi] *f* snack bar.

lancinante [lãnsi'nãntʃi] *adj* piercing.

languidez [lãŋgi'deʒ] *f* [debilitação] languor.

lânguido, da ['lãŋgidu, da] *adj* languid.

lanterna [lãn'texna] *f* **-1.** [aparelho] lantern; ~ **elétrica** torch UK, flashlight US. **-2.** AUTO light.

La Paz [la'paʃ] *n* La Paz.

lapela [la'pɛla] *f* lapel.

lapidar [lapi'da(x)] *vt* to polish.

lápide ['lapidʒi] *f* **-1.** [comemorativa] plaque. **-2.** [tumular] tombstone.

lápis ['lapiʃ] *m inv* pencil; ~ **de cera** wax crayon; ~ **de cor** colouring pencil; ~ **de olho** eye pencil.

lapiseira [lapi'zejra] *f* pencil case.

Lapônia [la'ponja] *f* Lapland.

lapso ['lapsu] *m* **-1.** [falta] mistake. **-2.** [espaço de tempo] lapse.

laptop ['lapitopi] (*pl* **laptops**) *m* COMPUT laptop.

laquê [la'ke] *m* hairspray.

lar ['la(x)] (*pl* **-es**) *m* home.

laranja [la'rãʒa] <> *f* [fruta] orange. <> *m* **-1.** [cor] orange. **-2.** *fam* [testa-de-ferro] scapegoat. <> *adj* (*inv*) [cor] orange.

laranjada [larãn'ʒada] *f* orangeade.

laranjal [larãn'ʒaw] (*pl* **-ais**) *m* orange grove.

laranjeira [larãn'ʒejra] *f* orange tree.

lareira [la'rejra] *f* fireplace.

larga ['laxga] *f* ⊳ **largo**.

largada [lax'gada] *f* [em corrida] start; **dar a** ~ to start.

largado, da [lax'gadu, da] *adj* neglected.

largar [lax'ga(x)] <> *vt* **-1.** [ger] to leave. **-2.** [soltar] to loosen. **-3.** [deixar cair] to drop. **-4.** [pôr em liberdade] to release. **-5.** [deixar em paz] to leave alone. **-6.** *fam* [dar] to give; ~ **a mão em alguém** to slap sb. <> *vi* **-1.** [deixar]: ~ **de algo/de ser algo** to stop doing sthg/being sthg. **-2.** NÁUT to set sail.
➡ **largar-se** *vp* **-1.** [desprender-se] to untie o.s. from. **-2.** [ir] to go.

largo, ga ['laxgu, ga] *adj* **-1.** [grande de lado a lado] wide. **-2.** [folgado] loose. **-3.** (*antes de subst*) [extenso] great, large. **-4.** (*antes de subst*) [prolongado] long. **-5.** (*antes de subst*) [abundante] abundant.
➡ **largo** *m* [praça] square.
➡ **ao largo** *loc adv*: **passar ao** ~ **(de)** to give a wide berth (to); **avistar algo ao** ~ to make something out in the distance.

largura [lax'gura] *f* width; **tem 3 metros de** ~ it is 3 metres wide; ~ **de banda** COMPUT bandwidth.

larica [la'rika] *f fam* [fome] hunger.

laringe [la'rĩʒi] *f* larynx.

laringite [larĩ'ʒitʃi] *f* laryngitis.

larva ['laxva] *f* larva.

lasanha [la'zãɲa] *f* lasagne.

lascivo, va [la'sivu, va] *adj* lascivious.

laser ['lejze(x)] (*pl* **-es**) <> *adj* (*inv*) ⊳ **raio**. <> *m* (*inv*) laser.

lástima ['laʃtʃima] *f* **-1.** [pessoa]: **ser/estar**

uma ~ to be pathetic; [coisa] to be a disgrace. -**2.** [pena]: **é uma ~ (que)** it is a pity (that); **que ~!** what a pity!

lastimar [laʃtʃi'ma(x)] vt -**1.** [lamentar] to regret. -**2.** [ter pena de] to pity.

➭ **lastimar-se** vp [lamentar-se]: **~-se (de algo)** to moan (about sthg).

lastimável [laʃtʃi'mavɛw] (pl -**eis**) adj -**1.** [lamentável] regrettable. -**2.** [deplorável] disgraceful.

lata ['lata] f -**1.** [material] tin. -**2.** [recipiente] can; **~ de conserva** tin; **~ de lixo** rubbish bin -**3.** fam **na ~** straight.

latão [la'tãw] (pl -**ões**) m [material] brass.

lataria [lata'ria] f -**1.** AUTO bodywork. -**2.** [latas] large quantity of tins.

latejar [late'ʒa(x)] vi to throb.

latente [la'tẽtʃi] adj latent.

lateral [late'raw] (pl -**ais**) ◇ adj lateral. ◇ m FUT outfielder. ◇ f ESP [linha] sideline.

látex ['latɛks] m inv latex.

latido [la'tʃidu] m bark.

latifundiário, ria [latʃifũn'dʒjarju, rja] ◇ adj landed. ◇ m, f landowner.

latifúndio [latʃi'fũndʒju] m large property.

latim [la'tʃĩ] m Latin; **gastar o seu ~** to waste one's breath.

latino, na [la'tʃinu, na] ◇ adj Latin. ◇ m, f Latin.

latino-americano, latino-americana [la,tʃinwameri'kanu, la,tʃinwameri'kana] ◇ adj Latin American. ◇ m, f Latin American.

latir [la'tʃi(x)] vi to bark.

latitude [latʃi'tudʒi] f -**1.** [ger] latitude. -**2.** [amplitude] capacity.

latrocínio [latro'sinju] m larceny.

laudo ['lawdu] m -**1.** [parecer] verdict. -**2.** [documento] written verdict.

lava ['lava] f lava.

lavabo [la'vabu] m -**1.** [pia] washbasin. -**2.** [local] bathroom.

lavadeira [lava'dejra] f -**1.** [trabalhadora] washerwoman. -**2.** [libélula] dragonfly.

lavadora [lava'dora] f washing machine.

lavagem [la'vaʒẽ] (pl -**ns**) f -**1.** [limpeza] washing; **~ a seco** dry-cleaning. -**2.** MED washout. -**3.** PSIC: **~ cerebral** brainwashing. -**4.** FIN: **~ de dinheiro** money laundering. -**5.** [comida de porcos] swill.

lavanda [la'vãnda] f -**1.** BOT lavender. -**2.** [colônia] lavender water. -**3.** [recipiente com água] finger bowl.

lavanderia [lavãnde'ria] f laundry.

lavar [la'va(x)] vt to wash.

➭ **lavar-se** vp to wash o.s.

lavatório [lava'tɔrju] m -**1.** [pia] washbasin. -**2.** [toalete] cloakroom.

lavoura [la'vora] f cultivation.

lavrador, ra [lavra'do(x), ra] (mpl -**es**, fpl -**s**) m, f ploughman.

laxante [la'ʃãntʃi] adj laxative.

lazer [la'ze(x)] m -**1.** [descanso] pleasure. -**2.** [tempo de folga] leisure.

LBV (abrev de **Legião da Boa Vontade**) f Brazilian charitable organization for support of the needy.

leal [le'aw] (pl -**ais**) adj loyal.

lealdade [leaw'dadʒi] f loyalty.

leão [le'ãw] (pl -**ões**) m, f lion.

➭ **Leão** m -**1.** [zodíaco] Leo; veja também **Virgem**. -**2.** fig [fisco]: **o Leão** the taxman.

leasing ['lisĩŋ] m ECON leasing.

lebre ['lɛbri] f hare.

lecionar [lesjo'na(x)] ◇ vt to teach. ◇ vi to teach.

legado [le'gadu] m -**1.** [herança] legacy. -**2.** [enviado] envoy.

legal [le'gaw] (pl -**ais**) ◇ adj -**1.** JUR legal. -**2.** fam [bom, bonito] cool. -**3.** [hora] official time. ◇ adv fam [bem] well.

legalidade [legali'dadʒi] f legality.

legalizar [legali'za(x)] vt to legalize.

legar [le'ga(x)] vt -**1.** JUR to bequeath. -**2.** [transmitir] to pass on.

legenda [le'ʒẽnda] f -**1.** [em foto, desenho etc.] caption. -**2.** CINE subtitle. -**3.** POL number identifying political party on ballot sheet; **votar na ~** to vote for the party.

legendado, da [leʒẽn'dadu, da] adj -**1.** [filme] subtitled. -**2.** [fotos] captioned.

legendar [le'ʒẽnda(x)] vt -**1.** [filme] to subtitle. -**2.** [fotos] to caption.

legendário, ria [leʒẽn'darju, rja] adj legendary.

legião [le'ʒjãw] (pl -**ões**) f [de fãs, leitores] legion.

legislação [leʒizla'sãw] (pl -**ões**) f legislation.

legislador, ra [leʒizla'do(x), ra] m, f legislator.

legislativo, va [leʒizla'tʃivu, va] adj legislative.

➭ **Legislativo** m: **o Legislativo** the legislature.

legislatura [leʒizla'tura] f -**1.** [corpo] legislature. -**2.** [período] term.

legitimar [leʒitʃi'ma(x)] vt [legalizar] to legitimize.

legítimo, ma [le'ʒitʃimu, ma] adj -**1.** [ger] legitimate; **em legítima defesa** in legitimate defense. -**2.** [autêntico] authentic.

legível [le'ʒivɛw] (*pl* **-eis**) *adj* **-1.** [nítido] legible. **-2.** [agradável de ler] readable.

légua ['lɛgwal] *f* [medida] league.

➤ **léguas** *fpl fig* [grande distância] miles.

legume [le'gumel] *m* vegetable.

leguminosa [legumi'nɔzal] *f* BOT leguminous plant.

➤ **leguminosas** *fpl* BOT leguminosae.

lei ['lejl] *f* [ger] law; ~ **da oferta e da procura** the law of supply and demand.

leigo, ga ['lejgu, gal] <> *adj* **-1.** RELIG secular. **-2.** *fig* [imperito]: **ser ~ em algo** to be a layperson in sthg. <> *m, f* [pessoa imperita] layperson.

leilão [lej'lãw] (*pl* **-ões**) *m* auction.

leiloar [lej'lwa(x)] *vt* to auction.

leiloeiro, ra [lej'lwejru, ral *m, f* auctioneer.

leitão, toa [lej'tãw, toal (*pl* **-ões**) *m, f* suckling pig.

leite ['lejtʃil *m* milk; ~ **em pó** powdered milk; ~ **de coco** coconut milk; ~ **condensado** condensed milk; ~ **desnatado** OU **magro** skimmed milk; ~ **integral** full-cream milk; ~ **de magnésia** Milk of Magnesia; ~ **de soja** soya milk.

leiteiro, ra [lej'tejru, ral <> *adj* [que produz leite] dairy. <> *m, f* [pessoa] milkman (*f* milkwoman).

➤ **leiteira** *f* **-1.** [para ferver leite] milk pan. **-2.** [para servir leite] milk jug.

leito ['lejtul *m* bed.

leitor, ra [lej'to(x), ral (*mpl* **-es**, *fpl* **-s**) *m, f* **-1.** [quem lê] reader. **-2.** UNIV visiting lecturer.

leitura [lej'tural *f* reading.

lema ['lemal *m* **-1.** [norma] maxim. **-2.** [político] motto.

lembrança [lẽn'brãnsal *f* **-1.** [recordação] souvenir. **-2.** [presente] gift.

➤ **lembranças** *fpl* [cumprimentos]: **(dê) ~s minhas à sua família** (give) my regards to your family.

lembrar [lẽm'bra(x)] <> *vt* **-1.** [recordar] to remember. **-2.** [parecer] to look like. **-3.** [trazer à memória]: ~ **algo a alguém** to remind sb of sthg. <> *vi* **-1.** [recordar]: ~ **(de alguém/algo)** to remember (sb/sthg). **-2.** [advertir]: ~ **a alguém de algo/de fazer algo** to remind sb of sthg/to do sthg; ~ **a alguém (de) que** to remind sb that.

➤ **lembrar-se** *vp*: ~**-se (de alguém/algo)** to remember (sb/sthg); ~**-se (de) que** to remember that.

lembrete [lẽn'bretʃil *m* memo.

leme ['lemil *m* **-1.** [ger] helm. **-2.** [dispositivo] rudder.

lenço ['lẽnsul *m* **-1.** [para limpar] handkerchief; ~ **de papel** paper handkerchief, tissue. **-2.** [de cabeça] headscarf. **-3.** [de pescoço] neckerchief.

lençol [lẽn'sɔwl (*pl* **-óis**) *m* sheet; ~ **d'água** water table; **estar em maus lençóis** *fig* to be in a fine mess.

lenda ['lẽndal *f* **-1.** [história] legend. **-2.** *fig* [mentira] tall story.

lendário, ria [lẽn'darju, rjal *adj* legendary.

lenha ['leɲal *f* [para queimar] firewood; **botar ~ na fogueira** *fig* to add fuel to the fire.

lenhador [leɲa'do(x)l *m* woodcutter.

lente ['lẽntʃil *f* lens; ~ **de aumento** magnifying glass; ~**s de contato** contact lenses.

lentidão [lẽntʃi'dãwl *f* slowness.

lentilha [lẽn'tʃiʎal *f* lentil.

lento, ta ['lẽntu, tal *adj* slow.

leoa [le'oal *f* ▷ **leão**.

leões [le'õjʃl *pl* ▷ **leão**.

leonino, na [leo'ninu, nal *adj* **-1.** [caráter] leonine; [contrato] fraudulent. **-2.** ASTRO Leo. <> *m, f* ASTRO Leo.

leopardo [ljo'paxdul *m* leopard.

lépido, da ['lɛpidu, dal *adj* **-1.** [ágil] nimble. **-2.** [contente] happy.

leporino, na [lepo'rinu, nal *adj* ▷ **lábio**.

lepra ['lɛpral *f* leprosy.

leprosário [lepro'zarjul *m* leper colony.

leproso, osa [le'prozu, ɔzal <> *adj* leprous. <> *m, f* [pessoa] leper.

leque ['lɛkil *m* **-1.** [abano] fan. **-2.** *fig* [conjunto]: **um ~ de** a range of.

ler ['le(x)l <> *vt* to read. <> *vi* to read.

lerdo, da ['lɛxdu, dal *adj* **-1.** [vagaroso] sluggish. **-2.** [idiota] slow.

lesado, da [le'zadu, dal *adj* [ferido] injured.

lesão [le'zãwl (*pl* **-ões**) *f* **-1.** MED lesion; ~ **corporal** grievous bodily harm. **-2.** JUR [violação] violation.

lesar [le'za(x)l *vt* **-1.** *fig* [prejudicar, enganar] to cheat. **-2.** JUR [violar] to violate.

lésbico, ca ['lɛʒbiku, kal *adj* lesbian.

➤ **lésbica** *f* lesbian.

lesma ['leʒmal *f* **-1.** [animal] slug. **-2.** *fig* [pessoa] sluggard.

leste ['lɛʃtʃil <> *m* (*inv*) [ger] east; **a ~ (de)** to the east (of); **para ~** eastward. <> *adj* (*inv*) easterly.

letal [le'tawl (*pl* **-ais**) *adj* lethal.

letargia [letax'ʒial *f* lethargy.

letárgico, ca [le'taxʒiku, kal *adj* lethargic.

letivo, va [le'tʃivu, val *adj* school (*antes de subst*); **ano ~** academic year, school year.

Letônia [le'tonja] *n* Latvia.

letra ['letra] *f* **-1.** [caractere] letter; ~ **de imprensa** print; ~ **maiúscula/minúscula** capital/small letter. **-2.** [caligrafia] handwriting; ~ **de mão** handwriting. **-3.** [de música] lyrics (*pl*). **-4.** COM: ~ **de câmbio** bill of exchange.

➡ **letras** *fpl* **-1.** [curso] arts. **-2.** [literatura] literature.

➡ **à letra, ao pé da letra** *loc adv* **-1.** [literalmente] literally. **-2.** [rigorosamente] to the letter.

letrado, da [le'tradu, da] *adj* **-1.** [culto] lettered. **-2.** [versado em literatura] well read.

letreiro [le'trejru] *m* notice.

léu ['lɛw] ➡ **ao léu** *loc adv* **-1.** [à toa] aimlessly. **-2.** [à mostra] uncovered.

leucemia [lewse'mia] *f* leukaemia *UK*, leukemia *US*.

levado, da [le'vadu, da] *adj*: ~ **(da breca)** unruly.

levantador, ra [levãnta'do(x), ra] *m, f ESP*: ~ **de pesos** weightlifter.

levantamento [levãnta'mẽntu] *m* **-1.** [pesquisa] survey. **-2.** [inventário] inventory. **-3.** ESP: ~ **de pesos** weightlifting.

levantar [levãn'ta(x)] <> *vt* **-1.** [ger] to raise. **-2.** [do chão] to lift; ~ **vôo** to take off. **-3.** [tornar mais alto] to lift up. **-4.** [coletar] to collect. **-5.** [inventariar] to count. <> *vi* **-1.** [ficar de pé] to stand. **-2.** [sair da cama] to get up. **-3.** [avivar] to cheer.

➡ **levantar-se** *vp* **-1.** [ficar de pé] to stand up. **-2.** [sair da cama] to get up.

levante [le'vãntʃi] *m* **-1.** [revolta] uprising. **-2.** [leste] east.

levar [le'va(x)] *vt* **-1.** [ger] to take; **isso leva algum tempo** that will take some time; ~ **adiante** to carry on; ~ **a cabo** to carry out. **-2.** [carregar] to carry. **-3.** [induzir] to lead; ~ **alguém a algo/a fazer algo** to bring sb to sthg/to do sthg; **deixar-se** ~ **por algo** to let o.s. be led by sthg. **-4.** [retirar] to take away. **-5.** [lidar com] to deal with. **-6.** [vida]: **ele leva uma vida dura** he has a hard life. **-7.** [susto, surra]: ~ **um susto** to get a fright; ~ **uma surra** to take a beating. **-8.** [ganhar] to win.

leve ['lɛvi] *adj* light; **de** ~ lightly.

levedo [le'vedu] *m*, **levedura** *f* [leve'dura] yeast.

leviandade [levjãn'dadʒi] *f* **-1.** [imprudência] rashness. **-2.** [falta de seriedade] frivolity.

leviano, na [le'vjanu, na] *adj* **-1.** [imprudente] rash. **-2.** [sem seriedade] frivolous.

léxico, ca ['lɛksiku, ka] *adj* [análise, família] lexical.

➡ **léxico** *m* [vocabulário] lexicon.

lexicógrafo, fa [leksi'kografu, fa] *m* lexicographer.

lexicólogo, ga [leksi'kologu, ga] *m* lexicologist.

lhama ['ʎama] *mf* llama.

lhe [ʎe] (*pl* **lhes**) *pron pess* **-1.** [a ele, ela] (to) him/her/it; **dei-** ~ **um presente** I gave him/her a present; **Maria** ~ **contou um segredo** Maria told him/her a secret; **acertaram-** ~ **um tiro** they shot him/her; **isto lhes custou caro** this cost them a lot of money **-2.** [a você] (to) you; **telefonei-** ~ **ontem** I phoned you yesterday; **o que** ~ **aconteceu?** what's happened to you?; **ouçam bem o que lhes digo!** listen carefully to what I say! **-3.** [indicando posse - dele, dela] his (*f* her); **roubaram-** ~ **o carro** they stole his/her car; **ardia-lhes a vista** their eyes were stinging; [- de você] your; **beijei-** ~ **as faces** I kissed your cheeks; **não lhes pesa a consciência?** doesn't your conscience trouble you? **-4.** [para enfatizar - a ele, ela] his (*f* her); **não sei como ele agüenta as confusões que sua namorada** ~ **apronta** I don't know how he puts up with his girlfriend's nonsense; [- a você] you; **não sei como você agüenta as confusões que sua namorada** ~ **apronta** I don't know how you put up with your girlfriend's nonsense.

Líbano ['libanu] *n*:o ~ Lebanon.

libelo [li'bɛlu] *m* **-1.** [ger] lampoon. **-2.** JUR indictment.

libélula [li'bɛlula] *f* dragonfly.

liberação [libera'sãw] *f* **-1.** [ger] release. **-2.** [libertação] liberation. **-3.** [de preços, câmbio] freedom from controls. **-4.** [de cheque] clearing. **-5.** [do aborto] legalization.

liberal [libe'raw] (*pl* **-ais**) <> *adj* liberal. <> *mf* POL liberal.

liberar [libe'ra(x)] *vt* **-1.** [ger] to release; ~ **alguém de algo** to release sb from sthg. **-2.** [libertar] to release. **-3.** [preço, câmbio] to free from controls. **-4.** [cheque] to clear. **-5.** [aborto] to legalize.

liberdade [libex'dadʒi] *f* freedom; **estar em** ~ to be free; **pôr em** ~ to set free; **ter** ~ **para fazer algo** to be at liberty to do sthg; **tomar a** ~ **de fazer algo** to take the liberty of doing sthg; **estar em** ~ **condicional** to be on parole; ~ **de expressão** freedom of speech; ~ **sob fiança** release on bail.

Libéria [li'bɛrja] *n* Liberia.

líbero ['liberu] *m* FUT sweeper.

libertação [libex'tasãw] (*pl* -ões) *f* liberation.

libertar [libex'ta(x)] *vt* [tornar livre] to liberate.

libertino, na [libex'tʃinu, na] <> *adj* libertine. <> *m*, *f* libertine.

Líbia ['libja] *n* Libya.

libido [li'bidul] *f* libido.

libra ['libra] *f* pound; ~ **(esterlina)** pound (sterling).
➡ **Libra** *m* [zodíaco] Libra; *veja também* **Virgem**.

libreto [li'bretu] *m* libretto.

lição [li'sãw] (*pl* -ões) *f* -1. *EDUC* lesson. -2. *fig* [ensinamento] lesson. -3. *fig* [repreensão]: **dar uma ~ em alguém** to teach sb a lesson.

licença [li'sẽnsa] *f* -1. [permissão] permission; **dar ~ a alguém (para fazer algo)** to give sb permission (to do sthg); **com ~ excuse** me. -2. [de trabalho] permit; **estar de ~** to be on leave. -3. [documento] licence *UK*, license *US*.

licença-maternidade [li'sẽnsa'matexni'dadʒil] (*pl* **licenças-maternidade**) *f* maternity leave.

licenciado, da [lisẽ'sjadu, da] <> *adj* -1. *UNIV* graduated. -2. [do trabalho] on leave. <> *m*, *f* *UNIV* graduate.

licenciar [lisẽn'sja(x)] *vt* [do trabalho] to allow time off work.
➡ **licenciar-se** *vp* -1. *UNIV*: ~-se **(em algo)** to obtain a degree (in sthg). -2. [do trabalho] to go on leave.

licenciatura [lisẽnsja'tural] *f* -1. [grau] degree. -2. [curso] degree course.

licitação [lisita'sãw] (*pl* -ões) *f* -1. [em leilão] bid. -2. [concorrência] tender; **vencer uma ~** to win a tender.

lícito, ta ['lisitu, ta] *adj* -1. [legal] lawful. -2. [correto] licit.

lições [li'sõiʃ] *pl* ⊳ **lição**.

licor [li'ko(x)] (*pl* -es) *m* liqueur.

lidar [li'da(x)] *vi*: ~ **com alguém/algo** [conviver com] to deal with sb/sthg; [tratar] to deal with sb/sthg; [trabalhar com] to deal with sb/sthg.

líder ['lide(x)] (*pl* -es) *mf* leader.

liderança [lide'rãnsa] *f* leadership.

liderar [lide'ra(x)] *vt* to lead.

lido, da ['lidu, da] *pp* ⊳ **ler**.

lifting ['liftĩŋ] *m* facelift.

liga ['liga] *f* -1. [associação] league. -2. [de meias] garter. -3. [de metais] alloy.

ligação [liga'sãw] (*pl* -ões) *f* -1. [ger] connection; **fazer a ~ entre algo e algo** to connect sthg with sthg. -2. *TELEC* (telephone) call; **a ~ caiu** we have been cut off; **completar a ~** to get through (on the phone); **fazer uma ~**

(para alguém) to make a call (to sb). -3. [relacionamento - amoroso] liaison; [- profissional] relationship.

ligado, da [li'gadu, da] *adj* -1. [ger] connected. -2. [absorto] immersed. -3. [afeiçoado] attached.
➡ **ligada** *f* *TELEC* phone call; **dar uma ~ para alguém** to call sb.

ligadura [liga'dura] *f* -1. [atadura] bandage. -2. *MÚS* ligature.

ligamento [liga'mẽntu] *m* -1. *ANAT* ligament. -2. *MED*: ~ **de trompas** tubal ligation.

ligar [li'ga(x)] <> *vt* -1. [ger] to connect. -2. [unir] to connect, to join. -3. [criar vínculos] to tie. -4. [dar importância a]: **não ~ a mínima (para alguém/algo)** to not pay the least bit of attention to sb/ sthg. <> *vi* -1. [telefonar] to call; ~ **para alguém/algum lugar** to call sb/somewhere (on the phone). -2. [dar importância] to care; ~ **para alguém/algo** to care about sb/sthg. -3. [dar atenção] to notice; ~ **para alguém/algo** to notice sb/sthg.
➡ **ligar-se** *vp* -1. [unir-se] to unite. -2. [afeiçoar-se] to become attached.

ligeireza [liʒej'reza] *f* -1. [rapidez] lightness. -2. [agilidade] agility.

ligeiro, ra [li'ʒejru, ra] *adj* -1. [rápido] light. -2. [ágil] agile. -3. [antes de subst] *fig* [sutil] slight:
➡ **ligeiro** *adv* -1. [rapidamente] swiftly. -2. [com agilidade] nimbly.

lilás [li'laʃ] (*pl* **lilases**) <> *adj* [cor] lilac. <> *m* lilac.

lima ['lima] *f* -1. [fruta] lime. -2. [ferramenta] file.

Lima ['lima] *n* Lima.

limão [li'mãw] (*pl* -ões) *m* lemon.

limbo ['lĩnbul] *m*: **estar no ~** *fig* to be in limbo.

limiar [li'mja(x)] *m* threshold.

limitação [limita'sãw] (*pl* -ões) *f* limitation.

limitado, da [limi'tadu, da] *adj* limited.

limitar [limi'ta(x)] *vt* [restringir] to limit.
➡ **limitar-se** *vp* [restringir-se]: ~-se **a fazer algo** to limit o.s. to doing sthg.

limite [li'mitʃi] *m* [ger] limit; **passar dos ~s** to go too far.

limítrofe [li'mitrofi] *adj* bordering.

limo ['limu] *m* *BOT* slime.

limoeiro [li'mwejru] *m* lemon tree.

limões [li'mõiʃ] *pl* ⊳ **limão**.

limonada [limo'nada] *f* lemonade *UK*, lemon soda *US*.

limpador [lĩnpa'do(x)] (*pl* -es) *m* cleaner; ~ **de pára-brisas** windscreen wiper *UK*, windshield wiper *US*.

limpar [lĩm'pa(x)] *vt* -1. [ger] to clean. -2. *fig* [elevar]: ~ **a imagem de alguém/ algo** to clean up sb's/sthg's image. -3. [enxugar] to dry. -4. [esvaziar] to clean. -5. [roubar] to clean out.

➤ **limpar-se** *vp* -1. [assear-se] to wash o.s. -2. [moralmente] to make a clean start.

limpeza [lĩm'peza] *f* -1. [estado] cleanliness. -2. [ato] cleaning; **fazer uma ~ em algo** [livrar de excessos] to clear sthg out; [livrar de maus elementos] to clean sthg up; [roubar] to clean sthg out; ~ **pública** refuse collection. -3. [esmero] neatness.

limpo, pa [ˈlĩpu, pal ◇ *pp* ▷ **limpar.** ◇ *adj* -1. [asseado] clean. -2. [esmerado] neat; **passar a ~ to** make a clean copy. -3. *fig* [honrado] blameless. -4. [desanuviado] clear. -5. [sem dinheiro] broke. -6. [sem descontos]: **recebi 100 mil ~s** I received 100,000 clear. -7. *loc*: **tirar a ~ to** get to the bottom of.

limusine [limu'zinil *f* limousine.

lince [ˈlĩsil *m* lynx.

linchamento [lĩ∫a'mẽntul *m* lynching.

linchar [lĩn'∫a(x)] *vt* to lynch.

lindo, da [ˈlĩdu, dal *adj* beautiful.

lingerie [lãnʒe'xil *f* lingerie.

língua [ˈlĩgwal *f* -1. [órgão] tongue; **dar com a ~ nos dentes** to spill the beans; **ficar de ~ de fora** to be exhausted; **estar na ponta da ~ to** be on the tip of one's tongue; **dobrar a ~ to** mind what one says. -2. [idioma] language; ~ **materna** mother tongue.

linguado [lĩŋ'gwadul *m* [peixe] (Brazilian) flounder.

linguagem [lĩŋ'gwaʒẽl (*pl* -ns) *f* language; ~ **de máquina** machine language; ~ **de programação** programming language.

linguarudo, da [lĩŋgwa'rudu, dal ◇ *adj* gossipy. ◇ *m, f* gossip.

língüeta [lĩŋ'gwetal *f* -1. [de fechadura] catch. -2. [balança] pointer.

lingüiça [lĩŋ'gwisal *f* chorizo.

lingüístico, ca [lĩŋ'gwi∫t∫iku, kal *adj* linguistic.

➤ **lingüística** *f* linguistics *(pl)*.

linha [ˈlĩɲal *f* -1. [ger] line; **em ~s gerais** in general terms; ~ **de mira** line of sight; ~ **de fogo** firing line; ~ **de montagem** assembly line; ~ **cruzada** crossed line; **não dar ~ to** be dead; **andar na ~** *fig* to toe the line. -2. [fio de costura] thread. -3. [via] route; ~ **aérea** airline. -4. [elegância] flair; **é um homem de ~** he has a flair for things; **perder a ~ to** lose face. -5. *COMPUT*: ~

de comando command line; ~ **dedicada** dedicated line; ~ **discada** dial-up line.

linho [ˈlĩɲul *m* -1. [tecido] linen. -2. [planta] flax.

link [ˈlĩɲki] (*pl* **links**) *m COMPUT* link.

linóleo [liˈnɔljul *m* linoleum.

lipoaspiração [lipu'a∫pirasãwl (*pl* -ões) *f* liposuction.

liquidação [likidaˈsãwl (*pl* -ões) *f* -1. [dissolução] settlement. -2. *FIN* liquidation. -3. *COM* clearance sale; **(estar) em ~** (to be) in liquidation. -4. [destruição] elimination.

liquidar [likiˈda(x)] ◇ *vt* -1. [ger] to liquidate. -2. [dissolver] to settle. -3. [destruir] to eliminate. ◇ *vi* -1. *COM* to hold a clearance sale. -2.: ~ **com alguém/algo** [destruir] to destroy sb/sthg.

liquidez [likiˈdeʃl *f ECON* liquidity.

liqüidificador [likwidʒifikaˈdo(x)] *m* blender.

líquido, da [ˈlikidu, ˈlikidal *adj* -1. [estado] liquid. -2. [valor] net; **peso ~** *COM* net weight.

➤ **líquido** *m* [fluido] liquid.

lira [ˈliral *f* -1. [instrumento] lyre. -2. [moeda] lira.

lírico, ca [ˈliriku, kal *adj* -1. [gênero] lyrical. -2. *fig* [romântico] romantic.

➤ **lírica** *f* [coleção de poesia] lyrical poetry.

lírio [ˈlirjul *m* lily.

Lisboa [liʒˈboal *n* Lisbon.

liso, sa [ˈlizu, ˈlizal *adj* -1. [superfície] smooth. -2. [cabelo] straight. -3. [tecido] plain. -4. *fam* [sem dinheiro] broke.

lisonja [liˈzõʒal *f* flattery.

lisonjeador, ra [lizõˈʒjaˈdo(x), ral ◇ *adj* flattering. ◇ *m, f* flatterer.

lisonjear [lizõˈʒja(x)] *vt* to flatter.

lisonjeiro, ra [lizõˈʒejru, ral *adj* flattering.

lista [ˈli∫tal *f* -1. [relação] list; ~ **negra** blacklist; ~ **de discussão** newsgroup; ~ **telefônica** telephone directory. -2. [listra] stripe.

listar [li∫ˈta(x)] *vt COMPUT* to list.

listra [ˈli∫tral *f* stripe.

listrado, da [li∫ˈtradu, dal, **listado, da** [li∫ˈtadu, dal *adj* striped.

literal [liteˈrawl (*pl* -ais) *adj* literal.

literário, ria [liteˈrarju, rjal *adj* literary.

literatura [literaˈtural *f* literature.

litígio [liˈt∫iʒjul *m* -1. *JUR* [questão] litigation. -2. *fig* [disputa] quarrel.

litogravura [ˌlitograˈvural *f* [gravura] lithograph.

litoral [litoˈrawl (*pl* -ais) ◇ *adj* [costeiro] coastal. ◇ *m* [beira-mar] coast.

litorâneo, nea [lito'ranju, nja] *adj* coastal.

litro ['litru] *m* [medida] litre *UK*, liter *US*.

Lituânia [li'twãnja] *f* Lithuania.

liturgia [litux'ʒia] *f* liturgy.

lívido, da ['lividu, da] *adj* pallid.

livrar [li'vra(x)] *vt* -**1.** [libertar] to free. -**2.** [salvar]: ~ **alguém/algo de algo** to save sb/sthg from sthg.

➜ livrar-se *vp* [libertar-se]: ~-**se (de alguém/algo)** to free o.s. (from sb/sthg).

livraria [livra'ria] *f* bookshop *UK*, bookstore *US*.

livre ['livri] *adj* -**1.** [ger] free. -**2.** [independente] independent; **de** ~ **e espontânea vontade** of one's own free will. -**3.** [permitido] free. -**4.** [solto] free. -**5.** [isento]: ~ **de impostos** tax-free.

livre-arbítrio [ˌlivrjax'bitrju] (*pl* **livres-arbítrios**) *m* free will.

livre-iniciativa ['livri'inisja'tʃiva] (*pl* -**s**) *m ECON* free enterprise.

livreiro, ra [liv'rejru, ra] *m,f* bookseller.

livro ['livru] *m* book; ~ **de bolso** pocketbook; ~ **de capa dura** hardback; ~ **didático** text book; ~ **de cabeceira** favourite reading.

livro-caixa [ˌlivro'kajʃa] (*pl* **livros-caixas**) *m* cash book.

lixa ['liʃa] *f* -**1.** [papel] sandpaper. -**2.** [de ferro] file; ~ **de unhas** nail file.

lixar [li'ʃa(x)] *vt* -**1.** [madeira] to sand. -**2.** [unhas] to file.

➜ lixar-se *vp fam* [não se incomodar]: **ele está se lixando com a demissão** he couldn't care less about the resignation.

lixeira [li'ʃejra] *f* -**1.** [em prédio] rubbish chute *UK*, garbage chute *US*. -**2.** [local] rubbish dump *UK*, garbage dump *US*.

lixeiro [li'ʃejru] *m* refuse collector *UK*, dustman *UK*, garbage collector *US*.

lixo ['liʃu] *m* -**1.** [restos] rubbish *UK*, garbage *US*; ~ **atômico** nuclear waste. -**2.** [coisa sem valor] rubbish *UK*, garbage *US*.

-lo [lu] *pron* [pessoa] him; [coisa] it; [você] you.

lobby ['lɔbi] (*pl* **lobbies**) *m POL* lobby.

lobista [lo'biʃta] *mf* lobbyist.

lobo ['lobu] *m* wolf.

lobo-do-mar [ˌlobudu'ma(x)] (*pl* **lobos-do-mar**) *m* sea dog, old salt.

lóbulo ['lɔbulu] *m* lobe.

locação [loka'sãw] (*pl* -**ões**) *f* -**1.** [de carro, vídeo] hire, rental. -**2.** [de telefone, imóvel] rental. -**3.** *CINE* location.

locador, ra [loka'do(x), ra] *m* -**1.** [de imóvel] landlord. -**2.** [de carro] lessor.

➜ locadora *f* [agência] hire *ou* rental

company; ~ **de vídeo** video hire *ou* rental shop.

local [lo'kaw] (*pl* -**ais**) <> *adj* local. <> *m* place.

localidade [lokali'dadʒi] *f* -**1.** [lugar] locality. -**2.** [povoado] town.

localizar [lokali'za(x)] *vt* -**1.** [encontrar] to find. -**2.** [limitar a certo local] to site.

➜ localizar-se *vp* [situar-se] to be sited.

loção [lo'sãw] (*pl* -**ões**) *f* lotion; ~ **após-barba** aftershave.

locatário, ria [loka'tarju, rja] *m* -**1.** [carro] lessee. -**2.** [imóvel] tenant.

locomotiva [lokomo'tʃiva] *f* locomotive.

locomover-se [lokomo'vexsi] *vp* to move.

locutor, ra [loku'to(x), ra] (*mpl* -**es**, *fpl* -**s**) *m,f* [profissional] presenter.

lodacento, ta [loda'sẽntu, ta] *adj* muddy.

lodo ['lodu] *m* mud.

lodoso, osa [lo'dozu, ɔza] *adj* = **lodacento**.

lógico, ca ['lɔʒiku, ka] *adj* logical; **(é)** ~! of course!

➜ lógica *f* -**1.** [ger] logic. -**2.** [raciocínio] reasoning.

log-in (*pl* **logins**) *m COMPUT* login.

logo ['logu] <> *adv* -**1.** [sem demora] at once; ~ **de saída** *ou* **de cara** straight away. -**2.** [em breve] soon; **até** ~! see you later!; ~ **mais** in a while. -**3.** [exatamente]: ~ **agora** right now; ~ **ali** right there. -**4.** [pouco]: ~ **antes/depois** just before/after. <> *conj* [portanto] therefore.

➜ logo que *loc adv* as soon as.

logomarca [logo'maxka] *f* logo.

logotipo [logo'tʃipu] *m* logo.

logradouro [logra'doru] *m* public area.

lograr [lo'gra(x)] *vt* -**1.** [conseguir] to achieve; ~ **fazer algo** to manage to do sthg. -**2.** [empulhar] to trick.

logro ['logru] *m* fraud.

loiro, ra ['lojru, ra] *adj* = **louro**.

loja ['lɔʒa] *f* -**1.** *COM* shop *UK*, store *US*; ~ **de departamentos** department store. -**2.** [maçônica] lodge.

lombada [lõn'bada] *f* -**1.** [de livro] spine. -**2.** [de boi] fillet. -**3.** [no solo] ridge.

lombar [lõn'ba(x)] *adj* lumbar.

lombinho [lõn'biɲu] *m* [carne de porco] pork fillet.

lombo ['lõnbu] *m* -**1.** [dorso] lower back. -**2.** [carne] loin. -**3.** [elevação] ridge.

lombriga [lõn'briga] *f* roundworm.

lona ['lona] *f* -**1.** [tecido] canvas. -**2.** [cobertura] tarpaulin. -**3.** [de pneu] layer.

Londres ['lõndriʃ] *n* London.

londrino, na ['lõn'drinu, na] <> *adj* London (*antes de subst*). <> *m, f* Londoner.

longa-metragem [ˌlõŋgame'traʒẽ] (*pl* **longas-metragens**) *m*: **(filme de)** ~ feature-length film.

longe ['lõʒi] <> *adv* far (away); **ir** ~ **demais** *fig* [exceder-se] to go too far; **ver** ~ *fig* [ter visão] to look far ahead. <> *adj* remote.
⚫ **ao longe** *loc adv* [no espaço] in the distance.
⚫ **de longe** *loc adv* -**1.** [no espaço] from far away. -**2.** [no tempo]: **vir de** ~ to be longstanding. -**3.** [sem comparação] by far.
⚫ **longe de** <> *loc conj* far from; ~ **disso** far from it. <> *loc prep* far from.

longevidade [lõʒevi'dadʒi] *f* longevity.

longevo, va [lõʒe'vu, va] *adj* -**1.** [muito idoso] elderly. -**2.** [duradouro] long-lived.

longínquo, qua [lõ'ʒĩŋkwu, kwa] *adj* -**1.** [no espaço] distant, remote. -**2.** [no tempo] distant.

longitude [lõʒi'tudʒi] *f GEOGR* longitude.

longo, ga ['lõŋgu, ga] *adj* -**1.** [ger] long. -**2.** (*antes de subst*) [duradouro] lasting.
⚫ **longo** *m* [vestido] long dress.
⚫ **ao longo de** *loc prep* -**1.** [no sentido longitudinal] along. -**2.** [à beira de] alongside. -**3.** [no tempo]: **ao** ~ **dos anos** over the years.

lontra ['lõntra] *f* otter.

loquacidade [lokwasi'dadʒi] *m* loquaciousness.

loquaz [lo'kwaʒ] *adj* -**1.** [falador] talkative. -**2.** [eloqüente] eloquent.

losango [lo'zãŋgu] *m* diamond, lozenge.

lotação [lota'sãw] (*pl* -**ões**) *f* -**1.** [capacidade] capacity; ~ **esgotada** [cinema, teatro] sold out, full house. -**2.** [quadro de pessoal] number of personnel. -**3.** [veículo] minibus.

lotado, da [lo'tadu, da] *adj* [cheio] full, crowded.

lotar [lo'ta(x)] <> *vt* [encher] to fill. <> *vi* [encher]: ~ **(de)** to fill (with).

lote ['lɔtʃi] *m* -**1.** [parte] parcel. -**2.** [conjunto] set. -**3.** [terreno] plot.

lotear [lo'tʃja(x)] *vt* to divide into plots.

loteria [lote'ria] *f* lottery; ~ **esportiva** (football) pools *UK*, lottery *US*.

loto ['lɔtu] *m* lottery.

louça ['losa] *f* china; **de** ~ china (*antes de subst*); **lavar/secar a** ~ to wash/dry the dishes.

louco, ca ['loku, ka] <> *adj* -**1.** [ger] crazy. -**2.** [insano] mad. -**3.** [transtornado] crazed; **deixar alguém** ~ to drive sb

mad. -**4.** [furioso]: ~ **(da vida com)** spitting mad (at). -**5.** [apaixonado]: **ser** ~ **por alguém/algo** to be crazy about sb/sthg. -**6.** [excêntrico] weird. -**7.** [intenso] extreme. <> *m, f* [insano] lunatic; ~ **varrido** *ou* **de pedra** *fam* stark raving mad.
⚫ **louca** *f*: **dar a louca em alguém** to go mad.

loucura [lo'kura] *f* -**1.** [insanidade] insanity. -**2.** [imprudência] lunacy, madness; **ser (uma)** ~ **fazer algo** to be madness to do sthg. -**3.** [extravagância] antics (*pl*); **fazer** ~**s** to get up to antics. -**4.** [paixão] passion.

louro, ra ['loru, ra] <> *adj* [cabelo, pessoa] fair. <> *m, f* [pessoa] fair-haired person.
⚫ **louro** *m* -**1.** [cor] fair, blond. -**2.** [árvore] laurel. -**3.** *CULIN* bay leaf. -**4.** [papagaio] polly parrot.

louvar [lo'va(x)] <> *vt* -**1.** [elogiar] to praise. -**2.** [glorificar] to exalt. <> *vi*: ~ **a Deus** to praise God.

louvável [lo'vavɛw] (*pl* -**eis**) *adj* praiseworthy.

louvor [lo'vo(x)] *m*: ~ **a alguém/algo** [elogio] praise for sb/sthg; [glorificação] glorification of sb/sthg.

Ltda. (*abrev de* **Limitada**) *f* Ltd.

lua ['lua] *f* moon; ~ **cheia/nova** full/new moon; **estar no mundo da** ~ to be daydreaming; **ser de** ~ to have mood swings.

lua-de-mel [ˌluadʒi'mɛw] (*pl* **luas-de-mel**) *f* honeymoon.

luar ['lwa(x)] *m* moonlight.

lubrificante [lubrifi'kãntʃi] <> *adj* lubricating. <> *m* lubricant.

lubrificar [lubrifi'ka(x)] *vt* to lubricate.

lucidez [lusi'deʒ] *f* lucidity.

lúcido, da ['lusidu, da] *adj* lucid.

lucrar [lu'kra(x)] <> *vt*: ~ **algo com** *ou* **em algo** [financeiramente] to make a profit of sthg from sthg; [tirar vantagem de] to enjoy sthg through sthg. <> *vi* [financeiramente] to make a profit; ~ **com algo** [tirar vantagem de] to benefit from sthg.

lucrativo, va [lukra'tʃivu, va] *adj* -**1.** [financeiramente] lucrative, profitable; **com/sem fins** ~**s** profit/non-profit-making. -**2.** [proveitoso] useful.

lucro ['lukru] *m* -**1.** [financeiro] profit; **participação nos** ~**s** profit-sharing. -**2.** [proveito] gain.

lúdico, da ['ludʒiku, ka] *adj* play (*antes de subst*).

lugar [lu'ga(x)] (*pl* -**es**) *m* -**1.** [ger] place; **em algum** ~ somewhere; **em** ~ **nenhum**

nowhere; **em outro** ~ somewhere
else; ~ **de nascimento** place of birth;
em primeiro ~ [em competição] in first
place; [em argumentação] in the first
place; **tirar o primeiro/segundo** ~ to
come first/second. **-2.** [espaço] room.
-3. [assento] seat. **-4.** [função, ocupação]
position; **colocar-se no** ~ **de alguém** to
put o.s. in sb else's shoes. **-5.** [situa-
ção]: **no seu** ~ **eu faria o mesmo** if I
were you, I would do the same. **-6.**
log: **dar** ~ **a** to give rise to.
➡ **em lugar de** *loc prep* instead of.
lugar-comum [lu,gaxku'mũl] (*pl* **lugares-
comuns**) *m* commonplace.
lugarejo [luga'reʒu] *m* small village.
lugar-tenente [lu,ga(x)te'nẽntʃi] *m* deputy.
lúgubre ['lugubri] *adj* gloomy.
lula ['lula] *f* squid.
luminária [lumi'narja] *f* lamp.
luminosidade [luminozi'dadʒi] *f* brightness.
luminoso, osa [lumi'nozu, ɔza] *adj* **-1.**
[que emite luz] luminous. **-2.** *fig* [racioci-
nio, idéia, talento] brilliant.
lunar [lu'na(x)] (*pl* **-es**) *adj* lunar.
lunático, ca [lu'natʃiku, ka] *adj* lunatic.
luneta [lu'neta] *f* telescope.
lupa ['lupa] *f* magnifying glass.
lusco-fusco [,luʃku'fuʃku] *m* twilight.
lusitano, na [luzi'tanu, na] ⟨⟩ *adj*
Lusitanian. ⟨⟩ *m, f* Lusitanian.
luso, sa [za, 'luzul ⟨⟩ *adj* Portuguese.
⟨⟩ *m, f* Portuguese person.
lusófono, na [na, lu'zɔfonu, na] ⟨⟩ *adj*
Portuguese-speaking. ⟨⟩ *m, f* Portuguese speaker.
lustrar [luʃ'tra(x)] *vt* [móvel] to polish.
lustre ['luʃtri] *m* **-1.** [polimento] polish;
dar um ~ **em algo** to give sthg a polish.
-2. [luminária] chandelier.
lustroso, osa [luʃ'trozu, ɔza] *adj* shiny.
luta ['luta] *f* **-1.** [ger] struggle. **-2.** [com-
bate] fight. **-3.** *ESP*: ~ **de boxe** boxing;
~ **livre** wrestling.
lutador, ra [luta'do(x), ra] ⟨⟩ *adj* [esfor-
çado] tough. ⟨⟩ *m, f* **-1.** [ger] fighter. **-2.**
BOXE boxer.
lutar [lu'ta(x)] ⟨⟩ *vi* **-1.** [combater]: ~
(com/contra alguém) to fight with/
against sb; ~ **por algo** to fight for
sthg. **-2.** *fig* [combater]: ~ **por/contra
algo** to fight for/against sthg. **-3.** [em-
penhar-se] to use all one's forces; ~
(por algo/para fazer algo) to fight (for
sthg/to do sthg). **-4.** [resistir] to fight;
~ **contra algo** to fight against sthg.
⟨⟩ *vt* [judô, caratê, capoeira, luta livre] to
fight.

luterano, na [lute'ranu, na] ⟨⟩ *adj* [pes-
soa, igreja, doutrina] Lutheran. ⟨⟩ *m, f*
[crente] Lutheran.
luto ['lutu] *m* mourning; **estar de** ~ to
be in mourning.
luva ['luva] *f* glove; **cair como uma** ~ to
fit like a glove.
➡ **luvas** *fpl* [pagamento] payment.
Luxemburgo [luʃẽn'buxgu] *n* Luxemburg.
luxemburguês, esa [luʃẽnbux'geʃ, eza]
⟨⟩ *adj* Luxemburg (*antes de subst*). ⟨⟩
m, f person from Luxemburg.
luxo ['luʃu] *m* **-1.** [pompa] ostentation;
de ~ luxury (*antes de subst*). **-2.** [extra-
vagância] luxury. **-3.** [afetação, cerimônia]
ceremony; **cheio de** ~ full of airs and
graces.
luxuoso, osa [lu'ʃwozu, ɔza] *adj* luxurious.
luxúria [lu'ʃurja] *f* [lascívia] lust.
luz ['luʃ] (*pl* **-es**) *f* **-1.** [claridade, fonte de
luz] light; **acender a** ~ to turn on the
light; **apagar a** ~ to turn off the light;
~ **do dia** daylight. **-2.** [eletricidade]
electricity; **falta** ~ **todos os dias aqui**
the electricity gets cut off here every
day. **-3.** *loc*: **dar à** ~ to give birth.
luzir [lu'zi(x)] *vi* to shine.
Lycra® ['lajkra] *f* Lycra®.

m, M ['emil *m* [letra] m, M.
má [ma] ⟶ **mau.**
MA (*abrev de* **Estado do Maranhão**) *m*
State of Maranhão.
maca ['maka] *f MED* trolley.
maçã [ma'sã] *f* apple; ~ **do rosto** cheek;
~ **do amor** toffee apple.
macabro, bra [ma'kabru, bra] *adj* maca-
bre.
macacão [maka'kãw] (*pl* **-ões**) *m* overalls
(*pl*) UK, coveralls (*pl*) US.
macaco, ca [ma'kaku, ka] *adj m, f* [animal]
monkey; ~ **velho** *fig* [pessoa experiente]
old hand.
➡ **macaco** *m AUTO* jack.
maçaneta [masa'neta] *f* handle.
maçante [ma'sãntʃi] *adj* boring.
macaquice [maka'kisi] *f*: **fazer** ~**s** to
monkey around.

maçarico [masaˈriku] *m* blow torch.

maçaroca [masaˈrɔka] *f* -1. [emaranhado] tangle. -2. [mixórdia] mess.

macarrão [makaˈxãw] *m* -1. [massa] pasta. -2. [em tiras] spaghetti.

macete [maˈsetʃi] *m* -1. [instrumento] mallet. -2. *fam* [truque] trick.

machadada [maʃaˈdadul] *f* axe blow.

machado [maˈʃadul] *m* axe.

machão, ona [maˈʃãw, ɔna] (*mpl* -ões, *fpl* -s) *adj* -1. *pej* [ger] macho. -2. [corajoso] brave.

machismo [maˈʃiʒmu] *m* machismo.

machista [maˈʃiʃta] ◇ *adj* macho. ◇ *m* male chauvinist.

macho [ˈmaʃul] ◇ *adj* -1. [ger] manly. -2. [gênero] male. ◇ *m* -1. [animal] male. -2. *TEC* tap. -3. [prega] box pleat.

machões [maˈʃõjʃ] *pl* ⊳ **machão**.

machona [maˈʃɔnal] *f* ⊳ **machão**.

machucado, da [maʃuˈkadu, dal] *adj* -1. [ferido] hurt. -2. [contundido] injured. -3. [esmagado] bruised. -4. [lascado] scratched. -5. [magoado] hurt.
➨ **machucado** *m* [ferida] wound.

machucar [maʃuˈkax] ◇ *vt* -1. [ferir] to hurt. -2. [contundir] to injure. -3. [esmagar] to bruise. -4. [lascar] to scratch. -5. [magoar] to hurt. ◇ *vi* to hurt.
➨ **machucar-se** *vp* -1. [ferir-se] to injure o.s. -2. [contundir-se] to hurt o.s.

maciço, ça [maˈsisu, sal] *adj* -1. [sólido] massive. -2. [em quantidade] massive. -3. *fig* [sólido] solid.
➨ **maciço** *m* [cadeia montanhosa] massif.

macieira [maˈsjejral] *f* apple tree.

maciez [maˈsjeʒ] *f* softness.

macio, cia [maˈsiu, sial] *adj* -1. [ger] smooth. -2. [fofo] soft.

maço [ˈmasul] *m* -1. [de notas, folhas] bundle. -2. [de cartas] pack. -3. [de cigarros] packet.

maçom [maˈsõ] (*pl* -ns) *m* [membro da maçonaria] Freemason.

maçonaria [masonaˈrial] *f* freemasonry.

maconha [maˈkɔɲal] *f* -1. *BOT* hemp. -2. [droga] cannabis, marijuana.

má-criação [ˌmakrjaˈsãw] *f* = **malcriação**.

macrobiótico, ca [makroˈbjɔtʃiku, kal] *adj* macrobiotic.
➨ **macrobiótica** *f* -1. [doutrina] macrobiotics. -2. [dieta] macrobiotic diet.

mácula [ˈmakulal] *f fig* [desonra, mancha] stain.

maculado, da [makuˈladu, dal] *adj* -1. [manchado] stained. -2. [desonrado] tarnished.

macumba [maˈkũbal] *f* [espirit- religião]

macumba, *Afro-Brazilian religion*; [- despacho] sacrificial offering.

macumbeiro, ra [makũˈbejru, ral] ◇ *adj* [relativo à macumba] macumba *(antes de subst).* ◇ *m, f* [adepto] macumba initiate.

madame [maˈdãmil, **madama** [maˈdamal *f* -1. [senhora] Madam. -2. *irôn* [mulher rica] lady. -3. *irôn* [esposa] ladyship. -4. [cafetina] madam.

madeira [maˈdejral] *f* wood; **de ~** wooden; **bater na ~** to touch wood.

madeireiro, ra [madejˈrejru, ral] ◇ *adj* timber *(antes de subst).* ◇ *m, f* timber merchant.
➨ **madeireira** *f* [empresa] timber merchant's.

madeixa [maˈdejʃal] *f* [mecha] lock.

madrasta [maˈdraʃtal] *f* -1. [esposa do pai] stepmother. -2. *fig* [mãe má] unfit mother.

madre [ˈmadril] *f* -1. [religiosa] nun. -2. [título] Mother.

madrepérola [ˌmadreˈpɛrulal] *f* mother-of-pearl.

madressilva [ˌmadreˈsiwval] *f BOT* honeysuckle.

Madri [maˈdril] *n* Madrid.

madrileno, na [madriˈlenu, nal] ◇ *adj* Madrid *(antes de subst).* ◇ *m & f* person from Madrid.

madrinha [maˈdriɲal] *f* -1. [RELIG - de batismo] godmother; [- de crisma] sponsor; [- de casamento] chief bridesmaid. -2. *fig* [protetora, patrocinadora] patroness.

madrugar [madruˈga(x)] *vi* -1. [acordar cedo] to wake up early. -2. [chegar cedo] to get in early.

maduro, ra [maˈduru, ral] *adj* -1. [fruto] ripe. -2. [pessoa, atitude, decisão] mature.

mãe [ˈmãj] *f* -1. [ger] mother; **~ adotiva** adoptive mother; **~ de criação** foster mother. -2. [como forma de tratamento] mother.

mãe-de-santo [ˌmãjʃdʒiˈsãntul] (*pl* **mães-de-santo**) *f* [espirit] *high priestess in Afro-Brazilian religion.*

maestro, trina [maˈɛʃtru, trinal] *m, f* maestro.

má-fé [ˌmaˈfɛl] *f inv* bad faith; **agir de ~** to act in bad faith.

máfia [ˈmafjal] *f* -1. [bando do crime organizado] Mafia. -2. [grupo de corruptos] mafia.

mafioso, osa [maˈfjozu, ɔzal] ◇ *adj* -1. [pessoa] Mafioso. -2. [ação] of the Mafia. ◇ *m, f* [membro da máfia] Mafioso.

magia [maˈʒial] *f* magic.

mágico, ca [ˈmaʒiku, kal] ◇ *adj* magic.

◇ *m, f* [prestidigitador] magician.
◆ **mágica** *f* -1. [prestidigitação] magic.
-2. [truque] trick; **fazer mágica** to perform magic; *fig* to work miracles.

magistério [maʒiʃ'tɛrju] *m* -1. [profissão] teaching. -2. [classe dos professores] teaching profession. -3. [ensino] teaching.

magistrado, da [maʒiʃ'tradu, da] *m* magistrate.

magistral [maʒiʃ'traw] (*pl* -ais) *adj* [exemplar] masterly.

magistratura [maʒiʃtra'tura] *f* [os magistrados] magistracy.

magnânimo, ma [mag'nanimu, ma] *adj* magnanimous.

magnata [mag'nata] *m* magnate.

magnésio [mag'nɛʒju] *m* magnesium.

magnético, ca [mag'nɛtʃiku, ka] *adj* magnetic.

magnetismo [magne'tʃiʒmu] *m* magnetism.

magnífico, ca [mag'nifiku, ka] *adj* magnificent.

magnitude [magni'tudʒi] *f* [dimensão] magnitude.

magnólia [mag'nɔlja] *f* magnolia.

mago, ga ['magu, ga] ◇ *m, f* wizard (*f* witch). ◇ *adj*: **os reis ~s** the Three Kings.

mágoa ['magwa] *f* -1. [ressentimento] grief. -2. [tristeza] sorrow.

magoado, da [ma'gwadu, da] *adj*: **estar/ ficar ~ (com algo)** [ressentido] to be/feel offended (by sthg); [triste] to be hurt (by sthg).

magoar [ma'gwa(x)] ◇ *vt* [ferir] to hurt. ◇ *vi* [ferir] to hurt.

magrela [ma'grɛla] *adj* skinny.

magricela [magri'sɛla] *adj* = magrela.

magro, gra ['magru, ra] *adj* -1. [franzino] slim. -2. [sem gordura - carne, presunto] lean; [- leite] skimmed. -3. (*antes de subst*) *fig* [parco] meagre *UK*, meager *US*.

mai. (*abrev de* maio) May.

mail [mejo] (*pl* mails) *m COMPUT* e-mail.

maio ['maju] *m* May; *veja também* setembro.

maiô [ma'jo] *m* swimming costume *UK*, swimsuit *US*.

maionese [majo'nɛzi] *f* mayonnaise.

maior [ma'jɔ(x)] (*pl* -es) ◇ *adj* -1. [comparativo]: **~ (do) que** [de tamanho] bigger than; [de importância] more important than; [de número] larger than. -2. [superlativo]: **o/a ~ ...** [de tamanho] the biggest ...; [de importância] the highest ...; [de número] the largest ...; **ser o ~ barato** [pessoa] to be really cool; [coisa] to be really great. -3. [adulto]: **ser ~**

(de idade) to be of age; **ser ~ de 21 anos** to be over 21. -4. *MÚS*: **em dó ~** in C major. ◇ *mf* -1. [de tamanho]: **o/a ~** the largest. -2. *fam* [superior]: **ser o/a ~** to be the best. -3. [adulto] adult; **ser de ~** to be an adult.

maioral [majo'raw] (*pl* -ais) *mf*: **o ~** the boss.

maioria [majo'ria] *f* majority; **a ~ de** the majority of; **a ~ das pessoas acha ...** the majority think ...

maioridade [majori'dadʒi] *f* age of majority.

mais ['majʃ] ◇ *adv* -1. [em comparações] more; **a Ana é ~ alta/inteligente** Ana is taller/more intelligent; **~ do que** more than; **~ ... do que ...** more ... than ...; **bebeu um copo a ~!** he's had one too many!; **deram-me dinheiro a ~** they gave me too much money; **é ~ alta do que eu** she's taller than me. -2. [como superlativo]: **o/a ~ ...** the most ...; **o ~ engraçado/inteligente** the funniest/ most intelligent. -3. [indica adição] any more; **não necessito de ~ trabalho** I don't need any more work; **não necessito de ~ ninguém** I don't need anyone else. -4. [indica intensidade]: **que dia ~ feliz!** what a great day!; **que casa ~ feia!** what a horrible house! -5. [indica preferência]: **vale ~ a pena ficar em casa** it would be better to stay at home; **gosto ~ de comida chinesa** I prefer Chinese food. -6. [em locuções]: **de ~ a ~** [ainda por cima] what's more; **~ ou menos** more or less; **por ~ que se esforce** however hard he tries; **sem ~ nem menos** for no apparent reason; **uma vez ~, ~ uma vez** once *ou* yet again. ◇ *adj inv* -1. [em comparações] more; **eles têm ~ dinheiro** they have more money; **está ~ calor hoje** it's hotter today; **~ ... do que** more ... than. -2. [como superlativo] (the) most; **a pessoa que ~ discos vendeu** the person who sold (the) most records; **os que ~ dinheiro têm** those who have (the) most money. -3. [indica adição] more; **~ água, por favor** I'd like some more water, please; **~ alguma coisa?** anything else?; **tenho ~ três dias de férias** I have another three days of vacation left. ◇ *conj* and; **quero uma sopa ~ pão com manteiga** I'd like some soup and some bread and butter. ◇ *prep* [indica soma] plus; **dois ~ dois são quatro** two plus two is four.

maisena [maj'zena] *f*: **de ~** cornflour *UK*, cornstarch *US*.

maître ['mɛtri] *m* head waiter.

maiúsculo, la [maˈjuʃkulu, la] *adj*: **letra maiúscula** capitals *(pl)*.
➤ **maiúscula** f capital letter.
➤ **majestade** [maʒeʃˈtadʒi] f majesty.
➤ **Majestade** f: **Sua Majestade** Your Majesty, His Majesty, Her Majesty.
majestoso, osa [maʒeʃˈtozu, ɔzal *adj* [grandioso] majestic.
major [maˈʒɔ(x)] *(pl -res)* m MIL major.
majoritário, ria [maʒoriˈtarju, rja] *adj* majority *(antes de subst)*; **a opinião majoritária é que ...** the majority opinion is that ...
mal [ˈmaw] *(pl -es)* m - **1.** [ger] evil; **cortar o ~ pela raiz** to stop things going from bad to worse; **a luta entre o bem e o ~** the fight between good and evil. - **2.** [dano] damage; **fazer ~ (a)** [à saúde] to damage; **o cigarro faz ~ à saúde** smoking damages your health; **fazer ~ a alguém** [afetar] to upset sb; [deflorar] to deflower sb; **você fez ~ em se divorciar** you did the wrong thing in getting divorced; **não faz ~** it doesn't matter. - **3.** [doença] illness. - **4.** [sofrimento] stress.
➤ **mal** <> *adv* - **1.** [ger] badly; **dar-se ~ (em algo)** to do badly (in sthg); **de ~ a pior** from bad to worse. - **2.** [quase não]: **ele ~ consegue dormir** he barely manages to sleep. - **3.** [injustamente] wrongly. - **4.** [rudemente] rudely. - **5.** [de maneira desfavorável] unfavourably; **não me leve a ~, mas ...** don't get me wrong, but ... - **6.** PSIC [doente] down; **passar ~** to feel sick. <> *conj* just; **~ cheguei, ele saiu** just as I arrived, he left.
mala [ˈmala] f - **1.** [recipiente] suitcase; **fazer as ~s** to pack one's bags. - **2.** AUTO boot UK, trunk US. - **3.** COM: **~ direta** mail order. - **4.** [serviço]: **~ postal** mail. - **5.** fam pej [pessoa chata]: **ser uma ~** to be a pain.
malabarismo [malabaˈriʒmul m - **1.** [arte] juggling. - **2.** fig [habilidade] deftness.
malabarista [malabaˈriʃtal mf juggler.
mal-acabado, da [ˌmawakaˈbadul *adj* - **1.** [construção, móvel] poorly finished. - **2.** [corpo] in poor shape.
mala-direta [ˌmaladʒiˈreta] *(pl malas-diretas)* f [marketing] direct marketing.
mal-agradecido, da [ˌmawagradeˈsidu, dal *(pl -s)* <> *adj* ungrateful. <> m, f: **o ~ nem sequer me agradeceu** he's so ungrateful he didn't even thank me.
malagueta [malaˈgetal m chilli pepper.
malandragem [malãnˈdraʒẽ] *(pl -ns)*, **malandrice** [malãnˈdrisil f - **1.** [patifaria] double-dealing. - **2.** [astúcia] cunning.

- **3.** [vadiagem] vagrancy. - **4.** [preguiça] laziness.
malandro, dra [maˈlãndru, dral <> *adj* - **1.** [patife] crooked. - **2.** [astuto] sharp. - **3.** [vadio] vagrant. - **4.** [preguiçoso] idle. <> m, f - **1.** [patife] crook. - **2.** [astuto] swindler. - **3.** [vadio] vagrant. - **4.** [preguiçoso] layabout.
malária [maˈlarja] f malaria.
mal-arrumado, da [mawaxuˈmadu, dal *(pl -s)* *adj* untidy.
mala-sem-alça [ˈmalasẽˈsaw] *(pl malas-sem-alça)* mf fam bore.
Malásia [maˈlazja] n Malaysia.
malbaratar [mawbaraˈta(x)] vt to squander.
malcomportado, da [mawkõmpoxˈtadu, dal *adj* badly behaved.
malcriação [mawkrjaˈsãw] *(pl -ões)*, **má-criação** [makrjaˈsãw] *(pl -ões)* f bad manners; **respondeu com ~** he replied rudely; **fazer ~** to behave badly.
malcriado, da [mawkriˈadu, dal <> *adj* ill-mannered. <> m, f yob.
maldade [mawˈdadʒil f - **1.** [ger] cruelty; **bater em criança é uma ~** it's cruel to hit children; **ser uma ~** to be cruel. - **2.** [malícia] malice.
maldição [mawdiˈsãw] *(pl -ões)* f curse.
maldito, ta [mawˈdʒitu, tal <> *pp* ▷ **maldizer.** <> *adj* - **1.** [amaldiçoado] damned. - **2.** [funesto] tragic. - **3.** [cruel] cruel. - **4.** *(antes de subst)* fam [para enfatizar]: **essa chuva maldita** this bloody rain.
maldizer [mawdʒiˈze(x)] vt to curse.
maldoso, osa [mawˈdozu, ɔzal *adj* - **1.** [malvado] nasty. - **2.** fig [mordaz] vicious.
maleável [maˈljavewl *(pl -eis)* *adj* malleable.
maledicência [malidʒiˈsẽnsjal f - **1.** [ação] slander. - **2.** [difamação] defamation.
mal-educado, da [ˌmaleduˈkadu, dal <> *adj* rude. <> m, f: **o ~** the rude man; **a malcriada** the rude woman.
malefício [maleˈfisjul m - **1.** [ação] wrong. - **2.** [dano] harm.
maléfico, ca [maˈlɛfiku, kal *adj* harmful.
mal-encarado, da [ˌmalẽŋkaˈradu, dal *(pl -s)* *adj* shady.
mal-entendido [ˌmawẽntẽnˈdʒidul *(pl mal-entendidos)* <> *adj* [mal interpretado] misunderstood. <> m misunderstanding.
males [ˈmaliʃ] *pl* ▷ **mal.**
mal-estar [maweʃˈta(x)] *(pl mal-estares)* m - **1.** [indisposição] upset. - **2.** fig [embaraço] uneasiness.
maleta [maˈleta] f small suitcase.

malevolente adj [male.vo'lẽntʃi] malevolent.

malévolo, la [ma'lɛvolu, la] adj malevolent.

malfeito, ta [mal'fejtu, ta] adj -1. [malacabado] sloppy. -2. [deforme] misshapen. -3. fig [injusto] unjust.

malfeitor, ra [mawfej'to(x), ra] (mpl -es, fpl -s) m -1. [quem comete delito] wrongdoer. -2. [bandido] criminal.

malgrado [maw'gradu] prep despite.

malha [ˈmaʎa] f -1. [tecido] jersey; de ~ jersey. -2. [de rede, tecido] mesh. -3. [de balé] leotard. -4. [suéter] sweatshirt.

malhação [maʎa'sãw] (pl -ões) f fam [crítica violenta] panning.

malhado, da [ma'ʎadu, ada] adj [animal] mottled.

malhar [ma'ʎa(x)] <> vt -1. [ger] to beat. -2. [criticar] to knock. <> vi [fazer ginástica] fam to work out.

malharia [maʎa'ria] f -1. [loja] knitwear shop. -2. [fábrica] textile mill. -3. [artigos] knitted goods.

malho [ˈmaʎu] m mallet.

mal-humorado, da [mawumo'radu, da] adj -1. [que tem mau humor] sullen. -2. [ranzinza] grumpy.

malícia [ma'lisja] f -1. [intenção maldosa] malice. -2. [intenção licenciosa] licentiousness. -3. [manha, marotice] cunning.

malicioso, osa [mali'sjozu, ɔza] adj -1. [maldoso] malicious. -2. [que vê licenciosidade] licentious. -3. [manhoso] sly.

maligno, gna [ma'lignu, gna] adj -1. [mau] malicious. -2. [nocivo] harmful. -3. MED malignant.

má-língua [ˌma'lĩngwa] (pl más-línguas) f scandalmonger; dizem as más-línguas que ... the scandalmongers are saying that ...

mal-intencionado, da [ˌmawĩntẽnsjo'nadu, da] (pl -s) adj malicious.

malogrado, da [malo'gradu, da] adj thwarted.

malograr [malo'gra(x)] <> vt to thwart. <> vi to fall through.

malogro [ma'logru] m failure.

malote [ma'lɔtʃi] m -1. [bolsa] pouch. -2. [correspondência] mail. -3. [serviço] courier.

malpassado, da [mawpa'sadu, da] adj rare.

malsucedido, da [mawsuse'dʒidu, da] adj unsuccessful.

Malta [ˈmawta] n Malta.

malte [ˈmawtʃi] m malt.

maltês, esa [maw'teʃ, eza] <> adj Maltese. <> m, f Maltese.

maltrapilho, lha [mawtra'piʎu, ʎa] <> adj ragged. <> m, f -1. [mendigo] beggar. -2. [criança] urchin.

maltratar [mawtra'ta(x)] vt -1. [fisicamente] to mistreat. -2. [verbalmente] to abuse. -3. [tratar com desleixo] to mishandle.

maluco, ca [ma'luku, ka] <> adj -1. PSIC crazy. -2. [adoidado] nuts. -3. [absurdo] mad. <> m, f PSIC insane person.

maluquice [malu'kisil] f PSIC madness.

malvadeza [mawva'deza], **malvadez** [mawva'deʒ] f wickedness.

malvado, da [maw'vadu, da] <> adj wicked. <> m, f thug.

malversação [mawvexsa'sãw] (pl -ões) f -1. [desvio]: ~ (de algo) embezzlement (of sthg). -2. [mau gerenciamento] mismanagement.

Malvinas [maw'vinaʃ] npl: as (ilhas) ~ the Falkland Islands, the Falklands.

mama [ˈmama] f breast.

mamadeira [mama'dejra] f baby's bottle.

mamãe [mã'mãj] f mummy, mum.

mamão [ma'mãw] (pl -ões) m papaya.

mamar [ma'ma(x)] <> vt [sugar] to suck. <> vi [alimentar-se] to feed; dar de ~ a alguém to breastfeed sb.

mamata [ma'mata] f -1. fam [proveito ilícito] racket. -2. [facilidade] breeze.

mamífero, ra [ma'miferu, ra] adj mammalian.

➡ **mamífero** m mammal.

mamilo [ma'milu] m nipple.

maminha [ma'miɲa] f [carne] rump steak.

mamoeiro [ma'mwejru] m papaya tree.

mamões [ma'mõjʃ] pl ⊳ **mamão**.

manada [ma'nada] f herd.

Manágua [ma'nagwa] n Managua.

manancial [manãn'sjaw] (pl -ais) m -1. [fonte] spring. -2. fig [origem] source.

Manaus [ma'nawʃ] n Manaus.

mancada [mãŋ'kada] f -1. [erro] mistake. -2. [gafe] gaffe; dar uma ~ to make a gaffe.

mancar [mãŋ'ka(x)] vi [coxear] to limp.

➡ **mancar-se** vp fam [desconfiar] to take a hint.

mancha [ˈmãnʃa] f -1. [ger] stain. -2. [em pintura] blotch. -3. [marca] mark.

manchado, da [mã'ʃadu, da] adj -1. [com manchas] stained. -2. [pintura] blotched. -3. [malhado] mottled.

manchar [mã'ʃa(x)] vt -1. [ger] to stain. -2. [deixar marca] to mark.

manchete [mãn'ʃɛtʃi] f headline; o acidente virou ~ em todo o país the accident hit the headlines nationwide.

manco, ca ['mãŋku, ka] <> *adj* lame. <> *m, f* disabled person.

mandachuva [mãnda'ʃuva] *mf* **-1.** [pessoa poderosa] boss. **-2.** [chefe, líder] chief.

mandado [mãn'dadu] *m* **-1.** [autorização] order. **-2.** *JUR* injunction; ~ **de prisão** arrest warrant; ~ **de segurança** injunction.

mandamento [mãnda'mẽntu] *m* **-1.** [preceito] order. **-2.** *RELIG* commandment.

mandão, ona [mãn'dãw, ɔna] (*mpl* -ões) *adj fam* [autoritário] bossy.

mandatário, ria [mãnda'tarju, rja] *m* **-1.** [representante] deputy, representative. **-2.** [procurador] defence lawyer *UK*, defense lawyer *US*, counsel for the defence *UK*, defense attorney *US*.

mandato [mãn'datu] *m* **-1.** [procuração] mandate. **-2.** [missão] duty. **-3.** [ordem] order. **-4.** *POL* term of office.

mandíbula [mãn'dʒibula] *f* jaw.

mandioca [mãn'dʒɔka] *f* cassava, manioc.

mandões [mãn'dõjʃ] *mpl* ▷ **mandão**.

mandona [mãn'dona] *f* ▷ **mandão**.

maneira [ma'nejra] *f* manner; à ~ (de) like; de ~ **nenhuma** *ou* **alguma** no way; **não volto àquele clube de** ~ **alguma!** no way am I going back to that club!; **de** ~ **que** so that; **de qualquer** ~ [sem cuidado] anyhow; [a qualquer preço] at whatever cost; [de todo modo] whatever; **de qualquer** ~ **será útil** it'll be useful, whatever.

◆ **maneiras** *fpl* manners; **boas** ~ **s** good manners.

manejar [mane'ʒa(x)] *vt* **-1.** [ger] to control. **-2.** [manusear] to handle. **-3.** [administrar] to manage.

manejável [mane'ʒavɛw] (*pl* -eis) *adj* **-1.** [fácil de usar] simple. **-2.** [controlável] controllable.

manequim [mane'kĩ] (*pl* -ns) <> *m* [boneco] dummy. <> *mf* [pessoa] model.

maneta [ma'neta] *adj* one-handed.

manga ['mãŋga] *f* **-1.** [de roupa] sleeve. **-2.** [fruto] mango. **-3.** [filtro] filter.

mangue ['mãŋgi] *m* **-1.** [terreno] mangrove swamp. **-2.** [planta] mangrove.

mangueira [mãŋ'gejra] *f* **-1.** *BOT* mango tree. **-2.** [cano] hose.

manha ['mãɲa] *f* **-1.** [habilidade] skill. **-2.** [esperteza] shrewdness. **-3.** *fam* [choro, birra] tantrum; **fazer** ~ to throw a tantrum.

manhã [ma'ɲã] (*pl* -s) *f* morning; **amanhã de** ~ tomorrow morning; **de** ~ *ou* **pela** ~ in the morning; **hoje de** ~ this

morning; **seis horas da** ~ six o'clock in the morning.

manhãzinha [mãɲã'ziɲa] *f*: **de** ~ early in the morning.

manhoso, osa [ma'ɲozu, ɔza] *adj* **-1.** [esperto] sly. **-2.** [chorão, birrento] whingeing.

mania [ma'nia] *f* **-1.** *PSIC* mania. **-2.** [gosto exagerado] obsession; ~ **de algo** obsession with sthg. **-3.** [hábito] habit; **ter** ~ **de fazer algo** to have a habit of doing sthg. **-4.** [mau hábito] bad habit. **-5.** [peculiaridade, excentricidade] quirk.

maníaco, ca [ma'niaku, ka] <> *adj* **-1.** *PSIC* maniacal. **-2.** [fanático]: **ser** ~ **por algo** to be manic about sthg. <> *m, f* *PSIC* maniac.

manicômio [mani'komju] *m* lunatic asylum.

manicure [mani'kuri] *f* manicure.

manifestação [manifeʃta'sãw] (*pl* -ões) *f* **-1.** [ger] manifestation. **-2.** [expressão] display.

manifestadamente [manifeʃtada'mẽntʃi] *adv* quite clearly.

manifestante [manifeʃ'tãntʃi] *mf* demonstrator.

manifestar [manifeʃ'ta(x)] *vt* **-1.** [exprimir] to express. **-2.** [revelar] to display.

◆ **manifestar-se** *vp* **-1.** [revelar-se] to reveal o.s. **-2.** [pronunciar-se]: ~-**se (sobre/a favor de/contra algo)** to express an opinion (on/in favour of/against sthg).

manifesto, ta [mani'fɛʃtu, ta] *adj* manifest.

◆ **manifesto** *m* manifesto.

manipulação [manipula'sãw] *f* **-1.** [com as mãos] handling. **-2.** [ger] manipulation. **-3.** *FARM* preparation.

manipular [manipu'la(x)] *vt* **-1.** [ger] to manipulate. **-2.** [com as mãos] to handle. **-3.** *FARM* to prepare.

maniqueísmo [manike'iʒmu] *m* Manicheism.

manivela [mani'vɛla] *f* crank.

manjado, da [mã'ʒadu, da] *adj fam* wellknown.

manjar [mã'ʒa(x)] <> *m* [iguaria] delicacy. <> *vt fam* **-1.** [compreender] to grasp. **-2.** [observar] to watch. <> *vi* [conhecer]: ~ **de algo** to know about sthg.

manjedoura [mãʒe'dora] *f* manger.

manjericão [mãʒeri'kãw] *m* basil.

mano, na ['manu, na] *m,f fam* **-1.** [irmão] brother (sister). **-2.** *fam* [camarada, amigo] buddy.

manobra [ma'nɔbra] *f* **-1.** [ger] manoeuvre *UK*, maneuver *US*. **-2.** *fig* [manipulação] manipulation.

manobrar [mano'bra(x)] <> vt -1. [manejar] to manoeuvre UK, to maneuver US. -2. [dirigir] to direct. -3. fig [manipular] to manipulate. <> vi MIL to manoeuvre UK, to maneuver US.

manobrista [mano'briʃta] mf -1. [de carro] valet UK, car jockey US. -2. [de trem] shunter.

mansão [mãn'sãw] (pl -ões) f mansion.

mansidão [mãnsi'dãw] f -1. [brandura] gentleness; **ele falava com ~** he spoke gently. -2. [tranqüilidade] calmness.

mansinho, nha [mã'siɲu, ɲal adj [diminutivo de manso] gentle.
➡ **de mansinho** loc adv -1. [de leve] gently. -2. [sorrateiramente]: **entrar/sair de ~** to creep in/out.

manso, sa ['mãsu, sal adj -1. [brando] gentle. -2. [tranqüilo] calm. -3. [domesticado] tame.

mansões [mãn'sõjʃ] pl ⊳ mansão.

manta ['mãntal f -1. [cobertor] blanket. -2. [xale] shawl. -3. [de carne seca] cut.

manteiga [mãn'tejgal f butter; **~ de cacau** cocoa butter.

manter [mãn'te(x)] vt -1. [ger] to keep. -2. [em bom estado - máquina] to service; [- casa, saúde] to keep. -3. [família] to support. -4. [opinião, posição] to hold. -5. [relações] to maintain; **~ boas relações com alguém** to maintain a good relationship with sb.
➡ **manter-se** vp -1. [sustentar-se] to support o.s. -2. [permanecer] to remain; **~-se a par de algo** to keep abreast of sthg.

mantimentos [mãntʃi'mẽntuʃ] m provisions (pl).

manto ['mãntul m -1. [vestimenta] cloak. -2. [de reis] robe. -3. fig [simulação] smokescreen.

manual [ma'nwaw] (pl -ais) <> adj manual. <> m manual.

manufatura [manufa'tural f [fabricação] manufacture.

manufaturar [manufatu'ra(x)] vt to manufacture.

manuscrito, ta [manuʃ'kritul adj handwritten.
➡ **manuscrito** m manuscript.

manusear [manu'zea(x)] vt -1. [manejar] to handle. -2. [folhear] to thumb.

manutenção [manutẽn'sãw] f -1. [ger] maintenance. -2. [da casa] upkeep. -3. [da família] support.

mão ['mãw] (pl mãos) f -1. [ger] hand; **à ~** [perto] at hand; [com a mão] by hand; **feito à ~** handmade; **à ~ armada** armed; **de ~ s dadas** hand in hand; **de segunda ~** second-hand; **entregar algo em ~ s** to deliver sthg by hand; **ter algo em ~** to have sthg to hand. -2. [no trânsito]: **esta rua dá ~ para a praia** this street takes you to the beach; **~ dupla** two-way; **~ única** one-way. -3. [de tinta] coat. -4. [habilidade]: **ter uma ~ boa para algo** to be good at sthg. -5. [poder, controle]: **estar nas ~ s de alguém** to be in sb's hands; **estar em boas ~ s** to be in good hands. -6. loc: **abrir ~ de algo** to give sthg up; **ficar na ~** to be duped; **lançar ~ de algo** to make use of sthg; **pedir a ~ de alguém (em casamento)** to ask for sb's hand (in marriage); **pôr a ~ no fogo por alguém** to stand up for sb; **de ~ beijada** buckshee; **dar uma ~ a alguém** to give sb a hand; **preciso de uma ~** I need a hand.

mão-aberta [,mãwa'bɛxtal (pl mãos-abertas) adj generous.

mão-de-obra [mãw'dʒjobral (pl mãos-de-obra) f -1. [trabalho, custo] labour UK, labor US; **ser uma ~ fig** to be hard work. -2. [trabalhadores] workforce.

mapa ['mapal m map; **sumir do ~ fam fig** to disappear off the face of the earth.

mapa-múndi [,mapa'mũndʒil (pl mapas-múndi) m world map.

maquete [ma'kɛtʃil f model.

maquiado, da [ma'kjadu, dal adj [com maquiagem] made-up.

maquiador, ra [makja'do(x), ral, **maquilador, ra** [makila'do(x), ral m, f make-up artist.

maquiagem [ma'kjaʒẽl (pl -ns) f -1. [ger] make-up; **ele se encarregou da ~** he was in charge of make-up. -2. [disfarce]: **~ financeira** financial cover-up.

maquiar [ma'kjax] vt -1. [pintar] to make up. -2. fig [mascarar] to cover up.
➡ **maquiar-se** vp [pintar-se] to put on one's make-up.

maquiavélico, ca [makja'vɛliku, kal adj Machiavellian.

maquilador, ra [makila'do(x), ral m, f = maquiador.

maquilagem [maki'laʒẽl f = maquiagem.

máquina ['makinal f -1. [ger] machine; **bater ou escrever à ~** to type; **feito à ~** machine-made; **~ de calcular** calculator; **~ de costura** sewing machine; **~ de escrever** typewriter; **~ fotográfica** camera; **~ de lavar (roupa)** washing machine. -2. [locomotora] engine; **~ a vapor** steam engine. -3. fig [de estado, partido etc.] machinery.

maquinação [makina'sãw] (pl -ões) f machination.

maquinar [maki'na(x)] <> *vt* to plot. <> *vi*: ~ **contra alguém/algo** to plot against sb/sthg.

maquinária [maki'narja], **maquinaria** [makina'ria] *f* [máquinas] machinery.

maquinário [maki'narju] *m* = **maquinária**.

maquinista [maki'niʃta] *mf* - 1. FERRO engine driver. - 2. TEATRO stagehand.

mar ['ma(x)] (*pl* -es) *m* sea; ~ **aberto** open sea; **por** ~ by sea; ~ **Morto** Dead Sea; ~ **Negro** Black Sea; ~ **do Norte** North Sea; ~ **de rosas** [mar calmo] calm sea; *fig* bed of roses; **nem tanto ao** ~ **nem tanto à terra** neither one way nor the other.

mar. (*abrev de* março) Mar.

maracujá [maraku'ʒa] *m* passion fruit.

maracutaia [maraku'taja] *f* dirty trick.

marajá [mara'ʒa] *m* - 1. [título] maharaja. - 2. *fig* [servidor] a person who has uses their position, not necessarily honestly, in order to become very rich.

Maranhão [mara'pãw] *n* Maranhão.

marasmo [ma'raʒmu] *m* - 1. [desânimo] lethargy. - 2. [estagnação] stagnation.

maratona [mara'tona] *m* marathon.

maravilha [mara'viʎa] *f* wonder; **às mil** ~ **s** wonderfully; **ser uma** ~ to be wonderful.

maravilhar [maravi'ʎa(x)] *vt* to astonish. ➡ **maravilhar-se** *vp*: ~ **-se (de algo)** to be amazed (at sthg).

maravilhoso, osa [maravi'ʎozu, ɔza] *adj* wonderful.

marca ['maxka] *f* - 1. [ger] mark. - 2. [COM - de carro] make; [- de café, queijo] brand; ~ **registrada** registered trademark. - 3. [de prata] hallmark. ➡ **de marca maior** *loc adj pej* of the first order.

marcação [maxka'sãw] (*pl* -ões) *f* - 1. [ato de marcar - enxoval] marking; [- gado] branding. - 2. ESP marking. - 3. [perseguição, vigilância] scrutiny; **estar de** ~ **com alguém** to pick on sb.

marcado, da [max'kadu, da] *adj* - 1. [assinalado - roupa, texto] marked; [- gado] branded. - 2. [reservado] booked. - 3. [com marca, mancha] marked. - 4. [pessoa - traumatizada] marked; [- em evidência] watched.

marcador [maxka'do(x)] *m* - 1. [de livro] bookmark. - 2. [ESP - quadro] scoreboard; [- jogador] scorer.

marcante [max'kãntʃi] *adj* marked.

marcapasso [maxka'pasu] *m* MED pacemaker.

marcar [max'ka(x)] *vt* - 1. [ger] to mark; ~ **época** to make history. - 2. [pôr marca

em - livro, roupa] to mark; [- animal] to brand. - 3. [data, hora, prazo] to fix; ~ **o tempo de algo** to time sthg. - 4. [almoço, encontro] to arrange; ~ **uma consulta** to make an appointment. - 5. [ESP - jogador] to mark; [- gol] to score. - 6. [suj: relógio] to say. - 7. [suj: termômetro] to show. - 8. [demarcar] to demarcate.

marceneiro, ra [maxse'nejru, ra] *m, f* cabinet-maker.

marcha ['maxʃa] *f* - 1. [ato] marching. - 2. [passo] pace. - 3. [ger] march. - 4. AUTO gear; ~ **à ré** reverse. - 5. [MÚS - tradicional] march; ~ **fúnebre** funeral march; [- popular] festive march. - 6. *fig* [progressão] course.

marchar [max'ʃa(x)] *vi* - 1. MIL to march. - 2. [ir]: ~ **para** to go to.

marchinha [max'ʃiɲa] *f* MÚS a satirical song in double time, in the main performed during carnival.

marcial [max'sjaw] (*pl* -ais) *adj* martial; **corte** ~ court martial.

marco ['maxku] *m* - 1. [ger] landmark. - 2. [moeda] mark. - 3. [da janela] frame.

março ['marsu] *m* March; *veja também* setembro.

maré [ma'rɛ] *f* - 1. [do mar] tide; ~ **alta/baixa** high/low tide; **remar contra a** ~ *fig* to swim against the tide. - 2. *fig* [ocasião] spell. - 3. *fig* [tendência] tendency. - 4. *fig* [multidão] sea.

marechal [mare'ʃaw] (*pl* -ais) *m* marshal.

maré-cheia [ma,rɛ'ʃeja] (*pl* **marés-cheias**) *f* high tide.

maremoto [mare'mɔtu] *m* tidal wave.

maresia [mare'zia] *f* sea air.

marfim [max'fĩ] *m* ivory; **de** ~ ivory (*antes de subst*).

margarida [maxga'rida] *f* BOT daisy.

margarina [maxga'rina] *f* margarine.

margem ['maxʒẽ] (*pl* -ns) *f* - 1. [ger] margin; ~ **de lucro** profit margin. - 2. [beira - de estrada, lago] edge; **à** ~ **de** alongside; [- de rio] bank; [- litoral] shore. - 3. [latitude] room; ~ **de erro** margin of error; ~ **de segurança** safety margin. - 4. [limites] edge; **à** ~ **da sociedade/lei** on the fringes of society/the law. - 5. [ocasião]: **dar** ~ **a alguém para fazer algo** to give sb the chance to do sthg.

marginal [maxʒi'naw] (*pl* -ais) <> *adj* - 1. [pessoa] delinquent. - 2. [nota] marginal. <> *mf* [pessoa] delinquent.

marginalidade [maxʒinali'dadʒi] *f* delinquency.

marginalizar [maxʒinali'za(x)] *vt* [excluir] to marginalize.

massagear

➤ **marginalizar-se** *vp* [tornar-se fora-da-lei] to marginalize o.s.

maria-fumaça [ma‚riafu'masa] (*pl* marias-fumaças) *m* & *f* steam train.

maria-sem-vergonha [ma‚riasẽnvex'goɲal (*pl* marias-sem-vergonha) *f BOT* busy lizzie.

marido [ma'ridul *m* husband.

marimbondo [marĩ'bõndul *m* hornet.

marina [ma'rinal *f* marina.

marinha [ma'riɲal *f* ▷ **marinho**.

marinheiro, ra [mari'ɲejru, ral ⬦ *adj* sailor's *(antes de subst)*. ⬦ *m, f* sailor; ~ **de primeira viagem** *fig* greenhorn.

marinho, nha [ma'riɲu, ɲal *adj* [do mar] marine.

➤ **marinho** ⬦ *adj inv* [cor] navy. ⬦ *m* [cor] navy blue.

➤ **marinha** *f* **-1.** [força] navy; **marinha (de guerra)** navy; **marinha mercante** merchant navy. **-2.** [pintura] seascape.

marionete [marjo'nɛtʃil *f* puppet.

mariposa [mari'pozal *f* moth.

marisco [ma'riʃkul *m* shellfish.

marital [mari'tawl (*pl* -ais) *adj* marital.

marítimo, ma [ma'ritʃimu, mal *adj* maritime.

marketing ['maxketʃĩŋl *m* marketing.

marmanjo [max'mãnʒul *m* grown man.

marmelada [maxme'ladal *f* -1. [doce] quince jam. **-2.** *fam* [mamata] racket.

marmelo [max'mɛlul *m* quince.

marmita [max'mital *f* -1. [recipiente] casserole. **-2.** [refeição] packed lunch.

mármore ['maxmoril *m* marble.

marmóreo, rea [max'mɔriu, rial *adj* marble.

marola [ma'rɔlal *f* small wave.

marquês, quesa [max'keʃ, ezal (*mpl* -eses, *fpl* -esas) *m, f* marquis (*f* marchioness).

marquise [max'kizil *f* canopy.

marra ['maxal *f*: **obedeceu na** ~ he obeyed under pressure; **invadiram na** ~ they invaded in strength.

marreco [ma'xɛkul *m* wigeon.

Marrocos [ma'xɔkuʃl *n* Morocco.

marrom [ma'xõl (*pl* -ns) ⬦ *adj* brown. ⬦ *m* brown.

marroquino, na [maxo'kinu, nal ⬦ *adj* Moroccan. ⬦ *m, f* Morroccan.

Marte ['maxtʃil *m* Mars.

martelar [maxte'la(x)l ⬦ *vt* -1. [com martelo] to hammer. **-2.** [afligir] to bother. **-3.** [repetir] to repeat. ⬦ *vi* [dar marteladas] to hammer.

martelo [max'tɛlul *m* hammer.

mártir ['maxti(x)l (*pl* -es) *mf* martyr.

martírio [max'tʃirjul *m* **-1.** [suplício] martyrdom. **-2.** *fig* [tormento] torment; **ser um** ~ to be a torment.

martirizar [maxtʃiri'za(x)l *vt* **-1.** [torturar] to torture. **-2.** *fig* [atormentar] to torment.

➤ **martirizar-se** *vp* [atormentar-se] to agonize.

marujo [ma'ruʒul *m* sailor.

marulho [ma'ruʎul *m* **-1.** [do mar] surge. **-2.** [das ondas] lapping.

marxismo [max'ksiʒmul *m* Marxism.

marzipã [maxzi'pãl *m* marzipan.

mas [ma(j)ʃl ⬦ *conj* but; ~ **que decepção!** how disappointing! ⬦ *cont* = **me + as**.

➤ **mas também** *loc conj* but also; **não só ...** ~ **também** not only ... but also.

mascar [maʃ'ka(x)l ⬦ *vt* to chew. ⬦ *vi* to chew.

máscara ['maʃkaral *f* -1. [ger] mask; **baile de** ~s masked ball; ~ **de oxigênio** oxygen mask; ~ **(de beleza)** face mask. **-2.** [fachada] disguise; **tirar a** ~ **de alguém** to unmask sb.

mascarado, da [maʃka'radu, dal *adj* [fantasiado] masked.

mascarar [maʃka'ra(x)l *vt* to mask.

mascavo [maʃ'kavul *adj* ▷ **açúcar**.

mascote [maʃ'kɔtʃil *f* mascot.

masculinidade [maʃkulini'dadʒil *f* masculinity.

masculinizar [maʃkulini'za(x)l *vt* to masculinize.

masculino, na [maʃku'linu, nal *adj* -1. [sexo, população] male. **-2.** [modos, voz]: **esta foi uma reação tipicamente masculina** that was a typically male response. **-3.** *GRAM* masculine.

másculo, la ['maʃkulu, lal *adj* [viril] manly.

masmorra [maʒ'moxal *f* -1. [calabouço] dungeon. **-2.** *fig* [aposento] hole.

masoquista [mazo'kiʃtal ⬦ *adj* masochistic. ⬦ *mf* masochist.

massa ['masal *f* -1. [ger] mass. **-2.** [culinária - de pão] dough; [- de bolo] mixture; [- de torta, empada] pastry; [- de tomate] paste. **-3.** [macarrão] pasta. **-4.** [grande quantidade]: **uma** ~ **de** a mass of.

➤ **massas** *fpl*: **as** ~ **s** the masses.

➤ **em massa** *loc adv* en masse.

massa-corrida ['masako'xidal (*pl* -s) *f* plaster skim applied before painting.

massacrar [masa'kra(x)l *vt* **-1.** [ger] to massacre. **-2.** [oprimir] to oppress. **-3.** *fig* [torturar] to torture.

massacre [ma'sakril *m* massacre.

massagear [masa'ʒea(x)l ⬦ *vt* to massage. ⬦ *vi* to do massage.

massagem [ma'saʒẽ] (*pl* -ns) *f* massage.

massagista [masa'ʒiʃta] *mf* masseur (*f* masseuse).

massificar [masifi'ka(x)] *vt* -1. [ensino universitário] to popularize. -2. [povo] to sell to the masses.

massudo, da [ma'sudu, da] *adj* -1. [pão, torta] heavy. -2. [documentação, livro] bulky.

mastigar [maʃtʃi'ga(x)] <> *vt* [triturar] to chew. <> *vi* [triturar] to chew.

mastro ['maʃtru] *m* -1. NÁUT mast. -2. [para bandeira] flagpole.

masturbar [maʃtux'ba(x)] *vt* to masturbate.

◆ **masturbar-se** *vp* to masturbate.

mata ['mata] *f* forest; ~ **virgem** virgin forest.

mata-baratas [mataba'rataʃ] *mpl* [inseticida] cockroach killer.

matadouro [mata'doru] *m* slaughterhouse.

matagal [mata'gaw] (*pl* -ais) *m* -1. [terreno] bush. -2. [mata espessa] thicket.

mata-moscas [,mata'moʃkaʃ] *m* (*inv*) fly-swat.

matança [ma'tãnsa] *f* -1. [de pessoas] massacre. -2. [de animais] slaughter.

matar [ma'ta(x)] <> *vt* -1. [ger] to kill. -2. [saciar - fome] to satisfy; [- sede] to quench; [- curiosidade] to quell. -3. [gazetear] to skip. -4. [executar mal] to do badly. -5. [decifrar] to guess. -6. [fazer desaparecer] to crush. <> *vi* [causar morte] to kill.

◆ **matar-se** *vp* -1. [suicidar-se] to kill o.s. -2. [cansar-se]: ~-se de algo/fazer algo to kill o.s. with sthg/doing sthg.

◆ **de matar** *loc adj fig* [terrível] terrible; **dor de** ~ excruciating pain; **ser de** ~ to be terrible.

mate ['matʃi] *m* [bebida] maté.

matelassê [matela'se] *adj* quilted.

matemático, ca [mate'matʃiku, ka] <> *adj* mathematical. <> *m, f* mathematician.

◆ **matemática** *f* [ciência] mathematics (*sg*).

matéria [ma'tɛrja] *f* -1. [ger] matter. -2. [assunto] subject; **em** ~ **de política/ esporte** in the area of politics/sports. -3. EDUC subject. -4. JORN article.

material [mate'rjaw] (*pl* -ais) <> *adj* material. <> *m* -1. [substância] material. -2. [utensílios] materials (*pl*); ~ **de limpeza** cleaning products (*pl*). -3. [bélico] armaments (*pl*). -4. [informativo, didático] teaching material.

materialista [materja'liʃta] <> *adj* materialistic. <> *mf* materialist.

matéria-prima [ma,tɛrja'prima] (*pl* matérias-primas) *f* raw material.

maternal [matex'naw] (*pl* -ais) <> *adj* maternal. <> *m* EDUC nursery school.

maternidade [matexni'dadʒi] *f* -1. [qualidade] motherhood. -2. [hospital] maternity hospital.

materno, na [ma'tɛxnu, na] *adj* -1. [ger] maternal. -2. [língua]: **língua** ~ mother tongue.

matilha [ma'tʃiʎa] *f* [cães] pack.

matinal [matʃi'naw] (*pl* -ais) *adj* morning (*antes de subst*).

matinê [matʃi'ne] *f* matinée.

matiz [ma'tʃiʒ] *m* -1. [tom] shade. -2. *fig* [traço] tinge.

matizar [matʃi'za(x)] *vt* -1. [dar nuances a] to tinge. -2. [colorir] to colour *UK*, to color *US*.

mato ['matu] *m* -1. [área] scrubland. -2. [plantas] weeds (*pl*). -3. [roça] countryside. -4. *loc*: **estar num** ~ **sem cachorro** *fam* to be up the creek without a paddle.

matreiro, ra [ma'trejru, ra] *adj fam* [astuto, ardiloso] crafty.

matriarcal [matrjax'kaw] (*pl* -ais) *adj* matriarchal.

matrícula [ma'trikula] *f* -1. [inscrição] enrolment *UK*, enrollment *US*; **fazer (a)** ~ to enrol *UK*, to enroll *US*; **qual é o seu número de** ~ what's your registration number? -2. [taxa] fee.

matricular [matriku'la(x)] *vt*: ~ **alguém (em algo)** to enrol sb (in sthg) *UK*, to enroll sb (in sthg) *US*.

◆ **matricular-se** *vp*: ~-se **(em algo)** to enrol (in sthg) *UK*, to enroll (in sthg) *US*.

matrimonial [matrimo'njaw] (*pl* -ais) *adj* matrimonial.

matrimônio [matri'monju] *m* marriage.

matriz [ma'triʃ] (*pl* -es) <> *adj* -1. [igreja, língua] mother (*antes de subst*). -2. [idéia] original. <> *f* -1. [de empresa] head office. -2. [de igreja] mother church. -3. [molde] mould *UK*, mold *US*. -4. MAT matrix.

matrona [ma'trona] *f pej* matron.

maturidade [maturi'dadʒi] *f* maturity.

matuto, ta [ma'tutu, ta] *m, f* [pessoa da roça] country bumpkin.

mau, má ['maw, 'ma] <> *adj* -1. (*antes de subst*) [ger] bad. -2. (*antes de subst*) [incapaz] poor. <> *m, f* -1. [pessoa] bad person. -2. [em filme etc.] baddy.

mau-caráter [,mawka'ratex] (*pl* maus-caráteres) <> *adj* disreputable. <> *mf* bad character.

mau-olhado [,mawo'ʎadu] (*pl* maus-olhados) *m* evil eye.

mausoléu [mawzɔ'lɛu] *m* mausoleum.

maus-tratos [mawʃ'tratuʃ] *mpl* abuse.

maxilar [maksi'la(x)] (*pl* **-es**) ◇ *m* jaw. ◇ *adj* maxillary.

máxima ['masima] *f* ▷ **máximo**.

máximo, ma ['masimu, ma] *adj* **-1.** [o maior possível] maximum. **-2.** [supremo] highest.

   ➡ **máximo** *m* [o mais alto grau] maximum; **ao ~** to the maximum; **no ~** at most; **ser o ~** [ser maravilhoso] to be the best.

   ➡ **máxima** *f* **-1.** [temperatura] maximum. **-2.** [sentença, princípio] maxim.

MB (*abrev de* **megabyte**) *m* MB.

MBA (*abrev de* **Master of Business Administration**) *m* MBA.

me [mi] *pron* [complemento direto] me; [complemento indireto] (to) me; [reflexo] myself; **eu nunca ~ engano** I'm never wrong; **eu ~ machuquei** I've hurt myself; **você já ~ contou essa história** you've already told me that story.

meado ['mjadu] *m*: **em ~s de setembro** in mid-September.

meandro ['mjãndru] *m* meander.

MEC (*abrev de* **Ministério da Educação e Cultura**) *m* Brazilian ministry of education and culture.

Meca ['mɛka] *n* Mecca.

mecânico, ca [me'kãniku, ka] ◇ *adj* mechanical. ◇ *m, f* [profissional] mechanic.

   ➡ **mecânica** *f* **-1.** [ger] mechanics (*pl*). **-2.** *fig* [mecanismo] workings (*pl*).

mecanismo [meka'niʒmu] *m* mechanism; **~ de defesa** defence mechanism; **~ de busca** *COMPUT* search engine.

mecenas [me'senaʃ] *m inv* patron.

mecha ['mɛʃa] *f* [de cabelo] strand.

medalha [me'daʎa] *f* medal.

média ['mɛdʒja] *f* ▷ **médio**.

mediação [medʒja'sãw] *f* mediation.

mediador, ra [medʒja'do(x), ra] *m, f* mediator.

mediano, na [me'dʒjãnu, na] *adj* **-1.** [ger] average. **-2.** [linha] median.

mediante [me'dʒjãntʃi] *prep* **-1.** [por meio de] through; **~ ajuda de** with the help of; **~ a graça de Deus** by the grace of God. **-2.** [a troco de] in exchange for.

mediar [me'dʒja(x)] ◇ *vt* [intervir em] to mediate; **~ um debate** to chair a debate. ◇ *vi* [intervir] to mediate.

medicamento [medʒika'mẽntu] *m* medicine.

medicar [medʒi'ka(x)] *vt* to medicate.

   ➡ **medicar-se** *vp* to take medicine.

medicina [medʒi'sina] *f* medicine.

medicinal [medʒisi'naw] (*pl* **-ais**) *adj* medicinal.

médico, ca ['mɛdʒiku, ka] ◇ *adj* medical. ◇ *m, f* doctor; **~ de família** family doctor, GP, general expert.

médico-hospitalar [ˌmɛdʒikwoʃpita'-la(x)] (*pl* **médico-hospitalares**) *adj* hospital and medical (*antes de subst*).

médico-legista, médica-legista [ˌmɛdʒikule'ʒiʃta] (*mpl* **médicos-legistas**, *fpl* **médicas-legistas**) *m, f* forensic expert.

medida [me'dʒida] *f* **-1.** [ger] measurement. **-2.** [tamanho] size; **feito sob ~** made to measure. **-3.** [grau] degree; **na ~ do possível** as far as possible. **-4.** [providência] measure; **~ provisória** *JUR* emergency measure; **~ de segurança** safety measure.

   ➡ **à medida que** *loc conj* as.

medieval [medʒje'vaw] (*pl* **-ais**) *adj* medieval.

médio, dia ['mɛdʒju, dja] *adj* **-1.** [entre dois pontos - ger] middle; [- tamanho] medium. **-2.** [resultado de cálculo] average. **-3.** [ensino] secondary.

   ➡ **média** *f* **-1.** *MAT* average; **em ~** on average. **-2.** *EDUC* secondary school. **-3.** [café com leite] white coffee.

medíocre [me'dʒiwkri] ◇ *adj* mediocre. ◇ *mf* mediocrity.

mediocridade [medʒiwkri'dadʒil] *f* mediocrity.

medir [me'dʒi(x)] *vt* **-1.** [ger] to measure. **-2.** [considerar, avaliar] to evaluate. **-3.** [moderar] to measure; **meça suas palavras!** watch what you say!

meditação [medʒita'sãw] (*pl* **-ões**) *f* meditation.

meditar [me'dʒita(x)] *vi* to meditate.

meditativo, va [medʒita'tʃivu, va] *adj* meditative.

mediterrâneo, nea [medʒite'xãnju, nja] *adj* Mediterranean.

   ➡ **Mediterrâneo** *n*: **o (mar) ~** the Mediterranean (Sea).

médium ['mɛdʒjũl] (*pl* **-ns**) [espírit] *mf* medium.

mediúnico, ca [me'dʒjuniku, ka] *adj* of a medium (*depois de subst*).

mediunidade [medʒjuni'dadʒil] *f* spiritualism.

medo ['medu] *m* **-1.** [pavor] fear; **estar com** *ou* **ter ~ (de)** to be afraid (of); **morrer de ~** to be frightened to death. **-2.** [receio]: **com ~ de/que** for fear of/that.

medroso, osa [medrozu, ɔza] ◇ *adj* [temeroso] scared. ◇ *m, f* coward.

medula [me'dula] *f* *ANAT* marrow, medulla; **~ óssea** bone marrow.

megabyte [mɛga'bajtʃi] *m COMPUT* mega-byte.

megafone [mɛga'foni] *m* megaphone.

megalomaníaco, ca [mɛgaloma'njaku, ka] ⟨⟩ *adj* megalomaniac. ⟨⟩ *m, f* megalomaniac.

megapixel [mɛga'piksew] *m* COMPUT megapixel.

megera [me'ʒɛra] *f* shrew.

meia ['meja] *f* ⟼ meio.

meia-calça [ˌmeja'kawsal (*pl* meias-cal-ças) *f* tights (*pl*) *UK*, pantyhose (*pl*) *US*.

meia-entrada [ˌmejaẽn'trada] (*pl* meias-entradas) *f* half-price ticket.

meia-idade [ˌmejej'dadʒi] (*pl* meias-ida-des) *f* middle age.

meia-lua [ˌmeja'lua] *f* -**1.** ASTRO half moon. -**2.** [semicírculo] semicircle.

meia-luz [ˌmeja'luʃ] (*pl* meias-luzes) *f* half light; à ~ in the gloom.

meia-noite [ˌmeja'nojtʃi] (*pl* meias-noi-tes) *f* midnight; à ~ at midnight.

meigo, ga ['mejgu, ga] *adj* gentle.

meio, meia ['meju, 'meja] *adj* half; a ~ caminho halfway; meia dúzia half a dozen; meia hora half an hour; ~ quilo half a kilo; são três e meia it's half past three.
➥ **meio** ⟨⟩ *adv* half- . ⟨⟩ *m* -**1.** [metade] half; ~ a ~ fifty-fifty. -**2.** [centro] middle; o filho do ~ the middle son. -**3.** [ambiente - social, profissional] circle; [- físico] milieu; ~ ambiente environment. -**4.** [modo] way; por ~ de through, by means of.
➥ **meios** *mpl* [recursos] means; os ~s de comunicação the media; ~s de transporte means of transport.
➥ **meia** ⟨⟩ *num* six. ⟨⟩ *f* -**1.** [meia - de seda] stocking; [- soquete] sock. -**2.** [entrada] half-price ticket.

meio-dia [ˌmeju'dʒia] (*pl* meios-dias) *m* midday; ao ~ at midday.

meio-fio [ˌmejo'fiw] (*pl* meios-fios) *m* kerb *UK*, curb *US*.

meio-tempo [ˌmeju'tẽnpu] (*pl* meios-tempos) *m* [ínterim]: nesse ~ mean-while.

meio-tom [ˌmeju'tõ] (*pl* meios-tons) *m* -**1.** MÚS semitone. -**2.** [de cor] half-tone.

mel ['mɛw] *m* honey.

melancia [melãn'sia] *f* watermelon.

melancolia [melãŋko'lia] *f* melancholy.

melancólico, ca [melãŋ'kɔliku, ka] *adj* melancholic.

melão [me'lãw] (*pl* -ões) *m* melon.

meleca [me'lɛka] *f* -**1.** *fam* [secreção] bogey; ele está tirando ~ do nariz he's picking his nose. -**2.** (*enfático*): essa ~ dessa chuva that damned rain.

melhor [me'ʎɔ(x)] (*pl* -es) ⟨⟩ *adj* -**1.** (*comparativo de bom*): ~ (do que) better (than); bem/muito ~ much better; é ~ você ... you had better ...; quanto mais ~ the more the better. -**2.** (*su-perlativo de bom*): o/a ~ the best. ⟨⟩ *adv* -**1.** (*comparativo de bem*): ~ (do que) better (than); estar ~ to be better. -**2.** (*superlativo de bem*) best. ⟨⟩ *m, f*: o/a ~ the best; levar a ~ to come off best.
➥ **ou melhor** *loc adv* or rather.

melhora [me'ʎɔra] *f* improvement; esti-mo suas ~s I hope you get better soon.

melhoramento [meʎora'mẽntu] *m* im-provement.

melhorar [meʎo'ra(x)] ⟨⟩ *vt* to im-prove. ⟨⟩ *vi* to improve; ~ de algo to improve in sthg; ~ de vida to get on in life.

melhoria [meʎo'ria] *f* improvement.

melindrar [melĩn'dra(x)] *vt* to offend.

melodia [melo'dʒia] *f* melody.

melódico, ca [me'lɔdʒiku, ka] *adj* melo-dic.

melodrama [melo'drama] *m* melodra-ma.

melodramático, ca [melodra'matʃiku, ka] *adj* melodramatic.

melões [me'lõjʃ] *pl* ⟼ melão.

melro ['mɛwxu] *m* blackbird.

membro ['mẽnbru] *m* -**1.** [ANAT - braços, pernas] limb; [- pênis] (male) member, penis. -**2.** [parte] member.

memorando [memo'rãndu] *m* -**1.** [comunicação] memo. -**2.** [nota diplomática] memorandum.

memorável [memo'ravew] (*pl* -eis) *adj* memorable.

memória [me'mɔrja] *f* -**1.** [ger] memory; de ~ by heart; ter ~ fraca to have a poor memory; vir à ~ to come to mind; ~ RAM/ROM RAM/ROM mem-ory. -**2.** [recordação] recollection; em ~ de in memory of.
➥ **memórias** *fpl* memoirs.

memorial [memo'rjaw] (*pl* -ais) *m* mem-orial.

memorização ['memori'zasãw] (*pl* -ões) *f* memorizing.

memorizar [memori'za(x)] *vt* to mem-orize.

menção [mẽn'sãw] (*pl* -ões) *f* -**1.** [referência] mention; fazer ~ a algo to make mention of sthg. -**2.** [intento]: fa-zer ~ de se levantar to make as if to get up. -**3.** [distinção]: ~ honrosa dis-tinction.

mencionar [mẽnsjo'na(x)] *vt* to mention;

(isso) sem mencionar ... not to mention ...

mendicância [mẽndʒi'kãnsja] f begging.

mendigar [mẽndʒi'ga(x)] ◇ vt **-1.** [esmola] to beg for. **-2.** [ajuda, favor] to beg. ◇ vi [pedir esmola] to beg.

mendigo, ga [mẽn'dʒigu, ga] m, f beggar.

menina [me'nina] f ▷ **menino**.

meninada [meni'nada] f kids (pl).

meningite [menĩn'ʒitʃi] f meningitis.

meninice [meni'nisi] f **-1.** [período] childhood. **-2.** [criancice] childishness.

menino, na [me'ninu, na] ◇ adj young. ◇ m, f **-1.** [criança] child; **nasceu um ∼** a baby was born; **∼ de rua** street child. **-2.** [jovem] youngster. **-3.** [como forma de tratamento] boy.

➤ **menina** f: **ser a menina dos olhos de alguém** to be the apple of sb's eye.

menopausa [meno'pawza] f menopause.

menor [me'nɔ(x)] (pl -es) ◇ adj **-1.** (comparativo): **∼ (do que)** [de tamanho] smaller (than); [de idade] younger (than); [de importância, número] less (than). **-2.** (superlativo): **o/a ∼ ...** [ger] the least; [de tamanho] the smallest. **-3.** [jovem]: **ser ∼ (de idade)** [para dirigir, votar] to be under age; JUR to be a minor, to be under age. **-4.** (antes de subst) [noção, paciência] slightest. ◇ mf **-1.** (superlativo): **o/a ∼** [de tamanho] the smallest; [de idade] the youngest; **proibido para ∼ es** prohibited to under 18s. **-2.** [jovem] young person. **-3.** JUR minor.

menoridade [menori'dadʒi] f minority.

menos ['menuʃ] ◇ adv **-1.** [em comparações] less; **a Ana é ∼ inteligente** Ana is less intelligent; **∼ do que** less than; **∼ ... do que ...** less ...than ...; **tenho ∼ trabalho do que ele** I have less work than him; **tenho um livro a ∼** I'm one book short; **deram-me 5 reais a ∼** they gave me 5 reals too little, they short-changed me by 5 reals. **-2.** [como superlativo]: **o/a ∼ ...** the least ...; **o ∼ caro/interessante** the least expensive/interesting. **-3.** [em locuções]: **a ∼ que** unless; **ao ∼, pelo ∼** at least; **isso é o de ∼** that's the least of it; **pouco ∼ de** just under. ◇ adj inv **-1.** [em comparações] less, fewer pl; **como ∼ carne** I eat less meat; **eles têm ∼ posses** they have fewer possessions; **está ∼ frio do que ontem** it's less cold than it was yesterday; **∼ ... do que** less ... than, fewer ... than pl. **-2.** [como superlativo] (the) least, (the) fewest pl; **as que ∼**

bolos comeram those who ate (the) fewest cakes; **os que ∼ dinheiro têm** those who have (the) least money. ◇ prep **-1.** [exceto] except (for); **todos gostaram ∼ ele** they all liked it except (for) him; **tudo ∼ isso** anything but that. **-2.** [indica subtração] minus; **três ∼ dois é igual a um** three minus two equals one.

menosprezado, da [menoʃpre'zadu, da] adj underestimated.

menosprezar [menoʃpre'za(x)] vt to disdain.

menosprezo [menoʃ'prezu] m: **∼ (por)** disdain (for).

mensageiro, ra [mẽsa'ʒejru, ra] m, f messenger.

mensagem [mẽnsa'ʒẽ] (pl -ns) f message; **∼ de texto** text message.

mensal [mẽn'saw] (pl -ais) adj monthly; **ganho 1.000 reais mensais** I earn 1,000 reals a month.

mensalidade [mẽnsali'dadʒi] f monthly payment.

mensalmente [mẽnsaw'mẽntʃi] adv monthly.

menstruação [mẽnʃtrwa'sãw] (pl -ões) f menstruation.

menstruada [mẽnʃ'trwada] adj f: **estar/ficar ∼** to be menstruating.

menstrual [mẽnʃ'trwaw] (pl -ais) adj menstrual.

menstruar [mẽnʃ'trwa(x)] vi to menstruate.

mensurável [mẽnsu'ravew] (pl -eis) adj measurable.

menta ['mẽnta] f mint; **de ∼** mint (antes de subst).

mental [mẽn'taw] (pl -ais) adj mental.

mentalidade [mẽntali'dadʒi] f mentality.

mentalizar [mẽntali'za(x)] vt **-1.** [pensar em] to think. **-2.** [conceber] to imagine.

mente ['mẽntʃi] f mind; **ter algo em ∼** to have sthg in mind.

mentecapto, ta [mẽnte'kaptu, ta] m, f insane, foolish.

mentir [mẽn'tʃi(x)] vi to lie.

mentira [mẽn'tʃira] f [falsidade] lie; **de ∼** [como brincadeira] as a joke; [falso] fake; **∼ deslavada** downright lie; **∼!** [mostrando surpresa] you don't say!

mentiroso, osa [mẽntʃi'rozu, ɔza] ◇ adj **-1.** [ger] untruthful. **-2.** [jornalista, artigo] lying. ◇ m, f [pessoa] liar.

mentolado, da [mẽnto'ladu, da] adj mentholated.

mentor, ra [mẽn'to(x), ra] m, f [autor intelectual]: **o/a ∼** the brains.

menu [me'nu] m menu.

meramente [mɛraˈmẽntʃi] *adv* merely.

mercado [mexˈkadu] *m* market; ~ negro black market; ~ de trabalho job market; ~ das pulgas flea market. ➤ Mercado Comum *m* Common Market.

mercador [mexkaˈdo(x)] *m* merchant.

mercadoria [mexkadoˈria] *f* commodity. ➤ mercadorias *fpl* merchandise, goods (*pl*).

mercante [mexˈkãntʃi] *adj* merchant (*antes de subst*).

mercantil [mexkãnˈtʃiw] (*pl* -is) *adj* mercantile.

mercantilismo [mexkãntʃiˈliʒmu] *m* mercantilism.

mercê [mexˈse] *f*: estar/ficar à ~ de alguém/algo to be at the mercy of sb/ sthg.

mercearia [mexsjaˈria] *f* grocery shop.

mercenário, ria [mexseˈnarju, rja] ◇ *adj* mercenary. ◇ *m, f* mercenary.

Mercosul [mexkoˈsuw] (*abrev de* Mercado do Cone Sul) *m* South American common market.

mercúrio [mexˈkurju] *m* mercury; ~ cromo merbromin, Mercurochrome®.

Mercúrio [mexˈkurju] *m* Mercury.

merda [ˈmɛxda] *mfam* ◇ *f* -1. [ger] crap, shit; ser/estar uma ~ to be crap; mandar alguém à ~ to tell sb to bugger off. -2. [excremento] shit. ◇ *interj*: (que) ~! what crap!

merecedor, ra [mereseˈdo(x), ra] *adj*: ~ de deserving of.

merecer [mereˈse(x)] ◇ *vt* to deserve. ◇ *vi*: ele ganhou o prêmio, mas não merecia he won the prize but he didn't deserve to.

merecido, da [mereˈsidu, da] *adj* deserved; foi um castigo bem ~ it was a well deserved punishment.

merecimento [meresiˈmẽntu] *m* [mérito, valor] merit.

merenda [meˈrẽnda] *f* snack; ~ escolar free school meal.

merendeira [merẽnˈdejra] *f* [lancheira] snack box.

merengue [meˈrẽngi] *m* meringue.

meretriz [mereˈtriʒ] *f* prostitute.

mergulhador, ra [mexguˈʎaˈdo(x), ra] (*mpl* -es, *fpl* -s) ◇ *adj* diving. ◇ *m, f* diver.

mergulhar [mexguˈʎa(x)] ◇ *vt* [afundar]: ~ algo (em algo) to dip sthg (in sthg). ◇ *vi* -1.: ~ (em algo) [afundar] to dive (into sthg); [saltar] to spring (from sthg). -2.: ~ em algo [penetrar] to plunge into sthg; *fig* [concentrar-se] to plunge o.s. in sthg.

mergulho [mexˈguʎu] *m* -1. [ger] dive; dar um ~ [na praia] to take a dip; [de trampolim] to spring. -2. *ESP* diving.

meridiano, na [meriˈdʒjãnu, na] *adj* meridian. ➤ meridiano *m* GEOGR meridian.

meridional [meridʒjoˈnaw] (*pl* -ais) *adj* southern.

meritíssimo, ma [meriˈtʃisimu, ma] *adj* highly deserving.

mérito [ˈmɛritu] *m* merit.

merluza [mexˈluza] *f* hake.

mero, ra [ˈmɛru, ra] *adj* mere.

merreca [meˈxɛka] *f*: uma ~ a trifle; custar/pagar uma ~ to cost/pay a trifle.

mês [ˈmeʃ] (*pl* meses) *m*: de ~ em ~ monthly.

mesa [ˈmeza] *f* -1. [móvel] table; pôr/tirar a ~ to lay/clear the table; ~ telefônica switchboard. -2. [de uma assembléia etc.] board. -3. *loc*: virar a ~ to turn the tables.

mesada [meˈzada] *f* -1. [pagamento] monthly payment. -2. [de criança] pocket money *UK*, allowance *US*.

mesa-de-cabeceira [ˌmezadʒikabiˈsejral] (*pl* mesas-de-cabeceira) *f* bedside table.

mesa-redonda [ˌmezaxeˈdõnda] (*pl* mesas-redondas) *f* round table.

mescla [ˈmɛʃkla] *f* -1. [mistura] mixture. -2. [tecido] blend.

mesclar [meʃˈkla(x)] *vt* -1. [misturar]: ~ algo (com algo) to mix sthg (with sthg). -2. [incorporar]: ~ algo a algo to combine sthg with sthg.

mesmo, ma [ˈmeʒmu, ma] ◇ *adj* -1. [ger] same; o ~ batom the same lipstick; na mesma hora [imediatamente] at once. -2. [próprio]: eu ~ fiz isso I made that myself; ela mesma herself; eles mesmos themselves. -3. [para enfatizar] very. ◇ *pron*: o ~ /a mesma the same. ➤ mesma ◇ *f*: continuar na mesma [não mudar] to be exactly the same. ◇ *m* [a mesma coisa]: o mesma the same; dá na mesma it's all the same. ➤ mesmo *adv* -1. [precisamente]: agora/ aqui ~ right now/here; é assim ~ that's just the way it is; por isso ~ for that very reason. -2. [realmente] really; é ~? really?; só ~ você consegue fazer isso only you can do it. -3. [até, ainda] even; ~ assim, assim ~ even so; nem ~ not even. ➤ mesmo que *loc conj* even though.

mesquinhez [meʃkiˈneʃ] *f* [] meanness.

mesquinho, nha [meʃˈkiɲu, ɲal] *adj* mean.

mesquita [meʃˈkita] f mosque.

messias [meˈsiaʃ] m fig messiah.

➤ **Messias** m: **o Messias** the Messiah.

mestiçagem [meʃtfiˈsaʒẽ] (pl -ns) f -1. [cruzamento] cross-breeding. -2. [miscigenação] miscegenation.

mestiço, ça [meʃˈtʃisu, sa] <> adj mestizo. <> m, f mestizo.

mestra [ˈmɛʃtra] f ➞ **mestre**.

mestrando, da [meʃˈtrãndu, da] m student about to complete a master's degree.

mestre, tra [ˈmɛʃtri, tra] <> adj -1. [extraordinário] fantastic. -2. [principal] master. <> m, f -1. [ger] master; **ser ~ em fazer algo** irôn to be a past master at doing sthg. -2. [fonte de ensinamento] teacher. -3. [músico] maestro.

mestre-de-cerimônias [ˌmɛʃtridʒiseriˈmonjaʃ] (pl mestres-de-cerimônias) m master of ceremonies.

mestre-de-obras [ˌmɛʃtriˈdʒjobraʃ] (pl mestres-de-obras) m foreman.

mestre-sala [ˌmɛʃtriˈsala] (pl mestres-sala) m [em escola de samba] leader of samba group display during carnival.

mesura [meˈzura] f reverence.

meta [ˈmɛta] f -1. [objetivo] aim, goal. -2. [gol] goal. -3. [na corrida] finishing line.

metabolismo [metaboˈliʒmu] m metabolism.

metade [meˈtadʒi] f half; **~ das pessoas** half the people; **deixar pela ~** to leave halfway through; **na ~ do caminho** halfway.

metáfora [meˈtafora] f metaphor.

metafórico, ca [metaˈfɔriku, ka] adj metaphorical.

metal [meˈtaw] (pl -ais) m metal.

➤ **metais** mpl MÚS brass instruments.

metálico, ca [meˈtaliku, ka] adj metallic.

metalurgia [metaluxˈʒia] f metallurgy.

metalúrgico, ca [metaˈluxʒiku, ka] <> adj metallurgic. <> m, f [operário] metallurgist.

➤ **metalúrgica** f [oficina] foundry.

meteórico, ca [meteˈɔriku, ka] adj meteoric.

meteorito [meteˈʃuˈritul m meteorite.

meteoro [meˈtjoru] m meteor.

meteorologia [meteʃoroloˈʒia] f meteorology.

meteorológico, ca [meteʃoroˈlɔʒiku, ka] adj meteorological.

meter [meˈte(x)] vt -1. [ger] to put. -2. [enfiar]: **~ algo em** ou **dentro de algo** to put sthg in/inside sthg. -3. [inspirar]: **ele**

me mete pena he makes me feel sorry for him; **ele é feio de ~ medo** he's so ugly it's frightening.

➤ **meter-se** vp -1. [ir, esconder-se] to hide. -2. [intrometer-se]: **~-se (em algo)** to stick one's nose in (in sthg); **não se meta!** don't interfere! -3. [desafiar]: **~ -se com alguém** to provoke sb. -4. [associar-se]: **~-se com alguém** to get mixed up with sb. -5. [fazer-se de]: **~-se a algo** to play at being sthg. -6. [aventurar-se]: **~-se a fazer algo** to start doing sthg.

meticuloso, osa [metʃikuˈlozu, ɔza] adj meticulous.

metido, da [meˈtʃidu, da] adj -1. [abelhudo] meddlesome, nosy. -2. [presumido]: **~ (a besta)** full of o.s. -3. [cheio de intimidades] inquisitive. -4. [envolvido]: **~ em algo** involved in sthg.

metodismo [metoˈdʒiʒmu] m -1. RELIG Methodism. -2. [procedimento] method.

metodista [metoˈdʒiʃta] RELIG <> adj Methodist. <> mf Methodist.

método [ˈmɛtodu] m method.

metodológico, ca [metodoˈlɔʒiku, ka] adj methodological.

metonímia [metoˈnimja] f metonymy.

metragem [meˈtraʒẽ] f -1. [medida] length in metres UK ou meters US. -2. CINE: **filme de curta/longa ~** short/feature-length film.

metralhadora [metraʎaˈdora] f machine gun.

métrico, ca [ˈmɛtriku, ka] adj -1. [do metro] metric; **fita métrica** tape measure. -2. LITER metrical.

metro [ˈmɛtrul m metre UK, meter US; **~ cúbico** cubic metre; **~ quadrado** square metre.

metrô [meˈtro] m underground UK, subway US.

metrópole [meˈtrɔpoli] f -1. [cidade principal] capital. -2. [cidade grande] metropolis. -3. [nação] mother country.

metropolitano, na [metropoliˈtãnu, na] adj metropolitan.

meu, minha [ˈmew, ˈmiɲa] <> adj -1. [ger] my; **este é o ~ carro** this is my car; **~ Deus!** my God!; **minha nossa!** oh me, oh my!, gosh! -2. [caro a mim] my; **como vai, ~ caro Affonso?** how are you, my dear Affonso?; **~ irmão** fam [tratamento] my friend. <> pron: **o ~ /a minha** mine; **um amigo ~** a friend of mine; **os ~s** [a minha família] my family; **este jeito de andar é bem ~** this manner of walking is quite me.

mexer [meˈʃe(x)] <> vt -1. [ger] to move. -2. [misturar] to mix. <> vi -1. [mover] to move. -2.: **~ em alguém/algo**

[tocar] to touch sb/sthg; [mudar de posição, remexer] to fiddle with sb/sthg. **- 3.:** ~ **com alguém** [caçoar] to tease sb; [provocar] to provoke sb; [afetar] to affect sb. **- 4.** [trabalhar]: ~ **com algo** to work with sthg.

◆ **mexer-se** *vp* **- 1.** [mover-se] to move. **- 2.** [agir] to move.

mexerica [meʃeˈrikal] *f* tangerine.

mexerico [meʃeˈrikul] *m* **- 1.** [ato] gossip. **- 2.** [intriga] intrigue.

mexicano, na [meʃiˈkãnu, na] ◇ *adj* Mexican. ◇ *m, f* Mexican.

México [ˈmɛʃikul] *n* Mexico.

mexido, da [meˈʃidu, da] *adj* **- 1.** [papéis] muddled. **- 2.** [ovos] scrambled.

mexilhão [meʃiˈʎãw] (*pl* **-ões**) *m* mussel.

mg (*abrev de* **miligrama**) *m* mg.

MG (*abrev de* **Estado de Minas Gerais**) *n* State of Minas Gerais.

mi [mi] *m* MÚS E, mi.

miado [ˈmjadu] *m* miaow.

miar [ˈmja(x)] *vi* to mew.

miçanga [miˈsãga] *f* **- 1.** [conta] glass bead. **- 2.** [ornato] beads (*pl*).

mico [ˈmiku] *m* ZOOL capuchin monkey.

mico-leão [mikuˈljãw] (*pl* **micos-leão**) *m* ZOOL golden lion tamarin.

micose [miˈkɔzi] *f* fungal infection, mycosis.

micro [ˈmikru] *m* COMPUT computer, PC.

micro- [mikru-] *prefixo* micro-.

micróbio [miˈkrɔbju] *m* microbe.

microbiologia [mikrobjoloˈʒia] *f* microbiology.

microcomputador [mikrokõnputaˈdo(x)] *m* microcomputer.

microempresa [mikrowẽnˈpreza] *f* small business.

microfilme [mikroˈfiwmi] *m* microfilm.

microfone [mikroˈfoni] *m* microphone.

microonda [mikroˈõnda] *f* microwave.

◆ **microondas** *mpl* [forno] microwave oven *(sg)*.

microônibus [mikroˈonibuʃ] *m inv* minibus.

microorganismo [mikrwoxgaˈniʒmul] *m* micro-organism.

microprocessador [mikruprosesaˈdo(x)] *m* microprocessor.

mictório [mikˈtɔrju] *m* urinal.

mídia [ˈmidʒja] *f* media.

migalha [miˈgaʎa] *f* [de pão, bolo] crumb.

◆ **migalhas** *fpl* [sobras] leftovers.

migrante [miˈgrãntʃi] ◇ *adj* **- 1.** [pássaro] migratory. **- 2.** [população] migrant. ◇ *mf* migrant.

migrar [miˈgra(x)] *vi* to migrate.

mijar [miˈʒa(x)] *vi fam* to pee.

mijo [ˈmiʒul] *m fam* pee.

mil [ˈmiw] *num* **- 1.** [número] thousand; **três** ~ three thousand. **- 2.** [grande número] a thousand; *veja também* **seis**.

milagre [miˈlagri] *m* miracle; **por** ~ miraculously.

milagroso, osa [milaˈgrozu, ɔza] *adj* miraculous.

milanesa [milaˈneza] *f*: **à** ~ in breadcrumbs.

milênio [miˈlenju] *m* millennium.

milésimo, ma [miˈlɛzimu, ma] *num* thousandth; **a milésima parte** the thousandth part.

mil-folhas [miwˈfoʎaʃ] *f inv* millefeuille.

milha [ˈmiʎa] *f* mile; ~ **marítima** nautical mile.

milhão [miˈʎãw] (*pl* **-ões**) *num* million; **três milhões** three million.

milhar [miˈʎa(x)] (*pl* **-es**) *m* thousand.

◆ **milhares** *mpl*: ~ **es de pessoas** thousands of people.

milho [ˈmiʎul] *m* **- 1.** [planta] maize UK, corn US. **- 2.** [grão] corn; ~ **de pipoca** popcorn.

milhões [miˈʎõjʃ] *pl* ⊳ **milhão**.

milícia [miˈlisja] *f* militia.

miligrama [miliˈgrãma] *m* milligram.

mililitro [miliˈlitru] *m* millilitre UK, milliliter US.

milímetro [miˈlimetru] *m* millimetre UK, millimeter US.

milionário, ria [miljoˈnarju, rja] ◇ *adj* millionaire. ◇ *m, f* millionaire.

militância [miliˈtãsja] *f* militancy.

militante [miliˈtãntʃi] ◇ *adj* militant. ◇ *mf* militant.

militar [miliˈta(x)] ◇ *adj* military. ◇ *mf* career soldier; **os** ~ **es** the military *(inv)*. ◇ *vi* **- 1.** [lutar]: ~ **(por/contra)** to fight for/against. **- 2.**: ~ **em** MIL to serve in; POL to be active in.

mim [ˈmĩ] *pron* **- 1.** [com preposição: complemento indireto] me; **ela comprou um presente para** ~ she bought a present for me, she bought me a present; **ele fez o serviço por** ~ he did the work for me; **a** ~ **ele não faria isto** he wouldn't do that to me; **falaram mal de** ~ they spoke ill of me; **o que você tem contra** ~? what have you got against me?; **eles foram embora sem** ~ they left without me; **para** ~, **este é o melhor quadro** [para expressar opinião] for me, this is the best painting; **por** ~, **você pode ficar aqui** [de minha parte] as far as I'm concerned, you can stay here. **- 2.** [com preposição: reflexo] myself; **a** ~, **você não engana** you don't fool me; **comprei-o para ~ (mesmo** OU **próprio)** I bought it for myself; **preciso cuidar mais de ~** I need to look after myself a bit better; **de ~ para ~** [comigo mesmo] to myself.

mimado, da [mi'madu, da] *adj* spoiled.

mimar [mi'ma(x)] *vt* **-1.** [fazer todas as vontades de] to spoil. **-2.** [tratar com carinho] to pamper.

mimeografar [mimjogra'fa(x)] *vt* to mimeograph.

mimeógrafo [mi'mjɔgraful] *m* mimeograph.

mímico, ca ['mimiku, ka] *adj* imitative. *m, f* **-1.** [pessoa] mimic. **-2.** [ator] mime artist.
➤ **mímica** *f* mime.

mimo ['mimu] *m* **-1.** [carinho] affection. **-2.** [pessoa ou coisa graciosa]: **ser um ~** to be a delight.

mimoso, osa [mi'mozu, ɔza] *adj* **-1.** [carinhoso] affectionate. **-2.** [gracioso] delightful. **-3.** [delicado] delicate.

mina ['mina] *f* **-1.** [ger] mine; **~ de carvão/ouro** coal/gold mine. **-2.** *fig*: **ser uma ~** [de lucros] to be a goldmine; [preciosidade] to be precious; **ser uma ~ de informações** to be a mine of information. **-3.** *fam* [garota] girl.

minar [mi'na(x)] *vt* **-1.** [pôr minas em] to mine. **-2.** [deteriorar, prejudicar] to undermine. *vi* [água]: **~ (de)** to stream (from).

mindinho [mĩn'dʒiɲul] *m fam* pinky.

mineiro, ra [mi'neʒru, ra] *adj* **-1.** [relativo a mina] mining. **-2.** [de Minas Gerais] from Minas Gerais. *m, f* **-1.** [operário] miner. **-2.** [de Minas Gerais] *person from Minas Gerais*.

mineração [minera'sãw] *f* **-1.** [exploração] mining. **-2.** [depuração] purifying.

minerador, ra [minera'do(x),ra] *adj* mining *(antes de subst)*. *m, f* miner.
➤ **mineradora** *f* mining company.

mineral [mine'raw] *(pl* **-ais)** *adj* mineral. *m* mineral.

minério [mi'nɛrju] *m* ore.

mingau [mĩŋ'gaw] *m* **-1.** [papa] porridge. **-2.** *fig* [coisa mole] mush.

míngua ['mĩŋgwa] *f* lack; **estar à ~ de algo** to be short of sthg; **viver à ~ de algo** to live with a shortage of sthg.

minguado, da [mĩŋ'gwadu, da] *adj* **-1.** [escasso] scarce. **-2.** [pouco desenvolvido] flat.

minguante [mĩŋ'gwãntʃi] *m* ASTRON [moon] waning, last quarter.

minguar [mĩŋ'gwa(x)] *vt* [reduzir] to reduce. *vi* [escassear] to dwindle.

minha ['miɲa] ➤ **meu**.

minhoca [mi'ɲɔka] *f* earthworm; **com ~ s na cabeça** with strange ideas.

míni ['minil] *adj inv* mini. *m* [vestido] minidress. *f* [saia] miniskirt.

miniatura [minja'tura] *f* miniature; **em ~** in miniature.

mínima ['minima] *f* ➤ **mínimo**.

minimizar [minimi'za(x)] *vt* **-1.** [tornar mínimo] to minimize. **-2.** [subestimar] to underestimate. **-3.** [fazer pouco caso de] to play down.

mínimo, ma ['minimu, ma] *adj* **-1.** [ger] minimal. **-2.** [muito pequeno] tiny. **-3.** [o menor possível] smallest. **-4.** *(antes de subst)* [nenhum] slightest.
➤ **mínimo** *m* [limite] least; **no ~** at least.
➤ **mínima** *f* **-1.** METEOR minimum (temperature). **-2.** MÚS minim. **-3.** *loc*: **não dar a mínima (para alguém/algo)** not to have the least concern (for sb/sthg).

minissaia [ˌmini'saja] *f* miniskirt.

minissérie [ˌmini'sɛrji] *f* miniseries.

ministério [miniʃ'tɛrju] *m* **-1.** [ger] ministry; **Ministério da Fazenda** ≃ HM Treasury *UK*, ≃ the Treasury *US*; **Ministério Público** public prosecution; **Ministério das Relações Exteriores** ≃ Foreign (and Commonwealth) Office *UK*, ≃ State Department *US*; **Ministério do Trabalho** ≃ Department of Employment *UK*, ≃ Department of Labor *US*; **Ministério da Educação e Cultura** ≃ Department of Education; **Ministério dos Transportes** ≃ Department of Transport. **-2.** [gabinete] cabinet.

ministro, tra [mi'niʃtru, tra] *m, f* minister; **~ da Educação e Cultura** ≃ Secretary for Education; **~ dos Transportes** ≃ Secretary for Transport.

minoria [mino'ria] *f* minority.

minoritário, ria [minori'tarju, rja] *adj* minority *(antes de subst)*.

minúcia [mi'nusja] *f* **-1.** [detalhe] detail. **-2.** [coisa sem importância] minutiae *(pl)*.

minucioso, osa [minu'sjozu, ɔza] *adj* meticulous.

minúsculo, la [mi'nuʃkulu, la] *adj* **-1.** [tamanho] minuscule. **-2.** [letra] lower case *(antes de subst)*.
➤ **minúscula** *f* [letra] lower case.

minuta [mi'nuta] *f* **-1.** [rascunho] draft. **-2.** [prato] cooked to order.

minuto [mi'nutu] *m* minute; **um ~ !** one minute!

miolo ['mjolu] *m* **-1.** [pão] crumb. **-2.** [fruta] pulp.
➤ **miolos** *mpl* **-1.** CULIN brains. **-2.** *fam* [cérebro] brains.

miopia [mju'pia] *f* myopia.

mira ['mira] *f* **-1.** [ger] aim. **-2.** [de arma] sight.

mirabolante [mirabo'lãntʃi] *adj* **-1.** [surpreendente] incredible. **-2.** [espalhafatoso] gaudy.

miraculoso, osa [miraku'lozu, ɔza] *adj* [espantoso] miraculous.

miragem [mi'raʒẽ] (*pl* **-ns**) *f* **-1.** [efeito ótico] mirage. **-2.** *fig* [ilusão] illusion.

mirante [mi'rãntʃi] *m* belvedere.

mirar [mi'ra(x)] ⟨⟩ *vt* **-1.** [fitar] to stare at. **-2.** [apontar para] to aim at. **-3.** [observar] to watch. ⟨⟩ *vi* [apontar]: ~ **(em algo)** to aim (at sthg).

mirim [mi'rĩ] (*pl* **-ns**) *adj* little.

miscelânea [mise'lãnja] *f* **-1.** [coletânea] miscellany. **-2.** *fig* [mistura] assortment.

miscigenação [misiʒena'sãw] *f* interbreeding.

miserável [mize'ravɛw] (*pl* **-eis**) ⟨⟩ *adj* **-1.** [ger] miserable. **-2.** [sovina] miserly. **-3.** [vil] despicable. **-4.** [terrível] dreadful. ⟨⟩ *mf* **-1.** [infeliz] miserable person. **-2.** [pessoa pobre] poor wretch. **-3.** [pessoa vil] despicable person.

miseravelmente [mizeravew'mẽntʃi] *adv* **-1.** [desgraçadamente] wretchedly. **-2.** [pobremente] in misery.

miséria [mi'zɛrja] *f* **-1.** [desgraça] misery. **-2.** [pobreza] poverty. **-3.** [sovinice] meanness. **-4.** [ninharia]: **custar/ganhar uma** ~ to cost/to earn a pittance.

misericórdia [mizeri'kɔrdʒja] *f*: ~ **(de/com)** mercy (on/for).

misericordioso, osa [mizerikox'dʒjozu, ɔza] *adj* compassionate.

mísero, ra ['mizeru, ra] *adj fig* [escasso] miserly.

misógino, na [mi'zɔʒinu, na] ⟨⟩ *adj* misogynous. ⟨⟩ *m, f* mysoginist.

missa ['misa] *f RELIG* mass.

missal [mi'saw] (*pl* **-ais**) *m* missal.

missão [mi'sãw] (*pl* **-ões**) *f* mission.

misse ['misi] *f* beauty queen.

míssil ['misiw] (*pl* **-eis**) *m* missile.

missionário, ria [misjo'narju, rja] ⟨⟩ *adj* missionary. ⟨⟩ *m, f* missionary.

missiva [mi'siva] *f* missive.

missões [mi'ʃõjʃ] *pl* ⟶ **missão**.

mister [miʃ'te(x)] *m* **-1.** [ofício] office. **-2.** [necessidade] need.

mistério [miʃ'tɛrju] *m* **-1.** [ger] mystery. **-2.** [segredo] secret.

misterioso, osa [miʃte'rjozu, ɔza] *adj* mysterious.

misticismo [miʃtʃi'siʒmu] *m* mysticism.

místico, ca ['miʃtʃiku, ka] ⟨⟩ *adj* mystic. ⟨⟩ *m, f* [pessoa] mystic.

mistificar [miʃtʃifi'ka(x)] *vt* to mystify.

misto, ta ['miʃtu, ta] *adj* mixed. ⟶ **misto** *m* mixture.

misto-quente [,miʃtu'kẽntʃi] (*pl* **mistos-quentes**) *m* toasted cheese and ham sandwich.

mistura [miʃ'tura] *f* mixture.

misturar [miʃtu'ra(x)] *vt* **-1.** [combinar, juntar] to mix. **-2.** [confundir] to mix up.

mítico, ca ['mitʃiku, ka] *adj* mythical.

mitificar [mitʃifi'ka(x)] *vt* to mythicize.

mito ['mitu] *m* **-1.** [ger] myth. **-2.** [pessoa] legend.

mitologia [mitolo'ʒia] *f* mythology.

mitológico, ca [mito'lɔʒiku, ka] *adj* mythological.

miúdo, da ['mjudu, da] *adj* [pequeno] small. ⟶ **miúdos** *mpl* **-1.** [dinheiro] small change. **-2.** [de animal] giblets. **-3.** *loc*: **trocar em** ~ **s** to put it simply.

mixagem [mik'saʒẽ] *f CINE & RÁDIO* mixing.

mixar¹ [mi'ʃa(x)] *vi fam* [gorar] to go down the drain.

mixar² [mi'ʃa(x)] *vt CINE & RÁDIO* to mix.

mixaria [miʃa'ria] *f* **-1.** *fam* [soma insignificante]: **uma** ~ peanuts. **-2.** [coisa sem valor] rubbish.

mixuruca [miʃu'ruka] *adj* **-1.** [presente] worthless. **-2.** [festa] lifeless.

ml (*abrev de* **mililitro**) *m* ml.

mm (*abrev de* **milímetro**) *m* mm.

mó ['mɔ] *f* **-1.** [de moinho] millstone. **-2.** [de afiar] whetstone.

mobília [mo'bilja] *f* furniture.

mobiliar [mobi'lja(x)] *vt* to furnish.

mobilização [mobiliza'sãw] *f* mobilization.

mobilizar [mobili'za(x)] *vt* to mobilize.

moça ['mosa] *f* ⟶ **moço**.

moçada [mo'sada] *f fam* group of young people.

moção [mo'sãw] *f* motion.

mocassim [moka'sĩ] (*pl* **-ns**) *m* moccasin.

mochila [mo'ʃila] *f* rucksack.

mocidade [mosi'dadʒi] *f* **-1.** [período] youth. **-2.** [os jovens]: **a** ~ the young.

mocinho, nha [mo'siɲu, ɲal *m, f* **-1.** [jovem] boy. **-2.** [herói] hero.

moço, ça ['mosu, sa] ⟨⟩ *adj* [pessoa] young. ⟨⟩ *m, f* **-1.** [jovem] young person. **-2.** [adulto] young boy (*f* young girl).

moções [mo'sõjʃ] *pl* ⟶ **moção**.

moda ['mɔda] *f* **-1.** [ger] fashion; **cair** *ou* **sair de** ~ to fall out of fashion; **fora de** ~ out of fashion. **-2.** [coqueluche] craze. **-3.** [maneira] way; **à** ~ **portuguesa** Portuguese-style. **-4.** *loc*: **inventar** ~ to create a new fad.

modalidade [modali'dadʒil] f -1. [tipo] mode. -2. ESP event.

modelagem [mode'laʒẽ] (pl -ns) f -1. [ato] modelling. -2. [produto] moulding UK, molding US. -3. [do corpo] shape.

modelar [mode'la(x)] vt -1. [ger] to mould UK, to mold US. -2. fig [moldar]: ~ algo por algo to model sthg on sthg.

modelista [mode'liʃta] mf designer.

modelo [mo'delu] ⇔ m model. ⇔ mf model; ~ **vivo** live model.

modem ['modẽ] (pl -ns) m COMPUT modem.

moderação [modera'sãw] f moderation.

moderado, da [mode'radu, da] adj moderate.

moderar [mode'ra(x)] vt to moderate.

➡ **moderar-se** vp [comedir-se] to control o.s.

modernidade [modexni'dadʒi] f modernity.

modernismo [modex'niʒmu] m modernism.

modernizar [modexni'za(x)] vt to modernize.

➡ **modernizar-se** vp to keep o.s. up to date.

moderno, na [mo'dɛxnu, na] adj modern.

modess® ['modeʃ] m inv sanitary towel UK, sanitary napkin US.

modéstia [mo'dɛʃtja] f modesty.

modesto, ta [mo'dɛʃtu, ta] adj modest.

módico, ca ['mɔdʒiku, ka] adj -1. [barato, parco] modest. -2. [moderado] moderate.

modificação [modʒifika'sãw] (pl -ões) f -1. [alteração] modification. -2. [transformação] transformation.

modismo [mo'dʒiʒmu] m -1. [tendência] trend. -2. [moda] fashion.

modo ['mɔdu] m -1. [ger] way; **de** ~ **algum** in no way. -2. [jeito] manner. -3. GRAM mood.

➡ **modos** mpl manners.

➡ **de modo que** loc conj -1. [de maneira que] so (that). -2. [assim sendo] so that.

modulação [modula'sãw] (pl -ões) f modulation.

modulado, da [modu'ladu, da] adj modular.

módulo ['mɔdulu] m -1. [unidade] module. -2. [veículo]: ~ **lunar** lunar module.

moeda ['mwɛda] f -1. [peça] coin; **uma** ~ **de 10 centavos** a 10 cent coin; **uma** ~ **falsa** a counterfeit coin. -2. [dinheiro] money; **pagar na mesma** ~ to pay sb back in their own coin; ⊳ **casa**.

moedor [mwe'do(x)] m -1. [de café,

pimenta] mill. -2. [de carne] mincer UK, grinder US.

moer ['mwe(x)l] ⇔ vt -1. [café, pimenta] to grind. -2. [carne] to mince UK, to grind US. -3. [para extrair suco] to mill. ⇔ vi [moinho] to grind.

mofado, da [mo'fadu, da] adj mouldy UK, moldy US.

mofar [mo'fa(x)] vi [criar mofo] to go mouldy UK ou moldy US.

mofo ['moful] m mould UK, mold US; **esta camisa está com cheiro de** ~ this shirt smells musty.

mogno ['mɔgnu] m mahogany.

moído, da ['mwidu, da] adj -1. [café, pimenta] ground. -2. [carne] minced UK, ground US. -3. fig [doído]: ~ **de algo** hurting from sthg.

moinho ['mwiɲul] m mill; ~ **de vento** windmill.

moita ['mojta] f thicket.

➡ **na moita** loc adv [às escondidas] in secret.

mola ['mɔla] f [dispositivo] spring.

molar [mo'la(x)] (pl -es) ⇔ adj [dente] molar. ⇔ m molar.

moldar [mow'da(x)] vt -1. [fazer o molde de] to make a mould UK ou mold US of. -2. [modelar] to mould UK, to mold US. -3. fig [dar forma a] to shape.

Moldávia [mow'davja] n Moldova, Moldavia.

molde ['mɔwdʒi] m mould UK, mold US.

moldura [mow'dura] f -1. [de quadro, espelho] frame. -2. ARQUIT moulding UK, molding US.

mole ['mɔli] ⇔ adj -1. [ger] soft. -2. [flácido] flabby. -3. [lento] languid. -4. [fraco] limp. -5. [indolente] lazy. -6. fam [fácil] a piece of cake. ⇔ adv [facilmente] easily.

moleca [mo'lɛka] f ⊳ **moleque**.

molecagem [mole'kaʒẽ] (pl -ns) f -1. [travessura] prank. -2. [brincadeira] trick.

molécula [mo'lɛkula] f molecule.

moleira [mo'lejra] f ANAT fontanelle UK, fontanel US.

molejo [mo'leʒu] m -1. [de veículo] suspension. -2. fam [de pessoa, corpo] wiggle.

moleque, leca [mo'lɛki, lɛka] ⇔ adj -1. [travesso] wild. -2. [brincalhão] mischievous. ⇔ m, f -1. [criança] youngster. -2. [criança travessa] rascal. -3. [patife] scoundrel.

molestar [moleʃ'ta(x)] vt -1. [importunar] to annoy. -2. [ofender] to offend. -3. [sexualmente] to molest.

moléstia [mo'lɛʃtja] f ailment.

moleza [mo'leza] f -1. [maciez] softness.

- 2. [lentidão] slowness. **- 3.** [fraqueza, falta de energia] limpness.

molhado, da [mo'ʎadu, da] *adj* wet.

molhar [mo'ʎa(x)] *vt* **- 1.** [banhar] to wet; ~ **algo em algo** *ou* **algo** to dip *ou* dunk sthg in sthg. **- 2.** [umedecer] to dampen. **- 3.** [regar] to water. **- 4.** *fam* [urinar] to wet.

molhe ['mɔʎi] *m* **- 1.** [de defesa] breakwater. **- 2.** [de atracação] jetty.

molho¹ ['mɔʎu] *m* sauce; ~ **pardo** *gravy made with chicken blood and vinegar.*

de molho <> *loc adv:* **pôr/deixar de** ~ [roupa, feijão] to put/leave to soak. <> *loc adj:* **ficar de** ~ *fig* [pessoa] to stay in bed.

molho² ['mɔʎu] *m* bunch.

molinete [moli'netʃi] *m PESCA* fishing reel.

molusco [mo'luʃku] *m* mollusc.

momentâneo, nea [momẽ'tãnju, nja] *adj* momentary.

momento [mo'mẽtu] *m* **- 1.** moment. **- 2.** [tempo presente]: **no** ~ at the moment.

Mônaco ['monaku] *n*: **(o principado de)** ~ (the principality of) Monaco.

monarca [mo'naxka] *mf* monarch.

monarquia [monax'kia] *f* monarchy.

monastério [monaʃ'tɛrju] *m* monastery.

monástico, ca [mo'naʃtʃiku, ka] *adj* monastic.

monção [mõn'sãw] (*pl* **-ões**) *f* [vento] monsoon.

monetário, ria [mone'tarju, rja] *adj* monetary; ⊳ **correção**.

monge, ja ['mõʒi, ʒa] *m, f* [monge] monk; [monja] nun.

mongolóide [mõngo'lɔjdʒi] *MED* <> *adj* Down's syndrome (*antes de subst*). <> *mf* (person with) Down's syndrome.

monitor, ra [moni'to(x), ra] (*mpl* **-es**, *fpl* **-s**) *m, f EDUC* monitor.

monitor *m* **- 1.** [ger] monitor. **- 2.** *TV* screen.

monja ['mõʒa] *f* ⊳ **monge**.

monocultura [monokuw'tura] *f* monoculture.

monogamia [monoga'mia] *f* monogamy.

monólogo [mo'nɔlogu] *m* monologue.

monopólio [mono'pɔlju] *m* monopoly.

monopolizar [monopoli'za(x)] *vt* to monopolize.

monotonia [monoto'nia] *f* monotony.

monótono, na [mo'nɔtonu, na] *adj* monotonous.

monóxido [mo'nɔksidu] *m* monoxide; ~ **de carbono** carbon monoxide.

monsenhor [mõnse'ɲo(x)] *m* Monsignor.

monstrengo, ga [mõnʃ'treŋgu, ga] *m, f* [pessoa, coisa] monstrosity.

monstro ['mõnʃtru] <> *adj inv* [enorme] huge. <> *m* [criatura disforme] monster; **ser um** ~ [ser um prodígio] to be a wizard; [ser cruel, enorme, horrendo] to be monstrous.

monstruosidade [mõnʃtrwozi'dadʒi] *f* monstrosity.

monstruoso, osa [mõnʃtrwozu, ɔza] *adj* **- 1.** [com conformação de monstro] deformed. **- 2.** [enorme] enormous. **- 3.** [horrendo] monstrous.

monta ['mõnta] *f*: **de pouca** ~ of little importance.

montagem [mõn'taʒẽ] (*pl* **-ns**) *f* **- 1.** [de equipamento, casa] assembly. **- 2.** *CINE* (film) editing. **- 3.** *TEATRO* (theatre) production.

montanha [mõn'tãɲa] *f* mountain.

montanha-russa [mõn,tãɲa'rusa] (*pl* **montanhas-russas**) *f* roller coaster.

montanhês, esa [mõnta'ɲeʃ, ezal (*pl* **-eses**) <> *adj* mountain (*antes de subst*). <> *m, f* highlander.

montanhismo [mõnta'ɲiʒmu] *m* mountaineering.

montanhista [mõnta'ɲiʃta] <> *adj* mountaineering. <> *mf* mountaineer.

montanhoso, osa [mõntã'ɲozu, ɔza] *adj* mountainous.

montante [mõn'tãntʃi] *m* **- 1.** [soma] amount, sum. **- 2.** [direção]: **a** ~ **de** upstream of.

montão [mõn'tãw] (*pl* **-ões**) *m* pile.

montar [mõn'ta(x)] <> *vt* **- 1.** [armar] to prime. **- 2.** [instalar] to ready. **- 3.** *CINE* to edit. **- 4.** *TEATRO* to produce. <> *vi* [cavalgar]: ~ **(a cavalo)** to ride (horseback).

montaria [mõnta'ria] *f* [cavalo] mount.

monte ['mõntʃi] *m* **- 1.** [elevação] hill. **- 2.** [pilha] pile. **- 3.** *fig* [grande quantidade]: **um** ~ **de** a load of; **comida aos** ~**s** loads of food.

Montevidéu [mõntevi'dɛw] *n* Montevideo.

montões [mõn'tõjʃ] *pl* ⊳ **montão**.

monumental [monumẽn'taw] (*pl* **-ais**) *adj* **- 1.** [enorme] monumental. **- 2.** [magnífico] magnificent.

monumento [monu'mẽntu] *m* monument.

moqueca [mo'kɛka] *f Brazilian fish or chicken stew made with coconut milk, onions and palm oil.*

moradia [mora'dʒia], **morada** [mo'rada] *f* dwelling.

morador, ra [mora'do(x), ra] (*mpl* -**es**, *fpl* -**s**) *m, f* resident.

moral [mo'raw] (*pl* -**ais**) <> *adj* moral. <> *m* [estado de espírito] morale; **levantar o ~ (de alguém)** to raise the morale (of sb). <> *f* -**1.** [ética] morals *(pl)*. -**2.** [de história, fato] moral. -**3.** [estado de espírito]: **estar de ~ baixa** to be demoralized.

moralidade [morali'dadʒi] *f* morality.

moralismo [mora'liʒmu] *m* moralism.

moralista [mora'liʃta] <> *adj* moralistic. <> *mf* moralist.

moralização [morali'zasãw] (*pl* -**ões**) *f* moralization.

moralizar [morali'za(x)] <> *vt* [tornar mais moral] to moralize. <> *vi* [pregar moral]: **~ (sobre)** to moralize (on).

morango [mo'rãŋgu] *m* strawberry.

morar [mo'ra(x)] *vi* -**1.** [habitar]: **~ (em)** to live (in). -**2.** *fam* [entender] to catch on; **morou?** got it?

moratória [mora'tɔrja] *f* moratorium.

mórbido, da [ˈmɔxbidu] *m* adj morbid.

morcego [mox'segu] *m* bat.

mordaça [mox'dasa] *f* -**1.** [de animal] muzzle. -**2.** *fig* [pano] gag.

mordaz [mox'daʒ] *adj* biting.

morder [mox'de(x)] <> *vt & vi* to bite.

mordomia [moxdo'mia] *f* -**1.** [num emprego] perks *(pl)*. -**2.** [conforto, luxo] comfort.

mordomo [mox'domu] *m* butler.

moreno, na [mo'renu, na] <> *adj* -**1.** [tipo - de pele] dark-skinned; [- de cabelo] dark-haired. -**2.** [bronzeado] tanned; **ficar ~** to tan; **estar ~** to be tanned. <> *m, f* -**1.** [de pele] dark-skinned person. -**2.** [de cabelo] dark-haired person. -**3.** [cor] tan.

morfina [mox'fina] *f* morphine.

moribundo, da [mori'bũndu, da] *adj* dying.

moringa [mo'rĩŋga] *f* water-cooler.

mormaço [mox'masu] *m* sultry weather.

mormente [mɔx'mẽntʃi] *adv* especially.

mórmon [ˈmɔxmõl] *mf* Mormon.

morno, na [ˈmoxnu, na] *adj* lukewarm.

moroso, osa [mo'rozu, ɔza] *adj* slow.

morrer [mo'xe(x)] *vi* -**1.** [ger] to die. -**2.** [cair no esquecimento] to be dead. -**3.** *AUTO* to die. -**4.** *fig* [sentir intensamente]: **estou morrendo de calor/fome/frio** I'm dying of heat/hunger/cold. -**5.** *fam* [desembolsar]: **~ em** to cough up.

morro [ˈmoxu] *m* -**1.** [monte] hill. -**2.** [favela] slum.

mortadela [moxta'dɛla] *f salami-type sausage*.

mortal [mox'taw] (*pl* -**ais**) <> *adj* -**1.** [ger] mortal. -**2.** [terrível - dor] dreadful; [- pecado] deadly. <> *mf* mortal.

mortalidade [moxtali'dadʒi] *f* mortality.

morte [ˈmɔxtʃi] *f* -**1.** [ger] death. -**2.** [fim] ending. -**3.** *loc*: **pensar na ~ da bezerra** *fig* to daydream; **ser de ~** *fam* to be impossible.

morteiro [mox'tejru] *m* mortar.

mortífero, ra [mox'tʃiferu, ra] *adj* lethal.

mortificar [moxtʃifi'ka(x)] *vt* -**1.** [torturar] to torture. -**2.** [atormentar] to torment.

morto, ta [ˈmoxtu, ta] <> *pp* ▷ **matar**. <> *adj* -**1.** [ger] dead; **nem ~** no way; **não ter onde cair ~** to have nowhere to lay one's head. -**2.** [sem atividades] deadly. -**3.** [desbotado] faded. -**4.** [sentindo intensamente]: **~ de fome** dying of hunger; **~ de raiva** seething with rage. <> *m, f* [falecido] deceased.

mosaico [mo'zajku] *m* mosaic.

mosca [ˈmoʃka] *f* fly; **acertar na ~** to hit the jackpot; **estar/viver às ~s** to be empty.

moscovita [moʃko'vita] <> *adj* Muscovite. <> *m, f* Muscovite.

Moscou [moʃ'kow] *n* Moscow.

mosquito [moʃ'kitul] *m* mosquito.

mostarda [moʃ'taxda] *f* mustard.

mosteiro [moʃ'tejru] *m* [de monges] monastery; [de monjas] convent.

mostra [ˈmoʃtra] *f* -**1.** [exposição] display. -**2.** [manifestação] sign.

mostrar [moʃ'tra(x)] *vt* -**1.** [ger] to show. -**2.** [apontar] to point out.

➡ **mostrar-se** *vp* -**1.** [revelar-se] to show o.s. to be. -**2.** [exibir-se] to show off.

mostruário [moʃ'trwarju] *m* display case.

motel [mo'tɛw] (*pl* -**éis**) *m* motel.

motim [mo'tʃĩl] (*pl* -**ns**) *m* -**1.** [do povo] riot. -**2.** [de tropas] mutiny.

motivação [motʃiva'sãw] (*pl* -**ões**) *f* motivation.

motivado, da [motʃiva'du, da] *adj* [incentivado] motivated.

motivar [motʃi'va(x)] *vt* -**1.** [estimular] to motivate. -**2.** [provocar] to provoke.

motivo [mo'tʃivul] *m* -**1.** [causa]: **~ (de/para)** cause (of/for); **por ~s de força maior** for reasons beyond our control; **sem ~** without reason. -**2.** [justificativa] reason. -**3.** *ARTE, MÚS* motif.

moto[1] [ˈmɔtul] *m* [lema] motto.

moto[2] [ˈmɔtul] *f* [motocicleta] motorbike.

motocicleta [ˌmotosi'klɛtal] *f* motorcycle, motorbike.

motociclismo [motosi'klizmu] *m* motorcycling.

motociclista [motosi'kliʃta] *mf* motorcyclist, biker.

motoneta [moto'neta] *f* motor scooter.

motoqueiro, ra [moto'kejru, ra] *m, f* -1. *fam* [motociclista] biker. -2. [entregador] deliveryman *(on a bike)*.

motor [mo'to(x)] *(pl -es)* <> *adj* -1. TEC driving. -2. ANAT motor. <> *m* engine.

motorista [moto'riʃta] *mf* driver.

motorizado, da [motori'zadu, da] *adj* motorized.

motorizar [motori'za(x)] *vt* to motorize.

motorneiro, ra [motox'nejru, ra] *m, f* tram driver *UK*, streetcar driver *US*.

motosserra [moto'sɛxal] *f* chainsaw.

mouro, ra ['moru, ra] <> *adj* Moorish. <> *m, f* Moor.

mouse [‚mawzil] *m* COMPUT mouse.

movediço, ça [move'dʒisu, sa] *adj* TEC moving; **areia movediça** quicksand.

móvel ['mɔvɛwl] *(pl -eis)* <> *adj* movable. <> *m* piece of furniture.

mover [mo've(x)] *vt* -1. [ger] to move. -2. [começar] to set in motion.

◆ mover-se *vp* to move.

movido, da [mo'vidu, da] *adj* -1. [impelido]: ~ **por algo** moved by sthg. -2. [promovido]: ~ **contra alguém/algo** started against sb/sthg. -3. [acionado]: ~ **a álcool/vapor** ethanol/steam-driven.

movimentado, da [movimẽn'tadu, da] *adj* -1. [bairro, loja, dia] busy. -2. [música, peça, show] lively.

movimentar [movimẽn'ta(x)] *vt* -1. [ger] to move. -2. *fig* [animar] to liven up.

movimento [movi'mẽntul] *m* -1. [ger] movement. -2. [animação] bustle.

MP <> *m* *(abrev de Ministério Público)* *Brazilian state government.* <> *f* *(abrev de Medida Provisória)* *emergency law.*

MPB *(abrev de Música Popular Brasileira)* *f generic term for all popular Brazilian music.*

MS *(abrev de Estado do Mato Grosso do Sul)* *m State of Mato Grosso do Sul.*

MS-DOS *(abrev de Microsoft Disk Operating System)* *m* MS-DOS.

MST *(abrev de Movimento dos Trabalhadores Sem-Terra)* *m Brazilian movement for landless workers.*

MT *(abrev de Estado do Mato Grosso)* *m State of Mato Grosso.*

muamba ['mwãnba] *f* -1. *fam* [mercadoria contrabandeada] contraband. -2. [mercadoria roubada] loot.

muambeiro, ra [mwãn'bejru, ra] *m, f* -1. [contrabandista] smuggler. -2. [vendedor de objetos roubados] fence.

muçulmano, na [musuw'mãnu, na] <> *adj* Muslim. <> *m, f* Muslim.

muda ['muda] *f* -1. BOT seedling. -2. ZOOL moult. -3. [vestuário]: ~ **(de roupa)** change (of clothes).

mudança [mu'dãnsa] *f* -1. [ger] move; **fazer a** ~ to move (house). -2. [modificação] change. -3. AUTO gear.

mudar [mu'da(x)] <> *vt* to change. <> *vi* [modificar] to change; ~ **de casa** to move house; ~ **de roupa** to change clothes.

mudez [mu'deʒ] *f* muteness.

mudo, da ['mudu, da] <> *adj* -1. [ger] silent. -2. MED mute. -3. [telefone] dead. <> *m, f* mute.

mugido [mu'ʒidul *m* moo.

muito, ta ['muĩntu, ta] <> *adj* -1. [grande quantidade - no sg] a lot of; **não tenho** ~ **tempo/** ~ **s alunos** I haven't much time/many pupils. -2. *(no sg)* [demais] too much. <> *pron (no sg)* much; *(no pl)* a lot.

◆ muito *adv* -1. [intensamente] a lot; **gostei** ~ **de ir ao cinema** I enjoyed going to the cinema very much; **não gosto** ~ I don't like it very much; ~ **mais** much more; **sinto** ~, **mas não posso** I'm very sorry, but I can't. -2. [muito tempo] a long time; ~ **antes/ depois** a long time before/afterwards; ~ **mais tarde** much later. -3. [freqüentemente] often. -4. *loc:* **quando** ~ at most.

mula ['mula] *f* mule.

mulato, ta [mu'latu, ta] <> *adj* mulatto. <> *m, f* mulatto.

muleta [mu'leta] *f* -1. [para andar] crutch. -2. *fig* [apoio] support.

mulher [mu'ʎɛ(x)] *(pl -es)* *f* -1. [ser] woman; ~ **de negócios** businesswoman; ~ **da vida** prostitute. -2. [esposa] wife.

mulheraço [muʎe'rasul *(pl -s)* **mulherão** [muʎe'rãw] *(pl -ões)* *f* fantastic woman.

mulherengo [muʎe'rẽngul <> *adj* womanizing. <> *m* womanizer.

mulher-feita [mu‚ʎɛx'fejta] *(pl mulheres-feitas)* *f* grown woman.

mulherio [muʎe'riwl *m* -1. [grupo de mulheres] group of women. -2. [as mulheres] women.

multa ['muwtal *f* fine; **dar uma** ~ to fine.

multar [muw'ta(x)] *vt:* ~ **alguém (em R$ 100)** to fine sb (100 R$).

multicolor [muwtʃico'lo(x)] adj multicoloured *UK*, multicolored *US*.

multidão [muwtʃi'dãw] (pl -ões) f -1. [de pessoas] crowd. -2. [grande quantidade] multitude.

multifacetado, da [muwtʃi'fasetadu, da] adj [personalidade, talento] multifaceted.

multiforme [muwtʃi'fɔxmi] adj multiform.

multimídia [muwtʃi'midʒa] adj COMPUT multimedia.

multimilionário, ria [muwtʃimiljo'narju, rja] <> adj multimillionaire (antes de subst). <> m, f multimillionaire.

multinacional [ˌmuwtʃinasjo'naw] (pl -ais) <> adj multinational. <> f multinational.

multiplicação [muwtʃiplika'sãw] (pl -ões) f -1. [ger] multiplication. -2. [aumento] increase.

multiplicar [muwtʃipli'ka(x)] <> vt -1. MAT to multiply. -2. [aumentar] to increase. <> vi MAT to multiply.
 multiplicar-se vp -1. [aumentar] to increase. -2. BIOL to multiply.

múltiplo, pla ['muwtʃiplu, pla] adj multiple.
 múltiplo m multiple.

multiprocessamento [muwtʃiprosesa'mẽntu] m COMPUT multiprocessing.

multirracial [muwtʃixa'sjaw] (pl -ais) adj multiracial.

multiuso [muwtʃi'uzu] adj inv multipurpose.

multiusuário, ria [muwtʃiuz'arju, rja] adj COMPUT multiuser.

múmia ['mumja] f -1. [cadáver] mummy. -2. fig [pessoa] moron.

mundano, na [mũn'dãnu, na] adj mundane.

mundial [mũn'dʒjaw] (pl -ais) <> adj -1. [política, guerra] world (antes de subst). -2. [organização, fama] worldwide. <> m [campeonato] world championship; [de futebol] World Cup.

mundo ['mũndu] m -1. [ger] world; o outro ~ the next world; vir ao ~ to come into the world. -2. [pessoas]: todo o ~ everyone. -3. [quantidade]: um ~ de loads of. -4. loc: estar no ~ da lua to be miles away; prometer ~s e fundos to promise the world; como este ~ é pequeno what a small world; desde que o ~ é ~ since time immemorial.
 Mundo m: Novo Mundo New World; Terceiro Mundo Third World.

munição [muni'sãw] (pl -ões) f ammunition.

municipal [munisi'paw] (pl -ais) adj municipal.

municipalizar [munisipali'za(x)] vt [instituições, serviços] to municipalize.

município [muni'sipju] m -1. [divisão administrativa] local authority. -2. [território] town.

munir [mu'ni(x)] vt: ~ alguém de algo to equip sb with sthg.
 munir-se vp: ~-se de algo to equip o.s. with sthg; ~-se de coragem to arm o.s. with courage; ~-se de paciência to arm o.s. with patience.

mural [mu'raw] (pl -ais) <> adj wall (antes de subst). <> m [pintura] mural.

muralha [mu'raʎa] f wall.

murchar [mux'ʃa(x)] <> vt -1. [planta] to wither. -2. [sentimento] to fade. -3. fig [retrair] to shrink. <> vi -1. [planta] to wilt. -2. fig [pessoa] to droop.

murcho, cha ['muxʃu, ʃa] adj -1. [planta] wilting. -2. [bola] soft. -3. [pessoa - sem energia] languid; [- triste] droopy.

murmurante [muxmu'rãntʃi] adj murmuring.

murmurar [muxmu'ra(x)] <> vt [sussurar] to whisper. <> vi [sussurar] to murmur.

murmurinho [muxmu'riɲu] m -1. [de vozes] murmuring. -2. [de folhas] rustling. -3. [som confuso] murmur.

murmúrio [mux'murju] m -1. [de vozes] murmuring. -2. [de folhas] rustling. -3. [de água] trickling.

muro ['muru] m wall.

murro ['muxu] m punch; dar ~ em ponta de faca fig to bang one's head against a brick wall.

musa ['muza] f muse.

musculação [muʃkula'sãw] f bodybuilding.

muscular [muʃku'la(x)] adj muscular.

musculatura [muʃkula'tura] f musculature.

músculo ['muʃkulu] m -1. ANAT muscle. -2. CULIN sinewy meat.

musculoso, osa [muʃku'lozu, ɔza] adj -1. [cheio de músculo - costas, pernas] muscular; [- carne de comer] tough. -2. fig [forte] tough.

museu [mu'zew] m museum.

musgo ['muʒgu] m moss.

música ['muzika] f ⊳ **músico**.

musical [muzi'kaw] (pl -ais) <> adj musical. <> m musical.

musicar [muzi'ka(x)] vt to set to music.

musicista [muzi'siʃta] mf -1. [músico] musician. -2. [especialista] musicologist.

músico, ca ['muziku, ka] <> adj [profissional] musical. <> m, f musician.

música f -1. [ger] music; ~ de câmara chamber music; ~ clássica classical music. -2. [canção] song.

musicologia [muzikolo'ʒial f musicology.

musicólogo, ga [muzi'kɔlogu, gal m musicologist.

musse ['musi] f CULIN mousse.

mutabilidade [mutabili'dadʒil f mutability.

mutilação [mutʃila'sãw] f -1. [orgânico] mutilation. -2. [de texto] cutting.

mutilado, da [mutʃi'ladu, dal ⬦ adj mutilated. ⬦ m, f cripple.

mutilar [mutʃi'la(x)] vt -1. [pessoa] to mutilate. -2. [texto] to cut.

mutirão [mutʃi'rãw] (pl -ões) m joint effort.

mutreta [mu'tretal f fam cheating; **fazer (uma)** ~ to cheat.

mutuamente [mutwa'mẽtʃil adv mutually.

mútuo, tua ['mutwu, twal adj mutual.

muxoxo [mu'ʃoʃul m tutting.

N

n, N ['enil m -1. [letra] n, N. -2. [quantidade indeterminada] n; **contamos** ~ **vezes a mesma história** we told the story for the nth time.

na [nal = em + a.

-na [nal pron [pessoa] her; [coisa] it; [você] you.

nabo ['nabul m turnip.

nação [na'sãw] (pl -ões) f nation.

nacional [nasjo'naw] (pl -ais) adj national.

nacionalidade [nasjonali'dadʒil f nationality.

nacionalismo [nasjona'liʒmul m nationalism.

nacionalista [nasjona'liʃtal ⬦ adj nationalist. ⬦ mf nationalist.

nacionalizar [nasjonali'za(x)] vt -1. [estatizar] to nationalize. -2. [naturalizar] to naturalize.

nações [na'sõjʃ] fpl ⬥ nação.
⬥ **Nações Unidas** fpl United Nations.

nada ['nadal ⬦ pron indef [coisa alguma] nothing; **não li** ~ **desse autor** I haven't read anything by this author; **antes de**

mais ~ first of all; **de** ~ ! [resposta a obrigado] not at all!, you're welcome!; ~ **de novo** nothing new; ~ **mais** nothing more; **não quero** ~ **mais com ele** I don't want anything more to do with him; ~ **mau** not bad; **não dizer** ~ to say nothing, not to say anything; **não foi** ~ [resposta a 'desculpa!'] don't mention it; **quase** ~ hardly anything, next to nothing; **que** ~ ! nonsense! ⬦ adv [de modo algum] not at all; **não gostei** ~ **do filme** I didn't enjoy the film at all; ~ **menos do que** nothing less than.

nadadeira [nada'dejral f -1. [de animal] fin. -2. [de mergulhador] flipper.

nadador, ra [nada'do(x), ral (mpl -es, fpl -s) m, f swimmer.

nadar [na'da(x)] vi -1. [em piscina, mar, rio] to swim. -2. [estar imerso] to be swimming; ~ **em dinheiro** fig to be rolling in money.

nádegas ['nadegaʃ] fpl buttocks.

nado ['nadul m swimming; **atravessar algo a** ~ to swim across sthg; ~ **borboleta** butterfly (stroke); ~ **de costas** backstroke; ~ **de peito** breaststroke; ~ **livre** freestyle.

NAFTA (abrev de **North American Free Trade Agreement**) f NAFTA.

náilon ['najlõl m nylon.

naipe ['najpil m -1. [cartas] suit. -2. fig [qualidade]: **de bom** ~ first class.

namorado, da [namo'radu, dal ⬦ adj enamoured. ⬦ m, f boyfriend (f girlfriend).

namorador, ra [namora'do(x), ral adj flirtatious.

namorar [namo'ra(x)] ⬦ vt -1. [manter namoro] to be going out with. -2. [cobiçar] to covet. -3. [fitar] to stare longingly at. ⬦ vi -1. [manter namoro] to be going out together. -2. [trocar carícias] to flirt.

namoro [na'morul m relationship.

nanquim [nãŋ'kĩl m Indian ink.

não [nãwl ⬦ adv -1. [resposta] no. -2. [negação] not; **ela é médica,** ~ **é?** she's a doctor, isn't she?; **agora** ~ not now; **como** ~ ? why not?; ~ **muito** not much; ~ **sei** I don't know; ~ **tem de quê** [resposta a 'obrigado'] not at all, you're welcome; **pois** ~ ! [como interj] of course! ⬦ m [recusa] refusal.

não-governamental [nãwgoverne-mẽ'tawl (pl -ais) adj non-governmental.

naquela [na'kɛlal = em + aquela.

naquele [na'kelil = em + aquele.

naquilo [na'kilul = em + aquilo.

narcisismo [naxsi'ziʒmu] *m* narcissism.

narcisista [naxsi'ziʃta] *adj* narcissistic.

narciso [nax'sizu] *m BOT* narcissus.

narcótico, ca [nax'kɔtʃiku, ka] *adj* narcotic.

◆ **narcótico** *m* narcotic.

narcotráfico [naxko'trafiku] *m* drug traffic.

narina [na'rina] *f* nostril.

nariz [na'riʃ] (*pl* -es) (*pl* -es) *f* -1. [ger] nose. - 2. *loc*: meter o ~ em to stick one's nose into; **sou dono do meu ~** I know my own mind.

narração [naxa'sãw] (*pl* -ões) *f* -1. [conto] story. - 2. [relato] narrative.

narrador, ra [naxa'do(x), ra] *m, f* narrator.

narrar [na'xa(x)] *vt* -1. [contar] to describe. - 2. [relatar] to recount.

narrativo, va [naxa'tʃivu, va] *adj* narrative.

◆ **narrativa** *f* = narração.

nas [naʃ] = em + as.

-nas [naʃ] *pron pl* [elas] them; [vocês] you.

NASA (*abrev de* National Aeronautics and Space Administration) *f* NASA.

nascença [na'sẽsa] *f* [nascimento] birth; de ~ from birth; ela é surda de ~ she has been deaf from birth; **marca de ~** birthmark.

nascente [na'sẽtʃi] ◇ *adj* -1. [interesse, povo] emerging. - 2. [planta] sprouting. ◇ *m* -1. [fonte] spring. - 2. [nascer do sol] sunrise. - 3. [leste] east.

nascer [na'se(x)] *vi* -1. [vir ao mundo] to be born. - 2. [brotar] to sprout. - 3. [originar-se] to originate. - 4. [surgir - sol, lua] to rise; [- dia] to dawn. - 5. [formar-se] to be born. - 6. [ter aptidão]: **ele nasceu para o comércio** he is a born businessman. - 7. [aparecer] to appear. - 8. *loc*: ~ em berço de ouro to be born with a silver spoon in one's mouth; ~ de novo to take on a new lease of life; **eu não nasci ontem** I wasn't born yesterday.

nascido, da [na'sidu, da] *adj* [pessoa] born; **bem ~** from a good family.

nascimento [nasi'mẽtu] *m* -1. [nascença] birth; de ~ since birth. - 2. *fig* [origem] origin.

NASDAQ (*abrev de* National Association of Securities Dealers Automated Quotation) *f* NASDAQ.

nata [na'tal] *f* cream.

natação [nata'sãw] *f* swimming.

natal [na'taw] (*pl* -ais) *adj* native; **terra ~** birthplace.

◆ **Natal** *m* Christmas; **Feliz Natal!** happy Christmas!, merry Christmas!

natalidade [natali'dadʒi] *f* birth rate.

natalino, na [nata'linu, na] *adj* Christmas (*antes de subst*).

nativo, va [na'tʃivu, va] ◇ *adj* native. ◇ *m, f* native.

nato, ta [na'tu, ta] *adj*: **ele é um escritor ~** he is a born writer.

natural [natu'raw] (*pl* -ais) ◇ *adj* -1. [ger] natural; **ao ~** *CULIN* uncooked. - 2. [nascido]: **ser ~ de** to be a native of. ◇ *m, f* [nativo] native.

naturalidade [naturali'dadʒi] *f* -1. [espontaneidade] spontaneity. - 2. [local de nascimento]: **ele é de ~ brasileira** he is Brazilian by birth.

naturalismo [natura'liʒmu] *m ARTE* naturalism.

naturalista [natura'liʃta] *mf* naturalist.

naturalização [naturaliza'sãw] *f* naturalization.

naturalizado, da [naturali'zadu, da] ◇ *adj* naturalized. ◇ *m, f* naturalized citizen.

naturalizar-se [naturali'zaxsi] *vp* to become naturalized.

naturalmente [naturaw'mẽtʃi] ◇ *adv* [evidentemente] naturally. ◇ *interj* of course!

natureza [natu'reza] *f* -1. [ger] nature. - 2. [espécie] kind.

natureza-morta [natuˌreza'mɔxta] (*pl* naturezas-mortas) *f* still life.

naufragar [nawfra'ga(x)] *vi* -1. [embarcação] to be wrecked. - 2. [pessoa] to be shipwrecked. - 3. *fig* [fracassar] to fail.

naufrágio [naw'fraʒju] *m* -1. [de embarcação, pessoa] shipwreck. - 2. *fig* [fracasso] failure.

náufrago, ga ['nawfragu, ga] *m* (shipwreck) survivor, castaway.

náusea ['nawzja] *f* nausea.

nausear [naw'zja(x)] ◇ *vt* -1. [enjoar] to make sick. - 2. [repugnar] to nauseate. ◇ *vi* [sentir náusea] to feel sick.

náutico, ca ['nawtʃiku, ka] *adj* nautical.

◆ **náutica** *f ESP* seamanship.

naval [na'vaw] (*pl* -ais) *adj* naval; **construção ~** shipbuilding.

navalha [na'vaʎa] *f* -1. [de barba] razor blade. - 2. [faca] blade.

navalhada [nava'ʎada] *f* stab.

nave ['navi] *f* -1. [de igreja] nave. - 2. *LITER* [embarcação] ship; ~ **espacial** spaceship.

navegação [navega'sãw] (*pl* -ões) *f* voyage; **companhia de ~** shipping line.

navegante [nave'gãtʃi] *mf* navigator.

navegável [nave'gavew] (*pl* -eis) *adj* navigable.

navio [na'viw] *m* ship; ~ **de guerra** warship; ~ **mercante** merchant ship;

ficar a ver ~ s to be left high and dry.

navio-petroleiro [na,viwpetro'lejrul (*pl* **navios-petroleiros**) *m* oil tanker.

nazismo [na'ziʒmul *m* Nazism.

nazista [na'ziʃta] ⟨⟩ *adj* Nazi. ⟨⟩ *mf* Nazi.

NBA (*abrev de* **National Basketball Association**) *f* NBA.

NE (*abrev de* **Nordeste**) *m* NE.

neblina [ne'blina] *f* mist.

nebulosa [nebu'lɔzal *f* ⟩ **nebuloso**.

nebulosidade [nebulozi'dadʒi] *f* cloudiness.

nebuloso, osa [nebu'lozu, ɔzal *adj* **-1.** [ger] cloudy. **- 2.** *fig* [sombrio] dark. **- 3.** *fig* [indefinido] nebulous. **- 4.** *fig* [obscuro] nebulous.

➡ **nebulosa** *f ASTRON* nebula.

necessário, ria [nese'sarju, rja] ⟨⟩ *adj* necessary. ⟨⟩ *m* necessities (*pl*); **o ~** the necessities.

necessidade [nesesi'dadʒi] *f* [o que se necessita] necessity; **em caso de ~** in case of necessity, if need be.

➡ **necessidades** *fpl* **-1.** [privação] need (*sg*). **- 2.:** **fazer suas ~** *fam* [defecar, urinar] to spend a penny.

necessitado, da [nesesi'tadu, dal *adj*: **~ (de)** in need (of).

➡ **necessitados** *mpl*: **os ~** [miseráveis] the needy.

necessitar [nesesi'ta(x)] ⟨⟩ *vt* to need. ⟨⟩ *vi* to be in need; **~ de** to need.

necrotério [nekro'tɛrju] *m* mortuary *UK*, morgue *US*.

néctar ['nɛkta(x)] (*pl* **-es**) *m* nectar.

nectarina [nekta'rina] *f* nectarine.

nefasto, ta [ne'faʃtu, tal *adj* **-1.** [agourento] ominous. **- 2.** [trágico] tragic. **- 3.** [nocivo] harmful.

negação [nega'sãw] (*pl* **-ões**) *f* **-1.** [recusa] refusal. **- 2.** [inaptidão]: **ser uma ~ em algo** to be hopeless at sthg. **- 3.** [desmentido] denial.

negar [ne'ga(x)] *vt* **-1.** [ger] to deny. **- 2.** [recusar, não permitir] to refuse.

➡ **negar-se** *vp* [recusar-se] to refuse.

negativo, va [nega'tʃivu, val ⟨⟩ *adj* negative. ⟨⟩ *adv*: **~!** nope!

➡ **negativo** *m FOT* negative.

➡ **negativa** *f* [recusa] refusal.

negligência [negli'ʒẽnsja] *f* negligence.

negligente [negli'ʒẽntʃil *adj* negligent.

negociação [negosja'sãw] (*pl* **-ões**) *f* **-1.** [transação] transaction. **- 2.** [entendimento] negotiation.

negociante [nego'sjãntʃil *mf* businessman (*f* businesswoman).

negociar [nego'sja(x)] ⟨⟩ *vi* **-1.** *COMM*: **~ (com algo)** to trade (in sthg); **~**

com alguém/algo to negotiate with sb/sthg. **- 2.** [discutir] to negotiate. ⟨⟩ *vt* **-1.** [combinar] to negotiate. **- 2.** *COM* to trade.

negociata [nego'sjatal *f* crooked deal.

negociável [nego'sjavew] (*pl* **-eis**) *adj inv* negotiable.

negócio [ne'gɔsju] *m* **-1.** *COM* business; **homem de ~s** businessman. **- 2.** [transação] deal; **fechar um ~** to make a deal; **~ da China** very profitable deal; **~ fechado!** it's a deal! **- 3.** [caso] matter; **o ~ é o seguinte** the deal is as follows. **- 4.** *fam* [coisa] thing; **que ~ é esse?** what's the big idea?

negro, gra ['negru, gral ⟨⟩ *adj* black. ⟨⟩ *m, f* black.

negrume [ne'grumil *m* darkness.

nela ['nɛlal = **em + ela**.

nele ['nelil = **em + ele**.

nem [nẽl *conj* nor; **nem ... nem ...** neither ... nor ...; **eles ~ (sequer) me convidaram** they didn't even invite me; **~ eu!** nor was I!; **ele foi agressivo mas ~ por isso você deveria ter retrucado** he was aggressive but that was no reason for you to retaliate; **~ sempre** not always; **~ tanto** not so much; **eles saíam sem ~ avisar** they would go out even without warning.

➡ **nem que** *loc conj* even if.

nenhum, ma [ne'nũ, mal (*mpl* **-ns**, *fpl* **-s**) ⟨⟩ *adj* **ele não tomou nenhuma decisão** he has made no decision; **em ~ momento** at no time. ⟨⟩ *pron* none; **não comprei livro ~** I didn't buy a single book; **não comprei ~** I didn't buy any; **não quero nenhuma bebida** I don't want anything to drink; **não tive problema ~** I didn't have a single problem; **~ professor é perfeito** no teacher is perfect; **todos os professores são pessoas, ~ é perfeito** all teachers are human; none is/are perfect; **~ de** none of, not one of; **~ dos dois** neither of them, neither of the two; **~ dos cinco** none of the five, not one of the five.

neoclássico, ca [nɛw'klasiku, kal *adj* neoclassical.

➡ **Neoclássico** *m* neoclassical period.

neófito, ta [ne'ɔfitu, tal *adj* [principiante] beginner.

neoliberal [neoliberawl (*pl* **-ais**) ⟨⟩ *adj* neoliberal. ⟨⟩ *mf* neoliberal.

neoliberalismo [nɛw'liberaliʒmul *m* neoliberalism.

neologismo [nɛwlo'giʒmul *m* neologism.

néon ['nɛõl, **neônio** [ne'onjul *m* neon.

neonazismo [nɛw'naziʒmul m neo-Naz-ism.

Nepal [ne'pawl n Nepal.

nervo ['nɛxvul m -1. ANAT nerve; **estar uma pilha de ~ s** to be a bag of nerves. -2. [na carne] sinew. -3. fig [força] driving force.

nervosismo [nexvo'ziʒmul m -1. [ger] nervousness. -2. [irritabilidade] irritability.

nervoso, osa [nex'vozu, ɔzal adj -1. [ger] nervous. -2. [irritado] irritable.

nessa ['nɛsal = em + essa.

nessas ['nɛsaʃl = em + essas.

nesse ['nesil = em + esse.

nesses ['nesiʃl = em + esses.

nesta ['nɛʃtal = em + esta.

nestas ['nɛʃtaʃl = em + estas.

neste ['neʃtʃil = em + este.

nestes ['neʃtʃiʃl = em + estes.

netiqueta [netʃi'ketal f COMPUT netiquette.

neto, ta ['nɛtu, tal m, f grandson (f granddaughter).

➤ **netos** mpl grandchildren.

Netuno [ne'tunul n Neptune.

neurologia [newrolo'ʒial f neurology.

neurologista [newrolo'ʒiʃtal mf neurologist.

neurose [new'rɔzil f neurosis.

neurótico, ca [new'rɔtʃiku, kal <> adj neurotic. <> m, f neurotic.

neutralidade [newtrali'dadʒil f neutrality.

neutralizar ['newtrali'za(x)] vt to neutralize.

neutro, tra ['newtru, tral adj neutral.

nevada [ne'vadal f snowfall.

nevado, da [ne'vadu, dal adj -1. [coberto de neve] snow-covered. -2. [branco] snow-white.

nevar [ne'va(x)] vi to snow.

nevasca [ne'vaʃkal f snowstorm.

neve ['nɛvil f snow; **branco feito ~** as white as snow.

névoa ['nɛvwal f fog.

nevoeiro [ne'vwejrul m thick fog.

nevralgia [nevraw'ʒial f neuralgia.

newsgroup [neuʃ'grupil (pl -s) m COMPUT newsgroup.

nexo ['nɛksul m -1. [ligação] connection. -2. [coerência] coherence; **sem ~** incoherent.

Nicarágua [nika'ragwal n Nicaragua.

nicaragüense [nikara'gwẽnsil <> adj Nicaraguan. <> mf Nicaraguan.

nicotina [niko'tʃinal f nicotine.

Nilo ['nilul n: **o ~** the Nile.

ninar [ni'na(x)] <> vt to sing to sleep. <> vi to fall asleep.

ninfeta [nĩn'fetal f nymphette.

ninfomaníaca [nĩnfoma'njakal f nymphomaniac.

ninguém [nĩŋ'gẽjl <> pron indef -1. [nenhuma pessoa] nobody; **~ vai descobrir** nobody will find out; **não conte a ~!** I don't tell anybody!, tell nobody!; **~ respeita mais ~** nobody respects anybody any more; **~ mais** nobody else. -2. fig [pessoa desimportante]: **ser ~** to be nobody. <> m fig [pessoa desimportante]: **esse (zé) ~** that nobody.

ninhada [ni'ɲadal f brood.

ninharia [niɲa'rial f trifle.

ninho ['niɲul m nest; **~ de rato** fam [bagunça] mess.

nipônico, ca [ni'poniku, kal <> adj Nipponese. <> m, f Nipponese.

níquel ['nikewl (pl -eis) m nickel.

nissei [ni'sejl mf child of Japanese parents born in Brazil.

nisso ['nisul = en + isso.

nisto ['niʃtul = em + isto.

nitidez [nitʃi'deʃl f -1. [precisão] sharpness. -2. [clareza] clarity. -3. [brilho] brightness.

nítido, da ['nitʃidu, dal f -1. [preciso] distinct. -2. [claro] clear. -3. [brilhante] bright.

nitrogênio [nitro'ʒenjul m nitrogen.

nível ['nivɛwl (pl -eis) m -1. [ger] level; **em ~ de** level with; **~ superior** UNIV higher education. -2. [condições] standard; **alto/baixo ~** high/low standard. -3. [ferramenta] spirit level.

nivelar [nive'la(x)] vt -1. [aplanar] to level. -2. [equiparar] to compare; **~ algo a** ou **por** ou **com algo** to put sthg on the same level as sthg. -3. [medir] to equal.

➤ **nivelar-se** vp [equiparar-se]: **~-se a** ou **por** ou **com alguém** to measure up to sb.

no [nul = em + o.

NO (abrev de **Noroeste**) m NW.

nó ['nɔl m -1. [laço] knot; **dar um ~** to tie a knot; **~ cego** fast knot; **~ do dedo** knuckle. -2. fig [dificuldade] knotty situation. -3. [ponto crucial] nub.

-no [nul pron [pessoa] him; [coisa] it; [você] you.

nobre ['nɔbril <> adj -1. [ger] noble; **bairro ~** smart area. -2. (antes de subst) [ilustre] honourable. -3. ▷ **horário**. <> m, f nobleman (f noblewoman).

nobreza [no'brezal f nobility.

noção [no'sãwl (pl -ões) f notion; **não ter a menor ~ de algo** not to have the slightest idea about sthg.

➤ **noções** fpl [rudimentos] basics.

nocaute [no'kawtʃi] m -1. BOXE knock-out; **levar alguém a ~/pôr alguém em ~** to knock sb out; fig [prostrar] to lay sb out. -2. [soco] punch.

nocivo, va [no'sivu, va] adj harmful.

noções [no'sõjʃ] pl ⊳ noção.

noctívago [nok'tʃivagu] adj & n = notívago.

nódoa ['nɔdwa] f stain.

nogueira [no'gejra] f walnut tree.

noitada [noj'tada] f -1. [período] night. -2. [de diversão] night out. -3. [de insônia] sleepless night.

noite ['nojtʃi] f -1. [período] night; **à ou de ~** at night; **boa ~!** [cumprimento] good evening!; [despedida] good night!; **da ~ para o dia** from one day to the next, overnight; **esta ~** [a noite passada] last night; [a próxima noite] this evening, tonight; **ontem/hoje/amanhã a ~** yesterday/this/tomorrow evening; **tarde da ~** late at night; **ao cair da ~** at nightfall. -2. [vida noturna] nightlife.

noitinha [noj'tʃiɲa] f: **à ou de ~** at dusk.

noivado [noj'vadu] m -1. [ger] engagement. -2. [festa] engagement party.

noivo, va ['nojvu, va] ⟨⟩ adj engaged. ⟨⟩ m, f -1. [comprometido]: **estar/ser ~ de alguém** to be sb's fiancé (f fiancée), to be engaged to sb. -2. [no altar] groom (f bride).
➡ **noivos** mpl: **os ~s** [no altar] the bride and groom; [na lua-de-mel] newlyweds.

nojento, ta [no'ʒẽtu, ta] adj -1. [que enoja] disgusting. -2. [antipático] loathsome.

nojo ['noʒu] m -1. [náusea] nausea. -2. [repulsa] disgust; **estar um ~** [estar sujo, ruim] to be filthy; **ser um ~** [ser antipático] to be loathsome.

nômade ['nomadʒi] ⟨⟩ adj nomadic. ⟨⟩ mf nomad.

nome ['nomi] m -1. [designação] name; **~ de batismo** Christian name; **~ de família** surname; **de ~** [renome] of renown; [reputação] well known. -2. [autoridade]: **em ~ de algo** in the name of sthg; **em ~ de alguém** on behalf of sb.

nomeação [nomja'sãw] (pl -ões) f -1. [denominação] naming. -2. [para cargo] nomination.

nomeado, da [nomea'du, da] adj nominated.

nomear [no'mja(x)] vt -1. [proferir o nome, conferir o nome a] to name. -2. [conferir cargo a] to appoint.

nonagésimo, ma [nona'ʒɛzimu, ma]

num ninetieth; veja também **sexto**.

nono, na ['nonu, na] num ninth; veja também **sexto**.

nora ['nɔra] f daughter-in-law.

nordeste [nox'dɛʃtʃi] ⟨⟩ adj northeast. ⟨⟩ m northeast.
➡ **Nordeste** m north-east region of Brazil.

nordestino, na [na, noxdɛʃ'tʃinu, na] ⟨⟩ adj -1. northeastern -2. of northeastern Brazil (depois de subst). ⟨⟩ -1. Northeasterner m, f -2. person from north-eastern Brazil.

nórdico, ca ['nɔxdʒiku, ka] ⟨⟩ adj Nordic. ⟨⟩ m, f Nordic.

norma ['nɔxma] f -1. [padrão] norm. -2. [regra] rule; **ter como ~** to have as a norm.

normal [nɔx'maw] (pl -ais) adj [ger] normal.

normalidade [noxmali'dadʒi] f normality.

normalizar [noxmali'za(x)] vt to bring back to normal.
➡ **normalizar-se** vp to return to normal.

normalmente [noxmaw'mẽtʃi] adv -1. [regularmente] as expected. -2. [geralmente] usually.

noroeste [no'rwɛʃtʃi] ⟨⟩ adj [relativo ao noroeste] north-west. ⟨⟩ m northwest.

norte ['nɔxtʃi] ⟨⟩ adj [relativo ao norte] north. ⟨⟩ m -1. [direção] north; **ao ~ de** to the north of. -2. [região] North. -3. [guia] guide.

norte-americano, na [ˌnɔxtʃjameri'kãnu, na] ⟨⟩ adj North American. ⟨⟩ m & f North American.

nortista [nox'tʃiʃta] ⟨⟩ adj [do norte] northern. ⟨⟩ mf [pessoa] northerner.

Noruega [no'rwɛga] n Norway.

norueguês, esa [norwe'geʃ, eza] ⟨⟩ adj Norwegian. ⟨⟩ m, f Norwegian.
➡ **norueguês** m [língua] Norwegian.

nos¹ [noʃ] = **em + os**.

nos² [noʃ] pron pess -1. (objeto direto) us; **convidaram-~ para a festa** they invited us to the party. -2. (objeto indireto) us; **ele ~ deu um presente** he gave us a present; **isto ~ saiu caro** that cost us a lot of money; [para enfatizar] us; **não ~ faça mais isto!** don't do that to us again! -3. (reflexivo) ourselves; **ontem ~ matriculamos na Universidade** yesterday we registered at University. -4. (reciprocamente) each other; **olha-mo-~ com ternura** we looked lovingly at each other. -5. [indicando posse] us; **ela ~ beijou as faces** she kissed us on the cheeks; **ardia-~ a vista** our eyes were stinging. **- 6.** [ao autor] us; **parece-~ ...** it seems to us ...; **neste caso, o que ~ chama a atenção é ...** in this case, what draws our attention is ...

nós [nɔʃ] *pron pess (com + nós = conosco)* **- 1.** [sujeito] we; **~ somos casados** we are married; **~, brasileiros/estudantes, somos ...** we Brazilians/students, are ...; **~, que gostamos de música, ...** we, who love music, ...; **não pude ver o jogo; ~ vencemos?** I couldn't watch the match; did we win?; **~ dois/quatro** the two/four of us, we two/four; **só ~ dois** just the two of us; **~ todos** all of us; **~ mesmos** *ou* **próprios** we ... ourselves; **~ mesmos pintaremos a casa** we shall paint the house ourselves. **- 2.** *(depois de prep)* us; **chegou un convite para ~** an invitation arrived for us, we received an invitation; **o que ele tem contra ~?** what does he have against us?; **você fica para jantar conosco?** are you staying with us for dinner?; **alguns de ~ serão premiados** some of us will be rewarded; **entre ~** [duas pessoas] between the two of us, between you and me; [mais de duas pessoas] among us. **- 3.** [o autor] we; **neste capítulo, o que ~ pretendemos é ...** in this chapter, what we are attempting to do is ... **- 4.** *loc*: **cá entre ~** between ourselves.

-nos [nɔʃ] *pron pl* [eles] them; [vocês] you ⊳ **nos**².

nosso, a [ˈnosu, a] ⟨⟩ *adj* our; **Nossa Senhora** Our Lady; **nossas coisas/brigas** our things/arguments; **um amigo ~ a** friend of ours; **este iate é ~** this yacht is ours. ⟨⟩ *pron*: **o ~ /a nossa** ours; **um amigo ~ a** friend of ours; **a nossa é maior** ours is bigger; **os ~s** [a nossa família] our family; [do nosso time] ours; **ser um dos ~s** *fam* [estar do nosso lado] to be one of ours; **à nossa!** here's to us!
    nossa *interj* [exprimindo espanto] God; **~ mãe!**, **~ senhora!** God!, Holy Mary!

nostalgia [noʃtawˈʒia] *f* **- 1.** [melancolia] nostalgia. **- 2.** [da pátria] homesickness.

nostálgico, ca [noʃˈtawʒiku, ka] *adj* nostalgic.

nota [ˈnɔtal] *f* **- 1.** [ger] note; **tomar ~** to take note; **~ de rodapé** footnote. **- 2.** *COM* bill; **~ fiscal** invoice. **- 3.** *EDUC* mark. **- 4.** [comunicado] notice; **~ oficial** official statement.

notar [noˈta(x)] *vt* [reparar] to note; **fazer ~** to indicate.
    notar-se *vp*: **nota-se que ...** it is clear that ...

notável [noˈtavɛwl] *(pl* **-eis)** *adj* notable.

notebook [ˈnɔtʃibukl] *(pl* **-s)** *m* COMPUT notebook.

notícia [noˈtʃisjal] *f* news *(sg)*; **ter ~s de alguém/algo** to have news of sb/sthg, to hear from sb/about sthg.

noticiário [notʃiˈsjarjul] *m* **- 1.** [de jornal] news section. **- 2.** [rádio, tv] news bulletin. **- 3.** [cinema] newsreel.

notificar [notʃifiˈka(x)l] *vt* **- 1.** [comunicar]: **~ algo a alguém** to notify sb of sthg. **- 2.** JUR to instruct.

notívago, ga [noˈtʃivagu, gal] ⟨⟩ *adj* nocturnal. ⟨⟩ *m, f* [pessoa] sleepwalker.

notoriedade [notorjeˈdadʒil] *f* **- 1.** [fama] fame. **- 2.** [evidência] blatancy.

notório, ria [noˈtɔrju, rjal] *adj* **- 1.** [famoso] famous, well-known. **- 2.** [evidente] blatant; **é público e ~ que ...** it is public knowledge and blatantly clear that ...

noturno, na [noˈtuxnu, nal] *adj* **- 1.** [trem, aula] night *(antes de subst)*; **vôo ~** night flight. **- 2.** [animais, plantas] nocturnal.
    noturno *m* **- 1.** MÚS nocturne. **- 2.** [trem] night train.

noutro [ˈnotrul] = **em + outro**.

nov. *(abrev de* **novembro)** Nov.

nova [ˈnɔval] *f* ⊳ **novo**.

nova-iorquino, na [ˌnovajoxˈkinu, nal] ⟨⟩ *adj* New York *(antes de subst)*. ⟨⟩ *m, f* New Yorker.

novamente [ˌnovaˈmẽtʃil] *adv* **- 1.** [outra vez] once again. **- 2.** [recentemente] recently.

novato, ta [noˈvatu, tal] ⟨⟩ *adj* inexperienced. ⟨⟩ *m, f* novice.

Nova York [ˌnovaˈjɔxkil] *n* New York.

Nova Zelândia [ˌnovazeˈlãdʒjal] *n* New Zealand.

nove [ˈnɔvil] *num* nine; *veja também* **seis**.

novecentos, tas [nɔveˈsẽtuʃ, taʃl] *num* nine hundred; *veja também* **seiscentos**.

novela [noˈvɛlal] *f* **- 1.** RÁDIO & TV soap opera. **- 2.** LITER story.

novelo [noˈvelul] *m* ball of yarn.

novembro [noˈvẽbrul] *m* November; *veja também* **setembro**.

noventa [noˈvẽtal] *num* ninety; *veja também* **sessenta**.

noviço, ça [noˈvisu, sal] *m, f* RELIG novice.

novidade [noviˈdadʒil] *f* **- 1.** [ger] novelty. **- 2.** [notícia] news *(sg)*.

novilho, lha [noˈviʎu, ʎal] *m, f* calf.

novo, nova [ˈnovu, ˈnɔval] ⟨⟩ *adj* **- 1.** [ger] new; **~ em folha** brand new; **o que há de ~?** what's new? **- 2.** [jovem] young. **- 3.** [outro] different. ⟨⟩ *m, f*: **a nova/o novo** the new one.
    de novo *loc adv* again.
    novo *m* unknown.

➤ **nova** *f*: **boa nova** good news; **nova economia** new economy.

novo-rico [novu'xikul (*pl* **novos-ricos**) *m,f* nouveau riche.

noz ['nɔʃ] (*pl* -es) *f* nut.

noz-moscada [ˌnɔʒmoʃ'kada] (*pl* **nozes-moscadas**) *f* nutmeg.

nu, nua ['nu, 'nua] *adj* -1. [ger] bare. -2. [sem roupa] naked. -3. [sem rodeios]: **a verdade nua e crua** the naked truth; **a realidade nua e crua** the stark reality.
➤ **nu** *m* ARTE nude.

nuança [nu'ãnsa], **nuance** [nu'ãsi] *f* nuance.

nublado, da [nu'bladu, da] *adj* cloudy.

nublar [nu'bla(x)] *vt* to cloud.
➤ **nublar-se** *vp* to become cloudy.

nuca ['nuka] *f* nape.

nuclear [nukle'a(x)] (*pl* -es) *adj* -1. TEC nuclear. -2. *fig* [central] central.

núcleo ['nuklju] *m* nucleus.

nudez [nu'deʃ] *f* -1. [de pessoa] nudity. -2. [de coisas] bareness.

nudista [nu'dʒiʃta] ⬦ *adj* nudist. ⬦ *mf* nudist.

nulidade [nuli'dadʒi] *f* insignificance.

nulo, la ['nulu, la] *adj* -1. [sem valor] invalid. -2. [nenhum] non-existent. -3. [inepto] useless.

num [nũ] = **em** + **um**.

núm. (*abrev de* **número**) *m* no.

numa ['numa] *cont* = **em** + **uma**.

numeração [numera'sãw] (*pl* -ões) *f* -1. [ato] numbering. -2. [sistema] numbers. -3. [de calçados, roupas] size.

numerado, da [nume'radu, da] *adj* numbered.

numeral [nume'raw] (*pl* -ais) *m* GRAM numeral.

numerar [nume'ra(x)] *vt* -1. [pôr número em] to number. -2. [pôr em ordem numérica] to place in numerical order.

numérico, ca [nu'mɛriku, ka] *adj* numerical.

número ['numeru] *m* -1. [ger] number; ~ **par/ímpar** even/odd number; **sem-**~ countless; **um sem-**~ **de vezes** countless times; ~ **de telefone/fax** telephone/fax number. -2. [tamanho]: **que** ~ **você calça?** what size shoe do you wear? -3. [edição] issue; ~ **atrasado** back number. -4. [quadro] act.

numeroso, osa [nume'rozu, ɔza] *adj* numerous.

nunca ['nũŋka] *adv* -1. [sentido negativo] never; ~ **mais** never again; **ele quase** ~ **sorri** he hardly ever smiles. -2. [sentido afirmativo]: **como** ~ as never

before; **mais do que** ~ more than ever.

nuns [nũʃ] = **em** + **uns**.

núpcias ['nupsjaʃ] *fpl* wedding.

nutrição [nutri'sãw] *f* nutrition.

nutricionista [nutrisjo'niʃta] *mf* nutritionist.

nutrido, da [nu'tridu, da] *adj* -1. [bem alimentado] well-fed. -2. [robusto] fit.

nutrir [nu'tri(x)] *vt* -1. [alimentar]: ~ **(com/de)** to nourish (with). -2. *fig* [acalentar]: ~ **algo por** to nurture sthg for. -3. *fig* [fornecer]: ~ **algo de** to provide sthg with.
➤ **nutrir-se** *vp* -1. [alimentar-se]: ~**-se de** to obtain nourishment from; ~**-se com** to feed on. -2. [prover-se] *fig*: ~**-se de algo** to supply o.s. with.

nutritivo, va [nutri'tʃivu, va] *adj* nourishing; **valor** ~ nutritional value.

nuvem ['nuvẽ] (*pl* -ns) *f* -1. [do céu] cloud. -2. *fig* [aglomeração - de pessoas] swarm; [- de insetos, gases, fumaça] cloud. -3. *loc*: **estar nas nuvens** to daydream; **passar em brancas nuvens** [data] to pass by unnoticed.

o¹, O [ɔ] *m* [letra] o, O.

o², a [u, a] (*mpl* **os**, *fpl* **as**) ⬦ *artigo definido* -1. [com substantivo genérico] the; **a casa** the house; **o hotel** the hotel; **os alunos** the students; **os noivos** the bride and groom. -2. [com substantivo abstrato]: **a vida** life; **o amor** love. -3. [com adjetivo substantivado]: **o melhor/pior** the best/worst; **vou fazer o possível** I'll do what I can. -4. [com nomes geográficos]: **a Inglaterra** England; **o Amazonas** the Amazon; **o Brasil** Brazil; **os Estados Unidos** the United States; **os Pireneus** the Pyrenees. -5. [indicando posse]: **quebrei o nariz** I broke my nose; **estou com os pés frios** my feet are cold. -6. [enfaticamente]: **ele pensa que é O gênio** he thinks he is THE genius; **ela é A supermãe** she is THE supermother; **Tentação, O perfume** Tentação, THE perfume. -7. [com nome de pessoa]: **o Alexandre** Alexandre; **a Helena** Helena; **o Sr. Mendes** Mr. Mendes.

- 8. [por cada] a, per; **3 reais a dúzia** 3 reals a dozen; **o linho é 5 reais o metro** linen is 5 reals per metre. **- 9.** [em datas, períodos] the; **o dois de abril** the second of April *UK*, April second *US*; **o pós-guerra** the post-war years. **-10.** [em títulos] the; **Alexandre, o Grande** Alexander, the Great; **D. Maria, a Louca** Queen Mary, the Madwoman. ◇ *pron pess* **-1.** [pessoa] him (f her), them *pl*; **eu a deixei ali** I left her there; **ela o amava muito** she loved him very much; **não os vi** I didn't see them. **- 2.** [você, vocês] you; **eu o chamei, Dirceu, mas você não ouviu** I called you, Dirceu, but you didn't hear; **prazer em conhecê-los, meus senhores** pleased to meet you, gentlemen. **-3.** [coisa] it, them *pl*; **onde estão as chaves?** não consigo achá-las where are the keys? I can't find them; **este paletó é novo, comprei-o no mês passado** this jacket is new, I bought it last month. **- 4.** [em locuções]: **o/a da esquerda** the one on the left; **os que desejarem vir terão de pagar** those who wish to come will have to pay; **o que (é que) ...?** what (is) ...?; **o que (é que) está acontecendo?** what's going on?; **era o que eu pensava** it's just as I thought; **o quê?** what? ◇ *pron dem* **-1.** [especificativo - com substantivo] the one; **feche a porta da frente e a dos fundos** close the front door and the one at the back; **compre o que for mais barato** buy the one that's cheapest; **2.** [- com adjetivo] the; **destas balas, adoro as vermelhas** out of these sweets, I prefer the red ones **3.** [indicando posse] one; **minha casa e a de Teresa** my house and Teresa's, mine and Teresa's house; **minha casa é grande e a de Teresa é pequena** my house is big and Teresa's one is small.

ó [ɔ] *interj* oh!

ô [o] *interj* oh!

OAB (*abrev de* Ordem dos Advogados do Brasil) *f Brazilian law society*.

oásis [ɔ'aziʃ] *m inv* oasis.

oba ['oba] *interj* **-1.** [de alegria] great! **-2.** [cumprimento] hi!

obcecado, da [obise'kadu, da] *adj* obsessive.

obedecer [obede'se(x)] ◇ *vt* to obey. ◇ *vi*: **~ a** (alguém/algo) to obey (sb/sth).

obediência [obe'dʒjẽnsja] *f* obedience.

obediente [obe'dʒjẽntʃi] *adj* obedient.

obeso, sa [o'bezu, za] ◇ *adj* obese. ◇ *m, f* obese person.

óbito ['ɔbitu] *m* death.

objeção [obʒe'sãw] (*pl* -ões) *f* **-1.**

[contestação] objection. **- 2.** [obstáculo] obstacle; **fazer** *ou* **pôr ~ a** to make an objection to.

objetivo, va [obʒe'tʃivu, va] *adj* objective.
➥ **objetivo** *m* objective, aim.

objeto [ob'ʒɛtul *m* **-1.** [coisa] object. **-2.** [de estudo] subject.

oblíquo, qua [o'blikwu, kwa] *adj* **-1.** [diagonal - luz, chuva, traço] slanting; [- terreno, reta] sloping; [- ângulo] oblique. **- 2.** *fig* [dissimulado] devious.

oblongo, ga [ob'lõŋgu, ga] *adj* oblong.

oboé [o'bwɛl *m* oboe.

obra ['ɔbra] *f* **-1.** [trabalho] work; **~ de arte** work of art; **ser ~ de alguém** *fig* to be the work of sb. **- 2.** *CONSTR* works (*pl*); **em ~s** under repair.

obra-prima [,ɔbra'prima] (*pl* obras-primas) *f* **-1.** [melhor obra] masterpiece. **-2.** [perfeição]: **ser/estar uma ~** to be a work of art.

obrigação [obriga'sãw] (*pl* -ões) *f* **-1.** [dever] obligation. **- 2.** *COM* bond.

obrigado, da [obri'gadu, da] *interj* [agradecimento]: **(muito) ~ (por)** thank you (very much) (for).

obrigar [obri'ga(x)] *vt*: **~ alguém a fazer algo** [forçar] to force sb to do sthg; [impor] to require sb to do sthg; [induzir] to compel sb to do sthg.
➥ **obrigar-se** *vp* to take it upon o.s.

obrigatoriedade [obrigatorje'dadʒi] *f* obligatory nature.

obrigatório, ria [obriga'tɔrju, rja] *adj* obligatory.

obsceno, na [obi'senu, na] *adj* obscene.

obscurecer [obiʃkure'se(x)] *vt* **-1.** [escurecer] to darken. **-2.** *fig* [entristecer] to trouble. **-3.** *fig* [prejudicar] to damage; *fig* [perturbar] to unsettle.

obscuridade [obiʃkuri'dadʒi] *f* **-1.** [escuridão] darkness. **- 2.** [anonimato] obscurity. **- 3.** *fig* [esquecimento] obscurity.

obscuro, ra [obi'ʃkuru, ra] *adj* **-1.** [escuro] dark. **- 2.** *fig* [desconhecido, confuso] obscure.

obséquio [obi'zɛkjul *m* favour *UK*, favor *US*; **por ~** please.

observação [obizexva'sãw] (*pl* -ões) *f* **-1.** [ato] observation. **- 2.** [comentário] remark. **- 3.** [cumprimento] observance.

observador, ra [obisexva'do(x), ra] (*pl* -es, *fpl* -s) ◇ *adj* [perspicaz] observant. ◇ *m, f* observer.

observar [obisex'va(x)] *vt* **-1.** [ger] to observe. **-2.** [contemplar] to look at. **-3.**: **~ que** [notar] to notice that; [comentar] to remark that.

observatório [obisexva'tɔrjul] *m* observatory.

obsessão [obse'sãwl] (*pl* -ões) *f* obsession.

obsessivo, va [obse'sivu, val *adj* obsessive.

obsoleto, ta [obso'letu, tal *adj* obsolete.

obstante [obiʃ'tãntʃil] ➤ **não obstante** ⋄ *loc conj* nevertheless. ⋄ *loc prep* in spite of.

obstetra [obʃ'tɛtral *mf* obstetrician.

obstinado, da [obiʃtʃi'nadu, dal *adj* -1. [perseverante] obdurate. -2. [teimoso] obstinate.

obstrução [obʃtru'sãwl] (*pl* -ões) *f* -1. [entupimento] blockage. -2. [impedimento] obstruction.

obstruir [obiʃ'trwi(x)l] *vt* -1. [entupir] to block. -2. [impedir] to obstruct.

obtenção [obitẽn'sãwl] (*pl* -ões) *f* -1. [aquisição] acquisition. -2. [consecução] achievement.

obter [obi'te(x)l] *vt* -1. [diploma, verbas, absolvição] to obtain. -2. [desempenho, sucesso] to achieve.

obturação [obtura'sãwl] (*pl* -ões) *f* [de dente] filling.

obturador [obtura'do(x)l] (*pl* -es) *m* FOT shutter.

obturar [obtu'ra(x)l] *vt* [dente] to fill.

obtuso, sa [obi'tuzu, zal *adj* -1. [arredondado] blunt. -2. [bronco] obtuse. -3. [obscuro] obscure.

óbvio, via [ˈɔbvju, vjal *adj* obvious; é ∼! of course!
➤ **óbvio** *m*: o ∼ the obvious; ser o ∼ ululante to be blatantly obvious.

ocasião [oka'zjãw] (*pl* -ões) *f* -1. [ger] time; **em certas ocasiões** sometimes. -2. [oportunidade]: **aproveitar a** ∼ to seize the moment; **ter** ∼ **de fazer algo** to have the opportunity to do sthg.

ocasional [okazjo'nawl (*pl* -ais) *adj* chance (*antes de subst*).

ocasionar [okazjo'na(x)l *vt* [proporcionar]: ∼ **algo a alguém** to afford sb sthg.

ocaso [o'kazul *m* -1. [do sol] sunset. -2. *fig* [fim] end. -3. *fig* [decadência] decline.

Oceania [osjã'nial *n* Oceania.

oceânico, ca [o'sjãniku, kal *adj* oceanic.

oceano [o'sjãnul *m* [mar] ocean; ∼ **Antártico** Antarctic Ocean; ∼ **Atlântico** Atlantic Ocean; ∼ **Ártico** Arctic Ocean; ∼ **Índico** Indian Ocean; ∼ **Pacífico** Pacific Ocean.

oceanografia [osjanogra'fial *f* oceanography.

ocidental [osidẽn'tawl (*pl* -ais) ⋄ *adj* western. ⋄ *m, f* westerner.

ocidentalizar [osidẽntali'za(x)l *vt* to westernize.
➤ **ocidentalizar-se** *vp* to become westernized.

ocidente [osi'dẽntʃil *m* west.
➤ **Ocidente** *m*: o **Ocidente** the West.

ócio [ˈɔsjul *m* -1. [tempo livre] free time. -2. [desocupação]: **estar no** ∼ to be unoccupied. -3. [indolência] idleness.

ocioso, sa [o'sjozu, zal *adj* -1. [desocupado] unoccupied. -2. [improdutivo] unproductive. -3. [indolente] idle. -4. [inútil] useless.

oco, oca [ˈoku, ˈokal *adj* -1. [vazio] hollow. -2. *fig* [fútil] empty.

ocorrência [oko'xẽnsjal *f* -1. [acontecimento] event; ∼ **policial** police matter. -2. [circunstância] circumstance.

ocorrer [oko'xe(x)l *vi* -1. [acontecer] to occur. -2. [vir à memória]: ∼ **a alguém** to occur to sb.

ocre [ˈɔkril ⋄ *adj* ochre *UK (antes de subst)*, ocher *US (antes de subst)*. ⋄ *m* ochre.

octógono [ok'tɔgonul *m* octagon.

ocular [oku'la(x)l *adj* ocular.

oculista [oku'liʃtal *mf* oculist, ophthalmologist.

óculo [ˈɔkulul *m* -1. [de navio] porthole. -2. ARQUIT oculus.
➤ **óculos** *mpl* glasses (*pl*); ∼**s escuros** sunglasses.

ocultar [okuw'ta(x)l *vt* to conceal.

ocultas [o'kuwtaʃl ➤ **às ocultas** *loc adv* secretly.

ocultismo [okuw'tʃiʒmul *m* occultism.

oculto, ta [o'kuwtu, tal *adj* -1. [secreto, desconhecido] hidden. -2. [sobrenatural] occult.

ocupação [okupa'sãwl (*pl* -ões) *f* -1. [ger] occupation. -2. [de um espaço] occupancy.

ocupado, da [oku'padu, dal *adj* -1. [ger] occupied. -2. [atarefado] busy. -3. TELEC engaged *UK*, busy *US*; **dar (sinal de)** ∼ to give the engaged tone *UK*, to give the busy signal *US*.

ocupante [oku'pãntʃil *mf* occupant.

ocupar [oku'pa(x)l *vt* -1. [ger] to occupy. -2. [atrair] to attract.
➤ **ocupar-se** *vp* -1. [preencher tempo] to keep o.s. occupied. -2. [cuidar de]: ∼**-se com alguém/algo** to look after sb/sthg.

odalisca [oda'liʃkal *f* odalisque.

odiar [o'dʒja(x)l ⋄ *vt* to hate. ⋄ *vi* to hate.
➤ **odiar-se** *vp* -1. [a si mesmo] to hate o.s. -2. [um ao outro] to hate one another.

ódio [ˈɔdʒjul *m* hatred, hate.

odioso, osa [oˈdʒjozu, ɔza] *adj* odious.

odisséia [odʒiˈsɛja] *f* odyssey.

odontologista [odõntoloˈʒiʃta] *mf* odontologist, dentist.

odor [oˈdo(x)] (*pl* -es) *m* odour.

OEA (*abrev de* Organização dos Estados Americanos) *f* OAS.

oeste [ˈwɛʃtʃi] <> *adj inv* west. <> *m*: a ~ de west of.

ofegante [ofeˈgãntʃi] *adj* -1. [arquejante] panting. -2. [cansado] breathless.

ofegar [ofeˈga(x)] *vi* to pant.

ofender [ofẽnˈde(x)] *vt* to offend.

ofender-se *vp* [sentir-se insultado] to be offended.

ofensa [oˈfẽnsa] *f* -1. [insulto] insult. -2. [desrespeito] offence *UK*, offense *US*.

ofensivo, va [ofẽnˈsivu, va] *adj* offensive.

ofensiva *f* offensive.

oferecer [ofereˈse(x)] *vt* to offer.

oferecer-se *vp* [propor seus serviços] to offer o.s.; ~-se para fazer algo to offer to do sthg.

oferecido, da [ofereˈsidu, da] *adj pej* easy.

oferenda [ofeˈrẽnda] *f RELIG* offering.

oferta [oˈfɛxta] *f* -1. [ger] offer; em ~ on offer. -2. *ECON* supply.

off-line [ˈɔflajni] *adv COMPUT* off-line.

oficializar [ofisjaliˈza(x)] *vt* to officialize.

oficina [ofiˈsina] *f* workshop; ~ mecânica garage.

ofício [oˈfisju] *m* -1. [profissão] profession. -2. [incumbência] job. -3. *RELIG* office. -4. [correspondência] official letter.

oficioso, osa [ofiˈsjozu, ɔza] *adj* [não oficial] unofficial.

oftalmológico, ca [oftawmoˈlɔʒiku, ka] *adj* ophthalmological.

oftalmologista [oftawmoloˈʒiʃta] *mf* ophthalmologist.

ofuscante [ofuʃˈkãntʃi] *adj* dazzling.

ofuscar [ofuʃˈka(x)] <> *vt* -1. [encobrir] to conceal. -2. [suplantar em brilho] to outshine. -3. [olhos] to dazzle. -4. *fig* [apagar] to overshadow. <> *vi* [turvar a vista] to dazzle.

ogum [oˈgũ] *m god of war in Afro-Brazilian cults*.

oh [ɔ] *interj* oh!

oi [oj] *interj* -1. [como saudação] hi! -2. [como resposta indagativa] mm?

oitavo, va [ojˈtavu, va] <> *num* eighth; a oitava parte the eighth part. <> *m* eighth; *veja também* sexto.

oitenta [ojˈtẽnta] *num* eighty; *veja também* sessenta.

oito [ˈojtu] *num* eight; *veja também* seis; ou ~ ou oitenta all or nothing.

oitocentos, tas [ojtuˈsẽntuʃ] *num* eight hundred; *veja também* seiscentos.

ola [ˈola] *f ESP* Mexican wave.

olá [oˈla] *interj* hello.

olaria [olaˈria] *f* [fábrica] pottery.

óleo [ˈɔlju] *m* oil; ~ de bronzear suntan oil; ~ diesel diesel oil.

oleoduto [oljoˈdutul] *m* pipeline.

oleoso, osa [oˈljozu, ɔza] *adj* greasy.

olfato [owˈfatul] *m* smell.

olhada [oˈʎada] *f* look; dar uma ~ (em) to take a look (at).

olhadela [oʎaˈdɛla] *f* glance.

olhar [oˈʎa(x)] <> *vt* -1. [ger] to look at. -2. [cuidar de] to keep an eye on. -3. [ponderar] to look at. <> *vi* [ver] to look; olha! look!; ~ por [cuidar de] to keep an eye on. <> *m* look.

olhar-se *vp* -1. [ver-se] to look at o.s. -2. [entreolhar-se] to look at each other.

olho [ˈoʎu] (*pl* olhos) *m* -1. [ger] eye; a ~ nu to the naked eye; ~ de sogra *CULIN* Brazilian plum pudding with caramelized topping; estar de ~ em alguém/algo to have one's eye on sb/sthg. -2. [vista] glance; dirigiu os ~ para todos durante o show she cast her eyes over everyone during the show; a ~s vistos in front of one's very eyes. -3. [de queijo] hole. -4. [de agulha] eye; ~ mágico magic eye. -5. *loc*: abrir os ~s de alguém to open sb's eyes; custar/pagar os ~s da cara to cost/pay an arm and a leg; não pregar o ~ not to sleep a wink; pôr alguém no ~ da rua to fire sb; ter o ~ maior do que a barriga to have eyes bigger than one's stomach.

oligarquia [oligaxˈkia] *f* oligarchy.

oligárquico, ca [oliˈgaxkiku, ka] *adj* oligarchical.

oligopólio [oligoˈpɔljul] *m* oligopoly.

olimpíada [olĩˈpjada] *f* Olympiad; as ~s the Olympics.

olímpico, ca [oˈlĩpiku, ka] *adj* Olympic.

olmo [ˈowmu] *m* elm.

OLP (Organização para Libertação da Palestina) *f* PLO.

ombro [ˈõnbrul] *m ANAT* shoulder; ~ a ~ shoulder to shoulder; encolher os ~s to shrug.

OMC (*abrev de* Organização Mundial de Comércio) *f* WTO.

omelete [omeˈlɛtʃil] *f* omelette *UK*, omelet *US*.

omissão [omiˈsãw] (*pl* -ões) *f* omission.

omisso, ssa [oˈmisu, sa] *adj* -1. [negligente, ausente] negligent. -2. [faltando] omitted.

omitir [omi'tʃi(x)] *vt* to omit.
◆ **omitir-se** *vp*: ~-se de algo to refrain from sthg.

omoplata [omo'platal *f* shoulder blade, scapula.

OMS (*abrev de* **Organização Mundial de Saúde**) *f* WHO.

onça [' õnsal *f* -1. [animal] jaguar; **estar/ficar uma** ~ to be wild. -2. [peso] ounce.

onça-pintada ['õnsapĩntada] (*pl* -s) *f ZOOL* jaguar.

onda ['õndal *f* -1. [ger] wave; **pegar** ~ [surfar] to surf. -2. [moda] vogue; **estar na** ~ to be in vogue. -3. *fam* [fingimento] lie. -4. *FÍSICA*: ~ **curta/média/longa** short/medium/long wave. -5. *loc*: **deixar de** ~ to stop messing about; **ir na** ~ **de alguém** to be taken in by sb.

onde ['õndʒi] (*a* + *onde* = *aonde*) ⟨⟩ *adv* (*interrogativo*) -1. where; ~ **fica o museu?** where is the museum?; **não sei** ~ **deixei meus óculos** I don't know where I've left my glasses; **aonde vamos esta noite?** where are we going tonight?; **por** ~ **vieram?** which way did you come?; ~ **quer que** wherever; **carregue sua carteira por** ~ **você for** keep your wallet with you wherever you go. -2. *loc*: **fazer por** ~ to do what's necessary. ⟨⟩ *pron* -1. (*relativo*) where; **a casa** ~ **moro** the house where I live; **o vale por** ~ **passa o rio** the valley where the river flows. -2. (*indefinido*) where; **eles não têm** ~ **morar** they have nowhere to live, they don't have anywhere to live; **pretendo voltar** ~ **estivemos ontem** I intend to go back to where we were yesterday; **até** ~ **eu sei** as far as I know.

ondulação [õndula'sãw] (*pl* -ões) *f* undulation.

ondulado, da [õndu'ladu, dal *adj* -1. [cabelo] wavy. -2. [folha] curled.

oneroso, osa [one'rozu, ɔzal *adj* -1. [dispendioso] costly. -2. [pesado] burdensome.

ONG (*abrev de* **Organização Não-Governamental**) *f* NGO.

ônibus ['onibuʃ] *m inv* bus.

onipotente [,onipo'tẽntʃil *adj* omnipotent.

onipresença [oni'prezẽnsal *f* omnipresence.

onírico, ca [o'niriku, kal *adj* dreamlike.

onisciência [oni'sjẽnsjal *f* omniscience.

onívoro, ra [o'nivuru, ral *adj* omnivorous.

ônix ['oniks] *m* (*inv*) onyx.

ontem ['õntẽ] *adv* yesterday; ~ **de**

manhã yesterday morning; ~ **à noite/à tarde** yesterday evening/afternoon.

ONU ['ɔnul (*abrev de* **Organização das Nações Unidas**) *f* UN.

ônus ['onuʃ] *m* -1. (*inv*) [peso] excess weight. -2. *fig* [encargo] obligation. -3. [imposto pesado] heavy tax.

onze ['õnzil *num* eleven; *veja também* **seis**.

opa ['opal *interj* [de admiração] wow!; [de saudação] hi!

opacidade [opasi'dadʒil *f* opacity.

opaco, ca [o'paku, kal *adj* opaque.

opala [o'palal *f* -1. [mineral] opal. -2. [tecido] *fine cotton material*.

opção [op'sãw] (*pl* -ões) *f* -1. [escolha] choice. -2. [preferência] preference.

opcional [opsjo'naw] (*pl* -ais) *adj* optional.

open market ['opẽn'maxkitʃ] *m* open market.

OPEP (*abrev de* **Organização dos Países Exportadores de Petróleo**) *f* OPEC.

ópera ['ɔperal *f* opera.

operação [opera'sãw] (*pl* -ões) *f* operation.

operacionalidade [operasjionali'dadʒil *f* operating efficiency.

operador, ra [opera'do(x), ral (*mpl* -es, *fpl* -s) *m, f* operator.

operar [ope'ra(x)] ⟨⟩ *vt* -1. [fazer funcionar] to operate. -2. *MED* to operate on. -3. [realizar] to perform. ⟨⟩ *vi* -1. [ger] to operate. -2. *MED* to operate.

operária [ope'rarjal *f* ⟩ **operário**.

operariado [opera'rjadul *m*: **o** ~ the working class.

operário, ria [ope'rarju, rjal ⟨⟩ *adj* -1. [greve] workers' (*antes de subst*). -2. [classe] working. -3. [abelha] worker (*antes de subst*). ⟨⟩ *m, f* [trabalhador] worker.

opereta [ope'retal *m* operetta.

opinar [opi'na(x)] *vi* [emitir opinião]: ~ (**sobre alguém/algo**) to give one's opinion (on sb/sthg).

opinião [opi'njãw] (*pl* -ões) *f* opinion; **a** ~ **pública** public opinion; **dar uma** ~ to give an opinion; **mudar de** ~ to change one's mind.

ópio ['ɔpjul *m* opium.

oponente [opo'nẽntʃil ⟨⟩ *adj* opposing. ⟨⟩ *mf* opponent.

opor [o'po(x)] *vt* -1. [resistência, objeção] to oppose. -2. [argumento, razão] to set.
◆ **opor-se** *vp* [ser contrário]: ~-se (**a algo**) to be opposed (to sthg).

oportunidade [opoxtuni'dadʒil *f* opportunity; **aproveitar a** ~ to seize the opportunity.

oportunista [opoxtu'niʃta] <> *adj* opportunistic. <> *mf* opportunist.

oportuno, na [opox'tunu, na] *adj* opportune; **momento** ~ opportune moment.

oposição [opozi'sãw] (*pl* -ões) *f* -1. [objeção] opposition; **fazer** ~ **a** to oppose. -2. POL: **a** ~ the opposition.

oposicionista [opozisjo'niʃta] <> *adj* opposition (*antes de subst*). <> *mf* member of the opposition.

oposto, ta [o'poʃtu, o'pɔʃta] *adj* -1. [contrário] opposite. -2. [em frente a] opposite.
    ◆ **oposto** *m* [inverso] opposite.

opressão [opre'sãw] (*pl* -ões) *f* -1. [ger] oppression. -2. [sufocação - no peito] tightness; [- no coração] oppression.

opressivo, va [opre'sivu, va] *adj* oppressive.

oprimido, da [opri'midu, da] *adj* oppressed.

oprimir [opri'mi(x)] *vt* -1. [ger] to oppress. -2. [comprimir] to crush.

optar [op'ta(x)] *vi*: ~ **(por/entre)** to opt (for/between); ~ **por fazer algo** to opt to do sthg, to choose to do sthg.

óptico, ca ['ɔptʃiku, ka] <> *adj* optical. <> *mf* optician.
    ◆ **óptica** *f* -1. FÍS optics (*sg*). -2. [loja] optician's. -3. [ponto de vista] point of view.

opulento, ta [opu'lẽtu, ta] *adj* opulent.

opúsculo [o'puʃkulu] *m* -1. [livreto] booklet. -2. [folheto] pamphlet.

ora ['ɔra] <> *adv* [agora] now; **ela** ~ **quer uma coisa,** ~ **quer outra** first she wants one thing, then she wants another; **por** ~ for now. <> *conj* now. <> *interj*: ~ **bolas!** oh hell!

oração [ora'sãw] (*pl* -ões) *f* -1. [reza] prayer. -2. GRAM clause.

oráculo [o'rakulu] *m* oracle.

oral [o'raw] (*pl* -ais) <> *adj* oral. <> *f* oral (exam).

orangotango [orãgu'tãgu] *m* orangutan.

orar [o'ra(x)] *vi*: ~ **(a/por)** to pray (to/for).

órbita ['ɔxbita] *f* -1. ASTRON orbit; **a lua está em** ~ **da Terra** the moon orbits the Earth; **o satélite entrou em** ~ the satellite entered into orbit; **estar fora de** ~ *fam fig* to be out of one's mind. -2. [de olho] socket. -3. *fig* [área] orbit.

orbitar [oxbi'ta(x)] *vt* -1. [descrever órbita] to orbit. -2. *fig* [em torno de alguém] to revolve around.

orçamentário, ria [oxsamẽ'tarju, rja] *adj* budget (*antes de subst*).

orçar [ox'sa(x)] <> *vt* [calcular] to estimate. <> *vi* [avaliar] to make an estimate; ~ **em** to estimate at.

ordeiro, ra [ox'dejru, ra] *adj* orderly.

ordem ['ɔxdẽ] (*pl* -ns) *f* -1. [ger] order; **estar em** ~ to be tidy; ~ **do dia** agenda; **manter a** ~ to maintain order; **tudo em** ~? everything OK?; ~ **pública/social** public/social order; **às suas ordens** at your service; **dar** ~ **a alguém para fazer algo** to tell sb to do sthg; ~ **de pagamento** money order; ~ **de prisão** prison order. -2. [categoria]: **foi um prejuízo da** ~ **de bilhões** there was damage in the order of billions; **de primeira/segunda** ~ first/ second rate.

ordenado, da [oxde'nadu, da] *adj* [organizado] organized.
    ◆ **ordenado** *m* [salário] salary, wages (*pl*).

ordenar [oxde'na(x)] *vt* to order.
    ◆ **ordenar-se** *vp* -1. RELIG to be ordained. -2. [organizar-se] to organize o.s.

ordenhar [oxde'ɲa(x)] *vt* to milk.

ordinal [oxdʒi'naw] (*pl* -ais) *adj* ordinal.

ordinário, ria [oxdʒi'narju, rja] *adj* -1. [ger] ordinary. -2. [de má qualidade] poor. -3. [comum, freqüente] usual.

orégano [o'reganu] *m* oregano.

orelha [o'reʎa] *f* -1. ANAT ear; **estar de** ~ **em pé** *fam fig* to have one's wits about one; **estar até as** ~s **com algo** to be up to one's ears in sthg. -2. [aba] flap.

orelhão [ore'ʎãw] (*pl* -ões) *m* [cabine de telefone público] open telephone booth.

orfanato [oxfa'natu] *m* orphanage.

órfão, ã ['ɔxfãw, fã] <> *adj* orphaned; ~ **de pai/mãe** fatherless/motherless. <> *m, f* orphan.

orgânico, ca [ox'gãniku, ka] *adj* organic.

organismo [oxga'niʒmu] *m* -1. [ger] organism. -2. *fig* [instituição] organization.

organização [oxganiza'sãw] (*pl* -ões) *f* organization.

organizacional [oxganiza'sjonaw] (*pl* -ais) *adj* organizational.

organizador, ra [oxganiza'do(x), ra] *m, f* organizer.

organizar [oxgani'za(x)] *vt* to organize.

órgão ['ɔxgãw] (*pl* -s) *m* -1. [ger] organ. -2. [instituição] body; ~ **de imprensa** news publication.

orgasmo [ox'gaʒmu] *m* orgasm.

orgia [ox'ʒial] *f* orgy.

orgulhar [oxgu'ʎa(x)] *vt* to make proud.

➡️ **orgulhar-se** *vp*: ~**-se de** to pride o.s. on.

orgulho [ox'guʎul] *m* **-1.** [ger] pride. **-2.** [arrogância] arrogance.

orgulhoso, osa [oxgu'ʎozu, ɔza] *adj* **-1.** [brioso] self-satisfied. **-2.** [satisfeito] proud. **-3.** [arrogante] arrogant.

orientação [orjẽta'sãw] (*pl* **-ões**) *f* **-1.** [ger] direction; ~ **profissional** careers guidance. **-2.** [supervisão] supervision. **-3.** *fig* [linha, tendência] orientation.

oriental [orjẽ'taw] (*pl* **-ais**) ◇ *adj* oriental. ◇ *mf* oriental.

orientar [orjẽ'ta(x)] *vt* **-1.** [situar] to orient. **-2.** [nortear] to put in the right direction. **-3.** [supervisionar] to supervise. **-4.** *fig* [aconselhar] to advise.

➡️ **orientar-se** *vp* **-1.** [nortear-se] to orient o.s. **-2.** [aconselhar-se, informar-se] to take advice.

oriente [o'rjẽtʃi] *m* east.

➡️ **Oriente** *m*: **o Oriente** the East; **Extremo Oriente** Far East; **Oriente Médio** Middle East.

orifício [ori'fisju] *m* orifice.

origem [o'riʒẽl] (*pl* **-ns**) *f* **-1.** [início] origin. **-2.** [ascendência] origin; **país de** ~ country of origin. **-3.** [causa] cause; **dar** ~ **a** to give rise to.

original [oriʒi'naw] (*pl* **-ais**) ◇ *adj* original. ◇ *m* [obra] original.

originalidade [oriʒinali'dadʒi] *f* **-1.** [origem] origin. **-2.** [excentricidade] originality.

originalmente [oriʒinaw'mẽtʃil] *adv* originally.

originário, ria [oriʒi'narju, rja] *adj* [proveniente]: ~ **de** native of.

oriundo, da [o'rjũndu, dal *adj*: ~ **de** from.

orixá [ori'ʃal] *m Orisha, a Yoruba divinity that symbolizes the forces of nature and acts as an intermediary between worshippers and the highest divinity.*

orla ['oxlal *f* [faixa] edge.

ornamentação [oxnamẽta'sãw] (*pl* **-ões**) *f* decoration.

ornamental [oxnamẽ'taw] (*pl* **-ais**) *adj* ornamental.

ornamento [oxna'mẽtul *m* ornament.

orquestra [ox'kɛʃtral *f* orchestra.

orquestrar [oxkeʃ'tra(x)] *vt* to orchestrate.

orquídea [ox'kidʒjal *f* orchid.

ortodoxia [oxtodok'sial *f* orthodoxy.

ortodoxo, xa [oxto'dɔksu, ksal ◇ *adj* orthodox. ◇ *m*, *f* RELIG orthodox person.

ortografia [oxtogra'fial *f* orthography, spelling.

ortopédico, ca [oxto'pɛdʒiku, kal *adj* orthopaedic *UK*, orthopedic *US*.

ortopedista [oxtope'dʒiʃtal *mf* orthopaedist *UK*, orthopedist *US*.

orvalho [ox'vaʎul *m* dew.

os [uʃ] ▷ **o²**.

oscilação [osila'sãw] (*pl* **-ões**) *f* **-1.** [movimento] swinging. **-2.** [variação] swing. **-3.** *fig* [hesitação] hesitation.

oscilar [osi'la(x)] *vi* **-1.** [ger] to swing. **-2.** *fig* [hesitar] to hesitate.

Oslo ['oʒlul *n* Oslo.

ósseo, óssea ['ɔsju, 'ɔsjal *adj* bone (*antes de subst*).

osso ['osul (*pl* **ossos**) *m* **-1.** ANAT bone. **-2.** *fig* [dificuldade]: ~**s do ofício** occupational hazards; **ser um** ~ **duro de roer** to be a tough nut to crack.

ostensivo, va [oʃtẽ'sivu, val *adj* **-1.** [pessoa, luxo] ostentatious. **-2.** [policiamento] overt.

ostentar [oʃtẽ'ta(x)] *vt* **-1.** [exibir] to show off. **-2.** [alardear] to display.

osteoporose [oʃtʃjopo'rɔzil *f* osteoporosis.

ostra ['oʃtral *f* oyster.

ostracismo [oʃtra'siʒmul *m* ostracism.

OTAN [o'tãl (*abrev de* **Organização do Tratado do Atlântico Norte**) *f* NATO.

otário, ria [o'tarju, rjal *m*, *f* sucker.

ótico, ca ['ɔtʃiku, kal ◇ *adj* optic, optical. ◇ *m*, *f* [especialista] optician.

➡️ **ótica** *f* **-1.** [loja] optician's. **-2.** *fig* [ponto de vista] viewpoint. **-3.** FÍSICA optics (*sg*).

otimismo [otʃi'miʒmul *m* optimism.

otimista [otʃi'miʃtal ◇ *adj* optimistic. ◇ *mf* optimist.

otimização [otʃimiza'sãw] (*pl* **-ões**) *f* optimization.

otimizar [otʃimi'za(x)] *vt* to optimize.

ótimo, ma ['ɔtʃimu, mal ◇ *adj* (*superl de bom*) best. ◇ *interj* great!

otite [o'tʃitʃil *f* otitis.

otorrinolaringologista [otoxinularĩngolo'ʒiʃtal *mf* ear, nose and throat specialist.

ou [owl *conj* or; ~ ..., ~ ... either ..., or ...; ~ **seja** in other words.

ouriçado, da [ori'sadu, dal *adj fam* prickly.

ouriço [o'risul *m* **-1.** [casca espinhosa] burr. **-2.** ZOOL hedgehog.

ouriço-do-mar [o,risudu'ma(x)] (*pl* **ouriços-do-mar**) *m* sea urchin.

ourives [o'riviʃl *mf inv* goldsmith.

ourivesaria [oriveza'rial *f* **-1.** [arte] goldworking. **-2.** [oficina, loja] goldsmith's.

ouro ['orul *m* **-1.** [metal] gold; **de** ~ *lit*

gold; *fig* [coração] of gold. **-2.** *fig* [dinheiro] money.

◆ **ouros** *mpl* [naipe] diamonds.

ousadia [oza'dʒial *f* daring.

ousado, da [o'zadu, da] *adj* **-1.** [audacioso] audacious. **-2.** [corajoso] daring.

ousar [o'za(x)] ⬦ *vt* to dare. ⬦ *vi* to be daring.

out. (*abrev de* **outubro**) Oct.

outonal [oto'naw] (*pl* **-ais**) *adj* autumnal.

outono [o'tonu] *m* autumn.

outorgado, da [owtox'gadu, da] *adj* granted.

outra [l'otra] *f* ➭ **outro.**

outrem [o'trĕ] *pron* **-1.** *inv (pl)* other people. **-2.** *(sg)* someone else.

outro, outra [l'otru, 'otra] ⬦ *adj* **-1.** [ger] other; ~ **dia** the other day. **-2.** [diferente] another; **de** ~ **modo** in another way; **entre outras coisas** among other things. **-3.** [novo, adicional] another; **no** ~ **dia** the next day; **outra vez** again. ⬦ *pron* another; **o** ~ the other; **nem um, nem** ~ neither one nor the other, neither of them; **os** ~ **s** [pessoas] others; [objetos] the others; **dos** ~ **s** [pessoas] other people's.

◆ **outra** *f*: **a outra** [amante] the other woman; **estar em outra** *fam* to be into something else.

outubro [o'tubru] *m* October; *veja também* **setembro.**

ouvido [o'vidu] *m* **-1.** ANAT ear. **-2.** [audição] hearing; **dar** ~ **s a algo/ alguém** to listen to sthg/sb; **de** ~ by ear.

ouvinte [o'vĩtʃi] *mf* **-1.** RÁDIO listener. **-2.** UNIV auditor.

ouvir [o'vi(x)] ⬦ *vt* **-1.** [pela audição] to hear. **-2.** [atentamente] to listen to. ⬦ *vi* **-1.** [pela audição] to hear; ~ **dizer que** to hear that; ~ **falar de algo/alguém** to hear of sthg/sb. **-2.** [atentamente] to listen. **-3.** [ser repreendido] to get a telling off.

ova [l'oval *f* roe; **uma** ~ ! *fam* no way!

ovação [ova'sãw] (*pl* **-ões**) *f* ovation.

oval [o'vaw] (*pl* **-ais**) *adj* oval.

ovário [o'varju] *m* ovary.

ovelha [o'veʎa] *f* sheep; ~ **negra** *fig* black sheep.

overdose [ˌovex'dɔzi] *f* overdose.

ovni [l'ɔvni] *m* (*abrev de* **Objeto Voador Não-Identificado**) UFO.

ovo [l'ovu] (*pl* **ovos**) *m* ANAT egg; ~ **de codorna** quail egg; ~ **cozido** hard-boiled egg; ~ **estalado** OU **frito** fried egg; ~ **de granja** free-range egg; ~ **mexido** scrambled egg; ~ **de Páscoa**

Easter egg; ~ **quente** boiled egg; **acordar/estar de** ~ **virado** *fam* to get out of bed on the wrong side; **pisar em** ~ **s** to tread on eggshells.

óvulo [l'ovulul *m* ovum.

oxalá [oʃa'lal ⬦ *interj* let's hope. ⬦ *m* RELIG highest Yoruba divinity in Afro-Brazilian cults.

oxidar [oksi'da(x)] *vt* **-1.** QUÍM to oxidize. **-2.** [enferrujar] to rust.

◆ **oxidar-se** *vp* [enferrujar] to rust.

óxido [l'ɔksidul *m* oxide; ~ **de carbono** carbon monoxide.

oxigenado, da [oksiʒe'nadu, da] *adj* **-1.** [cabelo] bleached. **-2.** QUÍM: **água oxigenada** (hydrogen) peroxide.

oxigenar [oksiʒe'na(x)] *vt* **-1.** [ger] to oxygenate. **-2.** [cabelo] to bleach.

oxum [o'ʃul *m* Yoruba water goddess worshipped in Afro-Brazilian cults.

ozônio [o'zonjul *m* ozone.

P

p, P [pel *m* [letra] p, P.

pá [l'pal *f* **-1.** spade; ~ **de lixo** dustpan. **-2.** [de hélice] blade. **-3.** *fam* [quantidade]: **uma** ~ **de** a mass of. **-4.** *loc*: **ser da** ~ **virada** to be of dubious character.

PA (*abrev de* **Estado do Pará**) *m* State of Pará.

PABX (*abrev de* **Private Automatic Branch Exchange**) *m* PABX.

paca [l'pakal ⬦ *mf* ZOOL paca. ⬦ *adv* *fam* bloody; **isso está bom** ~ this is bloody good.

pacato, ta [pa'katu, tal *adj* quiet.

pachorrento, ta [paʃo'ʃĕntu, tal *adj* lumbering.

paciência [pa'sjĕnsjal *f* patience; **perder a** ~ to lose patience.

paciente [pa'sjĕntʃil ⬦ *adj* patient. ⬦ *mf* MED patient.

pacificar [pasifi'ka(x)] *vt* to pacify.

pacífico, ca [pa'sifiku, kal *adj* **-1.** [tranqüilo] tranquil. **-2.** [indiscutível] indisputable.

Pacífico [pa'sifikul *n*: **o (oceano)** ~ the Pacific (Ocean).

pacifismo [pasi'fiʒmul *m* pacifism.

pacifista [pasi'fiʃtal ⬦ *adj* pacifist. ⬦ *mf* pacifist.

paçoca [pa'sɔka] f [doce] *sweet made with peanuts and brown sugar.*

pacote [pa'kɔtʃi] m **-1.** [embrulho] packet. **-2.** *ECON* package.

pacto ['paktul] m [acordo] pact.

padaria [pada'ria] f bakery.

padecer [pade'se(x)] ◇ vt to suffer. ◇ vi: ~ **de algo** to suffer from sthg.

padecimento [padesi'mẽntul] m suffering.

padeiro, ra [pa'dejru, ra] m baker.

padiola [pa'dʒjɔla] f stretcher.

padrão [pa'drãw] (pl **-ões**) ◇ adj [tamanho] standard. ◇ m **-1.** [ger] standard; ~ **de vida** standard of living. **-2.** [desenho] pattern.

padrasto [pa'draʃtul] m stepfather.

padre ['padril] m **-1.** [sacerdote] priest. **-2.** [como título] father.

padrinho [pa'drinul] m **-1.** [testemunha] godfather. **-2.** [paraninfo] guest of honour. **-3.** [protetor] protector.

➡ **padrinhos** mpl [padrinho e madrinha] godparents.

padroeiro, ra [pa'drwejru, ra] m, f patron saint.

padrões [pa'drõjʃ] pl ▷ **padrão**.

padronizar [padroni'za(x)] vt to standardize.

pães ['pãjʃ] pl ▷ **pão**.

pág. (abrev de **página**) f p.

pagã [pa'gã] f ▷ **pagão**.

pagador, ra [paga'do(x), ra] ◇ adj paying. ◇ m, f payer; **ser bom/mau** ~ to be a good/bad payer.

pagamento [paga'mẽntul] m **-1.** [ger] payment. **-2.** [salário]: **dia de** ~ pay day. **-3.** *COM* [prestação, de dívida] repayment; ~ **contra entrega** cash on delivery; ~ **à vista** cash payment.

pagão, gã [pa'gãw, gã] (mpl **-s**, fpl **-s**) ◇ adj pagan. ◇ m, f pagan.

pagar [pa'ga(x)] ◇ vt **-1.** [ger] to pay. **-2.** [compensar, reembolsar] to repay. ◇ vi: ~ **(a alguém)** to pay (sb); ~ **por algo** [desembolsar] to pay for sthg; fig [crime, pecado] to pay for; **você me paga!** fig you'll pay for this!

página ['paʒina] f page; ~ **de rosto** facing page.

pago, ga [pa'gu, ga] ◇ pp ▷ **pagar**. ◇ adj paid.

pagode [pa'gɔdʒi] m **-1.** [templo] pagoda. **-2.** *MÚS* type of samba. **-3.** [festa] party where pagode is danced.

págs. (abrev de **páginas**) fpl pp.

pai ['paj] m **-1.** [ger] father; ~ **adotivo** adoptive father. **-2.** [protetor] protector.

➡ **pais** mpl [pai e mãe] parents.

pai-de-santo [,pajdʒi'sãntul] (pl **pais-de-santo**) m religious and spiritual candomblé leader.

painel [paj'nɛwl] (pl **-éis**) m **-1.** [ger] panel. **-2.** [quadro, panorama] picture. **-3.** *ARQUIT* frame.

pai-nosso [,paj'nɔsul] (pl **pais-nossos**) m Our Father, the Lord's Prayer.

paio ['pajul] m salami-like pork sausage.

paiol [pa'jɔwl] (pl **-óis**) m **-1.** [celeiro] store. **-2.** [depósito] arsenal.

pairar [paj'ra(x)] vi **-1.** [sustentar-se]: ~ **em/sobre** to hover in/over. **-2.** [ameaçar]: ~ **sobre** to hang over.

país [pa'iʃ] (pl **-es**) m country.

paisagem [paj'zaʒẽl] (pl **-ns**) f **-1.** [vista] view. **-2.** [pintura] landscape.

paisano, na [paj'zãnu, na] m, f [civil] civilian.

➡ **à paisana** loc adv in mufti.

País Basco [pa,iʃ'baʃku] n: **o** ~ the Basque Country.

Países Baixos [pa,iziʃ'bajʃuʃ] n: **os** ~ the Netherlands.

paixão [paj'ʃãw] (pl **-ões**) f passion.

pajé [pa'ʒɛ] m Amerindian priest and medicine man.

PAL (abrev de **Phase Alternate Line**) m PAL.

palácio [pa'lasjul] m **-1.** [residência] palace. **-2.** [sede] headquarters (pl).

paladar [pala'da(x)] (pl **-es**) m **-1.** [ger] taste. **-2.** *ANAT* palate.

palafita [pala'fital] f **-1.** [habitação] house built on stilts. **-2.** [estacas] stilts (pl).

palanque [pa'lãŋkil] m **-1.** [de comício] seating. **-2.** [para espectadores] stand.

palavra [pa'lavral] f **-1.** [ger] word; ~ **s cruzadas** crossword (puzzle) (sg); ~ **de ordem** watchword; **ter** ~ to keep one's word; ~ **de honra** word of honour. **-2.** [fala] speaking. **-3.** [direito de falar] right to speak; **dar a** ~ **a alguém** to hand the floor to sb.

palavrão [pala'vrãw] (pl **-ões**) m swear word.

palco ['pawkul] m **-1.** *TEATRO* stage. **-2.** fig [cenário] scene.

paleolítico, ca [paljo'litʃiku, ka] adj paleolithic.

palerma [pa'lɛxma] ◇ adj foolish. ◇ mf fool.

Palestina [paleʃ'tʃina] n Palestine.

palestino, na [paleʃ'tʃinu, na] ◇ adj Palestinian. ◇ m, f Palestinian.

palestra [pa'lɛʃtra] f [conferência] lecture, talk.

paleta [pa'leta] f palette.

paletó [pale'tɔ] m overcoat.

palha ['paʎɐ] *f* straw; **não mexer uma ~** *fam fig* not to lift a finger.

palhaçada [paʎa'sada] *f* -1. [brincadeira] clowning. -2. [cena ridícula] ridiculous sight.

palhaço, ça [pa'ʎasu, sa] *m, f* -1. [artista] clown. -2. *fam* [bobo] clown.

palheiro [pa'ʎejru] *m* [celeiro] hayloft.

palheta [pa'ʎeta] *f* -1. *ARTE* palette. -2. [lâmina - de veneziana] slat; [- de ventilador] blade. -3. [*MÚS* - para dedilhar] plectrum; [- embocadura] reed.

palhoça [pa'ʎɔsa] *f* straw hut.

paliativo, va [palja'tʃivu, va] <> *adj* palliative. <> *m* palliative.

paliçada [pali'sada] *f* -1. [tapume] palisade. -2. *MIL* stockade.

palidez [pali'deʒ] *f* -1. [de cor] paleness. -2. [de pessoa, rosto] pallor.

pálido, da [ˈpalidu, da] *adj* pale.

paliteiro [pali'tejru] *m* toothpick holder.

palito [pa'litu] *m* -1. [para os dentes] toothpick. -2. [biscoito] straw. -3. [fósforo] matchstick. -4. [pessoa magra] matchstick.

PAL-M (*abrev de* **Phase Alternate Line-Modified**) *m* PAL-M.

palma ['pawma] *f* palm.
  ◆ **palmas** *fpl* [aplauso]: **bater ~** to clap.

palmada [paw'mada] *f* smack; **dar/levar umas ~s** to smack/be smacked.

Palmas ['pawmaʃ] *n* Palmas.

palmeira [paw'mejra] *f* palm tree.

palmilha [paw'miʎa] *f* inner sole.

palmito [paw'mitu] *m* Assai palm.

palmo ['pawmu] *m* handspan; **~ a ~** inch by inch.

palpável [paw'pavɛw] (*pl* -eis) *adj* [tangível] palpable.

pálpebra ['pawpebra] *f* eyelid.

palpitação [pawpita'sãw] (*pl* -ões) *f* throbbing.
  ◆ **palpitações** *fpl* palpitations.

palpitar [pawpi'ta(x)] *vi* -1. [pulsar] to throb. -2. [agitar-se] to quiver. -3. [opinar] to speculate.

palpite [paw'pitʃi] *m* -1. [opinião] speculation. -2. [turfe] tip.

palpiteiro, ra [pawpi'tejru, ra] <> *adj* opinionated. <> *m, f* opinionated person.

paludismo [palu'dʒiʒmu] *m* malaria.

pampa ['pãnpa] *m* -1. *GEOGR* pampas. -2.: **às ~s** [com substantivo] loads of; [com adjetivo] extremely; [com advérbio] really.

panaca [pa'naka] <> *adj* dim-witted. <> *mf* dimwit.

Panamá [pana'ma] *n* Panama.

panamenho, nha [pana'meɲu, ɲa] <> *adj* Panamanian. <> *m, f* Panamanian.

pança ['pãnsa] *f fam* paunch.

pancada [pãŋ'kada] <> *adj fam* nuts. <> *f* -1. [golpe] blow; **dar uma ~ em alguém** to hit sb. -2. [batida] hit. -3. [chuva]: **~ d'água** downpour.

pancadaria [pãŋkada'ria] *f* brawl.

pâncreas ['pãŋkrjaʃ] *m* pancreas.

panda ['pãnda] *m ZOOL* panda.

pandarecos [pãnda'rɛkuʃ] *mpl fam*: **em ~** [exausto] shattered; [destruído] in pieces; [moralmente] thoroughly dejected.

pandeiro [pãn'dejru] *m MÚS* tambourine.

pandemônio [pãnde'monju] *m* pandemonium.

pane ['pãni] *f* breakdown.

panela [pa'nɛla] *f* -1. [recipiente] saucepan; **~ de pressão** pressure cooker. -2. *fig* [conteúdo] saucepanful.

panelaço [pane'lasu] *m banging of pots and pans as a form of protest.*

panfleto [pãn'fletu] *m* pamphlet.

pangaré [pãŋga'rɛ] *m* nag.

pânico ['pãniku] *m* panic; **estar/entrar em ~** to panic.

panificação [panifika'sãw] *f* -1. [padaria] bakery. -2. [fabrico] bread making.

pano ['pãnu] *m* -1. [tecido] cloth; **~ de chão** floor cloth; **~ de prato** tea towel; **por baixo/debaixo do ~** *fig* on the quiet; **dar ~ para mangas** *fig* to get people talking. -2. *TEATRO* curtain; **~ de fundo** backdrop.

panorama [pano'rãma] *m* panorama.

panorâmico, ca [pano'rãmiku, ka] *adj* panoramic.

panqueca [pãŋ'kɛka] *f* pancake.

pantanal [pãnta'naw] (*pl* -ais) *m* large swamp.

pântano ['pãntanu] *m* swamp.

pantanoso, osa [pãnta'nozu, ɔza] *adj* swampy.

pantera [pãn'tɛra] *f ZOOL* panther.

pantomima [pãnto'mima] *f TEATRO* pantomime.

pantufa [pãn'tufa] *f* slipper.

pão ['pãw] (*pl* **pães**) *m* -1. [alimento] bread; **~ de forma** tin loaf; **~ de mel** honey bread; **~ dormido** stale bread; **~ francês** small baguette; **~ integral** wholemeal bread; **comer o ~ que o diabo amassou** to go through a bad patch; **com ele é ~, ~, queijo, queijo** you know where you stand with him. -2. [sustento] daily bread; **ganhar o**

~ to earn a crust. **-3.** RELIG Eucharist.

pão-duro [,pãw'durul (*pl* pães-duros) <> *adj* miserly. <> *m, f* miser.

pãozinho [pãw'ziɲul *m* roll.

papa ['papal *f* **-1.** [mingau] pap. **-2.** [pasta] mush; **não ter ~s na língua** to be outspoken.

➤ **Papa** *m* RELIG Pope.

papagaio [papa'gajul <> *m* **-1.** ZOOL parrot. **-2.** COM promissory note. **-4.** AUTO provisional licence. <> *interj fam:* **~ (s)!** golly!

papaguear [papa'gja(x)] <> *vt* [repetir] to parrot. <> *vi* [tagarelar] to chatter away.

papai [pa'pajl *m* daddy.

➤ **Papai Noel** *m*: **o Papai Noel** Father Christmas.

papaia [pa'pajal *m* papaya, pawpaw.

papar [pa'pa(x)] *fam* <> *vt* **-1.** [comer] to gobble. **-2.** [conseguir] to win. <> *vi* to eat.

papear [pa'pja(x)] *vi:* **~ (com/sobre)** to chat with/about).

papel [pa'pɛwl (*pl* -éis) *m* **-1.** [ger] role; **fazer ~ de bobo** *fig* to look like a fool. **-2.** [folha] paper; **~ crepon** crepe paper; **~ de carta** notepaper; **~ de embrulho** wrapping paper; **~ de seda** tissue paper; **~ higiênico** toilet paper; **~ laminado** OU **de alumínio** aluminium foil; **~ ofício** headed paper; **~ pardo** brown wrapping paper; **~ de pared** COMPUT wallpaper. **-3.** [documento] paper; **de ~ passado** officially. **-4.** FIN paper money. **-5.** *gír droga* twist.

papelada [pape'ladal *f* **-1.** [papéis] pile of paper. **-2.** [documentos] stack of papers.

papelão [pape'lãwl *m* **-1.** [papel] cardboard. **-2.** *fig* [fiasco] fiasco.

papelaria [papela'rial *f* stationer.

papel-bíblia [pa'pewbiblial (*pl* papéis-bíblia) *m* India paper.

papel-carbono [pa,pɛwkax'bonul (*pl* papéis-carbono) *m* carbon paper.

papel-manteiga [pa'pewmãntejgal (*pl* papéis-manteiga) *m* tracing paper.

papel-moeda [pa,pɛw'mwɛdal (*pl* papéis-moeda) *m* paper money.

papelote [pape'lɔtʃil *m* *gír droga* twist.

papiro [pa'pirul *m* papyrus.

papo ['papul *m* **-1.** [de ave] crop. **-2.** *fam* [de pessoa] double chin; **estar no ~** to be in the bag; **ficar de ~ para o ar** *fig* to sit on one's hands. **-3.** *fam* [conversa] chat; **~ furado** [mentira] hot air; **bater (um) ~** to (have a) natter.

papo-de-anjo [,papu'dʒjãnʒul (*pl* papos-de-anjo) *m* CULIN baked egg sweet.

papoula [pa'polal *f* poppy.

páprica ['paprikal *f* paprika.

paquera [pa'keral <> *f fam* [paqueração] casual affair. <> *mf* pick-up.

paquerar [pake'ra(x)] *fam* <> *vt* to flirt with. <> *vi* to pull.

Paquistão [pakiʃ'tãwl *n* Pakistan.

paquistanês, esa [pakiʃta'neʃ, ezal <> *adj* Pakistani. <> *m, f* Pakistani.

par ['pa(x)l (*pl* -es) <> *adj* **-1.** MAT even. **-2.** [parelho] paired. <> *m* **-1.** [dupla] pair; **sem ~** peerless. **-2.** [casal] couple. **-3.** [em dança] partner. <> *f* TELEC: **~ trançado** twisted pair.

➤ **a par** *loc adj*: **estar a ~ de algo** to be well informed about sth.

para ['paral *prep* **-1.** [exprime finalidade, destinação] for; **um telefonema ~ o senhor** a phone call for the gentleman; **esta água não é boa ~ beber** this water is not good for drinking; **eu queria algo ~ comer** I would like something to eat; **~ que serve isto?** what's this for? **-2.** [indica motivo, objetivo] (in order) to; **cheguei mais cedo ~ arranjar lugar** I arrived early (in order) to get a seat; **era só ~ lhe agradar** it was only to please you. **-3.** [indica direção] towards; **ela apontou ~ cima/baixo** she pointed upwards/downwards; **olhei ~ ela** I looked at her; **ele seguiu ~ o aeroporto** he headed for the airport; **vá ~ casa!** go home! **-4.** [relativo a tempo]: **de uma hora ~ a outra** from one hour to the next; **quero isso pronto ~ amanhã** I want it done by tomorrow; **estará pronto ~ a semana/o ano** it'll be ready next week/year; **são quinze ~ as três** it's a quarter of three US, it's a quarter to three UK. **-5.** [em comparações]: **é caro demais ~ as minhas posses** it's too expensive for my budget; **~ o que come, está magro** he's thin, considering how much he eats. **-6.** [relativo a opinião, sentimento]: **~ mim** as far as I'm concerned; **~ ele, você está errado** as far as he's concerned, you are wrong. **-7.** [exprime iminência]: **estar ~ fazer algo** to be about to do sth; **o ônibus está ~ sair** the bus is about to leave; **ele está ~ chegar** he'll be here any minute now. **-8.** [em locuções]: **~ com** towards; **~ mais de** well over; **~ que** so that; **é ~ já!** coming up!

Pará [pa'ral *n* Pará.

parabéns [para'bẽɲʃl *mpl* **-1.** [congratulações] congratulations; **dar ~ a alguém** to congratulate sb. **-2.** [por aniversário] congratulations.

parábola [pa'rabola] *f* -**1.** [narrativa] parable. -**2.** *MAT* parabola.

pára-brisa [,para'briza] (*pl* pára-brisas) *m* windscreen *UK*, windshield *US*.

pára-choque [,para'ʃɔki] (*pl* pára-choques) *m* *AUTO* bumper.

paradeiro [para'dejru] *m* whereabouts.

paradisíaco, ca [paradʒi'ziaku, ka] *adj fig* idyllic.

parado, da [pa'radu, da] *adj* -**1.** [imóvel] motionless. -**2.** [sem vida] dull. -**3.** [desativado] stopped. -**4.** [abandonado] axed. -**5.** [em greve] on strike. -**6.** [sem trabalhar] unemployed.
 ⇔ **parada** *f* -**1.** [de ônibus, trem] stop. -**2.** [pausa] break; ~ **cardíaca** cardiac arrest. -**3.** [desfile] parade. -**4.** *MÚS* ~ **de sucessos** hit parade. -**5.** *fam* [dificuldade] obstacle.

paradoxal [paradok'saw] (*pl* -ais) *adj* paradoxical.

paradoxo [para'dɔksu] *m* paradox.

parafernália [parafex'nalja] *f* -**1.** [tralha] paraphernalia. -**2.** [equipamento] equipment.

parafina [para'fina] *f* paraffin.

paráfrase [pa'rafrazi] *f* paraphrase.

parafrasear [parafra'zja(x)] *vt* to paraphrase.

parafuso [para'fuzu] *m* screw; **ter um** ~ **de menos** *fam* to have a screw loose.

parágrafo [pa'ragrafu] *m* paragraph.

Paraguai [para'gwaj] *n*: (**o**) ~ Paraguay.

paraguaio, ia [para'gwaju, ja] ⇔ *adj* Paraguayan. ⇔ *m, f* Paraguayan.

paraíso [para'izu] *m* paradise; ~ **fiscal** *ECON fam* tax haven.

pára-lama [,para'lãma] (*pl* pára-lamas) *m* mudguard.

paralela [para'lɛla] *f* ▷ paralelo.

paralelepípedo [paralele'pipedu] *m* paving stone.

paralelo, la [para'lɛlu, la] *adj* parallel.
 ⇔ **paralelo** *m* parallel.
 ⇔ **paralela** *f* parallel (line).

paralisar [parali'za(x)] *vt* [fazer parar] to paralyse.

paralisia [parali'zia] *f* paralysis.

paralítico, ca [para'litʃiku, ka] ⇔ *adj* paralytic. ⇔ *m, f* paralytic.

paramédico, ca [para'mɛdʒiku, ka] *adj* paramedic.

parâmetro [pa'rãmetru] *m* parameter.

paraninfo [para'nĩfu] *m* sponsor.

paranóia [para'nɔja] *f* -**1.** *PSIC* paranoia. -**2.** *fig* [coletiva] fear.

paranóico, ca [para'nɔiku, ka] *adj* paranoid.

paranormal [paranox'maw] (*pl* -ais) ⇔ *adj* paranormal. ⇔ *mf* psychic.

paranormalidade [paranoxmali'dadʒi] *f* paranormal nature.

parapeito [para'pejtu] *m* -**1.** [de janela] window sill. -**2.** [muro] parapet.

paraplégico, ca [para'plɛʒiku, ka] ⇔ *adj* paraplegic. ⇔ *m, f* paraplegic.

pára-quedas [,para'kɛdaʃ] *m inv* parachute.

pára-quedista [,parake'dʒiʃta] (*pl* pára-quedistas) *mf* -**1.** [quem salta] parachutist. -**2.** *MIL* paratrooper.

parar [pa'ra(x)] ⇔ *vi* -**1.** [deter-se] to stop; ~ **de fazer algo** to stop doing sthg; **sem** ~ non-stop. -**2.** [permanecer] to stay. -**3.** [acabar]: **ir** ~ to end up. -**4.** [interromper-se] to stop. ⇔ *vt* -**1.** [deter] to stop. -**2.** [paralisar] to bring to a standstill.

pára-raios [,para'xajuʃ] *m inv* lightning conductor *UK*, lightning rod *US*.

parasita [para'zita] ⇔ *adj* parasitic. ⇔ *mf* parasite.

parceiro, ra [pax'sejru, ra] *m, f* partner.

parcela [pax'sɛla] *f* -**1.** [parte] portion. -**2.** [de pagamento] instalment. -**3.** [de terreno] plot. -**4.** [do eleitorado] section. -**5.** *MAT* factor.

parcelado, da [paxse'ladu, da] *adj* [pagamento] in instalments.

parcelamento [paxsela'mẽtu] *m* -**1.** [de pagamento] payment by instalments. -**2.** [de terra] distribution.

parcelar [paxse'la(x)] *vt* to divide into instalments.

parceria [paxse'ria] *f* partnership.

parcial [pax'sjaw] (*pl* -ais) *adj* -**1.** [incompleto] partial. -**2.** [não-isento] biased.

parco, ca ['paxku, ka] *adj* [escasso] scanty.

pardal [pax'daw] (*pl* -ais) *m* sparrow.

pardieiro [pax'dʒjejru] *m* ruin.

pardo, da ['paxdu, da] *adj* -**1.** [escuro] dark. -**2.** [mulato] coloured.

parecer [pare'se(x)] ⇔ *m* judgement, opinion. ⇔ *vi* -**1.** [ger] to seem; ~ **a alguém** to seem to sb; ~ **a alguém que** to think that; ~ (**com**) **algo/alguém** to resemble sthg/sb. -**2.** [ser possível]: ~ **que** to look like. -**3.** [aparentar]: **ao que parece** apparently.
 ⇔ **parecer-se** *vp* [assemelhar-se] to resemble one another; ~**se com alguém** to resemble sthg/sb.

parecido, da [pare'sidu, da] *adj*: **ser** ~ (**com alguém/algo**) to be similar (to sb/sthg).

parede [pa'redʒi] *f* wall; **subir pelas** ~**s** to go up the wall.

parente, ta [pa'rẽntʃi, ta] <> *m, f* relative. <> *adj*: ser ~ de alguém to be related to sb.

parentesco [parẽn'teʃku] *m* kinship.

parêntese [pa'rẽntezi] *m* -1. [sinal] parenthesis; **abrir/fechar** ~s to open/close brackets. -2. [digressão] digression; **abrir um** ~ to go off at a tangent.

páreo ['parju] *m* -1. [turfe] race. -2. [disputa] competition; **um** ~ **duro** *fig* a hard nut to crack.

pária ['parja] *m* pariah.

parir [pa'ri(x)] <> *vt* to give birth to. <> *vi* to give birth.

Paris [pa'riʃ] *n* Paris.

parlamentar [paxlamẽn'ta(x)] <> *adj* parliamentary. <> *mf* member of parliament. <> *vi* to discuss.

parlamento [paxla'mẽntu] *m POL* parliament.

parmesão [paxme'zãw] *adj* parmesan.

pároco ['paroku] *m RELIG* parish priest.

paródia [pa'rɔdʒja] *f* parody.

paróquia [pa'rɔkja] *f* -1. *RELIG* parish. -2. *fig* [vizinhança] neighbourhood.

parque ['paxki] *m* park; ~ **de diversões** amusement park; ~ **industrial** industrial park.

parreira [pa'xejra] *f* grapevine.

parricida [paxi'sida] <> *adj* parricidal. <> *mf* parricide.

parte ['paxtʃi] *f* -1. [fração] part; **a maior** ~ **de** the majority of, most; **em grande** ~ largely; **em** ~ in parts; **fazer** ~ **de algo** to belong to sthg; **tomar** ~ **em** to take part in. -2. [lado] side; **à** ~ [separadamente] separately; **em alguma/qualquer** ~ somewhere; **em** ~ **alguma** anywhere; **por toda (a)** ~ everywhere. -3. [quinhão] share. -4. *JUR* party. -5. [denúncia]: **dar** ~ **de algo/alguém** to report sthg/sb.
◆ **da parte de** *loc prep* from.

parteira [pax'tejra] *f* midwife.

participação [paxtʃisipa'sãw] (*pl* -ões) *f* -1. [atuação]: ~ **em algo** participation in sthg. -2. [comunicação]: **fazer uma** ~ **(a alguém) sobre algo** to make a statement (to sb) about sthg. -3. *COM* share.

participante [paxtʃisi'pãntʃi] <> *adj* participating. <> *mf* participant.

participar [paxtʃisi'pa(x)] <> *vi* [tomar parte]: ~ **de algo** to take part in sthg. -2. [compartilhar]: ~ **de algo** to share in sthg. <> *vt* [anunciar]: ~ **algo (a alguém)** to announce sthg (to sb).

particípio [paxtʃi'sipju] *m* participle; ~ **passado/presente** past/present participle.

partícula [pax'tʃikula] *f* particle.

particular [paxtʃiku'la(x)] (*pl* -es) <> *adj* -1. [privado] private. -2. [especial] particular. <> *m* -1. [singularidade] detail. -2. *fam* [conversa] private talk.
◆ **em particular** *loc adv* in private.

particularidade [paxtʃikulari'dadʒi] *f* detail.

particularizar [paxtʃikulari'za(x)] *vt* -1. [especificar] to specify. -2. [detalhar] to go into the details of.

particularmente [paxtʃikulax'mẽntʃi] *adv* [especialmente] particularly.

partida [pax'tʃida] *f* -1. [saída] departure. -2. [ESP - largada] start; [- jogo] game. -3. [COM - quantidade] shipment; [- remessa] consignment.

partidário, ria [partʃi'darju, rja] *adj* -1. [de partido] party (antes de subst). -2. [seguidor] follower.

partido, da [pax'tʃidu, da] *adj* [quebrado] broken.
◆ **partido** *m* -1. [político] party. -2. [defesa]: **tomar o** ~ **de alguém** to take sb's side. -3. [vantagem]: **tirar** ~ **de algo** to make the most of sthg. -4. [pretendente] catch.

partilha [pax'tʃiʎa] *f* sharing.

partilhar [paxtʃi'ʎa(x)] <> *vt* -1. [dividir] to share. -2. [distribuir] to share out. <> *vi* [compartilhar]: ~ **de algo** to share in sthg.

partir [pax'tʃi(x)] <> *vt* to break. <> *vi* -1. [ir embora] to leave. -2. *fam* [recorrer]: ~ **para** to resort to.
◆ **a partir de** *loc prep* -1. [desde] from. -2. [dali em diante]: **a** ~ **daquele momento** from that moment on; **a** ~ **de agora** from now on.

partitura [paxtʃi'tura] *f* score.

parto ['paxtu] *m* childbirth; **estar em trabalho de** ~ to be in labour *UK*, to be in labor *US*; **ser um** ~ *fig* [ser difícil] to be heavy going.

Páscoa ['paʃkwa] *f* -1. *RELIG* Easter. -2. *GEOG*: **a ilha de** ~ Easter Island.

pasmar [paʒ'ma(x)] <> *vt* to amaze. <> *vi* to be amazed.

pasmo, ma ['paʒmu, ma] *adj* amazed.
◆ **pasmo** *m* amazement.

passa ['pasa] *f* raisin.

passada [pa'sada] *f* [passo] step; **dar uma** ~ **em** to drop by.

passadeira [pasa'dejra] *f* -1. [tapete] stair carpet. -2. [mulher] ironing woman.

passado, da [pa'sadu, da] *adj* -1. [que passou - tempo] past; [- semana, ano] last. -2. [ultrapassado]: **meio** ~ dated. -3. [fruta] overripe. -4. [carne]: **bem** ~

well done; **mal** ~ rare. **- 5.** [vexado] infuriated.

➡ **passado** m past.

passageiro, ra [pasa'ʒejru, ral <> adj passing. <> m, f passenger.

passagem [pasa'ʒẽl (pl **-ns**) f **-1.** [caminho] way; ~ **de nível** level crossing; ~ **de pedestres** pedestrian crossing; ~ **subterrânea** underpass. **-2.** [condução - preço] fare; [- bilhete] ticket; ~ **de ida** one-way ticket; ~ **de ida e volta** return ticket. **-3.** [trecho] passage. **- 4.** [transição] transition.

➡ **de passagem** loc adv in passing; **estar de** ~ to be passing through.

passaporte [pasa'pͻxtʃil m passport.

passar [pa'sa(x)] <> vt **-1.** [transpor] to cross. **- 2.** [ultrapassar] to overtake; ~ **a frente de alguém** to get in front of sb; ~ **alguém para trás** fig [enganar] to dupe sb; [trair] to deceive sb. **-3.** [padecer] to endure. **-4.** [tarefa escolar] to set. **- 5.** [reprimenda] to tell off. **- 6.** [expedir] to send. **-7.** [entregar] to pass. **- 8.** [deslizar]: ~ **algo em/por** to run sthg over/through. **- 9.** [tempo] to spend. **-10.** [espalhar] to spread. **-11.** [coar] to sieve. **-12.** [grelhar] to grill. **-13.** [a ferro] to iron. <> vi **-1.** [ger] to pass; ~ **por algo** to pass o.s. off as sthg ou as being sthg; ~ **(de ano)** to go up (a year). **-2.** [ir] to go past; ~ **em/por** to go in/through; ~ **pela cabeça de alguém** fig to cross one's mind; ~ **por cima de alguém** fig to go over sb's head. **-3.** [cruzar]: ~ **por alguém/algo** to go by sb/sthg. **- 4.** [sentir-se] to feel; **como está passando?** [cumprimentando] how do you do? **- 5.** [sofrer]: ~ **por algo** to go through sthg. **- 6.** [trocar de lado] to cross over. **-7.** [ser mais tarde que] to be past. **- 8.** [ter mais id] to be over; **ela já passou dos 40** she's over 40 now; **aos cinco anos, o menino não passara dos 18 quilos** at five years of age, the boy still didn't weigh more than 18kg. **-10.** [ser apenas]: **não** ~ **de** pej to be no more than. **-11.** [ser aceitável] to be passable.

➡ **passar-se** vp **-1.** [suceder-se] to happen. **- 2.** [transcorrer] to go by.

passarela [pasa'rɛla] f **-1.** [para pedestre] footbridge. **- 2.** [para manequim] catwalk.

passarinho [pasa'riɲul m birdie.

pássaro [pasarul m bird.

passatempo [,pasa'tẽpul m hobby.

passável [pa'savewl (pl **-eis**) adj passable.

passe [pasil m **-1.** [licença] permit. **-2.** [ESP - de bola] pass; [- de jogador] transfer. **-3.** [lance]: ~ **de mágica**

sleight of hand. **- 4.** REL laying on of hands.

passear [pa'sja(x)] vi **-1.** [ger] to go for a walk. **- 2.** [cavalo, carro] to ride.

passeata [pa'sjatal f [protesto] demonstration.

passeio [pa'sejul m **-1.** [a pé] walk; **dar** ou **fazer um** ~ to go for a walk. **- 2.** [a cavalo, de carro] ride; **fazer um** ~ to go for a ride. **-3.** [calçada] pavement **UK**, sidewalk **US**.

passional [pasjo'nawl (pl **-ais**) adj **-1.** [discurso, atitude, artista] passionate. **-2.** [crime] of passion.

passista [pa'siʃtal mf samba dancer.

passível [pa'sivewl (pl **-eis**) adj: ~ **de** **algo** liable to sthg.

passivo, va [pa'sivu, val adj passive.

➡ **passivo** m COM liabilities (pl).

passo ['pasul m **-1.** [ger] step. **- 2.** [medida]: **a uns seis** ~**s (de distância)** a short distance away; **a um** ~ **de** fig on the verge of. **-3.** [ruído de passos] footsteps. **- 4.** [pegada] footprint. **-5.** [marcha] step. **- 6.** [modo de andar] walk.

➡ **ao passo que** loc adv **-1.** [enquanto] whilst. **- 2.** [contudo] whereas.

pasta ['paʃtal f **-1.** [creme] paste; ~ **de dentes** toothpaste. **-2.** [de couro] briefcase. **-3.** [de cartolina] folder. **- 4.** POL portfolio.

pastagem [paʃ'taʒẽl (pl **-ns**) f pasture.

pastar [paʃ'ta(x)] vi to graze; **vá** ~**!** fig & pej get lost!

pastel [paʃ'tɛwl (pl **-éis**) <> adj [cor] pastel. <> m **-1.** [ger] pastel. **-2.** [comida] pasty.

pastelaria [paʃtela'rial f cake shop.

pasteurizar [paʃtewri'za(x)] vt to pasteurize.

pastilha [paʃ'tʃiʎal f **-1.** [bala] pastille. **- 2.** MED pill. **-3.** COMPUT chip. **- 4.** CONSTR mosaic piece.

pasto ['paʃtul m **-1.** [erva] grass. **-2.** [pastagem] pasture.

pastor, ra [paʃ'to(x), ral (mpl **-es**, fpl **-s**) m, f AGR shepherd (f shepherdess).

➡ **pastor** m RELIG pastor.

pastoso, osa [paʃ'tozu, ͻzal adj pasty.

pata ['patal f **-1.** [de animal - de cão, gato] paw; [- de cavalo] foot. **- 2.** [ave] (female) duck.

patamar [pata'ma(x)] (pl **-es**) m **-1.** [de escada] landing. **-2.** fig [nível] level.

patê [pa'tel m pâté.

patente [pa'tẽtʃil <> adj obvious. <> f **-1.** COM patent. **-2.** MIL rank; **altas/baixas** ~**s** high/low ranks.

paternal [patex'nawl (pl **-ais**) adj paternal, fatherly.

paternidade [patexni'dadʒi] f paternity.

paterno, na [pa'tɛxnu, na] adj paternal, father's (antes de subst).

pateta [pa'tɛta] <> adj foolish. <> mf fool.

patético, ca [pa'tɛtʃiku, ka] adj pathetic.

patife [pa'tʃifi] <> adj roguish. <> m scoundrel.

patim [pa'tʃi] (pl -ns) m skate; **patins de rodas** roller skates.

patinação [patʃina'sãw] f skating; ~ **artística** figure skating; ~ **no gelo** ice skating.

patinar [patʃi'na(x)] vi -1. [de patins] to skate. -2. [carro] to skid.

pátio ['patʃiu] m patio.

pato ['patu] m -1. ZOOL duck. -2. fam [otário] sucker; **cair como um** ~ to be a laughing stock. -3. loc: **pagar o** ~ to carry the can.

patológico, ca [pato'lɔʒiku, ka] adj pathological.

patologista [patolo'ʒiʃta] mf pathologist.

patrão, roa [pa'trãw, roa] (mpl -ões, fpl -oas) m, f -1. [empregador] boss. -2. [de criados] master. -3. [como forma de tratamento] sir.

➡ **patroa** f -1. [mulher do patrão] master's/boss's wife. -2. fam [esposa] missus.

pátria ['patrja] f fatherland; **salvar a** ~ fig to save the day.

patriarca [pa'trjaxka] m patriarch.

patriarcal [patrjax'kaw] (pl -ais) adj patriarchal.

patricinha [patri'sina] f pej posh girl.

patrimônio [patri'monju] m -1. [bens] patrimony. -2. [herança] inheritance; ~ **histórico** historical heritage.

patriota [pa'trjɔta] mf patriot.

patroa [pa'troa] f ▷ **patrão**.

patrocinador, ra [patrosina'do(x), ra] (mpl -es, fpl -s) <> adj sponsoring. <> m, f sponsor.

patrocinar [patrosi'na(x)] vt -1. [ger] to support. -2. [financiar] to sponsor.

patrocínio [patro'sinju] m -1. [financiamento] sponsorship. -2. [apoio] support.

patrões [pa'trõjʃ] pl ▷ **patrão**.

patrono [pa'tronu] m patron.

patrulha [pa'truʎa] f -1. [ronda] patrol. -2. [censura] censorship.

patrulhar [patru'ʎa(x)] vt -1. [vigiar] to patrol. -2. [censurar] to censure.

pau ['paw] m -1. [bastão] stick. -2. [madeira]: **de** ~ wooden. -3. [de bandeira] pole; **a meio** ~ at half mast. -4. fam [briga] brawl; **o** ~ **comeu** all hell broke loose. -5. fam [moeda] slang for Brazilian currency. -6. mfam [pênis] cock.

➡ **paus** mpl [naipe] clubs; **de** ~**s** of clubs.

➡ **pau a pau** loc adj on an equal footing.

pau-brasil [ˌpawbra'ziw] m Brazil wood.

pau-de-arara [ˌpawdʒja'rara] (pl paus-de-arara) mf [retirante do Nordeste] migrant from north-eastern Brazil.

➡ **pau-de-arara** m [tortura] form of torture where victim is suspended face down from a pole.

pau-de-sebo [ˌpawdʒi'sebu] (pl paus-de-sebo) m [mastro de cocanha] greasy pole.

Paulicéia [pawli'sɛja] n São Paulo.

paulista [paw'liʃta] <> adj São Paulo (antes de subst). <> mf person from São Paulo.

paupérrimo, ma [paw'pɛximu, ma] adj extremely poor.

pausa ['pawza] f -1. [interrupção, intervalo] break. -2. [descanso] rest.

pausado, da [paw'zadu, da] adj -1. [lento] leisurely. -2. [cadenciado] rythmic.

➡ **pausado** adv unhurriedly.

pauta ['pawta] f -1. [linha] guideline; **sem** ~ unruled. -2. [folha com linhas] ruled sheet. -3. [lista] list. -4. [ordem do dia] agenda; **em** ~ on the agenda. -5. MÚS stave.

pavão [pa'vãw] (pl -ões) mf peacock.

pavê [pa'vel m CULIN cream cake made of sponge soaked in liqueur.

pavilhão [pavi'ʎãw] (pl -ões) m -1. [prédio] annex. -2. [de exposições] stand. -3. [tenda, abrigo] tent. -4. fig [bandeira] banner.

pavimentar [pavimẽn'ta(x)] vt to pave.

pavimento [pavi'mẽntu] m -1. [andar] storey UK, story US. -2. [chão] floor. -3. [de rua] pavement.

pavio [pa'viw] m wick; **ter o** ~ **curto** [ser de briga] to have a short fuse.

pavões [pa'võjʃ] pl ▷ **pavão**.

pavor [pa'vo(x)] m fear; **ter** ~ **de alguém/algo** to dread sb/sthg.

pavoroso, osa [pavo'rozu, ɔza] adj -1. [repulsivo] appalling. -2. [muito ruim, feio] dreadful.

paz ['paʃ] (pl -es) f peace; **deixar alguém em** ~ to leave sb in peace; **fazer as pazes** to make up.

PB (abrev de Estado da Paraíba) n State of Paraíba.

PBX (abrev de Private Branch Exchange) PBX.

PC (abrev de **Personal Computer**) m PC.

Pça. (abrev de **Praça**) f Sq.

PC do B (abrev de **Partido Comunista do Brasil**) m Brazilian communist party.

PCI (abrev de **Placa de Circuito Interno**) f internal circuit board.

PDT (abrev de **Partido Democrático Trabalhista**) m Democratic Labour Party, the second largest left-wing party in Brazil.

PDV (abrev de **Programa de Demissão Voluntária**) m Brazilian voluntary redundancy scheme.

pé ['pɛ] m -1. [ger] foot; **não arredar o ~** not to budge; **a ~** on foot; **com um ~ nas costas** with the greatest of ease; **em** OU **de ~** standing; **dar no ~** fam [fugir] to do a runner; **cuidado que aquela parte da piscina não dá ~** be careful because you will be out of your depth in that part of the pool; **estar de ~** fam to still be on; **meter os ~s pelas mãos** to go haywire; **não chegar aos ~s de** to be nowhere near as good as; **não largar do ~ de alguém** to stick like glue to sb; **não ter ~ nem cabeça** not to make any sense. - 2. [base - de monumento, morro] foot; **ao ~ de** at the foot of. - 3. BOT plant. - 4. [de calçado, meia] sole. - 5. [situação] state of affairs; **em ~ de guerra/igualdade** on a war/equal footing.

➤ **ao pé da letra** loc adv to the letter.

PE (abrev de **Estado de Pernambuco**) n State of Pernambuco.

peão ['pjãw] (pl -ões) m -1. [trabalhador] labourer UK, laborer US. - 2. [xadrez] pawn.

peça ['pɛsa] f -1. [ger] piece. - 2. MEC part; **~ de reposição** OU **sobressalente** replacement OU spare part. - 3. [cômodo] room. - 4. [brincadeira]: **pregar uma ~ em alguém** to play a practical joke on sb. - 5. TEATRO play. - 6. JUR document.

pecado [pe'kadu] m -1. RELIG sin; **~ original** original sin; **pagar os seus ~s** to pay for one's sins. - 2. [pena]: **que ~!** what a sin!

pecador, ra [peka'do(x), ra] m, f sinner.

pecar [pe'ka(x)] vi -1. RELIG to sin. - 2. [errar]: **~ por algo** to err on the side of sthg.

pechincha [pe'ʃĩʃa] f bargain; **ser uma ~** to be a bargain.

pecuário, ria [pe'kwarju, rja] adj cattle.
➤ **pecuária** f [criação] cattle-raising.

peculiar [peku'lja(x)] (pl -es) adj -1. [característico] particular. - 2. [curioso] peculiar.

peculiaridade [pekuljari'dadʒi] f peculiarity.

pedaço [pe'dasu] m -1. [parte] piece; **aos ~s** in pieces; **estar caindo aos ~s** to be falling to pieces. - 2. [trecho] piece. - 3. [lugar] area.

pedágio [pe'daʒju] m toll.

pedagógico, ca [peda'gɔʒiku, ka] adj teaching (antes de subst).

pedagogo, ga [peda'gogu, ga] m, f educationalist.

pé-d'água [,pɛ'dagwa] (pl **pés-d'água**) m deluge.

pedal [pe'daw] (pl -ais) m pedal.

pedalar [peda'la(x)] <> vt to pedal. <> vi to pedal.

pedalinho [peda'liɲu] m pedalo.

pedante [pe'dãntʃi] <> adj pedantic. <> m, f pedant.

pé-de-galinha [,pɛdʒiga'liɲa] (pl **pés-de-galinha**) m crow's foot.

pé-de-moleque [,pɛdʒimu'lɛki] (pl **pés-de-moleque**) m -1. [doce] peanut brittle. - 2. [calçamento] crazy paving.

pé-de-pato [,pɛdʒi'patu] (pl **pés-de-pato**) m -1. [nadadeira] flipper. - 2. fam [diabo] Satan.

pedestal [pedeʃ'taw] (pl -ais) m pedestal.

pedestre [pe'dɛʃtri] mf pedestrian.

pediatra [pe'dʒjatra] mf paediatrician UK, pediatrician US.

pedicuro, ra [pedʒi'kuru, ra] m, f pedicurist.

pedido [pe'dʒidu] m -1. [ger] order. - 2. [solicitação] request; **a ~** to an encore; **~ de casamento** marriage proposal; **~ de demissão** resignation; **~ de divórcio** divorce petition.

pedigree [pedʒi'gril] m pedigree.

pedinte [pe'dʒĩntʃi] mf beggar.

pedir [pe'dʒi(x)] <> vt -1. [solicitar] to ask for; **~ algo a alguém** to ask sb for sthg; **~ a alguém que faça algo** to ask sb to do sthg; **~ algo emprestado** to borrow sthg; **~ desculpas** OU **perdão** (por algo) to apologize (for sthg). - 2. [cobrar] to charge. - 3. [necessitar] to call for. - 4. [encomendar] to order. - 5. [exigir, requerer] to demand. <> vi [fazer pedidos] to make demands; **~ por alguém** to pray for sb.

pedra ['pedra] f -1. [ger] stone. - 2. [fragmento] pebble; **~ de gelo** ice cube; **~ preciosa** precious stone; **dormir com uma ~** to sleep like a log. - 3. [de açúcar] sugar lump.

pedreira [pe'drejra] f stone quarry.

pedreiro [pe'drejru] m CONSTR mason.

pegada [pe'gada] f footprint.

pegado, da [pe'gadu, da] *adj* **-1.** [contíguo] next door. **-2.** [unido] close.

pegajoso, osa [pega'ʒozu, ɔza] *adj* sticky.

pegar [pe'ga(x)] <> *vt* **-1.** [ger] to pick up. **-2.** [surpreender] to catch. **-3.** [embarcar em] to catch. **-4.** [seguir por] to take. **-5.** [compreender] to take in. **-6.** [vivenciar] to experience. **-7.** [aceitar fazer] to take on. <> *vi* **-1.** [segurar] to catch; **~ em algo** to hold on to sthg. **-2.** [grudar]: **~ em algo** to stick to sthg. **-3.** [difundir-se - moda, mania] to catch on; [- doença] to be catching. **-4.** [fogo]: **a fogueira pega mais rápido com álcool** the fire lights quicker with alcohol; **ele pegou fogo na casa** he set fire to the house. **-5.** [planta] to take root. **-6.** *RÁDIO* & *TV*: **~ (bem/mal)** to have good/ poor reception. **-7.** [motor] to start. **-8.** [iniciar]: **~ em algo** to start sthg. **-9.** [atitude]: **~ bem/mal** to go down well/badly; **não pega bem** it doesn't do. **-10.** [decidir-se]: **~ a fazer algo** to make up one's mind and do sthg.

◆ **pegar-se** *vp* [brigar]: **~-se (com)** to come to blows (with).

peido ['pejdu] *m mfam* fart.

peito ['pejtu] *m* **-1.** *ANAT* chest; **~ do pé** instep; **meter o ~ fam** to put one's heart into it. **-2.** [de mulher, ave] breast; **dar o ~** to breastfeed. **-3.** *fig* [coragem] courage; **no ~ (e na raça)** fearlessly.

peitoril [pejto'riw] (*pl* **-is**) *m* windowsill.

peitudo, da [pej'tudu, da] *adj* **-1.** [de peito grande] big-chested. **-2.** [valente] plucky.

peixada [pej'ʃada] *f* fish stew.

peixaria [pejʃa'ria] *f* fishmonger.

peixe ['pejʃi] *m zool* fish; **vender o seu ~** [tratar de seus interesses] to look out for one's own interests; [opinar] to have one's say.

◆ **Peixes** *m* [zodíaco] Pisces; *veja também* **Virgem**.

pejorativo, va [peʒora'tʃivu, va] *adj* pejorative.

pela ['pela] = **por** + **a**.

pelada [pe'lada] *FUT f* **-1.** [jogo informal] (friendly) match. **-2.** [jogo ruim] wasted game.

pelado, da [pe'ladu, da] *adj* **-1.** [nu] naked. **-2.** [sem pêlos] shorn.

pelar [pe'la(x)] <> *vt* **-1.** [animal] to skin. **-2.** [cabeça] to shave. <> *vi*: **estar pelando** [estar quentíssimo] to be scalding.

pelas ['pelaʃ] = **por** + **as**.

pele ['pɛli] *f* **-1.** [de pessoa] skin; **~ e osso** skin and bone; **cair na ~ de** *fig fam* to pester; **salvar a ~ de alguém** *fig fam* to save sb's skin; **sentir algo na ~** *fig* to experience sthg first hand. **-2.** [animal] hide; **de ~** hide. **-3.** [couro] leather; **de ~** leather. **-4.** [agasalho] fur. **-5.** [de fruta, legume] skin, peel.

pelerine [pele'rini] *f* cape.

pelica [pe'lika] *f* kid leather.

pelicano [peli'kãnu] *m zool* pelican.

pelo ['pelu] = **por** + **o**.

pêlo ['pelu] *m* **-1.** [em pessoa] hair; **nu em ~** stark naked. **-2.** [de animal] fur.

pelos ['peluʃ] = **por** + **os**.

pelotão [pelo'tãw] (*pl* **-ões**) *m* platoon; **~ de fuzilamento** firing squad.

pelúcia [pe'lusja] *f* plush.

peludo, da [pe'ludu, da] *adj* hairy.

pena ['pena] *f* **-1.** [de ave] feather. **-2.** [pesar] sorrow; **que ~!** what a pity!; **ser uma ~** to be a pity; **valer a ~** *fig* [compensar] to be worthwhile; **a duras ~s** with great difficulty. **-3.** *JUR* punishment; **~ capital** *ou* **de morte** capital punishment *ou* death penalty; **cumprir ~** to serve a sentence; **sob ~ de** *fig* under penalty of. **-4.** [piedade] pity; **dar ~** to arouse pity; **ter ~ de** to be sorry for.

penal [pe'naw] (*pl* **-ais**) *adj JUR* penal.

penalidade [penali'dadʒi] *f* **-1.** *JUR* penalty. **-2.** [castigo] punishment. **-3.** *FUT*: **~ máxima** penalty (kick).

penalizar [penali'za(x)] *vt* **-1.** [dar pena a] to distress. **-2.** [castigar] to punish.

pênalti [pe'nawtʃi] *m FUT* penalty.

penar [pe'na(x)] <> *m* [sofrimento] suffering. <> *vt* [sofrer] to hurt, to distress. <> *vi* [sofrer] to suffer.

penca ['penka] *f* bunch; **em ~** *fig* [quantidade] loads of.

pendência [pẽn'dẽnsja] *f* **-1.** [contenda] dispute. **-2.** [algo por decidir] pending matter.

pendente [pẽn'dẽntʃi] <> *adj* **-1.** [ger] hanging. **-2.** [por decidir] pending. <> *m* [de jóia] pendant.

pender [pẽn'de(x)] *vi* [estar pendurado] to hang.

pêndulo ['pẽndulu] *m* pendulum.

pendurado, da [pẽndu'radu, da] *adj* **-1.** [pendente]: **~ (em)** hanging (on). **-2.** *fig* [conta] on tick.

pendurar [pẽndu'ra(x)] *vt* **-1.** [colocar] to hang. **-2.** *fig* [conta] to pay on tick.

◆ **pendurar-se** *vp* [pessoa] to hang.

penduricalho [pẽnduri'kaʎu], **pendurucalho** [pẽnduru'kaʎu] *m* trinket.

penedo [pe'nedu] *m* boulder.

peneira [pe'nejra] *f* [para peneirar] sieve.

peneirar [penej'ra(x)] <> *vt* [na peneira] to sieve. <> *vi fig* [chuviscar] to drizzle.

penetração [penetra'sãw] (pl -ões) f - 1. [ger] penetration. - 2. fig [difusão] circulation.

penetrante [pene'trãntʃi] adj penetrating.

penetrar [pene'tra(x)] <> vt to penetrate. <> vi - 1. [entrar, infiltrar-se]: ~ em/por/entre to penetrate. - 2. fam [em festa] to gatecrash.

penhasco [pe'ɲaʃku] m cliff.

penhor [pe'ɲo(x)] m pawn; **fazer o ~ de algo** to pawn ou hock sthg, to leave sthg in pawn ou hock; **casa de ~ es** pawnshop.

penicilina [penisi'lina] f penicillin.

península [pe'nĩsula] f peninsula.

pênis ['peniʃ] m inv penis.

penitência [peni'tẽsja] f RELIG - 1. [contrição] contrition. - 2. [expiação] penance.

penitenciário, ria [penitẽ'sjarju, rja] <> adj penitentiary. <> m, f prisoner.
➡ **penitenciária** f penitentiary.

penoso, osa [pe'nozu, ɔza] adj - 1. [assunto, trabalho] hard. - 2. [tratamento, correção] harsh.

pensador, ra [pẽsa'do(x), ra] m, f thinker.

pensamento [pẽsa'mẽntu] m - 1. [ger] thought; **fazer ~ positivo** to think positively. - 2. [mente, opinião] mind. - 3. [doutrina] thinking. - 4. [idéia] idea.

pensão [pẽ'sãw] (pl -ões) f - 1. [pequeno hotel] boarding house. - 2. [renda] pension; **~ alimentícia** maintenance allowance. - 3. [restaurante] boarding house. - 4. [refeição]: **~ completa** full board.

pensar [pẽ'sa(x)] <> vt to think. <> vi - 1. [ger] to think; **~ em/sobre algo** to think about sthg. - 2. [tencionar] to intend.

pensativo, va [pẽsa'tʃivu, va] adj thoughtful.

pensionato [pẽsjo'natu] m hostel.

pensionista [pẽsjo'niʃta] mf - 1. [beneficiário] pensioner. - 2. [morador] boarder.

pentacampeão [ˌpẽntakãn'pjãw] (pl -ões) m five-times champion.

pentágono [pẽ'tagunu] m GEOM pentagon.

pentatlo [pẽn'tatlu] m pentathlon.

pente ['pẽntʃi] m - 1. [de cabelo] comb. - 2. [de pistola] cartridge.

penteadeira [pẽntʃja'dejra] f dressing table.

penteado, da [pẽn'tʃjadu] adj well groomed.
➡ **penteado** m hairstyle.

pentear [pẽn'tʃja(x)] vt - 1. [cabelo] to

comb. - 2. [fazer penteado] to style.
➡ **pentear-se** vp [pessoa] to do one's hair.

Pentecostes [pẽnte'kɔstʃiʃ] m RELIG Pentecost.

penugem [pe'nuʒẽ] (pl -ns) f down.

penúltimo, ma [pe'nuwtʃimu, ma] adj penultimate, last but one.

penumbra [pe'nũbra] f - 1. [meia-luz] half-light. - 2. fig [obscuridade] obscurity.

penúria [pe'nurja] f penury.

peões ['pjõjʃ] pl ▷ **peão**.

pepino [pe'pinu] m - 1. [fruto] cucumber. - 2. fig [problema] bit of a problem.

pequeno, na [pe'kenu, na] <> adj - 1. [tamanho] small. - 2. [mesquinho] mean. <> m, f [criança] child.
➡ **pequena** f [namorada] girlfriend.

pequeno-burguês, pequeno-burguesa [peˌkenubux'geʃ, peˌkenabux'geza] (pl pequenos-burgueses) <> adj petit bourgeois. <> m, f petit bourgeois.

Pequim [pe'kĩ] n Beijing.

pêra ['pera] (pl peras) f pear.

perambular [perãnbu'la(x)] vi: **~ (por)** to wander (through).

perante [pe'rãntʃi] prep - 1. [no espaço] before; **jurar ~ a Bíblia** to swear on the Bible. - 2. [no sentido] faced with.

pé-rapado, da [ˌpɛxa'padu, da] (mpl pés-rapados, fpl pés-rapadas) m, f loser.

percalço [pex'kawsu] m pitfall.

per capita [pɛx'kapita] loc adj per capita.

perceber [pexse'be(x)] vt - 1. [através dos sentidos] to perceive. - 2. [compreender] to realize. - 3. [notar] to notice.

percentagem [pexsẽn'taʒẽ] (pl -ns) f percentage.

percepção [pexsep'sãw] f [dos sentidos] perception.

perceptível [pexsep'tʃivew] (pl -eis) adj perceptible.

perceptivo, va [pexsep'tʃivu, va] adj perceptive.

percevejo [pexse'veʒu] m - 1. ZOOL bedbug. - 2. [prego] drawing pin.

percorrer [pexko'xe(x)] vt - 1. [viajar] to travel through. - 2. [passar por] to pass through. - 3. [esquadrinhar] to search. - 4. [consultar] to search through.

percurso [pex'kuxsu] m route.

percussão [pexku'sãw] (pl -ões) f percussion.

percussionista [pexkusjo'niʃta] mf drummer.

percutir [pexku'tʃi(x)] vt to hit.

perda ['pexda] f - 1. [ger] loss. - 2. [desperdício]: **~ de tempo** waste of time. - 3.

[prejuízo] damage; ~s e danos damages.

perdão [pex'dãw] (*pl* -dões) *m* [escusa] pardon; pedir ~ a alguém to apologize to sb; perdão! sorry!

perdedor, ra [pexde'do(x), ral] <> *adj* losing. <> *m, f* [de competição] loser.

perder [pex'de(x)l] <> *vt* -1. [ger] to lose. -2. [não chegar a tempo, não comparecer] to miss. -3. [desperdiçar] to waste; pôr tudo a ~ to ruin everything. <> *vi* [ser vencido] to lose; ~ de ou para alguém to lose to ou against sb.
◆ **perder-se** *vp* -1. [extraviar-se] to get lost; ~-se de alguém to wander away from sb. -2. [arruinar-se] to waste one's life. -3. *ant* [mulher] to lose one's virginity. -4. [atrapalhar-se] to get bogged down. -5. [absorver-se] to lose o.s.

perdição [pexdʒi'sãw] *f* -1. [ruína] decay. -2. [mau caminho] evil. -3. [desonra] fall from grace.

perdido, da [pex'dʒidu, da] <> *adj* -1. [ger] lost. -2. [amorosamente]: ~ (de amor) por alguém desperately in love with sb. -3. [arruinado]: nem tudo está ~ all is not lost; meu pai descobriu que fui reprovado, estou ~! my father's found out I've failed, I'm done for!<> *m, f* [pervertido] pervert.

perdigão [pexdʒi'gãw] (*pl* -ões) *m* [macho] male partridge.

perdiz [pex'dʒiʃ] (*pl* -es) *f* [fêmea] female partridge.

perdoar [pex'dwa(x)l] <> *vt* -1. [desculpar] to forgive; ~ algo (a alguém) to forgive (sb for) sthg. -2. [eximir de] to pardon. -3. *fig* [desperdiçar]: não ~ to make the most of. <> *vi* [desculpar] to forgive.

perdurar [pexdu'ra(x)l] *vi* -1. [durar muito]: ~ (por/através de) to last (for/throughout). -2. [permanecer] to carry on.

perecer [pere'se(x)l] *vi* -1. [extingüir-se] to perish. -2. [morrer] to die.

perecível [pere'sivɛwl] (*pl* -eis) *adj* perishable.

peregrinação [peregrina'sãw] (*pl* -ões) *f* -1. [viagem] journey. -2. *RELIG* pilgrimage.

peregrino, na [pere'grinu, na] *m, f* -1. [viajante] traveller. -2. *RELIG* pilgrim.

peremptório, ria [perẽp'tɔrju, rja] *adj* -1. [final] decisive. -2. [taxativo] peremptory.

perene [pe'renil] *adj* -1. [eterno] eternal. -2. [incessante] unceasing. -3. *BOT* perennial.

perfeccionista [pexfeksjo'niʃtal] <> *adj* perfectionist. <> *mf* perfectionist.

perfeição [pexfej'sãw] *f* perfection; ser uma ~ to be perfect.

perfeitamente [pex,fejta'mẽntʃil] <> *adv* perfectly. <> *interj* [de acordo] of course!

perfeito, ta [pex'fejtu, tal] *adj* -1. [ger] perfect. -2. *(antes de subst)* [completo] perfect.

pérfido, da [ˈpɛxfidu, dal] *adj* treacherous.

perfil [pex'fiwl] (*pl* -is) *m* -1. [ger] profile; de ~ in profile. -2. *fig* [retrato] outline. -3. [caráter] personality.

performance [pex'fɔxmãnsil] *f* performance.

perfumado, da [pexfu'madu, dal] *adj* perfumed.

perfumar [pexfu'ma(x)l] *vt* to perfume.
◆ **perfumar-se** *vp* to put perfume on.

perfume [pex'fumil] *m* perfume.

perfurar [pexfu'ra(x)l] *vt* to perforate.

pergaminho [pexga'miɲul] *m* [documento] parchment.

pérgula [ˈpɛxgulal] *f* pergola.

pergunta [pex'gũntal] *f* question; fazer uma ~ a alguém to ask sb a question.

perguntar [pexgũn'ta(x)l] <> *vt* -1. [indagar] to ask; ~ algo a alguém to ask sb sthg. -2. [interrogar] to question. <> *vi* [indagar] to ask questions; ~ por alguém to ask after sb.
◆ **perguntar-se** *vp* to wonder.

perícia [pe'risjal] *f* -1. [ger] expertise. -2. [policial] investigation. -3. [examinadores] investigators.

periculosidade [perikulozi'dadʒil] *f* peril; de alta ~ highly perilous.

periferia [perife'rial] *f* -1. [contorno] periphery. -2. *GEOM* circumference. -3. [subúrbio] outskirts (*pl*).

periférico, ca [peri'fɛriku, kal] *adj* -1. [que contorna] peripheral. -2. *fig* [marginal] superficial.
◆ **periférico** *m* COMPUT peripheral.

perigoso, osa [peri'gozu, ɔzal] *adj* dangerous.

perímetro [pe'rimetrul] *m* perimeter; ~ urbano city limits (*pl*).

periódico, ca [pe'rjɔdʒiku, kal] *adj* periodic.
◆ **periódico** *m* -1. [jornal] periodical (newspaper). -2. [revista] periodical (magazine).

período [pe'riwdul] *m* -1. [ger] period. -2. *UNIV* semester.

peripécia [peri'pɛsjal] *f* -1. [aventura] adventure. -2. [incidente] incident.

periquito [peri'kitul] *m* budgerigar.

perito, ta [pe'ritu, tal] <> *adj* [experiente,

especialista] expert. <> *m, f*-1. [especialista] expert. -2. [quem faz perícia] investigator.

perjúrio [pex'ʒurju] *m* perjury.

permanecer [pexmane'se(x)] *vi* to remain.

permanência [pexma'nẽnsja] *f*-1. [continuação, constância] endurance. -2. [estada] stay.

permanente [pexma'nẽntʃi] <> *adj* permanent. <> *m* [cartão] pass. <> *m* [penteado] perm; **fazer um ~** to have a perm.

permissão [pexmi'sãw] (*pl* -ões) *f* permission.

permissível [pexmi'sivew] (*pl* -eis) *adj* permissible.

permissivo, va [pexmi'sivu, va] *adj* permissive.

permitir [pexmi'tʃi(x)] *vt* -1. [admitir] to allow; **~ a alguém fazer algo** to allow sb to do sthg. -2. [conceder]: **~ algo a alguém** to grant sb sthg.
    ➡ **permitir-se** *vp* [tomar a liberdade de] to allow o.s.

perna ['pɛxna] *f* leg; **~ de pau** wooden leg; **passar a ~ em alguém** *fig* [enganar] to con sb; [trair] to cheat on sb.

pernicioso, osa [pexni'sjozu, ɔza] *adj* -1. [nocivo] destructive. -2. *MED* pernicious.

pernil [pex'niw] (*pl* -is) *m* CULIN hock.

pernilongo [pexni'lõŋgu] *m* stilt.

pernoitar [pexnoj'ta(x)] *vi* to spend the night.

pernóstico, ca [pex'nɔʃtʃiku, ka] <> *adj* pretentious. <> *mf* pretentious person.

pérola ['pɛrola] *f*-1. [de ostra] pearl. -2. *fig* [pessoa, peça rara] gem.

perpassar [pexpa'sa(x)] *vt fig* [atravessar] to imbue.

perpendicular [pexpẽndʒiku'la(x)] (*pl* -es) <> *adj* perpendicular. <> *f* perpendicular.

perpetrar [pexpe'tra(x)] *vt* to perpetrate.

perpetuar [pexpe'twa(x)] *vt* to prolong.
    ➡ **perpetuar-se** *vp* to survive.

perpétuo, tua [pex'pɛtwu, twa] *adj* -1. [eterno] eternal. -2. [vitalício] permanent. -3. *JUR*: **prisão perpétua** life imprisonment. -4. *(antes de subst)* [freqüente] on-going.

perplexidade [pexpleksi'dadʒi] *f* perplexity.

perplexo, xa [pex'plɛksu, sa] *adj* perplexed; **estar/ficar ~** to be perplexed.

perseguição [pexsegi'sãw] (*pl* -ões) *f*-1. [ger] persecution. -2. *fig* [de um objetivo] pursuit.

perseguir [pexse'gi(x)] *vt* -1. [ger] to pursue. -2. *POL* & *RELIG* to persecute.

perseverante [pexseve'rãntʃi] *adj* persevering.

perseverar [pexseve'ra(x)] *vi* -1. [persistir]: **~ (em)** to persevere (with). -2. [permanecer] to last.

persiana [pex'sjãna] *f* blind.

persistência [pexsiʃ'tẽnsja] *f* persistence.

persistente [pexsiʃ'tẽntʃi] *adj* persistent.

persistir [pexsiʃ'tʃi(x)] *vi* [insistir]: **~ (em algo)** to persist (in sthg).

personagem [pexso'naʒẽ] (*pl* -ns) *m, f* -1. *CINE, LITER* & *TEATRO* character. -2. [celebridade] celebrity.

personalidade [pexsonali'dadʒi] *f* personality; **dupla ~** split personality.

personalizado, da [pexsonali'zadu, da] *adj* personalized.

personificação [pexsonifika'sãw] (*pl* -ões) *f* personification.

perspectiva [pexʃpek'tʃiva] *f*-1. [ger] perspective. -2. [probabilidade] prospect; **em ~** [em vista] in prospect; [a distância] in perspective.

perspicácia [pexʃpi'kasja] *f* insight.

perspicaz [pexʃpi'kaʃ] (*pl* -es) *adj* insightful.

persuadir [pexswa'dʒi(x)] <> *vt* -1. [convencer]: **~ alguém (a fazer algo)** to persuade sb (to do sthg). -2. [induzir]: **~ alguém a fazer algo** to persuade sb to do sthg. <> *vi* [induzir] to persuade.
    ➡ **persuadir-se** *vp* [convencer-se]: **~-se (de algo)** to be persuaded (of sthg).

persuasão [pexswa'zãw] *f* persuasion.

persuasivo, va [pexswa'zivu, va] *adj* persuasive.

pertencente [pextẽn'sẽntʃi] *adj*: **~ a algo/alguém** belonging to sthg/sb.

pertencer [pextẽn'se(x)] *vi*: **~ a** [ger] to belong to; [concernir] to refer to.

pertences [pex'tẽnsiʃ] *mpl* [objetos pessoais] belongings.

pertinaz [pextʃi'najʒ] *adj* persistent.

pertinência [pextʃi'nẽnsja] *f* pertinence.

pertinente [pextʃi'nẽntʃi] *adj* -1. [ger] pertinent. -2. [importante] relevant.

perto ['pɛxtu] <> *adj* nearby. <> *adv* near; **de ~** [a pouca distância] closely; *fig* [intimamente] first-hand; **~ de** [em comparação] next to.

perturbador, ra [pextuxba'do(x), ra] *adj* disturbing.

perturbar [pextux'ba(x)] <> *vt* -1. [ger] to perturb. -2. [atrapalhar] to disturb. -3. [envergonhar] to embarass. <> *vi* [atordoar] to pester.

peru, rua [pe'ru, rua] *m, f* [ave] turkey.
➡ **perua** *f* -**1.** [caminhonete] estate car *UK*, station wagon *US*. -**2.** *fam pej* [mulher] hussy.

Peru [pe'ru] *n*: (o) ~ Peru.

peruano, na [pe'rwãnu, na] ⟨⟩ *adj* Peruvian. ⟨⟩ *m, f* Peruvian.

peruca [pe'ruka] *f* wig.

perversão [pexvex'sãw] (*pl* -ões) *f* -**1.** [depravação] perversion. -**2.** [alteração] alteration.

perverso, sa [pex'vɛxsu, sa] *adj* perverse.

perverter [pexvex'te(x)] *vt* -**1.** [corromper] to pervert. -**2.** [alterar] to alter. -**3.** [deturpar] to distort.
➡ **perverter-se** *vp* [corromper-se] to become depraved.

pervertido, da [pexvex'tʃidu, da] ⟨⟩ *adj* [corrompido] depraved. ⟨⟩ *m, f* pervert.

pesadelo [peza'delu] *m* nightmare.

pesado, da [pe'zadu, da] *adj* -**1.** [ger] heavy. -**2.** [tenso] tense. -**3.** [grosseiro] coarse.

pêsames ['pezamiʃ] *mpl* condolences.

pesar [pe'za(x)] ⟨⟩ *m* sadness; **apesar dos** ~ **es** in spite of everything. ⟨⟩ *vt* to weigh. ⟨⟩ *vi* -**1.** [ger] to weigh. -**2.** [recair]: ~ **sobre alguém** to fall on sb. -**3.** [onerar] to be burdensome. -**4.** [influenciar]: ~ **em algo** to influence sthg. -**5.** [causar tristeza]: ~ **a alguém** to grieve sb. -**6.** [causar remorso] to weigh sb down.
➡ **pesar-se** *vp* [verificar o peso] to weigh o.s.

pesaroso, osa [peza'rozu, ɔza] *adj* -**1.** [triste] sorrowful. -**2.** [arrependido] sorry.

pesca ['pɛʃka] *f* -**1.** [ato] fishing; **ir à** ~ to go fishing. -**2.** [o que se pescou] catch.

pescado [peʃ'kadu] *m* catch (*of fish*).

pescador, ra [peʃka'do(x), ra] (*mpl* -es, *fpl* -s) *m, f* fisherman (*f* fisherwoman).

pescar [peʃ'ka(x)] *vt* -**1.** [apanhar] to fish. -**2.** *fig* [conseguir] to get. -**3.** *fig* [conquistar] to catch.

pescoço [peʃ'kosul] *m* neck; **até o** ~ *fig* up to one's neck.

peso ['pezul] *m* -**1.** [ger] weight; ~ **bruto/líquido** gross/net weight; ~ **pesado** heavyweight; **ele é um intelectual de** ~ he is a weighty intelectual. -**2.** [para papéis] paperweight. -**3.** [em atletismo] weights (*pl*). -**4.** [moeda] peso. -**5.** *fig* [carga] burden.
➡ **em peso** *loc adj* en masse.

pesponto [peʃ'põntul] *m* backstitch.

pesqueiro, ra [peʃ'kejru, ra] *adj* fishing (*antes de subst*).

pesquisa [peʃ'kizal] *f* -**1.** [investigação] search. -**2.**: ~ **de mercado** market research; ~ **de opinião** opinion poll. -**3.** [estudo] research; ~ **e desenvolvimento** research and development.

pesquisador, ra [peʃkiza'do(x), ra] ⟨⟩ *adj* research (*antes de subst*). ⟨⟩ *m, f* researcher.

pesquisar [peʃki'za(x)] ⟨⟩ *vt* -**1.** [investigar] to investigate. -**2.** [estudar] to research. ⟨⟩ *vi* [estudar] to do research.

pêssego ['pesegul] *m* peach.

pessimismo [pesi'miʒmul] *m* pessimism.

pessimista [pesi'miʃta] ⟨⟩ *adj* pessimistic. ⟨⟩ *mf* pessimist.

péssimo, ma ['pɛsimu, ma] *adj* (*superl de mau*) terrible; **ficou** ~ **com a notícia** the news made him feel terrible.

pessoa [pe'soa] *f* [ger] person; **em** ~ personally; ~ **física** *JUR* private individual; ~ **jurídica** *JUR* legal entity.

pessoal [pe'swawl] (*pl* -ais) ⟨⟩ *adj* personal. ⟨⟩ *m* -**1.** [empregados] personnel (*pl*), staff. -**2.** [grupo] people (*pl*).

pessoalmente [peswaw'mẽntʃil] *adv* personally.

pestana [peʃ'tãna] *f* -**1.** [cílio] eyelash. -**2.** *COST* flap. -**3.** *MÚS* barré.

pestanejar [peʃtane'ʒa(x)] *vi* to blink; **sem** ~ *fig* without batting an eyelid.

peste ['pɛʃtʃil] *f* -**1.** [ger] plague. -**2.** *fig* [pessoa] pest. -**3.** *fig* [coisa perniciosa] scourge.

pesticida [peʃtʃi'sida] *f* pesticide.

pestilento, ta [peʃtʃi'lẽntu, ta] *adj* -**1.** [fedorento] stinking. -**2.** [infectado] pestilent.

pétala ['pɛtala] *f* petal.

peteca [pe'tɛka] *f* [brinquedo] shuttlecock; **não deixar a** ~ **cair** *fam fig* to keep the ball rolling.

peteleco [pete'lɛkul] *m* flick.

petição [petʃi'sãw] (*pl* -ões) *f* -**1.** [requerimento] petition. -**2.** [súplica] plea. -**3.** [estado]: **em** ~ **de miséria** in a pitiful state.

petiscar [petʃiʃ'ka(x)] *vi* to snack; **quem não arrisca não petisca** he who dares wins.

petisco [pe'tʃiʃkul] *m* titbit *UK*, tidbit *US*.

petit-pois [petʃi'pwal] *m inv* pea.

petrificar [petrifi'ka(x)] *vt* -**1.** [tornar em pedra] to harden. -**2.** [insensibilizar] to numb. -**3.** [aterrorizar] to petrify.

Petrobras (*abrev de* Petróleo Brasileiro **S/A**) *f* Brazilian state-owned petroleum company.

petroleiro, ra [petro'lejrul] ⟨⟩ *adj*: **navio-** ~ (oil) tanker. ⟨⟩ *m, f* [pessoa] oilman.

pinho

petróleo [pe'trɔlju] *m* petroleum, oil; ~ **bruto** crude oil.

petrolífero, ra [petro'liferu, ra] *adj* oil.

petulância [petu'lãnsja] *f* petulance.

petulante [petu'lãntʃi] *adj* petulant.

PFL (*abrev de* **Partido da Frente Liberal**) *m* Party of the Liberal Front, *the largest, very right-wing party in Brazil.*

piada ['pjada] *f* joke.

pianista [pja'niʃta] *mf* pianist.

piano ['pjãnu] *m* piano.

pião ['pjãw] (*pl* -**ões**) *m* spinning top.

piar ['pja(x)] *vi* [ave - pinto] to cheep; [- passarinho] to chirp; [- coruja] to hoot.

PIB (*abrev de* **Produto Interno Bruto**) *m* GDP.

picada [pi'kada] *f* ▷ **picado**.

picadinho [pika'dʒiɲu] *m* CULIN **- 1.** [de carne] minced meat. **- 2.** [de legumes] vegetable stew.

picado, da [pi'kadu, da] *adj* **- 1.** [ger] stung; **ser ~ por algo** to be bitten by sthg. **- 2.** [em pedaços] chopped up. **- 3.** [mar] choppy. **- 4.** [vôo] nosediving.
➡ **picada** *f* **- 1.** [espetada] prick. **- 2.** [mordida] bite. **- 3.** [caminho] trail.

picanha [pi'kãɲa] *f* [carne bovina] rump.

picante [pi'kãntʃi] *adj* spicy.

pica-pau [,pika'paw] (*pl* **pica-paus**) *m* woodpecker.

picar [pi'ka(x)] *vt* **- 1.** [espetar] to prick. **- 2.** [morder] to bite. **- 3.** [cortar em pedaços] to chop. **- 4.** [lascar] to splinter. **- 5.** [bicar] to peck.

picareta [pika'reta] ◇ *f* [instrumento] pickaxe *UK*, pickax *US*. ◇ *mf* [mau-caráter] con artist.

pichação [piʃa'sãw] (*pl* -**ões**) *f* **- 1.** [grafite] graffiti. **- 2.** *fam* [crítica] smear.

picles ['pikleʃ] *mpl* pickles.

pico ['piku] *m* **- 1.** [cume] summit. **- 2.** [de faca etc.] point. **- 3.** *fam* [de droga] shot.

picolé [piko'lɛ] *m* ice lolly.

picotar [piko'ta(x)] *vt* to perforate.

picuinha [pi'kwiɲa] *f* [implicância] dispute; **estar de ~ com alguém** to be at odds with sb.

piedade [pje'dadʒi] *f* **- 1.** [compaixão] pity; **ter ~ de alguém** to have pity on sb. **- 2.** [religiosidade] piety.

piedoso, osa [pje'dozu, ɔza] *adj* pious.

piegas ['pjɛgaʃ] *adj inv* soppy.

píer ['pie(x)] *m* pier.

piercing ['pixsĩn] *m* body piercing.

pifão [pi'fãw] (*pl* -**ões**) *m fam* drunk; **tomar um ~** to have a skinful.

pifar [pi'fa(x)] *vi fam* **- 1.** [enguiçar] to break down. **- 2.** [gorar] to fall through.

pigméia [pig'mɛja] *f* ▷ **pigmeu**.

pigmento [pig'mẽntu] *m* pigment.

pigmeu, méia [pig'mew, mɛja] ◇ *adj* [pequeno] pygmy. ◇ *m, f* pygmy.

pijama [pi'ʒãma] *m* pyjamas (*pl*) *UK*, pajamas (*pl*) *US*.

pilantra [pi'lãntra] *mf* rogue.

pilar [pi'la(x)] (*pl* -**es**) ◇ *m* [coluna] pillar. ◇ *vt* to grind.

pilha ['piʎa] *f* **- 1.** [monte] pile. **- 2.** ELETR battery. **- 3.** [pessoa]: **estar/ser uma ~ (de nervos)** to be a bundle of nerves. **- 4.** COMPUT stack.

pilhar [pi'ʎa(x)] *vt* **- 1.** [saquear] to pillage. **- 2.** [roubar] to rob.

pilhéria [pi'ʎɛrja] *f* jest.

pilotar [pilo'ta(x)] ◇ *vt* to steer. ◇ *vi* to steer.

piloto [pi'lotu] ◇ *adj* [modelo] pilot. ◇ *m* **- 1.** [ger] pilot. **- 2.** [de corrida] driver. **- 3.** [bico de gás] pilot light.

pílula ['pilula] *f* pill; ~ **anticoncepcional** contraceptive pill.

pimenta [pi'mẽnta] *f* **- 1.** CULIN pepper. **- 2.** *fig* [malícia] spite.

pimenta-do-reino [pi,mẽntadu'xejnu] (*pl* **pimentas-do-reino**) *f* black pepper.

pimenta-malagueta [pi,mẽntamala'geta] (*pl* **pimentas-malagueta**) *f* chilli pepper *UK*, chili pepper *US*.

pimentão [pimẽn'tãw] (*pl* -**ões**) *m*: ~ **verde/vermelho** green/red pepper.

pimenteira [pimẽn'tejra] *f* **- 1.** BOT pepper tree. **- 2.** [recipiente] pepper pot.

pinacoteca [pinako'tɛka] *f* **- 1.** [coleção] art collection. **- 2.** [museu] art gallery.

pinça [pĩnsa] *f* **- 1.** MED forceps (*pl*). **- 2.** [de sobrancelha] tweezers (*pl*).

píncaro ['pĩŋkaru] *m* **- 1.** [cume] peak. **- 2.** *fig* [apogeu] height.

pincel [pĩn'sɛw] (*pl* -**éis**) *m* brush; ~ **de barba** shaving brush.

pincelar [pĩnse'la(x)] *vt* to paint.

pincenê [pĩnse'ne] *m* pince-nez.

pinga ['pĩŋga] *f fam* [cachaça] booze.

pingar [pĩn'ga(x)] *vi* **- 1.** [gotejar] to drip. **- 2.** [chover] to spit. **- 3.** [render] to trickle in.

pingente [pĩn'ʒẽntʃi] *m* [objeto] pendant.

pingo ['pĩŋgu] *m* **- 1.** [gota] drop. **- 2.** [sinal ortográfico] dot; **pôr os ~ s nos is** *fig* to dot the i's and cross the t's.

pingue-pongue [,pĩŋgi'põŋgi] (*pl* **pingue-pongues**) *m* ping-pong, table tennis.

pingüim [pĩŋ'gwĩ] (*pl* -**ns**) *m* penguin.

pinheiro [pi'ɲejru] *m* pine tree.

pinho ['piɲu] *m* **- 1.** BOT pine (tree). **- 2.** [madeira] pine wood. **- 3.** *fam* [violão] fiddle.

pino ['pinu] *m* -**1.** [peça] peg. -**2.** [AUTO - em motor] crankpin; [- tranca] lock; *fam fig* [estar mal] to fall apart. -**3.** [cume]: a ~ at the zenith.

pinta ['pĩnta] *f* -**1.** [sinal] mole. -**2.** *fam* [aparência]: **o rapaz é boa** ~ the boy is looking good; **essa comida está com boa** ~ that food looks good; **ter** ~ **de algo** to look like sthg. -**3.** *fam* [indício]: **estar com** ~ **de (ser) difícil** to look (like being) difficult; **ela deu na** ~ **que ia nos assaltar** [demonstrar] she looked like she was going to attack us.

pintado, da [pĩn'tadu, da] *adj* -**1.** [colorido - papel] coloured; [- parede, olhos, unhas] painted; [- face] painted, made-up; [- cabelo] dyed. -**2.** [sardento] freckled.

pintar [pĩn'ta(x)] ⇔ *vt* -**1.** [ger] to paint. -**2.** [com tinta - ger] to paint; [- cabelo] to dye. -**3.** *fig* [conceber] to paint as. ⇔ *vi* -**1.** ARTE to paint. -**2.** *fam* [aparecer] to turn up. -**3.** [exceder-se] to get overexcited; ~ **e bordar** *fig* to have a great time.

➡ **pintar-se** *vp* [maquilar-se] to make o.s. up.

pinto, ta ['pĩntu, ta] *m, f* -**1.** ZOOL chick; **ficar (molhado) como um** ~ to get soaked to the bone. -**2.** *mfam* [pênis] cock. -**3.** [coisa fácil]: **ser** ~ to be a pushover.

pintor, ra [pĩn'to(x), ra] (*mpl* -**es**, *fpl* -**s**) *m, f* painter.

pintura [pĩn'tura] *f* -**1.** ARTE painting; ~ **a óleo** oil painting. -**2.** [de casa etc.] paintwork. -**3.** [maquiagem] make-up.

pio, pia ['piw, 'pia] *adj* -**1.** [devota] pious. -**2.** [caridoso] charitable.

➡ **pio** *m* [de ave] peep; **não dê um** ~, **senão atiro** not a peep, or else I'll shoot.

piões ['pjõjʃ] *pl* ⊳ **pião**.

piolho ['pjoʎu] *m* louse.

pioneiro, ra [pjo'nejru, ra] ⇔ *adj* pioneering. ⇔ *m, f* pioneer.

pior ['pjɔ(x)] (*pl* -**es**) ⇔ *adj* -**1.** [comparativo]: ~ **(do que)** worse (than). -**2.** [superlativo]: **o/a** ~ **... the worst ...**⇔ *m*: **o** ~ **(de)** [inferior] the worst (of); **o** ~ **é que ...** the worst of it is that ...⇔ *f*: **o/ a** ~ **(de)** the worst (of); **estar na** ~ to be in a jam; **levar a** ~ to lose. ⇔ *adv* [comparativo]: ~ **(do que)** worse (than); **ela está** ~ **de saúde** her health is worse.

piorar [pjo'ra(x)] *vi* to deteriorate.

pipa ['pipa] *f* -**1.** [vasilhame] barrel. -**2.** [de papel] kite.

pipi [pi'pi] *m fam* wee-wee *UK*, pee-pee *US*; **fazer** ~ to wee *UK*, to go pee-pee *US*.

pipoca [pi'pɔka] *f* -**1.** [de milho] popcorn. -**2.** [em pele] blister.

pipocar [pipo'ka(x)] *vi* -**1.** [estourar] to burst out. -**2.** [espocar] to crackle. -**3.** [surgir] to sprout up.

pipoqueiro, ra [pipo'keiru, ra] *m, f* [vendedor] popcorn seller.

pique ['piki] *m* -**1.** [brincadeira] catch. -**2.** [disposição] enthusiasm; **perder o** ~ to lose one's momentum. -**3.** [corte] notch. -**4.** NÁUT: **ir a** ~ to sink.

piquenique [,piki'niki] *m* picnic.

pirado, da [pi'radu, da] *adj* crazy.

pirâmide [pi'ramidʒi] *f* pyramid.

piranha [pi'raŋa] *f* -**1.** [peixe] piranha. -**2.** *mfam pej* [mulher] hussy. -**3.** [prendedor de cabelo] hair clasp.

pirão [pi'rãw] (*pl* -**ões**) *m* CULIN cassava porridge.

pirar [pi'ra(x)] *vi* -**1.** [endoidar] to go insane. -**2.** [fugir] to scarper.

pirata [pi'ratal] ⇔ *adj* pirate. ⇔ *mf* pirate.

pirataria [pirata'rial] *f* piracy.

Pireneus [pire'newʃl] *n*: **os** ~ the Pyrenees.

pires ['piriʃ] *m inv* saucer.

pirraça [pi'xasa] *f*: **fazer algo por** ~ to do sthg out of spite.

pirralho, lha [pi'xaʎu, ʎa] *m, f* child.

pirueta [pi'rweta] *f* pirouette.

pirulito [piru'litu] *m* -**1.** [bala] lollipop. -**2.** *fam* [pênis] willy.

pisada [pi'zada] *f* -**1.** [passo] footstep. -**2.** [pegada] footprint.

pisar [pi'za(x)] ⇔ *vt* -**1.** to tread on. -**2.** [esmagar] to crush. -**3.** [percorrer] to set foot on. ⇔ *vi* -**1.** [andar]: ~ **(em)** to walk *ou* tread (on). -**2.**: ~ **em** [tocar com os pés] to step on; [ir, vir] to set foot in; [humilhar] to crush; ⊳ **bola, ovo**.

pisca-pisca [,piʃka'piʃka] (*pl* pisca-piscas) *m* AUTO indicator.

piscar [piʃ'ka(x)] ⇔ *vt* [olho] to blink. ⇔ *vi* -**1.** [pessoa, olho] to wink. -**2.** [trocar sinais]: ~ **para alguém** to wink at sb. -**3.** [tremeluzir] to twinkle. ⇔ *m* twinkling; **num** ~ **de olhos** in a twinkling of an eye.

piscina [pi'sinal] *f* swimming pool.

piso ['pizul] *m* -**1.** [ger] floor. -**2.** [revestimento] flooring. -**3.** [salário]: ~ **(salarial)** minimum (professional) wage.

pisotear [pizo'tʃja(x)] *vt* -**1.** [pisar] to trample (on). -**2.** [humilhar] to trample over.

pista ['piʃtal] *f* -**1.** [vestígio] trace. -**2.** [encalço]: **na** ~ **de** in pursuit of, on the

pleito

trail of. **- 3.** *fig* [informação] clue. **- 4.** [de rua, estrada] track. **- 5.** *AERON* runway. **- 6.** [*ESP* - de automobilismo, atletismo] track; [- de esqui] piste; [- de equitação] ring; [- de tênis] court. **- 7.** [de dança] floor.

pistola [piʃ'tɔla] *f* **- 1.** [arma] pistol. **- 2.** [para pintar] (spray) gun.

pistoleiro, ra [piʃto'lejru, ra] *m, f* [criminoso] gunman.

pistom [piʃ'tõ] (*pl* **-ns**) *m* **- 1.** [instrumento] trumpet. **- 2.** [de motor] piston.

pitada [pi'tada] *f* pinch.

pitanga [pi'tãŋga] *f* (red Brazil) cherry.

pitoresco, ca [pito'reʃku, ka] <> *adj* picturesque. <> *m* attraction.

pivete [pi'vɛtʃi] *m* child thief.

pivô [pi'vo] *m* **- 1.** [de dente] pivot. **- 2.** *fig* [suporte] pivot. **- 3.** *fig* [agente principal] central figure. **- 4.** [jogador] centre.

pixel ['piksew] *m* COMPUT pixel.

pixote [pi'ʃɔtʃi] *m* small child.

pizza ['pitsa] *f* pizza.

pizzaria [pitsa'ria] *f* pizzeria.

plá [pla] *m*: **ter** *ou* **bater um** ~ **com alguém** to have a chat with sb.

placa ['plaka] *f* **- 1.** [ger] plaque. **- 2.** [lâmina] sheet. **- 3.** [aviso] sign; ~ **de sinalização** road sign. **- 4.** *AUTO* number plate *UK*, license plate *US*. **- 5.** COMPUT & ELECTRON board; ~ **de vídeo** video card. **- 6.** [na pele] blotch.

placa-mãe ['plakamãj] (*pl* **placas-mãe** *ou* **placas-mães**) *f* COMPUT motherboard.

placar [pla'ka(x)] *m* **- 1.** [escore] score. **- 2.** [marcador] scoreboard.

plácido, da ['plasidu, da] *adj* **- 1.** [pessoa, olhar, semblante] placid. **- 2.** [lugar, dia, vida] quiet.

plagiador, ra [plaʒja'do(x), ra] *m, f* plagiarist.

plagiar [pla'ʒja(x)] *vt* to plagiarize.

plagiário, ria [pla'ʒjarju, rja] *m, f* plagiarist.

plágio ['plaʒju] *m* plagiarism.

planador [plana'do(x)] (*pl* **-es**) *m* glider.

planalto [pla'nawtu] *m* plateau.

➡ **Planalto** *m* [palácio presidencial] president's office.

planar [pla'na(x)] *vi* to glide.

planejamento [planeʒa'mẽtu] *m* planning; ~ **familiar** family planning.

planejar [plane'ʒa(x)] *vt* **- 1.** [ger] to plan. **- 2.** *ARQUIT* to design.

planeta [pla'neta] *m* planet.

planetário, a [plane'tarju] *adj* planetary.

➡ **planetário** *m* planetarium.

planície [pla'nisji] *f* plain.

planilha [pla'niʎa] *f* **- 1.** [formulário] table. **- 2.** COMPUT spreadsheet.

plano, na ['plãnu, na] <> *adj* **- 1.** [superfície] flat. **- 2.** [liso] smooth. <> *m* **- 1.** [ger] plan. **- 2.** [superfície plana] level surface. **- 3.** [posição]: **em primeiro/segundo** ~ **in** the foreground/background; **para ela isso fica em segundo** ~ *fig* for her this takes second place. **- 4.** [nível] level. **- 5.** [seguro]: ~ **de saúde** health plan. **- 6.** *GEOM* plane.

planta ['plãta] *f* **- 1.** *BIOL* plant. **- 2.** *ANAT*: ~ **do pé** sole of the foot. **- 3.** *ARQUIT* plan.

plantação [plãta'sãw] *m* **- 1.** [ato] planting. **- 2.** [terreno] plantation. **- 3.** [produtos] crops (*pl*).

plantão [plãn'tãw] (*pl* **-ões**) *m* **- 1.** [serviço - diurno] duty; [- noturno] night duty; **estar de** ~ to be on duty. **- 2.** [plantonista] person on duty.

plantar [plãn'ta(x)] *vt* **- 1.** [planta, árvore] to plant. **- 2.** [semear] to sow. **- 3.** [fincar] to drive in. **- 4.** *fig* [estabelecer] to establish. **- 5.** [incutir] to inspire. **- 6.** [pôr] to set up.

plantões [plãn'tõjʃ] *pl* ➡ **plantão**.

plantonista [plãnto'niʃta] *mf* person on duty.

plaqueta [pla'keta] *f* **- 1.** [placa pequena] small plaque, plaquette. **- 2.** *AUTO* licensing badge. **- 3.** COMPUT chip.

plástico, ca ['plaʃtʃiku, ka] *adj* plastic.

➡ **plástico** *m* [matéria] plastic; **de** ~ plastic.

➡ **plástica** *f* **- 1.** [cirurgia] plastic surgery; **fazer plástica** to have plastic surgery. **- 2.** [corpo] build.

plataforma [plata'fɔxma] *f* **- 1.** [ger] platform; ~ **de exploração de petróleo** oil rig; ~ **de lançamento** launch pad. **- 2.** *GEOGR* shelf.

platéia [pla'tɛja] *f* **- 1.** [espaço] stalls (*pl*) *UK*, orchestra *US*. **- 2.** [público] audience.

platina [pla'tʃina] *f* [metal] platinum.

platinado, da [platʃi'nadu, da] *adj* platinum blond (*antes de subst*).

➡ **platinado** *m* *AUTO* contact point.

platônico, ca [pla'toniku, ka] *adj* platonic.

plausível [plaw'zivɛw] (*pl* **-eis**) *adj* [aceitável] plausible.

playground [plej'grawndʒi] *m* playground.

plebeu, béia [ple'bew, bɛja] <> *adj* plebeian. <> *m, f* plebeian.

plebiscito [plebi'situ] *m* plebiscite.

pleitear [plej'tʃja(x)] *vt* **- 1.** [diligenciar] to strive for. **- 2.** *JUR* to contest. **- 3.** [concorrer a] to compete for.

pleito ['plejtu] *m* **- 1.** *JUR* legal dispute, lawsuit. **- 2.** [eleição]: ~ **(eleitoral)** election.

plenamente [,plena'mẽntʃi] adv fully.

plenário [ple'narjul] m -1. [assembléia] plenary session. -2. [local] chamber.

plenitude [pleni'tudʒi] f fulfilment.

pleno, na ['plenu, na] adj -1. [cheio]: ~ de full of. -2. [total] complete; **em plena luz do dia** in broad daylight; **em ~ verão** in high summer; ~s **poderes** full powers.

pluma ['pluma] f -1. [de ave] feather. -2. [para escrever] quill. -3. [adorno] plume.

plural [plu'raw] (pl -ais) <> adj plural. <> m plural.

pluralismo [plura'liʒmu] m -1. [diversidade] diversity. -2. POL pluralism.

Plutão [plu'tãw] n Pluto.

pluvial [plu'vjaw] (pl -ais) adj pluvial, rain (antes de subst).

PM (abrev de Polícia Militar) f state police (force).

PMDB (abrev de Partido do Movimento Democrático Brasileiro) m Brazilian Party for Democratic Movement, the largest party of the centre.

PNB (abrev de Produto Nacional Bruto) m GNP.

pneu [pi'new] m -1. AUTO tyre UK, tire US. -2. fam [gordura] spare tyre UK, spare tire US.

pneumonia [pinewmu'nia] f pneumonia.

pó ['pɔ] m -1. [poeira] dust; **tirar o ~ de algo** to dust sthg. -2. [substância pulverizada] powder; **em ~** powdered. -3. [pó-de-arroz] face powder. -4. fam [cocaína] snow.

pobre ['pɔbri] <> adj -1. [ger] poor. -2. [escasso]: ~ **de/em algo** lacking in sthg. -3. (antes do subst) [digno de pena] poor. <> m [pessoa] poor person; **os ~s** the poor.

pobreza [po'breza] m -1. [miséria] poverty. -2. [escassez]: ~ **de** OU **em algo** lack of sthg.

poça ['pɔsa] f: ~ **(d'água)** puddle.

poção [po'sãw] (pl -ões) f potion.

pocilga [po'siwga] f -1. [chiqueiro] pigsty. -2. fig [lugar imundo] hovel.

poço ['posu] f [cavidade] well; ~ **de petróleo** oil well; **ir ao fundo do ~** fig to sink to the depths of despair.

podar [po'da(x)] vt to prune.

pó-de-arroz [,pɔdʒja'xoʃ] (pl **pós-de-arroz**) m face powder.

poder [po'de(x)] <> m -1. [político, influência] power; **estar no ~** to be in power; ~ **de compra** purchasing power; **não tenho ~ nenhum** I'm powerless. -2. [possessão] power; **estar em ~ de alguém** to be in sb's power; **ter em**

seu ~ algo to have sthg within one's power. <> v aux -1. [ser capaz de]: ~ **fazer algo** to be able to do sthg; **posso fazê-lo** I can do it; **posso ajudar?** can I help?, may I help?; **você podia tê-lo feito antes** you could have done it earlier; **não posso mais!** [em relação a cansaço] I've had enough!; [em relação a comida] I'm full! -2. [estar autorizado para]: ~ **fazer algo** to be allowed to do sthg; **posso fumar?** may I smoke?; **você não pode estacionar aqui** you can't park here; **não pude sair ontem** I wasn't allowed (to go) out yesterday. -3. [ser capaz moralmente] can; **não podemos magoar o gato** we can't hurt the cat. -4. [exprime possibilidade]: **você podia ter vindo de ônibus** you could have come by bus; **cuidado que você pode se machucar!** be careful, you might hurt yourself! -5. [exprime indignação, queixa]: **não pode ser!** this is outrageous!; **você podia ter nos avisado** you could have warned us!; **pudera!** I wish! <> v impess [ser possível]: **pode não ser verdade** it might not be true; **pode acontecer a qualquer um** it could happen to anybody; **pode ser que chova** it might rain.
◆ **poder com** v + prep -1. [suportar] to bear; **não posso com mentirosos** I cannot bear liars. -2. [rival, adversário] to bear. -3. [peso] to carry; **você não pode com tanto peso** you can't carry all that weight.

poderio [pode'riw] m power.

podre ['podri] <> adj -1. [ger] rotten. -2. fig [corrupto] corrupt. -3. fig [cheio]: **estou ~ (de cansaço)** I am dog-tired; ~ **de gripe** full of flu; ~ **de rico** filthy rich. <> m -1. [parte]: **o ~ da maçã** the bad part of the apple. -2. fig [defeito] dark secret.

podridão [podri'dãw] (pl -ões) f -1. [estado de podre] decay. -2. fig [corrupção] corruption.

poeira ['pwejra] f dust; ~ **radioativa** fallout.

poeirento, ta [pwej'rẽntu, ta] adj dusty.

poema ['pwema] m poem.

poesia [pwi'zia] f -1. [arte] poetry. -2. [poema] poem. -3. [encanto] charm.

poeta, tisa ['pwɛta, tʃiza] m, f poet.

poético, ca ['pwɛtʃiku, ka] adj poetic.

pois ['pojʃ] conj -1. [portanto] therefore. -2. [mas] well. -3. [porque] as.
◆ **pois bem** loc adv well then.
◆ **pois é** loc adv indeed.
◆ **pois não** <> loc adv [em loja, restaurante]: ~ **não?** can I help you? <> interj of course!

ponteiro

pois sim *interj*: ~ **sim!** certainly not!, yeah right!

polaco, ca [po'laku, ka] <> *adj* Polish. <> *m, f* Pole.

polaco *m* [língua] Polish.

polar [po'la(x)] *adj* polar.

polegada [pole'gada] *f* inch.

polegar [pole'ga(x)] (*pl* -**es**) *m* thumb.

polêmico, ca [po'lemiku, ka] *adj* controversial.

polêmica *f* controversy.

polemizar [polemi'za(x)] *vi*: ~ **sobre al-**go to debate on sthg.

pólen ['pɔlɛ̃] *m* pollen.

polenta [po'lẽta] *f* polenta.

polia [po'lia] *f* pulley.

polícia [po'lisja] <> *f* [corporação] police, police force; ~ **federal** federal police; ~ **militar** state police (force). <> *mf* [policial] police officer.

policial [poli'sjaw] (*pl* -**ais**) <> *adj* police (*antes de subst*). <> *mf* police officer.

policiar [poli'sja(x)] *vt* -**1.** [vigiar] to police. -**2.** [controlar] to control.

policiar-se *vp* [controlar-se] to control o.s.

polidez [poli'deʒ] *f* [cortesia] politeness.

polido, da [po'lidu, da] *adj* -**1.** [cortês] polite. -**2.** [liso] polished. -**3.** [lustroso] shiny.

poliéster [po'ljɛste(x)] *m* polyester.

poliestireno [poljestʃi'renu] *m* polystyrene.

polietileno [poljetʃi'lenu] *m* polythene.

polígamo, ma [po'ligamu, ma] *adj* polygamous.

poliglota [poli'glɔta] <> *adj* polyglot. <> *m* polyglot.

polígono [po'ligonu] *m* GEOM polygon.

polimento [poli'mẽtu] *m* -**1.** [lustração] polishing. -**2.** *fig* [finura] refinement.

polir [po'li(x)] *vt* -**1.** [ger] to polish. -**2.** *fig* [aprimorar - pessoa] to refine; [- linguagem] to polish up.

politécnica [poli'tɛknika] *f* polytechnic.

política [po'litʃika] *f* > **político**.

politicagem [politʃi'kaʒẽ] *f* politicking.

político, ca [po'litʃiku, ka] *adj* -**1.** POL political. -**2.** *fig* [hábil] astute.

político *m* politician.

política *f* -**1.** [ciência] politics (*pl*). -**2.** [programa] policy; **política econômica** economic policy. -**3.** *fig* [habilidade] astuteness.

politizar [politʃi'za(x)] *vt* to politicize.

politizar-se *vp* to become politically aware.

polivalente [poliva'lẽtʃi] *adj* -**1.** [versátil] versatile. -**2.** MED polyvalent.

pólo ['pɔlu] *m* -**1.** [ger] pole. -**2.** *fig* [extremo] side. -**3.** ASTRON: ~ **magnético** magnetic pole. -**4.** [concentração] hub; ~ **petroquímico** petrochemicals complex. -**5.** ESP polo; ~ **aquático** water polo.

Polônia [po'lonja] *n* Poland.

polpa ['powpa] *f* pulp.

poltrona [pow'trona] *f* armchair.

poluente [po'lwẽtʃi] <> *adj* pollutant. <> *m* pollutant.

poluição [poluj'sãw] *f* pollution.

poluir [po'lwi(x)] *vt* -**1.** [sujar] to pollute. -**2.** *fig* [corromper] to corrupt.

polvilho [pow'viʎu] *m* -**1.** [pó] powder. -**2.** [farinha] manioc flour.

polvo ['powvu] *m* octopus.

pólvora ['powvora] *f* gunpowder; **descobrir a** ~ *fig irôn* to do sthg highly original.

polvorosa [powvo'rɔza] *f*: **em** ~ [agitado] in a flap; [desarrumado] in a mess.

pomada [po'mada] *f* ointment.

pomar [po'ma(x)] (*pl* -**es**) *m* orchard.

pombo, ba ['põbu, ba] *m, f* dove, pigeon.

pompa ['põpa] *f* splendour.

pomposo, osa [põ'pozu, ɔza] *adj* ostentatious.

ponche ['põʃi] *m* punch.

poncho ['põʃu] *m* poncho.

ponderado, da [põde'radu, da] *adj* cautious.

ponderar [põde'ra(x)] <> *vi* -**1.** [refletir] to reflect. -**2.** [argumentar] to hold forth. <> *vt* -**1.** [avaliar] to weigh up. -**2.** [considerar] to consider.

pônei ['ponej] *m* pony.

ponta ['põta] *f* -**1.** [extremidade] end; **na** ~ **do pé** on tiptoe. -**2.** [bico] point. -**3.** [canto] corner. -**4.** [vértice] apex. -**5.** *fig* [quantidade]: **estou com uma** ~ **de fome** I'm a touch hungry. -**6.** [de cigarro] cigarette end. -**7.** CINE & TEATRO: **fazer uma** ~ to have a walk-on part. -**8.** *loc*: **saber na** ~ **da língua** to have on the tip of one's tongue.

pontada [põ'tada] *f* [dor] twinge.

pontão [põ'tãw] (*pl* -**ões**) *m* [plataforma] pontoon.

pontapé [põta'pɛ] *m* -**1.** [chute] kick; **dar um** ~ **em alguém** to kick sb. -**2.** *fig* [rejeição]: **ele levou um** ~ **da namorada** his girlfriend kicked him out.

pontaria [põta'ria] *f* aim.

ponte ['põtʃi] *f* -**1.** [ger] bridge. -**2.** AERON: ~ **aérea** air lift. -**3.** MED: ~ **de safena** (heart) bypass operation.

ponteiro [põ'tejru] *m* -**1.** [de velocímetro] pointer. -**2.** [de bússola] needle. -**3.** [de relógio] hand.

pontiagudo, da [põntʃja'gudu, da] *adj* pointed.

pontífice [põn'tʃifisi] *m* pope.

pontilhado, da [põntʃi'ʎadu, da] <> *adj* dotted. <> *m* [conjunto de pontos] dotted line.

ponto ['põntul *m* -1. [ger] point; ~ final terminus; ~ de ônibus bus stop; ~ de táxi taxi rank. -2. [costura, operação] stitch; ~ de meia stocking stitch; ~ de tricô garter stitch. -3. [sinal] spot. -4. [pontuação]: ~ (final) full stop *UK*, period *US*; dois ~s colon; ~ de interrogação/exclamação question/exclamation mark. -5. [mancha] mark. -6. [de calda] consistency. -7. [matéria escolar] topic. -8. *MÚS* (religious) chant. -9. *GEOGR* ~ cardeal cardinal point. -10. [espírit] spirit. -11. [traço]: ~ fraco weak point. -12. *loc*: não dar ~ sem nó to look after number one.

➡ a ponto de *loc adv* on the point of.

pontões [põn'tõjʃ] *pl* ⊳ **pontão**.

ponto-e-vírgula [ˌpõntwi'vixgula] (*pl* ponto-e-vírgulas) *m* semicolon.

pontuação [põntwa'sãw] (*pl* -ões) *f* punctuation.

pontual [põn'twawl (*pl* -ais) *adj* punctual.

pontualidade [põntwali'dadʒi] *f* punctuality.

pontudo, da [põn'tudu, da] *adj* pointed.

poodle ['pudowl *m* poodle.

POP (*abrev de* Post Office Protocol) *m* POP.

popa ['popa] *f* stern.

população [popula'sãw] (*pl* -ões) *f* population; ~ operária working population; ~ escolar school population.

popular [popu'la(x)] (*pl* -es) <> *adj* popular. <> *m* [homem da rua] ordinary person.

popularidade [populari'dadʒi] *f* popularity.

popularizar [populari'za(x)] *vt* to popularize.

➡ **popularizar-se** *vp* to become popular.

populoso, osa [popu'lozu, ɔza] *adj* populous.

pôquer ['poke(x)] *m* poker.

por [po(x)] *prep* -1. [indica causa] because of, due to; foi ~ sua causa it was your fault; ~ falta de fundos due to lack of funds; ~ hábito through force of habit. -2. [indica objetivo] for; lutar ~ algo to fight for sth. -3. [indica meio, modo, agente] by; foi escrito pela Cristina it was written by Cristina; ~ correio/fax by post/fax; ~ escrito in writing; ~

avião [carta] (by) air mail. -4. [relativo a tempo] for; ele partiu ~ duas semanas he went away for two weeks. -5. [relativo a lugar] through; entramos no Brasil pelo Paraguai we crossed into Brazil via Paraguay; está ~ aí it's around there somewhere; ~ onde você vai? which way are you going?; vamos ~ aqui we're going this way. -6. [relativo a troca, preço] for; paguei apenas 20 reais ~ este casaco I only paid 20 reals for this coat; troquei o carro velho ~ um novo I exchanged my old car for a new one. -7. [indica distribuição] per; 25 ~ cento 25 per cent; são 100 reais ~ dia/mês it's 100 reals per day/month. -8. [em locuções]: ~ que why; ~ que (é que) ...? why (is it that) ...?; ~ mim tudo bem! that's fine by me!

pôr [po(x)] *vt* -1. [ger] to put; ~ a mesa to set the table; ~ a roupa to put on clothes; ~ defeito em tudo to find fault with everything; ~ a culpa em alguém to put the blame on sb. -2. [incutir]: não lhe ponha medo! don't frighten him! -3. [guardar] to keep. -4. [desovar] to lay.

➡ **pôr-se** *vp* -1. [colocar-se] to stand; ~-se de pé to stand up. -2. [sol] to set. -3. [começar]: ~-se a fazer algo to start doing sthg.

porão [po'rãw] (*pl* -ões) *f* -1. [de navio] hold. -2. [de casa] basement.

porca ['pɔxka] *f* -1. *ZOOL* sow. -2. [parafuso] nut.

porção [pox'sãw] (*pl* -ões) *f* [parte] portion; uma ~ de a portion of; [grande quantidade] a lot of.

porcaria [poxka'ria] <> *adj* [sem valor] rubbishy. <> *f* -1. [imundície] filth. -2. *fig* [coisa malfeita] piece of junk. -3. *fig* [coisa sem valor] rubbish.

porcelana [poxse'lãna] *f* porcelain.

porcentagem [poxsẽn'taʒẽ] (*pl* -ns) *f* percentage.

porco, ca ['poxku, kal <> *adj* -1. [suja] dirty. -2. [grosseiro] coarse. -3. [malfeito] shoddy. <> *m, f* -1. *ZOOL* pig. -2. *CULIN* pork. -3. [pessoa] *fam* pig.

porções [pox'sõjʃ] *pl* ⊳ **porção**.

pôr-do-sol [ˌpoxdu'sɔwl (*pl* pores-do-sol) *m* sunset.

porco-espinho [ˌpoxkwiʃ'piɲul (*pl* porcos-espinhos) *m* porcupine.

porém [po'rẽjl <> *conj* [contudo] but, however. <> *m* [obstáculo] snag.

pormenor [poxme'nɔ(x)] (*pl* -es) *m* detail.

pornô [pox'nol <> *adj inv fam* porn. <> *m CINE* porn film.

pornográfico, ca [poxno'grafiku, ka] *adj* pornographic.

poro ['porul *m* pore.

porões [po'rõjʃ] *pl* ▷ **porão**.

pororoca [poro'rokal *f* [onda] bore.

poroso, osa [po'rozu, ɔza] *adj* porous.

porquanto [pox'kwãntul *conj* since.

porque [pux'ke] *conj* because; **ela trabalha ~ precisa** she works because she needs to; **~ sim** just because.

porquê [pux'ke] *m*: **o ~ the reason (for); não entendo o ~ dessa atitude** I don't understand the reason for that attitude.

porquinho-da-índia [pox,kinuda-'índʒial (*pl* **porquinhos-da-índia**) *m* guinea pig.

porra ['poxal ⟨⟩ *f vulg* [esperma] spunk. ⟨⟩ *interj vulg* [exprime irritação] fucking hell!

porrada [po'xadal *mfam f* -1. [pancada] **ele deu uma ~ com o carro no muro** he smashed the car into the wall; **o garçom levou uma ~ do bêbado** the waiter took one hell of a beating from the drunkard. -2. [quantidade]: **uma ~ de** loads of. -3. *fig* [revés] fuck-up.

porre ['poxil *fam m* -1. [bebedeira] booze-up; **estar/ficar de ~** to be plastered; **tomar um ~** to get a skinful. -2.: **ser um ~** [pessoa, festa] to be a drag.

porrete [po'xetʃil *m* club.

porta ['poxtal *m* -1. [peça] door. -2. *fig* [possibilidade, saída] opportunity. -3. *COMPUT*: **~ paralela** parallel port; **~ serial** serial port.

porta-aviões [,poxta'vjõiʃ] *m inv* aircraft carrier.

porta-bandeira [,poxtabãn'dejral (*pl* **porta-bandeiras**) *mf* standard-bearer.

portador, ra [poxta'do(x), ral (*mpl* -es, *fpl* -s) ⟨⟩ *adj* -1. [de vírus, doença] carrying. -2. [de notícias] bearing. ⟨⟩ *m, f* -1. [de bagagem, AIDS] carrier. -2. [de títulos, letras de câmbio, notícias] bearer; **ao ~** [cheque, ação] to the bearer.

portal [pox'taw] (*pl* -ais) *m* -1. [pórtico] doorway. -2. *COMPUT* portal.

porta-luvas [,poxta'luvaʃ] *m inv AUTO* glove compartment.

porta-malas [,poxta'malaʃ] *m inv AUTO* boot *UK*, trunk *US*.

portanto [pox'tãntu] *conj* therefore.

portão [pox'tãw] (*pl* -ões) *m* gate.

portar [pox'ta(x)] *vt* [carregar] to carry.
◆ **portar-se** *vp* [comportar-se] to behave.

porta-retratos [,poxtaxe'tratuʃ] *m* (inv) photo frame.

porta-revistas [,poxtaxe'viʃtaʃ] *m* (inv) magazine rack.

portaria [poxta'rial *f* -1. [de edifício] entrance hall. -2. [documento oficial] order; **baixar uma ~** to issue a decree.

portátil [pox'tatʃiwl (*pl* -eis) *adj* portable.

porta-voz [,poxta'vɔjʃ] (*pl* **porta-vozes**) *mf* spokesperson.

porte ['poxtʃil *m* -1. [transporte] carriage. -2. [preço] charge; **~ pago** post paid. -3. [postura] bearing. -4. [tamanho] scale; **de grande/médio/pequeno ~** large/medium/small-sized. -5. [importância] stature. -6. [licença]: **~ de arma** gun permit.

porteiro, ra [pox'tejru, ral *m, f* [de edifício] caretaker *UK*, janitor *US*; **~ eletrônico** entryphone.

portentoso, osa [poxtẽn'tozu, ɔzal *adj* marvellous.

pórtico ['poxtʃikul *m* portico.

porto ['poxtul *m* port.

portões [pox'tõjʃ] *pl* ▷ **portão**.

portuário, ria [pox'twarju, rjal ⟨⟩ *adj* port (antes de subst). ⟨⟩ *m, f* [funcionário] port official.

Portugal [poxtu'gaw] *n* Portugal.

português, esa [poxtu'geʃ, ezal (*mpl* -eses, *fpl* -s) ⟨⟩ *adj* Portuguese. ⟨⟩ *m, f* Portuguese person.
◆ **português** *m* [língua] Portuguese.

porventura [poxvẽn'tural *adv* by chance; **se ~ você ...** if you happen to ...

posar [po'za(x)] *vi* -1. [fazer pose] to pose. -2. [bancar]: **~ de** to pose as.

pose ['pozil *f* -1. [de modelo etc.] pose. -2. *pej* [afetação] affectedness; **ela está com muita ~ desde sua promoção** she's full of airs and graces since being promoted; **fazer ~ de** to pretend to be.

pós-escrito [,pɔjʃiʃ'kritul (*pl* **pós-escritos**) *m* postscript, PS.

pós-graduação [,pɔjʃgradwa'sãwl (*pl* **pós-graduações**) *f* qualifying for a degree as a postgraduate *UK* or graduate *US* student.

pós-guerra [,pɔjʃ'gɛxal (*pl* **pós-guerras**) *m* post-war.

posição [pozi'sãw] (*pl* -ões) *f* -1. [ger] position. -2. [arranjo] positioning.

posicionar [pozisjo'na(x)] *vt* -1. [ger] to position. -2. [funcionário] to place.

positivo, va [pozi'tʃivu, val *adj* positive.

possante [po'sãntʃil *adj* powerful.

posse ['posil *f* -1. [de bens] ownership; **pessoa de ~s** person of means. -2. [ocupação] possession; **tomar ~ de** to take possession of. -3. [investidura] swearing-in; **tomar ~** to take office.
◆ **posses** *fpl* [bens] possessions.

possessão [pose'sãw] (pl -ões) f possession.

possessivo, va [pose'sivu, va] adj possessive.

possibilidade [posibili'dadʒi] f -1. [gen]
possibility. -2. [oportunidade] opportunity.

possibilitar [posibili'ta(x)] vt to make
possible.

possível [po'sivεw] (pl -eis) <> adj
possible. <> m: o ~ what is possible.

possuidor, ra [poswi'do(x), ra] adj: ser ~
de to be the owner of.

possuir [po'swi(x)] vt [ter] to have.

posta ['poʃta] f [pedaço] piece.

postal [poʃ'taw] (pl -ais) <> adj post,
postage. <> m postcard.

poste ['poʃtʃi] m -1. [haste] post. -2.
ELECTR: ~ de iluminação lamp post.

pôster ['poʃte(x)] (pl -es) m poster.

posteridade [poʃteri'dadʒi] f posterity.

posterior [poʃte'rjo(x)] (pl -es) adj -1.
[no tempo] later. -2. [traseiro] rear.

postiço, ça [poʃ'tʃisu, sa] adj false.

postigo [poʃ'tʃigu] m small door.

posto, ta ['poʃtu, 'poʃta] pp ▷ pôr.
◆ **posto** m -1. [ger] post; ~ de gasolina petrol station UK, gas station US; ~
de saúde health centre UK, health
center US. -2. [de polícia] station. -3. [di-
plomático] posting.
◆ **a postos** loc adv at the ready.
◆ **posto que** loc conj since.

póstumo, ma ['poʃtumu, ma] adj posthumous.

postura [poʃ'tura] f -1. [ger] posture.
-2. [municipal] position. -3. fig [atitude]
point of view.

potássio [po'tasju] m potassium.

potável [po'tavεw] (pl -eis) adj: água ~
drinking water.

pote ['potʃi] m pot, jar.

potência [po'tẽsja] m -1. [ger] power.
-2. [sexual] potency.

potencial [potẽ'sjaw] (pl -ais) <> adj
potential. <> m potential; o poder econômico em ~ do país é enorme the
country's potential economic power is
great.

potentado [potẽ'tadul] m potentate.

potente [po'tẽtʃi] adj powerful.

pot-pourri [pupu'xi] m pot-pourri.

potro ['potru] m colt.

pouca-vergonha [,pokavεx'goɲa] (pl
poucas-vergonhas) f -1. [ato] disgrace.
-2. [falta de vergonha] shamelessness.

pouco, ca ['poku, ka] <> adj little; de
pouca importância of little importance;
faz ~ tempo, ~ tempo (atrás) a short
time ago; (pl) few; poucas pessoas few

people. <> pron little; (pl) few; muito
~ s very few; ~ s [pessoas] few.
◆ **pouco** m: um ~ a little; um ~ de a
little; nem um ~ (de) not at all; aos ~ s
gradually.
◆ **pouco** adv little; dormi ~ I hardly
slept; isso é ~ comum that's uncommon, that's rare; há ~ a short time
ago; daqui a ~, dentro em ~ shortly;
por ~ o carro não me atropelou the
car nearly ran me over; ~ a ~ little
by little; fazer ~ de [zombar] to make
fun of; [menosprezar] to belittle.

poupador, ra [popa'do(x), ra] adj thrifty.

poupança [po'pãnsa] f -1. [economia]
saving. -2. [fundo]: (caderneta de) ~
savings account (book).

poupar [po'pa(x)] <> vt -1. [economizar]
to save. -2. [resguardar]: ~ alguém (de
algo) to spare sb (from sthg). -3. [res-
peitar] to spare. <> vi [economizar] to
save.
◆ **poupar-se** vp [eximir-se] to spare
o.s.

pouquinho [po'kiɲu] m: um ~ (de algo)
a little (sthg).

pouquíssimo, ma [po'kisimu, ma]
superl ▷ pouco.

pousada [po'zada] f -1. [hospedaria] inn.
-2. [hospedagem] lodging.

pousar [po'za(x)] <> vi -1. [aterrissar] to
land. -2. [baixar] to settle. -3. [pernoitar]
to spend the night. -4. [assentar] to rest.
<> vt to put.

pouso ['pozul] m -1. [aterrissagem] landing; ~ de emergência emergency
landing. -2. [lugar de descanso] bolt-hole.

povão [po'vãw] m hoi polloi (pl).

povo ['povu] m -1. [habitantes] people.
-2. [multidão] crowd. -3. [família, amigos]
family.

povoação [povwa'sãw] (pl -ões) f -1.
settlement. -2. [aldeia] village. -3. [habi-
tantes] population.

povoado, da [po'vwadu, da] <> adj
populated. <> m [aldeia] village.

povoar [po'vwa(x)] vt to populate.

poxa ['poʃa] interj gosh!

PPB (abrev de **Partido Progressista Brasileiro**) m Brazilian Progressive Party, a
right-wing party.

PPS (abrev de **Partido Popular Socialista**)
m Popular Socialist Party, a centre-
right party.

PR (abrev de **Estado do Paraná**) m State
of Paraná.

pra ['pra] fam = para, para a.

praça ['prasa] <> f -1. [largo] square. -2.
[mercado financeiro] market. -3. MIL: ~
de guerra fortress. -4. [de touros] bull

ring. ◇ *m* MIL [soldado] private (soldier).

prado ['pradu] *m* **-1.** [campo] meadow. **-2.** [hipódromo] racecourse.

pra-frente [,pra'frẽntʃi] *adj inv fam* trendy.

praga ['praga] *f* **-1.** [ger] curse; **rogar uma ~ a alguém** to curse sb. **-2.** [doença] scourge. **-3.** ZOOL plague. **-4.** [pessoa chata] pest.

Praga ['praga] *n* Prague.

pragmático, ca [prag'matʃiku, ka] *adj* pragmatic.

praguejar [prage'ʒa(x)] *vi:* **~ (contra)** to curse (at).

praia ['praja] *f* beach.

prancha ['prãʃa] *f* **-1.** [tábua] plank. **-2.** [de surfe] board. **-3.** NÁUT gangplank. **-4.** FERRO open wagon.

pranto ['prãntu] *m* weeping.

prata ['prata] *f* **-1.** [metal] silver; **de ~** silver *(antes de subst)*; **~ de lei** sterling silver. **-2.** *fam* [dinheiro] pennies *(pl)*.

prataria [prata'ria] *f* **-1.** [objetos de prata] silverware. **-2.** [pratos] crockery.

prateado, da [pra'tʃjadu, da] ◇ *adj* **-1.** [cor] silver *(antes de subst)*. **-2.** *fig* [brilhante] silvery. ◇ *m* silver.

prateleira [prate'lejra] *f* shelf.

prática ['pratʃika] *f* ▷ **prático**.

praticante [pratʃi'kãntʃi] ◇ *adj* practising *UK*, practicing *US*. ◇ *mf* practitioner.

praticar [pratʃi'ka(x)] ◇ *vt* **-1.** [cometer] to commit. **-2.** [exercer] to practise *UK*, to practice *US*. ◇ *vi* [exercitar] to practise *US*, to practice *US*.

praticável [pratʃi'kavew] *(pl* **-eis)** *adj* **-1.** [realizável] feasible. **-2.** [transitável] passable.

prático, ca ['pratʃiku, ka] ◇ *adj* practical. ◇ *m, f* NÁUT pilot.

◆ **prática** *f* practice; **na ~** in practice; **pôr em ~** to put into practice.

prato ['pratu] *m* **-1.** [louça] plate; **~ fundo** soup plate; **~ raso** dinner plate; **~ de sobremesa** dessert plate. **-2.** [comida] dish; **~ do dia** dish of the day; **~ principal/segundo ~** main/second course. **-3.** MÚS cymbal. **-4.** [de toca-disco] turntable. **-5.** [de balança] scale pan. **-6.** *loc:* **ser um ~ cheio** to be manna from heaven.

praxe ['praʃi] *f* habit; **ter como ~** to be in the habit of; **ser de ~** to be customary.

prazer [pra'ze(x)] *(pl* **-es)** *m* **-1.** pleasure. **-2.** [em apresentação]: **muito ~ (em conhecê-lo)** delighted (to meet you).

prazeroso, sa [prazeˈērozu, ɔza] *adj* pleasant.

prazo ['prazu] *m* **-1.** [tempo] period; **tenho um ~ de trinta dias para pagá-lo** I have thirty days in which to pay him, I have to pay him within thirty days; **a ~** on credit; **a curto/médio/longo ~** in the short/medium/long term. **-2.** [vencimento] deadline; **~ final** final deadline.

preamar [prea'ma(x)] *f* high tide.

preaquecer [prjake'se(x)] *vt* to preheat.

precário, ria [pre'karju, rja] *adj* **-1.** [ger] precarious. **-2.** [escasso] scarce.

precaução [prekaw'sãw] *(pl* **-ões)** *f* caution.

precaver-se [preka'vexsi] *vp* [prevenir-se]: **~ de** OU **contra algo** to be forearmed against sthg.

precavido, da [preka'vidu, da] *adj* cautious.

prece ['prɛsi] *f* **-1.** [oração] prayer. **-2.** [súplica] supplication.

precedência [presen'dẽsja] *f* precedence; **ter ~ sobre** to take precedence over.

precedente [prese'dẽntʃi] ◇ *adj* precedent. ◇ *m* precedent; **sem ~s** unprecedented.

preceder [prese'de(x)] *vt* to precede.

preceito [pre'sejtu] *m* precept.

preciosidade [presjozi'dadʒi] *f* gem.

precioso, osa [pre'sjozu, ɔza] *adj* **-1.** [ger] precious. **-2.** [importante] important. **-3.** [fino, rico] fine.

precipício [presi'pisju] *m* **-1.** [abismo] precipice. **-2.** *fig* [desgraça] hole.

precipitação [presipita'sãw] *(pl* **-ões)** *f* **-1.** [ger] haste. **-2.** METEOR precipitation.

precipitado, da [presipi'tadu, da] *adj* hasty.

precipitar [presipi'ta(x)] ◇ *vt* [antecipar] to precipitate. ◇ *vi* QUÍM to precipitate.

◆ **precipitar-se** *vp* **-1.** [ger] to rush. **-2.** [apressar-se] to hurry. **-3.** [despenhar-se] to drop.

precisamente [pre,siza'mẽntʃi] *adv* precisely.

precisão [presi'zãw] *f* [exatidão] precision, accuracy.

precisar [presi'za(x)] ◇ *vt* **-1.** [ger] to need; **~ fazer algo** to need to do sthg; **preciso que me ajudem** I need you to help me. **-2.** [indicar] to specify. ◇ *vi* **-1.** [necessitar] to be in need; **~ de alguém/algo** to be in need of sb/sthg. **-2.** [ser necessário]: **não precisa** there is no need; **fiz isso sem precisar** I did this when there was no need; '**precisam-se vendedores**' 'salespersons required'; **você precisa da chave para abrir a porta** you need a key to open the door.

preciso, sa [pre'sizu, za] *adj* **-1.** [ger] precise. **-2.** [necessário] necessary.

preço ['presu] *m* **-1.** [ger] price; ~ **de custo** cost price; ~ **à vista** [no comércio] cash price; [na bolsa] spot price; **a** ~ **de banana** for peanuts. **-2.** [importância] value.

precoce [pre'kɔsi] *adj* **-1.** [pessoa] precocious. **-2.** [fruto] early. **-3.** [calvície] premature.

preconcebido, da [prekõnse'bidu, da] *adj* preconceived.

preconceito [prekõn'sejtu] *m* prejudice.

preconizar [prekoni'za(x)] *vt* **-1.** [anunciar] to proclaim. **-2.** [propagar] to spread. **-3.** [elogiar] to praise.

precursor, ra [prekux'so(x), ra] (*mpl* **-es,** *fpl* **-s**) *m, f* precursor.

predador, ra [preda'do(x), ra] (*mpl* **-es,** *fpl* **-s**) <> *adj* predatory. <> *m, f* predator.

pré-datado, da [ˌprɛda'tadu, da] (*pl* **-s**) *adj* predated.

predatório, ria [preda'tɔrju, rja] *adj* predatory.

predecessor, ra [predese'so(x), ra] (*mpl* **-es,** *fpl* **-s**) *m* predecessor.

predestinado, da [predeʃtʃi'nadu, da] *adj* predestined.

predeterminado, da [predetermi'nadu, da] *adj* predetermined.

predial [pre'dʒjaw] (*pl* **-ais**) *adj* ⊳ imposto.

predição [predʒi'sãw] (*pl* **-ões**) *f* prediction.

predileção [predʒile'sãw] (*pl* **-ões**) *f*: ~ (**por**) predilection (for).

predileto, ta [predʒi'lɛtu, ta] <> *adj* favourite *UK*, favorite *US*. <> *m, f* favourite *UK*, favorite *US*.

prédio ['prɛdʒjul] *m* building; ~ **de apartamentos** block of flats *UK*, apartment house *US*; ~ **comercial** commercial building.

predispor [predʒiʃ'po(x)] <> *vt* to predispose. <> *vi*: ~ **a** to predispose to.
➡ **predispor-se** *vp*: ~**-se a fazer algo** to be predisposed to do sthg.

predisposição [predʒiʃpozi'sãw] *f* predisposition.

predisposto, osta [predʒiʃ'poʃtu, ɔʃta] *adj* **-1.** [ger] predisposed. **-2.** [à doença] prone.

predizer [predʒi'ze(x)] <> *vt* to predict, to forecast. <> *vi* [profetizar] to make predictions.

predominante [predomi'nãntʃi] *adj* predominant.

predominar [predomi'na(x)] *vi* to predominate.

predomínio [predo'minju] *m* **-1.** [supremacia] supremacy. **-2.** [influência] predominance.

pré-eleitoral [ˌprɛelejto'raw] (*pl* **-ais**) *adj* pre-election (*antes de subst*).

preeminente [preemi'nẽntʃi] *adj* preeminent.

preencher [preẽn'ʃe(x)] *vt* **-1.** [completar - formulário, lacunas] to fill in; [- buracos] to fill. **-2.** [ocupar - tempo, férias] to spend; [- cargo, vaga] to fill. **-3.** [satisfazer] to fulfil *UK*, to fulfill *US*.

preenchimento [preẽnʃi'mẽntu] *m* **-1.** [de formulário, espaço em branco] filling in. **-2.** [de cargo, vaga, buraco] filling. **-3.** [de requisitos] fulfilment.

preestabelecer [ˌpreeʃtabele'se(x)] *vt* to pre-establish.

pré-estréia [ˌprɛiʃ'treja] (*pl* **-s**) *f* preview.

pré-fabricado, da [ˌprɛfabri'kadu, da] *adj* prefabricated.

prefácio [pre'fasju] *m* preface.

prefeito, ta [pre'fejtu, ta] *m, f* mayor.

prefeitura [prefej'tura] *f* town hall.

preferência [prefe'rẽnsja] *f* **-1.** [precedência] priority; **dar** ~ **a** to give preference to. **-2.** [predileção] preference; **de** ~ preferably; **ter** ~ **por** to have a preference for.

preferencial [preferẽn'sjaw] (*pl* **-ais**) <> *adj* priority (*antes de subst*). <> *f* main road.

preferido, da [prefe'ridu, da] *adj* favourite *UK*, favorite *US*.

preferir [prefe'ri(x)] *vt*: ~ **algo (a algo)** to prefer sthg (to sthg); **prefiro que você fique** I would prefer you to stay.

prefixo [pre'fiksu] *m* prefix.

prega ['prɛga] *f* **-1.** [dobra - em papel, pano] fold; [- na saia] pleat. **-2.** [ruga] wrinkle.

pregador [prega'do(x)] *m* **-1.** [orador] preacher. **-2.** [utensílio]: ~ **de roupa** clothes peg.

pregão [pre'gãw] (*pl* **-ões**) *m* **-1.** [proclamação] cry. **-2.** *BOLSA* trading. **-3.** [em leilão] bidding.

pregar [pre'ga(x)] <> *vt* **-1.** [ger] to fix; ~ **não preguei os olhos a noite toda** I didn't sleep a wink all night. **-2.** [com prego] to nail. **-3.** [infligir]: ~ **algo em alguém** to inflict sthg on sb; ~ **um susto em alguém** to give sb a fright; ~ **uma mentira em alguém** to tell sb a lie; ~ **uma peça em alguém** to play a trick on sb. **-4.** *RELIG* [louvar] to preach. <> *vi* **-1.** [pronunciar sermão] to preach. **-2.** [cansar-se] to collapse.

prego ['prɛgu] *m* **-1.** [peça] nail. **-2.** [casa

de penhor] pawn shop; **pôr algo no** ~ to pawn sthg. - **3.** [cansaço] exhaustion.

pregões [pre'gõjʃ] *pl* ⊳ **pregão.**

pregresso, sa [pre'grɛsu, sa] *adj* earlier.

preguiça [pre'gisa] *f* - **1.** [indolência] laziness; **estar com** ~ **(de fazer algo)** to be too lazy (to do sthg). - **2.** [animal] sloth.

preguiçoso, osa [pregi'sozu, ɔza] <> *adj* lazy. <> *m, f* lazy person.

pré-história [ˌprɛiʃ'tɔrja] *f* prehistory.

pré-histórico, ca [ˌprɛiʃ'tɔriku, kal *adj* prehistoric.

prejudicar [preʒudʒi'ka(x)] *vt* - **1.** [afetar] to damage. - **2.** [transtornar] to disrupt. - **3.** [depreciar] to impair.

prejudicial [preʒudʒi'sjaw] (*pl* -**ais**) *adj* harmful.

prejuízo [pre'ʒwizu] *m* - **1.** [dano] damage. - **2.** [financeiro] loss.

preliminar [prelimi'na(x)] <> *adj* preliminary. <> *f* [partida] preliminary.

prelúdio [pre'ludʒju] *m* prelude.

prematuro, ra [prema'turu, ra] *adj* - **1.** [bebê] premature. - **2.** [colheita, fruta] early.

premeditado, da [premedʒi'tadu, da] *adj* premeditated.

premeditar [premedʒi'ta(x)] *vt* to premeditate.

premente [pre'mẽntʃi] *adj* urgent.

premiado, da [pre'mjadu, da] <> *adj* prize-winning. <> *m, f* prizewinner.

premiar [pre'mja(x)] *vt* - **1.** [dar prêmio] to award a prize to. - **2.** [recompensar] to reward.

premiê [pre'mje], **premier** [pre'mje] *m* premier.

prêmio ['premju] *m* - **1.** [em concurso, jogo] prize; ~ **de consolação** consolation prize. - **2.** [recompensa] reward. - **3.** [seguro] premium. - **4.** *ESP:* **Grande Prêmio** [de turfe, automobilismo] Grand Prix.

premonição [premuni'sãw] (*pl* -**ões**) *f* premonition.

pré-natal [ˌprɛna'taw] (*pl* **pré-natais**) *adj* antenatal *UK*, prenatal *US*.

prenda ['prẽnda] *f* - **1.** [presente] present. - **2.** [em jogo] forfeit.

◆ **prendas** *fpl:* ~**s domésticas** housework *(inv)*.

prendado, da [prẽn'dadu, da] *adj* gifted.

prendedor [prẽnde'do(x)] *m* peg; ~ **de papel** paper clip; ~ **de cabelo** hairgrip; ~ **de gravata** tie clip.

prender [prẽn'de(x)] *vt* - **1.** [pregar] to fasten. - **2.** [amarrar] to tie. - **3.** [reter] to keep. - **4.** [capturar] to arrest. - **5.** [atrair] to capture. - **6.** [afetivamente] to unite. - **7.** [impedir] to restrict.

◆ **prender-se** *vp* - **1.**: ~**-se a alguém** [afeiçoar-se] to grow attached to sb; [em relacionamento] to tie o.s. down to sb. - **2.** [preocupar-se]: ~**-se a algo** to get caught up in sthg.

prenome [pre'nomil *m* forename.

prensar [prẽn'sa(x)] *vt* - **1.** [na prensa] to compress. - **2.** [fruta] to squeeze.

prenunciar [prenũn'sja(x)] *vt* to forewarn.

prenúncio [pre'nũnsjo] *m* harbinger; **essas nuvens são um** ~ **de chuva** clouds are a sign of rain.

preocupação [preokupa'sãw] (*pl* -**ões**) *f* concern.

preocupante [preoku'pãntʃi] *adj* worrying.

preocupar [preoku'pa(x)] *vt* [inquietar] to worry.

◆ **preocupar-se** *vp:* ~**-se (com algo/alguém)** to worry (about sthg/sb).

preparação [prepara'sãw] (*pl* -**ões**) *f* [preparo] preparation.

preparar [prepa'ra(x)] *vt* to prepare.

◆ **preparar-se** *vp* - **1.** [aprontar-se] to get ready. - **2.** [instruir-se]: ~**-se para algo** to train for sthg.

preparativos [prepara'tʃivuʃ] *mpl* preparations, arrangements.

preparo [pre'paru] *m* - **1.** [preparação] preparation. - **2.** [condição]: ~ **físico** physical fitness.

preponderante [prepõnde'rãntʃi] *adj* preponderant, predominant.

preposição [prepozi'sãw] (*pl* -**ões**) *f* preposition.

prepotência [prepo'tẽnsja] *f* - **1.** [grande poder] forcefulness. - **2.** [despotismo] tyranny.

prepotente [prepo'tẽntʃi] *adj* - **1.** [poderoso] forceful. - **2.** [despótico] overbearing.

prerrogativa [prexoga'tʃiva] *f* prerogative.

presa ['preza] *f* - **1.** [na guerra] spoils *(pl).* - **2.** [preia] prey. - **3.** [dente] fang. - **4.** [garra] talon. - **5.** [vítima] slave. - **6.** [mulher encarcerada] (female) prisoner.

presbiteriano, na [preʒbite'rjãnu, na] <> *adj* Presbyterian. <> *m, f* Presbyterian.

prescindir [presĩn'dʒi(x)] *vi:* ~ **de algo** [dispensar] to do without sthg; [abstrair] to disregard sthg.

prescrever [preʃkre've(x)] <> *vt* - **1.** [ger] to prescribe. - **2.** [determinar] to decide. <> *vi* - **1.** [cair em desuso] to fall into disuse. - **2.** *JUR* to lapse.

prescrição [preʃkri'sãw] (*pl* -**ões**) *f* - **1.** [ordem] order. - **2.** *MED* prescription. - **3.** *JUR* lapse.

presença [pre'zẽnsa] *f-* **1.** [ger] presence; ~ **de espírito** presence of mind; **marcar** ~ to be present; **ter boa** ~ to be well turned out. **-2.** [em curso etc.] attendance.

presenciar [prezẽn'sja(x)] *vt* to witness.

presente [pre'zẽntʃi] <> *adj* **-1.** [ger] present. **-2.** [evidente] obvious. **-3.** [interessado] concerned. <> *m* **-1.** [ger] present. **-2.** [pessoa]: **(entre) os** ~**s** (among) those present. **-3.** [regalo] present, gift; **de** ~ as a present; ~ **de grego** *fig* unwelcome gift.

presentear [prezẽn'tʃja(x)] *vt*: ~ **alguém (com algo)** to give sb (sthg as) a present.

presépio [pre'zɛpju] *m* crib, Nativity scene.

preservação [prezexva'sãw] (*pl* **-ões**) *f* preservation.

preservar [prezex'va(x)] *vt* to preserve.
➧ **preservar-se** *vp* to protect o.s.

preservativo [prezexva'tʃivu] *m-* **1.** [substância] preservative. **-2.** [camisinha] condom.

presidência [prezi'dẽnsja] *f-* **1.** [de país] presidency; **assumir a** ~ to assume the presidency. **-2.** [de assembléia] chairmanship; **assumir a** ~ to take the chair. **-3.** [tempo em excercício] time in office.

presidente, ta [prezi'dẽntʃi, ta] *m, f-* **1.** [de país] president. **-2.** [de assembléia, empresa] chairman.
➧ **Presidente da República** *m* President of the Republic.

presidiário, ria [prezi'dʒjarju, rja] <> *adj* prison *(antes de subst)*. <> *m, f* convict.

presídio [pre'zidʒju] *m* prison.

presidir [prezi'dʒi(x)] <> *vt* **-1.** [dirigir] to lead. **-2.** [reger] to rule. <> *vi*: ~ **a algo** [dirigir] to preside over sthg; [reger] to rule sthg.

presilha [pre'ziʎa] *f-* **1.** [de suspensório, sapato] strap. **-2.** [de cabelo] hairslide.

preso, sa ['prezu, za] <> *adj* **-1.** [encarcerado] imprisoned. **-2.** [detido] detained, under arrest. **-3.** [atado] tied. **-4.** *fig* [em engarrafamento, casa] stuck. **-5.** *fig* [casado] spoken for. **-6.** *fig* [língua, voz] tongue-tied; **ele está com a voz presa** he has a catch in his voice. <> *m, f* [prisioneiro] prisoner.

pressa ['prɛsa] *f-* **1.** [velocidade] speed; **às** ~**s** quickly; **com** ~ in a hurry; **vir sem** ~ to take one's time. **-2.** [urgência] rush; **ter** ~ **de algo/de fazer algo** to be in a hurry for sthg/to do sthg. **-3.** [precipitação] hastiness.

presságio [pre'saʒju] *m-* **1.** [indício] sign. **-2.** [pressentimento] premonition.

pressão [pre'sãw] (*pl* **-ões**) *f-* **1.** [ger] pressure; ~ **contra algo** pressure against sthg. **-2.** [colchete] press stud. **-3.** *MED*: ~ **alta/baixa** high/low (blood) pressure.

pressentimento [presẽntʃi'mẽntu] *m* premonition.

pressentir [presẽn'tʃi(x)] *vt* **-1.** [pressagiar] to foresee. **-2.** [suspeitar] to suspect. **-3.** [perceber] to sense.

pressionar [presjo'na(x)] *vt* **-1.** [apertar] to press. **-2.** *fig* [coagir]: ~ **alguém (a fazer algo)** to pressurize sb (into doing sthg).

pressões [pre'sõjʃ] *pl* ➧ **pressão**.

pressupor [presu'po(x)] *vt* to assume.

pressuposto, osta [presu'poʃtu, ɔʃta] *pp* ➧ **pressupor**.
➧ **pressuposto** *m*: **partir de um** ~ to assume.

pressurizado, da [presuri'zadu, da] *adj* pressurized.

prestação [preʃta'sãw] (*pl* **-ões**) *f-* **1.** [ger] instalment *UK*, installment *US*; **ele só compra à** ~ he only buys on hire purchase. **-2.** [acerto]: ~ **de conta** accounts rendered. **-3.** [trabalho]: ~ **de serviço** services rendered.

prestar [preʃ'ta(x)] <> *vt* **-1.** [conceder]: ~ **algo (a alguém)** [favores] to grant sthg (to sb); [informações] to provide (sb with) sthg. **-2.** [apresentar]: ~ **algo (a alguém)** to present sthg (to sb). **-3.** [fazer]: ~ **algo (a alguém/algo)** to provide sthg (to sb/sthg); ~ **atenção** to pay attention. **-4.** [dedicar]: ~ **algo a alguém** to pay sthg to sb. <> *vi* **-1.** [ser útil]: **essa caneta não presta** this pen isn't any good. **-2.** [ter bom caráter]: **ele não presta!** he's no good!
➧ **prestar-se** *vp* [dispor-se]: ~**-se a algo** to accept sthg.

prestativo, va [preʃta'tʃivu, va] *adj* obliging.

prestes ['prɛʃtʃiʃ] *adj inv*: **estar** ~ **a fazer algo** to be about to do sthg.

prestígio [preʃ'tʃiʒju] *m* prestige; **é um escritor de** ~ he is an eminent writer.

prestigioso, osa [preʃtʃi'ʒjozu, ɔza] *adj* prestigious.

presumido, da [prezu'midu, da] *adj* [presunçoso] presumptuous.

presumir [prezu'mi(x)] *vt* [supor] to presume.

presunção [prezũn'sãw] (*pl* **-ões**) *f* presumption.

presunçoso, osa [prezũn'sozu, ɔza] *adj* presumptuous.

presunto [preˈzũntu] *m* **-1.** [de porco] ham. **-2.** *gír crime* [defunto] stiff.

prêt-à-porter [prɛtapoxˈte] *adj inv* ready-to-wear.

pretendente [pretẽnˈdẽntʃi] <> *mf* [candidato]: ~ **a algo** applicant for sthg. <> *m* [de uma mulher] suitor.

pretender [pretẽnˈde(x)] *vt* **-1.** [desejar]: ~ **fazer algo** to want to do sthg. **-2.** [ter a intenção de]: ~ **fazer algo** to intend to do sthg.

pretensão [pretẽnˈsãw] (*pl* **-ões**) *f* **-1.** [aspiração] pretension; ~ **salarial** proposed salary. **-2.** [arrogância] pretentions *(pl)*. **-3.** [intenção] aim.

pretensioso, osa [pretẽnˈsjozu, ɔza] *adj* pretentious.

pretérito, ta [preˈtɛritu] *adj* past.
➡ **pretérito** *m GRAM* preterite.

pretexto [preˈteʃtu] *m* [desculpa] pretext; **a** ~ **de** under the pretext of.

preto, ta [ˈpretu, ta] <> *adj* [cor] black. <> *m, f* [pessoa] black (person).
➡ **preto** *m* [cor] black.

preto-e-branco [ˌpretwiˈbrãŋku] *adj inv* black and white.

prevalecer [prevaleˈse(x)] *vi* **-1.** [predominar] to prevail. **-2.** [ter primazia]: ~ **(a/sobre)** to prevail (over).
➡ **prevalecer-se** *vp*: ~**-se de algo** [aproveitar-se] to avail o.s. of sthg.

prevenção [prevẽnˈsãw] (*pl* **-ões**) *f* [precaução]: ~ **(a/contra/de)** prevention (against/of).

prevenido, da [previˈnidu, da] *adj* **-1.** [precavido] precautious. **-2.** [com dinheiro]: **estar** ~ to be in pocket.

prevenir [previˈni(x)] *vt* **-1.** [avisar] to warn. **-2.** [evitar] to avoid. **-3.** [proibir] to prohibit.
➡ **prevenir-se** *vp* **-1.** [precaver-se]: ~ **-se contra alguém/algo** to protect o.s. against sb/sthg. **-2.** [equipar-se] ~**-se de** to equip o.s. with.

preventivo, va [prevẽnˈtʃivu, va] *adj* preventive.
➡ **preventivo** *m* [teste]: **(fazer um)** ~ to have a check-up.

prever [preˈve(x)] *vt* **-1.** [conjeturar] to foresee; ~ **que** to foresee (that). **-2.** [profetizar] to predict.

pré-vestibular [ˌprɛveʃtʃibuˈla(x)] (*pl* **pré-vestibulares**) <> *adj* preparing for university entrance exam. <> *m* [curso] *university entrance-exam preparatory course.*

prévia [ˈprɛvja] *f* ➡ **prévio**.

previamente [ˌprɛvjaˈmẽntʃi] *adv* previously.

previdência [previˈdẽnsja] *f* precaution; ~ **social** social security.

previdente [previˈdẽntʃi] *adj* **-1.** [que prevê] provident. **-2.** [cauteloso] cautious.

prévio, via [ˈprɛvju, vja] *adj* **-1.** [anterior] previous. **-2.** [preliminar] preliminary.

previsão [previˈzãw] (*pl* **-ões**) *f* prediction; ~ **do tempo** weather forecast.

previsto, ta [preˈviʃtu, ta] *pp* ➡ **prever**.

previsualização [previzwalizaˈsãw] *f COMPUT* preview.

prezado, da [preˈzadu, da] *adj* **-1.** [estimado] prized. **-2.** [em carta]: **Prezado Senhor** Dear Sir.

prezar [preˈza(x)] *vt* **-1.** [gostar muito] to cherish. **-2.** [respeitar] to respect.
➡ **prezar-se** *vp* [respeitar-se] to have self-respect.

primário, ria [priˈmarju, rja] *adj* **-1.** [ger] primary. **-2.** [primitivo] primitive.
➡ **primário** *m* [curso] primary education *UK*, elementary education *US*.

primata [priˈmata] *m* primate.

primavera [primaˈvɛra] *f* **-1.** [estação] spring. **-2.** *BOT* primrose.

primeira [priˈmejra] *f* ➡ **primeiro**.

primeira-dama [priˌmejraˈdãma] (*pl* **primeiras-damas**) *f* first lady.

primeiro, ra [priˈmejru, ra] <> *num* first. <> *adj* [inicial] first; ~ **grau** *EDUC* middle school; ~ **s socorros** first aid; **à primeira vista** at first sight. <> *m, f* **-1.** [em ordem]: **ele foi o** ~ **a chegar** he was the first to arrive. **-2.** [o melhor]: **é o** ~ **na turma** he is the top of the class.
➡ **primeiro** <> *adv* [em primeiro lugar] first. <> *m* [andar] first.
➡ **primeira** *f AUTO* first.
➡ **de primeira** *loc adj* **-1.** [hotel, restaurante] first-class. **-2.** [carne] prime.

primeiro-ministro, primeira-ministra [priˌmejrumiˈniʃtru, priˌmejramiˈniʃtra] (*mpl* **primeiros-ministros**, *fpl* **primeiras-ministras**) *m, f* prime minister.

primitivo, va [primiˈtʃivu, va] *adj* primitive.

primo, ma [ˈprimu, ma] <> *adj* [número] prime. <> *m, f* [parente] cousin; ~ **em segundo grau** second cousin.

primogênito, ta [primoˈʒenitu, ta] <> *adj* firstborn. <> *m, f* firstborn.

primo-irmão, prima-irmã [ˌprimwixˈmãw, ˌprimajxˈmã] (*mpl* **primos-irmãos**, *fpl* **primas-irmãs**) *m, f* first cousin.

primor [priˈmo(x)] *m* **-1.** [excelência] excellence. **-2.** [beleza] beauty. **-3.** [esmero]: **com** ~ thoroughly.

princesa [prĩnˈseza] *f* princess.

principal [prīnsi'paw] (pl **-ais**) <> adj
-1. [mais importante - ator] principal; [-
rua, praça, entrada] main. **-2.** [fundamental]
main. <> m principal.

príncipe ['prīnsipil m prince.

principiante [prīnsi'pjãntʃil <> adj
budding. <> mf beginner.

princípio [prīn'sipju] m **-1.** [ger] beginning; **a ~** at first. **-2.** [lei, norma, elemen-
to] principle. **-3.** [premissa]: **partir do ~**
to assume.

⇒ **princípios** mpl [morais] principles.

prioridade [prjori'dadʒi] f [primazia]
priority.

prisão [prizãw] (pl **-ões**) f **-1.** [captura]
arrest. **-2.** [encarceramento] imprisonment; **~ perpétua** life imprisonment.
-3. [cadeia] prison. **-4.** fig [sufoco] (holy)
deadlock. **-5.** MED: **~ de ventre** constipation.

prisioneiro, ra [prizjo'nejru, ra] m, f
prisoner.

prisões [pri'zõjʃ] pl ▷ **prisão**.

privação [priva'sãw] (pl **-ões**) f priva-
tion.

⇒ **privações** fpl [penúria] hardship.

privacidade [privasi'dadʒi] f privacy.

privada [pri'vada] f toilet.

privado, da [pri'vadu, da] adj **-1.** [parti-
cular] private. **-2.** [desprovido] deprived.

privar [pri'va(x)] vt: **~ alguém de algo** to
deprive sb of sthg.

privativo, va [priva'tʃivu, va] adj [exclusi-
vo] private.

privilegiado, da [privile'ʒjadu, da] adj
-1. [favorecido] privileged. **-2.** [excepcio-
nal] exceptional.

privilegiar [privile'ʒja(x)] vt to favour
UK, to favor US.

privilégio [privi'lɛʒju] m privilege.

pro [prul = para + o.

pró [prɔ] <> prep [a favor de] pro. <> m
[vantagem] pro; **os ~s e os contras** the
pros and cons.

pró- [prɔl prefixo pro-.

proa ['proal f bow.

probabilidade [probabili'dadʒi] f probability, likelihood.

problema [pro'blema] m problem.

problemático, ca [proble'matʃiku, ka]
adj problematic.

⇒ **problemática** f problematic.

procedência [prose'dẽnsja] f **-1.** [origem]
origin. **-2.** [lugar de saída] point of
departure. **-3.** [fundamento]: **não ter ~**
to be unfounded.

procedente [prose'dẽntʃil adj **-1.** [oriun-
do] originating. **-2.** [lógico] logical.

proceder [prose'de(x)] vi **-1.** [ger] to
proceed. **-2.** [prosseguir] to continue.

-3. [comportar-se] to behave; **~ mal/
bem** to behave badly/well. **-4.** [ter fun-
damento] to have foundation.

procedimento [prosedʒi'mẽntul m **-1.**
[comportamento] behaviour UK, behavior US. **-2.** [método] method. **-3.** JUR
proceedings (pl).

processador [prosesa'do(x)] (pl **-es**) m
COMPUT processor; **~ de texto** word
processor.

processar [prose'sa(x)] vt **-1.** JUR to sue,
to prosecute. **-2.** COMPUT to process.

processo [pro'sɛsul m **-1.** [JUR - ação]
legal proceedings (pl), lawsuit; **abrir
ou mover um ~ contra** to instigate
legal proceedings against, to file a
lawsuit against; [- documentação] evidence. **-2.** [método] process. **-3.** [está-
gio] course.

procissão [prosi'sãw] (pl **-ões**) f procession.

proclamar [prokla'ma(x)] vt to proclaim.

Procon (abrev de **Fundação de Proteção
e Defesa do Consumidor**) m Brazilian
organization for the protection of
consumers' rights.

procriar [pro'krja(x)] <> vt [gerar] to
engender. <> vi [multiplicar] to procrea-
te.

procura [pro'kural f **-1.** [busca] search;
estar à ~ de to be searching for. **-2.**
COM demand.

procurar [proku'ra(x)] <> vt **-1.** [buscar -
objeto, pessoa] to look for; [- verdade] to
seek. **-2.** [requerer] to look for. **-3.** [esfor-
çar-se por]: **~ fazer algo** to try to do
sthg. **-4.** [contatar] to call on. <> vi [bus-
car]: **~ (por)** to search (for).

prodígio [pro'dʒiʒjul m **-1.** [pessoa]
prodigy. **-2.** [maravilha] feat.

produção [produ'sãw] (pl **-ões**) f **-1.** [ger]
production. **-2.** [volume, obra] output; **~
em massa** ou **em série** mass production.

produtivo, va [produ'tʃivu, va] adj **-1.**
[fértil] productive. **-2.** [rendoso] profitable.

produto [pro'dutul m **-1.** [ger] product.
-2. AGR produce. **-3.** ECON: **~ interno
bruto** gross domestic product.

produtor, ra [produ'to(x), ra] (mpl **-es**,
fpl **-s**) <> adj producing. <> m, f
producer.

⇒ **produtora** f [empresa] production
company.

produzido, da [produ'zidu, da] adj [es-
merado] trendy.

proeminente [projmi'nẽntʃil adj prominent.

proeza [pro'ezal f feat.

profanar [profa'na(x)] *vt* to desecrate.
profano, na [pro'fãnu, na] *adj* profane.
profecia [profe'sia] *f* prophecy.
proferir [profe'ri(x)] *vt* **- 1.** [dizer] to utter. **- 2.** [decretar] to pronounce.
professar [profe'sa(x)] <> *vt* **- 1.** [exercer profissão] to practise *UK*, to practice *US*. **- 2.** [propagar] to profess. <> *vi RELIG* to take holy orders.
professor, ra [profe'so(x), ra] *(mpl* **-es**, *fpl* **-s**) *m, f* teacher.
profeta, tisa [pro'fɛta, 'tʃiza] *m, f* prophet.
profético, ca [pro'fɛtʃiku, ka] *adj* prophetic.
profetisa [profe'tʃiza] *f* ▷ **profeta**.
profetizar [profetʃi'za(x)] <> *vt* to prophesy. <> *vi* to predict the future.
proficiência [profi'sjẽsja] *f* proficiency.
proficiente [profi'sjẽtʃi] *adj* [capaz] proficient.
profissão [profi'sãw] *(pl* **-ões)** *f* **- 1.** [ofício] profession. **- 2.** [carreira] professional life. **- 3.** [declaração] statement.
profissional [profisjo'naw] *(pl* **-ais)** <> *adj* professional. <> *mf* professional; **~ liberal** *person in a liberal profession.*
profissionalizante [profisjonali'zãtʃi] *adj* [ensino] vocational.
profundidade [profũdʒi'dadʒi] *f* depth; **o mar aqui tem 20 metros de ~** here the sea is 20 metres deep.
profundo, da [pro'fũdu, da] *adj* **- 1.** [ger] deep. **- 2.** *fig* [intenso - sono, respeito, amor] deep; [- dor] intense; [- ódio] profound.
profusão [profu'zãw] *f* profusion.
progenitor, ra [proʒeni'to(x), ra] *m, f* progenitor.
🢂 **progenitores** *mpl* parents.
prognosticar [prognoʃtʃi'ka(x)] <> *vt* [predizer] to forecast. <> *vi MED* to make a prognosis.
prognóstico [prog'nɔʃtʃiku] *m* **- 1.** [predição] prediction. **- 2.** *MED* prognosis.
programa [pro'grãma] *m* **- 1.** [plano] programme *UK*, program *US*. **- 2.** *COMPUT* program.
programação [programa'sãw] *(pl* **-ões)** *f* **- 1.** [ger] programming; **~ orientada a objetos** object-orientated programming; **~ visual** graphic design. **- 2.** [organização] planning.
programador, ra [programa'do(x), ra] *m, f* **- 1.** [de rádio, empresa] programme planner. **- 2.** *COMPUT* programmer; **~ visual** graphic designer.
programar [progra'ma(x)] *vt* **- 1.** [planejar] to plan. **- 2.** *COMPUT* to program.

progredir [progre'dʒi(x)] *vi* **- 1.** [prosperar]: **~ (em algo)** to progress (in sthg). **- 2.** [agravar-se] to progress.
progressista [progre'siʃta] <> *adj* progressive. <> *mf* progressive.
progressivo, va [progre'sivu, va] *adj* progressive.
progresso [pro'grɛsu] *m* progress; **fazer ~ s em algo** to make progress in sthg.
proibição [projbi'sãw] *(pl* **-ões)** *f* prohibition.
proibir [proj'bi(x)] *vt* **- 1.** [impedir]: **~ alguém (de fazer algo)** to prohibit sb (from doing sthg). **- 2.** [interdizer] to ban. **- 3.** [vedar] to prevent.
proibitivo, va [projbi'tʃivu, va] *adj* prohibitive.
projeção [proʒe'sãw] *(pl* **-ões)** *f* **- 1.** [ger] projection. **- 2.** *fig* [notoriedade] prominence.
projetar [proʒe'ta(x)] *vt* **- 1.** [ger] to project. **- 2.** [planejar] to plan. **- 3.** *ARQUIT* to design.
projétil [pro'ʒɛtʃiw] *(pl* **-teis)** *m* projectile.
projeto [pro'ʒɛtu] *m* **- 1.** [ger] plan. **- 2.** [empreendimento] project. **- 3.** [esboço de texto] draft; **~ de lei** bill.
projetor [proʒe'to(x)] *(pl* **-es)** *m* **- 1.** [ger] projector. **- 2.** [holofote] searchlight.
prol [prɔw] *m*: **em ~ de** in favour of.
prole ['prɔli] *f* [filhos] offspring.
proletariado [proleta'rjadu] *m* proletariat.
proletário, ria [prole'tarju, rja] <> *adj* proletarian. <> *m, f* proletarian.
proliferação [prolifera'sãw] *(pl* **-ões)** *f* proliferation.
proliferar [prolife'ra(x)] *vi* to proliferate.
prolífico, ca [pro'lifiku, ka] *adj* prolific.
prolixo, xa [pro'liksu, ksa] *adj* **- 1.** [verboso] long-winded. **- 2.** [muito longo] lengthy.
prólogo ['prɔlogu] *m* prologue.
prolongado, da [prolõ'gadu, da] *adj* prolonged.
prolongamento [prolõga'mẽtu] *m* extension.
prolongar [prolõ'ga(x)] *vt* **- 1.** [duração] to prolong. **- 2.** [extensão] to extend. **- 3.** [adiar] to put off.
🢂 **prolongar-se** *vp* **- 1.** [estender-se] to stretch. **- 2.** [durar] to last.
promessa [pro'mɛsa] *f* promise.
prometer [prome'te(x)] <> *vt* **- 1.** [ger] to promise. **- 2.** [comprometer-se]: **~ algo a alguém** to promise sb sthg; **~ fazer algo** to promise to do sthg. **- 3.** [assegurar]: **~ algo a alguém** to promise sb sthg. <> *vi* **- 1.** [fazer promessa] to

promise. - **2.** [ter potencial] to be promising.

prometido, da [prome'tʃidu, da] adj promised.

➡ **prometido** m: aqui está o ~ here's what was promised; **cumprir o** ~ to keep one's promise.

promiscuidade [promiʃkwi'dadʒi] f promiscuity.

promíscuo, cua [pro'miʃkwu, kwa] adj - **1.** [sem ordem] disorderly. - **2.** [sexualmente] promiscuous.

promissor, ra [promi'so(x), ra] (mpl **-es**, fpl **-s**) adj promising.

promissória [promi'sɔrja] f [nota] promissory note.

promoção [promo'sãw] (pl **-ões**) f promotion; **em** ~ on special offer.

promotor, ra [promo'to(x), ra] <> adj promoting. <> m, f promoter; ~ **público** public prosecutor.

promover [promo've(x)] vt - **1.** [ger] to promote. - **2.** [funcionário]: ~ **alguém (a)** to promote sb (to).

➡ **promover-se** vp [favorecer-se] to make o.s. look good.

promulgar [promuw'ga(x)] vt to promulgate.

pronome [pro'nɔmi] m pronoun.

prontidão [prõtʃi'dãw] f - **1.** [alerta] readiness; **estar de** ~ to be on the alert. - **2.** [rapidez] promptness.

pronto, ta ['prõntu, ta] adj - **1.** [concluído, preparado] ready. - **2.** (antes de subst) [imediato] prompt. - **3.** [rápido] prompt. - **4.** [disposto]: ~ **a fazer algo** ready to do sthg. - **5.** fam [sem recursos] broke.

➡ **pronto** adv promptly; **de** ~ promptly.

pronto-socorro [,prõntuso'koxu] (pl **prontos-socorros**) m [hospital] casualty unit UK, emergency unit US.

prontuário [prõn'twarju] m - **1.** [ficha] file. - **2.** [manual] handbook.

pronúncia [pro'nũnsja] f - **1.** LING pronunciation. - **2.** JUR pronouncement.

pronunciamento [pronũnsja'mẽntu] m - **1.** [declaração] pronouncement. - **2.** JUR judgment.

pronunciar [pronũn'sja(x)] vt to pronounce.

➡ **pronunciar-se** vp [emitir juizo]: ~**-se sobre/a favor de** to express an opinion about/in favour of.

propaganda [propa'gãnda] f - **1.** [COM - publicidade] advertising; [- anúncio] advert, advertisement; **fazer ~ de algo** to advertise sthg. - **2.** POL propaganda. - **3.** [divulgação] spreading.

propagar [propa'ga(x)] vt - **1.** [disseminar]

to spread. - **2.** BIOL to propagate.

➡ **propagar-se** vp - **1.** [ger] to propagate. - **2.** [disseminar-se] to spread.

propensão [propẽ'sãw] (pl **-ões**) f inclination.

propenso, sa [pro'pẽnsu, sa] adj: ~ **a algo/a fazer algo** inclined to sthg/doing sthg.

propiciar [propi'sja(x)] vt - **1.** [permitir, favorecer] to favour UK, to favor US. - **2.** [proporcionar]: ~ **algo a alguém** to allow sb sthg.

propício, cia [pro'pisju, sja] adj - **1.** [favorável]: ~ **a algo** propitious for sthg. - **2.** [oportuno] propitious.

propina [pro'pina] f - **1.** [gratificação] tip. - **2.** [ilegal] bribe.

propor [pro'po(x)] vt - **1.** [ger] to propose; ~ **(a alguém) que** to propose (to sb) that. - **2.** JUR [ação] to move.

➡ **propor-se** vp: ~**-se a fazer algo** [visar] to aim to do sthg; [dispor-se] to offer to do sthg.

proporção [propox'sãw] (pl **-ões**) f proportion.

proporcional [propoxsjo'naw] (pl **-ais**) adj proportional; ~ **a algo** proportional to sthg.

proporcionar [propoxsjo'na(x)] vt [propiciar] to provide.

proporções [propox'sõjʃ] pl ▷ **proporção**.

proposital [propozi'taw] (pl **-ais**) adj intentional.

propósito [pro'pɔzitu] m intention; **de** ~ on purpose.

➡ **a propósito** loc adv [aliás] by the way.

➡ **a propósito de** loc prep concerning.

proposto, osta [pro'poʃtu, ɔʃta] <> pp ▷ **propor**. <> adj proposed.

➡ **proposta** f - **1.** [proposição] proposition. - **2.** [oferta] proposal.

propriamente [prɔprja'mẽntʃi] adv [exatamente] exactly; ~ **dito** per se; **o Estado** ~ **dito** the actual State.

propriedade [proprje'dadʒi] f - **1.** [ger] property; ~ **privada** private property. - **2.** [direito de propriedade] ownership.

proprietário, ria [proprje'tarju, rja] m, f - **1.** [dono] owner. - **2.** [de imóvel de aluguel] landlord.

próprio, pria ['prɔprju, prja] adj - **1.** [ger] proper. - **2.** [particular] own; **meu** ~ **apartamento/carro** my own flat/car. - **3.** [apropriado]: ~ **(para)** suitable (for). - **4.** [peculiar] characteristic. - **5.** [mesmo] - self; **o** ~ **cliente do banco** the customer of the bank himself; **falei com o** ~ **presidente** I spoke to the president himself; **eu** ~ I myself; **é o** ~ [ser ele mesmo] speaking.

propulsor, ra [propuw'so(x), ra] adj propelling.

→ **propulsor** m propellor.

prorrogação [proxoga'sãw] (pl -ões) f -1. [prolongação] deferment. - 2. FUT extra time.

prorrogar [proxo'ga(x)] vt to defer, to postpone.

prorrogável [proxo'gavew] (pl -eis) adj deferrable.

prosa ['prɔza] <> adj [cheio de si] puffed up. <> f -1. LITER prose. - 2. [conversa] chat. - 3. [conversa fiada] chit-chat.

proscrever [proʃkre've(x)] vt -1. [desterrar] to exile. - 2. [expulsar] to ban. - 3. [proibir] to prohibit. - 4. [abolir] to do away with.

proscrito, ta [proʃ'kritu, ta] <> pp ▷ **proscrever**. <> adj -1. [desterrado] banished. - 2. [expulso] outlawed. - 3. [proibido] forbidden. <> m, f [exilado] exile.

prospecção [proʃpek'sãw] (pl -ões) f GEOL prospecting; ~ **de petróleo** oil exploration.

prospector, ra [proʃpek'to(x), ra] m, f GEOL prospector.

prosperar [proʃpe'ra(x)] vi -1. [progredir]: ~ **(em algo)** [melhorar] to prosper (in sthg); [ter sucesso] to thrive (in sthg). - 2. [enriquecer] to prosper.

prosperidade [proʃperi'dadʒi] f -1. [progresso] prosperity. - 2. [sucesso] success.

próspero, ra ['prɔʃperu, ra] adj -1. [que progride] thriving. - 2. [bem-sucedido] prosperous.

prosseguir [prose'gi(x)] <> vt to continue. <> vi: ~ **(em algo)** to continue (in sthg); ~ **fazendo algo** to continue doing sthg.

prostíbulo [proʃ'tʃibulu] m brothel.

prostituição [proʃtʃitwi'sãw] f prostitution.

prostituta [prosʃtʃi'tuta] f prostitute.

prostrado, da [proʃ'tradu, da] adj prostrate.

protagonista [protago'niʃta] mf protagonist.

proteção [prote'sãw] (pl -ões) f -1. [resguardo] protection. - 2. [favorecimento] favour UK, favor US. - 3. [dispositivo] defence UK, defense US.

proteger [prote'ʒe(x)] vt to protect.

→ **proteger-se** vp [resguardar-se] to protect o.s.

protegido, da [prote'ʒidu, da] <> adj [resguardado] protected. <> m, f [favorito] protégé (f protégée).

proteína [prote'ina] f protein.

prótese ['prɔtezi] f MED prosthesis.

protestante [proteʃ'tãntʃi] <> adj Protestant. <> mf Protestant.

protestar [proteʃ'ta(x)] <> vt -1. [título, promissória] to contest. - 2. [declarar] to profess. <> vi [reclamar]: ~ **(contra/em favor de algo)** to protest (against/in favour of sthg); **protesto!** JUR I protest!

protesto [pro'tɛʃtu] m [ger] protest.

protetor, ra [prote'to(x), ra] (mpl -es, fpl -s) <> adj protective. <> m, f protector.

protocolo [proto'kɔlu] m -1. [ger & COMPUT] protocol. - 2. [registro] registration. - 3. [recibo] record. - 4. [setor] registry.

protótipo [pro'tɔtʃipu] m -1. [modelo] prototype. - 2. fig [exemplo]: **ser o** ~ **de algo** to be the epitome of sthg.

protuberância [protube'rãnsja] f protuberance.

prova ['prɔva] f -1. [ger] proof. - 2. EDUC exam. - 3. [teste] test; **à** ~ **de água** waterproof; **à** ~ **de bala** bulletproof; **à** ~ **de fogo** fireproof; **pôr algo à** ~ to put sthg to the test. - 4. ESP event. - 5. COST fitting. - 6. [de comida, bebida] taster.

provador [prova'do(x)] m -1. [em loja] fitting room. - 2. [de café, vinho] taster.

provar [pro'va(x)] <> vt -1. [demonstrar] to prove. - 2. [testar] to test. - 3. [roupa] to try on. - 4. [comida, bebida] to taste. <> vi: ~ **(de algo)** [comida, bebida] to have a taste (of sthg).

provável [pro'vavew] (pl -eis) adj [possível] probable; **é** ~ **que chova** it looks like rain; **é** ~ **que ela não chegue hoje** she's not likely to come today.

provedor, ra [prove'do(x), ra] m, f provider; ~ **de acesso** COMPUT Internet access provider.

proveito [pro'vejtu] m advantage; **em** ~ **de** in favour of; **tirar** ~ **de algo** to benefit from sthg.

proveitoso, osa [provej'tozu, ɔza] adj -1. [vantajoso] advantageous. - 2. [lucrativo] profitable. - 3. [útil] useful.

proveniência [prove'njẽnsja] f origin.

proveniente [prove'njẽntʃi] adj: ~ **de** [originário] originating from; [resultante] arising from; **esta uva é** ~ **da Itália** these grapes come from Italy.

prover [pro've(x)] vt -1. [ger]: ~ **algo/alguém de algo** to provide sthg/sb with sthg. - 2. [providenciar] to provide. - 3. [vaga, cargo] to fill.

→ **prover-se** vp [abastecer-se]: ~-**se de algo** to provide o.s. with sthg.

provérbio [pro'vɛrbju] m proverb.

proveta [pro'vetal *f* test tube; **bebê de**
~ test tube baby.

providência [provi'dẽnsjal *f* [medida] measure; **tomar** ~ **s** to take measures.

providencial [providẽn'sjaw] (*pl* **-ais**) *adj*
providential.

providenciar [providẽn'sja(x)] ⟨⟩ *vt* **-1.**
[prover] to provide. **-2.** [tomar providências para] to set into motion. ⟨⟩ *vi* [cui-
dar]: **vamos** ~ **para que tudo dê certo**
let's see to it that all works out.

provido, da [pro'vidu, dal *adj* [abasteci-
do]: ~ **de algo** supplied with sthg;
bem ~ well stocked; **uma conta bancária bem provida** a fat bank account.

província [pro'vĩnsjal *f* **-1.** [divisão admi-
nistrativa] province. **-2.** [interior] provin-
ces *(pl)*.

provinciano, na [provĩn'sjãnu, nal *adj*
pej provincial.

provisão [provi'zãw] (*pl* **-ões**) *f* supply.

◆ **provisões** *fpl* supplies.

provisório, ria [provi'zɔrju, rjal *adj* provisional.

provocador, ra [provoka'do(x), ral (*mpl*
-es, *fpl* **-s**) ⟨⟩ *adj* provocative. ⟨⟩ *m*,
f provoker.

provocante [provo'kãntʃil *adj* [sensual-
mente] provocative.

provocar [provo'ka(x)] *vt* **-1.** [ger] to
provoke. **-2.** [incitar]: ~ **alguém (a fazer
algo)** to provoke sb (into doing sthg).
-3. [chamar a atenção, atrair sensualmente]
to arouse. **-4.** [promover] to cause.

proximidade [prosimi'dadʒil *f* **-1.** [ger]
proximity. **-2.** [afinidade] closeness.

◆ **proximidades** *fpl* [arredores] proximity *(sg)*.

próximo, ma ['prɔsimu, mal ⟨⟩ *adj* **-1.**
[no espaço]: ~ **(a ou de) algo** close (to). **-2.**
[no tempo] recent. **-3.** *(antes de subst)* [se-
guinte] next. **-4.** [chegado] close. ⟨⟩ *m*, *f*
[em fila] next (one).

◆ **próximo** ⟨⟩ *m*: **o** ~ [o semelhante]
neighbour *UK*, neighbor *US*. ⟨⟩ *adv*
close.

◆ **próxima** *f* [a próxima vez]: **até a próxima!** [em despedida] see you soon!

proxy ['prɔʃil (*pl* **proxies**) *m* COMPUT
proxy.

prudência [pru'dẽnsjal *f* caution, prudence.

prudente [pru'dẽntʃil *adj* **-1.** [comedido]
prudent. **-2.** [cauteloso] cautious.

prurido [pru'ridul *m* **-1.** [comichão] itch.
-2. *fig* [desejo] urge.

PS *m* **-1.** *(abrev de* **Post Scriptum)** PS. **-2.**
(abrev de **Pronto-Socorro)** first aid.

PSB *(abrev de* **Partido Socialista Brasileiro)** *m Brazilian socialist party*.

PSDB *(abrev de* **Partido da Social Democracia Brasileira)** *m Brazilian social
democratic party, the second largest
right-wing party in Brazil*.

pseudônimo [psew'donimul *m* pseudonym.

psicanálise [psika'nalizil *f* psychoanalysis.

psicanalítico, ca [psikana'litʃiku, kal *adj*
psychoanalitical.

psicodélico, ca [psiko'dɛliku, kal *adj* psy-
chedelic.

psicologia [psikolo'ʒial *f* psychology.

psicológico, ca [psiko'lɔʒiku, kal *adj* psychological.

psicólogo, ga [psi'kɔlogu, gal *m*, *f* psychologist.

psicopata [psiko'patal *mf* psychopath.

psicose [psi'kɔzil *f* MED psychosis.

psicossomático, ca [psikoso'matʃiku,
kal *adj* psychosomatic.

psicótico, ca [psi'kɔtʃiku, kal *adj* psychotic.

psiquiátrico, ca [psi'kjatriku, kal *adj*
psychiatric.

psíquico, ca ['psikiku, kal *adj* psychic.

psiu [psiwl *interj* **-1.** [para chamar] hey! **-2.**
[para calar] hush!

PT *(abrev de* **Partido dos Trabalhadores)**
*m Brazilian workers' party, the lar-
gest left-wing party in Brazil*.

PTB *(abrev de* **Partido Trabalhista Brasileiro)** *m Brazilian Workers' Party, a
large party of the centre*.

puberdade [puber'dadʒil *f* puberty.

púbis ['pubiʃl *m inv* pubis.

publicação [publika'sãw] (*pl* **-ões**) *f* publication.

publicar [publi'ka(x)] *vt* **-1.** [ger] to
publish. **-2.** [divulgar] to broadcast.

publicidade [publisi'dadʒil *f* **-1.** [divulga-
ção] publicity. **-2.** COM advertising.

publicitário, ria [publisi'tarju, rjal ⟨⟩
adj advertising *(antes de subst)*. ⟨⟩ *m*, *f*
advertiser.

público, ca ['publiku, kal *adj* public.

◆ **público** *m* **-1.** [o povo] public. **-2.**
[platéia] audience; **em** ~ in public.

PUC *(abrev de* **Pontifícia Universidade
Católica)** *f Pontifical Catholic university*.

pudico, ca [pu'dʒiku, kal *adj* **-1.** [recata-
do] bashful. **-2.** *pej* prudish.

pudim [pu'dʒĩl (*pl* **-ns**) *m* pudding; ~ **de
leite** milk pudding.

pudor [pu'do(x)] *m* **-1.** [recato] modesty;
ter ~ **de** [ter vergonha] to be ashamed
of. **-2.** [decoro] decency.

pueril [pwe'riwl (*pl* **-is**) *adj* childish,
puerile.

pugilista [puʒi'liʃta] *m* boxer.
puído, da ['pwidu, da] *adj* frayed.
puir [pwi(x)] *vt* to fray.
pujante [pu'ʒãntʃi] *adj* powerful.
pular [pu'la(x)] ◇ *vt* **-1.** [saltar] to jump (over); ~ **corda** to skip. **-2.** [páginas, trechos] to skip. **-3.**: ~ **Carnaval** to celebrate carnival. ◇ *vi* **-1.** [saltar] to jump. **-2.** [palpitar] to skip a beat.
pulga ['puwga] *f* flea; **estar/ficar com a ~ atrás da orelha** to smell a rat.
pulha ['puʎa] *m* creep.
pulmão [puw'mãw] (*pl* **-ões**) *m* lung.
pulo ['pulu] *m* leap; **a um ~ de** *fig* [perto de] just a hop away from; **dar um ~ em** *fig* [ir] to stop off at.
pulôver [pu'love(x)] (*pl* **-es**) *m* pullover.
púlpito ['puwpitu] *m* pulpit.
pulsação [puwsa'sãw] (*pl* **-ões**) *f* **-1.** [batimento] pulsation. **-2.** MED [pulso] pulse.
pulsar [puw'sa(x)] *vi* [palpitar] to beat, to throb.
pulverizar [puwveri'za(x)] *vt* **-1.** [ger] to spray. **-2.** [reduzir a pó] [destruir] to pulverize.
pum [pũ] (*pl* **puns**) *m* *mfam* [peido] fart; **soltar um ~** to pass wind.
pungente [pũn'ʒẽntʃi] *adj* poignant.
punhado [pu'ɲadu] *m*: **um ~ de** a handful of.
punhal [pu'ɲaw] (*pl* **-ais**) *m* dagger.
punhalada [puɲa'lada] *f* stab.
punho ['puɲu] *m* **-1.** ANAT fist; **de próprio ~** in one's own handwriting. **-2.** [de manga] cuff. **-3.** [de espada, punhal] hilt.
punição [puni'sãw] (*pl* **-ões**) *f* punishment.
punir [pu'ni(x)] *vt* to punish.
punitivo, va [puni'tʃivu, va] *adj* punitive.
puns [pũnʃ] *mpl* ▷ **pum**.
pupila [pu'pila] *f* ANAT pupil.
pupilo, la [pu'pilu, la] *m, f* **-1.** [aluno] pupil. **-2.** [tutelado] ward.
purê [pu're] *m* purée, mash; **~ de batatas** mashed potato.
pureza [pu'reza] *f* purity.
purgante [pux'gãntʃi] *m* **-1.** [remédio] purgative. **-2.** *fam* [pessoa, trabalho] pain in the neck.
purgar [pux'ga(x)] *vt* [expiar] to purge.
purgatório [puxga'tɔrju] *m* RELIG purgatory.
purificar [purifi'ka(x)] *vt*: **~ algo (de algo)** [depurar] to cleanse sthg (of sthg).
◆ **purificar-se** *vp* to cleanse o.s.
puritano, na [puri'tãnu, na] ◇ *adj* puritanical. ◇ *m, f* puritan.
puro, ra ['puru, ra] *adj* **-1.** [ger] pure. **-2.** *(antes de subst)* [mero] pure. **-3.** *(antes de subst)* [absoluto] plain.
púrpura ['puxpura] *f* [cor] purple.
purpúreo, rea [pux'purju, rja] *adj* crimson.
pus ['puʃ] *m inv* pus.
pusilânime [puzi'lãnimi] *adj* pusillanimous.
puto, ta ['putu, ta] ***vulg adj*** **-1.** [devasso] rotten; **o ~ de ...** ***fam*** the bloody ... **-2.** [zangado] mad.
◆ **puta** ***vulg*** *f* [prostituta] whore; **puta que pariu!** fucking hell!
putrefato, ta [putre'fatu, ta] *adj* rotten.
putrefazer [putrefa'ze(x)] *vt* to putrefy.
◆ **putrefazer-se** *vp* to rot.
pútrido, da ['putridu, da] *adj* rotten.
puxa ['puʃa] *interj*: **~ (vida)!** goodness (me)!, gosh.
puxador [puʃa'do(x)] (*pl* **-es**) *mf* **-1.** [de samba] *the leading singer in an 'escola de samba', a group of musicians and samba dancers who perform in street parades during carnival celebrations in Brazil.* **-2.** [de fumo] (marijuana) smoker. **-3.** [ladrão] thief. ◇ *m* handle.
puxão [pu'ʃãw] (*pl* **-ões**) *m* tug; **dar um ~ em alguém** to pull s.b.
puxar [pu'ʃa(x)] ◇ *vt* **-1.** [ger] to pull. **-2.** [arrancar, sacar] to pull out. **-3.** [iniciar - conversa] to start (up); [- briga] to break into; [- samba] to start (up), to break into; **~ assunto** to bring up a subject. **-4.** [desencadear] to bring about. **-5.** [adular]: **~ o saco de alguém** ***fam fig*** to suck up to sb. **-6.** ***gír droga*** [fumo] to smoke. **-7.** ***gír crime*** [automóvel] to steal. ◇ *vi* **-1.** [impor esforço a]: **~ por** to strain. **-2.** [ser parecido com]: **~ a alguém** to take after sb. **-3.** [mancar]: **~ de uma perna** to limp.
puxa-saco [,puʃa'saku] (*pl* **puxa-sacos**) *fam* ◇ *adj* crawling. ◇ *mf* crawler.
puxões [pu'ʃõjʃ] *pl* ▷ **puxão**.
PV (*abrev de* **Partido Verde**) *m* *Brazilian green party.*
PVC (*abrev de* **Polyvinyl Chloride**) *m* PVC.

Q

q, Q [ke] *m* [letra] q, Q.
QG (*abrev de* **Quartel-General**) *m* HQ.
QI (*abrev de* **Quociente de Inteligência**) *m* IQ.

QT (*abrev de* **QualidadeTotal**) *f* TQM.

qua. (*abrev de* **quarta-feira**) *f* Wed.

quadra ['kwadra] *f* - **1.** [quarteirão] block. - **2.** [esportiva] court. - **3.** [em jogos] four. - **4.** [estrofe] quatrain.

quadragésimo, ma [kwadra'ʒɛzimu, mal *num* fortieth; *veja também* **sexto**.

quadriculado, da [kwadriku'ladu, dal *adj* - **1.** [camisa, padrão] checked. - **2.** [papel] squared.

quadril [kwa'driw] (*pl* -**is**) *m* hip.

quadrilha [kwa'driʎa] *f* - **1.** [de ladrões etc.] gang. - **2.** [dança] quadrille.

quadrimestral [kwadrimeʃ'traw] (*pl* -**ais**) *adj* quarterly.

quadrinho [kwa'driɲu] *m* [das tiras] (cartoon) drawing.
➡ **quadrinhos** *mpl*: **(história em)** ~ **s** cartoon strip.

quadro ['kwadru] *m* - **1.** [ger] frame. - **2.** [pintura] painting. - **3.** [quadro-negro] blackboard. - **4.** [mural] board. - **5.** [gráfico] chart. - **6.** *TEC* [painel] panel. - **7.** *TEATRO* & *TV* scene. - **8.** [situação] picture; ~ **clínico** clinical picture.

quadro-negro [ˌkwadru'negru] (*pl* **quadros-negros**) *m* blackboard.

quadrúpede [kwa'drupedʒil ◇ *adj* [animal] quadrupedal, four-footed. ◇ *mf* [animal] quadruped.

quadruplicar [kwadrupli'ka(x)] ◇ *vt* to quadruple. ◇ *vi* to quadruple.

quádruplo, pla ['kwadruplu, pla] ◇ *adj* quadruple. ◇ *m, f* [quadrigêmeo] quad, quadruplet.
➡ **quádruplo** *m* quadruple.

quaisquer ▷ **qualquer**.

qual [kwaw] (*pl* **quais**) ◇ *adj* which; ~ **perfume você prefere?** which perfume do you prefer?; **não sei** ~ **caminho devo seguir** I don't know which road I should follow. ◇ *conj fml* [como] like; **(tal)** ~ exactly like. ◇ *interj* what!; ~ **!** [exprimindo espanto] what!; [exprimindo negação] no; ~ **nada!**, ~ **o quê!** yeah right! ◇ *pron* - **1.** [em interrogativa] what; ~ **é o seu nome?** what's your name?; ~ **a cor dos seus cabelos?** what is the colour of your hair?; **quais são suas intenções?** what are your intentions? - **2.** [especificando] which (one); **perguntei** ~ **seria a melhor opção** I asked which (one) would be the better option; **o/a** ~ [suj: pessoa] who; [complemento: pessoa] whom; [suj, complemento: coisa] which; **ela teve três filhos, o mais velho dos quais tornou-se médico** she had three sons, the eldest of whom became a doctor; **este é o livro sobre o** ~ **lhe escrevi** this is the book (which/

that) I wrote to you about; **cada** ~ each and every one; ~ **deles ...?** which one (of them) ...?

qualidade [kwali'dadʒil *f* - **1.** [ger] quality; ~ **de vida** quality of life; **de** ~ good quality. - **2.** [tipo] grade. - **3.** *pej* [baixo nível] ilk. - **4.** [condição]: **na** ~ **de** in the capacity of.

qualificação [kwalifika'sãw] (*pl* -**ões**) *f* [avaliação] classification.
➡ **qualificações** *fpl* [formação, preparo] qualifications.

qualificado, da [kwalifi'kadu, dal *adj* - **1.** [preparado] qualified. - **2.** *JUR* [caracterizado] aggravated.

qualificar [kwalifi'ka(x)] *vt* - **1.** [classificar] to qualify. - **2.** [avaliar] to describe.
➡ **qualificar-se** *vp* [classificar-se] to qualify.

qualquer [kwaw'kɛ(x)] (*pl* **quaisquer**) ◇ *adj* - **1.** [algum]: **traga uma bebida** ~ bring me any old drink; **comprei um jornal** ~ I bought any old newspaper; **havia** ~ **coisa de errado** there was something wrong; **num ponto** ~ **da Sibéria** somewhere or other in Siberia; ~ **dia venha me visitar** come and see me some day; **a** ~ **momento** any minute now; **um outro** ~ [coisa] any other one; [pessoa] some; **ser** ~ **coisa** [ser ótimo, extraordinário] to be something else. - **2.** (*antes de subst*) [todo] any; **ele enfrenta quaisquer perigos** he braves all dangers; ~ **pessoa sabe fazer arroz** anybody can cook rice; ~ **que seja** whatever; ~ **um** anybody; **todo e** ~ each and every; **de** ~ **maneira** *ou* **jeito** [seja como for] somehow or other; [a todo custo] come what may. - **3.** *pej* [ordinário, sem importância]: **ele se contenta com** ~ **coisa** he's happy with any old thing; **de** ~ **maneira** *ou* **jeito** [sem cuidado] any (old) how. ◇ *pron* - **1.** [algum]: ~ **(de)** any (of); **como não posso ter todas, terei de escolher** ~ **as** I can't have them all, I'll have to chose any one; **prove quaisquer destas balas** try any one of these sweets; **um** ~ *pej* [pessoa] a nobody. - **2.** [todo - coisa]: ~ **(de)** any (of); ~ **destas substâncias é perigosa** any of these substances is dangerous; [- pessoa] anyone; ~ **de nós faria o mesmo** anyone of us would do the same.

quando ['kwãndul ◇ *adv* when. ◇ *conj* when; [ao passo que] while; **de** ~ **em** ~ from time to time; **de vez em** ~ from time to time; **desde** ~ how long; ~ **mais não seja** at least, if only; ~

muito at (the) most; ~ **quer que** whenever.

quanta ▷ **quanto**.

quantia [kwãn't∫ia] f sum.

quantidade [kwãnt∫i'dadʒi] f -1. [medida] amount. -2. [número] number. -3. [abundância]: **uma ~ de** a number of; **em ~** in large quantity.

quantitativo, va [kwãnt∫ita't∫ivu, va] adj quantitative.

quanto, ta ['kwãntu, ta] ◇ adj -1. (interrogativo) how; **quantas maças você quer?** how many apples do you want?; **há ~ tempo você está esperando?** how long have you been waiting? -2. (exclamativo) how; **quantos livros!** how many books!, so many books!; **quanta gente!** how many people!, so many people! ◇ pron -1. (interrogativo) how; **quantos fugiram?** how many got away? -2. (exclamativo) how; **quantos não morrem antes de chegar à idade adulta!** how many died before reaching adulthood! -3. (relativo): **tantos ... quantos** ... as many ... as ...; **faça tantas alterações quantas forem necessárias** make as many changes as necessary; **gosto de tudo ~ é verdura** I like all green vegetables; **tudo ~ é tipo de penteado** all kinds of hairstyles.

➡ **quanto** ◇ pron (interrogativo) [quantia, preço] how; ~ **custa este casaco?** how much does this coat cost?; **a ~ está o dólar?** how much is the dollar?; [quantidade]: ~ **de maionese devo acrescentar?** how much mayonnaise should I add?; ~ **de combustível ainda temos?** how much fuel do we still have? ◇ adv [indicando intensidade, proporção] much; **esforcei-me o ~ pude** I tried as much/hard as I could; **sei o ~ você me ama** I know how much you love me; **um tanto ~** [meio] somewhat; **tanto ~** as much as; **tanto um quanto o outro são incompetentes** [ambos] both are equally incompetent; **tão ... ~** as ... as ...; ~ **mais tem, mais quer** the more he has, the more he wants; ~ **mais rápido, melhor** the faster, the better; ~ **mais** [especialmente] especially; [muito menos] especially not.

➡ **quanto a** loc prep [com relação a] as for, as far as; ~ **a mim** as for me, as far as I'm concerned.

➡ **quanto antes** loc adv: **o ~ antes** as soon as possible.

➡ **quantos** pron pl fam: **um certo Carlos não sei dos quantos** a certain Carlos something or other.

➡ **quantas** pron pl fam: **a quantas** [em que situação] at what stage; **não sei a quantas anda esse processo** I don't know what stage the trial is at.

quão [kwãw] adv how.

quarenta [kwa'rẽnta] num forty; veja também **sessenta**.

quarentena [kwarẽn'tena] f quarantine.

quaresma [kwa'reʒma] f -1. RELIG Lent. -2. [flor] glory bush.

quarta ['kwaxta] f [quarta-feira] Wednesday; veja também **sábado**.

quarta-feira [ˌkwaxta'fejra] (pl quartas-feiras) f Wednesday; ~ **de cinzas** Ash Wednesday; veja também **sábado**.

quarteirão [kwaxtej'rãw] (pl -ões) m block.

quartel [kwax'tɛw] (pl -éis) m MIL barracks (pl).

quartel-general [kwaxˌtɛwʒene'raw] (pl quartéis-generais) m general headquarters (pl).

quarteto [kwax'tetu] m MÚS quartet; ~ **de cordas** string quartet.

quarto, ta ['kwaxtu, ta] num fourth; **a quarta parte** a quarter; veja também **sexto**.

➡ **quarto** m -1. [a quarta parte] quarter. -2. [aposento] bedroom; ~ **de casal** double room; ~ **de banho** bathroom. -3. MIL [plantão] watch. -4. [de boi] haunch. -5. ASTRON [da lua]: ~ **crescente/minguante** first/last quarter.

quarto-e-sala [ˌkwaxtwi'sala] (pl quarto-e-salas) m studio apartment.

quartzo ['kwaxtsu] m quartz.

quase ['kwazi] adv -1. [ger] nearly; **tropecei e ~ caí** I tripped and almost fell. -2. [pouco mais, ou menos] almost, nearly; **ela tem ~ dez anos** she is almost ou nearly ten years old; ~ **não trabalhei hoje** I hardly worked today; ~ **nada/tudo** almost nothing/everything; ~ **nunca** almost never, hardly ever; ~ **sempre** nearly always.

quatro ['kwatru] num four; **de ~** on all fours; **estar de ~ por alguém** [apaixonado] to be head over heels over sb; veja também **seis**.

quatrocentos, tas [ˌkwatru'sẽntuʃ, taʃ] num four hundred; veja também **seis**.

que [ki] ◇ adj inv -1. [em interrogativas] what, which; ~ **livros você quer?** which books do you want?; ~ **dia é hoje?** what day is it today?; ~ **horas são?** what time is it? -2. [em exclamações]: **mas ~ belo dia!** what a beautiful day!; ~ **fome!** I'm starving!; ~ **maravilha!** how wonderful! ◇ pron -1. [em interrogativas] what; ~ **é isso?** what's that?; **o ~ você quer?** what do you want?; **o ~ você vai comer?** what are you going to eat? **- 2.** [uso relativo: sujeito-pessoa] who; **o homem ~ está correndo** the man who's running; [-coisa] which, that; **a guerra ~ começou em 1939** the war that started in 1939. **- 3.** [uso relativo: complemento-pessoa] whom, that; **o homem ~ conheci** the man (whom) I met; [-coisa] which, that; **o bolo ~ comi era ótimo** the cake (that) I ate was great. ⋄ *conj* **- 1.** [com complemento direto] that; **ele disse-me ~ ia de férias** he told me (that) he was going on holiday. **- 2.** [em comparações]: **(do) ~ than; é mais caro (do) ~ o outro** it's more expensive than the other. **- 3.** [exprime causa]: **leva o guarda-chuva ~ está chovendo** take an umbrella because it's raining; **vai depressa ~ você está atrasado** you'd better hurry because you're late. **- 4.** [exprime conseqüência] that; **ele disse-me tanto ~ acabei por lhe dar** he asked me for it so much that I ended up giving it to him. **- 5.** [exprime tempo]: **há horas ~ estou à espera** I've been waiting for hours; **há muito ~ não vou lá** I haven't been there for ages. **- 6.** [indica desejo]: **espero ~ você se divirta** I hope (that) you have fun; **quero ~ você o faça** I want you to do it; **~ você seja feliz!** may you be happy! **- 7.** [em locuções]: **~ nem** like; **ele chorou ~ nem um bebê** he cried like a baby; **ele é feio ~ nem o irmão** he's as ugly as his brother.

quê ['ke] ⋄ *m* [algo]: **um ~** something; **um ~ de** [toque] a touch of; [sabor] slightly; **um não sei ~** a je ne sais quoi; **sem ~ nem por ~** [sem motivo] without rhyme or reason. ⋄ *interj* [exprimindo espanto] what! ⋄ *pron* ▷ **que.**

quebra ['kɛbra] *f* **- 1.** [ger] break. **- 2.** [despedaçamento] breakage. **- 3.** [falência] bankruptcy. **- 4.** COMPUT: **~ de página** page break.
◆ **de quebra** *loc adv* what's more.

quebra-cabeça [ˌkɛbraka'besa] (*pl* **quebra-cabeças**) *m* **- 1.** [jogo] puzzle. **- 2.** *fig* [problema] dilemma.

quebradiço, ça [kebra'dʒisu, sa] *adj* fragile.

quebrado, da [ke'bradu, da] *adj* **- 1.** [vaso, vidro, braço] broken. **- 2.** [enguiçado - carro, máquina] broken down; [- telefone] out of order. **- 3.** [cansado] worn out. **- 4.** [falido] bankrupt. **- 5.** *fam* [sem dinheiro] broke.

quebra-galho [ˌkɛbra'gaʎu] (*pl* **quebra-galhos**) *m* **- 1.** [pessoa] Mr Fixit. **- 2.** [objeto] contrivance.

quebra-molas [ˌkɛbra'mɔlaʃ] *m inv* speed bump *ou* hump, sleeping policeman.

quebra-nozes [ˌkɛbra'nɔziʃ] *m inv* nutcracker.

quebranto [ke'brãntu] *m* **- 1.** [mau- olhado] evil eye. **- 2.** [abatimento] run-down state.

quebra-quebra [ˌkɛbra'kɛbra] (*pl* **quebra-quebras**) *m* riot.

quebrar [ke'bra(x)] ⋄ *vt* **- 1.** [ger] to break; **~ algo ao meio** to split sthg in half. **- 2.** [espancar] to beat up. **- 3.** [enfraquecer] to weaken. **- 4.** [interromper] to halt. **- 5.** [desviar] to deflect. ⋄ *vi* **- 1.** [despedaçar-se] to break. **- 2.** [enguiçar] to break down. **- 3.** [falir] to go bankrupt. **- 4.** *fam* [ficar sem dinheiro] to be broke.
◆ **quebrar-se** *vp* **- 1.** [despedaçar-se] to break. **- 2.** [desfazer-se] to be broken.

queda ['kɛda] *f* **- 1.** [ger] fall; **~ livre** free fall; **~ de barreira** landslide; **em ~** falling. **- 2.** [declínio] fall. **- 3.** *fig* [inclinação]: **ter uma ~ para algo** to have a flair for sthg; **ter uma ~ por alguém** to have a soft spot for sb.

queda-d'água [ˌkɛda'dagwa] (*pl* **quedas-d'água**) *f* waterfall.

queijo ['kejʒu] *m* cheese; **~ prato** (form of) processed cheese; **~ ralado** grated cheese.

queima ['kejma] *f* **- 1.** [queimada] burning fire; **~ de fogos** fireworks display. **- 2.** COM & *fig* [liquidação] clearance sale.

queimado, da [kej'madu, da] *adj* **- 1.** [ger] burnt. **- 2.** [de sol - bronzeado] tanned; [- ferido] sunburnt. **- 3.** [plantas] scorched. **- 4.** *fam fig* [malquisto] ruined.
◆ **queimada** *f* slash-and-burn.

queimadura [kejma'dura] *f* **- 1.** [com fogo] burn. **- 2.** [de sol] sunburn.

queimar [kej'ma(x)] ⋄ *vt* **- 1.** [ger] to burn. **- 2.** [atear fogo a] to set on fire. **- 3.** [abrasar, ferir - fogo, choque, sol] to burn; [- líquido] to scald. **- 4.** [bronzear] to tan. **- 5.** COM & *fig* [liquidar] to liquidate. **- 6.** *fam fig* [tornar malquisto] to ruin. **- 7.** *fig* [dinheiro] to blow. ⋄ *vi* **- 1.** [ger] to burn. **- 2.** [abrasar] to be burning hot. **- 3.** [arder em febre] to burn (up). **- 4.** ESP to hit the net. **- 5.** [comida] to burn.
◆ **queimar-se** *vp* **- 1.** [ferir-se - ger] to burn o.s.; [- com líquido fervente] to scald o.s. **- 2.** [bronzear-se] to sunbathe. **- 3.**

fam fig [enfezar-se] to take offence. **- 4.** *fam fig* [tornar-se malquisto] to blow it.

queima-roupa [ˌkejmaˈxopa] *f*: à ~ [disparo] at point-blank range; *fig* [sem rodeios] point-blank.

queixa [ˈkejʃa] *f* **-1.** [reclamação] complaint. **-2.** [lamento] grievance.

queixar-se [kejˈʃaxsi] *vp* **-1.** [reclamar]: ~-**se (de algo/alguém)** to complain (about sthg/sb). **-2.** [lamentar-se] to moan.

queixo [ˈkejʃu] *m* chin; **estava com tanto frio que chegava a a bater o** ~ [de frio] I was so cold my teeth started chattering; **ele ficou de** ~ **caído** [ficar admirado] his jaw dropped in amazement.

queixoso, osa [kejˈʃozu, ɔzal] *adj* **-1.** [agravado] querulous. **-2.** [magoado] aggrieved.

quem [ˈkẽj] *pron* [interrogativo: sujeito] who; [interrogativo: complemento] who, whom; [indefinido] whoever; ~ **diria!** who would have thought it!; ~ **é?** [na porta] who's there?; ~ **fala?** [no telefone] who's calling?, who's speaking?; ~ **me dera ser rico!** if only I were rich!; ~ **quer que** whoever; **seja** ~ **for** no matter who it is, whoever it is.

quente [ˈkẽntʃi] <> *adj* **-1.** [ger] hot. **-2.** [roupa] warm. **-3.** [animado] vibrant. **-4.** *gír jornalismo* [notícia] reliable. <> *m* [moda]: **o** ~ **agora é usar cabelo comprido** the in thing now is to wear one's hair long.

quentinha [kẽnˈtʃiɲa] *f* **-1.** [embalagem] *insulated carton for food.* **-2.** [refeição] snack.

quentura [kẽnˈtural] *f* warmth.

quer [kɛ(x)] <> *conj*: ~ ..., ~ ... whether ... or ...; ~ **você queira,** ~ **não** whether you want to or not. <> *v* ⊳ **querer**.

⬥ **onde quer que** *loc pron* wherever.

⬥ **o que quer que** *loc pron* whatever.

⬥ **quem quer que** *loc pron* whoever.

querela [keˈrɛla] *f* **-1.** [contenda] quarrel. **-2.** *JUR* charge.

querer [keˈre(x)] <> *m* **-1.** [vontade] wanting. **-2.** [amor] love. <> *vt* **-1.** [ger] to want; **como queira/quiser** as you wish; **como quem não quer nada** casually; **não** ~ **nada com** to want nothing to do with; ~ **dizer** to mean; **quer dizer** [em outras palavras] that is to say. **-2.** [cobrar]: **quero dois mil pelo carro** I want two thousand for the car. **-3.** [ter afeição por] to love. **-4.** [conseguir]: **não** ~ **fazer algo** not to want to do

sthg. <> *vi* **-1.** [desejar, ter vontade]: **não vou porque não quero** I am not going because I don't want to; **por** ~ on purpose; **sem** ~ unintentionally. **-2.** [amar] to love; ~ **bem a alguém** to care about sb; ~ **mal a alguém** to wish sb ill.

⬥ **querer-se** *vp* [amar-se] to love one another.

querido, da [keˈridu, dal] <> *adj* **-1.** [caro] dear; **ele é muito** ~ **na cidade** he is much liked in town. **-2.** [em carta]: **Querido ...** Dear ... <> *m, f* **-1.** [preferido] favourite *UK*, favorite *US*. **-2.** [como forma de tratamento] darling.

querosene [keroˈzenil] *m* kerosene.

questão [keʃˈtãw] (*pl* **-ões**) *f* **-1.** [ger] question; ~ **de honra** question of honour; ~ **de tempo** question of time; **em** ~ in question; **fazer** ~ **(de algo)** *fig* [insistir em] to insist (on sthg). **-2.** *JUR* case.

questionar [keʃtʃjoˈna(x)] *vt* **-1.** [debater] to dispute. **-2.** [fazer perguntas] to question.

questionário [keʃtʃjoˈnarjul] *m* questionnaire.

questionável [keʃtʃjoˈnavewl] (*pl* **-eis**) *adj* questionable.

questões [keʃˈtõjʃ] *pl* ⊳ **questão**.

qui. (*abrev de* **quinta-feira**) *f* Thur.

quiabo [ˈkjabu] *m* okra.

quicar [kiˈka(x)] <> *vt* [bola] to bounce. <> *vi* [bola] to bounce.

quíchua [ˈkiʃwal] <> *adj* Quechuan. <> *m, f* Quechuan.

⬥ **quíchua** *m* [língua] Quechuan.

quieto, ta [ˈkjɛtu, tal] *adj* **-1.** [em silêncio] quiet. **-2.** [tranqüilo] calm. **-3.** [imóvel] still.

quietude [kjeˈtudʒil] *f* tranquillity.

quilate [kiˈlatʃil] *m* **-1.** [de ouro] carat. **-2.** *fig* [excelência] calibre *UK*, caliber *US*.

quilha [ˈkiʎal] *f* keel.

quilo [ˈkilul] *m* kilo; **a** ~ by the kilo.

quilobyte [kiloˈbajtʃil] *m COMPUT* kilobyte.

quilometragem [kilomeˈtraʒẽl] (*pl* **-ns**) *f* **-1.** [distância percorrida] distance in kilometres *UK ou* kilometers *US*, ≃ mileage. **-2.** [distância entre dois pontos] distance in kilometres *UK ou* kilometers *US*.

quilométrico, ca [kiloˈmɛtriku, kal] *adj fig* [longo] mile *(antes de subst).*

quilômetro [kiˈlometrul] *m* kilometre *UK*, kilometer *US*.

quimera [kiˈmɛral] *f* [fantasia, ilusão] chimera.

químico, ca ['kimiku, ka] <> *adj* chemical. <> *m, f* [profissional] chemist.

 química *f* -1. [ger] chemistry. -2. [substância] chemical. -3. *fig* [segredo] secret.

quina ['kina] *f* -1. [canto] corner; **de ~** side on. -2. [de jogo] jackpot.

quindim [kĩn'dʒĩ] (*pl* -ns) *m* sweet made of egg, sugar and coconut.

quinhão [ki'ɲãw] (*pl* -ões) *m* share.

quinhentos, tas [ki'ɲẽntuʃ, taʃ] *num* five hundred; **ser outros ~** to be a different kettle of fish; *veja também* **seis**.

quinhões [ki'ɲõjʃ] *pl* ▷ **quinhão**.

quinina [ki'nina] *f* quinine.

qüinquagésimo, ma [kwĩŋkwa'ʒɛzimu, ma] *num* fiftieth; *veja também* **sexto**.

quinquilharia [kĩŋkiʎa'rial] *f* -1. [bugiganga] junk. -2. [ninharia] trinket.

quinta ['kĩnta] *f* -1. [quinta-feira] Thursday. -2. [sítio] estate; *veja também* **sábado**.

quinta-feira [ˌkĩnta'fejra] (*pl* **quintas-feiras**) *f* Thursday; *veja também* **sábado**.

quintal [kĩn'taw] (*pl* -ais) *m* [de casa] backyard.

quinteto [kĩn'tetu] *m* MÚS quintet.

quinto, ta ['kĩntu, ta] *num* fifth; *veja também* **sexto**.

quíntuplo, pla ['kĩntuplu, pla] *adj* quintuple.

 quíntuplo *m* quintuple.

quinze ['kĩzi] *num* fifteen; *veja também* **seis**.

quinzena [kĩn'zena] *f* -1. [tempo] fortnight. -2. [salário] fortnight's wages.

quinzenal [kĩze'naw] (*pl* -ais) *adj* fortnightly.

quiosque ['kjɔʃki] *m* -1. [de jardim] gazebo. -2. [banca] kiosk.

qüiprocó [kwipro'kɔ] *m* [confusão] mix-up.

quiromante [kiro'mãntʃi] *mf* palm reader.

quisto ['kiʃtu] *m* cyst.

quitanda [ki'tãnda] *f* grocer's shop *UK*, grocery store *US*.

quitandeiro, ra [kitãn'dejru, ra] *m, f* greengrocer.

quitar [ki'ta(x)] *vt* -1. [pagar] to settle. -2. [perdoar] to cancel. -3. [devedor] to release.

quite ['kitʃi] *adj* -1. [com credor]: **estar/ficar ~ (com alguém)** to be quits (with sb). -2. [igualado] even.

Quito ['kitu] *n* Quito.

quitute [ki'tutʃi] *m* titbit *UK*, tidbit *US*.

quociente [kwo'sjẽntʃi] *m* MAT quotient; **~ de inteligência** intelligence quotient, IQ.

R

r, R ['exi] *m* [letra] r, R.

rã ['xã] *f* frog.

rabada [xa'bada] *f* CULIN oxtail stew.

rabanada [xaba'nada] *f* -1. CULIN French toast. -2. [golpe com rabo] whack with the tail.

rabanete [xaba'netʃi] *m* radish.

rabecão [xabe'kãw] (*pl* -ões) *m* [carro fúnebre] hearse.

rabino, na [xa'binu, na] *m* rabbi.

rabiscar [xabiʃ'ka(x)] <> *vt* -1. [encher com rabiscos] to scribble over. -2. [riscos] to scribble. -3. [escrever às pressas] to scrawl. -4. [desenhar] to sketch. <> *vi* [fazer rabiscos] to doodle.

rabisco [xa'biʃku] *m* -1. [risco] scribble. -2. [esboço] sketch.

rabo ['xabu] *m* -1. [cauda] tail; **~ de foguete** *fig* can of worms; **com o ~ do olho** out of the corner of one's eye; **meter o ~ entre as pernas** *fig* to be left with one's tail between one's legs. -2. *vulg* [nádegas] bum.

rabo-de-cavalo [ˌxabudʒika'valu] (*pl* **rabos-de-cavalo**) *m* ponytail.

rabugento, ta [xabu'ʒẽntu, ta] *adj* grumpy.

raça ['xasa] *f* -1. [etnia] race. -2. [estirpe] lineage. -3. *pej* [laia] breed; **acabar com a ~ de alguém** [matar] to do away with sb. -4. *fig* [coragem, determinação] guts; **(no peito e) na ~** by sheer guts. -5. [de animal] breed; **cão/cavalo de ~** pedigree dog/thoroughbred horse.

racha ['xaʃa] *m* -1. *fam* [discórdia] split. -2. [em parede etc.] crack.

rachadura [xaʃa'dura] *f* crack.

rachar [xa'ʃa(x)] <> *vt* -1. [fender] to crack; **frio de ~** bitterly cold; **ou vai ou racha** do or die. -2. [dividir]: **~ algo (com alguém)** to split sthg (with sb). -3. *fig* [dividir] to split. -4. [cortar] to split. <> *vi* [fender-se] to crack.

racial [xa'sjaw] (*pl* -ais) *adj* racial.

raciocinar [xasjosi'na(x)] *vi* to reason.

raciocínio [xasjo'sinju] *m* reasoning.

racional [xasjo'naw] (*pl* **-ais**) *adj* rational.

racionalizar [xasjonali'za(x)] *vt* to racionalize.

racionamento [xasjona'mẽntu] *m* rationing.

racionar [xasjo'na(x)] *vt* to ration.

racismo [xa'siʒmu] *m* racism.

racista [xa'siʃta] <> *adj* racist. <> *mf* racist.

rack [xɛk] *m* rack.

radar [xa'da(x)] (*pl* **-es**) *m* radar.

radiação [xadʒja'sãw] (*pl* **-ões**) *f* radiation.

radiador [xadʒja'do(x)] (*pl* **-es**) *m* AUTO radiator.

radiante [xa'dʒjãntʃi] *adj* **-1.** [objeto] radiant. **-2.** [de alegria] ecstatic.

radical [xadʒi'kaw] (*pl* **-ais**) <> *adj* radical. <> *mf* **-1.** [ger] root. **-2.** POL & QUÍM radical; ~ **livre** free radical.

radicalismo [xadʒika'liʒmu] *m* radicalism.

radicar-se [xadʒi'kaxsi] *vp* to settle.

rádio ['xadʒu] <> *m* **-1.** [aparelho] radio. **-2.** QUÍM radium. **-3.** ANAT [osso] radius. <> *f* [emissora] radio station.

radioamador, ra [xadʒjwama'do(x), da] *m, f* radio ham.

radioatividade [xadʒwatʃivi'dadʒi] *f* radioactivity.

radioativo, va [ˌxadʒwa'tʃivu, va] *adj* radioactive.

radiodifusão [xadʒodʒifu'zãw] *f* broadcasting.

radiografar [xadʒografa(x)] <> *vt* **-1.** MED to X-ray. **-2.** [notícia] to radio. <> *vi* [fazer contato] to radio.

radiografia [ˌxadʒjografia] *f* **-1.** MED X-ray. **-2.** *fig* [análise] in-depth analysis.

radiograma [xadʒjo'grãma] *m* cablegram.

radiogravador [xadʒjugrava'do(x)] *m* radio-cassette player.

radiojornal [xadʒjuʒox'naw] (*pl* **-ais**) *m* radio news (*sg*).

radiologia [xadʒjolo'ʒia] *f* radiology.

radionovela [xadʒjuno'vɛla] *f* radio soap.

radiopatrulha [xadʒjupa'truʎa] *f* **-1.** [serviço] radio patrol. **-2.** [viatura] patrol car.

radiotáxi [ˌxadʒjo'taksi] *m* radio cab.

radioterapia [xadʒjotera'pia] *f* radiotherapy.

raia ['xaja] *f* **-1.** [linha] line. **-2.** [limite] boundary; **às ~ s de algo** to the limits of sthg. **-3.** [pista - de piscina] (lane) marker. **-4.** [peixe] ray. **-5.** *loc*: **fugir da ~** to cut and run.

raiado, da [xa'jadu, da] *adj* **-1.** [pista] marked. **-2.** [cano] rifled. **-3.** [piscina] divided into lanes. **-4.** [bandeira] striped.

raiar [xa'ja(x)] <> *vi* **-1.** [brilhar] to shine. **-2.** [despontar] to dawn. <> *vt* [com raias - pista] to mark; [- cano] to rifle; [- piscina] to lane off; [- pintar] to mark with stripes.

rainha [xa'iɲa] *f* queen.

raio ['xaju] *m* **-1.** [ger] ray; ~ **laser** laser beam; ~ **X** X-ray. **-2.** [de luz] beam. **-3.** METEOR bolt of lightening. **-4.** *fam* [como ênfase]: **perdi o ~ da carteira** I lost my blasted wallet. **-5.** GEOM radius. **-6.**: ~ **de ação** [alcance] range; *fig* [área de atuação] range.

raiva ['xajva] *f* **-1.** [fúria] rage; **com ~ (de)** angry (at); **ter/tomar ~ de** to hate. **-2.** [doença] rabies (*sg*).

raivoso, osa [xaj'vozu, ɔza] *adj* **-1.** [furioso] furious. **-2.** [doente] rabid.

raiz [xa'iʒ] (*pl* **raízes**) *f* **-1.** [ger] root; **cortar o mal pela ~** *fig* to root it out; ~ **quadrada** square root. **-2.** [origem] roots (*pl*).

rajada [xa'ʒada] *f* **-1.** [de vento] gust. **-2.** [de tiros] volley.

ralado, da [xa'ladu, da] *adj* **-1.** [moído] grated. **-2.** [esfolado] grazed.

ralador [xala'do(x)] (*pl* **-es**) *m* grater.

ralar [xa'la(x)] *vt* **-1.** [com ralador] to grate. **-2.** [esfolar] to graze.

ralé [xa'lɛ] *f* [escória] riff-raff.

ralhar [xa'ʎa(x)] *vi*: ~ **(com alguém)** to tell (sb) off.

rali [xa'li] *m* rally.

ralo, la ['xalu, la] *adj* **-1.** [cabelo, café, sopa] thin. **-2.** [vegetação] sparse.
   ➡ **ralo** *m* drainpipe.

Ram. (*abrev de* ramal) *m* ext.

RAM (*abrev de* Random Access Memory) *f* RAM.

rama ['xãma] *f* foliage; **pela ~** *fig* [superficialmente] superficially.

ramagem [xa'maʒẽ] *f* BOT branches (*pl*).

ramal [xa'maw] (*pl* **-ais**) *m* **-1.** [de telefone] extension. **-2.** FERRO branch line. **-3.** [rodoviário] branch road.

ramalhete [xama'ʎetʃi] *m* [buquê] bunch.

ramificação [xamifika'sãw] (*pl* **-ões**) *f* [subdivisão] branch.

ramificar-se [xamifi'kaxsi] *vp* **-1.** [subdividir-se] to be subdivided. **-2.** [espalhar-se] to branch out.

ramo ['xãmu] *m* **-1.** [ger] branch. **-2.** [de flores] bouquet. **-3.** [área] field.

rampa ['xãnpa] *f* ramp.

ranço ['xãnsu] *m* **-1.** [sabor] rancid taste.

-2. [cheiro] rank smell. **-3.** *fig* [atraso] age-old habit.

rancor [xãŋˈko(x)] *m* **-1.** [ressentimento] resentment. **-2.** [ódio] hatred.

rancoroso, osa [xãŋkoˈrozu, ɔza] *adj* resentful.

rançoso, osa [xãˈsozu, ɔza] *adj* rancid.

ranger [xãˈʒe(x)] ⬦ *m* [ruído - de porta] creaking; [- de dentes] grinding. ⬦ *vt* [os dentes] to grind. ⬦ *vi* to creak.

Rangun [xãŋˈgũl] *n* Rangoon.

ranhura [xãˈnural] *f* **-1.** [entalhe] groove. **-2.** [canaleta] keyway. **-3.** [para moeda] slot.

ranzinza [xãˈzĩza] *adj* bolshy.

rapadura [xapaˈdura] *f* raw cane sugar.

rapar [xaˈpa(x)] ⬦ *vt* **-1.** [pelar] to shave. **-2.** *fam* [roubar] to nick. ⬦ *vi* *fam* [ir embora] to scarper.

rapaz [xaˈpaʒ] (*pl* **-es**) *m* **-1.** [jovem] boy. **-2.** *fam* [cara] man.

rapé [xaˈpɛl] *m* snuff.

rapidez [xapiˈdeʃ] *f* speed.

rápido, da [ˈxapidu, da] *adj* **-1.** [veloz] fast, quick. **-2.** [breve] brief.
➡ **rápido** *adv* [ligeiro] quickly.

rapina [xaˈpina] *f* violent robbery.

raposa [xaˈpoza] *f* **-1.** *ZOOL* vixen (*f* vixen). **-2.** *fig* [pessoa astuta] sly old fox.

raptar [xapˈta(x)] *vt* to kidnap.

rapto [ˈxaptul] *m* kidnapping.

raptor, ra [xapˈto(x), ra] *m*, *f* kidnapper.

raquete [xaˈkɛtʃi] *f* **-1.** [de tênis, squash] racket. **-2.** [de pingue-pongue] bat.

raquítico, ca [xaˈkitʃiku, ka] *adj* **-1.** *MED* rachitic. **-2.** [magro] scrawny. **-3.** [escasso] sparse.

raquitismo [xakiˈtʃiʒmul] *m MED* rickets (*sg or pl*).

raramente [ˌxaraˈmẽntʃi] *adv* rarely, seldom.

rarear [xaˈrja(x)] *vi* **-1.** [tornar-se raro] to become scarce. **-2.** [cabelos] to thin. **-3.** [vegetação, população] to thin out.

rarefeito, ta [xareˈfejtu, ta] *adj* **-1.** [pouco denso] rarefied. **-2.** [disperso] dispersed.

raro, ra [ˈxaru, ra] *adj* rare.

rasante [xaˈzãntʃi] ⬦ *adj* low-flying. ⬦ *adv*: o avião passou ~ the plane flew low.

rascunho [xaʃˈkuɲu] *m* draft.

rasgado, da [xaʒˈgadu, da] *adj* **-1.** [tecido, papel] torn. **-2.** *fig* [elogio, gesto] generous. **-3.** *fig* [ritmo, dança] flourishing.

rasgão [xaʒˈgãw] (*pl* **-ões**) *m* tear.

rasgar [xaʒˈga(x)] ⬦ *vt* **-1.** [romper] to tear. **-2.** *fig* [elogios] to heap. ⬦ *vi* [romper-se] to tear.

➡ **rasgar-se** *vp* **-1.** [romper-se] to be torn. **-2.** [pessoa] to be consumed.

rasgo [ˈxaʒgul] *m* **-1.** [rasgão] tear. **-2.** [traço] line. **-3.** *fig* [ação, ímpeto] burst.

rasgões [xaʒˈgõjʃ] *pl* ⯈ **rasgão**.

raso, sa [ˈxazu, za] *adj* **-1.** [pouco fundo] shallow. **-2.** [colher etc.] level. **-3.** [liso] even. **-4.** [rente] close-cropped. **-5.** [sapato] flat. **-6.** [soldado] private.
➡ **raso** *m* shallow end.

raspa [ˈxaʃpa] *f* **-1.** [lasca] shavings (*pl*). **-2.** [de panela] scrapings (*pl*).

raspão [xaʃˈpãw] (*pl* **-ões**) *m* scratch; o tiro pegou de ~ no braço the shot grazed his arm.

raspar [xaʃˈpa(x)] ⬦ *vt* **-1.** [alisar] to smooth down. **-2.** [pêlos] to shave. **-3.** [limpar] to scrape. **-4.** [arranhar] to scratch. **-5.** [de raspão] to graze. ⬦ *vi* [de raspão]: ~ em to strike a glancing blow at.

raspões [xaʃˈpõjʃ] *pl* ⯈ **raspão**.

rasteiro, ra [xaʃˈtejru, ra] *adj* **-1.** [vegetação] low-lying. **-2.** [vôo] low. **-3.** [que se arrasta] crawling. **-4.** *fig* [superficial] superficial.
➡ **rasteira** *f* trip; dar uma ~ em alguém [com pernada] to trip sb up; *fig* [trair] to double-cross sb.

rastejante [xaʃteˈʒãntʃi] *adj* **-1.** [que se arrasta - animal] crawling; [- planta] creeping. **-2.** *fig* [submisso] crawling.

rastejar [xaʃteˈʒa(x)] ⬦ *vi* **-1.** [arrastar-se - planta] to creep; [- animal] to crawl; [- cobra] to slide. **-2.** [andar de rastos] to crawl. **-3.** *fig* [rebaixar-se] to grovel. ⬦ *vt* [rastrear] to track.

rasto [ˈxaʃtul] *m* **-1.** [pegada] track. **-2.** [de veículo] trail. **-3.** *fig* [vestígios] tracks (*pl*).

rastrear [xaʃˈtrja(x)] ⬦ *vt* **-1.** [seguir o rasto de] to track. **-2.** [investigar] to search for. ⬦ *vi* [seguir o rasto] to track.

rastro [ˈxaʃtrul] *m* = **rasto**.

rasura [xaˈzura] *f* crossing out.

ratazana [xataˈzãna] *f* Norway rat.

ratear [xaˈtʃja(x)] ⬦ *vt* [dividir] to share out. ⬦ *vi* [motor] to stall.

ratificar [xatʃifiˈka(x)] *vt* **-1.** [confirmar] to ratify. **-2.** [comprovar] to confirm.

rato, ta [ˈxatu, ta] *m*, *f* rat; ~ de praia *fig* thief (*on the beach*).

ratoeira [xaˈtwejra] *f* **-1.** [para ratos] mousetrap. **-2.** *fig* [armadilha] trap.

ravina [xaˈvina] *f* ravine.

ravióli [xaˈvjɔli] *m* ravioli.

razão [xaˈzãw] (*pl* **-ões**) ⬦ *f* **-1.** [faculdade] reason; ~ de ser raison d'être; de viver reason for living; em ~ de on account of. **-2.** [bom senso] (common) sense. **-3.** [justiça]: **dar ~ a alguém** to side with sb; **estar coberto de ~** to be absolutely right; **ter/não ter ~ (de)** to be right/wrong (to); **com ~** with good reason; **sem ~** for no reason. **-4.** [MAT - proporção] ratio; [- quociente, fração] quotient; **à ~ de** at the rate of. **-5.** FIN account. ⬦ *m* COM ledger.

razoável [xa'zwavew] (*pl* **-eis**) *adj* **-1.** [ger] reasonable. **-2.** [significativo] significant.

ré ['xɛ] *f* AUTO reverse; **dar uma ~, dar marcha à ~** to reverse, to back up; ⮫ **réu.**

reabastecer [xejaba∫te'se(x)] *vt* **-1.** [tanque, carro, avião] to refuel. **-2.** [despensa, cozinha] to restock. **-3.** [energias] to rebuild.
⬤ **reabastecer-se** *vp*: **~-se de algo** to replenish one's supply of sthg.

reabilitação [xeabilita'sãw] (*pl* **-ões**) *f* **-1.** [ger] rehabilitation. **-2.** [da forma física] recovery.

reação [xea'sãw] (*pl* **-ões**) *f* **-1.** [ger] reaction; **~ em cadeia** chain reaction. **-2.** [recuperação] recovery.

reacionário, ria [xeasjo'narju, rja] ⬦ *adj* reactionary. ⬦ *m, f* [pessoa] reactionary.

readaptação [xeadapta'sãw] (*pl* **-ões**) *f* readjustment.

reafirmar [xeafix'ma(x)] *vt* to reaffirm.

reagir [xea'ʒi(x)] *vi* **-1.** [responder]: **~ (a)** to react (to). **-2.** [protestar, resistir]: **~ (a** OU **contra)** to resist. **-3.** [recuperar-se] to rally.

reajuste [xea'ʒu∫t∫i] *m* adjustment.

real [xe'aw] (*pl* **-ais**) ⬦ *adj* **-1.** [verdadeiro] true. **-2.** [régio] royal. ⬦ *m* [realidade] reality.

realçar [xeaw'sa(x)] *vt* to highlight.

realce [xe'awsi] *m* **-1.** [destaque] emphasis; **dar ~ a** to emphasize. **-2.** [brilho] highlight.

realeza [xea'leza] *f* **-1.** [dignidade de rei] royalty. **-2.** [grandeza] *fig* grandeur.

realidade [xeali'dadʒi] *f* reality; **na ~** actually.

realista [xea'li∫ta] ⬦ *adj* realistic. ⬦ *mf* **-1.** [pessoa] realist. **-2.** [adepto] royalist.

realização [xealiza'sãw] (*pl* **-ões**) *f* **-1.** [ger] realization. **-2.** [execução - de projeto, negócios] realization; [- de congresso, espetáculo] holding; [- de reforma] enactment. **-3.** [pessoal] fulfilment UK, fulfillment US.

realizado, da [xeali'zadu, da] *adj* **-1.** [pessoa] fulfilled. **-2.** [obra] carried out. **-3.** [sonho] realized.

realizador, ra [xealiza'do(x), ra] (*mpl* **-es**, *fpl* **-s**) ⬦ *adj* enterprising. ⬦ *m, f* [pessoa] producer.

realizar [xeali'za(x)] *vt* **-1.** [ger] to realize. **-2.** [executar] to carry out; **ser realizado** [conferência, festa] to take place.
⬤ **realizar-se** *vp* **-1.** [concretizar-se] to be realized. **-2.** [ocorrer] to be carried out. **-3.** [alcançar seu ideal] to be fulfilled.

realmente [xeaw'mẽnt∫i] ⬦ *adv* **-1.** [de fato] in fact. **-2.** [muito] really. ⬦ *interj* [expressando indignação] really!

reanimar [xeani'ma(x)] *vt* **-1.** [fisicamente] to revive. **-2.** [moralmente] to cheer up. **-3.** MED to resuscitate.
⬤ **reanimar-se** *vp* **-1.** [fisicamente] to come to. **-2.** [moralmente] to rally.

reapresentar [xeaprezẽ'ta(x)] *vt* to represent.
⬤ **reapresentar-se** *vp* to reappear.

reatar [xea'ta(x)] *vt* **-1.** [nó] to retie. **-2.** [amizade, conversa, negócios] to resume.

reator [xea'to(x)] *m* reactor; **~ nuclear** nuclear reactor.

reavaliação [xeavalja'sãw] *f* **-1.** [ger] reevaluation. **-2.** [de jóia] revaluation.

reaver [xea've(x)] *vt* to recover.

rebaixar [xebaj'∫a(x)] *vt* **-1.** [teto, terreno] to lower. **-2.** [preço] to cut. **-3.** [pessoa] to discredit. **-4.** FUT to relegate.
⬤ **rebaixar-se** *vp* [pessoa] to lower o.s.

rebanho [xe'baɲu] *m* **-1.** [de bois, cabras] herd. **-2.** [de ovelhas] flock. **-3.** *fig* [de fiéis] flock.

rebater [xeba'te(x)] ⬦ *vt* **-1.** [bola] to kick back. **-2.** [golpe] to counter. **-3.** [argumentos, acusações] to rebut. **-4.** [à máquina] to retype. ⬦ *vi* [chutar] to kick back.

rebelar-se [xebe'laxsi] *vp*: **~-se (contra)** to rebel (against).

rebelde [xe'bɛwdʒi] ⬦ *adj* rebellious. ⬦ *mf* rebel.

rebeldia [xebew'dʒia] *f* **-1.** [qualidade] rebelliousness. **-2.** *fig* [oposição] defiance. **-3.** *fig* [obstinação] stubbornness.

rebelião [xebe'ljãw] (*pl* **-ões**) *f* [sublevação] rebellion.

rebentar [xebẽn'ta(x)] ⬦ *vi* **-1.** [ger] to break. **-2.** [não se conter]: **~ de** to burst with. **-3.** [guerra] to break out. ⬦ *vt* **-1.** [romper] to tear. **-2.** [vidraça, louça] to smash.

rebobinar [xebobi'na(x)] *vt* [vídeo] to rewind.

rebocar [xebo'ka(x)] *vt* **-1.** [barco, carro] to tow. **-2.** [carro mal estacionado] to tow away. **-3.** CONSTR to plaster.

rebolado [xebo'ladu] *m* swing of the hips.

rebolar [xebo'la(x)] <> vt [corpo, quadris] to swing. <> vi -1. [pessoa, corpo] to sway. -2. *fam fig* [empenhar-se] to fight hard.

reboque [xe'bɔkil] m -1. [ger] tow. -2. [carro-guincho] towtruck.

rebuliço [xebu'lisul] m commotion.

rebuscado, da [xebuʃ'kadu, da] adj affected.

recado [xe'kadul] m message; **dar conta do ~** *fig* to deliver the goods.

recaída [xeka'idal] f relapse.

recalcar [xekaw'ka(x)] vt -1. [comprimir] to tread upon. -2. [reprimir] to repress. -3. *PSIC* to inhibit.

recalque [xe'kawkil] m *PSIC* inhibition.

recanto [xe'kãntul] m nook.

recapitular [xekapitu'la(x)] vt -1. [resumir] to recap. -2. [relembrar] to recall.

recatado, da [xeka'tadu, da] adj -1. [pudico] modest. -2. [prudente] restrained.

recauchutado, da [xekawʃu'tadu, da] adj [pneu] remoulded *UK*, remolded *US*.

recear [xe'sja(x)] vt -1. [temer] to fear; **~ fazer algo** to be afraid to do sthg. -2. [preocupar-se com]: **~ que** to be worried that.

receber [xese'be(x)] <> vt -1. [ger] to receive. -2. [recepcionar] to entertain. <> vi -1. [ser pago] to be paid; **a ~** owing. -2. [recepcionar] to entertain.

recebimento [xesebi'mẽntul] m receipt; **acusar o ~ de** to acknowledge receipt of.

receio [xe'sejul] m -1. [medo] fear. -2. [apreensão] concern; **ter ~ (de) que** to be afraid that.

receita [xe'sejtal] f -1. [renda - pessoal] income; [- do Estado] tax revenue. -2. *FIN* income. -3. *MED*: **~ (médica)** prescription. -4. *CULIN* recipe. -5. *fig* [fórmula] way.

➤ **Receita** f: **a Receita (federal)** *Brazilian tax office*, ≃ Inland Revenue *UK*, ≃ Internal Revenue Service *US*.

receitar [xesej'ta(x)] <> vt to prescribe. <> vi to issue prescriptions.

recém- [xesẽnl] prefixo newly.

recém-casado, da [xe,sẽnka'zadu, da] <> adj newly-wed. <> m, f newlywed; **os ~ s** the newly-weds.

recém-chegado, da [xe,sẽʃe'gadu, da] <> adj recently arrived. <> m, f newcomer.

recém-nascido, da [xe,sẽna'sidu, da] <> adj newborn. <> m, f newborn child.

recenseamento [xesẽnsja'mẽntul] m census.

recente [xe'sẽntʃil] <> adj -1. [tempo] recent. -2. [novo] new; **este é o meu mais ~ hobby** this is my latest hobby. <> adv recently.

receoso, osa [xe'sjozu, ɔza] adj -1. [medroso] afraid. -2. [apreensivo] apprehensive; **estar ~ de que** to be worried that.

recepção [xesep'sãw] (pl -ões) f reception.

recepcionista [xesepsjo'niʃtal] mf receptionist.

receptivo, va [xesep'tʃivu, va] adj receptive.

receptor [xesep'to(x)] (pl -res) m [aparelho] receiver.

recessão [xese'sãw] (pl -ões) f recession.

recesso [xe'sɛsul] m -1. [férias] recess. -2. [recanto] nook.

rechaçar [xeʃa'sa(x)] vt -1. [opor-se a] to reject. -2. [repelir] to repel. -3. [negar] to decline.

recheado, da [xe'ʃjadu, da] adj -1. [comida]: **~ (com ou de)** filled (with). -2. [repleto]: **~ de algo** stuffed with sthg.

rechear [xe'ʃja(x)] vt [comida] to fill.

recheio [xe'ʃejul] m -1. [de comida - de carne] stuffing; [- de bolo, pastel] filling. -2. *fig* [num texto] padding.

rechonchudo, da [xeʃõn'ʃudu, da] adj chubby.

recibo [xe'sibul] m receipt.

reciclagem [xesi'klaʒẽl] f -1. [de material] recycling. -2. [de pessoa] retraining.

reciclar [xesi'kla(x)] vt -1. [material] to recycle. -2. [pessoa] to retrain.

recife [xe'sifil] m reef.

recinto [xe'sĩntul] m area.

recipiente [xesi'pjẽntʃil] m recipient.

recíproca [xe'siprokal] f ▷ **recíproco**.

recíproco, ca [xe'siproku, kal] adj reciprocal.

➤ **recíproca** f: **a recíproca** the reverse.

récita ['xɛsital] f performance.

recital [xesi'taw] (pl -ais) m recital.

reclamação [xeklama'sãw] (pl -ões) f -1. [queixa] complaint. -2. *JUR* [petição] claim.

reclamar [xekla'ma(x)] <> vt [exigir] to demand. <> vi [protestar]: **~ (de/contra)** to complain (about/against).

reclame [xeklãmil] m advertisement.

reclinar [xekli'na(x)] vt [inclinar]: **~ algo (em ou sobre)** to rest sthg (against ou on).

➤ **reclinar-se** vp [recostar-se] to lie back.

reclinável [xekli'navewl] (pl -eis) adj reclining.

reclusão [xeklu'zĩwl] f -1. [isolamento]

seclusion. - **2.** [em prisão] imprisonment. - **3.** [pena] solitary confinement.

recluso, sa [xe'kluzu, za] ◇ *adj* **-1.** [isolado] reclusive. - **2.** [preso] shut up. ◇ *m, f* **-1.** [pessoa que se isola] recluse. - **2.** [prisioneiro] prisoner.

recobrar [xeko'bra(x)] *vt* to recover.
➡ **recobrar-se** *vp*: ~**-se de algo** to recover from sthg.

recolher [xeko'ʎe(x)] *vt* **-1.** [ger] to collect. - **2.** [do chão] to pick up. - **3.** [juntar] to gather (together). - **4.** [pôr ao abrigo] to bring in. - **5.** [levar] to gather. - **6.** [tirar de circulação] to withdraw. - **7.** [coligir] to gather. - **8.** [encolher] to pull back.

recolhido, da [xeko'ʎidu, da] *adj* **-1.** [lugar] secluded. - **2.** [absorvido] absorbed. - **3.** [dentro de casa] housebound.

recolhimento [xekoʎi'mẽntu] *m* **-1.** [ato de levar] reception. - **2.** [arrecadação] collection. - **3.** [de circulação] withdrawal. - **4.** [coleta] gathering. - **5.** [devido a doença] confinement. - **6.** [refúgio] refuge. - **7.** [retraimento] seclusion.

recomeçar [xekome'sa(x)] ◇ *vt* to restart. ◇ *vi* to start again.

recomeço [xeko'mesu] *m* restart.

recomendar [xekomẽn'da(x)] *vt* **-1.** [ger] to recommend; **recomenda-se o uso de produtos naturais** the use of natural products is recommended. - **2.** [pedir] to ask. - **3.** [enviar cumprimentos] to send one's regards.

recomendável [xekomẽn'davɛw] (*pl* **-eis**) *adj* advisable; **é ~ que ...** it's advisable that ...

recompensa [xekõn'pẽnsa] *f* reward.

recompensar [xekõnpẽn'sa(x)] *vt* [premiar] to reward.

recompor [xekõn'po(x)] *vt* **-1.** [restabelecer] to reorganise. - **2.** [reordenar] to rearrange.

recôncavo [xe'kõŋkavu] *m* wide bay.

reconciliação [xekõnsilja'sãw] (*pl* **-ões**) *f* reconciliation.

reconciliar [xekõnsi'lja(x)] *vt* to reconcile.
➡ **reconciliar-se** *vp*: ~**-se com** [pessoa] to be reconciled with; [situação] to become reconciled to.

reconhecer [xekoɲe'se(x)] *vt* **-1.** [ger] to recognize. - **2.** [mostrar-se agradecido por] [admitir] to acknowledge. - **3.** [constatar] to accept. - **4.** [autenticar] to authenticate; ~ **firma num documento** to authenticate officially the signature on a document. - **5.** [explorar] to reconnoitre *UK*, to reconnoiter *US*.

reconhecimento [xekoɲesi'mẽntu] *m* **-1.** [ger] recognition. - **2.** [admissão]

acknowledgement. - **3.** [autenticação] authentication. - **4.** [gratidão] gratitude. - **5.** [exploração] reconnaissance.

reconquistar [xekõŋkiʃ'ta(x)] *vt* **-1.** [território] to reconquer. - **2.** [pessoa, confiança] to regain.

reconsiderar [xekõnside'ra(x)] *vt* to reconsider.

reconstruir [xekõnʃ'trwi(x)] *vt* to rebuild, to reconstruct.

recontar [xekõn'ta(x)] *vt* to recount.

recordação [xekoxda'sãw] (*pl* **-ões**) *f* **-1.** [ato, lembrança] memory. - **2.** [objeto] souvenir.

recordar [xekox'da(x)] *vt* **-1.** [lembrar] to remember. - **2.** [por semelhança]: ~ **algo/alguém a alguém** to remind sb of sthg/sb. - **3.** [recapitular] to revise.
➡ **recordar-se** *vp* [lembrar]: ~**-se de alguém/algo** to remember sb/sthg; ~**-se (de) que** to remember that.

recorde [xe'kɔxdʒi] ◇ *adj inv* record (*antes de subst*); **em tempo ~** in record time. ◇ *m* record; **bater/deter um ~** to break/hold a record.

recordista [xekox'dʒiʃta] ◇ *adj* record-breaking. ◇ *mf* **-1.** [quem detém um recorde] record-holder. - **2.** [quem bate um recorde] record-breaker.

recorrer [xeko'xe(x)] *vi* **-1.:** ~ **a** to resort to. - **2.** *JUR* to appeal; ~ **de algo** to appeal against sthg.

recortar [xekox'ta(x)] *vt* to cut out.

recorte [xe'kɔxtʃi] *m* [de jornal etc.] cutting.

recostar [xekoʃ'ta(x)] *vt* **-1.** [encostar] to rest. - **2.** [pôr meio deitado] to recline.
➡ **recostar-se** *vp* **-1.** [encostar-se] to lean against. - **2.** [pôr-se meio deitado] to lie back.

recreação [xekrja'sãw] *f* recreation.

recreativo, va [xekrja'tʃivu, va] *adj* recreational.

recreio [xe'kreju] *m* **-1.** [entretenimento] entertainment. - **2.** *EDUC* playtime *UK*, recess *US*.

recriminar [xekrimi'na(x)] *vt* to reproach.

recrudescer [xekrude'se(x)] *vi* to intensify.

recruta [xe'kruta] *mf* recruit.

recrutamento [xekruta'mẽntu] *m* recruitment.

recrutar [xekru'ta(x)] *vt* to recruit.

recuar [xe'kwa(x)] ◇ *vi* **-1.** [andar para trás] to step back. - **2.** [retirar-se] to retreat. - **3.** [voltar atrás - em intenção, decisão] to back out of; [- no tempo] to go back. - **4.** [canhão] to recoil. ◇ *vt* [mover para trás] to move back.

recuo [xe'kuw] *m* -**1.** [afastamento]: **com o ~, evitou ser atropelada** by stepping backwards, she avoided being run over; **o ~ do móvel, deu mais espaço na sala** moving this piece of furniture back has given the room more space. -**2.** [retirada] retreat. -**3.** [reconsideração - em intenção, decisão] reassessment; [- no tempo] going back. -**4.** [de canhão] recoil. -**5.** [em rua, terreno] setting back.

recuperação [xekupera'sãw] *f* -**1.** [reaquisição] recovery. -**2.** [restabelecimento] recuperation. -**3.** [reabilitação] rehabilitation. -**4.** [indenização] compensation.

recuperar [xekupe'ra(x)] *vt* -**1.** [readquirir] to recover. -**2.** [restabelecer] to regain. -**3.** [reabilitar] to rehabilitate.

➡ recuperar-se *vp* [restabelecer-se] to recuperate.

recurso [xe'kuxsu] *m* -**1.** [ato]: **o ~ a algo** resorting to sthg. -**2.** [meio] recourse; **como** *ou* **em último ~** as a last resort.

➡ recursos *mpl* [dinheiro] means.

recusa [xe'kuza] *f*: **~ (a/de algo)** refusal (to/of sthg); **~ a** *ou* **em fazer algo** refusal to do sthg.

recusar [xeku'za(x)] *vt* -**1.** [não aceitar] to refuse. -**2.** [não conceder]: **~ algo (a alguém)** to deny (sb) sthg.

➡ recusar-se *vp* [negar-se a]: **~-se (a fazer algo)** to refuse (to do sthg).

redação [xeda'sãw] (*pl* -**ões**) *f* -**1.** [ato] writing. -**2.** [modo de redigir] composition. -**3.** *EDUC* essay. -**4.** [redatores] editorial staff. -**5.** [seção] editorial office.

redator, ra [xeda'to(x), ra] (*mpl* -**es**, *fpl* -**s**) *m, f* -**1.** *JORN* writer. -**2.** [de obra de referência] editor, compiler.

redator-chefe, redatora-chefe [xedatox ʃɛfi, xedatoraʃɛfi] (*mpl* **redatores-chefes**, *fpl* **redatoras-chefes**) *m, f* editor in chief.

rede ['xedʒi] *f* -**1.** [ger] network. -**2.** [para pesca, caça & *ESP*] net. -**3.** [para cabelo] hairnet. -**4.** [leito] hammock.

rédea ['xedʒja] *f* [correia] rein.

redemoinho [xedʒi'mwiɲu] *m* -**1.** [de água] whirlpool. -**2.** [de vento] whirlwind.

redenção [xedẽ'sãw] *f* redemption.

redentor, ra [xedẽ'to(x), ra] *m, f* [pessoa] redeemer.

redigir [xedʒi'ʒi(x)] *◇ vt* to write. *◇ vi* to write.

redobrar [xedo'bra(x)] *◇ vt* -**1.** [dobrar de novo] to fold again. -**2.** [reduplicar, intensificar] to redouble. *◇ vi* to intensify.

redondamente [xe,dõnda'mẽntʃi] *adv*

[totalmente]: **me enganei ~** I was utterly wrong.

redondeza [xedõn'deza] *f* [qualidade] roundness.

➡ redondezas *fpl* [arredores] surroundings.

redondo, da [xe'dõndu, da] *adj* -**1.** [circular] round. -**2.** [rechonchudo] plump.

redor [xe'dɔ(x)] *m*: **ao ~ de** around.

redução [xedu'sãw] (*pl* -**ões**) *f* -**1.** [ger] reduction. -**2.** [conversão] conversion.

redundância [xedũn'dãnsja] *f* redundancy.

redundante [xedũn'dãntʃi] *adj* redundant.

reduto [xe'dutu] *m* -**1.** [fortificação] fort. -**2.** *fig* [abrigo] shelter. -**3.** *fig* [lugar de reunião] meeting place.

reduzido, da [xedu'zidu, da] *adj* -**1.** [diminuído] reduced. -**2.** [pequeno] limited.

reduzir [xedu'zi(x)] *vt* -**1.** [ger] to reduce. -**2.** [transformar]: **~ alguém/algo a algo** to reduce sb/sthg to sthg. -**3.** [levar]: **~ alguém a algo** to reduce sb to sthg.

➡ reduzir-se *vp*: **~-se a algo** [resumir-se] to be reduced to sthg.

reeditar [xeedʒi'ta(x)] *vt* to republish.

reeleição [xeelej'sãw] *f* re-election.

reembolsar [xeẽbow'sa(x)] *vt* -**1.** [reaver] to recover. -**2.** [restituir]: **~ alguém (de algo)** to refund sb (sthg). -**3.** [indenizar]: **~ algo a alguém, ~ alguém de algo** to reimburse sb for sthg.

reembolso [xeẽbowsu] *m* -**1.** [recuperação] recovery. -**2.** [restituição] refund. -**3.** [indenização] reimbursement.

reencarnação [xeẽkaxna'sãw] *f* reincarnation.

reencontro [xeẽɲ'kõntru] *m* reunion.

reescrever [xees kre've(x)] *vt* to rewrite.

reexaminar [xeezami'na(x)] *vt* to re-examine.

refazer [xefa'ze(x)] *vt* -**1.** [fazer de novo] to redo. -**2.** [reconstruir] to rebuild. -**3.** [recuperar] to recover.

➡ refazer-se *vp* -**1.** [recuperar-se]: **~-se (de algo)** to recover (from sthg). -**2.** [indenizar-se]: **~-se de algo** to be compensated for sthg.

refeição [xefej'sãw] (*pl* -**ões**) *f* meal; **fazer uma ~** to have a meal.

refeito, ta [xe'fejtu, ta] *◇ pp ▷* **refazer**. *◇ adj* -**1.** [feito de novo] redone. -**2.** [reconstruído] rebuilt. -**3.** [recuperado] recovered.

refeitório [xefej'tɔrju] *m* dining hall.

refém [xe'fẽ] (*pl* -**ns**) *mf* hostage.

referência [xefe'rẽnsja] *f* reference; **fazer ~ a** to refer to.

referências fpl [informação] referen-ces.

referendum [xefe'rẽndũ] m POL referen-dum.

referente [xefe'rẽntʃi] adj: ~ a concer-ning.

referir [xefe'ri(x)] vt [narrar]: ~ algo a al-guém to tell sb sthg.

➡ **referir-se** vp: ~-se a [aludir] to allu-de to; [dizer respeito] to refer to.

refestelar-se [xefeʃte'laxsil vp [estender-se] to sprawl.

refil [xe'fiwl (pl -is) m refill.

refinado, da [xefi'nadu, da] adj refined.

refinamento [xefina'mẽntul m -1. [ato] refining. -2. [requinte] refinement.

refinar [xefi'na(x)] vt to refine.

refinaria [xefina'ria] f refinery.

refletir [xefle'tʃi(x)] <> vt to reflect. <> vi -1. [luz]: ~ de to reflect off. -2. [pensar]: ~ (em/sobre) to reflect on/about. -3. [repercutir]: ~ em to reflect on.

➡ **refletir-se** vp -1. [espelhar-se] to be reflected. -2. [repercutir] to reflect on.

refletor [xefle'to(x)] (pl -es) m reflector.

reflexão [xeflek'sãw] (pl -ões) f reflec-tion.

reflexivo, va [xeflek'sivu, va] adj reflec-tive.

reflexo, xa [xe'flɛksu, sa] adj -1. [luz] reflected. -2. [movimento] reflex.

➡ **reflexo** m -1. [ger] reflection. -2. ANAT reflex.

➡ **reflexos** mpl [no cabelo] highlights.

reflorestamento [xefloreʃta'mẽntul m reforestation.

reflorestar [xefloreʃ'ta(x)] vt to reforest.

refluxo [xe'fluksul m ebb.

refogado, da [xefo'gadu, da] adj sau-téed.

➡ **refogado** m -1. [molho] gravy. -2. [prato] stew.

refogar [xefo'ga(x)] vt to sauté.

reforçado, da [xefox'sadu, da] adj -1. [ger] reinforced. -2. [refeição] hearty.

reforçar [xefox'sa(x)] vt -1. [ger] to reinforce. -2. [ânimo] to invigorate.

reforço [xe'foxsul m -1. [ger] reinforcement. -2. [a tropa, equipe] reinforcements (pl). -3. [de vacina] booster.

reforma [xe'fɔxmal f -1. [modificação] reform; ~ ministerial ministerial re-shuffle; ~ agrária land reform. -2. AR-QUIT renovation. -3. MIL regrouping.

➡ **Reforma** f: a Reforma RELIG the Re-formation.

reformado, da [xefox'madu, da] adj -1. [modificado - ensino, instituição] reformed;

[- leis] amended; [- sofá] repaired. -2. ARQUIT renovated. -3. MIL regrouped.

reformar [xefox'ma(x)] vt -1. [modificar - ensino, constituição] to reform; [- sofá] to repair; [- lei] to amend; [- empresa] to restructure. -2. ARQUIT to renovate. -3. MIL to regroup. -4. JUR to amend.

➡ **reformar-se** vp MIL to retire.

reformatar [xefoxma'ta(x)] vt COMPUT to reformat.

reformatório [xefoxma'tɔrjul m young offender institution UK, reformatory US.

refrão [xe'frãw] (pl -ões) m -1. [estribilho] chorus. -2. [provérbio] saying.

refratário, ria [xefra'tarju, rja] adj -1. [material] heat-resistant. -2. [rebelde]: ser ~ a algo to be impervious to sthg; [imune] to be immune to sthg.

refrear [xefri'a(x)] vt [reprimir] to sup-press.

➡ **refrear-se** vp [conter-se] to contain o.s.

refrescante [xefreʃ'kãntʃi] adj refresh-ing.

refrescar [xefreʃ'ka(x)] <> vt -1. [tornar menos quente] to cool. -2. [avivar] to refresh. -3. [tranquilizar] to refresh. <> vi [tempo] to cool down.

➡ **refrescar-se** vp [pessoa] to refresh o.s.

refresco [xe'freʃkul m fruit squash.

refrigeração [xefriʒera'sãw] m [de ali-mentos] refrigeration; [de ambiente] air conditioning.

refrigerador [xefriʒera'do(x)] m -1. [de alimentos] refrigerator. -2. [de máquina] cooler.

refrigerante [xefriʒe'rãntʃi] m soft drink.

refrigerar [xefriʒe'ra(x)] vt -1. [bebidas, alimentos] to chill. -2. [ambiente] to cool. -3. [máquina] to refrigerate.

refugiado, da [xefu'ʒjadu, da] <> adj refugee. <> m, f refugee.

refugiar-se [xefu'ʒjaxsil vp [abrigar-se] to take refuge; ~ em [abrigar-se] to take cover in; [asilar-se] to take refuge in; fig [amparar-se] to seek solace in.

refúgio [xe'fuʒjul m -1. [local] hideaway. -2. fig [apoio] refuge.

refugo [xe'fugul m -1. [resto] waste. -2. [mercadoria] rubbish UK, garbage US.

refutar [xefu'ta(x)] vt to refute.

regaço [xe'gasul m [colo] lap.

regador [xega'do(x)] (pl -es) m watering can.

regalia [xega'lia] f privilege.

regalo [xe'galul m [presente] gift.

regar [xe'ga(x)] vt -1. [aguar] to water.

-2. [banhar] to wash., **-3.** [acompanhar] to wash down.

regatear [xega't∫ja(x)] ⟨⟩ *vt* to haggle over. ⟨⟩ *vi* to haggle.

regeneração [xeʒenera'sãw] *f* **-1.** [recomposição] regeneration. **-2.** [moral] reform.

regenerar [xeʒene'ra(x)] *vt* **-1.** [recompor] to regenerate. **-2.** [moralmente] to reform.

  ◆ **regenerar-se** *vp* **-1.** [recompor-se] to be regenerated. **-2.** [moralmente] to be reformed.

regente [xe'ʒẽnt∫i] *m* **-1.** POL regent. **-2.** MÚS conductor. **-3.** UNIV vice chancellor *UK*, president *US*.

reger [xe'ʒe(x)] ⟨⟩ *vt* **-1.** [governar] to govern. ⟨⟩ [regular] to rule. **-3.** MÚS to conduct. **-4.** UNIV to occupy. **-5.** GRAM to govern. ⟨⟩ *vi* **-1.** [governar] to rule. **-2.** MÚS to conduct.

região [xe'ʒjãw] (*pl* -ões) *f* **-1.** [território] region. **-2.** [de cidade, corpo] area.

regime [xe'ʒimil *m* **-1.** [ger] system. **-2.** [dieta] diet; **estar de** ~ to be on a diet. **-3.** [regras] rules (*pl*).

regimento [xeʒi'mẽntul *m* **-1.** [ger] regiment. **-2.** [normas] rules (*pl*).

regiões [xe'ʒjõj∫] *mpl* ▷ **região**.

regional [xeʒjo'naw] (*pl* -ais) *adj* regional.

registradora [xeʒi∫tra'doral *f*[caixa] cash register.

registrar [xeʒi∫'tra(x)] *vt* **-1.** [ger] to register. **-2.** [anotar] to record. **-3.** [memorizar] to remember.

registro [xe'ʒi∫trul *m* **-1.** [ger & LING] register. **-2.** [postal] registration. **-3.** [órgão]: ~ **civil** registry office. **-4.** [torneira] tap *UK*, faucet *US*. **-5.** [relógio] meter. **-6.** MÚS range.

regozijar-se [xegozi'ʒaxsil *vp*: ~ **com algo/por fazer algo** to be delighted with sthg/to do sthg.

regra ['xɛgral *f* **-1.** [norma] rule. **-2.** [rotina] routine.

regredir [xegre'dʒi(x)] *vi*: ~ **(a algo)** to regress (to sthg).

regressão [xegre'sãw] *f* **-1.** [retrocesso] regression. **-2.** PSIC relapse.

regressar [xegre'sa(x)] *vi*: ~ **(de/a)** to return from/to.

regressivo, va [xegre'sivu, val *adj* regressive.

regresso [xe'grɛsul *m* return.

régua ['xɛgwal *f* ruler.

regulador, ra [xegula'do(x), ral *adj*[força] regulating.

  ◆ **regulador** *m* [medicamento] regulator.

regulagem [xegu'laʒẽl (*pl* -ns) *f* tuning.

regulamento [xegula'mẽntul *m* rules (*pl*).

regular [xegu'la(x)] (*pl* -es) ⟨⟩ *adj* **-1.** [ger] regular. **-2.** [legal] legal. **-3.** [tamanho] medium. **-4.** [razoável] reasonable. ⟨⟩ *vt*-1. [ger] to regulate. **-2.** [ajustar] to adjust. ⟨⟩ *vi* **-1.** [máquina]: ~ **bem/mal** to be well/badly adjusted. **-2.** [pessoa]: **não** ~ **(bem)** to not be quite right in the head.

regularidade [xegulari'dadʒil *f* regularity.

regularizar [xegulari'za(x)] *vt* **-1.** [legalizar] to legalize. **-2.** [normalizar] to regularize.

  ◆ **regularizar-se** *vp* [normalizar-se] to return to normal.

rei ['xejl *m* **-1.** [ger] king. **-2.** *loc*: **ter o** ~ **na barriga** to be full of o.s.

Reikjavik [xejkʒa'vikil *n* Reykjavik.

reinado [xej'nadul *m* reign.

reinar [xej'na(x)] *vi* **-1.** [governar] to reign. **-2.** *fig* [dominar] to dominate.

reincidir [xẽjnsi'dʒi(x)] *vi* to recur; ~ **em algo** to commit sthg again.

reino ['xejnul *m* **-1.** [ger] kingdom. **-2.** *fig* [âmbito] realm.

reintegrar [xẽjnte'gra(x)] *vt* **-1.** [em cargo etc.] to reinstate. **-2.** [reconduzir] to readmit.

reiterar [xeite'ra(x)] *vt* to reiterate.

reitor, ra [xej'to(x), ral *m, f* vice chancellor *UK*, president *US*.

reitoria [xejto'rial *f* **-1.** [cargo] vice-chancellorship *UK*, presidency *US*. **-2.** [gabinete] vice chancellor's office *UK*, president's office *US*.

reivindicação [xejvĩndʒika'sãw] (*pl* -ões) *f* claim.

reivindicar [xejvĩndʒi'ka(x)] *vt* to claim.

rejeição [xeʒej'sãw] (*pl* -ões) *f* rejection.

rejeitar [xeʒej'ta(x)] *vt* **-1.** [recusar] to reject. **-2.** [vomitar] to vomit. **-3.** [desprezar] to ignore.

rejuvenescer [xeʒuvene'se(x)] ⟨⟩ *vt* to rejuvenate. ⟨⟩ *vi* to rejuvenating.

rejuvenescimento [xeʒuvenesi'mẽntul *m* rejuvenation.

relação [xela'sãw] (*pl* -ões) *f* **-1.** [ligação] relationship; **em** ~ **a** in relation to; ~ **entre/com** relationship between/with. **-2.** [listagem] list.

  ◆ **relações** *fpl* [relacionamento] relationship (*sg*); **ele não é pessoa de minhas relações** he's not sb I have anything to do with; **cortar relações com alguém** to break off with sb; **ter relações com alguém** [sexual] to sleep with sb; **relações públicas** public relations;

relações sexuais sex, sexual intercourse.

relacionar [xelasjo'na(x)] vt -1. [listar] to list. -2. [pessoa] to bring into contact with.

➡ **relacionar-se** vp -1. [ligar-se] to be related. -2. [pessoa]: ~-se com alguém to mix with sb.

relações-públicas [xela,sõjʃ'publikaʃ] mf inv [pessoa] PR officer.

relâmpago [xe'lãnpagul ◇ m METEOR flash of lightning. ◇ adj [rápido] lightning (antes de subst).

relampejar [xelãnpe'ʒa(x)] vi: relampejou esta noite there was lightening last night.

relance [xe'lãnsil m: ver de ~ to glance at.

relapso, sa [xe'lapsu, sal ◇ adj negligent. ◇ m, f negligent person.

relatar [xela'ta(x)] vt to relate.

relativo, va [xela'tʃivu, val adj relative; ~ a algo relative to sthg.

relato [xe'latul m account.

relatório [xela'tɔrjul m report.

relaxado, da [xela'ʃadu, dal adj -1. [desleixado] careless. -2. [descansado] relaxed.

relaxante [xela'ʃãntʃil adj relaxing.

relaxar [xela'ʃa(x)] ◇ vt to relax. ◇ vi -1. [desleixar-se]: ~ em algo to become careless with sthg. -2. [descansar] to relax.

relegar [xele'ga(x)] vt to relegate.

relembrar [xelẽn'bra(x)] vt to recall.

reles ['xɛliʃ] adj inv -1. [desprezível] despicable. -2. [mero] mere.

relevante [xele'vãntʃil adj -1. [saliente] prominent. -2. [importante] important.

relevo [xe'levul m -1. [em superfície] outstanding feature. -2. ARTE relief. -3. fig [destaque] importance.

religião [xeli'ʒjãwl (pl -ões) f religion.

religioso, osa [xeli'ʒozu, ɔzal ◇ adj religious. ◇ m, f [padre, freira] monk (f nun).

relinchar [xelĩn'ʃa(x)] vi to neigh.

relíquia [xe'likjal f relic; ~ de família family heirloom.

relógio [xe'lɔʒjul m -1. [instrumento] clock; ~ de ponto time clock; ~ de pulso wrist watch; ~ de sol sundial. -2. [registro] meter.

relojoeiro, ra [xelo'ʒwejru, ral m, f watchmaker.

relutante [xelu'tãntʃil adj reluctant.

relutar [xelu'ta(x)] vi: ~ (em fazer algo) to be reluctant (to do sthg); ~ (contra algo) to be reluctant (to accept sthg).

reluzente [xelu'zẽntʃil adj shining.

relva ['xɛwval f grass.

remanescente [xemane'sẽntʃil ◇ adj remaining; isto é ~ de práticas antigas this is what remains of ancient customs. ◇ m remainder.

remanso [xe'mãnsul m backwater.

remar [xe'ma(x)] ◇ vt to row. ◇ vi to row; ~ contra a maré fig to swim against the tide.

remarcação [xemaxka'sãwl (pl -ões) f adjustment.

rematar [xema'ta(x)] vt -1. [concluir] to conclude. -2. [fazer o acabamento] to finish.

remate [xe'matʃil m -1. [conclusão] end. -2. [acabamento] finishing touch. -3. [de piada] punchline.

remediar [xeme'dʒja(x)] vt -1. [corrigir, solucionar] to put right. -2. [atenuar] to alleviate. -3. [evitar] to avoid.

remédio [xe'mɛdʒjul m -1. [medicamento] remedy. -2. [solução] solution.

rememorar [xememo'ra(x)] vt to remember.

remendar [xemẽn'da(x)] vt -1. [roupa] to mend. -2. [erros] to rectify.

remendo [xe'mẽndul m -1. [de pano] patch. -2. [de metal, couro] repair. -3. [emenda] correction.

remessa [xe'mesal f -1. [ato] dispatch. -2. [de dinheiro] remittance; [de mercadorias] shipment.

remetente [xeme'tẽntʃil mf [de carta] sender.

remeter [xeme'te(x)] vt -1. [carta, encomenda] to send. -2. [dinheiro] to remit.

➡ **remeter-se** vp [referir-se] to refer to.

remexer [xeme'ʃe(x)] ◇ vt -1. [mexer] to move. -2. [misturar] to mix. -3. [sacudir - braços] to shake; [- papéis, folhas] to shuffle. -4. [revolver] to stir up. -5. fam [rebolar] to roll. ◇ vi [mexer]: ~ em algo to rummage through sthg.

➡ **remexer-se** vp -1. [mover-se] to stir. -2. [rebolar-se] to roll.

reminiscência [xemini'sẽnsjal f reminiscence.

remissão [xemi'sãwl (pl -ões) f -1. [ger] remission. -2. [em texto] cross-reference.

remo ['xemul m -1. [instrumento] oar. -2. [esporte] rowing.

remoção [xemo'sãwl (pl -ões) f removal.

remoçar [xemo'sa(x)] ◇ vt to rejuvenate. ◇ vi to be rejuvenated.

remorso [xe'mɔxsul m remorse.

remoto, ta [xe'mɔtu, tal adj remote.

removedor [xemove'do(x)] m remover.

remover [xemo've(x)] vt -1. [ger] to remove. -2. [transferir] to transfer. -3. [superar] to overcome.

remuneração [xemunera'sãw] (pl -ões) f remuneration.

remunerar [xemune'ra(x)] vt to remunerate.

rena ['xena] f reindeer.

renal [xe'naw] (pl -ais) adj renal.

Renascença [xena'sẽsa] f: a ~ the Renaissance.

renascer [xena'se(x)] vi -1. [nascer de novo] to spring up again. -2. fig [recuperar-se, ressurgir] to be reborn.

renascimento [xenasi'mẽntu] m rebirth.
◆ **Renascimento** m: o **Renascimento** the Renaissance.

render [xẽn'de(x)] <> vt -1. [dominar] to overpower. -2. [substituir] to relieve. -3. [lucrar] to yield. -4. [causar] to bring about. -5. [prestar] to render. <> vi -1. [dar lucro] to be profitable. -2. [trabalho] to be productive. -3. [comida]: **a comida rendeu para toda a semana** there was enough food for the whole week; **vamos fazer sopa porque rende mais** let's make soup because it goes further. -4. [durar] to last.
◆ **render-se** vp [entregar-se]: ~-se (a algo/alguém) to surrender (to sb/sthg).

rendição [xẽndʒi'sãw] f -1. [capitulação] surrender. -2. [substituição] changing.

rendimento [xẽndʒi'mẽntu] m -1. [renda] rental. -2. [lucro] profit. -3. [desempenho] performance. -4. [juro] interest.

renegado, da [xene'gadu, da] <> adj renegade. <> m, f renegade.

renegar [xene'ga(x)] vt -1. [ger] to renounce. -2. [negar] to deny. -3. [desprezar] to reject.

renitente [xeni'tẽntʃi] adj persistent.

renomado, da [xeno'madu, da] adj renowned.

renome [xe'nɔmi] m: de ~ renowned.

renovação [xenova'sãw] (pl -ões) f -1. [ger] renewal. -2. [de ensino, empresa] revamping. -3. ARQUIT renovation.

renovar [xeno'va(x)] vt -1. [ger] to renew. -2. [ensino, empresa] to revamp. -3. ARQUIT to renovate.

rentabilidade [xẽntabili'dadʒi] f -1. [lucro] profitability. -2. [proveito] productiveness.

rentável [xẽn'tavɛw] (pl -eis) adj profitable.

rente ['xẽntʃi] <> adj -1. [muito curto] close-cropped. -2. [junto]: ~ a right next to. <> adv -1. [muito curto] very short. -2. [junto]: **ele caiu ~ ao chão** he fell flat on the floor; **ele foi esmagado ~ ao muro** he was crushed right up against the wall.

renúncia [xe'nũnsja] f renouncement.

renunciar [xenũn'sja(x)] vi: ~ **a algo** to renounce sthg.

reorganização [xeoxganiza'sãw] f reorganization.

reorganizar [xeoxgani'za(x)] vt to reorganize.

reparação [xepara'sãw] (pl -ões) f -1. [conserto] repair. -2. [indenização] compensation. -3. [retratação] reparation.

reparar [xepa'ra(x)] <> vt -1. [consertar] to repair. -2. [indenizar] to compensate. -3. [retratar-se de] to admit. -4. [notar] to notice. <> vi [notar]: ~ **em algo/alguém** to notice sthg/sb; **não repare na bagunça** pay no attention to the mess.

reparo [xe'paru] m -1. [conserto] repair. -2. [crítica] criticism.

repartição [xepaxtʃi'sãw] (pl -ões) f -1. [partilha] distribution. -2. [órgão governamental] department.

repartir [xepax'tʃi(x)] vt -1. [dividir - em partes] to divide up; ~ **o cabelo** to part one's hair; [- entre vários] to distribute. -2. [compartilhar] to share.

repassar [xepa'sa(x)] vt -1. [passar de novo] to cross again. -2. [revisar] to revise. -3. [verbas] to transfer.

repasse [xe'pasi] m [de verba] transfer.

repatriar [xepa'trja(x)] vt to repatriate.
◆ **repatriar-se** vp to return home.

repelente [xepe'lẽntʃi] <> adj [repugnante] repellent. <> m [inseticida] repellent.

repelir [xepe'li(x)] vt -1. [fazer regressar] to drive away. -2. [expulsar] to repel. -3. [rechaçar, impedir de entrar] to refuse admission to. -4. [recusar] to refuse. -5. [repudiar] to reject. -6. [desmentir] to refute.

repensar [xepẽn'sa(x)] vt to reconsider.

repente [xe'pẽntʃi] m: num ~ **tudo escureceu** all of a sudden everything went dark; **um ~ de carinho** a sudden show of affection.
◆ **de repente** loc adv -1. [repentinamente] suddenly. -2. fam [talvez] maybe.

repentinamente [xepẽntʃina'mẽntʃi] adv suddenly.

repentino, na [xepẽn'tʃinu, na] adj sudden.

repercussão [xepexku'sãw] (pl -ões) f -1. fig [de som] reverberation. -2. [efeito] repercussion; **o CD teve boa ~ no exterior** the CD was very successful abroad.

repercutir [xepexku'tʃi(x)] <> vt [som] to re-echo. <> vi -1. [som] to reverberate. -2. fig [afetar]: ~ **em** to have repercussions on.

repertório [ʃepexˈtɔrjul] *m* **-1.** [conjunto] collection. **-2.** *MÚS* repertoire.

repetição [ʃepetʃiˈsãw] (*pl* **-ões**) *f* repetition.

repetido, da [ʃepeˈtʃidu, da] *adj* repeated; **repetidas vezes** repeatedly.

repetir [ʃepeˈtʃi(x)] <> *vt* **-1.** [ger] to repeat. **-2.** [roupa] to wear again. **-3.** [refeição] to have a second helping of, to have seconds. **-4.** [tocar de novo]: ~ **uma música** to play an encore. <> *vi* to repeat.
◆ **repetir-se** *vp* **-1.** [fenômeno] to be repeated. **-2.** [pessoa] to repeat o.s.

repetitivo, va [ʃepetʃiˈtʃivu, va] *adj* repetitive.

repique [ʃeˈpikil] *m* [de sino] peal.

replay [xiˈplejl] *m* replay.

repleto, ta [ʃeˈplɛtu, ta] *adj* [cheio]: ~ **(de)** full (of).

réplica [ˈʃɛplika] *f* **-1.** [cópia] replica. **-2.** [resposta] reply.

replicar [ʃepliˈka(x)] <> *vt* **-1.** [responder] to reply. **-2.** [contestar] to answer. <> *vi* **-1.** [responder] to reply. **-2.** [contestar] to respond.

repolho [ʃeˈpoʎul] *m* cabbage.

repor [ʃeˈpo(x)] *vt* **-1.** [recolocar] to replace. **-2.** [devolver] to repay.
◆ **repor-se** *vp* to recover.

reportagem [ʃepoxˈtaʒẽl] (*pl* **-ns**) *f* **-1.** [ato] report. **-2.** [matéria]: ~ **(sobre)** report (on). **-3.** [repórteres] reporters (*pl*), the press.

repórter [ʃeˈpɔxte(x)] (*pl* **-es**) *mf* reporter.

repórter-fotográfico, ca [ʃeˈpɔxte(x)fotoˈgrafiku, ka] (*pl* **-s**) *m* press photographer.

repousante [ʃepoˈzãntʃil] *adj* restful.

repousar [ʃepoˈza(x)] <> *vt* to rest. <> *vi* **-1.** [descansar] to rest. **-2.** [basear-se]: ~ **em/sobre algo** to be based on sthg. **-3.** [não produzir] to rest, to lie fallow.

repouso [ʃeˈpozul] *m* [descanso] rest; **em** ~ at rest.

repreender [ʃeprjẽnˈde(x)] *vt* to reprimand.

repreensão [ʃeprjẽnˈsãw] (*pl* **-ões**) *f* reprimand.

repreensível [ʃeprjẽnˈsivew] (*pl* **-eis**) *adj* reprehensible.

represa [ʃeˈpreza] *f* dam.

represália [ʃepreˈzalja] *f* reprisal; **em** ~ in reprisal.

representação [ʃeprezẽntaˈsãw] (*pl* **-ões**) *f* **-1.** [reprodução] representation. **-2.** [queixa]: ~ **contra algo/alguém** complaint against sthg/sb. **-3.** [delegação] representatives (*pl*). **-4.** *TEATRO*

performance. **-5.** *COM*: **ter a** ~ **de algo** to display sthg. **-6.** *fig* [fingimento] pretence *UK*, pretense *US*.

representante [ʃeprezẽnˈtãntʃi] <> *adj* representative. <> *mf* representative.

representar [ʃeprezẽnˈta(x)] <> *vt* **-1.** [ger] to represent. **-2.** [*TEATRO* - encenar] to perform; [- interpretar] to play. <> *vi* *TEATRO* [interpretar] to perform.

representatividade [ʃeprezẽntatʃiviˈdadʒil] *f* representation.

representativo, va [ʃeprezẽntaˈtʃivu, val] *adj* representative; ~ **de algo** representative of sthg.

repressão [ʃepreˈsãw] (*pl* **-ões**) *f* repression.

reprimido, da [ʃepriˈmidu, da] *adj* repressed.

reprimir [ʃepriˈmi(x)] *vt* **-1.** [conter - paixão] to contain; [- pensamento] to suppress. **-2.** [dissimular] to suppress. **-3.** *PSIC* to repress. **-4.** [proibir] to prohibit.
◆ **reprimir-se** *vp* [conter-se] to control o.s.

reprise [ʃeˈprizi] *f* repeat.

reprodução [ʃeproduˈsãw] (*pl* **-ões**) *f* reproduction.

reprodutor, ra [ʃeproduˈto(x), ra] *adj* reproductive.
◆ **reprodutor** *m* breeding animal.

reproduzir [ʃeproduˈzi(x)] *vt* **-1.** [copiar, repetir] to copy. **-2.** [procriar] to breed. **-3.** [reeditar] to republish.
◆ **reproduzir-se** *vp* **-1.** [procriar-se] to breed. **-2.** [repetir-se] to be repeated.

reprovado, da [ʃeproˈvadu, da] <> *adj* failed. <> *m, f* failure.

reprovar [ʃeproˈva(x)] <> *vt* **-1.** [censurar] to disapprove of. **-2.** [rejeitar] to reject. **-3.** [em exame, seleção] to fail. <> *vi* [em exame, seleção] to fail.

réptil [ˈʃɛptʃiw] (*pl* **-eis**) *m* reptile.

república [ʃeˈpublika] *f* **-1.** *POL* republic. **-2.** *EDUC* students' residence.

República da África do Sul [ʃepublikadaˌafrikaduˈsuwl] *n* Republic of South Africa.

República Dominicana [ʃeˌpublikadomiˈniˈkãnal] *n* Dominican Republic.

republicano, na [ʃepubliˈkãnu, na] <> *adj* republican. <> *m, f* republican.

República Tcheca [ʃeˌpublikaˈtʃɛkal] *n* Czech Republic.

repudiar [ʃepuˈdʒjar] *vt* to repudiate.

repúdio [ʃeˈpudʒjul] *m* repudiation.

repugnância [ʃepugˈnãʃjal] *f* **-1.** [ger] repugnance. **-2.** [oposição] opposition.

repugnante [xepug'nãntʃi] *adj* repugnant.

repulsa [xe'puwsa] *f* -1. [ato] repulsion. -2. [sentimento] repugnance. -3. [oposição] rejection.

repulsivo, va [xepuw'sivu, va] *adj* repulsive.

reputação [xeputa'sãw] (*pl* -ões) *f* reputation.

repuxar [xepu'ʃa(x)] <> *vt* [esticar - roupa, pele] to stretch; [- cabelo] to pull back tight. <> *vi* [retesar] to tense.

requebrado [xeke'bradu] *m* swaying.

requeijão [xekej'ʒãw] (*pl* -ões) *m* soft cheese.

requentar [xekẽn'ta(x)] *vt* to reheat.

requerer [xeke're(x)] <> *vt* -1. [pedir] to request. -2. [exigir] to demand. -3. [merecer] to deserve. -4. JUR to petition for. <> *vi* JUR to make a petition.

requerimento [xekeri'mẽntu] *m* -1. [ato de requerer] application. -2. [petição] petition.

requintado, da [xekĩn'tadu, da] *adj* refined.

requinte [xe'kĩntʃi] *m* -1. [refinamento] refinement. -2. [excesso] excess.

requisito [xeki'zitu] *m* requirement.

resenha [xe'zaɲa] *f* -1. [de livro] review. -2. [relatório] report. -3. [resumo] summary.

reserva [xe'zɛxva] <> *f* -1. [ger] reserve; ~s **internacionais** foreign reserves; ~ **natural** nature reserve; ~ **de mercado** protected market. -2. [em hotel, avião *etc.*] reservation; **fazer** ~ **de algo** to reserve sthg. -3. [restrição]: **ter** ~ **a** OU **para com** to have reservations about. -4. [discrição] discretion. <> *mf* ESP reserve.

reservado, da [xezex'vadu, da] *adj* -1. [ger] reserved. -2. [íntimo] private.

⇒ **reservado** *m* [privada] private room.

reservar [xezex'va(x)] *vt* -1. [fazer reserva] to reserve. -2. [poupar] to save. -3. [destinar] to allow; **a vida lhe reserva muitas alegrias** life has much joy in store for him.

⇒ **reservar-se** *vp* [preservar-se] to save o.s.

reservatório [xezexva'tɔrju] *m* -1. [depósito] tank. -2. [de água] reservoir.

resfriado, da [xeʃfri'adu, da] *adj* -1. [pessoa] cold; **ficar** ~ to catch cold. -2. [carne] chilled.

⇒ **resfriado** *m* cold; **pegar um** ~ to catch a cold.

resfriar [xeʃ'frja(x)] *vt* [esfriar] to cool.

resgatar [xeʒga'ta(x)] *vt* -1. [ger] to rescue. -2. [restituir] to recover. -3.

[pagar] to pay off. -4. [recuperar] to recoup. -5. [expiar] to redeem.

resgate [xeʒ'gatʃi] *m* -1. [dinheiro] ransom. -2. [libertação] release. -3. [salvamento] rescue. -4. FIN [retirada] withdrawal. -5. COM redemption.

resguardar [xeʒgwax'da(x)] *vt* -1. [proteger]: ~ **(de)** to protect (from). -2. [vigiar] to protect.

⇒ **resguardar-se** *vp* [proteger-se]: ~**-se de** to protect o.s. from.

resguardo [xeʒ'gwaxdu] *m* -1. [proteção] protection. -2. [cuidado] care. -3. [repouso] rest.

residência [xezi'dẽnsja] *f* residence.

residencial [xezidẽn'sjaw] (*pl* -ais) *adj* residential.

residente [xezi'dẽntʃi] <> *adj* resident. <> *mf* -1. [morador] resident. -2. [médico] senior registrar UK, resident US.

residir [xezi'dʒi(x)] *vi* to reside.

resíduo [xe'zidwu] *m* -1. [resto] residue. -2. [bancário] surplus.

resignação [xezigna'sãw] *f*: ~ **(a/com)** resignation to.

resignar-se [xezig'naxsi] *vp* to resign o.s.; ~ **com algo** to resign o.s. to sthg; ~ **a fazer algo** to resign o.s. to doing sthg.

resina [xe'zina] *f* resin.

resistência [xeziʃ'tẽnsja] *f* -1. [ger] resistance; **o carro não teve** ~ **para subir a ladeira** the car did not have the power to go up the slope. -2. [moral] stamina. -3. *fig* [oposição]: ~ **a** resistance to.

resistente [xeziʃ'tẽntʃi] *adj* -1. [forte] strong; ~ **ao calor** heat-resistant. -2. [durável] durable. -3. [que se opõe a]: ~ **a** resistant to.

resistir [xeziʃ'tʃi(x)] *vi*: ~ **a algo** to resist sthg.

resmungar [xeʒmũŋ'ga(x)] *vt* & *vi* to grumble.

resolução [xezolu'sãw] (*pl* -ões) *f* -1. [decisão] decision. -2. [solução] solution. -3. [firmeza] resolve. -4. [de imagem] resolution; **de alta** ~ high-resolution, hi-res.

resolver [xezow've(x)] <> *vt* -1. [solucionar] to solve. -2. [decidir]: ~ **fazer algo** to decide to do sthg. <> *vi* -1. [adiantar]: **a violência não resolve** violence doesn't solve anything. -2. [decidir] to decide.

respaldar [xeʃpaw'da(x)] *vt* [apoiar] to back.

respectivo, va [xeʃpek'tʃivu, va] *adj* respective.

respeitador, ra [xeʃpejtado(x), ra] *adj* respectful.

respeitar [xeʃpej'ta(x)] *vt* to respect.

respeitável [xeʃpej'tavew] (*pl* -eis) *adj* - 1. [digno de respeito] respectable. - 2. [considerável] considerable.

respeito [xeʃ'pejtu] *m* - 1. [deferência]: ~ a *ou* por respect for; **faltar ao** ~ **com alguém** to be rude to sb. - 2. [relação] respect; **dizer** ~ **a** to concern; **a** ~ **de** [sobre] about.

respeitoso, osa [xeʃpej'tozu, ɔza] *adj* respectful.

respingar [xeʃpĩ'ga(x)] *vi* to splash.

respingo [xeʃ'pĩgul *m* splash.

respiração [xeʃpira'sãw] *f* breathing.

respirar [xeʃpi'ra(x)] <> *vt* [ar] to breathe. <> *vi* - 1. [absorver o ar] to breathe. - 2. *fig* [sentir alívio] to breathe freely again.

resplandecente [xeʃplãnde'sẽntʃi] *adj* - 1. [jóia] resplendent. - 2. [dia] splendid.

resplandecer [xeʃplãnde'se(x)] *vi* - 1. [brilhar] to shine. - 2. [sobressair] to outshine.

resplendor [xeʃplẽn'do(x)] *m* brilliance.

responder [xeʃpõn'de(x)] <> *vt* [dar resposta] to reply. <> *vi* - 1. [dar resposta] ~ **(a algo/alguém)** to reply to sthg/sb. - 2. [replicar] to answer. - 3. [ser respondão] to answer back. - 4. [reagir]: ~ **a algo** to respond to sthg. - 5. [responsabilizar-se]: ~ **por algo/alguém** to answer for sthg/sb. - 6. [submeter-se a]: ~ **a algo** to undergo sthg.

responsabilidade [xeʃpõnsabili'dadʒi] *f* - 1. [obrigação] responsibility. - 2. *JUR* liability.

responsabilizar [xeʃpõnsabili'za(x)] *vt*: ~ **algo/alguém (por algo)** to hold sthg/sb responsible for sthg.

➤ **responsabilizar-se** *vp*: ~-se **(por algo/alguém)** to hold o.s. responsible (for sthg/sb).

responsável [xeʃpõn'savew] (*pl* -eis) <> *adj*: ~ **(por)** responsible (for). <> *mf* - 1. [encarregado] person in charge. - 2. [culpado] person responsible.

resposta [xeʃ'pɔʃta] *f* - 1. [de pergunta] answer. - 2. *fig* [reação] response.

resquício [xeʃ'kisjul *m* - 1. [vestígio] fragment. - 2. [fragmento] fragment.

ressabiado, da [xesa'bjadu, da] *adj* - 1. [desconfiado] suspicious. - 2. [ressentido] resentful.

ressaca [xe'saka] *f* - 1. [do mar] rough sea. - 2. *fig* [de bebida] hangover.

ressaltar [xesaw'ta(x)] *vt* to emphasize.

ressalva [xe'sawva] *f* - 1. [emenda] correction. - 2. [restrição] proviso.

ressarcir [xesax'si(x)] *vt* [compensar]: ~

algo (de) to compensate for sthg (with); ~ **alguém (de)** to compensate sb (with).

ressecado, da [xese'kadu, da] *adj* dried up.

ressecar [xese'ka(x)] *vt & vi* to dry up.

ressentido, da [xesẽn'tʃidu, da] *adj* resentful.

ressentimento [xesẽntʃi'mẽntul *m* resentment.

ressentir-se [xesẽn'tʃixsil *vp* - 1. [magoar-se]: ~ **(de algo)** to resent (sthg). - 2. [sofrer consequência]: ~ **de algo** to feel the effects of sthg.

ressoar [xe'swa(x)] *vi* to resound.

ressurgir [xesux'ʒi(x)] *vi* - 1. [reaparecer] to reappear. - 2. [revitalizar-se] to revive. - 3. [ressuscitar] to be resurrected.

ressurreição [xesuxej'sãw] (*pl* -ões) *f* resurrection.

ressuscitar [xesusi'ta(x)] <> *vt* - 1. [pessoa, animal] to resuscitate. - 2. [costume, moda] to revive. <> *vi* - 1. [pessoa, animal] to be resuscitated. - 2. [costume, moda] to be revived.

restabelecer [xeʃtabele'se(x)] *vt* to restore.

➤ **restabelecer-se** *vp* to recover.

restabelecimento [xeʃtabelesi'mẽntul *m* - 1. [de ordem, tradição] restoration. - 2. [de doente] recovery.

restar [xeʃ'ta(x)] *vi* - 1. [sobrar] to be left over. - 2. [sobreviver] to survive. - 3. [subsistir] to remain; **não me resta dúvida de que ...** I no longer have any doubt that ... - 4. [faltar]: **faltam duas páginas para terminar** there are two pages left to finish.

restauração [xeʃtawra'sãw] (*pl* -ões) *f* restoration.

restaurante [xeʃtaw'rãntʃi] *m* restaurant.

restaurar [xeʃtaw'ra(x)] *vt* - 1. [ger] to restore. - 2. [recuperar] to recover.

restituição [xeʃtʃitwi'sãw] (*pl* -ões) *f* - 1. [devolução] return. - 2. [pagamento] repayment.

restituir [xeʃtʃi'twi(x)] *vt* - 1. [devolver] to return. - 2. [pagar] to repay. - 3. [restabelecer] to restore.

resto ['xɛʃtul *m* - 1. [ger] remainder. - 2. [restante] rest.

➤ **restos** *mpl* [de comida] leftovers.

restrição [xeʃtri'sãw] (*pl* -ões) *f* restriction.

restringir [xeʃtrĩn'ʒi(x)] *vt* to restrict.

restrito, ta [xeʃ'tritu, ta] *adj* restricted.

resultado [xezuw'tadul *m* - 1. [ger] result. - 2. [proveito]: **dar** ~ to be effective; **o filme deu bom ~ publicitá-rio** the film was good publicity.

resultante [xezuw'tãntʃil] <> adj resulting; **~ de algo** resulting from sthg. <> f **-1.** [conseqüência] outcome. **-2.** FÍSICA result.

resumir [xezu'mi(x)] vt to summarize.
→ **resumir-se** vp: **~-se em** OU **a algo** to consist of sthg.

resumo [xe'zumu] m summary; **em ~** in short.

reta ['xɛta] f ▷ **reto**.

retaguarda [ˌxeta'gwaxda] f **-1.** [posição] rear. **-2.** MIL rearguard.

retalho [xe'taʎu] m remnant.

retaliação [xetalja'sãw] (pl **-ões**) f retaliation.

retaliar [xeta'lja(x)] <> vt to repay. <> vi to retaliate.

retângulo [xe'tãŋgulu] m rectangle.

retardar [xetax'da(x)] vt **-1.** [atrasar] to delay. **-2.** [adiar] to postpone.

retenção [xetẽn'sãw] f **-1.** [detenção] detention; **a ~ no trânsito é grande** there is a major traffic hold-up. **-2.** MED [de líquidos] retention.

reter [xe'te(x)] vt **-1.** [ger] to retain. **-2.** [segurar, prender - rédeas, corda] to hold; [- ladrão, suspeito] to detain. **-3.** [guardar] to keep. **-4.** [reprimir, deter] to hold back.

retesado, da [xete'zadu, da] adj taut.

retesar [xete'za(x)] vt to tense.
→ **retesar-se** vp to tense.

retidão [xetʃi'dãw] f [lisura] rectitude.

retificar [xetʃifi'ka(x)] vt **-1.** [corrigir] to rectify. **-2.** [purificar] to purify. **-3.** AUTO to repair.

retina [xe'tʃina] f ANAT retina.

retirado, da [xetʃi'radu, da] adj [pessoa] retiring; [vida] retired; [lugar, casa] isolated.
→ **retirada** f **-1.** [ger] withdrawal; **bater em retirada** [fugir] to beat a retreat. **-2.** [migração] migration.

retirar [xetʃi'ra(x)] vt **-1.** [ger] to remove. **-2.** [retratar-se de] to take back. **-3.** [ganhar] to make. **-4.** [livrar, salvar] to get out.
→ **retirar-se** vp **-1.** [ger] to leave. **-2.** [refugiar-se] to withdraw.

retiro [xe'tʃiru] m retreat.

reto, ta ['xɛtu, ta] adj **-1.** [ger] straight; **ângulo ~** right angle. **-2.** fig [justo] straightforward. **-3.** fig [honesto] honest.
→ **reto** m ANAT rectum.
→ **reta** f **-1.** MAT straight line. **-2.** [de estrada, pista] straight; **ele bateu na reta contra um caminhão** he hit a lorry on the straight.

retocar [xeto'ka(x)] vt **-1.** [pintura] to touch up. **-2.** [texto] to tidy up.

retomar [xeto'ma(x)] vt **-1.** [continuar] to resume. **-2.** [reaver] to take back.

retoque [xe'tɔki] m finishing touch; **dar um ~** to add a finishing touch.

retorcer [xetox'se(x)] vt **-1.** [torcer de novo] to re-twist. **-2.** [contorcer-se] to twist.
→ **retorcer-se** vp [contorcer-se] to writhe.

retórico, ca [xe'tɔriku, ka] adj **-1.** [sem conteúdo] rhetorical. **-2.** fig [afetado] affected.
→ **retórica** f **-1.** [discurso] rhetoric. **-2.** pej [afetação] affectation.

retornar [xetox'na(x)] vi [voltar] to return.

retorno [xe'toxnul] m **-1.** [ger] return. **-2.** [resposta] response; **dar um ~ (sobre algo)** to give one's response (to sthg). **-3.** [em estrada] turning place; **fazer o ~** to turn back.

retraído, da [xetra'idu, da] adj fig [reservado, tímido] reserved.

retraimento [xetraj'mẽntu] m [reserva, timidez] reserve.

retrair [xetra'i(x)] vt **-1.** [ger] to withdraw. **-2.** [tornar reservado] to make reserved.
→ **retrair-se** vp **-1.** [afastar-se] to withdraw. **-2.** [tornar-se reservado] to become withdrawn.

retrasado, da [xetra'zadu, da] adj [ano, semana] before last.

retratar [xetra'ta(x)] vt **-1.** [fazer retrato] to depict. **-2.** [descrever] to portray. **-3.** [desdizer] to retract. **-4.** [expressar] to express.
→ **retratar-se** vp **-1.** [representar-se] to portray o.s. **-2.** [desdizer-se]: **~-se de algo** to retract sthg. **-3.** [confessar erro] to admit one's mistake.

retrato [xe'tratul] m **-1.** [ger] portrait; **~ falado** Identikit® picture. **-2.** fig [exemplo] picture.

retribuir [xetri'bwi(x)] vt **-1.** [pagar] to pay. **-2.** [agradecer] to return. **-3.** [corresponder] to reciprocate.

retroceder [xetrose'de(x)] vi **-1.** [recuar] to step back. **-2.** [decair] to decline.

retrocesso [xetro'sɛsul] m **-1.** [retorno] return. **-2.** [declínio] step backwards. **-3.** [recaída] recurrence. **-4.** [tecla] backspace. **-5.** [na economia] slowdown.

retrógrado, da [xe'trɔgradu, da] adj **-1.** [idéia, movimento] retrograde, reactionary. **-2.** [pessoa] reactionary.

retrospectiva [xetroʃpek'tʃiva] f retrospective.

retrospecto [xetroʃ'pɛktu] *m* [retrospectiva] retrospect; **em** ~ in retrospect.

retrovisor [xetrovi'zo(x)] (*pl* -es) <> *adj* rear-view. <> *m* rear-view mirror.

réu [xew], **ré** [xɛ] *m*, *f* accused.

reumatismo [xewma'tʃiʒmu] *m* rheumatism.

reunião [xew'njãw] (*pl* -ões) *f* -1. [encontro] meeting; ~ **de cúpula** summit. -2. [festa] party. -3. [coletânea] collection.

reunir [xew'ni(x)] *vt* -1. [juntar] to gather. -2. [congregar] to join together. -3. [aliar] to combine. -4. [unir] to unite.

    ⬥ **reunir-se** *vp* -1. [juntar-se] to gather. -2. [aliar-se] to be combined. -3. [realizar reunião] to meet. -4. [incorporar-se] to join together.

revanche [xe'vãnʃi] *f* -1. [desforra] revenge. -2. ESP return match.

reveillon [xeve'jõn] *m* New Year's Eve.

revelação [xevela'sãw] (*pl* -ões) *f* -1. [ger] revelation. -2. FOT developing.

revelar [xeve'la(x)] *vt* -1. [ger] to reveal. -2. [mostrar, demonstrar] to show. -3. FOT to develop.

    ⬥ **revelar-se** *vp* [dar-se a conhecer] to turn out to be.

revelia [xeve'lia] *f* default.

    ⬥ **à revelia** *loc adv* -1. JUR in absentia. -2. [despercebidamente] without anybody knowing.

    ⬥ **à revelia de** *loc adv* without the knowledge/consent of.

revendedor, ra [xevẽnde'do(x), ral (*mpl* -es, *fpl* -s) <> *adj* resale *(antes de subst)*. <> *m*, *f* [de automóveis] dealer.

rever [xe've(x)] *vt* -1. [tornar a ver] to see again. -2. [examinar] to check. -3. [revisar] to revise.

reverência [xeve'rẽnsja] *f* -1. [respeito] reverence. -2. [saudação]: **fazer uma** ~ to bow.

reverenciar [xeverẽn'sja(x)] *vt* -1. [respeitar] to respect. -2. [saudar] to salute.

reverendo [xeve'rẽndu] *m* priest.

reverso, sa [xe'vɛxsu, sal <> *adj* reverse. <> *m* [lado contrário] reverse.

reverter [xevex'te(x)] *vi* -1. [retroceder]: ~ **a** to return to. -2. [redundar]: ~ **em favor de alguém** to revert in s.o.'s favour; ~ **em benefício de** to benefit.

revés [xe'vɛʃ] (*pl* -eses) *m* -1. [reverso] reverse; **ao** ~ [às avessas] inside out. -2. *fig* [infortúnio] setback.

    ⬥ **de revés** *loc adv* [olhar, sorrir] askance.

revestimento [xeveʃtʃi'mẽntul *m* covering.

revestir [xeveʃ'tʃi(x)] *vt* -1. [ger] to cover. -2. [vestir] to don, to put on.

revezamento [xeveza'mẽntul *m* -1. [ato]: **para cuidar do bebê, o casal fez um** ~ the couple took it in turns to look after the baby. -2. ESP relay.

revezar [xeve'za(x)] <> *vt* to swap. <> *vi*: ~ **(com)** to take turns (with).

    ⬥ **revezar-se** *vp* to alternate.

revidar [xevi'da(x)] <> *vt* -1. [responder] to return. -2. [contestar] to answer. <> *vi* [responder] to answer back.

revide [xe'vidʒi] *m* response.

revigorar [xevigo'ra(x)] *vt* to reinvigorate.

    ⬥ **revigorar-se** *vp* to regain one's strength.

revirado, da [xevi'radu, dal *adj* -1. [casa] untidy. -2. [revolto] choppy.

revirar [xevi'ra(x)] *vt* -1. [tornar a virar] to turn over. -2. [mudar] to change. -3. [os olhos] to roll. -4. [remexer em] to turn out.

    ⬥ **revirar-se** *vp* [virar-se] to toss and turn.

reviravolta [xe,vira'vɔwtal *f* -1. [mudança] turnabout. -2. [pirueta] pirouette.

revisão [xevi'zãw] (*pl* -ões) *f* -1. [de texto] revision. -2. [de máquina - ger] overhaul; [- carro, motor de carro] service. -3. [os revisores] review board. -4. JUR review.

revisar [xevi'za(x)] *vt* -1. [texto] to revise. -2. [máquina - ger] to overhaul; [- motor de carro] to service. -3. [recapitular] to review.

revista [xe'viʃta] *f* -1. [publicação] magazine; ~ **em quadrinhos** comic. -2. [acadêmica] journal. -3. MIL [inspeção] review. -4. [busca] search. -5. TEATRO revue.

revistar [xeviʃ'ta(x)] *vt* to search.

revisto, ta [xe'viʃtu, tal *pp* ⊳ **rever**.

revitalizar [xevitali'za(x)] *vt* to revitalize.

revogação [xevoga'sãw] (*pl* -ões) *f* repeal.

revogar [xevo'ga(x)] *vt* to repeal.

revolta [xe'vɔwta] *f* -1. [ger] revolt. -2. [rebeldia]: ~ **(contra)** rebellion (against). -3. [indignação]: ~ **(diante de** OU **com)** indignation (at).

revolto, ta [xe'vowtu, tal *adj* -1. [revirado] rough. -2. [conturbado] troubled. -3. [desarrumado] untidy.

revoltoso, osa [xevow'tozu, ɔzal *adj* rebellious.

    ⬥ **revoltoso** *m* rebel.

revolução [xevolu'sãw] (*pl* -ões) *f* revolution.

revolucionar [xevolusjo'na(x)] *vt* -1. [transformar] to revolutionize. -2. [sublevar] to stir up. -3. [agitar] to change completely.

revolucionário, ria [xevolusjo'narju, rjal
⬦ *adj* revolutionary. ⬦ *m, f* revolutionary.

revolver [xevow've(x)] *vt* **-1.** [remexer] to rummage through. **-2.** [examinar, investigar] to search. **-3.** [revirar - olhos] to roll; [- corpo, terra] to turn over. **-4.** [agitar] to blow about. **-5.** [relembrar] to recall.

➡ revolver-se *vp* **-1.** [mexer-se] to roll over. **-2.** [agitar-se] to blow about.

revólver [xe'vɔwve(x)] (*pl* **-es**) *m* revolver.

reza ['xɛza] *f* prayer.

rezar [xe'za(x)] ⬦ *vt* **-1.** [orar] to pray. **-2.** [missa] to say mass. **-3.** [afirmar, preceituar] to state. ⬦ *vi* [orar] to pray.

RG (*abrev de* **Registro Geral**) *m Brazilian identity card*, ≃ ID card.

RH (*abrev de* **Recursos Humanos**) *m* HR.

riacho ['xjaʃu] *m* stream.

ribeirão [xibej'rãw] (*pl* **-ões**) *m* stream.

ribeirinho, nha [xibej'riɲu, ɲal ⬦ *adj* riverside. ⬦ *m, f* riverside dweller.

ricamente [xika'mẽntʃi] *adv* richly.

rícino ['xisinul *m* castor-oil plant.

rico, ca ['xiku, kal ⬦ *adj* **-1.** [ger] rich. **-2.** [opulento] opulent. **-3.** [abundante]: ~ **em algo** rich in sthg. **-4.** [esplêndido] splendid. **-5.** [valiosa] precious. ⬦ *m, f* [pessoa] rich person.

ricota [xi'kɔtal *f* ricotta.

ridicularizar [xidʒikulari'za(x)] *vt* to ridicule.

ridículo, la [xi'dʒikulu, lal *adj* ridiculous.

➡ ridículo *m* ridicule.

rifa ['xifal *f* raffle.

rifle ['xifli] *m* rifle.

rigidez [xiʒi'deʒ] *f* **-1.** [dureza - de metais, parede] rigidity; [- de músculo, corpo] stiffness. **-2.** *fig* [severidade] harshness. **-3.** *fig* [inflexibilidade] strictness.

rígido, da ['xiʒidu, dal *adj* **-1.** [hirto] stiff. **-2.** [resistente] strong. **-3.** [severo - pessoa, rosto] severe; [- disciplina] strict.

rigor [xi'go(x)] (*pl* **-es**) *m* **-1.** [rigidez] rigour *UK*, rigor *US*. **-2.** [severidade] severity. **-3.** [exatidão] rigour *UK*, rigor *US*. **-4.** [meticulosidade] thoroughness; **com** ~ strictly. **-5.** [preceito] good manners (*pl*). **-6.** [auge] harshness.

➡ a rigor *loc adv* strictly speaking.

rigoroso, osa [xigo'rozu, ɔzal *adj* **-1.** [ger] strict. **-2.** [castigo] severe. **-3.** [exato] precise. **-4.** [meticuloso] meticulous. **-5.** *fig* [penoso] severe.

rijo, ja ['xiʒu, ʒal *adj* **-1.** [rígido] firm. **-2.** [severo] severe.

rim ['xĩ] (*pl* **-ns**) *m* ANAT kidney.

➡ rins *mpl fam* [região lombar] lower back (*sg*).

rima ['ximal *f* rhyme.

rimar [xi'ma(x)] *vi* to rhyme.

rímel ['ximɛw] (*pl* **-eis**) *m* mascara.

ringue ['xĩgul *m* ring.

rinoceronte [xinose'rõntʃi] *m* rhinoceros.

rins [xĩʃ] *pl* ⊳ **rim**.

rio ['xiw] *m* river; **gastar** ~ **s de dinheiro** to spend lots of money.

riqueza [xi'kezal *f* **-1.** [ger] richness. **-2.** [fortuna, bens] wealth. **-3.** [beleza] beauty; **essa igreja é uma** ~! this church is beautiful!

rir ['xi(x)] *vi* to laugh; ~ **de algo/alguém** to laugh at sthg/sb; **morrer de** ~ (**de algo/alguém**) to laugh one's head off (at sthg/sb), to laugh oneself silly (at sthg/sb).

risada [xi'zadal *f* **-1.** [riso] laughter. **-2.** [gargalhada] guffaw.

risca ['xiʃka] *f* **-1.** [listra] stripe. **-2.** [no cabelo] parting. **-3.** [traço] line.

➡ à risca *loc adv* to the letter.

riscar [xiʃ'ka(x)] *vt* **-1.** [fazer riscas em - porta, parede] to scratch; [- papel] to draw lines on. **-2.** [esboçar] to sketch. **-3.** [marcar] to draw. **-4.** [apagar] to cross out. **-5.** [acender] to scratch. **-6.** [eliminar]: ~ **alguém/algo de algo** to eliminate sb/sthg from sthg. **-7.** [atritar] to scrape.

risco ['xiʃku] *m* **-1.** [traço] scratch. **-2.** [esboço] sketch. **-3.** [perigo] risk; **correr** ~ **de** to run the risk of; **pôr algo/alguém em** ~ to put sthg/sb at risk.

risco-país [ˌxiʃkupa'jiʃ] *m* ECON country risk.

riso ['xizul *m* laugh; ~ **amarelo** forced laugh.

risonho, nha [xi'tʌwaʃ, ɲal *adj* **-1.** [que sorri] smiling. **-2.** [alegre] cheerful.

risoto [xi'zɔtul *m* risotto.

ríspido, da ['xiʃpidu, dal *adj* harsh.

rítmico, ca ['xitʃmiku, kal *adj* rhythmic.

ritmo ['xitʃimul *m* rhythm.

rito ['xitul *m* rite.

ritual [xi'twaw] (*pl* **-ais** [xi'twajʃl) ⬦ *adj* ritual. ⬦ *m* **-1.** [ger] ritual. **-2.** [livro] service book.

rival [xi'vaw] (*pl* **-ais**) ⬦ *adj* rival. ⬦ *mf* rival.

rivalidade [xivali'dadʒi] *f* rivalry.

rivalizar [xivali'za(x)] *vi*: ~ **com algo/alguém** to compete with sthg/sb.

rixa ['xiʃal *f* quarrel.

RJ (*abrev de* **Estado do Rio de Janeiro**) *n State of Rio de Janeiro*.

RN (*abrev de* **Estado do Rio Grande do Norte**) *n* State of Rio Grande do Norte.

RO (*abrev de* **Estado de Rondônia**) *n* State of Rondônia.

robô [ro'bo] *m* robot.

robusto, ta [xo'buʃtu, ta] *adj* robust.

roça ['xɔsa] *f* **-1.** [plantação] plantation. **-2.** [campo] country. **-3.** [mato] clearing.

rocambole [xokãn'bɔli] *m* roll.

roçar [xo'sa(x)] ⟨⟩ *vt* **-1.** [cortar] to clear. **-2.** [tocar de leve] to brush. **-3.** [atritar] to scrape. ⟨⟩ *vi* [tocar de leve]: ~ **em** to brush against.

rocha ['xɔʃa] *f* **-1.** [pedra] rock. **-2.** [rochedo] crag.

rochedo [xo'ʃedu] *m* crag.

rock ['xɔkil] *m* MÚS rock.

roda ['xɔda] *f* **-1.** [ger] wheel. **-2.** [círculo] circle; **alta** ~ high society; ~ **de samba** circle of samba dancers and musicians; **brincar de** ~ to play in a circle. **-3.** [de saia] hoop.

rodado, da [xo'dadu, da] *adj* **-1.** [que tem roda] full. **-2.** [percorrido] on the clock.

➡ **rodada** *f* **-1.** [giro] turn; **dar uma rodada** to turn round. **-2.** [de bebida] round. **-3.** ESP round.

roda-gigante [xɔdaʒi'gãntʃi] (*pl* **rodas-gigantes**) *f* big wheel, Ferris wheel.

rodamoinho [xɔda'mwiɲul] *m* **-1.** [de água] whirlpool. **-2.** [de cabelo] swirl.

rodapé [xɔda'pɛ] *m* **-1.** [de parede] skirting board. **-2.** [de página] foot; **nota de** ~ footnote. **-3.** [artigo] article.

rodar [xo'da(x)] ⟨⟩ *vt* **-1.** [fazer girar] to turn. **-2.** [percorrer] to travel. **-3.** [imprimir] to print. **-4.** [filmar] to film. **-5.** AUTO to do. **-6.** COMPUT to run. ⟨⟩ *vi* **-1.** [girar] to turn. **-2.** [ser impresso] to be printed. **-3.** [decorrer] to move on.

rodear [xo'dʒja(x)] *vt* **-1.** [contornar] to go round. **-2.** [cercar] to surround.

➡ **rodear-se** *vp* [cercar-se] to surround o.s.

rodeio [xo'deju] *m* **-1.** [circunlóquio] circumlocution. **-2.** [evasiva] evasiveness; **fazer** ~ **s** to beat about the bush; **sem** ~ **s** bluntly. **-3.** [de gado] rodeo.

rodela [xo'dɛla] *f* [pedaço] slice.

rodízio [xo'dʒiziju] *m* **-1.** [revezamento] turn; **fazer** ~ to take turns. **-2.** [em restaurante] *type of service in a restaurant where you are served at your table as much meat or, sometimes, pizza as you can eat, and normally accompanied by a free buffet of salad, etc.*

rodo ['xodul] *m* **-1.** [para puxar água] brush. **-2.** [agrícola] rake.

➡ **a rodo** *loc adv* a lot.

rodopiar [xodo'pja(x)] *vi* to spin around.

rodopio [xodo'piwl] *m* spin.

rodovia [xodo'vial] *f* motorway UK, highway US.

rodoviário, ria [xodo'vjarju, rja] *adj* road.

➡ **rodoviária** *f* [estação de ônibus] bus station.

roedor, ra [xwe'do(x), ra] *adj* gnawing.

➡ **roedor** *m* rodent.

roer [i'xwe(x)] *vt* **-1.** [com dentes] to gnaw; ~ **as unhas** to bite one's nails; **duro de** ~ *fam fig* a hard nut to crack. **-2.** [destruir] to eat away. **-3.** [corroer] to erode. **-4.** *fig* [atormentar] to eat away at, to gnaw at.

➡ **roer-se** *vp fig* [atormentar-se]: ~ **-se de algo** to be eaten up with sthg.

rogado, da [xo'gadu, da] *adj*: **fazer-se de** ~ to play hard to get.

rogar [xo'ga(x)] ⟨⟩ *vt* to ask; ~ **pragas (contra algo/alguém)** to curse (sthg/sb). ⟨⟩ *vi* to pray; ~ **a alguém que faça algo** to beg sb to do sthg.

rojão [xo'ʒãw] (*pl* **-ões**) *m* **-1.** [foguete] rocket. **-2.** *fig* [ritmo intenso] hectic pace; **aguentar o** ~ *fig* [resistir] to stand the pace.

rol [xɔwl] (*pl* **róis**) *m* list.

rolar [xo'la(x)] ⟨⟩ *vt* **-1.** [fazer girar] to roll. **-2.** *fig* [dívida] to run up. ⟨⟩ *vi* **-1.** [cair, deslizar] to roll. **-2.** [na cama] to toss and turn. **-3.** *fam* [estender-se] to roll on. **-4.** *fam* [ser servido] to be served. **-5.** *fam* [acontecer] to go on.

roldana [xow'dãna] *f* pulley.

roleta [xo'leta] *f* **-1.** [jogo] roulette. **-2.** [borboleta] turnstile.

roleta-russa [xo,leta'xusa] (*pl* **roletas-russas**) *f* Russian roulette.

rolha ['xoʎa] *f* **-1.** [peça] cork. **-2.** *fam fig* [censura] gag.

roliço, ça [xo'lisu, sa] *adj* **-1.** [redondo] round. **-2.** [gordo] chubby.

rolo ['xolul] *m* **-1.** [ger] roller; ~ **de pastel** rolling pin; ~ **compressor** steam roller. **-2.** [cilindro] roll. **-3.** [almofada] bolster. **-4.** *fam* [bafafá, confusão] brawl; **dar** ~ to cause trouble.

ROM (*abrev de* **Read Only Memory**) *f* ROM.

romã [xo'mã] *f* pomegranate.

Roma ['xomal] *n* Rome.

romance [xo'mãnsil] *m* **-1.** LITER novel; ~ **policial** detective story. **-2.** *fig* [amoroso] romance. **-3.** *fig* [saga] saga.

romancista [xomãn'siʃta] *mf* novelist.

romano, na [xo'mɐnu, na] <> adj Roman. <> m, f Roman.

romântico, ca [xo'mãntʃiku, ka] <> adj -1. ARQUIT & LITER Romantic. -2. [poético, sentimental] romantic. <> m, f -1. ARQUIT & LITER Romantic. -2. [pessoa] romantic.

romantismo [xomãn'tʃiʒmul m -1. ARQUIT & LITER Romanticism. -2. [sentimentalismo] romance.

romaria [xoma'ria] f -1. [peregrinação] pilgrimage. -2. [festa] popular festival. -3. fig [muita gente] flock.

rombo ['xõbu] m -1. [furo] hole. -2. fig [desfalque] embezzlement. -3. fig [prejuízo] deficit.

Romênia [xo'menja] n Rumania.

romeno, na [xo'menu, na] <> adj Rumanian. <> m, f Rumanian.

romeno m [língua] Rumanian.

romeu-e-julieta [xoˌmewiʒu'ljeta] m CULIN guava preserve on cheese.

rompimento [xõpi'mẽntul m -1. [de cano, barragem] bursting. -2. [de contrato, relações] breaking.

roncar [xõ'ka(x)] vi to snore.

ronco ['xõku] m -1. [no sono] snore. -2. MED rale. -3. [ruído] rumble. -4. [grunhido] grunt.

ronda ['xõda] f beat; fazer a ~ to be on patrol.

rondar [xõ'da(x)] <> vt -1. [andar vigiando] to patrol. -2. [espreitar] to prowl about. -3. [andar à volta de] to go round. -4. [cifra] to reach. <> vi: ~ (por) [andar vigiando] to be on patrol (throughout); [espreitar] to prowl (about).

Rondônia [xõ'donja] n Rondonia.

ronronar [xõnxo'na(x)] vi to purr.

roqueiro, ra [xo'kejru, ra] m, f -1. [músico] rock musician. -2. [cantor] rock singer.

Roraima [xo'rajma] n Roraima.

rosa ['xɔza] <> adj inv [cor] pink. <> f BOT rose. <> m [cor] pink.

rosado, da [xo'zadu, da] adj pink.

rosário [xo'zarjul m -1. [colar] string of beads. -2. [orações] rosary.

rosbife [xoʒ'bifil m roast beef.

rosca ['xoʃka] f -1. [de parafuso, porca] thread. -2. [pão] twist. -3. [biscoito] biscuit.

roseira [xo'zejra] f rose bush.

róseo, sea ['xozju, zja] adj rosy.

rosnar [xoʒ'na(x)] <> vi [cão] to growl. <> m [de cão] growl.

rosto ['xoʃtu] m face.

rota ['xɔta] f route.

ROTA (abrev de Rondas Ostensivas Tobias de Aguiar) f shock police force of São Paulo.

rotação [xota'sãw] (pl -ões) f rotation.

rotatividade [xotatʃivi'dadʒil f -1. [movimento] turning. -2. [rodízio] rotation.

roteador, ra [rotea'do(x),ra] m COMPUT router.

roteiro [xo'tejrul m -1. [ger] script. -2. [de viagem] guide book. -3. [de trabalho] schedule.

rotina [xo'tʃina] f routine.

rotineiro, ra [xotʃi'nejru, ra] adj routine.

roto, ta ['xotu, ta] adj -1. [rasgado] torn. -2. [maltrapilho] ragged.

rótula ['xɔtula] f ANAT kneecap.

rotular [xotu'la(x)] <> adj ANAT patellar. <> vt -1. [etiquetar] to label. -2. fig [qualificar]: ~ alguém/algo (de algo) to label sb/sthg (as sthg).

rótulo ['xɔtulul m label.

roubalheira [xoba'ʎejra] f (outright) robbery.

roubar [xo'ba(x)] <> vt -1. [ger] to steal. -2. [furtar] to rob. <> vi -1. [furtar] to steal. -2. [enganar] to cheat.

roubo ['xobul m -1. [ato] theft. -2. [produto roubado] stolen goods (pl). -3. fig [preço extorsivo]: ser um ~ to be exorbitant.

rouco, ca ['xoku, ka] adj hoarse.

round ['xawndʒil m ESP round.

roupa ['xopal f clothes (pl); ~ de baixo underwear; ~ de cama/mesa bed/table linen.

roupão [xo'pãw] (pl -ões) m dressing gown.

rouxinol [xoʃi'nɔwl (pl -óis) m nightingale.

roxo, xa ['xoʃu, ʃal adj -1. [cor] violet; ~ de inveja fig green with envy; estar ~ de saudades fig to have the blues. -2. MED purple.

roxo m [cor] violet.

royalty ['xɔjawtʃil (pl royalties) m royalty.

RP (abrev de Relações Públicas) f PR.

RPM (abrev de Rotações por Minuto) f RPM.

RR (abrev de Estado de Roraima) n State of Roraima.

RS (abrev de Estado do Rio Grande do Sul) n State of Rio Grande do Sul.

RSVP (abrev de répondez s'il vous plaît) RSVP.

rua ['xual f [ger] street; ~ sem saída dead end.

rubéola [xu'bɛwlal f German measles, rubella.

rubi [xu'bil m ruby.

rubor [xu'bo(x)] (pl -es) m -1. [na face] flush. -2. [vergonha] blush.

ruborizar [xubori'za(x)] *vt* [envergonhar] to embarrass.

◆ **ruborizar-se** *vp* to blush.

rubrica [xu'brika] *f* **-1.** [assinatura] initials *(pl).* **-2.** [indicação de assunto *etc.*] rubric.

rubricar [xubri'ka(x)] *vt* to initial.

rubro, bra ['xubru, bra] *adj* **-1.** [ger] bright red. **-2.** [faces] ruddy.

ruço, ça ['xusu, sa] *adj* **-1.** [desbotado, surrado] faded. **-2.** *fam* [difícil] tricky.

rude ['xudʒi] *adj* **-1.** [descortês] rude. **-2.** [primitivo] crude.

rudimentar [xudʒimẽn'ta(x)] *adj* rudimentary.

rudimentos [xudʒi'mẽntuʃ] *mpl* rudiments.

ruela [xwɛla] *f* alleyway.

ruga ['xuga] *f* **-1.** [na pele] wrinkle. **-2.** [na roupa] crease.

rúgbi ['xugbi] *m* rugby.

ruge ['xuʒi] *m* rouge.

rugido [xu'ʒidu] *m* roar.

rugir [xu'ʒi(x)] *vi* to roar.

ruído ['xwidu] *m* noise.

ruidoso, osa [xwi'dozu, ɔza] *adj* noisy.

ruim ['xuĩ] *(pl* **-ns)** *adj* **-1.** [nocivo] vile. **-2.** [malvado] wicked. **-3.** [imprestável, ineficiente] useless. **-4.** [podre] rotten. **-5.** [defeituoso] faulty. **-6.** [ordinário] poor. **-7.** [desagradável] bad; **achar ~** [zangar-se] to get upset.

ruína [xwina] *f* **-1.** [ger] ruin; **estar em ~ s** to be in ruins. **-2.** [causa de destruição, queda] ruination. **-3.** [decadência] downfall.

ruins [xu'ĩʃ] *pl* ⊳ **ruim.**

ruir ['xwi(x)] *vi* to collapse.

ruivo, va ['xuivu, va] ◇ *adj* **-1.** [pessoa] red-headed. **-2.** [cabelo, barba] red. ◇ *m, f* redhead.

rum ['xũ] *m* rum.

rumar [xu'ma(x)] ◇ *vt:* **~ algo para** to steer sthg towards. ◇ *vi:* **~ para** to head for.

ruminar [xumi'na(x)] ◇ *vt* to think over. ◇ *vi* to ruminate.

rumo ['xumu] *m* **-1.** [direção] course; **ir ~ a** to head for. **-2.** *fig* [destino] fate; **sem ~** *lit* adrift; *fig* aimless.

rumor [xu'mo(x)] *(pl* **-es)** *m* **-1.** [ruído] noise. **-2.** [boato] rumour.

ruptura [xup'tura] *f* **-1.** [ger] rupture. **-2.** [de fiação] break. **-3.** [de relações, negociações] break-up. **-4.** [de contrato] breach.

rural [xu'raw] *(pl* **-ais)** *adj* rural.

rush ['xãʃi] *m* heavy traffic; **a hora do ~** rush hour.

Rússia ['xusja] *n* Russia.

russo, sa ['xusu, sa] ◇ *adj* Russian. ◇ *m, f* Russian.

◆ **russo** *m* [língua] Russian.

rústico, ca ['xuʃtʃiku, ka] *adj* rustic.

S

s, S ['ɛsi] *m* [letra] s, S.

sã [sã] *f* ⊳ **são.**

S.A. *(abrev de* **Sociedade Anônima)** *f incorporated company,* ≈ Inc.

Saara [sa'ara] *n:* **o (deserto do) ~** the Sahara (Desert).

sáb. *(abrev de* **sábado)** *m* Sat.

sábado ['sabadu] *m* Saturday; **aos ~s** on Saturdays; **cair num ~** to fall on a Saturday; **(no) ~** (on) Saturday; **(no) ~ que vem/no próximo ~** (on) the coming, next Saturday; **~ de manhã** Saturday morning; **~ à tarde/noite** Saturday afternoon/evening; **~ passado** *ou* **retrasado** last Saturday, Saturday just gone; **~ sim, ~ não** every other Saturday; **todos os ~s** every Saturday.

sabão [sa'bãw] *(pl* **-ões)** *m* [produto] soap; **~ em pó** soap powder.

sabedoria [sabedo'ria] *f* wisdom.

saber [sa'be(x)] ◇ *m* knowledge. ◇ *vi* to know. ◇ *vt* to know; **~ de cor** to know (off) by heart; **~ (como) fazer algo** to know how to do sthg; **sei lá!** *fam* who knows!; **você que sabe** *fam* it's up to you. ◇ *vi* **-1.** [ter erudição] to know. **-2.** [estar a par de]: **~ (de algo)** to know (sthg).

sabiá [sa'bja] *m* song thrush.

sabido, da [sa'bidu, da] *adj* **-1.** [astuto] wise. **-2.** [conhecedor] knowledgeable.

sábio, bia ['sabju, bja] ◇ *adj* wise. ◇ *m, f* wise person.

sabões [sa'bõjʃ] *pl* ⊳ **sabão.**

sabonete [sabo'netʃi] *m* toilet soap.

sabor [sa'bo(x)] *(pl* **-es)** *m* taste; **ao ~ de** at the mercy of.

saborear [sabo'rja(x)] *vt* to savour.

saboroso, osa [sabo'rozu, ɔza] *adj* tasty.

sabotagem [sabo'taʒẽ] *(pl* **-ns)** *f* sabotage.

sabotar [sabo'ta(x)] *vt* to sabotage.

SAC *(abrev de* **Serviço de Atendimento ao Consumidor)** *m* Brazilian consumer telephone service.

saca ['saka] f [saco largo] sack.

sacada [sa'kada] f ARQUIT balcony.

sacal [sa'kaw] (pl -ais) adj boring.

sacana [sa'kana] adj mfam -1. [sujo]: ser ~ to be a bastard. -2. [esperto] sharp. -3. [libidinoso] randy. -4. [brincalhão] raffish.

sacanagem [saka'naʒẽ] (pl -ns) f mfam -1. [sujeira] dirty trick. -2. [libidinagem] screwing. -3. [brincadeira] joke.

sacar [sa'ka(x)] <> vt -1. [arma, carteira] to pull out. -2. [em banco] to draw. -3. fam [compreender] to twig. <> vi -1. [de arma]: ~ de algo to whip out sthg. -2. [em banco]: ~ (contra/sobre) to draw (against/from). -3. ESP to serve. -4. fam [compreender] to twig. -5. fam [mentir] to fib. -6. fam [falar sem saber] to talk through one's hat.

saca-rolha [ˌsaka'xoʎa] (pl saca-rolhas) m corkscrew.

sacerdócio [sasex'dɔsju] m priesthood.

sacerdote, tisa [sasex'dɔtʃi, tʃiza] m, f [pagão] priest (f priestess).

saciar [sa'sja(x)] vt to satisfy.

saco ['saku] m -1. [recipiente] bag. -2. [utensílio]: ~ de dormir sleeping bag. -3. [enseada] cove. -4. vulg [testículos] balls. -5. fam [amolação]: encher o ~ (de alguém) to get one's goat; estar de ~ cheio (de alguém/algo) to have a bellyful (of sb/sthg); que ~! what a bore! -6. fam [paciência]: haja ~! keep your knickers on!, don't get your knickers in a twist! -7. fam [disposição]: estar com/sem ~ de fazer algo to give/not to give a hoot about doing sthg.

sacola [sa'kɔla] f saddlebag.

sacolejar [sakole'ʒa(x)] vt -1. [sacudir] to shake. -2. [rebolar] to sway.

sacramento [sakra'mẽntu] m RELIG sacrament.

sacrificar [sakrifi'ka(x)] vt -1. [ger] to sacrifice. -2. [prejudicar] to damage. -3. [matar] to put down.
  ➡ **sacrificar-se** vp -1. [ger] to sacrifice o.s. -2. [sujeitar-se] to give in to.

sacrifício [sakri'fisju] m sacrifice.

sacrilégio [sakri'lɛʒju] m sacrilege.

sacro, cra ['sakru, kra] adj -1. [sagrado] sacred. -2. ANAT sacral.

sacudida [saku'dʒida] f shake.

sacudir [saku'dʒi(x)] vt to shake.
  ➡ **sacudir-se** vp -1. [tremer] to shake. -2. [saracotear] to waggle.

sádico, ca ['sadʒiku, ka] <> adj sadistic. <> m, f sadist.

sadio, dia [sa'dʒiu, dʒia] adj healthy.

sadismo [sa'dʒiʒmu] m sadism.

safadeza [safa'deza] f -1. [ger] mischief. -2. [devassidão] debauchery.

safado, da [sa'fadu, da] adj -1. [ger] mischievous. -2. [devasso] debauched.

safári [sa'faril] m safari.

safira [sa'fira] f sapphire.

safra ['safra] f -1. AGR harvest. -2. fig [de cantores etc.] crop.

saga ['saga] f saga.

sagaz [sa'gajʒ] adj shrewd.

sagitariano, na [saʒita'rjãnu, na] <> adj Sagittarian. <> m, f Sagittarian.

Sagitário [saʒi'tarju] <> m [zodíaco] Sagittarius. <> mf [pessoa] Sagittarian.

sagrado, da [sa'gradu, da] adj sacred.

saguão [sa'gwãw] (pl -ões) m -1. [entrada] lobby. -2. [pátio] courtyard.

saia ['saja] f -1. [roupa] skirt. -2. [de mesa] (floor-length) tablecloth. -3. fam fig [mulher] skirt; ~ justa tight spot.

saída [sa'ida] f -1. [ger] way out; ~ de emergência emergency exit. -2. [ato] leaving. -3. [COMPUT - de programa] exit; [- de dados] output.

saída-de-praia [sa.idadʒi'praja] (pl saídas-de-praia) f beach wrap.

saideira [saj'dejra] f one for the road.

sair [sa'i(x)] vi -1. [gen] to come out; ~ do armário fig to come out (as being homosexual). -2. [ir para fora - de ônibus, trem, avião] to get off; [- de carro] to get out of. -3. [ir para a rua] to go out. -4. [ir embora, deixar] to leave; ~ de fininho to sneak off. -5. [fugir] to get out. -6. [escapar]: ~ de to get out of. -7. [aparecer] to appear. -8. [desaparecer]: ~ de moda to go out of fashion. -9. [parecer-se]: ~ a alguém to take after sb. -10. [resultar] to turn out; ~ ganhando/perdendo to end up winning/losing. -11. [custar]: ~ (a ou por) to come to; ~ caro to be expensive. -12. COMPUT to exit.
  ➡ **sair-se** vp [obter resultado]: ~-se bem/mal to come out well/badly.

sal ['saw] (pl sais) m salt; sem ~ [manteiga etc.] unsalted; [precisando de mais sal] bland; ~ grosso rock salt.

sala ['sala] f -1. [aposento] room; ~ de espera waiting room; ~ de estar living room; ~ de operações operating theatre; ~ de bate-papo COMPUT chat room. -2. [de espetáculos] concert hall. -3. EDUC: ~ (de aula) classroom; [alunos] class.

salada [sa'lada] f -1. CULIN salad; ~ de frutas fruit salad. -2. fig [confusão]: fazer uma ~ de algo to make a muddle of sthg.

sala-e-quarto [ˌsalaj'kwaxtu] (pl sala-e-quartos) m studio (flat).

salame [sa'lãmi] *m* salami.

salaminho [salã'miɲu] *m* small salami.

salão [sa'lãw] (*pl* -**ões**) *m* -**1.** [aposento] lounge. -**2.** [estabelecimento]: ~ **de beleza** beauty salon; ~ **de chá** tea room. -**3.** [exposição] exhibition hall.

salarial [sala'rjaw] (*pl* -**ais**) *adj* pay (*antes de subst*).

salário [sa'larju] *m* wage; ~ **de fome** miserly wage; **décimo terceiro** ~ *Christmas bonus equal to one month's wages*; ~ **mínimo** minimum wage; ~ **líquido** net salary.

saldar [saw'da(x)] *vt* to settle.

saldo ['sawdu] *m* -**1.** [ger] balance; ~ **credor/devedor** credit/debit balance; ~ **negativo/positivo** debit/credit balance. -**2.** *fig* [resultado] outcome.

saleiro [sa'lejru] *m* -**1.** [recipiente] salt cellar. -**2.** [moedor] salt mill.

salgadinho [sawga'dʒiɲu] *m* canapé.

salgado, da [saw'gadu, da] *adj* -**1.** [comida - com sal] salted; [- com excesso de sal] salty. -**2.** [anedota] salty. -**3.** [preço] steep.

salgar [saw'ga(x)] *vt* to salt.

salgueiro [saw'gejru] *m* willow.

salientar [saljẽn'ta(x)] *vt* -**1.** [ressaltar] to highlight. -**2.** [enfatizar] to stress.
  salientar-se *vp* [distinguir-se] to distinguish o.s.

saliente [sa'ljẽntʃi] *adj* -**1.** [ressaltado] salient. -**2.** *fig* [espevitado] eager.

salino, na [sa'linu, na] *adj* saline.
  salina *f* -**1.** [terreno] salt bed. -**2.** [empresa] salt works.

saliva [sa'liva] *f* saliva.

salmão [saw'mãw] (*pl* -**ões**) <> *m* [peixe] salmon. <> *m inv* [cor] salmon. <> *adj inv* [cor] salmon-pink.

salmo ['sawmu] *m* psalm.

salmões [saw'mõjʃ] *pl* ⯈ **salmão**.

salmoura [saw'mora] *f* brine.

salobro, bra [sa'lobru, bra] *adj* brackish.

salões [sa'lõjʃ] *pl* ⯈ **salão**.

salpicão [sawpi'kãw] (*pl* -**ões**) *m* -**1.** [paio] smoked sausage. -**2.** [prato]: ~ **(de galinha)** *cold shredded chicken and vegetable dish*.

salpicar [sawpi'ka(x)] *vt* -**1.**: ~ **algo em algo**, ~ **algo de algo** [temperar] to season sthg with sthg; [sarapintar, sujar] to splash; ~ **alguém de algo** [sujar] to splash sb with sthg. -**2.** [entremear]: ~ **algo com** *ou* **de algo** to pepper sthg with sthg.

salsa ['sawsa] *f* -**1.** [erva] parsley. -**2.** *Mús* salsa.

salsicha [saw'siʃa] *f* sausage.

salsichão [sawsi'ʃãw] (*pl* -**chões**) *m* large sausage.

saltar [saw'ta(x)] <> *vt* -**1.** [ger] to jump. -**2.** *fam* [fazer vir] to send for. <> *vi* -**1.** [pular]: ~ **(de/sobre)** to jump (from/on). -**2.** [de ônibus, trem, cavalo]: ~ **(de)** to jump (from). -**3.** [rolha] to pop.

salteador, ra [sawtʃja'do(x), ra] *m, f* mugger.

saltimbanco [sawtʃĩn'bãŋku] *m* travelling acrobat.

salto ['sawtu] *m* -**1.** [pulo] jump; **dar um** ~ to leap. -**2.** *ESP*: ~ **em altura** high jump; ~ **em distância** long jump; ~ **de vara** pole vault. -**3.** [de sapato] heel; ~ **alto/baixo** high/low heel.

salto-mortal [ˌsawtumox'taw] (*pl* **saltos-mortais**) *m* somersault.

salubre [sa'lubri] *adj* salubrious.

salutar [salu'ta(x)] (*pl* -**es**) *adj* -**1.** [saudável] healthy. -**2.** *fig* [moralizador] salutary.

salva ['sawva] *f* -**1.** *MIL*: ~ **(de tiros)** salvo (of gunshots). -**2.** *fig*: **uma** ~ **de palmas** a round of applause. -**3.** [bandeja] tray.

salvação [sawva'sãw] *f* salvation.

salvador, ra [sawva'do(x), ra] *m, f* [pessoa] saviour.

salvadorenho, nha [sawvado'reɲu, ɲa] <> *adj* Salvadorean. <> *m, f* Salvadorean.

salvaguardar [ˌsawvagwax'da(x)] *vt* to safeguard.

salvamento [sawva'mẽntu] *m* rescue.

salvar [saw'va(x)] *vt* to save.
  salvar-se *vp* [escapar] to escape.

salva-vidas [ˌsalva'vidaʃ] <> *adj inv* lifeguard. <> *m* -**1.** *inv* [bóia] lifebelt. -**2.** [pessoa] lifeguard. -**3.** [jaqueta] life jacket.

salve ['sawvi] *interj* cheers!

salvo, va ['sawvu, va] <> *adj* safe; **estar a** ~ to be safe. <> *prep* except.

salvo-conduto [ˌsawvukõn'dutu] (*pl* **salvo-condutos, salvos-condutos**) *m* safe conduct.

samambaia [samãn'baja] *f* fern.

samba ['sãnba] *m* samba.

samba-canção [ˌsãnbakãn'sãw] (*pl* **sambas-canções**) *m* *MÚS* type of samba.

sambar [sãn'ba(x)] *vi* to samba.

sambista [sãn'biʃta] *mf* -**1.** [dançarino] samba dancer. -**2.** [compositor] composer of sambas.

sambódromo [sãn'bɔdromu] *m* track along which samba schools parade.

sanar [sa'na(x)] *vt* -**1.** [curar] to cure. -**2.** [remediar] to remedy.

sanatório [sana'tɔrju] *m* sanatorium.

sanção [sãn'sãw] (*pl* -**ões**) *f* -**1.** [ger] sanction. -**2.** [punição]: ~ **(contra)** sanction (against).

sancionar [sãnsjo'na(x)] *vt* [aprovar] to sanction.

sanções [sãn'sõjʃ] *pl* ▷ **sanção**.

sandália [sãn'dalja] *f* sandal.

sanduíche [sãn'dwiʃi] *m* sandwich.

saneamento [sanja'mẽntul *m* -1. [limpeza] sanitization. -2. *fig* [correção] purge.

sanear [sa'nja(x)] *vt* -1. [tornar salubre] to sanitize. -2. *fig* [corrigir] to purge.

sanfona [sãn'fona] *f* -1. *MÚS* concertina. -2. [em suéter] ribbing.

sangrar [sãŋ'gra(x)] ⬦ *vi* [verter sangue] to bleed. ⬦ *vt* -1. [ger] to bleed. -2. [açude, represa] to drain.

sangrento, ta [sãŋ'grẽntu, tal *adj* -1. [ger] bloody. -2. *CULIN* [carne] rare.

sangria [sãŋ'grial *f* -1. [bebida] sangria. -2. *MED* blood-letting. -3. *fig* [extorsão] extortion.

sangue ['sãŋgil *m* -1. [ger] blood; **come-çou a sair muito ~ do corte** the cut started to bleed a lot. -2. *fig* [raça]: **puro ~** thoroughbred.

sangue-frio [ˌsãŋgi'friwl *m* sangfroid.

sanguessuga [ˌsãŋgi'sugal *f* leech.

sanguinário, ria [sãŋgi'narju, rja] *adj* bloodthirsty.

sanguíneo, nea [sãŋ'g(w)inju, njal *adj* -1. [relativo ao sangue] blood *(antes de subst)*. -2. [pessoa] ruddy.

sanidade [sani'dadʒi] *f* [mental] sanity.

sanitário, ria [sani'tarju, rjal *adj* -1. [ger] sanitary. -2. [banheiro] bath *(antes de subst)*.

San José [ˌsãnxo'sel *n* San José.

San Salvador [ˌsãnsawva'do(x)] *n* San Salvador.

Santa Catarina [ˌsãntakata'rinal *n* Santa Catarina.

santidade [sãntʃi'dadʒi] *f* sanctity.

Santiago do Chile [sãnˌtʃagudu'ʃilil *n* Santiago de Chile.

santo, ta ['sãntu, tal ⬦ *adj* -1. [sagrado] holy; **todo o ~ dia** *fam fig* the whole blessed day long. -2. *(antes de subst)* [caridoso] kind. ⬦ *m, f* [ger] saint.

Santo Domingo [ˌsãntudo'mĩŋgul *n* Santo Domingo.

santuário [sãn'twarjul *m* sanctuary.

são, sã ['sãw, 'sãl *adj* -1. [ger] healthy. -2. *PSIC* sane. -3. [curado] well. -4. [ileso]: **~ e salvo** safe and sound. -5. [sensato] sensible.

São [sãwl *m* Saint.

São Luís [ˌsãwlu'iʒ] *n* São Luis.

São Paulo [ˌsãw'pawlul *n* São Paulo.

sapataria [sapata'rial *f* -1. [ofício] shoe trade. -2. [loja] shoe shop.

sapateado [sapa'tʃjadul *m* tap dance.

sapateiro, ra [sapa'tejru, ral *m, f* -1. [fabricante] shoemaker. -2. [quem conserta] cobbler.
▰ **sapateiro** *m* [loja] shoe shop.

sapatilha [sapa'tʃiʎal *f* -1. [de balé] ballet shoe. -2. [sapato baixo] slipper.

sapato [sa'patul *m* shoe.

sapiência [sa'pjẽnsjal *f* -1. [erudição] knowledge. -2. [bom julgamento] wisdom.

sapo ['sapul *m* toad.

saque ['sakil *m* -1. *FIN* withdrawal. -2. *ESP* serve. -3. [de cidade, loja] ransacking. -4. *fam* [mentira] fib.

saquear [sa'kja(x)] *vt* to ransack.

saraivada [saraj'vadal *f* hail storm; **uma ~ de** *fig* a shower of.

sarampo [sa'rãnpul *m* measles.

sarar [sa'ra(x)] ⬦ *vt* [pessoa, doença, ferida] to heal. ⬦ *vi* -1. [pessoa] to get better. -2. [ferida] to heal.

sarcasmo [sax'kaʒmul *m* sarcasm.

sarcástico, ca [sax'kaʃtʃiku, kal *adj* sarcastic.

sarda ['saxdal *f* freckle.

Sardenha [sax'deɲal *n* Sardinia.

sardinha [sax'dʒiɲal *f* sardine.

sardônico, ca [sax'doniku, kal *adj* sardonic.

sargento [sax'ʒẽntul *mf* sergeant.

sarjeta [sax'ʒetal *f* gutter.

sarna ['saxnal *f* scabies; **procurar ~ para se coçar** to look for trouble.

Satã [sa'tãl, **Satanás** [sata'naʃl *m* Satan.

satélite [sa'tɛlitʃil ⬦ *m* satellite. ⬦ *adj* [cidade, país] satellite *(antes de subst)*.

sátira ['satʃiral *f* satire.

satírico, ca [sa'tʃiriku, kal *adj* satirical.

satirizar [satʃiri'za(x)] *vt* to satirize.

satisfação [satʃiʃfa'sãwl *(pl -ões)* *f* -1. [alegria, prazer] pleasure. -2. [de desejos, necessidades] satisfaction. -3. [explicação] explanation; **dar uma ~ a alguém** to give sb an explanation; **tomar satis-fações de alguém** to get an explanation from sb.

satisfatório, ria [satʃiʃfa'torju, rjal *adj* satisfactory.

satisfazer [satʃiʃfa'ze(x)] ⬦ *vt* to satisfy. ⬦ *vi* -1. [ser satisfatório] to be satisfactory. -2. [contentar, convir]: **~ a** to satisfy.
▰ **satisfazer-se** *vp*: **~-se (com)** to be satisfied (with).

satisfeito, ta [satʃiʃ'fejtu, tal ⬦ *pp* ▷ **satisfazer**. ⬦ *adj* -1. [ger] satisfied. -2. [alegre] pleased.

saturado, da [satu'radu, dal *adj* -1.: **~ de algo** saturated with sthg. -2. *fig* [enfastiado]: **~ (de algo/alguém)** fed up (with sthg/sb).

saturar [satu'ra(x)] vt -**1.**: ~ algo (de algo) to saturate sthg (with sthg). -**2.** fig [enfastiar]: ~ alguém de algo to wear sb out with sthg. -**3.** [saciar] to fill.

Saturno [sa'tuxnul] m Saturn.

saudação [sawda'sãw] (pl -ões) f -**1.** [cumprimento] greeting. -**2.** [homenagem] homage.

saudade [saw'dadʒi] f -**1.** [de pessoa, país, família] pining. -**2.** [do passado, de época] nostalgia; **estar morrendo de ~ (s) de alguém** to be pining for sb; **matar as ~s de alguém** to catch up with sb; **estava louco de ~s da minha cama** I was dying to sleep in my own bed again; **sentir ~ (s) de alguém/algo** to pine for sb/sthg.

saudar [saw'da(x)] vt to greet.

saudável [saw'davɛw] (pl -eis) adj healthy.

saúde [sa'udʒi] ◇ f health; **estar bem/mal de ~** to be in good/bad health; **brindar à ~ de alguém** to drink to sb's health; **~ pública** public health; [órgão] health service. ◇ interj [para brindar] cheers!; [depois de um espirro] bless you!

saudosismo [sawdo'ziʒmul] m nostalgia.

saudoso, osa [saw'dozu, ɔzal adj -**1.** [que causa saudades] dearly missed. -**2.** [que sente saudades]: **estar ~ de alguém/algo** to miss sb/sthg. -**3.** [que denota saudades] grieving.

sauna ['sawnal f [ger] sauna.

saveiro [sa'vejrul m fishing boat.

saxofone [sakso'fonil m saxophone.

sazonal [sazo'nawl (pl -ais) adj seasonal.

SBT (abrev de Sistema Brasileiro de Televisão) m the second most popular Brazilian television station.

SC (abrev de Estado de Santa Catarina) n State of Santa Catarina.

se [sil ◇ pron -**1.** [reflexo: pessoa] himself (f herself); [você, vocês] yourself, yourselves pl; [impessoal] oneself; **lavar-~** to wash (oneself); **eles ~ perderam** they got lost; **vocês se perderam** you got lost. -**2.** [reflexo: coisa, animal] itself; **o vidro partiu-~** the glass broke. -**3.** [recíproco] each other; **escrevem-~ regularmente** they write to each other regularly. -**4.** [com sujeito indeterminado]: **'aluga-~ quarto'** 'room to let'; **'vende-~'** 'for sale'; **come-~ bem aqui** the food here is very good. ◇ conj -**1.** [indica condição] if; ~ **tiver tempo, escrevo** I'll write if I have time; ~ **fizer sol, iremos à praia** if it's sunny, we'll go to the beach. -**2.** [indica causa] if; ~ **você está com fome, coma alguma coisa** if you're hungry, have something to eat; ~ ...,

então ... if ..., then ...; ~ **diminui a oferta, então aumenta o preço** if demand diminishes, the cost goes up. -**3.** [indica comparação] if; ~ **um é feio, o outro ainda é pior** if you think he's ugly, you should see the other one. -**4.** [em interrogativas]: **que tal ~ fôssemos ao cinema?** how about going to the movies?; **e ~ ela não vier?** and what if she doesn't come? -**5.** [exprime desejo] if; ~ **pelo menos tivesse dinheiro!** if only I had the money! -**6.** [em interrogativa indireta] if, whether; **avisem-me ~ quiserem ir** let me know if you'd like to go; **perguntei-lhe ~ gostou** I asked him if he liked it. -**7.** [em locuções]: ~ **bem que** even though, although.

SE (abrev de Estado de Sergipe) n State of Sergipe.

sebo ['sebul m -**1.** [substância] sebum. -**2.** [livraria] second-hand bookshop.

seboso, osa [se'bozu, ɔzal adj -**1.** [ger] greasy. -**2.** fam fig [pessoa] conceited.

SEBRAE (abrev de Serviço de Apoio às Micro e Pequenas Empresas) m Brazilian support body for small and very small businesses.

seca ['sekal f ▷ seco.

secador [seka'do(x)l (pl -es) m dryer; ~ **(de cabelo)** hairdryer; ~ **de roupa** [varal] clothes line.

secadora [seka'doral f tumble-dryer.

seção [se'sãwl (pl -ões) f section.

secar [se'ka(x)l vt & vi to dry.

seccionar [seksjo'na(x)l vt -**1.** [cortar] to cut into sections. -**2.** [dividir] to divide.

seco, ca ['seku, kal adj -**1.** [ger] dry. -**2.** [magro] thin.

seções [se'sõjʃl pl ▷ seção.

secreção [sekre'sãwl (pl -ões) f secretion.

secretaria [sekreta'rial f secretariat.

secretária [sekre'tarjal f ▷ secretário.

secretário, ria [sekre'tarju, rjal m, f [ger] secretary; ~ **de Estado** Secretary of State.

    secretária f -**1.** [mesa] desk. -**2.** [aparelho]: ~ **eletrônica** answering machine.

secreto, ta [se'krɛtu, tal adj secret.

sectário, ria [sɛk'tarju, rjal ◇ adj sectarian. ◇ m, f [seguidor] sectarian.

secular [seku'la(x)l (pl -es) adj -**1.** [ger] secular. -**2.** [antigo] age-old.

século ['sɛkulul m century.

    séculos mpl fig [longo tempo] ages; **há ~ s** for ages.

secundário, ria [sekũn'darju, rjal adj secondary.

seda ['sedal *f* [material] silk; ~ **crua/pura** raw/pure silk.

sedar [se'da(x)] *vt* to sedate.

sedativo, va [seda'tʃivu, val *adj* MED sedative; *fig* [música, balanço, silêncio] soothing.

◆ **sedativo** *m* MED sedative.

sede¹ ['sedʒil *f* -1. [secura] thirst; **estar com** ~ to be thirsty; **matar a** ~ to quench one's thirst. -2. *fig* [desejo]: ~ **de algo** thirst for sthg.

sede² ['sedʒil *f* -1. [estabelecimento] headquarters. -2. [de governo] seat. -3. [centro, local] venue.

sedentário, ria [sedẽn'tarju, rjal *adj* sedentary.

sedento, ta [se'dẽntu, tal *adj* [de água] thirsty.

SEDEX (*abrev de* Serviço de Encomenda Expressa) *m Brazilian express mail delivery service.*

sediar [se'dʒja(x)] *vt* to base.

sedimento [sedʒi'mẽntul *m* sediment.

sedoso, osa [se'dozu, ɔzal *adj* silky.

sedução [sedu'sãwl (*pl* -ões) *f* [ato] seduction.

sedutor, ra [sedu'to(x), ral (*mpl* -es, *fpl* -s) ◇ *adj* seductive. ◇ *m, f* [sexualmente] seducer.

seduzir [sedu'zi(x)l *vt* -1. [ger] to seduce. -2. [induzir] to encourage.

seg. (*abrev de* segunda-feira) *f* Mon.

segmento [seg'mẽntul *m* segment.

segredo [se'gredul *m* -1. [ger] secret; **guardar** ~ to keep secret. -2. [discrição] secrecy; **em** ~ in secret. -3. [dispositivo] secret lock.

segregação [segrega'sãwl *f* segregation.

segregar [segre'ga(x)l *vt* -1. [ger] to segregate. -2. [expelir] to secrete.

seguidamente [se,gida'mẽntʃil *adv* -1. [com freqüência] often. -2. [continuamente] continuously.

seguido, da [se'gidu, dal *adj* -1. [consecutivo] consecutive; **cinco dias** ~s five days running; **horas seguidas** hours on end. -2. [adotado] widely adopted. -3. [acompanhado]: ~ **de/por** followed by.

◆ **em seguida** *loc adv* -1. [consecutivamente] shortly after. -2. [imediatamente] straight away, at once.

seguidor, ra [segi'do(x), ral *m, f* follower.

seguimento [segi'mẽntul *m* continuation; **dar** ~ **a algo** to continue with sthg.

seguinte [se'gĩntʃil ◇ *adj* -1. [subseqüente] following, next. -2. (*antes de subst*) [citando, explicando] following. ◇ *mf*: **o/a** ~ [numa fila, ordem] the next; [citando, explicando] as follows; **o negócio é o** ~ *fam* the matter is as follows; **pelo** ~ for the following reason.

seguir [se'gi(x)l ◇ *vt* -1. [ger] to follow. -2. [perseguir] to chase. -3. [continuar] to continue. ◇ *vi* -1. [ger] to follow. -2. [continuar] to carry on, to keep going. -3. [direção] to continue; ~ **reto** to go straight ahead.

◆ **seguir-se** *vp* -1. [suceder]: ~-**se (a algo)** to follow on (from sthg); **seguiram-se dias de euforia** there followed days of euphoria. -2. [em citações] to follow.

segunda [se'gũndal *f* ▷ **segundo**.

segunda-feira [se,gũnda'fejral (*pl* segundas-feiras) *f* Monday; *veja também* sábado.

segundo, da [se'gũndu, dal ◇ *num adj* second. ◇ *num m, f* second. ◇ *adj* [outro] second; **segundas intenções** ulterior motives; **de segunda mão** second-hand.

◆ **segundo** ◇ *m* [medida de tempo] second; **(só) um** ~! *fig* just a second!, (just) one second! ◇ *prep* according to. ◇ *conj* [conforme] according to.

◆ **segunda** *f* -1. AUTO second (gear). -2. [segunda-feira] Monday.

◆ **de segunda** *loc adj* second class.

segurador, ra [segura'do(x), ral *m, f* [agente] insurance broker.

◆ **seguradora** *f* [companhia] insurance company.

segurança [segu'rãnsal ◇ *f* -1. [proteção, estabilidade] security; **cinto de** ~ safety belt. -2. [ausência de perigo] safety. -3. [certeza, confiança] assurance. ◇ *mf* [pessoa] security guard.

segurar [segu'ra(x)l ◇ *vt* -1. [pegar] to hold. -2. [firmar] to fix. -3. [sustentar] to hold up. -4. [pôr no seguro]: ~ **algo/alguém (contra)** to insure sthg/sb (against). ◇ *vi* [apoiar-se]: ~ **(em)** to hold on (to).

◆ **segurar-se** *vp* -1. [apoiar-se]: ~-**se em** to hold on to. -2. [fazer seguro] to steady o.s. -3. [controlar-se] to control o.s.

seguro, ra [se'guru, ral *adj* -1. [ger] safe. -2. [certo] sure; **estar** ~ **de algo** to be sure of sthg. -3. [confiante, firme] secure. -4. [infalível] foolproof.

◆ **seguro** ◇ *m* [contrato] insurance policy; ~ **de automóvel** car insurance; ~ **de viagem** travel insurance; ~ **de vida** life insurance. ◇ *adv* steadily.

seguro-saúde [se,gurusa'udʒil (*pl* seguros-saúde) *m* health insurance.

seio ['seju] *m* **-1.** ANAT breast. **-2.** *fig* [meio] heart.

seis ['sejʃ] *num* **-1.** [ger] six; **o (número)** ~ the (number) six; **duzentos e** ~ **two** hundred and six; **trinta e** ~ thirty-six; **Rua das Acácias, (número)** ~ number six, Rua das Acácias; **pacotes de** ~ packets of six; ~ **de cada vez** six at a time; **somos** ~ we are six, there are six of us. **-2.** [hora]: **às** ~ **(horas)** at six o'clock; **são** ~ **horas** it is six o'clock; **são** ~ **e meia** it is half past six. **-3.** [data] sixth; **(no) dia** ~ **de janeiro** (on the) sixth of January. **-4.** [idade]: **ele tem** ~ **anos (de idade)** he is six years old. **-5.** ESP [resultado]: **empatar de** ~ **a** ~ to draw six all; ~ **a zero** six nil. **-6.** [em naipes]: ~ **de espadas** six of spades.

seiscentos, tas [sejʃ'sẽtuʃ, taʃ] *num* six hundred; *veja também* **seis.**

seita ['sejta] *f* sect.

seixo ['sejʃu] *m* pebble.

seja ['seʒa] *conj* whether it be; **ou** ~ that is.

sela ['sɛla] *f* saddle.

selar [se'la(x)] *vt* **-1.** [ger] to seal. **-2.** [cavalo] to saddle. **-3.** [carta] to stamp.

seleção [sele'sãw] (*pl* -ões) *f* **-1.** [escolha] selection. **-2.** [equipe] team.

selecionar [selesjo'na(x)] *vt* to select.

seletivo, va [sele'tʃivu, va] *adj* selective.

seleto, ta [se'lɛtu, ta] *adj* select.

selim [se'lĩ] (*pl* -ns) *m* saddle.

selo ['selu] *m* **-1.** [carimbo, sinete] seal. **-2.** [postal] stamp. **-3.** *fig* [cunho] seal of approval.

selva ['sɛwva] *f* jungle.

selvagem [sew'vaʒẽ] (*pl* -ns) *adj* **-1.** [ger] wild. **-2.** [bárbaro] savage. **-3.** [ermo] desolate. **-4.** *fig* [grosseiro] rude.

sem [sẽ] *prep* without; ~ **algo/fazer algo** without sthg/doing sthg; ~ **dúvida** without doubt.

➥ **sem que** *loc conj* without.

semáforo [se'maforu] *m* **-1.** AUTO traffic lights (*pl*). **-2.** FERRO signal.

semana [se'mãna] *f* week; **uma** ~ **atrás** a week ago; **a** ~ **passada** last week.

➥ **Semana Santa** *f* Holy Week.

semanal [sema'naw] (*pl* -ais) *adj* weekly.

semblante [sẽ'blãtʃi] *m* [rosto] countenance.

semeadura [semja'dura] *f* [semeação] sowing; **começaram a** ~ **do trigo** they began sowing the wheat.

semear [se'mja(x)] *vt* **-1.** [ger] to sow. **-2.** *fig* [espalhar] to spread.

semelhante [seme'ʎãtʃi] <> *adj* **-1.** [parecido]: ~ **(a)** similar (to). **-2.** [tal] such. <> *m* (*ger pl*) [próximo] fellow man.

sêmen ['semẽ] *m* semen.

semente [se'mẽtʃi] *f* seed.

semestral [semeʃ'traw] (*pl* -ais) *adj* half-yearly.

semestre [se'mɛʃtri] *m* semester; **todo o** ~ the whole semester.

semi-analfabeto, ta [semjanawfa'bɛtu, tal (*mpl* -s, *fpl* -s) *adj* semiliterate.

semicerrar [semi'sexa(x)] *vt* to half-close.

semicírculo [semi'sixkulu] *m* semicircle.

semifinal [semifi'naw] (*pl* -ais) *f* semifinal.

seminário [semi'narju] *m* **-1.** RELIG seminary. **-2.** EDUC seminar.

seminarista [semina'riʃta] *mf* seminarist.

seminu, nua [semi'nu, nua] *adj* half-naked.

semiprecioso, osa [semipre'sjozu, ɔza] *adj* semiprecious.

sem-número [sẽ'numeru] *m*: **um** ~ **de** a countless number of.

semolina [semo'lina] *f* semolina.

sem-par [sẽn'pa(x)] *adj inv* peerless.

sempre ['sẽpri] *adv* always; **como** ~ as always; **de** ~ usual; **para** ~ for ever.

➥ **sempre que** *loc conj* whenever.

sem-terra [sẽ'tɛxa] *mf inv* landless farm worker.

sem-teto [sẽ'tɛtu] *mf inv* homeless person.

sem-vergonha [sẽvex'goɲa] <> *adj inv* shameless. <> *mf inv* shameless person.

SENAC (*abrev de* **Serviço Nacional de Aprendizagem Comercial**) *m Brazilian training body for people working in the general business sector.*

senado [se'nadu] *m* senate.

senador, ra [sena'do(x), ra] *m, f* senator.

SENAI (*abrev de* **Serviço Nacional de Aprendizagem Industrial**) *m Brazilian training body for people working in industry.*

senão [se'nãw] (*pl* -ões) <> *prep* [exceto] apart from. <> *conj* [caso contrário] or else. <> *m* hiccup.

Senegal [sene'gaw] *n*: **(o)** ~ Senegal.

senha ['seɲa] *f* [palavra de acesso] password; [de caixa automático] PIN (number).

senhor, ra [se'ɲo(x), ɔra] (*mpl* -es, *fpl* -s) *adj* grand; **uma senhora indigestão** a bad case of indigestion.

➥ **senhor** *m* **-1.** [tratamento - antes de nome, cargo]: ~ **X** Mr X; [- você]: **o** ~ you; [mais formal] sir; [- em cartas]: **Prezado Senhor** Dear Sir. **-2.** [homem] man.

- **3.** [cavalheiro] gentleman. - **4.** [homem idoso]: ~ **(de idade)** elderly man. - **5.** [patrão] boss. - **6.** RELIG: **o Senhor** the Lord.

➡ **senhora** f - **1.** [tratamento - antes de nome, cargo]: **senhora X** Mrs X; [- você]: **a senhora** you; [mais formal] madam; **senhoras e ~ es!** ladies and gentlemen!; [- em cartas]: **Prezada Senhora** Dear Madam. - **2.** [mulher] woman. - **3.** [dama] lady. - **4.** [mulher idosa]: **senhora (de idade)** elderly woman. - **5.** [esposa] wife. - **6.** RELIG: **Nossa Senhora** Our Lady; **(Minha) Nossa (Senhora)!** fam Heavens (above)!, (My/Dear) Lord!

senhoria [seɲoˈrial] f ⊳ **senhorio**.

senhorio, ria [seɲoˈriu, rial] m, f [proprietário] landlord (f landlady).

➡ **Senhoria** f [em carta]: **Vossa Senhoria** Your Honour.

senhorita [seɲoˈrital] f - **1.** [tratamento - antes de nome]: ~ **X** Miss X; [- você]: **a ~** you. - **2.** [moça] young lady.

senil [seˈniwl] (pl -**is**) adj senile.

senões [seˈnõjʃ] mpl ⊳ **senão**.

sensação [sẽnsaˈsãw] (pl -**ões**) f [ger] feeling; **ter a ~ de que** to have the feeling that.

sensacional [sẽnsasjoˈnawl] (pl -**ais**) adj sensational.

sensacionalista [sẽnsasjonaˈliʃtal] adj sensationalist.

sensato, ta [sẽˈsatu, tal] adj sensible.

sensibilidade [sẽnsibiliˈdaȝil] f sensitivity.

sensível [sẽnˈsivɛwl] (pl -**eis**) adj - **1.** [ger] sensitive. - **2.** [evidente, considerável] marked.

senso [ˈsẽnsul] m [juízo] sense; ~ **de humor** sense of humour; **bom ~** good sense; ~ **comum** common sense.

sensual [sẽnˈswawl] (pl -**ais**) adj sensual.

sensualidade [sẽnswaliˈdaȝil] f sensuality.

sentado, da [sẽnˈtadu, dal] adj - **1.** [pessoa] sitting. - **2.** [jantar] sit-down.

sentar [sẽnˈta(x)] vt & vi to sit.

➡ **sentar-se** vp to sit down.

sentido, da [sẽnˈtʃidu, dal] adj - **1.** [ressentido] offended. - **2.** [triste] hurt. - **3.** [lamentoso] sorrowful.

➡ **sentido** m - **1.** [ger] sense; **sexto ~** sixth sense. - **2.** [significado] meaning; ~ **figurado** figurative sense; **ter/não ter ~** to make/not make sense. - **3.** [direção] direction; ~ **horário/anti-horário** clockwise/anticlockwise. - **4.** [aspecto] way. - **5.** [propósito] aim.

sentimental [sẽntʃimẽnˈtawl] (pl -**ais**) ⟨⟩ adj - **1.** [ger] sentimental. - **2.** [amoroso] love (antes de subst). ⟨⟩ mf sentimental person.

sentimento [sẽntʃiˈmẽntul] m - **1.** [ger] feeling. - **2.** [emoção]: **com ~** with feeling. - **3.** [senso] sense.

sentir [sẽnˈtʃi(x)] ⟨⟩ vt - **1.** [ger] to feel. - **2.** [pelos sentidos] to sense. - **3.** [sofrer com] to be upset by. - **4.** [melindrar-se com] to resent. - **5.** [lamentar] to regret. ⟨⟩ vi - **1.** [sofrer] to suffer. - **2.** [lamentar] to regret; **sinto muito** I am very sorry.

➡ **sentir-se** vp to feel.

senzala [sẽnˈzalal] f slave quarters (pl).

separação [separaˈsãw] (pl -**ões**) f separation; ~ **de bens** (contract of) separation of property (prior to marriage).

separado, da [sepaˈradu, dal] adj - **1.** [apartado] separate. - **2.** [do cônjuge] separated.

separar [sepaˈra(x)] vt - **1.** [ger] to separate. - **2.** [isolar] to isolate. - **3.** [reservar] to set aside.

➡ **separar-se** vp - **1.** [ger] to separate. - **2.** [cônjuges]: ~ **-se (de alguém)** to separate (from s.o.).

septuagésimo, ma [septwaˈȝɛzimu, mal num seventieth.

sepultamento [sepuwtaˈmẽntul m burial.

sepultar [sepuwˈta(x)] vt to bury.

sepultura [sepuwˈtural f tomb, grave.

seqüela [seˈkwɛlal f - **1.** [seqüência] sequel. - **2.** [conseqüência] consequence. - **3.** MED sequela.

seqüência [seˈkwẽnsjal f sequence.

sequer [seˈkɛ(x)] adv at least; **nem ~** not even; **não sabia ~ o nome de seus pais** he didn't even know his parents' name.

seqüestrador, ra [sekweʃtraˈdo(x), ral (mpl -**res**, fpl -**s**) m, f - **1.** [de pessoa] kidnapper. - **2.** [de avião] hijacker.

seqüestrar [sekweʃˈtra(x)] vt - **1.** [pessoa] to kidnap. - **2.** [avião] to hijack. - **3.** JUR [bens] to sequestrate.

séquito [ˈsɛkitul m retinue.

ser [ˈse(x)] (pl -**res**) ⟨⟩ m [criatura] being; ~ **humano** human being. ⟨⟩ vi - **1.** [para descrever] to be; **é longo demais** it's too long; **são bonitos** they're pretty; **sou médico** I'm a doctor. - **2.** [para designar lugar, origem] to be; **ele é do Brasil** he's from Brazil; **ele é em São Paulo** it's in São Paulo; **sou brasileira** I'm Brazilian. - **3.** [custar] to be; **quanto é? - são 100 reais** how much is it? - (it's) 100 reals. - **4.** [com data, dia, hora] to be; **hoje é sexta** it's Friday today; **que horas são?** what time is it?; **são seis horas** it's six o'clock. - **5.** [exprime possessão] to be; **é**

do Ricardo it's Ricardo's; **este carro é seu?** is this your car? **- 6.** [em locuções]: **a não ~ que** unless; **que foi?** what's wrong?; **ou seja** in other words; **será que ele vem?** will he be coming? ⬦ *v aux* [forma a voz passiva] to be; **ele foi visto na saída do cinema** he was seen on his way out of the cinema. ⬦ *v impess* **-1.** [exprime tempo] to be; **é de dia/noite** it's daytime/night-time; **é tarde/cedo** it's late/early. **- 2.** [com adjetivo] to be; **é difícil dizer** it's difficult to say; **é fácil de ver** it's easy to see; **eles são Fluminense** they're Fluminense fans.

➥ **ser de** *v + prep* [matéria] to be made of; [ser adepto de] to be a fan of.

➥ **ser para** *v + prep* to be for; **isto não é para comer** this isn't for eating.

sereia [se'reja] *f* mermaid.

serenar [sere'na(x)] ⬦ *vt* **-1.** [acalmar] to calm down. **- 2.** [suavizar] to relieve. ⬦ *vi* [acalmar] to calm down.

serenata [sere'nata] *f* serenade.

sereno, na [se'renu, na] *adj* **-1.** [tranqüilo] serene. **- 2.** [límpido] clear.

➥ **sereno** *m* night air.

seresta [se'rɛʃta] *f* serenade.

Sergipe [sex'ʒipi] *n* Sergipe.

seriado, da [seri'adu, da] *adj* serialized.

➥ **seriado** *m* TV series.

serial [seri'jaw] (*pl* -ais) *adj* COMPUT serial.

série ['sɛrji] *f* **-1.** [ger] series; **uma ~ de** a series of; **número de ~** serial number. **- 2.** EDUC year.

➥ **fora de série** *loc adj* [excepcional] exceptional.

seriedade [serje'dadʒi] *f* **-1.** [ger] seriousness. **- 2.** [circunspecção] sobriety. **- 3.** [honestidade] integrity.

seringa [se'rĩga] *f* syringe.

seringueiro, ra [serĩ'gejru, ra] *m, f* rubber tapper.

➥ **seringueira** *f* rubber tree.

sério, ria ['sɛrju, rja] ⬦ *adj* **-1.** [ger] serious. **- 2.** [sóbrio] sober. **- 3.** [sem rir] straight-faced. ⬦ *adv* really.

➥ **a sério** *loc adv* seriously; **levar a ~** [dedicar-se] to take seriously; [magoar-se com] to take seriously.

sermão [sex'mãw] (*pl* -ões) *m* sermon; **levar um ~ de alguém** to be given a sermon by sb.

serpente [sex'pẽtʃi] *f* **-1.** ZOOL serpent, snake. **- 2.** *fig* [pessoa] snake (in the grass).

serpentina [serpẽ'tʃinal] *f* **-1.** [de papel] streamer. **- 2.** [conduto] coil.

SERPRO (*abrev de* **Serviço Federal de Processamento de Dados**) *m Brazilian federal data-processing agency.*

serra ['sɛxa] *f* **-1.** [ferramenta] saw. **- 2.** [lâmina] serrated blade. **- 3.** [montanhas] mountain range, sierra.

Serra Leoa [ˌsexale'oa] *n* Sierra Leone.

serralheiro, ra [sexa'ʎejru, ra] *m, f* blacksmith.

serralheria [sexaʎe'rial] *f* **-1.** [ofício] smithery. **- 2.** [oficina] smithy.

serrano, na [se'xãnu, na] ⬦ *adj* mountain *(antes de subst).* ⬦ *m, f* mountain dweller.

serrar [se'xa(x)] *vt* to saw.

serrote [se'xɔtʃi] *m* saw.

sertanejo, ja [sextane'ʒu, ʒa] ⬦ *adj* of the sertão. ⬦ *m, f* person who lives in the sertão.

sertão [sex'tãw] *m* **-1.** [o interior do país] bush. **- 2.** [região agreste] wilderness.

servente [sex'vẽtʃi] *mf* **-1.** [faxineiro] caretaker UK, janitor US. **- 2.** [operário] labourer.

Sérvia ['sɛxvja] *n* Serbia.

serviçal [sexvi'saw] (*pl* -ais) ⬦ *adj* [prestativo] obliging. ⬦ *mf* [criado] servant.

serviço [sex'visu] *m* **-1.** [ger] service; **~ de bordo** ship's roster; **~ de informações** information service. **- 2.** [trabalho, local de trabalho] work; **prestar ~ s** [trabalhar] to render services; [fazer favores] to help out; **~ social** social services *(pl).* **- 3.** [iguarias] catering. **- 4.** *loc*: **não brincar em ~** [ser eficiente] to be a stickler; [não desperdiçar oportunidade] to not miss an opportunity.

➥ **de serviço** *loc adj* [entrada, elevador] tradesmen's *(antes de subst).*

servido, da [sex'vidu, da] *adj* **-1.** [que se serve] served. **- 2.** [provido]: **bem ~ de** well-supplied with.

servil [sex'viw] (*pl* -is) *adj* [subserviente]: **~ (a)** servile (to).

servir [sex'vi(x)] ⬦ *vt* **-1.** [jantar, bebida] to serve; **pedi para o garçom nos ~ duas cervejas** I asked the waiter to bring us a couple of beers; **~ algo a alguém**, **~ alguém de algo** to serve sthg to sb, to serve sb with sthg. **- 2.** [ajudar] to help. ⬦ *vi* **-1.** [ger] to serve. **- 2.** [prestar serviço]: **~ a** to serve. **- 3.** [prestar, ser útil] to be of use. **- 4.** [ser adequado] to be good; **qualquer trem serve** any train will do; **não ~ para algo** to be no good for. **- 5.** [caber] to fit. **- 6.** [fazer as vezes de]: **~ de algo** to act as. **- 7.** [ser apto] to be fit.

➥ **servir-se** *vp* [de comida, bebida]: **~ -se (de)** to help o.s. (to).

servo, va ['sɛxvu, va] *m, f* **-1.** [escravo] slave. **- 2.** [criado] servant.

SESC (*abrev de* Serviço Social do Comércio) *m Brazilian body providing social, sport and cultural facilities to people working in the general business sector.*

sessão [se'sãw] (*pl* -ões) *f* -**1**. [ger] session. -**2**. *CINE* performance.

sessenta [se'sẽnta] *num* sixty; **os anos** ~ the sixties; *veja também* **seis**.

sessões [se'sõjʃ] *pl* ▷ **sessão**.

sesta ['sɛʃta] *f* siesta, afternoon nap.

set. (*abrev de* setembro) Sept.

set ['sɛtʃi] *m ESP* set.

seta ['sɛta] *f* arrow.

sete ['sɛtʃi] *num* seven; **pintar o** ~ *fig* to get up to mischief; *veja também* **seis**.

setecentos, tas [sɛtʃi'sẽntuʃ, taʃ] *num* seven hundred; *veja também* **seis**.

setembro [se'tẽnbru] *m* September; **em** ~, **no mês de** ~ in September/in the month of September; **em** ~ **do ano que vem/do ano passado** in September next year/last year; **em meados de** ~ in mid-September; **dia primeiro/dois/ seis de** ~ first/second/sixth of September; **no início/fim de** ~ at the beginning/end of September.

setenta [se'tẽnta] *num* seventy; **os anos** ~ the seventies; *veja também* **seis**.

sétimo, ma ['sɛtʃimu, ma] *num* seventh; **a sétima parte** the seventh part.

setor [se'to(x)] (*pl* -es) *m* -**1**. [ger] sector. -**2**. [de repartição, estabelecimento] section.

seu, sua ['sew, 'sua] <> *adj* -**1**. [dele] his; [dela] her; [de você, vocês] your; [deles, delas] their; **ela trouxe o** ~ **carro** she brought her car; **onde estacionou a sua moto?** where did you park your motorcycle? -**2**. [de coisa, animal: singular] its; **o cachorro foi para o seu canil** the dog went into its kennel -**3**. [de coisa, animal: plural] their. <> *pron:* **o** ~ /**a sua** [dele] his; [dela] hers; [deles, delas] theirs; [de coisa, animal: singular] its; [de coisa, animal: plural] theirs; **um amigo** ~ a friend of his/hers; **os** ~ **s** [a família de cada um] his/her etc. family. <> *m*, *f*-**1**. *pej:* **como vai,** ~ **Pedro?** how are you, mister Pedro?; ~ **estúpido!** you fool!; ~ **s irresponsáveis!** you irresponsible lot! -**2**. [com malícia]: ~ **malandro!** you cheeky one!, cheeky thing!; **sua danadinha!** you rotter!, rotten thing!

Seul [se'uw] *n* Seoul.

seus [sewʃ] ▷ **seu**.

severidade [severi'dadʒi] *f* -**1**. [ger] severity. -**2**. [com filho] strictness.

severo, ra [se'vɛru, ra] *adj* -**1**. [castigo] severe. -**2**. [pessoa] strict.

sex. (*abrev de* sexta-feira) *f* Fri.

sexagenário, ria [seksaʒe'narjo, rja] <> *adj:* **ser** ~ to be a sexagenarian, to be in one's sixties. <> *m*, *f* sexagenarian.

sexagésimo, ma [seksa'ʒɛzimu, ma] *num* sixtieth.

sexo ['sɛksu] *m* sex.

sexta ['seʃta] *f* ▷ **sexto**.

sexta-feira [ˌseʃta'fejra] (*pl* sextas-feiras) *f* Friday; *veja também* **sábado**.
> **Sexta-Feira Santa** *f* Good Friday.

sexto, ta ['seʃtu, ta] *num* sixth; **a sexta parte** the sixth part.
> **sexta** *f* [sexta-feira] Friday.

sexual [sek'swaw] (*pl* -ais) *adj* -**1**. [ger] sexual. -**2**. [educação, vida] sex (*antes de subst*).

sexy ['sɛksi] *adj* sexy.

SFH (*abrev de* Sistema Financeiro de Habitação) *m Brazilian housing credit advisory service.*

shareware [ʃari'wari] (*pl* -s) *m COMPUT* shareware.

shopping ['ʃopĩŋ] *m* shopping centre *UK*, shopping mall *US*.

short ['ʃɔxtʃi] *m* shorts (*pl*).

show ['ʃow] *m* -**1**. [espetáculo] show; **ser/ estar um** ~ *fig* to be spectacular. -**2**. *fig* [atuação brilhante]: **dar um** ~ **(de algo)** to give a brilliant performance (of sthg).

Sibéria [si'bɛrja] *n:* **(a)** ~ Siberia.

Sicília [si'silja] *n* Sicily.

siderúrgico, ca [side'ruxʒiku, ka] *adj* iron and steel (*antes de sust*).
> **siderúrgica** *f* [usina] steelworks (*sg*).

sidra ['sidra] *f* cider.

sifão [si'fãw] (*pl* -ões) *m* -**1**. [tubo] siphon. -**2**. [de aparelho sanitário] U-bend. -**3**. [garrafa] soda siphon.

sífilis ['sifiliʃ] *f inv* syphilis.

sifões [si'fõjʃ] *pl* ▷ **sifão**.

sigilo [si'ʒilu] *m* secrecy.

sigiloso, osa [siʒi'lozu, ɔza] *adj* secret.

sigla ['sigla] *f* -**1**. [abreviatura] acronym. -**2**. [sinal] initial.

significado [signifi'kadu, da] *m* [sentido] meaning.

significar [signifi'ka(x)] <> *vt* -**1**. [ger] to mean. -**2**. [indicar] to signify. <> *vi* [ter importância] to mean.

significativo, va [signifika'tʃivu, va] *adj* significant.

signo ['signu] *m* sign.

sílaba ['silaba] *f* syllable.

silenciar [silẽn'sja(x)] <> *vt* -**1**. [calar] to silence. -**2**. [omitir] to conceal. <> *vi* [calar-se] to be quiet.

silêncio [si'lẽnsju] *m* silence; **ficar em** ~ to remain silent.

silencioso, osa [silẽn'sjozu, ɔza] *adj* silent.

silhueta [si'ʎwetal *f* -1. [ger] silhouette. -2. [corpo] outline.

silício [si'lisju] *m* silicon.

silicone [sili'koni] *m* silicone.

silo ['silu] *m* silo.

silvar [siw'va(x)] *vi* -1. [ger] to hiss. -2. [vento] to whistle.

silvestre [siw'vɛ∫tri] *adj* wild.

sim ['sĩ] *adv* yes; **acho** OU **creio que** ~ I think OU believe so; **dizer que** ~ to say yes; **quero**, ~ yes, I'd like to; **vou**, ~ yes, I'm going.

simbólico, ca [sĩn'bɔliku, ka] *adj* symbolic.

simbolizar [sĩnboli'za(x)] *vt* to symbolize.

símbolo ['sĩnbolu] *m* -1. [ger] symbol. -2. [insígnia] emblem.

simetria [sime'tria] *f* symmetry.

simétrico, ca [si'mɛtriku, ka] *adj* symmetrical.

similar [simi'la(x)] (*pl* -es) *adj*: ~ (a) similar (to).

similitude [simili'tudʒi] *f* similitude.

simpatia [sĩnpa't∫ia] *f* -1. [qualidade] warmth. -2. [atração - por outrem, lugar] liking; **sentir** ~ **por alguém** to like sb. -3. [pessoa]: **ser uma** ~ to be friendly. -4. [solidariedade] sympathy. -5. [espírit] charm.

simpático, ca [sĩn'pat∫iku, ka] *adj* -1. [pessoa - atraente] pleasant; [- amável] nice. -2. [agradável] pleasant. -3. [favorável]: ~ **a algo/alguém** favourable towards sthg/sb. -4. ANAT sympathetic.

simpatizante [sĩnpat∫i'zãnt∫i] *adj*: ~ **com** sympathetic towards.

simpatizar [sĩnpat∫i'za(x)] *vi*: ~ **com alguém/algo** to like sb/sthg; ~ **com uma causa** to sympathize with a cause.

simples ['sĩnpli∫] <> *adj* -1. [ger] simple. -2. (*antes de subst*) [mero] mere; [único] single. <> *adv* simply.

simplesmente [sĩnpli∫'mẽnt∫i] *adv* simply.

simplicidade [sĩnplisi'dadʒi] *f* simplicity.

simplificar [sĩnplifi'ka(x)] *vt* to simplify.

simplório, ria [sĩn'plɔrju, rja] *adj* simple.

simular [simu'la(x)] *vt* -1. [combate, salvamento] to simulate. -2. [sentimento, desmaio] to feign. -3. [animal, vozes] to imitate.

simultâneo, nea [simuw'tãnju, nja] *adj*: ~ (a OU com) simultaneous (with).

sina ['sina] *f* fate.

sinagoga [sina'gɔga] *f* synagogue.

sinal [si'naw] (*pl* -ais) *m* -1. [ger] sign; **fazer um** ~ **(para alguém)** to signal (to sb); **em** ~ **de** as a sign of. -2. [símbolo] signal; ~ **de pontuação** punctuation mark; ~ **de mais/menos** plus/minus sign. -3. TELEC tone; ~ **de discar** dialling tone; **dar** ~ **(de discar)** to give the (dialling) tone. -5. AUTO: ~ **(luminoso de tráfego)** traffic lights (*pl*); ~ **verde** green light; **avançar o** ~ to jump the lights. -6. [pinta] mole; [de nascença] birthmark. -7. COM deposit.
por sinal *loc adv* -1. [a propósito] by the way. -2. [aliás] besides.

sinalização [sinaliza'sãw] *f* -1. [sinais de tráfego - AUTO] traffic signs (*pl*); [- FERRO] signals (*pl*). -2. [indicação em estrada *etc.*] road sign.

sinalizar [sinali'za(x)] <> *vt* [avenida, estrada] to signpost. <> *vi* [pessoa] to signal.

sinceridade [sĩnseri'dadʒi] *f* sincerity.

sincero, ra [sĩn'sɛru, ra] *adj* sincere.

sincopado, da [sĩnko'padu, da] *adj* MÚS syncopated.

sincronizar [sĩnkroni'za(x)] *vt* -1. [combinar] to synchronize. -2. CINE to sync.

sindical [sĩndʒi'kaw] (*pl* -ais) *adj* trade union (*antes de subst*).

sindicalista [sĩndʒika'li∫ta] <> *adj* trade union (*antes de subst*). <> *mf* trade unionist.

sindicato [sĩndʒi'katu] *m* -1. [de profissionais] trade union. -2. [financeiro] syndicate.

síndico, ca [ˈsĩndʒiku, ka] *m,f* -1. [de prédio] residents' representative. -2. [de falência] receiver. -3. [de inquérito] leader.

síndrome ['sĩndromi] *f* syndrome; ~ **de abstinência** withdrawal symptoms (*pl*).

sinfonia [sĩnfo'nia] *f* symphony.

sinfônico, ca [sĩn'foniku, ka] *adj* symphonic.
sinfônica *f* [orquestra] symphonic orchestra.

singelo, la [sĩn'ʒɛlu, la] *adj* simple.

singular [sĩŋgu'la(x)] (*pl* -es) <> *adj* -1. [ger] singular. -2. [peculiar] strange. <> *m* GRAM singular.

sinistro, tra [si'ni∫tru, tra] *adj* sinister.
sinistro *m* -1. [acidente] disaster. -2. [dano] damage.

sino ['sinu] *m* bell.

sinônimo, ma [si'nonimu, ma] *adj* synonymous.
sinônimo *m* synonym.

sinopse [si'nɔpsi] *f* synopsis.

síntese ['sĩntezi] *f* -1. [ger] synthesis. -2. [resumo] summary; **em** ~ in short.

sintético, ca [sĩn'tɛtʃiku, ka] *adj* **-1.** [artificial] synthetic. **-2.** [conciso] concise.

sintetizador [sĩntetʃiza'do(x)] *m* synthesizer.

sintetizar [sĩntetʃi'za(x)] *vt* **-1.** [resumir] to summarize. **-2.** QUÍM to synthesize.

sintoma [sĩn'toma] *m* **-1.** MED symptom. **-2.** *fig* [indício] sign.

sintomático, ca [sĩnto'matʃiku, ka] *adj* symptomatic.

sinuca [si'nuka] *f* ESP snooker.

sinuoso, osa [si'nwozu, ɔza] *adj* **-1.** [linha] wavy. **-2.** [estrada, rio] meandering. **-3.** [recorte] wavy.

sionismo [sjo'niʒmu] *m* Zionism.

sirene [si'reni] *f* siren.

siri [si'ri] *m* crab; **casquinha de ~** CULIN *stuffed crab shells.*

Síria ['sirja] *n* Syria.

sísmico, ca ['siʒmiku, ka] *adj* seismic.

siso ['sizul] *m* **-1.** [juízo] wisdom. **-2.** [dente]: **(dente de) ~** wisdom tooth.

sistema [sij'tema] *m* **-1.** [ger] system; **~ nervoso** nervous system; **~ solar** solar system; **~ operacional** COMPUT operating system. **-2.** [maneira] method.

sistemático, ca [sij'te'matʃiku, ka] *adj* systematic.

sistematizar [sij'tematʃi'za(x)] *vt* to systematize.

sisudo, da [si'zudu, da] *adj* wise.

site ['sajtʃi] (*pl* **-s**) *m* COMPUT site.

sitiar [si'tʃja(x)] *vt* **-1.** [cercar] to besiege. **-2.** [assediar] to harrass.

sítio ['sitʃju] *m* **-1.** [propriedade] farm. **-2.** MIL siege; **em estado de ~** under siege.

situação [sitwa'sãw] (*pl* **-ões**) *f* **-1.** [ger] situation. **-2.** [localização] position.

situado, da [si'twadu, da] *adj* situated.

situar [si'twa(x)] *vt* to place.

➡ situar-se *vp* **-1.** [localizar-se - casa, filme] to be located; [- pessoa] to place o.s.; **tenho que me ~ para saber que rua seguir** I have to get my bearings in order to know which street to take. **-2.** [classificar-se] to be placed. **-3.** [em assunto, questão] to take a position.

skate [ij'kejtʃi] *m* **-1.** [esporte] skateboarding. **-2.** [prancha] skateboard.

slide [iʒ'lajdʒi] *m* slide, transparency.

slogan [iʒ'logãn] *m* slogan.

smoking [iʒ'mokĩŋ] *m* dinner jacket.

SNI (*abrev de* Serviço Nacional de Informações) *m Brazilian information service concerned particularly with state security*, ≃ MI5 *UK*, ≃ CIA *US*.

só ['sɔ] <> *adj* **-1.** [sozinho] alone; **a ~ s** alone. **-2.** [solitário] lonely. **-3.** [único] single. <> *adv* [somente] only.

SO (*abrev de* Sudoeste) *m* SW.

soalho ['swaʎu] *m* = assoalho.

soar ['swa(x)] <> *vi* **-1.** [ger] to sound. **-2.** [ser pronunciado] to be voiced. **-3.** [hora] to strike. <> *vt* [suj: horas] to strike.

sob ['sobi] *prep* under; **~ esse aspecto** from that perspective.

soberania [sobera'nia] *f* **-1.** [de nação] sovereignty. **-2.** *fig* [superioridade] supremacy.

soberano, na [sobe'rãnu, na] <> *adj* **-1.** [independente] sovereign. **-2.** [poderoso] powerful. **-3.** [supremo] supreme. **-4.** [altivo] haughty. <> *m, f* [monarca] sovereign.

soberbo, ba [so'bexbu, ba] *adj* **-1.** [arrogante] arrogant. **-2.** [magnífico] magnificent.

sobra ['sɔbra] *f* leftover; **ter algo de ~** to have sthg spare.

➡ sobras *fpl* leftovers.

sobrado [so'bradul] *m* floor.

sobrancelha [sobrãn'seʎa] *f* eyebrow.

sobrar [so'bra(x)] *vi* **-1.** [ger]: **~ to be left over**; **me sobra tempo para ir ao cinema** I have some free time to go to the cinema; **o médico examinou duas crianças, sobrou uma** the doctor examined two children, there was one still left; **isso dá e sobra** that is more than enough. **-2.** [ficar de fora] to be left out.

sobre ['sobri] *prep* **-1.** [ger] on. **-2.** [por cima de] over. **-3.** [a respeito de] about.

sobreaviso [sobrja'vizul] *m*: **estar/ficar de ~** to be on the alert.

sobrecarregar [sobrekaxe'ga(x)] *vt* **-1.** [com carga] to overload. **-2.** [pessoa] to overburden.

sobreloja [sobre'lɔʒa] *f* mezzanine.

sobremesa [sobre'meza] *f* dessert; **de ~** for dessert.

sobrenatural [ˌsobrenatu'raw] (*pl* **-ais**) *adj* supernatural.

sobrenome [ˌsobri'nɔmi] *m* surname.

sobrepor [sobre'po(x)] *vt* **-1.** [pôr em cima]: **~ algo a algo** to put sthg on top of sthg. **-2.** *fig* [antepor]: **~ algo a algo** to put sthg before sthg.

➡ sobrepor-se *vp* **-1.** [pôr-se em cima] to be put on top. **-2.** *fig* [antepor-se] to come before. **-3.** *fig* [a críticas] to overcome.

sobreposto, ta [sobre'poʃtu, ta] <> *pp* ▷ **sobrepor**. <> *adj* [posto em cima]: **~ a** placed on top of.

sobrepujar [sobrepu'ʒa(x)] *vt* **-1.** [ger] to overcome. **-2.** [ser superior a]: **~ algo/ /alguém (em algo)** to outdo sthg/s.o. (in sthg).

sobressalente [sobresa'lẽntʃi] <> adj spare. <> m spare.

sobressaltado, da [sobresaw'tadu, da] adj -1. [assustado] startled; **acordar** ~ to wake up with a start. -2. [apreensivo] worried.

sobressaltar [sobresaw'ta(x)] vt -1. [assustar] to startle. -2. [inquietar] to worry. ➥ **sobressaltar-se** vp -1. [assustar-se] to be startled. -2. [inquietar-se] to worry.

sobressalto [sobre'sawtul m -1. [ger] start. -2. [inquietação] concern.

sobretaxa [ˌsobre'taʃa] f surcharge.

sobretudo [sobre'tudu] <> m overcoat. <> adv especially.

sobrevivência [sobrevi'vẽsja] f: ~ (a) survival (from).

sobrevivente [sobrevi'vẽntʃi] <> adj surviving. <> mf survivor.

sobreviver [sobrevi've(x)] vi: ~ (a algo/ alguém) to survive (sthg/s.o.).

sobrevoar [sobre'vwa(x)] vt to fly over.

sobriedade [sobrje'dadʒi] f -1. [moderação] moderation. -2. [ausência de embriaguez] sobriety.

sobrinho, nha [so'briɲu, ɲal m, f nephew (f niece).

sóbrio, bria [ˈsɔbrju, brja] adj -1. [ger] sober. -2. [moderado]: ~ **(em)** moderate (in).

socar [so'ka(x)] vt -1. [dar socos em] to punch. -2. [esmagar] to crush. -3. [calcar] to grind. -4. [amassar] to knead. -5. [meter] to chuck.

social [so'sjaw] (pl **-ais**) adj -1. [ger] social. -2. [relativo a sócios] members' (antes de subst). -3. [via de acesso] front (antes de subst). -4. [banheiro] guest (antes de subst). -5. [camisa] dress.

socialdemocrata [so,sjawdemo'krata] <> adj social democratic. <> mf social democrat.

socialismo [sosja'liʒmul m socialism.

socialista [sosja'liʃta] <> adj socialist. <> mf socialist.

socializar [sosjali'za(x)] vt to socialize.

sociável [so'sjavew] (pl **-eis**) adj sociable.

sociedade [sosje'dadʒi] f -1. [ger] society; **a alta** ~ high society; **Sociedade Protetora dos Animais** society for the protection of animals, ≃ RSPCA **UK**. -2. [COM - empresa] company; [- entre sócios] partnership; ~ **anônima** limited company. -3. [parceria] partnership.

sócio, cia [ˈsɔsju, sjal m, f -1. [ger] partner. -2. [membro] member.

sociologia [sosjolo'ʒial f sociology.

sociólogo, ga [so'sjɔlogu, gal m, f sociologist.

sociopolítico, ca [sosjopo'litʃiku, kal (mpl **-s**, fpl **-s**) adj socio-political.

soco [ˈsokul m punch; **dar um** ~ **em al-go/alguém** to punch sthg/sb.

socorrer [soko'xe(x)] vt to rescue.

socorro [so'koxul m rescue; **equipe de** ~ rescue team; **pedir** ~ to ask for help; **socorro!** help!; **primeiros** ~ s first aid (sg).

soda [ˈsɔdal f -1. [bebida] soda. -2. [substância]: ~ **cáustica** caustic soda.

sódio [ˈsɔdʒjul m sodium.

sofá [so'fal m sofa.

sofá-cama [so,fa'kãmal (pl **sofás-camas**) m sofa bed.

Sófia [ˈsɔfjal n Sofia.

sofisticado, da [sofiʃtʃi'kadu, dal adj -1. [requintado] sophisticated. -2. [aprimorado] fancy. -3. [afetado] refined.

sofredor, ra [sofre'do(x), ral <> adj suffering. <> m, f [pessoa] sufferer.

sôfrego, ga [ˈsofregu, gal adj -1. [ávido] eager. -2. [ao comer, beber] greedy. -3. [impaciente] impatient; **o pai aguardava** ~ **notícias sobre o filho** the father waited impatiently for news of his son.

sofrer [so'fre(x)] <> vt -1. [ger] to suffer. -2. [suportar] to bear. -3. [receber] to undergo. <> vi [padecer] to suffer; ~ **de** MED to suffer from.

sofrido, da [so'fridu, dal adj long-suffering.

sofrimento [sofri'mẽntul m suffering.

soft [ˈsoftʃil, **software** [sof'twe(x)] m COMPUT software.

sogro, gra [sogru, gral m, f father-in-law (f mother-in-law).

sóis [ˈsɔjʃl pl ▷ **sol**.

soja [ˈsɔʒal f soya.

sol [ˈsɔwl (pl **sóis**) m -1. [ger] sun; **fazer** ~ to be sunny; **tomar (banho de)** ~ to sunbathe; **ao** ~ in the sun; **tapar o** ~ **com a peneira** to hide the truth. -2. MÚS [nota] soh, sol.

sola [ˈsɔlal f -1. [de sapato] sole. -2. ANAT: ~ **do pé** sole of the foot.

solar [so'la(x)] (pl **-es**) <> adj solar. <> m [moradia] manor house. <> vt [sapato] to sole. <> vi -1. [bolo] to fail to rise. -2. MÚS to perform a solo.

solda [ˈsowdal f -1. [substância] solder. -2. [soldadura] weld.

soldado [sow'dadul mf -1. MIL soldier. -2. [defensor] defender.

soldador, ra [sowda'do(x), ral m, f welder.

soldar [sow'da(x)] vt to weld.

soldo [ˈsowdul m MIL pay.

soleira [so'lejral f -1. [de porta] threshold. -2. [de ponte] foundation.

solene [so'lenɪ] *adj* solemn.

solenemente [soleni'mẽntʃi] *adv* solemnly.

solenidade [soleni'dadʒi] *f* -1. [qualidade] solemnity. -2. [cerimônia] ceremony.

soletrar [sole'tra(x)] *vt* -1. [letras] to spell. -2. [ler devagar] to read out slowly.

solicitação [solisita'sãw] (*pl* -ões) *f* [pedido] request.
◆ **solicitações** *fpl* [apelo] appeal (*sg*).

solicitar [solisi'ta(x)] *vt* -1. [pedir] to request; ~ **algo a alguém** to ask sb for sthg. -2. [requerer] to apply for. -3. [atenção, amizade] to seek.

solícito, ta [so'lisitu, ta] *adj* helpful.

solidão [soli'dãw] *f* -1. [isolamento] solitude. -2. [ermo] desolation. -3. [sentimento] loneliness.

solidariedade [solidarje'dadʒi] *f* solidarity.

solidário, ria [soli'darju, rja] *adj* -1. [na dor] united; **mostrar-se** ~ to show one's solidarity; **ser** ~ **com** to stand by. -2. [simpático]: **ser** ~ **a** to be sympathetic to.

solidificar [solidʒifi'ka(x)] *vt* -1. [fisicamente] to solidify. -2. *fig* [laços, amizade] to strengthen.
◆ **solidificar-se** *vp* -1. [fisicamente] to set. -2. *fig* [laços, amizade] to become strong.

sólido, da ['sɔlidu, da] *adj* -1. [ger] solid. -2. [moralmente] strong. -3. *fig* [firmeza] strong; [- conhecimento] firm; [- argumento] sound.
◆ **sólido** *m* MAT solid.

solista [so'liʃta] *m* MÚS soloist.

solitário, ria [soli'tarju, rja] <> *adj* solitary. <> *m, f* [eremita] solitary person.
◆ **solitário** *m* [diamante] solitaire.
◆ **solitária** *f* -1. [cela] solitary (confinement) cell. -2. [verme] tapeworm.

solo ['sɔlu] *m* -1. [chão] ground. -2. MÚS solo.

soltar [sow'ta(x)] *vt* -1. [libertar] to release; ~ **os cachorros** *fig* to lash out. -2. [desatar] to untie. -3. [afrouxar] to loosen. -4. [largar] to let go. -5. [deixar cair (das mãos)] to drop. -6. [emitir] to let out. -7. [pronunciar] to utter. -8. [lançar] to let off.
◆ **soltar-se** *vp* [desprender-se]: ~**-se (de algo)** to free o.s. (from sthg).

solteira [sow'tejra] *f* ▷ **solteiro**.

solteirão, rona [sowtej'rãw, rona] (*mpl* -ões, *fpl* -s) *m, f* bachelor (*f* spinster).

solteiro, ra [sow'tejru, ra] *adj* unmarried, single.

solteirona [sowtej'rona] *f* ▷ **solteirão**.

solto, ta ['sowtu, ta] <> *pp* ▷ **soltar**. <> *adj* [ger] loose.
◆ **à solta** *loc adv* on the loose.

solução [solu'sãw] (*pl* -ões) *f* solution; ~ **de continuidade** interruption; **sem** ~ **de continuidade** without interruption; ~ **de limpeza** [para lentes de contato] cleansing solution.

soluçar [solu'sa(x)] *vi* -1. [chorar] to sob. -2. MED to hiccup.

solucionar [solusjo'na(x)] *vt* to resolve.

soluço [su'lusu] *m* -1. [choro] sob; **aos** ~**s** sobbing. -2. MED hiccup.

solúvel [so'luvew] (*pl* -eis) *adj* soluble.

solvente [sow'vẽntʃi] <> *adj* -1. [substância] soluble. -2. FIN [devedor] solvent. <> *m* [substância] solvent.

som ['sõ] (*pl* -ns) *m* -1. [ger] sound; **fazer um** ~ *fam* to make music; **ao** ~ **de** to the sound of. -2. [aparelho] hi-fi.

soma ['soma] *f* -1. [ger] sum. -2. *fig* [conjunto] combination.

Somália [so'malja] *n* Somalia.

somar [so'ma(x)] <> *vt* -1. [adicionar] to add; ~ **algo a algo** to add sthg to sthg. -2. [totalizar] to add up to. <> *vi* to add (up).
◆ **somar-se** *vp* to gather together.

sombra ['sõbra] *f* -1. [projeção] shadow; **fazer** ~ **a alguém** *fig* to put sb in the shade. -2. [área] shade; **à** ~ **de** in the shade of; *fig* [sob a proteção de] under the protection of. -3. *fig* [sinal] shadow; **sem** ~ **de dúvida** without a shadow of a doubt. -4. *fig* [anonimato] in the shade.

sombrinha [sõ'briɲa] *f* umbrella.

sombrio, bria [sõ'briw, bria] *adj* -1. [escuro] dark. -2. [triste] gloomy. -3. [carrancudo] grim.

somente [sɔ'mẽntʃi] *adv* only.

sonambulismo [sonãbu'liʒmu] *m* sleepwalking.

sonâmbulo, la [so'nãbulu, la] <> *adj* sleepwalking. <> *m, f* sleepwalker.

sonda ['sõda] *f* -1. MED probe. -2. MED [de alimentação] drip. -3. NÁUT depth finder. -4. TEC [para mineiração] bore. -5. TEC [petrolífera] drill. -6. METEOR weather balloon.
◆ **sonda espacial** *f* space probe.

sondagem [sõ'daʒẽ] (*pl* -ns) *f* -1. [com sonda - biliar] exploration; [- marítima, meteorológica] sounding; [- petrolífera] drilling. -2. [de opinião] survey.

sondar [sõ'da(x)] *vt* -1. [ger] to probe. -2. NÁUT to sound. -3. TEC [terreno] to bore. -4. TEC [petróleo] to drill. -5. METEOR [atmosfera] to take soundings of. **- 6.** [opinião] to survey. **-7. fig** [investigar] to fathom.

soneca [so'nɛka] *f* nap; **tirar uma ~** to take a nap.

sonegação [sonega'sãw] *f* **-1.** [ocultação] withholding; **~ de impostos** *ou* **fiscal** tax evasion. **-2.** [roubo] theft.

sonegador, ra [sonega'do(x), ra] ◇ *adj* [de impostos] fraudulent. ◇ *m, f* [de impostos] tax dodger.

sonegar [sone'ga(x)] *vt* **-1.** [dinheiro, bens] to conceal. **-2.** [impostos] to dodge. **-3.** [roubar] to steal. **- 4.** [informações] to withhold.

soneto [so'netu] *m* sonnet.

sonhador, ra [soɲa'do(x), ra] (*mpl* **-es**, *fpl* **-s**) ◇ *adj* dreaming. ◇ *m, f* dreamer.

sonhar [so'ɲa(x)] ◇ *vt* [ter sonho com] to dream. ◇ *vi* **-1.** [ter sonho] to dream; **~ com algo/alguém** to dream about sthg/sb. **-2.** [desejar]: **~ com algo** to dream of sthg; **~ em fazer algo** to dream of doing sthg.

sonho ['soɲu] *m* **-1.** [ger] dream. **-2.** *CU-LIN* doughnut.

sono ['sonu] *m* **-1.** [período] sleep. **-2.** [vontade de dormir]: **estar com** *ou* **sentir ~ to** be *ou* feel sleepy; **estar sem ~** not to be sleepy.

sonolento, ta [sono'lẽntu, ta] *adj* sleepy.

sonorizar [sonori'za(x)] *vt* **-1.** [filme] to make the soundtrack for. **-2.** [sala] to set up the sound for.

sonoro, ra [so'nɔru, ra] *adj* **-1.** [de som] resonant. **-2.** *GRAM* voiced.

sons [sõʃ] *pl* ⊳ **som**.

sonso, sa ['sõsu, sa] *adj* sly.

sopa ['sopa] *f* **-1.** *CULIN* soup. **-2.** *fam* [facilidade] easy life; **ser ~** to be a piece of cake.

sopapo [so'papu] *m* slap.

sopé [so'pɛ] *m* foot.

sopeira [so'pejra] *f* (soup) tureen.

soporífero, ra [sopo'riferu, ra] *adj* **-1.** [que faz dormir] soporific. **-2.** *fig* [chato] boring.

    ➡ **soporífero** *m* [substância] soporific.

soporífico [sopo'rifiku] = **soporífero**

soprano [so'prãnu] ◇ *adj* soprano (*antes de subst*). ◇ *mf* soprano.

soprar [so'pra(x)] ◇ *vt* **-1.** [com sopro] to blow. **-2.** *fig* [segredar] to whisper. ◇ *vi* [vento] to blow.

sopro ['soprul *m* **-1.** [ar] puff. **-2.** [som de vento] sigh; [- de fole] puff; [- de saxofone] soft sound; **instrumento de ~** wind instrument. **-3.** [aragem] breeze. **- 4.** *fig* [ânimo] breath.

soquete [so'kɛtʃi] *f* [meia] ankle sock.

sórdido, da ['sɔrdʒidu, da] *adj* **-1.** [imundo] squalid. **-2.** [torpe] sordid.

soro ['soru] *m* **-1.** *MED* serum. **-2.** [de leite] whey.

soropositivo, va [soropozi'tʃivu, va] ◇ *adj* seropositive. ◇ *m, f* seropositive person.

sorrateiro, ra [soxa'tejru, ra] *adj* stealthy.

sorridente [soxi'dẽntʃi] *adj* smiling.

sorrir [so'xi(x)] *vi* to smile; **~ (para)** to smile (at); [destino, fortuna *etc.*] to smile on.

sorriso [so'xizu] *m* smile; **dar um ~ (para alguém)** to smile (at sb).

sorte ['sɔxtʃi] *f* **-1.** [ventura] luck; **boa ~!** good luck!; **dar ~ (para alguém)** to bring (sb) luck; **estar com** *ou* **ter ~** to be lucky; **má ~** bad luck; **que ~!** what luck!; **de ~** [sortudo] lucky; **tirar a ~ grande** [na loteria] to hit the jackpot; [enriquecer] to become rich; [ser afortunado] to do the right thing. **-2.** [acaso] chance; **por ~** by chance. **-3.** [sina] fate. **- 4.** [situação] lot. **-5.** [maneira]: **de ~ que** in such a way that. **- 6.** [espécie] sort; **toda ~ de iguarias** all sorts of delicacies.

sortear [sox'tʃja(x)] *vt -***1.** [pessoa, bilhete] to draw lots for. **-2.** [rifar] to raffle.

sorteio [sox'teju] *m* **-1.** [de pessoa, bilhete] draw. **-2.** [rifa] raffle.

sortido, da [sox'tʃidu, da] *adj* **-1.** [abastecido] stocked. **-2.** [variado] assorted.

sortimento [soxtʃi'mẽntu] *m* [provisão] stock.

sortudo, da [sox'tudu, da] ◇ *adj* lucky. ◇ *m, f* lucky person.

sorver [sox've(x)] *vt* **-1.** [ger] to inhale. **-2.** [beber] to sip. **-3.** [absorver] to absorb.

sorvete [sox'vetʃi] *m* **-1.** [com leite] ice cream. **-2.** [sem leite] sorbet.

sorveteiro, ra [soxve'tejru, ra] *m, f* ice-cream man.

sorveteria [soxvete'ria] *f* ice-cream parlour.

sósia ['sɔzja] *mf* double.

soslaio [soʒ'laju] ➡ **de soslaio** *loc adv* sideways.

sossegado, da [sose'gadu, da] *adj* quiet.

sossegar [sose'ga(x)] *vt & vi* to calm down.

sossego [so'segu] *m* peace (and quiet).

sótão ['sɔtãw] (*pl* **-ãos**) *m* attic.

sotaque [so'taki] *m* accent.

soterrar [sote'xa(x)] *vt* to bury.

soturno, na [so'tuxnu, na] *adj* **-1.** [triste] sad. **-2.** [amedrontador] frightening.

soutien [su'tʃjã] *m* = sutiã.

sova ['sɔva] *f* -1. [amassamento - uva, cacau] crushing; [- de massa] keading. -2. [surra] beating.

sovaco [so'vaku] *m* armpit.

sovina [so'vina] <> *adj* miserly. <> *mf* miser.

sovinice [sovi'nisi] *f* meanness; **ser pura** ~ to be utterly mean.

sozinho, nha [sɔ'ziɲu, ɲal *adj* -1. [desacompanhado] alone. -2. [solitário] all alone. -3. [único] by itself. -4. [por si só] by myself/yourself/himself etc.

SP (*abrev de* Estado de São Paulo) *n* State of São Paulo.

spam ['ijpãm] (*pl* -s) *m* COMPUT spam.

SPC (*abrev de* Serviço de Proteção ao Crédito) *m* Brazilian service providing information on credit credit rating.

spot [iʃ'pɔt] *m* spotlight.

spray [iʃ'prej] *m* spray.

SQL (*abrev de* Structured Query Language) *f* SQL.

Sr. (*abrev de* senhor) *m* ≃ Mr.

Sra. (*abrev de* senhora) *f* ≃ Mrs.

SRF (*abrev de* Secretaria da Receita Federal) *f* department of the Brazilian ministry of finance responsible for taxes and customs and excise.

Srs. (*abrev de* senhores) *mpl* Messrs, Mr and Mrs.

srta. (*abrev de* senhorita) *f* ≃ Miss.

status [iʃ'tatus] *m* status.

STF (*abrev de* Supremo Tribunal Federal) *m* Brazilian supreme federal tribunal responsible for the enforcement of the constitution and also heading the judiciary.

STJ (*abrev de* Superior Tribunal de Justiça) *m* Brazilian higher court of justice.

strip-tease [iʃ,tripi'tʃizi] *m* striptease; **fazer um** ~ to do a striptease.

sua ['sua] ⊳ **seu**.

suado, da ['swadu, dal *adj* -1. [da suor] sweaty. -2. *fam fig* [difícil de obter] hard-earned.

suar ['swa(x)] <> *vt* -1. [transpirar] to sweat. -2. [roupa] to make sweaty. <> *vi* -1. [transpirar] to sweat; ~ **frio** to come out in a cold sweat. -2. [verter umidade] to sweat. -3. *fam fig* [esforçar-se]: ~ **por algo/para fazer algo** to sweat blood for sthg/to do sthg; **ela suou por esse emprego** she had to work hard for that job.

suas ['suaʃ] ⊳ **seu**.

suástica ['swaʃtʃika] *f* swastika.

suave ['swavil *adj* -1. [ger] mild. -2. [vinho, pele, cabelos] smooth. -3. [brisa, ritmo] gentle. -4. [cor] delicate. -5.

[música, tecido] soft. -6. [terno - pessoa] charming; [- carícia] gentle; [- voz] soft. -7. [leve - trabalho] light; [- vida] easy.

suavidade [swavi'dadʒi] *f* -1. [ger] mildness. -2. [de pele, cabelos] smoothness. -3. [de brisa, música, ritmo] gentleness. -4. [de tecido, cor, brisa, música] softness. -5. [ternura] charm.

suavizar [swavi'za(x)] *vt* -1. [abrandar] to tone down. -2. [amenizar] to ease. -3. [amaciar - pele, cabelo] to smooth; [- tecido] to soften.

➤ **suavizar-se** *vp* [amenizar-se] to ease.

subalimentado, da [subalimẽn'tadu, dal *adj* undernourished.

subalterno, na [subaw'tɛxnu, nal <> *adj* subordinate. <> *m, f* subordinate.

subconsciente [subkõn'sjẽntʃil <> *adj* subconscious. <> *m* subconscious.

subdesenvolvido, da [subdʒizĩnvow'vidu, dal <> *adj* -1. [não desenvolvido] underdeveloped. -2. *pej* [atrasado] moronic. <> *m, f pej* [pessoa] moron.

subdesenvolvimento [subdʒizĩnvowvi'mẽntul *m* underdevelopment.

subemprego [subẽn'pregul *m* -1. [trabalho] underpaid job. -2. [condição] underpaid work.

subentender [subẽntẽn'de(x)] *vt* to infer.

➤ **subentender-se** *vp* to be inferred; **subentende-se que ...** it can be inferred that ...

subentendido, da [subẽntẽn'dʒidu, dal *adj* inferred.

➤ **subentendido** *m* innuendo.

subestimar [subeʃtʃi'ma(x)] *vt* to underestimate.

subida [su'bidal *f* -1. [ato] climb. -2. [ladeira] slope. -3. [de preços] rise.

subir [su'bi(x)] <> *vt* -1. [galgar] to climb (up). -2. [ir para cima, percorrer] to go up. -3. [escalar] to climb, to scale. -4. [aumentar] to raise. -5. [ascender] to climb. -6. [voz] to raise. <> *vi* -1. [ger] to go up; ~ **a** *ou* **até** to go up to; ~ **em** [árvore] to climb (up); [telhado, cadeira] to climb onto; ~ **por** to go up; ~ **à cabeça** *fig* to go to one's head. -2. [ascender - balão, neblina, fumaça] to rise; [- elevador, teleférico] to go up; [- em ônibus] to get on. -3. [socialmente] to go up in the world; ~ **a/ de** to rise from; ~ **na vida** to get on in life. -4. [aumentar] to rise. -5. *fam* [embriagar] to go to one's head.

súbito, ta ['subitu, tal *adj* sudden.

➤ **súbito** *adv* suddenly; **de** ~ suddenly.

subjetividade [subʒetʃivi'dadʒi] *f* subjectivity.

subjetivo, va [subʒɛ'tʃivu, va] adj subjective.

subjugar [subʒu'ga(x)] vt -**1.** [derrotar] to overpower. -**2.** [dominar] to dominate. -**3.** [impor-se a] to supplant. -**4.** [moralmente] to subdue.

subjuntivo [subʒũn'tʃivu] m subjunctive.

sublime [su'blimi] adj sublime.

sublinhar [subli'ɲa(x)] vt -**1.** [palavras] to underline. -**2.** [enfatizar] to emphasize.

sublocar [sublo'ka(x)] vt to sublet.

submarino, na [subma'rinu, na] adj underwater.
→ **submarino** m submarine.

submergir [submex'ʒi(x)] vt & vi to submerge.

submeter [subme'te(x)] vt -**1.** [dominar] to subdue. -**2.** [para apreciação]: ~ algo a to submit sthg to. -**3.** [sujeitar]: ~ alguém/algo a algo to subject sb/sthg to sthg.
→ **submeter-se** vp -**1.** [render-se] to surrender. -**2.** [sujeitar-se]: ~ a algo to undergo sthg; ~ a alguém to submit to sb.

submissão [submi'sãw] f -**1.** [sujeição, obediência] submission. -**2.** [apatia] lack of determination.

submisso, sa [sub'misu, sa] adj submissive.

submundo [sub'mũndu] m underworld.

subnutrição [subnutri'sãw] f malnutrition.

subnutrido, da [subnu'tridu, da] adj malnourished.

subordinado, da [suboxdʒi'nadu, da] ◇ adj subordinate. ◇ m,f [subalterno] subordinate.

subordinar [suboxdʒi'na(x)] vt -**1.** [ger] to subordinate. -**2.** [sujeitar] to subject.
→ **subordinar-se** vp [sujeitar-se]: ~-se a algo/alguém to subject o.s. to sthg/sb.

subornar [subox'na(x)] vt to bribe.

suborno [su'boxnu] m bribe.

subproduto [subpro'dutu] m by-product.

sub-reptício, cia [subxrep'tʃisju, sja] adj surreptitious.

subscrever [subʃkre've(x)] vt -**1.** [assinar] to sign. -**2.** [aprovar] to subscribe to. -**3.** [arrecadar] to collect. -**4.** [ações] to subscribe to.

subscrito, ta [subʃ'kritu, ta] ◇ pp ▷ subscrever. ◇ adj undersigned. ◇ m, f undersigned.

subseqüente [subse'kwẽntʃi] adj subsequent; ~ (a) subsequent (to).

subserviência [subsexvjẽnsja] f subservience.

subserviente [subsex'vjẽntʃi] adj subservient, servile; ~ (a) subservient (towards).

subsidiar [subzi'dʒja(x)] vt to subsidize.

subsidiário, ria [subzi'dʒjarju, rja] adj subsidiary.
→ **subsidiária** f [empresa] subsidiary.

subsídio [sub'zidʒju] m -**1.** [contribuição] contribution. -**2.** [estatal] subsidy.
→ **subsídios** mpl [dados, contribuições] information (sg).

subsistência [subziʃ'tẽnsja] f [sustento, sobrevivência] subsistence.

subsistir [subziʃ'tʃi(x)] vi -**1.** [existir] to exist. -**2.** [persistir] to remain. -**3.** [sobreviver] to survive.

subsolo [sub'sɔlu] m -**1.** [da terra] subsoil. -**2.** [de prédio] basement.

substância [subʃ'tãnsja] f substance.

substancial [subʃtãn'sjaw] (pl -ais) ◇ adj substantial. ◇ m [essência] essence.

substantivo, va [subʃtãn'tʃivu, va] adj -**1.** [essencial] essential. -**2.** GRAM substantive.
→ **substantivo** m GRAM noun.

substituição [subʃtʃitwi'sãw] (pl -ões) f substitution, replacement.

substituir [subʃtʃi'twi(x)] vt to substitute, to replace.

substituto, ta [subʃtʃi'tutu, ta] ◇ adj substitute (antes de subst), replacement (antes de subst). ◇ m, f substitute, replacement.

subterrâneo, nea [subte'xãnju, nja] adj underground.

subtrair [subtra'i(x)] ◇ vt -**1.** [furtar] to steal. -**2.** [deduzir] to deduct. -**3.** MAT to subtract. ◇ vi MAT to subtract.

subumano, na [subju'mãnu, na] adj subhuman.

suburbano, na [subux'bãnu, na] ◇ adj -**1.** [do subúrbio] suburban. -**2.** pej [atrasado] backward. ◇ m, f -**1.** [morador] suburbanite. -**2.** pej [atrasado] moron.

subúrbio [su'buxbju] m suburb.

subvenção [subvẽn'sãw] (pl -ões) f subsidy.

subversivo, va [subvex'sivu, va] ◇ adj subversive. ◇ m, f [pessoa] subversive.

subverter [subvex'te(x)] vt -**1.** [desordenar] to subvert. -**2.** [agitar] to incite. -**3.** [arruinar] to upset.

sucção [suk'sãw] f suction.

suceder [suse'de(x)] vi -**1.** [acontecer] to happen. -**2.** [seguir-se a]: ~ a algo/alguém to follow (on from) sthg/sb.
→ **suceder-se** vp -**1.** [seguir-se]: sucedem-se os governantes, mas nada muda rulers come and go but nothing

changes. **- 2.** [repetir-se]: **os dias se sucediam e ele não regressava** day followed day and still he didn't return.

sucedido, da [suse'dʒidu, da] *m*: **vou lhe contar o ~** I'll tell you what happened.

sucessão [suse'sãw] *(pl* **-ões)** *f* succession.

sucessivo, va [suse'sivu, va] *adj* successive; **crimes ~ s** a succession of crimes.

sucesso [su'sɛsu] *m* **- 1.** [êxito] success; **com/sem ~** successfully/unsuccessfully. **- 2.** [música, filme] hit.

sucinto, ta [su'sĩtu, ta] *adj* succinct.

suco ['suku] *m* juice.

suculento, ta [suku'lẽtu, ta] *adj* succulent.

sucumbir [sukũ'bi(x)] *vi* **- 1.** [vergar]: **~ a algo** to yield to sthg. **- 2.** [morrer]: **~ (a algo)** to succumb (to sthg).

SUDAM (Superintendência do Desenvolvimento da Amazônia) *f body overseeing the use of resources for the development of the Amazon region.*

Sudão [su'dãw] *n* Sudan.

SUDENE *(abrev de* **Superintendência do Desenvolvimento do Nordeste)** *f body responsible for overseeing economic and financial incentives in northeastern Brazil.*

sudeste [su'dɛʃtʃi] <> *adj* south-east. <> *m* south-east.

súdito, ta ['sudʒitu, ta] *m, f* subject.

sudoeste [su'dwɛʃtʃi] <> *adj* southwest. <> *m* south-west.

Suécia ['swɛsja] *n* Sweden.

sueco, ca ['swɛku, ka] <> *adj* Swedish. <> *m, f* Swede.
➡ **sueco** *m* [língua] Swedish.

suéter ['swɛte(x)] *(pl* **-es)** *m ou f* sweater.

suficiente [sufi'sjẽtʃi] <> *adj* sufficient. <> *m*: **tenho o ~ até amanhã** I have enough until tomorrow.

suflê [su'fle] *m* soufflé.

sufocar [sufo'ka(x)] <> *vt* **- 1.** [asfixiar] to suffocate. **- 2.** *fig* [oprimir] to oppress. **- 3.** *fig* [debelar] to crush. <> *vi* [asfixiarse] to be stifled.

sufoco [su'foku] *m* **- 1.** [aflição] dread; **que ~!** how dreadful! **- 2.** [dificuldade] hassle; **deixar alguém no ~** to leave sb in the lurch.

sufrágio [su'fraʒju] *m* **- 1.** [voto] vote. **- 2.** [apoio] support.

sugar [su'ga(x)] *vt* **- 1.** [por sucção] to suck. **- 2.** *fig* [extorquir] to extort.

sugerir [suʒe'ri(x)] *vt* to suggest.

sugestão [suʒeʃ'tãw] *(pl* **-ões)** *f* **- 1.** [ger] suggestion; **dar uma ~** to make a suggestion. **- 2.** [evocação, insinuação] hint.

sugestionar [suʒeʃtʃjo'na(x)] *vt*: **~ algo a alguém** to inspire sb with sthg.

sugestivo, va [suʒeʃ'tʃivu, va] *adj* **- 1.** [evocativo] evocative. **- 2.** [insinuante] suggestive.

Suíça ['swisa] *n* Switzerland.

suíças ['swisaʃ] *fpl* sideburns.

suicida [swi'sida] <> *adj* suicidal. <> *mf* [pessoa] suicidal person.

suicidar-se [swisi'daxsi] *vp* to commit suicide.

suicídio [swisi'dʒju] *m* suicide.

suíço, ça ['swisu, sa] <> *adj* Swiss. <> *m, f* Swiss.

suingar [swĩ'ga(x)] *vi* to dance the swing.

suingue ['swĩgi] *m* swing.

suíno, na ['swinu, na] *adj* pig *(antes de subst).*
➡ **suíno** *m* [porco] pig.

suíte ['switʃi] *f* suite.

sujar [su'ʒa(x)] <> *vt* **- 1.** [tornar sujo] to dirty. **- 2.** *fig* [macular] to disgrace. <> *vi fam* [dar errado] to go wrong.
➡ **sujar-se** *vp* **- 1.** [tornar-se sujo] to get dirty. **- 2.** *fig* [macular-se] to disgrace o.s.

sujeira [su'ʒejra] *f* **- 1.** [coisa suja] dirt. **- 2.** [estado] dirtiness; **a sala estava uma ~ quando cheguei** the room was a dirty mess when I arrived. **- 3.** *fam* [bandalheira] dirty trick.

sujeitar [suʒej'ta(x)] *vt* [submeter]: **~ algo/alguém a algo** to subject sthg/sb to sthg.
➡ **sujeitar-se** *vp* [submeter-se]: **~-se a algo** to subject o.s. to sthg.

sujeito, ta [su'ʒejtu, ta] <> *adj*: **~ a** subject to. <> *m, f* person.
➡ **sujeito** *m GRAM* subject.

sujo, ja ['suʒu, ʒa] <> *adj* **- 1.** [imundo] dirty. **- 2.** *fig* [mau-caráter] dishonest. <> *m, f fig* [pessoa] dishonest person.

sul ['suw] <> *adj* southern. <> *m* [região] south; **ao ~ de** to the south of.

sulco [suw'kul] *m* furrow.

sulista [su'liʃta] <> *adj* southern. <> *mf* southerner.

suma ['suma] ➡ **em suma** *loc adv* in short.

sumamente [suma'mẽtʃi] *adv* [extremamente] extremely.

sumário, ria [su'marju, rja] *adj* **- 1.** [breve] brief. **- 2.** [julgamento] summary. **- 3.** [traje] skimpy.
➡ **sumário** *m* **- 1.** [resumo] summary. **- 2.** [no início de livro] table of contents. **- 3.** *JUR*: **~ de culpa** indictment.

sumiço [su'misu] *m* disappearance; **dar (um) ~ em** to do away with.

sumido, da [su'midu, da] *adj* -**1.** [desaparecido] vanished; **andar** ~ to have disappeared. -**2.** [voz] low. -**3.** [apagado] faint.

sumir [su'mi(x)] *vi* to disappear; ~ **com algo** to disappear with sthg.

sumo, ma ['sumu, ma] *adj* extreme; ~ **sacerdote** high priest.
→ **sumo** *m* [suco] juice.

sundae ['sãndej] *m* sundae.

sunga ['sũŋga] *f* [de banho] (swimming) trunks.

suntuoso, osa [sũn'twozu, ɔza] *adj* sumptuous.

suor ['swɔ(x)] (*pl* -**es**) *m* -**1.** [transpiração] sweat. -**2.** *fig* [trabalho]: **fiz esta casa com o meu próprio** ~ I built this house by the sweat of my brow.

super ['supe(x)] *fam* <> *adj* [ótimo] super. <> *interj* super!

superado, da [supe'radu, da] *adj* -**1.** [ultrapassado] outmoded, old-fashioned. -**2.** [resolvido] overcome.

superalimentar [superalimẽn'ta(x)] *vt* -**1.** [animais, pacientes] to overfeed. -**2.** [indústria, sistema] to supercharge.

superaquecimento [,superakesi'mẽntu] *m* overheating.

superar [supe'ra(x)] *vt* -**1.** [sobrepujar]: ~ **alguém (em algo)** to outdo sb (in sthg); ~ **o inimigo** to defeat an enemy; **superou a todos em velocidade** he surpassed everyone in terms of speed. -**2.** [recorde] to beat. -**3.** [expectativa, objetivos *etc.*] to exceed. -**4.** [ultrapassar] to surpass. -**5.** [resolver] to overcome.
→ **superar-se** *vp* -**1.** [melhorar]: ~-**se (em algo)** to excel o.s. (in sthg). -**2.** [exceder-se] to excel o.s.

superávit [supe'ravitʃi] *m* COM surplus.

supercílio [super'silju] *m* eyebrow.

superdotado, da [,supexdo'tadu, da] <> *adj* -**1.** [em inteligência] (exceptionally) gifted. -**2.** *fam* [sexualmente] well endowed. <> *m, f* [em inteligência] (exceptionally) gifted person.

superestimar [,superestʃi'ma(x)] *vt* to overestimate.

superficial [supexfi'sjaw] (*pl* -**ais**) *adj* superficial.

superficialidade [supexfisjali'dadʒi] *f* superficiality.

superfície [supex'fisji] *f* -**1.** [parte externa] surface. -**2.** [extensão] area.

supérfluo, lua [su'pɛxflu, lua] *adj* superfluous.
→ **supérfluo** *m* [gasto]: **vamos cortar o** ~ we're going to cut out what is superfluous.

super-homem [,super'ɔmẽ] (*pl* -**ns**) *m* superman.

superintendência [,superĩntẽn'dẽnsja] *f* [órgão] management.

superintendente [,superĩntẽn'dẽntʃi] *mf* manager.

superior [supe'rjo(x)] (*pl* -**es**) <> *adj* RELIG superior. <> *m, f* [em hierarquia] superior.
→ **superior** *adj* -**1.** [de cima] upper. -**2.** [mais alto] higher. -**3.** [maior] greater. -**4.** [melhor] better; ~ **a** better than. -**5.** [excelente] first class. -**6.** EDUC higher; **escola** ~ senior school; **curso** ~ degree course.

superioridade [superjori'dadʒi] *f* superiority.

superlativo, va [supexla'tʃivu] *adj* superlative. → **superlativo** *m* GRAM superlative.

superlotado, da [,supexlo'tadu, da] *adj*: ~ **(de)** overcrowded (with).

supermercado [,supexmex'kadu] *m* supermarket.

superpotência [,supexpo'tẽnsja] *f* superpower.

superpovoado, da [,supexpo'vwadu, da] *adj* overpopulated.

superprodução [,supexprodu'sãw] (*pl* -**ões**) *f* -**1.** ECON overproduction. -**2.** CINE mega-production.

supersônico, ca [,supex'soniku, ka] *adj* supersonic.

superstição [supexʃtʃi'sãw] (*pl* -**ões**) *f* superstition.

supersticioso, osa [supexʃtʃi'sjozu, ɔza] <> *adj* superstitious. <> *m, f* superstitious person.

supervisão [,supexvi'zãw] (*pl* -**ões**) *f* -**1.** [ato] supervision. -**2.** [instância] supervisory authority.

supervisionar [,supexvizjo'na(x)] *vt* to supervise.

supervisor, ra [,supexvi'zo(x), ra] *m, f* supervisor.

suplantar [suplãn'ta(x)] *vt* [sobrepujar]: ~ **algo/alguém (em algo)** to supplant sthg/sb (in sthg).

suplementar [suplemẽn'ta(x)] <> *adj* extra. <> *vt* -**1.** [fornecer] to provide. -**2.** [servir de suplemento a] to supplement.

suplemento [suple'mẽntu] *m* -**1.** [suprimento] supply. -**2.** [complemento] supplement; ~ **policial** police reinforcement. -**3.** JORN supplement.

súplica ['suplika] *f* plea.

suplicar [supli'ka(x)] <> *vt* to beg for. <> *vi* to plead.

suplício [su'plisju] *m* torture.

supor [su'po(x)] vt -1. [ger] to suppose.
-2. [pressupor] to presuppose.
→ **supor-se** vp to be assumed.

suportar [supox'ta(x)] vt -1. [sustentar] to
support. -2. [resistir a] to withstand. -3.
[tolerar] to bear.

suportável [supox'tavew] (pl -eis) adj
bearable.

suporte [su'poxtʃi] m support.

suposição [supozi'sãw] (pl -ões) f [conje-
tura] assumption.

suposto, osta [su'poʃtu, oʃta] <> pp
⊳ **supor**. <> adj supposed.
→ **suposto** m [pressuposto] assumption.

supremo, ma [su'premu, ma] adj -1.
[amor, perdão, tribunal] supreme. -2.
[qualidade] superior.
→ **Supremo** m: o Supremo the Supreme Court.

supressão [supre'sãw] (pl -ões) f -1. [cor-
te] cutback. -2. [eliminação] deletion.
-3. [abolição] abolition. -4. [omissão]
suppression.

suprimento [supri'mẽntu] m supply.

suprimir [supri'mi(x)] vt -1. [cortar] to
cut back. -2. [eliminar] to delete. -3.
[abolir] to abolish. -4. [omitir] to suppress.

suprir [su'pri(x)] vt -1. [prover]: ~ alguém de ou com algo to supply sb with
sthg. -2. [substituir]: ~ algo por algo to
substitute sthg with sthg. -3. [fazer as
vezes de] to replace. -4. [preencher] to
meet; ~ a falta de algo to make up for
the lack of sthg. -5. [perfazer] to make
up.

surdez [sux'deʒ] f deafness.

surdina [sux'dʒina] f MÚS mute.
→ **em surdina** loc adv on the quiet.

surdo, da ['suxdu, da] <> adj -1. MED
deaf. -2. [som] muffled. -3. [consoante]
voiceless. <> m, f [pessoa] deaf person.
→ **surdo** m MÚS [de bateria] kind of
drum.

surdo-mudo, surda-muda ['suxdu'-
mudu, 'suxda'mudal (mpl surdos-mudos,
fpl surdas-mudas) <> adj [pessoa] deaf
and dumb. <> m, f [pessoa] deaf mute.

surfar [sux'fa(x)] vi to surf.

surfe ['suxfi] m surfing.

surfista [sux'fiʃta] mf surfer.

surgimento [suxʒi'mẽntu] m emergence.

surgir [sux'ʒi(x)] vi -1. [aparecer] to
appear. -2. [sobrevir] to arise; ~ de to
come from.

surpreendente [surprjẽn'dẽntʃi] adj
surprising.

surpreender [surprjẽn'de(x)] <> vt -1.

[ger] to surprise. -2. [apanhar em flagran-
te]: ~ alguém (fazendo algo) to catch
sb (doing sthg). <> vi [causar espanto] to
be surprising.
→ **surpreender-se** vp [espantar-se]: ~
-se de/com algo to be amazed by/at
sthg.

surpreso, sa [sux'prezu, za] <> pp ⊳
surpreender. <> adj surprised.
→ **surpresa** f -1. [espanto] amazement.
-2. [imprevisto] surprise; **fazer uma surpresa para alguém** to give sb a surprise;
que surpresa! [em encontro casual] what a
surprise!; **ser uma surpresa** to be a
surprise; **de surpresa** by surprise. -3.
[presente] surprise.

surra ['suxa] f thrashing; **dar uma ~ em
alguém** to give sb a thrashing; **levar
uma ~ (de alguém)** to get a thrashing
(from sb).

surrar [su'xa(x)] vt -1. [espancar] to beat
up. -2. ESP to thrash. -3. [usar muito] to
wear out.

surrealista [suxea'liʃta] <> adj -1. ARTE
surrealist. -2. fig [fora do normal]
surreal. <> mf ARTE surrealist.

surtar [sur'ta(x)] vi fam to go berserk.

surtir [sux'tʃi(x)] <> vt [produzir] to
bring about; ~ efeito to be effective.
<> vi [funcionar] to work out.

surto ['suxtu] m -1. [irrupção] outburst.
-2. [de doença] outbreak. -3. [de progresso, industrialização] surge.

suscetível [suse'tʃivew] (pl -eis) adj -1.
[melindroso] sensitive. -2. [propenso]:
~ a susceptible to.

suscitar [susi'ta(x)] vt -1. [provocar] to
provoke. -2. [fazer surgir] to arouse. -3.
[despertar] to awaken.

suspeita [suʃ'pejta] f ⊳ suspeito.

suspeitar [suʃpej'ta(x)] <> vt [crer, su-
por]: ~ que to suspect (that). <> vi
[desconfiar]: ~ de alguém to suspect sb.

suspeito, ta [suʃ'pejtu, ta] <> adj -1.
[que desperta suspeita] suspicious. -2.
[de ser tendencioso]: **sou ~ para falar,
mas ...** I'm biased in saying this but ...
<> m, f [pessoa]: ~ (de algo) suspect (of
sthg).
→ **suspeita** f suspicion; **estar com suspeita de algo** to be suspected of having
sthg.

suspender [suʃpẽn'de(x)] vt -1. [ger] to
suspend. -2. [levantar] to lift up. -3.
[adiar] to postpone. -4. [encomenda] to
cancel.

suspensão [suʃpẽn'sãw] (pl -ões) f -1.
[ger] suspension. -2. [adiamento] postponement. -3. [de encomenda]
cancellation. -4. [de sanções] lifting.

suspense [suʃ'pɛ̃nsi] *m* suspense; **estamos assistindo um (filme de)** ~ we are watching a thriller; **fazer** ~ to create suspense.

suspenso, sa [suʃ'pɛ̃nsu, sa] <> *pp* ▷ **suspender**. <> *adj* -**1.** [ger] suspended. -**2.** [levantado] held up. -**3.** [adiado] postponed. -**4.** [encomenda] cancelled. -**5.** [sanções] lifted.

suspensórios [suʃpɛ̃n'sɔrjuʃ] *mpl* braces *UK*, suspenders *US*.

suspirar [suʃpi'ra(x)] *vi* to sigh.

suspiro [suʃ'piru] *m* -**1.** [aspiração] sigh. -**2.** *CULIN* meringue.

sussurrar [susu'xa(x)] <> *vt* & *vi* to whisper.

sussurro [su'suxu] *m* whisper.

sustentar [suʃtẽn'ta(x)] *vt* -**1.** [ger] to support. -**2.** [afirmar]: ~ **que** to maintain (that). -**3.** [defender] to uphold.
➡ **sustentar-se** *vp* -**1.** [ger] to support o.s.; ~-**se no ar** to hover. -**2.** [alimentar-se] to sustain o.s.

sustento [suʃ'tẽntu] *m* -**1.** [alimento] sustenance. -**2.** [manutenção] support.

susto ['suʃtu] *m* fright; **levar** *ou* **tomar um** ~ to get a fright.

sutiã [su'tʃjã] *m* bra.

sutil [su'tʃiw] (*pl* -**is**) *adj* subtle.

sutileza [sutʃi'leza] *f* subtlety.

sutilmente [sutʃiw'mẽntʃi] *adv* subtly.

suvenir [suve'ni(x)] *m* souvenir.

T

t, T *m* [letra] t, T.

tá ['ta] *fam* = **está**.

tabacaria [tabaka'ria] *f* tobacconist's.

tabaco [ta'baku] *m* tobacco.

tabefe [ta'bɛfi] *m fam* slap; **dar um** ~ **em alguém** to slap sb; **levar um** ~ **de alguém** to be slapped by sb.

tabela [ta'bɛla] *f* -**1.** [quadro] table. -**2.** [lista] list; ~ **de preços** price list. -**3.: por** ~ [indiretamente] indirectly. -**4.** *loc*: **estar caindo pelas** ~**s** [estar fatigado, adoentado] to feel out of sorts; [estar em más condições] to be in a bad way.

tabelado, da [tabe'ladu, da] *adj* -**1.** [produtos] price-controlled. -**2.** [preços] controlled. -**3.** [dados] listed.

tabelamento [tabela'mẽntu] *m* [controle de preços]: ~ **de preços** price control.

tabelar [tabe'la(x)] *vt* -**1.** [fixar o preço de] to set the price of. -**2.** [dados] to list.

tabelião, liã [tabe'ljãw, ljã] (*mpl* -**ães**, *fpl* -**s**) *m, f* notary public.

taberna [ta'bɛxna] *f* public house *UK*, tavern *US*.

tablado [ta'bladu] *m* -**1.** [palco] stage. -**2.** [palanque] stand. -**3.** [estrado] dais.

tablete [ta'blɛtʃi] *m* -**1.** [de chocolate] bar. -**2.** [de manteiga] pat. -**3.** [medicamento] tablet.

tablóide [ta'blɔjdʒi] *m* tabloid.

tabu [ta'bu] <> *adj* taboo. <> *m* taboo.

tábua ['tabwa] *f* -**1.** [de madeira] board; ~ **de passar roupa** ironing board. -**2.** [de mesa] leaf. -**3.** *MAT* table.

tabuleiro [tabu'lejru] *m* -**1.** [bandeja] tray. -**2.** *CULIN* baking tray. -**3.** [de jogo] board.

tabuleta [tabu'leta] *f* notice board.

taça ['tasa] *f* -**1.** [copo] glass. -**2.** [troféu] cup.

tacada [ta'kada] *f* -**1.** *ESP* strike. -**2.** *fig*: **de uma** ~ **só** [de uma só vez] in one go.

tacanho, nha [ta'kãɲu, ɲal *adj* -**1.** [baixo] short. -**2.** [mesquinho] mean. -**3.** *fig* [sem visão] obtuse.

tacha ['taʃa] *f* -**1.** [prego] tack. -**2.** [em roupa, cadeira] stud.

tachar [ta'ʃa(x)] *vt*: ~ **alguém/algo de algo** to brand sb/sth as sthg.

tachinha [ta'ʃiɲa] *f* drawing pin *UK*, thumbtack *US*.

tacho ['taʃu] *m* [recipiente] pan, dish.

tácito, ta ['tasitu, ta] *adj* [implícito] tacit.

taciturno, na [tasi'tuxnu, na] *adj* [introverso, sério] taciturn.

taco ['taku] *m* -**1.** [*ESP* - bilhar] cue; [- golfe] club; [- hóquei] stick; [- pólo] mallet. -**2.** [de assoalho] block.

tagarela [taga'rɛla] <> *adj* prattling, chattering. <> *mf* chatterbox.

Tailândia [taj'lãndʒja] *n* Thailand.

tailleur [taj'ɛ(x)] *m* (woman's) suit.

tainha [ta'iɲa] *f* mullet.

tais [tajʃ] *pl* ▷ **tal**.

Taiti [taj'tʃi] *n* Tahiti.

Taiwan [taj'wã] *n* Taiwan.

tal ['taw] (*pl* **tais**) <> *adj* -**1.** [ger] such; **eu nunca diria** ~ **coisa** I would never say such a thing; **não me misturo com tais pessoas** I don't mix with such people; **isso nunca teve** ~ **repercussão** this never had such an effect; **a dor foi** ~, **que desmaiei** the pain was such that I fainted. -**2.** [este, aquele]: **não existe** ~ **hotel** there is no such hotel; **a** ~ **respeito** on that subject; **o** ~ **vizinho**

that neighbour. **-3.** [valor indeterminado]: **na avenida** ~ in such and such street. **-4.** [introduz um exemplo ou uma enumeração]: ~ **como** such as. **-5.** [introduz uma comparação]: ~ **qual** just like; ~ **pai,** ~ **filho** like father, like son. ◇ *pron indef* [isto, aquilo]: **por** ~ for that reason. ◇ *mf*: **ele se acha o** ~ he thinks he's it.

➡ **que tal** *loc* [pedindo opinião]: **que** ~ ? what do you think?; **que** ~ **(tomarmos) um drinque?** what about (us having) a drink?

➡ **e tal** *loc*: **ele é simpático e** ~ **, mas ineficiente** he's nice and all that, but inefficient.

➡ **um tal de** *loc*: **um** ~ **de João** John what's-his-name.

➡ **a tal ponto que** *loc conj* such a point that.

➡ **de tal maneira que** *loc conj* in such a way that.

tala ['talal *f MED* splint.

talão [ta'lãw] (*pl* -ões) *m* **-1.** [bloco] book; ~ **de cheques** cheque book *UK*, check book *US*. **-2.** [canhoto] stub.

talco ['tawku] *m* **-1.** [material] talc. **-2.** [produto de higiene] talcum powder.

talento [ta'lẽntu] *m* **-1.** [aptidão] ability. **-2.** [pessoa talentosa] talented person.

talentoso, osa [talẽn'tozu, ɔza] *adj* talented.

talhar [ta'ʎa(x)] ◇ *vt* [madeira] to carve. ◇ *vi* [leite] to curdle.

talharim [taʎa'rĩ] (*pl* -ns) *m* tagliatelle.

talhe ['taʎi] *m* [de roupa] cut.

talher [ta'ʎɛ(x)] (*pl* -es) *m* place setting; ~ **es** cutlery (*sg*).

talho ['taʎu] *m* [corte] cut.

talo ['talu] *m BOT* stalk, stem.

talvez [taw'veʒ] *adv* maybe, perhaps; ~ **ele esteja certo** maybe he is right.

tamanco [ta'mãŋku] *m* clog.

tamanduá [tamãn'dwa] *m* anteater.

tamanho, nha [ta'mãɲu, ɲal *adj* **-1.** [tão grande]: **seu erro foi** ~ **que ele pediu desculpas** his mistake was so great he apologized. **-2.** [tão notável]: **ele é um** ~ **escritor** he is such a great author.

➡ **tamanho** *m* size; **em** ~ **natural** life-size, life-sized.

tamanho-família [ta,mãɲufa'milja] *adj inv* **-1.** [garrafa, caixa] family-size. **-2.** *fig* [casa, carro] family (*antes de subst*).

tâmara ['tãmara] *f* date.

tamarindo [tama'rĩndu] *m* tamarind.

também [tãn'bẽ] ◇ *adv* **-1.** [igualmente] too; **ele** ~ **é inteligente** he's intelligent, too, he too is intelligent; **quero um café – eu** ~ I want a coffee – so do I *ou* me too; **sou do Rio, e ele** ~ **é**

I'm from Rio, and so is he; **ela não viajou, e eu** ~ **não** she didn't go, and neither did I; **ele não fala inglês, e eu** ~ **não** he doesn't speak English, and neither do I. **-2.** [além disso] too. ◇ *interj* [não é de surpreender] hardly surprising!

tambor [tãn'bo(x)] (*pl* -es) *m* drum.

tamborim [tãnbo'rĩ] (*pl* -ns) *m* tambourine.

Tâmisa ['tãmiza] *n*: **o** (rio) ~ the (river) Thames.

tampa ['tãnpa] *f* **-1.** [de caixa, privada, panela] lid. **-2.** [de garrafa] cap.

tampado, da [tãn'padu, da] *adj*: **a panela está tampada** the saucepan is covered.

tampão [tãn'pãw] (*pl* -ões) *m* **-1.** [de pia, banheira] plug. **-2.** *MED* compress. **-3.** [vaginal] tampon. **-4.** [de poço, esgoto] bung.

tampar [tãn'pa(x)] *vt* **-1.** [com tampa - ger] to put a lid on; [- em garrafa] to put a top on. **-2.** [tapar] to cover.

tampinha [tãn'piɲa] *mf fam* [pessoa baixa] dumpy person.

tampo ['tãnpu] *m* **-1.** [de privada] seat, lid. **-2.** [de mesa] top.

tampouco [,tãn'poku] *adv*: **não foi à reunião e** ~ **justificou sua ausência** he didn't turn up at the meeting, nor did he justify his absence.

tanga ['tãŋga] *f* **-1.** [roupa indígena] loincloth. **-2.** [biquíni] G-string.

tanger [tãn'ʒe(x)] ◇ *vt* [instrumento] to play; [sinos] to ring. ◇ *vi* **-1.** [sinos] to ring. **-2.** [dizer respeito]: **no que tange a** with regard to, as regards.

tangerina [tãnʒe'rina] *f* tangerine.

tangível [tãn'ʒivew] (*pl* -eis) *adj fig* **-1.** [alcançável] attainable. **-2.** [real] tangible.

tanque ['tãŋki] *m* **-1.** *MIL* tank. **-2.** [de lavar roupa] washtub. **-3.** [reservatório] reservoir.

tanto, ta ['tãntu, ta] ◇ *adj* **-1.** [tão grande] so much; ~ **tempo** so much time. **-2.** [tão numeroso] so many; **ele tem trinta e** ~ **s anos** he is thirty something; **tanta gente** so many people. ◇ *pron* so much; **pode ficar com o lápis, já tenho** ~ **s** you can keep the pencil, I already have so many.

➡ **tanto** *adv* so much; **ela trabalha** ~ she works so much; ~ **quanto** as much as; ~ **... como** both ... and; **se** ~ if that.

➡ **tantas** *fpl*: **às tantas** the early hours of the morning.

➡ **e tanto** *loc adj*: **é um professor e** ~ he's an amazing teacher.

tecer

➼ **tanto que** *loc conj* so much so that.

➼ **tanto faz** *loc adv* it's all the same.

tão [tãw] *adv* so; ~ ... **quanto** as... as; ~ **logo** as soon as.

tão-só [tãw'sɔ] *adv* only.

tão-somente [tãosɔ'mẽtʃi] *adv* only.

tapa ['tapa] *m* [tabefe] slap; **no** ~ by force.

tapar [ta'pa(x)] *vt* -1. [ger] to cover. -2. [garrafa] to put the lid back on.

tapear [ta'pja(x)] *vt* [enganar] to fool.

tapeçaria [tapesa'ria] *f* -1. [tapete - de chão] rug; [- de parede] tapestry, wall hanging. -2. [loja] carpet shop. -3. [arte - de chão] rug-making; [- de parede] tapestry.

tapeceiro, ra [tape'sejru, ra] *m, f* -1. [vendedor] *seller of carpets and soft furnishings.* -2. [fabricante] *manufacturer of carpets and soft furnishings.*

tapete [ta'petʃi] *m* -1. [solto] rug; ~ **de banheiro** bathmat. -2. [fixo] carpet.

tapioca [ta'pjɔka] *f* tapioca.

tapume [ta'pumi] *m* -1. [cerca de sebe] hedge. -2. [anteparo de madeira] fence. -3. [parede divisória] partition.

taquicardia [takikax'dʒia] *f* palpitations (*pl*), tachycardia.

taquigrafia [takigra'fia] *f* shorthand *UK*, stenography *US*.

taquígrafo, fa [ta'kigrafu, fa] *m, f* shorthand typist *UK*, stenographer *US*.

tara ['tara] *f* PSIC mania.

tarado, da [ta'radu, da] ◇ *adj* -1. [desequilibrado] unbalanced. -2. [sexualmente] depraved. -3. *fam fig* [fascinado]: **ser** ~ **por** to be mad about. ◇ *m, f* [desequilibrado] maniac; ~ **(sexual)** (sexual) pervert.

tardar [tax'da(x)] ◇ *vt* [retardar] to put off. ◇ *vi* [demorar-se, vir tarde] to delay; ~ **a fazer algo** to take a long time to do sthg; **o mais** ~ at the latest.

tarde ['taxdʒi] ◇ *f* afternoon; **às cinco da** ~ at five in the afternoon; **boa** ~! good afternoon!; **de** ou **à** ~ in the afternoon. ◇ *adv* late; ~ **demais** too late; **mais** ~ later; **antes** ~ **do que nunca** better late than never.

tardio, dia [tax'dʒiu, dʒia] *adj* late.

tarefa [ta'rɛfa] *f* -1. [trabalho em geral] task. -2. [empreitada] job.

tarifa [ta'rifa] *f* -1. [preço - de gás, água] tariff; ~ **alfandegária** customs duty; [- de transporte] fare. -2. [tabela de preços] price list.

tarifaço [tari'fasu] *m general price rise in publicly-owned utilities.*

tarimbado, da [tarĩ'badu, da] *adj:* ~ **(em)** highly-experienced (in).

tarô [ta'ro] *m* tarot.

tartaruga [taxta'ruga] *f* -1. [grande] turtle. -2. [pequena] tortoise; **pente de** ~ tortoiseshell comb.

tataravô, vó [tatara'vo, vɔ] *m, f* great-great grandfather (*f* grandmother).

tatear [ta'tʃja(x)] ◇ *vt* to feel. ◇ *vi* to feel one's way.

tático, ca ['tatʃiku, ka] *adj* tactical.

➼ **tática** *f* -1. MIL tactic. -2. [ciência] tactics (*sg*).

-3. *fam* [plano de ação] strategy.

tato ['tatu] *m* -1. [ger] touch. -2. *fig* [cautela]: **ter** ~ to be tactful.

tatu [ta'tu] *m* armadillo.

tatuagem [ta'twaʒẽ] (*pl* -ns) *f* -1. [desenho] tattoo. -2. [técnica] tattooing.

tatuar [ta'twa(x)] *vt* to tattoo.

taxa ['taʃa] *f* -1. [ger] rate; ~ **de natalidade/crescimento** birth/growth rate; ~ **de câmbio** exchange rate; ~ **de juros** interest rate; ~ **de inscrição** registration fee. -2. [imposto] tax; ~ **de embarque** airport tax.

taxar [ta'ʃa(x)] *vt* -1. [onerar com imposto] to tax. -2. [fixar o preço de] to fix.

taxativo, va [taʃa'tʃivu, va] *adj* [categórico] categorical.

táxi ['taksi] *m* taxi *UK*, cab *US*.

taxiar [tak'sja(x)] *vi* to taxi.

taxímetro [tak'simetru] *m* taxi meter.

tchau ['tʃaw] *interj fam* bye, ciao.

tcheco, ca ['tʃɛku, ka] ◇ *adj* Czech. ◇ *m, f* Czech.

➼ **tcheco** *m* [língua] Czech.

tchecoslovaco, ca [tʃɛkoʒlo'vaku, ka] ◇ *adj* Czechoslovakian. ◇ *m, f* Czechoslovak.

Tchecoslováquia [tʃɛkoʒlo'vakja] *n* Czechoslovakia.

te ['tʃi] *pron pess* -1. [você] you. -2. [a, para, em você]: ~ **mandei duas cartas** I sent you two letters.

tear [te'a(x)] (*pl* -es) *m* loom.

teatral [tʃja'traw] (*pl* -ais) *adj* -1. [ger] theatre (*antes de subst*) *UK*, theater (*antes de subst*) *US*. -2. *fig* [pessoa, comportamento] theatrical.

teatro ['tʃjatru] *m* -1. [ger] theatre *UK*, theater *US*; ~ **de arena** theatre in the round; ~ **de marionetes** puppet theatre. -2. [LITER - gênero] playwriting; [- obras de um autor] plays (*pl*). -3. [curso] drama. -4. MIL: ~ **de operações** theatre of war *UK*. -5. *fig* [palco] scene.

teatrólogo, ga [tʃja'trɔlogu, ga] *m, f* dramatist.

tecelão, lã [tese'lãw, lã] (*mpl* -ões, *fpl* -s) *m, f* weaver.

tecer [te'se(x)] *vt* [ger] to weave.

tecido [te'sidul *m* -1. [têxtil] material. -2. BIOL & ANAT tissue.

tecla ['tɛkla] *f* -1. [ger] key; ~ **de função** function key. -2. [de máquina de calcular, de gravador] button.

tecladista [tekla'dʒiʃtal *mf* MÚS keyboard player.

teclado [te'kladul *m* keyboard.

técnica ['tɛknika] *f* ⊳ técnico.

técnico, ca ['tɛkniku, ka] ◇ *adj* technical. ◇ *m, f* -1. [profissional] technician. -2. [especialista] expert. -3. ESP coach.

➡ **técnica** *f* -1. [procedimentos, métodos] technique. -2. [conhecimento prático] skill.

tecnocrata [tekno'krata] *mf* technocrat.

tecnologia [teknolo'ʒial *f* technology; ~ **da informação** information technology; ~ **de ponta** latest technology.

tecnológico, ca [tekno'lɔʒiku, ka] *adj* technological.

teco-teco [ˌtɛku'tɛkul (*pl* teco-tecos) *m* light aircraft.

tédio ['tɛdʒiul *m* tedium.

tedioso, osa [te'dʒjozu, ɔzal *adj* tedious.

Tegucigalpa [tegusi'kawpal *n* Tegucigalpa.

teia ['tejal *f* [ger] web; ~ **de aranha** spider's web, cobweb.

teimar [tej'ma(x)] ◇ *vt*: ~ **que** to insist that. ◇ *vi* [insistir] to persist.

teimosia [tejmo'zial *f* stubbornness; ~ **em fazer algo** obstinacy in doing sthg.

teimoso, osa [tej'mozu, ɔzal *adj* -1. [adulto] obstinate. -2. [criança] stubborn.

Tejo ['tɛʒul *n*: o (rio) ~ the (river) Tagus.

tel. [tɛll (*abrev de* telefone) *m* tel.

tela ['tɛlal *f* -1. [ger] canvas. -2. [de arame] wire netting. -3. CINE, COMPUT & TV screen.

telão [te'lãwl (*pl* -ões) *m* big screen.

tele ['tɛlɛl *pref* tele.

telecomunicação [ˌtɛlekomunika'sawl (*pl* -ões) *f* telecommunication.

➡ **telecomunicações** *fpl* telecommunications.

teleférico [tele'fɛrikul *m* -1. [de esqui] ski lift. -2. [bondinho] cable car.

telefonar [telefo'na(x)] *vi* to (tele)phone, to call; ~ **para alguém** to (tele)phone sb, to call sb.

telefone [tele'fɔnil *m* -1. [aparelho, linha] (tele)phone; ~ **celular** mobile phone *UK*, cellphone *US*; ~ **sem fio** cordless phone; ~ **público** public (tele)phone. -2. [número] (tele)phone number.

telefonema [telefo'nemal *m* (tele)phone call; **dar um** ~ **para alguém/algum lugar** to make a call to sb/somewhere.

telefônico, ca [tele'foniku, kal *adj* telephone (*antes de subst*).

telefonista [telefo'niʃtal *mf* telephonist.

telégrafo [te'lɛgraful *m* -1. [aparelho] telegraph. -2. [local] telegraph office.

telegrama [tele'grãmal *m* telegram; **passar um** ~ to send a telegram; ~ **fonado** telemessage.

teleguiado, da [tɛle'gjadu, dal *adj* [guiado a distância] remote-controlled; **míssil** ~ guided missile.

telejornal [ˌtɛleʒox'nawl (*pl* -ais) *m* TV television news (*sg*).

telejornalismo [tɛleʒoxna'liʒmul *m* television journalism.

telenovela [ˌtɛleno'vɛlal *f* TV soap opera.

teleobjetiva [ˌtɛljobʒe'tʃival *f* telephoto lens.

telepatia [telepa'tʃial *f* telepathy.

telepático, ca [tele'patʃiku, kal *adj* telepathic.

telescópico, ca [teleʃ'kɔpiku, kal *adj* telescopic.

telescópio [teleʃ'kɔpjul *m* telescope.

telespectador, ra [tɛleʃpekta'do(x), ral ◇ *adj* viewing. ◇ *m, f* viewer.

televisão [televi'zãwl (*pl* -ões) *f* -1. [ger] television; ~ **a cabo** cable television. -2. [empresa] television company.

televisivo, va [televi'zivu, val *adj* television (*antes de subst*).

televisor [televi'zo(x)] (*pl* -es) *m* television.

telex [tɛ'lɛkiʃl (*pl* -es) *m* telex; **passar um** ~ to send a telex.

telha ['tɛʎal *f* -1. [de casa *etc.*] tile. -2. *fam fig* [mente]: **dar na** ~ **de alguém** fazer algo to get it into sb's head to do sthg.

telhado [te'ʎadul *m* roof.

telnet [tel'netʃil (*pl* -s) *f* COMPUT telnet.

telões [tɛ'lõjʃl *pl* = telão.

tema ['temal *m* -1. [assunto - de redação, romance] theme; [- de palestra] subject. -2. MÚS theme. -3. [dever de casa] homework.

temático, ca [te'matʃiku, kal *adj* thematic.

➡ **temática** *f* thematics (*sg*).

temer [te'me(x)] ◇ *vt* to fear; ~ **que** to fear that; ~ **fazer algo** to be afraid to do sthg, to be afraid of doing sthg. ◇ *vi* to be afraid; ~ **por alguém/algo** to fear for sb/sthg.

temerário, ria [teme'rarju, rjal *adj* -1. [audacioso, destemido] fearless. -2. [perigoso, arriscado] reckless.

temeridade [temeri'dadʒi] *f*: **ser uma ~** [ser arriscado, perigoso] to be a foolhardy act; [ser atemorizador] to be terrifying.

temeroso, osa [teme'rozu, ɔza] *adj* **-1.** [medroso, receoso] afraid. **-2.** [amedrontador] dreadful.

temido, da [te'midu, da] *adj* [assustador] frightening.

temível [te'mivɛw] (*pl* **-eis**) *adj* fearsome.

temor [te'mo(x)] (*pl* **-es**) *m* fear.

temperado, da [tẽpe'radu, da] *adj* **-1.** [ferro, aço] hardened. **-2.** [clima] temperate. **-3.** [CULIN - condimentado] seasoned; [- marinado] marinated.

temperamental [tẽperamẽn'taw] (*pl* **-ais**) ⟨⟩ *adj* temperamental. ⟨⟩ *mf* temperamental person.

temperamento [tẽpera'mẽntu] *m* temperament.

temperar [tẽmpe'ra(x)] *vt* **-1.** [metal] to temper. **-2.** [CULIN - condimentar] to season; [- marinar] to marinate.

temperatura [tẽnpera'tura] *f* temperature.

tempero [tẽn'peru] *m* **-1.** [condimento] seasoning. **-2.** [vinha d'alho] marinade. **-3.** [sabor] flavour *UK*, flavor *US*.

tempestade [tẽnpeʃ'tadʒi] *f* storm; **fazer uma ~ em copo d'água** to make a mountain out of a molehill.

tempestuoso, osa [tẽnpeʃ'twozu, ɔza] *adj* [dia, tempo] stormy.

templo [tẽnplu] *m* **-1.** [pagão] temple. **-2.** [cristão] church.

tempo [tẽnpu] *m* **-1.** [ger] time; **quanto ~?** how long?; **há quanto ~ você mora aqui?** how long have you been living here?; **não a vejo há muito ~** it's a long time since I saw her; **não dá ~** there isn't (enough) time; **~ integral** full-time; **ganhar/perder ~** to gain/lose time; **em ~ hábil** in reasonable time; **a ~** on time; **nesse meio ~** in the meanwhile; **ao mesmo ~** at the same time; **de ~s em ~s** from time to time. **-2.** *METEOR* weather; **previsão do ~** weather forecast. **-3.** *GRAM* tense. **-4.** *ESP*: **primeiro/segundo ~** first/second half. **-5.** [MÚS - divisão de compasso] time; [- velocidade de execução] timing.

têmpora [tẽnpora] *f* *ANAT* temple.

temporada [tẽnpo'rada] *f* **-1.** [ger] season; **baixa/alta ~** high/low season. **-2.** [espaço de tempo] time.

temporal [tẽnpo'raw] (*pl* **-ais**) *m* storm.

temporário, ria [tẽnpo'rarju, rja] *adj* temporary.

tenacidade [tenasi'dadʒi] *f* tenacity.

tenaz [te'najʒ] *adj* [pessoa] tenacious.

tencionar [tẽnsjo'na(x)] *vt*: **~ algo/fazer zer algo** to be planning sthg/to do sthg.

tenda [tẽnda] *f* tent.

tendão [tẽn'dãw] (*pl* **-ões**) *m* tendon.

tendência [tẽn'dẽnsja] *f* **-1.** [propensão] tendency; **~ a** *ou* **para algo** tendency to *ou* towards sthg; **~ a fazer algo** tendency to do sthg. **-2.** [vocação] inclination. **-3.** [da moda, música] trend.

tendencioso, osa [tẽndẽn'sjozu, ɔza] *adj* tendentious.

tender [tẽn'de(x)] *vt* **-1.** [ter tendência]: **~ a** *ou* **para algo** to be inclined to *ou* towards sthg; **~ a fazer algo** to tend to do sthg. **-2.** [ter vocação]: **~ a** *ou* **para algo** to be inclined towards sthg; **~ a fazer algo** to intend to do sthg.

tenebroso, sa [tene'brozu, za] *adj* **-1.** [ger] dark. **-2.** *fig* [terrível, horrível] horrendous.

tenente [te'nẽntʃi] *mf* lieutenant.

tenho [ˈtẽɲu] ▷ **ter**.

tênis [ˈteniʃ] *m* **-1.** *inv* *ESP* tennis; **~ de mesa** table tennis. **-2.** [calçado] trainer *UK*, sneaker *US*.

tenista [te'niʃta] *mf* tennis player.

tenor [te'no(x)] ⟨⟩ *m* tenor. ⟨⟩ *adj inv* [instrumento] tenor (*antes de subst*).

tenro, ra [ˈtẽnxu, xa] *adj* **-1.** [ger] tender. **-2.** [recente, novo] new.

tensão [tẽn'sãw] (*pl* **-ões**) *f* **-1.** [ger] tension; **~ pré-menstrual** pre-menstrual tension, PMT. **-2.** [pressão] pressure. **-3.** [voltagem] voltage.

tenso, sa [ˈtẽnsu, sa] *adj* **-1.** [ger] taut. **-2.** [pessoa, ambiente] tense.

tentação [tẽnta'sãw] (*pl* **-ões**) *f* temptation.

tentáculo [tẽn'takulu] *m* tentacle.

tentador, ra [tẽnta'do(x), ra] (*mpl* **-es**, *fpl* **-s**) *adj* tempting.

tentar [tẽn'ta(x)] *vt* **-1.** [experimentar] to try. **-2.** [usar de meios para] to attempt; **~ fazer algo** to try to do sthg. **-3.** [atrair] to tempt.

tentativa [tẽnta'tʃiva] *f* attempt; **~ de roubo** attempted robbery.

tênue [ˈtẽnwi] *adj* **-1.** [fraco - luz, voz, desejo] faint; [- sentimento] slight; [- argumento] tenuous. **-2.** [fino] flimsy. **-3.** [leve] slight.

teologia [tʃolo'ʒial] *f* theology.

teor [ˈt'tʃjo(x)] *m* **-1.** [conteúdo, significado] tenor. **-2.** [proporção de uma substância] content.

teorema [teo'rema] *m* theorem.

teoria [teo'rial] *f* theory.

teoricamente [ˌtjɔrika'mẽntʃi] *adv* theoretically.

teórico, ca [te'ɔriku, ka] ⟨⟩ *adj* theoretical. ⟨⟩ *m, f* theorist.

tépido, da [ˈtɛpidu, dal *adj* tepid, luke-warm.

ter [ˈte(x)] ⟨⟩ *vt* -1. [ger] to have; ~ **razão** to be right. -2. [obter]: ~ **sucesso em algo** to be successful in sthg. -3. [sentir] to be; ~ **fome/pressa/calor** to be hungry/hurried/hot; **o que é que você tem?** what's wrong with you? -4. [contar]: **'quantos anos você tem?'** - **'tenho 30 anos'** [idade] 'how old are you?' - 'I'm 30'; **ele tem 2 metros de altura** [medida] he is 2 metres tall. -5. [proceder com]: ~ **cuidado** to be careful; **tenha calma!** calm down! ⟨⟩ *v impess* [haver]: **tem algo/alguém** there is sthg/sb; **não tem problema** (it's) no problem; **não tem de quê** you're welcome. ⟨⟩ *v aux*: ~ **que** *ou* **de fazer algo** to have to do sthg; ~ **como fazer algo** to be able to do sthg; ~ **a ver com** to have sthg to do with; **não tenho nada a ver com isso** I have nothing to do with it; **não** ~ **onde cair morto** to have nowhere to turn.

ter. (*abrev de* terça-feira) *f* Tue.

terabyte [texaˈbajtʃi] (*pl* **terabytes**) *m* terabyte.

terapeuta [teraˈpewta] *mf* therapist.

terapêutico, ca [teraˈpewtʃiku, ka] *adj* therapeutic.
➤ **terapêutica** *f* -1. [parte da medicina] therapeutics (*pl*). -2. [tratamento] therapy.

terapia [teraˈpia] *f* [ger] therapy.

terça [ˈtexsa], **terça-feira** [texsaˈfejra] (*pl* **terças-feiras** [texsaʃˈfejraʃ]) *f* Tuesday; ~ **gorda** Shrove Tuesday, Pancake Day; *veja também* sexta-feira.

terceiro, ra [texˈsejru, ra] ⟨⟩ *num* third; **o Terceiro Mundo** the Third World; *veja também* sexto. ⟨⟩ *m, f* -1. [ger] third party. -2. [aquele ou aquilo em terceiro lugar] third.
➤ **terceira** *f* AUTO third (gear).
➤ **terceiros** *mpl* [outras pessoas] others.

terço, ça [ˈtexsu, sa] *num*: **a terça parte** the third part.
➤ **terço** *m* [rosário] rosary.

terçol [texˈsɔw] (*pl* **-óis**) *m* stye.

termas [ˈtexmaʃ] *fpl* spa (*sg*).

térmico, ca [ˈtɛxmiku, ka] *adj* thermal.

terminal [texmiˈnaw] (*pl* **-ais**) ⟨⟩ *adj* terminal; **em estado** ~ terminally ill. ⟨⟩ *m* -1. [ger] terminal. -2. [fim da linha] terminus.

terminar [texmiˈna(x)] ⟨⟩ *vt* to finish. ⟨⟩ *aux*: ~ **de fazer algo** [finalmente] to finish doing sthg; [há pouco tempo] to have just done sthg. ⟨⟩ *vi* to finish; ~ **em algo** [em local, forma] to end in sthg.

término [ˈtexminu] *m* end.

terminologia [texminoloˈʒia] *f* terminology.

termo [ˈtexmu] *m* -1. [ger] term. -2. [fim] end; **pôr** ~ **a algo** to put an end to sthg; **a longo** ~ in the long term; **meio** ~ compromise.
➤ **termos** *mpl* terms; **em** ~**s de** in terms of.

termômetro [texˈmometru] *m* [instrumento] thermometer.

termostato [texmoʃˈtatu] *m* thermostat.

terno, na [ˈtexnu, na] *adj* tender.
➤ **terno** *m* [traje] suit.

ternura [texˈnura] *f* tenderness.

terra [ˈtexal] *f* -1. [ger] earth; ~ **batida** earth floor. -2. [por oposição ao mar] [terreno] land. -3. [região, país]: **já me habituei a viver nesta** ~ I've got used to living in this area; ~ **de ninguém** no-man's-land. -4. [pátria] homeland; ~ **natal** birthplace.

terraço [teˈxasul] *m* -1. [varanda] terrace. -2. [cobertura plana de um edifício] roof terrace.

terracota [texaˈkɔta] *f* [argila] terracotta.

terraplenar [texapleˈna(x)] *vt* to level.

terreiro [teˈxejru] *m* -1. [espaço de terra] yard. -2. [espirit] *place where Afro-Brazilian rites are performed*.

terremoto [texeˈmotu] *m* earthquake.

terreno, na [teˈxenu, na] *adj* [material, mundano] material.
➤ **terreno** *m* -1. [extensão de terra] land. -2. [para construção, plantação] site; ~ **baldio** wasteland. -3. GEOL terrain.

térreo, ea [ˈtexju, ja] *adj* [andar, casa] ground level (*antes de subst*).
➤ **térreo** *m* [andar térreo] ground floor *UK*, first floor *US*.

terrestre [teˈxɛʃtri] *adj* -1. [relativo ou pertencente à Terra - globo, crosta] earth's, of the earth; [- seres, fenômenos] earthly. -2. [por oposição a aquático] land (*antes de subst*).

territorial [texitoˈrjaw] *adj* territorial.

território [texiˈtɔrju] *m* -1. [ger] territory. -2. [parte de uma federação] district.

terrível [teˈxivew] (*pl* **-eis**) *adj* -1. [ger] terrible. -2. [muito forte, enorme] dreadful.

terror [teˈxo(x)] (*pl* **-es**) *m* [medo] terror.

terrorista [texoˈriʃta] ⟨⟩ *adj* terrorist (*antes de subst*). ⟨⟩ *mf* [pessoa] terrorist.

tesão [teˈsãw] (*pl* **-ões**) *m mfam* [desejo sexual] hots (*pl*); **sentir** ~ **por alguém** to have the hots for sb; **ser um** ~ [pessoa] to be sexy; [coisa] to be fantastic.

tese [ˈtɛzi] *f* thesis.

teso, sa [ˈtezu, za] *adj* -**1.** [esticado] taut.
-**2.** [ereto] stiff.

tesões [teˈzõjʃ] *pl* ⊳ **tesão**.

tesoura [teˈzoral *f* scissors *(pl)*.

tesouraria [tezoraˈrial *f* -**1.** [departamento] finance department. -**2.** [cargo] finance director.

tesoureiro, ra [tezoˈrejru, ral *m, f* -**1.** [de banco] treasurer. -**2.** [de empresa] financial director.

tesouro [teˈzorul *m* -**1.** [ger] treasure.
-**2.** [lugar onde são guardadas as riquezas] treasury.
➡ **Tesouro** *m*: **o Tesouro Nacional** the Treasury.

testa [ˈtɛʃtal *f* forehead.

testa-de-ferro [ˌtɛʃtadʒiˈfɛxul *(pl* **testas-de-ferro)** *mf* figurehead.

testamento [teʃtaˈmẽntul *m* will.
➡ **Novo Testamento** *m* New Testament.
➡ **Velho Testamento** *m* Old Testament.

testar [teʃˈta(x)] *vt* -**1.** [submeter a teste] to test. -**2.** [deixar em testamento] to bequeath.

teste [ˈtɛʃtʃil *m* test.

testemunha [teʃteˈmuɲal *f* witness; ~ **ocular** eye witness; ~ **de acusação** witness for the prosecution.

testemunhar [teʃteˈmuɲa(x)] ◇ *vt* -**1.** [ger] to witness. -**2.** *JUR* [depor sobre] to testify to. -**3.** [comprovar] to prove. -**4.** [manifestar] to display. ◇ *vi JUR* to testify.

testemunho [teʃteˈmuɲul *m* testimony.

testículo [teʃˈtʃikulul *m* testicle.

teta [ˈtetal *f* [ANAT - de mulher] breast; [- de animal] teat; [- de vaca] udder.

tétano [ˈtɛtanul *m* tetanus.

teto [ˈtɛtul *m* -**1.** [ger] ceiling. -**2.** [de peça da casa] roof; ~ **solar** AUTO sunroof.
-**3.** [habitação]: **sem** ~ homeless person.

tetracampeão, peã [tetrakãnˈpjãw, pjãl *m, f* four times champion.

tetraplégico, ca [tetraˈplɛʒiku, kal ◇ *adj* quadriplegic. ◇ *m, f* quadriplegic.

tétrico, ca [ˈtɛtriku, kal *adj* -**1.** [medonho, horrível] grim. -**2.** [triste, fúnebre] gloomy.

teu, tua [ˈtew, ˈtual ◇ *adj poss* your. ◇ *pron poss* yours.

tevê [teˈvel *f* = **televisão**.

têxtil [ˈteʃtʃiwl *(pl* **-teis)** *adj* textile.

texto [ˈteʃtul *m* text.

textura [teʃˈtural *f* texture.

texugo [teˈʃugul *m* ZOOL badger.

tez [ˈtɛʃl *f* [cútis] complexion.

ti [ˈtʃil *pron pess* you; **trouxe este presente para** ~ I brought this present for you.

tia [ˈtʃial *f* aunt.

tia-avó [ˌtʃiaˈvɔl *(pl* **tias-avós)** *f* greataunt.

tiara [ˈtʃjaral *f* tiara.

Tibete [tʃiˈbɛtʃil *n* Tibet.

tíbia [ˈtʃibjal *f* ANAT tibia.

tíbio, bia [ˈtʃibju, bjal *adj* lukewarm.

tição [tʃiˈsãwl *(pl* **-ões)** *m* -**1.** [lenha] ember. -**2.** [negro] *fig & pej* nigger.

tico-tico [ˌtʃikuˈtʃikul *(pl* **-s)** *m* ZOOL crown sparrow.

tido, da [ˈtʃidu, dal *adj* [considerado]: ~ **como** considered.
➡ **tido** *pp* ⊳ **ter**.

tiete [ˈtʃjetʃil *mf fam* fan.

tifo [ˈtʃiful *m* typhus.

tigela [tʃiˈʒɛlal *f* [vasilha] bowl.

tigre [ˈtʃigril *m* ZOOL tiger.

tijolo [tʃiˈʒolul *m* brick.

til [ˈtʃiwl *m* tilde.

timão [tʃiˈmãwl *(pl* **-ões)** *m* NÁUT helm, tiller.

timbre [ˈtʃĩbril *m* -**1.** [em papel de correspondência] heading. -**2.** [de voz] tone. -**3.** *MÚS* [tom] timbre. -**4.** [de vogal] sound.

time [ˈtʃimil *m* -**1.** [ger] team. -**2.** *fam loc*: **tirar o** ~ **de campo** to pull out.

timidez [tʃimiˈdeʃl *f* timidity.

tímido, da [ˈtʃimidu, dal *adj* -**1.** [avanço, governo] timid. -**2.** [pessoa, temperamento] timid, shy.

timões [tʃiˈmõjʃl *pl* ⊳ **timão**.

timoneiro, ra [tʃimoˈnejru, ral *m, f* NÁUT helmsman.

tímpano [ˈtʃĩpanul *m* -**1.** ANAT eardrum. -**2.** [em campainha] bell.

tina [ˈtʃinal *f* -**1.** [para lavar roupa] trough.
-**2.** [para banho] bathtub. -**3.** [para uso industrial] vat.

tingido, da [tʃĩˈʒidu, dal *adj* [tinto] dyed.

tingimento [tʃĩʒiˈmẽntul *m* dyeing.

tingir [tʃĩˈʒi(x)] *vt* -**1.** [ger] to dye. -**2.** [parede, corpo] to paint.

tinha [ˈtʃinal ⊳ **ter**.

tinhoso, osa [tʃiˈɲozu, ɔzal *adj* -**1.** [teimoso] obstinate. -**2.** [persistente] stubborn.

tinir [tʃiˈni(x)] *vi* -**1.** [ger] to ring. -**2.** *loc*: **estar tinindo** [estar em ótimo estado de limpeza] to be sparkling; [estar bem preparado] to be well-primed; [estar em ótimas condições] to be in excellent order; ~ **de fome/raiva** to be extremely hungry/furious.

tinjo [ˈtʃĩʒul *vb* ⊳ **tingir**.

tino [ˈtʃinu] *m* -1. [juízo] common sense; **perder o** ~ to lose one's common sense. -2. [prudência] care.

tinta [ˈtʃĩnta] *f* -1. [para imprimir, escrever] ink. -2. [para tingir] dye. -3. [para pintar] paint; ~ **a óleo** oil paint.

tinteiro [tʃĩnˈtejru] *m* inkwell.

tinto [ˈtʃĩntu] *adj* -1. [cabelos] dyed. -2.: **vinho** ~ red wine.

tintura [tʃĩnˈtura] *f* -1. [tinta] dye. -2. [ato] dyeing.

tinturaria [tʃĩntura'rial] *f* -1. [ramo] dyeing. -2. [lavanderia] dry-cleaner's. -3. [onde se faz tingimento] dyer's.

tio [ˈtʃiw] *m* uncle; **os meus** ~**s** [casal] my aunt and uncle.

tio-avô [ˈtʃiwaˈvol] (*pl* **tios-avôs**) *m* great-uncle.

tipicamente [tʃipikaˈmẽntʃil] *adv* typically.

típico, ca [ˈtʃipiku, ka] *adj* typical.

tipo [ˈtʃipu] *m* -1. [espécie] type; ~ **sangüíneo** blood group. -2. [pessoa] sort. -3. *fam* [sujeito] guy (*f* girl). -4. [TIP-peça] type; [- letra] font.

tipografia [tʃipograˈfial *f* -1. [arte] typography. -2. [estabelecimento] printer's.

tipógrafo, fa [tʃiˈpografu, fal *m, f* [profissional - que imprime] printer; [- que compõe] typesetter.

tipóia [tʃiˈpojal *f* [tira de pano] sling.

tique [ˈtʃikil *m* tick; ~ **nervoso** nervous tic.

tique-taque [ˌtʃikiˈtakil (*pl* **tique-taques**) *m* tick-tock.

tíquete [tʃiˈketʃil *m* ticket, voucher.

tíquete-restaurante [ˈtʃiketʃiʃeʃtawˈrãntʃil (*pl* **tíquetes-restaurantes**) *m* [vale-refeição] luncheon voucher.

tiquinho [tʃiˈkiɲul *m*: **um** ~ (**de**) a shred (of).

tira [ˈtʃiral ⇔ *f* [ger] strip. ⇔ *m gír* [agente de polícia] cop.

tiracolo [tʃiraˈkɔlul *m*: **a** ~ across the shoulder; **com os filhos a** ~ with the children in tow.

tiragem [tʃiˈraʒẽl (*pl* **-ns**) *f* -1. [operação de imprimir] print run. -2. [número de exemplares] circulation.

tira-gosto [ˈtʃiraˈgoʃtul (*pl* **tira-gostos**) *m* savoury *UK*, savory *US*.

Tirana [tʃiˈrãnal *n* Tirana.

tirânico, ca [tʃiˈrãniku, ka] *adj* tyrannical.

tirano, na [tʃiˈrãnu, nal ⇔ *adj* [cruel, injusto] tyrannical. ⇔ *m, f* tyrant.

tirar [tʃiˈra(x)] *vt* -1. [ger] to take. -2. [retirar] to take away. -3. [de cima] [despir, descalçar] to take off. -4. [de dentro]

[sacar] to take out, to withdraw. -5. [trazer abaixo] to take down. -6. [extrair] to extract. -7. [eliminar] to remove. -8. [obter] to get; ~ **proveito de** to make use of. -9. [mesa] to clear. -10. [para dançar] to ask. -11. *MÚS* to take down. -12. *TIP* [imprimir] to print. -13.: ~ **algo/alguém de algo** [afastar, fazer sair] to take sthg/sb away from sthg; -14. [loc]: **sem** ~ **nem pôr** exactly like; **ele é o pai sem** ~ **nem pôr** he's the spitting image of his father.

tiritar [tʃiriˈta(x)] *vi* to shiver; ~ **de frio** to shiver with cold.

tiro [ˈtʃirul *m* -1. [ger] shot; **dar um** ~ (**em**) to fire a shot (at); **trocar** ~**s** to exchange fire; ~ **ao alvo** target practice. -2. [loc]: **ser** ~ **e queda** to be sure-fire.

tiro-de-guerra [tʃirudʒiˈɡɛxal (*pl* **tiros-de-guerra**) *m army reserve training centre*.

tiroteio [tʃiroˈtejul *m* -1. [tiros amiudados] shooting. -2. [troca de tiros] shootout.

titia [tʃiˈtʃial *f fam* aunty.

titio [tʃiˈtʃiul *m fam* uncle.

titubear [tʃituˈbja(x)] *vi* -1. [hesitar] to hesitate. -2. [cambalear] to lurch.

titular [tʃituˈla(x)] ⇔ *adj* [efetivo - juiz] incumbent; [- professor] tenured; [- oficial] official. ⇔ *mf* -1. [ocupante efetivo de função ou cargo] incumbent. -2. *POL* [de ministério]: **o** ~ **do Ministério da Saúde** the Health Minister. -3. [possuidor] holder.

título [ˈtʃitulul *m* -1. [ger] title. -2. [documento] (title) deed; ~ **de propriedade** *JUR* title deed. -3. [motivo]: **a** ~ **de** by way of.

tive [ˈtʃivil *v* ⊳ ter.

TM (*abrev de* **Trademark**) *f* TM.

TO (*abrev de* **Estado de Tocantins**) *n State of Tocantins*.

toa [ˈtoal *f NÁUT* towline.
➔ **à toa** *loc adv* -1. [ger] for no reason. -2. [inutilmente] in vain. -3. [desocupado] at a loose end. -4. [sem rumo] aimlessly.

toalete [twaˈletʃil ⇔ *m* [banheiro] toilet. ⇔ *f* -1. [ato]: **fazer a** ~ to get washed and dressed. -2. [traje] outfit.

toalha [ˈtwaʎal *f* towel; ~ **de mesa** tablecloth.

toca [ˈtɔkal *f* -1. [covil] den. -2. *fig* [refúgio] bolt-hole.

toca-discos [ˌtɔkaˈdʒiʃkuʃl *m inv* record player.

toca-fitas [ˌtɔkaˈfitaʃl *m inv* cassette player.

tocaia [toˈkajal *f* ambush.

tocante [to'kãntʃi] *adj inv* [comovente] touching.

   ◆ **no tocante a** *loc prep* when it comes to.

tocar [to'ka(x)] <> *vt* **-1.** [ger] to touch. **-2.** *MÚS* to play. **-3.** [campainha, sino] to ring. **-4.** [buzina] to hoot. **-5.** [conduzir] to drive. **-6.** [fazer progredir]: ~ **algo (para frente)** to move (sthg) forward. <> *vi* **-1.** [ger] to ring. **-2.** [apalpar, encostar]: ~ **(em) algo/alguém** to touch sthg/sb.

   ◆ **tocar em** *vi* **-1.** [referir-se a] to touch (up)on. **-2.** [fazer escala em] to stop off in. **-3.** [caber a]: **toca a você fazer isso** it's up to you to do it.

   ◆ **tocar-se** *vp* **-1.** [pôr-se em contato] to touch. **-2.** [perceber] to notice. **-3.** [ofender-se] to be provoked.

tocha ['tɔʃa] *f* [facho] torch.

toco ['toku] *m* **-1.** [de árvore] stump. **-2.** [de cigarro, charuto] butt(-end), stub.

todavia [toda'via] *conj* however.

todo, da ['todu, da] <> *adj indef* [inteiro] all; **a Europa toda** the whole of Europe; **a equipe toda** the entire team; **o dia** ~, ~ **o dia** the whole day (long). <> *adv* [completamente] completely. <> *pron indef* [qualquer, cada] every; ~ **dia**, ~ **os dias** every day; **em** OU **por toda parte** everywhere; ~ **mundo** everyone; **em** ~ **caso** in any case.

   ◆ **todo** *m* whole; **ao** ~ in all.

   ◆ **todos** *pron pl* [todas as pessoas] everyone *(sg)*.

   ◆ **a toda (velocidade)** *loc adv* at top speed.

todo-poderoso, osa [ˌtodupode'rozu, ɔza] *adj* all-powerful.

toicinho [toj'siɲu] *m* = **toucinho**.

toldo ['towdu] *m* awning.

tolerância [tole'rãsja] *f* tolerance.

tolerante [tole'rãntʃi] *adj* tolerant.

tolerar [tole'ra(x)] *vt* **-1.** [ger] to tolerate. **-2.** [suportar] to bear.

tolher [to'ʎe(x)] *vt* [dificultar] to impede.

tolice [to'lisi] *f* **-1.** [ato] stupid thing. **-2.** [qualidade] idiocy. **-3.** [dito] rubbish.

tolo, la ['tolu, la] <> *adj* **-1.** [ger] stupid. **-2.** [pessoa - idiota] idiotic; [- ingênuo] foolish. <> *m, f* [pessoa] idiot.

tom ['tõ] *(pl* **-ns)** *m* **-1.** [ger] tone. **-2.** [altura de um som] pitch; ~ **agudo/grave** high/low pitch. **-3.** [matiz] shade. **-4.** [MÚS - intervalo entre duas notas] tone; [- escala] key; ~ **maior/menor** major/ minor key. **-5.** *loc:* **ser de bom** ~ to be polite.

tomada [to'mada] *f* **-1.** [ato] taking; ~ **de decisão** decision making; ~ **de posto** oficial taking office. **-2.** [ELETR - plugue] plug; [- na parede] socket. **-3.** [ocupação] taking. **-4.** *CINE* take.

tomar [to'ma(x)] *vt* **-1.** [ger] to take; ~ **alguém em/por algo** to take sb in/by sthg; ~ **emprestado** to borrow; **toma!** there you are!; ~ **um susto** to get a fright. **-2.** [ocupar] to take. **-3.** [beber] to have. **-4.** [ocupar aspecto] to take up. **-5.** [satisfação]: ~ **satisfação de alguém** to get an explanation from sb. **-6.** [considerar]: ~ **algo como algo** to take sthg as sthg; ~ **alguém por algo** to take sb for sthg.

tomara [to'mara] *interj* let's hope so!; ~ **que chova!** let's hope it rains!

tomate [to'matʃi] *m* tomato.

tombar [tõn'ba(x)] <> *vt* **-1.** [derrubar] to knock down. **-2.** [para preservar] to list *(for the preservation of buildings)*. <> *vi:* ~ **(em/de/para)** [cair] to fall on/off/towards; [cair rolando] to tumble on/off/towards.

tombo ['tõnbu] *m* [queda] fall.

tomilho [to'miʎu] *m* thyme.

tona ['tona] *f:* **à** ~ to the surface.

tonal [to'naw] *(pl* **-ais)** *adj MÚS* tonal.

tonalidade [tonali'dadʒi] *f* **-1.** [ger] shade. **-2.** [mus] tonality.

tonel [to'nɛw] *(pl* **-éis)** *m* [recipiente] cask.

tonelada [tone'lada] *f* **-1.** [medida] ton. **-2.** *fig* [grande quantidade de]: **uma** ~ **de** tons of.

tonelagem [tone'laʒẽ] *f* tonnage.

toner ['tone(x)] *m* TEC toner.

tônico, ca ['toniku, ka] *adj* tonic.

   ◆ **tônico** *m:* ~ **para o cabelo** hair tonic.

   ◆ **tonica** *f* **-1.** [água tônica] tonic water. **-2.** *MÚS* tonic. **-3.** *fig* [idéia, assunto principal] keynote.

tonificar [tonifi'ka(x)] *vt* to tone.

tons [tõʃ] *pl* ▷ **tom**.

tontear [tõn'tʃja(x)] <> *vt* **-1.** [suj: bebida, perfume] to make giddy. **-2.** [suj: pessoa, notícia, revelação] to stun. **-3.** [suj: barulho, confusão] to drive mad. <> *vi* **-1.** [bebida, perfume] to be intoxicating. **-2.** [notícia, revelação] to be shocking. **-3.** [barulho, confusão] to be maddening. **-4.** [pessoa - ficar tonto] to become dizzy; [- perturbar-se] to be stunned; [- ficar atordoado] to be maddened.

tonteira [tõn'tejra] *f* [vertigem] giddiness, dizziness; **ter** ~ to suffer a dizzy spell.

tonto, ta ['tõntu, ta] *adj* **-1.** [zonzo] dizzy. **-2.** [perturbado, atordoado] giddy. **-3.** [tolo] giddy.

tontura [tõn'tura] *f* = **tonteira**.

top ['tɔpil *m* **-1.** [bustiê] bodice. **-2.** [o melhor]: ~ **de linha** top-of-the-range.

topada [to'padal *f* trip; **dar uma** ~ **em algo** to trip over sthg.

topar [to'pa(x)] <> *vt* [aceitar, concordar com]: ~ **algo/fazer algo** to agree to sthg/to do sthg. <> *vi* [aceitar, concordar] to agree.
- **topar com** *vi* [encontrar] to come across.
- **topar em** *vi* [tropeçar em] to trip over.
- **topar-se** *vp* [deparar-se]: ~ **com algo/alguém** to come across sthg/sb.

topázio [to'pazju] *m* topaz.

topete [to'petʃil *m* [cabelo levantado] quiff; **ter o** ~ **de fazer algo** to have the nerve to do sthg.

tópico, ca ['tɔpiku, kal *adj* [questão, assunto] topical.
- **tópico** *m* [tema, assunto] topic.

topless [tɔpi'lɛʃl <> *adj inv* topless. <> *m inv* topless bikini.

topo ['topul *m* top.

topográfico, ca [topo'grafiku, kal *adj* topographical.

toque ['tɔkil <> *v* <> **tocar.** <> *m* **-1.** [ger] touch. **-2.** [de campainha] ring. **-3.** [de corneta] blast. **-4.** *fam*: **dar um** ~ **em alguém** to have a word with sb. **-5.** MIL: ~ **de recolher** curfew. **-6.** *loc*: **a** ~ **de caixa** hurriedly.

tora ['tɔral *f* **-1.** [de madeira] log. **-2.** [pedaço] piece.

tórax ['tɔrakiʃl *m inv* thorax.

torção [tɔx'sãw] *f* **-1.** [ato de torcer] twist(ing). **-2.** MED sprain.

torcedor, ra [tɔxse'do(x), ral *(mpl* **-es,** *fpl* **-s)** *m, f* ESP supporter; **sou** ~ **do Flamengo** I am a Flamengo supporter.

torcer [tɔx'se(x)] <> *vt* **-1.** [ger] to twist. **-2.** [espremer] to wring. **-3.** MED to sprain. <> *vi* **-1.** [ger] to twist. **-2.** [num jogo] to do one's bit as a supporter.
- **torcer para, torcer por** *vi* [desejar o êxito de] to back.

torcicolo [tɔxsi'kɔlul *m* MED stiff neck, wryneck; **estar com** ~ to have a stiff neck.

torcida [tɔx'sidal *f* [ESP - ato] support; [- torcedores] supporters *(pl).*

tormenta [tɔx'mẽntal *f* **-1.** METEOR storm. **-2.** *fig* [transtorno] upheaval.

tormento [tɔx'mẽntul *m* torment.

tornado [tɔx'nadul *m* tornado.

tornar [tɔx'na(x)] <> *vt* [fazer ser] to make. <> *vi*: ~ **a fazer algo** to do sthg again; **ela tornou a insistir** she again insisted.
- **tornar-se** *vp* [vir a ser] to become.

torneado, da [tɔx'njadu, dal *adj* [arredondado] turned; **bem** ~ *fig* [corpo, pernas] well-turned, shapely.

torneio [tɔx'neju] *m* [competição] tournament.

torneira [tɔx'nejral *f* tap *UK*, faucet *US*.

torniquete [tɔxni'ketʃil *m* MED tourniquet.

torno ['tɔxnul *m* TEC lathe.
- **en torno de** *loc prep* around.

tornozelo [tɔxnu'zelul *m* ankle.

toró [to'rɔ] *m* METEOR downpour; **caiu um** ~ there was a heavy downpour.

torpe ['tɔxpil *adj* **-1.** [vil] foul. **-2.** [desonesto] shameful. **-3.** [obsceno] disgraceful.

torpedo [tɔx'pedul *m* torpedo.

torpor [tɔx'po(x)] *m* **-1.** [entorpecimento] torpor. **-2.** [indiferença] inertia. **-3.** MED unresponsiveness.

torrada [to'xadal *f* toast.

torradeira [toxa'dejral *f* toaster.

torrão [to'xãw] *(pl* **-ões)** *m* **-1.** [de terra endurecida] clod. **-2.** [de açúcar] lump.

torrar [to'xa(x)] <> *vt* **-1.** [tostar] to toast. **-2.** [ressecar] to parch. **-3.** *fig* [mercadorias] to dump. **-4.** *fig* [dinheiro] to burn. <> *vi* to be irritating.

torre ['toxil *f* **-1.** [construção] tower; ~ **de controle** AERON control tower. **-2.** ELETR pylon. **-3.** RÁDIO & TV mast. **-4.** [xadrez] castle, rook.

torrencial [toxẽn'sjawl *adj* torrential.

torrente [to'xẽntʃil *f* torrent.

torresmo [to'xeʒmul *m* CULIN crackling, pork scratchings *(pl).*

tórrido, da ['tɔxidu, dal *adj* torrid.

torrone [to'xɔnil *m* nougat.

torso ['tɔxsul *m* torso.

torta ['tɔxtal *f* [empadão, doce] pie.

torto, ta ['tɔxtu, tal *adj* **-1.** [ger] crooked. **-2.** *loc*: **a** ~ **e a direito** left, right and centre; **cometer erros a** ~ **e a direito** to make mistakes left, right and centre.

tortuoso, osa [tɔx'twozu, ɔzal *adj* **-1.** [sinuoso] winding. **-2.** *(fig)* [que não segue uma linha reta] convoluted.

tortura [tɔx'tural *f* [ger] torture; [lance difícil]: **ser uma** ~ to be torture.

torturador, ra [tɔxtura'do(x), ral *m, f* torturer.

torturar [tɔxtu'ra(x)] *vt* [ger] to torment; [incomodar fisicamente] to kill.

torvelinho [tɔxve'liɲul *m* [confusão] turmoil.

tosa ['tɔzal *f* **-1.** [de pêlo] trimming. **-2.** [de lã] shearing.

tosar [to'za(x)] *vt* **-1.** [pêlo] to clip. **-2.** [cabelo] to crop.

tosco, ca ['toʃku, kal *adj* crude.

tosquiar [toʃ'kja(x)] *vt* [ovelha] to shear.

tosse ['tɔsi] *f* cough; ~ **de cachorro** *ou* **comprida** whooping cough.

tossir [to'si(x)] *vi* -1. [ger] to cough. -2. [expelir] to cough up.

tostado, da [toʃ'tadu, da] *adj* -1. [levemente queimado] browned. -2. [moreno] tanned.

tostão [toʃ'tãw] (*pl* -ões) *m* [dinheiro] cash; **estava sem um** ~ I didn't have a penny; **fiquei sem um** ~ I was left penniless.

tostar [toʃ'ta(x)] *vt* -1. [ger] to brown. -2. [pele] to tan.

total [to'taw] (*pl* -ais) <> *adj* total. <> *m* total.

totalitário, ria [totali'tarju, rja] *adj* totalitarian.

totalmente [totaw'mẽntʃil] *adv* entirely, totally.

touca ['tokal] *f* [de lã, malha] bonnet; ~ **de banho/natação** bathing/swimming cap.

toucinho [to'siɲul] *m* uncured bacon; ~ **defumado** smoked bacon.

toupeira [to'pejral] *f* -1. *zool* mole. -2. *fig* [ignorante] dimwit.

tourada [to'radal] *f* bullfight.

tourear [to'rja(x)] <> *vt* to fight (*bulls*). <> *vi* to be a bullfighter.

toureiro, ra [to'rejru, ral] *m, f* bullfighter.

touro ['torul] *m* -1. *zool* bull. -2. *fig*: **ser um** ~ [ser robusto] to be strong as an ox.
◆ **Touro** *m* [zodíaco] Taurus; *veja também* **Virgem**.

tóxico, ca ['tɔksiku, kal] *adj* toxic.
◆ **tóxico** *m* -1. [veneno] poison. -2. [droga] drug.

toxicômano, na [toksi'komanu, nal] *m, f* drug addict.

TPM (*abrev de* **Tensão Pré-Menstrual**) *f* PMT.

trabalhadeira [trabaʎa'dejral] *f* ▷ **trabalhador**.

trabalhador, ra [trabaʎa'do(x), ral] (*mpl* -es, *fpl* -s) <> *adj* [laborioso] hard-working. <> *m, f* worker; (~) **autônomo** freelance (worker).

trabalhão [traba'ʎãw] *m* = **trabalheira**.

trabalhar [traba'ʎa(x)] <> *vt* -1. [ger] to work. -2. [aprimorar] to work on. -3. [elaborar] to develop. <> *vi* to work; ~ **em algo** [em projeto] to work at sthg; *teatro* to perform in sthg; ~ **como algo** [exercer a profissão de] to work as sthg.

trabalheira [traba'ʎejral] *f* hard work.

trabalhista [traba'ʎiʃta] <> *adj* -1. [ger] labour *UK*, labor *US*. -2. [que é especialista em direito do trabalho] employment (*antes de subst*). <> *mf* [*pol* - partidário]

Labour Party supporter; [- membro] Labour Party member.

trabalho [tra'baʎul] *m* -1. [ger] work; ~ **braçal** manual work; ~ **doméstico** domestic work; ~ **de parto** labour *UK*, labor *US*. -2. [tarefa] job. -3. *econ* labour *UK*, labor *US*. -4. *educ* homework. -5. [espírit] spell; **fazer um** ~ to cast a spell. -6.: **dar** ~ (a alguém) [exigir esforço] to be a lot of work (for sb); [causar transtorno] to be a bother (to sb).

trabalhoso, osa [traba'ʎozu, ɔzal] *adj* arduous.

traça ['trasal] *f* -1. [de roupa] moth. -2. [de livro] bookworm.

traçado [tra'sadul] *m* -1. [conjunto de traços] sketch. -2. [planta] plan.

tração [tra'sãw] *f* traction; ~ **nas quatro rodas** four-wheel drive.

traçar [tra'sa(x)] *vt* -1. [fazer com traços] to sketch. -2. [planejar] to draw up. -3. [demarcar] to mark out. -4. *fam* [devorar] to devour.

traço ['trasul] *m* -1. [linha] line. -2. [sinal de pontuação] (en) dash. -3. [modo de desenhar] style. -4. [característica] trait.
◆ **traços** *mpl* -1. [feições] features. -2. *fig* [vestígio] traces. -3. *fig* [laivos] traces. -4. [pequena quantidade de substância] traces.

tradição [tradʒi'sãw] (*pl* -ões) *f* tradition.

tradicional [tradʒisjo'naw] (*pl* -ais) *adj* traditional.

tradicionalmente [tradʒisjonaw'mẽntʃil] *adv* traditionally.

tradução [tradu'sãw] (*pl* -ões) *f* [ger] translation.

tradutor, ra [tradu'to(x), ral] (*mpl* -es, *fpl* -s) <> *adj* translating. <> *m, f* translator; ~ **juramentado** accredited translator.

traduzir [tradu'zi(x)] <> *vt* -1. [texto, código] to translate. -2. [sentimento, pensamento] to express. <> *vi* -1. [saber traduzir] to translate. -2. [ser tradutor] to work as a translator.

trafegar [trafe'ga(x)] *vi* [transitar] to be driven.

tráfego ['trafegul] *m* traffic; ~ **engarrafado** traffic jam; ~ **aéreo** air traffic.

traficante [trafi'kãntʃil] *mf* trafficker; ~ **de drogas** drug trafficker *ou* dealer.

traficar [trafi'ka(x)] <> *vt* to traffic in. <> *vi* to traffic; ~ **com** to deal in.

tráfico ['trafikul] *m* traffic; ~ **de drogas** drug trafficking.

tragar [tra'ga(x)] <> *vt* -1. [engolir] to swallow. -2. [inalar] to inhale. -3. *fam* [tolerar] to tolerate. <> *vi* [inalar] to inhale.

tragédia [tra'ʒɛdʒia] f tragedy.

trágico, ca ['traʒiku, ka] <> adj -1. [ger] tragic. -2. fig [dado a fazer drama] over-dramatic. <> m, f [ator] tragic actor (f actress).

trago ['tragu] <> v ⊳ trazer. <> m -1. [gole] mouthful. -2. [dose pequena] drop. -3. [em cigarro] puff.

traguei [tra'gej] v ⊳ tragar.

traição [traj'sãw] (pl -ões) f -1. [deslealdade] disloyalty. -2. [infidelidade] infidelity. -3. POL treason.

traiçoeiro, ra [traj'swejru, ra] adj -1. [pessoa] disloyal. -2. [ação] treacherous. -3. [mar, passagem] treacherous.

traidor, ra [traj'do(x), ra] (mpl -es, fpl -s) <> adj -1. [infiel] unfaithful. -2. [comprometedor] betraying. <> m, f [pessoa] traitor.

trailer ['trejle(x)] m -1. [ger] trailer. -2. [tipo casa] caravan UK, trailer US.

traineira [traj'nejra] f NÁUT trawler.

training ['trejniŋ] m tracksuit.

trair [tra'i(x)] vt -1. [atraiçoar] to betray. -2. [ser infiel a] to be unfaithful to. -3. [não cumprir - promessa] to break; [- dever] to fail in. -4. [revelar] to betray.
 ⇒ **trair-se** vp: ~-se por algo/fazendo algo [denunciar-se] to give o.s. away by sthg/doing sthg.

trajar [tra'ʒa(x)] vt to wear.

traje ['traʒi] m dress; ~ **de banho** swimsuit; ~ **de passeio** smart dress; ~ **a rigor** evening dress.

trajeto [tra'ʒɛtu] m distance, journey.

trajetória [traʒe'tɔrja] f -1. [trajeto] path. -2. fig [caminho] course.

tralha ['traʎa] f [traste] junk.

trama ['trama] f -1. [ger] plot. -2. [de tecido] weft.

tramar [tra'ma(x)] <> vt -1. [tecer] to weave. -2. [maquinar] to plot. <> vi [conspirar]: ~ **contra** to plot against.

trambolhão [trambo'ʎãw] (pl -ões) m tumble; **levar um** ~ to be knocked down; **abrir caminho aos trambolhões** to push one's way through.

trambolho [tran'boʎu] m [objeto grande e incômodo] encumbrance.

trâmites ['tramitʃif] mpl fig [vias] procedures.

tramóia [tra'mɔja] f -1. [trama] scheme. -2. [trapaça] swindle.

trampolim [trãnpo'lĩ] (pl -ns) m -1. ESP diving board. -2. fig [meio] springboard.

tranca ['trãŋka] f -1. [de porta] bolt. -2. [de carro] lock; **passar a** ~ **em** to lock.

trança ['trãsa] f -1. [ger] plaited bread. -2. [trançado] braid.

trançado, da [trãn'sadu, da] adj -1. [cabelo] plaited. -2. [cinto, galão, fita] braided. -3. [cesto] woven.

trancado, da [trãŋka'du, da] adj [fechado] firmly shut.

trancafiar [trãŋka'fja(x)] vt to lock up.

trancar [trãŋ'ka(x)] vt -1. [chavear] to lock. -2. [prender] to lock up. -3. EDUC & UNIV [matrícula] to suspend. -4. FUT to shove (to one side).
 ⇒ **trancar-se** vp [fechar-se] to shut o.s. away.

trançar [trãn'sa(x)] vt-1. [cabelo] to plait. -2. [palha, fita] to weave.

tranco ['trãŋku] m -1. [esbarrão] shove. -2. [solavanco] jolt.
 ⇒ **aos trancos e barrancos** loc adv [com dificuldade] with great difficulty.

tranqüilamente [trãŋkwila'mẽntʃi] adv -1. [com calma] calmly. -2. [sossegadamente] peacefully. -3. [com facilidade, seguramente] easily.

tranqüilidade [trãŋkwili'dadʒi] f tranquillity; **preciso de** ~ **para fazer isso** I need peace and quiet to do this.

tranqüilizante [trãŋkwili'zãntʃi] <> adj soothing. <> m MED tranquillizer.

tranqüilizar [trãŋkwili'za(x)] vt-1. [acalmar] to calm (down). -2. [despreocupar] to reassure.
 ⇒ **tranqüilizar-se** vp to calm down.

tranqüilo, la [trãŋ'kwilu, la] adj -1. [mulher, criança] calm. -2. [lugar, sono] peaceful. -3. [consciência] clear. -4. [sem dificuldades] easy. -5. [certo] certain.

transa ['trãnza] f fam -1. [combinação] arrangement. -2. [relação] relationship. -3. [relação sexual] sex. -4. [assunto] matter. -5. [negócios] business.

transação [trãnza'sãw] (pl -ões) f -1. [combinação, acordo] agreement. -2. [negociação] deal. -3. COM business.

transar [trãn'za(x)] <> vt-1. fam [combinar] to arrange. -2. [arranjar] to obtain. -3. [drogas - tomar] to take; [- negociar] to deal in. <> vi -1. [ter relação sexual] to have sex; ~ **com** to have sex with. -2. [relacionar-se]: ~ **com** to hang out with. -3. [negociar, trabalhar]: ~ **com** to deal in.

transatlântico, ca [trãnza'tlãntʃiku, ka] adj transatlantic.
 ⇒ **transatlântico** m liner.

transbordar [trãnʒbox'da(x)] vi: ~ **(de)** to overflow (from); ~ **de felicidade** to be overjoyed.

transcendental [trãnsẽndẽn'taw] (pl -ais) adj transcendental.

transcender [trãnsẽn'de(x)] vt: ~ **(a)** algo to transcend sthg.

transcorrer [trãnʃko'xe(x)] vi -1. [decorrer] to go by. -2. [decorrer em certo estado ou condição] to pass off.

transcrito [trãnʃ'kritul] m transcript.

transe ['trãnzil] m -1. [espirit] anguish. -2. [situação difícil] ordeal. -3. [hipnótico] trance.

transeunte [trãn'zeũntʃil] mf passerby.

transferência [trãnʃfe'rẽnsjal] f -1. [ger] transfer. -2. PSIC transference. -3. [adiamento] postponement.

transferir [trãnʃfe'ri(x)] vt -1. [deslocar]: ~ algo/alguém para algum lugar to transfer sthg/sb somewhere. -2. [transmitir]: ~ algo para alguém to transfer sthg to sb; PSIC to transfer sthg onto sb. -3. [adiar] to postpone.

transformação [trãnʃfoxma'sãw] (pl -ões) f transformation.

transformador, ra [trãnʃfoxma'do(x), ral (mpl -es, fpl -s) m ELETR transformer.

transformar [trãnʃfox'ma(x)] vt -1. [dar nova forma, modificar] to transform. -2. [converter]: ~ algo/alguém em to turn sthg/sb into.
→ **transformar-se** vp -1. [mudar, transfigurar-se] to be transformed. -2. [converter-se]: ~-se em to turn into, to become.

transfusão [trãnʃfu'zãw] (pl -ões) f transfusion; ~ de sangue blood transfusion.

transgênico, ca [trãnʃ'zeniku, kal adj transgenic.

transgredir [trãnzgre'dʒi(x)] vt [infringir] to transgress.

transgressão [trãnzgre'sãw] (pl -ões) f transgression.

transgressor, ra [trãzgre'so(x), ral <> adj offending. <> m, f offender; ~ da lei offender.

transição [trãnzi'sãw] (pl -ões) f [passagem de um estado a outro] transition.

transitar [trãnzi'ta(x)] vi: ~ (por) [pessoa, carro] to travel (through).

transitivo, va [trãnzi'tʃivu, val adj GRAM transitive.

trânsito ['trãnzitul m -1. [ger] passage. -2. [tráfego] traffic; ~ impedido no entry. -3. [boa aceitação] acceptance; ter bom ~ em to be well-accepted in.

transitório, ria [trãnzi'tɔrju, rjal adj transitory.

translúcido, da [trãnz'lusidu, dal adj -1. [que deixa passar a luz] translucent. -2. fig [claro] clear.

transmissão [trãnzmi'sãw] (pl -ões) f -1. [ger] transmission. -2. [de ordem, notícia, recado] sending. -3. [de bens, cargo] transfer. -4. [RÁDIO & TV - programa] broadcast; [- ato de transmitir] broadcasting; ~ ao vivo live broadcast.

transmissível [trãnzmi'sivew] (pl -eis) adj [doença] transmittable.

transmissor, ra [trãnzmi'so(x), ral adj transmitting.
→ **transmissor** m -1. [ger] transmitter. -2. [de doença] carrier.

transmitir [trãnzmi'tʃi(x)] vt -1. [ger] to transmit. -2. [comunicar] to send. -3. [transferir] to transfer. -4. RÁDIO & TV to broadcast.

transparência [trãnʃpa'rẽnsjal f -1. [ger] transparency. -2. [usada em projetor] slide.

transparente [trãnʃpa'rẽntʃil adj -1. [ger] transparent. -2. [roupa] seethrough. -3. fig [claro, evidente - sentimentos, intenções] clear; o livro é de um moralismo ~ the book is clearly moralistic; [- pessoa] transparent.

transpassar [trãnʃpa'sa(x)] vt -1. [atravessar] to cross. -2. [penetrar, furar] to pierce. -3. [peça de vestuário] to overlap.

transpiração [trãnʃpira'sãw] f -1. [ato] perspiration. -2. [suor] perspiration.

transpirar [trãnʃpi'ra(x)] <> vt -1. [suar] to perspire. -2. [exprimir] to exude. <> vi -1. [suar] to perspire. -2. [revelar-se] to transpire. -3. [divulgar-se] to become known.

transplante [trãnʃ'plãntʃil m transplant.

transportadora [trãnʃpoxta'doral f haulage company.

transportar [trãnʃpox'ta(x)] vt [levar] to transport.

transporte [trãnʃ'pɔxtʃil m -1. [ato] transport. -2. [condução] haulage; ~ coletivo public transport. -3. [soma] amount carried forward.

transtornar [trãnʃtox'na(x)] vt -1. [abalar] to upset. -2. [alterar] to disrupt.
→ **transtornar-se** vp to get upset.

transtorno [trãnʃ'toxnul m -1. [perturbação] confusion. -2. [desordem, alteração] disruption. -3. [contrariedade, contratempo] upset.

transversal [trãnzvex'saw] (pl -ais) <> adj -1. [corte, linha] transverse. -2. [rua]: esta rua é ~ à avenida principal this street crosses the main avenue. <> f [rua transversal] cross street.

trapaça [tra'pasal f cheating; fazer ~s no jogo to cheat during the game.

trapacear [trapa'sja(x)] vt & vi to cheat.

trapaceiro, ra [trapa'sejru, ral <> adj cheating. <> m, f cheat.

trapalhão, ona [trapa'ʎãw, ʎona] (mpl -ões, fpl -s) adj clumsy.

trapézio [tra'pɛzju] m -1. [aparelho] trapeze. -2. GEOM trapezium. -3. [ANAT - no pescoço] trapezius; [- do carpo] trapezium.

trapezista [trape'ziʃta] mf trapeze artist.

trapezoidal [trapezoj'daw] (pl -ais) adj trapezoidal.

trapo ['trapu] m -1. [pedaço de pano] rag. -2. fig: estar um ~ [estar mal física ou moralmente] to be down and out; [estar muito cansado] to be washed out.

traquéia [tra'kɛja] f trachea, windpipe.

traquejo [tra'keʒu] m experience.

trarei [tra'rej] v ⊳ trazer.

traria [tra'ria] v ⊳ trazer.

trás ['trajʃ] adv & prep behind; de ~ para frente back to front; andar para ~ to walk backwards; ficar para ~ to fall behind; de ~ back; por ~ de behind.

traseira [tra'zejra] f -1. [parte posterior] rear. -2. fam [nádegas] bottom.

traseiro, ra [tra'zejru, ra] adj rear.
◆ **traseiro** m fam [nádegas] bottom.

traspassar [traʒpa'sa(x)] vt = transpassar.

traste ['traʃtʃil] m -1. [objeto de pouco valor] bauble. -2. [pessoa - inútil] no-hoper; [- de mau caráter] rogue; estar um ~ [estar mal fisicamente] to be a wreck.

tratado, da [tra'tadu, da] m -1. [acordo] treaty. -2. [obra] treatise.

tratamento [trata'mẽntu] m -1. [ger] treatment. -2. [de problema, tema] handling.

tratar [tra'ta(x)] vt -1. [ger] to treat. -2. [combinar] to deal with. -3. MED: ~ (de) alguém/algo to treat sb/sthg. -4. [negociar] to organize. -5. [abordar] to deal with. -6. [forma de tratamento]: ~ alguém de ou por algo to address sb as ou by sthg.
◆ **tratar de** vi -1. [cuidar de - pessoa, planta] to care for; [- caso, negócio] to look after. -2. [organizar] to organize. -3. [discorrer, versar sobre] to deal with. -4. [empenhar-se]: ~ de fazer algo to try to do sthg.
◆ **tratar-se** vp -1. [cuidar-se] to look after o.s. -2. MED: ~-se com alguém to be under sb's care. -3. loc: trata-se de ... it's a matter of ...; trata-se de uma moça de origem muito humilde she happens to be a girl from a very humble background; de que se trata? what's it about?

trato ['tratu] m -1. [tratamento] treatment. -2. [convivência, contato]

dealings (pl). -3. [acordo, combinação] agreement.

trator [tra'to(x)] (pl -es) m tractor.

trauma ['trawma] m -1. MED injury. -2. PSIC trauma.

traumatizante [trawmatʃi'zãntʃil] adj traumatizing.

traumatizar [trawmatʃi'za(x)] vt -1. MED to injure. -2. PSIC to traumatize. -3. fig [afetar] to affect.

trava ['trava] f [peça] stop.

travado, da [tra'vadu, da] adj -1. [preso] locked. -2. [freado] stopped.

travar [tra'va(x)] vt -1. [fazer parar] to stop. -2. [frear] to brake. -3. [iniciar, desencadear - conversa, amizade] to strike up; [- luta] to start. -4. [movimento] to hinder. -5. [segurar] to take hold of.

trave ['travi] f -1. CONSTR beam. -2. ESP crossbar.

travessa [tra'vɛsa] f -1. [rua] alleyway. -2. [prato] serving dish. -3. [prendedor de cabelo] slide.

travessão [trave'sãw] (pl -ões) m GRAM (em) dash.

travesseiro [trave'sejru] m pillow.

travessia [trave'sia] f -1. [ato] crossing. -2. [viagem] journey.

travesso, ssa [tra'vesu, sa] adj [criança] naughty.

travessura [trave'sura] f -1. [de criança] mischief; fazer ~s to get up to mischief. -2. [brincadeira] prank.

travesti [traveʃtʃil] m -1. [homossexual] transvestite. -2. [artista] drag artist.

trazer [tra'ze(x)] vt -1. [ger] to bring; ~ de volta to bring back. -2. [ter] to have. -3. [usar, trajar] to wear.

TRE (abrev de Tribunal Regional Eleitoral) m Regional Electoral Court.

trecho ['treʃu] m -1. [parte do espaço de um lugar] stretch. -2. LITER & MÚS passage.

treco ['trɛku] m fam [coisa] thing; ter um ~ [sentir-se mal] to have a nasty turn; [zangar-se] to have a fit.

trégua ['trɛgwa] f -1. MIL truce. -2. fig [descanso] rest.

treinado, da [trej'nadu, da] adj -1. [animal] trained. -2. [atleta] fit. -3. [acostumado] practised UK, practiced US.

treinador, ra [trejna'do(x), ra] (mpl -es, fpl -s) m, f trainer.

treinamento [trejna'mẽntu] m training.

treinar [trej'na(x)] ⟨⟩ vt -1. [ger] to train. -2. [praticar] to practise UK, to practice US. ⟨⟩ vi [praticar] to train.

treino ['trejnu] m -1. [ger] training. -2. [destreza] skill.

trejeito [tre'ʒejtu] m -1. [gesto] gesture. -2. [gesto cômico] funny face.

trela ['trɛla] f: dar ~ a *ou* para alguém [conversar com] to keep chatting to sb; [dar confiança a] to encourage sb.

treliça [tre'lisa] f [para porta, planta] trellis.

trem ['trẽ] (pl -ns) m -1. FERRO train; ir de ~ to go by train; **pegar um** ~ to take a train; ~ **de carga** goods train. -2. AERON: ~ **de aterrissagem** landing gear, undercarriage.

trema ['trema] m diaeresis UK, dieresis US.

trem-bala [ˌtrẽ'bala] (pl **trens-bala**) m high-speed train.

tremelique [treme'liki] m trembling.

tremendo, da [tre'mẽndu, da] adj -1. [imenso] enormous. -2. [terrível] terrible. -3. [fantástico] amazing.

tremer [tre'me(x)] vi to shake; ~ **de frio/ medo** to shake with cold/fear.

tremor [tre'mo(x)] (pl -es) m tremor; ~ **de terra** earthquake.

tremular [tremu'la(x)] vi -1. [bandeira] to flutter. -2. [luz] to flicker.

trêmulo, la ['tremulu, la] adj -1. [pessoa, mão] trembling. -2. [passo, voz] faltering.

trena ['trena] f [fita métrica] tape measure.

trenó [tre'nɔ] m sledge UK, sled US.

trepada [tre'pada] f mfam leg-over; **dar uma** ~ to get laid.

trepadeira [trepa'dejra] f creeper.

trepar [tre'pa(x)] vi -1. [subir]: ~ **(em algo)** to climb (up sthg). -2. mfam [ter relações sexuais]: ~ **(com alguém)** to get laid.

trepidação [trepida'sãw] f shaking.

trepidar [trepi'da(x)] vi to shake.

três ['trejʃ] <> num three. <> m three; *veja também* **seis**.

tresloucado, da [treʒlo'kadu, da] adj crazy.

Três-Marias [ˌtrejʒma'riaʃ] fpl -1. ASTRON Orion's Belt. -2. BOT bougainvillea.

trevas ['trɛvaʃ] fpl [escuridão] darkness (sg).

trevo ['trevu] m -1. BOT clover. -2. [de vias] intersection.

treze ['trezi] <> num thirteen. <> m [algarismo] thirteen; *veja também* **seis**.

trezentos, tas [tre'zẽntuʃ, taʃ] <> num three hundred. <> m [algarismo] three hundred; *veja também* **seis**.

triagem ['trjaʒẽ] f -1. [seleção] selection; **fazer uma** ~ to make a selection. -2. [separação] sorting.

triângulo ['trjãngulu] m triangle.

triathlon ['trjatlu] m triathlon.

tribal [tri'baw] adj tribal.

tribo ['tribu] m tribe.

tribulação [tribula'sãw] (pl -ões) f tribulation.

tribuna [tri'buna] f -1. [de orador] rostrum. -2. [em espetáculos públicos] platform; ~ **da imprensa** press gallery.

tribunal [tribu'naw] (pl -ais) m -1. [instituição] court; **Tribunal de Contas** Court of Accounts; **Tribunal de Justiça** Court of Justice. -2. [os magistrados] bench.

tributar [tribu'ta(x)] vt -1. [ger] to tax. -2. [pagar como tributo] to pay tax on. -3. fig [render, prestar] to pay.

tributário, ria [tribu'tarju, rja] adj -1. [relativo a tributo] tax (antes de subst). -2. [rio] tributary (antes de subst).

tributo [tri'butu] m -1. [imposto] tax. -2. fig [ônus] duty.

tricampeão, peã [trikãn'pjãw, pjã] m, f three-times champion.

triciclo [tri'siklu] m -1. [de criança] tricycle. -2. [usado para a entrega de mercadorias] (delivery) tricycle.

tricô [tri'ko] -1. m knitting; **de** ~ knitted. -2. ⊳ **ponto**.

tricolor [triko'lo(x)] adj -1. [desenho, bandeira] three-coloured UK, three-coloured US. -2. FUT tricolour UK, tricolor US.

tricotar [triko'ta(x)] vt & vi to knit.

tridimensional [tridʒimẽnsjo'naw] (pl -ais) adj three-dimensional.

trigal [tri'gaw] m wheat field.

trigêmeo, mea [tri'ʒemju, mja] <> adj [criança] triplet (antes de subst). <> m, f triplet.

trigésimo, ma [tri'ʒɛzimu, ma] <> num thirtieth. <> m thirtieth; *veja também* **sexto**.

trigo ['trigu] m wheat.

trilha ['triʎa] f -1. [caminho] path. -2. [rasto] trail. -3. fig [exemplo]: **seguir a** ~ **de alguém** to follow in sb's footsteps. -4. COMPUT track. -5. CINE: ~ **sonora** soundtrack.

trilhado, da [tri'ʎadu, da] adj [percorrido] well-trodden.

trilhão [tri'ʎãw] (pl -ões) num trillion.

trilho ['triʎu] m -1. FERRO rail. -2. [caminho] track.

trimestral [trimeʃ'traw] (pl -ais) adj quarterly.

trimestralidade [trimeʃtrawi'dadʒi] f quarterly payment.

trimestre [tri'mɛʃtri] m quarter.

trincar [trĩŋ'ka(x)] <> vt -1. [cortar com os dentes] to crunch. -2. [cerrar] to grit. -3. [rachar] to crack. <> vi [rachar] to crack.

trincheira [trĩn'ʃejra] f MIL trench.

trinco ['trĩŋkul] *m* **-1.** [ferrolho] latch. **-2.** [lingüeta] catch.

Trinidad e Tobago [trini,dadʒito'bagul] *n* Trinidad and Tobago.

trinta ['trĩtal] <> *num* thirty. <> *m* thirty; *veja também* **sessenta**.

trio ['triwl *m* trio; ~ **elétrico** music float.

tripa [tri'pal *f* **-1.** [intestino] intestine. **-2.** *CULIN* tripe *(inv)*.

tripé [tri'pɛl *m* [suporte] tripod.

triplicar [tripli'ka(x)l] <> *vt* **-1.** *MAT* to treble. **-2.** [aumentar muito] to triple. <> *vi* **-1.** [tornar-se triplo] to treble. **-2.** [aumentar muito] to triple.

triplo, pla ['triplu, plal *adj* triple.
➡ **triplo** *m*: 27 é o ~ de 9 27 is three times 9; **este sofá é o** ~ **daquele** this sofa is three times the size of that one.

tripulação [tripula'sãwl (*pl* **-ões**) *f* crew.

tripulado, da [tripula'du, dal *adj* **-1.** [nave] manned. **-2.** [barco] crewed.

tripulante [tripu'lãntʃil *mf* crew member.

tripular [tripu'la(x)l] *vt* **-1.** [prover de tripulação] to man. **-2.** [governar] to crew.

triste ['triʃtʃil *adj* **-1.** [ger] sad. **-2.** [entristecedor] depressing. **-3.** [sombrio, lúgubre] sombre. **-4.** *fam* [pessoa] sad.

tristeza [triʃ'tezal *f* **-1.** [de pessoa] sadness. **-2.** [de lugar] gloominess. **-3.:** **ser uma** ~ [ser terrível] to be appalling.

triturar [tritu'ra(x)l] *vt* **-1.** [reduzir a fragmentos] to grind. **-2.** *fig* [afligir] to crush.

triunfante [trjũn'fãntʃil *adj* triumphant.

triunfar [trjũn'fa(x)l] *vi* [vencer] to triumph.

triunfo ['trjũnful *m* triumph.

trivial [tri'vjawl] (*pl* **-ais**) <> *adj* **-1.** [comida] ordinary. **-2.** [assunto, preocupações] trivial. <> *m* [comida cotidiana] everyday food.

trivialidade [trivjali'dadʒil *f* triviality.

triz ['triʃl *m*: **por um** ~ by a whisker.

troça [tro'sal *f* [zombaria] ridicule; **fazer** ~ **de alguém** to make fun of sb.

trocadilho [troka'dʒiʎul *m* pun.

trocado, da [tro'kadu, dal *adj* **-1.** [errado] wrong. **-2.** [dinheiro] in coins.
➡ **trocado** *m* small change.

trocador, ra [troka'do(x), ral *m, f* [em ônibus] conductor.

trocar [tro'ka(x)l] <> *vt* **-1.** [ger] to change; ~ **alguém/algo de lugar** to change the place of sb/sthg; ~ **dinheiro** to change money. **-2.** [permutar] to swap. **-3.** [confundir] to mix up. **-4.** [cheque] to cash. **-5.** [reciprocar] to exchange. **-6.** [permutar]: ~ **algo/alguém por algo**, ~ **algo/alguém por alguém** to change sthg/sb for sthg, to

change sthg/sb for sb. **-7.** [dar preferência]: ~ **algo por algo** to exchange sthg for sthg. **-8.** *loc:* ~ **as pernas** *fig* to trip over one's (own) feet. <> *vi:* ~ **de algo** to change sthg.
➡ **trocar-se** *vp* [mudar de roupa] to get changed.

troçar [tro'sa(x)l] *vt* to ridicule.

troco ['trokul *m* **-1.** [dinheiro] change. **-2.** *fig* [revide] retort, rejoinder; **a** ~ **de que ela fez isso?** [por quê, para quê] what on earth did she do that for?

troço ['trosul *m fam* [coisa] thing; **ter um** ~ [sentir-se mal] to feel a pang; [ficar chocado, danado] to get a shock; **ser** ~ **em algum lugar/em algo** [ser influente] to have influence somewhere/in sthg; **ser um** ~ [ser muito bonito, bom] to be amazing.

troféu [tro'fɛwl *m* trophy.

tromba ['trõnbal *f* **-1.** [de elefante] trunk. **-2.** *fam* [cara amarrada] long face.

trombada [trõn'badal *f* crash; **dar uma** ~ to crash.

tromba-d'água [,trõnba'dagwal (*pl* **trombas-d'água**) *f* [chuva] downpour.

trombadinha [trõnba'dʒiɲal *mf gír* [pivete] very young thief.

trombeta [trõn'betal *f MÚS* [instrumento] trumpet.

trombone [trõn'bonil *m MÚS* trombone.

trombose [trõn'bɔzil *f* thrombosis.

trombudo, da [trõn'budu, dal *adj fig* [emburrado] sulky.

trompa ['trõnpal *f* **-1.** *MÚS* horn. **-2.** *ANAT:* ~ **de Falópio** Fallopian tube; **ligar as** ~**s** to have one's tubes tied, to undergo tubal ligation.

tronco ['trõŋkul *m* **-1.** [BOT - caule] trunk; [- ramo] branch. **-2.** *ANAT* trunk. **-3.** *TELEC* trunkline. **-4.** [de família, raça] lineage.

trono ['tronul *m* **-1.** [cadeira] throne. **-2.** *fig* [poder] driving seat. **-3.** *fam* [latrina] throne.

tropa ['trɔpal *f* **-1.** *MIL* army. **-2.** [conjunto de pessoas] troop. **-3.** [polícia]: ~ **de choque** riot squad.

tropeção [trope'sãwl (*pl* **-ões**) *m* trip.

tropeçar [trope'sa(x)l] *vi* to trip; ~ **em algo** [dar topada em] to trip over sthg; *fig* [esbarrar em] to stumble on sthg.

tropeções [trope'sõjʃl *pl* ▷ **tropeção**.

trôpego, ga ['tropegu, gal *adj* unsteady.

tropical [tropi'kawl] (*pl* **-ais**) *adj* tropical.

tropicalismo [tropika'liʒmul *m Brazilian musical movement*.

trópico ['trɔpikul *m* tropic; **Trópico de Câncer/Capricórnio** Tropic of Cancer/Capricorn.

troquei [tro'kej] v ⊳ **trocar**.

trotar [tro'ta(x)] vi to trot.

trote ['trɔtʃi] m -1. [de cavalo] trot. -2. [por telefone] hoax. -3. [em calouro] trick.

trouxa ['troʃa] ⟨⟩ adj fam [bobo] foolish. ⟨⟩ mf fam [bobo] fool. ⟨⟩ f bundle.

trouxe ['trosi] v ⊳ **trazer**.

trova ['trɔva] f -1. [cantiga] folksong. -2. [poesia] ballad.

trovão [tro'vãw] (pl -ões) m thunder.

trovejar [trove'ʒa(x)] vi METEOR to thunder.

trovoada [tro'vwada] f thunderstorm.

trucidar [trusi'da(x)] vt to slaughter, to massacre.

truculência [truku'lẽsja] f horror.

truculento, ta [truku'lẽntu, ta] adj gruesome.

trufa ['trufa] f truffle.

truncar [trũŋ'ka(x)] vt -1. [texto] to shorten. -2. [discurso] to cut off.

trunfo ['trũfu] m trump card.

truque ['truki] m trick.

truste ['truʃtʃi] m -1. [organização financeira] trust. -2. [grupo de empresas] corporation.

truta ['truta] f trout.

TSE [te'ɛsi ɛ] (abrev de **Tribunal Superior Eleitoral**) m Brazilian higher electoral tribunal.

TST [te'ɛsi te] (abrev de **Tribunal Superior do Trabalho**) m Brazilian higher employment tribunal.

tu ['tu] pron pess you.

tua ['tua] f ⊳ **teu**.

tuba ['tuba] f MÚS tuba.

tubarão [tuba'rãw] (pl -ões) m shark.

tuberculose [tubexku'lɔzi] f tuberculosis, TB.

tubo ['tubu] m -1. [ger] tube; ~ **de ensaio** test tube. -2. [canal] pipe.

tubulação [tubula'sãw] f -1. [conjunto de tubos] pipework. -2. [colocação de tubos] plumbing.

tucano [tu'kãnu] m -1. ZOOL toucan. -2. POL member of Brazilian Social Democratic Party.

tudo ['tudu] pron indef -1. [todas as coisas, a totalidade] everything; ~ **quanto é tipo de gente** all kinds of people. -2. [a coisa fundamental]: **ser** ~ to be everything.
  ➡ **acima de tudo** loc adv above all.
  ➡ **apesar de tudo** loc prep despite everything.
  ➡ **depois de tudo** loc adv after all.

tufão [tu'fãw] (pl -ões) m typhoon.

tulipa [tu'lipa] f -1. BOT tulip. -2. [chope servido em copo alto] tall glass of draught beer.

tumba ['tũba] f [sepultura] tomb.

tumor [tu'mo(x)] (pl -es) m tumour UK, tumor US.

túmulo ['tumulu] m -1. [monumento] tomb. -2. [cova] grave.

tumulto [tu'muwtu] m -1. [grande movimento] commotion. -2. [confusão, balbúrdia] hubbub. -3. [motim] riot.

tumultuado, da [tumuw'twadu, da] adj -1. [vida] turbulent. -2. [rua] noisy.

tumultuar [tumuw'twa(x)] ⟨⟩ vt [desordenar, agitar] to disrupt. ⟨⟩ vi -1. [fazer barulho] to make a noise. -2. [amotinar-se] to rise up.

túnel ['tunɛw] (pl -eis) m tunnel.

túnica ['tunika] f [vestimenta] tunic.

Túnis ['tuniʃ] n Tunis.

Tunísia [tu'nizja] f Tunisia.

tupi [tu'pi] ⟨⟩ adj Tupi. ⟨⟩ mf Tupi Indian. ⟨⟩ m [língua] Tupi.

tupiniquim [tupini'kĩ] ⟨⟩ adj -1. [relativo aos tupiniquins] Brazilian Indian. -2. pej [brasileiro] Brazilian. ⟨⟩ mf Brazilian Indian.

turbante [tux'bãntʃi] m turban.

turbilhão [tuxbi'ʎãw] (pl -ões) m -1. [de água] whirlpool. -2. [de ar] whirlwind. -3. fig [agitação] whirl.

turbina [tux'bina] f turbine.

turbinado, da [tuxbina'du, da] adj fam [motor, processador] turbocharged.

turbulência [tuxbu'lẽsja] f -1. METEOR turbulence. -2. [desordem, inquietação] unrest.

turbulento, ta [tuxbu'lẽntu, ta] adj -1. METEOR stormy. -2. [tumultuoso] turbulent. -3. [que cria desordem] disorderly.

turco, ca ['tuxku, ka] ⟨⟩ adj Turkish. ⟨⟩ m, f Turk.
  ➡ **turco** m [língua] Turkish.

turfe ['tuxfi] m ESP horse-racing.

turismo [tu'riʒmu] m tourism.

turista [tu'riʃta] mf [quem faz turismo] tourist.

turístico, ca [tu'riʃtʃiku, ka] adj tourist (antes de subst).

turma ['tuxma] f -1. [grupo] group. -2. [grupo de trabalhadores] shift. -3. EDUC class. -4. fam [grupo de amigos] gang.

turnê [tux'ne] f tour.

turno ['tuxnu] m -1. [turma] group. -2. [horário de trabalho] shift; [- de escola] class; ~ **da noite** night shift; ~ **da manhã** morning shift. -3. ESP round. -4. [de eleição] round. -5. [vez] turn.

turquesa [tux'keza] ⟨⟩ adj inv turquoise. ⟨⟩ m [cor] turquoise. ⟨⟩ f [pedra] turquoise.

Turquia [tux'kia] n Turkey.

turrão, ona [tu'xãw, ɔna] *adj fam* [teimoso, pertinaz] stubborn.

turvo, va ['tuxvu, va] *adj* cloudy.

tusso ['tusul *v* ⊳ **tossir**.

tutano [tu'tãnu] *m ANAT* marrow.

tutela [tu'tɛla] *f* **-1.** *JUR* guardianship. **-2.** [proteção] protection. **-3.** [supervisão] supervision.

tutor, ra [tu'to(x), ra] (*mpl* **-es**, *fpl* **-s**) *m, f* guardian.

tutu [tu'tul *m* **-1.** *CULIN* Brazilian dish consisting of beans, bacon and cassava flour. **-2.** *fam* [dinheiro] cash.

TV [te' ve] (*abrev de* **televisão**) *f* TV.

U

u, U *m* [letra] u, U.

uai ['waj] *interj* **-1.** [espanto, surpresa, terror] oh! **-2.** [reforço, confirmação] yeah!

úbere ['uberi] ⬦ *adj* [solo] fertile. ⬦ *m* [mama] udder.

Ubes (*abrev de* União Brasileira dos Estudantes Secundaristas) *f Brazilian union of secondary students.*

ué ['wɛ] *interj* **-1.** [exprimindo surpresa] what? **-2.** [exprimindo ironia] hey!

UE (*abrev de* União Européia) *f* EU.

UEM (*abrev de* União Econômica e Monetária) *f* EMU.

UERJ (*abrev de* Universidade Estadual do Rio de Janeiro) *f state university of Rio de Janeiro.*

UF (*abrev de* Unidade Federativa) *f state.*

ufanar-se [ufa'naxsil *vp*: ~ **de** to take inordinate pride in.

ufanismo [ufa'niʒmu] *m* **-1.** [por feitos pessoais] vainglory. **-2.** [pela pátria] national pride.

UFBA (*abrev de* Universidade Federal da Bahia) *f federal university of Bahia.*

UFMG (*abrev de* Universidade Federal de Minas Gerais) *f federal university of Minas Gerais.*

UFRGS (*abrev de* Universidade Federal do Rio Grande do Sul) *f federal university of Rio Grande do Sul.*

UFRJ (*abrev de* Universidade Federal do Rio de Janeiro) *f federal university of Rio de Janeiro.*

Uganda [u'gãnda] *n* Uganda.

UHF (*abrev de* **Ultra High Frequency**) *f* UHF.

ui ['uj] *interj* **-1.** [exprimindo dor] ouch! **-2.** [exprimindo surpresa] hey!

uísque ['wiʃki] *m* whisky.

uivada [uj'vada] *f* howl.

uivante [uj'vãntʃi] *adj* howling.

uivar [uj'va(x)] *vi* [ger] to howl; ~ **(de)** to howl (with).

uivo ['ujvu] *m* howl.

UK (*abrev de* **United Kingdom**) *m* UK.

úlcera ['uwsera] *f* ulcer.

ulterior [uwte'rjo(x)] *adj* [que ocorre depois] subsequent.

última ['uwtʃima] *f* ⊳ **último**.

ultimamente [ˌuwtʃima'mẽntʃi] *adv* lately.

últimas ['uwtʃimaʃ] *fpl* ⊳ **último**.

ultimato [uwtʃi'matul, **ultimátum** [uwtʃi'matũ] *m* ultimatum.

último, ma ['uwtʃimu, ma] ⬦ *adj* **-1.** [ger] last; **por** ~ [em último lugar] last; [finalmente] lastly. **-2.** [mais recente] latest. **-3.** [o pior] worst. **-4.** [gravíssimo] final. **-5.** [máximo] ultimate. ⬦ *m, f* [em fila, competição] last.
➡ **última** *f* **-1.** [novidade] latest. **-2.** [asneira] latest blunder.

ultrajar [uwtra'ʒa(x)] *vt* to outrage.

ultraje [uwtra'ʒi] *m* outrage.

ultraleve [ˌuwtra'lɛvi] *m* microlight.

ultramar [ˌuwtra'ma(x)] *m* overseas.

ultramarino, na [ˌuwtrama'rinu, na] *adj* overseas (*antes de subst*).

ultrapassado, da [ˌuwtrapa'sadu, da] *adj* out-of-date.

ultrapassagem [ˌuwtrapa'saʒẽ] (*pl* **-ns**) *f* overtaking *UK*, passing *US*.

ultrapassar [ˌuwtrapa'sa(x)] ⬦ *vt* **-1.** [passar à frente de] to overtake *UK*, to pass *US*. **-2.** [transpor] to cross. **-3.** [em qualidade]: ~ **alguém (em algo)** to surpass sb (in sthg). **-4.** [exceder] to exceed. ⬦ *vi* [passar à frente] to overtake *UK*, to pass *US*.

ultra-som [ˌuwtra'sõ] (*pl* **-s**) *m* ultrasound.

ultravioleta [ˌuwtravjo'leta] *adj* ultraviolet.

um, uma [ũ, 'uma] (*mpl* uns, *fpl* umas) ⬦ *artigo indefinido* a, an (*antes de vogal ou h mudo*); ~ **homem** a man; **uma casa** a house; **uma mulher** a woman; **uma hora** an hour; **uma maçã** an apple. ⬦ *adj* **-1.** [exprime quantidade, data indefinida] one, some *pl*; **comprei uns livros** I bought some books; **uma dia voltarei** I'll be back one day; **estou saindo umas semanas de férias** I'm going on holidays for a few weeks. **-2.** [para indicar quantidades] one; **trinta e** ~ **dias** thirty-one days; ~ **litro/metro/quilo** one litre/metre/kilo. **-3.** [aproximadamente] about, around; **esperei uns dez minutos** I waited for about ten minutes; **estavam lá umas cinquenta pessoas** there were about fifty people there. **- 4.** [para enfatizar]: **está** ~ **frio/calor** it's so cold/hot; **estou com uma sede** I'm so thirsty; **foi** ~ **daqueles dias!** it's been one of those days! ◇ *pron* [indefinido] one, some *pl*; **me dê** ~ give me one; **pede mais uma** ask for another one; ~ **deles** one of them; ~ **a** ~, ~ **por** ~ one by one; **uns e outros** some/other people. ◇ *num* one ▷ *veja também* **seis.**

umbanda [ũn'bãnda] *f* [espirit] *Afro-Brazilian cult.*

umbigo [ũn'bigu] *m* navel.

umbilical [ũnbili'kaw] (*pl* -ais) *adj* ▷ **cordão.**

umbral [ũn'braw] (*pl* -ais) *m* **-1.** [de porta] doorway. **-2.** [limiar] threshold.

umedecer [umide'se(x)] *vt* to dampen.
➡ **umedecer-se** *vp* to mist over.

umedecido, da [umide'sidu, da] *adj* damp.

umidade [umi'dadʒi] *f* **-1.** [de clima, ar] humidity. **-2.** [de parede, terra] damp.

úmido, da ['umidu, da] *adj* damp.

UN (*abrev de* **United Nations**) *f* UN.

UnB (*abrev de* **Universidade de Brasília**) *f university of Brasília.*

unânime [u'nãnimi] *adj* unanimous.

unanimidade [unãnimi'dadʒi] *f* unanimity.

UNE (*abrev de* **União Nacional dos Estudantes**) *f Brazilian national union of students,* ≃ NUS *UK.*

UNESCO (*abrev de* **United Nations Educational, Scientific and Cultural Organization**) *f* UNESCO.

ungir [ũn'ʒi(x)] *vt* RELIG to anoint.

ungüento [ũn'gwẽntu] *m* ointment.

unha ['uɲa] *f* nail; **fazer as** ~**s** [com manicure] to do one's nails; ~ **encravada** ingrowing nail.

unhada [u'ɲada] *f* scratch.

unha-de-fome [ˌuɲadʒi'fɔmi] (*pl* **unhas-de-fome**) ◇ *adj* miserly. ◇ *mf* miser.

unhar [u'ɲa(x)] *vt* to scratch.

união [u'ɲãjw] (*pl* -ões) *f* **-1.** [ger] union. **-2.** [junção] joining.
➡ **União** *f* **-1.** [o governo federal]: **a União** the Union. **-2.** [confederação]: **a União Européia** the European Union.

Unicamp (*abrev de* **Universidade Estadual de Campinas**) *f university of Campinas.*

UNICEF (*abrev de* **United Nations International Children's Emergency Fund**) *m* UNICEF.

único, ca ['uniku, ka] *adj* **-1.** [ger] unique. **-2.** [só] single; **ser filho** ~ to be an only child.

unidade [uni'dadʒi] *f* **-1.** [ger] unit; ~ **de CD-ROM** CD-ROM drive; ~ **de disco** disc drive. **-2.** [uniformidade, união, coesão] unity.

unido, da [u'nidu, da] *adj* **-1.** [ligado] joined. **-2.** *fig* [pessoas] united.

UNIFESP (*abrev de* **Universidade Federal de São Paulo**) *f federal university of São Paulo.*

unificar [unifi'ka(x)] *vt* **-1.** [unir] to unite. **-2.** [uniformizar] to unify.

uniforme [uni'fɔxmi] ◇ *adj* **-1.** [que só tem uma forma, semelhante] uniform. **-2.** [que não varia] regular. ◇ *m* [roupa] uniform; **de** ~ in uniform.

uniformizado, da [unifoxmi'zadu, da] *adj* **-1.** [de uniforme] uniformed. **-2.** [uniforme] uniform.

uniformizar [unifoxmi'za(x)] *vt* **-1.** [unificar] to standardize. **-2.** [pessoa] to put into uniform.
➡ **uniformizar-se** *vp* [vestir uniforme] to wear one's uniform.

unir [u'ni(x)] *vt* **-1.** [ger] to unite. **-2.** [juntar] [comunicar cidades] to join (together). **-3.** [combinar] to combine; ~ **o útil ao agradável** to mix business with pleasure.
➡ **unir-se** *vp* **-1.** [juntar-se] to unite; ~ -**se a algo/alguém** to join sthg/sb. **-2.** [afetivamente] to be united. **-3.** [conciliar-se] to be reconciled.

uníssono, na [u'nisonu, na] *adj* unison; **em** ~ in unison.

unitário, ria [uni'tarju, rja] *adj* **-1.** [preço] unit *(antes de subst).* **-2.** POL unitary.

universal [univex'saw] (*pl* -ais) *adj* universal.

universidade [univexsi'dadʒi] *f* **-1.** [ger] university. **-2.** [pessoal] faculty.

universitário, ria [univexsi'tarju, rja] ◇ *adj* university *(antes de subst).* ◇ *m, f* **-1.** [professor] faculty member, university lecturer. **-2.** [aluno] university student.

universo [uni'vɛxsu] *m* **-1.** ASTRON universe. **-2.** *fig* [mundo] world.

uno, una ['unu, 'una] *adj* single.

uns [ũnʃ] ▷ **um.**

untar [ũn'ta(x)] *vt* : ~ **algo (com)** [forma] to grease sthg (with); [corpo] to oil sthg (with).

update ['apdejtʃi] *m* COMPUT update.

upgrade [ˈapɡrejdʒi] *m* COMPUT: **fazer um ~ to** upgrade.

upload [ˈaplodʒi] *m* COMPUT: **fazer um ~ to** upload.

urânio [uˈrãnju] *m* uranium.

Urano [uˈrãnu] *n* Uranus.

urbanismo [uxbaˈniʒmu] *m* town planning.

urbanista [uxbaˈniʃta] *mf* town planner.

urbanização [uxbanizaˈsãw] *f* urbanization.

urbanizar [uxbaniˈza(x)] *vt* **-1.** [área] to urbanize. **-2.** [pessoa] to refine.

urbano, na [uxˈbãnu, na] *adj* **-1.** [da cidade] urban. **-2.** [pessoa - com hábitos citadinos] urban; [- cortês] urbane.

urdidura [uxdʒiˈdura] *f* **-1.** [conjunto de fios] warp. **-2.** [enredo] plot.

urdu [uxˈdu] *m* [língua] Urdu.

urgência [uxˈʒẽnsja] *f* urgency; **com ~** urgently.

urgente [uxˈʒẽntʃi] *adj* urgent.

úrico, ca [ˈuriku, ka] *adj* [ácido] uric.

urina [uˈrina] *f* urine.

urinar [uriˈna(x)] <> *vt* **-1.** [sangue] to pass. **-2.** [cama] to wet. <> *vi* [expelir urina] to urinate. ◆ **urinar-se** *vp* [com urina] to wet o.s.

urinol [uriˈnɔw] (*pl* **-óis**) *m* chamber pot.

URL (*abrev de* Universal Resources Locator) *f* URL.

urna [ˈuxna] *f* [caixa] urn; **~ eleitoral** ballot box; **~ eletrônica** computerized vote.

urrar [uˈxa(x)] <> *vt* [gritar] to scream. <> *vi* **-1.** [animal] to roar. **-2.** [gritar]: **~ de dor** to scream with pain.

urro [ˈuxu] *m* **-1.** [de animal] roar. **-2.** [grito] scream.

urso, sa [ˈuxsu, sa] *m, f* bear. ◆ **Ursa** *f*: **Ursa Maior/Menor** Ursa Major/Minor.

urso-branco [ˌuxsuˈbrãŋku] *m* polar bear.

urso-polar [ˌuxsuˈpola(x)] (*pl* **ursos-polares**) *m* polar bear.

urtiga [uxˈtʃiga] *f* nettle.

urubuzar [urubuˈza(x)] *vt fam* [com o olhar] to watch like a hawk.

Uruguai [uruˈgwaj] *n*: (o) **~** Uruguay.

uruguaio, ia [uruˈgwaju, ja] <> *adj* Uruguayan. <> *m, f* Uruguayan.

usado, da [uˈzadu, da] *adj* **-1.** [utilizado] used; **muito/pouco ~** much/little used. **-2.** [comum] usual. **-3.** [na moda] fashionable. **-4.** [gasto] worn out.

usar [uˈza(x)] <> *vt* **-1.** [ger] to use. **-2.** [gastar] to wear out. **-3.** [vestir, ter] to wear. **-4.** [costumar]: **~ fazer algo** to be in the habit of doing sthg. <> *vi*

[servir-se de]: **~ de algo** to use sthg.

username [uzexˈnejmi] (*pl* **usernames**) *m* COMPUT username.

usina [uˈzina] *f* **-1.** [industrial] factory; **~ de aço** steelworks *(pl)*. **-2.** [agrícola]: **~ de açúcar** sugar mill. **-3.** [de energia elétrica]: **~ hidrelétrica** hydroelectric power station; **~ termonuclear** nuclear power station.

uso [ˈuzu] *m* **-1.** [ger] use; **objetos de ~ pessoal** personal belongings; **fazer ~ de** to make use of; **para ~ externo/interno** FARM for external/internal use. **-2.** [vestir] wearing. **-3.** [costume] common practice. **-4.** [desgaste] wear. **-5.** LING usage.

USP (*abrev de* Universidade de São Paulo) *f* university of São Paulo.

usual [uˈzwaw] (*pl* **-ais**) *adj* usual.

usuário, ria [uˈzwarju, rja] *m, f* user.

úteis [ˈutejʃ] *pl* ▷ **útil**.

utensílio [utẽnˈsilju] *m* **-1.** [instrumento] tool. **-2.** [de cozinha, doméstico] utensil.

útero [ˈuteru] *m* uterus, womb.

UTI (*abrev de* Unidade de Terapia Intensiva) *f* ICU.

útil [ˈutʃiw] (*pl* **-eis**) *adj* **-1.** [ger] useful. **-2.** [reservado ao trabalho]: **dia ~** working day.

utilidade [utʃiliˈdadʒi] *f* **-1.** [ger] usefulness. **-2.** [utensílio]: **~s domésticas** domestic appliances.

utilitário, ria [utʃiliˈtarju, rja] *adj* **-1.** [objetivo, peça *etc.*] practical. **-2.** AUTO & COMPUT utility.

utilização [utʃilizaˈsãw] (*pl* **-ões**) *f* use.

utilizar [utʃiliˈza(x)] *vt* to use. ◆ **utilizar-se** *vp*: **~-se de** to make use of.

utopia [utoˈpia] *f* Utopia.

utópico, ca [uˈtɔpiku, ka] *adj* Utopian.

UV (*abrev de* Ultravioleta) *m* UV.

uva [ˈuva] *f* **-1.** [fruta] grape. **-2.** *fam* [pessoa, coisa]: **uma ~** a delight.

V

v, V *m* [letra] v, V.

vã [vã] *f* ▷ **vão**.

vaca [ˈvaka] *f* **-1.** ZOOL cow; **carne de ~** beef; **~ leiteira** dairy cow; **a ~ foi para o brejo** it went out the window. **-2.** *fam* *pej* [pessoa] lump. **-3.** *loc*: **no tempo das ~ s gordas** in times of plenty; **no tempo das ~ s magras** during lean times.

vacante [va'kãntʃi] *adj* vacant.

vacilante [vasi'lãntʃi] *adj* **-1.** [hesitante] hesitant. **-2.** [pouco firme] wobbly. **-3.** [luz] flickering.

vacilar [vasi'la(x)] *vi* **-1.** [hesitar] to hesitate; **~ em algo/em fazer algo** to hesitate in sthg/in doing sthg. **-2.** [oscilar] to sway. **-3.** [cambalear] to totter. **-4.** [luz] to flicker.

vacilo [va'silu] *m fam* **-1.** [hesitação] havering, shilly-shallying. **-2.** [erro, falha] howler, blunder.

vacina [va'sina] *f* vaccine.

vacinação [vasina'sãw] (*pl* **-ões**) *f* vaccination.

vacinar [vasi'na(x)] *vt MED*: **~ alguém (contra)** to vaccinate sb (against).

➡ **vacinar-se** *vp MED*: **~-se (contra)** to be vaccinated (against).

vácuo ['vakwu] *m* **-1.** *FÍSICA* vacuum. **-2.** *METEOR* low. **-3.** [espaço] space. **-4.** *fig* [vazio] void.

vadiar [va'dʒia(x)] *vi* **-1.** [viver na ociosidade] to lounge about. **-2.** [suj: aluno, professional] to skive. **-3.** [perambular] to roam.

vadio, dia [va'dʒiu, ʒia] *adj* **-1.** [ocioso] idle. **-2.** [aluno, professional] skiving. **-3.** [vagabundo] vagrant.

vaga ['vaga] *f* ⊳ **vago**.

vagabundo, da [vaga'bũndu, da] ◇ *adj* **-1.** [errante] vagabond. **-2.** [vadio] idle. **-3.** [safado] shameless. **-4.** [mulher] easy. **-5.** [produto] shoddy. ◇ *m, f* **-1.** [pessoa errante] tramp. **-2.** [vadio] idler. **-3.** [safado] rogue.

vaga-lume [ˌvaga'lumi] (*pl* **vaga-lumes**) *m* **-1.** *ZOOL* glow-worm. **-2.** [cine] usher.

vagão [va'gãw] (*pl* **-ões**) *m* **-1.** [de passageiros] carriage. **-2.** [de carga] wagon.

vagão-leito [vaˌgãw'lejtu] (*pl* **vagões-leito**) *m* sleeping car.

vagão-restaurante [vaˌgãwxeʃtaw'rãntʃi] (*pl* **vagões-restaurante**) *m* buffet car.

vagar [va'ga(x)] ◇ *vi* **-1.** [ficar desocupado] to be vacant. **-2.** [vaguear] to drift. ◇ *m* [lentidão] slowness; **com mais ~** at greater leisure.

vagaroso, osa [vaga'rozu, ɔza] *adj* slow.

vagem ['vaʒẽ] (*pl* **-ns**) *f* green bean.

vagina [va'ʒina] *f* vagina.

vago, ga ['vagu, ga] *adj* **-1.** [impreciso] vague. **-2.** [desocupado] vacant. **-3.** [desabitado] empty.

➡ **vaga** *f* **-1.** [em hotel] vacancy. **-2.** [em empresa *etc.*] vacancy. **-3.** [para carro] space. **-4.** [onda] wave.

vagões [va'gõjʃ] *pl* ⊳ **vagão**.

vaguear [va'gja(x)] *vi* **-1.** [perambular] to drift. **-2.** [passear] to ramble.

vaia ['vaja] *f* boo.

vaiar [va'ja(x)] *vt* & *vi* to boo.

vaidade [vaj'dadʒi] *f* **-1.** [orgulho] vanity. **-2.** [futilidade] futility.

vaidoso, osa [vaj'dozu, ɔza] *adj* vain; **ser ~ de alguém/algo** to be proud of sb/sthg.

vaivém [vaj'vẽl (*pl* **-ns**) *m* **-1.** [de pessoas] to-and-fro. **-2.** [de pêndulo] swinging. **-3.** [de barco] rocking.

vala ['vala] *f* [escavação] ditch.

vale ['vali] *m* **-1.** *GEOGR* valley. **-2.** [documento] receipt. **-3.** [postal] **~ postal** postal order.

valente [va'lẽntʃi] *adj* brave.

valentia [valẽn'tʃia] *f* **-1.** [coragem] courage. **-2.** [ação] feat.

valer [va'le(x)] ◇ *vt* **-1.** [ger] to be worth; **~ a pena** to be worthwhile. **-2.** [acarretar]: **~ algo a alguém** to bring sb sthg. ◇ *vi* **-1.** [ger] to be worth; **valeu!** *fam* cheers! **-2.** [equivaler]: **~ por** to be worth the same as; **ou coisa que o valha** or something similar. **-3.** [ser válido] to be valid; [em jogos] to be fair; **fazer ~ os direitos** to assert one's rights. **-4.** [vigorar] to be in force.

➡ **para valer** *loc adv* [muito]: **me diverti para ~** I had a really good time.

➡ **valer-se** *vp* [servir-se]: **~-se de** to make use of.

valete [va'lɛtʃi] *m* [carta] jack.

vale-transporte [ˌvalitrãnʃ'pɔxtʃi] (*pl* **vales-transporte**) *m* travel voucher.

valia [va'lia] *f* value.

validade [vali'dadʒi] *f* validity; **prazo de ~** [em comida] expiry date.

validar [vali'da(x)] *vt* to validate.

válido, da ['validu, da] *adj* valid.

valioso, osa [va'ljozu, ɔza] *adj* valuable.

valise [va'lizi] *f* case.

valor [va'lo(x)] (*pl* **-es**) *m* value; **no ~ de** to the value of; **dar ~ a algo/alguém** to value sthg/sb.

➡ **valores** *mpl* **-1.** [princípios] values. **-2.** *BOLSA* securities.

valorizar [valori'za(x)] *vt* **-1.** [imóvel, moeda] to push up the value of. **-2.** [pessoa, trabalho] to appreciate.

➡ **valorizar-se** *vp* to appreciate.

valsa ['vawsa] *f* waltz.

válvula ['vawvula] *f* valve; **~ de escape** *fig* safety valve; **~ de segurança** safety valve.

vampiro [vãm'piru] *m* **-1.** [personagem] vampire. **-2.** *ZOOL* vampire bat.

vandalismo [vãnda'liʒmu] *m* vandalism.

vândalo, la ['vãndalu, la] *m, f* vandal.

vangloriar-se [vãŋglo'rjaxsil] *vp*: ~ **-se (de)** to boast (about).

vanguarda [vãŋ'gwaxda] *f* **-1.** MIL front line. **-2.** [cultural] avant-garde.

vantagem [vãn'taʒẽl] *f* **-1.** [ger] advantage; **tirar ~ de** to take advantage from. **-2.** [superioridade]: **~ (sobre)** advantage (over); **levar ~ (sobre)** to have an advantage (over).

vantajoso, osa [vãnta'ʒozu, ɔza] *adj* **-1.** [benéfico] advantageous. **-2.** [lucrativo] profitable.

vão, vã ['vãw, 'vã] *adj* **-1.** [frívolo] empty. **-2.** [inútil] vain; **em ~** in vain. **-3.** [irreal] futile.
➡ **vão** *m* **-1.** [espaço] space. **-2.** [de porta etc.] opening.

vapor [va'po(x)] *(pl -es)* *m* **-1.** [de água] steam; **a ~** [máquina, ferro] steam *(antes de subst).* **-2.** FÍSICA vapour *UK*, vapor *US*.

vaporizador [vaporiza'do(x)] *(pl -es)* *m* **-1.** [de perfume *etc.*] spray. **-2.** MED vaporizer.

vaporoso, osa [vapo'rozu, ɔza] *adj* **-1.** [tecido, cortina] see-through, diaphanous. **-2.** [com vapor] steamy.

vapt-vupt [vapt∫i'vupt∫i] ⬦ *interj* zap! ⬦ *m* [lençol] fitted sheet.

vaqueiro [va'kejru] *m* cowherd *UK*, cowboy *US*.

vaquinha [va'kiɲa] *f*: **fazer uma ~** to have a whip-round.

vara ['vara] *f* **-1.** [pau] stick. **-2.** [para salto] pole. **-3.** TEC rod. **-4.** [de trombone] slide. **-5.** JUR jurisdiction. **-6.** [de porcos] herd.

varal [va'raw] *(pl -ais)* *m* [de roupas] clothes line.

varanda [va'rãnda] *f* **-1.** [sacada] verandah. **-2.** [balcão] balcony.

varar [va'ra(x)] ⬦ *vt* **-1.** [furar] to pierce. **-2.** [passar por] to cross. ⬦ *vi*: **~ por** [passar por] to pass through; [atravessar] to go through.

varejeira [vare'ʒejra] *f* [mosca] bluebottle.

varejista [vare'ʒi∫ta] ⬦ *adj* retail *(antes de subst).* ⬦ *mf* [vendedor] retailer.

varejo [va'reʒu] *m* COM retail trade; **a loja vende a ~** the shop sells retail.

variação [varja'sãw] *(pl -ões)* *f* [alteração] change, variation; **~ cambial** ECON exchange rate fluctuation.

variado, da [va'rjadu, da] *adj* **-1.** [diverso] varied. **-2.** [sortido] assorted.

variar [va'rja(x)] ⬦ *vt* [diversificar] to vary. ⬦ *vi* **-1.** [ger] to vary. **-2.** [diversificar] to make changes; **para ~** [para diversificar] for a change; *irôn* and just for a change. **-3.** *fam* [delirar] to unhinge.

variável [va'rjavew] *(pl -eis)* ⬦ *adj* changeable, variable. ⬦ *f* MAT variable.

varicela [vari'sɛla] *f* chickenpox.

variedade [varje'dadʒi] *f* **-1.** [diversidade] variety. **-2.** [tipo] type.
➡ **variedades** *fpl* variety *(sg)*; **espetáculo/teatro de ~s** variety show *OU* theatre *UK OU* theater *US*.

varinha [va'riɲa] *f* stick; **~ de condão** magic wand.

vário, ria ['varju, rja] *adj* [variado] diverse.
➡ **vários** ⬦ *adj pl* several. ⬦ *pron pl* several.

varizes [va'riziʃ] *fpl* varicose veins.

varredura [vaxe'dura] *f* **-1.** [ato] sweep. **-2.** COMPUT scan.

varrer [va'xe(x)] *vt* **-1.** [com vassoura] to sweep. **-2.** [arrastar] to sweep away. **-3.** *fig* [devastar] to raze.

Varsóvia [vax'sɔvja] *n* Warsaw.

várzea ['vaxʒja] *f* [vale] low, flat valley.

vascular [va∫ku'ʎa(x)] *vt* **-1.** [pesquisar] to research. **-2.** [revirar] to rummage through.

vasectomia [vazekto'mia] *f* vasectomy.

vaselina [vaze'lina] *f* [substância] vaseline.

vasilha [va'ziʎa] *f* vessel.

vaso ['vazu] *m* **-1.** [para plantas] pot. **-2.** [privada] toilet; **~ sanitário** toilet bowl.

vassalo, la [va'salu, la] *m, f* vassal.

vassoura [va'sora] *f* broom.

vasto, ta ['va∫tu, ta] *adj* **-1.** [extenso] vast. **-2.** *fig* [considerável] wide.

vaticano, na [vat∫i'kãnu, na] *adj* Vatican *(antes de subst).*

vaticínio [vat∫i'sinju] *m* prophecy.

vau [vaw] *m* **-1.** [de rio] ford. **-2.** NÁUT beam.

vazamento [vaza'mẽntu] *m* leakage.

vazão [va'zaw] *(pl -ões)* *f* **-1.** [vazamento] leak. **-2.** [escoamento] flow. **-3.** COM [venda] sale. **-4.** *loc*: **dar ~ a** [liberar] to give vent to; [atender a] to deal with; [solucionar] to sort out; COM to clear.

vazar [va'za(x)] ⬦ *vi* **-1.** [ger] to leak. **-2.** [maré] to go out. **-3.** *fig* [informação] to leak out. ⬦ *vt* **-1.** [esvaziar] to empty. **-2.** [olhos] to gouge out. **-3.** *fig* [moldar] to model.

vazio, zia [va'ziu, zia] *adj* **-1.** [ger] empty. **-2.** [com pouca gente] deserted.
➡ **vazio** *m* **-1.** [vácuo] vacuum. **-2.** [lacuna] blank space. **-3.** *fig* [sentimento] void.

vazões [va'zõj∫] *pl* ▷ **vazão**.

veado ['vjadu] *m* **-1.** [animal] deer; **carne de ~** venison. **-2.** *vulg pej* [homossexual] poof(ter) *UK*, fag(got) *US*.

vedado, da [ve'dadu, da] *adj* **-1.** [proibido, impedido] barred; **~ a** prohibited to.

-2. [hermeticamente fechado] sealed.

vedar [ve'da(x)] *vt* **-1.** [proibir, impedir] to prohibit, to bar. **-2.** [sangue]**: vedou o sangramento com um lenço** he stopped the flow of blood with a handkerchief. **-3.** [hermeticamente] to seal.

vedete [ve'dɛtʃi] *f* **-1.** [de teatro] star. **-2.** *fam fig* [destaque] star.

veemente [veje'mẽtʃi] *adj* vehement.

vegetação [veʒeta'sãw] (*pl* **-ões**) *f* vegetation.

vegetal [veʒe'taw] (*pl* **-ais**) <> *adj* plant (*antes de subst*). <> *m* plant.

vegetar [veʒe'ta(x)] *vi* **-1.** [planta] to grow. **-2.** *fig* [pessoa] to vegetate.

vegetariano, na [veʒeta'rjãnu, na] <> *adj* vegetarian. <> *m, f* vegetarian.

veia ['veja] *f* **-1.** [ger] vein. **-2.** *fig* [tendência] streak.

veiculação [vejkula'sãw] (*pl* **-ões**) *f* **-1.** [de mercadorias, visitantes] transport *UK*, transportation *US*. **-2.** [de doença] transmission. **-3.** [de idéias, mensagens, doutrinas] spreading.

veicular [vejku'la(x)] *vt* **-1.** [publicar, divulgar] to spread. **-2.** [anúncios] to distribute.

veículo [ve'ikulu] *m* **-1.** [de locomoção] vehicle. **-2.** [de informação] means *(sg)*.

veio ['veju] *m* **-1.** [de rocha] vein. **-2.** [de madeira] grain. **-3.** [em mina] seam.

vela ['vɛla] *f* **-1.** [de cera] candle. **-2.** *NÁUT* sail; à ~ sailing; **fazer-se à vela** to set sail. **-3.** [embarcação] yacht.

velame [velã'mil] *m NÁUT* sails (*pl*).

velar [ve'la(x)] <> *adj LING* velar. <> *vt LING* velar. <> *vt* **-1.** [cobrir]: ~ **algo (com algo)** to cover sthg (with sthg). **-2.** [ocultar] to hide. **-3.** [dissimular] to disguise. **-4.** [doente, sono] to watch over. **-5.** [defunto] to keep vigil for, to hold a wake for. <> *vi* **-1.** [cuidar]: ~ **por algo/alguém** to watch over sthg/sb. **-2.** *FOT* [filme] to be damaged by exposure to light.

veleiro [ve'lejru] *m NÁUT* sailing boat.

velejar [vele'ʒa(x)] *vi* to sail.

velhice [vɛ'ʎisi] *f* old age.

velho, lha ['vɛʎu, ʎa] <> *adj* old; **nos ~s tempos** in the old days. <> *m, f* **-1.** [pessoa] old person. **-2.** *fam* [pai] old man; **os ~s** [pai e mãe] one's folks. **-3.** *fam* [amigo]: **meu** ~ old chap.

velocidade [velosi'dadʒi] *f* [ger] speed; **em alta** ~ at high speed.

velocímetro [velo'simetru] *m* speedometer.

velocíssimo, ma [velo'sisimu, mal *adj superl* ▷ **veloz**.

velódromo [ve'lɔdrumul] *m* cycle track.

velório [ve'lɔrjul] *m* wake.

veloz [ve'lɔʃ] (*pl* **-es**) *adj* **-1.** [ger] fast. **-2.** [movimento] quick.

veludo [ve'ludul] *m* [tecido] velvet; ~ **cotelê** corduroy.

vencedor, ra [vẽse'do(x), ral (*pl* **-es**, *fpl* **-s**) <> *adj* winning. <> *m, f* winner.

vencer [vẽ'se(x)] <> *vt* **-1.** [ger] to win. **-2.** [superar, dominar, resistir a] to overcome. **-3.** [derrotar] to defeat. **-4.** [conter] to contain. **-5.** [percorrer] to cross. <> *vi* **-1.** [ganhar] to win. **-2.** [expirar - prazo, garantia, contrato, validade] to expire; [- pagamento, conta, promissória] to become due.

vencido, da [vẽ'sidu, dal *adj* **-1.** [derrotado] beaten. **-2.** [expirado] expired.

vencimento [vẽsi'mẽtul] *m* **-1.** [expiração] expiry. **-2.** [data] due date.
➤ **vencimentos** *mpl* [salário] earnings.

venda ['vẽdal *f* **-1.** [vendagem] sale; à ~ on *ou* for sale; ~ **a crédito** credit sale; ~ **a prazo** *ou* **prestação** sale in instalments. **-2.** [mercearia] general store. **-3.** [nos olhos] blindfold.

vendar [vẽ'da(x)] *vt*: ~ **(os olhos de) alguém** to blindfold sb.

vendaval [vẽda'vawl (*pl* **-ais**) *m* **-1.** [ventania] gale. **-2.** *fig* [turbilhão] whirlwind.

vendedor, ra [vẽde'do(x), ral (*mpl* **-es**, *fpl* **-s**) *m, f* **-1.** [dono] seller. **-2.** [em loja] sales assistant; ~ **ambulante** street vendor. **-3.** [de seguros] salesperson.

vender [vẽ'de(x)] <> *vt* **-1.** [pôr à venda] to sell; ~ **no varejo** to sell retail; ~ **no/por atacado** to sell wholesale. **-2.** [entregar em venda] to sell off; ~ **algo a/para alguém (por)** to sell sb sthg (for); ~ **algo a prazo** *ou* **prestação** to sell sthg on credit/in instalments; ~ **fiado** to give credit. <> *vi* to sell.
➤ **vender-se** *vp* **-1.** [estar à venda]: **vendem-se picolés** ice lollies for sale. **-2.** [deixar-se subornar]: **ele se vendeu por 30 mil dólares** he accepted a bribe of 30 thousand dollars.

veneno [ve'nenul] *m* **-1.** [peçonha] poison; **o cigarro é um** ~ **para a saúde** smoking is a health hazard. **-2.** [de cobra, inseto] venom. **-3.** *fig* [malícia] venom.

venenoso, osa [vene'nozu, ɔzal *adj* **-1.** [ger] poisonous. **-2.** *fig* [malicioso] venomous.

veneração [venera'sãw] *f*: ~ **(por)** veneration (for).

venerar [vene'ra(x)] *vt* **-1.** [adorar] to revere. **-2.** *RELIG* to worship.

venéreo, rea [ve'nɛrju, rjal *adj* venereal.

veneziana [vene'zjanal *f* **-1.** [porta] louvred door *UK*, louvered door *US*.

-2. [janela] louvred window *UK*, louvered window *US*.

Venezuela [vene'zwɛla] *n* Venezuela.

venezuelano, na [venezwɛ'lanu, na] <> *adj* Venezuelan. <> *m, f* Venezuelan.

ventania [vẽta'nia] *f* gale.

ventar [vẽ'ta(x)] *vi*: **venta muito aqui** it is very windy here; **estar ventando** to be windy.

ventarola [vẽta'rɔla] *f* fan.

ventilação [vẽtʃila'sãw] *f* **-1.** [de ambiente] ventilation. **-2.** *AUTO* [de motor] cooling.

ventilador [vẽtʃila'do(x)] *(pl* **-es)** *m* [elétrico] fan.

ventilar [vẽtʃi'la(x)] *vt* [arejar] to air.

vento ['vẽtu] *m* **-1.** [ar] air. **-2.** [brisa] wind. **-3.** *loc*: **ir de** ~ **em popa** to go very well.

ventoso, osa [vẽ'tozu, ɔza] *adj* windy.
◆ **ventosa** *f* **-1.** *MED* ventouse. **-2.** *ZOOL* sucker.

ventre ['vẽtri] *m* **-1.** *ANAT* belly. **-2.** *euf* [útero] womb.

ventríloquo, qua [vẽ'trilokwu, kwa] *m, f* ventriloquist.

ventura [vẽ'tura] *f* **-1.** [destino] fate; **por** ~ by chance. **-2.** [sorte] good fortune.

venturoso, osa [vẽtu'rozu, ɔza] *adj* [feliz] happy.

Vênus ['venuʃ] *n* Venus.

ver ['ve(x)] <> *vt* **-1.** [ger] to see; **já volto, viu?** I'll be back soon, OK? **-2.** [assistir] to watch. **-3.** [resolver] to see to. **-4.** [tomar cuidado em] to watch. **-5.** [em remissiva]: **veja ...** look ... <> *vi* **-1.** [enxergar] to see; **ela é bonita que só vendo** you wouldn't believe how pretty she is; ~ **em fig** [em situação, pessoa] to see in. **-2.** [ger]: **ter a** *ou* **que** ~ **com** to have to do with; [ter envolvimento com] to be involved with; **são pessoas muito diferentes, não têm nada a** ~ **uma com a outra** they are two very different people, they are not at all alike; **este trabalho tem muito a** ~ **com você** that work is right up your street. <> *m*: **a meu** ~ in my opinion.
◆ **ver-se** *vp* **-1.** [ger] to see o.s. **-2.** [avistar-se] to see one another. **-3.** [ter contato]: **há anos que não nos víamos** it's years since we saw each other, we hadn't seen each other for years. **-4.** [em dificuldade, lugar] to find o.s. **-5.** [entender-se]: **bem se vê que ...** it's obvious that ...
◆ **pelo visto** *loc adv* by the look of it.
◆ **vai ver que** *loc adv* [talvez] perhaps.

veracidade [verasi'dadʒi] *f* truthfulness.

veranear [vera'nja(x)] *vi* to spend the summer.

veraneio [vera'neju] *m* summer holidays *(pl) UK*, summer vacation *US*.

veranista [vera'niʃta] *mf* summer holidaymaker *UK*, summer vacationer *US*.

verão [ve'rãw] *(pl* **-ões)** *m* summer.

verba ['vɛxba] *f* funding.

verbal [vex'baw] *(pl* **-ais)** *adj* verbal.

verbete [vex'betʃi] *m* [em dicionário] entry.

verbo ['vɛxbu] *m* **-1.** *GRAM* verb; **soltar o** ~ *fam* to shoot one's mouth off. **-2.** *RELIG*: **o Verbo** the Word.

verborrágico, ca [vexbo'xaʒiku, ka] *adj* verbose.

verdade [vex'dadʒi] *f* truth; **não é** ~? *fam* isn't that right?; **na** ~ in fact; **para falar a** ~ to tell the truth.
◆ **verdades** *fpl* home truths; **dizer umas** ~ **s a alguém** *fam* to tell sb a few home truths.
◆ **de verdade** <> *loc adv* **-1.** [realmente]: **tudo o que relato aconteceu de** ~ everything I'm describing really happened. **-2.** [a sério] seriously. <> *loc adj* [autêntico]: **é um vencedor de** ~ he's a true winner.

verdadeiro, ra [vexda'dejru, ra] *adj* **-1.** [ger] true. **-2.** [autêntico] real.

verde ['vexdʒi] <> *adj* **-1.** [cor] green; ~ **de raiva** livid. **-2.** [fruta] unripe, green. <> *m* **-1.** [cor] green. **-2.** [natureza] country.

verde-claro, ra ['vexdʒi'klaru, ra] *(pl* **-s)** <> *adj* light green. <> *m* light green.

verde-escuro, ra ['vexdʒiʃ'kuru, ra] *(pl* **-s)** <> *adj* dark green. <> *m* dark green.

verdejante [vexde'ʒãtʃi] *adj* verdant.

verdejar [vexde'ʒa(x)] *vi* to become green.

verdor [vex'do(x)] *m* **-1.** [cor verde] greenness. **-2.** [as plantas verdes] greenery.

verdura [vex'dura] *f* [hortaliça] greens *(pl)*.

verdureiro, ra [vexdu'rejru, ra] *m, f* greengrocer.

vereador, ra [verja'do(x), ra] *m, f* councillor *UK*, councilor *US*.

vereda [ve'reda] *f* path.

veredicto [vere'dʒiktu] *m* verdict.

verga ['vexga] *f* **-1.** [vara] stick. **-2.** [metálica] rod.

vergar [vex'ga(x)] <> *vt* [dobrar] to bend. <> *vi* **-1.** [dobrar] to bend. **-2.** [com peso] to sag.

vergonha [vex'goɲa] *f* **-1.** [acanhamento] shyness; **que** ~! how embarrassing!; **ter** ~ **de fazer algo** to feel shy about doing sthg. **-2.** [brio, pudor] shame; **que falta de** ~! how disgraceful!; **ter** ~ **na cara** to be shameless. **-3.** [desonra] shame. **-4.** [vexame] outrage.

vergonhoso, osa [vexgo'nozu, ɔza] *adj* **-1.** [indigno] disgraceful. **-2.** [indecoroso] indecent. **-3.** [que dá vergonha] shameful.

verídico, ca [ve'ridʒiku, ka] *adj* true.

verificar [verifi'ka(x)] *vt* **-1.** [averiguar] to check. **-2.** [comprovar] to confirm.

➡ **verificar-se** *vp*: verifica-se um aumento na inflação an increase in inflation has been confirmed.

verme ['vɛxmi] *m* worm.

vermelho, lha [vex'meʎu, ʎa] *adj* [ger] red; **ficar ~ de raiva/vergonha** to flush with anger/embarrassment.

➡ **vermelho** *m* **-1.** [cor] red. **-2.** [déficit]: **estar no ~** to be in the red.

vermute [vex'mutʃi] *m* vermouth.

vernáculo, la [vex'nakulu, la] *adj* vernacular.

➡ **vernáculo** *m* vernacular.

vernissage [vexni'saʒi] *f* opening.

verniz [vex'niʃ] (*pl* -es) *m* **-1.** [solução] varnish. **-2.** [couro] patent leather. **-3.** *fig* [polidez] veneer.

verões [ve'rõjʃ] *pl* ⊳ verão.

verossímil [vero'simiw] (*pl* -eis) *adj* **-1.** [crível] credible. **-2.** [provável] likely.

verruga [ve'xuga] *f* wart.

versado, da [vex'sadu, da] *adj*: **~ em** versed in.

versão [vex'sãw] (*pl* -ões) *f* **-1.** [interpretação] version. **-2.** [tradução]: **~ (para)** translation (into).

versátil [vex'satʃiw] (*pl* -eis) *adj* versatile.

versículo [vex'sikulu] *m* **-1.** [de artigo] paragraph. **-2.** *RELIG* verse.

verso ['vɛxsu] *m* **-1.** [gênero] verse. **-2.** [linha de poema] line. **-3.** [poema] poem. **-4.** [de página] verso; **vide ~** see over(-leaf).

versões [vex'sõjʃ] *pl* ⊳ versão.

vértebra ['vɛxtebra] *f* vertebra.

vertebrado, da [vexte'bradu, da] *adj* vertebrate.

➡ **vertebrado** *m* vertebrate.

vertebral [vexte'braw] (*pl* -ais) *adj* vertebral.

vertente [vex'tẽntʃi] *f* **-1.** [declive] slope. **-2.** *fig* [aspecto] angle.

verter [vex'te(x)] *vt* **-1.** [despejar - líquido] to pour; [- recipiente] to tip. **-2.** [derramar] to spill. **-3.** [lágrimas, sangue] to shed. **-4.** [traduzir]: **~ (para)** to translate (into). *vi* [brotar]: **~ de** [água] to spring from; [rio] to rise from.

vertical [vexti'kaw] (*pl* -ais) *adj* vertical. *f* vertical.

vértice ['vɛxtʃisil] *m* **-1.** *GEOM* vertex. **-2.** [de montanha *etc.*] summit.

vertigem [vex'tʃiʒẽ] (*pl* -ns) *f* **-1.** *MED* vertigo. **-2.** [tonteira] giddiness, dizziness; **ter ~** to feel giddy, to feel dizzy.

vertiginoso, osa [vextʃiʒi'nozu, ɔza] *adj* vertiginous.

vesgo, ga ['veʒgu, ga] *adj* cross-eyed.

vesícula [ve'zikula] *f*: **~ (biliar)** gall bladder.

vespa ['veʃpa] *f* wasp.

véspera ['vɛʃpera] *f*: **na ~ de** the day before; **~ de Natal** Christmas Eve.

➡ **vésperas** *fpl* [um tempo antes]: **nas ~ s de** on the eve of.

veste ['vɛʃtʃi] *f* **-1.** [vestido] dress. **-2.** [eclesiástica] vestment.

vestiário [veʃ'tʃjarju] *m* **-1.** [onde se troca roupa] changing room. **-2.** [onde se deixa casacos *etc.*] cloakroom.

vestibular [veʃtʃibu'la(x)] *m* university entrance exam.

vestíbulo [veʃ'tʃibulu] *m* **-1.** [de casa] hall. **-2.** [de teatro] foyer.

vestido, da [veʃ'tʃidu, da] *adj* **-1.** [com roupa]: **~ (com/de)** dressed in. **-2.** [fantasiado]: **~ de** dressed as.

➡ **vestido** *m* dress; **~ de noiva** wedding dress.

vestígio [veʃ'tʃiʒju] *m* **-1.** [pegada] trail. **-2.** *fig* [indício] trace.

vestimenta [veʃtʃi'mẽnta] *f* **-1.** [roupa] garment. **-2.** *TEATRO* vestment.

vestir [veʃ'tʃi(x)] *vt* **-1.** [pôr sobre alguém] to put on. **-2.** [usar] to wear. **-3.** [costurar para] to make clothes for. **-4.** [dar vestuário para] to clothe. **-5.** [fronha] to cover. *vi* [ter caimento]: **~ bem/mal** to dress well/badly.

➡ **vestir-se** *vp* **-1.** [usar]: **ela só se veste de branco** she only wears white. **-2.** [aprontar-se] to get dressed. **-3.** [fantasiar-se]: **vestiu-se de pirata** he was dressed (up) as a pirate.

vestuário [veʃ'twarju] *m* **-1.** [roupas] clothing. **-2.** *TEATRO* costumes (*pl*).

vetar [ve'ta(x)] *vt* **-1.** [lei, proposta, candidato] to veto. **-2.** [acesso] to forbid.

veterano, na [vete'rãnu, na] *adj* veteran (*antes de subst*). *m, f* veteran.

veterinário, ria [veteri'narju, rja] *adj* veterinary. *m, f* vet, veterinary surgeon.

veto ['vɛtu] *m* veto.

véu ['vɛu] *m* [pano] veil.

vexame [ve'ʃãmi] *f* **-1.** [vergonha] shame. **-2.** [humilhação] humiliation. **-3.** [ultraje] outrage.

vez [veʃ] (*pl* -es) *f* **-1.** [freqüência, quantidade] time; **uma ~** once; **duas ~ es** twice; **três ~ es** three times; **algumas ~ es** a few times; **às ~ es** sometimes; **cada ~ mais** more and more; **cada ~ mais alto** higher and higher; **de ~ em quando** from time to time; **mais uma**

~, **outra** ~ (once) again; **uma** ~ **ou outra** once in a while; **várias** ~ **es** several times. - **2.** [ocasião] time; **você já sentiu isso alguma** ~? have you ever felt that?; **desta** ~ this time; **de uma** ~ **só** once only; **de** ~ once and for all; **era uma** ~ ... once·upon a time ...; **na maioria das** ~ **es** on most occasions, most times. - **3.** [turno] turn. - **4.** [multiplicação] times; **2** ~ **es 4** 2 times 4.

➡ **em vez de** *loc prep* instead of.

➡ **uma vez que** *loc conj* [já que] since.

VHF (*abrev de* Very High Frequency) *f* VHF.

VHS (*abrev de* Video Home System) *m* VHS.

via ['vial] <> *f* - **1.** [caminho, estrada] road; ~ **férrea** railway. - **2.** [transporte]: **por** ~ **aérea** by air; [postal] by airmail; **por** ~ **terrestre** by land, overland. - **3.** [meio] route; **por** ~ **oficial** through official means. - **4.** [processo]: **em** ~ **(s) de** on the way to. - **5.** [de documento] copy; **primeira/segunda** ~ original/ duplicate (copy). - **6.** [de drenagem *etc.*] channel. - **7.** *ANAT* tract; **por** ~ **oral** by mouth. <> *prep* via.

➡ **Via Láctea** *f* Milky Way.

➡ **por via das dúvidas** *loc adv* just in case.

viabilizar [vjabili'za(x)] *vt* to make possible.

viação [vja'sãw] (*pl* -ões) *f* - **1.** [conjunto de estradas] highways, roads (*pl*). - **2.** [companhia] bus company.

viaduto [vja'dutu] *m* viaduct.

viagem ['vjaʒẽl] (*pl* -ns) *f* - **1.** [ger] journey; **boa** ~! have a good journey!; ~ **de ida e volta** return trip; ~ **de negócios** business trip. - **2.** *fig* [sob efeito de droga] trip.

➡ **viagens** *fpl* travels.

viajante [vja'ʒãntʃi] <> *adj* travelling *UK*, traveling *US*. <> *mf* traveller *UK*, traveler *US*.

viajar [vja'ʒa(x)] *vi*: ~ **(por)** to travel (across/through).

viável ['vjavɛw] (*pl* -eis) *adj* viable, feasible.

víbora ['vibora] *f* - **1.** *ZOOL* viper. - **2.** *fig* [pessoa] snake in the grass.

vibração [vibra'sãw] (*pl* -ões) *f* - **1.** [tremor] vibration. - **2.** *fig* [entusiasmo] thrill.

vibrador, ra [vibra'do(x),ra] *adj* [vibratório] vibrating.

➡ **vibrador** *m* [estimulador] vibrator.

vibrante [vi'brãntʃi] *adj fig* [entusiasmado] vibrant.

vibrar [vi'bra(x)] <> *vt* - **1.** [fazer tremer] to shake. - **2.** [dedilhar] to vibrate. <> *vi*

- **1.** [tremer] to shake. - **2.** *fig* [entusiasmarse] to be thrilled.

vibrião [vi'brjãw] (*pl* -ões) *m* vibrio.

vice ['visil *mf* deputy.

vice- [visil *prefixo* vice-.

vice-presidente, ta [,visiprezi'dẽntʃi, tal (*mpl* -s, *fpl* -s) *m, f* - **1.** *POL* vice-president. - **2.** [de comitê, empresa] deputy chairman.

vice-versa [,visi'vɛxsal *adv* vice versa.

viciado, da [vi'sjadu, dal *adj* - **1.** [em droga *etc.*]: ~ **(em)** addicted (to). - **2.** [adulterado] vitiated.

viciar [vi'sja(x)] <> *vt* - **1.** [dar vício a] to addict. - **2.** [adulterar] to vitiate. <> *vi* [criar vício] to be addictive.

➡ **viciar-se** *vp* [tornar-se viciado]: ~ **-se (em)** to become addicted (to).

vício ['visjul *m* - **1.** [devassidão] vice. - **2.** [em droga, bebida] addiction. - **3.** [mau hábito] bad habit.

vicioso, osa [vi'sjozu, ɔzal *adj* - **1.** [sistema, hábito] corrupt. - **2.** [círculo] vicious.

viço ['visul *m* - **1.** [de planta] vigour *UK*, vigor *US*. - **2.** [de pele] freshness.

viçoso, osa [vi'sozu, ɔzal *adj* - **1.** [planta] luxuriant. - **2.** [pele] glowing.

vida ['vidal *f* - **1.** [ger] life; **dar a** ~ **por** *fig* to give anything for; **estar entre a** ~ **e a morte** to be at death's door; **feliz da** ~ delighted; ~ **conjugal** married life; ~ **útil** [de máquina *etc.*] useful life. - **2.** [subsistência]: **estar bem de** ~ to be well off; **ganhar a** ~ to earn one's living; **meio de** ~ means of living; **cheio de** ~ full of life; **sem** ~ lifeless. - **3.** [direção]: **seguir (reto) toda a** ~ to continue straight on as far as you can go. - **4.** [prostituição]: **cair na** ~ to go on the game.

vide ['vidʒil *vt* see; ~ **verso** see over(-leaf).

videira [vi'dejra] *f* grapevine.

vídeo ['vidʒjul *m* - **1.** [ger] video. - **2.** [tela] screen.

videocassete [,vidʒjuka'sɛtʃil *m* - **1.** [aparelho] video cassette recorder, VCR. - **2.** [fita] videotape.

videoclipe [,vidʒju'klipil *m* music video.

videoclube [,vidʒju'klubil *m* video club.

videoconferência ['vidʒjukõnʃe'rẽnsjal *f TELEC* video-conference.

videogame ['vidʒju'gejmil *m* video game.

videolocadora [,vidʒjuloka'doral *f* video rental.

videoteipe [,vidʒju'tejpil *m* - **1.** [fita] videotape. - **2.** [processo] videotaping.

vidraça [vi'drasal *f* window pane.

vidraçaria [vidrasa'rial *f* - **1.** [loja] glazier's. - **2.** [fábrica] glass factory. - **3.** [vidraças] glazing.

vidrado, da [vi'dradu, da] *adj* **-1.** [ger] glazed. **-2.** *fam* [encantado]: ~ **em** crazy about.

vidro ['vidru] *m* **-1.** [material] glass; ~ **fumê** smoked glass. **-2.** [frasco] bottle.

Viena ['vjɛna] *n* Vienna.

viés [vjɛʃ] *m* COST bias.
　　◆ de viés *loc adv* sideways.

Vietnã [vjɛt'nã] *n*: (o) ~ Vietnam.

vietnamita [vjɛtna'mita] <> *adj* Vietnamese. <> *mf* Vietnamese.
　　◆ vietnamita *m* [língua] Vietnamese.

viga ['viga] *f* **-1.** [de madeira] beam. **-2.** [de concreto, ferro] girder.

vigamento [viga'mẽtu] *m* rafters *(pl)*.

vigário [vi'garju] *m* vicar.

vigarista [viga'riʃta] *mf* swindler.

vigência [vi'ʒẽsja] *f* validity; **estar em** ~ to be in force.

vigente [vi'ʒẽtʃi] *adj* **-1.** [lei, contrato, norma] in force. **-2.** [situação política, costume] current.

vigésimo, ma [vi'ʒɛzimu, ma] *num* twentieth; *veja também* **sexto.**

vigia [vi'ʒia] <> *f* **-1.** [vigilância] surveillance. **-2.** NÁUT porthole. <> *mf* [pessoa] nightwatchman.

vigiar [vi'ʒja(x)] <> *vt* **-1.** [banco, presos] to guard. **-2.** [mala, criança] to keep an eye on. **-3.** [espreitar] to watch. <> *vi* to be on the lookout.

vigilância [viʒi'lãsja] *f* surveillance.

vigília [vi'ʒilja] *f* **-1.** [privação de sono]: **fez-se uma** ~ **para evitar ataques a** watch was kept in order to avoid attack. **-2.** [prática religiosa] vigil.

vigor [vi'go(x)] *m* **-1.** [energia - de corpo, espírito] vigour; [- para o trabalho] energy. **-2.** [veemência] vigour. **-3.** [vigência]: **em** ~ in force.

vigorar [vigo'ra(x)] *vi* to be in force.

vigoroso, osa [vigo'rozu, ɔza] *adj* vigorous.

vil ['viw] *(pl* **vis)** *adj* vile.

vila ['vila] *f* **-1.** [povoação] town. **-2.** [conjunto residencial] residential block. **-3.** [casa] villa.

vilã [vi'lã] *f* ▷ **vilão.**

vilão, lã [vi'lãw, lã] *(mpl* **-ãos, -ães,** *fpl* **-s)** *m, f* villain.

vilarejo [vila'reʒu] *m* hamlet.

vinagre [vi'nagri] *m* vinegar.

vinagrete [vina'grɛtʃi] *m* vinaigrette.

vinco ['vĩku] *m* **-1.** [em roupa, papel] crease. **-2.** [no rosto] wrinkle. **-3.** [sulco] furrow.

vinculação [vĩkula'sãw] *f* link, linking; **ele não quer a** ~ **do seu nome aos escândalos** he doesn't want his name to be linked to the scandals.

vincular [vĩku'la(x)] *vt* **-1.** [ligar] to tie. **-2.** [por obrigação] to bind.

vínculo ['vĩkulu] *m* **-1.** [pessoal, familiar] bond. **-2.** [profissional, entre países] tie; ~ **empregatício** work contract.

vinda ['vĩda] *f* ▷ **vindo.**

vindima [vĩ'dʒima] *f* grape harvest.

vindo, da ['vĩdu, da] <> *pp* ▷ **vir.** <> *adj*: ~ **(de)** originating (in).
　　◆ vinda *f* **-1.** [ger] arrival (in). **-2.** [regresso] return.

vindouro, ra [vĩ'doru, ra] *adj* **-1.** [ano, década] coming. **-2.** [geração] future.

vingança [vĩ'gãsa] *f* revenge.

vingar [vĩ'ga(x)] <> *vt* [tirar desforra de] to avenge. <> *vi* **-1.** [medrar] to thrive. **-2.** [dar certo] to be successful.
　　◆ vingar-se *vp* [tirar desforra]: ~ **-se (de)** to take revenge (on/for).

vingativo, va [vĩga'tʃivu, va] *adj* vindictive.

vinha ['viɲa] *f* **-1.** [vinhedo] vineyard. **-2.** [planta] vine.

vinhedo [vi'ɲedu] *m* vineyard.

vinho ['viɲu] <> *adj inv* [cor] burgundy. <> *m* **-1.** [cor] burgundy. **-2.** [bebida] wine; ~ **branco** white wine; ~ **do Porto** port; ~ **rosado** rosé (wine); ~ **tinto** red wine.

vinil [vi'niw] *m* vinyl.

vinte ['vĩtʃi] *num* twenty; *veja também* **seis.**

vintém [vĩ'tɛ̃] *(pl* **-ns)** *m* **-1.** [moeda antiga] old Brazilian coin. **-2.** [dinheiro]: **estar sem um** ~ to be penniless.

vintena [vĩ'tena] *f*: **uma** ~ **de** a score of.

viola ['vjɔla] *f* viola.

violação [vjola'sãw] *(pl* **-ões)** *f* **-1.** [de lei, pacto, direitos] violation. **-2.** [invasão]: ~ **de domicílio** housebreaking. **-3.** [de pessoa] violation, rape. **-4.** [de correspondência] interference. **-5.** [de local sagrado] violation, desecration.

violão [vjo'lãw] *(pl* **-ões)** *m* guitar.

violar [vjo'la(x)] *vt* **-1.** [lei, pacto, direitos] to violate. **-2.** [domicílio] to break in. **-3.** [pessoa] to violate, to rape. **-4.** [correspondência] to interfere with. **-5.** [local sagrado] to violate. **-6.** [segredo] to breach.

violeiro, ra [vjo'lejru, ra] *m, f* guitarist.

violência [vjo'lẽsja] *f* **-1.** [ato] violence. **-2.** [agressividade] vehemence. **-3.** [força - de vendaval] force; [- de paixões] violence.

violentar [vjolẽ'ta(x)] *vt* **-1.** [mulher] to violate, to rape. **-2.** [deturpar] to distort.

violento, ta [vjo'lẽtu, ta] *adj* violent.

violeta [vjo'leta] <> *f* [flor] violet. <> *adj inv* [cor] violet.

violinista [vjoli'niʃta] *mf* violinist.

violino [vjo'linu] *m* violin.

violoncelista [vjolõnse'liʃta] *mf* cellist.

violoncelo [vjolõn'sɛlu] *m* cello.

violonista [vjolo'niʃta] *mf* guitarist.

VIP (*abrev de* **Very Important Person**) [vipi] <> *adj* [pessoa, local] VIP. <> *mf* VIP.

vir [ˈvi(x)] *vi* -**1.** [apresentar-se] to come; **veio me ver** he came to see me; **venho visitá-lo amanhã** I'll come and see you tomorrow. -**2.** [chegar] to arrive; **ele veio atrasado/adiantado** he arrived late/early; **ela veio no ônibus das onze** she came on the eleven o'clock bus. -**3.** [a seguir no tempo] to come; **a semana/o ano que vem** next week/year, the coming week/year. -**4.** [estar] to be; **vem escrito em português** it's written in Portuguese; **vinha embalado** it came in a package. -**5.** [regressar] to come back; **eles vêm de férias amanhã** they're coming back from holidays tomorrow; **hoje, venho mais tarde** today, I'll be coming later than usual. -**6.** [surgir] to come; **o carro veio não sei de onde** the car came out of nowhere; **veio-me uma idéia** I've got an idea. -**7.** [provir]: ~ **de** to come from; **venho agora mesmo de lá** I've just come from there. -**8.** [em locuções]: ~ **a ser** to become; **que vem a ser isto?** what's the meaning of this?; ~ **abaixo** [edifício, construção] to collapse; ~ **ao mundo** [nascer] to come into the world, to be born; ~ **a saber (de algo)** to find out (about sthg); ~ **sobre** [arremeter contra] to lunge at; ~ **a tempo de algo** to arrive in time for sthg; ~ **a tempo de fazer algo** to arrive in time to do sthg.

virado, da [vi'radu, da] *adj* [voltado]: ~ **para** facing.

virada *f* -**1.** [viradela] turning. -**2.** [guinada] swerve. -**3.** *ESP* sudden turn-around.

vira-lata [ˌvira'lata] (*pl* **vira-latas**) *m* -**1.** [cachorro] mongrel. -**2.** [pessoa] down-and-out.

virar [vi'ra(x)] <> *vt* -**1.** [volver]: ~ **algo (para)** to turn sthg (towards); ~ **as costas** to turn one's back. -**2.** [mostrar pelo verso] to turn over. -**3.** [entornar] to tip. -**4.** [emborcar] to capsize. -**5.** [contornar] to turn. -**6.** [fazer mudar de opinião] to change. -**7.** [transformar-se] to turn into. <> *vi* -**1.** [volver] to turn; ~ **para** to turn towards; ~ **de bruços** to turn on to one's tummy; ~ **de costas** to turn on to one's back; ~ **do avesso** to turn inside out. -**2.** [emborcar] to capsize. -**3.** [contornar]: ~ **(em)** to turn (into); ~ **à direita/esquerda** to turn (to the) right/left.

-**4.** [mudar] to change. -**5.** [mudar de direção] to change direction.

virar-se *vp* -**1.** [volver-se] to turn around. -**2.** [rebelar-se] to rebel; ~ **-se contra** to turn against. -**3.** [defender-se] to stand up for o.s. -**4.** [empenhar-se] to struggle.

virgem [ˈvixʒẽ] (*pl* -**ns**) <> *adj* -**1.** [ger] virgin. -**2.** [fita, filme] blank. -**3.** [mel] pure. <> *f* [pessoa] virgin.

Virgem *f* -**1.** *RELIG* Virgin. -**2.** *ARTE* madonna. -**3.** [zodíaco] Virgo; **ser Virgem** to be a Virgo.

virgindade [vixʒĩ'dadʒi] *f* virginity.

virginiano, na [vixʒi'njãnu, na] <> *adj* Virgo (*antes de subst.*) <> *m, f* Virgo.

vírgula [ˈvixgula] *f* -**1.** [entre palavras] comma. -**2.** [entre números] (decimal) point. -**3.** [mecha] curl. -**4.** [objetando-se]: **uma** ~ ! *fam* my foot!

viril [vi'riw] (*pl* -**is**) *adj* virile.

virilha [vi'riʎa] *f* groin.

virose [vi'rɔzi] *f* viral infection.

virtualmente [vixtwaw'mẽtʃi] *adv* virtually.

virtude [vix'tudʒi] *f* -**1.** [qualidade] virtue. -**2.** [capacidade] knack. -**3.** [razão]: **em** ~ **de** due to.

virtuoso, osa [vix'twozu, ɔza] <> *adj* [íntegro] virtuous. <> *m, f* [gênio] virtuoso.

vis [viʃ] *pl* ⊳ **vil**.

visado, da [vi'zadu, da] *adj* -**1.** [cheque] valid. -**2.** [pessoa] watched.

visão [vi'zãw] (*pl* -**ões**) *f* -**1.** [sentido] vision, sight. -**2.** [o que se vê] sight. -**3.** [alucinação] vision. -**4.** [percepção, ponto de vista]: ~ **(de/sobre)** view (on/about). -**5.** [revelação] vision.

visar [vi'za(x)] <> *vt* -**1.** [cheque, passaporte] to stamp. -**2.** [objetivar] to look for; ~ **(a) fazer algo** to aim to do sthg. <> *vi* [objetivar]: ~ **a algo/a fazer algo** to aim for sthg/to aim to do sthg.

víscera [ˈviseral] *f* viscus.

viscoso, osa [viʃ'kozu, ɔza] *adj* viscous.

viseira [vi'zejra] *f* visor.

visibilidade [vizibili'dadʒi] *f* visibility.

visita [vi'zita] *f* -**1.** [ato] visit; **fazer uma** ~ **a alguém** to pay sb a visit. -**2.** [visitante] visitor; **ter** ~ **s** to have visitors. -**3.** [vistoria] inspection.

visitação [vizita'sãw] (*pl* -**ões**) *f* [visita] visit; **aberto à** ~ **pública** open to the public.

visitante [vizi'tãtʃi] *mf* visitor.

visitar [vizi'ta(x)] *vt* -**1.** [fazer visita a] to visit. -**2.** [vistoriar] to inspect.

visível [vi'zivew] (*pl* -**eis**) *adj* visible.

vislumbre [viʒ'lũbri] *m* glimpse.

visões [vi'zõjʃ] *pl* ⊳ **visão**.

visor [vi'zo(x)] (*pl* -**es**) *m* viewfinder.

vista [ˈviʃta] f ▷ **visto**.

visto, ta [ˈviʃtu, ta] ◇ *pp* ▷ **ver**. ◇ *adj* **-1.** [olhado]: ~ **(de)** seen (from). **-2.** [considerado] thought of. **-3.** [estudado] looked at.

➡ **visto** *m* **-1.** [em documento] stamp. **-2.** [em passaporte] visa.

➡ **vista** f **-1.** [ger] view. **-2.** [sentido] sight. **-3.** [olhos, olhar] eyesight; **à primeira vista** at first sight; **à vista** [visível] visible; [pagamento] in cash; **pôr à vista** to put on display; **até a vista!** see you later!; **conhecer de vista** to know by sight; **vista cansada** tired eyes. **-4.** *loc*: **saltar à vista** to be glaringly obvious, to stand out a mile.

➡ **em vista de** *loc prep* in view of.

➡ **pelo visto** *loc adv* by the look of it.

vistoria [viʃtoˈria] f inspection.

vistoriar [viʃtoˈrja(x)] vt to inspect.

vistoso, osa [viʃˈtozu, ɔza] *adj* eye-catching.

visual [viˈzwaw] (*pl* **-ais**) ◇ *adj* visual. ◇ *m fam* **-1.** [aspecto] appearance, look. **-2.** [vista] view.

visualizar [vizwaliˈza(x)] vt to visualize.

visualmente [vizuawˈmẽntʃi] *adv* visually; ~ **incapacitado** visually impaired.

vital [viˈtaw] (*pl* **-ais**) *adj* vital.

vitalício, cia [vitaˈlisju, sja] *adj* lifelong (*antes de subst*).

vitalidade [vitaliˈdadʒi] f vitality.

vitamina [vitaˈmina] f vitamin.

vitela [viˈtɛla] f **-1.** *ZOOL* calf. **-2.** [carne] veal.

vítima [ˈvitʃima] f [pessoa] victim.

vitória [viˈtɔrja] f victory.

vitorioso, osa [vitoˈrjozu, ɔza] *adj* victorious.

vitral [viˈtraw] (*pl* **-ais**) *m* stained-glass window.

vitrine [viˈtrini], **vitrina** [viˈtrina] f **-1.** [de loja] shop window. **-2.** [armário] display case.

viuvez [vjuˈveʒ] f widowhood.

viúvo, va [ˈvjuvu, va] ◇ *adj* widowed. ◇ *m, f* widower (f widow).

viva [ˈvival] ◇ *m* cheer. ◇ *interj* hooray!; ~ **a rainha!** long live the Queen!

viveiro [viˈvejru] *m* **-1.** [de plantas] nursery. **-2.** [de pássaros] aviary. **-3.** [de peixes] fish farm.

vivência [viˈvẽsja] f **-1.** [existência] existence. **-2.** [experiência] experience; **ter** ~ **em algo** to have experience in sthg.

vivenda [viˈvẽda] f (detached) house.

vivente [viˈvẽntʃi] ◇ *adj* living. ◇ *mf* living being.

viver [viˈve(x)] ◇ *vt* **-1.** [vida] to live.

-2. [fase, situação] to experience. ◇ *vi* **-1.** [ger] to live; ~ **bem** [economicamente] to live comfortably; [em harmonia] to live happily. **-2.** [estar vivo] to be alive. **-3.** [perdurar] to last. **-4.** [sustentar-se]: ~ **de** to live off; ~ **à custa de** to live off. **-5.** [conviver]: ~ **com** to mingle with; [maritalmente] to live with. **-6.** [dedicar-se completamente]: ~ **para** to live for. **-7.** [residir]: ~ **(em)** to live (in). **-8.** [freqüentar muito]: ~ **(em)** to live (in). **-9.** [estar sempre] to always be; ~ **doente/gripado** to always be ill/have a cold; ~ **trabalhando** to do nothing but work. ◇ *m* life.

víveres [ˈviveriʃ] *mpl* provisions.

vivido, da [viˈvidu, da] *adj* [pessoa] experienced.

vívido, da [ˈvividu, da] *adj* **-1.** [ger] vivid. **-2.** [expressivo] vivacious.

vivo, va [ˈvivu, va] *adj* **-1.** [ger] bright. **-2.** [existente] living; **estar** ~ to be alive. **-3.** [animado, buliçoso] lively. **-4.** [ardente] fervent.

➡ **ao vivo** *loc adv* live.

vizinhança [viziˈnãnsa] f neighbourhood *UK*, neighborhood *US*.

vizinho, nha [viˈziɲu, ɲa] ◇ *adj* neighbouring *UK*, neighboring *US*. ◇ *m, f* neighbour *UK*, neighbor *US*.

voador, ra [vwaˈdo(x), ra] *adj* flying.

voar [ˈvwa(x)] *vi* **-1.** [ger] to fly; ~ **fazer algo voando** *fig* to do sthg quickly. **-2.** [explodir]: ~ **pelos ares** to explode. **-3.** *loc*: ~ **alto** *fig* to aim high; ~ **para cima de alguém** [assediar] to mob sb; [atacar] to fly at sb.

vocabulário [vokabuˈlarju] *m* vocabulary.

vocábulo [voˈkabulu] *m* word.

vocação [vokaˈsãw] (*pl* **-ões**) f vocation.

vocacional [vokasjoˈnaw] (*pl* **-ais**) *adj* vocational.

vocal [voˈkaw] (*pl* **-ais**) *adj* vocal.

vocálico, ca [voˈkaliku, ka] *adj* vocal.

vocalista [vokaˈliʃta] *mf* vocalist.

você [voˈse] (*pl* **vocês**) *pron pess* **-1.** [tratamento] you; ~ **é médico?** are you a doctor?; ~ **está muito elegante** you're looking very elegant; **vocês precisam estudar** you need to study; ~ **mesmo** *ou* **próprio** you yourself. **-2.** (*depois de prep*): **isto pertence a** ~? is this yours?; **quero ir com vocês** I want to go with you; **penso muito em** ~ I think about you a lot; **esta carta é para** ~ this letter is for you. **-3.** [em anúncios]: '**o novo Fiat Regatta** ~ **vai adorar**' 'the new Fiat Regatta - you'll love it'; '**o melhor para** ~' 'the best thing for you'. **-4.** [alguém qualquer um] one; **na Universidade,** ~

tem que estudar muito at university, one has to study a lot.

vociferar [vosife'ra(x)] ◇ *vt* [bradar] to shout. ◇ *vi* [reclamar]: ~ **(contra)** to complain (about).

vodca ['vɔdʒka] *f* vodka.

voga ['vɔga] *f* **-1.** [ger] fashion. **-2.** NÁUT [cadência] rowing.

vogal [vo'gaw] (*pl* **-ais**) *f* LING vowel.

volante [vo'lãntʃi] *m* **-1.** AUTO steering wheel; **estar no** ~ to be at the wheel. **-2.** [motorista, piloto] driver. **-3.** [para apostas] betting slip. **-4.** [de máquina] flywheel.

volátil [vo'latʃiw] (*pl* **-eis**) *adj* volatile.

vôlei ['volej] *m* volleyball; ~ **de praia** beach volleyball.

voleibol [volei'bow] *m* = **vôlei**.

volt ['vɔwtʃi] *m* volt.

volta ['vɔwta] *f* **-1.** [giro] turn; **dar uma** ~ [sobre si mesmo] to turn round. **-2.** [retorno] return; **estar de** ~ to be back; **na** ~ [voltando] on the way back; [ao chegar] on arrival. **-3.** [passeio]: **dar uma** ~ [a pé] to go for a walk; [de carro] to go for a drive. **-4.** ESP lap. **-5.** MIL: **dar meia** ~ to about-turn *UK*, to about-face *US*. **-6.** AUTO: **fazer a** ~ to make a U-turn, to turn back. **-7.** [de espiral] twist. **-9.** [contorno] edge. **-10.** [curva] curve. **-11.** *fig* [troco] comeback. **-12.** *loc*: **dar a** ~ **por cima** *fig* to get over (it).
→ **às voltas com** *loc prep*: **estar/andar às** ~ **s com** to be struggling with.
→ **em volta de** *loc prep* around.
→ **por volta de** *loc prep* around.
→ **volta e meia** *loc adv* every now and again.

voltagem [vow'taʒẽ] *f* voltage.

voltar [vow'ta(x)] ◇ *vt* **-1.** [dirigir]: **algo para** to turn sthg towards. **-2.** [mudar a posição de] to turn. **-3.** [mostrar pelo verso] to turn over. ◇ *vi* **-1.** [ger] to return; ~ **a si** to come to; ~ **atrás** *fig* to back out. **-2.** [repetir-se] to come back. **-4.** [tratar novamente]: ~ **a algo** to return to sthg. **-5.** [recomeçar]: ~ **a fazer algo** to do sthg again.
→ **voltar-se** *vp* **-1.** [virar-se] to turn round. **-2.** [recorrer]: ~**-se para** to turn to. **-3.** [rebelar-se]: ~**-se contra** to turn against.

volteio [vow'teju] *m* **-1.** [rodopio] spin. **-2.** [volta] bend. **-3.** [de equilibrista] movement.

volume [vo'lumi] *m* **-1.** [ger] volume; **aumentar/diminuir o** ~ to turn the volume up/down. **-2.** [pacote] package.

volumoso, osa [volu'mozu, ɔza] *adj* bulky.

voluntário, ria [volũn'tarju, rja] ◇ *adj* voluntary. ◇ *m, f* volunteer.

voluntarioso, osa [volũnta'rjozu, ɔza] *adj* headstrong.

volúpia [vo'lupja] *f* **-1.** [sexual] pleasure. **-2.** [ambição] desire.

voluptuoso, osa [volup'twozu, ɔza] *adj* voluptuous.

volúvel [vo'luvew] (*pl* **-eis**) *adj* changeable.

volver [vow've(x)] ◇ *vt* to turn. ◇ *vi*: ~ **a** to return to.

vomitar [vomi'ta(x)] ◇ *vt* **-1.** [expelir] to vomit, to throw up. **-2.** [sujar com vômito] to vomit on, to be sick on. **-3.** *fig* [proferir] to spew out. ◇ *vi* [expelir vômito] to vomit, to be sick.

vômito ['vomitu] *m* **-1.** [ato] vomiting, throwing up. **-2.** [substância] vomit, sick.

vontade [võn'tadʒi] *f* **-1.** [determinação] will. **-2.** [desejo] wish; **dar** ~ **a alguém de fazer algo** to make sb feel like doing sthg; **me deu vontade de sair** I felt like going out; **o filme me deu vontade de viajar** the film made me feel like travelling; **fazer a** ~ **de alguém** to do what sb wants; **ter** ~ **de fazer algo** to feel like doing sthg; **contra a** ~ unwillingly. **-3.** [necessidade] need. **-4.** [empenho, interesse]: **boa/má** ~ good/ill will.
→ **vontades** *fpl* [caprichos]: **fazer todas as** ~ **s de alguém** to pander to sb.
→ **à vontade** *loc adv* **-1.** [sem cerimônia]: **ficar à** ~ to feel at ease; **fique à** ~ make yourself at home. **-2.** [em quantidade] loads. **-3.** [quanto se quiser] as much as one wants.
→ **com vontade** *loc adv* [comer *etc.*] heartily.

vôo ['vow] *m* flight; **levantar** ~ to take off; ~ **livre** ESP hang-gliding.

voraz [vo'raʃ] (*pl* **-es**) *adj* **-1.** [pessoa, apetite] voracious. **-2.** *fig* [fogo *etc.*] devastating.

vos [vuʃ] *pron pl* [complemento direto] you; [complemento indireto] (to) you; *fml* [reflexo] yourselves; *fml* [recíproco] each other, one another.

vós ['vɔʃ] *pron pess* [sujeito, complemento direto] you; [complemento indireto] (to) you; ~ **mesmos** *ou* **próprios** you, yourselves.

vosso, vossa ['vɔsu, 'vɔsa] ◇ *adj* your. ◇ *pron*: **o** ~ /**a vossa** yours; **um amigo** ~ a friend of yours; **os** ~ **s** [a vossa família] your family.

votação [vota'sãw] (*pl* **-ões**) *f* [ato] voting; [voto] vote.

votar [vo'ta(x)] ◇ *vt* **-1.** [eleger] to vote. **-2.** [submeter a votação] to take a vote on. **-3.** [aprovar] to pass. ◇ *vi* **-1.** [dar voto] to vote; ~ **em/contra/por** to vote on/ against/for; ~ **em branco** to abstain. **-2.** [ter direito a voto] to have a vote.

voto [ˈvɔtu] *m* **-1.** [votação] voting; ~ **nulo/em branco** invalid/blank vote; ~ **secreto** secret ballot. **-2.** [promessa] vow; ~ **de castidade/pobreza** vow of chastity/poverty. **-3.** [desejo] wish; **fazer** ~ **s que** to hope that.

vovó [voˈvɔ] *f* granny.

vovô [voˈvo] *m* grandpa.

voyeurismo [vojeˈriʒmu] *m* voyeurism.

voz [ˈvɔʃ] (*pl* **-es**) *f* **-1.** [ger] voice; **em** ~ **alta/baixa** in a loud/low voice. **-2.** [poder decisório, autoridade]: **ter** ~ **(ativa) em** to have a say in. **-3.** *fig* [conselho]: **a** ~ **da experiência** the voice of experience.

vozerio [vozeˈriw] *m* uproar.

vulcânico, ca [vuwˈkãniku, ka] *adj* volcanic.

vulcão [vuwˈkãw] (*pl* **-ões**) *m* volcano.

vulgar [vuwˈga(x)] (*pl* **-es**) *adj* **-1.** [comum] common. **-2.** [baixo, grosseiro] vulgar. **-3.** [medíocre] mediocre.

vulgaridade [vuwgariˈdadʒi] *f* vulgarity.

vulgarizar [vuwgariˈza(x)] *vt* [popularizar] to popularize.

➡ **vulgarizar-se** *vp* **-1.** [popularizar-se] to become commonplace. **-2.** [tornar-se reles] to coarsen.

vulgarmente [vuwgaxˈmẽntʃi] *adv* commonly.

vulgo [ˈvuwgul] <> *m* common people. <> *adv* otherwise known as.

vulnerabilidade [vuwnerabiliˈdadʒi] *f* vulnerability.

vulnerável [vuwneˈravɛw] (*pl* **-eis**) *adj* vulnerable.

vulto [ˈvuwtul] *m* **-1.** [figura, sombra] figure. **-2.** [semblante] face. **-3.** *fig* [importância] stature; **de** ~ important. **-4.**: **tomar** ~ [desenvolver-se] to take shape.

vultoso, osa [vuwˈtozu, ɔza] *adj* **-1.** [volumoso] bulky. **-2.** [obra, negócio] weighty. **-3.** [quantia] considerable.

vulva [ˈvuwva] *f* vulva.

W

w, W *m* [letra] w, W.

walkie-talkie [ˌwɔkiˈtɔki] (*pl* **walkie-talkies**) *m* walkie-talkie.

walkman® [ˈwɔkmən] *m* Walkman.

Washington [ˈwɔʃintõl] *n* Washington.

watt [ˈwɔtʃi] *m* watt.

WC (*abrev de* water closet) *m* WC.

windsurfe [wĩdʒiˈsuxfil] *m* windsurfing.

workshop [wɔxkiˈʃɔpil] *m* workshop.

WWW (*abrev de* **World Wide Web**) *f* WWW.

X

x, X *m* [letra] x, X.

xadrez [ʃaˈdreʃ] <> *m* **-1.** [jogo] chess. **-2.** [desenho] check. **-3.** [tecido] checked cloth. **-4.** *fam* [prisão] clink. <> *adj inv* checked.

xale [ˈʃali] *m* shawl.

xampu [ʃãnˈpul] *m* shampoo.

xarope [ʃaˈrɔpi] *m* syrup.

xenofobia [ʃenofoˈbia] *f* xenophobia.

xepa [ˈʃepal] *f fam* [de feira] scraps *(pl)*.

xeque [ˈʃɛki] *m* **-1.** [xadrez] check. **-2.** [xeique] sheikh. **-3.** *loc*: **pôr em** ~ to threaten.

xeque-mate [ˌʃɛkiˈmatʃil] (*pl* **xeque-mates**) *m* checkmate.

xereta [ʃeˈretal] *adj fam* [bisbilhoteiro] busybody.

xerez [ʃeˈreʃ] *m* sherry.

xerife [ʃeˈrifil] *m* sheriff.

xerocar [ʃeroˈka(x)l], *vt* to photocopy.

xerocópia [ʃeroˈkɔpjal] *f* photocopy.

xerocopiar [ʃerokoˈpja(x)] *vt* = xerocar.

xérox® [ʃeˈrɔks] *m* **-1.** [cópia] photocopy. **-2.** [máquina] photocopier.

xícara [ˈʃikaral] *f* cup; ~ **de chá** cup of tea.

xiita [ʃiˈital] <> *adj* [muçulmano] Shiite. <> *mf* **-1.** [muçulmano] Shiite. **-2.** *fig* [radical] extremist.

xilofone [ʃiloˈfonil] *m* xylophone.

xilografia [ʃilograˈfial] *f* **-1.** [técnica] wood engraving. **-2.** [gravura] woodcut.

xingamento [ʃĩgaˈmẽntul] *m* swearing.

xingar [ʃĩŋˈga(x)] <> *vt* to swear at; ~ **alguém de algo** to call sb sthg. <> *vi* to swear.

xixi [ʃiˈʃil] *m fam* pee; **fazer** ~ to pee.

xodó [ʃoˈdɔl] *m* [pessoa querida] sweetheart.

xucro, cra [ˈʃukru, kral] *adj* **-1.** [animal] untamed. **-2.** [grosseiro] coarse. **-3.** [ignorante] thick.

Z

z, Z *m* [letra] z, Z.
zaga ['zaga] *f* FUT fullback.
zagueiro [za'gejru] *m* FUT fullback.
Zaire ['zajri] *n* Zaire.
zanga ['zãŋga] *f* -**1.** [irritação] annoyance. -**2.** [briga] anger.
zangado, da [zãŋ'gadu, da] *adj* -**1.** [aborrecido] angry. -**2.** [irritado] annoyed. -**3.** [mal-humorado] cross.
zangão ['zãŋgãw] (*pl* -ões) *m* ZOOL drone.
zangar [zãŋ'ga(x)] <> *vt* [irritar] to annoy. <> *vi* -**1.** [irritar-se] to get angry. -**2.** [ralhar] to scold; ~ **com alguém** to tell sb off.
 ⬥ **zangar-se** *vp* -**1.** [aborrecer-se] to get angry. -**2.** [irritar-se] to get annoyed.
zangões [zãŋ'gõjʃ] *pl* ⊏⊐ **zangão**.
zanzar [zan'za(x)] *vi* to wander about.
zarpar [zax'pa(x)] *vi* -**1.** [embarcação] to weigh anchor. -**2.** [partir] to set off. -**3.** [fugir] to run away.
zebra ['zebra] *f* -**1.** ZOOL zebra. -**2.** [faixa para pedestres] zebra crossing. -**3.** *fam pej* [pessoa] dunce. -**4.** *loc*: **dar ~** to turn out badly.
zelador, ra [zela'do(x), ra] (*pl* -es, *fpl* -s) *m, f* [de prédio] caretaker *UK*, janitor *US*.
zelar [ze'la(x)] *vi*: ~ **por** to care for.
zelo ['zelu] *m* -**1.** [cuidado] care. -**2.** [empenho] zeal.
zeloso, osa [ze'lozu, za] *adj* [cuidadoso]: ~ **(de/por)** caring (for), careful (of).
zé-mané [,zɛma'nɛ] (*pl* -s) *m fam* [otário, bobalhão] idiot, airhead.
zen [zẽ] *adj inv* zen.
zen-budismo [zẽn bu'dʒiʒmu] *m* Zen Buddhism.
zé-ninguém [,zɛnĩ'gẽ] (*pl* zés-ninguém) *m*: um ~ a nobody.
zepelim [ze'pelĩ] (*pl* -ns) *m* [balão] zeppelin.
zerar [ze'ra(x)] *vt* -**1.** [reduzir a zero] to reduce to zero. -**2.** [liquidar] to wipe out.
zero ['zɛru] *num* -**1.** [ger] zero; ~ **erros** no mistakes; **abaixo/acima de** ~ below/above zero. -**2.** *ESP* nil; [em tênis] love. -**3.** *loc*: **ser um** ~ **à esquerda** to be a nothing.
 ⬥ **a zero** *loc adv*: **ficar a** ~ to end up broke; *veja também* **seis**.
zero-quilômetro [,zɛruki'lometru] <> *adj inv* brand new. <> *m inv* brand new car.
ziguezague [,zigi'zagi] *m* zigzag.
ziguezaguear [zigiza'gja(x)] *vi* to zigzag.
zinco ['zĩŋku] *m* zinc.
zipar [zi'pa(x)] *vt* COMPUT to zip.
zoada ['zwada] *f* = **zoeira**.
zoar ['zwa(x)] <> *vt* [caçoar] to make fun of. <> *vi* -**1.** [fazer grande ruído] to make a din. -**2.** [zumbir] to buzz. -**3.** [fazer troça] to make fun. -**4.** [promover confusão] to cause trouble.
zodiacal [zodʒja'kaw] *adj* of the zodiac (*depois de subst*).
zodíaco [zo'dʒiaku] *m* zodiac.
zoeira ['zwejra] *f* din.
zombar [zõm'ba(x)] *vi* -**1.** [debochar]: ~ **de alguém/algo** to make fun of sb/sthg. -**2.** [desdenhar]: ~ **de algo** to sneer at sthg.
zombaria [zõba'ria] *f* [deboche] ridicule.
zombeteiro, ra [zõbe'tejru, ra] <> *adj* [zombador] joking. <> *m, f* joker.
zona ['zona] *f* -**1.** [ger] zone; ~ **franca** free trade area. -**2.** *fam* [bagunça, confusão] mess.
zoneamento [zonja'mẽtu] *m* [divisão em zonas] zoning.
zonear [zo'nja(x)] <> *vt* -**1.** *fam* [bagunçar] to mess up. -**2.** [dividir em zonas] to zone. <> *vi fam* [bagunçar] to mess up.
zonzo, za ['zõzu, za] *adj* -**1.** [tonto] dizzy. -**2.** [atordoado, confuso] giddy.
zôo ['zow] *m* zoo.
zoologia [zwolo'ʒia] *f* zoology.
zoológico, ca [zo'lɔʒiku, ka] *adj* zoological.
 ⬥ **zoológico** *m* zoo.
zoom [zũ] *m* zoom.
zum [zũ] *m* zoom.
zumbido [zũn'bidu] *m* -**1.** [de inseto] buzz. -**2.** [de motor, vozes *etc*.] hum. -**3.** [no ouvido] ringing.
zumbir [zũn'bi(x)] *vi* -**1.** [inseto] to buzz. -**2.** [motor, vozes] to hum. -**3.** [bala, vento] to whistle. -**4.** [ouvido] to ring.
zunzum [zũn'zũ] (*pl* -ns) *m* -**1.** [ruído] humming. -**2.** [boato] rumour.

a¹ (*pl as OR* a's), **A** (*pl As OR* A's) [eɪ] *n* [letter] a, A *m*; **to get from A to B** ir de um lugar para outro.

▸ **A** *n* **-1.** MUS [note] lá *m* **-2.** SCH [mark] A *m*.

a² [*stressed* eɪ, *unstressed* ə] (*before vowel or silent 'h'* **an**) [*stressed* æn, *unstressed* ən] *indef art* **-1.** [non-specific] um *m*, uma *f*; ~ **boy** um garoto; ~ **table** uma mesa; **an orange** uma laranja **-2.** [referring to occupation]: **she's** ~ **teacher/actress** ela é professora/atriz **-3.** [one] um, uma; ~ **hundred/thousand pounds** cem/mil libras **-4.** [to express prices, ratios etc.] por; **£10** ~ **day/person** £10 por dia/pessoa; **twice** ~ **week/month** duas vezes por semana/mês; **50 km an hour** 50 km por hora **-5.** [to express prices, ratios etc.]: **20 cents** ~ **kilo** 20 centavos o quilo.

AA *n* **-1.** (*abbr of* **Automobile Association**) *associação britânica que presta serviço de emergência a seus filiados em situações de problemas e acidentes automobilísticos,* ≃ Touring *m* Club do Brasil **-2.** (*abbr of* **Alcoholics Anonymous**) AA *mpl*.

AAA *n* (*abbr of* **American Automobile Association**) *associação automobilística americana.*

AB *n* (*abbr of* **Bachelor of Arts**) (*titular de*) *graduação em ciências humanas nos Estados Unidos.*

aback [ə'bæk] *adv*: **to be taken** ~ (**by sthg**) ficar surpreso(sa) (com algo), ser surpreendido(da) (por algo).

abandon [ə'bændən] ⬦ *vt* **-1.** [leave, desert] abandonar **-2.** [give up] desistir de. ⬦ *n* (*U*): **with** ~ sem inibição, desenfreado(da).

abashed [ə'bæʃt] *adj* envergonhado(da).

abate [ə'beɪt] *vi fml* [storm, noise, wind] abrandar; [pain, fear, anxiety] diminuir.

abattoir ['æbətwɑːʳ] *n* matadouro *m*.

abbey ['æbɪ] *n* abadia *f*.

abbot ['æbət] *n* abade *m*.

abbreviate [ə'briːvɪeɪt] *vt* abreviar.

abbreviation [ə,briːvɪ'eɪʃn] *n* [short form] abreviatura *f*.

ABC *n* **-1.** [alphabet] abc *m* **-2.** *fig* [basics]: **the** ~ **of** o abc de.

abdicate ['æbdɪkeɪt] ⬦ *vi* abdicar. ⬦ *vt* [responsibility] abrir mão de.

abdomen ['æbdəmen] *n* abdome *m*.

abduct [əb'dʌkt] *vt* raptar.

aberration [,æbə'reɪʃn] *n* aberração *f*; **a mental** ~ um desatino.

abet [ə'bet] (*pt* & *pp* **-ted**, *cont* **-ting**) *vt* ▷ **aid.**

abeyance [ə'beɪəns] *n fml*: **in** ~ em estado jacente.

abhor [əb'hɔːʳ] (*pt* & *pp* **-red**, *cont* **-ring**) *vt* abominar.

abide [ə'baɪd] *vt* suportar.

▸ **abide by** *vt fus* sujeitar-se a.

ability [ə'bɪlətɪ] (*pl* **-ies**) *n* **-1.** (*U*) [capacity, level of capability] capacidade *f* **-2.** [skill, talent] habilidade *f*.

abject ['æbdʒekt] *adj* **-1.** [miserable, depressing] abjeto(ta) **-2.** [humble] servil.

ablaze [ə'bleɪz] *adj* [on fire] em chamas.

able ['eɪbl] *adj* **-1.** [capable] capaz; **to be** ~ **to do sthg** ser capaz de fazer algo; [in a position to] poder fazer algo; [manage to] conseguir fazer algo **-2.** [accomplished, talented] competente.

ably ['eɪblɪ] *adv* competentemente, habilmente.

abnormal [æb'nɔːml] *adj* anormal.

aboard [ə'bɔːd] ⬦ *adv* [on ship, plane] a bordo. ⬦ *prep* [ship, plane] a bordo de; [bus, train] em.

abode [ə'bəʊd] *n fml*: **of no fixed** ~ sem domicílio fixo.

abolish [ə'bɒlɪʃ] *vt* abolir.

abolition [,æbə'lɪʃn] *n* abolição *f*.

abominable [ə'bɒmɪnəbl] *adj* abominável.

aborigine [,æbə'rɪdʒənɪ] *n* aborígine *mf*.

abort [ə'bɔːt] *vt* & *vi* abortar.

abortion [ə'bɔːʃn] *n* [of pregnancy] aborto *m*; **to have an** ~ abortar.

abortive [ə'bɔ:tɪv] adj fracassado(da).

abound [ə'baʊnd] vi **-1.** [be plentiful] existir em abundância, abundar **-2.** [be full]: **to ~ with** or **in sthg** ser rico(ca) em algo, ser cheio(cheia) de algo.

about [ə'baʊt] ◇ adv **-1.** [approximately] cerca de; **~ fifty/a hundred/a thousand** quase or cerca de cinquenta/cem/mil; **to be just ~ ready** estar quase pronto(ta); **at ~ five o'clock** por volta das cinco horas **-2.** [referring to place] por perto; **to walk ~** andar por perto; **to jump ~** saltitar **-3.** [on the point of]: **to be ~ to do sthg** estar prestes a fazer algo. ◇ prep **-1.** [relating to, concerning] sobre; **a film ~ Paris** um filme sobre Paris; **what is it ~?** de que se trata?; **to talk ~ sthg** falar sobre algo **-2.** [referring to place] por; **to wander ~ the streets** vagar pelas ruas.

about-turn esp UK, **about-face** esp US n **-1.** MIL meia-volta f **-2.** fig [change of attitude] guinada f de 180 graus.

above [ə'bʌv] ◇ adv **-1.** [on top, higher up] de cima **-2.** [in text] acima; **the items mentioned ~** os itens acima mencionados **-3.** [more, over] acima de; **children aged five and ~** crianças de cinco anos ou mais. ◇ prep acima de.
➡ **above all** adv acima de tudo.

aboveboard [ə,bʌv'bɔ:d] adj **-1.** legítimo(ma) **-2.** limpo(pa).

abrasive [ə'breɪsɪv] adj **-1.** [cleaner, cloth] abrasivo(va) **-2.** fig [person, manner] mordaz.

abreast [ə'brest] adv lado a lado.
➡ **abreast of** prep: **to keep ~ of sthg** estar a par de algo.

abridged [ə'brɪdʒd] adj resumido(da), compacto(ta).

abroad [ə'brɔ:d] adv [overseas]: **to live ~** viver/morar no exterior; **to go ~** ir para o exterior.

abrupt [ə'brʌpt] adj **-1.** [sudden] repentino(na) **-2.** [brusque, rude] brusco(ca).

abscess ['æbsɪs] n abscesso m.

abscond [əb'skɒnd] vi esconder-se.

abseil ['æbseɪl] vi praticar rappel.

absence ['æbsəns] n **-1.** [of person] ausência f **-2.** [lack] falta f.

absent ['æbsənt] adj [not present]: **~ (from)** ausente (de).

absentee [æbsən'ti:] n ausente mf.

absent-minded [-'maɪndɪd] adj distraído(da).

absent-mindedness n distração f.

absolute ['æbsəlu:t] adj **-1.** [complete, utter] absoluto(ta) **-2.** [totalitarian] arbitrário(ria).

absolutely ['æbsəlu:tlɪ] ◇ adv [completely, utterly] absolutamente. ◇ excl [expressing agreement] sem dúvida.

absolve [əb'zɒlv] vt [free, clear]: **to ~ sb (of sthg)** absolver alguém (de algo).

absorb [əb'sɔ:b] vt **-1.** [soak up] absorver **-2.** fig [learn] assimilar **-3.** [interest] absorver; **to be ~ ed in sthg** estar absorvido(da) em algo **-4.** [take over] incorporar.

absorbent [əb'sɔ:bənt] adj absorvente.

absorption [əb'sɔ:pʃn] n **-1.** [soaking up] absorção f **-2.** [interest] concentração f **-3.** [taking over] incorporação f.

abstain [əb'steɪn] vi **-1.** [refrain]: **to ~ from sthg** abster-se de algo **-2.** [in vote] abster-se.

abstemious [æb'sti:mjəs] adj fml abstêmio(mia).

abstention [əb'stenʃn] n [in vote] abstenção f.

abstract ['æbstrækt] ◇ adj abstrato(ta). ◇ n [summary] resumo m.

absurd [əb'sɜ:d] adj absurdo(da).

ABTA (abbr of Association of British Travel Agents) n associação britânica de agentes de viagens, ≃ ABAV f.

abundant [ə'bʌndənt] adj abundante.

abundantly [ə'bʌndəntlɪ] adv **-1.** [manifestly] suficientemente; **it is ~ clear that ...** está suficientemente claro que ...; **he made it ~ clear that ...** ele deixou mais do que claro que ... **-2.** [in large amounts] em abundância.

abuse [n ə'bju:s, vb ə'bju:z] ◇ n **-1.** [offensive remarks] insultos mpl **-2.** [maltreatment, misuse] abuso m. ◇ vt **-1.** [insult] insultar **-2.** [maltreat] maltratar **-3.** [misuse] abusar de.

abusive [ə'bju:sɪv] adj abusivo(va).

abysmal [ə'bɪzml] adj abismal.

abyss [ə'bɪs] n **-1.** abismo m **-2.** fig [gap] abismo m.

a/c (abbr of account (current)) c.c. f.

AC (abbr of alternating current) n CA f.

academic [,ækə'demɪk] ◇ adj **-1.** [of college, university] acadêmico(ca) **-2.** [studious] intelectual **-3.** [hypothetical] conjetural. ◇ n [teacher, researcher] acadêmico m, -ca f.

academy [ə'kædəmɪ] (pl -ies) n **-1.** [school, college] academia f, escola f **-2.** [institution, society] academia f.

ACAS (abbr of Advisory Conciliation and Arbitration Service) n organização britânica para conciliação entre sindicatos e empregadores.

accede [æk'si:d] vi **-1.** fml [agree]: **to ~ to sthg** aceder a algo **-2.** [monarch]: **to ~ to the throne** subir ao trono.

accelerate [ək'seləreɪt] ⟨⟩ vt apressar. ⟨⟩ vi -1. [car, driver] acelerar -2. [inflation, growth] disparar.

acceleration [ək,selə'reɪʃn] n -1. [of car] aceleração f -2. [of inflation, growth] disparada f.

accelerator [ək'seləreɪtəʳ] n acelerador m.

accent ['æksent] n -1. [when speaking] sotaque m -2. [in writing] acento m.

accept [ək'sept] vt -1. [agree to take, receive] aceitar -2. [agree to follow] assentir -3. [recognize as satisfactory] aprovar -4. [get used to] reconhecer -5. [admit, recognize as one's own] assumir -6. [person - as part of group] acolher; [- for job, as member of club] aceitar -7. [agree, believe]: to ~ that aceitar que -8. [process] aceitar.

acceptable [ək'septəbl] adj -1. [permissible] aceitável -2. [passable] admissível.

acceptance [ək'septəns] n -1. [gen] aceitação f -2. [recognizing as satisfactory] aprovação f.

access ['ækses] n -1. [entry, way in] acesso m -2. [opportunity to use, see]: to have ~ to sthg ter acesso a algo.

access provider n COMPUT provedor de acesso.

accessible [ək'sesəbl] adj -1. [reachable, understandable] acessível -2. [available] disponível.

accessory [ək'sesərɪ] (pl -ies) n -1. [extra part, device] acessório m -2. JUR cúmplice mf.

accident ['æksɪdənt] n -1. acidente m; to have an ~ sofrer um acidente -2. (U) [chance]: by ~ por acaso; it was an ~ foi sem querer.

accidental [,æksɪ'dentl] adj acidental.

accidentally [,æksɪ'dentəlɪ] adv -1. [drop, break] sem querer -2. [meet, find, discover] acidentalmente.

accident-prone adj propenso(sa) a acidentes.

acclaim [ə'kleɪm] ⟨⟩ n (U) aclamação f. ⟨⟩ vt aclamar.

acclimatize, -ise [ə'klaɪmətaɪz], **acclimate** US ['æklɪmeɪt] vi: to ~ (to sthg) aclimatar-se (a algo).

accommodate [ə'kɒmədeɪt] vt -1. [provide room for] acomodar -2. [oblige] comprazer a.

accommodating [ə'kɒmədeɪtɪŋ] adj complacente.

accommodation UK [ə,kɒmə'deɪʃn] n, **accommodations** US [ə,kɒmə'deɪʃnz] npl [lodging] alojamento m, acomodação f.

accompany [ə'kʌmpənɪ] (pt & pp -ied) vt -1. acompanhar -2. MUS [with instrument]: to ~ sb (on sthg) acompanhar alguém (em algo).

accomplice [ə'kʌmplɪs] n cúmplice m.

accomplish [ə'kʌmplɪʃ] vt [achieve, manage] conseguir; [carry out, effect] realizar; [reach, attain] alcançar.

accomplishment [ə'kʌmplɪʃmənt] n -1. [achievement, finishing] realização f, conclusão f -2. [feat, deed] feito m.
◆ **accomplishments** npl [skills] habilidades fpl.

accord [ə'kɔːd] n -1. [settlement] acordo m -2. [agreement, harmony]: to do sthg of one's own ~ fazer algo por iniciativa própria.

accordance [ə'kɔːdəns] n: in ~ with sthg de acordo com algo.

according to prep -1. [as stated or shown by] segundo; to go ~ to plan sair conforme o planejado -2. [with regard to, depending on] conforme.

accordingly [ə'kɔːdɪŋlɪ] adv -1. [appropriately] de modo apropriado -2. [consequently] conseqüentemente.

accordion [ə'kɔːdjən] n acordeão m, sanfona f.

accost [ə'kɒst] vt abordar.

account [ə'kaʊnt] n -1. [with bank, company] conta f -2. [with shop]: I have an ~ at the butcher's tenho conta no açougue -3. [report]: to give an ~ of sthg fazer um relato de algo -4. phr: to take ~ of sthg, to take sthg into ~ levar algo em consideração; to be of no ~ não ter importância; on no ~ de modo algum.
◆ **accounts** npl [of business] contabilidade f.
◆ **by all accounts** adv de acordo com a opinião geral.
◆ **on account of** prep devido a; on my ~ por minha causa.
◆ **account for** vt fus -1. [explain] justificar; a theory that ~ s for all the facts uma teoria que justifique os fatos -2. [represent] representar.

accountable [ə'kaʊntəbl] adj [responsible]: to be held ~ for sthg ser responsabilizado(da) por algo.

accountancy [ə'kaʊntənsɪ] n [profession, business] contabilidade f.

accountant [ə'kaʊntənt] n contador m, -ra f.

accounts department n setor m de contabilidade.

accrue [ə'kruː] vt & vi FIN render.

accumulate [ə'kjuːmjʊleɪt] ⟨⟩ vt acumular. ⟨⟩ vi acumular-se.

accuracy ['ækjʊrəsɪ] n -1. [truth, correctness] exatidão f -2. [precision - of weapon, marksman] precisão f; [- of typing, figures, estimate] exatidão f.

accurate [ˈækjʊrət] adj -1. [true, correct] exato(ta) -2. [precise - shot, marksman] preciso(saı); [- typist, figures, estimate] exato(ta).

accurately [ˈækjʊrətlı] adv -1. [truthfully, correctly] com exatidão -2. [precisely - aim] com precisão; [- type, estimate] com exatidão.

accusation [ˌækjuː'zeıʃn] n -1. [charge, criticism] acusação f -2. JUR [formal charge] incriminação f.

accuse [ə'kjuːz] vt -1. [charge, criticize]: to ~ sb of sthg/of doing sthg acusar alguém de algo/de fazer algo -2. JUR : to ~ sb of sthg/of doing sthg incriminar alguém por algo/por fazer algo.

accused [ə'kjuːzd] n JUR: the ~ [defendant] o réu(a ré).

accustomed [ə'kʌstəmd] adj: to be ~ to sthg/to doing sthg estar acostumado(-da) a algo/a fazer algo.

ace [eıs] n -1. [playing card] ás m -2. TENNIS ace m.

ache [eık] ◇ n [dull pain] dor f. ◇ vi -1. [be painful] doer -2. fig [want]: to be aching for sthg/to do sthg estar morrendo de vontade de algo/de fazer algo.

achieve [ə'tʃiːv] vt [success] conseguir; [goal, ambition] realizar; [victory, fame] conquistar.

achievement [ə'tʃiːvmənt] n [feat, deed] conquista f.

Achilles' tendon n tendão m de Aquiles.

acid [ˈæsıd] ◇ adj -1. ácido(da) -2. fig [remark, tone] áspero(ra). ◇ n -1. ácido m -2. inf [LSD] ácido m.

acid rain n chuva f ácida.

acknowledge [ək'nɒlıdʒ] vt -1. [accept, recognize] reconhecer; to ~ sb as sthg reconhecer alguém como algo -2. [letter]: to ~ (receipt of) sthg acusar (o recebimento de) algo -3. [greet] cumprimentar.

acknowledg(e)ment [ək'nɒlıdʒmənt] n -1. [acceptance, recognition] reconhecimento m -2. [of letter] aviso m de recebimento -3. [thanks, gratitude] retribuição f.
  ➤ **acknowledg(e)ments** npl [in book] agradecimentos mpl.

acne [ˈæknı] n acne f.

acorn [ˈeıkɔːn] n bolota f, glande m.

acoustic [ə'kuːstık] adj acústico(ca).
  ➤ **acoustics** npl [of room, auditorium] acústica f.

acquaint [ə'kweınt] vt: to ~ sb with sthg [information] informar alguém sobre algo; to be ~ed with sthg [method, technique] estar por dentro de algo; to be ~ed with sb fml conhecer alguém.

acquaintance [ə'kweıntəns] n [personal associate] conhecido m, -da f.

acquire [ə'kwaıəʳ] vt -1. [obtain] [property, company, object] adquirir -2. [information, document] obter -3. [skill, knowledge, habit] adquirir.

acquisitive [ə'kwızıtıv] adj ambicioso(-sa), consumista.

acquit [ə'kwıt] (pt & pp -ted, cont -ting) vt [conduct]: to ~ o.s. well/badly desempenhar-se bem/mal.

acquittal [ə'kwıtl] n JUR absolvição f.

acre [ˈeıkəʳ] n [unit of measurement] acre m (4046,9 m²).

acrid [ˈækrıd] adj -1. [smoke, smell, taste] acre -2. fig [remark] mordaz.

acrimonious [ˌækrı'məʊnjəs] adj acrimonioso(sa).

acrobat [ˈækrəbæt] n [circus performer] acrobata mf.

across [ə'krɒs] ◇ adv -1. [from one side to the other]: they came ~ in a small boat eles atravessaram num barco pequeno -2. [in the direction of]: she looked ~ at me ela olhou em minha direção; he went ~ to speak to her ele foi em sua direção para lhe falar -3. [in measurements] de um lado a outro -4. [in crosswords] cruzado(da). ◇ prep -1. [from one side to the other] de um lado a outro; he drew a line ~ the page ele traçou uma linha de um lado a outro da página; there is a bridge ~ the river há uma ponte sobre o rio; she walked/ran ~ the road ela atravessou a estrada caminhando/correndo; he looked ~ the street ele olhou pela rua -2. [on the other side of] no outro lado de.
  ➤ **across from** prep na frente de.

acrylic [ə'krılık] ◇ adj [fibre, jumper, paint] acrílico(ca). ◇ n (U) [fibre] acrílico m.

act [ækt] ◇ n -1. [action, deed] ato m -2. JUR lei f -3. [of play, opera] ato m; [in cabaret etc.] número m -4. fig [pretence] fingimento m; to put on an ~ agir com fingimento -5. phr: to get one's ~ together organizar-se. ◇ vi -1. [gen] agir; to ~ as if/like agir como se/como -2. [in play, film] representar, atuar -3. fig [pretend] fingir -4. [fulfil function]: to ~ as sthg atuar como algo. ◇ vt [role] desempenhar.

ACT (abbr of American College Test) n exame realizado ao final do ensino médio em escolas norte-americanas.

acting ['æktɪŋ] <> *adj* [interim] interino(na). <> *n (U)* [in play, film] atuação *f*; **to enjoy ~** gostar de atuar.

action ['ækʃn] *n* -1. *(U)* [fact of doing sthg] ação *f*; **to take ~** agir; **to put sthg into ~** pôr algo em ação; **in ~** [person, machine] em atividade; **out of ~** [person] fora de combate; [machine] desativado(da) -2. [deed] atividade *f* -3. *(U)* [in battle, war] ação *f* -4. JUR ação *f* judicial -5. [in play, book, film] história *f* -6. [effect] efeito *m*.

action replay *n* replay *m*.

activate ['æktɪveɪt] *vt* [set off] ativar.

active ['æktɪv] *adj* -1. [lively, energetic] ativo(va) -2. [involved, hardworking] dinâmico(ca) -3. [positive] incessante -4. [volcano] ativo(va).

actively ['æktɪvlɪ] *adv* -1. [promote] ativamente -2. [seek, encourage] incessantemente.

activity [æk'tɪvətɪ] *(pl* -ies) *n (U)* atividade *f*.
 ◆ **activities** *npl* [actions, doings] ações *fpl*.

actor ['æktər] *n* ator *m*.

actress ['æktrɪs] *n* atriz *f*.

actual ['æktʃʊəl] *adj* real.

actually ['æktʃʊəlɪ] *adv* -1. [really, in truth] na verdade, realmente -2. [by the way] a propósito.

acumen ['ækjʊmen] *n (U)*: **business ~** tino para os negócios.

acupuncture ['ækjʊpʌŋktʃər] *n (U)* acupuntura *f*.

acupuncturist ['ækjʊpʌŋktʃərɪst] *n* acupuntor *m*, -ra *f*.

acute [ə'kjuːt] *adj* -1. [severe, extreme] agudo(da) -2. [perceptive, intelligent] engenhoso(sa) -3. [keen, sensitive] aguçado(da) -4. LING: **e ~** e agudo -5. MATH agudo(da).

ad *(abbr of* advertisement) *n fam* -1. [in newspaper] anúncio *m* -2. [on TV] propaganda *f*.

AD *(abbr of* Anno Domini) d.C.

adamant ['ædəmənt] *adj* [determined]: **to be ~ (about sthg/that)** estar inflexível (em relação a algo).

Adam's apple ['ædəmz-] *n* pomo-de-adão *m*.

adapt [ə'dæpt] <> *vt* adaptar. <> *vi*: **to ~ to sthg** adaptar-se a algo.

adaptable [ə'dæptəbl] *adj* [person] maleável.

adapter, adaptor [ə'dæptər] *n* ELEC adaptador *m*.

ADAS *(abbr of* Agricultural Development and Advisory Service) *n organização britânica de pesquisa e consultoria para as indústrias do setor agrícola.*

add [æd] *vt* -1.: **to ~ sthg to sthg** adicionar algo a algo -2. [total] somar; **6 ~ 3 equals 9** *US* 6 mais 3 é igual a 9 -3. [say as an afterthought] acrescentar.
 ◆ **add on** *vt sep*: **to ~ sthg on (to sthg)** [to building] anexar algo (a algo); [to bill, total] incluir algo (em algo).
 ◆ **add to** *vt fus* [increase] aumentar.
 ◆ **add up** *vt sep* [total up] adicionar.
 ◆ **add up to** *vt fus* [represent] representar.

adder ['ædər] *n* [snake] víbora *f*.

addict ['ædɪkt] *n* -1. [to drug, harmful substance] viciado *m*, -da *f*, dependente *mf* -2. [exercise, TV etc.] fanático *m*, -ca *f*.

addicted [ə'dɪktɪd] *adj* -1. [to drug, harmful substance]: **~ (to sthg)** viciado(da) (em algo), dependente de algo -2. *fig* [to exercise, TV] fanático(ca) (por algo).

addiction [ə'dɪkʃn] *n (U)* -1. [to drug, harmful substance] vício *m*, dependência *f*; **~ to sthg** vício em algo, dependência de algo -2. *fig* [to exercise, food, TV] fanatismo *m*; **~ to sthg** fanatismo por algo.

addictive [ə'dɪktɪv] *adj* -1. [drug, harmful substance] que vicia -2. *fig* [exercise, food, TV] que vicia.

addition [ə'dɪʃn] *n* -1. *(U)* MATH adição *f* -2. [extra thing] acréscimo *m* -3. *(U)* [act of adding] adicionamento *m*; **in ~** além disso; **in ~ to** além de.

additional [ə'dɪʃənl] *adj* [extra] adicional.

additive ['ædɪtɪv] *n* aditivo *m*.

address [ə'dres] <> *n* -1. [location] endereço *m* -2. [speech] discurso *m*. <> *vt* -1. [letter, parcel] endereçar -2. [give a speech to] discursar -3. [speak to, accost]: **to ~ sb** as dirigir-se a alguém como -4. [deal with] tratar.

address book *n* agenda *f* de endereços.

adenoids ['ædɪnɔɪdz] *npl* adenóides *fpl*.

adept ['ædept] *adj*: **to be ~ at sthg/at doing sthg** ser perito(ta) em algo/em fazer algo.

adequate ['ædɪkwət] *adj* -1. [sufficient] suficiente -2. [competent] adequado(-da).

adhere [əd'hɪər] *vi* -1. [to surface, principle]: **to ~ (to sthg)** aderir (a algo) -2. [to regulation, decision]: **to ~ to sthg** respeitar algo.

adhesive [əd'hiːsɪv] <> *adj* [sticky] adesivo(va). <> *n* [glue] cola *f*.

adhesive tape *n* fita *f* adesiva.

adjacent [ə'dʒeɪsənt] *adj* adjacente; **~ to sthg** adjacente a algo.

adjective ['ædʒɪktɪv] *n* adjetivo *m*.

adjoining [ə'dʒɔɪnɪŋ] ◇ adj [next-door] vizinho(nha). ◇ prep ao lado de.

adjourn [ə'dʒɜːn] ◇ vt [postpone] adiar. ◇ vi [come to a temporary close] ser/estar suspenso(sa).

adjudicate [ə'dʒuːdɪkeɪt] vi [serve as judge, arbiter in contest] julgar; to ~ on OR upon sthg deliberar sobre algo.

adjust [ə'dʒʌst] ◇ vt [alter, correct] ajustar. ◇ vi: to ~ (to sthg) adaptar-se (a algo).

adjustable [ə'dʒʌstəbl] adj [machine, chair] regulável.

adjustment [ə'dʒʌstmənt] n - 1. [to heat, speed, machine] ajuste m - 2. (U) [change of attitude] mudança f; ~ to sthg adaptação a algo.

ad lib [ˌæd'lɪb] (pt & pp ad-libbed, cont ad-libbing) ◇ adj [improvised] espontâneo(nea). ◇ adv [freely] de improviso. ◇ n [improvised joke, remark] improviso m.
➡ **ad-lib** vi [improvise] improvisar.

administer [əd'mɪnɪstər] vt - 1. [company, business] administrar - 2. [justice, punishment] aplicar - 3. [drug, medication] ministrar.

administration [əd,mɪnɪˈstreɪʃn] n - 1. (U) [of company, business] administração f - 2. (U) [of justice, punishment] aplicação f.

administrative [əd'mɪnɪstrətɪv] adj [job, work, staff] administrativo(va).

admirable ['ædmərəbl] adj admirável.

admiral ['ædmərəl] n almirante mf.

admiration [ˌædmə'reɪʃn] n admiração f.

admire [əd'maɪər] vt - 1. [respect, like] admirar; to ~ sb for sthg admirar alguém por algo - 2. [look at with pleasure] apreciar.

admirer [əd'maɪərər] n - 1. [suitor] pretendente mf - 2. [enthusiast, fan] fã mf.

admission [əd'mɪʃn] n - 1. [permission to enter] admissão f - 2. [cost of entrance] entrada f - 3. [confession] confissão f.

admit [əd'mɪt] (pt & pp -ted, cont -ting) ◇ vt - 1. [acknowledge, confess] confessar, admitir; to ~ that admitir que; to ~ doing sthg admitir/confessar ter feito algo; to ~ defeat fig dar-se por vencido(da) - 2. [allow to enter] admitir; to be admitted to hospital UK OR to the hospital US dar entrada no hospital - 3. [allow to join] admitir; to ~ sb to sthg admitir alguém em algo. ◇ vi: to ~ to sthg/to doing sthg admitir algo/ fazer algo.

admittance [əd'mɪtəns] n [right to enter, entrance]: 'no ~' 'entrada proibida'.

admittedly [əd'mɪtɪdlɪ] adv reconhecidamente.

admonish [əd'mɒnɪʃ] vt fml [tell off] repreender.

ad nauseam [ˌæd'nɔːzɪæm] adv exaustivamente.

ado [ə'duː] n: without further OR more ~ sem mais delongas OR preâmbulos.

adolescence [ˌædə'lesns] n adolescência f.

adolescent [ˌædə'lesnt] ◇ adj - 1. [teenage] adolescente - 2. pej [immature] imaturo(ra). ◇ n [teenager] adolescente mf.

adopt [ə'dɒpt] vt [recommendation, suggestion] aceitar.

adoption [ə'dɒpʃn] n (U) adoção f.

adore [ə'dɔːr] vt adorar.

adorn [ə'dɔːn] vt [decorate] adornar.

adrenalin [ə'drenəlɪn] n (U) adrenalina f.

Adriatic [ˌeɪdrɪ'ætɪk] n: the ~ (Sea) o (Mar) Adriático.

adrift [ə'drɪft] ◇ adj [boat, ship] à deriva. ◇ adv: to go ~ fig [go wrong] ir por água abaixo.

adult ['ædʌlt] ◇ adj - 1. [mature, responsible] adulto(ta) - 2. [for adults] para adultos, para maiores. ◇ n [person, animal] adulto m, -ta f.

adultery [ə'dʌltərɪ] n (U) adultério m.

advance [əd'vɑːns] ◇ n - 1. [gen] avanço m - 2. [money] adiantamento m. ◇ comp - 1. [early] antecipado(da) - 2. [prior]: ~ warning aviso prévio. ◇ vt - 1. [improve] progredir - 2. [bring forward in time] adiantar - 3. [money]: to ~ sb sthg adiantar algo a alguém. ◇ vi - 1. [go forward] avançar - 2. [improve] progredir.
➡ **advances** npl: to make ~s to sb [sexual] assediar alguém; [business] propor um bom negócio para alguém.
➡ **in advance** adv com antecedência; to book in ~ reservar antecipadamente; to know in ~ saber de antemão; half an hour in ~ meia hora antes.

advanced [əd'vɑːnst] adj avançado(da).

advantage [əd'vɑːntɪdʒ] n - 1. vantagem f; to be to one's ~ ser conveniente para alguém; to have OR hold the ~ (over sb) ter OR levar vantagem (sobre alguém) - 2. phr: to take ~ of sthg/sb aproveitar-se de algo/alguém.

advent ['ædvənt] n [of invention, person, period] advento m.
➡ **Advent** n RELIG Advento m.

adventure [əd'ventʃər] n aventura f; to have no sense of ~ não ter espírito de aventura.

adventure playground n área de lazer para crianças que oferece materiais diversos para montar e brincar.

adventurous [əd'ventʃərəs] adj - 1. [person] intrépido(da) - 2. [life, project] aventureiro(ra) - 3. [menu, programme etc.] atraente, interessante.

adverb ['ædvɜ:b] n advérbio m.

adverse ['ædvɜ:s] adj adverso(sa).

advert ['ædvɜ:t] n UK = advertisement.

advertise ['ædvətaɪz] ⬦ vt [job, car, product] anunciar. ⬦ vi [in newspaper, on TV, in shop window]: **they're advertising for sales representatives** estão anunciando vaga para representantes comerciais.

advertisement [əd'vɜ:tɪsmənt] n - 1. [in newspaper, on TV, in shop window] anúncio m - 2. fig [recommendation] propaganda f.

advertiser ['ædvətaɪzə'] n anunciante mf.

advertising ['ædvətaɪzɪŋ] n (U) - 1. [advertisements] propaganda f - 2. [industry] publicidade f.

advice [əd'vaɪs] n (U) conselho m; **to give sb ~** dar conselhos a alguém; **to take sb's ~** aceitar conselhos de alguém; **a piece of ~** um conselho.

advisable [əd'vaɪzəbl] adj aconselhável.

advise [əd'vaɪz] ⬦ vt - 1. [give advice to]: **to ~ sb to do sthg/not to do sthg** aconselhar alguém a fazer algo/a não fazer algo - 2. [professionally]: **to ~ sb on sthg** assessorar alguém em algo - 3. fml [inform] avisar; **to ~ sb of sthg** avisar alguém sobre algo. ⬦ vi - 1. [give advice]: **to ~ against sthg/against doing sthg** desaconselhar algo/a fazer algo - 2. [act as adviser]: **to ~ on sthg** assessorar em algo.

advisedly [əd'vaɪzɪdlɪ] adv deliberadamente.

adviser UK, **advisor** US [əd'vaɪzə'] n assessor m, -ra f.

advisory [əd'vaɪzərɪ] adj [group, organization] de assessoria.

advocate [n 'ædvəkət, vb 'ædvəkeɪt] ⬦ n - 1. Scot JUR advogado m, -da f - 2. [supporter] defensor m, -ra f. ⬦ vt fml [recommend] defender.

Aegean [i:'dʒi:ən] n: **the ~ (Sea)** o (Mar) Egeu; **in the ~** no Egeu.

aerial ['eərɪəl] ⬦ adj [of, from, in the air] aéreo(rea). ⬦ n UK [antenna] antena f.

aerobics [eə'rəʊbɪks] n (U) aeróbica f, ginástica f aeróbica.

aerodynamic [ˌeərəʊdaɪ'næmɪk] adj aerodinâmico(ca).

⬦ **aerodynamics** ⬦ n (U) SCIENCE aerodinâmica f. ⬦ npl [aerodynamic qualities] aerodinâmicas f.

aeroplane UK ['eərəpleɪn], **airplane** US ['eəpleɪn] n avião m.

aerosol ['eərəsɒl] n aerossol m.

aesthetic, esthetic US [i:s'θetɪk] adj estético(ca).

afar [ə'fɑ:'] adv: **from ~** à distância.

affable ['æfəbl] adj [pleasant] afável.

affair [ə'feə'] n - 1. [event] acontecimento m - 2. [concern] assunto m - 3. [extramarital relationship] caso m.

affect [ə'fekt] vt - 1. [influence, act upon] afetar - 2. [imitate, put on] imitar - 3. [feign] fingir.

affection [ə'fekʃn] n afeição f.

affectionate [ə'fekʃnət] adj afetuoso(sa).

affirm [ə'fɜ:m] vt afirmar.

affix [ə'fɪks] vt [stamp] afixar.

afflict [ə'flɪkt] vt afligir; **to be ~ed with sthg** sofrer de algo.

affluence ['æfluəns] n (U) riqueza f.

affluent ['æfluənt] adj rico(ca).

afford [ə'fɔ:d] vt - 1. [have enough money for]: **to be able to ~ sthg** poder pagar por algo - 2. [time, energy]: **to be able to ~ the time (to do sthg)** ter tempo (para fazer algo) - 3. [allow]: **we can't ~ to let this happen** não podemos nos dar ao luxo de deixar que isto aconteça - 4. fml [provide, give] oferecer.

affront [ə'frʌnt] ⬦ n afronta f. ⬦ vt ofender.

Afghanistan [æf'gænɪstæn] n Afeganistão.

afield [ə'fiəld] adv: **far ~** longe.

afloat [ə'fləʊt] adj - 1. [above water] flutuante - 2. fig [out of debt] em dia.

afoot [ə'fʊt] adj [present, happening] em ação.

afraid [ə'freɪd] adj - 1. [frightened] assustado(da); **to be ~ (of sb/sthg)** ter medo (de alguém/algo); **to be ~ of doing** OR **to do sthg** ter medo de fazer algo - 2. [reluctant, apprehensive] apreensivo(va); **to be ~ of sthg** ter medo de algo; **he was ~ of losing his job** tinha medo de perder seu emprego - 3. [in apologies]: **to be ~ (that)** ter receio (que); **I'm ~ so/not** receio que sim/não.

afresh [ə'freʃ] adv novamente.

Africa ['æfrɪkə] n África.

African ['æfrɪkən] ⬦ adj africano(na). ⬦ n africano m, -na f.

aft [ɑ:ft] adv à popa OR ré.

after ['ɑ:ftə'] ⬦ prep - 1. [following - in time] após; [- in order] após; **~ you!** atrás de você! - 2. [as a result of] depois - 3. [in spite of] apesar de **- 4.** *inf* [in search of, looking for] atrás de **- 5.** [with the name of] em homenagem a **- 6.** [directed at sb moving away] atrás de **- 7.** *ART* à moda de **- 8.** *US* [telling the time]: **it's twenty ~ three** são três e vinte. <> *adv* em seguida, depois. <> *conj* depois que/ de; **~ she left university ...** depois que deixou/de deixar a universidade, ela ...

➤ **afters** *npl UK* sobremesa *f.*

➤ **after all** *adv* **- 1.** [in spite of everything] apesar de tudo **- 2.** [it should be remembered] afinal.

after-effects *npl* efeitos *mpl* secundários, conseqüências *fpl.*

afterlife ['ɑ:ftəlaɪf] (*pl* **-lives** [-laɪvz]) *n* vida *f* após a morte.

aftermath ['ɑ:ftəmæθ] *n* conseqüências *fpl.*

afternoon [,ɑ:ftə'nu:n] *n* tarde *f*; **good ~** boa tarde.

➤ **afternoons** *adv esp US* à tarde.

after-sales service *n* serviço *m* pósvenda.

aftershave ['ɑ:ftəʃeɪv] *n* loção *f* após a barba.

aftersun (lotion) ['ɑ:ftəsʌn-] *n* creme *m* hidratante após o sol.

aftertaste ['ɑ:ftəteɪst] *n* [of food, drink] ressaibo *m*, mau sabor *m.*

afterthought ['ɑ:ftəθɔ:t] *n* pensamento *m* a posteriori.

afterwards, afterward *US* ['ɑ:ftəwəd(z)] *adv* posteriormente, depois.

again [ə'gen] *adv* **- 1.** [one more time] outra vez; **~ and ~** repetidas vezes; **all over ~** tudo de novo; **time and ~** mil vezes **- 2.** [once more as before] de novo **- 3.** [asking for information to be repeated]: **what was that ~?** o que foi mesmo que você disse? **- 4.** *phr:* **half as much ~** cinqüenta por cento a mais; **(twice) as much ~** (duas) vezes mais; **come ~?** *inf* o quê?; **then** *OR* **there ~** por outro lado.

against [ə'genst] <> *prep* **- 1.** [gen] contra **- 2.** [in contrast to]: **as ~** em comparação com, em vez de. <> *adv* contra.

age [eɪdʒ] (*cont* **ageing** *OR* **aging**) <> *n* **- 1.** [of person, animal, thing] idade *f*; **what ~ are you?** quantos anos você tem?; **to come of ~** atingir a maioridade; **to be under ~** ser menor de idade **- 2.** *(U)* [state or process of ageing - of person] idade *f*; [- of object, cheese, wine] tempo *m*; **wine improves with ~** o vinho melhora com o tempo **- 3.** [stage - of person's life]

idade *f*, hora *f*; [- of history] era *f.* <> *vt* envelhecer. <> *vi* envelhecer.

➤ **ages** *npl* [a long time]: **~s ago** séculos atrás; **for ~s** há séculos.

aged [eɪdʒd, *npl* 'eɪdʒɪd] <> *adj* **- 1.** [of the stated age] da idade de; **a person ~ 30** uma pessoa de 30 anos; **to be ~ 20** ter 20 anos (de idade) **- 2.** [very old] envelhecido(da), antigo(ga). <> *npl*: **the ~** [the elderly] os idosos.

age group *n* grupo *m* etário.

agency ['eɪdʒənsɪ] (*pl* **-ies**) *n* **- 1.** [gen] agência *f* **- 2.** [government organization] órgão *m.*

agenda [ə'dʒendə] (*pl* **-s**) *n* ordem *f* do dia, expediente *m.*

agent ['eɪdʒənt] *n* [person] agente *mf.*

aggravate ['ægrəveɪt] *vt* **- 1.** [make worse] agravar **- 2.** [annoy] irritar.

aggregate ['ægrɪgət] <> *adj* total. <> *n* [total] total *m.*

aggressive [ə'gresɪv] *adj* **- 1.** [belligerent] agressivo(va) **- 2.** [forceful - campaign] agressivo(va); [- person] audaz, empreendedor(ra).

aggrieved [ə'gri:vd] *adj* [upset, hurt] magoado(da).

aghast [ə'gɑ:st] *adj* [horrified] espantado(da); **~ at sthg** espantado(da) (com algo).

agile [*UK* 'ædʒaɪl, *US* 'ædʒəl] *adj* [body, person, mind] ágil.

agitate ['ædʒɪteɪt] <> *vt* **- 1.** [disturb, worry] perturbar **- 2.** [shake] agitar. <> *vi* [campaign actively]: **to ~ for/against sthg** fazer campanha pró/contra algo.

AGM (*abbr of* **annual general meeting**) *n UK* assembléia *f* geral anual *(de clube, empresa etc.).*

agnostic [æg'nɒstɪk] <> *adj* agnóstico(ca). <> *n* agnóstico *m*, -ca *f.*

ago [ə'gəʊ] *adv* atrás; **three days ~** três dias atrás; **years/long ~** anos/tempos atrás.

agog [ə'gɒg] *adj* ansioso(osa), impaciente; **to be all ~ (with)** estar ansioso(sa) (com).

agonizing ['ægənaɪzɪŋ] *adj* **- 1.** [decision, wait] angustiante **- 2.** [pain] agonizante.

agony ['ægənɪ] (*pl* **-ies**) *n* **- 1.** [physical pain] dores *fpl*, agonia *f*; **to be in ~** estar morrendo de dor **- 2.** [mental pain] angústia *f*; **to be in ~** estar angustiado(da).

agony aunt *n UK inf* conselheira *f* sentimental.

agree [ə'gri:] <> *vi* **- 1.** [concur] concordar; **to ~ with sb/sthg** concordar com alguém/algo; **to ~ on sthg** chegar a um acordo sobre algo; **to ~ about sthg**

concordar sobre algo - **2.** [consent] concordar; **to ~ to sthg** concordar com algo - **3.** [statements] conferir - **4.** [food]: **to ~ with sb** combinar com alguém - **5.** GRAMM : **to ~ (with)** concordar (com). ◇ vt - **1.** [price, terms] concordar - **2.** [concur]: **to ~ that** concordar que - **3.** [arrange]: **to ~ to do sthg** combinar para fazer algo - **4.** [concede]: **to ~ (that)** concordar (que).

agreeable [ə'gri:əbl] adj - **1.** [weather, experience] agradável - **2.** [willing]: **to be ~ to sthg** ser favorável a algo.

agreed [ə'gri:d] adj: **to be ~ on sthg** estar de acordo sobre algo.

agreement [ə'gri:mənt] n - **1.** [accord] acordo m; **to be in ~ with sb/sthg** estar de acordo com alguém/algo - **2.** [settlement, contract] acordo m - **3.** [consent] aceitação f - **4.** GRAMM concordância f.

agricultural [ˌægrɪ'kʌltʃərəl] adj agrícola.

agriculture [ˈægrɪkʌltʃəˡ] n [farming] agricultura f.

aground [ə'graʊnd] adv: **to run ~** encalhar.

ahead [ə'hed] adv - **1.** [in front] à frente; **right** OR **straight ~** direto em frente - **2.** [forwards] em frente - **3.** [in competition, game] à frente - **4.** [indicating success]: **to get ~** ir adiante, prosperar - **5.** [in time] à frente.
 ◆ **ahead of** prep - **1.** [gen] à frente de - **2.** [in time] antes de; **~ of schedule** adiantado(da).

aid [eɪd] ◇ n - **1.** [help] socorro m, assistência f; **in ~ of sb/sthg** em benefício de alguém/algo; **with the ~ of sb/sthg** com a ajuda de alguém/algo - **2.** [device - for teaching, learning] ferramenta f; [- for walking, hearing etc.] aparelho m. ◇ vt - **1.** [help] socorrer - **2.** JUR : **to ~ and abet** ser cúmplice de.

AIDS, Aids (abbr of acquired immune deficiency syndrome) ◇ n AIDS f. ◇ comp: **~ patient** aidético m, -ca f.

aid worker n pessoa que presta assistência em áreas atingidas por catástrofes ou guerras.

ailing [ˈeɪlɪŋ] adj - **1.** [ill] doente - **2.** fig [economy] debilitado(da).

ailment [ˈeɪlmənt] n [illness] doença f.

aim [eɪm] ◇ n - **1.** [objective] objetivo m - **2.** [in firing gun, arrow] mira f; **to take ~ at sthg** apontar para algo. ◇ vt - **1.** [gun, camera]: **to ~ sthg at sb/sthg** mirar algo em alguém/algo - **2.** [plan, programme]: **to be ~ed at doing sthg** ser OR estar voltado(da) para algo - **3.** [remark, criticism]: **to be ~ed at sb** ser

OR estar direcionado(da) para alguém. ◇ vi - **1.** [point weapon] mirar; **to ~ at sthg** mirar em algo - **2.** [intend]: **to ~ at** OR **for sthg** visar a algo; **to ~ to do sthg** pretender fazer algo.

aimless [ˈeɪmlɪs] adj [person, life, work] sem objetivo.

ain't [eɪnt] inf = am not, are not, is not, have not, has not.

air [eəˡ] ◇ n - **1.** [for breathing] ar m - **2.** [sky]: **to be seen from the ~** ser visto(ta) do alto OR de cima; **to throw sthg into the ~** mandar algo pelos ares; **by ~** [travel] de avião; **to be (up) in the ~** fig ser avoado(da) - **3.** [distinctive quality] ar m - **4.** RADIO & TV : **to be on the ~** estar no ar. ◇ comp aéreo(rea). ◇ vt - **1.** [washing, room, bed] arejar - **2.** [feelings, opinions] manifestar - **3.** [broadcast] anunciar. ◇ vi [washing] arejar.

airbag [ˈeəbæg] n AUT airbag m.

airbase [ˈeəbeɪs] n base f aérea.

airbed [ˈeəbed] n UK [inflatable mattress] colchão m inflável.

airborne [ˈeəbɔːn] adj - **1.** [troops, regiment] transportado(da) por via aérea - **2.** [plane] em vôo.

air-conditioned [-kən'dɪʃnd] adj climatizado(da).

air-conditioning [-kən'dɪʃnɪŋ] n ar-condicionado m.

aircraft [ˈeəkrɑːft] (pl inv) n aeronave f, avião m.

aircraft carrier n porta-aviões m inv.

airfield [ˈeəfiːld] n aeródromo m.

air force n força f aérea.

air freshener [-ˈfreʃnəˡ] n purificador m de ar.

airgun [ˈeəgʌn] n pistola f de ar comprimido.

air hostess n UK aeromoça f.

airlift [ˈeəlɪft] ◇ n transporte m aéreo. ◇ vt transportar por via aérea.

airline [ˈeəlaɪn] n companhia f aérea.

airliner [ˈeəlaɪnəˡ] n avião m de passageiros.

airlock [ˈeəlɒk] n - **1.** [in tube, pipe] retentor m de ar - **2.** [airtight chamber] câmara f de compressão.

airmail [ˈeəmeɪl] n correio m aéreo; **by ~** por via aérea.

airplane [ˈeəpleɪn] n US = aeroplane.

airport [ˈeəpɔːt] n aeroporto m.

airport tax n taxas fpl de embarque.

air raid n ataque m aéreo.

air rifle n espingarda f de ar comprimido.

airsick [ˈeəsɪk] adj: **to be ~** estar enjoado(da).

airspace [ˈeəspeɪs] n espaço m aéreo.

air steward n comissário m de bordo.

airstrip ['eəstrɪp] n campo m de pouso.

air terminal n terminal m aéreo.

airtight ['eətaɪt] adj hermético(ca).

air-traffic controller n controlador m de tráfego aéreo.

airy ['eərɪ] (compar -ier, superl -iest) adj -1. [room] arejado(da) -2. [notions, promises] leviano(na) -3. [nonchalant] indiferente.

aisle [aɪl] n -1. [in church] nave f lateral -2. [in plane, theatre, shop] corredor m.

ajar [ə'dʒɑː'] adj [door] entreaberto(ta).

aka (abbr of also known as) também conhecido(da) como.

akin [ə'kɪn] adj semelhante.

alacrity [ə'lækrətɪ] n fml [eagerness] prontidão f.

alarm [ə'lɑːm] <> n -1. [fear] susto m -2. [device] alarme m; **to raise** OR **sound the** ~ dar OR soar o alarme. <> vt [scare] alarmar.

alarm clock n despertador m.

alarming [ə'lɑːmɪŋ] adj alarmante.

alas [ə'læs] excl literary ai!

Albania [æl'beɪnjə] n Albânia.

Albanian [æl'beɪnjən] <> adj albanês(-nesa). <> n -1. [person] albanês m, -sa f -2. [language] albanês m.

albeit [ɔːl'biːɪt] conj fml embora.

alderman ['ɔːldəmən] (pl -men [-mən]) n vereador m.

ale [eɪl] n cerveja f.

alert [ə'lɜːt] <> adj -1. [vigilant, aware] alerta; **to be** ~ **to sthg** estar alerta para algo -2. [perceptive] atento(ta). <> n [warning] alerta f; **on the** ~ [watchful] em estado de alerta; **on** ~ MIL em estado de alerta. <> vt -1. [warn] alertar, avisar -2. [make aware]: **to** ~ **sb to sthg** alertar alguém sobre algo.

A level (abbr of Advanced level) n SCH exame feito ao final do ensino médio na Grã-Bretanha

alfresco [æl'freskəʊ] adj, adv [meal, eat] ao ar livre.

algae ['ældʒiː] npl algas fpl.

algebra ['ældʒɪbrə] n álgebra f.

Algeria [æl'dʒɪərɪə] n Argélia; **in** ~ na Argélia.

alias ['eɪlɪəs] (pl -es) <> adv vulgo. <> n nome m falso.

alibi ['ælɪbaɪ] n álibi m.

alien ['eɪljən] <> adj -1. [foreign] estrangeiro(ra) -2. [from outer space] alienígena -3. [unfamiliar] estranho(nha). <> n -1. [from outer space] alienígena mf -2. JUR [foreigner] estrangeiro m, -ra f.

alienate ['eɪljəneɪt] vt [estrange] alienar.

alight [ə'laɪt] (pt & pp -ed OR alit) <>

adj [on fire] em chamas. <> vi fml -1. [land] pousar -2. [from train, bus] descer; **to** ~ **from sthg** descer de algo.

align [ə'laɪn] vt [line up] alinhar.

alike [ə'laɪk] <> adj [two people, things] semelhante, parecido(da). <> adv [in a similar way] de forma semelhante; **they look** ~ eles são parecidos.

alimony ['ælɪmənɪ] n pensão f (alimentícia).

alive [ə'laɪv] adj [living] vivo(va); **to come** ~ ganhar vida.

alkali ['ælkəlaɪ] (pl -s OR -es) n álcali m.

all [ɔːl] <> adj -1. [with singular noun] todo(da) -, ~ **the money** o dinheiro todo; ~ **the time** sempre; **we were out** ~ **day** estivemos fora o dia inteiro -2. [with plural noun] todos(das); ~ **the houses** todas as casas; ~ **trains stop at Trenton** todos os trens param em Trenton. <> adv -1. [completely] completamente; **alone** completamente só -2. [in scores]: **it's two** ~ dois a dois (empate) -3. [in phrases]: ~ **but empty** quase vazio(zia); ~ **over** [finished] terminado(da). <> pron -1. [everything] tudo; [people, things] todos mpl, -das fpl; **is that** ~? [in store] mais alguma coisa?; **the best of** ~ o melhor de todos -2. [everybody] todos, todo o mundo; ~ **of us went** fomos todos -3. [in phrases]: **can I help you at** ~? posso ajudar em alguma coisa?; **in** ~ [in total] ao todo; **in** ~ **it was a great success** resumindo, foi um grande êxito.

Allah ['ælə] n Alá m.

all-around adj US = all-round.

allay [ə'leɪ] vt fml -1. [calm] abrandar -2. [solve, settle] dirimir.

all clear n -1. [signal] sinal de fim de estado de alerta -2. fig [go-ahead] permissão f para prosseguir.

allegation [,ælɪ'geɪʃn] n alegação f.

allege [ə'ledʒ] vt [claim] alegar; **to** ~ **that** alegar que.

allegedly [ə'ledʒɪdlɪ] adv supostamente.

allergic [ə'lɜːdʒɪk] adj alérgico(ca); ~ **to sthg** lit & fig alérgico(ca) a algo.

allergy ['ælədʒɪ] (pl -ies) n alergia f; **to have an** ~ **to sthg** ter alergia a algo.

alleviate [ə'liːvɪeɪt] vt [ease] aliviar.

alley(way) ['ælɪ(weɪ)] n [narrow path] beco m.

alliance [ə'laɪəns] n -1. [agreement] acordo m -2. [union] aliança f.

allied ['ælaɪd] adj -1. [powers, troops] aliado(da) -2. [related] relacionado(da).

alligator ['ælɪgeɪtə'] (pl inv OR -s) n aligátor m.

all-important adj [crucial] crucial.

all-in *adj UK* [price] tudo incluído.
➡ **all in** ◇ *adj inf* [tired] exausto(ta).
◇ *adv UK* [inclusive] com extras incluí-do.

all-night *adj* [party, vigil, session] que dura toda a noite; [chemist's, shop] 24 horas.

allocate ['æləkeɪt] *vt*: **to ~ sthg to sb/sthg** [money, resources, items] alocar algo para alguém/algo; [task] atribuir algo para alguém/algo.

allot [ə'lɒt] (*pt & pp* **-ted**, *cont* **-ting**) *vt* [allocate - task] distribuir; [- money, resources] repartir; [- time] dedicar.

allotment [ə'lɒtmənt] *n* **-1.** *UK* [garden] lote *m* **-2.** [sharing out - of tasks, resources] distribuição *f*; [- of money] partilha *f*; [- of time] dedicação *f* **-3.** [share - of money, resources] cota *f*; [- of time] alocação *f*.

all-out *adj* [effort] supremo(ma); [war] total; [attack] resoluto(ta).

allow [ə'laʊ] *vt* **-1.** [permit] permitir; **to ~ sb to do sthg** permitir *or* deixar alguém fazer algo **-2.** [allocate] destinar **-3.** [admit]: **to ~ (that)** admitir que.
➡ **allow for** *vt fus* levar em conta *or* consideração.

allowance [ə'laʊəns] *n* **-1.** [grant] subsí-dio *m*, auxílio *m* **-2.** *US* [pocket money] mesada *f* **-3.** [excuse]: **to make ~ s for sb/sthg** fazer concessões para alguém *or* algo.

alloy ['ælɔɪ] *n* [metal] liga *f*.

all right ◇ *adv* **-1.** [gen] bem **-2.** [indi-cating agreement] sim, o.k. **-3.** [do you un-derstand?]: **all right?** certo? **- 4.** [now then] certo, o.k. ◇ *adj* **-1.** [healthy, un-harmed]: **to be ~** estar bem **-2.** *inf* [ac-ceptable, satisfactory]: **how was the film? ~, I suppose** como foi o filme? - legal, imagino; **sorry I'm late - that's ~** descul-pe, estou atrasada - não tem impor-tância **-3.** [permitted]: **is it ~ if ...?** tudo bem se ...?, posso ...?

all-round *UK*, **all-around** *US adj* [ath-lete, worker] versátil.

all-terrain vehicle *n* (veículo) *m* fora-de-estrada *m*.

all-time *adj* [record, best]: **it was an ~ re-cord** foi um recorde insuperável; **one of the ~ greatest songs** uma das me-lhores canções de todos os tempos.

allude [ə'lu:d] *vi*: **to ~ to sthg** aludir a algo.

alluring [ə'ljʊərɪŋ] *adj* [attractive] fasci-nante, encantador(ra).

allusion [ə'lu:ʒn] *n* [reference] alusão *f*.

ally [*n* 'ælaɪ, *vb* ə'laɪ] (*pl* **-ies**, *pt & pp* **-ied**) ◇ *n* **-1.** MIL & POL aliado *m*, -da *f* **-2.** [associate, helper] associado *m*, -da *f*.
◇ *vt*: **to ~ o.s. with sb** aliar-se a alguém.

almighty [ɔ:l'maɪtɪ] *adj inf* [enormous] enorme.

almond ['ɑ:mənd] *n* [nut] amêndoa *f*.

almost ['ɔ:lməʊst] *adv* quase, pratica-mente.

alms [ɑ:mz] *npl dated* esmola *f*.

aloft [ə'lɒft] *adv* [in the air] no ar, nas alturas.

alone [ə'ləʊn] ◇ *adj* [without others] só, sozinho(nha). ◇ *adv* **-1.** [without others] só **-2.** [only] somente, só; **he ~ knows the answer** só *or* somente ele sabe a resposta **-3.** [untouched, un-changed]: **to leave sthg ~** deixar algo em paz, parar de mexer em algo; **leave me ~!** deixe-me em paz!
➡ **let alone** *conj* sem falar em.

along [ə'lɒŋ] ◇ *adv*: **they went ~ to the demonstration** eles foram *or* se dirigiram para a demonstração; **she insisted on coming ~** ela insistiu em vir junto *or* também; **I took her ~ to the concert** levei-a comigo ao concerto. ◇ *prep* **-1.** [from one end to the other] ao longo de **-2.** [beside] ao lado de, junto de **-3.** [in] em.
➡ **all along** *adv* o tempo todo.
➡ **along with** *prep* junto com.

alongside [ə,lɒŋ'saɪd] ◇ *prep* [next to] junto a; [beside] ao lado de. ◇ *adv* lado a lado.

aloof [ə'lu:f] ◇ *adj* [reserved] reserva-do(da). ◇ *adv* [distant]: **to remain ~ (from sthg)** ficar indiferente (a algo).

aloud [ə'laʊd] *adv* alto, em voz alta.

alphabet ['ælfəbet] *n* alfabeto *m*.

alphabetical [,ælfə'betɪkl] *adj* alfabéti-co(ca).

Alps [ælps] *npl*: **the ~** os Alpes.

already [ɔ:l'redɪ] *adv* já.

alright [,ɔ:l'raɪt] *adv & adj* = **all right**.

also ['ɔ:lsəʊ] *adv* [as well] também.

altar ['ɔ:ltə'] *n* altar *m*.

alter ['ɔ:ltə'] ◇ *vt* [change, modify] alterar. ◇ *vi* alterar-se.

alteration [,ɔ:ltə'reɪʃn] *n* **-1.** [act of chan-ging] alteração *f*, modificação *f* **-2.** [change] alteração *f*, mudança *f*.

alternate [*adj UK* ɔ:l'tɜ:nət, *US* 'ɒ:ltərnət, *vb* 'ɔ:ltərneɪt] ◇ *adj* alterna-do(da). ◇ *vt* alternar. ◇ *vi*: **to ~ (with)** alternar (com); **to ~ between sthg and sthg** alternar entre uma coisa e outra.

alternately [ɔ:l'tɜ:nətlɪ] *adv* [by turns] alternadamente.

alternating current ['ɔ:ltəneɪtɪŋ-] *n* ELEC corrente *f* alternada.

alternative [ɔːlˈtɜːnətɪv] <> *adj* alternativo(va). <> *n* alternativa *f*; **an ~ to sb/sthg** uma alternativa a alguém/algo; **to have no ~ (but to do sthg)** não ter alternativa (a não ser fazer algo).

alternatively [ɔːlˈtɜːnətɪvlɪ] *adv* por outro lado, de outro modo.

alternative medicine *n* medicina *f* alternativa.

alternator [ˈɔːltəneɪtəʳ] *n* ELEC alternador *m*.

although [ɔːlˈðəʊ] *conj* embora, apesar de.

altitude [ˈæltɪtjuːd] *n* altitude *f*.

altogether [ˌɔːltəˈɡeðəʳ] *adv* **-1.** [completely] completamente, totalmente **-2.** [in general] de modo geral, no geral **-3.** [in total] ao todo, no total.

aluminium UK [ˌæljʊˈmɪnɪəm], **aluminum** US [əˈluːmɪnəm] <> *n* alumínio *m*. <> *comp* de alumínio.

alumnus [əˈlʌmnəs] (*pl* **-ni** [-naɪ]) *n* ex-aluno *m*, -na *f*.

always [ˈɔːlweɪz] *adv* sempre.

am [æm] *vb* ⊳ be.

a.m. (ante meridiem): **at three ~** às três da manhã.

AM (*abbr of* amplitude modulation) *n* **-1.** AM *f*. **-2.** (*abbr of* Master of Arts) *(titular de) diploma de mestre em ciências humanas nos Estados Unidos*.

amalgamate [əˈmælɡəmeɪt] <> *vt* [unite] amalgamar, misturar. <> *vi* [unite] unir-se.

amass [əˈmæs] *vt* [fortune, power, information] acumular.

amateur [ˈæmətəʳ] <> *adj* amador(ra). <> *n* amador *m*, -ra *f*.

amateurish [ˌæməˈtɜːrɪʃ] *adj pej* [unprofessional] malfeito(ta), mal-acabado(da).

amaze [əˈmeɪz] *vt* [astonish] surpreender, assombrar.

amazed [əˈmeɪzd] *adj* surpreso(sa), assombrado(da).

amazement [əˈmeɪzmənt] *n* surpresa *f*, assombro *m*.

amazing [əˈmeɪzɪŋ] *adj* [incredible] incrível, surpreendente.

Amazon [ˈæməzən] *n* **-1.** [river]: **the ~** o Amazonas **-2.** [region]: **the ~ (Basin)** a bacia amazônica; **the ~ rainforest** a floresta amazônica **-3.** [woman] amazona *f*.

ambassador [æmˈbæsədəʳ] *n* embaixador *m*, -ra *f*.

amber [ˈæmbəʳ] *n* **-1.** [substance] âmbar *m* **-2.** UK [colour of traffic light] amarelo *m*.

ambiguous [æmˈbɪɡjʊəs] *adj* ambíguo(gua).

ambition [æmˈbɪʃn] *n* ambição *f*.

ambitious [æmˈbɪʃəs] *adj* ambicioso(sa).

amble [ˈæmbl] *vi* [walk] passear.

ambulance [ˈæmbjʊləns] *n* ambulância *f*.

ambush [ˈæmbʊʃ] <> *n* emboscada *f*. <> *vt* [attack] emboscar.

amenable [əˈmiːnəbl] *adj*: **~ (to sthg)** receptivo(va) (a algo).

amend [əˈmend] *vt* [change] emendar, corrigir.

◆ amends *npl*: **to make ~s (for sthg)** compensar (por algo).

amendment [əˈmendmənt] *n* **-1.** [change] correção *f* **-2.** [act of changing] emenda *f*.

amenities [əˈmiːnətɪz] *npl* comodidades *fpl*, conforto *m*.

America [əˈmerɪkə] *n* América, Estados Unidos (da América); **in ~** na América, nos Estados Unidos (da América).

American [əˈmerɪkn] <> *adj* americano(na), estadunidense. <> *n* americano *m*, -na *f*, estadunidense *mf*.

American football *n* UK futebol *m* americano.

American Indian *n* ameríndio *m*.

amiable [ˈeɪmjəbl] *adj* [pleasant, likable] amável.

amicable [ˈæmɪkəbl] *adj* [friendly] amigável.

amid(st) [əˈmɪd(st)] *prep fml* [among] entre, no meio de.

amiss [əˈmɪs] <> *adj* [wrong] errado(da). <> *adv* [wrongly]: **to take sthg ~** levar algo a mal.

ammonia [əˈməʊnjə] *n* [liquid] amônia *f*; [gas] amoníaco *m*.

ammunition [ˌæmjʊˈnɪʃn] *n* **-1.** [bombs, bullets] munição *f* **-2.** *fig* [information, argument] argumento *m*.

amnesia [æmˈniːzjə] *n* amnésia *f*.

amnesty [ˈæmnəstɪ] (*pl* **-ies**) *n* anistia *f*.

amok [əˈmɒk] *adv*: **to run ~** *correr cega e furiosamente com o intuito de matar*.

among(st) [əˈmʌŋ(st)] *prep* **-1.** [surrounded by, in middle of] no meio de, entre **-2.** [within, between, included in] entre.

amoral [ˌeɪˈmɒrəl] *adj* [person, behaviour] amoral.

amorous [ˈæmərəs] *adj* amoroso(sa).

amount [əˈmaʊnt] *n* **-1.** [quantity] quantidade *f*, volume *m* **-2.** [sum of money] quantia *f*.

◆ amount to *vt fus* **-1.** [total] totalizar, atingir a quantia de **-2.** [be equivalent to] equivaler.

amp *n* (*abbr of* ampere) A.

ampere [ˈæmpeə^r] n ampère m.

amphibious [æmˈfɪbɪəs] adj [animal, vehicle] anfíbio(bia).

ample [ˈæmpl] adj **-1.** [enough] suficiente **-2.** [large] amplo(pla).

amplifier [ˈæmplɪfaɪə^r] n [for radio, stereo] amplificador m.

amputate [ˈæmpjʊteɪt] <> vt [limb] amputar. <> vi [perform amputation] amputar.

Amsterdam [ˌæmstəˈdæm] n Amsterdã; **in** ~ em Amsterdã.

Amtrak [ˈæmtræk] n empresa pública de trens mais importante dos Estados Unidos no transporte de passageiros.

amuck [əˈmʌk] adv = amok.

amuse [əˈmjuːz] vt **-1.** [cause to laugh, smile] divertir **-2.** [entertain] entreter; **to** ~ **o.s. (by doing sthg)** entreter-se (fazendo algo).

amused [əˈmjuːzd] adj **-1.** [entertained, delighted] divertido(da), entretido(da); **to be** ~ **at OR by sthg** estar entretido(da) com algo **-2.** [entertained]: **to keep o.s.** ~ entreter-se.

amusement [əˈmjuːzmənt] n **-1.** [enjoyment] divertimento m **-2.** [diversion, game] diversão f, entretenimento m.

amusement arcade n fliperama m.

amusement park n parque m de diversões.

amusing [əˈmjuːzɪŋ] adj [funny] divertido(da).

an [stressed æn, unstressed ən] indef art ▷ a².

anabolic steroid [ˌænəˈbɒlɪk-] n esteróide m anabólico OR anabolizante.

anaemic UK, **anemic** US [əˈniːmɪk] adj [suffering from anaemia] anêmico(ca).

anaesthetic UK, **anesthetic** US [ˌænɪsˈθetɪk] n anestésico m; **under** ~ anestesiado(da).

analogue, analog US [ˈænəlɒg] adj [watch, clock] analógico(ca).

analogy [əˈnælədʒɪ] (pl -ies) n [similarity] analogia f; **by** ~ por analogia.

analyse UK, **analyze** US [ˈænəlaɪz] vt [examine] analisar.

analysis [əˈnæləsɪs] (pl analyses [əˈnæləsiːz]) n análise f.

analyst [ˈænəlɪst] n **-1.** [political, computer, statistics] analista mf **-2.** [psychoanalyst] psicanalista mf.

analytic(al) [ˌænəˈlɪtɪk(l)] adj [person, study, approach] analítico(ca).

analyze vt US = analyse.

anarchist [ˈænəkɪst] n POL anarquista mf.

anarchy [ˈænəkɪ] n [lawlessness, disorder] anarquia f.

anathema [əˈnæθəmə] n [object of dislike, disapproval] anátema m.

anatomy [əˈnætəmɪ] (pl -ies) n anatomia f.

ANC (abbr of African National Congress) n Congresso m Nacional Africano.

ancestor [ˈænsestə^r] n [person] ancestral mf, antepassado m, -da f.

anchor [ˈæŋkə^r] <> n **-1.** NAUT âncora f; **to drop/weigh** ~ lançar/içar âncora **-2.** TV [presenter] âncora mf. <> vt **-1.** [secure] assegurar **-2.** TV [present] apresentar. <> vi NAUT ancorar.

anchovy [ˈæntʃəvɪ] (pl inv OR -ies) n anchova f.

ancient [ˈeɪnʃənt] adj **-1.** [dating from distant past] antigo(ga) **-2.** hum [very old] pré-histórico(ca).

ancillary [ænˈsɪlərɪ] adj [staff, workers, device] auxiliar.

and [strong form ænd, weak form ənd, ən] conj **-1.** [as well as, in addition to] e **-2.** [in numbers] e **-3.** (with infinitive) [in order to]: **come** ~ **see!** venha ver!; **try** ~ **come!** tente vir!; **to wait** ~ **see** esperar para ver.

➡ **and all that** adv e (todas) essas coisas.

➡ **and so on, and so forth** adv e assim por diante.

Andes [ˈændiːz] npl: **the** ~ os Andes; **in** ~ nos Andes.

Andorra [ænˈdɔːrə] n Andorra f.

anecdote [ˈænɪkdəʊt] n anedota f.

anemic adj US = anaemic.

anesthetic etc. n US = anaesthetic etc.

anew [əˈnjuː] adv novamente.

angel [ˈeɪndʒəl] n **-1.** RELIG anjo m **-2.** fig inf [delightful person] anjo m.

anger [ˈæŋgə^r] <> n raiva f. <> vt irritar, zangar.

angina [ænˈdʒaɪnə] n angina f.

angle [ˈæŋgl] n **-1.** MATH ângulo m **-2.** [corner] canto m, ângulo m **-3.** [point of view] ângulo m **-4.** [slope] ladeira f; **at an** ~ [aslant] em ângulo.

Anglepoise (lamp)® [ˈæŋglpɔɪz-] n luminária f de mesa (flexível).

angler [ˈæŋglə^r] n pescador m, -ra f (de linha e anzol).

Anglican [ˈæŋglɪkən] <> adj anglicano(na). <> n anglicano m, -na f.

angling [ˈæŋglɪŋ] n [fishing] pesca f (com linha e anzol).

angry [ˈæŋgrɪ] (compar -ier, superl -iest) adj zangado(da), furioso(sa); **to be** ~ **(with sb)** estar zangado(da) (com alguém); **to get** ~ **(with sb)** zangar-se (com alguém).

anguish ['æŋgwɪʃ] n angústia f.

angular ['æŋgjʊlə'] adj [face, jaw, body] angular.

animal ['ænɪml] <> adj animal. <> n -1. [living creature] animal m -2. inf pej [brutal person] animal m.

animate ['ænɪmət] adj animado(da).

animated ['ænɪmeɪtɪd] adj animado(da).

aniseed ['ænɪsiːd] n semente f de anis.

ankle ['æŋkl] <> n tornozelo m. <> comp: ~ deep até o tornozelo.

annex ['æneks] vt anexar.

annexe ['æneks] n [building] anexo m.

annihilate [ə'naɪəleɪt] vt [destroy] aniquilar.

anniversary [,ænɪ'vɜːsərɪ] (pl -ies) n aniversário m (de casamento, de independência etc.).

announce [ə'naʊns] vt anunciar.

announcement [ə'naʊnsmənt] n [public statement] anúncio m.

announcer [ə'naʊnsə'] n: television/ radio ~ locutor de televisão/rádio.

annoy [ə'nɔɪ] vt [irritate] irritar, amolar.

annoyance [ə'nɔɪəns] n irritação f, aborrecimento m.

annoyed [ə'nɔɪd] adj irritado(da); to be ~ at sthg estar irritado(da) com algo; to be ~ with sb estar irritado(da) com alguém; to get ~ irritar-se.

annoying [ə'nɔɪɪŋ] adj irritante.

annual ['ænjʊəl] <> adj anual. <> n -1. [plant] planta f sazonal -2. [book] anuário m, publicação f anual.

annual general meeting n reunião f geral anual.

annul [ə'nʌl] (pt & pp -led, cont -ling) vt anular, invalidar.

annulment [ə'nʌlmənt] n anulação f.

annum ['ænəm] n: per ~ por ano.

anomaly [ə'nɒməlɪ] (pl -ies) n [different thing, person] anomalia f.

anonymous [ə'nɒnɪməs] adj anônimo(-ma).

anorak ['ænəræk] n esp UK anoraque m.

anorexia (nervosa) [,ænə'reksɪə(nɜː'vəʊsə)] n anorexia f nervosa.

anorexic [,ænə'reksɪk] <> adj anoréxico(ca). <> n anoréxico m, -ca f.

another [ə'nʌðə'] <> adj -1. [additional] outro(tra); in ~ few minutes ... dentro de alguns minutos ... -2. [different] outro(tra). <> pron -1. [an additional one] outro m, -tra f; one after ~ um(a) depois do(da) outro(tra) -2. [a different one] outro m, -tra f; to argue with one ~ discutir um com o outro/uma com a outra; to love one ~ amar-se.

answer ['ɑːnsə'] <> n [reply] resposta f; in ~ to sthg em resposta a algo. <> vt -1. responder -2. [respond to]: to ~ the door/phone atender a porta/o telefone. <> vi [reply] responder.

➡ **answer back** <> vt sep retrucar. <> vi retrucar.

➡ **answer for** vt fus responder por.

answerable ['ɑːnsərəbl] adj [accountable] responsável; ~ to sb adequado(da) a alguém; ~ for sthg responsável por algo.

answering machine, answerphone ['ɑːnsərɪŋ-] n secretária f eletrônica.

ant [ænt] n formiga f.

antagonism [æn'tægənɪzm] n antagonismo m.

antagonize, -ise [æn'tægənaɪz] vt hostilizar.

Antarctic [æn'tɑːktɪk] n: the ~ o Antártico.

antelope ['æntɪləʊp] (pl inv OR -s) n antílope m.

antenatal [,æntɪ'neɪtl] adj pré-natal.

antenatal clinic n clínica f pré-natal.

antenna [æn'tenə] (pl sense 1 -nae [-niː], pl sense 2 -s) n -1. [of insect, lobster] antena f-2. US [aerial] antena f.

anthem ['ænθəm] n [song, hymn] hino m.

anthology [æn'θɒlədʒɪ] (pl -ies) n antologia f.

antibiotic [,æntɪbaɪ'ɒtɪk] n [medicine] antibiótico m.

antibody ['æntɪ,bɒdɪ] (pl -ies) n BIOL anticorpo m.

anticipate [æn'tɪsɪpeɪt] vt -1. [expect, experience prematurely] prever -2. [preempt] antecipar-se a.

anticipation [æn,tɪsɪ'peɪʃn] n -1. [advance action] antecipação f -2. [expectation] expectativa f; in ~ of na expectativa de -3. [foresight] pressentimento m.

anticlimax [,æntɪ'klaɪmæks] n [disappointment] anticlímax m.

anticlockwise UK [,æntɪ'klɒkwaɪz] <> adj [direction] em sentido anti-horário. <> adv em sentido anti-horário.

antics ['æntɪks] npl -1. [of children, animals] palhaçadas fpl -2. pej [of politician etc.] trapaças fpl.

anticyclone [,æntɪ'saɪkləʊn] n METEOR anticiclone m.

antidepressant [,æntɪdɪ'presnt] <> adj antidepressivo(va). <> n [drug] antidepressivo m.

antidote ['æntɪdəʊt] n -1. [drug, medicine] antídoto m; ~ to sthg antídoto contra algo -2. fig [relief] antídoto.

antifreeze ['æntɪfriːz] n anticongelante m.

antihistamine [,æntɪ'hɪstəmɪn] <> adj

anti-histamínico(ca). <> n anti-histamínico m.

antiperspirant [ˌæntɪˈpɜːspərənt] n desodorante m.

antiquated [ˈæntɪkweɪtd] adj antiqua-
do(da).

antique [ænˈtiːk] <> adj [furniture, ob-
ject] antigo(ga). <> n [piece of furniture,
object] antiguidade f.

antique shop n loja f de antiguidades.

anti-Semitism [ˌæntɪˈsemɪtɪzm] n anti-
semitismo m.

antiseptic [ˌæntɪˈseptɪk] <> adj anti-
séptico(ca). <> n anti-séptico m.

antisocial [ˌæntɪˈsəʊʃl] adj anti-social.

antivirus software [ˌæntɪˈvaɪrəs-] n
COMPUT antivírus m inv.

antlers [ˈæntləz] npl cornos mpl.

anus [ˈeɪnəs] n ânus m.

anvil [ˈænvɪl] n bigorna f.

anxiety [æŋˈzaɪətɪ] (pl -ies) n -1. [worry]
ansiedade f-2. [cause of worry] angústia
f-3. [keenness] anseio m.

anxious [ˈæŋkʃəs] adj -1. [worried] preo-
cupado(da); to be ~ about sb/sthg estar
preocupado(da) com alguém/algo -2.
[keen]: to be ~ to do sthg estar ansio-
so(sa) por fazer algo; to be ~ that estar
ansioso(sa) para que.

any [ˈenɪ] <> adj -1. (with negative)
nenhum(ma); I haven't got ~ money
não tenho dinheiro nenhum; he never
does ~ work ele nunca faz trabalho
algum -2. [some] (with sg n) algum(ma);
(with pl n) alguns(mas); can I be of ~
help? posso ajudar (em algo)?; have you
got ~ money? você tem algum dinheiro? -3. [no matter which] qualquer; ~
box will do qualquer caixa serve. <>
pron -1. (with negative) nenhum(ma); I
didn't buy ~ of them não comprei
nenhum deles -2. [some] algum(ma);
do you have ~? você tem (algum)? -3.
[no matter which one or ones] qualquer um
(uma); take ~ you like pegue qualquer
um que você queira. <> adv -1. (with
negative): I don't want it ~ more não
quero mais isto; I can't stand it ~ longer
não agüento mais isto -2. [some, a little]
um pouco; is that ~ better/different?
está um pouco melhor/diferente?

anybody [ˈenɪˌbɒdɪ] pron = anyone.

anyhow [ˈenɪhaʊ] adv -1. [in spite of that]
assim mesmo -2. [carelessly] de qualquer jeito -3. [returning to topic in conver-
sation] seja como for.

anyone [ˈenɪwʌn] pron -1. (in negative
statements) ninguém -2. (in questions)
alguém -3. [someone] alguém -4. [any
person] qualquer pessoa.

anyplace adv US = anywhere.

anything [ˈenɪθɪŋ] pron -1. (in negative
statements) nada -2. (in questions) algo
-3. [something] algo, qualquer coisa -4.
[any object, event] qualquer coisa.

anyway [ˈenɪweɪ] adv [in any case] de
qualquer forma.

anywhere [ˈenɪweə˞], **anyplace** US
[ˈenɪpleɪs] adv -1. (in negative statements)
nenhum lugar -2. (in questions) em/a
algum lugar -3. [any place] (em) qualquer lugar.

apart [əˈpɑːt] adv -1. [separated in space] à
parte, separadamente, distante; we're
living ~ estamos vivendo separados;
the houses were only a few yards ~ from
each other as casas ficavam a apenas
algumas jardas de distância uma da
outra; I had to keep them ~ eu tinha
que mantê-los à distância -2. [to pieces]
em pedaços -3. [aside, excepted] à parte.
➤ **apart from** <> prep [except for]
exceto, a não ser (por). <> conj [in addition to] além de.

apartheid [əˈpɑːtheɪt] n apartheid m.

apartment [əˈpɑːtmənt] n apartamento
m.

apartment building n prédio m de
apartamentos.

apathy [ˈæpəθɪ] n apatia f.

ape [eɪp] <> n [animal] macaco m, -ca f.
<> vt pej [imitate] imitar.

aperitif [əperəˈtiːf] n aperitivo m.

aperture [ˈæpəˌtjʊə˞] n abertura f.

apex [ˈeɪpeks] (pl -es OR apices) n [top]
ápice m.

Apex (abbr of advance purchase excursion) n UK passagem comprada com
antecedência e que oferece descontos.

apices [ˈeɪpɪsiːz] pl ➤ apex.

apiece [əˈpiːs] adv [each] cada.

apocalypse [əˈpɒkəlɪps] n apocalipse
m.

apologetic [əˌpɒləˈdʒetɪk] adj arrepen-
dido(da); to be ~ about sthg estar
arrependido(da) em relação a algo,
desculpar-se por algo.

apologize, -ise [əˈpɒlədʒaɪz] vi [say sor-
ry]: to ~ to sb for sthg pedir desculpas
a alguém por algo.

apology [əˈpɒlədʒɪ] (pl -ies) n [spoken,
written] desculpa f.

apostle [əˈpɒsl] n RELIG apóstolo m.

apostrophe [əˈpɒstrəfɪ] n GRAMM após-
trofe f.

appal (UK pt & pp -led, cont -ling), **appall**
US [əˈpɔːl] vt [shock deeply] horrorizar.

appalling [əˈpɔːlɪŋ] adj -1. [shocking]
espantoso(sa) -2. inf [very bad] terrível.

apparatus [,æpə'reɪtəs] (*pl inv OR* **-es**) *n* **- 1.** [equipment] aparelho *m* **- 2.** [system, organization] organização *f.*

apparel [ə'pærəl] *n US* traje *m.*

apparent [ə'pærənt] *adj* aparente.

apparently [ə'pærəntlɪ] *adv* aparentemente.

appeal [ə'pi:l] ◇ *vi* **- 1.** [request] apelar; **to ~ to sb for sthg** apelar a alguém p'or algo **- 2.** [to sb's honour, common sense]: **to ~ to sthg** apelar para algo **- 3.** [contest a decision or verdict] recorrer; **to ~ against sthg** recorrer contra algo **- 4.** [attract, interest]: **to ~ (to sb)** agradar a alguém. ◇ *n* **- 1.** [request] apelo *m* **- 2.** [contesting a decision or verdict] apelação *m* **- 3.** [charm, interest] encanto *m.*

appealing [ə'pi:lɪŋ] *adj* [attractive] encantor(ra).

appear [ə'pɪəʳ] ◇ *vi* **- 1.** [gen] aparecer **- 2.** [act] atuar **- 3.** *JUR* comparecer. ◇ *vt* [seem]: **to ~ to be/do sthg** aparentar ser/fazer algo; **it would ~ that ...** pareceria que.

appearance [ə'pɪərəns] *n* **- 1.** [arrival] chegada *f* **- 2.** [becoming visible - of person] aparecimento *m*; [- of object] chegada *f*; [- of rash etc. on skin] surgimento *m*; **to make an ~** aparecer **- 3.** [outward aspect] aparência *f* **- 4.** [bodily features] aspecto *m* **- 5.** [in play, film, on TV] participação *f.*

appease [ə'pi:z] *vt* **- 1.** [placate] apaziguar **- 2.** [satisfy] saciar.

append [ə'pend] *vt fml* [add]: **to ~ sthg (to sthg)** anexar algo a algo.

appendices [ə'pendɪsi:z] *pl* ⊳ **appendix.**

appendicitis [ə,pendɪ'saɪtɪs] *n* apendicite *f.*

appendix [ə'pendɪks] (*pl* **-dixes** *OR* **-dices**) *n* apêndice *m*; **to have one's ~ out** *OR* **removed** sofrer a remoção do apêndice.

appetite ['æpɪtaɪt] *n* **- 1.** [for food] apetite *m*; **~ for sthg** desejo por algo **- 2.** *fig* [enthusiasm]: **~ for sthg** gosto por algo.

appetizer, -iser ['æpɪtaɪzəʳ] *n* [food] entrada *f*; [drink] aperitivo *m.*

appetizing, -ising ['æpɪtaɪzɪŋ] *adj* [food] apetitoso(sa).

applaud [ə'plɔ:d] ◇ *vt* **- 1.** [clap for] aplaudir **- 2.** *fig* [approve] aplaudir. ◇ *vi* [clap] aplaudir.

applause [ə'plɔ:z] *n* aplauso *m.*

apple ['æpl] *n* maçã *f.*

apple tree *n* macieira *f.*

appliance [ə'plaɪəns] *n* [device] utensílio *m.*

applicable [ə'plɪkəbl] *adj* apropriado(da);

~ to sb/sthg apropriado(da) a alguém/ algo.

applicant ['æplɪkənt] *n* candidato *m*, -ta *f*; **~ for sthg** [job] candidato(ta) a algo; [state benefit] pretendente a algo *m.*

application [,æplɪ'keɪʃn] *n* **- 1.** [gen] aplicação *f* **- 2.** [for job, college, club] inscrição *f*; **~ for sthg** inscrição para algo **- 3.** *COMPUT* aplicativo *m.*

application form *n* ficha *f* de inscrição.

applied [ə'plaɪd] *adj* [science] aplicado(da).

apply [ə'plaɪ] (*pt & pp* **-ied**) ◇ *vt* **- 1.** [rule, skill] aplicar **- 2.** [paint, ointment] aplicar **- 3.** [brakes] usar. ◇ *vi* **- 1.** [for work, grant] candidatar-se; **to ~ for sthg** candidatar-se a algo; **to ~ to sb for sthg** recorrer a alguém para algo **- 2.** [be relevant] aplicar-se; **to ~ to sb/sthg** aplicar-se a alguém/algo.

appoint [ə'pɔɪnt] *vt* **- 1.** [to job, position] nomear; **to ~ sb to/as sthg** nomear alguém para/como algo **- 2.** *fml* [time, place] marcar.

appointment [ə'pɔɪntmənt] *n* **- 1.** (*U*) [to job, position] nomeação *f* **- 2.** [job, position] posição *f* **- 3.** [with doctor, hairdresser, in business] hora *f* marcada; **to have an ~** ter uma hora marcada; **to make an ~** marcar uma hora; **the doctor only sees patients by ~** o médico só atende (pacientes) com hora marcada.

apportion [ə'pɔ:ʃn] *vt* [money, blame] dividir.

appraisal [ə'preɪzl] *n* [report, opinion] apreciação *f.*

appreciable [ə'pri:ʃəbl] *adj* [noticeable] apreciável.

appreciate [ə'pri:ʃɪeɪt] ◇ *vt* **- 1.** [value] valorizar **- 2.** [recognize, understand] reconhecer **- 3.** [be grateful for] reconhecer. ◇ *vi FIN* [increase in value] valorizar.

appreciation [ə,pri:ʃɪ'eɪʃn] *n* **- 1.** (*U*) [liking] apreciação *m* **- 2.** (*U*) [recognition, understanding] reconhecimento *f* **- 3.** (*U*) [gratitude] gratidão *m.*

appreciative [ə'pri:ʃjətɪv] *adj* apreciativo(va).

apprehensive [,æprɪ'hensɪv] *adj* [anxious]: **~ (about sthg)** apreensivo(va) com algo.

apprentice [ə'prentɪs] *n* [trainee] aprendiz *mf*, estagiário(ria).

apprenticeship [ə'prentɪʃɪp] *n* estágio *m.*

approach [ə'prəʊtʃ] ◇ *n* **- 1.** [arrival] chegada *f* **- 2.** [way in, access] acesso *m*

- **3.** [method] abordagem *m* - **4.** [proposal]: **to make an ~ to sb** fazer uma proposta a alguém. ⬦ *vt* - **1.** [come near to] aproximar-se de - **2.** [speak to]: **to ~ sb about sthg** abordar alguém sobre algo; *COMM* sondar alguém sobre algo - **3.** [deal with] abordar - **4.** [approximate, reach] alcançar. ⬦ *vi* aproximar-se.

approachable [ə'prəʊtʃəbl] *adj* acessível.

appropriate [*adj* ə'prəʊprɪət, *vb* ə'prəʊprɪeɪt] ⬦ *adj* [suitable] apropriado(da). ⬦ *vt* - **1.** [steal] apropriar-se de - **2.** [allocate] destinar.

approval [ə'pruːvl] *n* - **1.** [liking, admiration] aprovação *f* - **2.** [official agreement] sanção *f* - **3.** *COMM*: **on ~** sob condição.

approve [ə'pruːv] ⬦ *vi*: **to ~ (of sb/sthg)** ser a favor de alguém/algo. ⬦ *vt* [ratify] aprovar.

approx. (*abbr of* **approximately**) aprox.

approximate [ə'prɒksɪmət] *adj* aproximado(da).

approximately [ə'prɒksɪmətlɪ] *adv* aproximadamente.

apricot ['eɪprɪkɒt] *n* [fruit] damasco *m*.

April ['eɪprəl] *n* abril *m*; *see also* **September**.

apron ['eɪprən] *n* [clothing] avental *m*.

apt [æpt] *adj* - **1.** [pertinent] adequado(da) - **2.** [likely]: **to be ~ to do sthg** costumar fazer algo.

aptitude ['æptɪtjuːd] *n* [skill] aptidão *f*; **to have an ~ for sthg** ter aptidão para algo.

aptly ['æptlɪ] *adv* [suitably] apropriadamente.

aqualung ['ækwəlʌŋ] *n* aqualung *m*.

aquarium [ə'kweərɪəm] (*pl* **-riums** OR **-ria** [-rɪə]) *n* aquário *m*.

Aquarius [ə'kweərɪəs] *n* - **1.** [sign] Aquário *m* - **2.** [person] aquariano *m*, -na *f*.

aquatic [ə'kwætɪk] *adj* aquático(ca).

aqueduct ['ækwɪdʌkt] *n* aqueduto *m*.

Arab ['ærəb] ⬦ *adj* árabe. ⬦ *n* [person, horse] árabe *mf*.

Arabian [ə'reɪbjən] ⬦ *adj* árabe. ⬦ *n* [person] árabe *mf*.

Arabic ['ærəbɪk] ⬦ *adj* arábico(ca). ⬦ *n* [language] arábico *m*.

Arabic numeral *n* algarismo *m* arábico.

arable ['ærəbl] *adj* cultivável.

arbitrary ['ɑːbɪtrərɪ] *adj* [random] arbitrário(ria).

arbitration [,ɑːbɪ'treɪʃn] *n* arbitragem *f*; **to go to ~** ir à arbitragem.

arcade [ɑː'keɪd] *n* arcada *f*.

arch [ɑːtʃ] ⬦ *adj* [knowing] travesso(sa). ⬦ *n* arco *m*. ⬦ *vt* [back, eyebrow] arquear. ⬦ *vi* arquear-se.

archaeologist [,ɑːkɪ'ɒlədʒɪst] *n* arqueólogo *m*, -ga *f*.

archaeology [,ɑːkɪ'ɒlədʒɪ] *n* arqueologia *f*.

archaic [ɑː'keɪɪk] *adj* - **1.** [ancient] arcaico(ca) - **2.** [old-fashioned] antiquado(da).

archbishop [,ɑːtʃ'bɪʃəp] *n* arcebispo *m*.

archenemy [,ɑːtʃ'enɪmɪ] (*pl* **-ies**) *n* arquiinimigo *m*, -ga *f*.

archeology etc. [,ɑːkɪ'ɒlədʒɪ] *n* = **archaeology etc.**

archer ['ɑːtʃəʳ] *n* arqueiro *m*.

archery ['ɑːtʃərɪ] *n* arco-e-flecha *m*.

archetypal [,ɑːkɪ'taɪpl] *adj* [typical] arquetípico(ca).

architect ['ɑːkɪtekt] *n* - **1.** [of buildings] arquiteto *m*, -ta *f* - **2.** *fig* [of plan, event] idealizador *m*, -ra *f*.

architecture ['ɑːkɪtektʃəʳ] *n* arquitetura *f*.

archives ['ɑːkaɪvz] *npl* [of documents] arquivo *m*.

archway ['ɑːtʃweɪ] *n* passagem *f* em arco.

Arctic ['ɑːktɪk] ⬦ *adj* - **1.** *GEOGR* ártico(ca) - **2.** *inf* [very cold] gélido(da). ⬦ *n*: **the ~** o Ártico.

ardent ['ɑːdənt] *adj* [passionate] ardente.

arduous ['ɑːdjʊəs] *adj* [difficult] árduo(a).

are [*stressed* ɑːʳ, *unstressed* əʳ] *vb* ▷ **be**.

area ['eərɪə] *n* - **1.** [gen] área *f* - **2.** *fig* [approximate size, number]: **in the ~ of** ao redor de.

area code *n US* código *m* de área.

arena [ə'riːnə] *n* - **1.** *SPORT* estádio *m* - **2.** *fig* [area of activity] área *f*.

aren't [ɑːnt] = **are not**.

Argentina [,ɑːdʒən'tiːnə] *n* Argentina *f*.

Argentine ['ɑːdʒəntaɪn], **Argentinian** [,ɑːdʒən'tɪnɪən] ⬦ *adj* argentino(na). ⬦ *n* [person] argentino *m*, -na *f*.

arguably ['ɑːgjʊəblɪ] *adv* indubitavelmente.

argue ['ɑːgjuː] ⬦ *vi* - **1.** [quarrel] discutir; **to ~ (with sb about sthg)** discutir (com alguém sobre algo) - **2.** [reason] argumentar; **to ~ for/against sthg** argumentar a favor/contra algo. ⬦ *vt* [case, point] afirmar; **to ~ that** afirmar que.

argument ['ɑːgjəmənt] *n* - **1.** [quarrel] discussão *f*; **to have an ~ (with sb)** ter uma discussão (com alguém) - **2.** [reason] argumento *m* - **3.** [reasoning] argumentação *f*.

argumentative [,ɑːgjʊ'mentətɪv] *adj* questionador(ra).

arid ['ærɪd] *adj* - **1.** [land] árido(da) - **2.** *fig* [subject, writing] árido(da).

Aries ['eəri:z] n -1. [sign] Áries f-2. [person] ariano(na).

arise [ə'raɪz] (pt arose, pp arisen [ə'rɪzn]) vi [appear] surgir; to ~ from sthg surgir de algo; if the need ~s se houver necessidade.

aristocrat [UK 'ærɪstəkræt, US ə'rɪstəkræt] n aristocrata mf.

arithmetic [ə'rɪθmətɪk] <> adj aritmético(ca). <> n aritmética f.

ark [ɑːk] n [ship] arca f.

arm [ɑːm] <> n -1. [of person] braço m; ~ in ~ de braços dados; to keep sb at ~'s length manter alguém à distância; to welcome sb/sthg with open ~s fig receber alguém/algo de braços abertos; to twist sb's ~ fig forçar alguém a fazer algo; to cost an ~ and a leg fig custar os olhos da cara -2. [of garment] manga f -3. [of chair] braço m. <> vt [with weapons] armar.
♦ **arms** npl [weapons] armas fpl; to take up ~s pegar em armas; to be up in ~s (about sthg) estar furioso(sa) em relação a algo.

armaments ['ɑːməmənts] npl [weapons] armamento m.

armband ['ɑːmbænd] n braçadeira f.

armchair ['ɑːmtʃeəʳ] n poltrona f.

armed [ɑːmd] adj -1. [with weapon] armado(da) -2. fig [with information]: ~ with sthg munido(da) de algo.

armed forces npl forças fpl armadas.

armhole ['ɑːmhəʊl] n cava f.

armour UK, **armor** US ['ɑːməʳ] n -1. [for person] armadura f-2. [for military vehicle] blindagem f.

armoured car [ɑːməd-] n MIL carro m blindado.

armoury UK (pl -ies), **armory** US (pl -ies) ['ɑːmərɪ] n arsenal m.

armpit ['ɑːmpɪt] n axila f.

armrest ['ɑːmrest] n braço m.

arms control ['ɑːmz-] n controle m armamentista.

army ['ɑːmɪ] (pl -ies) n -1. MIL exército m -2. fig [large group] exército m.

A road n UK rodovia principal.

aroma [ə'rəʊmə] n [smell] aroma m.

arose [ə'rəʊz] pt ▷ arise.

around [ə'raʊnd] <> adv -1. [about, around] por aí -2. [on all sides] ao redor -3. [in circular movement] ao redor -4. phr: to have been ~ inf ter experiência. <> prep -1. [encircling] ao redor de -2. [through, throughout] por todo(da) -3. [near] perto -4. [approximately] cerca de.

arouse [ə'raʊz] vt -1. [excite - feeling] provocar; [- person] estimular -2. [wake] despertar.

arrange [ə'reɪndʒ] vt -1. [flowers, books, furniture] arrumar -2. [event, meeting, party] organizar; to ~ to do sthg combinar para fazer algo -3. MUS fazer um arranjo.

arrangement [ə'reɪndʒmənt] n -1. [agreement] acordo m; to come to an ~ chegar a um acordo -2. [of objects] arranjo m -3. MUS arranjo m.
♦ **arrangements** npl providências fpl.

array [ə'reɪ] <> n [of objects, people, ornaments] série f. <> vt [ornaments] enfeitar.

arrears [ə'rɪəz] npl [money owed] dívida f; in ~ [retrospectively] retroativamente; [late] em atraso.

arrest [ə'rest] <> n [by police] prisão f; under ~ preso(sa). <> vt -1. [subj: police] prender -2. fml [sb's attention] prender -3. fml [stop] deter.

arrival [ə'raɪvl] n [gen] chegada f; late ~ [of train, bus, mail] chegada atrasada; new ~ [person] recém-chegado(da); [baby] recém-nascido(da).

arrive [ə'raɪv] vi -1. [gen] chegar; to ~ at a conclusion/decision chegar a uma conclusão/decisão -2. [baby] nascer.

arrogant ['ærəgənt] adj arrogante.

arrow ['ærəʊ] n -1. [weapon] flecha f-2. [symbol] seta f.

arse UK [ɑːs], **ass** US [æs] n vulg [bottom] bunda f.

arsenic ['ɑːsnɪk] n arsênico m.

arson ['ɑːsn] n incêndio m premeditado.

art [ɑːt] n (U) arte f. <> comp de artes.
♦ **arts** npl -1. SCH & UNIV [humanities] artes fpl -2. [fine arts]: the ~s as belas-artes.

artefact ['ɑːtɪfækt] n = artifact.

artery ['ɑːtərɪ] (pl -ies) n artéria f.

art gallery n -1. [public] museu m de arte -2. [for selling paintings] galeria f de arte.

arthritis [ɑː'θraɪtɪs] n artrite f.

artichoke ['ɑːtɪtʃəʊk] n alcachofra f.

article ['ɑːtɪkl] n artigo m.

articulate [adj ɑː'tɪkjʊlət, vb ɑː'tɪkjʊleɪt] <> adj [eloquent - person] articulado(-da); [- speech] claro(ra). <> vt [give clear expression to] articular.

articulated lorry [ɑː'tɪkjʊleɪtɪd-] n UK caminhão m articulado.

artifact ['ɑːtɪfækt] n artefato m.

artificial [ˌɑːtɪ'fɪʃl] adj artificial.

artificial insemination [-ɪnˌsemɪ'neɪʃn] n inseminação f artificial.

artillery [ɑː'tɪlərɪ] n [guns] artilharia f.

artist ['ɑːtɪst] n artista mf.

artiste [ɑː'tiːst] n artista mf.

artistic [ɑːˈtɪstɪk] *adj* artístico(ca).

artistry [ˈɑːtɪstrɪ] *n* [creative skill] talento *m* artístico.

artless [ˈɑːtlɪs] *adj* [naive, simple] ingênuo(nua), simples.

as [*stressed* æz, *unstressed* əz] <> *conj* **-1.** [referring to time] enquanto; **she rang (just)** ~ **I was leaving** ela ligou (bem) na hora em que eu estava saindo; ~ **time goes by** com o passar do tempo **-2.** [referring to manner, way] como; **do** ~ **I say** faça como eu digo **-3.** [introducing a statement] como; ~ **you know, ...** como você sabe **-4.** [because] como. <> *prep* **-1.** [referring to function, characteristic]: **he lived in Africa** ~ **a boy** ele viveu na África quando garoto; **she works** ~ **a nurse** ela trabalha como enfermeira **-2.** [referring to attitude, reaction] como. <> *adv* (*in comparisons*): ~ **...** ~ tão ... quanto; ~ **red** ~ **a tomato** tão vermelho quanto um tomate; **he's** ~ **tall** ~ **I am** ele é tão alto quanto eu; ~ **much/ many** ~ tanto ... quanto; ~ **much wine/ chocolate** ~ **you want** tanto vinho/ chocolate quanto você queira.
  as for, as to *prep* quanto a.
  as from, as of *prep* a partir de.
  as if, as though *conj* como se.
  as to *prep* sobre.

asap (*abbr of* as soon as possible) o mais rápido possível.

asbestos [æsˈbestəs] *n* asbesto *m*.

ascend [əˈsend] <> *vt fml* [hill, staircase, ladder] subir. <> *vi* [climb] subir, elevar-se.

ascendant [əˈsendənt] *n*: **to be in the** ~ [rising in power] estar em ascensão.

ascent [əˈsent] *n* **-1.** [climb] escalada *f* **-2.** [upward slope] subida *f* **-3.** (*U*) *fig* [progress] escalada *f*.

ascertain [ˌæsəˈteɪn] *vt* averiguar.

ascribe [əˈskraɪb] *vt* [attribute]: **to** ~ **sthg to sthg/sb** atribuir algo a algo/alguém.

ash [æʃ] *n* **-1.** [from cigarette, fire] cinza *f* **-2.** [tree] freixo *m*.

ashamed [əˈʃeɪmd] *adj* [embarrassed] envergonhado(da); **to be** ~ **of** estar envergonhado(da) por alguém/ algo; **to be** ~ **to do sthg** estar com vergonha de fazer algo.

ashen-faced [ˈæʃnˌfeɪst] *adj* pálido(da).

ashore [əˈʃɔːʳ] *adv* [go, swim] em direção à costa.

ashtray [ˈæʃtreɪ] *n* cinzeiro *m*.

Ash Wednesday *n* Quarta-feira *f* de Cinzas.

Asia [ˈeɪʒə] *n* Ásia.

Asian [ˈeɪʒn] <> *adj* asiático(ca). <> *n* [person] asiático *m*, -ca *f*.

aside [əˈsaɪd] <> *adv* **-1.** [to one side] para o lado; **to take sb** ~ chamar alguém à parte **-2.** [apart] à parte; ~ **from** com exceção de. <> *n* **-1.** [in play] aparte *m* **-2.** [remark] observação *f*.

ask [ɑːsk] <> *vt* **-1.** [question] perguntar; **to** ~ **sb sthg** perguntar algo a alguém **-2.** [enquire] perguntar; **to** ~ **a question** fazer uma pergunta **-3.** [request] pedir; **to** ~ **sb for sthg** pedir algo a alguém; **to** ~ **sb to do sthg** pedir a alguém para fazer algo **-4.** [invite] convidar **-5.** [set a price of]: **how much are they asking?** quanto estão pedindo? <> *vi* **-1.** [enquire] perguntar **-2.** [request] pedir.
  ask after *vt fus*: **to** ~ **after sb** perguntar por alguém.
  ask for *vt fus* **-1.** [person] pedir por, chamar por **-2.** [thing] pedir por.

askance [əˈskæns] *adv* [disapprovingly]: **to look** ~ **at sb/sthg** olhar alguém/algo com desconfiança, olhar de soslaio para alguém/algo.

askew [əˈskjuː] *adj* [not straight] torto(ta).

asking price [ˈɑːskɪŋ-] *n* [for house, car, item in sale] preço *m* estipulado.

asleep [əˈsliːp] *adj* [sleeping] adormecido(da); **to fall** ~ pegar no sono.

asparagus [əˈspærəgəs] *n* asparago *m*.

aspect [ˈæspekt] *n* **-1.** aspecto *m* **-2.** ARCHIT posição *f*.

aspersions [əˈspɜːʃnz] *npl* : **to cast** ~ **(on sb)** levantar calúnias (sobre alguém); **to cast** ~ **(on sthg)** levantar suspeitas (sobre algo).

asphalt [ˈæsfælt] *n* asfalto *m*.

asphyxiate [əsˈfɪksɪeɪt] *vt* asfixiar.

aspiration [ˌæspəˈreɪʃn] *n* aspiração *f*.

aspire [əˈspaɪəʳ] *vi*: **to** ~ **to sthg/to do sthg** aspirar algo/fazer algo.

aspirin [ˈæsprɪn] *n* aspirina *f*.

ass [æs] *n* **-1.** [donkey] jumento *m* **-2.** *UK inf* [idiot] burro *m*, -ra *f* **-3.** *US vulg* = arse.

assailant [əˈseɪlənt] *n* [attacker] agressor *m*, -ra *f*.

assassin [əˈsæsɪn] *n* assassino *m*, -na *f*.

assassinate [əˈsæsɪneɪt] *vt* assassinar; **to be** ~ **ed** ser assassinado(da).

assassination [əˌsæsɪˈneɪʃn] *n* assassinato *m*.

assault [əˈsɔːlt] <> *n* **-1.** MIL ataque *m*; ~ **on sthg** ataque a algo **-2.** [physical attack] agressão *f*; ~ **on sb** agressão a alguém. <> *vt* [attack - physically] agredir; [- sexually] violentar, estuprar.

assemble [əˈsembl] <> *vt* **-1.** [gather] reunir **-2.** [fit together] montar. <> *vi* [gather] reunir.

assembly [əˈsemblɪ] (*pl* -ies) *n* **-1.** [meeting] reunião *f* **-2.** [law-making body] assembléia f, parlamento m -**3.** (U) [gathering together] assembléia f-**4.** (U) [fitting together] montagem f.

assembly line n linha f de montagem.

assent [ə'sent] <> n [agreement] acordo m, aprovação f. <> vi concordar; **to ~ to sthg** aceitar algo.

assert [ə'sɜːt] vt -**1.** [fact, belief] afirmar -**2.** [authority] impor.

assertive [ə'sɜːtɪv] adj positivo(va).

assess [ə'ses] vt -**1.** [judge] avaliar -**2.** [estimate] estimar.

assessment [ə'sesmənt] n -**1.** [judgment] avaliação f-**2.** [estimate] estimativa f.

assessor [ə'sesəʳ] n FIN analista mf.

asset ['æset] n ativo m.
⇒ **assets** npl COMM ativos mpl; **~s and liabilities** ativo m e passivo.

assign [ə'saɪn] vt -**1.** [allot, allocate]: **to ~ sthg (to sb/sthg)** designar algo (a alguém/algo) -**2.** [appoint]: **to ~ sb (to sthg/to do sthg)** designar alguém (para algo/fazer algo).

assignment [ə'saɪnmənt] n -**1.** [task] tarefa f-**2.** (U) [act of appointing] designação f-**3.** [law] partilha f, transferência f de bens.

assimilate [ə'sɪmɪleɪt] vt -**1.** [ideas, facts] assimilar -**2.** [people]: **to ~ sb (into sthg)** absorver alguém (em algo) -**3.** [nutrients, food] absorver.

assist [ə'sɪst] vt [help] auxiliar; **to ~ sb with sthg/in doing sthg** auxiliar alguém em algo/a fazer algo.

assistance [ə'sɪstəns] n [help] auxílio m, ajuda f; **to be of ~ (to sb)** ser de alguma ajuda (para alguém).

assistant [ə'sɪstənt] <> n -**1.** [helper] assistente mf -**2.** [in shop] balconista mf, atendente mf. <> comp assistente mf; **~ manager** gerente adjunto.

assistant referee n árbitro m assistente, árbitra f assistente.

associate [adj & n ə'səʊʃɪət, vb ə'səʊʃɪeɪt] <> adj [member] associado(da). <> n [business partner] sócio m, -cia f. <> vt [connect] associar-se; **to ~ o.s. with sb/sthg** associar-se a alguém/algo; **to ~ sthg with sb/sthg** associar algo a alguém/algo; **to be ~d with sb/sthg** ser associado a alguém/algo. <> vi: **to ~ with sb** relacionar-se com alguém.

association [ə,səʊsɪ'eɪʃn] n -**1.** [organization] associação f-**2.** (U) [relationship, of ideas] associação f; **in ~ with sb/sthg** em associação com alguém/algo.

assorted [ə'sɔːtɪd] adj [of various types] sortido(da), variado(da).

assortment [ə'sɔːtmənt] n [mixture] diversidade f.

assume [ə'sjuːm] vt -**1.** [suppose] supor -**2.** [take on] assumir.

assumed name [ə'sjuːmd-] n nome m falso.

assuming [ə'sjuːmɪŋ] conj: **~ that** supondo que.

assumption [ə'sʌmpʃn] n [supposition] suposição f.

assurance [ə'ʃʊərəns] n -**1.** [promise] promessa f-**2.** (U) [confidence] segurança f-**3.** (U) FIN [insurance] seguro m.

assure [ə'ʃʊəʳ] vt [reassure] assegurar; **to ~ sb of sthg** assegurar alguém de algo; **to be ~d of sthg** [be certain] estar seguro(ra de algo).

assured [ə'ʃʊəd] adj [confident] autoconfiante.

asterisk ['æstərɪsk] n asterisco m.

astern [ə'stɜːn] adv NAUT à popa.

asthma ['æsmə] n asma f.

astonish [ə'stɒnɪʃ] vt [amaze] surpreender.

astonishment [ə'stɒnɪʃmənt] n espanto m, surpresa f.

astound [ə'staʊnd] vt [amaze] pasmar.

astray [ə'streɪ] adv: **to go ~** [become lost] extraviar-se; **to lead sb ~** fig [into bad ways] levar alguém para o mau caminho.

astride [ə'straɪd] prep: sitting **~ a horse** montado(da) em um cavalo; sitting **~ a chair** sentado(da) numa cadeira com uma perna de cada lado.

astrology [ə'strɒlədʒɪ] n astrologia f.

astronaut ['æstrənɔːt] n astronauta mf.

astronomical [,æstrə'nɒmɪkl] adj -**1.** ASTRON astronômico(ca) -**2.** inf fig [very large] astronômico(ca).

astronomy [ə'strɒnəmɪ] n astronomia f.

astute [ə'stjuːt] adj [shrewd] perspicaz.

asylum [ə'saɪləm] n -**1.** dated [mental hospital] hospício m -**2.** (U) [protection] asilo m.

at [stressed æt, unstressed ət] prep -**1.** [indicating place, position] em; **~ work** no trabalho; **~ my father's** na casa do meu pai; **~ home** em casa; **~ the top of the house** em cima de casa; **~ the bottom of the hill** ao pé da colina -**2.** [indicating direction] para, em direção a; **to smile ~ sb** sorrir para alguém; **to stare ~ sb/sthg** olhar para alguém/algo; **to shoot ~ sb/sthg** atirar em (direção a) alguém/algo -**3.** [indicating a particular time] em; **~ midnight/noon** à meia-noite, ao meio-dia; **~ eleven o'clock** às onze horas; **~ Christmas** no Natal; **~ night** à noite -**4.** [indicating age, speed, rate] a, em; **~ your age** na sua idade; **~ high speed** em alta velocidade; **~ 52 (years**

of age) aos 52 anos (de idade); ~ **100 mph** a 100 milhas por hora **- 5.** [indicating price] a; ~ **£50** a OR por 50 libras **- 6.** [indicating particular state, condition] a, em; ~ **liberty** em liberdade; ~ **my invitation** a meu convite; ~ **peace/war** em paz/ guerra; ~ **lunch/dinner** no almoço/ jantar **- 7.** *(after adjectives)* com; **amused/appalled/puzzled** ~ **sthg** entretido(da)/apavorado(da)/embaraçado(da) com algo; **to be bad/good** ~ **sthg** ser ruim/bom (boa) em algo.

◆ **at all** *adv* **-1.** *(with negative):* **not** ~ **all** [when thanked] não há de que; [when answering a question] de forma alguma; **she's not** ~ **all happy** ela não está nem um pouco feliz **- 2.** [in the slightest]: **anything** ~ **all will do** qualquer coisa está bem; **do you know her** ~ **all?** você a conhece de algum lugar?

ate [UK et, US eɪt] pt ▷ **eat.**

atheist [ˈeɪθɪɪst] n ateu m, -téia f.

Athens [ˈæθɪnz] n Atenas; **in** ~ em Atenas.

athlete [ˈæθliːt] n atleta mf.

athletic [æθˈletɪk] adj atlético(ca).

◆ **athletics** npl atletismo m.

Atlantic [ətˈlæntɪk] ◇ adj atlântico(ca). ◇ n: **the** ~ **(Ocean)** o (Oceano) Atlântico.

atlas [ˈætləs] n atlas m inv.

atmosphere [ˈætmə.sfɪərˈ] n atmosfera f.

atmospheric [.ætməsˈferɪk] adj **-1.** [relating to the atmosphere] atmosférico(ca) **- 2.** [attractive, mysterious] envolvente.

atom [ˈætəm] n **-1.** TECH átomo m **- 2.** fig [tiny amount] ponta f pingo m.

atom bomb n bomba f atômica.

atomic [əˈtɒmɪk] adj atômico(ca).

atomic bomb n = atom bomb.

atomizer, -iser [ˈætəmaɪzəˈ] n vaporizador m.

atone [əˈtəʊn] vi: **to** ~ **for sthg** redimirse por algo.

A to Z n A a Z m.

atrocious [əˈtrəʊʃəs] adj **-1.** [cruel] desumano(na), atroz **- 2.** [very bad] atroz.

atrocity [əˈtrɒsɪtɪ] *(pl* -ies*)* n [terrible act] atrocidade f.

at (sign) n COMPUT arroba f.

attach [əˈtætʃ] vt **-1.** [fasten] prender; **to** ~ **sthg to sthg** prender algo em algo **- 2.** [to document] anexar; **to** ~ **sthg to sthg** anexar algo a algo **- 3.** [importance, blame] atribuir; **to** ~ **sthg to sthg** atribuir algo a algo **- 4.** COMPUT atachar, anexar.

attaché case [əˈtæʃeɪ-] n pasta f.

attached [əˈtætʃt] adj [fond]: ~ **to sb/**

sthg apegado(da) a alguém/algo.

attachment [əˈtætʃmənt] n **-1.** [device] dispositivo m **- 2.** [fondness]: ~ **(to sb/ sthg)** apego (a alguém/algo) **- 3.** COMPUT anexo m.

attack [əˈtæk] ◇ n **-1.** [gen] ataque f; ~ **on sb/sthg** ataque contra OR a alguém/algo **- 2.** [physical, verbal] agressão f; ~ **on sb** agressão a alguém ◇ vt **-1.** [gen] atacar **- 2.** [physically, verbally] agredir. ◇ vi atacar.

attacker [əˈtækəˈ] n **-1.** [assailant] agressor m, -ra f **- 2.** SPORT atacante mf.

attain [əˈteɪn] vt [reach] atingir.

attainment [əˈteɪnmənt] n **-1.** (U) [act of achieving] conquista f **- 2.** [skill] capacitação f, qualificação f.

attempt [əˈtempt] ◇ n [try] tentativa m; ~ **at sthg** tentativa de fazer algo; ~ **on sb's life** atentado contra a vida de alguém. ◇ vt [try] tentar; **to** ~ **to do sthg** tentar fazer algo.

attend [əˈtend] ◇ vt **-1.** [meeting, party] comparecer **- 2.** [school, church] freqüentar. ◇ vi **-1.** [be present] comparecer **- 2.** [pay attention]: **to** ~ **(to sthg)** prestar atenção (a algo).

◆ **attend to** vt fus **-1.** [deal with] cuidar de **- 2.** [look after] atender a.

attendance [əˈtendəns] n **-1.** [number of people present] audiência f **- 2.** (U) [presence] presença f.

attendant [əˈtendənt] ◇ adj [accompanying] relacionado(da). ◇ n [at museum, petrol station] atendente mf.

attention [əˈtenʃn] ◇ n **-1.** [gen] atenção f; **to attract sb's** ~ atrair a atenção de alguém; **to bring sthg to sb's** ~, **to draw sb's** ~ **to sthg** chamar a tenção de alguém para algo; **to pay** ~ **to sb/ sthg** prestar atenção a alguém/algo **- 2.** [care] atenção f, cuidados mpl **- 3.** COMM: **for the** ~ **of** aos cuidados de. ◇ excl MIL sentido!

attentive [əˈtentɪv] adj **-1.** [paying attention] atento(ta) **- 2.** [politely helpful] atencioso(sa).

attic [ˈætɪk] n sótão m.

attitude [ˈætɪtjuːd] n **-1.** [way of thinking/ acting] atitude f; ~ **to(wards) sb/sthg** atitude frente a alguém/algo **- 2.** [posture] postura f.

attn (abbr of for the attention of) a/c.

attorney [əˈtɜːnɪ] n US [lawyer] advogado m, -da f.

attorney general *(pl* attorneys general*)* n procurador m, -ra f público, -ca f.

attract [əˈtrækt] vt atrair.

attraction [əˈtrækʃn] n **-1.** (U) [liking] atração f; ~ **to sb** atração por alguém

- 2. *(U)* [appeal, charm] graça *f* **- 3.** [attractive feature, event] atração *f*.

attractive [ə'træktɪv] *adj* atraente.

attribute [*vb* ə'trɪbju:t, *n* 'ætrɪbju:t] ⬦ *vt*: **to ~ sthg to sb/sthg** atribuir algo a alguém/algo. ⬦ *n* [quality] atributo *m*.

attrition [ə'trɪʃn] *n* desgaste *m*.

aubergine ['əʊbəʒi:n] *n UK* beringela *f*.

auburn ['ɔ:bən] *adj* [hair] castanho avermelhado(da).

auction ['ɔ:kʃn] ⬦ *n* [sale] leilão *m*; **at** OR **by ~** em leilão; **to put sthg up for ~** pôr algo em leilão. ⬦ *vt* leiloar.
➡ **auction off** *vt sep* leiloar.

auctioneer [ˌɔ:kʃə'nɪəʳ] *n* leiloeiro *m*, -ra *f*.

audacious [ɔ:'deɪʃəs] *adj* [daring, impudent] audacioso(sa).

audible ['ɔ:dəbl] *adj* audível.

audience ['ɔ:djəns] *n* **- 1.** [of play, film, TV programme] platéia *f* **- 2.** [formal meeting] audiência *f*.

audio-visual ['ɔ:dɪəʊ-] *adj* audiovisual.

audit ['ɔ:dɪt] ⬦ *n* [of accounts] auditoria *f*. ⬦ *vt* [accounts] auditorar.

audition [ɔ:'dɪʃn] *n* audição *f*.

auditor ['ɔ:dɪtəʳ] *n* [of accounts] auditor *m*, -ra *f*.

auditorium [ˌɔ:dɪ'tɔ:rɪəm] *(pl* **-riums** OR **-ria** [-rɪə]) *n* auditório *m*.

augur ['ɔ:gəʳ] *vi*: **to ~ well/badly** ser um bom/mau sinal.

August ['ɔ:gəst] *n* agosto *m*; *see also* **September**.

Auld Lang Syne [ˌɔ:ldlæŋ'saɪn] *n* canção escocesa tradicionalmente cantada no ano-novo.

aunt [ɑ:nt] *n* tia *f*.

auntie, aunty ['ɑ:ntɪ] *(pl* **-ies)** *n inf* titia *f*.

au pair [ˌəʊ'peəʳ] *n* au pair *mf*.

aura ['ɔ:rə] *n* aura *f*.

aural ['ɔ:rəl] *adj* auditivo(va), auricular.

auspices ['ɔ:spɪsɪz] *npl*: **under the ~ of** sob o patrocínio de.

auspicious [ɔ:'spɪʃəs] *adj* [promising] promissor(ra).

Aussie ['ɒzɪ] *inf* ⬦ *adj* australiano(na). ⬦ *n* australiano *m*, -na *f*.

austere [ɒ'stɪəʳ] *adj* **- 1.** [person, life] duro(ra), austero(ra) **- 2.** [room, building] austero(ra).

austerity [ɒ'sterətɪ] *n* austeridade *f*.

Australia [ɒ'streɪljə] *n* Austrália *f*.

Australian [ɒ'streɪljən] ⬦ *adj* australiano(na). ⬦ *n* australiano *m*, -na *f*.

Austria ['ɒstrɪə] *n* Áustria *f*.

Austrian ['ɒstrɪən] ⬦ *adj* austríaco(ca). ⬦ *n* austríaco *m*, -ca *f*.

authentic [ɔ:'θentɪk] *adj* **- 1.** [genuine] autêntico(ca) **- 2.** [accurate] fidedigno(na).

author ['ɔ:θəʳ] *n* autor *m*, -ra *f*.

authoritarian [ɔ:ˌθɒrɪ'teərɪən] *adj* autoritário(ria).

authoritative [ɔ:'θɒrɪtətɪv] *adj* **- 1.** [person, voice] autoritário(ria) **- 2.** [report] oficial.

authority [ɔ:'θɒrətɪ] *(pl* **-ies)** *n* **- 1.** [gen] autoridade *f*; **~ on sthg** autoridade em algo **- 2.** *(U)* [power] autoridade *f*; **in ~ com** autoridade **- 3.** *(U)* [permission] autorização *f*.
➡ **authorities** *npl* [people in power]: **the authorities** as autoridades.

authorize, -ise ['ɔ:θəraɪz] *vt* autorizar; **to ~ sb to do sthg** autorizar alguém a fazer algo.

autistic [ɔ:'tɪstɪk] *adj* autista.

auto ['ɔ:təʊ] *(pl* **-s)** *n US* [car] auto *m*.

autobiography [ˌɔ:təbaɪ'ɒgrəfɪ] *(pl* **-ies)** *n* autobiografia *f*.

autocratic [ˌɔ:tə'krætɪk] *adj* autocrático(ca).

autograph ['ɔ:təgrɑ:f] ⬦ *n* autógrafo *m*. ⬦ *vt* autografar.

automate ['ɔ:təmeɪt] *vt* automatizar.

automatic [ˌɔ:tə'mætɪk] ⬦ *adj* **- 1.** [gen] automático(ca) **- 2.** [fine, right of appeal] imediato(ta). ⬦ *n* **- 1.** [car] carro *n* automático **- 2.** [gun] pistola *f* automática **- 3.** [washing machine] máquina *f* de lavar automática.

automatically [ˌɔ:tə'mætɪklɪ] *adv* automaticamente.

automation [ˌɔ:tə'meɪʃn] *n* [of process] automação *f*, automatização *f*.

automobile ['ɔ:təməbi:l] *n US* [car] automóvel *m*.

autonomy [ɔ:'tɒnəmɪ] *n* autonomia *f*.

autopsy ['ɔ:tɒpsɪ] *(pl* **-ies)** *n* autópsia *f*.

autumn ['ɔ:təm] *n* outono *m*.

auxiliary [ɔ:g'zɪljərɪ] *(pl* **-ies)** ⬦ *adj* auxiliar. ⬦ *n* [person] auxiliar *mf*.

avail [ə'veɪl] ⬦ *n*: **to no ~** em vão. ⬦ *vt*: **to ~ o.s. of sthg** aproveitar-se de algo.

available [ə'veɪləbl] *adj* disponível.

avalanche ['ævəlɑ:nʃ] *n* avalanche *f*.

avarice ['ævərɪs] *n* avareza *f*.

Ave. *(abbr of* **avenue)** Av.

avenge [ə'vendʒ] *vt* vingar.

avenue ['ævənju:] *n* [wide road] avenida *f*.

average ['ævərɪdʒ] ⬦ *adj* **- 1.** [mean] média(dio) **- 2.** [typical] comum **- 3.** *pej* [mediocre] mediano(na). ⬦ *n* [mean] média *f*; **on ~** em média. ⬦ *vt* [speed, distance, quantity]: **they ~ 300 cars a day**

eles atingem uma média de 300 carros por dia.

◆ **average out** *vi*: **to** ~ **out at** chegar à média de.

aversion [əˈvɜːʃn] *n* [dislike] aversão *f*; ~ **to sthg** aversão a algo.

avert [əˈvɜːt] *vt* [avoid] evitar.

aviary [ˈeɪvjərɪ] (*pl* -ies) *n* aviário *m*.

avid [ˈævɪd] *adj* [keen] ávido(da); ~ **for sthg** ávido(da) de/por algo.

avocado [ˌævəˈkɑːdəʊ] (*pl* -s OR -es) *n*: ~ **(pear)** abacate *m*.

avoid [əˈvɔɪd] *vt* evitar; **to** ~ **doing sthg** evitar fazer algo.

await [əˈweɪt] *vt* - 1. [wait for] esperar - 2. [be ready for] estar pronto(ta) para.

awake [əˈweɪk] (*pt* **awoke** OR **awaked**, *pp* **awoken**) ⟨⟩ *adj* [not sleeping] acordado(da). ⟨⟩ *vt* - 1. [wake up] acordar - 2. *fig* [provoke] despertar. ⟨⟩ *vi* [wake up] acordar.

awakening [əˈweɪknɪŋ] *n* - 1. [from sleep] despertar *m* - 2. *fig* [of feeling] despertar *m*.

award [əˈwɔːd] ⟨⟩ *n* [prize] prêmio *m*. ⟨⟩ *vt* [give] premiar; **to** ~ **sb sthg**, **to** ~ **sthg to sb** conceder algo a alguém.

aware [əˈweəʳ] *adj* - 1. [conscious]: ~ **of sthg** consciente de algo; ~ **that** ciente de que - 2. [informed, sensitive] consciente; ~ **of sthg** informado(da) sobre algo.

awareness [əˈweənɪs] *n* consciência *f*.

awash [əˈwɒʃ] *adj*: ~ **(with sthg)** cheio(a) (de algo).

away [əˈweɪ] ⟨⟩ *adv* - 1. [indicating movement] embora; ~ **from** longe de; **to look/turn** ~ virar-se - 2. [at a distance - in space]: **she lives 3 miles** ~ ela mora a três milhas daqui; **we live 4 miles** ~ **from the city centre** moramos a 4 milhas do centro da cidade; [- in time]: **the exams were only two days** ~ faltavam apenas dois dias para os exames - 3. [separate from]: **to be kept** ~ **from sthg** ser mantido(da) afastado(da) de algo; **to give sthg** ~ dar algo; **to take sthg** ~ levar algo - 4. [absent]: **to be** ~ estar fora - 5. [in a safe place]: **to put sthg** ~ guardar algo - 6. [indicating disappearance, cessation]: **the stain has faded** ~ a mancha desapareceu; **the wood had rotted** ~ a madeira tinha apodrecido - 7. [continuously]: **to sing/work** ~ cantar/trabalhar sem parar. ⟨⟩ *adj* SPORT: ~ **team** time *m* visitante; ~ **game** jogo fora de casa.

awe [ɔː] *n* temor *m*; **to be in** ~ **of sb** estar intimidado(da) por alguém.

awesome [ˈɔːsəm] *adj* [impressive] terrível.

awful [ˈɔːfʊl] *adj* - 1. [terrible] horrível - 2.

inf [very great]: **to have an** ~ **lot of work to do** ter um bocado de coisas para fazer.

awfully [ˈɔːflɪ] *adv inf* [very] pra caramba; **to be** ~ **difficult** ser difícil pra caramba.

awhile [əˈwaɪl] *adv literary* durante um tempo.

awkward [ˈɔːkwəd] *adj* - 1. [clumsy] desajeitado(da) - 2. [embarrassing] embaraçoso(sa) - 3. [embarrassed]: **to feel** ~ sentir-se embaraçado(da) - 4. [difficult to deal with] complicado(da) - 5. [inconvenient] inadequado(da).

awning [ˈɔːnɪŋ] *n* - 1. [of tent] cobertura *f* - 2. [of shop] toldo *m*.

awoke [əˈwəʊk] *pt* ▷ **awake**.

awoken [əˈwəʊkn] *pp* ▷ **awake**.

awry [əˈraɪ] ⟨⟩ *adj* [twisted] desajeitado(da). ⟨⟩ *adv*: **to go** ~ [wrong] dar errado.

axe UK, **ax** US [æks] ⟨⟩ *n* machado *m*. ⟨⟩ *vt* [project, jobs] cortar.

axes [ˈæksiːz] *pl* ▷ **axis**.

axis [ˈæksɪs] (*pl* **axes**) *n* eixo *m*.

axle [ˈæksl] *n* [shaft] eixo *m*.

aye [aɪ] ⟨⟩ *adv* [yes] sim. ⟨⟩ *n* [affirmative vote] sim *m*.

azalea [əˈzeɪljə] *n* azaléia *f*.

Azores [əˈzɔːz] *npl*: **the** ~ os Açores.

B

b (*pl* **b's** OR **bs**), **B** (*pl* **B's** OR **Bs**) [biː] *n* [letter] b, B *m*.

◆ **B** *n* - 1. MUS si *m* - 2. SCH [mark] B *m*.

BA *n* (*abbr of* **Bachelor of Arts**) *titular de graduação em ciências humanas*.

babble [ˈbæbl] ⟨⟩ *n* [noise] balbucio *m*. ⟨⟩ *vi* [person] balbuciar.

baboon [bəˈbuːn] *n* [animal] babuíno *m*.

baby [ˈbeɪbɪ] (*pl* -ies) *n* - 1. [child] bebê *mf*, nenê *mf* - 2. *pej* [feeble person]: **don't be such a** ~! não seja tão criança! - 3. *esp US inf* [term of affection] pequeno(-na).

baby buggy UK, **baby carriage** US *n* [foldable pushchair] carrinho *m* de bebê

baby food *n* comida *f* de nenê.

baby-sit *vi* tomar conta de crianças, trabalhar como babá.

baby-sitter [-'sitə^r] n babá f, baby-sitter f.

bachelor ['bætʃələ^r] n [unmarried man] solteirão m; **confirmed** ~ solteirão convicto.

Bachelor of Arts n bacharelado em Artes, Ciências Humanas ou Sociais.

Bachelor of Science n [person] Bacharel m em Ciências; [degree] bacharelado m em ciências.

back [bæk] <> adj (in compounds) **-1.** [rear] traseiro(ra); ~ **legs** patas traseiras **-2.** [at the back] de trás, dos fundos; ~ **seat** assento de trás; ~ **garden** jardim dos fundos **-3.** [overdue] atrasado(da). <> adv **-1.** [backwards] para trás **-2.** [indicating return to former position or state] de volta; **is he** ~ **yet?** ele já está de volta?, ele já voltou?; **to go** ~ **to sleep** voltar a dormir; **to go** ~ **and forth** ficar indo e vindo **-3.** [earlier]: ~ **in January** em janeiro passado **-4.** [in reply, in return] de volta; **to phone** ~ ligar de volta; **to pay** ~ reembolsar; **to write** ~ responder **-5.** [in fashion again]: **to be** ~ **(in fashion)** estar de volta (à moda). <> n **-1.** [of person, animal] costas fpl; **to do sthg behind sb's** ~ fazer algo pelas costas de alguém **-2.** [reverse side - of page, envelope] verso m; [- of head] parte f de trás, parte f anterior **-3.** [furthest point away from front - of room] fundos mpl; [- of cupboard, fridge]: **in the** ~ **of the fridge** na parte de trás geladeira; [- of car] traseira f; [- of chair] encosto m; **at the** ~ **of, in the** ~ **of** US atrás de **-4.** SPORT [player] zagueiro(ra). <> vt **-1.** [reverse] recuar **-2.** [support] apoiar **-3.** [bet on] apostar. <> vi [reverse] retornar; **to** ~ **into sthg** [walking] voltar-se para algo; [in vehicle] entrar de ré em algo.

◆ **back to back** adv [with backs touching]: **to stand** ~ **to** ~ ficar costas com costas.

◆ **back to front** adv [the wrong way round] de trás para frente, ao contrário.

◆ **back down** vi voltar atrás.

◆ **back out** vi [of promise, arrangement] dar para trás.

◆ **back up** <> vt sep **-1.** [support] apoiar **-2.** [reverse] dar marcha à ré **-3.** COMPUT fazer cópia de segurança de. <> vi [reverse] dar marcha à ré.

backache ['bækeik] n dor f nas costas.

backbencher [,bæk'bentʃə^r] n UK POL membro do Parlamento Britânico, sem cargo oficial no governo ou na oposição.

backbone ['bækbəʊn] n **-1.** [spine] coluna f vertebral **-2.** (U) fig [courage, force] tutano m **-3.** fig [main support]: **the** ~ **of** a espinha dorsal de.

backcloth ['bækklɒθ] n UK = **backdrop**.

backdate [,bæk'deit] vt antedatar.

back door n porta f dos fundos.

backdrop ['bækdrɒp] n **-1.** THEATRE pano m de fundo **-2.** fig [background] pano m de fundo.

backfire [,bæk'faiə^r] vi **-1.** [motor vehicle] engasgar **-2.** [go wrong] dar errado; **his plans** ~**d (on him)** seus planos não deram o resultado esperado.

backgammon ['bæk,gæmən] n (U) gamão m.

background ['bækgraʊnd] n **-1.** [in picture, view] fundo m; **in the** ~ lit ao fundo; fig [unnoticeable] em segundo plano **-2.** [of event, situation] cenário m **-3.** [upbringing] background m.

backhand ['bækhænd] n backhand m.

backhanded ['bækhændıd] adj fig [equivocal] falso(sa).

backhander ['bækhændə^r] n UK inf [bribe] suborno m.

backing ['bækıŋ] n **-1.** (U) [support] suporte m **-2.** [lining] forro m.

backing group n MUS grupo m de acompanhamento.

backlash ['bæklæʃ] n [adverse reaction] revolta f.

backlog ['bæklɒg] n acúmulo m.

back number n número m atrasado.

backpack ['bækpæk] n mochila f.

back pay n (U) salário m atrasado.

back seat n [in car] banco m de trás; **to take a** ~ fig desempenhar um papel secundário.

backside [,bæk'said] n inf traseiro m.

backstage [,bæk'steidʒ] adv nos bastidores.

back street n UK ruela f.

backstroke ['bækstrəʊk] n [in swimming] nado m (de) costas.

backup ['bækʌp] <> adj [reserve] de reserva. <> n **-1.** [support] suporte m **-2.** COMPUT backup m, cópia f de segurança.

backward ['bækwəd] <> adj **-1.** [directed towards the rear] para trás **-2.** pej [late in development - person] retardado(da); [- society, ideas] atrasado(da). <> adv US = **backwards**.

backwards ['bækwədz], **backward** US ['bækwəd] adv [towards the rear] de trás para a frente; ~ **and forwards** de um lado para outro.

backwater ['bæk,wɔːtə^r] n fig & pej [place behind the times] lugar m atrasado; **cultural** ~ atraso m cultural.

backyard [ˌbæk'jɑːd] n -1. UK [yard] pátio m, quintal m -2. US [garden] jardim m.

bacon ['beɪkən] n (U) bacon m.

bacteria [bæk'tɪərɪə] npl bactérias fpl.

bad [bæd] (compar worse, superl worst) ⋄ adj -1. [gen] ruim; not ~ nada mal; too ~ uma pena; to be ~ at sthg ser ruim em algo -2. [unfavourable] mau (má) -3. [severe] grave, severo(ra) -4. [inadequate] ruim -5. [guilty]: to feel ~ about sthg sentir-se mal por algum motivo -6. [food, milk, meat] mal; to go ~ ir mal. ⋄ adv US = badly.

badge [bædʒ] n -1. [metal, plastic] crachá m -2. [sewn on] distintivo m -3. [on car] selo m.

badger ['bædʒəʳ] ⋄ n [animal] texugo m. ⋄ vt [pester]: to ~ sb (to do sthg) convencer alguém (a fazer algo).

badly ['bædlɪ] (compar worse, superl worst) adv -1. [poorly] mal -2. [severely] gravemente -3. [improperly] indevidamente -4. [cruelly] mal -5. [very much]: to be ~ in need of sthg precisar muito de algo.

badly-off adj [poor] carente.

bad-mannered [-'mænəd] adj mal-educado(da).

badminton ['bædmɪntən] n (U) badminton m.

bad-tempered [-'tempəd] adj -1. [by nature] genioso(sa) -2. [in a bad mood] mal-humorado(da).

baffle ['bæfl] vt [puzzle] desnortear.

bag [bæg] (pt & pp -ged, cont -ging) ⋄ n -1. [container] saco m; to pack one's ~ fig [leave] fazer as malas -2. [handbag] bolsa f; [when travelling] mala f -3. [bagful] sacola f. ⋄ vt -1. UK inf [get] pegar -2. UK inf [reserve] marcar.
➡ **bags** npl -1. [under eyes] bolsas fpl -2. [lots]: ~s of sthg inf um montão de algo.

bagel ['beɪgəl] n pão m enrolado.

baggage ['bægɪdʒ] n (U) bagagem f.

baggage reclaim n esteira f de bagagem.

baggy ['bægɪ] (compar -ier, superl -iest) adj largo(ga).

bagpipes ['bægpaɪps] npl gaita f de foles.

baguette [bə'get] n [loaf] baguete f.

Bahamas [bə'hɑːməz] npl: the ~ as Bahamas.

bail [beɪl] n (U) JUR fiança f; on ~ sob fiança.
➡ **bail out** ⋄ vt sep -1. JUR [pay bail for] afiançar -2. [rescue] resgatar -3. [boat] tirar água. ⋄ vi [from plane] saltar de pára-quedas.

bailiff ['beɪlɪf] n -1. [in court] oficial mf de justiça -2. [in charge of repossession] administrador m, -ra f de propriedades.

bait [beɪt] ⋄ n (U) [food] isca f. ⋄ vt -1. [hook] pôr isca em -2. [mousetrap] armar -3. [tease, torment - person] atormentar; [- bear, badger] provocar.

bake [beɪk] ⋄ vt -1. [cook] assar -2. [dry, harden] queimar. ⋄ vi [food] assar.

baked beans [beɪkt-] npl feijão cozido em molho de tomate.

baked potato [beɪkt-] n batata grande assada com casca e servida com recheio.

baker ['beɪkəʳ] n padeiro m; ~'s (shop) padaria f.

bakery ['beɪkərɪ] (pl -ies) n padaria f.

baking ['beɪkɪŋ] n [process] cozimento m.

balaclava (helmet) [bælə'klɑːvə-] n UK balaclava f.

balance ['bæləns] ⋄ n -1. [equilibrium] equilíbrio m; to keep/lose one's ~ manter/perder o equilíbrio; off ~ desequilibrado(da) -2. fig [counterweight] contrapeso m -3. fig [weight, force]: ~ of evidence peso m da evidência -4. [scales] balança f -5. [remainder] restante m -6. [of bank account] saldo m. ⋄ vt -1. [keep in balance] balancear -2. [compare]: to ~ sthg against sthg contrabalançar algo em relação a algo -3. [in accounting]: to ~ the books/a budget fazer o balanço dos livros/do orçamento. ⋄ vi -1. [maintain equilibrium] equilibrar-se -2. [in accounting] fechar, bater.
➡ **on balance** adv de um modo geral.

balanced diet ['bælənst-] n dieta f equilibrada.

balance of payments n balança f de pagamentos.

balance of trade n balança f comercial.

balance sheet n balancete m.

balcony ['bælkənɪ] (pl -ies) n -1. [on building] sacada f, varanda f -2. [in theatre] balcão m, galeria f.

bald [bɔːld] adj -1. [head, man, tyre] careca -2. fig [unadorned] curto(ta) e grosso(-sa).

bale [beɪl] n fardo m.
➡ **bale out** UK vt sep = bail out.

Balearic Islands [ˌbælɪ'ærɪk-], **Balearics** [ˌbælɪ'ærɪks] npl: the ~ as Ilhas Baleares.

baleful ['beɪlfʊl] adj fulminante.

balk [bɔːk] vi [recoil]: to ~ (at sthg) [person] recusar-se (a fazer algo).

Balkans ['bɔːlkənz], **Balkan States** npl:
the ~ os Bálcãs.

ball [bɔːl] n -1. [in game] bola f; to be on
the ~ fig estar ligado(da) em tudo; to
play ~ with sb fig colaborar (com
alguém) -2. [sphere] novelo m -3. [of
foot] sola f -4. [dance] baile m.
➤ **balls** vulg ◇ n [nonsense] merda f.
◇ npl [testicles] saco m; fig [courage]:
to have ~ ter colhões. ◇ excl caralho!

ballad ['bæləd] n balada f.

ballast ['bæləst] n (U) lastro m.

ball bearing n rolamento m.

ball boy n gandula m.

ballerina [,bælə'riːnə] n bailarina f.

ballet ['bæleɪ] n (U) balé m.

ballet dancer n bailarino(na).

ball game n -1. US [baseball match] jogo
m de beisebol -2. fig [situation]: it's a
whole new ~ inf é outra história.

balloon [bə'luːn] n balão m.

ballot ['bælət] ◇ n -1. [voting paper]
voto m -2. [voting process] votação f. ◇
vt [canvass] caçar votos.

ballot box n -1. [container] urna f -2.
[voting process] urnas fpl.

ballot paper n cédula f de votação.

ball park n US estádio m de beisebol.

ballpoint (pen) ['bɔːlpɔɪnt-] n caneta f
esferográfica.

ballroom ['bɔːlrʊm] n salão m de baile.

ballroom dancing n (U) dança f de
salão.

balm [bɑːm] n bálsamo m.

balmy ['bɑːmɪ] (compar -ier, superl -iest)
adj suave.

balsa ['bɒlsə] n = balsawood.

balsawood ['bɒlsəwʊd] n balsa f.

Baltic ['bɔːltɪk] ◇ adj [port, coast]
báltico(ca). ◇ n: the ~ (Sea) o (mar)
Báltico.

Baltic Republic n: the ~s as Repúbli-
cas Bálticas.

Baltic State n: the ~s os Estados
Bálticos.

bamboo [bæm'buː] n bambu m.

bamboozle [bæm'buːzl] vt inf lograr.

ban [bæn] (pt & pp -ned, cont -ning) ◇
n proibição f; ~ on sthg proibição de
algo. ◇ vt banir; to ~ sb from doing
sthg proibir alguém de fazer algo.

banal [bə'nɑːl] adj pej banal.

banana [bə'nɑːnə] n banana f.

band [bænd] n -1. [musical group] banda f
-2. [gang] bando m -3. [long strip] correia
f -4. [broad stripe, range] faixa f.
➤ **band together** vi unir-se.

bandage ['bændɪdʒ] ◇ n faixa f. ◇
vt enfaixar.

Band-Aid® n band-aid® m.

b and b, B and B (abbr of bed and
breakfast) n tipo de acomodação
típica da Grã-Bretanha em que re-
sidências privadas oferecem serviço
de quarto e café-da-manhã.

bandit ['bændɪt] n bandido m.

bandstand ['bændstænd] n palanque m.

bandwagon ['bændwægən] n: to jump
on the ~ pegar carona na idéia.

bandy ['bændɪ] (compar -ier, superl -iest,
pt & pp -ied) adj [bandy-legged] cam-
baio(a).
➤ **bandy about, bandy around** vt sep
ficar repetindo.

bandy-legged [-,legd] adj = bandy.

bang [bæŋ] ◇ adv [right]: ~ in the middle bem no meio; ~ on certeiro(ra).
◇ n -1. [blow] golpe m -2. [loud noise]
estrondo m. ◇ vt -1. [hit] bater -2.
[move noisily] bater. ◇ vi -1. [knock]: to
~ on sthg dar pancadas -2. [make a
loud noise] bater -3. [crash]: to ~ into
sb/sthg bater em alguém/algo. ◇
excl bum.
➤ **bangs** npl US franjas fpl.

banger ['bæŋəʳ] n UK -1. inf [sausage]
salsicha f -2. inf [old car] carroça f -3.
[firework] rojão m.

bangle ['bæŋgl] n pulseira f.

banish ['bænɪʃ] vt banir.

banister ['bænɪstəʳ] n, **banisters**
['bænɪstəz] npl corrimão m.

bank [bæŋk] ◇ n -1. [gen & FIN] banco
m; blood/data ~ banco m de sangue/
dados -2. [alongside river, lake] margem m
-3. [slope] monte m -4. [of clouds, fog]
massa f. ◇ vt FIN depositar. ◇ vi -1.
FIN: to ~ with sb ser correntista de -2.
[plane] inclinar lateralmente.
➤ **bank on** vt fus contar com.

bank account n conta f corrente.

bank balance n saldo m bancário.

bank card n cartão m de garantia de
cheque.

bank charges npl tarifas fpl bancári-
as.

bank draft n ordem f bancária.

banker ['bæŋkəʳ] n FIN banqueiro m, -ra
f.

bank holiday n UK feriado m bancário.

banking ['bæŋkɪŋ] n (U) serviços mpl
bancários.

bank manager n gerente mf de banco.

bank note n cédula f.

bank rate n taxa f referencial de
juros.

bankrupt ['bæŋkrʌpt] adj [financially] fa-
lido(da); to go ~ ir à falência; to be

morally ~ *fig* estar desmoralizado(da).
bankruptcy ['bæŋkrəptsɪ] (*pl* **-ies**) *n* falência *f*; **moral** ~ *fig* desmoralização *f*.
bank statement *n* extrato *m* bancário.
banner ['bænə'] *n* [made of cloth] faixa *f*.
bannister ['bænɪstə'] *n*, **bannisters** ['bænɪstəz] *npl* = banister.
banquet ['bæŋkwɪt] *n* banquete *m*.
banter ['bæntə'] *n* (*U*) brincadeiras *fpl*.
bap [bæp] *n UK* bisnaguinha *f*.
baptism ['bæptɪzm] *n* batismo *m*.
Baptist ['bæptɪst] *n* batista *mf*.
baptize, -ise [*UK* bæp'taɪz, *US* 'bæptaɪz] *vt* batizar.
bar [bɑː'] (*pt* & *pp* **-red**, *cont* **-ring**) <> *n* **- 1.** [of wood, metal, chocolate, soap etc.] barra *f*; **to be behind** ~ **s** estar atrás das grades **- 2.** *fig* [obstacle] barreira *f* **- 3.** [drinking place] bar *m* **- 4.** [counter] balcão *m* **- 5.** *MUS* compasso *m*. <> *vt* **- 1.** [bolt] trancar **- 2.** [block off] bloquear; **to** ~ **sb's way** bloquear a passagem de alguém **- 3.** [ban] barrar. <> *prep* [except] exceto; ~ **none** sem exceção.
◆ **Bar** *n* **- 1.** *UK*: **the Bar** [barristers] o Magistrado; [profession] a Magistratura **- 2.** *US*: **the Bar** [lawyers] advogados(das); [profession] a Advocacia.
barbaric [bɑː'bærɪk] *adj pej* bárbaro(ra).
barbecue [bɑː'bɪkjuː] *n* **- 1.** [grill] churrasqueira *f* **- 2.** [party] churrasco *m*.
barbed wire [bɑː'bd-] *n UK* (*U*) arame *m* farpado.
barber ['bɑː'bə'] *n* barbeiro *m*; ~ **'s (shop)** barbearia *f*.
barbiturate [bɑː'bɪtjʊrət] *n* barbitúrico *m*.
bar code *n* código *m* de barras.
bare [beə'] <> *adj* **- 1.** [without covering] descoberto(ta) **- 2.** [basic] mínimo(ma) **- 3.** [empty] vazio(a). <> *vt* [reveal - chest, limbs] exibir, mostrar; **to** ~ **one's teeth** mostrar os dentes; **to** ~ **one's head** tirar o chapéu.
bareback ['beəbæk] *adv* em pêlo.
barefaced ['beəfeɪst] *adj* deslavado(da).
barefoot(ed) [,beə'fʊt(ɪd)] <> *adj* descalço(ça). <> *adv* descalço.
barely ['beəlɪ] *adv* [scarcely] mal.
bargain ['bɑːgɪn] <> *n* **- 1.** [agreement] barganha *f*; **into the** ~ ainda por cima **- 2.** [good buy] pechincha *f*. <> *vi* barganhar; **to** ~ **with sb for sthg** pechinchar com alguém por algo.
◆ **bargain for, bargain on** *vt fus* esperar.
barge [bɑːdʒ] <> *n* barca *f*. <> *vi inf* **to** ~ **into sb/sthg** esbarrar em alguém/

algo; **to** ~ **past sb/sthg** passar empurrando alguém/algo.
◆ **barge in** *vi*: **to** ~ **in (on sb/sthg)** interromper (alguém/algo).
baritone ['bærɪtəʊn] *n* barítono *m*.
bark [bɑːk] <> *n* **- 1.** [of dog] latido *m* **- 2.** [on tree] casca *f*. <> *vi* [dog] latir; **to** ~ **at sb/sthg** xingar alguém/algo.
barley ['bɑːlɪ] *n* (*U*) cevada *f*.
barley sugar *n UK* bala *feita com caramelo e cevada*.
barley water *n UK* (*U*) *bebida à base de cevada e suco de fruta*.
barmaid ['bɑːmeɪd] *n* garçonete *f*.
barman ['bɑːmən] (*pl* **-men** [-mən]) *n* barman *m*.
barn [bɑːn] *n* celeiro *m*.
barometer [bə'rɒmɪtə'] *n* **- 1.** [instrument] barômetro *m* **- 2.** *fig* [way of measuring] ≈ termômetro *m*.
baron ['bærən] *n* barão *m*; **oil/press** ~ *fig* magnata da imprensa/do petróleo.
baroness ['bærənɪs] *n* baronesa *f*.
barrack ['bærək] *vt UK* interromper com gritos.
◆ **barracks** *npl* quartel *m*.
barrage ['bærɑːʒ] *n* **- 1.** [of firing] bombardeio *m* **- 2.** [of questions] bombardeio *m* **- 3.** *UK* [dam] barragem *f*.
barrel ['bærəl] *n* **- 1.** [container] barril *m* **- 2.** [of gun] cano *m*.
barren ['bærən] *adj* **- 1.** [unable to have children] estéril **- 2.** [unable to produce crops] improdutivo(va).
barricade [,bærɪ'keɪd] *n* barricada *f*.
barrier ['bærɪə'] *n* **- 1.** [fence, wall] barreira *f* **- 2.** *fig* [obstacle] obstáculo *m*.
barring ['bɑːrɪŋ] *prep*: ~ **accidents** a menos que haja imprevistos; ~ **further complications** se não houver complicações.
barrister ['bærɪstə'] *n UK* advogado *m*, -da *f*.
barrow ['bærəʊ] *n* [market stall] carrinho *m* de frutas/verduras.
bartender ['bɑːtendə'] *n US* garçom *m*, -nete *f*.
barter ['bɑːtə'] <> *n* barganha *f*, troca *f*. <> *vt* trocar; **to** ~ **sthg for sthg** trocar algo por algo. <> *vi* barganhar.
base [beɪs] <> *n* base *f*. <> *vt* **- 1.** [use as starting point]: **to** ~ **sthg (up)on sthg** basear algo em algo **- 2.** [locate] estabelecer; **to be** ~ **d in** viver/trabalhar em; **a New York-based company** uma empresa sediada em Nova York. <> *adj pej* [dishonourable] desprezível.
baseball ['beɪsbɔːl] *n* (*U*) beisebol *m*.
baseball cap *n* boné *m* de beisebol.
basement ['beɪsmənt] *n* porão *m*.

base rate n taxa f de base.
bases ['beɪsi:z] pl ⊳ **basis**.
bash [bæʃ] inf ⬦ n **-1.** [painful blow] pancada f **-2.** [attempt]: **to have a ~ (at sthg)** tentar fazer (algo). ⬦ vt [hit] bater.
bashful ['bæʃful] adj tímido(da).
basic ['beɪsɪk] adj [fundamental] básico(-ca).
➡ **basics** npl [rudiments] princípios mpl básicos.
BASIC (abbr of Beginners' All-purpose Symbolic Instruction Code) n BASIC m.
basically ['beɪsɪklɪ] adv [essentially] basi-camente, no fundo.
basil ['bæzl] n (U) manjericão m.
basin ['beɪsn] n **-1.** UK [bowl, container] tigela f; [for washing] pia f **-2.** GEOGR bacia f.
basis ['beɪsɪs] (pl -ses) n **-1.** [gen] base f; **on the ~ that** com base no fato de que, considerando que **-2.** [arrangement]: **on a weekly/monthly ~** numa base semanal/mensal; **on the ~ of** com base em.
bask [bɑ:sk] vi [sunbathe]: **to ~ in the sun** tomar banho de sol.
basket ['bɑ:skɪt] n [container - for rubbish] cesto m; [- for shopping] cesta f.
basketball ['bɑ:skɪtbɔ:l] n (U) basquete m.
bass [beɪs] adj [part, singer] baixo(xa).
bass drum [beɪs-] n MUS tambor m baixo.
bass guitar [beɪs-] n MUS baixo m.
bassoon [bə'su:n] n MUS fagote m.
bastard ['bɑ:stəd] n **-1.** [illegitimate child] bastardo m, -da f **-2.** v inf pej [person] canalha mf, filho-da-mãe m.
bastion ['bæstɪən] n fig bastião m.
bat [bæt] (pt & pp -ted, cont -ting) n **-1.** [animal] morcego m **-2.** [SPORT - for cricket] pá f; [- for baseball] bastão m; [- for table tennis] raquete f **-3.** phr: **to do sthg off one's own ~** fazer algo sem auxílio.
batch [bætʃ] n **-1.** [of papers, letters] pilha f **-2.** [of work] porção f **-3.** [of products] lote m **-4.** [of people] grupo m **-5.** [of bread, cakes etc.] fornada f.
bated ['beɪtɪd] adj: **with ~ breath** [expectantly] segurando a respiração.
bath [bɑ:θ] ⬦ n **-1.** [bathtub] banheira f **-2.** [act of washing] banho m; **to have** OR **take a bath** tomar (um) banho. ⬦ vt dar banho em.
➡ **baths** npl UK [public] banhos mpl públicos.
bathe [beɪð] ⬦ vt **-1.** [wound] lavar **-2.** [in light, sweat] banhar; **to be ~d in sthg** estar coberto(ta) de algo. ⬦ vi **-1.**

[swim] nadar **-2.** US [take a bath] tomar (um) banho.
bathing ['beɪðɪŋ] n (U) banho m; **safe for ~** próprio(pria) para banho; **to go ~** dar um mergulho.
bathing cap n touca f de banho.
bathing costume, bathing suit n maiô m.
bathrobe ['bɑ:θrəub] n **-1.** [made of to-welling] roupão m de banho **-2.** [dressing gown] US chambre m.
bathroom ['bɑ:θrum] n UK banheiro m.
bath towel n toalha f de banho.
bathtub ['bɑ:θtʌb] n banheira f.
baton ['bætən] n **-1.** [of conductor] batuta f **-2.** [in relay race] bastão m **-3.** UK [of po-liceman] cassetete m.
batsman ['bætsmən] (pl -men [-mən]) n CRICKET batedor m.
battalion [bə'tæljən] n batalhão m.
batten ['bætn] n [piece of wood] tábua f.
batter ['bætə'] ⬦ n **-1.** CULIN massa f (mole) **-2.** SPORT batedor m, -ra f ⬦ vt [child, woman] surrar. ⬦ vi [beat] bater.
battered ['bætəd] adj **-1.** [child, woman] maltratado(da) **-2.** [old, worn-out - car] arruinado(da); [- hat] surrado(da) **-3.** CULIN misturado(da).
battery ['bætərɪ] (pl -ies) n **-1.** [gen] bateria f **-2.** [ELEC - of car] bateria f; [- of radio, torch etc.] pilha f **-3.** [group - of peo-ple] grupo m; [- of things] série f, conjunto m.
battle ['bætl] ⬦ n batalha f; **~ for/against/with sthg** batalha f por/contra/com algo. ⬦ vi [fight] lutar; **to ~ for/against/with sthg** lutar por/contra/com algo.
battlefield ['bætlfi:ld], **battleground** ['bætlgraund] n MIL & fig campo m de batalha.
battlements ['bætlmənts] npl [of castle] ameias fpl.
battleship ['bætlʃɪp] n couraçado m.
bauble ['bɔ:bl] n bugiganga f.
baulk [bɔ:k] vi = **balk**.
bawdy ['bɔ:dɪ] (compar -ier, superl -iest) adj obsceno(na).
bawl [bɔ:l] ⬦ vt [shout] gritar. ⬦ vi **-1.** [shout] gritar **-2.** [weep] berrar.
bay [beɪ] n **-1.** GEOGR baía f **-2.** [for loading] zona m de carga e descarga **-3.** [for parking] vaga f **-4.** phr: **to keep sb/sthg at ~** manter alguém/algo à distância.
bay leaf n folha f de louro.
Bay of Biscay n: **the ~** o Golfo de Biscaia.
bay window n bay window f, janela f saliente.

bazaar [bəˈzɑː.ʳ] n -1. [market] bazar m -2. UK [charity sale] bazar m beneficente.

B & B n abbr of bed and breakfast.

BBC (abbr of British Broadcasting Corporation) n companhia estatal britânica de rádio e televisão, BBC f.

BC (abbr of before Christ) a.C.

be [biː] (pt was OR were, pp been) ◇ aux vb -1. (in combination with ppr: to form cont tense) estar; what is he doing? o que ele está fazendo?; it's snowing está nevando -2. (in combination with pp: to form passive) ser; to ~ loved ser amado(da) -3. (in question tags) ser, estar; the meal was delicious, wasn't it? a comida estava deliciosa, não estava? -4. (followed by to + infin) dever; I'm to ~ promoted devo ser promovido(da); you're not to tell anyone você não deve contar a ninguém. ◇ copulative vb -1. (with adj, n) ser, estar; to ~ a doctor/lawyer/plumber ser médico/advogado/bombeiro; she's intelligent/attractive ela é inteligente/atraente; ~ quiet! fique quieto!; 1 and 1 are 2 1 e 1 são 2 -2. [referring to health] estar; how are you? como vai você? -3. [referring to age] ter; how old are you? quantos anos você tem? -4. [cost] custar; how much was it? quanto custou?; that will ~ £10, please são £10, por favor. ◇ vi -1. [exist] existir, haver, ser; ~ that as it may seja como for -2. [referring to place] estar; Toulouse is in France Toulouse fica na França; he will ~ here tomorrow ele estará aqui amanhã -3. [referring to movement] estar; I've been to the cinema/to France/to the butcher's fui ao cinema/para a França/ao açougue. ◇ v impers -1. [referring to time, dates] ser; it's two o'clock são duas horas -2. [referring to distance] ser; it's 3 km to the next town são 3 quilômetros até a próxima cidade -3. [referring to the weather] estar; it's hot/cold/windy está quente/frio/ventando -4. [for emphasis] ser; it's me sou eu; it's the milkman é o leiteiro.

beach [biːtʃ] ◇ n praia f. ◇ vt [boat, whale] encalhar.

beacon [ˈbiːkən] n -1. [warning fire] fogaréu m -2. [lighthouse] farol m -3. [radio beacon] radiofarol m.

bead [biːd] n -1. [of wood, glass] conta f -2. [of sweat] gota f.

beagle [ˈbiːgl] n bigle m.

beak [biːk] n [of bird] bico m.

beaker [ˈbiːkəʳ] n copo m (de plástico).

beam [biːm] ◇ n -1. [of wood, concrete] viga f -2. [of light] raio m, feixe m -3. US

AUT: high/low ~s luz alta/baixa. ◇ vt [signal, news] transmitir. ◇ vi [smile] irradiar-se.

bean [biːn] n CULIN feijão m, grão m; to be full of ~s inf estar cheio (cheia) de vida; to spill the ~s inf dar com a língua nos dentes.

beanbag [ˈbiːnbæg] n [seat] almofada grande e redonda, feita de flocos de espuma que se adapta ao corpo de quem senta.

beanshoot [ˈbiːnʃuːt], **beansprout** [ˈbiːnspraʊt] n broto m de feijão.

bear [beəʳ] (pt bore, pp borne) ◇ n [animal] urso m, -sa f. ◇ vt -1. [carry] carregar -2. [sustain] suportar -3. [accept] aceitar -4. [show] exibir -5. [tolerate] suportar -6. [feeling] guardar. ◇ vi -1. [turn] virar -2. [have effect]: to bring pressure/influence to ~ on sb exercer pressão/influência sobre alguém.

➤ **bear down** vi: to ~ down on sb/sthg abater-se sobre algo/alguém.

➤ **bear out** vt sep confirmar.

➤ **bear up** vi resistir.

➤ **bear with** vt fus tolerar.

beard [bɪəd] n [of man] barba f.

bearer [ˈbeərəʳ] n -1. [of stretcher, coffin] carregador m, -ra f -2. [of news, document] portador m, -ra f -3. [of name, title] detentor m, -ra f.

bearing [ˈbeərɪŋ] n -1. [connection] relação f; ~ on sthg relação com algo -2. [deportment] conduta f -3. TECH mancal m -4. [on compass] direção f; to get/lose one's ~s fig achar/perder o rumo.

beast [biːst] n -1. [animal] besta m -2. inf pej [person] besta f.

beastly [ˈbiːstlɪ] (compar -ier, superl -iest) adj dated abominável.

beat [biːt] (pt beat, pp beaten) ◇ n -1. [gen] batida f -2. [of heart, pulse] batimento m -3. MUS [rhythm] ritmo m -4. [of policeman] ronda f. ◇ vt -1. [hit] bater em -2. [defeat] derrotar; it ~s me inf isto acaba comigo -3. [be better than] superar -4. [eggs, wings] bater -5. MUS [time] marcar -6. phr: ~ it! inf [go away] caia fora! ◇ vi -1. [rain] cair -2. [heart, pulse] bater.

➤ **beat off** vt sep [resist] repelir.

➤ **beat up** vt sep inf [person] espancar.

beating [ˈbiːtɪŋ] n [defeat, punishment] surra f.

beautiful [ˈbjuːtɪfʊl] adj -1. [gen] bonito(ta) -2. [well executed] belo(la).

beautifully [ˈbjuːtəflɪ] adv -1. [attractively] belamente -2. inf [very well] esplendidamente.

beauty ['bju:tɪ] (pl -ies) n -1. (U) [attractiveness] beleza f -2. [beautiful woman] beldade f.

beauty parlour n salão m de beleza.

beauty salon n = beauty parlour.

beauty spot n -1. [place] recanto m -2. [on skin] sinal m.

beaver ['bi:vəʳ] n castor m.

became [bɪ'keɪm] pt ▷ become.

because [bɪ'kɒz] conj porque.
▸ **because of** prep por causa de.

beck [bek] n: to be at sb's ~ and call estar sempre à disposição de alguém.

beckon ['bekən] ◇ vt [make a signal to] acenar. ◇ vi [signal]: to ~ to sb acenar para alguém.

become [bɪ'kʌm] (pt became, pp become) vt -1. [grow] ficar. -2. [acquire post of] tornar-se -3. [suit, be appropriate to] combinar com, ficar bem em.

becoming [bɪ'kʌmɪŋ] adj -1. [attractive] elegante -2. [appropriate] adequado(da).

bed [bed] (pt & pp -ded, cont -ding) n -1. [to sleep on] cama f; to go to ~ ir para a cama; to go to ~ with sb euphemism ir para a cama com alguém -2. [flowerbed] canteiro m -3. [bottom - of sea] fundo m; [- of river] leito m.

bed and breakfast n -1. [service] hospedagem f com café da manhã -2. [hotel] bed and breakfast m, acomodação típica da Grã-Bretanha (geralmente em casa de família) acompanhada de café-da-manhã.

bedclothes ['bedkləʊðz] npl roupa f de cama.

bedlam ['bedləm] n [chaos] tumulto m.

bed linen n roupa f de cama.

bedraggled [bɪ'drægld] adj enlameado(da).

bedridden ['bed,rɪdn] adj acamado(da).

bedroom ['bedrum] n quarto m.

bedside ['bedsaɪd] n beira f da cama.

bedside table n mesa-de-cabeceira f, criado-mudo m.

bed-sit(ter) n UK conjugado m.

bedsore ['bedsɔːʳ] n assadura f.

bedspread ['bedspred] n colcha f.

bedtime ['bedtaɪm] n hora f de dormir.

bee [bi:] n abelha f.

beech [bi:tʃ] n faia f.

beef [bi:f] ◇ n (U) [meat] carne f de vaca. ◇ vi inf [complain]: to ~ about sthg reclamar de algo.

beefburger ['bi:f,bɜ:gəʳ] n hambúrguer m bovino.

Beefeater ['bi:f,i:təʳ] n guarda da Torre de Londres.

beefsteak ['bi:f,steɪk] n bife m.

beehive ['bi:haɪv] n [for bees] colméia f.

beeline ['bi:laɪn] n: to make a ~ for sb/sthg inf ir direto a alguém/algo.

been [bi:n] pp ▷ be.

beeper ['bi:pəʳ] n [device] bipe m.

beer [bɪəʳ] n cerveja f.

beer garden n terraço de um bar em que geralmente se admite a presença de crianças.

beer mat n bolacha f.

beet [bi:t] n -1. [sugar beet] acelga f -2. US [beetroot] beterraba f.

beetle ['bi:tl] n besouro m.

beetroot ['bi:tru:t] n beterraba f.

before [bɪ'fɔːʳ] ◇ adv [previously] antes. ◇ prep -1. [preceding in time] antes de -2. [in front of]: the road stretched out ~ them a estrada se abria diante OR à frente deles; ~ my very eyes diante de meus próprios olhos; standing ~ the door parado(da) em frente à porta. ◇ conj: ~ leaving the country antes de deixar o país; ~ he entered the house antes de entrar na casa.

beforehand [bɪ'fɔːhænd] adv [in advance] de antemão.

befriend [bɪ'frend] vt -1. [make friends with] fazer amizade com -2. [support] favorecer.

beg [beg] (pt & pp -ged, cont -ging) ◇ vt -1. [money, food] mendigar, pedir -2. [favour, forgiveness, mercy] pedir; I ~ your pardon desculpe-me; to ~ sb to do sthg pedir algo a alguém; to ~ sb to do sthg pedir a alguém para fazer algo. ◇ vi -1. [for money, food] mendigar, pedir; to ~ for sthg mendigar OR pedir algo -2. [for favour, forgiveness, mercy] pedir; to ~ for sthg pedir algo.

began [bɪ'gæn] pt ▷ begin.

beggar ['begəʳ] n mendigo m, -ga f.

begin [bɪ'gɪn] (pt began, pp begun, cont -ning) ◇ vt -1. [start] começar; to ~ doing OR to do sthg começar a fazer algo -2. [initiate] começar. ◇ vi [start] começar; to ~ with, ... para começar, ...

beginner [bɪ'gɪnəʳ] n [learner] principiante mf, aprendiz mf.

beginning [bɪ'gɪnɪŋ] n -1. [start] começo m -2. [origin] início m, origem f.

begrudge [bɪ'grʌdʒ] vt -1. [envy]: to ~ sb sthg invejar algo de alguém -2. [give, do unwillingly]: to ~ doing sthg fazer algo de má vontade.

begun [bɪ'gʌn] pp ▷ begin.

behalf [bɪ'hɑːf] n: on ~ of sb UK, in ~ of sb US em nome de alguém.

behave [bɪ'heɪv] ◇ v refl: to ~ o.s. comportar-se bem. ◇ vi -1. [in a particular way] comportar-se -2. [in an acceptable way] comportar-se bem.

benefit

behaviour *UK*, **behavior** *US* [bɪˈheɪvjəʳ] *n* comportamento *m*.

behead [bɪˈhed] *vt* degolar.

beheld [bɪˈheld] *pt & pp* ⊳ **behold**.

behind [bɪˈhaɪnd] ◇ *prep* **-1.** [at the back of] atrás de **-2.** [causing, responsible for] por trás de **-3.** [supporting]: **to be ~ sb** apoiar alguém, estar com alguém **-4.** [indicating deficiency, delay] atrás de; **to run ~ schedule** estar atrasado(-da). ◇ *adv* **-1.** [at, in the back] atrás **-2.** [late] para trás; **~ with sthg** com atraso em algo. ◇ *n inf* [buttocks] traseiro *m*.

behold [bɪˈhəʊld] (*pt & pp* **beheld**) *vt literary* contemplar.

beige [beɪʒ] ◇ *adj* bege. ◇ *n* bege *m*.

being [ˈbiːɪŋ] *n* **-1.** [creature] ser *m* **-2.** (*U*) [state of existing]: **in ~** em vigor; **to come into ~** nascer; **for the time ~** por enquanto.

Beirut [ˌbeɪˈruːt] *n* Beirute.

belated [bɪˈleɪtɪd] *adj* tardio(dia).

belch [beltʃ] ◇ *n* arroto *m*. ◇ *vt* [smoke, fire] expelir. ◇ *vi* [person] arrotar.

beleaguered [bɪˈliːgəd] *adj* **-1.** [MIL - city] sitiado(da); [- troops] cercado(da) **-2.** *fig* [harassed] assediado(da).

Belgian [ˈbeldʒən] ◇ *adj* belga. ◇ *n* belga *mf*.

Belgium [ˈbeldʒəm] *n* Bélgica; **in ~** na Bélgica.

Belgrade [ˌbelˈgreɪd] *n* Belgrado; **in ~** em Belgrado.

belie [bɪˈlaɪ] (*cont* **belying**) *vt* **-1.** [disprove] desmentir **-2.** [give false idea of] esconder, disfarçar.

belief [bɪˈliːf] *n* **-1.** (*U*) crença *f*; **~ in sthg** crença em algo **-2.** [opinion] opinião *f*.

believe [bɪˈliːv] ◇ *vt* **-1.** [think] achar; **I ~ so** acho que sim **-2.** [person, statement] acreditar em; **~ it or not** acredite ou não. ◇ *vi* **-1.** [be religious] crer em **-2.** [know to exist]: **to ~ in sb/sthg** acreditar em alguém/algo.

believer [bɪˈliːvəʳ] *n* **-1.** *RELIG* crente *mf* **-2.** [supporter]: **~ in sthg** partidário(ria) de algo.

belittle [bɪˈlɪtl] *vt* [disparage] depreciar.

bell [bel] *n* **-1.** [of church] sino *m* **-2.** [on door, bicycle] campainha *f*.

belligerent [bɪˈlɪdʒərənt] *adj* **-1.** [at war] beligerante **-2.** [aggressive] agressivo(-va).

bellow [ˈbeləʊ] *vi* **-1.** [person] gritar **-2.** [bull] mugir.

bellows [ˈbeləʊz] *npl* fole *m*.

belly [ˈbelɪ] (*pl* -ies) *n* barriga *f*.

bellyache [ˈbelɪeɪk] *n* [stomachache] dor *f* de estômago.

belly button *n inf* [navel] umbigo *m*.

belong [bɪˈlɒŋ] *vi* **-1.** [be property]: **to ~ to sb** pertencer a alguém **-2.** [be a member]: **to ~ to sthg** fazer parte *OR* ser membro de algo **-3.** [be situated in right place] encaixar-se.

belongings [bɪˈlɒŋɪŋz] *npl* pertences *mpl*.

beloved [bɪˈlʌvd] *adj* amado(da), querido(da).

below [bɪˈləʊ] ◇ *adv* **-1.** [in a lower position] de baixo **-2.** [in text or with numbers, quantities] abaixo **-3.** *NAUT*: **to go ~** descer. ◇ *prep* abaixo de.

belt [belt] ◇ *n* **-1.** [for clothing] cinto *m* **-2.** *TECH* correia *f*. ◇ *vt* **-1.** *inf* [hit with a belt] dar uma surra de cinto em **-2.** *inf* [punch, beat] meter o couro em.

beltway [ˈbeltˌweɪ] *n US* anel *m* viário, rodoanel *m*.

bemused [bɪˈmjuːzd] *adj* bestificado(-da).

bench [bentʃ] *n* **-1.** [seat] banco *m* **-2.** [in laboratory, workshop] bancada *f* **-3.** *UK JUR* magistratura *f*.

benchmark [ˈbentʃmɑːk] *n* **-1.** [standard] referência *f* **-2.** *COMPUT* padrão *m* de desempenho **-3.** *ECON* benchmark *m*, indicador *m*.

bend [bend] (*pt & pp* **bent**) ◇ *n* **-1.** curva *f* **-2.** *phr*: **round the ~** *inf* pirado(-da), maluco(ca); **to drive sb round the ~** deixar alguém maluco(ca). ◇ *vt* dobrar. ◇ *vi* **-1.** [arm, leg] dobrar-se; [tree, person] inclinar-se **-2.** [river, road] fazer uma curva.

➨ **bend down** *vi* curvar-se.

➨ **bend over** *vi* inclinar-se; **to ~ over backwards for sb** *fig* fazer todo o possível por alguém.

beneath [bɪˈniːθ] ◇ *adv* [below] debaixo. ◇ *prep* **-1.** [under] debaixo de, sob **-2.** [unworthy of]: **he felt the job was ~ him** ele sentia que o emprego estava aquém dele; **to be ~ sthg** não ser digno(na) de algo.

benefactor [ˈbenɪfæktəʳ] *n* benfeitor *m*.

beneficial [ˌbenɪˈfɪʃl] *adj* benéfico(ca); **~ to sb/sthg** benéfico(ca) para alguém/algo.

beneficiary [ˌbenɪˈfɪʃərɪ] (*pl* -ies) *n JUR* beneficiário *m*, -ria *f*.

benefit [ˈbenɪfɪt] ◇ *n* **-1.** [advantage] benefício *m*; **to be to sb's ~**, **to be of ~ to sb** ser benéfico(ca) para alguém; **for the ~ of** em benefício *OR* prol de **-2.** [good point] vantagem *f* **-3.** *ADMIN* [allowance of money] auxílio *m*. ◇ *vt* beneficiar. ◇ *vi*: **to ~ from sthg** beneficiar-se de algo.

Benelux [ˈbenɪlʌks] n Benelux.

benevolent [bɪˈnevələnt] adj [kind, generous] benevolente.

benign [bɪˈnaɪn] adj -1. [gen] benévolo(-la) -2. [influence, conditions] agradável, propício(cia) -3. MED benigno(na).

bent [bent] ⬧ pt & pp ⊳ **bend.** ⬧ adj -1. [wire, bar] torto(ta) -2. [person, body] curvado(da) -3. UK inf [dishonest] corrupto(ta) -4. [determined]: **to be ~ on sthg/on doing sthg** ter inclinação para algo/fazer algo. ⬧ n [natural aptitude] inclinação f; **to have a ~ for sthg** ter uma inclinação para algo.

bequeath [bɪˈkwiːð] vt -1. [money, property] deixar -2. fig [idea, system] passar.

bequest [bɪˈkwest] n [in will] herança f.

berate [bɪˈreɪt] vt [rebuke] repreender.

bereaved [bɪˈriːvd] (pl inv) ⬧ adj enlutado(da). ⬧ npl: **the ~** os enlutados.

beret [ˈbereɪ] n boina f.

berk [bɜːk] n UK inf palhaço m, -ça f.

Berlin [bɜːˈlɪn] n Berlim; **in ~** em Berlim.

berm [bɜːm] n US berma f.

Bermuda [bəˈmjuːdə] n (Ilhas) Bermudas fpl.

Bern [bɜːn] n Berna; **in ~** em Berna.

berry [ˈberɪ] (pl -ies) n baga f.

berserk [bəˈzɜːk] adj: **to go ~** ficar furioso(sa).

berth [bɜːθ] ⬧ n -1. [in harbour] ancoradouro m -2. [in ship, train] beliche m. ⬧ vi [ship] ancorar, atracar.

beseech [bɪˈsiːtʃ] (pt & pp besought OR beseeched) vt literary [implore] suplicar; **to ~ sb to do sthg** suplicar a alguém para que faça algo.

beset [bɪˈset] (pt & pp beset, cont -ting) ⬧ adj: **~ with OR by sthg** cercado(da) de algo. ⬧ vt envolver.

beside [bɪˈsaɪd] prep -1. [next to] ao lado de -2. [compared with] comparado(da) com -3. phr: **to be ~ o.s. with sthg** estar louco(ca) de algo.

besides [bɪˈsaɪdz] ⬧ adv além disso. ⬧ prep [in addition to] além de.

besiege [bɪˈsiːdʒ] vt -1. [town, fortress] sitiar -2. fig: **to be ~d** with calls/complaints ser bombardeado(da) com ligações/reclamações.

besotted [bɪˈsɒtɪd] adj: **~ (with sb)** obcecado(da) (por alguém).

besought [bɪˈsɔːt] pt & pp ⊳ **beseech.**

best [best] ⬧ adj [in quality] melhor. ⬧ adv -1. [better than all the others] melhor; **whoever does ~ in the exam** quem se sair melhor no exame -2. [more than all the others] mais; **which one did you like**

~? de qual deles você gostou mais? ⬧ n -1. [highest standard possible] melhor m; **to do one's ~** fazer o melhor possível; **he is the ~ of friends** ele é o melhor amigo do mundo -2. [utmost] máximo m; **she tried her ~** ela fez o tudo o que podia -3. [most outstanding person, thing etc.] melhor mf -4. phr: **to make the ~ of sthg** tirar o máximo de proveito de algo; **to be for the ~** ser melhor; **all the ~!** um abraço!
➡ **at best** adv na melhor das hipóteses.

best man n padrinho m de casamento.

bestow [bɪˈstəʊ] vt fml: **to ~ sthg on sb** outorgar OR conceder algo a alguém.

best-seller n -1. [article sold] mais vendido m, -da f -2. [book] best-seller m.

bet [bet] (pt & pp bet OR -ted, cont -ting) ⬧ n -1. [wager] aposta f -2. fig [prediction] aposta f; **it's a safe ~ that ...** é certo que ...; **your best ~ is to ...** o melhor a se fazer é ... ⬧ vt apostar. ⬧ vi apostar; **to ~ on sthg** apostar em algo; **you ~!** inf pode apostar!, com certeza!

betray [bɪˈtreɪ] vt -1. [person, principles] trair -2. [secret, emotion] revelar.

betrayal [bɪˈtreɪəl] n [of person, principles] traição f.

better [ˈbetə^r] ⬧ adj melhor; **to get ~** melhorar; **to get ~ and ~** ficar cada vez melhor. ⬧ adv -1. [gen] melhor -2. [when giving advice, stating intention]: **you'd ~ phone her** é melhor você ligar para ela; **I'd ~ go now** é melhor eu ir embora. ⬧ n -1. [best one] melhor mf; **to get the ~ of sb** apoderar-se OR tomar conta de alguém; **her emotions got the ~ of her** suas emoções tomaram conta dela. ⬧ vt [improve] melhorar; **to ~ o.s.** melhorar de vida, aprimorar-se.

better off adj -1. [financially] melhor de vida -2. [in a better situation] melhor; **you're ~ taking a taxi** será melhor você pegar um táxi.

betting [ˈbetɪŋ] n -1. [bets] apostar m -2. [odds] chance f.

betting shop n UK casa f de apostas.

between [bɪˈtwiːn] ⬧ prep entre. ⬧ adv: **(in ~)** entre.

beverage [ˈbevərɪdʒ] n fml [drink] bebida f.

beware [bɪˈweə^r] vi tomar cuidado, ter cautela; **to ~ of sthg** tomar cuidado com algo.

bewildered [bɪˈwɪldəd] adj [confused] confuso(sa), desnorteado(da).

bewitching [bɪˈwɪtʃɪŋ] adj encantador(-ra).

beyond [bɪˈjɒnd] ⬧ prep -1. além de;

it is ~ my responsibility vai além de minha responsabilidade - **2.** [outside the range of] fora de; **it is ~ my control** está fora de meu controle; **the town has changed ~ all recognition** a cidade ficou irreconhecível. ⬦ *adv* - **1.** [in space] mais além, mais adiante - **2.** [in time] mais além, mais um pouco.

bias ['baɪəs] *n* - **1.** [prejudice] preconceito *m* - **2.** [tendency] propensão *f*, tendência *f*.

biased ['baɪəst] *adj* - **1.** [prejudiced] preconceituoso(sa); **to be ~ against sthg/sb** ser preconceituoso(sa) em relação a algo/alguém - **2.** [tendentious] tendencioso(sa); **to be ~ towards sthg** ser tendencioso(sa) em relação a algo; **to be ~ towards sb** pender para o lado de alguém.

bib [bɪb] *n* [for baby] babador *m*.

Bible ['baɪbl] *n*: **the ~** a Bíblia.

bicarbonate of soda [baɪ'kɑ:bənət-] *n* bicarbonato *m* de sódio.

biceps ['baɪseps] (*pl inv*) *n* bíceps *m*.

bicker ['bɪkə'] *vi* [quarrel] brigar.

bicycle ['baɪsɪkl] ⬦ *n* bicicleta *f*. ⬦ *vi* andar de bicicleta.

bicycle path *n* ciclovia *f*.

bicycle pump *n* bomba *f* de ar *(para bicicleta)*.

bid [bɪd] (*pt & pp* bid, *cont* bidding) ⬦ *n* - **1.** [attempt] tentativa *f*, intento *m*; **a ~ for power** uma busca pelo poder - **2.** [at auction] licitação *f* - **3.** COMM proposta *f*. ⬦ *vt* - **1.** [at auction] licitar. ⬦ *vi* - **1.** [at auction]: **to ~ (for sthg)** abrir licitação (para algo) - **2.** [attempt]: **to ~ for sthg** tentar algo.

bidder ['bɪdə'] *n* [at auction] licitante *mf*.

bidding ['bɪdɪŋ] *n* [at auction] licitação *f*.

bide [baɪd] *vt*: **to ~ one's time** esperar a vez.

bifocals [baɪ'fəʊklz] *npl* lentes *fpl* bifocais.

big [bɪg] (*compar* -ger, *superl* -gest) *adj* - **1.** [gen] grande - **2.** [older] mais velho-(lha) - **3.** [successful] importante.

bigamy ['bɪgəmɪ] *n* (U) bigamia *f*.

big deal *inf* ⬦ *n* grande coisa *f*; **it's no ~** não é nada de mais; **what's the ~?** e daí? ⬦ *excl* grande coisa!

Big Dipper [-'dɪpə'] *n* - **1.** UK [rollercoaster] montanha-russa *f* - **2.** US ASTRON: **the ~** a Ursa Maior.

big-headed *adj inf* metido(da).

bigot ['bɪgət] *n* fanático *m*, -ca *f*.

bigoted ['bɪgətɪd] *adj* fanático(ca).

bigotry ['bɪgətrɪ] *n* (U) fanatismo *m*.

big time *n inf*: **the ~** o auge.

big toe *n* dedão *m* do pé.

big top *n* (lona do) circo *m*.

big wheel *n* UK [at fairground] roda-gigante *f*.

bike [baɪk] *n inf* - **1.** [cycle] bike *f*, bicicleta *f* - **2.** [motorcycle] moto *f*.

bikeway ['baɪkweɪ] *n* US ciclovia *f*.

bikini [bɪ'ki:nɪ] *n* biquíni *m*.

bile [baɪl] *n* - **1.** [fluid] bílis *f* - **2.** [anger] irritação *f*.

bilingual [baɪ'lɪŋgwəl] *adj* bilíngüe.

bill [bɪl] ⬦ *n* - **1.** [statement of cost] conta *f*; **~ for sthg** conta de algo - **2.** [in parliament] projeto *m* de lei - **3.** [of show, concert] programa *m* - **4.** US [bank note] nota *f* - **5.** [poster]: **'post OR stick no ~s'** 'proibido colar cartazes' - **6.** [beak] bico *m*. ⬦ *vt* [send a bill to]: **to ~ sb (for sthg)** cobrar (algo) de alguém.

billboard ['bɪlbɔ:d] *n* quadro *m* de anúncios.

billet ['bɪlɪt] *n* boleto *m*, alojamento *m*.

billfold ['bɪlfəʊld] *n* US carteira *f*.

billiards ['bɪljədz] *n* (U) bilhar *m*.

billion ['bɪljən] *num* - **1.** [thousand million] bilhão *m* - **2.** UK dated [million million] trilhão *m*.

Bill of Rights *n*: **the ~** *as dez primeiras emendas da Constituição norte-americana.*

bimbo ['bɪmbəʊ] (*pl* -s OR -es) *n inf pej* ≈ burra *f* gostosa.

bin [bɪn] (*pt & pp* -ned, *cont* -ning) *n* - **1.** UK [for rubbish] lixeira *f* - **2.** [for storage] lata *f*.

bind [baɪnd] (*pt & pp* bound) *vt* - **1.** [tie up] amarrar - **2.** [unite] ligar - **3.** [bandage] atar - **4.** [book] encadernar - **5.** [constrain] comprometer.

binder ['baɪndə'] *n* [cover] encadernação *f*.

binding ['baɪndɪŋ] ⬦ *adj* comprometedor(ra), obrigatório(ria). ⬦ *n* [of book - process] encadernação *f*; [- cover] capa *f*.

binge [bɪndʒ] *inf* ⬦ *n*: **to go on a ~** ir à farra. ⬦ *vi*: **to ~ on sthg** empanturrar-se de algo.

bingo ['bɪŋgəʊ] *n* bingo *m*.

binoculars [bɪ'nɒkjʊləz] *npl* binóculo *m*.

biochemistry [baɪəʊ'kemɪstrɪ] *n* (U) bioquímica *f*.

biodegradable [baɪəʊdɪ'greɪdəbl] *adj* biodegradável.

biodiversity [baɪəʊdaɪ'vɜ:sətɪ] *n* biodiversidade *f*.

bioethics [baɪəʊ'eθɪks] *n* (U) bioética *f*.

biography [baɪ'ɒgrəfɪ] (*pl* -ies) *n* biografia *f*.

biofuel ['baɪəfjʊəl] *n* biocombustível *m*.

biological [baɪə'lɒdʒɪkl] *adj* biológico(ca);

~ washing powder sabão em pó com enzimas.

biology [baɪˈɒlədʒɪ] n (U) biologia f.

biomass [ˈbaɪəʊˈmæs] n biomassa f.

biosphere [ˈbaɪəʊ͵sfɪəᵊ] n biosfera f.

biotech company [ˈbaɪəʊtek-] n empresa f de biotecnologia.

bioterrorism [͵baɪəʊˈterərɪzm] n bioterrorismo m.

birch [bɜːtʃ] n [tree] bétula f.

bird [bɜːd] n -1. [creature] pássaro m, ave f -2. inf [woman] perua f.

birdie [ˈbɜːdɪ] n -1. [bird] passarinho m -2. [in golf] birdie m.

bird's-eye view n vista f panorâmica.

biro® [ˈbaɪərəʊ] n caneta f esferográfica.

birth [bɜːθ] n nascimento m; **to give ~ (to)** dar à luz (a); fig [of idea, system, country] dar origem(a).

birth certificate n certidão f de nascimento.

birth control n (U) controle m de natalidade.

birthday [ˈbɜːθdeɪ] n aniversário m.

birthmark [ˈbɜːθmɑːk] n sinal m de nascença.

birthrate [ˈbɜːθreɪt] n taxa f de natalidade.

Biscay [ˈbɪskɪ] n: **the Bay of ~** a Baía de Biscaia.

biscuit [ˈbɪskɪt] n -1. UK [crisp] biscoito m, bolacha f -2. US [bread-like cake] bolacha f.

bisect [baɪˈsekt] vt -1. GEOM cortar ao meio -2. [cut in two] dividir em duas partes.

bishop [ˈbɪʃəp] n bispo m.

bison [ˈbaɪsn] (pl inv OR -s) n búfalo f.

bit [bɪt] <> pt <> bite. <> n -1. [small piece] pedaço m; **~s and pieces** UK inf bugigangas; **to ~s** aos pedaços -2. [unspecified amount]: **a ~ of** um pouco de; **quite a ~ of** um bocado de -3. [short time]: **for a ~** por um instante/momento -4. [of drill] broca f -5. [of bridle] freio m -6. COMPUT bit m.

➡ **a bit** adv um pouco.

➡ **bit by bit** adv pouco a pouco.

bitch [bɪtʃ] n -1. [female dog] cadela f -2. v inf pej [unpleasant woman] vaca f.

bitchy [ˈbɪtʃɪ] (compar -ier, superl -iest) adj inf malicioso(sa).

bite [baɪt] (pt bit, pp bitten) <> n -1. [act of biting] mordida f, dentada f -2. inf [food]: **a ~ (to eat)** algo (para beliscar) -3. [wound] picada f. <> vt -1. [subj: person, animal] morder; **to ~ one's nails** roer as unhas -2. [subj: insect, snake] picar. <> vi -1. [animal, person]

morder; **to ~ into sthg** morder algo; **to ~ off sthg** abocanhar algo -2. [insect, snake] picar -3. [tyres, clutch] furar -4. fig [sanction, law] morder.

biting [ˈbaɪtɪŋ] adj -1. [very cold] cortante -2. [caustic] mordaz.

bitten [ˈbɪtn] pp ▷ **bite**.

bitter [ˈbɪtəᵊ] <> adj -1. [gen] amargo(ga) -2. [acrimonious] pungente -3. [resentful] amargurado(da) -4. [icy] gelado(da). <> n UK [beer] cerveja f amarga.

bitter lemon n batida f de limão.

bitterness [ˈbɪtənɪs] n (U) -1. [gen] amargor m -2. [of wind, weather] rigor m.

bizarre [bɪˈzɑːᵊ] adj bizarro(ra), estranho(nha).

blab [blæb] (pt & pp -bed, cont -bing) vi inf fazer fofoca.

black [blæk] <> adj -1. [in colour] preto(ta) -2. [person, skin] negro(gra) -3. [without milk] puro(ra), preto(ta) -4. [grim] sombrio(a); **~ humour** humor negro. <> n -1. (U) [colour] preto m; **in ~ and white** [in writing] o preto no branco, por escrito; **in the ~** [solvent] sem dívidas -2. [person] negro m, -gra f. <> vt UK [boycott] boicotar.

➡ **black out** vi [faint] desmaiar.

blackberry [ˈblækbərɪ] (pl -ies) n amora f.

blackbird [ˈblækbɜːd] n melro m.

blackboard [ˈblækbɔːd] n quadro-negro m, lousa f.

blackcurrant [͵blækˈkʌrənt] n groselha-preta f.

blacken [ˈblækn] <> vt pretejar. <> vi [sky] escurecer.

black eye n olho m roxo.

Black Forest n: **the ~** a Floresta Negra.

blackhead [ˈblækhed] n cravo m.

black ice n (U) camada fina e transparente de gelo sobre as ruas que dificulta a passagem de carros.

blackleg [ˈblækleg] n pej fura-greve mf.

blacklist [ˈblæklɪst] <> n lista f negra. <> vt incluir na lista negra.

blackmail [ˈblækmeɪl] <> n lit & fig chantagem f. <> vt chantagear.

black market n mercado m negro.

blackout [ˈblækaʊt] n -1. [in wartime] blecaute m -2. [power cut] blecaute m, apagão m -3. [suppression of news] censura f -4. [fainting fit] desmaio m.

black pudding n UK morcela f preta.

Black Sea n: **the ~** o Mar Negro.

black sheep n fig ovelha f negra.

blacksmith [ˈblæksmɪθ] n ferreiro m.

bladder [ˈblædəᵊ] n ANAT bexiga f.

blade [bleɪd] *n* **-1.** [of knife, saw] lâmina *f* **-2.** [of propeller] pá *f* **-3.** [of grass] folha *f.*

blame [bleɪm] ⬦ *n (U)* [responsibility] culpa *f*; **to take the ~ for sthg** assumir a culpa por algo. ⬦ *vt* culpar; **to ~ sthg on sb/sthg, to ~ sb/sthg for sthg** culpar alguém/algo de alguma coisa; **to be to ~ for sthg** ser culpado(da por algo).

bland [blænd] *adj* **-1.** [person] agradável, meigo(ga) **-2.** [food] insosso(sa) **-3.** [music, style] suave.

blank [blæŋk] ⬦ *adj* **-1.** em branco **-2.** *fig* [look] vazio(a). ⬦ *n* **-1.** [empty space] espaço *m* em branco **-2.** MIL [cartridge] cartucho *m.*

blank cheque *n* **-1.** cheque *m* em branco **-2.** *fig* [free hand] carta *f* branca.

blanket [blæŋkɪt] *n* **-1.** [bed cover] cobertor *m*, colcha *f* **-2.** [layer] camada *f.*

blare [bleəʳ] *vi* soar.

blasphemy [blæsfəmɪ] (*pl* **-ies**) *n* blasfêmia *f.*

blast [blɑːst] ⬦ *n* **-1.** [of bomb] explosão *f* **-2.** [of air] corrente *f* **-3.** *US inf* [celebration] farra *f.* ⬦ *vt* [hole, tunnel] dinamitar. ⬦ *excl UK inf* diabos!

➤ **(at) full blast** *adv* **-1.** [maximum volume] a todo volume **-2.** [maximum effort, speed] a todo vapor.

blasted [blɑːstɪd] *adj inf* [for emphasis] maldito(ta).

blast-off *n (U)* SPACE decolagem *f.*

blatant [bleɪtənt] *adj* [shameless] descarado(da).

blaze [bleɪz] ⬦ *n* **-1.** [fire] incêndio *m* **-2.** *fig* [of colour, light] explosão *f.* ⬦ *vi* **-1.** [fire] arder **-2.** *fig* [with colour, emotion] resplandecer.

blazer [bleɪzəʳ] *n* [jacket] blazer *m.*

bleach [bliːtʃ] ⬦ *n* [chemical] alvejante *m.* ⬦ *vt* **-1.** [hair] clarear **-2.** [clothes] alvejar. ⬦ *vi* desbotar.

bleached [bliːtʃt] *adj* **-1.** [hair] descolorido(da), clareado(da) **-2.** [jeans] desbotado(da).

bleachers [bliːtʃəz] *npl US* SPORT arquibancadas *fpl.*

bleak [bliːk] *adj* **-1.** [future] sombrio(a) **-2.** [place] escuro(ra) **-3.** [weather] gélido(da) **-4.** [face, person] triste.

bleary-eyed [ˌblɪərɪˈaɪd] *adj* com os olhos turvos.

bleat [bliːt] ⬦ *n* [of sheep, goat] balido *m.* ⬦ *vi* **-1.** [sheep, goat] balir **-2.** *fig* [person - speak] tagarelar; [- complain] balbuciar.

bleed [bliːd] (*pt* & *pp* **bled**) ⬦ *vt* [drain] esvaziar. ⬦ *vi* sangrar.

bleeper [bliːpəʳ] *n* bipe *m.*

blemish [blemɪʃ] *n* **-1.** [flaw] mancha *f* **-2.** [pimple, scar] cicatriz *f* **-3.** *fig* [on name, reputation] mancha *f.*

blend [blend] ⬦ *n* mistura *f.* ⬦ *vt* [mix] misturar; **to ~ sthg with sthg** misturar algo com algo. ⬦ *vi* [colours, sounds] misturar-se; **to ~ with sthg** misturar com algo.

blender [blendəʳ] *n* [food mixer] liquidificador *m.*

bless [bles] (*pt* & *pp* **-ed** OR **blest**) *vt* RELIG & *fig* abençoar; **to be ~ed with sthg** ser abençoado(da) com algo; **~ you!** [after sneezing] saúde!; [thank you] obrigado(-da)!

blessing [blesɪŋ] *n* benção *f.*

blest [blest] *pt* & *pp* ⊳ **bless.**

blew [bluː] *pt* ⊳ **blow.**

blight [blaɪt] *vt* arruinar.

blimey [blaɪmɪ] *excl UK inf* minha nossa!, caramba!

blind [blaɪnd] ⬦ *adj* **-1.** [gen] cego(ga) **-2.** *fig* [unaware]: **~ to sthg** cego(ga) para algo. ⬦ *n* [for window] persiana *f.* ⬦ *npl*: **the ~** os cegos. ⬦ *vt* **-1.** cegar **-2.** *fig* [make unobservant] ofuscar; **to ~ sb to sthg** impedir alguém de ver algo.

blind alley *n* **-1.** [street] beco *m* **-2.** *fig* [dead end] beco *m* sem saída.

blind corner *n* curva *f* sem visibilidade.

blind date *n* encontro *m* às cegas.

blinders [blaɪndəz] *npl US* antolhos *mpl.*

blindfold [blaɪndfəʊld] ⬦ *adv* de olhos vendados. ⬦ *n* venda *f.* ⬦ *vt* vendar.

blindingly [blaɪndɪŋlɪ] *adv* [clearly]: **~ obvious** totalmente óbvio(via).

blindly [blaɪndlɪ] *adv* **-1.** [without seeing] às cegas **-2.** *fig* [without knowing] sem saber.

blindness [blaɪndnɪs] *n (U)* cegueira *f*; **~ to sthg** falta *f* de visão para algo.

blind spot *n* [when driving] ponto *m* cego.

blink [blɪŋk] ⬦ *n inf* [machine]: **on the ~** enguiçado(da). ⬦ *vt* [eyes] piscar. ⬦ *vi* **-1.** [person] piscar **-2.** [light] cintilar.

blinkered [blɪŋkəd] *adj fig* [view, attitude] bitolado(da).

blinkers [blɪŋkəz] *npl UK* [for horse] antolhos *mpl.*

bliss [blɪs] *n* êxtase *m*, bem-aventurança *f.*

blissful [blɪsfʊl] *adj* abençoado(da); **~ ignorance** santa ignorância.

blister [blɪstəʳ] ⬦ *n* [on skin] bolha *f.* ⬦ *vi* formar bolhas.

blithely [blaɪðlɪ] *adv* **-1.** [without a care]

despreocupadamente **-2.** [casually] tranqüilamente.

blitz [blɪts] n MIL bombardeio m aéreo.

blizzard ['blɪzəd] n nevasca f.

bloated ['bləʊtɪd] adj **-1.** [swollen] inchado(da) **-2.** [having eaten too much] empanturrado(da).

blob [blɒb] n **-1.** [drop] pingo m **-2.** [shapeless thing] borrão m, mancha f.

block [blɒk] <> n **-1.** [gen] bloco m **-2.** [of buildings] quadra f, quarteirão m **-3.** [obstruction] bloqueio m. <> vt **-1.** bloquear **-2.** [hinder] barrar.

blockade [blɒ'keɪd] <> n bloqueio m. <> vt bloquear.

blockage ['blɒkɪdʒ] n [obstruction] obstrução f.

blockbuster ['blɒkbʌstə'] n inf [book, film] estouro m.

block capitals npl maiúsculas fpl.

block letters npl maiúsculas fpl.

blog [blɒg] n COMPUT blog m.

bloke [bləʊk] n UK inf cara m.

blond [blɒnd] adj [hair, man] loiro(ra), claro(ra).

blonde [blɒnd] <> adj [hair, woman] loiro(ra), claro(ra). <> n [woman] loira f.

blood [blʌd] n sangue m; **in cold ~ a** sangue frio.

bloodbath ['blʌdbɑːθ] n banho m de sangue.

blood cell n glóbulo m sangüíneo.

blood donor n doador m, -ra f de sangue.

blood group n grupo m sangüíneo.

bloodhound ['blʌdhaʊnd] n cão m de Santo Humberto.

blood poisoning n septicemia f.

blood pressure n pressão f sangüínea OR arterial.

bloodshed ['blʌdʃed] n derramamento m de sangue.

bloodshot ['blʌdʃɒt] adj [eyes] injetado(da).

bloodstream ['blʌdstriːm] n corrente f sangüínea.

blood test n exame m de sangue.

bloodthirsty ['blʌdˌθɜːstɪ] adj sanguinário(ria).

blood transfusion n transfusão f de sangue.

bloody ['blʌdɪ] (compar **-ier**, superl **-iest**) <> adj **-1.** [war, conflict] sangrento(ta) **-2.** [face, hands] ensangüentado(da) **-3.** UK v inf [for emphasis]: that **~** ... essa droga de ...; **you ~ idiot!** seu imbecil! <> adv UK v inf: **~ good** bom pra caramba; **~ difficult** difícil para burro.

bloody-minded [-'maɪndɪd] adj UK inf do contra.

bloom [bluːm] <> n [flower] flor f. <> vi [plant, tree] florir.

blooming ['bluːmɪŋ] <> adj UK inf [for emphasis]: **~ heck!** esse inferno miserável! <> adv UK inf pra caramba.

blossom ['blɒsəm] <> n [of tree] flor f; **in ~** em flor. <> vi **-1.** [tree] florescer **-2.** fig [person] desabrochar.

blot [blɒt] (pt & pp **-ted**, cont **-ting**) <> n **-1.** [of ink etc.] borrão m **-2.** fig [- on character, reputation] mancha f; [- on landscape] estrago m. <> vt **-1.** [dry] secar **-2.** [stain with ink] borrar.

◆ **blot out** vt sep **-1.** [obscure] ocultar **-2.** [erase] apagar.

blotchy ['blɒtʃɪ] (compar **-ier**, superl **-iest**) adj manchado(da).

blotting paper ['blɒtɪŋ-] n papel m mata-borrão.

blouse [blaʊz] n blusa f.

blow [bləʊ] (pt blew, pp blown) <> vi **-1.** [wind] ventar **-2.** [through mouth] soprar **-3.** [fuse] estourar **-4.** [whistle] assoviar. <> vt **-1.** [subj: wind] soprar **-2.** [whistle, horn, trumpet] soar **-3.** [clear]: **to ~ one's nose** assoar o nariz. <> n **-1.** [hit] golpe m **-2.** [shock] choque m.

◆ **blow away** vi [in wind] voar longe, sair voando.

◆ **blow out** <> vt sep apagar. <> vi **-1.** [candle] apagar **-2.** [tyre] estourar.

◆ **blow over** vi **-1.** [storm] cessar **-2.** [argument] esquecer-se.

◆ **blow up** <> vt sep **-1.** [inflate] encher **-2.** [with bomb] explodir **-3.** [enlarge] ampliar. <> vi [explode] explodir.

blow-dry <> n secagem f. <> vt secar.

blowlamp UK ['bləʊlæmp], **blowtorch** ['bləʊtɔːtʃ] n maçarico m.

blown [bləʊn] pp ⊳ blow.

blowout ['bləʊaʊt] n [of tyre] furo m.

blowtorch n = blowlamp.

blubber ['blʌbə'] <> n [of whale] gordura f. <> vi pej [weep] choramingar.

bludgeon ['blʌdʒən] vt espancar; **to ~ sb into doing sthg** fig ameaçar alguém para que faça algo.

blue [bluː] <> adj **-1.** [in colour] azul **-2.** inf [sad] triste **-3.** [pornographic - film, movie] pornográfico(ca); [- joke] obsceno(na). <> n azul m; **out of the ~** inesperadamente.

◆ **blues** npl **the ~ s** MUS o blues; inf [sad feeling] a melancolia.

bluebell ['bluːbel] n campainha f (azul).

blueberry ['bluːbərɪ] (pl **-ies**) n mirtilo m.

bluebottle ['bluːˌbɒtl] n mosca-varejeira f.

blue channel n: the ~ acesso direto utilizado pelos membros da Comunidade Européia ao passar pelo controle de passaportes.

blue cheese n queijo m azul.

blue-collar adj operário(ria).

blue jeans npl US jeans m, calça f jeans.

blueprint ['blu:prınt] n -1. CONSTR planta f -2. fig [plan, programme] projeto m.

bluff [blʌf] <> adj [person, manner] expansivo(va). <> n -1. [deception] blefe m; **to call sb's** ~ pagar para ver (o que alguém está ameaçando fazer) -2. [cliff] penhasco m. <> vt: **to** ~ **one's way into/out of sthg** trapacear para entrar em/sair de algo. <> vi blefar.

blunder ['blʌndə^r] <> n gafe f. <> vi [make mistake] cometer um grande equívoco.

blunt [blʌnt] <> adj -1. [gen] obtuso(sa) -2. [pencil] sem ponta -3. [knife] cego(ga) -4. [forthright] direto(ta). <> vt -1. [knife] cegar -2. fig [enthusiam, interest etc.] murchar -3. [impact] amortecer.

blur [blɜ:^r] (pt & pp -red, cont -ring) <> n borrão m, névoa f. <> vt -1. [outline, photograph] desfocar -2. [distinction, memory, vision] embaçar -3. [confuse] obscurecer.

blurb [blɜ:b] n inf [on book] sinopse f.

blurt [blɜ:t] ◆ **blurt out** vt sep falar sem pensar.

blush [blʌʃ] <> n rubor m. <> vi corar.

blusher ['blʌʃə^r] n ruge m.

blustery ['blʌstərı] adj ventoso(sa).

BNP (abbr of **British National Party**) n partido britânico de extrema direita.

BO (abbr of **body odour**) n cê-cê m.

boar [bɔ:^r] n -1. [male pig] barrão m -2. [wild pig] javali m.

board [bɔ:d] <> n -1. [plank] tábua f -2. [for notices] quadro m (de avisos) -3. [for games] tabuleiro m -4. [blackboard] quadro-negro m -5. ADMIN direção f; ~ **of directors** conselho m de diretores; **examining** ~ banca f examinadora; ~ **of enquiry** comissão f de inquérito -6. UK [at hotel, guesthouse] pensão f; ~ **and lodging** casa e comida; **full** ~ pensão completa; **half** ~ meia pensão -7. phr: **above** ~ honesto(ta). <> vt [get onto] embarcar em.
◆ **across the board** <> adj generalizado(da). <> adv de forma generalizada.
◆ **on board** <> adj a bordo. <> adv a bordo; **to take sthg on** ~ aceitar algo.
◆ **board up** vt sep fechar com tábuas.

boarder ['bɔ:də^r] n -1. [lodger] pensionista mf -2. [at school] interno m, -na f.

boarding card ['bɔ:dıŋ-] n cartão m de embarque.

boarding house ['bɔ:dıŋ-] n hospedaria f.

boarding school ['bɔ:dıŋ-] n colégio m interno.

Board of Trade n UK: the ~ ≃ Câmara f do Comércio, na Inglaterra, comissão governamental responsável pela supervisão do comércio e pelo estímulo às exportações.

boardroom ['bɔ:drʊm] n sala f da diretoria.

boast [bəʊst] <> n alarde m. <> vi [show off] vangloriar-se; **to** ~ **about sthg** gabar-se de algo.

boastful ['bəʊstfʊl] adj presunçoso(sa).

boat [bəʊt] n [ship] barco m; [for rowing] bote m; [for sailing] veleiro m; **by** ~ de barco.

boater ['bəʊtə^r] n [hat] chapéu m de palha.

boatswain ['bəʊsn] n NAUT contramestre m.

bob [bɒb] (pt & pp -bed, cont -bing) <> n -1. [hairstyle] corte m chanel -2. UK inf dated [shilling] xelim m -3. = bobsleigh. <> vi [boat, ship] balouçar-se.

bobbin ['bɒbın] n [spool] bobina f.

bobby ['bɒbı] (pl -ies) n UK inf [policeman] tira m.

bobsleigh ['bɒbsleı] n trenó m de esporte.

bode [bəʊd] vi literary: **to** ~ **ill/well (for sb/sthg)** ser de mau/bom agouro (para alguém/algo).

bodily ['bɒdılı] <> adj [needs] físico(ca). <> adv [carry, lift] em peso.

body ['bɒdı] (pl -ies) n -1. [gen] corpo m -2. [corpse] cadáver m -3. [organization] entidade f -4. [of car] carroceria f -5. [of plane] fuselagem f -6. (U) [of wine] corpo m -7. [garment] body m.

body building n fisiculturismo m.

bodyguard ['bɒdıgɑ:d] n guarda-costas mf inv.

body odour UK, **body odor** US n odor m corporal.

body piercing [-'pıəsıŋ] n piercing m.

bodywork ['bɒdıwɜ:k] n [of car] carroçeria f.

bog [bɒg] n -1. [marsh] lodaçal m -2. UK v inf [toilet] privada f.

bogged down [,bɒgd-] adj atolado(-da).

boggle ['bɒgl] vi: **the mind** ~s! não dá para acreditar!

bog-standard adj inf comum.

bogus ['bəʊgəs] *adj* falso(sa).

boil [bɔɪl] ◇ *n* -1. MED [on skin] furúnculo *m* -2. [boiling point]: **to bring sthg to the ~** deixar algo ferver; **to come to the ~** começar a ferver. ◇ *vt* -1. [water, kettle] ferver -2. [food] cozinhar. ◇ *vi* [water, kettle] ferver.

➡ **boil down to** *vt fus fig* reduzir-se a.

➡ **boil over** *vi* -1. [liquid] derramar -2. *fig* [feelings] descontrolar-se.

boiled [bɔɪld] *adj* cozido(da); ~ **sweet** *UK* caramelo *m*; ~ **egg** ovo *m* cozido.

boiler ['bɔɪlə*r*] *n* boiler *m*.

boiler suit *n UK* macacão *m*.

boiling ['bɔɪlɪŋ] *adj* -1. [liquid] fervente -2. *inf* [hot - person] morto(ta) de calor; [- weather] abrasador(ra).

boiling point *n* ponto *m* de ebulição.

boisterous ['bɔɪstərəs] *adj* [child, behaviour] irrequieto(ta).

bold [bəʊld] *adj* -1. [confident] audacioso(sa) -2. [brave] corajoso(sa) -3. ART [lines, design] nítido(da) -4. [colour] nítido(da) -5. TYPO : **in ~ type** OR **print** em negrito.

bollard ['bɒlɑːd] *n* [on road] poste *m* de sinalização.

bollocks ['bɒləks] *UK vulg* ◇ *npl* saco *m*. ◇ *excl* saco!

bolster ['bəʊlstə*r*] ◇ *n* [pillow] travesseiro *m* longo. ◇ *vt* [encourage] alentar.

➡ **bolster up** *vt fus* [support] sustentar.

bolt [bəʊlt] ◇ *n* -1. [on door, window] ferrolho *m*, trinco *m* -2. [type of screw] parafuso *m*. ◇ *adv*: **to sit ~ upright** sentar direito. ◇ *vt* -1. [fasten together] aparafusar -2. [close] trancar -3. [food] devorar. ◇ *vi* [run] disparar.

bomb [bɒm] ◇ *n* [explosive device] bomba *f*. ◇ *vt* bombardear.

bombard [bɒm'bɑːd] *vt* MIL & *fig* bombardear; **to ~ sb with sthg** bombardear alguém com algo.

bombastic [bɒm'bæstɪk] *adj* bombástico(ca).

bomb disposal squad *n* esquadrão *m* antibombas.

bomber ['bɒmə*r*] *n* -1. [plane] bombardeiro *m* -2. [person] *pessoa que pratica atentados a bomba*.

bombing ['bɒmɪŋ] *n* bombardeio *m*.

bombshell ['bɒmʃel] *n fig* [unpleasant surprise] bomba *f*; **to come as a ~** cair como uma bomba.

bona fide ['bəʊnə'faɪdɪ] *adj* [genuine] legítimo(ma).

bond [bɒnd] ◇ *n* -1. [emotional link] laço *m* -2. [binding promise] compromisso *m* -3. FIN título *m*. ◇ *vt* -1. [glue]: **to**

~ **sthg to sthg** colar algo a algo -2. *fig* [people] unir.

bondage ['bɒndɪdʒ] *n literary* [servitude] servidão *f*.

bone [bəʊn] ◇ *n* [of body, material] osso *m*. ◇ *vt* [fish, meat] desossar.

bone-dry *adj* completamente seco(ca).

bone-idle *adj inf* encostado(da).

bonfire ['bɒn,faɪə*r*] *n* fogueira *f* ao ar livre.

bonfire night *n UK noite de 5 de novembro, quando os ingleses lançam fogos de artifício e queimam a figura de Guy Fawkes numa fogueira ao ar livre.*

bonk [bɒŋk] *inf* ◇ *vt* [have sex with] transar com. ◇ *vi* [have sex] transar.

Bonn [bɒn] *n* Bonn; **in ~** em Bonn.

bonnet ['bɒnɪt] *n* -1. *UK* [of car] capô *m* -2. [hat] touca *f*.

bonus ['bəʊnəs] (*pl* -es) *n* -1. [extra money] bônus *m inv* -2. *fig* [added treat] vantagem *f* adicional.

bony ['bəʊnɪ] (*compar* -ier, *superl* -iest) *adj* -1. [person, hand, face] ossudo(da) -2. [meat] com osso; [fish] cheio (cheia) de espinhas.

boo [buː] (*pl* -s) ◇ *excl* bu! ◇ *n* vaia *f*. ◇ *vt* & *vi* vaiar.

boob [buːb] *n inf* [mistake] gafe *f*.

➡ **boobs** *npl UK inf* [breasts] tetas *fpl*.

booby trap ['buːbɪ-] *n* -1. [bomb] bomba *f* camuflada -2. [prank] armadilha *f*.

book [bʊk] ◇ *n* -1. [for reading] livro *m* -2. [pack - of stamps] bloco *m*; [- of matches] caixa *f*; [- of cheques, tickets] talão *m*. ◇ *vt* -1. [reserve] reservar; **to be fully ~ed** estar totalmente cheio (cheia) OR esgotado(da) -2. *inf* [subj: police] autuar -3. *UK* FTBL dar cartão amarelo OR vermelho a. ◇ *vi* reservar, fazer uma reserva.

➡ **books** *npl* COMM registros *mpl*.

➡ **book up** *vt sep*: **to be ~ed up** [fully booked] estar completamente cheio (cheia); **the hotel is ~ed up** o hotel está lotado.

book bag *n US* = booksack.

bookcase ['bʊkkeɪs] *n* estante *f* (para livros).

bookie ['bʊkɪ] *n inf* bookmaker *m*.

booking ['bʊkɪŋ] *n* -1. *esp UK* [reservation] reserva *f* -2. *esp UK* FTBL cartão *m* amarelo OR vermelho.

booking office *n esp UK* bilheteria *f*.

bookkeeping ['bʊk,kiːpɪŋ] *n* COMM contabilidade *f*.

booklet ['bʊklɪt] *n* [pamphlet] folheto *m*.

bottle

bookmaker [ˈbʊkˌmeɪkəʳ] n bookmaker m.

bookmark [ˈbʊkmɑːk] n marcador m de páginas.

bookseller [ˈbʊkˌseləʳ] n vendedor m, -ra f de livros.

bookshelf [ˈbʊkʃelf] (pl -shelves [-ʃelvz]) n prateleira f OR estante f (para livros).

bookshop UK [ˈbʊkʃɒp], **bookstore** US [ˈbʊkstɔːʳ] n livraria f.

book token n esp UK vale-livro m.

boom [buːm] <> n -1. [loud noise] estrondo m - 2. [increase] boom m, crescimento m - 3. NAUT retranca f - 4. [for TV camera, microphone] bum m. <> vi -1. [make noise] ribombar - 2. ECON [grow] crescer rapidamente.

boon [buːn] n [help, advantage] ajuda f.

boost [buːst] <> n -1. [increase] incremento m - 2. [improvement] impulso m. <> vt -1. [increase] incrementar - 2. [improve] levantar - 3. US inf [steal] afanar.

booster [ˈbuːstəʳ] n MED [vaccine] reforço m.

boot [buːt] <> n -1. [footwear] bota f - 2. UK [of car] porta-bagagem m. <> vt -1. inf [kick] dar um pé na bunda de - 2. COMPUT inicializar, dar boot em.
 ◆ **to boot** adv também.
 ◆ **boot up** vi COMPUT inicializar, dar boot.

booth [buːð] n -1. [at fair] barraca f - 2. [telephone booth] cabine f (telefônica) - 3. [voting booth] cabine f eleitoral.

booty [ˈbuːtɪ] n literary butim m.

booze [buːz] inf <> n [alcohol] trago m. <> vi [drink alcohol] tomar umas e outras.

bop [bɒp] (pt & pp -ped, cont -ping) inf <> n [disco, dance] festa f dançante. <> vi [dance] dançar.

border [ˈbɔːdəʳ] <> n -1. [between countries] fronteira f - 2. [edge] borda f - 3. [hem] orla f - 4. [outer boundary] limite m - 5. [bank, shore] margem f - 6. [for flowers] bordadura f. <> vt -1. [country] limitar-se com - 2. [surround] cercar.
 ◆ **border on** vt fus [verge on] beirar em.

borderline [ˈbɔːdəlaɪn] <> adj: ~ case caso-limite m. <> n fig [division] limite m.

bore [bɔːʳ] <> pt ▷ bear. <> n -1. pej [tedious person] chato m, -ta f; [tedious situation, event] chatice f - 2. [of gun] calibre m. <> vt -1. [not interest] entediar; to ~ sb stiff OR to tears OR to death inf matar alguém de tédio - 2. [drill] furar.

bored [bɔːd] adj entediado(da); to be ~ with sthg estar entediado(da) com algo.

boredom [ˈbɔːdəm] n tédio m.

boring [ˈbɔːrɪŋ] adj chato(ta).

born [bɔːn] adj -1. [given life] nascido(da); to be ~ nascer - 2. [for emphasis] nato(-ta).

borne [bɔːn] pp ▷ bear.

borough [ˈbʌrə] n município m, distrito m.

borrow [ˈbɒrəʊ] vt [property, money] tomar emprestado(da); to ~ sthg from sb pegar algo emprestado de alguém.

Bosnia [ˈbɒznɪə] n Bósnia.

Bosnia-Herzegovina [-ˌhɜːtsəgəˈviːnə] n Bósnia-Herzegovina.

Bosnian [ˈbɒznɪən] <> adj bósnio(nia). <> n bósnio m, -nia f.

bosom [ˈbʊzəm] n -1. [of woman] peito m - 2. fig [centre] seio m; ~ friend amigo m, -ga f do peito.

boss [bɒs] <> n -1. [of company, department, organization] chefe mf - 2. fig [of gang] chefão m; you're the ~! você é quem manda! <> vt pej [give orders to] mandar.
 ◆ **boss about, boss around** vt sep mandar em.

bossy [ˈbɒsɪ] (compar -ier, superl -iest) adj mandão(ona).

bosun [ˈbəʊsn] n = boatswain.

botany [ˈbɒtənɪ] n botânica f.

botch [bɒtʃ] ◆ **botch up** vt sep inf fazer nas coxas.

both [bəʊθ] <> adj ambos(bas), os dois, as duas; we ~ left nós dois (duas) saímos, ambos saímos; ~ my brother and myself will be there tanto meu irmão quanto eu estaremos lá, nós dois estaremos lá. <> adv não apenas ... como; she is ~ witty and intelligent ela não só é espirituosa, como também inteligente. <> pron ambos mpl, -bas fpl; ~ of us nós dois (duas).

bother [ˈbɒðəʳ] <> vt -1. [worry] preocupar; I can't be ~ed to do that não me disponho a fazer isso - 2. [irritate, annoy] incomodar. <> vi [trouble o.s.] incomodar-se; to ~ about sthg incomodar-se com algo; to ~ doing OR to do sthg incomodar-se em fazer algo. <> n -1. (U) [inconvenience] aborrecimento m - 2. [nuisance] incômodo m - 3. [difficulty] dificuldade f - 4. [obstacle] estorvo m. <> excl (que) droga!

bothered [ˈbɒðəd] adj -1. [worried] preocupado(da) - 2. [annoyed] chateado(da).

bottle [ˈbɒtl] <> n -1. [gen] garrafa f - 2. [of medicine] frasco m - 3. [of perfume] vidro m - **4.** [for baby] mamadeira f - **5.** *(U) UK inf* [courage]: **he didn't have the ~ to do it** ele não teve coragem de fazer isso. $\Leftrightarrow$ vt - **1.** [wine] engarrafar - **2.** [fruit] enfrascar.

◆ **bottle up** vt sep [feelings] reprimir.

bottle bank n contêiner no qual se recolhem garrafas de vidro vazias para reciclagem.

bottleneck ['bɒtlnek] n - **1.** [in traffic] engarrafamento m - **2.** [in production] gargalo m.

bottle-opener n abridor m (de garrafa).

bottom ['bɒtəm] $\Leftrightarrow$ adj - **1.** [lowest] de baixo - **2.** [least successful] último(ma). $\Leftrightarrow$ n - **1.** [lowest part - of glass, bag, lake] fundo m; [- of page] fim m, final m; [- of mountain, hill] sopé m; **at the ~** embaixo; **at the ~ of** no fundo de - **2.** [far end] fim m, final m - **3.** [least successful level] nível m mais baixo - **4.** [buttocks] traseiro m - **5.** fig [root, cause]: **to get to the ~ of sthg** ir até o fundo de algo.

◆ **bottom out** vi [prices, recession] estabilizar-se.

bottom line n fig: **the ~ is that ...** a questão toda é que ...

bough [baʊ] n [of tree] galho m.

bought [bɔːt] pt & pp $\triangleright$ **buy**.

boulder ['bəʊldə'] n pedregulho m.

bounce [baʊns] $\Leftrightarrow$ vi - **1.** [ball] quicar - **2.** [person - with energy, enthusiasm]: **she was bouncing with energy/enthusiasm** ela estava pulando de alegria/entusiasmo; **she bounced into the room, singing** ela entrou na sala radiante, cantando; [- jump up and down]: **to ~ on sthg** saltar sobre algo - **4.** inf [cheque] ser devolvido(da). $\Leftrightarrow$ vt [ball] bater. $\Leftrightarrow$ n [of ball] pulo m.

bouncer ['baʊnsə'] n inf [at club etc.] leão-de-chácara m.

bound [baʊnd] $\Leftrightarrow$ pt & pp $\triangleright$ **bind**. $\Leftrightarrow$ adj - **1.** [certain]: **to be ~ to do sthg** fazer algo na certa - **2.** [forced, morally obliged]: **~ by sthg/to do sthg** obrigado(da) por algo/fazer algo; **I'm ~ to say/admit** devo dizer/admitir - **3.** [en route]: **to be ~ for** estar a caminho de. $\Leftrightarrow$ n [leap] salto m.

◆ **bounds** npl [limits] limites mpl; **out of ~s** interditado(da).

boundary ['baʊndərɪ] (pl -ies) n - **1.** [of area of land] fronteira f - **2.** fig [of science, knowledge] fronteiras fpl.

bouquet garni [ˌbuːkeɪɡɑːˈniː] n bouquet garni m (ervas para tempero).

bourbon ['bɜːbən] n bourbon m (uísque norte-americano).

bout [baʊt] n - **1.** [attack] ataque m - **2.** [session] período m - **3.** [boxing match] assalto m.

bow¹ [baʊ] $\Leftrightarrow$ n - **1.** [act of bowing] reverência f - **2.** [of ship] proa f. $\Leftrightarrow$ vt [lower] inclinar. $\Leftrightarrow$ vi - **1.** [make a bow] inclinar-se - **2.** [defer]: **to ~ to sthg** submeter-se a algo.

bow² [bəʊ] n - **1.** [gen & MUS] arco m - **2.** [knot] laço m.

bowels ['baʊəlz] npl - **1.** [intestines] intestinos mpl - **2.** fig [deepest part] entranhas fpl.

bowl [baʊl] $\Leftrightarrow$ n - **1.** [container - gen] tigela f; [- for sugar] açucareiro m; [- for fruit] fruteira f - **2.** [bowl-shaped part - of toilet, sink] bacia f; [- of pipe] fornilho m - **3.** [bowlful] prato m. $\Leftrightarrow$ vt & vi [in cricket] atirar.

◆ **bowls** n (U) jogo m de bocha.

◆ **bowl over** vt sep - **1.** [knock over] derrubar - **2.** fig [surprise, impress] surpreender.

bow-legged [ˌbəʊˈleɡɪd] adj cambota.

bowler ['bəʊlə'] n - **1.** [in cricket, bowls] lançador m - **2.** [headgear]: **~ (hat)** chapéu-coco m.

bowling ['bəʊlɪŋ] n: **(tenpin) ~** jogo m de boliche.

bowling alley n - **1.** [building] boliche m - **2.** [alley] pista f de boliche.

bowling green n cancha m de bocha.

bow tie [bəʊ-] n gravata-borboleta f.

box [bɒks] $\Leftrightarrow$ n - **1.** [gen] caixa f - **2.** [in theatre] camarote m - **3.** [in car races] box m - **4.** UK inf [television]: **the ~ a TV.** $\Leftrightarrow$ vi [fight] lutar.

boxer ['bɒksə'] n - **1.** [fighter] boxeador m, -ra f - **2.** [dog] boxer mf.

boxer shorts npl cuecas fpl samba-canção.

boxing ['bɒksɪŋ] n (U) boxe m.

Boxing Day n dia seguinte ao Natal em que é feriado nacional no Reino Unido. Tradicionalmente, era o dia em que os empregados recebiam os presentes dos patrões, geralmente uma caixinha em dinheiro.

boxing glove n luva f de boxe.

box office n bilheteria f.

boxroom ['bɒksrʊm] n UK quarto m de despejo.

boy [bɔɪ] $\Leftrightarrow$ n - **1.** [young male] menino m - **2.** [adult male] rapaz m - **3.** [son] filho m. $\Leftrightarrow$ excl: **(oh) ~!** inf nossa!

boycott ['bɔɪkɒt] $\Leftrightarrow$ n boicote m. $\Leftrightarrow$ vt boicotar.

boyfriend ['bɔɪfrend] n namorado m.

boyish ['bɔɪʃ] adj juvenil.

bra [brɑː] n sutiã f.

brace [breɪs] <> n MED aparelho m. <> vt lit & fig to ~ o.s. (for sthg): preparar-se (para algo).
➡ **braces** npl UK [for trousers] suspensórios mpl.

bracelet ['breɪslɪt] n bracelete m.

bracing ['breɪsɪŋ] adj revigorante.

bracken ['brækn] n (U) samambaia f.

bracket ['brækɪt] <> n -1. [support] suporte m, mão-francesa f -2. [parenthesis] parêntese m; in ~s entre parênteses -3. [group] faixa f. <> vt [enclose in brackets] colocar entre parênteses.

brag [bræg] (pt & pp -ged, cont -ging) vi [boast] gabar-se.

braid [breɪd] <> n -1. [on uniform] galão m -2. US [hairstyle] trança f. <> vt US trançar.

brain [breɪn] n -1. [organ] cérebro m -2. [mind] cabeça f -3. inf [clever person] gênio m.
➡ **brains** npl [intelligence] sabedoria f.

brainchild ['breɪntʃaɪld] n invenção f.

brainwash ['breɪnwɒʃ] vt fazer lavagem cerebral em.

brainwave ['breɪnweɪv] n idéia f luminosa.

brainy ['breɪnɪ] (compar -ier, superl -iest) adj inf sabichão(chona).

brake [breɪk] <> n -1. [on vehicle] freio m -2. fig [restraint] freio m. <> vi frear.

brake light n luz f de freio.

bramble ['bræmbl] n [bush] amoreira f silvestre; [fruit] amora f silvestre.

bran [bræn] n (U) farelo m.

branch [brɑ:ntʃ] <> n -1. [of tree] galho m -2. [of river] braço m -3. [of railway] ramal m -4. [of company, bank, organization] sucursal f -5. [of subject] ramo m. <> vi [road] bifurcar-se.
➡ **branch out** vi [person, company] expandir-se em nova direção.

brand [brænd] <> n -1. COMM marca f -2. fig [type] tipo m. <> vt -1. [cattle] marcar com ferro em brasa -2. fig [classify]: to ~ sb (as) sthg rotular alguém de algo.

brandish ['brændɪʃ] vt brandir.

brand name n marca f registrada.

brand-new adj novo(va) em folha.

brandy ['brændɪ] (pl -ies) n conhaque m.

brash [bræʃ] adj pej atrevido(da).

brass [brɑ:s] n -1. (U) [type of metal] latão m -2. MUS: the ~ os metais.
➡ **brasses** npl [ornaments] objetos mpl decorativos em latão.

brass band n fanfarra f.

brassiere [UK 'bræsɪəʳ, US brə'zɪr] n sutiã m.

brat [bræt] n inf pej capeta m.

bravado [brə'vɑ:dəʊ] n (U) bravata f.

brave [breɪv] <> adj corajoso(sa). <> n [warrior] guerreiro m índio, bravo m. <> vt enfrentar.

bravery ['breɪvərɪ] n (U) bravura f.

brawl [brɔ:l] n briga f.

brawn [brɔ:n] n (U) [muscle] músculo m

bray [breɪ] vi [donkey] zurrar.

brazen ['breɪzn] adj descarado(da).
➡ **brazen out** vt sep: to ~ it out encarar.

brazier ['breɪzjəʳ] n braseiro m.

Brazil [brə'zɪl] n Brasil.

Brazilian [brə'zɪljən] <> adj brasileiro(-ra). <> n brasileiro m, -ra f.

brazil nut n castanha-do-pará f.

breach [bri:tʃ] <> n -1. [act of disobedience] quebra f; a ~ of an agreement o rompimento de um acordo; a ~ of the law uma transgressão da lei; to be in ~ of sthg estar transgredindo algo -2. [opening, gap] brecha f. <> vt -1. [disobey] romper -2. [make hole in] abrir uma brecha em.

breach of the peace n atentado m à ordem pública.

bread [bred] n [food] pão m; ~ and butter [food] pão com manteiga; fig [main income] sustento m.

bread bin UK, **bread box** US n caixa f para pão.

breadcrumbs ['bredkrʌmz] npl farinha f de rosca.

breadline ['bredlaɪn] n: to be on the ~ estar no limite da pobreza.

breadth [bretθ] n -1. [in measurements] largura f -2. fig [scope] alcance f.

breadwinner ['bred,wɪnəʳ] n arrimo m (de família).

break [breɪk] (pt broke, pp broken) <> n -1. [interruption] interrupção f; a ~ in transmission uma queda na transmissão -2. [gap] brecha f -3. [fracture] fratura f -4. [pause] pausa f; tea/coffee/lunch ~ pausa para o chá/café/almoço; [rest] descanso m; a weekend ~ um feriado curto; give me a ~! me dá um tempo/uma trégua!; to have a ~ from sthg dar uma parada em algo; without a ~ sem parar -5. SCOL recreio m -6. inf [luck, chance] chance f; lucky ~ golpe de sorte. <> vt -1. [gen] quebrar -2. [fracture] fraturar -3. [cause to malfunction] danificar -4. [interrupt] interromper -5. [undermine, cause to fail] furar -6. [announce]: to ~ the news (of sthg to sb) dar a notícia (de algo a alguém). <> vi -1. [gen] quebrar -2. [split] partir-se -3. [burst through] romper -4. [pause]

parar **- 5.** [weather] mudar **- 6.** [escape]:
to ~ **loose** OR **free** escapar **- 7.** [voice -
with emotion] perturbar-se; [- at puberty]
mudar **- 8.** [become known] ser divulga-
do(da) **- 9.** phr: to ~ **even** ficar em ponto
de equilíbrio.
➡ **break away** vi [escape] escapar.
➡ **break down** ⬦ vt sep **-1.** [destroy,
demolish] derrubar **- 2.** [analyse] analisar.
⬦ vi **-1.** [stop working] estragar **- 2.** [end
unsuccessfully] concluir sem sucesso **- 3.**
[collapse, disintegrate] terminar **- 4.** [MED:
collapse] sofrer um colapso; to ~ **down**
in tears romper em lágrimas.
➡ **break in** ⬦ vi **-1.** [enter by force]
arrombar **- 2.** [interrupt] interromper;
to ~ **in on sb/sthg** interromper al-
guém/algo. ⬦ vt sep **-1.** [horse] domar
- 2. [person] acostumar.
➡ **break into** vt fus **-1.** [enter by force]
arrombar **- 2.** [begin suddenly] romper
em.
➡ **break off** ⬦ vt sep **-1.** [detach]
quebrar **- 2.** [put an end to] acabar. ⬦
vi **-1.** [become detached] quebrar-se **- 2.**
[stop talking] deter-se.
➡ **break out** vi **-1.** [begin suddenly] rebentar **- 2.** [escape]: to ~ **out (of)** fugir
(de).
➡ **break up** ⬦ vt sep **-1.** [separate into
smaller pieces - ice] partir; [- soil] repartir;
[- car] desmontar **- 2.** [bring to an end]
acabar. ⬦ vi **-1.** [separate into smaller
pieces] partir-se **- 2.** [come to an end]
acabar-se; to ~ **up with sb** acabar
com alguém **- 3.** [disperse] dispersar-se
- 4. [for school holiday] terminar.
breakage ['breɪkɪdʒ] n quebra f.
breakdown ['breɪkdaʊn] n **-1.** [failure,
ending] quebra f **- 2.** [analysis] detalha-
mento m **- 3.** MED **nervous ~** colapso m
nervoso.
breakfast ['brekfəst] n café-da-manhã
m.
breakfast television n UK programa
m de tv matutino.
break-in n arrombamento m.
breaking ['breɪkɪŋ] n (U): ~ **and enter-
ing** JUR invasão m de domicílio.
breakneck ['breɪknek] adj: **at ~ speed**
em altíssima velocidade.
breakthrough ['breɪkθruː] n avanço m.
breakup ['breɪkʌp] n [of relationship]
rompimento m.
breast [brest] n **-1.** [gen] peito m **- 2.** [of
woman] seio m.
breast-feed vt & vi amamentar.
breaststroke ['breststrəʊk] n (U) nado
m de peito.
breath [breθ] n **-1.** (U) [air taken into lungs]

respiração f; **out of ~** sem fôlego; **to
get one's ~ back** retomar o fôlego **- 2.**
[air breathed out] hálito m; **bad ~** mau
hálito.
breathalyse UK, **-yze** US ['breθəlaɪz] vt
aplicar o teste do bafômetro em.
breathe [briːð] ⬦ vi respirar. ⬦ vt
[inhale] inalar.
➡ **breathe in** ⬦ vi [inhale] respirar.
⬦ vt sep [inhale] inalar.
➡ **breathe out** vi [exhale] exalar.
breather ['briːðə'] n inf respirada f,
descanso m.
breathing ['briːðɪŋ] n (U) respiração f.
breathless ['breθlɪs] adj **-1.** [physically]
ofegante **- 2.** [with excitement] radiante.
breathtaking ['breθ,teɪkɪŋ] adj **-1.**
[beautiful] surpreendente **- 2.** [extreme]
incrível.
breed [briːd] (pt & pp **bred** [bred]) ⬦ n
-1. [of animal] raça f **- 2.** fig [sort, style] tipo
m. ⬦ vt **-1.** [cultivate] criar **- 2.** fig [pro-
voke] gerar. ⬦ vi [produce young] procriar.
breeding ['briːdɪŋ] n (U) **-1.** [raising animals, plants] criação f **- 2.** [manners] boa
educação f; **a person of good ~** uma
pessoa de berço.
breeze [briːz] n [light wind] brisa f.
breezy ['briːzɪ] (compar **-ier**, superl **-iest**)
adj **-1.** [windy] ventoso(sa) **- 2.** [cheerful]
alegre.
brevity ['brevɪtɪ] n **-1.** [shortness] brevidade f **- 2.** [conciseness] concisão f.
brew [bruː] ⬦ vt [beer] fermentar;
[tea] preparar. ⬦ vi **-1.** [infuse] preparar-se **- 2.** fig [develop - crisis, trouble]
armar-se; [- storm] formar-se.
brewer ['bruːə'] n fabricante mf de
cerveja.
brewery ['bruːərɪ] (pl **-ies**) n cervejaria f.
bribe [braɪb] ⬦ n suborno m. ⬦ vt
subornar; **to ~ sb to do sthg** subornar
alguém para fazer algo.
bribery ['braɪbərɪ] n (U) suborno m.
brick [brɪk] n [for building] tijolo m.
bricklayer ['brɪk,leɪə'] n pedreiro m.
bridal ['braɪdl] adj de noiva.
bride [braɪd] n noiva f.
bridegroom ['braɪdgrʊm] n noivo m.
bridesmaid ['braɪdzmeɪd] n dama f de
honra.
bridge [brɪdʒ] ⬦ n **-1.** [gen] ponte f **- 2.**
[on ship] ponte f de comando **- 3.** [of nose]
cavalete m **- 4.** [card game] bridge m **- 5.**
[for teeth] ponte f. ⬦ vt [gap] transpor.
bridle ['braɪdl] n [of horse] cabresto m.
bridle path n trilha f.
brief [briːf] ⬦ adj **-1.** [short, concise]
breve; **in ~** em suma **- 2.** [revealing,

skimpy] reduzido(da). <> *n* - **1.** *JUR* [statement] declaração *f* - **2.** *UK* [instructions] instrução *f*. <> *vt* informar; **to ~ sb on sthg** [bring up to date] pôr alguém a par de algo; [instruct] treinar alguém sobre/em algo.

<> **briefs** *npl* [underwear] cuecas *fpl*.

briefcase ['bri:fkeis] *n* pasta *f* executiva.

briefing ['bri:fɪŋ] *n* instruções *fpl*.

briefly ['bri:flɪ] *adv* - **1.** [for a short time] brevemente - **2.** [concisely] rapidamente.

brigade [brɪ'geɪd] *n* brigada *f*.

brigadier [,brɪgə'dɪə°] *n* brigadeiro *m*.

bright [braɪt] *adj* - **1.** [full of light] claro(ra) - **2.** [colour] vivo(va) - **3.** [lively, cheerful] alegre - **4.** [intelligent] inteligente - **5.** [hopeful, promising] radioso(sa).

<> **brights** *npl* *US* *inf* *AUT* luz *f* alta.

brighten ['braɪtn] *vi* - **1.** [become lighter] iluminar-se - **2.** [become more cheerful] alegrar-se.

<> **brighten up** <> *vt sep* alegrar. <> *vi* - **1.** [become more cheerful] alegrar-se - **2.** [weather] melhorar.

brilliance ['brɪljəns] *n* - **1.** [cleverness] inteligência *f* - **2.** [of light, colour] brilho *m*.

brilliant ['brɪljənt] *adj* - **1.** [clever, successful] brilhante - **2.** [colour] vivo(va) - **3.** [light] brilhante - **4.** *inf* [wonderful, enjoyable] genial.

Brillo pad® ['brɪləʊ-] *n* esfregão *m* (de aço com sabão).

brim [brɪm] (*pt* & *pp* -**med**, *cont* -**ming**) <> *n* - **1.** [edge] borda *f* - **2.** [of hat] aba *f*. <> *vi*: **to ~ with enthusiasm** transbordar de entusiasmo.

brine [braɪn] *n* (*U*) salmoura *f*.

bring [brɪŋ] (*pt* & *pp* **brought**) *vt* [gen] trazer; **to ~ sthg to an end** acabar com algo.

<> **bring about** *vt sep* produzir.

<> **bring around** *vt sep* [make conscious]: **to bring sb around** fazer alguém recuperar os sentidos.

<> **bring back** *vt sep* - **1.** [hand over] devolver - **2.** [carry, transport] trazer de volta - **3.** [recall] relembrar - **4.** [reinstate] trazer de volta.

<> **bring down** *vt sep* - **1.** [cause to fall] derrubar - **2.** [reduce] baixar.

<> **bring forward** *vt sep* - **1.** [in time] adiantar - **2.** [in bookkeeping] transportar.

<> **bring in** *vt sep* - **1.** [introduce] apresentar - **2.** [earn] render.

<> **bring off** *vt sep* conseguir.

<> **bring out** *vt sep* - **1.** [produce and sell] lançar - **2.** [reveal] ressaltar.

<> **bring round, bring to** *vt sep* = **bring around**.

<> **bring up** *vt sep* - **1.** [educate] educar - **2.** [mention] mencionar - **3.** [vomit] vomitar.

brink [brɪŋk] *n*: **on the ~ of** à beira de.

brisk [brɪsk] *adj* - **1.** [walk, swim] rápido(da) - **2.** [manner, tone] enérgico(ca).

bristle ['brɪsl] <> *n* - **1.** [hair] pêlo *m* - **2.** [on brush] cerda *f*. <> *vi* - **1.** [stand up] ficar em pé - **2.** [react angrily]: **to ~ (at sthg)** eriçar-se (diante de algo).

Britain ['brɪtn] *n* Grã-Bretanha; **in ~** na Grã-Bretanha.

British ['brɪtɪʃ] <> *adj* britânico(ca). <> *npl*: **the ~** os britânicos.

British Isles *npl*: **the ~** as Ilhas Británicas.

British Telecom *n* principal empresa británica de telecomunicações.

Briton ['brɪtn] *n* británico *m*, -ca *f*.

Britpop ['brɪtpɒp] *n* (*U*) tipo de música pop tocada por bandas británicas, muito popular em meados dos anos 90.

Brittany ['brɪtənɪ] *n* Bretanha.

brittle ['brɪtl] *adj* [easily broken] quebradiço(ça).

broach [brəʊtʃ] *vt* [subject] abordar.

broad [brɔ:d] <> *adj* - **1.** [physically wide] largo(ga) - **2.** [wide-ranging, extensive] amplo(pla) - **3.** [general, unspecific] geral - **4.** [hint] explícito(ta) - **5.** [accent] forte. <> *n* *US* *inf* [woman] sujeita *f*.

<> **in broad daylight** *adv* em plena luz do dia.

B road *n* *UK* estrada *f* secundária.

broadband ['brɔ:dbænd] *n* *COMPUT* banda *f* larga.

broad bean *n* fava *f*.

broadcast ['brɔ:dkɑ:st] (*pt* & *pp* **broadcast**) <> *n* transmissão *f*. <> *vt* transmitir.

broaden ['brɔ:dn] <> *vt* - **1.** [make physically wider] alargar - **2.** [make more general, wide-ranging] ampliar - <> *vi* [become physically wider] alargar-se.

broadly ['brɔ:dlɪ] *adv* [generally] em geral.

broadminded [,brɔ:d'maɪndɪd] *adj* tolerante.

broccoli ['brɒkəlɪ] *n* brócolis *mpl*.

brochure ['brəʊʃə°] *n* folheto *m*.

broil [brɔɪl] *vt* *US* grelhar.

broke [brəʊk] <> *pt* ⊳ **break**. <> *adj* *inf* [penniless] falido(da).

broken ['brəʊkn] <> *pp* ⊳ **break**. <> *adj* - **1.** [damaged, in pieces] quebrado(da) - **2.** [fractured] fraturado(da) - **3.** [not working] estragado(da) - **4.** [interrupted] interrompido(da) **-5.** [marriage; home] desfeito(ta).

broker ['brəʊkə^r] n corretor m, -ra f.

brolly ['brɒlɪ] (pl -ies) n UK inf guarda-chuva m.

bronchitis [brɒŋ'kaɪtɪs] n (U) bronquite f.

bronze [brɒnz] ◇ n (U) [metal] bronze m. ◇ adj [bronze-coloured] bronzeado(da).

brooch [brəʊtʃ] n broche m.

brood [bruːd] n [of animals] ninhada f.

brook [brʊk] n riacho m.

broom [bruːm] n [brush] vassoura f.

broomstick ['bruːmstɪk] n cabo m de vassoura.

Bros, bros (abbr of brothers) irmãos.

broth [brɒθ] n (U) caldo m.

brothel ['brɒθl] n bordel m.

brother ['brʌðə^r] n **-1.** [gen & RELIG] irmão m **-2.** fig [associate, comrade] irmão m.

brother-in-law (pl brothers-in-law) n cunhado m.

brought [brɔːt] pt & pp ▷ bring.

brow [braʊ] n **-1.** [forehead] testa f **-2.** [eyebrow] sobrancelha f **-3.** [of hill] topo m.

brown [braʊn] ◇ adj **-1.** [colour - hair, eyes] castanho(nha); [- object] marrom; ~ **bread** pão m integral **-2.** [tanned] bronzeado(da). ◇ n [colour] marrom m. ◇ vt [food] tostar.

Brownie (Guide) n escoteira júnior de sete a doze anos.

brown paper n (U) papel m pardo.

brown rice n (U) arroz m integral.

brown sugar n (U) açúcar m mascavo.

browse [braʊz] ◇ vt COMPUT: to ~ the Web navegar na Web. ◇ vi **-1.** [in shop] dar uma olhada **-2.** [read]: to ~ through sthg dar uma olhada em algo **-3.** [graze] pastar.

browser ['braʊzə^r] n COMPUT navegador m.

bruise [bruːz] ◇ n equimose f. ◇ vt **-1.** [leave a bruise on] machucar **-2.** fig [hurt, offend] ferir.

brunch [brʌntʃ] n brunch m, combinação de café-da-manhã e almoço servido ao meio-dia.

brunette [bruː'net] n morena f.

brunt [brʌnt] n: to bear OR take the ~ of sthg suportar OR sofrer a força de algo.

brush [brʌʃ] ◇ n **-1.** [for hair] escova f **-2.** [of artist, for shaving, paint] pincel m **-3.** [encounter] atrito m. ◇ vt **-1.** [clean with brush] escovar **-2.** [touch lightly] roçar.

◆ **brush aside** vt sep desprezar.

◆ **brush off** vt sep [dismiss] desprezar.

◆ **brush up** ◇ vt sep [revise] recapitular. ◇ vi: to ~ up on sthg treinar OR praticar algo.

brush-off n inf: to give sb the ~ dar um chega pra lá em alguém, botar alguém de escanteio.

brushwood ['brʌʃwʊd] n (U) graveto m.

brusque [bruːsk] adj brusco(ca).

Brussels ['brʌslz] n Bruxelas; in ~ em Bruxelas.

brussels sprout n couve-de-bruxelas f.

brutal ['bruːtl] adj brutal.

brute [bruːt] ◇ adj bruto(ta). ◇ n **-1.** [large animal] besta f **-2.** [bully] animal mf.

BSc (abbr of Bachelor of Science) n (titular de) graduação em ciências.

BT (abbr of British Telecom) n empresa de telefonia britânica.

bubble ['bʌbl] ◇ n bolha f. ◇ vi borbulhar.

bubble bath n **-1.** [liquid] espuma f de banho **-2.** [bath] banho m de espuma.

bubble gum n (U) chiclete m de bola.

bubblejet printer ['bʌbldʒet-] n impressora f a jato de tinta.

Bucharest [ˌbuːkə'rest] n Bucareste; in ~ em Bucareste.

buck [bʌk] (pl sense 1 inv OR -s) ◇ n **-1.** [male animal] macho m **-2.** US inf [dollar] dólar mf **-3.** inf [responsibility]: to pass the ~ passar OR transferir a responsabilidade. ◇ vi [horse] corcovear.

◆ **buck up** inf vi **-1.** [hurry up] apressar-se **-2.** [cheer up, become more positive] animar-se.

bucket ['bʌkɪt] n **-1.** [container] balde m **-2.** [bucketful] balde m.

Buckingham Palace ['bʌkɪŋəm-] n Palácio m de Buckingham.

buckle ['bʌkl] ◇ n fivela f. ◇ vt **-1.** [fasten] afivelar **-2.** [bend] arquear. ◇ vi [bend] arquear-se, vergar-se.

bud [bʌd] (pt & pp -ded, cont -ding) ◇ n botão m. ◇ vi florescer.

Budapest [ˌbjuːdə'pest] n Budapeste; in ~ em Budapeste.

Buddha ['bʊdə] n Buda m.

Buddhism ['bʊdɪzm] n (U) budismo m.

budding ['bʌdɪŋ] adj [aspiring] principiante.

buddy ['bʌdɪ] (pl -ies) n US inf [friend] camarada mf.

budge [bʌdʒ] ◇ vt **-1.** [move] mexer **-2.** [change mind of] dissuadir. ◇ vi **-1.** [move - object] mover-se; [- person] mudar-se **-2.** [change mind] mudar de opinião.

budgerigar ['bʌdʒərɪgɑː^r] n periquito m (australiano).

budget ['bʌdʒɪt] <> *adj* [cheap] econômico(ca). <> *n* orçamento *m*.
➡ **budget for** *vt fus* planejar os gastos com.

budgie ['bʌdʒɪ] *n inf* periquito *m* (australiano).

buff [bʌf] <> *adj* [brown] pardo(da). <> *n inf* [expert] expert *mf*.

buffalo ['bʌfələʊ] (*pl inv OR* -es *OR* -s) *n* búfalo *m*.

buffer ['bʌfə'] *n* -1. [for trains] párachoque *m* -2. [protection] proteção *f* -3. *COMPUT* buffer *m*.

buffet¹ [*UK* 'bʊfeɪ, *US* bə'feɪ] *n* -1. [meal] bufê *m* -2. [cafeteria] cantina *f*.

buffet² ['bʌfɪt] *vt* [physically] bater.

buffet car ['bʊfeɪ-] *n* vagão-restaurante *m*.

bug [bʌg] (*pt & pp* -ged, *cont* -ging) <> *n* -1. *US* [small insect] inseto *m* -2. *inf* [germ] vírus *m* -3. *inf* [listening device] grampo *m* -4. *COMPUT* [fault in program] bug *m*. <> *vt inf* -1. [spy on] grampear -2. *US* [annoy] chatear.

bugger ['bʌgə'] *UK v inf* <> *n* -1. [unpleasant person, task] porre *mf* -2. [particular type of person] infeliz *mf*. <> *excl* merda!
➡ **bugger off** *vi*: ~ **off!** vá à merda!

buggy ['bʌgɪ] (*pl* -ies) *n* [pushchair, stroller] carrinho *m* de bebê.

bugle ['bju:gl] *n* trombeta *f*.

build [bɪld] (*pt & pp* **built**) <> *vt* construir. <> *n* corpo *m*, constituição *f* física.
➡ **build on** <> *vt fus* [further] ampliar. <> *vt sep* [base on] alicerçar.
➡ **build up** <> *vt sep* [strengthen] fortalecer. <> *vi* [increase] intensificar.
➡ **build upon** *vt fus & vt sep* = **build on**.

builder ['bɪldə'] *n* construtor.

building ['bɪldɪŋ] *n* -1. [structure] edifício *m*, prédio *m* -2. (*U*) [profession] construção *f*.

building and loan association *n US* associação *f* de financiamento imobiliário, ≃ sistema *m* financeiro de habitação.

building site *n* canteiro *m* de obras.

building society *n UK* sociedade *f* de financiamento imobiliário.

build-up *n* [increase] intensificação *f*.

built [bɪlt] *pt & pp* ▷ **build**.

built-in *adj* -1. *CONSTR* embutido(da) -2. [inherent] embutido(da).

built-up *adj*: ~ **area** área *f* urbanizada.

bulb [bʌlb] *n* -1. [for lamp] lâmpada *f* -2. [of plant] bulbo *m*.

Bulgaria [bʌl'geərɪə] *n* Bulgária.

Bulgarian [bʌl'geərɪən] <> *adj* búlgaro(ra). <> *n* -1. [person] búlgaro *m*, -ra *f* -2. [language] búlgaro *m*.

bulge [bʌldʒ] <> *n* [lump] protuberância *f*. <> *vi*: **to** ~ **(with sthg)** estar estourando(de algo).

bulk [bʌlk] *n* -1. [mass] volume *m* -2. [of person] massa *f* -3. *COMM*: **in** ~ **a** granel -4. [majority, most of]: **the** ~ **of a** maior parte de. <> *adj* a granel.

bulky ['bʌlkɪ] (*compar* -ier, *superl* -iest) *adj* volumoso(osa).

bull [bʊl] *n* -1. [male cow] touro *m* -2. [male animal] macho *m*.

bulldog ['bʊldɒg] *n* buldogue *m*.

bulldozer ['bʊldəʊzə'] *n* escavadeira *f*.

bullet ['bʊlɪt] *n* [for gun] bala *f*.

bulletin ['bʊlətɪn] *n* -1. [brief report] boletim *m* -2. [regular publication] boletim *m*.

bullet-proof *adj* à prova de bala.

bullfight ['bʊlfaɪt] *n* tourada *f*.

bullfighter ['bʊl,faɪtə'] *n* toureiro *m*.

bullfighting ['bʊl,faɪtɪŋ] *n* touradas *fpl*.

bullion ['bʊljən] *n* (*U*) barras *fpl* de ouro ou prata.

bullock ['bʊlək] *n* boi *m*.

bullring ['bʊlrɪŋ] *n* arena *f* de touros.

bull's-eye *n* -1. [target] mosca *f* -2. [shot] mosca *f*.

bully ['bʊlɪ] (*pl* -ies, *pt & pp* -ied) <> *n* brigão *m*, -gona *f*. <> *vt* amedontrar; **to** ~ **sb into doing sthg** amedrontar alguém para que faça algo.

bum [bʌm] (*pt & pp* -med, *cont* -ming) *n* -1. *esp UK v inf* [bottom] traseiro *m* -2. *US inf pej* [tramp] vagabundo *m*.

bum bag *n inf* pochete *f*.

bumblebee ['bʌmblbi:] *n* abelhão *m*.

bump [bʌmp] <> *n* -1. [lump] elevação *f* -2. [head] galo *m* -3. [leg] inchaço *m* -4. [knock, blow] batida *f* -5. [noise] pancada *f*. <> *vt* [knock, damage] bater.
➡ **bump into** *vt fus* [meet by chance]: **to** ~ **into sb** topar com alguém.

bumper ['bʌmpə'] <> *adj* super-. <> *n* -1. [on car] pára-choque *m* -2. *US RAIL* pára-choque *m*.

bumptious ['bʌmpʃəs] *adj pej* presunçoso(sa).

bumpy ['bʌmpɪ] (*compar* -ier, *superl* -iest) *adj* -1. [surface] esburacado(da) -2. [ride, journey] turbulento(ta).

bun [bʌn] *n* -1. [cake] bolo *m* doce (*pequeno e com passas*) -2. [bread roll] pãozinho *m* -3. [hairstyle] coque *m*.

bunch [bʌntʃ] <> *n* [group - of people] grupo *m*; [- of flowers] ramalhete *m*; [- of fruit] cacho *m*; [- of keys] molho *m*. <> *vi* unir.

◆ **bunches** *npl* [hairstyle] maria-chiquinha *f*.

bundle ['bʌndl] ◇ *n* **-1.** [clothes] trouxa **-2.** [paper] maço **-3.** [wood] feixe. ◇ *vt* socar.

bung [bʌŋ] ◇ *n* tampo *m*. ◇ *vt UK inf* **-1.** [give] passar **-2.** [put] deixar **-3.** [toss] jogar.

bungalow ['bʌŋgələʊ] *n* [single-storey house] casa *f* térrea.

bungee jump *n* bungee jump *m*.

bungle ['bʌŋgl] *vt* fracassar.

bunion ['bʌnjən] *n* joanete *m*.

bunk [bʌŋk] *n* **-1.** [bed] beliche *m* **-2.** = **bunk bed**.

bunk bed *n* beliche *m*.

bunker ['bʌŋkə'] *n* **-1.** MIL [shelter] abrigo *m* **-2.** [for coal] carvoeira *f* **-3.** [in golf] bunker *m*.

bunny ['bʌnɪ] (*pl* **-ies**) *n*: ~ **(rabbit)** coelhinho *m*.

bunting ['bʌntɪŋ] *n* [flags] bandeirolas *fpl*.

buoy [*UK* bɔɪ, *US* 'bu:ɪ] *n* [float] bóia *f*.

◆ **buoy up** *vt sep* [encourage] animar.

buoyant ['bɔɪənt] *adj* **-1.** [able to float] capaz de flutuar, flutuante **-2.** [optimistic] otimista.

BUPA (*abbr of* **British United Provident Association**) *n* plano de saúde privado existente na Grã-Bretanha.

burden ['bɜ:dn] ◇ *n* **-1.** [physical load] carga **-2.** *fig* [heavy responsibility] fardo *m*; **to be a** ~ **on sb** ser um peso para alguém; **to relieve the** ~ **on sb** aliviar a carga sobre alguém. ◇ *vt*: **to** ~ **sb with sthg** sobrecarregar alguém com algo.

bureau ['bjʊərəʊ] (*pl* **-x**) *n* **-1.** [office, branch] agência *f*, escritório *m* **-2.** *UK* [desk] escrivaninha *f* **-3.** *US* [chest of drawers] cômoda *f*.

bureaucracy [bjʊə'rɒkrəsɪ] (*pl* **-ies**) *n* **-1.** [system] burocracia *f* **-2.** (*U*) *pej* [rules] burocracia *f*.

bureau de change [ˌbjʊərəʊdə'ʃɒndʒ] (*pl* **bureaux de change** [ˌbjʊərəʊdə'ʃɒndʒ]) *n* casa *f* de câmbio.

bureaux ['bjʊərəʊz] *pl* ▷ **bureau**.

burger ['bɜ:gə'] *n* [hamburger] hambúrguer *m*.

burglar ['bɜ:glə'] *n* ladrão *m*, -dra *f*.

burglar alarm *n* alarme *m* anti-roubo.

burglarize *vt US* = **burgle**.

burglary ['bɜ:glərɪ] (*pl* **-ies**) *n* **-1.** [event] roubo *m (de casa)*, arrombamento *m (de casa)* **-2.** [activity] roubo *m (de casa)*, arrombamento *m (de casa)*.

burgle ['bɜ:gl], **burglarize** ['bɜ:gləraɪz]

US vt roubar *(casa)*, arrombar *(casa)*.

burial ['berɪəl] *n* enterro *m*.

burly ['bɜ:lɪ] (*compar* **-ier**, *superl* **-iest**) *adj* robusto(ta).

Burma ['bɜ:mə] *n* Birmânia.

burn [bɜ:n] (*pt & pp* **burnt** OR **-ed**) ◇ *vt* **-1.** [gen] queimar; **to** ~ **o.s.** queimar-se **-2.** [destroy by fire] incendiar. ◇ *vi* **-1.** [gen] queimar **-2.** [be on fire] incendiar-se **-3.** *fig* [feel strong emotion]: **to** ~ **with sthg** arder de algo. ◇ *n* **-1.** [wound, injury] queimadura *f* **-2.** [mark] queimadura *f*.

◆ **burn down** ◇ *vt sep* [destroy by fire] incendiar. ◇ *vi* [be destroyed by fire] incendiar-se.

burner ['bɜ:nə'] *n* [on cooker] queimador *m*.

Burns Night *n* festa celebrada na Escócia em 25 de janeiro para comemorar o aniversário do poeta Robert Burns.

burnt [bɜ:nt] *pt & pp* ▷ **burn**.

burp [bɜ:p] *inf* ◇ *n* arroto *m*. ◇ *vi* arrotar.

burrow ['bʌrəʊ] ◇ *n* toca *f*. ◇ *vi* **-1.** [dig] entocar-se **-2.** *fig* [in order to search] remexer.

bursar ['bɜ:sə'] *n* tesoureiro *m*, -ra *f*.

bursary ['bɜ:sərɪ] (*pl* **-ies**) *n UK* [scholarship, grant] bolsa *f (de estudos)*.

burst [bɜ:st] (*pt & pp* **burst**) ◇ *vi* **-1.** [break open] estourar **-2.** [explode] explodir **-3.** [go suddenly] irromper. ◇ *vt* [break open] estourar. ◇ *n* [bout] estouro *m*.

◆ **burst into** *vt fus* irromper em.

◆ **burst out** *vt fus* **-1.** [say suddenly] exclamar **-2.** [begin suddenly]: **to** ~ **out laughing/crying** começar a gargalhar/chorar.

bursting ['bɜ:stɪŋ] *adj* **-1.** [full] repleto(ta) **-2.** [with emotion]: ~ **with sthg** repleto(ta) de algo **-3.** [eager]: **to be** ~ **to do sthg** estar morrendo de vontade de fazer algo.

bury ['berɪ] (*pt & pp* **-ied**) *vt* **-1.** [gen] enterrar **-2.** [hide - face, hands] esconder.

bus [bʌs] *n* ônibus *m*; **by** ~ **de** ônibus.

bush [bʊʃ] *n* **-1.** [plant] arbusto *m* **-2.** [open country]: **the** ~ **a** selva **-3.** *phr*: **to beat about the** ~ **fazer** rodeios.

bushy ['bʊʃɪ] (*compar* **-ier**, *superl* **-iest**) *adj* espesso(sa).

business ['bɪznɪs] *n* **-1.** (*U*) [commerce] negócios *mpl*; **on** ~ **a** negócios; **to mean** ~ *inf* falar sério; **to go out of** ~ ir à falência **-2.** [company] negócio *m* **-3.** (*U*) [concern, duty] assunto *m*; **mind your**

own ~! *inf* meta-se com sua vida! **- 4.** [affair, matter] negócio *m*, assunto *m*.
business class *n* (U) classe *f* executiva.
businesslike ['bɪznɪslaɪk] *adj* profissional.
businessman ['bɪznɪsmæn] (*pl* -men [-men]) *n* [occupation] empresário *m*, homem *m* de negócios.
business trip *n* viagem *f* de negócios.
businesswoman ['bɪznɪs,wʊmən] (*pl* -women [-,wɪmɪn]) *n* [occupation] empresária *f*, mulher *f* de negócios.
busker ['bʌskə'] *n* UK artista *mf* de rua.
bus shelter *n* abrigo *m* de ônibus.
bus station *n* estação *f* rodoviária.
bus stop *n* parada *f* OR ponto *m* de ônibus.
bust [bʌst] (*pt* & *pp* bust OR -ed) ⟨⟩ *adj inf* **- 1.** [broken] quebrado(da) **- 2.** [bankrupt]: **to go** ~ quebrar. ⟨⟩ *n* busto *m* ⟨⟩ *vi inf* [break] quebrar. ⟨⟩ *vi* quebrar.
bustle ['bʌsl] ⟨⟩ *n* [activity] movimento *m*. ⟨⟩ *vi* apressar-se.
busy ['bɪzɪ] (*compar* -ier, *superl* -iest) ⟨⟩ *adj* **- 1.** [gen & TELEC] ocupado(da); **to be** ~ **doing sthg** estar ocupado(da) fazendo algo **- 2.** [hectic - time] agitado(da); [- place] movimentado(da). ⟨⟩ *vt*: **to** ~ **o.s. (doing sthg)** ocupar-se fazendo algo.
busybody ['bɪzɪ,bɒdɪ] (*pl* -ies) *n pej* intrometido *m*, -da *f*.
busy signal *n* US TELEC sinal *m* de ocupado.
but [bʌt] ⟨⟩ *conj* mas. ⟨⟩ *prep* senão, a não ser; **you've been nothing** ~ **trouble** você só tem me dado trabalho; **the last** ~ **one** o penúltimo (a penúltima).
◆ **but for** *prep* se não fosse.
butcher ['bʊtʃə'] ⟨⟩ *n* **- 1.** [shopkeeper] açougueiro *m*, -ra *f*; ~'**s (shop)** açougue *m* **- 2.** *fig* [indiscriminate killer] carniceiro *m*, -ra *f*. ⟨⟩ *vt* **- 1.** [kill for meat] abater **- 2.** *fig* [kill indiscriminately] exterminar, fazer uma carnificina com.
butler ['bʌtlə'] *n* mordomo *m*.
butt [bʌt] ⟨⟩ *n* **- 1.** [of cigarette, cigar] bagana *f* **- 2.** [of rifle] coronha *f* **- 3.** [for water] tina *m* **- 4.** [target] alvo *m* **- 5.** *esp* US *inf* [bottom] traseiro *m*. ⟨⟩ *vt* [hit with head] dar cabeçada em.
◆ **butt in** *vi* [interrupt] atrapalhar, interromper; **to** ~ **in on sb/sthg** atrapalhar OR interromper alguém/algo.
butter ['bʌtə'] ⟨⟩ *n* (U) manteiga *f*. ⟨⟩ *vt* passar manteiga em.
buttercup ['bʌtəkʌp] *n* botão-de-ouro *m*.
butter dish *n* manteigueira *f*.

butterfly ['bʌtəflaɪ] (*pl* -ies) *n* **- 1.** [insect] borboleta *f* **- 2.** (U) [swimming style] nado *m* borboleta.
buttocks ['bʌtəks] *npl* nádegas *fpl*.
button ['bʌtn] ⟨⟩ *n* **- 1.** [on clothes] botão *m* **- 2.** [on machine] botão *m* **- 3.** US [badge] button *m*. ⟨⟩ *vt* = **button up**.
◆ **button up** *vt sep* [fasten] abotoar.
button-down *adj* abotoado(da).
button mushroom *n* cogumelo *m* de Paris.
buttress ['bʌtrɪs] *n* contraforte *m*.
buxom ['bʌksəm] *adj* de corpo e seios grandes.
buy [baɪ] (*pt* & *pp* bought) ⟨⟩ *vt lit* & *fig* comprar; **to** ~ **sthg from sb** comprar algo de alguém. ⟨⟩ *n* compra *f*, aquisição *f*.
◆ **buy out** *vt sep* **- 1.** [in business] comprar a parte de **- 2.** [from army] pagar para sair; **he bought himself out** ele comprou sua saída do exército.
◆ **buy up** *vt sep* comprar a totalidade de.
buyer ['baɪə'] *n* **- 1.** [purchaser] comprador *m*, -ra *f* **- 2.** [profession] gerente *mf* de compras.
buyout ['baɪaʊt] *n* compra *f* majoritária de ações.
buzz [bʌz] ⟨⟩ *n* [noise - of insect, machinery] zumbido *m*; [- of conversation] murmúrio *m*; **to give sb a** ~ *inf* [on phone] dar uma ligada para alguém. ⟨⟩ *vi* zunir; *lit* & *fig* **to** ~ **(with sthg)** zunir (de algo). ⟨⟩ *vt* [on intercom] ligar, chamar.
buzzer ['bʌzə'] *n* campainha *f*.
buzzword ['bʌzwɜːd] *n inf* palavra *f* da moda.
by [baɪ] ⟨⟩ *prep* **- 1.** [expressing cause, agent] por; **he's worried** ~ **her absence** está preocupado com a sua ausência; **he was hit** ~ **a car** ele foi atropelado por um carro; **a book** ~ **Stephen King** um livro de Stephen King; **funded** ~ **the government** financiado pelo governo. **- 2.** [expressing method, means]: ~ **car/bus/plane** de carro/ônibus/avião; ~ **phone/mail** pelo telefone/correio; **to pay** ~ **credit card/cheque** pagar com cartão de crédito/cheque; **to win** ~ **cheating** ganhar trapaceando. **- 3.** [near to, beside] junto a; ~ **the sea** à beira-mar, junto ao mar. **- 4.** [past] por; **a car went** ~ **the house** um carro passou pela casa. **- 5.** [via] por; **exit** ~ **the door on the left** saia pela porta do lado esquerdo. **- 6.** [with time]: **be there** ~ **nine** esteja lá às nove horas; ~ **day** de dia; **it should be ready** ~ **now** já deve

estar pronto. **-7.** [expressing quantity] a; sold ~ **the dozen** vende-se à dúzia; prices fell ~ **20%** os preços baixaram 20%; **we charge** ~ **the hour** cobramos por hora. **-8.** [expressing meaning] com; **what do you mean** ~ **that?** que quer dizer com isso? **-9.** [in division, multiplication] por; **about six feet** ~ **fifteen** aproximadamente dois metros por cinco. **-10.** [according to] segundo; ~ **law** segundo a lei; **it's fine** ~ **me** por mim tudo bem. **-11.** [expressing gradual process] a; **one** ~ **one** um a um; **day** ~ **day** dia a dia. **-12.** [in phrases]: ~ **mistake** por engano; ~ **oneself** sozinho; ~ **profession** por profissão. ◇ adv [past]: **to go/drive** ~ passar.

bye (-bye) [baɪ(baɪ)] excl inf tchau!

bye-election n = by-election.

byelaw [ˈbaɪlɔː] n = bylaw.

by-election n eleição suplementar realizada para substituir um político que renunciou ao cargo parlamentar ou morreu.

bygone [ˈbaɪgɒn] adj decorrido(da).
➡ **bygones** npl: **to let** ~ **s be** ~ **s** deixar o que passou para trás.

bylaw [ˈbaɪlɔː] n estatuto m.

bypass [ˈbaɪpɑːs] ◇ n **-1.** [road] rodoanel m **-2.** MED: ~ **(operation)** (cirurgia de) ponte f de safena. ◇ vt **-1.** [place] passar ao redor de **-2.** [issue, person] passar por cima de.

by-product n **-1.** [product] subproduto m **-2.** fig [consequence] subproduto m.

bystander [ˈbaɪˌstændəʳ] n espectador m, -ra f.

byte [baɪt] n COMPUT byte m.

byword [ˈbaɪwɜːd] n [symbol]: **to be a** ~ **for sthg** ser um exemplo de algo.

C

c (pl **c's** OR **cs**), **C** (pl **C's** OR **Cs**) [siː] n [letter] c, C m.
➡ **C** n **-1.** MUS dó m **-2.** SCH [mark] C m, regular m **-3.** (abbr of **celsius, centigrade**) C.

c., ca. (abbr of circa) c.

cab [kæb] n **-1.** [taxi] táxi m **-2.** [of lorry] cabine f.

cabaret [ˈkæbəreɪ] n cabaré m.

cabbage [ˈkæbɪdʒ] n [vegetable] repolho m.

cabin [ˈkæbɪn] n **-1.** [on ship] camarote m **-2.** [in aircraft] cabine f **-3.** [house] cabana f.

cabin class n classe f cabina.

cabin crew n tripulação f.

cabinet [ˈkæbɪnɪt] n **-1.** [cupboard] armário m **-2.** POL gabinete m.

cable [ˈkeɪbl] ◇ n **-1.** [rope] cabo m **-2.** [telegram] telegrama m **-3.** ELEC cabo m **-4.** TV = **cable television.** ◇ vt [telegraph] telegrafar.

cable car n teleférico m.

cable television, cable TV n (U) televisão f a cabo.

cache [kæʃ] n **-1.** [store] esconderijo m **-2.** COMPUT cache f.

cackle [ˈkækl] vi **-1.** [hen] cacarejar **-2.** [person] gargalhar.

cactus [ˈkæktəs] (pl **-tuses** OR **-ti** [-taɪ]) n cacto m.

cadet [kəˈdet] n [in police] cadete m.

cadge [kædʒ] UK inf ◇ vt: **to** ~ **sthg (off** OR **from sb)** filar algo (de alguém). ◇ vi: **to** ~ **off** OR **from sb** pedir esmolas a OR para alguém.

caesarean (section) UK, **cesarean (section)** US [sɪˈzeərɪən-] n cesariana f; **she had a** ~ ela fez uma cesariana.

cafe, café [ˈkæfeɪ] n café m.

cafeteria [ˌkæfɪˈtɪərɪə] n cantina f.

caffeine [ˈkæfiːn] n (U) cafeína f.

cage [keɪdʒ] n **-1.** [for animals] jaula f **-2.** [for birds] gaiola f.

cagey [ˈkeɪdʒɪ] (compar **-ier**, superl **-iest**) adj inf cauteloso(sa), cuidadoso(sa).

cagoule [kəˈguːl] n UK capa f de chuva.

cajole [kəˈdʒəʊl] vt: **to** ~ **sb into doing sthg** persuadir alguém a fazer algo.

cake [keɪk] n **-1.** [type of sweet food] bolo m; **a piece of** ~ inf uma moleza OR barbada **-2.** [of fish, potato] bolinho m (achatado) **-3.** [of soap] sabonete m.

caked [keɪkt] adj: ~ **with sthg** empastado(da) de algo, coberto(ta) de algo.

calcium [ˈkælsɪəm] n (U) cálcio m.

calculate [ˈkælkjʊleɪt] vt **-1.** [work out - figures, result etc.] calcular; [- consequences, risk etc.] medir **-2.** [plan, intend]: **to be** ~ **d to do sthg** ter o intuito de fazer algo.

calculating [ˈkælkjʊleɪtɪŋ] adj pej calculista.

calculation [ˌkælkjʊˈleɪʃn] n MATH cálculo m.

calculator [ˈkælkjʊleɪtəʳ] n calculadora f.

calendar [ˈkælɪndəʳ] n calendário m.

calendar year n ano m civil.

calf [kɑːf] (*pl* **calves**) *n* -1. [young animal - cow] bezerro *m*, -ra *f*; [- elephant, whale] filhote *m* -2. [of leg] panturrilha *f*, barriga *f* da perna.

calibre, caliber *US* ['kælɪbə'] *n* -1. [quality] nível *m* -2. [size] calibre *m*.

California [,kælɪ'fɔ:njə] *n* Califórnia.

calipers *npl US* = **callipers**.

call [kɔ:l] ⬦ *n* -1. [cry - of person] grito *m*; [- of animal, bird] canto *m* -2. [visit] visita *f*; **to pay a ~ on sb** fazer uma visita a alguém -3. [for flight] chamada *f*; **final ~** última chamada -4. [demand] pedido *m*; **~ for sthg** solicitação por algo; **there's no ~ for that** não há razão para isso -5. [summons] chamado *m* -6. [standby]: **on ~** de plantão -7. [telephone call] telefonema *m*, ligação *f*; **long-distance ~** chamada de longa distância. ⬦ *vt* -1. [gen] chamar; **disgraceful, I'd ~ it!** uma vergonha, eu diria!; **would you ~ what he does art?** você chamaria o que ele faz de arte?; **he ~ed me a liar** ele me chamou de mentiroso; **let's ~ it £10** a gente faz por £10 -2. [telephone] ligar para. ⬦ *vi* -1. [shout] chamar -2. [animal, bird] cantar -3. [by telephone] ligar -4. [visit] visitar.

⬥ **call back** ⬦ *vt sep* -1. [on telephone] ligar de volta -2. [ask to return] chamar de volta. ⬦ *vi* -1. [on phone] ligar de volta -2. [visit again] voltar outra vez.

⬥ **call for** *vt fus* -1. [collect] ir buscar -2. [demand] exigir.

⬥ **call in** ⬦ *vt sep* -1. [send for] chamar -2. *COMM* [goods] fazer um recall de; *FIN* [loan] resgatar. ⬦ *vi*: **could you ~ in at the butcher's on your way home?** você pode passar no açougue ao voltar para casa?

⬥ **call off** *vt sep* -1. [cancel] cancelar -2. [order not to attack] mandar voltar.

⬥ **call on** *vt fus* -1. [visit] visitar -2. [ask]: **to ~ on sb to do sthg** convocar alguém para fazer algo.

⬥ **call out** ⬦ *vt sep* -1. [gen] convocar -2. [cry out] gritar. ⬦ *vi* [cry out] gritar.

⬥ **call round** *vi* dar uma passada.

⬥ **call up** *vt sep* -1. *MIL* convocar -2. [on telephone] dar uma ligada -3. *COMPUT* chamar, buscar.

call box *n UK* cabine *f* telefônica, ≃ orelhão *m*.

caller ['kɔ:lə'] *n* -1. [visitor] visita *f* -2. [on telephone]: **I'm sorry ~, the number is engaged** sinto muito, senhor(ra), a linha está ocupada.

caller (ID) display *n* [on telephone] identificador *m* de chamadas.

call-in *n US RADIO & TV* programa com participação por telefone de ouvintes ou telespectadores.

calling ['kɔ:lɪŋ] *n* -1. [profession, trade] profissão *f* -2. [vocation] vocação *f*.

calling card *n US* cartão *m* de visita.

callipers *UK*, **calipers** *US* ['kælɪpəz] *npl* -1. *MATH* compasso *m* de calibre -2. *MED* aparelho *m* ortopédico.

callous ['kæləs] *adj* insensível.

callus ['kæləs] (*pl* **-es**) *n* calo *m*.

calm [kɑ:m] ⬦ *adj* [person, voice, weather] calmo(ma), tranquilo(la). ⬦ *n (U)* [peaceful state] tranquilidade *f*, calmaria *f*. ⬦ *vt* acalmar, tranquilizar.

⬥ **calm down** ⬦ *vt sep* acalmar, tranquilizar. ⬦ *vi* acalmar-se, tranquilizar-se.

Calor gas® ['kælə'-] *n UK (U)* ≃ butano *m*.

calorie ['kælərɪ] *n* [in food] caloria *f*.

calves [kɑ:vz] *pl* ⊳ **calf**.

camber ['kæmbə'] *n* inclinação *f*.

Cambodia [kæm'bəʊdjə] *n* Camboja.

camcorder ['kæm,kɔ:də'] *n* filmadora *f*.

came [keɪm] *pt* ⊳ **come**.

camel ['kæml] *n* [animal] camelo *m*.

cameo ['kæmɪəʊ] (*pl* **-s**) *n* -1. [piece of jewellery] camafeu *m* -2. [in writing] descrição *f* breve e inteligente -3. [in acting] ponta *f*.

camera ['kæmərə] *n* câmera *f*.

⬥ **in camera** *adv fml* em câmara.

cameraman ['kæmərəmæn] (*pl* **-men** [-men]) *n* cameraman *m*, câmera *m*.

Cameroon [,kæmə'ru:n] *n* Camarões.

camouflage ['kæməflɑ:ʒ] ⬦ *n* comuflagem *f* ⬦ *vt* camuflar.

camp [kæmp] ⬦ *n* -1. [gen] acampamento *m*; **holiday ~** acampamento de férias; **training ~** campo *m* de treinamento; **concentration/refugee ~** campo de concentração/refugiados -2. *fig* [faction] facção *f*. ⬦ *vi* acampar.

⬥ **camp out** *vi* acampar.

campaign [kæm'peɪn] ⬦ *n* campanha *f*. ⬦ *vi*: **to ~ (for/against sthg)** fazer campanha (a favor de/contra algo).

camp bed *n* cama *f* de armar.

camper ['kæmpə'] *n* -1. [person] campista *mf* -2. [vehicle]: **~ (van)** trailer *m*.

campground ['kæmpgraʊnd] *n US* camping *m*.

camping ['kæmpɪŋ] *n (U)* acampamento *m*; **to go ~** ir acampar.

camping site, campsite ['kæmpsaɪt] *n* camping *m*.

campus ['kæmpəs] (*pl* **-es**) *n* campus *m*.

can¹ [kæn] ⬦ *n* [container] lata *f*. ⬦ *vt* enlatar.

can² [*weak form* kən, *strong form* kæn] *pt*

& conditional could) aux vb -**1.** [be able to] poder; ~ **you help me?** pode me ajudar?; **I ~ see the mountains** posso ver as montanhas -**2.** [know how to] saber; ~ **you drive?** você sabe dirigir?; **I ~ speak Portuguese** eu sei falar português -**3.** [be allowed to] poder; **you can't smoke here** você não pode fumar aqui -**4.** [in polite requests] poder; ~ **you tell me the time?** pode me dizer as horas?; ~ **I speak to the manager?** posso falar com o gerente? -**5.** [expressing occasional occurrence] poder; **it ~ get cold at night** às vezes a temperatura diminui bastante à noite -**6.** [expressing possibility] poder; **they could be lost** eles podem estar perdidos.

Canada ['kænədə] n Canadá; **in ~** no Canadá.

Canadian [kə'neɪdjən] <> adj canadense. <> n canadense mf.

canal [kə'næl] n [waterway] canal m.

canary [kə'neərɪ] (pl -ies) n canário m.

cancel ['kænsl] (UK pt & pp -led, cont -ling, US pt & pp -ed, cont -ing) vt [call off, invalidate] cancelar.
 ➡ **cancel out** vt sep anular.

cancellation [ˌkænsə'leɪʃn] n cancelamento m.

cancer ['kænsəʳ] n [disease] câncer m.
 ➡ **Cancer** n [sign] Câncer m.

candelabra [ˌkændɪ'lɑːbrə] n candelabro m.

candid ['kændɪd] adj [frank] sincero(ra), franco(ca).

candidate ['kændɪdət] n -**1.** [for job]: ~ **for sthg** candidato(ta) a algo -**2.** [taking exam] candidato m, -ta f.

candle ['kændl] n vela f.

candlelight ['kændllaɪt] n (U) luz f de vela.

candlelit ['kændllɪt] adj à luz de velas.

candlestick ['kændlstɪk] n castiçal m.

candour UK, **candor** US ['kændəʳ] n (U) sinceridade f, franqueza f.

candy ['kændɪ] (pl -ies) n esp US (U) [confectionery] doce m, guloseima f.

candy bar n US barra f de doce.

candy box n US caixa f de doces.

candyfloss UK ['kændɪflɒs], **cotton candy** US n (U) algodão-doce m.

candy store n US confeitaria f.

cane [keɪn] n -**1.** (U) [for making furniture] palhinha f -**2.** [walking stick] bengala f -**3.** [for punishment]: **the ~** ≃ a palmatória -**4.** [for supporting plant] vara f. <> vt bater com vara em.

canine ['keɪnaɪn] <> adj canino(na). <> n: ~ **(tooth)** (dente m) canino m.

canister ['kænɪstəʳ] n lata f de metal; a

~ **of tear gas** uma bomba de gás lacrimogênio; **a smoke ~** uma bomba de fumaça.

cannabis ['kænəbɪs] n (U) maconha f.

canned [kænd] adj [tinned - food] enlatado(da); [- drink] em lata, de latinha.

cannibal ['kænɪbl] n canibal mf.

cannon ['kænən] (pl inv OR -s) n -**1.** [on ground] canhão m -**2.** [on aircraft] canhão m.

cannonball ['kænənbɔːl] n bala f de canhão.

cannot ['kænɒt] vb fml ▷ can².

canny ['kænɪ] (compar -ier, superl -iest) adj [shrewd] astuto(ta).

canoe [kə'nuː] n canoa f.

canoeing [kə'nuːɪŋ] n (U): **to go ~** praticar canoagem.

canon ['kænən] n -**1.** [clergyman] cônego m -**2.** [general principle] cânone m.

can opener n abridor m de lata.

canopy ['kænəpɪ] (pl -ies) n -**1.** [over bed, seat] dossel m -**2.** [of trees, branches] cobertura f.

can't [kɑːnt] = cannot.

cantaloup UK, **cantaloupe** US ['kæntəluːp] n cantalupo m.

cantankerous [kæn'tæŋkərəs] adj rabugento(ta).

canteen [kæn'tiːn] n -**1.** [restaurant] cantina f -**2.** [box of cutlery] faqueiro m.

canter ['kæntəʳ] <> n meio m galope. <> vi andar a meio galope.

cantilever ['kæntɪliːvəʳ] n viga f em balanço, cantiléver f.

canvas ['kænvəs] n -**1.** (U) [cloth] lona f -**2.** ART tela f.

canvass ['kænvəs] vt -**1.** POL pedir -**2.** [investigate] sondar.

canyon ['kænjən] n desfiladeiro m.

cap [kæp] (pt & pp -ped, cont -ping) <> n -**1.** [hat] boné m -**2.** [swimming, shower] touca f -**3.** [lid, top] tampa f. <> vt -**1.** [cover top of] cobrir -**2.** [improve on]: **to ~ it all** para arrematar.

capability [ˌkeɪpə'bɪlətɪ] (pl -ies) n -**1.** [ability] capacidade f -**2.** MIL poderio m.

capable ['keɪpəbl] adj -**1.** [able, having capacity]: **to be ~ of sthg/of doing sthg** ser capaz de algo/de fazer algo -**2.** [competent, skilful] competente, hábil.

capacity [kə'pæsɪtɪ] (pl -ies) n -**1.** (U) [limit, ability] capacidade f; ~ **for sthg** capacidade para algo; ~ **for doing** OR **to do sthg** capacidade para OR de fazer algo -**2.** [position] qualidade f; **in a ... ~** na condição de ...

cape [keɪp] n -**1.** GEOGR cabo m -**2.** [cloak] capa f.

caper ['keɪpəʳ] n -1. [for flavouring food] alcaparra f - 2. inf [escapade] mutreta f.

capital ['kæpɪtl] <> adj -1. [letter] maiúsculo(la) - 2. [punishable by death] capital. <> n -1. [of country]: ~ (city) capital f - 2. fig [centre] capital f - 3. TYPO: ~ (letter) (letra) maiúscula - 4. [money] capital m; to make ~ (out) of sthg fig aproveitar-se de algo.

capital expenditure n (U) dispêndio m com ativos fixos.

capital gains tax n imposto m sobre lucros de capital.

capital goods npl bens mpl de capital.

capitalism ['kæpɪtəlɪzm] n (U) capitalismo m.

capitalist ['kæpɪtəlɪst] <> adj capitalista. <> n capitalista mf.

capitalize, -ise ['kæpɪtəlaɪz] vi: to ~ on sthg [make most of] tirar proveito de algo, capitalizar algo.

capital punishment n (U) pena f de morte.

Capitol Hill ['kæpɪtl-] n congresso norte-americano.

capitulate [kə'pɪtjʊleɪt] vi: to ~ (to sthg) render-se (a algo), ceder (frente a algo).

Capricorn ['kæprɪkɔ:n] n [sign] Capricórnio m.

capsize [kæp'saɪz] <> vt emborcar. <> vi emborcar-se.

capsule ['kæpsju:l] n cápsula f.

captain ['kæptɪn] n -1. [gen] capitão m - 2. [of airliner] comandante mf.

caption ['kæpʃn] n legenda f.

captivate ['kæptɪveɪt] vt cativar.

captive ['kæptɪv] <> adj -1. [imprisoned] de cativeiro - 2. fig [unable to leave] cativo(va); ~ audience audiência cativa. <> n prisioneiro m, -ra f.

captor ['kæptəʳ] n capturador m, -ra f.

capture ['kæptʃəʳ] <> vt -1. [gen] capturar - 2. [gain, take control of] conquistar. <> n (U) captura f.

car [kɑ:ʳ] <> n -1. [motor car] carro m - 2. [on train] vagão m. <> comp de automóvel.

carafe [kə'ræf] n garrafa f de mesa.

car alarm n alarme m de carro.

caramel ['kærəmel] n -1. (U) [burnt sugar] caramelo m - 2. [sweet] caramelo m.

carat ['kærət] n UK quilate m.

caravan ['kærəvæn] n -1. UK [vehicle - towed by car] trailer m; [- towed by horse] carruagem m - 2. [travelling group] caravana f.

caravan site n UK área f para trailers.

carbohydrate [ˌkɑ:bəʊ'haɪdreɪt] n (U) [chemical substance] carboidrato m.

→ **carbohydrates** npl [food] carboidratos mpl.

carbon ['kɑ:bən] n (U) [element] carbono m.

carbonated ['kɑ:bəneɪtɪd] adj com gás.

carbon copy n -1. [document] cópia f em papel carbono - 2. fig [exact copy] cópia f perfeita.

carbon dioxide [-daɪ'ɒksaɪd] n (U) dióxido m de carbono.

carbon monoxide [-mɒ'nɒksaɪd] n monóxido m de carbono.

carbon paper n papel-carbono m.

car-boot sale n UK feira em que objetos usados são vendidos no porta-malas de um carro.

carburettor UK, **carburetor** US [ˌkɑ:bə'retəʳ] n carburador m.

carcass ['kɑ:kəs] n [of animal] carcaça f.

card [kɑ:d] n -1. [playing card] carta f - 2. [for information, greetings] cartão m - 3. [postcard] postal m, cartão-postal m. - 4. (U) [cardboard] papelão m.

→ **cards** npl [game] cartas fpl.

→ **on the cards** UK, **in the cards** US adv inf: to be on the ~ estar na cara.

cardboard ['kɑ:dbɔ:d] <> n (U) papelão m. <> comp [made of cardboard] de papelão m.

cardboard box n caixa f de papelão.

cardiac ['kɑ:dɪæk] adj cardíaco(ca), do coração.

cardigan ['kɑ:dɪgən] n cardigã m.

cardinal ['kɑ:dɪnl] <> adj primordial. <> n RELIG cardeal m.

card index n UK fichário m.

cardphone ['kɑ:dfəʊn] n telefone m (público) de cartão.

card table n mesa f de jogo.

care [keəʳ] <> n -1. (U) [protection, looking after] cuidado m; to take ~ of sb [look after] cuidar de alguém; to take ~ of sthg [deal with] cuidar de algo; take ~! inf [when saying goodbye] cuide-se! - 2. (U) [caution, carefulness] cuidado m; to take ~ to do sthg ter o cuidado de fazer algo; take ~! [be careful] tenha cuidado! - 3. [cause of worry] preocupação f. <> vi -1. [be concerned] preocupar-se; to ~ about sb/sthg preocupar-se com alguém/algo - 2. [mind] importar-se.

→ **care of** prep aos cuidados de.

→ **care for** vt fus [like] gostar de.

career [kə'rɪəʳ] <> n carreira f. <> vi desgovernar-se; to ~ into sthg ir desgovernado(da) em direção a algo.

careers adviser n orientador m, -ra f vocacional.

carefree ['keəfri:] adj despreocupado(da).

careful ['keəfʊl] *adj* -**1.** [cautious] cuidadoso(sa); ~ **with sthg** cuidadoso(sa) com algo; **to be** ~ **to do sthg** ter o cuidado de fazer algo -**2.** [thorough] cuidadoso(sa).

carefully ['keəflɪ] *adv* -**1.** [cautiously] cuidadosamente, com cuidado -**2.** [thoroughly] cuidadosamente.

careless ['keəlɪs] *adj* -**1.** [inattentive] desatento(ta), descuidado(da) -**2.** [unconcerned] despreocupado(da).

caress [kə'res] <> *n* carícia *f*. <> *vt* acariciar.

caretaker ['keə,teɪkəʳ] *n UK* zelador *m*, -ra *f*.

car ferry *n* balsa *f*.

cargo ['ka:gəʊ] (*pl* -**es** OR -**s**) *n* carregamento *m*.

car hire *n UK* (*U*) aluguel *m* de carros.

Caribbean [*UK* kærɪ'bɪən, *US* kə'rɪbɪən] *n* -**1.** [sea]: **the** ~ **(Sea)** o (Mar do) Caribe -**2.** [region]: **the** ~ o Caribe.

caring ['keərɪŋ] *adj* afetuoso(sa).

carnage ['ka:nɪdʒ] *n* (*U*) carnificina *f*.

carnal ['ka:nl] *adj literary* carnal.

carnation [ka:'neɪʃn] *n* craveiro *m*.

carnival ['ka:nɪvl] *n* -**1.** [festive occasion] carnaval *m* -**2.** [fair] parque *m* de diversões.

carnivorous [ka:'nɪvərəs] *adj* carnívoro(ra).

carol ['kærəl] *n*: **(Christmas)** ~ cântico *m* de Natal.

carousel [,kærə'sel] *n* -**1.** *esp US* [at fair] carrossel *m* -**2.** [at airport] esteira *f*.

carp [ka:p] (*pl inv* OR -**s**) <> *n* carpa *f*. <> *vi* queixar-se; **to** ~ **about sthg** queixar-se de algo.

car park *n UK* estacionamento *m*.

carpenter·['ka:pəntəʳ] *n* carpinteiro *m*, -ra *f*.

carpentry ['ka:pəntrɪ] *n* (*U*) carpintaria *f*.

carpet ['ka:pɪt] <> *n* [floor covering] carpete *m*. <> *vt* [fit with floor covering] acarpetar.

carpet slipper *n* pantufas *fpl*.

carpet sweeper [-'swi:pəʳ] *n* limpador *m* de carpete, feiticeira *f*.

car phone *n* telefone *m* para automóvel.

car radio *n* rádio *m* de carro.

car rental *n Am* aluguel *m* de carro.

carriage ['kærɪdʒ] *n* -**1.** [horsedrawn vehicle] carruagem *f* -**2.** *UK* [railway coach] vagão -**3.** (*U*) [transport of goods] carregamento *m*; ~ **paid** OR **free** *UK* frete pago.

carriageway ['kærɪdʒweɪ] *n UK* pista *f* simples.

carrier ['kærɪəʳ] *n* -**1.** COMM transportador *m*, -ra *f* -**2.** [of disease] portador *m*, -ra *f* -**3.** = **carrier bag**.

carrier bag *n* sacola *f*.

carrot ['kærət] *n* -**1.** [vegetable] cenoura *f* -**2.** *inf fig* [incentive] incentivo *m*.

carry ['kærɪ] (*pt* & *pp* -**ied**) <> *vt* -**1.** [transport - subj: person, animal] carregar; [- subj: water, wind, vehicle] levar -**2.** [be equipped with] dispor de; **all planes** ~ **lifejackets** todos os aviões dispõem de coletes salva-vidas -**3.** [weapon] portar -**4.** [disease] transmitir -**5.** [involve as a consequence] implicar; **the job carries considerable responsibility** o emprego implica em responsabilidades consideráveis -**6.** [motion, proposal] aprovar -**7.** [be pregnant with] carregar -**8.** MATH sobrar. <> *vi* [sound] projetar-se.

◆ **carry away** *vt sep*: **to get carried away** entrar no embalo.

◆ **carry forward** *vt sep* transportar.

◆ **carry off** *vt sep* -**1.** [make a success of] tornar um sucesso -**2.** [win] sair-se bem.

◆ **carry on** <> *vt fus* [continue] continuar; **to** ~ **on doing sthg** continuar a fazer algo. <> *vi* -**1.** [continue] continuar; **to** ~ **on with sthg** continuar algo -**2.** *inf* [make a fuss] criar caso.

◆ **carry out** *vt fus* -**1.** [task, plan, experiment] levar a cabo -**2.** [promise, order, threat] cumprir.

◆ **carry through** *vt sep* [accomplish] completar.

carryall ['kærɔ:l] *n US* bolsa *f* de viagem.

carrycot ['kærɪkɒt] *n esp UK* moisés *m inv*.

carsick ['ka:,sɪk] *adj* enjoado(da) *(em carro)*.

cart [ka:t] <> *n* -**1.** [vehicle] carroça *f* -**2.** *US* [for shopping]: **(shopping** OR **grocery)** ~ carrinho *m* (de compras). <> *vt inf* carregar.

carton ['ka:tn] *n* -**1.** [brick-shaped] caixa *f* -**2.** [plastic] frasco *m*.

cartoon [ka:'tu:n] *n* -**1.** [satirical drawing] cartum *m* -**2.** [comic strip] tira *f*, tirinha *f* -**3.** [film] desenho *m* animado.

cartridge ['ka:trɪdʒ] *n* -**1.** [for gun] cartucho *m* -**2.** [for pen] recarga *f* -**3.** [for camera] rolo *m* de filme.

cartwheel ['ka:twi:l] *n* [movement] pirueta *f*.

carve [ka:v] <> *vt* -**1.** [shape, sculpt] esculpir -**2.** [slice] fatiar -**3.** [cut into surface] gravar. <> *vi* [slice joint] fatiar a carne.

◆ **carve out** *vt sep* [create, obtain] criar.

◆ **carve up** *vt sep* [divide] dividir.

carving ['kɑ:vɪŋ] n [art, work, object] entalhe m.

carving knife n faca f de trinchar.

car wash n **-1.** [process] lavagem f de carro **-2.** [place] lava-rápido m.

case [keɪs] n **-1.** [gen] caso m; **to be the** ~ ser o caso; **in that** ~ nesse caso; **he may still come, in which** ~ **we can all leave together** pode ser que ele ainda venha, e neste caso todos podemos partir juntos; **as** OR **whatever the** ~ **may be** seja qual for o caso; **in** ~ **of** em caso de **-2.** [argument] razão fpl; ~ **for/against sthg** razões a favor de/contra algo **-3.** JUR [trial, inquiry] causa f- **4.** [container, holder] estojo m **-5.** UK [suitcase] mala f.

 in any case adv seja como for.

 in case ⟨⟩ conj caso. ⟨⟩ adv: (just) **in** ~ só por precaução.

cash [kæʃ] ⟨⟩ n (U) **-1.** [notes and coins] dinheiro m; **to pay (in)** ~ pagar em dinheiro **-2.** inf [money] dinheiro m **-3.** [payment]: **in** ~ **advance** pagamento m adiantado/antecipado; ~ **on delivery** pagamento contra entrega. ⟨⟩ vt descontar.

cash and carry n sistema f pague e leve.

cashbook ['kæʃbʊk] n livro-caixa m.

cash box n cofre m.

cash card n cartão m de saque.

cash desk n UK caixa m.

cash dispenser [-dɪ'spensə^r] n = **cashpoint**

cashew (nut) ['kæʃu:-] n castanha-de-caju f.

cashier [kæ'ʃɪə^r] n caixa mf.

cash machine n = **cashpoint**.

cashmere [kæʃ'mɪə^r] n (U) caxemira f.

cashpoint ['kæʃpɔɪnt] n caixa m automático.

cash register n caixa f registradora.

casing ['keɪsɪŋ] n [protective cover] invólucro m.

casino [kə'si:nəʊ] (pl -s) n cassino m.

cask [kɑ:sk] n barril m.

casket ['kɑ:skɪt] n **-1.** [for jewels] porta-jóias m inv **-2.** US [coffin] caixão m.

casserole ['kæsərəʊl] n **-1.** [stew] ensopado m (no forno) **-2.** [pot] prato f de ir ao forno.

cassette [kæ'set] n cassete f.

cassette player n toca-fitas m inv.

cassette recorder n gravador m.

cast [kɑ:st] (pt & pp cast) ⟨⟩ n **-1.** [of play, film] elenco m **-2.** MED gesso m. ⟨⟩ vt **-1.** [turn, direct] dar uma espiada em; **to** ~ **doubt on sthg** pôr algo em dúvida **-2.** [light, shadow] lançar **-3.** [throw] arremessar **-4.** [choose for play, film] dar o papel a; **she** ~ **him in the role of Hamlet** ela deu-lhe o papel de Hamlet **-5.** POL: **to** ~ **one's vote** votar **-6.** [metal] moldar.

 cast aside vt sep rejeitar.

 cast off ⟨⟩ vt **-1.** fml [old practices, habits, burden] livrar-se de **-2.** [in knitting] arrematar. ⟨⟩ vi **-1.** NAUT soltar as amarras **-2.** [in knitting] arrematar os pontos.

 cast on ⟨⟩ vt [in knitting] montar. ⟨⟩ vi [in knitting] montar os pontos.

castaway ['kɑ:stəweɪ] n náufrago m, -ga f.

caster ['kɑ:stə^r] n [wheel] rodízio m.

caster sugar n (U) UK açúcar m refinado.

casting vote ['kɑ:stɪŋ-] n voto m de minerva.

cast iron n (U) ferro m fundido.

castle ['kɑ:sl] n **-1.** [building] castelo m **-2.** [in chess] torre f.

castor ['kɑ:stə^r] n = **caster**.

castor oil n (U) óleo m de rícino.

castor sugar n = **caster sugar**.

castrate [kæ'streɪt] vt castrar.

casual ['kæʒʊəl] adj **-1.** [relaxed, uninterested] despreocupado(da) **-2.** pej [offhand] deselegante, informal **-3.** [chance] ocasional **-4.** [clothes] informal **-5.** [irregular] temporário(ria).

casually ['kæʒʊəlɪ] adv **-1.** [in a relaxed manner, without interest] casualmente **-2.** [dress] informalmente.

casualty ['kæʒʊəltɪ] (pl -ies) n **-1.** [dead or injured person] vítima mf; MIL baixa f **-2.** MED = **casualty department**.

casualty department n pronto-socorro m.

cat [kæt] n **-1.** [domestic animal] gato m, -ta f; **there's no room to swing a** ~ não há espaço nem para respirar; **to play** ~ **and mouse** brincar de gato e rato **-2.** [wild animal] felino m, -na f.

catalogue UK, **catalog** US ['kætəlɒg] ⟨⟩ n **-1.** [of items for sale] catálogo m **-2.** [in library, museum] catálogo m. ⟨⟩ vt catalogar.

catalyst ['kætəlɪst] n **-1.** CHEM catalisador m **-2.** fig [cause] motivo m.

catalytic converter n conversor m catalítico.

catapult UK ['kætəpʊlt] ⟨⟩ n **-1.** [handheld] atiradeira f, estilingue m **-2.** HIST [machine] catapulta f. ⟨⟩ vt **-1.** [hurl] catapultar **-2.** fig [promote] projetar.

cataract ['kætərækt] n catarata f.

catarrh [kə'tɑ:^r] n (U) catarro m.

catastrophe [kə'tæstrəfɪ] n catástrofe f.

catch [kætʃ] (pt & pp caught) ⟨⟩ vt **-1.**

[gen] pegar **- 2.** [ball etc.] apanhar **- 3.** [discover, surprise] flagrar; **to ~ sb doing sthg** flagrar alguém fazendo algo; **to ~ sb unawares** pegar alguém desprevenido(da) **- 4.** [hear clearly] compreender **- 5.** [interest, imagination, attention] despertar **- 6.** [sight]: **to ~ sight of sb/sthg, to ~ a glimpse of sb/sthg** conseguir avistar alguém/algo **- 7.** [on hook, in door, in trap] prender **- 8.** [strike] atingir. ◇ *vi* **-1.** [become hooked, get stuck] ficar preso(sa) em **- 2.** [start to burn] pegar. ◇ *n* **-1.** [of ball etc.] pegada *f* **- 2.** [thing or amount caught] pesca *f* **- 3.** [fastener] trinco *m* **- 4.** [snag] armadilha *f*.

← **catch on** *vi* **-1.** [become popular] pegar **- 2.** *inf* [understand] entender; **to ~ on to sthg** dar-se conta de algo.

← **catch out** *vt sep* [trick] apanhar em erro.

← **catch up** ◇ *vt sep* **-1.** [come level with] alcançar **- 2.** [involve]: **to get caught up in sthg** ser envolvido(da) em algo. ◇ *vi* alcançar; **to ~ up on sthg** pôr algo em dia.

← **catch up with** *vt fus* **-1.** [get to same point as] alcançar **- 2.** [catch, find] pegar.

catching ['kætʃɪŋ] *adj* [infectious] contagioso(sa).

catchment area ['kætʃmənt-] *n* região atendida por uma escola ou um hospital.

catchphrase ['kætʃfreɪz] *n* [of entertainer] bordão *m*.

catchy ['kætʃɪ] (*compar* **-ier**, *superl* **-iest**) *adj* que pega com facilidade.

categorically [ˌkætɪ'gɒrɪklɪ] *adv* categoricamente.

category ['kætəgərɪ] (*pl* **-ies**) *n* categoria *f*.

cater ['keɪtər] *vi* [provide food] fornecer comida.

← **cater for** *vt fus* *UK* **-1.** [provide for] satisfazer; **the magazine ~s for independent working women** a revista se destina a mulheres autônomas **- 2.** [anticipate] contar com.

← **cater to** *vt fus* servir de instrumento a.

caterer ['keɪtərər] *n* (serviço *m* de) bufê *m*.

catering ['keɪtərɪŋ] *n* bufê *m*; **a ~ college** uma escola de culinária.

caterpillar ['kætəpɪlər] *n* [insect] lagarta *f*.

cathedral [kə'θiːdrəl] *n* catedral *f*.

Catholic ['kæθlɪk] ◇ *adj* católico(ca). ◇ *n* católico *m*, -ca *f*.

← **catholic** *adj* [broad] eclético(ca).

cat litter *n* granulado *m* higiênico (para gatos).

Catseyes® ['kætsaɪz] *npl* *UK* olhos-de-gato *mpl*.

cattle ['kætl] *npl* gado *m*.

catty ['kætɪ] (*compar* **-ier**, *superl* **-iest**) *adj* *inf pej* [spiteful] rancoroso(sa).

catwalk ['kætwɔːk] *n* passarela *f*.

caucus ['kɔːkəs] *n* *POL* **-1.** *US* convenção ou reunião política. **- 2.** [interest group] ala *f*.

caught [kɔːt] *pt* & *pp* ▷ **catch**.

cauliflower ['kɒlɪˌflaʊər] *n* couve-flor *f*.

cause [kɔːz] ◇ *n* **-1.** [gen] causa *f* **- 2.** [grounds] razão *f*; **to have ~ for sthg** ter razão para algo; **to have ~ to do sthg** ter razão para fazer algo ◇ *vt* causar; **to ~ sb to do sthg** fazer com que alguém faça algo; **to ~ sthg to be done** fazer com que algo seja feito.

caustic ['kɔːstɪk] *adj* **-1.** *CHEM* cáustico(-ca) **- 2.** *fig* [comment] mordaz.

caution ['kɔːʃn] ◇ *n* **-1.** (*U*) [care] cuidado *m*; **to do sthg with ~** fazer algo com cautela **- 2.** [warning] aviso *m* **- 3.** *UK* *JUR* injunção *f*. ◇ *vt* **-1.** [warn]: **to ~ sb against doing sthg** prevenir alguém para não fazer algo **- 2.** *UK* *JUR* advertir; **to ~ sb for sthg** advertir alguém por algo.

cautious ['kɔːʃəs] *adj* cauteloso(sa).

cavalry ['kævlrɪ] *n* (*U*) **-1.** [on horseback] cavalaria *f* **- 2.** [in armoured vehicles] cavalaria *f*.

cave [keɪv] *n* gruta *f*, caverna *f*.

← **cave in** *vi* [physically collapse] desabar.

caveman ['keɪvmæn] (*pl* **-men** [-men]) *n* troglodita *mf*.

cavernous ['kævənəs] *adj* imenso(sa).

caviar(e) ['kævɪɑːʳ] *n* (*U*) caviar *m*.

cavity ['kævətɪ] (*pl* **-ies**) *n* **-1.** [in object, structure, body] cavidade *f*; **buccal ~** cavidade bucal; **nasal ~** fossas *fpl* nasais **- 2.** [in tooth] cárie *f*.

cavort [kə'vɔːt] *vi* saracotear.

CB *n* (*abbr of* **Citizens' Band**) CB, faixa *f* do cidadão.

CBI (*abbr of* **Confederation of British Industry**) *n* confederação britânica de empresários, ≃ CNI *f*.

cc ◇ *n* (*abbr of* **cubic centimetre**) *cm*. ◇ (*abbr of* **carbon copy**) cópia *f* carbono.

CD *n* (*abbr of* **compact disc**) CD *m*.

CD player *n* tocador *m* de CD.

CD-R (*abbr of* **compact disc (rewritable)**) *n* CD-R *m*.

CD-R drive *n* unidade *f* de CD-R.

CD rewriter ['siːdiːˈriːˌraɪtəʳ] = **CD-RW drive**.

CD-ROM (*abbr of* **compact disc read-only memory**) *n* CD-ROM *m*.

CD-RW (abbr of **compact disc rewritable**) n CD-RW m.

CD-RW drive n gravador m de CD.

CD tower n torre f para CDs.

cease [si:s] fml ⬥ vt cessar; **to ~ doing** OR **to do sthg** parar de fazer algo; **~ fire!** cessar fogo! ⬥ vi parar.

ceasefire ['si:sfaɪəʳ] n cessar-fogo m.

ceaseless ['si:slɪs] adj fml incessante.

cedar ['si:dəʳ] n cedro m.

ceiling ['si:lɪŋ] n **-1.** [of room] teto m **-2.** fig [limit] teto m máximo.

celebrate ['selɪbreɪt] ⬥ vt celebrar. ⬥ vi comemorar.

celebrated ['selɪbreɪtɪd] adj célebre, famoso(sa).

celebration [,selɪ'breɪʃn] n **-1.** (U) [activity, feeling] celebração f **-2.** [event] comemoração f.

celebrity [sɪ'lebrətɪ] (pl -ies) n [star] celebridade f.

celery ['selərɪ] n (U) aipo m.

celibate ['selɪbət] adj celibatário(ria).

cell [sel] n **-1.** BIOL & COMPUT célula f **-2.** [small room] cela f **-3.** [secret group] unidade f.

cellar ['seləʳ] n **-1.** [basement] porão m **-2.** [stock of wine] adega f.

cello ['tʃeləʊ] (pl -s) n [instrument] violoncelo m.

Cellophane® ['seləfeɪn] n (U) celofane® m.

Celsius ['selsɪəs] adj Célsius.

Celt [kelt] n celta mf.

Celtic ['keltɪk] ⬥ adj celta. ⬥ n [language] celta m.

cement [sɪ'ment] ⬥ n (U) [for concrete] cimento m, argamassa f. ⬥ vt **-1.** [cover with cement] cimentar **-2.** fig [reinforce] fortalecer.

cement mixer n betoneira f.

cemetery ['semɪtrɪ] (pl -ies) n cemitério m.

censor ['sensəʳ] ⬥ n [of films, books, letters] censor m, -ra f. ⬥ vt [film, book, letter] censurar.

censorship ['sensəʃɪp] n (U) censura f.

censure ['senʃəʳ] ⬥ n (U) repreensão f. ⬥ vt repreender.

census ['sensəs] (pl censuses) n [population survey] censo m.

cent [sent] n centavo m.

centenary UK [sen'ti:nərɪ] (pl -ies), **centennial** US [sen'tenjəl] n centenário m.

center n, adj & vt US = **centre**.

centigrade ['sentɪgreɪd] adj centígrado(da).

centilitre UK, **centiliter** US ['sentɪ,li:təʳ] n centilitro m.

centimetre UK, **centimeter** US ['sentɪ,mi:təʳ] n centímetro m.

centipede ['sentɪpi:d] n centopéia f.

central ['sentrəl] adj central.

Central America n América Central.

central heating n (U) aquecimento m central.

centralize, -ise ['sentrəlaɪz] vt centralizar.

central locking [-'lɒkɪŋ] n travamento f central (das portas).

central reservation n UK canteiro m central.

centre UK, **center** US ['sentəʳ] ⬥ n **-1.** [gen] centro m; **health/leisure ~** centro de saúde/lazer; **~ of attention** centro das atenções; **~ of gravity** centro de gravidade; **the ~** POL o centro **-2.** SPORT [player] pivô. ⬥ adj **-1.** [middle] central, do meio **-2.** POL de centro. ⬥ vt [place centrally] centralizar.

centre back n SPORT centromédio m.

centre forward n SPORT centroavante m.

centre half n = **centre back**.

century ['sentʃʊrɪ] (pl -ies) n **-1.** [one hundred years] século m **-2.** CRICKET: **to score a ~** marcar cem pontos.

ceramic [sɪ'ræmɪk] adj de cerâmica, cerâmico(ca).

➡ **ceramics** n [craft, objects] cerâmica f.

cereal ['sɪərɪəl] n [crop, breakfast food] cereal m.

ceremonial [,serɪ'məʊnjəl] ⬥ adj cerimonial, de cerimônia. ⬥ n **-1.** [event] cerimônia f OR m **-2.** [pomp, formality] cerimonial m.

ceremony ['serɪmənɪ] (pl -ies) n **-1.** [event] cerimônia f; **degree ~** cerimônia f de colação de grau **-2.** (U) [pomp, formality] formalidade f; **to stand on ~** fazer cerimônia.

certain ['sɜ:tn] adj [gen] certo(ta); **she is ~ to be late** ela certamente vai se atrasar; **to be ~ of sthg/of doing sthg** ter a certeza de algo/fazer algo; **to make ~ of sthg/of doing sthg** assegurar-se de algo/fazer algo; **for ~** com certeza; **to a ~ extent** até certo ponto.

certainly ['sɜ:tnlɪ] adv com certeza; **I ~ do** com certeza (que sim); **~ not!** de modo algum.

certainty ['sɜ:tntɪ] (pl -ies) n (U) certeza f.

certificate [sə'tɪfɪkət] n **-1.** [gen] certificado m **-2.** [of birth, marriage] certidão f; **death ~** atestado m de óbito.

certified ['sɜ:tɪfaɪd] adj **-1.** [professional person] habilitado(da) **-2.** [document] autenticado(da).

certified mail n US postagem f registrada.

certified public accountant n US peritocontador m, -ra f.

certify ['sɜːtɪfaɪ] (pt & pp -ied) vt -1. [declare true]: to ~ that certificar OR atestar que -2. [declare insane]: to be certified ser declarado(da) incapacitado(da).

cervical [sə'vaɪkl] adj cervical; ~ cancer câncer m de colo de útero.

cervical smear n exame f de lâmina.

cervix ['sɜːvɪks] (pl -ices [-ɪsiːz]) n colo m do útero.

cesarean (section) n US = caesarean (section).

cesspit ['sespɪt], **cesspool** ['sespuːl] n fossa f.

cf. (abbr of confer) cf., cfr.

CFC (abbr of chlorofluorocarbon) n CFC m.

ch. (abbr of chapter) cap.

chafe [tʃeɪf] vt [rub] roçar.

chaffinch ['tʃæfɪntʃ] n tentilhão m.

chain [tʃeɪn] <> n -1. [metal] corrente f -2. [of islands] série f; ~ of events rede f de acontecimentos -3. [of mountains] cadeia f -4. [of shops, hotels] cadeia f, rede f. <> vt -1. [prisoner, bicycle] acorrentar -2. [hands] algemar -3. [dog] amarrar.

chain reaction n reação f em cadeia.

chainsaw n serra f articulada.

chain-smoke vi fumar um cigarro atrás do outro.

chain-smoker n fumante mf inveterado, -da.

chain store n filial f.

chair [tʃeəʳ] <> n -1. [for sitting in] cadeira f -2. [university post] cátedra f -3. [of meeting, organization - position] presidência f; [- person] presidente mf. <> vt [meeting, discussion] presidir.

chairlift n teleférico m.

chairman ['tʃeəmən] (pl -men [-mən]) n presidente m.

chairperson ['tʃeə,pɜːsn] (pl -s) n presidente mf.

chalet ['ʃæleɪ] n chalé f.

chalk [tʃɔːk] n -1. (U) [mineral] greda f -2. [for drawing] giz m.

chalkboard ['tʃɔːkbɔːd] n UK quadronegro m.

challenge ['tʃælɪndʒ] <> n desafio m. <> vt -1. [to fight, competition]: to ~ sb (to sthg) desafiar alguém (para algo); to ~ sb to do sthg desafiar alguém a fazer algo -2. [question] questionar.

challenging ['tʃælɪndʒɪŋ] adj -1. [difficult] desafiador(ra) -2. [aggressive] provocador(ra).

chamber ['tʃeɪmbəʳ] n -1. [room] gabinete m; the council ~ o gabinete do conselho -2. [body] câmara f -3. [of gun] tambor m.

chambermaid ['tʃeɪmbəmeɪd] n camareira f.

chamber music n (U) música f de câmara.

chamber of commerce n câmara f de comércio.

chameleon [kə'miːljən] n [animal] camaleão m, -oa f.

champagne [,ʃæm'peɪn] n (U) champanha m.

champion ['tʃæmpjən] n -1. [of competition] campeão f, -ã -2. [of cause] defensor m, -ra f.

championship ['tʃæmpjənʃɪp] n campeonato m.

chance [tʃɑːns] <> n -1. (U) [luck] acaso m, sorte f; by ~ por acaso; by any ~ por acaso -2. [likelihood, opportunity] chance f; not to stand a ~ (of doing sthg) não ter a menor chance (de fazer algo); on the off-~ (that) na esperança de que -3. [risk] risco m; to take a ~ (on sthg/on doing sthg) arriscar-se (em algo/a fazer algo). <> adj acidental. <> vt [risk] arriscar.

chancellor ['tʃɑːnsələʳ] n -1. [chief minister] chanceler m -2. UNIV reitor m, -ra f.

Chancellor of the Exchequer n UK ≃ Ministro m, -tra f da Fazenda.

chandelier [,ʃændə'lɪəʳ] n lustre m.

change [tʃeɪndʒ] <> n -1. [alteration, difference] mudança f, alteração f; ~ in sb/sthg mudança em alguém/algo -2. [contrast, for variety] diferença f; Peter arriving on time? That makes a ~! Peter chegando na hora? Que mudança!; for a ~ para variar -3. [switch, replacement] mudança f; ~ of clothes muda f de roupa -4. (U) [money returned after payment, smaller units of money] troco m -5. (U) [coins] trocado m. <> vt -1. [gen] mudar; to ~ sthg into sthg transformar algo em algo; to ~ one's mind mudar de idéia; to get ~d mudar de roupa -2. [replace, exchange] trocar. <> vi -1. [gen] mudar; to ~ into sthg transformar-se em algo -2. [put on different clothes] trocar-se -3. [move to different train, bus] fazer conexão.

◆ **change over** vi [convert] trocar para; to ~ over to sthg trocar para algo.

changeable ['tʃeɪndʒəbl] adj -1. [mood] inconstante -2. [weather] instável.

change machine n máquina f de troco.

changeover [ˈtʃeɪndʒ,əʊvəʳ] n: ~ (to sthg) mudança f (para algo).

changing [ˈtʃeɪndʒɪŋ] adj variável, instável.

changing room n vestiário m.

channel [ˈtʃænl] (UK pt & pp **-led**, cont **-ling**, US pt & pp **-ed**, cont **-ing**) ◇ n canal m. ◇ vt canalizar.
➡ **Channel** n: **the (English) Channel** o Canal da Mancha.
➡ **channels** npl: **to go through the proper ~ s** seguir os trâmites legais.

Channel Islands npl: **the ~** as Ilhas Normandas.

Channel Tunnel n: **the ~** o Túnel do Canal da Mancha.

chant [tʃɑ:nt] n **-1.** RELIG [song] canto m **-2.** [repeated words] coro m.

chaos [ˈkeɪɒs] n caos m.

chaotic [keɪˈɒtɪk] adj caótico(ca).

chap [tʃæp] n UK inf [man] cara m, chapa m.

chapel [ˈtʃæpl] n capela f.

chaplain [ˈtʃæplɪn] n capelão m.

chapped [tʃæpt] adj rachado(da).

chapter [ˈtʃæptəʳ] n **-1.** capítulo m **-2.** phr: **to give sb ~ and verse on sthg** falar tudo a alguém sobre algo.

char [tʃɑ:ʳ] (pt & pp **-red**, cont **-ring**) vt [burn] carbonizar, torrar.

character [ˈkærəktəʳ] n **-1.** [nature - of place] jeito m; [- of person] caráter m; **in ~** típico **-2.** [unusual quality, style] estilo m **-3.** [in film, book, play] personagem mf **-4.** inf [unusual person] tipo m **-5.** [letter, symbol] caractere m.

characteristic [,kærəktəˈrɪstɪk] ◇ adj [typical] característico(ca). ◇ n [attribute] característica f.

characterize, -ise [ˈkærəktəraɪz] vt **-1.** [typify] caracterizar **-2.** [portray]: **to ~ sthg as** caracterizar algo como.

charade [ʃəˈrɑ:d] n charada f.
➡ **charades** n (U) mímica f.

charcoal [ˈtʃɑ:kəʊl] n carvão m (vegetal).

charge [tʃɑ:dʒ] ◇ n **-1.** [cost] preço m; **admission ~** entrada f; **telephone ~ s** tarifas fpl telefônicas; **delivery ~** taxa f de entrega; **free of ~** grátis **-2.** [command, control] responsabilidade f; **to have ~ of sthg** estar no comando de algo; **to take ~ (of sthg)** tomar conta (de algo); **in ~** encarregado(da); **in ~ of** no comando de **-3.** JUR acusação f **-4.** ELEC & MIL carga f. ◇ vt **-1.** [sum of money] cobrar; **to ~ sthg to sb/sthg** debitar algo de alguém/algo **-2.** [suspect, criminal] acusar; **to ~ sb with sthg** acusar alguém de algo **-3.** [attack] investir

contra **-4.** ELEC carregar. ◇ vi **-1.** [rush] correr **-2.** [attack] investir.

chargé d'affaires [,ʃa:zeɪdæˈfeə] (pl **chargés d'affaires** [,ʃa:zeɪdæˈfeə]) n encarregado m, -da f de negócios.

charger [ˈtʃɑ:dʒəʳ] n [for batteries] carregador m.

chariot [ˈtʃærɪət] n biga f.

charisma [kəˈrɪzmə] n carisma m.

charity [ˈtʃærətɪ] (pl **-ies**) n **-1.** (U) [gifts, money] caridade f **-2.** [organization] instituição f de caridade **-3.** [kindness] simpatia f.

charm [tʃɑ:m] ◇ n **-1.** (U) [appeal, attractiveness] charme m, encanto m **-2.** [spell] feitiço m **-3.** [on bracelet] amuleto m. ◇ vt encantar.

charming [ˈtʃɑ:mɪŋ] adj encantador(-ra).

chart [tʃɑ:t] ◇ n **-1.** [diagram] gráfico m **-2.** [map] mapa m, carta f; **a star/sea ~** uma carta celeste/marítima. ◇ vt **-1.** [plot, map] cartografar **-2.** fig [record] registrar.
➡ **charts** npl: **the ~ s** as paradas de sucesso.

charter [ˈtʃɑ:təʳ] ◇ n [document] carta f. ◇ vt [plane, boat] fretar.

chartered accountant [ˈtʃɑ:təd-] n UK contador m diplomado, contadora f diplomada.

charter flight n vôo m fretado.

charter plane n avião m fretado.

chase [tʃeɪs] ◇ n **-1.** [pursuit] perseguição f **-2.** [hunt] caça f. ◇ vt **-1.** [pursue] perseguir **-2.** [drive away] enxotar. ◇ vi: **to ~ after sb/sthg** correr atrás de alguém/algo.

chasm [ˈkæzm] n abismo m.

chassis [ˈʃæsɪ] (pl inv) n [of vehicle] chassi m.

chat [tʃæt] (pt & pp **-ted**, cont **-ting**) ◇ n bate-papo m, conversa f; **to have a ~** bater papo. ◇ vi bater papo, conversar.
➡ **chat up** vt sep UK inf bater papo.

chatiquette [ˈtʃætɪket] n COMPUT etiqueta f no bate-papo, chatiqueta f.

chat room n COMPUT sala f de bate-papo.

chat show n UK programa m de entrevistas.

chatter [ˈtʃætəʳ] ◇ n **-1.** [of person] tagarelice f **-2.** [of animal, bird] chilro m. ◇ vi **-1.** [person] tagarelar **-2.** [animal, bird] chilrar **-3.** [teeth] bater.

chatterbox [ˈtʃætəbɒks] n inf tagarela mf.

chattering classes npl UK: **the ~** os pseudoformadores de opinião.

chatty ['tʃætɪ] (*compar* -ier, *superl* -iest) *adj* -1. [person] tagarela -2. [letter] informal.

chauffeur ['ʃəʊfəʳ] *n* chofer *m*.

chauvinist ['ʃəʊvɪnɪst] *n* chauvinista *mf*.

cheap [tʃi:p] <> *adj* -1. [gen] barato(ta) -2. [despicable, vulgar] de mau gosto. <> *adv* barato.

cheapen ['tʃi:pn] *vt* [degrade] rebaixar; **to ~ o.s.** rebaixar-se.

cheaply ['tʃi:plɪ] *adv* [at a low price] barato.

cheat [tʃi:t] <> *n* trapaceiro *m*, -ra *f*. <> *vt* trapacear; **to ~ sb out of sthg** passar alguém para trás em algo. <> *vi* [be dishonest] trapacear.
➡ **cheat on** *vt fus inf* [be unfaithful to] trair.

check [tʃek] <> *n* -1. [gen]: **~ (on sthg)** checagem *f* (de algo) -2. [restraint]: **~ (on sthg)** controle *m* (sobre algo); **in ~** sob controle -3. *US* [bill] conta *f* -4. [pattern] xadrez *m* -5. [in chess] xeque *m*. <> *vt* -1. [test, verify] verificar, conferir -2. [restrain, stop] conter. <> *vi* verificar; **to ~ for sthg** verificar se há algo, procurar por algo; **to ~ on sthg** examinar algo.
➡ **check in** <> *vt sep* [luggage, coat] despachar. <> *vi* -1. [at hotel] registrar-se -2. [at airport] fazer check-in.
➡ **check out** <> *vt sep* -1. [luggage, coat] dar baixa em -2. [investigate] averiguar. <> *vi* [from hotel] fechar a conta e sair.
➡ **check up** *vi* informar-se; **to ~ up on sb/sthg** informar-se sobre alguém/algo.

checkbook *n US* = chequebook.

checked [tʃekt] *adj* [patterned] quadriculado(da).

checkered *adj US* = chequered.

checkers ['tʃekəz] *n US* (jogo *m* de) damas *fpl*.

check-in *n* check-in *m*.

checking account ['tʃekɪŋ-] *n US* conta *f* corrente.

checkmate ['tʃekmeɪt] *n* [in chess] xeque-mate *m*.

checkout ['tʃekaʊt] *n* [in supermarket] caixa *m*.

checkpoint ['tʃekpɔɪnt] *n* [place] posto *m* de controle.

check-up *n* check-up *m*.

Cheddar (cheese) ['tʃedəʳ-] *n* queijo *m* Cheddar.

cheek [tʃi:k] *n* -1. [of face] bochecha *f* -2. *inf* [impudence] audácia *f*.

cheekbone ['tʃi:kbəʊn] *n* osso *m* malar, maçã *f* do rosto.

cheeky ['tʃi:kɪ] (*compar* -ier, *superl* -iest) *adj* descarado(da).

cheer [tʃɪəʳ] <> *n* [shout] vivas *fpl*. <> *vt* -1. [shout approval, encouragement at] ovacionar -2. [gladden] animar. <> *vi* aclamar, aplaudir.
➡ **cheers** *excl* -1. [said before drinking] saúde! -2. *UK inf* [goodbye] tchau! -3. *UK inf* [thank you] valeu!
➡ **cheer up** <> *vt sep* animar. <> *vi* animar-se.

cheerful ['tʃɪəfʊl] *adj* alegre.

cheerio [,tʃɪərɪ'əʊ] *excl UK inf* tchau!

cheese [tʃi:z] *n* queijo *m*.

cheeseboard ['tʃi:zbɔ:d] *n* -1. [board] tábua *f* de queijos -2. [on menu] variedade *f* de queijos.

cheeseburger ['tʃi:z,bɜ:gəʳ] *n* xisburguer *m*.

cheesecake ['tʃi:zkeɪk] *n CULIN* torta *f* de queijo.

cheetah ['tʃi:tə] *n* guepardo *m*.

chef [ʃef] *n* cozinheiro *m*, -ra *f* -chefe.

chemical ['kemɪkl] <> *adj* químico(ca). <> *n* substância *f* química.

chemical weapon *n* arma *f* química.

chemist ['kemɪst] *n* -1. *UK* [pharmacist] farmacêutico *m*, -ca *f*; **~'s (shop)** farmácia *f* -2. [scientist] químico *m*, -ca *f*.

chemistry ['kemɪstrɪ] *n* química *f*.

cheque *UK*, **check** *US* [tʃek] *n* cheque *m*.

chequebook *UK*, **checkbook** *US* ['tʃekbʊk] *n* talão *m* de cheques.

cheque (guarantee) card *n UK* cartão *m* de garantia de cheque.

chequered *UK* ['tʃekəd], **checkered** *US* ['tʃekərd] *adj fig* [varied] cheio (cheia) de altos e baixos.

cherish ['tʃerɪʃ] *vt* [treasure - hope, memory] acalentar; [- privilege, right] apreciar; [- person, thing] acariciar.

cherry ['tʃerɪ] (*pl* -ies) *n* -1. [fruit] cereja *f* -2.: **~ (tree)** cerejeira *f*.

chess [tʃes] *n* xadrez *m*.

chessboard ['tʃesbɔ:d] *n* tabuleiro *m* de xadrez.

chessman ['tʃesmæn] (*pl* -men [-men]), **chess piece** *n* peça *f* do jogo de xadrez.

chest [tʃest] *n* -1. *ANAT* peito *m* -2. [box, trunk] caixa *f* -3. [coffer] baú *m*.

chestnut ['tʃesnʌt] <> *adj* [colour] castanho(nha). <> *n* -1. [nut] castanha *f* -2.: **~ (tree)** castanheiro *m*.

chest of drawers (*pl* **chests of drawers**) *n* [piece of furniture] cômoda *f*.

chew [tʃu:] <> *n* [biting] mastigação *f*. <> *vt* -1. [food] mastigar -2. [nails, carpet] roer.
➡ **chew up** *vt sep* [food, slippers] roer.

chewing gum ['tʃuːɪŋ-] n chiclete m.

chic [ʃiːk] <> adj chique. <> n elegância f.

chick [tʃɪk] n - 1. [baby bird] filhote m (de pássaro) - 2. inf [woman] garota f.

chicken ['tʃɪkɪn] n - 1. [bird] galinha f - 2. (U) [food] frango m - 3. inf [coward] galinha m.
  → **chicken out** vi inf: to ~ out (of sthg/ of doing sthg) acovardar-se (de algo/de fazer algo).

chickenpox ['tʃɪkɪnpɒks] n catapora f.

chickpea ['tʃɪkpiː] n grão-de-bico m.

chicory ['tʃɪkərɪ] n [vegetable] chicória f.

chief [tʃiːf] <> adj - 1. [most important] principal - 2. [head] chefe; ~ accountant contador m, -ra f chefe. <> n - 1. [of organization] chefe mf - 2. [of tribe] chefe m, cacique m.

chief executive n [head of company] presidente mf executivo, -va.

chiefly ['tʃiːflɪ] adv [mainly] principalmente.

chiffon ['ʃɪfɒn] n chiffon m.

chilblain ['tʃɪlbleɪn] n frieira f.

child [tʃaɪld] (pl children) n - 1. [boy, girl] criança f - 2. [son, daughter] filho m, -lha f.

child benefit n UK benefício pago pelo governo britânico a todas as famílias de acordo com o número de filhos.

childbirth ['tʃaɪldbɜːθ] n (U) parto m.

childhood ['tʃaɪldhʊd] n infância f.

childish ['tʃaɪldɪʃ] adj pej infantil.

childlike ['tʃaɪldlaɪk] adj ingênuo(nua).

childminder ['tʃaɪld,maɪndəʳ] n UK babá mf.

childproof ['tʃaɪldpruːf] adj seguro(ra) para crianças, à prova de crianças.

children ['tʃɪldrən] pl ▷ child.

Chile ['tʃɪlɪ] n Chile.

Chilean ['tʃɪlɪən] <> adj chileno(na). <> n chileno m, -na f.

chili ['tʃɪlɪ] n = chilli.

chill [tʃɪl] <> adj glacial. <> n - 1. [illness] resfriado m - 2. [in temperature]: a ~ in the air uma friagem - 3. [feeling of fear] calafrio m. <> vt - 1. [drink, food] gelar - 2. [person] arrepiar-se de. <> vi [drink, food] esfriar.

chilli ['tʃɪlɪ] (pl -ies) n [vegetable] pimenta-malagueta f.

chilling ['tʃɪlɪŋ] adj - 1. [very cold] gelado(da) - 2. [frightening] arrepiante.

chilly ['tʃɪlɪ] (compar -ier, superl -iest) adj frio (fria).

chime [tʃaɪm] <> n [of bell, clock] batida f. <> vt [time] bater. <> vi [bell, clock] tocar.
  → **chime in** vi concordar.

chimney ['tʃɪmnɪ] n chaminé f.

chimneypot ['tʃɪmnɪpɒt] n cano m de chaminé.

chimneysweep ['tʃɪmnɪswiːp] n limpador m, -ra f de chaminé.

chimp [tʃɪmp] inf, **chimpanzee** [,tʃɪmpən'ziː] n chimpanzé mf.

chin [tʃɪn] n queixo m.

china ['tʃaɪnə] n (U) - 1. [substance] porcelana f - 2. [crockery] louças fpl de porcelana.

China ['tʃaɪnə] n China.

Chinese [,tʃaɪ'niːz] <> adj chinês(esa). <> n [language] chinês m. <> npl: the ~ os chineses.

Chinese cabbage n repolho m chinês.

Chinese leaf n UK = Chinese cabbage.

chink [tʃɪŋk] n - 1. [narrow opening] fresta f - 2. [sound] tinido m.

chip [tʃɪp] (pt & pp -ped, cont -ping) n - 1. UK [hot, fried potato strip] batata f frita em palito - 2. US [snack] batata f frita de pacote - 3. [fragment] lasca f - 4. [flaw] defeito m - 5. COMPUT chip m - 6. [token] ficha f. <> vt [damage] lascar.
  → **chip in** vi inf - 1. [contribute] fazer uma vaquinha - 2. [interrupt] interromper.
  → **chip off** vt sep lascar.

chipboard ['tʃɪpbɔːd] n (U) compensado m.

chip shop n UK loja onde se compram peixe com batatas fritas.

chiropodist [kɪ'rɒpədɪst] n quiropodista mf.

chirp [tʃɜːp] vi chilrar, piar.

chirpy ['tʃɜːpɪ] (compar -ier, superl -iest) adj esp UK inf [cheerful] animado(da).

chisel ['tʃɪzl] (UK pt & pp -led, cont -ling, US pt & pp -ed, cont -ing) <> n - 1. [for wood] formão m - 2. [for stone] cinzel m. <> vt - 1. [wood] esculpir com formão - 2. [stone] cinzelar.

chit [tʃɪt] n [note] vale m.

chit-chat n (U) inf bate-papo m.

chivalry ['ʃɪvlrɪ] n - 1. literary [of knights] cavalaria f - 2. [courtesy] cavalheirismo m.

chives [tʃaɪvz] npl cebolinha f.

chlorine ['klɔːriːn] n (U) cloro m.

choc-ice ['tʃɒkaɪs] n UK bola de sorvete com cobertura de chocolate.

chock [tʃɒk] n calço m (para roda de veículo).

chock-a-block, chock-full adj inf: ~ (with) [people] apinhado(da) (de); [things] entupido(da) (de).

chocolate ['tʃɒkələt] <> n (U) chocolate m; plain/milk ~ chocolate amargo/ ao leite; a box of ~s uma caixa de bombons. ⬦ *comp* [biscuit, cake, mousse] de chocolate.

choice [tʃɔɪs] ⬦ *n* -**1.** [gen] escolha *f*, opção *f*; **it was my first** ~ foi a minha primeira opção -**2.** [variety, selection] variedade *f*. ⬦ *adj* selecionado(da).

choir [ˈkwaɪəʳ] *n* [singers] coro *m*.

choirboy [ˈkwaɪəbɔɪ] *n* menino *m* de coro.

choke [tʃəʊk] ⬦ *n* AUT afogador *m*. ⬦ *vt* -**1.** [subj: person] estrangular -**2.** [subj: smoke, fumes] asfixiar, sufocar -**3.** [block] entupir, obstruir. ⬦ *vi* [on food, water] engasgar.

cholera [ˈkɒlərə] *n* (*U*) cólera *f*.

choose [tʃuːz] (*pt* chose, *pp* chosen) ⬦ *vt* -**1.** [select] escolher -**2.** [opt]: **to** ~ **to do sthg** optar por fazer algo. ⬦ *vi* [select]: **to** ~ **(from sthg)** escolher (entre algo).

choos(e)y [ˈtʃuːzɪ] (*compar* -ier, *superl* -iest) *adj* exigente.

chop [tʃɒp] ⬦ *n* [meat] costeleta *f*. ⬦ *vt* -**1.** [wood] retalhar -**2.** [vegetables, apple] picar -**3.** *inf* [funding, budget] cortar -**4.** *phr*: **to** ~ **and change** ser inconstante.

➡ **chop down** *vt sep* derrubar.

➡ **chop up** *vt sep* -**1.** [vegetables, fruit] picar -**2.** [wood, meat] cortar.

chopper [ˈtʃɒpəʳ] *n* -**1.** [axe] machadinha *f* -**2.** *inf* [helicopter] helicóptero *m*.

choppy [ˈtʃɒpɪ] (*compar* -ier, *superl* -iest) *adj* [sea] agitado(da).

chopsticks [ˈtʃɒpstɪks] *npl* hashi *mpl*.

chord [kɔːd] *n* MUS acorde *m*.

chore [tʃɔːʳ] *n* afazeres *mpl*; **household** ~ **s** afazeres domésticos.

chortle [ˈtʃɔːtl] *vi* dar gargalhadas.

chorus [ˈkɔːrəs] *n* -**1.** [gen] coro *m* -**2.** [part of song] refrão *m*.

chose [tʃəʊz] *pt* ⊳ choose.

chosen [ˈtʃəʊzn] *pp* ⊳ choose.

Christ [kraɪst] ⬦ *n* Cristo *m*. ⬦ *excl* Jesus Cristo!, Minha Nossa!

christen [ˈkrɪsn] *vt* batizar.

christening [ˈkrɪsnɪŋ] *n* batizado *m*.

Christian [ˈkrɪstʃən] ⬦ *adj* cristão(tã). ⬦ *n* cristão *m*, -tã *f*.

Christianity [ˌkrɪstɪˈænətɪ] *n* (*U*) cristianismo *m*.

Christian name *n* nome *m* de batismo.

Christmas [ˈkrɪsməs] *n* Natal *m*; **Happy** OR **Merry** ~! Feliz Natal!

Christmas card *n* cartão *m* de Natal.

Christmas carol *n* cântico *m* de Natal.

Christmas Day *n* dia *m* de Natal.

Christmas Eve *n* noite *f* de Natal.

Christmas pudding *n* UK pudim rico e escuro feito com frutas secas,

condimentos e gordura animal, servido no Natal.

Christmas tree *n* árvore *f* de Natal.

chrome [krəʊm], **chromium** [ˈkrəʊmɪəm] ⬦ *n* (*U*) cromo *m*. ⬦ *comp* de cromo, cromado(da).

chronic [ˈkrɒnɪk] *adj* -**1.** [long-lasting] crônico(ca) -**2.** [habitual] inveterado(-da).

chronicle [ˈkrɒnɪkl] *n* crônica *f*.

chronological [ˌkrɒnəˈlɒdʒɪkl] *adj* cronológico(ca).

chrysanthemum [krɪˈsænθəməm] (*pl* -s) *n* crisântemo *m*.

chubby [ˈtʃʌbɪ] (*compar* -ier, *superl* -iest) *adj* rechonchudo(da).

chuck [tʃʌk] *vt inf* -**1.** [throw] jogar, atirar -**2.** *inf*: **to** ~ **sb** dar o fora em alguém; **to** ~ **sthg** largar algo.

➡ **chuck away, chuck out** *vt sep inf* jogar fora; **to** ~ **sthg out** botar algo fora; **to** ~ **sb out** botar alguém para fora.

chuckle [ˈtʃʌkl] *vi* rir discretamente.

chug [tʃʌg] (*pt & pp* -ged, *cont* -ging) *vi* ratear.

chum [tʃʌm] *n inf* camarada *mf*, companheiro *m*, -ra *f*.

chunk [tʃʌŋk] *n* -**1.** [piece] pedaço *m* -**2.** *inf* [large amount] grande parte *f*.

church [tʃɜːtʃ] *n* -**1.** [building] igreja *f*; **to go to** ~ freqüentar a igreja -**2.** [organization]: **the Church** a Igreja.

Church of England *n*: **the** ~ a Igreja Anglicana.

churchyard [ˈtʃɜːtʃjɑːd] *n* cemitério ao redor de uma igreja.

churlish [ˈtʃɜːlɪʃ] *adj* indelicado(da).

churn [tʃɜːn] ⬦ *n* -**1.** [for making butter] batedeira *f* de manteiga -**2.** [for transporting milk] latão *m*. ⬦ *vt* [stir up] agitar.

➡ **churn out** *vt sep inf* produzir em larga escala.

chute [ʃuːt] *n* -**1.** [waterfall] queda *f* d'água, cachoeira *f* -**2.** [for escape] rampa *f* -**3.** [for rubbish] calha *f* -**4.** [in a pool] tobogã *m*.

chutney [ˈtʃʌtnɪ] *n* (*U*) molho feito à base de frutas, sementes picantes e açúcar que se come com carne ou queijo.

CIA (*abbr of* **Central Intelligence Agency**) *n* CIA *f*.

CID (*abbr of* **Criminal Investigation Department**) *n* departamento de investigação criminal da polícia britânica.

cider [ˈsaɪdəʳ] *n* sidra *f*.

cigar [sɪˈgɑːʳ] *n* charuto *m*.

cigarette [ˌsɪgəˈret] *n* cigarro *m*.

cinder [ˈsɪndəʳ] *n* cinza *f*.

Cinderella [ˌsɪndəˈrelə] *n* Cinderela *f* gata borralheira *f*.

cinema [ˈsɪnəmə] *n* [place, art] cinema *m*.

cinnamon [ˈsɪnəmən] *n (U)* canela *f*.

cipher [ˈsaɪfəʳ] *n* **-1.** [secret writing system] cifra *f* **-2.** *fig* [person] nulidade *f*.

circa [ˈsɜːkə] *prep* cerca de, aproximadamente.

circle [ˈsɜːkl] ◇ *n* **-1.** [gen] círculo *m*; **to go round in ~s** andar em círculos **-2.** [seats in theatre, cinema] galeria *f*. ◇ *vt* **-1.** [draw a circle round] marcar com círculo **-2.** [move round] circundar. ◇ *vi* mover-se em círculos.

circuit [ˈsɜːkɪt] *n* **-1.** [gen] circuito *m* **-2.** [lap, movement round] volta *f*.

circuitous [səˈkjuːɪtəs] *adj* tortuoso(sa).

circular [ˈsɜːkjʊləʳ] ◇ *adj* **-1.** [shape, object] redondo(da) **-2.** [argument] circular. ◇ *n* circular *f*.

circulate [ˈsɜːkjʊleɪt] ◇ *vi* circular. ◇ *vt* circular.

circulation [ˌsɜːkjʊˈleɪʃn] *n* circulação *f*; **in ~** em circulação.

circumcision [ˌsɜːkəmˈsɪʒn] *n* circuncisão *f*.

circumference [səˈkʌmfərəns] *n* circunferência *f*.

circumflex [ˈsɜːkəmfleks] *n*: **~ (accent)** (acento) *m* circunflexo *m*.

circumspect [ˈsɜːkəmspekt] *adj* circunspecto(ta).

circumstances [ˈsɜːkəmstənsɪz] *npl* circunstâncias *fpl*; **under OR in no ~** sob OR em nenhuma circunstância; **under OR in the ~** nas OR nestas circunstâncias.

circumvent [ˌsɜːkəmˈvent] *vt* *fml* burlar.

circus [ˈsɜːkəs] *n* **-1.** [for entertainment] circo *m* **-2.** [in place names] *no Reino Unido, praça circular à qual convergem várias ruas.*

CIS (*abbr of* Commonwealth of Independent States) *n* CEI *f*.

cistern [ˈsɪstən] *n* **-1.** *UK* [in roof] cisterna *f* **-2.** [on lavatory] caixa *f* de descarga.

cite [saɪt] *vt* citar.

citizen [ˈsɪtɪzn] *n* [of country, of town] cidadão *m*, -dã *f*.

Citizens' Advice Bureau *n* Centro *m* de Apoio ao Cidadão.

citizenship [ˈsɪtɪznʃɪp] *n (U)* cidadania *f*.

citrus fruit [ˈsɪtrəs-] *n* fruta *f* cítrica.

city [ˈsɪtɪ] (*pl* -ies) *n* cidade *f*.

➡ **City** *n UK*: **the City** o *bairro financeiro de Londres.*

city centre *n* centro *m* da cidade.

city hall *n US* prefeitura *f*.

city technology college *n UK* centro de formação técnica profissional custeada por indústrias.

civic [ˈsɪvɪk] *adj* cívico(ca).

civic centre *n UK* centro *m* cívico.

civil [ˈsɪvl] *adj* **-1.** [involving ordinary citizens] civil **-2.** [polite] educado(da).

civil engineering *n (U)* engenharia *f* civil.

civilian [sɪˈvɪljən] ◇ *n* civil *mf*. ◇ *comp* civil.

civilization [ˌsɪvɪlaɪˈzeɪʃn] *n (U)* civilização *f*.

civilized [ˈsɪvɪlaɪzd] *adj* civilizado(da).

civil law *n (U)* [relating to private case] direito *m* civil.

civil liberties *npl* liberdades *fpl* civis.

civil rights *npl* direitos *mpl* civis.

civil servant *n* funcionário *m* público, funcionária *f* pública.

civil service *n* serviço *m* público.

civil war *n* guerra *f* civil.

CJD (*abbr of* Creutzfeldt-Jakob disease) *n* forma humana da doença da vaca louca, doença *f* de Creutzfeldt-Jakob.

cl (*abbr of* centilitre) *n* cl.

clad [klæd] *adj* *literary* [dressed]: **~ in sthg** vestido(da) de algo.

claim [kleɪm] ◇ *n* **-1.** [assertion] alegação *f* **-2.** [demand] reivindicação *f* **-3.** [rightful]: **to have a ~ on sb** ter direitos sobre alguém; **to have a ~ on sb's attention** reivindicar a atenção de alguém; **to lay ~ to sthg** reivindicar algo **-4.** [financial] reclamação *f*. ◇ *vt* **-1.** [assert, maintain] alegar; **to ~ (that)** alegar que **-2.** [apply for, assert one's rights to] reivindicar **-3.** [take] levar. ◇ *vi*: **to ~ on one's insurance** acionar o seguro; **to ~ for sthg** reclamar algo.

claimant [ˈkleɪmənt] *n* **-1.** [to the throne] pretendente *mf* **-2.** [of benefit, in law case] requerente *mf*.

clairvoyant [kleəˈvɔɪənt] *n* vidente *mf*.

clam [klæm] (*pt* & *pp* -med, *cont* -ming) *n* marisco *m*.

clamber [ˈklæmbəʳ] *vi* subir com dificuldade.

clammy [ˈklæmɪ] (*compar* -ier, *superl* -iest) *adj* *inf* melado(da).

clamour *UK*, **clamor** *US* [ˈklæməʳ] ◇ *n (U)* [noise] clamor *m*. ◇ *vi*: **to ~ for sthg** queixar-se por algo.

clamp [klæmp] ◇ *n* **-1.** [fastener] presilha *f*, braçadeira *f* **-2.** MED & TECH grampo *m*. ◇ *vt* **-1.** [with fastener] apertar **-2.** [parked car] pôr travas em.

➡ **clamp down** *vi*: **to ~ down (on sthg)** impor restrições (a algo).

clan [klæn] *n* clã *m*.

clandestine [klæn'destɪn] *adj* clandestino(na).

clang [klæŋ] *n* som *m* metálico, tinido *m*.

clap [klæp] (*pt* & *pp* **-ped**, *cont*-**ping**) ⟨⟩ *vt* **to** ~ **one's hands** bater palmas. ⟨⟩ *vi* aplaudir.

clapping ['klæpɪŋ] *n (U)* aplauso *m*.

claret ['klærət] *n* **-1.** [wine] clarete *m* **-2.** [colour] cor-de-vinho *f*.

clarify ['klærɪfaɪ] (*pt* & *pp* **-ied**) *vt* [explain, expand on] esclarecer.

clarinet [,klærə'net] *n* clarinete *m*.

clarity ['klærətɪ] *n (U)* clareza *f*.

clash [klæʃ] ⟨⟩ *n* **-1.** [of interests, personality] choque *m* **-2.** [disagreement] divergência *f* **-3.** [noise] estrépito *m*. ⟨⟩ *vi* **-1.** [be incompatible - ideas, beliefs] chocar-se; [- colours] destoar; **to** ~ **with sthg** destoar de algo **-2.** [fight] chocarse **-3.** [disagree] divergir **-4.** [coincide] coincidir.

clasp [klɑːsp] ⟨⟩ *n* [fastener] fecho *m*. ⟨⟩ *vt* [hold tight] apertar.

class [klɑːs] ⟨⟩ *n* **-1.** [gen] classe *f* **-2.** [lesson] aula *f* **-3.** [category] espécie *f*. ⟨⟩ *vt* classificar; **to** ~ **sb as sthg** classificar alguém como algo.

classic ['klæsɪk] ⟨⟩ *adj* clássico(ca). ⟨⟩ *n* clássico *m*.

classical ['klæsɪkl] *adj* clássico(ca).

classified ['klæsɪfaɪd] *adj* [secret] confidencial.

classified ad *n* (anúncio *m*) classificado *m*.

classify ['klæsɪfaɪ] (*pt* & *pp* **-ied**) *vt* classificar.

classmate ['klɑːsmeɪt] *n* colega *mf* de classe.

classroom ['klɑːsrʊm] *n* sala *f* de aula.

classy ['klɑːsɪ] (*compar* **-ier**, *superl* **-iest**) *adj inf* bacana, chique.

clatter ['klætəʳ] *n* **-1.** [of pans, dishes] tinido *m* **-2.** [of hooves] repique *m*.

clause [klɔːz] *n* **-1.** [in legal document] cláusula *f* **-2.** GRAMM oração *f*.

claw [klɔː] ⟨⟩ *n* **-1.** [of wild animal, bird] garra *f* **-2.** [of cat, dog] unha *f* **-3.** [of sea creature] pinça *f* **-4.** [of insect] ferrão *f*. ⟨⟩ *vt* arranhar; **to** ~ **one's way to** galgar seu caminho para. ⟨⟩ *vi*: **to** ~ **at sthg** agarrar-se a algo.

clay [kleɪ] *n* argila *f*, barro *m*.

clean [kliːn] ⟨⟩ *adj* **-1.** [gen] limpo(pa) **-2.** [blank] em branco **-3.** [inoffensive] inofensivo(va) **-4.** [cut, break] preciso(sa). ⟨⟩ *vt* [make clean] limpar; **to** ~ **one's teeth** *UK* escovar os dentes. ⟨⟩ *vi* fazer faxina.

➡ **clean out** *vt sep* [clear out] fazer uma limpeza (em).

➡ **clean up** *vt sep* [clear up] arrumar.

cleaner ['kliːnəʳ] *n* **-1.** [person] faxineiro *m*, **-ra** *f* **-2.** [substance] produto *m* de limpeza.

cleaning ['kliːnɪŋ] *n (U)* limpeza *f*, faxina *f*.

cleanliness ['klenlɪnɪs] *n (U)* limpeza *f*, asseio *m*.

clean-living *adj* de vida limpa.

cleanse [klenz] *vt* **-1.** [make clean] limpar **-2.** [make pure] purificar.

cleanser ['klenzəʳ] *n* **-1.** [for skin] creme *m* de limpeza **-2.** [detergent] detergente *m*.

cleansing solution ['klenzɪŋ-] *n* [for contact lenses] solução *f* de limpeza.

clean-shaven *adj* -'[eɪvn] *adj* de barba feita.

clear [klɪəʳ] ⟨⟩ *adj* **-1.** [gen] claro(ra); **to make sthg** ~ **(to sb)** tornar algo claro (para alguém); **to make it** ~ **that** deixar claro que; **to make o.s.** ~ fazer-se entender; **to be** ~ **about sthg** [understand] entender algo com clareza; [explain clearly] fazer-se entender sobre algo; ~ **head** mente *f* lúcida **-2.** [obvious, unmistakable] óbvio(via) **-3.** [transparent] transparente **-4.** [water] límpido(da) **-5.** [unobstructed, free] livre. ⟨⟩ *adv* [out of the way]: **to step** ~ ficar fora do caminho; **stand** ~! afaste-se!; **to stay** OR **steer** ~ **of sb/sthg** afastar-se de alguém/algo. ⟨⟩ *vt* **-1.** [remove obstacles from - way, path] desimpedir; [- pipe] limpar; [- table] tirar **-2.** [take out of the way] retirar **-3.** [jump] transpor **-4.** [pay] saldar **-5.** [authorize] autorizar **-6.** [prove not guilty] livrar de culpa; **to be** ~ **ed of sthg** ser declarado(da) inocente de algo **-7.** [customs] desembaraçar. ⟨⟩ *vi* **-1.** [disperse, diminish - fog, smoke] dissipar-se; [- headache] passar **-2.** [brighten up] clarear.

➡ **clear away** *vt sep* arrumar.

➡ **clear off** *vi UK inf* dar o fora.

➡ **clear out** ⟨⟩ *vt sep* [tidy up] arrumar. ⟨⟩ *vi inf* [leave] dar o fora.

➡ **clear up** ⟨⟩ *vt sep* **-1.** [tidy] arrumar **-2.** [solve, settle] resolver. ⟨⟩ *vi* **-1.** [weather] clarear **-2.** [tidy up] arrumar.

clearance ['klɪərəns] *n (U)* **-1.** [removal] retirada *f*; **the** ~ **of mines** a remoção de minas terrestres; **land** ~ a limpeza da terra **-2.** [of contents of house] desocupação *f* **-3.** [permission] autorização *f*; **customs** ~ desembaraço *m* alfandegário.

clear-cut *adj* bem definido(da).

clearing ['klɪərɪŋ] *n* [in forest] clareira *f*.

clearing bank *n UK* banco *m* compensador.

clearly ['klɪəlɪ] *adv* **-1.** [distinctly, lucidly]

claramente -2. [obviously] evidentemente.

clearway ['klɪəweɪ] n UK AUT via f expressa.

cleavage ['kli:vɪdʒ] n [between breasts] decote m.

cleaver ['kli:və'] n cutelo m de açougueiro.

clef [klef] n clave f.

cleft [kleft] n fenda f, rachadura f.

clench [klentʃ] vt cerrar; **to have sthg ~ed between one's teeth** ter algo preso entre os dentes.

clergy ['klɜ:dʒɪ] npl: **the ~** o clero.

clergyman ['klɜ:dʒɪmən] (pl -men [-mən]) n clérigo m.

clerical ['klerɪkl] adj -1. [in office] de escritório -2. [in church] clerical.

clerk [UK klɑ:k, US klɜ:rk] n -1. [in office] auxiliar mf de escritório -2. [in court] escriturário m, -ria f, escrevente mf -3. US [shop assistant] balconista mf.

clever ['klevə'] adj -1. [intelligent] inteligente -2. [ingenious] engenhoso(sa); **that's ~!** que engenhoso! -3. [skilful] hábil.

click [klɪk] <> n -1. [gen] clique m -2. [of tongue] estalo m. <> vt estalar. <> vi [gen] estalar; **the door ~ed shut** a porta se fechou com um clique.

client ['klaɪənt] n cliente mf.

cliff [klɪf] n penhasco m.

climate ['klaɪmɪt] n clima m.

climate change n mudança f climática.

climax ['klaɪmæks] n clímax m.

climb [klaɪm] <> n [ascent] escalada f. <> vt [go up - tree, ladder] subir em; [- hill, mountain] escalar; [- fence] transpor. <> vi -1. [person]: to ~ up/down/over sthg subir em/descer de/transpor algo; to ~ into/out of sthg subir em/ descer de algo -2. [plant] trepar -3. [road, plane, prices] subir.

climb-down n retratação f.

climber ['klaɪmə'] n [person] alpinista mf.

climbing ['klaɪmɪŋ] <> adj [plant] trepadeira. <> n (U) alpinismo m.

clinch [klɪntʃ] vt [settle] fechar.

cling [klɪŋ] (pt & pp clung) vi -1. [person]: to ~ to sb/sthg [physically] agarrar-se a alguém/algo; fig [emotionally: to person] apegar-se a alguém/algo; [to beliefs, ideas, principles] aferrar-se a alguém/ algo -2. [clothes]: to ~ (to sb) ajustar-se bem (a alguém).

clingfilm ['klɪŋfɪlm] n (U) UK filme m de PVC transparente.

clinic ['klɪnɪk] n [building] clínica f.

clinical ['klɪnɪkl] adj -1. MED clínico(ca) -2. pej [coldly rational] analítico(ca) -3. [functional] impessoal.

clink [klɪŋk] vi tilintar.

clip [klɪp] (pt & pp -ped, cont -ping) <> n -1. [fastener - for paper] clipe m; [- for hair] grampo m; [- for earring] fecho m -2. TV & CINEMA videoclipe m -3. inf [smack]: **to give sb a ~ around the ear** dar um tapa na orelha de alguém. <> vt -1. [fasten] prender -2. [cut - lawn, hedge, nails] cortar; [- newspaper cutting] recortar.

clipboard ['klɪpbɔ:d] n prancheta f com prendedor.

clip-on adj de prender; **~ earrings** brincos mpl de pressão; **~ badge** button m; **~ bow tie** gravata-borboleta f.

clippers ['klɪpəz] npl -1. [for hair] máquina f de cortar cabelo -2. [for nails] cortador m de unhas -3. [for plants, hedges] tesoura f de podar.

clipping ['klɪpɪŋ] n [newspaper cutting] recorte m.

clippings npl [small pieces] fragmentos mpl; **grass/nail ~s** restos mpl de grama/unha cortada.

cloak [kləʊk] n [garment] capa f.

cloakroom ['kləʊkrʊm] n -1. [for clothes] guarda-volumes m inv -2. UK [toilet - in public place] banheiro m; [- in house] lavabo m.

clock [klɒk] <> n -1. [timepiece] relógio m; **round the ~** dia e noite -2. [in vehicle - mileometer] hodômetro m; [- speedometer] velocímetro m. <> vt [reach time or speed] marcar.

clock in, clock on vi UK [at work] bater o ponto OR cartão-de-ponto na entrada.

clock off, clock out vi UK [at work] bater o ponto OR cartão-de-ponto na saída.

clockwise ['klɒkwaɪz] <> adj em sentido horário. <> adv em sentido horário.

clockwork ['klɒkwɜ:k] <> n (U): **to go like ~** funcionar como um relógio. <> comp de corda.

clog [klɒg] (pt & pp -ged, cont -ging) vt entupir, bloquear.

clogs npl tamancos mpl.

clog up <> vt sep -1. [drains] entupir -2. [nose] congestionar. <> vi [drains] entupir; [roads] bloquear; [pores] fechar.

clone [kləʊn] vt clonar.

cloning ['kləʊnɪŋ] n clonagem f.

close¹ [kləʊs] <> *adj* **-1.** [near] próxi-
mo(ma), perto; ~ **to sb/sthg** perto de
alguém/algo; **it was a ~ shave** foi por
um fio *OR* triz; ~ **up**, ~ **to** de perto; ~
by, ~ **at hand** bem perto **-2.** [in relation-
ship] íntimo(ma); ~ **to sb** apegado(da) a
alguém **-3.** [in degree of connection - resemblance, family] próximo(ma); [- link,
connection] estreito(ta) **-4.** [careful]: **a ~
watch** um olhar atento; **to pay ~ attention** prestar muita atenção; ~ **questioning** uma pergunta detalhada; **a
~r look** um olhar mais de perto; **a ~r
examination** um exame minucioso **-5.**
[oppressive] carregado(da) **-6.** [almost
equal] com uma pequena margem de
diferença. <> *adv* perto.
➡ **close on, close to** *prep* [almost] cerca
de.

close² [kləʊz] <> *vt* **-1.** [shut, shut down]
fechar **-2.** [bring to an end] encerrar,
concluir. <> *vi* **-1.** [shut] fechar **-2.** [end]
terminar. <> *n* [end] fim *m*, final *m*.
➡ **close down** <> *vt sep* [shut] fechar.
<> *vi* [shut down] fechar.

closed [kləʊzd] *adj* fechado(da).

close-knit [ˌkləʊs-] *adj* muito unido(-
da).

closely ['kləʊslɪ] *adv* **-1.** [in degree of con-
nection] intimamente; **to resemble sb/
sthg ~** parecer muito com alguém/
algo **-2.** [carefully] atentamente.

closet ['klɒzɪt] <> *adj inf* inconfesso(-
sa). <> *n* **-1.** *US* closet *m*, armário *m* **-2.**
fig: **to come out of the ~** sair do
armário.

close-up ['kləʊs-] *n* primeiro plano *m*.

closing time *n* horário *m* de fechamento.

closure ['kləʊʒə˞] *n* **-1.** [of business, com-
pany] fechamento *m* **-2.** [of road, railway
line: temporarily] interdição *f*.

clot [klɒt] (*pt & pp* **-ted**, *cont* **-ting**) <>
n **-1.** [of blood] coágulo *m* **-2.** *UK inf* [fool]
idiota *mf*. <> *vi* [blood] coagular.

cloth [klɒθ] *n* **-1.** (*U*) [fabric] tecido *m* **-2.**
[for cleaning] pano *m* **-3.** [tablecloth] toalha *f*.

clothe [kləʊð] *vt fml* [dress] vestir.

clothes [kləʊðz] *npl* roupa *f*; **to put one's
~ on** vestir-se; **to take one's ~ off** tirar
a roupa.

clothes brush *n* escova *f* de roupa.

clothesline ['kləʊðzlaɪn] *n* varal *m*.

clothes peg *UK*, **clothespin** *US*
['kləʊðzpɪn] *n* prendedor *m* de roupa.

clothing ['kləʊðɪŋ] *n* (*U*) roupa *f*; ~ **allowance** auxílio-vestuário *m*.

cloud [klaʊd] *n* [gen] nuvem *f*.
➡ **cloud over** *vi* [sky] encobrir-se.

cloudy ['klaʊdɪ] (*compar* **-ier**, *superl*
-iest) *adj* **-1.** [sky] nublado(da) **-2.** [liquid]
turvo(va).

clout [klaʊt] *inf* <> *n* (*U*) [influence]
influência *f*. <> *vt* [hit] dar um bofetão
em.

clove [kləʊv] *n*: **a ~ of garlic** um dente
de alho.
➡ **cloves** *npl* [spice] cravo-da-índia *m*.

clover ['kləʊvə˞] *n* (*U*) trevo *m*.

clown [klaʊn] <> *n* **-1.** [performer]
palhaço *m* **-2.** [fool] palhaço *m*, -ça *f*.
<> *vi* fazer palhaçadas.

cloying ['klɔɪɪŋ] *adj* enjoativo(va).

club [klʌb] (*pt & pp* **-bed**, *cont* **-bing**) <>
n **-1.** [association] clube *m* **-2.** [nightclub]
boate *f*, casa *f* noturna **-3.** [weapon]
bastão *m* **-4.** *SPORT* [equipment]: **(golf)
~** taco *m* (de golfe). <> *vt* [hit] espancar.
➡ **clubs** *npl* [playing cards] paus *mpl*.
➡ **club together** *vi UK* fazer vaquinha.

club car *n US RAIL* vagão-restaurante *m*.

clubhouse ['klʌbhaʊs] *n* clube *m*.

cluck [klʌk] *vi* [hen, person] cacarejar.

clue [kluː] *n* **-1.** [in crime] pista *f*, vestígio
m; **I haven't (got) a ~** não tenho (a
menor) idéia **-2.** [hint] dica *f* **-3.** [in cross-
word] pista *f*.

clued-up [kluːd-] *adj UK inf* antenado(-
da).

clump [klʌmp] *n* [group - of trees] arvoredo *m*; [- of bushes] moita *m*; [- of flow-
ers] ramalhete *m*.

clumsy ['klʌmzɪ] (*compar* **-ier**, *superl*
-iest) *adj* [gen] desajeitado(da).

clung [klʌŋ] *pt & pp* ⊳ **cling**.

cluster ['klʌstə˞] <> *n* [group - of people,
houses, trees] grupo *m*; [- of grapes] cacho
m; [- of flowers] ramalhete *m*. <> *vi* **-1.**
[people] agrupar-se, reunir-se **-2.**
[things] amontoar-se.

clutch [klʌtʃ] <> *n AUT* embreagem *f*.
<> *vt* [with hands - object] agarrar; [-
part of body] apertar. <> *vi*: **to ~ at sb/
sthg** agarrar-se a alguém/algo.

clutter ['klʌtə˞] <> *n* bagunça *f*. <> *vt*
bagunçar.

cm (*abbr of* **centimetre**) *n* cm.

CND (*abbr of* **Campaign for Nuclear Disarmament**) *n* organização britânica
*que realiza campanhas contra o
armamento nuclear*.

c/o (*abbr of* **care of**) a/c.

Co. -1. (*abbr of* **Company**) Cia. **-2.** (*abbr
of* **County**) *área administrativa britânica, usada, em alguns casos, na
representação de endereços*.

coach [kəʊtʃ] <> *n* **-1.** *UK* [bus] ônibus
m inv **-2.** *RAIL* vagão *m* **-3.** [horsedrawn]

carruagem f - **4.** SPORT treinador m, -ra f - **5.** [tutor] professor m, -ra f particular. ◇ vt - **1.** SPORT treinar - **2.** [tutor] preparar; **to ~ sb in sthg** preparar alguém em algo.

coach station n UK (estação f) rodoviária f.

coal [kəʊl] n (U) carvão m.

coalfield ['kəʊlfi:ld] n jazida f de carvão.

coalition [,kəʊə'lɪʃn] n POL coalizão f.

coal mine n mina f de carvão.

coarse [kɔ:s] adj - **1.** [rough] áspero(ra) - **2.** [vulgar] grosseiro(ra).

coast [kəʊst] ◇ n costa f. ◇ vi [car] ir em ponto morto.

coastal ['kəʊstl] adj costeiro(ra); **a ~ town** uma cidade litorânea.

coaster ['kəʊstə'] n - **1.** [small mat] descanso m para copos - **2.** UK [ship] navio m costeiro.

coastguard ['kəʊstgɑ:d] n - **1.** [person] guarda mf costeiro, -ra - **2.** [organization]: **the ~** a guarda costeira.

coastline ['kəʊstlaɪn] n litoral m.

coat [kəʊt] ◇ n - **1.** [garment] casaco m - **2.** [of animal] pêlo m - **3.** [of paint, varnish] demão f. ◇ vt: **to ~ sthg (with sthg)** revestir algo (com algo).

coat hanger n cabide m.

coating ['kəʊtɪŋ] n [covering - of chocolate, icing] cobertura f; [- of dust] camada f.

coat of arms (pl **coats of arms**) n brasão m.

coax [kəʊks] vt: **to ~ sb (to do** OR **into doing sthg)** persuadir alguém (a fazer algo); **to ~ sthg out of sb** conseguir algo de alguém com jeitinho.

cobbled ['kɒbld] adj de pedras arredondadas.

cobbler ['kɒblə'] n sapateiro m, -ra f.

cobbles ['kɒblz], **cobblestones** ['kɒblstəʊnz] npl pedras arredondadas (para pavimentação).

cobweb ['kɒbweb] n teia f de aranha.

Coca-Cola® [,kəʊkə'kəʊlə] n Coca-Cola® f.

cocaine [kəʊ'keɪn] n (U) cocaína f.

cock [kɒk] ◇ n - **1.** UK [male chicken] galo m - **2.** [male bird] pássaro m macho - **3.** vulg [penis] pinto m. ◇ vt - **1.** [gun] engatilhar - **2.** [head] virar.

➤ **cock up** vt sep UK vulg: **the project was going fine, but they ~ed it up** o projeto estava indo bem, mas eles acabaram fodendo tudo.

cockerel ['kɒkrəl] n frango m.

cockeyed ['kɒkaɪd] adj inf - **1.** [not straight] torto(ta) - **2.** [unlikely to succeed] absurdo(da).

cockle ['kɒkl] n [shellfish] berbigão m.

Cockney ['kɒknɪ] (pl **Cockneys**) n - **1.** [person] pessoa vinda da área leste de Londres, em geral da classe trabalhadora - **2.** [accent] cockney m.

cockpit ['kɒkpɪt] n - **1.** [in plane] cabine f de comando - **2.** [in F1 car] cockpit m.

cockroach ['kɒkrəʊtʃ] n barata f.

cocksure [,kɒk'ʃʊə'] adj convencido(da).

cocktail ['kɒkteɪl] n [drink] coquetel m.

cocktail party n coquetel m.

cock-up n vinf cagada f.

cocky ['kɒkɪ] (compar -ier, superl -iest) adj inf petulante.

cocoa ['kəʊkəʊ] n (U) - **1.** [powder] cacau m - **2.** [drink] chocolate m.

coconut ['kəʊkənʌt] n coco m.

cod [kɒd] (pl inv OR -s) n bacalhau m.

COD - **1.** (abbr of **cash on delivery**) entrega contra pagamento - **2.** (abbr of **collect on delivery**) entrega contra pagamento.

code [kəʊd] ◇ n código m. ◇ vt - **1.** [encode] codificar - **2.** [give identifier to] identificar como.

cod-liver oil n (U) óleo m de fígado de bacalhau.

coerce [kəʊ'ɜ:s] vt: **to ~ sb (into doing sthg)** coagir alguém(a fazer algo).

C. of E. (abbr of **Church of England**) n igreja anglicana.

coffee ['kɒfɪ] n [drink] café m.

coffee bar n UK lanchonete f.

coffee break n intervalo m para o café, coffee break m.

coffee morning n UK evento social, realizado durante o café-da-manhã, cuja finalidade é arrecadar dinheiro para organizações beneficentes.

coffee pot n bule m para café.

coffee shop n - **1.** UK [café] café m - **2.** US [restaurant] cafeteria f - **3.** [shop selling coffee] cafeteria f.

coffee table n mesinha f de centro.

coffin ['kɒfɪn] n caixão m.

cog [kɒg] n [tooth on wheel] dente m de engrenagem; [wheel] roda f dentada.

coherent [kəʊ'hɪərənt] adj coerente.

cohesive [kəʊ'hi:sɪv] adj [united] coeso(sa).

coil [kɔɪl] ◇ n - **1.** [of rope, wire] rolo m - **2.** [of smoke] espiral f - **3.** ELEC bobina f - **4.** UK [contraceptive device] DIU m. ◇ vt enrolar. ◇ vi enrolar-se, enroscar-se.

➤ **coil up** vt sep enrolar-se.

coin [kɔɪn] ◇ n moeda f. ◇ vt [invent] criar.

coinage [ˈkɔɪnɪdʒ] n -1. (U) [currency] moeda f -2. (U) [system] sistema m monetário.

coincide [ˌkəʊɪnˈsaɪd] vi -1. [occur simultaneously]: to ~ (with sthg) coincidir (com algo) -2. [be in agreement] coincidir.

coincidence [kəʊˈɪnsɪdəns] n [chance event] coincidência f.

coincidental [kəʊˌɪnsɪˈdentl] adj coincidente.

coke [kəʊk] n -1. [fuel] coque m -2. inf [cocaine] coca f.

Coke® [kəʊk] n Coca® f.

cola [ˈkəʊlə] n refrigerante m de cola.

colander [ˈkʌləndəʳ] n coador m.

cold [kəʊld] ⟨⟩ adj frio (fria); **to feel** ~ [person] sentir frio; **to be** ~ [person] estar com frio; **it's** ~ **today** está frio hoje; **to get** ~ [person] ficar com frio; [food] esfriar. ⟨⟩ n -1. [illness] resfriado m; **to catch (a)** ~ pegar um resfriado -2. (U) [low temperature]: **the** ~ o frio.

cold-blooded [-ˈblʌdɪd] adj -1. [unfeeling] frio (fria) -2. [ruthless - killer, murderer] de sangue frio; [- killing, murder] a sangue frio.

cold sore n herpes m inv bucal.

cold war n: **the** ~ a guerra fria.

coleslaw [ˈkəʊlslɔː] n (U) salada f de repolho.

colic [ˈkɒlɪk] n (U) cólica f.

collaborate [kəˈlæbəreɪt] vi -1. [work together] colaborar; **to** ~ **with sb** colaborar com alguém -2. pej [with enemy] conspirar; **to** ~ **with sb** conspirar com alguém.

collapse [kəˈlæps] ⟨⟩ n (U) -1. [gen] colapso m -2. [of building, roof] desmoronamento m. ⟨⟩ vi -1. [gen] desmoronar -2. [fail] fracassar -3. [person] ter um colapso; **his lung** ~d o pulmão dele entrou em falência; **to** ~ **with a heart attack** ter um ataque do coração; **I** ~d **into bed** desfaleci na cama -4. [folding table, chair] desmontar-se.

collapsible [kəˈlæpsəbl] adj desmontável.

collar [ˈkɒləʳ] ⟨⟩ n -1. [on garment - shirt] colarinho m; [- dress, jacket] gola f -2. [for dog] coleira f -3. TECH anel m. ⟨⟩ vt inf [detain] segurar.

collarbone [ˈkɒləbəʊn] n clavícula f.

collate [kəˈleɪt] vt -1. [compare] confrontar -2. [put in order] ordenar.

collateral [kɒˈlætərəl] n (U) garantia f de empréstimo, caução f.

colleague [ˈkɒliːg] n colega mf.

collect [kəˈlekt] ⟨⟩ vt -1. [gather together - wood, bottles, belongings] juntar; [- material for book] colher, coletar; **to** ~ **o.s.** OR **one's thoughts** recompor-se -2. [as a hobby] colecionar -3. [fetch, pick up] buscar -4. [money, taxes] cobrar. ⟨⟩ vi -1. [crowd, people] reunir-se -2. [dust, dirt] juntar -3. [for charity, gift] arrecadar. ⟨⟩ adv US TELEC: **to call (sb)** ~ ligar (para alguém) a cobrar.

collection [kəˈlekʃn] n -1. [of objects] coleção f -2. [anthology] antologia f -3. (U) [act of collecting] coleta f -4. [of money] arrecadação f, vaquinha f; **they made a** ~ **to buy flowers for her** fizeram uma vaquinha para comprar flores para ela.

collective [kəˈlektɪv] ⟨⟩ adj coletivo(-va). ⟨⟩ n cooperativa f.

collector [kəˈlektəʳ] n -1. [as a hobby] colecionador m, -ra f -2. [of taxes] coletor m, -ra f -3. [of debts, rent] cobrador m, -ra f.

college [ˈkɒlɪdʒ] n -1. [for further education] escola f; **a** ~ **of technology** um instituto de tecnologia; **art** ~ escola de artes; **community** ~ US escola politécnica -2. UK [of university] instituição dentro de certas universidades britânicas que possui corpo docente, instalações e estudantes próprios -3. [organized body] colégio m; **electoral** ~ colégio eleitoral.

college of education n faculdade f de educação.

collide [kəˈlaɪd] vi: **to** ~ **(with sb/sthg)** colidir (com alguém/algo).

collie [ˈkɒlɪ] n collie m.

colliery [ˈkɒljərɪ] (pl -ies) n UK mina f de carvão (incluindo suas instalações).

collision [kəˈlɪʒn] n [crash]: ~ **(with sb/ sthg)** colisão f (com alguém/algo); ~ **between** colisão de.

collision course n: **to be on a** ~ estar em rota de colisão.

colloquial [kəˈləʊkwɪəl] adj coloquial.

colloquialism [kəˈləʊkwɪəlɪzm] n coloquialismo m.

collude [kəˈluːd] vi: **to** ~ **with sb** entrar em conluio com alguém.

Colombia [kəˈlɒmbɪə] n Colômbia f.

colon [ˈkəʊlən] n -1. ANAT cólon m -2. [punctuation mark] dois-pontos mpl.

colonel [ˈkɜːnl] n coronel m.

colonial [kəˈləʊnjəl] adj [rule, power] colonial.

colonize, -ise [ˈkɒlənaɪz] vt colonizar.

colony [ˈkɒlənɪ] (pl -ies) n -1. [gen] colônia f -2. [of artists] retiro m.

color etc. US = colour etc.

colossal [kəˈlɒsl] adj colossal.

colour *UK*, **color** *US* [ˈkʌləʳ] ⬦ *n* cor *f*; red/blue in ~ na cor vermelha/azul; the photos are in ~ as fotos são coloridas. ⬦ *adj* colorido(da); ~ **television/diagram** televisão/diagrama em cores. ⬦ *vt* -**1.** [food, liquid] tingir; [with pen, crayon] pintar, colorir -**2.** [dye] tingir -**3.** *fig* [affect] influenciar. ⬦ *vi* [blush] corar.

colour bar *n* discriminação *f* racial.

colour blind *adj* -**1.** daltônico(ca) -**2.** *fig* [racially unprejudiced] que não faz discriminação racial.

coloured *UK*, **colored** *US* [ˈkʌləd] *adj* -**1.** [having colour] colorido(da) -**2.** [having stated colour]: a cream-~ed jacket uma jaqueta cor de creme; a brightly ~ed shirt uma camisa de cores vivas.

colourful *UK*, **colorful** *US* [ˈkʌləfʊl] *adj* -**1.** [brightly coloured] colorido(da) -**2.** [story] vivo(va) -**3.** [person] animado(da).

colouring *UK*, **coloring** *US* [ˈkʌlərɪŋ] *n* -**1.** [dye] corante *m* -**2.** *(U)* [complexion, hair] tonalidade *f* -**3.** [colours] cor *m*.

colour scheme *n* distribuição *f* de cores.

colt [kəʊlt] *n* [young horse] potro *m*.

column [ˈkɒləm] *n* -**1.** [gen] coluna *f* -**2.** [of people, vehicles] fila *f*.

columnist [ˈkɒləmnɪst] *n* colunista *mf*.

coma [ˈkəʊmə] *n* coma *m*.

comb [kəʊm] ⬦ *n* [for hair] pente *m*. ⬦ *vt* -**1.** [hair] pentear -**2.** *fig* [search] vasculhar.

combat [ˈkɒmbæt] ⬦ *n* combate *m*. ⬦ *vt* [fight] combater.

combination [ˌkɒmbɪˈneɪʃn] *n* combinação *f*.

combine [*vb* kəmˈbaɪn, *n* ˈkɒmbaɪn] ⬦ *vt* [join together] agrupar; to ~ sthg with sthg [two substances] combinar algo com algo; [two qualities] reunir; [two activities] conjugar. ⬦ *vi* [businesses, political parties]: to ~ (with sb/sthg) aliar-se (a alguém/algo). ⬦ *n* [group] associação *f*.

come [kʌm] (*pt* came, *pp* come) *vi* -**1.** [move] vir; [arrive] chegar; the news came as a shock a notícia foi um choque; coming! estou indo. -**2.** [reach]: to ~ up/down to chegar a -**3.** [happen] chegar a; ~ what may haja o que houver -**4.** [become]: to ~ true tornar-se realidade; to ~ undone/unstuck se desfazer/soltar -**5.** [begin gradually]: to ~ to do sthg passar a fazer algo -**6.** [be placed in order] classificar-se; P ~s before O o P vem antes do Q; she came second in the exam ela se classificou em segundo lugar no exame -**7.** *phr*: ~ to think of it pensando bem.

➡ **to come** *adv* vindouro(ra); in (the) days/years to ~ nos dias/anos vindouros.

➡ **come about** *vi* [happen] acontecer.

➡ **come across** *vt fus* [find] encontrar.

➡ **come along** *vi* -**1.** [arrive by chance] aparecer -**2.** [improve] desenvolver-se.

➡ **come apart** *vi* -**1.** [fall to pieces] desfazer-se -**2.** [come off] cair.

➡ **come at** *vt fus* [attack] avançar para.

➡ **come back** *vi* -**1.** [in talk, writing]: to ~ back to sthg voltar a algo -**2.** [memory]: to ~ back (to sb) lembrar(-se) de.

➡ **come by** *vt fus* [get, obtain] conseguir.

➡ **come down** *vi* -**1.** [unemployment, prices] baixar -**2.** [aeroplane, parachutist] descer -**3.** [rain] cair.

➡ **come down to** *vt fus* resumir-se a.

➡ **come down with** *vt fus* [cold, flu] apanhar.

➡ **come forward** *vi* [witnesses, volunteers] apresentar-se.

➡ **come from** *vt fus* vir de.

➡ **come in** *vi* [enter] entrar.

➡ **come in for** *vt fus* [criticism] receber.

➡ **come into** *vt fus* -**1.** [inherit] receber -**2.** [begin to be]: to ~ into being surgir.

➡ **come off** *vi* -**1.** [button, label, lid] abrir -**2.** [attempt, joke] dar certo -**3.** [stain] sair -**4.** *phr*: ~ off it! *inf* deixa disso!

➡ **come on** *vi* -**1.** [start] começar -**2.** [light, heating] ligar-se -**3.** [progress, improve] ir; how's the work coming on? como está indo o trabalho? -**4.** *phr*: ~ on! [expressing encouragement] vamos lá!; [hurry up] vamos; [expressing disbelief] que é isso.

➡ **come out** *vi* -**1.** [truth, fact] revelar-se -**2.** [product, book, film] ser lançado -**3.** [go on strike] entrar em greve -**4.** [declare publicly]: to ~ out for/against sthg manifestar-se a favor/contra algo -**5.** [sun, moon, stars] aparecer.

➡ **come out with** *vt fus* [remark] sair com.

➡ **come round** *vi* [regain consciousness] voltar a si.

➡ **come through** *vt fus* [survive] sobreviver a.

➡ **come to** ⬦ *vt fus* -**1.** [reach]: to ~ to an end chegar ao fim; to ~ to a decision chegar a uma decisão -**2.** [amount to] chegar a. ⬦ *vi* [regain consciousness] voltar a si.

➡ **come under** *vt fus* -**1.** [be governed by] ser de competência de -**2.** [suffer]: to ~ under attack (from) sofrer ataque (de).

come up *vi* **-1.** [gen] surgir **-2.** [be imminent] estar próximo.

come up against *vt fus* [opposition, difficulties] enfrentar.

come up to *vt fus* [in space] chegar até.

come up with *vt fus* [answer, idea, solution] aparecer com.

comeback ['kʌmbæk] *n* [return] reaparecimento *m*; **to make a ~** reaparecer.

comedian [kə'mi:djən] *n* [comic] comediante *m*.

comedown ['kʌmdaʊn] *n inf* [anticlimax] retrocesso *m*.

comedy ['kɒmədɪ] (*pl* **-ies**) *n* comédia *f*.

comet ['kɒmɪt] *n* cometa *m*.

come-uppance [ˌkʌm'ʌpəns] *n inf*: **to get one's ~** levar o troco.

comfort ['kʌmfət] <> *n* **-1.** (*U*) [ease] conforto *m* **-2.** [luxury] luxo *m* **-3.** [solace] consolo *m*. <> *vt* consolar.

comfortable ['kʌmftəbl] *adj* **-1.** [chair, room] confortável **-2.** [at ease] à vontade **-3.** [financially secure] bem de vida **-4.** [after operation, accident] bem **-5.** [ample] amplo(pla).

comfortably ['kʌmftəblɪ] *adv* **-1.** [sit, sleep] confortavelmente **-2.** [without financial difficulty] bem; **I can manage ~ on £50 a week** posso me virar bem com 50 libras por semana **-3.** [win] com facilidade.

comfort station *n US euph* banheiro *m* público.

comic ['kɒmɪk] <> *adj* [amusing] engraçado(da). <> *n* **-1.** [comedian] comediante *mf* **-2.** [magazine] história *f* em quadrinhos, gibi *m*.

comical ['kɒmɪkl] *adj* [amusing] engraçado(da).

comic strip *n* tira *f* em quadrinhos.

coming ['kʌmɪŋ] <> *adj* [future] próximo(ma). <> *n*: **~s and goings** idas *fpl* e vindas.

comma ['kɒmə] *n* vírgula *f*.

command [kə'mɑːnd] <> *n* **-1.** [order] comando *m* **-2.** (*U*) [control] comando *m* **-3.** [mastery] domínio *m*; **at one's ~** à disposição; **she has four languages at her ~** ela domina quatro idiomas **-4.** COMPUT comando *m*. <> *vt* **-1.** [order] mandar; **to ~ sb to do sthg** mandar alguém fazer algo **-2.** MIL [control] comandar **-3.** [deserve] merecer.

commandeer [ˌkɒmən'dɪər] *vt* confiscar.

commander [kə'mɑːndər] *n* **-1.** [in army] comandante *mf* **-2.** [in navy] capitão *m*, -tã *f*.

commando [kə'mɑːndəʊ] (*pl* **-s** OR **-es**) *n* **-1.** [unit] unidade *f* de assalto **-2.** [soldier] soldado *m* da unidade de assalto.

commemorate [kə'meməreɪt] *vt* homenagear.

commemoration [kəˌmeməˈreɪʃn] *n*: **in ~ of** em homenagem a.

commence [kə'mens] *fml* <> *vt* principiar; **to ~ doing sthg** principiar algo. <> *vi* principiar.

commend [kə'mend] *vt* **-1.** [praise]: **to ~ sb (on** OR **for sthg)** elogiar alguém (por algo) **-2.** [recommend]: **to ~ sthg (to sb)** recomendar algo (a alguém); **we ~ our souls to God** encomendamos nossas almas a Deus.

commensurate [kə'menʃərət] *adj fml*: **~ with sthg** proporcional a algo.

comment ['kɒment] <> *n* comentário *m*; **no ~** sem comentários. <> *vt*: **to ~ that** comentar que. <> *vi* comentar; **to ~ on sthg** comentar algo.

commentary ['kɒməntrɪ] (*pl* **-ies**) *n* **-1.** RADIO & TV comentário *m* **-2.** [written explanation, comment] crítica *f*.

commentator ['kɒmənteɪtər] *n* **-1.** [RADIO & TV - making comments] comentarista *mf*; [- describing] narrador *m*, -ra *f* **-2.** [expert] analista *mf*; **political ~** analista político.

commerce ['kɒmɜːs] *n* (*U*) comércio *m*.

commercial [kə'mɜːʃl] <> *adj* comercial. <> *n* [advertisement] comercial *m*.

commercial break *n* (intervalo *m*) comercial *m*.

commiserate [kə'mɪzəreɪt] *vi*: **to ~ (with sb)** compadecer-se (de alguém).

commission [kə'mɪʃn] <> *n* **-1.** [gen] comissão *f* **-2.** [piece of work] encomenda *f*. <> *vt* [work] encomendar; **to ~ sb (to do sthg)** encarregar alguém (de fazer algo).

commissionaire [kəˌmɪʃəˈneər] *n UK* porteiro *m*, -ra *f*.

commissioner [kə'mɪʃnər] *n* [high-ranking public official] comissário *m*, -ria *f*.

commit [kə'mɪt] (*pt* & *pp* **-ted**, *cont* **-ting**) *vt* **-1.** [carry out] cometer **-2.** [promise] comprometer; **to ~ o.s. (to sthg/ to doing sthg)** comprometer-se (a algo/a fazer algo) **-3.** [person to institution] confinar **-4.**: **to ~ sthg to memory** confiar algo à memória.

commitment [kə'mɪtmənt] *n* **-1.** (*U*) [dedication] dedicação *f* **-2.** [responsibility] compromisso *m*.

committee [kə'mɪtɪ] *n* comitê *m*.

commodity [kə'mɒdətɪ] (*pl* **-ies**) *n* **-1.** [gen] mercadoria *f* **-2.** ECON commodity *f*.

common ['kɒmən] ◇ adj -1. [gen] comum; ~ **to** comum a -2. UK pej [vulgar] vulgar. ◇ n [land] área f pública.
◆ **in common** adv em comum.

common law n direito m consuetudinário, lei f comum.
◆ **common-law** adj concubinário(ria).

commonly ['kɒmənlɪ] adv [generally] geralmente.

commonplace ['kɒmənpleɪs] ◇ adj [everyday] trivial. ◇ n [frequent phenomenon] lugar-comum m.

common room n [in school, college] sala f de recreação.

Commons ['kɒmənz] npl UK: **the** ~ a Câmara dos Comuns.

common sense n (U) senso m comum.

Commonwealth ['kɒmənwelθ] n [former British colonies]: **the** ~ a Comunidade Britânica.

Commonwealth of Independent States n: **the** ~ a Comunidade dos Estados Independentes.

commotion [kə'məʊʃn] n comoção f.

communal ['kɒmjʊnl] adj comum.

commune [n 'kɒ'mju:n, vb kə'mju:n] ◇ n [group of people] comuna f. ◇ vi: **to** ~ **with** comungar com.

communicate [kə'mju:nɪkeɪt] ◇ vt comunicar. ◇ vi comunicar-se, relacionar-se; **to** ~ **with** comunicar-se com.

communication [kə,mju:nɪ'keɪʃn] n (U) comunicação f.

communications technology n tecnologia f de comunicação.

communion [kə'mju:njən] n (U) [communication] comunhão f.
◆ **Communion** n (U) RELIG comunhão f.

communism ['kɒmjʊnɪzm] n (U) comunismo m.

communist ['kɒmjʊnɪst] ◇ adj comunista. ◇ n comunista mf.

community [kə'mju:nətɪ] (pl -ies) n [group] comunidade f; **the** ~ a comunidade.

community centre n centro m comunitário.

commutation ticket [,kɒmju:'teɪʃn-] n US passagem f integrada.

commute [kə'mju:t] ◇ vt JUR comutar. ◇ vi [to work] viajar regularmente entre a casa e o trabalho, especialmente de trem.

commuter [kə'mju:tə'] n pessoa que viaja regularmente entre a casa e o trabalho, especialmente de trem.

compact [adj kəm'pækt, n 'kɒmpækt] ◇ adj [small and neat] compacto(ta). ◇ n -1. [for face powder] estojo m -2. US AUT: ~ **(car)** carro m de médio porte.

compact disc n disco m compacto, CD m.

compact disc player n CD-player m, toca-CD m.

companion [kəm'pænjən] n -1. [gen] companheiro m, -ra f -2. [book] compêndio m.

companionship [kəm'pænjənʃɪp] n (U) camaradagem f.

company ['kʌmpənɪ] (pl -ies) n -1. [gen] companhia f; **to keep sb** ~ fazer companhia a alguém -2. [business] companhia f, empresa f.

company secretary n secretário m, -ria f geral da empresa OR companhia.

comparable ['kɒmprəbl] adj comparável; ~ **to** OR **with** comparável a OR com.

comparative [kəm'pærətɪv] adj -1. [relative] relativo(va) -2. [study, literature] comparado(da) -3. GRAM comparativo(-va).

comparatively [kəm'pærətɪvlɪ] adv [relatively] relativamente.

compare [kəm'peə'] ◇ vt comparar; **to** ~ **sb/sthg with** OR **to** comparar alguém/algo com OR a; ~**d with** OR **to** comparado com OR a. ◇ vi: **to** ~ **(with sb/sthg)** comparar-se (com alguém/algo).

comparison [kəm'pærɪsn] n comparação f; **in** ~ **(with** OR **to)** em comparação (com OR a).

compartment [kəm'pɑ:tmənt] n compartimento m.

compass ['kʌmpəs] n [for finding direction] bússola f.
◆ **compasses** npl compasso m; **a pair of** ~**es** um compasso.

compassion [kəm'pæʃn] n (U) compaixão f.

compassionate [kəm'pæʃənət] adj compassível.

compassionate leave n tempo que o empregador permite que o funcionário se ausente do trabalho por razões pessoais.

compatible [kəm'pætəbl] adj ~ **(with)** compatível (com).

compel [kəm'pel] (pt & pp -led, cont -ling) vt [force] compelir; **to** ~ **sb to do sthg** compelir alguém a fazer algo.

compelling [kəm'pelɪŋ] adj -1. [argument, reason] convincente -2. [book, film, performance] envolvente.

compensate ['kɒmpenseɪt] ◇ vt: **to** ~ **sb for sthg** [financially] compensar alguém por algo. ◇ vi: **to** ~ **for sthg** compensar algo.

compensation [,kɒmpen'seɪʃn] n: ~ **(for sthg)** compensação f (por algo).

compete [kəm'piːt] *vi* - **1.** [vie]: **to ~ (for sthg)** competir (por algo); **to ~ with** OR **against sb (for sthg)** competir com OR contra alguém (por algo) - **2.** COMM: **to ~ (with sb/sthg)** concorrer (com alguém/algo); **to ~ for sthg** disputar algo.

competence ['kɒmpɪtəns] *n (U)* [proficiency] competência *f*.

competent ['kɒmpɪtənt] *adj* competente.

competition [ˌkɒmpɪ'tɪʃn] *n* - **1.** [gen] competição *f* - **2.** *(U)* COMM concorrência *f*.

competitive [kəm'petətɪv] *adj* competitivo(va).

competitor [kəm'petɪtəʳ] *n* - **1.** [in business] concorrente *mf* - **2.** [in race, contest] competidor *m*, -ra *f*.

compile [kəm'paɪl] *vt* compilar.

complacency [kəm'pleɪsnsɪ] *n (U)* complacência *f*.

complain [kəm'pleɪn] *vi* [moan] queixar-se; **to ~ about sthg** queixar-se de algo.

complaint [kəm'pleɪnt] *n* queixa *f*.

complement [*n* 'kɒmplɪmənt, *vb* 'kɒmplɪˌment] ⇔ *n* - **1.** [gen & GRAM] complemento *m* - **2.** [accompaniment] acompanhamento *m*. ⇔ *vt* - **1.** [gen] complementar - **2.** [accompany] acompanhar.

complementary [ˌkɒmplɪ'mentərɪ] *adj* complementar.

complete [kəm'pliːt] ⇔ *adj* - **1.** [total, thorough] completo(ta); **~ with sthg** completo(ta) com - **2.** [finished, ended] concluído(da). ⇔ *vt* - **1.** [collection, set, form] completar - **2.** [work, painting, book] concluir.

completely [kəm'pliːtlɪ] *adv* [totally] completamente.

completion [kəm'pliːʃn] *n (U)* [of work] conclusão *f*.

complex ['kɒmpleks] ⇔ *adj* complexo(xa). ⇔ *n* complexo *m*.

complexion [kəm'plekʃn] *n* - **1.** [of face] aparência *f* - **2.** [aspect] caráter *m*.

compliance [kəm'plaɪəns] *n (U)* [obedience] cumprimento *m*; **~ with sthg** de acordo com algo.

complicate ['kɒmplɪkeɪt] *vt* complicar.

complicated ['kɒmplɪkeɪtɪd] *adj* complicado(da).

complication [ˌkɒmplɪ'keɪʃn] *n* complicação *f*.

compliment [*n* 'kɒmplɪmənt, *vb* 'kɒmplɪment] ⇔ *n* cumprimento *m*, elogio *m*. ⇔ *vt*: **to ~ sb (on sthg)** cumprimentar alguém (por algo).

➡ compliments *npl* *fml* cumprimentos *mpl*.

complimentary [ˌkɒmplɪ'mentərɪ] *adj* - **1.** [admiring] lisonjeiro(ra) - **2.** [free] gratuito(ta).

complimentary ticket *n* bilhete *m* gratuito.

comply [kəm'plaɪ] *(pt & pp -ied)* *vi*: **to ~ with sthg** cumprir algo.

component [kəm'pəʊnənt] *n* componente *m*.

compose [kəm'pəʊz] *vt* - **1.** [constitute] compor; **to be ~ d of sthg** ser composto(ta) por algo - **2.** [write, create] escrever - **3.** [make calm]: **to ~ o.s.** recompor-se.

composed [kəm'pəʊzd] *adj* [calm] tranqüilo(la).

composer [kəm'pəʊzəʳ] *n* compositor *m*, -ra *f*.

composition [ˌkɒmpə'zɪʃn] *n* composição *f*.

compost [*UK* 'kɒmpɒst, *US* 'kɒmpəʊst] *n (U)* adubo *m*.

composure [kəm'pəʊzəʳ] *n (U)* compostura *f*.

compound ['kɒmpaʊnd] *n* - **1.** [gen] composto *m* - **2.** [enclosed area] complexo *m*.

compound fracture *n* MED fratura *f* exposta.

comprehend [ˌkɒmprɪ'hend] *vt* [understand] compreender.

comprehension [ˌkɒmprɪ'henʃn] *n* - **1.** *(U)* [understanding] compreensão *f* - **2.** SCH [exercise] interpretação *f*.

comprehensive [ˌkɒmprɪ'hensɪv] ⇔ *adj* - **1.** [wide-ranging] abrangente - **2.** [insurance] total. ⇔ *n UK* [school] = **comprehensive school**.

comprehensive school *n* escola estadual de ensino médio que abrange todas as habilidades.

compress [kəm'pres] ⇔ *n* MED compressa *f*. ⇔ *vt* - **1.** [squeeze, press] comprimir - **2.** [condense] sintetizar.

comprise [kəm'praɪz] *vt* - **1.** [consist of]: **to be ~ d of** ser constituído(da) de - **2.** [constitute] constituir.

compromise ['kɒmprəmaɪz] ⇔ *n* [concession, agreement] meio-termo *m*. ⇔ *vt* [undermine integrity of] comprometer. ⇔ *vi* [make concessions] fazer concessões.

compulsion [kəm'pʌlʃn] *n* - **1.** [strong desire] compulsão *f* - **2.** *(U)* [force] coação *f*.

compulsive [kəm'pʌlsɪv] *adj* - **1.** [behaviour, gambler, liar] compulsivo(va) - **2.** [compelling] envolvente.

compulsory [kəm'pʌlsəri] *adj* compulsório(ria).

computer [kəm'pju:tə^r] <> *n* computador *m*. <> *comp* de computador.

computer game *n* jogo *m* de computador.

computer graphics *npl* infografia *f*.

computerized [kəm'pju:təraizd] *adj* informatizado(da).

computer science *n* ciência *f* da computação.

computing [kəm'pju:tıŋ] *n (U)* computação *f*, informática *f*.

comrade ['kɒmreıd] *n* companheiro *m*, -ra *f*.

concave [,kɒn'keıv] *adj* côncavo(va).

conceal [kən'si:l] *vt* [hide - object, substance] esconder; [- information, feelings] ocultar; **to ~ sthg from sb** esconder algo de alguém.

concede [kən'si:d] <> *vt* [admit] conceder. <> *vi* aceitar.

conceit [kən'si:t] *n (U)* [arrogance] presunção *f*.

conceited [kən'si:tıd] *adj* presunçoso(sa).

conceive [kən'si:v] <> *vt* conceber. <> *vi* **-1.** MED conceber **-2.** [imagine]: **to ~ of sthg** conceber algo.

concentrate ['kɒnsəntreıt] <> *vt* concentrar. <> *vi* concentrar-se; **to ~ on sthg** concentrar-se em algo.

concentration [,kɒnsən'treıʃn] *n* concentração *f*.

concentration camp *n* campo *m* de concentração.

concept ['kɒnsept] *n* conceito *m*.

concern [kən'sɜ:n] <> *n* **-1.** [worry, anxiety] preocupação *f* **-2.** COMM [company] negócio *m*. <> *vt* **-1.** [worry]: **to be ~ed (about sb/sthg)** estar preocupado(da) (com alguém/algo) **-2.** [involve] dizer respeito(a); **to be ~ed with sthg** [subj: person] estar envolvido(da) com algo; **to ~ o.s. with sthg** preocupar-se com algo; **as far as ... is ~ed** no que diz respeito a ... **-3.** [subj: book, report, film] tratar de.

concerning [kən'sɜ:nıŋ] *prep* acerca de, sobre.

concert ['kɒnsət] *n* concerto *m*.

concerted [kən'sɜ:tıd] *adj* [effort] conjunto(ta).

concert hall *n* casa *f* de concertos.

concertina [,kɒnsə'ti:nə] *n* concertina *f*.

concerto [kən'tʃeətəʊ] (*pl* **-s**) *n* concerto *m*.

concession [kən'seʃn] *n* **-1.** [allowance, point won] concessão *f* **-2.** COMM [franchise] franquia *f* **-3.** [special price] desconto *m*.

conciliatory [kən'sıliətrı] *adj* conciliatório(ria).

concise [kən'saıs] *adj* conciso(sa).

conclude [kən'klu:d] <> *vt* **-1.** [bring to an end] concluir **-2.** [deduce]: **to ~ (that)** concluir (que) **-3.** [agree on] firmar. <> *vi* [finish] concluir.

conclusion [kən'klu:ʒn] *n* [ending, decision] conclusão *f*.

conclusive [kən'klu:sıv] *adj* conclusivo(va).

concoct [kən'kɒkt] *vt* **-1.** [story, excuse, alibi] forjar **-2.** [mixture, drink] preparar.

concoction [kən'kɒkʃn] *n* [mixture, drink] mistura *f*.

concourse ['kɒŋkɔ:s] *n* [hall] hall *m*.

concrete ['kɒŋkri:t] <> *adj* concreto(ta). <> *n (U)* [building material] concreto *m*. <> *comp* [made of concrete] de concreto.

concur [kən'kɜ:^r] (*pt* & *pp* **-red**, *cont* **-ring**) *vi* [agree]: **to ~ (with sthg)** concordar (com algo).

concurrently [kən'kʌrəntlı] *adv* simultaneamente, concomitantemente.

concussion [kən'kʌʃn] *n (U)* concussão *f*.

condemn [kən'dem] *vt* **-1.** condenar; **to ~ sb for sthg** condenar alguém por algo **-2.** [force]: **to ~ sb to sthg/to do sthg** condenar alguém a algo/a fazer algo **-3.** JUR [sentence]: **to ~ sb to sthg** condenar alguém a algo.

condensation [,kɒnden'seıʃn] *n (U)* condensação *f*.

condense [kən'dens] <> *vt* condensar. <> *vi* [gas, liquid] condensar-se.

condensed milk [kən'denst-] *n (U)* leite *m* condensado.

condescending [,kɒndı'sendıŋ] *adj* condescendente.

condition [kən'dıʃn] <> *n* **-1.** [of person] forma *f*; **out of ~** fora de forma **-2.** [of car] estado *m*; **in good/bad ~** em bom/mau estado **-3.** MED [disease, complaint] problema *m* **-4.** [provision] condição *f*; **on one ~** sob OR com uma condição; **on ~ that** desde que; **to agree to do sthg on one ~** concordar em fazer algo sob OR com uma condição. <> *vt* **-1.** condicionar **-2.** [hair] hidratar.

conditional [kən'dıʃənl] <> *adj* condicional. <> *n* GRAM condicional *m*.

conditioner [kən'dıʃnə^r] *n* **-1.** [for hair] condicionador *m* **-2.** [for clothes] amaciante *m*.

condolences [kən'dəʊlənsız] *npl* condolências *fpl*, pêsames *mpl*.

condom ['kɒndəm] *n* camisinha *f*, preservativo *m*.

condominium [ˌkɒndəˈmɪnɪəm] *n US* [apartment, building] condomínio *m*.

condone [kənˈdəʊn] *vt* tolerar.

conducive [kənˈdjuːsɪv] *adj*: ~ to sthg/ to doing sthg conducente a algo/a fazer algo.

conduct [*n* ˈkɒndʌkt, *vb* kənˈdʌkt] ⟨⟩ *n* (U) conduta *f*. ⟨⟩ *vt* -1. [research, survey & PHYS] conduzir -2. [behave]: to ~ o.s. well/badly comportar-se bem/mal -3. MUS reger.

conducted tour [kənˈdʌktɪd-] *n* excursão *f* guiada.

conductor [kənˈdʌktəʳ] *n* -1. [on bus] cobrador *m* -2. [on train] *US* condutor *m* -3. PHYS condutor *m* -4. MUS maestro *m*, -trina *f*.

conductress [kənˈdʌktrɪs] *n* [on bus] cobradora *f*.

cone [kəʊn] *n* -1. [gen] cone *m* -2. [for ice cream] casquinha *f* -3. [from tree] pinha *f*.

confectioner [kənˈfekʃnəʳ] *n* confeiteiro *m*, -ra *f*; ~ 's (shop) confeitaria *f*.

confectionery [kənˈfekʃnərɪ] *n* (U) confeito *m*.

confederation [kənˌfedəˈreɪʃn] *n* [group] confederação *f*.

Confederation of British Industry *n*: the ~ a Confederação das Indústrias Britânicas.

confer [kənˈfɜːʳ] (*pt & pp*-red, *cont*-ring) ⟨⟩ *vt fml*: to ~ sthg (on sb) conferir algo (a alguém). ⟨⟩ *vi*: to ~ (with sb on OR about sthg) confabular (com alguém sobre OR a respeito de algo).

conference [ˈkɒnfərəns] *n* conferência *f*.

confess [kənˈfes] ⟨⟩ *vt* confessar; to ~ (that) confessar que. ⟨⟩ *vi* confessar; to ~ to sthg confessar OR admitir algo.

confession [kənˈfeʃn] *n* confissão *f*.

confetti [kənˈfetɪ] *n* (U) confete *m*.

confide [kənˈfaɪd] *vi*: to ~ in sb confiar em alguém.

confidence [ˈkɒnfɪdəns] *n* -1. (U) [assurance] autoconfiança *f* -2. (U) [trust] confiança *f*; to have ~ in sb ter confiança em alguém -3. [secrecy]: in ~ em segredo -4. [secret] confidência *f*.

confidence trick *n* conto-do-vigário *m*.

confident [ˈkɒnfɪdənt] *adj* -1. [assured] autoconfiante -2. [sure] confiante; ~ of sthg confiante em algo.

confidential [ˌkɒnfɪˈdenʃl] *adj* confidencial.

confine [kənˈfaɪn] *vt* confinar; to be ~ d to estar confinado(da) a; to ~ o.s. to

sthg/to doing sthg confinar-se a algo/a fazer algo.

 ➡ **confines** *npl* confins *mpl*.

confined [kənˈfaɪnd] *adj* [space, area] confinado(da).

confinement [kənˈfaɪnmənt] *n* (U) [imprisonment] confinamento *m*.

confirm [kənˈfɜːm] *vt* -1. [gen] confirmar -2. RELIG crismar.

confirmation [ˌkɒnfəˈmeɪʃn] *n* -1. [gen] confirmação *f* -2. RELIG crisma *f*.

confirmed [kənˈfɜːmd] *adj* [habitual] convicto(ta).

confiscate [ˈkɒnfɪskeɪt] *vt* confiscar.

conflict [*n* ˈkɒnflɪkt, *vb* kənˈflɪkt] ⟨⟩ *n* [fighting, clash] conflito *m*. ⟨⟩ *vi* [clash] entrar em conflito; to ~ with sb/sthg entrar em conflito com alguém/algo.

conflicting [kənˈflɪktɪŋ] *adj* [contradictory] conflitante.

conform [kənˈfɔːm] *vi* -1. [behave as expected] conformar-se -2. [be in accordance]: to ~ (to OR with sthg) conformar-se (com algo).

confound [kənˈfaʊnd] *vt* [confuse, defeat] confundir.

confront [kənˈfrʌnt] *vt* -1. [person] defrontar-se com -2. [task, problem] enfrentar -3. [present]: to ~ sb (with sthg) confrontar alguém (com algo).

confrontation [ˌkɒnfrʌnˈteɪʃn] *n* confrontação *f*.

confuse [kənˈfjuːz] *vt* -1. [bewilder] confundir -2. [mix up]: to ~ sb/sthg (with) confundir alguém/algo (com) -3. [complicate, make less clear] complicar.

confused [kənˈfjuːzd] *adj* confuso(sa).

confusing [kənˈfjuːzɪŋ] *adj* confuso(sa).

confusion [kənˈfjuːʒn] *n* confusão *f*.

congeal [kənˈdʒiːl] *vi* -1. [blood] coagular -2. [food] congelar.

congenial [kənˈdʒiːnjəl] *adj* agradável.

congested [kənˈdʒestɪd] *adj* congestionado(da).

congestion [kənˈdʒestʃn] *n* (U) -1. [overcrowding] congestionamento *m* -2. MED congestão *f*.

conglomerate [kənˈɡlɒmərət] *n* COMM conglomerado *m*.

congratulate [kənˈɡrætʃʊleɪt] *vt*: to ~ sb (on) felicitar alguém (por).

congratulations [kənˌɡrætʃʊˈleɪʃənz] ⟨⟩ *npl* felicitações *fpl*. ⟨⟩ *excl* parabéns!

congregate [ˈkɒnɡrɪɡeɪt] *vi* congregar-se.

congregation [ˌkɒnɡrɪˈɡeɪʃn] *n* RELIG congregação *f*.

congress [ˈkɒnɡres] *n* [meeting] congresso *m*.

 ➡ **Congress** *n US* POL Congresso *m*.

congressman ['kɒŋgresmən] (*pl* -men [-mən]) *n US POL* congressista *m*.

conifer ['kɒnɪfə'] *n* conífera *f*.

conjugation [ˌkɒndʒʊ'geɪʃn] *n* conjugação *f*.

conjunction [kən'dʒʌŋkʃn] *n* -1. *GRAM* conjunção *f* -2. [combination] combinação *f*; in ~ with em conjunto com.

conjunctivitis [kənˌdʒʌŋktɪ'vaɪtɪs] *n* (*U*) conjuntivite *f*.

conjure ['kʌndʒə'] *vi* [by magic] fazer truques.

  ◆ **conjure up** *vt sep* [evoke] evocar.

conjurer ['kʌndʒərə'] *n* [magician] mágico *m*, -ca *f*.

conjuror ['kʌndʒərə'] *n* = conjurer.

conk [kɒŋk] *n inf* [nose] narigão *m*.

  ◆ **conk out** *vi inf* -1. [person] estar em frangalhos -2. [car, machine] escangalhar-se.

conker ['kɒŋkə'] *n UK* castanha-da-índia *f*.

con man (*pl* -men) *n* vigarista *m*.

connect [kə'nekt] ◇ *vt* -1. [gen] ligar, conectar; to ~ sthg (to sthg) ligar algo (a algo); **I'm just ~ing you** [on telephone] estou completando sua ligação -2. [associate]: to ~ sb/sthg to OR with relacionar alguém/algo a OR com -3. *ELEC* [to power supply]: to ~ sthg to conectar algo a. ◇ *vi* [train, plane, bus]: to ~ (with) conectar com.

connected [kə'nektɪd] *adj* [related, associated] relacionado(da); ~ with conectado(da) com.

connection [kə'nekʃn] *n* -1. [relationship] conexão *f*, relação *f*; ~ between/with sthg relação entre/com algo; in ~ with em relação a -2. [plane, train, bus & *ELEC*] conexão *f* -3. [on telephone] ligação *f* -4. [influential contact] contato *m*.

connive [kə'naɪv] *vi* -1. [plot] conspirar -2. [allow to happen]: to ~ at sthg ser conivente em algo.

connoisseur [ˌkɒnə'sɜː'] *n* conhecedor *m*, -ra *f*, especialista *mf*.

conquer ['kɒŋkə'] *vt* -1. [take by force] conquistar -2. *fig* [overcome] dominar.

conqueror ['kɒŋkərə'] *n* conquistador *m*, -ra *f*.

conquest ['kɒŋkwest] *n* conquista *f*.

conscience ['kɒnʃəns] *n* consciência *f*.

conscientious [ˌkɒnʃɪ'enʃəs] *adj* conscencioso(sa).

conscious ['kɒnʃəs] *adj* consciente; ~ of sthg consciente de algo; **fashion-~** conhecedor(ra) da moda.

consciousness ['kɒnʃəsnɪs] *n* (*U*) consciência *f*; to lose/regain ~ perder/recobrar os sentidos.

conscript ['kɒnskrɪpt] *n MIL* recruta *mf*.

conscription [kən'skrɪpʃn] *n* (*U*) serviço *m* militar obrigatório.

consecutive [kən'sekjʊtɪv] *adj* consecutivo(va).

consent [kən'sent] ◇ *n* (*U*) consentimento *m*. ◇ *vi*: to ~ (to sthg) consentir (em algo).

consequence ['kɒnsɪkwəns] *n* -1. [result] conseqüência *f*; to face the ~s encarar as conseqüências; in ~ em conseqüência -2. [importance] importância *f*; to be of little ~ não ter importância.

consequently ['kɒnsɪkwəntlɪ] *adv* conseqüentemente.

conservation [ˌkɒnsə'veɪʃn] *n* conservação *f*.

conservative [kən'sɜːvətɪv] ◇ *adj* -1. [traditional] conservador(ra) -2. [cautious] cauteloso(sa). ◇ *n* conservador *m*, -ra *f*.

  ◆ **Conservative** *POL UK* ◇ *adj* conservador(ra). ◇ *n* conservador *m*, -ra *f*.

Conservative Party *n UK*: the ~ o Partido Conservador.

conservatory [kən'sɜːvətrɪ] (*pl* -ies) *n* estufa *f*.

conserve [*n* 'kɒnsɜːv, *vb* kən'sɜːv] ◇ *n* conserva *f*. ◇ *vt* conservar.

consider [kən'sɪdə'] *vt* -1. [gen] considerar; all things ~ed considerando tudo -2. [believe] achar.

considerable [kən'sɪdrəbl] *adj* considerável.

considerably [kən'sɪdrəblɪ] *adv* consideravelmente.

considerate [kən'sɪdərət] *adj* [thoughtful] atencioso(sa); that's very ~ of you é muita consideração de sua parte.

consideration [kənˌsɪdə'reɪʃn] *n* -1. (*U*) [gen] consideração *f*; to take sthg into ~ levar algo em consideração; to show no ~ for others não mostrar consideração pelos outros -2. [factor] fator *m* -3. [discussion]: under ~ em consideração; your proposal is under ~ sua proposta está sendo considerada.

considering [kən'sɪdərɪŋ] ◇ *prep* considerando, em vista de. ◇ *conj* considerando que. ◇ *adv* apesar de tudo, pensando bem.

consign [kən'saɪn] *vt* [relegate]: to ~ sb/sthg to sthg consignar alguém/algo a algo.

consignment [ˌkən'saɪnmənt] *n* [load] remessa *f*, despacho *m*.

consist [kən'sɪst] ◆ **consist in** *vt fus*: to ~ in sthg/in doing sthg consistir em algo/em fazer algo.

  ◆ **consist of** *vt fus* consistir em.

consistency [kən'sɪstənsɪ] (*pl* -ies) *n* -1.
(*U*) [coherence] consistência *f*, coerência *f* -2. [texture] consistência *f*.

consistent [kən'sɪstənt] *adj* -1. [gen]
constante -2. [growth, improvement] consistente -3. [argument, facts, position]: ~
(with) coerente (com).

consolation [,kɒnsə'leɪʃn] *n* consolação
f.

console [*n* 'kɒnsəʊl, *vt* kən'səʊl] <> *n*
[control panel] console *m*. <> *vt* consolar.

consonant ['kɒnsənənt] *n* consoante
f.

consortium [kən'sɔːtjəm] (*pl* -tiums OR
-tia [-tjə]) *n* consórcio *m*.

conspicuous [kən'spɪkjʊəs] *adj* conspí-
cuo(cua).

conspiracy [kən'spɪrəsɪ] (*pl* -ies) *n* conspiração *f*.

conspire [kən'spaɪəʳ] *vt* : to ~ to do sthg
conspirar para fazer algo.

constable ['kʌnstəbl] *n* UK [policeman]
guarda *m*.

constabulary [kən'stæbjʊlərɪ] (*pl* -ies) *n*
UK força *f* policial.

constant ['kɒnstənt] *adj* [gen] constante.

constantly ['kɒnstəntlɪ] *adv* constante-
mente.

consternation [,kɒnstə'neɪʃn] *n* (*U*)
consternação *f*.

constipated ['kɒnstɪpeɪtɪd] *adj* consti-
pado(da).

constipation [,kɒnstɪ'peɪʃn] *n* (*U*) constipação *f*, prisão *f* de ventre.

constituency [kən'stɪtjʊənsɪ] (*pl* -ies) *n*
-1. [area] distrito *m* eleitoral -2. [group]
eleitorado *m*.

constituent [kən'stɪtjʊənt] *n* -1. [voter]
eleitor *m*, -ra *f* -2. [element] constituinte
m.

constitute ['kɒnstɪtjuːt] *vt* constituir.

constitution [,kɒnstɪ'tjuːʃn] *n* -1.
[health] constituição *f* (física) -2. [com-
position] constituição *f*.

constraint [kən'streɪnt] *n* -1. [restriction]
restrição *f*; ~ on sthg restrição a algo
-2. (*U*) [control] força *f* -3. [coercion]
coação *f*.

construct [kən'strʌkt] *vt* [edifice, object]
construir.

construction [kən'strʌkʃn] <> *n* -1.
[gen] construção *f* -2. (*U*) [building indus-
try] construção *f* (civil).

constructive [kən'strʌktɪv] *adj* constru-
tivo(va).

construe [kən'struː] *vt* fml [interpret]: to
~ sthg as interpretar algo como.

consul ['kɒnsəl] *n* [envoy] cônsul *m*,
consulesa *f*.

consulate ['kɒnsjʊlət] *n* [building] consulado *m*.

consult [kən'sʌlt] <> *vt* consultar. <>
vi: to ~ with sb consultar-se com
alguém.

consultancy [kən'sʌltənsɪ] *n* empresa *f*
de consultoria.

consultant [kən'sʌltənt] *n* -1. [expert]
consultor *m*, -ra *f* -2. UK [medical specia-
list] especialista *mf*.

consultation [,kɒnsəl'teɪʃn] *n* consulta
f.

consulting room [kən'sʌltɪŋ-] *n* consultório *m*.

consume [kən'sjuːm] *vt* consumir.

consumer [kən'sjuːməʳ] *n* consumidor
m, -ra *f*.

consumer goods *npl* bens *mpl* de
consumo.

consumer society *n* (*U*) sociedade *f*
de consumo.

consummate ['kɒnsəmeɪt] *vt* consumar.

consumption [kən'sʌmpʃn] *n* (*U*) [use]
consumo *m*.

cont. (*abbr of* continued): ~ on page 10
continua na página 10.

contact ['kɒntækt] <> *n* -1. (*U*) [physi-
cal, eye, communication] contato *m*; to lose
~ with sb perder contato com alguém;
to make ~ with sb fazer contato com
alguém; in ~ em contato; in ~ with sb
em contato com alguém -2. [person]
contato *m*. <> *vt* contatar, entrar em
contato com.

contact lens *n* lente *f* de contato.

contagious [kən'teɪdʒəs] *adj* -1. MED
contagioso(sa) -2. fig [laughter, good hu-
mour] contagiante.

contain [kən'teɪn] *vt* conter.

container [kən'teɪnəʳ] *n* -1. [box, bottle
etc.] recipiente *m* -2. COMM [for transporting goods] contêiner *m*.

contaminate [kən'tæmɪneɪt] *vt* contaminar.

cont'd (*abbr of* continued) cont.

contemplate ['kɒntempleɪt] <> *vt* -1.
[scheme, idea, proposal] considerar -2. literary [sunset, flower] contemplar. <> *vi*
[meditate] contemplar.

contemporary [kən'tempərərɪ] (*pl* -ies)
<> *adj* contemporâneo(nea). <> *n*
contemporâneo *m*, -nea *f*.

contempt [kən'tempt] *n* (*U*) -1. [gen]
desprezo *m*; ~ for sb/sthg desprezo
por alguém/algo -2. JUR : ~ (of court)
desacato *m* (à autoridade do tribunal).

contemptuous [kən'temptʃʊəs] *adj*
desdenhoso(sa); to be ~ of sthg fazer
pouco caso de algo.

contend [kən'tend] <> vt -1. [deal]: to ~ with sthg lidar com algo; to have enough to ~ with ter muitos problemas para resolver -2. [compete]: to ~ for sthg disputar algo; to ~ against sb disputar com alguém. <> vt fml [claim]: to ~ that sustentar que.

contender [kən'tendə^r] n -1. [in fight, race] oponente mf -2. [for political office] candidato m, -ta f.

content [n 'kɒntent, adj & vb kən'tent] <> adj contente; ~ with sthg contente com algo; to be ~ to do sthg estar a fim de fazer algo. <> n -1. [amount contained] teor m -2. [subject matter] conteúdo m. <> vt: to ~ o.s. with sthg/with doing sthg contentar-se com algo/em fazer algo.

➡ **contents** npl -1. [of container, document] conteúdo m -2. [at front of book] sumário m.

contented [kən'tentɪd] adj satisfeito(-ta).

contention [kən'tenʃn] n -1. [argument, assertion] argumentação f -2. (U) [disagreement] discussão f.

contest [n 'kɒntest, vb kən'test] <> n -1. [competition] concurso m -2. [for power, control] disputa f. <> vt -1. [compete for] concorrer -2. [dispute] questionar.

contestant [kən'testənt] n concorrente mf.

context ['kɒntekst] n contexto m.

continent ['kɒntɪnənt] n GEOGR continente m.

➡ **Continent** n UK: the Continent o Continente Europeu (excluindo-se a Grã-Bretanha).

continental [ˌkɒntɪ'nentl] adj GEOGR continental.

continental breakfast n café-da-manhã m continental.

contingency [kən'tɪndʒənsɪ] (pl -ies) n contingência f.

contingency plan n plano m de contingência.

continual [kən'tɪnjʊəl] adj contínuo(-nua).

continually [kən'tɪnjʊəlɪ] adv continuamente.

continuation [kənˌtɪnjʊ'eɪʃn] n -1. (U) [act of extending] prolongamento m -2. [sequel] continuação f.

continue [kən'tɪnjuː] <> vt -1. [carry on] continuar, prosseguir; to ~ doing OR to do sthg continuar a fazer algo -2. [begin again] recomeçar -3. [resume speaking] prosseguir. <> vi -1. [carry on] continuar; to ~ with sthg continuar com algo -2. [begin again] recomeçar -3.

[resume speaking, travelling] prosseguir.

continuous [kən'tɪnjʊəs] adj [uninterrupted] contínuo(nua).

continuously [kən'tɪnjʊəslɪ] adv [without interruption] continuamente.

contort [kən'tɔːt] vt contorcer.

contortion [kən'tɔːʃn] n contorção f.

contour ['kɒnˌtʊə^r] n -1. [outline] contorno m -2. [on map] relevo m.

contraband ['kɒntrəbænd] <> adj contrabandeado(da). <> n (U) contrabando m.

contraception [ˌkɒntrə'sepʃn] n (U) contracepção f.

contraceptive [ˌkɒntrə'septɪv] <> adj anticoncepcional. <> n anticoncepcional m.

contract [n 'kɒntrækt, vb kən'trækt] <> n contrato m. <> vt -1. [through legal agreement] contratar; to ~ to do sthg contratar para fazer algo -2. COMM: to ~ sb (to do sthg) contratar alguém (para fazer algo) -3. fml [illness, disease] contrair. <> vi [metal, plastic] contrair-se.

contraction [kən'trækʃn] n contração f.

contractor [kən'træktə^r] n contratante mf.

contradict [ˌkɒntrə'dɪkt] vt -1. [challenge] contradizer -2. [conflict with]: to ~ each other contradizer-se.

contradiction [ˌkɒntrə'dɪkʃn] n contradição f.

contraflow ['kɒntrəfləʊ] n contrafluxo m.

contraption [kən'træpʃn] n geringonça f.

contrary ['kɒntrərɪ] <> adj [opposing] contrário(ria); ~ to sthg contrário(ria) a algo. <> n contrário m; on the ~ pelo contrário.

➡ **contrary to** prep contrário a.

contrast [n 'kɒntrɑːst, vb kən'trɑːst] <> n -1. [difference]: ~ (between/with) contraste m (entre/com); by OR in ~ em comparação, por outro lado; in ~ with OR to sthg em comparação com algo -2. [something different]: ~ (to sb/sthg) oposto m, -ta f (a alguém/algo). <> vt: to ~ sthg with sthg contrastar algo com algo. <> vi: to ~ (with sthg) contrastar OR dar contraste (com algo).

contravene [ˌkɒntrə'viːn] vt violar.

contribute [kən'trɪbjuːt] <> vt -1. [give] contribuir com. <> vi -1. [give money]: to ~ (to sthg) contribuir (para algo) -2. [be part of cause]: to ~ to sthg contribuir para algo -3. [write material]: to ~ to sthg colaborar com algo.

contribution [ˌkɒntrɪ'bjuːʃn] n -1. [gen]: ~ **(to sthg)** contribuição f (para algo) -2. [written article] colaboração f.

contributor [kən'trɪbjʊtəʳ] n -1. [of money] contribuinte mf -2. [to magazine, newspaper] colaborador m, -ra f.

contrive [kən'traɪv] fml vt -1. [manoeuvre to put in place] manipular -2. [manage]: **to ~ to do sthg** dar um jeito de fazer algo -3. [invent, construct] improvisar.

contrived [kən'traɪvd] adj pej arranjado(da).

control [kən'trəʊl] (pt & pp -led, cont -ling) <> n -1. [gen] controle m; **in ~ of** no controle de, no comando de; **under ~** sob controle; **to lose ~** [of emotions] perder o controle -2. COMPUT comando m. <> vt controlar.
  ➡ **controls** npl [of machine, vehicle] controles mpl.

controller [kən'trəʊləʳ] n [person responsible] controller mf, diretor m, -ra f; **financial ~** contador m, -ra f.

control panel n painel m de controle.

control tower n torre f de controle.

controversial [ˌkɒntrə'vɜːʃl] adj controverso(sa), polêmico(ca).

controversy ['kɒntrəvɜːsɪ, UK kən'trɒvəsɪ] (pl -ies) n controvérsia f, polêmica f.

convalesce [ˌkɒnvə'les] vi convalescer.

convene [kən'viːn] <> vt [meeting, conference] convocar. <> vi [court, parliament] reunir-se.

convenience [kən'viːnjəns] n (U) [gen] conveniência f; **at your earliest ~** assim que possível.

convenience store n US loja f de conveniências.

convenient [kən'viːnjənt] adj -1. [suitable] conveniente -2. [handy] cômodo(da); ~ **for sthg** conveniente para algo.

convent ['kɒnvənt] n [building] convento m.

convention [kən'venʃn] n convenção f.

conventional [kən'venʃnl] adj convencional; ~ **person** pej pessoa f sem graça; ~ **weapons** armas fpl não-nucleares.

converge [kən'vɜːdʒ] vi convergir; **to ~ on sb/sthg** [to move towards] dirigir-se para alguém/algo.

convergence [kən'vɜːdʒəns] n [in EU] convergência f; ~ **criteria** critérios mpl de convergência.

conversant [kən'vɜːsənt] adj fml: ~ **with** sthg familiarizado(da) com algo.

conversation [ˌkɒnvə'seɪʃn] n conversação f, conversa f.

converse [n 'kɒnvɜːs, vb kən'vɜːs] <> n

[opposite]: **the ~** o inverso. <> vi fml [talk] conversar; **to ~ with sb** conversar com alguém.

conversely [kən'vɜːslɪ] adv fml inversamente.

conversion [kən'vɜːʃn] n -1. [gen] conversão f -2. [converted building, room] reforma f.

convert [vb kən'vɜːt, n 'kɒnvɜːt] <> vt: **to ~ sthg (in)to sthg** converter algo em algo; **to ~ sb (to sthg)** converter alguém (para algo); **I didn't like jazz much but she ~ed me to it** eu não gostava muito de jazz, mas ela me converteu. <> vi [change]: **she's ~ed to Catholicism** ela se converteu ao catolicismo; **the seating ~s to a double bed** o sofá se transforma numa cama de casal. <> n convertido m, -da f.

convertible [kən'vɜːtəbl] <> adj [bed, sofa] dobrável. <> n [car] conversível m.

convex [kɒn'veks] adj convexo(xa).

convey [kən'veɪ] vt -1. fml [people, cargo] conduzir -2. [feelings, ideas, thoughts] expressar; **to ~ sthg to sb** transmitir algo a alguém.

conveyer belt [kən'veɪəʳ-], **conveyor belt** n esteira f transportadora.

convict [n 'kɒnvɪkt, vb kən'vɪkt] <> n condenado m, -da f. <> vt JUR: **to ~ sb of sthg** condenar alguém por algo.

conviction [kən'vɪkʃn] n -1. [gen] convicção f -2. JUR condenação f.

convince [kən'vɪns] vt [persuade] convencer; **to ~ sb of sthg** convencer alguém de algo; **to ~ sb to do sthg** convencer alguém a fazer algo.

convincing [kən'vɪnsɪŋ] adj convincente.

convoluted ['kɒnvəluːtɪd] adj [tortuous] enrolado(da).

convoy ['kɒnvɔɪ] n [group] comboio m.

convulse [kən'vʌls] vt: **to be ~d with** [laughter, pain] dobrar-se de.

convulsion [kən'vʌlʃn] n MED convulsão f.

coo [kuː] vi -1. [bird] arrulhar -2. [person] sussurrar.

cook [kʊk] <> n cozinheiro m, -ra f. <> vt -1. [food, meal] cozinhar; **I'll ~ dinner** vou preparar o jantar -2. inf [books, accounts] falsificar. <> vi cozinhar.

cookbook ['kʊkbʊk] n = cookery book.

cooker ['kʊkəʳ] n esp UK [stove] fogão m.

cookery ['kʊkərɪ] n (U) culinária f.

cookery book n livro m de receitas.

cookie ['kʊkɪ] n -1. esp US [biscuit] biscoito m -2. COMPUT cookie m.

cooking [ˈkʊkɪŋ] n (U) -**1.** [activity] culi-nária f; **do you like ~?** você gosta de cozinhar? -**2.** [food] cozinha f; **her ~ is awful!** ela cozinha mal pra caramba!

cool [kuːl] ⟨⟩ adj -**1.** [not warm] frio (fria) -**2.** [calm] tranqüilo(la) -**3.** [un-friendly] frio (fria) -**4.** inf [excellent] legal -**5.** inf [trendy] bacana. ⟨⟩ vt esfriar. ⟨⟩ vi [food, liquid, room] esfriar. ⟨⟩ n inf [calm]: **to keep/lose one's ~** manter/perder a calma.
  ◆ **cool down** vi [become less warm] esfriar.

cool bag n bolsa f térmica.

cool box UK, **cooler** US n caixa f de gelo.

coop [kuːp] n gaiola f; **chicken ~** gali-nheiro m.
  ◆ **coop up** vt sep inf trancafiar.

co-op (abbr of **cooperative**) n fam coop.

cooperate [kəʊˈɒpəreɪt] vi cooperar; **to ~ with sb/sthg** cooperar com alguém/algo.

cooperation [kəʊˌɒpəˈreɪʃn] n (U) coo-peração f.

cooperative [kəʊˈɒpərətɪv] ⟨⟩ adj co-operativo(va). ⟨⟩ n [enterprise] coope-rativa f.

coordinate [n kəʊˈɔːdɪnət, vt kəʊˈɔːdɪneɪt] ⟨⟩ n [on map, graph] coor-denada f. ⟨⟩ vt coordenar.
  ◆ **coordinates** npl [clothes] conjuntos mpl.

coordination [kəʊˌɔːdɪˈneɪʃn] n (U) co-ordenação f.

cop [kɒp] (pt & pp -**ped**, cont -**ping**) n inf [policeman] tira m.

cope [kəʊp] vi suportar; **to ~ with sthg** lidar com algo.

Copenhagen [ˌkəʊpənˈheɪgən] n Cope-nhague.

copier [ˈkɒpɪəʳ] n [photocopier] copiado-ra f.

cop-out n inf desculpa f furada.

copper [ˈkɒpəʳ] n -**1.** (U) [metal] cobre m -**2.** UK inf [policeman] tira m.

coppice [ˈkɒpɪs], **copse** [kɒps] n capão m.

copy [ˈkɒpɪ] (pt & pp -**ied**) ⟨⟩ n cópia f. ⟨⟩ vt copiar.

copyright [ˈkɒpɪraɪt] n (U) direitos mpl autorais, copyright m.

coral [ˈkɒrəl] n (U) coral m.

cord [kɔːd] n -**1.** [string] cordão m -**2.** [wire] fio m -**3.** [fabric] veludo m cotelê.
  ◆ **cords** npl inf calça f de veludo cotelê.

cordial [ˈkɔːdjəl] ⟨⟩ adj cordial. ⟨⟩ n cordial m.

cordon [ˈkɔːdn] n [barrier] cordão m de isolamento.
  ◆ **cordon off** vt sep isolar (com cordão).

corduroy [ˈkɔːdərɔɪ] n veludo m cotelê.

core [kɔːʳ] ⟨⟩ n -**1.** [gen] centro m -**2.** [of apple, pear] caroço m -**3.** [of argument, policy] âmago m -**4.** phr: **to be English/royalist to the ~** ser inglês(esa)/monar-quista até morrer; **to be shaken to the ~** ficar muito comovido(da). ⟨⟩ vt [fruit] descaroçar.

Corfu [kɔːˈfuː] n Corfu.

corgi [ˈkɔːgɪ] (pl -**s**) n pequeno cão do País de Gales de nariz alongado e pernas curtas.

coriander [ˌkɒrɪˈændəʳ] n (U) -**1.** [herb] coriandro m -**2.** [spice] coentro m.

cork [kɔːk] n -**1.** (U) [material] cortiça f -**2.** [stopper] rolha f.

corkscrew [ˈkɔːkskruː] n saca-rolhas m.

corn [kɔːn] n -**1.** (U) UK [wheat, barley, oats] cereais mpl -**2.** (U) esp Am [maize] milho m -**3.** [callus] calo m.

cornea [ˈkɔːnɪə] (pl -**s**) n córnea f.

corned beef [kɔːnd-] n (U) carne f bovina enlatada.

corner [ˈkɔːnəʳ] ⟨⟩ n -**1.** [gen] canto m; **to cut ~s** fig pular etapas -**2.** [in street, road] esquina f -**3.** FTBL escanteio m. ⟨⟩ vt -**1.** [trap] encurralar -**2.** [monopolize] monopolizar.

corner shop n pequeno armazém de esquina que vende comida e artigos de limpeza.

cornerstone [ˈkɔːnəstəʊn] n fig [basis] fundamento m.

cornet [ˈkɔːnɪt] n -**1.** [instrument] corneta f -**2.** UK [ice-cream cone] casquinha f.

cornflakes [ˈkɔːnfleɪks] npl flocos mpl de cereais.

cornflour UK [ˈkɔːnflaʊəʳ], **cornstarch** US [ˈkɔːnstɑːtʃ] n (U) amido m de milho.

corn oil n óleo m de milho.

corn on the cob n milho m cozido.

Cornwall [ˈkɔːnwɔːl] n Cornualha f; **in ~** na Cornualha.

corny [ˈkɔːnɪ] (compar -**ier**, superl -**iest**) adj inf batido(da).

coronary [ˈkɒrənrɪ] (pl -**ies**), **coronary thrombosis** [-θrɒmˈbəʊsɪs] (pl coro-nary thromboses [-θrɒmˈbəʊsiːz]) n trom-bose f coronária.

coronation [ˌkɒrəˈneɪʃn] n coroação f.

coroner [ˈkɒrənəʳ] n oficial responsável por investigar as mortes das pessoas que morreram de forma violenta, brusca ou incomum.

corporal [ˈkɔːpərəl] n cabo m.

corporal punishment n (U) castigo m corporal.

corporate [ˈkɔːpərət] adj -**1.** [business]

corporativo(va) **-2.** [collective] coletivo(-va).

corporation [ˌkɔːpəˈreɪʃn] n **-1.** [council] associação f **-2.** [large company] corporação f.

corps [kɔːʳ] (pl inv) n **-1.** MIL unidade f **-2.** [group] corpo m.

corpse [kɔːps] n cadáver m.

correct [kəˈrekt] ◇ adj **-1.** [right, accurate] certo(ta) **-2.** [appropriate, suitable] adequado(da). ◇ vt corrigir.

correction [kəˈrekʃn] n **-1.** (U) [act of correcting] correção f **-2.** [change] emenda f.

correlation [ˌkɒrəˈleɪʃn] n: ~ (between) correlação (entre).

correspond [ˌkɒrɪˈspɒnd] vi **-1.** [be equivalent]: to ~ (with OR to sthg) corresponder (com OR a algo) **-2.** [tally]: to ~ (with OR to sthg) ajustar-se (a algo) **-3.** [write letters]: to ~ (with sb) corresponder-se (com alguém).

correspondence [ˌkɒrɪˈspɒndəns] n **-1.** [letters] correspondência f **-2.** [letter-writing]: ~ with/between sb correspondência com/entre alguém **-3.** [relationship, similarity]: ~ with sthg relação com algo.

correspondence course n curso m por correspondência.

correspondent [ˌkɒrɪˈspɒndənt] n [reporter] correspondente mf.

corridor [ˈkɒrɪdɔːʳ] n [in building] corredor m.

corroborate [kəˈrɒbəreɪt] vt corroborar.

corrode [kəˈrəʊd] ◇ vt corroer. ◇ vi corroer-se.

corrosion [kəˈrəʊʒn] n (U) [of metal] corrosão f.

corrugated [ˈkɒrəgeɪtɪd] adj ondulado(-da).

corrugated iron n (U) ferro m corrugado.

corrupt [kəˈrʌpt] ◇ adj **-1.** [dishonest] corrupto(ta) **-2.** [depraved] depravado(-da) **-3.** COMPUT [damaged] corrompido(-da). ◇ vt corromper.

corruption [kəˈrʌpʃn] n (U) **-1.** [gen] corrupção f **-2.** [depravity] depravação f.

corset [ˈkɔːsɪt] n [undergarment] espartilho m.

Corsica [ˈkɔːsɪkə] n Córsega.

cosh [kɒʃ] ◇ n cacete m. ◇ vt dar cacetadas.

cosmetic [kɒzˈmetɪk] ◇ adj fig [superficial] superficial. ◇ n cosmético m.

cosmopolitan [ˌkɒzməˈpɒlɪtn] adj cosmopolita.

cosset [ˈkɒsɪt] vt acarinhar.

cost [kɒst] (pt & pp cost, pt & pp sense 2 -ed) ◇ n custo m; at all ~ s a qualquer custo. ◇ vt **-1.** [in financial transactions - sum of money] custar; [- person] custar a **-2.** COMM [estimate price of] orçar; to ~ a product orçar um produto; the work was ~ ed at £65 o trabalho foi orçado em £65.

➡ **costs** npl JUR custas fpl.

co-star [ˈkəʊ-] n coadjuvante mf.

Costa Rica [ˌkɒstəˈriːkə] n Costa Rica.

cost-effective adj rentável, lucrativo(-va).

costing [ˈkɒstɪŋ] n estimativa f de custos.

costly [ˈkɒstlɪ] (compar -ier, superl -iest) adj **-1.** [expensive] oneroso(sa) **-2.** fig [involving loss, damage] dispendioso(-sa).

cost of living n: the ~ o custo da vida.

cost price n preço m de custo.

costume [ˈkɒstjuːm] n **-1.** THEATRE roupa f; lion ~ fantasia de leão; in ~ and make-up vestido(da) e maquiado(da) **-2.** (U) [dress] traje m; swimming ~ maiô m.

costume jewellery n (U) bijuteria f.

cosy UK, **cozy** US [ˈkəʊzɪ] (compar -ier, superl -iest) adj [person] aconchegado(-da); to feel ~ sentir-se aconchegado(-da).

cot [kɒt] n **-1.** UK [for child] berço m **-2.** US [folding bed] cama f de campanha.

cottage [ˈkɒtɪdʒ] n cabana f, chalé m; a country ~ uma casa de campo.

cottage cheese n (U) requeijão m.

cottage pie n UK bolo de carne picada coberto com purê de batata.

cotton [ˈkɒtn] ◇ n (U) **-1.** [fabric, plants] algodão m **-2.** [thread] linha f. ◇ comp de algodão.

➡ **cotton on** vi inf: to ~ on (to sthg) sacar (algo).

cotton candy n US = candyfloss.

cotton wool n (U) chumaço m de algodão.

couch [kaʊtʃ] n **-1.** [gen] sofá m **-2.** [psychiatrist's] divã m.

cough [kɒf] ◇ n **-1.** [noise] tossida f **-2.** [illness] tosse f. ◇ vi tossir.

cough mixture n UK xarope m para a tosse.

cough sweet n UK pastilha f para a tosse.

cough syrup n = cough mixture.

could [kʊd] pt ▷ can².

couldn't [ˈkʊdnt] = could not.

could've [ˈkʊdəv] = could have.

council [ˈkaʊnsl] n **-1.** [local authority]

câmara f municipal - **2**. [group, organization] conselho m - **3**. [meeting] assembléia f.

council estate n UK conjunto de casas de propriedade do município destinado à locação.

council flat n UK apartamento de propriedade do município para ser alugado a baixo custo.

council house n UK casa de propriedade do município para ser alugada a baixo custo.

councillor [ˈkaʊnsələʳ] n vereador m, -ra f.

council tax n UK ≃ imposto m territorial urbano.

counsel [ˈkaʊnsl] (UK pt & pp -led, cont -ling, US pt & pp -ed, cont -ing) n - **1**. (U) fml [advice] parecer m - **2**. [lawyer] conselheiro m, -ra f, advogado m, -da f.

counsellor UK, **counselor** US [ˈkaʊnsələʳ] n - **1**. [adviser, helper] conselheiro m, -ra f, orientador(ra) ra - **2**. US [lawyer] advogado m, -da f.

count [kaʊnt] ⬦ n - **1**. [total] conta f; to keep ~ of sthg registrar algo; to lose ~ of sthg perder a conta de algo - **2**. [aristocrat] conde m. ⬦ vt - **1**. [add up] contar - **2**. [consider, include]: to ~ sb/sthg as sthg considerar alguém/algo como algo. ⬦ vi contar; to ~ (up) to contar até; to ~ as sthg contar como algo.

➡ **count against** vt fus pesar contra.

➡ **count on** vt fus [rely on, expect] contar com.

➡ **count up** vt fus contar.

➡ **count upon** vt fus = count on.

countdown [ˈkaʊntdaʊn] n contagem f regressiva.

counter [ˈkaʊntəʳ] ⬦ n - **1**. [in shop, kitchen] balcão m - **2**. [in board game] ficha f - **3**. [in post office, bank] guichê m. ⬦ vt: to ~ sthg with sthg [respond to] responder algo com algo. ⬦ vi: to ~ with sthg/by doing sthg responder com/fazendo sthg.

➡ **counter to** adv ao contrário de; to run ~ to sthg ir contra algo/ser contrário a algo.

counteract [ˌkaʊntəˈrækt] vt neutralizar.

counter-attack vt & vi contra-atacar.

counterclockwise US [ˌkaʊntəˈklɒkwaɪz] ⬦ adj anti-horário(ria). ⬦ adv em sentido anti-horário.

counterfeit [ˈkaʊntəfɪt] ⬦ adj falsificado(da). ⬦ vt falsificar.

counterfoil [ˈkaʊntəfɔɪl] n canhoto m.

countermand [ˌkaʊntəˈmɑːnd] vt revogar.

counterpart [ˈkaʊntəpɑːt] n contraparte f.

counter-productive adj contraproducente.

countess [ˈkaʊntɪs] n condessa f.

countless [ˈkaʊntlɪs] adj inúmero(ra).

country [ˈkʌntrɪ] (pl -ies) n - **1**. [nation] país m; to go to the ~ UK POL fazer uma eleição - **2**. [countryside]: the ~ o campo - **3**. [area of land, region] região f.

country dancing n (U) dança f tradicional.

country house n casa f de campo.

countryman [ˈkʌntrɪmən] (pl -men [-mən]) n [from same country] compatriota m.

country park n UK parque m regional.

countryside [ˈkʌntrɪsaɪd] n (U) campo m.

county [ˈkaʊntɪ] (pl -ies) n condado m.

county council n UK conselho m regional.

coup [kuː] n - **1**. [rebellion]: ~ (d'état) golpe de estado - **2**. [masterstroke] golpe m de mestre.

couple [ˈkʌpl] ⬦ n - **1**. [in relationship] casal m - **2**. [small number]: a ~ alguns, algumas; a ~ of dois, duas. ⬦ vt [join]: to ~ sthg (to sthg) unir algo (a algo).

coupon [ˈkuːpɒn] n - **1**. [voucher] vale m - **2**. [form] cupom m.

courage [ˈkʌrɪdʒ] n (U) coragem f; to take ~ (from sthg) tirar coragem (de algo).

courgette [kɔːˈʒet] n UK abobrinha f.

courier [ˈkʊrɪəʳ] n - **1**. [on holiday tour] representante de uma agência de viagens que cuida das pessoas que estão a passeio - **2**. [delivering letters, packages] mensageiro m, -ra f, courier m.

course [kɔːs] n - **1**. [gen] curso m - **2**. MED [of treatment] tratamento m - **3**. [path, route] rota f; to be on ~ for [ship, plane] estar rumando para; fig [on target] em curso; off ~ fora de curso - **4**. [plan]: ~ (of action) curso (de ação) - **5**. [of time]: in due ~ no tempo devido; in the ~ of no decorrer de - **6**. [in meal] prato m - **7**. SPORT campo m.

➡ **of course** adv - **1**. [inevitably, not surprisingly] evidentemente - **2**. [certainly] claro que sim; of ~ you can! claro que pode!; 'do you want the job?' - 'of ~ I do!' 'você quer o trabalho?' - 'claro que quero!'; of ~ not claro que não.

coursebook [ˈkɔːsbʊk] n livro m de curso.

coursework [ˈkɔːswɜːk] n (U) trabalho m de curso.

court [kɔːt] ⬦ n -1. JUR tribunal m; the ~ o tribunal -2. SPORT quadra f -3. [courtyard] pátio m -4. [of king, queen etc.] corte f. ⬦ vi dated [go out together] cortejar.

courteous ['kɜːtjəs] adj cortês.

courtesy ['kɜːtɪsɪ] n (U) [polite behaviour] cortesia f.
➡ **(by) courtesy of** prep [thanks to] por cortesia de.

courthouse ['kɔːthaʊs] n US palácio m da justiça.

courtier ['kɔːtjər] n cortesão m.

court-martial (pl **court-martials** OR **courts-martial**) n corte m marcial.

courtroom ['kɔːtrʊm] n sala f de tribunal.

courtyard ['kɔːtjɑːd] n pátio m.

cousin ['kʌzn] n primo m, -ma f.

cove [kəʊv] n [bay] enseada f.

covenant ['kʌvənənt] n [promise of money] convênio m.

Covent Garden [ˌkɒvənt-] n área comercial e artística coberta no centro de Londres, que também inclui o Royal Opera House.

cover ['kʌvər] ⬦ n -1. [covering] capa f -2. [lid] tampa f -3. [blanket] coberta f -4. [protection, shelter] abrigo m; to take ~ [from weather] abrigar-se; [from gunfire] proteger-se; under ~ [from weather] abrigado(da); under ~ of darkness sob o manto da escuridão -5. [disguise, front or insurance] cobertura f. ⬦ vt cobrir; to ~ sthg with sthg cobrir algo com algo; to ~ sb against sthg [give insurance] cobrir alguém contra algo.
➡ **cover up** vt sep fig [story, scandal] encobrir.

coverage ['kʌvərɪdʒ] n (U) [of news] cobertura f.

cover charge n couvert m.

covering ['kʌvərɪŋ] n cobertura f.

covering letter UK, **cover letter** US n carta ou nota contendo explicações ou informações adicionais que acompanha uma encomenda ou outra carta.

cover note n UK nota f de cobertura.

covert ['kʌvət] adj secreto(ta), oculto(-ta).

cover-up n encobrimento m.

covet ['kʌvɪt] vt fml ambicionar.

cow [kaʊ] ⬦ n -1. [female type of cattle] vaca f -2. [female elephant, whale, seal] fêmea f. ⬦ vt intimidar.

coward ['kaʊəd] n covarde mf.

cowardly ['kaʊədlɪ] adj covarde.

cowboy ['kaʊbɔɪ] n [cattlehand] vaqueiro.

cower ['kaʊər] vi encolher-se de medo.

cox [kɒks], **coxswain** ['kɒksən] n timoneiro m, -ra f.

coy [kɔɪ] adj recatado(da).

cozy adj US = cosy.

CPA (abbr of **certified public accountant**) n contador público certificado nos Estados Unidos.

crab [kræb] n -1. [sea creature] caranguejo m -2. [food] siri m.

crab apple n -1. [fruit] maçã f silvestre -2. [tree] macieira f silvestre.

crack [kræk] ⬦ n -1. [fault - in cup, glass, mirror] trinca f; [- in wall, ceiling] rachadura f; [- in skin] arranhão m -2. [small opening, gap] fresta f -3. [sharp noise] estalo m -4. inf [attempt]: to have a ~ at sthg tentar (fazer) algo -5. [cocaine] crack m. ⬦ adj de primeira. ⬦ vt -1. [damage - gen] arranhar; [- cup, glass] trincar; [- wall, ceiling] rachar -2. [cause to make sharp noise] estalar -3. [bang, hit] bater -4. [solve - problem] resolver; [- code] decifrar -5. inf [make]: to ~ a joke soltar uma piada. ⬦ vi -1. [split, be damaged - gen] arranhar; [- cup, glass] trincar; [- wall, ceiling] rachar -2. [give way, collapse] ruir.
➡ **crack down** vi: to ~ down (on sb/sthg) fazer linha dura (contra alguém/algo).
➡ **crack up** vi ter um colapso nervoso.

cracker ['krækər] n -1. [biscuit] biscoito m -2. UK [for Christmas] tubo colorido que faz barulho ao abrir e contém um presente surpresa.

crackers ['krækəz] adj UK inf [mad] doido(da).

crackle ['krækl] vi -1. [fire, cooking] crepitar -2. [phone, radio] estar com interferência.

cradle ['kreɪdl] ⬦ n -1. [baby's bed, birthplace] berço m -2. [hoist] pedestal m. ⬦ vt -1. [person] embalar -2. [object] segurar cuidadosamente.

craft [krɑːft] (pl sense 2 inv) n -1. [trade, skill] arte f -2. [boat] barco m.

craftsman ['krɑːftsmən] (pl -men [-mən]) n artesão m.

craftsmanship ['krɑːftsmənʃɪp] n destreza f, habilidade f.

craftsmen pl ➡ craftsman.

crafty ['krɑːftɪ] (compar -ier, superl -iest) adj astuto(ta).

crag [kræg] n penhasco m.

cram [kræm] (pt & pp -med, cont -ming) ⬦ vt abarrotar; to ~ sthg with sthg abarrotar algo com algo; to be crammed (with sthg) estar abarrotado(-da) (de algo). ⬦ vi [study hard] rachar de estudar.

cramp [kræmp] <> n -1. [in leg, arm] cãibra f - 2. [in stomach] cólica f. <> vt [restrict, hinder] limitar.

cranberry ['krænbərı] (pl -ies) n uva-do-monte f.

crane [kreın] n [machine] guindaste m.

crank [kræŋk] <> n -1. TECH manivela f - 2. inf [eccentric] extravagante mf. <> vt [gen] dar manivela em.

crankshaft ['kræŋkʃɑːft] n virabrequim m.

crap [kræp] n (U) vulg -1. [excrement] bosta f - 2. fig [rubbish] asneira f.

crash [kræʃ] <> n -1. [accident] acidente m - 2. [loud noise] estrépito m. <> vt [cause to collide] bater com. <> vi -1. [collide] colidir; **to ~ into** sthg colidir em algo - 2. FIN [collapse] entrar em colapso.

crash course n curso m intensivo.

crash helmet n elmo m.

crash-land vi aterrisar forçosamente.

crass [kræs] adj crasso(sa).

crate [kreıt] n -1. [for carrying things] caixote m - 2. [crateful] engradado m.

crater ['kreıtər] n cratera f.

cravat [krə'væt] n cachecol m.

crave [kreıv] <> vt ansiar. <> vi: **to ~ for** sthg ansiar por algo.

crawl [krɔːl] <> vi -1. [on hands and knees] engatinhar - 2. [move slowly - insect] rastejar; [- vehicle, traffic] arrastar-se - 3. inf: **to be ~ing with** sthg estar infestado(da) de algo. <> n (U) [swimming stroke]: **the ~** o crawl.

crayfish ['kreıfıʃ] (pl inv OR -es) n -1. [fish] lagostim m - 2. [food] camarão-d'água-doce m.

crayon ['kreıɒn] n lápis m de cera.

craze [kreız] n [fashion] moda f.

crazy ['kreızı] (compar -ier, superl -iest) adj inf [mad, enthusiastic] louco(ca); **to be ~ about** sthg/sb ser/estar louco(ca) por algo/alguém.

creak [kriːk] vi ranger.

cream [kriːm] <> adj [in colour] creme. <> n creme m.

cream cake n UK bolo m de creme.

cream cheese n (U) queijo m cremoso.

cream cracker n UK bolacha f cream cracker.

cream tea n UK chá acompanhado de bolinhos com presunto, geléia e creme, comum na Inglaterra.

crease [kriːs] <> n [in fabric - deliberate] friso m; [- accidental] dobra f. <> vt [deliberately] amassar; [accidentally] amarrotar. <> vi [fabric] amassar.

create [kriː'eıt] vt -1. [gen] criar - 2. [noise, fuss, impression] causar.

creation [kriː'eıʃn] n criação f.

creative [kriː'eıtıv] adj criativo(va); **~ writing** produção f literária.

creature ['kriːtʃər] n [animal] criatura f.

crèche [kreʃ] n UK creche f.

credence ['kriːdns] n (U) credibilidade f; **to give** OR **lend ~ to** sthg conferir credibilidade a algo.

credentials [krɪ'denʃlz] npl -1. [papers] credenciais fpl - 2. fig [qualifications] credenciais fpl - 3. [references] referências fpl.

credibility [ˌkredə'bɪlətɪ] n (U) credibilidade f.

credit ['kredıt] <> n -1. (U) [financial aid] crédito m; **in ~** com saldo positivo; **on ~** a prazo - 2. (U) [praise] honras fpl; **to give sb ~ for** sthg crer que alguém seja capaz de algo - 3. SCH & UNIV crédito m - 4. FIN [money credited] saldo m positivo. <> vt -1. FIN creditar - 2. inf [believe] acreditar -3. [attribute]: **to ~ sb with** sthg atribuir a alguém o mérito por algo.

➤ **credits** npl CINEMA créditos mpl.

credit card n cartão m de crédito.

credit note n -1. COMM nota f promissória - 2. FIN letra f de câmbio.

creditor ['kredıtər] n credor m, -ra f.

creed [kriːd] n -1. [political] doutrina f - 2. RELIG credo m.

creek [kriːk] n -1. [inlet] enseada f - 2. US [stream] riacho m.

creep [kriːp] (pt & pp crept) <> vi -1. [move slowly] arrastar-se - 2. [move stealthily] andar furtivamente. <> n inf [person] pegajoso m, -sa f.

➤ **creeps** npl: **to give sb the ~s** inf dar arrepios mpl em alguém.

creeper ['kriːpər] n [plant] trepadeira f.

creepy ['kriːpı] (compar -ier, superl -iest) adj inf horripilante.

creepy-crawly [-'krɔːlı] (pl creepy-crawlies) n inf bicho m rastejante.

cremate [krɪ'meıt] vt cremar.

cremation [krɪ'meıʃn] n (U) cremação f.

crematorium UK [ˌkremə'tɔːrɪəm] (pl -riums OR -ria [-rɪə]), **crematory** US ['kremətrı] (pl -ies) n crematório m.

crepe [kreıp] n crepe m.

crepe bandage n UK atadura f.

crepe paper n (U) papel m crepom.

crept [krept] pt & pp ➤ creep.

crescent ['kresnt] n -1. [shape] crescente mf - 2. [street] rua f em forma de arco.

cress [kres] n (U) agrião m.

crest [krest] n -1. [on bird's head, of wave] crista f - 2. [of hill] cume m - 3. [on coat of arms] brasão m.

crestfallen ['krestˌfɔːln] adj desanimado(da).

Crete [kri:t] *n* Creta.

cretin ['kretɪn] *n inf offensive* [idiot] cretino *m*, -na *f*.

crevice ['krevɪs] *n* fenda *f*, rachadura *f*.

crew [kru:] *n* -1. [of ship, plane, ambulance] tripulação *f* -2. CINEMA & TV equipe *f* -3. *inf* [gang] bando *m*.

crew cut *n* corte *m* de cabelo à escovinha.

crew neck *n* [on sweater] gola *f* redonda.

crew-neck(ed) [-nek(t)] *adj* de gola redonda.

crib [krɪb] (*pt* & *pp* -bed, *cont* -bing) ⬦ *n* berço *m*. ⬦ *vt inf* [copy]: to ~ sthg off OR from sb copiar algo de alguém.

crick [krɪk] *n* [in neck] torcicolo *m*.

cricket ['krɪkɪt] *n* -1. (U) [game] críquete *m* -2. [insect] grilo *m*.

crime [kraɪm] *n* crime *m*.

criminal ['krɪmɪnl] ⬦ *adj* -1. [JUR - act] criminal; [- lawyer] criminalista; [offence] penal -2. *inf* [shameful] vergonhoso(sa). ⬦ *n* criminoso *m*, -sa *f*.

crimson ['krɪmzn] ⬦ *adj* -1. [in colour] carmesim -2. [with embarrassment] vermelho(lha). ⬦ *n* carmesim *mf*.

cringe [krɪndʒ] *vi* -1. [out of fear] encolher-se -2. *inf* [with embarrassment]: to ~ (at sthg) encolher-se de vergonha (por algo).

crinkle ['krɪŋkl] *vt* enrugar.

cripple ['krɪpl] ⬦ *n offensive* aleijado *m*, -da *f*. ⬦ *vt* -1. MED [disable] aleijar -2. [put out of action] inutilizar -3. *fig* [bring to a halt] paralisar.

crisis ['kraɪsɪs] (*pl* crises ['kraɪsi:z]) *n* crise *f*.

crisp [krɪsp] *adj* -1. [pastry, bacon] crocante; [fruit, vegetables] fresco(ca); [banknote] liso(sa); [snow] quebradiço(ça) -2. [weather] revigorante -3. [manner, toner] seco(ca).
➡ **crisps** *npl* UK batatas *fpl* fritas (em pacote).

criss-cross ⬦ *adj* [pattern] xadrez. ⬦ *vt* [subj: roads] entrecruzar.

criterion [kraɪ'tɪərɪən] (*pl* -ria [-rɪə], -rions) *n* critério *m*.

critic ['krɪtɪk] *n* crítico *m*, -ca *f*.

critical ['krɪtɪkl] *adj* -1. [serious] crítico(ca), grave -2. [crucial] fundamental -3. [analytical, disparaging] crítico(ca); to be ~ of sb/sthg criticar alguém/algo.

critically ['krɪtɪklɪ] *adv* -1. [seriously] criticamente, gravemente -2. [crucially] fundamentalmente -3. [analytically, disparagingly] criticamente.

criticism ['krɪtɪsɪzm] *n* crítica *f*.

criticize, -ise ['krɪtɪsaɪz] ⬦ *vt* [judge unfavourably] criticar. ⬦ *vi* [make unfavourable comments] criticar.

croak [krəʊk] ⬦ *vt* grunhir. ⬦ *vi* -1. [animal] coaxar -2. [bird] granir -3. [person] ter rouquidão.

Croat ['krəʊæt], **Croatian** [krəʊ'eɪʃn] ⬦ *adj* croata. ⬦ *n* -1. [person] croata *mf* -2. [language] croata *m*.

Croatia [krəʊ'eɪʃə] *n* Croácia.

crochet ['krəʊʃeɪ] *n* (U) crochê *m*.

crockery ['krɒkərɪ] *n* (U) louça *f* (de barro).

crocodile ['krɒkədaɪl] (*pl inv* OR -s) *n* [animal] crocodilo *m*.

crocus ['krəʊkəs] (*pl* -cuses) *n* açafrão *m*.

croft [krɒft] *n* UK sítio *m*.

crony ['krəʊnɪ] (*pl* -ies) *n inf* [friend] camarada *mf*.

crook [krʊk] *n* -1. [criminal] vigarista *mf* -2. [angle] curvatura *f* -3. [shepherd's staff] cajado *m*.

crooked ['krʊkɪd] *adj* -1. [not straight - back] arqueado(da); [- teeth, smile] torto(ta); [- path] sinuoso(sa) -2. *inf* [dishonest] desonesto(ta).

crop [krɒp] (*pt* & *pp* -ped, *cont* -ping) *n* -1. [kind of plant] cultura *f* -2. [harvested produce] colheita *f* -3. [whip] chicote *m* -4. [of bird] papo *m* -5. [haircut] cabelo *m* curto.
➡ **crop up** *vi* surgir.

croquette [krɒ'ket] *n* croquete *m*.

cross [krɒs] ⬦ *adj* zangado(da). ⬦ *n* -1. [gen] cruz *f* -2. [mixture] cruzamento *m*; a ~ between two things uma mistura de duas coisas. ⬦ *vt* -1. [gen] cruzar -2. [move across - street, room] atravessar; [- subj: expression] trespassar; a look of distaste ~ed her face um olhar de desagrado trespassou-lhe o rosto -3. UK [cheque] cruzar. ⬦ *vi* [intersect] cruzar-se.
➡ **cross off, cross out** *vt sep* riscar.

crossbar ['krɒsbɑ:ʳ] *n* -1. [of goal] trave *f* -2. [of bicycle] barra *f* transversal.

cross-Channel *adj* [ferry, route] do Canal da Mancha; ~ travel viagem pelo Canal da Mancha.

cross-country ⬦ *adj* & *adv* através do campo. ⬦ *n* [race, running] esporte praticado através dos campos.

cross-examine *vt* -1. JUR interrogar (para confirmar veracidade) -2. *fig* [question closely] interrogar.

cross-eyed ['krɒsaɪd] *adj* vesgo(ga).

crossfire ['krɒsˌfaɪəʳ] *n* (U) fogo *m* cruzado.

crossing ['krɒsɪŋ] *n* -1. [place to cross]

faixa f de segurança **-2.** [sea journey] travessia f.

cross-legged ['krɒslegd] *adv* de pernas cruzadas.

cross-purposes *npl* mal-entendido m; **to be at ~** não se entender.

cross-reference n referência f cruzada.

crossroads ['krɒsrəʊdz] (*pl inv*) n cruzamento m, encruzilhada f.

cross-section n **-1.** [drawing] corte m transversal **-2.** [of population] amostra f representativa.

crosswalk ['krɒswɔːk] n US faixa f de segurança.

crossways ['krɒsweɪz] *adv* = **crosswise**.

crosswind ['krɒswɪnd] n vento m contrário.

crosswise ['krɒswaɪz] *adv* em diagonal, transversalmente.

crossword (puzzle) ['krɒswɜːd-] n palavras *fpl* cruzadas.

crotch [krɒtʃ] n **-1.** [of person] entreperna f **-2.** [of garment] gancho m.

crotchety ['krɒtʃɪtɪ] *adj UK inf* rabugento(ta).

crouch [kraʊtʃ] vi **-1.** [person] agachar-se **-2.** [animal] armar o bote.

crow [krəʊ] <> n corvo m; **as the ~ flies** em linha reta. <> vi **-1.** [cock] cantar **-2.** *inf* [gloat] gabar-se.

crowbar ['krəʊbɑː] n pé-de-cabra m.

crowd [kraʊd] <> n [mass of people] multidão f. <> vi aglomerar-se. <> vt **-1.** [fill] lotar **-2.** [force into small space] empurrar; **to ~ everyone in** colocar todo mundo para dentro.

crowded ['kraʊdɪd] *adj* cheio (cheia), lotado(da); **~ with** cheio (cheia) de, repleto(ta) de.

crown [kraʊn] <> n **-1.** [gen] coroa f **-2.** [top - of hat] copa f; [- of head] topo m; [- of hill] cume m. <> vt **-1.** [monarch] coroar **-2.** [tooth] pôr uma coroa em **-3.** [cover top of] cobrir.

    ➤ **Crown** n: **the Crown** [monarchy] a Coroa.

Crown Jewels *npl*: **the ~** as jóias da Coroa.

crown prince n príncipe m herdeiro.

crow's feet *npl* pés-de-galinha *mpl*.

crucial ['kruːʃl] *adj* [vital] crucial.

crucifix ['kruːsɪfɪks] n crucifixo m.

Crucifixion [ˌkruːsɪ'fɪkʃn] n: **the ~** a Crucificação.

crude [kruːd] *adj* **-1.** [commodity] cru (crua) **-2.** [joke, person] grosseiro(ra) **-3.** [sketch] tosco(ca) **-4.** [method, shelter] primitivo(va).

crude oil n (U) petróleo m bruto.

cruel [kruəl] (*compar* **-ler**, *superl* **-lest**) *adj* **-1.** [sadistic] cruel **-2.** [painful, harsh - disappointment] doloroso(sa); [- winter] rigoroso(sa).

cruelty ['kruəltɪ] n (U) crueldade f.

cruet ['kruːɪt] n galheta f.

cruise [kruːz] <> n cruzeiro m. <> vi **-1.** [sail] fazer um cruzeiro **-2.** [drive] ir à velocidade de cruzeiro **-3.** [fly] voar.

cruiser ['kruːzə'] n **-1.** [warship] cruzador m **-2.** [cabin cruiser] iate m.

crumb [krʌm] n [of food] migalha f.

crumble ['krʌmbl] <> n doce de frutas coberto com uma mistura de farinha, manteiga e açúcar e cozido no forno. <> vt esmigalhar. <> vi **-1.** [disintegrate - bread, cheese] esmigalhar-se; [- building, cliff] desmoronar **-2.** *fig* [collapse] desmoronar.

crumbly ['krʌmblɪ] (*compar* **-ier**, *superl* **-iest**) *adj* farelento(ta).

crumpet ['krʌmpɪt] n [food] fatias de bolo tostadas que se come com manteiga.

crumple ['krʌmpl] vt amassar.

crunch [krʌntʃ] <> n [sound] mastigação f barulhenta; **if/when it comes to the ~** *inf* se/quando chegar a hora da verdade. <> vt **-1.** [with teeth] mastigar ruidosamente **-2.** [underfoot] esmagar com o pé ao caminhar.

crunchy ['krʌntʃɪ] (*compar* **-ier**, *superl* **-iest**) *adj* **-1.** [food] crocante **-2.** [snow, gravel] que estala.

crusade [kruː'seɪd] n **-1.** [war] cruzada f **-2.** *fig* [campaign] campanha f.

crush [krʌʃ] <> n **-1.** [crowd] aglomeração f **-2.** *inf* [infatuation]: **to have a ~ on sb** estar obcecado(da) por alguém. <> vt **-1.** [squash, press, smash] esmagar **-2.** *fig* [destroy] acabar com.

crust [krʌst] n **-1.** [on bread] casca f **-2.** [on pie] crosta f torrada **-3.** [hard covering] crosta f.

crutch [krʌtʃ] n **-1.** [stick] muleta f **-2.** *fig* [support] apoio m.

crux [krʌks] n ponto m crucial.

cry [kraɪ] (*pl* **cries**, *pt* & *pp* **cried**) <> n **-1.** [shout] grito m; **to be a far ~ from** não se parecer em nada com **-2.** [of bird] canto m. <> vi **-1.** [weep] chorar **-2.** [shout] gritar.

    ➤ **cry off** vi desistir de.

    ➤ **cry out** <> vt gritar. <> vi [call out] gritar.

cryptic ['krɪptɪk] *adj* [mysterious] enigmático(ca).

crystal ['krɪstl] n cristal m.

crystal clear *adj* [motive, meaning] claro(ra).

CSE (*abbr of* **Certificate of Secondary Education**) *n antigo certificado de conclusão de ensino médio na Grã-Bretanha.*

CTC (*abbr of* **city technology college**) *n escola de ensino médio que tem parceria com empresas e com o governo para ensino de tecnologia na Grã-Bretanha.*

cub [kʌb] *n* -1. [young animal] filhote *m* -2. [boy scout] lobinho *m*.

Cuba ['kjuːbə] *n* Cuba.

Cuban ['kjuːbən] <> *adj* cubano(na). <> *n* cubano *m*, -na *f*.

cubbyhole ['kʌbɪhəʊl] *n* cubículo *m*.

cube [kjuːb] <> *n* cubo *m*. <> *vt* MATH elevar ao cubo.

cubic ['kjuːbɪk] *adj* cúbico(ca).

cubicle ['kjuːbɪkl] *n* -1. [shower] boxe *m* -2. [in shop] provador *m*.

Cub Scout *n* lobinho *m*.

cuckoo ['kʊkuː] *n* cuco *m*.

cuckoo clock *n* [relógio *m* de] cuco *m*.

cucumber ['kjuːkʌmbəʳ] *n* pepino *m*.

cuddle ['kʌdl] <> *n* abraço *m*. <> *vt* abraçar. <> *vi* abraçar-se.

cuddly toy ['kʌdlɪ-] *n* bicho *m* de pelúcia.

cue [kjuː] *n* -1. RADIO, THEATRE & TV deixa *f*; **on** ~ no momento certo -2. [in snooker, pool] taco *m*.

cuff [kʌf] *n* -1. [of sleeve] punho *m* -2. US [of trouser] barra *f* -3. [blow] tapa *m*.

cufflink *n* abotoadura *f*.

cul-de-sac ['kʌldəsæk] *n* beco *m* sem saída.

cull [kʌl] <> *n* [kill] extermínio *m*. <> *vt* -1. [kill] exterminar -2. *fml* [gather] reunir.

culminate ['kʌlmɪneɪt] *vi*: **to** ~ **in sthg** culminar em algo.

culmination [,kʌlmɪ'neɪʃn] *n* culminação *f*.

culottes [kjuː'lɒts] *npl* saia-calça *f*.

culpable ['kʌlpəbl] *adj fml* culpável; ~ **homicide** homicídio *m* culposo.

culprit ['kʌlprɪt] *n* culpado *m*, -da *f*.

cult [kʌlt] <> *n* -1. RELIG culto *m* -2. [book, film] objeto *m* de culto. <> *comp* [book, film] de culto.

cultivate ['kʌltɪveɪt] *vt* -1. [gen] cultivar -2. [get to know] fazer amizade com.

cultivation [,kʌltɪ'veɪʃn] *n* (*U*) [farming] cultivo *m*.

cultural ['kʌltʃərəl] *adj* cultural.

culture ['kʌltʃəʳ] *n* cultura *f*.

cultured ['kʌltʃəd] *adj* [educated] culto(-ta).

cumbersome ['kʌmbəsəm] *adj* [object] de difícil manejo.

cunning ['kʌnɪŋ] <> *adj* -1. [person] astuto(ta) -2. [method, idea] engenhoso(-sa). <> *n* (*U*) astúcia *f*.

cup [kʌp] *n* -1. [gen] xícara *f* -2. [as prize, of bra] taça *f* -3. [competition] copa *f*.

cupboard ['kʌbəd] *n* armário *m*.

cupcake ['kʌpkeɪk] *n* bolinho *m* coberto com glacê.

Cup Final *n*: **the** ~ o jogo final da copa.

cup tie *n* UK jogo *m* eliminatório.

curate ['kjʊərət] <> *n* RELIG coadjutor *m*, -ra *f*. <> *vt* [exhibition] organizar.

curator [,kjʊə'reɪtəʳ] *n* [of museum] curador *m*, -ra *f*.

curb [kɜːb] <> *n* -1. [control]: ~ **(on sthg)** controle *m* (sobre algo) -2. US [of road] meio-fio *m*. <> *vt* controlar.

curdle ['kɜːdl] *vi* -1. [milk] coalhar -2. [blood] coagular.

cure [kjʊəʳ] <> *n* -1. MED: ~ **(for sthg)** cura *f* (de algo) -2. [solution]: ~ **(for sthg)** solução *f* (para algo). <> *vt* -1. MED curar -2. [solve] remediar -3. [rid]: **to** ~ **sb of sthg** *fig* livrar alguém de algo -4. [preserve] curtir.

cure-all *n* panacéia *f*.

curfew ['kɜːfjuː] *n* toque *m* de recolher.

curio ['kjʊərɪəʊ] (*pl* -s) *n* raridade *f*, curiosidade *f*.

curiosity [,kjʊərɪ'ɒsətɪ] *n* -1. (*U*) [inquisitiveness] curiosidade *f* -2. [rarity] raridade *f*.

curious ['kjʊərɪəs] *adj* curioso(sa); ~ **about sb/sthg** curioso(sa) sobre alguém/algo.

curl [kɜːl] <> *n* [of hair] cacho *m*. <> *vt* -1. [hair] encrespar, encaracolar -2. [tail, ribbon] enrolar. <> *vi* -1. [hair] encrespar, encaracolar -2. [paper, leaf, road, smoke, snake] enrolar.

➤ **curl up** *vi* [person, animal] enrolar-se.

curler ['kɜːləʳ] *n* rolo *m*.

curling tongs *npl* ferros *mpl* de frisar.

curly ['kɜːlɪ] (*compar* -**ier**, *superl* -**iest**) *adj* [hair] encaracolado(da).

currant ['kʌrənt] *n* [dried grape] uva *f* passa.

currency ['kʌrənsɪ] (*pl* -**ies**) *n* -1. [money] moeda *f* corrente; **foreign** ~ moeda *f* estrangeira -2. *fml* [acceptability]: **to gain** ~ ganhar aceitação.

current ['kʌrənt] <> *adj* atual; **in** ~ **use** de uso corrente. <> *n* corrente *f*.

current account *n* UK conta *f* corrente.

current affairs *npl* atualidades *fpl*.

currently ['kʌrəntlɪ] *adv* atualmente.

curriculum [kə'rɪkjələm] (*pl* -**lums** OR -**la** [-lə]) *n* [course of study] currículo *m*.

curriculum vitae [-'viːtaɪ] (*pl* **curricula**

vitae) n currículo m, curriculum m (vitae).

curry ['kʌrɪ] (pl -ies) n caril m.

curse [kɜ:s] <> n -1. [evil charm]: ~ (on sb/sthg) maldição f OR praga f (sobre alguém/algo) -2. [swearword] palavrão m -3. [source of problems] desgraça f. <> vt -1. [wish misfortune on] maldizer -2. [complain about] xingar. <> vi [swear] praguejar.

cursor ['kɜ:sə'] n COMPUT cursor m.

cursory ['kɜ:sərɪ] adj apressado(da); a ~ glance um olhada por cima.

curt [kɜ:t] adj brusco(ca).

curtail [kɜ:'teɪl] vt [cut short] encurtar.

curtain ['kɜ:tn] n cortina f.

curts(e)y ['kɜ:tsɪ] (pt & pp curtsied) <> n reverência f (feita por mulher). <> vi fazer reverência.

curve [kɜ:v] <> n curva f. <> vi fazer uma curva.

cushion ['kʊʃn] <> n [for sitting on] almofada f. <> vt amortecer.

cushy ['kʊʃɪ] (compar -ier, superl -iest) adj inf mole.

custard ['kʌstəd] n [sauce] creme m (para doces).

custodial adj [sentence] custódio(dia).

custodian [kʌ'stəʊdjən] n [of building, museum] guarda m.

custody ['kʌstədɪ] n (U) -1. [of child] custódia f -2. [of suspect]: in ~ sob custódia.

custom ['kʌstəm] n -1. [tradition, habit] costume m, hábito m -2. (U) COMM [trade] preferência f; thank you for your ~ agradecemos a preferência.

➠ **customs** n (U) [place, organization] alfândega f; to go through ~ passar pela alfândega.

customary ['kʌstəmrɪ] adj costumeiro(-ra), habitual.

customer ['kʌstəmə'] n -1. [client] cliente mf -2. inf [person] tipo m; an awkward ~ um tipo complicado.

customize, -ise ['kʌstəmaɪz] vt -1. [gen] personalizar -2. COMPUT customizar.

Customs and Excise n (U) UK departamento do governo britânico responsável por coletar impostos sobre a compra e venda de bens e serviços ou sobre bens importados.

customs duty n (U) imposto m alfandegário.

customs officer n fiscal mf de alfândega.

cut [kʌt] (pt & pp cut, cont -ting) <> n [gen] corte m; ~ (in sthg) corte (em algo). <> vt -1. [gen] cortar -2. inf [miss] matar -3. phr: to ~ sb dead fazer que

não se vê alguém; ~ and dried definitivo(va). <> vi -1. cortar -2. phr: to ~ both ways ser uma faca de dois gumes.

➠ **cut back** <> vt sep -1. [tree, bush] podar -2. [expenditure, budget] reduzir, diminuir. <> vi: to ~ back (on sthg) reduzir (algo).

➠ **cut down** <> vt sep -1. [chop down] cortar, derrubar -2. [reduce] reduzir, diminuir. <> vi: to ~ down on sthg reduzir algo.

➠ **cut in** vi -1. [interrupt]: to ~ in (on sb) interromper (alguém) -2. [in car] cortar (a frente de), fechar.

➠ **cut off** vt sep -1. [sever] cortar fora -2. [sever supply of] cortar; I got ~ off [on telephone] cortaram meu telefone -3. [isolate]: to be ~ off (from sb/sthg) ficar isolado(da) (de alguém/algo).

➠ **cut out** vt sep [gen] cortar; to ~ out the light cortar a entrada de luz; ~ it out! pare com isso!

➠ **cut up** vt sep [chop up] picar.

cutback ['kʌtbæk] n: ~ (in sthg) corte m (em algo).

cute [kju:t] adj esp US [appealing] bonitinho(nha).

cuticle ['kju:tɪkl] n cutícula f.

cutlery ['kʌtlərɪ] n (U) talheres mpl.

cutlet ['kʌtlɪt] n costeleta f.

cut-out n -1. [on machine] disjuntor m -2. [shape] figura f para recortar.

cut-price, cut-rate US adj com desconto.

cut-throat adj [ruthless] acirrado(da).

cutting ['kʌtɪŋ] <> adj [sarcastic] mordaz. <> n -1. [of plant] chantão m -2. [from newspaper] recorte m -3. UK [for road, railway] corte m.

CV (abbr of curriculum vitae) n UK CV m.

cwt. abbr of hundredweight.

cyanide ['saɪənaɪd] n (U) cianeto m, cianureto m.

cybercafé n COMPUT cibercafé m.

cyberspace ['saɪbəspeɪs] n COMPUT ciberespaço m.

cycle ['saɪkl] <> n -1. [process] ciclo m -2. [bicycle] bicicleta f. <> comp: ~ path ciclovia f; ~ track pista f para ciclismo; ~ race corrida f de bicicletas. <> vi andar de bicicleta.

cycling ['saɪklɪŋ] n (U) ciclismo m; to go ~ andar de bicicleta.

cyclist ['saɪklɪst] n ciclista mf.

cygnet ['sɪgnɪt] n filhote m de cisne.

cylinder ['sɪlɪndə'] n -1. [gen] cilindro m -2. [container] tambor m.

cymbals ['sɪmblz] npl címbalos mpl.

cynic ['sɪnɪk] n cético m, -ca f.

cynical ['sɪnɪkl] adj cético(ca).

cynicism ['sɪnɪsɪzml] n (U) ceticismo m.

cypress ['saɪprəs] n cipreste m.

Cypriot ['sɪprɪət] ◇ adj cipriota. ◇ n cipriota mf.

Cyprus ['saɪprəs] n Chipre.

cyst [sɪst] n cisto m.

cystitis [sɪs'taɪtɪs] n (U) cistite f.

czar [zɑːʳ] n czar m.

Czech [tʃek] ◇ adj tcheco(ca). ◇ n -1. [person] tcheco m, -ca f - 2. [language] tcheco m.

Czechoslovak adj & n = Czechoslovakian.

Czechoslovakia [ˌtʃekəslə'vækɪə] n Tchecoslováquia.

Czechoslovakian [ˌtʃekəslə'vækɪən] ◇ adj tchecoslovaco(ca). ◇ n tchecoslovaco m, -ca f.

Czech Republic n: the ~ a República Tcheca.

D

d (pl d's OR ds), **D** (pl D's OR Ds) [diː] n [letter] d,D m.

➨ **D** n -1. MUS ré m - 2. SCH [mark] D m.

DA (abbr of district attorney) n promotor nos Estados Unidos.

D/A (abbr of digital to analogue) adj D/A.

dab [dæb] (pt & pp -bed, cont -bing) ◇ n [small amount - of powder, ointment] pitada f; [- of paint] pincelada f. ◇ vt -1. [skin, wound] aplicar de leve - 2. [eyes] tocar de leve - 3. [cream, ointment]: to ~ sthg on(to) sthg aplicar algo em algo.

dabble ['dæbl] vi: to ~ (in sthg) atuar como amador (em algo).

dachshund ['dækshʊnd] n dachshund m.

dad [dæd] n inf pai m.

daddy ['dædɪ] (pl -ies) n inf papai m.

daddy longlegs [-'lɒŋlegz] (pl inv) n pernilongo m.

daffodil ['dæfədɪl] n narciso m.

daft [dɑːft] adj UK inf bobo(ba).

dagger ['dægəʳ] n adaga f.

daily ['deɪlɪ] (pl -ies) ◇ adj diário(-ria). ◇ adv diariamente; **twice** ~ duas vezes por dia. ◇ n [newspaper] diário m.

dainty ['deɪntɪ] (compar -ier, superl -iest) adj delicado(da).

dairy ['deərɪ] (pl -ies) n leiteria f.

dairy products npl lacticínios mpl.

dais ['deɪs] n estrado m.

daisy ['deɪzɪ] (pl -ies) n margarida f.

daisy-wheel printer n impressora f de margarida.

dale [deɪl] n literary vale m.

dam [dæm] (pt & pp -med, cont -ming) ◇ n [across river] represa f, barragem f. ◇ vt [river] represar.

damage ['dæmɪdʒ] ◇ n: ~ **(to sthg)** [gen] dano m (a algo); [to health, skin] mal m (a algo). ◇ vt -1. [object] danificar - 2. [person] machucar - 3. fig [chances, reputation] prejudicar.

➨ **damages** npl JUR danos mpl.

damn [dæm] ◇ adj inf maldito(ta). ◇ adv inf muito. ◇ n inf: **not to give** OR **care a ~ (about sthg)** não estar nem aí (para algo). ◇ vt RELIG [condemn] condenar. ◇ excl inf droga!

damned [dæmd] inf ◇ adj maldito(ta); **well I'll be** OR **I'm ~** ! ora veja só! ◇ adv muito.

damning ['dæmɪŋ] adj condenatório(-ria), incriminatório(ria).

damp [dæmp] ◇ adj úmido(da). ◇ n (U) umidade f. ◇ vt [make wet] umedecer.

dampen ['dæmpən] vt -1. [make wet] umedecer - 2. fig [emotion] esfriar.

damson ['dæmzn] n abrunheiro m.

dance [dɑːns] ◇ n -1. [gen] dança f; **shall we have a ~** ? vamos dançar? - 2. [social event] baile m. ◇ vt dançar. ◇ vi dançar.

dancer ['dɑːnsəʳ] n dançarino m, -na f.

dancing ['dɑːnsɪŋ] n (U) dança f; **to go ~** ir dançar.

dandelion ['dændɪlaɪən] n dente-de-leão m.

dandruff ['dændrʌf] n (U) caspa f.

Dane [deɪn] n dinamarquês m, -esa f.

danger ['deɪndʒəʳ] n perigo m; **in ~** em perigo; **out of ~** fora de perigo; ~ **to sb/sthg** perigo para alguém/algo; **to be in ~ of doing sthg** perigar fazer algo.

dangerous ['deɪndʒərəs] adj perigoso(-sa).

dangle ['dæŋgl] vt, vi balançar.

Danish ['deɪnɪʃ] ◇ adj dinamarquês(-quesa). ◇ n -1. [language] dinamarquês m - 2. US = Danish pastry. ◇ npl: **the** ~ os dinamarqueses.

Danish pastry, Danish US n torta recheada com maçãs, glacê e marzipã.

dank [dæŋk] adj úmido e frio, úmida e fria.

Danube ['dænju:b] *n*: the ~ o Danúbio.

dapper ['dæpə'] *adj* garboso(sa).

dappled ['dæpld] *adj* -**1.** [animal] pintado(da), malhado(da) -**2.** [shade] pintado(da).

dare [deə'] ◇ *vt* -**1.** [be brave enough]: to ~ to do sthg ousar fazer algo -**2.** [challenge]: to ~ sb to do sthg desafiar alguém a fazer algo -**3.** *phr*: I ~ say ouso dizer (que). ◇ *vi* atrever-se; how ~ you! como se atreve! ◇ *n* desafio *m*.

daredevil ['deə,devl] *n* intrépido *m*, -da *f*.

daring ['deərɪŋ] ◇ *adj* ousado(da). ◇ *n* (U) ousadia *f*.

dark [dɑ:k] ◇ *adj* [gen] escuro(ra). ◇ *n* -**1.** (U) [darkness]: **the** ~ a escuridão, o escuro; **to be in the** ~ **about sthg** estar às escuras sobre algo -**2.** [night]: **before/after** ~ antes/depois de escurecer.

darken ['dɑ:kn] ◇ *vt* escurecer. ◇ *vi* escurecer.

dark glasses *npl* óculos *m inv* escuros.

darkness ['dɑ:knɪs] *n* (U) escuridão *f*, trevas *fpl*.

darkroom ['dɑ:krʊm] *n* câmara *f* escura.

darling ['dɑ:lɪŋ] ◇ *adj* [dear] querido(-da). ◇ *n* -**1.** [loved person] querido *m*, -da *f*; **she's a little** ~ é uma graça de criança -**2.** [favourite] preferido *m*, -da *f*.

darn [dɑ:n] ◇ *adj inf* maldito(ta). ◇ *adv inf* pra caramba. ◇ *vt* [repair] remendar, cerzir.

dart [dɑ:t] ◇ *n* [arrow] dardo *m*. ◇ *vi* [move quickly] lançar-se.

➤ **darts** *n* (U) [game] dardos *mpl*.

dartboard ['dɑ:tbɔ:d] *n* alvo *m* para dardos.

dash [dæʃ] ◇ *n* -**1.** [of liquid] pingo *m* -**2.** [in punctuation] travessão *m* -**3.** [rush]: **to make a** ~ **for sthg** sair em disparada por algo. ◇ *vt* -**1.** *literary* [hurl] arremessar -**2.** [hopes] frustar. ◇ *vi* correr.

dashboard ['dæʃbɔ:d] *n* painel *m* de instrumentos.

dashing ['dæʃɪŋ] *adj* [handsome, energetic] atraente.

data ['deɪtə] *n* dados *mpl*, informações *fpl*.

database ['deɪtəbeɪs] *n* base *f* de dados.

data management *n* COMPUT gerenciamento *m* de dados.

data processing *n* (U) processamento *m* de dados.

data protection *n* COMPUT proteção *f* de dados.

data recovery *n* COMPUT recuperação *f* de dados.

date [deɪt] ◇ *n* -**1.** [in time] data *f*; **what's today's** ~? que dia é hoje?; **at a later** ~ um outro dia; **to bring sb/sthg up to** ~ atualizar alguém/algo; **to keep sb/sthg up to** ~ manter alguém/algo atualizado(da); **to be out of** ~ [dictionary, database] estar desatualizado(da); [passport] estar vencido(da); **to** ~ até agora -**2.** [appointment] encontro *m* -**3.** [person] par *m* -**4.** [fruit] tâmara *f*, datil *m*. ◇ *vt* -**1.** [put a date on] datar -**2.** [go out with] sair com. ◇ *vi* [go out of fashion] cair de moda.

datebook *n* US agenda *f*.

dated ['deɪtɪd] *adj* antiquado(da).

date of birth *n* data *f* de nascimento.

daub [dɔ:b] *vt*: **to** ~ **sthg with sthg** manchar algo.

daughter ['dɔ:tə'] *n* filha *f*.

daughter-in-law (*pl* **daughters-in-law**) *n* nora *f*.

daunting ['dɔ:ntɪŋ] *adj* desalentador(ra).

dawdle ['dɔ:dl] *vi* fazer cera.

dawn [dɔ:n] ◇ *n* -**1.** [of day] amanhecer *m*, alvorada *f* -**2.** *fig* [of era, period] aurora *f*. ◇ *vi* -**1.** [day] amanhecer -**2.** *fig* [era, period] despertar.

➤ **dawn (up)on** *vt fus* dar-se conta de; **it finally** ~**ed on me that ...** finalmente me dei conta de que ...

day [deɪ] *n* -**1.** [gen] dia *m*; **the** ~ **before** a véspera; **the** ~ **after** o dia seguinte; **the** ~ **before Christmas** a véspera de Natal; **the** ~ **before yesterday** anteontem; **the** ~ **after tomorrow** depois de amanhã; **any** ~ **now** qualquer dia destes; **to make sb's** ~ ganhar o dia, guardar algo para dias mais difíceis -**2.** [age, era] tempo *m*; **one** ~, **some** ~, one of these ~s um dia (desses).

➤ **days** *adv* [work] durante o dia.

daybreak ['deɪbreɪk] *n* romper *m* do dia; **at** ~ ao romper do dia.

day care *n* assistência diurna proporcionada a idosos e/ou portadores de deficiência.

day centre *n* UK centro assistencial que proporciona cuidados e recreação durante o dia a idosos e/ou portadores de deficiência.

daydream ['deɪdri:m] *vi* devanear, sonhar acordado(da).

daylight ['deɪlaɪt] *n* -**1.** (U) [light] luz *f* do dia -**2.** [dawn] amanhecer *m*.

day off (*pl* **days off**) *n* dia *m* de folga.

day return *n* UK passagem *f* de ida e volta (no mesmo dia).

daytime ['deɪtaɪm] ◇ *n* dia *m*; **in the**

~ durante o dia. ⬦ *comp* de dia; ~ **flight** vôo *m* diurno.

day-to-day *adj* diário(ria).

daytrader ['deitreidə'] *n* STEX day-trader *mf.*

day trip *n* viagem *f* de um dia.

daze [deiz] ⬦ *n*: in a ~ atordoado(da). ⬦ *vt* atordoar.

dazzle ['dæzl] *vt* -1. [blind] ofuscar -2. [impress] deslumbrar.

DC *n* (*abbr of* direct current) CC *f.*

D-day ['di:dei] *n* dia *m* D.

DEA (*abbr of* Drug Enforcement Administration) *n departamento da polícia norte-americana encarregado do controle de questões relacionadas a drogas,* ≃ DENARC *m.*

deacon ['di:kn] *n* -1. [minister] diácono *m* -2. [lay assistant] acólito *m.*

deactivate [ˌdi:'æktiveit] *vt* desativar.

dead [ded] ⬦ *adj* -1. [not alive] morto(ta); to shoot sb ~ matar alguém com um tiro -2. [numb] dormente, adormecido(da) -3. [ELEC - battery] descarregado(da); [- radio, TV] quebrado(da); [- telephone line] mudo(da) -4. [complete]: ~ silence silêncio *m* mortal; ~ stop parada *f* repentina -5. [not lively] morto(ta). ⬦ *adv* -1. [directly, precisely] diretamente; ~ on time bem na hora -2. *inf* [completely, very] totalmente; to be ~ against sthg/doing sthg ser totalmente contra algo/fazer algo -3. [suddenly]: to stop ~ parar repentinamente. ⬦ *npl*: the ~ os mortos.

deaden ['dedn] *vt* -1. [noise] amortecer -2. [feeling] abrandar.

dead end *n* -1. [street] rua *f* sem saída -2. *fig* [course of action] impasse *m.*

dead heat *n* empate *m.*

deadline ['dedlain] *n* prazo *m* final.

deadlock ['dedlɒk] *n* impasse *m.*

dead loss *n inf* -1. [person] traste *m* -2. [thing] porcaria *f.*

deadly ['dedli] (*compar* -ier, *superl* -iest) ⬦ *adj* -1. [lethal] letal -2. [mortal] mortal -3. [fatally precise] fatal. ⬦ *adv* [extremely] terrivelmente.

deadpan ['dedpæn] ⬦ *adj* supostamente sério(ria). ⬦ *adv* afetadamente sério(ria).

deaf [def] ⬦ *adj* -1. [unable to hear] surdo(da) -2. *fig* [unwilling to hear]: to be ~ to sthg ser surdo(da) a algo. ⬦ *npl*: the ~ os surdos.

deaf-aid *n UK* aparelho *m* de surdez.

deafen ['defn] *vt* ensurdecer.

deaf mute ⬦ *adj* surdo-mudo(da). ⬦ *n* surdo-mudo *m*, -da *f.*

deafness ['defnis] *n (U)* surdez *f.*

deal [di:l] (*pt* & *pp* dealt) ⬦ *n* -1. [business agreement] transação *f*, acordo *m*; to do OR strike a ~ with sb fazer um acordo com alguém -2. *inf* [treatment] tratamento *m* -3. [quantity]: a good OR great ~ muito; a good OR great ~ of work muito trabalho. ⬦ *vt* -1. [strike]: to ~ sb/sthg a blow dar um golpe em alguém/algo; to ~ a blow to sthg *fig* ser um golpe em/para algo -2. [cards] repartir. ⬦ *vi* -1. [in cards] repartir -2. [trade] negociar.

➡ **deal in** *vt fus* COMM negociar.

➡ **deal out** *vt sep* repartir.

➡ **deal with** *vt fus* -1. [handle, cope with, be faced with] lidar com -2. [be concerned with] tratar de.

dealer ['di:lə'] *n* -1. [trader] negociante *m* -2. [in cards] carteador *m*, -ra *f.*

dealings *npl* [relations]: ~s with sb relações *mpl* com alguém.

dealt [delt] *pt* & *pp* ⊳ **deal**.

dean [di:n] *n* -1. [of church, cathedral] deão *m* -2. [of university] decano *m*, -na *f.*

dear [diə'] ⬦ *adj* -1. [loved] querido(da); to be ~ to sb ser precioso(sa) para alguém -2. [in letter]: Dear Sir/Madam Prezado Senhor/Prezada Senhora -3. *esp UK* [expensive] caro(ra). ⬦ *n*: my ~ meu querido, minha querida. ⬦ *excl*: oh ~! oh céus!

dearly ['diəli] *adv* -1.: to love sb ~ amar muito alguém -2. [very much] muito; I would ~ love to know ... eu adoraria saber ... -3. [pay, cost] caro.

death [deθ] *n* morte *f*; to frighten/worry sb to ~ quase matar alguém de susto/preocupação; to be sick to ~ of sthg/of doing sthg *inf* estar de saco cheio de algo/de fazer algo.

death certificate *n* certidão *f* de óbito.

death duty *UK*, **death tax** *US n* imposto *m* de transmissão causa mortis.

deathly ['deθli] (*compar* -ier, *superl* -iest) *adj* [silence, hush] mortal.

death penalty *n* pena *f* de morte.

death rate *n* taxa *f* de mortalidade.

death tax *n US* = death duty.

death trap *n inf*: this car is a ~ este carro é um perigo.

debar [di:'bɑ:'] (*pt* & *pp* -red, *cont* -ring) *vt*: to ~ sb (from somewhere/from doing sthg) privar alguém (do acesso a algum lugar/de fazer algo).

debase [di'beis] *vt* [person, sport] degradar; to ~ o.s. degradar-se.

debate [di'beit] ⬦ *n (U)* debate *m*; open to ~ aberto(ta) ao debate. ⬦ *vt* [issue] debater; **to ~ whether to do sthg** discutir sobre o que fazer. <> *vi* debater.

debating society [dɪ'beɪtɪŋ-] *n* grupo *m* de discussão.

debauchery [dɪ'bɔːtʃərɪ] *n (U)* depravação *f*.

debit ['debɪt] <> *n* débito *m*. <> *vt* [account, sum of money] debitar.

debit card *n* cartão *m* de débito.

debris ['deɪbriː] *n* **-1.** escombros *mpl* **-2.** GEOL fragmento *m* de rocha.

debt [det] *n* **-1.** dívida *f*; **to be in ~** estar endividado(da) **-2.** [feeling of gratitude] dívida *f*; **to be in sb's ~** estar em débito com alguém.

debt collector *n* cobrador *m*, -ra *f* de dívidas.

debtor ['detə'] *n* devedor *m*, -ra *f*.

debug [ˌdiː'bʌg] (*pt & pp* **-ged**, *cont* **-ging**) *vt* COMPUT [program] depurar.

debunk [ˌdiː'bʌŋk] *vt* derrubar.

debut ['deɪbjuː] *n* debute *m*.

dec. (*abbr of* **deceased**) m.

decade ['dekeɪd] *n* década *f*.

decadence ['dekədəns] *n* decadência *f*.

decadent ['dekədənt] *adj* decadente.

decaffeinated [dɪ'kæfɪneɪtɪd] *adj* descafeinado(da).

decanter [dɪ'kæntə'] *n* [container] licoreira *f*.

decathlon [dɪ'kæθlɒn] *n* decatlo *m*.

decay [dɪ'keɪ] <> *n* **-1.** [of tooth] cárie *f* **-2.** [of body, plant] decomposição *f* **-3.** *fig* [of building, society]: **to fall into ~** [building] cair em ruínas; [system] entrar em decadência; [society] entrar em declínio; **urban ~** decadência *f* urbana. <> *vi* **-1.** [tooth] criar cáries **-2.** [body, plant] decompor-se **-3.** *fig* [building, society] entrar em declínio.

deceased [dɪ'siːst] (*pl inv*) *fml* <> *adj* falecido(da). <> *n*: **the ~** o falecido, a falecida. <> *npl*: **the ~** os mortos.

deceit [dɪ'siːt] *n* engano *m*.

deceitful [dɪ'siːtful] *adj* enganoso(sa).

deceive [dɪ'siːv] *vt* enganar; **to ~ o.s.** enganar-se.

December [dɪ'sembə'] *n* dezembro; *see also* **September**.

decency ['diːsnsɪ] *n* **-1.** [respectability] decência *f* **-2.** [consideration]: **to have the ~ to do sthg** ter a decência de fazer algo.

decent ['diːsnt] *adj* decente.

deception [dɪ'sepʃn] *n* **-1.** [lie, pretence] engano *m*, trapaça *f* **-2.** [act of lying, pretending] embuste *m*.

deceptive [dɪ'septɪv] *adj* enganoso(sa).

decide [dɪ'saɪd] <> *vt* **-1.** [resolve, determine] decidir; **to ~ to do sthg** decidir fazer algo; **to ~ that** decidir que **-2.** [settle] decidir, resolver. <> *vi* [make up one's mind] decidir-se.

decide (up)on *vt fus* decidir-se por.

decided [dɪ'saɪdɪd] *adj* **-1.** [distinct] evidente **-2.** [resolute] decidido(da).

decidedly [dɪ'saɪdɪdlɪ] *adv* decididamente.

deciduous [dɪ'sɪdjʊəs] *adj* decíduo(dua).

decimal ['desɪml] <> *adj* decimal. <> *n* (número *m*) decimal *m*.

decimal point *n* vírgula *f* decimal.

decimate ['desɪmeɪt] *vt* dizimar.

decipher [dɪ'saɪfə'] *vt* decifrar.

decision [dɪ'sɪʒn] *n* **-1.** [gen] decisão *f* **-2.** [decisiveness] determinação *f*.

decisive [dɪ'saɪsɪv] *adj* **-1.** [person] decidido(da) **-2.** [factor, event] decisivo(va).

deck [dek] *n* **-1.** [of ship] convés *m* **-2.** [of bus] piso *m* **-3.** [of cards] baralho *m* **-4.** *US* [of house] *área com piso e sem telhado junto a uma casa*.

deckchair ['dektʃeə'] *n* espreguiçadeira *f*.

declaration [ˌdeklə'reɪʃn] *n* declaração *f*.

Declaration of Independence *n*: **the ~** *a declaração da independência norte-americana em 1776*.

declare [dɪ'kleə'] *vt* declarar.

decline [dɪ'klaɪn] <> *n* declínio *m*; **to be in ~** estar em declínio; **on the ~** em declínio. <> *vt* [refuse] recusar, declinar; **to ~ to do sthg** recusar-se a fazer algo. <> *vi* **-1.** [deteriorate] decair **-2.** [refuse] recusar-se.

decode [ˌdiː'kəʊd] *vt* decodificar.

decompose [ˌdiːkəm'pəʊz] *vi* [decay] decompor.

decongestant [ˌdiːkən'dʒestənt] *n* descongestionante *m*.

decorate ['dekəreɪt] *vt* **-1.** [gen] decorar **-2.** [with medal] condecorar.

decoration [ˌdekə'reɪʃn] *n* **-1.** [ornament] enfeite *m* **-2.** [activity, appearance] decoração *f* **-3.** [medal] condecoração *f*.

decorator ['dekəreɪtə'] *n* decorador *m*, -ra *f*.

decoy [*n* 'diːkɔɪ, *vb* dɪ'kɔɪ] <> *n* chamariz *m*, isca *f*. <> *vt* atrair.

decrease [*n* 'diːkriːs, *vb* dɪ'kriːs] <> *n* diminuição *f*; **~ in sthg** diminuição de algo. <> *vt* diminuir. <> *vi* diminuir.

decree [dɪ'kriː] <> *n* **-1.** [order, decision] decreto *m* **-2.** *US* [judgment] sentença *f*. <> *vt* decretar; **to ~ that** decretar que.

decree nisi [-'naɪsaɪ] (*pl* **decrees nisi**) *n*

UK JUR sentença *f* provisória de divórcio.

decrepit [dɪ'krepɪt] *adj* decrépito(ta).

dedicate ['dedɪkeɪt] *vt* -1. [book, song, poem]: **to ~ sthg to sb** dedicar algo a alguém -2. [life, career] dedicar.

dedication [,dedɪ'keɪʃn] *n* dedicação *f*.

deduce [dɪ'dju:s] *vt* deduzir; **to ~ sthg from sthg** deduzir algo de algo.

deduct [dɪ'dʌkt] *vt* deduzir; **to ~ sthg from sthg** descontar OR deduzir algo de algo.

deduction [dɪ'dʌkʃn] *n* -1. [conclusion] dedução *f* -2. [sum deducted] desconto *m*.

deed [di:d] *n* -1. [action] ação *f*, feito *m* -2. JUR escritura *f*.

deem [di:m] *vt fml* julgar; **the building was ~ed to be unsafe** o edifício foi considerado inseguro; **to ~ it wise to do sthg** julgar sensato fazer algo.

deep [di:p] <> *adj* -1. [gen] profundo(da) -2. [in measurements] de profundidade -3. [colour] intenso(sa) -4. [sound, voice] grave. <> *adv* fundo; **to go ~ into the forest** embrenhar-se floresta adentro; **to know ~ down** *fig* saber bem no fundo.

deepen ['di:pn] *vi* -1. [river, sea] aprofundar-se -2. [crisis, recession, feeling] agravar-se.

deep freeze *n* freezer *m*.

deep-fry *vt* fritar *(com muito óleo)*.

deeply ['di:plɪ] *adv* -1. [dig, sigh] fundo -2. [profoundly, sincerely] profundamente.

deep-sea *adj* submarino(na).

deer [dɪəʳ] *(pl inv)* *n* veado *m*, cervo *m*.

deface [dɪ'feɪs] *vt* danificar.

defamatory [dɪ'fæmətrɪ] *adj fml* difamatório(ria).

default [dɪ'fɔ:lt] *n* -1. JUR falta *f*; **to declare s.o. in ~** declarar alguém inadimplente; **by ~** à revelia -2. COMPUT default *m*, padrão *m*.

defeat [dɪ'fi:t] <> *n* [gen] derrota *f*; **to admit ~** admitir a derrota. <> *vt* -1. [team, opponent] derrotar -2. [motion, proposal] rechaçar.

defeatist [dɪ'fi:tɪst] <> *adj* derrotista. <> *n* derrotista *mf*.

defect [*n* 'di:fekt, *vb* dɪ'fekt] <> *n* [fault] defeito *m*. <> *vi* POL: **to ~ to the other side** ≃ passar para o outro lado, virar a casaca.

defective [dɪ'fektɪv] *adj* defeituoso(sa).

defence, **defense** *US* [dɪ'fens] *n* -1. [gen & SPORT] defesa *f*; **~ against sb/sthg** defesa contra alguém/algo -2. [protective device, system] proteção *f*; **~ against**

sb/sthg proteção *f* contra alguém/algo -3. [JUR - lawyers]: **the ~** a defesa; [- denial of charge] defesa *f*.

defenceless *UK*, **defenseless** *US* [dɪ'fenslɪs] *adj* indefeso(sa).

defend [dɪ'fend] *vt* defender; **to ~ sb/ sthg against sb/sthg** defender alguém/ algo de alguém/algo.

defendant [dɪ'fendənt] *n* réu *m*, ré *f*.

defender [dɪ'fendəʳ] *n* -1. [gen] defensor *m*, -ra *f* - [SPORT - player] zagueiro *m*, -ra *f*; [- of title] defensor *m*, -ra *f*.

defense *n US* = **defence**.

defenseless *adj US* = **defenceless**.

defensive [dɪ'fensɪv] <> *adj* -1. [weapons, tactics] defensivo(va) -2. [person] receoso(sa). <> *n*: **on the ~** na defensiva.

defer [dɪ'fɜ:ʳ] *(pt & pp* -red, *cont* -ring*)* <> *vt* adiar, protelar. <> *vi*: **to ~ to sb** deferir a alguém.

deferential [,defə'renʃl] *adj* deferente.

defiance [dɪ'faɪəns] *n* desafio *m*; **in ~ of sb/sthg** a despeito de alguém/algo.

defiant [dɪ'faɪənt] *adj* desafiador(ra).

deficiency [dɪ'fɪʃnsɪ] *(pl* -ies*)* *n* -1. [lack] deficiência *f* -2. [inadequacy] deficiência *f*, imperfeição *f*.

deficient [dɪ'fɪʃnt] *adj* -1. [lacking]: **~ in sthg** deficiente em algo -2. [inadequate] deficiente.

deficit ['defɪsɪt] *n* déficit *m*.

defile [dɪ'faɪl] *vt* -1. [grave, church] profanar -2. [mind, purity] corromper.

define [dɪ'faɪn] *vt* definir.

definite ['defɪnɪt] *adj* -1. [date, plan] definido(da) -2. [improvement, difference] claro(ra) -3. [person] seguro(ra).

definitely ['defɪnɪtlɪ] *adv* sem dúvida.

definition [defɪ'nɪʃn] *n* -1. [of word, expression, concept] definição *f* -2. [of problem, function] explicação *f* -3. [clarity] nitidez *f*.

deflate [dɪ'fleɪt] <> *vt* [balloon, tyre] esvaziar. <> *vi* [balloon, tyre] esvaziar-se.

deflation [dɪ'fleɪʃn] *n* ECON deflação *f*.

deflect [dɪ'flekt] *vt* desviar.

defogger [,di:'fɒgəʳ] *n US* AUT desembaçador *m*.

deformed [dɪ'fɔ:md] *adj* deformado(da).

DEFRA *(abbr of* **Department for the Environment, Food and Rural Affairs***) n* divisão do governo britânico que trata de questões agrárias e do meio ambiente.

defraud [dɪ'frɔ:d] *vt* fraudar.

defrost [,di:'frɒst] <> *vt* -1. [fridge] degelar -2. [frozen food] descongelar

- 3. US [AUT-de-ice] descongelar. ⟨⟩ vi **-1.** [fridge] degelar **- 2.** [frozen food] descongelar.

deft [deft] adj **-1.** [movement, fingers] ágil **- 2.** [handling of situation] hábil.

defunct [dɪˈfʌŋkt] adj extinto(ta).

defuse [ˌdiːˈfjuːz] vt UK **-1.** [bomb] desativar **- 2.** fig [situation] acalmar.

defy [dɪˈfaɪ] (pt & pp -ied) vt **-1.** [disobey] desafiar **- 2.** [challenge]: to ~ sb to do sthg desafiar alguém a fazer algo **-3.** fig [elude - description] impossibilitar; [- efforts] tornar inútil.

degenerate [adj dɪˈdʒenərət, vb dɪˈdʒenəreɪt] ⟨⟩ adj degenerado(da). ⟨⟩ vi degenerar; to ~ into degenerar para.

degrading [dɪˈgreɪdɪŋ] adj [debasing] degradante.

degree [dɪˈgriː] n **-1.** [unit of measurement, amount] grau m; by ~s gradualmente **- 2.** [qualification] título m universitário; to have/take a ~ (in sthg) ter/obter graduação (em algo).

dehydrated [ˌdiːhaɪˈdreɪtɪd] adj desidratado(da).

de-ice [diːˈaɪs] vt descongelar.

deign [deɪn] vi: to ~ to do sthg dignar-se a fazer algo.

deity [ˈdiːɪtɪ] (pl -ies) n divindade f, deidade f.

dejected [dɪˈdʒektɪd] adj abatido(da), desanimado(da).

delay [dɪˈleɪ] ⟨⟩ n atraso m. ⟨⟩ vt **-1.** [cause to be late] atrasar **- 2.** [postpone] adiar; to ~ doing sthg adiar (fazer) algo. ⟨⟩ vi demorar-se; to ~ in doing sthg demorar-se para fazer algo.

delayed [dɪˈleɪd] adj atrasado(da).

delectable [dɪˈlektəbl] adj **-1.** [food] delicioso(sa) **- 2.** [person] fabuloso(sa).

delegate [n ˈdelɪgət, vb ˈdelɪgeɪt] ⟨⟩ n delegado m, -da f. ⟨⟩ vt **-1.** [appoint to do job] delegar; to ~ sb to do sthg delegar alguém para fazer algo **- 2.** [hand over responsibility for sthg]: to ~ sthg to sb delegar algo a alguém.

delegation [ˌdelɪˈgeɪʃn] n delegação f.

delete [dɪˈliːt] vt **-1.** [remove] apagar **- 2.** COMPUT deletar.

deli [ˈdelɪ] (abbr of delicatessen) n fam loja onde se vendem bebidas, frios, conservas e pães.

deliberate [adj dɪˈlɪbərət, vb dɪˈlɪbəreɪt] ⟨⟩ adj **-1.** [intentional] deliberado(da) **- 2.** [slow] pausado(da). ⟨⟩ vi fml deliberar.

deliberately [dɪˈlɪbərətlɪ] adv [on purpose] deliberadamente.

delicacy [ˈdelɪkəsɪ] (pl -ies) n **-1.** (U) [gracefulness, tact] delicadeza f **- 2.** [food] iguaria f.

delicate [ˈdelɪkət] adj **-1.** [gen] delicado(da) **- 2.** [flavour, colour] suave **-3.** [instrument] delicado(da), sensível.

delicatessen [ˌdelɪkəˈtesn] n delicatessen f.

delicious [dɪˈlɪʃəs] adj [tasty] delicioso(sa).

delight [dɪˈlaɪt] ⟨⟩ n [great pleasure] prazer m, deleite m; to take ~ in doing sthg ter prazer em fazer algo. ⟨⟩ vt encantar. ⟨⟩ vi: to ~ in sthg/in doing sthg encantar-se em algo/em fazer algo.

delighted [dɪˈlaɪtɪd] adj muito contente; ~ by OR with sthg encantado(da) com algo; to be ~ to do sthg estar muito feliz por fazer algo.

delightful [dɪˈlaɪtfʊl] adj encantador(ra).

delinquent [dɪˈlɪŋkwənt] ⟨⟩ adj delinquente. ⟨⟩ n delinquente mf.

delirious [dɪˈlɪrɪəs] adj delirante; to be ~ estar delirando.

deliver [dɪˈlɪvəʳ] vt **-1.** [distribute]: to ~ sthg (to sb) entregar algo (a alguém) **- 2.** [give - speech, lecture] proferir; [- message] entregar; [- warning, ultimatum] dar **- 3.** [blow] desferir **- 4.** [baby] trazer ao mundo **- 5.** fml [liberate]: to ~ sb (from sthg) libertar alguém (de algo) **- 6.** US POL [votes] captar.

delivery [dɪˈlɪvərɪ] (pl -ies) n **-1.** [of goods, letters] entrega f **- 2.** [goods delivered] remessa f **- 3.** [way of speaking] elocução f **- 4.** [birth] parto m.

delude [dɪˈluːd] vt enganar; to ~ o.s. enganar-se.

delusion [dɪˈluːʒn] n ilusão f.

delve [delv] vi **-1.** [into mystery] pesquisar; to ~ into sthg investigar algo **- 2.** [in bag, cupboard] remexer; to ~ into OR inside sthg revolver dentro de algo.

demand [dɪˈmɑːnd] ⟨⟩ n **-1.** [gen] exigência f; on ~ a pedido; COMM sob demanda **- 2.** [need & COMM]: ~ for sthg demanda f por algo; in ~ solicitado(da). ⟨⟩ vt **-1.** [gen] exigir; to ~ to do sthg exigir fazer algo **- 2.** [enquire forcefully] inquirir.

demanding [dɪˈmɑːndɪŋ] adj **-1.** [exhausting] que exige muito esforço **- 2.** [not easily satisfied] exigente.

demean [dɪˈmiːn] vt rebaixar.

demeaning [dɪˈmiːnɪŋ] adj humilhante.

demeanour UK, **demeanor** US [dɪˈmiːnəʳ] n fml comportamento m.

demented [dɪˈmentɪd] adj demente.

demise [dɪ'maɪz] n fml - **1.** [death] falecimento m - **2.** fig [end] fim m.

demister [,di:'mɪstə^r] n UK AUT desembaçador m.

demo ['deməʊ] (pl -s) (abbr of demonstration) n - **1.** fam [protest] manifestação f. - **2.** [tape, video] demo f.

democracy [dɪ'mɒkrəsɪ] (pl -ies) n democracia f.

democrat ['deməkræt] n democrata mf.
◆ **Democrat** n US democrata mf.

democratic [demə'krætɪk] adj democrático(ca).
◆ **Democratic** adj US democrata.

Democratic Party n US: the ~ o Partido Democrata (dos Estados Unidos).

demolish [dɪ'mɒlɪʃ] vt - **1.** [knock down] demolir - **2.** [prove wrong] destruir, acabar com.

demonstrate ['demənstreɪt] <> vt - **1.** [gen] demonstrar - **2.** [appliance, machine] mostrar o funcionamento de. <> vi manifestar-se; to ~ for/against sthg manifestar-se a favor de/contra algo.

demonstration [demən'streɪʃn] n [protest gathering, march] manifestação f.

demonstrator ['demənstreɪtə^r] n - **1.** [of machine, product] demonstrador m, -ra f - **2.** [protester] manifestante mf.

demoralized [dɪ'mɒrəlaɪzd] adj desmoralizado(da).

demote [,di:'məʊt] vt rebaixar (na carreira profissional).

demure [dɪ'mjʊə^r] adj recatado(da).

den [den] n [lair] toca f.

denial [dɪ'naɪəl] n - **1.** [refutation] contestação f - **2.** (U) [refusal] negação f.

denier ['denɪə^r] n [of stockings, tights] denier m, medida da espessura do fio de náilon ou de seda usado na fabricação de roupas.

denigrate ['denɪgreɪt] vt fml difamar, denegrir.

denim ['denɪm] n brim m.
◆ **denims** npl jeans m inv.

denim jacket n jaqueta f jeans.

Denmark ['denmɑːk] n Dinamarca f.

denomination [dɪ,nɒmɪ'neɪʃn] n - **1.** RELIG denominação f, seita f - **2.** FIN valor m.

denounce [dɪ'naʊns] vt denunciar.

dense [dens] adj - **1.** [thick - trees, undergrowth] denso(sa); [- mist, fog] espesso(sa) - **2.** inf [stupid] estúpido(da).

dent [dent] <> n amassado m. <> vt [surface] amassar.

dental ['dentl] adj dentário(ria); a ~ problem um problema nos dentes.

dental floss n (U) fio m dental.

dental surgeon n cirurgião-dentista m, cirurgiã-dentista f.

dental surgery n cirurgia f dentária.

dentist ['dentɪst] n dentista mf; to go to the ~'s ir ao dentista.

dentures ['dentʃəz] npl dentadura f.

deny [dɪ'naɪ] (pt & pp -ied) vt negar; to ~ sb sthg negar algo a alguém.

deodorant [di:'əʊdərənt] n desodorante m.

depart [dɪ'pɑːt] vi fml - **1.** [leave] partir; to ~ from partir de - **2.** [differ]: to ~ from sthg afastar-se de algo.

department [dɪ'pɑːtmənt] n - **1.** [gen] departamento m - **2.** [of government] ministério m.

department store n loja f de departamentos.

departure [dɪ'pɑːtʃə^r] n - **1.** [leaving] partida f - **2.** [variation]: ~ (from sthg) abandono m (de algo) - **3.** [orientation] início m.

departure lounge n sala f de embarque.

depend [dɪ'pend] vi - **1.** [rely - financially]: to ~ on sb/sthg depender de alguém/algo; [- emotionally]: to ~ on sb confiar em alguém - **2.** [be determined]: it ~s depende; it ~s on depende de; ~ing on dependendo de.

dependable [dɪ'pendəbl] adj confiável.

dependant [dɪ'pendənt] n dependente mf.

dependent [dɪ'pendənt] adj - **1.** [reliant]: to be ~ (on sb/sthg) ser dependente (de alguém/algo) - **2.** [addicted] dependente - **3.** [determined by]: to be ~ on sb/sthg depender de alguém/algo.

depict [dɪ'pɪkt] vt - **1.** [show in picture] retratar - **2.** [describe]: to ~ sb/sthg as sthg retratar alguém/algo como algo.

deplete [dɪ'pliːt] vt reduzir.

deplorable [dɪ'plɔːrəbl] adj deplorável.

deplore [dɪ'plɔː^r] vt deplorar.

deploy [dɪ'plɔɪ] vt dispor.

depopulation [di:,pɒpjʊ'leɪʃn] n (U) despovoamento m.

deport [dɪ'pɔːt] vt deportar.

depose [dɪ'pəʊz] vt [king, ruler] depor.

deposit [dɪ'pɒzɪt] <> n - **1.** GEOL [of gold, oil] jazida f - **2.** [of sediment, silt] depósito m - **3.** [fin] depósito m; to make a ~ fazer um depósito - **4.** [down payment - on house, car] entrada f; [- on hotel room] depósito m - **5.** [returnable payment - on hired goods] caução f; [- on bottle, container] depósito m. <> vt - **1.** [gen] depositar - **2.** [bag, case, shopping] colocar.

deposit account n UK conta f remunerada.

depot ['depəʊ] n -**1.** [storage facility - for goods] armazém m; [- for vehicles] garagem f -**2.** US [bus or train terminus] terminal m.

depreciate [dɪ'priːʃɪeɪt] vi depreciar.

depress [dɪ'pres] vt -**1.** [sadden, discourage] deprimir -**2.** ECON depreciar -**3.** [slow down, reduce] reduzir.

depressed [dɪ'prest] adj -**1.** [person] deprimido(da) -**2.** [area]: ~ **point** ponto inferior.

depressing [dɪ'presɪŋ] adj deprimente.

depression [dɪ'preʃn] n depressão f.

deprivation [ˌdeprɪ'veɪʃn] n [privation] privação f.

deprive [dɪ'praɪv] vt: to ~ sb of sthg privar alguém de algo.

depth [depθ] n -**1.** profundidade f; to be out of one's ~ [lit & fig] não dar pé para alguém; in ~ em profundidade -**2.** [severity] gravidade f; the ~ of sthg a gravidade de algo.
> **depths** npl: the ~s [of sea, memory] as profundezas; [of winter] o auge; to be in the ~s of despair estar no auge do desespero.

deputation [ˌdepjʊ'teɪʃn] n delegação f.

deputize, -ise ['depjʊtaɪz] vi: to ~ (for sb) substituir oficialmente (alguém).

deputy ['depjʊtɪ] (pl -ies) <> adj adjunto(ta); ~ **head** subdiretor m, -ra f; ~ **chairman** vice-presidente m. <> n -**1.** [second-in-command] suplente mf -**2.** US [deputy sheriff] ajudante mf do delegado.

derail [dɪ'reɪl] vt [train] descarrilhar.

deranged [dɪ'reɪndʒd] adj perturbado(da), transtornado(da).

derby [UK 'dɑːbɪ, US 'dɜːbɪ] (pl -ies) n -**1.** [sports event] jogo m local -**2.** US [hat] chapéu-coco m.

derelict ['derəlɪkt] adj abandonado(da).

deride [dɪ'raɪd] vt escarnecer de, zombar de.

derisory [də'raɪzərɪ] adj -**1.** [ridiculous] irrisório(ria) -**2.** [scornful] zombeteiro(ra).

derivative [dɪ'rɪvətɪv] <> adj pej pouco original. <> n derivado m.

derive [dɪ'raɪv] <> vt -**1.** [pleasure]: to ~ sthg from sthg encontrar algo em algo -**2.** [word, expression]: to be ~d from sthg derivar de algo. <> vi [word, expression]: to ~ from sthg derivar-se de algo.

derogatory [dɪ'rɒgətrɪ] adj depreciativo(va).

derv [dɜːv] n UK gasóleo m.

descend [dɪ'send] <> vi -**1.** fml [go down] descer -**2.** [fall]: to ~ (on sb/sthg) recair (sobre alguém/algo) -**3.** [stoop, lower o.s.]: to ~ to sthg/to doing sthg rebaixar-se a algo/a fazer algo. <> vt fml [go down] descer.

descendant [dɪ'sendənt] n [family member] descendente mf.

descended [dɪ'sendɪd] adj: to be ~ from sb ser descendente OR descender de alguém.

descent [dɪ'sent] n -**1.** [downwards movement] descida f -**2.** (U) [origin] ascendência f.

describe [dɪ'skraɪb] vt [recount] descrever.

description [dɪ'skrɪpʃn] n -**1.** [account] descrição f -**2.** [type] tipo m.

desecrate ['desɪkreɪt] vt profanar.

desert [n 'dezət, vb & npl dɪ'zɜːt] <> n GEOGR deserto m. <> vt abandonar. <> vi MIL desertar.
> **deserts** npl: to get one's just ~s receber aquilo que se merece.

deserted [dɪ'zɜːtɪd] adj [place] deserto(ta), abandonado(da).

deserter [dɪ'zɜːtə'] n desertor m, -ra f.

desert island ['dezət-] n ilha f deserta.

deserve [dɪ'zɜːv] vt merecer; to ~ sthg merecer algo; we ~ to win merecemos vencer.

deserving [dɪ'zɜːvɪŋ] adj merecedor(ra).

design [dɪ'zaɪn] <> n -**1.** [plan, drawing] projeto m -**2.** (U) [art] design m -**3.** [pattern, motif] padrão m -**4.** [structure, shape] modelo m -**5.** fml [intention] intenção f; by ~ por intenção; to have ~s on sb/sthg ter más intenções com relação a alguém/algo. <> vt -**1.** [building, car] projetar -**2.** [clothes, costumes] desenhar -**3.** [plan, system, test] projetar, criar; to be ~ed for sthg/to do sthg ser projetado(da) para algo/para fazer algo.

designate [adj 'dezɪgnət, vb 'dezɪgneɪt] <> adj designado(da). <> vt [appoint] designar.

designer [dɪ'zaɪnə'] <> adj [jeans, glasses, stubble] de marca. <> n -**1.** [of building, machine] projetista mf -**2.** [of theatre set] cenógrafo m, -fa f -**3.** [of clothes] estilista mf.

desirable [dɪ'zaɪərəbl] adj -**1.** fml [appropriate] apropriado(da) -**2.** [attractive] agradável -**3.** [sexually attractive] desejável.

desire [dɪ'zaɪə'] <> n -**1.** [wish] desejo m, vontade f; ~ **for sthg/to do sthg** desejo por algo/de fazer algo, vontade de algo/de fazer algo -**2.** (U) [sexual longing] desejo m. <> vt desejar.

desist [dɪ'zɪst] *vi fml*: to ~ **(from doing sthg)** desistir (de fazer algo).

desk [desk] *n* **-1.** [piece of furniture - in office, study] escrivaninha *f*; [- in school] carteira *f* **-2.** [service point] balcão *m*.

desk diary *n* agenda *f (de mesa)*.

desktop publishing *n (U)* editoração *f* eletrônica.

desolate ['desələt] *adj* desolado(da).

despair [dɪ'speə^r] ◇ *n (U)* desespero *m*. ◇ *vi* desesperar-se; **to ~ of sb/ sthg** perder a esperança com alguém/algo; **to ~ of doing sthg** perder a esperança de fazer algo.

despairing [dɪ'speərɪŋ] *adj* desesperador(ra).

despatch [dɪ'spætʃ] *n & vt* = dispatch.

desperate ['desprət] *adj* **-1.** [gen] desesperado(da); **to feel ~** sentir-se desesperado(da) **-2.** [situation, problem] desesperador(ra) **-3.** [criminal] implacável **-4.** [in great need]: **to be ~ for sthg** estar louco(ca) por algo.

desperately ['desprətlɪ] *adv* **-1.** [gen] desesperadamente **-2.** [busy, sorry, in love] muito.

desperation [ˌdespə'reɪʃn] *n (U)* desespero *m*; **in ~** em desespero.

despicable [dɪ'spɪkəbl] *adj* desprezível.

despise [dɪ'spaɪz] *vt* desprezar.

despite [dɪ'spaɪt] *prep* apesar de.

despondent [dɪ'spɒndənt] *adj* desanimado(da).

dessert [dɪ'zɜ:t] *n* sobremesa *f*.

dessertspoon [dɪ'zɜ:tspu:n] *n* [spoon] colher *f* de sobremesa.

destination [ˌdestɪ'neɪʃn] *n* destino *m*.

destined ['destɪnd] *adj* **-1.** [intended]: **~ for sthg/to do sthg** predestinado(da) a algo/a fazer algo **-2.** [bound]: **to be ~ for** estar indo para.

destiny ['destɪnɪ] (*pl* **-ies**) *n* destino *m*.

destitute ['destɪtjuːt] *adj* [extremely poor] necessitado(da), miserável.

destroy [dɪ'strɔɪ] *vt* [gen] destruir.

destruction [dɪ'strʌkʃn] *n (U)* destruição *f*.

detach [dɪ'tætʃ] *vt* **-1.** [remove] tirar; **to ~ sthg from sthg** tirar algo de algo; [tear off] destacar **-2.** [dissociate]: **to ~ o.s. from sthg** afastar-se de algo.

detached [dɪ'tætʃt] *adj* [unemotional] imparcial.

detached house *n* casa *f* separada.

detachment [dɪ'tætʃmənt] *n* **-1.** *(U)* [aloofness] desinteresse *m*, desapego *m* **-2.** MIL destacamento *m*.

detail ['diːteɪl] ◇ *n* **-1.** [small point] detalhe *m* **-2.** *(U)* [collection of facts, points] detalhe *m*, particularidade *f*;

to go into ~ entrar em detalhes; **in ~** detalhadamente **-3.** MIL destacamento *m*. ◇ *vt* [list] detalhar.

➡ **details** *npl* **-1.** [information] dados *mpl* **-2.** [personal information] dados *mpl* (pessoais).

detailed ['diːteɪld] *adj* detalhado(da).

detain [dɪ'teɪn] *vt* **-1.** [in hospital, police station] deter **-2.** [delay] retardar.

detect [dɪ'tekt] *vt* **-1.** [subj: person] perceber **-2.** [subj: device] detectar.

detection [dɪ'tekʃn] *n* **-1.** *(U)* [discovery] detecção *f* **-2.** [investigation] investigação *f*.

detective [dɪ'tektɪv] *n* detetive *mf*.

detective novel *n* romance *m* policial.

detention [dɪ'tenʃn] *n* **-1.** *(U)* [of suspect, criminal] detenção *f* **-2.** [at school] castigo *m (depois da aula)*.

deter [dɪ'tɜː^r] (*pt & pp* **-red**, *cont* **-ring**) *vt* dissuadir; **to ~ sb from doing sthg** dissuadir alguém de fazer algo.

detergent [dɪ'tɜːdʒənt] *n* detergente *m*.

deteriorate [dɪ'tɪərɪəreɪt] *vi* piorar.

determination [dɪˌtɜːmɪ'neɪʃn] *n* **-1.** *(U)* [resolve] determinação *f* **-2.** [establishing, fixing] definição *f*.

determine [dɪ'tɜːmɪn] *vt* **-1.** [gen] determinar **-2.** *fml* [resolve]: **to ~ to do sthg** determinar-se a fazer algo **-3.** [fix, settle] definir.

determined [dɪ'tɜːmɪnd] *adj* [person, effort] determinado(da); **~ to do sthg** determinado(da) a fazer algo.

deterrent [dɪ'terənt] *n* dissuasão *f*.

detest [dɪ'test] *vt* detestar.

detonate ['detəneɪt] ◇ *vt* detonar. ◇ *vi* detonar.

detour ['diːˌtʊə^r] *n* desvio *m*.

detract [dɪ'trækt] *vi*: **to ~ from** [quality, achievement] depreciar; [enjoyment] perturbar.

detriment ['detrɪmənt] *n*: **to the ~ of sb/sthg** em detrimento de alguém/algo.

detrimental [ˌdetrɪ'mentl] *adj* prejudicial.

deuce [djuːs] *n* TENNIS empate *m*.

devaluation [ˌdiːvæljʊ'eɪʃn] *n* FIN desvalorização *f*.

devastated ['devəsteɪtɪd] *adj* **-1.** [place] devastado(da) **-2.** *fig* [person] arrasado(da).

devastating ['devəsteɪtɪŋ] *adj* **-1.** [disastrous] devastador(ra) **-2.** [very effective, attractive] avassalador(ra).

develop [dɪ'veləp] ◇ *vt* **-1.** [gen] desenvolver **-2.** [land, area, resources] explorar **-3.** [illness] contrair **-4.** PHOT revelar. ◇ *vi* **-1.** [gen] desenvolver **-2.** [problem, illness] aparecer.

developing country [dɪ'veləpɪŋ-] *n* país *m* em desenvolvimento.

development [dɪ'veləpmənt] *n* -1. (U) [expansion, growth, conception - gen] desenvolvimento *m*; [- of business, company] crescimento *m* -2. (U) [of land, area] exploração *f* -3. [developed land] loteamento *m* -4. [further incident] acontecimento *m* -5. (U) [of illness, fault, habit] desenvolvimento *m* -6. *PHOT* revelação *f*.

deviate ['di:vɪeɪt] *vi*: to ~ (from sthg) desviar-se (de algo).

device [dɪ'vaɪs] *n* -1. [apparatus] dispositivo *m*, aparelho *m* -2. [plan, method] artifício *m* -3. [bomb]: **(incendiary) ~** bomba *f* incendiária.

devil ['devl] *n* -1. [evil spirit] demônio *m* -2. *inf* [person] diabo *m*, -ba *f*; **poor ~!** pobre diabo! -3. [for emphasis]: **who/where/why the ~ ...?** que/onde/por que diabos ...?

    ➡ **Devil** *n* [Satan]: **the Devil** o Diabo.

devious ['di:vjəs] *adj* -1. [gen] desonesto(ta) -2. [route] sinuoso(sa).

devise [dɪ'vaɪz] *vt* conceber.

devoid [dɪ'vɔɪd] *adj fml*: ~ **of sthg** desprovido(da) de algo.

devolution [ˌdi:və'lu:ʃn] *n* (U) *POL* descentralização *f*.

devote [dɪ'vəʊt] *vt*: to ~ **sthg to sthg** dedicar algo a algo.

devoted [dɪ'vəʊtɪd] *adj* [person] dedicado(da); ~ **to sb/sthg** dedicado(da) a alguém/algo.

devotee [ˌdevə'ti:] *n* -1. [disciple] devoto *m*, -ta *f* -2. [fan] fã *mf* -3. [enthusiast] entusiasta *mf*.

devotion [dɪ'vəʊʃn] *n* -1. (U) [commitment]: ~ **to sb/sthg** dedicação *f* a alguém/algo -2. *RELIG* devoção *f*.

devour [dɪ'vaʊə^r] *vt* -1. [eat, read avidly] devorar -2. *fig* [subj: fire] consumir.

devout [dɪ'vaʊt] *adj RELIG* devoto(ta).

dew [dju:] *n* (U) orvalho *m*.

diabetes [ˌdaɪə'bi:ti:z] *n* (U) diabete *f*.

diabetic [ˌdaɪə'betɪk] <> *adj* [person] diabético(ca). <> *n* diabético *m*, -ca *f*.

diabolic(al) [ˌdaɪə'bɒlɪk(l)] *adj* -1. [evil] diabólico(ca) -2. *inf* [very bad] horroroso(sa).

diagnose ['daɪəgnəʊz] *vt* diagnosticar.

diagnosis [ˌdaɪəg'nəʊsɪs] (*pl* -oses [-əʊsi:z]) *n* diagnóstico *m*.

diagonal [daɪ'ægənl] <> *adj* [line] diagonal. <> *n* diagonal *f*.

diagram ['daɪəgræm] *n* diagrama *m*.

dial ['daɪəl] (*UK pt & pp* -led, *cont* -ling, *US pt & pp* -ed, *cont* -ing) <> *n* -1. [of watch, clock, meter] mostrador *m* -2. [of radio] dial *m* -3. [of telephone] teclado *m*. <> *vt* [number] discar.

dialect ['daɪəlekt] *n* dialeto *m*.

dialling code *UK*, **dialing code** *US* ['daɪəlɪŋ-] *n* código *m* de discagem.

dialling tone *UK* ['daɪəlɪŋ-], **dial tone** *US* *n* linha *f* (no telefone).

dialogue *UK*, **dialog** *US* ['daɪəlɒg] *n* diálogo *m*.

dial tone *n US* = dialling tone.

dialysis [daɪ'ælɪsɪs] *n* (U) diálise *f*.

diameter [daɪ'æmɪtə^r] *n* diâmetro *m*.

diamond ['daɪəmənd] *n* -1. [gem] diamante *m* -2. [shape] losango *m*.

    ➡ **diamonds** *npl* [cards] ouros *mpl*.

diaper ['daɪpə^r] *n US* fralda *f*.

diaphragm ['daɪəfræm] *n* diafragma *m*.

diarrh(o)ea [ˌdaɪə'rɪə] *n* (U) diarréia *f*.

diary ['daɪərɪ] (*pl* -ies) *n* -1. [appointment book] agenda *f* -2. [personal record] diário *m*.

dice [daɪs] (*pl inv*) <> *n* [for games] dado *m*. <> *vt* cortar em cubinhos.

dictate [*vb* dɪk'teɪt, *n* 'dɪkteɪt] <> *vt* -1. [letter] ditar -2. [conditions, terms] ditar, impor. <> *n* ditado *m*.

dictation [dɪk'teɪʃn] *n* ditado *m*.

dictator [dɪk'teɪtə^r] *n POL* ditador *m*, -ra *f*.

dictatorship [dɪk'teɪtəʃɪp] *n* ditadura *f*.

dictionary ['dɪkʃənrɪ] (*pl* -ies) *n* dicionário *m*.

did [dɪd] *pt* ⊳ do.

diddle ['dɪdl] *vt UK inf* passar a perna em.

didn't ['dɪdnt] = did not.

die [daɪ] (*pt & pp* died, *cont* dying) <> *vi* -1. [person, animal, plant] morrer; **to be dying** estar morrendo; **to be dying for sthg/to do sthg** *inf* estar morrendo de vontade de algo/de fazer algo -2. *fig* [love, anger, memory] morrer. <> *n* [dice] dado *m*.

    ➡ **die away** *vi* [sound, wind] desvanecer-se.

    ➡ **die down** *vi* -1. [fire] arrefecer -2. [sound, wind] abrandar.

    ➡ **die out** *vi* -1. [family, custom] desaparecer -2. [species] ser extinto(ta).

diehard ['daɪhɑːd] *n* teimoso(sa).

diesel ['di:zl] *n* -1. (U) [fuel, oil] diesel *m* -2. [vehicle] veículo *m* a diesel.

diesel engine *n* motor *m* a diesel.

diesel fuel, diesel oil *n* óleo *m* diesel.

diet ['daɪət] <> *n* -1. [gen] dieta *f* -2. [in order to lose weight] dieta *f*, regime *m*; **to be/go on a ~** estar de/entrar em dieta. <> *comp* [low-calorie] de baixa caloria; **a ~ Coke®** uma Coca® light. <> *vi* [in order to lose weight] fazer regime.

differ ['dɪfə'] *vi* **-1.** [be different] diferir; to ~ from sb/sthg diferir/distinguir-se de alguém/algo **-2.** [disagree]: **to ~ with sb (about sthg)** discordar de alguém (sobre algo).

difference ['dɪfrəns] *n* diferença *f*; **it doesn't make any ~** não faz a menor diferença.

different ['dɪfrənt] *adj* diferente; ~ **from** diferente de.

differentiate [ˌdɪfə'renʃɪeɪt] <> *vt*: **to ~ sthg from sthg** diferenciar algo de algo. <> *vi*: **to ~ (between)** diferenciar (entre).

difficult ['dɪfɪkəlt] *adj* difícil.

difficulty ['dɪfɪkəltɪ] (*pl* -ies) *n* dificuldade *f*; **to have ~ in doing sthg** ter dificuldade em fazer algo.

diffident ['dɪfɪdənt] *adj* acanhado(da).

diffuse [dɪ'fjuːz] *vt* **-1.** [light] difundir **-2.** [information] divulgar.

dig [dɪg] (*pt* & *pp* **dug**, *cont* **digging**) <> *n* **-1.** *fig* [unkind remark] zombaria *f* **-2.** ARCHAEOL escavação *f*. <> *vt* [in ground] cavar. <> *vi* **-1.** [in ground] enterrar-se **-2.** [press, jab]: **to ~ into sthg** cravar-se em algo; **my strap's ~ging into me** a alça do vestido está me apertando.

➡ **dig out** *vt sep inf* [letter, document] desencavar.

➡ **dig up** *vt sep* **-1.** [from ground] desenterrar **-2.** *inf* [information] desencavar.

digest [*n* 'daɪdʒest, *vb* dɪ'dʒest] <> *n* [book] resenha *f*. <> *vt* [food, information] digerir.

digestion [dɪ'dʒestʃn] *n* digestão *f*.

digestive biscuit [dɪ'dʒestɪv-] *n UK* biscoito liso levemente adocicado muito comum na Grã-Bretanha.

digestive system *n* sistema *m* digestivo.

digger *n* [machine] escavadeira *f*.

digit ['dɪdʒɪt] *n* **-1.** [figure] dígito *m* **-2.** [finger, toe] dedo *m*.

digital ['dɪdʒɪtl] *adj* [watch, readout] digital.

digital camera *n* câmera *f* digital.

digital television, digital TV *n* televisão *f* digital.

digital watch *n* relógio *m* digital.

dignified ['dɪgnɪfaɪd] *adj* digno(na).

dignity ['dɪgnɪtɪ] *n* dignidade *f*.

digress [daɪ'gres] *vi* fugir do assunto, divagar; **to ~ (from sthg)** desviar-se (de algo).

digs [dɪgz] *npl UK inf* quarto *m* alugado.

dike [daɪk] *n* **-1.** [wall, bank] dique *m* **-2.** *inf pej* [lesbian] sapatão *m*.

dilapidated [dɪ'læpɪdeɪtɪd] *adj* em ruínas.

dilate [daɪ'leɪt] <> *vt* dilatar. <> *vi* dilatar-se.

dilemma [dɪ'lemə] *n* dilema *m*.

diligent ['dɪlɪdʒənt] *adj* diligente, aplicado(da).

dilute [daɪ'luːt] <> *adj* diluído(da). <> *vt*: **to ~ sthg (with sthg)** diluir algo(com algo).

dim [dɪm] (*compar* -**mer**, *superl* -**mest**, *pt* & *pp* -**med**, *cont* -**ming**) <> *adj* **-1.** [dark] sombrio(bria) **-2.** [indistinct - shape] indistinto(ta); [- sight, sound] fraco(ca); [- memory] vago(ga) **-3.** [weak] fraco(ca) **-4.** *inf* [stupid] idiota. <> *vt* [light] diminuir. <> *vi* [beauty, hope, memory] extinguir-se.

dime [daɪm] *n US* moeda de 10 centavos de dólar.

dimension [dɪ'menʃn] *n* dimensão *f*.

➡ **dimensions** *pl* [of room, object] dimensões *fpl*.

diminish [dɪ'mɪnɪʃ] <> *vt* [make less important] diminuir. <> *vi* diminuir.

diminutive [dɪ'mɪnjʊtɪv] <> *adj fml* [tiny] diminuto(ta). <> *n GRAMM* diminutivo *m*.

dimmer ['dɪmə'] *n* [switch] dimmer *m*.

➡ **dimmers** *npl US* **-1.** [dipped headlights] faróis *mpl* baixos **-2.** [parking lights] pisca-alerta *m*.

dimmer switch *n* = dimmer.

dimple ['dɪmpl] *n* covinha *f* (no rosto).

din [dɪn] *n inf* zoeira *f*.

dine [daɪn] *vi fml* jantar.

➡ **dine out** *vi* jantar fora.

diner ['daɪnə'] *n* **-1.** [person] cliente *mf* (de restaurante) **-2.** *US* [restaurant] lanchonete *f* (em beira de estrada).

dinghy ['dɪŋgɪ] (*pl* -ies) *n* [for sailing] barco *m* a vela (pequeno); [for rowing] bote *m* a remo.

dingy ['dɪndʒɪ] (*compar* -ier, *superl* -iest) *adj* [dirty, drab] sujo(ja).

dining car ['daɪnɪŋ-] *n* vagão-restaurante *m*.

dining room ['daɪnɪŋ-] *n* sala *f* de jantar.

dinner ['dɪnə'] *n* **-1.** [meal - in evening] jantar *m*; [- at midday] almoço *m* **-2.** [formal event] jantar *m*.

dinner jacket *n UK* smoking *m*.

dinner party *n* jantar *m* (para poucas pessoas).

dinnertime ['dɪnətaɪm] *n* hora *f* do jantar.

dinosaur ['daɪnəsɔː'] *n* [reptile] dinossauro *m*.

dint [dɪnt] *n fml*: **by ~ of** por meio de.

dip [dɪp] (*pt* & *pp* -ped, *cont* -ping) ⬦ *n* - **1.** [in road, ground] depressão *f* - **2.** [sauce] molho *m* cremoso - **3.** [swim]: **to go for a ~** dar um mergulho. ⬦ *vt* - **1.** [into liquid]: **to ~ sthg in (to) sthg** mergulhar algo em algo - **2.** *UK* [headlights] baixar. ⬦ *vi* - **1.** [sun, wing] baixar - **2.** [road, ground] descer.

Dip. Ed. (*abbr of* Diploma in Education) (*titular de*) *diploma em educação na Grã-Bretanha.*

diploma [dɪˈpləʊmə] (*pl* -s) *n* diploma *m.*

diplomacy [dɪˈpləʊməsɪ] *n* diplomacia *f.*

diplomat [ˈdɪpləmæt] *n* diplomata *mf.*

diplomatic [ˌdɪpləˈmætɪk] *adj* diplomático(ca).

dipstick [ˈdɪpstɪk] *n* AUT vareta *f* do nível do óleo.

dire [ˈdaɪəʳ] *adj* [serious] terrível.

direct [dɪˈrekt] ⬦ *adj* [gen] direto(ta). ⬦ *vt* - **1.** [aim]: **to ~ sthg at sb** dirigir algo a alguém - **2.** [person to place] guiar - **3.** [group, project, film, play] dirigir - **4.** [order]: **to ~ sb to do sthg** mandar alguém fazer algo. ⬦ *adv* direto.

direct current *n* corrente *f* contínua.

direct debit *n* UK débito *m* automático (*em conta corrente*).

direction [dɪˈrekʃn] *n* - **1.** [spatial] direção *f* - **2.** *fig* [orientation] rumo *m* - **3.** [of group, project, play, film] direção *f*; **under the ~** of sob a direção de.
➤ **directions** *npl* - **1.** [instructions to place] indicações *fpl* - **2.** [instructions for use] instruções *fpl.*

directly [dɪˈrektlɪ] *adv* - **1.** [in straight line] diretamente, direto - **2.** [frankly, openly] diretamente - **3.** [exactly] logo, bem - **4.** [very soon] imediatamente.

director [dɪˈrektəʳ] *n* diretor *m*, -ra *f.*

directory [dɪˈrektərɪ] (*pl* -ies) *n* - **1.** [book, list] lista *f* - **2.** COMPUT diretório *m.*

directory enquiries *n* UK (serviço *m* de) auxílio *m* à lista.

dire straits *npl*: **in ~** em apuros.

dirt [dɜːt] *n* - **1.** [mud, dust] sujeira *f* - **2.** [earth] terra *f.*

dirt cheap *inf* ⬦ *adj* bem barato(ta). ⬦ *adv* bem barato; **this was ~** isso foi uma ninharia.

dirty [ˈdɜːtɪ] (*compar* -ier, *superl* -iest, *pt* & *pp* -ied) ⬦ *adj* - **1.** [not clean] sujo(ja) - **2.** [unfair] baixo(xa) - **3.** [smutty] obsceno(na). ⬦ *vt* sujar.

disability [ˌdɪsəˈbɪlətɪ] (*pl* -ies) *n* deficiência *f.*

disabled [dɪsˈeɪbld] ⬦ *adj* [person] incapacitado(da). ⬦ *npl*: **the ~** os deficientes.

disadvantage [ˌdɪsədˈvɑːntɪdʒ] *n* desvantagem *f*; **to be at a ~** estar em desvantagem.

disagree [ˌdɪsəˈgriː] *vi* - **1.** [have different opinions] discordar, não estar de acordo; **to ~ with sb** discordar de alguém; **to ~ with sthg** discordar de algo - **2.** [differ] divergir - **3.** [subj: food, drink]: **to ~ with sb** fazer mal a alguém.

disagreeable [ˌdɪsəˈgriːəbl] *adj* desagradável.

disagreement [ˌdɪsəˈgriːmənt] *n* - **1.** [of opinions, records] divergência *f* - **2.** [argument] discussão *f.*

disallow [ˌdɪsəˈlaʊ] *vt* - **1.** *fml* [appeal, claim] rejeitar - **2.** [goal] anular.

disappear [ˌdɪsəˈpɪəʳ] *vi* desaparecer.

disappearance [ˌdɪsəˈpɪərəns] *n* - **1.** [of person, object] desaparecimento *m* - **2.** [of species, civilization] extinção *f.*

disappoint [ˌdɪsəˈpɔɪnt] *vt* [fail to satisfy] desapontar, decepcionar.

disappointed [ˌdɪsəˈpɔɪntɪd] *adj* desapontado(da), decepcionado(da); **~ in** OR **with sthg** decepcionado(da) com algo.

disappointing [ˌdɪsəˈpɔɪntɪŋ] *adj* desapontador(ra), decepcionante.

disappointment [ˌdɪsəˈpɔɪntmənt] *n* - **1.** *(U)* [feeling] desapontamento *m* - **2.** [letdown] decepção *f.*

disapproval [ˌdɪsəˈpruːvl] *n* *(U)* desaprovação *f.*

disapprove [ˌdɪsəˈpruːv] *vi*: **to ~ (of sb/ sthg)** desaprovar (algo/alguém).

disarm [dɪsˈɑːm] *vt* & *vi* desarmar.

disarmament [dɪsˈɑːməmənt] *n* *(U)* desarmamento *m.*

disarray [ˌdɪsəˈreɪ] *n* *(U)*: **in ~** *fml* [clothes, hair] em desalinho; [room] em desordem; POL em desacordo.

disaster [dɪˈzɑːstəʳ] *n* - **1.** [gen] desastre *m*; **natural ~** desastre *m* natural - **2.** *(U)* [misfortune] azar *m.*

disastrous [dɪˈzɑːstrəs] *adj* [catastrophic] desastroso(sa).

disband [dɪsˈbænd] ⬦ *vt* dispersar. ⬦ *vi* dispersar-se.

disbelief [ˌdɪsbɪˈliːf] *n* *(U)*: **in** OR **with ~** com descrença.

discard [dɪˈskɑːd] *vt* desfazer-se de, pôr fora.

discern [dɪˈsɜːn] *vt* - **1.** [see] discernir - **2.** [detect] perceber.

discerning [dɪˈsɜːnɪŋ] *adj* perspicaz.

discharge [*n* ˈdɪstʃɑːdʒ, *vb* dɪsˈtʃɑːdʒ] ⬦ *n* - **1.** [of patient] alta *f*; [of prisoner, defendant] libertação *f*; [from armed forces] dispensa *f* - **2.** [toxic emission] descarga *f* - **3.** MED [from nose, wound] secreção *f.*

$\diamond$ *vt* **-1.** [allow to leave - patient] dar alta para; [- prisoner, defendant] libertar; [- from armed forces] dispensar **-2.** *fml* [fulfil] cumprir **-3.** [emit] emitir.

disciple [dɪ'saɪpl] *n* **-1.** *RELIG* apóstolo *m* **-2.** *fig* [follower] discípulo *m*, -la *f.*

discipline ['dɪsɪplɪn] $\diamond$ *n* disciplina *f.* $\diamond$ *vt* **-1.** [train] disciplinar **-2.** [punish] punir.

disc jockey *n* disc-jóquei *mf.*

disclaim [dɪs'kleɪm] *vt fml* negar.

disclose [dɪs'kləʊz] *vt* divulgar.

disclosure [dɪs'kləʊʒə'] *n* **-1.** *(U)* [act of disclosing] divulgação *f* **-2.** [revealed fact] revelação *f.*

disco ['dɪskəʊ] *(pl* **-s)** *(abbr of* **discotheque)** *n* casa *f* noturna.

discomfort [dɪs'kʌmfət] *n* **-1.** [gen] desconforto *m* **-2.** *(U)* [physical pain] mal-estar *m.*

disconcert [ˌdɪskən'sɜ:t] *vt* desconcertar.

disconnect [ˌdɪskə'nekt] *vt* **-1.** [detach] desconectar **-2.** [from gas, electricity - appliance] desconectar, desligar; [- house, building] cortar **-3.** [on phone] cortar.

disconsolate [dɪs'kɒnsələt] *adj* inconsolável.

discontent [ˌdɪskən'tent] *n (U):* $\sim$ **(with** **sthg)** descontentamento *m* (com algo).

discontented [ˌdɪskən'tentɪd] *adj:* $\sim$ **(with sthg)** descontente (com algo).

discontinue [ˌdɪskən'tɪnju:] *vt* suspender.

discord ['dɪskɔ:d] *n* **-1.** *(U) fml* [conflict] discórdia *f* **-2.** *MUS* dissonância *f.*

discotheque ['dɪskəʊtek] *n* discoteca *f.*

discount [*n* 'dɪskaʊnt, *vb UK* dɪs'kaʊnt, *US* 'dɪskaʊnt] $\diamond$ *n* [price reduction] desconto *m.* $\diamond$ *vt* **-1.** [disregard] desconsiderar **-2.** *COMM* [offer at lower price] dar desconto em; [price] abater.

discourage [dɪs'kʌrɪdʒ] *vt* **-1.** [dishearten] desencorajar **-2.** [dissuade] dissuadir; **to** $\sim$ **sb from doing sthg** desestimular alguém de fazer algo.

discover [dɪ'skʌvə'] *vt* **-1.** [gen] descobrir **-2.** [realize] perceber, dar-se conta de.

discovery [dɪ'skʌvərɪ] *(pl* **-ies)** *n* **-1.** [gen] descoberta *f;* **the** $\sim$ **of America** o descobrimento da América **-2.** [realization] compreensão *f.*

discredit [dɪs'kredɪt] $\diamond$ *n (U)* [shame] descrédito *m.* $\diamond$ *vt* **-1.** [person] desonrar **-2.** [idea, belief, theory] desacreditar.

discreet [dɪ'skri:t] *adj* discreto(ta).

discrepancy [dɪ'skrepənsɪ] *(pl* **-ies)** *n:* $\sim$ **(in/between)** discrepância *f* (em/entre).

discretion [dɪ'skreʃn] *n* **-1.** [tact] discrição *f* **-2.** [judgment] ponderação *f;* **at the** $\sim$ **of** a critério de.

discriminate [dɪ'skrɪmɪneɪt] *vi* **-1.** [distinguish] discriminar; **to** $\sim$ **between** fazer distinção entre **-2.** [treat unfairly]: **to** $\sim$ **against sb** discriminar alguém.

discriminating [dɪ'skrɪmɪneɪtɪŋ] *adj* [discerning] criterioso(sa).

discrimination [dɪ,skrɪmɪ'neɪʃn] *n (U)* **-1.** [prejudice] discriminação *f* **-2.** [good judgment] discernimento *m.*

discus ['dɪskəs] *(pl* **-es)** *n* [sport] disco *m.*

discuss [dɪ'skʌs] *vt* discutir; **to** $\sim$ **sthg with sb** discutir algo com alguém.

discussion [dɪ'skʌʃn] *n (U)* [act of discussing] discussão *f;* **under** $\sim$ em discussão **-2.** [talk] debate *f.*

disdain [dɪs'deɪn] *fml n (U)* desdém *m;* $\sim$ **for sb/sthg** desprezo *m* por alguém/algo.

disease [dɪ'zi:z] *n* doença *f.*

disembark [ˌdɪsɪm'bɑ:k] *vi* desembarcar.

disenchanted [ˌdɪsɪn'tʃɑ:ntɪd] *adj:* $\sim$ **(with sthg)** desencantado(da) (com algo).

disengage [ˌdɪsɪn'geɪdʒ] *vt* **-1.** [release]: **to** $\sim$ **sthg (from sthg)** desprender algo (de algo) **-2.** *TECH* [gears, mechanism] desengatar.

disfavour *UK,* **disfavor** *US* [dɪs'feɪvə'] *n:* **to look on sthg with** $\sim$ olhar para algo com desaprovação; **to fall into** $\sim$ **with sb** cair em desgraça com alguém.

disfigure [dɪs'fɪgə'] *vt* desfigurar.

disgrace [dɪs'greɪs] $\diamond$ *n* **-1.** *(U)* [shame] desgraça *f;* **in** $\sim$ com vergonha **-2.** [cause for shame - thing] desgraça *f;* [- person] vergonha *f.* $\diamond$ *vt* envergonhar; **to** $\sim$ **o.s.** envergonhar-se.

disgraceful [dɪs'greɪsfʊl] *adj* vergonhoso(sa).

disgruntled [dɪs'grʌntld] *adj* decepcionado(da).

disguise [dɪs'gaɪz] $\diamond$ *n* disfarce *m;* **in** $\sim$ disfarçado(da). $\diamond$ *vt* disfarçar.

disgust [dɪs'gʌst] $\diamond$ *n* nojo *m;* $\sim$ **at sthg** nojo de algo.

disgusting [dɪs'gʌstɪŋ] *adj* [very unpleasant] nojento(ta).

dish [dɪʃ] *n* [container, food] prato *m.*
$\Rightarrow$ **dishes** *npl* louça *f;* **to do** OR **wash the** $\sim$ **es** lavar a louça.
$\Rightarrow$ **dish out** *vt sep inf* distribuir.
$\Rightarrow$ **dish up** *vt sep inf* pôr na mesa.

dish aerial *UK,* **dish antenna** *US n* antena *f* parabólica.

dishcloth ['dɪʃklɒθ] *n* pano *m* de prato.

disheartened [dɪs'hɑːtnd] *adj* desanimado(da).

dishevelled *UK*, **disheveled** *US* [dɪ'ʃevəld] *adj* desalinhado(da).

dishonest [dɪs'ɒnɪst] *adj* desonesto(ta).

dishonor *n* & *vt US* = **dishonour**.

dishonorable *adj US* = **dishonourable**.

dishonour *UK*, **dishonor** *US* [dɪs'ɒnə^r] *fml* ◇ *n* desonra *f*. ◇ *vt* desonrar.

dishonourable *UK*, **dishonorable** *US* [dɪs'ɒnərəbl] *adj* desonroso(sa).

dish soap *n US* detergente *m (para lavar louça)*.

dish towel *n US* pano *m* de prato.

dishwasher ['dɪʃ,wɒʃə^r] *n* [machine] lava-louças *fpl inv*.

disillusioned [,dɪsɪ'luːʒnd] *adj* desiludido(da); ~ **with sb/sthg** desiludido(da) com alguém/algo.

disincentive [,dɪsɪn'sentɪv] *n* desestímulo *m*.

disinclined [,dɪsɪn'klaɪnd] *adj*: **to be** ~ **to do sthg** estar pouco disposto(ta) a fazer algo.

disinfect [,dɪsɪn'fekt] *vt* desinfetar.

disinfectant [,dɪsɪn'fektənt] *n* desinfetante *m*.

disintegrate [dɪs'ɪntɪgreɪt] *vi* [object] desintegrar-se.

disinterested [,dɪs'ɪntrəstɪd] *adj* - **1.** [objective] neutro(tra) - **2.** [uninterested]: ~ **(in sb/sthg)** desinteressado(da) (em alguém/algo).

disjointed [dɪs'dʒɔɪntɪd] *adj* desconjuntado(da).

disk [dɪsk] *n COMPUT*: **floppy** ~ disquete *m*; **hard** ~ disco *m* rígido.

disk drive *UK*, **diskette drive** *US n COMPUT* drive *m*, unidade *f* de disco.

diskette [dɪsk'et] *n COMPUT* disquete *m*.

diskette drive *n US* = **disk drive**.

dislike [dɪs'laɪk] ◇ *n* - **1.** (U) [feeling] aversão *f*; ~ **of sb/sthg** aversão a alguém/algo; **to take a** ~ **to sb** não simpatizar com alguém; **to take a** ~ **to sthg** ter aversão a algo. - **2.** [thing not liked] desgosto *m*. ◇ *vt* não gostar de.

dislocate ['dɪsləkeɪt] *vt* - **1.** *MED* deslocar - **2.** [disrupt] desorganizar.

dislodge [dɪs'lɒdʒ] *vt* [remove - person]: **to** ~ **sb (from)** desalojar alguém (de); [- thing]: **to** ~ **sthg (from)** remover algo (de).

disloyal [,dɪs'lɔɪəl] *adj*: ~ **(to sb)** desleal (a alguém).

dismal ['dɪzml] *adj* - **1.** [gloomy, depressing] sombrio(bria), deprimente - **2.** [unsuccessful] frustrante.

dismantle [dɪs'mæntl] *vt* [machine, structure] desmantelar.

dismay [dɪs'meɪ] ◇ *n* (U) consternação *f*. ◇ *vt* consternar.

dismiss [dɪs'mɪs] *vt* - **1.** [from job]: **to** ~ **sb (from sthg)** despedir alguém (de algo) - **2.** [refuse to take seriously] descartar - **3.** [allow to leave] dispensar - **4.** [JUR - case] encerrar; [- jury] dispensar.

dismissal [dɪs'mɪsl] *n* - **1.** [from job] demissão *f* - **2.** [refusal to take seriously] descartamento *m* - **3.** [JUR - of case] encerramento *m*; [- of jury] dispensa *f*.

dismount [,dɪs'maʊnt] *vi*: **to** ~ **(from sthg)** descer (de algo).

disobedience [,dɪsə'biːdjəns] *n* desobediência *f*.

disobedient [,dɪsə'biːdjənt] *adj* desobediente.

disobey [,dɪsə'beɪ] *vt* [person, rule] desobedecer a.

disorder [dɪs'ɔːdə^r] *n* - **1.** [disarray]: **in** ~ em desordem - **2.** [rioting] tumulto *m* - **3.** *MED* distúrbio *m*.

disorderly [dɪs'ɔːdəlɪ] *adj* - **1.** [untidy] desordenado(da) - **2.** [unruly] indisciplinado(da).

disorganized, -ised [dɪs'ɔːgənaɪzd] *adj* desorganizado(da).

disorientated *UK* [dɪs'ɔːrɪənteɪtɪd], **disoriented** *US* [dɪs'ɔːrɪəntɪd] *adj* desorientado(da).

disown [dɪs'əʊn] *vt* renegar.

disparaging [dɪ'spærɪdʒɪŋ] *adj* depreciativo(va).

dispassionate [dɪ'spæʃnət] *adj* imparcial.

dispatch [dɪ'spætʃ] ◇ *n* [message] envio *m*. ◇ *vt* [send] enviar, despachar.

dispel [dɪ'spel] (*pt* & *pp* **-led**, *cont* **-ling**) *vt* [feeling] dissipar.

dispensary [dɪ'spensərɪ] (*pl* **-ies**) *n* dispensário *m*.

dispense [dɪ'spens] *vt* - **1.** [justice] administrar - **2.** [advice] oferecer - **3.** [drugs, medicine] preparar.

◆ **dispense with** *vt fus* dispensar.

dispensing chemist *UK*, **dispensing pharmacist** *US* [dɪ'spensɪŋ-] *n* farmacêutico *m*, -ca *f*.

disperse [dɪ'spɜːs] ◇ *vt* - **1.** [crowd] dispersar - **2.** [knowledge, news] disseminar - **3.** [substance, gas, oil slick] dispersar. ◇ *vi* [crowd] dispersar-se.

dispirited [dɪ'spɪrɪtɪd] *adj* desalentado(da).

displace [dɪs'pleɪs] *vt* - **1.** [supplant] substituir - **2.** *CHEM* & *PHYS* deslocar.

display [dɪ'spleɪ] ◇ *n* - **1.** [of goods, merchandise, ornaments] exposição *f*; **window** ~ vitrine *f* - **2.** [of feeling, courage, skill] demonstração *f* - **3.** [performance]

displease

exibição f - **4.** *COMPUT* exibição f. <> vt - **1.** [gen] expor - **2.** [feeling, courage, skill] demonstrar.

displease [dɪs'pliːz] vt descontentar.

displeasure [dɪs'pleʒəʳ] n (U) descontentamento m.

disposable [dɪ'spəʊzəbl] adj - **1.** [to be thrown away after use] descartável; ~ nappy *UK*, ~ diaper *US* fralda f descartável - **2.** [available] disponível.

disposal [dɪ'spəʊzl] n (U) - **1.** [getting rid] descarte f - **2.** [availability]: at sb's ~ à disposição de alguém.

dispose ◆ **dispose of** vt fus [get rid of - rubbish, nuclear waste] descartar-se de; [- problem] livrar-se de.

disposed [dɪ'spəʊzd] adj - **1.** [willing]: to be ~ to do sthg estar disposto(ta) a fazer algo - **2.** [positive]: to be well-~ to OR towards sb estar bem-intencionado(da) com/em relação a alguém.

disposition [ˌdɪspə'zɪʃn] n - **1.** [temperament] temperamento m - **2.** [willingness, tendency]: ~ to do sthg disposição f para fazer algo.

disprove [ˌdɪs'pruːv] vt [theory, ideal]: to ~ sthg mostrar que algo está errado.

dispute [dɪ'spjuːt] <> n - **1.** [quarrel] disputa f - **2.** (U) [disagreement] discussão f. <> vt - **1.** [question, challenge] discutir - **2.** [fight for] disputar.

disqualify [ˌdɪs'kwɒlɪfaɪ] (pt & pp -ied) vt - **1.** [subj: authority, illness, criminal record]: to ~ sb (from doing sthg) desqualificar alguém (para fazer algo) - **2.** *SPORT* desqualificar - **3.** *UK* [from driving] ser proibido de.

disquiet [dɪs'kwaɪət] n (U) inquietação f.

disregard [ˌdɪsrɪ'gɑːd] <> n: ~ (for sthg) desconsideração f OR indiferença f (por algo). <> vt desconsiderar.

disrepair [ˌdɪsrɪ'peəʳ] n (U) mau estado m de conservação; to fall into ~ estar caindo aos pedaços.

disreputable [dɪs'repjʊtəbl] adj desacreditado(da).

disrepute [ˌdɪsrɪ'pjuːt] n: to bring sthg into ~ desacreditar algo; to fall into ~ cair em descrédito.

disrupt [dɪs'rʌpt] vt transtornar.

dissatisfaction ['dɪsˌsætɪs'fækʃn] n (U) insatisfação f.

dissatisfied [ˌdɪs'sætɪsfaɪd] adj insatisfeito(ta); ~ with sthg insatisfeito(ta) com algo.

dissect [dɪ'sekt] vt dissecar.

dissent [dɪ'sent] <> n (U) [disagreement] divergência f. <> vi: to ~ (from sthg) divergir (de algo).

dissertation [ˌdɪsə'teɪʃn] n dissertação f.

disservice [ˌdɪs'sɜːvɪs] n: to do sb a ~ fazer um desserviço a alguém.

dissimilar [ˌdɪ'sɪmɪləʳ] adj diferente; ~ to diferente de.

dissipate ['dɪsɪpeɪt] vt - **1.** [heat] dissipar - **2.** [efforts, money] dispersar.

dissociate [dɪ'səʊʃɪeɪt] vt dissociar; to ~ o.s. from sthg dissociar-se de algo.

dissolute ['dɪsəluːt] adj dissoluto(ta).

dissolve [dɪ'zɒlv] <> vt dissolver. <> vi - **1.** [substance] dissolver-se - **2.** fig [disappear] desaparecer.

dissuade [dɪ'sweɪd] vt: to ~ sb (from doing sthg) dissuadir alguém (de fazer algo).

distance ['dɪstəns] n - **1.** [between two places] distância f - **2.** [distant point]: at a ~ à distância; from a ~ de longe; in the ~ ao longe.

distant ['dɪstənt] adj distante; ~ from distante de.

distaste [dɪs'teɪst] n (U) repugnância f; ~ for sthg repugnância a algo.

distasteful [dɪs'teɪstfʊl] adj [unpleasant] desagradável, repugnante.

distended [dɪ'stendɪd] adj dilatado(da).

distil *UK* (pt & pp -led, cont -ling), **distill** *US* [dɪ'stɪl] vt destilar.

distillery [dɪ'stɪlərɪ] (pl -ies) n destilaria f.

distinct [dɪ'stɪŋkt] adj - **1.** [different] distinto(ta); ~ from distinto(ta de); as ~ from em oposição a - **2.** [clear] nítido(da).

distinction [dɪ'stɪŋkʃn] n - **1.** [difference, excellence] distinção f; to draw OR make a ~ between fazer uma distinção entre - **2.** [in exam result] destaque m.

distinctive [dɪ'stɪŋktɪv] adj [flavour, voice] característico(ca).

distinguish [dɪ'stɪŋgwɪʃ] <> vt - **1.** [tell apart]: to ~ sthg from sthg distinguir algo de algo - **2.** [discern, perceive, make different] distinguir. <> vi: to ~ between distinguir-se entre.

distinguished [dɪ'stɪŋgwɪʃt] adj ilustre.

distinguishing [dɪ'stɪŋgwɪʃɪŋ] adj [feature, mark] peculiar.

distort [dɪ'stɔːt] vt distorcer.

distract [dɪ'strækt] vt [person, attention]: to ~ sb (from sthg) distrair alguém (de algo).

distracted [dɪ'stræktɪd] adj [preoccupied] atordoado(da).

distraction [dɪ'strækʃn] n [gen] distração f.

distraught [dɪ'strɔːt] adj transtornado(-da).

distress [dɪ'stres] <> n [suffering - mental]

aflição f; [- physical] agonia f, dor f. ⟨⟩ vt [upset] afligir.

distressing [dɪˈstresɪŋ] adj [news, account, image] angustiante.

distribute [dɪˈstrɪbjuːt] vt distribuir.

distribution [ˌdɪstrɪˈbjuːʃn] n distribuição f.

distributor [dɪˈstrɪbjʊtəʳ] n **-1.** comm distribuidor m, -ra f **- 2.** aut distribuidor m.

district [ˈdɪstrɪkt] n **-1.** [of country] distrito m **- 2.** [of town] bairro m.

district attorney n US jur promotor m público, promotora f pública.

district council n UK admin conselho m de bairro.

district nurse n UK enfermeira encarregada de atender a domicílio os pacientes de uma área.

distrust [dɪsˈtrʌst] ⟨⟩ n desconfiança f. ⟨⟩ vt desconfiar.

disturb [dɪˈstɜːb] vt **-1.** [interrupt] incomodar **- 2.** [upset, worry] preocupar **- 3.** [cause to change] mexer em.

disturbance [dɪˈstɜːbəns] n **-1.** [fight] distúrbio m **- 2.** [interruption, disruption]: ~ of the peace jur perturbação f da ordem **- 3.** [distress, upset] perturbação f.

disturbed [dɪˈstɜːbd] adj perturbado(-da).

disturbing [dɪˈstɜːbɪŋ] adj [news, image] perturbador(ra).

disuse [ˌdɪsˈjuːs] n: to fall into ~ cair em desuso.

disused [ˌdɪsˈjuːzd] adj [factory, railway line] abandonado(da).

ditch [dɪtʃ] ⟨⟩ n fosso m. ⟨⟩ vt inf **-1.** [boyfriend, girlfriend] livrar-se de **- 2.** [plan] descartar **- 3.** [old car, clothes] desfazer-se de.

dither [ˈdɪðəʳ] vi [be indecisive] hesitar.

ditto [ˈdɪtəʊ] adv idem.

dive [daɪv] (UK pt & pp -d, US pt & pp -d OR **dove**) ⟨⟩ vi **-1.** [gen] mergulhar; to ~ (into sthg) mergulhar (em algo) **- 2.** [as sport] mergulhar, saltar **- 3.** [into pocket, bag]: to ~ into sthg enfiar a mão em algo. ⟨⟩ n **-1.** [gen] mergulho m **- 2.** [sudden movement] movimento m brusco **- 3.** inf pej [bar, restaurant] espelunca f.

diver [ˈdaɪvəʳ] n mergulhador m, -ra f.

diverge [daɪˈvɜːdʒ] vi **-1.** [opinions, interests] divergir; to ~ from sthg divergir de algo **- 2.** [roads, paths] separar-se.

diversify [daɪˈvɜːsɪfaɪ] (pt & pp -ied) ⟨⟩ vt [products] diversificar. ⟨⟩ vi [in industry] diversificar-se.

diversion [daɪˈvɜːʃn] n **-1.** (U) [gen] desvio m **- 2.** [distraction] diversão f.

diversity [daɪˈvɜːsətɪ] n (U) diversidade f.

divert [daɪˈvɜːt] vt **-1.** [gen] desviar **- 2.** [distract] distrair.

divide [dɪˈvaɪd] ⟨⟩ vt **-1.** dividir **- 2.** [split up]: to ~ sthg into dividir algo em **- 3.** math: to ~ sthg by dividir algo por. ⟨⟩ vi [split into two] dividir-se.

dividend [ˈdɪvɪdend] n [profit] dividendo m.

divine [dɪˈvaɪn] adj divino(na).

diving [ˈdaɪvɪŋ] n [from board] salto m (de trampolim); [underwater] mergulho m.

diving board n trampolim m.

divinity [dɪˈvɪnətɪ] (pl -ies) n **-1.** (U) [godliness] divindade f **- 2.** (U) [study] teologia f **- 3.** [god, goddess] deidade f.

division [dɪˈvɪʒn] n **-1.** [gen] divisão f **- 2.** (U) [sharing out, distribution] repartição f **- 3.** [disagreement] discórdia f.

divorce [dɪˈvɔːs] ⟨⟩ n jur divórcio m. ⟨⟩ vt jur [husband, wife] divorciar-se de.

divorced [dɪˈvɔːst] adj **-1.** jur divorciado(da) **- 2.** fig [separated]: to be ~ from sthg estar distante de algo.

divorcee [dɪvɔːˈsiː] n divorciado m, -da f.

divulge [daɪˈvʌldʒ] vt [information, secret] divulgar.

DIY (abbr of do-it-yourself) n UK conceito utilizado para atividades do tipo faça-você-mesmo, como montar objetos ou fazer reparos em casa.

dizzy [ˈdɪzɪ] (compar -ier, superl -iest) adj [giddy] tonto(ta).

DJ n (abbr of disc jockey) DJ mf.

DNA (abbr of deoxyribonucleic acid) n DNA m.

DNS (abbr of Domain Name System) n comput DNS m.

do [duː] (pt did, pp done) ⟨⟩ aux vb **-1.** [in negatives]: don't ~ that! não faça isso!; she didn't see it ela não o viu. **- 2.** [in questions]: ~ you like it? você gosta?; how ~ you do it? como é que se faz? **- 3.** [referring to previous verb]: ~ you smoke? - yes, I ~ /no, I don't você fuma? sim/não; I eat more than you ~ eu como mais do que você; no, I didn't do it! não fiz, não!; so ~ I eu também. **- 4.** [in question tags]: so, you like Scotland, ~ you? então você gosta da Escócia, não gosta?; the train leaves at five o'clock, doesn't it? o trem sai às cinco, não é (verdade)? **- 5.** [for emphasis]: I ~ like this bedroom eu realmente gosto deste quarto; ~ come in! faça o favor de entrar! ⟨⟩ vt **-1.** [perform] fazer; to ~

one's homework fazer o dever de casa; **what is she doing?** o que ela está fazendo?; **what can I ~ for you?** em que posso ajudá-lo? **- 2.** [clean, brush etc.]: **to ~ one's hair** pentear-se; **to ~ one's make-up** maquiar-se; **to ~ one's teeth** escovar os dentes. **- 3.** [cause] fazer; **to ~ damage** fazer estragos; **to ~ sb good** fazer bem a alguém. **- 4.** [have as job]: **what do you ~?** o que você faz? **- 5.** [provide, offer] fazer; **we ~ pizzas for under $5** vendemos pizzas por menos de 5 dólares. **- 6.** [subj: vehicle] ir a; **the car was ~ ing 50mph** o carro ia a 80 km/h. **- 7.** inf [visit] visitar; **we're doing Scotland next week** para a semana vamos visitar a Escócia. <> vi **- 1.** [behave, act] fazer; **~ as I say** faça como eu lhe digo. **- 2.** [progress]: **he did badly/well on his test** ele foi mal/bem no exame; **how did you ~?** como é que foi? **- 3.** [be sufficient] chegar; **will $10 ~?** 10 dólares chega? **- 4.** [in phrases]: **how ~ you ~?** [greeting] (muito) prazer (em conhecê-lo); **how are you ~ing?** como é que vão as coisas?; **what does that have to ~ with it?** o que é que isso tem a ver? <> n [party] festa f; **~ s and don'ts** o que fazer e não fazer.

◆ **do up** vt sep [coat, shirt] abotoar; [shoes, laces] apertar, atar; [zip] fechar; [decorate] renovar.

◆ **do with** vt fus [need]: **I could ~ with a drink** eu bem que beberia alguma coisa.

◆ **do without** vt fus passar sem.

Doberman ['dəʊbəmən] (pl -s) n: **~ (pinscher)** dobermann m pinscher.

docile [UK 'dəʊsaɪl, US 'dɒsəl] adj dócil.

dock [dɒk] <> n **- 1.** [in harbour] doca f **- 2.** [in court] banco m dos réus. <> vi **- 1.** [ship] atracar **- 2.** [passengers] chegar.

docker ['dɒkər] n estivador m, -ra f.

docklands ['dɒkləndz] npl UK região f das docas.

dock worker n = docker.

dockyard ['dɒkjɑːd] n estaleiro m.

doctor ['dɒktər] <> n **- 1.** [of medicine] médico m, -ca f; **to go to the ~'s** ir ao médico **- 2.** [holder of PhD] doutor m, -ra f. <> vt [change, tamper with] adulterar.

doctorate ['dɒktərət], **doctor's degree** n doutorado m.

Doctor of Medicine n doutor m, -ra f em medicina.

doctrine ['dɒktrɪn] n doutrina f.

document [n 'dɒkjʊmənt] n documento m.

documentary [ˌdɒkjʊ'mentərɪ] (pl -ies) <> adj [evidence] documental. <> n documentário m.

dodge [dɒdʒ] <> n inf mutreta f; **a ~** uma mutreta para não pagar impostos. <> vt [avoid] fugir de. <> vi esquivar-se.

dodgy ['dɒdʒɪ] adj UK inf **- 1.** [dishonest] desonesto(ta) **- 2.** [risky, unreliable] arriscado(da) **- 3.** [weak, unhealthy] fraco(ca).

doe [dəʊ] n **- 1.** [female deer] corça f **- 2.** [female rabbit] coelha f.

does [weak form dəz, strong form dʌz] vb ▷ do.

doesn't ['dʌznt] = does not.

dog [dɒg] (pt & pp -ged, cont -ging) <> n [animal] cão m, cachorro m; **let sleeping ~s lie** não mexa em casa de marimbondo. <> vt **- 1.** [follow closely] seguir **- 2.** [subj: problems, bad luck] atormentar.

dog collar n **- 1.** [of dog] coleira f de cachorro **- 2.** [of clergyman] gola f de padre.

dog-eared [-ɪəd] adj [book, page] com orelhas.

dog food n ração f para cachorro.

dogged ['dɒgɪd] adj [resistance, perseverance] persistente.

dogsbody ['dɒgzˌbɒdɪ] (pl -ies) n UK inf faz-tudo mf, burro m de carga.

doing ['duːɪŋ] n: **is this your ~?** foi você que fez isso?

◆ **doings** npl [activities] atividades fpl.

do-it-yourself n (U) sistema m faça-você-mesmo.

doldrums ['dɒldrəmz] npl: **to be in the ~** fig estar estagnado(da).

dole [dəʊl] n UK [unemployment benefit] ≃ seguro-desemprego m; **to be on the ~** estar recebendo seguro-desemprego.

◆ **dole out** vt sep [food, money] repartir.

doleful ['dəʊlfʊl] adj lúgubre.

doll [dɒl] n [toy] boneca f.

dollar ['dɒlər] n dólar m.

dollop ['dɒləp] n inf monte m.

dolphin ['dɒlfɪn] n golfinho m.

domain [də'meɪn] n [sphere of interest, land] domínio m.

domain name n COMPUT nome m de domínio.

dome [dəʊm] n ARCHIT domo m.

domestic [də'mestɪk] <> adj **- 1.** [genflight] doméstico(ca); [- production] nacional **- 2.** [person] caseiro(ra). <> n doméstico m, -ca f.

domestic appliance n eletrodoméstico m.

dominant ['dɒmɪnənt] adj **- 1.** [colour] predominante **- 2.** [personality, group] influente.

dominate ['dɒmɪneɪt] vt dominar.

domineering [ˌdɒmɪ'nɪərɪŋ] adj [person, personality] dominador(ra).

dominion [də'mɪnjən] n -1. (U) [power] dominação f -2. [land] domínio m.

domino ['dɒmɪnəʊ] (pl -es) n peça f de dominó.

◆ **dominoes** npl [game] dominó m.

don [dɒn] (pt & pp -ned, cont -ning) n UK UNIV professor m, -ra f universitário, -ria f.

donate [də'neɪt] vt [give] doar.

done [dʌn] ◇ pp ▷ **do**. ◇ adj -1. [finished] pronto(ta) -2. [cooked] assado(-da). ◇ excl [to conclude deal] combinado!

donkey ['dɒŋkɪ] (pl donkeys) n burro m, -ra f.

donor ['dəʊnə'] n doador m, -ra f.

donor card n carteira f de doador.

don't [dəʊnt] = do not.

doodle ['du:dl] ◇ n rabisco m. ◇ vi rabiscar.

doom [du:m] n destino m.

doomed [du:md] adj [plan, mission] condenado(da); **to be ~ to sthg/to do sthg** estar destinado(da) a algo/a fazer algo; **to be ~ to failure** estar fadado(da) ao fracasso.

door [dɔ:'] n porta f; **the next ~ neighbour** o vizinho do lado; **the house next ~** a casa ao lado; **she showed him the ~** ela pediu para que ele saísse; **out of ~s** ao ar livre; **it's three miles ~ to ~** são três milhas de um ponto a outro; **as one ~ closes another one opens** quando se fecha uma porta, se abre uma janela.

doorbell ['dɔ:bel] n campainha f.

doorknob ['dɔ:nɒb] n maçaneta f.

doorman ['dɔ:mən] (pl -men [-mən]) n porteiro m.

doormat ['dɔ:mæt] n -1. [mat] capacho m -2. fig [person] capacho m.

doorstep ['dɔ:step] n [step] degrau m; **there's a cinema right on the ~** há um cinema bem próximo de casa.

doorway ['dɔ:weɪ] n vão m da porta.

dope [dəʊp] ◇ n -1. drugs sl [cannabis] maconha f -2. [for athlete, horse] estimulante m -3. inf [fool] babaca mf. ◇ vt [drug] dopar.

dopey ['dəʊpɪ] (compar -ier, superl -iest) adj inf -1. [groggy] grogue -2. [stupid] tonto(ta).

dormant ['dɔ:mənt] adj inativo(va).

dormitory ['dɔ:mətrɪ] (pl -ies) n -1. [room] dormitório m -2. US [in university] casa f de estudante.

Dormobile® ['dɔ:mə,bi:l] n motocasa f.

DOS [dɒs] (abbr of disk operating system) n DOS m.

dose [dəʊs] n -1. [of medicine, drug] dose f -2. [of illness] ataque f.

dosser ['dɒsə'] n UK inf pessoa que não tem onde morar e dorme na rua ou em pensões baratas.

dosshouse ['dɒshaʊs, pl -haʊzɪz] n UK inf pensão f barata (para os sem-teto).

dot [dɒt] (pt & pp -ted, cont -ting) ◇ n -1. [on material] mancha f -2. [in punctuation] ponto m; **since the year ~** desde que o mundo é mundo. ◇ vt [scatter - over surface] salpicar; [- over town, area, country] espalhar.

◆ **on the dot** adv em ponto.

dotcom ['dɒtkɒm] adj ponto-com.

dote ◆ **dote on** vt fus adorar; **to ~ on sb/sthg** babar por alguém/algo.

dot-matrix printer n impressora f matricial.

dotted line ['dɒtɪd-] n linha f pontilhada.

double ['dʌbl] ◇ adj duplo(pla). ◇ adv -1. [twice] dobro -2. [two of the same] em dobro -3. [in two] em dois; **to bend ~** dobrar ao meio. ◇ n -1. [twice the amount] dobro m -2. [of alcohol] duplo m, -pla f -3. [look-alike] cópia f -4. CINEMA dublê mf. ◇ vt [increase twofold] dobrar. ◇ vi [increase twofold] duplicar.

◆ **doubles** npl TENNIS dupla f.

double-barrelled UK, **double-barreled** US [-'bærəld] adj -1. [shotgun] de dois canos -2. [plan, question] de duplo sentido -3. [name]: **a ~ surname** um sobrenome composto.

double bass [-beɪs] n contrabaixo m.

double bed n cama f de casal.

double-breasted [-'brestɪd] adj [jacket] trespassado(da).

double-check ◇ vt verificar duas vezes. ◇ vi verificar duas vezes.

double chin n papada f.

double-click COMPUT ◇ n duplo clique m. ◇ vt dar um duplo clique em. ◇ vi dar um duplo clique.

double cream n UK creme m muito espesso.

double-cross vt passar para trás.

double-decker [-'dekə'] n [bus] ônibus m inv de dois andares.

double-dutch n UK hum: **to talk ~** falar grego.

double fault n TENNIS falta f dupla.

double-glazing [-'gleɪzɪŋ] n vidros mpl duplos.

double-park vi AUT estacionar em fila dupla.

double room n quarto m de casal.

double vision n visão f dupla.

doubly ['dʌblɪ] adv duplamente.

doubt [daʊt] <> n dúvida f; **there is no ~ that** não há dúvida de que; **to cast ~ on sthg** lançar dúvida sobre algo; **no ~** sem dúvida; **without (a) ~** sem dúvida; **in ~** em dúvida. <> vt -1. [distrust] desconfiar de -2. [consider unlikely] duvidar; **to ~ whether** OR **if** duvidar se.

doubtful ['daʊtfʊl] adj -1. [unlikely] improvável -2. [uncertain] incerto(ta) -3. [dubious] duvidoso(sa).

doubtless ['daʊtlɪs] adv sem dúvida.

dough [dəʊ] n (U) -1. [for baking] massa f -2. inf [money] grana f.

doughnut ['dəʊnʌt] n -1. [without hole] sonho m -2. [with hole] rosca f.

douse [daʊs] vt -1. [put out] jogar água em -2. [drench] encharcar.

dove¹ [dʌv] n [bird] pomba f.

dove² [dəʊv] pt US > dive.

dovetail ['dʌvteɪl] vi combinar.

dowdy ['daʊdɪ] (compar -ier, superl -iest) adj deselegante.

down [daʊn] <> adv -1. [downwards] para baixo; **to fall ~** cair -2. [along]: **I'm going ~** to the shops estou indo fazer compras; **we walked ~** to the park fomos até o parque -3. [southwards]: **we flew ~ from Recife to Rio** viajamos para o sul, do Recife até o Rio -4. [reduced, lower] baixo; **prices are coming ~** os preços estão baixando; **to the last detail** até o último detalhe. <> prep -1. [downwards] para baixo; **they ran ~ the hill** eles correram morro abaixo -2. [along]: **we walked ~ the street** caminhamos pela rua. <> adj -1. inf [depressed] desanimado(da) -2. [not in operation] fora de operação. <> n (U) [feathers, hair] penugem f. <> vt -1. [knock over] abater -2. [swallow] engolir.
◆ **down with** excl: **~ with the king!** abaixo o rei!

down-and-out <> adj sem futuro. <> n mendigo m, -ga f.

down-at-heel adj esp UK desleixado(da).

downbeat ['daʊnbiːt] adj inf [gloomy] sombrio(bria).

downcast ['daʊnkɑːst] adj fml [person] abatido(da).

downfall ['daʊnfɔːl] n -1. (U) [ruin] queda f -2. [cause of ruin] ruína f.

downhearted [,daʊn'hɑːtɪd] adj desacorçoado(da).

downhill [,daʊn'hɪl] <> adj [path] íngreme. <> adv -1. [downwards] para baixo -2. fig [from bad to worse] de mau a pior. <> n SKIING descida f.

Downing Street ['daʊnɪŋ-] n rua no centro de Londres onde fica a resi-

dência oficial do primeiro-ministro inglês, governo m britânico.

download [,daʊn'ləʊd] COMPUT <> vt baixar, fazer download de. <> n download m.

down payment n entrada f.

downpour ['daʊnpɔːʳ] n aguaceiro m.

downright ['daʊnraɪt] <> adj [lie, fool] inequívoco(ca). <> adv completamente.

downstairs [,daʊn'steəz] <> adj andar de baixo. <> adv: **to come ~** vir para OR andar de baixo; **to go ~** ir para OR andar de baixo; **to live ~** morar no andar de baixo.

downstream [,daʊn'striːm] adv a jusante, rio abaixo.

down-to-earth adj realista.

downtown [,daʊn'taʊn] esp US <> adj do centro; **~ New York** Nova York central. <> adv: **to go ~** ir ao centro; **to live ~** viver no centro.

downturn ['daʊntɜːn] n decréscimo m; **~ in sthg** queda em algo.

down under adv na OR para Austrália/Nova Zelândia.

downward ['daʊnwəd] <> adj -1. [towards ground] para baixo -2. [decreasing] descendente. <> adv US = **downwards**.

downwards ['daʊnwədz] adv [look, move] para baixo; **the overall trend is ~** a tendência geral é de baixa.

dowry ['daʊərɪ] (pl -ies) n dote m.

doz. (abbr of **dozen**) dz.

doze [dəʊz] <> n soneca f; **to have a ~** tirar uma soneca. <> vi dormitar.
◆ **doze off** vi cochilar.

dozen ['dʌzn] <> num adj dúzia f. <> n [twelve] dúzia f; **50p a ~** 50p a dúzia.
◆ **dozens** npl inf: **~s of** um montão de.

dozy ['dəʊzɪ] (compar -ier, superl -iest) adj -1. [sleepy] sonolento(ta) -2. UK inf [stupid] retardado(da).

Dr (abbr of **Doctor**) Dr. (Dra.).

Dr. (abbr of **Drive**) usado em nomes de rua na Grã-Bretanha.

drab [dræb] (compar -ber, superl -best) adj -1. [buildings] sombrio(bria) -2. [colour, garment] apagado(da) -3. [life] monótono(na).

draft [drɑːft] <> n -1. [early version] rascunho m -2. [money order] ordem f de pagamento -3. US MIL: **the ~** o destacamento -4. US = **draught**. <> vt -1. [write] rascunhar, fazer um rascunho de -2. US MIL recrutar -3. [transfer] deslocar.

draftsman n US = **draughtsman**.

drafty adj US = **draughty**.

dream

drag [dræg] (*pt* & *pp* **-ged**, *cont* **-ging**) ⬦ *vt* **-1.** [gen] arrastar **-2.** [search] dragar. ⬦ *vi* **-1.** [trail] arrastar **-2.** [pass slowly] arrastar-se. ⬦ *n* **-1.** *inf* [bore] chatice *f*; **what a ~!** que pé no saco! **-2.** *inf* [on cigarette] tragada *f* **-3.** *(U)* [cross-dressing]: **in ~** vestido como mulher.

⬥ **drag on** *vi* arrastar-se.

dragon ['drægən] *n* **-1.** [beast] dragão *m* **-2.** *inf* [woman] bruxa *f*.

dragonfly ['drægnflaɪ] (*pl* **-ies**) *n* libélula *f*.

drain [dreɪn] ⬦ *n* **-1.** [pipe] cano *m* de esgoto; **to go down the ~** ir para o brejo; [grating in street] bueiro *m* **-2.** [depletion]: **~ on sthg** sorvedouro de algo; **it's a ~ on my energy** esgota todas as minhas forças. ⬦ *vt* **-1.** [remove water from] drenar **-2.** [deplete] esgotar, exaurir **-3.** [drink, glass] beber até o fim. ⬦ *vi* [dry] escoar.

drainage ['dreɪnɪdʒ] *n* **-1.** [pipes, ditches] esgoto *m* **-2.** [draining] drenagem *f*.

draining board *UK* ['dreɪnɪŋ-], **drainboard** *US* ['dreɪnbɔːrd] *n* escorredor *m* de louça.

drainpipe ['dreɪnpaɪp] *n* cano *m* de esgoto.

dram [dræm] *n* [of whisky] trago *m*.

drama ['drɑːmə] *n* **-1.** [play, excitement] drama *f* **-2.** *(U)* [art] teatro *m*.

dramatic [drə'mætɪk] *adj* **-1.** [concerned with theatre] teatral **-2.** [exciting] dramático(ca) **-3.** [sudden, noticeable] drástico(ca).

dramatist ['dræmətɪst] *n* dramaturgo *m*, -ga *f*.

dramatize, -ise ['dræmətaɪz] *vt* **-1.** [rewrite as play] dramatizar **-2.** *pej* [make exciting] tornar dramático(ca).

drank [dræŋk] *pt* ⊳ **drink**.

drape [dreɪp] *vt* colocar suavemente; **to be ~d with** *OR* **in sthg** estar/ser coberto(ta) com algo.

⬥ **drapes** *npl* *US* cortinas *fpl*.

drastic ['dræstɪk] *adj* drástico(ca).

draught *UK*, **draft** *US* [drɑːft] *n* **-1.** [air current] corrente *f* **-2.** [from barrel]: **on ~** [beer] de barril.

⬥ **draughts** *n* *UK* damas *fpl*.

draught beer *n* *UK* chope *m*.

draughtboard ['drɑːftbɔːd] *n* *UK* tabuleiro *m* de damas.

draughtsman *UK*, **draftsman** *US* ['drɑːftsmən] (*pl* **-men** [-mən]) *n* [of technical drawings] desenhista *m* industrial.

draughtswoman *UK*, **draftswoman** *US* (*pl* **-women** [-wɪmɪn]) *n* [of technical drawings] desenhista *f* industrial.

draughty *UK* (*compar* **-ier**, *superl* **-iest**), **drafty** *US* (*compar* **-ier**, *superl* **-iest**) ['drɑːftɪ] *adj* pouco protegido(da) do frio.

draw [drɔː] (*pt* **drew**, *pp* **drawn**) ⬦ *vt* **-1.** [sketch] desenhar **-2.** [pull] puxar **-3.** [breath] inalar **-4.** [pull out] sacar **-5.** [arrive at, form] chegar a **-6.** [formulate] estabelecer **-7.** [attract] atrair; **to ~ sb's attention to sthg** chamar a atenção de alguém para algo. ⬦ *vi* **-1.** [sketch] esboçar **-2.** [move]: **to ~ near** aproximar-se; **to ~ away** afastar-se **-3.** *SPORT* empatar; **to ~ with sb** empatar com alguém. ⬦ *n* **-1.** *SPORT* [result] empate *m* **-2.** [lottery] sorteio *m* **-3.** [attraction] atração *f*.

⬥ **draw out** *vt* *sep* **-1.** [encourage] desinibir **-2.** [prolong] prolongar **-3.** [withdraw] sacar.

⬥ **draw up** ⬦ *vt* *sep* [draft] redigir, preparar. ⬦ *vi* [stop] parar.

drawback ['drɔːbæk] *n* inconveniente *m*.

drawbridge ['drɔːbrɪdʒ] *n* ponte *f* levadiça.

drawer [drɔːr] *n* [in desk, chest] gaveta *f*.

drawing ['drɔːɪŋ] *n* **-1.** [picture] desenho *m*, croqui *m* **-2.** *(U)* [skill, act] ato *m* de desenhar.

drawing board *n* prancheta *f* de desenho.

drawing pin *n* *UK* percevejo *m*.

drawing room *n* [living room] sala *f* de estar.

drawl [drɔːl] ⬦ *n* fala *f* arrastada. ⬦ *vi* falar de forma arrastada.

drawn [drɔːn] *pp* ⊳ **draw**.

dread [dred] ⬦ *n* *(U)* medo *m*, pavor *m*. ⬦ *vt* temer; **to ~ doing sthg** ter medo de fazer algo.

dreadful ['dredfʊl] *adj* **-1.** [terrible] terrível **-2.** [unpleasant] desagradável **-3.** [ill] horrível **-4.** [embarrassed] envergonhado(da) **-5.** [poor] fraco(ca) **-6.** [for emphasis] horroroso(sa).

dreadfully ['dredfʊlɪ] *adv* **-1.** [badly] terrivelmente **-2.** [extremely] extremamente.

dream [driːm] (*pt* & *pp* **-ed** *OR* **dreamt**) ⬦ *n* **-1.** [during sleep] sonho *m*; **bad ~** pesadelo *m* **-2.** [aspiration] sonho *m*. ⬦ *adj* almejado(da). ⬦ *vt* [during sleep]: **to ~ (that)** sonhar que. ⬦ *vi* **-1.** [during sleep] sonhar; **to ~ of** *OR* **about sthg** sonhar com algo; **I wouldn't ~ of it** *fig* nem pensar, de maneira nenhuma **-2.** [aspire]: **to ~ of sthg/of doing sthg** sonhar com algo/em fazer algo.

⬥ **dream up** *vt* *sep* bolar.

dreamt [dremt] *pt* & *pp* ⊳ **dream**.

dreamy ['dri:mɪ] (*compar* -**ier**, *superl* -**iest**) *adj* -**1.** [look, smile] distraído(da), sonhador(ra) -**2.** [music, feeling] sentimental.

dreary ['drɪərɪ] (*compar* -**ier**, *superl* -**iest**) *adj* -**1.** [gloomy, depressing] sombrio(a) -**2.** [dull, boring] chato(ta).

dredge [dredʒ] *vt* [lake, harbour, river] dragar.
➡ **dredge up** *vt sep* -**1.** [with dredger] dragar -**2.** *fig* [from past] trazer à tona.

dregs [dregz] *npl* -**1.** [of liquid] borra *f* -**2.** *fig* [of society] ralé *f*.

drench [drentʃ] *vt* encharcar; **to be ~ ed in** OR **with sthg** estar encharcado(da) de algo.

dress [dres] ⟨⟩ *n* -**1.** [frock] vestido *m* -**2.** [type of clothing] roupa *f*. ⟨⟩ *vt* -**1.** [clothe] vestir; **to be ~ ed** estar vestido(-da); **to be ~ ed in** estar vestido(da) de; **to get ~ ed** vestir-se -**2.** [bandage] fazer curativo em -**3.** CULIN temperar. ⟨⟩ *vi* vestir-se.
➡ **dress up** *vi* -**1.** [in costume] fantasiar-se -**2.** [in best clothes] vestir-se elegantemente -**3.** [in formal clothes] vestir-se a rigor.

dress circle *n* THEATRE balcão *m* nobre.

dresser ['dresəʳ] *n* -**1.** [for dishes] aparador *m* -**2.** US [chest of drawers] cômoda *f* -**3.** THEATRE camareiro *m*, -ra *f*.

dressing ['dresɪŋ] *n* -**1.** [bandage] curativo *m* -**2.** [for salad] tempero *m*, molho *m* -**3.** US [for turkey etc.] molho *m*.

dressing gown *n* -**1.** [man's] roupão *m* -**2.** [woman's] robe *f*.

dressing room *n* SPORT vestiário *m* -**2.** THEATRE camarim *m*.

dressing table *n* penteadeira *f*.

dressmaker ['dres,meɪkəʳ] *n* costureiro *m*, -ra *f*.

dressmaking ['dres,meɪkɪŋ] *n (U)* costura *f*.

dress rehearsal *n* THEATRE ensaio *m* geral.

dressy ['dresɪ] (*compar* -**ier**, *superl* -**iest**) *adj* [smart] chique.

drew [dru:] *pt* ⊳ **draw**.

dribble ['drɪbl] ⟨⟩ *n* -**1.** *(U)* [of saliva] filete *m* -**2.** [of other liquid] gota *f*. ⟨⟩ *vt* SPORT [ball] driblar. ⟨⟩ *vi* -**1.** [drool] babar -**2.** [trickle] derramar.

dried [draɪd] ⟨⟩ *pt* & *pp* ⊳ **dry**. ⟨⟩ *adj* -**1.** [powdered] em pó -**2.** [fruit, herbs, flowers] seco(ca).

drier ['draɪəʳ] *n* = **dryer**.

drift [drɪft] ⟨⟩ *n* -**1.** [movement, trend] tendência *f* -**2.** [of current] fluxo *m* -**3.** [geol] pressão *f* -**4.** [of people] curso *m* -**5.** [of snow, leaves, sand] monte *m* -**6.** [meaning] sentido *m*; **to get the general ~** pegar a idéia geral. ⟨⟩ *vi* -**1.** [boat] estar à deriva -**2.** [snow, sand, leaves] acumular-se.

driftwood ['drɪftwʊd] *n (U)* madeira *f* flutuante.

drill [drɪl] ⟨⟩ *n* -**1.** [tool] furadeira *f* -**2.** [industrial] perfuradora *f* -**3.** [dentist's] broca *f* -**4.** [exercise, training] treinamento *m*. ⟨⟩ *vt* -**1.** [metal, wood, hole] perfurar *f* -**2.** [instruct] instruir.

drink [drɪŋk] (*pt* **drank**, *pp* **drunk**) ⟨⟩ *n* -**1.** [non-alcoholic beverage] bebida *f* -**2.** [alcoholic beverage] bebida *f* alcoólica; **to have a ~** tomar um drinque -**3.** *(U)* [alcohol] bebida *f*. ⟨⟩ *vt* beber. ⟨⟩ *vi* beber.

drink-driving UK, **drunk-driving** US *n (U)* ato *m* de dirigir bêbado, -da *f*.

drinker ['drɪŋkəʳ] *n* -**1.** [of alcohol] beberrão *m*, -rona *f* -**2.** [of tea, coffee]: **he's a great tea/coffee ~** ele gosta muito de tomar chá/café.

drinking companion *n* companheiro *m*, -ra *f* de bebida.

drinking water ['drɪŋkɪŋ-] *n (U)* água *f* potável.

drip [drɪp] (*pt* & *pp* -**ped**, *cont* -**ping**) ⟨⟩ *n* -**1.** [drop] gota *f* -**2.** MED aparelho *m* de soro. ⟨⟩ *vi* -**1.** [gen] pingar -**2.** [nose] escorrer.

drip-dry *adj* que não amarrota ao secar.

drive [draɪv] (*pt* **drove**, *pp* **driven**) ⟨⟩ *n* -**1.** [journey] passeio *m*, volta *f* de carro -**2.** [urge] ímpulso *m* -**3.** [campaign] campanha *f* -**4.** *(U)* [energy] ímpeto *m* -**5.** [road to house] caminho *m (de entrada)* -**6.** SPORT [stroke] tacada *f* -**7.** US AUT [in automatic car] transmissão *f* automática. ⟨⟩ *vt* -**1.** [vehicle] dirigir; [passenger] levar *(de carro)* -**2.** TECH [operate] operar -**3.** [chase] seguir -**4.** [motivate] motivar -**5.** [force]: **to ~ sb to sthg/to do sthg** levar alguém a algo/a fazer algo; **to ~ sb mad** OR **crazy** [make insane] deixar alguém louco(ca) OR maluco(-ca); [irritate] deixar alguém furioso(sa) -**6.** [hammer] bater. ⟨⟩ *vi* AUT -**1.** [driver] dirigir -**2.** [travel by car] viajar.

drivel ['drɪvl] *n inf* bobagem *f*.

driven ['drɪvn] *pp* ⊳ **drive**.

driver ['draɪvəʳ] *n* [of vehicle] motorista *mf*.

driver's license *n* US = **driving licence**.

drive shaft *n* eixo *m* de transmissão.

driveway ['draɪvweɪ] *n* acesso *m*.

driving ['draɪvɪŋ] ⟨⟩ *adj* [rain, wind] forte; **~ rain** chuva *f* torrencial. ⟨⟩ *n (U)* direção *f*.

dubious

driving instructor n instrutor m, -ra f de direção.

driving lesson n aula f de direção.

driving licence UK, **driver's license** US n carteira f de motorista.

driving mirror n (espelho m) retrovisor m.

driving school n auto-escola f.

driving test n exame m de direção.

drizzle ['drɪzl] <> n garoa f, chuvisco m. <> v impers garoar, chuviscar.

droll [drəʊl] adj engraçado(da).

drone [drəʊn] n -1. [sound] zunido m -2. [bee] zangão m.

drool [druːl] vi -1. [dribble] babar -2. fig [admire]: **to ~ over sb/sthg** babar por alguém/algo.

droop [druːp] vi [hang down - shoulders] encurvar-se; [- head] inclinar-se; [- eyelids] fechar-se; [- flowers] murchar-se.

drop [drɒp] (pt & pp -ped, cont -ping) <> n -1. [of liquid - water, blood, rain] gota f; [- tea, coffee, milk] gole m; [- alcohol] dose f -2. [sweet] bala f -3. [decrease] queda f; **~ in sthg** queda de algo -4. [vertical distance] descida f. <> vt -1. [let fall - gen] deixar cair; [- bombs] lançar; [- stitch]: **she ~ped a stitch** escapou um ponto -2. [decrease, lower] reduzir -3. [voice] baixar -4. [leave, abandon] deixar -5. [leave out] excluir -6. [hint, remark] lançar -7. [write]: **to ~ sb a line** OR **note** escrever a alguém umas linhas OR um bilhete. <> vi -1. [fall] cair; **to ~ to one's knees** ajoelhar-se; **~ dead!** vai tomar banho! -2. [fall] baixar -3. [wind, attendance] diminuir.

◆ **drops** npl MED gotas fpl.

◆ **drop in** vi inf passar na casa de; **to ~ in on sb** passar na casa de alguém.

◆ **drop off** <> vt sep deixar. <> vi -1. [fall asleep] cair no sono -2. [grow less] diminuir.

◆ **drop out** vi [withdraw] retirar-se; **to ~ out of** OR **from sthg** desligar-se de algo.

dropout ['drɒpaʊt] n -1. [from society] marginalizado m, -da f -2. [from university] pessoa f que largou os estudos.

droppings ['drɒpɪŋz] npl excremento m (de animais).

drought [draʊt] n seca f.

drove [drəʊv] pt <> **drive**.

drown [draʊn] <> vt [kill] afogar. <> vi afogar-se.

drowsy ['draʊzɪ] (compar -ier, superl -iest) adj [person] sonolento(ta).

drudgery ['drʌdʒərɪ] n (U) trabalho m pesado.

drug [drʌg] (pt & pp -ged, cont -ging) <> n -1. [medication] remédio m -2. [illegal substance] droga f. <> vt -1. [person, animal] drogar -2. [food, drink] adicionar droga a.

drug abuse n (U) abuso m de drogas.

drug addict n drogado m, -da f, viciado m, -da f em drogas.

druggist ['drʌgɪst] n US farmacêutico m, -ca f.

drugstore ['drʌgstɔː'] n US farmácia f, drogaria f.

drum [drʌm] (pt & pp -med, cont -ming) <> n -1. [instrument] tambor m -2. [container, cylinder] barril m. <> vt [fingers] tamborilar. <> vi -1. [on drums] tocar -2. [rain, fingers] tamborilar -3. [hooves] bater.

◆ **drums** npl [set of drums] bateria f.

◆ **drum up** vt sep angariar.

drummer ['drʌmə'] n baterista mf.

drumstick ['drʌmstɪk] n -1. [for drum] baqueta f -2. [food] coxa f.

drunk [drʌŋk] <> pp <> **drink**. <> adj [on alcohol] bêbado(da); **to get ~** embebedar-se. <> n bêbado m, -da f.

drunkard ['drʌŋkəd] n beberrão m, -rona f.

drunk-driving n US = drink-driving.

drunken ['drʌŋkən] adj -1. [person] bêbado(da) -2. [state, event] = de bêbado.

drunken driving n = drink-driving.

dry [draɪ] (compar -ier, superl -iest, pt & pp dried) <> adj -1. [gen] seco(ca) -2. [climate] árido(da) -3. [sense of humour] sarcástico(ca) -4. [tedious] monótono(na). <> vt & vi secar.

◆ **dry up** <> vt sep [dishes] secar. <> vi -1. [gen] secar -2. [supplies, inspiration] esgotar-se -3. [actor, speaker] calar-se.

dry cleaner n: **~'s** tinturaria f.

dryer ['draɪə'] n [for clothes] secadora f.

dry land n terra f firme.

dry rot n (U) apodrecimento m da madeira (de casa).

dry ski slope n rampa f de esqui artificial.

DTI (abbr of Department of Trade and Industry) n ministério britânico da indústria e do comércio, ≃ MDIC m.

DTP (abbr of desktop publishing) n DTP f.

dual ['djuːəl] adj duplo(pla).

dual carriageway n UK pista f dupla.

dubbed [dʌbd] adj -1. CINEMA dublado(da) -2. [nicknamed] apelidado(da).

dubious ['djuːbjəs] adj -1. [suspect, questionable] duvidoso(sa) -2. [uncertain, undecided]: **to be ~ about doing' sthg** estar indeciso(sa) sobre fazer algo.

Dublin ['dʌblɪn] *n* Dublin; **in ~** em Dublin.

duchess ['dʌtʃɪs] *n* duquesa *f*.

duck [dʌk] ◇ *n* **-1.** [bird] pato *m*, -ta *f* **-2.** (U) [food] pato *m*. ◇ *vt* **-1.** [lower] curvar **-2.** [try to avoid] esquivar-se de; **to ~ the issue** evitar a questão. ◇ *vi* [lower head] curvar-se.

duckling ['dʌklɪŋ] *n* **-1.** [animal] patinho *m*, -nha *f* **-2.** [food] pato *m* novo.

duct [dʌkt] *n* **-1.** [pipe - heating] tubo *m*; [- water] canal *m* **-2.** ANAT ducto *m*.

dud [dʌd] *adj* **-1.** [banknote, coin, cheque] falso(sa) **-2.** [machine, idea] imprestável **-3.** [bomb, shell, bullet] que falhou.

dude [dju:d] *n US inf* [man] cara *m*.

due [dju:] *adj* **-1.** [expected] previsto(ta); **she's ~ back** shortly espera-se que ela volte logo; **when is the next train ~?** quando chega o próximo trem? **-2.** [proper] devido(da); **in ~ course** no tempo devido **-3.** [owed, owing]: **the rent is ~** o aluguel venceu; **she's ~ a pay rise** ela deve ganhar um aumento de salário; **how much are you ~?** quanto te devem? ◇ *n* [deserts] direito *m*. ◇ *adv* exatamente; **~ north** bem ao norte.
◆ **dues** *npl* direitos *mpl*.
◆ **due to** *prep* devido a.

duel ['dju:əl] *n* duelo *m*.

duet [dju:'et] *n* dueto *m*.

duffel bag ['dʌfl-] *n* mochila *f*.

duffel coat ['dʌfl-] *n* casaco *m* grosso (com capuz).

duffle bag ['dʌfl-] *n* = **duffel bag**.

duffle coat ['dʌfl-] *n* = **duffel coat**.

dug [dʌg] *pt & pp* ▷ **dig**.

duke [dju:k] *n* duque *m*.

dull [dʌl] ◇ *adj* **-1.** [boring] entediante **-2.** [colour, light] opaco(ca) **-3.** [day, weather] nublado(da) **-4.** [thud, boom] surdo(da) **-5.** [ache, pain] incômodo(da). ◇ *vt* **-1.** [deaden - pain] aliviar; [- senses, memory] enfraquecer; [- pleasure] diminuir **-2.** [make less bright] embaçar.

duly ['dju:lɪ] *adv* **-1.** [properly] devidamente **-2.** [as expected] como era de se esperar.

dumb [dʌm] *adj* **-1.** [unable to speak] mudo(da) **-2.** *esp US inf* [stupid] estúpido(da).

dumbfound [dʌm'faʊnd] *vt* pasmar; **to be ~ed** ficar pasmado(da).

dummy ['dʌmɪ] (*pl* -ies) ◇ *adj* [fake] falso(sa). ◇ *n* **-1.** [model of human figure - tailor's] manequim *m*; [- ventriloquist's] boneco *m* **-2.** [copy, fake object] imitação *f* **-3.** *UK* [for baby] chupeta *f* **-4.** SPORT drible *m*.

dump [dʌmp] ◇ *n* **-1.** [for rubbish] lixeira *f* **-2.** [for ammunition] depósito *m*. ◇ *vt* **-1.** [put down] deixar cair **-2.** [dispose of] descarregar **-3.** *inf* [jilt] romper com.

dumper (truck) ['dʌmpə^r-] *UK*, **dump truck** *US n* caminhão *m* basculante.

dumping ['dʌmpɪŋ] *n* (U) descarregamento *m*; **'no ~'** 'proibido jogar lixo'.

dumpling ['dʌmplɪŋ] *n* CULIN bolinho *m* de massa de pão.

dump truck *n US* = **dumper (truck)**.

dumpy ['dʌmpɪ] (*compar* -ier, *superl* -iest) *adj inf* atarracado(da).

dunce [dʌns] *n* burro *m*, -ra *f*, ignorante *mf*.

dune [dju:n] *n* duna *f*.

dung [dʌŋ] *n* (U) esterco *m*.

dungarees [,dʌŋgə'ri:z] *npl UK* macacão *m*.

dungeon ['dʌndʒən] *n* masmorra *f*.

Dunkirk [dʌn'kɜ:k] *n* Dunquerque.

duo ['dju:əʊ] *n* **-1.** MUS dueto *m* **-2.** [couple] casal *m*.

duplex ['dju:pleks] *n US* dúplex *m inv*.

duplicate [*adj & n* 'dju:plɪkət, *vb* 'dju:plɪkeɪt] ◇ *adj* [document] duplicado(da); **~ key** cópia *f* de chave. ◇ *n* [of document] cópia *f*; **in ~** em duplicata. ◇ *vt* [document] copiar.

durable ['djʊərəbl] *adj* durável, duradouro(ra).

duration [djʊ'reɪʃn] *n* (U) duração *f*; **for the ~ of** durante.

duress [djʊ'res] *n* (U): **under ~** sob coerção.

Durex® ['djʊəreks] *n* [condom] preservativo *m*, camisinha *f*.

during ['djʊərɪŋ] *prep* durante.

dusk [dʌsk] *n* (U) crepúsculo *m*, anoitecer *m*.

dust [dʌst] ◇ *n* (U) **-1.** [gen] pó *m*; *fig* [be ignored] ser privado(da); **to let the ~ settle** deixar a poeira baixar; **to have bitten the ~** ser derrubado(da) por terra **-2.** [earth, sand] poeira *f*, pó *m*. ◇ *vt* **-1.** [clean] tirar o pó de **-2.** [cover]: **to ~ sthg with sthg** polvilhar algo com algo.

dustbin ['dʌstbɪn] *n UK* lata *f* de lixo.

dustcart ['dʌstkɑ:t] *n UK* caminhão *m* de lixo.

dust cover *n* [for book] = **dust jacket**

duster ['dʌstə^r] *n* [cloth] espanador *m* de pó.

dust jacket, dust cover *n* [on book] sobrecapa *f*.

dustman ['dʌstmən] (*pl* -men [-mən]) *n UK* lixeiro *m*.

dustpan ['dʌstpæn] *n* pá *f* de lixo.

dusty [ˈdʌstɪ] (*compar* **-ier**, *superl* **-iest**) *adj* [covered in dust] empoeirado(da).

Dutch [dʌtʃ] ⬥ *adj* holandês(esa). ⬥ *n* [language] holandês *m*. ⬥ *npl*: **the ~** os holandeses. ⬥ *adv*: **let's go ~** cada um paga a sua parte.

Dutch elm disease *n (U)* doença *f* do olmo holandês.

dutiful [ˈdjuːtɪfʊl] *adj* zeloso(sa).

duty [ˈdjuːtɪ] (*pl* **-ies**) *n* **-1.** (*U*) [moral, legal responsibility] dever *m*; **to do one's ~** cumprir com o dever **-2.** (*U*) [work] obrigação *f*; **to be on/off ~** estar de plantão/folga **-3.** [tax] imposto *m*.
◆ **duties** *npl* [tasks, part of job] funções *fpl*.

duty-free ⬥ *n* **-1.** [goods] artigo *m* isento de impostos **-2.** [shop] loja *f* duty-free. ⬥ *adj* [whisky, cigarettes] isento(ta) de impostos.

duvet [ˈduːveɪ] *n UK* edredom *m*, acolchoado *m*.

duvet cover *n UK* capa *f* do edredom.

DVD (*abbr of* Digital Versatile Disk) *n* DVD *m*.

DVD player *n* (reprodutor *m* de) DVD *m*.

DVD ROM (*abbr of* Digital Versatile Disk read only memory) *n* DVD-ROM *m*.

DVLA (*abbr of* Driver and Vehicle Licensing Agency) *n* órgão britânico responsável pelo registro de automóveis e emissão de carteiras de motorista. ≃ DENATRAN *m*.

dwarf [dwɔːf] (*pl* **-s** OR **dwarves** [dwɔːvz]) ⬥ *n* anão *m*, anã *f*. ⬥ *vt* [tower over] sobrepujar.

dwell [dwel] (*pt* & *pp* **dwelt** OR **-ed**) *vi literary* [live] morar.
◆ **dwell on** *vt fus* [past, problem] ficar dando voltas com.

dwelling [ˈdwelɪŋ] *n literary* morada *f*.

dwelt [dwelt] *pt* & *pp* ▷ **dwell**.

dwindle [ˈdwɪndl] *vi* [decrease, grow smaller] ir diminuindo.

dye [daɪ] ⬥ *n* [colouring] tintura *f*. ⬥ *vt* [change colour of] tingir.

dying [ˈdaɪɪŋ] ⬥ *cont* ▷ **die**. ⬥ *adj* **-1.** [about to die - person] agonizante; [- species] em vias de extinção **-2.** *fig* [declining] que está desaparecendo.

dyke [daɪk] *n* = **dike**.

dynamic [daɪˈnæmɪk] *adj* [energetic] dinâmico(ca).

dynamite [ˈdaɪnəmaɪt] ⬥ *n (U)* **-1.** [explosive] dinamite *f* **-2.** *inf fig* [person, story, news]: **to be ~** ser uma bomba **-3.** *inf fig* [excellent] excelente.

dynamo [ˈdaɪnəməʊ] (*pl* **-s**) *n TECH* dínamo *m*.

dynasty [*UK* ˈdɪnəstɪ, *US* ˈdaɪnəstɪ] (*pl* **-ies**) *n* [ruling family] dinastia *f*.

dyslexia [dɪsˈleksɪə] *n (U)* dislexia *f*.

dyslexic [dɪsˈleksɪk] *adj* disléxico(ca).

E

e (*pl* **e's** OR **es**), **E** (*pl* **E's** OR **Es**) [iː] *n* [letter] e, E *m*.
◆ **E** *n* **-1.** *MUS* mi *m* **-2.** (*abbr of* **east**) l **-3.** (*abbr of* **ecstasy**) ecstasy *m*.

each [iːtʃ] ⬥ *adj* [every] cada. ⬥ *pron* [every one] cada um (uma); **two of ~** dois de cada; **~ other** um ao outro; **we know ~ other** nós nos conhecemos.

eager [ˈiːgəʳ] *adj* [keen, enthusiastic] animado(da); **to be ~ for sthg/to do sthg** estar ansioso(sa) por algo/para fazer algo.

eagle [ˈiːgl] *n* [bird] águia *f*.

ear [ɪəʳ] *n* **-1.** [of person, animal] orelha *f*; **to play it by ~** *fig* nadar de acordo com a maré **-2.** [of corn] espiga *f*.

earache [ˈɪəreɪk] *n* dor *f* de ouvido.

eardrum [ˈɪədrʌm] *n* tímpano *m*.

earl [ɜːl] *n* conde *m*.

earlier [ˈɜːlɪəʳ] ⬥ *adj* **-1.** [previous] anterior **-2.** [according to clock]: **let's take the ~ train** vamos pegar o trem que tem antes. ⬥ *adv* antes; **~ on** antes; **that day mais cedo naquele dia; they arrived ~ than expected** eles chegaram antes do esperado.

earliest [ˈɜːlɪəst] ⬥ *adj* **-1.** [first] primeiro(ra); **at your ~ convenience** assim que puder **-2.** [according to clock] primeiro(ra). ⬥ *adv*: **at the ~** no mínimo.

earlobe [ˈɪələʊb] *n* lóbulo *m* da orelha.

early [ˈɜːlɪ] (*compar* **-ier**, *superl* **-iest**) ⬥ *adj* **-1.** [gen] adiantado(da); **the ~ train** o primeiro trem; **to make an ~ start** começar na primeira hora **-2.** [of the beginning of a period of time - old] antigo(ga); [- period]: **this chair is ~ Victorian** esta cadeira é do início da era Vitoriana; [- in career, life] os primeiros anos de; [- in time] no começo de; **~-morning** da madrugada; **the ~ chapters** os primeiros capítulos. ⬥ *adv* **-1.** [before expected time] antes da hora **-2.** [in the morning, in a period of time] cedo; **to get up ~** madrugar; **as ~ as 1950** já em 1950; **~ on** cedo.

early closing n meio-feriado m (para as lojas).

early retirement n aposentadoria f antecipada.

earmark ['ɪəmɑːk] vt: to be ~ed for sthg ser destinado(da) para algo.

earn [ɜːn] vt -1. [as salary] ganhar -2. COMM gerar -3. fig [respect, praise] merecer.

earnest ['ɜːnɪst] adj [serious, sincere] sério(ria), sincero(ra).
◆ **in earnest** <> adj convicto(ta). <> adv para valer.

earnings ['ɜːnɪŋz] npl [of person, business] rendimentos mpl.

earphones ['ɪəfəʊnz] npl [headset] fones mpl de ouvido.

earpiece n audiofone m.

earplugs ['ɪəplʌgz] npl protetores mpl de ouvido.

earring ['ɪərɪŋ] n brinco m.

earshot ['ɪəʃɒt] n: within/out of ~ dentro/fora do alcance do ouvido.

earth [ɜːθ] <> n -1. [gen] terra f; how/what on ~ ...? como/o que é que ...?; where/why on ~ ...? onde/por que diabos ...?; to cost the ~ UK custar uma fortuna -2. (U) [soil] solo m -3. UK [in electric plug, appliance] terra m. <> vt UK: to be ~ed estar aterrado(da).

earthenware ['ɜːθnweə'] n (U) cerâmica f.

earthquake ['ɜːθkweɪk] n terremoto m.

earthworm ['ɜːθwɜːm] n minhoca f.

earthy ['ɜːθɪ] (compar -ier, superl -iest) adj -1. [humour, person] direto(ta) -2. [taste, smell] de terra.

earwig ['ɪəwɪg] n lacraia f.

ease [iːz] <> n (U) -1. [lack of difficulty] facilidade f; to do sthg with ~ fazer algo com facilidade -2. [comfort] comodidade f; at ~ à vontade; ill at ~ pouco(ca) à vontade. <> vt -1. [make less severe - pain, restrictions] aliviar; [- problems] atenuar -2. [move carefully] ajeitar; to ~ sthg open abrir algo com cuidado. <> vi [become less severe] aliviar; to show signs of easing mostrar sinais de alívio.
◆ **ease off** vi diminuir.
◆ **ease up** vi -1. [rain] acalmar -2. [relax] relaxar.

easel ['iːzl] n cavalete m.

easily ['iːzɪlɪ] adv -1. [without difficulty] facilmente -2. [undoubtedly] sem sombra de dúvida -3. [in a relaxed manner] tranqüilamente.

east [iːst] <> adj -1. [in the east, facing the east] oriental -2. [from the east] leste. <> adv a leste; ~ of ao leste de. <> n -1. [direction] leste m -2. [region]: the ~ o leste.
◆ **East** n: the East [of country] o leste; [Asia, Eastern bloc] o Oriente.

East End n: the ~ o leste de Londres.

Easter ['iːstə'] n Páscoa f.

Easter egg n ovo m de Páscoa.

easterly ['iːstəlɪ] adj -1. [towards the east, in the east] a leste -2. [from the east] do leste.

eastern ['iːstən] adj [part of country, continent] oriental, do leste.
◆ **Eastern** adj oriental.

East German <> adj da Alemanha Oriental. <> n [person] alemão m, -mã f oriental.

East Germany n: (the former) ~ (a antiga) Alemanha Oriental.

eastward ['iːstwəd] <> adj ao leste. <> adv = eastwards.

eastwards ['iːstwədz] adv em direção ao leste.

easy ['iːzɪ] (compar -ier, superl -iest) <> adj -1. [not difficult] fácil -2. [comfortable] cômodo(da) -3. [relaxed] sossegado(da). <> adv: to take it OR things ~ inf levar isso OR as coisas com calma.

easy chair n [armchair] poltrona f.

easygoing [ˌiːzɪ'gəʊɪŋ] adj [person, manner] descontraído(da).

eat [iːt] (pt ate, pp eaten) vt & vi comer.
◆ **eat away** vt sep, **eat into** vt fus -1. [corrode away] corroer -2. [deplete] destruir.

eaten ['iːtn] pp ⊳ eat.

eaves ['iːvz] npl [of house] beirado m.

eavesdrop ['iːvzdrɒp] (pt & pp -ped, cont -ping) vi [listen, spy] bisbilhotar; to ~ on sb bisbilhotar alguém.

ebb [eb] <> n (U) [of tide, sea] vazante f. <> vi [tide, sea] baixar.

ebony ['ebənɪ] <> adj literary [colour] da cor do ébano. <> n (U) [wood] ébano m.

e-business n -1. [company] empresa f de e-business -2. [electronic commerce] e-business m.

EC (abbr of European Community) n CE f.

e-cash n COMPUT dinheiro m eletrônico.

ECB (abbr of European Central Bank) n BCE m.

eccentric [ɪk'sentrɪk] <> adj [odd] excêntrico(ca). <> n [person] excêntrico m, -ca f.

echo ['ekəʊ] (pl -es, pt & pp -ed, cont -ing) <> n eco m. <> vt [repeat - words] repetir; [- opinion] repercutir. <> vi ecoar.

eclipse [ɪ'klɪps] <> n -1. [of sun, moon] eclipse m -2. fig [decline] declínio m. <> vt fig [overshadow] eclipsar.

eco-friendly [ˈiːkəʊˈfrendlɪ] adj ecológico(ca).

ecological [ˌiːkəˈlɒdʒɪkl] adj ecológico(ca).

ecology [ɪˈkɒlədʒɪ] n (U) ecologia f.

e-commerce n comércio m eletrônico.

economic [ˌiːkəˈnɒmɪk] adj econômico(ca).

economical [ˌiːkəˈnɒmɪkl] adj econômico(ca).

Economic and Monetary Union n União f Monetária e Econômica.

economics [ˌiːkəˈnɒmɪks] <> n (U) [study] economia f. <> npl [of plan, business, trade] aspectos mpl econômicos.

economy [ɪˈkɒnəmɪ] (pl -ies) n economia f; **economies of scale** economias de escala.

economy class n classe f econômica.

economy-size(d) adj [pack, jar] de tamanho econômico.

ecotax [ˈiːkəʊtæks] n ecotaxa f.

ecotourism [ˌiːkəʊˈtʊərɪzm] n ecoturismo m.

ecotourist [ˌiːkəʊˈtʊərɪst] n ecotourista mf.

ecstasy [ˈekstəsɪ] (pl -ies) n -1. (U) [great happiness] êxtase m -2. [drug] ecstasy m.

ecstatic [ekˈstætɪk] adj extasiado(da).

ECU, Ecu [ˈekjuː] (abbr of European Currency Unit) n Unidade f Monetária Européia.

eczema [ˈeksmə] n (U) eczema m.

Eden [ˈiːdn] n: **(the Garden of)** ~ (o Jardim do) Éden.

edge [edʒ] <> n -1. [outer limit] borda f; **to be on the** ~ **of sthg** estar à beira de algo -2. [of blade] fio m -3. [advantage]: **to have an** ~ **over sb/sth, to have the** ~ **on sb/sthg** levar ligeira vantagem sobre alguém/algo. <> vi [move slowly] avançar lentamente.
◆ **on edge** adj -1. [person] nervoso(sa) -2. [nerves] à flor da pele.

edgeways [ˈedʒweɪz], **edgewise** [ˈedʒwaɪz] adv [sideways] de lado.

edgy [ˈedʒɪ] (compar -ier, superl -iest) adj impaciente.

edible [ˈedɪbl] adj [safe to eat] comestível.

edict [ˈiːdɪkt] n [decree] edital m.

Edinburgh [ˈedɪnbrə] n Edimburgo.

edit [ˈedɪt] vt [correct] revisar; **to need** ~ **ing** precisar de revisão.

edition [ɪˈdɪʃn] n edição f.

editor [ˈedɪtəʳ] n -1. [gen] editor m, -ra f -2. [copy editor] revisor m, -ra f -3. COMPUT editor m (de texto).

editorial [ˌedɪˈtɔːrɪəl] <> adj editorial. <> n editorial m.

educate [ˈedʒʊkeɪt] vt -1. SCH & UNIV educar -2. [inform] informar.

education [ˌedʒʊˈkeɪʃn] n (U) -1. [activity, sector] educação f, ensino m -2. [process or result of teaching] educação f.

educational [ˌedʒʊˈkeɪʃənl] adj -1. [establishment, policy] educacional -2. [toy, experience] educativo(va).

EEC (abbr of European Economic Community) n CEE f.

eel [iːl] n enguia f.

eerie [ˈɪərɪ] adj lúgubre, sinistro(tra).

efface [ɪˈfeɪs] vt apagar.

effect [ɪˈfekt] <> n [gen] efeito m; **to have an** ~ **on sb/sthg** ter um efeito sobre alguém/algo; **to take** ~ [law, rule] entrar em vigor; [drug] fazer efeito; **to put sthg into** ~ pôr algo em prática; **for** ~ para impressionar. <> vt -1. [recovery, change] causar -2. [reconciliation, comeback, repairs] fazer.
◆ **effects** npl -1. : (special) ~s efeitos (especiais) -2. [property] bens mpl.
◆ **in effect** adv na prática; **the law is in** ~ a lei está em vigor.

effective [ɪˈfektɪv] adj -1. [successful] eficaz -2. [actual, real] efetivo(va) -3. [in operation] em vigor.

effectively [ɪˈfektɪvlɪ] adv -1. [well, successfully] eficazmente -2. [in fact] efetivamente.

effectiveness [ɪˈfektɪvnɪs] n (U) [success, efficiency] eficácia f.

effeminate [ɪˈfemɪnət] adj pej efeminado(da).

effervescent [ˌefəˈvesənt] adj [liquid] efervescente.

efficiency [ɪˈfɪʃənsɪ] n (U) eficiência f.

efficient [ɪˈfɪʃənt] adj eficiente.

effluent [ˈefluənt] n efluente m.

effort [ˈefət] n -1. (U) [physical or mental exertion] esforço m; **to be worth the** ~ valer o esforço; **to make the** ~ **to do sthg** esforçar-se para fazer algo; **with** ~ com esforço -2. [attempt] esforço m, tentativa f; **to make an/no** ~ **to do sthg** empenhar-se/não se empenhar em fazer algo.

effortless [ˈefətlɪs] adj fácil, com desenvoltura.

effusive [ɪˈfjuːsɪv] adj efusivo(va).

e.g. (abbr of exempli gratia) adv e.g.

egg [eg] n -1. [gen] ovo m -2. [of woman] óvulo m.
◆ **egg on** vt sep instigar.

eggcup [ˈegkʌp] n oveiro m.

eggplant [ˈegplɑːnt] n US berinjela f.

eggshell [ˈegʃel] n casca f de ovo.

egg white n clara f de ovo.

egg yolk [-jəʊk] n gema f de ovo.

ego ['i:gəʊ] (*pl* -s) *n* [opinion of self] ego *m*.

egoism ['i:gəʊızm] *n* (*U*) [self-interest] egoísmo *m*.

egoistic [ˌi:gəʊ'ıstık] *adj* [self-centred] egoísta.

egotistic(al) [ˌi:gə'tıstık(l)] *adj* egotista, egoísta.

Egypt ['i:dʒıpt] *n* Egito.

Egyptian [ı'dʒıpʃn] <> *adj* egípcio(cia). <> *n* [person] egípcio *m*, -cia *f*.

eiderdown ['aıdədaʊn] *n UK* [bed cover] edredom *m*.

eight [eıt] *num* oito; *see also* **six**.

eighteen [ˌeı'ti:n] *num* dezoito; *see also* **six**.

eighth [eıtθ] *num* oitavo(va); *see also* **sixth**.

eighty ['eıtı] (*pl* -ies) *num* oitenta; *see also* **sixty**.

Eire ['eərə] *n* (República da) Irlanda.

either ['aıðəʳ, 'i:ðəʳ] <> *adj* -1. [one or the other] qualquer; ~ **side could win** qualquer um dos lados poderia ganhar; **she couldn't find** ~ **jumper** ela não conseguiu achar nenhuma das blusas; ~ **way** de qualquer jeito; **I don't mind** ~ **way** por mim tanto faz -2. [each] cada; **on** ~ **side** de cada lado. <> *pron*: ~ **(of them) will do** qualquer um (deles) serve; **I don't like** ~ **(of them)** não gosto de nenhum (dos dois). <> *adv (after negative)* também não; **they don't smoke** ~ eles também não fumam. <> *conj*: ~ ... **or** ... [in positive sentence] ou ...ou ...; [in negative sentence] nem ...nem ...; ~ **he leaves or I do** ou ele sai ou saio eu; **you are not being** ~ **clever or funny** você não está sendo nem inteligente nem engraçado.

eject [ı'dʒekt] *vt* -1. [object] ejetar -2. [person]: **to** ~ **sb (from)** expulsar alguém (de).

eke [i:k] ◆ **eke out** *vt sep* [save - money] esticar; [- food, supply] racionar.

elaborate [*adj* ı'læbrət, *vb* ı'læbəreıt] <> *adj* [complicated, detailed] elaborado(da). <> *vi*: **to** ~ **(on sthg)** detalhar (algo).

elapse [ı'læps] *vi* [time] transcorrer.

elastic [ı'læstık] <> *adj* -1. [material, skin] elástico(ca) -2. *fig* [plan, timetable] elástico(ca). <> *n* (*U*) [material] elástico *m*.

elasticated [ı'læstıkeıtıd] *adj* [waistband] elástico(ca).

elastic band *n UK* elástico *m*.

elated [ı'leıtıd] *adj* exultante.

elbow ['elbəʊ] *n* cotovelo *m*.

elder ['eldəʳ] <> *adj* [older] mais velho(lha), primogênito(ta). <> *n* -1. [older person] velho *m*, -lha *f*- 2. [of tribe] ancião

m, -ã *f* - 3. [of church] presbítero *m* - 4. *BOT*: ~ **(tree)** sabugueiro *m*.

elderly ['eldəlı] <> *adj* [old - person] idoso(sa); [- thing] velho(lha), antigo(ga). <> *npl*: **the** ~ os idosos.

eldest ['eldıst] *adj* [oldest] mais velho(lha).

elect [ı'lekt] <> *adj* eleito(ta). <> *vt*-1. [by voting] eleger; **to** ~ **sb (as) sthg** eleger alguém (como) algo -2. *fml* [choose]: **to** ~ **to do sthg** escolher fazer algo.

election [ı'lekʃn] *n* eleição *f*; **to have** OR **hold an** ~ ter OR fazer uma eleição.

electioneering [ıˌlekʃə'nıərıŋ] *n* (*U*) *pej* propaganda *f* eleitoral, eleitoralismo *m*.

elector [ı'lektəʳ] *n* [voter] eleitor *m*, -ra *f*.

electorate [ı'lektərət] *n*: **the** ~ o eleitorado.

electric [ı'lektrık] *adj* -1. [using or producing electricity] elétrico(ca) -2. *fig* [exciting] eletrizante.

◆ **electrics** *npl UK inf* [in car, machine] partes *fpl* elétricas.

electrical [ı'lektrıkl] *adj* elétrico(ca).

electrical engineering *n* (*U*) engenharia *f* elétrica.

electrical shock *n US* = **electric shock**.

electric blanket *n* cobertor *m* elétrico.

electric cooker *n* fogão *m* elétrico.

electric drill *n* furadeira *f* elétrica.

electric fence *n* cerca *f* elétrica.

electric fire *n* estufa *f* elétrica.

electrician [ˌılek'trıʃn] *n* eletricista *mf*.

electricity [ˌılek'trısətı] *n* ELEC eletricidade *f*.

electric shock *UK*, **electrical shock** *US n* choque *m* elétrico.

electrify [ı'lektrıfaı] (*pt* & *pp* -ied) *vt* -1. [convert to electric power] eletrificar -2. *fig* [excite] deixar eletrizado(da).

electrocute [ı'lektrəkju:t] *vt* eletrocutar; **to** ~ **o.s** eletrocutar-se.

electrolysis [ˌılek'trɒləsıs] *n* (*U*) eletrólise *f*.

electron [ı'lektrɒn] *n* elétron *m*.

electronic [ˌılek'trɒnık] *adj* eletrônico(ca).

◆ **electronics** <> *n* (*U*) [technology] eletrônica *f*. <> *npl* [equipment] componentes *mpl* eletrônicos.

electronic banking *n* serviço *m* bancário via internet.

electronic data processing *n* (*U*) processamento *m* eletrônico de dados.

electronic mail *n* (*U*) correio *m* eletrônico.

electronic organizer n agenda f eletrônica.

elegant ['elɪgənt] adj -1. [stylish, beautiful] elegante -2. [clever, neat] brilhante.

element ['elɪmənt] n -1. SCIENCE elemento m -2. [small amount, proportion] parcela f -3. [in heater, kettle] resistência f -4. pej [in society, group] elemento m.
  ◆ **elements** npl -1. [basics] conhecimentos mpl básicos -2. [weather]: the ~ s os fenômenos atmosféricos.

elementary [ˌelɪ'mentərɪ] adj elementar.

elementary school n US escola f primária.

elephant ['elɪfənt] (pl inv OR -s) n elefante m.

elevate ['elɪveɪt] vt -1. [give importance to, promote]: to ~ sb/sthg to sthg, to ~ sb/sthg into sthg elevar alguém/algo a algo -2. [raise physically] levantar.

elevated railway n ferrovia f elevada.

elevator ['elɪveɪtə'] n US elevador m.

eleven [ɪ'levn] num onze; see also six.

elevenses [ɪ'levnzɪz] n (U) UK lanche m rápido (às 11 da manhã).

eleventh [ɪ'levnθ] num décimo primeiro, décima primeira; see also sixth.

elicit [ɪ'lɪsɪt] vt fml -1. [response, reaction]: to ~ sthg (from sb) obter algo (de alguém) -2. [information]: to ~ sthg (from sb) extrair algo (de alguém).

eligible ['elɪdʒəbl] adj [suitable, qualified] elegível; to be ~ for sthg/to do sthg estar habilitado(da) a algo/a fazer algo.

eliminate [ɪ'lɪmɪneɪt] vt -1. [remove]: to ~ sb/sthg (from) eliminar alguém/algo (de) -2. [in sport, competition]: to be ~ d from sthg ser eliminado(da) de algo.

elite [ɪ'liːt] ⬦ adj de elite. ⬦ n elite f.

elitist [ɪ'liːtɪst] pej ⬦ adj elitista. ⬦ n elitista mf.

elk [elk] (pl inv OR -s) n alce m.

elm [elm] n: ~ (tree) olmo m.

elocution [ˌelə'kjuːʃn] n (U) elocução f.

elongated ['iːlɒŋgeɪtɪd] adj alongado(-da).

elope [ɪ'ləʊp] vi: to ~ (with sb) fugir para casar (com alguém).

eloquent ['eləkwənt] adj eloqüente.

El Salvador [ˌel'sælvədɔː'] n El Salvador m.

else [els] adv: anything ~ mais alguma coisa; he doesn't need anything ~ ele não precisa de nada mais; everyone ~ todos os outros, todas as outras; nothing ~ nada mais; someone ~ alguma outra pessoa; something ~ outra coisa; somewhere ~ outro lugar; who/what/where ~ ? quem/que/onde mais?
  ◆ **or else** conj [or if not] ou então, senão.

elsewhere [els'weə'] adv em outro lugar.

elude [ɪ'luːd] vt escapar de; his name ~ s me completely o nome dele me escapa totalmente.

elusive [ɪ'luːsɪv] adj esquivo(va), evasivo(va).

emaciated [ɪ'meɪʃɪeɪtɪd] adj emagrecido (da).

e-mail n e-mail m, correio m eletrônico.

e-mail address n endereço m (de correio) eletrônico, e-mail m.

emanate ['emaneɪt] fml vi: to ~ from emanar de.

emancipate [ɪ'mænsɪpeɪt] vt: to ~ sb (from sthg) emancipar alguém (de algo).

embankment [ɪm'bæŋkmənt] n -1. [along road, railway] barreira f -2. [along river] margem f.

embark [ɪm'bɑːk] vi -1. [board ship]: to ~ (on) embarcar(em) -2. [start]: to ~ (up)on sthg dar início (a algo).

embarkation [ˌembɑː'keɪʃn] n embarque m.

embarrass [ɪm'bærəs] vt [shame] envergonhar.

embarrassed [ɪm'bærəst] adj [self-conscious] envergonhado(da).

embarrassing [ɪm'bærəsɪŋ] adj [shameful] embaraçoso(sa).

embarrassment [ɪm'bærəsmənt] n vergonha f.

embassy ['embəsɪ] (pl -ies) n embaixada f.

embedded [ɪm'bedɪd] adj -1. [buried]: ~ in sthg enterrado(da) em algo -2. COMPUT: ~ in sthg embutido(da) em algo -3. fig [ingrained] enraizado(da).

embellish [ɪm'belɪʃ] vt -1. [room, garment]: to ~ sthg with sthg embelezar algo com algo -2. fig [story, account] enfeitar.

embers ['embəz] npl brasa f.

embezzle [ɪm'bezl] vt [money] desviar.

embittered [ɪm'bɪtəd] adj amargurado(da).

emblem ['embləm] n [symbolic design] emblema m.

embody [ɪm'bɒdɪ] (pt & pp -ied) vt -1. [epitomize] personificar -2. [include]: to be embodied in sthg estar incorporado(da) em algo.

embossed [ɪm'bɒst] adj -1. [material] em relevo -2. [design, lettering]: ~ (on sthg) em relevo (sobre algo).

embrace [ɪm'breɪs] <> n abraço m. <> vt -1. [person] abraçar -2. fml [religion, way of life] converter-se a. <> vi abraçar-se.

embroider [ɪm'brɔɪdə'] <> vt -1. SEWING bordar -2. pej [embellish] enfeitar. <> vi SEWING bordar.

embroidery [ɪm'brɔɪdərɪ] n (U) bordado m.

embroil [ɪm'brɔɪl] vt : to get/be ~ ed (in sthg) envolver-se/ser envolvido(da) (em algo).

embryo ['embrɪəʊ] (pl -s) n BIOL embrião m.

emerald ['emərəld] <> adj [colour] esmeralda. <> n [stone] esmeralda f.

emerge [ɪ'mɜːdʒ] <> vi -1. [come out] aparecer; to ~ from sthg surgir de algo -2. [from experience, situation]: to ~ from surgir de -3. [become known - facts, truth] vir à tona; [- writer, movement] surgir. <> vt : it ~ s that vem à tona que.

emergence [ɪ'mɜːdʒəns] n (U) surgimento m, aparecimento m.

emergency [ɪ'mɜːdʒənsɪ] (pl -ies) <> adj de emergência. <> n emergência f.

emergency brake n US [of car] freio m de mão.

emergency exit n saída f de emergência.

emergency landing n pouso m de emergência.

emergency number n número m de emergência.

emergency room n US [in hospital] sala f de emergência.

emergency services npl serviços mpl de emergência.

emery board ['emərɪ-] n lixa f (de unhas).

emigrant ['emɪgrənt] n emigrante mf.

emigrate ['emɪgreɪt] vi emigrar; to ~ to/from emigrar para/de.

eminent ['emɪnənt] adj [distinguished] eminente.

emission [ɪ'mɪʃn] n fml emissão f.

emit [ɪ'mɪt] (pt & pp -ted, cont -ting) vt fml emitir.

emoticon [ɪ'məʊtɪkɒn] n COMPUT emoticon m.

emotion [ɪ'məʊʃn] n emoção f.

emotional [ɪ'məʊʃənl] adj -1. [easily moved] emotivo(va) -2. [charged with emotion] emocionado(da) -3. [appealing to the emotions] comovente.

emperor ['empərə'] n imperador m.

emphasis ['emfəsɪs] (pl -ases [-əsiːz]) n: ~ (on sthg) ênfase f (em algo); to lay OR place ~ on sthg dar ênfase a algo.

emphasize, -ise ['emfəsaɪz] vt enfatizar.

emphatic [ɪm'fætɪk] adj [forceful] enfático(ca).

emphatically [ɪm'fætɪklɪ] adv -1. [with emphasis] enfaticamente -2. [definitely] terminantemente.

empire ['empaɪə'] n império m.

employ [ɪm'plɔɪ] vt -1. [give work to] empregar; to be ~ed as sthg estar empregado(da) como algo -2. fml [use] empregar; to ~ sthg as sthg/to do sthg empregar algo como algo/para fazer algo.

employee [ɪm'plɔiː] n empregado m, -da f.

employer [ɪm'plɔɪə'] n empregador m, -ra f.

employment [ɪm'plɔɪmənt] n -1. [being in work] emprego m; to be in ~ estar empregado(da) -2. [work] trabalho m.

employment agency n agência f de empregos.

emporium [em'pɔːrɪəm] n empório m.

empower [ɪm'paʊə'] vt fml: to be ~ed to do sthg receber autoridade para fazer algo.

empress ['emprɪs] n imperatriz f.

empty ['emptɪ] (compar -ier, superl -iest, pt & pp -ied, pl -ies) <> adj vazio(zia). <> vt esvaziar; to ~ sthg into/out of sthg despejar algo em/de dentro de algo. <> vi [become empty] esvaziar. <> n inf casco m.

empty-handed [-'hændɪd] adv de mãos vazias.

EMS (abbr of European Monetary System) n SMT m.

EMU (abbr of Economic and Monetary Union) n UME f.

emulate ['emjʊleɪt] vt -1. [gen] imitar -2. COMPUT emular.

emulsion [ɪ'mʌlʃn] n ~ (paint) tinta f plástica.

enable [ɪ'neɪbl] vt : to ~ sb to do sthg permitir que alguém faça algo.

enact [ɪ'nækt] vt -1. JUR promulgar -2. [act] representar.

enamel [ɪ'næml] n (U) esmalte m.

encampment [ɪn'kæmpmənt] n [of soldiers, gipsies] acampamento m.

encapsulate [ɪn'kæpsjʊleɪt] vt fig [philosophy, idea]: to ~ sthg (in) resumir algo (em).

encase [ɪn'keɪs] vt : ~d in sthg envolvido(da) em algo.

enchanted [ɪn'tʃɑːntɪd] adj -1. [delighted]: ~ (by OR with sthg) encantado(da) (por OR com algo) -2. [under a spell] encantado(da).

enchanting [ɪn'tʃɑ:ntɪŋ] *adj* encantador(ra).

encircle [ɪn'sɜ:kl] *vt* cercar.

enclose [ɪn'kləʊz] *vt* **-1.** [surround, contain] cercar; **~d by** OR **with sthg** cercado(da) por OR com algo **-2.** [put in envelope] anexar; **please find ~d ...** segue anexo(xa) ...

enclosure [ɪn'kləʊʒə^r] *n* **-1.** [place] cercado *m* **-2.** [in letter] anexo *m*.

encompass [ɪn'kʌmpəs] *vt fml* **-1.** [include] abranger **-2.** [surround] cercar.

encore ['ɒŋkɔ:^r] ⬦ *n* [by singer, performer] bis *m*. ⬦ *excl* bis!

encounter [ɪn'kaʊntə^r] ⬦ *n* encontro *m*. ⬦ *vt fml* **-1.** [person] encontrar, encontrar-se com **-2.** [problem, difficulty etc.] deparar-se com.

encourage [ɪn'kʌrɪdʒ] *vt* **-1.** [give confidence to]: **to ~ sb (to do sthg)** incentivar alguém (a fazer algo) **-2.** [foster] incentivar, estimular.

encouragement [ɪn'kʌrɪdʒmənt] *n (U)* incentivo *m*, estímulo *m*.

encroach [ɪn'krəʊtʃ] *vi*: **to ~ (up)on sthg** apossar-se de algo; [rights] abusar de algo; [privacy] invadir algo.

encrypt [ɪn'krɪpt] *vt* COMPUT criptografar.

encyclop(a)edic [ɪn,saɪkləʊ'pi:dɪk] *adj* enciclopédico(ca).

end [end] ⬦ *n* **-1.** [last part, finish] fim *m*, final *m*; **to be at an ~** estar no fim; **to come to an ~** acabar, chegar ao fim; **to put an ~ to sthg** pôr fim a algo; **at the ~ of the day** *fig* no final das contas; **in the ~** [finally] finalmente **-2.** [tip, edge] extremidade *f* **-3.** [point, final section] ponta *f* **-4.** [side, one of two ends, of phone line] lado *m*; **which ~ does it open?** de que lado abre?; **to make ~s meet** conseguir que o dinheiro chegue **-5.** *fml* [purpose] fim *m*, objetivo *m* **-6.** *literary* [death] fim *m*. ⬦ *vt* acabar, terminar; **to ~ sthg with** acabar OR terminar algo com. ⬦ *vi* [finish] acabar, terminar; **to ~ in** acabar em; **to ~ with** acabar OR terminar com.

➡ on end *adv* **-1.** [upright] em pé **-2.** [continuously] a fio.

➡ end up *vi* acabar, terminar; **to ~ up doing sthg** acabar fazendo algo.

endanger [ɪn'deɪndʒə^r] *vt* pôr em perigo.

endearing [ɪn'dɪərɪŋ] *adj* simpático(ca).

endeavour UK, **endeavor** US [ɪn'devə^r] *fml* ⬦ *n* tentativa *f*, esforço *m*. ⬦ *vt*: **to ~ to do sthg** tentar fazer algo.

ending ['endɪŋ] *n* **-1.** [gen] final *m* **-2.** GRAMM terminação *f*.

endive ['endaɪv] *n* **-1.** [salad vegetable] endívia *f* **-2.** [chicory] chicória *f*.

endless ['endlɪs] *adj* **-1.** [unending] interminável **-2.** [inexhaustible] inesgotável **-3.** [vast] sem fim.

endorse [ɪn'dɔ:s] *vt* [approve] endossar.

endorsement [ɪn'dɔ:smənt] *n* **-1.** *(U)* [gen] endosso *m* **-2.** UK [on driving licence] pontos *mpl*.

endow [ɪn'daʊ] *vt* **-1.** [equip]: **to be ~ed with sthg** ser dotado(da) de algo **-2.** [donate money to] dotar.

endurance [ɪn'djʊərəns] *n (U)* resistência *f*.

endure [ɪn'djʊə^r] ⬦ *vt* resistir, suportar. ⬦ *vi fml* perdurar.

endways UK ['endweɪz], **endwise** US ['endwaɪz] *adv* **-1.** [lengthways] de frente **-2.** [end to end] ponta a ponta.

enemy ['enɪmɪ] *(pl* **-ies)** ⬦ *n* **-1.** [person] inimigo *m*, -ga *f* **-2.** MIL: **the ~** o inimigo. ⬦ *comp* inimigo(ga).

energetic [,enə'dʒetɪk] *adj* **-1.** [lively] ativo(va) **-2.** [physically taxing] vigoroso(sa) **-3.** [enthusiastic] ativo(va).

energy ['enədʒɪ] *(pl* **-ies)** *n (U)* energia *f*.

enforce [ɪn'fɔ:s] *vt* **-1.** [law] fazer cumprir, aplicar **-2.** [standards, discipline] impor.

enforced [ɪn'fɔ:st] *adj* **-1.** [obligatory] compulsório(ria) **-2.** [unavoidable] inevitável.

engage [ɪn'geɪdʒ] ⬦ *vt* **-1.** [attract] atrair **-2.** TECH engrenar **-3.** *fml* [employ] contratar; **to be ~d in** OR **on sthg** dedicar-se a algo; [busy with] estar ocupado(da) em algo. ⬦ *vi* [be involved]: **to ~ in** envolver-se em.

engaged [ɪn'geɪdʒd] *adj* **-1.** [couple] noivo(va); **to ~ to sb** noivo(va) de alguém; **to get ~** noivar **-2.** [busy, occupied] ocupado(da); **~ in sthg** envolvido(da) em algo **-3.** [phone, toilet] ocupado(da).

engaged tone *n* UK sinal *m* de ocupado.

engagement [ɪn'geɪdʒmənt] *n* **-1.** [of couple] noivado *m* **-2.** [appointment] compromisso *m*.

engagement ring *n* anel *m* de noivado.

engaging [ɪn'geɪdʒɪŋ] *adj* atraente.

engender [ɪn'dʒendə^r] *vt fml* gerar.

engine ['endʒɪn] *n* **-1.** [of car, plane, ship] motor *m* **-2.** RAIL locomotiva *f*.

engine driver *n* UK maquinista *mf*.

engineer [,endʒɪ'nɪə^r] *n* **-1.** [of roads, machines, bridges] engenheiro *m*, -ra *f* **-2.** [on ship] técnico *m*, -ca *f* **-3.** US [engine driver] maquinista *mf*.

engineering [ˌendʒɪ'nɪərɪŋ] n engenharia f.

England ['ɪŋglənd] n Inglaterra; **in ~** na Inglaterra.

English ['ɪŋglɪʃ] <> adj inglês(esa). <> n [language] inglês m. <> npl: **the ~** os ingleses.

English Channel n: **the ~** o Canal da Mancha.

Englishman ['ɪŋglɪʃmən] (pl -men [-mən]) n inglês m.

Englishwoman ['ɪŋglɪʃˌwʊmən] (pl -women [-ˌwɪmɪn]) n inglesa f.

engrave [ɪn'greɪv] vt **-1.** [metal, glass] gravar **-2.** [design]: **to ~ sthg (on sthg)** gravar algo (em algo) **-3.** fig [on memory] gravar.

engraving [ɪn'greɪvɪŋ] n **-1.** [design] gravura f **-2.** (U) [skill] gravação f.

engrossed [ɪn'grəʊst] adj: **to be ~ (in sthg)** estar absorto(ta) (em algo).

engulf [ɪn'gʌlf] vt **-1.** [cover, surround - subj:fire] devorar; [- subj:water] tragar **-2.** fig [overwhelm] tomar conta de.

enhance [ɪn'hɑːns] vt **-1.** [increase] aumentar **-2.** [improve] melhorar **-3.** [heighten: beauty, graphics] realçar.

enjoy [ɪn'dʒɔɪ] vt **-1.** [like] gostar de; **to ~ doing sthg** gostar de fazer algo; **to ~ o.s.** divertir-se **-2.** fml [possess] desfrutar de.

enjoyable [ɪn'dʒɔɪəbl] adj agradável.

enjoyment [ɪn'dʒɔɪmənt] n (U) prazer m.

enlarge [ɪn'lɑːdʒ] vt ampliar.
➡ enlarge (up)on vt fus desenvolver.

enlargement [ɪn'lɑːdʒmənt] n **-1.** (U) [gen] ampliação f **-2.** MED dilatação f.

enlighten [ɪn'laɪtn] vt fml esclarecer.

enlightened [ɪn'laɪtnd] adj esclarecido(da).

enlightenment [ɪn'laɪtnmənt] n (U) esclarecimento m.
➡ Enlightenment n: **the Enlightenment** o Iluminismo.

enlist [ɪn'lɪst] <> vt **-1.** MIL [recruit] recrutar **-2.** [support, help] angariar. <> vi MIL: **to ~ (in)** alistar-se(em).

enmity ['enmətɪ] (pl -ies) n (U) inimizade f.

enormity [ɪ'nɔːmətɪ] n (U) enormidade f.

enormous [ɪ'nɔːməs] adj enorme.

enough [ɪ'nʌf] <> adj suficiente. <> pron suficiente; **to have had ~ (of sthg)** [expressing annoyance] estar farto(ta) (de algo); **more than ~** mais que suficiente <> adv **-1.** [sufficiently] suficientemente, bastante; **to suffer ~** sofrer o bastante; **he hasn't tried hard ~** ele ainda não

tentou o suficiente; **to be good ~ to do sthg** fml ter a bondade de fazer algo **-2.** [rather] bastante; **strangely ~** curiosamente.

enquire [ɪn'kwaɪə'] vt & vi = **inquire**.

enquiry [ɪn'kwaɪərɪ] (pl -ies) n = **inquiry**.

enraged [ɪn'reɪdʒd] adj enfurecido(da).

enrol UK (pt & pp -led, cont -ling), **enroll** US [ɪn'rəʊl] <> vt matricular. <> vi: **to ~ (on OR in sthg)** matricular-se (em algo).

ensign ['ensaɪn] n [flag] bandeira f.

ensue [ɪn'sjuː] vi fml resultar.

ensure [ɪn'ʃʊə'] vt assegurar; **to ~ (that)** assegurar que.

ENT (abbr of ear, nose and throat) n otorrino mf.

entail [ɪn'teɪl] vt [involve] implicar.

enter ['entə'] <> vt **-1.** [come or go into] entrar em **-2.** [join - competition, race, the church] entrar em; [- school, politics, parliament] ingressar em; [- armed forces] alistar-se em; [- university] matricular-se em **-3.** [register]: **to ~ sb/sthg for sthg** inscrever alguém/algo em algo **-4.** [write down] registrar **-5.** COMPUT inserir; **your name, please** insira seu nome. <> vi **-1.** [come or go in] entrar **-2.** [register]: **to ~ (for sthg)** inscrever-se (para algo).
➡ enter into vt fus **-1.** [begin] iniciar **-2.** [become involved in] comprometer-se em.

enter key n COMPUT tecla f enter.

enterprise ['entəpraɪz] n **-1.** [company, business] empresa f **-2.** [venture] aventura f **-3.** (U) [initiative] empreendimento m.

enterprise zone n UK zona do Reino Unido na qual se fomenta a atividade de cultural e empresarial.

enterprising ['entəpraɪzɪŋ] adj empreendedor(ra).

entertain [ˌentə'teɪn] <> vt **-1.** [amuse] entreter **-2.** [have as guest] receber **-3.** fml [consider] considerar **-4.** fml [harbour] nutrir.

entertainer [ˌentə'teɪnə'] n animador m, -ra f.

entertaining [ˌentə'teɪnɪŋ] adj divertido(da).

entertainment [ˌentə'teɪnmənt] <> n **-1.** (U) [amusement] divertimento m, entretenimento m **-2.** [show] espetáculo m.

enthral (pt & pp -led, cont -ling), **enthrall** US [ɪn'θrɔːl] vt fascinar.

enthrone [ɪn'θrəʊn] vt fml entronizar.

enthusiasm [ɪn'θjuːzɪæzm] n **-1.** (U) [passion, eagerness] entusiasmo m; **~**

for sthg entusiasmo por algo **-2.** [interest, hobby] paixão *f*, interesse *m*.

enthusiast [ɪn'θju:zɪæst] *n* [fan] entusiasta *mf*.

enthusiastic [ɪn,θju:zɪ'æstɪk] *adj* entusiástico(ca).

entice [ɪn'taɪs] *vt* atrair; **to ~ sb away from sthg** desviar alguém de algo; **to ~ sb into sthg** instigar alguém a algo.

entire [ɪn'taɪə^r] *adj* inteiro(ra).

entirely [ɪn'taɪəlɪ] *adv* inteiramente; **that's ~ different** isso é completamente diferente.

entirety [ɪn'taɪrətɪ] *n (U) fml*: **in its ~** em sua totalidade.

entitle [ɪn'taɪtl] *vt* [allow]: **to ~ sb to sthg** dar a alguém o direito a algo; **to ~ sb to do sthg** autorizar alguém a fazer algo.

entitled [ɪn'taɪtld] *adj* **-1.** [having a right to]: **to be ~ to sthg/to do sthg** ter direito a algo/a fazer algo **-2.** [called] intitulado(da).

entitlement [ɪn'taɪtlmənt] *n* direito *m*.

entrance [*n* 'entrəns, *vb* ɪn'trɑ:ns] <> *n* **-1.** [arrival] entrada *f* **-2.** [way in]: **~ (to sthg)** entrada (para OR de algo) **-3.** (U) [entry]: **to gain ~ to sthg** *fml* [to building] obter acesso a algo; [to society, university] ingressar em algo. <> *vt* [delight] encantar.

entrance examination *n* [for school, profession] exame *m* de admissão ; [for university] ≃ vestibular *m*.

entrance fee *n* **-1.** [gen] (preço *m* do) ingresso *m* **-2.** [to club] taxa *f* de admissão.

entrant ['entrənt] *n* [gen] participante *mf*.

entreat [ɪn'tri:t] *vt*: **to ~ sb (to do sthg)** suplicar a alguém (para que faça algo).

entrenched *adj* [firm] arraigado(da).

entrepreneur [,ɒntrəprə'nɜ:^r] *n* empresário *m*, -ria *f*.

entrust [ɪn'trʌst] *vt*: **to ~ sthg to sb, to ~ sb with sthg** confiar algo a alguém.

entry ['entrɪ] (*pl* **-ies**) *n* **-1.** [gen] entrada *f*; **~ (into)** entrada (em) **-2.** (U) [admission]: **~ (to)** acesso *m* (a); **to gain ~ to** conseguir acesso a; **'no ~'** [to room, building] 'proibida a entrada'; AUT 'não entre' **-3.** [in competition] inscrição *f* **-4.** [in diary] anotação *f* **-5.** [in ledger] lançamento *m* **-6.** *fig* [joining] ingresso *m*.

entry form *n* ficha *f* de inscrição.

entry phone *n* porteiro *m* eletrônico.

envelop [ɪn'veləp] *vt*: **to ~ sb/sthg in sthg** envolver alguém/algo em algo.

envelope ['envələʊp] *n* [for letter] envelope *m*.

envious ['envɪəs] *adj* invejoso(sa); **~ (of sb/sthg)** invejoso(sa) (de alguém/algo).

environment [ɪn'vaɪərənmənt] *n* **-1.** [gen] ambiente *m* **-2.** [natural world]: **the ~** o meio ambiente.

environmental [ɪn,vaɪərən'mentl] *adj* ambiental.

environmentalist [ɪn,vaɪərən'mentəlɪst] *n* ambientalista *mf*.

environmentally [ɪn,vaɪərən'mentəlɪ] *adv* ecologicamente; **~ friendly** que não prejudica o meio ambiente, ecológico(ca).

envisage [ɪn'vɪzɪdʒ], **envision** US [ɪn'vɪʒn] *vt* prever.

envoy ['envɔɪ] *n* enviado *m*, -da *f*.

envy ['envɪ] (*pt* & *pp* **-ied**) <> *n (U)* inveja *f*. <> *vt* invejar; **to ~ sb sthg** invejar algo a alguém.

eon *n* US = aeon.

epic ['epɪk] <> *adj* épico(ca). <> *n* [book, film] épico *m*.

epidemic [,epɪ'demɪk] *n* [of disease] epidemia *f*.

epileptic [,epɪ'leptɪk] <> *adj* [fit, person] epilético(ca). <> *n* epilético *m*, -ca *f*.

episode ['epɪsəʊd] *n* episódio *m*.

epistle [ɪ'pɪsl] *n literary* [letter] epístola *f*.

epitaph ['epɪtɑ:f] *n* epitáfio *m*.

epitome [ɪ'pɪtəmɪ] *n*: **the ~ of sb/sthg** [person] o exemplo vivo de alguém/algo, a personificação de alguém/algo; **this hotel is the ~ of luxury** este hotel é o número um em termos de luxo.

epitomize, -ise [ɪ'pɪtəmaɪz] *vt* personificar, representar o paradigma de.

epoch ['i:pɒk] *n* época *f*.

equable ['ekwəbl] *adj* [calm, reasonable] calmo(ma).

equal ['i:kwəl] (*UK pt* & *pp* **-led**, *cont* **-ling**, *US pt* & *pp* **-ed**, *cont* **-ing**) <> *adj* **-1.** igual; **~ to sthg** [sum] igual a algo; **on ~ terms** em igualdade de condições **-2.** [capable]: **to be ~ to sthg** estar à altura de algo. <> *n* [person] igual *mf*; **he's her ~ in everything** ele é igual a ela em tudo. <> *vt* **-1.** MATH ser igual a **-2.** [in standard] igualar-se a.

equality [i:'kwɒlətɪ] *n (U)* igualdade *f*.

equalize, -ise ['i:kwəlaɪz] <> *vt* igualar. <> *vi SPORT* empatar.

equalizer ['i:kwəlaɪzə^r] *n SPORT* gol *m* de empate.

equally ['i:kwəlɪ] *adv* **-1.** [to the same extent] igualmente **-2.** [in equal amounts] por igual **-3.** [by the same token] da mesma forma.

equal opportunities *npl* oportunidades *fpl* iguais.

equanimity [,ekwə'nɪmətɪ] *n (U)* equanimidade *f.*

equate [ɪ'kweɪt] *vt*: **to ~ sthg with sthg** equiparar algo com algo.

equation [ɪ'kweɪʒn] *n* MATH equação *f.*

equator [ɪ'kweɪtə] *n*: **the ~** o equador.

equilibrium [,iːkwɪ'lɪbrɪəm] *n* equilíbrio *m.*

equip [ɪ'kwɪp] (*pt* & *pp* -**ped**, *cont* -**ping**) *vt* -**1.** [provide with equipment] equipar; **~ sb/sthg with sthg** equipar alguém/algo com algo -**2.** [prepare mentally]: **~ sb for sthg** preparar alguém psicologicamente para algo.

equipment [ɪ'kwɪpmənt] *n (U)* equipamento *m.*

equity ['ekwətɪ] *n* FIN [market value] patrimônio *m* líquido.

➡ **equities** *npl* ST EX ações *fpl* ordinárias.

equivalent [ɪ'kwɪvələnt] ◇ *adj* equivalente; **to be ~ to sthg** ser equivalente a algo. ◇ *n* equivalente *m.*

equivocal [ɪ'kwɪvəkl] *adj* -**1.** [statement, remark] ambíguo(gua) -**2.** [behaviour, event] duvidoso(sa).

er [ɜː] *excl* -**1.** [in hesitation] ãhn! -**2.** [to attract attention] ei!

era ['ɪərə] (*pl* -**s**) *n* era *f.*

eradicate [ɪ'rædɪkeɪt] *vt* erradicar.

erase [ɪ'reɪz] *vt* -**1.** [rub out] apagar -**2.** *fig* [drive away, eliminate] eliminar, extinguir.

eraser [ɪ'reɪzə] *n* US borracha *f.*

erect [ɪ'rekt] ◇ *adj* ereto(ta). ◇ *vt* -**1.** [building, statue] erigir -**2.** [tent, roadblock] montar.

erection [ɪ'rekʃn] *n* -**1.** (*U*) [of building, statue] construção *f* -**2.** [erect penis] ereção *f.*

ergonomic [,ɜːgə'nɒmɪk] *adj* ergonômico(ca).

ERM (*abbr of* **Exchange Rate Mechanism**) *n* MTC *m.*

ermine ['ɜːmɪn] *n (U)* [fur] arminho *m.*

erode [ɪ'rəʊd] ◇ *vt* -**1.** GEOL causar erosão em -**2.** *fig* [destroy] destruir. ◇ *vi* -**1.** GEOL sofrer erosão -**2.** *fig* [be destroyed] ser destruído(da).

erosion [ɪ'rəʊʒn] *n* -**1.** GEOL erosão *f* -**2.** *fig* [destruction] destruição *f.*

erotic [ɪ'rɒtɪk] *adj* erótico(ca).

err [ɜː] *vi* errar.

errand ['erənd] *n* -**1.** [task] tarefa *f*; **to go on** OR **run an ~ (for sb)** encarregar-se de alguma tarefa (para alguém) -**2.** [message] recado *m.*

erratic [ɪ'rætɪk] *adj* irregular.

error ['erə] *n* -**1.** [mistake] erro *m*; **~ of judgment** erro de julgamento; **in ~** por engano -**2.** FIN: **~s and omissions excepted** salvo erro ou omissão.

erupt [ɪ'rʌpt] *vi* -**1.** [volcano] entrar em erupção -**2.** *fig* [violence, war] explodir.

eruption [ɪ'rʌpʃn] *n* -**1.** [of volcano] erupção *f* -**2.** [of violence, war] explosão *f.*

escalate ['eskəleɪt] *vi* -**1.** [conflict, violence] intensificar-se -**2.** [costs, prices] aumentar.

escalator ['eskəleɪtə] *n* escada *f* rolante.

escapade [,eskə'peɪd] *n* escapada *f.*

escape [ɪ'skeɪp] ◇ *n* -**1.** [gen] fuga *f*; **~ (from sb/ sthg)** fuga (de alguém/algo); **to make an** OR **one's ~ (from)** fugir (de); **we had a narrow ~** escapamos por um triz -**2.** [leakage] escapamento *m* -**3.** COMPUT tecla *f* Esc. ◇ *vt* -**1.** [gen] fugir de -**2.** [death, injury] escapar a -**3.** [subj: fact, name] escapar. ◇ *vi* -**1.** [from person, place, situation]: **to ~ (from sb/sthg)** fugir (de alguém/algo) -**2.** [from danger] escapar -**3.** [leak] vazar.

escapism [ɪ'skeɪpɪzm] *n (U)* escapismo *m.*

escort [*n* 'eskɔːt, *vb* ɪ'skɔːt] ◇ *n* -**1.** [guard] escolta *f*; **under ~** sob escolta -**2.** [companion] acompanhante *mf.* ◇ *vt* [accompany] acompanhar.

Eskimo ['eskɪməʊ] (*pl* -**s**) *n* -**1.** [person] esquimó *mf.*

espadrille [,espə'drɪl] *n* alpargata *f.*

especially [ɪ'speʃəlɪ] *adv* -**1.** [in particular, specifically] especialmente -**2.** [more than usually] excepcionalmente.

espionage [,espɪə'nɑːʒ] *n (U)* espionagem *f.*

esplanade [,esplə'neɪd] *n* esplanada *f.*

Esquire [ɪ'skwaɪə] *n*: **James Smith, ~** Sr. James Smith.

essay ['eseɪ] *n* -**1.** SCH & UNIV trabalho *m* -**2.** LITERATURE ensaio *m.*

essence ['esns] *n* essência *f*; **in ~** em essência.

essential [ɪ'senʃl] *adj* essencial; **~ (to** OR **for sthg)** essencial (para algo).

➡ **essentials** *npl* -**1.** [basic commodities] o essencial -**2.** [most important elements] fundamentos *mpl*, elementos *mpl* essenciais.

essentially [ɪ'senʃəlɪ] *adv* [basically] essencialmente, basicamente.

essential oil *n* óleo *m* essencial.

establish [ɪ'stæblɪʃ] *vt* -**1.** [create, found] criar, estabelecer -**2.** [initiate]: **to ~ contact with sb** estabelecer contato com alguém -**3.** [ascertain] provar -**4.** [cause to be accepted] firmar.

establishment [ɪ'stæblɪʃmənt] n -**1.** (U) [creation, foundation] fundação f, criação f -**2.** [shop, business] estabelecimento m.

➡ **Establishment** n [status quo]: **the Establishment** a classe governante.

estate [ɪ'steɪt] n -**1.** [land, property] propriedade f -**2.** : **housing** ~ loteamento m -**3.** : **industrial** ~ zona f industrial -**4.** JUR [inheritance] herança f.

estate agency n UK agência f imobiliária.

estate agent n UK corretor m, -ra f de imóveis; ~'s agência f imobiliária.

estate car n UK van f, perua f.

esteem [ɪ'sti:m] ◇ n estima f. ◇ vt [respect] estimar.

esthetic etc. US = aesthetic etc.

estimate [n 'estɪmət, vb 'estɪmeɪt] ◇ n -**1.** [calculation, reckoning] cálculo m, estimativa f -**2.** COMM orçamento m. ◇ vt calcular, estimar.

estimation [,estɪ'meɪʃn] n -**1.** [opinion] opinião f -**2.** [calculation] cálculo m, estimativa f.

Estonia [e'stəʊnɪə] n Estônia f.

estranged [ɪ'streɪndʒd] adj separado(da); **his** ~ **son** o filho com o qual ele não fala.

estuary ['estjʊərɪ] (pl -ies) n estuário m.

e-tailer ['i:teɪləʳ] n varejista mf eletrônico(ca), e-tailer mf.

etc. (abbr of et cetera) etc.

etching ['etʃɪŋ] n gravura f de água-forte.

eternal [ɪ'tɜ:nl] adj -**1.** [gen] eterno(na) -**2.** [truth, value] absoluto(ta).

eternity [ɪ'tɜ:nətɪ] n (U) eternidade f.

ethic ['eθɪk] n ética f.

➡ **ethics** ◇ n (U) [study] ética f. ◇ npl [morals] moral f.

ethical ['eθɪkl] adj [morally right] ético(ca).

Ethiopia [,i:θɪ'əʊpɪə] n Etiópia f.

ethnic ['eθnɪk] adj -**1.** [traditions, groups, conflict] étnico(ca) -**2.** [clothes, food] folclórico(ca).

ethnic cleansing [-'klensɪŋ] n limpeza f étnica.

ethos ['i:θɒs] n sistema m de valores.

etiquette ['etɪket] n etiqueta f.

ETV (abbr of Educational Television) n rede norte-americana de televisão especializada em programas culturais e educacionais.

EU (abbr of European Union) n UE f.

eulogy ['ju:lədʒɪ] (pl -ies) n fml elogio m.

euphemism ['ju:fəmɪzm] n eufemismo m.

euphoria [ju:'fɔ:rɪə] n euforia f.

euro ['jʊərəʊ] n euro m.

Eurocheque ['jʊərəʊ,tʃek] n eurocheque m.

Euro MP n membro m do Parlamento Europeu.

Europe ['jʊərəp] n Europa f.

European [,jʊərə'pi:ən] ◇ adj europeu(péia). ◇ n europeu m, -péia f.

European Central Bank n: **the** ~ o Banco Central Europeu.

European Community n: **the** ~ a Comunidade Européia.

European Monetary System n: **the** ~ o Sistema Monetário Europeu.

European Parliament n: **the** ~ o Parlamento Europeu.

European Union n: **the** ~ a União Européia.

Eurosceptic ['ʊərəʊ,skeptɪk] ◇ adj eurocético(ca). ◇ n eurocético m, -ca f.

Eurostar ['ʊərəʊstɑ:ʳ] n Eurostar m, trem de alta velocidade que vai da Inglaterra à França passando sob o Canal da Mancha.

euthanasia [,ju:θə'neɪzjə] n eutanásia f.

evacuate [ɪ'vækjʊeɪt] vt evacuar.

evade [ɪ'veɪd] vt -**1.** [pursuers, capture] fugir a -**2.** [issue, question] fugir de -**3.** [subj: love, success] escapar de.

evaluate [ɪ'væljʊeɪt] vt avaliar.

evaporate [ɪ'væpəreɪt] vi -**1.** [liquid] evaporar -**2.** fig [feeling] evaporar-se, dissipar-se.

evaporated milk [ɪ'væpəreɪtɪd-] n tipo de leite condensado por evaporação que não contém açúcar.

evasion [ɪ'veɪʒn] n -**1.** (U) [of responsibility, payment etc.] evasão f -**2.** [lie] evasiva f.

evasive [ɪ'veɪsɪv] adj -**1.** [to avoid question, subject] evasivo(va) -**2.** [to avoid being hit]: **to take** ~ **action** tomar uma ação defensiva.

eve [i:v] n [day before] véspera f.

even ['i:vn] ◇ adj -**1.** [regular] regular -**2.** [calm] equilibrado(da) -**3.** [flat, level] plano(na) -**4.** [equal] igual; **to get** ~ **with sb** ficar quite com alguém -**5.** : **number** número par. ◇ adv -**1.** [for emphasis] mesmo; ~ **I** mesmo eu; ~ **now** mesmo agora; ~ **then** [at that time] mesmo então; [in spite of that] mesmo assim -**2.** [in comparisons] ainda -**3.** [indeed] até.

➡ **even if** conj mesmo se.

➡ **even so** adv [in spite of that] mesmo assim.

➡ **even though** conj ainda que.

➡ **even out** ◇ vt sep nivelar. ◇ vi nivelar-se.

evening ['i:vnɪŋ] n -1. [end of day - from 5 pm until 8pm] tardinha f; **good** ~ **boa tarde**; **in the** ~ à tarde; [- from 8 pm onwards] noite f; **good** ~ **boa noite**; **in the** ~ à noite, ao anoitecer -2. [event, entertainment] noite f.
➡ **evenings** adv US à noite.

evening class n aula f noturna.

evening dress n -1. (U) [formal clothes] traje m a rigor -2. [woman's garment] vestido m de gala.

event [ɪ'vent] n -1. [happening] acontecimento m; **social** ~ evento m social -2. SPORT evento m -3. [case] caso m; **in the** ~ **of** em caso de; **in the** ~ **that the train is cancelled** na eventualidade de o trem ser cancelado.
➡ **in any event** adv [all the same] em todo o caso.
➡ **in the event** adv UK na realidade.

eventful [ɪ'ventfʊl] adj movimentado(-da), agitado(da).

eventual [ɪ'ventʃʊəl] adj final.

eventuality [ɪ,ventʃʊ'ælətɪ] (pl -ies) n eventualidade f.

eventually [ɪ'ventʃʊəlɪ] adv finalmente, no fim.

ever ['evər] adv -1. [already, at some time] já, alguma vez; **have you** ~ **been to Scotland?** você já/alguma vez foi para a Escócia?; **the worst film I've** ~ **seen** o pior filme que eu já vi -2. [with negative-gen] nunca; **no one** ~ **calls these days** ninguém nunca telefona por esses dias; **hardly** ~ quase nunca; [- emphatic] jamais; **don't** ~ **speak to me like that!** jamais fale comigo desse jeito -3. [all the time] sempre; **as** ~ como sempre; **for** ~ para sempre -4. [for emphasis]: **why** ~ **did you do that?** por que cargas d'água você fez isso?; **how** ~ **did he get back?** como será que ele voltou?; ~ **so kind** tão gentil; ~ **such a mess** tamanha bagunça.
➡ **ever since** ⬦ adv desde então. ⬦ conj desde que. ⬦ prep desde.

evergreen ['evəgri:n] ⬦ adj sempre-verde. ⬦ n sempre-verde m.

everlasting [,evə'lɑ:stɪŋ] adj [lasting forever] eterno(na).

every ['evrɪ] adj -1. [each] cada -2. [to express frequency]: ~ **three hours** a cada três horas; ~ **day** cada dia.
➡ **every now and then, every so often** adv de vez em quando.
➡ **every other** adj [every alternate]: ~ **other day** dia sim, dia não; ~ **other week** cada duas semanas.
➡ **every which way** adv US para todos os lados.

everybody ['evrɪ,bɒdɪ] pron = everyone.

everyday ['evrɪdeɪ] adj diário(ria).

everyone ['evrɪwʌn] pron todo mundo, todos mpl -das fpl.

everyplace adv US = everywhere.

everything ['evrɪθɪŋ] pron tudo.

everywhere ['evrɪweər], **everyplace** US ['evrɪ,pleɪs] adv para todo o lado; [with verbs of motion] para todo o lado; ~ **you go it's the same** onde quer que se vá é o mesmo.

evict [ɪ'vɪkt] vt: **to** ~ **sb (from)** despejar alguém (de).

evidence ['evɪdəns] n -1. [proof] evidência f -2. JUR prova f; **to give** ~ prestar depoimento.

evident ['evɪdənt] adj evidente.

evidently ['evɪdəntlɪ] adv evidentemente.

evil ['i:vl] ⬦ adj [morally bad] mau(má). ⬦ n -1. (U) [wicked behaviour] maldade f -2. [wicked thing] mal m.

evoke [ɪ'vəʊk] vt -1. [call up, summon] chamar -2. [elicit, provoke] evocar.

evolution [,i:və'lu:ʃn] n evolução f.

evolve [ɪ'vɒlv] ⬦ vt [develop] desenvolver. ⬦ vi BIOL: **to** ~ **(into/from)** evoluir (para/de) -2. [develop] desenvolver-se.

ewe [ju:] n ovelha f.

ex- [eks] prefix ex-.

exacerbate [ɪg'zæsəbeɪt] vt exacerbar.

exact [ɪg'zækt] ⬦ adj [precise] exato(ta); **to be** ~ para ser exato(ta). ⬦ vt: **to** ~ **sthg (from sb)** exigir algo (de alguém).

exacting [ɪg'zæktɪŋ] adj [demanding, rigorous] exigente.

exactly [ɪg'zæktlɪ] ⬦ adv [precisely] exatamente; **not** ~ [not really] não exatamente. ⬦ excl exatamente!

exaggerate [ɪg'zædʒəreɪt] ⬦ vt exagerar. ⬦ vi exagerar.

exaggeration [ɪg,zædʒə'reɪʃn] n exagero m.

exalted [ɪg'zɔ:ltɪd] adj [important] sublime.

exam [ɪg'zæm] (abbr of **examination**) n -1. SCH prova f; **to take** OR **sit an** ~ fazer uma prova. -2. MED US exame m.

examination [ɪg,zæmɪ'neɪʃn] n -1. [gen] exame m -2. [inspection] investigação f -3. [consideration] análise f -4. JUR [of witness, suspect] interrogatório m.

examine [ɪg'zæmɪn] vt -1. [gen] examinar -2. [consider] estudar -3. JUR interrogar.

examiner [ɪg'zæmɪnər] n examinador m, -ra f.

example [ɪg'zɑːmpl] n exemplo m; **for ~** por exemplo.

exasperate [ɪg'zæspəreɪt] vt exasperar.

exasperation [ɪg,zæspə'reɪʃn] n (U) exasperação f.

excavate ['ekskəveɪt] vt escavar.

exceed [ɪk'siːd] vt **-1.** [be bigger than] exceder **-2.** [go beyond, go over - limit] ultrapassar; [- expectations] superar.

exceedingly [ɪk'siːdɪŋlɪ] adv extremamente.

excel [ɪk'sel] (pt & pp **-led**, cont **-ling**) <> vi: **to ~ (in** OR **at sthg)** sobressair-se (em algo). <> vt: **to ~ o.s.** UK superar-se.

excellence ['eksələns] n (U) excelência f.

excellent ['eksələnt] <> adj excelente. <> excl excelente!

except [ɪk'sept] <> prep exceto. <> conj exceto. <> vt: **to ~ sb (from sthg)** excluir alguém (de algo).
~ except for <> prep com exceção de. <> conj exceto.

excepting [ɪk'septɪŋ] prep & conj = except.

exception [ɪk'sepʃn] n **-1.** [exclusion] exceção f; **~ to sthg** exceção a algo; **with the ~ of** com a exceção de **-2.** [offence]: **to take ~ to sthg** ofender-se com algo.

exceptional [ɪk'sepʃənl] adj [unusually clever, talented] excepcional.

excerpt ['eksɜːpt] n: **~ (from sthg)** excerto m (de algo).

excess [ɪk'ses, before nouns 'ekses] <> adj excessivo(va). <> n excesso m.

excess baggage n excesso m de bagagem.

excess fare n UK sobretaxa f.

excessive [ɪk'sesɪv] adj excessivo(va).

exchange [ɪks'tʃeɪndʒ] <> n **-1.** (U) [act of swapping] troca f, intercâmbio m; **in ~** em troca; **in ~ for** em troca de **-2.** [swap] troca f **-3.** FIN: **stock ~** bolsa f (de valores) **-4.** FIN: **(foreign) ~** câmbio m, divisas fpl **-5.** TELEC: **(telephone) ~** central f telefônica **-6.** [educational visit] intercâmbio m. <> vt [swap] trocar; **to ~ sthg for sthg** trocar algo por algo; **to ~ sthg with sb** trocar algo com alguém.

exchange rate n FIN taxa f de câmbio.

Exchequer [ɪks'tʃekəʳ] n UK: **the ~** o Ministério da Fazenda britânico.

excise ['eksaɪz] n (U) imposto m; **Customs and Excise** ≃ a Receita Federal.

excite [ɪk'saɪt] vt **-1.** [person] entusiasmar **-2.** [nerves, heart] agitar **-3.** [interest, suspicion] despertar.

excited [ɪk'saɪtɪd] adj **-1.** [enthused] entusiasmado(da) **-2.** [agitated] agitado(-da).

excitement [ɪk'saɪtmənt] n (U) [state - enthusiasm] entusiasmo m; [- agitation] agitação f.

exciting [ɪk'saɪtɪŋ] adj emocionante.

exclaim [ɪk'skleɪm] <> vt & vi exclamar.

exclamation [,eksklə'meɪʃn] n exclamação f.

exclamation mark UK, **exclamation point** US n ponto m de exclamação.

exclude [ɪk'skluːd] vt excluir; **to ~ sb/sthg (from sthg)** excluir alguém/algo (de algo).

excluding [ɪk'skluːdɪŋ] prep excluindo.

exclusive [ɪk'skluːsɪv] <> adj exclusivo(va). <> n PRESS artigo m exclusivo.
~ exclusive of prep: **~ of sales tax** imposto sobre vendas não-incluído.

excrement ['ekskrɪmənt] n fml excremento m.

excruciating [ɪk'skruːʃɪeɪtɪŋ] adj **-1.** [pain] insuportável **-2.** [emotion, performance] terrível.

excursion [ɪk'skɜːʃn] n [trip] excursão f.

excuse [n ɪk'skjuːs, vb ɪk'skjuːz] <> n **-1.** [reason, explanation] desculpa f **-2.** [justification]: **~ (for sthg)** desculpa (para algo). <> vt **-1.** desculpar; **to ~ sb for sthg/for doing sthg** desculpar alguém por algo/por fazer algo **-2.** [let off, free] dispensar; **to ~ sb from sthg** dispensar alguém de algo **-3.** [allow to leave] dar licença **-4.** phr: **~ me** [to attract attention] com licença; [forgive me] desculpe; US [sorry] perdão.

ex-directory adj UK que não consta na lista telefônica.

execute ['eksɪkjuːt] vt executar.

execution [,eksɪ'kjuːʃn] n execução f.

executioner [,eksɪ'kjuːʃnəʳ] n carrasco m, -ca f.

executive [ɪg'zekjʊtɪv] <> adj executivo(va). <> n **-1.** COMM executivo m, -va f **-2.** [of government] executivo m **-3.** [of political party] executiva f.

executive director n diretor m executivo, diretora f executiva.

executor [ɪg'zekjʊtəʳ] n [of will] testamenteiro m, -ra f.

exemplify [ɪg'zemplɪfaɪ] (pt & pp **-ied**) vt **-1.** [typify] ilustrar **-2.** [give example of] exemplificar.

exempt [ɪg'zempt] <> adj: **to be ~ (from sthg)** [tax] estar isento(ta) (de algo); [duty, rules] estar livre (de algo); [military service] estar dispensado(da) (de algo). <> vt: **to ~ sb/sthg (from**

sthg) [tax] isentar alguém/algo (de algo); [duty, rules, military service] dispensar alguém/algo (de algo).

exercise ['eksəsaɪz] ⬦ *n* exercício *m*; an ~ in sthg um exercício de algo. ⬦ *vt* -1. exercitar; to ~ sb's mind exercitar a mente de alguém -2. *fml* [use, practise] exercer. ⬦ *vi* exercitar-se.

exercise book *n* -1. [for notes] caderno *m (de anotações)* -2. [published book] livro *m* de exercícios.

exert [ɪg'zɜːt] *vt* exercer; to ~ o.s. esforçar-se.

exertion [ɪg'zɜːʃn] *n* -1. [physical effort] esforço *m* -2. *fig* [committed effort] empenho *m* -3. (U) [of power, influence] exercício *m*.

exhale [eks'heɪl] ⬦ *vt* exalar. ⬦ *vi* exalar.

exhaust [ɪg'zɔːst] ⬦ *n* -1. [fumes] descarga *f*, escapamento *m* -2. [tube]: ~ (pipe) [cano *m* de) descarga *f*. ⬦ *vt* -1. [person, patience, subject] esgotar -2. [supply, money] usar.

exhausted [ɪg'zɔːstɪd] *adj* exausto(ta).

exhausting [ɪg'zɔːstɪŋ] *adj* exaustivo(-va).

exhaustion [ɪg'zɔːstʃn] *n* (U) exaustão *f*.

exhaustive [ɪg'zɔːstɪv] *adj* exaustivo(-va).

exhibit [ɪg'zɪbɪt] ⬦ *n* -1. *ART* objeto *m* exposto -2. *JUR* [piece of evidence] prova *f*, evidência *f*. ⬦ *vt* -1. *fml* [demonstrate] demonstrar -2. *ART* expor.

exhibition [,eksɪ'bɪʃn] *n* -1. *ART* exposição *f* -2. [demonstration] demonstração *f* -3. *phr*: to make an ~ of o.s. *UK* fazer um escândalo.

exhilarating [ɪg'zɪləreɪtɪŋ] *adj* estimulante.

exile ['eksaɪl] ⬦ *n* -1. [condition] exílio *m*; in ~ no exílio -2. [person] exilado *m*, -da *f*. ⬦ *vt*: to ~ sb (from/to) exilar alguém (de/para).

exist [ɪg'zɪst] *vi* existir.

existence [ɪg'zɪstəns] *n* (U) existência *f*; to come into ~ entrar em vigor; to be in ~ existir.

existing [ɪg'zɪstɪŋ] *adj* existente, atual.

exit ['eksɪt] ⬦ *n* saída *f*. ⬦ *vi* sair.

exodus ['eksədəs] *n* êxodo *m*.

exonerate [ɪg'zɒnəreɪt] *vt*: to ~ sb (from sthg) exonerar alguém (de algo).

exorbitant [ɪg'zɔːbɪtənt] *adj* exorbitante.

exotic [ɪg'zɒtɪk] *adj* exótico(ca).

expand [ɪk'spænd] ⬦ *vt* -1. [gen] expandir -2. [department, area] ampliar -3. [influence] aumentar. ⬦ *vi* -1. [gen]

expandir-se -2. [influence] aumentar -3. *PHYS* dilatar.

➤ **expand (up)on** *vt fus* entrar em detalhes.

expanse [ɪk'spæns] *n* vastidão *f*.

expansion [ɪk'spænʃn] *n* -1. (U) [gen] expansão *f* -2. [of department, area] ampliação *f* -3. [of influence] aumento *m* -4. *PHYS* dilatação *f*.

expect [ɪk'spekt] ⬦ *vt* -1. [gen] esperar; to ~ to do sthg esperar fazer algo; to ~ sb to do sthg esperar que alguém faça algo; to ~ sthg from sb esperar algo de alguém -2. [suppose]: to ~ (that) supor que; I ~ so suponho que sim; what do you ~? e o que você queria? ⬦ *vi* [be pregnant]: to be ~ing estar esperando bebê.

expectancy *n* ⬡ life expectancy.

expectant [ɪk'spektənt] *adj* [crowd, person] ansioso(sa).

expectant mother *n* gestante *f*.

expectation [,ekspek'teɪʃn] *n* -1. [hope] expectativa *f* -2. [belief] convicção *f*; against *OR* contrary to all ~ (s) ao contrário de todas as expectativas.

expedient [ɪk'spiːdjənt] *fml* ⬦ *adj* pertinente, conveniente. ⬦ *n* expediente *m*.

expedition [,ekspɪ'dɪʃn] *n* -1. [organized journey] expedição *f* -2. [short trip, outing] passeio *m*.

expel [ɪk'spel] (*pt* & *pp* -led, *cont* -ling) *vt* [from school, country]: to ~ sb (from) expulsar alguém (de).

expend [ɪk'spend] *vt*: to ~ sthg (on sthg) gastar algo (com/em algo).

expendable [ɪk'spendəbl] *adj* -1. [person] dispensável -2. [resources] consumível.

expenditure [ɪk'spendɪtʃəʳ] *n* -1. [of money] gastos *mpl* -2. [of energy, resource] gasto *m*.

expense [ɪk'spens] *n* -1. [amount spent] despesa *f*, gasto *m* -2. (U) [cost] custo *m*; at the ~ of em detrimento de, à custa de; at his/her own ~ [financial] do seu próprio bolso; at sb's ~ *fig* [in order to mock] às custas de alguém.

➤ **expenses** *npl* *COMM* despesas *fpl*.

expense account *n* relatório *m* de despesas.

expensive [ɪk'spensɪv] *adj* [financially] caro(ra).

experience [ɪk'spɪərɪəns] ⬦ *n* experiência *f*. ⬦ *vt* experimentar.

experienced [ɪk'spɪərɪənst] *adj* [well-practised] experiente; ~ at *OR* in sthg experiente em algo.

experiment [ɪk'sperɪmənt] ⬦ *n* -1. *SCIENCE* experimento *m*; to carry out an

~ conduzir um experimento **- 2.** [exploratory attempt] tentativa *f.* ⬥ *vi* SCIENCE fazer experiências; **to ~ with sthg** fazer experiências com algo.

expert ['ekspɜ:t] ⬥ *adj* especializado(da), perito(ta). ⬥ *n* especialista *mf*, perito *m*, -ta *f.*

expertise [,ekspɜ:'ti:z] *n (U)* excelência *f*, perícia *f.*

expire [ɪk'spaɪə'] *vi* [run out] vencer.

expiry [ɪk'spaɪərɪ] *n (U)* vencimento *m.*

explain [ɪk'spleɪn] ⬥ *vt* **- 1.** [describe, clarify] explicar; **to ~ sthg to sb** explicar algo a alguém **- 2.** [account for] justificar. ⬥ *vi* explicar-se; **to ~ to sb (about sthg)** justificar-se (para alguém) sobre algo.

explanation [,eksplə'neɪʃn] *n* **- 1.** (U) [act of explaining] explicação *f* **- 2.** [account]: ~ **(for sthg)** justificativa *f* (por algo) **- 3.** [description, clarification] explanação *f.*

explicit [ɪk'splɪsɪt] *adj* [clearly expressed] explícito(ta).

explode [ɪk'spləʊd] ⬥ *vt* [set off] explodir. ⬥ *vi* **- 1.** [blow up] explodir **- 2.** *fig* [with feeling] explodir.

exploit [*n* 'eksplɔɪt, *vb* ɪk'splɔɪt] ⬥ *n* façanha *f.* ⬥ *vt* explorar.

exploitation [,eksplɔɪ'teɪʃn] *n (U)* [of workers, resources] exploração *f.*

exploration [,eksplə'reɪʃn] *n* [of space, countries] exploração *f.*

explore [ɪk'splɔ:'] ⬥ *vt* explorar. ⬥ *vi* explorar.

explorer [ɪk'splɔ:rə'] *n* explorador *m*, -ra *f.*

explosion [ɪk'spləʊʒn] *n* explosão *f.*

explosive [ɪk'spləʊsɪv] ⬥ *adj* **- 1.** [gen] explosivo(va) **- 2.** [controversial] controverso(sa). ⬥ *n* explosivo *m.*

exponent [ɪk'spəʊnənt] *n* [supporter] defensor *m*, -ra *f.*

export [*n & comp* 'ekspɔ:t, *vb* ɪk'spɔ:t] ⬥ *n (U)* exportação *f.* ⬥ *comp* de exportação. ⬥ *vt* exportar.

exporter [ek'spɔ:tə'] *n* exportador *m*, -ra *f.*

expose [ɪk'spəʊz] *vt* **- 1.** [gen] expor; **to be ~d to sthg** estar exposto(ta) a algo **- 2.** [unmask] desmascarar.

exposed [ɪk'spəʊzd] *adj* [unsheltered] desprotegido(da).

exposure [ɪk'spəʊʒə'] *n* **- 1.** [gen] exposição *f* **- 2.** MED [hypothermia]: **to die from ~** morrer de frio **- 3.** [PHOT - time] exposição *f*; [- photograph] pose *f.*

exposure meter *n* fotômetro *m.*

expound [ɪk'spaʊnd] *fml* ⬥ *vt* expor. ⬥ *vi*: **to ~ on sthg** explanar sobre algo.

express [ɪk'spres] ⬥ *adj* **- 1.** *UK* [urgent letter, parcel] expresso(sa) **- 2.** [transport] expresso(sa) **- 3.** *fml* [specific] explícito(-ta). ⬥ *adv* por correio expresso. ⬥ *n*: ~ **(train)** (trem *m*) expresso *m.* ⬥ *vt* [show, state] expressar, exprimir.

expression [ɪk'spreʃn] *n* expressão *f.*

expressive [ɪk'spresɪv] *adj* [full of feeling] expressivo(va).

expressly [ɪk'spreslɪ] *adv* [specifically] expressamente.

expressway [ɪk'spreweɪ] *n* via *f* expressa.

exquisite [ɪk'skwɪzɪt] *adj* **- 1.** [beautiful] fino(na), requintado(da) **- 2.** [very pleasing] delicado(da).

ext., extn. (*abbr of* extension) extens.

extend [ɪk'stend] ⬥ *vt* **- 1.** [make bigger] ampliar **- 2.** [make longer - in space] estender; [- in time] prolongar **- 3.** [postpone] prorrogar **- 4.** [make more wide-ranging] estender **- 5.** *fml* [stretch out] esticar **- 6.** [offer - welcome, help] estender; [- credit] conceder. ⬥ *vi* **- 1.** [stretch, reach] estender-se **- 2.** [rule, law]: **to ~ to sb/ sthg** estender-se a alguém/algo.

extension [ɪk'stenʃn] *n* **- 1.** [gen] aumento *m* **- 2.** [longer time limit] prorrogação *f* **- 3.** [development, growth] expansão *f* **- 4.** TELEC & ELEC extensão *f.*

extension cable, extension lead *n* ELEC extensão *f.*

extensive [ɪk'stensɪv] *adj* **- 1.** [in amount] amplo(pla) **- 2.** [in area, range] extenso(-sa).

extensively [ɪk'stensɪvlɪ] *adv* **- 1.** [in amount] amplamente **- 2.** [in range] extensivamente.

extent [ɪk'stent] *n* **- 1.** [gen] extensão *f* **- 2.** [degree]: **to what ~ ...?** até que ponto ...?; **to the ~ that** [in that, in so far as] na medida em que; [to the point where] até o ponto em que; **to a certain ~** até um certo ponto; **to a large** OR **great ~** em grande parte; **to some ~** até certo ponto.

extenuating circumstances [ɪk'stenj-ʊeɪtɪŋ-] *npl* circunstâncias *fpl* atenuantes.

exterior [ɪk'stɪərɪə'] ⬥ *adj* externo(-na). ⬥ *n* exterior *m.*

exterminate [ɪk'stɜ:mɪneɪt] *vt* exterminar.

external [ɪk'stɜ:nl] *adj* **- 1.** [outside] externo(na) **- 2.** [foreign] exterior(ra).

extinct [ɪk'stɪŋkt] *adj* extinto(ta).

extinguish [ɪk'stɪŋwɪʃ] *vt* *fml* [put out] apagar.

extinguisher [ɪk'stɪŋwɪʃə'] *n*: **(fire) ~** extintor *m* (de incêndio).

extol (*pt* & *pp* **-led**, *cont* **-ling**), **extoll** *US* [ɪk'stəʊl] *vt* enaltecer.

extort [ɪk'stɔːt] *vt*: **to ~ sthg from sb** extorquir algo de alguém.

extortionate [ɪk'stɔːʃnət] *adj* extorsivo(va).

extra ['ekstrə] <> *adj* [additional] extra; **~ charge** sobrecarga *f*. <> *n* **-1.** [addition] acessório *m* **-2.** CINEMA & THEATRE extra *mf*. <> *adv* extra.
➡ **extras** *npl* [in price] extras *mpl*.

extra- ['ekstrə] *prefix* extra.

extract [*n* 'ekstrækt, *vb* ɪk'strækt] <> *n* **-1.** [excerpt] trecho *m* **-2.** CHEM & CULIN extrato *m*. <> *vt* **-1.** [take out]: **to ~ sthg (from sthg)** extrair algo (de algo) **-2.** [obtain, elicit]: **to ~ sthg (from sb)** arrancar algo (de alguém).

extradite ['ekstrədaɪt] *vt*: **to ~ sb (from/to)** extraditar alguém (de/para).

extramarital [ˌekstrə'mærɪtl] *adj* extraconjugal.

extramural [ˌekstrə'mjʊərəl] *adj* UNIV de extensão universitária.

extraordinary [ɪk'strɔːdnrɪ] *adj* **-1.** [special] extraordinário(ria) **-2.** [strange] esquisito(ta).

extraordinary general meeting *n* assembléia *f* geral extraordinária.

extravagance [ɪk'strævəgəns] *n* **-1.** [luxury] extravagância *f* **-2.** (U) [excessive spending] gasto *m* excessivo.

extravagant [ɪk'strævəgənt] *adj* **-1.** [excessive] extravagante **-2.** [elaborate] caprichado(da).

extreme [ɪk'striːm] <> *adj* extremo(ma). <> *n* [furthest limit] extremo *m*.

extremely [ɪk'striːmlɪ] *adv* [very] extremamente.

extreme sports *npl* esportes *mpl* radicais.

extremist [ɪk'striːmɪst] <> *adj* extremista. <> *n* extremista *mf*.

extricate ['ekstrɪkeɪt] *vt*: **to ~ sthg (from)** soltar algo (de); **to ~ o.s. (from)** livrar-se (de).

extrovert ['ekstrəvɜːt] <> *adj* extrovertido(da). <> *n* extrovertido *m*, -da *f*.

exuberance [ɪg'zjuːbərəns] *n* (U) exuberância *f*.

exultant [ɪg'zʌltənt] *adj* exultante.

eye [aɪ] (*cont* **eyeing** OR **eying**) <> *n* **-1.** [gen & ANAT] olho *m*; **to cast** OR **run one's ~ over sthg** passar os olhos em algo; **to catch sb's ~** chamar a atenção de alguém; **to have one's ~ on sb/sthg** ter os olhos sobre alguém/algo; **to keep one's ~s open (for), to keep an ~ out (for)** ficar de olhos abertos (em); **to keep an ~ on sb/sthg** dar uma olhada em alguém/algo **-2.** [of needle] buraco *m*. <> *vt* olhar.

eyeball ['aɪbɔːl] *n* globo *m* ocular.

eyebath ['aɪbɑːθ] *n* copinho *m* para lavar os olhos.

eyebrow ['aɪbraʊ] *n* sobrancelha *f*.

eyebrow pencil *n* lápis *m inv* de sobrancelha.

eyedrops ['aɪdrɒps] *npl* colírio *m*.

eyeglasses ['aɪglɑːsɪz] *npl* US óculos *m inv*.

eyelash ['aɪlæʃ] *n* cílio *m*.

eyelid ['aɪlɪd] *n* pálpebra *f*.

eyeliner ['aɪˌlaɪnəʳ] *n* delineador *m (para os olhos)*.

eye-opener *n inf* revelação *f*.

eye shadow *n* sombra *f (para os olhos)*.

eyesight ['aɪsaɪt] *n* visão *f*.

eyesore ['aɪsɔːʳ] *n* horror *m*, monstruosidade *f*.

eyestrain ['aɪstreɪn] *n* vista *f* cansada.

eyewitness [ˌaɪ'wɪtnɪs] *n* testemunha *mf* ocular.

e-zine ['iːziːn] *n* revista *f* eletrônica.

F

f (*pl* **f's** OR **fs**), **F** (*pl* **F's** OR **Fs**) [ef] *n* [letter] f, F *m*.
➡ **F** *n* **-1.** MUS fá *m* **-2.** (*abbr of* **Fahrenheit**) F.

fable ['feɪbl] *n* [traditional story] fábula *f*.

fabric ['fæbrɪk] *n* **-1.** [cloth] tecido *m* **-2.** *fig* [of building, society] estrutura *f*.

fabrication [ˌfæbrɪ'keɪʃn] *n* **-1.** [lie, lying] invenção *f* **-2.** (U) [manufacture] fabricação *f*.

fabulous ['fæbjʊləs] *adj* fabuloso(sa).

facade [fə'sɑːd] *n* fachada *f*.

face [feɪs] <> *n* **-1.** [of person] rosto *m*, cara *f*; **~ to ~** cara a cara; **to say sthg to sb's ~** dizer algo na cara de alguém **-2.** [expression] expressão *f*; **to make** OR **pull a ~** fazer careta **-3.** [of building] fachada *f* **-4.** [of coin] lado *m* **-5.** [of clock, watch] mostrador *m* **-6.** [appearance, nature] cara *f* **-7.** [surface] face *f*; **on the ~ of it** à primeira vista **-8.** [respect]: **to lose ~** perder a reputação; **to save**

~ **livrar a cara.** <> *vt* **-1.** [gen] encarar - **2.** [look on to, point towards] dar para - **3.** [confront] enfrentar.

➤ **face down** *adv* [person] de bruços; [object] para baixo.

➤ **face up** *adv* [person] de costas; [object] para cima.

➤ **in the face of** *prep* [confronted with] diante de.

➤ **face up to** *vt fus* enfrentar.

facecloth ['feɪsklɒθ] *n UK* toalhinha *f* de rosto.

face cream *n* (*U*) creme *m* para o rosto.

facelift *n* **-1.** [on face] lifting *m* - **2.** *fig*: to give sthg a ~ dar uma cara nova para algo.

face powder *n* (*U*) pó-de-arroz *m*.

face-saving [-ˈseɪvɪŋ] *adj* para salvar as aparências.

facet [ˈfæsɪt] *n* faceta *f*.

facetious [fəˈsiːʃəs] *adj* brincalhão(lhona).

face value *n* [of coin, stamp] valor *m* nominal; **to take sthg at** ~ *fig* levar algo ao pé da letra.

facility [fəˈsɪlətɪ] (*pl* -ies) *n* [feature] recurso *m*.

➤ **facilities** *npl* **-1.** [amenities] instalações *fpl* - **2.** [services] serviços *mpl*.

facing [ˈfeɪsɪŋ] *adj* [opposite] oposto(ta).

facsimile [fækˈsɪmɪlɪ] *n* fac-símile *m*; **a** ~ **edition** uma edição fac-similar.

fact [fækt] *n* fato *m*; **to know sthg for a** ~ ter certeza de algo.

➤ **in fact** <> *conj* na verdade. <> *adv* na verdade.

fact of life *n* fato *m* consumado.

➤ **facts of life** *npl euphemism*: to tell sb (about) the ~s of life contar a alguém como nascem as crianças.

factor [ˈfæktər] *n* fator *m*.

factory [ˈfæktərɪ] (*pl* -ies) *n* fábrica *f*.

fact sheet *n UK* informativo *m*.

factual [ˈfæktʃʊəl] *adj* real, concreto(ta).

faculty [ˈfækltɪ] (*pl* -ies) *n* **-1.** [gen] faculdade *f* - **2.** *US* [in college]: **the** ~ o corpo docente.

fad [fæd] *n* mania *f*, capricho *m*.

fade [feɪd] <> *vt* [remove colour] desbotar. <> *vi* **-1.** [colour] desbotar - **2.** [sound] diminuir - **3.** [hope, memory, feeling] esvaecer.

faeces *UK*, **feces** *US* [ˈfiːsiːz] *npl* fezes *fpl*.

fag [fæg] *n* **-1.** *UK inf* [cigarette] cigarro *m* - **2.** *US inf pej* [homosexual] bicha *f*.

Fahrenheit [ˈfærənhaɪt] *adj* Fahrenheit *inv*.

fail [feɪl] <> *vt* **-1.** [not succeed in]: **to** ~ **to do sthg** não conseguir fazer algo - **2.** [SCH & UNIV - exam, test] não passar em; [- candidate] rodar - **3.** [neglect]: **to** ~ **to do sthg** deixar de fazer algo. <> *vi* **-1.** [not succeed] não conseguir - **2.** *SCH & UNIV* rodar - **3.** [stop functioning] falhar - **4.** [weaken] enfraquecer.

failing [ˈfeɪlɪŋ] <> *n* [weakness] fraqueza *f*. <> *prep* na falta de; **or,** ~ **that,** ... ou, caso contrário, ...

failure [ˈfeɪljər] *n* **-1.** fracasso *m* - **2.** [breakdown, malfunction] falha *f* - **3.** *MED*: **heart** ~ falência *f* do coração.

faint [feɪnt] <> *adj* **-1.** [slight] vago(ga) - **2.** [half-hearted] desmaiado(da) - **3.** [dizzy] fraco(ca). <> *vi* desmaiar.

fair [feər] <> *adj* **-1.** [just] justo(ta); **it's not** ~! não é justo! - **2.** [quite large] considerável - **3.** [quite good] bom (boa) - **4.** [hair, person] loiro(ra) - **5.** [skin, complexion] claro(ra) - **6.** [weather] claro(ra), bom (boa). <> *n* **-1.** *UK* [funfair] parque *m* de diversões - **2.** [trade fair] feira *f*. <> *adv* [fairly] limpo.

➤ **fair enough** *excl UK inf* tudo bem.

fair-haired [-ˈheəd] *adj* [person] loiro(ra).

fairly [ˈfeəlɪ] *adv* **-1.** [rather] bastante - **2.** [justly] justamente.

fairness [ˈfeənɪs] *n* (*U*) [justness] imparcialidade *f*, justiça *f*.

fairy [ˈfeərɪ] (*pl* -ies) *n* [imaginary creature] fada *f*.

fairy tale *n* conto *m* de fadas.

faith [feɪθ] *n* **-1.** (*U*) [trust] fé *f* - **2.** [religion] crença *f*, fé *f*.

faithful [ˈfeɪθfʊl] *adj* fiel.

faithfully [ˈfeɪθfʊlɪ] *adv* [loyally] fielmente; **Yours** ~ *UK* [in letter] atenciosamente, cordialmente.

fake [feɪk] <> *adj* falso(sa). <> *n* **-1.** [object, painting] falsificação *f* - **2.** [person] falsário *m*, -ria *f*. <> *vt* **-1.** [falsify] falsificar - **2.** [simulate] fingir. <> *vi* [pretend] fingir.

falcon [ˈfɔːlkən] *n* falcão *m*.

Falkland Islands [ˈfɔːklənd-], **Falklands** [ˈfɔːkləndz] *npl*: **the** ~ as (Ilhas) Malvinas.

fall [fɔːl] (*pt* fell, *pp* fallen) <> *vi* **-1.** [gen] cair; **to** ~ **flat** [joke] não surtir efeito - **2.** [become] ficar; **to** ~ **in love** apaixonar-se - **3.** [occur]: **to** ~ **on** cair em. <> *n* **-1.** [accident] tombo *m*, caída *f* - **2.** [of snow] nevasca *f* - **3.** [from power] queda *f* - **4.** [decrease] queda *f*; ~ **in sthg** queda de algo - **5.** *US* [autumn] outono *m*.

➤ **falls** *npl* [waterfall] cataratas *fpl*.

➤ **fall apart** *vi* **-1.** [book, chair] cair aos

pedaços -**2.** *fig* [country, person] desmoronar.

→ **fall back** *vi* -**1.** [retreat, recede] retroceder -**2.** [lag behind] recuar.

→ **fall back on** *vt fus* [resort to] recorrer
a.

→ **fall behind** *vi* -**1.** [in race] ficar para
trás -**2.** [with rent, with work] atrasar-se.

→ **fall for** *vt fus* -**1.** *inf* [fall in love with]
ficar caído(da) por -**2.** [be deceived by]
deixar-se enganar por.

→ **fall in** *vi* -**1.** [roof, ceiling] desabar -**2.**
MIL entrar em forma.

→ **fall off** *vi* -**1.** [drop off] desprender-
se -**2.** [diminish] diminuir.

→ **fall out** *vi* -**1.** [drop out] cair -**2.** [quar-
rel]: **to ~ out (with sb)** brigar (com
alguém) -**3.** *MIL* sair de forma.

→ **fall over** ◇ *vt fus* tropeçar em. ◇
vi [lose balance] cair.

→ **fall through** *vi* [plan, deal] fracassar.

fallacy [ˈfæləsɪ] (*pl* -ies) *n* [misconception]
falácia *f*.

fallen [ˈfɔːln] *pp* ▷ **fall**.

fallible [ˈfæləbl] *adj* falível.

fallout [ˈfɔːlaʊt] *n (U)* [radiation] chuva *f*
radioativa.

fallout shelter *n* abrigo *m* antinuclear.

fallow [ˈfæləʊ] *adj* [land] alqueivado(da);
to lie ~ ficar sem cultivo.

false [fɔːls] *adj* -**1.** [gen] falso(sa) -**2.** [arti-
ficial] postiço(ça).

false alarm *n* alarme *m* falso.

falsely [ˈfɔːlslɪ] *adv* -**1.** [wrongly] erroneamente -**2.** [insincerely] falsamente.

false teeth *npl* dentadura *f* postiça.

falsify [ˈfɔːlsɪfaɪ] (*pt & pp* -ied) *vt* [facts,
accounts] falsificar.

falter [ˈfɔːltəʳ] *vi* -**1.** [gen] vacilar -**2.** [hes-
itate, lose confidence] hesitar.

fame [feɪm] *n (U)* fama *f*.

familiar [fəˈmɪljəʳ] *adj* -**1.** [known] familiar -**2.** [conversant]: **~ with sthg** fami-
liarizado(da) com algo -**3.** *pej* [overly
informal - person] que se dá muitas
liberdades; [- tone, manner] amigável
em excesso.

familiarity [fə͵mɪlɪˈærətɪ] *n* [with book,
rules, subject]: **~ with sthg** conhecimento *m* de algo.

familiarize, -ise [fəˈmɪljəraɪz] *vt*: **to ~
o.s. with sthg** familiarizar-se com algo;
to ~ sb with sthg familiarizar alguém
com algo.

family [ˈfæmlɪ] (*pl* -ies) *n* família *f*.

family credit *n (U) UK* auxílio-família
m.

family doctor *n* médico *m*, -ca *f*
de família.

family planning *n (U)* planejamento
m familiar.

famine [ˈfæmɪn] *n* fome *f* extrema e
coletiva.

famished [ˈfæmɪʃt] *adj inf* [very hungry]
faminto(ta), morto(ta) de fome.

famous [ˈfeɪməs] *adj* famoso(sa); **~ for**
sthg famoso(sa) por algo.

famously [ˈfeɪməslɪ] *adv dated*: **to get on**
OR **along ~with sb** ficar íntimo(ma) de
alguém.

fan [fæn] (*pt & pp* -ned, *cont* -ning) ◇
n -**1.** [of paper, silk] leque *m* -**2.** [electric or
mechanical] ventilador *m* -**3.** [enthusiast]
fã *mf*, admirador *m*, -ra *f*. ◇ *vt* -**1.**
[cool] abanar.

→ **fan out** *vi* [army, search party] espalhar-se.

fanatic [fəˈnætɪk] *n* fanático *m*, -ca *f*.

fan belt *n* correia *f* do ventilador.

fanciful [ˈfænsɪfʊl] *adj* -**1.** [odd] estapa-
fúrdio(dia) -**2.** [elaborate] extravagante.

fancy [ˈfænsɪ] (*compar* -ier, *superl* -iest,
pl -ies, *pt & pp* -ied) ◇ *adj* -**1.** [elabo-
rate] caprichado(da) -**2.** [expensive] extravagante. ◇ *n* -**1.** [liking] gosto *m*; **to
take a ~** to sb/sthg ter simpatia por
alguém/algo; **to take sb's ~** cair nas
graças de alguém -**2.** [whim] capricho
m. ◇ *vt* -**1.** *inf* [want] querer; **I ~ going
to the cinema** me agrada a idéia de ir
ao cinema -**2.** [like] agradar-se de.

fancy dress *n (U)* fantasia *f*.

fancy-dress party *n* festa *f* à fantasia.

fanfare [ˈfænfeəʳ] *n MUS* fanfarra *f*.

fang [fæŋ] *n* -**1.** [of snake] presa *f* -**2.** [of
carnivore] colmilho *m*.

fan heater *n* aquecedor *m* de ventoi-
nha.

fanny [ˈfænɪ] *n US inf* [backside] bunda *f*.

fantasize, -ise [ˈfæntəsaɪz] *vi* fantasiar;
to ~ about sthg/about doing sthg fantasiar sobre algo/sobre fazer algo.

fantastic [fænˈtæstɪk] *adj inf* [gen] fan-
tástico(ca).

fantasy [ˈfæntəsɪ] (*pl* -ies) *n* fantasia *f*.

fao (*abbr of* for the attention of) a/c.

far [fɑːʳ] (*compar* **farther** *OR* **further**,
superl **farthest** *OR* **furthest**) ◇ *adv*
-**1.** [in distance] longe; **how ~ is it?** a
que distância fica?; **how ~ have you
come?** até onde você veio?; **is it ~?** é
longe?; **~ away** *OR* **off** muito longe; **~
and wide** por todo o lugar; **as ~ as até;
we walked as ~ as the river** caminhamos
até o rio -**2.** [in time]: **~ away** *OR* **off**
muito longe -**3.** [in degree or extent]
muito; **how ~ have you got with your novel?** até onde você já foi no romance?;
as ~ as I know até onde eu sei; **as ~ as**

fault

I'm concerned no que me diz respeito; as ~ as possible até onde é possível; ~ and away, by ~ de longe; ~ from it pelo contrário. <> *adj* [distant, extreme] extremo(ma).

faraway ['fɑːrəweɪ] *adj* -1. [distant] distante -2. [dreamy] ausente.

farce [fɑːs] *n* farsa *f*.

farcical ['fɑːsɪkl] *adj* ridículo(la).

fare [feəʳ] *n* -1. [payment, rate] tarifa *f* -2. [price of ticket] preço *m* -3. [person] passageiro *m*, -ra *f* -4. *fml* [food] comida *f*.

Far East *n*: the ~ o Extremo Oriente.

farewell [,feə'wel] <> *n* despedida *f*, adeus *m*. <> *excl literary* adeus!

farm [fɑːm] <> *n* fazenda *f*. <> *vt* cultivar.

farmer ['fɑːməʳ] *n* fazendeiro *m*, -ra *f*.

farmhand ['fɑːmhænd] *n* peão *m*, -oa *f*.

farmhouse ['fɑːmhaʊs, *pl* -haʊzɪz] *n* granja *f*, quinta *f*.

farming ['fɑːmɪŋ] *n (U)* -1. [activity] agricultura *f* -2. [of animals] criação *f* -3. [of crops] cultivo *m*.

farmland ['fɑːmlænd] *n (U)* terra *f* cultivada.

farmstead ['fɑːmsted] *n US* granja *f*.

farmyard ['fɑːmjɑːd] *n* terreiro *m (de fazenda)*.

far-reaching [-'riːtʃɪŋ] *adj* -1. [implications] de longo alcance -2. [changes] abrangente.

far-sighted *adj* -1. [person] prudente; [plan] perspicaz -2. *US* [longsighted] hipermetrope.

fart [fɑːt] *vulg* <> *n* [wind] peido *m*. <> *vi* peidar.

farther ['fɑːðəʳ] *compar* ▷ far.

farthest ['fɑːðəst] *superl* ▷ far.

fascia ['feɪʃə] *n* [of mobile phone] capa *f* frontal.

fascinate ['fæsɪneɪt] *vt* fascinar.

fascinating ['fæsɪneɪtɪŋ] *adj* fascinante.

fascination [,fæsɪ'neɪʃn] *n (U)* fascinação *f*.

fascism ['fæʃɪzm] *n (U)* fascismo *m*.

fashion ['fæʃn] <> *n* -1. [current style] moda *f*; ~ **model** modelo *mf* (de passarela); **in/out of** ~ [vogue] na/fora de moda -2. [manner] maneira *f*; **after a** ~ até certo ponto. <> *vt fml* [shape] moldar.

fashionable ['fæʃnəbl] *adj* [in vogue] da moda.

fashion show *n* desfile *m* de modas.

fast [fɑːst] <> *adj* -1. [rapid] rápido(da) -2. [clock, watch] adiantado(da) -3. [dye] permanente. <> *adv* -1. [rapidly] depressa; **how** ~ **does this car go?** a que

velocidade este carro chega?; **I need help** ~ preciso de ajuda rápido -2. [firmly] firmemente; **to hold** ~ **to sthg** [grip firmly] segurar firme algo; *fig* [stick to] manter-se firme em algo; **to be** ~ **asleep** dormir profundamente. <> *n* jejum *m*. <> *vi* jejuar.

fasten ['fɑːsn] <> *vt* -1. [close - jacket, bag] fechar; [- seat belt] apertar -2. [attach]: **to** ~ **sthg to sthg** fixar algo em algo. <> *vi*: **to** ~ **on to sb/sthg** agarrar-se a alguém/algo.

fastener ['fɑːsnəʳ] *n* -1. [dress, bag] fecho *m* -2. [necklace] presilha *f* -3. [door] fechadura *f*.

fastening ['fɑːsnɪŋ] *n* -1. [gen] fechadura *f* -2. [on window] trinco *m*.

fast food *n (U)* fast-food *m*.

fastidious [fə'stɪdɪəs] *adj* [fussy] meticuloso(sa).

fat [fæt] (*compar* -ter, *superl* -test) <> *adj* -1. [person, animal, face, legs, meat] gordo(da); **to get** ~ engordar -2. [volume, file, wallet] pesado(da) -3. [*FIN* - profit, fee] avultado(da); [- cheque, bank account] gordo(da). <> *n* -1. *(U) ANAT* gordura *f* -2. *(U)* [in food - raw] banha *f*; [- cooked] sebo *m*; [- in cooking, diet] gordura *f*.

fatal ['feɪtl] *adj* -1. [ruinous] fatal -2. [mortal] mortal.

fatality [fə'tælətɪ] (*pl* -ies) *n* [accident victim] fatalidade *f*; [fatalism] fatalismo *m*.

fate [feɪt] *n* -1. *(U)* [destiny] destino *m*; **to tempt** ~ brincar com a sorte -2. [of person, thing] sina *f*.

fateful ['feɪtfʊl] *adj* [decisive] fatídico(ca).

father ['fɑːðəʳ] *n lit, fig* pai *m*.

Father Christmas *n UK* Papai *m* Noel.

father-in-law (*pl* **father-in-laws** OR **fathers-in-law**) *n* sogro *m*.

fatherly ['fɑːðəlɪ] *adj* paternal.

fathom ['fæðəm] <> *n* braça *f*. <> *vt*: **to** ~ **sthg (out)** desvendar algo; **to** ~ **sb (out)** compreender alguém.

fatigue [fə'tiːg] *n (U)* fadiga *f*.

fatten ['fætn] *vt* engordar.

fattening ['fætnɪŋ] *adj* que engorda; **to be very** ~ engordar muito.

fatty ['fætɪ] (*compar* -ier, *superl* -iest, *pl* -ies) <> *adj* -1. [food] gorduroso(sa) -2. *BIOL* [tissue] adiposo(sa). <> *n inf pej* gorducho *m*, -cha *f*.

fatuous ['fætjʊəs] *adj* fátuo(tua).

fatwa ['fætwə] *n* mandado *m* religioso islâmico.

faucet ['fɔːsɪt] *n US* torneira *f*.

fault [fɔːlt] <> *n* -1. [responsibility] culpa *f* -2. [defect] defeito *m* -3. [mistake, imperfection] falha *f*; **to find** ~ **with sb/sthg**

criticar algo/alguém; **to be at ~** equivocar-se **- 4.** GEOL falha f **- 5.** [in tennis] falta f. ⬦ vt: **to ~ sb (on sthg)** criticar alguém (em algo).

faultless ['fɔːltlɪs] adj impecável.

faulty ['fɔːltɪ] (compar **-ier**, superl **-iest**) adj **- 1.** [machine, system] defeituoso(sa) **- 2.** [reasoning, logic] falho(lha).

fauna ['fɔːnə] n fauna f.

favour UK, **favor** US ['feɪvə^r] ⬦ n **- 1.** (U) [approval] aprovação f; **in sb's ~** em favor de alguém; **to be in ~ (with sb)** contar com o apoio de alguém; **to be out of ~ (with sb)** não contar com o apoio (de alguém); **to curry ~ with sb** puxar o saco de alguém **- 2.** [kind act] favor m; **to do sb a ~** fazer um favor a alguém **- 3.** (U) [favouritism] favoritismo m. ⬦ vt [gen] favorecer.

➡ **in favour** adv [in agreement] a favor.

➡ **in favour of** prep **- 1.** [in preference to] em favor de **- 2.** [in agreement with]: **to be in ~ of sthg/of doing sthg** estar a favor de algo/de fazer algo.

favourable UK, **favorable** US ['feɪvrəbl] adj favorável.

favourite UK, **favorite** US ['feɪvrɪt] ⬦ adj [preferred] favorito(ta). ⬦ n favorito(ta).

favouritism UK, **favoritism** US ['feɪvrɪtɪzm] n (U) favoritismo m.

fawn [fɔːn] ⬦ adj castanho(nha) claro(ra). ⬦ n [animal] cervato m. ⬦ vi: **to ~ on sb** bajular alguém.

fax [fæks] ⬦ n fax m. ⬦ vt **- 1.** [send fax to] enviar um fax para **- 2.** [send by fax] enviar por fax.

fax machine n (máquina f de) fax m.

FBI (abbr of **Federal Bureau of Investigation**) n FBI m.

FC (abbr of **Football Club**) n FC.

fear [fɪə^r] ⬦ n **- 1.** [gen] medo m **- 2.** [risk] risco m, perigo m; **for ~ of** por medo de. ⬦ vt **- 1.** [be afraid of] ter medo de, temer **- 2.** [anticipate] temer, recear; **to ~ (that)** recear que.

fearful ['fɪəfʊl] adj **- 1.** fml [frightened] temeroso(sa); **~ of sthg/of doing sthg** temeroso(sa) de algo/de fazer algo **- 2.** [frightening] terrível, pavoroso(sa).

fearless ['fɪəlɪs] adj sem medo, destemido(da).

feasible ['fiːzəbl] adj [plan] viável.

feast [fiːst] ⬦ n [meal] banquete m. ⬦ vi: **to ~ on** OR **off sthg** banquetear-se com algo.

feat [fiːt] n façanha f.

feather ['feðə^r] n pena f.

feature ['fiːtʃə^r] ⬦ n **- 1.** [characteristic - of house] característica f; [- of machine]

recurso m; [- of style, landscape] aspecto m; [- of face, personality] traço m **- 2.** [article] reportagem f especial **- 3.** RADIO & TV [programme] especial m **- 4.** CINEMA longa-metragem m. ⬦ vt [subj: film, exhibition] ter como atração principal; **a film featuring Juliette Binoche** um filme estrelando Juliette Binoche. ⬦ vi: **to ~ (in sthg)** [appear, figure] figurar (em algo).

feature film n longa-metragem m.

February ['februərɪ] n fevereiro m; see also **September**.

feces npl US = faeces.

fed [fed] pt & pp ⊳ feed.

federal ['fedrəl] adj federal.

federation [ˌfedə'reɪʃn] n **- 1.** [country] federação f **- 2.** [association] liga f.

fed up adj farto(ta), cheio(a); **to be ~ with sb/sthg** estar cheio de alguém/algo.

fee [fiː] n [payment - school] (taxa f de) matrícula f; [- doctor] preço m da consulta; [- lawyer] honorários mpl; [- monthly membership] mensalidade f; [- annual membership] anuidade f; [- entrance] taxa f de admissão.

feeble ['fiːbl] adj **- 1.** [weak] fraco(ca) **- 2.** [lacking conviction] débil.

feed [fiːd] (pt & pp fed) ⬦ vt **- 1.** [give food to] alimentar **- 2.** [put, insert]: **to ~ sthg into sthg** inserir algo em algo. ⬦ vi [take food] alimentar-se; **to ~ on** OR **off sthg** alimentar-se de algo. ⬦ n **- 1.** [meal] comida f **- 2.** (U) [animal food] ração f.

feedback ['fiːdbæk] n (U) **- 1.** [reaction] reação f **- 2.** ELEC feedback m.

feeding bottle ['fiːdɪŋ-] n UK mamadeira f.

feel [fiːl] (pt & pp felt) ⬦ vt **- 1.** [touch] tocar **- 2.** [believe, think] achar, acreditar; **to ~ (that)** achar que **- 3.** [experience, be aware of] sentir; **to ~ o.s. doing sthg** sentir-se fazendo algo **- 4.** phr: **I'm not ~ing myself today** não estou me sentindo bem hoje. ⬦ vi **- 1.** [have sensation, emotion] sentir-se; **to ~ like sthg/like doing sthg** [be in mood for] ter vontade de algo/de fazer algo **- 2.** [seem] parecer **- 3.** [by touch]: **to ~ for sthg** procurar algo com as mãos. ⬦ n **- 1.** [sensation, touch] sensação f **- 2.** [atmosphere] clima m.

feeler ['fiːlə^r] n [of insect, snail] antena f.

feeling ['fiːlɪŋ] n **- 1.** [emotion] sensação f **- 2.** [physical - of nausea, vertigo etc.] sensação f; [- sensation] sensibilidade f **- 3.** [awareness, impression] impressão f **- 4.** [understanding] disposição f.

➡ **feelings** npl sentimentos mpl; **to**

fiddle

hurt sb's ~s magoar alguém, magoar os sentimentos de alguém.
feet [fiːt] *pl* ⊳ **foot**.
feign [feɪn] *vt fml* fingir.
fell [fel] ⟨⟩ *pt* ⊳ **fall**. ⟨⟩ *vt* **-1.** [tree] cortar **-2.** [person] derrubar.
➡ **fells** *npl GEOGR* charneca *f*.
fellow ['feləʊ] ⟨⟩ *adj* companheiro *m*, -ra *f*. ⟨⟩ *n* **-1.** *dated* [man] cara *mf* **-2.** [comrade, peer] camarada *mf* **-3.** [of society or college] membro *m* honorário.
fellowship ['feləʊʃɪp] *n* **-1.** (U) [comradeship] companheirismo *m* **-2.** [organization] sociedade *f* **-3.** [in university - grant] bolsa *f* de pesquisa; [- post] pesquisador *m*, -ra *f*.
felony ['felənɪ] (*pl* **-ies**) *n JUR* delito *m* grave.
felt [felt] ⟨⟩ *pt & pp* ⊳ **feel**. ⟨⟩ *n* (U) [textile] feltro *m*.
felt-tip pen *n* pincel *m* atômico.
female ['fiːmeɪl] ⟨⟩ *adj* **-1.** [gen] feminino(na) **-2.** [plant] fêmeo(mea). ⟨⟩ *n* **-1.** [female animal] fêmea *f* **-2.** *inf pej* [woman] fêmea *f*.
feminine ['femɪnɪn] ⟨⟩ *adj* feminino(na). ⟨⟩ *n GRAMM* feminino *m*.
feminist ['femɪnɪst] *n* feminista.
fence [fens] ⟨⟩ *n* [barrier] cerca *f*; **to sit on the ~** *fig* ficar em cima do muro. ⟨⟩ *vt* cercar.
fencing ['fensɪŋ] *n* (U) **-1.** *SPORT* esgrima *f* **-2.** [fences] cerca *f* **-3.** [material] material *m* para fazer cerca.
fend [fend] *vi*: **to ~ for o.s.** saber se virar.
➡ **fend off** *vt sep* rechaçar.
fender ['fendəʳ] *n* **-1.** [round fireplace] guarda-fogo *m* **-2.** [on boat] proteção *f* **-3.** *US* [on car] pára-lama *f*.
ferment [*n* 'fɜːment, *vb* fə'ment] ⟨⟩ *n* (U) [unrest] grande agitação *f*, polvorosa *f*. ⟨⟩ *vi* [change chemically] fermentar.
fern [fɜːn] *n* samambaia *f*.
ferocious [fə'rəʊʃəs] *adj* feroz.
ferret ['ferɪt] *n* [animal] furão *m*.
➡ **ferret about, ferret around** *vi inf* vasculhar.
ferris wheel ['ferɪs-] *n esp US* roda-gigante *f*.
ferry ['ferɪ] (*pl* **-ies**, *pt & pp* **-ied**) ⟨⟩ *n* balsa *f*. ⟨⟩ *vt* transportar.
ferryboat ['ferɪbəʊt] *n* = **ferry**.
fertile ['fɜːtaɪl] *adj* fértil.
fertilizer ['fɜːtɪlaɪzəʳ] *n* fertilizante *m*.
fervent ['fɜːvənt] *adj* **-1.** [admirer, believer] fervoroso(sa) **-2.** [belief, desire, hope] ardente.
fester ['festəʳ] *vi* [wound] inflamar, inflamar-se.

festival ['festəvl] *n* **-1.** [series of organized events] festival *m* **-2.** [holiday] feriado *m*, dia *m* festivo.
festive ['festɪv] *adj* festivo(va).
festive season *n*: **the ~** a época do Natal.
festivities [fes'tɪvətɪz] *npl* festividades *fpl*.
festoon [fe'stuːn] *vt* enfeitar; **to be ~ed with sthg** estar enfeitado(da) com algo.
fetch [fetʃ] *vt* **-1.** [go and get] ir buscar **-2.** [sell for] alcançar.
fetching ['fetʃɪŋ] *adj* atraente.
fete, fête [feɪt] ⟨⟩ *n* festa *f* beneficente. ⟨⟩ *vt* festejar (em honra de alguém).
fetid ['fetɪd] *adj* fétido(da).
fetish ['fetɪʃ] *n* **-1.** [sexual obsession] fetiche *m* **-2.** [mania] mania *f* **-3.** [object] amuleto *m*.
fetus ['fiːtəs] *n* = **foetus**.
feud [fjuːd] ⟨⟩ *n* contenda *f*. ⟨⟩ *vi* brigar.
feudal ['fjuːdl] *adj* feudal.
fever ['fiːvəʳ] *n* **-1.** *MED* febre *f* **-2.** *fig* [frenzy] frenesi *m*.
feverish ['fiːvərɪʃ] *adj* **-1.** *MED* febril **-2.** [frenzied] frenético(ca).
few [fjuː] ⟨⟩ *adj* [not many] pouco(ca); **a ~** alguns(mas); **a ~ more** mais alguns(mas); **quite a ~**, **a good ~** bastante; **~ and far between** pouquíssimos(mas). ⟨⟩ *pron* poucos *mpl*, -cas *fpl*; **a ~** poucos(cas); **quite a ~**, **a good ~** bastante.
fewer ['fjuːəʳ] ⟨⟩ *adj* menos ⟨⟩ *pron* menos.
fewest ['fjuːəst] *adj* o menos possível.
fiancé [fɪ'ɒnseɪ] *n* noivo *m*.
fiancée [fɪ'ɒnseɪ] *n* noiva *f*.
fiasco [fɪ'æskəʊ] (*UK pl* **-s**, *US pl* **-s** *OR* **-es**) *n* fiasco *m*.
fib [fɪb] (*pt & pp* **-bed**, *cont* **-bing**) *inf* ⟨⟩ *n* lorota *f*. ⟨⟩ *vi* contar lorotas.
fibre *UK*, **fiber** *US* ['faɪbəʳ] *n* **-1.** (U) [material, substance] fibra *f* **-2.** [thread] filamento *m* **-3.** (U) [strength] força *f*.
fibreglass *UK*, **fiberglass** *US* ['faɪbəglɑːs] *n* (U) fibra *f* de vidro.
fibre optics *UK*, **fiber optics** *US* *n* fibra *f* óptica.
fickle ['fɪkl] *adj* inconstante, volúvel.
fiction ['fɪkʃn] *n* **-1.** (U) [literature] ficção *f* **-2.** [fabrication, lie] invenção *f*.
fictional ['fɪkʃənl] *adj* **-1.** [literary] ficcional **-2.** [invented] imaginário(ria).
fictitious [fɪk'tɪʃəs] *adj* [false] fictício(cia).
fiddle ['fɪdl] ⟨⟩ *n* **-1.** [violin] rabeca *f* **-2.** *UK inf* [fraud] embuste *m*. ⟨⟩ *vt UK*

inf falsificar. <> *vi* **-1.** [fidget]: **to ~ (about** OR **around)** enrolar; **to ~ (about** OR **around) with sthg** mexer em algo **- 2.** [waste time]: **to ~ about** OR **around** perder tempo.

fiddly ['fɪdlɪ] (*compar* **-ier,** *superl* **-iest**) *adj UK inf* trabalhoso(sa).

fidget ['fɪdʒɪt] *vi* estar irrequieto(ta), mover-se sem parar.

field [fi:ld] <> *n* **-1.** [gen] campo *m* **- 2.** [of knowledge] área *f.* <> *vt* [avoid answering] responder.

field day *n* [for study, sport] dia *m* de atividades externas; **to have a ~** *fig* fazer a festa.

field glasses *npl* binóculos *mpl.*

field marshal *n* marechal-de-campo *m.*

field trip *n* viagem *f* de estudos.

fieldwork ['fi:ldwɜ:k] *n* (*U*) pesquisa *f* de campo.

fiend [fi:nd] *n* **-1.** [cruel person] demônio *m* **-2.** *inf* [fanatic] fanático *m*, -ca *f.*

fiendish ['fi:ndɪʃ] *adj* **-1.** [evil] diabólico(ca) **-2.** *inf* [very difficult] cabeludo(-da).

fierce [fɪəs] *adj* **-1.** [aggressive, ferocious] feroz **- 2.** [wild, uncontrolled] violento(ta) **- 3.** [intense - competition, battle] árduo(a); [- heat] intenso(sa); [- criticism] ferrenho(nha).

fiery ['faɪərɪ] (*compar* **-ier,** *superl* **-iest**) *adj* **-1.** [burning] ardente **-2.** [volatile] explosivo(va).

fifteen [fɪf'ti:n] *num* quinze; *see also* **six.**

fifth [fɪfθ] *num* quinto, quinta; *see also* **sixth.**

Fifth Amendment *n*: **the ~** a Quinta Emenda, *emenda constitucional americana que estabelece direitos civis aos criminosos.*

fifty ['fɪftɪ] (*pl* **-ies**) *num* cinqüenta; *see also* **sixty.**

fifty-fifty <> *adj*: **to have a ~ chance** ter cinqüenta por cento de chance. <> *adv*: **to split sthg ~** dividir algo meio a meio.

fig [fɪg] *n* figo *m.*

fight [faɪt] (*pt & pp* **fought**) <> *n* **-1.** [physical] briga *f*, luta *f*; **to have a ~ (with sb)** ter uma briga (com alguém); **to put up a ~** desencadear uma luta **- 2.** *fig* [battle, struggle] luta *f*, batalha *f* **- 3.** [argument] discussão *f*; **to have a ~ (with sb)** ter uma discussão (com alguém). <> *vt* **-1.** [gen] lutar (com), combater; [physically] brigar com **- 2.** [combat, struggle against] lutar contra. <> *vi* **-1.** [physically, in war] lutar **- 2.** *fig*

[battle, struggle]: **to ~ for/against sthg** lutar por/contra algo **- 3.** [argue] discutir sobre; **to ~ about** OR **over sthg** discutir sobre algo.

➡ **fight back** <> *vt fus* segurar. <> *vi* revidar.

fighter ['faɪtə'] *n* **-1.** [plane] caça *m* **- 2.** [soldier] guerreiro *m*, -ra *f* **- 3.** [combative person] lutador *m*, -ra *f.*

fighting ['faɪtɪŋ] *n* (*U*) [in war, punch-up] luta *f.*

figment ['fɪgmənt] *n*: **a ~ of sb's imagination** um produto da imaginação de alguém.

figurative ['fɪgərətɪv] *adj* [language, art] figurado(da).

figure [*UK* 'fɪgə', *US* 'fɪgjər] <> *n* **-1.** [statistic] índice *m* **- 2.** [symbol of number] número *m*; **in single/double ~s** em valores até dez/acima de dez **- 3.** [human shape, outline] silhueta *f* **- 4.** [diagram, representative personality] figura *f* **- 5.** [famous person] personalidade *f* **- 6.** [aesthetic shape of body] forma *f.* <> *vt esp US* [suppose] supor. <> *vi* [feature] figurar.

➡ **figure out** *vt sep* compreender.

figurehead ['fɪgəhed] *n* **-1.** [on ship] carranca *f* de proa **- 2.** [leader without real power] testa-de-ferro *m.*

figure of speech *n* figura *f* de linguagem.

Fiji ['fi:dʒi:] *n* Fiji.

file [faɪl] <> *n* **-1.** [folder] pasta *f* **- 2.** [report] relatório *m*; **on ~, on the ~s** em arquivo, arquivado(da) **- 3.** COMPUT arquivo *m* **- 4.** [tool] lixa *f* **- 5.** [line]: **in single ~** em fila indiana. <> *vt* **-1.** [put in folder] pôr na pasta **- 2.** JUR dar entrada em **- 3.** [shape, smooth] lixar. <> *vi* **-1.** [walk in single file] andar em fila única **- 2.** JUR: **to ~ for divorce** dar entrada no divórcio.

file clerk *n US* = **filing clerk.**

filet *n US* = **fillet.**

filing cabinet ['faɪlɪŋ-] *n* fichário *m.*

fill [fɪl] <> *vt* **-1.** [make full - container] encher; [- room, street] ocupar; **to ~ sthg (with sthg)** encher algo com algo **- 2.** [fulfill] preencher **- 3.** [tooth] obturar. <> *vi* encher-se.

➡ **fill in** <> *vt sep* **-1.** [form] preencher **- 2.** [hole] tapar **- 3.** [inform]: **to ~ sb in (on sthg)** informar alguém (sobre algo). <> *vi* [substitute]: **to ~ in (for sb)** substituir alguém.

➡ **fill out** *vt sep* [complete] completar. <> *vi* [get fatter] engordar.

➡ **fill up** <> *vt sep* encher. <> *vi* lotar.

fillet *UK*, **filet** *US* ['fɪlɪt] *n* -1. [piece of meat] filé *m* -2. *(U)* [type of meat] lombo *m*.

fillet steak *n* filé *m*.

filling ['fɪlɪŋ] ◇ *adj* [satisfying] que satisfaz. ◇ *n* -1. [in tooth] obturação *f* -2. [in cake, sandwich] recheio *m*.

filling station *n* posto *m* de gasolina.

film [fɪlm] ◇ *n* -1. [cinema, TV, photographic] filme *m* -2. *(U)* [footage] cobertura *f* -3. [layer] película *f*. ◇ *vt* filmar. ◇ *vi* filmar.

film star *n* astro *m* de cinema, estrela *f* de cinema.

Filofax® ['faɪləʊfæks] *n* agenda *f* (de folhas descartáveis).

filter ['fɪltə'] ◇ *n* filtro *m*. ◇ *vt* -1. [water, petrol] filtrar -2. [coffee] coar.

filter coffee *n* café *m* coado.

filter lane *n* *UK* faixa *f* de conversão (à direita ou esquerda).

filter-tipped [-'tɪpt] *adj* com filtro.

filth [fɪlθ] *n (U)* -1. [dirt] sujeira *f* -2. [obscenity] obscenidade *f*.

filthy ['fɪlθɪ] (compar **-ier**, superl **-iest**) *adj* -1. [very dirty] imundo(da) -2. [obscene] obsceno(na).

fin [fɪn] *n* -1. [on fish] barbatana *f* -2. *US* [for swimmer] nadadeira *f*.

final ['faɪnl] ◇ *adj* -1. [last in order] último(ma) -2. [at end, definitive] final. ◇ *n* final *f*.

◆ **finals** *npl* *UNIV* exames *mpl* finais; **to sit one's ~s** prestar os exames finais.

finale [fɪ'nɑːlɪ] *n* final *m*.

finalize, -ise ['faɪnəlaɪz] *vt* finalizar.

finally ['faɪnəlɪ] *adv* -1. [at last] finalmente -2. [lastly] finalmente, por fim.

finance [*n* 'faɪnæns, *vb* faɪ'næns] ◇ *n* *(U)* -1. [money] financiamento *m* -2. [money management] finanças *fpl*. ◇ *vt* financiar.

◆ **finances** *npl* finanças *fpl*.

financial [fɪ'nænʃl] *adj* financeiro(ra).

find [faɪnd] (pt & pp **found**) ◇ *vt* -1. [gen] encontrar, achar -2. [realize, discover]: **to ~ (that)** descobrir que -3. *JUR*: **to be found guilty/not guilty of sthg** ser declarado(da) culpado(da)/inocente de algo. ◇ *n* descoberta *f*.

◆ **find out** ◇ *vi* descobrir. ◇ *vt fus* -1. [information] informar-se -2. [truth] desmascarar. ◇ *vt sep* [person] descobrir.

findings ['faɪndɪŋz] *npl* constatações *fpl*.

fine [faɪn] ◇ *adj* -1. [good, high-quality] excelente -2. [perfectly satisfactory] ótimo(ma) -3. [healthy] bem -4. [not rainy] bom(boa) -5. [thin, smooth] fino(na) -6.

[minute, exact] sutil. ◇ *adv* [quite well] bem. ◇ *n* multa *f*. ◇ *vt* multar.

fine arts *npl* belas-artes *fpl*.

finery ['faɪnərɪ] *n (U)* refinamento *m*.

fine-tune ['faɪntjuːn] *vt* ajustar.

finger ['fɪŋgə'] ◇ *n* dedo *m*; **to slip through one's ~s** escorrer pelos dedos. ◇ *vt* [feel] tocar com os dedos.

fingernail ['fɪŋgəneɪl] *n* unha *f* (dos dedos da mão).

fingerprint ['fɪŋgəprɪnt] *n* impressão *f* digital.

fingertip ['fɪŋgətɪp] *n* ponta *f* do dedo; **at one's ~s** ao alcance da mão.

finicky ['fɪnɪkɪ] *adj pej* [- person] meticuloso(sa); [- task] minucioso(sa).

finish ['fɪnɪʃ] ◇ *n* -1. [end] final *m* -2. [texture] acabamento *m*. ◇ *vt* -1. [conclude, complete] terminar; **to ~ doing sthg** terminar de fazer algo -2. [consume] acabar -3. [leave] terminar, acabar. ◇ *vi* -1. [gen] terminar -2. [complete task] terminar, acabar.

◆ **finish off** *vt sep* [conclude, complete, consume] terminar.

◆ **finish up** *vi* acabar, terminar.

finishing line ['fɪnɪʃɪŋ-] *n* linha *f* de chegada.

finishing school ['fɪnɪʃɪŋ-] *n* ≃ colégio privado no qual se preparam as alunas da alta classe para entrar na sociedade.

finite ['faɪnaɪt] *adj* -1. [limited] finito(ta) -2. *GRAMM* conjugado(da).

Finland ['fɪnlənd] *n* Finlândia.

Finn [fɪn] *n* [inhabitant of Finland] finlandês *m*, -esa *f*.

Finnish ['fɪnɪʃ] ◇ *adj* [of or relating to Finland] finlandês(esa). ◇ *n* [language] finlandês *m*.

fir [fɜː'] *n* abeto *m*.

fire ['faɪə'] ◇ *n* -1. *(U)* [flames, burning] fogo *m*; **on ~** em chamas; **to catch ~** pegar fogo; **to set ~ to sthg** pôr fogo em algo -2. [for warmth, cooking] fogueira *f* -3. [blaze, conflagration] incêndio *m* -4. *UK* [heater, apparatus] aquecedor *m*, estufa *f* -5. *(U)* [shooting] fogo *m*; **to open ~ (on sb)** abrir fogo (contra alguém). ◇ *vt* -1. [shoot] disparar -2. *esp US* [dismiss] demitir, despedir. ◇ *vi*: **to ~ (on** *OR* **at)** atirar em.

fire alarm *n* alarme *m* contra incêndio.

firearm ['faɪərɑːm] *n* arma *f* de fogo.

firebomb ['faɪəbɒm] ◇ *n* bomba *f* incendiária. ◇ *vt* lançar bombas incendiárias em.

fire brigade *UK*, **fire department** *US* *n* corpo *m* de bombeiros.

fire door n porta f corta-fogo.

fire engine n carro m de bombeiros.

fire escape n escada f de incêndio.

fire extinguisher n extintor m de incêndio.

fireguard ['faɪəɡɑːd] n guarda-fogo m.

firelighter ['faɪəlaɪtə'] n acendedor m de fogo.

fireman ['faɪəmən] (pl -men [-mən]) n bombeiro m.

fireplace ['faɪəpleɪs] n lareira f.

fireproof ['faɪəpruːf] adj à prova de fogo.

fireside ['faɪəsaɪd] n: by the ~ ao calor da lareira.

fire station n posto m de bombeiros.

firewall ['faɪəwɔːl] n COMPUT firewall m.

firewood ['faɪəwʊd] n (U) lenha f.

firework ['faɪəwɜːk] n fogo m de artifício.
  ◆ **fireworks** npl fig [outburst of anger] fogos mpl de artifício.

firing ['faɪərɪŋ] n (U) MIL tiroteio m.

firing squad n pelotão m de fuzilamento.

firm [fɜːm] ◇ adj -1. [gen] firme; to stand ~ manter-se firme -2. [definite] claro(ra) -3. [investment, rate] estável. ◇ n empresa f.

first [fɜːst] ◇ adj primeiro(ra); for the ~ time pela primeira vez; ~ thing (in the morning) à primeira hora (da manhã). ◇ adv -1. [before anyone, anything else] primeiro; ~ of all antes de mais nada, em primeiro lugar -2. [for the first time] pela primeira vez -3. [firstly, in list of points] primeiramente. ◇ n -1. [person] primeiro m, -ra f -2. [unprecedented event] acontecimento m sem precedentes -3. UK UNIV diploma m universitário -4. AUT: ~ (gear) primeira f (marcha).
  ◆ **at first** adv no princípio.
  ◆ **at first hand** adv em primeira mão.

first aid n (U) primeiros socorros mpl.

first-aid kit n kit m de primeiros socorros.

first-class adj -1. [excellent] de primeira -2. [letter, ticket] de primeira classe.

first course n entrada f.

first floor n -1. UK [above ground level] primeiro andar m -2. US [at ground level] andar m térreo.

firsthand [,fɜːst'hænd] ◇ adj de primeira mão. ◇ adv em primeira mão.

first lady n POL primeira-dama f.

firstly ['fɜːstlɪ] adv primeiramente.

first name n nome m de batismo, nome m..

first-rate adj de primeira.

firtree ['fɜːtriː] n = fir.

fish [fɪʃ] (pl inv) ◇ n peixe m. ◇ vt pescar em. ◇ vi [try to catch fish] pescar; to ~ for sthg pescar algo.

fish and chips npl UK peixe m frito com batatas fritas.

fish and chip shop n UK barraca f de peixe frito com batatas fritas.

fishbowl ['fɪʃbəʊl] n aquário m.

fishcake ['fɪʃkeɪk] n bolinho m de peixe.

fisherman ['fɪʃəmən] (pl -men [-mən]) n pescador m.

fish farm n viveiro m de peixes.

fish fingers UK, **fish sticks** US npl porções fpl de peixe empanado.

fishing ['fɪʃɪŋ] n (U) pesca f; to go ~ ir pescar.

fishing boat n barco m de pesca.

fishing line n linha f de pesca.

fishing rod n vara f de pescar.

fishmonger ['fɪʃ,mʌŋɡə'] n esp UK peixeiro m; ~'s (shop) peixaria f.

fish shop n peixaria f.

fish sticks npl US = fish fingers.

fish tank n aquário m (usado como viveiro).

fishy ['fɪʃɪ] (compar -ier, superl -iest) adj -1. [like fish] de peixe -2. fig [suspicious] duvidoso(sa).

fist [fɪst] n punho m.

fit [fɪt] (pt & pp -ted, cont -ting) ◇ adj -1. [suitable] adequado(da); to be ~ for sthg estar apto(ta) para algo; to be ~ to do sthg estar apto(ta) a fazer algo; do as you think ~ faça como você achar melhor -2. [healthy] em forma; to keep ~ manter-se em forma. ◇ n -1. [of clothes, shoes etc.] tamanho m; it's a good ~ fica bem; it's a tight ~ fica justo -2. [epileptic seizure] ataque m; to have a ~ MED ter um ataque; fig [be angry] ter um ataque (de fúria) -3. [bout - of crying, depression] crise f; [- of rage, sneezing, giggles] acesso m; in ~s and starts aos trancos e barrancos. ◇ vt -1. [be correct size for] servir -2. [place]: to ~ sthg into sthg encaixar algo em algo -3. [provide]: to ~ sthg with sthg equipar algo com algo; to have sthg ~ted instalar algo -4. [be suitable for] adequar-se. ◇ vi -1. [be correct size] servir -2. [go] encaixar -3. [into container] caber.
  ◆ **fit in** ◇ vt sep [accommodate] arranjar tempo para. ◇ vi adaptar-se; to ~ in with sb/sthg adaptar-se com alguém/algo; that ~s in with what she told me isso vem ao encontro do que ela me contou.

fitful ['fɪtfʊl] *adj* intermitente.

fitment ['fɪtmənt] *n* móvel *m* (*da casa*).

fitness ['fɪtnɪs] *n* (*U*) -1. [health] bom estado *m* físico -2. [suitability] aptidão *f*; ~ **for** sthg aptidão para algo.

fitted carpet ['fɪtəd-] *n* carpete *m*.

fitted kitchen ['fɪtəd-] *n* *UK* cozinha *f* de módulos.

fitter ['fɪtə'] *n* [mechanic] mecânico *m*, -ca *f*.

fitting ['fɪtɪŋ] <> *adj fml* apropriado(-da). <> *n* -1. [part] acessório *m* -2. [for clothing] prova *f*.
fittings *npl* acessórios *mpl*.

fitting room *n* provador *m*.

five [faɪv] *num* cinco; *see also* **six**.

fiver ['faɪvə'] *n inf* -1. *UK* [amount] cinco libras; [note] *cédula de cinco libras* -2. *US* [amount] *cinco dólares*; [note] *cédula de cinco dólares*.

fix [fɪks] <> *vt* -1. [attach, concentrate] fixar; **to** ~ **sthg to sthg** fixar algo em algo -2. [set, arrange] arranjar -3. [repair] consertar -4. *inf* [rig] manipular -5. *esp US* [food, drink] preparar. <> *n* -1. *inf* [difficult situation]: **to be in a** ~ estar em apuro -2. *drugs sl* dose *f* de entorpecente.
fix up *vt sep* -1. [provide]: **to** ~ **sb up with sthg** arranjar algo para alguém -2. [arrange] organizar, preparar.

fixation [fɪk'seɪʃn] *n* fixação *f*; ~ **on** *OR* **about sb/sthg**, ~ fixação em *OR* por alguém/algo.

fixed [fɪkst] *adj* fixado(da).

fixture ['fɪkstʃə'] *n* -1. [in building] instalação *f* -2. *fig* [permanent feature] figura *f* constante -3. [sports event] encontro *m*.

fizz [fɪz] *vi* -1. [drink] espumar -2. [firework] crepitar.

fizzle ['fɪzl] **fizzle out** *vi* -1. [firework] falhar -2. *fig* [interest] sumir.

fizzy ['fɪzɪ] (*compar* -**ier**, *superl* -**iest**) *adj* gasoso(sa).

flabbergasted ['flæbəgɑːstɪd] *adj* estarrecido(da), pasmado(da).

flabby ['flæbɪ] (*compar* -**ier**, *superl* -**iest**) *adj* flácido(da), gordo(da).

flag [flæg] (*pt* & *pp* -**ged**, *cont* -**ging**) <> *n* [banner] bandeira *f*. <> *vi* -1. [person] desanimar -2. [spirts] decair -3. [conversation] acabar.
flag down *vt sep* fazer sinal para.

flagpole ['flægpəʊl] *n* mastro *m* de bandeira.

flagrant ['fleɪgrənt] *adj* flagrante.

flagstone ['flægstəʊn] *n* laje *f*.

flair [fleə'] *n* -1. [talent] dom *m* -2. (*U*) [stylishness] habilidade *f*.

flak [flæk] *n* (*U*) -1. [gunfire] fogo *m* antiaéreo -2. *inf* [criticism] críticas *fpl*.

flake [fleɪk] <> *n* [small piece - of snow] floco *m*; [- of paint, plaster] lasca *f*; [- of skin] pedaço *m*. <> *vi* descascar.

flamboyant [flæm'bɔɪənt] *adj* -1. [person, behaviour] extravagante -2. [clothes, design] chamativo(va).

flame [fleɪm] *n* chama *f*; **in** ~**s** em chamas; **to burst into** ~**s** irromper em chamas.

flamingo [flə'mɪŋgəʊ] (*pl* -**s** *OR* -**es**) *n* flamingo *m*.

flammable ['flæməbl] *adj* inflamável.

flan [flæn] *n* torta *f*.

flank [flæŋk] <> *n* -1. [of animal] lado *m* -2. [of army] flanco *m*. <> *vt*: **to be** ~ **ed by sb/sthg** ser ladeado(da) por alguém/algo.

flannel ['flænl] *n* -1. (*U*) [fabric] flanela *f* -2. *UK* [facecloth] luva *f* de banho.

flap [flæp] (*pt* & *pp* -**ped**, *cont* -**ping**) <> *n* -1. [piece] dobra *f* -2. *inf* [state of panic]: **to get in a** ~ ficar histérico(ca). <> *vt* -1. [wings] bater -2. [arms] agitar, mexer. <> *vi* [wave - skirt, jacket] ondear, agitar-se; [- wings, bird] bater.

flapjack ['flæpdʒæk] *n* -1. *UK* [biscuit] biscoito *m* de aveia -2. *US* [pancake] panqueca *f*.

flare [fleə'] <> *n* [distress signal] sinal *m* luminoso. <> *vi* -1.: **to** ~ (**up**) [fire] chamejar; [person] enfurecer-se; [war, revolution, disease] deflagrar-se -2. [trousers, skirt] alargar-se -3. [nostrils] abrir-se.
flares *npl UK* [trousers] calças *fpl* boca-de-sino.

flash [flæʃ] <> *n* -1. [of light, colour] brilho *m* -2. *PHOT* flash *m* -3. [sudden moment] instante *m*; **in a** ~ num instante. <> *vt* -1. [light, torch] brilhar (*numa direção específica*) -2. [look, smile]: **she flashed a smile at him** ela sorriu rapidamente para ele -3. [show on screen] projetar -4. [show briefly] mostrar rapidamente. <> *vi* -1. [gen] reluzir -2. [move fast] irromper; **it** ~**ed through his mind that ...** imediatamente lhe ocorreu que ...; **to** ~ **past** passar feito um raio.

flashback ['flæʃbæk] *n* flashback *m*.

flashbulb ['flæʃbʌlb] *n* (lâmpada *f* de) flash *m*.

flashgun ['flæʃgʌn] *n* disparador *m* de flash.

flashlight ['flæʃlaɪt] *n* [torch] lanterna *f* (elétrica).

flashy ['flæʃɪ] (*compar* -**ier**, *superl* -**iest**) *adj inf* ostentoso(sa).

flask [flɑ:sk] *n* -1. [to keep drinks hot] garrafa *f* térmica -2. [used in chemistry] frasco *m* -3. [hip flask] cantil *m*.

flat [flæt] (*compar* -ter, *superl* -test) ◇ *adj* -1. [level] plano(na); ~ **feet** pés *mpl* chatos -2. [shoes] sem salto -3. [punctured] vazio(zia) -4. [categorical] categórico(ca) -5. [business, trade] estagnado(da) -6. [monotonous - voice] monótono(na); [- performance, writing] uniforme -7. [MUS - lower than correct note] abaixo do tom; [- lower than stated note] abemolado(da) -8. COMM [fare, fee] único(ca) -9. [no longer fizzy - beer] choco(ca); [- lemonade] que passou do ponto -10. [battery] descarregado(da). ◇ *adv* -1. [level] horizontalmente -2. [exactly] precisamente. ◇ *n* -1. UK [apartment] flat *m* -2. MUS bemol *m*.

➡ **flat out** *adv* a todo vapor.

flatly ['flætlɪ] *adv* -1. [absolutely] categoricamente -2. [dully] de forma monótona.

flatmate ['flætmeɪt] *n* UK colega *mf* que divide o apartamento com outro.

flat rate *n* preço *m* único.

flatscreen television, flatscreen TV ['flæt,skri:n] *n* tv *f* de tela plana.

flatten ['flætn] *vt* -1. [make flat - steel, bumps] aplanar; [- wrinkles] esticar; [- paper] alisar -2. [building] demolir.

➡ **flatten out** ◇ *vi* aplanar-se, nivelar-se. ◇ *vt sep* [wrinkles] esticar; [lumps, bumps] aplanar.

flatter ['flætəʳ] *vt* -1. [compliment] adular, bajular; I'm ~ **ed** sinto-me lisonjeado(da) -2. [suit] cair bem.

flattering ['flætərɪŋ] *adj* [remark, offer] lisonjeiro(ra); [dress, colour, neckline] que cai bem.

flattery ['flætərɪ] *n* (U) bajulação *f*.

flaunt [flɔ:nt] *vt* ostentar.

flavour UK, **flavoring** US ['fleɪvəʳ] ◇ *n* -1. [taste] sabor *m* -2. *fig* [atmosphere] ar *m*, toque *m*. ◇ *vt* [food, drink] condimentar.

flavouring UK, **flavoring** US ['fleɪvərɪŋ] *n* (U) condimento *m*.

flaw [flɔ:] *n* [fault] imperfeição *f*; ~ **in** sthg imperfeição em algo.

flawless ['flɔ:lɪs] *adj* impecável.

flax [flæks] *n* linho *m*.

flea [fli:] *n* pulga *f*.

flea market *n* mercado *m* das pulgas.

fleck [flek] ◇ *n* mancha *f*. ◇ *vt*: ~ **ed with** sthg manchado(da) com algo.

fled [fled] *pt* & *pp* ➪ **flee**.

flee [fli:] (*pt* & *pp* **fled**) ◇ *vt* [country, enemy] fugir de. ◇ *vi* fugir.

fleece [fli:s] ◇ *n* -1. [material, of sheep] velo *m* -2. [garment] sobretudo *m* de lã. ◇ *vt inf* [cheat] trapacear.

fleet [fli:t] *n* frota *f*.

fleeting ['fli:tɪŋ] *adj* fugaz.

Flemish ['flemɪʃ] ◇ *adj* flamengo(ga). ◇ *n* [language] flamengo *m*. ◇ *npl*: the ~ os flamengos.

flesh [fleʃ] *n* -1. [of body] carne *f*; to be only ~ **and blood** ser de carne e osso; to be sb's own ~ **and blood** ser sangue do sangue de alguém -2. [of fruit, vegetable] polpa *f*.

flesh wound *n* ferimento *m* superficial.

flew [flu:] *pt* ➪ **fly**.

flex [fleks] ◇ *n* ELEC fio *m*, cabo *m*. ◇ *vt* [bend] flexionar.

flexible ['fleksəbl] *adj* flexível.

flexitime ['fleksɪtaɪm] *n* (U) horário *m* flexível.

flick [flɪk] ◇ *n* -1. [of whip, towel] pancada leve -2. [with finger] peteleco *m*. ◇ *vt* [switch - turn on] ligar; [- turn off] desligar.

➡ **flick through** *vt fus* folhear.

flicker ['flɪkəʳ] *vi* -1. [candle, light] tremeluzir -2. [shadow, eyelids] tremer.

flick knife *n* UK canivete *f* de mola.

flight [flaɪt] *n* -1. [gen] vôo *m* -2. [of steps, stairs] lance *m* -3. [escape] fuga *f*.

flight attendant *n* comissário *m*, -ria *f* de bordo.

flight crew *n* tripulação *f* de vôo.

flight deck *n* -1. [of aircraft carrier] pista *f* de aterrissagem -2. [of aircraft] cabine *f* de comando.

flight recorder *n* caixa-preta *f*.

flimsy ['flɪmzɪ] (*compar* -ier, *superl* -iest) *adj* -1. [fabric, structure] frágil -2. [excuse, argument] furado(da).

flinch [flɪntʃ] *vi* encolher-se; to ~ **from** sthg/from doing sthg vacilar diante de algo/em fazer algo; without ~ **ing** sem pestanejar.

fling [flɪŋ] (*pt* & *pp* **flung**) ◇ *n* [affair] caso *m*. ◇ *vt* [throw] atirar.

flint [flɪnt] *n* -1. (U) [rock] sílex *m* -2. [in lighter] pedra *f*.

flip [flɪp] (*pt* & *pp* -**ped**, *cont* -**ping**) ◇ *vt* -1. [move with a flick] mover rapidamente, sacudir; to ~ **a coin** tirar cara ou coroa; to ~ **sthg open** abrir algo de supetão; to ~ **sthg over** virar algo bruscamente; to ~ **through** sthg folhear algo -2. [switch]: to ~ **on** ligar; to ~ **off** desligar. ◇ *vi inf* [become angry] perder o controle. ◇ *n* -1. [of coin] arremesso *m* rápido -2. [somersault]

piparote m -**3.** *phr:* at the ~ of a switch ao toque de um interruptor.

flip-flop n *UK* [shoe] sandália f de dedo.

flippant ['flɪpənt] *adj* leviano(na).

flipper ['flɪpə^r] n -**1.** [of animal] barbatana f -**2.** [for swimmer, diver] pé-de-pato m.

flirt [flɜːt] <> n [person] paquerador m, -ra f. <> vi [with person] flertar; **to ~ with sb** flertar com alguém.

flirtatious [flɜː'teɪʃəs] *adj* galanteador(-ra).

flit [flɪt] (*pt* & *pp* **-ted,** *cont* **-ting**) vi [move quickly - bird] esvoaçar.

float [fləʊt] <> n -**1.** [on fishing line, net] bóia f -**2.** [in procession] carro m alegórico -**3.** [money] caixa m. <> vt [on water] fazer boiar. <> vi -**1.** [on water] boiar -**2.** [through air] flutuar.

flock [flɒk] n -**1.** [of birds, people] bando m -**2.** [of sheep] rebanho m.

flog [flɒg] (*pt* & *pp* **-ged,** *cont* **-ging**) vt -**1.** [whip] chicotear -**2.** *UK inf* [sell] pôr no prego.

flood [flʌd] n -**1.** [of water] enchente f -**2.** *fig* [great amount] dilúvio m. <> vt -**1.** [with water] inundar -**2.** *fig* [overwhelm]: **to ~ sthg (with)** inundar algo (com) -**3.** [with light] encher -**4.** *AUT* [engine] afogar.

flooding ['flʌdɪŋ] n (U) [from river, rain] enchente f, inundação f.

floodlight ['flʌdlaɪt] n holofote m.

floor [flɔː^r] <> n -**1.** [of room] piso m, chão m -**2.** [bottom] fundo m -**3.** [storey] andar m; **first** *US OR* **ground** *UK* ~ andar térreo -**4.** [at meeting, debate]: **from the ~** da platéia; **to have/give the ~** ter/dar a palavra -**5.** [for dancing] pista f. <> vt -**1.** [knock down] nocautear -**2.** [baffle] confundir.

floorboard ['flɔːbɔːd] n tábua f de assoalho.

floor show n espetáculo m noturno (*em bar, restaurante, cabaré*).

flop [flɒp] *inf* n [failure] fracasso m.

floppy ['flɒpɪ] (*compar* **-ier,** *superl* **-iest**) *adj* desengonçado(da).

floppy (disk) n disquete m.

flora ['flɔːrə] n flora f.

florid ['flɒrɪd] *adj* -**1.** [face, complexion] corado(da) -**2.** [style] florido(da).

florist ['flɒrɪst] n florista *mf*; ~'**s (shop)** floricultura f.

flotsam ['flɒtsəm] n (U): ~ **and jetsam** [debris] entulho m; [people] gente f desocupada.

flounder ['flaʊndə^r] (*pl inv OR* **-s**) vi -**1.** [in water, mud] debater-se -**2.** [in conversation, speech] atrapalhar-se.

flour ['flaʊə^r] n (U) farinha f.

flourish ['flʌrɪʃ] <> vi -**1.** [grow healthily - plants, garden] florescer; [- child] crescer -**2.** [be successful] prosperar. <> vt movimentar. <> n -**1.** [movement]: **to do sthg with a** ~ fazer algo de maneira a ser notado(da) -**2.** [of trumpets] fanfarra f.

flout [flaʊt] vt desrespeitar.

flow [fləʊ] <> n fluxo m. <> vi -**1.** [liquid, electricity, air] correr f -**2.** [traffic, words, ideas] fluir -**3.** [hair, dress] ondear.

flow chart, flow diagram n fluxograma m.

flower ['flaʊə^r] <> n *BOT* flor f; **in** ~ em flor. <> vi florescer.

flowerbed ['flaʊəbed] n canteiro m de flores.

flowerpot ['flaʊəpɒt] n vaso m de flores.

flowery ['flaʊərɪ] (*compar* **-ier,** *superl* **-iest**) *adj* -**1.** [patterned] florido(da) -**2.** *pej* [elaborate] floreado(da).

flown [fləʊn] *pp* ▷ **fly.**

flu [fluː] n (U) gripe m.

fluctuate ['flʌktʃʊeɪt] vi oscilar, flutuar.

fluency ['fluːənsɪ] n (U) [in a foreign language] fluência f.

fluent ['fluːənt] *adj* fluente; **he speaks ~ Spanish** ele fala espanhol fluentemente.

fluff [flʌf] n (U) [downy] macio(cia).

fluffy ['flʌfɪ] (*compar* **-ier,** *superl* **-iest**) *adj* [downy] macio(cia).

fluid ['fluːɪd] <> n fluido m. <> *adj* -**1.** [flowing] fluido(da) -**2.** [unfixed] mutável.

fluid ounce n onça f fluida (*0,028 litro*).

fluke [fluːk] n *inf* [chance] obra f do acaso.

flummox ['flʌməks] vt *esp UK inf* bestificar.

flung [flʌŋ] *pt* & *pp* ▷ **fling.**

flunk [flʌŋk] *esp US inf* vt [*SCH* & *UNIV* - exam, test] não passar em; [- student] reprovar.

fluorescent [flʊə'resnt] *adj* [colour] fluorescente.

fluoride ['flʊəraɪd] n fluoreto m.

flurry ['flʌrɪ] (*pl* **-ies**) n -**1.** [shower] lufada f -**2.** [sudden burst] erupção f.

flush [flʌʃ] <> *adj* [level]: ~ **with sthg** nivelado(da) com. <> n -**1.** [in toilet] descarga f -**2.** [blush] rubor m -**3.** [sudden feeling] acesso m. <> vt [with water]: **to ~ the toilet** dar a descarga na privada. <> vi -**1.** [toilet] dar a descarga -**2.** [blush] ruborizar.

flushed [flʌʃt] *adj* -**1.** [red-faced] ruborizado(da) -**2.** [excited]: ~ **with sthg** empolgado(da) com algo.

flustered ['flʌstəd] *adj* atrapalhado(da).

flute [fluːt] *n* MUS flauta *f*.

flutter ['flʌtə'] ⇔ *n* -1. [of wings] bater *m* -2. [of eyelashes] pestanejo *m* -3. *inf* [sudden feeling] agito *m* -4. *inf* [bet] aposta *f.* ⇔ *vi* -1. [bird, insect, wings] agitar -2. [flag] tremular -3. [dress] esvoaçar.

flux [flʌks] *n* -1. (*U*) [change] fluxo *m*; to be in a state of ~ mudar continuamente -2. TECH fundente *m*.

fly [flaɪ] (*pl* flies, *pt* flew, *pp* flown) ⇔ *n* -1. [insect] mosca *f* -2. [of trousers] braguilha *f.* ⇔ *vt* -1. [cause to fly] fazer voar -2. [transport by air] transportar em avião -3. [flag] tremular. ⇔ *vi* -1. [bird, insect, plane] voar -2. [pilot] pilotar -3. [travel by plane] ir de avião -4. [move fast] voar -5. [flag] tremular.

➡ **fly away** *vi* ir-se embora.

fly-fishing *n* (*U*) pesca *f* com iscas artificiais.

flying ['flaɪɪŋ] ⇔ *adj* -1. [able to fly] voador(ra) -2. [running] veloz. ⇔ *n* [in plane]: I hate ~ odeio viajar de avião.

flying colours *npl*: to pass (sthg) with ~ passar (em algo) com louvor.

flying saucer *n* disco *m* voador.

flying squad *n* UK radiopatrulha *f*.

flying start *n*: to get off to a ~ começar muito bem.

flying visit *n* visita *f* rápida.

flyover ['flaɪˌəʊvə'] *n* UK viaduto *m*.

flysheet ['flaɪʃiːt] *n* [on tent] teto *m* duplo.

fly spray *n* inseticida *f*.

FM (*abbr of* **frequency modulation**) FM *f*.

foal [fəʊl] *n* potro *m*.

foam [fəʊm] ⇔ *n* -1. [bubbles] espuma *f* -2. [material]: ~ **rubber** espuma de borracha. ⇔ *vi* espumar.

fob [fɒb] (*pt* & *pp* **-bed**, *cont* **-bing**) ➡ **fob off** *vt sep*: to ~ sthg off on sb empurrar algo para alguém; to ~ sb off with sthg enrolar alguém com algo.

focal point ['fəʊkl-] *n* -1. [of view, room] ponto *m* central -2. *fig* [of report, study] foco *m*.

focus ['fəʊkəs] (*pl* **-cuses** OR **-ci** [-saɪ]) ⇔ *n* [gen] foco *m*; out of/in ~ fora de/em foco. ⇔ *vt* -1. [lens, camera] focar -2. [mentally]: to ~ one's attention on sb/ sthg concentrar a atenção em alguém/algo. ⇔ *vi* -1. : to ~ on sb/sthg enfocar alguém/algo -2. [mentally]: to ~ on sthg concentrar-se em algo.

focussed *adj* [mentally] concentrado(-da).

fodder ['fɒdə'] *n* [feed] forragem *f*.

foe [fəʊ] *n literary* inimigo *m*, -ga *f*, antagonista *mf*.

foetus ['fiːtəs] *n* feto *m*.

fog [fɒg] *n* [mist] nevoeiro *m*, neblina *f*.

foggy ['fɒgɪ] (*compar* **-ier**, *superl* **-iest**) *adj* [misty] nevoento(ta).

foghorn ['fɒghɔːn] *n* buzina *f* de nevoeiro.

fog lamp *n* farol *m* de neblina.

foible ['fɔɪbl] *n* ponto *m* fraco.

foil [fɔɪl] ⇔ *n* (*U*) [metal sheet] papel *m* alumínio. ⇔ *vt* frustrar.

fold [fəʊld] ⇔ *vt* -1. [gen] dobrar; to ~ one's arms cruzar os braços -2. [wrap] abraçar. ⇔ *vi* -1. [bed, chair] dobrar -2. *inf* [newspaper, play] fracassar -3. *inf* [business] falir. ⇔ *n* -1. [in material, paper] dobra *f* -2. [for animals] curral *m* -3. *fig* [group of people]: the ~ o grupo.

➡ **fold up** ⇔ *vt sep* dobrar. ⇔ *vi* -1. dobrar -2. *inf* [newspaper, play] fracassar -3. *inf* [business] falir.

folder ['fəʊldə'] *n* [gen & COMPUT] pasta *f*.

folding ['fəʊldɪŋ] *adj* [chair, table] dobrável.

foliage ['fəʊlɪdʒ] *n* (*U*) folhagem *f*.

folk [fəʊk] ⇔ *adj* popular. ⇔ *npl* [people] gente *f*.

➡ **folks** *npl inf* [relatives] parentes *mpl*.

folklore ['fəʊklɔː'] *n* (*U*) folclore *m*.

folk music *n* (*U*) música *m* folk.

folk song *n* canção *f* folk.

folksy ['fəʊksɪ] (*compar* **-ier**, *superl* **-iest**) *adj* US *inf* amigável.

follow ['fɒləʊ] ⇔ *vt* -1. [gen] seguir; ~ that taxi! siga aquele táxi! -2. [pursue] perseguir -3. [go along with, understand] acompanhar. ⇔ *vi* -1. [come after] seguir-se -2. [happen as logical result] vir em seguida -3. [be logical] proceder; it ~ s that isso quer dizer que -4. [understand] acompanhar.

➡ **follow up** *vt sep* -1. [pursue] acompanhar -2. [supplement]: to ~ sthg up with responder a algo com.

follower ['fɒləʊə'] *n* [disciple, believer] seguidor *m*, -ra *f*.

following ['fɒləʊɪŋ] ⇔ *adj* seguinte. ⇔ *n* [group of supporters, fans] séquito *m*. ⇔ *prep* [after] depois de.

folly ['fɒlɪ] *n* (*U*) [foolishness] loucura *f*.

fond [fɒnd] *adj* [affectionate] carinhoso(-sa); to be ~ of sb gostar muito de alguém; to be ~ of sthg/of doing sthg gostar muito de algo/de fazer algo.

fondle ['fɒndl] *vt* acariciar.

font [fɒnt] *n* -1. [in church] pia *f* batismal -2. COMPUT & TYPO fonte *f*.

food [fuːd] *n* comida *f*.

food mixer *n* batedeira *f*.

food poisoning [-'pɔɪznɪŋ] n (U) into-xicação f alimentar.

food processor [-,prəʊsesə^r] n multi-processador m.

foodstuffs ['fu:dstʌfs] npl gêneros mpl alimentícios.

fool [fu:l] <> n -1. [idiot] idiota mf - 2. UK [dessert] musse f. <> vt enganar; to ~ sb into doing sthg enrolar alguém para que faça algo. <> vi brincar.

◆ **fool about, fool around** vi -1. [behave foolishly]: to ~ about (with sthg) fazer-se de bobo (em relação a algo) -2. [be unfaithful]: to ~ about (with sb) pular a cerca (com alguém) -3. US [tamper]: to ~ around with sthg brincar com algo.

foolhardy ['fu:l,hɑːdɪ] adj temerário(ria).

foolish ['fu:lɪʃ] adj -1. [unwise, silly] bo-bo(ba), idiota -2. [laughable, undignified] tolo(la).

foolproof ['fu:lpru:f] adj infalível.

foot [fʊt] (pl senses 1 and 2 **feet**, pl sense 3 inv OR **feet**) <> n -1. [of animal] pata f - 2. [of person] pé m; on ~ a pé; to be on one's feet, to get to one's feet ficar de pé; to have/get cold feet não ter coragem suficiente; to put one's ~ in it meter os pés pelas mãos; to put one's feet up descansar -3. [bottom] pé m -4. [of hill] sopé m -5. [unit of measurement] pé m (30,48 cm). <> vt inf: to ~ the bill (for sthg) pagar a conta (por algo).

footage ['fʊtɪdʒ] n (U) metragem f.

football ['fʊtbɔːl] n -1. UK [game] futebol m - 2. US [American football] futebol m americano -3. [ball] bola f de futebol.

footballer ['fʊtbɔːlə^r] n UK jogador m, -ra f de futebol, futebolista mf.

football ground n UK campo m de futebol.

football player n jogador m, -ra f de futebol.

footbrake ['fʊtbreɪk] n freio m de pé.

footbridge ['fʊtbrɪdʒ] n passarela f.

foothills ['fʊthɪlz] npl contraforte m.

foothold ['fʊthəʊld] n apoio m para os pés.

footing ['fʊtɪŋ] n -1. [foothold] lugar m onde pôr o pé; to lose one's ~ escorregar, perder a base -2. [basis] base f.

footlights ['fʊtlaɪts] npl ribalta f.

footnote ['fʊtnəʊt] n nota f de rodapé.

footpath ['fʊtpɑːθ, pl -pɑːðz] n trilha f.

footprint ['fʊtprɪnt] n pegada f.

footsie n: to play ~ tocar o pé de alguém com o próprio pé demonstrando interesse afetivo ou sexual.

footstep ['fʊtstep] n -1. [sound] passo m - 2. [footprint] pegada f.

footwear ['fʊtweə^r] n (U) calçado m.

for [fɔːr] prep -1. [expressing intention, purpose, reason] para; this book is ~ you este livro é para você; what did you do that ~? para que você fez isso?; what's it ~? para que é?; to go ~ a walk ir dar um passeio; '~ sale' 'vende-se'; a town famous ~ its wine uma cidade famosa pelo vinho; ~ this reason por esta razão -2. [during] durante; I'm going away ~ a while vou estar fora durante OR por algum tempo; I've lived here ~ ten years vivo aqui há dez anos; we talked ~ hours falamos horas e horas -3. [by, before] para; it'll be ready ~ to-morrow estará pronto (para) amanhã; be there ~ 8 p.m. esteja lá antes das oito da noite -4. [on the occasion of] por; I got socks ~ Christmas ganhei meias de Natal; ~ the first time pela primeira vez; what's ~ dinner? o que há para jantar?; ~ the moment no momento -5. [on behalf of] por; to do sthg ~ sb fazer algo para alguém; to work ~ sb trabalhar para alguém -6. [with time and space] para; there's no room ~ it não há espaço para isso; to have time ~ sthg ter tempo para algo -7. [expressing distance]: roadwork ~ 20 miles obras na estrada ao longo de 32 quilômetros; we drove ~ miles dirigimos quilôme-tros e mais quilômetros -8. [expressing destination] para; a ticket ~ Boston um bilhete para Boston; this train is ~ Newark only este trem só vai até Newark -9. [expressing price] por; I bought it ~ five dollars comprei-o por cinco dólares -10. [expressing meaning]: what's the Portuguese ~ boy? como é que se diz boy em português? -11. [with regard to] para; it's warm ~ Novem-ber para novembro está quente; it's easy ~ you para você é fácil; respect ~ human rights respeito pelos direitos humanos; I feel sorry ~ them sinto pena deles; it's too far ~ us to walk é longe demais para irmos a pé; it's time ~ dinner está na hora do jantar.

forage ['fɒrɪdʒ] vi [search] procurar; to ~ for sthg sair à procura de algo.

foray ['fɒreɪ] n -1. [raid] incursão f - 2. fig [excursion] incursão f; ~ into sthg in-cursão em algo.

forbad [fə'bæd], **forbade** [fə'beɪd] pt ⊳ forbid.

forbid [fə'bɪd] (pt -bade OR -bad, pp for-bid OR -bidden, cont -bidding) vt [not al-low] proibir; to ~ sb to do sthg proibir alguém de fazer algo.

forbidden [fə'bɪdn] <> pp ⊳ forbid. <> adj proibido(da).

forbidding [fə'bɪdɪŋ] *adj* -**1.** [severe] repulsivo(va) -**2.** [threatening] ameaçador(ra).

force [fɔ:s] ⬦ *n* -**1.** [gen] força *f*; **by ~ à força** -**2.** [power, influence] poder *m*; **a ~ to be reckoned with** um poder a ser reconhecido -**3.** [effect]: **to be in/come into ~** estar/entrar em vigor. ⬦ *vt* -**1.** [compel] forçar; **to ~ sb to do sthg** obrigar alguém a fazer algo; **to ~ sthg on sb** impor algo a alguém -**2.** [break open] forçar -**3.** [push] empurrar; **to ~ sthg open** forçar algo.
➡ **forces** *npl*: **the ~s** as Forças Armadas; **to join ~s (with sb)** unir forças (com alguém).

force-feed *vt* alimentar à força.

forceful ['fɔ:sfʊl] *adj* -**1.** [strong, powerful] forte -**2.** [words, ideas] contundente -**3.** [support, recommendation] enérgico(ca).

forceps ['fɔ:seps] *npl* fórceps *m*.

forcibly ['fɔ:səblɪ] *adv* -**1.** [using physical force] à força -**2.** [powerfully] eficazmente -**3.** [eagerly] energicamente.

ford [fɔ:d] *n* vau *m*.

fore [fɔ:ʳ] ⬦ *adj* NAUT dianteiro(ra). ⬦ *n*: **to come to the ~** *fig* tornar-se influente.

forearm ['fɔ:rɑ:m] *n* antebraço *m*.

foreboding [fɔ:'bəʊdɪŋ] *n* mau pressentimento *m*.

forecast ['fɔ:kɑ:st] (*pt & pp* **forecast** OR **-ed**) ⬦ *n* [prediction] previsão *f*. ⬦ *vt* [predict] prever.

foreclose [fɔ:'kləʊz] ⬦ *vt* executar. ⬦ *vi*: **to ~ on sb** privar alguém do direito de resgatar uma hipoteca.

forecourt ['fɔ:kɔ:t] *n* área *f* para estacionamento.

forefront ['fɔ:frʌnt] *n*: **in** OR **at the ~ of sthg** em primeiro plano de algo.

forego [fɔ:'gəʊ] *vt* = **forgo**.

foregone conclusion ['fɔ:gɒn-] *n*: **it's a ~** é um resultado inevitável.

foreground ['fɔ:graʊnd] *n* primeiro plano *m*.

forehand ['fɔ:hænd] *n* [tennis stroke] golpe *m* com a frente da mão.

forehead ['fɔ:hed] *n* testa *f*.

foreign ['fɒrən] *adj* -**1.** [from abroad] estrangeiro(ra) -**2.** [external] exterior.

foreign affairs *npl* relações *fpl* exteriores.

foreign currency *n* moeda *m* estrangeira.

foreigner ['fɒrənəʳ] *n* [from abroad] estrangeiro *m*, -ra *f*.

Foreign Legion *n*: **the ~** a Legião Estrangeira.

foreign minister *n* ministro *m* de relações exteriores.

Foreign Office *n* UK: **the ~** ≃ o Ministério das Relações Exteriores.

Foreign Secretary *n* UK ≃ Ministro *m* das Relações Exteriores.

foreleg ['fɔ:leg] *n* perna *f* dianteira.

foreman ['fɔ:mən] (*pl* **-men** *n* -**1.** [of workers] capataz *m* -**2.** [of jury] primeiro jurado *m*.

foremost ['fɔ:məʊst] ⬦ *adj* principal. ⬦ *adv*: **first and ~** antes de mais nada.

forensic [fə'rensɪk] *adj* forense.

forensic medicine *n* (U) medicina *f* legal.

forensic science *n* (U) ciência *f* forense.

forerunner ['fɔ:ˌrʌnəʳ] *n* [precursor] precursor *m*, -ra *f*.

foresee [fɔ:'si:] (*pt* **-saw** [-'sɔ:], *pp* **-seen**) *vt* prever.

foreseeable [fɔ:'si:əbl] *adj* previsível; **for/in the ~ future** num futuro próximo.

foreseen [fɔ:'si:n] *pp* ▷ **foresee**.

foreshadow [fɔ:'ʃædəʊ] *vt* prenunciar.

foresight ['fɔ:saɪt] *n* (U) previdência *f*.

forest ['fɒrɪst] *n* floresta *f*.

forestall [fɔ:'stɔ:l] *vt* prevenir.

forestry ['fɒrɪstrɪ] *n* (U) silvicultura *f*.

foretaste ['fɔ:teɪst] *n* [sample] amostra *f*.

foretell [fɔ:'tel] (*pt & pp* **-told**) *vt* predizer, prenunciar.

foretold [fɔ:'təʊld] *pt & pp* ▷ **foretell**.

forever [fə'revəʳ] *adv* [eternally] para sempre.

forewarn [fɔ:'wɔ:n] *vt* prevenir.

foreword ['fɔ:wɜ:d] *n* apresentação *f*.

forfeit ['fɔ:fɪt] ⬦ *n* -**1.** [penalty] prenda *f* -**2.** [fine] multa *f*. ⬦ *vt* [lose] perder.

forgave [fə'geɪv] *pt* ▷ **forgive**.

forge [fɔ:dʒ] ⬦ *n* [place] forja *f*. ⬦ *vt* -**1.** [industry] forjar -**2.** *fig* [create] forjar -**3.** [make illegal copy of] falsificar.
➡ **forge ahead** *vi* avançar continuamente.

forger ['fɔ:dʒəʳ] *n* falsificador *m*, -ra *f*.

forgery ['fɔ:dʒərɪ] (*pl* **-ies**) *n* falsificação *f*.

forget [fə'get] (*pt* **-got**, *pp* **-gotten**, *cont* **-getting**) ⬦ *vt* -**1.** [gen] esquecer; **to ~ to do sthg** esquecer-se de fazer algo -**2.** [leave behind] esquecer-se de. ⬦ *vi* esquecer-se; **to ~ about sthg** esquecer-se de algo.

forgetful [fə'getfʊl] *adj* esquecido(da).

forget-me-not *n* não-te-esqueças-de-mim *f*, miosótis *f*.

forgive [fə'gɪv] (pt -gave, pp -given) vt perdoar; to ~ sb for sthg/for doing sthg perdoar alguém por algo/por fazer algo.

forgiveness [fə'gɪvnɪs] n (U) perdão m.

forgo [fɔː'gəʊ] (pt -went, pp -gone [-'gɒn]) vt renunciar a, abrir mão de.

forgot [fə'gɒt] pt ▷ forget.

forgotten [fə'gɒtn] pp ▷ forget.

fork [fɔːk] ◇ n -1. [for food] garfo m -2. [for gardening] forquilha f -3. [in road, river] bifurcação f. ◇ vi bifurcar-se.
➡ **fork out** inf ◇ vt fus desembolsar. ◇ vi: to ~ out (for sthg) desembolsar uma grana (para algo).

forklift truck ['fɔːklɪft-] n empilhadeira f.

forlorn [fə'lɔːn] adj -1. [face, expression, cry] desesperado(da) -2. [desolate - person] desolado(da); [- place] abandonado(da) -3. [hope, attempt] desesperançado(da).

form [fɔːm] ◇ n -1. [shape] forma f; in the ~ of na forma de -2. [type] tipo m -3. (U) [fitness] aparência f; on ~ UK, in ~ US em forma; off ~ fora de forma -4. [questionnaire] formulário m -5. [figure] imagem f -6. UK SCH [class] série f. ◇ vt -1. [gen] formar -2. [constitute] constituir. ◇ vi formar-se.

formal ['fɔːml] adj -1. [gen] formal -2. [official] oficial.

formality [fɔː'mælətɪ] (pl -ies) n formalidade f.

format ['fɔːmæt] (pt & pp -ted, cont -ting) ◇ n -1. [of book, magazine] formato m -2. [of meeting] estilo m -3. COMPUT formato. ◇ vt COMPUT formatar.

formation [fɔː'meɪʃn] n -1. [gen] formação f -2. (U) [establishment] estrutura f.

formative ['fɔːmətɪv] adj formativo(va).

former ['fɔːmə'] ◇ adj -1. [earlier, previous] ex-; ~ husband ex-marido m -2. [first] anterior. ◇ n: the ~ o primeiro.

formerly ['fɔːmlɪ] adv antigamente.

formidable ['fɔːmɪdəbl] adj -1. [frightening] pavoroso(sa) -2. [impressive] impressionante.

formula ['fɔːmjʊlə] (pl -as OR -ae [-iː]) n fórmula f.

formulate ['fɔːmjʊleɪt] vt formular.

forsake [fə'seɪk] (pt -sook, pp -saken) vt literary abandonar.

forsaken [fə'seɪkn] adj abandonado(da).

forsook [fə'sʊk] pt ▷ forsake.

fort [fɔːt] n forte m.

forte ['fɔːtɪ] n forte m.

forth [fɔːθ] adv literary [outwards, onwards] adiante.

forthcoming [fɔː'θkʌmɪŋ] adj -1. [imminent] próximo(ma) -2. [helpful] prestimoso(sa).

forthright ['fɔːθraɪt] adj franco(ca).

forthwith [fɔːθ'wɪθ] adv fml incontinenti.

fortified wine ['fɔːtɪfaɪd-] n vinho m licoroso.

fortify ['fɔːtɪfaɪ] (pt & pp -ied) vt -1. [place] fortificar -2. fig [person, resolve] fortalecer.

fortnight ['fɔːtnaɪt] n quinzena f.

fortnightly ['fɔːt,naɪtlɪ] ◇ adj quinzenal. ◇ adv quinzenalmente.

fortress ['fɔːtrɪs] n fortaleza f.

fortunate ['fɔːtʃnət] adj feliz; it's ~ that ... por sorte ...

fortunately ['fɔːtʃnətlɪ] adv felizmente.

fortune ['fɔːtʃuːn] n -1. [large amount of money] fortuna f -2. [luck] sorte f -3. [future]: to tell sb's ~ ler a sorte de alguém.

fortune-teller [-,telə'] n -1. adivinho m, -nha f -2. [using cards] cartomante mf.

forty ['fɔːtɪ] num quarenta; see also sixty.

forward ['fɔːwəd] ◇ adj -1. [position] dianteiro(ra) -2. [movement] para frente -3. [advanced] avançado(da) -4. [impudent] impudente. ◇ adv -1. [in space] para a frente -2. [to earlier time]: to bring sthg ~ trazer algo à baila. ◇ n SPORT atacante mf. ◇ vt [send on - letter] remeter; [- parcels, goods] expedir; [- information] enviar; please ~ favor enviar para novo endereço.

forwarding address ['fɔːwədɪŋ-] n endereço m para envio.

forwards ['fɔːwədz] adv = forward.

forward slash n TYPO barra f inclinada (para frente).

forwent [fɔː'went] pt ▷ forgo.

fossil ['fɒsl] n GEOL fóssil m.

foster ['fɒstə'] ◇ adj de criação; ~ brother irmão de criação. ◇ vt -1. [child] criar, cuidar de -2. [idea, hope] fomentar.

foster child n filho m, -lha f de criação.

foster parent n pais mpl de criação.

fought [fɔːt] pt & pp ▷ fight.

foul [faʊl] ◇ adj -1. [dirty - linen] enlameado(da); [- water] imundo(da); [- air] poluído(da) -2. [food] estragado(da), podre; [taste] nojento(ta); [smell, breath] fétido(da) -3. [very unpleasant] péssimo(ma), horrível -4. [obscene] obsceno(na). ◇ n SPORT falta f. ◇ vt -1. [make dirty] sujar -2. SPORT cometer falta em.

found [faʊnd] ◇ *pt & pp* ▷ **find**. ◇ *vt* -**1**. [provide funds for] fundar -**2**. [start building] assentar os alicerces de -**3**. [base]: **to ~ sthg on** basear algo em.

foundation [faʊn'deɪʃn] *n* -**1**. (U) [gen] fundação *f* -**2**. [basis] base *f* -**3**. (U) [cosmetic]: **~ (cream)** base *f*.
➡ **foundations** *npl* CONSTR alicerces *mpl*.

founder ['faʊndə'] ◇ *n* [person] fundador *m*, -ra *f*. ◇ *vi* [sink] afundar.

foundry ['faʊndrɪ] (*pl* -ies) *n* fundição *f*.

fountain ['faʊntɪn] *n* [man-made] chafariz *m*.

fountain pen *n* caneta-tinteiro *f*.

four [fɔː'] *num* quatro; *see also* **six**; **on all ~ s** de quatro.

four-letter word *n* palavrão *m*.

four-poster (bed) *n* cama *f* com dossel.

foursome ['fɔːsəm] *n* quarteto *m*.

fourteen [ˌfɔː'tiːn] *num* quatorze; *see also* **six**.

fourth [fɔːθ] *num* quarto(ta); *see also* **sixth**.

Fourth of July *n*: **the ~** o 4 de Julho (*dia da Independência norte-americana*).

four-wheel drive *n* -**1**. [vehicle] veículo *m* com tração nas quatro rodas -**2**. [system] tração *f* nas quatro rodas.

fowl [faʊl] (*pl inv* OR -**s**) *n* -**1**. CULIN ave *f* -**2**. [bird] ave *f* (doméstica).

fox [fɒks] ◇ *n* [animal] raposa *f*. ◇ *vt* -**1**. [outwit] lograr -**2**. [baffle] deixar atordoado(da).

foxcub *n* [animal] filhote *m* de raposa.

foxglove ['fɒksglʌv] *n* dedaleira *f*.

foyer ['fɔɪeɪ] *n* -**1**. [of hotel, theatre] saguão *m* -**2**. US [of house] vestíbulo *m*.

fracas ['fræka:, US 'freɪkəs] (*UK pl inv*, *US pl* **fracases**) *n* rixa *f*.

fraction ['frækʃn] *n* -**1**. [gen] fração *f* -**2**. [a little bit]: **it's a ~ too big** é um pouquinho maior.

fractionally ['frækʃnəlɪ] *adv* levemente.

fracture ['fræktʃə'] MED ◇ *n* fratura *f*. ◇ *vt* fraturar.

fragile ['frædʒaɪl] *adj* frágil.

fragment [*n* 'frægmənt] *n* fragmento *m*.

fragrance ['freɪgrəns] *n* fragrância *f*.

fragrant ['freɪgrənt] *adj* perfumado(da).

frail [freɪl] *adj* frágil.

frame [freɪm] ◇ *n* -**1**. [of picture] moldura *f* -**2**. [of glasses] armação *f* -**3**. [structure - of door] marco *m*; [- of boat] estrutura *f*; [- of window, bicycle] quadro *m*; [- of bed, chair] armação *f* -**4**. [physique] constituição *f*. ◇ *vt* -**1**. [put in a frame] emoldurar -**2**. *fig* [surround]

cercar -**3**. [formulate, express] expressar -**4**. *inf* [falsely incriminate] incriminar falsamente.

frame of mind *n* estado *m* de espírito.

framework ['freɪmwɜːk] *n* -**1**. [physical structure] estrutura *f* -**2**. [basis] base *f*.

France [frɑːns] *n* França; **in ~** na França.

franchise ['fræntʃaɪz] *n* -**1**. POL [right to vote] direito *m* de voto -**2**. COMM [right to sell goods] franquia *f*.

frank [fræŋk] ◇ *adj* franco(ca). ◇ *vt* franquear.

frankly ['fræŋklɪ] *adv* francamente.

frantic ['fræntɪk] *adj* frenético(ca); **she was ~** ela estava fora de si.

fraternity [frə'tɜːnətɪ] (*pl* -ies) *n* -**1**. [community] comunidade *f* -**2**. US [of students] fraternidade *f* -**3**. (U) [friendship] fraternidade *f*.

fraternize, -ise ['frætənaɪz] *vi* [be on friendly terms] confraternizar; **to ~ with sb** confraternizar-se com alguém.

fraud [frɔːd] *n* -**1**. (U) [crime] fraude *f* -**2**. [deceitful act] trapaça *f* -**3**. *pej* [impostor] impostor *m*, -ra *f*.

fraught [frɔːt] *adj* -**1**. [full]: **~ with sthg** repleto(ta) de algo -**2**. UK [frantic] preocupado(da); **a ~ weekend** um fim de semana enlouquecido.

fray [freɪ] ◇ *vi* -**1**. [clothing, fabric, rope] esfiapar-se -**2**. *fig* [nerves, temper] desgastar-se. ◇ *n literary* rixa *f*.

frayed [freɪd] *adj* -**1**. [clothing, fabric, rope] esfiapado(da) -**2**. *fig* [nerves, temper] desgastado(da).

freak [friːk] ◇ *adj* imprevisto(ta). ◇ *n* -**1**. [strange creature - in appearance] aberração *f*; [- in behaviour] excêntrico *m*, -ca *f* -**2**. [unusual event] anomalia *f* -**3**. *inf* [fanatic] fanático *m*, -ca *f*.
➡ **freak out** *inf vi* -**1**. [get angry] baratinar-se -**2**. [panic] apavorar-se.

freckle ['frekl] *n* sarda *f*.

free [friː] (*compar* **freer**, *superl* **freest**, *pt & pp* **freed**) ◇ *adj* -**1**. [gen] livre; **to be ~ to do sthg** ser livre para fazer algo; **feel ~!** sinta-se à vontade!; **to set sb/sthg ~** libertar alguém/algo; **to give sb a ~ hand** dar a alguém carta branca -**2**. [not paid for] grátis; **~ of charge** sem despesas. ◇ *adv* -**1**. [without payment] gratuitamente; **for ~** de graça -**2**. [without restraint] livremente. ◇ *vt* -**1**. [release] pôr em liberdade, libertar -**2**. [make available] liberar -**3**. [remove] livrar.

freedom ['friːdəm] *n* liberdade *f*; **~ from sthg** ausência *f* de algo; **the right to ~ from hunger** o direito de não se passar fome.

Freefone® [ˈfriːfəʊn] *n UK (U)* discagem *f* gratuita.

free-for-all *n* **-1.** [brawl] tumulto *m* generalizado **-2.** [argument] discussão *f* generalizada.

free gift *n* oferta *f*.

freehand [ˈfriːhænd] <> *adj* à mão livre. <> *adv* à mão livre.

freehold [ˈfriːhəʊld] *n* propriedade *f* alodial.

free house *n bar não-controlado por uma única cervejaria*.

free kick *n* tiro *m* livre; **to take a ~** bater OR cobrar um tiro livre.

freelance [ˈfriːlɑːns] <> *adj* frila, autônomo(ma). <> *n* frila *mf*, autônomo *m*, -ma *f*.

freely [ˈfriːlɪ] *adv* **-1.** [without constraint] livremente; **~ available** fácil de obter **-2.** [generously] generosamente.

Freemason [ˈfriːˌmeɪsn] *n* maçom *m*.

freephone [ˈfriːfəʊn] *n* = freefone.

freepost *n (U)* porte *m* pago.

free-range *adj UK* caipira; **~ eggs** ovos caipira.

freestyle [ˈfriːstaɪl] *n* [in swimming] estilo *m* livre.

free time *n* tempo *m* livre.

free trade *n (U)* livre comércio *m*.

freeway [ˈfriːweɪ] *n US* auto-estrada *f*.

freewheel [ˌfriːˈwiːl] *vi* **-1.** [cyclist] andar sem pedalar **-2.** [motorist] ir em ponto morto.

free will *n (U)* vontade *f* própria; **to do sthg of one's own ~** fazer algo por vontade própria.

freeze [friːz] (*pt* froze, *pp* frozen) <> *vt* **-1.** [gen] congelar **-2.** [engine, lock] emperrar **-3.** [pipes] entupir. <> *vi* **-1.** [turn to ice] congelar-se **-2.** METEOR esfriar muito **-3.** [stop moving] parar **-4.** *inf* [be cold] congelar. <> *n* **-1.** [cold weather] frio *m* intenso **-2.** [of wages, prices] congelamento *m*.

freeze-dried [-ˈdraɪd] *adj* congelado(-da) a vácuo.

freezer [ˈfriːzəʳ] *n* **-1.** [machine] freezer *m*, frízer *m* **-2.** [part of fridge] congelador *m*.

freezing [ˈfriːzɪŋ] <> *adj* gelado(da); **it's ~ in here** está um gelo aqui; **I'm ~** estou congelando. <> *n* congelamento *m*; **5 degrees below ~** *inf* 5 graus abaixo de zero.

freezing point *n* ponto *m* de congelamento.

freight [freɪt] *n (U)* [goods] carga *f*.

freight train *n* trem *m* de carga.

French [frentʃ] <> *adj* francês(esa). <> *n* francês *m*, -esa *f*. <> *npl*: **the ~** os franceses.

French bean *n* vagem *f*.

French bread *n (U)* pão *m* francês, bisnaga *f*.

French Canadian <> *adj* franco-canadense. <> *n* [person] franco-canadense *mf*.

French doors *npl* = French windows.

French dressing *n* **-1.** [in UK] molho *m* vinagrete **-2.** [in US] molho *m* rosé.

French fries *npl esp US* batatas *fpl* fritas.

Frenchman [ˈfrentʃmən] (*pl* -men [-mən]) *n* francês *m*.

French stick *n UK* baguete *f*.

French windows *npl* janela *f* de batente.

Frenchwoman [ˈfrentʃˌwʊmən] (*pl* -women [ˌwɪmɪn]) *n* francesa *f*.

frenetic [frəˈnetɪk] *adj* frenético(ca).

frenzy [ˈfrenzɪ] (*pl* -ies) *n* frenesi *m*.

frequency [ˈfriːkwənsɪ] (*pl* -ies) *n* frequência *f*.

frequent [*adj* ˈfriːkwənt, *vb* frɪˈkwent] <> *adj* freqüente. <> *vt* freqüentar.

frequently [ˈfriːkwəntlɪ] *adv* freqüentemente.

fresh [freʃ] *adj* **-1.** [gen] fresco(ca) **-2.** [water] doce **-3.** [another] novo(va) **-4.** [refreshing] refrescante **-5.** [original] original **-6.** *inf dated* [cheeky] atrevido(-da).

freshen [ˈfreʃn] <> *vt* [refresh] renovar. <> *vi* [wind] tornar-se mais frio (fria). **◆ freshen up** *vi* [person] refrescar-se *(com água)*.

fresher [ˈfreʃəʳ] *n UK inf* calouro *m*, -ra *f*.

freshly [ˈfreʃlɪ] *adv* [recently] recentemente, recém-.

freshman [ˈfreʃmən] (*pl* -men [-mən]) *n* calouro *m*.

freshness [ˈfreʃnɪs] *n* **-1.** [gen] frescor *m* **-2.** [originality] originalidade *f*.

freshwater [ˈfreʃˌwɔːtəʳ] *adj* de água doce.

fret [fret] (*pt* & *pp* -ted, *cont* -ting) *vi* [worry] preocupar-se.

friar [ˈfraɪəʳ] *n* frei *m*.

friction [ˈfrɪkʃn] *n (U)* **-1.** [rubbing] fricção *f* **-2.** [conflict] atrito *m*.

Friday [ˈfraɪdɪ] *n* sexta-feira *f*; *see also* Saturday.

fridge [frɪdʒ] *n esp UK* refrigerador *m*.

fridge-freezer *n UK* refrigerador *m* com freezer.

fried [fraɪd] <> *pt* & *pp* ▷ fry. <> *adj* frito(ta); **~ egg** ovo frito.

friend [frend] *n* amigo *m*, -ga *f*; **to be ~s (with sb)** ser amigo(ga) (de alguém); **to make ~s (with sb)** fazer amizade (com alguém).

friendly ['frendlɪ] (compar -ier, superl -iest, pl -ies) adj -1. [kind, pleasant] amável; to be ~ with sb ser amigável com alguém -2. [not enemy] amigo(ga) -3. [not serious] amistoso(sa).

friendship ['frendʃɪp] n -1. [between people] amizade f -2. [between countries] boas relações fpl.

fries [fraɪz] npl = French fries.

frieze [fri:z] n friso m.

fright [fraɪt] n -1. (U) [fear] medo m; to take ~ ter medo -2. [shock] susto m; to give sb a ~ dar um susto em alguém.

frighten ['fraɪtn] vt assustar; to ~ sb into doing sthg forçar alguém a fazer algo por medo.

frightened ['fraɪtnd] adj amedrontado(da); to be ~ of sthg/of doing sthg ter medo de algo/de fazer algo.

frightening ['fraɪtnɪŋ] adj assustador(ra).

frightful ['fraɪtfʊl] adj dated horrendo(da).

frigid ['frɪdʒɪd] adj [sexually cold] frígido(da).

frill [frɪl] n -1. [decoration] babado m -2. inf [extra] frescura f.

fringe [frɪndʒ] n -1. [gen] franja f -2. fig [edge] orla f, margem f -3. fig [extreme] facção f.

fringe benefit n benefício m adicional.

frisk [frɪsk] vt [search] revistar.

frisky ['frɪskɪ] (compar -ier, superl -iest) adj inf brincalhão(lhona).

fritter ['frɪtər] n CULIN bolinho m frito.
➤ **fritter away** vt sep desperdiçar.

frivolous ['frɪvələs] adj frívolo(la).

frizzy ['frɪzɪ] (compar -ier, superl -iest) adj crespo(pa).

fro [frəʊ] adv ▷ to.

frock [frɒk] n dated vestido m.

frog [frɒg] n [animal] rã f; to have a ~ in one's throat estar com a garganta irritada.

frogman ['frɒgmən] (pl -men [-mən]) n homem-rã m.

frolic ['frɒlɪk] (pt & pp -ked, cont -king) vi brincar.

from [frɒm] prep -1. [expressing origin, source] de; I'm ~ California sou da Califórnia; the train ~ Chicago o trem de Chicago; I bought it ~ a supermarket comprei-o num supermercado -2. [expressing removal, deduction] de; away ~ home longe de casa; to take sthg (away) ~ sb tirar algo de alguém; 10% will be deducted ~ the total será deduzido 10% do total -3. [expressing distance] de; five miles ~ here a oito

quilômetros daqui; it's not far ~ here não é longe daqui -4. [expressing position] de; ~ here you can see the valley daqui se vê o vale -5. [expressing what sthg is made with] de; it's made ~ stone é feito de pedra -6. [expressing starting time] desde; ~ the moment you arrived desde que chegou; ~ now on de agora em diante; ~ next year a partir do próximo ano; open ~ nine to five aberto das nove às cinco -7. [expressing change] de; the price has gone up ~ $1 to $2 o preço subiu de um dólar para dois; to translate ~ German into English traduzir do alemão para o inglês -8. [expressing range] de; it could take ~ two to six months pode levar de dois a seis meses -9. [as a result of] de; I'm tired ~ walking estou cansado de andar -10. [expressing protection] de; sheltered ~ the wind protegido do vento -11. [in comparisons]: different ~ diferente de.

front [frʌnt] ◇ n -1. [gen] frente f; at the ~ of à frente de -2. MIL front m, frente f -3. [promenade]: (sea) ~ orla f marítima -4. [outward appearance] fachada f -5. [of book] capa f. ◇ adj [at front] da frente; ~ page primeira página; ~ cover capa.
➤ **in front** adv -1. [further forward] na frente -2. [winning]: to be in ~ estar na frente.
➤ **in front of** prep -1. [close to front of] em frente de -2. [in the presence of] na frente de.

frontbench [frʌnt'bentʃ] n cadeiras dianteiras no parlamento britânico nas quais se sentam os líderes do governo e da oposição.

front door n porta f da frente.

frontier ['frʌn.tɪər, US frʌn'tɪər] n -1. [border] fronteira f -2. fig [furthest limit] fronteira f.

front man n -1. [of group] representante mf -2. [of programme] apresentador m, -ra f.

front room n sala f de estar.

front-runner n favorito m, -ta f.

front-wheel drive n -1. [vehicle] veículo m com tração dianteira -2. [system] tração f dianteira.

frost [frɒst] n -1. (U) [layer of ice] geada f -2. [weather] frio m intenso.

frostbite ['frɒstbaɪt] n (U) enregelamento m.

frosted ['frɒstɪd] adj -1. [opaque] fosco(ca) -2. US CULIN coberto(ta) com glacê.

frosting ['frɒstɪŋ] n (U) US CULIN cobertura f (de glacê).

frosty ['frɒstɪ] (compar -ier, superl -iest)

adj -1. [very cold] gelado(da) **-2.** [covered with frost] coberto(ta) de geada **-3. fig** [unfriendly] glacial.

froth [frɒθ] n (U) espuma f.

frown [fraʊn] vi franzir as sobrancelhas.

➡ **frown (up)on** vt fus não ver com bons olhos.

froze [frəʊz] pt ⊳ **freeze**.

frozen [frəʊznl] ⊳ pp ⊳ **freeze**. ⊳ adj **-1.** [gen] congelado(da) **-2.** [feeling very cold] gelado(da) **-3.** [prices, salaries, assets] congelado(da).

frugal ['fru:gl] adj **-1.** [small] frugal **-2.** [careful] regrado(da).

fruit [fru:t] (pl inv OR fruits) n **-1.** [food] fruta f **-2. fig** [result] fruto m; **to bear ~** dar resultados.

fruitcake ['fru:tkeɪk] n **-1.** bolo m com passas **-2.** inf [mad person] maluco m, -ca f.

fruiterer ['fru:tərəᵣ] n UK fruteiro m, -ra f; **~'s (shop)** fruteira f.

fruitful ['fru:tfʊl] adj [successful] produtivo(va), proveitoso(sa).

fruition [fru:'ɪʃn] n (U): **to come to ~** realizar-se.

fruit juice n suco m de fruta.

fruitless ['fru:tlɪs] adj [wasted] infrutífero(ra), vão (vã).

fruit machine n UK caça-níqueis m inv.

fruit salad n salada f de frutas.

frumpy ['frʌmpɪ] (compar -ier, superl -iest) adj inf antiquado(da).

frustrate [frʌ'streɪt] vt frustrar.

frustrated [frʌ'streɪtɪd] adj frustrado(da).

frustration [frʌ'streɪʃn] n frustração f.

fry [fraɪ] (pt & pp fried) ⊳ vt [food] fritar. ⊳ vi [food] fritar.

frying pan ['fraɪŋ-] n frigideira f.

ft. abbr of foot, feet.

FTSE (abbr of Financial Times Stock Exchange) n FTSE m; **the ~ index** o índice FTSE; **the ~ 100** as ações das 100 maiores empresas britânicas ponderadas com base em seu valor de mercado.

fuck [fʌk] vulg ⊳ vt [have sex with] trepar OR foder com. ⊳ vi trepar, foder.

➡ **fuck off** excl vulg vá se foder!

fudge [fʌdʒ] n (U) [sweet] fondant m, doce de açúcar, leite e manteiga.

fuel [fjʊəl] (UK pt & pp -led, cont -ling, US pt & pp -ed, cont -ing) ⊳ n combustível m. ⊳ vt **-1.** [supply with fuel] abastecer **-2.** [increase] aumentar.

fuel pump n bomba f de combustível.

fuel tank n tanque m de combustível.

fugitive ['fju:dʒətɪv] n fugitivo m, -va f.

fulfil (pt & pp -led, cont -ling), **fulfill** US [fʊl'fɪl] vt **-1.** [carry out] cumprir; **to ~ one's role** desempenhar seu papel **-2.** [satisfy] satisfazer.

fulfilment, fulfillment US [fʊl'fɪlmənt] n (U) **-1.** [satisfaction] satisfação f **-2.** [carrying through - of ambition, dream] realização f; [- of role] desempenho m; [- of need, promise] cumprimento m.

full [fʊl] ⊳ adj **-1.** [gen] cheio (cheia); **~ of** cheio (cheia) de **-2.** [with food] satisfeito(ta) **-3.** [complete - employment, use] integral; [- explanation, name, day, recovery] completo(ta), efetivo(va); [- member, professor] titular **-4.** [maximum] máximo(ma) **-5.** [sound] forte **-6.** [flavour] rico(ca) **-7.** [plump - mouth] cheio (cheia); [- figure] voluptuoso(sa) **-8.** [ample, wide] largo(ga). ⊳ adv [very]: **to know ~ well that ...** saber muito bem que ... ⊳ n: **in ~** [payment] na totalidade; [write] por extenso.

full-blown [-'bləʊn] adj bem-caracterizado(da); **a ~ disease** uma doença bem-desenvolvida.

full board n (U) diária f completa.

full-fledged adj US = **fully-fledged**.

full moon n lua f cheia.

full-scale adj **-1.** [model, drawing, copy] em tamanho natural **-2.** [inquiry] completo(ta) **-3.** [war] total **-4.** [attack] maciço(ça).

full stop n ponto m final.

full time n UK SPORT final m de jogo.

➡ **full-time** ⊳ adj de tempo integral. ⊳ adv em tempo integral.

full up adj **-1.** [after meal] cheio(cheia) **-2.** [bus, train] lotado(da).

fully ['fʊlɪ] adv **-1.** [completely] completamente, totalmente; **to be ~ booked** estar com as reservas esgotadas **-2.** [in detail] em detalhes.

fully-fledged UK, **full-fledged** US [-'fledʒd] adj fig [doctor, lawyer] experiente.

fulsome ['fʊlsəm] adj exagerado(da).

fumble ['fʌmbl] vi tatear; **to ~ for sthg** procurar desajeitadamente por algo; **he ~d in his pockets for his keys** ele vasculhou os bolsos desajeitadamente à procura das chaves.

fume [fju:m] vi [with anger] fumegar.

➡ **fumes** npl [gas - from car, fire] fumaça f; [- of paint] vapor m.

fumigate ['fju:mɪgeɪt] vt desinfetar.

fun [fʌn] n (U) **-1.** [pleasure, amusement] diversão f; **we really had ~ at the party** nós realmente nos divertimos na festa; **what ~!** que divertido!; **for ~, for**

the ~ of it por prazer, por brincadeira
- 2. [playfulness] alegria *f* - 3. [ridicule]: to
make ~ of sb caçoar de alguém; to
poke ~ at sb zombar de alguém.

function [ˈfʌŋkʃn] ◇ *n* - 1. [gen] função *f* - 2. [formal social event] cerimônia *f*.
◇ *vi* funcionar; to ~ as sthg funcionar
como algo.

functional [ˈfʌŋkʃnəl] *adj* - 1. [furniture,
design] funcional - 2. [machine, system]
operacional.

fund [fʌnd] ◇ *n* - 1. [amount of money]
fundo *m* - 2. *fig* [reserve] reserva *f*. ◇
vt financiar.
◆ **funds** *npl* recursos *mpl*.

fundamental [ˌfʌndəˈmentl] *adj* - 1. [ba-
sic] básico(ca), fundamental - 2. [vital]
fundamental; ~ to sthg fundamental
para algo.

funding [ˈfʌndɪŋ] *n (U)* recursos *mpl*.

funeral [ˈfjuːnərəl] *n* funeral *m*.

funeral parlour *n* casa *f* funerária.

funfair [ˈfʌnfeəˈ] *n* parque *m* de diversões.

fungus [ˈfʌŋgəs] (*pl* -gi [-gaɪ], -es) *n* BOT
fungo *m*.

funnel [ˈfʌnl] *n* [tube] funil *m* - 2. [on ship]
chaminé *f*.

funny [ˈfʌnɪ] (*compar* -ier, *superl* -iest)
adj - 1. [amusing] engraçado(da) - 2. [odd]
esquisito(ta) - 3. [ill]: to feel ~ não se
sentir bem.
◆ **funnies** *npl US* quadrinhos *mpl*.

fur [fɜːˈ] *n* - 1. [on animal] pêlo *m* - 2. [gar-
ment] pele *f*.

fur coat *n* casaco *m* de pele.

furious [ˈfjʊərɪəs] *adj* - 1. [very angry]
furioso(sa) - 2. [violent] violento(ta).

furlong [ˈfɜːlɒŋ] *n* medida correspondente a um oitavo de milha.

furnace [ˈfɜːnɪs] *n* [fire] fornalha *f*.

furnish [ˈfɜːnɪʃ] *vt* - 1. [fit out] mobiliar
- 2. *fml* [provide] fornecer; to ~ sb with
sthg fornecer algo a alguém.

furnished [ˈfɜːnɪʃt] *adj* [fitted out] mobi-
liado(da).

furnishings [ˈfɜːnɪʃɪŋz] *npl* mobiliário *m*.

furniture [ˈfɜːnɪtʃəˈ] *n (U)* móvel *m*.

furrow [ˈfʌrəʊ] *n* - 1. [in field] sulco *m* - 2.
[on forehead] ruga *f*.

furry [ˈfɜːrɪ] (*compar* -ier, *superl* -iest) *adj*
- 1. [animal] peludo(da) - 2. [material, toy]
de pelúcia.

further [ˈfɜːðəˈ] ◇ *compar* ▷ far.
◇ *adv* - 1. [gen] mais adiante; how
much ~ is it? a que distância fica?; ~
on/back mais adiante/atrás - 2. [compli-
cate, develop, enquire] mais; to take sth ~
levar algo adiante; to go ~ ir adiante
- 3. [in addition] além disso. ◇ *adj*

adicional, novo(va); until ~ notice até
novas ordens. ◇ *vt* [career, cause, aims]
impulsionar.

further education *n UK* educação
para adultos após deixar a escola
excluindo-se a universidade.

furthermore [ˌfɜːðəˈmɔːˈ] *adv* além do
mais, além disso.

furthest [ˈfɜːðɪst] ◇ *superl* ▷ far.
◇ *adj* - 1. [in distance] mais afastado(da)
- 2. [greatest] maior. ◇ *adv* - 1. [in dis-
tance] mais longe - 2. [to greatest degree,
extent] maior.

furtive [ˈfɜːtɪv] *adj* furtivo(va).

fury [ˈfjʊərɪ] *n* fúria *f*.

fuse *esp UK*, **fuze** *US* [fjuːz] ◇ *n* - 1. ELEC
fusível *m* - 2. [of bomb, firework] detona-
dor *m*. ◇ *vt* - 1. [gen] fundir - 2. ELEC
queimar. ◇ *vi* - 1. [gen] fundir-se - 2.
ELEC queimar.

fusebox *n* caixa *f* de fusíveis.

fused [fjuːzd] *adj* ELEC [fitted with a fuse]
com fusível.

fuselage [ˈfjuːzəlɑːʒ] *n* fuselagem *f*.

fuss [fʌs] ◇ *n* [bother, agitation] alvoroço *m*; to make a ~ fazer um estardalhaço. ◇ *vi* [become agitated]
alvoroçar-se.

fussy [ˈfʌsɪ] (*compar* -ier, *superl* -iest) *adj*
- 1. [fastidious] exigente - 2. [over-ornate]
exagerado(da).

futile [ˈfjuːtaɪl] *adj* fútil.

futon [ˈfuːtɒn] *n* colchão japonês.

future [ˈfjuːtʃəˈ] ◇ *n* - 1. [time ahead]
futuro *m*; in (the) ~ no futuro - 2.
GRAMM: ~ (tense) futuro *m*. ◇ *adj*
futuro(ra).

fuze *US* = fuse.

fuzzy [ˈfʌzɪ] (*compar* -ier, *superl* -iest) *adj*
- 1. [hair] encrespado(da) - 2. [image,
ideas] difuso(sa).

G

g¹ (*pl* g's OR gs), **G** (*pl* G's OR Gs) [dʒiː] *n*
[letter] g, G *m*.
◆ **G** ◇ *n* MUS sol *m*. ◇ (*abbr of* **good**)
B *m*.

g² (*abbr of* gram) g.

gab [gæb] *n* ▷ gift.

gabble [ˈgæbl] ◇ *vt* tagarelar. ◇ *vi*
tagarelar. ◇ *n* tagarelice *f*.

gable ['geɪbl] *n* oitão *m*.

gadget ['gædʒɪt] *n* aparelho *m*.

Gaelic ['geɪlɪk] <> *adj* gaélico(ca). <> *n* gaélico *m*, -ca *f*.

gag [gæg] (*pt* & *pp* **-ged**, *cont* **-ging**) <> *n* **-1.** [for mouth] mordaça *f* **-2.** *inf* [joke] piada *f*. <> *vt* [put gag on] amordaçar.

gage *n* & *vt US* = **gauge**.

gaiety ['geɪətɪ] *n* (*U*) alegria *f*.

gaily ['geɪlɪ] *adv* **-1.** [cheerfully] alegremente **-2.** [without thinking] despreocupadamente.

gain [geɪn] <> *n* **-1.** [profit] ganho *m* **-2.** (*U*) [making a profit] lucro *m* **-3.** [increase] aumento *m*. <> *vt* [gen] ganhar. <> *vi* **-1.** [increase]: to ~ in sthg crescer em algo **-2.** [profit] lucrar; to ~ from/by sthg lucrar com algo **-3.** [watch, clock] adiantar-se.

◆ **gain on** *vt fus* aproximar-se de.

gait [geɪt] *n* maneira *f* de andar.

gal. *abbr of* **gallon**.

gala ['gɑːlə] *n* [celebration] festival *m*.

galaxy ['gæləksɪ] (*pl* **-ies**) *n* [group of planets and stars] galáxia *f*.

gale [geɪl] *n* [wind] ventania *f*.

gall [gɔːl] *n* [nerve]: **to have the ~ to do sthg** ter a audácia de fazer algo.

gallant [*sense 1* 'gælənt, *sense 2* gə'lænt] *adj* **-1.** [courageous] valente **-2.** [polite to women] galante.

gall bladder *n* vesícula *f* biliar.

gallery ['gælərɪ] (*pl* **-ies**) *n* galeria *f*.

galley ['gælɪ] (*pl* **galleys**) *n* **-1.** [ship] galé *f* **-2.** [kitchen] cozinha *f* (*de navio ou avião*) **-3.** *TYPO*: ~ (proof) prova *f* de granel.

Gallic ['gælɪk] *adj* gaulês(lesa).

galling ['gɔːlɪŋ] *adj* **-1.** [annoying] irritante **-2.** [humiliating] vergonhoso(sa).

gallivant [,gælɪ'vænt] *vi inf* perambular.

gallon ['gælən] *n* galão *m*.

gallop ['gæləp] <> *n* **-1.** [pace of horse] galope *m* **-2.** [horse ride] galopada *f*. <> *vi* galopar.

gallows ['gæləʊz] (*pl inv*) *n* forca *f*.

gallstone ['gɔːlstəʊn] *n* cálculo *m* biliar.

galore [gə'lɔːʳ] *adv* em abundância.

galvanize, -ise ['gælvənaɪz] *vt* **-1.** *TECH* galvanizar **-2.** [impel]: **to ~ sb into action** estimular alguém a uma ação.

gambit ['gæmbɪt] *n* **-1.** [remark, ploy] lábia *f* **-2.** [in chess] tática *f*, estratégia *f*.

gamble ['gæmbl] <> *n* [calculated risk] aposta *f*. <> *vi* **-1.** [bet] apostar; **to ~ on sthg** apostar em algo **-2.** [take risk]: **to ~ on sthg** arriscar em algo.

gambler ['gæmbləʳ] *n* jogador *m*, -ra *f*.

gambling ['gæmblɪŋ] *n* (*U*) jogo *m* (*de azar*).

game [geɪm] <> *n* **-1.** [sport, amusement] jogo *m*; **a children's** ~ uma brincadeira de criança **-2.** [contest, match] jogo *m*, partida *f* **-3.** [division of match - in tennis] game *m* **-4.** [playing equipment] brinquedo *m* **-5.** (*U*) [hunted animals] caça *f* **-6.** *phr*: **the** ~'s up acabou a brincadeira; **to give the** ~ **away** entregar o jogo. <> *adj* **-1.** [brave] corajoso(sa) **-2.** [willing] disposto(ta); ~ **for sthg/to do sthg** pronto(ta) para algo/para fazer algo.

◆ **games** <> *n SCH* [physical education] jogos *mpl*. <> *npl* [sporting contest] jogos *mpl*.

gamekeeper ['geɪm,kiːpəʳ] *n* guarda-caça *mf*.

game reserve *n* reserva *f* de caça.

gamma rays ['gæmə-] *npl* raios *mpl* gama.

gammon ['gæmən] *n* (*U*) presunto *m*.

gamut ['gæmət] *n* gama *f*.

gang [gæŋ] *n* **-1.** [of criminals] quadrilha *f*, gangue *f* **-2.** [of young people] turma *f*.

◆ **gang up** *vi inf* mancomunar-se; **to ~ up on sb** mancomunar-se contra alguém.

gangland ['gæŋlænd] *n* (*U*) submundo *m* (*do crime*).

gangrene ['gæŋgriːn] *n* (*U*) gangrena *f*.

gangster ['gæŋstəʳ] *n* gângster *mf*.

gangway ['gæŋweɪ] *n* **-1.** *UK* [aisle] corredor *m* **-2.** [gangplank] passadiço *m*.

gantry ['gæntrɪ] (*pl* **-ies**) *n* [for crane] cavalete *m*.

gaol [dʒeɪl] *n* & *vt UK* = **jail**.

gap [gæp] *n* **-1.** [empty space] espaço *m*, brecha *f*; **her death left a** ~ **in our lives** sua morte deixou um vazio em nossas vidas; **fill in the** ~s preencher as lacunas **-2.** [in time] intervalo *m* **-3.** *fig* [in knowledge, report] falha *f* **-4.** *fig* [between theory and practice etc.] disparidade *f*.

gape [geɪp] *vi* **-1.** [person]: **to ~ (at sb/sthg)** ficar boquiaberto(ta) (diante de alguém/algo) **-2.** [hole, shirt] abrir.

gaping ['geɪpɪŋ] *adj* **-1.** [person] boquiaberto(ta) **-2.** [hole, shirt, wound] todo aberto, toda aberta.

garage [*UK* 'gærɑːʒ, *US* gə'rɑːʒ] *n* **-1.** [for keeping car] garagem *f* **-2.** *UK* [for fuel] posto *m* de gasolina **-3.** [for car repair] oficina *f* (*mecânica*) **-4.** [for selling cars] revendedora *f*.

garbage ['gɑːbɪdʒ] *n esp US* (*U*) **-1.** [refuse] lixo *m* **-2.** *inf* [nonsense] besteira *f*.

garbage can *n US* lata *f* de lixo.

garbage truck *n US* caminhão *m* de lixo.

garbled ['gɑːbld] *adj* [message, account] adulterado(da).

Garda (Síochána) *n Irish*: the ~ a polícia irlandesa.

garden ['gɑːdn] <> *n* jardim *m.* <> *vi* jardinar.

garden centre *n* loja *f* de jardinagem.

gardener ['gɑːdnəʳ] *n* jardineiro *m*, -ra *f.*

gardening ['gɑːdnɪŋ] *n* (*U*) jardinagem *f.*

gargle ['gɑːgl] *vi* gargarejar.

gargoyle ['gɑːgɔɪl] *n* gárgula *f.*

garish ['geərɪʃ] *adj* espalhafatoso(sa).

garland ['gɑːlənd] *n* guirlanda *f* (*de flores*).

garlic ['gɑːlɪk] *n* alho *m.*

garlic bread *n* pão *m* de alho.

garment ['gɑːmənt] *n* peça *f* de roupa.

garnish ['gɑːnɪʃ] CULIN <> *n* decoração *f.* <> *vt* decorar.

garrison ['gærɪsn] *n* [soldiers] guarnição *f.*

garrulous ['gærələs] *adj* tagarela.

garter ['gɑːtəʳ] *n* - **1.** [band round leg] liga *f* - **2.** *US* [suspender] suspensório *m.*

gas [gæs] (*pl* **gases** OR **gasses**, *pt* & *pp* -**sed**, *cont* -**sing**) <> *n* - **1.** CHEM gás *m* - **2.** [domestic fuel] gás *m* (*de cozinha*) - **3.** *US* [fuel for vehicle] gasolina *f*; to step on the ~ *inf* pisar no acelerador. <> *vt* [poison] envenenar (com gás).

gas cooker *n UK* fogão *m* a gás.

gas cylinder *n* botijão *m* de gás.

gas fire *n UK* aquecedor *m* a gás.

gas gauge *n US* medidor *m* de gás.

gash [gæʃ] <> *n* corte *m* (*na pele*), ferida *f.* <> *vt* cortar (*a pele*), ferir.

gasket ['gæskɪt] *n* gaxeta *f.*

gasman ['gæsmæn] (*pl* -**men** [-menl]) *n* vendedor *m*, -ra *f* de gás.

gas mask *n* máscara *f* antigás.

gasmen *pl* > **gasman**.

gas meter *n* medidor *m* de gás.

gasoline ['gæsəliːn] *n US* (*U*) gasolina *f.*

gasp [gɑːsp] <> *n* arfada *f.* <> *vi* ofegar.

gas pedal *n US* acelerador *m.*

gas station *n US* posto *m* de gasolina.

gas stove *n* = **gas cooker**.

gas tank *n US* tanque *m* de gasolina.

gas tap *n* torneira *f* de gás.

gastroenteritis ['gæstrəʊ,entə'raɪtɪs] *n* (*U*) gastroenterite *f.*

gastronomy [gæs'trɒnəmɪ] *n* (*U*) gastronomia *f.*

gasworks ['gæswɜːks] (*pl inv*) *n* fábrica *f* de gás.

gate [geɪt] *n* portão *m.*

gatecrash ['geɪtkræʃ] *inf* <> *vt* entrar

como penetra em. <> *vi* entrar como penetra.

gateway ['geɪtweɪ] *n* - **1.** [entrance] portão *m* - **2.** *fig* [means of access]: ~ to entrada *f* para.

gather ['gæðəʳ] <> *vt* - **1.** [collect - gen] colher; [- courage, strength] reunir: to ~ together reunir - **2.** [speed, momentum] ganhar - **3.** [understand]: to ~ (that) compreender que - **4.** [into folds] franzir. <> *vi* [come together] reunir.

gathering ['gæðərɪŋ] *n* [meeting] assembléia *f.*

gaudy ['gɔːdɪ] (*compar* -**ier**, *superl* -**iest**) *adj* chamativo(va).

gauge, gage *US* [geɪdʒ] <> *n* - **1.** [measuring instrument - for rain] pluviômetro *m*; [- for tyre pressure] calibrador *m*; [- for fuel] medidor *m* de combustível - **2.** [calibre] calibre *m* - **3.** [of rail] bitola *f.* <> *vt* - **1.** [estimate, measure] estimar, calcular - **2.** [predict] prever.

Gaul [gɔːl] *n* - **1.** [country] Gália - **2.** [person] gaulês *m*, -lesa *f.*

gaunt [gɔːnt] *adj* - **1.** [person, face] esquelético(ca) - **2.** [landscape, building] desolado(da).

gauntlet ['gɔːntlɪt] *n* [medieval glove] manopla *f*; [for motorcyclist] luva *f* (*de material resistente e punho largo*); to run the ~ of sthg expor-se a algo; to throw down the ~ (to sb) lançar um desafio (a alguém).

gauze [gɔːz] *n* (*U*) [fabric] gaze *f.*

gave [geɪv] *pt* > **give**.

gawky ['gɔːkɪ] (*compar* -**ier**, *superl* -**iest**) *adj* desengonçado(da).

gawp [gɔːp] *vi* embasbacar-se; to ~ at sb/sthg embasbacar-se diante de alguém/algo.

gay [geɪ] <> *adj* - **1.** [homosexual] gay - **2.** [cheerful, brightly coloured] alegre. <> *n* [homosexual] gay *mf.*

gaze [geɪz] <> *n* olhar *m* fixo. <> *vi*: to ~ (at sb/sthg) olhar fixamente (para alguém/algo).

gazelle [gə'zell] (*pl inv* OR -**s**) *n* gazela *f.*

gazetteer [,gæzɪ'tɪəʳ] *n* dicionário *m* geográfico.

gazump [gə'zʌmp] *vt UK inf* concordar em vender uma casa a alguém e depois vendê-la a outro por um preço mais alto; to be ~ed ser passado(da) pra trás na compra de um imóvel.

GB (*abbr of* Great Britain) *n* GB.

GCE (*abbr of* General Certificate of Education) *n* antigo exame final do ensino médio na Grã-Bretanha.

GCSE (*abbr of* General Certificate of Secondary Education) *n* exame final do *ensino médio na Grã-Bretanha, em substituição ao nível O do GCE.*

GDP (*abbr of* **gross domestic product**) *n* PIB *m*.

gear [gɪə'] ⬦ *n* **-1.** TECH [mechanism] engrenagem *f* **-2.** [on car, bicycle] marcha *f*; **in ~** engatado(da), engrenado(da); **out of ~** desengatado(da), fora de funcionamento **-3.** (U) [equipment, clothes] apetrechos *mpl*. ⬦ *vt*: **to ~ sthg to sb/sthg** encaminhar algo a alguém/algo.

➡ **gear up** *vi*: **to ~ up for sthg/to do sthg** preparar-se para algo/para fazer algo.

gearbox ['gɪəbɒks] *n* caixa *f* de câmbio.

gear lever, gear stick UK, **gear shift** US *n* alavanca *f* de mudança.

gear wheel *n* roda *f* de engrenagem.

geese [giːs] *pl* ➪ **goose**.

gel [dʒel] (*pt & pp* **-led**, *cont* **-ling**) ⬦ *n* [for hair] gel *m*. ⬦ *vi* **-1.** *fig* [idea, plan] tomar forma **-2.** [liquid] engrossar.

gelatin ['dʒelətɪn], **gelatine** [,dʒelə'tiːn] *n* gelatina *f*.

gelignite ['dʒelɪgnaɪt] *n* (U) gelignite *f*.

gem [dʒem] *n* **-1.** [jewel] gema *f*, pedra *f* preciosa **-2.** *fig* [person, thing] jóia *f*.

Gemini ['dʒemɪnaɪ] *n* **-1.** [sign] Gêmeos.

gender ['dʒendə'] *n* **-1.** [sex] sexo *m* **-2.** GRAMM gênero *m*.

gene [dʒiːn] *n* gene *m*.

general ['dʒenərəl] ⬦ *adj* geral. ⬦ *n* MIL general *mf*.

➡ **in general** *adv* **-1.** [as a whole] em geral **-2.** [usually] geralmente.

general anaesthetic *n* anestesia *f* geral.

general delivery *n* (U) US posta-restante *f*.

general election *n* eleições *fpl* gerais.

generalization [,dʒenərəlaɪ'zeɪʃn] *n* generalização *f*.

general knowledge *n* (U) cultura *m* geral.

generally ['dʒenərəlɪ] *adv* **-1.** [usually] geralmente **-2.** [by most people] comumente **-3.** [in a general way] em geral.

general practitioner *n* clínico *m*, -ca *f* geral.

general public *n*: **the ~** o público em geral.

general strike *n* greve *f* geral.

generate ['dʒenəreɪt] *vt* **-1.** [energy, power, heat] gerar **-2.** [interest, excitement] provocar ; [jobs, employment] gerar.

generation [,dʒenə'reɪʃn] *n* geração *f*.

generator ['dʒenəreɪtə'] *n* gerador *m*.

generic [dʒɪ'nerɪk] *adj* genérico(ca).

generic drug *n* (medicamento *m*) genérico *m*.

generosity [,dʒenə'rɒsətɪ] *n* (U) generosidade *f*.

generous ['dʒenərəs] *adj* generoso(sa).

genetic [dʒɪ'netɪk] *adj* genético(ca).

➡ **genetics** *n* (U) genética *f*.

genetically modified [dʒɪ'netɪkəlɪ'mɒdɪfaɪd] *adj* geneticamente modificado(da).

Geneva [dʒɪ'niːvə] *n* Genebra; **in ~** em Genebra.

genial ['dʒiːnjəl] *adj* cordial, simpático(ca).

genitals ['dʒenɪtlz] *npl* genitais *mpl*.

genius ['dʒiːnjəs] (*pl* **-es**) *n* **-1.** [person] gênio *m* **-2.** [special ability]: **a stroke of ~** um golpe de mestre.

genome ['dʒiːnəʊm] *n* genoma *m*.

gent [dʒent] *n* UK dated inf cavalheiro *m*.

➡ **gents** *n* UK [toilets] banheiro *m* masculino.

genteel [dʒen'tiːl] *adj* **-1.** [refined] fino(na), refinado(da) **-2.** [affected] afetado(da).

gentle ['dʒentl] *adj* **-1.** [gen] suave **-2.** [kind] gentil **-3.** [discreet] leve.

gentleman ['dʒentlmən] (*pl* **-men** [-mən]) *n* **-1.** [well-bred man] cavalheiro *m*, gentleman *m* [man] senhor *m*.

gently ['dʒentlɪ] *adv* **-1.** [gen] suavemente **-2.** [kindly] delicadamente, gentilmente **-3.** [slowly] lentamente.

gentry ['dʒentrɪ] *n* alta burguesia *f*.

genuine ['dʒenjʊɪn] *adj* **-1.** [antique, work of art] genuíno(na) **-2.** [person, feeling, mistake] autêntico(ca).

geography [dʒɪ'ɒgrəfɪ] *n* geografia *f*.

geology [dʒɪ'ɒlədʒɪ] *n* geologia *f*.

geometric(al) [,dʒɪə'metrɪk(l)] *adj* geométrico(ca).

geometry [dʒɪ'ɒmətrɪ] *n* (U) geometria *f*.

geranium [dʒɪ'reɪnjəm] (*pl* **-s**) *n* gerânio *m*.

gerbil ['dʒɜːbɪl] *n* gerbo *m*.

geriatric [,dʒerɪ'ætrɪk] *adj* **-1.** [of old people] geriátrico(ca) **-2.** *pej* [very old, inefficient] ultrapassado(da).

germ [dʒɜːm] *n* **-1.** BIO germe *m* **-2.** MED bactéria *f* **-3.** *fig* [of idea, plan] embrião *m*.

German ['dʒɜːmən] ⬦ *adj* alemão(mã). ⬦ *n* **-1.** [person] alemão *m*, -mã *f* **-2.** [language] alemão *m*.

German measles *n* (U) rubéola *f*.

Germany ['dʒɜːmənɪ] (*pl* **-ies**) *n* Alemanha.

germinate ['dʒɜːmɪneɪt] *vi* germinar.

gerund [ˈdʒerənd] n GRAMM gerúndio m.

gesticulate [dʒesˈtɪkjʊleɪt] vi gesticular.

gesture [ˈdʒestʃəʳ] <> n gesto m. <> vi: to ~ to OR towards sb fazer gestos a alguém

get [get] (pt & pp got, US pp gotten) vt -1. [obtain] obter; [buy] comprar; **she got a job** ela arranjou emprego -2. [receive] receber; **I got a book for Christmas** ganhei um livro no Natal -3. [means of transportation] apanhar; **let's ~ a taxi** vamos apanhar um táxi -4. [find] ir buscar; **could you ~ me the manager?** [in store] podia chamar o gerente?; [on phone] pode me passar o gerente? -5. [illness] apanhar; **I got the flu over Christmas** peguei uma gripe no Natal -6. [cause to become]: **to ~ sthg done** mandar fazer algo; **to ~ sthg ready** preparar algo; **can I ~ my car repaired here?** posso mandar consertar o meu carro aqui? -7. [ask, tell]: **to ~ sb to do sthg** arranjar alguém para fazer algo -8. [move]: **to ~ sthg out of sthg** tirar algo de algo; **I can't ~ it through the door** não consigo passar com isso na porta -9. [understand] compreender; **to ~ a joke** contar uma piada -10. [time, chance] ter; **we didn't ~ the chance to see everything** não tivemos oportunidade de ver tudo -11. [idea, feeling] ter; **I ~ a lot of enjoyment from it** me divirto à beça com isso -12. [phone] atender -13. [in phrases]: **you ~ a lot of rain here in winter** chove muito aqui no inverno; ▷ **have.** <> vi -1. [become] ficar; **it's getting late** está ficando tarde; **to ~ ready** preparar-se; **to ~ lost** perder-se; **~ lost!** não enche o saco!, desapareça! -2. [into particular state, position] meter-se; **how do you ~ to El Paso from here?** como se vai daqui para El Paso?; **to ~ into the car** entrar no carro -3. [arrive] chegar; **when does the train ~ here?** quando é que o trem chega aqui? -4. [in phrases]: **to ~ to do sthg** ter a oportunidade de fazer algo. <> aux vb ser; **to ~ delayed** atrasar-se; **to ~ killed** ser morto.

◆ **get along (with sb)** vi dar-se bem (com alguém).

◆ **get back** vi [return] voltar.

◆ **get in** vi [arrive] chegar; (enter) entrar.

◆ **get off** vi [leave] sair.

◆ **get on** vi [enter train, bus] entrar.

◆ **get out** vi [of car, bus, train] sair.

◆ **get through** vi [on phone] completar a ligação.

◆ **get up** vi levantar-se.

getaway [ˈgetəweɪ] n fuga f; **to make one's ~** escapar.

get-together n inf encontro m informal (entre amigos).

geyser [ˈgiːzəʳ] n [hot spring] gêiser m.

Ghana [ˈgɑːnə] n Gana.

ghastly [ˈgɑːstlɪ] (compar -ier, superl -iest) adj -1. inf [very bad, unpleasant] horrível -2. [horrifying, macabre] macabro(bra), horroroso(sa).

gherkin [ˈgɜːkɪn] n pepino m em conserva.

ghetto [ˈgetəʊ] (pl -s OR -es) n gueto m.

ghetto blaster [-ˈblɑːstəʳ] n inf minisystem portátil de grande potência.

ghost [gəʊst] n [spirit] fantasma m.

giant [ˈdʒaɪənt] <> adj gigantesco(ca). <> n [gen] gigante m.

gibberish [ˈdʒɪbərɪʃ] n (U) asneira f.

gibe [dʒaɪb] n zombaria f.

Gibraltar [dʒɪˈbrɔːltəʳ] n Gibraltar.

giddy [ˈgɪdɪ] (compar -ier, superl -iest) adj [dizzy] tonto(ta).

gift [gɪft] n -1. [present] presente m -2. [talent] dom m; **to have a ~ for sthg/for doing sthg** ter o dom para algo/para fazer algo; **to have the ~ of the gab** ter o dom da fala; pej ter lábia.

gift certificate n US = gift token.

gifted [ˈgɪftɪd] adj -1. [gen] talentoso(sa), de talento -2. [child] superdotado(da).

gift token, gift voucher UK, **gift certificate** US n vale-presente m.

gift wrap n papel m de presente.

gig [gɪg] n inf [concert] show m.

gigabyte [ˈgaɪgəbaɪt] n COMPUT gigabyte m.

gigantic [dʒaɪˈgæntɪk] adj gigantesco(ca).

giggle [ˈgɪgl] <> n -1. [laugh] risadinha f, risada f -2. UK inf [fun] diversão f; **to do sthg for a ~** divertir-se fazendo algo tolo; **to have the ~s** ter um ataque de riso. <> vi [laugh] dar risadinhas bobas.

gilded [ˈgɪldɪd] adj = gilt.

gill [dʒɪl] n [unit of measurement] 0,142 litro.

gills [gɪlz] npl [of fish] guelras fpl.

gilt [gɪlt] <> adj [covered in gold] dourado(da). <> n (U) [gold layer] dourado m.

gimmick [ˈgɪmɪk] n pej artimanha f.

gin [dʒɪn] n [drink] gim m; **~ and tonic** gim-tônica m.

ginger [ˈdʒɪndʒəʳ] <> adj UK [colour - of hair] ruivo(va); [- of cat] avermelhado(-da). <> n (U) -1. [root] gengibre m -2. [powder] gengibre m em pó.

ginger ale n [mixer] jinjibirra f.

ginger beer n [slightly alcoholic] cerveja f de gengibre.

gingerbread ['dʒɪndʒəbred] n (U) **-1.** [cake] pão m de gengibre **-2.** [biscuit] biscoito m de gengibre.

ginger-haired [-'heəd] adj ruivo(va).

gingerly ['dʒɪndʒəlɪ] adv cuidadosamente.

gipsy ['dʒɪpsɪ] (pl -ies) <> adj cigano(-na). <> n [nomad] cigano m, -na f.

giraffe [dʒɪ'rɑːf] (pl inv OR -s) n girafa f.

girder ['gɜːdəʳ] n viga f.

girdle ['gɜːdl] n [corset] espartilho m.

girl [gɜːl] n **-1.** [young female child] menina f, garota f **-2.** [young woman] moça f **-3.** [daughter] menina f **-4.** [female friend]: the ~s as amigas, as meninas.

girlfriend ['gɜːlfrend] n **-1.** [female lover] namorada f **-2.** [female friend] amiga f.

girl guide UK, **girl scout** US n [individual] escoteira f, bandeirante f.

giro ['dʒaɪrəʊ] (pl -s) n UK **-1.** (U) [system] transferência f de crédito **-2.**: inf ~ (cheque) seguro-desemprego m.

girth [gɜːθ] n **-1.** [circumference] circunferência f **-2.** [of horse] cincha f.

gist [dʒɪst] n essência f; to get the ~ (of sthg) pegar a essência (de algo).

give [gɪv] (pt gave, pp given) <> vt **-1.** [gen] dar; to ~ sb sthg dar algo para OR a alguém **-2.** [hand over, pass] entregar; to ~ sb sthg, to ~ sthg to sb entregar algo para OR a alguém. <> vi [collapse, break] ceder. <> n (U) [elasticity] elasticidade f.

◆ **give or take** prep mais ou menos.

◆ **give away** vt sep **-1.** [get rid of] desfazer-se de **-2.** [reveal] revelar.

◆ **give back** vt sep [return] devolver.

◆ **give in** vi **-1.** [admit defeat] render-se, dar-se por vencido(da) **-2.** [agree unwillingly]: to ~ in to sthg ceder frente a algo.

◆ **give off** vt fus [produce] exalar.

◆ **give out** <> vt sep [distribute] distribuir. <> vi **-1.** [be exhausted] esgotar-se **-2.** [fail] falhar, não funcionar.

◆ **give up** <> vt sep **-1.** [stop, abandon] abandonar; to ~ up smoking parar de fumar; to ~ up chocolate deixar de comer chocolate **-2.** [surrender]: to ~ o.s. up (to sb) render-se (a alguém). <> vi [admit defeat] render-se.

given ['gɪvn] <> adj **-1.** [set, fixed] dado(da) **-2.** [prone]: to be ~ to sthg/to doing sthg ser dado(da) a algo/a fazer algo. <> prep [taking into account] dado(da); ~ the circumstances dadas as circunstâncias; ~ that dado que.

given name n US prenome m.

glacier ['glæsjəʳ] n geleira f.

glad [glæd] (compar -der, superl -dest)

adj **-1.** [happy, pleased] feliz; to be ~ about sthg estar feliz por algo **-2.** [willing]: to be ~ to do sthg ter vontade de fazer algo, desejar fazer algo **-3.** [grateful]: to be ~ of sthg ficar agradecido(da) por algo.

gladly ['glædlɪ] adv **-1.** [happily, eagerly] com prazer, alegremente **-2.** [willingly] com satisfação.

glamor n US = glamour.

glamorous ['glæmərəs] adj [gen] glamouroso(sa); [job] atraente.

glamour UK, **glamor** US ['glæməʳ] n (U) [gen] glamour m; [of job] encanto m.

glance [glɑːns] <> n [quick look] olhadela f; at a ~ de relance; at first ~ à primeira vista. <> vi [look quickly]: to ~ at sb/sthg olhar alguém/algo de relance.

◆ **glance off** vt fus **-1.** [light] desviar **-2.** [ball] rebater **-3.** [bullet] ricochetear.

glancing ['glɑːnsɪŋ] adj [oblique] oblíquo(qua).

gland [glænd] n glândula f.

glandular fever ['glændjʊlə-] n (U) mononucleose f infecciosa.

glare [gleəʳ] <> n **-1.** [scowl] olhar m penetrante, encarada f **-2.** (U) [blaze, dazzle] brilho m **-3.** [of publicity] foco m. <> vi **-1.** [scowl]: to ~ at sb/sthg fulminar alguém/algo com o olhar, lançar um olhar fulminante sobre alguém/algo **-2.** [blaze, dazzle] ofuscar.

glaring ['gleərɪŋ] adj **-1.** [very obvious] evidente **-2.** [blazing, dazzling] ofuscante.

glasnost ['glæznɒst] n (U) glasnost f.

glass [glɑːs] <> n **-1.** (U) [material] vidro m **-2.** [for drinking] copo m **-3.** (U) [glassware] objetos mpl de cristal. <> comp de vidro.

◆ **glasses** npl [spectacles] óculos m inv; [binoculars] binóculos mpl.

glassware ['glɑːsweəʳ] n (U) objetos mpl de cristal.

glassy ['glɑːsɪ] (compar -ier, superl -iest) adj **-1.** [smooth, shiny] cristalino(na) **-2.** [blank, lifeless] vidrado(da).

glaze [gleɪz] <> n **-1.** [on pottery] verniz m, esmalte m **-2.** CULIN glacê m. <> vt **-1.** [pottery] envernizar **-2.** CULIN cristalizar.

glazier ['gleɪzjəʳ] n vidraceiro m, -ra f.

gleam [gliːm] <> n **-1.** [glow] lampejo m **-2.** [fleeting expression] olhar m. <> vi **-1.** [surface, object] reluzir **-2.** [light] brilhar **-3.** [face, eyes] olhar.

gleaming ['gliːmɪŋ] adj **-1.** [surface, object] reluzente **-2.** [light] brilhante **-3.** [face, eyes] reluzente.

glean [gliːn] vt [gather] coletar.

glee [gli:] n (U) [joy, delight] alegria f; [gloating] regozijo m.

glen [glen] n Scot & Irish vale m.

glib [glɪb] (compar -ber, superl -best) adj pej -1. [answer, excuse] de momento -2. [person] de muita lábia.

glide [glaɪd] vi -1. [move smoothly] deslizar -2. [fly] planar.

glider ['glaɪdəʳ] n [plane] planador m.

gliding ['glaɪdɪŋ] n (U) [sport] vôo m sem motor; **to go** ~ voar de planador.

glimmer ['glɪməʳ] n -1. [faint light] luz f fraca -2. fig [trace, sign] sinal m mínimo.

glimpse [glɪmps] <> n -1. [sight, look] vislumbre m -2. [perception, idea, insight] noção f. <> vt -1. [catch sight of] ver de relance -2. [perceive] vislumbrar.

glint [glɪnt] <> n brilho m. <> vi -1. [metal, sunlight] brilhar -2. [eyes - greed, anger] faiscar; [- amusement] brilhar.

glisten ['glɪsn] vi brilhar.

glitter ['glɪtəʳ] <> n [gen] brilho m. <> vi -1. [object, light] brilhar -2. [eyes - with excitement] cintilar; [- with fury] faiscar.

gloat [gləʊt] vi: **to** ~ **(over sthg)** tripudiar (de algo).

global ['gləʊbl] adj [worldwide] mundial.

globalization [ˌgləʊbəlaɪ'zeɪʃn] n globalização f.

global warming [-'wɔːmɪŋ] n (U) aquecimento m global.

globe [gləʊb] n -1. [Earth]: **the** ~ o globo -2. [spherical shape] globo m.

gloom [glu:m] n -1. [darkness] escuro m, escuridão f -2. [unhappiness] desânimo m.

gloomy ['glu:mɪ] (compar -ier, superl -iest) adj -1. [place, landscape] sombrio(bria) -2. [weather] sombrio(bria), escuro(ra) -3. [atmosphere] deprimente; [mood] pessimista -4. [outlook, news] desanimador(ra).

glorious ['glɔːrɪəs] adj -1. [illustrious] glorioso(sa) -2. [wonderful] magnífico(ca).

glory ['glɔːrɪ] (pl -ies) n -1. [gen] glória f -2. (U) [splendour] esplendor m.
➡ **glory in** vt fus [relish] desfrutar de.

gloss [glɒs] n -1. (U) [shine - of wood, furniture] lustre m; [- of hair] brilho m -2.: ~ **(paint)** esmalte m.
➡ **gloss over** vt fus falar por alto sobre.

glossary ['glɒsərɪ] (pl -ies) n glossário m.

glossy ['glɒsɪ] (compar -ier, superl -iest) adj lustroso(sa).

glove [glʌv] n luva f.

glove compartment n porta-luvas m inv.

glow [gləʊ] <> n [light] fulgor m, brilho m. <> vi -1. [fire] arder -2. [sky, light, brass] brilhar.

glower ['glaʊəʳ] vi: **to** ~ **(at sb/sthg)** olhar ameaçadoramente (para alguém/algo).

glucose ['glu:kəʊs] n (U) glicose f.

glue [glu:] (cont glueing OR gluing) <> n (U) cola f. <> vt [stick with glue] colar; **to** ~ **sthg to sthg** colar algo em algo.

glum [glʌm] (compar -mer, superl -mest) adj [unhappy] melancólico(ca).

glut [glʌt] n excesso m.

glutton ['glʌtn] n [greedy person] glutão m, -tona f; **to be a** ~ **for punishment** gostar de sofrer.

GM foods npl alimentos mpl geneticamente modificados.

GMO (abbr of genetically modified organism) <> adj OGM. <> n OGM m.

gnarled [nɑːld] adj -1. [tree] nodoso(sa) -2. [hands] áspero(ra).

gnash [næʃ] vt: **to** ~ **one's teeth** ranger os dentes.

gnat [næt] n mosquito m.

gnaw [nɔː] <> vt [chew] roer. <> vi [worry] atormentar-se; **to** ~ **(away) at sb** atormentar alguém.

gnome [nəʊm] n gnomo m.

GNP (abbr of gross national product) n PNB m.

GNVQ (abbr of General National Vocational Qualification) n EDUC curso de formação profissional com duração de dois anos para maiores de 16 anos na Inglaterra e no País de Gales.

go [gəʊ] (pt went, pp gone, pl goes) vi -1. [move, travel] ir; **to** ~ **home** ir para casa; **to** ~ **to Brazil** ir ao Brasil; **to** ~ **by bus** ir de ônibus; **to** ~ **for a walk** fazer um passeio; **to** ~ **and do sthg** ir fazer algo; **to** ~ **in** entrar; **to** ~ **out** sair -2. [leave] ir-se; **it's time for us to** ~ é hora de irmos embora; **when does the bus** ~? quando é que ônibus sai?; ~ **away!** vá embora! -3. [attend] ir; **to** ~ **to school** ir para a escola; **which school do you** ~ **to?** para que escola você vai? -4. [become] ficar; **she went pale** empalideceu; **the milk has gone sour** o leite azedou -5. [expressing future tense]: **to be going to do sthg** ir fazer algo -6. [function] funcionar; **the car won't** ~ o carro não pega -7. [stop working] ir-se; **the fuse has gone** o fusível queimou -8. [time] passar -9. [progress] correr; **to** ~ **well** correr bem -10. [bell, alarm] tocar -11. [match] condizer; **to** ~ **with** condizer com; **red wine doesn't** ~ **with fish** vinho tinto não combina com peixe

-12. [be sold] ser vendido; **'everything must ∼'** 'liquidação total' **-13.** [fit] caber **-14.** [lead] ir; **where does this path ∼?** aonde vai dar este caminho? **-15.** [belong] ir, ser **-16.** [in phrases]: **to let ∼ of sthg** [drop] largar algo; **there are two days to ∼** faltam dois dias; **to ∼ US** [to take away] para levar. ⋄ n **-1.** [turn] vez f; **it's your ∼** é a sua vez **-2.** [attempt] tentativa f; **to have a ∼ at sthg** experimentar algo; **'50 cents a ∼'** [for game] '50 centavos cada vez'.

➡ **go ahead** vi [take place] realizar-se; **∼ ahead!** vá em frente!

➡ **go around** vi [revolve] rodar; **there isn't enough cake to ∼ around** não tem bolo (suficiente) para todo mundo.

➡ **go back** vi voltar.

➡ **go down** vi [decrease] diminuir; [sun] pôr-se; [tire] esvaziar-se.

➡ **go in** vi entrar.

➡ **go off** vi [alarm, bell] tocar, soar; [go bad] azedar; [light, heating] apagar-se.

➡ **go on** vi [happen] passar-se; [light, heating] acender-se; **to ∼ on doing sthg** continuar a fazer algo.

➡ **go out** vi [leave house] sair; [light, fire, cigarette] apagar-se; [have relationship]: **to ∼ out with sb** sair com alguém; **to ∼ out to eat** ir comer fora.

➡ **go over** vt fus [check] rever.

➡ **go through** vt fus [experience] passar por; [spend] gastar; [search] revistar.

➡ **go up** vi [increase] subir.

➡ **go without** vt fus passar sem.

goad [gəʊd] vt [provoke] provocar.

go-ahead ⋄ adj [dynamic] dinâmico(-ca), empreendedor(ra). ⋄ n [permission] permissão f.

goal [gəʊl] n **-1.** SPORT gol m **-2.** [aim] meta f, objetivo m.

goalkeeper ['gəʊl,ki:pəʳ] n goleiro m, -ra f.

goalmouth ['gəʊlmaʊθ, pl -maʊðz] n boca f do gol.

goalpost ['gəʊlpəʊst] n trave f.

goat [gəʊt] n [animal] cabra f, bode m; **to get (on) sb's ∼** encher o saco de alguém.

goat's cheese n queijo m de cabra.

gob [gɒb] (pt & pp -bed, cont -bing) v inf ⋄ n **-1.** UK [mouth] matraca f, bico m **-2.** UK [spit] escarro m. ⋄ vi [spit] escarrar.

gobble ['gɒbl] vt devorar.

➡ **gobble down, gobble up** vt sep engolir rapidamente.

go-between n intermediário m, -ria f.

gobsmacked ['gɒbsmækt] adj UK v inf embasbacado(da).

go-cart n = go-kart.

god [gɒd] n deus m.

➡ **God** ⋄ n Deus m; **God knows** só Deus sabe; **for God's sake!** pelo amor de Deus!; **thank God** graças a Deus; **God willing** se Deus quiser. ⋄ excl: **(my) God!** (meu) Deus!

➡ **gods** npl UK inf: **the ∼s** THEATRE as galerias.

godchild ['gɒdtʃaɪld] (pl **-children** [-,tʃɪldrən]) n afilhado m, -da f.

goddaughter ['gɒd,dɔ:təʳ] n afilhada f.

goddess ['gɒdɪs] n deusa f.

godfather ['gɒd,fɑːðəʳ] n padrinho m.

godforsaken ['gɒdfə,seɪkn] adj abandonado(da) por Deus, que Deus esqueceu.

godmother ['gɒd,mʌðəʳ] n madrinha f.

godsend ['gɒdsend] n dádiva f de Deus.

godson ['gɒdsʌn] n afilhado m.

goes [gəʊz] vb ⊳ **go**.

goggles ['gɒglz] npl óculos m de proteção.

going ['gəʊɪŋ] ⋄ adj **-1.** [rate, salary] em vigor, atual **-2.** UK [available, in existence] disponível; **she's the biggest fool ∼** ela é a maior trouxa do mundo. ⋄ n **-1.** [progress] avanço m, marcha f; **that's good ∼** isso é que é andar rápido; **it was slow ∼** estava indo devagar; **to be heavy ∼** ser pesado(da); **to be easy ∼** ser fácil (de lidar) **-2.** [in riding, horse-racing] condições fpl (do chão de corrida).

go-kart [-kɑːt] n UK kart m.

gold [gəʊld] ⋄ adj [gold-coloured] dourado(da). ⋄ n **-1.** (U) [metal] ouro m **-2.** (U) [gold jewellery, ornaments, coins] riquezas fpl. ⋄ comp [made of gold] de ouro.

golden ['gəʊldən] adj **-1.** [made of gold] de ouro **-2.** [gold-coloured] dourado(da).

goldfish ['gəʊldfɪʃ] (pl inv) n peixe-dourado m.

gold leaf n (U) ouro m em folha.

gold medal n medalha f de ouro.

goldmine ['gəʊldmaɪn] n lit, fig mina f de ouro.

gold-plated [-'pleɪtɪd] adj banhado(da) a ouro.

gold standard adj padrão-ouro m.

goldsmith ['gəʊldsmɪθ] n ourives mf.

golf [gɒlf] n (U) golfe m.

golf ball n **-1.** [for golf] bola f de golfe **-2.** [for typewriter] esfera f.

golf club n **-1.** [association, place] clube m de golfe **-2.** [stick] taco m de golfe.

golf course n campo m de golfe.

golfer ['gɒlfəʳ] n jogador m, -ra f de golfe.

gone [gɒn] <> *pp* ⊳ **go**. <> *adj* [no longer here] que já se foi. <> *prep* [past]: **it's just ~ midday** já passa do meio-dia; **she's ~ fifty** ela já passou dos cinquenta.

gong [gɒŋ] *n* gongo *f*.

good [gʊd] (*compar* **better**, *superl* **best**) <> *adj* **-1.** [gen] bom, boa; **it feels ~ to be in the fresh air** faz bem estar ao ar livre; **it's ~ that ...** é bom que ...; **to be ~ at** sthg ser bom em algo, ser boa em algo; **to be ~ with** [children, animals] ter jeito com; [one's hands] ter habilidade com **-2.** [kind] gentil; **to be ~ to sb** ser bom para alguém, ser boa para alguém; **to be ~ enough to do sthg** fazer o favor de fazer algo; **a ~ number of people** um bom número de pessoas **-3.** [morally correct] correto(ta) **-4.** [well-behaved] bem-comportado(da); **be ~!** comporte-se bem! **-5.** [beneficial]: **it's ~ for you** faz bem para você. <> *n* **-1.** (U) [benefit, welfare] bem *m*; **it will do him ~** fará bem a ele **-2.** [use]: **it's no ~** não adianta; **what's the ~ of ...?** qual é a vantagem de ...? **-3.** [morality, virtue] bem *m*; **to be up to no ~** estar com más intenções. <> *excl* que bom!

➡ **goods** *npl* [merchandise] mercadorias *fpl*.

➡ **as good as** *adv* quase; **it's as ~ as new** está praticamente novo.

➡ **for good** *adv* [forever] para sempre.

➡ **good afternoon** *excl* boa tarde!

➡ **good evening** *excl* boa noite!

➡ **good morning** *excl* bom dia!

➡ **good night** *excl* boa noite!

good behaviour *n* bom comportamento *m*.

goodbye [ˌgʊd'baɪ] <> *excl* até logo! <> *n* adeus *m*.

good deed *n* boa ação *f*.

good fortune *n* boa sorte *f*.

Good Friday *n* Sexta-Feira *f* Santa.

good-humoured [-'hjuːməd] *adj* bem-humorado(da).

good-looking [-'lʊkɪŋ] *adj* [person] bonito(ta).

good-natured [-'neɪtʃəd] *adj* **-1.** [person] de bom coração **-2.** [rivalry, argument] amigável.

goodness ['gʊdnɪs] <> *n* **-1.** [kindness] bondade *f* **-2.** [nutritive quality] valor *m* nutritivo. <> *excl*: **(my) ~!** minha nossa!; **for ~ sake!** pelo amor de Deus!; **thank ~** graças a Deus!; **~ gracious!** Santo Deus!

goods train [gʊdz-] *n* UK trem *m* de carga.

goodwill [ˌgʊd'wɪl] *n* **-1.** [kind feelings] boa vontade *f* **-2.** COMM fundo *m* de comércio.

goody ['gʊdɪ] (*pl* **-ies**) <> *n* inf [good person] mocinho *m*, -nha *f*. <> *excl* que ótimo!

➡ **goodies** *npl* inf **-1.** [delicious food] guloseimas *fpl* **-2.** [desirable objects] coisas *fpl* atraentes.

goose [guːs] (*pl* **geese** [giːsl]) *n* [bird] ganso *m*, -sa *f*.

gooseberry ['gʊzbərɪ] (*pl* **-ies**) *n* **-1.** [fruit] groselha *f* **-2.** UK inf [unwanted person]: **to play ~** segurar a vela.

gooseflesh ['guːsfleʃ], **goose pimples** UK *n*, **goosebumps** US ['guːsbʌmps] *npl* arrepio *m*.

gore [gɔːʳ] <> *n* (U) *literary* [blood] sangue *m* (*derramado*). <> *vt* [subj: bull] ferir com os chifres.

gorge [gɔːdʒ] <> *n* garganta *f*, desfiladeiro *m*. <> *vt*: **to ~ o.s. on** OR **with** sthg empanturrar-se com algo.

gorgeous ['gɔːdʒəs] *adj* **-1.** [place, present, weather] magnífico(ca), maravilhoso(sa) **-2.** inf [person] deslumbrante.

gorilla [gə'rɪlə] *n* gorila *m*.

gormless ['gɔːmlɪs] *adj* UK inf burro(ra).

gorse [gɔːs] *n* (U) tojo *m*.

gory ['gɔːrɪ] (*compar* **-ier**, *superl* **-iest**) *adj* sangrento(ta).

gosh [gɒʃ] *excl* inf por Deus!

go-slow *n* UK operação *f* tartaruga.

gospel ['gɒspl] *n* [doctrine] evangelho *m*.

➡ **Gospel** *n* [in Bible] Evangelho *m*.

gossip ['gɒsɪp] <> *n* **-1.** [conversation] conversa *f*, bate-papo *m*; **to have a ~** bater papo **-2.** [person] fofoca *f*. <> *vi* fofocar.

gossip column *n* coluna *f* social.

got [gɒt] *pt* & *pp* ⊳ **get**.

gotten ['gɒtn] *pp* US ⊳ **get**.

goulash ['guːlæʃ] *n* (U) gulash *m* (*prato típico húngaro*).

gourmet ['gʊəmeɪ] <> *n* gourmet *m*. <> *comp* gastrônomo *m*, -ma *f*.

gout [gaʊt] *n* (U) gota *f*.

govern ['gʌvən] <> *vt* **-1.** POL governar **-2.** [determine] controlar. <> *vi* POL governar.

governess ['gʌvənɪs] *n* governanta *f*.

government ['gʌvnmənt] *n* **-1.** [group of people] governo *m* **-2.** (U) [process] governo *m*; **the art of ~** a arte de governar.

governor ['gʌvənəʳ] *n* **-1.** POL governador *m*, -ra *f* **-2.** [of school] diretor *m*, -ra *f* **-3.** [of prison] diretor *m*, -ra *f*.

gown [gaʊn] *n* **-1.** [dress] vestido *m* **-2.** UNIV & JUR beca *f* **-3.** MED avental *m*.

GP (*abbr of* **general practitioner**) *n* clínico *m* geral.

grab [græb] (*pt* & *pp* **-bed**, *cont* **-bing**) ◇ *vt* **-1.** [with hands - person, arm] agarrar; [- money] pegar **-2.** *fig* [opportunity, sandwich] pegar; **to ~ the chance to do sthg** aproveitar a oportunidade de fazer algo **-3.** *inf* [appeal to] arrebatar; **how does this ~ you?** o que você me diz disso? ◇ *vi*: **to ~ at sthg** [with hands] tentar agarrar.

grace [greɪs] ◇ *n* **-1.** (*U*) [elegance] graça *f*, elegância *f* **-2.** (*U*) [extra time] prazo *m* **-3.** [prayer] graças *fpl*. ◇ *vt* **-1.** *fml* [honour] agraciar **-2.** [adorn] enfeitar.

graceful ['greɪsfʊl] *adj* **-1.** [beautiful] elegante **-2.** [gracious] amável.

gracious ['greɪʃəs] ◇ *adj* [polite] afável. ◇ *excl*: **good) ~!** Santo Deus!, Nossa (Senhora)!

grade [greɪd] ◇ *n* **-1.** [level] nível *m* **-2.** [quality] qualidade *f*; **high-~** de alta qualidade; **low-~** de baixa qualidade **-3.** *US* [in school] série *f* **-4.** [mark] classificação *f* **-5.** *US* [gradient] declive *m*. ◇ *vt* **-1.** [classify] classificar **-2.** [mark, assess] avaliar.

grade crossing *n US* passagem *f* de nível.

grade school *n US* escola *f* primária.

grade school teacher *n US* professor *m*, -ra *f* de nível primário.

gradient ['greɪdjənt] *n* **-1.** [of road] declive *m* **-2.** *MATH* gradiente *m*.

gradual ['grædʒʊəl] *adj* gradual.

gradually ['grædʒʊəlɪ] *adv* gradualmente.

graduate [*n* 'grædʒʊət, *vb* 'grædʒʊeɪt] ◇ *n* **-1.** [person with a degree] graduado *m*, -da *f*, licenciado *m*, -da *f* **-2.** *US*: **to be a high-school ~** ter completado o segundo grau. ◇ *vi* **-1.** [with a degree]: **to ~** graduar-se **-2.** *US* [from high school]: **to ~** formar-se.

graduation [,grædʒʊ'eɪʃn] *n* **-1.** [completion of course] formatura *f* **-2.** [ceremony - at university] colação *f* de grau; *US* [at high school] formatura *f*.

graffiti [grə'fi:tɪ] *n* (*U*) pichação *f*.

graft [grɑ:ft] ◇ *n* **-1.** [gen] enxerto *m* **-2.** *UK inf* [hard work] labuta *f* **-3.** *US inf* [corruption] suborno *m*. ◇ *vt* enxertar.

grain [greɪn] *n* **-1.** [of corn, rice, salt] grão *m* **-2.** (*U*) [crops] cereais *mpl* **-3.** (*U*) [of wood] veio *m*.

gram [græm] *n* grama *f*.

grammar ['græmə'] *n* gramática *f*.

grammar school *n* **-1.** [in UK] ginásio *m* **-2.** [in US] escola *f* primária.

grammatical [grə'mætɪkl] *adj* gramatical.

gramme [græm] *n UK* = **gram**.

gramophone ['græməfəʊn] *dated n* gramofone *m*.

gran [græn] *n UK inf* vovó *f*.

granary bread *n* pão *m* de trigo.

grand [grænd] (*pl inv*) ◇ *adj* **-1.** [impressive, imposing] magnífico(ca) **-2.** [ambitious, large-scale] ambicioso(sa) **-3.** [socially important] ilustre **-4.** *inf dated* [excellent] excelente. ◇ *n inf* [thousand pounds] mil libras *fpl*; [thousand dollars] mil dólares *mpl*.

grandad *n inf* vovô *m*.

grandchild ['græntʃaɪld] (*pl* **-children** [-,tʃɪldrən]) *n* neto *m*, -ta *f*.

granddad ['grændæd] *n inf* = **grandad**.

granddaughter ['græn,dɔ:tə'] *n* neta *f*.

grandeur ['grændʒə'] *n* grandeza *f*.

grandfather ['grænd,fɑ:ðə'] *n* avô *m*.

grandma ['grænmɑ:] *n inf* vovó *f*, vó *f*.

grandmother ['græn,mʌðə'] *n* avó *f*.

grandpa ['grænpɑ:] *n inf* vovô *m*, vô *m*.

grandparents ['græn,peərənts] *npl* avós *mpl*.

grand piano *n* piano *m* de cauda.

grand slam *n SPORT* grand slam *m*.

grandson ['grænsʌn] *n* neto *m*.

grandstand ['grændstænd] *n* tribuna *f* de honra.

grand total *n* total *m* geral.

granite ['grænɪt] *n* (*U*) granito *m*.

granny ['grænɪ] (*pl* **-ies**) *n inf* vovó *f*, vó *f*.

grant [grɑ:nt] ◇ *n* [money - for renovations] subsídio *m*; [- for study] bolsa *f*. ◇ *vt fml* **-1.** [agree to] conceder **-2.** [accept as true] admitir. **-3.** *phr*: **to take sb/sthg for ~ed** não dar o devido valor a alguém/algo.

granulated sugar ['grænjʊleɪtɪd-] *n* (*U*) açúcar-cristal *m*.

granule ['grænjuːl] *n* grânulo *m*.

grape [greɪp] *n* uva *f*.

grapefruit ['greɪpfruːt] (*pl inv OR* **-s**) *n* pomelo *m*.

grapevine ['greɪpvaɪn] *n* **-1.** [plant] parreira *f* **-2.** *fig* [information channel]: **I heard on the ~ that ...** um passarinho me contou que ...

graph [grɑːf] *n* gráfico *m*.

graphic ['græfɪk] *adj* **-1.** [vivid] vívido(da) **-2.** *ART* pitoresco(ca).
➤ **graphics** *npl* [pictures] artes *fpl* gráficas.

graphic artist *n* artista *mf* gráfico, -ca.

graphite ['græfaɪt] *n* (*U*) grafita *f*.

graph paper *n* (*U*) papel *m* quadriculado.

grapple ['græpl] ➤ **grapple with** *vt fus*

grasp

154

grasp

-1. [physically] atracar-se com **-2.** *fig* [mentally] estar às voltas com.

grasp [grɑːsp] ◇ *n* **-1.** [grip] agarramento *m* **-2.** [understanding] compreensão *f*; **to have a good ~ of sthg** ter um bom domínio de algo. ◇ *vt* **-1.** [with hands] segurar **-2.** [understand] compreender **-3.** *fig* [seize] agarrar.

grasping ['grɑːspɪŋ] *adj pej* [greedy - person] ganancioso(sa); [- attitude] avaro(ra).

grass [grɑːs] ◇ *n* **-1.** [common green plant] grama *f* **-2.** *(U)* [drugs] *sl* [marijuana] maconha *f*. ◇ *vi UK crime sl*: **to ~ (on sb)** dedurar alguém.

grasshopper ['grɑːsˌhɒpəʳ] *n* gafanhoto *m*.

grass roots ◇ *npl* [ordinary people] plebe *f*. ◇ *comp* popular.

grass snake *n* cobra *f* d'água.

grate [greɪt]. ◇ *n* [fireplace] grade *f*. ◇ *vt CULIN* ralar. ◇ *vi* [irritate] irritar.

grateful ['greɪtfʊl] *adj* agradecido(da); **to be ~ to sb (for sthg)** ser grato(ta) a alguém (por algo).

grater ['greɪtəʳ] *n* ralador *m*.

gratify ['grætɪfaɪ] *(pt & pp* -ied*)* *vt* **-1.** [please]: **to be gratified** sentir-se gratificado(da) **-2.** [satisfy] satisfazer.

grating ['greɪtɪŋ] ◇ *adj* áspero(ra). ◇ *n* [grille] grade *f*.

gratitude ['grætɪtjuːd] *n (U)* gratidão *f*; **~ to sb (for sthg)** gratidão por alguém (por algo).

gratuitous [grəˈtjuːɪtəs] *adj fml* [unjustified] gratuito(ta).

grave [greɪv] ◇ *adj* grave. ◇ *n* túmulo *m*; **to dig one's own ~** cavar a própria sepultura.

gravel ['grævl] *n (U)* cascalho *m*.

gravestone ['greɪvstəʊn] *n* lápide *f*.

graveyard ['greɪvjɑːd] *n* cemitério *m*.

gravity ['grævətɪ] *n* **-1.** [force] gravidade *f* **-2.** *fml* [seriousness, worrying nature] seriedade *f*, gravidade *f*.

gravy ['greɪvɪ] *n* [meat juice] molho *m* de carne; [sauce] caldo *m* de carne.

gray *adj & n US* = **grey**.

graze [greɪz] ◇ *n* [wound] machucado *m*, ferimento *m*. ◇ *vt* **-1.** [feed on] pastar **-2.** [cause to feed] pastorear **-3.** [break surface of] esfolar **-4.** [touch lightly] tocar de leve. ◇ *vi* [animals] pastar.

grease [griːs] ◇ *n* **-1.** [animal fat] gordura *f* **-2.** [lubricant] graxa *f* **-3.** [dirt] sebo *m*. ◇ *vt* **-1.** [gen] engraxar **-2.** [baking tray] untar.

greaseproof paper [ˌgriːsˈpruːf-] *n (U) UK* papel *m* parafinado.

greasy ['griːzɪ] *(compar* -ier*, superl* -iest*)*

adj **-1.** [food] gorduroso(sa); [tools] engordurado(da); [hair, hands, skin] seboso(sa) **-2.** [clothes] sujo(ja) **-3.** [road] escorregadio(dia).

great [greɪt] ◇ *adj* **-1.** [gen] grande **-2.** *inf* [really good, really nice] ótimo(ma). ◇ *excl* ótimo!

Great Britain *n* Grã-Bretanha.

greatcoat ['greɪtkəʊt] *n* sobretudo *m* pesado.

Great Dane *n* dogue *m* alemão.

great-grandchild *n* bisneto *m*, -ta *f*.

great-grandfather *n* bisavô *m*.

great-grandmother *n* bisavó *f*.

greatly ['greɪtlɪ] *adv* imensamente; **~ exaggerated** muito exagerado(da); **~ different** extremamente diferente.

greatness ['greɪtnɪs] *n* grandeza *f*.

Greece [griːs] *n* Grécia.

greed [griːd] *n* **-1.** [for food] gula *f* **-2.** *fig* [for money, power]: **~ (for sthg)** ganância (por algo).

greedy ['griːdɪ] *(compar* -ier*, superl* -iest*)* *adj* **-1.** [for food] guloso(sa) **-2.** *fig* [for money, power]: **~ for sthg** ganancioso(sa) por algo.

Greek [griːk] ◇ *adj* grego(ga). ◇ *n* **-1.** [person] grego *m*, -ga *f* **-2.** [language] grego *m*.

green [griːn] ◇ *adj* **-1.** [gen] verde **-2.** *inf* [with nausea, fear] pálido(da) **-3.** *inf* [inexperienced] novato(ta). ◇ *n* **-1.** [colour] verde **-2.** [in village] praça *f* **-3.** *GOLF* green *m*.

➤ **Green** *n POL* Verde; **the Greens** os Verdes.

➤ **greens** *npl* [vegetables] verduras *fpl*.

greenback ['griːnbæk] *n US inf* [banknote] nota *f* de dólar.

green belt *n UK* área *f* verde.

green card *n* **-1.** *UK* [for insuring vehicle] *seguro que protege veículos e motoristas no exterior* **-2.** *US* [resident's permit] green card *m*, visto *m* permanente *(nos Estados Unidos)*.

greenery ['griːnərɪ] *n (U)* folhagem *f*.

greenfly ['griːnflaɪ] *(pl inv OR* -ies*)* *n* pulgão *m*.

greengage ['griːngeɪdʒ] *n* rainha-cláudia *f*.

greengrocer ['griːnˌgrəʊsəʳ] *n* verdureiro(ra); **~'s (shop)** quitanda *f*.

greenhouse ['griːnhaʊs, *pl* -haʊzɪz] *n* estufa *f*.

greenhouse effect *n*: **the ~** o efeito estufa.

greenhouse gas *n* gás *m* de efeito estufa.

Greenland ['griːnlənd] *n* Groenlândia.

green salad *n* salada *f* verde.

greet [griːt] vt **-1.** [say hello to] cumprimentar **-2.** [speech, announcement, remark] saudar.

greeting ['griːtɪŋ] n [salutation] cumprimento m, saudação f.

➡ **greetings** npl [on card] votos mpl.

greetings card UK ['griːtɪŋz-], **greeting card** US n cartão m de comemoração.

grenade [grəˈneɪd] n: **(hand)** ~ granada f (de mão).

grew [gruː] pt ▷ **grow**.

grey UK, **gray** US [greɪ] ◇ adj **-1.** [colour, weather] cinzento(ta) **-2.** [hair, beard] grisalho(lha); **to go** ~ ficar grisalho(lha) **-3.** fig [life, situation] preto(ta). ◇ n cinza m.

grey-haired [-ˈheəd] adj grisalho(lha).

greyhound ['greɪhaʊnd] n galgo m.

grid [grɪd] n **-1.** [grating] gradeamento m **-2.** [system of squares] grade f **-3.** ELEC rede f.

griddle ['grɪdl] n chapa f de ferro (para assar).

gridlock ['grɪdlɒk] n empasse m.

grief [griːf] n **-1.** [sorrow] pesar m, tristeza f **-2.** inf [trouble] chateação f **-3.** phr: **to come to** ~ fracassar; **good** ~! credo!

grievance ['griːvns] n [complaint] queixa m, agravo m.

grieve [griːv] vi: **to** ~ **(for sb/sthg)** estar de luto por alguém/algo.

grievous ['griːvəs] adj fml [serious, harmful] doloroso(sa).

grievous bodily harm n (U) lesão f corporal.

grill [grɪl] ◇ n [for cooking] grelha f. ◇ vt **-1.** [cook on grill] grelhar **-2.** inf [interrogate] interrogar.

grille [grɪl] n grade f.

grim [grɪm] (compar -mer, superl -mest) adj **-1.** [stern] severo(ra), rígido(da) **-2.** [gloomy] deprimente.

grimace [grɪˈmeɪs] ◇ n careta f. ◇ vi fazer caretas.

grime [graɪm] n (U) sujeira f.

grimy ['graɪmɪ] (compar -ier, superl -iest) adj imundo(da).

grin [grɪn] (pt & pp -ned, cont -ning) ◇ n sorriso m aberto. ◇ vi: **to** ~ **(at sb/sthg)** abrir um sorriso (para alguém/algo).

grind [graɪnd] (pt & pp ground) ◇ vt [coffee, pepper, grain] moer; **freshly ground coffee** café moído na hora. ◇ vi [scrape] arranhar. ◇ n [hard, boring work] rotina f.

➡ **grind down** vt sep [oppress] oprimir.

➡ **grind up** vt sep **-1.** [bottles] triturar **-2.** [knife] afiar **-3.** US [meat] picar **-4.** [gemstone] lapidar.

grinder ['graɪndər] n [machine] moedor m.

grip [grɪp] (pt & pp -ped, cont -ping) ◇ n **-1.** [physical hold]: **to have a** ~ **on sb/sthg** ter o controle sobre alguém/algo; **to keep a** ~ **on the handrail** segurar-se no corrimão; **to get a good** ~ dar um bom aperto; **to release one's** ~ **on sb/sthg** deixar de controlar alguém/algo **-2.** [control, domination] domínio m; ~ **on sb/sthg** controle sobre alguém/algo; **to get to** ~ **s with sthg** encarar algo; **to get a** ~ **on o.s.** controlar-se **-3.** (U) [adhesion] aderência f **-4.** [handle] punho m **-5.** dated [bag] valise f. ◇ vt **-1.** [grasp] agarrar **-2.** [subj: tyres] ter aderência a **-3.** [imagination, attention] controlar.

gripe [graɪp] inf ◇ n [complaint] queixa f; **the** ~ **s** cólicas fpl. ◇ vi: **to** ~ **(about sthg)** resmungar (por causa de algo).

gripping ['grɪpɪŋ] adj [story, film] emocionante.

grisly ['grɪzlɪ] (compar -ier, superl -iest) adj [horrible, macabre] horrendo(da), medonho(nha).

gristle ['grɪsl] n (U) cartilagem f.

grit [grɪt] (pt & pp -ted, cont -ting) ◇ n **-1.** [stones] areia f **-2.** inf [courage] coragem f. ◇ vt [road, steps] pôr areia em.

gritty ['grɪtɪ] (compar -ier, superl -iest) adj **-1.** [stony] arenoso(sa) **-2.** inf [brave] corajoso(sa).

groan [grəʊn] ◇ n gemido m. ◇ vi **-1.** [moan] gemer **-2.** [creak] ranger **-3.** [complain] resmungar.

grocer ['grəʊsər] n dono m, -na f de mercearia; ~ **'s (shop)** mercearia f.

groceries ['grəʊsərɪz] npl [foods] comestíveis mpl.

grocery ['grəʊsərɪ] (pl -ies) n [shop] mercearia f.

groggy ['grɒgɪ] (compar -ier, superl -iest) adj grogue.

groin [grɔɪn] n ANAT virilha f.

groom [gruːm] ◇ n **-1.** [of horses] cavalariço m **-2.** [bridegroom] noivo m. ◇ vt **-1.** [horse, dog] tratar **-2.** [candidate]: **to** ~ **sb (for sthg)** preparar alguém (para algo).

groomed adj: **well/badly** ~ bem/mal tratado(da).

groove [gruːv] n **-1.** [in metal, wood] entalhe m **-2.** [in record] ranhura f.

grope [grəʊp] vi: **to** ~ **(about) for sthg** [object] tatear por algo.

gross [grəʊs] (pl inv OR -es) ◇ adj **-1.** [total] bruto(ta) **-2.** fml [serious,

inexcusable] grave **-3.** inf [coarse, vulgar] indecente **-4.** inf [obese] balofo(fa). <> n grosa f.

grossly ['grəʊslı] adv [for emphasis] extremamente.

grotesque [grəʊ'tesk] adj [strange, unnatural] grotesco(ca).

grotto ['grɒtəʊ] (pl -es OR -s) n gruta f.

grotty ['grɒtı] (compar -ier, superl -iest) adj UK inf asqueroso(sa).

ground [graʊnd] <> pt & pp ⊳ grind. <> n -1. [surface of earth] terra f, chão m; above/below ~ em cima/embaixo da terra; on the ~ no chão -2. (U) [area of land] terreno m -3. [area used for a particular purpose] campo m -4. [subject area] área f -5. [advantage]: to gain/lose ~ ganhar/perder terreno. <> vt -1. [base]: to be ~ ed on OR in sthg ter algo como base; to be well-~ ed in sthg estar bem baseado em algo -2. [aircraft, pilot] ficar retido(da) -3. esp US inf [child] ficar de castigo -4. US ELEC: to be ~ ed ter um fio-terra.

➡ **grounds** npl -1. [reason] razão f, motivo m; ~ s for sthg/for doing sthg motivo para algo/para fazer algo -2. [land round building] jardins mpl -3. [of coffee] borra f.

ground crew n equipe f de terra.

ground floor n (andar m) térreo m.

grounding ['graʊndıŋ] n: ~ (in sthg) conhecimentos mpl básicos (sobre algo).

groundless ['graʊndlıs] adj infundado(da).

groundsheet ['graʊndʃi:t] n lona f.

ground staff n -1. [at sports ground] equipe f de campo -2. UK [at airport] pessoal m de terra.

groundswell ['graʊndswel] n [of feeling] acirramento m.

groundwork ['graʊndwɜ:k] n (U) base f, fundamento m.

group [gru:p] <> n -1. [gen] grupo m -2. MUS banda f. <> vt agrupar; [classify] classificar. <> vi: to ~ (together) agrupar-se.

groupie ['gru:pı] n inf tiete mf.

grouse [graʊs] (pl -s) <> n [bird] galo-silvestre m. <> vi inf queixar-se.

grove [grəʊv] n -1. [of trees] arvoredo m -2. [of fruit trees] pomar m.

grovel ['grɒvl] (UK pt & pp -led, cont -ling, US pt & pp -ed, cont -ing) vi pej [humble o.s.] humilhar-se; to ~ to sb humilhar-se diante de alguém.

grow [grəʊ] (pt grew, pp grown) <> vt -1. [plants] cultivar -2. [hair, beard] deixar crescer. <> vi -1. [plant, hair, person]

crescer; [company, city, economy, plan] desenvolver-se -2. [increase] aumentar -3. [become] tornar-se; to ~ tired of sthg cansar-se de algo.

➡ **grow on** vt fus inf [please more and more]: this book is growing on me gosto cada vez mais deste livro.

➡ **grow out of** vt fus -1. [clothes, shoes]: he's grown out of all his clothes as roupas dele ficaram pequenas -2. [habit] perder.

➡ **grow up** vi crescer.

grower ['grəʊə'] n [person] produtor m, -ra f, agricultor m, -ra f.

growl [graʊl] vi -1. [dog] rosnar -2. [lion] rugir -3. [engine] ranger -4. [person] resmungar.

grown [grəʊn] <> pp ⊳ grow. <> adj crescido(da).

grown-up <> adj -1. [fully grown, full-sized] crescido(da) -2. [mature, sensible] maduro(ra). <> n adulto m, -ta f.

growth [grəʊθ] n -1. (U) [development, increase] crescimento m -2. MED [lump] tumor m, abscesso m.

grub [grʌb] n -1. [insect] larva f -2. (U) inf [food] rango m.

grubby ['grʌbı] (compar -ier, superl -iest) adj encardido(da).

grudge [grʌdʒ] <> n ressentimento m; to bear sb a ~, to bear a ~ against sb guardar rancor contra alguém. <> vt ressentir, lamentar; to ~ sb sthg invejar alguém por algo.

gruelling UK, **grueling** US ['grʊəlıŋ] adj árduo(dua).

gruesome ['gru:səm] adj horrível.

gruff [grʌf] adj -1. [hoarse] rouco(ca) -2. [rough, unfriendly] brusco(ca).

grumble ['grʌmbl] vi -1. [complain] resmungar; to ~ about sthg resmungar por algo -2. [rumble - thunder, stomach] roncar; [- train] reboar.

grumpy ['grʌmpı] (compar -ier, superl -iest) adj -1. inf [person] resmungão(ona) -2. inf [face] rabugento(ta).

grunt [grʌnt] <> n -1. [of pig] grunhido m -2. [of person] resmungo m. <> vi -1. [pig] grunhir -2. [person] resmungar.

G-string n -1. MUS corda f G -2. [clothing] tanga f tapa-sexo.

guarantee [ˌgærən'ti:] <> n garantia f. <> vt -1. COMM dar garantia para -2. [promise] garantir.

guard [gɑ:d] <> n -1. [person] guarda mf -2. [group of guards] guarda f -3. [supervision] proteção f; to be on ~ estar em guarda; to catch sb off ~ pegar alguém desprevenido(da) -4. UK RAIL chefe mf de trem -5. [protective device] dispositivo m de segurança - **6.** [in boxing] proteção f. ⬦ vt - **1.** [protect] proteger - **2.** [prevent from escaping] vigiar.

guard dog n cão m de guarda.

guarded ['gɑ:dɪd] adj [careful] cauteloso(sa).

guardian ['gɑ:djən] n - **1.** JUR [of child] guardião m, -diã f - **2.** [protector] curador m, -ra f.

guard rail n US [on road] proteção f lateral.

guard's van n UK vagão m de freio.

guerilla [gə'rɪlə] n = guerrilla.

Guernsey ['gɜ:nzɪ] n [place] Guernsey.

guerrilla [gə'rɪlə] n guerrilheiro m, -ra f; **urban ~** guerrilheiro urbano, guerrilheira urbana.

guerrilla warfare n (U) guerrilha f.

guess [ges] ⬦ n - **1.** [at facts, figures] suposição f - **2.** [hypothesis] hipótese f. ⬦ vt [assess correctly] adivinhar; **~ what!** adivinha! ⬦ vi - **1.** [attempt to answer] chutar; **to ~ at sthg** tentar adivinhar algo - **2.** [think, suppose]: **I ~ (so)** eu acho (que sim).

guesswork ['geswɜ:k] n (U) adivinhação f.

guest [gest] n - **1.** [visitor - at home] visita mf; [- at club, restaurant, concert] convidado m, -da f - **2.** [at hotel] hóspede mf.

guesthouse ['gesthaʊs, pl -haʊzɪz] n pensão f.

guestroom ['gestrʊm] n quarto m de hóspedes.

guffaw [gʌ'fɔ:] ⬦ n gargalhada f. ⬦ vi gargalhar, dar gargalhadas.

guidance ['gaɪdəns] n - **1.** [help] orientação f - **2.** [leadership] liderança f.

guide [gaɪd] ⬦ n - **1.** [person, book for tourist] guia mf - **2.** [manual] manual m - **3.** [indication] estimativa f (aproximada) - **4.** = **girl guide**. ⬦ vt - **1.** [show by leading] guiar; **the waiter ~d them to a table** o garçom os conduziu até a mesa - **2.** [plane, missile] orientar - **3.** [influence]: **to be ~d by sb/sthg** ser orientado(da) por alguém/algo.

Guide Association n: **the ~** as Escoteiras.

guide book n guia m.

guide dog n cão-guia m.

guided tour n - **1.** [of city] excursão f guiada - **2.** [of cathedral, museum etc.] visita f guiada.

guidelines ['gaɪdlaɪnz] npl princípios mpl, diretrizes fpl.

guild [gɪld] n - **1.** HIST guilda f - **2.** [association] associação f.

guile [gaɪl] n (U) literary astúcia f.

guillotine ['gɪlə,ti:n] ⬦ n guilhotina f. ⬦ vt guilhotinar.

guilt [gɪlt] n culpa f.

guilty ['gɪltɪ] (compar -ier, superl -iest) adj - **1.** [remorseful] culpado(da) - **2.** [causing remorse] condenável, que causa remorso - **3.** JUR culpado(da); **to be found ~ /not ~** ser declarado culpado(da)/inocente - **4.** fig [culpable] culpável; **to be ~ of sthg** ser culpado(da) de algo.

guinea pig ['gɪnɪ-] n - **1.** [animal] porquinho-da-India m - **2.** [subject of experiment] cobaia mf.

guise [gaɪz] n fml aparência f, aspecto m.

guitar [gɪ'tɑ:ʳ] n violão m, guitarra f.

guitarist [gɪ'tɑ:rɪst] n violonista mf, guitarrista mf.

gulf [gʌlf] n - **1.** [sea] golfo m - **2.** [deep hole]: **~ (between)** abismo (entre) - **3.** fig [separation] abismo m.

➡ **Gulf** n: **the Gulf** o Golfo Pérsico.

gull [gʌl] n [bird] gaivota f.

gullet ['gʌlɪt] n esôfago m.

gullible ['gʌləbl] adj ingênuo(nua).

gully ['gʌlɪ] (pl -ies) n - **1.** [valley] barranco m - **2.** [ditch] vala f.

gulp [gʌlp] ⬦ n gole m. ⬦ vt engolir. ⬦ vi engolir em seco.

➡ **gulp down** vt sep engolir.

gum [gʌm] (pt & pp -med, cont -ming) ⬦ n - **1.** (U) [chewing gum] chiclete m - **2.** [adhesive] goma f. ANAT gengiva f. ⬦ vt - **1.** [cover with adhesive] passar goma em - **2.** [stick] colar.

gumboots ['gʌmbu:ts] npl UK galocha f.

gummed adj adesivo(va).

gun [gʌn] (pt & pp -ned, cont -ning) n - **1.** [gen] arma f - **2.** [specific type - revolver] revólver m; [- pistol] pistola f; [- shotgun] espingarda m; [- rifle] rifle m; [- cannon] canhão m - **3.** SPORT [starting pistol] revólver m - **4.** [tool] pistola f.

➡ **gun down** vt sep balear.

gunboat ['gʌnbəʊt] n canhoeira f.

gunfire ['gʌnfaɪəʳ] n (U) tiroteio m.

gunman ['gʌnmən] (pl -men [-mən]) n pistoleiro m.

gunpoint ['gʌnpɔɪnt] n: **at ~** na mira.

gunpowder ['gʌn,paʊdəʳ] n (U) pólvora f.

gunshot ['gʌnʃɒt] n [firing of gun] tiro m.

gunsmith ['gʌnsmɪθ] n armeiro m, -ra f.

gurgle ['gɜ:gl] vi - **1.** [water] gorgolejar - **2.** [baby] fazer gugu.

guru ['gʊru:] n [spiritual leader] guru m.

gush [gʌʃ] ⬦ n jorro m. ⬦ vi - **1.** [flow out] verter - **2.** pej [enthuse] entusiasmar-se.

gusset ['gʌsɪt] n -1. SEWING nesga f- 2. [in tights] entreperna m.

gust [gʌst] n rajada f.

gusto ['gʌstəu] n (U): with ~ com garra.

gut [gʌt] (pt & pp -ted, cont -ting) <> n -1. MED intestino m -2. inf [stomach] bucho m. <> vt -1. [remove organs from] destripar -2. [destroy] destruir.
➡ **guts** npl inf -1. [intestines] tripas fpl; to hate sb's ~ s ter alguém atravessado(-da) na garganta - 2. [courage] coragem f.

gutter ['gʌtəʳ] n -1. [ditch] sarjeta f - 2. [on roof] calha f.

gutter press n pej imprensa-marrom f.

guy [gaɪ] n -1. inf [man] cara mf- 2. esp US [person] galera f inv -3. UK [dummy] boneco que se queima na Grã-Bretanha na Noite da Conspiração da Pólvora.

Guy Fawkes Night n Noite f da Conspiração da Pólvora.

guy rope n amarra f.

guzzle ['gʌzl] <> vt pej - [food] devorar com gula;[- drink] beber com gula. <> vi engolir com gula.

gym [dʒɪm] n inf -1. [gymnasium - in school] ginásio m; [- in hotel, health club] sala f de ginástica - 2. (U) [exercises] ginástica f, ginásio m.

gymnasium [dʒɪm'neɪzjəm] (pl -siums OR -sia [-zjə]) n ginásio m.

gymnast ['dʒɪmnæst] n ginasta mf.

gymnastics [dʒɪm'næstɪks] n (U) ginástica f.

gym shoes npl sapatilha f de ginástica.

gymslip ['dʒɪm,slɪp] n UK bata f escolar.

gynaecologist UK, **gynecologist** US [,gaɪnə'kɒlədʒɪst] n ginecologista mf.

gynaecology UK, **gynecology** US [,gaɪnə'kɒlədʒɪ] n (U) ginecologia f.

gypsy ['dʒɪpsɪ] (pl -ies) adj & n = gipsy.

gyrate [dʒaɪ'reɪt] vi girar.

H

h (pl h's OR hs), **H** (pl H's OR Hs) [eɪtʃ] n [letter] h, H m.

haberdashery ['hæbədæʃərɪ] (pl -ies) n -1. (U) [goods] materiais mpl de costura, artigos mpl de armarinho -2. [shop] armarinho m.

habit ['hæbɪt] n -1. [customary practice] hábito m, costume m; to make a ~ of sthg tornar algo um hábito; to make a ~ of doing sthg ter por hábito fazer algo - 2. [drug addiction] vício m - 3. [garment] hábito m.

habitat ['hæbɪtæt] n hábitat m.

habitual [hə'bɪtʃuəl] adj -1. [customary] habitual, costumeiro(ra) -2. [offender, smoker, drinker] inveterado(da).

hack [hæk] <> n pej [writer] escritorzinho m, -razinha f. <> vt -1. [cut] cortar - 2. inf [cope with] enfrentar.
➡ **hack into** vt fus COMPUT invadir ilegalmente.

hacker ['hækəʳ] n COMPUT: (computer) ~ hacker mf (de computador).

hackneyed ['hæknɪd] adj pej batido(da), banal.

hacksaw ['hæksɔ:] n serra f para metais.

had [weak form həd, strong form hæd] pt & pp ⊳ have.

haddock ['hædək] (pl inv) n hadoque m.

hadn't ['hædnt] = had not.

haemophiliac [,hi:mə'fɪliæk] n = hemophiliac.

haemorrhage ['hemərɪdʒ] n & vi = hemorrhage.

haemorrhoids ['hemərɔɪdz] npl = hemorrhoids.

haggard ['hægəd] adj abatido(da).

haggis ['hægɪs] n lingüiça escocesa, normalmente com o formato de uma bola, feita de carne de carneiro picada e embutida na pele do estômago do carneiro.

haggle ['hægl] vi pechinchar, regatear; to ~ over OR about sthg pechinchar acerca de algo.

Hague [heɪg] n: The ~ Haia.

hail [heɪl] <> n -1. (U) [frozen rain] granizo m -2. fig [torrent - of bullets] rajada f; [- of criticism] chuva f; [- of abuse] onda f. <> vt -1. [call] chamar - 2. [acclaim]: to ~ sb/sthg as sthg aclamar alguém/algo como algo. <> v impers METEOR chover granizo.

hailstone ['heɪlstəun] n granizo m.

hailstorm n chuva f de granizo.

hair [heəʳ] <> n -1. (U) [on human head] cabelo m; to do one's ~ pentear-se -2. [on animal, insect, plant] pêlo m -3. [on human skin] pêlo m. <> comp -1. [oil, lotion] capilar -2. [conditioner] de cabelos.

hairbrush ['heəbrʌʃ] n escova f de cabelo.

haircut ['heəkʌt] n corte m de cabelo.

hairdo ['heədu:] (pl -s) n inf penteado m.

hairdresser ['heə,dresəʳ] n cabeleireiro m, -ra f; ~'s **(salon)** (salão m de) cabeleireiro m.

hairdryer ['heə,draɪəʳ] n secador m de cabelos.

hair gel n (U) gel m fixador.

hairgrip ['heəgrɪp] n UK grampo m de cabelo.

hairpin ['heəpɪn] n grampo m de cabelo.

hairpin bend n curva f fechada.

hair-raising [-,reɪzɪŋ] adj assustador(-ra); a ~ story uma história de deixar os cabelos em pé.

hair remover [-rɪ,muːvəʳ] n (creme m) depilatório m.

hair slide n UK passador m, presilha f.

hairspray ['heəspreɪ] n laquê m.

hairstyle ['heəstaɪl] n penteado m.

hairy ['heərɪ] (compar **-ier**, superl **-iest**) adj **-1.** [covered in hair - person] cabeludo(da); [- animal, legs] peludo(da) **-2.** inf [dangerous] arriscado(da).

Haiti ['heɪtɪ] n Haiti.

hake [heɪk] (pl inv OR **-s**) n merluza f.

half [UK haːf, US hæf] (pl **halves**) <> adj meio (meia); ~ **my salary** metade f do meu salário. <> adv **-1.** [partly, almost] meio, quase; **I ~ expected him to say yes** eu meio que esperava que ele dissesse sim **-2.** [by half]: **to increase sthg by ~** acrescentar a metade ao valor de algo **-3.** [in equal measure] meio; ~**-and-~** meio a meio **-4.** [in telling the time]: ~ **past ten** UK, ~ **after ten** US dez e meia; **it's ~ past ten/one** são dez e meia/é uma e meia. <> n **-1.** [one of two equal parts] metade f; **to go halves (with sb)** rachar as despesas (com alguém) **-2.** [fraction] meio m **-3.** SPORT [of sports match] tempo m **-4.** SPORT [halfback] meio-campo mf **-5.** [of beer] meia cerveja f **-6.** [child's ticket] meia entrada f. <> pron [one of two equal parts] metade de; ~ **of** metade do.

halfback ['haːfbæk] n meio-campo mf.

half board n (U) UK meia pensão f.

half-breed <> adj mestiço(ça). <> n mestiço m, -ça f.

half-caste [-kaːst] <> adj mestiço(ça). <> n mestiço m, -ça f.

half-fare n meia passagem f.

half-hearted [-'haːtɪd] adj desanimado(da).

half hour n meia hora f.

half-mast n UK: **at ~** [flag] a meio pau.

half moon n meia-lua f.

half note n US MUS mínima f.

halfpenny ['heɪpnɪ] (pl **-pennies** OR **-pence**) n meio pêni m.

half-price adj a metade do preço.

half term n UK recesso m escolar.

half time n (U) meio-tempo m.

halfway [haːf'weɪ] <> adj no meio do caminho. <> adv **-1.** [in space] a meio caminho **-2.** [in time] no meio.

halibut ['hælɪbət] (pl inv OR **-s**) n halibute m.

hall [hɔːl] n **-1.** [in house] entrada f, hall m **-2.** [meeting room] salão m **-3.** [public building] sala f; **town ~** prédio m da prefeitura **-4.** UK [UNIV & hall of residence] alojamento m, casa f do estudante **-5.** [country house] mansão m.

hallmark ['hɔːlmaːk] n **-1.** [typical feature] marca f distintiva **-2.** [on metal] selo m de autenticidade.

hallo [hə'ləʊ] excl = hello.

hall of residence (pl **halls of residence**) n UK UNIV casa f do estudante.

Hallowe'en, Halloween, [,hæləʊ'iːn] n Dia m das Bruxas.

hallucinate [hə'luːsɪneɪt] vi alucinar.

hallway ['hɔːlweɪ] n **-1.** [at entrance of house] saguão m, hall m **-2.** [corridor] corredor m.

halo ['heɪləʊ] (pl **-es** OR **-s**) n [of saint, angel] auréola f.

halt [hɔːlt] <> n [stop]: **to come to a ~** [vehicle, horse] fazer uma parada; [development, activity] interromper-se; **to call a ~ to sthg** pôr fim a algo. <> vt [stop - person] deter; [- development, activity] interromper. <> vi [stop - person, train] parar; [- development, activity] interromper-se.

halterneck ['hɔːltənek] adj: ~ **dress** vestido m de frente única.

halve [UK haːv, US hæv] vt **-1.** [reduce by half] reduzir à metade **-2.** [divide] partir ao meio.

halves [UK haːvz, US hævz] pl ⊳ **half**.

ham [hæm] (pt & pp **-med**, cont **-ming**) <> n [meat] presunto m. <> comp de presunto.

hamburger ['hæmbɜːgəʳ] n **-1.** [burger] hambúrguer m **-2.** US [mince] carne f moída.

hamlet ['hæmlɪt] n aldeia f.

hammer ['hæməʳ] <> n [tool] martelo m. <> vt **-1.** [with tool] martelar **-2.** [with fist] bater em **-3.** inf fig [fact, order]: **to ~ sthg into sb** meter algo na cabeça de alguém **-4.** inf fig [defeat] dar uma surra em. <> vi [with fist]: **to ~ (on sthg)** bater com insistência (em algo).

➡ **hammer out** <> vt fus [draw up] alcançar com muito esforço. <> vt sep [with tool] malhar.

hammock ['hæmək] n rede f de dormir.

hamper ['hæmpə'] <> n -1. [for picnic] cesta f -2. US [for laundry] cesto m de roupa. <> vt [impede] dificultar.

hamster ['hæmstə'] n hamster m.

hamstring ['hæmstrɪŋ] n ANAT tendão m do jarrete.

hand [hænd] <> n -1. [part of body] mão f; **to hold ~s** dar as mãos; **by ~** à mão; **to get** OR **lay one's ~s on sb** colocar OR pôr as mãos em alguém -2. [help] mão f; **to give** OR **lend sb a ~** (with sthg) dar uma mão para alguém (em algo) -3. [control, management] mão f -4. [worker - on farm] peão m, -ona f; [- on ship] tripulante mf -5. [of clock, watch] ponteiro m -6. [handwriting] caligrafia f -7. [of cards] mão f. <> vt: **to ~ sthg to sb**, **to ~ sb sthg** entregar algo a alguém.

◆ **(close) at hand** adv próximo.
◆ **in hand** adv -1. [time, money]: **to have sthg in ~** ter algo sobrando -2. [problem, situation]: **to have sb/sthg in ~** ter alguém/algo sob controle.
◆ **on hand** adv em prontidão.
◆ **on the one hand** adv por um lado.
◆ **on the other hand** adv por outro lado.
◆ **out of hand** <> adj [situation]: **to get out of ~** sair de controle. <> adv [completely] completamente.
◆ **to hand** adv à mão.
◆ **hand down** vt sep [to next generation] legar.
◆ **hand in** vt sep entregar.
◆ **hand out** vt sep distribuir.
◆ **hand over** <> vt sep -1. [baton, money] entregar -2. [responsibility, power] transferir, ceder -3. TELEC passar a ligação. <> vi [government minister, chairman] transferir; **to ~ over to sb** transferir para alguém.

handbag ['hændbæg] n bolsa f.

handball ['hændbɔːl] n (U) [game] handebol m.

handbook ['hændbʊk] n manual m.

handbrake ['hændbreɪk] n freio m de mão.

handcuffs ['hændkʌfs] npl algemas fpl.

handful ['hændfʊl] n lit & fig punhado m.

handgun ['hændgʌn] n arma f de mão.

handheld PC ['hændheld-] n computador m de bolso, handheld m.

handicap ['hændɪkæp] (pt & pp **-ped**, cont **-ping**) <> n -1. [physical or mental disability] deficiência f -2. fig [disadvantage] obstáculo m -3. SPORT handicap m. <> vt [hinder] estorvar, atrapalhar.

handicapped ['hændɪkæpt] <> adj [physically or mentally disabled] deficiente. <> npl: **the ~** os deficientes.

handicraft ['hændɪkrɑːft] n [skill] artesanato m.

handiwork ['hændɪwɜːk] n (U) [work produced by o.s.] trabalho m manual.

handkerchief ['hæŋkətʃɪf] (pl **-chiefs** OR **-chieves** [-tʃiːvz]) n lenço m.

handle ['hændl] <> n -1. [for opening and closing - of window] trinco m; [- of door] maçaneta f -2. [for holding] cabo m -3. [for carrying] alça f. <> vt -1. [with hands] manusear -2. [control, operate - car] guiar; [- ship] comandar; [- gun] manejar; [- words] articular -3. [manage, process] manejar -4. [cope with] tratar de.

handlebars ['hændlbɑːz] npl guidom m.

handler ['hændlə'] n -1. [of animal] treinador m, -ra f -2. [of luggage]: **(baggage) ~** carregador m, -ra f (de bagagem) -3. [of stolen goods] receptador m, -ra f.

hand luggage n UK bagagem f de mão.

handmade [,hænd'meɪd] adj feito(ta) à mão.

handout ['hændaʊt] n -1. [gift] donativo m -2. [leaflet] folheto m informativo -3. [for lecture, discussion] polígrafo m.

handrail ['hændreɪl] n corrimão m.

handset ['hændset] n TELEC fone m (do telefone).

handshake ['hændʃeɪk] n aperto m de mão.

handsome ['hænsəm] adj -1. [man] bonito(ta) -2. [reward, profit] considerável.

handstand ['hændstænd] n: **to do a ~** plantar bananeira.

hand towel n toalha f de mão.

handwriting ['hænd,raɪtɪŋ] n letra f, caligrafia f.

handy ['hændɪ] (compar **-ier**, superl **-iest**) adj inf -1. [useful] prático(ca); **to come in ~** vir a calhar -2. [skilful] hábil -3. [near] à mão.

handyman ['hændɪmæn] (pl **-men** [-men]) n faz-tudo mf.

hang [hæŋ] (pt & pp sense 1 **hung**, pt & pp sense 2 **hung** OR **hanged**) <> vt -1. [suspend] pendurar -2. [execute] enforcar. <> vi -1. [be suspended] estar suspenso(sa) -2. [be executed] ser enforcado(da). <> n: **to get the ~ of sthg** inf pegar o jeito de algo.

◆ **hang about, hang around** vi -1. [loiter] demorar-se -2. [wait] rondar.
◆ **hang down** vi pender.
◆ **hang on** vi -1. [keep hold]: **to ~ on (to sb/sthg)** segurar-se (em alguém/

algo) **- 2.** *inf* [continue waiting] aguardar **- 3.** [persevere] resistir, agüentar.

➤ **hang out** *vi inf* [spend time] passar um tempo, frequentar.

➤ **hang round** *vi* = **hang about.**

➤ **hang up** ◇ *vt sep* [suspend] pendurar. ◇ *vi* [on telephone] desligar.

➤ **hang up on me** *vt fus* TELEC desligar; **he hung up on me** ele desligou o telefone na minha cara.

hangar ['hæŋəʳ] *n* hangar *m*.

hanger ['hæŋəʳ] *n* [coat hanger] cabide *m*.

hanger-on (*pl* hangers-on) *n* bajulador *m*, -ra *f*, aproveitador *m*, -ra *f*.

hang gliding *n (U)* vôo *m* livre *(com asa delta)*.

hangover ['hæŋ,əʊvəʳ] *n* [from drinking] ressaca *f*; **to have a ~** estar de ressaca.

hang-up *n inf* PSYCH complexo *m*.

hanker ['hæŋkəʳ] ➤ **hanker after, hanker for** *vt fus* ansiar por, desejar ardentemente.

hankie, hanky ['hæŋkɪ] (*pl* -ies) (*abbr of* **handkerchief**) *n inf* lencinho *m*.

hanky-panky *n inf* [sexual behaviour] sem-vergonhice *f*.

haphazard [,hæp'hæzəd] *adj* caótico(-ca), desordenado(da).

hapless ['hæplɪs] *adj literary* desafortunado(da).

happen ['hæpən] *vi* **- 1.** [occur] acontecer; **to ~ to sb** acontecer com alguém **- 2.** [chance]: **I ~ed to see him yesterday** por acaso eu o vi ontem; **do you ~ to have a pen on you?** você não teria por acaso uma caneta?; **as it ~s** por acaso.

happening ['hæpənɪŋ] *n* [occurrence] acontecimento *m*.

happily ['hæpɪlɪ] *adv* **- 1.** [contentedly]: **to be ~ doing sthg** fazer algo alegremente **- 2.** [fortunately] felizmente **- 3.** [willingly] com satisfação.

happiness ['hæpɪnɪs] *n (U)* felicidade *f*.

happy ['hæpɪ] (*compar* -ier, *superl* -iest) *adj* **- 1.** [contented] feliz, contente **- 2.** [causing contentment] feliz; **Happy Christmas/New Year/Birthday!** Feliz Natal/Ano Novo/Aniversário!; **to be ~ with** OR **about sthg** estar feliz com algo; **to be ~ to do sthg** estar muito disposto(ta) a fazer algo; **I'd be ~ to do it** eu faria isso com muito gosto.

happy-go-lucky *adj* despreocupado(-da).

happy medium *n* meio-termo *m*.

harangue [hə'ræŋ] ◇ *n* arenga *f*, ladainha *f*. ◇ *vt* arengar.

harass ['hærəs] *vt* [pester - with questions,

problems] atormentar; [- sexually] molestar.

harbour UK, **harbor** US ['hɑ:bəʳ] ◇ *n* porto *m*. ◇ *vt* **- 1.** [feeling] abrigar **- 2.** [person] dar refúgio a.

hard [hɑ:d] ◇ *adj* **- 1.** [very firm, not soft] duro(ra) **- 2.** [difficult] difícil **- 3.** [strenuous, stressful] duro(ra), pesado(da) **- 4.** [forceful] forte **- 5.** [harsh, unkind] ríspido(-da); **to be ~ on sb/sthg** ser duro com alguém/algo **- 6.** [winter, frost] rigoroso(-sa) **- 7.** [water] duro(ra) **- 8.** [fact, news] concreto(ta) **- 9.** UK POL [extreme]: **~ left/right** extrema esquerda/direita. ◇ *adv* **- 1.** [strenuously] muito, duro **- 2.** [forcefully] com força **- 3.** [rain, snow] intensamente **- 4.** *phr*: **to be ~ pushed** OR **put** OR **pressed to do sthg** ver-se em apuros para fazer algo; **to feel ~ done by** sentir-se injustiçado(da) por.

hardback ['hɑ:dbæk] ◇ *adj* de capa dura. ◇ *n* [book] edição *f* de capa dura.

hardboard ['hɑ:dbɔ:d] *n (U)* madeira *f* compensada.

hard-boiled *adj* [egg] cozido(da).

hard cash *n (U)* dinheiro *m* vivo.

hard copy *n* COMPUT cópia *f* impressa.

hard disk *n* disco *m* rígido.

harden ['hɑ:dn] ◇ *vt* **- 1.** [steel, arteries] endurecer **- 2.** *fig* [person] endurecer **- 3.** [attitude, ideas, opinion] fortalecer. ◇ *vi* **- 1.** [glue, concrete, arteries] endurecer, endurecer-se **- 2.** [attitude, ideas, opinion] fortalecer-se.

hard-headed [-'hedɪd] *adj* realista.

hard-hearted [-'hɑ:tɪd] *adj* insensível; **a ~ person** uma pessoa sem coração.

hard labour *n (U)* trabalhos *mpl* forçados.

hard-liner *n* linha-dura *mf*.

hardly ['hɑ:dlɪ] *adv* **- 1.** [scarcely, not really] dificilmente; **~ ever/anything** quase nunca/nada; **I can ~ move/wait** mal posso me mover/esperar **- 2.** [only just] apenas.

hardness ['hɑ:dnɪs] *n* **- 1.** [firmness, also of water] dureza *f* **- 2.** [difficulty] dificuldade *f*.

hard return *n* COMPUT retorno *m* de hardware.

hardship ['hɑ:dʃɪp] *n* **- 1.** *(U)* [difficult conditions] privações *fpl* **- 2.** [difficult circumstance] dificuldade *f*.

hard shoulder *n* UK AUT acostamento *m*.

hard up *adj inf* desprovido(da); **~ for sthg** desprovido(da) de algo.

hardware ['hɑ:dweəʳ] *n* **- 1.** [tools, equipment] ferragens *fpl* **- 2.** COMPUT hardware *m*.

hardware shop n ferragem f.

hardwearing [ˌhɑːdˈweərɪŋ] adj UK resistente.

hardworking [ˌhɑːdˈwɜːkɪŋ] adj trabalhador(ra).

hardy ['hɑːdɪ] (compar -ier, superl -iest) adj -1. [person, animal] forte, robusto(ta) -2. [plant] resistente.

hare [heəʳ] n lebre f.

harebrained ['heəˌbreɪnd] adj inf tolo(la).

harelip [ˌheəˈlɪp] n lábio m leporino.

haricot (bean) ['hærɪkəʊ-] n feijão m.

harm [hɑːm] ◇ n [physical] mal m; [psychological] dano m; to do ~ to sb/sthg, to do sb/sthg ~ fazer mal a alguém/algo; to be out of ~'s way estar a salvo. ◇ vt [physically] ferir; [psychologically] danificar, prejudicar.

harmful ['hɑːmfʊl] adj [physically] nocivo(va); [psychologically] prejudicial.

harmless ['hɑːmlɪs] adj inofensivo(va).

harmonica [hɑːˈmɒnɪkə] n gaita-de-boca f.

harmonize, -ise ['hɑːmənaɪz] ◇ vt harmonizar. ◇ vi harmonizar; to ~ with sthg harmonizar-se com algo.

harmony ['hɑːmənɪ] (pl -ies) n harmonia f.

harness ['hɑːnɪs] ◇ n -1. [for horse] arreio m -2. [for person, child] andador m. ◇ vt -1. [horse] arrear, pôr arreios em -2. [energy, solar power] aproveitar.

harp [hɑːp] n MUS harpa f.
➤ **harp on** vi: to ~ on (about sthg) bater sempre na mesma tecla (sobre algo).

harpoon [hɑːˈpuːn] ◇ n arpão m. ◇ vt arpoar.

harpsichord ['hɑːpsɪkɔːd] n clavicórdio m.

harrowing ['hærəʊɪŋ] adj angustiante.

harsh [hɑːʃ] adj -1. [cruel, severe] severo(ra), duro(ra) -2. [conditions, weather] duro(ra) -3. [cry, voice] áspero(ra) -4. [colour, contrast, light] forte -5. [landscape] desolado(da) -6. [taste] azedo(da).

harvest ['hɑːvɪst] ◇ n colheita f. ◇ vt [crops] colher.

has [weak form həz, strong form hæz] vb ➤ have.

has-been n inf pej: that man is a ~ aquele homem já era.

hash [hæʃ] n -1. (U) [meat] picadinho m -2. inf [mess]: to make a ~ of sthg fazer uma confusão em algo.

hashish ['hæʃiːʃ] n (U) haxixe m.

hasn't ['hæznt] = has not.

hassle ['hæsl] inf ◇ n [annoyance] amolação f. ◇ vt amolar, aborrecer.

haste [heɪst] n (U) -1. [rush] pressa f; to do sthg in ~ fazer algo às pressas -2. [speed] rapidez f; to make ~ dated apressar-se.

hasten ['heɪsn] ◇ vt acelerar. ◇ vi apressar-se; I ~ to add that ... apressome a acrescentar que ...

hastily ['heɪstɪlɪ] adv -1. [rashly] apressadamente -2. [quickly] rapidamente, às pressas.

hasty ['heɪstɪ] (compar -ier, superl -iest) adj -1. [rash] precipitado(da) -2. [quick] breve.

hat [hæt] n chapéu m.

hatch [hætʃ] ◇ vt -1. [chick] incubar -2. [egg] chocar -3. fig [scheme, plot] conceber, idealizar. ◇ vi -1. [chick] sair do ovo -2. [egg] chocar. ◇ n [for serving food] portinhola f, janela f de comunicação.

hatchback ['hætʃˌbæk] n carro m com porta traseira.

hatchet ['hætʃɪt] n machadinha f.

hatchway ['hætʃˌweɪ] n escotilha f.

hate [heɪt] ◇ n -1. [emotion] ódio m -2. [person, thing hated] aversão f. ◇ vt [dislike] detestar, odiar; to ~ doing sthg odiar fazer algo.

hateful ['heɪtfʊl] adj detestável.

hatred ['heɪtrɪd] n (U) ódio m.

hat trick n SPORT série de três pontos marcados pelo mesmo jogador na mesma partida.

haughty ['hɔːtɪ] (compar -ier, superl -iest) adj arrogante.

haul [hɔːl] ◇ n -1. [of drugs, stolen goods] carregamento m -2. [distance]: long ~ longo trajeto m. ◇ vt [pull] arrastar, puxar.

haulage ['hɔːlɪdʒ] n -1. [gen] transporte m -2. [cost] gasto m com transporte.

haulier UK ['hɔːlɪəʳ], **hauler** US ['hɔːlər] n -1. [business] transportadora f -2. [person] transportador m, -ra f.

haunch [hɔːntʃ] n -1. [of person] quadril m -2. [of animal] lombo m.

haunt [hɔːnt] ◇ n [place] lugar m preferido. ◇ vt -1. [subj: ghost] assombrar -2. [subj: memory, fear, problem] perseguir.

have [hæv] (pt & pp had) ◇ aux vb -1. [to form perfect tenses]: I ~ finished acabei; ~ you been there? - no, I ~ n't você já esteve lá? - não; they hadn't seen it não o tinham visto; we had already left nós já tínhamos saído -2. [must]: to ~ (got) to do sthg ter de fazer algo; do you ~ to pay? - é preciso pagar? ◇ vt -1. [possess]: to ~ (got) ter; do you ~ OR ~ you got a double

room? você tem um quarto de casal?; **she's got brown hair** ela tem o cabelo castanho **-2.** [experience] ter; **to ~ a cold** estar resfriado; **to ~ a great time** divertir-se a valer **-3.** [replacing other verbs] ter; **to ~ breakfast** tomar o café da manhã; **to ~ dinner** jantar; **to ~ lunch** almoçar; **to ~ a bath** tomar banho; **to ~ a drink** tomar qualquer coisa, tomar um drinque; **to ~ a shower** tomar um banho; **to ~ a swim** nadar **-4.** [feel] ter; **I ~ no doubt about it** não tenho dúvida alguma OR nenhuma sobre isso **-5.** [cause to be]: **to ~ sthg done** mandar fazer algo; **to ~ one's hair cut** cortar o cabelo **-6.** [be treated in a certain way]: **I've had my wallet stolen** roubaram a minha carteira.

haven ['heɪvn] n [refuge] abrigo m.

haven't ['hævnt] = **have not**.

haversack ['hævəsæk] n dated mochila f.

havoc ['hævək] n (U) destruição f, estragos mpl; **to play ~ with sthg** causar estragos em algo.

Hawaii [hə'waɪi:] n Havaí; **in ~** no Havaí.

hawk [hɔːk] n [bird] falcão m.

hawker ['hɔːkə'] n **-1.** [street vendor] camelô mf **-2.** [door-to-door] vendedor m, -ra f ambulante.

hay [heɪ] n (U) feno m.

hay fever n (U) febre f do feno.

haystack ['heɪˌstæk] n feixe m de feno.

haywire ['heɪˌwaɪə'] adj inf: **to go ~** ficar louco(ca).

hazard ['hæzəd] <> n [danger] perigo m. <> vt **-1.** [life, reputation] arriscar, pôr em perigo **-2.** [guess, suggestion] atrever-se a fazer.

hazardous ['hæzədəs] adj perigoso(sa), arriscado(da).

hazard warning lights npl UK pisca-alerta m.

haze [heɪz] n **-1.** [mist] neblina f **-2.** [state of confusion] confusão f mental.

hazel ['heɪzl] adj castanho-claro.

hazelnut ['heɪzlˌnʌt] n avelã f.

hazy ['heɪzɪ] (compar -ier, superl -iest) adj **-1.** [misty] nebuloso(sa) **-2.** [vague, confused - ideas, memory] vago(ga); [- person, facts] confuso(sa).

HCA (abbr of **health care assistant**) n auxiliar mf de enfermagem.

he [hiː] pers pron ele; **~'s tall** ele é alto.

head [hed] <> n **-1.** [gen] cabeça f; **a** OR **per ~** por pessoa, por cabeça; **to laugh/sing/shout one's ~ off** rir/cantar/gritar a plenos pulmões; **to be off one's ~** UK, **to be out of one's ~** US estar

fora de seu juízo; **to go to one's ~** subir à cabeça; **to keep one's ~** manter a cabeça no lugar; **to lose one's ~** perder a cabeça; **to be soft in the ~** ter o miolo mole **-2.** [of table, bed, river] cabeceira f **-3.** [of page] cabeçalho m **-4.** [of stairs] topo m **-5.** [of queue, procession] frente f **-6.** [of flower] corola f **-7.** [head teacher] diretor m, -ra f **-8.** ELEC cabeçote m. <> vt **-1.** [be at front of, top of] encabeçar **-2.** [be in charge of] comandar **-3.** FTBL cabecear. <> vi dirigir-se, ir; **we gave up and ~ed home** nós desistimos e fomos para casa; **the ship was ~ing due north** o navio rumava para o norte.

➤ **heads** npl [on coin] cara f; **~s or tails?** cara ou coroa?

➤ **head for** vt fus **-1.** [place] dirigir-se para **-2.** fig [trouble, disaster] encaminhar-se para.

headache ['hedeɪk] n dor f de cabeça; **to have a ~** ter uma dor de cabeça.

headband ['hedbænd] n faixa f (para a cabeça).

head boy n UK [at school] representante m discente.

headdress ['hedˌdres] n touca f.

header ['hedə'] n **-1.** FTBL cabeçada f **-2.** [at top of page] cabeçalho m.

headfirst [ˌhed'fɜːst] adv de cabeça.

headgear ['hedˌgɪə'] n proteção f para a cabeça.

head girl n UK [in school] representante f discente.

heading ['hedɪŋ] n título m, cabeçalho m.

headlamp ['hedlæmp] n UK farol m (de carro).

headland ['hedlənd] n promontório m.

headlight ['hedlaɪt] n farol m (de carro).

headline ['hedlaɪn] n **-1.** [in newspaper] manchete f **-2.** [of news broadcast] notícia f principal.

headlong ['hedlɒŋ] <> adv **-1.** [at great speed] apressadamente **-2.** [impetuously] precipitadamente **-3.** [dive, fall] abruptamente.

headmaster [ˌhed'mɑːstə'] n diretor m (de colégio).

headmistress [ˌhed'mɪstrɪs] n diretora f (de colégio).

head office n sede f.

head-on <> adj frontal, de frente. <> adv de frente.

headphones ['hedfəʊnz] npl fones mpl de ouvido.

headquarters [ˌhed'kwɔːtəz] npl **-1.** FIN sede f, matriz f **-2.** MIL quartel-general m.

headrest ['hedrest] n apoio m para a cabeça.

headroom ['hedrʊm] n (U) **-1.** [in car] espaço m (entre a cabeça e o teto) **-2.** [below bridge] altura f livre.

headscarf ['hedskɑːf] (pl **-scarves** [-skɑːvz] OR **-scarfs**) n lenço m (para a cabeça).

headset ['hedset] n fones mpl de ouvido com microfone.

head start n vantagem f inicial; ~ **on** OR **over sb** vantagem sobre alguém.

headstrong ['hedstrɒŋ] adj cabeça-dura, obstinado(da).

head waiter n maître m.

headway ['hedweɪ] n: **to make** ~ fazer progressos.

headwind ['hedwɪnd] n vento m contrário.

headword n [in dictionary, reference book] entrada f, verbete m.

heady ['hedɪ] (compar **-ier**, superl **-iest**) adj **-1.** [exciting] emocionante **-2.** [causing giddiness] inebriante, estonteante.

heal [hiːl] ⋄ vt **-1.** [mend, cure - person] curar; [- wound] cicatrizar **-2.** fig [breach, division] cicatrizar. ⋄ vi [be mended, cured] cicatrizar.

healing ['hiːlɪŋ] ⋄ adj curativo(va). ⋄ n (U) cura f.

health [helθ] n (U) **-1.** [condition of body] saúde f **-2.** fig [of country, organization] bom estado m.

health centre n centro m de saúde.

health food n alimentos mpl naturais.

health food shop n loja f de alimentos naturais.

health service n serviço m de saúde.

healthy ['helθɪ] (compar **-ier**, superl **-iest**) adj **-1.** [gen] saudável **-2.** fig [thriving] saneado(da) **-3.** [substantial] substancial.

heap [hiːp] ⋄ n monte m, pilha f. ⋄ vt **-1.** [pile up] amontoar; **to** ~ **sthg on (to) sthg** amontoar algo sobre algo.
➡ **heaps** npl inf: ~**s of** montes OR pilhas de.

hear [hɪəʳ] (pt & pp **heard** [hɜːd]) ⋄ vt **-1.** [perceive] ouvir **-2.** [learn of] escutar; **to** ~ **(that)** ouvir dizer que **-3.** JUR [listen to] ver. ⋄ vi **-1.** [perceive sound] ouvir **-2.** [know]: **to** ~ **from sb** ter notícias de; **to** ~ **about sthg** ouvir falar sobre algo **-3.** [receive news] ter notícias de; **to** ~ **from sb** ter notícias de alguém **-4.** phr: **I've never heard of him/it!** nunca ouvi falar dele/disto!; **I won't** ~ **of it!** não quero saber nada sobre isto!

hearing ['hɪərɪŋ] n **-1.** [sense] audição f; **hard of** ~ com problemas de audição **-2.** JUR [trial] audiência f, julgamento m.

hearing aid n aparelho m auditivo.

hearsay ['hɪəseɪ] n (U) rumor m, boato m.

hearse [hɜːs] n carro m funerário.

heart [hɑːt] n **-1.** [gen] coração m; **from the** ~ de coração; **to break sb's** ~ partir o coração de alguém **-2.** (U) [courage]: **to have the** ~ **to do sthg** ter coragem de fazer algo; **to lose** ~ perder o ímpeto **-3.** [of problem] centro m **-4.** [of cabbage, celery, lettuce] miolo m.
➡ **hearts** npl [playing cards] copas fpl.
➡ **at heart** adv de coração.
➡ **by heart** adv de cor.

heartache ['hɑːteɪk] n sofrimento m, angústia f.

heart attack n ataque m cardíaco.

heartbeat ['hɑːtbiːt] n pulsação f.

heartbroken ['hɑːt,brəʊkn] adj de coração partido.

heartburn ['hɑːtbɜːn] n (U) azia f.

heart failure n (U) parada f cardíaca.

heartfelt ['hɑːtfelt] adj sincero(ra), de todo coração.

hearth [hɑːθ] n **-1.** [of fireplace] base f **-2.** [fireplace] lareira f.

heartless ['hɑːtlɪs] adj desumano(na); ~ **person** pessoa sem coração.

heartwarming ['hɑːt,wɔːmɪŋ] adj enternecedor(ra), gratificante.

hearty ['hɑːtɪ] (compar **-ier**, superl **-iest**) adj **-1.** [loud, energetic] caloroso(sa) **-2.** [substantial - meal] farto(ta); [- appetite] bom (boa).

heat [hiːt] ⋄ n **-1.** (U) [gen] calor m **-2.** (U) [specific temperature] temperatura f **-3.** (U) [fire, source of heat] fogo m **-4.** (U) fig: **in the** ~ **of the moment** no calor do momento **-5.** [eliminating round] rodada f **-6.** ZOOL: **on** ~ UK, **in** ~ no cio. ⋄ vt esquentar.
➡ **heat up** ⋄ vt sep [make warm] esquentar. ⋄ vi [become warm] ficar quente, esquentar.

heated ['hiːtɪd] adj **-1.** [room, swimming pool] aquecido(da) **-2.** [argument, discussion, person] esquentado(da).

heater ['hiːtəʳ] n aquecedor m.

heath [hiːθ] n [open place] charneca f.

heathen ['hiːðn] ⋄ adj pagão(gã). ⋄ n pagão m, -gã f.

heather ['heðəʳ] n (U) urze f.

heating ['hiːtɪŋ] n (U) calefação f.

heatstroke ['hiːtstrəʊk] n (U) insolação f.

heat wave n onda f de calor.

heave [hiːv] ⋄ vt **-1.** [pull] puxar, arrastar; [push] empurrar **-2.** inf [throw] atirar, arremessar **-3.** [give out]: **to** ~ **a sigh** dar um suspiro. ⋄ vi **-1.** [pull]

puxar **-2.** [rise and fall - boat, shoulders] sacudir-se; [- waves] ondular; [- chest] arfar **-3.** [retch] embrulhar.

heaven ['hevn] *n* [Paradise] paraíso *m*.
◆ **heavens** ◇ *npl*: **the ~ s** *literary* os céus. ◇ *excl*: **(good) ~ s!** céus!

heavenly ['hevnlɪ] *adj inf dated* [delightful] divino(na).

heavily ['hevɪlɪ] *adv* **-1.** [for emphasis - to rain, smoke, drink, tax] excessivamente; [- laden, booked, dependent] totalmente; [- in debt] seriamente; [- populated] densamente **-2.** [solidly] solidamente **-3.** [noisily, ponderously] pesadamente **-4.** [deeply] profundamente.

heavy ['hevɪ] (*compar* **-ier**, *superl* **-iest**) *adj* **-1.** [gen] pesado(da); **how ~ is it?** quanto pesa? **-2.** [intense, deep] intenso(sa); **to be a ~ sleeper** ter o sono muito profundo **-3.** [in quantity] em grande número **-4.** [person - fat] gordo(da); [- solidly built] sólido(da) **-5.** [ponderous - movement] brusco(ca); [- fall] feio (feia) **-6.** [oppressive] carregado(da) **-7.** [grave, serious] grande **-8.** [busy] cheio (cheia).

heavy cream *n US* nata *f* para enfeitar.

heavy goods vehicle *n UK* veículo *m* de carga pesada.

heavyweight ['hevɪweɪt] ◇ *adj SPORT* peso pesado. ◇ *n* peso *m* pesado.

Hebrew ['hi:bru:] ◇ *adj* hebraico(ca). ◇ *n* **-1.** [person] hebraico *m*, -ca *f* **-2.** [language] hebraico *m*.

Hebrides ['hebrɪdi:z] *npl*: **the ~** as Hébridas.

heck [hek] *excl*: **what/where/why the ~ ...?** o que/onde/por que diabos ...?; **a ~ of a lot of** uma montanha de; **a ~ of a nice guy** um cara e tanto.

heckle ['hekl] ◇ *vt* ficar interrompendo. ◇ *vi* ficar interrompendo.

hectic ['hektɪk] *adj* muito agitado(da).

he'd [hi:d] = **he had**, **he would**.

hedge [hedʒ] ◇ *n* [shrub] cerca *f* viva. ◇ *vi* [prevaricate] dar evasivas.

hedgehog ['hedʒhɒg] *n* porco-espinho *m*.

heed [hi:d] ◇ *n*: **to take ~ of sthg** levar em consideração. ◇ *vt fml* ter em conta.

heedless ['hi:dlɪs] *adj*: **to be ~ of sthg** não fazer caso de algo.

heel [hi:l] *n* **-1.** [of foot] calcanhar *m* **-2.** [of shoe] salto *m*.

hefty ['heftɪ] (*compar* **-ier**, *superl* **-iest**) *adj inf* **-1.** [person] robusto(ta) **-2.** [salary, fee, fine] vultoso(sa), alto(ta).

heifer ['hefə^r] *n* vitela *f*, novilha *f*.

height [haɪt] *n* **-1.** [gen] altura *f*; **in ~** de

altura; **what ~ is it/are you?** que altura tem isto/você tem? **-2.** [zenith] apogeu *m*; **the ~ of** [fight, fame, tourist season] o auge de; [stupidity, ignorance, bad manners] o cúmulo de.

heighten ['haɪtn] ◇ *vt* intensificar. ◇ *vi* intensificar-se.

heir [eə^r] *n* herdeiro *m*.

heiress ['eərɪs] *n* herdeira *f*.

heirloom ['eəlu:m] *n* herança *f* de família.

heist [haɪst] *n inf* roubo *m*.

held [held] *pt & pp* ⊳ **hold**.

helicopter ['helɪkɒptə^r] *n* helicóptero *m*.

helium ['hi:lɪəm] *n* (U) hélio *m*.

hell [hel] ◇ *n* **-1.** inferno *m* **-2.** *inf* [for emphasis]: **what/where/why the ~ ...?** o que/onde/por que diabos ...?; **it was one ~ of a mess** estava uma bagunça total; **he's a ~ of a nice guy** ele é um cara simpático e tanto **-3.** *phr*: **to do sthg for the ~ of it** *inf* fazer algo por gosto; **to give sb ~** *inf* [verbally] fazer alguém passar poucas e boas; **go to ~!** *v inf* vá para o inferno! ◇ *excl inf* diabos!, droga!

he'll [hi:l] = **he will**.

hellish ['helɪʃ] *adj inf* infernal.

hello [hə'ləʊ] *excl* [greeting] olá!, oi!; [answering telephone, attracting attention] alô!

helm [helm] *n* **-1.** [of ship] leme *m*, timão *m* **-2.** *fig* [of company, organization] direção *f*.

helmet ['helmɪt] *n* capacete *m*.

help [help] ◇ *n* **-1.** (U) [assistance] ajuda *f*; **to be of ~** ajudar; **with the ~ of sb/ sthg** com a ajuda de alguém/algo **-2.** (U) [in an emergency] socorro *m* **-3.** [useful person or object]: **to be a ~** ser útil. ◇ *vt* **-1.** [gen] ajudar; **to ~ sb (to) do sthg** ajudar alguém a fazer algo; **to ~ sb with sthg** ajudar alguém em algo. **-2.** [avoid] evitar; **I can't ~ feeling sad** não posso evitar ficar triste; **I couldn't ~ laughing** eu não conseguia parar de rir **-3.** *phr*: **to ~ o.s. (to sthg)** servir-se (de algo). ◇ *vi* [gen] ajudar; **to ~ with sthg** ajudar em algo. ◇ *excl* socorro!
◆ **help out** ◇ *vt sep* dar uma mão para. ◇ *vi* dar uma mão.

helper ['helpə^r] *n* ajudante *mf*.

helpful ['helpfʊl] *adj* **-1.** [willing to help] prestativo(va) **-2.** [useful] proveitoso(sa).

helping ['helpɪŋ] *n* porção *f* (de comida); **would you like a second ~?** quer repetir?

helpless ['helplɪs] *adj* indefeso(sa).

helpline ['helplaɪn] n (linha f de) suporte m.

Helsinki ['helsɪŋkɪ] n Helsinque; **in ~** em Helsinque.

hem [hem] (pt & pp -med, cont -ming) ◇ n bainha f. ◇ vt abainhar, fazer a bainha de.
◆ **hem in** vt sep cercar.

hemisphere ['hemɪ,sfɪər] n [of Earth] hemisfério m.

hemline ['hemlaɪn] n (altura f da) bainha f.

hemophiliac [,hi:mə'fɪliæk] n hemofílico m, -ca f.

hemorrhage ['hemərɪdʒ] n hemorragia f.

hemorrhoids ['hemərɔɪdz] npl hemorróidas fpl.

hen [hen] n -1. [female chicken] galinha f -2. [female bird] fêmea f.

hence [hens] adv fml -1. [therefore] por isso, assim -2. [from now]: **ten years ~** daqui a dez anos.

henceforth [,hens'fɔ:θ] adv fml doravante.

henchman ['hentʃmən] (pl -men [-mən]) n pej capanga m, jagunço m.

henna ['henə] ◇ n (U) hena f. ◇ vt passar OR aplicar hena em.

henpecked ['henpekt] adj pej submisso(sa), dominado(da).

her [hɜ:r] ◇ pers pron -1. (direct) a; **I know ~** eu a conheço -2. (indirect) lhe; **send it to ~** mande isso para ela; **tell ~** diga-lhe -3. (after prep) ela; **Lucy brought it with ~** a Lucy trouxe-o consigo OR com ela. ◇ poss adj o seu (a sua), dela; **~ books** o livros dela, os seus livros.

herald ['herəld] ◇ n [messenger] mensageiro m, -ra f. ◇ vt fml -1. [signify, usher in] anunciar -2. [proclaim] conclamar.

herb [UK hɜ:b, US ɜ:b] n erva f.

herd [hɜ:d] ◇ n -1. [gen] rebanho m; [of elephants] manada f -2. [of people] multidão f. ◇ vt -1. [drive] pastorear -2. fig [push] conduzir (em grupo).

here [hɪər] adv [in, at this place] aqui; **~ he is/they are** aqui está ele/estão eles; **~ it is** aqui está; **~ you are!** toma!; **Christmas is nearly ~** o Natal está próximo; **~ and there** aqui e acolá.

hereabouts UK ['hɪərə,baʊts], **hereabout** US [,hɪərə'baʊt] adv por aqui.

hereafter [,hɪər'ɑ:ftər] ◇ adv fml de agora em diante, a partir de agora. ◇ n: **the ~** o além.

hereby [,hɪə'baɪ] adv -1. fml [in documents] por meio deste (desta) -2. fml [when speaking]: **I ~ declare this theatre open** neste momento, declaro este teatro aberto.

hereditary [hɪ'redɪtrɪ] adj hereditário(-ria).

heresy ['herəsɪ] (pl -ies) n heresia f.

herewith [,hɪə'wɪð] adv fml [with letter]: **please find ~ ...** segue anexo ...

heritage ['herɪtɪdʒ] n (U) herança f.

hermetically [hɜ:'metɪklɪ] adv: **~ sealed** hermeticamente fechado(da).

hermit ['hɜ:mɪt] n eremita mf.

hernia ['hɜ:njə] n hérnia f.

hero ['hɪərəʊ] (pl -es) n [gen] herói m.

heroic [hɪ'rəʊɪk] adj heróico(ca).
◆ **heroics** npl pej patetices fpl.

heroin ['herəʊɪn] n [drug] (U) heroína f.

heroine ['herəʊɪn] n heroína f.

heron ['herən] (pl inv OR -s) n garça-real f.

herring ['herɪŋ] (pl inv OR -s) n arenque m.

hers [hɜ:z] poss pron o seu (a sua), (o/a) dela; **a friend of ~** um amigo dela OR seu; **those shoes are ~** estes sapatos são dela OR seus; **these are mine - where are ~?** estes são os meus - onde estão os delas?

herself [hɜ:'self] pron -1. (reflexive) se; **she hurt ~** ela se machucou -2. (after prep) si própria OR mesma; **she did it ~** foi ela mesma que o fez.

he's [hi:z] = he is, he has.

hesitant ['hezɪtənt] adj hesitante.

hesitate ['hezɪteɪt] vi [pause] hesitar; **to ~ to do sthg** hesitar em fazer algo.

hesitation [,hezɪ'teɪʃn] n hesitação f.

heterogeneous [,hetərə'dʒi:njəs] adj fml heterogêneo(nea).

heterosexual [,hetərəʊ'sekʃʊəl] ◇ adj heterossexual. ◇ n heterossexual mf.

het up [het-] adj inf nervoso(sa), como uma pilha de nervos.

hexagon ['heksəgən] n hexágono m.

hey [heɪ] excl ei!

heyday ['heɪdeɪ] n auge m, apogeu m.

HGV (abbr of heavy goods vehicle) n veículos pesados, como ônibus e caminhão; **an ~ licence** ≃ uma carteira categoria C.

hi [haɪ] excl inf [hello] oi!, olá!

hiatus [haɪ'eɪtəs] (pl -es) n fml [pause] pausa f.

hibernate ['haɪbəneɪt] vi hibernar.

hiccough, hiccup ['hɪkʌp] (pt & pp -ped, cont -ping) ◇ n -1. [sound] soluço m; **to have ~s** estar com soluços -2. fig [difficulty] contratempo m. ◇ vi soluçar.

hid [hɪd] *pt* ⊳ **hide.**

hidden ['hɪdn] ⟨⟩ *pp* ⊳ **hide.** ⟨⟩ *adj* **-1.** [from view] escondido(da) **-2.** [not apparent - disadvantages, dangers] escondido(da); [- problems] não aparente; [- cost] embutido(do) **-3.** [deliberately concealed - weapons] secreto; [- feelings] oculto.

hide [haɪd] (*pt* hid, *pp* hidden) ⟨⟩ *n* **-1.** [animal skin] pele *f* **-2.** [for watching birds, animals] esconderijo *m*. ⟨⟩ *vt* **-1.** [conceal] esconder; **to ~ sthg (from sb)** esconder algo (de alguém) **-2.** [cover] cobrir. ⟨⟩ *vi* [conceal o.s.] esconder-se.

hide-and-seek *n* (*U*) esconde-esconde *m*; **to play ~** brincar de esconde-esconde.

hideaway ['haɪdəweɪ] *n inf* refúgio *m*.

hideous ['hɪdɪəs] *adj* horrível.

hiding ['haɪdɪŋ] *n* **-1.** (*U*) [concealment]: **to be in ~** estar escondido(da) **-2.** *inf* [beating]: **to give sb a (good) ~** dar uma (boa) surra em alguém; **to get a (good) ~ from sb** levar uma (boa) surra de alguém.

hiding place *n* esconderijo *m*.

hierarchy ['haɪərɑːkɪ] (*pl* -ies) *n* hierarquia *f*.

hi-fi ['haɪfaɪ] *n* sistema *m* hi-fi.

high [haɪ] ⟨⟩ *adj* **-1.** [gen] alto(ta); **how ~ is it?** qual é a altura? **-2.** [greater than normal - speed] alto(ta); [- wind] forte; [- prices, unemployment] elevado(da); **temperatures in the ~ twenties** temperaturas bem acima dos 20 graus **-3.** [important, influential] importante **-4.** [honourable] nobre **-5.** [high-pitched] agudo(da) **-6.** *drugs sl* [on drugs] baratinado(da) **-7.** *inf* [drunk] alto(ta). ⟨⟩ *adv* **-1.** [above ground level] a grande altura **-2.** [in degrees] em alto grau; **to search ~ and low** procurar em tudo quanto é lugar. ⟨⟩ *n* [highest point] pico *m*.

highbrow ['haɪbraʊ] *adj* erudito(ta).

high chair *n* cadeira *f* de bebê.

high-class *adj* [superior - person] de alta classe; [- hotel, restaurant] de alta categoria; [- performance] de alto nível.

high commission *n* alta comissão *f*.

High Court *n UK* JUR Corte *f* Suprema.

higher ['haɪəʳ] *adj* [exam, qualification] superior(ra).

◆ **Higher** *n*: **Higher (Grade)** SCH na Escócia, exame realizado ao final da escola secundária.

higher education *n* (*U*) ensino *m* superior.

high-handed [-'hændɪd] *adj* despótico(ca).

high jump *n* SPORT salto *m* em altura.

Highland Games ['haɪlənd-] *npl* Jogos *mpl* das Terras Altas.

Highlands ['haɪləndz] *npl*: **the ~** [of Scotland] as Terras Altas.

highlight ['haɪlaɪt] ⟨⟩ *n* [of event, occasion] ponto *m* alto, destaque *m*. ⟨⟩ *vt* **-1.** [with pen] realçar **-2.** [emphasize] enfatizar.

◆ **highlights** *npl* [in hair] realces *mpl*.

highlighter (pen) ['haɪlaɪtəʳ-] *n* caneta *f* marca-texto.

highly ['haɪlɪ] *adv* **-1.** [very, extremely] altamente **-2.** [very well, at high level] muito bem **-3.** [favourably] favoravelmente; **I ~ recommend it** realmente recomendo isso.

highly-strung *adj* irritadiço(ça).

Highness ['haɪnɪs] *n*: **His/Her/Your (Royal) ~** Sua Alteza (Real); **Their (Royal) ~es** Suas Altezas (Reais).

high-pitched [-'pɪtʃt] *adj* [shrill] agudo(da).

high point *n* [of occasion] ponto *m* alto.

high-powered [-'paʊəd] *adj* **-1.** [powerful] de alta potência **-2.** [dynamic] dinâmico(ca).

high-ranking [-'ræŋkɪŋ] *adj* de destaque.

high-rise *adj* de muitos andares; **a ~ building** um espigão.

high school *n* **-1.** *UK* [for 11- to 18-year-olds] ≃ escola *f* secundária **-2.** *US* [for 15- to 18-year-olds] ≃ segundo grau *m*.

high season *n* alta estação *f*.

high spot *n* ponto *m* de relevo.

high street *n UK* avenida *f* principal.

high-tech *adj* [method, industry] de alta tecnologia.

high tide *n* (*U*) [of sea] maré *f* alta.

highway ['haɪweɪ] *n* **-1.** *US* [main road between cities] auto-estrada *f* **-2.** *UK* [any main road] rodovia *f*.

Highway Code *n UK*: **the ~** ≃ o Código Nacional de Trânsito.

hijack ['haɪdʒæk] ⟨⟩ *n* [of aircraft, car] seqüestro *m*. ⟨⟩ *vt* [aircraft, car] seqüestrar.

hijacker ['haɪdʒækəʳ] *n* seqüestrador *m*, -ra *f*.

hike [haɪk] ⟨⟩ *n* [long walk] caminhada *f*. ⟨⟩ *vi* [go for a long walk] caminhar.

hiker ['haɪkəʳ] *n* caminhante *mf*, andarilho *m*.

hiking ['haɪkɪŋ] *n* (*U*) excursões *fpl* a pé; **to go ~** fazer excursões.

hilarious [hɪ'leərɪəs] *adj* hilariante, engraçado(da).

hill [hɪl] *n* **-1.** [mound] colina *f* **-2.** [slope] ladeira *f*.

hillside ['hɪlsaɪd] *n* encosta *f*.

hilly ['hɪlɪ] (*compar* -**ier**, *superl* -**iest**) *adj* montanhoso(sa).

hilt [hɪlt] *n* punho *m*; **to the ~** ao extremo; **to support/defend sb to the ~** apoiar/defender alguém com unhas e dentes.

him [hɪm] *pers pron* -**1.** (*direct*) o; **I know ~** eu o conheço -**2.** (*indirect*) lhe; **tell ~ diga-lhe** -**3.** (*after prep*) ele; **send it to ~** mande isso para ele; **Tony brought it with ~** Tony trouxe-o consigno OR com ele.

Himalayas [ˌhɪmə'leɪəz] *npl*: **the ~** as montanhas do Himalaia.

himself [hɪm'self] *pron* -**1.** (*reflexive*) se; **he hurt ~** machucou-se -**2.** (*after prep*) si próprio OR mesmo; **he did it ~** foi ele mesmo que o fez.

hind [haɪnd] (*pl inv* OR -**s**) <> *adj* traseiro(ra). <> *n* [deer] corça *f*.

hinder ['hɪndəʳ] *vt* retardar, atrapalhar.

Hindi ['hɪndɪ] *n* (*U*) [language] hindi *m*.

hindrance ['hɪndrəns] *n* -**1.** [obstacle] obstáculo *m* -**2.** (*U*) [delay] atrasos *mpl*.

hindsight ['haɪndsaɪt] *n* (*U*): **with the benefit of ~** olhando em retrospecto.

Hindu ['hɪnduː] (*pl* -**s**) <> *adj* hindu. <> *n* hindu *m*.

hinge [hɪndʒ] (*cont* **hingeing**) *n* [on door, window, lid] dobradiça *f*.

➤ **hinge (up)on** *vt fus* [depend on] depender de.

hint [hɪnt] <> *n* -**1.** [indirect suggestion] alusão *f*; **to drop a ~** dar uma indireta -**2.** [useful suggestion, tip] dica *f* -**3.** [small amount, trace] sinal *m*. <> *vi*: **to ~ at sthg** fazer alusão a algo. <> *vt*: **to ~ that** insinuar que.

hip [hɪp] *n* [part of body] quadril *m*.

hippie ['hɪpɪ] *n* hippie *m*.

hippo ['hɪpəʊ] (*pl* -**s**) *n* hipopótamo *m*.

hippopotamus [ˌhɪpə'pɒtəməs] (*pl* -**muses** OR -**mi** -**maɪ**) *n* hipopótamo *m*.

hippy ['hɪpɪ] (*pl* -**ies**) *n* = **hippie**.

hire ['haɪəʳ] <> *n* (*U*) [of car, equipment] aluguel *m*; **for ~** a aluga-se; **bicycles for ~** alugam-se bicicletas; **taxi for ~** táxi livre. <> *vt* -**1.** [rent] alugar -**2.** [employ] contratar.

➤ **hire out** *vt sep* alugar.

hire car *n* UK: **to have a ~** alugar um carro.

hire purchase *n* (*U*) UK compra *f* a prazo.

his [hɪz] <> *poss pron* o seu (a sua), (o/a) dele; **~ books** os livros dele, os seus livros <> *poss adj* o seu (a sua), dele; **a friend of ~** um amigo dele OR seu; **these shoes are ~** estes sapatos são dele OR

seus; **these are mine - where are ~?** estes são os meus - onde estão os dele?

hiss [hɪs] <> *n* -**1.** [of animal, person] silvo *m* -**2.** [of audience] vaia *f* -**3.** [of steam, gas] assobio *m*. <> *vi* -**1.** [animal, person] silvar; **she ~ed angrily at him** ela o vaiou irritada -**2.** [steam, gas] assobiar.

historic [hɪ'stɒrɪk] *adj* [significant] histórico(ca).

historical [hɪ'stɒrɪkəl] *adj* histórico(ca).

history ['hɪstərɪ] *n* -**1.** [gen] história *f*; **to go down in ~** entrar para a história -**2.** [past record] histórico *m*.

hit [hɪt] (*pt* & *pp* **hit**, *cont* -**ting**) <> *n* -**1.** [blow] golpe *m*, pancada *f* -**2.** [successful strike] tiro *m* certeiro -**3.** [success] sucesso *m* -**4.** COMPUT [of website] visita *f*. <> *comp* de sucesso. <> *vt* -**1.** [strike a blow at] bater em -**2.** [crash into] bater contra -**3.** [reach] alcançar; **the thought suddenly ~ me that ...** de repente me dei conta de que ... -**4.** [affect badly] atingir -**5.** *phr*: **to ~ it off (with sb)** dar-se bem (com alguém).

hit-and-miss *adj* = **hit-or-miss**.

hit-and-run <> *adj* -**1.** [driver] que não presta socorro -**2.** [accident] em que não se presta socorro. <> *n* [accident] acidente no qual não se presta socorro.

hitch [hɪtʃ] <> *n* [problem, snag] dificuldade *f*. <> *vt* -**1.** [solicit]: **to ~ a lift** pegar carona -**2.** [fasten]: **to ~ sthg on(to) sthg** amarrar algo em algo. <> *vi* [hitchhike] viajar de carona.

➤ **hitch up** *vt sep* [pull up] levantar.

hitchhike ['hɪtʃhaɪk] *vi* viajar de carona.

hitchhiker ['hɪtʃhaɪkəʳ] *n* caroneiro *m*, -ra *f*.

hi-tech [ˌhaɪ'tek] *adj* = **high-tech**.

hitherto [ˌhɪðə'tuː] *adv* *fml* até agora.

hit-or-miss *adj* aleatório(ria).

HIV (*abbr of* **human immunodeficiency virus**) *n* (*U*) HIV *m*; **to be ~-positive** ser soropositivo(va).

hive [haɪv] *n* [for bees] colméia *f*; **a ~ of activity** *fig* um centro de atividades.

➤ **hive off** *vt sep* [separate] transferir.

HNC (*abbr of* **Higher National Certificate**) *n certificado de qualificação em disciplinas técnicas na Grã-Bretanha.*

HND (*abbr of* **Higher National Diploma**) *n diploma de qualificação em disciplinas técnicas na Grã-Bretanha.*

hoard [hɔːd] <> *n* [store] provisão *f*. <> *vt* [collect, save] estocar.

hoarding ['hɔːdɪŋ] *n* UK [for advertisements, posters] outdoor *m*.

hoarfrost ['hɔːfrɒst] n (U) geada f.

hoarse [hɔːs] adj rouco(ca).

hoax [həʊks] n trote m.

hob [hɒb] n UK [on cooker] mesa f.

hobble ['hɒbl] vi [limp] coxear.

hobby ['hɒbɪ] (pl -ies) n [leisure activity] hobby m.

hobby horse n -1. [toy] cavalinho-de-pau m -2. [favourite topic] assunto m favorito.

hobo ['həʊbəʊ] (pl -es OR -s) n US [tramp] vagabundo m, -da f.

hockey ['hɒkɪ] n -1. [on grass] hóquei m -2. US [ice hockey] hóquei m no gelo.

hockey stick n bastão m de hóquei.

hoe [həʊ] <> n enxada f. <> vt capinar.

hog [hɒg] (pt & pp -ged, cont -ging) <> n -1. US lit & fig porco m, -ca f -2. phr: to go the whole ~ ir até o fim. <> vt inf [monopolize] monopolizar.

Hogmanay ['hɒgməneɪ] n denominação escocesa para a Noite de Ano Novo.

hoist [hɔɪst] <> n guindaste f. <> vt -1. [load, person] levantar -2. [sail, flag] içar.

hold [həʊld] (pt & pp held) <> n -1. [grasp, grip]: **to have a firm ~ on sthg** segurar algo firme; **to keep ~ of sthg** segurar algo; **to take** OR **lay ~ of sthg** começar a ter efeito de algo; **to get ~ of sthg** [obtain] arranjar algo; **to get ~ of sb** [find] encontrar -2. [of ship, aircraft] porão m -3. [control, influence] influência f. <> vt -1. [in hand, arms] segurar -2. [maintain in position] manter; **to ~ sb prisoner** manter alguém como prisioneiro(ra); **to ~ sb hostage** tomar alguém como refém -3. [have, possess] ter, possuir -4. [conduct, stage] conduzir -5. fml [consider] julgar; **to ~ (that)** sustentar que; **to ~ sb responsible for sthg** responsabilizar alguém por algo -6. [on telephone]: **please ~ the line** aguarde na linha, por favor -7. [keep, sustain] manter -8. MIL ocupar -9. [support, have space for] guardar -10. [contain] guardar -11. phr: **~ it!**, **~ everything!** espera aí!; **to ~ one's own** virar-se. <> vi -1. [remain unchanged] manter-se; **to ~ still** OR **steady** segurar firme -2. [on phone] esperar.

➧ **hold back** vt sep [gen] reter.

➧ **hold down** vt sep [job] manter.

➧ **hold off** <> vt sep [fend off] manter à distância.

➧ **hold on** vi -1. [gen] esperar -2. [grip]: **to ~ on (to sthg)** segurar-se firme (em algo).

➧ **hold out** <> vt sep [hand, arms]

estender. <> vi -1. [last] durar -2. [resist]: **to ~ out (against sb/sthg)** resistir (a alguém/algo).

➧ **hold up** vt sep -1. [raise] levantar -2. [delay] atrasar.

holdall ['həʊldɔːl] n UK mochila f.

holder ['həʊldə'] n -1. [gen] suporte m, recipiente m; **cigarette ~** boquilha f; **candle ~** castiçal m -2. [owner - gen] titular mf; [- of ticket] portador m, -ra f; [- position, title] detentor m, -ra f.

holding ['həʊldɪŋ] n -1. [investment] participação f acionária -2. [farm] propriedade f.

hold-up n -1. [robbery] assalto m à mão armada -2. [delay] empecilho m, atraso m.

hole [həʊl] n -1. [gen] buraco m; **~ in one** um buraco numa só tacada -2. inf [horrible place] buraco m -3. inf [predicament] apuro m.

holiday ['hɒlɪdeɪ] n -1. [vacation] férias fpl; **to be/go on ~** estar de/sair de férias -2. [public holiday] feriado m.

holiday camp n UK colônia f de férias.

holidaymaker ['hɒlɪdeɪˌmeɪkə'] n UK excursionista mf.

holiday pay n UK férias fpl remuneradas.

holiday resort n UK cidade f turística.

holistic [həʊˈlɪstɪk] adj holístico(ca).

Holland ['hɒlənd] n Holanda f.

holler ['hɒlə'] inf <> vt gritar. <> vi esp US gritar.

hollow ['hɒləʊ] <> adj -1. [gen] oco (oca), vazio(zia) -2. [gaunt - eyes] fundo(da); [- cheeks] magro(gra) -3. [empty of meaning or value - laugh, optimism] falso(sa); [- promise, victory] vão (vã). <> n -1. [gen] buraco m -2. [in ground, pillow] buraco m, cavidade f.

➧ **hollow out** vt sep -1. [make hollow] tornar oco (oca) -2. [make by hollowing] escavar.

holly ['hɒlɪ] n (U) azevinho m.

holocaust ['hɒləkɔːst] n [destruction] holocausto m.

➧ **Holocaust** n: **the Holocaust** o Holocausto.

holster ['həʊlstə'] n coldre m.

holy ['həʊlɪ] (compar -ier, superl -iest) adj -1. [sacred] sagrado(da), santo(ta); **~ water** água-benta f -2. [pure and good] puro(ra).

Holy Ghost n: **the ~** o Espírito Santo.

Holy Land n: **the ~** a Terra Santa.

Holy Spirit n: **the ~** o Espírito Santo.

home [həʊm] <> adj -1. [not foreign] nacional -2. SPORT interno(na). <> adv -1. [to or at one's house] para casa -2.

[from abroad] para casa (do exterior).
<> n -1. [one's house, place of residence]
casa f; to make one's ~ fazer a casa
-2. [place of origin] terra f natal -3. [family
unit, Institution] lar m; to leave ~ sair de
casa.
◆ at home adv -1. [gen] em casa; at ~
with sthg à vontade com algo; to make
o.s. at ~ sentir-se à vontade OR em
casa -2. [in one's own country] no meu
país.

home address n endereço m residencial.

home brew n (U) [beer] cerveja f
caseira.

home computer n computador m
pessoal.

home cooking n comida f caseira.

Home Counties npl UK: the ~ os
condados ao redor de Londres.

home delivery n entrega m a domicílio.

home economics n (U) economia f
doméstica.

home help n UK empregada que
auxilia pessoas idosas ou doentes.

home improvements npl reformas
fpl na casa.

homeland ['hǝʊmlænd] n -1. [country of
birth] terra f natal -2. [in South Africa]
gueto m.

homeless ['hǝʊmlɪs] <> adj sem-teto.
<> npl: the ~ os sem-teto, os desabrigados.

homely ['hǝʊmlɪ] adj -1. [simple, unpretentious] simples -2. [ugly] feio (feia).

home-made adj caseiro(ra); ~ bread
pão m feito em casa.

Home Office n UK: the ~ ≃ o Ministério do Interior.

homeopathy [ˌhǝʊmɪ'ɒpǝθɪ] n (U) homeopatia f.

home page n COMPUT homepage f,
página f inicial.

Home Secretary n UK ≃ Ministro m,
-tra f do Interior.

homesick ['hǝʊmsɪk] adj com saudade
de casa; to feel ~ estar com saudades
de casa.

hometown ['hǝʊmtaʊn] n cidade f
natal.

homeward ['hǝʊmwǝd] adj de regresso.
<> adv = homewards.

homewards ['hǝʊmwǝdz] adv para casa.

homework ['hǝʊmwɜːk] n -1. SCH dever
m de casa, tema m -2. inf fig [preparation] dever m de casa.

homey, homy ['hǝʊmɪ] US adj US
familiar.

homicide ['hɒmɪsaɪd] n fml (U) homicídio m.

homoeopathy etc. n = homeopathy
etc.

homogeneous [ˌhɒmǝ'dʒiːnjǝs] adj homogêneo(nea).

homophobic ['hǝʊmǝʊ'fǝʊbɪk] adj homofóbico(ca).

homosexual [ˌhɒmǝ'sekʃʊǝl] <> adj
homossexual. <> n homossexual mf.

homy adj US = homey.

hone [hǝʊn] vt -1. [knife, sword] afiar -2.
[intellect, wit] aprimorar.

honest ['ɒnɪst] <> adj -1. [trustworthy]
honesto(ta) -2. [frank, truthful] sincero(ra); to be ~, ... para ser franco(ca), ...
-3. [legal] legal. <> adv inf: I didn't steal
your pencil, ~! eu não roubei o seu
lápis, juro!

honestly ['ɒnɪstlɪ] <> adv -1. [in a trustworthy manner] honestamente -2.
[frankly, truthfully] sinceramente. <>
excl [expressing impatience, disapproval]
ora, francamente!

honesty ['ɒnɪstɪ] n -1. (U) [trustworthiness] honestidade f -2. [frankness, truthfulness] sinceridade f.

honey ['hʌnɪ] n -1. (U) [food] mel m -2.
esp US [dear] querido m, -da f.

honeycomb ['hʌnɪkǝʊm] n -1. [in wax]
favo m (de mel) -2.: ~ pattern formato m de favo de mel.

honeymoon ['hʌnɪmuːn] <> n lit & fig
lua-de-mel f. <> vi sair em lua-de-mel.

honeysuckle ['hʌnɪˌsʌkl] n madressilva
f.

Hong Kong [ˌhɒŋ'kɒŋ] n Hong Kong.

honk [hɒŋk] <> vi -1. [motorist] buzinar
-2. [goose] grasnar. <> vt: to ~ a horn
tocar a buzina.

honor etc. n & vt US = honour etc.

honorary [UK 'ɒnǝrǝrɪ, US ɒnǝ'reǝrɪ] adj
honorário(ria).

honour UK, **honor** US ['ɒnǝʳ] <> n
honra f; in ~ of sb/sthg em honra de
alguém/algo. <> vt honrar.
◆ **honours** npl -1. [gen] honras fpl -2.
UNIV tipo de grau universitário concedido por universidades britânicas.

honourable UK, **honorable** US
['ɒnrǝbl] adj honrado(da).

honours degree n UK [univ] = honours
2.

Hon. Sec. (abbr of honorary secretary)
n secretário m honorário, secretária f
honorária.

hood [hʊd] n -1. [on cloak, jacket] capuz m
-2. US [of car] capota f -3. [of pram] toldo
m -4. [of cooker] aba f -5. US [car bonnet]
capô m.

hoodlum ['hu:dləm] *n* [youth] *US inf* arruaceiro *m*, -ra *f*; [gangster] gângster *mf*.

hoof [hu:f, hʊf] (*pl* -s OR **hooves**) *n* pata *f*, casco *m*.

hook [hʊk] <> *n* -1. [for coat, picture, curtain] gancho *m* -2. [for catching fish] anzol *m* -3. [fastener] fecho *m*. <> *vt* -1. [fasten with hook] enganchar -2. [fish] fisgar.

➡ **off the hook** *adv* -1. [phone] fora do gancho -2. [out of trouble] sem problemas.

➡ **hook up** *vt sep*: to ~ sthg up to sthg COMPUT & TELEC conectar algo em algo.

hooked [hʊkt] *adj* -1. [shaped like a hook] curvado(da) -2. *inf* [addicted]: to be ~ (on sthg) ser viciado(da) (em algo).

hook(e)y ['hʊkɪ] *n* (U) *US inf*: to play ~ matar aula.

hooligan ['hu:lɪgən] *n* arruaceiro *m*, -ra *f*, hooligan *m*.

hoop [hu:p] *n* argola *f*.

hooray [hʊ'reɪ] *excl* = **hurray**.

hoot [hu:t] <> *n* -1. [of owl] pio *m* -2. [of horn] buzinada *f* -3. *UK inf* [amusing thing, person]: she's a real ~ ela é o máximo. <> *vi* -1. [owl] piar -2. [horn] buzinar. <> *vt* [horn] buzinar.

hooter ['hu:təᵊ] *n* [horn - of car] buzina *f*; [- of factory] sirene *f*.

Hoover® ['hu:vəᵊ] *n UK* aspirador *m*.

➡ **hoover** *vt* passar o aspirador em.

hooves [hu:vz] *pl* ▷ **hoof**.

hop [hɒp] (*pt & pp* -ped, *cont* -ping) <> *n* -1. [of person] pulo *m* num pé só -2. [of small animal, bird] pulinho *m*. <> *vt inf phr*: ~ it! dê o fora. <> *vi* -1. [jump on one leg] pular com um pé só -2. [small animal, bird] dar pulinhos -3. *inf* [move nimbly] pular; she ~ped on a plane to New York ela foi dar um pulo em Nova York.

➡ **hops** *npl* [for making beer] lúpulos *mpl*.

hope [həʊp] <> *n* esperança *f*; in the ~ of na esperança de. <> *vt*: to ~ (that) esperar que; to ~ to do sthg esperar fazer algo. <> *vi* esperar; to ~ for sthg esperar (por) algo; I ~ so/ not espero que sim/não.

hopeful ['həʊpfʊl] <> *adj* -1. [full of hope] esperançoso(sa), otimista; to be ~ of sthg/of doing sthg ter esperanças de algo/de fazer algo -2. [encouraging] promissor(ra).

hopefully ['həʊpfəlɪ] *adv* -1. [in a hopeful way] esperançosamente -2. [with luck] com sorte.

hopeless ['həʊplɪs] *adj* -1. [despairing] desesperado(da) -2. [impossible] impossível -3. *inf* [useless] inútil.

hopelessly ['həʊplɪslɪ] *adv* -1. [despairingly] desesperançosamente -2. [completely] totalmente.

horizon [hə'raɪzn] *n* [of sky] horizonte *m*; on the ~ no horizonte.

horizontal [,hɒrɪ'zɒntl] <> *adj* horizontal. <> *n*: the ~ a horizontal.

hormone ['hɔ:məʊn] *n* hormônio *m*.

horn [hɔ:n] *n* -1. [of animal] chifre *m* -2. MUS [instrument] trompa *f* -3. [of car] buzina *f* -4. [of ship] apito *m*.

hornet ['hɔ:nɪt] *n* vespão *m*.

horny ['hɔ:nɪ] (*compar* -ier, *superl* -iest) *adj* -1. [scale, body, armour] feito(ta) de chifre -2. [hand] calejado(da) -3. *vinf* [sexually excited] com tesão.

horoscope ['hɒrəskəʊp] *n* horóscopo *m*.

horrendous [hɒ'rendəs] *adj* horrendo(-da).

horrible ['hɒrəbl] *adj* horrível.

horrid ['hɒrɪd] *adj* -1. *esp UK* [person] antipático(ca) -2. [idea, place] horroroso(sa).

horrific [hɒ'rɪfɪk] *adj* horroroso(sa), horrível.

horrify ['hɒrɪfaɪ] (*pt & pp* -ied) *vt* horrorizar.

horror ['hɒrəᵊ] *n* [gen] horror *m*.

horror film *n* filme *m* de terror.

horse [hɔ:s] *n* [animal] cavalo *m*.

horseback ['hɔ:sbæk] <> *adj*: ~ riding *US* equitação *f*. <> *n*: on ~ a cavalo.

horse chestnut *n* -1. [tree]: ~ (tree) castanheiro-da-índia *m* -2. [nut] castanha-da-índia *f*.

horseman ['hɔ:smən] (*pl* -men [-mən]) *n* -1. [non-professional] cavaleiro *m* -2. [professional] ginete *m*.

horsepower ['hɔ:s,paʊəᵊ] *n* (U) cavalo-vapor *m*.

horse racing *n* (U) corrida *f* de cavalos.

horseradish ['hɔ:s,rædɪʃ] *n* (U) [plant] raiz-forte *f*.

horse riding *n* (U) equitação *f*; to go ~ andar a cavalo, montar.

horseshoe ['hɔ:sʃu:] *n* ferradura *f*.

horsewoman ['hɔ:s,wʊmən] (*pl* -women [-,wɪmɪn]) *n* amazona *f*.

horticulture ['hɔ:tɪkʌltʃəᵊ] *n* (U) horticultura *f*.

hose [həʊz] <> *n* [hosepipe] mangueira *f*. <> *vt* regar com mangueira.

hosepipe ['həʊzpaɪp] *n* mangueira *f*.

hosiery ['həʊzɪərɪ] *n* (U) artigos *mpl* de malha, lingeries *fpl*.

hospitable [hɒ'spɪtəbl] *adj* hospitalei-ro(ra).

hospital ['hɒspɪtl] *n* hospital *m*.

hospitality [ˌhɒspɪ'tælətɪ] *n (U)* hospitalidade *f*.

host [həʊst] ◇ *n* -1. [at private party] anfitrião *m*, -ã *f* -2. [place, organization] sede *f* -3. [compere] apresentador *m*, -ra *f* -4. *literary* [large number]: **a ~ of sthg** um monte de algo. ◇ *vt* apresentar.

hostage ['hɒstɪdʒ] *n* refém *mf*.

hostel ['hɒstl] *n* albergue *m*, alojamento *m*; **(youth) ~** albergue (da juventude).

hostess ['həʊstes] *n* [at party] anfitriã *f*.

hostile [*UK* 'hɒstaɪl, *US* 'hɒstl] *adj* -1. [gen] hostil; **~ to sb/sthg** hostil com alguém/algo -2. [unfavourable] adverso(sa), desfavorável.

hostility [hɒ'stɪlətɪ] *n (U)* [antagonism, unfriendliness] hostilidade *f*.

➡ **hostilities** *npl* hostilidades *fpl*.

hot [hɒt] (*compar* -**ter**, *superl* -**test**) *adj* -1. [gen] quente; **I'm ~** estou com calor -2. [spicy] picante -3. *inf* [expert] bom (boa); **to be ~ on** *OR* **at sthg** ser bom (boa) em algo -4. [recent] recente, quente -5. [temper] veemente.

hot-air balloon *n* balão *m* de ar quente.

hotbed ['hɒtbed] *n fig* [centre] foco *m*.

hot-cross bun *n* pão doce feito com passas e enfeitado com uma cruz que se come na Semana Santa.

hot dog *n* cachorro-quente *m*.

hotel [həʊ'tel] *n* hotel *m*.

hot flush *UK*, **hot flash** *US n* calorão *m* (da menopausa).

hotfoot *adv literary* apressadamente.

hotheaded [ˌhɒt'hedɪd] *adj* temerário(-ria).

hothouse ['hɒthaʊs, *pl* -haʊzɪz] *n* [greenhouse] estufa *f*.

hot line *n* -1. [between government heads] linha *f* direta -2. [24-hour phone line] linha *f* de emergência.

hotly ['hɒtlɪ] *adv* -1. [argue, debate] calorosamente -2. [deny] veementemente -3. [pursue] **to be ~ pursued** ser seguido(da) de perto.

hotplate ['hɒtpleɪt] *n* chapa *f* elétrica.

hot-tempered *adj* esquentado(da).

hot-water bottle *n* bolsa *f* de água quente.

hound [haʊnd] ◇ *n* [dog] cão *m* de caça. ◇ *vt* -1. [persecute] perseguir -2. [drive out]: **to ~ sb out (of somewhere)** conseguir tirar alguém (de algum lugar).

hour ['aʊə'] *n* -1. [gen] hora *f*; **half an ~** meia hora; **per** *OR* **an ~** por hora; **on the ~** nas horas cheias, nas horas fechadas.

➡ **hours** *npl* -1. [of business] expediente *m*; **bank ~** expediente bancário -2. [routine] horário *m*; **to work long ~** trabalhar por horas a fio.

hourly ['aʊəlɪ] ◇ *adj* -1. [happening every hour] de hora em hora, a cada hora -2. [per hour] por hora. ◇ *adv* -1. [every hour] a cada hora -2. [per hour] por hora.

house [*n & adj* haʊs, *pl* 'haʊzɪz, *vb* haʊz] ◇ *adj* -1. *COMM* caseiro(ra) -2. [wine] da casa. ◇ *n* -1. [gen] casa *f*; **it's on the ~** é oferta da casa; **to bring the ~ down** *inf* fazer a casa vir abaixo, ser muito aplaudido(da) -2. [people in house] família *f* -3. *POL* câmara *f* -4. [in debates]: **this ~ believes that ...** os participantes do debate acreditam que ... -5. [in school] dormitório *m*. ◇ *vt* [accommodate - people, family] alojar; [- department, library, office] abrigar.

house arrest *n (U)*: **under ~** sob prisão domiciliar.

houseboat ['haʊsbəʊt] *n* casa *f* flutuante.

housebreaking ['haʊsˌbreɪkɪŋ] *n (U)* arrombamento *m* da casa.

housecoat ['haʊskəʊt] *n* chambre *m*.

household ['haʊshəʊld] ◇ *adj* -1. [domestic] doméstico(ca) -2. [familiar] familiar. ◇ *n* família *f*, lar *m*.

housekeeper ['haʊsˌkiːpə'] *n* governanta *f*.

housekeeping ['haʊsˌkiːpɪŋ] *n* -1. [work] tarefas *fpl* domésticas -2. [budget]: **~ (money)** dinheiro *m* para os gastos da casa.

house music *n* house music *f*.

House of Commons *n UK*: **the ~** a Câmara dos Comuns.

House of Lords *n UK*: **the ~** a Câmara dos Lordes.

House of Representatives *n US*: **the ~** a Câmara dos Representantes.

houseplant ['haʊsplɑːnt] *n* planta *f* de interior.

Houses of Parliament *npl UK*: **the ~** o Parlamento britânico.

housewarming (party) ['haʊsˌwɔːmɪŋ-] *n* festa *f* de inauguração de uma casa.

housewife ['haʊswaɪf] (*pl* -**wives** [-waɪvz]) *n* dona *f* de casa.

housework ['haʊswɜːk] *n (U)* afazeres *mpl* domésticos.

housing ['haʊzɪŋ] *n* -1. *(U)* [accommodation] alojamento *m* - **2.** *(U)* [topic, study] habitação *f*.

housing association *n UK* organização que possui casas e ajuda seus membros a alugá-las ou comprá-las por um preço mais barato.

housing benefit *n UK* auxílio-moradia *m*.

housing estate *UK*, **housing project** *US* *n* conjunto *m* habitacional.

hovel ['hɒvl] *n* [house] choupana *f*.

hover ['hɒvə^r] *vi* [fly] pairar, flutuar no ar.

hovercraft ['hɒvəkrɑːft] *(pl inv OR* -**s**) *n* aerodeslizador *m*.

how [haʊ] *adv* - **1.** [referring to way or manner] como; ~ **do you get there?** como se chega lá?; ~ **does it work?** como funciona?; **tell me** ~ **to do it** me diga como fazer isso. - **2.** [referring to health, quality] como; ~ **are you?** como vai?; ~ **are you doing?** como vai você?; ~ **are things?** como vão as coisas?; ~ **is your room?** como é o seu quarto? - **3.** [referring to degree, amount] quanto; ~ **far?** a que distância?; ~ **long?** quanto tempo?; ~ **many?** quantos?; ~ **much?** quanto?; ~ **much is it?** quanto custa?; ~ **old are you?** quantos anos você tem? - **4.** [in phrases]: ~ **about a drink?** que tal uma bebida?; ~ **lovely!** que lindo!

however [haʊ'evə^r] ⟨⟩ *conj* [in whatever way] como quer que; ~ **you want** como quiser. ⟨⟩ *adv* - **1.** [nevertheless] contudo, no entanto - **2.** [no matter how]: ~ **difficult it is** por mais difícil que seja; ~ **many/much** não importa quantos/quanto - **3.** [how] de que modo, como.

howl [haʊl] ⟨⟩ *n* - **1.** [of pain, anger] grito *m* - **2.** [of laughter] gargalhada *f*. ⟨⟩ *vi* - **1.** [animal, wind] uivar - **2.** [person - in pain] gritar; [- with laughter] gargalhar.

hp *(abbr of* horsepower*) n* hp *m*.

HP *n* - **1.** *UK (abbr of* hire purchase*)* a prazo; **to buy sthg on** ~ comprar algo a prazo - **2.** = **hp**.

HQ *(abbr of* headquarters*) n* QG.

hr *(abbr of* hour*)* h.

hrs *(abbr of* hours*)* h.

hub [hʌb] *n* - **1.** [of wheel] cubo *m* - **2.** [of activity] centro *m*.

hubbub ['hʌbʌb] *n* algazarra *f*.

hubcap ['hʌbkæp] *n* calota *f*.

huddle ['hʌdl] ⟨⟩ *vi* - **1.** [crouch, curl up] amontoar-se - **2.** [crowd together] apertar-se um contra os outros. ⟨⟩ *n* [of people] amontoado *m*.

hue [hjuː] *n* [colour] matiz *f*.

huff [hʌf] *n*: **in a** ~ com raiva.

hug [hʌg] *(pt & pp* -**ged**, *cont* -**ging**) ⟨⟩ *n*

abraço *m*; **to give sb a** ~ dar um abraço em alguém. ⟨⟩ *vt* - **1.** [embrace] abraçar - **2.** [stay close to] manter-se perto de.

huge [hjuːdʒ] *adj* enorme.

hulk [hʌlk] *n* - **1.** [of ship] carcaça *f* - **2.** [person] brutamontes *mpl*.

hull [hʌl] *n* [of ship] casco *m*.

hullo [hə'ləʊ] *excl* = **hello**.

hum [hʌm] *(pt & pp* -**med**, *cont* -**ming**) *vi* - **1.** [buzz] zumbir - **2.** [sing] cantarolar - **3.** [be busy] estar em atividade. ⟨⟩ *vt* [tune] zunir.

human ['hjuːmən] ⟨⟩ *adj* humano(na). ⟨⟩ *n*: ~ **(being)** (ser *m*) humano *m*.

humane [hjuː'meɪn] *adj* [compassionate] humano(na), humanitário(ria).

humanitarian [hjuːˌmænɪ'teərɪən] *adj* humanitário(ria).

humanity [hjuː'mænətɪ] *n* humanidade *f*.

➡ **humanities** *npl*: **the humanities** as humanidades.

human race *n*: **the** ~ a raça humana.

human resources *npl* recursos *mpl* humanos.

human rights *npl* direitos *mpl* humanos.

humble ['hʌmbl] ⟨⟩ *adj* humilde. ⟨⟩ *vt* humilhar.

humbug ['hʌmbʌg] *n* - **1.** *(U) dated* [hypocrisy] hipocrisia *f* - **2.** *UK* [sweet] caramelo *m* de menta.

humdrum ['hʌmdrʌm] *adj* monótono(na).

humid ['hjuːmɪd] *adj* úmido(da).

humidity [hjuː'mɪdətɪ] *n (U)* umidade *f*.

humiliate [hjuː'mɪlɪeɪt] *vt* humilhar.

humiliation [hjuːˌmɪlɪ'eɪʃn] *n (U)* humilhação *f*.

humility [hjuː'mɪlətɪ] *n (U)* humildade *f*.

humor *n & vt US* = **humour**.

humorous ['hjuːmərəs] *adj* humorístico(ca).

humour *UK*, **humor** *US* ['hjuːmə^r] ⟨⟩ *(U)* [gen] humor *m*; **in bad/good** ~ *dated* de mau/bom humor. ⟨⟩ *vt* fazer a vontade de.

hump [hʌmp] *n* - **1.** [hill] elevação *f* - **2.** [on back of animal, person] corcova *f*.

humpbacked bridge ['hʌmpbækt-] *n* ponte *f* encurvada.

hunch [hʌntʃ] *n inf* pressentimento *m*.

hunchback ['hʌntʃbæk] *n* corcunda *mf*.

hunched [hʌntʃt] *adj* encurvado(da).

hundred ['hʌndrəd] *num* cem; **a** OR **one hundred** cem; *see also* **six**.

➡ **hundreds** *npl* centenas *fpl*.

hundredth ['hʌndrətθ] *num* centésimo(ma); *see also* **sixth**.

hundredweight [ˈhʌndrədweɪt] n -1. [in UK] quintal m métrico *(50,8 kg)* -2. [in US] quintal m métrico *(45,3 kg)*.

hung [hʌŋ] pt & pp ▷ **hang**.

Hungarian [hʌŋˈgeərɪən] ◇ adj húngaro(ra). ◇ n -1. [person] húngaro m, -ra f -2. [language] húngaro m.

Hungary [ˈhʌŋgərɪ] n Hungria.

hunger [ˈhʌŋgəʳ] n -1. [desire for food, starvation] fome f -2. *literary* [strong desire] sede f.
‣ **hunger after, hunger for** vt fus *literary* ter fome de.

hunger strike n greve f de fome.

hung over adj inf: to be ~ estar com ressaca.

hungry [ˈhʌŋgrɪ] *(compar -ier, superl -iest)* adj -1. [for food] faminto(ta) -2. *literary* [eager]: to be ~ for sthg ter sede de algo.

hung up adj inf: to be ~ (on sb/sthg), to be ~ (about sb/sthg) ficar complexado(da) (por causa de alguém/algo).

hunk [hʌŋk] n -1. [large piece] naco m -2. *inf* [attractive man] pedaço m de mau caminho.

hunt [hʌnt] ◇ n -1. [SPORT - activity] caça f; [- hunters] grupo m de caçadores -2. [search] busca f. ◇ vi -1. [for food, sport] caçar -2. [search]: to ~ (for sthg) procurar (algo). ◇ vt -1. [animals, birds] caçar -2. [person] procurar.

hunting [ˈhʌntɪŋ] n -1. *SPORT* caça f -2. *UK* [foxhunting] caça f à raposa.

hurdle [ˈhɜːdl] ◇ n -1. [in race] barreira f -2. [obstacle] obstáculo m. ◇ vt [jump over] saltar.
‣ **hurdles** npl *SPORT* corrida f de obstáculos.

hurl [hɜːl] vt -1. [throw] arremessar -2. [shout] proferir.

hurray [hʊˈreɪ] excl viva!

hurricane [ˈhʌrɪkən] n furacão m.

hurried [ˈhʌrɪd] adj [hasty] apressado(da), precipitado(da).

hurriedly [ˈhʌrɪdlɪ] adv apressadamente, precipitadamente.

hurry [ˈhʌrɪ] *(pt & pp -ied)* ◇ vt apressar. ◇ vi apressar-se; to ~ to do sthg apressar-se para fazer algo. ◇ n [rush] pressa f; to be in a ~ estar com pressa; to do sthg in a ~ fazer algo com pressa.
‣ **hurry up** vi apressar-se; hurry! vamos de uma vez!

hurt [hɜːt] *(pt & pp hurt)* ◇ vt -1. [cause physical pain to] machucar -2. [injure] ferir -3. [upset] magoar -4. [be detrimental to] prejudicar. ◇ vi -1. [gen] doer; my feet ~ os meus pés doem;

ouch, you're ~ing! ai, você está me machucando -2. [be detrimental] prejudicar. ◇ adj -1. [injured] machucado(da) -2. [upset] magoado(da).

hurtful [ˈhɜːtfʊl] adj ofensivo(va).

hurtle [ˈhɜːtl] vi precipitar-se; to ~ over precipitar-se por; to ~ past passar como um raio.

husband [ˈhʌzbənd] n marido m.

hush [hʌʃ] ◇ n [quietness] silêncio m. ◇ excl silêncio!
‣ **hush up** vt sep -1. [affair] silenciar a respeito de -2. [noisy person] ficar quieto(ta).

husk [hʌsk] n [of seed, grain] casca f.

husky [ˈhʌskɪ] *(compar -ier, superl -iest)* ◇ adj [hoarse] rouco(ca). ◇ n [dog] husky m.

hustle [ˈhʌsl] ◇ vt [hurry] empurrar. ◇ n (U) [business]: ~ and bustle grande atividade f.

hut [hʌt] n -1. [rough house] cabana f -2. [shed] barraca f.

hutch [hʌtʃ] n arapuca f.

hyacinth [ˈhaɪəsɪnθ] n jacinto m.

hydrant [ˈhaɪdrənt] n hidrante m.

hydraulic [haɪˈdrɔːlɪk] adj hidráulico(ca).

hydroelectric [ˌhaɪdrəʊˈlektrɪk] adj hidrelétrico(ca).

hydrofoil [ˈhaɪdrəfɔɪl] n embarcação f com hidrofólio.

hydrogen [ˈhaɪdrədʒən] n (U) hidrogênio m.

hyena [haɪˈiːnə] n hiena f.

hygiene [ˈhaɪdʒiːn] n (U) higiene f.

hygienic [haɪˈdʒiːnɪk] adj higiênico(ca).

hymn [hɪm] n hino m.

hype [haɪp] inf ◇ n (U) propaganda f exagerada. ◇ vt fazer propaganda exagerada de.

hyperactive [ˌhaɪpərˈæktɪv] adj hiperativo(va).

hyperlink [ˈhaɪpəˌlɪŋk] n *COMPUT* hyperlink m.

hypermarket [ˈhaɪpəˌmɑːkɪt] n hipermercado m.

hyphen [ˈhaɪfn] n hífen m.

hypnosis [hɪpˈnəʊsɪs] n (U) hipnose f.

hypnotic [hɪpˈnɒtɪk] adj hipnótico(ca).

hypnotize, -ise [ˈhɪpnətaɪz] vt hipnotizar.

hypocrisy [hɪˈpɒkrəsɪ] n (U) hipocrisia f.

hypocrite [ˈhɪpəkrɪt] n hipócrita mf.

hypocritical [ˌhɪpəˈkrɪtɪkl] adj hipócrita.

hypothesis [haɪˈpɒθɪsɪs] *(pl -theses [-θɪsiːz])* n hipótese f.

hypothetical [ˌhaɪpəˈθetɪkl] adj hipotético(ca).

hysteria [hɪsˈtɪərɪə] n histeria f.

hysterical [hɪs'terɪkl] adj - **1.** [gen] histérico(ca) - **2.** inf [very funny] hilariante.
hysterics [hɪs'terɪks] npl - **1.** [panic, excitement] crise f histérica, histeria f - **2.** inf [fits of laughter] ataque m de riso; **to be in** ~ arrebentar-se de tanto rir.

i (pl **i's** OR **is**), **I¹** (pl **I's** OR **Is**) [aɪ] n [letter] i, I m.
I² [aɪ] pers pron - **1.** (unstressed) [referring to o.s.] eu; **she and** ~ **were at college together** eu e ela fomos ao colégio juntos(tas); **it is** ~ fml sou eu - **2.** (stressed) [referring to o.s.] eu; ~ **can't do it** eu não posso fazer isso.
ice [aɪs] <> n - **1.** (U) [gen] gelo m - **2.** UK [ice cream] sorvete m. <> vt UK [cover with icing] cobrir com glacê.
◆ **ice over, ice up** vi congelar.
iceberg [aɪsbɜːg] n iceberg m.
iceberg lettuce n alface f americana.
icebox [aɪsbɒks] n - **1.** UK [in refrigerator] congelador m - **2.** US [refrigerator] geladeira f, refrigerador m.
ice cream n sorvete m.
ice cream bar n US picolé m com casquinha de chocolate.
ice cube n cubo m de gelo.
ice hockey n (U) hóquei m sobre o gelo.
Iceland [aɪslənd] n Islândia f.
Icelandic [aɪs'lændɪk] <> adj islandês(esa). <> n [language] islandês m.
ice lolly n UK picolé m.
ice pick n picador m de gelo.
ice rink n rinque m (de patinação).
ice skate n patim m para o gelo.
◆ **ice-skate** vi patinar sobre o gelo.
ice-skating n (U) patinação f sobre o gelo; **to go** ~ praticar patinação.
icicle [aɪsɪkl] n pingente m de gelo.
icing [aɪsɪŋ] n (U) glacê m.
icing sugar n UK açúcar m de confeiteiro.
icon [aɪkɒn] n ícone m.
icy [aɪsɪ] (compar -ier, superl -iest) adj - **1.** [very cold] gelado(da) - **2.** [covered in ice] coberto(ta) de gelo - **3.** fig [unfriendly] frio (fria).
I'd [aɪd] = I would, I had.

ID n (abbr of identification) identificação f; ~ **card** (carteira f de) f identidade, ≃ RG m.
idea [aɪ'dɪə] n - **1.** [gen] idéia f; **to get the** ~ inf pegar a idéia; **to have an** ~ **that** ter a sensação de que; **to have no** ~ não ter idéia - **2.** [suspicion] impressão f.
ideal [aɪ'dɪəl] <> adj [perfect] ideal; **to be** ~ **for sthg** ser ideal para algo. <> n [principle] ideal m.
ideally [aɪ'dɪəlɪ] adv - **1.** [perfectly] perfeitamente - **2.** [preferably] idelmente.
identical [aɪ'dentɪkl] adj idêntico(ca).
identification [aɪ,dentɪfɪ'keɪʃn] n identificação f; ~ **with sb/sthg** identificação com alguém/algo.
identify [aɪ'dentɪfaɪ] (pt & pp -ied) <> vt - **1.** [gen] identificar - **2.** [connect]: **to** ~ **sb with sthg** relacionar alguém a algo. <> vi [empathize]: **to** ~ **with sb/sthg** identificar-se com alguém/algo.
Identikit picture® [aɪ'dentɪkɪt-] n retrato m falado.
identity [aɪ'dentətɪ] (pl -ies) n identidade f.
identity card n (carteira f de) identidade f.
identity parade n identificação f (de um criminoso).
ideology [,aɪdɪ'ɒlədʒɪ] (pl -ies) n ideologia f.
idiom [ɪdɪəm] n - **1.** [phrase] expressão f idiomática - **2.** fml [style, language] linguagem f.
idiomatic [,ɪdɪə'mætɪk] adj [natural-sounding] idiomático(ca).
idiosyncrasy [,ɪdɪə'sɪŋkrəsɪ] (pl -ies) n idiossincrasia f.
idiot [ɪdɪət] n [fool] idiota mf.
idiotic [,ɪdɪ'ɒtɪk] adj idiota.
idle [aɪdl] <> adj - **1.** [person - inactive] ocioso(sa); [- lazy] preguiçoso(sa) - **2.** [not in use] parado(da) - **3.** [empty] vão (vã) - **4.** [casual] casual - **5.** [futile] inútil. <> vi [engine] estar em ponto morto.
◆ **idle away** vt sep desperdiçar.
idol [aɪdl] n ídolo m.
idolize, -ise [aɪdəlaɪz] vt idolatrar.
idyllic [ɪ'dɪlɪk] adj idílico(ca).
i.e. (abbr of id est) i.e.
IEE (abbr of Institution of Electrical Engineers) n instituto britânico de engenheiros eletricistas.
if [ɪf] conj - **1.** [gen] se; ~ **I were you** se eu fosse você - **2.** [though] ainda que; **a good,** ~ **rather expensive, restaurant** um bom restaurante, ainda que caro - **3.** [that] que.
◆ **if not** conj se não.
◆ **if only** <> conj - **1.** [providing a reason]

ao menos, nem que seja; **let's stop at the next services, ~ to stretch our legs** vamos parar no próximo posto, ao menos OR nem que seja para esticar as pernas **- 2.** [expressing regret] se ao menos. ◇ *excl* quem dera!

igloo ['ɪgluː] (*pl* **-s**) *n* iglu *m*.

ignite [ɪg'naɪt] ◇ *vt* acender. ◇ *vi* acender, acender-se.

ignition [ɪg'nɪʃn] *n* ignição *f*.

ignition key *n* chave *f* de ignição.

ignorance ['ɪgnərəns] *n* (*U*) ignorância *f*.

ignorant ['ɪgnərənt] *adj* **-1.** [uneducated] ignorante; [lacking information] desinformado(da) **- 2.** *fml* [unaware]: **to be ~ of sthg** ignorar algo **- 3.** *inf* [rude] ignorante.

ignore [ɪg'nɔː^r] *vt* [take no notice of] ignorar.

ilk [ɪlk] *n* *fml*: **of that ~** [of that sort] do mesmo tipo.

ill [ɪl] ◇ *adj* **-1.** [sick, unwell] doente; **to feel ~** sentir-se doente; **to be taken ~, to fall ~** ficar doente **- 2.** [bad, unfavourable] mau (má). ◇ *adv* mal; **to speak/ think ~ of sb** falar/pensar mal de alguém; **we can ~ afford such luxuries** mal conseguimos pagar esses luxos.

I'll [aɪl] = **I will, I shall**.

ill at ease *adj*: **he always felt shy and ~ at parties** ele sempre se sentia intimidado e pouco à vontade nas festas.

illegal [ɪ'liːgl] *adj* ilegal.

illegible [ɪ'ledʒəbl] *adj* ilegível.

illegitimate [,ɪlɪ'dʒɪtɪmət] *adj* ilegítimo(ma).

ill-equipped [-ɪ'kwɪpt] *adj* despreparado(da).

ill-fated [-'feɪtɪd] *adj* malfadado(da).

ill feeling *n* (*U*) ressentimento *f*, rancor *m*.

ill health *n* (*U*) má saúde *f*.

illicit [ɪ'lɪsɪt] *adj* ilícito(ta).

illiteracy [ɪ'lɪtərəsɪ] *n* (*U*) analfabetismo *m*.

illiterate [ɪ'lɪtərət] ◇ *adj* analfabeto(ta). ◇ *n* analfabeto *m*, -ta *f*.

illness ['ɪlnɪs] *n* doença *f*.

illogical [ɪ'lɒdʒɪkl] *adj* ilógico(ca).

ill-suited *adj* inadequado(da); **an ~ couple** um casal desajustado; **to be ~ to sthg** ser inadequado(da) para algo.

ill-timed [-'taɪmd] *adj* inoportuno(na).

ill-treat *vt* maltratar.

illuminate [ɪ'luːmɪneɪt] *vt* **-1.** [light up] iluminar **- 2.** [explain] ilustrar, esclarecer.

illumination [ɪ,luːmɪ'neɪʃn] *n* (*U*) [lighting] iluminação *f*.

◆ **illuminations** *npl* *UK* luzes *fpl* decorativas.

illusion [ɪ'luːʒn] *n* [gen] ilusão *f*; **to have no ~s about sb/sthg** não ter ilusões com alguém/algo; **to be under the ~ that** estar com a ilusão de que.

illustrate ['ɪləstreɪt] *vt* ilustrar.

illustration [,ɪlə'streɪʃn] *n* ilustração *f*.

illustrious [ɪ'lʌstrɪəs] *adj* *fml* ilustre.

ill will *n* (*U*) animosidade *f*.

I'm [aɪm] = **I am**.

image ['ɪmɪdʒ] *n* [gen] imagem *f*.

imagery ['ɪmɪdʒrɪ] *n* imagens *fpl*.

imaginary [ɪ'mædʒɪnrɪ] *adj* imaginário(ria).

imagination [ɪ,mædʒɪ'neɪʃn] *n* imaginação *f*.

imaginative [ɪ'mædʒɪnətɪv] *adj* imaginativo(va).

imagine [ɪ'mædʒɪn] *vt* imaginar; **to ~ doing sthg** imaginar fazer algo; **~ (that)!** imagine!

imbalance [,ɪm'bæləns] *n* desequilíbrio *m*.

imbecile ['ɪmbɪsiːl] *n* imbecil *mf*.

IMF (*abbr of* **International Monetary Fund**) *n* FMI *m*.

imitate ['ɪmɪteɪt] *vt* imitar.

imitation [,ɪmɪ'teɪʃn] ◇ *n* imitação *f*. ◇ *adj* de imitação.

immaculate [ɪ'mækjʊlət] *adj* **-1.** [clean and tidy] imaculado(da) **- 2.** [impeccable] impecável.

immaterial [,ɪmə'tɪərɪəl] *adj* [irrelevant, unimportant] irrelevante.

immature [,ɪmə'tjʊə^r] *adj* **-1.** [childish] imaturo(ra) **- 2.** *BOT & ZOOL* jovem.

immediate [ɪ'miːdjət] *adj* **-1.** [gen] imediato(ta) **- 2.** [closest in relationship] próximo(ma).

immediately [ɪ'miːdjətlɪ] ◇ *adv* **-1.** [gen] imediatamente **- 2.** [directly, closely] diretamente. ◇ *conj* [as soon as] assim que.

immense [ɪ'mens] *adj* imenso(sa).

immerse [ɪ'mɜːs] *vt* **-1.** [plunge into liquid]: **to ~ sthg in sthg** mergulhar algo em algo **- 2.** *fig* [involve]: **to ~ o.s. in sthg** envolver-se em algo.

immersion heater [ɪ'mɜːʃn-] *n* ebulidor *m*.

immigrant ['ɪmɪgrənt] *n* imigrante *mf*.

immigration [,ɪmɪ'greɪʃn] *n* (*U*) imigração *f*.

imminent ['ɪmɪnənt] *adj* iminente.

immobilize, -ise [ɪ'məʊbɪlaɪz] *vt* imobilizar.

immobilizer *n* *AUT* corta-corrente *m*.

immoral [ɪ'mɒrəl] *adj* imoral.

immortal [ɪ'mɔːtl] ◇ *adj* imortal. ◇

n -**1.** [god] deus *m* -**2.** [hero] imortal *mf*.

immortalize, -ise [ɪ'mɔːtəlaɪz] *vt* imortalizar.

immovable [ɪ'muːvəbl] *adj* -**1.** [fixed] fixo(xa) -**2.** [obstinate] inflexível.

immune [ɪ'mjuːn] *adj* -**1.** MED imune; to be ~ to sthg ser imune a algo -**2.** *fig* [impervious]: **to be** ~ **to** sthg não ser suscetível a algo -**3.** [exempt] isento(ta), livre; **to be** ~ **from** sthg estar protegido(da) de algo.

immunity [ɪ'mjuːnətɪ] *n* -**1.** (*U*) MED: ~ **(to** sthg) imunidade *f* (a algo) -**2.** (*U*) *fig* [imperviousness]: ~ **to** sthg falta *f* de suscetibilidade a algo -**3.** [exemption] isenção *f*; ~ **from** sthg proteção *f* contra algo.

immunize, -ise ['ɪmjuːnaɪz] *vt*: **to** ~ **sb (against** sthg) MED imunizar alguém (contra algo).

imp [ɪmp] *n* -**1.** [creature] diabinho *m* -**2.** [naughty child] diabinho *m*, -nha *f*.

impact [*n* 'ɪmpækt, *vb* ɪm'pækt] ◇ *n* impacto *m*; to make an ~ on sb/sthg causar impacto em alguém/algo. ◇ *vt* -**1.** [collide with] colidir com -**2.** [influence] influenciar.

impair [ɪm'peə*r*] *vt* prejudicar, debilitar.

impart [ɪm'pɑːt] *vt fml* -**1.** [information]: **to** ~ sthg **(to** sb) transmitir algo (a alguém) -**2.** [feeling, quality] conferir; **to** ~ **flavour to the dish** conferir sabor ao prato.

impartial [ɪm'pɑːʃl] *adj* imparcial.

impassable [ɪm'pɑːsəbl] *adj* intransitável.

impassioned [ɪm'pæʃnd] *adj* veemente.

impassive [ɪm'pæsɪv] *adj* impassível.

impatience [ɪm'peɪʃns] *n* impaciência *f*.

impatient [ɪm'peɪʃnt] *adj* impaciente; **to be** ~ **to do** sthg estar impaciente para fazer algo; **to be** ~ **for** sthg esperar algo com impaciência.

impeccable [ɪm'pekəbl] *adj* impecável.

impede [ɪm'piːd] *vt* impedir.

impediment [ɪm'pedɪmənt] *n* impedimento *m*; **a speech** ~ um defeito de fala.

impel [ɪm'pell] (*pt & pp* -led, *cont* -ling) *vt*: **to** ~ sb **to do** sthg impelir alguém a fazer algo.

impending [ɪm'pendɪŋ] *adj* iminente.

imperative [ɪm'perətɪv] ◇ *adj* [essential] indispensável. ◇ *n* imperativo *m*.

imperfect [ɪm'pɜːfɪkt] ◇ *adj* [not perfect] imperfeito(ta). ◇ *n* GRAMM: ~ **(tense)** (pretérito *m*) imperfeito *m*.

imperial [ɪm'pɪərɪəl] *adj* -**1.** [of an empire or emperor] imperial -**2.** [system of measurement]: ~ **system** *sistema britânico de medidas*.

imperil [ɪm'perɪl] (*UK pt & pp* -led, *cont* -ling, *US pt & pp* -ed, *cont* -ing) *vt fml* pôr em perigo.

impersonal [ɪm'pɜːsnl] *adj* impessoal.

impersonate [ɪm'pɜːsəneɪt] *vt* -**1.** [mimic, imitate] imitar -**2.** [pretend to be] fazer-se passar por.

impersonation [ɪm͵pɜːsə'neɪʃn] *n* [by mimic] imitação *f*; **to do** ~**s (of** sb) fazer imitações (de alguém).

impertinent [ɪm'pɜːtɪnənt] *adj* [rude] impertinente.

impervious [ɪm'pɜːvjəs] *adj* [not influenced]: ~ **to** sthg imune a algo.

impetuous [ɪm'petʃʊəs] *adj* impetuoso(sa).

impetus ['ɪmpɪtəs] *n* -**1.** [momentum] ímpeto *m* -**2.** [stimulus] estímulo *m*.

impinge [ɪm'pɪndʒ] *vi*: **to** ~ **on** sb/sthg afetar alguém/algo.

implant [*n* 'ɪmplɑːnt, *vb* ɪm'plɑːnt] ◇ *n* implante *m*. ◇ *vt*: **to** ~ sthg **in(to)** sb implantar algo em alguém.

implausible [ɪm'plɔːzəbl] *adj* implausível.

implement [*n* 'ɪmplɪmənt, *vt* 'ɪmplɪment] ◇ *n* [tool] ferramenta *f*. ◇ *vt* implementar.

implication [͵ɪmplɪ'keɪʃn] *n* -**1.** (*U*) [involvement] implicação *f*, envolvimento *m* -**2.** [inference] implicação *f*; **by** ~ por conseqüência.

implicit [ɪm'plɪsɪt] *adj* -**1.** [inferred] implícito(ta) -**2.** [complete] absoluto(ta).

implore [ɪm'plɔː*r*] *vt*: **to** ~ sb **(to do** sthg) implorar a alguém (para que faça algo).

imply [ɪm'plaɪ] (*pt & pp* -ied) *vt* -**1.** [suggest] pressupor -**2.** [involve] implicar.

impolite [͵ɪmpə'laɪt] *adj* descortês, indelicado(da).

import [*n* 'ɪmpɔːt, *vt* ɪm'pɔːt] ◇ *n* COMM importação *f*. ◇ *vt* importar.

importance [ɪm'pɔːtns] *n* (*U*) importância *f*.

important [ɪm'pɔːtnt] *adj* importante; **to be** ~ **to** sb ser importante para alguém.

importer [ɪm'pɔːtə*r*] *n* importador *m*, -ra *f*.

impose [ɪm'pəʊz] ◇ *vt* [force]: **to** ~ sthg **(on** sb/sthg) impor algo (a alguém/algo). ◇ *vi* [cause trouble]: **to** ~ **(on** sb) causar problemas (para alguém).

imposing [ɪm'pəʊzɪŋ] *adj* imponente.

imposition [ˌɪmpə'zɪʃn] n imposição f.

impossible [ɪm'pɒsəbl] adj impossível.

impostor, imposter US [ɪm'pɒstə'] n impostor m, -ra f.

impotent ['ɪmpətənt] adj impotente.

impound [ɪm'paʊnd] vt JUR apreender.

impoverished [ɪm'pɒvərɪʃt] adj lit & fig empobrecido(da).

impractical [ɪm'præktɪkl] adj pouco prático(ca).

impregnable [ɪm'pregnəbl] adj -1. [impenetrable] invulnerável -2. fig [in very strong position] imbatível.

impregnate ['ɪmpregneɪt] vt -1. [introduce substance into]: to ~ sthg with sthg impregnar algo de algo -2. fml [fertilize] fecundar.

impress [ɪm'pres] vt -1. [influence, affect] impressionar -2. [make clear]: to ~ sthg on sb convencer alguém da importância de algo.

impression [ɪm'preʃn] n -1. [gen] impressão f; to make an ~ impressionar; to be under the ~ (that) ter a impressão de que -2. [impersonation] imitação f.

impressive [ɪm'presɪv] adj impressionante.

imprint ['ɪmprɪnt] ⟨⟩ n -1. [mark] marca f, impressão f -2. [publisher's name] ≃ selo m da editora. ⟨⟩ vt [mark] imprimir, marcar.

imprison [ɪm'prɪzn] vt [put in prison] aprisionar.

improbable [ɪm'prɒbəbl] adj [unlikely] improvável.

impromptu [ɪm'prɒmptjuː] adj de improviso, improvisado(da).

improper [ɪm'prɒpə'] adj -1. [unsuitable] inadequado(da) -2. [dishonest] desonesto(ta) -3. [rude, shocking] impróprio(pria).

improve [ɪm'pruːv] ⟨⟩ vi [get better] melhorar; to ~ (up)on sthg melhorar algo. ⟨⟩ vt -1. [gen] melhorar -2. [cultivate] desenvolver.

improvement [ɪm'pruːvmənt] n melhoria f; ~ in/on sthg melhoria em algo.

improvise ['ɪmprəvaɪz] vt & vi improvisar.

impudence n impudência f.

impudent ['ɪmpjʊdənt] adj impudente.

impulse ['ɪmpʌls] n impulso m; on ~ sem pensar.

impulsive [ɪm'pʌlsɪv] adj impulsivo(va).

impunity [ɪm'pjuːnətɪ] n impunidade f; with ~ impunemente.

impurity [ɪm'pjʊərətɪ] (pl -ies) n impureza f.

in [ɪn] ⟨⟩ prep -1. [indicating place, position] em; it comes ~ a box vem numa caixa; ~ the hospital no hospital; ~ Scotland na Escócia; ~ Boston em Boston; ~ the middle no meio; ~ the sun/rain no sol/na chuva; ~ here/there aqui/ali (dentro); ~ front à frente. -2. [appearing in] em; who's ~ the play? quem está na peça? -3. [indicating arrangement] em; they come ~ packs of three vêm em embalagens de três; ~ a row em fila; cut it ~ half corte-o ao meio. -4. [during]: ~ April em abril; ~ the afternoon à OR de tarde; ~ the morning de manhã; ten o'clock ~ the morning dez (horas) da manhã; ~ 1994 em 1994; ~ summer/winter no verão/inverno. -5. [within] em; [after] dentro de, daqui a; it'll be ready ~ an hour estará pronto daqui a OR dentro de uma hora; she did everything ~ ten minutes ela fez tudo em dez minutos; they're arriving ~ two weeks chegam dentro de OR daqui a duas semanas. -6. [indicating means]: ~ writing por escrito; they were talking ~ English estavam falando (em) inglês; write ~ ink escreva a tinta. -7. [wearing] de; dressed ~ red vestido de vermelho; the man ~ the blue suit o homem com o terno azul. -8. [indicating state] em; to be ~ a hurry estar com pressa; to be ~ pain ter dores; to cry out ~ pain gritar de dor OR com dores; ~ ruins em ruínas; ~ good health com boa saúde. -9. [with regard to]: de; a rise ~ prices uma subida dos preços; to be 50 metres ~ length ter 50 metros de comprimento. -10. [with numbers]: one ~ ten um em cada dez. -11. [indicating age]: she's ~ her twenties ela está na casa dos vinte. -12. [with colours]: it comes ~ green or blue vem em verde ou azul. -13. [with superlatives] de; the best ~ the world o melhor do mundo. ⟨⟩ adv -1. [inside] dentro; you can go ~ now pode entrar agora. -2. [at home, work]: she's not ~ (ela) não está; to stay ~ ficar em casa. -3. [train, bus, plane]: the train's not ~ yet o trem ainda não chegou. -4. [tide]: the tide is ~ a maré está cheia. ⟨⟩ adj inf [fashionable] na moda, in (inv).

in. abbr of inch.

inability [ˌɪnə'bɪlətɪ] n incapacidade f; ~ to do sthg incapacidade para fazer algo.

inaccessible [ˌɪnək'sesəbl] adj inacessível.

inaccurate [ɪn'ækjʊrət] adj impreciso(sa).

inadequate [ɪn'ædɪkwət] adj -1. [insufficient] insuficiente -2. [person] incapaz.

inconsequential

inadvertently [ˌməd'vɜːtəntlɪ] adv acidentalmente.

inadvisable [ˌməd'vaɪzəbl] adj desaconselhável.

inane [ɪ'neɪn] adj vazio(zia), fútil.

inanimate [ɪn'ænɪmət] adj inanimado(da).

inappropriate [ˌɪnə'prəʊprɪət] adj inapropriado(da).

inarticulate [ˌɪnɑː'tɪkjʊlət] adj -1. [person] incapaz de se expressar (bem) -2. [words, sounds] inarticulado(da).

inasmuch [ˌɪnəz'mʌtʃ] ◆ inasmuch as conj fml [because] visto que; [to the extent that] na medida em que.

inaudible [ɪ'nɔːdɪbl] adj inaudível.

inaugural [ɪ'nɔːgjʊrəl] adj [opening] inaugural.

inauguration [ɪˌnɔːgjʊ'reɪʃn] n -1. [of leader, president] posse f -2. [of building, system] inauguração f.

in-between adj intermediário(ria).

inborn [ˌɪn'bɔːn] adj inato(ta).

inbound ['ɪnbaʊnd] adj US: an ~ ship um navio que se aproxima; the ~ flight from Miami o vôo que chega de Miami.

inbred [ˌɪn'bred] adj -1. [family, group] endogâmico(ca), consangüíneo(nea) -2. [characteristic, quality] inato(ta).

inbuilt [ˌɪn'bɪlt] adj [quality, defect] inerente.

inc. (abbr of inclusive) inclusive.

Inc. [ɪŋk] (abbr of incorporated) ≈ S.A.

incapable [ɪn'keɪpəbl] adj -1. [unable]: to be ~ of sthg/of doing sthg ser incapaz de algo/de fazer algo -2. [incompetent] incompetente.

incapacitated [ˌɪnkə'pæsɪteɪtɪd] adj incapacitado(da).

incarcerate [ɪn'kɑːsəreɪt] vt fml encarcerar.

incendiary device [ɪn'sendjərɪ-] n artefato m incendiário.

incense [n 'ɪnsens, vt ɪn'sens] ⟨⟩ n (U) [perfume] incenso m. ⟨⟩ vt [anger] enfurecer, enraivecer.

incentive [ɪn'sentɪv] n incentivo m.

incentive scheme n plano m de incentivos.

inception [ɪn'sepʃn] n fml começo m, origem f.

incessant [ɪn'sesnt] adj incessante.

incessantly [ɪn'sesntlɪ] adv incessantemente.

incest ['ɪnsest] n incesto m.

inch [ɪntʃ] ⟨⟩ n polegada f. ⟨⟩ vi avançar gradualmente.

incidence ['ɪnsɪdəns] n incidência f.

incident ['ɪnsɪdənt] n [occurrence, event] incidente m.

incidental [ˌɪnsɪ'dentl] adj [minor] acessório(ria), secundário(ria).

incidentally [ˌɪnsɪ'dentəlɪ] adv -1. [by chance] por acaso -2. [by the way] a propósito.

incinerate [ɪn'sɪnəreɪt] vt incinerar.

incipient [ɪn'sɪpɪənt] adj fml incipiente.

incisive [ɪn'saɪsɪv] adj incisivo(va).

incite [ɪn'saɪt] vt incitar; to ~ sb to do sthg incitar alguém a fazer algo.

inclination [ˌɪnklɪ'neɪʃn] n -1. (U) [liking, preference] vontade f -2. [tendency]: ~ to do sthg tendência f OR inclinação f para fazer algo.

incline [n 'ɪnklaɪn, vb ɪn'klaɪn] ⟨⟩ n [slope] ladeira f. ⟨⟩ vt [lean, bend] inclinar.

inclined [ɪn'klaɪnd] adj -1. [tending] inclinado(da), propenso(sa); to be ~ to sthg estar propenso(sa) a algo; to be ~ to do sthg estar inclinado(da) a fazer algo -2. [wanting, willing]: to be ~ to do sthg estar disposto(ta) a fazer algo -3. [sloping] inclinado(da).

include [ɪn'kluːd] vt -1. [contain] abranger -2. [add, count] incluir.

included [ɪn'kluːdɪd] adj incluído(da).

including [ɪn'kluːdɪŋ] prep inclusive; six died, ~ a child seis morreram, incluindo uma criança.

inclusive [ɪn'kluːsɪv] adj inclusive; 1 to 9, ~ de um a nove, inclusive; £150 ~ £150, tudo incluído; ~ of incluindo.

incoherent [ˌɪnkəʊ'hɪərənt] adj incoerente.

income ['ɪnkʌm] n -1. [earnings] renda f -2. [profit] lucro m.

income support n UK auxílio dado pelo governo a pessoas desempregadas ou de renda muito baixa.

income tax n imposto m de renda.

incompatible [ˌɪnkəm'pætɪbl] adj incompatível; ~ with sb/sthg incompatível com alguém/algo.

incompetent [ɪn'kɒmpɪtənt] adj incompetente.

incomplete [ˌɪnkəm'pliːt] adj incompleto(ta).

incomprehensible [ɪnˌkɒmprɪ'hensəbl] adj incompreensível.

inconceivable [ˌɪnkən'siːvəbl] adj inconcebível.

inconclusive [ˌɪnkən'kluːsɪv] adj -1. [meeting, outcome, debate] sem conclusões claras -2. [evidence, argument] pouco convincente.

incongruous [ɪn'kɒŋgrʊəs] adj incongruente.

inconsequential [ˌɪnkɒnsɪ'kwenʃl] adj [insignificant] insignificante.

inconsiderable [ˌɪnkən'sɪdərəbl] adj: not ~ nada desprezível.

inconsiderate [ˌɪnkən'sɪdərət] adj -1. [attitude, treatment] impensado(da), irrefletido(da) -2. [person] sem consideração.

inconsistency [ˌɪnkən'sɪstənsɪ] (pl-ies) n -1. (U) [state of being inconsistent] inconsistência f -2. [contradictory point] contradição f.

inconsistent [ˌɪnkən'sɪstənt] adj -1. [not agreeing, contradictory] inconsistente; ~ with sthg contraditório(ria) com algo -2. [erratic] irregular.

inconspicuous [ˌɪnkən'spɪkjʊəs] adj discreto(ta).

inconvenience [ˌɪnkən'viːnjəns] <> n -1. (U) [difficulty, discomfort] incômodo m -2. [inconvenient thing] inconveniência f. <> vt incomodar.

inconvenient [ˌɪnkən'viːnjənt] adj inconveniente.

incorporate [ɪn'kɔːpəreɪt] vt -1. [include] incorporar; to ~ sb/sthg in (to) sthg incluir alguém/algo em algo -2. [blend] combinar.

incorporated company n COMM sociedade f anônima.

incorrect [ˌɪnkə'rekt] adj incorreto(ta).

incorrigible [ɪn'kɒrɪdʒəbl] adj incorrigível.

increase [n 'ɪnkriːs, vb ɪn'kriːs] <> n: ~ (in sthg) aumento m (de algo); to be on the ~ estar aumentando, estar em crescimento. <> vt & vi aumentar.

increasing [ɪn'kriːsɪŋ] adj crescente.

increasingly [ɪn'kriːsɪŋlɪ] adv cada vez mais.

incredible [ɪn'kredəbl] adj inf incrível.

incredulous [ɪn'kredjʊləs] adj incrédulo(la).

increment ['ɪnkrɪmənt] n incremento m.

incriminating [ɪn'krɪmɪneɪtɪŋ] adj incriminatório(ria).

incubator ['ɪnkjʊbeɪtə] n [for baby] incubadora f.

incumbent [ɪn'kʌmbənt] fml <> adj: to be ~ (up)on sb to do sthg incumbir alguém de fazer algo. <> n [postholder] titular mf.

incur [ɪn'kɜː] (pt & pp -red, cont -ring) vt -1. [wrath, criticism] incorrer em -2. [expenses] contrair.

indebted [ɪn'detɪd] adj [grateful]: to be ~ to sb estar em dívida com alguém.

indecent [ɪn'diːsnt] adj -1. [obscene] indecente -2. [unreasonable] inadequado(da).

indecent assault n atentado m contra o pudor.

indecent exposure n (U) ato m obsceno.

indecisive [ˌɪndɪ'saɪsɪv] adj indeciso(sa).

indeed [ɪn'diːd] adv -1. [certainly] realmente, certamente -2. [in fact] na verdade -3. [for emphasis] realmente; very big ~ estupidamente grande; very few ~ pouquíssimos(mas) -4. [to express surprise, disbelief] mesmo; ~? é mesmo?

indefinite [ɪn'defɪnɪt] adj -1. [indeterminate] indefinido(da) -2. [imprecise] impreciso(sa).

indefinitely [ɪn'defɪnətlɪ] adv [for indeterminate period] indefinidamente.

indemnity [ɪn'demnətɪ] n -1. (U) [insurance] garantia f -2. [compensation] indenização f.

indent [ɪn'dent] vt -1. [text] recuar -2. [edge, surface] recortar.

independence [ˌɪndɪ'pendəns] n independência f.

Independence Day n festa nos Estados Unidos em comemoração à sua independência, no dia 4 de julho em 1776.

independent [ˌɪndɪ'pendənt] adj independente; ~ of sb/sthg independente de alguém/algo.

independent school n UK escola f privada.

in-depth adj em profundidade, exaustivo(va).

indescribable [ˌɪndɪ'skraɪbəbl] adj indescritível.

indestructible [ˌɪndɪ'strʌktəbl] adj indestrutível.

index ['ɪndeks] (pl senses 1 and 2 -es, pl sense 3 -es OR indices) n -1. [of book] índice m remissivo -2. [in library] catálogo m -3. ECON [value system] índice m.

index card n ficha f de indexação.

index finger n (dedo m) indicador m.

index-linked [-lɪŋkt] adj indexado(da).

India ['ɪndjə] n Índia.

Indian ['ɪndjən] <> adj -1. [from India] indiano(na) -2. [from the Americas] índio(dia). <> n -1. [from India] indiano m, -na f -2. [from the Americas] índio m, -dia f.

Indian Ocean n: the ~ o Oceano Índico.

indicate ['ɪndɪkeɪt] <> vt -1. [gen] indicar -2. [suggest] sugerir. <> vi [when driving]: to ~ left/right sinalizar à esquerda/direita.

indication [ˌɪndɪ'keɪʃn] n -1. [suggestion] indicação f -2. [sign] indício m.

indicative [ɪnˈdɪkətɪv] ◇ adj: ~ of sthg indicativo(va) de algo. ◇ n GRAMM indicativo m.

indicator [ˈɪndɪkeɪtəʳ] n -1. [sign] indicador m -2. [on car] pisca-pisca m.

indices [ˈɪndɪsiːz] pl ⊳ index.

indict [ɪnˈdaɪt] vt indiciar; to ~ sb for sthg indiciar alguém por algo.

indictment [ɪnˈdaɪtmənt] n -1. JUR indiciamento m -2. [criticism] crítica f dura.

indifference [ɪnˈdɪfrəns] n (U) indiferença f.

indifferent [ɪnˈdɪfrənt] adj -1. [uninterested] indiferente; ~ to sthg indiferente a algo -2. [mediocre] medíocre.

indigenous [ɪnˈdɪdʒɪnəs] adj nativo(va), indígena.

indigestion [ˌɪndɪˈdʒestʃn] n (U) indigestão f.

indignant [ɪnˈdɪgnənt] adj indignado(da); to be ~ at sthg estar indignado(da) com algo.

indignity [ɪnˈdɪgnətɪ] (pl -ies) n -1. (U) [feeling of humiliation] afronta f -2. [humiliating situation] indignidade f.

indigo [ˈɪndɪgəʊ] ◇ adj [in colour] da cor de anil. ◇ n [colour] anil m.

indirect [ˌɪndɪˈrekt] adj indireto(ta).

indiscreet [ˌɪndɪˈskriːt] adj indiscreto(ta); [tactless] indelicado(da).

indiscriminate [ˌɪndɪˈskrɪmɪnət] adj indiscriminado(da).

indispensable [ˌɪndɪˈspensəbl] adj indispensável.

indisputable [ˌɪndɪˈspjuːtəbl] adj inquestionável.

indistinguishable [ˌɪndɪˈstɪŋgwɪʃəbl] adj indistinguível; ~ from sb/sthg indistinguível de alguém/algo.

individual [ˌɪndɪˈvɪdʒʊəl] ◇ adj -1. [gen] individual -2. [private] particular -3. [distinctive] pessoal. ◇ n indivíduo m.

individually [ˌɪndɪˈvɪdʒʊəlɪ] adv [separately] individualmente.

indoctrination [ɪnˌdɒktrɪˈneɪʃn] n (U) doutrinação f.

Indonesia [ˌɪndəˈniːzjə] n Indonésia.

indoor [ˈɪndɔːʳ] adj -1. [plant] de interior -2. [shoes] para dentro de casa -3. [sports] em local coberto; ~ swimming pool piscina f coberta.

indoors [ˌɪnˈdɔːz] adv dentro de casa; to go ~ entrar, ir para dentro.

induce [ɪnˈdjuːs] vt: to ~ sb to do sthg induzir alguém a fazer algo.

inducement [ɪnˈdjuːsmənt] n [incentive] estímulo m, incentivo m.

induction [ɪnˈdʌkʃn] n -1. [into official position]: ~ into sthg posse m em algo

-2. [introduction to job] apresentação f.

induction course n curso m de integração OR de iniciação.

indulge [ɪnˈdʌldʒ] ◇ vt -1. [whim, passion] satisfazer -2. [child, person] fazer a vontade de. ◇ vi: to ~ in sthg permitir-se algo.

indulgence [ɪnˈdʌldʒəns] n -1. (U) [tolerance, kindness] indulgência f -2. [special treat] vício m, prazer m.

indulgent [ɪnˈdʌldʒənt] adj [liberal, kind] indulgente.

industrial [ɪnˈdʌstrɪəl] adj -1. [of industry] industrial -2. [industrialized] industrializado(da).

industrial action n: to take ~ declarar-se em greve.

industrial estate UK, **industrial park** US n parque m industrial.

industrialist [ɪnˈdʌstrɪəlɪst] n industrialista mf.

industrial park n US = industrial estate.

industrial relations npl relações fpl de trabalho.

industrial revolution n revolução f industrial.

industrious [ɪnˈdʌstrɪəs] adj trabalhador(ra), diligente.

industry [ˈɪndəstrɪ] (pl -ies) n -1. [gen] indústria f; the coal ~ o setor carvoeiro -2. (U) [hard work] laboriosidade f.

inebriated [ɪˈniːbrɪeɪtɪd] adj fml inebriado(da).

inedible [ɪnˈedɪbl] adj -1. [unpleasant to eat] não-comestível -2. [poisonous] venenoso(sa).

ineffective [ˌɪnɪˈfektɪv] adj ineficaz, inútil.

ineffectual [ˌɪnɪˈfektʃʊəl] adj ineficaz, inútil.

inefficiency [ˌɪnɪˈfɪʃnsɪ] n (U) ineficiência f.

inefficient [ˌɪnɪˈfɪʃnt] adj ineficiente.

ineligible [ɪnˈelɪdʒəbl] adj inelegível; to be ~ for sthg não estar qualificado(da) para algo.

inept [ɪˈnept] adj -1. [incompetent] inepto(ta); ~ at sthg incapaz de algo -2. [clumsy] malfeito(ta).

inequality [ˌɪnɪˈkwɒlətɪ] (pl -ies) n desigualdade f.

inert [ɪˈnɜːt] adj inerte.

inertia [ɪˈnɜːʃə] n inércia f.

inescapable [ˌɪnɪˈskeɪpəbl] adj inevitável.

inevitable [ɪnˈevɪtəbl] adj inevitável. ◇ n: the ~ o inevitável.

inevitably [ɪnˈevɪtəblɪ] adv inevitavelmente.

inexcusable [,ınık'skju:zəbl] *adj* imperdoável.

inexhaustible [,ınıg'zɔ:stəbl] *adj* inesgotável.

inexpensive [,ınık'spensıv] *adj* barato(ta), econômico(ca).

inexperienced [,ınık'spıərıənst] *adj* inexperiente.

inexplicable [,ınık'splıkəbl] *adj* inexplicável.

infallible [ın'fæləbl] *adj* infalível.

infamous ['ınfəməs] *adj* infame.

infancy ['ınfənsı] *n (U)* primeira infância *f*; **to be in its ~** *fig* estar engatinhando.

infant ['ınfənt] *n* **-1.** [baby] bebê *m* **-2.** [young child] criança *f* pequena.

infantry ['ınfəntrı] *n (U)* infantaria *f*.

infant school *n UK na Grã-Bretanha, escola para crianças entre 5 e 7 anos.*

infatuated [ın'fætjʊeıtıd] *adj*: **~ (with sb/sthg)** obcecado(da) (por alguém/algo).

infatuation [ın,fætjʊ'eıʃn] *n*: **~ (with sb/sthg)** obsessão *f* (por alguém/algo).

infect [ın'fekt] *vt* **-1.** *MED* infectar; **to become ~ed** [wound] infeccionar; **to ~ sb with sthg** infectar alguém com algo **-2.** *fig* [spread to] contagiar.

infection [ın'fekʃn] *n* **-1.** [disease] infecção *f* **-2.** *(U)* [spreading of germs] contágio *m*.

infectious [ın'fekʃəs] *adj* **-1.** [disease] infeccioso(sa) **-2.** *fig* [feeling, laugh] contagioso(sa).

infer [ın'fɜ:'] *(pt & pp* -red, *cont* -ring) *vt* **-1.** [deduce]: **to ~ (that)** inferir que; **to ~ sthg (from sthg)** deduzir OR inferir algo (de algo) **-2.** *inf* [insinuate] insinuar.

inferior [ın'fıərıə'] <> *adj* [gen] inferior; **~ to sb/sthg** inferior a alguém/algo. <> *n* [in status] inferior *mf*.

inferiority [ın,fıərı'ɒrətı] *n (U)* inferioridade *f*.

inferiority complex *n* complexo *m* de inferioridade.

inferno [ın'fɜ:nəʊl] *(pl* -s*) n* inferno *m*, incêndio *m* incontrolável.

infertile [ın'fɜ:taıl] *adj* **-1.** [woman, animal] estéril **-2.** [soil] infértil.

infested [ın'festıd] *adj*: **~ with sthg** infestado(da) por algo.

infighting ['ın,faıtıŋ] *n (U)* disputa *f* interna.

infiltrate ['ınfıltreıt] *vt* infiltrar.

infinite ['ınfınət] *adj* infinito(ta).

infinitive [ın'fınıtıv] *n GRAMM* infinitivo *m*.

infinity [ın'fınətı] *n* **-1.** *(U)* [gen] infinito *m* **-2.** *MATH* [incalculable number] infinidade *f*.

infirm [ın'fɜ:m] <> *adj* [unhealthy] enfermo(ma). <> *npl*: **the ~** os enfermos.

infirmary [ın'fɜ:mərı] *(pl* -ies*) n* **-1.** [hospital] hospital *m* **-2.** [room] enfermaria *f*.

infirmity [ın'fɜ:mətı] *(pl* -ies*) n* enfermidade *f*.

inflamed [ın'fleımd] *adj MED* inflamado(da).

inflammable [ın'flæməbl] *adj* [burning easily] inflamável.

inflammation [,ınflə'meıʃn] *n MED* inflamação *f*.

inflatable [ın'fleıtəbl] *adj* inflável.

inflate [ın'fleıt] *vt* **-1.** [fill with air] inflar **-2.** *ECON* [increase] inflacionar.

inflation [ın'fleıʃn] *n (U) ECON* inflação *f*.

inflationary [ın'fleıʃnrı] *adj ECON* inflacionário(ria).

inflation rate *n ECON* taxa *f* de inflação.

inflict [ın'flıkt] *vt*: **to ~ sthg on sb** infligir algo a alguém.

influence ['ınflʊəns] <> *n* **-1.** *(U)* [power]: **~ (on sb/sthg)** influência *f* (sobre alguém/algo); **under the ~ of** [person, group] sob a influência de; [alcohol, drugs] sob o efeito de **-2.** [influential person, thing]: **~ (on sb/sthg)** influência para alguém/algo. <> *vt* influenciar.

influential [,ınflʊ'enʃl] *adj* influente.

influenza [,ınflʊ'enzə] *n (U) fml* influenza *f*.

influx ['ınflʌks] *n* afluxo *m*.

inform [ın'fɔ:m] *vt* informar; **to ~ sb of/about sthg** informar alguém de/sobre algo.

➨ inform on *vt fus* denunciar, delatar.

informal [ın'fɔ:ml] *adj* informal.

informant [ın'fɔ:mənt] *n* informante *mf*.

information [,ınfə'meıʃn] *n (U)* informações *fpl*; **to give sb ~** dar informações a alguém; **to get ~** obter informações; **that's a useful piece of ~** esta é uma informação útil; **to have some ~ on** OR **about sthg** ter alguma informação sobre algo; **'Information'** 'Informações'; **for your ~** para seu conhecimento.

information desk *n* (balcão *m* de) informações *fpl*.

information technology *n* tecnologia *f* da informação.

informative [ın'fɔ:mətıv] *adj* instrutivo(va).

informer [ın'fɔ:mə'] *n* [denouncer] informante *mf*, delator *m*, -ra *f*.

infrared [,ınfrə'red] *adj* infravermelho(lha).

infrastructure [ˈɪnfrəˌstrʌktʃəʳ] *n* infra-estrutura *f*.

infringe [ɪnˈfrɪndʒ] (*cont* **infringeing**) <> *vt* **-1.** [right] transgredir, violar **-2.** [law, agreement] infringir. <> *vi* **-2.** [on right]: **to ~ on sthg** transgredir OR violar algo **-2.** [on law, agreement]: **to ~ on sthg** infringir algo.

infringement [ɪnˈfrɪndʒmənt] *n* **-1.** [of right] transgressão *f*, violação *f* **-2.** [of law, agreement] infração *f*.

infuriating [ɪnˈfjʊərɪeɪtɪŋ] *adj* enfurecedor(ra).

ingenious [ɪnˈdʒiːnjəs] *adj* engenhoso(-sa).

ingenuity [ˌɪndʒɪˈnjuːətɪ] *n* (*U*) engenhosidade *f*.

ingenuous [ɪnˈdʒenjʊəs] *adj fml* ingênuo(nua).

ingot [ˈɪŋgət] *n* lingote *m*.

ingrained [ˌɪnˈgreɪnd] *adj* **-1.** [ground in] entranhado(da) **-2.** [deeply rooted] arraigado(da).

ingratiating [ɪnˈgreɪʃɪeɪtɪŋ] *adj* insinuante, lisonjeiro(ra).

ingredient [ɪnˈgriːdjənt] *n* ingrediente *m*.

inhabit [ɪnˈhæbɪt] *vt* habitar.

inhabitant [ɪnˈhæbɪtənt] *n* habitante *mf*.

inhale [ɪnˈheɪl] <> *vt* inalar. <> *vi* [breathe in - smoker] tragar; [- patient] inspirar.

inhaler [ɪnˈheɪləʳ] *n* MED inalador *m*.

inherent [ɪnˈhɪərənt, ɪnˈherənt] *adj* inerente; **~ in sthg** inerente a algo.

inherently [ɪnˈhɪərəntlɪ, ɪnˈherəntlɪ] *adv* intrinsecamente.

inherit [ɪnˈherɪt] <> *vt*: **to ~ sthg (from sb)** herdar algo (de alguém). <> *vi* herdar.

inheritance [ɪnˈherɪtəns] *n* herança *f*.

inhibit [ɪnˈhɪbɪt] *vt* **-1.** [restrict] impedir **-2.** PSYCH [repress] inibir.

inhibition [ˌɪnhɪˈbɪʃn] *n* inibição *f*.

inhospitable [ˌɪnhɒˈspɪtəbl] *adj* **-1.** [unwelcoming] inospitaleiro(ra) **-2.** [climate, area] inóspito(ta).

in-house <> *adj* **-1.** [journal, report, magazine] de circulação interna **-2.** [staff, group] interno(na), da casa; **~ staff** quadro *m* interno. <> *adv* internamente.

inhuman [ɪnˈhjuːmən] *adj* **-1.** [cruel] desumano(na) **-2.** [not human] inumano(-na).

initial [ɪˈnɪʃl] (*UK pt* & *pp* -**led**, *cont* -**ling**, *US pt* & *pp* -**ed**, *cont* -**ing**) <> *adj* inicial. <> *vt* rubricar.
➨ **initials** *npl* iniciais *fpl*.

initially [ɪˈnɪʃəlɪ] *adv* inicialmente.

initiate [ɪˈnɪʃɪeɪt] *vt* **-1.** [start] iniciar **-2.** [teach]: **to ~ sb (into sthg)** iniciar alguém (em algo).

initiative [ɪˈnɪʃətɪv] *n* **-1.** [gen] iniciativa *f* **-2.** [advantage]: **to have the ~** ter a vantagem.

inject [ɪnˈdʒekt] *vt* **-1.** MED: **to ~ sb with sthg, to ~ sthg into sb** injetar algo em alguém **-2.** *fig* [add]: **to ~ sthg into sthg** injetar algo em algo.

injection [ɪnˈdʒekʃn] *n* injeção *f*.

injure [ˈɪndʒəʳ] *vt* **-1.** [hurt physically] machucar **-2.** [reputation, chances] prejudicar **-3.** [offend] ferir.

injured [ˈɪndʒəd] <> *adj* [physically hurt] machucado(da), ferido(da). <> *npl*: **the ~** os feridos.

injury [ˈɪndʒərɪ] (*pl* -**ies**) *n* **-1.** (*U*) [physical harm] lesão *f* **-2.** [wound] ferimento *m*; **to do o.s. an ~** machucar-se **-3.** (*U*) [to one's reputation] dano *m* **-4.** [to one's pride, feelings] golpe *m*.

injury time *n* (*U*) tempo *m* de desconto (*num jogo*).

injustice [ɪnˈdʒʌstɪs] *n* injustiça *f*; **to do sb an ~** fazer uma injustiça a alguém.

ink [ɪŋk] *n* (*U*) tinta *f*.

ink cartridge *n* COMPUT cartucho *m* de tinta.

ink-jet printer *n* impressora *f* jato de tinta.

inkwell [ˈɪŋkwel] *n* tinteiro *m*.

inlaid [ˌɪnˈleɪd] *adj* incrustado(da); **~ with sthg** incrustado(da) de algo.

inland [*adj* ˈɪnlənd, *adv* ɪnˈlænd] <> *adj* interior. <> *adv* **-1.** [drive, head, walk] para o interior **-2.** [be positioned] no interior.

Inland Revenue *n* UK: **the ~** o fisco, ≃ a Receita Federal.

in-laws *npl inf* sogros *mpl*.

inlet [ˈɪnlet] *n* **-1.** [stretch of water] enseada *f* **-2.** [way in] entrada *f*.

inmate [ˈɪnmeɪt] *n* **-1.** [mental hospital] interno *m*, -na *f* **-2.** [prison] preso *m*, -sa *f*.

inn [ɪn] *n* pousada *f*.

innate [ˌɪˈneɪt] *adj* inato(ta).

inner [ˈɪnəʳ] *adj* **-1.** [most central] interno(na); **Inner London** o centro de Londres **-2.** [unexpressed, secret - feelings, doubts] íntimo(ma); [- peace, meaning] interior.

inner city *n*: **the ~** o centro urbano decadente.

inner tube *n* câmara *f* de ar.

innings [ˈɪnɪŋz] (*pl inv*) *n* UK [in cricket] turno *m*.

innocence [ˈɪnəsəns] *n* (*U*) **-1.** JUR [gen]

inocência f - 2. [naivety] ingenuidade f.

innocent [ˈɪnəsənt] ◇ adj -1. [gen] inocente; ~ of sthg inocente de algo -2. [harmless] ingênuo(nua). ◇ n [naive person] inocente mf.

innocuous [ɪˈnɒkjʊəs] adj [harmless] inócuo(cua).

innovation [ˌɪnəˈveɪʃn] n inovação f.

innovative [ˈɪnəvətɪv] adj inovador(ra).

innuendo [ˌɪnjuːˈendəʊ] (pl -es OR -s) n -1. [individual remark] insinuação f, indireta f - 2. (U) [style of speaking] insinuações fpl.

innumerable [ɪˈnjuːmərəbl] adj inumerável.

inoculate [ɪˈnɒkjʊleɪt] vt inocular; to ~ sb with sthg inocular algo em alguém.

inordinately [ɪˈnɔːdɪnətlɪ] adv fml [extremely] de forma desmesurada.

in-patient n paciente mf interno, -na.

input [ˈɪnpʊt] (pt & pp input OR -ted, cont -ting) ◇ n (U) -1. [contribution] contribuição f - 2. COMPUT, ELEC entrada f. ◇ vt COMPUT entrar.

inquest [ˈɪnkwest] n JUR inquérito m.

inquire [ɪnˈkwaɪəʳ] ◇ vt: to ~ when/whether/if/how... inquirir quando/se/como ... ◇ vi [ask for information] informar-se; to ~ about sthg pedir informações sobre algo.
  ◆ inquire after vt fus perguntar por.
  ◆ inquire into vt fus investigar.

inquiry [ɪnˈkwaɪərɪ] (pl -ies) n -1. [question] pergunta f; 'Inquiries' 'Informações' -2. [investigation] investigação f, inquérito m.

inquiry desk n (balcão m de) informações fpl.

inquisitive [ɪnˈkwɪzətɪv] adj curioso(sa).

inroads [ˈɪnrəʊdz] npl: to make ~ into sthg abrir caminho em algo.

insane [ɪnˈseɪn] adj -1. MED [mad] insano(na) -2. fig [very stupid] louco(ca).

insanity [ɪnˈsænətɪ] n (U) -1. MED [madness] insanidade f - 2. fig [great stupidity] loucura f.

insatiable [ɪnˈseɪʃəbl] adj insaciável.

inscription [ɪnˈskrɪpʃn] n -1. [gen] inscrição f - 2. [in book] dedicatória f.

inscrutable [ɪnˈskruːtəbl] adj inescrutável, impenetrável.

insect [ˈɪnsekt] n inseto m.

insecticide [ɪnˈsektɪsaɪd] n inseticida m.

insect repellent n repelente m para insetos.

insecure [ˌɪnsɪˈkjʊəʳ] adj -1. [not confident] inseguro(ra) -2. [not safe] pouco seguro(ra).

insensible [ɪnˈsensəbl] adj -1. [unconscious] inconsciente -2. [unaware]: to be

~ of sthg não ter consciência de algo -3. [unable to feel]: to be ~ to sthg ser insensível a algo.

insensitive [ɪnˈsensətɪv] adj -1. [unkind, thoughtless] insensível -2. [unresponsive]: ~ to sthg indiferente a algo -3. [unable to feel]: ~ to sthg insensível a algo.

inseparable [ɪnˈseprəbl] adj -1. [subjects, facts]: ~ (from sthg) inseparável (de algo) -2. [people] inseparável.

insert [vb ɪnˈsɜːt, n ˈɪnsɜːt] ◇ n encarte m. ◇ vt [put in]: to ~ sthg (in OR into sthg) inserir algo (em algo).

insertion [ɪnˈsɜːʃn] n (U) inserção f.

in-service training n UK treinamento m no serviço.

inshore [adj ˈɪnʃɔːʳ, adv ɪnˈʃɔːʳ] ◇ adj costeiro(ra). ◇ adv -1. [towards shore] em direção à costa -2. [close to shore] perto da costa.

inside [ɪnˈsaɪd] ◇ adj [interior, near centre] interno(na). ◇ adv -1. [in, within - place, object, building] para dentro; there was sthg ~ havia alguma coisa dentro; [- body, mind] por dentro -2. [prison] sl preso(sa). ◇ prep dentro de; get some food ~ you! coma alguma coisa!; ~ three weeks em menos de três semanas. ◇ n -1. [interior, inner part]: the ~ o lado de dentro; ~ out [clothes] do avesso; to know sthg ~ out fig conhecer algo de cabo a rabo; to turn sthg ~ out virar algo do avesso -2. AUT: the ~ [in UK] a faixa da esquerda; [in mainland Europe, US, Brazil etc.] a faixa da direita.
  ◆ insides npl inf [intestines] tripas fpl.
  ◆ inside of prep US [building, object] dentro de.

inside lane n AUT -1. [in UK] faixa f da esquerda -2. [in mainland Europe, US, Brazil etc.] faixa f da direita.

insight [ˈɪnsaɪt] n -1. (U) [wisdom]: ~ (into sthg) discernimento m (sobre algo) -2. [glimpse]: ~ (into sthg) insight m (sobre algo); the book gave me an ~ into the problem o livro me fez ter algumas idéias sobre o problema.

insignificant [ˌɪnsɪgˈnɪfɪkənt] adj insignificante.

insincere [ˌɪnsɪnˈsɪəʳ] adj insincero(ra).

insinuate [ɪnˈsɪnjʊeɪt] pej vt [imply]: to ~ (that) insinuar que.

insipid [ɪnˈsɪpɪd] adj pej -1. [dull, boring] insosso(sa) -2. [flavourless - drink] insípido(da); [- food] insosso(sa).

insist [ɪnˈsɪst] ◇ vt: to ~ (that) insistir que. ◇ vi: to ~ on sthg insistir em algo; to ~ on doing sthg insistir em fazer algo.

insistent [ɪn'sɪstənt] *adj* insistente; ~ on sthg insistente em algo.

insofar [ˌɪnsəʊ'fɑːʳ] ➡ **insofar as** *conj* na medida em que.

insole ['ɪnsəʊl] *n* [in shoe] palmilha *f*.

insolent ['ɪnsələnt] *adj* insolente.

insolvable *adj US* insolúvel.

insolvent [ɪn'sɒlvənt] *adj* insolvente.

insomnia [ɪn'sɒmnɪə] *n* (U) insônia *f*.

inspect [ɪn'spekt] *vt* - **1.** [letter, person] examinar - **2.** [factory] inspecionar, vistoriar - **3.** [troops] passar revista em.

inspection [ɪn'spekʃn] *n* - **1.** [examination] exame *m* - **2.** [official check] inspeção *f*, vistoria *f*.

inspector [ɪn'spektəʳ] *n* - **1.** [official] fiscal *mf* - **2.** [of police] inspetor *m*, -ra *f*.

inspiration [ˌɪnspə'reɪʃn] *n* - **1.** (U) [source of ideas] inspiração *f*; ~ **(for sthg)** inspiração (para algo) - **2.** [brilliant idea] idéia *f*.

inspire [ɪn'spaɪəʳ] *vt* [stimulate, encourage]: **to ~ sb (to do sthg)** inspirar alguém (a fazer algo); **to ~ sb with sthg, to ~ sthg in sb** inspirar algo a alguém.

install *UK*, **instal** *US* [ɪn'stɔːl] *vt* [machinery, equipment] instalar.

installation [ˌɪnstə'leɪʃn] *n* instalação *f*.

instalment *UK*, **installment** *US* [ɪn'stɔːlmənt] *n* - **1.** [payment] prestação *f*; **in ~s** em prestações - **2.** [episode] episódio *m*.

instance ['ɪnstəns] *n* [example, case] caso *m*, exemplo *m*; **for ~** por exemplo.

instant ['ɪnstənt] ⟷ *adj* instantâneo(nea). ⟷ *n* [moment] instante *m*; **the ~ (that)** ... no mesmo instante em que ...

instantly ['ɪnstəntlɪ] *adv* instantaneamente.

instead [ɪn'sted] *adv* em vez disso. ➡ **instead of** *prep* em vez de, em lugar de.

instep ['ɪnstep] *n* [of foot] peito *m* do pé.

instigate ['ɪnstɪgeɪt] *vt* [initiate] instigar.

instil *UK* (*pt* & *pp* -led, *cont* -ling), **instill** *US* (*pt* & *pp* -ed, *cont* -ing) [ɪn'stɪl] *vt*: **to ~ sthg in(to) sb** instilar algo em alguém.

instinct ['ɪnstɪŋkt] *n* instinto *m*; **first ~** primeiro impulso *m*.

instinctive [ɪn'stɪŋktɪv] *adj* instintivo(va).

institute ['ɪnstɪtjuːt] ⟷ *n* [establishment] instituto *m*. ⟷ *vt* instituir.

institution [ˌɪnstɪ'tjuːʃn] *n* instituição *f*.

institutionalize *vt* institucionalizar.

instruct [ɪn'strʌkt] *vt* - **1.** [tell, order]: **to ~ sb to do sthg** instruir alguém a fazer algo - **2.** [teach] instruir; **to ~ sb in sthg** instruir alguém em algo.

instruction [ɪn'strʌkʃn] *n* instrução *f*. ➡ **instructions** *npl* [for use] instruções *fpl*.

instructor [ɪn'strʌktəʳ] *n* - **1.** [in driving, skiing] instrutor *m* - **2.** [in swimming] professor *m*.

instrument ['ɪnstrʊmənt] *n* - **1.** instrumento *m* - **2.** *literary* [means] instrumento *m*.

instrumental [ˌɪnstrʊ'mentl] *adj* [important, helpful]: **to be ~ in sthg** desempenhar um papel fundamental em algo.

instrument panel *n* painel *m* de instrumentos.

insubordinate [ˌɪnsə'bɔːdɪnət] *adj fml* insubordinado(da).

insubstantial [ˌɪnsəb'stænʃl] *adj* - **1.** [fragile] frágil - **2.** [unsatisfying] pouco substancioso(sa).

insufficient [ˌɪnsə'fɪʃnt] *adj fml* insuficiente; ~ **for sthg/to do sthg** insuficiente para algo/para fazer algo.

insular ['ɪnsjʊləʳ] *adj* [narrow-minded] limitado(da).

insulate ['ɪnsjʊleɪt] *vt* isolar; **to ~ sb against OR from sthg** isolar alguém de algo.

insulating tape ['ɪnsjʊleɪtɪŋ-] *n* (U) *UK* fita *f* isolante.

insulation [ˌɪnsjʊ'leɪʃn] *n* (U) [material, substance] isolamento *m*.

insulin ['ɪnsjʊlɪn] *n* (U) insulina *f*.

insult [*vt* ɪn'sʌlt, *n* 'ɪnsʌlt] ⟷ *n* insulto *m*. ⟷ *vt* insultar, ofender.

insuperable [ɪn'suːprəbl] *adj fml* insuperável.

insurance [ɪn'ʃʊərəns] *n* - **1.** [against fire, accident, theft] seguro *m*; ~ **against sthg** seguro contra algo - **2.** *fig* [safeguard, protection] proteção *f*; ~ **against sthg** proteção contra algo.

insurance policy *n* apólice *f* de seguros.

insure [ɪn'ʃʊəʳ] ⟷ *vt* - **1.** [against fire, accident, theft]: **to ~ sb/sthg against sthg** segurar alguém/algo contra algo - **2.** *US* [make certain] assegurar. ⟷ *vi* [protect]: **to ~ against sthg** prevenir-se contra algo.

insurer [ɪn'ʃʊərəʳ] *n* segurador *m*, -ra *f*.

insurmountable [ˌɪnsə'maʊntəbl] *adj* intransponível.

intact [ɪn'tækt] *adj* intacto(ta).

intake ['ɪnteɪk] *n* - **1.** [amount consumed] ingestão *f* - **2.** [people recruited - SCH, UNIV] ingresso *m*; [- MIL] recrutamento *m* - **3.** [inlet] entrada *f*.

integral ['ɪntɪgrəl] *adj* [essential] essencial; **to be ~ to sthg** ser parte integrante de algo.

integrate ['ɪntɪgreɪt] <> vi integrar. <> vt integrar.

integrity [ɪn'tegrɪtɪ] n (U) **-1.** [honour] integridade f **-2.** fml [wholeness] integridade f.

intellect ['ɪntəlekt] n **-1.** [gen] inteligência f, intelecto m **-2.** [mind] inteligência f.

intellectual [ˌɪntə'lektjʊəl] <> adj intelectual. <> n [person] intelectual mf.

intelligence [ɪn'telɪdʒəns] n (U) **-1.** [ability to think and reason] inteligência f **-2.** [information service] serviço m de inteligência **-3.** [information] informações fpl secretas.

intelligent [ɪn'telɪdʒənt] adj [clever] inteligente.

intelligent card n cartão m inteligente.

intend [ɪn'tend] vt [mean] pretender, propor-se a; **to be ~ ed for/as sthg** ser destinado(da) para algo; **to be ~ ed for sb** ser destinado(da) a alguém; **it wasn't ~ ed to be a criticism** não pretendia ser uma crítica; **it was ~ ed to be a surprise** era para ser uma surpresa; **to ~ doing sthg/to do sthg** pretender fazer algo.

intended [ɪn'tendɪd] adj [planned] planejado(da); **the ~ victim** a vítima almejada.

intense [ɪn'tens] adj **-1.** [gen] intenso(sa) **-2.** [person - serious] muito sério(ria); [- emotional] forte.

intensely [ɪn'tenslɪ] adv **-1.** [very] enormemente **-2.** [very much] intensamente.

intensify [ɪn'tensɪfaɪ] (pt & pp -ied) <> vt intensificar. <> vi intensificar-se.

intensity [ɪn'tensɪtɪ] n **-1.** [gen] intensidade f **-2.** [of person - seriousness] seriedade f; [- of emotional nature] força f.

intensive [ɪn'tensɪv] adj [concentrated] intensivo(va).

intensive care n (U) tratamento m intensivo.

intent [ɪn'tent] <> adj **-1.** [absorbed] atento(ta) **-2.** [determined]: **to be ~ (up)on doing sthg** estar determinado(da) a fazer algo. <> n fml [intention] intenção f; **to all ~ s and purposes** para todos os efeitos.

intention [ɪn'tenʃən] n intenção f.

intentional [ɪn'tenʃənl] adj intencional.

intently [ɪn'tentlɪ] adv atentamente.

interact [ˌɪntər'ækt] vi **-1.** [people]: **to ~ (with sb)** interagir (com alguém) **-2.** [forces, ideas]: **to ~ (with sthg)** interagir (com algo).

interactive [ˌɪntər'æktɪv] n COMPUT interativo(va).

intercede [ˌɪntə'siːd] vi fml: **to ~ (with/**

for sb) interceder (junto a/em favor de alguém).

intercept [ˌɪntə'sept] vt [message, missile] interceptar.

interchange [n 'ɪntətʃeɪndʒ, vb ˌɪntə'tʃeɪndʒ] <> n **-1.** [exchange] intercâmbio m **-2.** [road junction] trevo m rodoviário. <> vt trocar, intercambiar; **to ~ sthg with sb/sthg** trocar algo com alguém/algo.

interchangeable [ˌɪntə'tʃeɪndʒəbl] adj: **~ (with sb/sthg)** intercambiável (com alguém/algo).

intercity [ˌɪntə'sɪtɪ] adj UK intermunicipal.

intercom ['ɪntəkɒm] n interfone m.

intercourse ['ɪntəkɔːs] n (U) [sexual] relação f sexual.

interest ['ɪntrəst] <> n **-1.** [gen] interesse m; **~ in sb/sthg** interesse em alguém/algo **-2.** [hobby] hobby m; **in the ~ s of peace** em nome da paz **-3.** (U) [financial charge] juro m **-4.** [share in company] participação f. <> vt [appeal to] interessar; **can I ~ you in a drink?** posso te convidar para um drinque?

interested ['ɪntrəstɪd] adj interessado(da); **to be ~ in sb/sthg** estar interessado(da) em alguém/algo; **to be ~ in doing sthg** estar interessado(da) em fazer algo.

interesting ['ɪntrəstɪŋ] adj interessante.

interest rate n taxa f de juros.

interface [n 'ɪntəfeɪs] n **-1.** COMPUT interface f **-2.** [junction, boundary] zona f de interação.

interfere [ˌɪntə'fɪəʳ] vi **-1.** [meddle] interferir, intrometer-se; **to ~ in sthg** interferir em algo, intrometer-se em algo **-2.** [cause disruption] interferir; **to ~ with sthg** interferir em algo.

interference [ˌɪntə'fɪərəns] n (U) **-1.** [meddling]: **~ (with OR in sthg)** intrometimento m (em algo) **-2.** RADIO & TV interferência f.

interim ['ɪntərɪm] <> adj provisório(ria). <> n: **in the ~** neste ínterim.

interior [ɪn'tɪərɪəʳ] <> adj **-1.** [inner] interno(na), interior **-2.** POL do interior. <> n [inside] interior m.

interlock [ˌɪntə'lɒk] vi **-1.** TECH encaixar; **to ~ with sthg** encaixar com algo **-2.** [entwine] entrelaçar.

interloper ['ɪntələʊpəʳ] n intruso m, -sa f.

interlude ['ɪntəluːd] n [gen] intervalo m.

intermediary [ˌɪntə'miːdjərɪ] (pl -ies) n intermediário m, -ria f, mediador m, -ra f.

intermediate [ˌɪntəˈmiːdjət] *adj* intermediário *m*, -ria *f*.

interminable [ɪnˈtɜːmɪnəbl] *adj* interminável.

intermission [ˌɪntəˈmɪʃn] *n* intervalo *m*.

intermittent [ˌɪntəˈmɪtənt] *adj* intermitente.

intern [*vb* ɪnˈtɜːn, *n* ˈɪntɜːn] ◇ *n US* [trai-
nee - teacher] estagiário *m*, -ria *f*; [- doc-
tor] interno *m*, -na *f*. ◇ *vt* internar.

internal [ɪnˈtɜːnl] *adj* interno(na); ~ af-
fairs relações *fpl* interiores.

internally [ɪnˈtɜːnəlɪ] *adv* internamente.

Internal Revenue *n US*: **the** ~ a receita
pública.

international [ˌɪntəˈnæʃənl] ◇ *adj* internacional. ◇ *n UK SPORT* **-1.** [match]
partida *f* internacional **-2.** [player] atleta *mf* da seleção.

Internet [ˈɪntənet] *n*: **the** ~ a Internet.

Internet access *n* acesso *m* à Internet.

Internet café *n* cibercafé *m*.

Internet connection *n* conexão *f* com
a Internet.

Internet Service Provider *n* provedor *m* de serviços de Internet.

Internet start-up company *n* empresa *f* eletrônica que surgiu com a
Internet.

Internet television, Internet TV *n*
televisão *f* via Internet.

interpret [ɪnˈtɜːprɪt] ◇ *vt* [understand]
interpretar; **to** ~ **sthg as** interpretar
algo como. ◇ *vi* [translate] interpretar.

interpreter [ɪnˈtɜːprɪtəʳ] *n* [person] intérprete *mf*.

interpreting [ɪnˈtɜːprɪtɪŋ] *n* [occupation]
interpretação *f*.

interracial [ˌɪntəˈreɪʃl] *adj* inter-racial.

interrelate [ˌɪntərɪˈleɪt] ◇ *vt* correla-
cionar. ◇ *vi*: **to** ~ **(with sthg)** corre-
lacionar-se (com algo).

interrogate [ɪnˈterəgeɪt] *vt* [question]
interrogar.

interrogation [ɪnˌterəˈgeɪʃn] *n* **-1.** *(U)*
[questioning] interrogação *f* **-2.** [inter-
view] interrogatório *m*.

interrogation mark *n US* ponto *m* de
interrogação.

interrogative [ˌɪntəˈrɒgətɪv] *GRAM* ◇
adj interrogativo(va). ◇ *n* **-1.** [form]:
the ~ a forma interrogativa **-2.** [word]
pronome *m* interrogativo.

interrupt [ˌɪntəˈrʌpt] ◇ *vt* interromper. ◇ *vi* interromper, incomodar.

interruption [ˌɪntəˈrʌpʃn] *n* interrupção *f*.

intersect [ˌɪntəˈsekt] ◇ *vi* cruzar-se.
◇ *vt* cruzar.

intersection [ˌɪntəˈsekʃn] *n* [junction] interseção *f*.

intersperse [ˌɪntəˈspɜːs] *vt*: **to be** ~**ed
with sthg** ser entremeado(da) por
algo.

interstate (highway) *n US* rodovia *f*
interestadual.

interval [ˈɪntəvl] *n* **-1.** [period of time]: ~
(between) intervalo *m* (entre); **at** ~**s**
em intervalos; **at monthly/yearly** ~**s**
em intervalos de um mês/um ano **-2.**
UK [at play, concert] intervalo *m*.

intervene [ˌɪntəˈviːn] *vi* **-1.** [gen] intervir;
to ~ **in sthg** intervir em algo **-2.** [inter-
rupt] interferir.

intervention [ˌɪntəˈvenʃn] *n* intervenção *f*.

interview [ˈɪntəvjuː] ◇ *n* entrevista *f*.
◇ *vt* entrevistar.

interviewer [ˈɪntəvjuːəʳ] *n* entrevista-
dor *m*, -ra *f*.

intestine [ɪnˈtestɪn] *n* intestino *m*.

intimacy [ˈɪntɪməsɪ] *(pl* -ies) *n (U)* [close-
ness]: ~ **(between/with)** intimidade *f*
(entre/com).

  ➡ **intimacies** *npl* [personal thoughts] in-
timidades *fpl*.

intimate [*adj & n* ˈɪntɪmət, *vb* ˈɪntɪmeɪt]
◇ *adj* **-1.** íntimo(ma) **-2.** [personal]
pessoal **-3.** [thorough] profundo(da).
◇ *vt fml* [hint, imply] insinuar; **to** ~ **that**
insinuar que, dar a entender que.

intimately [ˈɪntɪmətlɪ] *adv* intimamente.

intimidate [ɪnˈtɪmɪdeɪt] *vt* intimidar.

into [ˈɪntʊ] *prep* **-1.** [inside - referring to
object] em; [- referring to place, vehicle]
em direção a; **to get** ~ **a car** entrar
num carro **-2.** [against] contra; **to bump**
~ **sb/sthg** tropeçar em alguém/algo;
to crash ~ **sb/sthg** chocar-se com al-
guém/algo **-3.** [indicating transformation,
change] em; **to translate** ~ **Spanish** traduzir para o espanhol **-4.** [concerning,
about] sobre **-5.** *MATH* [indicating division]
por; **6** ~ **2 is 3** 6 dividido por 2 é 3 **-6.**
[indicating elapsed time]: ~ **the night** noite
adentro; **I was a week** ~ **my holiday
when ...** eu estava há uma semana de
férias quando ... **-7.** *inf* [interested in]: **to
be** ~ **sthg** gostar de algo.

intolerable [ɪnˈtɒlrəbl] *adj fml* intolerável.

intolerance [ɪnˈtɒlərəns] *n (U)* [lack of re-
spect] intolerância *f*.

intolerant [ɪnˈtɒlərənt] *adj* intolerante.

intoxicated [ɪnˈtɒksɪkeɪtd] *adj* **-1.**
[drunk]: **to be** ~ estar embriagado(da)
-2. *fig* [excited]: **to be** ~ **by** OR **with sthg**
estar inebriado(da) com algo.

intoxication [ɪnˌtɒksɪˈkeɪʃn] *n* embriaguez *f*.

intractable [ɪnˈtræktəbl] *adj fml* -**1.** [stubborn] intratável -**2.** [insoluble] insolúvel.

intramural *adj* intramuros.

Intranet *n* COMPUT Intranet *f*.

intransitive [ɪnˈtrænzətɪv] *adj* intransitivo(va).

intravenous [ˌɪntrəˈviːnəs] *adj* intravenoso(sa).

in-tray *n* bandeja *f* de entrada *(para documentos em escritório)*.

intricate [ˈɪntrɪkət] *adj* intricado(da).

intrigue [ɪnˈtriːg] <> *n* intriga *f*. <> *vt* intrigar.

intriguing [ɪnˈtriːgɪŋ] *adj* intrigante.

intrinsic [ɪnˈtrɪnsɪk] *adj* intrínseco(ca).

introduce [ˌɪntrəˈdjuːs] *vt* -**1.** [present, make aware of] apresentar; to ~ sb to sb/sthg apresentar alguém a alguém/algo -**2.** [bring in]: to ~ sthg (to OR into) introduzir algo (em).

introduction [ˌɪntrəˈdʌkʃn] *n* -**1.** [start, initiation] introdução *f*; ~ to sthg introdução a algo -**2.** [presentation]: ~ (to sb) apresentação *f* (a alguém).

introductory [ˌɪntrəˈdʌktrɪ] *adj* introdutório(ria).

introvert [ˈɪntrəvɜːt] *n* introvertido *m*, -da *f*.

introverted [ˈɪntrəvɜːtɪd] *adj* introvertido(da).

intrude [ɪnˈtruːd] *vi* intrometer-se; to ~ (up)on sb/sthg intrometer-se em alguém/algo.

intruder [ɪnˈtruːdəʳ] *n* intruso *m*, -sa *f*.

intrusive [ɪnˈtruːsɪv] *adj* -**1.** [person] intrometido(da) -**2.** [presence, interest] inoportuno(na).

intuition [ˌɪntjuːˈɪʃn] *n* intuição *f*.

inundate [ˈɪnʌndeɪt] *vt* inundar; to be ~d with sthg estar cheio (cheia) de algo.

invade [ɪnˈveɪd] *vt* invadir.

invalid [*adj* ɪnˈvælɪd *n* & *vb* ˈɪnvəlɪd] <> *adj* [not acceptable] inválido(da). <> *n* [ill person] inválido *m*, -da *f*.

invaluable [ɪnˈvæljʊəbl] *adj*: ~ (to sb/sthg) inestimável (para alguém/algo).

invariably [ɪnˈveərɪəblɪ] *adv* [always] invariavelmente.

invasion [ɪnˈveɪʒn] *n* invasão *f*.

invent [ɪnˈvent] *vt* inventar.

invention [ɪnˈvenʃn] *n* invenção *f*.

inventive [ɪnˈventɪv] *adj* inventivo(va).

inventor [ɪnˈventəʳ] *n* inventor *m*, -ra *f*.

inventory [ˈɪnventrɪ] (*pl* -ies) *n* -**1.** [list] inventário *m* -**2.** US [goods] estoque *m*.

invert [ɪnˈvɜːt] *vt fml* inverter.

inverted commas [ɪnˈvɜːtɪd-] *npl* UK aspas *fpl*; in ~ entre aspas.

invest [ɪnˈvest] <> *vt* [gen]: to ~ sthg in sthg/in doing sthg investir algo em algo/para fazer algo. <> *vi* -**1.** [financially] investir; to ~ in sthg investir em algo -**2.** *fig* [in sthg useful]: to ~ in sthg investir em algo.

investigate [ɪnˈvestɪgeɪt] *vt* & *vi* investigar.

investigation [ɪnˌvestɪˈgeɪʃn] *n*: ~ (into sthg) investigação *f* (sobre algo).

investment [ɪnˈvestmənt] *n* investimento *m*.

investor [ɪnˈvestəʳ] *n* investidor *m*, -ra *f*.

inveterate [ɪnˈvetərət] *adj* inveterado(da).

invidious [ɪnˈvɪdɪəs] *adj* -**1.** [unfair] injusto(ta) -**2.** [unpleasant] desagradável.

invigilate [ɪnˈvɪdʒɪleɪt] UK <> *vt* fiscalizar *(um exame)*. <> *vi* fiscalizar um exame.

invigorating [ɪnˈvɪgəreɪtɪŋ] *adj* -**1.** [gen] revigorante -**2.** [experience] estimulante.

invincible [ɪnˈvɪnsɪbl] *adj* [unbeatable] invencível.

invisible [ɪnˈvɪzɪbl] *adj* invisível.

invitation [ˌɪnvɪˈteɪʃn] *n* convite *m*; an ~ to sthg/to do sthg um convite para algo/para fazer algo.

invite [ɪnˈvaɪt] *vt* -**1.** [request to attend] convidar; to ~ sb to sthg convidar alguém para algo -**2.** [ask politely]: to ~ sb to do sthg convidar alguém para fazer algo -**3.** [encourage] estimular.

inviting [ɪnˈvaɪtɪŋ] *adj* convidativo(va), tentador(ra).

invoice [ˈɪnvɔɪs] <> *n* fatura *f*. <> *vt* -**1.** [send an invoice to] enviar uma fatura para -**2.** [prepare an invoice for] faturar.

invoke [ɪnˈvəʊk] *vt* -**1.** *fml* [quote as justification] invocar -**2.** [cause] evocar, suscitar.

involuntary [ɪnˈvɒləntrɪ] *adj* [unintentional] involuntário(ria).

involve [ɪnˈvɒlv] *vt* -**1.** [entail, require] envolver; to ~ doing sthg envolver fazer algo -**2.** [concern, affect] atingir, afetar; to be ~ed in sthg estar envolvido(da) em algo -**3.** [make part of sthg]: to ~ sb in sthg envolver alguém em algo.

involved [ɪnˈvɒlvd] *adj* -**1.** [complex] complicado(da) -**2.** [participating]: to be ~ in sthg estar metido(da) em algo -**3.** [in a relationship]: to be/get ~ with sb envolver-se com alguém -**4.** [entailed]: ~ (in sthg) envolvido(da) (em algo).

involvement [ɪnˈvɒlvmənt] *n* (U) [gen] envolvimento *m*; ~ in sthg envolvimento em algo.

inward ['ɪnwəd] <> adj -1. [feelings, satisfaction] interno(na), interior -2. [flow, movement] para dentro.

iodine [UK 'aɪədi:n, US 'aɪədaɪn] n (U) iodo m.

iota [aɪ'əʊtə] n pouquinho m; not an ~ nem um pouquinho.

IOU (abbr of I owe you) n documento assinado no qual se reconhece uma dívida.

IQ (abbr of intelligence quotient) n QI m.

IRA (abbr of Irish Republican Army) n IRA m.

Iran [ɪ'rɑːn] n Irã.

Iranian [ɪ'reɪnjən] <> adj iraniano(na). <> n [person] iraniano m, -na f.

Iraq [ɪ'rɑːk] n Iraque.

Iraqi [ɪ'rɑːkɪ] <> adj iraquiano(na). <> n [person] iraquiano m, -na f.

irate [aɪ'reɪt] adj irado(da).

Ireland ['aɪələnd] n Irlanda.

iris ['aɪərɪs] (pl -es) n MED, BOT íris f inv.

Irish ['aɪrɪʃ] <> adj irlandês(esa). <> n [language] gaélico-irlandês m. <> npl: the ~ os irlandeses.

Irishman ['aɪrɪʃmən] (pl -men [-mən]) n irlandês m.

Irish Sea n: the ~ o Mar da Irlanda.

Irishwoman ['aɪrɪʃˌwʊmən] (pl -women [-ˌwɪmɪn]) n irlandesa f.

irksome ['ɜːksəm] adj fml aborrecido(da).

iron ['aɪən] <> adj -1. [made of iron] de ferro -2. fig [very strict] duro(ra). <> n -1. (U) [metal] ferro m -2. [for clothes] ferro m (de passar roupa) -3. [golf club] ferro m. <> vt passar (a ferro).
   iron out vt sep fig [overcome] resolver.

ironic(al) [aɪ'rɒnɪk(l)] adj irônico(ca); how ~! que ironia!

ironing ['aɪənɪŋ] n (U) [clothes to be ironed] roupa f para passar.

ironing board n tábua f de passar roupa.

ironmonger ['aɪənˌmʌŋgə'] n UK ferrageiro m, -ra f; ~'s (shop) ferragem f.

irony ['aɪərənɪ] (pl -ies) n ironia f; the ~ of it all is that ... o curioso disso tudo é que ...

irrational [ɪ'ræʃənl] adj irracional.

irreconcilable [ɪˌrekən'saɪləbl] adj [completely different] irreconciliável.

irregular [ɪ'regjʊlə'] adj irregular.

irrelevant [ɪ'reləvənt] adj irrelevante.

irreparable [ɪ'repərəbl] adj irreparável.

irreplaceable [ˌɪrɪ'pleɪsəbl] adj insubstituível.

irrepressible [ˌɪrɪ'presəbl] adj irreprimível.

irresistible [ˌɪrɪ'zɪstəbl] adj irresistível.

irrespective <> irrespective of prep independente de.

irresponsible [ˌɪrɪ'spɒnsəbl] adj irresponsável.

irrigate ['ɪrɪgeɪt] vt [land] irrigar.

irrigation [ˌɪrɪ'geɪʃn] <> n (U) [of land] irrigação f. <> comp de irrigação.

irritable ['ɪrɪtəbl] adj [bad-tempered] irritável.

irritate ['ɪrɪteɪt] vt irritar.

irritated adj irritado(da).

irritating ['ɪrɪteɪtɪŋ] adj irritante.

irritation [ɪrɪ'teɪʃn] n -1. [gen] irritação f -2. [cause of anger] motivo m de irritação.

IRS (abbr of Internal Revenue Service) n departamento norte-americano de arrecadação de impostos, ≃ Secretaria f da Fazenda.

is [ɪz] vb ▷ be.

ISDN (abbr of Integrated Services Delivery Network) n COMPUT RDSI f, ISDN f.

Islam ['ɪzlɑːm] n (U) [religion] Islã m.

island ['aɪlənd] n -1. [in water] ilha f -2. [in traffic] passagem m para pedestres.

islander ['aɪləndə'] n ilhéu m, ilhoa f.

isle [aɪl] n ilha f, ilhota f.

Isle of Man n: the ~ a Ilha de Man.

Isle of Wight [-waɪt] n: the ~ a Ilha de Wight.

isn't ['ɪznt] = is not.

isobar ['aɪsəbɑː'] n METEOR isóbara f.

isolate ['aɪsəleɪt] vt: to ~ sthg/sb (from sthg) isolar algo/alguém (de algo).

isolated ['aɪsəleɪtɪd] adj isolado(da).

Israel ['ɪzreɪəl] n Israel.

Israeli [ɪz'reɪlɪ] <> adj israelense. <> n israelense mf.

issue ['ɪʃuː] <> n -1. [important subject] assunto m, questão f; at ~ em questão; to make an ~ of sthg dar importância demasiada a algo -2. [edition] número m, edição f -3. [bringing out] emissão f. <> vt -1. [statement, decree, warning] expedir -2. [stamps, bank notes, shares] emitir, pôr em circulação -3. [passport, documents, uniforms] expedir.

isthmus ['ɪsməs] n istmo m.

it [ɪt] pron -1. [referring to specific thing, subject after prep] ele m, ela f -2. [direct object] o m, a f -3. [indirect object] lhe; a free book came with ~ veio acompanhado de um livro grátis; give ~ to me me dê isso; he gave ~ a kick ele deu um chute nele; ~'s big é grande; ~'s here está aqui; she hit ~ ela deu uma pancada nele; she lost ~ ela o perdeu. -4. [referring to situation, fact]: ~'s a difficult question é uma questão

difícil; **I can't remember** ~ não me
lembro; **tell me about** ~ conte-me. **- 5.**
[used impersonally]: ~**'s hot** está calor;
~**'s six o'clock** são seis horas; ~**'s Sun-**
day é domingo. **- 6.** [referring to person]:
~**'s me** sou eu; **who is** ~**?** quem é?

IT (*abbr of* **information technology**) *n* TI
f.

Italian [ɪ'tæljən] ⟨⟩ *adj* italiano(na).
⟨⟩ *n* **-1.** [person] italiano *m*, -na *f* **- 2.**
[language] italiano *m*.

italic [ɪ'tælɪk] *adj* itálico *m*.
⟶ **italics** *npl*: **in** ~ em itálico.

Italy ['ɪtəlɪ] *n* Itália.

itch [ɪtʃ] ⟨⟩ *n* coceira f. ⟨⟩ *vi* **-1.** [be
itchy] coçar **- 2.** *fig* [be impatient]: **to be**
~**ing to do sthg** estar se coçando para
fazer algo.

itchy ['ɪtʃɪ] (*compar* **-ier**, *superl* **-iest**) *adj*
que coça.

it'd ['ɪtəd] = **it would**, **it had**.

item ['aɪtəm] *n* **-1.** [single thing] item *m*
- 2. [article in newspaper] artigo *m*.

itemize, -ise ['aɪtəmaɪz] *vt* detalhar,
especificar.

itinerary [aɪ'tɪnərərɪ] (*pl* **-ies**) *n* itinerário *m*.

it'll [ɪtl] = **it will**.

its [ɪts] *poss adj* o seu (a sua), dele
(dela).

it's [ɪts] = **it is**, **it has**.

itself [ɪt'self] *pron* **-1.** *(reflexive)* se **- 2.**
(after prep) si mesmo *m*, -ma *f* **- 3.**
(stressed): **the house** ~ **is fine** a casa
em si é boa.

ITV (*abbr of* **Independent Television**) *n*
canal privado de televisão na Grã-
Bretanha.

I've [aɪv] = **I have**.

ivory ['aɪvərɪ] *n (U)* marfim *m*.

ivy ['aɪvɪ] *n (U)* hera *f*.

Ivy League *n US grupo formado pelas*
oito universidades mais prestigiadas
do leste norte-americano.

J

j (*pl* **j's** OR **js**) **J** (*pl* **J's** OR **Js**) [dʒeɪ] *n* [letter] j,
J *m*.

jab [dʒæb] (*pt* & *pp* **-bed**, *cont* **-bing**) ⟨⟩
n **-1.** [push] golpe *m* **- 2.** *UK inf* [injection]
injeção *f*. ⟨⟩ *vt*: **to** ~ **sthg at sb/sthg**

espetar algo em alguém/algo; **to** ~
sthg into sb/sthg cravar algo em al-
guém/algo.

jabber ['dʒæbə'] ⟨⟩ *vt* algaraviar. ⟨⟩
vi tagarelar.

jack [dʒæk] *n* **-1.** [device] macaco *m* **- 2.**
[playing card] valete *m*.
⟶ **jack up** *vt sep* **-1.** [lift with a jack]
macaquear **- 2.** [force up] aumentar.

jackal ['dʒækəl] *n* chacal *m*.

jackdaw ['dʒækdɔ:] *n* gralha *f*.

jacket ['dʒækɪt] *n* **-1.** [garment] casaco *m*,
jaqueta *f* **- 2.** [potato skin] casca *f* **- 3.**
[book cover] sobrecapa *f* **- 4.** *US* [of record]
capa *f* **- 5.** [of boiler] camisa *f*.

jacket potato *n* batata *f* assada com
pele.

jackhammer ['dʒæk,hæmə'] *n US* brita-
deira *f*.

jack knife *n* [tool] canivete *m* grande.
⟶ **jack-knife** *vi* [truck, lorry] derrapar a
parte dianteira.

jack plug *n* pino *m*.

jackpot ['dʒækpɒt] *n* bolada *f*.

jaded ['dʒeɪdɪd] *adj* estafado(da).

jagged ['dʒægɪd] *adj* dentado(da).

jail [dʒeɪl] ⟨⟩ *n* prisão *f*, cadeia *f*. ⟨⟩
vt prender.

jailer ['dʒeɪlə'] *n* carcereiro *m*, -ra *f*.

jam [dʒæm] (*pt* & *pp* **-med**, *cont* **-ming**)
⟨⟩ *n* **-1.** *(U)* [preserve] geléia *f* **- 2.** [of
traffic] engarrafamento *m* **- 3.** *inf* [diffi-
cult situation]: **to get into/be in a** ~
meter-se/estar em apuros. ⟨⟩ *vt* **-1.**
[place roughly]: **to** ~ **sthg onto sthg**
enfiar algo em algo **- 2.** [fix, cause to stick
- window]: **to** ~ **the window shut** trancar a janela; [- mechanism] emperrar
- 3. [fill, pack tightly] apinhar, abarrotar;
to ~ **sthg into sthg** socar algo em algo
- 4. *TELEC* bloquear **- 5.** *RADIO* interferir.
⟨⟩ *vi* [stick] emperrar.
⟶ **jam on** *vt* [brakes] pisar.

Jamaica [dʒə'meɪkə] *n* Jamaica; **in** ~ na
Jamaica.

jam-packed [-'pækt] *adj inf* apinhado(-
da).

jangle ['dʒæŋgl] ⟨⟩ *vt* fazer soar de
forma estridente. ⟨⟩ *vi* retinir.

janitor ['dʒænɪtə'] *n US & Scot* [caretaker]
zelador *m*, -ra *f*.

January ['dʒænjʊərɪ] *n* janeiro; *see also*
September.

Japan [dʒə'pæn] *n* Japão.

Japanese [,dʒæpə'ni:z] (*pl inv*) ⟨⟩ *adj*
japonês(esa). ⟨⟩ *n* **-1.** [person] japonês
m, -esa *f* **- 2.** [language] japonês *m*. ⟨⟩
npl [people]: **the** ~ os japoneses.

jar [dʒɑ:'] (*pt* & *pp* **-red**, *cont* **-ring**) ⟨⟩ *n*
pote *m*. ⟨⟩ *vt* [shake] sacudir. ⟨⟩ *vi* **-1.**

[noise, voice]: **to ~ (on sb)** dar nos nervos (de alguém) **- 2.** [colours] destoar.

jargon ['dʒɑːgən] n (U) jargão m.

jaundice ['dʒɔːndɪs] n (U) icterícia f.

jaundiced ['dʒɔːndɪst] adj fig [attitude, view] pessimista.

jaunt [dʒɔːnt] n excursão f.

jaunty ['dʒɔːntɪ] (compar -ier, superl -iest) adj **- 1.** [hat, wave] vistoso(sa) **- 2.** [person] animado(da).

javelin ['dʒævlɪn] n dardo m.

jaw [dʒɔː] n **- 1.** [of person] maxilar m **- 2.** [of animal] mandíbula f.

jawbone ['dʒɔːbəʊn] n osso m maxilar.

jay [dʒeɪ] n gaio m.

jaywalker ['dʒeɪwɔːkəʳ] n pedestre mf imprudente.

jazz [dʒæz] n MUS jazz m.

➤ **jazz up** vt sep inf alegrar, animar.

jazzy ['dʒæzɪ] (compar -ier, superl -iest) adj [bright] chamativo(va).

jealous ['dʒeləs] adj [envious]: **to be ~ (of sb/sthg)** ter inveja (de alguém/ algo).

jealousy ['dʒeləsɪ] n (U) **- 1.** [envy] inveja f **- 2.** [resentment] ciúmes mpl.

jeans [dʒiːnz] npl jeans m inv.

Jeep® n jipe m.

jeer [dʒɪəʳ] ⟨⟩ vt **- 1.** [mock] zombar de **- 2.** [boo] vaiar. ⟨⟩ vi **- 1.** [boo] vaiar; **to ~ at sb** vaiar alguém **- 2.** [mock] zombar; **to ~ at sb** zombar de alguém.

Jehovah's Witness [dʒɪ'həʊvəz-] n Testemunha f de Jeová.

Jello® n (U) US ≃ gelatina f.

jelly ['dʒelɪ] (pl -ies) n **- 1.** [dessert] gelatina f **- 2.** [jam] geléia f.

jellyfish ['dʒelɪfɪʃ] (pl inv OR -es) n água-viva f.

jeopardize, -ise ['dʒepədaɪz] vt pôr em perigo, arriscar.

jerk [dʒɜːk] ⟨⟩ n **- 1.** [movement] guinada f, movimento m brusco **- 2.** inf pej [fool] estúpido m, -da f. ⟨⟩ vi dar solavancos.

jersey ['dʒɜːzɪ] (pl jerseys) n **- 1.** [sweater] suéter m **- 2.** (U) [cloth] jérsei m.

Jersey ['dʒɜːzɪ] n Jersey.

jest [dʒest] n brincadeira f; **in ~** de brincadeira.

Jesus (Christ) ['dʒiːzəs-] ⟨⟩ n Jesus Cristo. ⟨⟩ interj inf Jesus Cristo!

jet [dʒet] (pt & pp -ted, cont -ting) n **- 1.** [gen] jato m **- 2.** [nozzle, outlet] cano m de descarga.

jet-black adj da cor de azeviche.

jet engine n motor m a jato.

jetfoil ['dʒetfɔɪl] n hidroavião m.

jet lag n (U) jet lag m.

jetsam ['dʒetsəm] n ▷ **flotsam**.

jettison ['dʒetɪsən] vt **- 1.** [cargo, bombs] alijar **- 2.** fig [discard] descartar.

jetty ['dʒetɪ] (pl -ies) n quebra-mar m.

Jew [dʒuː] n judeu m.

jewel ['dʒuːəl] n **- 1.** [gemstone] pedra f preciosa **- 2.** [piece of jewellery] jóia f **- 3.** [in watch] rubi m.

jeweller UK, **jeweler** US ['dʒuːələʳ] n joalheiro m, -ra f; **~'s (shop)** joalheria f.

jewellery UK, **jewelry** US ['dʒuːəlrɪ] n (U) jóias fpl.

Jewish ['dʒuːɪʃ] adj judeu(dia).

jib [dʒɪb] (pt & pp -bed, cont -bing) n **- 1.** [NAUT - beam] vau m; [- sail] bujarrona f **- 2.** [of crane] braço m de guindaste.

jibe [dʒaɪb] n zombaria f.

jiffy ['dʒɪfɪ] n inf: **in a ~** num instante.

Jiffy bag® n envelope m acolchoado.

jig [dʒɪg] n [dance] jiga f.

jigsaw (puzzle) ['dʒɪgsɔː-] n quebra-cabeça m.

jilt [dʒɪlt] vt deixar plantado(da).

jingle ['dʒɪŋgl] ⟨⟩ n **- 1.** [sound] tilintar m **- 2.** [song] jingle m. ⟨⟩ vi tilintar.

jinx [dʒɪŋks] n pé-frio m.

jitters ['dʒɪtəz] npl inf: **to have the ~** ficar com os nervos à flor da pele.

job [dʒɒb] n **- 1.** [paid employment] emprego m **- 2.** [task, piece of work] trabalho m **- 3.** [difficult time]: **to have a ~ doing sthg** ter trabalho para fazer algo **- 4.** inf [crime] trabalho m **- 5.** phr: **that's just the ~** UK inf isso vem bem a calhar.

job centre n UK agência f de empregos.

jobless ['dʒɒblɪs] adj desempregado(da).

Job Seekers Allowance n UK seguro-desemprego concedido a pessoas que comprovadamente estão buscando um novo trabalho.

jobsharing ['dʒɒbʃeərɪŋ] n (U) prática de dividir um trabalho de tempo integral entre duas pessoas de forma que cada uma cumpra apenas meio turno, especialmente para permitir que mulheres com filhos possam trabalhar.

jockey ['dʒɒkɪ] (pl -s) ⟨⟩ n jóquei m. ⟨⟩ vi: **to ~ for position** competir por uma melhor posição.

jocular ['dʒɒkjʊləʳ] adj **- 1.** [person] divertido(da) **- 2.** [remark] engraçado(da).

jodhpurs ['dʒɒdpəz] npl culote m.

jog [dʒɒg] (pt & pp -ged, cont -ging) ⟨⟩ n [run] corrida f, jogging m. ⟨⟩ vt [nudge] cutucar; **to ~ the table** sacudir a mesa; **to ~ sb's memory** refrescar a memória de alguém. ⟨⟩ vi [run] fazer cooper.

jogging ['dʒɒgɪŋ] n [running] cooper m.

john [dʒɒn] n US inf [toilet] banheiro m.

join [dʒɔɪn] ⬦ n junção f. ⬦ vt -1. [connect] juntar -2. [get together with] juntar-se a; **do ~ us for lunch** venha almoçar com a gente -3. [become a member of - political party] filiar-se a; [- club] associar-se a; [- army] alistar-se em -4. [take part in] unir-se a; **to ~ a queue** UK, **to ~ a line** US entrar numa fila; **to ~ forces** juntar forças; **~ the club!** juntem-se ao clube! ⬦ vi -1. [connect - rivers] unir-se; [- pieces] encaixar-se -2. [become a member - of library] inscrever-se; [- of club] associar-se.
➡ **join in** vt fus & vi participar.
➡ **join up** vi MIL alistar-se.

joiner ['dʒɔɪnəʳ] n marceneiro m, -ra f.

joinery ['dʒɔɪnərɪ] n (U) marcenaria f.

joint [dʒɔɪnt] ⬦ adj conjunto(ta). ⬦ n -1. ANAT articulação f -2. [where things are joined] encaixe m -3. UK [of meat] corte m -4. inf pej [place] espelunca f -5. drugs sl [cannabis cigarette] baseado m.

joint account n conta f conjunta.

jointly ['dʒɔɪntlɪ] adv conjuntamente.

joist [dʒɔɪst] n viga f de madeira.

joke [dʒəʊk] ⬦ n [funny story or action] piada f, anedota f; **to play a ~ on sb** pregar uma peça em alguém; **it's no ~** [not easy] não é fácil. ⬦ vi brincar; **to ~ about sthg** brincar em relação a algo.

joker ['dʒəʊkəʳ] n -1. [person] brincalhão m, -lhona f -2. [playing card] curinga m.

jolly ['dʒɒlɪ] (compar -ier, superl -iest) ⬦ adj alegre, divertido(da). ⬦ adv UK inf muito; **~ easy!** barbada!; **~ good!** excelente!

jolt [dʒəʊlt] ⬦ n -1. [jerk] empurrão m, solavanco m -2. [shock] sacudida f. ⬦ vt -1. [jerk] sacudir -2. [shock] chocar.

Jordan ['dʒɔ:dn] n Jordânia.

jostle ['dʒɒsl] ⬦ vt acotovelar. ⬦ vi acotovelar-se.

jot [dʒɒt] (pt & pp -ted, cont -ting) n tiquinho m; **there isn't a ~ of truth in ...** não há um pingo de verdade em ...; **I don't care a ~ what the rest of you think** não ligo a mínima para o que vocês pensam.
➡ **jot down** vt sep anotar.

jotter ['dʒɒtəʳ] n bloco m de anotações.

journal ['dʒɜ:nl] n -1. [magazine] revista f especializada -2. [diary] diário m.

journalism ['dʒɜ:nəlɪzm] n (U) jornalismo m.

journalist ['dʒɜ:nəlɪst] n jornalista mf.

journey ['dʒɜ:nɪ] (pl -s) n jornada f.

jovial ['dʒəʊvjəl] adj jovial.

jowls [dʒaʊlz] npl bochechas fpl.

joy [dʒɔɪ] n -1. (U) [happiness] alegria f -2. [cause of happiness] prazer m, deleite m.

joyful ['dʒɔɪfʊl] adj alegre.

joyride ['dʒɔɪraɪd] vi andar num carro roubado.

joystick ['dʒɔɪstɪk] n -1. [in aircraft] manche m -2. [for computers, video games] joystick m.

JP n abbr of Justice of the Peace.

Jr. (abbr of Junior) Jr.

jubilant ['dʒu:bɪlənt] adj jubilante.

jubilee ['dʒu:bɪli:] n jubileu m.

judge [dʒʌdʒ] ⬦ n juiz m, -za f. ⬦ vt -1. JUR julgar -2. [decide result of] sentenciar -3. [estimate] estimar. ⬦ vi [decide] julgar; **to ~ from** OR **by** a julgar por, julgando-se por.

judg(e)ment ['dʒʌdʒmənt] n -1. JUR julgamento m -2. [opinion] parecer m -3. (U) [ability to form opinion] opinião f -4. [punishment] sentença f.

judicial [dʒu:'dɪʃl] adj judicial.

judiciary [dʒu:'dɪʃərɪ] n: **the ~** o judiciário.

judicious [dʒu:'dɪʃəs] adj judicioso(sa).

judo ['dʒu:dəʊ] n (U) judô m.

jug [dʒʌg] n [container] jarro m.

juggernaut ['dʒʌgənɔ:t] n [truck] jamanta f.

juggle ['dʒʌgl] ⬦ vt -1. [throw] fazer malabarismos com -2. [rearrange] reorganizar -3. [commitments] equilibrar -4. [figures, ideas] maquiar. ⬦ vi [as entertainment] fazer malabarismos.

juggler ['dʒʌgləʳ] n malabarista mf.

jugular (vein) ['dʒʌgjʊləʳ-] n (veia f) jugular f.

juice [dʒu:s] n [from fruit, vegetables] suco m.

juicy ['dʒu:sɪ] (compar -ier, superl -iest) adj [full of juice] suculento(ta).

jukebox ['dʒu:kbɒks] n juke-box f.

July [dʒu:'laɪ] n julho; see also **September**.

jumble ['dʒʌmbl] ⬦ n [mixture] mistura f. ⬦ vt: **to ~ (up)** confundir.

jumble sale n UK venda f de objetos usados.

jumbo jet ['dʒʌmbəʊ-] n jumbo m.

jumbo-sized ['dʒʌmbəʊsaɪzd] adj gigantesco(ca).

jump [dʒʌmp] ⬦ n -1. [leap] salto m -2. [rapid increase] alta m -3. phr: **to keep one ~ ahead of sb** manter um passo à frente de alguém. ⬦ vt -1. [cross by leaping] pular; **the train ~ed the rails** o trem descarrilhou -2. inf [attack] atacar. ⬦ vi -1. [leap] saltar -2. [make a sudden movement] sobressaltar; **the noise**

made me ~ o barulho me fez dar um sobressalto - **3.** [increase rapidly] ter uma alta.

➤ **jump at** vt fus fig agarrar.

➤ **jump in** vi [get in quickly]: ~ **in!** entra rápido!

➤ **jump out** vi [get out quickly]: ~ **out!** salta fora!

➤ **jump up** vi [rise hurriedly] levantar-se rapidamente.

jumper ['dʒʌmpəʳ] n - **1.** UK [pullover] suéter m - **2.** US [dress] avental m.

jump leads npl cabos mpl para ligação da bateria.

jump-start vt fazer ligação direta.

jumpsuit ['dʒʌmpsu:t] n macacão m.

jumpy ['dʒʌmpɪ] (compar -ier, superl -iest) adj nervoso(sa).

junction ['dʒʌŋkʃn] n [meeting point] junção f, entroncamento m.

June [dʒu:n] n junho; see also **September**.

jungle ['dʒʌŋgl] n selva f; **the Amazon** ~ a floresta amazônica.

junior ['dʒu:njəʳ] ◇ adj - **1.** [younger] jovem - **2.** [lower in rank] júnior - **3.** US [after name] júnior. ◇ n - **1.** [person of lower rank] júnior mf - **2.** [younger person] jovem mf; **he's five years her** ~ ele é cinco anos mais jovem que ela - **3.** US SCH & UNIV aluno m, -na f do penúltimo ano.

junior high school n US escola f de ensino intermediário (para alunos de 13 a 15 anos).

junior school n UK escola f primária.

junk [dʒʌŋk] n - **1.** inf [unwanted things] traste m - **2.** [boat] junco m.

junk food n pej comida pronta e pouco saudável.

junkie ['dʒʌŋkɪ] n drugs sl drogado m, -da f.

junk mail n pej junk mail m.

junk shop n brechó m, brique m.

Jupiter ['dʒu:pɪtəʳ] n [planet] Júpiter.

jurisdiction [,dʒʊərɪs'dɪkʃn] n (U) jurisdição f.

jurisprudence [,dʒʊərɪs'pru:dəns] n (U) jurisprudência f.

juror ['dʒʊərəʳ] n jurado m, -da f.

jury ['dʒʊərɪ] (pl -ies) n júri m.

jury box n tribunal f do júri.

just [dʒʌst] ◇ adj [fair] justo(ta). ◇ adv - **1.** [recently] agora mesmo; **he's** ~ **left** ele acabou de sair - **2.** [at this or that moment]: **I was** ~ **about to go out** eu estava quase saindo; **I'm** ~ **going to do it** vou fazer isso agora mesmo; ~ **then** there was a knock at the door naquele momento houve uma batida na porta; **she arrived** ~ **as I was leaving** ela chegou

no exato momento em que eu estava saindo; **why do you always arrive** ~ **as I'm leaving?** por que você sempre chega justamente quando estou saindo? - **3.** [only, simply] apenas, simplesmente; **in** ~ **a minute** OR **moment** OR **second** num minuto OR um instante OR segundo; ~ **a minute!** espera aí um pouquinho! - **4.** [barely, almost not] mal; **I can only** ~ **hear you** mal consigo ouvir você; **I only** ~ **caught the train** quase perdi o trem; **we have** ~ **enough time** quase não temos tempo - **5.** [for emphasis] simplesmente; **I** ~ **can't believe it!** simplesmente não consigo acreditar!; ~ **look at this mess!** dá só uma olhada na bagunça! - **6.** [exactly, precisely] precisamente; ~ **here** exatamente aqui - **7.** [in requests]: **could I** ~ **borrow your pen?** poderia me emprestar sua caneta, por favor?

➤ **just about** adv mais ou menos.

➤ **just as** adv [in comparisons]: ~ **as well as you** tão bem quanto você; ~ **as bad as ever** mal como sempre.

➤ **just now** adv - **1.** [a short time ago] agora mesmo - **2.** [at this moment] neste momento.

justice ['dʒʌstɪs] n - **1.** [gen] justiça f - **2.** [of a cause, claim] razão f.

Justice of the Peace (pl **Justices of the Peace**) n Juiz m, -za f de Paz.

justify ['dʒʌstɪfaɪ] (pt & pp -ied) vt - **1.** [give reasons for] justificar - **2.** COMPUT & TYPO justificar.

justly ['dʒʌstlɪ] adv merecidamente, imparcialmente.

jut [dʒʌt] (pt & pp -ted, cont -ting) vi: **to** ~ **(out)** projetar-se.

juvenile ['dʒu:vənaɪl] ◇ adj - **1.** JUR juvenil - **2.** pej [childish] infantil. ◇ n JUR [young person] menor mf.

juxtapose [,dʒʌkstə'pəʊz] vt: **to** ~ **sthg with sthg** justapor algo com algo.

K

k (pl **k's** OR **ks**), **K** (pl **K's** OR **Ks**) [keɪ] n [letter] k, K m.

➤ **K** n - **1.** (abbr of **kilobyte**) K - **2.** (abbr of **thousand**) mil.

kaleidoscope [kə'laɪdəskəʊp] n caleidoscópio m.

kangaroo [ˌkæŋɡəˈruː] n canguru m.

kaput [kəˈpʊt] adj inf acabado(da).

karaoke [kɑːrəˈəʊki] n karaokê m.

karat [ˈkærət] n US quilate m.

karate [kəˈrɑːtɪ] n (U) karatê m.

kayak [ˈkaɪæk] n caiaque m.

KB (abbr of kilobyte(s)) n COMPUT KB.

KBE (abbr of Knight Commander of the Order of the British Empire) n (titular de) distinção britânica.

kcal (abbr of kilocalorie) Kcal.

kebab [kɪˈbæb] n churrasquinho picante servido com pão árabe e acompanhado de vegetais picados, kebab m.

keel [kiːl] n quilha f; **on an even ~** em perfeito equilíbrio.

♦ **keel over** vi -1. [ship] emborcar -2. [person] desmaiar.

keen [kiːn] adj -1. [enthusiastic] entusiasta; **to be ~ on sthg** gostar muito de algo, ser aficionado(da) por algo; **to be ~ on sb** gostar muito de alguém; **to be ~ to do** OR **on doing sthg** estar muito a fim de fazer algo; **I'm not madly ~ on going** não estou com toda essa vontade de ir -2. [intense] intenso(sa) -3. [sharp, well-developed] apurado(da) -4. [wind] forte.

keep [kiːp] (pt & pp kept) ⬦ vt -1. [maintain in a particular place or state or position] manter; **to ~ sb waiting** fazer alguém esperar -2. [retain] ficar com; **please ~ the change** pode ficar com o troco; **they're ~ing the house in Scotland** eles estão mantendo a casa na Escócia -3. [continue]: **to ~ doing sthg** continuar fazendo algo; **to ~ talking** continuar falando -4. [put aside, store] guardar -5. [prevent]: **to ~ sb/sthg from doing sthg** impedir alguém/algo de fazer algo -6. [detain] manter; **to ~ sb (from sthg)** privar alguém (de algo); **what kept you?** o que te segurou aqui? -7. [fulfil, observe] cumprir; **to ~ a secret** guardar um segredo -8. [withhold news or fact of]: **to ~ sthg from sb** ocultar algo de alguém; **~ it to yourself for the moment** não conta isso para ninguém por enquanto -9. [diary, record, account] ter -10. [own - farm animals] criar; [- shop, car] ter -11. phr: **they ~ themselves to themselves** eles são muito reservados. ⬦ vi -1. [remain, stay] manter-se -2. [continue moving] manter-se a -3. [last, stay fresh] conservar-se -4. UK [in health] manter-se. ⬦ n (U) [food, board etc.] sustento.

♦ **for keeps** adv para valer.

♦ **keep back** vt sep conter.

♦ **keep off** ⬦ vt sep [fend off] manter afastado(da). ⬦ vt fus [avoid] evitar; **'~ off the grass'** 'não pise na grama'.

♦ **keep on** vi -1. [continue] continuar -2. [talk incessantly]: **to ~ on (about sthg)** falar incessantemente (sobre algo). ⬦ vt [continue]: **to ~ on doing sthg** [without stopping] continuar fazendo algo; [repeatedly] continuar fazendo algo sem parar.

♦ **keep out** ⬦ vt sep manter-se fora. ⬦ vi: **'~ out'** 'entrada proibida'.

♦ **keep to** vt fus -1. [observe, respect] respeitar -2. [not deviate from] manter-se em.

♦ **keep up** ⬦ vt sep -1. [prevent from falling] segurar -2. [maintain, continue] manter -3. [prevent from going to bed] manter acordado(da). ⬦ vi [maintain pace, level] acompanhar; **to ~ up with sb/sthg** acompanhar alguém/algo.

keeper [ˈkiːpər] n -1. [in zoo] zelador m, -ra f, guarda mf -2. [curator] curador m, -ra f.

keep-fit UK n (U) ginástica f.

keeping [ˈkiːpɪŋ] n -1. [care] cuidado m -2. [conformity, harmony]: **in/out of ~ with sthg** [rules, regulations, decision] em acordo/desacordo com algo; [clothes, furniture, style] combinando/não combinando com algo.

keepsake [ˈkiːpseɪk] n lembrança f.

keg [keg] n barrilote m.

kennel [ˈkenl] n -1. [shelter for dog] canil m -2. US = kennels.

♦ **kennels** npl UK [for boarding pets] canil m.

Kenya [ˈkenjə] n Quênia m.

Kenyan [ˈkenjən] ⬦ adj queniano(na). ⬦ n queniano m, -na f.

kept [kept] pt & pp ➭ keep.

kerb [kɜːb] n UK meio-fio m.

kernel [ˈkɜːnl] n [of nut] amêndoa f; **the ~ of the issue** o cerne da questão.

kerosene [ˈkerəsiːn] n (U) querosene f.

ketchup [ˈketʃəp] n (U) ketchup m.

kettle [ˈketl] n chaleira f.

key [kiː] ⬦ n -1. [for lock] chave f -2. [of typewriter, computer] tecla f -3. [explanatory list] legenda f -4. [solution, answer]: **~ (to sthg)** chave (para algo) -5. [MUS - of piano, organ] tom m; [- scale of notes] clave f. ⬦ adj [main] principal; **~ position** posição-chave; **~ issue** questão-chave.

keyboard [ˈkiːbɔːd] n teclado m.

keyed up [kiːd-] adj excitado(da).

keyhole [ˈkiːhəʊl] n buraco m da fechadura.

keynote ['ki:nəʊt] ◇ n [main point] tônica f. ◇ comp: ~ **speech** conferência f de abertura.

keypad ['ki:pæd] n COMPUT teclado m.

key ring n chaveiro m.

kg (abbr of **kilogram**) kg.

khaki ['kɑ:kı] ◇ adj cáqui inv. ◇ n [colour] cáqui m.

kHz (abbr of **kilohertz**) n kHz.

kick [kık] ◇ n -1. [with foot] chute m - 2. inf [excitement]: **to do sthg for** ~ **s** fazer algo para se divertir; **to get a** ~ **from sthg** desfrutar de algo. ◇ vt -1. [with foot] chutar; **to** ~ **o.s.** fig morder-se de raiva -2. inf [give up] largar. ◇ vi [person, baby, animal] dar pontapés.
   ◆ **kick about, kick around** vi UK inf [lie around] rodear.
   ◆ **kick in** vi fazer efeito.
   ◆ **kick off** vi -1. FTBL dar o pontapé inicial - 2. inf fig [start] começar.
   ◆ **kick out** vt sep inf expulsar.

kid [kıd] (pt & pp -ded, cont -ding) ◇ n -1. inf [child, young person] criança f; **I've got four** ~ **s** tenho quatro filhos -2. [young goat] cabrito m -3. [leather] pelica f. ◇ comp inf [brother, sister]: **my** ~ **brother** meu irmão mais novo; **my** ~ **sister** minha irmã mais nova. ◇ vt inf -1. [tease] caçoar -2. [delude]: **to** ~ **o.s.** iludir-se. ◇ vi inf: **to be kidding** estar brincando.

kidnap ['kıdnæp] (UK pt & pp -ped, cont -ping, US pt & pp -ed, cont -ing) vt seqüestrar.

kidnapper UK, **kidnaper** US ['kıdnæpəʳ] n seqüestrador m, -ra f.

kidnapping UK, **kidnaping** US ['kıdnæpıŋ] n seqüestro m.

kidney ['kıdnı] (pl -s) n rim m.

kidney bean n feijão m roxo.

kill [kıl] ◇ n [of animal] abate m; **to move** OR **close in for the** ~ dar o bote; fig dar o bote. ◇ vt -1. [gen] matar; **my feet are** ~ **ing me** meus pés estão me matando; **to** ~ **o.s.** matar-se -2. [murder] assassinar -3. fig [cause to end, fail] acabar com. ◇ vi aniquilar.

killer ['kıləʳ] n -1. [person] assassino m, -na f - 2. [animal] matador m, -ra f.

killing ['kılıŋ] n -1. [of one person] assassinato m - 2. [of several people] matança f - 3. inf [profit]: **to make a** ~ faturar uma grana.

killjoy ['kıldʒɔı] n estraga-prazer mf.

kiln [kıln] n fornalha f.

kilo ['ki:ləʊ] (pl -s) (abbr of **kilogram**) n quilo m.

kilobyte ['kıləbaıt] n quilobyte m.

kilogram(me) ['kıləgræm] n quilograma m.

kilohertz ['kıləhз:tz] (pl inv) n quilohertz m.

kilometre UK ['kılə,mi:təʳ], **kilometer** US [kı'lɒmıtəʳ] n quilómetro m.

kilowatt ['kıləwɒt] n quilowatt m.

kilt [kılt] n kilt m.

kin [kın] n ⊳ **kith**.

kind [kaınd] ◇ adj gentil, amável. ◇ n espécie f, tipo m; **a** ~ **of** uma espécie de; ~ **of** inf de certo modo; **I** ~ **of thought that ...** eu meio que achei que ...; **of a** ~ [sort of] do estilo; **an agreement of a** ~ um acordo do estilo; [of same kind] do mesmo tipo; **in** ~ [payment] em espécie; **nothing of the** ~! de jeito nenhum!; **it's one of a** ~ é um em um milhão; **they're two of a** ~ os dois são muito semelhantes.

kindergarten ['kındə,gɑ:tn] n jardim-de-infância m.

kind-hearted [-'hɑ:tıd] adj de bom coração.

kindle ['kındl] vt -1. [fire] pôr fogo em - 2. fig [idea, feeling] inflamar.

kindly ['kaındlı] (compar -ier, superl -iest) ◇ adj bondoso(sa), gentil. ◇ adv -1. [gen] bondosamente, gentilmente - 2. [in sarcasm]: ~ **leave the room!** faça o favor de sair da sala!; **will you** ~ **stop calling me that name!** pode fazer o favor de parar de me chamar por esse nome!

kindness ['kaındnıs] n -1. (U) [gentleness] gentileza f, bondade f - 2. [helpful act] generosidade f.

kindred ['kındrıd] adj [similar] afim; ~ **spirit** alma f gêmea.

king [kıŋ] n rei m.

kingdom ['kıŋdəm] n reino m.

kingfisher ['kıŋ,fıʃəʳ] n martim-pescador m.

king-size(d) [-saız(d)] adj de tamanho grande; ~ **bed** cama f king-size.

kinky ['kıŋkı] (compar -ier, superl -iest) adj -1. inf [idea, behaviour] excêntrico(ca) - 2. [sex] pervertido(da).

kiosk ['ki:ɒsk] n -1. [small shop] banca f - 2. UK [telephone box] cabine f telefônica.

kip [kıp] (pt & pp -ped, cont -ping) UK inf ◇ n sesta f. ◇ vi sestear.

kipper ['kıpəʳ] n arenque m defumado.

kiss [kıs] ◇ n beijo m; **to give sb a** ~ dar um beijo em alguém. ◇ vt beijar. ◇ vi beijar-se.

kiss of death n fig: **the** ~ o beijo da morte.

kiss of life n [to resuscitate sb]: **to give sb**

the ~ fazer respiração boca-a-boca em alguém.

kit [kɪt] (*pt* & *pp* **-ted**, *cont* **-ting**) *n* -1. [set] estojo *m* -2. (*U*) [clothes] equipamento *m* -3. [to be assembled] kit *m*, modelo *m*.

kit bag *n* mochila *f* de viagem.

kitchen ['kɪtʃɪn] *n* cozinha *f*.

kitchen roll *n* papel-toalha *m*.

kitchen sink *n* pia *f* de cozinha.

kitchen unit *n* módulo *m* de cozinha.

kite [kaɪt] *n* -1. [toy] pipa *f*.

kith [kɪθ] *n*: ~ and kin amigos *mpl* e parentes.

kitten ['kɪtn] *n* gatinho *m*, -nha *f*.

kitty ['kɪtɪ] (*pl* **-ies**) *n* [shared fund - for bills, drinks] vaquinha *f*; [- in card games] bolo *m*.

kiwi ['ki:wi:] *n* -1. [bird] quivi *m* -2. *inf* [New Zealander] neozelandês *m*, -esa *f*.

kiwi fruit *n* quivi *m*.

km (*abbr of* **kilometre**) km.

km/h (*abbr of* **kilometres per hour**) km/h.

knack [næk] *n* inclinação *m*, queda *f*; to have the ~ (of doing sthg) levar jeito (para fazer algo); to have a ~ (for doing sthg) ter uma queda (para fazer algo).

knackered ['nækəd] *adj UK vinf* [tired, broken] acabado(da).

knapsack ['næpsæk] *n* mochila *f*.

knead [ni:d] *vt* [dough, clay] misturar.

knee [ni:] *n* ANAT joelho *m*.

kneecap ['ni:kæp] *n* rótula *f*.

kneel [ni:ll] (*UK pt* & *pp* **knelt**, *US pt* & *pp* **knelt** *OR* **-ed**) *vi* ajoelhar-se.

➡ **kneel down** *vi* ajoelhar, ajoelhar-se.

knelt [nelt] *pt* & *pp* ▷ **kneel**.

knew [nju:] *pt* ▷ **know**.

knickers ['nɪkəz] *npl* -1. *UK* [underwear] calcinha *f* -2. *US* [knickerbockers] calções *mpl* (presos à altura dos joelhos).

knick-knack ['nɪknæk] *n* penduricalho *m*.

knife [naɪf] (*pl* **knives**) ◇ *n* faca *f*. ◇ *vt* esfaquear.

knight [naɪt] ◇ *n* -1. [gen] cavaleiro *m* -2. [in chess] cavalo *m*. ◇ *vt* nomear cavaleiro(ra).

knighthood ['naɪthʊd] *n* título *m* da classe dos cavaleiros.

knit [nɪt] (*pt* & *pp* **knit** *OR* **-ted**, *cont* **-ting**) ◇ *adj*: closely *OR* tightly ~ *fig* fortemente unido(da). ◇ *vt* [make with wool] tricotar. ◇ *vi* -1. [with wool] fazer tricô, tricotar -2. [join] juntar-se.

knitting ['nɪtɪŋ] *n* (*U*) -1. [activity] trabalho *m* de tricô -2. [work produced] tricô *m*.

knitting needle *n* agulha *f* de tricô.

knitwear ['nɪtweəʳ] *n* (*U*) roupa *f* de tricô.

knives [naɪvz] *pl* ▷ **knife**.

knob [nɒb] *n* -1. [on door] maçaneta *f* -2. [on drawer] puxador *m* -3. [on walking stick, furniture] nó *m* -4. [on TV, radio] botão *m*.

knock [nɒk] ◇ *n* -1. [blow] pancada *f*, batida *f* -2. *inf* [piece of bad luck] azar *m*. ◇ *vt* -1. [gen] bater contra; to ~ one's head on sthg bater com a cabeça em algo; to ~ a hole in the wall abrir um buraco na parede; to ~ a nail into sthg pregar um prego em algo -2. *inf fig* [criticize] criticar. ◇ *vi* -1. [on door]: to ~ at *OR* on sthg bater em algo -2. [car engine] bater.

➡ **knock down** *vt sep* -1. [subj: car, driver] atropelar -2. [building] derrubar.

➡ **knock off** *vi inf* [stop working] parar de trabalhar.

➡ **knock out** *vt sep* -1. [make unconscious - subj: person, punch] pôr a nocaute; [- subj: drug] derrubar -2. [from competition] eliminar.

➡ **knock over** *vt sep* -1. [push over] derrubar -2. [in car] atropelar.

knocker ['nɒkəʳ] *n* [on door] aldrava *f*.

knock-kneed [-'ni:d] *adj* de pernas tortas.

knock-on effect *n UK* efeito *m* dominó.

knockout ['nɒkaʊt] *n* -1. [in boxing] nocaute *m* -2. *inf* [sensation]: she's a real ~ ela é de arrasar.

knockout competition *n UK* competição *f* com eliminatórias.

knot [nɒt] (*pt* & *pp* **-ted**, *cont* **-ting**) ◇ *n* -1. [gen] nó *m*; to tie/untie a ~ fazer/desfazer um nó -2. [of people] grupo *m*. ◇ *vt* [rope, string] dar um nó em.

knotty ['nɒtɪ] (*compar* **-ier**, *superl* **-iest**) *adj* [difficult] cabeludo(da).

know [nəʊ] (*pt* **knew**, *pp* **known**) ◇ *vt* -1. [become acquainted with] conhecer; to get to ~ sb conhecer alguém -2. [fact, information] saber; to ~ (that) saber que; to get to ~ sthg saber algo -3. [language, skill] ter conhecimento de; to ~ how to do sthg saber fazer algo -4. [recognize] reconhecer -5. [distinguish] diferenciar -6. [nickname, call]: to be known as ser conhecido(da) como. ◇ *vi* saber; to ~ of sthg saber de algo; to ~ about sthg [be aware of] saber sobre algo; [be expert in] saber de algo; you ~ [for emphasis, to add information] você sabe. ◇ *n*: to be in the ~ estar bem-informado(da) sobre.

ladle

know-all *n UK* sabichão *m*, -ona *f*.

know-how *n* experiência *f*, know-how *m*.

knowing ['nəʊɪŋ] *adj* [look, smile] de cumplicidade.

knowingly ['nəʊɪŋlɪ] *adv* -1. [look, smile] conscientemente -2. [act] de propósito.

know-it-all *n* = know-all.

knowledge ['nɒlɪdʒ] *n* conhecimento *m*.

knowledgeable ['nɒlɪdʒəbl] *adj* entendido(da).

known [nəʊn] *pp* ▷ know.

knuckle ['nʌkl] *n* -1. *ANAT* nó *m* (do dedo) -2. [of meat] mocotó *m*.

knuckle-duster *n* soqueira *f* de metal.

koala (bear) [kəʊ'ɑ:lə-] *n* coala *m*.

Koran [kɒ'rɑ:n] *n*: the ~ o Alcorão.

Korea [kə'rɪə] *n* Coréia.

Korean [kə'rɪən] ◇ *adj* coreano(na). ◇ *n* -1. [person] coreano *m*, -na *f* -2. [language] coreano *m*.

kosher ['kəʊʃəʳ] *adj* -1. [meat] kosher -2. *fig inf* [reputable] limpo(pa), puro(-ra).

Kosovo ['kɒsəvəʊl] *n* Kosovo.

Koweit *n* = Kuwait; **in ~** no Kuwait.

kung fu [,kʌŋ'fu:] *n (U)* kung fu *m*.

Kurd [kɜ:d] *n* curdo *m*, -da *f*.

Kuwait [kju:'weɪt] *n* -1. [country] Kuwait -2. [city] Kuwait.

l¹ (*pl* l's *OR* ls), **L** (*pl* L's *OR* Ls) [el] *n* [letter] l, L *m*.

l² (*abbr of* litre) l.

lab [læb] *n inf* laboratório *m*.

label ['leɪbl] (*UK pt* & *pp* -led, *cont* -ling, *US pt* & *pp* -ed, *cont* -ing) ◇ *n* -1. [identification - on bottle] rótulo *m*; [- on luggage, clothing] etiqueta *f* -2. [of record] selo *m*. ◇ *vt* -1. [fix label to - bottle] rotular; [- luggage, clothing] etiquetar -2. [describe] descrever; **to ~ sb as sthg** rotular alguém de algo.

labor *etc*. *n US* = labour.

laboratory [*UK* lə'bɒrətrɪ, *US* 'læbrə,tɔ:rɪ] (*pl* -ies) *n* laboratório *m*.

laborious [lə'bɔ:rɪəs] *adj* trabalhoso(sa).

labor union *n US* sindicato *m* (*de trabalhadores*).

labour *UK*, **labor** *US* ['leɪbəʳ] ◇ *n* -1. [work] trabalho *m*; **manual ~** trabalho manual; **to withdraw one's ~** abandonar o trabalho -2. [effort] esforço *m* -3. *(U)* [work force] mão-de-obra *f*; **parts and ~** peças e mão-de-obra -4. *MED* [giving birth] trabalho *m* de parto. ◇ *vi* -1. [work] trabalhar -2. [struggle]: **to ~ at** *OR* **over sthg** trabalhar em algo.
➡ **Labour** *UK POL* ◇ *adj* trabalhista. ◇ *n UK* o Partido Trabalhista.

laboured *UK*, **labored** *US* ['leɪbəd] *adj* -1. [breathing] forçado(da) -2. [style] elaborado(da).

labourer *UK*, **laborer** *US* ['leɪbərəʳ] *n* peão *m*.

Labour Party *n UK*: **the ~** o Partido Trabalhista.

Labrador ['læbrədɔ:ʳ] *n* -1. [dog] labrador *m*.

labyrinth ['læbərɪnθ] *n* labirinto *m*.

lace [leɪs] ◇ *n* -1. *(U)* [fabric] renda *f* -2. [shoelace] cadarço *m*. ◇ *vt* -1. [shoe, boot] amarrar -2. [drink, food] misturar álcool em.
➡ **lace up** *vt sep* amarrar.

lace-up *n UK* sapato *m* de amarrar.

lack [læk] ◇ *n* falta *f*; **for** *OR* **through ~ of** por falta de; **with no ~ of** sem falta de. ◇ *vt* sentir falta de, carecer de. ◇ *vi*: **you're ~ing in experience** te falta experiência; **to be ~ing** estar faltando.

lackadaisical [,lækə'deɪzɪkl] *adj pej* desinteressado(da), apático(ca).

lacklustre *UK*, **lackluster** *US* ['læk,lʌstəʳ] *adj* sem brilho.

laconic [lə'kɒnɪk] *adj* lacônico(ca).

lacquer ['lækəʳ] ◇ *n* -1. [for wood, metal] verniz *m* -2. [for hair] fixador *m*. ◇ *vt* -1. [wood, metal] envernizar -2. [hair] aplicar fixador em.

lacrosse [lə'krɒs] *n (U)* jogo canadense semelhante ao hóquei.

lad [læd] *n inf* -1. [young boy] rapaz *m* -2. [male friend] amigo *m*; **he went out for a drink with the ~s** ele saiu para beber com a rapaziada.

ladder ['lædəʳ] ◇ *n* -1. [for climbing] escada *f* de mão -2. *UK* [in tights] defeito *m*. ◇ *vt UK* [tights] puxar fio em. ◇ *vi UK* [tights] puxar fio.

laden ['leɪdn] *adj* carregado(da); **~ with sthg** carregado com algo.

ladies *UK* ['leɪdɪz], **ladies room** *US n* senhoras *fpl*, damas *fpl*.

ladle ['leɪdl] ◇ *n* concha *f*. ◇ *vt* servir com concha.

lady ['leɪdɪ] (pl -ies) ⬦ n -1. [woman] senhora f -2. [by birth or upbringing] dama f. ⬦ comp: ~ **doctor** médica f.
◆ **Lady** n [member of nobility] Lady f.

ladybird UK ['leɪdɪbɜːd], **ladybug** US ['leɪdɪbʌg] n joaninha f.

lady-in-waiting [-'weɪtɪŋ] (pl **ladies-in-waiting**) n dama f de companhia.

ladylike ['leɪdɪlaɪk] adj elegante, refinado(da).

Ladyship ['leɪdɪʃɪp] n: **her/your** ~ Vossa Senhoria.

lag [læg] (pt & pp -ged, cont -ging) ⬦ n [in time] atraso m, demora f. ⬦ vt revestir com material isolante. ⬦ vi [move more slowly]: **to** ~ **(behind)** ficar (para trás).

lager ['lɑːgəʳ] n cerveja m tipo Pilsen.

lagoon [lə'guːn] n lagoa f.

laid [leɪd] pt & pp ⊳ **lay**.

laid-back adj inf descontraído(da).

lain [leɪn] pp ⊳ **lie**.

lair [leəʳ] n toca f.

laity ['leɪətɪ] n RELIG: **the** ~ os laicos.

lake [leɪk] n lago m.

Lake District n: **the** ~ a Região dos Lagos.

Lake Geneva n o Lago de Genebra.

lamb [læm] n [animal, meat] cordeiro m.

lambswool ['læmzwʊl] ⬦ n (U) lã f de cordeiro. ⬦ comp de lã de cordeiro.

lame [leɪm] adj -1. [person, horse] manco(ca) -2. [excuse, argument] pouco convincente.

lament [lə'ment] ⬦ n lamento m. ⬦ vt lamentar.

lamentable ['læməntəbl] adj lamentável.

laminated ['læmɪneɪtɪd] adj laminado(da).

lamp [læmp] n lâmpada f.

lampoon [læm'puːn] ⬦ n sátira f. ⬦ vt satirizar.

lamppost ['læmppəʊst] n poste m de iluminação.

lampshade ['læmpʃeɪd] n quebra-luz m.

lance [lɑːns] ⬦ n [spear] lança f. ⬦ vt MED lancetar.

lance corporal n UK ≃ cabo m.

land [lænd] ⬦ n -1. [gen] terra f -2. [property, estate] terreno m -3. [nation] país m. ⬦ vt -1. [plane] aterrissar -2. [cargo, passengers] desembarcar -3. [fish] recolher -4. inf [job, contract] fechar -5. inf [put, place]: **to** ~ **sb in trouble** pôr alguém em apuros; **to** ~ **sb in jail** fazer com que alguém acabe na cadeia -6. inf [encumber]: **to** ~ **sb with sb/sthg** incomodar alguém com alguém/algo.
⬦ vi -1. [plane, passenger] aterrissar -2. [fall] cair.
◆ **land up** vi inf acabar; **to** ~ **up in serious debt** acabar com um monte de dívidas; **to** ~ **up in** OR **at** [place] acabar em, ir parar em.

landing ['lændɪŋ] n -1. [of stairs] patamar m -2. [of aeroplane] aterrissagem f -3. [of goods from ship] desembarque m.

landing card n cartão m de desembarque.

landing gear n (U) trem m de aterrissagem.

landing stage n cais m inv de desembarque.

landing strip n pista f de aterrissagem.

landlady ['lænd,leɪdɪ] (pl -ies) n [gen] senhoria f; [in guesthouse, pub] proprietária f.

landlord ['lændlɔːd] n -1. [in lodgings] senhorio m -2. [of pub] proprietário m.

landmark ['lændmɑːk] n -1. [prominent feature] ponto m de referência -2. fig [in history] marco m divisório.

landowner ['lænd,əʊnəʳ] n proprietário m, -ria f de terras.

landscape ['lændskeɪp] n paisagem f.

landslide ['lændslaɪd] n -1. [of earth, rocks] desmoronamento m -2. POL vitória f esmagadora.

lane [leɪn] n -1. [road - in country] senda f; [- in town, village] ruela f -2. [division of road] pista f, faixa f; **'get/keep in** ~' 'entrar/manter-se na pista' -3. [in swimming pool, on racetrack] raia f -4. [for shipping, aircraft] pista f.

language ['læŋgwɪdʒ] n -1. [spoken, foreign] língua f -2. [style, mode of communication] linguagem f.

language laboratory n laboratório m de línguas.

languid ['læŋgwɪd] adj lânguido(da).

languish ['læŋgwɪʃ] vi -1. [suffer] sofrer -2. [become weak] debilitar-se.

lank [læŋk] adj liso(sa).

lanky ['læŋkɪ] (compar -ier, superl -iest) adj magricela.

lantern ['læntən] n lanterna f.

lap [læp] (pt & pp -ped, cont -ping) ⬦ n -1. [knees] colo m -2. SPORT volta f. ⬦ vt -1. [subj: animal] lamber -2. SPORT [runner, car] estar uma volta à frente de. ⬦ vi [water, waves] marulhar.

lapel [lə'pel] n lapela f.

Lapland ['læplænd] n Lapônia; **in** ~ na Lapônia.

lapse [læps] ⬦ n -1. [failing] lapso m -2. [in behaviour] deslize m -3. [of time]

intervalo m. $\diamond$ vi **-1.** [custom, licence]
caducar **-2.** [passport] expirar **-3.** [law]
prescrever **-4.** [deteriorate] decair **-5.**
[subj: person]: **to ~ into** [coma] entrar
em; [silence, dialect] mergulhar em; [bad
habits] adquirir.

lap-top (computer) n (computador
m) lap-top m.

larceny ['lɑ:sənɪ] n (U) furto m.

lard [lɑ:d] n (U) toicinho m, banha f (de
porco).

larder ['lɑ:də'] n despensa f.

large [lɑ:dʒ] adj grande.
$\Rightarrow$ **at large** $\diamond$ adj [escaped prisoner, ani-
mal] em liberdade. $\diamond$ adv [as a whole]
em geral.

largely ['lɑ:dʒlɪ] adv em grande parte.

lark [lɑ:k] n **-1.** [bird] cotovia f **-2.** inf
[joke] brincadeira f.
$\Rightarrow$ **lark about** vi fazer palhaçadas.

laryngitis [,lærɪn'dʒaɪtɪs] n (U) laringite
f.

larynx ['lærɪŋks] (pl -es) n laringe f.

lasagna, lasagne [lə'zænjə] n (U) lasanha f.

laser ['leɪzə'] n laser m.

laser printer n impressora f a laser.

lash [læʃ] $\diamond$ n **-1.** [eyelash] cílio m **-2.**
[blow with whip] chicotada f. $\diamond$ vt **-1.**
[whip] chicotear **-2.** [subj: wind, rain,
waves] fustigar **-3.** [tie] atar; **to ~ sthg
to sthg** atar algo em algo.
$\Rightarrow$ **lash out** vi **-1.** [physically]: **to ~ out
(at OR against sb)** atacar alguém com
extrema violência **-2.** [verbally]: **to ~
out (at OR against sb)** atacar alguém
verbalmente **-3.** UK inf [spend money]: **to
~ out (on sthg)** esbanjar dinheiro (em
algo).

lass [læs] n [girl] moça f.

lasso [læ'su:] (pl **-s**, pt & pp **-ed**, cont
-ing) $\diamond$ n laço m. $\diamond$ vt laçar.

last [lɑ:st] $\diamond$ adj **-1.** [gen] último(ma);
~ but one penúltimo(ma); **~ but two**
antepenúltimo(ma) **-2.** [with dates, time
of day] último(ma), passado(da); **~
week** na semana passada, na última
semana; **~ year** no ano passado **-3.**
[least likely]: **you're the ~ person I expected to see** você é a última pessoa
que eu esperava ver. $\diamond$ adv **-1.** [in final
place] em último lugar **-2.** [most recently]:
when did you ~ visit them? quando
você os visitou pela última vez?; **at ~**
finalmente; **at ~!** até que enfim! $\diamond$
pron o último, a última; **to leave sthg
till ~** deixar algo para o fim; **the week
before ~** na semana retrasada; **the day
before ~** anteontem. $\diamond$ n [final thing]:
the ~ I saw/heard of him a última coisa

que eu soube dele. $\diamond$ vi **-1.** [gen]
durar; **they only had food to ~ another
week** eles só tinham comida para mais
uma semana **-2.** [survive] sobreviver.
$\Rightarrow$ **at (long) last** adv por fim.

last-ditch adj derradeiro(ra).

lasting ['lɑ:stɪŋ] adj duradouro(ra).

lastly ['lɑ:stlɪ] adv **-1.** [to conclude] por
fim **-2.** [at the end] finalmente.

last-minute adj de última hora.

last name n sobrenome m.

latch [lætʃ] n trinco m.
$\Rightarrow$ **latch onto** vt fus inf agarrar-se a.

late [leɪt] $\diamond$ adj **-1.** [delayed] atrasado(-
da); **to be ~ for sthg** estar atrasado(da)
para algo **-2.** [later than normal] tarde **-3.**
[near end of]: **in ~ December** no final de
dezembro **-4.** [dead] falecido(da). $\diamond$
adv [not on time] tarde; **he arrived 20 minutes ~** ele chegou 20 minutos atrasado; **~ in December** no final de
dezembro; **to work ~** trabalhar até
tarde.
$\Rightarrow$ **of late** adv recentemente.

latecomer ['leɪt,kʌmə'] n retardatário
m, -ria f.

lately ['leɪtlɪ] adv ultimamente.

latent ['leɪtənt] adj latente.

later ['leɪtə'] $\diamond$ adj **-1.** [last, final]
último(ma) **-2.** [subsequent, following]
posterior **-3.** [train, bus, boat] que sai
mais tarde. $\diamond$ adv [at a later time]: **~
(on)** mais tarde.

lateral ['lætərəl] adj lateral.

latest ['leɪtɪst] $\diamond$ adj [most recent] últi-
mo(ma). $\diamond$ n: **at the ~** no mais
tardar.

lathe [leɪð] n torno m mecânico.

lather ['lɑ:ðə'] $\diamond$ n espuma f. $\diamond$ vt
ensaboar.

Latin ['lætɪn] $\diamond$ adj latino(na). $\diamond$ n
[language] latim m.

Latin America n América Latina.

Latin American $\diamond$ adj latino-ameri-
cano(na). $\diamond$ n [person] latino-americano m, -na f.

latitude ['lætɪtju:d] n **-1.** GEOGR latitude f
-2. fml [freedom] liberdade f (de expressão).

latter ['lætə'] $\diamond$ adj **-1.** [later] último(-
ma) **-2.** [second] segundo(da). $\diamond$ n: **the
~** o último, a última; **we prefer the ~
house to the former** preferimos esta
casa àquela.

latterly ['lætəlɪ] adv recentemente.

lattice ['lætɪs] n [fence, frame] treliça f.

Latvia ['lætvɪə] n Letônia f.

laudable ['lɔ:dəbl] adj louvável.

laugh [lɑ:f] $\diamond$ n **-1.** [sound] riso m,
risada f **-2.** inf [fun, joke] piada f; **to do**

sthg for ~s OR a ~ fazer algo por prazer. ⬦ *vi* rir, gargalhar.

◆ **laugh at** *vt fus* [mock] rir-se de, gozar com.

◆ **laugh off** *vt sep* [dismiss] disfarçar com um sorriso.

laughable ['lɑ:fəbl] *adj pej* [absurd] risível.

laughingstock *n* motivo *m* de riso.

laughter ['lɑ:ftə'] *n* (U) risada *f*, risos *mpl*.

launch [lɔ:ntʃ] ⬦ *n* -1. [gen] lançamento *m* -2. [start, initiation] início *m*. ⬦ *vt* -1. [gen] lançar -2. [start, initiate] iniciar.

launch(ing) pad ['lɔ:ntʃ(ɪŋ)-] *n* [for rocket, missile, satellite] plataforma *f* de lançamento.

launder ['lɔ:ndə'] *vt* -1. [clothes] lavar e passar -2. *inf* [money] lavar.

laund(e)rette [lɔ:n'dret], **Laundromat®** US ['lɔ:ndrəmæt] *n* lavanderia *f* automatizada.

laundry ['lɔ:ndrɪ] (*pl* -ies) *n* -1. (U) [clothes - about to be washed] roupa *f* suja; [- newly washed] roupa *f* lavada -2. [room, business] lavanderia *f*.

laurel *n* louro *m*.

lava ['lɑ:və] *n* (U) lava *f*.

lavatory ['lævətrɪ] (*pl* -ies) *n* -1. [receptacle] privada *f*.

lavender ['lævəndə'] *n* [plant] alfazema *f*, lavanda *f*.

lavish ['lævɪʃ] ⬦ *adj* -1. [generous] generoso(sa); to be ~ with sthg ser generoso(sa) com algo -2. [sumptuous] suntuoso(sa). ⬦ *vt*: to ~ sthg on sb/sthg encher alguém/algo de algo.

law [lɔ:] *n* -1. [gen] lei *f*; to break the ~ transgredir a lei; against the ~ contra a lei; ~ and order lei e ordem -2. [system, subject] direito *m*.

law-abiding [-ə,baɪdɪŋ] *adj* obediente à lei.

law court *n* tribunal *m* de justiça.

lawful ['lɔ:fʊl] *adj fml* lícito(ta).

lawn [lɔ:n] *n* [grass] gramado *m*.

lawnmower ['lɔ:n,məʊə'] *n* cortador *m* de grama.

lawn tennis *n* tênis *m inv* de gramado.

law school *n* escola *f* de direito.

lawsuit ['lɔ:su:t] *n* ação *f* judicial.

lawyer ['lɔ:jə'] *n* advogado *m*, -da *f*.

lax [læks] *adj* negligente.

laxative ['læksətɪv] *n* laxante *m*.

lay [leɪ] (*pt & pp* laid) ⬦ *pt* ⊳ **lie**. ⬦ *vt* -1. [in specified position] colocar -2. [prepare - trap, snare] armar; [- plans] traçar; to ~ the table pôr a mesa -3. [bricks] assentar; [carpet] colocar; [cable]

afixar; [pipes, foundations] preparar -4. [egg] pôr -5. [blame, emphasis] aplicar. ⬦ *adj* -1. RELIG leigo(ga) -2. [untrained, unqualified] desqualificado(da).

◆ **lay aside** *vt sep* -1. [save] poupar -2. [put down, abandon] abandonar.

◆ **lay down** *vt sep* -1. [formulate] formular -2. [put down] depor.

◆ **lay off** ⬦ *vt sep* [make redundant] dispensar. ⬦ *vt fus inf* -1. [leave alone] deixar sozinho(nha) -2. [stop, give up] parar de.

◆ **lay on** *vt sep* UK [provide, supply] providenciar.

◆ **lay out** *vt sep* -1. [arrange, spread out] dispor -2. [plan, design] projetar.

layabout ['leɪəbaʊt] *n* UK *inf* vadio *m*, -dia *f*.

lay-by (*pl* -s) *n* UK acostamento *m*.

layer ['leɪə'] *n* -1. [of substance, material] camada *f* -2. *fig* [level] nível *m*.

layman ['leɪmən] (*pl* -men [-mən]) *n* leigo *m*; in ~'s terms em termos gerais.

layout ['leɪaʊt] *n* [design] leiaute *m*.

laze [leɪz] *vi*: to ~ (about OR around) vadiar.

lazy ['leɪzɪ] (*compar* -ier, *superl* -iest) *adj* -1. [person] preguiçoso(sa) -2. [action] ocioso(sa).

lazybones ['leɪzɪbəʊnz] (*pl inv*) *n inf* preguiçoso *m*, -sa *f*.

lb *abbr of* pound.

LCD (*abbr of* liquid crystal display) *n* tela *f* de cristal líquido, LCD *m*.

Ld (*abbr of* Lord) Lorde.

lead¹ [li:d] (*pt & pp* led) ⬦ *n* -1. (U) [winning position] dianteira *f*; to be in OR have the ~ estar na frente -2. [amount ahead] vantagem *f* -3. (U) [initiative, example] exemplo *m*; to take the ~ [do sthg first] tomar a iniciativa -4. (U) [most important role]: the ~ o papel principal -5. [clue] pista *f* -6. [for dog] correia *f* -7. [wire, cable] fio *m*. ⬦ *adj* [most important] principal. ⬦ *vt* -1. [be in front of] dirigir -2. [take, guide] conduzir -3. [head, be in charge of] chefiar, comandar -4. [organize] organizar -5. [life, existence] reger -6. [cause, influence]: to ~ sb to do sthg induzir alguém a fazer algo. ⬦ *vi* -1. [go] levar -2. [give access to]: that door ~s to the kitchen aquela porta dá para a cozinha -3. [be winning] estar na frente -4. [result in]: to ~ to sthg resultar em algo.

◆ **lead up to** *vt fus* -1. [precede] conduzir a -2. [in conversation] levar a.

lead² [led] ⬦ *n* -1. (U) [metal] chumbo *m* -2. [in pencil] grafite *m*. ⬦ *comp* [made of or with lead] de chumbo.

leaded ['ledɪd] *adj* **-1.** [petrol] com chumbo **-2.** [window] com almofada de vidro.

leader ['li:dəʳ] *n* **-1.** [gen] líder *mf* **-2.** UK [in newspaper] editorial *m*.

leadership ['li:dəʃɪp] *n* **-1.** [people in charge]: **the ~** a liderança **-2.** [position of leader] liderança *f*.

lead-free [led-] *adj* sem chumbo.

leading ['li:dɪŋ] *adj* **-1.** [prominent] destacado(da) **-2.** SPORT [at front] primeiro(-ra).

leading light *n* figura *f* central.

leaf [li:f] (*pl* **leaves**) *n* **-1.** [gen] folha *f* **-2.** [of table] aba *f*.

◆ **leaf through** *vt fus* folhear.

leaflet ['li:flɪt] *n* folder *m*, folheto *m*.

league [li:g] *n* liga *f*; **to be in ~ with sb** [work with] estar confabulado(da) com alguém.

leak [li:k] ◇ *n* **-1.** [gen] vazamento *m*; **a ~ in the roof** uma goteira **-2.** *fig* [disclosure] vazamento *m (de informações)*. ◇ *vt* [make known] vazar. ◇ *vi* **-1.** [gen] vazar; [boat, shoe]: **to be ~ing** estar com infiltração **-2.** [roof] ter goteiras.

◆ **leak out** *vi* [gen] vazar; **to ~ (out) from sthg** vazar de dentro de algo.

leakage ['li:kɪdʒ] *n* vazamento *m*.

lean [li:n] (*pt & pp* **leant** OR **-ed**) ◇ *adj* **-1.** [gen] magro(gra) **-2.** *fig* [harvest, year] improdutivo(va). ◇ *vt* [support, prop]: **to ~ sthg against sthg** apoiar algo contra algo. ◇ *vi* **-1.** [bend, slope] inclinar-se **-2.** [rest]: **to ~ on/against sthg** apoiar-se em/contra algo.

◆ **lean back** *vi* [person] recostar-se.

leaning ['li:nɪŋ] *n*: **~ (towards sthg)** inclinação *f* (para algo).

leant [lent] *pt & pp* ▷ **lean**.

lean-to (*pl* **-s**) *n* alpendre *m*.

leap [li:p] (*pt & pp* **leapt** OR **-ed**) ◇ *n* **-1.** [jump] salto *m*, pulo *m* **-2.** [increase] pulo *m*; **in ~s and bounds** com extrema rapidez. ◇ *vi* **-1.** [jump] saltar, pular **-2.** [increase] disparar; **to ~ to the eye** saltar aos olhos.

leapfrog ['li:pfrɒg] (*pt & pp* **-ged**, *cont* **-ging**) ◇ *n (U)* jogo *m* de pular carniça; **to play ~** brincar de pular carniça. ◇ *vi* **-1.** [jump]: **to ~ over sthg** saltar por cima de algo **-2.** *fig* aproveitar-se de.

leapt [lept] *pt & pp* ▷ **leap**.

leap year *n* ano *m* bissexto.

learn [lɜ:n] (*pt & pp* **-ed** OR **learnt**) ◇ *vt* **-1.** [gen] aprender; **to ~ (how) to do sthg** aprender a fazer algo **-2.** [hear] ouvir; **to ~ that** ficar sabendo que.

◇ *vi* **-1.** [acquire knowledge, skill] aprender **-2.** [hear]: **to ~ of** OR **about sthg** ficar sabendo de algo.

learned ['lɜ:nɪd] *adj* **-1.** [person] culto(-ta), erudito(ta) **-2.** [journal, paper, book] erudito(ta).

learner ['lɜ:nəʳ] *n* aprendiz *mf*.

learner (driver) *n* aprendiz *mf* de direção.

learning ['lɜ:nɪŋ] *n* **-1.** [knowledge] erudição *f* **-2.** [study] aprendizagem *f*.

learnt [lɜ:nt] *pt & pp* ▷ **learn**.

lease [li:s] ◇ *n* JUR arrendamento *m*, contrato *m* de locação. ◇ *vt* [premises] arrendar, alugar; **to ~ sthg from/to sb** arrendar algo de/para alguém; [car] fazer um leasing.

leasehold ['li:shəʊld] ◇ *adj* arrendado(da). ◇ *adv* em arrendamento.

leash [li:ʃ] *n* [for dog] coleira *f*.

least [li:st] ◇ *adj* (*superl of little*) [smallest in amount, degree]: **the ~ o (a)** menor; **he earns the ~ money of all** de todos ele é o que ganha menos. ◇ *pron* (*superl of little*) [smallest amount]: **the ~ o** mínimo; **it's the ~ we'll have to spend** é o mínimo que teremos de gastar; **that's the ~ of my worries!** essa é a menor das minhas preocupações!; **it's the ~ (that) he can do** é o mínimo que ele podia fazer; **not in the ~** em absoluto, de modo algum; **to say the ~** para não dizer outra coisa. ◇ *adv* [to the smallest amount, degree] menos; **to aim for the ~ possible expenditure** desejar alcançar o menor gasto possível.

◆ **at least** *adv* **-1.** [gen] pelo menos, no mínimo **-2.** [qualifying sthg one has said] pelo menos.

◆ **least of all** *adv* muito menos.

◆ **not least** *adv fml* em especial.

leather ['leðəʳ] ◇ *n (U)* couro *m*. ◇ *comp* de couro.

leave [li:v] (*pt & pp* **left**) ◇ *n* **-1.** [time off] licença *f*; **to be on ~** estar de licença **-2.** *fml* [permission] licença *f*, permissão *f*. ◇ *vt* **-1.** [gen] deixar; **~ me alone!** me deixa em paz!; **it ~s a lot to be desired** isso deixa muito a desejar **-2.** [depart from] sair de **-3.** [entrust]: **to ~ it to sb to do sthg** deixar que alguém faça algo; **to ~ sthg/with sb** deixar algo com alguém; **~ it with me!** deixa (isso) comigo!; **to ~ sb sthg**, **to ~ sthg to sb** deixar algo para alguém **-4.** [husband, wife] deixar, largar. ◇ *vi* **-1.** [gen] partir, ir embora **-2.** [end relationship] ir embora.

leave behind *vt sep* -1. [abandon] abandonar - 2. [forget] esquecer.

leave out *vt sep* [omit] excluir, deixar de fora.

leave of absence *n* licença *f*.

leaves [li:vz] *pl* ⊳ **leaf**.

Lebanon ['lebənən] *n* Líbano.

lecherous ['letʃərəs] *adj* lascivo(va).

lecture ['lektʃə'] ⟨⟩ *n* -1. [talk - at university] aula *f*; [- at conference] palestra *f*, conferência *f* - 2. [criticism, reprimand] sermão *m*. ⟨⟩ *vt* [scold] dar um sermão em. ⟨⟩ *vi* [university]: **to ~ (on/in sthg)** dar uma aula (sobre algo); [at conference] dar uma palestra (sobre algo).

lecturer ['lektʃərə'] *n* -1. [teacher] professor *m*, -ra *f* - 2. [speaker] palestrante *mf*, conferencista *mf*.

led [led] *pt & pp* ⊳ **lead**[1].

ledge [ledʒ] *n* -1. [of window] parapeito *m* - 2. [of mountain] saliência *f*.

ledger ['ledʒə'] *n* livro *m* contábil.

leech [li:tʃ] *n* -1. [creature] sanguessuga *f* - 2. *fig & pej* [person] sanguessuga *f*.

leek [li:k] *n* alho-poró *m*.

leer [lɪə'] ⟨⟩ *n* olhar *m* malicioso. ⟨⟩ *vi*: **to ~ at sb** olhar maliciosamente para alguém.

leeway ['li:weɪ] *n* (U) [room to manoeuvre] liberdade *f* de ação.

left [left] ⟨⟩ *pt & pp* ⊳ **leave**. ⟨⟩ *adj* -1. [remaining] sobrando; **do you have any money ~?** tem algum dinheiro sobrando?; **to be ~** sobrar; **there's no milk ~** não sobrou leite - 2. [side, hand, foot] esquerdo(da). ⟨⟩ *adv* para a esquerda. ⟨⟩ *n* (U) [direction]: **on/to the ~** à esquerda; **keep ~** mantenha-se à esquerda.

Left *n* POL: **the Left** a esquerda.

left-hand *adj* esquerdo(da); **~ side** lado *m* esquerdo.

left-hand drive *adj* com direção do lado esquerdo.

left-handed [-'hændɪd] *adj* -1. [person] canhoto(ta) - 2. [implement] para canhotos.

left luggage (office) *n* UK guarda-bagagem *m*.

leftover ['leftəʊvə'] *adj* restante.

leftovers *npl* sobras *fpl*.

left wing *n* POL esquerda *f*.

left-wing *adj* POL esquerdista, de esquerda.

leg [leg] *n* -1. [gen] perna *f*; **to pull sb's ~** pegar no pé de alguém; [of animal, bird, insect] pata *f* - 2. [CULIN - of chicken] coxa *f*; [- of frog, lamb] perna *f*; [- of pork] pernil *m* - 3. [of journey, tournament] etapa *f*.

legacy ['legəsɪ] (*pl* -ies) *n* -1. [gift of money] legado *m* - 2. *fig* [consequence] herança *f*.

legal ['li:gl] *adj* -1. [concerning the law] jurídico(ca) - 2. [lawful] legal.

legalize, -ise ['li:gəlaɪz] *vt* legalizar.

legal tender *n* (U) moeda *f* corrente.

legend ['ledʒənd] *n* -1. [myth] lenda *f* - 2. *fig* [person] lenda *f*.

leggings ['legɪnz] *npl* calças *fpl* stretch.

legible ['ledʒəbl] *adj* legível.

legislation [,ledʒɪs'leɪʃn] *n* (U) legislação *f*.

legislature ['ledʒɪsleɪtʃə'] *n* legislatura *f*.

legitimate [lɪ'dʒɪtɪmət] *adj* legítimo(-ma).

legless ['leglɪs] *adj* UK inf [drunk] bêbado(da) como um gambá.

legroom ['legrʊm] *n* (U) espaço *m* para as pernas.

leg-warmers [-,wɔ:məz] *npl* polainas *fpl*.

leisure [UK 'leʒə', US 'li:ʒər] *n* (U) lazer *m*; **do it at (your) ~** faça quando puder.

leisure centre *n* centro *m* de lazer.

leisurely [UK 'leʒəlɪ, US 'li:ʒərlɪ] ⟨⟩ *adj* calmo(ma). ⟨⟩ *adv* calmamente.

leisure time *n* (tempo *m* de) lazer *m*.

lemon ['lemən] *n* [fruit] limão *m*.

lemonade [,lemə'neɪd] *n* -1. UK [fizzy] soda *f* limonada - 2. [made with fresh lemons] limonada *f*.

lemon juice *n* suco *m* de limão.

lemon sole *n* solha-limão *m*.

lemon squash *n* UK suco *m* de limão.

lemon squeezer [-'skwi:zə'] *n* espremedor *m* de limão.

lemon tea *n* chá *m* com limão.

lend [lend] (*pt & pp* lent) *vt* -1. [money, book] emprestar; **to ~ sb sthg, to ~ sthg to sb** emprestar algo para alguém - 2. [support, assistance]: **to ~ sthg (to sb)** dar algo (a alguém) - 3. [credibility, quality]: **to ~ sthg to sthg** conferir algo a algo.

lending rate ['lendɪn-] *n* taxa *f* de empréstimo.

length [leŋθ] *n* -1. [gen] comprimento *m*; **what ~ is it?** quanto tem de comprimento?; **it's five metres in ~** são cinco metros de comprimento - 2. [of swimming pool] piscina *f* - 3. [piece] pedaço *m* - 4. (U) [duration] duração *f* - 5. *phr*: **to go to great ~s to do sthg** não medir esforços para fazer algo.

at length *adv* -1. [eventually] no final das contas - 2. [in detail] detalhadamente.

lengthen ['leŋθən] ⟨⟩ *vt* -1. [skirt] alongar - 2. [life] prolongar. ⟨⟩ *vi* alongar-se, ficar mais longo(ga).

lengthways ['leŋθweɪz] *adv* ao compri-do.

lengthy ['leŋθɪ] (*compar* **-ier**, *superl* **-iest**) *adj* longo(ga).

lenient ['li:njənt] *adj* leniente, indulgente.

lens [lenz] *n* -**1.** [made of glass] lente *f* - **2.** [contact lens] lente *f* (de contato).

lent [lent] *pt* & *pp* ⊳ **lend**.

Lent [lent] *n* (*U*) quaresma *f*.

lentil ['lentɪl] *n* lentilha *f*.

Leo ['li:əʊ] *n* [sign] leão *m*.

leopard ['lepəd] *n* leopardo *m*.

leotard ['li:ətɑ:d] *n* malha *f* (*usada por dançarinos, acrobatas*).

leper ['lepəʳ] *n* [person with leprosy] lepro-so *m*, -sa *f*.

leprosy ['leprəsɪ] *n* (*U*) lepra *f*.

lesbian ['lezbɪən] *n* lésbica *f*.

less [les] (*compar of little*) ◇ *adj* [not as much] menos; ~ ... than menos ... (do) que; ~ **and** ~ cada vez menos. ◇ *pron* [not as much] menos; ~ **than** menos (do) que; **the** ~ **you work the** ~ **you earn** quanto menos você trabalha, menos você ganha; **no** ~ **than** nada menos que. ◇ *adv* [to a smaller extent] menos; ~ **and** ~ cada vez menos. ◇ *prep* [minus] menos.

lessen ['lesn] *vt* & *vi* diminuir.

lesser ['lesəʳ] *adj* menor; **to a** ~ **extent** OR **degree** em menor grau.

lesson ['lesn] *n* -**1.** [class] aula *f* - **2.** [example] lição *f*; **to teach sb a** ~ ensinar uma lição a alguém.

let [let] (*pt* & *pp* **let**, *cont* **-ting**) *vt* -**1.** [allow]: **to** ~ **sb do sthg** deixar alguém fazer algo; **she** ~ **her hair grow** ela deixou o cabeço crescer; **to** ~ **go of sb/ sthg, to** ~ **sb/sthg go** soltar alguém/ algo; [release] soltar alguém/algo; **to** ~ **sb know sthg** informar alguém de algo, informar algo a alguém -**2.** (*in verb forms*): ~**'s go!** vamos!; ~**'s see** agora vejamos; ~ **them wait!** eles que esperem! - **3.** [rent out] alugar; **'to** ~**' 'aluga-se'.**

➥ **let alone** *conj* [much less]: **he couldn't walk**, ~ **alone jump** ele não conseguia caminhar, que dirá pular.

➥ **let down** *vt sep* -**1.** [deflate] esvaziar - **2.** [disappoint] desapontar.

➥ **let in** *vt sep* -**1.** [admit] deixar entrar - **2.** [air, water] deixar entrar.

➥ **let off** *vt sep* -**1.** [excuse, allow not to do]: **to** ~ **sb off sthg** eximir alguém de algo -**2.** [criminal, pupil, child] deixar impune -**3.** [bomb, explosive] detonar - **4.** [firework] estourar.

➥ **let on** *vi* contar (*um segredo*); **don't** ~ **on!** não conta nada!

➥ **let out** *vt sep* -**1.** [gen] deixar sair - **2.** [sound, cry, laugh] emitir -**3.** [garment] alargar.

➥ **let up** *vi* -**1.** [heat, rain] cessar -**2.** [person] relaxar.

letdown ['letdaʊn] *n inf* decepção *f*.

lethal ['li:θl] *adj* letal.

lethargic [lə'θɑ:dʒɪk] *adj* letárgico(ca).

let's [lets] = **let us**.

letter ['letəʳ] *n* -**1.** [written message] carta *f* - **2.** [of alphabet] letra *f*.

letter bomb *n* carta-bomba *f*.

letterbox ['letəbɒks] *n UK* -**1.** [in door] portinhola *f* para cartas -**2.** [in street] caixa *f* de correio.

letter of credit *n* carta *f* de crédito.

lettuce ['letɪs] *n* alface *f*.

letup ['letʌp] *n* pausa *f*, intervalo *m*.

leuk(a)emia [lu:'ki:mɪə] *n* leucemia *f*.

level ['levl] (*UK* *pt* & *pp* **-led**, *cont* **-ling**, *US* *pt* & *pp* **-ed**, *cont* **-ing**) ◇ *adj* -**1.** [equal in height] nivelado(da); **to be** ~ **(with sthg)** estar nivelado(da) (com algo) -**2.** [equal in standard] em pé de igualdade -**3.** [flat - floor, field] plano(na); [- spoon, cup] raso(sa). ◇ *n* -**1.** [gen] nível *m* - **2.** *US* [spirit level] nível *m* (de bolha) -**3.** [storey] andar *m* - **4.** *phr*: **to be on the** ~ *inf* ser sincero(ra). ◇ *vt* -**1.** [make flat] nivelar, aplainar -**2.** [demolish] derrubar.

➥ **level off, level out** *vi* estabilizar-se.

➥ **level with** *vt fus inf* [be honest with] ser sincero(ra) com.

level crossing *n UK* passagem *f* de nível.

level-headed [-'hedɪd] *adj* equilibrado(da), sensato(ta).

lever [*UK* 'li:vəʳ, *US* 'levəʳ] *n* alavanca *f*.

leverage [*UK* 'li:vərɪdʒ, *US* 'levərɪdʒ] *n* (*U*) -**1.** *fig* [influence] influência *f* - **2.** [force] alavancagem *f*, força *f*.

levy ['levɪ] (*pt* & *pp* **-ied**) ◇ *n* [financial contribution, tax]: ~ **(on sthg)** taxa *f* (sobre algo). ◇ *vt* [demand, collect] arrecadar.

lewd [lju:d] *adj* [behaviour] lascivo(va), obsceno(na).

liability [ˌlaɪə'bɪlətɪ] (*pl* **-ies**) *n* -**1.** [hindrance] estorvo *m* - **2.** *JUR* (*U*) [legal responsibility]: ~ **(for sthg)** responsabilidade *f* (por algo).

➥ **liabilities** *npl FIN* [debts] passivos *mpl*, obrigações *fpl*.

liable ['laɪəbl] *adj* -**1.** [likely]: **she is** ~ **to do something stupid** é bem provável que ela faça algo estúpido -**2.** [prone]: **to be** ~ **to sthg** estar propenso(sa) a algo -**3.** *JUR*: **to be** ~ **(for sthg)** [legally responsible] ser legalmente responsável (por algo); **to be ~ to** sthg [punishable] estar sujeito(ta) a algo.

liaise [lɪ'eɪz] vi: **to ~ (with)** fazer contato (com); **to ~ (between)** criar vínculos (entre).

liar ['laɪəʳ] n mentiroso m, -sa f.

libel ['laɪbl] (UK pt & pp -**led**, cont -**ling**, US pt & pp -**ed**, cont -**ing**) ◇ n libelo m. ◇ vt difamar.

liberal ['lɪbərəl] ◇ adj -**1.** [tolerant] liberal -**2.** [generous] generoso(sa). ◇ n liberal mf.

→ **Liberal** POL ◇ adj liberal. ◇ n liberal mf.

Liberal Democrat ◇ adj liberal democrata. ◇ n liberal democrata mf.

liberate ['lɪbəreɪt] vt libertar.

liberation [ˌlɪbə'reɪʃn] n (U) -**1.** [release] libertação f -**2.** fig [emancipation] libertação f.

liberty ['lɪbətɪ] (pl -**ies**) n [gen] liberdade f; at ~ em liberdade; **to be at ~ to do** sthg ter liberdade para fazer algo; **to take liberties (with** sb) tomar liberdades (com alguém).

Libra ['liːbrə] n [sign] Libra f.

librarian [laɪ'breərɪən] n bibliotecário m, -ria f.

library ['laɪbrərɪ] (pl -**ies**) n biblioteca f.

library book n livro m de biblioteca.

libretto [lɪ'bretəʊ] (pl -**s**) n libreto m.

Libya ['lɪbɪə] n Líbia f.

lice [laɪs] pl ⊳ **louse**.

licence ['laɪsəns] ◇ n -**1.** [permit - gen] licença f; [- for marriage] autorização f; [- for pilot] brevê m -**2.** COMM licença f. ◇ vt US = **license**.

license ['laɪsəns] ◇ vt COMM autorizar. ◇ n US = **licence**.

licensed ['laɪsənst] adj -**1.** [person]: **to be ~ to do** sthg estar autorizado(da) a fazer algo -**2.** [object - car, dog] com licença; [- gun] registrado(da) -**3.** UK [premises] autorizado(da) a vender álcool.

license plate n US placa f (de automóvel).

lick [lɪk] vt [with tongue] lamber.

licorice ['lɪkərɪs] n = **liquorice**.

lid [lɪd] n -**1.** [cover] tampa f -**2.** [eyelid] pálpebra f.

lie [laɪ] (pt sense 1 **lied**, pt senses 2-4 **lay**, pp sense 1 **lied**, pp senses 2-4 **lain**, cont all senses **lying**) ◇ n mentira f; **to tell ~s** contar mentiras. ◇ vi -**1.** [tell untruth] mentir; **to ~ to** sb mentir para alguém -**2.** [to be lying down] estar deitado(da) -**3.** [lie down] deitar -**4.** [be situated] encontrar-se -**5.** phr: **to ~ low** ficar escondido(da).

→ **lie about, lie around** vi -**1.** [people] andar sem fazer nada, vadiar -**2.** [things] estar jogado(da).

→ **lie down** vi deitar-se.

→ **lie in** vi UK ficar na cama até tarde.

Liechtenstein ['lɪktən,staɪn] n Liechtenstein.

lie-down n UK: **to have a ~** repousar.

lie-in n UK: **to have a ~** ficar na cama até tarde.

lieutenant [UK lef'tenənt, US luː'tenənt] n tenente m.

life [laɪf] (pl **lives**) n -**1.** [gen] vida f; **to come to ~** criar vida; **that's ~!** é a vida!; **to scare the ~ out of** sb quase matar alguém do coração -**2.** (U) inf [life imprisonment] prisão f perpétua.

life assurance n = **life insurance**.

life belt n cinto m salva-vidas.

lifeboat ['laɪfbəʊt] n -**1.** [on ship] bote m salva-vidas -**2.** [on shore] lancha f de salvamento.

life buoy n bóia f salva-vidas.

life cycle n ciclo m vital.

life expectancy n espectativa f de vida.

lifeguard ['laɪfgɑːd] n salva-vidas mf inv.

life imprisonment [-ɪm'prɪznmənt] n prisão f perpétua.

life insurance n (U) seguro m de vida.

life jacket n colete m salva-vidas.

lifeless ['laɪflɪs] adj -**1.** [dead] sem vida, morto(ta) -**2.** [listless] apagado(da).

lifelike ['laɪflaɪk] adj -**1.** [statue, doll] realista -**2.** [portrait] fiel.

lifeline ['laɪflaɪn] n -**1.** [rope] corda f de segurança -**2.** fig [with outside] cordão m umbilical.

lifelong ['laɪflɒŋ] adj de toda a vida.

life preserver [-prɪ,zɜːvəʳ] n US -**1.** [belt] cinto m salva-vidas -**2.** [jacket] colete m salva-vidas.

life raft n balsa f salva-vidas.

lifesaver ['laɪf,seɪvəʳ] n [person] salvavidas mf inv.

life sentence n pena f de prisão perpétua.

life-size(d) [-saɪz(d)] adj em tamanho natural.

lifespan ['laɪfspæn] n -**1.** [of person, animal, plant] vida f -**2.** [of product, machine] vida f útil.

lifestyle ['laɪfstaɪl] n estilo m de vida.

life-support system n sistema m de respiração artificial.

lifetime ['laɪftaɪm] n [length of time] vida f.

lift [lɪft] ◇ n -**1.** [ride] carona f -**2.** UK [elevator] elevador m. ◇ vt -**1.** [gen]

levantar; **he ~ ed the books off the shelf** ele tirou os livros da estante **- 2.** [ban, embargo] revogar **- 3.** [plagiarize] plagiar **- 4.** *inf* [steal] levantar. ⬦ *vi* **- 1.** [lid, top] levantar **- 2.** [mist, fog, clouds] dissipar-se.

lift-off *n* decolagem *f*.

light [laɪt] (*pt* & *pp* **lit** *OR* **-ed**) ⬦ *adj* **- 1.** [gen] leve **- 2.** [not dark] claro(ra). ⬦ *adv*: **to travel ~** viajar com pouca bagagem. ⬦ *n* **- 1.** [gen] luz *f* **- 2.** [for cigarette, pipe] fogo *m*; **to set ~ to sthg** atear fogo em algo **- 3.** [perspective]: **in the ~ of** *UK*, **in ~ of** *US* à luz de **- 4.** *phr*: **to come to ~** vir à luz; **there's a ~ at the end of the tunnel** há uma luz no fim do túnel; **to make ~ of sthg** não dar a devida importância a algo. ⬦ *vt* **- 1.** [ignite] acender **- 2.** [illuminate] iluminar. ➡ **light up** ⬦ *vt sep* **- 1.** [illuminate] iluminar **- 2.** [start smoking] acender. ⬦ *vi* **- 1.** [look happy] iluminar-se **- 2.** *inf* [start smoking] pôr-se a fumar.

light bulb *n* lâmpada *f*.

lighten [laɪtn] ⬦ *vt* **- 1.** [make brighter] clarear **- 2.** [make less heavy] aliviar. ⬦ *vi* **- 1.** [brighten] iluminar-se **- 2.** [become happier, more relaxed] alegrar-se.

lighter [laɪtər] *n* [cigarette lighter] isqueiro *m*.

light-headed [-ˈhedɪd] *adj* tonto(ta).

light-hearted [-ˈhɑːtɪd] *adj* **- 1.** [cheerful] despreocupado(da) **- 2.** [amusing] alegre.

lighthouse [laɪthaʊs, *pl* -haʊzɪz] *n* farol *m*.

lighting [laɪtɪŋ] *n* (*U*) iluminação *f*.

light meter *n PHOT* fotômetro *m*.

lightning [laɪtnɪŋ] *n* (*U*) raio *m*, relâmpago *m*.

lightweight [laɪtweɪt] ⬦ *adj* [object] leve. ⬦ *n* [boxer] peso *m* leve.

likable [laɪkəbl] *adj* simpático(ca), agradável.

like [laɪk] ⬦ *prep* **- 1.** [similar to] como; **to look ~ sb/sthg** parecer-se com alguém/algo, parecer alguém/algo; **what did it taste ~?** tinha gosto de quê?; **what did it look ~?** como era?; **what did it sound ~?** como era o barulho?; **~ this/that** assim **- 2.** [such as] (tal) como. ⬦ *vt* **- 1.** [enjoy, find pleasant, approve of] gostar; **to ~ doing** *OR* **to do sthg** gostar de fazer algo **- 2.** [want, wish] querer; **to ~ to do sthg** desejar fazer algo; **to ~ sb to do sthg** desejar que alguém faça algo; **I'd ~ you to come** gostaria que você viesse. ⬦ *n*: **the ~ of sb/sthg** alguém/algo do estilo. ➡ **likes** *npl* [things one likes] gostos *mpl*.

likeable [laɪkəbl] *adj* = likable.

likelihood [laɪklɪhʊd] *n* (*U*) probabilidade *f*.

likely [laɪklɪ] *adj* **- 1.** [probable] provável; **rain is ~ later on** é provável que chova mais tarde; **to be ~ to do sthg** ser provável que algo aconteça; **he's ~ to come** é provável que ele venha; **a ~ story!** *iro* pura invenção! **- 2.** [suitable] indicado(da).

liken [laɪkn] *vt*: **to ~ sb/sthg to** comparar alguém/algo a.

likeness [laɪknɪs] *n* semelhança *f*; **~ to sb/sthg** semelhança com alguém/algo.

likewise [laɪkwaɪz] *adv* [similarly] da mesma maneira; **to do ~** fazer o mesmo.

liking [laɪkɪŋ] *n*: **~ for sb/sthg** afeição *f* por alguém/algo; **to have a ~ for sb/ sthg** ter afeição por alguém/algo; **to be to sb's ~** estar ao gosto de alguém.

lilac [laɪlək] ⬦ *adj* [colour] lilás. ⬦ *n* **- 1.** [tree] lilás *m* **- 2.** (*U*) [colour] lilás *m*.

Lilo® [laɪləʊ] (*pl* -s) *n UK* colchão *m* inflável.

lily [lɪlɪ] (*pl* -ies) *n* lírio *m*.

lily of the valley (*pl* lilies of the valley) *n* lírio-do-vale *m*.

Lima [liːmə] *n* Lima.

limb [lɪm] *n* **- 1.** [of body] membro *m* **- 2.** [of tree] ramo *m*.

limber [lɪmbər] ➡ **limber up** *vi* fazer aquecimento, aquecer.

limbo [lɪmbəʊ] (*pl* -s) *n* (*U*) [uncertain state]: **to be in ~** estar no limbo.

lime [laɪm] *n* **- 1.** [fruit] lima *f*; **~ (juice)** (suco *m* de) lima *f* **- 2.** [linden tree] tília *f* **- 3.** (*U*) [substance] cal *f*.

limelight [laɪmlaɪt] *n*: **to be in the ~** estar no/ser o centro das atenções.

limerick [lɪmərɪk] *n poema humorístico de cinco linhas*.

limestone [laɪmstəʊn] *n* (*U*) calcário *m*, pedra *f* calcária.

limey [laɪmɪ] (*pl* -s) *n US inf termo pejorativo que designa um inglês*.

limit [lɪmɪt] ⬦ *n* limite *m*; **to be off ~s** ser/estar proibido(da); **within ~s** [to a certain extent] até certo ponto. ⬦ *vt* limitar, restringir.

limitation [ˌlɪmɪˈteɪʃn] *n* limitação *f*.

limited [lɪmɪtɪd] *adj* [restricted] limitado(da).

limited company *n* companhia *f* limitada.

limited liability company *n* = limited company.

limousine [lɪməziːn] *n* limusine *f*.

limp [lɪmp] ⬦ *adj* **- 1.** [hand, handshake]

sem firmeza **- 2.** [body, lettuce] murcho(-cha) **- 3.** [excuse] mole. $\diamond$ *n* manqueira *f.* $\diamond$ *vi* mancar.

limpet ['lɪmpɪt] *n* lapa *f.*

line [laɪn] $\diamond$ *n* **- 1.** [gen] linha *f;* **washing ~** corda *f* de varal; **power ~** cabo *m* de força; **to draw the ~ at doing sthg** *fig* estabelecer limites para fazer algo **- 2.** [row] fileira *f,* linha *f* **- 3.** [queue] fila *f;* **to stand** OR **wait in ~** ficar OR esperar em fila **- 4.** [alignment] alinhamento *m;* **in ~ with** em linha com; **to step out of ~** sair da linha **- 5.** [RAIL - railway track] linha *f (férrea);* [- route] linha *f* **- 6.** [in writing - of text] linha *f* **- 7.** [wrinkle] ruga *f* **- 8.** TELEC [telephone connection] linha *f (telefônica)* **- 9.** *inf* [short letter]: **to drop sb a ~** escrever umas linhas para alguém **- 10.** *inf* [field of activity] ramo *m.* $\diamond$ *vt* [cover inside surface of] forrar.

$\blacktriangleright$ **out of line** *adj* inaceitável.

$\blacktriangleright$ **line up** $\diamond$ *vt sep* **- 1.** [in rows] alinhar **- 2.** *inf* [organize] arranjar, organizar. $\diamond$ *vi* **- 1.** [in a row] alinhar-se **- 2.** [in a queue] pôr-se na fila.

lined [laɪnd] *adj* **- 1.** [paper] pautado(da) **- 2.** [face] enrugado(da).

linen ['lɪnɪn] *(U) n* **- 1.** [cloth] linho *m* **- 2.** [sheets] roupa *f* de cama **- 3.** [tablecloths] toalha *f (de mesa).*

liner ['laɪnə'] *n* [ship] transatlântico *m.*

linesman ['laɪnzmən] *(pl* **-men** [-mən]) *n* SPORT juiz *m* de linha.

line-up *n* **- 1.** [of players, competitors] seleção *f* **- 2.** US [identification parade] fila *f* de identificação.

linger ['lɪŋgə'] *vi* **- 1.** [dawdle] demorar-se **- 2.** [persist] persistir.

lingo ['lɪŋgəʊ] *(pl* **-es**) *n inf* idioma *f.*

linguist ['lɪŋgwɪst] *n* **- 1.** [someone good at languages] pessoa *f* com facilidade para os idiomas **- 2.** [student or teacher of linguistics] lingüista *mf.*

lining ['laɪnɪŋ] *n* **- 1.** [of coat, curtains, box] forro *m* **- 2.** [of stomach, nose] paredes *fpl* internas **- 3.** AUT [of brakes] revestimento *m.*

link [lɪŋk] $\diamond$ *n* **- 1.** [of chain] elo *m* **- 2.** COMPUT [conexão] *m* **- 3.** [connection] conexão *f;* **~ between sb/sthg** vínculo *m* OR ligação *f* entre alguém/algo; **~ with sb/sthg** vínculo OR ligação com alguém/algo. $\diamond$ *vt* **- 1.** [relate] ligar, relacionar; **to ~ sb/sthg with** OR **to sb/sthg** ligar alguém/algo com OR a alguém/algo, relacionar alguém/algo com OR a alguém/algo **- 2.** [connect physically] enlaçar.

$\blacktriangleright$ **link up** $\diamond$ *vt sep* [connect] conectar;

to ~ sthg up with sthg conectar algo a algo.

links [lɪŋks] *(pl inv) n* SPORT campo *m* de golfe.

lino ['laɪnəʊ], **linoleum** [lɪ'nəʊljəm] *n (U)* linóleo *m.*

lintel ['lɪntl] *n* verga *f (de porta ou janela).*

lion ['laɪən] *n* leão *m.*

lioness ['laɪənes] *n* leoa *f.*

lip [lɪp] *n* **- 1.** [of mouth] lábio *m;* **to keep a stiff upper ~** manter-se firme **- 2.** [of container] borda *f.*

liposuction ['lɪpəʊˌsʌkʃn] *n* lipoaspiração *f.*

lip-read *vi* ler nos lábios.

lip salve [-sælv] *n UK* pomada *f* para lábios.

lip service *n*: **to pay ~ to sthg** concordar com algo da boca para fora.

lipstick ['lɪpstɪk] *n* batom *m.*

liqueur [lɪ'kjʊə'] *n* licor *m.*

liquid ['lɪkwɪd] $\diamond$ *adj* [fluid] líquido(-da). $\diamond$ *n* [fluid] líquido *m.*

liquidation [ˌlɪkwɪ'deɪʃn] *n (U)* FIN falência *f;* **to go into ~** abrir falência.

liquidize, -ise ['lɪkwɪdaɪz] *vt UK* CULIN liquidificar.

liquidizer ['lɪkwɪdaɪzə'] *n UK* liquidificador *m.*

liquor ['lɪkə'] *n US* [alcohol] álcool *m;* [spirits] bebida *f* alcoólica.

liquorice ['lɪkərɪs, 'lɪkərɪʃ] *n (U)* alcaçuz *m.*

liquor store *n US* armazém *m* de bebidas alcoólicas.

Lisbon ['lɪzbən] *n* Lisboa; **in ~** em Lisboa.

lisp [lɪsp] $\diamond$ *n* ceceio *m.* $\diamond$ *vi* cecear.

list [lɪst] $\diamond$ *n* lista *f.* $\diamond$ *vt* [in writing, speech] listar.

listed building [ˌlɪstɪd-] *n UK* prédio *m* tombado.

listen ['lɪsn] *vi* **- 1.** [give attention] escutar, ouvir; **to ~ to sb/sthg** escutar alguém/algo; **to ~ for sthg** estar atento(ta) a algo **- 2.** [heed advice] dar atenção; **to ~ to sb/sthg** escutar alguém/algo.

listener ['lɪsnə'] *n* ouvinte *mf.*

listless ['lɪstlɪs] *adj* apático(ca).

lit [lɪt] *pt & pp* $\triangleright$ **light.**

liter *n US* = **litre.**

literacy ['lɪtərəsɪ] *n (U)* alfabetização *f.*

literal ['lɪtərəl] *adj* literal.

literally ['lɪtərəlɪ] *adv* literalmente; **to take sthg ~** levar algo ao pé da letra.

literary ['lɪtərərɪ] *adj* literário(ria); **a ~ man** um literato.

literate ['lɪtərət] *adj* **- 1.** [able to read and write] alfabetizado(da); **computer-~**

que tem conhecimentos de informáti-ca - **2.** [well-read] letrado(da), culto(ta).

literature ['lɪtrətʃəʳ] *n (U)* -**1.** [novels, plays, poetry] literatura *f* - **2.** [books on a particular subject] literatura *f*, bibliografia *f* - **3.** [printed information] informações *fpl*.

lithe [laɪð] *adj* ágil.

Lithuania [ˌlɪθjʊ'eɪnɪə] *n* Lituânia.

litigation [ˌlɪtɪ'geɪʃn] *n fml* litígio *m*.

litre *UK*, **liter** *US* ['liːtəʳ] *n* -**1.** [metric unit] litro *m* - **2.** [capacity of engine] cilindrada *f*.

litter ['lɪtəʳ] <> *n* -**1.** *(U)* [waste material] lixo *m* - **2.** [newborn animals] ninhada *f* - **3.** [for litter tray]: **(cat)** ~ areia *f* química *(para fezes de gato).* <> *vt*: to be ~ **ed with sthg** estar coberto(ta) de algo.

litter bin *n UK* cesto *m* de lixo.

little ['lɪtl] <> *adj* -**1.** [gen] pequeno(na) - **2.** [younger] menor; **my ~ brother** meu irmão mais novo - **3.** [short in time or distance] curto(ta) - **4.** [not much] pouco(ca); **she has a ~ money left** ela tem pouco dinheiro sobrando. <> *pron* [small amount] pouco(ca); **a ~ um** pouco; **a ~ (bit)** um pouquinho. <> *adv* -**1.** [to a limited extent] pouco; **he's ~ more than a waiter** ele é pouco mais do que um garçom; ~ **by** ~ pouco a pouco - **2.** [rarely] raramente; **we go there as ~ as possible** vamos à o mínimo possível.

little finger *n* dedo *m* mínimo, mingui-nho *m*.

live [lɪv] <> *vi* -**1.** [gen] viver - **2.** [reside] morar, viver. <> *vt* viver; **to ~ it up** *inf* curtir a vida.

● **live down** *vt sep* redimir-se de.

● **live off** *vt fus* -**1.** [savings] viver de - **2.** [parents, family] viver às custas de.

● **live on** <> *vt fus* -**1.** [money] viver - **2.** [food] viver de. <> *vi* [memory, feeling, works] perdurar.

● **live together** *vi* [cohabit] viver jun-tos(tas).

● **live up to** *vt fus* estar à altura de.

● **live with** *vt fus* -**1.** [cohabit with] viver com - **2.** *inf* [accept] conviver com.

livelihood ['laɪvlɪhʊd] *n* meio *m* de vida, sustento *m*.

lively ['laɪvlɪ] *(compar* -**ier**, *superl* -**iest)** *adj* -**1.** [gen] animado(da) - **2.** [mind, curiosity, imagination] sagaz, perspicaz.

liven ['laɪvn] ● **liven up** <> *vt sep* animar. <> *vi* [person] animar-se.

liver ['lɪvəʳ] *n* fígado *m*.

livery ['lɪvərɪ] *(pl* -**ies)** *n* -**1.** [uniform] libré *f* - **2.** [of a company] marca *f* distintiva.

lives [laɪvz] *pl* ⊳ **life**.

livestock ['laɪvstɒk] *n (U)* animais *mpl* de uma fazenda.

livid ['lɪvɪd] *adj* -**1.** *inf* [angry] furioso(sa) - **2.** [blue-grey] roxo(xa).

living ['lɪvɪŋ] <> *adj* vivo(va); ~ **proof** prova *f* viva. <> *n* -**1.** [people]: **the ~ os vivos** - **2.** [means of earning money]: **what do you do for a ~?** o que você faz para ganhar a vida?; **to scrape a ~** mal ganhar a vida - **3.** *(U)* [lifestyle] (estilo *m* de) vida *f*; **healthy ~** vida *f* saudável.

living conditions *npl* condições *fpl* de vida.

living room *n* sala *f* de estar.

living standards *npl* padrão *m* de vida.

living wage *n* salário *m* básico.

lizard ['lɪzəd] *n* -**1.** [large] lagarto *m* - **2.** [small] lagartixa *f*.

llama ['lɑːmə] *(pl inv OR* -**s)** *n* lhama *m*.

load [ləʊd] <> *n* -**1.** [gen] carga *f*; **to take a ~ off one's mind** tirar um peso da consciência - **2.** [burden] fardo *m* - **3.** [large amount]: ~ **s of,** **a ~ of** *inf* um monte de; **a ~ of rubbish** *inf* um monte de bobagem. <> *vt* -**1.** [container, vehicle, person] carregar; **to ~ sb/sthg with sthg** carregar alguém/algo de algo - **2.** [gun]: **to ~ sthg (with sthg)** carregar algo (com algo) - **3.** [in camera, video recorder]: **to ~ a film** colocar filme *(na câmera);* **to ~ a tape** colocar fita *(na filmadora)* - **4.** *COMPUT* [program] carregar.

▶ **load up** <> *vt sep* carregar. <> *vi* [with furniture, boxes] carregar.

loaded ['ləʊdɪd] *adj* -**1.** [question, statement] com duplo sentido - **2.** [gun, camera] carregado(da) - **3.** *inf* [rich] forrado(da).

loading bay ['ləʊdɪŋ-] *n* zona *f* de carga e descarga.

loaf [ləʊf] *(pl* **loaves)** *n* [of bread] (pedaço *m* de) pão *m*.

loafer ['ləʊfəʳ] *n* -**1.** [shoe] mocassim *m* - **2.** [lazy person] vadio *m*, -dia *f*.

loan [ləʊn] <> *n* empréstimo *m*; **on** ~ por empréstimo. <> *vt* emprestar; **to ~ sthg to sb,** **to ~ sb sthg** emprestar algo a alguém.

loath [ləʊθ] *adj*: **to be ~ to do sthg** estar pouco inclinado(a) a fazer algo.

loathe [ləʊð] *vt* odiar, detestar; **to ~ doing sthg** odiar fazer algo.

loathsome ['ləʊðsəm] *adj* repugnante.

loaves [ləʊvz] *pl* ⊳ **loaf**.

lob [lɒb] *(pt & pp* -**bed,** *cont* -**bing)** <> *n* *TENNIS* lob *m*. <> *vt* -**1.** [throw] lançar - **2.** [*TENNIS* - ball] rebater com um lob.

lobby ['lɒbɪ] (*pl* -ies, *pt* & *pp* -ied) ⟨⟩ *n* -1. [hall] saguão *m* -2. [pressure group] lobby *m*, grupo *m* de pressão. ⟨⟩ *vt* pressionar.

lobe [ləʊb] *n* ANAT lóbulo *m*.

lobster ['lɒbstə'] *n* lagosta *f*.

local ['ləʊkl] ⟨⟩ *adj* local. ⟨⟩ *n inf* -1. [person]: **the ~ s** os habitantes do lugar -2. *UK* [pub] pub *m* local.

local authority *n UK* autoridade *f* local.

local call *n* chamada *f* local.

local government *n (U)* governo *m* local.

locality [ləʊ'kælətɪ] (*pl* -ies) *n* localidade *f*.

localized, -ised ['ləʊkəlaɪzd] *adj* localizado(da).

locally ['ləʊkəlɪ] *adv* [in region] localmente ; [in neighbourhood] na região.

locate [*UK* ləʊ'keɪt, *US* 'ləʊkeɪt] *vt* localizar.

location [ləʊ'keɪʃn] *n* -1. [place] localização *f* -2. CINEMA: **on ~** em locação.

loch [lɒk] *n Scot* lago *m*.

lock [lɒk] ⟨⟩ *n* -1. [of door, window, box] fechadura *f* -2. [on canal] eclusa *f* -3. AUT [steering lock] ângulo *m* de giro -4. [of hair] mecha *f*. ⟨⟩ *vt* -1. [fasten securely] fechar com chave -2. [keep safely] trancar -3. [immobilize] bloquear. ⟨⟩ *vi* -1. [fasten securely] fechar com chave, chavear -2. [become immobilized] trancar.

⇒ **lock away** *vt sep* trancar a sete chaves.

⇒ **lock in** *vt sep* encerrar.

⇒ **lock out** *vt sep* -1. [accidentally] trancar do lado de fora -2. [deliberately] deixar na rua.

⇒ **lock up** *vt sep* -1. [person] trancafiar -2. [house] trancar -3. [valuables] fechar com chave -4. [with padlock] fechar com cadeado.

locker ['lɒkə'] *n* [for clothes, luggage, books] compartimento *m* com chave.

locker room *n US* vestiário *m*.

locket ['lɒkɪt] *n* medalhão *m*.

locksmith ['lɒksmɪθ] *n* serralheiro *m*, -ra *f*.

locomotive ['ləʊkə,məʊtɪv] *n* locomotiva *f*.

locum ['ləʊkəm] (*pl* -s) *n* interino *m*, -na *f*.

locust ['ləʊkəst] *n* gafanhoto *m*.

lodge [lɒdʒ] ⟨⟩ *n* -1. [caretaker's room] portaria *f* -2. [of manor house] guarita *f* -3. [of Freemasons] loja *f* -4. [for hunting] região *f* de caça. ⟨⟩ *vt fml* [register] apresentar. ⟨⟩ *vi* -1. [stay, live]: **to ~**

with sb hospedar-se na casa de alguém -2. [become stuck] alojar-se -3. *fig* [in mind] gravar-se na mente.

lodger ['lɒdʒə'] *n* pensionista *mf* (*em casa de família*).

lodging ['lɒdʒɪŋ] *n* ⊳ **board**.

⇒ **lodgings** *npl* alojamentos *mpl*.

loft [lɒft] *n* [attic] sótão *m*; **~ (apartment)** *apartamento transformado na cobertura de um armazém ou de uma fábrica, em geral amplo e sem divisórias internas*.

lofty ['lɒftɪ] (*compar* -ier, *superl* -iest) *adj* -1. [noble] elevado(da), nobre -2. *pej* [haughty] arrogante -3. *literary* [high] elevado(da).

log [lɒg] (*pt* & *pp* -ged, *cont* -ging) ⟨⟩ *n* -1. [of wood] tronco *m* -2. [written record - of ship] diário *m* de bordo; [- of plane] diário *m* de vôo. ⟨⟩ *vt* -1. [information - on paper] registrar; [- in computer] registrar em log -2. [speed, distance, time] anotar.

⇒ **log in** *vi* COMPUT entrar (no sistema), efetuar login.

⇒ **log out** *vi* COMPUT sair (do sistema), efetuar logout.

logbook ['lɒgbʊk] *n* -1. [of ship] diário *m* de bordo -2. [of plane] diário *m* de vôo -3. [of car] documentação *f*.

loggerheads ['lɒgəhedz] *n*: **at ~ with** em desavença com.

logic ['lɒdʒɪk] *n* lógica *f*.

logical ['lɒdʒɪkl] *adj* lógico(ca).

logistics [lə'dʒɪstɪks] ⟨⟩ *n* MIL logística *f*. ⟨⟩ *npl fig* [organization] logística *f*.

logo ['ləʊgəʊ] (*pl* -s) *n* logotipo *m*.

loin [lɔɪn] *n* lombo *m*.

loiter ['lɔɪtə'] *vi* -1. [hang about] demorar-se -2. [dawdle] vadiar.

loll [lɒl] *vi* -1. [sit, lie about] recostar-se, refestelar-se -2. [hang down] estar pendente.

lollipop ['lɒlɪpɒp] *n* pirulito *m*.

lollipop lady *n UK* guarda *f* escolar.

lollipop man *n UK* guarda *m* escolar.

lolly ['lɒlɪ] (*pl* -ies) *n* -1. [lollipop] pirulito *m* -2. *UK* [ice cream] picolé *m*.

London ['lʌndən] *n* Londres; **in ~** em Londres.

Londoner ['lʌndənə'] *n* londrino *m*, -na *f*.

lone [ləʊn] *adj* solitário(ria).

loneliness ['ləʊnlɪnɪs] *n (U)* solidão *f*.

lonely ['ləʊnlɪ] (*compar* -ier, *superl* -iest) *adj* -1. [gen] solitário(ria), só -2. [place] isolado(da).

loner ['ləʊnə'] *n* solitário *m*, -ria *f*.

lonesome ['ləʊnsəm] *adj US inf* -1. [person] solitário(ria), só -2. [place] isolado(da).

loosely

long [lɒŋ] ◇ adj -**1.** [in time] longo(ga); **two days ~** de dois dias de duração; **how ~ will it take?** quanto tempo vai demorar? - **2.** [in space] comprido(da), longo(ga); **10 metres ~** com 10 metros de comprimento; **it's five hundred pages ~** tem quinhentas páginas. ◇ adv [for a long time] por muito tempo; **how ~ have you been waiting?** há quanto tempo você está esperando?; **as OR so ~ as** desde que; **before ~** agora; **no ~er** não mais; **I can't wait any ~er** não posso mais esperar; **so ~!** inf até logo! ◇ vt: **to ~ to do sthg** ansiar por fazer algo.

◆ **as long as, so long as** conj [if] desde que; **as ~ as you're happy about it** desde que você esteja feliz com isso.

◆ **long for** vt fus ansiar por.

long-distance adj de longa distância.

long-distance call n chamada f de longa distância.

longhand ['lɒŋhænd] n (U) escrita f à mão.

long-haul adj de grande distância.

longing ['lɒŋɪŋ] ◇ adj ansioso(sa). ◇ n desejo m; **~ (for sthg)** ânsia f (por algo).

longitude ['lɒndʒɪtjuːd] n GEOGR (U) longitude f.

long jump n salto m em distância.

long-life adj longa-vida.

long-playing record [-'pleɪŋ-] n LP m.

long-range adj -**1.** [missile, bomber] de longo alcance - **2.** [plan, forecast] a longo prazo.

long shot n fig possibilidade f remota.

long-sighted adj MED presbita.

long-standing adj de longa data.

long-suffering adj sofrido(da).

long term n: **in the ~** a longo prazo.

long-winded adj cansativo(va).

loo [luː] n (pl -s) UK inf toalete m.

look [lʊk] ◇ n -**1.** [with eyes] olhada f; **to give sb a ~** dar uma olhada em alguém; **to have a ~ (for sthg)** dar uma olhada (procurando algo); **to take OR have a ~ (at sthg)** dar uma olhada (em algo) - **2.** [appearance] aparência f; **by the ~ (s) of things** pelo jeito. ◇ vi -**1.** [with eyes] olhar; **to ~ at sb/sthg** olhar alguém/algo - **2.** [search] procurar - **3.** [have stated appearance] parecer; **to ~ like** parecer como; **it ~s like rain** parece que vai chover; **to ~ as if** parecer como se; **you ~ as if you haven't slept** parece que você não dormiu.

◆ **looks** npl [attractiveness] aparência f, beleza f.

◆ **look after** vt fus [take care of] cuidar de.

◆ **look at** vt fus -**1.** [examine] examinar - **2.** [analise] analisar - **3.** [regard, consider] olhar para.

◆ **look down on** vt fus [condescend to] desdenhar de, depreciar.

◆ **look for** vt fus procurar (por).

◆ **look forward to** vt fus aguardar (ansiosamente).

◆ **look into** vt fus [examine] analisar, examinar.

◆ **look on** vi [watch] observar.

◆ **look onto** vi [face] ter vista para, dar para.

◆ **look out** vi [take care] tomar cuidado; **~ out!** cuidado!

◆ **look out for** vt fus [try to spot] estar atento(ta) a.

◆ **look round** ◇ vt fus [visit] visitar. ◇ vi -**1.** [look at surroundings] percorrer com o olhar ao redor - **2.** [turn] virar-se.

◆ **look to** vt fus -**1.** [depend on] contar com - **2.** [think about] pensar em.

◆ **look up** ◇ vt sep -**1.** [in book] consultar - **2.** [visit] visitar. ◇ vi [improve] melhorar.

◆ **look up to** vt fus [admire] prezar, respeitar.

lookout ['lʊkaʊt] n -**1.** [place] posto m de observação, guarita f - **2.** [person] vigia mf - **3.** [search]: **to be on the ~ for sthg** estar à espreita de algo.

loom [luːm] vi -**1.** [rise up] erguer-se - **2.** fig [be imminent] aproximar-se, ser iminente.

◆ **loom up** vi despontar sombriamente.

loony ['luːnɪ] (compar -ier, superl -iest, pl -ies) inf ◇ adj lunático(ca). ◇ n lunático m, -ca f.

loop [luːp] n -**1.** [shape] laço m - **2.** [contraceptive] DIU m - **3.** COMPUT loop m, laço m.

loophole ['luːphəʊl] n furo m (na lei).

loose [luːs] adj -**1.** [not firmly fixed] frouxo(xa) - **2.** [unattached, unpackaged - sheets of paper] avulso(sa); [- sweets, nails] solto(ta) - **3.** [not tight-fitting] folgado(da) - **4.** [free, not restrained] solto(ta) - **5.** pej & dated [promiscuous] promíscuo(cua) - **6.** [inexact] impreciso(sa).

loose change n (U) trocado m.

loose end n ponta f solta; **yet another ~ we can't explain** outra incógnita que a gente não consegue explicar; **to be at a ~** UK, **to be at ~s** US estar entediado(da), não ter o que fazer.

loosely ['luːslɪ] adv -**1.** [not firmly] sem apertar - **2.** [inexactly] imprecisamente.

loosen ['lu:sn] *vt* [make less tight] afrouxar.

◆ **loosen up** *vi* -**1.** [before game, race] aquecer-se -**2.** *inf* [relax] relaxar.

loot [lu:t] ⬦ *n* (*U*) saque *m*. ⬦ *vt* saquear.

looting ['lu:tɪŋ] *n* (*U*) saque *m*.

lop [lɒp] (*pt & pp* **-ped**, *cont* **-ping**) *vt* podar.

◆ **lop off** *vt sep* cortar.

lop-sided [-'saɪdɪd] *adj* [uneven] assimétrico(ca).

lord [lɔːd] *n UK* [man of noble rank] lorde *m*.

◆ **Lord** *n* -**1.** *RELIG*: **the Lord** [God] o Senhor; **good Lord!** *UK* Deus meu! -**2.** [in titles] lorde *m* -**3.** [as form of address]: **my Lord** [bishop] Reverendíssimo *m*; [judge] Meritíssimo *m*, -ma *f*.

◆ **Lords** *npl UK POL*: **the (House of) Lords** a Câmara dos Lordes.

Lordship ['lɔːdʃɪp] *n*: **your/his** ~ Vossa/ Sua Senhoria.

lore [lɔːˈ] *n* (*U*) crença *f* popular.

lorry ['lɒrɪ] (*pl* **-ies**) *n UK* caminhão *m*.

lorry driver *n UK* motorista *mf* de caminhão.

lose [luːz] (*pt & pp* **lost**) ⬦ *vt* -**1.** [gen] perder; **to** ~ **sight of sb/sthg** perder alguém/algo de vista; **to** ~ **one's way** [get lost] perder-se; **to** ~ **weight** emagrecer, perder peso; **you have nothing to** ~ *inf* você não tem nada a perder -**2.** [subj: clock, watch]: **my watch** ~**s 5 minutes a day** meu relógio atrasa 5 minutos por dia -**3.** [elude, shake off] escapar de. ⬦ *vi* -**1.** [fail to win] perder -**2.** [time] atrasar-se.

◆ **lose out** *vi* sair perdendo.

loser ['luːzəˈ] *n* [gen] perdedor *m*, -ra *f*.

loss [lɒs] *n* -**1.** [gen] perda *f* -**2.** [failure to win] derrota *f* -**3.** *phr*: **to be at a** ~ **to explain sthg** não saber como explicar algo.

lost [lɒst] ⬦ *pt & pp* ▷ **lose**. ⬦ *adj* [gen] perdido(da); **to get** ~ [lose way] perder-se; **get** ~! *inf* te some!

lost-and-found office *n US* setor *m* de achados e perdidos.

lost property office *n UK* setor *m* de achados e perdidos.

lot [lɒt] *n* -**1.** [large amount]: **a** ~ **of**, ~**s of** muito(ta); **a** ~ **of people** muita gente, muitas pessoas; ~**s of problems** muitos problemas; **he talks a** ~ ele fala muito -**2.** *inf* [group of things]: **I bought two** ~**s of shares last week** comprei dois lotes de ações na semana passada; **put this** ~ **in my office** *inf* coloca tudo isso no meu escritório -**3.** [destiny] destino *m*,

sorte *f* -**4.** [at auction] lote *m* -**5.** [entire amount]: **the** ~ tudo -**6.** *US* [of land] lote *m*; [car park] estacionamento *m* -**7.** *phr*: **to draw** ~**s** tirar à sorte.

◆ **a lot** *adv* muito; ~ **better** muito melhor.

lotion ['ləʊʃn] *n* loção *f*.

lottery ['lɒtərɪ] (*pl* **-ies**) *n* loteria *f*.

LOTTO® ['lɒtəʊ] *n* loteria *f* nacional (britânica), ≃ loto *f*.

loud [laʊd] ⬦ *adj* -**1.** [person] barulhento(ta) -**2.** [voice, music, TV] alto(ta) -**3.** [bang] forte -**4.** [garish] espalhafatoso(sa). ⬦ *adv* alto.

loudhailer [ˌlaʊd'heɪləˈ] *n UK* megafone *m*.

loudly ['laʊdlɪ] *adv* -**1.** [shout] alto -**2.** [talk] em voz alta -**3.** [garishly] de forma espalhafatosa.

loudspeaker [ˌlaʊd'spiːkəˈ] *n* alto-falante *m*.

lough *n Irish* lago *m*.

lounge [laʊndʒ] (*cont* **loungeing**) ⬦ *n* -**1.** [in house] sala *f* de estar -**2.** [in airport] sala *f* de espera -**3.** *UK* [bar] = **lounge bar**. ⬦ *vi* recostar-se.

lounge bar *n UK* sala *f* mais confortável (*num bar*).

louse [laʊs] (*pl sense 1* **lice**, *pl sense 2* **-s**) *n* -**1.** [insect] piolho *m* -**2.** *inf pej* [person] canalha *mf*.

lousy ['laʊzɪ] (*compar* **-ier**, *superl* **-iest**) *adj inf* [poor-quality] péssimo(ma); **his performance was** ~ a apresentação dele foi uma porcaria.

lout [laʊt] *n* mal-educado *m*.

louvre *UK*, **louver** *US* ['luːvəˈ] *n*: ~ **door** porta *f* de veneziana; ~ **window** veneziana *f*.

lovable ['lʌvəbl] *adj* amável, encantador(ra).

love [lʌv] ⬦ *n* -**1.** (*U*) [affection for person] amor *m*; **give her my** ~ dá um abraço nela por mim; ~ **from** [at end of letter] um abraço, um beijo; **to be in** ~ estar apaixonado(da); **to fall in** ~ apaixonar-se; **to make** ~ fazer amor -**2.** [liking for sthg, for activity] paixão *f* -**3.** [beloved person, thing] amor *m* -**4.** *inf* [term of address] amor *m* -**5.** (*U*) *TENNIS*: **30** ~ **30** a zero. ⬦ *vt* -**1.** [gen] amar -**2.** [like] adorar; **to** ~ **to do sthg** OR **doing sthg** adorar fazer algo.

love affair *n* caso *m* (de amor).

love life *n* vida *f* amorosa.

lovely ['lʌvlɪ] (*compar* **-ier**, *superl* **-iest**) *adj* -**1.** [person, child - in looks] encantador(ra); [- in character] amável -**2.** [view, day, weather] adorável ; [dress, surprise, holiday] maravilhoso(sa), adorável.

lover ['lʌvəʳ] n -1. [sexual partner] amante mf -2. [enthusiast] amante mf, apaixonado m, -da f.

loving ['lʌvɪŋ] adj carinhoso(sa), afetuoso(sa).

low [ləʊ] <> adj -1. [gen] baixo(xa) -2. [poor - intelligence] pouco(ca); [- opinion] pobre; [- standard, quality, esteem] baixo(xa); [- health] debilitado(da) -3. [not loud or high] baixo(xa) -4. [light] fraco(ca) -5. [neckline] decotado(da) -6. [depressed] deprimido(da) -7. [vulgar] baixo(xa). <> adv -1. [gen] baixo -2. [situated, built] embaixo. <> n -1. [low point] baixa f -2. METEOR área f de baixa pressão.

low-calorie adj de baixa caloria.

low-cut adj decotado(da).

lower ['ləʊəʳ] adj inferior. <> vt -1. [gen] baixar -2. [reduce] reduzir.

low-fat adj com baixo teor de gordura.

low-key adj discreto(ta).

lowly ['ləʊlɪ] (compar -ier, superl -iest) adj humilde.

low-lying adj [land] baixo(xa).

loyal ['lɔɪəl] adj leal, fiel.

loyalty ['lɔɪəltɪ] (pl -ies) n lealdade f, fidelidade f.

loyalty card n cartão f de fidelização.

lozenge ['lɒzɪndʒ] n -1. [tablet] pastilha f -2. [shape] losango m.

LP (abbr of long-playing record) n LP m.

L-plate n UK ≃ auto-escola f (indicação no veículo), placa que contém a letra L em vermelho fixada no veículo conduzido por pessoa que está aprendendo a dirigir.

Ltd, ltd (abbr of limited) Ltda.

lubricant ['lu:brɪkənt] n lubrificante m.

lubricate ['lu:brɪkeɪt] vt lubrificar.

lucid ['lu:sɪd] adj -1. [easily understood] nítido(da) -2. [clear-headed] lúcido(da).

luck [lʌk] n (U) sorte f; good ~! boa sorte!; bad ~ [misfortune] azar m; bad ~ ! [said to commiserate] que azar!; hard ~ ! azar!; to be in ~ estar com sorte; with (any) ~ com (um pouco de) sorte.

luckily ['lʌkɪlɪ] adv afortunadamente.

lucky ['lʌkɪ] (compar -ier, superl -iest) adj -1. [fortunate - person] sortudo(da), com sorte; [- event] feliz -2. [bringing good luck] da sorte.

lucrative ['lu:krətɪv] adj lucrativo(va).

ludicrous ['lu:dɪkrəs] adj -1. [appearance, situation] ridículo(la) -2. [decision, suggestion] absurdo(da).

lug [lʌg] (pt & pp -ged, cont -ging) vt inf arrastar, tirar com dificuldade.

luggage ['lʌgɪdʒ] n (U) UK bagagem f.

luggage rack n UK porta-bagagem m.

lukewarm ['lu:kwɔ:m] adj -1. [tepid]

morno(na) -2. [unenthusiastic] desanimado(da), indiferente.

lull [lʌl] <> n -1. [in activity] pausa f -2. [in fighting] trégua f. <> vt -1. [make sleepy]: to ~ sb to sleep ninar alguém para dormir -2. [reassure]: to ~ sb into a false sense of security passar a alguém uma falsa sensação de segurança.

lullaby ['lʌləbaɪ] (pl -ies) n cantiga f de ninar.

lumber ['lʌmbəʳ] n -1. US [timber] madeira f serrada, tábua f -2. UK [bric-a-brac] trastes mpl.

  ◆ **lumber with** vt sep UK inf [encumber] encarregar.

lumberjack ['lʌmbədʒæk] n lenhador m, -ra f.

luminous ['lu:mɪnəs] adj luminoso(sa).

lump [lʌmp] <> n -1. [piece - of coal] pedaço m; [- earth, sugar] torrão m; [- in sauce, soup] caroço m -2. MED [on body] tumor m. <> vt: to ~ sth together agrupar algo; you'll just have to ~ it inf! você vai ter de engolir isso!

lump sum n soma f global.

lunacy ['lu:nəsɪ] n (U) loucura f.

lunar ['lu:nəʳ] adj lunar.

lunatic ['lu:nətɪk] <> adj pej lunático(ca). <> n -1. pej [fool] idiota mf -2. [insane person] lunático m, -ca f.

lunch [lʌntʃ] <> n almoço m; to have ~ almoçar. <> vi almoçar.

luncheon ['lʌntʃən] n fml almoço m.

luncheon meat n (U) fiambre m.

luncheon voucher n UK tíquete-refeição m.

lunch hour n hora f do almoço.

lunchtime ['lʌntʃtaɪm] n hora f do almoço.

lung [lʌŋ] n pulmão m.

lunge [lʌndʒ] vi arremessar-se; to ~ at sb investir contra alguém.

lurch [lɜ:tʃ] <> n [movement] cambaleio m, solavanco m; to leave sb in the ~ deixar alguém na mão. <> vi [in movement] cambalear, balançar.

lure [ljʊəʳ] <> n [attraction] fascínio m. <> vt [tempt] fascinar.

lurid ['ljʊərɪd] adj -1. [brightly coloured] sensacional -2. [shockingly unpleasant] chocante.

lurk [lɜ:k] vi espreitar.

luscious ['lʌʃəs] adj -1. [fruit] suculento(ta) -2. [colour] vistoso(sa).

lush [lʌʃ] adj -1. [healthy, thick] viçoso(sa) -2. inf [sumptuous] luxuoso(sa).

lust [lʌst] n -1. (U) [sexual desire] luxúria f -2. [greed]: ~ for sthg cobiça f por algo.

  ◆ **lust after, lust for** vt fus -1. [money,

power] cobiçar **-2.** [person] desejar.

lusty ['lʌstɪ] (*compar* **-ier**, *superl* **-iest**) *adj*
vigoroso(sa), forte.

Luxembourg ['lʌksəm,bɜːg] *n* Luxemburgo.

luxurious [lʌg'ʒʊərɪəs] *adj* **-1.** [expensive]
luxuoso(sa) **-2.** [voluptuous] esplêndi-
do(da).

luxury ['lʌkʃərɪ] (*pl* **-ies**) ⟨⟩ *n* luxo *m*.
⟨⟩ *comp* de luxo.

LW (*abbr of* **long wave**) *n* onda *f* longa.

Lycra® ['laɪkrə] ⟨⟩ *n* (*U*) lycra® *f*. ⟨⟩
comp de lycra.

lying ['laɪɪŋ] ⟨⟩ *adj* [dishonest] mentiro-
so(sa), falso(sa). ⟨⟩ *n* [dishonesty] mentiras *fpl*.

lynch [lɪntʃ] *vt* linchar.

lyric ['lɪrɪk] *adj* lírico(ca).
➤ **lyrics** *npl* letra *f (de música)*.

lyrical ['lɪrɪkl] *adj* **-1.** [poetic] lírico(ca)
-2. [enthusiastic] entusiasmado(da).

M

m¹ (*pl* m's *OR* ms), **M** (*pl* M's *OR* Ms) [em] *n*
[letter] m, M *m*.
➤ **M -1.** *UK* (*abbr of* **motorway**) rodovia *f*.

m² -1. (*abbr of* **metre**) m **-2.** (*abbr of* **million**) milhão *m*. **-3.** *abbr of* **mile**.

MA *n* (*abbr of* **Master of Arts**) (*titular
de*) *diploma de mestre em ciências
humanas*.

mac [mæk] (*abbr of* **mackintosh**) *n UK inf*
[coat] capa *f* de chuva.

macaroni [,mækə'rəʊnɪ] *n (U)* macarrão
m.

mace [meɪs] *n* **-1.** [ornamental rod] maça *f*
-2. (*U*) [spice] macis *m inv*.

machine [mə'ʃiːn] ⟨⟩ *n* máquina *f*. ⟨⟩
vt **-1.** *SEWING* costurar à máquina **-2.** *TECH*
usinar.

machinegun [mə'ʃiːngʌn] (*pt & pp*
-ned, *cont* **-ning**) *n* metralhadora *f*.

machine language *n* *COMPUT* linguagem *f* de máquina.

machinery [mə'ʃiːnərɪ] *n* (*U*) **-1.** [ma-
chines] maquinário *m* **-2.** *fig* [system]
mecanismo *m*.

macho ['mætʃəʊ] *adj inf* machista.

mackerel ['mækrəl] (*pl inv OR* **-s**) *n*
cavala *f*.

mackintosh ['mækɪntɒʃ] *n UK* capa *f* de
chuva.

mad [mæd] (*compar* **-der**, *superl* **-dest**)
adj **-1.** [insane] louco(ca); **to go ~** enlouquecer **-2.** *pej* [foolish] maluco(ca) **-3.**
[furious] doido(da); **to go ~ at** sb ficar
louco(ca) com alguém **-4.** [hectic] exas-
perado(da) **-5.** [very enthusiastic]: **to be
~ about** sb/sthg ser louco(ca) por al-
guém/algo.

Madagascar [,mædə'gæskə'] *n* Madagascar.

madam ['mædəm] *n fml* [form of address]
senhora *f*.

madcap ['mædkæp] *adj* doido(da).

madden ['mædn] *vt* enfurecer, exasperar.

made [meɪd] *pt & pp* ⟨⟩ **make**.

-made [meɪd] *suffix*: French **~** feito(ta)
na França.

Madeira [mə'dɪərə] *n* **-1.** (*U*) [wine] madeira *m* **-2.** *GEOGR* Ilha *f* da Madeira.

made-to-measure *adj* feito(ta) sob
medida.

made-up *adj* **-1.** [with make-up] maquia-
do(da) **-2.** [invented] falso(sa), esfarra-
pado(da).

madly ['mædlɪ] *adv* [frantically] alucina-
damente; **~ in love** loucamente apai-
xonado(da).

madman ['mædmən] (*pl* **-men** [-mən]) *n*
louco *m*.

madness ['mædnɪs] *n* (*U*) loucura *f*.

Madrid [mə'drɪd] *n* Madrid; **in ~** em
Madrid.

Mafia ['mæfɪə] *n*: **the ~** a Máfia.

magazine [,mægə'ziːn] *n* **-1.** [periodical]
revista *f* **-2.** [news programme] programa
m de variedades **-3.** [on a gun] câmara
f.

maggot ['mægət] *n* larva *f*.

magic ['mædʒɪk] ⟨⟩ *adj* **-1.** [gen] mági-
co(ca) **-2.** [referring to conjuring] de mágica. ⟨⟩ *n* (*U*) **-1.** [gen] magia *f* **-2.**
[conjuring] mágica *f*.

magical ['mædʒɪkl] *adj* [using sorcery]
mágico(ca).

magician [mə'dʒɪʃn] *n* **-1.** [conjurer] mágico *m*, -ca *f* **-2.** [wizard] mago *m*, -ga *f*.

magistrate ['mædʒɪstreɪt] *n* magistrado
m, -da *f*.

magistrates' court *n UK* tribunal *m*.

magnanimous [mæg'nænɪməs] *adj*
magnânimo(ma).

magnate ['mægneɪt] *n* magnata *mf*.

magnesium [mæg'niːzɪəm] *n* (*U*) magnésio *m*.

magnet ['mægnɪt] *n* **-1.** *PHYSICS* ímã *m* **-2.**
fig [attraction] atrativo *m*.

magnetic [mæg'netɪk] *adj* **-1.** *PHYSICS*

magnético(ca) **-2.** *fig* [personality] atraente, carismático(ca).

magnetic tape *n (U)* fita *f* magnética.

magnificent [mæg'nıfısənt] *adj* **-1.** [clothes, splendour, building] grandioso(sa) **-2.** [idea, book, game] magnífico(ca), brilhante.

magnify ['mægnıfaı] *(pt & pp* -ied) *vt* **-1.** [TECH - image] ampliar; [- sound] amplificar **-2.** *fig* [exaggerate] exagerar.

magnifying glass ['mægnıfaıŋ-] *n* lupa *f*, lente *f* de aumento.

magnitude ['mægnıtju:d] *n* magnitude *f*.

magpie ['mægpaı] *n* pega *f (ave)*.

maid [meıd] *n* [servant] empregada *f* doméstica.

maiden ['meıdn] <> *adj* [voyage, speech] de estréia, inaugural. <> *n literary* [young girl] donzela *f*.

maiden aunt *n* tia *f* solteirona.

maiden name *n* nome *m* de solteira.

mail [meıl] <> *n* **-1.** [letters, parcels] correio *m*; by ~ pelo correio **-2.** [system] correios *mpl*. <> *vt* **-1.** [send] mandar pelo correio **-2.** [put in mail box] postar.

mailbox ['meılbɒks] *n* **-1.** *US* [for letters] caixa *f* de correio **-2.** *COMPUT* caixa *f* de entrada.

mailing list ['meılıŋ-] *n* lista *f* de endereços.

mailman ['meılmən] *(pl* -men [-mən]) *n US* carteiro *m*.

mail order *n (U)* pedido *m* por reembolso postal.

mailshot ['meılʃɒt] *n* mala-direta *f*.

maim [meım] *vt* mutilar.

main [meın] <> *adj* principal. <> *n* [pipe] tubulação *f*.

➡ **mains** *npl*: the ~s [gas, water] as tubulações; [electric] a rede elétrica.

➡ **in the main** *adv* em geral.

main course *n* prato *m* principal.

mainframe (computer) ['meınfreım-] *n* computador *m* mainframe.

mainland ['meınlənd] <> *adj* continental. <> *n*: the ~ o continente.

mainly ['meınlı] *adv* principalmente.

main road *n* rodovia *f* principal.

mainstay ['meınsteı] *n* meio *m* de subsistência.

mainstream ['meınstri:m] <> *adj* predominante. <> *n*: the ~ a tendência geral.

maintain [meın'teın] *vt* **-1.** [gen] manter **-2.** [support, provide for] sustentar, manter **-3.** [look after] manter em bom estado **-4.** [assert]: to ~ (that) sustentar que.

maintenance ['meıntənəns] *n (U)* **-1.** [gen] manutenção *f* **-2.** [money] pensão *f*.

maize [meız] *n (U)* milho *m*.

majestic [mə'dʒestık] *adj* majestoso(sa).

majesty ['mædʒəstı] *(pl* -ies) *n* [grandeur] majestade *f*.

➡ **Majesty** *n*: His OR Her/Your Majesty Sua/Vossa Majestade.

major ['meıdʒəʳ] <> *adj* **-1.** [gen] principal **-2.** *MUS* maior. <> *n* [MIL - in army] major *m*; [- in air force] major-aviador *m*.

Majorca [mə'jɔ:kə, mə'dʒɔ:kə] *n* Maiorca.

majority [mə'dʒɒrətı] *(pl* -ies) *n* maioria *f*; in a OR the ~ na maioria; age of ~ maioridade *f*.

make [meık] *(pt & pp* made) *vt* **-1.** [produce, manufacture] fazer; to be made of ser feito de; to ~ lunch/dinner fazer o almoço/jantar; made in Japan fabricado no Japão. **-2.** [perform, do] fazer; to ~ a mistake cometer um erro, enganar-se; to ~ a phone call dar um telefonema. **-3.** [cause to be] tornar **-4.** [cause to do, force] fazer; to ~ sb do sthg obrigar alguém a fazer algo; it made her laugh isso a fez rir. **-5.** [amount to, total] ser; that ~ s $5 são 5 dólares. **-6.** [calculate]: I ~ it seven o'clock calculo que sejam sete horas; I ~ it $4 segundo os meus cálculos são 4 dólares. **-7.** [profit, loss] ter. **-8.** *inf* [arrive in time for]: we didn't ~ the 10 o'clock train não conseguimos apanhar o trem das 10. **-9.** [friend, enemy] fazer. **-10.** [have qualities for] dar; this would ~ a lovely bedroom isto dava um lindo quarto. **-11.** [bed] fazer. **-12.** [in phrases]: to ~ do contentar-se; [damage] reparar; to ~ it [arrive on time] conseguir chegar a tempo; [be able to go] poder ir; [survive a crisis] recuperar-se.

<> *n* [of product] marca *f*.

➡ **make out** *vt sep* [check, receipt] passar; [form] preencher; [see] distinguir; [hear] perceber, entender.

➡ **make up** *vt sep* [invent] inventar; [comprise] constituir; [difference, extra] cobrir.

➡ **make up for** *vt fus* compensar.

make-believe *n (U)* faz-de-conta *m*.

makeover ['meıkəʊvəʳ] *n* **-1.** [for person] tratamento *m* **-2.** [for company] aperfeiçoamento *m*.

maker ['meıkəʳ] *n* **-1.** [of film] produtor *m*, -ra *f* **-2.** [of product] fabricante *mf*.

makeshift ['meıkʃıft] *adj* **-1.** [temporary] provisório(ria) **-2.** [improvised] improvisado(da).

make-up n (U) **-1.** [cosmetics] maquiagem f; ~ **remover** removedor m de maquiagem **-2.** [person's character] caráter m **-3.** [composition] composição f.

making ['meɪkɪŋ] n [of cake] fabricação f; [of film] produção f; **in the** ~ em desenvolvimento; **this is history in the** ~ isto passará para a história; **your problems are of your own** ~ teus problemas são todos coisas da tua cabeça; **you have the** ~**s of a diplomat** você tem tudo para ser um diplomata.

malaise [mæ'leɪz] n (U) fml [unease] mal-estar m.

malaria [mə'leərɪə] n (U) malária f.

Malaya [mə'leɪə] n Malásia.

Malaysia [mə'leɪzɪə] n Malásia.

male [meɪl] <> adj **-1.** [animal] macho; ~ **kangaroo** canguru m macho **-2.** [human] masculino(na) **-3.** [concerning men] do homem, masculino(na). <> n **-1.** [animal] macho m **-2.** [human] homem m.

male nurse n enfermeiro m.

malevolent [mə'levələnt] adj malévolo(la).

malfunction [mæl'fʌŋkʃn] <> n mau funcionamento m. <> vi funcionar mal.

malice ['mælɪs] n (U) malícia f.

malicious [mə'lɪʃəs] adj malicioso(sa).

malign [mə'laɪn] <> adj maligno(na). <> vt difamar, falar mal de.

malignant [mə'lɪgnənt] adj MED maligno(na).

mall [mɔːl] n esp US: (shopping) ~ shopping m (center).

mallet ['mælɪt] n [hammer] marreta f.

malnutrition [ˌmælnjuː'trɪʃn] n (U) subnutrição f.

malpractice [ˌmæl'præktɪs] n (U) JUR falta f profissional.

malt [mɔːlt] n (U) [grain] malte m.

Malta ['mɔːltə] n Malta.

mammal ['mæml] n mamífero m.

mammoth ['mæməθ] <> adj gigantesco(ca), descomunal. <> n mamute m.

man [mæn] (pl **men**, pt & pp **-ned**, cont **-ning**) <> n **-1.** [gen] homem m; **the** ~ **in the street** o homem comum **-2.** [as form of address] cara m. <> vt **-1.** [ship, plane] tripular **-2.** [machine, switchboard, telephone] manejar.

manage ['mænɪdʒ] <> vi **-1.** [cope] arranjar-se **-2.** [financially] virar-se. <> vt **-1.** [be responsible for, control - organization, business] dirigir, gerenciar; [- money] administrar; [- another person] representar; [- time] organizar **-2.** [succeed]: **to** ~ **to do sthg** conseguir fazer algo **-3.** [be available for]: **I can only** ~ **an** hour tonight eu só disponho de uma hora esta noite.

manageable ['mænɪdʒəbl] adj **-1.** [hair, inflation] controlável **-2.** [children] dominável **-3.** [task, operation] viável.

management ['mænɪdʒmənt] n **-1.** (U) [control, running] administração f, gestão f **-2.** [people in control] gerência f, direção f.

manager ['mænɪdʒəˈ] n **-1.** [of organization] gerente mf, diretor m, -ra f **-2.** [of popstar] empresário m, -ria f **-3.** SPORT treinador m, -ra f.

manageress [ˌmænɪdʒə'res] n UK gerente f.

managerial [ˌmænɪ'dʒɪərɪəl] adj gerencial.

managing director ['mænɪdʒɪŋ-] n diretor-gerente m, diretora-gerente f.

mandarin ['mændərɪn] n [fruit] tangerina f.

mandate ['mændeɪt] n **-1.** [elected right or authority] mandato m **-2.** [task] incumbência f, missão f.

mandatory ['mændətrɪ] adj obrigatório(ria).

mane [meɪn] n **-1.** [of horse] crina f **-2.** [of lion] juba f.

maneuver US = manoeuvre.

manfully ['mænfʊlɪ] adv valentemente.

mangle ['mæŋgl] <> n [for washing] calandra f. <> vt [body, car] destroçar.

mango ['mæŋgəʊ] (pl **-es** OR **-s**) n manga f.

mangy ['meɪndʒɪ] (compar **-ier**, superl **-iest**) adj sarnento(ta).

manhandle ['mæn,hændl] vt maltratar.

manhole ['mænhəʊl] n poço m de inspeção, boca-de-lobo m.

manhood ['mænhʊd] n (U) **-1.** [age] idade f adulta **-2.** [virility] virilidade f.

man-hour n hora-homem f.

mania ['meɪnjə] n **-1.** (U) PSYCH mania f **-2.** [excessive liking]: ~ **(for sthg)** gosto m excessivo (por algo).

maniac ['meɪnɪæk] n **-1.** [madman] maníaco m, -ca f **-2.** [fanatic] fanático m, -ca f.

manic ['mænɪk] adj **-1.** [overexcited] doido(da) **-2.** PSYCH maníaco(ca).

manicure ['mænɪ,kjʊəˈ] n [individual treatment]: **to give sb a** ~ fazer as unhas de alguém.

manifest ['mænɪfest] fml <> adj manifesto(ta). <> vt manifestar.

manifesto [ˌmænɪ'festəʊ] (pl **-s** OR **-es**) n manifesto m.

manipulate [mə'nɪpjʊleɪt] vt **-1.** [control for personal benefit] manipular **-2.** [operate - machine, controls] operar; [- lever] acionar.

manipulative [mə'nɪpjʊlətɪv] *adj* manipulador(ra).

mankind [mæn'kaɪnd] *n* (U) humanidade *f*.

manly ['mænlɪ] (*compar* -ier, *superl* -iest) *adj* másculo(la), viril.

man-made *adj* -1. [problem, disaster] produzido(da) pelo homem -2. [fibre, environment] artificial.

manner ['mænə'] *n* -1. [method] maneira *f*, forma *f* -2. [bearing, attitude] jeito *m*, comportamento *m*.
  ◆ **manners** *npl* maneiras *fpl*; **to be good/bad ~s to do sthg** ser de boa/má educação fazer algo.

mannerism ['mænərɪzm] *n* trejeito *m*.

mannish ['mænɪʃ] *adj* [woman] masculino(na).

manoeuvre UK, **maneuver** US [mə'nu:və'] ⬦ *n* -1. [movement] manobra *f* -2. *fig* [clever move] manobra *f*. ⬦ *vt* [control physically] manobrar, manejar. ⬦ *vi* [move physically] manobrar.

manor ['mænə'] *n* [house] solar *m*.

manpower ['mæn,paʊə'] *n* (U) mão-de-obra *f*.

mansion ['mænʃn] *n* mansão *f*.

manslaughter ['mæn,slɔ:tə'] *n* (U) homicídio *m* involuntário.

mantelpiece ['mæntlpi:s] *n* consolo *m* de lareira.

manual ['mænjʊəl] ⬦ *adj* manual. ⬦ *n* [handbook] manual *m*.

manual worker *n* operário *m*, -ria *f*.

manufacture [,mænjʊ'fæktʃə'] ⬦ *n* (U) manufatura *f*, fabricação *f*. ⬦ *vt* [make] manufaturar, fabricar.

manufacturer [,mænjʊ'fæktʃərə'] *n* fabricante *mf*.

manure [mə'njʊə'] *n* (U) esterco *m*.

manuscript ['mænjʊskrɪpt] *n* manuscrito *m*.

many ['menɪ] (*compar* **more**, *superl* **most**) ⬦ *adj* [a lot of, plenty of] muitos(tas); **~ people** muitas pessoas, muita gente; **how ~ ...?** quantos(tas) ...?; **too ~ ...** demais; **there are too ~ books for me to read** há livros demais para eu ler; **as ~ ... as** tantos ... quantos, tantas ... quantas; **bring as ~ cups as you can** traga tantas xícaras quantas você puder; **so ~ ...** tantos(tas) ...; **a good** OR **great ~ ...** muitíssimos(mas) ..., um grande número de ... ⬦ *pron* [a lot, plenty] muitos(tas); **how ~?** quantos(tas)?; **too ~** muitos(tas); **as ~ as** tantos(tas) quanto; **so ~** tantos(tas).

map [mæp] (*pt* & *pp* **-ped**, *cont* **-ping**) ⬦ *n* mapa *m*; **to put sb/sthg on the ~** colocar alguém/algo no mapa. ⬦ *vt* -1. [chart] fazer o mapa de -2. COMPUT associar.
  ◆ **map out** *vt sep* planejar, planificar.

maple ['meɪpl] *n* bordo *m*.

marathon ['mærəθn] ⬦ *adj* exaustivo(va). ⬦ *n* maratona *f*.

marauder [mə'rɔ:də'] *n* gatuno *m*, -na *f*, saqueador *m*, -ra *f*.

marble ['mɑ:bl] *n* -1. (U) [stone] mármore *m* -2. [for game] bolinha *f* de gude.

march [mɑ:tʃ] ⬦ *n* -1. [gen] marcha *f* -2. [steady progress] avanço *m*. ⬦ *vi* -1. [gen] marchar -2. [approach] avançar.

March [mɑ:tʃ] *n* março; *see also* **September**.

marcher ['mɑ:tʃə'] *n* [protester] manifestante *mf*.

mare [meə'] *n* égua *f*.

margarine [,mɑ:dʒə'ri:n, ,mɑ:gə'ri:n] *n* (U) margarina *f*.

marge [mɑ:dʒ] *n* (U) *inf* margarina *f*.

margin ['mɑ:dʒɪn] *n* -1. [gen] margem *f* -2. [of desert, forest] limite *m*.

marginal ['mɑ:dʒɪnl] *adj* -1. [unimportant] secundário(ria) -2. UK POL: **~ seat** OR **constituency** *cadeira f ganha por uma pequena maioria de votos*.

marginally ['mɑ:dʒɪnəlɪ] *adv* ligeiramente.

marigold ['mærɪgəʊld] *n* calêndula *f*.

marihuana, marijuana [,mærɪ'wɑ:nə] *n* (U) maconha *f*.

marine [mə'ri:n] ⬦ *adj* -1. [underwater] marinho(nha) -2. [seafaring] marítimo(ma). ⬦ *n* MIL fuzileiro *m* naval.

marital ['mærɪtl] *adj* conjugal.

marital status *n* estado *m* civil.

maritime ['mærɪtaɪm] *adj* marítimo(ma).

mark [mɑ:k] ⬦ *n* -1. [stain] mancha *f*; [scratch] marca *f* -2. [in exam] nota *f* -3. [stage, level]: **the halfway ~** o meio caminho; **beyond the billion ~** acima de um bilhão -4. [sign, indication] sinal *f* -5. [currency] marco *m* -6. CULIN nível *m* de temperatura. ⬦ *vt* -1. [gen] marcar -2. [exam, essay] corrigir -3. [commemorate] comemorar, celebrar -4. [stain] manchar.
  ◆ **mark off** *vt sep* [cross off] assinalar.

marked [mɑ:kt] *adj* [noticeable] notável.

marker ['mɑ:kə'] *n* [sign] indicador *m*.

marker pen *n* caneta *f* marcadora.

market ['mɑ:kɪt] ⬦ *n* [gen] mercado *m*. ⬦ *vt* comercializar, vender.

market garden *n esp UK* horta *f*.

marketing ['mɑ:kɪtɪŋ] *n* (U) COMM marketing *m*.

marketplace ['mɑ:kɪtpleɪs] *n* mercado *m*.

market research n (U) pesquisa f de mercado.

market value n COMM valor m de mercado.

marking ['mɑːkɪŋ] n (U) SCH & UNIV correção f.

◆ **markings** npl - **1.** [of flower] manchas fpl - **2.** [of animal] pintas fpl - **3.** [of road] sinais mpl.

marksman ['mɑːksmən] (pl -men [-mən]) n atirador m.

marmalade ['mɑːməleɪd] n (U) geléia f.

maroon [mə'ruːn] adj castanho-avermelhado.

marooned [mə'ruːnd] adj abandonado(da).

marquee [mɑː'kiː] n toldo m.

marriage ['mærɪdʒ] n casamento m.

marriage bureau n UK agência f matrimonial.

marriage certificate n certidão m de casamento.

marriage guidance n (U) orientação f para casais.

married ['mærɪd] adj - **1.** [having a spouse] casado(da) - **2.** [of marriage] de casado.

marrow ['mærəʊ] n - **1.** UK [vegetable] abóbora f - **2.** (U) [in bones] medula f.

marry ['mærɪ] (pt & pp -ied) ◇ vt casar; will you ~ me? quer se casar comigo? ◇ vi [get married] casar-se.

Mars [mɑːz] n [planet] Marte.

marsh [mɑːʃ] n pântano m.

marshal ['mɑːʃl] (UK pt & pp -led, cont -ling, US pt & pp -ed, cont -ing) ◇ n - **1.** MIL marechal m - **2.** [assistant] oficial m - **3.** US [law officer] oficial mf de justiça. ◇ vt - **1.** [people] dirigir, conduzir - **2.** [support, thoughts] ordenar, organizar.

martial arts [ˌmɑːʃl-] npl artes fpl marciais.

martial law [ˌmɑːʃl-] n (U) lei f marcial.

martyr ['mɑːtəʳ] n mártir mf.

martyrdom ['mɑːtədəm] n (U) martírio m.

marvel ['mɑːvl] (UK pt & pp -led, cont -ling, US pt & pp -ed, cont -ing) ◇ n - **1.** [gen] maravilha f - **2.** [surprise, miracle] milagre m. ◇ vi: to ~ (at sthg) maravilhar-se (com algo).

marvellous UK, **marvelous** US ['mɑːvələs] adj maravilhoso(sa).

Marxism ['mɑːksɪzm] n (U) marxismo m.

Marxist ['mɑːksɪst] ◇ adj marxista. ◇ n marxista mf.

marzipan ['mɑːzɪpæn] n (U) maçapão m.

mascara [mæs'kɑːrə] n (U) rímel m.

masculine ['mæskjʊlɪn] adj masculino(-na).

mash [mæʃ] vt triturar, amassar.

mashed potatoes [mæʃt-] npl purê m de batatas.

mask [mɑːsk] ◇ n - **1.** [covering face] máscara f - **2.** fig [dissimulation] máscara f. ◇ vt - **1.** [cover] mascarar - **2.** [conceal] disfarçar.

masochist ['mæsəkɪst] n masoquista mf.

mason ['meɪsn] n - **1.** [stonemason] pedreiro m, -ra f - **2.** [Freemason] maçom m.

masonry ['meɪsnrɪ] n (U) [stones] alvenaria f.

masquerade [ˌmæskə'reɪd] vi: to ~ as fazer-se passar por.

mass [mæs] ◇ n [large amount] grande quantidade f. ◇ adj em massa. ◇ vi concentrar-se.

◆ **Mass** n RELIG missa f.

◆ **masses** npl - **1.** inf [lots, plenty] montes mpl; ~ es of sthg montes de algo - **2.** [ordinary people]: the ~ es as massas.

massacre ['mæsəkəʳ] ◇ n massacre m. ◇ vt massacrar.

massage [UK 'mæsɑːʒ, US mə'sɑːʒ] ◇ n massagem f. ◇ vt massagear.

massive ['mæsɪv] adj [size, amount] enorme; ~ majority maioria em massa.

mass media n or npl: the ~ os meios de comunicação de massas.

mass production n (U) produção f em série.

mast [mɑːst] n - **1.** [on boat] mastro m - **2.** RADIO & TV antena f.

master ['mɑːstəʳ] ◇ n - **1.** [person in charge] senhor m; a ~ and his servants um amo e seus servos - **2.** fig [of subject, situation] dono m - **3.** UK [teacher] mestre m - **4.** [of ship] capitão m - **5.** [original copy] original m. ◇ adj - **1.** [in trade] mestre - **2.** [original] original. ◇ vt - **1.** [gain control of] dominar, controlar - **2.** [perfect] dominar.

master key n chave-mestra f.

masterly ['mɑːstəlɪ] adj magistral.

mastermind ['mɑːstəmaɪnd] ◇ n cabeça mf; he is the ~ behind the plan ele é o cabeça do plano. ◇ vt ser o cabeça de.

Master of Arts (pl **Masters of Arts**) n - **1.** [degree] mestrado m em ciências humanas, diploma de mestre em ciências humanas - **2.** [person] mestre mf em ciências humanas, titular de diploma de mestre em ciências humanas.

Master of Science (pl **Masters of Science**) n - **1.** [degree] mestrado m em ciências exatas, diploma de mestre *em ciências exatas* - **2.** [person] mestre *mf* em ciências exatas, *titular de diploma de mestre em ciências exatas.*

masterpiece ['mɑːstəpiːs] *n* obra-prima *f*.

master's degree *n* mestrado *m*.

mastery ['mɑːstərɪ] *n (U)* domínio *m*.

mat [mæt] *n* - **1.** [on floor] tapete *m*; **door ~** capacho *m* - **2.** [on table]: **beer ~** porta-copos *m inv*; **table ~** jogo *m* americano.

match [mætʃ] ⋄ *n* - **1.** [game] partida *f* - **2.** [for lighting] fósforo *m* - **3.** [equal]: **to be no ~ for sb** não ser páreo para alguém. ⋄ *vt* - **1.** [be the same as] coincidir com - **2.** [coordinate with] combinar com - **3.** [equal] equiparar-se a. ⋄ *vi* [be the same] combinar.

matchbox ['mætʃbɒks] *n* caixa *f* de fósforos.

matching ['mætʃɪŋ] *adj* que combina bem.

mate [meɪt] ⋄ *n* - **1.** *inf* [friend] amigo *m*, -ga *f*, companheiro *m*, -ra *f* - **2.** *UK inf* [form of address] colega *mf* - **3.** [of animal] parceiro *m*, -ra *f* - **4.** NAUT: **(first) ~** contramestre *m*. ⋄ *vi* [animals] acasalar-se; **to ~ with** acasalar-se com.

material [mə'tɪərɪəl] ⋄ *adj* - **1.** material - **2.** [important] substancial. ⋄ *n* material *m*.
      ➤ **materials** *npl* materiais *mpl*.

materialistic [mə,tɪərɪə'lɪstɪk] *adj* materialista.

materialize, -ise [mə'tɪərɪəlaɪz] *vi* - **1.** [happen] concretizar-se - **2.** [appear] materializar-se.

maternal [mə'tɜːnl] *adj* maternal.

maternity [mə'tɜːnətɪ] *n (U)* maternidade *f*.

maternity dress *n* vestido *m* de gestante.

maternity hospital *n* maternidade *f (no hospital)*.

maternity leave *n* licença-maternidade *f*.

maternity ward *n* maternidade *f*.

math *n US* = **maths**.

mathematical [,mæθə'mætɪkl] *adj* matemático(ca).

mathematics [,mæθə'mætɪks] *n (U)* [subject] matemática *f*.

maths *UK* [mæθs], **math** *US* [mæθ] *(abbr of* **mathematics)** *inf n (U)* [subject] matemática *f*.

matinée ['mætɪneɪ] *n* matinê *f*.

mating season ['meɪtɪŋ-] *n* época *f* de acasalamento.

matrices ['meɪtrɪsiːz] *pl* ▷ **matrix**.

matriculation [mə,trɪkjʊ'leɪʃn] *n (U)* UNIV matrícula *f*.

matrimonial [,mætrɪ'məʊnjəl] *adj* matrimonial.

matrimony ['mætrɪmənɪ] *n (U)* matrimônio *m*.

matrix ['meɪtrɪks] *(pl* **matrices** OR **-es)** *n* - **1.** [gen] matriz *f* - **2.** TECH molde *m* para fundição.

matron ['meɪtrən] *n* - **1.** *UK* [in hospital] enfermeira-chefe *f* - **2.** [in school] enfermeira *f*.

matronly ['meɪtrənlɪ] *adj euph* matronal.

matt *UK*, **matte** *US* [mæt] *adj* fosco(ca).

matted ['mætɪd] *adj* embaraçado(da).

matter ['mætəʳ] ⋄ *n* - **1.** [question, situation] questão *f*, assunto *m*; **that's another** OR **a different ~** isso é outra questão/coisa; **a ~ of opinion** uma questão de opinião; **to make ~s worse** piorar as coisas; **and to make ~s worse, ...** e para piorar (ainda mais) as coisas, ...; **as a ~ of course** como algo natural - **2.** [trouble, cause of pain] problema *m*; **what's the ~?** qual é o problema?, o que (é que) houve?; **what's the ~ with it/her?** qual é o problema com isso/ela? - **3.** *(U)* PHYSICS matéria *f* - **4.** *(U)* [material] material *m*; **vegetable ~** matéria vegetal. ⋄ *vi* [be important] importar; **it doesn't ~** não importa; **it doesn't ~ what you decide** não interessa o que você decidir.
      ➤ **as a matter of fact** *adv* aliás, na verdade.
      ➤ **for that matter** *adv* quanto a isso.
      ➤ **no matter** *adv*: **no ~ how hard I try ...** não importa quanto eu tente ...; **no ~ what** aconteça o que acontecer.

Matterhorn ['mætə,hɔːn] *n*: **the ~** a Montanha Matterhorn.

matter-of-fact *adj* sem sentimento, prosaico(ca).

mattress ['mætrɪs] *n* colchão *m*.

mature [mə'tjʊəʳ] ⋄ *adj* - **1.** [person] maduro(ra) - **2.** [food, drink] envelhecido(da), maturado(da) - **3.** [cheese] curado(da). ⋄ *vi* - **1.** [gen] amadurecer - **2.** [animal, plant] crescer - **3.** [wine, spirit] envelhecer - **4.** [cheese] curar - **5.** [insurance policy] vencer.

mature student *n UK* UNIV estudante *mf* adulto, -ta.

maul [mɔːl] *vt* [attack, savage] atacar gravemente.

mauve [məʊv] ⋄ *adj* da cor de malva. ⋄ *n (U)* malva *f*.

max. [mæks] *(abbr of* **maximum)** máx.

maxim ['mæksɪm] *(pl* **-s)** *n* máxima *f*.

maxima ['mæksɪmə] pl ▷ **maximum**.
maximum ['mæksɪməm] (pl **maxima** OR **-s**) ◇ adj [highest, largest] máximo(ma). ◇ n [upper limit] máximo m.
may [meɪ] modal vb **-1.** [poder; you ~ like it talvez você goste; he ~ well have said that ele pode muito bem ter dito aquilo; it ~ rain pode ser que chova; be that as it ~ seja como for; I would like to add, if I ~ ... eu gostaria de acrescentar, se possível ... **-2.** fml [to express wish, hope]: **long ~ it last!** que dure por muito tempo!; **~ they be very happy!** que eles sejam muito felizes!; ▷ **might**.
May [meɪ] n maio; see also **September**.
maybe ['meɪbi] adv talvez.
mayhem ['meɪhem] n (U) caos m inv.
mayonnaise [ˌmeɪə'neɪz] n (U) maionese f.
mayor [meəʳ] n prefeito m.
mayoress ['meərɪs] n [female mayor] prefeita f; [wife of mayor] esposa f do prefeito.
maze [meɪz] n **-1.** [system of paths] labirinto m **-2.** fig [tangle] confusão f.
MB ◇ n (abbr of **Bachelor of Medicine**) (titular de) bacharelado em medicina. ◇ (abbr of **megabyte**) MB.
MD n **-1.** (abbr of **Doctor of Medicine**) (titular de) doutorado em medicina **-2.** (abbr of **managing director**) diretor-gerente m.
me [miː] pers pron **-1.** (direct, indirect) me; she knows ~ ela me conhece; it's ~ sou eu; send it to ~ mande-o para mim; **tell ~** diga-me; **-2.** (after prep) mim; with ~ comigo; it's for ~ é para mim.
meadow ['medəʊ] n campina f.
meagre UK, **meager** US ['miːgəʳ] adj magro(gra), insuficiente.
meal [miːl] n refeição f; **to go out for a ~** sair para jantar.
mealtime ['miːltaɪm] n hora f da refeição.
mean [miːn] (pt & pp **meant**) ◇ adj **-1.** [miserly] mesquinho(nha); **to be ~ with sthg** ser avarento com algo **-2.** [unkind] grosseiro(ra); **to be ~ to sb** ser malvado(da) com alguém **-3.** [average] médio(dia). ◇ n [average] meio-termo m; ▷ **means**. ◇ vt **-1.** [signify, represent] significar **-2.** [have in mind, intend] querer dizer; **to ~ to do sthg** ter a intenção de fazer algo, tencionar fazer algo; **to be meant for sb/sthg** ser feito(ta) para alguém/algo; **they're not meant to be there** eles não deveriam estar lá; **it was meant as a compliment** era para ser

um elogio; **to be meant to do sthg** dever fazer algo; **to ~ well** ter boa vontade **-3.** [be serious about] falar sério; **she meant every word she said** tudo o que ela disse era a sério **-4.** [entail] acarretar **-5.** phr: I ~ quer dizer.
meander [mɪ'ændəʳ] vi **-1.** [river, road] serpentear **-2.** [in walking] vagar **-3.** [in speaking] divagar.
meaning ['miːnɪŋ] n **-1.** [sense] sentido m, significado m **-2.** (U) [purpose, importance] sentido m.
meaningful ['miːnɪŋfʊl] adj **-1.** [expressive] significativo(va) **-2.** [deep, profound] sério(ria).
meaningless ['miːnɪŋlɪs] adj **-1.** [devoid of sense] sem sentido **-2.** [futile] fútil.
means [miːnz] (pl inv) ◇ n [method, way] meio m; **by ~ of** por meio de. ◇ npl [money] recursos mpl.
➤ **by all means** adv claro que sim.
➤ **by no means** adv de modo algum.
meant [ment] pt & pp ▷ **mean**.
meantime ['miːnˌtaɪm] n: **in the ~** enquanto isso.
meanwhile ['miːnˌwaɪl] adv **-1.** [at the same time] enquanto isso **-2.** [between two events] nesse ínterim.
measles ['miːzlz] n: **to catch ~** pegar sarampo.
measly ['miːzlɪ] (compar **-ier**, superl **-iest**) adj inf miserável.
measure ['meʒəʳ] ◇ n **-1.** [step, action] medida f **-2.** [of alcohol] dose f **-3.** [indication] indicação f **-4.** [device] régua f. ◇ vt [determine size of, gauge] medir.
measurement ['meʒəmənt] n **-1.** [figure, amount] medida f **-2.** (U) [act of measuring] medição f.
➤ **measurements** npl [of sb's body] medidas fpl.
meat [miːt] n (U) carne f.
meatball ['miːtbɔːl] n almôndega f.
meat pie n UK torta f de carne.
meaty ['miːtɪ] (compar **-ier**, superl **-iest**) adj fig [full of ideas] rico(ca), sólido(da).
Mecca ['mekə] n GEOGR Meca.
mechanic [mɪ'kænɪk] n mecânico m, -ca f.
➤ **mechanics** ◇ n (U) [study] mecânica f. ◇ npl [way sthg works] mecânica f.
mechanical [mɪ'kænɪkl] adj mecânico(-ca).
mechanism ['mekənɪzm] n mecanismo m.
medal ['medl] n medalha f.
medallion [mɪ'dæljən] n medalhão m.
meddle ['medl] vi meter-se; **to ~ in/with sthg** meter-se em/com algo.

media ['mi:djə] ⟨⟩ *pl* ▷**medium**. ⟨⟩ *n or npl*: **the** ~ a mídia.

mediaeval [ˌmedɪ'i:vl] *adj* = **medieval**.

median ['mi:djən] *n US* [of road] canteiro *m* divisor.

mediate ['mi:dɪeɪt] ⟨⟩ *vt* [produce by arbitration] negociar. ⟨⟩ *vi* [arbitrate]: **to** ~ **between** ser mediador(ra) entre.

mediator ['mi:dɪeɪtə'] *n* mediador *m*, -ra *f*.

Medicaid ['medɪkeɪd] *n (U) US* auxílio-saúde *m*.

medical ['medɪkl] ⟨⟩ *adj* médico(ca). ⟨⟩ *n* [checkup] exame *m* médico, check-up *m*.

Medicare ['medɪkeə'] *n (U) US* seguro-saúde *m (para idosos)*.

medicated ['medɪkeɪtɪd] *adj* medicinal.

medicine ['medsɪn] *n* -1. (U) [treatment of illness] medicina *f* -2. [substance] medicamento *m*, remédio *m*.

medieval [ˌmedɪ'i:vl] *adj* medieval.

mediocre [ˌmi:dɪ'əʊkə'] *adj* medíocre.

meditate ['medɪteɪt] *vi* -1. [reflect, ponder] refletir; **to** ~ **(up)on sthg** refletir sobre algo -2. [practise meditation] meditar.

Mediterranean [ˌmedɪtə'reɪnjən] ⟨⟩ *n* -1. [sea]: **the** ~ **(Sea)** o (Mar) Mediterrâneo -2. [area around sea]: **the** ~ o mediterrâneo. ⟨⟩ *adj* mediterrâneo(nea).

medium ['mi:djəm] (*pl sense 1* -**dia**, *pl sense 2* -**diums**) ⟨⟩ *adj* [middle, average] médio(dia). ⟨⟩ *n* -1. [way of communicating] meio *m* de comunicação -2. [spiritualist] médium *mf*.

medium-size(d) [-saɪzd] *adj* de tamanho médio.

medium wave *n (U)* onda *f* média.

medley ['medlɪ] (*pl* -**s**) *n* -1. [mixture] mistura *f* -2. [selection of music] coletânea *f*.

meek [mi:k] *adj* dócil, meigo(ga).

meet [mi:t] (*pt & pp* **met**) ⟨⟩ *n US* [meeting] encontro *m*, competição *f*. ⟨⟩ *vt* -1. [gen] encontrar; **she met his gaze defiantly** ela encarou o olhar dele de forma desafiadora -2. [by arrangement] encontrar-se com, reunir-se com -3. [make acquaintance of] conhecer; **I met a really interesting guy** conheci um cara muito interessante -4. [wait for - person] ir esperar; [- train, plane, bus, boat] esperar -5. [fulfil, satisfy] satisfazer, cumprir -6. [deal with] enfrentar -7. [pay] pagar em dia. ⟨⟩ *vi* -1. [gen] encontrar-se; **their eyes met across the room** os olhos deles se cruzaram na sala -2. [committee] reunir-se -3. [become acquainted] conhecer-se -4. [hit, touch] bater-se.

➤ **meet up** *vi* [by arrangement] encontrar-se; **to** ~ **up with sb** encontrar-se com alguém.

➤ **meet with** *vt fus* -1. [encounter] experimentar -2. *US* [by arrangement] encontrar.

meeting ['mi:tɪŋ] *n* -1. [gen] reunião *f* -2. [coming together] encontro *m*.

meeting place *n* ponto *m* de encontro.

megabyte ['megəbaɪt] *n COMPUT* megabyte *m*.

megaphone ['megəfəʊn] *n* megafone *m*.

megapixel [ˌmega'pɪksl] *n* megapixel *m*.

melancholy ['melənkəlɪ] ⟨⟩ *adj* [sad] melancólico(ca). ⟨⟩ *n (U)* melancolia *f*.

mellow ['meləʊ] ⟨⟩ *adj* -1. [gen] suave -2. [smooth, pleasant] melodioso(sa) -3. [gentle, relaxed] alegre, tranqüilo(la). ⟨⟩ *vi* [become more gentle or relaxed] suavizar-se, tranqüilizar-se.

melody ['melədɪ] (*pl* -**ies**) *n* [tune] melodia *f*.

melon ['melən] *n* melão *m*.

melt [melt] ⟨⟩ *vt* [make liquid] derreter. ⟨⟩ *vi* -1. [become liquid] derreter -2. *fig* [soften] amolecer -3. *fig* [disappear]: **to** ~ **away** dissipar-se; **his savings** ~ **ed away** suas economias se acabaram.

➤ **melt down** *vt sep* fundir-se.

meltdown ['meltdaʊn] *n* -1. (U) [act of melting] fusão *f* -2. [incident] acidente *m* nuclear.

melting pot ['meltɪŋ-] *n fig* [of cultures, races, ideas] cadinho *m* cultural.

member ['membə'] ⟨⟩ *n* membro *m*.

Member of Congress (*pl* **Members of Congress**) *n US* Membro *m* do Congresso.

Member of Parliament (*pl* **Members of Parliament**) *n* [in UK] Membro *m* do Parlamento.

membership ['membəʃɪp] *n* -1. [gen - of party, union] associação *f*; [- of club] qualidade *f* de sócio; **I have to renew my** ~ tenho que renovar o meu título -2. [number of members] número *m* de sócios -3. [people themselves]: **the** ~ os sócios, os membros.

membership card *n* carteira *f* de sócio.

memento [mɪ'mentəʊ] (*pl* -**s**) *n* lembrança *f*.

memo ['meməʊ] (*pl* -**s**) *n* [at work] memorando *m*.

memoirs ['memwɑ:z] *npl* memórias *fpl*.

memorandum [,memə'rændəm] (*pl* -da, ~-dums) *n fml* memorando *m*.

memorial [mɪ'mɔ:rɪəl] ◇ *adj* comemorativo(va). ◇ *n* memorial *m*.

memorize, -ise ['meməraɪz] *vt* memorizar, decorar.

memory ['memərɪ] (*pl* -ies) *n* -1. [gen] memória *f*; **from ~** de memória -2. [sthg remembered] lembrança *f*.

men [men] *pl* ▷ **man**.

menace ['menəs] ◇ *n* -1. [gen] ameaça *f* -2. *inf* [nuisance, pest] praga *f*. ◇ *vt* ameaçar.

menacing ['menəsɪŋ] *adj* ameaçador(-ra).

mend [mend] ◇ *n* (U) *inf*: **to be on the ~** estar convalescendo. ◇ *vt* [repair] consertar.

menial ['mi:njəl] *adj* simplório(ria), baixo(xa).

meningitis [,menɪn'dʒaɪtɪs] *n* (U) MED meningite *f*.

menopause ['menəpɔ:z] *n* (U): **the ~** a menopausa.

men's room *n* US: **the ~** o banheiro dos homens.

menstruation [,menstru'eɪʃn] *n* (U) menstruação *f*.

menswear ['menzweə'] *n* (U) roupa *f* masculina.

mental ['mentl] *adj* mental.

mental hospital *n* hospital *m* psiquiátrico.

mentality [men'tælətɪ] *n* (U) [way of thinking] mentalidade *f*.

mentally handicapped ['mentəlɪ-] *npl*: **the ~** os deficientes mentais.

mention ['menʃn] ◇ *vt* [say, talk about] mencionar; **to ~ sthg to sb** mencionar algo para alguém; **not to ~** sem falar em; **don't ~ it!** não tem de quê! ◇ *n* [reference] menção *f*.

menu ['menju:] *n* -1. [in restaurant] menu *m*, cardápio *m* -2. COMPUT menu *m*.

meow *n* & *vi* US = miaow.

MEP (*abbr of* Member of the European Parliament) *n* membro do parlamento europeu.

mercenary ['mɜ:sɪnrɪ] (*pl* -ies) ◇ *adj* mercenário(ria). ◇ *n* [soldier] mercenário *m*.

merchandise ['mɜ:tʃəndaɪz] *n* (U) COMM mercadoria *f*.

merchant ['mɜ:tʃənt] *n* comerciante *mf*.

merchant bank *n* UK banco *m* mercantil.

merchant navy UK, **merchant marine** US *n* marinha *f* mercante.

merciful ['mɜ:sɪfʊl] *adj* -1. [person] piedoso(sa) -2. [death, release] misericordioso(sa).

merciless ['mɜ:sɪlɪs] *adj* impiedoso(sa).

mercury ['mɜ:kjʊrɪ] *n* (U) mercúrio *m*.

Mercury ['mɜ:kjʊrɪ] *n* [planet] Mercúrio.

mercy ['mɜ:sɪ] (*pl* -ies) *n* -1. (U) [kindness, pity] piedade *f*; **at the ~ of** *fig* à mercê de -2. [blessing] bênção *f*.

mere [mɪə'] *adj* -1. [just, no more than] mero(ra); **she's a ~ child!** ela é só uma criança! -2. [for emphasis] simples, mero(ra) -3. [amount, quantity] apenas.

merely ['mɪəlɪ] *adv* -1. [simply, just, only] meramente, simplesmente -2. [of amount, quantity] apenas.

merge [mɜ:dʒ] ◇ *n* COMPUT intercalamento *m*. ◇ *vt* -1. COMM fundir -2. COMPUT intercalar. ◇ *vi* -1. COMM fundir-se; **to ~ with sthg** unir-se com algo -2. [roads, lines] unir-se -3. [blend, melt] misturar; **to ~ into sthg** incorporar-se em algo.

merger ['mɜ:dʒə'] *n* COMM fusão *f*.

meringue [mə'ræŋ] *n* merengue *m*.

merit ['merɪt] ◇ *n* (U) [value] mérito *m*. ◇ *vt* merecer.
➤ **merits** *npl* [advantages, qualities] méritos *mpl*.

mermaid ['mɜ:meɪd] *n* sereia *f*.

merry ['merɪ] (*compar* -ier, *superl* -iest) *adj* -1. *literary* [laugh, joke, person] alegre, divertido(da) -2. [fire, party] agradável; **Merry Christmas!** Feliz Natal! -3. *inf* [tipsy] alegre.

merry-go-round *n* carrossel *m*.

mesh [meʃ] ◇ *n* (U) [netting] malha *f*. ◇ *vi* -1. [fit together] combinar -2. TECH encaixar.

mesmerize, -ise ['mezməraɪz] *vt*: **to be ~d by sb/sthg** ser hipnotizado(da) por alguém/algo.

mess [mes] *n* -1. [gen] bagunça *f* -2. [muddle, problem] confusão *f* -3. MIL rancho *m*.
➤ **mess about, mess around** *inf* ◇ *vt sep* embromar. ◇ *vi* -1. [gen] matar tempo -2. [tinker]: **to ~ about with sthg** mexer em algo.
➤ **mess up** *vt sep inf* -1. [make untidy, dirty - room, papers, objects] bagunçar; [- clothes] sujar -2. [spoil] estragar.

message ['mesɪdʒ] *n* -1. [piece of information] mensagem *f* -2. [idea, moral] moral *m*.

messenger ['mesɪndʒə'] *n* mensageiro *m*, -ra *f*.

Messrs, Messrs. ['mesəz] (*abbr of* messieurs) Srs.

messy ['mesɪ] (*compar* -ier, *superl* -iest)

adj **-1.** [dirty, untidy] desarrumado(da) **-2.** [person, activity] confuso(sa) **-3.** [job] sujo(ja) **-4.** *inf* [complicated, confused] complicado(da).

met [met] *pt* & *pp* ▷ **meet.**

metal ['metl] ◇ *n* metal *m*. ◇ *adj* de metal.

metallic [mɪ'tælɪk] *adj* **-1.** [gen] metálico(ca) **-2.** *TECH* [of metal] metalífero(ra).

metalwork ['metəlwɜːk] *n* (*U*) [craft] trabalho *m* em metal.

metaphor ['metəfəʳ] *n* metáfora *f*.

mete [miːt] ◆ **mete out** *vt sep*: to ~ sthg out to sb impor algo a alguém.

meteor ['miːtɪəʳ] *n* meteoro *m*.

meteorology [ˌmiːtjə'rɒlədʒi] *n* (*U*) meteorologia *f*.

meter ['miːtəʳ] ◇ *n* **-1.** [device] medidor *m*; **taxi ~** taxímetro *m*; **electricity ~** relógio *m* de luz; **parking ~** parquímetro *m* **-2.** *US* = **metre.** ◇ *vt* [measure] medir.

method ['meθəd] *n* [way, system] método *m*.

methodical [mɪ'θɒdɪkl] *adj* metódico(-ca).

Methodist ['meθədɪst] ◇ *adj* metodista. ◇ *n* metodista *mf*.

meths [meθs] *n* *UK* *inf* álcool *m* metilado.

methylated spirits ['meθɪleɪtɪd-] *n* (*U*) álcool *m* metilado.

meticulous [mɪ'tɪkjʊləs] *adj* meticuloso(sa).

metre *UK*, **meter** *US* ['miːtəʳ] *n* [unit of measurement] metro *m*.

metric ['metrɪk] *adj* métrico(ca).

metronome ['metrənəʊm] *n* metrônomo *m*.

metropolitan [ˌmetrə'pɒlɪtn] *adj* [of a metropolis] metropolitano(na).

Metropolitan Police *npl*: the ~ a Polícia de Londres.

mettle ['metl] *n* (*U*): to be on one's ~ estar preparado(da) para agir da melhor forma possível; to show OR prove one's ~ provar seu próprio valor.

mew [mjuː] *n* & *vi* = **miaow.**

mews [mjuːz] (*pl inv*) *n* *UK* estrebaria *f*.

Mexican ['meksɪkn] ◇ *adj* mexicano(-na). ◇ *n* mexicano *m*, -na *f*.

Mexico ['meksɪkəʊ] *n* México *m*.

MI5 (*abbr of* Military Intelligence 5) *n* órgão do serviço secreto britânico de contra-espionagem.

MI6 (*abbr of* Military Intelligence 6) *n* órgão do serviço secreto britânico de espionagem.

miaow *UK* [miːˈaʊ], **meow** *US* [mɪˈaʊ] ◇ *n* miado *m*, miau *m*. ◇ *vi* miar.

mice [maɪs] *pl* ▷ **mouse.**

mickey ['mɪkɪ] *n*: to take the ~ out of sb *UK* *inf* tirar sarro de alguém.

microbusiness ['maɪkrəʊˌbɪznɪs] *n* microempresa *f*.

microchip ['maɪkrəʊtʃɪp] *n* microchip *m*.

microcomputer [ˌmaɪkrəʊkəm'pjuːtəʳ] *n* microcomputador *m*.

microfilm ['maɪkrəʊfɪlm] *n* microfilme *m*.

microlight ['maɪkrəlaɪt] *n* ultraleve *m*.

microphone ['maɪkrəfəʊn] *n* microfone *m*.

micro scooter *n* patinete *m*.

microscope ['maɪkrəskəʊp] *n* microscópio *m*.

microscopic [ˌmaɪkrə'skɒpɪk] *adj* **-1.** [very small] microscópico(ca) **-2.** [detailed] minucioso(sa).

microwave (oven) *n* forno *m* de microondas.

mid- [mɪd] *prefix*: ~**height** de meia altura; **in** ~**morning** no meio da manhã; **in** ~**August** em meados de agosto; **in** ~**winter** em pleno inverno; **she's in her** ~ **twenties** ela tem uns vinte e poucos anos.

midair [mɪd'eəʳ] ◇ *adj* no ar. ◇ *n* (*U*): **in** ~ no ar.

midday ['mɪddeɪ] *n* (*U*) meio-dia *m*.

middle ['mɪdl] ◇ *adj* [centre] do meio. ◇ *n* **-1.** [centre] meio *m*, centro *m*; **in the** ~ **(of sthg)** no meio (de algo) **-2.** [in time] meio *m*; **to be in the** ~ **of doing sthg** estar fazendo algo; **in the** ~ **of the night** no meio da noite, em plena madrugada; **in the** ~ **of September** em meados de setembro **-3.** [waist] cintura *f*.

middle-aged *adj* de meia-idade.

Middle Ages *npl*: **the** ~ a Idade Média.

middle-class *adj* da classe média.

middle classes *npl*: **the** ~ a classe média.

Middle East *n*: **the** ~ o Oriente Médio.

middleman ['mɪdlmæn] (*pl* **-men** [-men]) *n* intermediário *m*.

middle name *n* segundo nome *m* (*num nome composto*).

middleweight ['mɪdlweɪt] *n* peso *m* médio.

middling ['mɪdlɪŋ] *adj* médio(dia), regular.

Mideast *n* *US*: **the** ~ o Oriente Médio.

midfield [ˌmɪd'fiːld] *n* *FTBL* meio-campo *m*.

midge [mɪdʒ] *n* mosquito-pólvora *m*.

midget ['mɪdʒɪt] *n* anão *m*, -nã *f*.

midi system ['mɪdɪ-] n sistema m MIDI.

Midlands ['mɪdləndz] npl: the ~ a região central da Inglaterra.

midnight ['mɪdnaɪt] ⋄ n (U) meia-noite f.

midriff ['mɪdrɪf] n diafragma m.

midst [mɪdst] n [in space, time]: **in the ~ of** literary no meio de.

midsummer ['mɪd͵sʌmə'] n (U) pleno verão m.

Midsummer Day n Dia m de São João (24 de junho).

midway [͵mɪd'weɪ] adv -1. [in space]: ~ (between) a meio caminho (entre) -2. [in time]: ~ (through) na metade (de).

midweek [adj ͵mɪd'wiːk, adv 'mɪdwiːk] ⋄ adj do meio da semana. ⋄ adv no meio da semana.

midwife ['mɪdwaɪf] (pl -wives [-waɪvz]) n parteira f.

midwifery ['mɪd͵wɪfərɪ] n (U) trabalho m de parteira.

might [maɪt] ⋄ modal vb -1. [expressing possibility]: **I think I ~ go to the pub tonight** acho que é possível eu ir ao bar hoje; **he ~ be armed** ele poderia estar armado -2. [expressing suggestion]: **you ~ have told me** você poderia ter me contado; **it ~ be better to wait** talvez fosse melhor esperar -3. (past tense of may) fml [asking permission]: **he asked if he ~ leave the room** ele me pediu permissão para sair da sala -4. [in polite questions, suggestions]: ~ **I ...?** podia ...? -5. [contradicting a point of view]: **you ~ well be right, but ...** é bem possível que você tenha razão, mas ... -6. phr: **I ~ have known** OR **guessed** eu deveria ter suspeitado. ⋄ n -1. [power] poder m -2. [physical strength] força f.

mighty [compar -ier, superl -iest] ⋄ adj [powerful] poderoso(sa). ⋄ adv US inf muito.

migraine ['miːgreɪn, 'maɪgreɪn] n enxaqueca f.

migrant ['maɪgrənt] ⋄ adj -1. [bird, animal] migratório(ria) -2. [worker] migrante. ⋄ n -1. [bird, animal] migratório m, -ria f -2. [person] emigrante mf.

migrate [UK maɪ'greɪt, US 'maɪgreɪt] vi -1. [bird, animal] migrar -2. [person] emigrar.

mike [maɪk] (abbr of **microphone**) n inf mike m.

mild [maɪld] adj -1. [food, shampoo, sedative] suave -2. [person, manner] sereno(na) -3. [weather] temperado(da) -4. [surprise, criticism, reproach] moderado(da) -5. [illness] leve.

mildew ['mɪldjuː] n -1. (U) [gen] mofo m -2. (U) BOT míldio m.

mildly ['maɪldlɪ] adv -1. [talk, complain, criticize] moderadamente; **to put it ~** para não dizer coisa pior -2. [slightly] bastante.

mile [maɪl] n milha f; **to be ~s away** fig estar bem longe.

◆ **miles** adv (in comparisons) muito; **this is ~ better** sem dúvida alguma isto é realmente melhor.

mileage ['maɪlɪdʒ] n -1. [distance travelled] quilometragem f -2. (U) inf [advantage] vantagem f.

mileometer [maɪ'lɒmɪtə'] n odômetro m.

milestone ['maɪlstəʊn] n -1. [marker stone] marco m miliário -2. fig [event] marco m.

militant ['mɪlɪtənt] ⋄ adj militante. ⋄ n militante mf.

military ['mɪlɪtrɪ] ⋄ adj militar. ⋄ n: the ~ as forças armadas, os militares.

militia [mɪ'lɪʃə] n milícia f.

milk [mɪlk] ⋄ n leite m. ⋄ vt -1. [get milk from] ordenhar -2. fig [use for one's own ends] explorar.

milk chocolate n (U) chocolate m ao leite.

milkman ['mɪlkmən] (pl -men [-mən]) n leiteiro m.

milk shake n milk-shake m.

milky ['mɪlkɪ] (compar -ier, superl -iest) adj -1. UK [with milk] com leite -2. [like milk] leitoso(sa) -3. [pale white] pálido(-da).

Milky Way n: the ~ a Via Láctea.

mill [mɪl] ⋄ n -1. [flour mill] moinho m -2. [factory] fábrica f -3. [grinder] moedor m. ⋄ vt [grain] moer.

◆ **mill about, mill around** vi aglomerar-se.

millennium [mɪ'lenɪəm] (pl -nnia [-nɪə]) n [thousand years] milênio m.

miller ['mɪlə'] n moleiro m, -ra f.

millet ['mɪlɪt] n painço m.

milligram(me) ['mɪlɪgræm] n miligrama m.

millimetre UK, **millimeter** US ['mɪlɪ͵miːtə'] n milímetro m.

millinery ['mɪlɪnrɪ] n (U) chapelaria f (para senhoras).

million ['mɪljən] n -1. [1,000,000] milhão m -2. [enormous number]: **a ~, ~s of** milhões de.

millionaire [͵mɪljə'neə'] n milionário m, -ria f.

millstone ['mɪlstəʊn] n [for grinding] pedra f de moinho.

milometer [maɪˈlɒmɪtə^r] n = mileometer.

mime [maɪm] ◇ n (U) mímica f. ◇ vt imitar. ◇ vi fazer mímica.

mimic [ˈmɪmɪk] (pt & pp **-ked**, cont **-king**) ◇ n [person] imitador m, -ra f. ◇ vt [person, voice, gestures] imitar.

mimicry [ˈmɪmɪkrɪ] n (U) imitação f.

min. [mɪn] **-1.** (abbr of **minute**) min. **-2.** (abbr of **minimum**) mín.

mince [mɪns] ◇ n (U) UK carne f picada. ◇ vt picar; **not to ~ one's words** não ter papas na língua. ◇ vi andar com passinhos.

mincemeat [ˈmɪnsmiːt] n (U) **-1.** [fruit] iguaria feita de sebo, frutas cristalizadas e passas **-2.** US [minced meat] picadinho m.

mince pie n torta com recheio de frutas secas preparada geralmente no Natal.

mincer [ˈmɪnsə^r] n moedor m de carne.

mind [maɪnd] ◇ n **-1.** [gen] mente f; **state of ~** estado m de espírito **-2.** [thoughts] memória f; **to come into/cross sb's ~** passar pela cabeça de alguém; **to have sthg on one's ~** estar preocupado(da) com algo **-3.** [attention]: **to concentrate the ~** concentrar a mente; **to keep one's ~ on sthg** concentrar-se em algo; **to put one's ~ to sthg** colocar empenho em algo **-4.** [opinion]: **to my ~** na minha opinião; **to change one's ~** mudar de idéia; **to keep an open ~** manter a mente aberta; **to make one's ~ up** tomar uma decisão; **to speak one's ~** dizer o que se pensa; **to be in two ~s about sthg** estar com dois corações sobre algo **-5.** [memory] memória f; **to bear sthg in ~** ter algo em mente **-6.** [intention]: **to have sthg in ~** ter algo em mente; **to have a ~ to do sthg** estar pensando em fazer algo. ◇ vi [care, worry] importar-se; **do you ~ if ...?** você se importaria se ...?; **I don't ~** eu não me importo; **never ~** [don't worry] não faz mal; [it's not important] não tem importância. ◇ vt **-1.** [object to] importar-se em; **I don't ~ waiting** não me importo em esperar; **I wouldn't ~ a ...** eu aceitaria um ... **-2.** [bother about] preocupar-se com **-3.** [pay attention to] prestar atenção com **-4.** [take care of] tomar conta de.
  ◆ **mind you** adv: **he didn't give me a Christmas present this year - ~, he never does** ele não me deu um presente de Natal neste ano - bom, mas ele nunca dá mesmo.

minder [ˈmaɪndə^r] n UK [bodyguard] guarda-costas m inv.

mindful [ˈmaɪndfʊl] adj: **~ of sthg** ciente de algo.

mindless [ˈmaɪndlɪs] adj **-1.** [stupid] absurdo(da), sem sentido **-2.** [not requiring thought] tedioso(sa).

mine[1] [maɪn] ◇ n [gen] mina f. ◇ vt **-1.** [excavate] extrair **-2.** [lay mines in] minar.

mine[2] [maɪn] poss pron o meu (a minha); **a friend of mine** um amigo meu; **those shoes are mine** esses sapatos são meus; **mine are here - where are yours?** os meus estão aqui - onde estão os seus?

minefield [ˈmaɪnfiːld] n **-1.** [area containing mines] campo m minado **-2.** fig [dangerous topic] campo m minado.

miner [ˈmaɪnə^r] n mineiro m, -ra f.

mineral [ˈmɪnərəl] ◇ adj GEOL mineral. ◇ n GEOL mineral m.

mineral water n (U) água f mineral.

minesweeper [ˈmaɪnˌswiːpə^r] n caça-minas m inv.

mingle [ˈmɪŋgl] vi **-1.** [combine] misturar-se; **to ~ with sthg** misturar-se com algo **-2.** [socially] misturar-se; **to ~ with sb** misturar-se com alguém.

miniature [ˈmɪnətʃə^r] ◇ adj [reduced-scale] em miniatura. ◇ n **-1.** [painting] miniatura f **-2.** [of alcohol] garrafa f em miniatura **-3.** [small scale]: **in ~** em miniatura.

minibus [ˈmɪnɪbʌs] (pl **-es**) n microônibus m inv.

minicab [ˈmɪnɪkæb] n UK radiotáxi m.

MiniDisc® [ˈmɪnɪdɪsk] n MiniDisc® m.

MiniDisc player® n reprodutor m de MiniDisc®.

minidish [ˈmɪnɪdɪʃ] n miniparabólica f.

minima [ˈmɪnɪmə] pl ▷ **minimum**.

minimal [ˈmɪnɪml] adj mínimo(ma).

minimum [ˈmɪnɪməm] (pl **-mums** OR **-ma**) ◇ adj mínimo(ma). ◇ n mínimo m.

mining [ˈmaɪnɪŋ] ◇ adj mineiro(ra); **~ engineer** engenheiro m, -ra f de minas. ◇ n mineração f.

miniskirt [ˈmɪnɪskɜːt] n minissaia f.

minister [ˈmɪnɪstə^r] n **-1.** POL: **~ (for sthg)** ministro m, -tra f (de algo) **-2.** RELIG pastor m, -ra f.
  ◆ **minister to** vt fus **-1.** [person] atender **-2.** [needs] atender a.

ministerial [ˌmɪnɪˈstɪərɪəl] adj POL ministerial.

minister of state n: **~ (for sthg)** secretário m, -ria f de estado (para algo).

ministry [ˈmɪnɪstrɪ] (pl **-ies**) n **-1.** POL ministério m; **Ministry of Defence** Ministério da Defesa **-2.** RELIG [clergy]: **the ~** o sacerdócio.

mink [mɪŋk] (pl inv) n -1. (U) [fur] pele f de visom -2. [animal] visom m.

minnow ['mɪnəʊ] n [fish] peixinho m (de água doce).

minor ['maɪnər] ⟨⟩ adj [gen] menor. ⟨⟩ n [in age] menor mf de idade.

Minorca [mɪ'nɔːkə] n Minorca f; in ~ em Minorca.

minority [maɪ'nɒrətɪ] (pl -ies) ⟨⟩ adj minoritário(ria). ⟨⟩ n [gen] minoria f.

mint [mɪnt] ⟨⟩ n -1. (U) [herb] hortelã f -2. [sweet] bala f de hortelã -3. [for coins]: **the Mint** a Casa da Moeda; **in ~ condition** novo(va) em folha. ⟨⟩ vt [coins] cunhar.

minus ['maɪnəs] (pl -es) ⟨⟩ prep -1. MATH [less]: **4 ~ 2 is 2** 4 menos 2 é 2 -2. [in temperatures]: **it's ~ 5 degrees** está fazendo 5 graus abaixo de zero. ⟨⟩ adj -1. MATH [less than zero] negativo(va) -2. SCH [in grades] menos. ⟨⟩ n -1. MATH sinal m de menos -2. [disadvantage] desvantagem f.

minus sign n sinal m de menos.

minute[1] ['mɪnɪt] n [gen] minuto m; **at any ~** a qualquer momento; **this ~** agora mesmo.
➤ **minutes** npl [of meeting] ata f.

minute[2] [maɪ'njuːt] adj [tiny] mínimo(-ma).

miracle ['mɪrəkl] n milagre m.

miraculous [mɪ'rækjʊləs] adj milagroso(sa).

mirage [mɪ'rɑːʒ] n miragem f.

mire [maɪər] n (U) lamaçal m.

mirror ['mɪrər] ⟨⟩ n espelho m. ⟨⟩ vt [copy] espelhar.

mirth [mɜːθ] n (U) literary alegria f.

misadventure [ˌmɪsəd'ventʃər] n fml [unfortunate accident] desventura f; **death by ~** JUR morte f acidental.

misapprehension ['mɪsˌæprɪ'henʃn] n mal-entendido m.

misappropriation ['mɪsəˌprəʊprɪ'eɪʃn] n desvio m.

misbehave [ˌmɪsbɪ'heɪv] vi comportar-se mal.

miscalculate [ˌmɪs'kælkjʊleɪt] vt & vi calcular mal.

miscarriage [ˌmɪs'kærɪdʒ] n aborto m natural.

miscarriage of justice n erro m judicial.

miscellaneous [ˌmɪsə'leɪnjəs] adj diverso(sa).

mischief ['mɪstʃɪf] n (U) -1. [playfulness] malícia f -2. [naughty behaviour] travessuras fpl -3. [harm] dano m.

mischievous ['mɪstʃɪvəs] adj -1. [playful]

cheio (cheia) de malícia -2. [naughty] travesso(sa).

misconception [ˌmɪskən'sepʃn] n conceito m falho, idéia f equivocada.

misconduct [ˌmɪs'kɒndʌkt] n [bad behaviour] má conduta f.

misconstrue [ˌmɪskən'struː] vt fml interpretar erroneamente.

miscount [ˌmɪs'kaʊnt] vt & vi contar mal.

misdeed [ˌmɪs'diːd] n literary delito m.

misdemeanour UK, **misdemeanor** US [ˌmɪsdɪ'miːnər] n JUR contravenção f.

miser ['maɪzər] n avarento m, -ta f.

miserable ['mɪzrəbl] adj -1. [unhappy] infeliz, triste -2. [depressing - conditions, life] miserável; [- weather, holiday, evening] horrível -3. [failure] lamentável.

miserly ['maɪzəlɪ] adj mesquinho(nha), miserável.

misery ['mɪzərɪ] (pl -ies) n -1. [unhappiness] tristeza f -2. [poverty] miséria f.

misfire [ˌmɪs'faɪər] vi -1. [gun] não disparar -2. [car engine] não dar partida -3. [plan] fracassar.

misfit ['mɪsfɪt] n desajustado m, -da f.

misfortune [mɪs'fɔːtʃuːn] n -1. (U) [bad luck] azar m -2. [piece of bad luck] infortúnio m, desgraça f.

misgivings [mɪs'gɪvɪŋz] npl receio m, desconfiança f.

misguided [ˌmɪs'gaɪdɪd] adj -1. [person] desencaminhado(da) -2. [attempt, opinion] equivocado(da).

mishandle [ˌmɪs'hændl] vt -1. [person, animal] maltratar -2. [negotiations, business] administrar mal.

mishap ['mɪshæp] n [unfortunate event] incidente m, percalço m.

misinterpret [ˌmɪsɪn'tɜːprɪt] vt interpretar mal.

misjudge [ˌmɪs'dʒʌdʒ] vt -1. [calculate wrongly] calcular mal -2. [appraise wrongly] julgar mal.

mislay [ˌmɪs'leɪ] (pt & pp -laid) vt perder, extraviar.

mislead [ˌmɪs'liːd] (pt & pp -led) vt enganar.

misleading [ˌmɪs'liːdɪŋ] adj enganoso(sa).

misled [ˌmɪs'led] pt & pp ⊳ **mislead**.

misnomer [ˌmɪs'nəʊmər] n termo m impróprio.

misplace [ˌmɪs'pleɪs] vt extraviar, perder.

misprint ['mɪsprɪnt] n erro m de impressão.

miss [mɪs] ⟨⟩ vt -1. [gen] perder -2. [fail to see] não ver, perder -3. [fail to hit] errar; **to ~ the target** não acertar o alvo **- 4.** [feel absence of - person, home, family] sentir/estar com saudades de; [- things] sentir falta de **- 5.** [fail to be present at] faltar a **- 6.** [escape] evitar; **I just ~ ed being run over** escapei de ser atropelado por pouco. ◇ *vt* [fail to hit] não acertar. ◇ *n*: **to give sthg a ~** *inf* deixar algo.

◆ **miss out** ◇ *vt sep* omitir. ◇ *vi*: **to ~ out (on sthg)** perder (algo).

Miss [mɪs] *n* Senhorita *f*.

misshapen [ˌmɪsˈʃeɪpn] *adj* **-1.** [hands, fingers] deformado(da) **- 2.** [object] disforme.

missile [*UK* ˈmɪsaɪl, *US* ˈmɪsəl] *n* **-1.** [weapon] míssil *m* **- 2.** [thrown object] projétil *m*.

missing [ˈmɪsɪŋ] *adj* **-1.** [object] perdido(da) **- 2.** [person] desaparecido(da) **- 3.** [not present] que falta; **who's ~?** quem está faltando?

mission [ˈmɪʃn] *n* missão *f*.

missionary [ˈmɪʃənrɪ] (*pl* -ies) *n* missionário *m*, -ria *f*.

misspend (*pt & pp* -spent) *vt* [money, talent, youth] desperdiçar.

mist [mɪst] *n* neblina *f*.

◆ **mist over, mist up** *vi* embaçar.

mistake [mɪˈsteɪk] (*pt* -took, *pp* -taken) ◇ *n* erro *m*; **to make a ~** cometer um erro, equivocar-se; **by ~** por engano. ◇ *vt* **- 1.** [misunderstand] entender mal **- 2.** [fail to distinguish]: **to ~** sb/sthg **for** confundir alguém/algo com.

mistaken [mɪˈsteɪkn] ◇ *pp* ⇨ **mistake.** ◇ *adj* **-1.** [person] equivocado(da), enganado(da); **to be ~ about** sb/sthg estar enganado(da) sobre alguém/algo **- 2.** [belief, idea] equivocado(da).

mister [ˈmɪstəʳ] *n inf* amigo *m*.

◆ **Mister** *n* Senhor *m*.

mistletoe [ˈmɪsltəʊ] *n* (*U*) visco *m*.

mistook [mɪˈstʊk] *pt* ⇨ **mistake.**

mistreat [ˌmɪsˈtriːt] *vt* maltratar.

mistress [ˈmɪstrɪs] *n* **-1.** [of house, situation] dona *f* **- 2.** [female lover] amante *f* **- 3.** [schoolteacher] professora *f*.

mistrust [ˌmɪsˈtrʌst] ◇ *n* (*U*) desconfiança *f*, receio *m*. ◇ *vt* desconfiar de.

misty [ˈmɪstɪ] (*compar* -ier, *superl* -iest) *adj* nebuloso(sa).

misunderstand [ˌmɪsʌndəˈstænd] (*pt & pp* -stood) *vt & vi* entender mal.

misunderstanding [ˌmɪsʌndəˈstændɪŋ] *n* **-1.** (*U*) [lack of understanding] equívoco *m* **- 2.** [wrong interpretation] mal-entendido *m* **- 3.** [disagreement] desentendimento *m*.

misunderstood [ˌmɪsʌndəˈstʊd] *pt & pp* ⇨ **misunderstand.**

misuse [*n* ˌmɪsˈjuːs, *vb* ˌmɪsˈjuːz] ◇ *n* **-1.** (*U*) [wrong use] uso *m* indevido **- 2.** [abuse] abuso *m*. ◇ *vt* **-1.** [use wrongly] usar indevidamente **- 2.** [abuse] abusar de.

miter *n US* = **mitre.**

mitigate [ˈmɪtɪgeɪt] *vt fml* mitigar.

mitre *UK*, **miter** *US* [ˈmaɪtəʳ] *n* **-1.** [hat] mitra *f* **- 2.** [joint] meia-esquadria *f*.

mitt [mɪt] *n* **-1.** = **mitten - 2.** [in baseball] luva *f*.

mitten [ˈmɪtn] *n* [with fingers joined] luva *f* (*com separação somente para o polegar*); [with fingers cut off] mitene *f*.

mix [mɪks] ◇ *vi* misturar-se, combinar-se; **to ~ with** sb misturar-se com alguém. ◇ *n* **-1.** [gen] mistura *f* **- 2.** COMM: **marketing ~** mix *m* de marketing, composto *m* mercadológico.

◆ **mix up** *vt sep* **-1.** [confuse] confundir **- 2.** [disorder] misturar.

mixed [mɪkst] *adj* **-1.** [of different kinds] misturado(da) **- 2.** [of different sexes] misto(ta).

mixed-ability *adj UK* de vários níveis.

mixed grill *n* prato grelhado com carnes e vegetais.

mixed up *adj* **-1.** [confused] confuso(sa) **- 2.** [involved]: **to be ~ in** sthg estar envolvido(da) em algo.

mixer [ˈmɪksəʳ] *n* **-1.** [machine - for food] *f* batedeira; [- for drinks] misturador *m*; [- for cement] betoneira *f* **- 2.** [soft drink] *bebida não-alcoólica usada para se misturar com bebidas alcoólicas*.

mixture [ˈmɪkstʃəʳ] *n* mistura *f*.

mix-up *n inf* engano *m*, confusão *f*.

ml (*abbr of* **millilitre**) *n* ml.

mm (*abbr of* **millimetre**) mm.

MMR (*abbr of* **measles, mumps, and rubella**) *n* MMR *f*, SCR *f*.

moan [məʊn] ◇ *n* [of pain, sadness] gemido *m*. ◇ *vi* **-1.** [in pain, sadness] gemer **- 2.** *inf* [complain] resmungar, queixar-se; **to ~ about** sb/sthg resmungar OR queixar-se sobre alguém/algo.

moat [məʊt] *n* fosso *m*.

mob [mɒb] (*pt & pp* -bed, *cont* -bing) ◇ *n* **-1.** multidão *f* **- 2.** *pej*: **the ~** a ralé, a plebe. ◇ *vt* cercar, amontoar-se ao redor de.

mobile [ˈməʊbaɪl] ◇ *adj* **-1.** [able to move] móvel **- 2.** *inf* [having transport] motorizado(da). ◇ *n* **-1.** [phone] (telefone) celular *m* **- 2.** [decoration] móbile *m*.

mobile home *n* trailer *m*.

mobile phone *n* (telefone) celular *m*.

mobilize, -ise ['məʊbɪlaɪz] <> vt mobilizar. <> vi mobilizar-se.

mock [mɒk] <> adj falso(sa); a ~ exam um simulado. <> vt [deride] zombar de. <> vi zombar.

mockery ['mɒkərɪ] n - 1. (U) [scorn] zombaria f - 2. [travesty] paródia f.

mod cons [,mɒd-] (abbr of **modern conveniences**) npl UK inf: all ~ todas as comodidades modernas.

mode [məʊd] n - 1. [gen] modo m - 2. [of transport] meio m.

model ['mɒdl] (UK pt & pp -led, cont -ling, US pt & pp -ed, cont -ing) <> adj - 1. [miniature] em miniatura - 2. [exemplary] modelo. <> n [gen] modelo m. <> vt - 1. [shape] moldar - 2. [in fashion show] desfilar com - 3. [copy]: to ~ o.s. on sb ter alguém como modelo, espelhar-se em alguém. <> vi [in fashion show] desfilar.

modem ['məʊdem] COMPUT n modem m.

moderate [adj & n 'mɒdərət, vb 'mɒdəreɪt] <> adj moderado(da). <> n POL moderado m, -da f. <> vt moderar. <> vi moderar-se.

moderation [,mɒdə'reɪʃn] n moderação f; in ~ com moderação.

modern ['mɒdən] adj moderno(na).

modernize, -ise ['mɒdənaɪz] <> vt modernizar. <> vi modernizar-se.

modern languages npl línguas fpl modernas.

modest ['mɒdɪst] adj modesto(ta).

modesty ['mɒdɪstɪ] n (U) modéstia f.

modicum ['mɒdɪkəm] n fml quantia f módica; a ~ of um mínimo de.

modify ['mɒdɪfaɪ] (pt & pp -ied) vt - 1. [alter] modificar - 2. [tone down] moderar.

module ['mɒdjuːl] n módulo m.

mogul ['məʊgl] n [magnate] magnata m.

mohair ['məʊheəʳ] n mohair m.

moist [mɔɪst] adj úmido(da); ~ cake bolo m fofo.

moisten ['mɔɪsn] vt umedecer.

moisture ['mɔɪstʃəʳ] n (U) umidade f.

moisturizer ['mɔɪstʃəraɪzəʳ] n (creme) hidratante m.

molar ['məʊləʳ] n molar m.

molasses [mə'læsɪz] n (U) melaço m.

mold etc n & vt US = mould.

mole [məʊl] n - 1. [animal] toupeira f - 2. [on skin] sinal m - 3. [spy] espião m, -ã f.

molecule ['mɒlɪkjuːl] n molécula f.

molest [mə'lest] vt - 1. [attack sexually - child] molestar; [- person] assediar - 2. [bother] incomodar.

mollusc, mollusk US ['mɒləsk] n molusco m.

mollycoddle ['mɒlɪ,kɒdl] vt inf mimar.

molt vt & vi US = moult.

molten ['məʊltn] adj derretido(da), fundido(da).

mom [mɒm] n US inf mãe f.

moment ['məʊmənt] n [gen] momento m; at any ~ a qualquer momento; at the ~ no momento; for the ~ por enquanto.

momentarily ['məʊməntərɪlɪ] adv - 1. [for a short time] momentaneamente - 2. US [immediately] imediatamente.

momentary ['məʊməntrɪ] adj momentâneo(nea).

momentous [mə'mentəs] adj significativo(va).

momentum [mə'mentəm] n - 1. PHYSICS momento m - 2. fig [speed, force] força f.

momma ['mɒmə], **mommy** ['mɒmɪ] n US mamãe f, mãezinha f.

Monaco ['mɒnəkəʊ] n Mônaco; in ~ em Mônaco.

monarch ['mɒnək] n monarca mf.

monarchy ['mɒnəkɪ] (pl -ies) n monarquia f; the ~ a monarquia.

monastery ['mɒnəstrɪ] (pl -ies) n monastério m.

Monday ['mʌndɪ] n segunda-feira f; see also Saturday.

monetary ['mʌnɪtrɪ] adj monetário(ria).

money ['mʌnɪ] n (U) dinheiro m; to make ~ ganhar dinheiro; to get one's ~'s worth fazer o dinheiro OR investimento valer a pena.

moneybox ['mʌnɪbɒks] n cofrinho m.

moneylender ['mʌnɪ,lendəʳ] n prestamista mf.

money order n ordem f de pagamento.

money-spinner [-,spɪnəʳ] n esp UK inf mina f (de ouro).

mongol ['mɒngəl] dated & offensive n mongolóide m.

Mongolia [mɒŋ'gəʊliə] n Mongólia.

mongrel ['mʌngrəl] n [dog] vira-lata m.

monitor ['mɒnɪtəʳ] <> n TECH monitor m. <> vt monitorar.

monk [mʌŋk] n monge m.

monkey ['mʌŋkɪ] (pl -s) n [animal] macaco m, -ca f.

monkey nut n amendoim m.

monkey wrench n chave f inglesa.

mono ['mɒnəʊ] <> adj monofônico(ca), mono inv. <> n inf [sound] som m mono.

monochrome ['mɒnəkrəʊm] adj [TV, photograph] monocromo(ma).

monocle ['mɒnəkl] n monóculo m.

monologue, monolog US ['mɒnəlɒg] n THEATRE monólogo m.

monopolize, -ise [mə'nɒpəlaɪz] vt monopolizar.

monopoly [mə'nɒpəlɪ] (pl -ies) n monopólio m.

monotone ['mɒnətəʊn] n: **he speaks in a** ~ ele fala com uma voz monótona.

monotonous [mə'nɒtənəs] adj [voice, job, life] monótono(na).

monotony [mə'nɒtənɪ] n (U) monotonia f.

monsoon [mɒn'suːn] n [rainy season] monção f.

monster ['mɒnstə^r] n monstro m.

monstrosity [mɒn'strɒsətɪ] (pl -ies) n monstruosidade f.

monstrous ['mɒnstrəs] adj -1. [appalling] espantoso(sa) -2. [hideous] monstruoso(sa) -3. [very large] gigantesco(ca).

Mont Blanc [mɒnt] n Monte m Branco.

month [mʌnθ] n mês m.

monthly ['mʌnθlɪ] (pl -ies) <> adj mensal. <> adv mensalmente. <> n [publication] revista f mensal.

Montreal [mɒntrɪ'ɔːl] n Montreal; **in** ~ em Montreal.

monument ['mɒnjʊmənt] n monumento m.

monumental [ˌmɒnjʊ'mentl] adj -1. [gen] monumental -2. [extremely bad] descomunal.

moo [muː] (pl -s) <> n mugido m. <> vi mugir.

mood [muːd] n [state of feelings] humor m; **in a (bad)** ~ de mau humor; **in a good** ~ de bom humor.

moody ['muːdɪ] (compar -ier, superl -iest) adj pej -1. [changeable] temperamental, de humor variável -2. [bad-tempered] mal-humorado(da).

moon [muːn] n lua f.

moonlight ['muːnlaɪt] (pt & pp -ed) <> n (U) luar m, luz f da lua. <> vi inf [have second job] ter um trabalho extra.

moonlighting ['muːnlaɪtɪŋ] n (U) [illegal work] trabalho m extra, bico m.

moonlit ['muːnlɪt] adj enluarado(da).

moor [mɔː^r] vt & vi atracar, ancorar.

moorland ['mɔːlənd] n (U) esp UK charneca f.

moose [muːs] (pl inv) n [North American] alce m.

mop [mɒp] (pt & pp -ped, cont -ping) <> n -1. [for cleaning] esfregão m -2. inf [of hair] mecha f. <> vt -1. [floor] esfregar, passar o esfregão em -2. [brow, face] enxugar.

➤ **mop up** vt sep -1. [clean up] limpar (com esfregão) -2. fig [clear away] eliminar.

mope [məʊp] vi pej lastimar-se.

moped ['məʊped] n bicicleta f motorizada.

moral ['mɒrəl] <> adj moral. <> n [lesson] moral f.

➤ **morals** npl [principles] princípios mpl.

morale [mə'rɑːl] n (U) moral m.

morality [mə'rælətɪ] (pl -ies) n moralidade f.

morass [mə'ræs] n [mass] emaranhado m, confusão f.

morbid ['mɔːbɪd] adj [unhealthy] mórbido(da).

more [mɔː^r] <> adj -1. [a larger amount of] mais; **there are** ~ **tourists than usual** há mais turistas que o normal. -2. [additional] mais; **is there any** ~ **cake?** tem mais bolo?; **I'd like two** ~ **bottles** queria mais duas garrafas; **there's no** ~ **wine** já não tem mais vinho. <> adv -1. [in comparatives] mais; **it's** ~ **difficult than before** é mais difícil do que antes; **speak** ~ **clearly** fale de forma mais clara; **we go there** ~ **often now** agora vamos lá mais freqüentemente. -2. [to a greater degree] mais; **we ought to go to the movies** ~ **deviamos ir mais vezes ao cinema.** -3. [in phrases]: **once** ~ mais uma vez; **we'd be** ~ **than happy to help** teríamos muito prazer em ajudar.

➤ **more and more** adv, adj & pron cada vez mais.

➤ **more or less** adv mais ou menos.

moreover [mɔː'rəʊvə^r] adv fml além disso.

morgue [mɔːg] n [mortuary] necrotério m.

Mormon ['mɔːmən] n mórmon mf.

morning ['mɔːnɪŋ] n -1. [first part of day] manhã f; **in the** ~ [before lunch] de OR pela manhã; [tomorrow morning] pela manhã -2. [between midnight and noon] manhã f.

➤ **mornings** adv US de manhã.

Moroccan [mə'rɒkən] <> adj marroquino(na). <> n marroquino m, -na f.

Morocco [mə'rɒkəʊ] n Marrocos f.

moron ['mɔːrɒn] n inf [stupid person] idiota mf, imbecil mf.

morose [mə'rəʊs] adj melancólico(ca).

morphing n morphing m.

morphine ['mɔːfiːn] n (U) morfina f.

Morse (code) [mɔːs-] n (U) código m Morse.

morsel ['mɔːsl] n pedacinho m.

mortal ['mɔːtl] <> adj mortal. <> n mortal mf.

mortality [mɔː'tælətɪ] n (U) mortalidade f.

mortar ['mɔːtə^r] n -1. (U) [cement mixture]

argamassa f - **2.** [gun] morteiro m - **3.** [bowl] almofariz m.

mortgage ['mɔ:gɪdʒ] ◇ n hipoteca f. ◇ vt hipotecar.

mortified ['mɔ:tɪfaɪd] adj mortificado(-da).

mortify vt mortificar.

mortuary ['mɔ:tʃuəri] (pl -ies) n necrotério m.

mosaic [mə'zeɪɪk] n mosaico m.

Moscow ['mɒskəu] n Moscou; in ~ em Moscou.

Moslem ['mɒzləm] adj & n = **Muslim**.

mosque [mɒsk] n mesquita f.

mosquito [mə'ski:təu] (pl -es OR -s) n mosquito m.

moss [mɒs] n (U) musgo m.

most [məust] ◇ adj (superl of many & much) - **1.** [the majority of] a maioria de; ~ **people** a maioria das pessoas - **2.** [largest amount of]: (the) ~ mais; **who's got (the)** ~ **money?** quem é que tem mais dinheiro?; **what gave me (the)** ~ **satisfaction was ...** o que me deu a maior satisfação foi ... ◇ pron - **1.** [the majority] a maioria; ~ **of a maioria de;** ~ **of the time** a maior parte do tempo - **2.** [largest amount]: (the) ~ o máximo; at ~ no máximo - **3.** phr: **to make the** ~ **of** sthg tirar o máximo de algo. ◇ adv - **1.** [to the greatest extent]: **what I like (the)** ~ o que eu mais gosto - **2.** fml [very] muito; ~ **certainly** com toda a certeza - **3.** US [almost] quase.

mostly ['məustli] adv - **1.** [in the main] principalmente - **2.** [usually] normalmente.

MOT n (abbr of Ministry of Transport (test)) vistoria anual obrigatória realizada pelo Ministério dos Transportes britânico em carros com mais de 3 anos de fabricação.

motel [məu'tel] n hotel m de beira de estrada.

moth [mɒθ] n - **1.** ZOOL mariposa f - **2.** [in clothes] traça f.

mothball ['mɒθbɔ:l] n (bola de) naftalina f.

mother ['mʌðər] ◇ n mãe f ◇ vt pej [spoil] mimar.

mother-in-law (pl mothers-in-law OR mother-in-laws) n sogra f.

motherly ['mʌðəli] adj maternal, materno(na).

mother-of-pearl n (U) madrepérola f.

mother-to-be (pl mothers-to-be) n futura mãe f.

mother tongue n língua f materna.

motif [məu'ti:f] n motivo m.

motion ['məuʃn] ◇ n - **1.** (U) [process of moving] movimento m; **to set sthg in** ~ colocar algo em marcha - **2.** [proposal] proposta f. ◇ vt: **to** ~ **sb to do sthg** fazer sinal para alguém fazer algo. ◇ vi: **to** ~ **to sb** fazer sinal (com a mão) para alguém.

motionless ['məuʃənlɪs] adj imóvel.

motion picture n US filme m.

motivated ['məutɪveɪtɪd] adj motivado(-da).

motivation [ˌməutɪ'veɪʃn] n - **1.** [cause] razão f - **2.** (U) [sense of purpose] motivação f.

motive ['məutɪv] n motivo m, razão f.

motley ['mɒtlɪ] adj pej heterogêneo(-nea).

motor ['məutər] ◇ adj UK [relating to cars - industry, accident] automobilístico(-ca); [- mechanic] de automóveis. ◇ n [engine] motor m.

motorbike ['məutəbaɪk] n moto f.

motorboat ['məutəbəut] n barco m a motor.

motorcar ['məutəkɑ:r] n UK fml automóvel m.

motorcycle ['məutəˌsaɪkl] n motocicleta f.

motorcyclist ['məutəˌsaɪklɪst] n motociclista mf.

motoring ['məutərɪŋ] ◇ adj UK automobilístico(ca); ~ **offence** infração f de trânsito. ◇ n (U) dated automobilismo m.

motorist ['məutərɪst] n motorista mf.

motor racing n (U) corrida f automobilística.

motor scooter n lambreta f.

motor vehicle n veículo m motorizado.

motorway ['məutəweɪ] n UK auto-estrada f.

mottled ['mɒtld] adj com manchas, pintado(da).

motto ['mɒtəu] (pl -s OR -es) n [maxim] lema m.

mould, mold US [məuld] ◇ n - **1.** (U) BOT mofo m - **2.** [shape] fôrma f, molde m. ◇ vt - **1.** [influence] moldar - **2.** [shape physically] moldar, modelar.

moulding, molding US ['məuldɪŋ] n [decoration] cornija f.

mouldy, moldy US (compar -ier, superl -iest) ['məuldɪ] adj mofado(da).

moult, molt US [məult] vi - **1.** [bird] trocar as penas - **2.** [dog] trocar o pêlo.

mound [maund] n - **1.** [small hill] morro m - **2.** [untidy pile] montanha f.

mount [maunt] ◇ n - **1.** [support, frame] moldura f - **2.** [horse, pony] montaria f

- 3. [mountain] monte *m.* ⟨⟩ *vt* **-1.** [climb onto] montar **- 2.** *fml* [climb up] subir **- 3.** [organize] montar **- 4.** [photograph] emoldurar **- 5.** [trophy] pôr em posição de destaque **- 6.** [jewel] engastar. ⟨⟩ *vi* **-1.** [increase] aumentar **- 2.** [climb on horse] montar.

mountain [ˈmaʊntɪn] *n* [gen] montanha *f.*

mountain bike *n* mountain bike *f.*

mountaineer [ˌmaʊntɪˈnɪəʳ] *n* montanhista *mf,* alpinista *mf.*

mountaineering [ˌmaʊntɪˈnɪərɪŋ] *n (U)* montanhismo *m,* alpinismo *m.*

mountainous [ˈmaʊntɪnəs] *adj* [full of mountains] montanhoso(sa).

mourn [mɔːn] ⟨⟩ *vt* **-1.** [the loss of] lamentar **- 2.** [the death of] lamentar a morte de. ⟨⟩ *vi:* **to ~ for sb** fazer luto por alguém.

mourner [ˈmɔːnəʳ] *n* enlutado *m,* -da *f.*

mournful [ˈmɔːnfʊl] *adj* lamuriento(ta), desolado(da).

mourning [ˈmɔːnɪŋ] *n* **-1.** [period] luto *m* **- 2.** [clothes] traje *m* de luto; **in ~** em luto.

mouse [maʊs] *(pl* **mice)** *n* **-1.** [animal] camundongo *m* **- 2.** *COMPUT* mouse *m.*

mouse mat, mouse pad *n COMPUT* mouse pad *m.*

mousetrap [ˈmaʊstræp] *n* ratoeira *f.*

mousse [muːs] *n* **-1.** [food] musse *f* **- 2.** [for hair] mousse *m.*

moustache *UK* [məˈstɑːʃ], **mustache** *US* [ˈmʌstæʃ] *n* bigode *m.*

mouth [*n* maʊθ] *n* **-1.** *ANAT* boca *f* **- 2.** [entrance - of cave, hole] boca *f;* [- of river] foz *f.*

mouthful [ˈmaʊθfʊl] *n* [amount - of food] bocado *m;* [- of water] gole *m* .

mouthorgan [ˈmaʊθˌɔːɡən] *n* harmônica *f,* gaita-de-boca *f.*

mouthpiece [ˈmaʊθpiːs] *n* **-1.** [of object] bocal *m* **- 2.** [spokesperson] porta-voz *mf.*

mouth ulcer *n* úlcera *f* bucal.

mouthwash [ˈmaʊθwɒʃ] *n* anti-séptico *m* bucal.

mouth-watering [-ˌwɔːtərɪŋ] *adj* de dar água na boca.

movable [ˈmuːvəbl] *adj* móvel.

move [muːv] ⟨⟩ *n* **-1.** [movement] movimento *m;* **to get a ~ on** *inf* apressar-se **- 2.** [change] mudança *f* **- 3.** [in board game - turn to play] vez *f;* [- action] jogada *f* **- 4.** [course of action] medida *f.* ⟨⟩ *vt* **-1.** [shift] mudar, mexer; **to ~ the car** tirar o carro **- 2.** [change - job, office] mudar de; [- house] mudar-se de **- 3.** [affect emotionally] tocar, comover **- 4.** [in debate]: **to ~ that ...** sugerir que ... **- 5.**

fml [cause]: **to ~ sb to do sthg** impelir alguém a fazer algo. ⟨⟩ *vi* **-1.** [shift] mover-se, mexer-se **- 2.** [act] agir **- 3.** [to new house, job] mudar-se.

⬤ **move about** *vi* **-1.** [fidget] remexer-se, ir de lá para cá **- 2.** [travel] viajar.

⬤ **move along** ⟨⟩ *vt sep* circular. ⟨⟩ *vi* continuar andando.

⬤ **move around** *vi* = **move about.**

⬤ **move away** *vi* **-1.** [go in opposite direction] afastar-se **- 2.** [live elsewhere] ir-se embora.

⬤ **move in** *vi* **-1.** [to new house] instalar-se **- 2.** [take control, attack] preparar-se para o ataque.

⬤ **move on** *vi* **-1.** [after stopping] prosseguir **- 2.** [in discussion] passar para outro tema.

⬤ **move out** *vi* [from house] mudar-se.

⬤ **move over** *vi* chegar mais para lá/cá.

⬤ **move up** *vi* [on seat] chegar mais para lá/cá.

moveable *adj* = **movable.**

movement [ˈmuːvmənt] *n* **-1.** [gen] movimento *m* **- 2.** [transportation] movimentação *f.*

movie [ˈmuːvɪ] *n esp US* filme *m.*

movie camera *n* câmara *f* cinematográfica.

moving [ˈmuːvɪŋ] *adj* **-1.** [touching] tocante, comovente **- 2.** [not fixed] móvel.

mow [məʊ] *(pt* **-ed,** *pp* **-ed** *OR* **mown)** *vt* [cut - grass, lawn] cortar; [- corn, wheat] ceifar.

⬤ **mow down** *vt sep* dizimar.

mower [ˈməʊəʳ] *n* [machine] ceifadeira *f.*

mown [məʊn] *pp* ⊳ **mow.**

MP *n* **-1.** *(abbr of* **Member of Parliament)** *membro do Parlamento Britânico* **- 2.** *(abbr of* **Military Police)** *polícia militar,* ≃ PE *f.*

MP3 *(abbr of* **MPEG-1 Audio Layer-3)** *COMPUT* MP3 *m.*

MPEG *(abbr of* **Moving Pictures Expert Group)** *n COMPUT* MPEG *m.*

mpg *(abbr of* **miles per gallon)** *n* milhas *fpl* por galão.

mph *(abbr of* **miles per hour)** *n* milhas *fpl* por hora.

Mr [ˈmɪstəʳ] *(abbr of* **Mister)** *n* Sr.

Mrs [ˈmɪsɪz] *(abbr of* **Missus)** *n* Sra.

Ms [mɪz] *n abreviatura usada diante do nome de mulher quando não se quer especificar seu estado civil, válida para senhora ou senhorita.*

MS *n (abbr of* **multiple sclerosis)** *esclerose f* múltipla.

MSc *(abbr of* **Master of Science)** *n (titular de) mestrado em ciências.*

much [mʌtʃ] (*compar* more, *superl* most)
⟨⟩ *adj* muito(ta); **as ~ (...) as** tanto (...)
quanto; **how ~ ...?** quanto ...?; **too ~ ...**
demais. ⟨⟩ *pron* muito; **how ~ have
you got?** quanto você tem?; **I don't think
~ of it** não me parece grande coisa; **as
~ as** tanto quanto; **how ~?** quanto?;
too ~ demais; **this isn't ~ of a party**
essa festa não está grande coisa; **I'm
not ~ of a cook** não sou um grande
cozinheiro; **so ~ for my hard work!**
tanto desgaste por meu trabalho!; **I
thought as ~** já imaginava. ⟨⟩ *adv*
muito; **thank you very ~** muito obriga-
do(da); **it's ~ too cold** está frio demais;
it's ~ the same é praticamente a
mesma coisa; **'what did you think of the
film?' - 'not ~'** 'o que você achou do
filme?' - 'não gostei muito'; **he's not so
~ stupid as lazy** ele é muito mais
preguiçoso que bobo; **too ~** demais;
without so ~ as ... sem nem sequer ...;
~ as (exatamente) como; **nothing ~**
nada de mais.

muck [mʌk] *n inf* **-1.** [dirt] sujeira *f* **-2.**
[manure] esterco *m*.
◆ **muck about, muck around** *UK inf* ⟨⟩
vt sep fazer perder tempo. ⟨⟩ *vi* fazer
cera.
◆ **muck up** *vt sep UK inf* estragar.

mucky ['mʌkɪ] (*compar* -ier, *superl* -iest)
adj inf sujo(ja).

mucus ['mju:kəs] *n* (U) muco *m*.

mud [mʌd] *n* (U) lama *f*, barro *m*.

muddle ['mʌdl] ⟨⟩ *n* **-1.** [disorder]
desordem *f* **-2.** [confusion] confusão *f*.
⟨⟩ *vt* **-1.** [put into disorder] desordenar
-2. [confuse] confundir, misturar.
◆ **muddle along** *vi* prosseguir de forma confusa.
◆ **muddle through** *vi* conseguir de
qualquer jeito.
◆ **muddle up** *vt sep* misturar.

muddy ['mʌdɪ] (*compar* -ier, *superl*
-iest, *pt & pp* -ied) ⟨⟩ *adj* [covered with
mud - floor, boots] embarrado(da); [- riv-
er] lamacento(ta). ⟨⟩ *vt fig* [issue, situa-
tion] complicar.

mudguard ['mʌdgɑ:d] *n* pára-lama *m*.

mud-slinging *n* (U) *fig* difamação *f*.

muesli ['mju:zlɪ] *n UK* granola *f*.

muff [mʌf] ⟨⟩ *n* [for hands] regalo *m*;
[for ears] protetor *m* de orelhas (*contra
o frio*). ⟨⟩ *vt inf* perder.

muffin ['mʌfɪn] *n* **-1.** *UK* [bread roll]
*pãozinho redondo e chato que se
come quente com manteiga* **-2.** *US*
[cake] bolinho *m* doce com frutas/
chocolate.

muffle ['mʌfl] *vt* [quieten] abafar.

muffler ['mʌflər] *n US* [for car] silenciador *m*.

mug [mʌg] (*pt & pp* -ged, *cont* -ging) ⟨⟩
n **-1.** caneca *f* **-2.** *inf* [fool] tolo *m*, -la *f.*
⟨⟩ *vt* [attack and rob] assaltar.

mugging ['mʌgɪŋ] *n* assalto *m*.

muggy ['mʌgɪ] (*compar* -ier, *superl* -iest)
adj mormacento(ta), quente e úmido(-
da).

mule [mju:l] *n* **-1.** [animal] mula *f* **-2.** [slip-
per] tamanco *m*.

mull [mʌl] ◆ **mull over** *vt sep* refletir
sobre.

mullah ['mʌlə] *n* mulá *m*.

mulled [mʌld] *adj*: **~ wine** quentão *m*.

multicoloured *UK*, **multicolored** *US*
[,mʌltɪ'kʌləd] *adj* multicor.

multilateral [,mʌltɪ'lætərəl] *adj* multilateral.

multilingual *adj* multilíngue.

multimedia [,mʌltɪ'mi:djə] *adj* COMPUT
multimídia.

multinational [,mʌltɪ'næʃənl] *n* multinacional *f.*

multiple ['mʌltɪpl] ⟨⟩ *adj* múltiplo(-
pla). ⟨⟩ *n* MATH múltiplo *m.*

multiple sclerosis [-sklɪ'rəusɪs] *n* (U)
esclerose *f* múltipla.

multiplex cinema ['mʌltɪpleks-] *n* cinema *m* multissalas, cinema *m* multiplex.

multiplication [,mʌltɪplɪ'keɪʃn] *n* multiplicação *f.*

multiplication table *n* tabuada *f.*

multiply ['mʌltɪplaɪ] (*pt & pp* -ied) ⟨⟩
vt multiplicar. ⟨⟩ *vi* **-1.** MATH multiplicar **-2.** [increase] multiplicar-se.

multi-storey *UK*, **multistory** *US* ⟨⟩
adj com muitos andares. ⟨⟩ *n* edifí-
cio-garagem *m.*

multitude ['mʌltɪtju:d] *n* **-1.** [large num-
ber] multiplicidade *f* **-2.** [crowd] multidão *f.*

mum [mʌm] *UK inf* ⟨⟩ *n* [mother]
mamãe *f.* ⟨⟩ *adj*: **to keep ~** não dar
um pio.

mumble ['mʌmbl] *vt & vi* murmurar.

mummy ['mʌmɪ] (*pl* -ies) *n* **-1.** *UK inf*
[mother] mamãe *f*, mãe *f* **-2.** [preserved
body] múmia *f.*

mumps [mʌmps] *n* (U) caxumba *f.*

munch [mʌntʃ] *vt & vi* mascar.

mundane [mʌn'deɪn] *adj* trivial.

municipal [mju:'nɪsɪpl] *adj* municipal.

municipality [mju:,nɪsɪ'pælətɪ] (*pl* -ies) *n*
[city, district] município *m.*

mural [mju:ərəl] *n* (pintura *f*) mural *m.*

murder ['mɜ:dər] ⟨⟩ *n* assassinato *m.*
⟨⟩ *vt* assassinar.

murderer ['mɜ:dərər] *n* assassino *m.*

murderous ['mɜːdərəs] *adj* assassino(-na), homicida.

murky ['mɜːkɪ] (*compar* -ier, *superl* -iest) *adj* -1. [gen] sombrio(bria) -2. [water] turvo(va).

murmur ['mɜːməʳ] ◇ *n* -1. [low sound] murmúrio *m* -2. MED [of heart] sopro *m*. *vt & vi* murmurar.

muscle ['mʌsl] *n* -1. músculo *m* -2. (U) *fig* [power] poder *m*.
◆ **muscle in** *vi* intrometer-se.

muscular ['mʌskjʊləʳ] *adj* -1. [of muscles] muscular -2. [strong] musculoso(sa).

muse [mjuːz] ◇ *n* [source of inspiration] musa *f*. ◇ *vi* meditar, refletir.

museum [mjuː'ziːəm] *n* museu *m*.

mushroom ['mʌʃrʊm] ◇ *n* cogumelo *m*. ◇ *vi* [grow quickly] expandir-se rapidamente.

music ['mjuːzɪk] *n* -1. [gen] música *f* -2. [written set of notes] partitura *f*.

musical ['mjuːzɪkl] ◇ *adj* -1. [relating to music] [melodious] musical -2. [talented in music] com talento para música. ◇ *n* musical *m*.

musical instrument *n* instrumento *m* musical.

music centre *n* [machine] aparelho *m* de som.

music hall *n* UK -1. [theatre] sala *f* de espetáculo -2. (U) [variety entertainment] teatro *m* de variedades.

musician [mjuː'zɪʃn] *n* músico *m*, -ca *f*.

Muslim ['mʊzlɪm] ◇ *adj* muçulmano(na). ◇ *n* muçulmano *m*, -na *f*.

muslin ['mʌzlɪn] *n* (U) musselina *f*.

mussel ['mʌsl] *n* mexilhão *m*.

must [mʌst] ◇ *modal vb* -1. [have to] dever, ter que; **I → go** eu preciso ir -2. [intend to] ter que -3. [as suggestion] precisar, ter que -4. [to express likelihood] dever. ◇ *n* (U) *inf* [necessity]: **the film is a →** você tem que ver o filme.

mustache *n* US = **moustache.**

mustard ['mʌstəd] *n* (U) mostarda *f*.

muster ['mʌstəʳ] ◇ *vt* -1. [assemble] reunir -2. [summon - strength, energy] juntar; [- support] reunir. ◇ *vi* reunir-se.

mustn't ['mʌsnt] = **must not.**

must've ['mʌstəv] = **must have.**

musty ['mʌstɪ] (*compar* -ier, *superl* -iest) *adj* -1. [gen] mofado(da) -2. [smell] com cheiro de mofo.

mute [mjuːt] ◇ *adj* mudo(da). *n* [person who cannot speak] mudo *m*, -da *f*.

muted ['mjuːtɪd] *adj* -1. [soft] suave -2. [less strong - reaction] discreto(ta); [- feelings] contido(da).

mutilate ['mjuːtɪleɪt] *vt* mutilar.

mutiny ['mjuːtɪnɪ] (*pl* -ies, *pt & pp* -ied) ◇ *n* motim *m*. ◇ *vi* amotinar-se.

mutter ['mʌtəʳ] ◇ *vt* murmurar. ◇ *vi* resmungar; **to → to sb** sussurrar para alguém.

mutton ['mʌtn] *n* (U) (carne *f* de) carneiro *m*.

mutual ['mjuːtʃʊəl] *adj* -1. [reciprocal] mútuo(tua) -2. [common] comum.

mutually ['mjuːtʃʊəlɪ] *adv* [reciprocally] mutuamente.

muzzle ['mʌzl] ◇ *n* -1. [dog's nose and jaws] focinho *m* -2. [wire guard] focinheira *f* -3. [of gun] boca *f*. ◇ *vt* -1. [put guard on] colocar focinheira em -2. *fig* [silence] amordaçar.

MW (*abbr of* **medium wave**) onda *f* média.

my [maɪ] *poss adj* meu (minha); **→ books** os meus livros; **→ name is Joe** o meu nome é Joe.

myriad ['mɪrɪəd] *literary* ◇ *adj* incontável. ◇ *n* miríade *f*.

myself [maɪ'self] *pron* -1. (*reflexive*) me; **I hurt →** machuquei-me -2. (*after prep*) mim -3. (*stressed*) eu mesmo (eu mesma); **I did it →** eu mesmo o fiz.

mysterious [mɪ'stɪərɪəs] *adj* misterioso(sa).

mystery ['mɪstərɪ] (*pl* -ies) *n* mistério *m*.

mystical ['mɪstɪkl] *adj* [spiritual] místico(-ca).

mystified ['mɪstɪfaɪd] *adj* [puzzled] perplexo(xa), desconcertado(da).

mystifying ['mɪstɪfaɪɪŋ] *adj* [puzzling] desconcertante.

mystique [mɪ'stiːk] *n* (U) mística *f*.

myth [mɪθ] *n* mito *m*.

mythical ['mɪθɪkl] *adj* -1. [imaginary] mítico(ca) -2. [untrue] falso(sa).

mythology [mɪ'θɒlədʒɪ] (*pl* -ies) *n* -1. (U) [collection of myths] mitologia *f* -2. [set of false beliefs] mito *m*.

N

n (*pl* **n's** OR **ns**), **N** (*pl* **N's** OR **Ns**) [en] *n* [letter] n, N *m*.
◆ **N** (*abbr of* **north**) N.

n/a, N/A -1. (*abbr of* **not applicable**) não-aplicável -2. (*abbr of* **not available**) n/d.

nab [næb] (*pt* & *pp* **-bed**, *cont* **-bing**) *vt inf* **-1.** [arrest] pegar **-2.** [claim quickly] pegar rapidamente.

nag [næg] (*pt* & *pp* **-ged**, *cont* **-ging**) ⬥ *n inf UK* [horse] rocim *m*. ⬥ *vt* [pester, find fault with] incomodar; **to ~ sb to do sthg/into doing sthg** incomodar alguém para fazer algo.

nagging ['nægɪŋ] *adj* **-1.** [thought, doubt, pain] perturbador(ra), persistente **-2.** [person] briguento(ta).

nail [neɪl] ⬥ *n* **-1.** [for fastening] prego *m* **-2.** [of finger, toe] unha *f*. ⬥ *vt* [fasten]: **to ~ sthg to sthg** pregar algo em algo.
➠ **nail down** *vt sep* **-1.** [fasten] pregar **-2.** *fig* [person]: **to ~ sb down to a date** pressionar alguém a fixar uma data.

nail brush *n* escova *f* de unhas.

nail clippers *npl* cortador *m* de unhas.

nail file *n* lixa *f* de unha.

nail polish *n* (*U*) esmalte *m* de unhas.

nail scissors *npl* tesoura *f* para unhas.

nail varnish *n* (*U*) esmalte *m* de unhas.

nail varnish remover [-rɪ'muːvə[r]] *n* (*U*) removedor *m* de esmalte.

naive, naïve [naɪ'iːv] *adj* ingênuo(nua).

naked ['neɪkɪd] *adj* **-1.** [nude] nu (nua), pelado(da) **-2.** [exposed] descoberto(ta); **~ truth** verdade *f* nua e crua; **~ flame** chama *f* sem proteção; **with the ~ eye** a olho nu **-3.** [obvious, blatant - emotions] óbvio(via); [- aggression] aberto(ta).

name [neɪm] ⬥ *n* nome *m*; **what's your ~?** como você se chama?; **by ~** pelo nome; **in the ~ of** em nome de; **in my/ his ~** em meu/seu nome; **to call sb ~s** chamar alguém de tudo. ⬥ *vt* **-1.** [christen] batizar; **to ~ sb after sb** *UK*, **to ~ sb for sb** *US* dar nome a alguém em homenagem a alguém; **to ~ sthg after sthg** *UK*, **to ~ sthg for sthg** *US* dar um nome a algo em homenagem a algo **-2.** [reveal identity of] dizer o nome de **-3.** [choose] escolher.

nameless ['neɪmlɪs] *adj* **-1.** [unknown - person] anônimo(ma); [- disease] desconhecido(da) **-2.** [indescribable] indescritível.

namely ['neɪmlɪ] *adv* a saber.

namesake ['neɪmseɪk] *n* [with same name] xará *mf*.

nanny ['nænɪ] (*pl* **-ies**) *n* [childminder] babá *f*.

nap [næp] (*pt* & *pp* **-ped**, *cont* **-ping**) ⬥ *n* [sleep] soneca *f*, cochilo *m*; **to take** OR **have a ~** tirar uma soneca OR um cochilo. ⬥ *vi* [sleep] cochilar; **to be caught napping** *inf* ser pego de surpresa.

nape [neɪp] *n*: **~ (of the neck)** nuca *f*.

napkin ['næpkɪn] *n* [serviette] guardanapo *m*.

nappy ['næpɪ] (*pl* **-ies**) *n* *UK* fralda *f*.

nappy liner *n* espécie de papel descartável que mantém o bebê seco quando o restante da fralda está molhado.

narcissi [nɑː'sɪsaɪ] *pl* ▷ **narcissus**.

narcissus [nɑː'sɪsəs] (*pl* **-cissuses** OR **-cissi** [-saɪ]) *n* narciso *m*.

narcotic [nɑː'kɒtɪk] *n* narcótico *m*.

narrative ['nærətɪv] ⬥ *adj* narrativo(va). ⬥ *n* narrativa *f*.

narrator [*UK* nə'reɪtə[r], *US* 'næreɪtər] *n* [speaker] narrador *m*, -ra *f*.

narrow ['nærəʊ] ⬥ *adj* **-1.** [thin, not wide] estreito(ta) **-2.** [limited, restricted] limitado(da) **-3.** [marginal, close - victory, majority] apertado(da); [- escape]: **to have a ~ escape** escapar por um triz. ⬥ *vt* **-1.** [eyes] apertar **-2.** [difference] diminuir, reduzir. ⬥ *vi* **-1.** [road, river] estreitar-se **-2.** [eyes] estreitar-se **-3.** [difference] diminuir, reduzir.
➠ **narrow down** *vt sep* [restrict] diminuir, reduzir.

narrowly ['nærəʊlɪ] *adv* **-1.** [win, lose, miss] por muito pouco **-2.** [escape, miss] por um triz.

narrow-minded [-'maɪndɪd] *adj* de visão limitada.

nasal ['neɪzl] *adj* nasal.

nasty ['nɑːstɪ] (*compar* **-ier**, *superl* **-iest**) *adj* **-1.** [unkind, unpleasant] mal-intencionado(da) **-2.** [disgusting, unattractive] horrível, desagradável; **cheap and ~** barato(ta) e de mau gosto **-3.** [tricky] complicado(da) **-4.** [serious - injury, disease] sério(ria); [- fall, accident] feio (feia).

nation ['neɪʃn] *n* [country] nação *f*.

national ['næʃənl] ⬥ *adj* nacional. ⬥ *n* cidadão *m*, -dã *f*.

national anthem *n* hino *m* nacional.

national curriculum *n*: **the ~** o currículo nacional do ensino na Inglaterra e no País de Gales.

national dress *n* (*U*) roupas *fpl* típicas (de um país).

National Front *n UK* Frente *f* Nacional, partido político minoritário de extrema direita na Grã-Bretanha.

National Health Service *n* (*U*) *UK*: **the ~** o Serviço Nacional de Saúde, órgão britânico gestor da saúde pública.

National Insurance *n* (*U*) *UK* **-1.** [system] ≃ Instituto Nacional de Seguro Social **-2.** [payments] contribuição *f* para a previdência social.

nationalism ['næʃnəlɪzm] n (U) nacionalismo m.

nationalist ['næʃnəlɪst] <> adj [pro-independence] nacionalista. <> n [supporter of independence movement] nacionalista mf.

nationality [,næʃə'nælətɪ] (pl -ies) n nacionalidade f.

nationalize, -ise ['næʃnəlaɪz] vt [company, industry] nacionalizar.

national park n parque m nacional.

national service n (U) UK MIL serviço m militar.

National Trust n (U) UK: the ~ organização britânica que promove a preservação e o acesso público a edifícios de interesse histórico ou arquitetônico e a locais de beleza natural, ≃ o Patrimônio Nacional.

nationwide ['neɪʃənwaɪd] <> adj em âmbito nacional. <> adv -1. [travel] por todo o país -2. [being shown] em todo o país -3. [being broadcast] para todo o país.

native ['neɪtɪv] <> adj -1. [country, area] natal -2. nativo(va); ~ language língua f materna; ~ to nativo(va) de. <> n -1. [person born in area, country] natural mf -2. offensive [original inhabitant] nativo m, -va f.

Nativity [nə'tɪvətɪ] n: the ~ a Natividade.

NATO ['neɪtəʊ] (abbr of North Atlantic Treaty Organization) n OTAN f.

natural ['nætʃrəl] adj -1. [gen] natural -2. [inborn, instinctive] nato(ta).

natural gas n (U) gás m natural.

naturalize, -ise ['nætʃrəlaɪz] vt [make citizen] naturalizar; **to be ~d** naturalizar-se.

naturally ['nætʃrəlɪ] adv -1. [as expected, understandably] naturalmente -2. [unaffectedly] com naturalidade -3. [instinctively] por natureza.

natural wastage n demissão f voluntária.

natural yoghurt n iogurte m natural.

nature ['neɪtʃəʳ] n natureza f; **by ~** por natureza.

nature reserve n reserva f natural.

naughty ['nɔːtɪ] (compar -ier, superl -iest) adj -1. [badly behaved] malcriado(da) -2. [rude, indecent] obsceno(na), atrevido(da).

nausea ['nɔːsjə] n (U) náusea f.

nauseam ['nɔːzɪæm] ▷ **ad nauseam.**

nauseating ['nɔːsɪeɪtɪŋ] adj -1. [sickening] enjoativo(va) -2. fig [disgusting] repugnante.

nautical ['nɔːtɪkl] adj náutico(ca).

naval ['neɪvl] adj naval.

nave [neɪv] n nave f (da igreja).

navel ['neɪvl] n umbigo m.

navigate ['nævɪgeɪt] <> vt -1. [steer - plane] pilotar; [- ship] comandar -2. [travel safely across] navegar por. <> vi -1. [ship] comandar -2. [car] ser co-piloto(-ta) -3. [plane] pilotar.

navigation [,nævɪ'geɪʃn] n (U) [piloting, steering - plane] pilotagem f; [- ship] navegação.

navigator ['nævɪgeɪtəʳ] n -1. [on a ship] navegador m, -ra f -2. [on a plane] comandante mf.

navvy ['nævɪ] (pl -ies) n UK inf operário m (em escavações).

navy ['neɪvɪ] (pl -ies) <> adj [in colour] azul-marinho. <> n -1. [armed force] marinha f (de guerra) -2. = navy blue.

navy blue <> adj azul-marinho. <> n azul-marinho m.

Nazi ['nɑːtsɪ] (pl -s) <> adj nazista. <> n nazista mf.

NB (abbr of nota bene) NB.

near [nɪəʳ] <> adj -1. [in space] perto -2. [in time, relationship] próximo(ma); **in the ~ future** em breve; **the nearest thing to sthg** o mais próximo de algo -3. [almost happened] quase; **it was a ~ thing** faltou pouco. <> adv -1. [in space] perto; **come ~er!** chegue mais perto! -2. [in time] próximo(ma) -3. [almost] quase; **we're nowhere ~ finding a solution** não estamos nem perto de encontrar uma solução. <> prep -1. : ~ **(to)** perto de; **phone ~er the time** ligue quando chegar a hora -2. [on the point of]: ~ **(to)** à beira de -3. [similar to]: ~ **(to)** próximo(ma) de. <> vt aproximar-se de. <> vi aproximar-se.

nearby [nɪə'baɪ] <> adj próximo(ma). <> adv perto, nas redondezas.

nearly ['nɪəlɪ] adv [almost] quase; **I ~ cried** quase chorei; **not ~** nem de longe; **not ~ enough** muito pouco; **you don't make ~ enough effort** você não se esforça o suficiente OR o bastante; **he doesn't study ~ enough** ele não estuda o suficiente.

near miss n [nearly a collision] quase-colisão f.

nearside ['nɪəsaɪd] n lado m oposto ao do condutor.

nearsighted [,nɪə'saɪtɪd] adj US míope.

neat [niːt] adj -1. [tidy] arrumado(da) -2. [skilful] hábil -3. [undiluted] puro(ra) -4. US inf [very good] ótimo(ma), maravilhoso(sa).

neatly ['niːtlɪ] adv -1. [tidily] com capricho -2. [skilfully] habilmente.

nebulous ['nebjʊləs] adj fml nebuloso(sa).

necessarily [UK 'nesəsərɪlɪ, ˌnesə'serəlɪ] adv inevitavelmente, necessariamente; **not ~** não necessariamente.

necessary ['nesəsrɪ] adj -1. [required] necessário(ria) -2. [inevitable] inevitável.

necessity [nɪ'sesətɪ] (pl -ies) n necessidade f; **of ~** por necessidade.

neck [nek] ◇ n -1. ANAT pescoço m -2. [of shirt, dress] gola f -3. [of bottle] gargalo m. ◇ vi inf agarrar-se.
◆ **neck and neck** adj -1. [horses] cabeça a cabeça -2. [competitors] emparelhado(da).

necklace ['neklɪs] n colar m.

neckline ['neklaɪn] n decote m.

necktie ['nektaɪ] n US gravata f.

nectarine ['nektərɪn] n [fruit] nectarina f.

need [ni:d] ◇ n necessidade f; **~ for** sthg necessidade por algo; **~ to do** sthg necessidade de fazer algo; **to be in** OR **have ~ of** sthg necessitar de algo; **if ~ be** se necessário for; **in ~** em necessidade. ◇ vt precisar de, necessitar de; **to ~ to do** sthg precisar fazer algo. ◇ modal vb: **~ we go?** precisamos ir mesmo?; **it ~ not happen** não tem que ser assim.

needle ['ni:dl] ◇ n agulha f. ◇ vt inf alfinetar, importunar.

needless ['ni:dlɪs] adj desnecessário(ria); **~ to say ...** desnecessário dizer que ...

needlework ['ni:dlwɜ:k] n (U) -1. [work produced] bordado m -2. [activity] costura f.

needn't ['ni:dnt] = need not.

needy ['ni:dɪ] (compar -ier, superl -iest) adj necessitado(da), carente.

negative ['negətɪv] ◇ adj negativo(va). ◇ n -1. PHOT negativo m -2. LING negação f; **to answer in the ~** dizer não.

neglect [nɪ'glekt] ◇ n -1. [of duty] não-cumprimento m -2. [of work, children] desleixo m, descuido m; **in a state of ~** num estado de total abandono. ◇ vt -1. [not take care of] abandonar -2. [not do - duty] não cumprir com; [- work] não fazer; **to ~ to do** sthg deixar de fazer algo.

neglectful [nɪ'glektfʊl] adj negligente.

negligee ['neglɪʒeɪ] n chambre m.

negligence ['neglɪdʒəns] n (U) negligência f.

negligible ['neglɪdʒəbl] adj insignificante.

negotiate [nɪ'gəʊʃɪeɪt] ◇ vt -1. [obtain through negotiation] negociar -2. [get over] transpor -3. [get around - obstacle] contornar; [- bend] tomar. ◇ vi negociar; **to ~ with sb for** sthg negociar algo com alguém.

negotiation [nɪˌgəʊʃɪ'eɪʃn] n (U) [talking, discussion] negociação f.
◆ **negotiations** npl negociações fpl.

neigh [neɪ] vi relinchar.

neighbor etc. n US = neighbour etc.

neighbour UK, **neighbor** US ['neɪbəʳ] n vizinho m, -nha f.

neighbourhood UK, **neighborhood** US ['neɪbəhʊd] n -1. [of town] vizinhança f -2. [approximate area]: **in the ~ of** [approximately] por volta de.

neighbouring UK, **neighboring** US ['neɪbərɪŋ] adj vizinho(nha).

neighbourly UK, **neighborly** US ['neɪbəlɪ] adj de boa vizinhança; **to be ~** ser um bom vizinho.

neither ['naɪðəʳ, 'ni:ðəʳ] ◇ adj nenhum(ma). ◇ adv nem; **~ ... nor ...** nem ... nem ...; **that's ~ here nor there** isso não importa. ◇ pron nenhum(ma) dos dois; **~ of us** nenhum de nós dois. ◇ conj: **~ do I** nem eu.

neon ['ni:ɒn] n (U) neônio m.

neon light n lâmpada f OR luz f de néon.

nephew ['nefju:] n sobrinho m.

Neptune ['neptju:n] n [planet] Netuno m.

nerd n pessoa estúpida e ridícula.

nerve [nɜ:v] n -1. ANAT nervo m -2. [courage] coragem f; **to lose one's ~** perder a coragem -3. [cheek] petulância f.
◆ **nerves** npl nervos mpl; **to get on sb's ~s** dar nos nervos de alguém.

nerve-racking [-ˌrækɪŋ] adj angustiante.

nervous ['nɜ:vəs] adj nervoso(sa); **to be ~ of sthg/of doing** sthg ter medo de algo/de fazer algo; **to be ~ about** sthg ficar nervoso(sa) por algo.

nervous breakdown n crise f nervosa.

nest [nest] ◇ n -1. [gen] ninho m -2. [of ants] formigueiro m -3. [of wasps] vespeiro m -4. [of tables] conjunto m. ◇ vi [make a nest] fazer um ninho, aninhar-se.

nest egg n pé-de-meia m.

nestle ['nesl] vi -1. [make o.s. comfortable] aconchegar-se -2. [be sheltered] estar abrigado(da).

net [net] (pt & pp -ted, cont -ting) ◇ adj -1. [gen] líquido(da) -2. [final] final. ◇ n -1. [gen] rede f -2. [type of fabric] malha f. ◇ vt -1. [catch] enredar -2.

fig [acquire because of skill] alcançar - **3.** [bring in as profit] render.

➤ **Net** n: **the Net** COMPUT a Rede.

netball ['netbɔ:l] n (U) *esporte feminino semelhante ao basquete*, bola-ao-cesto m.

net curtains npl cortinas fpl de voile.

Netherlands ['neðələndz] npl: **the ~** os Países Baixos.

netiquette ['netɪket] n COMPUT netiqueta f.

net profit n lucro m líquido.

net revenue n receita f líquida.

nett adj = **net**.

netting ['netɪŋ] n (U) - **1.** [of metal, plastic] tela f - **2.** [fabric] voile m.

nettle ['netl] n urtiga f.

network ['netwɜ:k] ◇ n - **1.** [gen] rede f - **2.** [group of people] grupo m; **a ~ of contacts** uma rede de contatos. ◇ vt RADIO & TV [broadcast] transmitir em rede.

neurosis [ˌnjʊə'rəʊsɪs] (pl -ses [-si:z]) n neurose f.

neurotic [ˌnjʊə'rɒtɪk] ◇ adj [person] neurótico(ca). ◇ n neurótico m, -ca f.

neuter ['nju:tər] ◇ adj - **1.** GRAM neutro(tra) - **2.** [sexless] castrado(da). ◇ vt castrar.

neutral ['nju:trəl] ◇ adj - **1.** [non-allied] [pale grey-brown & ELEC] neutro(tra) - **2.** [inexpressive] indiferente - **3.** [colourless] incolor. ◇ n - **1.** (U) AUT ponto m morto - **2.** [POL - country] país m neutro; [- person] pessoa f neutra.

neutrality [nju:'trælətɪ] n (U) POL neutralidade f.

neutralize, -ise ['nju:trəlaɪz] vt [effects] neutralizar.

never ['nevər] adv - **1.** [at no time] nunca; **~ ever** jamais - **2.** inf [in surprise, disbelief] nunca; **you ~ did!** não (me diga)! - **3.** phr: **well I ~!** não acredito!

never-ending adj interminável.

nevertheless [ˌnevəðə'les] adv contudo, todavia.

new [nju:] adj novo(va); **as good as ~** como se fosse novo.

➤ **news** n (U) - **1.** [information] notícia f; **the ~s** as notícias; **a piece of ~s** uma notícia; **that's ~s to me** isto é novidade para mim - **2.** RADIO & TV noticiário m.

newborn ['nju:bɔ:n] adj recém-nascido(da).

newcomer ['nju:ˌkʌmər] n: **~ (to sthg)** novato m, -ta f (em algo); **~ (to somewhere)** recém-chegado m, -da f (em algum lugar).

newfangled [ˌnju:'fæŋgld] adj inf pej modernoso(sa).

new-found adj recém-descoberto(ta); **~ friend** amigo m recente.

newly ['nju:lɪ] adv recém-.

newly-weds npl recém-casados mpl, -das fpl.

new moon n lua f nova.

news agency n agência f de notícias.

newsagent UK ['nju:zeɪdʒənt], **newsdealer** US ['nju:zdi:lər] n [person] jornaleiro m, -ra f; **~'s (shop)** banca f de jornais.

newscaster ['nju:zkɑ:stər] n - **1.** [television] apresentador m, -ra f de jornal - **2.** [radio] locutor(ra).

newsdealer n US = **newsagent**.

newsflash ['nju:zflæʃ] n plantão m de notícias.

newsgroup ['nju:zgru:p] n COMPUT grupo m de notícias.

newsletter ['nju:zˌletər] n boletim m de notícias.

newspaper ['nju:zˌpeɪpər] n jornal m.

newsprint ['nju:zprɪnt] n (U) papel m jornal.

newsreader ['nju:zˌri:dər] n - **1.** [TV] apresentador m, -ra f de jornal - **2.** [radio] locutor(ra).

newsreel ['nju:zri:l] n cinejornal m.

news-stand n banca f de revistas.

newt [nju:t] n tritão m.

new town n UK cidade f planejada.

New Year n Ano m Novo; **Happy ~!** Feliz Ano Novo!

New Year's Day n dia m de Ano Novo, primeiro m do ano.

New Year's Eve n véspera f de Ano Novo.

New York [-'jɔ:k] n - **1.** [city] Nova Iorque; **~ (City)** (cidade f de) Nova Iorque - **2.** [state]: **~ (State)** (Estado m de) Nova Iorque.

New Zealand [-'zi:lənd] n Nova Zelândia; **in ~** na Nova Zelândia.

New Zealander [-'zi:ləndər] n neozelandês(esa).

next [nekst] ◇ adj - **1.** [in time] próximo(ma); **~ week** semana que vem; **the ~ week** na semana que vem; **the day after ~** depois de amanhã; **the week after ~** sem ser a próxima semana, na outra - **2.** [in space - turning, page, street] próximo(ma); [- room] ao lado. ◇ adv - **1.** [afterwards] depois; **when are you ~ going to Brazil?** quando você irá novamente ao Brasil? - **2.** [next time] da próxima vez (que); **when we ~ meet** da próxima vez que nos encontrarmos - **3.** (with superlatives): **~ best/biggest** o segundo melhor/maior. ◇ prep US ao lado de. ◇ n próximo m, -ma f.

next to prep **-1.** [physically near] ao lado de, junto a **-2.** (in comparisons) próximo(ma) de **-3.** [almost] quase; ~ **to nothing** quase nada.

next-door <> adj: ~ **neighbour** vizinho m, -nha f do lado. <> adv ao lado.

next of kin n parente m mais próximo.

NF n (abbr of National Front) pequeno partido político britânico de extrema direita.

NHS (abbr of National Health Service) n órgão estatal britânico de saúde pública.

NI (abbr of National Insurance) sistema britânico de seguridade social, ≃ INSS m.

nib [nɪb] n pena f (de caneta).

nibble ['nɪbl] vt **-1.** [subj: person, caterpillar] beliscar ; [subj: rodent, goat, sheep] roer **-2.** [playfully] mordiscar.

Nicaragua [ˌnɪkə'ræɡjuə] n Nicarágua.

nice [naɪs] adj **-1.** [expressing approval - dress, picture] belo(la); [- day, weather] agradável; [- car, food] bom (boa) **-2.** [kind, pleasant] gentil; **it was** ~ **of you to help** foi muita gentileza de sua parte ajudar.

nice-looking [-'lʊkɪŋ] adj [attractive] bonito(ta); ~ **person** pessoa f atraente.

nicely ['naɪslɪ] adv **-1.** [well, attractively, satisfactorily] bem; **that will do** ~ será o suficiente **-2.** [politely] educadamente.

niche [niːʃ] n **-1.** [gen] nicho m **-2.** [in life] boa colocação f.

nick [nɪk] <> n **-1.** [cut] talha f, corte m **-2.** inf [condition]: **in good/bad** ~ UK em bom/mau estado **-3.** phr: **in the** ~ **of time** em cima da hora. <> vt **-1.** [cut] talhar, cortar **-2.** UK inf [steal] passar a mão em **-3.** UK inf [arrest] enjaular.

nickel ['nɪkl] n **-1.** (U) [metal] níquel m **-2.** US [coin] moeda f de 5 centavos.

nickname ['nɪkneɪm] <> n apelido m. <> vt apelidar.

nicotine ['nɪkətiːn] n (U) nicotina f.

niece [niːs] n sobrinha f.

Nigeria [naɪ'dʒɪərɪə] n Nigéria.

niggle ['nɪgl] vt **-1.** [worry] preocupar **-2.** [criticize] incomodar.

night [naɪt] n **-1.** [not day] noite f; **at** ~ à OR de noite **-2.** phr: **to have an early/a late** ~ ir dormir cedo/tarde.

nights adv **-1.** US [at night] à OR noite **-2.** UK [night shift]: **to work** ~**s** trabalhar durante a noite.

nightcap ['naɪtkæp] n [drink] bebida que se toma antes de se ir dormir.

nightclub ['naɪtklʌb] n casa f noturna, nightclub m.

nightdress ['naɪtdres] n camisola f.

nightfall ['naɪtfɔːl] n (U) anoitecer m.

nightgown ['naɪtgaʊn] n camisola f.

nightie ['naɪtɪ] n inf camisola f.

nightingale ['naɪtɪŋgeɪl] n rouxinol m.

nightlife ['naɪtlaɪf] n (U) vida f noturna.

nightly ['naɪtlɪ] <> adj noturno(na). <> adv à noite.

nightmare ['naɪtmeəʳ] n lit & fig pesadelo m.

night porter n porteiro m, -ra f do turno da noite.

night school n (U) escola f noturna.

night shift n [period] turno m da noite.

nightshirt ['naɪtʃɜːt] n camisolão m.

night-time n (U) noite f.

nil [nɪl] n (U) **-1.** [nothing] nada m **-2.** UK SPORT zero m.

Nile [naɪl] n: **the** ~ o Nilo.

nimble ['nɪmbl] adj ágil.

nine [naɪn] num nove; see also six.

nineteen [ˌnaɪn'tiːn] num dezenove; see also six.

ninety ['naɪntɪ] num noventa; see also sixty.

ninth [naɪnθ] num nono(na); see also sixth.

nip [nɪp] (pt & pp -ped, cont -ping) <> n **-1.** [pinch] beliscão m **-2.** [bite] mordiscada f **-3.** [of drink] trago m. <> vt **-1.** [pinch] beliscar **-2.** [bite] mordiscar.

nipple ['nɪpl] n **-1.** [of breast] mamilo m **-2.** [of baby's bottle] bico m.

nit [nɪt] n **-1.** [in hair] lêndea f **-2.** UK inf [idiot] idiota m.

nit-picking inf n (U) detalhismo m.

nitrogen ['naɪtrədʒən] n (U) nitrogênio m.

nitty-gritty [ˌnɪtɪ'grɪtɪ] n inf: **to get down to the** ~ ir ao que interessa.

no [nəʊ] (pl -es) <> adv [gen] não; ~, **thanks** não obrigado(da). <> adj nenhum(ma), algum(ma); **I have** ~ **money left** não tenho mais um tostão. <> n não m.

No., no. (abbr of number) n°.

nobility [nə'bɪlətɪ] n **-1.** [aristocracy]: **the** ~ a nobreza **-2.** (U) [nobleness] nobreza f.

noble ['nəʊbl] <> adj [aristocratic, distinguished] nobre. <> n nobre mf.

nobody ['nəʊbədɪ] (pl -ies) <> pron ninguém. <> n pej [insignificant person] joão-ninguém m.

no-claim(s) bonus n bonificação f de seguro.

nocturnal [nɒk'tɜːnl] adj noturno(na).

nod [nɒd] (pt & pp -ded, cont -ding) <> vt [in agreement]: **to** ~ **one's head** assentir com a cabeça; [as greeting] cumprimentar com a cabeça. <> vi **-1.** [in

agreement] assentir com a cabeça - 2. [to indicate sthg] indicar com a cabeça **- 3.** [as greeting]: **to ~ to sb** cumprimentar alguém com a cabeça.

◆ **nod off** vi cabecear.

noise [nɔɪz] n [sound] barulho m.

noisy ['nɔɪzɪ] (compar **-ier**, superl **-iest**) adj barulhento(ta).

no-man's-land n (U) terra f de ninguém.

nom de plume n pseudônimo m.

nominal ['nɒmɪnl] adj **- 1.** [in name only] apenas no nome; **a ~ Catholic** um católico só no nome; **a ~ leader** um líder de fachada **- 2.** [very small] simbólico(ca).

nominate ['nɒmɪneɪt] vt **- 1.** [propose]: **to ~ sb (for/as sthg)** designar alguém (para algo) **- 2.** [appoint]: **to ~ sb (to sthg)** nomear alguém (algo); **to ~ sb (to sthg)** nomear alguém (para algo).

nominee [ˌnɒmɪ'niː] n nomeado m, -da f.

non- [nɒn] prefix [not] não-.

non-alcoholic adj não alcoólico(ca).

non-aligned adj não-alinhado(da).

nonchalant [UK 'nɒnʃələnt, US ˌnɒnʃə'lɑːnt] adj indiferente.

non-committal adj evasivo(va).

nonconformist [ˌnɒnkən'fɔːmɪst] ⬦ adj inconformista. ⬦ n inconformista mf.

nondescript [UK 'nɒndɪskrɪpt, US ˌnɒndɪ'skrɪpt] adj desinteressante.

none [nʌn] pron nehum m, -ma f; **there's ~ left** não resta nada; **~ of this is your fault** nada disso foi culpa sua.

nonentity [nɒ'nentətɪ] (pl **-ies**) n nulidade f, zero mf à esquerda.

nonetheless [ˌnʌnðə'les] adv contudo, não obstante.

non-event n decepção f, fracasso m.

non-existent adj inexistente.

non-fiction n (U) não-ficção f.

no-nonsense adj prático(ca).

non-payment n (U) inadimplência f, não-pagamento m.

nonplussed, nonplused US [ˌnɒn'plʌst] adj perplexo(xa).

non-returnable adj [bottle] não-retornável, sem retorno.

nonsense ['nɒnsəns] ⬦ n (U) **- 1.** [meaningless words] bobagem f, asneira f **- 2.** [foolish idea] besteira f; **it is ~ to suggest that ...** é um absurdo sugerir que ... **- 3.** [foolish behaviour] idiotice f; **stop this ~ at once** pára com essas criancices agora mesmo; **to make (a) ~ of sthg** ridicularizar algo. ⬦ excl bobagem!, que nada!

nonsensical [nɒn'sensɪkl] adj sem sentido, absurdo(da).

non-smoker n não-fumante mf.

non-stick adj antiaderente.

non-stop ⬦ adj **- 1.** [gen] contínuo(-nua), incessante **- 2.** [flight] sem escalas. ⬦ adv sem parar, continuamente.

noodles ['nuːdlz] npl talharim m.

nook [nʊk] n [of room] canto m; **every ~ and cranny** todos os cantos.

noon [nuːn] n (U) meio-dia m.

no one pron = **nobody**.

noose [nuːs] n [lasso] nó m corrediço.

no-place adv US = **nowhere**.

nor [nɔːʳ] conj **- 1.** ⬐ **neither - 2.** [and not] nem; **I don't smoke - ~ do I** eu não fumo – nem eu; **I don't know, ~ do I care** não sei, nem quero saber.

norm [nɔːm] n norma f; **the ~** o normal.

normal ['nɔːml] adj normal.

normality [nɔː'mælɪtɪ], **normalcy** US ['nɔːmlsɪ] n (U) normalidade f.

normally ['nɔːməlɪ] adv normalmente.

Normandy ['nɔːməndɪ] n Normandia; **in ~** na Normandia.

north [nɔːθ] ⬦ adj norte; **North London** o norte de Londres. ⬦ adv para o norte; **~ of** ao norte de. ⬦ n [direction] norte m.

North Africa n África do Norte.

North America n América do Norte; **in ~** na América do Norte.

North American ⬦ adj **- 1.** da América do Norte **- 2.** [of USA] norte-americano(na). ⬦ n **- 1.** pessoa f da América do Norte **- 2.** [of USA] norte-americano m, -na f.

North Country n: **the ~** UK a região norte da Inglaterra.

northeast [ˌnɔːθ'iːst] ⬦ adj nordeste. ⬦ n [direction] nordeste m. ⬦ adv para o nordeste; **~ of** ao nordeste de.

northerly ['nɔːðəlɪ] adj **- 1.** [towards north, in north] ao norte **- 2.** [from north] do norte.

northern ['nɔːðən] adj do norte.

Northern Ireland n Irlanda do Norte.

northernmost ['nɔːðənməʊst] adj mais setentrional, mais ao norte.

North Korea n Coréia do Norte; **in ~** na Coréia do Norte.

North Pole n: **the ~** o Pólo Norte.

North Sea n: **the ~** o Mar do Norte.

northward ['nɔːθwəd] ⬦ adj para o norte. ⬦ adv = **northwards**.

northwards ['nɔːθwədz] adv para o norte.

northwest [ˌnɔːθ'west] ⬦ adj **- 1.** [in

the northwest, facing the northwest] noroeste **-2.** [from the northwest] do
noroeste. $\diamond$ *n* [direction] noroeste *m*.
$\diamond$ *adv* para noroeste; $\sim$ **of** a noroeste
de.

Norway ['nɔ:weɪ] *n* Noruega.

Norwegian [nɔ:'wi:dʒən] $\diamond$ *adj* no-
rueguês(esa). $\diamond$ *n* **-1.** [person] norueguês *m*, -esa *f* **-2.** [language] norueguês
m.

nose [nəʊz] *n* ANAT nariz *m*; **to keep one's
$\sim$ out of sthg** não meter o nariz em
algo; **to look down one's $\sim$ at sb/sthg** *fig*
olhar de cima para alguém/algo; **to
poke** OR **stick one's $\sim$ into sthg** *inf* meter
o nariz em algo; **to turn up one's $\sim$ at
sthg** torcer o nariz para algo.
$\Rrightarrow$ **nose about, nose around** *vi* bisbilhotar.

nosebleed ['nəʊzbli:d] *n* hemorragia *f*
nasal.

nosedive ['nəʊzdaɪv] $\diamond$ *n* [of plane]
mergulho *m*. $\diamond$ *vi* **-1.** [plane] mergulhar **-2.** *fig* [prices, popularity] despencar.

nose ring *n* argola *f* de nariz.

nose stud *n* piercing *m* de nariz.

nosey ['nəʊzɪ] *adj* = **nosy**.

nostalgia [nɒ'stældʒə] *n* (U): $\sim$ **(for
sthg)** nostalgia *f* (de algo).

nostril ['nɒstrəl] *n* narina *f*.

nosy ['nəʊzɪ] (*compar* **-ier**, *superl* **-iest**)
adj curioso(sa), abelhudo(da).

not [nɒt] *adv* não; $\sim$ **a** nem um (uma);
$\sim$ **all/every** nem todos(das); $\sim$ **always**
nem sempre; **it's $\sim$ every day we get
sunshine** não é todo dia que tem sol;
it's $\sim$ that I'm jealous, but ... não que eu
seja ciumento, mas ...; $\sim$ **at all** em
absoluto, de maneira nenhuma; [to acknowledge thanks] de nada.

notable ['nəʊtəbl] *adj* notável; **to be $\sim$
for sthg** destacar-se por algo.

notably ['nəʊtəblɪ] *adv* **-1.** [in particular]
especialmente **-2.** [noticeably] claramente, obviamente.

notary ['nəʊtərɪ] (*pl* **-ies**) *n*: $\sim$ **(public)**
notário *m*, -ria *f*.

notch [nɒtʃ] *n* **-1.** [cut] corte *m*, entalhe
m **-2.** *fig* [on scale] ponto *m*.

note [nəʊt] $\diamond$ *n* **-1.** [gen] nota *f* **-2.**
[written reminder, record] anotação *f*, nota
f; **to take $\sim$ of sthg** prestar atenção em
algo **-3.** [short letter] bilhete *m* **-4.** [tone]
tom *m*. $\diamond$ *vt* **-1.** [observe] notar, observar **-2.** [mention] apontar, mencionar.
$\Rrightarrow$ **notes** *npl* [in book] anotações *fpl*.
$\Rrightarrow$ **note down** *vt sep* anotar.

notebook ['nəʊtbʊk] *n* **-1.** [for writing in]
caderno *m* **-2.** COMPUT notebook *m*.

noted ['nəʊtɪd] *adj* conhecido(da), des-
tacado(da); $\sim$ **for sthg** conhecido(da)
por algo.

notepad ['nəʊtpæd] *n* bloco *m* de notas.

notepaper ['nəʊtpeɪpəʳ] *n* (U) papel *m*
de carta.

noteworthy ['nəʊt,wɜ:ðɪ] (*compar* **-ier**,
superl **-iest**) *adj* digno(na) de menção.

nothing ['nʌθɪŋ] $\diamond$ *pron* nada; $\sim$
new/interesting nada de novo/interes-
sante; **she did $\sim$** ela não fez nada; **for
$\sim$** [free] de graça; [in vain] para nada.

notice ['nəʊtɪs] $\diamond$ *n* **-1.** (U) [attention]
atenção *f*; **to take $\sim$ (of sb/sthg)** dar
bola (para alguém/algo); **to take no $\sim$
(of sb/sthg)** não dar bola (para al-
guém/algo), fazer pouco caso (de
alguém/algo) **-2.** (U) [warning, announce-
ment] aviso *m*; **at short $\sim$** em cima da
hora; **until further $\sim$** até segunda
ordem **-3.** (U) [at work]: **to be given one's
$\sim$** receber aviso prévio; **to hand in
one's $\sim$** apresentar pedido de demissão. $\diamond$ *vt* perceber, notar; **to $\sim$ sb
doing sthg** ver que alguém está fazen-
do algo.

noticeable ['nəʊtɪsəbl] *adj* notável, dig-
no(na) de nota.

notice board *n* quadro *m* de avisos.

notify ['nəʊtɪfaɪ] (*pt & pp* **-ied**) *vt*: **to
$\sim$ sb (of sthg)** notificar alguém (de
algo).

notion ['nəʊʃn] *n* [concept, idea] noção *f*.
$\Rrightarrow$ **notions** *npl* US [haberdashery] avia-
mentos *mpl*.

notorious [nəʊ'tɔːrɪəs] *adj* notório(ria).

notwithstanding [,nɒtwɪθ'stændɪŋ] *fml*
$\diamond$ *prep* não obstante. $\diamond$ *adv* no
entanto, não obstante.

nought [nɔ:t] *num* zero *m*; $\sim$ **s and
crosses** jogo *m* da velha.

noun [naʊn] *n* substantivo *m*.

nourish ['nʌrɪʃ] *vt* [feed] nutrir.

nourishing ['nʌrɪʃɪŋ] *adj* nutritivo(va).

nourishment ['nʌrɪʃmənt] *n* (U) alimento *m*.

novel ['nɒvl] $\diamond$ *adj* original. $\diamond$ *n*
romance *m*.

novelist ['nɒvəlɪst] *n* romancista *mf*.

novelty ['nɒvltɪ] (*pl* **-ies**) *n* **-1.** (U) [quality]
originalidade *f* **-2.** [unusual object, event]
novidade *f* **-3.** [cheap object] bugiganga
f.

November [nə'vembəʳ] *n* novembro *m*;
see also **September**.

novice ['nɒvɪs] *n* **-1.** [inexperienced per-
son] novato *m*, -ta *f*, principiante *mf*
-2. RELIG noviço *m*, -ça *f*.

now [naʊ] $\diamond$ *adv* **-1.** [at this time] agora;
from $\sim$ on I'm in charge de agora em

diante eu estou no comando; **any day ~** qualquer dia destes; **any time ~** a qualquer momento; **~ and then** OR **again** de vez em quando **- 2.** [already, before this time] já; **they should be here by ~** eles já deveriam estar aqui; **he's been away for two weeks ~** já faz duas semanas que ele foi embora **- 3.** [at a particular time in the past] então; **we were all singing ~** estávamos todos cantando naquele momento **- 4.** [to introduce statement] agora **- 5.** [nowadays] atualmente; **~ many people use computers to work** atualmente muitas pessoas usam computadores para trabalhar. <> **conj**: **~ (that)** agora que.

nowadays ['naʊədeɪz] adv hoje em dia, atualmente.

nowhere UK ['nəʊweə'], **no-place** US adv em nenhum lugar; **~ near** nem de longe; **to be getting ~** indo a lugar nenhum.

nozzle ['nɒzl] n bocal m, bico m.

nuance [nju:'ɑ:ns] n [of word, meaning] nuança f.

nuclear ['nju:klɪə'] adj nuclear.

nuclear bomb n bomba f nuclear.

nuclear disarmament n (U) desarmamento m nuclear.

nuclear energy n (U) energia f nuclear.

nuclear power n (U) energia f nuclear.

nuclear reactor n reator m nuclear.

nuclear war n guerra f nuclear.

nucleus ['nju:klɪəs] (pl -lei [-lɪaɪ]) n núcleo m.

nude [nju:d] <> adj nu (nua). <> n [figure, painting] nu m - em pêlo.

nudge [nʌdʒ] vt - 1. [with elbow] cutucar - 2. fig [to encourage] empurrar; **to ~ sb's memory** puxar a memória de alguém.

nudist ['nju:dɪst] <> adj nudista. <> n nudista mf.

nugget ['nʌgɪt] n - 1. [of gold] pepita f - 2. fig [valuable piece] pérola f.

nuisance ['nju:sns] n - 1. [annoying thing, situation] chatice f - 2. [annoying person] chato m, -ta f de galocha; **to make a ~ of o.s.** amolar.

nuke [nju:k] inf <> n arma f nuclear. <> vt bombardear com armas nucleares.

null [nʌl] adj: **~ and void** nulo e sem valor.

numb [nʌm] <> adj [shoulder, hand] adormecido(da); [person] paralisado(da); **to be ~ with cold** estar congelado(da) de frio. <> vt [subj: cold, anaesthetic] paralisar.

number ['nʌmbə'] <> n - 1. [gen] número m; **a ~ of** vários(as); **I've told you any ~ of times ...** já te disse um milhão de vezes ... - 2. [of car] placa f - 3. [song] música f. <> vt - 1. [amount to] chegar a - 2. [give a number to] numerar - 3. [include]: **to be ~ed among** figurar entre.

number one <> adj [main] número um, principal. <> n inf [oneself]: **to look after ~** cuidar de si mesmo(ma).

numberplate ['nʌmbəpleɪt] n placa f do carro.

Number Ten n: **~ (Downing Street)** a casa número 10 de Downing Street, residência oficial do primeiro ministro britânico; fig o governo britânico.

numeral ['nju:mərəl] n algarismo m.

numerate ['nju:mərət] adj UK que sabe fazer cálculos elementares.

numerical [nju:'merɪkl] adj numérico(ca).

numerous ['nju:mərəs] adj inúmero(ra).

nun [nʌn] n freira f.

nurse [nɜ:s] <> n enfermeiro m, -ra f. <> vt - 1. MED [care for] cuidar de, atender - 2. [harbour, foster] nutrir - 3. [breast-feed] amamentar.

nursery ['nɜ:səri] (pl -ies) n - 1. [for children] creche f - 2. [for plants, trees] viveiro m - 3. [at home] quarto m das crianças.

nursery rhyme n cantiga f infantil.

nursery school n pré-escola f.

nursery slopes npl SKIING pista f para principiantes.

nursing ['nɜ:sɪŋ] n - 1. [profession] enfermagem f - 2. [care] cuidados mpl.

nursing home n - 1. [for old people] clínica f de repouso - 2. [for childbirth] maternidade f (privada).

nurture ['nɜ:tʃə'] vt - 1. [children, plants] criar - 2. [hope, desire, plan] alimentar.

nut [nʌt] n - 1. [to eat] noz f - 2. TECH porca f - 3. inf [mad person] maluco m, -ca f. **→ nuts** inf <> adj: **to be ~s** estar louco(ca). <> excl US maldito seja!

nutcrackers ['nʌt,krækəz] npl quebra-nozes m.

nutmeg ['nʌtmeg] n (U) noz-moscada f.

nutritious [nju:'trɪʃəs] adj nutritivo(va).

nutshell ['nʌtʃel] n casca f de noz; **in a ~** em poucas palavras.

nuzzle ['nʌzl] <> vt [with nose] fuçar. <> vi [nestle]: **to ~ (up) against sb/sthg** aconchegar-se em alguém/algo.

NVQ (abbr of National Vocational Qualification) n na Inglaterra e no País de Gales, certificado de qualificação *vocacional obtido pelos estudantes de 15 a 16 anos,* ≃ diploma *m* de segundo grau.

nylon ['naɪlɒn] ⇔ *n (U)* [fabric] náilon *m.* ⇔ *comp* de náilon.

O

o (*pl* o's OR os), **O** (*pl* O's OR Os) [əʊ] *n* - **1.** [letter] o, O *m* - **2.** [zero] zero *m.*

oak [əʊk] ⇔ *n:* ~ (**tree**) carvalho *m.* ⇔ *comp* de carvalho.

OAP (*abbr of* old age pensioner) *n* UK idoso que recebe pensão do estado.

oar [ɔː[r]] *n* remo *m.*

oasis [əʊ'eɪsɪs] (*pl* oases [əʊ'eɪsɪːz]) *n* - **1.** [in desert] oásis *m inv* - **2.** *fig* [pleasant place] oásis *m inv.*

oatcake ['əʊtkeɪk] *n* biscoito *m* de aveia.

oath [əʊθ] *n* - **1.** [promise] juramento *m*; on OR under ~ sob juramento - **2.** [swearword] blasfêmia *f.*

oatmeal ['əʊtmiːl] *n* [food] farinha *f* de aveia.

oats [əʊts] *npl* [grain] aveia *f.*

obedience [ə'biːdjəns] *n (U):* ~ (to sb) obediência *f* (a alguém).

obedient [ə'biːdjənt] *adj* obediente.

obese [əʊ'biːs] *adj* obeso(sa).

obey [ə'beɪ] ⇔ *vt* obedecer a. ⇔ *vi* obedecer.

obituary [ə'bɪtʃʊərɪ] (*pl* -ies) *n* obituário *m.*

object [*n* 'ɒbdʒɪkt, *vb* ɒb'dʒekt] ⇔ *n* - **1.** [gen] objeto *m* - **2.** [aim] objetivo *m* - **3.** GRAMM objeto *m*, complemento *m.* ⇔ *vt:* to ~ (that) objetar (que). ⇔ *vi* objetar; to ~ to sthg/to doing sthg opor a algo/a fazer algo.

objection [əb'dʒekʃn] *n* [argument against] objeção *f*; to have no ~ to sthg/to doing sthg não ter nenhuma objeção a algo/a fazer algo.

objectionable [əb'dʒekʃənəbl] *adj* desagradável.

objective [əb'dʒektɪv] ⇔ *adj* objetivo(va). ⇔ *n* objetivo *m.*

obligation [ˌɒblɪ'geɪʃn] *n* obrigação *f.*

obligatory [ə'blɪgətrɪ] *adj* obrigatório(ria).

oblige [ə'blaɪdʒ] *vt* - **1.** [force]: to ~ sb to do sthg obrigar alguém a fazer algo - **2.** *fml* [do a favour to] fazer um favor a.

obliging [ə'blaɪdʒɪŋ] *adj* prestativo(va).

oblique [ə'bliːk] ⇔ *adj* - **1.** [indirect - look] enviesado(da); [- reference, hint, compliment] indireto(ta) - **2.** [slanting] oblíquo(qua). ⇔ *n* TYPO barra *f.*

obliterate [ə'blɪtəreɪt] *vt* [destroy] obliterar.

oblivion [ə'blɪvɪən] *n (U)* - **1.** [unconsciousness] inconsciência *f* - **2.** [state of being forgotten] esquecimento *m.*

oblivious [ə'blɪvɪəs] *adj* inconsciente; to be ~ to OR of sthg não ter consciência de algo.

oblong ['ɒblɒŋ] ⇔ *adj* oblongo(ga). ⇔ *n* retângulo *m.*

obnoxious [əb'nɒkʃəs] *adj* repulsivo(va), repugnante.

oboe ['əʊbəʊ] *n* oboé *m.*

obscene [əb'siːn] *adj* obsceno(na).

obscure [əb'skjʊə[r]] ⇔ *adj* - **1.** [not well-known] desconhecido(da) - **2.** [difficult to see/understand] obscuro(ra). ⇔ *vt* - **1.** [make difficult to understand] obscurecer - **2.** [hide] esconder.

observance [əb'zɜːvns] *n (U)* observância *f*, cumprimento *m.*

observant [əb'zɜːvnt] *adj* observador(ra).

observation [ˌɒbzə'veɪʃn] *n* observação *f.*

observatory [əb'zɜːvətrɪ] (*pl* -ies) *n* observatório *m.*

observe [əb'zɜːv] *vt* observar.

observer [əb'zɜːvə[r]] *n* - **1.** [gen] observador *m*, -ra *f* - **2.** [political commentator] analista *mf.*

obsess [əb'ses] *vt* obsedar, obcecar; to be ~ ed by OR with sb/sthg estar obcecado(da) com OR por alguém/algo.

obsessive [əb'sesɪv] *adj* obsessivo(va).

obsolescent [ˌɒbsə'lesnt] *adj* antiquado(da).

obsolete ['ɒbsəliːt] *adj* obsoleto(ta).

obstacle ['ɒbstəkl] *n* obstáculo *m.*

obstetrics [ɒb'stetrɪks] *n (U)* obstetrícia *f.*

obstinate ['ɒbstənət] *adj* - **1.** [stubborn] obstinado(da), teimoso(sa) - **2.** [persistent] persistente.

obstruct [əb'strʌkt] *vt* - **1.** [road, path, traffic] obstruir, bloquear - **2.** [progress, justice] impedir.

obstruction [əb'strʌkʃn] *n* - **1.** [blockage, obstacle] obstrução *f*, obstáculo *m* - **2.** *(U)* [act of impeding] impedimento *m* - **3.** SPORT obstrução *f.*

obtain [əb'teɪn] *vt* [get] obter.

obtainable [əb'teɪnəbl] *adj* disponível.

obtrusive [əb'truːsɪv] *adj* -**1.** [person, behaviour] inconveniente -**2.** [smell] penetrante -**3.** [colour] gritante.

obtuse [əb'tjuːs] *adj* obtuso(sa).

obvious ['ɒbvɪəs] *adj* -**1.** [evident] óbvio(via) -**2.** [unsubtle] evidente.

obviously ['ɒbvɪəslɪ] *adv* -**1.** [of course] evidentemente, obviamente; ~ **not** claro que não -**2.** [clearly] evidentemente; **he's** ~ **lying** é óbvio que ele está mentindo.

occasion [ə'keɪʒn] <> *n* -**1.** [circumstance, time] ocasião *f*; **to rise to the** ~ mostrar-se à altura da ocasião -**2.** *fml* [reason, motive] razão *f*. <> *vt fml* [cause] ocasionar.

occasional [ə'keɪʒənl] *adj* ocasional.

occasionally [ə'keɪʒnəlɪ] *adv* de vez em quando, ocasionalmente.

occult [ɒ'kʌlt] *adj* oculto(ta).

occupant ['ɒkjʊpənt] *n* ocupante *mf*.

occupation [ˌɒkjʊ'peɪʃn] *n* -**1.** [job] ocupação *f*, emprego *m* -**2.** [pastime] passatempo *m* -**3.** *(U)* MIL ocupação *f*.

occupational disease *n* MED doença *f* ocupacional.

occupational hazard *n* risco *m* da profissão.

occupational therapy *n (U)* terapia *f* ocupacional.

occupier ['ɒkjʊpaɪər] *n* ocupante *mf*.

occupy ['ɒkjʊpaɪ] *(pt & pp -ied)* *vt* -**1.** [gen] ocupar -**2.** [keep busy]: **to** ~ **o.s.** ocupar-se.

occur [ə'kɜːr] *(pt & pp -red, cont -ring)* *vi* -**1.** [happen] ocorrer -**2.** [exist] existir -**3.** [be found] ser encontrado(da) -**4.** [come to mind]: **to** ~ **to sb** ocorrer a alguém.

occurrence [ə'kʌrəns] *n* [event] acontecimento *m*.

ocean ['əʊʃn] *n* oceano *m*.

oceangoing ['əʊʃnˌgəʊɪŋ] *adj* de grande autonomia.

ochre UK, **ocher** US ['əʊkər] *adj* [colour] ocre.

o'clock [ə'klɒk] *adv*: **five** ~ cinco horas; **it's four** ~ são quatro horas; **it's one** ~ é uma hora.

octave ['ɒktɪv] *n* MUS oitava *f*.

October [ɒk'təʊbər] *n* outubro *m*; *see also* **September**.

octopus ['ɒktəpəs] *(pl -puses OR -pi [-paɪ])* *n* polvo *m*.

OD <> *n inf (abbr of overdose)* overdose *f*. <> *vi* -**1.** *inf (abbr of overdose)* tomar uma overdose -**2.** *fig, hum* exagerar. <> *adj (abbr of overdrawn)* no negativo, referente a conta bancária.

odd [ɒd] *adj* -**1.** [strange] estranho(nha) -**2.** [not part of pair] sem par -**3.** [number]

ímpar -**4.** [leftover] avulso(sa) -**5.** [occasional] ocasional -**6.** *inf* [approximately]: **20** ~ **years** 20 e tantos anos.

➡ **odds** *npl* -**1.** [probability] probabilidades *fpl*; **the** ~ **s are that ...** as previsões são de que ...; **against the** ~ **s** apesar de todas as dificuldades -**2.** [bits]: ~ **s and ends** miudezas *fpl* -**3.** *phr*: **to be at** ~ **s with sb/sthg** discordar de algo/alguém.

oddity ['ɒdɪtɪ] *(pl -ies)* *n* -**1.** [strange person, thing] esquisitice *f* -**2.** *(U)* [strangeness] estranheza *f*.

odd jobs *npl* biscates *mpl*.

oddly ['ɒdlɪ] *adv* [strangely] estranhamente; ~ **enough, I didn't care** surpreendentemente, não me importei.

oddments ['ɒdmənts] *npl* retalhos *mpl*.

odds-on ['ɒdz-] *adj inf*: **the** ~ **favourite** o grande favorito.

odometer [əʊ'dɒmɪtər] *n* [in car] velocímetro *m*.

odor *n US* = **odour**.

odour UK, **odor** US ['əʊdər] *n* odor *m*.

of [ɒv] *prep* -**1.** [belonging to] de; **the colour** ~ **the car** a cor do carro. -**2.** [expressing amount] de; **a piece** ~ **cake** uma fatia de bolo; **a fall** ~ **20%** uma queda de 20%; **lots** ~ **people** muita gente. -**3.** [containing, made from] de; **a glass** ~ **beer** um copo de cerveja; **a house** ~ **stone** uma casa de pedra; **it's made** ~ **wood** é de madeira. -**4.** [regarding, relating to, indicating cause] de; **fear** ~ **spiders** medo de aranhas; **he died** ~ **cancer** ele morreu de câncer. -**5.** [referring to time] de; **the summer** ~ **1969** o verão de 1969; **the 26th** ~ **August** o 26 de agosto. -**6.** [with cities, countries] de; **the city** ~ **San Francisco** a cidade de San Francisco. -**7.** [on the part of] de; **that was very kind** ~ **you** foi muito amável da sua parte. -**8.** *US* [in telling the time] menos, para; **it's ten** ~ **four** são dez para as quatro.

off [ɒf] <> *adv* -**1.** [away]: **to drive/walk** ~ ir-se embora; **to get** ~ [from bus, train, etc.] descer; **we're** ~ **to Austria next week** vamos para a Áustria na próxima semana. -**2.** [expressing removal]: **to take sthg** ~ tirar algo. -**3.** [so as to stop working]: **to turn sthg** ~ [TV, radio, engine] desligar algo; [tap] fechar algo. -**4.** [expressing distance or time away]: **it's a long way** ~ [in distance] é muito longe; [in time] ainda falta muito; **it's two months** ~ é daqui a dois meses. -**5.** [not at work] de folga; **I'm taking a week** ~ vou tirar uma semana de férias. <> *prep* -**1.** [away from]: **to get** ~ **sthg** descer de algo; ~ **the coast** ao largo da costa; **just** ~ **the main road** perto da estrada principal. **- 2.** [indicating removal]: **take the lid ~ the jar** tire a tampa do frasco; **we'll take $20 ~ the price** descontaremos 20 dólares do preço. **- 3.** [absent from]: **to be ~ work** não estar trabalhando. **- 4.** *inf* [from] a; **I bought it ~ her** eu comprei isso dela. *<> adj* **-1.** [TV, radio, light] apagado(da), desligado(da); [tap] fechado(da); [engine] desligado(da). **- 2.** [cancelled] cancelado(da).

offal ['ɒfl] *n (U)* vísceras *fpl (do animal abatido)*.

off-chance *n*: **he called on the ~ of seeing her** ele ligou com a remota esperança de vê-la.

off-colour *adj* **-1.** [ill] indisposto(ta) **- 2.** [rude, offensive] ofensivo(va).

off duty *adv*: **when do you get ~?** quando você fica de folga?
➤ **off-duty** *adj* de folga.

offence *UK*, **offense** *US* [ə'fens] *n* **-1.** [crime] infração *f*, delito *m* **- 2.** [displeasure, hurt] insulto *m*, ofensa *f*; **to take ~** ofender-se.

offend [ə'fend] *vt* [upset] ofender.

offender [ə'fendə^r] *n* **-1.** [criminal] transgressor *m*, -ra *f* **- 2.** [culprit] infrator *m*, -ra *f*.

offense [*sense 2* 'ɒfens] *n US* **-1.** = **offence** **- 2.** *SPORT* ataque *m*.

offensive [ə'fensɪv] *<> adj* **-1.** [causing offence] ofensivo(va) **- 2.** [aggressive] agressivo(va). *<> n MIL* ofensiva *f*.

offer ['ɒfə^r] *<> n* **-1.** [something offered] oferta *f*; **on ~** [available] em oferta **- 2.** [bid, proposal] proposta *f*. *<> vt* **-1.** [present, give] oferecer; **to ~ sthg to sb, to ~ sb sthg** oferecer algo a alguém **- 2.** [propose]: **to ~ to do sthg** oferecer-se para fazer algo. *<> vi* oferecer-se.

offering ['ɒfərɪŋ] *n* **-1.** [something offered] oferta *f* **- 2.** *RELIG* [sacrifice] oferenda *f*.

off guard *adv* desprevenido(da).

off-hand *<> adj* [unfriendly] brusco(ca). *<> adv* [at this moment] de imediato.

office ['ɒfɪs] *n* **-1.** [room] escritório *m*, gabinete *m* **- 2.** [building] edifício *m* de escritórios **- 3.** [staff] pessoal *m* **- 4.** [government department] departamento *m* **- 5.** [distribution point - for tickets] bilheteria *f*; [- for information] guichê *m*; [- for enquiries] serviço *m* de informações **- 6.** [position of authority] cargo *m*; **in ~** no poder; **to take ~** tomar posse.

office automation *n* automatização *f*.

office block *n* prédio *m* de escritórios.

office hours *npl* horário *m* de expediente.

officer ['ɒfɪsə^r] *n* **-1.** *MIL* oficial *mf* **- 2.** [in

organization] diretor *m*, -ra *f* **- 3.** [in police force] (agente) policial *m*.

office worker *n* funcionário *m*, -ria *f* de escritório.

official [ə'fɪʃl] *<> adj* oficial. *<> n* [public] funcionário *m*, -ria *f*; *SPORT* oficial *mf*.

officialdom [ə'fɪʃəldəm] *n (U)* burocracia *f*.

offing ['ɒfɪŋ] *n*: **in the ~** num futuro próximo.

off-licence *n UK* loja *f* de bebidas alcoólicas.

off-line *adj COMPUT* off-line, desconectado(da).

off-peak *adj* de tarifa reduzida.

off-putting [-ˌpʊtɪŋ] *adj* desconcertante.

off season *n*: **the ~** a baixa temporada.

offset ['ɒfset] (*pt & pp* **offset**, *cont* **-ting**) *vt* contrabalançar.

offshoot ['ɒfʃuːt] *n* [spin-off] ramificação *f*; **to be an ~ of sthg** ser uma ramificação de algo.

offshore ['ɒfʃɔː^r] *<> adj* **-1.** [in or on the sea] em alto-mar **- 2.** [near coast] costeiro(ra). *<> adv* **-1.** [out at sea] ao largo **- 2.** [near coast] a pouca distância da costa.

offside [*adj & adv* ˌɒf'saɪd, *n* 'ɒfsaɪd] *<> adj* **-1.** [part of vehicle] do lado do motorista **- 2.** *SPORT* impedido(da). *<> n* [of vehicle] lado *m* do motorista.

offspring ['ɒfsprɪŋ] (*pl inv*) *n* **-1.** *fml or hum* [of people] descendência *f* **- 2.** [of animals] prole *f*.

offstage [ˌɒf'steɪdʒ] *<> adj* dos bastidores. *<> adv* nos bastidores.

off-the-cuff *<> adj* improvisado(da). *<> adv* de improviso.

off-the-peg *adj UK* pronto(ta), confeccionado(da).

off-the-record *<> adj* extra-oficial. *<> adv* extra-oficialmente.

off-white *adj* de cor não totalmente branca.

often ['ɒfn, 'ɒftn] *adv* **-1.** [many times] muitas vezes; **how ~?** quantas vezes?; **how ~ do you visit her?** com que freqüência você a visita? **- 2.** [in many cases] freqüentemente.
➤ **as often as not** *adv* geralmente.
➤ **every so often** *adv* de vez em quando.
➤ **more often than not** *adv* freqüentemente.

ogle ['əʊgl] *vt pej* comer com os olhos.

oh [əʊ] *excl* **-1.** [to introduce comment] ah!; **~ really?** é mesmo? **- 2.** [expressing emotion] ah!; **~ no!** essa não!

oil [ɔɪl] ◇ n -1. [gen] óleo m -2. (U) [petroleum] petróleo m -3. (U) [olive oil] azeite m. ◇ vt [lubricate] lubrificar.

oilcan [ˈɔɪlkæn] n almotolia f.

oilfield [ˈɔɪlfiːld] n campo m petrolífero.

oil filter n filtro m de óleo.

oil-fired [-ˌfaɪəd] adj a óleo.

oil painting n -1. [art] pintura f a óleo -2. [picture] quadro m a óleo.

oilrig [ˈɔɪlrɪg] n plataforma f petrolífera.

oilskins [ˈɔɪlskɪnz] npl capa f de oleado.

oil slick n mancha f de óleo.

oil tanker n -1. [ship] petroleiro m -2. [lorry] caminhão m -tanque.

oil well n poço m de petróleo.

oily [ˈɔɪlɪ] (compar -ier, superl -iest) adj [covered in oil] gorduroso(sa).

ointment [ˈɔɪntmənt] n pomada f.

OK (pl OKs, pt & pp OKed, cont OKing), **okay** [ˌəʊˈkeɪ] inf ◇ adj: are you ~? você está bem?; to be ~ with OR by sb estar tudo bem com alguém. ◇ adv [well] bem. ◇ excl -1. [asking for, expressing agreement] está bem!, tá (bem/ bom)! -2. [fair enough] certo! -3. [to introduce new topic] bom! ◇ vt aprovar.

old [əʊld] ◇ adj -1. [aged, ancient, long-standing] velho(lha) -2. [referring to age]: how ~ are you? quantos anos você tem? -3. [former, ancient, out-of-date] antigo(ga) -4. inf [for emphasis]: any ~ clothes will do qualquer roupa serve; any ~ how de qualquer jeito. ◇ npl: the ~ os idosos.

old age n (U) velhice f.

old age pensioner n UK aposentado m, -da f por idade.

Old Bailey [-ˈbeɪlɪ] n: the ~ o prédio do Tribunal Criminal (de Londres).

old-fashioned [-ˈfæʃnd] adj -1. [outmoded] antiquado(da) -2. [traditional] tradicional.

old people's home n lar m de idosos.

O level (abbr of ordinary level) n UK até há pouco tempo, primeira etapa do GCE, exame prestado pelos estudantes britânicos aos 16 anos, agora substituído pelo GCSE.

olive [ˈɒlɪv] ◇ adj da cor de oliva. ◇ n [fruit] azeitona f.

olive green adj verde-oliva.

olive oil n (U) azeite m de oliva.

Olympic [əˈlɪmpɪk] adj olímpico(ca).

◆ **Olympics** npl: the ~s as Olimpíadas.

Olympic Games npl: the ~ os Jogos Olímpicos.

ombudsman [ˈɒmbʊdzmən] (pl -men [-mən]) n ombudsman mf.

omelet(te) [ˈɒmlɪt] n omelete f.

omen [ˈəʊmen] n presságio m.

ominous [ˈɒmɪnəs] adj -1. [ominoso(sa) -2. [threatening] ameaçador(ra).

omission [əˈmɪʃn] n omissão f.

omit [əˈmɪt] (pt & pp -ted, cont -ting) vt omitir; to ~ to do sthg deixar de fazer algo.

omnibus [ˈɒmnɪbəs] n -1. [book] antologia f -2. UK RADIO & TV programa f de variedades.

on [ɒn] ◇ prep -1. [expressing position, location] em, sobre; it's ~ the table está na mesa, está sobre a mesa; put it ~ the table ponha-o em OR sobre a mesa; ~ my right à minha direita; ~ the right à direita; a picture ~ the wall um quadro na parede; the exhaust ~ the car o cano de descarga do carro; we stayed ~ a farm ficamos numa fazenda. -2. [with forms of transportation]: ~ the plane no avião; to get ~ a bus subir num ônibus. -3. [expressing means, method] em; ~ foot a pé; ~ the radio no rádio; ~ TV na televisão; paid ~ an hourly basis pago por hora. -4. [using] a; it runs ~ unleaded gas funciona com gasolina sem chumbo; to be ~ drugs drogar-se; to be ~ medication estar tomando medicamentos. -5. [about] sobre; a book ~ Germany um livro sobre a Alemanha. -6. [expressing time]: ~ arrival ao chegar; ~ Tuesday na terça-feira; ~ August 25th no dia 25 de agosto. -7. [with regard to] em, sobre; a tax ~ imports um imposto sobre as importações; the effect ~ the country o impacto no país. -8. [describing activity, state]: ~ vacation de férias; ~ sale à venda. -9. [in phrases]: do you have any money ~ you? inf você tem dinheiro?; the drinks are ~ me as bebidas são por minha conta. ◇ adv -1. [in place, covering]: to put one's clothes ~ vestir-se; to put the lid ~ tapar. -2. [movie, play, programme]: the news is ~ está passando no telejornal; what's ~ at the movies? o que é que está passando no cinema? -3. [with transportation]: to get ~ subir. -4. [functioning]: to turn sthg ~ [TV, radio, light] ligar OR acender algo; [tap] abrir algo; [engine] pôr algo para trabalhar. -5. [taking place]: how long is the festival ~? quanto tempo dura o festival?; the game is already ~ o jogo já começou. -6. [farther forward]: to drive ~ continuar a dirigir. -7. [in phrases]: I already have something ~ tonight já tenho planos para esta noite. ◇ adj [TV, radio, light] ligado(da), aceso(sa); [tap] aberto(ta); [engine] funcionando.

once [wʌns] ◇ adv -1. [on one occasion] uma vez; ~ again OR more [one more time] outra vez; [yet again] novamente; ~ and for all de uma vez por todas; ~ in a while de vez em quando; ~ or twice uma vez ou duas; for ~ ao menos uma vez -2. [previously, formerly] outrora; ~ upon a time era uma vez. ◇ conj assim que, quando.

➤ **at once** adv -1. [immediately] imediatamente -2. [at the same time] ao mesmo tempo; all at ~ de repente.

oncoming [ˈɒnˌkʌmɪŋ] adj -1. [traffic, vehicle] em sentido contrário -2. [danger] iminente.

one [wʌn] ◇ num um (uma); thirty-~ trinta e um; ~ fifth um quinto. ◇ adj [only] único(ca); ~ day um dia. ◇ pron [referring to a particular thing or person] um m, uma f; the green ~ o verde; that ~ aquele m, aquela f.

one-armed bandit n caça-níqueis m.

one-man adj individual, solo.

one-man band n [musician] homem-orquestra m.

one-off inf ◇ adj único(ca). ◇ n -1. [unique event, person] único m, -ca f -2. [unique product] exemplar m único.

one-on-one adj US = one-to-one.

one-parent family n família f que possui apenas um dos pais.

oneself [wʌnˈself] pron fml -1. (reflexive) se -2. (after prep) si próprio(pria), si mesmo(ma).

one-sided [-ˈsaɪdɪd] adj -1. [unequal] desigual, unilateral -2. [biased] parcial.

one-to-one UK, **one-on-one** US adj -1. [discussion] entre dois -2. [tuition] individual.

one-touch dialling UK, **one-touch dialing** US n discagem f automática.

one-upmanship [ˌwʌnˈʌpmənʃɪp] n (U) capacidade de parecer ser melhor que os outros.

one-way adj -1. [moving in one direction] de mão única -2. [for outward travel only] só de ida.

ongoing [ˈɒnˌɡəʊɪŋ] adj em andamento, atual.

onion [ˈʌnjən] n cebola f.

online [ˈɒnlaɪn] COMPUT adj & adv on-line.

online banking n serviço m de banco on-line.

online shopping n compras fpl on-line.

onlooker [ˈɒnˌlʊkəʳ] n espectador m, -ra f.

only [ˈəʊnlɪ] ◇ adj único(ca); an ~

child um filho único. ◇ adv -1. [exclusively] só -2. [merely, just] apenas, só -3. [for emphasis] só; I was ~ too willing to help eu queria tanto ajudar; it's ~ natural you should be upset é bastante natural que você fique perturbado; not ~ ... but also não apenas ... mas também; ~ just por pouco. ◇ conj só que.

onset [ˈɒnset] n começo m.

onshore [ˈɒnʃɔːʳ] ◇ adj -1. [on land] terrestre -2. [moving towards land] em direção à costa. ◇ adv -1. [on land] em terra -2. [towards land] para a praia.

onslaught [ˈɒnslɔːt] n investida f.

onto [unstressed before consonant ˈɒntə, unstressed before vowel ˈɒntʊ, stressed ˈɒntuː] prep = on.

onus [ˈəʊnəs] n ônus m.

onward [ˈɒnwəd] ◇ adj [advancing - in time] para a frente; [- in space] adiante, para a frente. ◇ adv = onwards.

onwards [ˈɒnwədz] adv [forwards - in space] para a frente; [- in time] em diante.

ooze [uːz] ◇ vt fig exalar. ◇ vi exsudar; to ~ from OR out of sthg transpirar por algo; sweat ~d from every pore o suor transpirava-lhe por todos os poros.

opaque [əʊˈpeɪk] adj -1. [not transparent] opaco(ca) -2. fig [obscure] obscuro(ra).

OPEC [ˈəʊpek] (abbr of Organization of the Petroleum Exporting Countries) n OPEP f.

open [ˈəʊpn] ◇ adj -1. [gen] aberto(ta); to be ~ to sthg [ready to accept] ser aberto(ta) a algo; to be ~ to sb [opportunity, choice] estar aberto(ta) a alguém -2. [frank] franco(ca) -3. [unfastened] desdobrado(da) -4. [meeting, competition, invitation] aberto(ta) a todos -5. [unconcealed] manifesto(ta). ◇ n: in the ~ [in the fresh air] ao ar livre; to bring sthg out into the ~ pôr algo para fora. ◇ vt -1. [gen] abrir -2. [inaugurate] inaugurar. ◇ vi abrir.

➤ **open on to** vt fus [subj: room, door] dar para.

➤ **open up** ◇ vt [unlock door] destrancar a porta. ◇ vi -1. [gen] abrir-se -2. [shop, house] abrir.

opener [ˈəʊpnəʳ] n abridor m.

opening [ˈəʊpnɪŋ] ◇ adj [first] primeiro(ra). ◇ n -1. [beginning] lançamento m -2. [gap] abertura f -3. [opportunity] oportunidade f; ~ for sthg oportunidade para algo -4. [job vacancy] vaga f.

opening hours npl horário m de funcionamento.

openly [ˈəʊpənlɪ] adv abertamente.

open-minded [-ˈmaɪndɪd] adj compreensivo(va), sem preconceitos.

open-plan adj sem divisórias.

Open University n UK: the ~ universidade britânica para alunos adultos que estudam em casa, através de uma combinação de programas de rádio e televisão e ensino à distância.

opera [ˈɒprə] n ópera f.

opera house n teatro m lírico.

operate [ˈɒpəreɪt] <> vt -1. [cause to work] operar -2. COMM [manage] dirigir. <> vi -1. [function] funcionar -2. COMM dirigir -3. MED operar; to ~ on sb/sthg operar alguém/algo.

operating theatre UK, **operating room** US [ˈɒpəreɪtɪŋ-] n sala f de operações.

operation [ˌɒpəˈreɪʃn] n -1. [gen] operação f -2. MIL manobra f -3. COMM administração f -4. (U) [functioning] funcionamento m; in ~ [machine, device] em funcionamento; [law, system] em vigor -5. MED operação f, cirurgia f; to have an ~ on one's knee ser operado(da) no joelho; to perform a kidney transplant ~ fazer uma cirurgia de transplante renal.

operational [ˌɒpəˈreɪʃənl] adj operacional.

operative [ˈɒprətɪv] <> adj [law] em vigor; [system] vigente. <> n [in factory] operário m, -ria f.

operator [ˈɒpəreɪtər] n -1. TELEC telefonista mf -2. [technician] operador m, -ra f -3. COMM [person in charge] encarregado m, -da f.

opinion [əˈpɪnjən] n opinião f; to be of the ~ that ser da opinião de que; in my ~ na minha opinião.

opinionated [əˈpɪnjəneɪtɪd] adj pej teimoso(sa), cabeça-dura.

opinion poll n pesquisa f de opinião.

opponent [əˈpəʊnənt] n adversário m, -ria f.

opportune [ˈɒpətjuːn] adj oportuno(na).

opportunist [ˌɒpəˈtjuːnɪst] n oportunista mf.

opportunity [ˌɒpəˈtjuːnətɪ] (pl -ies) n oportunidade f; to take the ~ to do OR of doing sthg aproveitar a oportunidade para fazer algo.

oppose [əˈpəʊz] vt opor-se a.

opposed [əˈpəʊzd] adj oposto(ta); to be ~ to sthg opor-se a algo; as ~ to em oposição a, em vez de; I like beer ~ to wine prefiro vinho a cerveja.

opposing [əˈpəʊzɪŋ] adj oposto(ta), contrário(ria).

opposite [ˈɒpəzɪt] <> adj -1. [facing] em frente; the ~ side (of the street/house/door) o outro lado (da rua/casa/porta) -2. [very different]: ~ (to sthg) oposto(ta) (a algo). <> adv [lá] em frente. <> prep [facing] em frente a. <> n [contrary] contrário m.

opposite number n número m equivalente.

opposition [ˌɒpəˈzɪʃn] n -1. (U) [gen] oposição f -2. [opposing team] adversário m, -ria f.

Opposition n UK POL: the Opposition a Oposição.

oppress [əˈpres] vt -1. [tyrannize] oprimir -2. [subj: anxiety, atmosphere] deprimir.

oppressive [əˈpresɪv] adj -1. [gen] opressivo(va) -2. [heat, weather] sufocante.

opt [ɒpt] <> vt: to ~ to do sthg optar por OR preferir fazer algo. <> vi: to ~ for sthg optar por OR escolher algo.

opt in vi: to ~ in (to sthg) optar por participar (de algo).

opt out vi: to ~ out (of sthg) optar por não participar (de algo); [give up] abrir mão (de algo).

optical [ˈɒptɪkl] adj -1. [relating to light] óptico(ca) -2. [visual] visual.

optician [ɒpˈtɪʃn] n oculista mf; ~'s óptica f.

optimist [ˈɒptɪmɪst] n otimista mf.

optimistic [ˌɒptɪˈmɪstɪk] adj otimista.

optimum [ˈɒptɪməm] adj ótimo(ma).

option [ˈɒpʃn] n [choice] opção f; to have the ~ to do OR of doing sthg ter a opção de fazer algo.

optional [ˈɒpʃənl] adj opcional.

or [ɔːr] conj -1. [gen] ou -2. [after negative] nem; he can't read ~ write ele não sabe ler nem escrever -3. [otherwise] senão; I'd better go now ~ I'll miss my plane acho melhor eu ir logo, senão vou perder o vôo.

oral [ˈɔːrəl] <> adj -1. [spoken] oral -2. [relating to the mouth] bucal. <> n exame m oral.

orally [ˈɔːrəlɪ] adv -1. [in spoken form] oralmente -2. [via the mouth] por via oral.

orange [ˈɒrɪndʒ] <> adj [colour] laranja. <> n -1. [fruit] laranja f -2. (U) [colour] laranja m inv.

orange juice n suco m de laranja.

orator [ˈɒrətər] n orador m, -ra f.

orbit [ˈɔːbɪt] <> n órbita f. <> vt orbitar.

orbital road n UK estrada que circunda uma cidade.

orchard ['ɔ:tʃəd] n pomar m.

orchestra ['ɔ:kɪstrə] n orquestra f.

orchestral [ɔ:'kestrəl] adj orquestral.

orchid ['ɔ:kɪd] n orquídea f.

ordain [ɔ:'deɪn] vt -1. fml [decree] ordenar, decretar -2. RELIG: to be ~ ed ser ordenado(da).

ordeal [ɔ:'di:l] n experiência f traumática, provação f.

order ['ɔ:dəʳ] <> n -1. [gen] ordem f; to be under ~ s to do sthg receber ordens para fazer algo; in ~ em ordem; in working ~ em funcionamento; to be out of ~ [not working] estar fora de operação, não estar funcionando; [in meeting, debate] agir de forma inaceitável; [behaviour] ser improcedente -2. COMM [request] pedido m; to place an ~ with sb for sthg encomendar algo com alguém; to ~ sob encomenda -3. US [portion] porção f. <> vt -1. [command] ordenar; to ~ sb to do sthg ordenar alguém a fazer algo; to ~ that ordenar que -2. [request - drink, food, shopping item] pedir; [- taxi] chamar.
➡ in the order of UK, on the order of US prep da ordem de.
➡ in order that conj a fim de que, para que.
➡ in order to conj para.
➡ order about, order around vt sep: he's always ~ ing people about ele está sempre mandando nas pessoas.

order form n formulário m de encomenda.

orderly ['ɔ:dəlɪ] (pl -ies) <> adj -1. [person] obediente -2. [room, office] ordenado(da). <> n [in hospital] assistente mf.

ordinarily ['ɔ:dənrəlɪ] adv [normally] geralmente.

ordinary ['ɔ:dənrɪ] <> adj -1. [normal] comum, normal -2. pej [unexceptional] medíocre. <> n: out of the ~ fora do comum.

ordnance ['ɔ:dnəns] n -1. [military supplies] arsenal f bélico -2. [artillery] artilharia f.

ore [ɔ:ʳ] n minério m.

oregano [ˌɒrɪ'gɑ:nəʊ] n (U) orégano m.

organ ['ɔ:gən] n -1. [gen] órgão m -2. fig [mouthpiece] órgão m.

organic [ɔ:'gænɪk] adj orgânico(ca).

organic farming n agricultura f orgânica.

organization [ˌɔ:gənaɪ'zeɪʃn] n organização f.

organize, -ise ['ɔ:gənaɪz] vt organizar.

organizer ['ɔ:gənaɪzəʳ] n [person] organizador m, -ra f.

orgasm ['ɔ:gæzm] n orgasmo m.

orgy ['ɔ:dʒɪ] (pl -ies) n orgia f.

Orient ['ɔ:rɪənt] n: the ~ o Oriente.

oriental [ˌɔ:rɪ'entl] adj oriental.

orienteering [ˌɔ:rɪən'tɪərɪŋ] n (U) esporte no qual as pessoas utilizam um mapa e uma bússola para se orientar, corrida f de orientação.

origami [ˌɒrɪ'gɑ:mɪ] n (U) origami m.

origin ['ɒrɪdʒɪn] n origem f; country of ~ país m de origem.
➡ origins npl origens fpl.

original [ə'rɪdʒənl] <> adj original. <> n original m.

originally [ə'rɪdʒənəlɪ] adv [initially] originalmente.

originate [ə'rɪdʒəneɪt] <> vt originar, produzir. <> vi: to ~ (in) originar-se (em), surgir (de); to ~ from originar-se de.

Orkney Islands ['ɔ:knɪ-], **Orkneys** ['ɔ:knɪz] npl: the ~ as Ilhas Órcadas.

ornament ['ɔ:nəmənt] n ornamento m.

ornamental [ˌɔ:nə'mentl] adj ornamental.

ornate [ɔ:'neɪt] adj ornado(da).

ornithology [ˌɔ:nɪ'θɒlədʒɪ] n (U) ornitologia f.

orphan ['ɔ:fn] <> n órfão m, -fã f. <> vt: to be ~ ed ficar órfão(fã).

orphanage ['ɔ:fənɪdʒ] n orfanato m.

orthodox ['ɔ:θədɒks] adj ortodoxo(xa).

orthopaedic [ˌɔ:θə'pi:dɪk] adj ortopédico(ca).

orthopedic etc. [ˌɔ:θə'pi:dɪk] adj = orthopaedic etc.

oscillate ['ɒsɪleɪt] vi -1. [from side to side] oscilar -2. fig [vacillate]: to ~ between oscilar entre.

Oslo ['ɒzləʊ] n Oslo; in ~ em Oslo.

ostensible [ɒ'stensəbl] adj ostensivo(va).

ostentatious [ˌɒsten'teɪʃəs] adj ostentoso(sa).

osteopath ['ɒstɪəpæθ] n osteopático m, -ca f.

ostracize, -ise ['ɒstrəsaɪz] vt condenar ao ostracismo.

ostrich ['ɒstrɪtʃ] n avestruz mf.

other ['ʌðəʳ] <> adj -1. [gen] outro(tra); the ~ one o outro, a outra -2. phr: the ~ day no outro dia; the ~ week na outra semana. <> adv: ~ than a não ser; to be none ~ than ser nem mais nem menos que. <> pron: the ~ o outro, a outra; ~ s outros(tras); the ~ s os outros, as outras; one after the ~ um atrás do outro, uma atrás da outra; one or ~ of you must help me um de vocês dois deve me ajudar.

➤ **something or other** *pron* uma coisa ou outra.

➤ **somehow or other** *adv* de um jeito ou de outro.

otherwise ['ʌðəwaɪz] ◇ *adv* **-1.** [apart from that] de resto, tirando isso **-2.** [differently, in a different way] de outra maneira; **deliberately or** ~ intencionalmente ou não. ◇ *conj* [or else] senão, do contrário.

otter ['ɒtə'] *n* lontra *f*.

ouch [aʊtʃ] *excl* ai!

ought [ɔːt] *aux vb* dever; **I really** ~ **to go** eu realmente deveria ir; **you** ~ **not to have done that** você não deveria ter feito isso; **she** ~ **to pass her exam** ela tem chance de passar no exame.

ounce [aʊns] *n* **-1.** [unit of measurement] onça *f* **-2.** *fig* [small amount]: **an** ~ **of**, um pouco de.

our ['aʊə'] *poss adj* nosso(a); ~ **books** os nossos livros.

ours ['aʊəz] *poss pron* o nosso (a nossa); **a friend of** ~ um amigo nosso; **those shoes are** ~ estes sapatos são (os) nossos; ~ **are here - where are yours?** os nossos estão aqui - onde estão os seus?

ourselves [aʊə'selvz] *pron pl* **-1.** (*reflexive*) nos **-2.** (*after prep*) nós mesmos(-mas), nós próprios(prias); **we did it** ~ nós mesmos *or* próprios o fizemos.

oust [aʊst] *vt fml*: **to** ~ **sb (from sthg)** expulsar alguém (de algo).

out [aʊt] ◇ *adj* [light, cigarette] apagado(da); [not in fashion] fora de moda; **cargo pants are so** ~ **as calças cargo estão** tão fora de moda. ◇ *adv* **-1.** [outside] fora; **to get/go** ~ **(of)** sair (de); **it's cold** ~ **today** está frio lá fora hoje; **he looked** ~ ele olhou para fora. **-2.** [not at home, work] fora; **to be** ~ não estar em casa; **to go** ~ sair. **-3.** [so as to be extinguished]: **to turn sthg** ~ apagar algo; **put your cigarette** ~ apague o cigarro. **-4.** [expressing removal]: **to pour sthg** ~ despejar algo, jogar algo fora; **to take money** ~ [from cashpoint] retirar dinheiro; **to take sthg** ~ **(of)** tirar algo (de). **-5.** [outwards]: **to stick** ~ sobressair. **-6.** [expressing distribution]: **to hand sthg** ~ distribuir algo. **-7.** [in phrases]: **to get enjoyment** ~ **of sthg** divertir-se com algo; **stay** ~ **of the sun** não se exponha ao sol; **made** ~ **of wood** (feito) de madeira; **five** ~ **of ten women** cinco em cada dez mulheres; **I'm** ~ **of cigarettes** não tenho cigarros.

out-and-out *adj* completo(ta), absoluto(ta).

outback ['aʊtbæk] *n*: **the** ~ o interior da Austrália.

outboard (motor) ['aʊtbɔːd-] *n* motor *m* de popa.

outbreak ['aʊtbreɪk] *n* **-1.** [of crime, violence] explosão *f* **-2.** [of disease] surto *m* **-3.** [of war] deflagração *f*.

outburst ['aʊtbɜːst] *n* **-1.** [of emotion] manifestação *f* **-2.** [sudden occurrence] explosão *f*.

outcast ['aʊtkɑːst] *n* rejeitado *m*, -da *f*.

outcome ['aʊtkʌm] *n* resultado *m*.

outcrop ['aʊtkrɒp] *n* afloramento *m*.

outcry ['aʊtkraɪ] (*pl* -**ies**) *n* protestos *mpl*.

outdated [,aʊt'deɪtɪd] *adj* ultrapassado(da), fora de moda.

outdid [,aʊt'dɪd] *pt* ▷ **outdo**.

outdo [,aʊt'duː] (*pt* -**did**, *pp* -**done** [-dʌn]) *vt* ultrapassar, superar.

outdoor ['aʊtdɔː'] *adj* ao ar livre.

outdoors [aʊt'dɔːz] *adv* ao ar livre; **let's eat** ~ vamos comer fora.

outer ['aʊtə'] *adj* externo(na); **Outer London** a Grande Londres.

outer space *n* (*U*) espaço *m* exterior.

outfit ['aʊtfɪt] *n* **-1.** [clothes] vestimenta *f*; [fancy dress] traje *m* **-2.** *inf* [organization] agrupamento *m*, grupo *m*.

outfitters ['aʊt,fɪtəz] *n UK dated* confecção *f*.

outgoing ['aʊt,gəʊɪŋ] *adj* **-1.** [leaving] de partida **-2.** [friendly, sociable] extrovertido(da), aberto(ta).

➤ **outgoings** *npl UK* despesas *fpl*.

outgrow [,aʊt'grəʊ] (*pt* -**grew**, *pp* -**grown**) *vt* **-1.** [grow too big for]: **he has** ~ **n his shirts** as camisas ficaram pequenas para ele **-2.** [grow too old for] ser muito grande para.

outhouse ['aʊthaʊs, *pl* -haʊzɪz] *n* dependência *f*.

outing ['aʊtɪŋ] *n* [trip] excursão *f*.

outlandish [aʊt'lændɪʃ] *adj* estranho(-nha), extravagante.

outlaw ['aʊtlɔː] ◇ *n* fora-da-lei *mf*. ◇ *vt* [make illegal] declarar ilegal.

outlay ['aʊtleɪ] *n* despesa *f*, desembolso *m*.

outlet ['aʊtlet] *n* **-1.** [for feelings] escape *m* **-2.** [hole, pipe] saída *f* **-3.** [shop] ponto *m* de venda **-4.** *US ELEC* tomada *f*.

outline ['aʊtlaɪn] ◇ *n* **-1.** [brief description] linhas *fpl* gerais, esboço *m*; **in** ~ em linhas gerais **-2.** [silhouette] contorno *m*. ◇ *vt* [describe briefly] resumir, esboçar.

outlive [,aʊt'lɪv] *vt* [subj: person] viver mais que.

outlook ['aʊtlʊk] *n* **-1.** [attitude, disposition]

postura *f*, atitude *f* **- 2.** [prospect] perspectiva *f*.

outlying [ˌaʊtˈlaɪɪŋ] *adj* distante, remoto(ta).

outmoded [ˌaʊtˈməʊdɪd] *adj* antiquado(da), fora de moda.

outnumber [ˌaʊtˈnʌmbəʳ] *vt* exceder em número.

out-of-date *adj* **- 1.** [passport, season ticket] expirado(da) **- 2.** [clothes, belief] antiquado(da).

out of doors *adv* ao ar livre.

out-of-the-way *adj* [isolated] remoto(-ta).

outpatient [ˈaʊtˌpeɪʃnt] *n* paciente *mf* ambulatorial.

outpost [ˈaʊtpəʊst] *n* fig [bastion] posto *m* avançado.

output [ˈaʊtpʊt] *n* **- 1.** [production] produção *f* **- 2.** [COMPUT - printing out] saída *f*; [- printout] cópia *f* impressa.

outrage [ˈaʊtreɪdʒ] ◇ *n* **- 1.** *(U)* [anger, shock] indignidade *f* **- 2.** [atrocity] atrocidade *f*, ultraje *m*. ◇ *vt* ultrajar.

outrageous [aʊtˈreɪdʒəs] *adj* **- 1.** [offensive, shocking] ultrajante **- 2.** [extravagant, wild] extravagante.

outright [*adj* ˈaʊtraɪt, *adv* ˌaʊtˈraɪt] ◇ *adj* **- 1.** [categoric, direct] claro(ra), categórico(ca) **- 2.** [total, complete - disaster] completo(ta); [- victory, winner] indiscutível. ◇ *adv* **- 1.** [ask] abertamente, francamente **- 2.** [win, fail] indiscutivelmente, completamente **- 3.** [deny] categoricamente.

outset [ˈaʊtset] *n*: at the ~ no princípio; from the ~ desde o princípio.

outside [*adv* ˌaʊtˈsaɪd, *adj, prep & n* ˈaʊtsaɪd] ◇ *adj* **- 1.** [gen] externo(na) **- 2.** [unlikely] remoto(ta). ◇ *adv* [lá] fora; to look ~ olhar para fora; to run ~ correr lá fora; to go ~ ir lá para fora. ◇ *prep* **- 1.** [not inside] fora de; we live half an hour ~ London moramos a meia hora de Londres **- 2.** [beyond] além de. ◇ *n* [exterior] exterior *m*.
➡ **outside of** *prep US* [apart from] exceto.

outside lane *n AUT* **- 1.** [in UK] faixa *f* da direita **- 2.** [in mainland Europe, US, Brazil etc.] faixa *f* da esquerda.

outside line *n* linha *f* externa.

outsider [ˌaʊtˈsaɪdəʳ] *n* **- 1.** *SPORT* azarão *m* **- 2.** [from outside social group] estranho *m*, -nha *f*, desconhecido *m*, -da *f*.

outsize [ˈaʊtsaɪz] *adj* **- 1.** [book, portion] enorme **- 2.** [clothes] extra-grande.

outskirts [ˈaʊtskɜːts] *npl*: the ~ os arredores.

outsource [ˈaʊtsɔːs] *vt COMM* terceirizar.

outsourcing [ˈaʊtsɔːsɪŋ] *n COMM* terceirização *f*.

outspoken [ˌaʊtˈspəʊkn] *adj* franco(ca).

outstanding [ˌaʊtˈstændɪŋ] *adj* **- 1.** [excellent] destacado(da), notável **- 2.** [very obvious, important] notável **- 3.** [pending] pendente.

outstay [ˌaʊtˈsteɪ] *vt*: to ~ one's welcome abusar da hospitalidade de alguém.

outstretched [ˌaʊtˈstretʃt] *adj* estendido(da).

outstrip [ˌaʊtˈstrɪp] (*pt & pp* **-ped**, *cont* **-ping**) *vt* **- 1.** [do better than] superar **- 2.** [run faster than] ultrapassar, deixar para trás.

out-tray *n* bandeja *f* de saída.

outward [ˈaʊtwəd] ◇ *adj* **- 1.** [going away] de ida **- 2.** [apparent] aparente **- 3.** [visible] visível.

outwardly [ˈaʊtwədlɪ] *adv* [apparently] aparentemente.

outweigh [ˌaʊtˈweɪ] *vt* pesar mais que.

outwit [ˌaʊtˈwɪt] (*pt & pp* **-ted**, *cont* **-ting**) *vt* ser mais esperto(ta) que.

oval [ˈəʊvl] ◇ *adj* oval. ◇ *n* oval *m*.

Oval Office *n*: the ~ o Salão Oval.

ovary [ˈəʊvərɪ] (*pl* -ies) *n ANAT* ovário *m*.

ovation [əʊˈveɪʃn] *n* ovação *f*; a standing ~ ovação com o público de pé.

oven [ˈʌvn] *n* [for cooking] forno *m*.

ovenproof [ˈʌvnpruːf] *adj* refratário(-ria).

over [ˈəʊvəʳ] ◇ *prep* **- 1.** [gen] sobre; put your coat ~ that chair ponha o seu casaco naquela cadeira; to rule ~ a country governar um país **- 2.** [directly above] sobre, em cima de **- 3.** [on the far side of] ao outro lado de **- 4.** [across the surface of] por; she walked ~ the lawn ela caminhou pelo gramado **- 5.** [across the top or edge of] por cima de **- 6.** [more than] mais de; ~ and above bem acima de **- 7.** [by means of] por **- 8.** [concerning, due to] por; it was a fight ~ a woman, I think era uma disputa por uma mulher, acho eu **- 9.** [during] durante **- 10.** [recovered from] recuperado(da) (de). ◇ *adv* **- 1.** [distance away] lá; ~ here/there por aqui, lá **- 2.** [across]: to cross ~ cruzar; they flew ~ to America eles voaram para a América; ~ at mum's na casa da minha mãe; to ask sb ~ convidar alguém para ir lá em casa **- 3.** [to face a different way]: to turn sth ~ virar algo **- 4.** [more] mais **- 5.** [remaining]: that leaves £2 ~ isso nos sobra £2; I ate the piece of cake left ~ comi o pedaço de bolo que sobrou **- 6.** *RADIO* câmbio; ~ and out! câmbio e desligo! **- 7.** [involving repetitions]: **(all)** ~ **again** (tudo) novamente; ~ **and** ~ **(again)** várias e várias vezes. ◇ *adj* [finished] acabado(da); **the meeting was** ~ **by seven** a reunião acabou às sete horas.

➡ **all over** ◇ *adv* [everywhere] por todas as partes. ◇ *adj* [finished] acabado(da).

overall [*adj & n* 'əʊvərɔːl, *adv* ,əʊvər'ɔːl] ◇ *adj* [total] global, total. ◇ *adv* -**1.** [in total] no geral -**2.** [in general] normalmente, em geral. ◇ *n* -**1.** [coat] avental *m*, guarda-pó *m* -**2.** *US* [with trousers] macacão *m*.

➡ **overalls** *npl* macacão *m*.

overawe [,əʊvər'ɔː] *vt* intimidar.

overbalance [,əʊvə'bæləns] *vi* perder o equilíbrio.

overbearing [,əʊvə'beərɪŋ] *adj pej* arrogante.

overboard ['əʊvəbɔːd] *adv* NAUT: **to fall** ~ cair ao mar.

overbook [,əʊvə'bʊk] *vi* ter mais reservas que lugares; **the plane was** ~ deu overbook no avião.

overcame [,əʊvə'keɪm] *pt* ▷ **overcome**.

overcast ['əʊvəkɑːst] *adj* carregado(da), nublado (da).

overcharge [,əʊvə'tʃɑːdʒ] *vt*: **to** ~ **sb (for sthg)** cobrar de alguém em excesso (por algo).

overcoat ['əʊvəkəʊt] *n* sobretudo *m*.

overcome [,əʊvə'kʌm] (*pt* -**came**, *pp* -**come**) *vt* -**1.** [control, deal with] superar, vencer -**2.** [overwhelm]: **to be** ~ **(by** OR **with sthg)** [emotion] estar tomado(da) (por algo); [smoke, fumes] estar asfixiado(da) (por algo).

overcrowded [,əʊvə'kraʊdɪd] *adj* -**1.** [room, building] superlotado(da) -**2.** [city, country] superpovoado(da).

overcrowding [,əʊvə'kraʊdɪŋ] *n* -**1.** (U) [of room, building] superlotação *f* -**2.** (U) [of city, country] superpovoamento *m*.

overdo [,əʊvə'duː] (*pt* -**did** [-dɪd], *pp* -**done**) *vt* -**1.** pej [exaggerate] exagerar -**2.** [do too much]: **to** ~ **the walking** caminhar demais; **the doctor told her not to** ~ **it** o médico disse para ela pegar leve OR não exagerar -**3.** [overcook] cozinhar demais.

overdone [,əʊvə'dʌn] ◇ *pp* ▷ **overdo**. ◇ *adj*: **it's** ~ cozinhou demais.

overdose ['əʊvədəʊs] *n* overdose *f*.

overdraft ['əʊvədrɑːft] *n* saldo *m* negativo.

overdrawn [,əʊvə'drɔːn] *adj* -**1.** [person]: **to be** ~ ter saldo negativo -**2.** [account] no negativo.

overdue [,əʊvə'djuː] *adj* -**1.** [gen] atrasado(da); **I'm** ~ **for a dental checkup** já está na hora de eu fazer a revisão no dentista -**2.** [needed, awaited]: **(long)** ~ (há muito) esperado(da).

overestimate [,əʊvər'estɪmeɪt] *vt* superestimar.

overflow [*vb* ,əʊvə'fləʊ, *n* 'əʊvəfləʊ] ◇ *vi* transbordar; **to be** ~**ing (with sthg)** estar transbordando (de algo). ◇ *n* ladrão *m*.

overgrown [,əʊvə'grəʊn] *adj* coberto(-ta) de mato.

overhaul [*n* 'əʊvəhɔːl, *vb* ,əʊvə'hɔːl] ◇ *n* revisão *f*. ◇ *vt* -**1.** [service] fazer a revisão de -**2.** [revise] revisar.

overhead [*adv* ,əʊvə'hed, *adj & n* 'əʊvəhed] ◇ *adj* aéreo(rea). ◇ *adv* por cima, pelo alto. ◇ *n* US despesas *fpl* gerais, gastos *mpl* gerais.

➡ **overheads** *npl* UK despesas *fpl* gerais, gastos *mpl* gerais.

overhead projector *n* retroprojetor *m*.

overhear [,əʊvə'hɪə[r]] (*pt & pp* -**heard** [-hɜːd]) *vt* entreouvir.

overheat [,əʊvə'hiːt] ◇ *vt* superaquecer. ◇ *vi* superaquecer-se.

overjoyed [,əʊvə'dʒɔɪd] *adj*: **to be** ~ **(at sthg)** estar contentíssimo(ma) (com algo).

overkill ['əʊvəkɪl] *n* (U) exagero *m*.

overladen [,əʊvə'leɪdn] ◇ *pp* ▷ **overload**. ◇ *adj* sobrecarregado(da).

overland ['əʊvəlænd] ◇ *adj* terrestre. ◇ *adv* por terra.

overlap [*n* 'əʊvəlæp, *vb* ,əʊvə'læp] (*pt & pp* -**ped**, *cont* -**ping**) *vi* -**1.** [cover each other] sobrepor-se -**2.** [be similar] coincidir; **to** ~ **(with sthg)** coincidir em parte (com algo).

overleaf [,əʊvə'liːf] *adv* no verso.

overload [,əʊvə'ləʊd] (*pp* -**loaded** OR -**laden**) *vt* sobrecarregar; **to be** ~**ed (with sthg)** estar sobrecarregado(da) de algo.

overlook [,əʊvə'lʊk] *vt* -**1.** [look over] dar para -**2.** [disregard, miss] fazer vista grossa para -**3.** [excuse] desculpar.

overnight [*adj* 'əʊvənaɪt, *adv* ,əʊvə'naɪt] ◇ *adj* -**1.** [stay, guest, parking] por uma noite -**2.** [clothes] para uma noite -**3.** [journey] de uma noite; ~ **bag** bolsa *f* de viagem -**4.** [very sudden] da noite para o dia. ◇ *adv* -**1.** [for all of night] durante a noite -**2.** [very suddenly] da noite para o dia.

overpass ['əʊvəpɑːs] *n* US viaduto *m*.

overpower [,əʊvə'paʊə[r]] *vt* -**1.** [in fight] subjugar -**2.** fig [overwhelm] vencer, sobrepujar.

overpowering [ˌəʊvəˈpaʊərɪŋ] *adj* -1. [desire, feeling] dominante -2. [smell] asfixiante -3. [heat, sensation] sufocante -4. [personality] opressor(ra).

overran [ˌəʊvəˈræn] *pt* ▷ **overrun.**

overrated [ˌəʊvəˈreɪtɪd] *adj* superestimado(da).

override [ˌəʊvəˈraɪd] (*pt* -**rode**, *pp* -**ridden**) *vt* -1. [be more important than] passar por cima de, não fazer caso de -2. [overrule] desautorizar.

overriding [ˌəʊvəˈraɪdɪŋ] *adj* predominante.

overrode [ˌəʊvəˈrəʊd] *pt* ▷ **override.**

overrule [ˌəʊvəˈruːl] *vt* -1. [person, decision] desautorizar -2. [objection] negar.

overrun [ˌəʊvəˈrʌn] (*pt* -**ran**, *pp* -**run**, *cont* -**running**) ◇ *vt* -1. MIL [occupy] invadir -2. *fig* [cover, fill]: **to be ~ with sthg** estar repleto(ta) de algo. ◇ *vi* passar do tempo previsto.

oversaw [ˌəʊvəˈsɔː] *pt* ▷ **oversee.**

overseas [*adj* ˈəʊvəsiːz, *adv* ˌəʊvəˈsiːz] ◇ *adj* -1. [market] exterior -2. [network, branches] no exterior -3. [sales, aid] para o exterior -4. [from abroad] estrangeiro(ra). ◇ *adv* -1. [travel, sell] para o exterior -2. [study, live] no exterior.

oversee [ˌəʊvəˈsiː] (*pt* -**saw**, *pp* -**seen** [-ˈsiːn]) *vt* supervisionar.

overseer [ˈəʊvəˌsiːəˈ] *n* supervisor *m*, -ra *f*.

overshadow [ˌəʊvəˈʃædəʊ] *vt* -1. [make darker] fazer sombra em -2. *fig* [outweigh, eclipse]: **to be ~ed by sb/sthg** ser eclipsado(da) por alguém/algo -3. *fig* [mar, cloud]: **to be ~ed by sthg** ser ofuscado(da) por algo.

overshoot [ˌəʊvəˈʃuːt] (*pt* & *pp* -**shot**) *vt* passar.

oversight [ˈəʊvəsaɪt] *n* deslize *m*, descuido *m*.

oversleep [ˌəʊvəˈsliːp] (*pt* & *pp* -**slept** [-ˈslept]) *vi* dormir demais, ficar dormindo.

overspill [ˈəʊvəspɪl] *n* (*U*) excesso *m* de população.

overstep [ˌəʊvəˈstep] (*pt* & *pp* -**ped**, *cont* -**ping**) *vt* passar por cima de; **to ~ the mark** passar dos limites.

overt [ˈəʊvɜːt] *adj* aberto(ta), manifesto(ta).

overtake [ˌəʊvəˈteɪk] (*pt* -**took**, *pp* -**taken** [-ˈteɪkn]) ◇ *vt* -1. AUT ultrapassar -2. [subj: disaster, misfortune] surpreender, pegar de surpresa. ◇ *vi* AUT ultrapassar.

overthrow [*n* ˈəʊvəθrəʊ, *vb* ˌəʊvəˈθrəʊ]

(*pt* -**threw**, *pp* -**thrown**) ◇ *n* deposição *f*, destituição *f*. ◇ *vt* [government, president] depor, destituir.

overtime [ˈəʊvətaɪm] ◇ *n* -1. [extra time worked] hora *f* extra -2. US SPORT prorrogação *f*. ◇ *adv*: **to work ~** fazer hora extra.

overtones [ˈəʊvətəʊnz] *npl* insinuações *fpl*.

overtook [ˌəʊvəˈtʊk] *pt* ▷ **overtake.**

overture [ˈəʊvəˌtjʊəˈ] *n* MUS abertura *f*.

overturn [ˌəʊvəˈtɜːn] ◇ *vt* -1. [turn over] virar -2. [overrule] invalidar -3. [overthrow] depor. ◇ *vi* -1. [boat] virar -2. [lorry, car] capotar.

overweight [ˌəʊvəˈweɪt] *adj* obeso(sa), gordo(da).

overwhelm [ˌəʊvəˈwelm] *vt* -1. [make helpless] subjugar -2. MIL [gain control of] dominar, passar a controlar.

overwhelming [ˌəʊvəˈwelmɪŋ] *adj* -1. [feeling, quality] impressionante -2. [victory, defeat, majority] esmagador(ra).

overwork [ˌəʊvəˈwɜːk] ◇ *n* (*U*) trabalho *m* excessivo. ◇ *vt* [give too much work to] fazer trabalhar demais.

overwrought [ˌəʊvəˈrɔːt] *adj* muito nervoso(sa).

owe [əʊ] *vt*: **to ~ sthg to sb, to ~ sb sthg** dever algo a alguém.

owing [ˈəʊɪŋ] *adj* que se deve.

◆ **owing to** *prep* por causa de, devido a.

owl [aʊl] *n* coruja *f*.

own [əʊn] ◇ *adj* [indicating possession] próprio(pria); **my/your ~ car** meu/teu próprio carro; **he doesn't need a lift, he has his ~ car** ele não precisa de carona, tem seu próprio carro; **she has her ~ style** ela tem um estilo próprio. ◇ *pron* [indicating possession]: **my ~** o(a) meu(minha); **your ~** o(a) seu(sua); **a house of my ~** minha própria casa; **the city has a special atmosphere of its ~** a cidade tem uma atmosfera especial que lhe é própria; **on one's ~** [alone] sozinho(nha); **to get one's ~ back** dar o troco, vingar-se. ◇ *vt* possuir, ter.

◆ **own up** *vi*: **to ~ up (to sthg)** confessar (algo), admitir (algo).

owner [ˈəʊnəˈ] *n* proprietário *m*, -ria *f*, dono *m*, -na *f*.

ownership [ˈəʊnəʃɪp] *n* (*U*) posse *f*, propriedade *f*.

ox [ɒks] (*pl* **oxen**) *n* boi *m*.

Oxbridge [ˈɒksbrɪdʒ] *n* (*U*) as universidades de Oxford e Cambridge.

oxen [ˈɒksn] *pl* ▷ **ox.**

oxtail soup [ˈɒksteɪl-] *n* (*U*) rabada *f*.

oxygen [ˈɒksɪdʒən] *n* (*U*) oxigênio *m*.

oxygen mask *n* máscara *f* de oxigênio.

oxygen tent *n* tenda *f* de oxigênio.

oyster ['ɔɪstə'] *n* ostra *f*.

oz. *abbr of* **ounce**.

ozone ['əʊzəʊn] *n* ozônio *m*.

ozone-friendly *adj* não-prejudicial à camada de ozônio.

ozone layer *n* camada *f* de ozônio.

P

p¹ (*pl* **p's** OR **ps**), **P** (*pl* **P's** OR **Ps**) [pi:] *n* [letter] p, P *m*.

p² -1. (*abbr of* **page**) p. -2. *abbr of* **penny, pence**.

P45 *n documento oficial que o empregado recebe do empregador na Grã-Bretanha ao deixar o emprego e repassa ao próximo empregador, contendo informações salariais.*

P60 *n documento oficial fornecido pelo empregador ao empregado na Grã-Bretanha com informações sobre salário recebido e impostos pagos durante aquele ano,* ≃ *declaração f de rendimentos.*

pa [pɑ:] *n inf esp US* pai *m*.

p.a. (*abbr of* **per annum**) p.a.

PA *n* -1. *UK* (*abbr of* **personal assistant**) assessor *m*, -ra *f* pessoal -2. (*abbr of* **public address system**) sistema *m* de alto-falantes.

pace [peɪs] ◇ *n* -1. (*U*) [speed, rate] ritmo *m*, andamento *m*; **to keep ~ (with sb/sthg)** acompanhar o ritmo (de alguém/algo) -2. [step] passo *m*. ◇ *vi* andar de um tado para o outro.

pacemaker ['peɪs,meɪkə'] *n* -1. MED marca-passo *m* -2. [in race] *competidor que estabelece o ritmo da corrida.*

Pacific [pə'sɪfɪk] ◇ *adj* do Pacífico. ◇ *n*: **the ~ (Ocean)** o (Oceano) Pacífico.

pacifier ['pæsɪfaɪə'] *n US* bico *m*.

pacifist ['pæsɪfɪst] *n* pacifista *mf*.

pacify ['pæsɪfaɪ] (*pt & pp* **-ied**) *vt* -1. [person] acalmar -2. [country, region] pacificar.

pack [pæk] ◇ *n* -1. [rucksack] mochila *f* -2. [bundle] pacote *m*, embrulho *m* -3. [of cigarettes] maço *m* -4. *esp US* [washing powder, tissues] caixa *f* -5. [of cards] baralho *m* -6. [of animals - dogs] matilha

f; [- wolves] alcatéia *f*; [- of thieves] quadrilha *f*. ◇ *vt* -1. [bag, suitcase] fazer -2. [clothes etc.] colocar na mala -3. [put in container, parcel] embalar -4. [crowd into] lotar; **to be ~ed into sthg** estar socado(da) em algo. ◇ *vi* [for journey, holiday] fazer as malas.

◆ **pack in** ◇ *vt sep UK inf* [job, boyfriend, smoking] deixar; **~ it in!** [stop annoying me] pare com isso!, chega!; [shut up] boca fechada! ◇ *vi inf* pifar.

◆ **pack off** *vt sep inf* enviar, mandar.

package ['pækɪdʒ] ◇ *n* -1. [gen] pacote *m* -2. [box] caixa *f* -3. *US* [of cigarettes] maço *m*, carteira *f* OR *m* -4. [set, group] pacote *m*. ◇ *vt* embalar, empacotar.

package deal *n* pacote *m* de acordo.

package tour *n* pacote *m* turístico.

packaging ['pækɪdʒɪŋ] *n* (*U*) embalagem *f*.

packed [pækt] *adj* -1. [place]: **~ (with)** lotado(da) (de) -2. [magazine, information pack]: **~ with** repleto(ta) de.

packed lunch *n UK* -1. [for school] *f* merenda *f* -2. [for work] marmita *f*.

packet ['pækɪt] *n* -1. [gen] pacote *m* -2. [box] caixa *f* -3. [of cigarettes] maço *m*, carteira *f*.

packing ['pækɪŋ] *n* (*U*) -1. [protective material] embalagem *f* -2. [for journey, holiday]: **to do the ~** fazer as malas.

packing case *n* caixote *m* de embalagem.

pact [pækt] *n* pacto *m*.

pad [pæd] (*pt & pp* **-ded**, *cont* **-ding**) ◇ *n* -1. [for clothes, body]: **shoulder ~** ombreira *f*; **knee ~** joelheira *f*; **shin ~** tornozeleira *f* -2. [notepad] bloco *m* de anotações -3. [for absorbing liquid - cotton wool] chumaço *m*; [- sanitary] absorvente *m* higiênico -4. *SPACE*: **(launch) ~** plataforma *f* (de lançamento) -5. [of cat or dog] almofadinha *f* -6. *inf dated* [home] casa *f*. ◇ *vt* -1. [clothing, furniture] revestir, forrar -2. [wound] cobrir. ◇ *vi* andar com suavidade.

padding ['pædɪŋ] *n* (*U*) -1. [in jacket] revestimento *m* -2. [in shoulders] ombreira *f* -3. [in chair] enchimento *m* -4. [in speech, essay, letter] enrolação *f*.

paddle ['pædl] ◇ *n* -1. [for canoe, dinghy] remo *m* -2. [wade]: **to have a ~** patinhar na água. ◇ *vi* -1. [in canoe, dinghy] remar -2. [wade] patinhar.

paddle boat, paddle steamer *n* vapor *m* movido a rodas.

paddling pool ['pædlɪŋ-] *n* -1. [in park] piscina *f* infantil -2. [inflatable] piscina *f* inflável.

paddock ['pædək] n -1. [small field] manejo m -2. [at racecourse] paddock m.
paddy field ['pædɪ-] n arrozal m.
padlock ['pædlɒk] ◇ n cadeado m. ◇ vt fechar com cadeado.
paediatrics [,piːdɪ'ætrɪks] n = pediatrics.
pagan ['peɪgən] ◇ adj pagão(gã). ◇ n pagão m, -gã f.
page [peɪdʒ] ◇ n página f. ◇ vt chamar (pelo alto-falante).
page [peɪdʒ] vt [using pager]: to be ~d receber chamadas pelo pager; to ~ sb chamar alguém pelo pager.
pageant ['pædʒənt] n desfile m, cortejo m cívico.
pageantry ['pædʒəntrɪ] n (U) fausto m, pompa f.
page break n COMPUT quebra f de página.
paid [peɪd] ◇ pt & pp ▷ **pay**. ◇ adj pago(ga).
pail [peɪl] n balde m.
pain [peɪn] n -1. dor f; to be in ~ sentir dor -2. (U) [mental suffering] sofrimento m, pena f -3. inf [annoyance]: it's such a ~! é tão chato!; he is a real ~! ele é um saco!
➤ **pains** npl esforços mpl; to be at ~s to do sthg empenhar-se para fazer algo; to take ~s to do sthg esforçar-se para fazer algo.
pained [peɪnd] adj aflito(ta), consternado(da).
painful ['peɪnfʊl] adj -1. [sore] dolorido(da) -2. [causing pain] doloroso(sa) -3. [distressing] penoso(sa), doloroso(sa).
painfully ['peɪnfʊlɪ] adv -1. [distressingly] dolorosamente -2. [for emphasis] terrivelmente.
painkiller ['peɪn,kɪləʳ] n analgésico m, calmante m.
painless ['peɪnlɪs] adj indolor, fácil.
painstaking ['peɪnz,teɪkɪŋ] adj meticuloso(sa), minucioso(sa).
paint [peɪnt] ◇ n tinta f. ◇ vt pintar; to ~ the wall white pintar o teto de branco. ◇ vi pintar.
paintbrush ['peɪntbrʌʃ] n -1. [of artist] pincel m -2. [of decorator] broxa f.
painter ['peɪntəʳ] n pintor m, -ra f.
painting ['peɪntɪŋ] n -1. [picture] pintura f, quadro m -2. (U) ACTIVITY pintura f.
paint stripper n (U) removedor m (de tinta).
paintwork ['peɪntwɜːk] n (U) pintura f.
pair [peəʳ] n par m; a ~ of idiots uma dupla de idiotas; a ~ of scissors uma tesoura; a ~ of trousers uma calça; a ~ of spectacles um óculos m.
pajamas [pə'dʒɑːməz] npl US = pyjamas.

Pakistan [UK ,pɑːkɪ'stɑːn, US ,pækɪ'stæn] n Paquistão.
Pakistani [UK ,pɑːkɪ'stɑːnɪ, US ,pækɪ'stænɪ] ◇ adj paquistanês(esa). ◇ n paquistanês, -esa f.
pal [pæl] n inf -1. [friend] camarada mf, companheiro m, -ra f -2. [as term of address]: now wait a minute, ~, I was first! espera um pouco, meu chapa, eu cheguei primeiro!
palace ['pælɪs] n palácio m.
palatable ['pælətəbl] adj -1. [pleasant to taste] saboroso(sa) -2. [acceptable] aceitável, admissível.
palate ['pælət] n -1. ANAT palato m -2. [sense of taste] paladar m.
palaver [pə'lɑːvəʳ] n inf -1. [talk] palavrório m -2. [fuss] bagunça f, rebuliço m.
pale [peɪl] adj -1. [colour] fosco(ca) -2. [light] tênue -3. [clothes] claro(ra) -4. [face, complexion] pálido(da).
Palestine ['pælɪ,staɪn] n Palestina; in ~ na Palestina.
Palestinian [,pælə'stɪnɪən] ◇ adj palestino(na). ◇ n palestino m, -na f.
palette ['pælət] n paleta f.
palings ['peɪlɪŋz] npl cerca f.
pall [pɔːl] ◇ n -1. [of smoke] nuvem f, cortina f -2. US [coffin] caixão m. ◇ vi perder a graça.
pallet ['pælɪt] n palete m, plataforma f de carga.
pallor ['pæləʳ] n palor m.
palm [pɑːm] n -1. [tree] palmeira f -2. [of hand] palma f.
➤ **palm off** vt sep inf: to ~ sthg off on sb empurrar algo para alguém; to ~ sb off with sthg enganar alguém com algo.
Palm Sunday n Domingo m de Ramos.
palmtop ['pɑːmtɒp] n COMPUT palmtop m.
palm tree n palmeira f.
palpable ['pælpəbl] adj palpável.
paltry ['pɔːltrɪ] (compar -ier, superl -iest) adj irrisório(ria).
pamper ['pæmpəʳ] vt mimar.
pamphlet ['pæmflɪt] n panfleto m.
pan [pæn] (pt & pp -ned, cont -ning) ◇ n -1. [for frying] fridigeira f -2. [for boiling] panela f -3. US [for baking] assadeira f -4. [of scales] prato m -5. [of toilet] vaso m sanitário. ◇ vt inf esculachar.
panacea [,pænə'sɪə] n fig: a ~ (for sthg) uma panacéia (para algo).
panama n: ~ (hat) panamá m.
Panama ['pænə,mɑː] n Panamá.
Panama Canal n: the ~ o Canal do Panamá.

pancake ['pænkeɪk] n panqueca f.

Pancake Day n UK ≃ Terça-feira f de Carnaval.

Pancake Tuesday n = Pancake Day.

panda ['pændə] (pl inv OR **-s**) n panda m.

Panda car n UK patrulha f policial.

pandemonium [ˌpændɪ'məʊnjəm] n (U) pandemônio m.

pander ['pændəʳ] vi: to ~ to sb/sthg fazer concessões a alguém/algo.

pane [peɪn] n vidraça f, vidro m de vidraça.

panel ['pænl] n **-1.** [group of people] equipe f **-2.** TECH painel m.

panelling UK, **paneling** US ['pænəlɪŋ] n (U) apainelamento m.

pang [pæŋ] n acesso m (de fome, de culpa etc.).

panic ['pænɪk] (pt & pp **-ked**, cont **-king**) ⬦ n (U) pânico m. ⬦ vi entrar em pânico.

panicky ['pænɪkɪ] adj **-1.** [person] aterrorizado(da) **-2.** [feeling] aterrorizante.

panic-stricken adj em pânico.

panorama [ˌpænə'rɑːmə] n panorama m.

pansy (pl **-ies**) n **-1.** [flower] amorperfeito m **-2.** inf pej [man] veado m.

pant [pænt] vi ofegar.
⬦ **pants** npl **-1.** UK [underpants] calcinha f **-2.** US [trousers] calças fpl.

panther ['pænθəʳ] (pl inv OR **-s**) n pantera f.

panties ['pæntɪz] npl inf calcinha f.

pantihose ['pæntɪhəʊz] npl = panty hose.

pantomime ['pæntəmaɪm] n UK peça de teatro para crianças realizada no Reino Unido no Natal.

pantry ['pæntrɪ] (pl **-ies**) n despensa f.

panty hose ['pæntɪ-] npl US meia-calça f.

papa [UK pə'pɑː, US 'pæpə] n papá m.

paper ['peɪpəʳ] ⬦ n **-1.** (U) [material] papel m; a **piece of** ~ uma folha de papel; **on** ~ [written down] no papel; [in theory] teoricamente **-2.** [newspaper] jornal m **-3.** [in exam] trabalho m **-4.** [essay] ensaio m **-5.** [at conference] apostila f, polígrafo m. ⬦ adj **-1.** [cup, napkin, hat] de papel **-2.** [theoretical] no papel. ⬦ vt empapelar.
⬦ **papers** npl **-1.** [identity papers] documentos mpl (de identidade) **-2.** [documents] documentação f.

paperback ['peɪpəbæk] n: ~ **(book)** brochura f.

paper bag n saco m de papel.

paper clip n clipe m.

paper handkerchief n lenço m de papel.

paper knife n abridor m de cartas.

paper shop n UK banca f de jornais.

paperweight ['peɪpəweɪt] n peso m para papel.

paperwork ['peɪpəwɜːk] n (U) papelada f.

paprika ['pæprɪkə] n (U) páprica f.

par [pɑːʳ] n **-1.** [parity]: **on a** ~ **with** sb/sthg no mesmo nível que alguém/algo **-2.** (U) GOLF par m **-3.** [good health]: **below** OR **under** ~ indisposto(ta) **-4.** FIN valor m (ao par).

parable ['pærəbl] n parábola f.

parachute ['pærəʃuːt] ⬦ n pára-quedas m inv. ⬦ vi saltar de pára-quedas.

parade [pə'reɪd] ⬦ n **-1.** [procession] desfile m **-2.** MIL parada f **-3.** [street, path] passeio m público. ⬦ vt **-1.** [MIL - soldiers] fazer desfilar; [- prisoners] apresentar **-2.** [object] exibir **-3.** fig [flaunt] fazer alarde de, mostrar-se com. ⬦ vi desfilar.

paradise ['pærədaɪs] n paraíso m.
⬦ **Paradise** n Paraíso m.

paradox ['pærədɒks] n paradoxo m.

paradoxically [ˌpærə'dɒksɪklɪ] adv paradoxalmente.

paraffin ['pærəfɪn] n (U) parafina f.

paragliding ['pærəˌglaɪdɪŋ] n vôo m de paraglider.

paragon n modelo m.

paragraph ['pærəgrɑːf] n parágrafo m.

Paraguay ['pærəgwaɪ] n Paraguai.

parallel ['pærəlel] (pt & pp **-led**, cont **-ling**) ⬦ adj [gen] paralelo(la); ~ **to** OR **with** sthg paralelo(la) a algo. ⬦ n paralelo m; **to have no** ~ não ter precedente OR paralelo.

paralyse UK, **paralyze** US ['pærəlaɪz] vt paralisar.

paralysis [pə'rælɪsɪs] (pl **-lyses** [-lɪsiːz]) n **-1.** MED paralisia f **-2.** [of industry, traffic] imobilidade f.

paralyze vt US = paralyse.

paramedic [ˌpærə'medɪk] n paramédico m, -ca f.

parameter [pə'ræmɪtəʳ] n parâmetro m.

paramount ['pærəmaʊnt] adj vital, fundamental; **of** ~ **importance** de suma importância.

paranoid ['pærənɔɪd] adj **-1.** [person] paranóico(ca) **-2.** [disorder] paranóico(ca).

paraphernalia [ˌpærəfə'neɪljə] n (U) parafernália f.

parascending [ˌpærə'sendɪŋ] n vôo m de parapente.

parasite ['pærəsaɪt] n parasita m.

parasol ['pærəsɒl] *n* sombrinha *f.*

paratrooper ['pærətruːpə^r] *n* pára-quedista *mf (do exército).*

parcel ['pɑːsl] *(UK pt & pp* -**led**, *cont* -**ling**, *US pt & pp* -**ed**, *cont* -**ing**) *n* pacote *m*, encomenda *f.*
➡ **parcel up** *vt sep* empacotar.

parched [pɑːtʃt] *adj* -**1.** [grass, plain] seco(ca) -**2.** [throat, lips] ressecado(da) -**3.** *inf* [very thirsty] seco(ca).

parchment ['pɑːtʃmənt] *n (U)* pergaminho *m.*

pardon ['pɑːdn] ⬦ *n* -**1.** *JUR* indulto *m* -**2.** *(U)* [forgiveness] perdão *m*; **I beg your ~ ?** [showing surprise or offence] como é?, o que foi?; [what did you say?] como?, o que você disse?; **I beg your ~ !** [to apologize] perdão!, desculpe! ⬦ *vt* -**1.** *JUR* indultar -**2.** [forgive] perdoar; **to ~ sb for sthg** perdoar alguém por algo; **~ me!** me desculpe!

parent ['peərənt] *n* -**1.** [mother] mãe *f* -**2.** [father] pai *m.*
➡ **parents** *npl* pais *mpl.*

parental [pə'rentl] *adj* dos pais.

parenthesis [pə'renθɪsɪs] *(pl* -**theses** [-θɪsiːz]) *n* parêntese *m.*

Paris ['pærɪs] *n* Paris; **in ~** em Paris.

parish ['pærɪʃ] *n* -**1.** [of church] paróquia *f* -**2.** *UK* [area of local government] distrito *m.*

Parisian [pə'rɪzjən] ⬦ *adj* parisiense. ⬦ *n* parisiense *mf.*

parity ['pærətɪ] *n (U)* igualdade *f*; **~ with** igualdade com; **~ between** paridade *f* de *OR* entre.

park [pɑːk] ⬦ *n* -**1.** [public] parque *m* -**2.** *US AUT* posição da alavanca de carro hidramático usada para estacionar. ⬦ *vt & vi* estacionar.

parking ['pɑːkɪŋ] *n (U)* estacionamento *m*; **I find ~ very difficult** acho muito difícil estacionar; **'no ~'** 'proibido estacionar'.

parking lot *n US* área *f* de estacionamento.

parking meter *n* parquímetro *m.*

parking ticket *n* multa *f* por estacionamento proibido.

parlance ['pɑːləns] *n (U)*: **in common/legal ~** em linguagem coloquial/legal.

parliament ['pɑːləmənt] *n* -**1.** [gen] parlamento *m* -**2.** [session] legislatura *f.*

parliamentary [ˌpɑːlə'mentərɪ] *adj* parlamentar.

parlour *UK*, **parlor** *US* ['pɑːlə^r] *n* -**1.** *dated* [in house] sala *f* de visitas -**2.** [cafe]: **ice cream ~** sorveteria *f.*

parochial [pə'rəʊkjəl] *adj pej* provinciano(na).

parody ['pærədɪ] *(pl* -**ies**, *pt & pp* -**ied**) ⬦ *n* paródia *f.* ⬦ *vt* parodiar.

parole [pə'rəʊl] *n (U)* liberdade *f* condicional; **on ~** em liberdade condicional.

parrot ['pærət] *n* papagaio *m.*

parry ['pærɪ] *(pt & pp* -**ied**) *vt* -**1.** [blow] desviar -**2.** [question] esquivar-se de.

parsley ['pɑːslɪ] *n (U)* salsa *f.*

parsnip ['pɑːsnɪp] *n* chirivia *f.*

parson ['pɑːsn] *n* pároco *m.*

part [pɑːt] ⬦ *n* -**1.** [gen] parte *f*; **for the most ~** em sua maioria; **the best** *OR* **better ~ of** a maior parte de -**2.** [component] peça *f* -**3.** [acting role] papel *m* -**4.** [involvement]: **~ in sthg** participação *f* em algo; **to take ~ in sthg** participar de algo; **to play an important ~ in sthg** ter um papel importante em algo; **for my/your** etc. **~** por minha/sua parte -**5.** *US* [hair parting] linha *f.* ⬦ *adv* em parte. ⬦ *vt* -**1.** [separate] separar -**2.** [move apart, open] abrir -**3.** [hair] repartir. ⬦ *vi* -**1.** [leave one another] separar-se -**2.** [move apart, open] abrir-se.
➡ **parts** *npl* terras *fpl.*
➡ **part with** *vt fus* desfazer-se de.

part exchange *n* -**1.** [deal] *negociação em que se paga parte do valor de um produto com um artigo usado* -**2.** *(U)* [system] *sistema através do qual se paga parte do valor do produto com um artigo usado*; **in ~** como parte do pagamento.

partial ['pɑːʃl] *adj* -**1.** [gen] parcial -**2.** [fond]: **~ to sthg** afeiçoado(da) a algo.

participant [pɑː'tɪsɪpənt] *n* participante *mf.*

participate [pɑː'tɪsɪpeɪt] *vi* participar; **to ~ in sthg** participar de algo.

participation [pɑːˌtɪsɪ'peɪʃn] *n (U)* participação *f.*

participle ['pɑːtɪsɪpl] *n* particípio *m.*

particle ['pɑːtɪkl] *n* partícula *f.*

parti-coloured *adj* multicor, matizado(da).

particular [pə'tɪkjʊlə^r] *adj* -**1.** [gen] especial -**2.** [fussy] exigente.
➡ **particulars** *npl* particularidades *fpl.*
➡ **in particular** *adv* em especial, em particular.

particularly [pə'tɪkjʊləlɪ] *adv* -**1.** [in particular] especialmente -**2.** [very] muito.

parting ['pɑːtɪŋ] *n* -**1.** *(U)* [leaving] despedida *f* -**2.** *UK* [in hair] repartição *f.*

partisan [ˌpɑːtɪ'zæn] ⬦ *adj* partidário(ria). ⬦ *n* guerrilheiro *m*, -ra *f.*

partition [pɑː'tɪʃn] ⬦ *n* -**1.** [wall] divisória *f* -**2.** [screen] separação *f.* ⬦ *vt*

-1. [room] separar com divisórias **-2.** [country] dividir.

partly ['pɑːtlɪ] *adv* em parte.

partner ['pɑːtnə'] ⬦ *n* parceiro *m*, -ra *f*. ⬦ *vt* ser parceiro de.

partnership ['pɑːtnəʃɪp] *n* parceria *f*.

partridge ['pɑːtrɪdʒ] (*pl inv* OR **-s**) *n* perdiz *f*.

part-time ⬦ *adj* de meio período. ⬦ *adv* em meio período.

party ['pɑːtɪ] (*pl* **-ies**, *pt* & *pp* **-ied**) ⬦ *n* **-1.** POL partido *m* **-2.** [social gathering] festa *f* **-3.** [group] grupo *m* **-4.** JUR, COMM [individual] parte *f*. ⬦ *vi inf* festejar.

party line *n* **-1.** POL linha *f* (política) do partido **-2.** TELEC extensão *f* de linha telefônica.

pass [pɑːs] ⬦ *n* **-1.** [gen] passe *m* **-2.** UK [successful result] aprovação *f*; **to get a ~** ser aprovado *m*, -da *f* em algo **-3.** [route between mountains] desfiladeiro *m* **-4.** *phr*: **to make a ~ at sb** *inf* passar-se com alguém. ⬦ *vt* **-1.** [gen] passar; **to ~ sthg to sb, to ~ sb sthg** passar algo a alguém **-2.** [move past] passar por **-3.** AUT [overtake] ultrapassar **-4.** [exceed] passar de **-5.** [exam, test] passar em **-6.** [approve] aprovar **-7.** [express - opinion, judgment] formular; [- sentence] ditar. ⬦ *vi* **-1.** [gen] passar **-2.** AUT [overtake] ultrapassar **-3.** SPORT fazer passes.

➡ **pass as** *vt fus* passar por.

➡ **pass away** *vi* falecer.

➡ **pass by** ⬦ *vt sep fig* passar desapercebido(da) por. ⬦ *vi* passar.

➡ **pass for** *vt fus* = **pass as**.

➡ **pass on** ⬦ *vt sep* **-1.** [object]: **to pass sthg on (to sb)** passar algo adiante (para alguém) **-2.** [characteristic, tradition, information] transmitir. ⬦ *vi* **-1.** [move on]: **to ~ on to the next question** passar para a próxima questão **-2.** = **pass away**.

➡ **pass out** *vi* **-1.** [faint] desmaiar **-2.** UK MIL graduar-se.

➡ **pass over** *vt fus* passar por cima.

➡ **pass up** *vt sep* deixar passar.

passable ['pɑːsəbl] *adj* **-1.** [satisfactory] passável, aceitável **-2.** [not blocked] livre.

passage ['pæsɪdʒ] *n* **-1.** [gen] passagem *f* **-2.** ANAT trato *m* **-3.** [sea journey] travessia *f*.

passageway ['pæsɪdʒweɪ] *n* passagem *f*, corredor *m*.

passbook ['pɑːsbʊk] *n* caderneta *f* de conta bancária.

passenger ['pæsɪndʒə'] *n* passageiro *m*, -ra *f*.

passerby [,pɑːsə'baɪ] (*pl* **passersby** [,pɑːsəz'baɪ]) *n* passante *mf*, transeunte *mf*.

passing ['pɑːsɪŋ] *adj* passageiro(ra).

➡ **in passing** *adv* de passagem.

passion ['pæʃn] *n* (U) paixão *f*; **~ for** sthg paixão por algo.

➡ **passions** *npl* paixões *fpl*.

passionate ['pæʃənət] *adj* apaixonado(-da).

passive ['pæsɪv] *adj* passivo(va).

Passover ['pɑːs,əʊvə'] *n*: **(the) ~** a Páscoa Judia.

passport ['pɑːspɔːt] *n* [document] passaporte *m*.

passport control *n* controle *m* de passaportes.

password ['pɑːswɜːd] *n* senha *f*.

past [pɑːst] ⬦ *adj* **-1.** [former] passado(da) **-2.** [last] último(ma); **over the ~ week** durante a última semana **-3.** [finished] terminado(da), passado(da); **our problems are now ~** nossos problemas terminaram. ⬦ *adv* **-1.** [telling the time]: **it's ten ~ eleven** são onze e dez **-2.** [by] por; **to walk ~** passar por; **to run ~** passar correndo por; **he didn't see me as I drove ~** ele não me viu quando passei por ele de carro. ⬦ *n* **-1.** [time]: **the ~** o passado; **in the ~** no passado **-2.** [personal history] passado *m*. ⬦ *prep* **-1.** [telling the time]: **at five ~ nine** às nove e cinco; **it's half ~ eight** são oito e meia **-2.** [by] pela frente de **-3.** [beyond] além de; **the post office is ~ the bank** o correio é passando o banco.

pasta ['pæstə] *n* (U) massa *f*, macarrão *m*.

paste [peɪst] ⬦ *n* **-1.** [smooth mixture] pasta *f* **-2.** (U) [glue] patê *m* **-3.** (U) [glue] cola *f*. ⬦ *vt* colar.

pastel ['pæstl] ⬦ *adj* pastel. ⬦ *n* pastel *m*.

pasteurize, -ise ['pɑːstʃəraɪz] *vt* pasteurizar.

pastille ['pæstɪl] *n* pastilha *f*.

pastime ['pɑːstaɪm] *n* passatempo *m*.

pastor ['pɑːstə'] *n* pastor *m*.

past participle *n* particípio *m* passado.

pastry ['peɪstrɪ] (*pl* **-ies**) *n* **-1.** (U) [mixture] massa *f* **-2.** [cake] torta *f*.

past tense *n* passado *m*.

pasture ['pɑːstʃə'] *n* pasto *m*.

pasty¹ ['peɪstɪ] (*compar* **-ier**, *superl* **-iest**) *adj* pálida(da).

pasty² ['pæstɪ] (*pl* **-ies**) *n* UK CULIN pastelão *m* de carne.

pat [pæt] (*compar* **-ter**, *superl* **-test**, *pt* & *pp* **-ted**, *cont* **-ting**) ⬦ *adv*: **to have sthg off ~** ter algo na ponta da língua.

◇ *n* **-1.** [light stroke] palmadinha *f* **-2.** [small portion] porção *f* pequena. ◇ *vt* **-1.** [surface] bater de leve em **-2.** [dog] acariciar **-3.** [back, shoulder, hand] dar uma palmadinha em.

patch [pætʃ] ◇ *n* **-1.** [piece of material] remendo *m* **-2.** [to cover eye] venda *f* **-3.** [small area] área *f* **-4.** [of land] pedaço *m* **-5.** [period of time] período *m*.

◆ **patch up** *vt sep* **-1.** [mend] consertar, remendar **-2.** *fig* [resolve] resolver.

patchwork ['pætʃwɜːk] *n* **-1.** colcha *f* de retalhos **-2.** *fig* [mixed collection - of fields] mosaico *m*; [- cultures, religions] mistura *m*; *inf* [hotchpotch] salada *m*.

patchy ['pætʃɪ] (*compar* **-ier**, *superl* **-iest**) *adj* **-1.** [gen] irregular **-2.** [incomplete] incompleto(ta).

pâté ['pæteɪ] *n* patê *m*.

patent [*UK* 'peɪtənt, *US* 'pætənt] ◇ *adj* evidente. ◇ *n* patente *f*. ◇ *vt* patentear.

patent leather *n* (*U*) couro *m* envernizado.

paternal [pə'tɜːnl] *adj* **-1.** [love, attitude] paternal **-2.** [relation] paterno(na).

path [pɑːθ, *pl* pɑːðz] *n* **-1.** [track] trilha *f* **-2.** [way ahead] caminho *m* **-3.** [trajectory] trajetória *f* **-4.** [course of action] curso *m*.

pathetic [pə'θetɪk] *adj* **-1.** [causing pity] patético(ca) **-2.** [useless] inútil, infeliz.

pathological [ˌpæθə'lɒdʒɪkl] *adj* patológico(ca).

pathology [pə'θɒlədʒɪ] *n* (*U*) patologia *f*.

pathos ['peɪθɒs] *n* (*U*) patos *m*.

pathway ['pɑːθweɪ] *n* caminho *m*.

patience ['peɪʃns] *n* (*U*) paciência *f*.

patient ['peɪʃnt] ◇ *adj* paciente. ◇ *n* paciente *mf*.

patio ['pætɪəʊ] (*pl* **-s**) *n* pátio *m*.

patriotic [*UK* ˌpætrɪ'ɒtɪk, *US* ˌpeɪtrɪ'ɒtɪk] *adj* patriótico(ca).

patrol [pə'trəʊl] (*pt* & *pp* **-led**, *cont* **-ling**) ◇ *n* patrulha *f*. ◇ *vt* patrulhar.

patrol car *n* radiopatrulha *f*.

patrolman [pə'trəʊlmən] (*pl* **-men** [-mən]) *n* *US* patrulheiro *m*, policial *m*.

patron ['peɪtrən] *n* **-1.** [gen] patrono *m*, -nesse *f* **-2.** *fml* [customer] cliente *mf*.

patronize, -ise ['pætrənaɪz] *vt* **-1.** *pej* [talk down to] tratar com condescendência **-2.** *fml* [be a customer of] ser cliente de **-3.** *fml* [back financially] patrocinar.

patronizing ['pætrənaɪzɪŋ] *adj pej* condescendente.

patter ['pætəʳ] ◇ *n* **-1.** [sound of feet] passinhos *mpl* **-2.** *fig*: the ~ of raindrops on the roof o barulhinho da chuva no

telhado **-3.** [talk] arenga *f*. ◇ *vi* **-1.** [dog] dar passinhos rápidos **-2.** [rain] tamborilar.

pattern ['pætən] *n* **-1.** [gen] padrão *m* **-2.** [for sewing, knitting] molde *m* **-3.** [model] modelo *m*.

paunch [pɔːntʃ] *n* pança *f*, barriga *f*.

pauper ['pɔːpəʳ] *n* indigente *mf*.

pause [pɔːz] ◇ *n* **-1.** [short silence] pausa *f* **-2.** [break, rest] interrupção *f*. ◇ *vi* fazer uma pausa.

pave [peɪv] *vt* pavimentar; **to ~ the way for sb/sthg** preparar o terreno para alguém/algo.

pavement ['peɪvmənt] *n* **-1.** *UK* [at side of road] calçada *f* **-2.** *US* [roadway] rua *f*.

pavilion [pə'vɪljən] *n* pavilhão *m*.

paving ['peɪvɪŋ] *n* (*U*) **-1.** [material] material *m* para pavimentação **-2.** [paved surface] pavimento *m*, calçamento *m*.

paving stone *n* paralelepípedo *m*.

paw [pɔː] *n* pata *f*.

pawn [pɔːn] *n* **-1.** [chesspiece] peão *m* **-2.** [unimportant person] joguete *m*, marionete *f*. ◇ *vt* empenhar.

pawnbroker ['pɔːnˌbrəʊkəʳ] *n* penhorista *mf*.

pawnshop ['pɔːnʃɒp] *n* casa *f* de penhores.

pay [peɪ] (*pt* & *pp* **paid**) ◇ *vt* **-1.** [gen] pagar; **to ~ sb/sth for sthg** pagar alguém/algo por algo **-2.** *UK* [into bank account]: **to ~ sthg into sthg** depositar algo em algo **-3.** [be profitable to] ser rentável para; **it won't ~ you to sell just now** não vale a pena vender agora **-4.** [be advantageous to] ser proveitoso(sa) para; **it will ~ you not to say anything** é melhor você não dizer nada **-5.** [compliment, respects, attention] prestar; [visit, call] fazer. ◇ *vi* **-1.** [gen] pagar; **to ~ for sthg** pagar algo; **the work ~s well** o trabalho é bem remunerado; **crime doesn't ~** o crime não compensa **-2.** *fig* [suffer] pagar; **to ~ dearly for sthg** pagar caro por algo. ◇ *n* **-1.** [wage] paga *f* **-2.** [salary] salário *m*.

◆ **pay back** *vt sep* **-1.** [return loan of money to] devolver **-2.** [revenge o.s. on]: **to ~ sb back (for sthg)** pagar a alguém na mesma moeda (por algo).

◆ **pay off** ◇ *vt sep* **-1.** [repay] saldar, liquidar **-2.** [dismiss] despedir com indenização **-3.** [bribe] subornar, comprar. ◇ *vi* obter êxito.

◆ **pay up** *vi* saldar dívida.

payable ['peɪəbl] *adj* **-1.** [to be paid] a pagar **-2.** [on cheque]: ~ **to sb** para crédito de alguém.

pay-as-you-go n [for mobile phone, Internet etc.] *sistema de pagamento por tempo de uso.*

paycheck ['peɪtʃek] n US [cheque] contracheque m; [money] salário m.

pay cheque n UK contracheque m.

payday ['peɪdeɪ] n (U) dia m de pagamento.

payee [peɪ'i:] n beneficiário m, -ria f.

pay envelope n US envelope m de pagamento.

payment ['peɪmənt] n pagamento m.

pay packet n UK **-1.** [envelope] envelope m de pagamento **-2.** [wages] pagamento m.

pay-per-view ◇ adj [channel] pay-per-view. ◇ n pay-per-view m.

pay phone, pay station US n telefone m público.

payroll ['peɪrəʊl] n folha f de pagamento.

payslip UK ['peɪslɪp], **paystub** US n contracheque m.

pay station n US = pay phone.

paystub ['peɪstʌb] n US = payslip.

pc (abbr of per cent) por cento.

PC ◇ n **-1.** (abbr of personal computer) PC m **-2.** (abbr of police constable) policial mf.

PDA (abbr of personal digital assistant) n COMPUT PDA m.

PDF (abbr of portable document format) n COMPUT PDF m.

PE (abbr of physical education) n UK ≃ Ed.Fís.

pea [pi:] n CULIN ervilha f.

peace [pi:s] n (U) **-1.** [gen] paz f; to make (one's) ∼ with sb/sthg fazer as pazes com alguém/algo **-2.** [law and order] paz f, ordem f.

peaceable ['pi:səbl] adj pacífico(ca).

peaceful ['pi:sfʊl] adj **-1.** [tranquil] tranqüilo(la) **-2.** [non-violent] pacífico(ca).

peacetime ['pi:staɪm] n (U) tempo m de paz.

peach [pi:tʃ] ◇ adj da cor de pêssego. ◇ n **-1.** [fruit] pêssego m **-2.** [colour] cor f de pêssego.

peacock ['pi:kɒk] n pavão m.

peak [pi:k] ◇ adj **-1.** [time] de pico **-2.** [productivity, condition] máximo(ma). ◇ n **-1.** [mountain top] pico m **-2.** [highest point] cume m, apogeu m **-3.** [of cap] viseira f. ◇ vi atingir o máximo.

peaked [pi:kt] adj com viseira; ∼ cap boné m (com viseira).

peak hour n hora f de pico.

peak period n período m de pico.

peak rate n tarifa f máxima.

peal [pi:l] ◇ n **-1.** [of bells] repique m

-2. [of thunder] estrondo m; ∼ (of laughter) gargalhada f. ◇ vi repicar.

peanut ['pi:nʌt] n amendoim m.

peanut butter n (U) manteiga f de amendoim.

pear [peəʳ] n pêra f.

pearl [pɜ:l] n pérola f.

peasant ['peznt] n [in countryside] camponês m, -esa f.

peat [pi:t] n (U) turfa f.

pebble ['pebl] n cascalho m, seixo m.

peck [pek] ◇ n **-1.** [with beak] bicada f **-2.** [kiss] bicota f. ◇ vt **-1.** [with beak] bicar **-2.** [kiss] dar uma bicota.

pecking order ['pekɪŋ-] n hierarquia f.

peckish ['pekɪʃ] adj UK inf esfomeado(-da).

peculiar [pɪ'kju:ljəʳ] adj **-1.** [odd] esquisito(ta) **-2.** [slightly ill] estranho(nha) **-3.** [characteristic]: to be ∼ to sb/sthg ser característico(ca) de alguém/algo.

peculiarity [pɪ,kju:lɪ'ærətɪ] (pl -ies) n **-1.** [strange habit] peculiaridade f **-2.** [individual characteristic] singularidade f **-3.** [oddness] excentricidade f.

pedal ['pedl] (UK pt & pp -led, cont -ling, US pt & pp -ed, cont -ing) ◇ n pedal m; brake ∼ freio m. ◇ vi pedalar.

pedal bin n lixeira f com pedal.

pedantic [pɪ'dæntɪk] adj pej pedante.

peddle ['pedl] vt **-1.** [sell] traficar **-2.** [spread] espalhar.

pedestal ['pedɪstl] n pedestal m.

pedestrian [pɪ'destrɪən] ◇ adj pej enfadonho(nha). ◇ n pedestre mf.

pedestrian crossing n UK faixa f para pedestres.

pedestrian precinct UK, **pedestrian zone** US n área f só para pedestres.

pediatrics [,pi:dɪ'ætrɪks] n (U) pediatria f.

pedigree ['pedɪgri:] ◇ adj com pedigree. ◇ n **-1.** [of animal] pedigree m **-2.** [of person] linhagem f.

pedlar UK, **peddler** US ['pedləʳ] n vendedor m, -ra f ambulante.

pee [pi:] inf ◇ n xixi m; to have a ∼ fazer xixi. ◇ vi fazer xixi.

peek [pi:k] inf ◇ n espiadela f. ◇ vi espiar.

peel [pi:l] ◇ n (U) casca f. ◇ vt & vi descascar.

peelings ['pi:lɪŋz] npl cascas fpl.

peep [pi:p] ◇ n **-1.** [look] espiada f **-2.** inf [sound] pio m. ◇ vi dar uma espiada em.

◆ **peep out** vi surgir.

peephole ['pi:phəʊl] n vigia f (em porta).

peer [pɪəʳ] ◇ n **-1.** [noble] nobre m **-2.** [equal] par m. ◇ vi: to ∼ at observar;

to ~ **through the clouds** observar por entre as nuvens.

peerage [ˈpɪərɪdʒ] *n* pariato *m*; **the** ~ o pariato.

peer group *n grupo de mesma faixa etária ou classe social.*

peeved [piːvd] *adj inf* aborrecido(da).

peevish [ˈpiːvɪʃ] *adj* irritadiço(ça), mal-humorado(da).

peg [peg] (*pt* & *pp* **-ged**, *cont* **-ging**) ◇ *n* **-1.** [hook] cabide *m* **-2.** [for washing line] prendedor *m* (de roupa) **-3.** [for tent] pino *m.* ◇ *vt* [price, increase] fixar.

pejorative [prˈdʒɒrətɪv] *adj* pejorativo(va).

pekinese (*pl inv OR* **-s**) *n* [dog] pequinês *m.*

Peking [piːˈkɪŋ] *n* Pequim; **in** ~ em Pequim.

pekingese (*pl inv OR* **-s**) *n* = **pekinese**.

pelican [ˈpelɪkən] (*pl inv OR* **-s**) *n* pelicano *m.*

pelican crossing *n UK* faixa *f* de segurança *(com semáforo acionado pelo pedestre).*

pellet [ˈpelɪt] *n* **-1.** [small ball - of paper] bolinha *f*; [- of food, mud] bolo *m* **-2.** [for gun] chumbinho *m.*

pelmet [ˈpelmɪt] *n UK* bandô *m.*

pelt [pelt] ◇ *n* [animal skin] pele *f.* ◇ *vt:* **to** ~ **sb with sthg** arremessar algo em alguém. ◇ *vi* **-1.** [rain] chover a cântaros **-2.** [run very fast] correr a toda.

pelvis [ˈpelvɪs] (*pl* **-vises** *OR* **-ves** [-viːz]) *n* pélvis *f inv.*

pen [pen] (*pt* & *pp* **-ned**, *cont* **-ning**) ◇ *n* **-1.** [for writing] caneta *f* **-2.** [enclosure] curral *m.* ◇ *vt* [enclose - livestock] cercar; [- people] encurralar.

penal [ˈpiːnl] *adj JUR* penal.

penalize, ise [ˈpiːnəlaɪz] *vt* **-1.** [gen] penalizar **-2.** [put at a disadvantage] prejudicar.

penalty [ˈpenltɪ] (*pl* **-ies**) *n* **-1.** [punishment] penalidade *f*; **to pay the** ~ **(for sthg)** *fig* pagar pena (por algo) **-2.** [fine] pena *f* **-3.** *SPORT* pênalti *m*; ~ **(kick)** pênalti.

penance [ˈpenəns] *n (U)* penitência *f.*

pence [pens] *UK pl* ▷ **penny**.

penchant [*UK* pãʃã , *US* ˈpentʃənt] *n:* **to have a** ~ **for sthg/for doing sthg** ter uma queda por algo/por fazer algo.

pencil [ˈpensl] (*UK pt* & *pp* **-led**, *cont* **-ling**, *US pt* & *pp* **-ed**, *cont* **-ing**) ◇ *n* lápis *m inv*; **in** ~ a lápis. ◇ *vt* escrever a lápis.

➤ **pencil in** *vt sep* **-1.** [person] inscrever provisoriamente **-2.** [date] marcar provisoriamente.

pencil case *n* estojo *m* (de canetas).

pencil sharpener *n* apontador *m* de lápis.

pendant [ˈpendənt] *n* pendente *m.*

pending [ˈpendɪŋ] *fml* ◇ *adj* **-1.** [about to happen] iminente **-2.** [waiting to be dealt with] pendente. ◇ *prep* à espera de.

pendulum [ˈpendjʊləm] (*pl* **-s**) *n* pêndulo *m.*

penetrate [ˈpenɪtreɪt] *vt* **-1.** [get through - subj: person, object] penetrar em, adentrar-se em; [- rain] infiltrar-se em **-2.** [infiltrate - party] entrar sorrateiramente em; [- terrorist group, spy ring] infiltrar-se em.

penfriend [ˈpenfrend] *n* amigo *m*, -ga *f* por correspondência.

penguin [ˈpeŋgwɪn] *n* pingüim *m.*

penicillin [ˌpenɪˈsɪlɪn] *n (U)* penicilina *f.*

peninsula [pəˈnɪnsjʊlə] (*pl* **-s**) *n* península *f.*

penis [ˈpiːnɪs] (*pl* **penises** [ˈpiːnɪsɪz]) *n* pênis *m inv.*

penitentiary [ˌpenɪˈtenʃərɪ] (*pl* **-ies**) *n US* penitenciária *f.*

penknife [ˈpennaɪf] (*pl* **-knives** [-naɪvz]) *n* canivete *m*, navalha *f.*

pen-name *n* pseudônimo *m.*

pennant [ˈpenənt] *n* bandeirola *f.*

penniless [ˈpenɪlɪs] *adj* sem dinheiro.

penny [ˈpenɪ] (*pl senses* **1** & **2** **-ies**, *pl sense* **3 pence**) *n* **-1.** *UK* [coin] pêni *m* **-2.** *US* [coin] centavo *m* **-3.** *UK* [value] centavo *m.*

pen pal *n inf* amigo *m*, -ga *f* por correspondência.

pension [ˈpenʃn] *n* **-1.** *UK* [on retirement - state scheme] pensão *f*; [- private scheme] previdência *f* privada **-2.** [for disability] pensão *f* por invalidez.

pensioner [ˈpenʃənə^{r}] *n UK:* **(old-age)** ~ pensionista *mf.*

pensive [ˈpensɪv] *adj* pensativo(va).

pentagon [ˈpentəgən] *n* pentágono *m.*

➤ **Pentagon** *n US:* **the Pentagon** o Pentágono.

pentathlete [penˈtæθliːtl] *n* pentatleta *mf.*

Pentecost [ˈpentɪkɒstl] *n* Pentecostes *m inv.*

penthouse [ˈpenthaʊs, *pl* -haʊzɪz] *n* cobertura *f.*

pent up [pent-] *adj* contido(da), reprimido(da).

penultimate [peˈnʌltɪmətl] *adj* penúltimo(ma).

people [ˈpiːpl] ◇ *n* [nation, race] povo *m.* ◇ *npl* **-1.** [gen] pessoas *fpl*; ~ **say that ...** dizem que ... **-2.** [inhabitants] habitantes *mpl* **-3.** *POL:* **the** ~ o povo.

◇ *vt*: **to be ~d by** OR **with** ser povoado(da) por.

people carrier *n* monovolume *m*.

pep [pep] (*pt* & *pp* **-ped**, *cont* **-ping**) *n* pep vigor *m*, vitalidade *f*.
➭ **pep up** *vt sep* **-1.** [person] revigorar **-2.** [party, event] animar.

pepper ['pepə^r] *n* **-1.** (U) [spice] pimenta *f* **-2.** [vegetable] pimentão *m*.

pepperbox *n US* = pepper pot.

peppermint ['pepəmɪnt] *n* **-1.** [sweet] menta *f* **-2.** (U) [herb] hortelã-pimenta *f*.

pepper pot UK, **pepperbox** US ['pepəbɒks] *n* pimenteira *f*.

pep talk *n inf* palavras *fpl* de ânimo OR incentivo.

per [pɜ:^r] *prep* por; **~ hour/day/kilo/person** por hora/dia/quilo/pessoa; **as ~ instructions** conforme/segundo as instruções.

per annum *adv* por ano.

per capita [pə'kæpɪtə] *adj*, *adv* per capita.

perceive [pə'si:v] *vt* **-1.** [see] distinguir **-2.** [notice, realize] perceber, ver **-3.** [conceive, consider]: **to ~ sb/sthg as** ver alguém/algo como.

per cent *adv* por cento.

percentage [pə'sentɪdʒ] *n* porcentagem *f*.

perception [pə'sepʃn] *n* **-1.** (U) [gen] distinção *f* **-2.** (U) [insight, understanding] percepção *f*, perspicácia *f*.

perceptive [pə'septɪv] *adj* perspicaz.

perch [pɜ:tʃ] (*pl sense 3 only inv* OR **-es**) ◇ *n* **-1.** [for bird] poleiro *m* **-2.** [high position] posição *f* elevada **-3.** [fish] perca *f*. ◇ *vi*: **to ~ (on sthg)** [bird] pousar (em algo); [person] empoleirar-se (em algo).

percolator ['pɜ:kəleɪtə^r] *n* cafeteira *f*.

percussion [pə'kʌʃn] *n* (U) MUS percussão *f*.

perennial [pə'renjəl] ◇ *adj* perene. ◇ *n* BOT planta *f* perene.

perfect [*adj* & *n* 'pɜ:fɪkt, *vb* pə'fekt] ◇ *adj* perfeito(ta); **it makes ~ sense** é perfeitamente lógico (ca). ◇ *n* GRAMM: **~ (tense)** o perfeito. ◇ *vt* aperfeiçoar.

perfection [pə'fekʃn] *n* perfeição *f*; **to ~** à perfeição.

perfectionist [pə'fekʃənɪst] *n* perfeccionista *mf*.

perfectly ['pɜ:fɪktlɪ] *adv* perfeitamente; **~ honest/ridiculous** totalmente honesto/ridículo, totalmente honesta/ridícula.

perforate ['pɜ:fəreɪt] *vt* perfurar.

perforations [,pɜ:fə'reɪʃnz] *npl* perfurações *fpl*.

perform [pə'fɔ:m] ◇ *vt* **-1.** [carry out] realizar, levar a cabo **-2.** [in front of audience - play] representar, interpretar; [- music, dance] apresentar. ◇ *vi* **-1.** [function - car, machine] funcionar; [- person, team] sair-se **-2.** [in front of audience] apresentar-se, atuar.

performance [pə'fɔ:məns] *n* **-1.** (U) [carrying out, doing] execução *f*, realização *f* **-2.** [show] apresentação *f* **-3.** [rendition] performance *f*, desempenho *m* **-4.** (U) [of car, engine] desempenho *m*, rendimento *m*.

performer [pə'fɔ:mə^r] *n* performer *mf*.

perfume ['pɜ:fju:m] *n* **-1.** [for woman] perfume *m* **-2.** [pleasant smell] aroma *f*.

perfunctory [pə'fʌŋktərɪ] *adj* superficial, feito(ta) às pressas.

perhaps [pə'hæps] *adv* talvez; **~ you're right** talvez você esteja certo; **~ so/not** talvez sim/não; **~ you should go and see her?** quem sabe você vai dar uma olhada nela?

peril ['perɪl] *n* (U) *literary* perigo *m*.

perimeter [pə'rɪmɪtə^r] *n* perímetro *m*; **~ fence/wall** alambrado *m*, cerca *f*.

period ['pɪərɪəd] ◇ *n* **-1.** [gen] período *m*; **free ~** período livre **-2.** HISTORY era *f* **-3.** [menstruation] período *m* menstrual **-4.** US [full stop] ponto *m*. ◇ *comp* [dress, furniture] de época.

periodic [,pɪərɪ'ɒdɪk] *adj* periódico(ca).

periodical [,pɪərɪ'ɒdɪkl] ◇ *adj* = periodic. ◇ *n* periódico *m*.

peripheral [pə'rɪfərəl] ◇ *adj* **-1.** [of little importance] secundário(ria) **-2.** [at edge] periférico(ca). ◇ *n* COMPUT periférico *m*.

perish ['perɪʃ] *vi* **-1.** [die] perecer **-2.** [decay] deteriorar-se.

perishable ['perɪʃəbl] *adj* perecível.
➭ **perishables** *npl* produtos *mpl* perecíveis.

perjury ['pɜ:dʒərɪ] *n* (U) JUR perjúrio *m*.

perk [pɜ:k] *n inf* mordomia *m*, regalia *f*.
➭ **perk up** *vi* animar-se.

perky ['pɜ:kɪ] (*compar* **-ier**, *superl* **-iest**) *adj inf* animado(da), alegre.

perm [pɜ:m] *n* permanente *m*.

permanent ['pɜ:mənənt] ◇ *adj* **-1.** [not temporary - job] fixo(xa); [- damage, feature] permanente **-2.** [continuous, constant] permanente, constante. ◇ *n US* permanente *m*.

permeate ['pɜ:mɪeɪt] *vt* permear.

permissible [pə'mɪsəbl] *adj* permissível.

permission [pə'mɪʃn] *n* (U) permissão *f*.

permissive [pə'mɪsɪv] *adj* permissivo(-va), tolerante.

permit [*vb* pə'mɪt, *n* 'pɜːmɪt] (*pt & pp* -ted, *cont* -ting) ◇ *n* autorização *f*. ◇ *vt* permitir; **to ~ sb to do sthg** permitir que alguém faça algo; **my mother won't ~ me to go out** minha mãe não vai me deixar sair; **to ~ sb sthg** permitir algo a alguém.

pernicious [pə'nɪʃəs] *adj fml* pernicioso(sa).

pernickety *UK*, **persnickety** *US* [pə'(s)nɪkətɪ] *adj inf* meticuloso(sa).

perpendicular [,pɜːpən'dɪkjələ˞] ◇ *adj* -1. *MATH* perpendicular; **~ to sthg** perpendicular a algo - 2. [upright] vertical. ◇ *n MATH* perpendicular *f*.

perpetrate ['pɜːpɪtreɪt] *vt fml* perpetrar.

perpetual [pə'petʃʊəl] *adj* -1. *pej* [continuous] constante - 2. [everlasting - darkness] perpétuo(tua); [- hunger] eterno(na).

perplex [pə'pleks] *vt* desconcertar, deixar perplexo(xa).

perplexing [pə'pleksɪŋ] *adj* desconcertante.

persecute ['pɜːsɪkjuːt] *vt* perseguir, oprimir.

perseverance [,pɜːsɪ'vɪərəns] *n* (U) perseverança *f*.

persevere [,pɜːsɪ'vɪə˞] *vi* -1. [with difficulty] perseverar; **to ~ with sthg** persistir em algo - 2. [with determination]: **to ~ in doing sthg** insistir em fazer algo.

Persian ['pɜːʃn] *adj* persa.

Persian cat *n* gato *m*, -ta *f* persa.

persist [pə'sɪst] *vi* -1. [problem, situation, rain] persistir - 2. [person]: **to ~ in doing sthg** insistir em fazer algo.

persistence [pə'sɪstəns] *n* (U) -1. [continuation] persistência *f* - 2. [determination] obstinação *f*, determinação *f*.

persistent [pə'sɪstənt] *adj* -1. [constant] constante - 2. [determined] obstinado(-da) determinado(da).

person ['pɜːsn] (*pl* people OR persons *fml*) *n* -1. [man or woman] pessoa *f*; **in ~** pessoalmente, em pessoa - 2. [body]: **about one's ~** em seu corpo -3. *GRAMM* pessoa *f*.

personable ['pɜːsnəbl] *adj* bem-apessoado(da).

personal ['pɜːsənl] *adj* -1. [gen] pessoal - 2. [letter, message] particular -3. *pej* [rude] ofensivo (va).

personal assistant *n* assistente *mf* particular.

personal column *n* seção *f* de recados *(em jornal)*.

personal computer *n* computador *m* pessoal.

personality [,pɜːsə'nælətɪ] (*pl* -ies) *n* personalidade *f*.

personally ['pɜːsnəlɪ] *adv* pessoalmente; **to take sthg ~** levar algo para o lado pessoal.

personal organizer *n* agenda *f* pessoal.

personal property *n* (U) *JUR* bens *mpl* móveis.

personal stereo *n* walkman *m*.

personify [pə'sɒnɪfaɪ] (*pt & pp* -ied) *vt* personificar.

personnel [,pɜːsə'nel] ◇ *n* (U) [in firm, organization] equipe *f*. ◇ *npl* [staff] funcionários *mpl*.

perspective [pə'spektɪv] *n* perspectiva *f*.

Perspex® ['pɜːspeks] *n UK* plexiglas *m*.

perspiration [,pɜːspə'reɪʃn] *n* transpiração *f*.

persuade [pə'sweɪd] *vt* persuadir; **to ~ sb to do sthg** persuadir alguém a fazer algo; **to ~ sb that** convencer alguém de que; **to ~ sb of sthg** convencer alguém de algo.

persuasion [pə'sweɪʒn] *n* -1. (U) [act of persuading] persuasão *f* - 2. [belief] crença *f*.

persuasive [pə'sweɪsɪv] *adj* persuasivo(-va).

pert [pɜːt] *adj* [person, reply] vivo(va), atrevido(da).

pertain [pə'teɪn] *vi fml*: **~ing to sb/sthg** relacionado(da) a alguém/algo.

pertinent ['pɜːtɪnənt] *adj* pertinente, relevante.

perturb [pə'tɜːb] *vt fml* perturbar.

Peru [pə'ruː] *n* Peru.

peruse [pə'ruːz] *vt* -1. [read thoroughly] ler com atenção - 2. [read quickly] ler por cima.

pervade [pə'veɪd] *vt* impregnar.

perverse [pə'vɜːs] *adj* perverso(sa).

perversion [*UK* pə'vɜːʃn, *US* pə'vɜːrʒn] *n* perversão *f*.

pervert [*n* 'pɜːvɜːt, *vb* pə'vɜːt] ◇ *n* pervertido *m*, -da *f*. ◇ *vt* -1. [distort] distorcer - 2. [corrupt morally] perverter.

pessimist ['pesɪmɪst] *n* pessimista *mf*.

pessimistic [,pesɪ'mɪstɪk] *adj* pessimista.

pest [pest] *n* [gen] praga *f*, peste *f*.

pester ['pestə˞] *vt* importunar, incomodar.

pet [pet] (*pt & pp* -ted, *cont* -ting) ◇ *adj* [favourite] predileto(ta), preferido(da). ◇ *n* -1. [domestic animal] animal *m* de estimação - 2. [favourite person] preferido *m*, -da *f*. ◇ *vt* acariciar, afagar. ◇ *vi* acariciar-se.

petal ['petl] *n* pétala *f*.

peter ['piːtə^r] ◆ **peter out** *vi* -**1.** [food, interest] esgotar-se -**2.** [path] desaparecer.

petite [pə'tiːt] *adj* diminuto(ta).

petition [pı'tıʃn] ◇ *n* -**1.** [supporting campaign] abaixo-assinado *m* -**2.** JUR petição *f*. ◇ *vt* peticionar.

petrified ['petrıfaıd] *adj* petrificado(da).

petrol ['petrəl] *n (U) UK* gasolina *f*.

petrol bomb *n UK* coquetel *m* molotov.

petrol can *n UK* lata *f* de gasolina.

petrol cap *n UK* tampa *f* do tanque de combustível.

petroleum [pı'trəʊljəm] *n (U)* petróleo *m*.

petrol pump *n UK* bomba *f* de gasolina.

petrol station *n UK* posto *m* de gasolina.

petrol tank *n UK* tanque *m* de gasolina.

pet shop *n* pet shop *f*, loja *f* de produtos para animais de estimação.

petticoat ['petıkəʊt] *n* anágua *f*.

petty ['petı] (*compar* -**ier**, *superl* -**iest**) *adj* -**1.** [small-minded] mesquinho(nha) -**2.** [trivial] insignificante.

petty cash *n (U)* dinheiro *m* para pequenas despesas, trocado *m*.

petty officer *n* suboficial *mf*.

petulant ['petjʊlənt] *adj* petulante.

pew [pjuː] *n* banco *m* (*de igreja*).

pewter ['pjuːtə^r] *n (U)* peltre *m*.

pH (*abbr of* **potential of hydrogen**) *n* CHEM ph.

phantom ['fæntəm] ◇ *adj* [imaginary] ilusório(ria). ◇ *n* [ghost] fantasma *m*.

pharmaceutical [ˌfɑːmə'sjuːtıkl] *adj* farmacêutico(ca).

pharmacist ['fɑːməsıst] *n* farmacêutico *m*, -ca *f*.

pharmacology [ˌfɑːmə'kɒlədʒı] *n (U)* farmacologia *f*.

pharmacy ['fɑːməsı] (*pl* -**ies**) *n* farmácia *f*.

phase [feız] *n* fase *f*.

◆ **phase in** *vt sep* introduzir gradualmente.

◆ **phase out** *vt sep* retirar gradualmente.

PhD (*abbr of* **Doctor of Philosophy**) *n* (*titular de*) doutorado *em* ciências *humanas*.

pheasant ['feznt] (*pl inv OR* -**s**) *n* faisão *m*.

phenomena [fı'nɒmınə] *pl* ▷ **phenomenon**.

phenomenal [fı'nɒmınl] *adj* fenomenal.

phenomenon [fı'nɒmınən] (*pl* -**mena**) *n* fenômeno *m*.

phial ['faıəl] *n* frasco *m*.

philanthropist [fı'lænθrəpıst] *n* filantropo *m*.

philately [fı'lætəlı] *n (U)* filatelia *f*.

Philippine ['fılıpiːn] *adj* filipino(na).

◆ **Philippines** *npl*: **the ~ s** as Filipinas.

philosopher [fı'lɒsəfə^r] *n* filósofo *m*, -fa *f*.

philosophical [ˌfılə'sɒfıkl] *adj* filosófico(ca).

philosophy [fı'lɒsəfı] (*pl* -**ies**) *n* filosofia *f*.

phlegm [flem] *n (U)* fleuma *f*.

phlegmatic [fleg'mætık] *adj* fleumático(ca).

phobia ['fəʊbjə] *n* fobia *f*.

phone [fəʊn] ◇ *n* telefone *m*; **to be on the ~** [speaking] estar no telefone; *UK* [connected to network] ter telefone. ◇ *comp* telefônico(ca). ◇ *vt* telefonar, ligar para. ◇ *vi* telefonar, ligar.

◆ **phone back** *vt sep* & *vi* ligar de volta.

◆ **phone up** *vt sep* & *vi* ligar.

phone book *n* lista *f* telefônica.

phone booth *n US* cabine *f* telefônica.

phone box *n UK* cabine *f* telefônica.

phone call *n* ligação *f*, chamada *f* telefônica; **to make a ~** fazer uma ligação.

phonecard ['fəʊnkɑːd] *n* cartão *m* telefônico.

phone-in *n* RADIO, TV programa *para o qual as pessoas ligam e suas perguntas ou opiniões vão para o ar*.

phone number *n* número *m* de telefone.

phonetics [fə'netıks] *n (U)* fonética *f*.

phoney *UK*, **phony** *US* ['fəʊnı] (*compar* -**ier**, *superl* -**iest**, *pl* -**ies**) ◇ *adj* falso(sa). ◇ *n* farsante *mf*.

phosphorus ['fɒsfərəs] *n (U)* fósforo *m*.

photo ['fəʊtəʊ] *n* foto *f*; **to take a ~** (**of sb/sthg**) tirar OR bater uma foto (de alguém/algo).

photocopier ['fəʊtəʊˌkɒıə^r] *n* fotocopiadora *f*.

photocopy ['fəʊtəʊˌkɒpı] (*pl* -**ies**, *pt* & *pp* -**ied**) ◇ *n* fotocópia *f*. ◇ *vt* fotocopiar.

photograph ['fəʊtəgrɑːf] ◇ *n* fotografia *f*; **to take a ~** (**of sb/sthg**) tirar OR bater uma fotografia (de alguém/algo). ◇ *vt* fotografar.

photographer [fə'tɒgrəfə^r] *n* fotógrafo *m*, -fa *f*.

photography [fə'tɒgrəfɪl] n (U) fotografia f.

photovoltaic cell [ˌfəʊtəʊvɒl'teɪk-] n célula f fotovoltaica.

phrasal verb ['freɪzl-] n combinação de um verbo e de uma preposição ou um advérbio, que juntos possuem sentido único.

phrase [freɪz] ◇ n -1. [part of sentence] frase f -2. [expression] expressão f. ◇ vt [express - letter] redigir; [- apology, refusal] expressar; **sorry, I've ~d that badly** desculpe, eu me expressei mal.

phrasebook ['freɪzbʊk] n manual m de conversação.

physical ['fɪzɪkl] ◇ adj físico(ca). ◇ n exame m médico.

physical education n (U) SCH educação f física.

physically ['fɪzɪklɪ] adv fisicamente.

physically handicapped ◇ adj portador(ra) de deficiência física. ◇ npl: **the ~** os portadores de deficiência física.

physician [fɪ'zɪʃn] n médico m, -ca f.

physicist ['fɪzɪsɪst] n físico m, -ca f.

physics ['fɪzɪks] n (U) física f.

physiotherapy [ˌfɪzɪəʊ'θerəpɪ] n (U) fisioterapia f.

physique [fɪ'ziːk] n físico m.

pianist ['pɪənɪst] n pianista mf.

piano [pɪ'ænəʊ] (pl -s) n piano m; **to play the ~** tocar piano.

pick [pɪk] ◇ n -1. [tool] picareta f -2. [selection]: **to take one's ~** escolher o que quiser -3. [best]: **the ~ of** o melhor de. ◇ vt -1. [select, choose] escolher -2. [gather] colher -3. [remove] tirar -4. [nose]: **to ~ one's nose** pôr o dedo no nariz -5. [teeth]: **to ~ one's teeth** palitar os dentes -6. [provoke] provocar; **to ~ a fight (with sb)** arranjar briga (com alguém) -7. [lock] forçar (com instrumento ou ferramenta).

  ⬥ **pick on** vt fus meter-se com.

  ⬥ **pick out** vt sep -1. [recognize] reconhecer -2. [select, choose] escolher.

  ⬥ **pick up** ◇ vt sep -1. [lift up] pegar, apanhar -2. [collect] pegar -3. [acquire] adquirir; **to ~ up speed** pegar velocidade -4. inf [start relationship with] dar em cima de -5. [detect, receive] captar -6. [resume] retomar. ◇ vi -1. [improve] melhorar -2. [resume] retomar.

pickaxe UK, **pickax** US ['pɪkæks] n picareta f.

picket ['pɪkɪt] ◇ n [at place of work - person] piqueteiro m, -ra f; [- instance of picketing] piquete m. ◇ vt fazer piquete em.

picket line n piquete m de grevistas.

pickle ['pɪkl] ◇ n -1. [food] picles m inv -2. inf [difficult situation]: **to be in a ~** estar numa enrascada. ◇ vt fazer conserva de.

pickpocket ['pɪkˌpɒkɪt] n batedor m, -ra f de carteiras.

pick-up n -1. [of record player] pickup f -2. [truck] picape f.

picnic ['pɪknɪk] (pt & pp -ked, cont -king) ◇ n piquenique m. ◇ vi fazer piquenique.

pictorial [pɪk'tɔːrɪəl] adj ilustrado(da).

picture ['pɪktʃəʳ] ◇ n -1. [painting, drawing] quadro m -2. [photograph] fotografia f -3. [image] imagem f -4. [movie] filme m -5. [prospect] cenário m -6. phr: **to get the ~** inf entender; **to put sb in the ~** colocar alguém a par. ◇ vt -1. [in mind] imaginar -2. [in photo] fotografar -3. [in painting, drawing] retratar.

  ⬥ **pictures** npl UK: **the ~** s o cinema.

picture book n livro m ilustrado.

picturesque [ˌpɪktʃə'resk] adj pitoresco(ca).

pie [paɪ] n -1. [sweet] torta f -2. [savoury] pastelão m.

piece [piːs] n -1. [gen] pedaço m; **to fall to ~s** ficar em pedaços; **to take sthg to ~s** desmontar algo; **in ~s** em pedaços; **in one ~** [intact] sem um arranhão, intacto(ta); [unharmed] são e salvo, sã e salva -2. [of food] pedaço f -3. (with uncountable noun) [gen] peça f; **~ of paper** folha f de papel; **~ of luck** golpe m de sorte; **~ of information** informação f -4. [of journalism] artigo m -5. [coin] moeda f.

  ⬥ **piece together** vt sep reunir.

piecemeal ['piːsmiːl] ◇ adj pouco sistemático(ca). ◇ adv aos poucos, gradualmente.

piecework ['piːswɜːk] n (U) trabalho m por tarefas.

pie chart n gráfico m circular.

pier [pɪəʳ] n píer m.

pierce [pɪəs] vt -1. [subj: bullet, needle] furar; **to have one's ears ~d** furar as orelhas -2. [subj: noise, light, pain] romper.

piercing ['pɪəsɪŋ] ◇ adj -1. [sound, voice] agudo(da), estridente -2. [wind] cortante -3. [look, eyes] penetrante. ◇ n piercing m.

pig [pɪg] (pt & pp -ged, cont -ging) n -1. [animal] porco m, -ca f -2. inf pej [greedy eater] glutão m, -ona f -3. inf pej [unkind person] grosseirão m, -rona f.

pigeon ['pɪdʒɪn] (pl inv OR -s) n pomba f.

pigeonhole ['pɪdʒɪnhəʊl] ⟨> n [compartment] escaninho m. ⟨> vt [classify] classificar.

piggybank ['pɪgɪbæŋk] n porquinho m (de moedas).

pig-headed adj cabeçudo(da).

pigment ['pɪgmənt] n pigmento m.

pigpen n US = pigsty.

pigskin ['pɪgskɪn] n (U) couro m de porco.

pigsty ['pɪgstaɪ] (pl -ies), **pigpen** US ['pɪgpen] n chiqueiro m.

pigtail ['pɪgteɪl] n trança f.

pike [paɪk] (pl sense 1 only inv OR -s) n -1. [fish] lúcio m -2. [spear] pique m.

pilchard ['pɪltʃəd] n sardinha f.

pile [paɪl] ⟨> n -1. [heap] monte m; a ~ OR ~s of sthg inf um monte de algo -2. [neat stack] pilha f -3. [of carpet, fabric] felpa f. ⟨> vt empilhar; **to be ~d with sthg** estar entulhado(da) de algo.

  ◆ **piles** npl MED hemorróidas fpl.

  ◆ **pile into** vt fus inf amontoar-se.

  ◆ **pile up** ⟨> vt sep amontoar, empilhar. ⟨> vi acumular-se.

pile-up n engavetamento m.

pilfer ['pɪlfəʳ] ⟨> vt: to ~ sthg (from) furtar algo (de). ⟨> vi: to ~ (from) furtar (de), surrupiar (de).

pilgrim ['pɪlgrɪm] n peregrino m, -na f.

pilgrimage ['pɪlgrɪmɪdʒ] n peregrinação f.

pill [pɪl] n -1. MED pílula f -2. [contraceptive]: **the ~** a pílula anticoncepcional; **to be on the ~** tomar pílula (anticoncepcional).

pillage ['pɪlɪdʒ] vt pilhar.

pillar ['pɪləʳ] n -1. ARCHIT pilar m -2. fig [of community, church etc.] bastião m; **to be a ~ of strength** ser uma fortaleza; **to be a ~ of the church** ser um bastião da igreja.

pillar box n UK caixa f coletora (do correio).

pillion ['pɪljən] n assento m traseiro; **to ride ~** ir na garupa.

pillow ['pɪləʊ] n -1. [for bed] travesseiro m -2. US [on sofa, chair] almofada f.

pillowcase ['pɪləʊkeɪs], **pillowslip** ['pɪləʊslɪp] n fronha f.

pilot ['paɪlət] ⟨> n piloto m. ⟨> comp [trial] piloto; ~ **project** projeto-piloto m. ⟨> vt -1. [gen] pilotar -2. [bill] pôr em prática -3. [scheme] aplicar.

pilot light, pilot burner n [on gas appliance] piloto m.

pilot study n estudo m piloto.

pimp [pɪmp] n inf cafetão m.

pimple ['pɪmpl] n espinha f.

pin [pɪn] (pt & pp -ned, cont -ning) ⟨> n -1. [for sewing] alfinete m; **to have ~s and needles** fig estar com formigamento -2. [drawing pin] percevejo m -3. [safety pin] alfinete m de segurança -4. [of plug, grenade] pino m -5. TECH pino m, cavilha f -6. US [brooch] broche m; [badge] bottom m. ⟨> vt -1. [attach]: **to ~ sthg to OR on sthg** prender OR colocar algo em algo -2. [immobilize]: **to ~ sb against OR to sthg** prender alguém contra/em algo -3. [apportion]: **to ~ sthg on sb** botar a culpa de algo em alguém, culpar alguém de algo.

  ◆ **pin down** vt sep -1. [identify] determinar, identificar -2. [force to make a decision] obrigar a se decidir.

pinafore ['pɪnəfɔːʳ] n -1. [apron] avental m -2. UK [dress] jardineira f.

pinball ['pɪnbɔːl] n (U) fliperama f.

pincers ['pɪnsəz] npl -1. [tool] torquês f -2. [front claws] pinças fpl.

pinch [pɪntʃ] ⟨> n -1. [nip] beliscão m -2. [small quantity] pitada f. ⟨> vt -1. [nip] beliscar -2. inf [steal - money, clothes] passar a mão em; [- car] pegar.

  ◆ **at a pinch** UK, **in a pinch** US adv em último caso.

pincushion ['pɪn,kʊʃn] n alfineteira f.

pine [paɪn] ⟨> n -1. [tree] pinheiro m -2. (U) [wood] pinho m. ⟨> vi: **to ~ for sb/sthg** suspirar por alguém/algo.

  ◆ **pine away** vi consumir-se (de desgosto).

pineapple ['paɪnæpl] n abacaxi m.

pine tree n pinheiro m.

ping [pɪŋ] n tinido m.

Ping-Pong® [-pɒŋ] n (U) pingue-pongue m.

pink [pɪŋk] ⟨> adj -1. [in colour] cor-de-rosa -2. [with embarrassment] vermelho(lha); **to turn ~** ficar vermelho(lha). ⟨> n [colour] rosa m.

pink pound UK, **pink dollar** US n: **the ~** poder aquisitivo da comunidade gay.

pinnacle ['pɪnəkl] n -1. fig [of career, success] auge m -2. [mountain peak] topo m -3. ARCHIT [spire] pináculo m.

pinpoint ['pɪnpɔɪnt] vt -1. [difficulty, cause] determinar, identificar -2. [position, target, leak] identificar.

pin-striped [-,straɪpt] adj riscado(da).

pint [paɪnt] n -1. UK [unit of measurement] quartilho m (0,568 litro) -2. US [unit of measurement] pint m (0,473 litro) -3. UK [beer] cerveja f.

pioneer [,paɪə'nɪəʳ] ⟨> n -1. [first settler] pioneiro m, -ra f -2. [innovator] pioneiro m, -ra f. ⟨> vt lançar, ser pioneiro(na) de.

pious

pious ['paɪəs] adj -1. [religious] piedoso(-sa) -2. pej [sanctimonious] devoto(ta).

pip [pɪp] n -1. [seed] semente f -2. UK [bleep] sinal m.

pipe [paɪp] ◇ n -1. [for gas, water] tubo m, cano m -2. [for smoking] cachimbo m. ◇ vt canalizar.
➡ pipes npl MUS [bagpipes] gaita f de foles.
➡ pipe down vi inf fechar a matraca.
➡ pipe up vi inf: there was silence and then she ~d up with a suggestion fez-se silêncio e então ela saiu com uma sugestão.

pipe cleaner n limpador m para cachimbo.

pipe dream n castelo m no ar, sonho m impossível.

pipeline ['paɪplaɪn] n -1. [for oil] oleoduto m -2. [for gas] gasoduto m.

piper ['paɪpər] n MUS tocador m, -ra f de gaita de foles.

piping hot ['paɪpɪŋ-] adj extremamente quente.

pique [piːk] n (U) ressentimento m.

piracy ['paɪrəsɪ] n pirataria f.

pirate ['paɪrət] ◇ adj [illegally copied] pirateado(da). ◇ n -1. [sailor] pirata m -2. [illegal copy] cópia f pirata. ◇ vt piratear.

pirate radio n UK rádio f pirata.

pirouette [ˌpɪru'et] ◇ n pirueta f. ◇ vi fazer pirueta.

Pisces ['paɪsiːz] n [sign] Peixes m.

piss [pɪs] vulg ◇ n [urine] mijo m. ◇ vi [urinate] mijar.

pissed [pɪst] adj vulg -1. UK [drunk] mamado(da) -2. US [annoyed] puto(ta) da cara.

pissed off adj vulg de saco cheio.

pistol ['pɪstl] n pistola f.

piston ['pɪstən] n pistom m.

pit [pɪt] (pt & pp -ted, cont -ting) ◇ n -1. [large hole] cova f -2. [small, shallow hole] marca f -3. [for orchestra] fosso m da orquestra -4. [mine] mina f -5. US [of fruit] caroço m. ◇ vt: to be ~ted against sb ser incitado(da) contra alguém.
➡ pits npl [in motor racing]: the ~s o box.

pitch [pɪtʃ] ◇ n -1. SPORT campo m -2. MUS tom m -3. (U) [level, degree] grau m -4. [street vendor's place] ponto m -5. inf [spiel]: sales ~ papo m de vendedor -6. [of slope, roof] [grau m de] inclinação f. ◇ vt -1. [throw] arremessar -2. [set level of - price] estabelecer um preço para; [- speech] dar um tom a -3. [camp, tent] armar. ◇ vi -1. [fall over] despencar;

to ~ forward precipitar-se para frente -2. [ship, plane] arfar.

pitch-black adj preto(ta) como carvão.

pitched battle [ˌpɪtʃt-] n batalha f campal.

pitcher ['pɪtʃər] n US -1. [jug] jarro m -2. [in baseball] lançador m.

pitchfork ['pɪtʃfɔːk] n forcado m.

piteous ['pɪtɪəs] adj lastimável, comovente.

pitfall ['pɪtfɔːl] n armadilha f, perigo m.

pith [pɪθ] n (U) parte branca da casca de uma fruta.

pithy ['pɪθɪ] (compar -ier, superl -iest) adj denso(sa), contundente.

pitiful ['pɪtɪfʊl] adj -1. [arousing pity] lastimável -2. [arousing contempt] lastimoso(sa).

pitiless ['pɪtɪlɪs] adj impiedoso(sa).

pit stop n pit stop m.

pittance ['pɪtəns] n miséria f.

pity ['pɪtɪ] (pt & pp -ied) ◇ n -1. [sympathy, sorrow] compaixão f; to take ou have ~ on sb ficar com pena de alguém -2. [shame] pena f; what a ~! que pena! ◇ vt sentir pena de.

pivot ['pɪvət] n -1. TECH eixo m -2. fig [crux] centro m, eixo m.

pixel ['pɪksl] n pixel m.

pizza ['piːtsə] n pizza f.

pl. abbr of please.

placard ['plækɑːd] n cartaz m.

placate [plə'keɪt] vt aplacar, acalmar.

place [pleɪs] ◇ n -1. [gen] lugar m; ~ of birth local de nascimento -2. [suitable occasion] momento m -3. [home] casa f; decimal ~ MATH casa decimal -4. [post, vacancy] vaga f -5. [role, function] papel m -6. [rank] posição f -7. [instance]: why didn't you say so in the first ~? por que você não disse isso logo?; in the first ~ ..., and in the second ~ ... em primeiro lugar ..., e em segundo lugar ... -8. phr: the market takes ~ every Sunday a feira acontece todos os domingos; the events that took ~ that day became infamous os acontecimentos que tiveram lugar naquele dia tornaram-se notórios; to take the ~ of sb/sthg tomar o lugar de alguém/algo, substituir alguém/algo. ◇ vt -1. [position, put] colocar -2. [lay, apportion]: to ~ blame on sb/sthg colocar a culpa em alguém/algo; to ~ emphasis on sb/sthg dar ênfase a alguém/algo; to ~ pressure on sb/sthg exercer pressão sobre alguém/algo; to ~ responsibility on sb/sthg pôr a responsabilidade em alguém/algo -3. [identify] identificar -4. [make]: to ~ an order COMM fazer um pedido; **to ~ a bet** fazer uma aposta - **5.** [situate] situar; **how are we ~d for money?** como estamos de dinheiro? - **6.** [in race]: **to be ~d** classificar-se.

all over the place *adv* por todo lado.

in place *adv* - **1.** [in proper position] no lugar - **2.** [established, set up] estabelecido(da).

in place of *prep*: **in ~ of me** em meu lugar.

out of place *adv* - **1.** [in wrong position] fora do lugar - **2.** [unsuitable] fora de propósito.

place mat *n* toalha *f* de mesa individual.

placement ['pleismənt] *n* - **1.** *(U)* [positioning] disposição *f* - **2.** [work experience] estágio *m*.

placid ['plæsɪd] *adj* - **1.** [even-tempered] plácido(da) - **2.** [peaceful] sereno(na).

plagiarize, -ise ['pleɪdʒəraɪz] *vt* plagiar.

plague [pleɪg] *n* praga *f*. *vt*: **to ~ sb with sthg** importunar alguém com algo; **to be ~d by sthg** ser/estar atormentado(da) por algo.

plaice [pleɪs] *(pl inv)* *n* linguado *m*.

plaid [plæd] *n (U)* tecido *m* em xadrez da Escócia.

Plaid Cymru [ˌplaɪdˈkʌmrɪ] *n UK POL* Plaid Cymru *(partido nacionalista galês)*.

plain [pleɪn] *adj* - **1.** [not patterned] liso(sa) - **2.** [simple, not fancy] simples; **~ yoghurt** iogurte *m* natural - **3.** [clear] claro(ra) - **4.** [blunt] direto(ta) - **5.** [absolute] absoluto(ta) - **6.** [not pretty] sem atrativos. *adv inf* [completely] claramente. *n GEOGR* planície *f*.

plain chocolate *n UK* chocolate *m* meio amargo.

plain-clothes *adj* à paisana.

plain flour *n UK* farinha *f* sem fermento.

plainly ['pleɪnlɪ] *adv* - **1.** [upset, angry] completamente - **2.** [remember, hear] claramente - **3.** [frankly] francamente, abertamente - **4.** [simply] de forma simples.

plaintiff ['pleɪntɪf] *n* querelante *mf*.

plait [plæt] *n* trança *f*. *vt* trançar.

plan [plæn] *(pt & pp -ned, cont -ning)* *n* - **1.** [strategy] plano *m*; **to go according to ~** sair de acordo com o planejado - **2.** [outline] esboço *m* - **3.** [diagram, map of garden, building] planta *f*; [of inside of a machine] esquema *m* de montagem. *vt* - **1.** [organize] planejar - **2.** [intend] pretender; **to ~ to do sthg** pensar em fazer algo - **3.** [design, devise]

projetar. *vi* fazer planos; **to ~ for sthg** fazer planos para algo.

plans *npl* planos *mpl*; **to have ~s for** ter planos para.

plan on *vt fus*: **to ~ on doing sthg** pretender fazer algo.

plane [pleɪn] *adj* plano(na). *n* - **1.** [aircraft] avião *m* - **2.** *GEOM* plano *m* - **3.** *fig* [level] patamar *m* - **4.** [tool] plaina *f* - **5.** [tree] plátano *m*.

planet ['plænɪt] *n* planeta *f*.

plank [plæŋk] *n* - **1.** [piece of wood] tábua *f* - **2.** *POL* [main policy] item *m*.

planning ['plænɪŋ] *n* planejamento *m*.

planning permission *n (U)* autorização *f* para construir.

plant [plɑ:nt] *n* - **1.** *BOT* planta *f* - **2.** [factory] fábrica *f*; **nuclear ~** usina *f* nuclear - **3.** *(U)* [heavy machinery] maquinários *mpl*. *vt* - **1.** [seed, tree] plantar; [field, garden] semear - **2.** [blow, kiss] dar - **3.** [place - oneself] plantar-se; [- object] fincar - **4.** [spy] infiltrar - **5.** [bomb, microphone] colocar secretamente - **6.** [thought, idea] incutir.

plantation [plænˈteɪʃn] *n* plantação *f*.

plaque [plɑ:k] *n* placa *f*.

plaster ['plɑ:stə^r] *n* - **1.** [gen] gesso *m* - **2.** *UK* [for cut]: (sticking) **~** esparadrapo *m*, Band-Aid® *m*. *vt* - **1.** [put plaster on] revestir com gesso - **2.** [cover]: **to ~ sthg with sthg** cobrir algo com algo.

plaster cast *n* molde *m* de gesso.

plastered ['plɑ:stəd] *adj inf* [drunk] de porre.

plasterer ['plɑ:stərə^r] *n* rebocador *m*, -ra *f*.

plaster of paris *n* gesso *m* de Paris.

plastic ['plæstɪk] *adj* de plástico. *n* [material] plástico *m*.

Plasticine® *UK* ['plæstɪsi:n], **play dough** *US n (U)* plasticina *f*.

plastic surgery *n (U)* cirurgia *f* plástica.

plastic wrap *n US* filme *m* de PVC transparente.

plate [pleɪt] *n* - **1.** [gen] prato *m* - **2.** [on wall, door or surgical] placa *f* - **3.** *(U)* [gold, silver etc.] baixela *f* - **4.** [photograph] chapa *f* - **5.** [in dentistry] dentadura *f* - **6.** [in baseball] base *f*. *vt*: **to be ~d (with sthg)** ser banhado (a algo).

plateau ['plætəʊ] *(pl -s OR -x [-z])* *n* - **1.** *GEOGR* planalto *m* - **2.** *fig* [steady level] nível *m* estável.

plate-glass *adj* de vidro laminado.

platform ['plætfɔ:m] *n* - **1.** [gen] plataforma *f* - **2.** [for speaker, performer] palanque *m*.

platform ticket n UK bilhete m de plataforma.

platinum ['plætɪnəm] n platina f.

platoon [plə'tu:n] n pelotão m.

platter ['plætəʳ] n travessa f.

plausible ['plɔ:zəbl] adj [reason, excuse] plausível; [person] convincente.

play [pleɪ] ◇ n -1. (U) [amusement] brincadeira f; **children at ~** crianças brincando - 2. [piece of drama] peça f - 3. [pun]: **~ on words** trocadilho - 4. TECH folga f. ◇ vt -1. [gen] jogar; **to ~ hide-and-seek** brincar de esconde-esconde - 2. [opposing player or team] jogar contra - 3. [joke, trick] pregar - 4. [perform] desempenhar, representar; **to ~ a part** OR **role in sthg** fig desempenhar um papel em algo - 5. [MUS - instrument, CD] tocar; [- tune] executar - 6. [pretend to be] fingir. ◇ vi -1. [amuse o.s.] brincar; **to ~ with sb/sthg** brincar com alguém/algo - 2. SPORT jogar; **to ~ for sb** jogar para alguém; **to ~ against sb** jogar contra alguém - 3. PER-FORM: **to ~ in sthg** atuar em algo - 4. [music] tocar - 5. phr: **to ~ safe** não se arriscar.
➤ **play along** vi: **to ~ along (with sb)** fazer o jogo (de alguém).
➤ **play down** vt sep menosprezar.
➤ **play up** ◇ vt sep enfatizar. ◇ vi -1. [cause problems] dar trabalho - 2. [mis-behave] comportar-se mal.

play-act vi fazer fita.

playboy ['pleɪbɔɪ] n playboy m.

play dough US = **Plasticine®**.

player ['pleɪəʳ] n -1. [of game, sport] jogador m, -ra f - 2. MUS músico m, -ca f; **guitar ~** guitarrista mf; **saxophone ~** saxofonista mf - 3. dated & THEATRE ator m, atriz f.

playful ['pleɪfʊl] adj -1. [good-natured] divertido(da) - 2. [frisky] brincalhão(lho-na).

playground ['pleɪgraʊnd] n [at school] pátio m de recreio; [in park] parque m de diversões.

playgroup ['pleɪgru:p] n jardim-de-in-fância m.

playing card ['pleɪŋ-] n carta f de baralho.

playing field ['pleɪŋ-] n quadra f de esportes.

playmate ['pleɪmeɪt] n amigo m, -ga f de infância.

play-off n partida f de desempate.

playpen ['pleɪpen] n cercadinho m para crianças, chiqueirinho m.

playschool ['pleɪsku:l] n jardim-de-in-fância m.

plaything ['pleɪθɪŋ] n -1. [toy] brinque-do m - 2. fig [person] joguete m.

playtime ['pleɪtaɪm] n (U) (hora f do) recreio m.

playwright ['pleɪraɪt] n dramaturgo m, -ga f.

plc (abbr of public limited company) UK companhia f pública limitada.

plea [pli:] n -1. [appeal] apelo m - 2. JUR contestação f.

plead [pli:d] (pt & pp -ed OR pled) ◇ vt -1. JUR defender; **to ~ insanity** alegar insanidade mental; **to ~ guilty** decla-rar culpado(da) - 2. [give as excuse] ale-gar. ◇ vi -1. [beg] implorar; **to ~ with sb to do sthg** implorar a alguém que faça algo; **to ~ for sthg** implorar algo - 2. JUR responder a uma acusação.

pleasant ['plezɪnt] adj agradável.

pleasantry ['plezntrɪ] (pl -ies) n: **to ex-change pleasantries** trocar amabi-lidades.

please [pli:z] ◇ adv por favor. ◇ vt agradar; **to ~ o.s.** fazer o que se deseja; **~ yourself!** como queira! ◇ vi -1. [give satisfaction] agradar - 2. [choose]: **to do as one ~s** fazer como quiser.

pleased [pli:zd] adj contente, feliz; **to be ~ about sthg** estar satisfeito(ta) com algo; **to be ~ with sb/sthg** estar satis-feito(ta) com alguém/algo; **~ to meet you!** prazer em conhecê-lo(-la)!

pleasing ['pli:zɪŋ] adj agradável.

pleasure ['pleʒəʳ] n -1. (U) [feeling of hap-piness] alegria f; **with ~** com (muito) prazer - 2. [enjoyment] prazer m; **it's a ~** OR **my ~!** é um prazer!, não tem de quê!

pleat [pli:t] ◇ n prega f. ◇ vt fazer prega em.

pled [pled] pt & pp ▷ **plead**.

pledge [pledʒ] ◇ n -1. [promise] pro-messa f - 2. [token] símbolo m - 3. [as a security] garantia f. ◇ vt -1. [promise to provide] prometer - 2. [commit]: **to be ~d to sthg** estar comprometido(da) com algo; **to ~ o.s. to sthg** comprometer-se com algo - 3. [pawn] penhorar.

plentiful ['plentɪfʊl] adj abundante.

plenty ['plentɪ] ◇ n (U) fartura f. ◇ pron bastante; **~ of** bastante; **~ of time** bastante tempo; **~ of reasons** inúmeras razões. ◇ adv US [very] muito.

pliable ['plaɪəbl], **pliant** ['plaɪənt] adj -1. [supple] flexível - 2. [adaptable] dócil.

pliers ['plaɪəz] npl alicate m.

plight [plaɪt] n péssima situação f; **in a ~** em apuros.

plimsoll ['plɪmsəl] n UK calçados mpl para prática de esportes.

plinth [plɪnθ] n plinto m.

PLO (abbr of Palestine Liberation Organization) n OLP f.

plod [plɒd] (pt & pp -ded, cont -ding) vi -1. [walk slowly] arrastar-se -2. [work slowly] trabalhar vagarosamente.

plodder ['plɒdə'] n pej trabalhador m lerdo e pouco criativo.

plonk [plɒŋk] n UK inf vinho m fajuto.

➡ **plonk down** vt sep inf deixar cair.

plot [plɒt] (pt & pp -ted, cont -ting) n -1. [conspiracy] complô m -2. [story] enredo m, trama f -3. [of land] lote m. ⬦ vt -1. [conspire] tramar; **to ~ to do sthg** tramar para fazer algo -2. [chart] traçar -3. MATH traçar, plotar. ⬦ vi conspirar; **to ~ against sb** conspirar contra alguém.

plotter ['plɒtə'] n [schemer] conspirador m, -ra f.

plough UK, **plow** US [plaʊ] ⬦ n arado m. ⬦ vt -1. AGR arar, lavrar -2. [invest]: **to ~ money into sthg** investir muito dinheiro em algo. ⬦ vi: **to ~ into sthg** colidir contra algo.

ploughman's ['plaʊmənz] (pl inv) n UK: **~ (lunch)** refeição que consiste em pão, queijo, cebola e picles.

plow etc. n & vt US = plough etc.

ploy [plɔɪ] n estratagema f.

pluck [plʌk] ⬦ vt -1. [flower, fruit] colher -2. [pull] apanhar; **the helicopter ~ed the survivors off the ship** o helicóptero resgatou os sobreviventes do navio -3. [chicken] depenar -4. [eyebrows] depilar -5. [musical instrument] dedilhar. ⬦ n (U) dated [courage] garra f.

➡ **pluck up** vt fus: **to ~ up the courage to do sthg** criar coragem para fazer algo.

plucky ['plʌkɪ] (compar -ier, superl -iest) adj dated valente.

plug [plʌg] (pt & pp -ged, cont -ging) ⬦ n -1. ELEC tomada f; [socket] plugue m -2. [for bath or sink] tampa f, válvula f. ⬦ vt -1. [block] tampar -2. inf [advertise] fazer propaganda de.

➡ **plug in** vt sep ligar.

plughole ['plʌghəʊl] n ralo m.

plum [plʌm] ⬦ adj -1. [colour] da cor de ameixa -2. [choice]: **a ~ job** uma jóia de emprego. ⬦ n [fruit] ameixa m.

plumb [plʌm] ⬦ adv -1. UK [exactly] exatamente -2. US [completely] totalmente. ⬦ vt: **to ~ the depths of sthg** atingir o auge de algo.

plumber ['plʌmə'] n encanador m, -ra f.

plumbing ['plʌmɪŋ] n (U) -1. [fittings] encanamento m -2. [work] trabalho m do encanador.

plume [pluːm] n -1. [on bird] pluma f -2. [on hat, helmet] penacho m -3. [column]: **a ~ of smoke** um penacho de fumaça.

plummet ['plʌmɪt] vi -1. [dive] mergulhar (em direção ao solo) -2. [decrease rapidly] despencar.

plump [plʌmp] ⬦ adj roliço(ça). ⬦ vi: **to ~ for sthg** optar por algo.

➡ **plump up** vt sep afofar.

plum pudding n pudim m de passas.

plunder ['plʌndə'] ⬦ n -1. [pillaging] pilhagem f -2. [booty] saque m. ⬦ vt saquear.

plunge [plʌndʒ] ⬦ n -1. [rapid decrease] caída f -2. [dive] mergulho; **to take the ~** mergulhar de cabeça, dar um passo decisivo. ⬦ vt -1. [immerse]: **to ~ sthg into sthg** mergulhar algo em algo -2. fig [thrust]: **to ~ sthg into sthg** enfiar algo em algo; **the room was ~d into darkness** a sala mergulhou na escuridão. ⬦ vi -1. [dive, throw o.s.] mergulhar -2. [decrease rapidly] despencar.

plunger ['plʌndʒə'] n desentupidor m.

pluperfect [ˌpluː'pɜːfɪkt] n: **the ~ (tense)** o (tempo) mais-que-perfeito.

plural ['plʊərəl] ⬦ adj plural. ⬦ n plural m.

plus [plʌs] (pl -es OR -ses) ⬦ adj mais; **thirty-five ~** trinta e cinco ou mais. ⬦ n -1. MATH sinal m de adição, sinal m de mais -2. inf [bonus] vantagem f. ⬦ prep mais. ⬦ conj [moreover] além disso.

plush [plʌʃ] adj suntuoso(sa).

plus sign n sinal m de mais.

Pluto ['pluːtəʊ] n Plutão.

plutonium [pluː'təʊnɪəm] n (U) plutônio m.

ply [plaɪ] (pt & pp plied) ⬦ n espessura. ⬦ vt -1. [work at] trabalhar em -2. [supply, provide]: **to ~ sb with sthg** prover alguém com algo. ⬦ vi [travel] navegar em.

-ply adj de espessura.

plywood ['plaɪwʊd] n (U) compensado m.

p.m., pm (abbr of post meridiem): **at three ~** às três da tarde.

PM (abbr of prime minister) n primeiro-ministro m, primeira-ministra f.

PMT (abbr of premenstrual tension) n TPM f.

pneumatic [njuː'mætɪk] adj -1. [air-powered] pneumático(ca) -2. [air-filled] de ar.

pneumatic drill n perfuratriz f.

pneumonia [njuː'məʊnjə] n (U) pneumonia f.

poach [pəʊtʃ] ⟨⟩ *vt* [hunt illegally] caçar ilegalmente - **2.** [copy] plagiar - **3.** [*CULIN - salmon*] escaldar; [- egg] escalfar. ⟨⟩ *vi* caçar ilegalmente.

poacher ['pəʊtʃə'] *n* [person] caçador *m* furtivo, caçadora *f* furtiva.

poaching ['pəʊtʃɪŋ] *n* (*U*) caça *f* ilegal.

PO Box (*abbr of* Post Office Box) *n* caixa *f* postal.

pocket ['pɒkɪt] ⟨⟩ *n* - **1.** [in clothes] bolso *m*; **the deal left us £10 out of ~** o negócio nos deu um prejuízo de £10; **to pick sb's ~** roubar do bolso de alguém - **2.** [in car door etc.] porta-mapas *m* - **3.** [small area] foco *m* - **4.** [of snooker, pool table] caçapa *f.* ⟨⟩ *adj* [pocket-sized] de bolso. ⟨⟩ *vt* - **1.** [place in pocket] pôr no bolso - **2.** [steal] embolsar - **3.** [in snooker, pool] encaçapar.

pocketbook ['pɒkɪtbʊk] *n* - **1.** [notebook] livro *m* de bolso - **2.** *US* [handbag] carteira *f*.

pocketknife ['pɒkɪtnaɪf] (*pl* **-knives** [-naɪvz]) *n* canivete *m*.

pocket money *n* (*U*) mesada *m*.

pockmark ['pɒkmɑːk] *n* sinal *m* de varíola.

pod [pɒd] *n* - **1.** [of plants] vagem *f* - **2.** [of spacecraft] módulo *m*.

podgy ['pɒdʒɪ] (*compar* **-ier**, *superl* **-iest**) *adj inf* atarracado(da).

podiatrist [pə'daɪətrɪst] *n US* podiatra *mf*.

podium ['pəʊdɪəm] (*pl* **-diums** OR **-dia** [-dɪə]) *n* pódio *m*.

poem ['pəʊɪm] *n* poema *f*.

poet ['pəʊɪt] *n* poeta *mf*, poetisa *f*.

poetic [pəʊ'etɪk] *adj* poético(ca).

poetry ['pəʊɪtrɪ] *n* (*U*) [poems] poesia *f*.

poignant ['pɔɪnjənt] *adj* comovente.

point [pɔɪnt] ⟨⟩ *n* - **1.** [gen] ponto *m*; **to make a ~** fazer uma observação; **to make one's ~** dar sua opinião - **2.** [tip] ponta *f* - **3.** [essence, heart] parte *f* essencial; **to get** OR **come to the ~** ir ao ponto principal; **beside the ~** irrelevante; **to the ~** objetivo(va) - **4.** [feature, characteristic] característica *f* - **5.** [purpose] propósito *m*, razão *f* - **6.** [of compass] ponto *m* cardeal - **7.** *UK* ELEC ponto *m* - **8.** *US* [full stop] ponto *m* final - **9.** *phr*: **to make a ~ of doing sthg** fazer questão de fazer algo. ⟨⟩ *vt*: **to ~ sthg (at sb/sthg)** apontar algo (para alguém/algo); **to ~ the way (to sthg)** mostrar a direção (para algo). ⟨⟩ *vi* apontar; **to ~ at sb/sthg, to ~ to sb/ sthg** apontar para alguém/algo.

➡ **points** *npl UK* RAIL pontos *mpl*.

➡ **up to a point** *adv* até certo ponto.

➡ **on the point of** *prep* prestes a.

➡ **point out** *vt sep* - **1.** [indicate] indicar - **2.** [call attention to] salientar.

point-blank *adv* - **1.** [directly] categoricamente - **2.** [at close range] à queima-roupa.

pointed ['pɔɪntɪd] *adj* - **1.** [sharp] pontiagudo(da) - **2.** [meaningful] sugestivo(va).

pointer ['pɔɪntə'] *n* - **1.** [tip, hint] dica *f* - **2.** [needle on dial] agulha *f* - **3.** [stick] indicador *m* - **4.** COMPUT ponteiro *m*.

pointless ['pɔɪntlɪs] *adj* inútil.

point of view (*pl* **points of view**) *n* ponto *m* de vista.

poise [pɔɪz] *n* (*U*) compostura *f*.

poised [pɔɪzd] *adj* - **1.** [ready] pronto(ta), preparado(da); **to be ~ to do sthg** estar pronto(ta) para fazer algo; **to be ~ for sthg** estar pronto(ta) para algo - **2.** [calm and dignified] equilibrado(da).

poison ['pɔɪzn] ⟨⟩ *n* veneno *m*. ⟨⟩ *vt* - **1.** [gen] envenenar - **2.** [pollute] poluir - **3.** *fig* [spoil, corrupt] corromper.

poisoning ['pɔɪznɪŋ] *n* (*U*) envenenamento *m*, intoxicação *f*.

poisonous ['pɔɪznəs] *adj* - **1.** [gas, chemical] tóxico (ca) - **2.** [snake, mushroom, plant] venenoso(sa).

poke [pəʊk] ⟨⟩ *vt* - **1.** [prod, jab] remexer, cutucar - **2.** [stick, thrust] enfiar em - **3.** [fire] atiçar, remexer. ⟨⟩ *vi* projetar-se; **his head ~d round the corner** a cabeça dele apareceu na esquina.

➡ **poke about, poke around** *vi inf* escarafunchar.

poker ['pəʊkə'] *n* - **1.** [game] pôquer *m* - **2.** [for fire] atiçador *m*.

poker-faced [-ˌfeɪst] *adj* de rosto inexpressivo.

poky ['pəʊkɪ] (*compar* **-ier**, *superl* **-iest**) *adj pej* apertado(da).

Poland ['pəʊlənd] *n* Polônia *f*.

polar ['pəʊlə'] *adj* GEOGR polar.

Polaroid® ['pəʊlərɔɪd] *n* polaróide *f*.

pole [pəʊl] *n* - **1.** [gen] pólo *m* - **2.** [rod, post] poste *m*.

Pole [pəʊl] *n* polonês *m*, -esa *f*.

poleaxed ['pəʊlækst] *adj* atordoado(da).

pole vault *n*: **the ~** o salto com vara.

police [pə'liːs] ⟨⟩ *npl* - **1.** [police force]: **the ~** a polícia - **2.** [policemen, policewomen] policial *mf*. ⟨⟩ *vt* policiar.

police car *n* radiopatrulha *f*.

police constable *n UK* policial *mf*.

police force *n* força *f* policial.

policeman [pə'liːsmən] (*pl* **-men** [-mən]) *n* policial *m*.

police officer *n* oficial *mf* de polícia.

police record *n* ficha *f* policial.

police station n UK delegacia f.

policewoman [pəˈliːsˌwʊmən] (pl -women [-ˌwɪmɪn]) n policial f.

policy [ˈpɒləsɪ] (pl -ies) n -1. [plan, practice] política f -2. [document, agreement] apólice f.

polio [ˈpəʊlɪəʊ] n (U) poliomielite f, paralisia f infantil.

polish [ˈpɒlɪʃ] ⬦ n -1. [cleaning material] polidor m -2. [shine] polimento m -3. fig [refinement] requinte m. ⬦ vt -1. polir -2. fig [perfect]: **to ~ sthg (up)** refinar algo.

⬥ **polish off** vt sep inf -1. [meal] comer/beber rapidamente -2. [job, book] dar um fim rápido em.

Polish [ˈpəʊlɪʃ] ⬦ adj polonês(esa). ⬦ n [language] polonês m. ⬦ npl: **the ~** os poloneses.

polished [ˈpɒlɪʃt] adj -1. [gen] polido(da) -2. [performer, performance] elegante.

polite [pəˈlaɪt] adj [person, remark] educado(da), cortês(tesa).

politic [ˈpɒlətɪk] adj fml prudente.

political [pəˈlɪtɪkl] adj político(ca).

politically correct [pəˌlɪtɪklɪ-] adj politicamente correto(ta).

politician [ˌpɒlɪˈtɪʃn] n político m, -ca f.

politics [ˈpɒlətɪks] ⬦ n política f. ⬦ npl [of a person, group] política f.

polka [ˈpɒlkə] n polca f; **to do the ~** dançar a polca.

polka dot n bolinhas fpl (em um padrão de tecido).

poll [pəʊl] ⬦ n -1. [election] eleição f -2. [survey] pesquisa f. ⬦ vt -1. [people] entrevistar -2. [votes] receber, obter.

⬥ **polls** npl: **to go to the ~s** ir às urnas.

pollen [ˈpɒlən] n (U) pólen m.

polling booth [ˈpəʊlɪŋ-] n cabine f de votação.

polling day [ˈpəʊlɪŋ-] n UK dia f de eleição.

polling station [ˈpəʊlɪŋ-] n zona f eleitoral.

pollute [pəˈluːt] vt poluir.

pollution [pəˈluːʃn] n poluição f.

polo [ˈpəʊləʊ] n (U) pólo m.

polo neck n UK -1. [collar] gola f alta -2. [jumper] blusão m de gola alta.

polo shirt n camisa f pólo.

polyethylene n US = polythene.

Polynesia [ˌpɒlɪˈniːʒə] n Polinésia f.

polystyrene [ˌpɒlɪˈstaɪriːn] n (U) poliestireno m, isopor m.

polytechnic [ˌpɒlɪˈteknɪk] n UK politécnica f.

polythene UK [ˈpɒlɪθiːn], **polyethylene** US [ˈpɒlɪˈeθɪliːn] n (U) polietileno m.

polythene bag n UK saco m de polietileno.

pomegranate [ˈpɒmɪˌɡrænɪt] n romã f.

pomp [pɒmp] n (U) pompa f.

pompom [ˈpɒmpɒm] n pompom m.

pompous [ˈpɒmpəs] adj [pretentious - speech, style] pomposo(sa); [- person] pretensioso(sa).

pond [pɒnd] n lago m (natural ou artificial); **the ~** inf o Atlântico.

ponder [ˈpɒndər] vt ponderar.

ponderous [ˈpɒndərəs] adj -1. [dull, solemn] ponderoso(sa) -2. [large and heavy] pesado(da).

pong [pɒŋ] UK inf n fedor m.

pontoon [pɒnˈtuːn] n -1. [bridge] barcaça f -2. UK [game] vinte-e-um m.

pony [ˈpəʊnɪ] (pl -ies) n pônei m.

ponytail [ˈpəʊnɪteɪl] n rabo-de-cavalo m.

pony-trekking [-ˌtrekɪŋ] n (U) excursão f em pôneis.

poodle [ˈpuːdl] n poodle m.

pool [puːl] ⬦ n -1. [natural] lago m -2. [swimming pool] piscina f -3. [of liquid, light] poça f -4. [of workers, cars, talent] grupo m -5. (U) SPORT bilhar m. ⬦ vt juntar.

⬥ **pools** npl UK: **the ~s** ≃ a loteria esportiva.

poor [pɔːr] ⬦ adj pobre. ⬦ npl: **the ~** os pobres.

poorly [ˈpɔːlɪ] ⬦ adj UK inf [ill] mal. ⬦ adv mal.

pop [pɒp] (pt & pp -ped, cont -ping) ⬦ n -1. (U) [music] pop m -2. (U) inf [fizzy drink] gasosa f -3. esp US inf [father] pai m -4. [noise] estouro m. ⬦ vt -1. [burst] estourar -2. [put quickly] pôr rapidamente. ⬦ vi -1. [burst] estourar -2. [spring, fly off] soltar-se -3. [eyes] arregalar.

⬥ **pop in** vi entrar por um momento.

⬥ **pop up** vi aparecer de repente.

pop concert n concerto m pop.

popcorn [ˈpɒpkɔːn] n (U) pipoca f.

pope [pəʊp] n papa m.

pop group n grupo m pop.

poplar [ˈpɒplər] n choupo m.

poppy [ˈpɒpɪ] (pl -ies) n papoula f.

Popsicle® [ˈpɒpsɪkl] n US picolé m.

populace [ˈpɒpjʊləs] n: **the ~** o populacho.

popular [ˈpɒpjʊlər] adj popular.

popularize, -ise [ˈpɒpjʊləraɪz] vt popularizar.

population [ˌpɒpjʊˈleɪʃn] n população f.

porcelain [ˈpɔːsəlɪn] n (U) porcelana f.

porch [pɔːtʃ] n -1. [entrance] átrio m -2. US [veranda] alpendre m.

porcupine ['pɔːkjʊpaɪn] n porco-espinho m.

pore [pɔː^r] n poro m.

➡ **pore over** vt fus examinar minuciosamente.

pork [pɔːk] n (U) carne f de porco.

pork pie n pastelão m de porco.

pornography [pɔː'nɒgrəfɪl] n (U) pornografia f.

porous ['pɔːrəs] adj poroso(sa).

porridge ['pɒrɪdʒ] n (U) mingau m com cereais.

port [pɔːt] n -1. [gen] porto m -2. (U) NAUT bombordo m -3. (U) [drink] vinho m do Porto -4. COMPUT porta f.

portable ['pɔːtəbl] adj portátil.

portal ['pɔːtl] n COMPUT portal m.

portent ['pɔːtənt] n literary prognóstico m.

porter ['pɔːtə^r] n -1. UK [doorman] porteiro m, -ra f -2. [for luggage] carregador m, -ra f -3. US [on train] cabineiro m, -ra f.

portfolio [ˌpɔːt'fəʊljəʊ] (pl -s) n -1. [case] pasta f -2. [sample of work] portfólio m -3. FIN carteira f.

porthole ['pɔːthəʊl] n vigia mf.

portion ['pɔːʃn] n -1. [part, share] porção f -2. [set amount of food] parte f.

portly ['pɔːtlɪ] (compar -ier, superl -iest) adj corpulento(ta).

portrait ['pɔːtrɪt] n retrato m.

portray [pɔː'treɪ] vt -1. [in a play, film] interpretar -2. [describe, represent] descrever -3. [subj: artist] retratar.

Portugal ['pɔːtʃʊgl] n Portugal.

Portuguese [ˌpɔːtʃʊ'giːz] (pl inv) ◇ adj português(guesa). ◇ n [language] português m. ◇ npl: the ~ os portugueses.

pose [pəʊz] ◇ n -1. [position, stance] pose f -2. pej [pretence, affectation] pose f. ◇ vt -1. [problem, danger, threat] constituir -2. [question] fazer. ◇ vi -1. [model] posar -2. pej [behave affectedly] fazer-se -3. [pretend to be]: to ~ as sb/sthg fazer-se passar por alguém/algo.

posh [pɒʃ] adj inf -1. [hotel, clothes] chique -2. [upper-class] chique.

position [pə'zɪʃn] ◇ n -1. [gen] posição f -2. [job] cargo m -3. [state, situation] posição f, situação f -4. [stance, opinion]: ~ on sthg posição sobre algo. ◇ vt posicionar.

positive ['pɒzətɪv] adj -1. [gen] positivo(va); to be ~ about sthg ser positivo(va) sobre algo; be ~ about the exam! seja otimista em relação à prova! -2. [irrefutable] irrefutável -3. [for emphasis]: a ~ joy uma ótima brincadeira; a ~ nightmare um pesadelo terrível.

posse ['pɒsɪ] n -1. [of sheriff] US destacamento m -2. inf [gang] bando m armado.

possess [pə'zes] vt -1. [gen] possuir -2. [subj: emotion] levar a.

possession [pə'zeʃn] n (U) posse f.

➡ **possessions** npl posses fpl, bens mpl.

possessive [pə'zesɪv] ◇ adj -1. pej [clinging] possessivo(va). -2. GRAMM possessivo(va). ◇ n GRAMM possessivo m.

possibility [ˌpɒsə'bɪlətɪ] (pl -ies) n possibilidade f.

possible ['pɒsəbl] ◇ adj possível; as soon as ~ o mais cedo possível; as much as ~ o máximo possível. ◇ n possível m.

possibly ['pɒsəblɪ] adv -1. [perhaps, maybe] possivelmente -2. [conceivably]: I'll do all I ~ can vou fazer tudo que estiver ao meu alcance; how could he ~ do that? como ele foi capaz de fazer isso?; I can't ~ take the money! simplesmente não posso aceitar o dinheiro!

post [pəʊst] n -1. [mail service]: the ~ o correio; by ~ pelo correio -2. (U) [letters etc.] correio m -3. [delivery] mala f -postal -4. UK [collection] coleta f -5. [pole] poste m -6. [position, job] posto m -7. MIL guarnição f. ◇ vt -1. [by mail] postar, pôr no correio -2. [transfer] transferir.

post [pəʊst] vt COMPUT [message, query] enviar.

postage ['pəʊstɪdʒ] n (U) franquia f; ~ and packing despesas fpl de envio.

postal ['pəʊstl] adj postal.

postal order n vale m postal.

postbox ['pəʊstbɒks] n UK caixa f de correio.

postcard ['pəʊstkɑːd] n cartão-postal m.

postcode ['pəʊstkəʊd] n UK código m (de endereçamento) postal.

post-date vt pós-datar.

poster ['pəʊstə^r] n cartaz m, pôster m.

poste restante [ˌpəʊst'restɑːnt] n (U) esp UK posta-restante f.

posterior [pɒ'stɪərɪə^r] ◇ adj posterior. ◇ n hum traseiro m.

postgraduate [ˌpəʊst'grædʒʊət] ◇ adj pós-graduado(da). ◇ n pós-graduado m, -da f.

posthumous ['pɒstjʊməs] adj póstumo(ma).

postman ['pəʊstmən] (pl -men [-mən]) n carteiro m.

postmark ['pəʊstmɑːk] ◇ n carimbo m (postal). ◇ vt carimbar.

postmaster ['pəʊstˌmɑːstə^r] n agente m de correio.

postmortem [ˌpəʊst'mɔːtəm] n -1. [autopsy] autópsia f -2. fig [analysis] análise f detalhada.

post office n -1. [organization]: **the Post Office** a Agência dos Correios -2. [building] correio m.

post office box n caixa f postal.

postpone [pəs'pəʊn] vt adiar.

postscript ['pəʊstskrɪpt] n -1. [to letter] pós-escrito m -2. fig [additional information] adendo m.

posture ['pɒstʃə'] n postura f.

postwar [ˌpəʊst'wɔː'] adj pós-guerra.

posy ['pəʊzɪ] (pl -ies) n ramalhete m.

pot [pɒt] (pt & pp -ted, cont -ting) <> n -1. [for cooking] panela f; **to go to ~** ir para o brejo; **the ~ calling the kettle black** rir-se o roto do esfarrapado -2. [for tea, coffee] bule m -3. [for paint, jam] frasco m -4. [flowerpot] vaso m -5. (U) drugs sl [cannabis] maconha f. <> vt -1. [plant] plantar (em vaso) -2. [billiards ball] encaçapar.

potassium [pə'tæsiəm] n (U) potássio m.

potato [pə'teɪtəʊ] (pl -es) n batata f.

potato peeler [-ˌpiːlə'] n descascador m de batatas.

potent ['pəʊtənt] adj -1. [argument] forte -2. [drink, drug] de alto teor, poderoso(sa) -3. [virile] potente, viril.

potential [pə'tenʃl] <> adj potencial, em potencial. <> n [of person] potencial m; **to have ~** ter potencial.

potentially [pə'tenʃəlɪ] adv potencialmente.

pothole ['pɒthəʊl] n buraco m.

potholing ['pɒtˌhəʊlɪŋ] n UK espeleologia; **to go ~** explorar cavernas.

potion ['pəʊʃn] n poção f.

potluck [ˌpɒt'lʌk] n: **to take ~** [at meal] contentar-se com o que houver para comer; [in choice] arriscar OR tentar a sorte.

potshot ['pɒtˌʃɒt] n: **to take a ~ (at sthg)** atirar a esmo (em algo).

potted ['pɒtɪd] adj -1. [grown in pot] de vaso -2. [preserved] em conserva.

potter ['pɒtə'] n oleiro m, -ra f.

  ◆ **potter about, potter around** vi UK ocupar-se em trabalhos pequenos.

pottery ['pɒtərɪ] (pl -ies) n -1. [gen] cerâmica f -2. [factory] olaria f.

potty ['pɒtɪ] (compar -ier, superl -iest, pl -ies) UK inf <> adj doido(da); **to be ~ about sb/sthg** ser doido(da) por alguém/algo. <> n [for children] penico m.

pouch [paʊtʃ] n bolsa f.

poultry ['pəʊltrɪ] <> n (U) [meat] carne f de aves (domésticas). <> npl [birds] aves fpl domésticas.

pounce [paʊns] vi -1. [subj: animal, bird]: **to ~ (on OR upon sthg)** agarrar (algo) -2. [subj: person, police]: **to ~ (on OR upon sb)** lançar-se (sobre alguém).

pound [paʊnd] <> n -1. UK [unit of money] libra f -2. UK [currency system]: **the ~** a libra -3. [unit of weight] libra f -4. [for dogs] canil -5. [for cars] depósito m (para automóveis apreendidos). <> vt -1. [strike loudly] esmurrar -2. [pulverize] pulverizar. <> vi -1. [strike loudly]: **to ~ on sthg** esmurrar algo -2. [beat, throb - heart] palpitar; [- head] latejar.

pound coin n moeda f de libra.

pound sterling n libra f esterlina.

pour [pɔː'] <> vt [cause to flow] despejar; **to ~ sthg into sthg** despejar algo em algo; **to ~ sb a drink, to ~ a drink for sb** servir um drinque a alguém. <> vi -1. [flow quickly] fluir, correr -2. fig [rush] correr. <> v impers [rain hard] chover a cântaros.

  ◆ **pour in** vi vir em enxurrada.

  ◆ **pour out** vt sep -1. [empty] esvaziar -2. [serve] servir.

pouring ['pɔːrɪŋ] adj [rain] torrencial.

pout [paʊt] vi fazer beiço.

poverty ['pɒvətɪ] n (U) -1. [hardship] miséria f.

poverty-stricken adj carente, necessitado(da).

powder ['paʊdə'] <> n [tiny particles] pó m; **face ~** pó-de-arroz m; **gun ~** pólvora f; **washing ~** detergente m. <> vt [make-up] maquiar.

powder compact n estojo m (de pó-de-arroz).

powdered ['paʊdəd] adj [in powder form] em pó.

powder puff n esponja f de pó-de-arroz.

powder room n toalete m.

power ['paʊə'] <> n -1. (U) [control, influence] poder m; **to be in ~** estar no poder; **to come to ~** chegar ao poder; **to take ~** assumir o poder -2. [ability, capacity] força f; **mental ~s** poderes mpl mentais; **to be (with)in one's ~ to do sthg** competir a alguém fazer algo -3. [legal authority] autoridade f; **to have the ~ to do sthg** ter autoridade para fazer algo -4. [strength] força f -5. (U) TECH energia f -6. (U) [electricity] luz f. <> vt alimentar.

powerboat ['paʊəbəʊt] n powerboat m, pequeno barco de corrida muito veloz.

power cut n corte m de energia.

power failure n falha f no sistema elétrico.

powerful ['pauəfull] adj -1. [influential] poderoso(sa) -2. [strong] poderoso(sa), forte -3. [very convincing, very moving] vigoroso(sa).

powerless ['pauəlıs] adj fraco(ca); **to be ~ to do sthg** ser impotente para fazer algo.

power point n UK ponto m de força, tomada f.

power station n estação f de força.

power steering n (U) direção f hidráulica.

pp (abbr of per procurationem) p/.

p & p (abbr of postage and packing) n postagem f e empacotamento.

PR ◇ n -1. (abbr of public relations) RP mf -2. (abbr of proportional representation) representação f proporcional. ◇ abbr of Puerto Rico.

practicable ['præktıkəbl] adj praticável.

practical ['præktıkl] ◇ adj -1. [gen] prático(ca) -2. [practicable] praticável. ◇ n prática f.

practicality [,præktı'kælətı] n (U) praticabilidade f.

practical joke n peça f, trote m.

practically ['præktıklı] adv praticamente.

practice ['præktıs], **practise** US n -1. (U) [gen] prática f; **to be out of ~** estar destreinado(da); **the athlete is out of ~** estar fora de forma -2. (U) [implementation]: **to put sthg into ~** pôr algo em prática; **in ~** [in fact] na prática -3. [training session] sessão f de treino.

practicing adj US = practising.

practise, practice US ['præktıs] ◇ vt praticar. ◇ vi -1. [train] treinar -2. [professional] exercer.

practising, practicing US ['præktısıŋ] adj -1. [doctor, lawyer] que exerce -2. [Christian, Catholic] praticante -3. [homosexual] assumido(da).

practitioner [præk'tıʃnər] n MED: **a medical ~** um profissional da área médica.

Prague [prɑːg] n Praga.

prairie ['preərı] n pradaria f.

praise [preız] ◇ n -1. (U) [commendation] elogio m -2. RELIG louvor m; **~ be to God!** louvado seja Deus! ◇ vt -1. [commend] elogiar -2. RELIG louvar.

praiseworthy ['preız,wɜːðı] adj louvável.

pram [præm] n UK carrinho m de bebê.

prance [prɑːns] vi empinar-se.

prank [præŋk] n peça f.

prawn [prɔːn] n pitu m.

pray [preı] vi RELIG rezar; **to ~ to sb** rezar para alguém; **to ~ for sthg** rezar por algo.

prayer [preər] n -1. (U) [act of praying] prece f -2. [set of words] oração f -3. fig [strong hope] pedido m.

prayer book n missal m.

preach [priːtʃ] ◇ vt pregar. ◇ vi -1. RELIG pregar; **to ~ to sb** fazer sermões a alguém -2. pej [pontificate] dar sermões em; **to ~ at sb** dar sermões em alguém.

preacher ['priːtʃər] n pregador m, -ra f.

precarious [prı'keərıəs] adj precário(ria).

precaution [prı'kɔːʃn] n precaução f.

precede [prı'siːd] vt -1. [gen] preceder -2. [walk in front of] adiantar-se.

precedence ['presıdəns] n: **to take ~ over sthg** ter prioridade sobre algo; **to take ~ over sb** ter precedência sobre alguém.

precedent ['presıdənt] n precedente m.

precinct ['priːsıŋkt] n -1. UK [shopping area] zona f comercial -2. US [district] distrito m.

  ⇒ precincts npl [around building] arredores mpl.

precious ['preʃəs] adj -1. [friendship, moment, time] precioso(sa), querido(da) -2. [jewel, object, material] precioso(sa) -3. inf iro [damned] maldito(ta) -4. [affected] afetado(da).

precipice ['presıpıs] n precipício m.

precipitate [adj prı'sıpıtət, vb prı'sıpıteıt] fml ◇ adj precipitado(da). ◇ vt precipitar.

precise [prı'saıs] adj preciso(sa), exato(ta).

precisely [prı'saıslı] adv exatamente; **to describe/explain sthg ~** descrever/explicar algo com precisão.

precision [prı'sıʒn] n (U) precisão f.

preclude [prı'kluːd] vt fml impedir, evitar; **to ~ sb/sthg from doing sthg** impedir alguém/algo de fazer algo.

precocious [prı'kəuʃəs] adj precoce.

preconceived [,priːkən'siːvd] adj preconcebido(da).

precondition [,priːkən'dıʃn] n fml precondição f, condição f prévia.

predator ['predətər] n -1. [animal, bird] predador m, -ra f -2. fig [exploitative person] explorador m, -ra f.

predecessor ['priːdısesər] n -1. [person] predecessor m, -ra f, antecessor m, -ra f -2. [thing] antecessor m, -ra f.

predicament [prı'dıkəmənt] n aperto m; **to be in a ~** estar num aperto.

predict [prı'dıkt] vt prever.

predictable [prı'dıktəbl] adj previsível.

prediction [prɪ'dɪkʃn] n -1. [something foretold] previsão f, prognóstico m -2. (U) [foretelling] previsão f.

predispose [ˌpriːdɪs'pəʊz] vt: **to be ~d to sthg/to do sthg** estar predisposto(ta) a algo/a fazer algo.

predominant [prɪ'dɒmɪnənt] adj predominante.

predominantly [prɪ'dɒmɪnəntlɪ] adv predominantemente.

pre-empt [-'empt] vt antecipar-se a.

pre-emptive [-'emptɪv] adj preventivo(va).

preen [priːn] vt -1. [subj: bird] alisar com o bico -2. fig [subj: person]: **to ~ o.s.** arrumar-se, ajeitar-se.

prefab ['priːfæb] n inf casa f pré-fabricada.

preface ['prefɪs] n [in book] prefácio m; **~ to sthg** [to text] prefácio a algo; [to speech] preâmbulo m.

prefect ['priːfekt] n UK monitor m, -ra f, prefeito m, -ta f (em escola).

prefer [prɪ'fɜːʳ] (pt & pp -red, cont -ring) vt preferir; **to ~ sthg to sthg** preferir algo a algo; **to ~ to do sthg** preferir fazer algo.

preferable ['prefrəbl] adj: **to be ~ (to sthg)** ser preferível(a algo).

preferably ['prefrəblɪ] adv preferivelmente.

preference ['prefərəns] n: **~ (for sthg)** preferência f (por algo); **to give sb/sthg ~, to give ~ to sb/sthg** dar preferência a alguém/algo.

preferential [ˌprefə'renʃl] adj preferencial.

prefix ['priːfɪks] n GRAMM prefixo m.

pregnancy ['pregnənsɪ] (pl -ies) n gravidez f.

pregnant ['pregnənt] adj [carrying unborn baby - human] grávido(da); [- animal] prenho(ha).

prehistoric [ˌpriːhɪ'stɒrɪk] adj pré-histórico(ca).

prejudice ['predʒʊdɪs] <> n -1. [bias] preconceito m; **~ in favour of sb/sthg** tendência f de favorecer alguém/algo; **~ against sb/sthg** preconceito contra alguém/algo -2. [harm] prejuízo m. <> vt -1. [bias] ter preconceito em relação a; **to ~ sb in favour of/against sthg** predispor alguém a favor de/contra algo -2. [jeopardize] prejudicar.

prejudiced ['predʒʊdɪst] adj preconceituoso(sa), parcial; **to be ~ in favour of sb/sthg** favorecer alguém/algo; **to be ~ against sb/sthg** ser preconceituoso(-sa) em relação a alguém/algo.

prejudicial [ˌpredʒʊ'dɪʃl] adj prejudicial;

to be ~ to sb/sthg ser prejudicial para alguém/algo.

preliminary [prɪ'lɪmɪnərɪ] (pl -ies) adj preliminar.

prelude ['preljuːd] n: **~ to sthg** prelúdio m de algo.

premarital [ˌpriː'mærɪtl] adj pré-marital, antes do casamento.

premature ['premə,tjʊəʳ] adj prematuro(ra).

premeditated [ˌpriː'medɪteɪtɪd] adj premeditado(da).

premenstrual syndrome, premenstrual tension [priː'menstrʊəl-] n síndrome f pré-menstrual.

premier ['premjəʳ] <> adj principal, primeiro(ra). <> n [prime minister] primeiro-ministro m, primeira-ministra f.

premiere ['premɪeəʳ] n estréia f.

premise ['premɪs] n premissa f; **on the ~** that com a premissa de que.

➡ **premises** npl [site] local m; **on the ~s** no local.

premium ['priːmjəm] n [gen] prêmio m; **at a ~** [above usual value] a um valor superior ao nominal; [in great demand] muito disputado(da).

premium bond n UK obrigação emitida pelo governo que dá direito a prêmios mensais em dinheiro mediante sorteio.

premonition [ˌpremə'nɪʃn] n premonição f.

preoccupied [priː'ɒkjʊpaɪd] adj preocupado(da); **to be ~ with sthg** estar preocupado(da) com algo.

prep [prep] n UK inf [homework]: **to do one's ~** fazer o dever de casa.

prepaid ['priːpeɪd] adj com porte pago.

prepaid card n cartão m pré-pago.

preparation [ˌprepə'reɪʃn] n -1. [act of preparing] preparação f -2. [prepared mixture] preparado m.

➡ **preparations** npl [plans] preparativos mpl; **to make ~s for sthg** fazer preparativos para algo.

preparatory [prɪ'pærətrɪ] adj preparatório(ria).

preparatory school n -1. [in UK] colégio pago para crianças de 7 a 13 anos -2. [in US] escola particular que prepara alunos para entrar na universidade.

prepare [prɪ'peəʳ] <> vt preparar; **to ~ to do sthg** preparar-se para fazer algo. <> vi: **to ~ for sthg** preparar-se para algo.

prepared [prɪ'peəd] adj [organized, done beforehand] preparado(da); **to be ~** OR

for sthg OR **to do sthg** estar preparado(-da) para algo/para fazer algo.

preposition [ˌprepəˈzɪʃn] *n* preposição *f.*

preposterous [prɪˈpɒstərəs] *adj* absurdo(da).

prep school (*abbr of* **preparatory school**) *n* escola particular primária para crianças de 7 a 12 anos na Grã-Bretanha.

prerequisite [ˌpriːˈrekwɪzɪt] *n* pré-requisito *m*; ~ **of** OR **for sthg** pré-requisito para algo.

prerogative [prɪˈrɒgətɪv] *n* prerrogativa *f.*

Presbyterian [ˌprezbɪˈtɪərɪən] ◇ *adj* presbiteriano(na). ◇ *n* presbiteriano *m*, -na *f.*

pre-school ◇ *adj* pré-escolar. ◇ *n* US pré-escola *f.*

prescribe [prɪˈskraɪb] *vt* -1. MED prescrever -2. [order] ordenar, mandar.

prescription [prɪˈskrɪpʃn] *n* [after - written form] receita *f* (médica); [- medicine] prescrição *f.*

prescriptive [prɪˈskrɪptɪv] *adj* GRAMM prescritivo(va).

presence [ˈprezns] *n* presença *f*; **in the** ~ **of sb** na presença de alguém.

presence of mind *n* presença *f* de espírito.

present [*adj* & *n* ˈpreznt, *vb* prɪˈzent] ◇ *adj* -1. [gen] presente, atual -2. [in attendance] presente; **to be** ~ **at sthg** estar presente em algo. ◇ *n* -1.: **the** ~ o presente; **at** ~ atualmente -2. GRAMM: ~ (**tense**) presente *m.* ◇ *vt* -1. [gen] apresentar; **to** ~ **sb to sb** apresentar alguém para alguém -2. [give] presentear; **to** ~ **sb with sthg, to** ~ **sthg to sb** presentear alguém com algo -3. [provide, pose] deparar-se com; **to** ~ **sb with sthg, to** ~ **sthg to sb** representar algo para alguém -4. [arrive, go]: **to** ~ **o.s.** apresentar-se.

presentable [prɪˈzentəbl] *adj* apresentável.

presentation [ˌpreznˈteɪʃn] *n* -1. [gen] apresentação *f* -2. [ceremony] cerimônia *f* -3. [performance] representação *f.*

present day *n*: **the** ~ o momento atual.

◆ **present-day** *adj* atual, de hoje em dia.

presenter [prɪˈzentər] *n* UK apresentador *m*, -ra *f.*

presently [ˈprezntlɪ] *adv* -1. [soon] em breve, daqui a pouco -2. [now] atualmente.

preservation [ˌprezəˈveɪʃn] *n* (U) -1.

[gen] preservação *f* -2. [of food] conservação *f.*

preservative [prɪˈzɜːvətɪv] *n* -1. [for food] conservante *m* -2. [for wood] revestimento *m.*

preserve [prɪˈzɜːv] ◇ *n* [jam] compota *f*, conserva *f.* ◇ *vt* -1. [gen] preservar -2. [food] conservar.

preset [ˌpriːˈset] (*pt* & *pp* **preset**, *cont* -**ting**) *vt* programar.

president [ˈprezɪdənt] *n* presidente *mf.*

President-elect *n* presidente *mf* eleito, -ta.

presidential [ˌprezɪˈdenʃl] *adj* presidencial.

press [pres] ◇ *n* -1. [push] pressionamento *m* -2. [journalism]: **the** ~ a imprensa; **to get a bad** ~ ser criticado(da) na/pela imprensa. -3. [printing machine] imprensa *f* -4. [pressing machine] prensa *f.* ◇ *vt* -1. [push firmly - switch] ligar; [- accelerator] pisar em; **to** ~ **sthg against sthg** prensar algo contra algo -2. [squeeze] espremer -3. [iron] passar -4. [press person, button] pressionar; **he didn't need much** ~ **and readily agreed** ele não precisava de muita pressão e concordou prontamente; **to** ~ **sb to do sthg** OR **into doing sthg** pressionar alguém a fazer algo -5. [pursue] insistir em. ◇ *vi* -1. [push hard]: **to** ~ **(on sthg)** apertar (algo) com força -2. [surge] comprimir-se; **to** ~ **forwards** empurrar para frente.

◆ **press on** *vi* [continue] continuar; **to** ~ **on with sthg** continuar com algo.

press agency *n* assessoria *f* de imprensa.

press conference *n* entrevista *f* coletiva.

pressed [prest] *adj*: **to be** ~ **(for time/money)** estar meio apertado(da) (de tempo/dinheiro).

pressing [ˈpresɪŋ] *adj* urgente, premente.

press officer *n* acessor *m*, -ra *f* de imprensa.

press release *n* press-release *m*, comunicado *m* de imprensa.

press-stud *n* UK botão *m* de pressão.

press-up *n* UK flexão *f*, apoio *m* (*como exercício*).

pressure [ˈpreʃər] *n* pressão *f*; **to put** ~ **on sb (to do sthg)** pressionar alguém (a fazer algo OR para que faça algo), exercer pressão sobre alguém (para fazer algo).

pressure cooker *n* panela *f* de pressão.

pressure gauge *n* manômetro *m.*

pressure group n grupo m de pressão.

pressurize, -ise [ˈpreʃəraɪz] vt -**1.** TECH pressurizar -**2.** UK [force]: to ~ sb to do OR into doing sthg pressionar alguém a fazer algo.

prestige [preˈstiːʒ] n (U) prestígio m.

presumably [prɪˈzjuːməblɪ] adv presumivelmente; ~ you've read the book suponho que você já tenha lido o livro.

presume [prɪˈzjuːm] vt presumir, supor; to be ~d dead/innocent ser julgado(da) morto/inocente; to ~ (that) supor OR imaginar que.

presumption [prɪˈzʌmpʃn] n -**1.** [assumption] pressuposição f, suposição f -**2.** (U) [audacity] presunção f.

presumptuous [prɪˈzʌmptʃʊəs] adj presunçoso(sa).

pretence, pretense US [prɪˈtens] n fingimento m; under false ~s com falsos pretextos.

pretend [prɪˈtend] <> vt -**1.** [make believe]: to ~ to be/to do sthg fingir ser/fazer algo; to ~ (that) fingir (que), fazer de conta (que) -**2.** [claim]: to ~ to do sthg fingir fazer algo. <> vi fingir.

pretense n US = pretence.

pretension [prɪˈtenʃn] n pretensão f.

pretentious [prɪˈtenʃəs] adj pretencioso(sa).

pretext [ˈpriːtekst] n pretexto m; on OR under the ~ that com o pretexto de que; on OR under the ~ of doing sthg com o pretexto de estar fazendo algo.

pretty [ˈprɪtɪ] (compar -ier, superl -iest) <> adj bonito(ta). <> adv [quite, rather] bastante; ~ much OR well mais ou menos.

prevail [prɪˈveɪl] vi -**1.** [be widespread] prevalecer, predominar -**2.** [triumph] prevalecer; to ~ over sb/sthg prevalecer sobre alguém/algo -**3.** [persuade]: to ~ (up)on sb to do sthg persuadir alguém a fazer algo OR para que faça algo.

prevailing [prɪˈveɪlɪŋ] adj predominante.

prevalent [ˈprevələnt] adj predominante, prevalecente.

prevent [prɪˈvent] vt evitar, impedir; to ~ sb (from) doing sthg impedir alguém de fazer algo; to ~ sthg (from) doing sthg evitar que algo faça algo; they tried to ~ any pain to the animal eles tentaram não causar nenhuma dor ao animal.

preventive [prɪˈventɪv] adj preventivo(va).

preview [ˈpriːvjuː] n -**1.** [early showing]

pré-estréia f -**2.** [trailer] trailer m -**3.** COMPUT pré-visualização f.

previous [ˈpriːvjəs] adj -**1.** [earlier, prior] anterior, prévio(via); ~ convictions antecedentes mpl criminais; it was the ~ President who did it foi o ex-presidente que fez isso -**2.** [days and dates] anterior.

previously [ˈpriːvjəslɪ] adv -**1.** [formerly] anteriormente, antes -**2.** [with days and dates] antes.

prewar [ˌpriːˈwɔː] adj anterior à guerra.

prey [preɪ] n (U) presa f, vítima f.

➡ **prey on** vt fus -**1.** [live off] caçar, alimentar-se de -**2.** [trouble]: to ~ on sb's mind atormentar alguém.

price [praɪs] <> n preço m. <> vt pôr preço em; it was ~d highly seu preço era muito elevado.

priceless [ˈpraɪslɪs] adj -**1.** [very valuable] inestimável, que não tem preço -**2.** inf [funny] impagável.

price list n lista f de preços.

price tag n -**1.** [label] etiqueta f de preço -**2.** [sacrifice] fig preço m.

pricey [ˈpraɪsɪ] (compar -ier, superl -iest) adj inf caro(ra).

prick [prɪk] <> n -**1.** [scratch, wound] picada f -**2.** vulg [penis] cacete m, caralho m -**3.** vulg [stupid person] pau-no-cu m. <> vt -**1.** [jab, pierce] espetar -**2.** [sting] arder.

➡ **prick up** vt fus: to ~ up one's ears [subj: animal] levantar as orelhas; [subj: person] aguçar os ouvidos.

prickle [ˈprɪkl] <> n -**1.** [thorn] espinho m -**2.** [sensation] formigamento m, comichão f. <> vi formigar, comichar.

prickly [ˈprɪklɪ] (compar -ier, superl -iest) adj -**1.** [thorny] espinhoso(sa), espinhento(ta) -**2.** fig [touchy] suscetível.

prickly heat n (U) brotoeja f.

pride [praɪd] <> n orgulho m; to take ~ in sthg/in doing sthg sentir-se orgulhoso(sa) em algo/ao fazer algo. <> vt: to ~ o.s. on sthg orgulhar-se de algo.

priest [priːst] n -**1.** [Christian] padre m, sacerdote m -**2.** [non-Christian] homem m religioso.

priestess [ˈpriːstɪs] n sacerdotisa f.

priesthood [ˈpriːsthʊd] n (U) -**1.** [position, office]: the ~ o sacerdócio -**2.** [priests collectively]: the ~ o clero.

prig [prɪg] n moralista mf, puritano m, -na f.

prim [prɪm] (compar -mer, superl -mest) adj afetado(da), empertigado(da).

primarily [ˈpraɪmərɪlɪ] adv primeiramente, principalmente.

primary ['praɪmərɪ] (pl -ies) ◇ adj primário(ria). ◇ n US POL prévias fpl.

primary school n escola f primária.

primary teacher n [in UK] professor m primário, professora f primária.

primate ['praɪmeɪt] n -1. ZOOL primata m -2. RELIG primaz m.

prime [praɪm] ◇ adj -1. [main] primeiro(ra) principal -2. [excellent] excelente, de primeira. ◇ n [peak] auge m, plenitude f; in one's ~ na flor da idade. ◇ vt -1. [inform]: to ~ sb about sthg instruir alguém sobre algo -2. [paint] imprimar, preparar para pintura -3. [make ready - gun] carregar; [- machine] aprontar; [- pump] escorvar.

prime minister n primeiro-ministro m, primeira-ministra f.

primer ['praɪmə'] n -1. [paint] imprimadura f -2. [textbook] manual m.

primeval [praɪ'miːvl] adj primitivo(va).

primitive ['prɪmɪtɪv] adj -1. [not civilized, of an early type] primitivo(va) -2. [simple, basic] rudimentar.

primrose ['prɪmrəʊz] n prímula f.

Primus stove® ['praɪməs-] n fogareiro m.

prince [prɪns] n príncipe m.

princess [prɪn'ses] n princesa f.

principal ['prɪnsəpl] ◇ adj principal. ◇ n -1. [of school] diretor m, -ra f -2. [of college] reitor m, -ra f.

principle ['prɪnsəpl] n -1. princípio m -2. (U) [integrity] princípios mpl; he lacks ~ ele não tem princípios; (to do sthg) on ~ OR as a matter of ~ fazer algo por (uma questão de) princípios.
◆ in principle adv em princípio.

print [prɪnt] ◇ n -1. (U) [type] caracteres mpl (de imprensa); the book is still in ~ o livro ainda está disponível (não esgotado); he saw his name in ~ ele viu seu nome impresso; to be out of ~ estar esgotado(da) -2. ART gravura f -3. [photograph] cópia f -4. [fabric] estampado m -5. [footprint] pegada f; [fingerprint] impressão f digital. ◇ vt -1. [produce by printing] imprimir -2. [publish] publicar -3. [on fabric] estampar -4. [write clearly] escrever em letra de forma ◇ vi [printer] imprimir.
◆ print out vt sep COMPUT imprimir.

printed matter ['prɪntɪd-] n (U) impresso m.

printer ['prɪntə'] n -1. [person, firm] impressor m, -ra f -2. COMPUT impressora f.

printing ['prɪntɪŋ] n impressão f.

printout ['prɪntaʊt] n saída f de impressora, impressão f.

prior ['praɪə'] ◇ adj -1. [previous] prévio(via), anterior -2. [more important] mais importante. ◇ n [monk] prior m.
◆ prior to prep antes de; ~ to doing sthg antes de fazer algo.

prioress ['praɪəres] n prioresa f.

priority [praɪ'ɒrətɪ] (pl -ies) n prioridade f; to have OR take ~ (over sthg) ter prioridade (sobre algo).

prise [praɪz] vt: to ~ sthg open abrir algo com força; to ~ sthg away separar algo usando força.

prison ['prɪzn] n prisão f.

prisoner ['prɪznə'] n prisioneiro m, -ra f.

prisoner of war (pl prisoners of war) n prisioneiro m, -ra f de guerra.

privacy [UK 'prɪvəsɪ, US 'praɪvəsɪ] n privacidade f.

private ['praɪvɪt] ◇ adj -1. [confidential, not for the public] privado(da) -2. [not state-controlled] privado (da), particular -3. [personal] privado(da), pessoal -4. [secluded] afastado(da), retirado(da) -5. [reserved] reservado(da). ◇ n -1. [soldier] soldado m raso -2. [secrecy]: (to do sthg) in ~ fazer algo em particular.

private enterprise n (U) empresa f privada.

private eye n detetive mf particular.

private limited company n COMM companhia f privada limitada.

privately ['praɪvɪtlɪ] adv -1. [not by the state] de forma privada; ~ owned de propriedade privada; ~ educated educado(da) em escola particular -2. [confidentially] privadamente, em particular -3. [personally] no fundo.

private property n propriedade f privada.

private school n escola f particular.

privatize, -ise ['praɪvɪtaɪz] vt privatizar.

privet ['prɪvɪt] n (U) alfena f.

privilege ['prɪvɪlɪdʒ] n -1. [special advantage] privilégio m -2. [honour] privilégio m, honra f.

privy ['prɪvɪ] adj: to be ~ to sthg fml inteirar-se de algo.

Privy Council n UK: the ~ conselho privado que aconselha o monarca em questões políticas.

prize [praɪz] ◇ adj -1. [prizewinning] premiado(da) -2. [perfect] perfeito(ta) -3. [valued] de estimação. ◇ n prêmio m. ◇ vt apreciar, valorizar.

prize-giving [-,gɪvɪŋ] n UK entrega f de prêmios.

prizewinner ['praɪz,wɪnə'] n premiado m, -da f.

pro [prəʊl] (pl **-s**) n **-1.** inf [professional] profissional mf **-2.** [advantage]: **the ~ s and cons** os prós e os contras.

probability [ˌprɒbəˈbɪlətɪ] (pl **-ies**) n probabilidade f.

probable [ˈprɒbəbl] adj provável.

probably [ˈprɒbəblɪ] adv provavelmente.

probation [prəˈbeɪʃn] n (U) **-1.** [of prisoner] liberdade f condicional; **to put sb on ~** colocar alguém em liberdade condicional **-2.** [trial period] período m de experiência; **to be on ~** estar em período de experiência.

probe [prəʊb] <> n **-1.** [investigation] sindicância f, investigação f; **~ into** sthg sindicância sobre algo **-2.** MED, TECH sonda f. <> vt **-1.** [investigate] investigar **-2.** [prod] explorar.

problem [ˈprɒbləm] <> n problema f; **no ~!** inf sem problema! <> comp problemático(ca).

problem page n página f com perguntas dos leitores (em revistas, jornais).

procedure [prəˈsiːdʒəʳ] n procedimento m.

proceed [vb prəˈsiːd, npl ˈprəʊsiːdz] <> vt [do subsequently]: **to ~ to do sthg** passar a fazer algo. <> vi **-1.** [continue] prosseguir, continuar; **to ~ with sthg** prosseguir com algo **-2.** fml [go, advance] dirigir-se para.
 ➤ **proceeds** npl proventos mpl.

proceedings [prəˈsiːdɪŋz] npl **-1.** [series of events] ação f **-2.** [legal action] processo m.

process [ˈprəʊses] <> n processo m; **in the ~** no decorrer; **to be in the ~ of doing sthg** estar em vias de fazer algo. <> vt processar.

processing [ˈprəʊsesɪŋ] n processamento m.

procession [prəˈseʃn] n **-1.** [ceremony] cortejo m **-2.** [demonstration] passeata f **-3.** [continuous line] procissão f.

proclaim [prəˈkleɪm] vt **-1.** [declare] proclamar, declarar **-2.** [law] promulgar.

procrastinate [prəˈkræstɪneɪt] vi procrastinar, protelar.

procure [prəˈkjʊəʳ] vt conseguir, obter.

prod [prɒd] (pt & pp **-ded**, cont **-ding**) vt [push, poke] cutucar, empurrar.

prodigal [ˈprɒdɪgl] adj pródigo(ga).

prodigy [ˈprɒdɪdʒɪ] (pl **-ies**) n prodígio m.

produce [n ˈprɒdjuːs, vb prəˈdjuːs] <> n **-1.** [goods] produtos mpl **-2.** [fruit and vegetables] produtos mpl agrícolas. <> vt **-1.** [gen] produzir **-2.** BIOL gerar **-3.** [yield -

raw materials, crop] produzir; [- interest, profit] gerar **-4.** [present, show] apresentar.

producer [prəˈdjuːsəʳ] n **-1.** [gen] produtor m, -ra f **-2.** [theatre] diretor m, -ra f.

product [ˈprɒdʌkt] n [thing manufactured or grown] produto m.

production [prəˈdʌkʃn] n produção f.

production line n linha f de produção.

productive [prəˈdʌktɪv] adj produtivo(va).

productivity [ˌprɒdʌkˈtɪvətɪ] n (U) produtividade f.

profane [prəˈfeɪn] adj obsceno(na).

profession [prəˈfeʃn] n **-1.** [career] profissão f; **by ~** por profissão **-2.** [body of people] categoria f (profissional).

professional [prəˈfeʃənl] <> adj profissional. <> n profissional mf.

professor [prəˈfesəʳ] n **-1.** UK [head of department] chefe mf de departamento **-2.** US & Can [teacher, lecturer] professor m (universitário), professora f (universitária).

proficiency [prəˈfɪʃnsɪ] n (U) proficiência f; **~ in sthg** proficiência em algo.

profile [ˈprəʊfaɪl] n perfil m.

profit [ˈprɒfɪt] <> n **-1.** [financial gain] lucro m; **to make a ~** ter lucro **-2.** (U) [advantage] proveito m, benefício m. <> vi: **to ~ (from** OR **by sthg)** tirar proveito (de algo).

profitability [ˌprɒfɪtəˈbɪlətɪ] n (U) lucratividade f, rentabilidade f.

profitable [ˈprɒfɪtəbl] adj **-1.** [making a profit] lucrativo(va), rentável **-2.** [beneficial] proveitoso(sa).

profiteering [ˌprɒfɪˈtɪərɪŋ] n (U) especulação f.

profound [prəˈfaʊnd] adj profundo(da).

profusely [prəˈfjuːslɪ] adv **-1.** [abundantly] abundantemente **-2.** [generously, extravagantly] profusamente.

profusion [prəˈfjuːʒn] n profusão f.

progeny [ˈprɒdʒənɪ] (pl **-ies**) n fml progênie f.

prognosis [prɒgˈnəʊsɪs] (pl **-noses** [-ˈnəʊsiːz]) n prognóstico m.

program [ˈprəʊgræm] (pt & pp **-med** OR **-ed**, cont **-ming** OR **-ing**) <> n **-1.** COMPUT programa m **-2.** US = **programme**. <> vt **-1.** COMPUT programar **-2.** US = **programme**.

programer n US = **programmer**.

programme UK, **program** US [ˈprəʊgræm] <> n programa m. <> vt programar; **to ~ sthg to do sthg** programar algo para fazer algo OR para que faça algo.

programmer *UK*, **programer** *US*
[ˈprəʊgræməʳ] *n COMPUT* programador
m, -ra *f*.

programming [ˈprəʊgræmɪŋ] *n COMPUT*
programação *f*.

progress [*n* ˈprəʊgres, *vb* prəˈgres] ◇ *n*
-1. [gen] progresso *m*;**to make ~** [im-
prove] fazer progresso; **to make ~ in
sthg** [get on] progredir em algo; **in ~**
em andamento -2. [physical movement]
avanço *m*. ◇ *vi* [gen] progredir.

progressive [prəˈgresɪv] *adj* -1. [forward-
looking] progressista -2. [gradual] pro-
gressivo(va).

prohibit [prəˈhɪbɪt] *vt* proibir; **to ~ sb
from doing sthg** proibir alguém de fazer
algo.

project [*n* ˈprɒdʒekt, *vb* prəˈdʒekt] ◇ *n*
-1. [plan, idea] projeto *m* -2. *SCH* projeto
m, estudo *m*;**~ on sthg** projeto estudo
sobre algo. ◇ *vt* -1. [gen] projetar -2.
[estimate] projetar, estimar -3. [present]
apresentar, dar uma imagem de. ◇
vi projetar.

projectile [prəˈdʒektaɪl] *n* projétil *m*.

projection [prəˈdʒekʃn] *n* -1. [gen] projeção *f* -2. [protrusion] saliência *f*.

projector [prəˈdʒektəʳ] *n* projetor *m*.

proletariat [ˌprəʊlɪˈteərɪət] *n* proletariado *m*.

prolific [prəˈlɪfɪk] *adj* prolífico(ca).

prologue, prolog *US* [ˈprəʊlɒg] *n* -1.
[introduction] prólogo *m* -2. *fig* [preceding
event]: **~ to sthg** preâmbulo *m* para
algo.

prolong [prəˈlɒŋ] *vt* prolongar.

prom [prɒm] *n* -1. *UK inf* (*abbr of* **promenade**) [at seaside] *caminho junto ao
mar* -2. *US* [ball] *baile de gala estudantil* -3. *UK inf* (*abbr of* **promenade
concert**): **the Proms** *concertos que
acontecem no Albert Hall, em
Londres, no verão.*

promenade [ˌprɒməˈnɑːd] *n UK* [at sea-
side] calçadão *m*.

promenade concert *n UK* concerto
sinfônico ao qual boa parte das
pessoas assiste de pé.

prominent [ˈprɒmɪnənt] *adj* -1. [impor-
tant - person, politician] destacado(da); [-
ideas, issues] proeminente -2. [noticeable
- building, landmark] em evidência; [-
cheekbones] saliente.

promiscuous [prɒˈmɪskjʊəs] *adj* pro-
míscuo(cua).

promise [ˈprɒmɪs] ◇ *n* promessa *f*.
◇ *vt* -1. [pledge]: **to ~ (sb) sthg**
prometer algo (a alguém); **to ~ (sb)
to do sthg** prometer (a alguém) fazer
algo -2. [indicate]: **to ~ sthg** prometer

algo; **it ~s to be a wonderful day**
promete ser um dia maravilhoso. ◇
vi prometer.

promising [ˈprɒmɪsɪŋ] *adj* promissor(-
ra).

promontory [ˈprɒməntrɪ] (*pl* **-ies**) *n*
promontório *m*.

promote [prəˈməʊt] *vt* -1. [foster] promover, fomentar -2. [push, advertise]
promover -3. [in job]: **to ~ sb (to sthg)**
promover alguém (a algo) -4. *SPORT*: **to
be ~ d to the First Division** subir para a
Primeira Divisão.

promoter [prəˈməʊtəʳ] *n* -1. [organizer]
patrocinador *m*, -ra *f* -2. [supporter]
defensor *m*, -ra *f*.

promotion [prəˈməʊʃn] *n* promoção
f.

prompt [prɒmpt] ◇ *adj* -1. [quick]
pronto(ta), rápido(da) -2. [punctual]
pontual. ◇ *adv* pontualmente. ◇ *n*
[*THEATRE* - line] deixa *f*; [- person] ponto *m*.
◇ *vt* -1. [provoke, persuade]: **to ~ sb (to
do sthg)** levar alguém (a fazer algo) -2.
THEATRE dar a deixa.

promptly [ˈprɒmptlɪ] *adv* -1. [quickly]
prontamente, rapidamente -2. [punc-
tually] pontualmente.

prone [prəʊn] *adj* -1. [susceptible]: **to be
~ to sthg/to do sthg** ser propenso(sa)
a algo/a fazer algo -2. [lying flat] (deita-
do(da)) de bruços.

prong [prɒŋ] *n* dente *m* (*de garfo*).

pronoun [ˈprəʊnaʊn] *n* pronome *m*.

pronounce [prəˈnaʊns] ◇ *vt* -1. [say
aloud] pronunciar -2. [declare, state] declarar. ◇ *vi*: **to ~ on sthg** pronunciar-se sobre algo.

pronounced [prəˈnaʊnst] *adj* pronun-
ciado(da), marcado(da).

pronouncement [prəˈnaʊnsmənt] *n*
pronunciamento *m*.

pronunciation [prəˌnʌnsɪˈeɪʃn] *n* pronúncia *f*.

proof [pruːf] *n* -1. [gen] prova *f* -2. [of
alcohol] teor *m* alcoólico.

prop [prɒp] (*pt* & *pp* **-ped**, *cont* **-ping**)
◇ *n* -1. [physical support] escora *f*,
estaca *f* -2. *fig* [supporting thing, person]
apoio *m* -3. *RUGBY* pilar *m*. ◇ *vt*: **to ~
sthg against sthg** apoiar algo em *OR*
contra algo.

➡ **props** *npl* [in film, play] acessórios
mpl.

➡ **prop up** *vt sep* -1. [support physically]
escorar, sustentar -2. *fig* [sustain]
apoiar.

propaganda [ˌprɒpəˈgændə] *n* (*U*) propaganda *f*.

propel [prəˈpel] (*pt* & *pp* **-led**, *cont* **-ling**) *vt* **-1.** [drive forward] impulsionar **-2.** *fig* [urge] impelir.

propeller [prə'pelə^r] *n* hélice *f*.

propelling pencil [prə'peliŋ-] *n* UK lapiseira *f*.

propensity [prə'pensətɪ] (*pl* -ies) *n* fml: ~ for OR to sthg propensão *f* a algo; ~ to do sthg propensão para fazer algo.

proper ['prɒpə^r] *adj* **-1.** [real] verdadeiro(ra) **-2.** [correct] correto(ta), exato(ta) **-3.** [decent] decente, apropriado(da).

properly ['prɒpəlɪ] *adv* **-1.** [satisfactorily] adequadamente, bem **-2.** [correctly] direito **-3.** [decently] adequadamente.

proper noun *n* nome *m* próprio.

property ['prɒpətɪ] (*pl* -ies) *n* **-1.** [gen] propriedade *f* **-2.** (U) [buildings] imóveis *mpl* **-3.** (U) [land] terrenos *mpl*.

property owner *n* proprietário *m*, -ria *f* de um imóvel.

prophecy ['prɒfɪsɪ] (*pl* -ies) *n* profecia *f*.

prophesy ['prɒfɪsaɪ] (*pt* & *pp* -ied) *vt* profetizar.

prophet ['prɒfɪt] *n* profeta *mf*.

proportion [prə'pɔ:ʃn] *n* **-1.** [part] parte *f* **-2.** [ratio, comparison] proporção *f* a **-3.** (U) ART: in ~ proporcional; out of ~ fora de proporção; a sense of ~ *fig* senso *m* de proporção.

proportional [prə'pɔ:ʃnl] *adj* proporcional, em proporção a; to be ~ to sthg ser proporcional a algo.

proportional representation *n* (U) representação *f* proporcional.

proportionate [prə'pɔ:ʃnət] *adj* proporcional; ~ to sthg proporcional a algo.

proposal [prə'pəʊzl] *n* proposta *f*; marriage ~ proposta *f* (de casamento).

propose [prə'pəʊz] <> *vt* **-1.** [suggest] propor **-2.** [introduce] apresentar **-3.** [toast] brindar a **-4.** [intend]: to ~ doing OR to do sthg ter a intenção de fazer algo. <> *vi* [make offer of marriage] pedir em casamento; to ~ to sb pedir a mão de alguém em casamento.

proposition [,prɒpə'zɪʃn] *n* **-1.** [statement of theory] proposição *f* **-2.** [suggestion] proposta *f*.

proprietor [prə'praɪətə^r] *n* proprietário *m*, -ria *f*.

propriety [prə'praɪətɪ] *n* (U) fml retidão *f*.

pro rata [-'rɑ:tə] *adj* & *adv* pro rata.

prose [prəʊz] *n* (U) prosa *f*.

prosecute ['prɒsɪkju:t] <> *vt* JUR processar; to be ~d for sthg ser processado(da) por algo. <> *vi* **-1.** [bring a charge] promover ação penal **-2.** [represent in court] sustentar acusação em juizo.

prosecution [,prɒsɪ'kju:ʃn] *n* **-1.** [criminal charge] acusação *f* **-2.** [lawyers]: the ~ a acusação.

prosecutor ['prɒsɪkju:tə^r] *n* promotor *m*, -ra *f*.

prospect [*n* 'prɒspekt, *vb* prə'spekt] <> *n* **-1.** [hope] possibilidade *f* **-2.** [probability] perspectiva *f*. <> *vi* prospectar; to ~ for sthg prospectar algo.
➡ **prospects** *npl* [chances of success]: ~ s (for sthg) perspectivas *fpl* (de algo).

prospecting [prə'spektɪŋ] *n* (U) prospecção *f*.

prospective [prə'spektɪv] *adj* provável, possível.

prospector [prə'spektə^r] *n* prospector *m*, -ra *f*.

prospectus [prə'spektəs] (*pl* -es) *n* prospecto *m*, folheto *m* informativo.

prosper ['prɒspə^r] *vi* prosperar.

prosperity [prɒ'sperətɪ] *n* (U) prosperidade *f*.

prosperous ['prɒspərəs] *adj* próspero(ra).

prostitute ['prɒstɪtju:t] *n* prostituta *f*; male ~ prostituto *m*.

prostrate ['prɒstreɪt] *adj* prostrado(da).

protagonist [prə'tægənɪst] *n* protagonista *mf*.

protect [prə'tekt] *vt* proteger; to ~ sb/ sthg from, to ~ sb/sthg against proteger alguém/algo de/contra.

protection [prə'tekʃn] *n* (U) proteção *f*; ~ from sb/sthg, ~ against sb/sthg proteção de OR contra alguém/algo.

protective [prə'tektɪv] *adj* protetor(ra).

protein ['prəʊti:n] *n* (U) proteína *f*.

protest [*n* 'prəʊtest, *vb* prə'test] <> *n* protesto *m*. <> *vt* **-1.** [state] declarar **-2.** US [protest against] protestar contra. <> *vi* [complain] protestar; to ~ about/against sthg protestar por/contra algo.

Protestant ['prɒtɪstənt] <> *adj* protestante. <> *n* protestante *mf*.

protester [prə'testə^r] *n* manifestante *mf*.

protest march *n* marcha *f* de protesto, manifestação *f*.

protocol ['prəʊtəkɒl] *n* (U) protocolo *m*.

prototype ['prəʊtətaɪp] *n* protótipo *m*.

protracted [prə'træktɪd] *adj* prolongado(da).

protrude [prə'tru:d] *vi* salientar-se, sobressair-se; to ~ from sthg sobressair-se em algo.

protuberance [prə'tju:bərəns] *n* protuberância *f*.

proud [praʊd] *adj* **-1.** [gen] orgulhoso(sa); to be ~ of sb/sthg estar orgulhoso(sa) de alguém/algo - **2.** *pej* [arrogant] orgulhoso(sa), arrogante.

prove [pru:v] (*pp* -**d** OR **proven**) *vt* - **1.** [show to be true] provar, demonstrar - **2.** [show o.s. to be]: **to ~ (to be) sthg** demonstrar ser algo; **to ~ o.s. to be** sthg mostrar-se algo.

proven ['pru:vn, 'prəʊvn] ⟨⟩ *pp* ⊳ **prove**. ⟨⟩ *adj* comprovado(da).

proverb ['prɒvɜ:bl] *n* provérbio *m*.

provide [prə'vaɪd] *vt* fornecer, prover; **to ~ sb with sthg** proporcionar algo a alguém; **to ~ sthg for sb** oferecer algo a alguém.

➡ **provide for** *vt fus* - **1.** [support] sustentar, manter - **2.** *fml* [make arrangements for] prever, tomar medidas para.

provided [prə'vaɪdd] ➡ **provided (that)** *conj* desde que, contanto que.

providing [prə'vaɪdɪŋ] ➡ **providing (that)** *conj* desde que.

province ['prɒvɪns] *n* - **1.** [part of country] província *f* - **2.** [specialist subject] campo *m*, ramo *m* do conhecimento; [area of responsibility] alçada *f*.

provincial [prə'vɪnʃl] *adj* - **1.** [of a province] da província - **2.** *pej* [narrowminded] provinciano(na).

provision [prə'vɪʒn] *n* - **1.** (*U*) [act of supplying] provisão *f* - **2.** (*U*) [arrangement] providência *f*; **to make ~ for/sthg** tomar providências para algo; **to make ~ for/sb** garantir o sustento de alguém - **3.** [in agreement, law] cláusula *f*.

➡ **provisions** *npl* [supplies] provisões *fpl*.

provisional [prə'vɪʒənl] *adj* provisório(ria).

proviso [prə'vaɪzəʊ] (*pl* -s) *n* condição *f*; **with the ~ that** com a condição de que.

provocative [prə'vɒkətɪv] *adj* - **1.** [controversial] provocativo(va) - **2.** [sexy] provocante.

provoke [prə'vəʊk] *vt* provocar.

prow [praʊ] *n* proa *f*.

prowess ['praʊɪs] *n* (*U*) *fml* façanha *f*.

prowl [praʊl] ⟨⟩ *n*: **on the ~** de ronda, rondando. ⟨⟩ *vt* rondar por. ⟨⟩ *vi* fazer a ronda.

prowler ['praʊlə'] *n* gatuno *m*, -na *f*.

proxy ['prɒksɪ] (*pl* -**ies**) *n*: **by ~** por procuração.

prudent ['pru:dnt] *adj* prudente.

prudish ['pru:dɪʃ] *adj* pudico(ca).

prune [pru:n] ⟨⟩ *n* ameixa *f* seca. ⟨⟩ *vt* podar.

pry [praɪ] (*pt* & *pp* **pried**) *vi* bisbilhotar; **to ~ into sthg** intrometer-se em algo.

PS (*abbr of* **postscript**) *n* PS.

psalm [sɑ:m] *n* salmo *m*.

pseudonym ['sju:dənɪm] *n* pseudônimo *m*.

psyche ['saɪkɪ] *n* psique *f*.

psychiatric [ˌsaɪkɪ'ætrɪk] *adj* psiquiátrico(ca).

psychiatrist [saɪ'kaɪətrɪst] *n* psiquiatra *mf*.

psychiatry [saɪ'kaɪətrɪ] *n* (*U*) psiquiatria *f*.

psychic ['saɪkɪk] ⟨⟩ *adj* - **1.** [clairvoyant] paranormal - **2.** [mental] psíquico(ca). ⟨⟩ *n* paranormal *mf*, médium *mf*.

psychoanalysis [ˌsaɪkəʊə'næləsɪs] *n* (*U*) psicanálise *f*.

psychoanalyst [ˌsaɪkəʊ'ænəlɪst] *n* psicanalista *mf*.

psychological [ˌsaɪkə'lɒdʒɪkl] *adj* psicológico(ca).

psychologist [saɪ'kɒlədʒɪst] *n* psicólogo *m*, -ga *f*.

psychology [saɪ'kɒlədʒɪ] *n* psicologia *f*.

psychopath ['saɪkəpæθ] *n* psicopata *mf*.

psychotic [saɪ'kɒtɪk] ⟨⟩ *adj* psicótico(ca). ⟨⟩ *n* psicótico *m*, -ca *f*.

pt - **1.** *abbr of* **pint** - **2.** (*abbr of* **point**) pt.

PT (*abbr of* **physical training**) *n* treinamento *m* físico.

PTO (*abbr of* **please turn over**) vide verso.

pub [pʌb] *n* pub *m*, bar *m*.

puberty ['pju:bətɪ] *n* (*U*) puberdade *f*.

pubic ['pju:bɪk] *adj* pubiano(na).

public ['pʌblɪk] ⟨⟩ *adj* [gen] público(ca); **to go ~ on sthg** *inf* levar a público. ⟨⟩ *n*: **the ~** o público; **in ~** em público.

public-address system *n* sistema *m* de auto-falantes.

publican ['pʌblɪkən] *n* UK dono *m*, -na *f* de um pub.

publication [ˌpʌblɪ'keɪʃn] *n* publicação *f*.

public company *n* sociedade *f* anônima (*com ações na Bolsa*).

public convenience *n* UK sanitário *m* público.

public holiday *n* feriado *m* nacional.

public house *n* UK *fml* bar *m*, pub *m*.

publicity [pʌb'lɪsɪtɪ] *n* publicidade *f*.

publicize, -ise ['pʌblɪsaɪz] *vt* divulgar.

public limited company *n* sociedade *f* anônima (*com ações na Bolsa*).

public opinion *n* (*U*) opinião *f* pública.

public prosecutor *n* promotor *m* público, promotora *f* pública.

public relations ⟨⟩ *n* (*U*) relações *fpl* públicas. ⟨⟩ *npl* relações *f* públicas.

public school *n* - **1.** UK [private school]

escola f particular - **2.** *US & Scot* [state school] escola f pública.

public-spirited *adj* com espírito cívico.

public transport n (U) transporte m público.

publish ['pʌblɪʃ] vt - **1.** [gen] publicar - **2.** [make known] divulgar, tornar público(-ca).

publisher ['pʌblɪʃə'] n - **1.** [company] editora f - **2.** [person] editor m, -ra f.

publishing ['pʌblɪʃɪŋ] n (U) setor m editorial.

pub lunch n almoço servido em um pub.

pucker ['pʌkə'] vt franzir.

pudding ['pʊdɪŋ] n - **1.** [food - sweet] pudim m; [- savoury] pastelão m - **2.** (U) UK [part of meal] sobremesa f.

puddle ['pʌdl] n poça f.

puff [pʌf] ⬦ n - **1.** [of cigarette, pipe] baforada f - **2.** [of air, smoke] golfada f. ⬦ vt baforar. ⬦ vi - **1.** [smoke]: to ~ at OR on sthg dar tragadas em algo - **2.** [pant] ofegar.
➤ **puff out** vt sep - **1.** [chest, cheeks] inflar - **2.** [feathers] eriçar.

puffed [pʌft] adj [swollen]: ~ up inchado(da)

puffin ['pʌfɪn] n papagaio-do-mar m.

puff pastry, puff paste US n (U) massa f folhada.

puffy ['pʌfɪ] (compar -ier, superl -iest) adj inchado(da).

pugnacious [pʌg'neɪʃəs] adj fml belicoso(sa).

pull [pʊl] ⬦ n - **1.** [tug with hand] puxão m - **2.** [influence] prestígio m. ⬦ vt - **1.** [gen] puxar; **to ~ sthg to pieces** despedaçar algo - **2.** [curtains - open] abrir; [- close] puxar - **3.** [take out - cork, tooth] arrancar; [- gun] sacar; **she ~ ed herself out of the water** ela se afastou da água - **4.** [muscle, hamstring] distender - **5.** [attract] atrair. ⬦ vi [tug with hand] puxar.
➤ **pull apart** vt sep desmontar.
➤ **pull at** vt fus puxar, dar puxões em.
➤ **pull away** vi - **1.** [from roadside]: **to ~ away (from)** afastar-se (da margem da estrada) - **2.** [in race]: **to ~ away (from)** disparar na frente (de).
➤ **pull down** vt sep demolir.
➤ **pull in** vi [vehicle] encostar.
➤ **pull off** vt sep - **1.** [take off] tirar rapidamente - **2.** [succeed in] conseguir levar a cabo.
➤ **pull out** ⬦ vt sep retirar. ⬦ vi - **1.** [train] partir - **2.** [vehicle] entrar na estrada - **3.** [withdraw] retirar.

➤ **pull over** vi [vehicle, driver] encostar.
➤ **pull through** vi [patient] restabelecer-se, recuperar-se.
➤ **pull together** vt sep: **to ~ o.s. together** acalmar-se.
➤ **pull up** ⬦ vt sep - **1.** [raise] levantar - **2.** [move closer] aproximar. ⬦ vi parar, deter.

pulley ['pʊlɪ] (pl pulleys) n roldana f.

pullover ['pʊl,əʊvə'] n pulôver m.

pulp [pʌlp] ⬦ adj barato(ta), de má qualidade. ⬦ n - **1.** [soft mass] pasta f - **2.** [of fruit] polpa f - **3.** [of wood] cerne m.

pulpit ['pʊlpɪt] n púlpito m.

pulsate [pʌl'seɪt] vi - **1.** [heart] pulsar, palpitar - **2.** [air, sound] vibrar; **pulsating rhythm** ritmo m vibrante.

pulse [pʌls] ⬦ n - **1.** [in body] pulso m - **2.** TECH impulso m. ⬦ vi [throb - blood] pulsar; [- music, room] vibrar.
➤ **pulses** npl [food] grãos mpl.

puma ['pju:mə] (pl inv OR -s) n puma m.

pumice (stone) ['pʌmɪs-] n (U) pedra-pomes f.

pummel ['pʌml] (UK pt & pp -led, cont -ling, US pt & pp -ed, cont -ing) vt esmurrar.

pump [pʌmp] ⬦ n bomba f. ⬦ vt - **1.** [convey by pumping] bombear - **2.** inf [interrogate] sondar. ⬦ vi - **1.** [machine] bater - **2.** [person] arfar - **3.** [heart] palpitar.
➤ **pumps** npl [shoes] sapatilhas fpl.

pumpkin ['pʌmpkɪn] n abóbora f.

pun [pʌn] n jogo m de palavras.

punch [pʌntʃ] ⬦ n - **1.** [blow] soco m - **2.** [tool] punção m - **3.** (U) [drink] ponche m. ⬦ vt - **1.** [hit] esmurrar, soquear - **2.** [perforate - paper, ticket] picar; [- hole] perfurar.

Punch-and-Judy show [-'dʒu:dɪ-] n teatro de fantoches para crianças apresentado normalmente na praia.

punch ball n saco m de pancadas.

punch(ed) card [pʌntʃ(t)-] n cartão m perfurado.

punch line n frase f final, arremate m (de uma história).

punch-up n UK inf briga f.

punchy ['pʌntʃɪ] (compar -ier, superl -iest) adj inf incisivo(va).

punctual ['pʌŋktʃʊəl] adj pontual.

punctuation [,pʌŋktʃʊ'eɪʃn] n (U) pontuação f.

punctuation mark n sinal m de pontuação.

puncture ['pʌŋktʃə'] ⬦ n furo m. ⬦ vt - **1.** [tyre, ball] furar - **2.** [lung, skin] perfurar.

pundit ['pʌndɪt] n especialista mf, autoridade f (em algum assunto).

pungent ['pʌndʒənt] *adj* **-1.** [strong-smelling] forte, penetrante **-2.** *fig* [powerful] pujante.

punish ['pʌnɪʃ] *vt* punir; **to ~ sb for sthg/for doing sthg** punir alguém por algo/por fazer algo.

punishing ['pʌnɪʃɪŋ] *adj* penoso(sa).

punishment ['pʌnɪʃmənt] *n* [gen] punição *f*, castigo *m*.

punk [pʌŋk] <> *adj* punk. <> *n* **-1.** (U) [music]: **~ (rock)** rock *m* punk **-2.** [person]: **~ (rocker)** roqueiro *m*, -ra *f* punk **-3.** *US inf* [lout] rebelde *mf*.

punt [pʌnt] *n* **-1.** [boat] barco *m* a remo **-2.** [Irish currency] libra *f* irlandesa.

punter ['pʌntə'] *n* **-1.** [someone who bets] apostador *m*, -ra *f* **-2.** *UK inf* [customer] cliente *mf*.

puny ['pju:nɪ] (*compar* **-ier**, *superl* **-iest**) *adj* **-1.** [person] raquítico(ca) **-2.** [limbs] fraco(ca) **-3.** [effort] débil.

pup [pʌp] *n* **-1.** [young dog] cachorrinho *m*, -nha *f* **-2.** [young seal, otter] filhote *m*.

pupil ['pju:pl] *n* **-1.** [student] aluno *m*, -na *f* **-2.** [of eye] pupila *f*.

puppet ['pʌpɪt] *n* **-1.** [string puppet] marionete *f* **-2.** [glove puppet] fantoche *m* **-3.** *pej* [person, country] fantoche *mf*.

puppy ['pʌpɪ] (*pl* **-ies**) *n* cachorrinho *m*, -nha *f*.

purchase ['pɜ:tʃəs] *fml* <> *n* **-1.** (U) [act of buying] compra *f*, aquisição *f* **-2.** [thing bought] aquisição *f* **-3.** [grip] apoio *m*. <> *vt* comprar, adquirir.

purchaser ['pɜ:tʃəsə'] *n* comprador *m*, -ra *f*.

purchasing power ['pɜ:tʃəsɪŋ-] *n* (U) poder *m* de compra.

pure [pjʊə'] *adj* **-1.** [gen] puro(ra) **-2.** [clear] cristalino(na) **-3.** *literary* [chaste] puro(ra) **-4.** [for emphasis] mero(ra), puro(ra).

puree ['pjʊəreɪ] *n* purê *m*.

purely ['pjʊəlɪ] *adv* puramente.

purge [pɜ:dʒ] <> *n* POL expurgo *m*. <> *vt* **-1.** POL purgar **-2.** [rid]: **to ~ sthg (of sthg)** livrar algo (de algo); **to ~ o.s. (of sthg)** livrar-se (de algo).

purify ['pjʊərɪfaɪ] (*pt & pp* **-ied**) *vt* purificar.

purist ['pjʊərɪst] *n* purista *mf*.

puritan ['pjʊərɪtən] <> *adj* puritano(na). <> *n* puritano *m*, -na *f*.

purity ['pjʊərətɪ] *n* (U) **-1.** pureza *f* **-2.** *literary* [chastity] pureza *f*.

purl [pɜ:l] <> *n* laçada *f*. <> *vt* dar uma laçada.

purple ['pɜ:pl] <> *adj* purpúreo(rea). <> *n* púrpura *f*.

purport [pə'pɔ:t] *vi fml*: **to ~ to do/be sthg** pretender fazer/ser algo.

purpose ['pɜ:pəs] *n* **-1.** [objective, reason] objetivo *m*, propósito *m* **-2.** [use] propósito *m*; **to no ~** em vão **-3.** [determination] determinação *f*.
◆ **on purpose** *adv* de propósito.

purposeful ['pɜ:pəsfʊl] *adj* determinado(da), resoluto(ta).

purr [pɜ:'] *vi* **-1.** [gen] roncar **-2.** [cat] ronronar.

purse [pɜ:s] <> *n* **-1.** [for money] carteira *f* **-2.** *US* [handbag] bolsa *f*. <> *vt* franzir (*em desagrado*).

purser ['pɜ:sə'] *n* comissário *m*, -ria *f* de bordo.

pursue [pə'sju:] *vt* **-1.** [follow] perseguir **-2.** [hobby] dedicar-se a **-3.** [interest, aim] buscar, ir atrás de **-4.** [take further] aprofundar-se em.

pursuer [pə'sju:ə'] *n* perseguidor *m*, -ra *f*.

pursuit [pə'sju:t] *n* **-1.** [gen] perseguição *f* **-2.** [of happiness, security etc.] *fml* busca *f* **-3.** [occupation, activity] atividade *f*.

pus [pʌs] *n* (U) pus *m*.

push [pʊʃ] <> *n* **-1.** [shove] empurrão *m* **-2.** [on button, bell] pressionamento *m* **-3.** [campaign] pressão *f*. <> *vt* **-1.** [press, move - door, person] empurrar; [- button] apertar **-2.** [encourage] incitar; **to ~ sb to do sthg** incitar alguém a fazer algo **-3.** [force] impelir; **to ~ sb into doing sthg** impelir alguém a fazer algo **-4.** *inf* [promote] promover. <> *vi* **-1.** [shove] empurrar; **to ~ through** abrir caminho aos empurrões em **-2.** [on button, bell] apertar **-3.** [campaign]: **to ~ for sthg** fazer pressão por algo.
◆ **push around** *vt sep inf fig* [bully] mandar.
◆ **push in** *vi* [in queue] furar.
◆ **push off** *vi inf* [go away] largar-se.
◆ **push on** *vi* [continue] seguir em frente sem parar.
◆ **push through** *vt sep* [force to be accepted] conseguir que se aprove.

pushchair ['pʊʃtʃeə'] *n UK* carrinho *m* de bebê.

pushed [pʊʃt] *adj inf*: **to be ~ for sthg** andar meio curto(ta) de algo; **to be hard ~ to do sthg** estar com dificuldades para fazer algo.

pusher ['pʊʃə'] *n drugs sl* traficante *mf*, vendedor *m*, -ra *f* de drogas.

pushover ['pʊʃ,əʊvə'] *n inf* otário *m*, -ria *f*.

push-up *n US* flexão *f*.

pushy ['pʊʃɪ] (*compar* **-ier**, *superl* **-iest**) *adj pej* agressivo(va).

puss [pʊs], **pussy (cat)** ['pʊsɪ-] n inf gatinho m, bichano m.

put [pʊt] (pt & pp put, cont -ting) vt -1. [gen] colocar, pôr -2. [express] colocar, expressar -3. [ask] colocar, perguntar -4. [cause to be] colocar; to ~ sb out of work deixar alguém sem trabalho -5. [estimate]: to ~ sthg at avaliar algo em -6. [invest]: to ~ sthg into sthg investir algo em algo, colocar algo em algo -7. [apply - responsibility]: to ~ pressure on sb/sthg pressionar alguém/algo; to ~ tax on sthg colocar impostos sobre algo -8. [write] escrever.

  ◆ **put across** vt sep expor.

  ◆ **put away** vt sep -1. [tidy away] colocar no lugar, organizar -2. inf [lock up] encerrar (na prisão).

  ◆ **put back** vt sep -1. [replace] repor no lugar -2. [postpone] adiar -3. [clock, watch] atrasar.

  ◆ **put by** vt sep [money] poupar.

  ◆ **put down** vt sep -1. [lay down] largar, pôr no chão -2. [quell] sufocar -3. [write down] apontar -4. UK [kill] sacrificar.

  ◆ **put down to** vt sep atribuir a.

  ◆ **put forward** vt sep -1. [propose] apresentar, propor -2. [advance] adiar -3. [clock, watch] adiantar.

  ◆ **put in** vt sep -1. [spend] dedicar -2. [submit] apresentar.

  ◆ **put off** vt sep -1. [postpone] adiar -2. [switch off - radio, light] desligar; [- brake] soltar -3. [cause to wait] fazer esperar -4. [discourage] desanimar, dissuadir -5. [disturb] distrair -6. [cause to dislike] desanimar, desestimular; to ~ sb off sthg desestimular alguém de algo.

  ◆ **put on** vt sep -1. [wear - trousers, hat] vestir; [- shoes] calçar -2. [arrange] montar -3. [gain in weight]: to ~ on weight engordar -4. [switch on - radio, light] ligar; [- brake] acionar -5. [play] tocar, pôr -6. [start cooking] colocar no fogo -7. [pretend] fingir -8. [bet] apostar -9. [add] acrescentar.

  ◆ **put out** vt sep -1. [place outside] colocar or pôr para fora -2. [issue] tornar público(ca) -3. [extinguish] apagar -4. [switch off] desligar -5. [extend] espichar -6. [annoy, upset]: to be ~ out ficar chateado(da) -7. [inconvenience] importunar, incomodar.

  ◆ **put through** vt sep TELEC transferir.

  ◆ **put up** ◇ vt sep -1. [build] erguer -2. [raise and open - umbrella] abrir; [- flag] hastear -3. [fix to wall] afixar -4. [provide] pôr -5. [propose] indicar -6. [increase] aumentar -7. [provide accommodation for]

hospedar. ◇ vt fus [offer, present] manifestar.

  ◆ **put up with** vt fus suportar, agüentar.

putrid ['pju:trɪd] adj fml putrefato(ta).

putt [pʌt] ◇ n tacada f leve (no golfe). ◇ vt dar uma tacada leve em. ◇ vi dar uma tacada leve.

putting green ['pʌtɪŋ-] n minicampo m sem obstáculos (para jogar golfe).

putty ['pʌtɪ] n (U) massa f de vidraceiro.

puzzle ['pʌzl] ◇ n -1. [toy, game] quebra-cabeça m -2. [mystery] enigma m. ◇ vt deixar perplexo(xa). ◇ vi: to ~ over sthg quebrar a cabeça com algo.

  ◆ **puzzle out** vt sep decifrar.

puzzling ['pʌzlɪŋ] adj desconcertante.

pyjamas [pə'dʒɑ:məz] npl pijama m.

pylon ['paɪlən] n ELEC torre f (de eletricidade).

pyramid ['pɪrəmɪd] n pirâmide f.

Pyrenees [,pɪrə'ni:z] npl: the ~ os Pireneus.

python ['paɪθn] (pl inv OR -s) n píton m.

Q

q (pl q's OR qs), **Q** (pl Q's OR Qs) [kju:] n [letter] q OR m.

quack [kwæk] n -1. [noise] grasnido m -2. inf pej [doctor] curandeiro m charlatão, curandeira f charlatona.

quad [kwɒd] n (abbr of quadrangle) pátio cercado por edifícios, em geral em escola ou universidade.

quadrangle ['kwɒdræŋgl] n -1. [figure] quadrângulo m -2. [courtyard] pátio m.

quadruple [kwɒ'dru:pl] ◇ adj quadruplicado (da). ◇ vt & vi quadruplicar.

quadruplets ['kwɒdrʊplɪts] npl quadrigêmeos mpl, -meas fpl.

quads [kwɒdz] npl inf quadrigêmeos mpl, -meas fpl.

quagmire ['kwægmaɪə'] n pântano m.

quail [kweɪl] (pl inv OR -s) ◇ n codorna f. ◇ vi literary amedrontar-se.

quaint [kweɪnt] adj pitoresco(ca), singular.

quake [kweɪk] ◇ n (abbr of earthquake) inf terremoto m. ◇ vi tremer.

Quaker ['kweɪkəʳ] n quacre m.

qualification [ˌkwɒlɪfɪ'keɪʃn] n -1. [examination, certificate] qualificação f, título m -2. [quality, skill] qualificação f -3. [qualifying statement] restrição f, ressalva f.

qualified ['kwɒlɪfaɪd] adj -1. [trained] qualificado(da) -2. [able]: **to be ~ to do sthg** estar qualificado(da) para fazer algo -3. [limited] com ressalvas.

qualify ['kwɒlɪfaɪ] (pt & pp -ied) <> vt -1. [modify] restringir -2. [entitle]: **to ~ sb to do sthg** qualificar alguém para fazer algo. <> vi -1. [pass exams] habilitar-se -2. [be entitled]: **to ~ (for sthg)** qualificar-se(para algo) -3. SPORT classificar-se.

quality ['kwɒlətɪ] (pl -ies) <> n qualidade f. <> comp de qualidade.

qualms [kwɑːmz] npl receio m, escrúpulos mpl.

quandary ['kwɒndərɪ] (pl -ies) n dilema m; **to be in a ~ about OR over sthg** estar num dilema sobre algo.

quantify ['kwɒntɪfaɪ] (pt & pp -ied) vt quantificar.

quantity ['kwɒntətɪ] (pl -ies) n quantidade f.

quantity surveyor n calculista mf de obra.

quarantine ['kwɒrəntiːn] <> n quarentena f. <> vt pôr em quarentena.

quark [kwɑːk] n -1. PHYSICS quark m -2. CULIN queijo m tipo quark.

quarrel ['kwɒrəl] (UK pt & pp -led, cont -ling, US pt & pp -ed, cont -ing) <> n discussão f. <> vi discutir; **to ~ with sb** discutir com alguém; **to ~ with sthg** não estar de acordo sobre algo.

quarrelsome ['kwɒrəlsəm] adj briguento(ta).

quarry ['kwɒrɪ] (pl -ies, pt & pp -ied) n -1. [place] pedreira f -2. [prey] presa f.

quart [kwɔːt] n -1. UK [unit of measurement] quarto m de galão (1,14 litro) -2. US [unit of measurement] quarto m de galão (0,95 litro).

quarter ['kwɔːtəʳ] n -1. [fraction] quarto m -2. [in telling time]: **it's a ~ past two** UK, **it's a ~ after two** US são duas e quinze; **it's a ~ to two** UK, **it's a ~ of two** US faltam quinze para as duas -3. [of year] trimestre m -4. US [coin] moeda f de 25 centavos -5. [four ounces] quarto m de libra (113,396 g) -6. [area in town] quarteirão m -7. [direction] lugar m, parte f; **they came from all ~s of the globe** eles vieram de todos os cantos da terra.

➡ **quarters** npl [rooms] alojamentos mpl.

➡ **at close quarters** adv de perto.

quarter-final n quarta-de-final f.

quarterly ['kwɔːtəlɪ] (pl -ies) <> adj trimestral. <> adv trimestralmente. <> n revista f trimestral.

quartermaster ['kwɔːtəˌmɑːstəʳ] n MIL quartel-mestre m.

quartet [kwɔː'tet] n quarteto m.

quartz [kwɔːts] n (U) quartzo m.

quartz watch n relógio m de quartzo.

quash [kwɒʃ] vt -1. [reject] revogar, anular -2. [quell] sufocar, reprimir.

quasi- ['kweɪzaɪ] prefix quase-.

quaver ['kweɪvəʳ] <> n -1. MUS colcheia f -2. [in voice] tremor m. <> vi tremer.

quay [kiː] n cais m.

quayside ['kiːsaɪd] n cais m.

queasy ['kwiːzɪ] (compar -ier, superl -iest) adj enjoado(da).

Quebec [kwɪ'bek] n Quebec.

queen [kwiːn] n -1. [gen] rainha f -2. [playing card] dama f.

queen bee n (abelha f) rainha f.

queen mother n: **the ~** a rainha-mãe.

queer [kwɪəʳ] <> adj [odd] esquisito(ta), estranho(nha). <> n inf pej [homosexual] veado m, bicha f.

quell [kwel] vt -1. [rebellion] sufocar, reprimir -2. [unease, anger] dominar, conter.

quench [kwentʃ] vt: **to ~ one's thirst** matar a sede.

querulous ['kwerʊləs] adj fml lamuriante.

query ['kwɪərɪ] (pl -ies, pt & pp -ied) <> n pergunta f, dúvida f. <> vt pôr em dúvida.

quest [kwest] n literary busca f; **~ for sthg** busca por algo.

question ['kwestʃn] <> n -1. [gen] questão f -2. [query] pergunta f; **to ask (sb) a ~** fazer uma pergunta a alguém -3. [doubt] dúvida f; **to OR call sthg into ~** por OR colocar algo em dúvida; **to OR bring sthg into ~** colocar algo em questão; **beyond ~** sem nenhuma dúvida -4. phr: **there's no ~ of ...** não há dúvida de (que) ... <> vt -1. [interrogate] interrogar -2. [express doubt about] questionar.

➡ **in question** adv: **the matter in ~** o assunto em questão.

➡ **out of the question** adj fora de questão.

questionable ['kwestʃənəbl] adj questionável.

question mark n ponto m de interrogação.

questionnaire [,kwestʃə'neəʳ] n questionário m.

queue [kju:] UK ◇ n fila f. ◇ vi fazer fila; **to ~ (up) for sthg** fazer fila para algo.

quibble ['kwɪbl] pej ◇ n chorumela f. ◇ vi queixar-se por bobagem, lamuriar-se; **to ~ over** OR **about sthg** queixar-se por bobagem sobre algo.

quiche [ki:ʃ] n quiche f.

quick [kwɪk] ◇ adj rápido(da). ◇ adv depressa, rápido.

quicken ['kwɪkn] ◇ vt [make faster] apressar, acelerar. ◇ vi [get faster] acelerar(-se).

quickly ['kwɪklɪ] adv -1. [rapidly] rapidamente -2. [without delay] depressa, rápido.

quicksand ['kwɪksænd] n areia f movediça.

quick-witted [-'wɪtɪd] adj arguto(ta).

quid [kwɪd] (pl inv) n UK inf libra f (esterlina).

quiet ['kwaɪət] ◇ adj -1. [gen] quieto(ta); **in a ~ voice** numa voz baixa; **to keep ~ about sthg** guardar silêncio sobre algo; **be ~!** fique quieto(ta)! -2. [tranquil] tranqüilo(la) -3. [not busy] parado(da) -4. [discreet] suave, discreto(ta); **to have a ~ word with sb** falar discretamente com alguém -5. [intimate] íntimo(ma). ◇ n (U) tranqüilidade f, silêncio m; **on the ~** inf na surdina, às escondidas. ◇ vt US acalmar, tranqüilizar.

◆ **quiet down** ◇ vt sep US acalmar, tranqüilizar. ◇ vi acalmar-se, tranqüilizar-se.

quieten ['kwaɪətn] vt acalmar, tranqüilizar.

◆ **quieten down** ◇ vt sep acalmar, tranqüilizar. ◇ vi acalmar-se, tranqüilizar-se.

quietly ['kwaɪətlɪ] adv -1. [without noise] sem fazer barulho -2. [without excitement] tranqüilamente -3. [without fuss] discretamente.

quilt [kwɪlt] n acolchoado m, edredom m.

quinine [kwɪ'ni:n] n (U) quinina f.

quins UK [kwɪnz], **quints** US [kwɪnts] npl inf quíntuplos mpl, -plas fpl.

quintet [kwɪn'tet] n quinteto m.

quints npl US = quins.

quintuplets [kwɪn'tju:plɪts] npl quíntuplos mpl, -plas fpl.

quip [kwɪp] (pt & pp -ped, cont -ping) ◇ n gracejo m. ◇ vi gracejar.

quirk [kwɜ:k] n -1. [habit] mania f, esquisitice f -2. [strange event] estranha coincidência f; **by a ~ of fate** por um capricho do destino.

quit [kwɪt] (UK pt & pp quit OR -ted, cont -ting, US pt & pp quit, cont -ting) ◇ vt -1. [resign from] abandonar, deixar -2. [stop]: **to ~ smoking** deixar de fumar. ◇ vi -1. [resign] demitir-se -2. [give up] desistir.

quite [kwaɪt] adv -1. [completely] completamente, totalmente -2. [fairly] bem; **~ a lot of people** bastante gente; **~ a few times** várias vezes -3. [after negative]: **I don't ~ understand** não entendo muito bem; **this room is not ~ big enough** essa sala não é tão grande quanto deveria ser -4. [for emphasis]: **she's ~ a singer** ela é uma cantora e tanto -5. [to express agreement]: **~ (so)!** exatamente!

quits [kwɪts] adj inf: **to be ~ (with sb)** estar quite(com alguém); **to call it ~** ficar quite.

quiver ['kwɪvəʳ] ◇ n -1. [shiver] estremecimento m -2. [for arrows] aljava f. ◇ vi estremecer.

quiz [kwɪz] (pl -zes, pt & pp -zed, cont -zing) ◇ n -1. [competitions, game] jogo m de perguntas e respostas -2. US SCH exame m. ◇ vt: **to ~ sb (about sthg)** interrogar alguém (sobre algo).

quizzical ['kwɪzɪkl] adj interrogativo(va).

quota ['kwəʊtə] n cota f.

quotation [kwəʊ'teɪʃn] n -1. [citation] citação f -2. COMM cotação f.

quotation marks npl aspas fpl; **in ~** entre aspas.

quote [kwəʊt] ◇ n -1. [citation] citação f -2. COMM cotação f. ◇ vt -1. [cite] citar -2. COMM cotar; **she ~d £100** ela fixou um preço de £100. ◇ vi -1. [cite] citar; **to ~ from sthg** citar de algo -2. COMM: **to ~ for sthg** estabelecer um preço para algo.

quotient ['kwəʊʃnt] n quociente m.

R

r (pl **r's** OR **rs**), **R** (pl **R's** OR **Rs**) [ɑ:ʳ] n [letter] r, R m.

rabbi ['ræbaɪ] n rabino m.

rabbit ['ræbɪt] n -1. [animal] coelho m, -lha f -2. (U) [food] coelho m.

rabbit hutch n coelheira f.

rabble ['ræbl] n -1. [disorderly crowd] povaréu m -2. [riffraff] gentalha f.

rabies ['reɪbiːz] n (U) raiva f.

RAC (abbr of Royal Automobile Club) n automóvel clube britânico.

race [reɪs] <> n -1. [ethnicity] raça f -2. [competition] corrida f; **a ~ against time** uma corrida contra o tempo. <> vt competir com (em corrida). <> vi -1. [compete]: **to ~ against sb** bater uma corrida com alguém -2. [rush] ir correndo -3. acelerar.

race car n US = racing car.

racecourse ['reɪskɔːs] n hipódromo m.

race driver n US = racing driver.

racehorse ['reɪshɔːs] n cavalo m de corrida.

racetrack ['reɪstræk] n autódromo m.

racial ['reɪʃl] adj racial.

racial discrimination n (U) discriminação m racial.

racing ['reɪsɪŋ] n (U) SPORT corrida f.

racing car UK, **race car** US n carro m de corrida.

racing driver UK, **race driver** US n piloto m de corrida.

racism ['reɪsɪzm] n (U) racismo m.

racist ['reɪsɪst] <> adj racista. <> n racista mf.

rack [ræk] n -1. [frame - for plates] escorredor m de louça; [- for toast] prateleira f; [- for bottles] porta-garrafas m inv -2. [for luggage] porta-bagagens m inv.

racket ['rækɪt] n -1. [noise] algazarra f, zoeira f -2. [illegal activity] golpe m, fraude f -3. SPORT raquete f.

racquet ['rækɪt] n raquete f.

racy ['reɪsɪ] (compar -ier, superl -iest) adj vivaz.

radar ['reɪdɑːʳ] n (U) radar m.

radiant ['reɪdjənt] adj -1. [happy] radiante -2. literary [brilliant] brilhante.

radiate ['reɪdɪeɪt] <> vt irradiar. <> vi -1. [be emitted] irradiar -2. [spread from centre] sair, partir do centro.

radiation [,reɪdɪ'eɪʃn] n radiação f.

radiator ['reɪdɪeɪtəʳ] n -1. [in house] aquecedor m -2. AUT radiador m.

radical ['rædɪkl] <> adj radical. <> n POL radical mf.

radically ['rædɪklɪ] adv radicalmente.

radii ['reɪdɪaɪ] pl ▷ radius.

radio ['reɪdɪəʊ] (pl -s) <> n -1. [gen] rádio m -2. [station] rádio f. <> comp de rádio. <> vt transmitir por rádio.

radioactive [,reɪdɪəʊ'æktɪv] adj radioativo(va).

radioactivity [,reɪdɪəʊæk'tɪvətɪ] n (U) radioatividade f.

radio alarm n rádio-relógio m.

radio-controlled [-kən'trəʊld] adj de controle remoto.

radiography [,reɪdɪ'ɒgrəfɪ] n (U) radiografia f.

radiology [,reɪdɪ'ɒlədʒɪ] n (U) radiologia f.

radiotherapy [,reɪdɪəʊ'θerəpɪ] n (U) radioterapia f.

radish ['rædɪʃ] n rabanete m.

radius ['reɪdɪəs] (pl radii) n -1. MATH raio m -2. ANAT rádio m.

RAF [ɑːreɪ'ef, ræf] (abbr of Royal Air Force) n força aérea real britânica.

raffle ['ræfl] <> n rifa f. <> vt rifar.

raffle ticket n bilhete m de rifa.

raft [rɑːft] n -1. [of wood] jangada f -2. [of rubber, plastic] bote m.

rafter ['rɑːftəʳ] n viga f.

rag [ræg] n -1. [piece of cloth] trapo m -2. pej [newspaper] jornaleco m.
◆ **rags** npl [clothes] trapos mpl.

rag-and-bone man n pessoa que compra e vende roupas e móveis velhos na rua.

rag doll n boneca f de pano.

rage [reɪdʒ] <> n -1. [fury] fúria f; **to fly into a ~** ficar enraivecido(da) -2. inf [fashion]: **all the ~** a última moda. <> vi -1. [person] enfurecer-se -2. [storm, argument] recrudescer.

ragged ['rægɪd] adj -1. [wearing torn clothes] maltrapilho(lha) -2. [torn] esfarrapado(da) -3. [wavy] irregular -4. [poor-quality] pobre.

rag week n UK semana em que as universidades britânicas organizam atividades divertidas para fins beneficentes.

raid [reɪd] <> n -1. MIL [attack] incursão f -2. [forced entry - by robbers] assalto m; [- by police] batida f. <> vt -1. MIL [attack] atacar de surpresa -2. [enter by force - robbers] assaltar; [- police] fazer uma batida em.

raider ['reɪdəʳ] n -1. [attacker] invasor m, -ra f -2. [thief] ladrão m, -dra f, assaltante mf.

rail [reɪl] <> n -1. [on staircase] corrimão m -2. [on walkway] ferro m de proteção -3. [on bridge] parapeito m -4. [on ship] amurada f -5. [bar] barra f -6. [of railway line] trilho m -7. (U) [form of transport] trem m. <> comp ferroviário(a).

railcard ['reɪlkɑːd] n UK cartão m de desconto (no trem).

railing ['reɪlɪŋ] n -1. [round basement] grade f -2. [on walkway] ferro m de

proteção - 3. [on ship] amurada *f* - **4.** [on bridge] parapeito *m*.

railway *UK* ['reɪlweɪ], **railroad** *US* ['reɪlrəʊd] *n* - **1.** [track] estrada *f* de ferro - **2.** [company] companhia *f* ferroviária - **3.** [system] sistema *m* ferroviário.

railway line *n* - **1.** [route] linha *f* de trem - **2.** [track] via *f* férrea, trilhos *mpl*.

railwayman ['reɪlweɪmən] (*pl* -men [-mən]) *n UK* ferroviário *m*.

railway station *n* estação *f* de trem.

railway track *n* via *f* férrea, trilhos *mpl*.

rain [reɪn] ◇ *n (U)* chuva *f*. ◇ *v impers* METEOR chover. ◇ *vi* [fall like rain] cair como chuva.

rainbow ['reɪnbəʊ] *n* arco-íris *m*.

rain check *n US*: to take a ~ (on sthg) deixar(algo) para outra hora OR para a próxima.

raincoat ['reɪnkəʊt] *n* capa *f* de chuva.

raindrop ['reɪndrɒp] *n* pingo *m* de chuva.

rainfall ['reɪnfɔːl] *n (U)* precipitação *f*.

rain forest *n* floresta *f* tropical.

rainy ['reɪnɪ] (*compar* -ier, *superl* -iest) *adj* chuvoso(sa).

raise [reɪz] ◇ *n US* aumento *m*. ◇ *vt* - **1.** [gen] levantar - **2.** [lift up] levantar, erguer; to ~ o.s. levantar-se - **3.** [increase] aumentar; to ~ one's voice levantar a voz - **4.** [improve] elevar - **5.** [evoke] evocar - **6.** [child, animals] criar - **7.** [crop] cultivar - **8.** [build] erguer.

raisin ['reɪzn] *n* passa *f (de uva)*.

rake [reɪk] ◇ *n* - **1.** [implement] rastelo *m* - **2.** *dated & literary* [immoral man] devasso *m*, libertino *m*. ◇ *vt* - **1.** [smooth] rastelar - **2.** [gather] juntar com o rastelo.

rally ['rælɪ] (*pl* -ies, *pt & pp* -ied) ◇ *n* - **1.** [gen] rali *m* - **2.** [meeting] comício *m*. ◇ *vt* reunir. ◇ *vi* - **1.** [come together] reunir-se - **2.** [recover] recuperar-se.
➡ **rally round** ◇ *vt fus* mobilizar. ◇ *vi* mobilizar-se.

ram [ræm] (*pt & pp* -med, *cont* -ming) ◇ *n* carneiro *m*. ◇ *vt* - **1.** [crash into] bater contra OR em - **2.** [force] enfiar.

RAM [ræm] (*abbr of* random-access memory) *n* RAM *f*.

ramble ['ræmbl] ◇ *n* passeio *m* no campo. ◇ *vi* - **1.** [walk] passear - **2.** [talk] divagar.

rambler ['ræmblər] *n* excursionista *mf*.

rambling ['ræmblɪŋ] *adj* - **1.** [building] cheio (cheia) de voltas e curvas - **2.** [conversation, book] desconexo(xa).

ramp [ræmp] *n* - **1.** [slope] rampa *f* - **2.** *AUT* [in road] viaduto *m*.

rampage [ræm'peɪdʒ] *n*: to go on the ~ sair em debandada, debandar-se.

rampant ['ræmpənt] *adj* desenfreado(da).

ramparts ['ræmpɑːts] *npl* muralha *f*.

ramshackle ['ræm.ʃækl] *adj* desmantelado(da).

ran [ræn] *pt* ▷ run.

ranch [rɑːntʃ] *n* fazenda *m*, rancho *m*.

rancher ['rɑːntʃər] *n* fazendeiro *m*, -ra *f*.

rancid ['rænsɪd] *adj* rançoso(sa).

rancour *UK*, **rancor** *US* ['ræŋkər] *n (U)* rancor *m*.

random ['rændəm] ◇ *adj* aleatório(ria). ◇ *n*: at ~ aleatoriamente.

random access memory *n (U)* COMPUT memória *f* de acesso aleatório, memória *f* RAM.

R and R (*abbr of* rest and recreation) *n US termo militar norte-americano para licença.*

randy ['rændɪ] (*compar* -ier, *superl* -iest) *adj inf* tarado(da).

rang [ræŋ] *pt* ▷ ring.

range [reɪndʒ] ◇ *n* - **1.** [distance covered - of telescope, gun] alcance *m*; [- of ship, plane] autonomia *f*; at close ~ à queima-roupa - **2.** [variety] variedade *f* - **3.** [bracket] faixa *f* - **4.** [of mountains, hills] cadeia *f* - **5.** [shooting area] linha *f* - **6.** *MUS* alcance *m*. ◇ *vt* [place in row] enfileirar. ◇ *vi* - **1.** [vary]: to ~ from ... to ... variar de ... a ...; to ~ between ... and ... oscilar entre ... e ... - **2.** [deal with, include]: to ~ over sthg passar por algo.

ranger ['reɪndʒər] *n* guarda-florestal *mf*.

rank [ræŋk] ◇ *adj* - **1.** [utter, absolute - disgrace, stupidity] completo(ta); [- injustice, bad luck] total - **2.** [offensive] rançoso(sa). ◇ *n* - **1.** [in army, police] posto *m*; the ~ and file *MIL* soldados rasos; [of political party, organization] bases *fpl* - **2.** [social class] nível *m* - **3.** [row, line] fila *f*. ◇ *vt* [classify] classificar. ◇ *vi* classificar-se; to ~ as/among classificar-se como/entre.
➡ **ranks** *npl* - **1.** *MIL*: the ~ s os soldados rasos - **2.** *fig* [members] filas *fpl*.

rankle ['ræŋkl] *vi* causar dor; it still ~ s with me! isso ainda me dói!

ransack ['rænsæk] *vt* - **1.** [plunder] saquear - **2.** [search] revistar.

ransom ['rænsəm] *n* resgate *m*; to hold sb to ~ [keep prisoner] pedir resgate por alguém; *fig* [put in impossible position] chantagear alguém.

rant [rænt] *vi* falar asneira.

rap [ræp] (*pt & pp* -ped, *cont* -ping) ◇ *n* - **1.** [knock] batidinha *f* - **2.** *MUS* rap *m*. ◇ *vt* [knock] dar batidinhas em.

rape [reɪp] ⬦ n -1. [gen] estupro m -2. *fig* [destruction] destruição f -3. *(U)* [plant] colza f. ⬦ vt estuprar.

rapeseed n semente f de colza.

rapid ['ræpɪd] adj rápido(da).
 ➤ **rapids** npl corredeira f.

rapidly ['ræpɪdlɪ] adv rapidamente.

rapist ['reɪpɪst] n estuprador m, -ra f.

rapport [ræ'pɔːʳ] n afinidade f; **a ~ with/between** uma afinidade com/entre.

rapture ['ræptʃəʳ] n arrebatamento m.

rapturous ['ræptʃərəs] adj arrebatador(ra).

rare [reəʳ] adj -1. [gen] raro(ra) -2. *CULIN* [underdone] malpassado(da).

rarely ['reəlɪ] adv raramente.

raring ['reərɪŋ] adj: **to be ~ to go** estar ansioso(sa) para começar.

rarity ['reərətɪ] (*pl* -ies) n raridade f.

rascal ['rɑːskl] n patife mf, malandro m, -dra f.

rash [ræʃ] ⬦ adj precipitado(da). ⬦ n -1. *MED* erupção f -2. [spate] onda f.

rasher ['ræʃəʳ] n fatia f fina *(de bacon)*.

rasp [rɑːsp] n rangido m.

raspberry ['rɑːzbərɪ] (*pl* -ies) n -1. [fruit] framboesa f -2. [rude noise]: **to blow a ~** debochar fazendo barulho com a boca.

rat [ræt] n -1. [animal] rato m, ratazana f -2. *pej* [person] tratante mf.

rate [reɪt] ⬦ n -1. [speed] velocidade f; **at this ~** nesse ritmo -2. [ratio, proportion - birth, death, inflation] taxa f; [- unemployment] índice m -3. [price] tarifa f. ⬦ vt -1. [consider]: **to ~ sb/sthg (as)** considerar alguém/algo; **to ~ sb/sthg (among)** classificar alguém/algo (entre) -2. [deserve] merecer.
 ➤ **at any rate** adv pelo menos.

ratepayer ['reɪt,peɪəʳ] n *UK* contribuinte mf.

rather ['rɑːðəʳ] adv -1. [slightly, a bit] um pouco -2. [for emphasis] bem, bastante -3. [expressing a preference]: **I would ~ wait** eu preferiria esperar -4. [more exactly]: **or ~ ...** ou melhor ... -5. [on the contrary]: **(but) ~ ...** (senão) pelo contrário ...
 ➤ **rather than** conj em vez de.

ratify ['rætɪfaɪ] (*pt & pp* -ied) vt ratificar.

rating ['reɪtɪŋ] n [standing - high, low, popularity] índice m; [- opinion poll] posição f.

ratio ['reɪʃɪəʊ] (*pl* -s) n razão f, proporção f.

ration ['ræʃn] ⬦ n ração f. ⬦ vt [goods] racionar.
 ➤ **rations** npl ração f.

rational ['ræʃənl] adj racional.

rationale [,ræʃə'nɑːl] n lógica f, fundamento m lógico.

rationalize, -ise ['ræʃənəlaɪz] vt racionalizar.

rat race n competição f acirrada *(no mundo dos negócios)*.

rattle ['rætl] ⬦ n -1. [noise] barulho m, ruído m -2. [toy] chocalho m. ⬦ vt -1. [make rattling noise with] chacoalhar -2. [unsettle] desconcertar. ⬦ vi [make rattling noise] chacoalhar.

rattlesnake ['rætlsneɪk], **rattler** *US* ['rætləʳ] n cascavel f.

raucous ['rɔːkəs] adj -1. [laughter, voice] rouco(ca) e estridente -2. [behaviour] escandaloso(sa).

ravage ['rævɪdʒ] vt devastar.
 ➤ **ravages** npl estragos mpl.

rave [reɪv] ⬦ adj entusiasmado(da). ⬦ n *UK inf* [party] rave f. ⬦ vi -1. [talk angrily]: **to ~ at sb** xingar alguém; **to ~ against sthg** vociferar contra algo -2. [talk enthusiastically]: **to ~ about sthg** falar com entusiasmo sobre algo.

raven ['reɪvn] n corvo m.

ravenous ['rævənəs] adj -1. [person, animal] faminto(ta) -2. [appetite] voraz.

ravine [rə'viːn] n ravina f.

raving ['reɪvɪŋ] adj [for emphasis] delirante; **~ lunatic** doido m varrido, doida f varrida.

ravioli [,rævɪ'əʊlɪ] n *(U)* ravióli m.

ravishing ['rævɪʃɪŋ] adj -1. [sight, beauty] extasiante -2. [person] belíssimo(ma).

raw [rɔː] adj -1. [uncooked] cru (crua) -2. [untreated] bruto(ta) -3. [painful] em carne viva -4. [inexperienced] inexperiente -5. [cold] frio (fria).

raw deal n: **to get a ~** receber um tratamento injusto.

raw material n -1. [natural substance] matéria-prima f -2. *(U) fig* [basis] base f.

ray [reɪ] n -1. [beam] raio m -2. *fig* [glimmer] resquício m.

rayon ['reɪɒn] n *(U)* raiom m.

raze [reɪz] vt destruir completamente, arrasar.

razor ['reɪzəʳ] n -1. [electric] barbeador m elétrico -2. [disposable] barbeador m, aparelho m de barbear.

razor blade n lâmina f de barbear.

RC (*abbr of* **Roman Catholic**) adj católico romano, católica romana.

Rd (*abbr of* **Road**) estrada f.

R & D (*abbr of* **research and development**) n P & D.

re [riː] prep referente a.

RE n (*abbr of* **religious education**) educação f religiosa.

reach [riːtʃ] ⟨⟩ *n* [of arm, boxer] alcance *m*; **within (sb's)** ⟨⟩ [easily touched] ao alcance (de alguém); [easily travelled to] a pouca distância (de alguém); **out of** OR **beyond sb's** ⟨⟩ [not easily touched] fora/além do alcance de alguém; [not easily travelled to] fora/além do alcance de alguém. ⟨⟩ *vt* -**1.** [arrive at] chegar a, alcançar -**2.** [be able to touch] alcançar -**3.** [contact] contatar, entrar em contato com -**4.** [extend as far as] atingir -**5.** [attain, achieve] chegar a. ⟨⟩ *vi* -**1.** [person]: **to** ~ **out/across** alcançar; **to** ~ **down** abaixar-se -**2.** [land] alcançar, ir até.

react [riˈækt] *vi* -**1.** [rebel]: **to** ~ **against sthg** reagir contra algo -**2.** CHEM: **to** ~ **with sthg** reagir com algo.

reaction [riˈækʃn] *n* -**1.** reação *f* -**2.** [response]: ~ **(to sthg)** reação *f*(a algo) -**3.** [rebellion]: ~ **(against sthg)** reação *f* (contra algo).

reactionary [riˈækʃənrɪ] ⟨⟩ *adj* reacionário(ria). ⟨⟩ *n* reacionário *m*, -ria *f*.

reactor [riˈæktəʳ] *n* [nuclear reactor] reator *m*.

read [riːd] (*pt* & *pp* **read** [red]) ⟨⟩ *vt* -**1.** [gen] ler; **to** ~ **sb's mind** ler os pensamentos de alguém; **to** ~ **events** ver os acontecimentos; **the man came to** ~ **the electricity meter** o funcionário veio fazer a leitura da luz; **to be well** ~ **in a subject** conhecer bem um assunto -**2.** [subj: sign, notice] dizer; [subj: gauge, meter, barometer] marcar -**3.** *UK UNIV* estudar. ⟨⟩ *vi* -**1.** [person] ler; **to** ~ **(to sb)** ler (para alguém); **to** ~ **between the lines** ler nas entrelinhas; **to** ~ **sb like a book** compreender alguém perfeitamente -**2.** [text]: **it** ~**s well/badly** isto está bem/mal escrito.

◆ read out *vt sep* ler em voz alta.

◆ read up on *vt fus* estudar.

readable [ˈriːdəbl] *adj* [book] interessante de se ler.

reader [ˈriːdəʳ] *n* leitor *m*, -ra *f*.

readership [ˈriːdəʃɪp] *n* público *m* leitor.

readily [ˈredɪlɪ] *adv* -**1.** [willingly] de boa vontade -**2.** [easily] facilmente.

reading [ˈriːdɪŋ] *n* -**1.** [gen] leitura *f* -**2.** [recital] recital *m* -**3.** [from gauge, meter, thermometer] marcação *f* -**4.** POL [of bill] revisão *f*.

readjust [ˌriːəˈdʒʌst] ⟨⟩ *vt* reajustar. ⟨⟩ *vi*: **to** ~ **(to sthg)** reorganizar-se (para algo).

readout [ˈriːdaʊt] *n* COMPUT exibição *f* de dados.

ready [ˈredɪ] (*pt* & *pp* -**ied**) ⟨⟩ *adj* -**1.** [prepared] pronto(ta); **to be** ~ **to do sthg** estar pronto(ta) para fazer algo; **to be** ~ **for sthg** estar pronto(ta) para algo; **to get** ~ preparar-se; **to get sthg** ~ preparar algo -**2.** [willing]: **to be** ~ **to do sthg** estar disposto(ta) a fazer algo -**3.** [in need of]: **to be** ~ **for sthg** precisar de algo -**4.** [likely]: **to be** ~ **to do sthg** estar prestes a fazer algo -**5.** [easily accessible] à mão. ⟨⟩ *vt* preparar.

ready cash *n* (U) dinheiro *m* em mão.

ready-made *adj* pronto(ta).

ready money *n* (U) dinheiro *m* à vista.

ready-to-wear *adj* prêt-à-porter.

reafforestation [ˈriːəˌfɒrɪˈsteɪʃn] *n* (U) reflorestamento *m*.

real [rɪəl] ⟨⟩ *adj* -**1.** [gen] real; **in** ~ **terms** em termos reais -**2.** [authentic - problem, situation] real; [- gold, jewels, legítimo(ma); **the** ~ **thing** a verdade; **a** ~ **job** um emprego de verdade; **it's for** ~ é real -**3.** [for emphasis] verdadeiro(ra). ⟨⟩ *adv* US bem.

real estate *n* (U) bens *mpl* imobiliários.

realign [ˌriːəˈlaɪn] *vt* -**1.** POL reorganizar -**2.** [brakes] realinhar.

realism [ˈrɪəlɪzm] *n* (U) -**1.** [common sense] bom senso *m* -**2.** [artistic style] realismo *m*.

realistic [ˌrɪəˈlɪstɪk] *adj* realista; ~ **chance** chance real; **to be** ~ **about sthg** ser realista em relação a algo.

reality [rɪˈælətɪ] (*pl* -**ies**) *n* [gen] realidade *f*.

reality TV *n* (U) reality shows *mpl*.

realization [ˌrɪəlaɪˈzeɪʃn] *n* (U) -**1.** [awareness, recognition] percepção *f* -**2.** [achievement] realização *f*.

realize, -ise [ˈrɪəlaɪz] *vt* -**1.** [become aware of, understand] perceber, dar-se conta de -**2.** [achieve] concretizar -**3.** COMM atingir.

really [ˈrɪəlɪ] ⟨⟩ *adv* -**1.** [gen] realmente -**2.** [to reduce force of negative statements] na real. ⟨⟩ *excl* -**1.** [expressing doubt]: **really?** é mesmo?, não é mesmo? -**2.** [expressing surprise, disbelief]: **really?** mesmo? -**3.** [expressing disapproval]: **really!** francamente!

realm [relm] *n* -**1.** [field] domínio *m* -**2.** [kingdom] reino *m*.

realtor [ˈrɪəltəʳ] *n* US corretor *m*, -ra *f* de imóveis.

reap [riːp] *vt* colher; **you** ~ **what you sow** você colhe o que planta.

reappear [ˌriːəˈpɪəʳ] *vi* reaparecer.

rear [rɪəʳ] ⟨⟩ *adj* -**1.** [door, window] dos fundos -**2.** [wheel] traseiro(ra). ⟨⟩ *n* -**1.** [back - of building] fundos *mpl*; [- of vehicle] traseira *f*; **to bring up the** ~ fechar a raia- **2.** *inf* [buttocks] bunda *f.* <> *vt* [children, animals, plants] criar. <> *vi*: **to ~ (up)** empinar, empinar-se.

rearm [riːˈɑːm] *vt* & *vi* rearmar.

rearmost [ˈrɪəməʊst] *adj* último(ma).

rearrange [ˌriːəˈreɪndʒ] *vt* - **1.** [arrange differently] reorganizar - **2.** [reschedule] reajustar.

rearview mirror [ˈrɪəvjuː-] *n* espelho *m* retrovisor.

reason [ˈriːzn] <> *n* - **1.** [cause] razão *f*, motivo *m*; ~ **for sthg** razão para algo; **for some** ~ por alguma razão - **2.** *(U)* [justification]: **to have ~ to do sthg** ter razões para fazer algo - **3.** *(U)* [rationality, common sense] razão *f*; **to listen to** ~ ouvir a razão; **it stands to** ~ é lógico. <> *vt* concluir. <> *vi* raciocinar.

➡ **reason with** *vt fus* argumentar com.

reasonable [ˈriːznəbl] *adj* - **1.** [sensible] sensato(ta) - **2.** [acceptable] razoável - **3.** [fairly large] aceitável.

reasonably [ˈriːznəblɪ] *adv* - **1.** [quite] razoavelmente - **2.** [sensibly] sensatamente.

reasoned [ˈriːznd] *adj* racional.

reasoning [ˈriːznɪŋ] *n* *(U)* raciocínio *m*.

reassess [ˌriːəˈses] *vt* reavaliar.

reassurance [ˌriːəˈʃɔːrəns] *n* - **1.** *(U)* [comfort] reconforto *m* - **2.** [promise] nova garantia *f*.

reassure [ˌriːəˈʃɔː] *vt* tranqüilizar.

reassuring [ˌriːəˈʃɔːrɪŋ] *adj* tranqüilizador(ra).

rebate [ˈriːbeɪt] *n* restituição *f*.

rebel [*n* ˈrebl, *vb* rɪˈbel] (*pt* & *pp* -**led**, *cont* -**ling**) <> *n* rebelde *mf.* <> *vi* - **1.** [revolt]: **to ~ (against sb/sthg)** rebelar-se (contra alguém/algo) - **2.** [not conform]: **to ~ (against sb/sthg)** revoltar-se (contra alguém/algo).

rebellion [rɪˈbeljən] *n* - **1.** [armed revolt] rebelião *f* - **2.** [opposition] oposição *f* - **3.** *(U)* [nonconformity] revolta *f.*

rebellious [rɪˈbeljəs] *adj* rebelde.

rebound [*n* ˈriːbaʊnd, *vb* ˌriːˈbaʊnd] <> *n*: **on the ~** [ball] no ricochete; [person] no impulso. *vi* - **1.** [ball] ricochetear.

rebuff [rɪˈbʌf] *n* recusa *f.*

rebuild [ˌriːˈbɪld] (*pt* & *pp* -**built**) *vt* reconstruir.

rebuke [rɪˈbjuːk] <> *n* reprimenda *f.* <> *vt*: **to ~ sb (for sthg)** repreender alguém (por algo).

recalcitrant [rɪˈkælsɪtrənt] *adj* obstinado(da).

recall [rɪˈkɔːl] <> *n* - **1.** *(U)* [memory] recordação *f* - **2.** [on faulty goods] recall *m.* <> *vt* - **1.** [remember] relembrar-se

de - **2.** [summon back - parliament] reconvocar; [- ambassador] chamar de volta.

recant [rɪˈkænt] *vi* retratar-se.

recap [ˈriːkæp] (*pt* & *pp* -**ped**, *cont* -**ping**) *inf* <> *n* recapitulação *f.* <> *vt* [summarize] recapitular. <> *vi* [summarize] recapitular.

recapitulate [ˌriːkəˈpɪtjʊleɪt] *vt* & *vi* recapitular.

recd, rec'd (*abbr of* received) recebido.

recede [riːˈsiːd] *vi* - **1.** [move away] afastar-se - **2.** *fig* [disappear, fade] desaparecer.

receding [rɪˈsiːdɪŋ] *adj* - **1.** [hair]: ~ **hairline** entrada *f* (no cabelo) - **2.** [chin]: ~ **chin** queixo *m* retraído.

receipt [rɪˈsiːt] *n* - **1.** [piece of paper] recibo *m* - **2.** *(U)* [act of receiving] recebimento *m.*

➡ **receipts** *npl* receita *f.*

receive [rɪˈsiːv] *vt* - **1.** [gen] receber - **2.** [welcome] recepcionar - **3.** [greet]: **to be well/badly ~d** ser bem/mal recebido(da).

receiver [rɪˈsiːvə] *n* - **1.** [of telephone] fone *m* - **2.** [radio, TV set] receptor *m* - **3.** [criminal] receptador *m*, -ra *f* - **4.** *FIN* [official] curador *m*, -ra *f.*

recent [ˈriːsnt] *adj* recente.

recently [ˈriːsntlɪ] *adv* recentemente; **until ~, no one knew of his existence** até pouco tempo atrás, ninguém sabia da existência dele.

receptacle [rɪˈseptəkl] *n* recipiente *m.*

reception [rɪˈsepʃn] *n* recepção *f.*

reception desk *n* recepção *f.*

receptionist [rɪˈsepʃənɪst] *n* recepcionista *mf.*

recess [ˈriːses, *UK* rɪˈses] *n* - **1.** [vacation] recesso *m*; **to be in/go into ~** estar/entrar em recesso - **2.** [alcove] reentrância *f*, vão *m* - **3.** [of mind, memory] refluxo *m* - **4.** *US SCH* recreio *m*, intervalo *m.*

recession [rɪˈseʃn] *n* recessão *f.*

recharge [ˌriːˈtʃɑːdʒ] *vt* recarregar.

recipe [ˈresɪpɪ] *n* receita *f.*

recipient [rɪˈsɪpɪənt] <> *adj* recebedor(ra), receptor(ra). <> *n* - **1.** [of letter] destinatário(ria) - **2.** [of cheque] beneficiário(ria) - **3.** [of award] ganhador(ra).

reciprocal [rɪˈsɪprəkl] *adj* recíproco(ca).

recital [rɪˈsaɪtl] *n* recital *m.*

recite [rɪˈsaɪt] *vt* - **1.** [perform aloud] recitar - **2.** [list] enumerar.

reckless [ˈrekləs] *adj* imprudente.

reckon [ˈrekn] *vt* - **1.** *inf* [think] achar - **2.** [consider, judge]: **he was ~ed to be too old for the job** ele foi considerado velho demais para o trabalho - **3**. [calculate] calcular.

◆ **reckon on** *vt fus* contar com.

◆ **reckon with** *vt fus* [expect] esperar.

reckoning [ˈrekənɪŋ] *n* cálculo *m*.

reclaim [rɪˈkleɪm] *vt* - **1**. [claim back] recuperar - **2**. [make fit for use] desbravar.

recline [rɪˈklaɪn] *vi* reclinar-se.

reclining [rɪˈklaɪnɪŋ] *adj* reclinável.

recluse [rɪˈkluːs] *n* recluso *m*, -sa *f*.

recognition [ˌrekəɡˈnɪʃn] *n* - **1**. [identification] reconhecimento *m*; **beyond** OR **out of all** ~ irreconhecível - **2**. [acknowledgment] identificação *f*; **in** ~ **of** em reconhecimento a.

recognizable [ˈrekəɡnaɪzəbl] *adj* reconhecível; **he was barely** ~ mal dava para reconhecê-lo.

recognize, -ise [ˈrekəɡnaɪz] *vt* reconhecer.

recoil [*vb* rɪˈkɔɪl, *n* ˈriːkɔɪl] ◇ *n* coice *m*. ◇ *vi* recuar; **to** ~ **from/at sthg** recuar diante de algo; **she** ~**ed at his suggestion** ela recuou diante da sugestão dele.

recollect [ˌrekəˈlekt] *vt* recordar-se de, lembrar-se de.

recollection [ˌrekəˈlekʃn] *n* recordação *f*, lembrança *f*.

recommend [ˌrekəˈmend] *vt* - **1**. [commend, speak in favour of] : **to** ~ **sb/sthg (to sb)** recomendar alguém/algo (para alguém) - **2**. [advise] recomendar.

recompense [ˈrekəmpens] ◇ *n*: ~ **(for sthg)** recompensa (por algo). ◇ *vt*: **to** ~ **sb (for sthg)** recompensar alguém (por algo).

reconcile [ˈrekənsaɪl] *vt* - **1**. [beliefs, ideas] conciliar; **to** ~ **sthg with sthg** conciliar algo com algo - **2**. [people] reconciliar - **3**. [resign] : **to** ~ **o.s. to sthg** resignar-se a algo.

reconditioned [ˌriːkənˈdɪʃnd] *adj* recondicionado(da).

reconnaissance [rɪˈkɒnɪsəns] *n* (*U*) reconhecimento *m*.

reconnoitre UK, **reconnoiter** US [ˌrekəˈnɔɪtəʳ] ◇ *vt* reconhecer. ◇ *vi* fazer um reconhecimento.

reconsider [ˌriːkənˈsɪdəʳ] *vt* & *vi* reconsiderar.

reconstruct [ˌriːkənˈstrʌkt] *vt* reconstruir.

record [*n* & *adj* ˈrekɔːd, *vb* rɪˈkɔːd] ◇ *adj* recorde. ◇ *n* - **1**. [gen] registro *m*; **off the** ~ em off; **on** ~ [on file] em registro; [ever recorded] já registrado(da) - **2**. [vinyl disc] disco *m* - **3**. [best achievement] recorde *m*. ◇ *vt* - **1**. [write down] registrar - **2**. [put on tape etc.] gravar.

recorded delivery [rɪˈkɔːdɪd-] *n* (*U*): **to send sthg by** ~ enviar algo como carta registrada.

recorder [rɪˈkɔːdəʳ] *n* - **1**. [machine] gravador *m* - **2**. [musical instrument] flauta *f* doce.

record holder *n* detentor *m*, -ra *f* do recorde.

recording [rɪˈkɔːdɪŋ] *n* gravação *f*.

record player *n* toca-discos *m*.

recount [*n* ˈriːkaʊnt, *vt sense 1* rɪˈkaʊnt, *sense 2* ˌriːˈkaʊnt] ◇ *n* recontagem *f*. ◇ *vt* - **1**. [narrate] relatar - **2**. [count again] recontar.

recoup [rɪˈkuːp] *vt* recuperar.

recourse [rɪˈkɔːs] *n* (*U*) *fml*: **to have** ~ **to sthg** recorrer a algo.

recover [rɪˈkʌvəʳ] ◇ *vt* - **1**. [stolen goods, money] recuperar; **to** ~ **sthg (from sb/somewhere)** recuperar algo (de alguém/algum lugar) - **2**. [consciousness, one's breath] recobrar. ◇ *vi* - **1**. [from illness, accident] [finances]: **to** ~ **(from sthg)** recuperar-se (de algo) - **2**. [from shock, setback, sb's death]: **to** ~ **(from sthg)** refazer-se (de algo).

recovery [rɪˈkʌvərɪ] (*pl* -ies) *n* - **1**.: **(from sthg)** recuperação (de algo) - **2**. recuperação *f*.

recreation [ˌrekrɪˈeɪʃn] *n* (*U*) recreação *f*, divertimento *f*.

recrimination [rɪˌkrɪmɪˈneɪʃn] *n* (*U*) recriminação *f*.

◆ **recriminations** *npl* recriminações *fpl*.

recruit [rɪˈkruːt] ◇ *n* recruta *mf*. ◇ *vt* recrutar; **to** ~ **sb (for sthg/to do sthg)** recrutar alguém (para algo/para fazer algo). ◇ *vi* [take on new staff] recrutar gente.

recruitment [rɪˈkruːtmənt] *n* (*U*) recrutamento *m*.

rectangle [ˈrekˌtæŋɡl] *n* retângulo *m*.

rectangular [rekˈtæŋɡjʊləʳ] *adj* retangular.

rectify [ˈrektɪfaɪ] (*pt* & *pp* -ied) *vt fml* retificar.

rector [ˈrektəʳ] *n* - **1**. [priest] pároco *m* - **2**. *Scot* [head - of school] diretor *m*, -ra *f*; [- of college, university] reitor *m*, -ra *f*.

rectory [ˈrektərɪ] (*pl* -ies) *n* residência *f* paroquial.

recuperate [rɪˈkuːpəreɪt] *vi fml*: **to** ~ **(from sthg)** restabelecer-se (de algo).

recur [rɪˈkɜːʳ] (*pt* & *pp* -red, *cont* -ring) *vi* repetir-se.

recurrence [rɪˈkʌrəns] *n fml* recorrência *f*.

recurrent [rɪˈkʌrənt] *adj* recorrente.

recycle [ˌriːˈsaɪkl] *vt* reciclar.

red [red] (*compar* -**der**, *superl* -**dest**) ⟨⟩ *adj* -**1.** [gen] vermelho(lha) -**2.** [hair] ruivo(va). ⟨⟩ *n* (U) [colour] vermelho *m*; **to be in the** ~ *inf* estar no vermelho.

red card *n* FTBL: **to be shown the** ~, **to get a** ~ receber cartão vermelho.

red carpet *n*: **to roll out the** ~ **for sb** estender o tapete vermelho para alguém.

➤ **red-carpet** *adj*: **to give sb the red-carpet treatment** dar tratamento VIP para alguém.

Red Cross *n*: **the** ~ a Cruz Vermelha.

redcurrant ['redkʌrənt] *n* -**1.** [fruit] groselha *f* -**2.** [bush] groselheira *f*.

redden ['redn] ⟨⟩ *vt* [make red] avermelhar. ⟨⟩ *vi* [flush] ruborizar-se, ficar ruborizado(da).

redecorate [,ri:'dekəreɪt] ⟨⟩ *vt* redecorar. ⟨⟩ *vi* redecorar a casa.

redeem [rɪ'di:m] *vt* -**1.** [save, rescue] redimir -**2.** [from pawnbroker] resgatar.

redeemer *n* RELIG: **the Redeemer** o Redentor.

redeeming [rɪ'di:mɪŋ] *adj* redentor, que redime.

redeploy [,ri:dɪ'plɔɪ] *vt* remanejar.

red-faced [-'feɪst] *adj* -**1.** [after exercise, with heat] vermelho(lha) -**2.** [with embarrassment] corado(da).

red-haired [-'heəd] *adj* ruivo(va).

red-handed [-'hændɪd] *adj*: **to catch sb** ~ pegar alguém com a mão na massa.

redhead ['redhed] *n* ruiva *f*.

red herring *n fig* pista *f* falsa.

red-hot *adj* -**1.** [extremely hot] em brasa -**2.** [very enthusiastic] apaixonado(da) -**3.** *inf* [very good] supimpa.

redid [,ri:'dɪd] *pt* ⊳ **redo**.

redirect [,ri:dɪ'rekt] *vt* -**1.** [mail] redirecionar -**2.** [traffic, aircraft] desviar -**3.** [one's energies, money, aid] direcionar.

rediscover [,ri:dɪs'kʌvəʳ] *vt* -**1.** [re-experience] redescobrir -**2.** [make popular, famous again]: **to be** ~**ed** ser redescoberto(ta).

red light *n* [traffic signal] luz *f* vermelha.

red-light district *n* zona *f* do baixo meretrício.

redo [,ri:'du:] (*pt* -**did**, *pp* -**done**) *vt* [do again] refazer.

redolent ['redələnt] *adj literary* -**1.** [reminiscent]: ~ **of sthg** rememorativo(va) de algo -**2.** [smelling]: ~ **of sthg** com aroma de algo.

redone *pp* ⊳ **redo**.

redouble [,ri:'dʌbl] *vt*: **to** ~ **one's efforts (to do sthg)** redobrar os esforços (para fazer algo).

redraft [,ri:'drɑːft] *vt* reescrever.

redress [rɪ'dres] *fml* ⟨⟩ *n* (U) retificação *f*. ⟨⟩ *vt*: **to** ~ **the balance** compensar.

Red Sea *n*: **the** ~ o Mar Vermelho.

reduce [rɪ'dju:s] ⟨⟩ *vt* -**1.** [make smaller, less] reduzir; **to** ~ **sthg to a pulp** reduzir algo à essência -**2.** [force, bring]: **to be** ~**d to doing sthg** ser forçado(da) a fazer algo; **to be** ~**d to sthg** estar reduzido(da) a algo. ⟨⟩ *vi* US [lose weight] emagrecer.

reduction [rɪ'dʌkʃn] *n* -**1.** [decrease]: ~ **(in sthg)** redução (em algo) -**2.** [amount of decrease]: ~ **(of)** redução de.

redundancy [rɪ'dʌndənsɪ] (*pl* -**ies**) *n UK* -**1.** [job loss] demissão *f* -**2.** (U) [jobless state] desemprego *m*.

redundant [rɪ'dʌndənt] *adj* -**1.** *UK* [jobless]: **to be made** ~ ficar desempregado(da) -**2.** [superfluous] supérfluo(a).

reed [ri:d] *n* -**1.** [plant] junco *m* -**2.** [of musical instrument] palheta *f*.

reef [ri:f] *n* recife *m*.

reek [ri:k] ⟨⟩ *n* fedor *m*. ⟨⟩ *vi*: **to** ~ **(of sthg)** feder (a algo).

reel [ri:l] ⟨⟩ *n* -**1.** [roll] rolo *m* -**2.** [on fishing rod] molinete *m*. ⟨⟩ *vi* [stagger] cambalear.

➤ **reel in** *vt sep* enrolar.

➤ **reel off** *vt sep* [list] enumerar.

re-enact *vt* reviver.

ref [ref] *n* -**1.** *inf* (*abbr of* **referee**) SPORT árbitro *m* -**2.** (*abbr of* **reference**) ADMIN ref.

refectory [rɪ'fektərɪ] (*pl* -**ies**) *n* -**1.** [in school, college] cantina *f* -**2.** [in monastery] refeitório *m*.

refer [rɪ'fɜːʳ] (*pt* & *pp* -**red**, *cont* -**ring**) *vt* -**1.** [person]: **to** ~ **sb to sthg** encaminhar alguém para algo -**2.** [report, case, decision]: **to** ~ **sthg to sb/sthg** encaminhar algo para alguém/algo.

➤ **refer to** *vt fus* -**1.** [mention, speak about] referir-se a -**2.** [apply to, concern] aplicar-se a -**3.** [consult] consultar.

referee [,refə'ri:] ⟨⟩ *n* -**1.** SPORT árbitro *m*, -**tra** *f* -**2.** *UK* [for job application] referência *f*. ⟨⟩ *vt* & *vi* SPORT apitar.

reference ['refrəns] *n* -**1.** [gen] referência *f* -**2.** (U) [act of mentioning]: **to make** ~ **to sb/sthg** referência a alguém/algo; **with** ~ **to** *fml* com referência a -**3.** [mention]: ~ **(to sb/sthg)** menção a alguém/algo -**4.** (U) [for advice, information]: ~ **(to sb/sthg)** referência a alguém/algo -**5.** COMM [in letter] referências *fpl*.

reference book *n* livro *m* de consulta.

reference number *n* número *m* de referência.

referendum [ˌrefəˈrendəm] (*pl* -s *OR* -da [-də]) *n POL* plebiscito *m*.

refill [*n* ˈriːfil, *vb* ˌriːˈfil] <> *n* -1. [for pen, lighter] carga *f* nova - 2. *inf* [drink] dose *f* extra. <> *vt* [fill again - bottle, glass] encher novamente; [- petrol tank] reabastecer.

refine [rɪˈfaɪn] *vt* -1. [purify] refinar - 2. [details, speech] aprimorar.

refined [rɪˈfaɪnd] *adj* refinado(da).

refinement [rɪˈfaɪnmənt] *n* -1. [improvement]: ~ (on sthg) refinamento (de algo) - 2. (*U*) [gentility] requinte *m*.

reflect [rɪˈflekt] <> *vt* refletir; to ~ that ... refletir que ... <> *vi* [think, consider]: to ~ (on *OR* upon sthg) refletir (sobre algo).

reflection [rɪˈflekʃn] *n* -1. [gen] reflexo *m* - 2. [comment, thought] reflexão *f*; ~ on sthg reflexão sobre algo; on ~ pensando bem.

reflector [rɪˈflektəʳ] *n* refletor *m*.

reflex [ˈriːfleks] *n*: ~ (action) (ato) reflexo *m*.

reflexive [rɪˈfleksɪv] *adj GRAMM* reflexivo(va).

reforestation [riːˌfɒrɪˈsteɪʃn] *n esp US* = reafforestation.

reform [rɪˈfɔːm] <> *n* reforma *f*. <> *vt* -1. [change] reformar - 2. [improve behaviour of] corrigir. <> *vi* corrigir-se.

Reformation [ˌrefəˈmeɪʃn] *n*: the ~ a Reforma.

reformer [rɪˈfɔːməʳ] *n* reformador *m*, -ra *f*.

refrain [rɪˈfreɪn] <> *n* refrão *m*. <> *vi fml*: to ~ from doing sthg abster-se de fazer algo.

refresh [rɪˈfreʃ] *vt* refrescar.

refreshed [rɪˈfreʃt] *adj* revigorado(da).

refresher course [rɪˈfreʃəʳ-] *n* curso *m* de aperfeiçoamento *OR* atualização.

refreshing [rɪˈfreʃɪŋ] *adj* -1. [pleasantly different] reconfortante - 2. [cooling, energy-giving] refrescante.

refreshments [rɪˈfreʃmənts] *npl* comes *mpl* e bebes, lanche *m*.

refrigerator [rɪˈfrɪdʒəreɪtəʳ] *n* geladeira *f*, refrigerador *m*.

refuel [ˌriːˈfjʊəl] (*UK pt* & *pp* -led, *cont* -ling, *US pt* & *pp* -ed, *cont* -ing) <> *vt* reabastecer. <> *vi* reabastecer-se (*de combustível*).

refuge [ˈrefjuːdʒ] *n* -1. [place of safety] refúgio *m* - 2. (*U*) [safety]: to seek *OR* take ~ [hide] procurar refúgio, refugiar-se; to seek *OR* take ~ in sthg *fig* procurar *OR* buscar refúgio em algo, refugiar-se em algo.

refugee [ˌrefjʊˈdʒiː] *n* refugiado *m*, -da *f*.

refund [*n* ˈriːfʌnd, *vb* rɪˈfʌnd] <> *n* reembolso *m*. <> *vt*: to ~ sthg to sb, to ~ sb sthg reembolsar algo a alguém.

refurbish [ˌriːˈfɜːbɪʃ] *vt* -1. [shop, office] reformar - 2. [building] restaurar.

refusal [rɪˈfjuːzl] *n* recusa *f*; her ~ to accept the conditions o fato de ela não ter aceitado as condições; to meet with ~ ser rechaçado(da).

refuse[1] [rɪˈfjuːz] <> *vt* -1. [withhold, deny]: to ~ sb sthg, to ~ sthg to sb negar algo a alguém - 2. [decline] recusar; to ~ to do sthg recusar-se a fazer algo, negar-se a fazer algo. <> *vi* negar-se, dizer que não.

refuse[2] [ˈrefjuːs] *n* (*U*) lixo *m*, refugo *m*.

refuse collection [ˈrefjuːs-] *n* coleta *f* de lixo.

refute [rɪˈfjuːt] *vt fml* refutar.

regain [rɪˈgeɪn] *vt* recuperar.

regal [ˈriːgl] *adj* régio(gia).

regalia [rɪˈgeɪljə] *n* (*U*) *fml* insígnias *fpl* reais.

regard [rɪˈgɑːd] <> *n* -1. (*U*) *fml* [respect, esteem] respeito *m*, estima *f*; ~ (for sb/sthg) respeito *OR* estima (por alguém/algo) - 2. [aspect]: in this/that ~ a este respeito. <> *vt* considerar; to ~ o.s. intelligent considerar-se inteligente; to be highly ~ed ser muito bem considerado(da).

→ **regards** *npl* [in greetings] lembranças *fpl*; with my best ~s cordialmente.

→ **as regards** *prep* em relação a, no que se refere a.

→ **in regard to, with regard to** *prep* a respeito de, em relação a.

regarding [rɪˈgɑːdɪŋ] *prep* a respeito de, em relação a.

regardless [rɪˈgɑːdlɪs] *adv* apesar de tudo.

→ **regardless of** *prep* independentemente de; ~ the cost custe o que custar.

regime [reɪˈʒiːm] *n pej* regime *m*.

regiment [ˈredʒɪmənt] *n MIL* regimento *m*.

region [ˈriːdʒən] *n* -1. [gen] região *f* - 2. [range]: in the ~ of por volta de.

regional [ˈriːdʒənl] *adj* regional.

register [ˈredʒɪstəʳ] <> *n* registro *f*. <> *vt* -1. registrar - 2. [express] expressar, mostrar. <> *vi* -1. [enrol]: to ~ as/for sthg inscrever-se como/para algo - 2. [book in] registrar-se - 3. *inf* [be properly understood] assimilar.

registered ['redʒɪstəd] adj -1. [officially listed] oficialmente inscrito(ta) -2. [letter, parcel] registrado(da).

registered trademark n marca f registrada.

registrar ['redʒɪstrɑː'] n -1. [keeper of records] escrivão m, -vã f, oficial mf de registro -2. UNIV [administrator] secretário m, -ria f-geral -3. UK [doctor] médico m, -ca f em estágio de especialização.

registration [,redʒɪ'streɪʃn] n -1. [course enrolment] matrícula f -2. [of births, marriages and deaths] registro m -3. AUT = **registration number**.

registration number n AUT número m de licença.

registry ['redʒɪstrɪ] (pl -ies) n registro m.

registry office n registro m civil.

regret [rɪ'gret] (pt & pp -ted, cont -ting) <> n -1. (U) fml [sorrow] pesar m -2. [sad feeling]: to have no ~ a about sthg não lamentar algo em absoluto. <> vt: to ~ sthg/doing sthg lamentar algo/ter feito algo; we ~ to announce ... lamentamos comunicar ...

regretfully [rɪ'gretfʊlɪ] adv pesarosamente; ~ we have to announce ... lamentamos ter que anunciar ...

regrettable [rɪ'gretəbl] adj fml lamentável.

regroup [,ri:'gru:p] vi reagrupar-se.

regular ['regjʊlə'] <> adj -1. [gen] regular -2. [frequent - occurrence] freqüente; [- customer] habitual; [- visitor] assíduo(dua) -3. [usual] habitual, normal -4. US [in size] médio(dia) -5. US [pleasant] amigável -6. US [normal] normal. <> n [customer, client] cliente mf habitual.

regularly ['regjʊləlɪ] adv -1. [equally spaced] de maneira uniforme -2. [repeated at expected time] regularmente.

regulate ['regjʊleɪt] vt regular.

regulation [,regjʊ'leɪʃn] <> adj regulamentar. <> n -1. [rule] regra f, lei f -2. (U) [control] regulamento m, regulamentação f.

rehabilitate [,ri:ə'bɪlɪteɪt] vt -1. [convict, addict] reabilitar -2. [patient, invalid] recuperar.

rehearsal [rɪ'hɜ:sl] n ensaio m.

rehearse [rɪ'hɜ:s] <> vt ensaiar. <> vi: to ~ (for sthg) ensaiar (para algo).

reheat [,ri:'hi:t] vt reaquecer, esquentar de novo.

reign [reɪn] <> n reinado m. <> vi: to ~ (over sb/sthg) reinar (sobre alguém/algo).

reimburse [,ri:ɪm'bɜ:s] vt: to ~ sb (for sthg) reembolsar alguém (por algo).

rein [reɪn] n fig: to give (a) free ~ to sb, to give sb free ~ dar carta branca a alguém.
◆ **reins** npl [for horse] rédeas fpl.

reindeer ['reɪn,dɪə'] (pl inv) n rena f.

reinforce [,ri:ɪn'fɔ:s] vt: to ~ sthg (with sthg) reforçar algo (com algo).

reinforced concrete [,ri:ɪn'fɔ:st-] n (U) concreto m armado.

reinforcement [,ri:ɪn'fɔ:smənt] n reforço m.
◆ **reinforcements** npl reforços mpl.

reinstate [,ri:ɪn'steɪt] vt -1. [person - in job] readmitir; [- in position, office] reempossar, reintegrar -2. [payment, idea, policy] restabelecer.

reissue [ri:'ɪʃu:] <> n reedição f, reimpressão f. <> vt reeditar, reimprimir.

reiterate [ri:'ɪtəreɪt] vt fml reiterar.

reject [n 'ri:dʒekt, vb rɪ'dʒekt] <> n [in factory, shop] refugo m, rejeito m. <> vt -1. [not agree to] rejeitar, não concordar com -2. [dismiss, not accept] rejeitar -3. [for job] recusar.

rejection [rɪ'dʒekʃn] n -1. (U) [act of refusal] rejeição f -2. [for job] recusa f.

rejoice [rɪ'dʒɔɪs] vi: to ~ (at OR in sthg) regozijar-se OR alegrar-se (por algo).

rejuvenate [rɪ'dʒu:vəneɪt] vt rejuvenescer.

rekindle [,ri:'kɪndl] vt fig reacender, reavivar.

relapse [rɪ'læps] <> n recaída f. <> vi: to ~ into [coma] entrar novamente em; [drunken stupor, old ways] voltar a cair em; [crime] reincidir em.

relate [rɪ'leɪt] <> vt -1. [connect]: to ~ sthg to sthg relacionar algo a algo -2. [tell] contar. <> vi -1. [connect]: to ~ to sthg relacionar-se a algo -2. [concern]: to ~ to sthg referir-se a algo -3. [empathize]: to ~ (to sb/sthg) ter muito em comum (com alguém/algo).
◆ **relating to** prep sobre, acerca de.

related [rɪ'leɪtɪd] adj -1. [in same family] aparentado(da); to be ~ to sb ser aparentado(da) de alguém -2. [connected] relacionado(da).

relation [rɪ'leɪʃn] n -1. (U) [connection]: ~ (to/between) relação f (com/entre); to bear no ~ to não ter nada a ver com -2. [family member] parente mf, familiar mf.
◆ **relations** npl [relationship] relações fpl; ~ between/with relações entre/com.

relationship [rɪ'leɪʃnʃɪp] n -1. [gen] relação f -2. [relations] relação f, relacionamento m -3. [connection] ligação f.

relative ['relətɪv] ◇ *adj* relativo(va). ◇ *n* parente *mf*, familiar *mf*.
➡ **relative to** *prep fml* **- 1.** [compared to] em comparação com **- 2.** [connected with] relativo(va) a, com relação a.

relatively ['relətɪvlɪ] *adv* relativamente.

relax [rɪ'læks] ◇ *vt* **- 1.** [gen] relaxar **- 2.** [loosen, free up] afrouxar. ◇ *vi* **- 1.** [person] relaxar, descontrair-se; ~ **!** It's OK! relaxe! Está tudo bem! **- 2.** [grip] afrouxar-se.

relaxation [,ri:læk'seɪʃn] *n* (U) **- 1.** [rest] relaxamento *m* **- 2.** [of rule, discipline, regulation] afrouxamento *m*.

relaxed [rɪ'lækst] *adj* **- 1.** [person] relaxado(da), descontraído(da) **- 2.** [meeting, evening, mood] descontraído(da).

relaxing [rɪ'læksɪŋ] *adj* relaxante.

relay ['ri:leɪ] (*pt* & *pp* senses 1 & 2 **-ed**, *pt* & *pp* sense 3 **relaid**) ◇ *n* **- 1.** SPORT: ~ **(race)** corrida *f* de revezamento; **in** ~ **s** *fig* em turnos **- 2.** [broadcast] retransmissão *f*. ◇ *vt* **- 1.** [broadcast] retransmitir **- 2.** [message, news]: **to** ~ **sthg (to sb)** transmitir algo (a alguém).

release [rɪ'li:s] ◇ *n* **- 1.** (U) [from captivity] soltura *f*, libertação *f* **- 2.** (U) [from pain, suffering] alívio *m* **- 3.** [statement] comunicado *m* **- 4.** (U) [of gas, fumes] escapamento *m*, emissão *f* **- 5.** (U) [of film, video, CD] lançamento *m* **- 6.** [film, video, CD]: **new** ~ novo lançamento. ◇ *vt* **- 1.** [set free] soltar, libertar; **to** ~ **sb from prison/captivity** libertar OR soltar alguém da prisão/do cativeiro; **to** ~ **sb from sthg** [promise, contract] liberar alguém de algo **- 2.** [make available] liberar **- 3.** [control, grasp, mechanism] soltar **- 4.** [let out, emit]: **heat is** ~ **d from the liquid into the air** o calor é liberado do líquido para o ar **- 5.** [film, video, CD] lançar; [statement, news story] divulgar.

relegate ['relɪgeɪt] *vt* **- 1.** [demote]: **to** ~ **sb/sthg (to)** relegar alguém/algo (a) **- 2.** SPORT: **to be** ~ **d** UK ser rebaixado(da).

relent [rɪ'lent] *vi* **- 1.** [person] condescender **- 2.** [wind, storm] abrandar-se, acalmar-se.

relentless [rɪ'lentlɪs] *adj* implacável.

relevant ['reləvənt] *adj* **- 1.** [pertinente; ~ **(to sb/sthg)** relevante (a alguém/algo) **- 2.** [important]: ~ **(to sb/sthg)** importante (a alguém/algo).

reliable [rɪ'laɪəbl] *adj* **- 1.** [dependable] confiável **- 2.** [correct, true] seguro(ra).

reliably [rɪ'laɪəblɪ] *adv* **- 1.** [dependably] de forma confiável **- 2.** [correctly, truly]: **to be** ~ **informed that ...** saber de fonte segura que ...

reliant [rɪ'laɪənt] *adj*: ~ **on sb/sthg** dependente de alguém/algo.

relic ['relɪk] *n* relíquia *f*.

relief [rɪ'li:f] *n* **- 1.** [comfort] alívio *m*; **she sighed with** ~ ela suspirou aliviada **- 2.** (U) [for poor, refugees] auxílio *m* **- 3.** US [social security] subsídio *m*.

relieve [rɪ'li:v] *vt* **- 1.** [ease, lessen] aliviar; **to** ~ **sb of sthg** aliviar alguém de algo **- 2.** [take over from] substituir **- 3.** [give help to] auxiliar.

religion [rɪ'lɪdʒn] *n* religião *f*.

religious [rɪ'lɪdʒəs] *adj* religioso(sa).

relinquish [rɪ'lɪŋkwɪʃ] *vt* **- 1.** [power, post, claim] renunciar a **- 2.** [hold] soltar.

relish ['relɪʃ] ◇ *n* **- 1.** (U) [enjoyment]: **with (great)** ~ com(grande)satisfação **- 2.** [pickle] picles *mpl*. ◇ *vt* desfrutar de; **to** ~ **the thought** OR **idea** OR **prospect of doing sthg** desfrutar de antemão da idéia OR da perspectiva de fazer algo.

relocate [,ri:ləʊ'keɪt] ◇ *vt* realocar, transferir. ◇ *vi* transferir-se.

reluctance [rɪ'lʌktəns] *n* (U) relutância *f*.

reluctant [rɪ'lʌktənt] *adj* relutante; **to be** ~ **to do sthg** estar pouco disposto(ta) a fazer algo.

reluctantly [rɪ'lʌktəntlɪ] *adv* relutantemente.

rely [rɪ'laɪ] (*pt* & *pp* **-ied**) ➡ **rely on** *vt fus* **- 1.** [count on] contar com; **to** ~ **on sb/sthg to do sthg** estar certo(ta) de que alguém/algo fará algo **- 2.** [be dependent on]: **to** ~ **on sb/sthg for sthg** depender de alguém/algo para algo.

remain [rɪ'meɪn] *vi* **- 1.** [stay] permanecer, ficar; **to** ~ **the same** continuar sendo igual **- 2.** [be left] ficar; **the problem** ~ o problema continua; **to** ~ **to be done** ficar para ser feito(ta). ➡ **remains** *npl* **- 1.** [of meal, fortune, body] restos *mpl* **- 2.** [corpses] corpos *mpl* **- 3.** [of ancient civilization, buildings] ruínas *fpl*.

remainder [rɪ'meɪndə'] *n* **- 1.** [rest]: **the** ~ o resto **- 2.** MATH resto *m*; **three into ten goes three** ~ **one** dez (dividido) por três é igual a três e sobra um.

remaining [rɪ'meɪnɪŋ] *adj* restante; **it's my last** ~ **pound!** é a última libra que eu tenho!

remand [rɪ'mɑ:nd] JUR ◇ *n*: **on** ~ sob prisão preventiva. ◇ *vt* recolocar em prisão preventiva; **to be** ~ **ed in custody** estar sob custódia.

remark [rɪ'mɑ:k] ◇ *n* comentário *m*. ◇ *vt*: **to** ~ **(that)** comentar que.

remarkable [rɪ'mɑ:kəbl] *adj* excepcional, extraordinário(ria).

remarry [,ri:'mærɪ] (*pt* & *pp* **-ied**) *vi* casar-se de novo.

remedial [rɪ'miːdjəl] *adj* -**1.** [pupil] atrasado(da) -**2.** [teacher, class] de reforço -**3.** [corrective] corretivo (va).

remedy ['remədɪ] (*pl* -**ies**, *pt & pp* -**ied**) ◇ *n* -**1.** [for ill health]: ~ (for sthg) remédio *m* (para algo) -**2.** *fig* [solution]: ~ (for sthg) OR solução *f* (para algo). ◇ *vt* remediar.

remember [rɪ'membəʳ] ◇ *vt* lembrar-se de, lembrar; to ~ doing sthg lembrar-se de ter feito algo; to ~ to do sthg lembrar-se de fazer algo. ◇ *vi* lembrar(-se).

remembrance [rɪ'membrəns] *n* (*U*) *fml*: in ~ of em memória de.

Remembrance Day *n* na Grã-Bretanha, dia em memória das pessoas mortas nas duas guerras mundiais.

remind [rɪ'maɪnd] *vt* -**1.** [tell]: to ~ sb (about sthg/to do sthg) lembrar alguém (de algo/de fazer algo) -**2.** [be reminiscent of]: to ~ sb of sb/sthg fazer alguém se lembrar de alguém/algo; she ~s me of my sister ela me faz lembrar a minha irmã.

reminder [rɪ'maɪndəʳ] *n* -**1.** [to jog memory]: ~ of sthg/to do sthg lembrança *f* de algo/de fazer algo -**2.** [for bill, membership, licence] lembrete *m*.

reminisce [ˌremɪ'nɪs] *vi*: to ~ (about sthg) rememorar(algo).

reminiscent [ˌremɪ'nɪsnt] *adj*: ~ of sb/sthg que faz lembrar alguém/algo.

remiss [rɪ'mɪs] *adj* descuidado(da), negligente.

remit ['riːmɪt] (*pt & pp* -**ted**, *cont* -**ting**) ◇ *n* UK alçada *f*; that's outside my ~ isto está fora da minha alçada. ◇ *vt* remeter.

remittance [rɪ'mɪtns] *n* -**1.** [payment] remessa *f* -**2.** COMM [settlement of invoice] remessa *f* de valores.

remnant ['remnənt] *n* [of cloth] sobra *f*; [of beauty, culture] resto *m*.

remold *n* US = remould.

remorse [rɪ'mɔːs] *n* (*U*) remorso *m*.

remorseful [rɪ'mɔːsfʊl] *adj* cheio (cheia) de remorso.

remorseless [rɪ'mɔːslɪs] *adj* -**1.** [pitiless] desapiedado(da) -**2.** [unstoppable] impiedoso(sa), implacável.

remote [rɪ'məʊt] *adj* -**1.** [gen] remoto(ta) -**2.** [unconnected, detached]: ~ from distante de.

remote control *n* controle *m* remoto.

remotely [rɪ'məʊtlɪ] *adv* remotamente.

remould UK, **remold** US ['riːməʊld] *n* pneu *m* recauchutado.

removable [rɪ'muːvəbl] *adj* desmontável.

removal [rɪ'muːvl] *n* -**1.** UK [change of house] mudança *f* -**2.** (*U*) [act of removing] remoção *f*.

removal van *n* UK caminhão *m* de mudança.

remove [rɪ'muːvl] *vt* -**1.** [gen]: to ~ sthg (from) remover algo (de) -**2.** [take off garment] tirar -**3.** [from a job, post]: to ~ sb (from) demitir alguém de -**4.** [injustice, difficulty] eliminar -**5.** [problem] resolver -**6.** [suspicion] dissipar.

remuneration [rɪˌmjuːnə'reɪʃn] *n fml* (*U*) remuneração *f*.

Renaissance [rə'neɪsəns] *n*: the ~ o Renascimento.

render ['rendəʳ] *vt* -**1.** [make, change] tornar; to ~ sthg useless tornar algo inútil; to ~ sb speechless deixar alguém boquiaberto(ta) -**2.** [give] dar, prestar; to ~ good services prestar bons serviços -**3.** COMPUT exibir.

rendering ['rendərɪŋ] *n* -**1.** [performance - of play] interpretação *f*; [- of song, piece of music] execução *f* -**2.** [translation] tradução *f* -**3.** COMPUT exibição *f*.

rendezvous ['rɒndɪvuː] (*pl inv*) *n* -**1.** [meeting] encontro *m* -**2.** [place] ponto *m* de encontro.

renegade ['renɪgeɪd] *n* renegado *m*, -da *f*.

renew [rɪ'njuː] *vt* -**1.** [gen] renovar -**2.** [start again] reiniciar.

renewable [rɪ'njuːəbl] *adj* renovável.

renewal [rɪ'njuːəl] *n* renovação *f*.

renounce [rɪ'naʊns] *vt* renunciar a.

renovate ['renəveɪt] *vt* renovar, reformar.

renown [rɪ'naʊn] *n* (*U*) renome *m*.

renowned [rɪ'naʊnd] *adj*: ~ (for sthg) renomado(da) (por algo).

rent [rent] ◇ *n* aluguel *m*. ◇ *vt* alugar.

rental ['rentl] ◇ *adj* de aluguel. ◇ *n* [money] aluguel *m*.

renunciation [rɪˌnʌnsɪ'eɪʃn] *n* (*U*) renúncia *f*.

reorganize, -ise [ˌriː'ɔːgənaɪz] *vt* reorganizar.

rep [rep] *n* -**1.** (*abbr of* representative) *inf* representante *mf* -**2.** (*abbr of* repertory) *apresentação de uma série de peças teatrais em sequência por uma mesma companhia teatral em um mesmo teatro.*

repaid [riː'peɪd] *pt & pp* ⊳ repay.

repair [rɪ'peəʳ] ◇ *n* -**1.** (*U*) [act of mending] reparo *m*, conserto *m*; it's beyond ~ não tem conserto; in good/bad ~ em bom/mau estado -**2.** [instance of mending] reparo *m*. ◇ *vt* reparar.

repair kit n caixa f de ferramentas (de bicicleta).

repartee [,repɑː'tiː] n (U) troca f de réplicas engenhosas.

repatriate [,riː'pætrɪeɪt] vt repatriar.

repay [riː'peɪ] (pt & pp **repaid**) vt -1. [money] reembolsar, devolver; to ~ sb sthg, to ~ sthg to sb reembolsar OR devolver algo a alguém -2. [favour] retribuir.

repayment [riː'peɪmənt] n -1. (U) [act of paying back] reembolso m, devolução f -2. [sum] pagamento m.

repeal [rɪ'piːl] <> n revogação f. <> vt revogar.

repeat [rɪ'piːt] <> vt -1. [gen] repetir -2. [broadcast] reprisar. <> n [broadcast] reprise f.

repeatedly [rɪ'piːtɪdlɪ] adv repetidamente.

repel [rɪ'pel] (pt & pp -led, cont -ling) vt -1. [disgust] repugnar -2. [drive away] repelir.

repellent [rɪ'pelənt] <> adj repugnante. <> n repelente m.

repent [rɪ'pent] <> vt arrepender-se de. <> vi: to ~ of sthg arrepender-se de algo.

repentance [rɪ'pentəns] n (U) arrependimento m.

repercussions [,riːpə'kʌʃnz] npl repercussões fpl.

repertoire ['repətwɑːʳ] n repertório m.

repertory ['repətrɪ] n (U) repertório m.

repetition [,repɪ'tɪʃn] n repetição f.

repetitious [,repɪ'tɪʃəs], **repetitive** [rɪ'petɪtɪv] adj repetitivo(va).

replace [rɪ'pleɪs] vt -1. [take the place of] substituir; to ~ sthg (with sthg) substituir OR trocar algo (por algo); to ~ sb (with sb) substituir alguém (por alguém); if I lose your book, I'll ~ it se eu perder o teu livro, eu te dou outro -2. [put back] recolocar no lugar.

replacement [rɪ'pleɪsmənt] n -1. (U) [act of replacing] reposição f, substituição f -2. [new person, object]: ~ (for sthg) substituto m, -ta f (para algo); ~ (for sb) suplente mf (para alguém).

replay [n 'riː:pleɪ, vb ,riː'pleɪ] <> n -1. [recording] replay m -2. [game] partida f de desempate. <> vt -1. [match, game] jogar de novo -2. [film, tape] reprisar.

replenish [rɪ'plenɪʃ] vt fml: to ~ sthg (with sthg) reabastecer OR prover novamente algo (com algo).

replica ['replɪkə] n réplica f, cópia f.

reply [rɪ'plaɪ] (pl -ies, pt & pp -ied) <> n resposta f. <> vt responder; to ~ that responder que. <> vi responder; to ~ to sb/sthg responder a alguém/algo.

reply coupon n cupom m de resposta.

report [rɪ'pɔːt] <> n -1. [description, account] relatório m -2. PRESS reportagem f -3. UK SCH boletim m de avaliação. <> vt -1. [news, crime] informar, comunicar -2. [make known]: to ~ that informar que; to ~ sthg (to sb) relatar algo (a alguém) -3. [complain about]: to ~ sb (to sb) denunciar alguém (a alguém); to ~ sb for sthg denunciar alguém por algo. <> vi -1. [give account] relatar; to ~ on sthg fazer um relatório sobre algo -2. PRESS: to ~ on sthg fazer uma reportagem sobre algo -3. [present o.s.]: to ~ to apresentar-se a; to ~ for sthg apresentar-se para algo.

report card n US SCH boletim m, caderneta f escolar.

reportedly [rɪ'pɔːtɪdlɪ] adv segundo se diz; he is ~ not intending to return to this country sabe-se que ele não pretende voltar a este país.

reporter [rɪ'pɔːtəʳ] n repórter mf.

repose [rɪ'pəʊz] n (U) literary repouso m.

repossess [,riːpə'zes] vt retomar a posse de.

reprehensible [,reprɪ'hensəbl] adj fml repreensível.

represent [,reprɪ'zent] vt representar.

representation [,reprɪzen'teɪʃn] n (U) representação f.
 ◆ **representations** npl fml: to make ~ s to sb apresentar reclamações a alguém.

representative [,reprɪ'zentətɪv] <> adj representativo(va); ~ (of sb/sthg) representativo(va) (de alguém/algo). <> n -1. [of company, organization, group] representante mf -2. COMM: (sales) ~ representante mf (de vendas) -3. US POL deputado m, -da f.

repress [rɪ'pres] vt reprimir.

repression [rɪ'preʃn] n (U) repressão f.

reprieve [rɪ'priːv] <> n -1. [of death sentence] indulto m -2. [respite] trégua f. <> vt indultar.

reprimand ['reprɪmɑːnd] <> n reprimenda f, repreensão f. <> vt repreender.

reprisal [rɪ'praɪzl] n retaliação f, represália f.

reproach [rɪ'prəʊtʃ] <> n -1. (U) [disapproval] censura f, repreensão f -2. [words of blame] acusação f. <> vt: to ~ sb (for OR with sthg) censurar OR repreender alguém (por algo).

reproachful [rɪ'prəʊtʃfʊl] adj de reprovação.

reproduce [,riːprə'djuːs] <> vt reproduzir. <> vi reproduzir-se.

reproduction [ˌriːprəˈdʌkʃn] n reprodução f.

reproof [rɪˈpruːf] n -1. [words of blame] censura f -2. (U) [disapproval] reprovação f.

reprove [rɪˈpruːf] vt: to ~ sb (for sthg) reprovar alguém (por algo).

reptile [ˈreptaɪl] n réptil m.

republic [rɪˈpʌblɪk] n república f.

republican [rɪˈpʌblɪkən] <> adj republicano(na). <> n republicano m, -na f.

➤ **Republican** <> adj -1. [in USA] republicano(na); **the Republican Party** o Partido Republicano -2. [in Northern Ireland] independentista. <> n -1. [in USA] republicano m, -na f -2. [in Northern Ireland] independentista mf.

repudiate [rɪˈpjuːdɪeɪt] vt fml repudiar.

repulse [rɪˈpʌls] vt repelir.

repulsive [rɪˈpʌlsɪv] adj repulsivo(va).

reputable [ˈrepjʊtəbl] adj de boa reputação.

reputation [ˌrepjʊˈteɪʃn] n reputação f.

repute [rɪˈpjuːt] n (U) fml [reputation]: of good/ill ~ de boa/má reputação.

reputed [rɪˈpjuːtɪd] adj de renome; to be ~ to be/do sthg ter fama de ser/fazer algo.

reputedly [rɪˈpjuːtɪdlɪ] adv supostamente, segundo dizem.

request [rɪˈkwest] <> n: ~ (for sthg) solicitação f (de algo); on ~ através de solicitação. <> vt solicitar, pedir; to ~ sb to do sthg solicitar a alguém que faça algo.

request stop n UK parada f de ônibus não-obrigatória.

require [rɪˈkwaɪəʳ] vt -1. [need] requerer, necessitar de -2. [demand] exigir; to ~ sb to do sthg exigir que alguém faça algo; **employees are ~d to wear a uniform** exige-se que os funcionários usem uniformes.

required [rɪˈkwaɪəd] adj necessário(ria); **formal dress is ~d** exigem-se trajes formais.

requirement [rɪˈkwaɪəmənt] n -1. [need] necessidade f -2. [condition] requisito m, condição f.

requisition [ˌrekwɪˈzɪʃn] vt requisitar.

reran [ˌriːˈræn] pt ➤ rerun.

rerun [n ˈriːˌrʌn , vb riːˈrʌn] (pt reran, pp rerun, cont -ning) <> n -1. [film, programme] reprise f -2. [similar situation] repetição f. <> vt -1. [race, competition] voltar a participar de -2. [film, programme] reprisar -3. [tape] pôr novamente.

resat [ˌriːˈsæt] pt & pp ➤ resit.

rescind [rɪˈsɪnd] vt [JUR - contract] rescindir; [- law] revogar.

rescue [ˈreskjuː] <> n -1. [help] auxílio f -2. [successful attempt] resgate m, salvamento m. <> vt resgatar, salvar; to ~ sb from sb/sthg resgatar OR salvar alguém de alguém/algo; to ~ sthg from sb/sthg salvar algo de alguém/algo.

rescuer [ˈreskjʊəʳ] n resgatador m, -ra f.

research [ˌrɪˈsɜːtʃ] <> n (U): ~ (on OR into sthg) pesquisa f (sobre algo); ~ and development pesquisa e desenvolvimento. <> vt pesquisar, fazer uma pesquisa sobre.

researcher [rɪˈsɜːtʃəʳ] n pesquisador m, -ra f.

resemblance [rɪˈzembləns] n semelhança f; ~ to sb/sthg semelhança com alguém/algo; ~ between semelhança entre.

resemble [rɪˈzembl] vt assemelhar-se a, parecer-se com.

resent [rɪˈzent] vt ofender-se com, ressentir-se de.

resentful [rɪˈzentfʊl] adj ressentido(da).

resentment [rɪˈzentmənt] n (U) ressentimento m.

reservation [ˌrezəˈveɪʃn] n -1. [gen] reserva f; without ~ sem reserva -2. US [for Native Americans] reserva f (indígena).

➤ **reservations** npl [doubts] reservas fpl, dúvidas fpl.

reserve [rɪˈzɜːv] <> n reserva f; in ~ de reserva. <> vt -1. [keep for particular purpose]: to ~ sthg for sb/sthg reservar algo para alguém/algo -2. [retain]: to ~ the right to do sthg reservar-se o direito de fazer algo.

reserved [rɪˈzɜːvd] adj reservado(da).

reservoir [ˈrezəvwɑːʳ] n [lake] reservatório m natural.

reset [ˌriːˈset] (pt & pp reset, cont -ting) vt -1. [clock, meter, controls] reajustar -2. COMPUT reinicializar.

reshape [ˌriːˈʃeɪp] vt reformar, remodelar.

reshuffle [ˌriːˈʃʌfl] <> n POL reorganização f, reforma f; **cabinet** ~ reforma f do gabinete. <> vt ADMIN & POL reformar.

reside [rɪˈzaɪd] vi fml residir; **happiness does not** ~ **in wealth** a felicidade não reside na riqueza.

residence [ˈrezɪdəns] n -1. [house] residência f -2. (U) [fact of residing]: to apply for ~ solicitar visto de residência; to take up ~ fml estabelecer residência (em), instalar-se -3. (U) UNIV: writer in ~

escritor(ra) residente *(que atua temporariamente numa universidade)*.

residence permit n visto m de residência.

resident ['rezɪdənt] <> *adj* residente; **she's been ~ in France for two years** faz dois anos que ela está morando na França. <> *n* residente *mf*.

residential [ˌrezɪ'denʃl] *adj* em regime de internato.

residential area n zona f residencial.

residue ['rezɪdjuː] n CHEM resíduo m.

resign [rɪ'zaɪn] <> *vt* **-1.** [give up - job] demitir-se de; [- post] renunciar a **-2.** [accept calmly]: **to ~ o.s. to sthg** resignar-se a algo. <> *vi* pedir demissão, demitir-se; **to ~ (from sthg)** pedir demissão OR demitir-se (de algo).

resignation [ˌrezɪg'neɪʃn] n **-1.** [from job] demissão f **-2.** [from post] renúncia f **-3.** (U) [calm acceptance] resignação f.

resigned [rɪ'zaɪnd] *adj*: **~ (to sthg)** resignado(da) (a algo).

resilient [rɪ'zɪlɪənt] *adj* **-1.** [rubber, metal] elástico(ca) **-2.** [person] que se recupera rapidamente, resistente.

resin ['rezɪn] n (U) resina f.

resist [rɪ'zɪst] *vt* **-1.** [gen] resistir a **-2.** [oppose] opor-se a.

resistance [rɪ'zɪstəns] n (U) **-1.** [to enemy, attack, infection] resistência f; **~ to sthg** resistência a algo **-2.** [to change, proposal, attempt] oposição f.

resit [n 'riːsɪt, vb ˌriː'sɪt] (pt & pp resat, cont -ting) UK <> *n* exame *m* de recuperação. <> *vt* fazer de novo *(um exame)*.

resolute ['rezəluːt] *adj* resoluto(ta), determinado(da).

resolution [ˌrezə'luːʃn] n **-1.** [gen] resolução f **-2.** [vow, promise] promessa f.

resolve [rɪ'zɒlv] <> n (U) resolução f. <> *vt* [solve] resolver; [vow, promise]: **to ~ that** prometer que; **to ~ to do sthg** resolver fazer algo.

resort [rɪ'zɔːt] n **-1.** [for holidays] estância f de férias **-2.** [solution]: **as a last ~** como último recurso; **in the last ~** em última instância.

➤ **resort to** *vt fus* apelar para.

resound [rɪ'zaʊnd] *vi* **-1.** [noise] ressoar, retumbar **-2.** [place]: **the room ~ed with laughter** as risadas ressoavam em toda a sala.

resounding [rɪ'zaʊndɪŋ] *adj* **-1.** [gen] retumbante **-2.** [extremely loud] estrondoso(sa) **-3.** [unequivocal] clamoroso(sa).

resource [rɪ'sɔːs] n recurso m.

resourceful [rɪ'sɔːsfʊl] *adj* versátil, habilidoso(sa).

respect [rɪ'spekt] <> n (U) respeito m; **~ (for sb/sthg)** respeito m OR admiração f (por alguém/algo); **with ~, ...** com todo o respeito, ...; **in this ~** a este respeito; **in that ~** quanto a isso. <> *vt* respeitar; **to ~ sb for sthg** respeitar alguém por algo.

➤ **respects** *npl* saudações *fpl*, cumprimentos *mpl*.

➤ **with respect to** *prep* com respeito a.

respectable [rɪ'spektəbl] *adj* respeitável.

respectful [rɪ'spektfʊl] *adj* respeitoso(sa).

respective [rɪ'spektɪv] *adj* respectivo(va).

respectively [rɪ'spektɪvlɪ] *adv* respectivamente.

respite ['respaɪt] n **-1.** [pause] descanso m **-2.** [delay] adiamento m, novo prazo m.

resplendent [rɪ'splendənt] *adj literary* resplandescente.

respond [rɪ'spɒnd] *vi*: **to ~ (to sthg)** responder (a algo); **to ~ by doing sthg** responder fazendo algo.

response [rɪ'spɒns] n resposta f.

responsibility [rɪˌspɒnsə'bɪlətɪ] (pl -ies) n: **~ (for sthg)** responsabilidade f (por algo); **~ (to sb)** responsabilidade f (diante de alguém).

responsible [rɪ'spɒnsəbl] *adj* **-1.** [gen]: **~ (for sthg)** responsável (por algo) **-2.** [answerable]: **~ to sb** que presta contas a alguém **-3.** [requiring sense] de responsabilidade.

responsibly [rɪ'spɒnsəblɪ] *adv* de forma responsável.

responsive [rɪ'spɒnsɪv] *adj* que responde muito bem; **~ (to sthg)** sensível OR atencioso(sa) (a algo).

rest [rest] <> n **-1.** [remainder]: **the ~** o resto; **the ~ of** o resto de **-2.** (U) [relaxation] descanso m **-3.** [break] pausa f, descanso m **-4.** [support] apoio m. <> *vt* **-1.** [relax] descansar **-2.** [support, lean]: **to ~ sthg on/against sthg** apoiar OR descansar algo em algo **-3.** *phr*: **~ assured (that)** fique descansado(da) que. <> *vi* **-1.** [relax, be still] descansar **-2.** [depend]: **to ~ (up)on sb/sthg** depender de alguém/algo **-3.** [be supported]: **to ~ on/against sthg** apoiar-se em/contra algo.

restaurant ['restərɒnt] n restaurante m.

restaurant car n UK vagão-restaurante m.

restful ['restfʊl] *adj* tranqüilo(la), sossegado(da).

rest home n - 1. [for the elderly] lar m de idosos - 2. [for the sick] casa f de repouso.

restive ['restɪv] adj inquieto(ta).

restless ['restlɪs] adj - 1. [bored, dissatisfied] impaciente - 2. [fidgety] inquieto(ta), agitado(da) - 3. [sleepless]: **a ~ night** uma noite em claro.

restoration [,restə'reɪʃn] n (U) restauração f.

restore [rɪ'stɔ:ʳ] vt - 1. [reestablish, bring back] restabelecer; **the king was ~ed to power** o rei foi reconduzido ao poder; **I feel completely ~ed to health** sinto-me totalmente recuperado(da); **to ~ sthg to sb/sthg** devolver algo a alguém/algo - 2. [renovate] restaurar - 3. [give back] restituir.

restrain [rɪ'streɪn] vt - 1. [gen] reprimir; **to ~ o.s. from doing sthg** conter-se para não fazer algo - 2. [overpower, bring under control] controlar.

restrained [rɪ'streɪnd] adj comedido(da).

restraint [rɪ'streɪnt] n - 1. [rule, check] restrição f, limitação f - 2. (U) [control] controle m.

restrict [rɪ'strɪkt] vt restringir, limitar; **to ~ sb to sthg** restringir alguém a algo; **to ~ sthg to sb/sthg** restringir algo a alguém/algo.

restriction [rɪ'strɪkʃn] n - 1. [limitation, regulation] restrição f - 2. (U) [impediment, hindrance] limitação f.

restrictive [rɪ'strɪktɪv] adj restritivo(va).

rest room n US banheiro m.

result [rɪ'zʌlt] <> n resultado m; **as a ~** como resultado, por conseguinte; **as a ~ of sthg** como resultado de algo. <> vi: **to ~ in sthg** ter algo como resultado; **to ~ from sthg** ser resultado de algo.

resume [rɪ'zju:m] <> vt - 1. [activity] recomeçar - 2. fml [place, position] retomar. <> vi recomeçar, continuar.

résumé ['rezju:meɪ] n - 1. [summary] resumo m - 2. US [of career, qualifications] currículo m.

resumption [rɪ'zʌmpʃn] n (U) retomada f.

resurgence [rɪ'sɜ:dʒəns] n (U) ressurgimento m.

resurrection [,rezə'rekʃn] n (U) ressurreição f.

resuscitation [rɪ,sʌsɪ'teɪʃn] n (U) ressuscitação f, reanimação f.

retail ['ri:teɪl] <> n (U) varejo m. <> adv no varejo. <> vi: **to ~ at** ser vendido(da) no varejo.

retailer ['ri:teɪləʳ] n varejista mf.

retail price n preço m no varejo.

retain [rɪ'teɪn] vt reter.

retainer [rɪ'teɪnəʳ] n [fee] adiantamento m.

retaliate [rɪ'tælɪeɪt] vi retaliar.

retaliation [rɪ,tælɪ'eɪʃn] n retaliação f.

retarded [rɪ'tɑ:dɪd] adj mentalmente retardado(da).

retch [retʃ] vi fazer força para vomitar.

retentive [rɪ'tentɪv] adj retentivo(va).

reticent ['retɪsənt] adj reticente.

retina ['retɪnə] (pl -nas OR -nae [-ni:]) n retina f.

retinue ['retɪnju:] n séquito m.

retire [rɪ'taɪəʳ] vi - 1. [from work] aposentar-se - 2. fml [to another place] retirar-se - 3. fml [to bed] recolher-se.

retired [rɪ'taɪəd] adj aposentado(da).

retirement [rɪ'taɪəmənt] n aposentadoria f.

retiring [rɪ'taɪərɪŋ] adj [shy] retraído(da), tímido(da).

retort [rɪ'tɔ:t] <> n réplica f. <> vt: **to ~ (that)** retrucar (que).

retrace [rɪ'treɪs] vt: **to ~ one's steps** refazer o mesmo caminho.

retract [rɪ'trækt] <> vt - 1. [take back] retratar - 2. [draw in] recolher. <> vi [be drawn in] recolher-se.

retrain [,ri:'treɪn] vt reabilitar.

retraining [,ri:'treɪnɪŋ] n (U) reciclagem f.

retread ['ri:tred] n pneu m recauchutado.

retreat [rɪ'tri:t] <> n - 1. MIL [withdrawal]: **~ (from)** retirada f (de) - 2. [refuge] refúgio m. <> vi: **to ~ (to/from)** retirar-se (para/de).

retribution [,retrɪ'bju:ʃn] n (U) castigo m merecido.

retrieval [rɪ'tri:vl] n (U) COMPUT recuperação f.

retrieve [rɪ'tri:v] vt - 1. [get back] reaver - 2. COMPUT recuperar - 3. [rescue, rectify] reparar, remediar.

retriever [rɪ'tri:vəʳ] n [dog] perdigueiro m; [of specific breed] labrador m.

retrograde ['retrəgreɪd] adj fml retrógrado(da); **a ~ step** um passo para trás.

retrospect ['retrəspekt] n (U): **in ~** em retrospecto.

retrospective [,retrə'spektɪv] adj - 1. [mood, look] retrospectivo(va) - 2. [law, pay rise] retroativo(va).

return [rɪ'tɜ:n] <> n - 1. (U) [arrival back] volta f, regresso m; **~ (to)** regresso m (para); **~ to sthg** fig volta a algo - 2. [giving back] devolução f - 3. TENNIS rebatida f - 4. UK [ticket] passagem f de ida e volta - 5. [profit] retorno m - 6. COMPUT [on keyboard] tecla f Return. <> vt - 1. [gen]

devolver - 2. [reciprocate, give in exchange] retribuir **- 3.** *JUR* dar **- 4.** *POL* eleger. <> *vi*: **to ~ (from/to)** voltar (de/a). <> **returns** *npl* **-1.** *COMM* retorno *m*, rendimentos *mpl* **- 2.** [on birthday]: **many happy ~s (of the day)!** que a data se repita por muitos e muitos anos! <> **in return** *adv* em troca. <> **in return for** *prep* em troca de.

return ticket *n UK* passagem *f* de ida e volta.

reunification [ˌriːjuːnɪfɪˈkeɪʃn] *n (U)* reunificação *f*.

reunion [ˌriːˈjuːnjən] *n* reunião *f*.

reunite [ˌriːjuːˈnaɪt] *vt* reunir; **to be ~d with sb/sthg** estar reunido com alguém/algo.

rev [rev] (*pt & pp* **-ved**, *cont* **-ving**) *inf* <> *n* (*abbr of* revolution) rotação *f*. <> *vt*: **to ~ sthg (up)** acelerar algo. <> *vi*: **to ~ (up)** acelerar o motor.

revamp [ˌriːˈvæmp] *vt inf* **- 1.** [reorganize] reformar **- 2.** [redecorate] redecorar.

reveal [rɪˈviːl] *vt* revelar.

revealing [rɪˈviːlɪŋ] *adj* **-1.** [clothes]: **a ~ dress** um vestido que mostra tudo **- 2.** [comment] revelador(ra), esclarecedor(ra).

reveille [*UK* rɪˈvælɪ, *US* ˈrevəlɪ] *n* toque *m* de alvorada.

revel [ˈrevl] (*UK pt & pp* **-led**, *cont* **-ling**, *US pt & pp* **-ed**, *cont* **-ing**) *vi*: **to ~ in sthg** desfrutar de algo, deleitar-se com algo.

revelation [ˌrevəˈleɪʃn] *n* **- 1.** [surprising fact] revelação *f* **- 2.** [surprising experience] surpresa *f*.

revenge [rɪˈvendʒ] <> *n (U)* vingança *f*; **to take ~ (on sb)** vingar-se (de alguém). <> *vt* vingar; **to ~ o.s. on sb/sthg** vingar-se de alguém/algo.

revenue [ˈrevənjuː] *n* **- 1.** [income] receita *f* **- 2.** [from investment] rendimento *f* **- 3.** *UK FIN*: **the Inland Revenue** a Receita Federal.

reverberate [rɪˈvɜːbəreɪt] *vi* **- 1.** [re-echo] ressoar, retumbar **- 2.** [have repercussions] repercutir.

reverberations [rɪˌvɜːbəˈreɪʃnz] *npl* **- 1.** [echoes] reverberação *f* **- 2.** [repercussions] repercussões *fpl*.

revere [rɪˈvɪəʳ] *vt fml* reverenciar, venerar.

reverence [ˈrevərəns] *n (U) fml* reverência *f*.

Reverend [ˈrevərənd] *n* reverendo *m*.

reverie [ˈrevərɪ] *n fml* devaneio *m*.

reversal [rɪˈvɜːsl] *n* **- 1.** [of trend, policy, decision] reviravolta *f* **- 2.** [of roles, order, position] inversão *f* **- 3.** [piece of ill luck] contratempo *m*.

reverse [rɪˈvɜːs] <> *adj* reverso(sa), inverso(sa). <> *n* **-1.** *AUT*: **~ (gear)** marcha *f* à ré **- 2.** [opposite]: **the ~** o contrário **- 3.** [back, other side - of paper] verso *m*; [- of coin] outro lado *m*. <> *vt* **- 1.** *AUT* dar marcha à ré em **- 2.** [trend, policy, decision] reverter **- 3.** [roles, order, position] inverter **- 4.** [turn over] virar **- 5.** *UK TELEC*: **to ~ the charges** fazer uma ligação a cobrar. <> *vi AUT* dar marcha à ré.

reverse-charge call *n UK* chamada *f* a cobrar.

reversing light [rɪˈvɜːsɪŋ-] *n UK* luz *f* de ré.

revert [rɪˈvɜːt] *vi*: **to ~ to sthg** voltar a algo.

review [rɪˈvjuː] <> *n* **- 1.** [examination] revisão *f*, reavaliação *f* **- 2.** [critique] crítica *f*, resenha *f*. <> *vt* **- 1.** [reassess] reavaliar *OR* **- 2.** [write an article on] fazer resenha *OR* crítica de **- 3.** [troops] passar em revista **- 4.** *US* [study] revisar.

reviewer [rɪˈvjuːəʳ] *n* crítico *m*, -ca *f*.

revile [rɪˈvaɪl] *vt literary* insultar, injuriar.

revise [rɪˈvaɪz] <> *vt* **- 1.** [reconsider] revisar **- 2.** [rewrite] corrigir, alterar **- 3.** *UK* [study] revisar. <> *vi UK*: **to ~ (for sthg)** fazer revisão (para algo).

revision [rɪˈvɪʒn] *n* **- 1.** [alteration] alteração *f*, correção *f* **- 2.** *(U)* [study] revisão *f*.

revitalize, -ise [ˌriːˈvaɪtəlaɪz] *vt* revitalizar.

revival [rɪˈvaɪvl] *n* **- 1.** *COMM* reativação *f* **- 2.** [of interest, cultural activity] renovação *f* **- 3.** [of play] revival *m*.

revive [rɪˈvaɪv] <> *vt* **- 1.** [resuscitate] ressuscitar **- 2.** [revitalize - plant, economy] revitalizar; [- interest, hopes] despertar **- 3.** [bring back into use, being - tradition] restabelecer; [- musical, play] reviver; [- memories] trazer à baila. <> *vi* **- 1.** [regain consciousness] voltar a si, recobrar os sentidos **- 2.** [be revitalized - plant, economy] revitalizar-se; [- interest, hopes] renovar-se.

revolt [rɪˈvəʊlt] <> *n* revolta *f*, rebelião *f*. <> *vt* revoltar. <> *vi*: **to ~ (against sb/sthg)** revoltar-se *OR* rebelar-se (contra alguém/algo).

revolting [rɪˈvəʊltɪŋ] *adj* revoltante, repugnante.

revolution [ˌrevəˈluːʃn] *n* revolução *f*; **~ in sthg** revolução em algo.

revolutionary [ˌrevəˈluːʃnərɪ] (*pl* **-ies**) <> *adj* revolucionário(ria). <> *n POL* revolucionário *m*, -ria *f*.

revolve [rɪˈvɒlv] *vi* girar, dar voltas; **to**

~ **(a)round** sthg girar em torno de algo; **to** ~ **(a)round** sb girar em torno de alguém.

revolver [rɪ'vɒlvə^r] n revólver m.

revolving [rɪ'vɒlvɪŋ] adj giratório(ria).

revolving door n porta f giratória.

revue [rɪ'vjuː] n teatro m de revista.

revulsion [rɪ'vʌlʃn] n (U) repugnância f, asco m.

reward [rɪ'wɔːd] <> n **-1.** [recompense] recompensa f **-2.** [sum of money] recompensa f, gratificação f. <> vt recompensar; **to** ~ **sb for/with** sthg recompensar alguém por/com algo.

rewarding [rɪ'wɔːdɪŋ] adj gratificante.

rewind [,riː'waɪnd] (pt & pp **rewound**) vt rebobinar.

rewire [,riː'waɪə^r] vt trocar a fiação elétrica de.

reword [,riː'wɜːd] vt expressar com outras palavras.

rewound [,riː'waʊnd] pt & pp ⊳ **rewind**.

rewrite [,riː'raɪt] (pt **rewrote** [,riː'rəʊt], pp **rewritten** [,riː'rɪtn]) vt reescrever.

Reykjavik ['rekjəvɪk] n Reykjavik.

rhapsody ['ræpsədɪ] (pl -ies) n **-1.** MUS rapsódia f **-2.** [strong approval] entusiasmo m.

rhetoric ['retərɪk] n (U) retórica f.

rhetorical question [rɪ'tɒrɪkl-] n pergunta f retórica.

rheumatism ['ruːmətɪzm] n (U) reumatismo m.

Rhine [raɪn] n: **the** ~ o Reno.

rhino ['raɪnəʊ] (pl inv OR -s) n inf rino m.

rhinoceros [raɪ'nɒsərəs] (pl inv OR -es) n rinoceronte m.

rhododendron [,rəʊdə'dendrən] n rododendro m.

Rhone n: **the (River)** ~ o rio Ródano.

rhubarb ['ruːbɑːb] n (U) ruibarbo m.

rhyme [raɪm] <> n **-1.** [word] rima f **-2.** [poem] poesia f, versos mpl. <> vi rimar; **to** ~ **with** sthg rimar com algo.

rhythm ['rɪðm] n ritmo m.

rib [rɪb] n **-1.** ANAT costela f **-2.** [of metal or wood] vareta f.

ribbed [rɪbd] adj canelado(da).

ribbon ['rɪbən] n fita f.

rice [raɪs] n (U) arroz m.

rice pudding n arroz-doce m, arroz-de-leite m.

rich [rɪtʃ] <> adj **-1.** [gen] rico(ca); **to be** ~ **in** sthg ser rico(ca) em algo **-2.** [indigestible] pesado(da). <> npl: **the** ~ os ricos.

◆ **riches** npl **-1.** [natural resources] riquezas fpl **-2.** [wealth] riqueza f.

richly ['rɪtʃlɪ] adv [gen] ricamente.

richness ['rɪtʃnɪs] n (U) **-1.** [gen] riqueza f **-2.** [of food] peso m.

rickets ['rɪkɪts] n (U) raquitismo m.

rickety ['rɪkətɪ] adj instável, sem solidez.

rickshaw ['rɪkʃɔː] n jinriquixá m.

ricochet ['rɪkəʃeɪ] (pt & pp **-ed** OR **-ted**, cont **-ing** OR **-ting**) <> n ricochete m. <> vi ricochetear; **to** ~ **off** sthg ricochetear em algo.

rid [rɪd] (pt **rid** OR **-ded**, pp **rid**, cont **-ding**) vt: **to** ~ **sb/sthg of** sthg livrar alguém/algo de algo; **to** ~ **o.s. of** sthg livrar-se de algo; **to get** ~ **of sb/sthg** livrar-se de alguém/algo.

ridden ['rɪdn] pp ⊳ **ride**.

riddle ['rɪdl] n **-1.** [verbal puzzle] adivinhação f **-2.** [mystery] enigma m.

riddled ['rɪdld] adj **-1.** [holes, errors] cheio (cheia) **-2.** [bullet holes] crivado(-da) **-3.** [woodworm] infestado(da).

ride [raɪd] (pt **rode**, pp **ridden**) <> n **-1.** [gen] passeio m; **to go for a** OR **horse/bike** ~ dar um passeio a cavalo/de bicicleta; **to go for a car** ~ dar uma volta OR um passeio de carro **-2.** phr: **to take sb for a** ~ inf [trick] levar alguém no bico. <> vt **-1.** [horse] montar em **-2.** [bicycle, motorbike] andar de **-3.** [distance] percorrer **-4.** US [travel in] ir de. <> vi **-1.** [on horseback] montar **-2.** [on bicycle] andar de bicicleta **-3.** [on motorbike] andar de moto **-4.** [in car, bus]: **to** ~ **in** sthg andar de algo.

rider ['raɪdə^r] n **-1.** [on horseback - male] cavaleiro m; [- female] amazona f **-2.** [on bicycle] ciclista mf **-3.** [on motorbike] motoqueiro m, -ra f.

ridge [rɪdʒ] n **-1.** [on mountain] crista f **-2.** [on flat surface - in sand, of muscles] saliência f; [- in fabric] ruga f.

ridicule ['rɪdɪkjuːl] <> n (U) zombaria f. <> vt ridicularizar.

ridiculous [rɪ'dɪkjʊləs] adj ridículo(-la).

riding ['raɪdɪŋ] n (U) equitação f.

riding school n escola f de equitação.

rife [raɪf] adj muito comum.

riffraff ['rɪfræf] n (U) gentalha f, ralé f.

rifle ['raɪfl] <> n rifle m. <> vt roubar.

rifle range n estande m de tiro ao alvo.

rift [rɪft] n **-1.** GEOL fenda f **-2.** [quarrel] desavença f; ~ **between/in** desavença entre/em.

rig [rɪg] (pt & pp **-ged**, cont **-ging**) <> n [structure - onshore] torre f de perfuração; [- offshore] plataforma f petrolífera. <> vt manipular.

◆ **rig up** vt sep armar, construir.

rigging ['rɪgɪŋ] *n* **-1.** [of ship] *(U)* corda-me *m* **-2.** [of votes] fraude *f* em uma votação.

right [raɪt] ◇ *adj* **-1.** [gen] certo(ta), correto(ta); **to be ~ about sthg** estar certo(ta) sobre algo, ter razão sobre algo; **to be ~ to do sthg** estar certo(ta) ao fazer algo **-2.** [going well] bem **-3.** [socially desirable, appropriate] apropriado(-da) **-4.** [not left] direito(ta) **-5.** *UK inf* [complete] perfeito(ta). ◇ *adv* **-1.** [correctly] corretamente, bem **-2.** [not left] para a direita **-3.** [emphatic use]: **~ here** aqui mesmo; **~ down** bem para baixo; **~ in the middle** bem no meio **-4.** [immediately]: **I'll be ~ back** eu já volto; **~ after Christmas** logo depois do Natal; **~ now** [immediately] agora; [at this very moment] já; **~ away** em seguida. ◇ *n* **-1.** *(U)* [moral correctness] certo *m*; **to be in the ~** ter razão **-2.** [entitlement, claim] direito *m*; **by ~s** por direito **-3.** [right-hand side] direita *f*; **on the ~** à direita. ◇ *vt* **-1.** [correct] corrigir **-2.** [make up-right] endireitar. ◇ *excl* certo!
➡ **Right** *n* POL: **the Right** a direita.

right angle *n* ângulo *m* reto; **at ~s to sthg** em ângulo reto com algo.

righteous ['raɪtʃəs] *adj* **-1.** [anger, indignation] justo(ta) **-2.** [person] honrado(-da).

rightful ['raɪtfʊl] *adj* legítimo(ma).

right-hand *adj* direito(ta); **~ side** o lado direito.

right-hand drive *adj* com direção do lado direito.

right-handed [-'hændɪd] *adj* destro(-tra).

right-hand man *n* braço *m* direito.

rightly ['raɪtlɪ] *adv* **-1.** [gen] corretamente **-2.** [justifiably] com razão.

right of way *n* **-1.** AUT preferência *f* **-2.** [access] direito *m* de passagem.

right wing *n*: **the ~** a direita.
➡ **right-wing** *adj* de direita.

rigmarole ['rɪgmərəʊl] *n inf pej* **-1.** [process] ritual *m* **-2.** [story] ladainha *f*.

rigor *n US* = rigour.

rigorous ['rɪgərəs] *adj* rigoroso(sa).

rigour *UK*, **rigor** *US* ['rɪgəʳ] *n (U)* rigor *m*.
➡ **rigours** *npl* rigores *mpl*.

rile [raɪl] *vt* irritar.

rim [rɪm] *n* **-1.** [top edge of container] borda *f* **-2.** [outer edge of round object - of spectacles, glass] moldura *f*; [- of wheel] aro *m*.

rind [raɪnd] *n* casca *f*.

ring [rɪŋ] (*pt* rang, *pp vt senses* 1 & 2 & *vi* rung, *pt* & *pp vt senses* 3 & 4 *only* ringed)
◇ *n* **-1.** [telephone call]: **to give sb a ~** dar uma ligada para alguém **-2.** [sound of bell] toque *m* **-3.** [quality, tone]: **it has a familiar ~** soa familiar **-4.** [circular object - for curtains, napkin] argola *f*; **napkin ~** argola *f* para guardanapo; [- hoop] aro *m* **-5.** [piece of jewellery] anel *m* **-6.** [of people, trees] círculo *m* **-7.** [for boxing] ringue *m* **-8.** [people working together] cartel *m*. ◇ *vt* **-1.** *UK* [phone] telefonar para, ligar para **-2.** [bell, doorbell] tocar **-3.** [draw a circle round] fazer um círculo ao redor de **-4.** [surround] cercar, rodear; **to be ~ed with sthg** estar cercado(da) de algo. ◇ *vi* **-1.** *UK* [phone] telefonar, ligar **-2.** [bell, doorbell] tocar **-3.** [to attract attention]: **to ~ (for sb/sthg)** chamar (por alguém/algo) **-4.** [resound]: **to ~ with sthg** ressoar com algo.
➡ **ring back** *UK* ◇ *vt sep* voltar a ligar para. ◇ *vi* voltar a ligar.
➡ **ring off** *vi UK* desligar.
➡ **ring up** *vt sep UK* ligar.

ring binder *n* fichário *m* com aros de metal.

ringing ['rɪŋɪŋ] *n* **-1.** *(U)* [of bell] toque *m* **-2.** *(U)* [in ears] zumbido *m*.

ringing tone *n UK* TELEC tom *m* de discagem.

ringleader ['rɪŋ,li:dəʳ] *n* cabeça *m*.

ringlet ['rɪŋlɪt] *n* anel *m* de cabelo.

ring road *n UK* anel *m* rodoviário.

ring tone *n* [for mobile phone] toque *m* musical.

rink [rɪŋk] *n* rinque *m*.

rinse [rɪns] *vt* enxaguar; **to ~ one's mouth out** enxaguar a boca.

riot ['raɪət] ◇ *n* desordem *f*; **to run ~** descontrolar-se. ◇ *vi* amotinar-se.

rioter ['raɪətəʳ] *n* desordeiro *m*, -ra *f*.

riotous ['raɪətəs] *adj* **-1.** [party] barulhento(ta) **-2.** [behaviour, mob] desordeiro(ra).

riot police *npl* tropa *f* de choque.

rip [rɪp] (*pt* & *pp* -ped, *cont* -ping) ◇ *n* rasgão *m*. ◇ *vt* **-1.** [tear, shred] rasgar **-2.** [remove] arrancar. ◇ *vi* rasgar.

RIP (*abbr of* rest in peace) descanse em paz.

ripe [raɪp] *adj* maduro(ra); **to be ~ (for sthg)** *fig* estar pronto(ta) (para algo).

ripen ['raɪpn] *vt* & *vi* amadurecer.

rip-off *n inf* **-1.** [swindle] assalto *m* **-2.** [imitation] imitação *f* barata.

ripple ['rɪpl] ◇ *n* **-1.** [in water] ondulação *f* **-2.** [of laughter, applause] onda *f*. ◇ *vt* ondular.

rise [raɪz] (*pt* rose, *pp* risen ['rɪzn]) ◇ *n* **-1.** *UK* [increase in amount] aumento *m*, subida *f* - **2.** UK [increase in salary] aumento *m* - **3.** [to power, fame] ascensão *f* - **4.** [slope] ladeira *f* - **5.** *phr*: **to give ~ to** sthg originar algo. ⬦ *vi* - **1.** [gen] elevar-se - **2.** [sun, moon] nascer, sair - **3.** UK [increase] aumentar, subir - **4.** [stand up] levantar-se - **5.** *literary* [get out of bed] levantar-se - **6.** [to a challenge]: **to ~ to** sthg mostrar-se à altura de algo; **to ~ to the occasion** elevar-se à altura (de algo) - **7.** [rebel] sublevar-se - **8.** [in status] ascender; **to ~ to** sthg ascender a algo - **9.** [bread, soufflé] crescer.

rising ['raɪzɪŋ] ⬦ *adj* - **1.** [gen] em ascensão - **2.** [sloping upwards] em aclive - **3.** [tide] que sobe. ⬦ *n* [rebellion] levante *m*, rebelião *f*.

risk [rɪsk] ⬦ *n* risco *m*; **to run the ~ of** sthg/of doing sthg correr o risco de algo/de fazer algo; **to take a ~** arriscar-se; **it's at your own ~** é por sua conta e risco; **at ~** em perigo. ⬦ *vt* - **1.** [put in danger] arriscar - **2.** [take the chance of]: **to ~ doing** sthg arriscar-se a fazer algo; **go on, ~ it!** vamos, arrisque-se!

risky ['rɪskɪ] (*compar* **-ier**, *superl* **-iest**) *adj* arriscado(da).

risqué ['riːskeɪ] *adj* picante.

rissole ['rɪsəʊl] *n* UK bolinho *m* de carne, rissole *m*.

rite [raɪt] *n* rito *m*.

ritual ['rɪtʃʊəl] ⬦ *adj* ritual. ⬦ *n* ritual *m*.

rival ['raɪvl] (UK *pt* & *pp* **-led**, *cont* **-ling**, US *pt* & *pp* **-ed**, *cont* **-ing**) ⬦ *adj* - **1.** [gen] rival - **2.** [company] concorrente. ⬦ *n* - **1.** [gen] rival *mf* - **2.** [company] concorrente *mf*. ⬦ *vt* rivalizar OR competir com.

rivalry ['raɪvlrɪ] *n* rivalidade *f*.

river ['rɪvəʳ] *n* rio *m*.

river bank *n* margem *f* do rio.

riverbed ['rɪvəbed] *n* leito *m* do rio.

riverside ['rɪvəsaɪd] *n*: **the ~** a margem do rio.

rivet ['rɪvɪt] ⬦ *n* rebite *m*. ⬦ *vt* - **1.** [fasten with rivets] rebitar - **2.** *fig* [fascinate]: **to be ~ed by** sthg estar fascinado(da) por algo.

Riviera [ˌrɪvɪ'eərə] *n*: **the French ~** a Riviera Francesa; **the Italian ~** a Riviera Italiana.

road [rəʊd] *n* - **1.** [major] estrada *f*; **by ~** por estrada; **on the ~ to** *fig* a caminho de - **2.** [minor] caminho *m* - **3.** [street] rua *f*.

roadblock ['rəʊdblɒk] *n* barreira *f* policial.

road hog *n* *inf* *pej* dono *m*, -na *f* da estrada.

road map *n* mapa *m* rodoviário.

road rage *n* raiva *f* no trânsito.

road safety *n* (U) segurança *f* no trânsito.

roadside ['rəʊdsaɪd] *n*: **the ~** a beira da estrada.

road sign *n* placa *f* de trânsito.

road tax *n* ≃ imposto *m* sobre veículos automotores, ≃ IPVA *m*.

roadway ['rəʊdweɪ] *n* pista *f* (da estrada).

road works *npl* obras *fpl* na pista.

roadworthy ['rəʊd,wɜːðɪ] *adj* em condições de tráfego.

roam [rəʊm] ⬦ *vt* vagar por. ⬦ *vi* vagar.

roar [rɔːʳ] ⬦ *vi* - **1.** [lion] rugir - **2.** [traffic, plane, engine] roncar - **3.** [person] urrar; **to ~ with laughter** rir às gargalhadas - **4.** [wind] bramir. ⬦ *vt* bradar. ⬦ *n* - **1.** [of lion] rugido *m* - **2.** [of engine] ronco *m* - **3.** [of traffic] barulho *m* - **4.** [of wind] sopro *m* - **5.** [of person] urro *m*.

roaring ['rɔːrɪŋ] *adj* - **1.** [traffic, wind] barulhento(ta) - **2.** [fire] crepitante - **3.** [for emphasis] estrondoso(sa); **a ~ success** um sucesso estrondoso; **to do a ~ trade** vender bem. ⬦ *adv* [for emphasis] completamente.

roast [rəʊst] ⬦ *adj* assado(da). ⬦ *n* assado *m*. ⬦ *vt* - **1.** [meat, potatoes] assar - **2.** [coffee beans, nuts] torrar.

roast beef *n* (U) rosbife *m*.

rob [rɒb] (*pt* & *pp* **-bed**, *cont* **-bing**) *vt* roubar; **to ~ sb of** sthg [of money, goods] roubar algo de alguém; *fig* [of opportunity, glory] privar alguém de algo.

robber ['rɒbəʳ] *n* ladrão *m*, -dra *f*.

robbery ['rɒbərɪ] (*pl* **-ies**) *n* roubo *m*.

robe [rəʊb] *n* - **1.** [of priest] túnica *f* - **2.** [judge] toga *f* - **3.** [monarch] manto *m* - **4.** US [dressing gown] robe *m*.

robin ['rɒbɪn] *n* pintarroxo *m*.

robot ['rəʊbɒt] *n* robô *m*.

robust [rəʊ'bʌst] *adj* [person] - **1.** robusto(ta) - **2.** [economy] forte - **3.** [health] de ferro - **4.** [criticism, defence] vigoroso(sa).

rock [rɒk] ⬦ *n* - **1.** (U) [substance] rocha *f* - **2.** [boulder] rochedo *m*, penhasco *m* - **3.** US [pebble] pedregulho *m* - **4.** (U) [music] rock *m* - **5.** (U) UK [sweet] barra *f* de caramelo. ⬦ *comp* [music] de rock. ⬦ *vt* - **1.** [cause to move] balançar - **2.** [shock] abalar. ⬦ *vi* balançar-se.

➤ **on the rocks** *adv* - **1.** [drink] com gelo, on the rocks - **2.** [marriage, relationship] que vai mal.

rock-and-roll *n* (U) rock-and-roll *m*.

rock bottom n (U) nível m baixíssimo; to hit ~ atingir o fundo do poço.
 ◆ **rock-bottom** adj baixíssimo(ma).

rockery ['rɒkərɪ] (pl -ies) n jardim m de pedras.

rocket ['rɒkɪt] <> n foguete m. <> vi disparar.

rocket launcher [-,lɔ:ntʃəʳ] n lança-foguetes m inv.

rocking chair ['rɒkɪŋ-] n cadeira f de balanço.

rocking horse ['rɒkɪŋ-] n cavalinho m de balanço.

rock-'n'-roll n = rock-and-roll.

rocky ['rɒkɪ] (compar -ier, superl -iest) adj -1. [full of rocks] rochoso(sa) -2. [unsteady] instável.

Rocky Mountains npl: the ~ as Montanhas Rochosas.

rod [rɒd] n -1. [wooden] vara f -2. [metal] barra f.

rode [rəʊd] pt > ride.

rodent ['rəʊdənt] n roedor m.

roe [rəʊ] n ova f (de peixe).

roe deer n corço m, -ça f.

rogue [rəʊg] n -1. [likable rascal] malandro m, -dra f -2. dated [dishonest person] vigarista mf.

role [rəʊl] n -1. [position, function] função f, papel m -2. CINEMA, THEATRE papel m.

roll [rəʊl] <> n -1. [of material, paper, film] rolo m -2. [of banknotes] maço m -3. [of cloth] peça f -4. [of bread] pãozinho m -5. [list] lista f -6. [sound - of drum] rufar m; [- of thunder] estrondo m. <> vt -1. [turn over] rolar -2. [make into cylinder] enrolar; ~ed into one fig tudo num só. <> vi -1. [of a round object] rolar -2. [move] andar.
 ◆ **roll about, roll around** vi rolar.
 ◆ **roll over** vi virar-se.
 ◆ **roll up** <> vt sep -1. [make into cylinder] enrolar -2. [sleeves] arregaçar. <> vi -1. [vehicle] chegar -2. inf [person] pintar.

roll call n toque m de chamada.

roller ['rəʊləʳ] n -1. [cylinder] cilindro m -2. [curler] rolo m.

Rollerblades® ['rəʊlə,bleɪdz] npl patins mpl em linha.

rollerblading ['rəʊlə,bleɪdɪŋ] n patinação f (com patins em linha); to go ~ praticar patinação (com patins em linha).

roller coaster n montanha-russa f.

roller skate n patim m de rodas.

rolling ['rəʊlɪŋ] adj -1. [undulating] ondulado(da) -2. phr: to be ~ in it inf estar nadando em dinheiro.

rolling pin n rolo m de massa.

rolling stock n (U) material m rodante.

roll-on adj de rolo, roll-on.

ROM [rɒm] (abbr of read-only memory) n ROM f.

Roman ['rəʊmən] <> adj romano(na). <> n romano m, -na f.

Roman candle n pistolão m.

Roman Catholic <> adj católico (romano), católica (romana). <> n católico m (romano), católica f (romana).

romance [rəʊ'mæns] n -1. [gen] romance m -2. (U) [romantic quality] romantismo m.

Romania [rə'meɪnjə] n Romênia.

Romanian [rə'meɪnjən] <> adj romeno(na). <> n -1. [person] romeno m, -na f -2. [language] romeno m.

Roman numerals npl algarismos mpl romanos.

romantic [rəʊ'mæntɪk] adj romântico(ca).

Rome [rəʊm] n Roma.

romp [rɒmp] <> n travessura f. <> vi brincar ruidosamente.

rompers ['rɒmpəz] npl, **romper suit** ['rɒmpəʳ-] n macacão m de criança.

roof [ru:f] n -1. [covering - of vehicle] capota f; [- of building] telhado m; not under my ~ ! não na minha casa!; to go through OR hit the ~ subir pelas paredes -2. [upper part - of cave] teto m; [- of mouth] céu m da boca.

roofing ['ru:fɪŋ] n (U) material m para cobertura.

roof rack n bagageiro m (na capota do carro).

rooftop ['ru:ftɒp] n telhado m.

rook [rʊk] n -1. [bird] gralha f -2. [chess piece] torre f.

rookie ['rʊkɪ] n US inf novato m, -ta f.

room [ru:m, rʊm] n -1. [in building] sala f -2. [bedroom] quarto m -3. (U) [space] espaço m; to make ~ for sb/sthg abrir espaço para alguém/algo -4. (U) [opportunity, possibility] possibilidade f.

rooming house ['ru:mɪŋ-] n US pensão f.

roommate ['ru:mmeɪt] n companheiro m, -ra f de quarto.

room service n serviço m de quarto.

roomy ['ru:mɪ] (compar -ier, superl -iest) adj espaçoso(sa), amplo(pla).

roost [ru:st] <> n o poleiro m. <> vi empoleirar-se.

rooster ['ru:stəʳ] n galo m.

root [ru:t] <> n [gen] raiz f; to take ~ [plant] pegar; [idea] consolidar-se. <> vi remexer.
 ◆ **roots** npl raízes fpl.

root for vt fus esp US inf torcer por.

root out vt sep arrancar até a raiz, extirpar.

rope [rəʊp] ◇ n corda f; **to know the ~s** estar por dentro do assunto. ◇ vt amarrar com corda.

rope in vt sep inf arrastar para.

rosary ['rəʊzərɪ] (pl -ies) n rosário m.

rose [rəʊz] ◇ pt ▷ **rise**. ◇ adj [pink] rosa, cor-de-rosa. ◇ n [flower] rosa f; **it's not a bed of ~s** não é um leito de rosas.

rosé ['rəʊzeɪ] n (U) vinho m rosé.

rosebud ['rəʊzbʌd] n botão m de rosa.

rose bush n roseira f.

rose-coloured adj cor-de-rosa.

rosemary ['rəʊzmərɪ] n (U) alecrim m.

rose-tinted adj: **to look through ~ glasses** ver tudo cor-de-rosa.

rosette [rəʊ'zet] n roseta f.

roster ['rɒstəʳ] n lista f.

rostrum ['rɒstrəm] (pl -trums OR -tra [-trə]) n tribuna f, rostro m.

rosy ['rəʊzɪ] (compar -ier, superl -iest) adj -1. [pink] rosado(da) -2. [hopeful] promissor(ra).

rot [rɒt] (pt & pp -ted, cont -ting) ◇ n -1. [decay - of wood, food] putrefação f; [- in society, organization] decadência f -2. UK dated [nonsense] besteira f, bobagem f. ◇ vt [cause to decay] corroer, decompor. ◇ vi apodrecer.

rota ['rəʊtə] n lista f de turnos.

rotary ['rəʊtərɪ] ◇ adj rotatório(ria). ◇ n US [roundabout] rotatória f.

rotate [rəʊ'teɪt] ◇ vt -1. [gen] alternar -2. [turn] girar. ◇ vi [turn] girar, dar voltas.

rotation [rəʊ'teɪʃn] n [turning movement] rotação f.

rote [rəʊt] n (U): **by ~** de cor OR memória.

rotten ['rɒtn] adj -1. [decayed] podre -2. inf [poor-quality, unskilled] péssimo(ma) -3. inf [unpleasant, nasty] perverso(sa), ruim -4. inf [unenjoyable] detestável -5. inf [unwell]: **to feel ~** sentir-se péssimo(ma).

rouge [ruːʒ] n (U) ruge m.

rough [rʌf] ◇ adj -1. [not smooth - surface] áspero(ra); [- road] acidentado(da) -2. [violent] rude, grosseiro(ra) -3. [crude, basic - people, manners] rústico(ca); [- shelter, conditions, situation] precário(ria) -4. [approximate - not detailed] rudimentar; [- not exact] aproximado(da) -5. [unpleasant, tough - life, time] duro(ra), difícil; [- area, town etc.] tumultuoso(sa) -6. [stormy - weather] tormentoso(sa);

[- crossing] movimentado(da); [- sea] agitado(da); [- wind] violento(ta); [- day] tempestuoso(sa) -7. [sounding harsh] áspero(ra) -8. [tasting harsh] azedo(da). ◇ adv: **to sleep ~** dormir na rua. ◇ n -1. GOLF: **the ~** o rough -2. [undetailed form]: **in ~** em rascunho. ◇ vt phr: **to ~ it** viver sem comodidades.

roughage ['rʌfɪdʒ] n fibras fpl.

rough and ready adj rústico(ca), feito(ta) às pressas.

roughcast n (U) reboco m grosso.

roughen ['rʌfn] vt tornar áspero(ra).

roughly ['rʌflɪ] adv -1. [not gently] bruscamente -2. [crudely] rusticamente -3. [approximately] aproximadamente, mais ou menos.

roulette [ruː'let] n (U) roleta f.

round [raʊnd] ◇ adj -1. [gen] redondo(da) -2. [fat, curved - cheeks, hips] roliço(ça), redondo(da); [- bulge] redondo(da). ◇ prep -1. [surrounding] ao redor de -2. [near] em volta de; **~ here** por aqui -3. [all over] por todo(da) -4. [in circular movement, in circumference] ao redor de; **she measures 70 cm ~ the waist** ela mede OR tem 70 cm de cintura -5. [to/on the other side of]: **to drive ~ the corner** dobrar a esquina; **I live just ~ the corner** eu moro logo ali -6. [so as to avoid - hole, obstacle]: **to go ~ an obstacle** contornar um obstáculo; [- problem]: **to find a way ~ sthg** achar um jeito de contornar algo. ◇ adv -1. [surrounding]: **all ~** por toda a volta, por todos os lados -2. [near]: **~ about** [in distance] por perto; [in number, amount] aproximadamente -3. [all over]: **to travel ~** viajar por aí -4. [in circular movement]: **~ (and ~)** em círculos; **to go ~** circular; **to spin ~** girar -5. [in circumference]: **it's at least 3 km ~** tem no mínimo 3 km de circunferência -6. [to the other side or direction] ao redor; **to turn ~** virar; **to go ~** dar a volta -7. [on a visit]: **come ~ sometime!** apareçam uma hora dessas! ◇ n -1. [gen] rodada f; **a ~ of applause** uma salva de palmas -2. [professional visit] percurso m -3. [of ammunition] cartucho m -4. BOXING assalto m -5. GOLF partida f. ◇ vt [turn] dobrar, virar.

rounds npl [professional visits] percurso m; **to do** OR **go the ~s** fig espalhar-se, propagar-se.

round off vt sep encerrar, terminar.

round up vt sep -1. [gather together] reunir -2. MATH arredondar.

roundabout ['raʊndəbaʊt] ◇ adj

indireto(ta). ◇ *n UK* **-1.** [on road] rotatória *f* **-2.** [at fairground] carrossel *m.*

rounders ['raʊndəz] *n (U) UK* bete *m.*

roundly ['raʊndlɪ] *adv* totalmente, terminantemente.

round-shouldered [-'ʃəʊldəd] *adj* de ombros caídos.

round trip *n* viagem *f* de ida e volta.

round-up *n* resumo *m.*

rouse [raʊz] *vt* **-1.** [wake up] despertar **-2.** [impel]: **to ~ sb to do sthg** animar alguém a fazer algo; **to ~ o.s. to do sthg** animar-se a fazer algo **-3.** [excite] estimular **-4.** [give rise to] suscitar.

rousing ['raʊzɪŋ] *adj* estimulante.

rout [raʊt] ◇ *n* derrota *f* esmagadora. ◇ *vt* derrotar de forma esmagadora.

route [ru:t] ◇ *n* **-1.** [line of travel - of journey] rota *f*; [- of or person, procession] trajeto *m*, percurso *m* **-2.** [of bus, train] linha *f* **-3.** [of plane, ship] rota *f* **-4.** *fig* [to achievement] caminho *m.* ◇ *vt* **-1.** [flight, traffic] direcionar **-2.** [goods] enviar.

route map *n* mapa *m (de localização).*

routine [ru:'ti:n] ◇ *adj* **-1.** [normal] de rotina **-2.** *pej* [humdrum, uninteresting] rotineiro(ra). ◇ *n* **-1.** *(U)* [normal pattern of activity] rotina *f* **-2.** *pej* [boring repetition] rotina *f.*

rove [rəʊv] *literary* ◇ *vt* errar, vagar por. ◇ *vi*: **to ~ around** vagar.

roving ['rəʊvɪŋ] *adj* itinerante; **~ eyes** olhar *m* errante.

row¹ [rəʊ] ◇ *n* **-1.** [gen] fileira *f* **-2.** [succession] seqüência *f*, série *f*; **four in a ~** quatro seguidos. ◇ *vt* **-1.** [boat] remar **-2.** [person] conduzir de barco a remo. ◇ *vi* [in boat] remar.

row² [raʊ] ◇ *n* **-1.** [quarrel] briga *f* **-2.** *inf* [noise] alvoroço *m*, barulho *m.* ◇ *vi* [quarrel] discutir, brigar.

rowboat ['rəʊbəʊt] *n US* barco *m* a remo.

rowdy ['raʊdɪ] *(compar* -ier, *superl* -iest*) adj* **-1.** [person] brigão(gona) **-2.** [party, atmosphere] barulhento(ta).

row house [rəʊ-] *n US* casa *f* geminada.

rowing ['rəʊɪŋ] *n (U)* remo *m.*

rowing boat *n UK* barco *m* a remo.

royal ['rɔɪəl] ◇ *adj* real. ◇ *n inf* membro *m* da família real.

Royal Air Force *n (U)*: **the ~** a Força Aérea Britânica.

royal family *n* família *f* real.

royal jelly *n (U)* geléia *f* real.

Royal Mail *n UK*: **the ~** os Correios da Grã-Bretanha.

Royal Navy *n*: **the ~** a Marinha Real Británica.

royalty ['rɔɪəltɪ] *n (U)* realeza *f.*
   ◆ **royalties** *npl* direitos *mpl* autorais.

rpm *(abbr of* **revolutions per minute)** *npl* rpm.

RSPCA *(abbr of* **Royal Society for the Prevention of Cruelty to Animals)** *n* sociedade británica protetora de animais.

RSVP *(abbr of* **répondez s'il vous plaît)** RSVP.

rub [rʌb] *(pt & pp* -bed, *cont* -bing) ◇ *vt* esfregar; **to ~ shoulders with** acotovelar-se com; **to ~ sthg in (to) sthg** esfregar algo em algo; **to ~ sb up the wrong way** *UK*, **to ~ sb the wrong way** *US* ofender alguém sem intenção. ◇ *vi*: **to ~ (against** *or* **on sthg)** roçar (em algo); **to ~ (together)** esfregar-se; **to ~ along** dar-se bem com.
   ◆ **rub off on** *vt fus* influir em.
   ◆ **rub out** *vt sep* apagar.

rubber ['rʌbə'] ◇ *adj* de borracha. ◇ *n* **-1.** *(U)* [substance] borracha *f* **-2.** *UK* [eraser] borracha *f* **-3.** [in bridge] rubber *m* **-4.** *US inf* [condom] camisinha *f.*

rubber band *n* atilho *m*, borrachinha *f (para papel).*

rubber plant *n* goma-elástica *f.*

rubber stamp *n* carimbo *m.*
   ◆ **rubber-stamp** *vt* aprovar sem questionar.

rubbish ['rʌbɪʃ] ◇ *n* **-1.** [refuse] lixo *m* **-2.** *inf fig* [worthless matter] porcaria *f* **-3.** *inf* [nonsense] besteira *f*, bobagem *f.* ◇ *vt inf* rebaixar. ◇ *excl* bobagem!

rubbish bag *n UK* saco *m* de lixo.

rubbish bin *n UK* lata *f* de lixo.

rubbish dump, rubbish tip *n UK* depósito *m* de lixo.

rubble ['rʌbl] *n (U)* entulho *m.*

ruby ['ru:bɪ] *(pl* -ies*) n* rubi *m.*

rucksack ['rʌksæk] *n* mochila *f.*

ructions ['rʌkʃnz] *npl inf* alvoroço *m*, tumulto *m.*

rudder ['rʌdə'] *n* leme *m.*

ruddy ['rʌdɪ] *(compar* -ier, *superl* -iest*) adj* **-1.** [reddish] corado(da) **-2.** *UK dated* [for emphasis] maldito(ta).

rude [ru:d] *adj* **-1.** [impolite] rude, grosseiro(ra) **-2.** [dirty, naughty - joke] sujo(ja); [- word] grosseiro(ra); [- noise] violento(ta) **-3.** [unexpected] brusco(ca); **~ awakening** um despertar brusco.

rudimentary [ˌru:dɪ'mentərɪ] *adj* rudimentar.

rueful ['ru:fʊl] *adj* arrependido(da).

ruffian ['rʌfjən] *n* rufião *m*, -ona *f.*

ruffle ['rʌfl] vt -1. [mess up - hair, fur] revolver; [- water] agitar -2. [upset] enervar.

rug [rʌg] n -1. [carpet] tapete m (pequeno) -2. [blanket] manta f.

rugby ['rʌgbɪ] n (U) rúgbi m.

rugged ['rʌgɪd] adj -1. [rocky, uneven] acidentado(da) -2. [sturdy] potente -3. [roughly handsome] rústico(ca) e atraente.

rugger ['rʌgə'] n (U) UK inf rúgbi m.

ruin ['ruːɪn] ◇ n ruína f. ◇ vt -1. [spoil] arruinar, estragar -2. [bankrupt] arruinar.
➡ **in ruin(s)** adv em ruínas.

rule [ruːl] ◇ n -1. [regulation - SPORT] regra f; [- SCH] norma f -2. [convention, guideline] regra f; **as a ~ of thumb** por experiência (própria) -3. [norm]: **the ~** a regra, a norma; **as a ~** via de regra -4. (U) [control] domínio m. ◇ vt -1. [control, guide] comandar -2. [govern] governar -3. [decide]: **to ~ that** ordenar OR decretar que. ◇ vi -1. [give decision] deliberar -2. fml [be paramount] dominar -3. [govern] governar.
➡ **rule out** vt sep -1. [reject as unsuitable] descartar -2. [prevent, make impossible - possibility, circumstances] descartar; [- event, decision] impedir.

ruled [ruːld] adj pautado(da).

ruler ['ruːlə'] n -1. [for measurement] régua f -2. [leader] soberano m, -na f.

ruling ['ruːlɪŋ] ◇ adj no poder, dominante. ◇ n sentença f, parecer m.

rum [rʌm] (compar -mer, superl -mest) n (U) rum m.

Rumania [ruːˈmeɪnjə] n = **Romania**.

Rumanian [ruːˈmeɪnjən] adj & n = **Romanian**.

rumble ['rʌmbl] ◇ n [noise - of thunder] estrondo m; [- of stomach, train] ronco m; [- of traffic] barulho m. ◇ vi -1. [thunder] trovejar -2. [stomach, train] roncar -3. [traffic] fazer barulho.

rummage ['rʌmɪdʒ] vi escarafunchar.

rumour UK, **rumor** US ['ruːmə'] n rumor m, boato m.

rumoured UK, **rumored** US ['ruːməd] adj: **to be ~ed that** comenta-se que.

rump [rʌmp] n -1. [of animal] anca f, garupa f -2. inf [of person] nádegas fpl.

rump steak n filé m de alcatra.

rumpus ['rʌmpəs] n inf bafafá m, rolo m.

run [rʌn] (pt ran, pp run, cont -ning) ◇ n -1. [on foot] corrida f; **to go for a ~** ir dar uma corrida; **to break into a ~** sair em disparada; **to take the dog for a ~** levar o cão para um passeio; **on the ~** em fuga -2. [in car] passeio f -3. [series - of luck] alternância f; [- of disasters, wins]

série f -4. THEATRE temporada f -5. [great demand]: **~ on sthg** procura f OR demanda f por algo -6. [in tights] fio m puxado -7. [in cricket, baseball] ponto m -8. [sports track] pista f -9. [term, period]: **in the short/long ~** a curto/longo prazo. ◇ vt -1. [on foot] correr -2. [manage, control] dirigir, administrar -3. [machine] operar -4. [car] dirigir, fazer andar -5. [water, bath, tap] abrir -6. [publish] publicar -7. inf [drive] levar -8. [move, pass]: **to ~ sthg along/over sthg** passar algo em/sobre algo. ◇ vi -1. [gen] passar -2. [on foot] correr -3. US [in election]: **to ~ (for sthg)** concorrer (a algo) -4. [progress, develop]: **to ~ smoothly** ir bem -5. [machine, factory, engine] funcionar; **to ~ on** OR **off sthg** funcionar com algo -6. [liquid, river] escorrer -7. [nose] escorrer -8. [tap] pingar -9. [colour] borrar -10. [continue] continuar; **feelings are ~ning high** os ânimos estão exaltados.
➡ **run about** vi -1. [from place to place] correr (de um lugar para outro) -2. [associate] andar.
➡ **run across** vt fus encontrar-se com.
➡ **run around** vi = **run about**.
➡ **run away** vi [flee]: **to ~ away (from sb/sthg)** fugir (de alguém/algo).
➡ **run down** ◇ vt sep -1. [in vehicle] atropelar -2. [criticize] falar mal de -3. [allow to decline] enfraquecer. ◇ vi perder força.
➡ **run into** vt fus -1. [encounter - problem] deparar-se com; [- person] topar com -2. [in vehicle] chocar-se com OR contra.
➡ **run off** ◇ vt sep [a copy] imprimir. ◇ vi [abscond, elope]: **to ~ off (with sb/sthg)** fugir (com alguém/algo).
➡ **run out** vi -1. [become used up] esgotar -2. [expire] vencer, caducar.
➡ **run out of** vt fus ficar sem.
➡ **run over** vt sep atropelar.
➡ **run through** vt fus -1. [practise] ensaiar, praticar -2. [read through] passar os olhos em.
➡ **run to** vt fus [amount to] chegar a.
➡ **run up** vt fus contrair.
➡ **run up against** vt fus deparar-se com.

runaway ['rʌnəweɪ] ◇ adj [out of control - train, inflation] descontrolado(da); [- victory] fácil. ◇ n fugitivo m, -va f.

rundown ['rʌndaʊn] n -1. [report] relatório m detalhado -2. [decline] desmantelamento m gradual.
➡ **run-down** adj -1. [dilapidated] arruinado(da), em ruínas -2. [tired] esgotado(da).

rung [rʌŋ] ◇ pp ▷ **ring**. ◇ n degrau m.

runner ['rʌnəʳ] n -1. [athlete] corredor m, -ra f -2. [smuggler - guns] contrabandista mf; [- drugs] traficante mf -3. [wood or metal strip - of sledge, skate] lâmina f; [- of drawer] corrediça f.

runner bean n UK feijão-trepador m.

runner-up (pl runners-up) n segundo colocado m, segunda colocada f.

running ['rʌnɪŋ] ◇ adj -1. [continuous] constante -2. [consecutive] consecutivo(-va) -3. [water - not stagnant] corrente; [- in pipes] encanado(da). ◇ n -1. (U) SPORT corrida f; she loves ~ in the park ela gosta de correr no parque -2. [management, control] gestão f, direção f -3. [of machine] funcionamento m -4. phr: to be in/out of the ~ (for sthg) ter/não ter possibilidades (de algo).

runny ['rʌnɪ] (compar -ier, superl -iest) adj -1. [food - eggs] malpassado(da); [- jam, honey] mole; [- butter, chocolate] derretido(da) -2. [nose] escorrendo -3. [eyes] lacrimejante.

run-of-the-mill adj corriqueiro(ra).

runt [rʌnt] n -1. [animal] filhote m mais fraco -2. pej [person] tampinha mf.

run-up n -1. [preceding time] período m anterior -2. SPORT impulso m.

runway ['rʌnweɪ] n pista f (de pouso/decolagem).

rupture ['rʌptʃəʳ] n -1. MED hérnia f -2. [of relationship] rompimento m.

rural ['ruərəl] adj rural.

ruse [ru:z] n ardil m.

rush [rʌʃ] ◇ n -1. [hurry] pressa f -2. [demand]: ~ (for OR on sthg) procura f excessiva (por algo) -3. [busiest period] corre-corre m -4. [surge - physical] fluxo m; ~ of air corrente m de ar; [- mental, emotional] torrente f. ◇ vt -1. [hurry] apressar -2. [send quickly] levar com urgência -3. [attack suddenly] investir repentinamente contra. ◇ vi -1. [hurry] apressar-se; to ~ into sthg entrar de cabeça em algo -2. [crowd] correr.

➤ **rushes** npl BOT juncos mpl.

rush hour n hora f do rush.

rusk [rʌsk] n biscoito m seco.

Russia ['rʌʃə] n Rússia f.

Russian ['rʌʃn] ◇ adj russo(sa). ◇ n -1. [person] russo m, -sa f -2. [language] russo m.

rust [rʌst] ◇ n (U) ferrugem f. ◇ vi enferrujar.

rustic ['rʌstɪk] adj rústico(ca).

rustle ['rʌsl] ◇ vt -1. [paper, leaves] farfalhar -2. US [cattle] roubar. ◇ vi farfalhar.

rusty ['rʌstɪ] (compar -ier, superl -iest) adj enferrujado(da).

rut [rʌt] n -1. [furrow] sulco m; to get into/be in a ~ tornar-se/ser escravo(-va) da rotina -2. [animal] cio m.

ruthless ['ru:θlɪs] adj impiedoso(sa).

RV n (abbr of recreational vehicle) US motor-home m.

rye [raɪ] n (U) centeio m.

rye bread n (U) pão m de centeio.

S

s (pl ss OR s's), **S** (pl Ss OR S's) [es] n [letter] s, S m.

➤ **S** (abbr of south) S.

Sabbath ['sæbəθ] n: the ~ o sabá.

sabbatical [sə'bætɪkl] n período m sabático; on ~ em período sabático.

sabotage ['sæbətɑ:ʒ] ◇ n (U) sabotagem f. ◇ vt sabotar.

saccharin(e) ['sækərɪn] n (U) sacarina f.

sachet ['sæʃeɪ] n sachê m.

sack [sæk] ◇ n -1. [bag] saco m -2. UK inf [dismissal]: to get OR be given the ~ ser despedido(da). ◇ vt UK inf [dismiss] despedir, mandar embora.

sacking ['sækɪŋ] n (U) linhagem f.

sacred ['seɪkrɪd] adj sagrado(da).

sacrifice ['sækrɪfaɪs] ◇ n sacrifício m. ◇ vt sacrificar.

sacrilege ['sækrɪlɪdʒ] n (U) sacrilégio m.

sacrosanct ['sækrəʊsæŋkt] adj sacrossanto(ta).

sad [sæd] (compar -der, superl -dest) adj triste.

sadden ['sædn] vt entristecer.

saddle ['sædl] ◇ n -1. [for horse] sela f -2. [of bicycle, motorcycle] selim m. ◇ vt -1. [put saddle on] selar -2. fig [burden]: to ~ sb with sthg encarregar alguém de algo.

saddlebag ['sædlbæg] n -1. [for horse] alforje m -2. [for bicycle, motorcycle] bolsa f.

sadistic [sə'dɪstɪk] adj sádico(ca).

sadly ['sædlɪ] adv -1. [sorrowfully] tristemente -2. [regrettably] lamentavelmente.

sadness ['sædnɪs] n tristeza f.

s.a.e., sae (abbr of stamped addressed envelope) n envelope-resposta com porte pago.

safari [sə'fɑːrɪ] *n* safári *m*.

safe [seɪf] <> *adj* **-1.** [not causing harm or danger] seguro(ra) **-2.** [not in danger] protegido(da); **to be ~ from** attack estar a salvo de ataques; **~ and sound** são e salvo, sã e salva **-3.** [not causing disagreement] pacífico(ca); **it's ~ to say that ...** pode-se dizer com segurança que ... **-4.** [not involving any risk] seguro(ra); **to be on the ~ side** por precaução. <> *n* cofre *m*.

safe-conduct *n* **-1.** [document giving protection] salvo-conduto *m* **-2.** (*U*) [protection] salvaguarda *f*.

safe-deposit box *n* caixa-forte *f*.

safeguard ['seɪfgɑːd] <> *n* salvaguarda *f*, proteção *f*; **~ against** sthg proteção contra algo. <> *vt*: **to ~ sb/sthg (against sthg)** proteger *OR* salvaguardar alguém/algo (de algo).

safe keeping *n* (*U*) proteção *f*, custódia *f*; **in sb's ~** aos cuidados de alguém.

safely ['seɪflɪ] *adv* **-1.** [gen] com segurança **-2.** [unharmed] ileso(sa), a salvo **-3.** [for certain]: **I can ~ say (that) ...** posso dizer seguramente que ...

safe sex *n* (*U*) sexo *m* seguro.

safety ['seɪftɪ] *n* segurança *f*.

safety belt *n* cinto *m* de segurança.

safety pin *n* alfinete *m* de segurança.

saffron ['sæfrən] *n* (*U*) **-1.** [spice] açafrão *m*.

sag [sæg] (*pt* & *pp* **-ged**, *cont* **-ging**) *vi* [sink downwards] afundar, ceder.

sage [seɪdʒ] <> *adj* [wise] sábio(bia). <> *n* **-1.** (*U*) [herb] sálvia *f* **-2.** [wise man] sábio *m*.

Sagittarius [ˌsædʒɪ'teərɪəs] *n* [sign] Sagitário *m*.

Sahara [sə'hɑːrə] *n*: **the ~ (Desert)** o (Deserto do) Saara.

said [sed] *pt* & *pp* ▷ **say**.

sail [seɪl] <> *n* **-1.** [of boat] vela *f*; **to set ~** zarpar **-2.** [journey by boat]: **let's go for a ~** vamos velejar. <> *vt* **-1.** [boat] governar **-2.** [sea] cruzar. <> *vi* **-1.** [to depart] zarpar **-2.** [sport] velejar **-3.** [to travel, move - person] navegar; [- boat] singrar **-4.** *fig* [through air] voar.
   ⬦ **sail through** *vt fus* passar fácil por.

sailboat *n US* = **sailing boat**.

sailing ['seɪlɪŋ] *n* **-1.** (*U*) *SPORT* navegação *f* a vela, vela *f*; **I like to go ~** eu gosto de (ir) velejar; **plain ~** sem maiores dificuldades **-2.** [trip by ship] travessia *f*.

sailing boat *UK*, **sailboat** *US* ['seɪlbəʊt] *n* barco *m* a vela.

sailing ship *n* veleiro *m*.

sailor ['seɪlə'] *n* marinheiro *m*, -ra *f*.

saint [seɪnt] *n* **-1.** *RELIG* santo *m*, -ta *f* **-2.** *inf* [very good person] santo *m*, -ta *f*.

saintly ['seɪntlɪ] (*compar* **-ier**, *superl* **-iest**) *adj* santo(ta), santificado(da).

sake [seɪk] *n* **-1.** [benefit, advantage]: **for the ~ of** para o bem de; **for my ~** por mim **-2.** [purpose]: **for the ~ of** pelo bem de; **let us say, for the ~ of argument, that ...** digamos, só para argumentar, que ... **-3.** *phr*: **for God's** *OR* **Heaven's ~!** pelo amor de Deus!

salad ['sæləd] *n* salada *f*.

salad bowl *n* saladeira *f*.

salad cream *n* (*U*) *UK* molho *m* para salada (*à base de maionese*).

salad dressing *n* (*U*) molho *m* para salada (*à base de vinagre, óleo e ervas*).

salami [sə'lɑːmɪ] *n* (*U*) salame *m*.

salary ['sælərɪ] (*pl* **-ies**) *n* salário *m*.

sale [seɪl] *n* **-1.** [gen] venda *f*; **on ~** à venda; **(up) for ~** à venda; **'for ~'** 'vende-se' **-2.** [at reduced prices] liquidação *f*, saldo *m* **-3.** [auction] leilão *m*.
   ⬦ **sales** <> *npl* **-1.** [quantity sold] vendas *fpl* **-2.** [at reduced prices]: **the ~ s** os saldos.

saleroom *UK* ['seɪlrʊm], **salesroom** *US* ['seɪlzrʊm] *n* sala *f* de leilão.

sales assistant ['seɪlz-], **salesclerk** *US* ['seɪlzklɑːrk] *n* balconista *mf*, vendedor *m*, -ra *f* (*em loja*).

salesman ['seɪlzmən] (*pl* **-men** [-mən]) *n* [gen] vendedor *m*; [representative] representante *m* de vendas.

sales rep *n inf* representante *mf* de vendas.

salesroom *n US* = **saleroom**.

saleswoman ['seɪlzˌwʊmən] (*pl* **-women** [-ˌwɪmɪn]) *n* vendedora *f*; [representative] representante *f* de vendas.

salient ['seɪljənt] *adj fml* evidente, notável.

saliva [sə'laɪvə] *n* (*U*) saliva *f*.

sallow ['sæləʊ] *adj* amarelado(da).

salmon ['sæmən] (*pl inv OR* **-s**) *n* salmão *m*.

salmonella [ˌsælmə'nelə] *n* (*U*) salmonela *f*.

salon ['sælɒn] *n* **-1.** [hairdresser's] salão *m* **-2.** [clothes shop] butique *f*.

saloon [sə'luːn] *n* **-1.** *UK* [car] sedã *m* **-2.** *US* [bar] bar *m* **-3.** *UK* [in pub]: **~ (bar)** *em alguns pubs e hotéis, bar finamente decorado e de preços mais altos do que os do public bar* **-4.** [on ship] salão *m*.

salt [sɔːlt, sɒlt] <> *n* sal *m*. <> *vt* **-1.** [food] salgar **-2.** [roads] jogar sal em (*para derreter o gelo*).
   ⬦ **salt away** *vt sep inf* guardar.

SALT [so:lt] (abbr of Strategic Arms Limitation Talks/Treaty) n SALT m.

salt cellar UK, **salt shaker** US [-ˌʃeɪkəʳ] n saleiro m.

saltwater [ˈsɔ:lt,wɔ:təʳ] <> adj de água salgada. <> n (U) água f salgada, água f do mar.

salty [ˈsɔ:ltɪ] (compar -ier, superl -iest) adj salgado(da).

salutary [ˈsæljʊtrɪ] adj salutar.

salute [səˈlu:t] <> n -1. MIL [with hand] continência f -2. MIL [firing of guns] salva f -3. (U) [act of saluting] cumprimento m -4. [formal acknowledgment] saudação f. <> vt -1. MIL [with hand] fazer continência a -2. [acknowledge formally, honour] cumprimentar. <> vi MIL [with hand] fazer continência.

salvage [ˈsælvɪdʒ] <> n -1. [rescue of ship] salvamento m -2. [property rescued] objetos mpl recuperados. <> vt -1. [rescue]: **to ~ sthg (from)** salvar algo (de) -2. fig [gain from failure]: **to ~ sthg (from)** preservar algo (de).

salvation [sælˈveɪʃn] n salvação f.

Salvation Army n: **the ~** o Exército da Salvação.

same [seɪm] <> adj [gen] mesmo(ma); **at the ~ time** [simultaneously] ao mesmo tempo; [yet] mesmo assim; **one and the ~** o mesmo, a mesma. <> adv: **the ~** o mesmo, a mesma. <> pron [unchanged, identical]: **the ~** o mesmo, a mesma; **the hats they were wearing were the ~** os chapéus que eles estavam usando eram iguais; **all OR just the ~** [nevertheless, anyway] mesmo assim; **it's all the ~ to me** para mim dá no mesmo, para mim tanto faz; **it's not the ~** não é a mesma coisa.

sample [ˈsɑ:mpl] <> n amostra f. <> vt -1. [taste] provar -2. [try out, test] experimentar.

sanatorium (pl -riums OR -ria [-rɪə]), **sanitorium** US (pl -riums OR -ria [-rɪə]) [ˌsænəˈtɔ:rɪəm] n sanatório m.

sanctimonious [ˌsæŋktɪˈməʊnjəs] adj pej santarrão(rrona).

sanction [ˈsæŋkʃn] <> n sanção f. <> vt sancionar.

sanctity [ˈsæŋktətɪ] n (U) santidade f.

sanctuary [ˈsæŋktʃʊərɪ] (pl -ies) n -1. [gen] santuário m -2. [place of safety] abrigo m -3. (U) [safety, refuge] refúgio m.

sand [sænd] <> n (U) areia f. <> vt lixar.

sandal [ˈsændl] n sandália f.

sandalwood [ˈsændlwʊd] n (U) sândalo m.

sandbox n US = **sandpit**.

sandcastle [ˈsænd,kɑ:sl] n castelo m de areia.

sand dune n duna f.

sandpaper [ˈsænd,peɪpəʳ] <> n (U) lixa f. <> vt lixar.

sandpit UK [ˈsændpɪt], **sandbox** US [ˈsændbɒks] n caixa f de areia.

sandstone [ˈsændstəʊn] n (U) arenito m.

sandwich [ˈsænwɪdʒ] <> n sanduíche m. <> vt fig: **to be ~ed between** ser prensado(da) entre.

sandwich course n UK curso universitário que inclui um certo tempo de experiência profissional.

sandy [ˈsændɪ] (compar -ier, superl -iest) adj -1. [made of sand] arenoso(sa) -2. [sand-coloured] cor-de-areia.

sane [seɪn] adj -1. [not mad] são(sã) -2. [sensible] sensato(ta).

sang [sæŋ] pt ▷ sing.

sanitary [ˈsænɪtrɪ] adj -1. [connected with health] sanitário(ria) -2. [clean, hygienic] higiênico(ca).

sanitary towel, sanitary napkin US n absorvente m higiênico.

sanitation [ˌsænɪˈteɪʃn] n -1. [in streets] saneamento m -2. [in houses] instalações fpl sanitárias.

sanitorium n US = **sanatorium**.

sanity [ˈsænɪtɪ] n -1. [saneness] sanidade f -2. [good sense] sensatez f.

sank [sæŋk] pt ▷ sink.

Santa (Claus) [ˈsæntə(ˌklɔ:z)] n Papai m Noel.

sap [sæp] (pt & pp -ped, cont -ping) <> n (U) [of plant] seiva m. <> vt enfraquecer, consumir.

sapling [ˈsæplɪŋ] n árvore m nova, arvorezinha f.

sapphire [ˈsæfaɪəʳ] n safira f.

sarcastic [sɑ:ˈkæstɪk] adj sarcástico(ca).

sarcophagus [sɑ:ˈkɒfəgəs] (pl -gi [-gaɪ], -es) n sarcófago m.

sardine [sɑ:ˈdi:n] n sardinha f.

Sardinia [sɑ:ˈdɪnjə] n Sardenha f.

sardonic [sɑ:ˈdɒnɪk] adj mordaz.

SAS (abbr of Special Air Service) n unidade especial do exército britânico encarregada de operações de antiterrorismo e sabotagem.

SASE (abbr of self-addressed stamped envelope) n US envelope auto-endereçado e já selado.

sash [sæʃ] n faixa f.

sat [sæt] pt & pp ▷ sit.

SAT [sæt] n -1. (abbr of Standard Assessment Test) exames de aptidão que os estudantes da Inglaterra e do País de Gales prestam aos 7, 11 e 14 anos de *idade* **-2.** (*abbr of* **Scholastic Aptitude Test**) *exame prestado por estudantes no último ano da escola secundária nos Estados Unidos, importante ao se ingressar na universidade.*

Satan ['seɪtn] *n* Satã *m*, Satanás *m*.

satchel ['sætʃəl] *n* pasta *f*, mochila *f* escolar.

satellite ['sætəlaɪt] <> *n* satélite *m*. <> *comp* **-1.** TELEC por satélite **-2.** [dependent]: ~ **city** cidade-satélite *f*.

satellite dish *n* [for TV] antena *f* parabólica.

satellite TV *n* tevê *f* via satélite.

satin ['sætɪn] <> *n* (U) cetim *m*. <> *comp* **-1.** [made of satin] de cetim **-2.** [smooth] acetinado(da).

satire ['sætaɪər] *n* sátira *f*.

satisfaction [ˌsætɪs'fækʃn] *n* **-1.** [gen] satisfação *f* **-2.** (U) [fulfilment of need] atendimento *m*, cumprimento *m*.

satisfactory [ˌsætɪs'fæktərɪ] *adj* satisfatório(ria).

satisfied ['sætɪsfaɪd] *adj* [happy] satisfeito(ta); **to be** ~ **with sthg** estar satisfeito(ta) com algo.

satisfy ['sætɪsfaɪ] (*pt* & *pp* **-ied**) *vt* **-1.** [make happy] satisfazer **-2.** [convince] convencer; **to** ~ **sb that** convencer alguém de que **-3.** [fulfil] satisfazer, atender a.

satisfying ['sætɪsfaɪɪŋ] *adj* satisfatório(ria), agradável.

satsuma [ˌsæt'suːmə] *n* tipo de tangerina proveniente do Japão.

saturate ['sætʃəreɪt] *vt* **-1.** [drench] ensopar, empapar; **to** ~ **sthg with sthg** ensopar OR empapar algo com algo **-2.** [fill completely, swamp] inundar; **to** ~ **sthg with sthg** saturar algo com algo.

saturated *adj* **-1.** [drenched] ensopado(da), empapado(da) **-2.** [fat] saturado(da).

Saturday ['sætədɪ] <> *n* sábado *m*; **what day is it? - it's** ~ que dia é hoje? - é sábado; **on** ~ no sábado; **on** ~ **s** aos sábados; **last** ~ sábado passado; **this** ~ este sábado; **next** ~ sábado da semana que vem; **every** ~ todos os sábados; **every other** ~ um sábado sim, outro não; **the** ~ **before** no sábado anterior; **the** ~ **before last** há dois sábados; **the** ~ **after next**, ~ **week, a week on** ~ não no próximo sábado, no outro. <> *comp* aos sábados; ~ **morning/afternoon/night** sábado de manhã/tarde/noite; ~ **evening** no fim da tarde de sábado.

sauce [sɔːs] *n* CULIN molho *m*.

saucepan ['sɔːspən] *n* panela *f* com cabo.

saucer ['sɔːsər] *n* pires *m inv*.

saucy ['sɔːsɪ] (*compar* **-ier**, *superl* **-iest**) *adj inf* atrevido(da).

Saudi Arabia [ˌsaʊdɪə'reɪbjə] *n* Arábia Saudita.

Saudi (Arabian) ['saʊdɪ-] <> *adj* árabe-saudita. <> *n* árabe-saudita *mf*.

sauna ['sɔːnə] *n* sauna *f*.

saunter ['sɔːntər] *vi* passear (*tranqüilamente*).

sausage ['sɒsɪdʒ] *n* **-1.** (U) [meat] lingüiça *f* **-2.** [shaped piece of meat] salsicha *f*.

sausage roll *n* UK enroladinho *m* de salsicha.

sauté [UK 'səʊteɪ, US səʊ'teɪ] (*pt* & *pp* **sautéed** OR **sautéd**) <> *adj* sauté. <> *vt* fritar levemente.

savage ['sævɪdʒ] <> *adj* selvagem. <> *n* selvagem *mf*. <> *vt* [attack physically] atacar ferozmente.

save [seɪv] <> *n* SPORT defesa *f*. <> *prep fml*: ~ **(for)** exceto. <> *vt* **-1.** [gen] salvar; **to** ~ **sb from sthg/from doing sthg** salvar alguém de algo/de fazer algo; **to** ~ **sb's life** salvar a vida de alguém **-2.** [prevent waste of] economizar **-3.** [set aside] guardar **-4.** [make unnecessary] poupar; **to** ~ **sb/sthg from doing sthg** poupar alguém/algo de fazer algo **-5.** SPORT defender. <> *vi* economizar.

➡ **save up** *vi* economizar.

saving grace ['seɪvɪŋ-] *n* mérito *m*.

savings ['seɪvɪŋz] *npl* economias *fpl*.

savings account *n* US (caderneta *f* de) poupança *f*.

savings and loan association *n* US sociedade *f* de empréstimos imobiliários.

savings bank *n* caixa *f* econômica, banco *m* só de cadernetas de poupança.

saviour UK, **savior** US ['seɪvjər] *n* salvador *m*, -ra *f*.

savour UK, **savor** US ['seɪvər] *vt* **-1.** [enjoy taste of] saborear **-2.** fig [enjoy greatly] saborear, aproveitar.

savoury UK (*pl* **-ies**), **savory** (*pl* **-ies**) US ['seɪvərɪ] <> *adj* **-1.** [not sweet] condimentado(da) **-2.** [respectable, pleasant] agradável. <> *n* tira-gosto *m*.

savoy (cabbage) *n* repolho *m* crespo.

saw [sɔː] (UK *pt* **-ed**, *pp* **sawn**, US *pt* & *pp* **-ed**) <> *pt* > **see**. <> *n* serra *f*. <> *vt* serrar.

sawdust ['sɔːdʌst] *n* (U) serragem *f*.

sawed-off shotgun *n* US = **sawn-off shotgun**.

sawmill ['sɔːmɪl] *n* serraria *f*.

sawn [sɔːn] *pp* UK > **saw**.

sawn-off shotgun *UK*, **sawed-off shotgun** *US* [sɔːd-] *n* arma *f* de cano serrado.

say [seɪ] (*pt* & *pp* **said**) ⬦ *vt* **-1.** [gen] dizer; **to ~ (that)** dizer que **-2.** [giving information] mostrar **-3.** [assume, suppose] supor **-4.** *phr:* **that goes without ~ing** nem precisa dizer isso; **it has a lot to be said for it** tem muitos pontos em seu favor; **what have you got to ~ for yourself?** o que você tem a dizer para se defender?; **you don't ~!** não diga!, não é verdade! ⬦ *n* [power of decision]: **to have a/no ~ (in sthg)** ter/não ter voz nem vez (em algo); **let me have my ~** deixe-me dizer o que eu penso.

◆ **that is to say** *adv* quer dizer.

saying [ˈseɪɪŋ] *n* ditado *m* popular, dito *m*.

scab [skæb] *n* **-1.** [of wound] casca *f*, crosta *f* **-2.** *pej* [non-striker] fura-greve *mf*.

scaffold [ˈskæfəʊld] *n* **-1.** [frame] andaime *m* **-2.** [for executions] cadafalso *m*, patíbulo *m*.

scaffolding [ˈskæfəldɪŋ] *n (U)* andaime *m*.

scald [skɔːld] ⬦ *n* escaldadura *f*. ⬦ *vt* escaldar.

scale [skeɪl] ⬦ *n* **-1.** [gen] escala *f*; **to ~ em escala -2.** [size, extent] tamanho *m* **-3.** [of fish, snake] escama *f* **-4.** *US* = **scales.** ⬦ *vt* **-1.** [climb] escalar **-2.** [remove scales from] escamar.

◆ **scales** *npl* balança *f*.

◆ **scale down** *vt fus* reduzir.

scale model *n* maquete *f*.

scallop [ˈskɒləp] ⬦ *n* [shellfish] vieira *f*. ⬦ *vt* [decorate edge of] guarnecer.

scalp [skælp] ⬦ *n* **-1.** ANAT couro *m* cabeludo **-2.** [removed from head] escalpo *m*. ⬦ *vt* escalpelar.

scalpel [ˈskælpəl] *n* bisturi *m*.

scamper [ˈskæmpər] *vi* fugir rapidamente.

scampi [ˈskæmpɪ] *n (U)* camarão-castanho *m*.

scan [skæn] (*pt* & *pp* **-ned**, *cont* **-ning**) ⬦ *n* MED & TECH exame *m*, escaneamento *m*. ⬦ *vt* **-1.** [gen] escanear **-2.** [examine carefully] examinar cuidadosamente **-3.** [glance at] correr os olhos por.

scandal [ˈskændl] *n* escândalo *m*.

scandalize, ise [ˈskændəlaɪz] *vt* escandalizar.

Scandinavia [ˌskændɪˈneɪvjəl] *n* Escandinávia.

Scandinavian [ˌskændɪˈneɪvjənl] ⬦ *adj* escandinavo(va). ⬦ *n* escandinavo *m*, -va *f*.

scant [skænt] *adj* insuficiente, escasso(sa).

scanty [ˈskæntɪ] (*compar* **-ier**, *superl* **-iest**) *adj* **-1.** [dress] mínimo(ma) **-2.** [amount, resources] escasso(sa) **-3.** [meal] insuficiente.

scapegoat [ˈskeɪpɡəʊt] *n* bode *m* expiatório.

scar [skaːʳ] (*pt* & *pp* **-red**, *cont* **-ring**) *n* [physical] cicatriz *f*.

scarce [skeəs] *adj* escasso(sa).

scarcely [ˈskeəslɪ] *adv* apenas.

scare [skeəʳ] ⬦ *n* **-1.** [sudden fright] susto *m* **-2.** [public panic] ameaça *f*; **bomb ~** ameaça de bomba. ⬦ *vt* assustar.

◆ **scare away, scare off** *vt sep* afugentar.

scarecrow [ˈskeəkrəʊ] *n* espantalho *m*.

scared [ˈskeəd] *adj* [very frightened] apavorado(da); **to be ~ stiff** OR **to death** estar morrendo de medo.

scarf [skaːf] (*pl* **-s** OR **scarves**) *n* **-1.** [long - to keep warm] cachecol *m*; [- as accessory] echarpe *f* **-2.** [square] lenço *m*.

scarlet [ˈskaːlət] ⬦ *adj* escarlate. ⬦ *n* escarlate *m*.

scarlet fever *n (U)* escarlatina *f*.

scarves [skaːvz] *pl* ⊳ **scarf**.

scathing [ˈskeɪðɪŋ] *adj* mordaz.

scatter [ˈskætəʳ] ⬦ *vt* espalhar. ⬦ *vi* dispersar-se.

scatterbrained [ˈskætəbreɪnd] *adj inf* desmiolado(da), avoado(da).

scavenger [ˈskævɪndʒəʳ] *n* **-1.** [animal] animal *que se alimenta de carniça* **-2.** *fig* [person] catador *m*, -ra *f* de lixo.

scenario [sɪˈnaːrɪəʊ] (*pl* **-s**) *n* cenário *m*.

scene [siːn] *n* **-1.** [gen] cena *f*; **behind the ~s** nos bastidores **-2.** [picture of place] paisagem *f*, cenário *m* **-3.** [sight, impression] vista *f* **-4.** [area of activity] área *f* **-5.** [embarrassing fuss] cena *f*, escândalo *m* **-6.** *phr:* **to set the ~** [for person] descrever a cena; [for event] preparar o cenário.

scenery [ˈsiːnərɪ] *n (U)* **-1.** [of countryside] paisagem *f* **-2.** THEATRE cenário *m*.

scenic [ˈsiːnɪk] *adj* **-1.** [view] pitoresco(ca) **-2.** [tour] turístico(ca).

scent [sent] *n* **-1.** [smell - of flowers] perfume *m*, fragrância *f*; [- of animal] cheiro *m*, odor *m* **-2.** *(U)* [perfume] perfume *m*.

scepter *n US* = **sceptre**.

sceptic *UK*, **skeptic** *US* [ˈskeptɪk] *n* céptico(ca).

sceptical *UK*, **skeptical** *US* [ˈskeptɪkl] *adj* cético(ca); **to be ~ about sthg** ser cético(ca) em relação a algo.

sceptre *UK*, **scepter** *US* ['septə^r] *n* cetro *m*.

schedule [*UK* 'ʃedju:l, *US* 'skedʒʊl] ◇ *n* **-1.** [plan] plano *m*; **to be ahead of** ~ estar adiantado(da); **to be behind** ~ estar atrasado(da); **on** ~ sem atraso **-2.** [written list - of prices, contents] lista *f*; [- of times] horários *mpl*. ◇ *vt*: **to** ~ **sthg (for)** marcar algo(para).

scheduled flight [*UK* 'ʃedju:ld-, *US* 'skedʒʊld-] *n* vôo *m* regular.

scheme [ski:m] ◇ *n* **-1.** [plan] projeto *m* **-2.** *pej* [dishonest plan] esquema *f* **-3.** [arrangement, decoration] disposição *f*; **colour** ~ combinação *f* de cores. ◇ *vi pej* tramar.

scheming ['ski:mɪŋ] *adj* que faz intriga.

schism ['sɪzm, 'skɪzm] *n* cisma *m*.

schizophrenic [ˌskɪtsə'frenɪk] ◇ *adj* esquizofrênico(ca). ◇ *n* esquizofrênico *m*, -ca *f*.

scholar ['skɒlə^r] *n* **-1.** [expert]: **he's a Greek** ~ ele é perito em grego **-2.** *dated* [student] aluno *m*, -na *f* **-3.** [holder of scholarship] bolsista *mf*.

scholarship ['skɒləʃɪp] *n* **-1.** [grant] bolsa *f* **-2.** *(U)* [learning] erudição *f*.

school [sku:l] *n* **-1.** [place of education] escola *f*, colégio *m* **-2.** [hours spent in school] escola *f* **-3.** *UNIV* [department] faculdade *f* **-4.** *US* [university] universidade *f* **-5.** [group of fish] cardume *m* **-6.** [of whales, dolphins] grupo *m*.

school age *n (U)* idade *f* escolar.

schoolbook ['sku:lbʊk] *n* livro *m* escolar.

schoolboy ['sku:lbɔɪ] *n* aluno *m*.

schoolchild ['sku:ltʃaɪld] (*pl* **-children** [-tʃɪldrən]) *n* aluno *m*, -na *f*.

schooldays ['sku:ldeɪz] *npl* tempos *mpl* de colégio *OR* escola.

schoolgirl ['sku:lgɜ:l] *n* aluna *f*.

schooling ['sku:lɪŋ] *n (U)* educação *f*, ensino *m*.

school-leaver [-ˌli:və^r] *n UK* jovem que concluiu o ensino obrigatório.

schoolmaster ['sku:lˌmɑːstə^r] *n dated* mestre *m*.

schoolmistress ['sku:lˌmɪstrɪs] *n dated* mestra *f*.

school of thought *n* escola *f* de pensamento.

schoolteacher ['sku:lˌti:tʃə^r] *n* professor *m*, -ra *f*.

school year *n* ano *m* letivo.

schooner ['sku:nə^r] *n* **-1.** [ship] escuna *f* **-2.** *UK* [sherry glass] caneca *f (para xerez)*.

sciatica [saɪ'ætɪkə] *en (U)* ciática *f*.

science ['saɪəns] *n* ciência *f*.

science fiction *n (U)* ficção *f* científica.

scientific [ˌsaɪən'tɪfɪk] *adj* científico(ca).

scientist ['saɪəntɪst] *n* cientista *mf*.

scintillating ['sɪntɪleɪtɪŋ] *adj* brilhante.

scissors ['sɪzəz] *npl* tesoura *f*; **a pair of** ~ uma tesoura.

sclerosis *n* ⊳ **multiple sclerosis**.

scoff [skɒf] ◇ *vt UK inf* devorar, engolir. ◇ *vi* zombar; **to** ~ **at sb/sthg** zombar de alguém/algo.

scold [skəʊld] *vt* repreender, xingar.

scone [skɒn] *n* bolinho geralmente tomado à hora do chá com manteiga ou geléia.

scoop [sku:p] ◇ *n* **-1.** [kitchen implement - for sugar] colher *f*; [- for ice cream] pá *f* **-2.** [scoopful] concha *f*, colher *f* grande; **two** ~ **s of ice cream** duas bolas de sorvete **-3.** [news report] furo *m*. ◇ *vt* **-1.** [with hands] tirar com as mãos **-2.** [with implement] tirar com colher.

◆ **scoop out** *vt sep* tirar com colher.

scooter ['sku:tə^r] *n* **-1.** [toy] patinete *f* **-2.** [motorcycle] lambreta *f*.

scope [skəʊp] *n (U)* **-1.** [opportunity] possibilidades *fpl* **-2.** [range] escopo *m*.

scorch [skɔ:tʃ] *vt* **-1.** [clothes, food, skin] chamuscar **-2.** [grass, fields] queimar.

scorching ['skɔ:tʃɪŋ] *adj inf* escaldante.

score [skɔ:^r] ◇ *n* **-1.** *SPORT* placar *m* **-2.** [in test, competition] nota *f* **-3.** *dated* [twenty] vintena *f* **-4.** *MUS* partitura *f* **-5.** [subject]: **on that** ~ a esse respeito. ◇ *vt* **-1.** *SPORT* marcar **-2.** [achieve] conseguir, obter **-3.** [win in an argument] ganhar **-4.** [cut] gravar, entalhar. ◇ *vi SPORT* marcar.

◆ **score out** *vt sep UK* riscar.

scoreboard ['skɔ:bɔ:d] *n* placar *m*.

scorer ['skɔ:rə^r] *n* **-1.** [official] anotador *m*, -ra *f* de pontos **-2.** [player - football] goleador *m*, -ra *f*; [- basketball] cestinha *mf*; [- sports in general] jogador(ra) que marca mais pontos.

scorn [skɔ:n] ◇ *n (U)* desdém *m*, menosprezo *m*. ◇ *vt* **-1.** [despise] desprezar **-2.** *fml* [refuse to accept] desdenhar.

scornful ['skɔ:nfʊl] *adj* desdenhoso(osa); **to be** ~ **of sthg** desdenhar de algo.

Scorpio ['skɔ:pɪəʊ] (*pl* **-s**) *n* [sign] Escorpião *m*.

scorpion ['skɔ:pjən] *n* escorpião *m*.

Scot [skɒt] *n* escocês *m*, -esa *f*.

scotch [skɒtʃ] *vt* **-1.** [idea] acabar com **-2.** [rumour] desmentir.

Scotch [skɒtʃ] ◇ *adj* escocês(esa). ◇ *n* [whisky] uísque *m* escocês.

Scotch (tape)® *n US* fita *f* adesiva, durex® *m*.

scribble

scot-free adj inf: **to get off ~** sair impune.

Scotland ['skɒtlənd] n Escócia.

Scots [skɒts] <> adj escocês(esa). <> n (U) [dialect] escocês m.

Scotsman ['skɒtsmən] (pl -men [-mən]) n escocês m.

Scotswoman ['skɒtswʊmən] (pl -women [-,wɪmɪn]) n escocesa f.

Scottish ['skɒtɪʃ] adj escocês(esa).

scoundrel ['skaʊndrəl] n dated canalha mf.

scour [skaʊəʳ] vt -1. [clean] esfregar -2. [search] esquadrinhar.

scourge [skɜːdʒ] n -1. [cause of suffering] flagelo m -2. [critic] tormento m.

scout [skaʊt] n MIL batedor m, explorador m.

➭ **Scout** n escoteiro m.

➭ **scout around** vi: **to ~ around (for sthg)** explorar a área (em busca de algo).

scowl [skaʊl] <> n carranca f, cara f feia. <> vi franzir o cenho; **to ~ at sb** fazer cara feia para alguém.

scrabble ['skræbl] vi -1. [scramble] escalar com dificuldade; **to ~ up/down** subir/descer escalando -2. [scrape]: **to ~ at sthg** arranhar algo -3. [feel around] escarafunchar; **to ~ around for sthg** escarafunchar à procura de algo.

scraggy ['skrægɪ] (compar -ier, superl -iest) adj inf magricela.

scramble ['skræmbl] <> n briga f. <> vi -1. [climb] trepar em -2. [move clumsily] caminhar cambaleando; **she ~d for her handbag in the crush** ela teve que brigar pela bolsa no meio do tumulto.

scrambled eggs ['skræmbld-] npl ovos mpl mexidos.

scrap [skræp] (pt & pp -ped, cont -ping) <> n -1. [small piece] pedaço m; ~ **of conversation** trecho m; ~ **of information** uma informação; **there isn't a ~ of evidence** não há prova alguma -2. [metal] sucata f -3. inf [fight, quarrel] briga f. <> vt abandonar.

➭ **scraps** npl sobras fpl.

scrapbook ['skræpbʊk] n álbum m de recortes.

scrap dealer n ferro-velho m, sucateiro m, -ra f.

scrape [skreɪp] <> n -1. [scraping noise] rangido m, arranhão m -2. dated [difficult situation] enrascada f. <> vt -1. [remove]: **to ~ sthg off sthg** raspar algo de algo -2. [peel] raspar -3. [rub against - car, bumper, glass] riscar; [- knee, elbow, skin] arranhar. <> vi [rub]: **to ~**

against/on sthg raspar contra/em algo.

➭ **scrape through** vt fus passar com as calças na mão.

scraper ['skreɪpəʳ] n raspador m.

scrap merchant n UK sucateiro m, -ra f.

scrap paper UK, **scratch paper** US n (U) papel m rascunho.

scrapyard ['skræpjɑːd] n ferro-velho m.

scratch [skrætʃ] <> n -1. [gen] arranhão m -2. phr: **to do sthg from ~** fazer algo começando do nada; **to be up to ~** estar à altura. <> vt -1. [wound] arranhar -2. [surface] riscar -3. [rub] coçar. <> vi -1. [branch, knife, thorn]: **to ~ at/against sthg** roçar em algo -2. [person, animal] coçar-se.

scratch paper n US = **scrap paper**.

scrawl [skrɔːl] <> n rabisco m. <> vt rabiscar.

scrawny ['skrɔːnɪ] (compar -ier, superl -iest) adj esquelético(ca).

scream [skriːm] <> n -1. [of person] grito m; ~**s of laughter** gargalhadas fpl. <> vt gritar. <> vi [person] gritar, vociferar.

scree [skriː] n (U) acúmulo de pedras soltas na encosta de uma montanha.

screech [skriːtʃ] <> n -1. [gen] guincho m -2. [of person] grito m; **a ~ of laughter** gargalhadas fpl. <> vt berrar, gritar. <> vi -1. [gen] guinchar -2. [person] gritar, berrar.

screen [skriːn] <> n -1. [viewing surface] tela f -2. CINEMA: **the (big) ~** a tela de cinema -3. [protective or dividing panel] biombo m. <> vt -1. [gen] exibir -2. [hide, shield] proteger; **to ~ sb/sthg (from sb/sthg)** proteger alguém/algo (de alguém/algo).

screening ['skriːnɪŋ] n -1. [in cinema] exibição f, projeção f -2. [on TV] exibição f -3. (U) [for security] triagem f -4. (U) MED [examination] exame m médico.

screenplay ['skriːnpleɪ] n roteiro m.

screen print n serigrafia f.

screw [skruː] <> n parafuso m. <> vt -1. [fix with screws]: **to ~ sthg to sthg** aparafusar algo em algo -2. [twist] enroscar -3. vulg [have sex with] trepar com, foder. <> vi [fix together] enroscar.

➭ **screw up** vt sep -1. [crumple up] amassar -2. [contort, twist] contrair -3. inf [ruin] ferrar.

screwdriver ['skruː,draɪvəʳ] n chave f de fenda.

scribble ['skrɪbl] <> n rabisco m, garrancho m. <> vt & vi rabiscar.

script [skrɪpt] n -1. [of play, film] script m, roteiro m -2. [system of writing] escrita f -3. [handwriting] letra f.

Scriptures ['skrɪptʃəz] npl: the ~ as Escrituras.

scriptwriter ['skrɪptˌraɪtə'] n roteirista mf.

scroll [skrəʊl] ◇ n rolo m de papel OR pergaminho. ◇ vt COMPUT rolar.

scrounge [skraʊndʒ] inf vt: to ~ sthg (off sb) filar algo (de alguém).

scrounger ['skraʊndʒə'] n inf parasita mf.

scrub [skrʌb] (pt & pp -bed, cont -bing) ◇ n -1. [rub] esfregação f; give it a good ~ dá uma boa esfregada (nisso) -2. [of undergrowth] moita f. ◇ vt esfregar.

scruff [skrʌf] n ANAT: by the ~ of the neck pelo cangote.

scruffy ['skrʌfɪ] (compar -ier, superl -iest) adj -1. [gen] sujo(ja) -2. [room, part of town] bagunçado(da).

scrum(mage) ['skrʌm(ɪdʒ)] n RUGBY disputa f de bola.

scrunchy ['skrʌntʃɪ] (pl -ies) n rabicó m.

scruples ['skru:plz] npl escrúpulos mpl.

scrutinize, -ise ['skru:tɪnaɪz] vt escrutinar.

scrutiny ['skru:tɪnɪ] n (U) escrutínio m.

scuff [skʌf] vt -1. [drag] arrastar -2. [damage - shoes] gastar; [- surface] riscar.

scuffle ['skʌfl] n briga f.

scullery ['skʌlərɪ] (pl -ies) n copa f (para lavar e guardar louça).

sculptor ['skʌlptə'] n escultor m, -ra f.

sculpture ['skʌlptʃə'] ◇ n escultura f. ◇ vt esculpir.

scum [skʌm] n -1. [froth] espuma f -2. v inf pej [worthless people] escória f.

scupper ['skʌpə'] vt -1. NAUT [sink] afundar -2. UK fig [ruin] arruinar.

scurrilous ['skʌrələs] adj fml difamatório(ria).

scurry ['skʌrɪ] (pt & pp -ied) vi: to ~ off escapulir-se.

scuttle ['skʌtl] ◇ n balde m para carvão. ◇ vi correr.

scythe [saɪð] n foice f.

SDLP (abbr of Social Democratic and Labour Party) n partido político da Irlanda do Norte que defende a integração pacífica com a República da Irlanda.

sea [si:] ◇ n mar m; to be at ~ [ship, sailor] estar no mar; to be all at ~ fig [person] estar totalmente perdido(da); by ~ pelo mar; by the ~ junto ao mar; out to ~ [away from land] para alto-mar. ◇ comp -1. [travel, voyage] marítimo(ma) -2. [animal] marinho(nha).

seabed ['si:bed] n: the ~ o fundo do mar.

seaboard ['si:bɔ:d] n fml litoral m.

sea breeze n brisa f do mar.

seafood ['si:fu:d] n (U) frutos mpl do mar.

seafront ['si:frʌnt] n orla f marítima.

seagull ['si:gʌl] n gaivota f.

seal [si:l] (pl sense 1 only inv OR -s) ◇ n -1. [gen] selo m -2. [animal] foca f. ◇ vt -1. [stick down] selar -2. [block up] vedar.
➤ **seal off** vt sep interditar.

sea level n (U) nível m do mar.

sea lion (pl inv OR -s) n leão-marinho m.

seam [si:m] n -1. SEWING costura f -2. [of coal] veio m.

seaman ['si:mən] (pl -men [-mən]) n marinheiro m.

seamy ['si:mɪ] (compar -ier, superl -iest) adj sórdido(da).

séance ['seɪɒns] n sessão f espírita.

seaplane ['si:pleɪn] n hidroavião m.

seaport ['si:pɔ:t] n porto m de mar.

search [sɜ:tʃ] ◇ n -1. [for lost person, object] procura f, busca f; ~ for sthg busca OR procura por algo; in ~ of a procura de, em busca de -2. [of person, luggage, house] procura f. ◇ vt -1. [gen] procurar -2. [mind, memory] vasculhar -3. [frisk] revistar. ◇ vi -1. [look for] procurar; to ~ for sb/sthg procurar (por) alguém/algo -2. [try to recall]: to ~ for sthg tentar lembrar algo.

search engine n COMPUT mecanismo m de busca.

searching ['sɜ:tʃɪŋ] adj -1. [question] perspicaz -2. [examination, review] minucioso(sa) -3. [look] penetrante.

searchlight ['sɜ:tʃlaɪt] n holofote m.

search party n equipe f de busca.

search warrant n mandado m de busca.

seashell ['si:ʃel] n concha f (marinha).

seashore ['si:ʃɔ:'] n: the ~ o litoral.

seasick ['si:sɪk] adj mareado(da).

seaside ['si:saɪd] n: the ~ a praia.

seaside resort n local m de veraneio (na praia).

season ['si:zn] ◇ n -1. [time of year] estação f -2. [for particular activity] período m, época f -3. [of holiday] temporada f; out of ~ fora de temporada -4. [of food]: in ~ da estação; out of ~ fora da estação -5. [series - of films] festival m; [- of lectures] série f. ◇ vt temperar.

seasonal ['si:zənl] adj sazonal.

seasoned ['si:znd] adj experiente.

seasoning ['si:znɪŋ] n tempero m.

season ticket n bilhete m para a temporada.

seat [si:t] <> n -**1.** [gen] assento m -**2.** [place to sit] banco m -**3.** [of clothing] fundilho m -**4.** POL [in parliament] cadeira f. <> vt [sit down] sentar.

seat belt n cinto m de segurança.

seating ['si:tɪŋ] n (U) acomodação f.

seawater ['si:ˌwɔ:tə^r] n (U) água f do mar.

seaweed ['si:wi:d] n (U) alga f marinha.

seaworthy ['si:ˌwɜ:ðɪ] adj em condições de navegar.

sec. (abbr of second) n seg.

secede [sɪ'si:d] vi fml separar-se; **to ~ from sthg** separar-se de algo.

secluded [sɪ'klu:dɪd] adj isolado(da), afastado(da).

seclusion [sɪ'klu:ʒn] n (U) isolamento m.

second ['sekənd] n -**1.** [gen] segundo m -**2.** UK UNIV diploma m com louvor -**3.** AUT: **~ (gear)** segunda f. <> num segundo(da); **~ only to Boris** ... perdendo apenas para Boris; **he is ~ to none** ele não perde para ninguém; see also **sixth**.
◆ **seconds** npl -**1.** COMM artigos mpl de segunda linha -**2.** [of food] repetição f.

secondary ['sekəndrɪ] adj secundário(-ria); **to be ~ to sthg** ser secundário para algo.

secondary school n escola f secundária.

second-class ['sekənd-] adj -**1.** [gen] de segunda classe -**2.** pej [less important] de segunda classe -**3.** UK UNIV tipo de grau universitário com louvor concedido por universidades britânicas.

second-hand ['sekənd-] adj -**1.** [gen] de segunda mão -**2.** [shop] de objetos usados. <> adv [not new] de segunda mão.

second hand ['sekənd-] n ponteiro m dos segundos.

secondly ['sekəndlɪ] adv em segundo lugar.

secondment [sɪ'kɒndmənt] n UK transferência f temporária.

second-rate ['sekənd-] adj pej de segunda categoria.

second thought ['sekənd-] n: **to have ~s about sthg** estar em dúvida sobre algo; **on ~s** UK, **on ~** US pensando bem.

secrecy ['si:krəsɪ] n (U) sigilo m.

secret ['si:krɪt] adj secreto(ta); **to keep sthg ~** manter algo em segredo. <> n segredo m; **in ~** em segredo.

secretarial [ˌsekrə'teərɪəl] adj -**1.** [course] de secretário -**2.** [staff] de secretários -**3.** [training] para secretariado.

secretary [UK 'sekrətrɪ, US 'sekrəˌterɪ] (pl -ies) n -**1.** [gen] secretário m, -ria f -**2.** POL [minister] ministro m, -tra f.

Secretary of State n -**1.** UK [minister]: **~ (for sthg)** ministro m (de algo) -**2.** US [in charge of foreign affairs] secretário m, -ria f das relações exteriores.

secretive ['si:krətɪv] adj -**1.** [person] reservado(da) -**2.** [organization] secreto(-ta).

secretly ['si:krɪtlɪ] adv secretamente, em segredo.

sect [sekt] n seita f.

sectarian [sek'teərɪən] adj sectário(-ria).

section ['sekʃn] <> n seção f. <> vt -**1.** GEOM seccionar -**2.** fml [cut] seccionar.

sector ['sektə^r] n setor m.

secular ['sekjʊlə^r] adj secular.

secure [sɪ'kjʊə^r] <> adj -**1.** [tightly locked up] seguro(ra), protegido(da) -**2.** [fixed in place] seguro(ra), firme -**3.** [safe, not likely to change] garantido(da) -**4.** [strong, solid] firme -**5.** [free of anxiety, confident] confiante. <> vt -**1.** [obtain] conseguir, obter -**2.** [make safe] proteger -**3.** [fasten] fechar bem.

security [sɪ'kjʊərətɪ] (pl -ies) n -**1.** [gen] segurança f -**2.** (U) [legal protection] segurança f, garantia f; **~ of tenure** cargo m vitalício.
◆ **securities** npl FIN papéis mpl negociáveis.

security guard n (guarda mf de) segurança mf.

sedan [sɪ'dæn] n US sedã m.

sedate [sɪ'deɪt] <> adj calmo(ma), sossegado(da). <> vt sedar.

sedation [sɪ'deɪʃn] n (U) sedação f.

sedative ['sedətɪv] n sedativo m.

sediment ['sedɪmənt] n sedimento m.

seduce [sɪ'dju:s] vt seduzir; **to ~ sb into doing sthg** persuadir alguém a fazer algo.

seductive [sɪ'dʌktɪv] adj sedutor(ra).

see [si:] (pt saw, pp seen) <> vt -**1.** [gen] ver; **we're going to ~ each other tonight** vamos nos ver hoje à noite; **~ you!** até mais!; **~ you soon/later/tomorrow!** até breve/mais tarde/amanhã! -**2.** [friend, doctor] visitar -**3.** [realize]: **to ~ (that)** perceber que -**4.** [understand] entender -**5.** [accompany] levar, acompanhar -**6.** [find out, ascertain] descobrir -**7.** [make sure]: **I'll ~ (that the work gets done)** vou providenciar (para que o trabalho fique pronto) -**8.** [judge, consider] ver, considerar. <> vi -**1.** [perceive with eyes] enxergar -**2.** [understand] entender; **I ~** entendo; **you ~,** ... veja bem, ... -**3.** [find out] ver; **let's ~**, **let me ~** vamos ver, vejamos.

➤ **seeing as, seeing that** *conj inf* já que, como.

➤ **see about** *vt fus* **-1.** [organize]: **I'll ~ about getting you some work** vou dar um jeito de te arrumar algum trabalho - **2.** [think about] ver.

➤ **see off** *vt sep* **-1.** [say goodbye to] despedir-se de - **2.** *UK* [chase away] afugentar.

➤ **see through** ◇ *vt fus* [not be deceived by] não se deixar enganar por. ◇ *vt sep* [to conclusion] levar a termo.

➤ **see to** *vt fus* cuidar de.

seed [siːd] *n* **-1.** [of plant] semente *f* - **2.** *SPORT* pré-selecionado *m*, -da *f*.

➤ **seeds** *npl fig* [beginnings] semente *f*.

seedling ['siːdlɪŋ] *n* muda *f*.

seedy ['siːdɪ] (*compar* **-ier**, *superl* **-iest**) *adj* **-1.** [person] maltrapilho(lha) - **2.** [room, area] usado(da).

seek [siːk] (*pt & pp* **sought**) *fml vt* procurar; **to ~ to do sthg** procurar fazer algo.

seem [siːm] ◇ *vi* parecer; **it ~s too good to be true** parece bom demais para ser verdade; **I ~ to remember that ... parece que eu me lembro de que ...; I can't ~ to do that** por mais que eu tente, não consigo fazer isso. ◇ *v impers*: **it ~s (that)** parece que.

seemingly ['siːmɪŋlɪ] *adv* aparentemente.

seen [siːn] *pp* ⊳ **see.**

seep [siːp] *vi* infiltrar-se, penetrar.

seesaw ['siːsɔː] *n* gangorra *f*.

seethe [siːð] *vi* fervilhar; **to be seething with sthg** estar fervilhando com algo.

see-through *adj* transparente.

segment ['segmənt] *n* **-1.** [of market, report, audience] segmento *m* - **2.** [of fruit] gomo *m*.

segregate ['segrɪgeɪt] *vt* segregar.

Seine [seɪn] *n*: **the (River) ~** o (rio) Sena.

seize [siːz] *vt* **-1.** [grab] agarrar, pegar - **2.** [win, capture] tomar - **3.** [arrest] prender, deter - **4.** [take advantage of] aproveitar.

➤ **seize (up)on** *vt fus* valer-se de.

➤ **seize up** *vi* **-1.** [body] enrijecer - **2.** [engine] emperrar.

seizure ['siːʒəʳ] *n* **-1.** *MED* ataque *m* - **2.** (*U*) [taking, capturing] tomada *f*.

seldom ['seldəm] *adv* raramente.

select [sɪ'lekt] ◇ *adj* **-1.** [carefully chosen] selecionado(da) - **2.** [exclusive] seleto(ta). ◇ *vt* selecionar.

selection [sɪ'lekʃn] *n* **-1.** [gen] seleção *f* - **2.** [range of goods] coleção *f*.

selective [sɪ'lektɪv] *adj* seletivo(va).

self [self] (*pl* **selves**) *n*: **she's her old ~** ela volta a ser ela mesma; **the ~** o eu.

self-assured *adj* confiante em si mesmo(ma), seguro(ra) de si.

self-catering *adj* sem refeições incluídas.

self-centred [-'sentəd] *adj* egocêntrico(ca).

self-confessed [-kən'fest] *adj* assumido(da).

self-confidence *n* autoconfiança *f*.

self-confident *adj* **-1.** [person] seguro(ra) de si - **2.** [remark, attitude] que passa segurança.

self-conscious *adj* inibido(da).

self-contained [-kən'teɪnd] *adj* **-1.** [person] reservado(da) - **2.** [flat] independente.

self-control *n* (*U*) autocontrole *m*.

self-defence *n* (*U*) legítima defesa *f*.

self-discipline *n* (*U*) autodisciplina *f*.

self-employed [-ɪm'plɔɪd] *adj* autônomo(ma), que trabalha por conta própria.

self-esteem *n* (*U*) amor-próprio *m*.

self-evident *adj* óbvio(via).

self-explanatory *adj* claro(ra), manifesto(ta).

self-government *n* (*U*) governo *m* autônomo.

self-important *adj pej* presunçoso(sa), convencido(da).

self-indulgent *adj pej* comodista, que se permite excessos.

self-interest *n* (*U*) *pej* interesse *m* pessoal OR próprio.

selfish ['selfɪʃ] *adj* egoísta.

selfishness ['selfɪʃnɪs] *n* (*U*) egoísmo *m*.

selfless ['selflɪs] *adj* desinteressado(da).

self-made *adj* que se fez por si mesmo(ma).

self-opinionated *adj pej* presunçoso(sa).

self-pity *n* (*U*) *pej* autocomiseração *f*.

self-portrait *n* auto-retrato *m*.

self-possessed [-pə'zest] *adj* dono de si mesmo, dona de si mesma.

self-preservation *n* autopreservação *f*.

self-raising flour *UK* [-,reɪzɪŋ-], **self-rising flour** *US* *n* (*U*) farinha *f* com fermento.

self-reliant *adj* independente.

self-respect *n* (*U*) amor-próprio *m*.

self-respecting [-rɪs'pektɪŋ] *adj* que se presta, digno(na).

self-restraint *n* (*U*) autocontrole *m*.

self-righteous *adj pej* hipócrita.

self-rising flour n US = **self-raising flour**.

self-sacrifice n (U) abnegação f.

self-satisfied adj pej convencido(da).

self-service n (U) auto-serviço m, self-service m.

self-sufficient adj: ~ **(in sthg)** auto-suficiente (em algo).

self-taught adj autodidata.

sell [sel] (pt & pp **sold**) ⬦ vt **-1.** vender; **to ~ sthg to sb, to ~ sb sthg** vender algo para alguém; **to ~ sthg for** vender algo por; **to ~ o.s.** vender-se; **to ~ o.s. short** desmerecer-se **-2.** fig [make enthusiastic about]: **to ~ sthg to sb, to ~ sb sthg** vender algo para alguém; **to ~ sb an idea** vender uma idéia a alguém; **I'm not really sold on the idea** não consigo comprar essa idéia. ⬦ vi vender; **to ~ for** OR **at** ser vendido(da) por OR a.

⬥ **sell off** vt sep liquidar.

⬥ **sell out** ⬦ vt sep: **to be sold out** estar esgotado(da). ⬦ vi **-1.** [shop, ticket office]: **to ~ out (of sthg)** vender todo o estoque (de algo) **-2.** [betray one's principles] vender-se.

sell-by date n UK prazo m de validade.

seller [ˈselǝʳ] n vendedor m, -ra f.

selling price [ˈselɪŋ-] n preço m de venda.

Sellotape® [ˈselǝteɪp] n UK fita f adesiva, durex® m.

sell-out n **-1.** [performance, match] sucesso m de bilheteria **-2.** [of principles] traição f.

selves [selvz] pl ⬥ **self**.

semaphore [ˈsemǝfɔːʳ] n (U) semáforo m.

semblance [ˈsemblǝns] n fml aparência f.

semen [ˈsiːmǝn] n (U) sêmen m.

semester [sɪˈmestǝʳ] n semestre m.

semicircle [ˈsemɪˌsɜːkl] n semicírculo m.

semicolon [ˌsemɪˈkǝʊlǝn] n ponto-e-vírgula m.

semi-detached ⬦ adj UK geminado(do). ⬦ n UK casa f geminada.

semi-final n semifinal f.

seminar [ˈsemɪnɑːʳ] n seminário m.

seminary [ˈsemɪnǝrɪ] (pl -ies) n RELIG seminário m.

semi-skilled adj semi-especializado(-da).

semolina [ˌsemǝˈliːnǝ] n (U) semolina f.

Senate [ˈsenɪt] n POL: **the ~** o Senado; **the United States ~** o Senado dos Estados Unidos.

senator [ˈsenǝtǝʳ] n senador m, -ra f.

send [send] (pt & pp **sent**) vt **-1.** [letter, message, money] enviar, mandar; **to ~ sb sthg, to ~ sthg to sb** enviar OR

mandar algo para alguém **-2.** [tell to go]: **to ~ sb (to)** mandar alguém (para); **to ~ sb for sthg** mandar alguém buscar algo **-3.** [into a specific state] deixar; **to ~ sb mad** deixar alguém louco(ca); **to ~ sb to sleep** dar sono em alguém; **to ~ sb flying** arremessar alguém longe.

⬥ **send back** vt sep devolver; **to ~ sb back** fazer alguém voltar.

⬥ **send for** vt fus **-1.** [person] mandar chamar **-2.** [by post] encomendar.

⬥ **send in** vt sep **-1.** [visitor] fazer entrar **-2.** [troops, police] enviar, mandar **-3.** [submit] enviar.

⬥ **send off** vt sep **-1.** [by post] enviar (pelo correio) **-2.** SPORT expulsar.

⬥ **send off for** vt fus encomendar (pelo correio).

⬥ **send up** vt sep inf UK [imitate] arremedar, imitar.

sender [ˈsendǝʳ] n remetente mf.

send-off n despedida f.

senile [ˈsiːnaɪl] adj senil.

senior [ˈsiːnjǝʳ] ⬦ adj **-1.** [highest-ranking] superior(ra) **-2.** [higher-ranking]: **~ to sb** superior a alguém **-3.** SCH [pupils, classes] veterano(na). ⬦ n **-1.** [older person] mais velho(lha); **I'm five years his ~** sou cinco anos mais velho do que ele **-2.** SCH & UNIV veterano m, -na f.

senior citizen n idoso m, -sa f.

sensation [senˈseɪʃn] n sensação f.

sensational [senˈseɪʃǝnl] adj **-1.** [causing a stir] sensacional **-2.** inf [wonderful] sensacional.

sensationalist [senˈseɪʃnǝlɪst] adj pej sensacionalista.

sense [sens] ⬦ n **-1.** [gen] sentido m; **to make ~** [have clear meaning] fazer sentido; [be logical] ser lógico(ca) **-2.** [feeling, sensation - of guilt, terror, honour] sentimento m; [- of justice, duty, urgency] senso m **-3.** [natural ability]: **~ of direction** senso m de direção; **~ of style** idéia f de estilo **-4.** (U) [wisdom, reason] bom senso m, sabedoria f **-5.** phr: **to come to one's ~s** [be sensible again] recobrar o juízo; [regain consciousness] recobrar os sentidos; **to be out of one's ~s** perder o juízo. ⬦ vt sentir; **to ~ that** sentir que.

⬥ **in a sense** adv de certo modo, em certo sentido.

senseless [ˈsenslɪs] adj **-1.** [stupid] sem sentido, estúpido(da) **-2.** [unconscious] inconsciente; **to knock sb ~** bater em alguém até ficar inconsciente.

sensibilities [ˌsensɪˈbɪlǝtɪz] npl sensibilidade f.

sensible ['sensəbl] *adj* -1. [reasonable, practical] prático(ca) -2. [person] sensato(ta).

sensitive ['sensɪtɪv] *adj* -1. [eyes, skin]: ~ **(to sthg)** sensível (a algo) -2. [understanding, aware]: ~ **(to sthg)** compreensivo(va) (com algo) -3. [easily hurt, touchy]: ~ **(to/about sthg)** sensível OR suscetível (a algo) -4. [controversial] delicado(da) -5. [instrument] sensível.

sensual ['sensjʊəl] *adj* sensual.

sensuous ['sensjʊəs] *adj* sensual.

sent [sent] *pt* & *pp* ▷ **send**.

sentence ['sentəns] ◇ *n* -1. [group of words] frase *f*, oração *f* -2. JUR sentença *f*. ◇ *vt*: **to** ~ **sb (to sthg)** condenar alguém (a algo).

sentiment ['sentɪmənt] *n* -1. [feeling] sentimento *m* -2. [opinion] opinião *f*.

sentimental [ˌsentɪˈmentl] *adj* -1. *pej* [over-emotional] sentimental -2. [emotional] sentimental.

sentry ['sentrɪ] (*pl* -ies) *n* sentinela *mf*.

separate [*adj* & *n* 'seprət, *vb* 'sepəreɪt] ◇ *adj* -1. [not joined, apart] separado(da); ~ **from sthg** separado(da) de algo -2. [individual] separado(da), diferente -3. [distinct] distinto(ta). ◇ *vt* separar; **to** ~ **sb/sthg from** separar alguém/algo de; **to** ~ **sb/sthg into** separar alguém/algo em; **to** ~ **sb/sthg from** separar alguém/algo de. ◇ *vi* -1. [gen] separar-se -2. [go different ways]: **to** ~ **(from sb/sthg)** separar-se (de alguém/algo).
➡ **separates** *npl* UK peças *fpl* avulsas (*de roupa*).

separately ['seprətlɪ] *adv* separadamente.

separation [ˌsepəˈreɪʃn] *n* separação *f*; ~ **(from sb/sthg)** separação (de alguém/algo).

September [sepˈtembəʳ] *n* setembro; **in** ~ em setembro; **last/this/next** ~ em setembro do ano passado/deste ano/do ano que vem; **by** ~ até setembro; **every** ~ todos os anos em setembro; **during** ~ em setembro, durante o mês de setembro; **at the beginning/end of** ~ no início/fim de setembro; **in the middle of** ~ em meados de setembro, no meio do mês de setembro.

septic ['septɪk] *adj* séptico(ca); **to go** ~ infeccionar.

septic tank *n* fossa *f* séptica.

sequel ['si:kwəl] *n* -1. [book, film]: ~ **to sthg** continuação *f* de algo -2. [consequence]: ~ **to sthg** seqüela *f* de algo.

sequence ['si:kwəns] *n* -1. [gen] seqüência *f* -2. [series] seqüência *f*, sucessão *f*.

Serb *adj* & *n* = **Serbian**.

Serbia ['sɜːbjə] *n* Sérvia.

Serbian ['sɜːbjən], **Serb** [sɜːb] ◇ *adj* sérvio(via). ◇ *n* -1. [person] sérvio *m*, -via *f* -2. [language] sérvio *m*.

serene [sɪˈriːn] *adj* sereno(na).

sergeant ['sɑːdʒənt] *n* -1. MIL sargento *m* -2. POLICE tenente *m*.

sergeant major *n* primeiro-sargento *m*.

serial ['sɪərɪəl] *n* série *f*, seriado *m*.

serial number *n* número *m* de série.

series ['sɪəriːz] (*pl inv*) *n* -1. [sequence] série *f* -2. RADIO & TV série *f*, seriado *m*.

serious ['sɪərɪəs] *adj* -1. [gen] sério(ria); **are you** ~? fala sério? -2. [problem, illness] grave.

seriously ['sɪərɪəslɪ] *adv* -1. [earnestly] seriamente; **to take sb/sthg** ~ levar alguém/algo a sério -2. [very badly] gravemente.

seriousness ['sɪərɪəsnɪs] *n* (*U*) -1. [of person, expression, voice] seriedade *f* -2. [of illness, situation, loss] gravidade *f*.

sermon ['sɜːmən] *n* -1. RELIG sermão *m* -2. *fig* & *pej* [lecture] sermão *m*.

serrated [sɪˈreɪtɪd] *adj* serrilhado(da), dentado(da).

servant ['sɜːvənt] *n* criado *m*, -da *f*, empregado *m*, -da *f*.

serve [sɜːv] ◇ *n* SPORT serviço *m*, saque *m*. ◇ *vt* -1. [gen] servir; **to** ~ **sthg to sb, to** ~ **sb sthg** servir algo a alguém -2. [have effect]: **to** ~ **to do sthg** servir para fazer algo; **to** ~ **a purpose** cumprir o propósito -3. [provide] abastecer; **which motorway** ~**s Birmingham** que rodovia atende à região de Birmingham? -4. JUR: **to** ~ **sb with sthg, to** ~ **sthg on sb** entregar algo a alguém -5. [complete, carry out] cumprir; **he's serving time** ele está cumprindo pena -6. SPORT servir, sacar -7. *phr*: **it** ~**s you right** bem feito! ◇ *vi* -1. [be employed - as soldier] servir o exército -2. [function]: **to** ~ **as sthg** servir como algo -3. [in shop, bar etc.] servir -4. SPORT sacar.
➡ **serve out, serve up** *vt sep* servir.

service ['sɜːvɪs] ◇ *n* -1. [gen] serviço *m*; **in** ~ em funcionamento; **out of** ~ fora de serviço -2. (*U*) [in shop, bar etc.] atendimento *m* -3. [mechanical check] revisão *f* -4. RELIG serviço *m*, culto *m* -5. [set of tableware] jogo *m*; **dinner** ~ aparelho *m* de jantar -6. SPORT serviço *m*, saque *m* -7. [use, help]: **to be of** ~ **(to sb)** servir (a alguém). ◇ *vt* [car, machine] fazer a revisão de.
➡ **services** *npl* -1. [on motorway] estação *f* de serviços -2. [armed forces]: **the** ~**s**

as forças armadas **-3.** [help] serviços *mpl.*

serviceable [ˈsɜːvɪsəbl] *adj* resistente, prático(ca).

service area *n* estação *f* de serviços.

service charge *n* taxa *f* de serviço.

serviceman [ˈsɜːvɪsmən] (*pl* **-men** [-mən]) *n* MIL militar *m*.

service provider *n* COMPUT provedor *m*.

service station *n* posto *m* de gasolina, posto *m* de serviços.

serviette [ˌsɜːvɪˈet] *n* guardanapo *m*.

sesame [ˈsesəmɪ] *n* (*U*) gergelim *m*, sésamo *m*; **open ~!** abre-te, sésamo!

session [ˈseʃn] *n* **-1.** [gen] sessão *f* **-2.** US [school term] período *m* letivo.

set [set] (*pt* & *pp* set, *cont* **-ting**) ◇ *adj* **-1.** [specified, prescribed] estabelecido(-da) **-2.** [fixed, rigid] fixo(xa); **~ phrase** frase *f* feita **-3.** [ready] pronto(ta); **~ for sthg/to do sthg** pronto(ta) para algo/para fazer algo **-4.** [determined]: **to be ~ on sthg/on doing sthg** estar empenhado(da) em algo/em fazer algo; **to be dead ~ against sthg** ser completamente contra algo. ◇ *n* **-1.** [collection, group - stamps] série *f*; [- chess, tea] jogo *m* (de); [- keys, tyres, saucepans] conjunto *m*; [- books] coleção *f* (de) **-2.** [apparatus] aparelhagem *f* **-3.** [of film, play] cenário *m* **-4.** TENNIS set *m.* ◇ *vt* **-1.** [put in specified position, place] pôr, colocar **-2.** [fix, insert]: **to ~ sthg in(to) sthg** fixar algo em algo **-3.** [indicating change of state or activity] pôr; **to ~ sb free** pôr alguém em liberdade; **to ~ sb's mind at rest** tranqüilizar alguém; **to ~ sthg in motion** pôr algo em movimento; **to ~ sthg right** emendar algo; **to ~ sb thinking** fazer alguém pensar; **to ~ sthg on fire** pôr fogo em algo **-4.** [lay, prepare in advance] pôr, colocar **-5.** [adjust] ajustar, botar; **she ~ the meter at zero** ela ajustou o medidor para zero **-6.** [decide on] estabelecer, fixar **-7.** [establish, create - example] dar; [- precedent] abrir; [- trend] impor; [- record] estabelecer **-8.** [assign - target, problem] determinar; [- school work] passar; [- exam, test work] aplicar **-9.** MED [mend] recompor **-10.** [story] passar-se; **the film is ~ in Scotland** o filme se passa na Escócia **-11.** [hair] fazer mise-en-plis. ◇ *vi* **-1.** [sun] pôr-se **-2.** [solidify - jelly] endurecer; [- glue, cement] secar.

◆ **set about** *vt fus*: **to ~ about sthg** começar algo; **to ~ about doing sthg** pôr-se a fazer algo.

◆ **set aside** *vt sep* **-1.** [keep, save] guardar **-2.** [not consider] deixar de lado.

◆ **set back** *vt sep* [delay] atrasar.

◆ **set off** ◇ *vt sep* **-1.** [initiate, cause] provocar **-2.** [ignite] fazer explodir. ◇ *vi* pôr-se a caminho.

◆ **set out** ◇ *vt sep* **-1.** [arrange, spread out] dispor **-2.** [clarify, explain] expor. ◇ *vt fus*: **to ~ out to do sthg** propor-se a fazer algo. ◇ *vi* pôr-se a caminho.

◆ **set up** *vt sep* **-1.** [gen] montar **-2.** [establish, arrange - company] montar, fundar; [- committee, organization] criar; [- interview, meeting] organizar **-3.** *inf* [make appear guilty] convencer; **to ~ sb up** armar contra alguém; **I was ~ up!** me armaram uma!

setback [ˈsetbæk] *n* contratempo *m*.

set menu *n* cardápio *m* a preço fixo.

settee [seˈtiː] *n* sofá *m.*

setting [ˈsetɪŋ] *n* **-1.** [surroundings] cenário *m* **-2.** [of dial, control] posição *f.*

settle [ˈsetl] ◇ *vt* **-1.** [conclude, decide] resolver **-2.** [pay] saldar **-3.** [make comfortable] acomodar **-4.** [calm] acalmar, tranqüilizar. ◇ *vi* **-1.** [go to live] instalar-se **-2.** [make o.s. comfortable] acomodar-se **-3.** [come to rest] depositar-se; **to ~ on sthg** pousar em algo.

◆ **settle down** *vi* **-1.** [give one's attention]: **to ~ down (to sthg/to doing sthg)** dedicar-se (a algo/a fazer algo) **-2.** [become stable] estabelecer-se **-3.** [make o.s. comfortable] acomodar-se; **to ~ down (for sthg)** preparar-se (para algo) **-4.** [become calm] acalmar-se.

◆ **settle for** *vt fus* conformar-se com.

◆ **settle in** *vi* **-1.** [new house] instalar-se **-2.** [in new job] adaptar-se.

◆ **settle on** *vt fus* decidir-se por.

◆ **settle up** *vi*: **to ~ up (with sb)** ajustar as contas (com alguém).

settlement [ˈsetlmənt] *n* **-1.** [agreement] acordo *m* **-2.** [village] povoado *m* **-3.** [payment] pagamento *m.*

settler [ˈsetlər] *n* colonizador *m*, -ra *f.*

set-up *n inf* **-1.** [system, organization] estrutura *f* **-2.** [deception to incriminate] armação *f.*

seven [ˈsevn] *num* sete; *see also* **six.**

seventeen [ˌsevnˈtiːn] *num* dezessete; *see also* **six.**

seventeenth [ˌsevnˈtiːnθ] *num* décimo sétimo, décima sétima; *see also* **sixth.**

seventh [ˈsevnθ] *num* sétimo(ma); *see also* **sixth.**

seventy [ˈsevntɪ] *num* setenta; *see also* **sixty.**

sever [ˈsevər] *vt* **-1.** [rope, limb] cortar **-2.** [relationship] romper.

several [ˈsevrəl] ◇ *adj* vários(rias). ◇ *pron* vários *mpl*, -rias *fpl.*

severance [ˈsevrəns] n (U) fml rompimento m.

severance pay n (U) indenização m por demissão.

severe [sɪˈvɪəʳ] adj **-1.** [extreme, bad - shock] forte; [- weather] ruim; [- pain] agudo(da); [- injury, illness] grave **-2.** [stern] severo(ra).

severity [sɪˈverətɪ] n (U) **-1.** [seriousness] gravidade f **-2.** [strength] força f **-3.** [sternness] severidade f.

sew [səʊ] (UK pp **sewn**, US pp **sewed** OR **sewn**) vt & vi costurar.
◆ **sew up** vt sep [join] costura.

sewage [ˈsuːɪdʒ] n (U) águas fpl residuais.

sewage works n estação f de tratamento de esgoto.

sewer [ˈsʊəʳ] n esgoto m; **the city's ~ system** o sistema de esgotos da cidade.

sewing [ˈsəʊɪŋ] n (U) **-1.** [activity] trabalho m de costura **-2.** [items] costura f.

sewing machine n máquina f de costura.

sewn [səʊn] pp ▷ **sew**.

sex [seks] n sexo m; **to have ~ (with sb)** fazer sexo (com alguém).

sexist [ˈseksɪst] ⟨⟩ adj sexista. ⟨⟩ n sexista mf.

sexual [ˈsekʃʊəl] adj sexual.

sexual discrimination n discriminação f sexual.

sexual harassment n (U) assédio m sexual.

sexual intercourse n (U) relações fpl sexuais.

sexually transmitted disease n doença f sexualmente transmissível.

sexy [ˈseksɪ] (compar-ier, superl-iest) adj inf sexy, sexualmente atraente.

shabby [ˈʃæbɪ] (compar-ier, superl-iest) adj **-1.** [in bad condition - clothes, briefcase] em mau estado; [- street] abandonado(da) **-2.** [wearing old clothes] esfarrapado(da) **-3.** [mean] mesquinho(nha).

shack [ʃæk] n cabana f.

shackle [ˈʃækl] vt **-1.** [chain] algemar **-2.** literary [restrict] impedir.
◆ **shackles** npl **-1.** [metal restraints] algemas pl **-2.** literary [restrictions] impedimentos mpl.

shade [ʃeɪd] ⟨⟩ n **-1.** (U) [shadow] sombra f **-2.** [lampshade] abajur m, quebra-luz m **-3.** [colour] tonalidade f **-4.** [nuance] tom m. ⟨⟩ vt **-1.** [from light] fazer sombra em, proteger do sol **-2.** [by drawing lines] sombrear.
◆ **shades** npl inf óculos mpl escuros.

shadow [ˈʃædəʊ] n **-1.** [dark area] sombra f **-2.** [under eyes] olheiras fpl **-3.** phr:

there's not a OR the ~ of a doubt não há sombra de dúvida.

shadow cabinet n gabinete-sombra m, gabinete do principal partido de oposição na Grã-Bretanha.

shadowy [ˈʃædəʊɪ] adj **-1.** [dark] escuro(ra) **-2.** [unknown, sinister] obscuro(ra).

shady [ˈʃeɪdɪ] (compar-ier, superl-iest) adj **-1.** [sheltered from sun] sombreado(da) **-2.** [providing shade] que dá sombra **-3.** inf [dishonest, sinister] suspeito(ta).

shaft [ʃɑːft] n **-1.** [vertical passage] poço m **-2.** [rod] haste f **-3.** [of light] feixe m.

shaggy [ˈʃægɪ] (compar-ier, superl-iest) adj **-1.** [hair, beard] desgrenhado(da) **-2.** [dog] peludo(da) **-3.** [carpet, rug] felpudo(da).

shake [ʃeɪk] (pt **shook**, pp **shaken** [ˈʃeɪkən]) ⟨⟩ vt **-1.** [gen] abalar **-2.** [move vigorously] sacudir; **to ~ sb's hand** apertar a mão de alguém; **to ~ hands** apertar as mãos; **to ~ one's head** [to say no] negar com a cabeça. ⟨⟩ vi tremer.
⟨⟩ n sacudida f.
◆ **shake off** vt sep livrar-se de.
◆ **shake up** vt sep abalar.

shaken [ˈʃeɪkn] pp ▷ **shake**.

shaky [ˈʃeɪkɪ] (compar-ier, superl-iest) adj **-1.** [unsteady - chair, table] frágil, instável; [- hand, writing, voice] trêmulo(la); [- person] abalado(da) **-2.** [weak, uncertain] débil.

shall [weak form ʃəl, strong form ʃæl] aux vb **-1.** [to express future tense]: **we ~ be in Scotland in June** estaremos na Escócia em junho; **I ~ ring next week** vou ligar semana que vem **-2.** [in questions]: **~ we have our tea now?** vamos tomar nosso chá agora?; **where ~ I put this?** onde eu coloco isto?; **~ I give her a ring, then?** ligo para ela, então?; **I'll do that, ~ I?** eu faço isso, pode ser? **-3.** [in orders]: **you ~ tell me what happened!** você deve me contar o que aconteceu!

shallow [ˈʃæləʊ] adj **-1.** [in size] raso(sa) **-2.** pej [superficial] superficial.

sham [ʃæm] ⟨⟩ adj falso(sa), fingido(da). ⟨⟩ n farsa f.

shambles [ˈʃæmblz] n **-1.** [disorder] confusão f **-2.** [fiasco] fiasco m.

shame [ʃeɪm] ⟨⟩ n **-1.** (U) [remorse] vergonha f **-2.** (U) [dishonour]: **to bring ~ (up)on sb** trazer desonra OR vergonha a alguém **-3.** [pity]: **it's a ~ (that)** é uma pena OR lástima que; **what a ~!** que pena! ⟨⟩ vt **-1.** [fill with shame] envergonhar **-2.** [force by making ashamed]: **I ~d him into telling the truth** eu o forcei a dizer a verdade ao fazê-lo sentir-se envergonhado por não dizer.

shamefaced [ˌʃeɪm'feɪst] *adj* envergonhado(da).

shameful ['ʃeɪmfʊl] *adj* vergonhoso(sa).

shameless ['ʃeɪmlɪs] *adj* desavergonhado(da).

shampoo [ʃæm'puː] (*pl* -s, *pt* & *pp* -ed, *cont* -ing) <> *n* -1. [liquid - for hair] xampu *m*; [- for carpet] detergente *m* -2. [act of shampooing] lavada *f* com xampu. <> *vt* lavar.

shamrock ['ʃæmrɒk] *n* (U) trevo *m*.

shandy ['ʃændɪ] (*pl* -ies) *n* shandy *m*, bebida preparada com limonada e cerveja.

shan't [ʃɑːnt] = shall not.

shanty town *n* ≃ favela *f*.

shape [ʃeɪp] <> *n* -1. [form] forma *f*; to take ~ tomar forma -2. [figure, silhouette] silhueta *f* -3. [form, health]: to be in good/bad ~ estar em boa/má forma. <> *vt* -1. [mould physically]: to ~ sthg (into) dar a algo forma (de); a birthmark ~d like a strawberry uma marca de nascença com a forma de morango -2. [influence] influenciar.

◆ **shape up** *vi* desenvolver-se.

SHAPE [ʃeɪp] (*abbr of* Supreme Headquarters Allied Powers Europe) *n* quartel-general das potências aliadas na Europa.

-shaped ['ʃeɪpt] *suffix* com forma de; star ~ em forma de estrela.

shapeless ['ʃeɪplɪs] *adj* sem forma.

shapely ['ʃeɪplɪ] (*compar* -ier, *superl* -iest) *adj* bem formado(da); ~ legs pernas *fpl* bem torneadas.

share [ʃeəʳ] <> *n*: everyone must do his ~ of the work todo mundo deve fazer a parte que lhe toca do trabalho; to have a ~ in the profits ter participação nos lucros. <> *vt* -1. [gen] compartilhar -2. [reveal] revelar. <> *vi* dividir, compartilhar; to ~ in sthg compartilhar algo.

◆ **shares** *npl* FIN ações *fpl*.

◆ **share out** *vt sep* dividir, compartilhar.

shareholder ['ʃeəˌhəʊldəʳ] *n* acionista *mf*.

shark [ʃɑːk] (*pl inv OR* -s) *n* [fish] tubarão *m*.

sharp [ʃɑːp] <> *adj* -1. [not blunt - teeth, pencil] apontado(da); [- needle] pontudo(da); [- knife, razor] afiado(da) -2. [well-defined] claro(ra), bem-definido(da) -3. [intelligent, keen - person, mind] inteligente, esperto(ta); [- eyesight] penetrante; [- hearing] atento(ta) -4. [abrupt, sudden] abrupto(ta), brusco(ca) -5. [angry, severe] seco(ca) -6. [sound, pain] agudo(da)

-7. [cold, wind] cortante -8. [bitter] acre -9. MUS sustenido(da); C ~ dó sustenido. <> *adv* -1. [punctually] pontualmente; at eight o'clock ~ pontualmente às oito horas -2. [quickly, suddenly] de repente. <> *n* MUS sustenido *m*.

sharpen ['ʃɑːpn] *vt* [make sharp - knife, tool] afiar; [- pencil] apontar.

sharpener ['ʃɑːpnəʳ] *n* -1. [for pencil] apontador *m* -2. [for knife] amolador *m*.

sharp-eyed [-'aɪd] *adj* perspicaz.

sharply ['ʃɑːplɪ] *adv* -1. [distinctly] claramente -2. [suddenly] de repente, repentinamente -3. [harshly] duramente.

shat [ʃæt] *pt* & *pp* ⊳ shit.

shatter ['ʃætəʳ] <> *vt* -1. [glass, window] estilhaçar -2. *fig* [beliefs, hopes, dreams] destruir, arrasar. <> *vi* estilhaçar-se.

shattered ['ʃætəd] *adj* -1. [shocked, upset] arrasado(da) -2. *UK inf* [very tired] podre.

shave [ʃeɪv] <> *n*: to have a ~ fazer a barba. <> *vt* -1. [with razor - face] barbear, fazer a barba de; [- body] depilar, raspar -2. [cut pieces off] cortar. <> *vi* barbear-se, fazer a barba.

shaver ['ʃeɪvəʳ] *n* barbeador *m*, aparelho *m* de barbear.

shaving brush ['ʃeɪvɪŋ-] *n* pincel *m* de barba.

shaving cream ['ʃeɪvɪŋ-] *n* (U) creme *m* de barbear.

shaving foam ['ʃeɪvɪŋ-] *n* (U) espuma *f* de barbear.

shavings ['ʃeɪvɪŋz] *npl* -1. [of wood] cavacos *mpl*, lascas *fpl* -2. [of metal] cisalha *f*.

shawl [ʃɔːl] *n* xale *m*.

she [ʃiː] *pers pron* ela; ~'s tall ela é alta.

sheaf [ʃiːf] (*pl* sheaves) *n* -1. [of papers, letters] maço *m* -2. [of corn, grain] feixe *m*.

shear [ʃɪəʳ] (*pt* -ed, *pp* -ed *OR* shorn) *vt* tosquiar.

◆ **shears** *npl* -1. [for garden] tesoura *f* de podar -2. [for dressmaking] tesoura *f*.

◆ **shear off** <> *vt sep* romper. <> *vi* romper-se.

sheath [ʃiːθ] (*pl* -s) *n* -1. [for sword, dagger] bainha *f* -2. *UK* [condom] camisinha *f*.

sheaves [ʃiːvz] *pl* ⊳ sheaf.

shed [ʃed] (*pt* & *pp* shed, *cont* -ding) <> *n* galpão *m*. <> *vt* -1. [lose naturally] perder -2. [discard, get rid of] desfazer-se de; the company decided to ~ 100 employees a empresa decidiu despedir 100 funcionários; after a drink she ~ s

any inhibition depois de um drinque, ela deixa de lado qualquer inibição - **3.** [tears, blood] derramar.

she'd [weak form ʃɪd, strong form ʃiːd] = she had, she would.

sheen [ʃiːn] n brilho m.

sheep [ʃiːp] (pl inv) n [animal] ovelha f.

sheepdog [ˈʃiːpdɒg] n cão m pastor.

sheepish [ˈʃiːpɪʃ] adj encabulado(da).

sheepskin [ˈʃiːpskɪn] n (U) pele f de carneiro.

sheer [ʃɪəʳ] adj - **1.** [absolute] puro(ra) - **2.** [very steep - cliff] escarpado(da); [- drop] vertical - **3.** [delicate] diáfano(na).

sheet [ʃiːt] n - **1.** [for bed] lençol m - **2.** [of paper] folha f - **3.** [of glass, metal, wood] lâmina f.

sheik(h) [ʃeɪk] n xeque m.

shelf [ʃelf] (pl shelves) n prateleira f.

shell [ʃel] <> n - **1.** [gen] casca f - **2.** [of tortoise] carapaça - **3.** [on beach] concha f - **4.** [of building] estrutura f - **5.** [of boat] casco m - **6.** [of car] chassi m - **7.** MIL granada f. <> vt - **1.** [remove covering] descascar - **2.** MIL [fire shells at] bombardear.

she'll [ʃiːl] cont = she will, she shall.

shellfish [ˈʃelfɪʃ] (pl inv) n - **1.** [creature] molusco m, crustáceo m - **2.** (U) [food] marisco m.

shell suit n UK conjunto de calça e jaqueta de náilon à prova d'água.

shelter [ˈʃeltəʳ] <> n - **1.** [building, structure] abrigo m, refúgio m - **2.** (U) [cover, protection] abrigo m, proteção f - **3.** (U) [accommodation] abrigo m. <> vt - **1.** [from rain, sun, bombs]: **to be ~ed by/from sthg** estar protegido(da) por/de algo - **2.** [give asylum to] abrigar. <> vi: **to ~ from/in sthg** abrigar-se de/em algo.

sheltered [ˈʃeltəd] adj - **1.** [protected] protegido(da) - **2.** [supervised] assistencial.

shelve [ʃelv] vt engavetar.

shelves [ʃelvz] pl ▷ shelf.

shepherd [ˈʃepəd] <> n pastor m. <> vt fig acompanhar.

shepherd's pie [ˈʃepədz-] n (U) gratinado de carne moída temperada com ervas e coberto com purê de batatas.

sheriff [ˈʃerɪf] n - **1.** US [law officer] xerife m - **2.** Scot [judge] juiz m, -íza f.

sherry [ˈʃerɪ] (pl -ies) n xerez m.

she's [ʃiːz] = she is, she has.

Shetland [ˈʃetlənd] n: ~, **the ~ Islands** as Ilhas Shetland.

shield [ʃiːld] <> n - **1.** [armour] escudo m - **2.** UK [sports trophy] troféu m (na forma de escudo) - **3.** [protection]: ~ **against sthg** proteção f contra algo. <> vt: **to ~ sb (from sthg)** proteger alguém (de algo).

shift [ʃɪft] <> n - **1.** [gen] turno m - **2.** [slight change] mudança f. <> vt - **1.** [move, put elsewhere] mover, mudar de lugar - **2.** [change slightly] mudar de - **3.** US AUT [gear] trocar. <> vi - **1.** [move] mover-se - **2.** [change slightly] mudar - **3.** US AUT trocar de marcha.

shiftless [ˈʃɪftlɪs] adj folgado(da).

shifty [ˈʃɪftɪ] (compar -ier, superl -iest) adj inf matreiro(ra).

shilling [ˈʃɪlɪŋ] n UK xelim m.

shilly-shally [ˈʃɪlɪˌʃælɪ] (pt & pp -ied) vi vacilar, titubear.

shimmer [ˈʃɪməʳ] <> n reflexo m trêmulo, cintilação f. <> vi cintilar, tremeluzir.

shin [ʃɪn] (pt & pp -ned, cont -ning) n canela f (na perna).

shin bone n tíbia f.

shine [ʃaɪn] (pt & pp shone) <> n brilho m. <> vt - **1.** [focus] direcionar - **2.** [polish] lustrar. <> vi [give out light] brilhar.

shingle [ˈʃɪŋgl] n (U) cascalhos m, pedrinhas fpl.

➡ **shingles** n MED herpes-zoster m.

shiny [ˈʃaɪnɪ] (compar -ier, superl -iest) adj brilhante.

ship [ʃɪp] (pt & pp -ped, cont -ping) <> n navio m, barco m. <> vt enviar por via marítima.

shipbuilding [ˈʃɪpˌbɪldɪŋ] n (U) construção f naval.

shipment [ˈʃɪpmənt] n carregamento m.

shipper [ˈʃɪpəʳ] n - **1.** [person] exportador(ra) - **2.** [company] empresa f exportadora.

shipping [ˈʃɪpɪŋ] n (U) - **1.** [transport] envio m, transporte m - **2.** [ships] navegação f.

shipshape [ˈʃɪpʃeɪp] adj em ordem.

shipwreck [ˈʃɪprek] <> n - **1.** [destruction of ship] naufrágio m - **2.** [wrecked ship] navio m naufragado. <> vt: **to be ~ed** naufragar.

shipyard [ˈʃɪpjɑːd] n estaleiro m.

shire [ʃaɪəʳ] n condado m.

shirk [ʃɜːk] vt escapar a.

shirt [ʃɜːt] n camisa f.

shirtsleeves [ˈʃɜːtsliːvz] npl: **to be in (one's) ~** estar em mangas de camisa.

shit [ʃɪt] (pt & pp shit OR -ted OR shat, cont -ting) vulg <> n merda f. <> vi cagar. <> excl merda!

shiver [ˈʃɪvəʳ] <> n tremer. <> vi: **to ~ (with sthg)** tremer (de algo).

shoal [ʃəʊl] n cardume m.

shock [ʃɒk] ⬦ n -1. [gen] choque m - 2. (U) MED: **to be suffering from** ~, **to be in (a state of)** ~ estar em estado de choque. ⬦ vt -1. [upset] chocar - 2. [offend] ofender.

shock absorber [-əb,zɔ:bə^r] n amortecedor m.

shocking [ʃɒkɪŋ] adj -1. [very bad] péssimo(ma) - 2. [scandalous] escandaloso(sa) - 3. [horrifying] chocante.

shod [ʃɒd] ⬦ pt & pp ⬧ shoe. ⬦ adj calçado(da).

shoddy [ʃɒdɪ] (compar -ier, superl -iest) adj -1. [badly done or made] de segunda qualidade - 2. fig [poor, unworthy] inferior.

shoe [ʃu:] (pt & pp -ed OR shod, cont -ing) ⬦ n [for person] sapato m. ⬦ vt ferrar.

shoebrush [ʃu:brʌʃ] n escova f para sapato.

shoehorn [ʃu:hɔ:n] n calçadeira f.

shoelace [ʃu:leɪs] n cadarço m.

shoe polish n graxa f de sapato.

shoe shop n sapataria f.

shoestring [ʃu:strɪŋ] n fig: **on a** ~ com orçamento mínimo.

shone [ʃɒn] pt & pp ⬧ shine.

shoo [ʃu:] ⬦ vt enxotar. ⬦ excl xô!

shook [ʃʊk] pt ⬧ shake.

shoot [ʃu:t] (pt & pp shot) ⬦ vt -1. [fire gun at - killing] matar a tiros, balear; [- wounding] ferir a tiros, balear; **to** ~ **o.s.** [kill o.s.] dar-se um tiro, atirar em si mesmo(ma) - 2. UK [hunt] caçar - 3. [arrow, question] disparar - 4. CINEMA filmar, rodar. ⬦ vi -1. [fire gun]: **to** ~ (**at sb/ sthg**) atirar (em alguém/algo) - 2. UK [hunt] caçar - 3. [move quickly]: **to** ~ **in/ out/past** entrar/sair/passar rapidamente; **to** ~ **ahead** sair na frente; **to** ~ **off** partir rapidamente - 4. CINEMA filmar, rodar - 5. [SPORT - football] chutar; [- basketball, netball etc.] arremessar. ⬦ n -1. UK [hunting expedition] caçada f - 2. [new growth] brote m.

⬥ **shoot down** vt sep -1. [person] matar a tiros - 2. [plane] derrubar.

⬥ **shoot up** vi -1. [grow quickly] dar um pulo - 2. [increase quickly] disparar.

shooting [ʃu:tɪŋ] n -1. [firing of gun] tiroteio m - 2. (U) [hunting] caça f.

shooting star n estrela f cadente.

shop [ʃɒp] (pt & pp -ped, cont -ping) ⬦ n -1. [store] loja f - 2. [workshop] oficina f, seminário m. ⬦ vi comprar; **to go shopping** fazer compras.

shop assistant n UK vendedor m, -ra f (de loja).

shop floor n: **the** ~ o chão de fábrica, os operários.

shopkeeper [ʃɒp,ki:pə^r] n lojista mf.

shoplifting [ʃɒp,lɪftɪŋ] n (U) roubo m numa loja.

shopper [ʃɒpə^r] n comprador m, -ra f.

shopping [ʃɒpɪŋ] n compras fpl; **to go** ~ fazer compras.

shopping bag n sacola f de compras.

shopping basket n UK -1. [in supermarket] cesta f - 2. [for online shopping] cesta f de compras.

shopping cart n US -1. [in supermarket] carrinho m - 2. [for online shopping] carrinho m de compras.

shopping centre UK, **shopping mall** US, **shopping plaza** US [-,plɑ:zə] n shopping (center) m, centro m comercial.

shopsoiled UK [ʃɒpsɔɪld], **shopworn** US [ʃɒpwɔ:n] adj deteriorado(da) por ficar exposto numa loja.

shop steward n representante mf sindical.

shopwindow [,ʃɒp'wɪndəʊ] n vitrina f.

shopworn adj US = shopsoiled.

shore [ʃɔ:^r] n -1. [land by water] beira f, margem f; sea ~ litoral m - 2. (U) [not at sea]: **on** ~ em terra.

⬥ **shore up** vt sep -1. [prop up] reforçar, sustentar - 2. fig [sustain] sustentar.

shorn [ʃɔ:n] ⬦ pp ⬧ shear. ⬦ adj -1. [grass] cortado(da) - 2. [hair] raspado(da); ~ **of** fig desprovido(da) de, despojado(da) de; **she was shorn of her responsibility** retiraram todo o poder dela.

short [ʃɔ:t] ⬦ adj -1. [in length, distance] curto(ta) - 2. [in height] baixo(xa) - 3. [in time] curto(ta), breve; **in two** ~ **days we'll be in Spain!** em apenas dois dias, estaremos na Espanha! - 4. [curt]: **to be** ~ (**with sb**) ser seco(ca) (com alguém) - 5. [lacking]: **money is always** ~ **around** Christmas o dinheiro anda sempre curto no Natal; **we're a pound** ~ falta (-nos) uma libra; **she's a bit** ~ **on brain power** falta a ela um pouco de agilidade mental; **to be** ~ **of sthg** andar mal de algo - 6. [abbreviated]: **to be** ~ **for sthg** ser o diminutivo de algo. ⬦ adv -1. [lacking]: **we're running** ~ **of food** está acabando a comida - 2. [suddenly, abruptly]: **to cut sthg** ~ interromper algo antes do tim; **to stop** ~ parar de repente. ⬦ n -1. UK [alcoholic drink] drinque m (**bebida forte**) - 2. CINEMA [film] curta f.

⬥ **shorts** npl -1. [short trousers] shorts mpl - 2. US [underwear] cuecas fpl.

➤ **for short** adv para abreviar, para simplificar.

➤ **in short** adv enfim.

➤ **nothing short of** prep: **it was nothing ~ of madness** foi uma verdadeira loucura.

➤ **short of** prep: **~ of doing sthg** a não ser fazendo algo.

shortage [ˈʃɔːtɪdʒ] n falta f, escassez f.

shortbread [ˈʃɔːtbred] n (U) biscoito m amanteigado.

short-change vt -1. [in shop, restaurant] dar mal o troco a - 2. fig [reward unfairly] passar para trás.

short circuit n curto-circuito m, curto m.

shortcomings [ˈʃɔːtˌkʌmɪŋz] npl defeitos mpl.

shortcrust pastry [ˈʃɔːtkrʌst-] n (U) massa f podre.

short cut n -1. [quick route] atalho m - 2. [quick method] método m rápido.

shorten [ˈʃɔːtn] ⬦ vt encurtar; 'Robert' can be ~ed to 'Bob' Bob é a forma reduzida de Robert. ⬦ vi encurtar.

shortfall [ˈʃɔːtfɔːl] n déficit m; ~ in OR of sthg déficit em OR de algo.

shorthand [ˈʃɔːthænd] n (U) [writing system] taquigrafia f, estenografia f.

shorthand typist n UK taquígrafo m, -fa f, estenógrafo m, -fa f.

short list n UK -1. [for job] lista f de candidatos selecionados - 2. [for prize] relação f dos finalistas.

shortly [ˈʃɔːtlɪ] adv [soon] em breve, logo; ~ before/after pouco antes/depois de.

shortsighted [ˌʃɔːtˈsaɪtɪd] adj -1. [myopic] míope - 2. fig [lacking foresight] de visão curta.

short-staffed [-ˈstɑːft] adj: **to be ~** estar com falta de pessoal.

short-stay adj: **a ~ car park** estacionamento para curtos períodos de tempo, geralmente 2-3 horas; **~ accommodation** acomodação para poucos dias; **a ~ patient** paciente hospitalizado por três dias ou menos.

short story n conto m.

short-tempered [-ˈtempəd] adj irritadiço(ça).

short-term adj -1. [happening soon] a curto prazo - 2. [of short duration] de curto prazo.

short wave n onda f curta.

shot [ʃɒt] ⬦ pt & pp ⊳ **shoot**. ⬦ n -1. [gunshot] tiro m; **like a ~** [quickly] como um raio - 2. [marksman] atirador m, -ra f - 3. SPORT chute m - 4. [photograph] foto f - 5. CINEMA tomada f - 6. inf [try, go] tentativa f - 7. [injection] injeção f.

shotgun [ˈʃɒtgʌn] n espingarda f.

should [ʃʊd] aux vb -1. [indicating duty, necessity]: **we ~ leave now** deveríamos ir agora - 2. [seeking advice, permission]: **~ I go too?** eu vou também? - 3. [as suggestion]: **I ~ deny everything** eu negaria tudo - 4. [indicating probability]: **she ~ be home soon** ela deve chegar em casa logo - 5. [was or were expected to]: **they ~ have won the match** eles deveriam ter ganhado o jogo - 6. (as conditional): **I ~ like to come with you** eu gostaria de ir com você; **how ~ I know?** como é que eu poderia saber?; **~ you be interested, ...** caso você esteja interessado, ... - 7. (in subordinate clauses): **we decided that you ~ meet him** decidimos que você deveria encontrá-lo - 8. [expressing uncertain opinion]: **I ~ think he's about 50 years old** eu diria que ele tem uns 50 anos - 9. (after who or what) [expressing surprise]: **and who ~ I see but Ann!** e então quem é que eu vejo? A Ann!

shoulder [ˈʃəʊldəʳ] ⬦ n -1. [part of body] ombro m - 2. [part of clothing] ombreira f - 3. CULIN [joint] quarto m dianteiro. ⬦ vt -1. [load] carregar nos ombros - 2. [responsibility] arcar com.

shoulder blade n omoplata f.

shoulder strap n alça f.

shouldn't [ˈʃʊdnt] = should not.

should've [ˈʃʊdəv] = should have.

shout [ʃaʊt] ⬦ n grito m. ⬦ vt gritar. ⬦ vi gritar; **to ~ at sb** [tell off] gritar com alguém.

➤ **shout down** vt sep calar com gritos.

shouting [ˈʃaʊtɪŋ] n (U) gritos mpl; **a lot of ~** uma gritaria.

shove [ʃʌv] inf ⬦ n: **to give sb/sthg a ~** dar um empurrão em alguém/ algo. ⬦ vt empurrar; **to ~ sb in** colocar alguém para dentro aos empurrões; **to ~ sb out** tirar alguém aos empurrões.

➤ **shove off** vi -1. [in boat] afastar-se da costa - 2. inf [go away] cair fora.

shovel [ˈʃʌvl] (UK pt & pp -led, cont -ling, US pt & pp -ed, cont -ing) ⬦ n pá f. ⬦ vt -1. [with a shovel] tirar com pá - 2. fig [food, meal] devorar; **they ~led down their food and left** eles engoliram a janta e saíram.

show [ʃəʊ] (pt -ed, pp shown OR -ed) ⬦ n -1. [piece of entertainment - theatre] espetáculo m; [- TV, radio] show m, programa m - 2. CINEMA sessão f - 3.

[exhibition] exposição *f* - **4.** [display] demonstração *f*. ◇ *vt* - **1.** [gen] mostrar; to ~ sb sthg, to ~ sthg to sb mostrar algo para alguém - **2.** [reveal] mostrar, revelar; to ~ sb sthg demostrar algo por alguém - **3.** [escort]: to ~ sb to sthg levar OR acompanhar alguém até algo - **4.** [broadcast] apresentar, passar - **5.** [profit, loss] registrar - **6.** [work of art, produce] mostrar, exibir. ◇ *vi* - **1.** [indicate, make clear] mostrar, indicar - **2.** [be visible] aparecer; inside he was very angry but it didn't ~ por dentro ele estava muito bravo mas não aparentava - **3.** CINEMA passar.

➡ **show off** ◇ *vt sep* exibir. ◇ *vi* exibir-se.

➡ **show up** ◇ *vt sep*: to ~ sb up in public fazer alguém passar vergonha em público. ◇ *vi* - **1.** [stand out] destacar-se - **2.** [arrive] aparecer.

show business *n (U)* showbusiness *m*, mundo *m* dos espetáculos.

showdown ['ʃəʊdaʊn] *n*: to have a ~ with sb ter um acerto final de contas com alguém.

shower ['ʃaʊə'] ◇ *n* - **1.** [gen] chuva *f* - **2.** [device] chuveiro *m* - **3.** [wash]: to have OR take a ~ tomar uma ducha - **4.** [for a baby] chá *m* de fralda. ◇ *vt* - **1.** [sprinkle] jogar; the newlyweds were ~ ed with confetti os recém-casados ganharam uma chuva de confetes - **2.** [bestow]: to ~ sb with sthg, to ~ sthg (up)on sb encher alguém de algo. ◇ *vi* tomar banho.

shower cap *n* touca *f* de banho.

showing ['ʃəʊɪŋ] *n* sessão *f*.

show jumping [-,dʒʌmpɪŋ] *n (U)* concurso *m* hípico de saltos.

shown [ʃəʊn] *pp* ▷ **show**.

show-off *n inf* exibido(da).

showpiece ['ʃəʊpi:s] *n* atração *f* principal.

showroom ['ʃəʊrʊm] *n* salão *m* de exposição.

shrank [ʃræŋk] *pt* ▷ **shrink**.

shrapnel ['ʃræpnl] *n (U)* metralha *f*.

shred [ʃred] (*pt & pp* -ded, *cont* -ding) ◇ *n* - **1.** [small piece] pedaço *m* - **2.** fig [scrap]: there was not a ~ of evidence that ... não havia a mais remota evidência de que ...; a ~ of truth um pingo de verdade. ◇ *vt* - **1.** CULIN picar - **2.** [paper] picar, rasgar.

shredder ['ʃredə'] *n* - **1.** CULIN [in food processor] triturador *m* - **2.** [for documents] picadora *f* de papel.

shrewd [ʃru:d] *adj* perspicaz, astuto(ta).

shriek [ʃri:k] ◇ *n* grito *m*; a ~ of

laughter uma gargalhada. ◇ *vi*: to ~ with laughter gargalhar.

shrill [ʃrɪl] *adj* agudo(da).

shrimp [ʃrɪmp] *n* camarão *m*.

shrine [ʃraɪn] *n* santuário *m*.

shrink [ʃrɪŋk] (*pt* shrank, *pp* shrunk) ◇ *vt* encolher. ◇ *vi* - **1.** [become smaller] encolher - **2.** fig [contract, diminish] diminuir - **3.** [recoil]: to ~ away from sthg recuar frente a algo - **4.** [be reluctant]: to ~ from sthg/from doing sthg fugir de algo/de fazer algo. ◇ *n inf* [psychoanalyst] psicanalista *mf*.

shrinkage ['ʃrɪŋkɪdʒ] *n (U)* - **1.** [loss in size] encolhimento *m* - **2.** fig [contraction] redução *f*.

shrink-wrap *vt* embalar com plástico termorretrátil.

shrivel ['ʃrɪvl] (*UK pt & pp* -led, *cont* -ling, *US pt & pp* -ed, *cont* -ing) ◇ *vt*: to ~ (up) secar, murchar. ◇ *vi*: to ~ (up) secar, murchar.

shroud [ʃraʊd] ◇ *n* mortalha *f*. ◇ *vt*: to be ~ ed in sthg [darkness, fog] estar encoberto(ta) em algo; [mystery] estar envolto(ta) em algo.

Shrove Tuesday ['ʃrəʊv-] *n* Terça-feira *f* de Carnaval.

shrub [ʃrʌb] *n* arbusto *m*.

shrubbery ['ʃrʌbərɪ] (*pl* -ies) *n* arbustos *mpl*.

shrug [ʃrʌg] (*pt & pp* -ged, *cont* -ging) ◇ *vt* encolher. ◇ *vi* dar de ombros, encolher os ombros.

➡ **shrug off** *vt sep* não dar bola para.

shrunk [ʃrʌŋk] *pp* ▷ **shrink**.

shudder ['ʃʌdə'] *vi* - **1.** [person]: to ~ (with sthg) estremecer-se (de algo) - **2.** [machine, vehicle] tremer, balançar.

shuffle ['ʃʌfl] *vt* - **1.** [feet] arrastar - **2.** [cards] embaralhar - **3.** [papers] mudar de lugar.

shun [ʃʌn] (*pt & pp* -ned, *cont* -ning) *vt* evitar.

shunt [ʃʌnt] *vt* RAIL manobrar, trocar de via férrea.

shut [ʃʌt] (*pt & pp* shut, *cont* -ting) ◇ *adj* fechado(da). ◇ *vt & vi* fechar.

➡ **shut away** *vt sep* - **1.** [criminal] trancafiar - **2.** [valuables] guardar.

➡ **shut down** ◇ *vt sep & vi* fechar.

➡ **shut out** *vt sep* [of building, room] não deixar entrar.

➡ **shut up** ◇ *vt sep* - **1.** [shop, factory] fechar - **2.** [silence] calar, fazer calar. ◇ *vi* - **1.** inf [be quiet] calar a boca - **2.** [close] fechar.

shutter ['ʃʌtə'] *n* - **1.** [on window] veneziana *f* - **2.** [in camera] obturador *m*.

shuttle ['ʃʌtl] <> adj: ~ **service** [of planes] ponte f aérea; [of buses, train] linha f regular; [of buses, train] linha f regular - **2.** [plane] avião m da ponte aérea.

shuttlecock ['ʃʌtlkɒk] n peteca f.

shy [ʃaɪ] (pt & pp **shied**) <> adj tímido(da); **to be ~ of doing sthg** não se atrever a fazer algo. <> vi espantar-se.

Siberia [saɪ'bɪərɪə] n Sibéria f.

sibling ['sɪblɪŋ] n irmão m, -mã f.

Sicily ['sɪsɪlɪ] n Sicília.

sick [sɪk] adj - **1.** [unwell] doente - **2.** [nauseous]: **to feel ~** sentir-se mal - **3.** [vomiting]: **to be ~** UK vomitar - **4.** [fed up]: **to be ~ of sthg/of doing sthg** estar farto(ta) de algo/de fazer algo - **5.** [offensive] de mau gosto.

sickbay ['sɪkbeɪ] n enfermaria f.

sicken ['sɪkn] <> vt deixar doente. <> vi UK: **to be ~ing for sthg** estar ficando doente de algo.

sickening ['sɪknɪŋ] adj - **1.** [disgusting] repugnante - **2.** hum [infuriating] irritante, exasperante.

sickle ['sɪkl] n foice f.

sick leave n (U) licença f de saúde.

sickly ['sɪklɪ] (compar **-ier**, superl **-iest**) adj - **1.** [unhealthy] doentio(tia) - **2.** [nauseating] nauseante.

sickness ['sɪknɪs] n - **1.** (U) [general illness] doença f, enfermidade f - **2.** UK (U) [nausea, vomiting] náusea f, enjôo m - **3.** [specific illness] doença f.

sick pay n (U) espécie de auxílio-doença pago pelo empregador.

side [saɪd] <> n - **1.** [gen] lado m; **on every ~**, **on all ~s** por todos os lados; **from ~ to ~** de um lado a outro; **at** OR **by sb's ~** ao lado de alguém; **~ by ~** lado a lado; **my mother's ~** por parte da minha mãe - **2.** [surface] lateral f - **3.** [of table, river] borda f, beira f - **4.** [slope] ladeira f, encosta f - **5.** [in sport] equipe f - **6.** [viewpoint] ponto m de vista; **to take sb's ~** ficar do lado de alguém - **7.** [aspect] aspecto m; **to be on the safe ~** por via das dúvidas. <> adj lateral.
◆ **side with** vt fus pôr-se ao lado de.

sideboard ['saɪdbɔːd] n armário m, guarda-louça m.

sideboards UK ['saɪdbɔːdz], **sideburns** US ['saɪdbɜːnz] npl suíças fpl, costeletas fpl.

side effect n efeito m colateral.

sidelight ['saɪdlaɪt] n luz f lateral.

sideline ['saɪdlaɪn] n - **1.** [extra business] ocupação f secundária - **2.** SPORT [painted line] linha f lateral.

sidelong ['saɪdlɒŋ] <> adj de lado. <> adv: **to look ~ at sb/sthg** olhar de lado para alguém/algo.

sidesaddle ['saɪd,sædl] adv: **to ride ~** montar de silhão.

sideshow ['saɪdʃəʊ] n área de jogos ou de espetáculos paralelos numa feira ou num circo.

sidestep ['saɪdstep] (pt & pp **-ped**, cont **-ping**) vt - **1.** [step to one side to avoid] desviar, evitar - **2.** fig [problem, question] esquivar-se de.

side street n rua f secundária.

sidetrack ['saɪdtræk] vt: **to be ~ed** desviar (dos objetivos).

sidewalk ['saɪdwɔːk] n US calçada f.

sideways ['saɪdweɪz] <> adj - **1.** [movement] lateral - **2.** [look] de soslaio. <> adv - **1.** [move] de lado - **2.** [look] de soslaio.

siding ['saɪdɪŋ] n - **1.** UK [for shunting] via f morta - **2.** US [loop line] tapume m.

sidle ['saɪdl] ◆ **sidle up** vi: **to ~ up to sb** aproximar-se furtivamente de alguém.

siege [siːdʒ] n cerco m.

sieve [sɪv] <> n peneira f. <> vt peneirar.

sift [sɪft] <> vt - **1.** [sieve] peneirar - **2.** fig [examine carefully] examinar cuidadosamente. <> vi: **to ~ through sthg** analisar algo minuciosamente.

sigh [saɪ] <> n suspiro m. <> vi suspirar.

sight [saɪt] <> n - **1.** [vision] visão f; **his first ~ of the sea** a primeira vez que ele viu o mar; **in ~** à vista; **out of ~** longe de vista; **at first ~** à primeira vista - **2.** [spectacle] espetáculo m - **3.** [on gun] mira f; **to set one's ~ on sthg** botar algo na cabeça. <> vt avistar, divisar.
◆ **sights** npl pontos mpl turísticos.

sightseeing ['saɪt,siːɪŋ] n (U) turismo m; **to do some ~** fazer turismo.

sightseer ['saɪt,siːəʳ] n turista mf.

sign [saɪn] <> n - **1.** [gen] sinal m - **2.** [in music] símbolo m - **3.** [notice] placa f. <> vt [document] assinar.
◆ **sign on** vi - **1.** [enrol]: **to ~ on (for sthg)** [for course] inscrever-se (em algo); MIL alistar-se (em algo) - **2.** [register as unemployed] cadastrar-se para receber o seguro desemprego.
◆ **sign up** <> vt sep - **1.** [employee] contratar - **2.** [soldier] recrutar. <> vi [enrol]: **to ~ up (for sthg)** [for course] inscrever-se (em algo); MIL alistar-se (em algo).

signal ['sɪgnl] (UK pt & pp **-led**, cont **-ling**, US pt & pp **-ed**, cont **-ing**) <> n sinal m. <> vt - **1.** [send signals to] enviar sinais a **- 2.** [indicate - a turn] sinalizar; [- a warning] indicar; **to ~ sb (to do sthg)** fazer sinal para alguém (fazer algo) **- 3. fig** marcar, anunciar. ◇ *vi* **-1.** AUT sinalizar **- 2.** [indicate]: **to ~ to sb (to do sthg)** fazer sinal para alguém (fazer algo).

signalman ['sɪgnlmən] (*pl* **-men** [-mən]) *n* sinaleiro *m*.

signature ['sɪgnətʃəʳ] *n* assinatura *f*.

signature tune *n* tema *m*.

signet ring ['sɪgnɪt-] *n* anel *m* com sinete.

significance [sɪg'nɪfɪkəns] *n* (U) **-1.** [importance] importância *f* **- 2.** [meaning] significado *m*.

significant [sɪg'nɪfɪkənt] *adj* significativo(va).

signify ['sɪgnɪfaɪ] (*pt* & *pp* **-ied**) *vt* significar.

signpost ['saɪnpəʊst] *n* placa *f* de sinalização.

Sikh [si:k] ◇ *adj* sique. ◇ *n* sique *mf*.

silence ['saɪləns] ◇ *n* silêncio *m*. ◇ *vt* silenciar, calar.

silencer ['saɪlənsəʳ] *n* **-1.** [on gun] silenciador *m* **- 2.** AUT silenciador *m*, silencioso *m*.

silent ['saɪlənt] *adj* **-1.** [gen] silencioso(sa) **- 2.** [taciturn] silencioso(sa), taciturno(na) **- 3.** CINEMA & LING mudo(da).

silhouette [ˌsɪlu:'et] *n* silhueta *f*.

silicon chip [ˌsɪlɪkən-] *n* chip *m* de silício.

silk [sɪlk] ◇ *n* (U) seda *f*. ◇ *comp* de seda.

silky ['sɪlkɪ] (*compar* **-ier**, *superl* **-iest**) *adj* sedoso(sa).

sill [sɪl] *n* peitoril *m*.

silly ['sɪlɪ] (*compar* **-ier**, *superl* **-iest**) *adj* **-1.** [foolish] bobo(ba) **- 2.** [comical] bobo(ba), ridículo(la).

silo ['saɪləʊ] (*pl* **-s**) *n* silo *m*.

silt [sɪlt] *n* (U) sedimento *m*, lodo *m*.

silver ['sɪlvəʳ] ◇ *adj* prateado(da). ◇ *n* (U) **- 1.** [metal] prata *f* **- 2.** [coins] moedas *fpl* **- 3.** [silverware] prataria *f*. ◇ *comp* [made of silver] de prata.

silver-plated [-'pleɪtɪd] *adj* prateado(da).

silversmith ['sɪlvəsmɪθ] *n* prateiro *m*, -ra *f*.

silverware ['sɪlvəweəʳ] *n* **-1.** [objects made of silver] prataria *f* **- 2.** US [cutlery] prataria *f*.

similar ['sɪmɪləʳ] *adj* parecido(da), semelhante; **~ to sthg** parecido(da) OR similar a algo.

similarly ['sɪmɪləlɪ] *adv* igualmente, da mesma forma.

simmer ['sɪməʳ] *vt* & *vi* cozinhar em fogo baixo.

simpering ['sɪmpərɪŋ] *adj* **-1.** [person] que sorri com cara de bobo(ba) **- 2.** [smile] bobo(ba).

simple ['sɪmpl] *adj* **-1.** [gen] simples **- 2.** *inf* [mentally retarded] simplório(ria).

simple-minded [-'maɪndɪd] *adj* simplório(ria).

simplicity [sɪm'plɪsətɪ] *n* simplicidade *f*.

simplify ['sɪmplɪfaɪ] (*pt* & *pp* **-ied**) *vt* simplificar.

simply ['sɪmplɪ] *adv* **-1.** [gen] simplesmente; **you ~ must go and see the film** você só tem que ir ver o filme **- 2.** [in an uncomplicated way] de forma simples.

simulate ['sɪmjʊleɪt] *vt* **-1.** [feign] simular, fingir **- 2.** [produce effect, appearance of] simular.

simultaneous [UK ˌsɪməl'teɪnjəs, US ˌsaɪməl'teɪnjəs] *adj* simultâneo(nea).

sin [sɪn] (*pt* & *pp* **-ned**, *cont* **-ning**) ◇ *n* pecado *m*. ◇ *vi*: **to ~ (against sb/ sthg)** pecar (contra alguém/algo).

since [sɪns] ◇ *adv*: **~ (then)** desde então. ◇ *prep* desde. ◇ *conj* **-1.** [in time]: **it's ages ~ I saw him** faz séculos que eu não o vejo **- 2.** [because] já que, como.

sincere [sɪn'sɪəʳ] *adj* sincero(ra).

sincerely [sɪn'sɪəlɪ] *adv* sinceramente; **Yours ~** [at end of letter] atenciosamente.

sincerity [sɪn'serətɪ] *n* (U) sinceridade *f*.

sinew ['sɪnju:] *n* tendão *m*.

sinful ['sɪnfʊl] *adj* **-1.** [guilty of sin] pecador(ra) **- 2.** [wicked, immoral] pecaminoso(sa).

sing [sɪŋ] (*pt* **sang**, *pp* **sung**) *vt* & *vi* cantar.

Singapore [ˌsɪŋə'pɔ:ʳ] *n* Cingapura.

singe [sɪndʒ] (*cont* **singeing**) *vt* chamuscar.

singer ['sɪŋəʳ] *n* cantor *m*, -ra *f*.

singing ['sɪŋɪŋ] *n* canto *m*.

single ['sɪŋgl] ◇ *adj* **-1.** [sole] único(ca); **to sweep up every ~ leaf** varrer todas as folhas, sem deixar nenhuma; **every ~ day** todo santo dia **- 2.** [unmarried] solteiro(ra) **- 3.** UK [one-way] de ida. ◇ *n* **-1.** UK [one-way ticket] passagem *f* de ida **- 2.** MUS single *m*.

➡ **singles** *npl* TENNIS simples *f inv*.

➡ **single out** *vt sep*: **to ~ sb out (for sthg)** escolher alguém (para algo).

single bed *n* cama *f* de solteiro.

single-breasted [-'brestɪd] *adj* não trespassado(da).

single cream *n* (U) UK creme *m* leve.

single file *n*: **in ~** em fila indiana.

single-handed [-'hændɪd] *adv* sem ajuda.

single-minded [-'maɪndɪd] *adj* determinado(da), resoluto(ta).

single parent *n* pai *m* solteiro, mãe *f* solteira.

single-parent family *n* família *f* em que falta um dos pais.

single room *n* quarto *m* simples.

singlet ['sɪŋglɪt] *n* camiseta *f* (sem mangas).

singular ['sɪŋgjələʳ] ◇ *adj* -1. GRAMM no singular -2. [unusual, remarkable] singular. ◇ *n* singular *m*.

sinister ['sɪnɪstəʳ] *adj* sinistro(tra).

sink [sɪŋk] (*pt* sank, *pp* sunk) ◇ *n* pia *f.* ◇ *vt* -1. [cause to go underwater] afundar -2. [cause to penetrate]: **to ~ sthg into** sthg cravar algo em algo. ◇ *vi* -1. [gen] afundar; **to ~ without trace** sumir sem deixar vestígio -2. [below ground - person] afundar-se; [- sun] pôr-se -3. [slump]: **he sank back into his chair** ele se afundou na cadeira; **she sank to her knees** ela caiu sobre os joelhos -4. *fig* [heart, spirits] congelar -5. [fall] baixar; **her voice sank to a whisper** sua voz foi baixando até ficar um sussurro -6. *fig* [slip]: **to ~ into sthg** [despair, poverty] cair em algo; [depression, coma] entrar em algo.

◆ **sink in** *vi*: **it hasn't sunk in yet** ainda não caiu a ficha.

sink unit *n* pia *f.*

sinner ['sɪnəʳ] *n* pecador *m*, -ra *f.*

sinus ['saɪnəs] (*pl* -es) *n* seio *m* (*paranasal*)*.*

sip [sɪp] (*pt* & *pp* -ped, *cont* -ping) ◇ *n* gole *m.* ◇ *vt* bebericar.

siphon ['saɪfn] ◇ *n* sifão *m.* ◇ *vt* -1. [draw off] tirar com sifão -2. *fig* [transfer] desviar.

◆ **siphon off** *vt sep* -1. [draw off] tirar com sifão -2. *fig* [transfer] desviar.

sir [sɜːʳ] *n* -1. [form of address] senhor *m* -2. [in titles] sir *m.*

siren ['saɪərən] *n* sirene *f.*

sirloin (steak) ['sɜːlɔɪn] *n* bife *m* de lombo de vaca.

sissy ['sɪsɪ] (*pl* -ies) *n* inf fresco *m.*

sister ['sɪstəʳ] *n* -1. [gen] irmã *f* -2. [nun] irmã *f*, freira *f* -3. UK [senior nurse] (enfermeira *f*) supervisora *f.*

sister-in-law (*pl* sisters-in-law OR sister-in-laws) *n* cunhada *f.*

sit [sɪt] (*pt* & *pp* sat, *cont* -ting) ◇ *vt* -1. [place] sentar -2. UK [examination] fazer. ◇ *vi* -1. [gen] sentar-se -2. [be member]: **to ~ on sthg** integrar algo, fazer parte de algo -3. [be in session] reunir-se.

◆ **sit about, sit around** *vi* ver o tempo passar.

◆ **sit down** *vi* sentar-se.

◆ **sit in on** *vt fus* estar presente (sem tomar parte).

◆ **sit through** *vt fus* agüentar até o final.

◆ **sit up** *vi* -1. [be sitting upright] sentarse reto(ta); [move into upright position] endireitar-se -2. [stay up] ficar acordado(da).

sitcom ['sɪtkɒm] *n* inf comédia *f* de situação, sitcom *f.*

site [saɪt] ◇ *n* -1. [piece of land - archaeology] sítio *m*; [- building] lote *m*; [- missile] campo *m*; [- camp] área *f* -2. [location, place] local *m* -3. COMPUT site *m.* ◇ *vt* localizar-se, situar-se.

sit-in *n* greve *f* branca.

sitting ['sɪtɪŋ] *n* -1. [serving of meal] turno *m* para as refeições -2. [session] sessão *f.*

sitting room *n* sala *f* de estar.

situated ['sɪtjʊeɪtɪd] *adj*: **to be ~** estar localizado(da), localizar-se.

situation [,sɪtjʊ'eɪʃn] *n* -1. [gen] situação *f* -2. [location] localização *f* -3. [job] emprego *m*, colocação *f*; **'Situations Vacant'** UK 'Empregos'.

six [sɪks] ◇ *num adj* -1. [numbering six] seis -2. [referring to age]: **she's ~ (years old)** ela tem seis anos (de idade). ◇ *num pron* seis; **I want ~** quero seis; **there were ~ of us** éramos seis; **groups of ~** grupos *mpl* de seis. ◇ *num n* -1. [gen] seis; **two hundred and ~** duzentos e seis -2. [six o'clock] seis (*horas*); **we arrived at ~** chegamos às seis -3. [in addresses]: **~ Peyton Place** Praça Peyton, casa OR número 6; **~-nil** seis a zero.

sixteen [sɪks'tiːn] *num* dezesseis; *see also* **six**.

sixteenth [sɪks'tiːnθ] *num* décimo sexto, décima sexta; *see also* **sixth**.

sixth [sɪksθ] ◇ *num adj* sexto(ta). ◇ *num adv* sexto. ◇ *num pron* sexto(ta). ◇ *n* -1. [fraction] sexto *m* -2. [in dates]: **the ~** o dia seis; **the ~ of September** o dia seis de setembro.

sixth form *n* UK SCH curso opcional de dois anos no ensino secundário britânico oferecido aos alunos de 16 anos a fim de ingressarem na universidade.

sixth form college *n* UK escola pública na Inglaterra para adolescentes de 16 a 18 anos na qual se preparam para ingressar na universidade ou para fazer testes de formação profissional.

sixty ['sɪkstɪ] (*pl* -ies) *num* sessenta; *see also* **six**.

◆ **sixties** *npl* -1. [decade]: **the sixties** os anos sessenta -2. [in ages]: **to be in one's sixties** estar na casa dos sessenta.

size [saɪz] *n* tamanho *m*; **an organization of that** ~ uma organização daquele porte.

◆ **size up** *vt sep* -1. [situation] avaliar -2. [person] julgar.

sizeable ['saɪzəbl] *adj* considerável.

sizzle ['sɪzl] *vi* chiar.

skate [skeɪt] (*pl sense 2 only inv OR* -s) *n* -1. [gen] patim *m* -2. [fish] raia *f*. ◇ *vi* -1. [on ice skates] patinar no gelo -2. [on roller skates] patinar, andar de patins.

skateboard ['skeɪtbɔ:d] *n* skate *m*.

skater ['skeɪtə'] *n* patinador *m*, -ra *f*.

skating ['skeɪtɪŋ] *n* (*U*) -1. [on ice] patinação *f* no gelo; **to go** ~ patinar no gelo -2. [on roller skates] patinação *f*; **to go** ~ andar de patins.

skating rink *n* [for ice skating] pista *f* de patinação no gelo; [for roller skating] rinque *m*, pista *f* de patinação.

skeleton ['skelɪtn] *n* esqueleto *m*.

skeleton key *n* chave-mestra *f*.

skeleton staff *n* contingente *m* mínimo de pessoal.

skeptic etc. *n US* = **sceptic** etc.

sketch [sketʃ] ◇ *n* -1. [drawing] esboço *m*, croqui *m* -2. [brief description] resumo *m* -3. [on TV, radio, stage] esquete *m*. ◇ *vt* -1. [draw] fazer um esboço de -2. [describe] resumir.

sketchbook ['sketʃbʊk] *n* caderno *m* de desenhos.

sketchpad ['sketʃpæd] *n* bloco *m* de desenhos.

sketchy ['sketʃɪ] (*compar* -ier, *superl* -iest) *adj* incompleto(ta), pouco detalhado(da).

skewer ['skjʊə'] ◇ *n* espeto *m*. ◇ *vt* espetar.

ski [ski:] (*pt & pp* **skied**, *cont* **skiing**) ◇ *n* esqui *m*. ◇ *vi* esquiar.

ski boots *npl* botas *fpl* de esqui.

skid [skɪd] (*pt & pp* -**ded**, *cont* -**ding**) ◇ *n AUT* derrapagem *f*; **to go into a** ~ derrapar. ◇ *vi* derrapar.

skier ['ski:ə'] *n* esquiador *m*, -ra *f*.

skiing ['ski:ɪŋ] *n* (*U*) esqui *m*; **to go** ~ ir esquiar.

ski jump *n* -1. [slope] rampa *f* para saltos de esqui -2. [sporting event] salto *m* de esqui.

skilful, skillful *US* ['skɪlfʊl] *adj* hábil.

ski lift *n* teleférico *m*.

skill [skɪl] *n* -1. (*U*) [expertise] experiência *f*, destreza *f* -2. [craft, technique] habilidade *f*.

skilled [skɪld] *adj* -1. [skilful] habilidoso(sa); **to be** ~ **in** *OR* **at doing sthg** ter muito jeito para fazer algo -2. [trained] especializado(da), qualificado(da).

skillful *adj US* = **skilful**.

skim [skɪm] (*pt & pp* -**med**, *cont* -**ming**) ◇ *vt* -1. [remove - cream] tirar a nata de; [- fat] tirar a gordura de; [- sap] extrair -2. [glide over] roçar. ◇ *vi* -1. : **to** ~ **over sthg** [bird] dar uma rasante em algo; [stone] ricochetear em algo -2. [read]: **to** ~ **through sthg** ler algo por cima.

skim(med) milk [skɪm(d)mɪlk] *n* (*U*) leite *m* desnatado.

skimp [skɪmp] *vi*: **to** ~ **on sthg** [food, material, time] restringir algo; [money] economizar em algo; [work] fazer algo correndo.

skimpy ['skɪmpɪ] (*compar* -ier, *superl* -iest) *adj* -1. [meal] parco(ca) -2. [clothes] justo(ta) -3. [facts] insuficiente.

skin [skɪn] (*pt & pp* -**ned**, *cont* -**ning**) ◇ *n* -1. (*U*) [gen] pele *f* -2. [of fruit, vegetable, on paint, pudding] casca *f* -3. [on milk] nata *f*. ◇ *vt* -1. [remove skin from - fruit] descascar; [- dead animal] pelar -2. [graze] esfolar.

skin-deep *adj* superficial.

skin diving *n* (*U*): **to go** ~ praticar mergulho *m* livre.

skinny ['skɪnɪ] (*compar* -ier, *superl* -iest) *adj inf* magricela.

skin-tight *adj* muito justo(ta).

skip [skɪp] (*pt & pp* -**ped**, *cont* -**ping**) ◇ *n* -1. [little jump] pulinho *m* -2. *UK* [large container] caçamba *f* (*para entulho*). ◇ *vt* -1. [page] pular -2. [class] perder -3. [meal] faltar a. ◇ *vi* -1. [move in little jumps] ir pulando -2. *UK* [using rope] pular.

ski pants *npl* calças *fpl* de esqui.

ski pole *n* bastão *m* de esqui.

skipper ['skɪpə'] *n* capitão *m*, -tã *f*.

skipping rope ['skɪpɪŋ-] *n UK* corda *f* de pular.

skirmish ['skɜ:mɪʃ] *n* -1. *MIL* escaramuça *f* -2. *fig* [disagreement] desavença *f*.

skirt [skɜ:t] ◇ *n* [garment] saia *f*. ◇ *vt* -1. [go round] contornar -2. [avoid dealing with] evitar.

◆ **skirt round** *vt fus* -1. [go round]: **to** ~ **round sb/sthg** desviar de alguém/algo -2. [avoid dealing with]: **to** ~ **round sthg** evitar algo.

skit [skɪt] *n*: ~ **on sthg** sátira *f OR* paródia *f* sobre algo.

ski tow *n* ski lift *m*.

skittle ['skɪtl] *n UK* pino *m* de boliche.

◆ **skittles** *n* (*U*) *UK* boliche *m*.

skive [skaɪv] *vi UK inf*: to ~ (off) [at school]
matar aula; [at work] matar o serviço.

skulk [skʌlk] *vi* esconder-se.

skull [skʌl] *n* -1. ANAT crânio *m* -2. [on
skeleton] caveira *f*.

skunk [skʌŋk] *n* gambá *m*.

sky [skaɪ] (*pl* **skies**) *n* céu *m*.

skylight ['skaɪlaɪt] *n* clarabóia *f*.

skyscraper ['skaɪˌskreɪpəʳ] *n* arranha-
céu *m*.

slab [slæb] *n* -1. [of concrete, stone] laje *f*
-2. [of meat, cake] fatia *f* -3. [of chocolate]
barra *f*.

slack [slæk] ◇ *adj* -1. [not tight] frou-
xo(xa) - 2. [not busy] parado(da) - 3. [not
efficient] desleixado(da), negligente.
◇ *n* (U) ponta *f* solta.

slacken ['slækn] ◇ *vt* -1. [make slower]
reduzir - 2. [make looser] afrouxar. ◇ *vi*
-1. [become slower] reduzir - 2. [become
looser] afrouxar.

slag [slæg] *n* -1. (U) [waste material]
escombros *mpl* - 2. *inf pej* [promiscuous
woman] vagabunda *f*.

slagheap ['slæghiːp] *n* monte *m* de
entulho.

slain [sleɪn] *pp* ▷ slay.

slam [slæm] (*pt & pp* -med, *cont* -ming)
◇ *vt* -1. [shut] bater - 2. [place roughly]:
to ~ sthg on (to) sthg jogar algo com
violência sobre algo. ◇ *vi* [shut] bater.

slander ['slɑːndəʳ] ◇ *n* (U) calúnia *f*.
◇ *vt* caluniar.

slang [slæŋ] *n* (U) gíria *f*.

slant [slɑːnt] ◇ *n* -1. [diagonal angle - of
table, shelf] inclinação *f*; [- of land]
declive *m* - 2. [point of view] perspectiva
f, enfoque *m*. ◇ *vt* [bias] distorcer. ◇
vi [slope] inclinar-se.

slanting ['slɑːntɪŋ] *adj* inclinado(da).

slap [slæp] (*pt & pp* -ped, *cont* -ping) ◇
n -1. [on face] bofetada *f* - 2. [on back]
tapa *m*. ◇ *vt* -1. [smack - on face]
esbofetear; [- on back] dar um tapa
em - 2. [put]: to ~ sthg on dar uma
retocada em. ◇ *adv inf* [exactly] em
cheio; ~ in the middle of the city bem no
meio da cidade.

slapdash ['slæpdæʃ], **slaphappy** ['slæp-
ˌhæpɪ] *adj* relaxado(da).

slapstick ['slæpstɪk] *n* (U) pastelão *m*;
the film is pure ~ este filme é um
pastelão só.

slap-up *adj UK inf* farto(ta); a ~ dinner
um jantar formidável.

slash [slæʃ] ◇ *n* -1. [long cut] rasgão *m*,
corte *m* - 2. [oblique stroke] barra *f*
oblíqua; forward ~ barra *f* (inclinada)
-3. *UK inf* [pee]: to have a ~ fazer xixi.
◇ *vt* -1. [cut - material, tyres] rasgar;

[- wrists] cortar - 2. *inf* [reduce drastically]
cortar.

slat [slæt] *n* ripa *f*, sarrafo *m*.

slate [sleɪt] ◇ *n* -1. (U) [material] ardósia *f* - 2. [on roof] telha *f* de ardósia; to
wipe the ~ clean sacudir a poeira; put it
on the ~ põe na conta. ◇ *vt* [criticize]
malhar.

slaughter ['slɔːtəʳ] ◇ *n* -1. [of animals]
matança *f* - 2. [of people] chacina *f*. ◇
vt -1. [animals] matar, carnear - 2. [peo-
ple] chacinar.

slaughterhouse ['slɔːtəhaʊs, *pl* -haʊzɪz]
n matadouro *m*.

slave [sleɪv] ◇ *n* escravo *m*, -va *f*; to be
a ~ to sthg ser escravo(va) de algo. ◇
vi [work hard]: to ~ (over sthg) trabalhar
como um escravo em algo, trabalhar
como uma escrava em algo.

slavery ['sleɪvərɪ] *n* (U) escravidão *f*.

slay [sleɪ] (*pt* slew, *pp* slain) *vt literary*
assassinar.

sleaze *n* sujeira *f*.

sleazy ['sliːzɪ] (*compar* -ier, *superl* -iest)
adj sujo(ja).

sledge [sledʒ], **sled** US [sled] *n* trenó *m*.

sledgehammer ['sledʒˌhæməʳ] *n* marreta *f*.

sleek [sliːk] *adj* -1. [hair] sedoso(sa) - 2.
[fur] brilhoso(sa) - 3. [animal, bird] lustro-
so(sa) - 4. [car, plane] vistoso(sa) - 5. [per-
son] polido(da).

sleep [sliːp] (*pt & pp* slept) ◇ *n* -1. (U)
[rest] sono *m*; to go to ~ [doze off]
adormecer; [go numb] ficar dormente
- 2. [period of sleeping] sono *m*. ◇ *vi*
dormir.

◆ sleep in *vi* dormir até mais tarde.

◆ sleep with *vt fus euphemism* dormir
com.

sleeper ['sliːpəʳ] *n* -1. [person]: to be a
heavy/light ~ ter sono pesado/leve
- 2. [sleeping compartment] leito *m* - 3.
[train] trem-leito *m* - 4. *UK* [on railway
track] dormente *m*.

sleeping bag ['sliːpɪŋ-] *n* saco *m* de
dormir.

sleeping car ['sliːpɪŋ-] *n* vagão-leito *m*.

sleeping pill ['sliːpɪŋ-] *n* pílula *f* para
dormir.

sleepless ['sliːplɪs] *adj* em claro, sem
dormir.

sleepwalk ['sliːpwɔːk] *vi* sonambular.

sleepy ['sliːpɪ] (*compar* -ier, *superl* -iest)
adj [person] sonolento(ta).

sleet [sliːt] ◇ *n* (U) granizo *m*. ◇ *v*
impers chover granizo.

sleeve [sliːv] *n* -1. [of garment] manga *f*
- 2. [for record] capa *f*.

sleigh [sleɪ] *n* trenó *m*.

sleight of hand [ˌslaɪt-] n (U) -**1.** [skill with hands] prestidigitação f -**2.** fig [deception] artimanha f.

slender ['slendə^r] adj -**1.** [thin - person, figure] esbelto(ta); [- legs] delgado(da) -**2.** [scarce] escasso(sa).

slept [slept] pt & pp ▷ sleep.

slew [slu:] ◇ pt ▷ slay. ◇ vi: the car ~ed off the road o carro rodopiou para fora da estrada.

slice [slaɪs] ◇ n -**1.** [gen] fatia f -**2.** [of lemon] rodela f -**3.** [proportion] parte f -**4.** SPORT cortada f. ◇ vt -**1.** [cut into slices] fatiar -**2.** SPORT cortar.

◆ **slice off** vt sep [sever] arrancar fora.

slick [slɪk] ◇ adj -**1.** [smoothly efficient - performance, teamwork] talentoso(sa); [- technique, crime] engenhoso(sa) -**2.** pej [glib] ardiloso(sa). ◇ n local m escorregadio.

slide [slaɪd] (pt & pp slid [slɪd]) ◇ n -**1.** PHOT eslaide m -**2.** [in playground] escorregador m -**3.** UK [for hair] passador m -**5.** [decline] declínio m. ◇ vt [move smoothly] deslizar. ◇ vi -**1.** [on ice, slippery surface] escorregar -**2.** [move quietly] deslizar -**3.** [decline gradually] sucumbir a.

sliding door [ˌslaɪdɪŋ-] n porta f de correr.

sliding scale [ˌslaɪdɪŋ-] n escala f móvel.

slight [slaɪt] ◇ adj -**1.** [minor] ligeiro(ra); not in the ~est nem de leve; I haven't got the ~est interest in his car eu não tenho o menor interesse no carro dele -**2.** [slender] de aspecto frágil. ◇ n menosprezo m. ◇ vt [offend] menosprezar.

slightly ['slaɪtlɪ] adv [to small extent] ligeiramente, levemente.

slim [slɪm] (compar -mer, superl -mest, pt & pp -med, cont -ming) ◇ adj -**1.** [person] esbelto(ta) -**2.** [object] fino(na) -**3.** [chance, possibility] remoto(ta). ◇ vi emagrecer; I'm ~ming estou de dieta.

slime [slaɪm] n (U) muco m.

slimming ['slɪmɪŋ] ◇ n (U) emagrecimento m. ◇ adj -**1.** [magazine] de dieta -**2.** [product] para emagrecer.

sling [slɪŋ] (pt & pp slung) ◇ n -**1.** [for injured arm] tipóia f -**2.** [for carrying things] linga f. ◇ vt -**1.** [hang roughly] pendurar -**2.** inf [throw] atirar, jogar -**3.** [hang by both ends] pendurar.

slip [slɪp] (pt & pp -ped, cont -ping) ◇ n -**1.** [mistake] deslize m, descuido m; a ~ of the pen um erro de ortografia; a ~ of the tongue um lapso verbal -**2.** [form] formulário m -**3.** [of paper] folha

f -**4.** [underwear] combinação f, anágua f -**5.** phr: to give sb the ~ inf safar-se de alguém. ◇ vt -**1.** [slide] enfiar, meter -**2.** [clothes]: to ~ sthg on vestir algo rapidamente; ~ your clothes off tira fora essas tuas roupas -**3.** [escape] fugir; it ~ped my mind me esqueci. ◇ vi -**1.** [lose balance] escorregar -**2.** [move unexpectedly] escapulir -**3.** [move gradually] entrar em -**4.** [decline] baixar -**5.** [move discreetly] escapulir-se; to ~ into/out of sthg [clothes] vestir/tirar algo -**6.** AUT [clutch] patinar.

◆ **slip away** vi [leave] ir embora.

◆ **slip on** vt sep [clothes, shoes] enfiar.

◆ **slip up** vi [make a mistake] cometer um deslize.

slipped disc [ˌslɪpt-] n hérnia f de disco.

slipper ['slɪpə^r] n pantufa f.

slippery ['slɪpərɪ] adj -**1.** [surface, soap] escorregadio(dia) -**2.** pej [person] evasivo(va).

slip road n UK acesso m (na estrada).

slipshod ['slɪpʃɒd] adj desleixado(da).

slip-up n inf mancada f.

slipway ['slɪpweɪ] n carreira f (para navios).

slit [slɪt] (pt & pp slit, cont -ting) ◇ n -**1.** [opening] fenda f -**2.** [cut] corte m. ◇ vt -**1.** [cut open] cortar -**2.** [cut through] fender.

slither ['slɪðə^r] vi -**1.** [car, person] arrastar-se -**2.** [snake] rastejar.

sliver ['slɪvə^r] n -**1.** [gen] caco f -**2.** [of ice, wood] lasca f.

slob [slɒb] n inf [disgusting person - in habits] porcalhão m, -lhona f; [- in appearance] porco m, -ca f.

slog [slɒg] (pt & pp -ged, cont -ging) inf ◇ n [tiring work] chatice f. ◇ vi [work]: to ~ (away) at sthg trabalhar sem descanso em algo.

slogan ['sləʊgən] n slogan m.

slop [slɒp] (pt & pp -ped, cont -ping) ◇ vt derramar. ◇ vi transbordar.

slope [sləʊp] ◇ n -**1.** [of roof, ground] inclinação f -**2.** [hill] encosta f. ◇ vi inclinar-se.

sloping ['sləʊpɪŋ] adj inclinado(da).

sloppy ['slɒpɪ] (compar -ier, superl -iest) adj [careless] desleixado(da), relaxado(da).

slot [slɒt] n -**1.** [opening] abertura f -**2.** [groove] ranhura f -**3.** [place in schedule] espaço m -**4.** COMPUT slot m.

slot machine n -**1.** [vending machine] máquina f automática (de bebidas, cigarros etc.) -**2.** [arcade machine] caçaníqueis m inv.

slouch [slaʊtʃ] *vi* [in posture] ter má postura.

Slovakia [slə'vækɪə] *n* Eslováquia.

slovenly ['slʌvnlɪ] *adj* **-1.** [person, work] desmazelado(da) **-2.** [appearance] desleixado(da) **-3.** [dress] desalinhado(da).

slow [sləʊ] ◇ *adj* **-1.** [not fast] lento(ta) **-2.** [clock, watch] atrasado(da) **-3.** [not intelligent] lerdo(da). ◇ *adv*: **to go** ~ [driver] ir devagar; [workers] fazer operação-tartaruga. ◇ *vt* retardar. ◇ *vi* ir mais devagar, desacelerar.

➤ **slow down, slow up** ◇ *vt sep* **-1.** [growth] retardar **-2.** [car] reduzir a velocidade de. ◇ *vi* **-1.** [car] reduzir a velocidade de **-2.** [walker] diminuir a marcha.

slowdown ['sləʊdaʊn] *n* desaceleração f.

slowly ['sləʊlɪ] *adv* devagar.

slow motion *n* (U) câmera f lenta.

sludge [slʌdʒ] *n* **-1.** [mud] lama f **-2.** [sediment] lodo m.

slug [slʌg] *n* **-1.** ZOOL lesma f **-2.** *inf* [of alcohol] trago m **-3.** US *inf* [bullet] bala f (de revólver).

sluggish ['slʌgɪʃ] *adj* **-1.** [lethargic] vagaroso(sa) **-2.** [reaction, business] moroso(sa).

sluice [slu:s] *n* [lock] comporta f.

slum [slʌm] *n* [area of poor housing] favela f, cortiço m.

slumber ['slʌmbə'] *literary* ◇ *n* (U) sono m. ◇ *vi* adormecer.

slump [slʌmp] ◇ *n* **-1.** [decline]: ~ (in sthg) queda f (em algo) **-2.** ECON crise f econômica. ◇ *vi* **-1.** [business, prices, market] cair **-2.** [person] afundar-se.

slung [slʌŋ] *pt & pp* ⊳ **sling**.

slur [slɜ:'] (*pt & pp* **-red**, *cont* **-ring**) ◇ *n* [insult]: ~ (on sb/ sthg) ultraje m OR afronta f (a alguém/algo). ◇ *vt* [speech] balbuciar; **to** ~ **one's words** engolir as palavras.

slush [slʌʃ] *n* (U) neve f meio derretida.

slush fund, slush money US *n* caixa m dois.

slut [slʌt] *n* **-1.** *inf* [dirty or untidy woman] mulher f relaxada **-2.** *v inf* [sexually immoral woman] rameira f.

sly [slaɪ] (*compar* **slyer** OR **slier**, *superl* **slyest** OR **sliest**) *adj* **-1.** [look, smile, grin] dissimulado(da) **-2.** [cunning] astuto(ta).

smack [smæk] ◇ *n* **-1.** [slap] palmada f **-2.** [impact] batida f. ◇ *vt* **-1.** [slap] dar uma palmada em **-2.** [put] colocar bruscamente **-3.** [make sound]: **to** ~ **one's lips** estalar os lábios.

small [smɔ:l] *adj* **-1.** [gen] pequeno(na) **-2.** [person] baixo(xa) **-3.** [importance]

pouco(ca) **-4.** [matter, alteration] de pouca importância.

small ads [-ædz] *npl* UK classificados mpl.

small change *n* (U) trocado m.

smallholder ['smɔ:lˌhəʊldə'] *n* UK minifundiário m, -ria f.

small hours *npl* primeiras horas fpl da manhã.

smallpox ['smɔ:lpɒks] *n* (U) varíola f.

small print *n*: **the** ~ as letras miúdas (de um contrato).

small talk *n* (U): **to make** ~ conversar amenidades.

smarmy ['smɑ:mɪ] (*compar* **-ier**, *superl* **-iest**) *adj inf* adulador(ra).

smart [smɑ:t] ◇ *adj* **-1.** [elegant] elegante **-2.** [clever] inteligente **-3.** [fashionable, exclusive] chique, elegante **-4.** [rapid] rápido(da). ◇ *vi* **-1.** [sting] pungir, arder **-2.** [feel anger, humiliation] ofender-se.

smarten ['smɑ:tn] ➤ **smarten up** *vt sep* arrumar; **to** ~ **o.s. up** arrumar-se.

smash [smæʃ] ◇ *n* **-1.** [sound] estilhaço m **-2.** *inf* [car crash] acidente m **-3.** TENNIS cortada f. ◇ *vt* **-1.** [break into pieces] quebrar **-2.** [hit, crash] bater em; **to** ~ **one's fist into sthg** dar um soco em algo **-3.** *fig* [defeat] derrotar. ◇ *vi* **-1.** [break into pieces] quebrar-se **-2.** [crash, collide]: **to** ~ **through/into sthg** espatifar-se contra/em algo.

smashing ['smæʃɪŋ] *adj inf* fabuloso(sa), fenomenal.

smattering ['smætərɪŋ] *n* noções fpl: **to have a** ~ **of Welsh** falar meia dúzia de palavras de galês.

smear [smɪə'] ◇ *n* **-1.** [dirty mark] mancha f (de gordura) **-2.** MED esfregaço m **-3.** [slander] calúnia f. ◇ *vt* **-1.** [smudge - page] manchar; [- painting] borrar **-2.** [spread]: **to** ~ **sthg onto sthg** espalhar algo sobre algo; **to** ~ **sthg with sthg** untar algo com algo **-3.** [slander] caluniar.

smell [smel] (*pt & pp* **-ed** OR **smelt**) ◇ *n* **-1.** [odour] cheiro m, odor m **-2.** (U) [sense of smell] olfato m. ◇ *vt* **-1.** [notice an odour of] sentir cheiro de **-2.** [sniff at] cheirar **-3.** *fig* [sense] pressentir. ◇ *vi* **-1.** [have sense of smell] sentir cheiro **-2.** [have particular smell]: **to** ~ **of sthg** cheirar a algo; **to** ~ **like sthg** cheirar como algo; **to** ~ **good/bad** cheirar bem/mal **-3.** [smell unpleasantly] feder.

smelly ['smelɪ] (*compar* **-ier**, *superl* **-iest**) *adj* fedorento(ta).

smelt [smelt] ◇ *pt & pp* ⊳ **smell**. ◇ *vt* TECH fundir.

smile [smaɪl] ⬦ n sorriso m. ⬦ vi sorrir.

smiley ['smaɪlɪ] n COMPUT smiley m.

smirk [smɜːk] n sorriso m afetado.

smock [smɒk] n avental m, guarda-pó m.

smog [smɒg] n (U) bruma f.

smoke [sməʊk] ⬦ n (U) [from burning] fumaça f. ⬦ vt -1. [cigarette, cigar] fumar -2. [fish, meat, cheese] defumar. ⬦ vi -1. [chimney, engine, lamp] fumegar -2. [person] fumar.

smoked [sməʊkt] adj [food] defumado(da).

smoker ['sməʊkəʳ] n -1. [person who smokes] fumante mf -2. inf RAIL [compartment] vagão m para fumantes.

smokescreen ['sməʊkskriːn] n fig cortina f de fumaça.

smoke shop n US tabacaria f.

smoking ['sməʊkɪŋ] n (U): ~ is bad for you fumar não te faz bem; 'no ~' é proibido fumar'.

smoky ['sməʊkɪ] (compar -ier, superl -iest) adj -1. [full of smoke] enfumaçado(da) -2. [resembling smoke - taste] com gosto de fumaça; [- colour] cinzento(ta).

smolder vi US = smoulder.

smooth [smuːð] ⬦ adj -1. [surface - skin, fabric] macio(cia); [- stone] liso(sa); [- water, sea] calmo(ma) -2. CULIN [texture] uniforme -3. [flow, supply] fluido(da) -4. [pace] tranqüilo(la) -5. [taste, ride] suave -6. [engine] macio(cia) -7. pej [person, manner] lisonjeiro(ra) -8. [trouble-free] tranqüilo(la), sem problemas. ⬦ vt -1. [gen] alisar -2. [rub] passar.

  ➡ **smooth out** vt sep -1. [gen] alisar -2. fig [difficulties] resolver-se.

smother ['smʌðəʳ] vt -1. [cover thickly]: to ~ sthg in OR with sthg cobrir algo de algo -2. [suffocate] sufocar -3. [extinguish] abafar -4. fig [repress] reprimir -5. [suffocate with love] mimar demais.

smoulder UK, **smolder** US ['sməʊldəʳ] vi -1. [fire] fumegar -2. fig [feelings] arder.

SMS (abbr of short message service) n COMPUT SMS m, mensagens fpl curtas de texto.

smudge [smʌdʒ] ⬦ n [dirty mark] borrão m. ⬦ vt [spoil - by blurring] borrar; [- by dirtying] manchar.

smug [smʌg] (compar -ger, superl -gest) adj pej presunçoso(sa).

smuggle ['smʌgl] vt [across frontiers] contrabandear.

smuggler ['smʌgləʳ] n contrabandista mf.

smuggling ['smʌglɪŋ] n (U) contrabando m.

smutty ['smʌtɪ] (compar -ier, superl -iest) adj inf pej obsceno(na), indecente.

snack [snæk] ⬦ n lanche m.

snack bar n lanchonete f.

snag [snæg] (pt & pp -ged, cont -ging) ⬦ n -1. [small problem] dificuldade f -2. [in nail, tights, fabric] ponta f saliente. ⬦ vi: to ~ (on sthg) enganchar-se (em algo).

snail [sneɪl] n caracol m.

snail mail n correio m tradicional.

snake [sneɪk] n cobra f, serpente f.

snap [snæp] (pt & pp -ped, cont -ping) ⬦ adj atropelado(da), repentino(na). ⬦ n -1. [act or sound of snapping] estalo m -2. inf [photograph] foto f -3. [card game] jogo de cartas semelhante ao burro mecânico. ⬦ vt -1. [break] partir (em dois) -2. [make cracking sound with]: to ~ sthg open/shut abrir/fechar algo com um golpe; to ~ one's fingers estalar os dedos -3. [speak sharply] falar bruscamente. ⬦ vi -1. [break] partir (em dois) -2. [attempt to bite]: to ~ (at sb/sthg) tentar morder (alguém/algo) -3. [speak sharply]: to ~ (at sb) ficar bravo(va) (com alguém).

  ➡ **snap up** vt sep não deixar escapar.

snap fastener n esp US botão m de pressão.

snappy ['snæpɪ] (compar -ier, superl -iest) adj inf -1. [stylish] chique -2. [quick] rápido(da); **make it ~!** anda logo!

snapshot ['snæpʃɒt] n instantânea f.

snare [sneəʳ] ⬦ n armadilha f. ⬦ vt pegar numa armadilha.

snarl [snɑːl] ⬦ n rosnado m. ⬦ vi -1. [animal] rosnar -2. [person] resmungar.

snatch [snætʃ] ⬦ n [fragment] trecho m. ⬦ vt [grab] agarrar.

sneak [sniːk] (US pt snuck) ⬦ n UK inf mexeriqueiro m, -ra f. ⬦ vt levar escondido(da); to ~ a look at sb/sthg espiar alguém/algo. ⬦ vi [move quietly] esgueirar-se.

sneakers ['sniːkəz] npl US tênis m inv.

sneaky ['sniːkɪ] (compar -ier, superl -iest) adj inf sorrateiro(ra).

sneer [snɪəʳ] ⬦ n escárnio m. ⬦ vi [smile unpleasantly] sorrir com escárnio.

sneeze [sniːz] ⬦ n espirro m. ⬦ vi espirrar.

snide [snaɪd] adj sarcástico(ca).

sniff [snɪf] ⬦ vt -1. [smell] fungar -2. [drug] cheirar. ⬦ vi [to clear nose] assoar.

snigger ['snɪgəʳ] ⬦ n escárnio m. ⬦ vi rir por dentro.

snip [snɪp] (*pt* & *pp* **-ped**, *cont* **-ping**) ◇ *n inf* [bargain] pechincha *f.* ◇ *vt* [cut] cortar (em pedaços).

sniper ['snaɪpə'] *n* franco-atirador *m*, -ra *f.*

snippet ['snɪpɪt] *n* fragmento *m.*

snivel ['snɪvl] (*UK pt* & *pp* **-led**, *cont* **-ling**, *US pt* & *pp* **-ed**, *cont* **-ing**) *vi* choramingar.

snob [snɒb] *n* esnobe *mf.*

snobbish ['snɒbɪʃ], **snobby** ['snɒbɪ] (*compar* **-ier**, *superl* **-iest**) *adj* esnobe.

snooker ['snu:kə'] *n* (*U*) snooker *m.*

snoop [snu:p] *vi inf* bisbilhotar.

snooty ['snu:tɪ] (*compar* **-ier**, *superl* **-iest**) *adj* presunçoso(sa).

snooze [snu:z] ◇ *n* cochilo *m*, soneca *f*; **to have a ~** tirar uma soneca OR um cochilo. ◇ *vi* cochilar.

snore [snɔ:'] ◇ *n* ronco *m.* ◇ *vi* roncar.

snoring ['snɔ:rɪŋ] *n* (*U*) roncos *mpl.*

snorkel ['snɔ:kl] *n* (tubo *m*) snorkel *m.*

snort [snɔ:t] ◇ *n* bufo *m.* ◇ *vi* bufar.

snout [snaʊt] *n* focinho *m.*

snow [snəʊ] ◇ *n* (*U*) neve *f.* ◇ *v impers* nevar.

snowball ['snəʊbɔ:l] ◇ *n* bola *f* de neve. ◇ *vi fig* [increase rapidly] crescer como bola de neve.

snowboard ['snəʊbɔ:d] *n* snowboard *m.*

snowboarding ['snəʊbɔ:dɪŋ] *n* snowboard *m*; **to go ~** praticar snowboard.

snowbound ['snəʊbaʊnd] *adj* bloqueado(da) pela neve.

snowdrift ['snəʊdrɪft] *n* monte *m* de neve.

snowdrop ['snəʊdrɒp] *n* campainha-branca *f.*

snowfall ['snəʊfɔ:l] *n* **-1.** [fall of snow] nevada *f* **-2.** [amount of snow over time] quantidade *f* de neve.

snowflake ['snəʊfleɪk] *n* floco *m* de neve.

snowman ['snəʊmæn] (*pl* **-men** [-men]) *n* boneco *m* de neve.

snowplough *UK*, **snowplow** *US* ['snəʊplaʊ] *n* [vehicle] limpa-neve *m.*

snowshoe ['snəʊʃu:] *n* raquete *f* de neve.

snowstorm ['snəʊstɔ:m] *n* nevasca *f.*

SNP (*abbr of* **Scottish National Party**) *n* partido nacional escocês que prega a independência da Grã-Bretanha.

Snr, snr (*abbr of* **senior**) sênior.

snub [snʌb] (*pt* & *pp* **-bed**, *cont* **-bing**) ◇ *n* repulsa *f.* ◇ *vt* desprezar.

snuck [snʌk] *pt US* ▷ **sneak**.

snuff [snʌf] *n* (*U*) [tobacco] rapé *m.*

snug [snʌg] (*compar* **-ger**, *superl* **-gest**) *adj* **-1.** [person, feeling] agradável **-2.** [place] confortável **-3.** [close-fitting] cômodo(da).

snuggle ['snʌgl] *vi* aconchegar-se; **to ~ down** cobrir-se (com coberta).

so [səʊ] ◇ *adv* **-1.** [emphasizing degree] tão; **don't be ~ stupid!** não seja tão idiota!; **it's ~ difficult (that ...)** é tão difícil (que ...); **~ much** tanto(ta); **~ many** tantos(tas). **-2.** [referring back]: **I don't think ~** acho que não; **I'm afraid ~** receio que sim; **~ you knew already** então você já sabia; **if ~** nesse caso. **-3.** [also] também; **~ do I** eu também. **-4.** [in this way] deste modo, assim. **-5.** [expressing agreement]: **~ there is** pois é, é verdade. **-6.** [in phrases]: **or ~** mais ou menos; **~ as** para; **~ that** para. ◇ *conj* **-1.** [therefore] por isso; **I'm away next week ~ I won't be there** viajo na semana que vem, portanto não estarei lá. **-2.** [summarizing] então; **~ what have you been up to?** então, o que é que você tem feito? **-3.** [in phrases]: **~ what?** *inf* daí?; **~ there!** *inf* pronto!, nada a fazer!

soak [səʊk] ◇ *vt* **-1.** [leave immersed] pôr de molho **-2.** [wet thoroughly] ensopar; **to be ~ed with sthg** estar ensopado(da) de algo. ◇ *vi* **-1.** [become thoroughly wet]: **to leave sthg to ~**, **let sthg ~** deixar algo de molho **-2.** [spread]: **to ~ into sthg** espalhar-se por algo; **to ~ through (sthg)** infiltrar-se em algo.

➤ **soak up** *vt sep* [liquid] absorver.

soaking ['səʊkɪŋ] *adj* ensopado(da).

so-and-so *n inf* **-1.** [to replace a name] fulano *m*, -na *f* **-2.** [annoying person] filho *m*, -lha *f* da mãe.

soap [səʊp] *n* **-1.** (*U*) [for washing] sabão *m* **-2.** *TV* novela *f.*

soap dish *n* saboneteira *f.*

soap flakes *npl* sabão *m* em flocos.

soap opera *n* novela *f.*

soap powder *n* (*U*) sabão *m* em pó.

soapy ['səʊpɪ] (*compar* **-ier**, *superl* **-iest**) *adj* **-1.** [full of soap] ensaboado(da) **-2.** [resembling soap] de sabão.

soar [sɔ:'] *vi* **-1.** [bird] levantar vôo **-2.** [rise into the sky] subir **-3.** [increase rapidly] aumentar rapidamente.

sob [sɒb] (*pt* & *pp* **-bed**, *cont* **-bing**) ◇ *n* soluço *m.* ◇ *vi* [cry] soluçar.

sober ['səʊbə'] *adj* **-1.** [not drunk] sóbrio(bria) **-2.** [serious] sério(ria) **-3.** [plain] simples.

➤ **sober up** *vi* ficar sóbrio(bria).

sobering ['səʊbərɪŋ] *adj* que faz refletir.

so-called [-kɔ:ld] *adj* **-1.** [misleadingly

named] suposto(ta) **-2.** [widely known as] chamado(da).

soccer ['sɒkə^r] *n (U)* futebol *m.*

sociable ['səʊʃəbl] *adj* sociável.

social ['səʊʃl] *adj* social.

social club *n* clube *m* social.

socialism ['səʊʃəlɪzm] *n (U)* socialismo *m.*

socialist ['səʊʃəlɪst] <> *adj* socialista. <> *n* socialista *mf.*

socialize, -ise ['səʊʃəlaɪz] *vi*: **to ~ (with sb)** socializar-se (com alguém).

social security *n (U)* previdência *f* social.

social services *npl* assistência *f* social.

social worker *n* assistente *mf* social.

society [sə'saɪətɪ] *(pl* -ies*)* *n* sociedade *f.*

sociology [,səʊsɪ'ɒlədʒɪ] *n (U)* sociologia *f.*

sock [sɒk] *n* meia *f.*

socket ['sɒkɪt] *n* **-1.** *ELEC* tomada *f* **-2.** [de lâmpada] soquete *m* **-3.** [*ANAT* - of arm, hip-bone] concavidade *f*; [- of eye] órbita *f.*

sod [sɒd] *n* **-1.** [of turf] torrão *m* **-2.** *vinf* [person] sujeito *m.*

soda ['səʊdə] *n* **-1.** [gen] soda *f* **-2.** *US* [fizzy drink] refrigerante *m.*

soda water *n (U)* soda *f*, água *f* com gás.

sodden ['sɒdn] *adj* encharcado(da).

sodium ['səʊdɪəm] *n (U)* sódio *m.*

sofa ['səʊfə] *n* sofá *m.*

Sofia ['səʊfjə] *n* Sofia.

soft [sɒft] *adj* **-1.** [gen] mole **-2.** [to touch] macio(cia) **-3.** [gentle] suave **-4.** [kind, caring] meigo(ga), bondoso(sa) **-5.** [not strict] flexível.

softball *n SPORT* espécie de beisebol que se joga com uma bola mais macia e maior.

soft drink *n* **-1.** [fruit juice] refresco *m* **-2.** [fizzy drink] refrigerante *m.*

soften ['sɒfn] <> *vt* **-1.** [substance] suavizar **-2.** [blow, impact, effect] amortecer **-3.** [attitude] enternecer. <> *vi* **-1.** [substance] amaciar **-2.** [attitude] amolecer **-3.** [eyes, voice, expression] suavizar.

softhearted [,sɒft'hɑːtɪd] *adj* de bom coração.

softly ['sɒftlɪ] *adv* **-1.** [gently, without violence] com delicadeza **-2.** [quietly] suavemente **-3.** [dimly] tenuamente **-4.** [fondly] carinhosamente.

soft return *n COMPUT* quebra *f* de linha condicional.

soft-spoken *adj* de voz suave.

software ['sɒftweə^r] *n (U)* *COMPUT* software *m.*

soggy ['sɒgɪ] *(compar* -ier, *superl* -iest*)* *adj* empapado(da), encharcado(da).

soil [sɔɪl] <> *n* **-1.** [earth] terra *f*, solo *m* **-2.** *fig* [territory] solo *m.* <> *vt* [dirty] sujar.

soiled [sɔɪld] *adj* sujo(ja).

solace ['sɒləs] *n literary* consolo *m.*

solar ['səʊlə^r] *adj* solar.

solar energy *n* energia *f* solar.

solar power *n* energia *f* solar.

sold [səʊld] *pt & pp* ⊳ **sell.**

solder ['səʊldə^r] <> *n (U)* solda *f.* <> *vt* soldar.

soldier ['səʊldʒə^r] *n* soldado(da).

sold out *adj* esgotado(da).

sole [səʊl] *(pl sense 2 only inv OR* -s*)* <> *adj* **-1.** [only] único(ca) **-2.** [exclusive] exclusivo(va). <> *n* **-1.** [of foot] sola *f* **-2.** [fish] linguado *m.*

solemn ['sɒləm] *adj* solene.

solicit [sə'lɪsɪt] <> *vt fml* [request] solicitar. <> *vi* [prostitute] oferecer seus serviços.

solicitor [sə'lɪsɪtə^r] *n UK* solicitador *m*, -ra *f.*

solid ['sɒlɪd] <> *adj* **-1.** [gen] sólido(da) **-2.** [of a single substance] maciço(ça) **-3.** [reliable, respectable] coerente **-4.** [unbroken, continuous] ininterrupto(ta). <> *adv*: **to be packed ~** estar superlotado(da). <> *n* [not liquid or gas] sólido *m.*
➥ **solids** *npl* [food] sólidos *mpl*; **she can't eat ~s** ela não pode comer nada sólido.

solidarity [,sɒlɪ'dærətɪ] *n (U)* solidariedade *f.*

solitaire [,sɒlɪ'teə^r] *n* **-1.** [jewel] solitário *m* **-2.** [card game] paciência *f.*

solitary ['sɒlɪtrɪ] *adj* **-1.** [gen] solitário(-ria) **-2.** [single] isolado(da).

solitary confinement *n (U)* solitária *f.*

solitude ['sɒlɪtjuːd] *n (U)* solidão *f.*

solo ['səʊləʊ] *(pl* -s*)* <> *adj* **-1.** *MUS* solo *inv* **-2.** [attempt, flight] único(ca). <> *n* *MUS* solo *m.* <> *adv* **-1.** *MUS* em solo **-2.** [fly, climb] sozinho(nha).

soloist ['səʊləʊɪst] *n* solista *mf.*

soluble ['sɒljʊbl] *adj* **-1.** [substance] solúvel **-2.** [problem] solucionável.

solution [sə'luːʃn] *n* **-1.** [to problem, puzzle]: **~ (to sthg)** solução *f* (para algo) **-2.** [liquid] solução *f.*

solve [sɒlv] *vt* resolver.

solvent ['sɒlvənt] <> *adj FIN* solvente. <> *n* [substance] solvente *m.*

Somalia [sə'mɑːlɪə] *n* Somália.

sombre *UK*, **somber** *US* ['sɒmbə^r] *adj* **-1.** [person, mood] lúgubre **-2.** [colour, place] sombrio(bria).

some [sʌm] <> *adj* **-1.** [certain, large amount of] algum (alguma); **~ meat** um pouco de carne; **~ money** um pouco de dinheiro; **I had ~ difficulty getting here** tive algumas dificuldades para chegar aqui. **- 2.** [certain, large number of] alguns (algumas); **~ sweets** alguns doces; **~ people** algumas pessoas; **I've known him for ~ years** já o conheço há alguns anos. **- 3.** [not all] alguns (algumas); **~ jobs are better paid than others** alguns empregos são mais bem pagos que outros. **- 4.** [in imprecise statements] um (uma) ... qualquer; **~ woman phoned** telefonou uma mulher. ◇ *pron* **-1.** [certain amount] algum *m*, alguma *f*, parte *f*; **can I have ~ ?** posso ficar com uma parte?; **~ of the money** algum dinheiro, parte do dinheiro. **- 2.** [certain number] alguns *mpl*, algumas *fpl*; **can I have ~ ?** posso ficar com alguns?; **~ (of them) left early** alguns (deles) foram embora cedo. ◇ *adv* [approximately] aproximadamente; **there were ~ 7,000 people there** havia umas 7.000 pessoas.

somebody ['sʌmbədɪ] *pron* alguém.

someday ['sʌmdeɪ] *adv* algum dia.

somehow ['sʌmhaʊ], **someway** *US* ['sʌmweɪ] *adv* **-1.** [by some action] de alguma maneira **- 2.** [for some reason] por alguma razão; **~ I don't think he'll come** tenho a impressão de que ele não virá.

someone ['sʌmwʌn] *pron* = somebody.

someplace *adv US* = somewhere.

somersault ['sʌməsɔːlt] ◇ *n* salto *m* mortal. ◇ *vi* dar um salto mortal.

something ['sʌmθɪŋ] ◇ *pron* **-1.** algo, alguma coisa; **or ~** *inf* ou (qualquer) coisa parecida **- 2.** *phr*: **it's really ~!** é demais! ◇ *adv* [in approximations]: **~ like** uns(umas), qualquer coisa como.

sometime ['sʌmtaɪm] *adv*: **~ in June** em junho.

sometimes ['sʌmtaɪmz] *adv* às OR por vezes.

someway *adv US* = somehow.

somewhat ['sʌmwɒt] *adv* um tanto.

somewhere *UK* ['sʌmweəʳ], **someplace** *US* ['sʌmpleɪs] *adv* **-1.** [unknown place] em algum lugar, em alguma parte **- 2.** [specific place] a alguma parte **- 3.** [in approximations]: **~ around** OR **between** aproximadamente.

son [sʌn] *n* filho *m*.

song [sɒŋ] *n* **-1.** [piece of music] música *f*; **- 2.** (U) [act of singing]: **they burst into ~** desataram a cantar **- 3.** [of bird] canto *m*.

sonic ['sɒnɪk] *adj* sônico(ca).

son-in-law (*pl* sons-in-law OR son-in-laws) *n* genro *m*.

sonnet ['sɒnɪt] *n* soneto *m*.

sonny ['sʌnɪ] *n inf* filhinho *m*.

soon [suːn] *adv* **-1.** [in a short time] logo **- 2.** [early] cedo; **how ~ can you finish it?** para quando você consegue terminar?; **as ~ as** assim que; **as ~ as possible** o quanto antes.

sooner ['suːnəʳ] *adv* **-1.** [earlier] mais cedo; **no ~ did he arrive than ...** ele tinha acabado de chegar quando ...; **~ or later** mais cedo ou mais tarde; **the ~ the better** quanto mais cedo, melhor **- 2.** [expressing preference]: **I'd ~ ...** preferiria ...

soot [sʊt] *n* (U) fuligem *f*.

soothe [suːð] *vt* **-1.** [relieve] aliviar **- 2.** [calm] acalmar.

sophisticated [səˈfɪstɪkeɪtɪd] *adj* **-1.** [stylish] sofisticado(da) **- 2.** [intelligent] inteligente **- 3.** [complicated] complicado(da).

sophomore ['sɒfəmɔːʳ] *n US* estudante do segundo ano de faculdade.

soporific [ˌsɒpəˈrɪfɪk] *adj* soporífero(ra).

sopping ['sɒpɪŋ] *adj*: **~ (wet)** encharcado(da).

soppy ['sɒpɪ] (*compar* -ier, *superl* -iest) *adj inf pej* sentimentalóide.

soprano [səˈprɑːnəʊ] (*pl* -s) *n* **-1.** [person] soprano *mf* **- 2.** [voice] soprano *f*.

sorbet ['sɔːbeɪ] *n* sorbet *m*.

sorcerer ['sɔːsərəʳ] *n* feiticeiro *m*.

sorceress *n* feiticeira *f*.

sordid ['sɔːdɪd] *adj* sórdido(da).

sore [sɔːʳ] ◇ *adj* **-1.** [painful] dolorido(da); **a ~ throat** uma dor de garganta **- 2.** *US inf* [angry] zangado(da). ◇ *n MED* inflamação *f*.

sorely ['sɔːlɪ] *adv literary* imensamente.

sorrow ['sɒrəʊ] *n* **-1.** (U) [feeling of sadness] mágoa *f* **- 2.** [cause of sadness] desgosto *m*.

sorry ['sɒrɪ] (*compar* -ier, *superl* -iest) ◇ *adj* **-1.** [expressing apology]: **I'm ~** desculpe; **to be ~ about sthg** lamentar algo; **to be ~ for sthg** estar arrependido(da) por algo; **to be ~ to do sthg** desculpar-se por fazer algo **- 2.** [expressing disappointment]: **to be ~ (that)** lamentar que; **to be ~ about sthg** ficar sentido(da) por algo **- 3.** [expressing regret]: **I'm ~ to have to say that ...** lamento ter que dizer que ...; **to be ~ to do sthg** estar triste por fazer algo **- 4.** [expressing sympathy]: **to be** OR **feel ~ for sb** estar com/sentir pena de alguém **- 5.** [expressing polite disagreement]: **I'm ~, but I think that ...** me desculpa, mas eu acho que ... **- 6.** [poor, pitiable] lamentável. ◇ *excl* **-1.** [expressing apology] desculpe! **- 2.** [asking for repetition] como! **- 3.**

[to correct o.s.]: **a boy, ~, a man** um garoto, quer dizer, um homem.

sort [sɔːt] ⬦ *n* **-1.** [gen] tipo *m*; **a ~ of** um tipo de, uma espécie de **-2.** [act of sorting out] escolha *f*. ⬦ *vt* [classify, separate] classificar.

➨ **sort of** *adv* [rather] mais ou menos.

➨ **sort out** *vt sep* **-1.** [into groups] classificar **-2.** [tidy up] pôr em ordem **-3.** [solve] resolver **-4.** [work out] concluir.

sorting office ['sɔːtɪŋ-] *n* centro *f* de triagem.

SOS (*abbr of* **save our souls**) *n* SOS *f*.

so-so *inf adj, adv* mais ou menos.

sought [sɔːt] *pt & pp* ⮕ **seek**.

soul [səʊl] *n* **-1.** [gen] alma *f* **-2.** [emotional depth] sentimento *m* **-3.** [perfect example] exemplo *m* perfeito **-4.** (*U*) [music] (música *f*) soul *m*.

soul-destroying [-dɪ,strɔɪɪŋ] *adj* [boring] massante; [discouraging] desmoralizador(ra).

soulful ['səʊlfʊl] *adj* cheio (cheia) de sentimentos.

sound [saʊnd] ⬦ *adj* **-1.** [healthy] sadio(dia) **-2.** [sturdy] sólido(da) **-3.** [reliable] confiável, seguro(ra) **-4.** [thorough] completo(ta). ⬦ *adv*: **to be ~ asleep** estar num sono profundo. ⬦ *n* **-1.** [particular noise] barulho *m* **-2.** (*U*) [in general] som *m* **-3.** (*U*) [volume] volume *m* **-4.** [impression, idea] tom *m*. ⬦ *vt* [alarm, bell, horn] tocar. ⬦ *vi* **-1.** [make a noise] fazer barulho; **to ~ like sthg** soar como algo **-2.** [seem] parecer; **to ~ like sthg** parecer algo.

➨ **sound out** *vt sep*: **to ~ sb out (on** OR **about sthg)** sondar alguém(sobre algo).

sound barrier *n* barreira *f* do som.

sound card *n* COMPUT placa *f* de som.

sound effects *npl* efeitos *mpl* sonoros.

sounding ['saʊndɪŋ] *n* **-1.** NAUT [measurement] prumada *f* **-2.** *fig* [investigation] sondagem *f*.

soundly ['saʊndlɪ] *adv* **-1.** [thoroughly] completamente **-2.** [deeply] profundamente.

soundproof ['saʊndpruːf] *adj* à prova de som.

soundtrack ['saʊndtræk] *n* trilha *f* sonora.

soup [suːp] *n* sopa *f*, caldo *m*.

soup plate *n* prato *m* fundo.

soup spoon *n* colher *f* de sopa.

sour [saʊəʳ] ⬦ *adj* **-1.** [acidic] ácido(da) **-2.** [milk] azedo(da) **-3.** [ill-tempered] mal-humorado(da). ⬦ *vt & vi* [person, relationship] azedar.

source [sɔːs] *n* **-1.** [gen] fonte *f* **-2.** [cause] origem *f* **-3.** [of river] nascente *f*.

sour grapes *n* (*U*) *inf* inveja *f* pura.

south [saʊθ] ⬦ *adj* sul. ⬦ *adv* para o sul; **~ of** ao sul de. ⬦ *n* **-1.** [direction] sul *m* **-2.** [region]: **the ~** o sul.

South Africa *n* África *f* do Sul.

South African ⬦ *adj* sul-africano(-na). ⬦ *n* [person] sul-africano *m*, -na *f*.

South America *n* América *f* do Sul.

South American ⬦ *adj* sul-americano(na). ⬦ *n* [person] sul-americano *m*, -na *f*.

south-east ⬦ *adj* sudeste. ⬦ *adv* para o sudeste; **~ of** a sudeste de. ⬦ *n* **-1.** [direction] sudeste *m* **-2.** [region]: **the ~** o sudeste.

southerly ['sʌðəlɪ] *adj* **-1.** [in the south] ao sul **-2.** [towards the south] para o sul **-3.** [from the south] do sul.

southern ['sʌðən] *adj* sulista.

South Korea *n* Coréia *f* do Sul.

South Pole *n*: **the ~** o Pólo Sul.

southward ['saʊθwəd] ⬦ *adj* sul. ⬦ *adv* = **southwards**.

southwards ['saʊθwədz] *adv* para o sul.

south-west ⬦ *adj* sudoeste. ⬦ *adv* para o sudoeste; **~ of** a sudoeste de. ⬦ *n* **-1.** [direction] sudoeste *m* **-2.** [region]: **the ~** o sudoeste.

souvenir [,suːvə'nɪəʳ] *n* suvenir *m*, lembrança *f*.

sovereign ['sɒvrɪn] ⬦ *adj* [state, territory] soberano(na). ⬦ *n* **-1.** [ruler] soberano *m*, -na *f* **-2.** [coin] soberano *m*.

soviet *n* soviético(ca).

➨ **Soviet** ⬦ *adj* soviético *m*, -ca *f*. ⬦ *n* [person] soviético *m*, -ca *f*.

Soviet Union *n*: **the (former) ~** a (antiga) União Soviética.

sow[1] [saʊ] (*pt* **-ed**, *pp* **sown** OR **-ed**) *vt* semear.

sow[2] [saʊ] *n* [pig] porca *f*.

sown [səʊn] *pp* ⮕ **sow[1]**.

soya [sɔɪə] *n* (*U*) soja *f*.

soy(a) bean ['sɔɪ(ə)-] *n* grão *m* de soja.

spa [spɑː] *n* **-1.** [mineral spring] termas *fpl* **-2.** [for health care] spa *m*.

space [speɪs] ⬦ *n* **-1.** [gen] espaço *m* **-2.** [gap] lugar *m*, espaço *m* **-3.** [period of time] intervalo *m* **-4.** [seat, place] lugar *m*. ⬦ *comp* espacial. ⬦ *vt* espaçar.

➨ **space out** *vt sep* [arrange] espaçar.

spacecraft ['speɪskrɑːft] (*pl inv*) *n* espaçonave *f*.

spaceman ['speɪsmæn] (*pl* **-men** [-men]) *n inf* [astronaut] astronauta *m*.

spaceship ['speɪsʃɪp] *n* nave *f* espacial, astronave *f*.

space shuttle *n* ônibus *m inv* espacial.

spacesuit ['speɪssu:t] *n* roupa *f* espacial.

spacing ['speɪsɪŋ] *n (U)* TYPO espaçamento *m*.

spacious ['speɪʃəs] *adj* espaçoso(sa).

spade [speɪd] *n* **-1.** [tool] pá *f* **-2.** [playing card] espada *f*.

➤ **spades** *npl* espadas *fpl*.

spaghetti [spə'getɪ] *n (U)* espaguete *m*.

Spain [speɪn] *n* Espanha *f*.

spam [spæm] (*pt* & *pp* **-med**, *cont* **-ming**) COMPUT ⋄ *n* spam *m*. ⋄ *vt* enviar spam para.

span [spæn] (*pt* & *pp* **-ned**, *cont* **-ning**) ⋄ *pt* ▷ **spin**. ⋄ *n* **-1.** [in. time] período *m*; **concentration ~** tempo *m* de concentração **-2.** [range] gama *f* **-3.** [of hand] palmo *m* **-4.** [of arms] braçada *f* **-5.** [of wings] envergadura *f* **-6.** [of bridge, arch] extensão *f*. ⋄ *vt* **-1.** [encompass] cobrir um período de **-2.** [cross] atravessar, cruzar.

Spaniard ['spænjəd] *n* espanhol *m*, -la *f*.

spaniel ['spænjəl] *n* cocker *m* spaniel.

Spanish ['spænɪʃ] ⋄ *adj* espanhol(la). ⋄ *n* [language] espanhol *m*. ⋄ *npl*: **the ~** os espanhóis.

spank [spæŋk] *vt* dar palmadas em.

spanner ['spænəʳ] *n* chave *f* inglesa.

spar [spɑ:ʳ] (*pt* & *pp* **-red**, *cont* **-ring**) *vi* BOXING treinar boxe.

spare [speəʳ] ⋄ *adj* **-1.** [surplus] sobressalente, de sobra; **have you got a ~ pencil?** você tem um lápis sobrando? **-2.** [free] livre. ⋄ *n* [surplus object] sobressalente *mf*. ⋄ *vt* **-1.** [put aside, make available] dispor de; **to have sthg to ~** [extra] ter algo de sobra **-2.** [not harm] preservar **-3.** [economize] poupar; **to ~ no expense** não poupar despesas **-4.** [save, protect from]: **to ~ sb sthg** poupar alguém de algo.

spare time *n (U)* tempo *m* livre.

sparing ['speərɪŋ] *adj*: **to be ~ with** OR **of sthg** ser econômico(ca) em algo.

sparingly ['speərɪŋlɪ] *adv* com moderação.

spark [spɑ:k] *n* **-1.** [from fire] fagulha *f* **-2.** [from electricity] faísca *f* **-3.** *fig* [of interest, humour *etc*.] lampejo *m*.

sparking plug ['spɑ:kɪŋ-] *n* UK = spark plug.

sparkle [spɑ:kl] ⋄ *n* [gen] brilho *m*. ⋄ *vi* [gen] brilhar.

sparkling *adj* **-1.** [mineral water] com gás, gaseificado(da) **-2.** [wit] brilhante.

sparkling wine ['spɑ:klɪŋ-] *n* vinho *m* espumante.

spark plug *n* vela *f* (*de ignição*).

sparrow ['spærəʊ] *n* pardal *m*.

sparse [spɑ:s] *adj* esparso(sa).

spasm ['spæzm] *n* **-1.** MED [muscular contraction] espasmo *m* **-2.** [fit] acesso *m*.

spastic ['spæstɪk] MED *n* espasmofílico *m*, -ca *f*.

spat [spæt] *pt* & *pp* ▷ **spit**.

spate [speɪt] *n* série *f*, sucessão *f*.

spatter ['spætəʳ] *vt* & *vi* respingar.

spawn [spɔ:n] ⋄ *n (U)* [of frogs, fish] ovas *fpl*. ⋄ *vt* *fig* [produce] gerar. ⋄ *vi* ZOOL desovar.

speak [spi:k] (*pt* **spoke**, *pp* **spoken**) ⋄ *vt* **-1.** [say] dizer **-2.** [language] falar. ⋄ *vi* **-1.** [say words] falar; **to ~ to** OR **with sb** falar com alguém; **to ~ to sb about sthg** falar com alguém sobre algo; **to ~ about sb/sthg** falar sobre alguém/algo **-2.** [make a speech] discursar; **to ~ to sb** discursar para alguém; **to ~ on sthg** falar OR discursar sobre algo **-3.** [in giving an opinion]: **generally ~ing** falando em termos gerais; **personally ~ing** pessoalmente falando.

➤ **so to speak** *adv* por assim dizer.

➤ **speak for** *vt fus* [represent] falar em nome de.

➤ **speak up** *vi* **-1.** [say something] falar claro; **to ~ up for sb/sthg** sair em defesa de alguém/algo **-2.** [speak louder] falar mais alto.

speaker ['spi:kəʳ] *n* **-1.** [person talking, of a language] falante *mf* **-2.** [in lecture] orador *m*, -ra *f*, conferencista *mf* **-3.** [loudspeaker] alto-falante *m* **-4.** [in stereo system] caixa *f* de som.

➤ **Speaker** *n* UK [in House of Commons] Presidente *mf* da Câmara dos Comuns.

spear [spɪəʳ] ⋄ *n* [weapon] lança *f*. ⋄ *vt* lancear.

spearhead ['spɪəhed] ⋄ *n* ponta-de-lança *f*. ⋄ *vt* encabeçar.

spec [spek] *n* UK *inf*: **to buy sthg on ~** comprar algo sem garantia; **to go on ~** ir sem ter feito reserva.

special ['speʃl] *adj* especial.

special delivery *n (U)* [service] entrega *f* especial.

specialist ['speʃəlɪst] ⋄ *adj* especializado(da). ⋄ *n* [expert] especialista *mf*.

speciality [,speʃɪ'ælətɪ] (*pl* **-ies**), **specialty** US ['speʃltɪ] (*pl* **-ies**) *n* especialidade *f*.

specialize, -ise ['speʃəlaɪz] *vi* especializar-se; **to ~ in sthg** especializar-se em algo.

specially ['speʃəlɪ] *adv* **-1.** [on purpose, specifically] especialmente **-2.** [really] realmente; **do you want to go? - not ~** quer ir? - na verdade não.

specialty n US = speciality.

species ['spi:ʃi:z] (pl inv) n espécie f.

specific [spə'sıfık] adj [particular, precise] específico(ca); ~ **to sb/sthg** específico(ca) de alguém/algo.

specifically [spə'sıfıklı] adv especificamente.

specify ['spesıfaı] (pt & pp -ied) vt especificar.

specimen ['spesımən] n -1. [example] espécime m, exemplar m -2. [sample] amostra f.

speck [spek] n -1. [small stain] mancha f pequena -2. [small particle] partícula f.

speckled ['spekld] adj manchado(da); ~ **with sthg** pintado(da) de algo.

specs [speks] npl inf [glasses] óculos m inv.

spectacle ['spektəkl] n -1. [sight] visão f -2. [event] espetáculo m.
➡ **spectacles** npl UK [glasses] óculos m inv.

spectacular [spek'tækjələʳ] adj espetacular.

spectator [spek'teıtəʳ] n espectador m, -ra f.

spectre UK, **specter** US ['spektəʳ] n -1. fml [ghost] espectro m -2. fig [frightening prospect]: **the ~ of famine** o fantasma da fome.

spectrum ['spektrəm] (pl -tra [-trə]) n -1. PHYS espectro m -2. fig [range] gama f.

speculation [ˌspekjʊ'leıʃn] n especulação f.

sped [sped] pt & pp ▷ speed.

speech [spi:tʃ] n -1. [gen] fala f -2. [manner of speaking] maneira f de falar -4. (U) [dialect] dialeto m, maneira f de falar -5. GRAMM discurso m.

speechless ['spi:tʃlıs] adj: **to be ~ (with sthg)** ficar emudecido(da) (de algo).

speed [spi:d] (pt & pp -ed OR sped) ◇ n -1. [rate, pace] velocidade f; **at ~ a** grande velocidade -2. (U) [rapid rate] rapidez f -3. [gear] marcha f. ◇ vi -1. [move fast]: **to ~ (along/away/by)** ir/acelerar/passar a toda velocidade -2. AUT [go too fast] exceder a velocidade.
➡ **speed up** ◇ vt sep acelerar. ◇ vi acelerar.

speedboat ['spi:dbəʊt] n lancha f.

speed-dial button n [on phone, fax] tecla m de discagem rápida.

speeding ['spi:dıŋ] n (U) excesso m de velocidade.

speed limit n limite m de velocidade.

speedometer [spı'dɒmıtəʳ] n velocímetro m.

speedway ['spi:dweı] n -1. SPORT corrida f de motos -2. US [road] pista f de corrida.

speedy ['spi:dı] (compar -ier, superl -iest) adj rápido(da).

spell [spel] (UK pt & pp **spelt** OR -ed, US pt & pp -ed) ◇ n -1. [period of time] período m -2. [enchantment] feitiço m, encanto m -3. [magic words] palavras fpl mágicas. ◇ vt -1. [write] soletrar -2. fig [signify] significar. ◇ vi escrever corretamente.
➡ **spell out** vt sep -1. [read aloud] soletrar -2. [explain]: **to ~ sthg out (for** OR **to sb)** explicar algo em detalhes (para alguém).

spellbound ['spelbaʊnd] adj encantado(da).

spellcheck ['speltʃek] vt COMPUT passar o corretor ortográfico em.

spellchecker ['speltʃekəʳ] n COMPUT corretor m ortográfico.

spelling ['spelıŋ] n ortografia f.

spelt [spelt] pt & pp UK ▷ spell.

spend [spend] (pt & pp spent) vt -1. [pay out] gastar; **to ~ sthg on sb/sthg** gastar algo em alguém/algo -2. [time, life] passar -3. [energy] gastar.

spendthrift ['spendθrıft] n perdulário m, -ria f.

spent [spent] ◇ pt & pp ▷ spend. ◇ adj [consumed, burned out - matches, ammunition] usado(da); [- force, patience, energy] esgotado(da).

sperm [spɜ:m] (pl inv OR -s) n esperma m.

spew [spju:] ◇ vt [cause to flow, spread] expelir, cuspir. ◇ vi [flow, spread]: **to ~ (out) from sthg** lançar-se (para fora) de algo; **flames ~ed out of the volcano** o vulcão cuspia chamas.

sphere [sfıəʳ] n esfera f.

spice [spaıs] n tempero m.

spick-and-span [ˌspıkən'spæn] adj asseado(da).

spicy ['spaısı] (compar -ier, superl -iest) adj picante.

spider ['spaıdəʳ] n aranha f.

spike [spaık] ◇ n -1. [on railings] prego m -2. [on shoe] cravo m -3. [on plant] espigão m -4. [of hair] corte m escovinha. ◇ vt reforçar com mais álcool.

spill [spıl] (UK pt & pp **spilt** OR -ed, US pt & pp -ed) ◇ vt derramar. ◇ vi -1. [liquid] derramar; **the wine ~ed all over the carpet** o vinho esparramou por todo o carpete -2. [salt, sugar etc.] esparramar.

spilt [spılt] pt & pp UK ▷ spill.

spin [spın] (pt **span** OR **spun**, pp **spun**, cont -ning) ◇ n -1. [turn] giro m, volta f -2. AERON parafuso m -3. inf [in car] volta f -4. SPORT [on ball] efeito m. ◇ vt -1.

[cause to rotate] rodar, girar **-2.** [in spin-dryer] centrifugar **-3.** [thread, cloth, wool] fiar **-4.** *SPORT* [ball] fazer girar. <> *vi* **-1.** [rotate] girar, dar voltas **-2.** [spinner] fiar **-3.** [in spin-dryer] centrifugar.

➤ **spin out** *vt sep* **-1.** [story, explanation] prorrogar **-2.** [food, money] esticar.

spinach ['spɪnɪdʒ] *n (U)* espinafre *m*.

spinal column ['spaɪnl-] *n* coluna *f* vertebral.

spinal cord *n* medula *f* espinhal.

spindly ['spɪndlɪ] (*compar* **-ier**, *superl* **-iest**) *adj* longo e fino, longa e fina.

spin-dryer *n UK* centrifugadora *f (de roupas)*.

spine [spaɪn] *n* **-1.** *ANAT* espinha *f* dorsal **-2.** [of book] lombada *f* **-3.** [spike, prickle] espinho *m*.

spinning ['spɪnɪŋ] *n (U)* fiação *f*.

spinning top *n* pião *m*.

spin-off *n* [by-product] subproduto *m*.

spinster ['spɪnstə'] *n* solteirona *f*.

spiral ['spaɪərəl] (*UK pt* & *pp* **-led**, *cont* **-ling**, *US pt* & *pp* **-ed**, *cont* **-ing**) <> *adj* espiral. <> *n* **-1.** [curve] espiral *f* **-2.** [increase] escalada *f* **-3.** [decrease] queda *f*. <> *vi* [move in spiral curve] mover-se em espiral.

spiral staircase *n* escada *f* caracol.

spire [spaɪə'] *n* pináculo *m*.

spirit ['spɪrɪt] <> *n* espírito *m*.

➤ **spirits** *npl* **-1.** [mood] astral *m*; **to be in high/low** ∼ **s** estar de alto/baixo astral **-2.** [alcohol] bebidas *fpl* destiladas.

spirited ['spɪrɪtɪd] *adj* animado(da).

spirit level *n* nível *m* de pedreiro *OR* bolha.

spiritual ['spɪrɪtʃʊəl] *adj* espiritual.

spit [spɪt] (*UK pt* & *pp* **spat**, *cont* **-ting**, *US pt* & *pp* **spit**, *cont* **-ting**) <> *n* **-1.** *(U)* [saliva] cuspe *m* **-2.** [skewer] espeto *m*. <> *vi* [from mouth] cuspir. <> *v impers UK* [rain lightly] chuviscar.

spite [spaɪt] <> *n (U)* rancor *m*. <> *vt* magoar.

➤ **in spite of** *prep* apesar de.

spiteful ['spaɪtfʊl] *adj* maldoso(sa), mal-intencionado(da).

spittle ['spɪtl] *n (U)* cuspe *m*.

splash [splæʃ] <> *n* **-1.** [sound] chape *m*, pancada *f* na água **-2.** [patch] mancha *f*. <> *vt* **-1.** [subj: person] respingar **-2.** [subj: water] molhar **-3.** [apply haphazardly] espalhar. <> *vi* **-1.** [person]: **to** ∼ **about** *OR* **around** patinhar **-2.** [water, liquid]: **to** ∼ **on/against sthg** espirrar em/contra algo.

➤ **splash out** *inf vi*: **to** ∼ **out (on sthg)** gastar um dinheirão (em algo).

spleen [spliːn] *n* **-1.** *ANAT* baço *m* **-2.** *(U) fig* [anger] cólera *f*.

splendid ['splendɪd] *adj* **-1.** [very good] esplêndido(da) **-2.** [magnificent, beautiful] esplendoroso(sa).

splint [splɪnt] *n* tala *f*.

splinter ['splɪntə'] <> *n* lasca *f*. <> *vi* [glass, bone, wood] lascar.

split [splɪt] (*pt* & *pp* **split**, *cont* **-ting**) <> *n* **-1.** [crack] racha *f*, fenda *f*; ∼ **(in sthg)** fenda (em algo) **-2.** [tear] rasgão *m*; ∼ **in sthg** rasgão em algo **-3.** [division, schism] separação *f*; ∼ **in sthg** racha *m* em algo; ∼ **between** divisão *f* entre. <> *vt* **-1.** [crack] rachar, partir **-2.** [tear] rasgar **-3.** [divide - group, organization] rachar; [- road] dividir-se. <> *vi* **-1.** [crack] rachar-se **-2.** [tear] rasgar-se **-3.** [divide - group, organisation] rachar; [road] dividir-se.

➤ **split up** *vi* separar-se; **to** ∼ **up with sb** romper com alguém.

split screen *n* **-1.** *CINEMA* & *TV* tela *f* múltipla **-2.** *COMPUT* divisão *f* de tela.

split second *n* fração *f* de segundo.

splutter ['splʌtə'] *vi* **-1.** [person] balbuciar **-2.** [car, engine] estalar **-3.** [spit] crepitar.

spoil [spɔɪl] (*pt* & *pp* **-ed** *OR* **spoilt**) *vt* **-1.** [ruin] estragar **-2.** [pamper] mimar; **to** ∼ **sb** fazer um agrado a alguém.

➤ **spoils** *npl* butim *m*; ∼ **of war** despojos *mpl* de guerra.

spoiled [spɔɪld] *adj* = **spoilt**.

spoilsport ['spɔɪlspɔːt] *n* desmancha-prazeres *mf inv*.

spoilt [spɔɪlt] <> *pt* & *pp* ⊳ **spoil**. <> *adj* **-1.** [child] mimado(da) **-2.** [food, dinner] estragado(da).

spoke [spəʊk] <> *pt* ⊳ **speak**. <> *n* raio *m (da roda)*.

spoken ['spəʊkn] *pp* ⊳ **speak**.

spokesman ['spəʊksmən] (*pl* **-men** [-mən]) *n* porta-voz *m*.

spokeswoman ['spəʊks,wʊmən] (*pl* **-women** [-,wɪmɪn]) *n* porta-voz *f*.

sponge [spʌndʒ] (*UK cont* **spongeing**, *US cont* **sponging**) <> *n* **-1.** [for cleaning, washing] esponja *f* **-2.** [cake] pão-de-ló *m*. <> *vt* limpar com esponja. <> *vi inf*: **to** ∼ **off sb** viver às custas de alguém.

sponge bag *n UK* nécessaire *m*.

sponge cake *n* pão-de-ló *m*.

sponsor ['spɒnsə'] <> *n* patrocinador *m*, -ra *f*. <> *vt* **-1.** patrocinar **-2.** [bill, appeal, proposal] dar o respaldo a.

sponsored walk [,spɒnsəd-] *n* marcha *f* beneficente.

sponsorship ['spɒnsəʃɪp] *n (U)* patrocínio *m*.

spontaneous [spɒn'teɪnjəs] *adj* espontâneo(nea).

spooky ['spu:kɪ] (*compar* **-ier**, *superl* **-iest**) *adj* **-1.** *inf* [place, house] assombrado(da) **-2.** *inf* [film] aterrorizante.

spool [spu:l] *n* **-1.** [of thread, tape, film] carretel *m* **-2.** COMPUT spool *m*.

spoon [spu:n] *n* **-1.** [piece of cutlery] colher *f* **-2.** [spoonful] colherada *f*.

spoon-feed *vt* **-1.** [feed with spoon] dar de comer com colher a **-2.** *fig* [give too much help to] dar mastigado OR de mão beijada a.

spoonful ['spu:nfʊl] (*pl* **-s** OR **spoonsful** ['spu:nzfʊl]) *n* colherada *f*.

sporadic [spə'rædɪk] *adj* esporádico(ca).

sport [spɔ:t] *n* **-1.** [gen] esporte *m* **-2.** *dated* [cheerful person] pessoa *f* amável.

sporting ['spɔ:tɪŋ] *adj* **-1.** [relating to sport] esportivo(va) **-2.** [generous, fair] nobre; **that's very ~ of you** é muita bondade sua.

sports car ['spɔ:ts-] *n* carro *m* esporte.

sports jacket ['spɔ:ts-] *n* jaqueta *f* esportiva.

sportsman ['spɔ:tsmən] (*pl* **-men** [-mən]) *n* esportista *m*.

sportsmanship ['spɔ:tsmənʃɪp] *n* (U) espírito *m* esportivo.

sportswear ['spɔ:tsweəʳ] *n* (U) roupas *fpl* esportivas.

sportswoman ['spɔ:ts,wʊmən] (*pl* **-women** [-,wɪmɪn]) *n* esportista *f*.

sporty ['spɔ:tɪ] (*compar* **-ier**, *superl* **-iest**) *adj* *inf* [person] aficionado(da) por esportes.

spot [spɒt] (*pt* & *pp* **-ted**, *cont* **-ting**) ◇ *n* **-1.** [mark, dot] mancha *f* **-2.** [pimple] sinal *m* **-3.** *inf*: **a ~ of sleep** uma dormida; **a ~ of work** um pouco de trabalho; [- of milk, liquid] gole *m*; [- of rain] pingo *m*, gota *f* **-4.** [place] local *m*; **on the ~** no local; **to do sthg on the ~** fazer algo no ato **-5.** RADIO & TV espaço *m*. ◇ *vt* [notice] enxergar.

spot check *n* controle *m* aleatório.

spotless ['spɒtlɪs] *adj* [clean] impecável.

spotlight ['spɒtlaɪt] *n* [bright light] refletor *m*; **to be in the ~** *fig* ser o centro das atenções.

spotted ['spɒtɪd] *adj* de bolinhas.

spotty ['spɒtɪ] (*compar* **-ier**, *superl* **-iest**) *adj* UK [skin] sardento(ta).

spouse [spaʊs] *n* esposo *m*, -sa *f*.

spout [spaʊt] ◇ *n* **-1.** [of container] bico *m* **-2.** [of water - from fountain, geyser] jorro *m*; [- from whale] esguicho *m*. ◇ *vi*: **to ~ from** OR **out of sthg** jorrar de algo.

sprain [spreɪn] ◇ *n* torção *f*, distensão *f*. ◇ *vt* torcer, distender.

sprang [spræŋ] *pt* ▷ **spring**.

sprawl [sprɔ:l] *vi* **-1.** [person] estirar-se **-2.** [city, suburbs] expandir-se.

spray [spreɪ] ◇ *n* **-1.** (U) [droplets] borrifo *m* **-2.** [pressurized liquid] spray *m* **-3.** [insect] pulverizador *m* **-4.** [can, container] vaporizador *m* **-5.** [of flowers] ramo *m*. ◇ *vt* & *vi* **-1.** [treat] pulverizar **-2.** [apply] borrifar.

spread [spred] (*pt* & *pp* **spread**) ◇ *n* **-1.** (U) CULIN [paste] pasta *f* **-2.** [diffusion, growth] propagação *f* **-3.** [range] extensão *f* **-4.** US [bedspread] colcha *f*. ◇ *vt* **-1.** [open out, unfold - map, tablecloth, rug] estender; [- arms, legs, fingers] abrir **-2.** [apply - butter, jam] untar; **to ~ sthg over sthg** untar algo com algo; [- glue] passar; **to ~ sthg over sthg** passar algo em algo **-3.** [diffuse, disseminate] espalhar **-4.** [over an area] espalhar; **the floor was ~ with straw** o chão estava coberto de palha **-6.** [distribute evenly] expandir. ◇ *vi* [gen] espalhar-se; [disease, infection] alastrar-se.

◆ **spread out** *vi* [disperse] dispersar-se.

spread-eagled [-,i:gld] *adj* de braços e pernas abertos.

spreadsheet ['spredʃi:t] *n* COMPUT panilha *f* eletrônica.

spree [spri:] *n* farra *f*.

sprightly ['spraɪtlɪ] (*compar* **-ier**, *superl* **-iest**) *adj* ativo(va).

spring [sprɪŋ] (*pt* **sprang**, *pp* **sprung**) ◇ *n* **-1.** [season] primavera *f*; **in ~** na primavera **-2.** [coil] mola *f* **-3.** [water source] fonte *f*. ◇ *vi* **-1.** [leap] saltar **-2.** [be released] soltar-se; **to ~ shut/open** fechar/abrir rapidamente **-3.** [originate]: **to ~ from sthg** originar-se de algo.

◆ **spring up** *vi* **-1.** [get up] levantar-se **-2.** [grow in size, height] elevar-se **-3.** [appear] surgir de repente.

springboard ['sprɪŋbɔ:d] *n* *fig* [launch pad]: **~ for/to sthg** trampolim *m* para algo.

spring-clean *vt* fazer uma faxina geral em.

spring onion *n* UK cebolinha *f* verde.

springtime ['sprɪŋtaɪm] *n* (U): **in (the) ~** na primavera.

springy ['sprɪŋɪ] (*compar* **-ier**, *superl* **-iest**) *adj* **-1.** [carpet, mattress, ground] flexível **-2.** [rubber] elástico(ca).

sprinkle ['sprɪŋkl] *vt* **-1.** salpicar; **to ~ sthg over** OR **on sthg** salpicar algo sobre OR em algo; **to ~ sthg with sthg** regar algo com algo - **2.** [powder] polvilhar - **3.** [liquid] borrifar.

sprinkler ['sprɪŋklə[r]] n - **1.** [for gardens] regador m - **2.** [for extinguishing fires] extintor m.

sprint [sprɪnt] ⟨⟩ n SPORT [race] corrida f de velocidade. ⟨⟩ vi correr a toda (velocidade).

sprout [spraʊt] ⟨⟩ n - **1.** CULIN: (brussels) ~s couve-de-bruxelas f - **2.** [shoot] broto m. ⟨⟩ vt - **1.** [germinate] germinar - **2.** [bud] brotar - **3.** [grow] crescer. ⟨⟩ vi - **1.** [germinate] germinar - **2.** [bud] brotar - **3.** [grow] crescer.

spruce [spru:s] ⟨⟩ adj alinhado(da). ⟨⟩ n [tree] abeto m.
⇒ **spruce up** vt sep arrumar.

sprung [sprʌŋ] pp ▷ **spring**.

spry [spraɪ] (compar -ier, superl -iest) adj ativo(va).

spun [spʌn] pt & pp ▷ **spin**.

spur [spɜ:[r]] (pt & pp -red, cont -ring) ⟨⟩ n - **1.** [incentive]: ~ (to sthg) estímulo m (a algo) - **2.** [on rider's boot] espora f. ⟨⟩ vt - **1.** [encourage]: to ~ sb to do sthg incentivar alguém a fazer algo - **2.** [horse] esporear.
⇒ **on the spur of the moment** adv sem pensar duas vezes.
⇒ **spur on** vt sep [encourage] estimular.

spurious ['spʊərɪəs] adj - **1.** [not genuine] espúrio(ria) - **2.** [based on false reasoning] falso(sa).

spurn [spɜ:n] vt rejeitar, desprezar.

spurt [spɜ:t] ⟨⟩ n - **1.** [of steam] jato m - **2.** [of water] jorro m - **3.** [of flame] labareda f - **4.** [of activity, energy] acesso m - **5.** [burst of speed] acelerada f. ⟨⟩ vi [water]: to ~ (out of OR from sthg) jorrar (de algo); [steam] sair um jato de vapor (de algo); [flame] sair uma labareda (de algo)

spy [spaɪ] (pl spies, pt & pp spied) ⟨⟩ n espião m, -ã f. ⟨⟩ vt inf espionar. ⟨⟩ vi - **1.** [work as spy] espionar - **2.** [watch secretly]: to ~ on sb espionar alguém.

spying ['spaɪɪŋ] n (U) espionagem f.

Sq., sq. (abbr of **square**) pça.

squabble ['skwɒbl] ⟨⟩ n rinha f, discussão f. ⟨⟩ vi: to ~ (about OR over sthg) discutir (sobre algo).

squad [skwɒd] n - **1.** [of police] esquadrão m - **2.** MIL pelotão m - **3.** [SPORT, group of players - of club] time m; [- of national team] seleção f.

squadron ['skwɒdrən] n esquadrão m.

squalid ['skwɒlɪd] adj - **1.** [filthy] esquálido(da), sórdido(da) - **2.** [base, dishonest] depreciável.

squall [skwɔ:l] n [storm] tempestade f.

squalor ['skwɒlə[r]] n (U) sordidez f, miséria f.

squander ['skwɒndə[r]] vt desperdiçar.

square [skweə[r]] ⟨⟩ adj - **1.** quadrado(da) - **2.** [not owing money]: we're ~ now estamos quites agora. ⟨⟩ n - **1.** [shape] quadrado m - **2.** [in town, city] praça f - **3.** inf [unfashionable person] quadrado m, -da f. ⟨⟩ vt - **1.** MATH [multiply by itself] elevar ao quadrado - **2.** [balance, reconcile]: to ~ sthg with sthg conciliar algo com algo.
⇒ **square up** vi [settle up]: to ~ up with sb acertar-se com alguém, acertar as contas com alguém.

squarely ['skweəlɪ] adv - **1.** [directly] exatamente - **2.** [honestly] honestamente, abertamente.

square meal n boa refeição f.

squash [skwɒʃ] ⟨⟩ n - **1.** (U) SPORT squash m - **2.** UK [drink]: lemon/orange ~ refresco m de limão/laranja - **3.** US [vegetable] abóbora f. ⟨⟩ vt [squeeze, flatten] esmagar.

squat [skwɒt] (compar -ter, superl -test, pt & pp -ted, cont -ting) ⟨⟩ adj atarracado(da). ⟨⟩ vi [crouch]: to ~ (down) agachar-se.

squatter ['skwɒtə[r]] n UK [in empty building] posseiro m, -ra f.

squawk [skwɔ:k] n [of bird] grasnado m.

squeak [skwi:k] n - **1.** [of animal] guincho m - **2.** [of door, hinge] rangido m.

squeal [skwi:l] vi [person, animal] gritar.

squeamish ['skwi:mɪʃ] adj apreensivo(va).

squeeze [skwi:z] ⟨⟩ n [pressure] aperto m. ⟨⟩ vt - **1.** [press firmly] apertar - **2.** [extract, press out] espremer - **3.** [cram]: to ~ sthg into sthg [into place] espremer algo dentro de algo; [into time] virar-se para fazer algo em algo.

squelch [skweltʃ] vi chapinhar.

squid [skwɪd] (pl inv OR -s) n lula f.

squiggle ['skwɪgl] n rabisco m.

squint [skwɪnt] ⟨⟩ n MED estrabismo m. ⟨⟩ vi - **1.** MED ser estrábico(ca) - **2.** [half-close one's eyes]: to ~ at sthg olhar com os olhos semicerrados para algo.

squire ['skwaɪə[r]] n [landowner] proprietário m, -ria f rural.

squirm [skwɜ:m] vi [wriggle] contorcer-se.

squirrel [UK 'skwɪrəl, US 'skwɜ:rəl] n esquilo m.

squirt [skwɜ:t] ⟨⟩ vt [force out] esguichar. ⟨⟩ vi: to ~ (out of sthg) esguichar (para fora de algo).

Sr (abbr of **senior**) forma utilizada após o nome de um homem para indicar *que ele é pai de alguém com o mesmo nome.*

Sri Lanka [ˌsriːˈlæŋkə] n Sri Lanka.

St (abbr of **saint**) Sto.

stab [stæb] (pt & pp **-bed**, cont **-bing**) ⬦ n **-1.** [with knife] punhalada f **-2.** inf [attempt]: **to have a ~ (at sthg)** ter uma experiência (em algo) **-3.** [twinge] pontada f. ⬦ vt **-1.** apunhalar, esfaquear **-2.** [jab] fincar.

stable [steɪbl] ⬦ adj **-1.** [gen] estável **-2.** [solid, anchored] firme. ⬦ n [building] estábulo m **-2.** [horses] cavalariça f.

stack [stæk] ⬦ n [pile] pilha f. ⬦ vt [pile up] empilhar.

stadium [ˈsteɪdjəm] (pl **-diums** OR **-dia** [-djəl]) n estádio m.

staff [stɑːf] ⬦ n [employees] pessoal m, quadro m. ⬦ vt: **the shop was ~ ed by women** a equipe da loja era composta de mulheres.

stag [stæg] (pl inv OR **-s**) n ZOOL veado m.

stage [steɪdʒ] ⬦ n **-1.** [period, phase] etapa f, estágio m **-2.** [platform] palco m **-3.** [acting profession]: **the ~** o teatro. ⬦ vt **-1.** THEATRE representar **-2.** [organize] organizar.

stagecoach [ˈsteɪdʒkəʊtʃ] n diligência f.

stage fright n (U) medo m do palco.

stage-manage vt **-1.** THEATRE dirigir **-2.** fig [orchestrate] orquestrar.

stagger [ˈstægəʳ] ⬦ vt **-1.** [astound] abalar, chocar **-2.** [arrange at different times] escalonar. ⬦ vi [totter] cambalear.

stagnant [ˈstægnənt] adj **-1.** [water, air] estancado(da) **-2.** [business, career, economy] estagnado(da).

stagnate [stægˈneɪt] vi **-1.** [water, air] estancar **-2.** [business, career, economy] estagnar-se.

stag night OR **party** n despedida f de solteiro.

staid [steɪd] adj sério(ria), recatado(da).

stain [steɪn] ⬦ n [mark] mancha f. ⬦ vt [discolour] manchar.

stained glass [ˌsteɪnd-] n (U) vitral m.

stainless steel [ˌsteɪnlɪs-] n (U) aço m inoxidável.

stain remover [-rɪˌmuːvəʳ] n removedor m de manchas.

stair [steəʳ] n [step] degrau m.

➡ **stairs** npl [flight] escada f.

staircase [ˈsteəkeɪs] n escadas fpl.

stairway [ˈsteəweɪ] n escadas fpl, escadaria f.

stairwell [ˈsteəwell] n vão m OR poço m das escadas.

stake [steɪk] ⬦ n **-1.** [share]: **to have a ~ in sthg** ter interesses em algo **-2.**

[wooden post] estaca f **-3.** [in gambling] aposta f. ⬦ vt **-1.** [risk]: **to ~ sthg (on** OR **upon sthg)** arriscar algo (com algo) **-2.** [in gambling] apostar.

➡ **at stake** adv: **to be at ~** estar em jogo.

stale [steɪl] adj **-1.** [food] passado(da) **-2.** [air] viciado(da) **-3.** [bread] amanhecido(da) **-4.** [breath] velho(lha).

stalemate [ˈsteɪlmeɪt] n **-1.** [deadlock] impasse m **-2.** CHESS empate m.

stalk [stɔːk] ⬦ n **-1.** [of flower, plant] caule m **-2.** [of leaf] talo m **-3.** [of fruit] cabo m. ⬦ vt [hunt] tocaiar. ⬦ vi [walk] andar de forma irritada.

stall [stɔːl] ⬦ n **-1.** [table] estande m, banca f **-2.** [in stable] baia f. ⬦ vt AUT fazer morrer. ⬦ vi **-1.** AUT morrer **-2.** [delay] ganhar tempo.

➡ **stalls** npl UK platéia f.

stallion [ˈstæljən] n garanhão m.

stalwart [ˈstɔːlwət] n leal partidário m, -ria f.

stamina [ˈstæmɪnə] n (U) resistência f.

stammer [ˈstæməʳ] ⬦ n gagueira f. ⬦ vi gaguejar.

stamp [stæmp] ⬦ n **-1.** [postage stamp] selo m **-2.** [rubber stamp] carimbo m **-3.** fig [hallmark] selo m. ⬦ vt **-1.** [mark, word, sign] carimbar **-2.** [pattern] timbrar **-3.** [stomp]: **to ~ one's foot** bater com o pé no chão **-4.** fig [with characteristic quality] estampar. ⬦ vi **-1.** [walk] andar com passos pesados **-2.** [with one foot]: **to ~ on sthg** pisar em algo.

stamp album n álbum m de selos.

stamp-collecting n (U) filatelia f.

stamped addressed envelope [ˈstæmptəˌdrest-] n UK envelope selado e endereçado ao remetente, que o usa para enviar algo a si próprio através de outra pessoa.

stampede [stæmˈpiːd] n **-1.** [of animals] debandada f **-2.** [of people] fuga f em pânico.

stance [stæns] n **-1.** [posture] atitude f, postura f **-2.** [attitude]: **~ (on sthg)** postura (sobre algo).

stand [stænd] (pt & pp **stood**) ⬦ n **-1.** [stall] banca f, barraca f **-2.** [for umbrella, hat] cabide m **-3.** [for bicycle, lamp] suporte m **-4.** SPORT arquibancada f **-5.** MIL posição f; **to make a ~** resistir ao inimigo **-6.** [position] posição f **-7.** US JUR depoimento m. ⬦ vt **-1.** [place] colocar **-2.** [withstand] agüentar **-3.** [put up with] suportar. ⬦ vi **-1.** [be on one's feet] ficar em pé **-2.** [rise to one's feet] levantar-se **-3.** [be located] estar **-4.** [be left undisturbed] repousar **-5.** [be valid] seguir de pé **- 6.** [indicating current situation]: **as things ~ ...** do jeito que as coisas andam; **unemployment ~s at three million** o desemprego já atinge três milhões de pessoas **- 7.** *UK* POL [be a candidate], candidatar-se (a) **- 8.** *US* [stop]: **'no ~ing'** proibido parar e estacionar.

➡ **stand back** *vi* [get out of way] afastar-se.

➡ **stand by** ◇ *vt fus* **-1.** [person] estar ao lado de **- 2.** [promise, decision, offer] manter. ◇ *vi* **-1.** [in readiness]: **to ~ by (for sthg/to do sthg)** estar preparado (da) (a algo/a fazer algo) **- 2.** [not intervene] ficar de lado.

➡ **stand down** *vi* [resign] retirar-se.

➡ **stand for** *vt fus* **-1.** [signify] significar, representar **- 2.** [tolerate] agüentar.

➡ **stand in** *vi*: **to ~ in (for sb)** substituir (alguém).

➡ **stand out** *vi* **-1.** [be clearly visible] sobressair **- 2.** [be distinctive] destacar-se.

➡ **stand up** ◇ *vt sep inf* [miss appointment with] deixar plantado(da) **- 1.** [be on one's feet, upright] ficar de pé **- 2.** [rise to one's feet] levantar-se.

➡ **stand up for** *vt fus* sair em defesa de.

➡ **stand up to** *vt fus* **-1.** [weather, heat, bad treatment] resistir a **- 2.** [person, boss] peitar.

standard ['stændəd] ◇ *adj* **-1.** [gen] normal **- 2.** [type, feature] comum **- 3.** [size] padronizado **- 4.** [text, work] -padrão; **~ practice** prática-padrão *f.* ◇ *n* **-1.** [level] nível *m* **- 2.** [point of reference] padrão *m*, critério *m* **- 3.** [flag] estandarte *m.*

➡ **standards** *npl* [principles] valores *mpl* morais.

standard lamp *n UK* abajur *m* de pé.

standard of living (*pl* standards of living) *n* padrão *m* de vida.

standby ['stændbaɪ] (*pl* standbys) ◇ *n* [substitute] reserva *f*; **to be on ~** estar a postos. ◇ *comp* stand-by.

stand-in *n* **-1.** [replacement] suplente *mf*, **- 2.** [stunt person] dublê *mf.*

standing ['stændɪŋ] ◇ *adj* [permanent] permanente; **a ~ joke** uma piada manjada; **a ~ invitation** um convite em aberto. ◇ *n* **-1.** [reputation] reputação *f* **- 2.** [duration] duração *f*; **friends of 20 years' ~** amigos há mais de 20 anos.

standing order *n* débito *m* automático em conta.

standing room *n (U)* lugar *m* em pé.

standoffish [ˌstænd'ɒfɪʃ] *adj* reservado(da).

standpoint ['stændpɔɪnt] *n* ponto *m* de vista.

standstill ['stændstɪl] *n*: **at a ~** [not moving] parado(da); *fig* [not active] paralisado(da); **to come to a ~** [stop moving] parar; *fig* [cease] estancar.

stand-up *adj*: **~ comedian** comediante *mf* de platéia; **~ fight** briga *f* violenta.

stank [stæŋk] *pt* ▷ stink.

staple ['steɪpl] ◇ *adj* [principal] básico(ca), de primeira necessidade. ◇ *n* **-1.** [for paper] grampo *m* **- 2.** [principal commodity] produto *m* de primeira necessidade. ◇ *vt* grampear.

stapler ['steɪplə'] *n* grampeador *m.*

star [stɑː'] (*pt & pp* -red, *cont* -ring) ◇ *n* [gen] estrela *f.* ◇ *comp* de estrela. ◇ *vi* [actor]: **to ~ (in sthg)** ser protagonista(de algo).

➡ **stars** *npl* [horoscope] horóscopo *m.*

starboard ['stɑːbəd] ◇ *adj* de estibordo. ◇ *n (U)* estibordo *m*; **to ~ a** estibordo.

starch [stɑːtʃ] *n* **-1.** [stiffening substance] goma *f* **- 2.** [in food] amido *m.*

stardom ['stɑːdəm] *n (U)* estrelato *m.*

stare [steə'] ◇ *n* olhar *m* fixo. ◇ *vi*: **to ~ (at sb/sthg)** olhar fixamente (para alguém/algo).

stark [stɑːk] ◇ *adj* **-1.** [bare, bleak] desolado(da) **- 2.** [rock] áspero(ra) **- 3.** [decoration] desguarnecido(da) **- 4.** [room] sem mobília **- 5.** [contrast] duro(ra) **- 6.** [reality] nu(a) e cru(a) **- 7.** [fact] às claras. ◇ *adv*: **~ naked** em pêlo.

starling ['stɑːlɪŋ] *n* estorninho *m.*

starry ['stɑːrɪ] (*compar* -ier, *superl* -iest) *adj* estrelado(da).

starry-eyed [-'aɪd] *adj* [naive] iludido(da).

Stars and Stripes *n*: **the ~** a *bandeira dos Estados Unidos.*

start [stɑːt] ◇ *n* **-1.** [beginning] início *m*, começo *m* **- 2.** [jump] sobressalto *m*, susto *m* **- 3.** SPORT [lead] saída *f* **- 3.** [lead] vantagem *f.* ◇ *vt* **-1.** [begin] começar; **to ~ doing** OR **to do sthg** começar a fazer algo **- 2.** [turn on] ligar **- 3.** [set up - gen] criar, formar; [- business] montar **- 4.** [initiate, instigate] iniciar. ◇ *vi* **-1.** [begin] começar; **to ~ with sb/sthg** começar com alguém/algo; **to ~ with,** ... [at first] para começar, ... **- 2.** [car] pegar **- 3.** [engine] pôr-se em funcionamento **- 4.** [tape] ligar **- 5.** [set out] sair **- 6.** [jump] sobressaltar-se, assustar-se.

➡ **start off** ◇ *vt sep* [cause to start - person] pôr-se a caminho; **this should**

be enough work to ~ **you off** com isso já tem trabalho suficiente para começar; [- meeting] começar; [- rumour, discussion] desencadear. <> *vi* -1. [begin] começar -2. [set out] sair.

◆ **start out** *vi* -1. [in life, career] começar -2. [set out] partir.

◆ **start up** <> *vt sep* -1. [set up - business] montar; [- shop] botar; [- women's group] criar, formar -2. [car, engine, machine] ligar. <> *vi* -1. [guns, music, noise] começar -2. [car, engine, machine] ligar -3. [set up business] estabelecer-se.

starter ['stɑ:tə'] *n* -1. *UK* [hors d'oeuvre] entrada *f*, primeiro prato *m* -2. *AUT* (motor *m* de) arranque *m* -3. [*SPORT* - official] juiz *m*, -íza *f*; [- competitor] corredor *m*, -ra *f*.

starting point ['stɑ:tɪŋ-] *n* ponto *m* de partida.

startle ['stɑ:tl] *vt* assustar.

startling ['stɑ:tlɪŋ] *adj* assustador(ra), surpreendente.

starvation [stɑ:'veɪʃn] *n (U)* fome *f*, inanição *f*.

starve [stɑ:v] <> *vt* [deprive of food] não dar comida para. <> *vi* -1. [have no food] passar fome -2. *inf* [be hungry]: **I'm starving to death!** estou morrendo de fome!

state [steɪt] <> *n* -1. [condition] estado *m*; **to be in a** ~ estar com os nervos à flor da pele -2. [authorities]: **the** ~ o Estado. <> *comp* de estado. <> *vt* [declare] afirmar, declarar; **to** ~ **that** afirmar que; [specify] estabelecer.

◆ **State** *n* [government]: **the State** o Estado.

◆ **States** *npl* [USA]: **the States** os Estados Unidos.

State Department *n US* ≃ Ministério *m* das Relações Exteriores.

stately ['steɪtlɪ] (*compar* **-ier**, *superl* **-iest**) *adj* [dignified] majestoso(sa).

statement ['steɪtmənt] *n* -1. [declaration] afirmação *f*, declaração *f* -2. *JUR* declaração *f* -3. [from bank] extrato *m*.

state of mind (*pl* **states of mind**) *n* estado *m* de espírito.

statesman ['steɪtsmən] (*pl* **-men** [-mən]) *n* estadista *m*, homem *m* de estado.

static ['stætɪk] <> *adj* [unchanging] estável. <> *n (U)* *ELEC* estática *f*.

static electricity *n (U)* eletricidade *f* estática.

station ['steɪʃn] <> *n* -1. [gen] estação *f*; **police** ~ delegacia *f*; **fire** ~ corpo *m* de bombeiros -2. [position] posto *m* -3. *fml* [rank] posição *f*. <> *vt* -1. [position] situar, colocar -2. *MIL* estacionar.

stationary ['steɪʃnərɪ] *adj* estacionário(-ria).

stationer *n* dono *m*, -na *f* de papelaria; ~ '**s (shop)** papelaria *f*.

stationery ['steɪʃnərɪ] *n (U)* artigos *mpl* de escritório.

stationmaster ['steɪʃn,mɑ:stə'] *n* chefe *mf* da estação.

station wagon *n US* perua *f* (*camioneta*).

statistic [stə'tɪstɪk] *n* [number] estatística *f*.

◆ **statistics** *n (U)* [science] estatística *f*.

statistical [stə'tɪstɪkl] *adj* estatístico(-ca).

statue ['stætʃu:] *n* estátua *f*.

stature ['stætʃə'] *n (U)* -1. [height, size] estatura *f* -2. [importance] categoria *f*.

status ['steɪtəs] *n (U)* -1. [legal or social position] condição *f*, estado *m* -2. [prestige] status *m inv*.

status bar *n COMPUT* barra *f* de status.

status symbol *n* símbolo *m* de status.

statute ['stætʃu:t] *n* estatuto *m*.

statutory ['stætjʊtrɪ] *adj* estatutário(-ria).

staunch [stɔ:ntʃ] <> *adj* leal, fiel. <> *vt* estancar.

stave [steɪv] (*pt & pp* **-d** *OR* **stove**) *n MUS* pauta *f*.

◆ **stave off** *vt sep* afastar temporariamente.

stay [steɪ] <> *n* [visit] estada *f*, estadia *f*. <> *vi* -1. [remain] ficar -2. [reside temporarily] ficar, permanecer -3. [continue to be] permanecer; **I don't want to** ~ **a teacher all my life** não quero ser professor toda a minha vida; **she** ~ **ed awake till midnight** ficou acordada até a meia-noite.

◆ **stay in** *vi* [stay at home] ficar em casa.

◆ **stay on** *vi* ficar, permanecer.

◆ **stay out** *vi* -1. [not come home] ficar fora -2. [not get involved]: **to** ~ **out of sthg** ficar fora de algo.

◆ **stay up** *vi* -1. [not go to bed] ficar acordado(da) -2. [not fall] ficar de pé.

staying power ['steɪɪŋ-] *n (U)* resistência *f*.

stead [sted] *n*: **to stand sb in good** ~ servir muito a alguém.

steadfast ['stedfɑ:st] *adj* -1. [supporter] fiel -2. [resolve] resoluto(ta) -3. [gaze] fixo(xa).

steadily ['stedɪlɪ] *adv* -1. [gradually] gradualmente -2. [regularly] normalmente -3. [calmly - look, stare] fixamente; [- say] calmamente.

steady ['stedɪ] (*compar* **-ier**, *superl* **-iest**,

pt & pp **-ied**) ⋄ adj **-1.** [gradual] gradual **-2.** [regular, constant] constante **-3.** [not shaking] firme **- 4.** [calm - voice] calmo(ma); [- stare] fixo(xa) **-5.** [stable - boyfriend, girlfriend] firme; [- relationship] sério(ria); [- job] estável **- 6.** [sensible] sensato(ta). ⋄ vt **-1.** [stabilize] estabilizar **- 2.** [calm] controlar; **to ~ o.s.** acalmar-se, controlar os nervos.

steak [steɪk] n **- 1.** (U) [meat] bife m **- 2.** [piece of meat or fish] filé m.

steal [stiːl] (pt **stole**, pp **stolen**) ⋄ vt roubar. ⋄ vi [move stealthily] mover-se furtivamente.

stealthy [ˈstelθɪ] (compar **-ier**, superl **-iest**) adj furtivo(va).

steam [stiːm] ⋄ n (U) vapor m. ⋄ vt CULIN cozinhar no vapor. ⋄ vi largar vapor.

➡ **steam up** ⋄ vt sep fig [get angry]: **to get ~ed up about sthg** soltar fumaça pelas ventas por causa de algo. ⋄ vi [window, glasses] embaçar.

steamboat [ˈstiːmbəʊt] n barco m a vapor.

steam engine n máquina f a vapor.

steamer [ˈstiːməʳ] n [ship] navio m a vapor.

steamroller [ˈstiːmˌrəʊləʳ] n rolo m compressor.

steamy [ˈstiːmɪ] (compar **-ier**, superl **-iest**) adj **- 1.** [full of steam] cheio (cheia) de vapor **- 2.** inf [erotic] quente.

steel [stiːl] n (U) aço m. ⋄ comp de aço.

steelworks [ˈstiːlwɜːks] (pl inv) n (usina f) siderúrgica f.

steep [stiːp] ⋄ adj **- 1.** [hill, road] íngreme **- 2.** [increase, fall] acentuado(da) **- 3.** inf [expensive] abusivo(va). ⋄ vt **- 1.** [soak] embeber, molhar **- 2.** [fruit] macerar.

steeple [ˈstiːpl] n agulha f (do campanário).

steeplechase [ˈstiːpltʃeɪs] n corrida f de obstáculos.

steer [stɪəʳ] ⋄ n [bullock] boi m. ⋄ vt conduzir, guiar. ⋄ vi conduzir; **the car ~s well** é um carro bom de dirigir; **the bus ~ed into the hedge** o ônibus foi direto para a cerca viva; **to ~ clear (of sb/sthg)** fig ficar longe (de alguém/algo).

steering [ˈstɪərɪŋ] n (U) AUT direção f.

steering wheel n volante m, direção f.

stem [stem] (pt & pp **-med**, cont **-ming**) ⋄ n **- 1.** [of plant] caule m **- 2.** [of glass] pé m, base f **-3.** [of pipe] tubo m **- 4.** GRAMM raiz f. ⋄ vt [stop - flow] conter; [- blood] estancar.

➡ **stem from** vt fus derivar-se de, ser o resultado de.

stem cell n MED célula-tronco f.

stench [stentʃ] n fedor m.

stencil [ˈstensl] (UK pt & pp **-led**, cont **-ling**, US pt & pp **-ed**, cont **-ing**) ⋄ n [template] matriz f. ⋄ vt reproduzir com matriz.

stenographer [stəˈnɒgrəfəʳ] n estenógrafo m, -fa f.

step [step] (pt & pp **-ped**, cont **-ping**) ⋄ n **- 1.** [pace] passo m; **in ~ with** fig [in touch with] em acordo com; **out of ~ with** fig [out of touch with] em desacordo com **- 2.** [action] medida f **-3.** [stage, degree] grau m; **~ by ~** passo a passo **- 4.** [stair, ladder] degrau m. ⋄ vi **-1.** [take a single step] dar um passo; **to ~ forward** dar um passo à frente; **watch where you ~** olhe onde você pisa; **to ~ off sthg** descer de algo; **to ~ over sthg** pisar em algo **- 2.** [put one's foot down]: **to ~ on sthg** pisar em algo; **~ on it!** [drive fast, hurry up] acelera!; **to ~ in sthg** meter o pé em algo.

➡ **steps** npl **- 1.** [stairs] escadas fpl **- 2.** UK [stepladder] escada f de mão.

➡ **step down** vi [resign] renunciar.

➡ **step in** vi [intervene] intervir.

➡ **step up** vt sep [increase] aumentar.

step aerobics n step m.

stepbrother [ˈstepˌbrʌðəʳ] n meio-irmão m.

stepdaughter [ˈstepˌdɔːtəʳ] n enteada f.

stepfather [ˈstepˌfɑːðəʳ] n padrasto m.

stepladder [ˈstepˌlædəʳ] n escada f de mão.

stepmother [ˈstepˌmʌðəʳ] n madrasta f.

stepping-stone [ˈstepɪŋ-] n **- 1.** [in river] passadeira f **- 2.** fig [way to success] trampolim m.

stepsister [ˈstepˌsɪstəʳ] n meia-irmã f.

stepson [ˈstepsʌn] n enteado m.

stereo [ˈsterɪəʊ] (pl **-s**) ⋄ adj estéreo(rea). ⋄ n **- 1.** [stereo system] (aparelho m de) som m **- 2.** (U) [stereo sound] estéreo m.

stereotype [ˈsterɪətaɪp] n estereótipo m.

sterile [ˈsteraɪl] adj **- 1.** [germ-free] esterilizado(da) **- 2.** [unable to produce offspring] estéril.

sterilize, -ise [ˈsteraɪlaɪz] vt esterilizar.

sterling [ˈstɜːlɪŋ] ⋄ adj **- 1.** [of British money] esterlino(na) **- 2.** [excellent] excelente. ⋄ n (U) libra f esterlina.

sterling silver n (U) prata f de lei.

stern [stɜːn] ⋄ adj severo(ra). ⋄ n popa f.

steroid [ˈstɪərɔɪd] n esteróide m.

stethoscope ['steθəskəʊp] n estetoscópio m.

stew [stju:] ⟨⟩ n ensopado m, refogado m. ⟨⟩ vt ensopar, refogar.

steward ['stjʊəd] n -1. UK [on plane] comissário m de bordo -2. UK [ship, train] camareiro m -3. UK [marshal] coordenador m, -ra f (de uma corrida, um desfile etc.).

stewardess ['stjʊədɪs] n comissária f de bordo.

stick [stɪk] (pt & pp stuck) ⟨⟩ n -1. [piece of wood] graveto m -2. [of chalk] (pedaço m de) giz m -3. [of dynamite] (banana f) de dinamite -4. [of celery] talho m de aipo -5. [walking stick] bastão m -6. SPORT taco m. ⟨⟩ vt -1. [jab]: to ~ sthg in(to) sthg fincar or espetar algo em algo -2. [with adhesive] colar; to ~ sthg on or to sthg colar algo em algo -3. inf [put] socar -4. UK inf [tolerate] agüentar. ⟨⟩ vi -1. [arrow, dart, spear]: I've got a splinter stuck in my finger há uma felpa enfiada no meu dedo -2. [adhere]: to ~ (to sthg) colar (em algo) -3. [become jammed] emperrar.

⟿ **stick out** ⟨⟩ vt sep -1. [extend] colocar para fora; to ~ one's tongue out at sb botar a língua (para alguém) -2. inf [endure]: to ~ it out agüentar. ⟨⟩ vi -1. [protrude] sobressair -2. inf [be noticeable] destacar-se, chamar a atenção.

⟿ **stick to** vt fus -1. [person, path] não abandonar -2. [principles, decision] ser fiel a; if I were you, I'd ~ to French se eu fosse tu, ficaria apenas com o francês -3. [promise] cumprir.

⟿ **stick up** vi sobressair; to be ~ ing up estar espetado(da).

⟿ **stick up for** vt fus defender.

sticker ['stɪkəʳ] n [piece of paper] adesivo m.

sticking plaster ['stɪkɪŋ-] n -1. (U) [bandaging material] esparadrapo m -2. [bandage] curativo m.

stickler ['stɪkləʳ] n: ~ for sthg obsessivo(va) por algo.

stick shift n US [gear lever] alavanca f da marcha or mudança; [car] carro m com câmbio manual.

stick-up n inf assalto m à mão armada.

sticky ['stɪkɪ] (compar -ier, superl -iest) adj -1. [tacky] grudento(ta) -2. [adhesive] adesivo(va) -3. inf [awkward] chato(ta).

stiff [stɪf] ⟨⟩ adj -1. [inflexible] duro(ra) -2. [difficult to move] emperrado(da) -3. [difficult to stir] consistente -4. [aching] dolorido(da); ~ neck torcicolo m -5. [formal] formal -6. [severe] severo(ra) -7. [difficult] duro(ra). ⟨⟩ adv inf [for emphasis] muito; to be bored ~ estar completamente entediado(da); to be scared/frozen ~ estar morrendo de medo/de frio.

stiffen ['stɪfn] ⟨⟩ vt -1. [paper, fabric] endurecer -2. [resistance, resolve] reforçar. ⟨⟩ vi -1. [tense up - people] ficar tenso(sa); [- joints, muscles, back] enrijecer -2. [become difficult to move] emperrar -3. [become more severe, intense - competition] ficar mais acirrado(da); [- resistance, resolve] fortalecer-se.

stifle ['staɪfl] ⟨⟩ vt -1. [suffocate] sufocar -2. [suppress] sufocar, reprimir. ⟨⟩ vi [suffocate] sufocar.

stifling ['staɪflɪŋ] adj sufocante.

stigma ['stɪgmə] n estigma m.

stile [staɪl] n escada f para passar sobre uma cerca.

stiletto (heel) [stɪ'letəʊ-] n UK salto m alto.

still [stɪl] ⟨⟩ adv -1. [in time] ainda; do you ~ live in ...? você ainda mora em ...? -2. [all the same] ainda assim -3. (with comparatives) ainda; more interesting ~, ... ainda mais interessante que isso, ... -4. [motionless] sem se mover; sit ~ ! te senta e fica quieto! ⟨⟩ adj -1. [not moving] parado(da) -2. [calm, quiet] calmo(ma), tranqüilo(la) -3. [not windy] sem vento -4. [not fizzy] sem gás. ⟨⟩ n -1. PHOT foto f fixa -2. [for making alcohol] alambique m.

stillborn ['stɪlbɔːn] adj natimorto(ta).

still life (pl -s) n natureza-morta f.

stilted ['stɪltɪd] adj forçado(da).

stilts [stɪlts] npl -1. [for person] pernas fpl de pau -2. [for building] estacas fpl.

stimulate ['stɪmjʊleɪt] vt -1. [gen] estimular -2. [physically] excitar.

stimulating ['stɪmjʊleɪtɪŋ] adj estimulante.

stimulus ['stɪmjʊləs] (pl -li [-laɪ]) n estímulo m.

sting [stɪŋ] (pt & pp stung) ⟨⟩ n -1. [from bee] ferroada f -2. [from insect] picada f -3. [from nettle] urticária f -4. [part of bee, wasp, scorpion] ferrão m. ⟨⟩ vt [subj: bee, wasp, scorpion] picar; [subj: nettle] queimar; [subj: smoke, acid] irritar. ⟨⟩ vi -1. [bee, wasp, scorpion] picar; [nettle] queimar; [smoke, acid] irritar -2. [eyes, skin] arder.

stingy ['stɪndʒɪ] (compar -ier, superl -iest) adj -1. inf [person] sovina -2. inf [amount] escasso(sa).

stink [stɪŋk] (pt stank or stunk, pp stunk) ⟨⟩ n fedor m. ⟨⟩ vi [smell] feder.

stinking ['stɪŋkɪŋ] *inf* <> *adj* **-1.** [smelly] fedorento(ta) **-2.** *fig* [for emphasis] maldito(ta).

stint [stɪnt] <> *n* [period of time] período *m*. <> *vi*: **to ~ on** sthg pechinchar algo.

stipulate ['stɪpjuleɪt] *vt* estipular.

stir [stɜːʳ] (*pt* & *pp* -**red**, *cont* -**ring**) <> *n* **-1.** [public excitement] agitação *f*, alvoroço *m*. <> *vt* **-1.** [mix] mexer, misturar **-2.** [move physically] mexer **-3.** [rouse, excite] instigar. <> *vi* **-1.** [move gently] mover-se, mexer-se **-2.** [awaken] despertar.

➤ **stir up** *vt sep* **-1.** [dust, mud] levantar **-2.** [trouble, dissent, feelings, memories] provocar.

stirrup ['stɪrəp] *n* estribo *m*.

stitch [stɪtʃ] <> *n* **-1.** [gen] ponto *m* **-2.** [pain]: **to have a ~** sentir pontadas de dor. <> *vt* costurar.

stoat [stəut] *n* arminho *m*.

stock [stɒk] <> *n* **-1.** [gen] estoque *m*; **in ~** em estoque; **out of ~** esgotado(da) **-2.** [FIN - of company] capital *m*; [- of government] títulos *mpl* do governo; **~s and shares** títulos *mpl* mobiliários, ações *fpl* **-3.** (U) [ancestry] estirpe *f*, linhagem *f* **-4.** CULIN caldo *m* **-5.** (U) [livestock] rebanho *m* **-6.** [of gun] coronha *f* **-7.** *phr*: **to take ~ (of sthg)** refletir (sobre algo). <> *adj* [typical] típico(ca). <> *vt* **-1.** COMM ter em estoque **-2.** [fill] encher (de); **to be ~ed with** estar cheio (cheia) de.

➤ **stock up** *vi*: **to ~ up (on** OR **with sthg)** fazer estoque (de algo).

stockbroker ['stɒk,brəukəʳ] *n* corretor *m*, -ra *f* da bolsa.

stock cube *n* UK caldo *m* em cubo.

stock exchange *n* bolsa *f* de valores.

stockholder ['stɒk,həuldəʳ] *n* US acionista *mf*.

Stockholm ['stɒkhəum] *n* Estocolmo *m*; **in ~** em Estocolmo.

stocking ['stɒkɪŋ] *n* meia *f*.

stockist ['stɒkɪst] *n* UK varejista *mf*.

stock market *n* mercado *m* de ações.

stock phrase *n* frase *f* feita.

stockpile ['stɒkpaɪl] <> *n* estoque *m*. <> *vt* estocar, armazenar.

stocktaking ['stɒk,teɪkɪŋ] *n* (U) inventário *m*.

stocky ['stɒkɪ] (*compar* -**ier**, *superl* -**iest**) *adj* reforçado(da), corpulento(ta).

stodgy ['stɒdʒɪ] (*compar* -**ier**, *superl* -**iest**) *adj* [indigestible] pesado(da).

stoical ['stəuɪkl] *adj* estóico(ca).

stoke [stəuk] *vt* [keep burning] alimentar.

stole [stəul] <> *pt* ▷ **steal**. <> *n* [shawl] estola *f*.

stolen ['stəuln] *pp* ▷ **steal**.

stolid ['stɒlɪd] *adj* impassível.

stomach ['stʌmək] <> *n* **-1.** [organ] estômago *m* **-2.** [abdomen] ventre *m*. <> *vt* [tolerate] tolerar.

stomach ache *n* dor *f* de estômago.

stomach upset [-'ʌpset] *n* indigestão *f*.

stone [stəun] (*pl sense 5 only inv* OR -**s**) <> *n* **-1.** [gen] pedra *f*; **a ~'s throw from** bem perto de **-2.** [in fruit] caroço *m* **-3.** [unit of measurement] *equivalente a 6,35kg*. <> *comp* de pedra. <> *vt* apedrejar.

stone-cold *adj* gelado(da) como pedra.

stonewashed ['stəunwɒʃt] *adj* estonado(da).

stonework ['stəunwɜːk] *n* (U) cantaria *f*.

stood [stud] *pt* & *pp* ▷ **stand**.

stool [stuːl] *n* [seat] mocho *m*, banquinho *m*.

stoop [stuːp] <> *n* [bent back]: **to walk with a ~** caminhar encurvado(da). <> *vi* **-1.** [bend forwards and down] abaixar-se **-2.** [hunch shoulders] encurvar-se.

stop [stɒp] (*pt* & *pp* -**ped**, *cont* -**ping**) <> *n* **-1.** [gen] parada *f* **-2.** [end]: **to put a ~ to sthg** dar um basta em algo **-3.** [in punctuation] ponto *m* **-5.** TECH trava *f*, ferrolho *m*. <> *vt* **-1.** [gen] parar; **to ~ doing sthg** parar de fazer algo **-2.** [prevent] impedir; **to ~ sb/sthg from doing sthg** impedir alguém/algo de fazer algo **-3.** [hole, gap] tapar. <> *vi* **-1.** [gen] parar **-2.** [stay] ficar.

➤ **stop off** *vi* dar uma parada.

➤ **stop up** *vt sep* [block] entupir.

stopgap ['stɒpgæp] *n* quebra-galho *m*.

stopover ['stɒp,əuvəʳ] *n* parada *f*.

stoppage ['stɒpɪdʒ] *n* **-1.** [strike] paralisação *f* **-2.** UK [deduction] dedução *f*.

stopper ['stɒpəʳ] *n* rolha *f*.

stop press *n* notícias *fpl* de última hora.

stopwatch ['stɒpwɒtʃ] *n* cronômetro *m*.

storage ['stɔːrɪdʒ] *n* (U) armazenamento *m*.

storage heater *n* UK *aquecedor que acumula calor à noite, quando a eletricidade é mais barata, e libera calor durante o dia.*

store [stɔːʳ] <> *n* **-1.** *esp* US [shop] loja *f* **-2.** [supply] reserva *f*, provisão *f* **-3.** [storage place] depósito *m*. <> *vt* **-1.** [gen] armazenar **-2.** [details, address, ideas] guardar.

➤ **store up** *vt sep* **-1.** [objects] armazenar **-2.** [facts, information] guardar.

store card n cartão m de crédito (de lojas).

storekeeper ['stɔː,kiːpəʳ] n US lojista mf.

storeroom ['stɔːrʊm] n -1. [gen] almoxarifado m -2. [for food] despensa f.

storey UK (pl storeys), **story** US (pl -ies) ['stɔːrɪ] n andar m.

stork [stɔːk] n cegonha f.

storm [stɔːm] <> n -1. [bad weather] temporal m, tempestade f -2. [violent reaction] torrente f. <> vt -1. MIL tomar de assalto -2. [say angrily] esbravejar. <> vi [go angrily]: **to ~ into/out of** entrar/sair intempestivamente.

stormy ['stɔːmɪ] (compar -ier, superl -iest) adj -1. [weather, sea] tempestuoso(sa) -2. fig [relationship, meeting] turbulento(ta).

story ['stɔːrɪ] (pl -ies) n -1. [tale] história f, conto m -2. HIST & euphemism história f -3. [article - newspaper] artigo m; [- TV, radio] reportagem f -4. US = storey.

storybook ['stɔːrɪbʊk] adj de novela.

storyteller ['stɔːrɪ,teləʳ] n -1. [teller of story] contador m, -ra f de histórias -2. euphemism [liar] mentiroso m, -sa f.

stout [staʊt] <> adj -1. [corpulent] corpulento(ta) -2. [strong] forte, resistente -3. [brave] firme, forte. <> n (U) cerveja f escura, stout f.

stove [staʊv] <> pt & pp ▷ **stave**. <> n -1. [for cooking] forno m -2. [for heating] estufa f.

stow [staʊ] vt: **to ~ sthg (away)** guardar algo.

stowaway ['staʊəweɪ] n clandestino m, -na f.

straddle ['strædl] vt -1. [subj: person] escarranchar-se em -2. [subj: bridge, town] atravessar, cruzar.

straggle ['strægl] vi -1. [buildings, hair, plant] espalhar-se -2. [person, group] ficar para trás.

straggler ['stræglə'] n retardatário m, -ria f.

straight [streɪt] <> adj -1. [gen] reto(ta) -2. [not curly] liso(sa) -3. [honest, frank] direto(ta), franco(ca) -4. [tidy] arrumado(da) -5. [simple] fácil, simples -6. [undiluted] puro(ra) -7. phr: **to get something ~** deixar uma coisa clara. <> adv -1. [in a straight line]: **~ ahead** bem na frente; **I couldn't see ~** não podia ver direito -2. [upright] reto(ta); **why won't that painting hang ~** por que aquele quadro não fica reto? -3. [directly, immediately] imediatamente; **I'll go ~ to bed** vou direto para a cama -4. [honestly, frankly] com toda a franqueza -5.

[undiluted]: **I drink my whisky ~** tomo meu uísque puro.
　◆ **straight off** adv no ato.
　◆ **straight out** adv sem rodeios.

straightaway adv em seguida.

straighten ['streɪtn] vt -1. [tidy] arrumar, organizar -2. [make straight] endireitar -3. [make level] pôr reto(ta), endireitar.
　◆ **straighten out** vt sep [sort out - mess] arrumar; [- problem] resolver.

straight face n: **to keep a ~** ficar sério(ria).

straightforward [,streɪt'fɔːwəd] adj -1. [easy] simples -2. [honest, frank - answer] direto(ta); [- person] aberto(ta), franco(ca).

strain [streɪn] <> n -1. [mental] tensão f -2. MED [of muscle, back] distensão f -3. [TECH - weight] peso m; [- pressure] pressão f; [- force] força f. <> vt -1. [work hard] forçar -2. MED [injure] distender -3. [overtax - resources, budget] esticar; [- enthusiasm] acabar; [- patience] esgotar -4. [drain - vegetables] escorrer; [- tea] coar -5. TECH [rope, girder, ceiling] estirar. <> vi [try very hard]: **to ~ to do sthg** esforçar-se para fazer algo.
　◆ **strains** npl literary [of music] acordes mpl.

strained [streɪnd] adj -1. [forced] forçado(da) -2. [tense] tenso(sa) -3. MED [sprained] distendido(da) -4. [CULIN - liquid] coado(da); [- vegetables] escorrido(da).

strainer ['streɪnəʳ] n coador m.

strait [streɪt] n GEOGR estreito m.
　◆ **straits** npl: **in dire** OR **desperate ~s** em sérios apuros.

straitjacket ['streɪt,dʒækɪt] n [garment] camisa-de-força f.

straitlaced [,streɪt'leɪst] adj pej puritano(na).

strand [strænd] n -1. [of hair, cotton, wool] mecha f; **a ~ of hair** um fio de cabelo -2. [of story, argument, plot] linha f.

stranded ['strændɪd] adj -1. [person] preso(sa) -2. [car] atolado(da) -3. [boat] encalhado(da).

strange [streɪndʒ] adj -1. [unusual, unexpected] estranho(nha) -2. [unfamiliar] desconhecido(da), estranho(nha).

stranger ['streɪndʒəʳ] n -1. [unknown person] estranho m, -nha f -2. [person from elsewhere] forasteiro m, -ra f.

strangle ['stræŋgl] vt -1. [kill - person] estrangular; [- chicken] torcer o pescoço de -2. fig [stifle] sufocar.

stranglehold ['stræŋglhəʊld] n -1. [round neck] gravata f -2. fig [strong influence]: **~**

(on sb/sthg) controle *m* total (sobre alguém/algo).

strap [stræp] *(pt & pp* **-ped,** *cont* **-ping)** ◇ *n* **-1.** [for carrying] correia *f,* tira *f* **-2.** [for fastening] alça *f* **-3.** [of watch] pulseira *f.* ◇ *vt* [fasten] prender *(com correia).*

strapping ['stræpɪŋ] *adj* robusto(ta).

Strasbourg ['stræzbɜːg] *n* Estrasburgo; **in ~** em Estrasburgo.

strategic [strə'tiːdʒɪk] *adj* estratégico(-ca).

strategy ['strætɪdʒɪ] *(pl* **-ies)** *n* estratégia *f.*

straw [strɔː] *n* **-1.** (U) [dried corn] palha *f* **-2.** [for drinking] canudinho *m.*

strawberry ['strɔːbərɪ] *(pl* **-ies)** ◇ *n* [fruit] morango *m.* ◇ *comp* de morango.

stray [streɪ] ◇ *adj* perdido(da). ◇ *vi* **-1.** [from group] perder-se **-2.** [from path] desviar-se **-3.** [thoughts, mind]: **to ~ from the point** desviar-se do tema.

streak [striːk] ◇ *n* **-1.** [of grease] faixa *f* **-2.** [of lightning] raio *m* **-3.** [in hair] listra *f* **-4.** [in character] traço *m.* ◇ *vi* [move quickly] passar como um raio.

stream [striːm] ◇ *n* **-1.** [brook] riacho *m* **-2.** [of liquid] curso *m* **-3.** [of air] corrente *f* **-4.** [of light] raio *m,* faixa *f* **-5.** [of liquid, air, light] rio *m* **-6.** [of people, traffic] torrente *f* **-7.** [of abuse, queries, complaints, books] série *f*- **8.** UK SCH grupo *m.* ◇ *vt* UK SCH agrupar de acordo com o rendimento escolar. ◇ *vi* **-1.** [gen] jorrar **-2.** [air] fluir **-3.** [people]: **to ~ in/out** entrar/sair em massa **-4.** [traffic] mover-se rapidamente.

streamer ['striːməʳ] *n* [for party] serpentina *f,* flâmula *f.*

streamlined ['striːmlaɪnd] *adj* **-1.** [aerodynamic] aerodinâmico(ca) **-2.** [efficient] racional.

street [striːt] *n* rua *f.*

streetcar ['striːtkɑːʳ] *n* US bonde *m.*

street lamp, street light *n* lâmpada *f* de rua.

street plan *n* mapa *m* viário.

strength [streŋθ] *n* **-1.** (U) [gen] força *f* **-2.** (U) [power, influence] poder *m* **-3.** [quality, ability] ponto *m* forte **-4.** (U) [solidity] solidez *f*- **5.** [intensity - gen] intensidade *f;* [- of alcohol] teor *m* alcoólico; [- of drug] potência *f*- **6.** FIN [of currency] solidez *f.*

strengthen ['streŋθn] *vt* **-1.** [gen] fortalecer **-2.** [reinforce] reforçar **-3.** [intensify] intensificar **-4.** [make braver, more confident] encorajar.

strenuous ['strenjʊəs] *adj* extenuante.

stress [stres] ◇ *n* **-1.** [emphasis]: **~ (on sthg)** ênfase *f* (em algo) **-2.** [tension, anxiety] estresse *m* **-3.** TECH [physical pressure]: **~ (on sthg)** pressão *f* (sobre algo) **-4.** LING [on word, syllable] acento *m* tônico. ◇ *vt* **-1.** [emphasize] enfatizar, realçar **-2.** LING [word, syllable] acentuar *(na pronúncia).*

stressful ['stresfʊl] *adj* estressante.

stretch [stretʃ] ◇ *n* **-1.** [area] extensão *f*- **2.** [period of time] período *m.* ◇ *vt* **-1.** [gen] esticar **-2.** [pull taut] estirar **-3.** [rules, meaning, truth] distorcer **-4.** [challenge] fazer render ao máximo. ◇ *vi* **-1.** [gen] esticar-se **-2.** [area]: **to ~ over** estender-se por; **to ~ from ... to** estender-se de ... até **-3.** [person] espreguiçar-se.

➡ **stretch out** ◇ *vt sep* estender, esticar. ◇ *vi* esticar-se *(deitando).*

stretcher ['stretʃəʳ] *n* maca *f.*

strew [struː] *(pt* **-ed,** *pp* **strewn** [struːn], **-ed)** *vt:* **to be strewn with sthg** estar coberto(ta) de algo.

stricken ['strɪkn] *adj:* **to be ~ by** OR **with sthg** [grief] estar abalado(da) por algo; [doubt, horror, panic] ser tomado(da) por algo; [illness, complaint] estar atacado(-da) por algo.

strict [strɪkt] *adj* **-1.** [severe] rígido(da) **-2.** [exact, precise] exato(ta), preciso(sa).

strictly ['strɪktlɪ] *adv* **-1.** [severely] rigidamente **-2.** [rigidly, absolutely] estritamente **-3.** [precisely, exactly] exatamente, precisamente; **~ speaking** a rigor **-4.** [exclusively] exclusivamente.

stride [straɪd] *(pt* **strode,** *pp* **stridden** ['strɪdn]) ◇ *n* passada *f;* **to take sthg in one's ~** *fig* encarar algo com tranqüilidade. ◇ *vi* caminhar a passos largos.

strident ['straɪdnt] *adj* **-1.** [voice, sound] estridente **-2.** [demand] rigoroso(sa).

strife [straɪf] *n* (U) *fml* conflitos *mpl.*

strike [straɪk] *(pt & pp* **struck**) ◇ *n* **-1.** [gen] greve *f;* **to be (out) on ~** estar em greve; **to go on ~** entrar em greve **-2.** MIL [attack] ataque *m* **-3.** [find] descoberta *f.* ◇ *vt* **-1.** [hit - deliberately] bater, golpear; [- accidentally] atingir, pegar em **-2.** [subj: hurricane, disaster, lightning] atingir **-3.** [subj: thought] ocorrer; **to ~ sb as sthg** parecer algo a alguém **-4.** [reach, arrive at] fechar **-5.** [ignite] acender **-6.** [chime] bater. ◇ *vi* **-1.** [stop working] entrar em greve **-2.** [hit accidentally]: **to ~ against sthg** bater em algo **-3.** [happen suddenly - hurricane, disaster] ocorrer; [- lightning] cair **-4.** [attack] atacar **-5.**

[chime]: **the clock struck seven** o relógio bateu sete horas.

◆ **strike down** *vt sep* derrubar.

◆ **strike out** ◇ *vt sep* rasurar. ◇ *vi* **-1.** [head out] partir, pôr-se a caminho **-2.** [do sthg different] partir para outra.

◆ **strike up** ◇ *vt fus* **-1.** [friendship, conversation] travar **-2.** [music] começar a tocar.

striker ['straɪkə^r] *n* **-1.** [person on strike] grevista *mf* **-2.** FTBL atacante *mf*.

striking ['straɪkɪŋ] *adj* **-1.** [noticeable, unusual] impressionante, chocante **-2.** [attractive] que chama a atenção.

string [strɪŋ] (*pt & pp* **strung**) *n* **-1.** (U) [thin rope] cordão *m*, barbante *m* **-2.** [piece of thin rope] cordel *m*; **to pull ~ s** mexer os pauzinhos **-3.** [row, chain - of beads, pearls] colar *m* **-4.** [series] série *f*, sucessão *f* **-5.** [for bow, tennis racket] corda *f*; **to be highly strung** *fig* ter o pavio curto **-6.** COMPUT string *m*.

◆ **strings** *npl* MUS: **the ~ s** as cordas.

◆ **string out** *vt sep*: **to be strung out** estar disperso(sa).

◆ **string together** *vt sep fig* juntar.

string bean *n* vagem *f*.

stringed instrument ['strɪŋd-] *n* instrumento *m* de corda.

stringent ['strɪndʒənt] *adj* rigoroso(sa).

strip [strɪp] (*pt & pp* **-ped**, *cont* **-ping**) ◇ *n* **-1.** [of fabric, paper, carpet] tira *f* **-2.** [of land, water, forest] faixa *f* **-3.** UK SPORT camiseta *f (de time)*. ◇ *vt* **-1.** [undress] despir; **~ ped to the waist** nu (nua) até o peito **-2.** [remove layer of] descascar. ◇ *vi* [undress] despir-se.

◆ **strip off** *vi* despir-se.

strip cartoon *n* UK tira *f* em quadrinhos.

stripe [straɪp] *n* **-1.** [band of colour] lista *f*, faixa *f* **-2.** [sign of rank] galão *m*.

striped [straɪpt] *adj* listado(da).

strip lighting *n* (U) iluminação *f* fluorescente.

stripper ['strɪpə^r] *n* **-1.** [performer of striptease] stripper *mf* **-2.** [tool, liquid] removedor *m*.

striptease ['strɪptiːz] *n* striptease *m*.

strive [straɪv] (*pt* **strove**, *pp* **striven** ['strɪvn]) *vi fml*: **to ~ for sthg/to do sthg** lutar por algo/para fazer algo.

strode [strəʊd] *pt* ▷ **stride**.

stroke [strəʊk] ◇ *n* **-1.** MED derrame *m* cerebral **-2.** [of brush] pincelada *f* **-3.** [of pen] traço *m* **-4.** [in swimming - movement] braçada *f*; [- style] nado *m* **-5.** [movement in rowing] remada *f* **-6.** [in tennis] raquetada *f* **-7.** [in golf] tacada *f* **-8.** [of clock] batida *f* **-9.** [of bell] dobre *m* **-10.**

UK TYPO [slash] barra *f* **-11.** [piece]: **a ~ of genius** um lance de gênio; **a ~ of luck** um golpe de sorte; **at a ~** de um golpe só. ◇ *vt* acariciar.

stroll [strəʊl] ◇ *n* passeio *m*. ◇ *vi* passear.

stroller ['strəʊlə^r] *n* US [for baby] carrinho *m* de bebê.

strong [strɒŋ] *adj* **-1.** [gen] forte; **~ point** ponto forte; **~ nerves** nervos *mpl* de aço **-2.** [solid, sturdy] reforçado(da) **-3.** [in number] de ... pessoas; **the crowd was 2000 ~** a multidão tinha 2000 pessoas.

strongbox ['strɒŋbɒks] *n* caixa-forte *f*.

stronghold ['strɒŋhəʊld] *n fig* baluarte *m*.

strongly ['strɒŋlɪ] *adv* **-1.** [sturdily, solidly-built] solidamente; [- protected] fortemente **-2.** [in degree or intensity] intensamente; **the kitchen smells ~ of onions** tem um cheiro forte de cebola na cozinha **-3.** [very definitely] totalmente; **to feel ~ about sthg** ter uma opinião firme sobre algo.

strong room *n* casa-forte *f*.

strove [strəʊv] *pt* ▷ **strive**.

struck [strʌk] *pt & pp* ▷ **strike**.

structure ['strʌktʃə^r] *n* **-1.** [organization, arrangement] estrutura *f* **-2.** [building, construction] construção *f*.

struggle ['strʌgl] ◇ *n* **-1.** [gen]: **~ (for sthg/to do sthg)** luta *f* (por algo/por fazer algo) **-2.** [fight] briga *f* ◇ *vi* **-1.** [try hard, strive] esforçar-se; **to ~ free** lutar para ser solto(ta); **to ~ (for sthg/to do sthg)** lutar (por algo/para fazer algo) **-2.** [fight]: **to ~ (with sb)** brigar (com alguém).

strum [strʌm] (*pt & pp* **-med**, *cont* **-ming**) *vt* dedilhar.

strung [strʌŋ] *pt & pp* ▷ **string**.

strut [strʌt] (*pt & pp* **-ted**, *cont* **-ting**) ◇ *n* CONSTR escora *f*. ◇ *vi* andar empertigado(da).

stub [stʌb] (*pt & pp* **-bed**, *cont* **-bing**) ◇ *n* **-1.** [of cigarette, pencil] toco *m* **-2.** [of ticket, cheque] canhoto *m*. ◇ *vt*: **to ~ one's toe (on)** dar uma topada com o dedo no pé (em).

◆ **stub out** *vt sep* apagar.

stubble ['stʌbl] *n* (U) **-1.** [in field] restolho *m* **-2.** [on chin] barba *f* curta.

stubborn ['stʌbən] *adj* **-1.** [person] teimoso(sa), cabeçudo(da) **-2.** [stain] persistente, difícil.

stuck [stʌk] ◇ *pt & pp* ▷ **stick**. ◇ *adj* **-1.** [gen] preso(sa) **-2.** [window] emperrado(da) **-3.** [stumped]: **can you help with this problem? I'm ~** pode me ajudar com esse problema? (eu) empaquei.

stuck-up adj inf pej convencido(da), metido(da).

stud [stʌd] n - **1.** [metal decoration] tachão m - **2.** [earring] pingente m - **3.** UK [on boot, shoe] salto m; - **4.** (U) [of horses] plantel m.

studded ['stʌdɪd] adj: ~ **(with sthg)** adornado(da) (com algo); **a ~ jacket** uma jaqueta adornada; ~ **with precious stones** cravejado(da) de pedras preciosas.

student ['stju:dnt] <> n - **1.** [at college, university] estudante mf - **2.** [scholar] estudioso m, -sa f. <> comp - **1.** [nurse, teacher] em estágio - **2.** [politics] estudantil - **3.** [lifestyle] de estudante - **4.** [disco] para estudantes.

student loan n UK crédito m educativo.

studio ['stju:dɪəʊ] (pl -s) n estúdio m.

studio flat UK, **studio apartment** US n quitinete f.

studious ['stju:djəs] adj estudioso(sa).

studiously ['stju:djəslɪ] adv cuidadosamente.

study ['stʌdɪ] (pl -ies, pt & pp -ied) <> n - **1.** (U) [gen] estudo m - **2.** [room] sala f de estudos. <> vt - **1.** [learn] estudar - **2.** [examine] examinar, estudar. <> vi estudar.
　studies npl estudos mpl.

stuff [stʌf] <> n (U) inf - **1.** [matter, things] coisa f - **2.** [substance]: **what's that ~ in your pocket?** o que é isso aí no seu bolso? - **3.** [belongings] coisas fpl. <> vt - **1.** [push, put] enfiar - **2.** [fill, cram]: **to ~ sthg (with sthg)** encher algo (com algo) - **3.** CULIN rechear.

stuffed [stʌft] adj - **1.** [filled, crammed]: ~ **with sthg** atulhado(da) de algo - **2.** inf [with food] empanturrado(da) - **3.** CULIN recheado(da) - **4.** [animal] empalhado(da).

stuffing ['stʌfɪŋ] n (U) - **1.** [filling - for furniture] estofamento m; [- for toys] enchimento m - **2.** CULIN recheio m.

stuffy ['stʌfɪ] (compar -ier, superl -iest) adj - **1.** [room] abafado(da) - **2.** [formal, old-fashioned] retrógrado(da).

stumble ['stʌmbl] vi - **1.** [trip] tropeçar - **2.** [hesitate, make mistake] equivocar-se.
　stumble across, stumble on vt fus - **1.** [person] topar com - **2.** [objects] encontrar por acaso.

stumbling block ['stʌmblɪŋ-] n pedra f no caminho, obstáculo m.

stump [stʌmp] <> n - **1.** [of tree] toco m - **2.** [of limb] coto m. <> vt deixar perplexo(xa).

stun [stʌn] (pt & pp -ned, cont -ning) vt - **1.** [bring under strict control] sujeitar,

- **1.** [knock unconscious] deixar sem sentidos - **2.** [shock, surprise] atordoar.

stung [stʌŋ] pt & pp ⊳ **sting**.

stunk [stʌŋk] pt & pp ⊳ **stink**.

stunning ['stʌnɪŋ] adj - **1.** [very beautiful] imponente - **2.** [very shocking, surprising] espantoso(sa).

stunt [stʌnt] <> n - **1.** [for publicity] golpe m publicitário - **2.** CINEMA cena f arriscada, cena f perigosa. <> vt inibir.

stunted ['stʌntɪd] adj mirrado(da).

stunt man n dublê m.

stupefy ['stju:pɪfaɪ] (pt & pp -ied) vt - **1.** [tire, bore] entorpecer - **2.** [surprise] deixar estupefato(ta).

stupendous [stju:'pendəs] adj inf - **1.** [wonderful] estupendo(da) - **2.** [very large] enorme.

stupid ['stju:pɪd] adj - **1.** [foolish] estúpido(da) - **2.** inf [wretched, damned] idiota.

stupidity [stju:'pɪdətɪ] n (U) estupidez f.

sturdy ['stɜ:dɪ] (compar -ier, superl -iest) adj - **1.** [person] forte, robusto(ta) - **2.** [furniture, platform] sólido(da), firme.

stutter ['stʌtə²] vi gaguejar.

sty [staɪ] (pl sties) n chiqueiro m.

stye [staɪ] n terçol m.

style [staɪl] <> n - **1.** [manner] estilo m; **in the ~ of** ao estilo de - **2.** (U) [smartness, elegance] classe f - **3.** [fashion, design] modelo m. <> vt pentear de acordo com a moda.

stylish ['staɪlɪʃ] adj de estilo.

stylist ['staɪlɪst] n estilista mf.

suave [swɑ:v] adj afável.

sub [sʌb] n inf - **1.** SPORT (abbr of substitute) reserva mf - **2.** (abbr of submarine) submarino m - **3.** UK (abbr of subscription) assinatura f - **4.** UK [advance payment] adiantamento m.

subconscious [,sʌb'kɒnʃəs] <> adj subconsciente. <> n: **the ~** o subconsciente.

subcontract [,sʌbkən'trækt] vt subcontratar.

subdivide [,sʌbdɪ'vaɪd] vt subdividir.

subdue [səb'dju:] vt - **1.** [enemy, rioters, crowds] subjugar - **2.** [feelings, passions] conter, dominar.

subdued [səb'dju:d] adj - **1.** [person] desanimado(da) - **2.** [feelings] reprimido(da) - **3.** [light, sound, colour] fraco(ca).

subject [adj, n & prep 'sʌbdʒekt, vt səb'dʒekt] <> adj: ~ **(to sthg)** sujeito(ta) (a algo). <> n - **1.** [topic, person under consideration] assunto m, tema m - **2.** GRAMM sujeito m - **3.** SCH & UNIV cadeira f - **4.** [citizen] súdito m, -ta f. <> vt - **1.** [bring under strict control] sujeitar,

dominar **- 2.** [force to experience]: **to ~ sb to sthg** sujeitar alguém a algo.
➣ **subject to** prep sujeito(ta) a; **~ to the budget** dependendo do orçamento.

subjective [səb'dʒektɪv] adj subjetivo(-va).

subject matter ['sʌbdʒekt-] n (U) temática f, tema m.

subjunctive [səb'dʒʌŋktɪv] n GRAMM: **~ (mood)** (modo m) subjuntivo m.

sublet [ˌsʌb'let] (pt & pp sublet, cont -ting) vt sublocar.

sublime [sə'blaɪm] adj sublime.

submachine gun [ˌsʌbmə'ʃiːn-] n metralhadora f.

submarine [ˌsʌbmə'riːn] n submarino m.

submerge [səb'mɜːdʒ] <> vt **- 1.** [flood] inundar **- 2.** [plunge into liquid] submergir. <> vi mergulhar.

submission [səb'mɪʃn] n (U) **- 1.** [obedience, capitulation] submissão f **- 2.** [presentation] apresentação f.

submissive [səb'mɪsɪv] adj submisso(-sa).

submit [səb'mɪt] (pt & pp -ted, cont -ting) <> vt submeter. <> vi: **to ~ (to sb)** render-se (a alguém); **to ~ (to sthg)** submeter-se (a algo).

subnormal [ˌsʌb'nɔːml] adj subnormal.

subordinate [ˌsə'bɔːdɪnət] <> adj fml: **~ (to sthg)** subordinado(da) (a algo). <> n subordinado m, -da f.

subpoena [sə'piːnə] (pt & pp -ed) JUR n intimação f (para comparecimento em juízo). <> vt intimar (para comparecimento em juízo).

subscribe [səb'skraɪb] vi **- 1.** [to magazine, newspaper]: **to ~ (to sthg)** fazer assinatura (de algo) **- 2.** [to view, belief]: **to ~ to sthg** concordar com algo.

subscriber [səb'skraɪbə[r]] n **- 1.** [to magazine, newspaper] assinante mf **- 2.** [to service] usuário m, -ria f.

subscription [səb'skrɪpʃn] n **- 1.** [to newspaper, magazine] assinatura f **- 2.** [to club, organization - monthly] mensalidade f; [- yearly] anuidade f.

subsequent ['sʌbsɪkwənt] adj subseqüente.

subsequently ['sʌbsɪkwəntlɪ] adv subseqüentemente, por conseguinte.

subservient [səb'sɜːvjənt] adj **- 1.** [servile]: **~ (to sb)** subserviente (a alguém) **- 2.** [less important]: **~ (to sthg)** subordinado(da) (a algo).

subside [səb'saɪd] vi **- 1.** [storm, anger] acalmar; [pain, grief] passar **- 2.** [floods] baixar; [swelling] diminuir **- 3.** CONSTR ceder.

subsidence [səb'saɪdns, 'sʌbsɪdns] n (U) CONSTR: **the problems were caused by ~** os problemas foram causados pelo fato de o terreno ter cedido.

subsidiary [səb'sɪdjərɪ] (pl -ies) <> adj subsidiário(ria). <> n: **~ (company)** (empresa f) subsidiária f.

subsidize, -ise ['sʌbsɪdaɪz] vt subsidiar.

subsidy ['sʌbsɪdɪ] (pl -ies) n subsídio m.

substance ['sʌbstəns] n **- 1.** [gen] substância f **- 2.** [essence, gist] essência f **- 3.** (U) [importance] importância f.

substantial [səb'stænʃl] adj **- 1.** [large, considerable] substancial **- 2.** [solid, well-built] sólido(da).

substantially [səb'stænʃəlɪ] adv **- 1.** [quite a lot] substancialmente, consideravelmente **- 2.** [mainly] basicamente.

substantiate [səb'stænʃɪeɪt] vt fml fundamentar.

substitute ['sʌbstɪtjuːt] <> n **- 1.** [replacement]: **~ (for sb/sthg)** substituto m, -ta f (de alguém/algo) **- 2.** SPORT reserva mf, suplente mf. <> vt: **to ~ sb for sb** substituir alguém por alguém; **to ~ sthg for sthg** substituir algo por algo.

subtitle ['sʌbˌtaɪtl] n subtítulo m.
➣ **subtitles** npl CINEMA legenda f.

subtle ['sʌtl] adj sutil.

subtlety ['sʌtltɪ] n **- 1.** [gen] sutileza f **- 2.** [delicacy, understatement] delicadeza f.

subtotal ['sʌbˌtəʊtl] n subtotal m.

subtract [səb'trækt] vt: **to ~ sthg (from sthg)** subtrair algo (de algo).

subtraction [səb'trækʃn] n subtração f.

suburb ['sʌbɜːb] n periferia f.
➣ **suburbs** npl: **the ~ s** a periferia.

suburban [sə'bɜːbn] adj **- 1.** [of suburbs] da periferia **- 2.** pej [boring] suburbano(-na).

suburbia [sə'bɜːbɪə] n (U) bairros mpl residenciais.

subversive [səb'vɜːsɪv] <> adj subversivo(va). <> n subversivo m, -va f.

subway ['sʌbweɪ] n **- 1.** UK [underground walkway] passagem f subterrânea **- 2.** US [underground railway] metrô m.

succeed [sək'siːd] <> vt **- 1.** [person] suceder a **- 2.** [event, emotion]: **to be ~ed by sthg** ser sucedido(da) por algo. <> vi **- 1.** [achieve desired result]: **to ~ in sthg/in doing sthg** conseguir algo/fazer algo **- 2.** [work well, come off] dar bons resultados, sair-se bem **- 3.** [go far in life] triunfar.

succeeding [sək'siːdɪŋ] adj seguinte.

success [sək'ses] n sucesso m.

successful [sək'sesfʊl] adj **- 1.** [attempt] bem-sucedido(da) **- 2.** [film, book etc.] de sucesso **- 3.** [person] bem-sucedido(da), de sucesso.

succession [sək'seʃn] n **-1.** [series] sucessão f **-2.** (U) fml [to high position] sucessão f.

successive [sək'sesɪv] adj sucessivo(va).

succinct [sək'sɪŋkt] adj sucinto(ta).

succumb [sə'kʌm] vi: to ~ (to sthg) sucumbir (a algo).

such [sʌtʃ] <> adj **-1.** [referring back] tal, semelhante; **I never heard ~ nonsense!** nunca ouvi tal absurdo! **-2.** [referring forward] assim; **have you got ~ a thing as a tin opener?** você teria algo como um abridor de latas?; ~ **words as 'duty' and 'honour'** palavras como dever e honra **-3.** [whatever]: **I've spent ~ as I had** gastei o pouco dinheiro que eu tinha **-4.** [so great, so extreme]: ~ ... **that** tal ... que; **the state of the economy is ~ that ...** tal é o estado da economia que ... <> adv tão; ~ **nice people** essas pessoas tão gentis; ~ **a lot of books** tantos livros; ~ **a long time** tanto tempo. <> pron [referring back]: **and ~ (like)** e coisas do gênero.
as such adv propriamente dito(ta).
such and such adj: **at ~ and ~ a time** de tal em tal hora.

suck [sʌk] vt **-1.** [by mouth] chupar **-2.** [draw in] aspirar, sugar.

sucker ['sʌkə'] n **-1.** [suction pad] ventosa f **-2.** inf [gullible person] trouxa mf.

suction ['sʌkʃn] n (U) **-1.** [drawing in] sucção f **-2.** [adhesion] adesão f.

Sudan [su:'dɑ:n] n Sudão m.

sudden ['sʌdn] adj **-1.** [quick] repentino(na); **all of a ~** de repente **-2.** [unforeseen] inesperado(da).

suddenly ['sʌdnlɪ] adv de repente.

suds [sʌdz] npl espuma f de sabão.

sue [su:] vt: **to ~ sb (for sthg)** processar alguém (por algo).

suede [sweɪd] n (U) camurça f.

suet ['soɪt] n (U) sebo m.

suffer ['sʌfə'] <> vt sofrer. <> vi **-1.** [feel physical pain] sofrer de; **to ~ from** sthg MED sofrer de algo **-2.** [experience difficulties or loss] sair prejudicado(da).

sufferer ['sʌfrə'] n paciente mf.

suffering ['sʌfrɪŋ] n sofrimento m.

suffice [sə'faɪs] vi fml ser suficiente, bastar.

sufficient [sə'fɪʃnt] adj suficiente.

sufficiently [sə'fɪʃntlɪ] adv suficientemente.

suffocate ['sʌfəkeɪt] <> vt sufocar, asfixiar. <> vi sufocar-se, asfixiar-se.

suffrage ['sʌfrɪdʒ] n (U) sufrágio m.

suffuse [sə'fju:z] vt: ~ d **with** sthg banhado(da) de algo.

sugar ['ʃʊgə'] <> n (U) açúcar m. <> vt adoçar.

sugar beet n (U) beterraba f (açucareira).

sugarcane ['ʃʊgəkeɪn] n (U) cana-de-açúcar f.

sugary ['ʃʊgərɪ] adj [high in sugar] açucarado(da), muito doce.

suggest [sə'dʒest] vt **-1.** [propose] sugerir, propor; **to ~ that sb do sthg** sugerir que alguém faça algo **-2.** [imply] insinuar.

suggestion [sə'dʒestʃn] n **-1.** [gen] sugestão f **-2.** (U) [implication] insinuação f.

suggestive [sə'dʒestɪv] adj **-1.** [implying sexual connotation] insinuante, provocante **-2.** [implying a certain conclusion]: ~ **(of sthg)** indicativo(va) (de algo) **-3.** [reminiscent]: ~ **of** sthg evocativo(va) de algo.

suicide ['su:ɪsaɪd] n suicídio m; **to commit ~** cometer suicídio, suicidar-se.

suit [su:t] n **-1.** [of matching clothes - for man] terno m; [- for woman] conjunto m **-2.** [in cards] naipe m; **to follow ~** seguir no mesmo naipe; fig seguir o exemplo **-3.** JUR processo m. <> vt **-1.** [look attractive on] cair bem **-2.** [be convenient or agreeable to] convir **-3.** [be appropriate to]: **that job ~s you perfectly!** este trabalho é a sua cara! <> vi [be convenient or agreeable to]: **does that ~?** está bom para ti?

suitable ['su:təbl] adj adequado(da), apropriado(da); **the most ~ person** a pessoa mais indicada.

suitably ['su:təblɪ] adv adequadamente, apropriadamente.

suitcase ['su:tkeɪs] n mala f.

suite [swi:t] n **-1.** [of rooms] suíte f **-2.** [of furniture] conjunto m.

suited ['su:tɪd] adj **-1.** [suitable]: ~ **to/for** sthg adequado(da) para algo **-2.** [compatible]: **they are well ~** eles combinam muito bem.

suitor ['su:tə'] n dated pretendente m.

sulfur n US = sulphur.

sulk [sʌlk] vi emburrar.

sulky ['sʌlkɪ] (compar -ier, superl -iest) adj emburrado(da).

sullen ['sʌlən] adj mal-humorado(da), atacado(da).

sulphur UK, **sulfur** US ['sʌlfə'] n (U) enxofre m.

sultana [səl'tɑ:nə] n UK [dried grape] passa f branca.

sultry ['sʌltrɪ] (compar -ier, superl -iest)

adj -1. [hot] abafado(da), mormacento(ta) -2. [sexy] quente.

sum [sʌm] (*pt* & *pp* -med, *cont* -ming) *n* soma *f.*

◆ **sum up** *vt sep* [summarize] resumir. ◇ *vi* recapitular.

summarize, -ise [ˈsʌməraɪz] *vt* resumir. ◇ *vi* resumir.

summary [ˈsʌmərɪ] (*pl* -ies) *n* resumo *m.*

summer [ˈsʌməʳ] *n* verão *m*; **in ~** no verão. ◇ *comp* de verão.

summer house *n* -1. [in garden] quiosque *m* (em jardim) -2. [for holidays] casa *f* de veraneio.

summer school *n* escola *f* de verão.

summertime [ˈsʌmətaɪm] *n*: (the) **~** o verão.

summit [ˈsʌmɪt] *n* -1. [mountaintop] topo *m*, cume *m* -2. [meeting] reunião *f* de cúpula.

summon [ˈsʌmən] *vt* convocar.

◆ **summon up** *vt sep* armar-se de.

summons [ˈsʌmənz] (*pl* **summonses**) *JUR* *n* intimação *f.* ◇ *vt* intimar.

sump [sʌmp] *n* *AUT* cárter *m.*

sumptuous [ˈsʌmptʃʊəs] *adj* suntuoso(sa).

sun [sʌn] *n*: the **~** o sol.

sunbathe [ˈsʌnbeɪð] *vi* tomar (banho de) sol.

sunbed [ˈsʌnbed] *n* câmara *f* de bronzeamento artificial.

sunburn [ˈsʌnbɜːn] *n* (U) queimadura *f* de sol.

sunburned [ˈsʌnbɜːnd], **sunburnt** [ˈsʌnbɜːnt] *adj* queimado(da) de sol.

Sunday [ˈsʌndɪ] *n* domingo *m; see also* Saturday.

Sunday school *n* catequese *f.*

sundial [ˈsʌndaɪəl] *n* relógio *m* de sol.

sundown [ˈsʌndaʊn] *n* (U) crepúsculo *m.*

sundry [ˈsʌndrɪ] *adj fml* diversos(sas); all and **~** todos(das) sem exceção.

◆ **sundries** *npl fml* artigos *mpl* diversos.

sunflower [ˈsʌnˌflaʊəʳ] *n* girassol *m.*

sung [sʌŋ] *pp* ▷ **sing**.

sunglasses [ˈsʌnˌglɑːsɪz] *npl* óculos *mpl* escuros *OR* de sol.

sunk [sʌŋk] *pp* ▷ **sink**.

sunlight [ˈsʌnlaɪt] *n* (U) luz *f* do sol *OR* solar.

sunny [ˈsʌnɪ] (*compar* -ier, *superl* -iest) *adj* -1. [full of sun] ensolarado(da) -2. *fig* [cheerful] luminoso(sa).

sunrise [ˈsʌnraɪz] *n* -1. [time of day] amanhecer *m* -2. [event] nascer *m* do sol.

sunroof [ˈsʌnruːf] *n* teto *m* solar.

sunset [ˈsʌnset] *n* -1. (U) [time of day] anoitecer *m* -2. [event] pôr-do-sol *m*, crepúsculo *m.*

sunshade [ˈsʌnʃeɪd] *n* guarda-sol *m.*

sunshine [ˈsʌnʃaɪn] *n* (U) (luz *f* do) sol *m.*

sunstroke [ˈsʌnstrəʊk] *n* (U) insolação *f.*

suntan [ˈsʌntæn] *n* bronzeado *m.* ◇ *comp* bronzeador(ra).

suntrap [ˈsʌntræp] *n* local *m* muito ensolarado.

super [ˈsuːpəʳ] *adj inf* excelente. ◇ *n* [petrol] gasolina *f* premium.

superannuation [ˌsuːpəˌrænjʊˈeɪʃn] *n* -1. (U) [pension] aposentadoria *f*, pensão *f* -2. [contribution] contribuição *f* para a previdência.

superb [suːˈpɜːb] *adj* soberbo(ba).

supercilious [ˌsuːpəˈsɪlɪəs] *adj* convencido(da), arrogante.

superficial [ˌsuːpəˈfɪʃl] *adj* superficial.

superfluous [suːˈpɜːflʊəs] *adj* supérfluo(flua).

superhuman [ˌsuːpəˈhjuːmən] *adj* sobre-humano(na).

superimpose [ˌsuːpərɪmˈpəʊz] *vt*: to **~** sthg on sthg sobrepor algo a algo.

superintendent [ˌsuːpərɪnˈtendənt] *n* -1. *UK* [of police] chefe *mf* de polícia -2. *fml* [of department] superintendente *mf.*

superior [suːˈpɪərɪəʳ] *adj* -1. [gen] superior; **~** to sthg/sb superior a algo/alguém -2. *pej* [arrogant] arrogante. ◇ *n* superior *m*, -ra *f.*

superlative [suːˈpɜːlətɪv] *adj* [of the highest quality] excelente. ◇ *n* *GRAMM* superlativo *m.*

supermarket [ˈsuːpəˌmɑːkɪt] *n* supermercado *m.*

supernatural [ˌsuːpəˈnætʃrəl] *adj* sobrenatural.

superpower [ˈsuːpəˌpaʊəʳ] *n* superpotência *f.*

supersede [ˌsuːpəˈsiːd] *vt* suplantar.

supersonic [ˌsuːpəˈsɒnɪk] *adj* supersônico(ca).

superstitious [ˌsuːpəˈstɪʃəs] *adj* supersticioso(sa).

superstore [ˈsuːpəstɔːʳ] *n* hipermercado *m.*

supertanker [ˈsuːpəˌtæŋkəʳ] *n* superpetroleiro *m.*

supervise [ˈsuːpəvaɪz] *vt* supervisionar.

supervisor [ˈsuːpəvaɪzəʳ] *n* supervisor *m*, -ra *f.*

supper [ˈsʌpəʳ] *n* -1. [main evening meal] jantar *m* -2. [snack before bedtime] lanche *m* antes de dormir.

supple [ˈsʌpl] *adj* flexível.

supplement [*n* ˈsʌplɪmənt, *vb*

'sʌplɪmentl *n* -**1.** [addition] acréscimo *m* -**2.** [in book] suplemento *m*; [of newspaper] suplemento *m*, encarte *m*. ⬦ *vt* complementar.

supplementary [ˌsʌplɪ'mentərɪ] *adj* suplementar.

supplier [sə'plaɪəʳ] *n* fornecedor *m*, -ra *f*.

supply [sə'plaɪ] (*pl* -ies, *pt* & *pp* -ied) *n* -**1.** [store, reserve] estoque *m* -**2.** (*U*) [network] abastecimento *m* -**3.** (*U*) ECON oferta *f*. ⬦ *vt*: to ~ sthg (to sb) fornecer algo (a alguém); if you ~ the food, I'll bring the drink se você entrar com a comida, eu trago a bebida; to ~ sb (with sthg) prover alguém (com algo); to ~ sthg with sthg abastecer algo com algo.
➡ **supplies** *npl* -**1.** [food] provisões *fpl* -**2.** [office equipment] material *m* -**3.** MIL apetrechos *mpl*.

support [sə'pɔ:t] *n* -**1.** [gen] apoio *m* -**2.** (*U*) [financial] ajuda *f* -**3.** [object, person] suporte *m*. ⬦ *vt* -**1.** [physically] sustentar, apoiar -**2.** [back, back up] apoiar -**3.** [financially] ajudar -**4.** [theory] fundamentar -**5.** SPORT torcer para.

supporter [sə'pɔ:təʳ] *n* -**1.** [of person, plan] partidário *m*, -ria *f* -**2.** SPORT torcedor *m*, -ra *f*.

suppose [sə'pəʊz] *vt* -**1.** [assume] supor -**2.** [concede reluctantly] supor, achar. ⬦ *vi* -**1.** [assume] crer; I ~ (so) suponho que sim; I ~ not suponho que não -**2.** [admit] admitir; I ~ so/not admito que sim/que não.

supposed [sə'pəʊzd] *adj* -**1.** [doubtful] suposto(posta) -**2.** [intended]: you weren't ~ to be outside não era para você estar na rua -**3.** [reputed]: he was ~ to be here at eight era para ele estar aqui às oito horas; it's ~ to be very good dizem que é muito bom.

supposedly [sə'pəʊzɪdlɪ] *adv* supostamente.

supposing [sə'pəʊzɪŋ] *conj*: ~ we went out? que tal OR e se a gente saísse?

suppress [sə'pres] *vt* -**1.** [uprising, revolt] reprimir -**2.** [information, report] ocultar -**3.** [emotions] conter.

supreme [sʊ'pri:m] *adj* -**1.** [highest in rank] supremo(ma) -**2.** [great] extraordinário(ria).

Supreme Court *n* [in US]: the ~ a Suprema Corte.

surcharge ['sɜ:tʃɑ:dʒ] *n*: ~ (on sthg) sobretaxa *f* (a algo).

sure [ʃʊəʳ] *adj* -**1.** [reliable] confiável, seguro(ra) -**2.** [certain] certo(ta); to be ~ about sthg ter certeza sobre algo;

to be ~ of sthg estar certo de algo; to be ~ of doing sthg ter certeza de que vai fazer algo; to make ~ (that) ... certificar-se de que ...; I'm ~ (that) ... tenho certeza de que ... -**3.** [confident]: to be ~ of o.s. estar seguro(ra) de si mesmo(ma). ⬦ *adv* -**1.** *inf* [yes] com certeza, claro -**2.** US [really] realmente.
➡ **for sure** *adv* com (toda) certeza.
➡ **sure enough** *adv* de fato.

surely ['ʃʊəlɪ] *adv* com certeza; ~ you can't be serious! você não pode estar falando a verdade!

surety ['ʃʊərətɪ] *n* garantia *f*, fiança *f*.

surf [sɜ:f] *n* (*U*) espuma *f* (*das ondas do mar*).

surface ['sɜ:fɪs] *n* superfície *f*; on the ~ à primeira vista. ⬦ *vi* -**1.** [from water] emergir, vir à tona -**2.** [become generally known] vir à tona.

surface mail *n* correio *m* terrestre OR marítimo.

surfboard ['sɜ:fbɔ:d] *n* prancha *f* de surfe.

surfeit ['sɜ:fɪt] *n fml* excesso *m*.

surfing ['sɜ:fɪŋ] *n* (*U*) surfe *m*; to go ~ ir surfar.

surge [sɜ:dʒ] ⬦ *n* -**1.** [gen] onda *f*; [of electricity] sobretensão *f* -**2.** [of water] torrente *f* -**3.** [of sales, applications] onda *f*, aumento *m*. ⬦ *vi* -**1.** [people, vehicles] avançar em massa -**2.** [water] subir.

surgeon ['sɜ:dʒən] *n* cirurgião *m*, -giã *f*.

surgery ['sɜ:dʒərɪ] (*pl* -ies) *n* -**1.** (*U*) MED [activity, operation] cirurgia *f* -**2.** UK MED [place] consultório *m*.

surgical ['sɜ:dʒɪkl] *adj* -**1.** [connected with surgery] cirúrgico(ca) -**2.** [worn as treatment] ortopédico(ca).

surgical spirit *n* (*U*) UK anti-séptico *m*.

surly ['sɜ:lɪ] (*compar* -ier, *superl* -iest) *adj* ríspido(da).

surmount [sɜ:'maʊnt] *vt* superar, vencer.

surname ['sɜ:neɪm] *n* sobrenome *m*.

surpass [sə'pɑ:s] *vt fml* ultrapassar, superar.

surplus ['sɜ:pləs] *adj* excedente; he was ~ to requirements ele estava além do que se precisava. ⬦ *n* -**1.** [gen] excedente *m* -**2.** [in budget] superávit *m*.

surprise [sə'praɪz] *n* surpresa *f*. ⬦ *vt* surpreender.

surprised [sə'praɪzd] *adj* surpreso(sa).

surprising [sə'praɪzɪŋ] *adj* surpreendente.

surprisingly [sə'praɪzɪŋlɪ] *adv* surpreendentemente.

surrender [sə'rendəʳ] *n* rendição *f*. ⬦

vi -1. [stop fighting]: **to ~ (to sb)** render-se (a alguém) -2. *fig* [give in]: **to ~ (to sthg)** sucumbir *OR* ceder (a algo).

surreptitious [ˌsʌrəpˈtɪʃəs] *adj* clandestino(na), furtivo(va).

surrogate [ˈsʌrəgeɪt] *adj* suplente. <> *n* substituto *m*, -ta *f*.

surrogate mother *n* mãe *f* de aluguel.

surround [səˈraʊnd] *vt* -1. [encircle] circundar, rodear -2. [trap] cercar -3. *fig* [be associated with] rondar.

surrounding [səˈraʊndɪŋ] *adj* -1. [all around] circundante -2. [associated] relacionado(da).

➟ **surroundings** *npl* -1. [physical] arredores *mpl* -2. [social] ambiente *m*.

surveillance [sɜːˈveɪləns] *n (U)* vigilância *f*.

survey [*n* ˈsɜːveɪ, *vb* səˈveɪ] *n* -1. [statistical investigation] pesquisa *f*, levantamento *m* -2. [physical examination - of land] medição *f*; [- of building] vistoria *f*, inspeção *f*. <> *vt* -1. [contemplate] contemplar -2. [investigate statistically] fazer um levantamento de -3. [examine, assess - land] medir; [- building] vistoriar, inspecionar.

surveyor [səˈveɪər] *n* [of land] agrimensor *m*, -ra *f*; [of building] vistoriador *m*, -ra *f*.

survival [səˈvaɪvl] *n (U)* [continuing to live] sobrevivência *f*.

survive [səˈvaɪv] *vt* -1. [live through] sobreviver a -2. [live longer than] sobreviver. <> *vi* -1. [gen] sobreviver -2. *inf* [cope successfully] sobreviver.

survivor [səˈvaɪvər] *n* -1. [gen] sobrevivente *mf* -2. *fig* [fighter] lutador *m*, -ra *f*.

susceptible [səˈseptəbl] *adj* -1. [likely to be influenced]: **~ (to sthg)** suscetível (a algo) -2. *MED*: **~ (to sthg)** propenso(sa) (a algo).

suspect [*adj & n* ˈsʌspekt, *vb* səˈspekt] *adj* suspeito(ta). <> *n* suspeito *m*, -ta *f*. <> *vt* -1. suspeitar; **I ~ corruption in the system** imagino que haja corrupção no sistema -2. [consider guilty]: **to ~ sb (of sthg)** suspeitar de alguém (em algo).

suspend [səˈspend] *vt* -1. [gen] suspender -2. [temporarily discontinue] suspender, interromper.

suspended sentence [səˈspendɪd-] *n* condenação *f* condicional.

suspender belt [səˈspendər-] *n UK* cinta-liga *f*.

suspenders [səˈspendəz] *npl* -1. *UK* [for stockings] cintas-ligas *fpl* -2. *US* [for trousers] suspensórios *mpl*.

suspense [səˈspens] *n (U)* suspense *m*.

suspension [səˈspenʃn] *n* suspensão *f*.

suspension bridge *n* ponte *f* suspensa.

suspicion [səˈspɪʃn] *n* suspeita *f*.

suspicious [səˈspɪʃəs] *adj* -1. [having suspicions] desconfiado(da) -2. [causing suspicion] suspeito(ta).

sustain [səˈsteɪn] *vt* -1. [gen] manter -2. [nourish spiritually] sustentar -3. [suffer] sofrer -4. [withstand] suportar.

sustainable development [səˈsteɪnabl-] *n* desenvolvimento *m* sustentável.

sustenance [ˈsʌstɪnəns] *n (U) fml* subsistência *f*.

SW *(abbr of* short wave*)* OC *f*.

swab [swɒb] *n* [bucha *f* de) algodão *m*.

swagger [ˈswægər] *vi* andar com ar garboso.

Swahili [swɑːˈhiːlɪ] *n* [language] suaíli *m*.

swallow [ˈswɒləʊ] *n* -1. [bird] andorinha *f* -2. [of drink] gole *m*. <> *vt* -1. [gen] engolir -2. *fig* [hold back] engolir em seco. <> *vi* engolir.

swam [swæm] *pt* ➪ **swim**.

swamp [swɒmp] *n* pântano *m*, brejo *m*. <> *vt* -1. [flood] inundar -2. [overwhelm]: **to ~ sb/sthg (with sthg)** sobrecarregar alguém/algo (de algo).

swan [swɒn] *n* cisne *m*.

swap [swɒp] *(pt & pp* -ped, *cont* -ping) *vt*: **to ~ sthg (with sb)** trocar algo com alguém; **to ~ sthg (over *OR* round)** trocar algo; **to ~ sthg for sthg** trocar algo por algo.

swarm [swɔːm] *n fig* [of people] mundaréu *m*. <> *vi* -1. *fig* [people] apinhar-se -3. *fig* [place]: **to be ~ing (with)** estar fervilhando de.

swarthy [ˈswɔːðɪ] *(compar* -ier, *superl* -iest) *adj* moreno(na).

swastika [ˈswɒstɪkə] *n* suástica *f*.

swat [swɒt] *(pt & pp* -ted, *cont* -ting) *vt* golpear.

sway [sweɪ] *vt* [influence] persuadir, convencer. <> *vi* oscilar.

swear [sweər] *(pt* swore, *pp* sworn) *vt* [gen] jurar; **to ~ to do sthg** jurar fazer algo *inf* [state emphatically] jurar. <> *vi* -1. [state emphatically] jurar -2. [use swearwords] praguejar.

swearword [ˈsweəwɜːd] *n* blasfêmia *f*, palavrão *m*.

sweat [swet] *n (U)* [perspiration] suor *m*. <> *vi* -1. [perspire] suar -2. *inf* [worry] preocupar-se com.

sweater [ˈswetər] *n* suéter *m*.

sweatshirt [ˈswetʃɜːt] *n* moletom *m*.

sweaty [ˈswetɪ] *(compar* -ier, *superl* -iest) *adj* -1. [skin, clothes] suado(da) -2. [activity] exaustivo(va).

swede [swiːd] *n UK* rutabaga *f.*

Swede [swiːd] *n* sueco *m*, -ca *f.*

Sweden [ˈswiːdn] *n* Suécia *f.*

Swedish [ˈswiːdɪʃ] *adj* sueco(ca). ◇ *n* [language] sueco *m*. ◇ *npl*: **the ~** os suecos.

sweep [swiːp] (*pt* & *pp* **swept**) *n* **-1.** [sweeping movement] movimento *m* (circular) **-2.** [with brush] varrida *f* **-3.** [chimneysweep] limpador *m*, -ra *f* de chaminé. ◇ *vt* **-1.** [gen] varrer **-2.** [with eyes] examinar **-3.** [spread through] disseminar.
- **sweep away** *vt sep* varrer do mapa.
- **sweep up** *vt sep* & *vi* escovar.

sweeping [ˈswiːpɪŋ] *adj* **-1.** [effect] radical **-2.** [statement] muito genérico(ca).

sweet [swiːt] *adj* **-1.** [gen] doce **-2.** [smell] doce, perfumado(da) **-3.** [sound] doce, melodioso(sa) **-4.** [gentle, kind] amável; **that's very ~ of you** é muita gentileza de sua parte **-5.** [attractive] meigo(ga). ◇ *n UK* **-1.** [candy] doce *m* **-2.** [dessert] sobremesa *f.*

sweet corn *n (U)* milho *m* verde.

sweeten [ˈswiːtn] *vt* adoçar.

sweetheart [ˈswiːthɑːt] *n* **-1.** [term of endearment] querido *m*, -da *f* **-2.** [boyfriend or girlfriend] namorado *m*, -da *f.*

sweetness [ˈswiːtnɪs] *n (U)* **-1.** [gen] doçura *f* **-2.** [of feelings] prazer *f* **-3.** [of smell] aroma *f* **-4.** [of sound] melodia *f.*

sweet pea *n* ervilha-de-cheiro *f.*

swell [swel] (*pt* -ed, *pp* **swollen** OR -ed) *vi* **-1.** [become larger]: **to ~ (up)** inchar **-2.** [fill with air] inflar **-3.** [increase in number] aumentar **-4.** [become louder] intensificar-se **-5.** [with pride] encher-se. ◇ *vt* aumentar. ◇ *n* elevação *f*; **sea ~** vaivém *m* do mar. ◇ *adj US inf* genial, excelente.

swelling [ˈswelɪŋ] *n* **-1.** *(U)* [swollenness] inchamento *m* **-2.** [swollen area] inchaço *m.*

sweltering [ˈsweltərɪŋ] *adj* **-1.** [weather] abafado(da) **-2.** [person] sufocado(da).

swept [swept] *pt* & *pp* ▷ **sweep**.

swerve [swɜːv] *vi* **-1.** [car, lorry] dar uma guinada **-2.** [person] desviar repentinamente.

swift [swɪft] *adj* **-1.** [fast] veloz **-2.** [prompt, ready] rápido(da). ◇ *n* [bird] andorinhão *m* preto.

swig [swɪg] *n inf* trago *m.*

swill [swɪl] *n (U)* lavagem *f.* ◇ *vt UK* enxaguar.

swim [swɪm] (*pt* **swam**, *pp* **swum**, *cont* -ming) *n* banho *m (de mar, de piscina)*; **to have a ~** nadar; **to go for a ~** ir nadar OR tomar banho *(de mar, de piscina)*. ◇ *vi* **-1.** [move through water] nadar; **can you ~?** você sabe nadar? **-2.** [feel dizzy] dar voltas; **my head was ~ming** minha cabeça estava girando.

swimmer [ˈswɪməʳ] *n* nadador *m*, -ra *f.*

swimming [ˈswɪmɪŋ] *n* [bathing] natação *f*; **to go ~** ir nadar.

swimming cap *n* touca *f* de natação.

swimming costume *n UK* traje *m* de banho.

swimming pool *n* piscina *f.*

swimming trunks *npl* sunga *m.*

swimsuit [ˈswɪmsuːt] *n* traje *m* de banho.

swindle [ˈswɪndl] *n* logro *m*, fraude *f.* ◇ *vt* lograr; **to ~ sb out of sthg** lograr alguém em algo.

swine [swaɪn] *n inf pej* [person] porco *m*, -ca *f.*

swing [swɪŋ] (*pt* & *pp* **swung**) *n* **-1.** [child's toy] balanço *m* **-2.** [change] virada *f*, mudança *f* **-3.** [swaying movement] rebolado *m* **-4.** *phr*: **to be in full ~** estar a todo vapor. ◇ *vt* **-1.** [move back and forth] balançar **-2.** [turn] virar bruscamente. ◇ *vi* **-1.** [move back and forth] balançar **-2.** [turn] girar; **to ~ open** abrir-se **-3.** [change] virar, mudar.

swing bridge *n* ponte *f* giratória.

swing door *n* porta *f* corrediça.

swingeing [ˈswɪndʒɪŋ] *adj* severo(ra).

swipe [swaɪp] ◇ *vt* **-1.** *inf* [steal] roubar **-2.** [plastic card] passar. ◇ *vi*: **to ~ at sthg** tentar golpear algo.

swirl [swɜːl] ◇ *n* **-1.** [swirling movement] rodopio *m* **-2.** [eddy] redemoinho *m.* ◇ *vi* girar.

swish [swɪʃ] ◇ *adj inf* [posh] bacana. ◇ *vt* [tail] balançar, agitar.

Swiss [swɪs] ◇ *adj* suíço(ça). ◇ *n* [person] suíço *m*, -ça *f.* ◇ *npl*: **the ~** os suíços.

switch [swɪtʃ] ◇ *n* **-1.** [control device] chave *f*, interruptor *m* **-2.** [change] mudança *f*, virada *f.* ◇ *vt* **-1.** [transfer] trocar; **to ~ one's attention to sthg** dirigir a atenção a algo **-2.** [swap, exchange] trocar de; **to ~ sthg round** trocar algo de lugar.
- **switch off** *vt sep* desligar.
- **switch on** *vt sep* ligar.

Switch® [swɪtʃ] *n UK cartão de débito automático.*

switchboard [ˈswɪtʃbɔːd] *n* mesa *f* telefônica.

Switzerland [ˈswɪtsələnd] *n* Suíça *f.*

swivel [ˈswɪvl] (*UK pt* & *pp* -led, *cont* -ling, *US pt* & *pp* -ed, *cont* -ing) *vt* & *vi* girar.

swivel chair *n* cadeira *f* giratória.

swollen ['swəʊln] <> pp ▷ swell. <>
adj -1. [ankle, arm] inchado(da) -2. [river]
cheio (cheia).

swoop [swu:p] <> n [raid] ataque-
surpresa m. <> vi -1. [fly downwards]
precipitar-se, mergulhar -2. [pounce]
atacar de surpresa.

swop [swɒp] n, vt & vi = swap.

sword [sɔ:d] n espada f.

swordfish ['sɔ:dfɪʃ] (pl inv OR -es) n
peixe-espada m.

swore [swɔ:ʳ] pt ▷ swear.

sworn [swɔ:n] <> pp ▷ swear. <>
adj JUR sob juramento.

swot [swɒt] (pt & pp -ted, cont -ting) UK
inf <> n pej cê-dê-efe mf. <> vi: to ~
(for sthg) matar-se de estudar (para
algo).

swum [swʌm] pp ▷ swim.

swung [swʌŋ] pt & pp ▷ swing.

sycamore ['sɪkəmɔ:ʳ] n falso-plátano m.

syllable ['sɪləbl] n sílaba f.

syllabus ['sɪləbəs] (pl-buses OR -bi [-baɪ])
n programa m da disciplina.

symbol ['sɪmbl] n símbolo m.

symbolize, -ise ['sɪmbəlaɪz] vt simbolizar.

symmetry ['sɪmətrɪ] n (U) simetria f.

sympathetic [ˌsɪmpə'θetɪk] adj -1. [un-
derstanding] compreensivo(va) -2. [will-
ing to support] favorável; ~ to sthg
favorável a algo.

sympathize, -ise ['sɪmpəθaɪz] vi -1. [feel
sorry] compadecer-se; to ~ with sb
solidarizar-se com alguém, compadecer-se de alguém -2. [understand] compreender; to ~ with sthg compreender
algo -3. [support]: to ~ with sthg apoiar
algo.

sympathizer, -iser ['sɪmpəθaɪzəʳ] n simpatizante mf.

sympathy ['sɪmpəθɪ] n -1. [understand-
ing] empatia f; ~ for sb empatia por
alguém -2. [agreement] simpatia f; in ~
(with sthg) de acordo (com algo).
▸ **sympathies** npl -1. [approval] simpa-
tias fpl -2. [condolences] pêsames mpl.

symphony ['sɪmfənɪ] (pl-ies) n sinfonia
f.

symposium [sɪm'pəʊzjəm] (pl-siums OR
-sia [-zjə]) n fml simpósio m.

symptom ['sɪmptəm] n sintoma m.

synagogue ['sɪnəgɒg] n sinagoga f.

syndicate ['sɪndɪkət] n sindicato m.

syndrome ['sɪndrəʊm] n síndrome f.

synonym ['sɪnənɪm] n sinônimo m; ~
for OR **of sthg** sinônimo para OR de algo.

synopsis [sɪ'nɒpsɪs] (pl -ses [-si:z]) n
sinopse f.

syntax ['sɪntæks] n LING sintaxe f.

synthesis ['sɪnθəsɪs] (pl -ses [-si:z]) n
síntese f.

synthetic [sɪn'θetɪk] adj -1. [man-made]
sintético(ca) -2. pej [insincere] artificial.

syphilis ['sɪfɪlɪs] n (U) sífilis f inv.

syphon ['saɪfn] n & vt = siphon.

Syria ['sɪrɪə] n Síria f.

syringe [sɪ'rɪndʒ] n seringa f.

syrup ['sɪrəp] n (U) -1. [sugar and water]
calda f -2. UK [golden syrup] melado m
-3. [medicine] xarope m.

system ['sɪstəm] n -1. [gen] sistema m
-2. [network, structure - road] rede f; [-
railway] malha f -3. (U) [methodical ap-
proach] sistemática f.

systematic [ˌsɪstə'mætɪk] adj sistemáti-
co(ca).

system disk n COMPUT disco m de
sistema.

systems analyst ['sɪstəmz-] n COMPUT
analista mf de sistemas.

T

t (pl t's OR ts), **T** (pl T's OR Ts) [ti:] n t, T m.

ta [ta:] excl UK inf brigado(da)!; ~ **very
much** brigado(da)!

tab [tæb] n -1. [of cloth] etiqueta f -2. [of
metal] lingüeta f -3. US [bill] conta f; to
pick up the ~ pagar a conta -4. phr:
to keep ~s on sb ficar de olho em
alguém.

tabby ['tæbɪ] (pl -ies) n: ~ (cat) gato m
tigrado.

table ['teɪbl] <> n -1. [piece of furniture]
mesa f -2. [diagram] tabela f. <> vt UK
[propose] apresentar.

tablecloth ['teɪblklɒθ] n toalha f de
mesa.

table football n pebolim m.

table lamp n luminária f.

table mat n descanso m para panelas.

table of contents n sumário m.

tablespoon ['teɪblspu:n] n -1. [spoon]
colher f (de sopa) -2. [spoonful] colherada f de sopa.

tablet ['tæblɪt] n -1. [pill] comprimido m,
pastilha f -2. [piece of stone] pedra f
lascada -3. [piece of soap] barra f.

table tennis n (U) tênis m inv de mesa.

table wine n (U) vinho m de mesa.

tabloid ['tæblɔɪd] n: ~ **(newspaper)**

tablóide *m*; **the ~ press** a imprensa sensacionalista.

tabulate ['tæbjʊleɪt] *vt* dispor em formato de tabela.

tacit ['tæsɪt] *adj fml* tácito(ta).

taciturn ['tæsɪtɜːn] *adj fml* taciturno(na).

tack [tæk] <> *n* -1. [nail] tacha *f* -2. NAUT rumo *m* -3. *fig* [course of action] tática *f*. <> *vt* -1. [fasten with nail] afixar (com tachas) -2. [in sewing] alinhavar. <> *vi* NAUT virar.

tackle ['tækl] <> *n* -1. FTBL entrada *f* -2. RUGBY obstrução *f* -3. [equipment, gear] apetrechos *mpl* -4. [for lifting] guincho *m*. <> *vt* -1. [job] lidar com -2. [problem] atacar -3. FTBL roubar a bola de -4. RUGBY derrubar -5. [attack] enfrentar.

tacky ['tækɪ] (*compar* -ier, *superl* -iest) *adj* -1. *inf* [cheap and nasty] barato(ta) -2. [sticky] grudento(ta), pegajoso(sa).

tact [tækt] *n* (*U*) tato *m*.

tactful ['tæktfʊl] *adj* discreto(ta); **that wasn't very ~ of you** você não agiu com muito tato.

tactic ['tæktɪk] *n* tática *f*.
  ➤ tactics *n* (*U*) MIL tática *f*.

tactical ['tæktɪkl] *adj* -1. [gen] estratégico(ca) -2. MIL tático(ca).

tactile *adj* tátil.

tactless ['tæktlɪs] *adj* indiscreto(ta); **he's so ~** falta tato nele.

tadpole ['tædpəʊl] *n* girino *m*.

taffy ['tæfɪ] (*pl* -ies) *n US* puxa-puxa *m*.

tag [tæg] *n* etiqueta *f*.

tail [teɪl] <> *n* -1. [gen] rabo *m* -2. [of coat, shirt] fralda *f* -3. [of car] parte *f* traseira. <> *vt inf* ir atrás de.
  ➤ tails <> *adv* [when tossing a coin] coroa *f*. <> *npl* [coat] fraque *m*.
  ➤ tail off *vi* diminuir.

tailback ['teɪlbæk] *n UK* fila *f* (*de carros*).

tailcoat ['teɪl.kəʊt] *n* fraque *m*.

tail end *n* final *m*, parte *f* final.

tailgate ['teɪlgeɪt] *n* tampa *f* traseira.

tailor ['teɪlə^r] <> *n* alfaiate *m*. <> *vt* adaptar.

tailor-made *adj fig* [role, job] sob medida.

tailwind ['teɪlwɪnd] *n* vento *m* de cauda.

tainted ['teɪntɪd] *adj* -1. [reputation] manchado(da) -2. *US* [food] estragado(da).

Taiwan [.taɪ'wɑːn] *n* Taiwan.

take [teɪk] (*pt* took, *pp* taken) *vt* -1. [gen] levar -2. [accompany] levar, acompanhar -3. [capture, undergo, swallow, measure] tomar -4. [receive] receber -5. [rent] alugar -6. [object, hand, road, means of transport] pegar -7. [accept, take on]

aceitar; **~ my word for it** acredita em mim; **what batteries does it ~?** que pilha vai aí? -8. [contain] suportar -9. [bear] agüentar -10. [require] precisar; **it could ~ years** pode levar anos -11. [holiday] tirar; **to ~ a walk** dar uma caminhada; **to ~ a bath** tomar um banho; **to ~ a photo** tirar OR bater uma foto -12. [pity, interest] ter; **to ~ offence** ofender-se; **I ~ the view that ...** sou da opinião de que ...; **to ~ sthg seriously/badly** levar algo a sério/a mal -13. [wear as a particular size - shoe] calçar; [- dress] vestir -14. [consider] pensar em, considerar -15. [assume]: **I ~ it (that) ...** presumo que ...
  ➤ take after *vt fus* parecer-se com.
  ➤ take apart *vt sep* desmontar.
  ➤ take away *vt sep* -1. [remove] levar embora -2. [deduct] subtrair, tirar.
  ➤ take back *vt sep* -1. [return] devolver -2. [accept] aceitar de volta -3. [statement, accusation] retirar.
  ➤ take down *vt sep* -1. [dismantle] desmontar -2. [write down] escrever, tomar nota de -3. [lower] baixar.
  ➤ take in *vt sep* -1. [deceive] enganar -2. [understand] compreender -3. [include] incluir -4. [provide accommodation for] acolher.
  ➤ take off <> *vt sep* -1. [remove] tirar -2. [have as holiday] tirar de folga; **she took the afternoon off** ela tirou a tarde de folga -3. *UK inf* [imitate] imitar. <> *vi* -1. [gen] decolar -2. [go away suddenly] mandar-se (embora), ir-se embora.
  ➤ take on *vt sep* -1. [accept - work, job] aceitar; [- responsibility] assumir -2. [employ] admitir -3. [confront] desafiar.
  ➤ take out *vt sep* -1. [from container] tirar -2. [go out with] convidar para sair.
  ➤ take over <> *vt sep* -1. [take control of] tomar o controle de, assumir -2. [job, role] assumir. <> *vi* -1. [take control] tomar o poder -2. [in job] assumir.
  ➤ take to *vt fus* -1. [feel a liking for - person] ter afeição especial por; [- activity] gostar de -2. [begin]: **to ~ to doing sthg** começar a fazer algo.
  ➤ take up *vt fus* -1. [begin - acting, singing] começar a se dedicar a; [- post, job] assumir -2. [use up - time] tomar; [- space] ocupar; [- effort] exigir.
  ➤ take up on *vt sep* [an offer] aceita.

takeaway *UK* ['teɪkə.weɪ], **takeout** *US* ['teɪkaʊt] <> *n* [food] comida *f* para levar. <> *comp* [food] para levar.

taken ['teɪkn] *pp* ▷ **take**.

takeoff ['teɪkɒf] *n* decolagem *f*.

takeout *n US* = **takeaway**.

takeover ['teɪk,əʊvə^r] n -1. [of company] aquisição f -2. [of government] tomada f do poder.

takings npl féria f, arrecadação f.

talc [tælk], **talcum (powder)** ['tælkəm-] n (U) talco m.

tale [teɪl] n -1. [fictional story] conto m -2. [anecdote] história f.

talent ['tælənt] n: ~ (for sthg) talento m (para algo).

talented ['tæləntɪd] adj talentoso(sa).

talk [tɔːk] ◇ n -1. [conversation] conversa f -2. (U) [gossip] boatos mpl, falatório m -3. [lecture] palestra f. ◇ vi -1. [gen] falar; to ~ to sb falar OR conversar com alguém; to ~ about sb/sthg falar sobre alguém/algo; ~ing of sb/sthg, ... falando de alguém/algo, ..., por falar em alguém/algo, ... -2. [gossip] fofocar -3. [make a speech] dar palestra; to ~ on OR about sthg falar sobre algo. ◇ vt -1. [discuss] tratar de -2. [spout] falar.

◆ **talks** npl negociações fpl.

◆ **talk into** vt sep: to ~ sb into sthg/into doing sthg convencer alguém de algo/a fazer algo.

◆ **talk out of** vt sep: to ~ sb out of sthg/out of doing sthg dissuadir alguém de algo/de fazer algo.

◆ **talk over** vt sep discutir.

talkative ['tɔːkətɪv] adj loquaz.

talk show US n programa m de entrevistas, talk-show m.

talk time n (U) [on mobile phone] tempo m de conversação.

tall [tɔːl] adj [in height] alto(ta); **she's two metres** ~ ela mede dois metros (de altura); **how** ~ **are you?** qual é a sua altura?

tall story n história f fantasiosa.

tally ['tælɪ] (pl -ies, pt & pp -ied) ◇ n [record] conta f; **to keep** ~ **of sthg** manter registro de algo. ◇ vi [correspond] fechar.

talon ['tælən] n garra f.

tambourine [,tæmbə'riːn] n pandeiro m.

tame [teɪm] ◇ adj -1. [animal, bird] domesticado(da) -2. pej [person] parado(da) -3. pej [unexciting] monótono(na). ◇ vt -1. [animal, bird] domesticar -2. [person] dominar.

tamper ['tæmpə^r] ◆ **tamper with** vt fus -1. [gen] mexer em -2. [lock] forçar.

tampon ['tæmpɒn] n absorvente m interno.

tan [tæn] (pt & pp -ned, cont -ning) ◇ adj castanho(nha). ◇ n bronzeado m; **to get a** ~ bronzear-se. ◇ vi bronzear-se.

tang [tæŋ] n [smell] cheiro m forte; [taste] gosto m forte.

tangent ['tændʒənt] n GEOM tangente f; **to go off at a** ~ fig sair pela tangente.

tangerine [,tændʒə'riːn] n tangerina f.

tangible ['tændʒəbl] adj tangível.

Tangier [tæn'dʒɪə^r] n Tânger f.

tangle ['tæŋgl] n -1. [mass] emaranhado m -2. fig [mess] rolo m; **they got into a** ~ eles se meteram num rolo.

tank [tæŋk] n tanque m.

tanker ['tæŋkə^r] n -1. [ship] navio-tanque m; **oil** ~ petroleiro m -2. [truck] caminhão-tanque m -3. [train] vagão-tanque m.

tanned [tænd] adj bronzeado(da).

Tannoy® ['tænɔɪ] n alto-falante m.

tantalizing ['tæntəlaɪzɪŋ] adj tentador(ra).

tantamount ['tæntəmaʊnt] adj: ~ to sthg equivalente a algo.

tantrum ['tæntrəm] (pl -s) n acesso m de fúria.

Tanzania [,tænzə'nɪə] n Tanzânia.

tap [tæp] (pt & pp -ped, cont -ping) ◇ n -1. [device] torneira f -2. [knock] batida f leve, palmadinha f. ◇ vt -1. [knock] bater de leve; **to** ~ **one's fingers on sthg** tamborilar em algo -2. [make use of] utilizar -3. [listen secretly to] grampear.

tap dance n sapateado m.

tape [teɪp] ◇ n -1. [gen] fita f -2. [adhesive material] fita f adesiva. ◇ vt -1. [record] gravar -2. [fasten with adhesive tape] juntar com fita adesiva.

tape measure n fita f métrica.

taper ['teɪpə^r] vi estreitar-se, afilar-se.

tape recorder n gravador m.

tapestry ['tæpɪstrɪ] (pl -ies) n tapeçaria f.

tar [tɑː^r] n (U) alcatrão m.

target ['tɑːgɪt] ◇ n -1. [gen] alvo m -2. fig [goal] meta f. ◇ vt -1. [as object of attack] mirar -2. [as customer] visar.

tariff ['tærɪf] n -1. [tax] tarifa f -2. UK [price list] tabela f de preços.

Tarmac® ['tɑːmæk] n alcatrão m.

◆ **tarmac** n AERON: **the tarmac** a pista.

tarnish ['tɑːnɪʃ] vt -1. [make dull] embaciar -2. fig [damage] manchar.

tarpaulin [tɑː'pɔːlɪn] n -1. (U) [material] encerado m -2. [sheet] lona f alcatroada.

tart [tɑːt] ◇ adj -1. [bitter-tasting] azedo(da) -2. [sarcastic] mordaz. ◇ n -1. [sweet pastry] torta f -2. UK vinf [prostitute] piranha f.

◆ **tart up** vt sep UK inf pej [smarten up]: **to** ~ **o.s. up** emperiquitar-se.

tartan ['tɑːtn] <> n -1. [pattern] xadrez m -2. (U) [cloth] tartan m. <> comp de tartan.

tartar(e) sauce ['tɑːtəʳ-] n (U) molho m tártaro.

task [tɑːsk] n tarefa f.

task force n força-tarefa f.

tassel ['tæsl] n borla f.

taste [teɪst] <> n -1. [gen] gosto m; in bad/good ~ de mau/bom gosto -2. fig [liking, preference]: ~ (for sthg) gosto (por algo) -3. fig [experience]: I've had a ~ of success eu senti o gostinho do sucesso -4. (U) [sense of taste] paladar m -5. [try]: have a ~ dá uma provada. <> vt -1. [gen] sentir o gosto de -2. [test, try] provar. <> vi: it ~s horrible tem um gosto horrível; to ~of/like sthg ter gosto de algo.

tasteful ['teɪstfʊl] adj de bom gosto.

tasteless ['teɪstlɪs] adj -1. [cheap and unattractive] sem graça -2. [offensive] de mau gosto -3. [without flavour] sem gosto.

tasty ['teɪstɪ] (compar -ier, superl -iest) adj saboroso(sa).

tatters ['tætəz] npl: in ~ [clothes] em farrapos; fig [confidence, reputation] em frangalhos.

tattle-tale n US = telltale.

tattoo [təˈtuː] (pl -s) <> n -1. [design] tatuagem f -2. UK [military display] parada f OR desfile m militar. <> vt tatuar.

tatty ['tætɪ] (compar -ier, superl -iest) adj UK inf pej -1. [clothes] surrado(da) -2. [area] enxovalhado(da).

taught [tɔːt] pt & pp ⊳ teach.

taunt [tɔːnt] <> n insulto m. <> vt insultar.

Taurus ['tɔːrəs] n [sign] Touro m.

taut [tɔːt] adj retesado(da).

tawdry ['tɔːdrɪ] (compar -ier, superl -iest) adj pej de mau gosto.

tax [tæks] <> n imposto m. <> vt -1. [gen] tributar -2. [strain, test] esgotar.

taxable ['tæksəbl] adj tributável.

tax allowance n limite m de isenção fiscal.

taxation [tækˈseɪʃn] n (U) -1. [system] sistema m tributário -2. [amount] tributação f.

tax avoidance [-əˈvɔɪdəns] n (U) dedução f fiscal.

tax collector n cobrador m, -ra f de impostos.

tax disc n UK disco fixado no pára-brisa do veículo para mostrar que o imposto já foi pago.

tax evasion n (U) sonegação f de impostos.

tax-free UK, **tax-exempt** US adj isento(ta) de imposto.

taxi ['tæksɪ] <> n táxi m. <> vi taxiar.

taxi driver n motorista mf de táxi, taxista mf.

tax inspector n inspetor m, -ra f da Receita.

taxi rank UK, **taxi stand** n ponto m de táxi.

taxpayer ['tæks,peɪəʳ] n contribuinte mf.

tax relief n (U) dedução f tributária.

tax return n declaração f de renda.

TB (abbr of tuberculosis) n tuberculose f.

tea [tiː] n -1. [gen] chá m -2. UK [afternoon meal] lanche m -3. UK [evening meal] chá m.

teabag ['tiːbæg] n saquinho m de chá.

teach [tiːtʃ] (pt & pp taught) <> vt -1. [instruct] ensinar; to ~ sb sthg, to ~ sthg to sb ensinar algo a alguém; to ~ sb to do sthg ensinar alguém a fazer algo; to ~ (sb) that ensinar (a alguém) que -2. [give lessons in] dar aulas de -3. [advocate] preconizar. <> vi lecionar.

teacher ['tiːtʃəʳ] n professor m, -ra f.

teacher training college UK, **teachers college** US n curso f de licenciatura.

teaching ['tiːtʃɪŋ] n -1. (U) [profession, work] magistério m -2. [thing taught] ensinamento m.

tea cloth n -1. [tablecloth] toalha f de mesa -2. [tea towel] pano m de prato.

tea cosy UK, **tea cozy** US n abafador m (de chá).

teacup ['tiːkʌp] n xícara f de chá.

teak [tiːk] n (U) teca f.

team [tiːm] n -1. SPORT time m -2. [group] equipe f.

teammate ['tiːmmeɪt] n companheiro m, -ra f de equipe.

teamwork ['tiːmwɜːk] n (U) trabalho m em equipe.

teapot ['tiːpɒt] n bule m de chá.

tear¹ [tɪəʳ] n lágrima f; to burst into ~s debulhar-se em lágrimas.

tear² [teəʳ] (pt tore, pp torn) <> vt -1. [rip] rasgar -2. [remove roughly] arrancar. <> vi -1. [rip] rasgar -2. inf [move quickly] ir a toda. <> n [rip] rasgão m.

    ⮞ **tear apart** vt sep -1. [rip up] destroçar -2. fig [disrupt greatly] desmantelar -3. [upset greatly] magoar.

    ⮞ **tear down** vt sep -1. [demolish] demolir -2. [remove] remover.

    ⮞ **tear up** vt sep despedaçar, fazer em pedaços.

teardrop ['tɪədrɒp] n lágrima f.

tearful ['tɪəfʊl] adj [person] choroso(rosa)

tear gas [tɪəʳ-] n (U) gás m lacrimogêneo.

tearoom ['tiːrʊm] n salão f de chá.

tease [tiːz] ⟨⟩ n inf - **1.** [joker] gozador m, -ra f - **2.** [sexually] provocador m, -ra f. ⟨⟩ vt: **to ~ sb (about sthg)** gozar de alguém (sobre algo).

teaspoon ['tiːspuːn] n colher f de chá.

teat [tiːt] n - **1.** [of animal] teta f - **2.** [of bottle] bico m.

teatime ['tiːtaɪm] n (U) UK hora f do chá.

tea towel n pano m de prato.

technical ['teknɪkl] adj técnico(ca).

technical college n UK escola f técnica.

technicality [,teknɪ'kælətɪ] (pl -ies) n detalhe m técnico.

technically ['teknɪklɪ] adv tecnicamente.

technician [tek'nɪʃn] n [worker] técnico m, -ca f.

technique [tek'niːk] n técnica f.

techno ['teknəʊ] n MUS tecno m.

technological [,teknə'lɒdʒɪkl] adj tecnológico(ca).

technology [tek'nɒlədʒɪ] (pl -ies) n tecnologia f.

teddy ['tedɪ] (pl -ies) n: **~ (bear)** ursinho m de pelúcia.

tedious ['tiːdjəs] adj tedioso(sa).

tee [tiː] n GOLF - **1.** [area] tee m, ponto m de partida - **2.** [for ball] tee m.

teem [tiːm] vi - **1.** [rain] chover torrencialmente; **the rain ~ ed down** caiu uma chuva torrencial - **2.** [be busy]: **to be ~ ing with** estar inundado(da) de.

teenage ['tiːneɪdʒ] adj adolescente.

teenager ['tiːn,eɪdʒəʳ] n adolescente mf.

teens [tiːnz] npl adolescência f.

tee shirt n camiseta f.

teeter ['tiːtəʳ] vi - **1.** [wobble] balançar, oscilar - **2.** fig [be in danger]: **to ~ on the brink of bankruptcy** estar à beira da falência.

teeth [tiːθ] pl ⊳ tooth.

teethe [tiːð] vi começar a ter dentes.

teething troubles ['tiːðɪŋ-] npl fig dificuldades fpl iniciais.

teetotaller UK, **teetotaler** US [tiː'təʊtləʳ] n abstêmio m, -mia f.

TEFL ['tefl] (abbr of **teaching of English as a foreign language**) n ensino de inglês para estrangeiros.

tel. (abbr of **telephone**) tel. m.

telecommunications ['telɪkə,mjuːnɪ-keɪʃnz] npl telecomunicações fpl.

telegram ['telɪgræm] n telegrama m.

telegraph ['telɪgrɑːf] ⟨⟩ n telégrafo m. ⟨⟩ vt telegrafar.

telegraph pole, telegraph post UK n poste m de telégrafo.

telepathy [tɪ'lepəθɪ] n (U) telepatia f.

telephone ['telɪfəʊn] ⟨⟩ n (U) telefone m; **to be on the ~** UK [have a telephone line] ter telefone; [be talking on the telephone] estar no telefone. ⟨⟩ vt telefonar. ⟨⟩ vi telefonar.

telephone banking n serviço m de banco por telefone.

telephone book n lista f telefônica.

telephone booth n UK telefone m público.

telephone box n UK cabine f telefônica.

telephone call n telefonema m.

telephone directory n lista f telefônica.

telephone line n linha f de telefone.

telephone number n número m de telefone.

telephonist [tɪ'lefənɪst] n UK telefonista mf.

telephoto lens [,telɪ'fəʊtəʊ-] n (lente f) teleobjetiva f.

telescope ['telɪskəʊp] n telescópio m.

teleshopping n telecompras fpl.

teletext ['telɪtekst] n (U) teletexto m.

televideo [telɪ'vɪdɪəʊ] n televisor m com videocassete.

televise ['telɪvaɪz] vt televisionar.

television ['telɪ,vɪʒn] n televisão f; **on ~** na televisão.

television set n (aparelho m de) televisão f.

teleworker ['telɪwɜːkəʳ] n teletrabalhador m, -ra f.

telex ['teleks] ⟨⟩ n telex m. ⟨⟩ vt transmitir por telex.

tell [tel] (pt & pp told) ⟨⟩ vt - **1.** [gen] contar; **to ~ sb (that)** contar a alguém que; **to ~ sb sthg, to ~ sthg to sb** contar algo a alguém - **2.** [instruct, judge, reveal] dizer; **do as you're told!** faça como lhe disseram!; **to ~ sb to do sthg** dizer para alguém fazer algo; **to ~ sb (that)** dizer a alguém que; **to ~ what sb is thinking** saber o que alguém está pensando ⟨⟩ vi - **1.** [speak] falar - **2.** [judge] dizer - **3.** [have effect] surtir efeito.

➡ **tell apart** vt sep distinguir, diferenciar.

➡ **tell off** vt sep repreender.

telling ['telɪŋ] adj - **1.** [relevant] contundente - **2.** [revealing] revelador(ra).

telltale ['telteɪl] ⟨⟩ adj revelador(ra). ⟨⟩ n mexeriqueiro m, -ra f.

telly ['telɪ] (pl -ies) n UK inf televisão f; **on ~** na televisão.

temp *UK* [temp] *inf* ⬦ *n* (*abbr of* **temporary (employee)**) funcionário *m* temporário, funcionária *f* temporária. ⬦ *vi* trabalhar em emprego temporário.

temper ['tempə'] ⬦ *n* **-1.** [state of mind, mood] humor *m*; **to be in a good/bad ~** estar de bom/mau humor; **to lose one's ~** perder a cabeça; **-2.** [temperament] temperamento *m*. ⬦ *vt fml* controlar, conter.

temperament ['temprəmənt] *n* temperamento *m*.

temperamental [,temprə'mentl] *adj* temperamental.

temperate ['temprət] *adj* temperado(-da).

temperature ['temprətʃə'] *n* temperatura *f*; **to have a ~** ter febre.

tempestuous [tem'pestjʊəs] *adj* **-1.** *literary* [stormy] turbulento(ta) **-2.** *fig* [emotional] tempestuoso(sa).

template ['templɪt] *n* [of shape, pattern] molde *m*, modelo *m*.

temple ['templ] *n* **-1.** *RELIG* templo *m* **-2.** *ANAT* têmpora *f*.

temporarily [,tempə'rerəlɪ] *adv* temporariamente.

temporary ['tempərərɪ] *adj* temporário(ria).

tempt [tempt] *vt* tentar; **to ~ sb to do sthg** tentar alguém a fazer algo.

temptation [temp'teɪʃn] *n* tentação *f*.

tempting ['temptɪŋ] *adj* tentador(ra).

ten [ten] *num* dez; *see also* **six.**

tenable ['tenəbl] *adj* [reasonable, credible] sustentável.

tenacious [tɪ'neɪʃəs] *adj* tenaz.

tenancy ['tenənsɪ] (*pl* -ies) *n* **-1.** [period] aluguel *m* **-2.** (*U*) [possession] locação *f*.

tenant ['tenənt] *n* **-1.** [of a house] inquilino *m*, -na *f* **-2.** [of a pub] locatário *m*, -ria *f*.

tend [tend] *vt* **-1.** [have tendency]: **to ~ to do sthg** ter a tendência a fazer algo **-2.** [look after] cuidar.

tendency ['tendənsɪ] (*pl* -ies) *n* **-1.** [gen]: **~ towards sthg/to do sthg** tendência a algo/a fazer algo **-2.** [leaning, habit] tendência *f*.

tender ['tendə'] ⬦ *adj* **-1.** [caring, gentle] terno(na), meigo(ga) **-2.** [meat] macio(cia) **-3.** [sore] dolorido(da). ⬦ *n* *COMM* proposta *f*, oferta *f*. ⬦ *vt fml* oferecer.

tendon ['tendən] *n* tendão *m*.

tenement ['tenəmənt] *n* cortiço *m*.

Tenerife *n* Tenerife.

tenet ['tenɪt] *n fml* dogma *m*.

tennis ['tenɪs] *n* (*U*) tênis *m*.

tennis ball *n* bola *f* de tênis.

tennis court *n* quadra *f* de tênis..

tennis racket *n* raquete *f* de tênis.

tenor ['tenə'] *n* [singer] tenor *m*.

tense [tens] ⬦ *adj* tenso(sa). ⬦ *n* *GRAMM* tempo *m* (verbal). ⬦ *vt* tensionar, retesar.

tension ['tenʃn] *n* tensão *f*.
➤ **tensions** *npl* conflitos *mpl*.

tent [tent] *n* tenda *f*, barraca *f*.

tentacle ['tentəkl] *n* tentáculo *m*.

tentative ['tentətɪv] *adj* **-1.** [unconfident, hesitant - person] indeciso(sa); [- handshake] vacilante **-2.** [temporary, not final] provisório(ria).

tenterhooks ['tentəhʊks] *npl*: **to be on ~** estar com os nervos à flor da pele.

tenth [tenθ] *num* décimo(ma); *see also* **sixth.**

tent peg *n* estaca *f* de barraca.

tent pole *n* mastro *m* de barraca.

tenuous ['tenjʊəs] *adj* **-1.** [argument] pouco convincente **-2.** [connection] de pouca importância **-3.** [hold] tênue.

tenure ['tenjə'] *n* (*U*) *fml* **-1.** [of property] posse *f* **-2.** [of job] estabilidade *f*.

tepid ['tepɪd] *adj* [liquid] tépido(da), morno(na).

term [tɜːm] ⬦ *n* **-1.** [word, expression] termo *m* **-2.** *SCH & UNIV* [third of school year] semestre *m* **-3.** [stretch of time] período *m*; **in the long/short ~** a longo/curto prazo. ⬦ *vt* designar.
➤ **terms** *npl* **-1.** [of contract, agreement] termos *mpl* **-2.** [conditions]: **in international/real ~s** em termos internacionais/reais **-3.** [of relationship]: **to be on good ~s (with sb)** dar-se bem (com alguém) **-4.** *phr*: **to come to ~s with sthg** aceitar algo.
➤ **in terms of** *prep* no que diz respeito a.

terminal ['tɜːmɪnl] ⬦ *adj* terminal. ⬦ *n* terminal *m*.

terminate ['tɜːmɪneɪt] ⬦ *vt* **-1.** [agreement, discussion] *fml* pôr fim a, encerrar **-2.** [pregnancy] interromper **-3.** [contract] rescindir. ⬦ *vi* **-1.** [bus, train]: **this bus ~s in the city centre** este ônibus pára no centro na cidade **-2.** [contract] terminar.

terminus ['tɜːmɪnəs] (*pl* -ni *OR* -nuses) *n* terminal *m*.

terrace ['terəs] *n* **-1.** *UK* [of houses] fileira *f* de casas geminadas **-2.** [patio] terraço *m* **-3.** [on hillside] terraço *m*, socalco *m*.
➤ **terraces** *npl* *FTBL*: **the ~s** as arquibancadas.

terraced ['terəst] *adj* escalonado(da).

terraced house *n UK* casa *f* geminada.

terrain [te'reɪn] *n* (*U*) terreno *m*.

terrible ['terəbl] *adj* terrível.

terribly ['terəblı] *adv* -**1.** [very badly] terrivelmente -**2.** [extremely] imensamente.

terrier ['terɪə'] *n* terrier *m*.

terrific [tə'rɪfɪk] *adj* -**1.** [wonderful] fabuloso(sa), maravilhoso(so) -**2.** [enormous] enorme.

terrified ['terɪfaɪd] *adj*: ~ (of sb/sthg) aterrorizado(da) (com alguém/algo); to be ~ of sthg ter horror a algo.

terrifying ['terɪfaɪɪŋ] *adj* aterrorizante.

territory ['terətrɪ] (*pl* -ies) *n* -**1.** [political area] território *m* -**2.** [terrain] terreno *m* -**3.** [area of knowledge] campo *m*, área *f*.

terror ['terə'] *n* -**1.** (*U*) [fear] terror *m* -**2.** [something feared] horror *m* -**3.** *inf* [rascal] pestinha *mf*.

terrorism ['terərɪzm] *n* (*U*) terrorismo *m*.

terrorist ['terərɪst] *n* terrorista *mf*.

terrorize, -ise ['terəraɪz] *vt* aterrorizar.

terry (cloth) *n* (*U*) tecido *m* atoalhado.

terse [tɜːs] *adj* seco(ca).

Terylene® ['terɪliːn] *n* (*U*) tergal® *m*.

test [test] ⇔ *n* -**1.** [trial] teste *m* -**2.** [MED, examination of knowledge, skill] exame *m*; *SCH* prova *f*, teste *m*. ⇔ *vt* -**1.** [try out] testar -**2.** [examine, check] examinar; to ~ sb on sthg examinar algo de alguém.

testament ['testəmənt] *n* testamento *m*.

test-drive *vt* test-drive *m*.

testicles ['testɪklz] *npl* testículos *mpl*.

testify ['testɪfaɪ] (*pt* & *pp* -ied) ⇔ *vt* declarar; to ~ that testemunhar que. ⇔ *vi* -**1.** *JUR* declarar sob juramento -**2.** [be proof]: to ~ to sthg evidenciar algo.

testimony [UK 'testɪmənɪ, US 'testəməʊnɪ] *n* (*U*) *JUR* depoimento *m*, testemunho *m*; to bear ~ testemunhar.

testing ['testɪŋ] *adj* [trying, difficult] duro(ra).

test match *n* UK partida *f* internacional.

testosterone *n* testosterona *f*.

test pilot *n* piloto *m* de prova.

test tube *n* tubo *m* de ensaio, proveta *f*.

test-tube baby *n* bebê *m* de proveta.

tetanus ['tetənəs] *n* (*U*) tétano *m*.

tether ['teðə'] ⇔ *vt* -**1.** [horse] apear -**2.** [dog] amarrar. ⇔ *n*: to be at the end of one's ~ estar no limite.

text [tekst] *n* texto *m*.

textbook ['tekstbʊk] *n* livro-texto *m*.

textile ['tekstaɪl] *n* tecido *m*.

texting ['tekstɪŋ] *n* *inf* mensagens *fpl* de texto.

text message *n* [on mobile phone] mensagem *m* de texto.

text messaging [-'mesɪdʒɪŋ] *n* [on mobile phone] mensagem *f* de texto.

texture ['tekstʃə'] *n* textura *f*.

Thai [taɪ] ⇔ *adj* tailandês(esa). ⇔ *n* -**1.** [person] tailandês *m*, -esa *f* -**2.** [language] tailandês *m*.

Thailand ['taɪlænd] *n* Tailândia.

Thames [temz] *n*: the ~ o Tâmisa.

than [weak form ðən, strong form ðæn] *conj* que; more ~ ten mais de dez; I'd rather stay in ~ go out prefiro ficar em casa a sair.

thank [θæŋk] *vt*: to ~ sb (for sthg) agradecer alguém (por algo); ~ God OR goodness OR heavens! graças a Deus/aos céus!
◆ **thanks** ⇔ *npl* agradecimento *m*. ⇔ *excl* obrigado(da)!
◆ **thanks to** *prep* graças a.

thankful ['θæŋkfʊl] *adj* agradecido(da); ~ for sthg agradecido(da) por algo.

thankless ['θæŋklɪs] *adj* ingrato(ta).

thanksgiving *n* ação *f* de graças.
◆ **Thanksgiving (Day)** *n* Dia *m* de Ação de Graças.

thank you *excl* obrigado(da); ~ for obrigado(da) por.

that [ðæt, weak form of pron & conj ðət] (*pl* those) ⇔ *adj* -**1.** [referring to thing, person mentioned] esse (essa); I prefer ~ book prefiro esse livro. -**2.** [referring to thing, person farther away] aquele (aquela); ~ book at the back aquele livro lá atrás; I'll have ~ one quero aquele (ali) OR esse. ⇔ *pron* -**1.** [referring to thing, person mentioned] esse *m*, essa *f*; [indefinite] isso; what's ~? o que é isso?; who's ~? [on the phone] quem fala?; [pointing] e esse, quem é?; ~'s interesting que interessante. -**2.** [referring to thing, person farther away] aquele *m*, aquela *f*; [indefinite] aquilo; is ~ Lucy? [pointing] aquela é a Lucy?; I want those at the back quero aqueles lá atrás; what's ~ on the roof? o que é aquilo no telhado? -**3.** [introducing relative clause] que; a shop ~ sells antiques uma loja que vende antiguidades; the movie ~ I saw o filme que eu vi; the room ~ I slept in o quarto onde OR em que dormi. ⇔ *adv* assim tão; it wasn't ~ bad/good não foi assim tão mau/bom; it didn't cost ~ much não custou tanto assim. ⇔ *conj* que; tell him ~ I'm going to be late diga-lhe que vou chegar atrasado.

thatched [θætʃt] *adj* com telhado de palha.

that's [ðæts] = that is.

thaw [θɔ:] ◇ vt -1. [ice] derreter -2. [frozen food] descongelar. ◇ vi -1. [ice] derreter -2. [food] descongelar -3. fig [people, relations] tornar-se um pouco mais amistoso. ◇ n [warm spell] degelo m.

the [weak form ðə, before vowel ði, strong form ði:] definite article -1. [gen] o (a), os (as) (pl); ~ book o livro; ~ apple a maçã; ~ girls as meninas; ~ Wilsons os Wilson; to play ~ piano tocar piano. -2. [with an adjective to form a noun] o (a), os (as) (pl); ~ British os britânicos; ~ young os jovens; ~ impossible o impossível. -3. [in dates]: ~ twelfth o dia doze; ~ forties os anos quarenta. -4. [in titles]: Elizabeth ~ Second Elizabeth Segunda.

theatre, theater US ['θɪətəʳ] n -1. [building] teatro m -2. [art, industry]: the ~ o teatro -3. [in hospital] sala f de cirurgia -4. US [cinema] cinema m.

theatregoer, theatergoer US ['θɪətə,gəʊəʳ] n aficionado m, -da f por teatro.

theatrical [θɪ'ætrɪkl] adj teatral.

theft [θeft] n roubo m.

their [ðeəʳ] adj seu (sua), deles (delas); ~ house a sua casa, a casa deles.

theirs [ðeəz] pron o(a) deles (o/a delas); a friend of ~ um amigo deles; these books are ~ estes livros são (os) deles; these are ours - where are ~? estes são os nossos - onde estão os deles?

them [weak form ðəm, strong form ðem] pron -1. (direct) os mpl, as fpl; I know ~ eu os conheço -2. (indirect) lhes; send this to ~ mande-lhes isso; tell ~ diga-lhes -3. (after prep) eles mpl, elas fpl; Anna and Sam brought it with ~ a Anna e o Sam trouxeram-no com eles.

theme [θi:m] n -1. [gen] tema m -2. [signature tune] sintonia f.

theme tune n música-tema f, tema f musical.

themselves [ðem'selvz] pron -1. (reflexive) se; they hurt ~ eles machucaram-se -2. (after prep) eles mpl próprios, elas fpl próprias, si mpl próprios, si fpl próprias; they blame ~ eles culpam-se a si próprios; they did it ~ fizeram-no eles mesmos OR próprios.

then [ðen] ◇ adv -1. [later, as a result] então; if you help me out now, ~ I'll return the favour se você me ajudar agora, eu te devolvo o favor; it starts at eight - I'll see you ~ começa às oito - te vejo a essa hora -2. [next, afterwards] depois -3. [in that case] então, neste caso; all right ~ então, tudo certo -4.

[therefore] então, portanto -5. [furthermore, also] além disso. ◇ adj então.

theology [θɪ'ɒlədʒɪ] n teologia f.

theoretical [θɪə'retɪkl] adj teórico(ca).

theorize, -ise ['θɪəraɪz] vi: to ~ (about sthg) teorizar (sobre algo).

theory ['θɪərɪ] (pl -ies) n teoria f; in ~ em teoria.

therapist ['θerəpɪst] n terapeuta mf.

therapy ['θerəpɪ] n (U) terapia f.

there [ðeəʳ] ◇ pron [indicating existence of sthg]: ~ is/are há; ~'s someone at the door tem alguém na porta ◇ adv -1. [in existence, available] lá, ali; is Sam ~, please? [when telephoning] o Sam está? -2. [referring to place] lá; I'm going ~ next week vou lá para a semana; over ~ ali; it's right ~ by the phone está aí bem ao lado do telefone.

➤ **there you are** adv handing sthg to sb] aqui está.

thereabouts [,ðeərə'baʊts], **thereabout** US [,ðeərə'baʊt] adv: or ~ ou por ali; by 1998 or ~ mais ou menos em 1998.

thereafter [,ðeər'ɑ:ftəʳ] adv fml conse-qüentemente, depois disso.

thereby [,ðeər'baɪ] adv fml desse modo.

therefore ['ðeəfɔ:ʳ] adv portanto, por isso.

there's [ðeəz] cont = there is.

thermal ['θɜ:ml] adj térmico(ca); ~ waters águas fpl termais.

thermometer [θə'mɒmɪtəʳ] n termô-metro m.

Thermos (flask)® ['θɜ:məs-] n garrafa f térmica.

thermostat ['θɜ:məstæt] n termostato m.

thesaurus [θɪ'sɔ:rəs] (pl -es) n tesauro m.

these [ði:z] pl ⊳ this.

thesis ['θi:sɪs] (pl theses ['θi:si:zl]) n tese f.

they [ðeɪ] pers pron pl eles mpl, elas fpl.

they'd [ðeɪd] = they had, they would.

they'll [ðeɪl] = they shall, they will.

they're [ðeəʳ] = they are.

they've [ðeɪv] = they have.

thick [θɪk] ◇ adj -1. [bulky] grosso(sa); it's 6 cm ~ tem 6 cm de espessura; how ~ is that wall? qual é a espessura da parede? -2. [dense] denso(sa) -3. inf [stupid] estúpido(da) -4. [viscous] espes-so(sa) -5. [voice - with anger] enraiveci-do(da); [- with emotion] embargado(da); [- with drink] enrolado(da). ◇ n: to be in the ~ of sthg estar no centro de algo.

thicken ['θɪkn] ◇ vt engrossar. ◇ vi

-1. [become denser] ficar mais denso(-sa) **-2.** [become more solid] engrossar.

thicket ['θɪkɪt] *n* moita *f*.

thickness ['θɪknɪs] *n* **-1.** [width, depth] espessura *f* **-2.** [density - of forest, hedge] densidade *f*; [- of hair] grossura *f* **-3.** [of soup, sauce] consistência *f*.

thickset [ˌθɪk'set] *adj* robusto(ta).

thick-skinned [-'skɪnd] *adj* insensível.

thief [θi:f] (*pl* **thieves**) *n* ladrão *m*, -dra *f*.

thieve [θi:v] <> *vt* roubar. <> *vi* roubar.

thieves [θi:vz] *pl* ➣ **thief**.

thigh [θaɪ] *n* coxa *f*.

thimble ['θɪmbl] *n* dedal *m*.

thin [θɪn] (*compar* -ner, *superl* -nest, *pt* & *pp* -ned, *cont* -ning) *adj* **-1.** [in width, depth] fino(na) **-2.** [skinny] magro(gra) **-3.** [watery] ralo(la), aguado(da) **-4.** [sparse - crowd, vegetation] disperso(sa); [- hair] ralo(la) **-5.** [excuse] fraco(ca).
➣ **thin down** *vt sep* diluir.

thing [θɪŋ] *n* **-1.** [gen] coisa *f*; **you poor ~!** coitadinho(nha); **the next ~ on the list** o próximo item da lista; **the (best) ~ to do would be ...** o melhor a fazer seria ...; **the ~ is ...** a questão é ..., acontece que ... **-2.** [anything]: **not a ~** nada; **I don't know a ~ (about)** não sei nada (sobre *OR* de).
➣ **things** *npl* **-1.** [clothes, possessions] coisas *fpl* **-2.** *inf* [life] coisas *fpl*.

think [θɪŋk] (*pt* & *pp* **thought**) <> *vt* **-1.** [believe]: **to ~ (that)** achar *OR* acreditar que; **I ~ so** acho que sim; **I don't ~ so** acho que não **-2.** [have in mind] pensar **-3.** [imagine] entender, imaginar **-4.** [in polite requests]: **do you ~ you could help me?** você acha que pode me ajudar? <> *vi* **-1.** [use mind] pensar **-2.** [have stated opinion]: **what do you ~ of *OR* about his new film?** o que você acha do novo filme dele?; **I don't ~ much of them/it** não tenho uma opinião muito boa sobre eles/ele; **to ~ a lot of sb/sthg** ter alguém/algo em grande estima **-3.** *phr*: **to ~ twice** pensar duas vezes.
➣ **think about** *vt fus* [consider] pensar em; **I'll have to ~ about it** vou ter que pensar sobre isso.
➣ **think of** *vt fus* **-1.** [gen] pensar em; **to ~ of doing sthg** pensar em fazer algo **-2.** [remember] lembrar-se de.
➣ **think over** *vt sep* refletir sobre.
➣ **think up** *vt sep* imaginar, bolar.

think tank *n* assessoria *f* técnica.

third [θɜ:d] <> *num* terceiro(ra). <> *n* **-1.** [fraction] terço *m* **-2.** *UK UNIV* ≃ nota *f* C (*num título universitário*); *see also* **sixth**.

thirdly ['θɜ:dlɪ] *adv* em terceiro lugar.

third party insurance *n* seguro *m* contra terceiros.

third-rate *adj pej* de terceira categoria.

Third World *n*: **the ~** o Terceiro Mundo.

thirst [θɜ:st] *n* sede *f*; **~ for sthg** *fig* sede de algo.

thirsty ['θɜ:stɪ] (*compar* -ier, *superl* -iest) *adj* **-1.** [parched]: **to be** *OR* **feel ~** estar com *OR* sentir sede **-2.** [causing thirst] que dá sede.

thirteen [ˌθɜ:'ti:n] *num* treze; *see also* **six**.

thirty ['θɜ:tɪ] (*pl* -ies) *num* trinta; *see also* **sixty**.

this [ðɪs] (*pl* **these**) <> *adj* **-1.** [referring to thing, person] este (esta); **these chocolates are delicious** estes chocolates são deliciosos; **~ morning/week** esta manhã/semana; **I prefer ~ book** prefiro este livro; **I'll take ~ one** quero este. **-2.** *inf* [used when telling a story]: **there was ~ man ...** havia um homem ... <> *pron* [referring to thing, person] este *m*, esta *f*; [indefinite] isto; **~ is for you** isto é para você; **what are these?** o que é isto?, o que é que são estas coisas?; **~ is David Gregory** [introducing someone] este é o David Gregory; [on telephone] aqui fala David Gregory. <> *adv*: **it was ~ big** era deste tamanho; **I don't remember it being ~ tiring** não me lembro de ser tão cansativo assim.

thistle ['θɪsl] *n* cardo *m*.

thong [θɒŋ] *n* **-1.** [piece of leather] correia *f*, tira *f* de couro **-2.** [bikini] tanga *f*.

thorn [θɔ:n] *n* **-1.** [prickle] espinho *m* **-2.** [bush, tree] espinheiro *m*.

thorny ['θɔ:nɪ] (*compar* -ier, *superl* -iest) *adj* **-1.** [prickly] espinhoso(sa), cheio (cheia) de espinhos **-2.** *fig* [tricky, complicated] espinhoso(sa).

thorough ['θʌrə] *adj* **-1.** [gen] completo(ta) **-2.** [meticulous] minucioso(sa).

thoroughbred ['θʌrəbred] *n* puro-sangue *m*.

thoroughfare ['θʌrəfeəʳ] *n fml* via *f* pública.

thoroughly ['θʌrəlɪ] *adv* **-1.** [fully, in detail] a fundo, exaustivamente **-2.** [completely, utterly] completamente, totalmente.

those [ðəʊz] *pl* ➣ **that**.

though [ðəʊ] <> *conj* **-1.** [in spite of the fact that] embora **-2.** [even if] ainda que; **even ~** embora. <> *adv* no entanto.

thought [θɔ:t] <> *pt* & *pp* ➣ **think**. <> *n* **-1.** [notion] idéia *f* **-2.** (*U*) [act of thinking] reflexão f -3. (U) [philosophy] pensamento m -4. [gesture] intenção f.

➤ **thoughts** npl -1. [reflections] opiniões fpl; she keeps her ~ to herself ela não expressa o que pensa -2. [views] opiniões fpl, idéias fpl.

thoughtful ['θɔːtfʊl] adj -1. [pensive] pensativo(va) -2. [considerate] atencioso(sa).

thoughtfulness ['θɔːtfʊlnɪs] n (U) -1. [pensiveness] ar m pensativo -2. [considerateness] atenção f, consideração f.

thoughtless ['θɔːtlɪs] adj indelicado(da).

thousand ['θaʊznd] num: a ~ mil; two ~ dois mil; ~s of milhares de.

thousandth ['θaʊznθ] num -1. milésimo(ma) -2. [fraction] milésimo(ma); see also sixth.

thrash [θræʃ] vt -1. [beat, hit] surrar, dar uma surra em -2. inf [trounce] dar uma surra em.

➤ **thrash about, thrash around** vi debater-se; to be ~ing about in one's sleep ter um sono agitado.

➤ **thrash out** vt sep esgotar (um assunto).

thread [θred] ◇ n -1. [of cotton, wool] fio m -2. [of screw] rosca f -3. fig [theme] fio m da meada. ◇ vt [pass thread through] enfiar.

threadbare ['θredbeəʳ] adj -1. [clothes, carpet] surrado(da) -2. [argument, joke] manjado(da).

threat [θret] n -1. [warning] ameaça f -2. [menace]: ~ (to sb/sthg) ameaça (a alguém/algo) -3. [risk]: ~ (of sthg) ameaça (de algo).

threaten ['θretn] ◇ vt -1. [issue threat]: to ~ sb (with sthg) ameaçar alguém (com algo); to ~ to do sthg ameaçar fazer algo -2. [endanger] ameaçar. ◇ vi ameaçar.

three [θriː] num três; see also six.

three-dimensional [-dɪ'menʃənl] adj tridimensional.

threefold ['θriːfəʊld] ◇ adj triplo(pla). ◇ adv três vezes; to increase ~ triplicar.

three-piece adj de três peças.

three-ply adj -1. [wood] com três espessuras -2. [wool] com três fios.

thresh [θreʃ] vt debulhar.

threshold ['θreʃhəʊld] n -1. [doorway] soleira f -2. [level] limiar m.

threw [θruː] pt ▷ throw.

thrift shop n US loja f beneficente.

thrifty ['θrɪftɪ] (compar -ier, superl -iest) adj econômico(ca).

thrill [θrɪl] ◇ n -1. [sudden feeling - of joy]

vibração f; [- of horror] estremecimento m -2. [exciting experience] emoção f. ◇ vt emocionar, entusiasmar.

thrilled [θrɪld] adj: ~ (with sthg/to do sthg) encantado(da) (com algo/por fazer algo).

thriller ['θrɪləʳ] n suspense m (enquanto obra).

thrilling ['θrɪlɪŋ] adj emocionante.

thrive [θraɪv] (pt -d OR throve, pp -d) vi -1. [person, plant] desenvolver-se -2. [business] prosperar.

thriving ['θraɪvɪŋ] adj -1. próspero(ra) -2. [plant] que se desenvolve.

throat [θrəʊt] n -1. [inside mouth] garganta f -2. [front of neck] pescoço m.

throb [θrɒb] (pt & pp -bed, cont -bing) vi -1. [beat - pulse, blood] pulsar; [- heart] palpitar; [- engine, machine] vibrar; [- music, drums] vibrar, ressoar -2. [be painful] latejar.

throes [θrəʊz] npl: to be in the ~ of sthg estar no meio de algo.

throne [θrəʊn] n -1. [chair] trono m -2. [position, authority]: the ~ o trono.

throng [θrɒŋ] ◇ n aglomeração f. ◇ vt aglomerar.

throttle ['θrɒtl] ◇ n -1. [valve] válvula f de estrangulamento -2. [lever] alavanca f (da válvula de estrangulamento); [pedal] afogador m. ◇ vt estrangular.

through [θruː] ◇ adj [finished] terminado(da); to be ~ with sthg ter terminado algo; to be ~ with sb terminar com alguém. ◇ adv -1. [from one end to another] até o fim; they let us ~ nos deixaram passar -2. [until] até; I slept ~ till ten dormi até as dez. ◇ prep -1. [from one side to another] através de; to cut ~ cortar algo; to get ~ sthg passar por algo -2. [during, throughout] durante; to go ~ an experience passar por uma experiência -3. [because of] por; to happen ~ sthg acontecer devido a algo -4. [by means of] graças a -5. US [up till and including]: Monday ~ Friday de segunda a sexta.

➤ **through and through** adv -1. [completely] dos pés à cabeça -2. [thoroughly]: to know sthg ~ and ~ conhecer algo de cima a baixo.

throughout [θruː'aʊt] ◇ prep -1. [during] durante todo(da) -2. [everywhere in] por todo(da). ◇ adv -1. [all the time] o tempo todo -2. [everywhere] por todo o lado.

throve [θrəʊv] pt ▷ thrive.

throw [θrəʊ] (pt threw, pp thrown) ◇ vt -1. [gen] atirar -2. [move suddenly]: to

~ **o.s.** jogar-se, atirar-se **- 3.** [rider] derrubar, desmontar **- 4.** *fig* [force into]: **we were all thrown into confusion** ficamos todos muito confusos; **he was thrown into the job at short notice** largaram o trabalho nas costas dele sem avisar **- 5.** *fig* [confuse] deixar confuso(-sa). <> *n* [toss, pitch] arremesso *m*, lançamento *m*.

➡ **throw away** *vt sep* jogar fora.

➡ **throw out** *vt sep* **- 1.** [discard] jogar fora **- 2.** *fig* [reject] rejeitar **- 3.** [force to leave] expulsar.

➡ **throw up** *vi inf* [vomit] vomitar, botar para fora.

throwaway ['θrǝʊǝ,weɪl] *adj* **- 1.** [disposable] descartável **- 2.** [casual] fortuito(ta), casual.

throw-in *n UK FTBL* arremesso *m* lateral.

thrown [θrǝʊn] *pp* ⊳ **throw**.

thru [θru:] *adj*, *adv* & *prep US inf* = **through**.

thrush [θrʌʃ] *n* **- 1.** [bird] tordo *m* **- 2.** *MED* cândida *f*.

thrust [θrʌst] (*pt* & *pp* **thrust**) <> *n* **- 1.** [forward movement - of knife, sword] golpe *m*; [- of army] investida *f*; [- of body] impulso *m* **- 2.** [main aspect] essência *f*. <> *vt* [shove, jab] empurrar.

thud [θʌd] (*pt* & *pp* **-ded**, *cont* **-ding**) <> *n* baque *m*. <> *vi* dar um baque seco.

thug [θʌg] *n* marginal *mf*.

thumb [θʌm] <> *n* [of hand] polegar *m*. <> *vt inf* [hitch]: **to ~ a lift** pedir carona (com o dedo).

➡ **thumb through** *vt fus* folhear.

thumbs down [,θʌmz-] *n*: **to get** *OR* **be given the ~** ser recebido(da) com desaprovação, não ser bem recebido(da).

thumbs up [,θʌmz-] *n* [go-ahead]: **to give sb/sthg the ~** dar luz verde a alguém/algo.

thumbtack ['θʌmtæk] *n US* percevejo *m* (para fixar).

thump [θʌmp] <> *n* **- 1.** [blow] soco *m* **- 2.** [thud] baque *m*. <> *vt* [punch] dar um soco em. <> *vi* [pound - heart] palpitar; [- head] latejar.

thunder ['θʌndǝ⁰] <> *n* (*U*) **- 1.** *METEOR* trovão *m* **- 2.** *fig* [loud sound] estrondo *m*. <> *v impers METEOR* trovejar.

thunderbolt ['θʌndǝbǝʊlt] *n* **- 1.** *METEOR* raio *m* **- 2.** *fig* [shock] choque *m*.

thunderclap ['θʌndǝklæp] *n* trovão *m*.

thunderstorm ['θʌndǝstɔ:m] *n* temporal *m*.

thundery ['θʌndǝrɪ] *adj* carregado(da).

Thursday ['θɜ:zdɪ] *n* quinta-feira *f*; *see also* **Saturday**.

thus [ðʌs] *adv fml* **- 1.** [as a consequence] assim, por isso **- 2.** [in this way] desse modo **- 3.** [as follows] assim.

thwart [θwɔ:t] *vt* frustrar, impedir.

thyme [taɪm] *n* (*U*) tomilho *m*.

thyroid ['θaɪrɔɪd] *n* tireóide *f*.

tiara [tɪ'ɑ:rǝ] *n* tiara *f*.

Tibet [tɪ'betl] *n* Tibete *f*.

tic [tɪk] *n* tique *m*.

tick [tɪk] <> *n* **- 1.** [written mark] (sinal *m* de) visto *m* **- 2.** [sound] tiquetaque *m*; **I shan't be a ~** não vou demorar **- 3.** [insect] carrapato *m*. <> *vt* marcar (com sinal de visto). <> *vi* [make ticking sound] fazer tiquetaque

➡ **tick off** *vt sep* **- 1.** [mark off] marcar (com sinal de visto) **- 2.** [tell off]: **to ~ sb off (for sthg)** dar uma bronca em alguém (por algo).

➡ **tick over** *vi* funcionar em marcha lenta.

ticket ['tɪkɪt] *n* **- 1.** [for entry, access - plane] bilhete *m*; [- bus, train] passagem *f*; [- for footbal match, concert] entrada *f*, ingresso *m* **- 2.** [label on product] etiqueta *f* **- 3.** [notice of traffic offence] multa *f*.

ticket collector *n UK* cobrador *m*, -ra *f* (no trem).

ticket inspector *n UK* cobrador *m*, -ra *f* (no trem).

ticket machine *n* máquina *f* automática que vende ingressos.

ticket office *n* **- 1.** [in theatre] bilheteria *f* **- 2.** [in station] guichê *m* de venda.

tickle ['tɪkl] <> *vt* **- 1.** [touch lightly] fazer cócegas em **- 2.** *fig* [amuse] divertir. <> *vi*: **my feet are tickling** sinto cócegas nos pés.

ticklish ['tɪklɪʃ] *adj* [sensitive to touch]: **to be ~** sentir cócegas.

tidal ['taɪdl] *adj* da maré.

tidal wave *n* maremoto *m*.

tidbit *n US* = **titbit**.

tiddlywinks ['tɪdlɪwɪŋks], **tiddledywinks** *US* ['tɪdldɪwɪŋks] *n* (*U*) [game] jogo *m* da pulga.

tide [taɪd] *n* **- 1.** [of sea] maré *f* **- 2.** *fig* [trend] tendência *f*; **the ~ of history** o curso da história **- 3.** *fig* [large quantity] corrente *f*.

tidy ['taɪdɪ] (*compar* **-ier**, *superl* **-iest**, *pt* & *pp* **-ied**) <> *adj* **- 1.** [gen] arrumado(da) **- 2.** [in habits] asseado(da). <> *vt* arrumar.

➡ **tidy up** <> *vt sep* arrumar. <> *vi*: **I'll have to ~ up before going out** [objects] vou ter que arrumar tudo antes de sair.; [hair, appearance] vou ter que me arrumar antes de sair.

tie [taɪ] (*pt* & *pp* **tied**, *cont* **tying**) ⬦ *n*
-1. [necktie] gravata *f* - **2.** [in game, compe-
tition] empate *m*. ⬦ *vt* **-1.** [attach]: **to ~
sthg (on)sthg** amarrar algo (em
algo); **to ~ sthg round sthg** amarrar
algo em volta de algo; **to ~ sthg with
sthg** amarrar algo com algo **- 2.** [do up,
fasten - shoelaces] atar, amarrar; [- knot]
dar **- 3.** *fig* [link]: **to be ~d to sb/sthg**
estar ligado(da) a alguém/algo. ⬦ *vi*
[draw]: **to ~ (with sb)** empatar (com
alguém).

➡ **tie down** *vt sep fig* [restrict] prender;
to feel tied down by sthg sentir-se
preso(sa) a algo.

➡ **tie in with** *vt fus* concordar com,
ajustar-se com.

➡ **tie up** *vt sep* **-1.** [secure with string,
rope] amarrar **- 2.** *fig* [restrict use of]
limitar o uso de **- 3.** *fig* [link]: **to be ~d
up with sthg** estar ligado(da) a algo.

tiebreak(er) ['taɪbreɪk(ə^r)] *n* **- 1.** TENNIS
tie-break *m* **- 2.** [extra question] desempate *m*.

tiepin ['taɪpɪn] *n* alfinete *m* de gravata.

tier [tɪə^r] *n* **- 1.** [of seats, shelves] fileira *f*
- 2. [cake] camada *f*.

tiff [tɪf] *n* desavença *f*, briguinha *f*.

tiger ['taɪgə^r] *n* tigre *m*.

tight [taɪt] ⬦ *adj* **-1.** [gen] apertado(-
da); **a ~ fit** justo(ta) **- 2.** [taut] esticado(-
da), teso(sa) **- 3.** [close together]
comprimido(da) **- 4.** [strict] rigoroso(sa)
- 5. [at sharp angle] cerrado(da) **- 6.** *inf*
[drunk] bêbado(da) **- 7.** *inf* [miserly] sovina.
⬦ *adv* **-1.** [firmly, securely] com força; **to
hold ~** segurar bem; **to shut** OR **close
sthg ~** fechar bem algo **- 2.** [tautly]
bem esticado(da).

➡ **tights** *npl* meia-calça *f*.

tighten ['taɪtn] ⬦ *vt* **- 1.** [knot, belt,
rules] apertar **- 2.** [make tauter] esticar
- 3. [strengthen]: **to ~ one's hold** OR **grip
on sthg** agarrar OR segurar algo com
força **- 4.** [security] intensificar. ⬦ *vi*
[make tighter] apertar.

tightfisted [,taɪt'fɪstɪd] *adj inf pej* pão-
duro.

tightly ['taɪtlɪ] *adv* [firmly, securely] com
força; [fasten, tie] bem.

tile [taɪl] *n* **- 1.** [on roof] telha *f* - **2.** [on
floor] piso *m* - **3.** [on wall] azulejo *m*.

tiled [taɪld] *adj* **-1.** [roof] telhado(da) **- 2.**
[floor] ladrilhado(da) **- 3.** [wall] azuleja-
do(da).

till [tɪl] ⬦ *prep* até; **~ now** até agora.
⬦ *conj* até; **wait ~ I come back** espere
até eu voltar OR que eu volte. ⬦ *n*
caixa *f* (registradora).

tiller ['tɪlə^r] *n* cana *f* do leme.

tilt [tɪlt] ⬦ *vt* inclinar. ⬦ *vi* inclinar-
se.

timber ['tɪmbə^r] *n* **- 1.** (U) [wood] madeira *f* (*para a construção*) **- 2.** [beam -
of ship] viga *f* mestra; [- of house]
madeiramento *m*.

timbered ['tɪmbəd] *adj* revestido(da)
com madeira.

time [taɪm] ⬦ *n* **- 1.** (U) [general measurement, spell] tempo *m*; **to take ~** levar
tempo; **to have no ~ for sb/sthg** não ter
tempo a perder com alguém/algo; **to
pass the ~** passar o tempo; **to play for
~** tentar ganhar tempo; **it was a long
~ before he came** passou muito tempo
antes que ele viesse; **for a ~** por um
tempo **- 2.** [as measured by clock, moment]
hora *f*; **the ~ is three o'clock** são três
horas; **what ~ is it?, what's the ~?** que
horas são?, tem horas?; **in a week's/
year's ~** daqui a uma semana/um
mês; **to lose ~** atrasar; **to tell the ~**
dizer as horas; **now would be a good ~
to ask** agora seria uma boa hora para
perguntar **- 3.** [point in time in past] época
f; **at that ~** naquela época **- 4.** [era] era
f; **in ancient ~s** na antiguidade; **before
my ~** [before I was born] antes de eu
nascer; [before I worked here] antes de eu
trabalhar ali **- 5.** [occasion] vez *f*; **from ~
to ~** de vez em quando; **~ after ~, ~
and again** uma e outra vez **- 6.** [experi-
ence]: **we had a good ~** nos divertimos
muito; **we had a terrible ~** foi uma
situação horrível; **to have a hard ~ trying to do sthg** ter dificuldade tentando
fazer algo **- 7.** [degree of lateness]: **in good
~** na hora certa; **ahead of ~** cedo; **on
~** na hora **- 8.** MUS compasso *m*. ⬦ *vt*
-1. [schedule] marcar **- 2.** [measure duration, speed of] cronometrar **- 3.** [choose
appropriate moment for] escolher o momento certo para.

➡ **times** ⬦ *npl*: **four ~s as much as me**
quatro vezes mais do que eu. ⬦ *prep*
MATH: **four ~s five is twenty** quatro vezes
cinco é vinte.

➡ **about time** *adv*: **it's about ~** já era
hora.

➡ **at a time** *adv*: **for months at a ~** por
meses seguidos; **one at a ~** um (uma)
por vez; **I always read several maganizes
at a ~** sempre leio várias revistas ao
mesmo tempo.

➡ **at times** *adv* às vezes.

➡ **at the same time** *adv* ao mesmo
tempo.

➡ **for the time being** *adv* por enquanto.

➡ **in time** *adv* **-1.** [not late]: **in ~ (for**

to

sthg) a tempo (para algo) **-2.** [eventually] com o tempo.

time bomb n bomba-relógio f.

time lag n intervalo m.

timeless ['taɪmlɪs] adj eterno(na).

time limit n prazo m, limite m de tempo.

timely ['taɪmlɪ] (compar -ier, superl -iest) adj oportuno(na).

time off n (U) (tempo m de) folga f; **I'm owed** ~ me devem alguns dias de folga.

time-out (pl time-outs OR times-out) n US SPORT intervalo m.

timer ['taɪmə'] n temporizador m.

time scale n escala f de tempo.

time-share n UK propriedade f comprada em sociedade.

time switch n temporizador m (numa máquina).

timetable ['taɪm,teɪbl] n **-1.** [gen] horário m **-2.** [schedule] programação f, programa m.

time zone n fuso m horário.

timid ['tɪmɪd] adj tímido(da).

timing ['taɪmɪŋ] n (U) **-1.** [of actor, musician, tennis player] timing m **-2.** [chosen moment]: **she made her comment with perfect** ~ ela fez seu comentário no momento certo **-3.** SPORT [measuring] cronometragem f.

timpani ['tɪmpənɪ] npl timbales mpl, tímpanos mpl.

tin [tɪn] n **-1.** (U) [metal] estanho m; ~ **plate** folha-de-flandres f **-2.** UK [for food, storage] lata f.

tin can n lata f.

tinfoil ['tɪnfɔɪl] n (U) papel m OR folha f de estanho.

tinge [tɪndʒ] n **-1.** [of colour] tom m, matiz m **-2.** [of feeling] rápida sensação f; **a** ~ **of guilt** uma ponta de culpa.

tinged [tɪndʒd] adj **-1.** [colour]: ~ **with sthg** com um toque de algo **-2.** [feeling]: ~ **with sthg** com uma pontinha de algo.

tingle ['tɪŋgl] vi formigar.

tinker ['tɪŋkə'] <> n pej [gipsy] cigano m, -na f. <> vi atamancar; **to** ~ **with sthg** fuçar em algo.

tinkle ['tɪŋkl] vi **-1.** [bell] tilintar **-2.** [phone] tocar.

tinned [tɪnd] adj UK enlatado(da), em conserva.

tin opener n UK abridor m de lata.

tinsel ['tɪnsl] n (U) lantejoula f, ouropel m.

tint [tɪnt] n matiz m.

tinted ['tɪntɪd] adj **-1.** [window, glass] colorido(da) **-2.** [hair] tingido(da).

tiny ['taɪnɪ] (compar -ier, superl -iest) adj minúsculo(la), diminuto(ta).

tip [tɪp] (pt & pp -ped, cont -ping) <> n **-1.** [end] ponta f **-2.** UK [dump]: **rubbish** ~ lixão m, depósito m de lixo **-3.** [gratuity] gorjeta f **-4.** [piece of advice] dica f. <> vt **-1.** [tilt] inclinar **-2.** [spill] derramar **-3.** [give a gratuity to] dar gorjeta a. <> vi **-1.** [tilt] inclinar-se **-2.** [spill] derramar. ◆ **tip over** vt sep & vi virar.

tip-off n informação f (secreta).

tipped [tɪpt] adj **-1.** [spear] com ponta de aço **-2.** [cigarette] com filtro **-3.** [pen]: **felt-** ~ **pen** caneta f hidrográfica.

tipsy ['tɪpsɪ] (compar -ier, superl -iest) adj inf alto(ta) (por ingerir bebida alcoólica), tocado(da).

tiptoe ['tɪptəʊ] <> n: **on** ~ nas pontas dos pés. <> vi andar nas pontas dos pés.

tip-top adj inf dated ótimo(ma).

tire ['taɪə'] <> n US = **tyre**. <> vt cansar. <> vi **-1.** [get tired] cansar-se, ficar cansado(da) **-2.** [get fed up]: **to** ~ **of sb/sthg** cansar-se de alguém/algo.

tired ['taɪəd] adj **-1.** [sleepy] cansado(da) **-2.** [fed up]: ~ **of sthg/of doing sthg** cansado(da) de algo/de fazer algo.

tireless ['taɪəlɪs] adj incansável.

tiresome ['taɪəsəm] adj cansativo(va), enfadonho(nha).

tiring ['taɪərɪŋ] adj cansativo(va).

tissue ['tɪʃuː] n **-1.** [paper handkerchief] lenço m de papel **-2.** (U) BIOL tecido m.

tissue paper n (U) papel m de seda.

tit [tɪt] n **-1.** [bird] chapim m **-2.** vulg [breast] teta f.

titbit UK ['tɪtbɪt], **tidbit** US ['tɪdbɪt] n **-1.** [of food] petisco m **-2.** fig [of news]: **a** ~ **of gossip** uma pequena fofoca.

tit for tat [-'tæt] n: **it's** ~ é olho por olho.

titillate ['tɪtɪleɪt] vt excitar.

title ['taɪtl] n título m.

title deed n título m de propriedade.

title role n papel m principal.

titter ['tɪtə'] vi rir baixinho.

TM <> abbr of **trademark**.

to [unstressed before consonant tə, unstressed before vowel tʊ, stressed tuː] <> prep **-1.** [indicating direction] para; **to go** ~ **Brazil** ir ao Brasil; **to go** ~ **school** ir para a escola. **-2.** [indicating position] a; ~ **the left/right** à esquerda/direita. **-3.** [expressing indirect object] a; **to give sthg** ~ **sb** dar algo a alguém; **give it** ~ **me** dê-me isso; **to listen** ~ **the radio** ouvir rádio. **-4.** [indicating reaction, effect]: ~ **my surprise** para surpresa minha; **it's** ~ **your advantage** é em seu benefício. **-5.** [until] até; **to count** ~ **ten** contar até dez; **we work from nine ~ five** trabalhamos das nove (até) às cinco. **- 6.** [in stating opinion] para; **~ me, he's lying** para mim, ele está mentindo. **- 7.** [indicating change of state]: **to turn ~ sthg** transformar-se em algo; **it could lead ~ trouble** pode vir a dar problemas. **- 8.** *UK* [in expressions of time] para; **it's ten ~ three** são dez para as três; **at quarter ~ seven** às quinze para as sete. **- 9.** [in ratios, rates]: **40 miles ~ the gallon** 40 milhas por galão. **-10.** [of, for]: **the answer ~ the question** a resposta à pergunta; **the key ~ the car** a chave do carro; **a letter ~ my daughter** uma carta para a minha filha. **-11.** [indicating attitude] (para) com; **to be rude ~ sb** ser grosseiro com alguém. <> *with infinitive* **-1.** [forming simple infinitive]: **~ walk** andar; **~ laugh** rir. **- 2.** [following another verb]: **to begin ~ do sthg** começar a fazer algo; **to try ~ do sthg** tentar fazer algo. **- 3.** [following an adjective]: **difficult ~ do** difícil de fazer; **pleased ~ meet you** prazer em conhecê-lo; **ready ~ go** pronto para partir. **- 4.** [indicating purpose] para; **we came here ~ look at the castle** viemos para ver o castelo.

toad [təʊd] *n* sapo *m*.

toadstool ['təʊdstu:l] *n* cogumelo *m* venenoso.

toast [təʊst] <> *n* **-1.** *(U)* [bread] torrada *f*, pão *m* torrado **- 2.** [drink] brinde *m*. <> *vt* **-1.** [bread] tostar, torrar **- 2.** [person] brindar a.

toasted sandwich [ˌtəʊstɪd-] *n* misto-quente *m*.

toaster ['təʊstə^r] *n* torradeira *f*.

tobacco [tə'bækəʊ] *n* tabaco *m*.

tobacconist *n* charuteiro *m*, -ra *f*, vendedor *m*, -ra *f* de fumo *OR* tabaco; **~'s (shop)** tabacaria *f*.

toboggan [tə'bɒgən] *n* tobogã *m*.

today [tə'deɪ] <> *adv (U)* **-1.** [this day] hoje **- 2.** [nowadays] de hoje, atual; **~'s technology** a tecnologia hoje em dia. <> *adv* **-1.** [this day] hoje **-2.** [nowadays] hoje (em dia).

toddler ['tɒdlə^r] *n* criança *f* pequena *(que começa a andar)*.

toddy ['tɒdɪ] *(pl* -ies*) n* ponche *m*.

to-do *(pl* -s*) n inf dated* tumulto *m*, alvoroço *m*.

toe [təʊ] <> *n* **-1.** [of foot] dedo *m (do pé)* **- 2.** [of sock] ponta *f* **- 3.** [of shoe] biqueira *f*. <> *vt*: **to ~ the line** cumprir as normas.

toenail ['təʊneɪl] *n* unha *f* do pé.

toffee ['tɒfɪ] *n* **-1.** [sweet] tofe *m*, caramelo *m* **- 2.** *(U)* [substance] tofe *m*.

toga ['təʊgə] *n* toga *f*.

together [tə'geðə^r] *adv* juntos(tas); **to go ~** combinar.
➦ **together with** *prep* junto com.

toil [tɔɪl] *fml* <> *n* trabalho *m* duro. <> *vi* trabalhar duro.

toilet ['tɔɪlɪt] *n* vaso *m* sanitário; **to go to the ~** ir ao banheiro.

toilet bag *n* nécessaire *m*.

toilet paper *n (U)* papel *m* higiênico.

toiletries ['tɔɪlɪtrɪz] *npl* artigos *mpl* de toalete.

toilet roll *n* **-1.** *(U)* [paper] papel *m* higiênico **- 2.** [roll] rolo *m* de papel higiênico.

toilet water *n (U)* água-de-colônia *f*, colônia *f*.

token ['təʊkn] <> *adj* simbólico(ca). <> *n* **-1.** [voucher, disc - for machines] ficha *f*; [- for books, records] vale *m* **- 2.** [symbol] símbolo *m*, mostra *f*.
➦ **by the same token** *adv* da mesma forma.

told [təʊld] *pt & pp* ⊳ **tell**.

tolerably ['tɒlərəblɪ] *adv* razoavelmente.

tolerance ['tɒlərəns] *n* tolerância *f*.

tolerant ['tɒlərənt] *adj* **-1.** [not bigoted]: **~ of sb/sthg** tolerante com alguém/algo **- 2.** [resistant]: **~ to sthg** resistente a algo.

tolerate ['tɒləreɪt] *vt* **-1.** [put up with] suportar, tolerar **- 2.** [permit] tolerar.

toll [təʊl] <> *n* **-1.** [number]: **death ~** número *m* de vítimas fatais **- 2.** [fee] pedágio *m* **- 3.** *phr*: **to take its ~** ter suas implicações. <> *vt* [bell] tocar, badalar.

toll-free *US adv*: **to call ~** telefonar *OR* ligar gratuitamente.

tomato [*UK* tə'mɑːtəʊ, *US* tə'meɪtəʊ] *(pl* -es*) n* tomate *m*.

tomb [tu:m] *n* túmulo *m*, tumba *f*.

tomboy ['tɒmbɔɪ] *n* menina que gosta de jogos e brincadeiras de meninos.

tombstone ['tu:mstəʊn] *n* lápide *f*.

tomcat ['tɒmkæt] *n* gato *m (macho)*.

tomorrow [tə'mɒrəʊ] <> *n* **-1.** [day after today] amanhã *m* **- 2.** *fig* [future] futuro *m*. <> *adv* **-1.** [the day after today] amanhã; **~ week** uma semana a contar de amanhã **- 2.** [in future] no futuro.

ton [tʌn] *(pl inv OR* -s*) n* **-1.** *UK* [imperial unit of measurement] tonelada *f* inglesa *OR* longa *(1016,05 kg)* **- 2.** *US* [unit of measurement] tonelada *f (907,19 kg)* **- 3.** [metric unit of measurement] tonelada *f* métrica.
➦ **tons** *npl UK inf*: **~s (of)** um monte de.

tone [təʊn] *n* **-1.** [gen] tom *m* **- 2.** *TELEC*

sinal *m*; **dialling** ~ linha *f* de discagem.

➤ **tone down** *vt sep* suavizar, moderar.

➤ **tone up** *vt sep* pôr em forma.

tone-deaf *adj* que não tem ouvido musical.

tongs [tɒŋz] *npl* **-1.** [for sugar] pinça *f* para açúcar **-2.** [for hair] pinças *fpl*.

tongue [tʌŋ] *n* **-1.** [gen] língua *f*; **to hold one's** ~ *fig* fechar o bico **-2.** *fml* [language] língua *f* **-3.** [of shoe] lingüeta *f*.

tongue-in-cheek *adj* em tom de brincadeira.

tongue-tied [-ˌtaɪd] *adj* mudo(da) *(por timidez ou nervosismo)*.

tongue twister [-ˌtwɪstə'] *n* trava-língua *m*.

tonic [ˈtɒnɪk] *n* **-1.** [gen] tônico *m* **-2.** *(U)* [tonic water] (água *f*) tônica *f*.

tonic water *n (U)* (água *f*) tônica *f*.

tonight [təˈnaɪt] <> *n (U)* esta noite *f*. <> *adv* hoje à noite, esta noite.

tonnage [ˈtʌnɪdʒ] *n (U)* NAUT **-1.** [weight] tonelagem *f* **-2.** [amount of cargo] tonelagem *f* (de arqueação).

tonne [tʌn] *(pl inv OR -s) n* tonelada *f* métrica.

tonsil [ˈtɒnsl] *n* amígdala *f*.

tonsil(l)itis [ˌtɒnsɪˈlaɪtɪs] *n (U)* amigdalite *f*.

too [tuː] *adv* **-1.** [also] também **-2.** [excessively]: ~ much demais; ~ old velho demais; ~ many things muitas e muitas coisas; ~ long a book um livro longo demais; **all** ~ soon cedo demais; **only** ~ ... muito ...; **I'd be only** ~ happy to help eu adoraria ajudar **-3.** *(with negatives)*: **not** ~ bad nada mal; **I wasn't** ~ impressed não fiquei muito impressionado.

took [tʊk] *pt* ▷ **take**.

tool [tuːl] *n* **-1.** [implement] ferramenta *f* **-2.** *fig* [means] ferramenta *f*, instrumento *m*.

tool box *n* caixa *f* de ferramentas.

tool kit *n* jogo *m* de ferramentas.

toot [tuːt] <> *n* buzinada *f*. <> *vi* buzinar.

tooth [tuːθ] *(pl teeth) n* dente *m*.

toothache [ˈtuːθeɪk] *n (U)* dor *f* de dente.

toothbrush [ˈtuːθbrʌʃ] *n* escova *f* de dentes.

toothpaste [ˈtuːθpeɪst] *n (U)* pasta *f* de dentes.

toothpick [ˈtuːθpɪk] *n* palito *m*.

top [tɒp] *(pt & pp -ped, cont -ping)* <> *adj* **-1.** [highest] de cima, superior **-2.** [most important, successful] importante; **she got the** ~ **mark** ela tirou a melhor nota **-3.** [maximum] máximo(ma). <> *n* **-1.** [gen] topo *m*, parte *f* de cima; **at the** ~ **of one's voice** a toda voz **-2.** [highest point - of list, class] primeiro(ra); [- of tree] copa *f*; [- of hill] cume *m*; [- of page] topo *m* **-3.** [lid, cap] tampa *f* **-4.** [upper side] superfície *f* **-5.** [clothing - bikini, pyjama] parte *f* de cima; [- blouse] blusa *f* **-6.** [toy] pião *m* **-7.** [highest rank - of an organization] topo *m*; [- of a league, class] primeiro(ra). <> *vt* **-1.** [to be first in - league, poll] liderar, estar em primeiro lugar em; [- table, chart] liderar, encabeçar **-2.** [better] superar **-3.** [exceed] passar de **-4.** [put on top of] cobrir.

➤ **on top of** *prep* **-1.** [in space] em cima de **-2.** [in addition to] além de; **on** ~ **of that** como se não bastasse.

➤ **top up** *UK*, **top off** *US vt sep* encher novamente.

top floor *n* último andar *m*.

top hat *n* cartola *f*.

top-heavy *adj* muito pesado(da) na parte de cima.

topic [ˈtɒpɪk] *n* tópico *m*.

topical [ˈtɒpɪkl] *adj* atual, da atualidade.

topless [ˈtɒplɪs] *adj* [barebreasted] topless; **to go** ~ fazer topless.

top-level *adj* do mais alto nível.

topmost [ˈtɒpməʊst] *adj* mais alto(ta).

topping [ˈtɒpɪŋ] *n* cobertura *f*.

topple [ˈtɒpl] <> *vt* derrubar. <> *vi* vir abaixo.

top-secret *adj* ultra-secreto(ta).

topspin *n (U)* topspin *m*.

topsy-turvy [ˌtɒpsɪˈtɜːvɪ] *adj* **-1.** [messy] de pernas para o ar **-2.** [haywire] louco(ca).

top-up card *n* [for mobile phone] cartão *m* de recarga.

torch [tɔːtʃ] *n* **-1.** *UK* [electric] lanterna *f* **-2.** [flaming stick] tocha *f*.

tore [tɔː'] *pt* ▷ **tear** ².

torment [*n* 'tɔːment, *vb* tɔːˈment] <> *n* tormento *m*. <> *vt* atormentar.

torn [tɔːn] *pp* ▷ **tear** ².

tornado [tɔːˈneɪdəʊ] *(pl -es OR -s) n* tornado *m*.

torpedo [tɔːˈpiːdəʊ] *(pl -es) n* torpedo *m*.

torrent [ˈtɒrənt] *n* torrente *f*.

torrid [ˈtɒrɪd] *adj* tórrido(da).

tortoise [ˈtɔːtəs] *n* tartaruga *f* terrestre.

tortoiseshell [ˈtɔːtəʃel] <> *adj* [cat] escama-de-tartaruga. <> *n (U)* [material] tartaruga *f*.

torture [ˈtɔːtʃə'] <> *n* tortura *f*. <> *vt* torturar.

Tory ['tɔ:rɪ] (*pl* -ies) ◇ *adj* tóri, do partido conservador britânico. ◇ *n* tóri *mf*, membro *m* do partido conservador britânico.

toss [tɒs] *vt* -1. [throw carelessly] atirar, jogar -2. [head] sacudir -3. [food] misturar -4. [coin] jogar *(ao ar)*; **to ~ a coin** tirar no cara ou coroa -5. [throw about] jogar, arremessar.

➙ **toss up** *vi* disputar no cara ou coroa.

tot [tɒt] *n* -1. *inf* [small child] nenezinho *f*, -nha -2. [of drink] golinho *m*.

total ['təʊtl] (*UK pt* & *pp* -led, *cont* -ling, *US pt* & *pp* -ed, *cont* -ing) ◇ *adj* total. ◇ *n* total *m*. ◇ *vt* -1. [add up] somar -2. [amount to] totalizar.

totalitarian [ˌtəʊtælɪ'teərɪən] *adj* totalitário(ria).

totally ['təʊtəlɪ] *adv* totalmente.

totter ['tɒtər] *vi* cambalear.

touch [tʌtʃ] ◇ *n* -1. [gen] toque *m* -2. [contact]: **to get in ~ (with sb)** entrar em contato (com alguém); **to keep in ~ (with sb)** manter contato (com alguém); **to lose ~ (with sb)** perder o contato (com alguém); **to be out of ~ with sthg** estar por fora de algo -3. [small amount]: **a ~ (of sthg)** um pouco (de algo) -4. *SPORT*: **in ~** na lateral -5. *(U)* [sense] tato *m*; **soft to the ~** suave ao toque; **the ~ of her lips** o toque de seus lábios. ◇ *vt* -1. [make contact with] tocar -2. [move emotionally] tocar, comover -3. [eat] comer -4. [drink] beber. ◇ *vi* -1. [make contact] tocar -2. [be in contact] tocar-se.

➙ **touch down** *vi* [plane] aterrissar.

➙ **touch on** *vt fus* tocar por cima.

touch-and-go *adj* incerto(ta), duvidoso(sa).

touchdown ['tʌtʃdaʊn] *n* -1. [on land, sea] aterrissagem *f* -2. [in American football] touchdown *m*.

touched [tʌtʃt] *adj* -1. [grateful] comovido(da), emocionado(da) -2. *inf* [slightly mad] tantã.

touching ['tʌtʃɪŋ] *adj* tocante, comovente.

touchline ['tʌtʃlaɪn] *n SPORT* linha *f* lateral.

touch screen *n* tela *f* tátil.

touchy ['tʌtʃɪ] (*compar* -ier, *superl* -iest) *adj* -1. [person] suscetível -2. [subject, question] delicado(da).

tough [tʌf] *adj* -1. [gen] duro(ra) -2. [person, character] forte -3. [material] resistente -4. [decision, life] difícil -5. [criminal, neighbourhood] da pesada.

toughen ['tʌfn] *vt* endurecer.

toupee ['tu:peɪ] *n* peruca *f*.

tour [tʊər] ◇ *n* -1. [trip] excursão *f*, viagem *f* -2. [of building, town, museum] visita *f*; **guided ~** visita *f* guiada -3. [official journey] turnê *f*. ◇ *vt* -1. [visit] visitar -2. *SPORT* & *THEATRE* fazer uma turnê por.

touring ['tʊərɪŋ] *n (U)* viagens *fpl* turísticas; **to go ~** fazer turismo.

tourism ['tʊərɪzm] *n (U)* turismo *m*.

tourist ['tʊərɪst] *n* turista *mf*.

tourist (information) office *n* (serviço *m* de) informações *fpl* turísticas.

tournament ['tɔ:nəmənt] *n CHESS* & *SPORT* torneio *m*.

tour operator *n* agência *f* de viagens.

tousle *vt* -1. [hair] despentear -2. [fur, feathers] desarrumar.

tout [taʊt] ◇ *n* cambista *mf*. ◇ *vt* [tickets, goods] revender *(como cambista)*. ◇ *vi*: **to ~ for sthg** angariar algo; **to ~ for trade** tentar obter algo; **to ~ for clients** aliciar algo; **to ~ for investment** buscar algo.

tow [təʊ] ◇ *n* reboque *m*; **on ~** *UK* a reboque. ◇ *vt* rebocar.

towards *UK* [tə'wɔ:dz], **toward** *US* [tə'wɔ:d] *prep* -1. [in the direction of] para, em direção a -2. [indicating attitude] em relação a -3. [near in time, space] perto de -4. [as contribution to] para.

towel ['taʊəl] *n* toalha *f*.

towelling *UK*, **toweling** *US* ['taʊəlɪŋ] *n (U)* tecido *m* atoalhado.

towel rail *n* toalheiro *m*.

tower ['taʊər] ◇ *n* torre *f*. ◇ *vi* destacar-se; **to ~ over sb** ser muito mais alto(ta) do que alguém; **to ~ over sthg** destacar-se por cima de algo.

tower block *n UK* prédio *m* alto de escritórios.

towering ['taʊərɪŋ] *adj* [very tall] altíssimo(ma).

town [taʊn] *n* -1. [population centre] cidade *f* -2. *(U)* [centre of town, city] centro *m* (da cidade); **to go out on the ~** ir divertir-se; **to go to ~** *fig* botar para quebrar.

town centre *n* centro *m* (da cidade).

town council *n* câmara *f* municipal.

town hall *n* -1. [building] prefeitura *f* -2. *(U) fig* [council] prefeitura *f*.

town plan *n* -1. [map] mapa *m* da cidade -2. [project, plan] projeto *m* de urbanização.

town planning *n (U)* -1. [study] urbanismo *m* -2. [practice] urbanização *f*.

township ['taʊnʃɪp] *n* -1. [in South Africa] zona urbana atribuída antigamente pelo governo à população negra -2. [in US] ≃ município *m*.

towpath ['təʊpɑ:θ, *pl* -pɑ:ðz] *n* caminho *m* de sirga.

towrope ['təʊrəʊp] *n* cabo *m* para reboque.

tow truck *n US* guincho *m*, reboque *m*.

toxic ['tɒksɪk] *adj* tóxico(ca).

toy [tɔɪ] *n* brinquedo *m*.
→ **toy with** *vt fus* -1. [idea]: **to ~ with** sthg pensar em algo -2. [play]: **to ~ with** sthg brincar com algo.

toy shop *n* loja *f* de brinquedos.

trace [treɪs] <> *n* -1. [evidence, remains] vestígio *m* -2. [small amount] vestígio *m*. <> *vt* -1. [find] localizar -2. [follow progress of] traçar -3. [mark outline of] traçar; [with tracing paper] decalcar.

tracing paper ['treɪsɪŋ-] *n (U)* papel *m* de decalque.

track [træk] <> *n* -1. [path] trilha *f* -2. *SPORT* pista *f* -3. *RAIL* trilho *m* -4. [mark, trace] pegada *f* -5. [on record, tape, CD] faixa *f* -6. *phr*: **to lose ~ of sb/sthg** perder alguém/algo de vista; **to be on the right/wrong ~** estar no caminho certo/errado. <> *vt* [follow] seguir a pista de.
→ **track down** *vt sep* localizar.

track record *n* histórico *m* (*de reputação*).

tracksuit ['træksu:t] *n* abrigo *m* esportivo.

tract [trækt] *n* -1. [pamphlet] panfleto *m* -2. [of land, forest] extensão *f*.

traction ['trækʃn] *n (U)* -1. *PHYSICS* tração *f* -2. *MED* tração *f*.

tractor ['træktəʳ] *n* trator *m*.

trade [treɪd] <> *n* -1. *(U)* [commerce] comércio *m* -2. [job] profissão *f*, ofício *m*; **by ~** por formação. <> *vt* [exchange] negociar; **to ~ sthg for sthg** trocar algo por algo. <> *vi COMM* [do business] negociar; **to ~ with sb** negociar com alguém.
→ **trade in** *vt sep* [exchange] dar como entrada.

trade fair *n* feira *f* industrial.

trade-in *n* objeto ou artigo que se entrega como entrada ao se comprar um novo, base *f* de troca.

trademark ['treɪdmɑ:k] *n* -1. *COMM* marca *f* registrada -2. *fig* [characteristic] marca *f* registrada.

trade name *n COMM* razão *f* social.

trader ['treɪdəʳ] *n* comerciante *mf*.

tradesman ['treɪdzmən] (*pl* -men [-mən]) *n* [shopkeeper, trader] comerciante *m*.

trades union *n UK* = trade union.

Trades Union Congress *n UK*: **the ~** *a* associação britânica dos sindicatos.

trades unionist *n UK* = trade unionist.

trade union *n* sindicato *m*.

trade unionist *n* sindicalista *mf*.

trading ['treɪdɪŋ] *n (U)* comércio *m*.

trading estate *n UK* distrito *m* industrial.

tradition [trə'dɪʃn] *n* -1. *(U)* [system of customs] tradição *f* -2. [established practice] costume *m*.

traditional [trə'dɪʃənl] *adj* tradicional.

traffic ['træfɪk] (*pt & pp* -ked, *cont* -king) <> *n (U)* -1. [vehicles] tráfego *m* -2. [illegal trade] tráfico *m*; **~ in sthg** tráfico de algo. <> *vi*: **to ~ in sthg** traficar algo.

traffic circle *n US* rotatória *f*.

traffic jam *n* congestionamento *m*.

trafficker ['træfɪkəʳ] *n* traficante *mf*; **~ in sthg** traficante de algo.

traffic lights *npl* semáforo *m*.

traffic warden *n UK* guarda *mf* de trânsito.

tragedy ['trædʒədɪ] (*pl* -ies) *n* -1. *(U)* [ill fate, dramatic form] tragédia *f* -2. [terrible event, play] tragédia *f*.

tragic ['trædʒɪk] *adj* trágico(ca).

trail [treɪl] <> *n* -1. [path] trilha *f* -2. [traces] rastro *m*. <> *vt* -1. [drag behind, tow] arrastar -2. [lag behind] estar atrás de. <> *vi* -1. [drag behind] arrastar -2. [move slowly] andar lentamente -3. *SPORT* [lose] perder.
→ **trail away, trail off** *vi* apagar-se.

trailer ['treɪləʳ] *n* -1. [vehicle for luggage] reboque *m* -2. *esp US* [for living in] trailer *m* -3. *CINEMA* trailer *m*.

train [treɪn] <> *n* -1. *RAIL* trem *m* -2. [of dress] cauda *f* -3. [connected sequence]: **~ of thought** linha *f* de raciocínio. <> *vt* -1. [teach] treinar; **to ~ sb to do sthg** treinar alguém para fazer algo; **to ~ sb in sthg** treinar alguém em algo -2. [for job]: **to ~ sb as sthg** preparar OR formar alguém para ser algo -3. *SPORT* treinar; **to ~ sb for sthg** treinar alguém para algo -4. [gun, camera] apontar. <> *vi* -1. [for job] preparar-se; **to ~ as sthg** estudar para algo -2. *SPORT* treinar; **to ~ for sthg** treinar para algo.

train driver *n* maquinista *mf*.

trained [treɪnd] *adj* -1. [psychologist] formado(da) -2. [singer] profissional -3. [cartographer] qualificado(da) -4. [doctor] especializado(da).

trainee [treɪ'ni:] *n* estagiário *m*, -ria *f*, trainee *mf*.

trainer ['treɪnəʳ] *n* -1. [of animals] amestrador *m*, -ra *f* -2. *SPORT* treinador *m*, -ra *f*.
→ **trainers** *npl UK* [shoes] tênis *m inv* para a prática desportiva.

training ['treɪnɪŋ] n (U) - **1.** [for job]: ~ in sthg formação f em algo, treinamento m para algo - **2.** SPORT treinamento m.

training college n UK escola f profissionalizante.

training shoes npl UK tênis m inv para a prática desportiva.

traipse [treɪps] vi vaguear.

trait [treɪt] n traço m.

traitor ['treɪtər] n traidor m, -ra f.

trajectory [trə'dʒektərɪ] (pl -ies) n TECH trajetória f.

tram [træm], **tramcar** ['træmkɑːr] n UK bonde m.

tramp [træmp] <> n vagabundo m, -da f. <> vi andar com passos pesados.

trample ['træmpl] vt esmagar com os pés, pisar em.

trampoline ['træmpəliːn] n trampolim m.

trance [trɑːns] n [hypnotic state] transe m.

tranquil ['træŋkwɪl] adj literary plácido(da).

transaction [træn'zækʃn] n transação f.

transcend [træn'send] vt fml [go beyond] transcender.

transcript ['trænskrɪpt] n [of speech, conversation] transcrição f.

transfer [n 'trænsfɜːr, vb træns'fɜːr] (pt & pp -red, cont -ring) <> n - **1.** [gen] transferência f - **2.** [design] decalcomania f. <> vt transferir. <> vi transferir-se.

transfix [træns'fɪks] vt [immobilize] paralisar.

transform [træns'fɔːm] vt transformar; to ~ sb/sthg into sthg transformar alguém/algo em algo.

transfusion [træns'fjuːʒn] n transfusão f.

transgenic [trænz'dʒenɪk] adj transgênico(ca).

transient ['trænzɪənt] adj fml [fleeting] transitório(ria).

transistor [træn'zɪstər] n ELECTRON transistor m.

transistor radio n dated (rádio m) transistor m.

transit ['trænsɪt] n: in ~ de passagem.

transition [træn'zɪʃn] n - **1.** [change] transição f - **2.** (U) [act of changing] transição f; ~ from sthg to sthg transição de algo para algo.

transitive ['trænzɪtɪv] adj GRAMM transitivo(va).

transitory ['trænzɪtrɪ] adj transitório(ria).

translate [træns'leɪt] vt - **1.** [languages] traduzir - **2.** fig [transform]: to ~ sthg into sthg transformar algo em algo.

translation [træns'leɪʃn] n tradução f.

translator [træns'leɪtər] n tradutor m, -ra f.

transmission [trænz'mɪʃn] n transmissão f.

transmit [trænz'mɪt] (pt & pp -ted, cont -ting) vt transmitir.

transmitter [trænz'mɪtər] n ELECTRON transmissor m.

transparency [trans'pærənsɪ] (pl -ies) n transparência f.

transparent [træns'pærənt] adj - **1.** [gen] transparente - **2.** [obvious] óbvio(via).

transpire [træn'spaɪər] fml <> vt: it ~ s that ... descobre-se que ... <> vi [happen] acontecer, ocorrer.

transplant [n 'trænsplɑːnt, vb træns'plɑːnt] <> n transplante m. <> vt [gen] transplantar.

transport [n 'trænspɔːt, vb træn'spɔːt] <> n transporte m. <> vt [goods, people] transportar.

transportation [ˌtrænspɔː'teɪʃn] n (U) esp US = transport.

transport cafe ['trænspɔːt-] n UK lanchonete f de estrada.

transpose [træns'pəʊz] vt [change round] inverter.

trap [træp] (pt & pp -ped, cont -ping) <> n - **1.** [for animal, bird] armadilha f - **2.** fig [trick] cilada f. <> vt - **1.** [animal, bird] apanhar em armadilha - **2.** fig [trick] armar uma cilada - **3.** [retain] guardar.

trapdoor [ˌtræp'dɔːr] n alçapão m.

trapeze [trə'piːz] n trapézio m.

trappings ['træpɪŋz] npl pompas fpl.

trash [træʃ] n (U) - **1.** US [refuse] lixo m - **2.** inf pej [sthg of poor quality] lixo m, porcaria f.

trashcan ['træʃkæn] n US lata f de lixo.

traumatic [trɔː'mætɪk] adj traumático(ca).

travel ['trævl] (UK pt & pp -led, cont -ling, US pt & pp -ed, cont -ing) <> n (U) viagem f; I'm keen on ~ eu adoro viajar. <> vt - **1.** [place] viajar por - **2.** [distance] viajar. <> vi - **1.** [gen] viajar - **2.** [news] voar.

travel agency n agência f de viagens.

travel agent n agente mf de viagens; ~'s agência f de viagens.

travel brochure n catálogo m de viagens.

travel card n passe m.

travel insurance n seguro m de viagem.

traveller UK, **traveler** US ['trævlər] n - **1.** [gen] viajante mf - **2.** [sales representative] representante mf comercial.

traveller's cheque n cheque m de viagem, traveler's cheque m.

travelling *UK*, **traveling** *US* ['trævlɪŋ] *adj* **-1.** [itinerant] itinerante, ambulante **-2.** [portable, of travel] de viagem.

travelsick ['trævəlsɪk] *adj* enjoado(da) *(pela viagem)*.

travesty ['trævəstɪ] *(pl* **-ies)** *n* paródia *f*.

trawler ['trɔ:lə ʳ] *n* traineira *f*.

tray [treɪ] *n* bandeja *f*.

treacherous ['tretʃərəs] *adj* **-1.** [person] traidor(ra) **-2.** [plan, behaviour] traiçoeiro(ra) **-3.** [dangerous] perigoso(sa).

treachery ['tretʃərɪ] *n (U)* traição *f*.

treacle ['tri:kl] *n UK* melado *m*.

tread [tred] *(pt* **trod**, *pp* **trodden)** ⟨⟩ *n* **-1.** [on tyre] banda *f* de rodagem **-2.** [shoe] sola *f* **-3.** [sound or way of walking] passos *mpl*. ⟨⟩ *vi* [place foot]: **to ~ on sthg** pisar em algo.

treadmill ['tredmɪl] *n* esteira *f*.

treason ['tri:zn] *n (U)* traição *f*.

treasure ['treʒə ʳ] ⟨⟩ *n lit* & *fig* tesouro *m*. ⟨⟩ *vt* dar valor a.

treasurer ['treʒərə ʳ] *n* tesoureiro *m*, -ra *f*.

treasury ['treʒərɪ] *(pl* **-ies)** *n* [room] sala *f* do tesouro.

➡ **Treasury** *n*: **the Treasury** ≃ o Ministério da Fazenda.

treat [tri:t] ⟨⟩ *vt* **-1.** [handle, deal with] tratar **-2.** [give sthg special]: **to ~ sb (to sthg)** convidar alguém (para algo) **-3.** [*MED*, process] tratar. ⟨⟩ *n* **-1.** [food] delícia *f* **-2.** [gift] prazer *m*.

treatise ['tri:tɪs] *n fml*: **~ (on sthg)** tratado *m* (sobre algo).

treatment ['tri:tmənt] *n* tratamento *m*.

treaty ['tri:tɪ] *(pl* **-ies)** *n* [written agreement] tratado *m*.

treble ['trebl] ⟨⟩ *adj* **-1.** *MUS* de soprano **-2.** [with numbers]: **my phone extension is ~ 4** meu ramal é 444. ⟨⟩ *n MUS* soprano *m*. ⟨⟩ *vt* & *vi* triplicar.

treble clef *n* clave *f* de sol.

tree [tri:] *n* árvore *f*.

treetop ['tri:tɒp] *n* copa *f* (de árvore).

tree-trunk *n* tronco *m* (de árvore).

trek [trek] *n* expedição *f*.

trellis ['trelɪs] *n* treliça *f*.

tremble ['trembl] *vi* tremer.

tremendous [trɪ'mendəs] *adj* **-1.** [impressive, large] tremendo(da), enorme **-2.** *inf* [really good] fabuloso(sa).

tremor ['tremə ʳ] *n* tremor *m*.

trench [trentʃ] *n* **-1.** [narrow channel] vala *f* **-2.** *MIL* trincheira *f*.

trench coat *n* capa *f* de chuva.

trend [trend] *n* [tendency] tendência *f*.

trendy ['trendɪ] *(compar* **-ier**, *superl* **-iest**, *pl* **-ies)** *inf adj* **-1.** [person] moderno(na) **-2.** [clothes, music] da moda.

trepidation [ˌtrepɪ'deɪʃn] *n (U) fml*: **in** *OR* **with ~** com ansiedade.

trespass ['trespəs] *vi* [on sb's land] invadir; **'no ~ing'** 'entrada proibida'.

trespasser ['trespəsə ʳ] *n* invasor *m*, -ra *f*.

trestle ['tresl] *n* cavalete *m*.

trestle table *n* mesa *f* de cavalete.

trial ['traɪəl] *n* **-1.** *JUR* julgamento *m*; **to be on ~ (for sthg)** ser processado(da) (por algo) **-2.** [test, experiment] teste *m*; **on ~** em testes; **by ~ and error** por tentativa e erro **-3.** [unpleasant experience] suplício *m*.

triangle ['traɪæŋgl] *n* triângulo *m*.

tribe [traɪb] *n* [social group] tribo *f*.

tribunal [traɪ'bju:nl] *n* tribunal *m*.

tributary ['trɪbjʊtrɪ] *(pl* **-ies)** *n GEOGR* afluente *m*.

tribute ['trɪbju:t] *n* **-1.** [act of respect, admiration] tributo *m*; **to be a ~ to sb/sthg** ser um tributo para alguém/algo **-2.** [evidence] prova *f* **-3.** *(U)* [respect, admiration] homenagem *f*; **to pay ~ (to sb/sthg)** prestar homenagem (a alguém/algo).

trice [traɪs] *n*: **in a ~** num abrir e fechar de olhos.

trick [trɪk] ⟨⟩ *n* **-1.** [to deceive] trapaça *f*; **to play a ~ on sb** pregar uma peça em alguém **-2.** [to entertain] truque *m* **-3.** [ability, knack] hábito *m*; **to do the ~** dar resultado. ⟨⟩ *vt* enganar; **to ~ sb into sthg** enrolar alguém sobre algo; **to ~ sb into doing sthg** enrolar alguém para que faça algo.

trickery ['trɪkərɪ] *n (U)* trapaça *f*.

trickle ['trɪkl] ⟨⟩ *n* [of liquid] fio *m*. ⟨⟩ *vi* **-1.** [liquid] gotejar, pingar **-2.** [people, things]: **to trickle in/out** entrar/sair aos poucos.

tricky ['trɪkɪ] *(compar* **-ier**, *superl* **-iest)** *adj* [difficult] enrolado(da), complicado(da).

tricycle ['traɪsɪkl] *n* triciclo *m*.

tried [traɪd] *adj*: **~ and tested** testado e aprovado, testada e aprovada.

trifle ['traɪfl] *n* **-1.** *CULIN* sobremesa de biscoito feita com gelatina, creme, frutas e nata **-2.** [unimportant thing] ninharia *f*.

➡ **a trifle** *adv fml* ligeiramente, um pouco.

trifling ['traɪflɪŋ] *adj pej* insignificante.

trigger ['trɪgə ʳ] *n* [on gun] gatilho *m*.

trill [trɪl] *n* **-1.** *MUS* tremolo *m* **-2.** [of birds] trinado *m*.

trim [trɪm] *(compar* **-mer**, *superl* **-mest**, *pt* & *pp* **-med**, *cont* **-ming)** ⟨⟩ *adj* **-1.** [neat and tidy] bem cuidado(da) **-2.** [slim]

esbelto(ta). ◇ *n* -**1.** [cut - hair] corte *m*; [- hedge] poda *f*. ◇ *vt* -**1.** [cut - hair, nails, lawn] cortar; [- hedge] podar; [- moustache] aparar -**2.** [decorate] enfeitar; **to ~ sthg with sthg** enfeitar algo com algo.

trimming *n* [on clothing] enfeite *m*.
 ➨ **trimmings** *npl* -**1.** CULIN guarnição *f* -**2.** [scraps] aparas *fpl*.

trinket ['trɪŋkɪt] *n* adorno *m*.

trio ['tri:əʊ] (*pl* -s) *n* trio *m*.

trip [trɪp] (*pt* & *pp* -**ped**, *cont* -**ping**) ◇ *n* -**1.** [journey] viagem *f* -**2.** drugs *sl* [experience] viagem *f*. ◇ *vt* [make stumble] fazer tropeçar, passar uma rasteira em. ◇ *vi* [stumble]: **to ~ (over)** tropeçar (em); **to ~ over sthg** tropeçar em algo.
 ➨ **trip up** *vt sep* [make stumble] fazer tropeçar.

tripe [traɪp] *n* (U) -**1.** CULIN dobradinha *f* -**2.** inf [nonsense] bobajada *f*.

triple ['trɪpl] ◇ *adj* triplo(pla). ◇ *vt* & *vi* triplicar.

triple jump *n*: **the ~** o salto triplo.

triplets ['trɪplɪts] *npl* trigêmeos *mpl*, -meas *fpl*.

triplicate ['trɪplɪkət] *n*: **in ~** em três vias.

tripod ['traɪpɒd] *n* tripé *m*.

trite [traɪt] *adj pej* banal.

triumph ['traɪəmf] ◇ *n* -**1.** [success] triunfo *m* -**2.** (U) [satisfaction] triunfo *m*. ◇ *vi* triunfar; **to ~ over sb/sthg** triunfar sobre alguém/algo.

trivia ['trɪvɪə] *n* (U) trivialidades *fpl*.

trivial ['trɪvɪəl] *adj* trivial.

trod [trɒd] *pt* ⊳ **tread**.

trodden ['trɒdn] *pp* ⊳ **tread**.

trolley ['trɒlɪ] (*pl* **trolleys**) *n* -**1.** UK [gen] carrinho *m* -**2.** US [vehicle] bonde *m*.

trolley case *n* mala *f* com rodinhas.

trombone [trɒm'bəʊn] *n* trombone *m*.

troop [tru:p] ◇ *n* [band] bando *m*, grupo *m*. ◇ *vi* [march] andar em bando; **to ~ in/out** entrar/sair em bando.
 ➨ **troops** *npl* MIL tropas *fpl*.

trophy ['trəʊfɪ] (*pl* -**ies**) *n* SPORT troféu *m*.

tropical ['trɒpɪkl] *adj* tropical.

tropics ['trɒpɪks] *npl*: **the ~** os trópicos.

trot [trɒt] (*pt* & *pp* -**ted**, *cont* -**ting**) ◇ *n* [of horse] trote *m*. ◇ *vi* [horse] trotar.
 ➨ **on the trot** *adv inf*: **four times on the ~** quatro vezes seguidas.

trouble ['trʌbl] ◇ *n* -**1.** (U) [difficulty] problema *m*; **to be in ~** [having problems] estar com problemas -**2.** [bother] incômodo *m*; **to take the ~ to do sthg** dar-se

ao trabalho de fazer algo -**3.** (U) [pain, illness] problema *m* -**4.** (U) [fighting] confusão *f* -**5.** POL [unrest] agitação *f*. ◇ *vt* -**1.** [worry, upset] preocupar -**2.** [interrupt, disturb] importunar -**3.** [cause pain to] incomodar.
 ➨ **troubles** *npl* -**1.** [worries] problemas *mpl*, preocupações *fpl* -**2.** POL [unrest] conflitos *mpl*.

troubled ['trʌbld] *adj* -**1.** [worried, upset] preocupado(da) -**2.** [disturbed - sleep] agitado(da); [- life, place, time] tumultuado(da).

troublemaker ['trʌbl,meɪkə^r] *n* agitador *m*, -ra *f*.

troubleshooter ['trʌbl,ʃu:tə^r] *n* solucionador *m*, -ra *f* de problemas; **he's the ~ here** é ele quem resolve os problemas aqui.

troublesome ['trʌblsəm] *adj* problemático(ca).

trough [trɒf] *n* -**1.** [for animals] cocho *m* -**2.** [low point] baixa *f*.

troupe [tru:p] *n* trupe *f*.

trousers ['traʊzəz] *npl* calças *fpl*.

trout [traʊt] (*pl inv* OR -s) *n* truta *f*.

trowel ['traʊəl] *n* -**1.** [for the garden] pá *f* de jardim -**2.** [for cement, plaster] colher *f* de pedreiro.

truant ['tru:ənt] *n* [child] criança *f* que mata as aulas; **to play ~** gazear OR matar aula.

truce [tru:s] *n* trégua *f*.

truck [trʌk] *n* -**1.** *esp* US [lorry] caminhão *m* -**2.** RAIL vagão *m*.

truck driver *n esp* US motorista *mf* de caminhão.

trucker ['trʌkə^r] *n* US caminhoneiro *m*, -ra *f*.

truck farm *n* US chácara *f*.

truculent ['trʌkjʊlənt] *adj* truculento(ta).

trudge [trʌdʒ] *vi* arrastar-se.

true [tru:] *adj* -**1.** [factual] verdadeiro(ra); **I can't believe it's ~** não acredito que seja verdade; **to come ~** tornar-se realidade -**2.** [faithful, genuine] verdadeiro(ra); [- friend] de verdade -**3.** [precise, exact] exato(ta).

truffle ['trʌfl] *n* trufa *f*.

truly ['tru:lɪ] *adv* -**1.** [in fact] verdadeiramente -**2.** [sincerely] realmente; **~, I didn't do it** com toda sinceridade eu não fiz isso -**3.** [for emphasis] realmente -**4.** *phr*: **yours ~** [at end of letter] cordialmente; **and who do you think did that? - yours ~, of course!** e quem em você acha que fez isso? - euzinho em pessoa, obviamente!

trump [trʌmp] *n* [card] trunfo *m*.

trumped-up ['trʌmpt-] *adj pej* forjado(-da).

trumpet ['trʌmpɪt] *n MUS* trompete *m*.

truncheon ['trʌntʃən] *n* cassetete *m*.

trundle ['trʌndl] *vi* rodar lentamente.

trunk [trʌŋk] *n* -1. [gen] tronco *m* -2. [of elephant] tromba *f* -3. [box] baú *m* (de viagem) -4. *US* [of car] porta-malas *m inv*.

➡ **trunks** *npl* [for swimming] calção *m* de banho, sunga *f*.

trunk road *n UK* ≃ rodovia *f* nacional.

truss [trʌs] *n MED* funda *f OR* cinta *f* para hérnia.

trust [trʌst] ◇ *vt* -1. [have confidence in] confiar em; **to ~ sb to do sthg** confiar em alguém para fazer algo -2. [entrust]: **to ~ sb with sthg** confiar algo a alguém -3. *fml* [hope]: **to ~ (that)** esperar que. ◇ *n* -1. *(U)* [faith] confiança *f*; **~ in sb/sthg** confiança em alguém/algo -2. *(U)* [responsibility] confiança *f* -3. *FIN* fideicomisso *m*; **in ~** em fideicomisso -4. *COMM* truste *m*.

trusted ['trʌstɪd] *adj* de confiança.

trustee [trʌs'tiː] *n* -1. *FIN & JUR* fideicomissário *m*, -ria *f* -2. [of institution] curador *m*, -ra *f*.

trust fund *n* fundo *m* fiduciário.

trusting ['trʌstɪŋ] *adj* crédulo(la).

trustworthy ['trʌst,wɜːðɪ] *adj* (digno(-na)) de confiança.

truth [truːθ] *n* -1. [gen]: **the ~** a verdade; **to tell the ~,** ... para dizer a verdade,... -2. *(U)* [veracity] veracidade *f*; **in (all) ~** em verdade, na realidade.

truthful ['truːθfʊl] *adj* -1. [person] sincero(ra), verdadeiro(ra) -2. [story] verídico(ca).

try [traɪ] (*pt & pp* -**ied**, *pl* -**ies**) ◇ *vt* -1. [attempt] tentar; **to ~ to do sthg** tentar fazer algo -2. [sample, test] experimentar -3. *JUR* levar a julgamento -4. [tax, strain] cansar; **to ~ sb's patience** esgotar a paciência de alguém. ◇ *vi* tentar; **to ~ for sthg** tratar de conseguir algo. ◇ *n* -1. [attempt] tentativa *f*; **to give sthg a ~** provar algo -2. *RUGBY* ato de levar a bola até a linha de fundo do adversário e posicioná-la no solo para se marcar pontos.

➡ **try on** *vt sep* [clothes] experimentar.

➡ **try out** *vt sep* -1. [car, machine] testar -2. [plan] pôr à prova.

trying ['traɪɪŋ] *adj* difícil, árduo(dua).

T-shirt *n* camiseta *f*.

T-square *n* régua-tê *f*.

tub [tʌb] *n* -1. [container - for ice cream, margarine] pote *m*; [- for water] tina *f* -2. *inf* [bath] banheira *f*.

tubby ['tʌbɪ] (*compar* -**ier**, *superl* -**iest**) *adj inf* rolha-de-poço, gorducho(cha).

tube [tjuːb] *n* -1. [gen] tubo *m* -2. *UK* [underground train] metrô *m*; [underground system]: **the ~** o metrô; **by ~** de metrô.

tuberculosis [tjuː,bɜːkjʊ'ləʊsɪs] *n (U)* tuberculose *f*.

tubing ['tjuːbɪŋ] *n (U)* tubulação *f*.

tubular ['tjuːbjʊləʳ] *adj* tubular.

TUC (*abbr of* **Trades Union Congress**) *n* federação *dos* sindicatos na Grã-Bretanha, ≃ CUT *f*.

tuck [tʌk] *vt* [place neatly] enfiar, meter.

➡ **tuck away** *vt sep* [store] guardar.

➡ **tuck in** ◇ *vt sep* -1. [child, patient in bed] ajeitar na cama -2. [clothes] meter para dentro. ◇ *vi inf* comer com apetite.

➡ **tuck up** *vt sep* enfiar, meter.

tuck shop *n UK* confeitaria *f (perto de um colégio)*.

Tuesday ['tjuːzdɪ] *n* terça-feira *f*; *see also* **Saturday**.

tuft [tʌft] *n* tufo *m*.

tug [tʌg] (*pt & pp* -**ged**, *cont* -**ging**) ◇ *n* -1. [pull] puxão *m* -2. [boat] rebocador *m*. ◇ *vt* dar um puxão em. ◇ *vi* dar um puxão; **to ~ at sthg** dar um puxão em algo.

tug-of-war *n* cabo-de-guerra *m*.

tuition [tjuː'ɪʃn] *n (U)* ensino *m*; **private ~** aulas *fpl* particulares.

tulip ['tjuːlɪp] *n* tulipa *f*.

tumble ['tʌmbl] ◇ *vi* -1. [person] tombar -2. [water] jorrar -3. *fig* [prices] despencar. ◇ *n* tombo *m*.

➡ **tumble to** *vt fus UK inf* sacar, tocar-se de.

tumbledown ['tʌmbldaʊn] *adj* em ruínas.

tumble-dryer [-,draɪəʳ] *n* secadora *f* (de roupa).

tumbler ['tʌmbləʳ] *n* [glass] copo *m*.

tummy ['tʌmɪ] (*pl* -**ies**) *n inf* barriga *f*.

tumour *UK*, **tumor** *US* ['tjuːməʳ] *n* tumor *m*.

tuna [*UK* 'tjuːnə, *US* 'tuːnə] (*pl inv OR* -**s**), **tuna fish** (*pl* **tuna fish**) *n* -1. [fish] atum *m* -2. *(U)* [food] atum *m*.

tune [tjuːn] ◇ *n* [song, melody] melodia *f*. ◇ *vt* -1. *MUS* afinar -2. *RADIO & TV* sintonizar -3. [engine] ajustar, regular.

➡ **tune in** *vi RADIO & TV* sintonizar-se; **to ~ in to sthg** sintonizar-se em algo.

➡ **tune up** *vi MUS* afinar *OR* consertar os instrumentos.

➡ **in tune** ◇ *adj MUS* afinado(da). ◇ *adv* -1. *MUS* harmonicamente -2. [in agreement]: **in ~ with sb/sthg** em sintonia com alguém/algo.

◆ **out of tune** ◇ *adj* MUS desafinado(-da). ◇ *adv* **-1.** MUS desarmonicamente **-2.** [not in agreement]: **out of ~ with** sb/sthg fora de sintonia com alguém/algo.

tuneful ['tju:nful] *adj* melodioso(sa).

tuner ['tju:nə^r] *n* **-1.** RADIO & TV sintonizador *m* **-2.** MUS afinador *m*.

tunic ['tju:nık] *n* [clothing] túnica *f*.

tuning fork ['tju:nıŋ-] *n* diapasão *m*.

Tunisia [tju:'nızıə] *n* Tunísia *f*.

tunnel ['tʌnl] (*UK pt & pp* **-led**, *cont* **-ling**, *US pt & pp* **-ed**, *cont* **-ing**) ◇ *n* túnel *m*. ◇ *vi*: **to ~ through** sthg atravessar um túnel por algo.

turban ['tɜ:bən] *n* [man's headdress] turbante *m*.

turbine ['tɜ:baın] *n* turbina *f*.

turbocharged ['tɜ:bəutʃɑ:dʒd] *adj* com turbo; **~ car** carro-turbo *m*.

turbulence ['tɜ:bjuləns] *n* (U) turbulência *f*.

turbulent ['tɜ:bjulənt] *adj* turbulento(-ta).

tureen [tə'ri:n] *n* sopeira *f*.

turf [tɜ:f] (*pl* **-s** OR **turves**) ◇ *n* **-1.** (U) [grass surface] gramado *m* **-2.** [clod] turfa *f*. ◇ *vt* [with grass] gramar.

◆ **turf out** *vt sep UK inf* **-1.** [evict] chutar, dar patadas em **-2.** [throw away] jogar fora.

turgid ['tɜ:dʒıd] *adj fml* [style, prose] empolado(da).

Turk [tɜ:k] *n* turco *m*, -ca *f*.

turkey ['tɜ:kı] (*pl* **turkeys**) *n* **-1.** [bird] peru *m* **-2.** (U) [meat] peru *m*.

Turkey ['tɜ:kı] *n* Turquia *f*.

Turkish ['tɜ:kıʃ] ◇ *adj* turco(ca). ◇ *n* [language] turco *m*. ◇ *npl*: **the ~** os turcos.

Turkish delight *n* (U) doce feito de substância gelatinosa em cubos com cobertura de açúcar ou chocolate.

turmoil ['tɜ:mɔıl] *n* (U) desordem *f*.

turn [tɜ:n] ◇ *n* **-1.** [in road, river] curva *f* **-2.** [revolution, twist] volta *f* **-3.** [change] reviravolta *f* **-4.** [in game]: **it's my ~** é a minha vez **-5.** [in order] vez *f*; **in ~** por vez **-6.** [performance] número *m*, apresentação *f* **-7.** MED ataque *m*, crise *f* **-8.** *phr*: **to do** sb **a good ~** fazer uma boa ação a alguém. ◇ *vt* **-1.** [cause to rotate] girar **-2.** [move round, turn over] virar **-3.** [go round] dobrar **-4.** [direct]: **to ~** sthg **to** sb/sthg voltar algo para alguém/algo **-5.** [change]: **to ~** sthg **into** sthg transformar algo em algo **-6.** [make, cause to become] deixar; **to ~** sthg **inside out** virar algo pelo avesso. ◇ *vi* **-1.** [change direction] virar, dobrar; **to ~ to**

sb/sthg voltar-se para alguém/algo **-2.** [rotate] girar **-3.** [move round] voltar-se **-4.** [in book]: **~ to page 102** vão até a página 102 **-5.** [for consolation]: **to ~ to** sb/sthg buscar consolo em alguém/algo **-6.** [become] tornar-se; **my hair's ~ing grey** meu cabelo está ficando branco; **to ~ into** sthg transformar-se em algo.

◆ **turn around** *vt sep & vi* = **turn round**.

◆ **turn away** ◇ *vt sep* [refuse entry to] não deixar entrar. ◇ *vi* distanciar-se.

◆ **turn back** ◇ *vt sep* **-1.** [force to return] fazer voltar **-2.** [fold back] dobrar. ◇ *vi* [return] voltar atrás.

◆ **turn down** *vt sep* **-1.** [reject] recusar **-2.** [heating, lighting] diminuir **-3.** [sound] abaixar.

◆ **turn in** *vi inf* [go to bed] ir dormir.

◆ **turn off** ◇ *vt fus* [road, path] sair de. ◇ *vt sep* [switch off - appliance, engine] desligar; [- gas, tap] fechar. ◇ *vi* [leave road, path] dobrar.

◆ **turn on** ◇ *vt sep* **-1.** [make work - appliance, engine] ligar; [- gas, tap] abrir; [- light] acender **-2.** *inf* [excite sexually] acender. ◇ *vt fus* [attack] avançar em.

◆ **turn out** ◇ *vt sep* **-1.** [switch off] apagar **-2.** [empty] esvaziar. ◇ *vt fus*: **to ~ out to be** acabar sendo, vir a ser; **it ~s out that ...** acontece que ... ◇ *vi* **-1.** [end up] acabar, terminar **-2.** [attend]: **to ~ out (for** sthg**)** comparecer (em algo).

◆ **turn over** ◇ *vt sep* **-1.** [playing card, stone, page] virar **-2.** [consider]: **I ~ed his ideas over in my mind** fiquei com as idéias dele dando voltas na minha cabeça **-3.** [hand over] entregar; **to ~** sb/sthg **over to** sb entregar alguém/algo para alguém. ◇ *vi* **-1.** [roll over] revirar-se **-2.** *UK* TV mudar de canal.

◆ **turn round** ◇ *vt sep* **-1.** [chair, picture] virar **-2.** [wheel] girar **-3.** [words, sentence] expressar de outra maneira **-4.** [quantity of work] aliviar. ◇ *vi* [person] virar-se.

◆ **turn up** ◇ *vt sep* [heat, lighting, radio, TV] aumentar. ◇ *vi inf* **-1.** [gen] aparecer **-2.** [opportunity, solution] surgir.

turning ['tɜ:nıŋ] *n* [side road]: **the first ~ to the left** a primeira (rua) à esquerda.

turning point *n* momento *m* decisivo.

turnip ['tɜ:nıp] *n* nabo *m*.

turnout ['tɜ:naut] *n* [attendance] comparecimento *m*, número *m* de participantes.

turnover ['tɜːnˌəʊvə'] n (U) - **1.** [of person-nel] rotatividade f - **2.** FIN volume m de vendas.

turnpike ['tɜːnpaɪk] n US rodovia f com pedágio.

turnstile ['tɜːnstaɪl] n borboleta f (em ônibus).

turntable ['tɜːnˌteɪbl] n [on record player] prato m (giratório).

turn-up n UK - **1.** [on trousers] bainha f - **2.** inf [surprise]: **a ~ for the books** inf uma surpresa total.

turpentine ['tɜːpəntaɪn] n (U) terebentina f.

turquoise ['tɜːkwɔɪz] <> adj turquesa. <> n - **1.** (U) [mineral, gem] turquesa f - **2.** [colour] turquesa m.

turret ['tʌrɪt] n [on castle] torre f pequena.

turtle ['tɜːtl] (pl inv OR -s) n tartaruga f.

turtleneck ['tɜːtlnek] n - **1.** [garment] blusa f de gola olímpica - **2.** [neck] gola f olímpica.

turves [tɜːvz] UK pl ⊳ turf.

tusk [tʌsk] n [of animal] presa f.

tussle ['tʌsl] <> n briga f. <> vi brigar; **to ~ over sthg** brigar por algo.

tutor ['tjuːtə'] n - **1.** [private] professor m, -ra f particular - **2.** UNIV professor m universitário, professora f universitária.

tutorial [tjuːˈtɔːrɪəl] n aula f para grupos pequenos.

tuxedo [tʌkˈsiːdəʊ] (pl -s) n US smoking m.

TV (abbr of television) n [medium, industry, apparatus] TV f.

twang [twæŋ] n - **1.** [sound - of guitar] som m metálico; [- of string, elastic] som m vibrante - **2.** [accent] som m nasalado.

tweed [twiːd] n (U) tweed m.

tweezers ['twiːzəz] npl pinças fpl.

twelfth [twelfθ] num décimo segundo, décima segunda; see also sixth.

twelve [twelv] num doze; see also six.

twentieth ['twentɪəθ] num vigésimo(-ma); see also sixth.

twenty ['twentɪ] (pl -ies) num vinte; see also sixty.

twice [twaɪs] adv duas vezes; **~ a week** duas vezes por semana; **he earns ~ as much as me** ele ganha o dobro que eu.

twiddle ['twɪdl] <> vt girar (entre os dedos). <> vi: **to ~ with sthg** brincar com algo entre os dedos.

twig [twɪg] n graveto m.

twilight ['twaɪlaɪt] n [in evening] crepúsculo m vespertino.

twin [twɪn] <> adj - **1.** [child, sibling] gêmeo(mea) - **2.** [beds] duplo(pla) - **3.** [towns, towers] gêmeos(meas). <> n [sibling] gêmeos mpl, -meas fpl.

twin-bedded [-ˈbedɪd] adj com duas camas.

twine [twaɪn] <> n (U) barbante m. <> vt: **to ~ sthg round sthg** enrolar algo em algo.

twinge [twɪndʒ] n - **1.** [of pain] pontada f - **2.** [of guilt] remorso m.

twinkle ['twɪŋkl] vi - **1.** [star, light] cintilar - **2.** [eyes] brilhar.

twin room n quarto m com duas camas.

twin town n cidade-irmã f.

twirl [twɜːl] <> vt - **1.** [spin] girar - **2.** [twist] torcer. <> vi rodopiar.

twist [twɪst] <> n - **1.** [gen] volta f - **2.** fig [in plot] reviravolta f. <> vt - **1.** [gen] retorcer - **2.** [face, frame] torcer - **3.** [head] voltar - **4.** [lid, knob, dial] girar - **5.** [words, meaning] distorcer. <> vi - **1.** [road, river] dar voltas - **2.** [body, part of body] torcer.

twit [twɪt] n UK inf idiota mf, imbecil mf.

twitch [twɪtʃ] <> n espasmo m; **nervous ~** tique m nervoso. <> vi contrair-se.

two [tuː] num dois (duas); **in ~** em dois; see also **six**.

two-door adj [car] de duas portas.

twofaced [ˌtuːˈfeɪst] adj pej de duas caras.

twofold ['tuːfəʊld] <> adj duplo(pla). <> adv: **to increase ~** duplicar-se.

two-piece adj [suit, swimsuit] de duas peças.

twosome ['tuːsəm] n inf dupla f.

two-way adj - **1.** [traffic] de mão dupla - **2.** [discussion, debate] de duas vias - **3.** [cooperation] mútuo(tua).

tycoon [taɪˈkuːn] n magnata mf.

type [taɪp] <> n - **1.** [gen] tipo m - **2.** (U) TYPO: **in bold/italic ~** em negrito/itálico. <> vt & vi - **1.** [on typewriter] datilografar - **2.** [on computer] digitar.

typecast ['taɪpkɑːst] (pt & pp typecast) vt escalar sempre para o mesmo tipo de papel; **to be ~ as sthg** ser sempre escalado(da) (para atuar) como algo.

typeface ['taɪpfeɪs] n TYPO tipo m, letra f.

typescript ['taɪpskrɪpt] n cópia f datilografada.

typeset ['taɪpset] (pt & pp typeset, cont -ting) vt TYPO compor.

typesetting n composição f (para impressão).

typewriter ['taɪpˌraɪtə'] n máquina f de escrever.

typhoid (fever) ['taɪfɔɪd-] n (U) febre f tifóide.

typhoon [taɪˈfuːn] n tufão m.

typical ['tɪpɪkl] *adj* típico(ca); ~ **of sb/ sth** típico(ca) de alguém/algo.

typing ['taɪpɪŋ] *n* -**1.** (*U*) [on typewriter] datilografia *f* -**2.** (*U*) [on computer] digitação *f*.

typist ['taɪpɪst] *n* -**1.** [on typewriter] datilógrafo *m*, -fa *f* -**2.** [on computer] digitador *m*, -ra *f*.

typography [taɪ'pɒgrəfɪ] *n* -**1.** (*U*) [process, job] tipografia *f* -**2.** [format] composição *f* tipográfica.

tyranny ['tɪrənɪ] *n* (*U*) [of person, government] tirania *f*.

tyrant ['taɪrənt] *n* tirano *m*, -na *f*.

tyre *UK*, **tire** *US* ['taɪəʳ] *n* pneu *m*.

tyre pressure *n* (*U*) pressão *f* do pneu.

U

u (*pl* **u's** OR **us**), **U** (*pl* **U's** OR **Us**) [juː] *n* [letter] u, U *m*.
➤ **U** (*abbr of* **universal**) *filme de censura livre.*

U-bend *n* sifão *m*.

udder ['ʌdəʳ] *n* úbere *m*.

UFO (*abbr of* **unidentified flying object**) *n* OVNI *m*.

Uganda [juː'gændə] *n* Uganda.

ugh [ʌg] *excl* puf!

ugly ['ʌglɪ] (*compar* -**ier**, *superl* -**iest**) *adj* -**1.** [unattractive] feio (feia) -**2.** *fig* [unpleasant] desagradável.

UHF (*abbr of* **ultra-high frequency**) *n* UHF *m*.

UK (*abbr of* **United Kingdom**) *n* RU *m*.

UKAEA (*abbr of* **United Kingdom Atomic Energy Authority**) *n* *órgão responsável pelo controle da energia atômica no Reino Unido.*

Ukraine [juː'kreɪn] *n*: **the** ~ **a** Ucrânia.

ulcer ['ʌlsəʳ] *n* -**1.** [in stomach] úlcera *f* -**2.** [in mouth] afta *f*.

ulcerated ['ʌlsəreɪtɪd] *adj* ulcerado(da).

Ulster ['ʌlstəʳ] *n* Irlanda *f* do Norte.

ulterior [ʌl'tɪərɪəʳ] *adj*: ~ **motive** motivo *m* ulterior.

ultimata [ˌʌltɪ'meɪtə] *pl* ▷ **ultimatum**.

ultimate ['ʌltɪmət] ◇ *adj* -**1.** [success, objetive] final, definitivo(va) -**2.** [failure] último(ma) -**3.** [most powerful] máximo(ma). ◇ *n*: **the** ~ **in sth** a última palavra em algo.

ultimately ['ʌltɪmətlɪ] *adv* -**1.** [finally, in the long term] finalmente, por fim -**2.** [fundamentally] no fundo.

ultimatum [ˌʌltɪ'meɪtəm] (*pl* -**tums** OR -**ta**) *n* ultimato *m*.

ultrasound ['ʌltrəsaʊnd] *n* (*U*) ultrasom *m*.

ultraviolet [ˌʌltrə'vaɪələt] *adj* ultravioleta.

umbilical cord [ʌm'bɪlɪkl-] *n* cordão *m* umbilical.

umbrella [ʌm'brelə] ◇ *n* -**1.** [gen] guarda-chuva *m*; -**2.** [fixed] guarda-sol *m*. ◇ *adj* guarda-chuva; ~ **word** palavra guarda-chuva.

umpire ['ʌmpaɪəʳ] ◇ *n* árbitro *m*. ◇ *vt* & *vi* arbitrar, apitar.

umpteen [ˌʌmp'tiːn] *num adj inf*: ~ **times** um milhão de vezes.

umpteenth [ˌʌmp'tiːnθ] *num adj inf* enésimo(ma).

UN (*abbr of* **United Nations**) *n*: **the** ~ **a** ONU.

unabated [ˌʌnə'beɪtɪd] *adj* incessante.

unable [ʌn'eɪbl] *adj* incapaz; **to be** ~ **to do sth** não poder fazer algo.

unacceptable [ˌʌnək'septəbl] *adj* inaceitável.

unaccompanied [ˌʌnə'kʌmpənɪd] *adj* -**1.** [child] sozinho(nha) -**2.** [luggage] desacompanhado(da) -**3.** [song] sem acompanhamento.

unaccountably [ˌʌnə'kaʊntəblɪ] *adv* [inexplicably] inexplicavelmente.

unaccounted [ˌʌnə'kaʊntɪd] *adj*: ~ **for** desaparecido(da).

unaccustomed [ˌʌnə'kʌstəmd] *adj* [unused]: **to be** ~ **to sth/to doing sth** estar desacostumado(da) a algo/a fazer algo.

unadulterated [ˌʌnə'dʌltəreɪtɪd] *adj* -**1.** [unspoiled] não-adulterado(da) -**2.** [absolute] puro(ra).

unanimous [juː'nænɪməs] *adj* unânime.

unanimously [juː'nænɪməslɪ] *adv* unanimemente.

unanswered [ˌʌn'ɑːnsəd] *adj* não-respondido(da).

unappetizing, -ising [ˌʌn'æpɪtaɪzɪŋ] *adj* -**1.** [food] pouco apetitoso(sa) -**2.** [sight, thought] pouco apetecível.

unarmed [ˌʌn'ɑːmd] *adj* desarmado(da).

unarmed combat *n* (*U*) combate *m* sem armas.

unashamed [ˌʌnə'ʃeɪmd] *adj* descarado(da).

unassuming [ˌʌnə'sjuːmɪŋ] *adj* despretensioso(sa).

unattached [ˌʌnə'tætʃt] *adj* -**1.** [not fastened, linked] independente; ~ **to sth**

separado(da) de algo **- 2.** [without partner] sem compromisso.

unattended [ˌʌnə'tendɪd] adj **- 1.** [luggage, children] desacompanhado(da) **- 2.** [fire, shop] sem vigilância.

unattractive [ˌʌnə'træktɪv] adj **- 1.** [person, building, place] sem atrativos **- 2.** [idea, prospect] sem brilho.

unauthorized, -ised [ˌʌn'ɔ:θəraɪzd] adj não-autorizado(da).

unavailable [ˌʌnə'veɪləbl] adj que não está disponível.

unaware [ˌʌnə'weəʳ] adj desconhecedor(ra); **to be ~ of sb/sthg** não estar consciente de alguém/algo.

unawares [ˌʌnə'weəz] adv: **to catch** OR **take sb ~** pegar alguém desprevenido(da).

unbalanced [ˌʌn'bælənst] adj **- 1.** [biased] parcial **- 2.** [deranged] desequilibrado(da).

unbearable [ʌn'beərəbl] adj insuportável, insustentável.

unbeatable [ˌʌn'bi:təbl] adj imbatível.

unbeknown(st) [ˌʌnbɪ'nəʊn(st)] adv: **~ to sem** o conhecimento de.

unbelievable [ˌʌnbɪ'li:vəbl] adj **- 1.** [amazing] incrível **- 2.** [not believable] inacreditável.

unbending [ʌn'bendɪŋ] adj [intransigent] resoluto(ta).

unbia(s)sed [ˌʌn'baɪəst] adj imparcial.

unborn [ˌʌn'bɔ:n] adj [child] nascituro(ra).

unbreakable [ˌʌn'breɪkəbl] adj inquebrável.

unbridled [ˌʌn'braɪdld] adj desenfreado(da).

unbutton [ˌʌn'bʌtn] vt desabotoar.

uncalled-for [ʌn'kɔ:ld-] adj injusto(ta), desnecessário(ria).

uncanny [ʌn'kænɪ] (compar **-ier**, superl **-iest**) adj sinistro(tra).

unceasing [ˌʌn'si:sɪŋ] adj fml incessante.

unceremonious [ˈʌnˌserɪ'məʊnjəs] adj [abrupt] abrupto(ta).

uncertain [ʌn'sɜ:tn] adj **- 1.** [gen] incerto(ta) **- 2.** [person] indeciso(sa); **in no ~ terms** sem meias palavras.

unchanged [ˌʌn'tʃeɪndʒd] adj sem alterar.

unchecked [ˌʌn'tʃekt] ◇ adj [unrestrained] desenfreado(da). ◇ adv [unrestrained] sem restrições.

uncivilized [ˌʌn'sɪvɪlaɪzd] adj [barbaric] não-civilizado(da).

uncle ['ʌŋkl] n tio m.

unclear [ˌʌn'klɪəʳ] adj **- 1.** [meaning, instructions] confuso(sa), pouco claro(ra)

- 2. [future] obscuro(ra) **- 3.** [motives, details] confuso(sa) **- 4.** [person]: **to be ~ about sthg** não ter algo claro.

uncomfortable [ˌʌn'kʌmftəbl] adj **- 1.** [giving discomfort] desconfortável **- 2.** fig [awkward] desagradável **- 3.** [person - in physical discomfort] desconfortável; [- ill at ease] incomodado(da).

uncommon [ʌn'kɒmən] adj **- 1.** [rare] raro(ra) **- 2.** fml [extreme] fora do comum.

uncompromising [ˌʌn'kɒmprəmaɪzɪŋ] adj resoluto(ta), inflexível.

unconcerned [ˌʌnkən'sɜ:nd] adj [not anxious] indiferente.

unconditional [ˌʌnkən'dɪʃənl] adj incondicional.

unconscious [ʌn'kɒnʃəs] ◇ adj **- 1.** [gen] inconsciente **- 2.** fig [unaware]: **to be ~ of sthg** não estar ciente de algo. ◇ n PSYCH: **the ~** o inconsciente.

unconsciously [ʌn'kɒnʃəslɪ] adv inconscientemente.

uncontrollable [ˌʌnkən'trəʊləbl] adj incontrolável.

unconventional [ˌʌnkən'venʃənl] adj não-convencional.

unconvinced [ˌʌnkən'vɪnst] adj não-convencido(da).

uncouth [ʌn'ku:θ] adj grosseiro(ra).

uncover [ʌn'kʌvəʳ] vt **- 1.** [saucepan] destampar **- 2.** [corruption, truth] revelar, expor.

undecided [ˌʌndɪ'saɪdɪd] adj **- 1.** [person] indeciso(sa) **- 2.** [issue] pendente.

undeniable [ˌʌndɪ'naɪəbl] adj inegável.

under ['ʌndəʳ] ◇ prep **- 1.** [beneath, below] embaixo de; **they walked ~ the bridge** passaram por baixo da ponte **- 2.** [less than] menos de **- 3.** [indicating conditions or circumstances]: **~ the circumstances** dadas as circunstâncias; **I'm ~ the impression that ...** tenho a impressão de que ... **- 4.** [undergoing]: **~ discussion** em discussão **- 5.** [directed, governed by]: **he has ten people ~ him** tem dez pessoas trabalhando sob seu comando **- 6.** [according to] de acordo com **- 7.** [in classification, name, title]: **he filed it ~ 'D'** arquivou na letra D; **~ an alias** sob outro nome. ◇ adv **- 1.** [beneath] embaixo; **to go ~** fracassar **- 2.** [less]: **children of five years and ~** crianças de cinco anos ou menos.

underage [ˌʌndər'eɪdʒ] adj **- 1.** [person] menor de idade **- 2.** [drinking, sex] para menor de idade.

undercarriage ['ʌndəˌkærɪdʒ] n trem m de aterrissagem.

undercharge [ˌʌndə'tʃɑ:dʒ] vt cobrar menos que o estipulado.

underclothes [ˈʌndəkləʊðz] *npl* roupas *fpl* íntimas OR de baixo.

undercoat [ˈʌndəkəʊt] *n* [of paint] primeira demão *f*.

undercover [ˈʌndəˌkʌvəʳ] *adj* secreto(ta).

undercurrent [ˈʌndəˌkʌrəntl] *n* *fig* [tendency] sentimento *m* oculto.

undercut [ˌʌndəˈkʌt] (*pt & pp* undercut, *cont* -ting) *vt* [in price] vender mais barato que.

underdeveloped [ˌʌndədɪˈveləpt] *adj* subdesenvolvido(da), em desenvolvimento.

underdog [ˈʌndədɒg] *n*: the ~ os menos favorecidos.

underdone [ˌʌndəˈdʌn] *adj* [food] meio cru (crua).

underestimate [ˌʌndərˈestɪmeɪtl] *vt* subestimar.

underexposed [ˌʌndərɪkˈspəʊzd] *adj* PHOT subexposto(ta).

underfoot [ˌʌndəˈfʊtl] *adv* debaixo dos pés; **the ground is wet** ~ o chão está molhado.

undergo [ˌʌndəˈgəʊ] (*pt* -went, *pp* -gone) *vt* -1. [change, difficulties] passar por -2. [operation, examination] submeter-se a.

undergraduate [ˌʌndəˈgrædʒʊət] *n* universitário *m*, -ria *f (que ainda não colou grau)*.

underground [*adj & n* ˈʌndəgraʊnd, *adv* ˌʌndəˈgraʊnd] <> *adj* -1. [below the ground] subterrâneo(nea) -2. *fig* [secret, illegal] clandestino(na). <> *adv*: **to go** ~ passar à clandestinidade; **to be forced** ~ ter de passar à clandestinidade. <> *n* -1. UK [transport system] metrô *m* -2. [activist movement] resistência *f*.

undergrowth [ˈʌndəgrəʊθ] *n* (U) vegetação *f* rasteira *(numa floresta)*.

underhand [ˌʌndəˈhænd] *adj* clandestino(na).

underline [ˌʌndəˈlaɪn] *vt* -1. [draw line under] sublinhar -2. *fig* [stress] salientar.

underlying [ˌʌndəˈlaɪɪŋ] *adj* subjacente.

undermine [ˌʌndəˈmaɪn] *vt* *fig* [weaken] minar.

underneath [ˌʌndəˈniːθ] <> *prep* debaixo de. <> *adv* -1. [beneath] por baixo -2. *fig* [within oneself] por dentro, no fundo. <> *adj inf* de baixo. <> *n* [underside]: **the** ~ a parte de baixo; **on the** ~ **of the box** na parte de baixo da caixa.

underpaid [ˈʌndəpeɪd] *adj* mal pago(-ga).

underpants [ˈʌndəpænts] *npl* cueca *f*.

underpass [ˈʌndəpɑːs] *n* passagem *f* subterrânea.

underprivileged [ˌʌndəˈprɪvɪlɪdʒd] *adj* [children] desamparado(da).

underrated [ˌʌndəˈreɪtɪd] *adj* subestimado(da).

undershirt [ˈʌndəʃɜːt] *n* US camiseta *f*.

underside [ˈʌndəsaɪd] *n*: **the** ~ a parte de baixo.

underskirt [ˈʌndəskɜːt] *n* anágua *f*.

understand [ˌʌndəˈstænd] (*pt & pp* -stood) <> *vt* -1. entender, compreender -2. *fml* [believe]: **to** ~ **that** acreditar que. <> *vi* entender, compreender.

understandable [ˌʌndəˈstændəbl] *adj* compreensível.

understanding [ˌʌndəˈstændɪŋ] <> *n* -1. [knowledge, insight] compreensão *f*, entendimento *m* -2. (U) [sympathy] compreensão *f* mútua -3. [interpretation, conception]: **it is my** ~ **that ...** tenho a impressão de que ... -4. [informal agreement] entendimento *m* <> *adj* [sympathetic] compreensivo(va).

understated *adj* [elegance, clothes] sóbrio(bria).

understatement [ˌʌndəˈsteɪtmənt] *n* -1. [inadequate statement] atenuação *f* -2. (U) [quality of understating] atenuação *f*; **he is a master of** ~ ele é o rei dos eufemismos.

understood [ˌʌndəˈstʊd] *pt & pp* ▷ understand.

understudy [ˈʌndəˌstʌdɪ] (*pl* -ies) *n* ator *m* substituto, atriz *f* substituta.

undertake [ˌʌndəˈteɪk] (*pt* -took, *pp* -taken) *vt* -1. [take on - responsibility, control] assumir; [- task] incumbir-se de -2. [promise]: **to** ~ **to do sthg** comprometer-se a fazer algo.

undertaker [ˈʌndəˌteɪkəʳ] *n* agente *mf* funerário, -ria.

undertaking [ˌʌndəˈteɪkɪŋ] *n* -1. [task] incumbência *f* -2. [promise] promessa *f*.

undertone [ˈʌndətəʊn] *n* -1. [quiet voice] voz *f* baixa -2. [vague feeling] traço *m*; **an** ~ **of sadness** um traço de tristeza.

undertook [ˌʌndəˈtʊk] *pt* ▷ undertake.

underwater [ˌʌndəˈwɔːtəʳ] <> *adj* submarino(na). <> *adv* debaixo d'água.

underwear [ˈʌndəweəʳ] *n* (U) roupa *f* íntima OR de baixo.

underwent [ˌʌndəˈwent] *pt* ▷ undergo.

underwired *adj* [bra] com suporte.

underworld [ˈʌndəˌwɜːld] *n* [criminal society]: **the** ~ o submundo.

underwriter [ˈʌndəˌraɪtəʳ] *n* segurador *m*, -ra *f*.

undid [ˌʌnˈdɪd] pt ▷ **undo**.

undies [ˈʌndɪz] npl inf roupas fpl ínti-mas or de baixo.

undisputed [ˌʌndɪˈspjuːtɪd] adj indiscu-tível.

undistinguished [ˌʌndɪˈstɪŋgwɪʃt] adj sem graça.

undo [ʌnˈduː] (pt -did, pp -done) vt -1. [knot] desfazer, desatar -2. [buttons] desabotoar -3. [garment] desamarrar -4. [good work, efforts] anular.

undoing [ˌʌnˈduːɪŋ] n (U) fml ruína f, perdição f.

undone [ʌnˈdʌn] ⟨⟩ pp ▷ **undo**. ⟨⟩ adj -1. [coat] desabotoado(da) -2. [shoe] desamarrado(da) -3. fml [not done] por fazer.

undoubted [ʌnˈdaʊtɪd] adj indubitável.

undoubtedly [ʌnˈdaʊtɪdlɪ] adv indubi-tavelmente.

undress [ˌʌnˈdres] ⟨⟩ vt despir. ⟨⟩ vi despir-se.

undue [ˌʌnˈdjuː] adj fml desmedido(da).

undulate [ˈʌndjʊleɪt] vi fml ondular.

unduly [ˌʌnˈdjuːlɪ] adv fml demasiada-mente.

unearth [ˌʌnˈɜːθ] vt -1. [dig up] desen-terrar -2. fig [discover] descubrir.

unearthly [ʌnˈɜːθlɪ] adj inf [time of day]: at an ~ hour in the morning num horário absurdo da manhã.

unease [ʌnˈiːz] n (U) inquietação f, apreensão f.

uneasy [ʌnˈiːzɪ] (compar -ier, superl -iest) adj -1. [troubled] apreensivo(va) -2. [em-barrassed] constrangido(da); an ~ si-lence um silêncio constrangedor -3. [peace, truce] duvidoso(sa).

uneconomic [ˈʌnˌiːkəˈnɒmɪk] adj pouco rentável.

uneducated [ˌʌnˈedjʊkeɪtɪd] adj -1. [person] inculto(ta), sem instrução -2. [behaviour, manners, speech] em que se percebe falta de instrução.

unemployed [ˌʌnɪmˈplɔɪd] ⟨⟩ adj [out-of-work] desempregado(da). ⟨⟩ npl: the ~ os desempregados.

unemployment [ˌʌnɪmˈplɔɪmənt] n de-semprego m.

unemployment benefit UK, **unem-ployment compensation** US n (U) ≃ seguro-desemprego m.

unerring [ˌʌnˈɜːrɪŋ] adj infalível.

uneven [ˌʌnˈiːvn] adj -1. [surface] irregu-lar -2. [road] acidentado(da) -3. [perfor-mance, coverage etc.] desigual, desparelho(lha) -4. [competition] injus-to(ta).

unexpected [ˌʌnɪkˈspektɪd] adj inespe-rado(da).

unexpectedly [ˌʌnɪkˈspektɪdlɪ] adv inesperadamente.

unfailing [ʌnˈfeɪlɪŋ] adj [loyalty, support, good humour] infalível.

unfair [ˌʌnˈfeəʳ] adj injusto(ta).

unfaithful [ˌʌnˈfeɪθfʊl] adj [sexually] in-fiel.

unfamiliar [ˌʌnfəˈmɪljəʳ] adj -1. [not well-known] desconhecido(da) -2. [not ac-quainted]: to be ~ with sb/sthg desco-nhecer alguém/algo.

unfashionable [ˌʌnˈfæʃnəbl] adj ultra-passado(da).

unfasten [ˌʌnˈfɑːsn] vt -1. [garment, buttons] desabotoar -2. [rope] desamar-rar.

unfavourable UK, **unfavorable** US [ˌʌnˈfeɪvrəbl] adj desfavorável.

unfeeling [ʌnˈfiːlɪŋ] adj insensível.

unfinished [ˌʌnˈfɪnɪʃt] adj inacabado(-da).

unfit [ˌʌnˈfɪt] adj -1. [not in good shape] fora de forma -2. [not suitable]: ~ (for sthg) inadequado(da) (para algo).

unfold [ʌnˈfəʊld] ⟨⟩ vt [open out] des-dobrar. ⟨⟩ vi [become clear] esclarecer-se.

unforeseen [ˌʌnfɔːˈsiːn] adj imprevisto(-ta).

unforgettable [ˌʌnfəˈgetəbl] adj ines-quecível.

unforgivable [ˌʌnfəˈgɪvəbl] adj imper-doável.

unfortunate [ʌnˈfɔːtʃnət] adj -1. [un-lucky] azarento(ta) -2. [regrettable] la-mentável.

unfortunately [ʌnˈfɔːtʃnətlɪ] adv infe-lizmente.

unfounded [ˌʌnˈfaʊndɪd] adj infunda-do(da).

unfriendly [ˌʌnˈfrendlɪ] (compar -ier, superl -iest) adj hostil.

unfurnished [ˌʌnˈfɜːnɪʃt] adj desmobi-liado(da), sem móveis.

ungainly [ʌnˈgeɪnlɪ] adj desajeitado(-da).

ungodly [ˌʌnˈgɒdlɪ] adj inf [unreasonable]: why are you phoning me at this ~ hour? por que você está me ligando nesta hora da madrugada?

ungrateful [ʌnˈgreɪtfʊl] adj mal-agra-decido(da).

unhappy [ʌnˈhæpɪ] (compar -ier, superl -iest) adj -1. [sad] triste -2. [uneasy]: to be ~ (with or about sthg) estar des-contente(com algo) -3. fml [unfortunate] lamentável, infeliz.

unharmed [ˌʌnˈhɑːmd] adj ileso(sa).

unhealthy [ʌnˈhelθɪ] (compar -ier, superl -iest) adj -1. [in bad health] doentio(tia)

-2. [causing bad health] insalubre **-3.** *fig* [undesirable] prejudicial.

unheard-of [ʌn'hɜːd-l] *adj* **-1.** [unknown, completely absent] inaudito(ta) **-2.** [unprecedented] sem precedente.

unhook [ˌʌn'hʊk] *vt* **-1.** [unfasten hooks of] desenganchar **-2.** [remove from hook] desprender.

unhurt [ˌʌn'hɜːt] *adj* ileso(sa).

unhygienic [ˌʌnhaɪ'dʒiːnɪk] *adj* anti-higiênico(ca).

uni (*abbr of* **university**) *n UK inf* universidade *f*.

unidentified flying object *n* objeto *m* voador não-identificado.

unification [ˌjuːnɪfɪ'keɪʃn] *n* (U) unificação *f*.

uniform ['juːnɪfɔːml] <> *adj* uniforme. <> *n* uniforme *m*.

unify ['juːnɪfaɪ] (*pt & pp* -ied) *vt* unificar.

unilateral [ˌjuːnɪ'lætərəl] *adj* unilateral.

unimportant [ˌʌnɪm'pɔːtənt] *adj* insignificante, sem importância.

uninhabited [ˌʌnɪn'hæbɪtɪd] *adj* desabitado(da).

uninjured [ˌʌn'ɪndʒəd] *adj* ileso(sa).

unintelligent [ˌʌnɪn'telɪdʒənt] *adj* pouco inteligente.

unintentional [ˌʌnɪn'tenʃənl] *adj* involuntário(ria).

union ['juːnjən] <> *n* **-1.** [trade union] sindicato *m* **-2.** [alliance] união *f*. <> *comp* sindical.

unionized, -ised *adj* sindicalizado(da).

Union Jack *n*: the ~ *a* bandeira do Reino Unido.

unique [juː'niːk] *adj* **-1.** [unparalleled] incomparável, único(ca) **-2.** *fml* [peculiar, exclusive]: ~ **to sb/sthg** peculiar a alguém/algo.

unison ['juːnɪzn] *n* (U) [agreement] harmonia *f*; **in** ~ [simultaneously] em uníssono.

unit ['juːnɪt] *n* **-1.** [gen] unidade *f* **-2.** [piece of furniture] módulo *m*.

unite [juː'naɪt] <> *vt* unificar. <> *vi* unir-se, juntar-se.

united [juː'naɪtɪd] *adj* **-1.** [in harmony] unido(da) **-2.** [unified] unificado(da).

United Kingdom *n*: the ~ o Reino Unido.

United Nations *n*: the ~ as Nações Unidas.

United States *n*: the ~ (of America) os Estados Unidos (da América); **in the** ~ nos Estados Unidos.

unit trust *n UK* fundo *m* de investimento.

unity ['juːnɪtɪ] *n* **-1.** [union] união *f*, unidade *f* **-2.** [harmony] união *f*.

universal [ˌjuːnɪ'vɜːsl] *adj* [belief, truth] universal.

universe ['juːnɪvɜːs] *n ASTRON* universo *m*.

university [ˌjuːnɪ'vɜːsətɪ] (*pl* -ies) <> *n* universidade *f*. <> *comp* universitário(ria); ~ **student** estudante *m* universitário, -ria *f*.

unjust [ˌʌn'dʒʌst] *adj* injusto(ta).

unkempt [ˌʌn'kempt] *adj* [hair, beard, appearance] desajeitado(da).

unkind [ʌn'kaɪnd] *adj* [gen] indelicado(da).

unknown [ˌʌn'nəʊn] *adj* desconhecido(da).

unlawful [ˌʌn'lɔːfʊl] *adj* ilegal.

unleaded [ˌʌn'ledɪd] *adj* sem chumbo.

unleash [ˌʌn'liːʃ] *vt literary* desencadear.

unless [ən'les] *conj* a menos que; ~ **I'm mistaken, ...** a não ser que eu esteja enganado, ...

unlike [ˌʌn'laɪk] *prep* **-1.** [different from] diferente de **-2.** [in contrast to] ao contrário de **-3.** [not typical of] atípico(ca); **it's very** ~ **you to complain** você não é de reclamar.

unlikely [ʌn'laɪklɪ] *adj* **-1.** [not probable] improvável **-2.** [bizarre] estranho(nha).

unlisted [ʌn'lɪstɪd] *adj US* [phone number] fora da lista.

unload [ˌʌn'ləʊd] *vt* [gen] descarregar.

unlock [ˌʌn'lɒk] *vt* destrancar, abrir (*com chave*).

unlucky [ʌn'lʌkɪ] (*compar* -ier, *superl* -iest) *adj* **-1.** [unfortunate] infeliz **-2.** [bringing bad luck] de mau agouro.

unmarried [ˌʌn'mærɪd] *adj* solteiro(ra).

unmistakable [ˌʌnmɪ'steɪkəbl] *adj* inconfundível.

unmitigated [ʌn'mɪtɪgeɪtɪd] *adj* completo(ta), absoluto(ta); **he's talking** ~ **nonsense!** ele não está dizendo coisa com coisa!

unnatural [ʌn'nætʃrəl] *adj* **-1.** [unusual, strange] estranho(nha) **-2.** [affected] pouco natural.

unnecessary [ʌn'nesəsərɪ] *adj* desnecessário(ria).

unnerving [ʌn'nɜːvɪŋ] *adj* enervante.

unnoticed [ˌʌn'nəʊtɪst] *adj* desapercebido(da).

unobtainable [ˌʌnəb'teɪnəbl] *adj* inacessível.

unobtrusive [ˌʌnəb'truːsɪv] *adj* discreto(ta).

unofficial [ˌʌnə'fɪʃl] *adj* não-oficial.

unorthodox [ˌʌn'ɔːθədɒks] *adj* não-ortodoxo(xa).

unpack [ˌʌn'pæk] <> vt -1. [bag, suitcase] desfazer -2. [clothes, books, shopping] desembrulhar. <> vi desfazer as malas.

unpalatable [ʌn'pælətəbl] adj -1. [unpleasant to taste] intragável -2. fig [difficult to accept] desagradável.

unparalleled [ʌn'pærəleld] adj sem paralelo.

unpleasant [ʌn'pleznt] adj desagradável.

unplug [ʌn'plʌg] (pt & pp -ged, cont -ging) vt ELEC desligar.

unpopular [ˌʌn'pɒpjʊləʳ] adj impopular.

unprecedented [ʌn'presɪdəntɪd] adj sem precedente.

unpredictable [ˌʌnprɪ'dɪktəbl] adj imprevisível.

unprofessional [ˌʌnprə'feʃənl] adj não-profissional.

unqualified [ˌʌn'kwɒlɪfaɪd] adj -1. [not qualified] desqualificado(da) -2. [total, complete] absoluto(ta).

unquestionable [ʌn'kwestʃənəbl] adj inquestionável.

unquestioning [ʌn'kwestʃənɪŋ] adj incondicional.

unravel [ʌn'rævl] (UK pt & pp -led, cont -ling, US pt & pp -ed, cont -ing) vt -1. [undo] desembaraçar -2. fig [solve] elucidar.

unreal [ˌʌn'rɪəl] adj [strange] irreal.

unrealistic [ˌʌnrɪə'lɪstɪk] adj pouco realista.

unreasonable [ʌn'riːznəbl] adj -1. [unfair, not sensible] injusto(ta) -2. [not justifiable] absurdo(da), irracional.

unrelated [ˌʌnrɪ'leɪtɪd] adj: to be ~ (to sthg) não estar relacionado(da) (a algo).

unrelenting [ˌʌnrɪ'lentɪŋ] adj -1. [pressure] contínuo(nua) -2. [questions] implacável.

unreliable [ˌʌnrɪ'laɪəbl] adj inconfiável.

unremitting [ˌʌnrɪ'mɪtɪŋ] adj incessante.

unrequited [ˌʌnrɪ'kwaɪtɪd] adj não-correspondido(da).

unresolved [ˌʌnrɪ'zɒlvd] adj sem solução.

unrest [ˌʌn'rest] n (U) agitação f.

unrivalled UK, **unrivaled** US [ʌn'raɪvld] adj incomparável.

unroll [ˌʌn'rəʊl] vt [unfold] desenrolar.

unruly [ʌn'ruːlɪ] (compar -ier, superl -iest) adj -1. [wayward] indisciplinado(-da) -2. [untidy] desarrumado(da).

unsafe [ˌʌn'seɪf] adj -1. [dangerous] perigoso(sa) -2. [in danger] inseguro(ra).

unsaid [ˌʌn'sed] adj: to leave sthg ~ não falar algo.

unsatisfactory [ˈʌnˌsætɪs'fæktərɪ] adj insatisfatório(ria).

unsavoury, unsavory US [ˌʌn'seɪvərɪ] adj -1. [behaviour, person, habits] (moralmente) ofensivo(va) -2. [smell] repugnante.

unscathed [ˌʌn'skeɪðd] adj ileso(sa), são e salvo, sã e salva.

unscrew [ˌʌn'skruː] vt -1. [lid, bottle top] desenroscar -2. [sign, mirror] desparafusar.

unscrupulous [ʌn'skruːpjʊləs] adj inescrupuloso(sa).

unseemly [ʌn'siːmlɪ] (compar -ier, superl -iest) adj inconveniente.

unselfish [ʌn'selfɪʃ] adj desinteressado(da).

unsettled [ˌʌn'setld] adj -1. [unstable - person] inquieto(ta); [- weather] instável -2. [unfinished, unresolved - argument] incerto(ta); [- issue] vago(ga) -3. [account, bill] duvidoso(sa) -4. [area, region] despovoado(da).

unshak(e)able [ʌn'ʃeɪkəbl] adj inabalável.

unshaven [ˌʌn'ʃeɪvn] adj [face, chin] com a barba por fazer.

unsightly [ʌn'saɪtlɪ] adj de péssima aparência.

unskilled [ˌʌn'skɪld] adj não-especializado(da).

unsociable [ʌn'səʊʃəbl] adj [person, place] anti-social.

unsocial [ˌʌn'səʊʃl] adj: to work ~ hours trabalhar fora de hora.

unsound [ˌʌn'saʊnd] adj -1. [based on false ideas] equivocado(da) -2. [in poor condition] inseguro(ra).

unspeakable [ʌn'spiːkəbl] adj terrível.

unstable [ˌʌn'steɪbl] adj instável.

unsteady [ˌʌn'stedɪ] (compar -ier, superl -iest) adj -1. [person, step, voice] inseguro(ra) -2. [chair, ladder] pouco seguro(-ra).

unstoppable [ʌn'stɒpəbl] adj inevitável.

unstuck [ˌʌn'stʌk] adj: to come ~ [notice, stamp, label] descolar-se; fig [plan, system] degringolar; fig [person] dar-se mal.

unsuccessful [ˌʌnsək'sesfʊl] adj malsucedido(da).

unsuccessfully [ˌʌnsək'sesfʊlɪ] adv em vão.

unsuitable [ˌʌn'suːtəbl] adj inconveniente; to be ~ for sthg ser inapropriado(da) para algo.

unsure [ˌʌn'ʃɔːʳ] adj -1. [not confident]: to

be ~ **(of o.s.)** não ser seguro(ra) (de si) **- 2.** [not certain]: **to be ~ (about/of sthg)** não ter certeza (sobre/de algo).

unsuspecting [ˌʌnsə'spektɪŋ] *adj* insuspeitável.

unsympathetic [ˈʌnˌsɪmpə'θetɪk] *adj* [unfeeling] insensível.

untangle [ˌʌn'tæŋgl] *vt* [disentangle] desemaranhar.

untapped [ˌʌn'tæpt] *adj* [unexploited] inexplorado(da).

untenable [ˌʌn'tenəbl] *adj* insustentável.

unthinkable [ʌn'θɪŋkəbl] *adj* [inconceivable] inconcebível.

untidy [ʌn'taɪdɪ] (*compar* **-ier**, *superl* **-iest**) *adj* **-1.** [gen] desarrumado(da) **-2.** [person, work] desleixado(da).

untie [ˌʌn'taɪ] (*cont* **untying**) *vt* [string, knot, bonds] desatar; [prisoner] soltar.

until [ʌn'tɪl] <> *prep* **-1.** [up to, till] até **- 2.** *(after negative)* antes de; **I can't come ~ tomorrow** eu não posso vir antes de amanhã. <> *conj* **-1.** [up to, till] até; **we were told to wait ~ he arrived** pediram-nos para esperar até que ele chegasse *OR* até ele chegar **-2.** *(after negative)* antes de, até; **they never help ~ I tell them to** eles só ajudam quando eu peço; **don't sign ~ you've checked everything** não assine nada antes de ter verificado tudo.

untimely [ʌn'taɪmlɪ] *adj* **-1.** [premature] prematuro(ra) **-2.** [inopportune] inoportuno(na).

untold [ˌʌn'təʊld] *adj* [incalculable, vast] inimaginável.

untoward [ˌʌntə'wɔːd] *adj* [unfortunate] inconveniente.

untrue [ˌʌn'truː] *adj* [inaccurate] falso(sa).

unused [*sense 1* ˌʌn'juːzd, *sense 2* ˌʌn'juːst] *adj* **-1.** [new] novo(va) **-2.** [unaccustomed]: **to be ~ to sthg/to doing sthg** não estar acostumado(da) a algo/a fazer algo.

unusual [ʌn'juːʒl] *adj* [rare] raro(ra).

unusually [ʌn'juːʒəlɪ] *adv* [exceptionally] excepcionalmente.

unveil [ˌʌn'veɪl] *vt* **-1.** [remove covering from] desvelar **- 2.** *fig* [reveal, divulge] expor.

unwanted [ˌʌn'wɒntɪd] *adj* indesejado(da).

unwelcome [ʌn'welkəm] *adj* **-1.** [news, experience] desagradável **-2.** [visitor] desconfortável.

unwell [ˌʌn'wel] *adj*: **to be/feel ~** estar/ sentir-se indisposto(ta).

unwieldy [ʌn'wiːldɪ] (*compar* **-ier**, *superl* **-iest**) *adj* **-1.** [cumbersome] pesado(da) **- 2.** *fig* [inefficient] ineficiente.

unwilling [ˌʌn'wɪlɪŋ] *adj* [reluctant] relutante; **to be ~ to do sthg** estar relutante para/em fazer algo.

unwind [ˌʌn'waɪnd] (*pt* & *pp* **-wound**) <> *vt* desenrolar. <> *vi fig* [person] relaxar.

unwise [ˌʌn'waɪz] *adj* imprudente.

unwitting [ʌn'wɪtɪŋ] *adj fml* inadvertido(da), impremeditado(da).

unworkable [ˌʌn'wɜːkəbl] *adj* impraticável.

unworthy [ʌn'wɜːðɪ] (*compar* **-ier**, *superl* **-iest**) *adj* [undeserving]: **to be ~ of sb/sthg** ser indigno(na) de alguém/ algo.

unwound [ˌʌn'waʊnd] *pt* & *pp* ⊳ **unwind**.

unwrap [ˌʌn'ræp] (*pt* & *pp* **-ped**, *cont* **-ping**) *vt* desembrulhar.

unwritten law [ˌʌn'rɪtn-] *n* lei *f* não-escrita.

unzip [ˌʌn'zɪp] *vt* descompactar.

up [ʌp] <> *adv* **-1.** [toward higher position, level] para cima; **we walked ~ to the top** subimos até o topo **-2.** [in higher position]: **she's ~ in her bedroom** está lá em cima no seu quarto; **~ there** ali *OR* lá em cima. **-3.** [into upright position]: **to stand ~** pôr-se em pé; **to sit ~** [from lying position] sentar-se; [sit straight] sentar-se direito. **- 4.** [northward]: **~ in Canada** no Canadá. **-5.** [in phrases]: **to walk ~ and down** andar de um lado para o outro; **to jump ~ and down** dar pulos; **~ to six weeks** até seis semanas; **~ to ten people** até dez pessoas; **are you ~ to travelling?** você está em condições de viajar?; **what are you ~ to?** o que você está tramando?; **it's ~ to you** depende de você; **~ until ten o'clock** até às dez horas. <> *prep* **-1.** [toward higher position]: **to walk ~ a hill** subir um monte; **I went ~ the stairs** subi as escadas. **- 2.** [in higher position] no topo de; **~ a hill** no topo de um monte; **~ a ladder** no topo de uma escada. **-3.** [at end of]: **they live ~ the block from us** eles vivem no final da nossa rua. <> *adj* **-1.** [out of bed] levantado(da); **I got ~ at six today** levantei-me às seis hoje. **- 2.** [at an end]: **time's ~** acabou-se o tempo. **- 3.** [rising]: **the ~ escalator** a escada rolante ascendente. <> *n*: **~s and downs** altos e baixos *mpl*.

up-and-coming *adj* promissor(ra).

upbringing ['ʌpˌbrɪŋɪŋ] *n (U)* educação *f*.

update [ˌʌp'deɪt] *vt* [bring up-to-date] atualizar.

upheaval [ʌp'hiːvl] *n* convulsão *f*.

upheld [ʌp'held] pt & pp ⊳ **uphold**.
uphill [,ʌp'hɪl] ◇ adj **-1.** [rising] íngreme **-2.** fig [difficult] árduo(dua). ◇ adv para cima.
uphold [ʌp'həʊld] (pt & pp **-held**) vt [support] apoiar.
upholstery [ʌp'həʊlstərɪ] n (U) estofamento m.
upkeep ['ʌpkiːp] n (U) manutenção f.
uplifting [ʌp'lɪftɪŋ] adj [cheering] extasiante, edificante.
up-market adj de alta categoria.
upon [ə'pɒn] prep fml **-1.** [gen] sobre; **the weekend is ~ us** o final de semana já está em cima da gente; **summer is ~ us** o verão está chegando **-2.** [when] após.
upper ['ʌpə'] ◇ adj **-1.** [gen] superior **-2.** GEOGR [inland] alto(ta). ◇ n [of shoe] gáspea f.
upper class n: **the ~** a alta classe.
➡ **upper-class** adj de alta classe.
upper-crust adj da alta roda.
upper hand n: **to have the ~** ter a palavra final; **to gain** OR **get the ~** obter o controle.
Upper House n UK POL Câmara f dos Lordes.
uppermost ['ʌpəməʊst] adj **-1.** [highest] mais alto(ta) **-2.** [most important]: **to be ~ in one's mind** ser o mais importante na cabeça de alguém.
upright [adj ,ʌp'raɪt, ʌp'ʌpraɪt] ◇ adj **-1.** [erect] vertical **-2.** fig [honest] honesto(ta). ◇ adv verticalmente. ◇ n **-1.** [of door] marco m **-2.** [of bookshelf] pilar m **-3.** [of goal] poste m.
uprising ['ʌp,raɪzɪŋ] n revolta f rebelião f.
uproar ['ʌprɔː'] n **-1.** [commotion] algazarra f **-2.** [protest] protesto m.
uproot [ʌp'ruːt] vt **-1.** [force to leave] arrancar; **to ~ o.s.** desarraigar-se **-2.** BOT [tear out of ground] arrancar.
upset [ʌp'set] (pt & pp **upset**, cont **-ting**) ◇ adj **-1.** [distressed] descontrolado(da); [offended] chateado(da) **-2.** MED: **to have an ~ stomach** ter um estômago fraco. ◇ n **-1.** MED: **to have a stomach ~** ficar com dor de estômago **-2.** [surprise result] surpresa f. ◇ vt **-1.** [distress] deixar nervoso(sa), irritar **-2.** [mess up] atrapalhar **-3.** [overturn, knock over] virar.
upshot ['ʌpʃɒt] n desfecho m.
upside down [,ʌpsaɪd-] ◇ adj [inverted] invertido(da), ao contrário. ◇ adv de cabeça para baixo; **to turn sthg ~** fig [disorder] virar algo de pernas para o ar.

upstairs [,ʌp'steəz] ◇ adj de cima. ◇ adv **-1.** [not downstairs] em cima **-2.** [on one of the floors above] de cima. ◇ n andar de cima.
upstart ['ʌpstɑːt] n novo-rico m, nova-rica f.
upstream [,ʌp'striːm] ◇ adj: **the bridge is a few miles ~ (from here)** a ponte fica poucas milhas rio acima (a partir daqui). ◇ adv correnteza acima.
upsurge ['ʌpsɜːdʒ] n: **~ of/in sthg** aumento m de/em algo.
uptake ['ʌpteɪk] n: **to be quick/slow on the ~** ter um raciocínio rápido/lento.
uptight [ʌp'taɪt] adj inf nervoso(sa).
up-to-date adj **-1.** [machinery, methods] moderno(na) **-2.** [news, information] atualizado(da); **to keep ~ with sthg** manter-se a par de algo.
upturn ['ʌptɜːn] n: **~ (in sthg)** melhoria f (em algo).
upward ['ʌpwəd] adj [movement, trend] para cima.
uranium [jʊ'reɪnjəm] n (U) urânio m.
urban ['ɜːbən] adj urbano(na).
urbane [ɜː'beɪn] adj gentil.
Urdu ['ʊəduː] n (U) urdu m.
urge [ɜːdʒ] ◇ n impulso m; **to have an ~ to do sthg** ter um impulso de fazer algo. ◇ vt **-1.** [try to persuade]: **to ~ sb to do sthg** incitar alguém a fazer algo **-2.** [advocate] defender.
urgency ['ɜːdʒənsɪ] n (U) urgência f.
urgent ['ɜːdʒənt] adj **-1.** [pressing] urgente **-2.** [desperate] insistente.
urinal [jʊə'raɪnl] n [receptacle] urinol m; [room] mictório m.
urinate ['jʊərɪneɪt] vi urinar.
urine ['jʊərɪn] n (U) urina f.
URL (abbr of **uniform resource locator**) n COMPUT URL f.
urn [ɜːn] n **-1.** [for ashes] urna f funerária **-2.** [for tea, coffee] chaleira f.
Uruguay ['jʊərəgwaɪ] n Uruguai m.
us [ʌs] pers pron (direct) nos; (indirect, after prep) they know ~ conhecem-nos; **it's ~** somos nós; **send it to ~** envie-nos isso; **tell ~** diga-nos; **we brought it with ~** trouxemo-lo conosco.
US (abbr of **United States**) n: **the ~** os EUA.
USA n (abbr of **United States of America**): **the ~** os EUA.
usage ['juːzɪdʒ] n **-1.** (U) [use of language] uso m **-2.** [meaning] sentido m **-3.** (U) [handling, treatment] uso m.
USB (abbr of **Universal Serial Bus**) n COMPUT USB m.

USB port *n COMPUT* porta *f* USB.

use [*n & aux vb* juːs, *vt* juːz] ◇ *n* **-1.** [gen]
uso *m*; **to be in** ~ estar em uso; **to be
out of** ~ estar fora de uso; **to make** ~
of sthg fazer uso de algo; **to let sb have
the** ~ **of** sthg deixar que alguém utilize
algo **-2.** [purpose, usefulness] utilidade *f*;
to be of ~ ser útil; **to be no** ~ ser inútil;
what's the ~ **(of doing sthg)?** qual é a
utilidade (de se fazer algo)? ◇ *aux vb*
costumar; **I** ~ **d to live in London** eu
morava em Londres; **there** ~ **d to be a
tree here** havia uma árvore aqui. ◇
vt **-1.** [utilize] usar, utilizar **-2.** *pej* [exploit]
usar.
◆ **use up** *vt sep* esgotar.

used [*sense 1* juːzd, *sense 2* juːst] *adj* **-1.**
[object, car *etc.*] usado(da) **-2.** [accus-
tomed]: **to be** ~ **to** sthg/to doing sthg
estar acostumado(da) a algo/a fazer
algo; **to get** ~ **to** sthg acostumar-se a
algo.

useful ['juːsful] *adj* útil.

useless ['juːslɪs] *adj* **-1.** [gen] inútil **-2.** *inf*
[hopeless] incorrigível.

user ['juːzə'] *n* usuário *m*, -ria *f*.

user-friendly *adj* de fácil utilização.

usher ['ʌʃə'] ◇ *n* **-1.** [at wedding]
recepcionista *mf* **-2.** [at theatre, concert]
lanterninha *mf*. ◇ *vt* conduzir.

usherette [ˌʌʃə'ret] *n* **-1.** [at wedding]
recepcionista *f* **-2.** [at theatre, concert]
lanterninha *f*.

USSR (*abbr of* Union of Soviet Socialist
Republics) *n*: **the (former)** ~ a (ex-)
URSS.

usual ['juːʒəl] *adj* usual, habitual; **as** ~
[as normal] como de costume; [as often
happens] como sempre.

usually ['juːʒəlɪ] *adv* geralmente, normalmente.

usurp [juːˈzɜːp] *vt fml* usurpar.

utensil [juːˈtensl] *n* utensílio *m*.

uterus ['juːtərəs] (*pl* -**ri** [-raɪ], -**ruses**) *n*
útero *m*.

utility [juːˈtɪlətɪ] (*pl* -**ies**) *n* **-1.** (U) [useful-
ness] utilidade *f* **-2.** [public service] serviço *m* público **-3.** *COMPUT* utilitário *m*.

utility room *n* área *f* de serviços.

utilize, -ise ['juːtəlaɪz] *vt* utilizar.

utmost ['ʌtməust] ◇ *adj* máximo(ma),
supremo(ma). ◇ *n* **-1.** [best effort]: **to
do one's** ~ fazer o impossível **-2.** [max-
imum] máximo *m*; **to the** ~ ao máximo,
até não poder mais.

utter ['ʌtə'] ◇ *adj* total, completo(ta).
◇ *vt* **-1.** [sound, cry] emitir **-2.** [word]
proferir.

utterly ['ʌtəlɪ] *adv* totalmente, completamente.

U-turn *n* **-1.** [turning movement] retorno
m **-2.** *fig* [complete change] guinada *f* de
180 graus.

v¹ (*pl* v's OR vs), **V** (*pl* V's OR Vs) [viː] *n*
[letter] v, V *m*.

v² **-1.** (*abbr of* verse) v. **-2.** (*abbr of* vide)
[cross-reference] vide **-3.** (*abbr of* versus)
versus **-4.** (*abbr of* volt) v.

vacancy ['veɪkənsɪ] (*pl* -**ies**) *n* **-1.** [job, po-
sition] vaga *f* **-2.** [room available] quarto *m*
livre; **'vacancies'** 'há vagas'; **'no vacancies'** 'lotação esgotada'.

vacant ['veɪkənt] *adj* **-1.** [gen] vago(ga)
-2. [look, expression] distraído(da).

vacant lot *n* lote *m* disponível.

vacate [vəˈkeɪt] *vt* **-1.** [give up, resign]
deixar vago(ga) **-2.** [leave empty, stop
using] desocupar.

vacation [vəˈkeɪʃn] *n* **-1.** *UNIV* [period
when closed] férias *fpl* **-2.** *US* [holiday]
férias *fpl*.

vacationer [vəˈkeɪʃənə'] *n US* veranista
mf.

vaccinate ['væksɪneɪt] *vt*: **to** ~ **sb
(against** sthg) vacinar alguém (contra
algo).

vaccine [*UK* 'væksiːn, *US* væk'siːn] *n*
vacina *f*.

vacuum ['vækjʊəm] ◇ *n* **-1.** [gen]
vácuo *m* **-2.** [machine]: ~ **(cleaner)**
aspirador *m* (de pó). ◇ *vt* aspirar,
passar o aspirador em.

vacuum cleaner *n* aspirador *m* de
pó.

vacuum-packed *adj* embalado(da) a
vácuo.

vagina [vəˈdʒaɪnə] *n* vagina *f*.

vagrant ['veɪɡrənt] *n* vagabundo *m*, -da
f.

vague [veɪɡ] *adj* **-1.** [imprecise] vago(ga),
impreciso(sa) **-2.** [feeling] leve **-3.** [eva-
sive] evasivo(va) **-4.** [absent-minded] dis-
traído(da) **-5.** [indistinct] vago(ga).

vaguely ['veɪɡlɪ] *adv* **-1.** [imprecisely] va-
gamente **-2.** [slightly, not very] levemente
-3. [absent-mindedly] distraidamente **-4.**
[indistinctly]: **I could** ~ **make out a ship on
the horizon** mal dava para distinguir
um navio no horizonte.

vain [veɪn] *adj* **-1.** *pej* [conceited] vaidoso(sa) **- 2.** [futile, worthless] vão (vã).
➟ **in vain** *adv* em vão.
valentine card ['væləntaɪn-] *n* cartão *m* de dia dos namorados.
Valentine's Day ['væləntaɪnz-] *n*: **(St)** ~ Dia *m* dos Namorados.
valet ['væleɪ, 'vælɪt] *n* [manservant] camareiro *m*.
valid ['vælɪd] *adj* válido(da).
valley ['vælɪ] (*pl* **valleys**) *n* vale *m*.
valuable ['væljʊəbl] *adj* valioso(sa).
➟ **valuables** *npl* objetos *mpl* de valor.
valuation [ˌvæljʊ'eɪʃn] *n* avaliação *f*.
value ['vælju:] <> *n* **-1.** *(U)* [gen] valor *m* **- 2.** [financial] valor *m*; **to be good** ~ estar com o preço muito bom; **to be** ~ **for money** estar bem em conta. <> *vt* **-1.** [estimate price of] avaliar **- 2.** [cherish] valorizar.
➟ **values** *npl* [morals] valores *mpl* morais, princípios *mpl*.
value added tax *n* ≃ imposto *m* sobre circulação de mercadorias e serviços.
valued ['vælju:d] *adj* estimado(da).
valve [vælv] *n* válvula *f*.
van [væn] *n* **-1.** *AUT* caminhonete *f*, van *f* **- 2.** *UK RAIL* vagão *m* de carga.
vandal ['vændl] *n* vândalo *m*, -la *f*.
vandalism ['vændəlɪzm] *n* *(U)* vandalismo *m*.
vandalize, -ise ['vændəlaɪz] *vt* destruir.
vanilla [və'nɪlə] *n* *(U)* baunilha *f*.
vanish ['vænɪʃ] *vi* desaparecer.
vanity ['vænətɪ] *n* *(U)* *pej* vaidade *f*.
vapour *UK*, **vapor** *US* ['veɪpə'] *n* *(U)* vapor *m*.
variable ['veərɪəbl] *adj* variável.
variation [ˌveərɪ'eɪʃn] *n* **-1.** *(U)* [fact of difference] variação *f*; ~ **in sthg** variação em algo **- 2.** [degree of difference] variação *f*; ~ **in sthg** variação em algo **- 3.** [different version & *MUS*] variação *f*.
varicose veins ['værɪkəʊs-] *npl* varizes *fpl*.
varied ['veərɪd] *adj* variado(da).
variety [və'raɪətɪ] (*pl* **-ies**) *n* **-1.** *(U)* [difference in type] variedade *f* **- 2.** [selection] variedade *f* **- 3.** [type] tipo *m* **- 4.** *(U)* *THEATRE* (teatro *m* de) variedades *fpl*.
variety show *n* programa *m* de variedades.
various ['veərɪəs] *adj* **-1.** [several] vários(-rias) **- 2.** [different] variados(das).
varnish ['vɑ:nɪʃ] <> *n* **-1.** [for wood] verniz *m* **- 2.** [for nails] esmalte *m*. <> *vt* **-1.** [wood] envernizar **- 2.** [nails] pintar.
vary ['veərɪ] (*pt* & *pp* **-ied**) <> *vt* variar. <> *vi*; **to** ~ **in sthg** variar em algo; **to** ~ **with sthg** variar de acordo com algo.

vase [*UK* vɑ:z, *US* veɪz] *n* vaso *m*.
Vaseline® ['væsəli:n] *n* *(U)* vaselina *f*.
vast [vɑ:st] *adj* enorme, imenso(sa).
vat [væt] *n* tina *f*.
Vatican ['vætɪkən] *n*: **the** ~ o Vaticano.
vault [vɔ:lt] <> *n* **-1.** [in bank] caixa-forte *f* **- 2.** [in church] cripta *f* **- 3.** [roof] abóbada *f*. <> *vt* saltar. <> *vi*: **to** ~ **over sthg** pular por cima de algo.
veal [vi:l] *n* *(U)* vitela *f*.
veer [vɪə'] *vi* **-1.** [vehicle, road, wind] virar **- 2.** *fig* [conversation, mood] alternar-se.
vegan ['vi:gən] <> *adj* vegan. <> *n* vegan *mf*.
vegetable ['vedʒtəbl] <> *n* **-1.** *BOT* vegetal *m* **- 2.** [food] hortaliças *fpl*, legume *m* <> *adj* **-1.** [protein] vegetal **- 2.** [soup] de legumes.
vegetarian [ˌvedʒɪ'teərɪən] <> *adj* vegetariano(na). <> *n* vegetariano *m*, -na *f*.
vegetation [ˌvedʒɪ'teɪʃn] *n* *(U)* vegetação *f*.
vehement ['vi:əmənt] *adj* **-1.** [gesture, attack] violento(ta) **- 2.** [person, denial] veemente.
vehicle ['vi:əkl] *n* **-1.** [for transport] veículo *m* **- 2.** *fig* [medium]: **a** ~ **for sthg** um meio para algo.
veil [veɪl] *n* **-1.** [for face] véu *m* **- 2.** *fig* [obscuring thing] manto *m*.
vein [veɪn] *n* **-1.** *ANAT* veia *f* **- 2.** [of leaf] nervura *f* **- 3.** [of mineral] veio *m*.
velocity [vɪ'lɒsətɪ] (*pl* **-ies**) *n* *PHYSICS* velocidade *f*.
velvet ['velvɪt] *n* *(U)* veludo *m*.
vendetta [ven'detə] *n* vendeta *f*.
vending machine ['vendɪŋ-] *n* máquina *f* de venda automática.
vendor ['vendɔ:'] *n* vendedor *m*, -ra *f*.
veneer [və'nɪə'] *n* **-1.** *(U)* [of wood] compensado *m* **- 2.** *fig* [appearance] aparência *f*.
venereal disease [vɪ'nɪərɪəl-] *n* *(U)* doença *f* venérea.
venetian blind *n* persiana *f*.
Venezuela [ˌvenɪz'weɪlə] *n* Venezuela.
vengeance ['vendʒəns] *n* *(U)* vingança *f*; **it started raining with a** ~ começou a chover para valer.
venison ['venɪzn] *n* *(U)* carne *f* de veado.
venom ['venəm] *n* *(U)* **-1.** [poison] veneno *m* **- 2.** *fig* [spite, bitterness] veneno *m*.
vent [vent] <> *n* saída *f* de ar, abertura *f* de ar; **to give** ~ **to sthg** dar vazão a algo. <> *vt* [express] descarregar; **to** ~ **sthg on sb/sthg** descarregar algo em alguém/algo.
ventilate ['ventɪleɪt] *vt* ventilar.

ventilator ['ventɪleɪtəʳ] n ventilador m.

ventriloquist [ven'trɪləkwɪst] n ventrí-loquo m, -qua f.

venture ['ventʃəʳ] ⋄ n empreendi-mento m. ⋄ vt [proffer] arriscar; **to ~ to do sthg** arriscar-se a fazer algo. ⋄ vi **-1.** [go somewhere dangerous] aventu-rar-se **-2.** [embark]: **to ~ into sthg** lançar-se em algo.

venue ['venju:] n local m (em que se realiza algo).

veranda(h) [vəˈrændə] n varanda f.

verb [vɜ:b] n verbo m.

verbal ['vɜ:bl] adj verbal.

verbatim [vɜ:'beɪtɪm] ⋄ adj literal. ⋄ adv literalmente, palavra por pa-lavra.

verdict ['vɜ:dɪkt] n **-1.** JUR veredito m **-2.** [opinion] parecer m; **~ on sthg** parecer sobre algo.

verge [vɜ:dʒ] n **-1.** [edge, side] acosta-mento m **-2.** [brink]: **on the ~ of sthg** à beira de algo; **on the ~ of doing sthg** a ponto de fazer algo.

◆ verge (up)on vt fus beirar.

verify ['verɪfaɪ] (pt & pp -ied) vt **-1.** [check] verificar **-2.** [confirm] confirmar.

veritable ['verɪtəbl] adj fml or hum legí-timo(ma).

vermin ['vɜ:mɪn] npl **-1.** [ZOOL - rodents] bichos mpl; [- insects] insetos mpl nocivos **-2.** pej [people] parasita mf.

vermouth ['vɜ:məθ] n (U) vermute m.

versa ▷ vice-versa.

versatile ['vɜ:sətaɪl] adj **-1.** [multitalented] versátil **-2.** [multipurpose] multifuncio-nal.

verse [vɜ:s] n **-1.** (U) [poetry] versos mpl, poesia f **-2.** [stanza] estrofe m **-3.** [in Bi-ble] versículo m.

versed [vɜ:st] adj: **to be well ~ in sthg** ser bem versado(da) em algo.

version ['vɜ:ʃn] n [gen] versão f.

versus ['vɜ:səs] prep **-1.** SPORT contra **-2.** [as opposed to] em oposição a.

vertebra ['vɜ:tɪbrə] (pl -brae [-bri:]) n vértebra f.

vertical ['vɜ:tɪkl] adj vertical.

vertigo ['vɜ:tɪɡəʊ] n (U) vertigem f.

verve [vɜ:v] n (U) vivacidade f, entu-siasmo m.

very ['verɪ] ⋄ adv **-1.** [for emphasis] muito; **to like sthg ~ much** gostar muito de algo **-2.** [as euphemism]: **he's not ~ intelligent** ele não é muito inteligente. ⋄ adj mesmíssimo(ma); **the ~ book I've been looking for** justo o livro que eu estava procurando; **the ~ thought make us bad** só de pensar eu já fico mal; **fighting for his ~ life** lutando por

sua própria vida; **the ~ best** o melhor de todos; **a house of my ~ own** minha própria casa.

◆ very well adv muito bem; **you can't ~ well stop him now** é um pouco tarde para impedi-lo.

vessel ['vesl] n fml **-1.** [boat] embarcação f **-2.** [container] recipiente m, vasilha f.

vest [vest] n **-1.** UK [undershirt] camiseta f **-2.** US [waistcoat] colete m.

vested interest ['vestɪd-] n capital m investido; **~ in sthg** capital investido em algo.

vestibule ['vestɪbju:l] n fml [entrance hall] vestíbulo m.

vestige ['vestɪdʒ] n fml vestígio m.

vestry ['vestrɪ] (pl -ies) n sacristia f.

vet [vet] (pt & pp -ted, cont -ting) ⋄ n UK (abbr of veterinary surgeon) vete-rinário m, -ria f. ⋄ vt UK [check] submeter a uma investigação.

veteran ['vetrən] ⋄ adj [experienced] veterano(na). ⋄ n veterano m, -na f.

veterinarian [‚vetərɪ'neərɪən] n US ve-terinário m, -ria f.

veterinary surgeon ['vetərɪnrɪ-] n UK fml veterinário m, -ria f.

veto ['vi:təʊ] (pl -es, pt & pp -ed, cont -ing) ⋄ n **-1.** (U) [power to forbid] veto m **-2.** [act of forbidding] veto m. ⋄ vt vetar.

vex [veks] vt fml [annoy] importunar.

vexed question [‚vekst-] n pomo m de discórdia.

via ['vaɪə] prep **-1.** [travelling through] via; **they flew to China ~ Karachi** eles viaja-ram para a China (passando) por Karachi **-2.** [by means of] através de; **~ satellite** via satélite.

viable ['vaɪəbl] adj viável.

vibrate [vaɪ'breɪt] vi vibrar.

vicar ['vɪkəʳ] n vigário m, pároco m.

vicarage ['vɪkərɪdʒ] n casa f paroquial.

vicarious [vɪ'keərɪəs] adj indireto(ta).

vice [vaɪs] n **-1.** (U) [immorality] vício m **-2.** [moral fault] vício m **-3.** [tool] torno m de mesa.

vice-chairman n vice-presidente m.

vice-chancellor n UK UNIV reitor m, -ra f.

vice-president n vice-presidente mf.

vice versa [‚vaɪs'vɜ:sə] adv vice-versa.

vicinity [vɪ'sɪnətɪ] n **-1.** [neighbourhood] proximidades fpl, redondezas fpl; **in the ~ (of)** nas proximidades OR re-dondezas(de) **-2.** [approximate figures]: **in the ~ of** cerca de.

vicious ['vɪʃəs] adj **-1.** [attack, blow] violento(ta) **-2.** [person, gossip] cruel **-3.** [dog] feroz, bravo(va).

vicious circle n círculo m vicioso.
victim ['vɪktɪm] n vítima f.
victimize, -ise ['vɪktɪmaɪz] vt vitimar.
victor ['vɪktə'] n vencedor m, -ra f.
victorious [vɪk'tɔːrɪəs] adj [winning] vitorioso(sa).
victory ['vɪktərɪ] (pl -ies) n -1. (U) [act of winning] vitória f -2. [win] vitória f; ~ over sb/sthg vitória sobre alguém/algo.
video ['vɪdɪəʊ] (pl -s, pt & pp -ed, cont -ing) <> n -1. (U) [medium] vídeo m -2. [recording, machine] vídeo m -3. [cassette] videocassete m. <> comp de vídeo. <> vt -1. [using videorecorder] gravar em vídeo -2. [using camera] gravar um vídeo de.
video camera n câmera f de vídeo.
video cassette n videocassete m, vídeo m.
video conference n videoconferência f.
video game n videogame m.
videorecorder ['vɪdɪəʊrɪˌkɔːdə'] n videocassete m, vídeo m.
video shop n videolocadora f.
videotape ['vɪdɪəʊteɪp] n -1. [cassette] videoteipe m -2. (U) [ribbon] fita f.
vie [vaɪ] (pt & pp vied, cont vying) vi: to ~ for sthg competir por algo; to ~ with sb (for sthg/to do sthg) competir com alguém (por algo/para fazer algo).
Vienna [vɪ'enə] n Viena f.
Vietnam [UK ˌvjet'næm, US ˌvjet'nɑːm] n Vietnã.
Vietnamese [ˌvjetnə'miːz] <> adj vietnamita. <> n [language] vietnamita m. <> npl: the ~ os vietnamitas.
view [vjuː] <> n -1. [opinion] visão f, opinião f; in my ~ na minha opinião -2. [vista] vista f -3. [ability to see] visão f; to come into ~ aparecer. <> vt -1. [consider] ver -2. fml [house] visitar -3. [solar system] observar.
◆ **in view of** prep em vista de.
◆ **with a view to** conj com o intuito de.
viewer ['vjuːə'] n -1. [person] telespectador m, -ra f -2. [apparatus] visor m.
viewfinder ['vjuːˌfaɪndə'] n visor m.
viewpoint ['vjuːpɔɪnt] n -1. [opinion] ponto m de vista -2. [place] mirante m.
vigil ['vɪdʒɪl] n vigília f.
vigilante [ˌvɪdʒɪ'læntɪ] n vigilante mf.
vigorous ['vɪgərəs] adj -1. [gen] vigoroso(sa) -2. [attempt] enérgico(ca) -3. [person, animal] vivaz -4. [plant] viçoso(sa).
vigour UK, **vigor** US ['vɪgə'] n (U) vigor m.
vile [vaɪl] adj -1. [person] vil -2. [mood]

muito ruim -3. [act] desprezível -4. [food] repugnante.
villa ['vɪlə] n casa f de campo, chalé m.
village ['vɪlɪdʒ] n vilarejo m povoado m.
villager ['vɪlɪdʒə'] n população f de um vilarejo.
villain ['vɪlən] n -1. [of film, book, play] vilão m, -lã f -2. dated [criminal] criminoso m, -sa f.
vindicate ['vɪndɪkeɪt] vt [confirm] vindicar; [justify] justificar.
vindictive [vɪn'dɪktɪv] adj vingativo(va).
vine [vaɪn] n [grapevine] videira f, parreira f.
vinegar ['vɪnɪgə'] n (U) vinagre m.
vineyard ['vɪnjəd] n vinhedo m.
vintage ['vɪntɪdʒ] <> adj -1. [wine] de boa safra -2. fig [classic] clássico(ca). <> n [wine] safra f.
vintage wine n vinho m de uma boa safra.
vinyl ['vaɪnɪl] n (U) vinil m.
viola [vɪ'əʊlə] n -1. MUS viola f -2. BOT violeta f.
violate ['vaɪəleɪt] vt -1. [disregard] violar -2. [disrupt] invadir -3. [break into] profanar.
violence ['vaɪələns] n (U) -1. [physical force] violência f -2. [of words, reaction] violência f.
violent ['vaɪələnt] adj -1. [gen] violento(ta) -2. [emotion, colour] intenso(sa).
violet ['vaɪələt] <> adj violeta. <> n -1. [flower] violeta f -2. (U) [colour] violeta f.
violin [ˌvaɪə'lɪn] n violino m.
violinist [ˌvaɪə'lɪnɪst] n violinista mf.
viper ['vaɪpə'] n víbora f.
virgin ['vɜːdʒɪn] <> adj literary -1. [sexually] virgem -2. [forest, snow, soil] virgem. <> n virgem mf.
Virgo ['vɜːgəʊ] (pl -s) n [sign] Virgem m.
virile ['vɪraɪl] adj viril.
virtually ['vɜːtʃʊəlɪ] adv [almost] praticamente.
virtual reality n realidade f virtual.
virtue ['vɜːtjuː] n -1. (U) [goodness] virtude f -2. [merit, quality] virtude f -3. [benefit] vantagem f; ~ in sthg vantagem em algo.
◆ **by virtue of** prep fml em virtude de.
virtuous ['vɜːtʃʊəs] adj virtuoso(sa).
virus ['vaɪrəs] n vírus m inv.
visa ['viːzə] n visto m.
vis-à-vis [ˌviːzɑː'viː] prep fml em relação a.
viscose ['vɪskəʊs] n (U) -1. [solution] viscose f -2. [material] viscose f.
visibility [ˌvɪzɪ'bɪlətɪ] n visibilidade f.
visible ['vɪzəbl] adj visível.
vision ['vɪʒn] n -1. (U) [ability to see] visão

f, vista f - **2.** (U) fig [foresight] visão f - **3.** [impression, dream] visão f.

visit ['vızıt] ⟨⟩ n visita f; **on a ~ to** numa visita a. ⟨⟩ vt visitar.

visiting hours ['vızıtıŋ-] npl hora f de visita.

visitor ['vızıtə'] n - **1.** [to person] visita mf - **2.** [to place] visitante mf.

visitors' book n livro m de visitantes.

visitor's passport n UK passaporte m temporário.

visor ['vaızə'] n [on helmet] viseira f.

vista ['vıstə] n [view] vista f, perspectiva f.

visual ['vıʒʊəl] adj - **1.** [gen] visual - **2.** [examination] de vista.

visual aids npl recursos mpl visuais.

visual display unit n monitor m.

visualize, -ise ['vıʒʊəlaız] vt visualizar; **to ~** (sb) **doing sthg** imaginar (alguém) fazendo algo.

vital ['vaıtl] adj - **1.** [essential] vital, essencial - **2.** [full of life] cheio (cheia) de vida.

vitally ['vaıtəlı] adv extremamente.

vital statistics npl inf [of figure] medidas fpl (do corpo de uma mulher).

vitamin [UK 'vıtəmın, US 'vaıtəmın] n vitamina f.

vivacious [vı'veıʃəs] adj vivaz, animado(da).

vivid ['vıvıd] adj - **1.** [bright] vivo(va) - **2.** [clear] vívido(da).

vividly ['vıvıdlı] adv - **1.** [brightly] com cores muito vivas - **2.** [clearly] vividamente.

vixen ['vıksn] n raposa f (fêmea).

VLF (abbr of very low frequency) n VLF f.

V-neck n - **1.** [sweater, dress] decote m em V - **2.** [neck] gola f em V.

vocabulary [və'kæbjʊlərı] (pl -ies) n vocabulário m.

vocal ['vəʊkl] adj - **1.** [outspoken] sincero(ra) - **2.** [of the voice] vocal.

vocal cords npl cordas fpl vocais.

vocation [vəʊ'keıʃn] n [calling] vocação f.

vocational [vəʊ'keıʃənl] adj vocacional.

vociferous [və'sıfərəs] adj fml vociferante.

vodka ['vɒdkə] n vodca f.

vogue [vəʊg] n moda f; **in ~** na moda, em voga.

voice [vɔıs] ⟨⟩ n [gen] voz f. ⟨⟩ vt [opinion, emotion] manifestar.

voice mail n correio m de voz.

void [vɔıd] ⟨⟩ adj - **1.** [invalid] inválido(da) ⟨⟩ **null** - **2.** fml [empty]: **~ of sthg** desprovido(da) de algo. ⟨⟩ n literary vazio m.

volatile [UK 'vɒlətaıl, US 'vɒlətl] adj [un-

predictable - situation] imprevisível; [- person] volúvel; [- market] volátil.

volcano [vɒl'keınəʊ] (pl -es OR -s) n vulcão m.

volition [və'lıʃn] n fml: **of one's own ~** por vontade própria.

volley ['vɒlı] (pl **volleys**) ⟨⟩ n - **1.** [of gunfire] rajada f, saraivada f - **2.** fig [rapid succession] torrente f - **3.** SPORT voleio m. ⟨⟩ vt dar de voleio em.

volleyball ['vɒlıbɔːl] n (U) voleibol m, vôlei m.

volt [vəʊlt] n volt m.

voltage ['vəʊltıdʒ] n voltagem f.

volume ['vɒljuːm] n (U) volume m.

voluntarily [UK 'vɒləntrılı, US ˌvɒlən'terəlı] adv voluntariamente.

voluntary ['vɒləntrı] adj voluntário(-ria); **~ organization** organização f beneficente.

voluntary work n trabalho m voluntário.

volunteer [ˌvɒlən'tıə'] ⟨⟩ n voluntário m, -ria f. ⟨⟩ vt - **1.** [offer of one's free will]: **to ~ to do sthg** oferecer-se de livre e espontânea vontade) para fazer algo - **2.** [information, advice] oferecer. ⟨⟩ vi - **1.** [freely offer one's services]: **to ~** (for sthg) oferecer-se (para algo) - **2.** MIL alistar-se como voluntário(ria).

vomit ['vɒmıt] ⟨⟩ n (U) vômito m. ⟨⟩ vi vomitar.

vote [vəʊt] ⟨⟩ n - **1.** [individual decision] voto m; **~ for sb/sthg** voto em alguém/algo; **~ against sb/sthg** voto contra alguém/algo - **2.** [session, ballot] votação f; **to put sthg to the ~** levar algo à votação - **3.** [result of ballot]: **the ~** a votação - **4.** [section of voters] eleitorado m - **5.** [suffrage] voto m. ⟨⟩ vt - **1.** [declare, elect] eleger - **2.** [choose in ballot] votar em; **they ~ed to return to work** eles votaram pela volta ao trabalho - **3.** [suggest] votar. ⟨⟩ vi [express one's choice] votar; **to ~ for/against sb** votar em/contra alguém; **to ~ for/against sthg** votar a favor de/contra algo.

vote of thanks (pl **votes of thanks**) n: **to give a ~** fazer um discurso de agradecimento.

voter ['vəʊtə'] n votante mf.

voting ['vəʊtıŋ] n votação f.

vouch [vaʊtʃ] ➔ **vouch for** vt fus - **1.** [take responsibility for] responsabilizar-se por - **2.** [declare belief in] dar testemunho de.

voucher ['vaʊtʃə'] n [for restaurant, purchase, petrol] vale m.

vow [vaʊ] ⟨⟩ n - **1.** juramento m, promessa f solene - **2.** RELIG voto m. ⟨⟩

vt: **to ~ to do sthg** jurar fazer algo; **to ~ (that)** jurar que.

vowel ['vaʊəl] *n* vogal *f*.

voyage ['vɔɪdʒ] *n* viagem *f*.

vs (*abbr of* **versus**) vs.

VSO (*abbr of* **Voluntary Service Overseas**) *n* organização britânica de voluntários para ajuda a países em desenvolvimento.

vulgar ['vʌlgəʳ] *adj* **-1.** [common] comum **-2.** [rude] vulgar, baixo(xa).

vulnerable ['vʌlnərəbl] *adj* **-1.** [easily hurt] vulnerável; **~ to sthg** [to being hurt] vulnerável a algo **-2.** [easily influenced]: **~ (to sthg)** facilmente influenciável (por algo).

vulture ['vʌltʃəʳ] *n* **-1.** [bird] abutre *m*, urubu *m* **-2.** *fig* [exploitative person] abutre *m*.

w (*pl* **w's** OR **ws**), **W** (*pl* **W's** OR **Ws**) ['dʌblju:] *n* w, W *m*.

◆ **W -1.** (*abbr of* **west**) O. **-2.** (*abbr of* **watt**) W *m*.

wad [wɒd] *n* **-1.** [of cotton wool] chumaço *m*; [of paper, bank notes, documents] pilha *f*; [of tobacco] masca *f*.

waddle ['wɒdl] *vi* caminhar se balançando.

wade [weɪd] *vi* patinhar.

◆ **wade through** *vt fus* *fig*: he was wading through the documents ele penava muito para ler os documentos.

wading pool ['weɪdɪŋ-] *n* US piscina *f* para crianças.

wafer ['weɪfəʳ] *n* [thin biscuit] wafer *m*.

waffle ['wɒfl] ◇ *n* **-1.** CULIN waffle *m* **-2.** (U) UK *inf* [vague talk] lengalenga *f*, ladainha *f*. ◇ *vi* *inf* enrolar.

wag [wæg] (*pt* & *pp* **-ged**, *cont* **-ging**) ◇ *vt* sacudir. ◇ *vi* [tail] abanar.

wage [weɪdʒ] ◇ *n* salário *m*. ◇ *vt*: **to ~ war against sb/sthg** guerrear com alguém/algo.

◆ **wages** *npl* [of worker] pagamento *m*, salário *m*; **I always get my ~ s at the end of the week** eu recebo sempre nos finais de semana.

wage earner [-ˌɜːnəʳ] *n* assalariado *m*, -da *f*.

wager ['weɪdʒəʳ] *n* aposta *f*.

waggle ['wægl] *inf* *vt* & *vi* balançar.

wagon ['wægən], **waggon** UK *n* **-1.** [horse-drawn vehicle] carroça *f* **-2.** UK RAIL vagão *m*.

wail [weɪl] ◇ *n* lamento *m*, gemido *m*. ◇ *vi* **-1.** [baby] choramingar **-2.** [person] gemer.

waist [weɪst] *n* cintura *f*.

waistcoat ['weɪskəʊt] *n* colete *m*.

waistline ['weɪstlaɪn] *n* cintura *f*.

wait [weɪt] ◇ *n* espera *f*. ◇ *vi* esperar; **to ~ and see** esperar para ver. ◇ *vt* I/he etc. **couldn't ~ to do sthg** eu/ele mal podia esperar para fazer algo.

◆ **wait for** *vt fus* esperar; **to ~ for sb to do sthg** esperar que alguém faça algo.

◆ **wait on** *vt fus* [serve food to] servir; **she ~ s on her family hand and foot** ela responde a todas as necessidades da família.

◆ **wait up** *vi* ficar acordado(da) esperando.

waiter ['weɪtəʳ] *n* garçom *m*.

waiting list ['weɪtɪŋ-] *n* lista *f* de espera.

waiting room ['weɪtɪŋ-] *n* sala *f* de espera.

waitress ['weɪtrɪs] *n* garçonete *f*.

waive [weɪv] *vt* **-1.** *fml* [rule] não aplicar **-2.** *fml* [entrance fee] abrir mão de.

wake [weɪk] (*pt* **woke** OR **-d**, *pp* **woken** OR **-d**) ◇ *n* [of ship, boat] esteira *f*. ◇ *vt* acordar. ◇ *vi* acordar-se.

◆ **wake up** ◇ *vt sep* acordar. ◇ *vi* [wake] acordar-se.

waken ['weɪkən] *fml* ◇ *vt* despertar. ◇ *vi* despertar-se.

Wales [weɪlz] *n* País de Gales.

walk [wɔːk] ◇ *n* **-1.** [stroll] passeio *m*, caminhada *f*; **to go for a ~** dar um passeio **-2.** [gait] jeito *m* de andar. ◇ *vt* **-1.** [escort] acompanhar **-2.** [take out for exercise] levar para passear **-3.** [cover on foot] caminhar. ◇ *vi* caminhar, andar.

◆ **walk out** *vi* **-1.** [leave suddenly] sair **-2.** [go on strike] entrar em greve branca.

◆ **walk out on** *vt fus* deixar, abandonar.

walkie-talkie [ˌwɔːkɪˈtɔːkɪ] *n* walkie-talkie *m*.

walking ['wɔːkɪŋ] *n* [for pleasure, sport] caminhada *f*; **to go ~** dar uma caminhada.

walking stick *n* bengala *f*.

Walkman® ['wɔːkmən] *n* walkman® *m*.

walk of life (*pl* **walks of life**) *n* **-1.** [job]

profissão f - **2.** [social position] posição f social.

walkout ['wɔːkaut] n [of members, spectators, workers] greve f branca.

walkover ['wɔːkˌəuvəʳ] n UK inf [victory] barbada f, vitória f fácil.

walkway ['wɔːkweɪ] n passadiço m, passagem f.

wall [wɔːl] n - **1.** [interior] parede f - **2.** [exterior] muro m - **3.** ANAT parede f.

wallchart ['wɔːltʃɑːt] n mural m.

walled [wɔːld] adj cercado(da) (com muros).

wallet ['wɒlɪt] n carteira f.

wallflower ['wɔːlˌflauəʳ] n - **1.** [plant] aleli m - **2.** inf fig [person] azeite m.

wallow ['wɒləu] vi - **1.** [in water] mergulhar - **2.** [in mud] chafurdar.

wallpaper ['wɔːlˌpeɪpəʳ] <> n (U) papel m de parede. <> vt forrar com papel de parede.

Wall Street n Wall Street; on ~ em Wall Street.

walnut ['wɔːlnʌt] n - **1.** [nut] noz m - **2.** [tree, material] nogueira f.

walrus ['wɔːlrəs] (pl inv OR -es) n morsa f.

waltz [wɔːls] <> n valsa f. <> vi [dance] dançar uma valsa.

wand [wɒnd] n varinha f mágica.

wander ['wɒndəʳ] vi - **1.** [person] perambular - **2.** [mind, thoughts] divagar.

wane [weɪn] vi - **1.** [influence, interest] declinar - **2.** [moon] minguar.

want [wɒnt] <> n - **1.** [need] necessidade f - **2.** [lack] falta f; for ~ of por falta de - **3.** (U) [deprivation] penúria f; to be in ~ passar necessidades. <> vt - **1.** [desire] querer; to ~ to do sthg querer fazer algo; to ~ sb to do sthg querer que alguém faça algo - **2.** inf [need] precisar.

wanted ['wɒntɪd] adj: to be ~ (by the police) ser procurado(da) (pela polícia).

wanton ['wɒntən] adj fml [malicious] gratuito(ta), sem motivo.

WAP [wæp] (abbr of wireless application protocol) n WAP m.

WAP phone n telefone m WAP.

war [wɔːʳ] n guerra f; at ~ em guerra.

ward [wɔːd] n - **1.** [in hospital] ala f - **2.** UK POL distrito m eleitoral - **3.** JUR tutelado m, -da f.

♦ **ward off** vt fus proteger-se de.

warden ['wɔːdn] n - **1.** [of park] guarda mf - **2.** UK [of youth hostel, hall of residence] diretor m, -ra f - **3.** US [prison governor] diretor m, -ra f.

warder ['wɔːdəʳ] n [in prison] carcereiro m, -ra f.

wardrobe ['wɔːdrəub] n - **1.** [piece of furniture] guarda-roupa m, armário m - **2.** [collection of clothes] guarda-roupa m.

warehouse ['weəhaus, pl -hauzɪz] n armazém m, depósito m.

warfare ['wɔːfeəʳ] n combate m; **gang** ~ disputa f entre gangues.

warhead ['wɔːhed] n MIL ogiva f.

warily ['weərəlɪ] adv com desconfiança.

warm [wɔːm] <> adj - **1.** [gen] quente; I'm ~ estou com calor; are you ~ enough? não está com frio, certo? - **2.** [clothing, blanket] que protege do frio - **3.** [sound] cálido(da) - **4.** [person] afetuoso(sa), caloroso(sa) - **5.** [friendly - congratulations] efusivo(va); [- attitude, smile, handshake] caloroso(sa). <> vt [heat gently] aquecer.

♦ **warm to** vt fus tomar simpatia por.

♦ **warm up** <> vt sep - **1.** [heat] esquentar - **2.** [audience] esquentar. <> vi - **1.** [get warmer - gen] esquentar; [- person] esquentar-se - **2.** [prepare - for exercise] aquecer, aquecer-se; [- for performance] preparar-se.

warmly ['wɔːmlɪ] adv - **1.** [in warm clothes]: to dress ~ agasalhar-se bem - **2.** [in a friendly way] calorosamente, efusivamente.

warmth [wɔːmθ] n (U) - **1.** [of temperature] calor m - **2.** [of welcome, smile, support] cordialidade f.

warn [wɔːn] vt - **1.** [advise] advertir, prevenir; to ~ sb of OR about sthg advertir alguém de/sobre algo; to ~ sb not to do sthg avisar a alguém para que não faça algo - **2.** [inform] avisar.

warning ['wɔːnɪŋ] n - **1.** [official caution] advertência f - **2.** [prior notice] aviso m.

warning light n luz f de advertência.

warrant ['wɒrənt] <> n JUR [written order] mandado m (judicial). <> vt fml [justify] merecer.

warranty ['wɒrəntɪ] (pl -ies) n garantia f.

warren ['wɒrən] n [of rabbit] toca f.

warrior ['wɒrɪəʳ] n literary guerreiro m, -ra f.

Warsaw ['wɔːsɔː] n Varsóvia; in ~ em Varsóvia.

warship ['wɔːʃɪp] n navio m de guerra.

wart [wɔːt] n verruga f.

wartime ['wɔːtaɪm] n (U) tempos mpl de guerra; in ~ em tempos de guerra.

wary ['weərɪ] (compar -ier, superl -iest) adj receoso(sa); ~ of sthg/of doing sthg receoso(sa) de algo/de fazer algo.

was [weak form wəz, strong form wɒz] pt ⊳ **be**.

wash [wɒʃ] <> n - **1.** [act of washing]

lavada f; **to have a** ~ lavar-se; **to give sthg a** ~ dar uma lavada em algo -**2.** [clothes to be washed] roupa f para lavar OR suja -**3.** [from boat] esteira f. ◇ vt [clean] lavar. ◇ vi [clean o.s.] lavar-se.

➤ **wash away** vt sep levar, arrastar.

➤ **wash up** ◇ vt sep UK [dishes] lavar. ◇ vi -**1.** UK [wash the dishes] lavar os pratos -**2.** US [wash o.s.] lavar-se.

washable ['wɒʃəbl] adj lavável.

washbasin UK ['wɒʃ,beɪsɪn], **washbowl** US ['wɒʃbəʊl] n lavatório m.

washcloth ['wɒʃ,klɒθ] n US toalha f de rosto.

washing ['wɒʃɪŋ] n (U) -**1.** [act] lavagem f -**2.** [clothes] roupa f para lavar OR suja.

washing line n varal m.

washing machine n lavadora f (de roupa).

washing powder n (U) UK sabão m em pó.

Washington ['wɒʃɪŋtən] n [city]: ~ **D.C.** Washington D.C.

washing-up n -**1.** UK [crockery, pans etc.] louça f para lavar OR suja -**2.** [act]: **to do the** ~ lavar a louça.

washing-up liquid n UK detergente m.

washout ['wɒʃaʊt] n inf fracasso m, desastre m.

washroom ['wɒʃrʊm] n US lavabo m.

wasn't ['wɒznt] = was not.

wasp [wɒsp] n [insect] vespa f.

waste [weɪst] ◇ adj -**1.** [material, fuel] de sobra -**2.** [area of land] improdutivo(-va). ◇ n -**1.** [misuse] desperdício m; **a** ~ **of time** uma perda de tempo -**2.** [refuse] resíduos mpl. ◇ vt [misuse] desperdiçar; **it would be** ~**d on me** eu não saberia aproveitar isso.

➤ **wastes** npl literary [wastelands] desertos mpl.

wastebasket n US cesto m de lixo.

waste disposal unit n triturador m de lixo.

wasteful ['weɪstfʊl] adj: **to be very** ~ **to do sthg** ser muito desperdício fazer algo.

waste ground n (U) terra f improdutiva, descampados mpl.

wastepaper basket [,weɪst'peɪpə^r-], **wastepaper bin** [,weɪst'peɪpə^r-], **wastebasket** US ['weɪst,bɑ:skɪt] n cesto m para papel.

waste segregation n coleta f seletiva.

watch [wɒtʃ] ◇ n -**1.** [timepiece] relógio m -**2.** [act of guarding]: **to keep** ~ ficar de guarda; **to keep** ~ **on sb/sthg** vigiar alguém/algo -**3.** [guard] guarda mf. ◇ vt -**1.** [look at - television, programme, match] ver; [- scene, activity] contemplar -**2.** [spy on] vigiar -**3.** [be careful about] cuidar; ~ **what you're doing** presta atenção no que você está fazendo. ◇ vi [observe] observar.

➤ **watch for** vt fus esperar.

➤ **watch out** vi -**1.** [be careful]: **to** ~ **out (for sthg)** ter cuidado (com algo); ~ **out!** cuidado! -**2.** [keep a lookout]: **to** ~ **out for sthg** prestar atenção em algo.

watchful ['wɒtʃfʊl] adj [vigilant] atento(-ta).

watchmaker ['wɒtʃ,meɪkə^r] n relojoeiro m, -ra f.

watchman ['wɒtʃmən] (pl **-men** [-mən]) n segurança m, vigia m.

water ['wɔ:tə^r] ◇ n [gen] água f. ◇ vt [plants, soil] regar. ◇ vi -**1.** [eyes] lacrimejar -**2.** [mouth]: **it makes my mouth** ~ fico com água na boca.

➤ **waters** npl águas fpl.

➤ **water down** vt sep -**1.** [dilute] diluir -**2.** usu pej [moderate] suavizar, moderar.

water bottle n garrafa f d'água, cantil m.

watercolour ['wɔ:tə,kʌlə^r] n aquarela f.

watercress ['wɔ:təkres] n (U) agrião m.

waterfall ['wɔ:təfɔ:l] n queda-d'água f, cachoeira f.

water heater n aquecedor m de água.

waterhole ['wɔ:təhəʊl] n cacimba f.

watering can ['wɔ:tərɪŋ-] n regador m.

water level n nível m de água.

water lily n nenúfar m.

waterline ['wɔ:təlaɪn] n NAUT linha-d'água f.

waterlogged ['wɔ:təlɒgd] adj -**1.** [land] alagado(da) -**2.** [vessel] inundado(da).

water main n adutora f.

watermark ['wɔ:təmɑ:k] n -**1.** [in paper] marca f d'água -**2.** [showing water level] linha-d'água f.

watermelon ['wɔ:tə,melən] n melancia f.

water polo n (U) pólo m aquático.

waterproof ['wɔ:təpru:f] ◇ adj à prova d'água. ◇ n capa f impermeável; ~**s** roupa f à prova d'água.

water skiing n (U) esqui m aquático.

water tank n caixa-d'água f.

watertight ['wɔ:tətaɪt] adj -**1.** [waterproof] hermético(ca) -**2.** fig [faultless] infalível.

waterway ['wɔ:təweɪ] n via f navegável, canal m.

waterworks ['wɔ:təwɜ:ks] (pl inv) n [building] instalações fpl para a distribuição de água.

watery ['wɔ:tərɪ] *adj* **-1.** [food, drink] aguado(da) **-2.** [light, sun, moon] pálido(-da).

watt [wɒt] *n* watt *m*.

wave [weɪv] ⋄ *n* **-1.** [gen] onda *f* **-2.** [of people] leva *f* **-3.** [in hair] ondulação *f* **-4.** [gesture] aceno *m*. ⋄ *vt* **-1.** [brandish - hand, flag] agitar; [- baton] manejar; [- stick, pistol, gun] empunhar **-2.** [gesture to] fazer sinal para. ⋄ *vi* **-1.** [with hand] abanar; **to ~ at** OR **to sb** abanar para alguém **-2.** [flag] tremular.

wavelength ['weɪvleŋθ] *n* comprimento *m* de onda; **to be on the same ~** *fig* estar em sintonia.

wavy ['weɪvɪ] (*compar* **-ier**, *superl* **-iest**) *adj* **-1.** [hair] ondulado(da) **-2.** [line] sinuoso(sa).

wax [wæks] *n* [gen] cera *f*. ⋄ *vt* **-1.** [floor, table] encerar; [skis] passar cera em **-2.** [legs] depilar com cera. ⋄ *vi* [moon] crescer.

wax paper *n* US papel *m* encerado.

waxworks ['wækswɜ:ks] (*pl inv*) *n* [museum] museu *m* de cera.

way [weɪ] ⋄ *n* **-1.** [means, method] maneira *f*, modo *m* **-2.** [manner, style] jeito *m*, maneira *f*; **in the same ~** da mesma forma; **this/that ~** dessa/daquela forma; **in a ~** de certa forma OR maneira; **to fall for sb in a big ~** apaixonar-se loucamente por alguém **-3.** [thoroughfare, path] caminho *m*; **'give ~'** UK AUT dê passagem **-4.** [route leading to a specified place] caminho *m*; **do you know the ~ to the cathedral?** sabe como se faz para chegar na catedral?; **to lose one's ~** perder-se; **out of one's ~** [place] fora do caminho de alguém; **can you post this letter on the** OR **one's ~ (to the shops)** quando você for (fazer compras), pode colocar esta carta no correio?; **to be under ~** [ship] estar navegando; [project, meeting] estar em andamento; **to get under ~** [ship] zarpar; [project, meeting] estar em andamento; **to be in the ~** estar na passagem OR frente; **if you put your suitcase over there, it will be out of the ~** se colocar sua mala lá, ela não vai ficar atrapalhando; **to go out of one's ~ to do sthg** não poupar esforços para fazer algo; **to keep out of sb's ~** não cruzar o caminho de alguém; **keep out of the ~!** saia do caminho!; **to make ~ for sb/sthg** abrir espaço para alguém/algo; **to stand in sb's ~** *fig* ficar no caminho de alguém **-5.** [route leading in a specified direction]: **come this ~** vem por aqui; **~ in** entrada *m*; **~ out** saída *m* **-6.** [side] lado *m*; **the right/wrong ~ round** do jeito certo/errado; **the right/wrong ~ up** com o lado certo/errado para cima **-7.** [distance]: **all the ~** todo o caminho; **a long ~** um longo caminho **-8.** *phr*: **to give ~** [under weight, pressure] ceder; **no ~!** de maneira alguma! ⋄ *adv inf* [by far] muito; **it's ~ too big!** é enorme de grande!

➤ **ways** *npl* [customs, habits] costumes *mpl*, hábitos *mpl*.

➤ **by the way** *adv* a propósito, aliás.

WC (*abbr of* **water closet**) *n* WC *m*.

we [wi:] *pers pron pl* nós **~'re young** (nós) somos jovens.

weak [wi:k] *adj* **-1.** [gen] fraco(ca) **-2.** [lacking knowledge, skill]: **to be ~ on sthg** ser fraco(ca em algo).

weaken ['wi:kn] ⋄ *vt* **-1.** [gen] enfraquecer; FIN [devalue] desvalorizar **-2.** [debilitate] debilitar. ⋄ *vi* **-1.** [person - physically] debilitar-se; [- morally] desgastar-se; **no signs of ~ing** nenhum sinal de desgaste **-2.** [influence, power] diminuir **-3.** [structure] enfraquecer-se **-4.** FIN [dollar, mark] desvalorizar-se.

weakness ['wi:knɪs] *n* **-1.** (*U*) [of person - physical] fraqueza *f*; [- moral] ponto *m* fraco **-2.** [of government, structure, plan] debilidade *f* **-3.** FIN [of currency] fragilidade *f*.

wealth [welθ] *n* **-1.** (*U*) [riches] riqueza *f* **-2.** [abundance]: **a ~ of sthg** uma profusão de algo.

wealthy ['welθɪ] (*compar* **-ier**, *superl* **-iest**) *adj* rico(ca).

wean [wi:n] *vt* [from mother's milk] desmamar.

weapon ['wepən] *n* arma *f*.

wear [weə[r]] (*pt* **wore**, *pp* **worn**) ⋄ *n* **-1.** [type of clothes] roupa *f* **-2.** [damage] desgaste *m*; **~ and tear** desgaste **-3.** [use] uso *m*. ⋄ *vt* **-1.** [gen] usar **-2.** [clothes] vestir **-3.** [shoes] calçar **-4.** [damage - permanently] danificar; [- holes] abrir. ⋄ *vi* **-1.** [deteriorate] gastar **-2.** [last]: **to ~ well/badly** durar bastante/pouco.

➤ **wear away** ⋄ *vt sep* desgastar. ⋄ *vi* desgastar-se.

➤ **wear down** *vt sep* **-1.** [reduce size of] gastar **-2.** [weaken] esgotar.

➤ **wear off** *vi* passar.

➤ **wear out** ⋄ *vt sep* **-1.** [clothing, machinery] usar até estragar **-2.** [patience, strength, reserves] esgotar **-3.** [person] ficar esgotado(da). ⋄ *vi* [clothing, shoes] gastar.

weary ['wɪərɪ] (*compar* **-ier**, *superl* **-iest**) *adj* **-1.** [exhausted] exausto(ta) **-2.** [fed up]: **to be ~ of** sthg/of doing sthg estar farto(ta) de algo/de fazer algo.

weasel ['wi:zl] *n* doninha *f.*

weather ['weðə^r] ⬦ *n* tempo *m*; **to be under the ~** estar se sentindo um pouco indisposto(ta). ⬦ *vt* [survive] superar.

weather-beaten [-ˌbi:tn] *adj* [face, skin] desgastado(da) pelo tempo.

weather forecast *n* previsão *f* do tempo.

weatherman ['weðəmæn] (*pl* **-men** [-men]) *n* meteorologista *m.*

weather vane [-veɪn] *n* cata-vento *m.*

weave [wi:v] (*pt* **wove**, *pp* **woven**) ⬦ *vt* [using loom] tecer. ⬦ *vi* [move]: **to ~ in and out** ziguezaguear.

weaver ['wi:və^r] *n* tecelão *m*, -lã *f.*

web [web] *n* **-1.** [cobweb] teia *f* **-2.** *fig* [of lies, intrigue] rede *f* **-3.** COMPUT Web *f*, Rede *f.*

web browser *n* COMPUT navegador *m.*

webcam ['webkæm] *n* câmera *f* web, webcam *f.*

webcast ['webka:st] *n* transmissão *f* ao vivo pela Internet.

web designer *n* web designer *mf.*

web page *n* página *f* da Web.

webphone ['webfəʊn] *n* webphone *m.*

website ['websaɪt] *n* site *m* da Web.

wed [wed] (*pt* & *pp* **wed** OR **-ded**) *literary* ⬦ *vt* [marry] desposar. ⬦ *vi* casar.

we'd [wi:d] = **we had**, **we would**.

wedding ['wedɪŋ] *n* casamento *m (cerimônia).*

wedding anniversary *n* aniversário *m* de casamento.

wedding cake *n* bolo *m* de casamento.

wedding dress *n* vestido *m* de noiva.

wedding ring *n* aliança *f.*

wedge [wedʒ] ⬦ *n* **-1.** [gen] cunha *f* **-2.** [of cheese, cake, pie] fatia *f*, porção *f.* ⬦ *vt* **-1.** [make fixed or steady] calçar com cunha **-2.** [squeeze, push] enfiar; **she sat ~d between us** ela se sentou enfiada entre nós.

Wednesday ['wenzdɪ] *n* quarta-feira *f*; *see also* **Saturday.**

wee [wi:] ⬦ *adj Scot* pequenino(na). ⬦ *n inf* xixi *m.* ⬦ *vi inf* fazer xixi.

weed [wi:d] ⬦ *n* **-1.** [wild plant] erva *f* daninha **-2.** *UK inf* [feeble person] fracote *m*, -ta *f.* ⬦ *vt* capinar.

weedkiller ['wi:dˌkɪlə^r] *n* herbicida *m.*

week [wi:k] *n* [gen] semana *f*; **during the ~** durante a semana; **in three ~s' time** dentro de três semanas; **a ~ last Saturday** uma semana antes de sábado.

weekday ['wi:kdeɪ] *n* dia *m* da semana.

weekend [ˌwi:k'end] *n* fim *m* de semana; **at the ~** no fim de semana.

weekly ['wi:klɪ] (*pl* **-ies**) ⬦ *adj* semanal. ⬦ *adv* semanalmente. ⬦ *n* semanário *m.*

weep [wi:p] (*pt* & *pp* **wept**) ⬦ *vt* derramar. ⬦ *vi* chorar.

weeping willow [ˌwi:pɪŋ-] *n* salgueiro-chorão *m.*

weigh [weɪ] ⬦ *vt* **-1.** [gen] pesar **-2.** [raise]: **to ~ anchor** levantar âncora. ⬦ *vi* [have specific weight] pesar.
➤ **weigh down** *vt sep* **-1.** [physically] sobrecarregar **-2.** [mentally]: **to be ~ ed down by** OR **with sthg** estar prostrado(da) por algo.
➤ **weigh up** *vt sep* [situation, pros and cons] pesar; [person, opposition] fazer uma idéia de.

weight [weɪt] *n* **-1.** [gen] peso *m*; **to put on** OR **gain ~** engordar; **to lose ~** perder peso **-2.** *fig* [power, influence]: **the ~ of public opinion** a opinião pública em peso.

weighted ['weɪtɪd] *adj*: **to be ~ in favour of/against sb** pesar a favor de/contra alguém; **to be ~ in favour of/ against sthg** pesar a favor de/contra algo.

weight lifting *n* (*U*) levantamento *m* de peso.

weighty ['weɪtɪ] (*compar* **-ier**, *superl* **-iest**) *adj* [serious, important] de peso.

weird [wɪəd] *adj* estranho(nha), esquisito(ta).

welcome ['welkəm] ⬦ *adj* **-1.** [gen] bem-vindo(da) **-2.** [free]: **to be ~ to do sthg** ter toda a liberdade para fazer algo **-3.** [in reply to thanks]: **you're ~** de nada. ⬦ *n* acolhida *f.* ⬦ *vt* [gen] acolher. ⬦ *excl* bem-vindo(da)!

welfare ['welfeə^r] ⬦ *adj* de assistência social. ⬦ *n* **-1.** [state of wellbeing] bem-estar *m* **-2.** *US* [income support] assistência *f* social (*do governo*).

welfare state *n* estado *m* de bem-estar social.

well [wel] (*compar* **better**, *superl* **best**) ⬦ *adj* bem; **to get ~** ficar bem; **all is ~** está tudo bem; **just as ~** ainda bem que. ⬦ *adv* **-1.** [gen] bem; **to go ~** ir bem; **~ done!** muito bem!; **~ and truly** completamente **-2.** [definitely, certainly] certamente, definitivamente; **it was ~ worth it** claro que valeu a pena; **she's ~ over 40** ela tem muito mais de 40 **-3.** [easily, possibly] (muito) bem. ⬦ *n* [water, oil] poço *m.* ⬦ *excl* **-1.** [in hesitation] bem!, bom! **-2.** [to correct o.s.] bem

- 3. [to express resignation]: **oh ~!** enfim!
- 4. [in surprise] quem diria!, olha só!
➤ **as well** adv [in addition] também; **you may/might as ~ tell the truth** e por que você não conta a verdade.
➤ **as well as** conj além de.
➤ **well up** vi brotar.

we'll [wi:l] = we shall, we will.
well-advised [-əd'vaɪzd] adj prudente; **he/you would be ~ to do sthg** seria prudente que ele/você fizesse algo.
well-behaved [-bɪ'heɪvd] adj bem-comportado(da).
wellbeing [ˌwel'bi:ɪŋ] n (U) bem-estar m.
well-built adj [person] robusto(ta), fornido(da).
well-done adj [thoroughly cooked] bem passado(da).
well-dressed [-'drest] adj bem vestido(da).
well-earned [-'ɜ:nd] adj merecido(da).
wellington (boot) n bota f impermeável.
well-kept adj **- 1.** [garden, village] bem cuidado(da) **- 2.** [secret] bem guardado(da).
well-known adj conhecido(da).
well-mannered [-'mænəd] adj: **to be ~** ter boas maneiras.
well-meaning adj bem-intencionado(da).
well-off adj **- 1.** [financially] rico(ca), próspero(ra) **- 2.** [in a good position]: **to be ~ for sthg** estar bem de algo.
well-read [-'red] adj instruído(da), culto(ta).
well-timed adj oportuno(na).
well-to-do adj abastado(da), de dinheiro.
well-wisher n simpatizante mf.
Welsh [welʃ] ◇ adj galês(esa). ◇ n (U) [language] galês m. ◇ npl: **the ~** os galeses.
Welshman ['welʃmən] (pl -men [-mən]) n galês m.
Welshwoman ['welʃˌwʊmən] (pl -women [-ˌwɪmɪn]) n galesa f.
went [went] pt ▷ go.
wept [wept] pt & pp ▷ weep.
were [wɜ:ʳ] vb ▷ be.
we're [wɪəʳ] = we are.
weren't [wɜ:nt] = were not.
west [west] ◇ n **- 1.** [direction] oeste m; **the ~** o oeste **- 2.** [region]: **the ~** o Oeste. ◇ adj oeste. ◇ adv para o oeste; **~ of** ao oeste de.
➤ **West** n POL: **the West** o Ocidente.
West Bank n: **the ~** a Cisjordânia.
West Country n: **the ~** o sudoeste da Inglaterra.

westerly ['westəlɪ] adj **- 1.** [towards the west]: **in a ~ direction** para o oeste **- 2.** [in the west] ocidental **- 3.** [from the west] oeste.
western ['westən] ◇ adj **- 1.** [part of country, continent] ocidental **- 2.** POL [relating to the West] do Ocidente. ◇ n [book, film] western m.
West Indian ◇ adj antilhano(na). ◇ n [person] antilhano m, -na f.
West Indies [-'ɪndɪz] npl: **the ~** as Antilhas.
Westminster ['westmɪnstəʳ] n **- 1.** [area] Westminster **- 2.** fig [British parliament] parlamento m britânico.
westward ['westwəd] ◇ adj para o oeste. ◇ adv = **westwards**.
westwards ['westwədz] adv para o oeste.
wet [wet] (compar -ter, superl -test, pt & pp wet OR -ted, cont -ting) ◇ adj **- 1.** [damp] úmido(da) **- 2.** [soaked] molhado(da) **- 3.** [rainy] chuvoso(sa) **- 4.** [ink, concrete] fresco(ca) **- 5.** UK inf pej [weak, feeble] fraco(ca). ◇ vt **- 1.** [soak] molhar **- 2.** [dampen] umedecer **- 3.** [bed]: **to ~ the bed** fazer xixi na cama.
wet suit n roupa f de mergulho.
we've [wi:v] = we have.
whack [wæk] ◇ n **- 1.** [hit] pancada f **- 2.** inf [share]: **one's ~ of the profits** a sua parte nos lucros. ◇ vt dar pancadas em.
whale [weɪl] n [animal] baleia f.
wharf [wɔ:f] (pl -s OR wharves [wɔ:vz]) n cais m inv.
what [wɒt] ◇ adj **- 1.** [in questions] que; **~ colour is it?** de que cor é?; **he asked me ~ colour it was** ele perguntou-me de que cor era. **- 2.** [in exclamations] que; **a surprise!** mas que surpresa!; **~ a beautiful day!** mas que dia lindo! ◇ pron **- 1.** [in questions] o que; **~ is going on?** o que é que está acontecendo?; **~ is that?** o que é isso?; **~ is that thing called?** como é que se chama aquilo?; **~ is the problem?** qual é o problema?; **she asked me ~ had happened** ela perguntou-me o que é que tinha acontecido; **she asked me ~ I had seen** ela perguntou-me o que é que eu tinha visto. **- 2.** [in questions: after prep] que; **~ are they talking about?** de que é que eles estão falando?; **~ is it for?** para que é isso?; **she asked me ~ I was thinking about** ela me perguntou em que eu estava pensando. **- 3.** [introducing relative clause] o que; **I didn't see ~ happened** não vi o que aconteceu; **you can't have ~ you want** você não pode

ter o que quer. **- 4.** [in phrases]: ~ **for?** para quê?; ~ **about going out for a meal?** que tal irmos comer fora? <> *excl* o quê!

whatever [wɒt'evə'] <> *adj* qualquer; **eat ~ food you find** come o que encontrar; **no chance** ~ nem a mais remota chance; **nothing** ~ absolutamente nada. <> *pron* **-1.** [no matter what] o que quer que; ~ **they may offer** ofereçam o que oferecerem **- 2.** [indicating surprise]: ~ **did you say?** o que foi que você disse? **- 3.** [indicating lack of precision]: ~ **that is** seja lá o que for; **or** ~ ou o que seja.

what's-her-name *n inf* a tal fulana.

what's-his-name *n inf* o tal fulano.

whatsoever [ˌwɒtsəʊ'evə'] *adj* absolutamente.

wheat [wi:t] *n* trigo *m*.

wheel [wi:l] <> *n* **- 1.** [of bicycle, car, train] roda *f* **- 2.** *AUT* [steering wheel] direção *f* (do carro). <> *vt* empurrar *(algo com rodas)*. <> *vi* [turn round]: **to ~ round** dar a volta.

wheelbarrow ['wi:lˌbærəʊ] *n* carrinho *m* de mão.

wheelchair ['wi:lˌtʃeə'] *n* cadeira *f* de rodas.

wheeze [wi:z] <> *n* [sound of wheezing] respiração *f* ofegante. <> *vi* resfolegar.

when *adv & conj* quando.

whenever [wen'evə'] <> *conj* sempre que. <> *adv* **- 1.** [indicating surprise] quando é que **- 2.** [indicating lack of precision]: **or** ~ ou quando quiser.

where [weə'] *adv & conj* onde.

whereabouts [*adv* ˌweərə'baʊts, *n* 'weərəbaʊts] <> *adv* por onde. <> *npl* paradeiro *m*.

whereas [weər'æz] *conj* enquanto que, ao passo que.

whereby [weə'baɪ] *conj fml* através do (da) qual, pelo(la) qual.

whereupon [ˌweərə'pɒn] *conj fml* depois do que.

wherever [weər'evə'] <> *conj* **- 1.** [no matter where, everywhere] em todo o lugar que **- 2.** [anywhere, in whatever place] onde quer que; **sit ~ you like** senta onde quiser **- 3.** [in any situation] sempre que **- 4.** [indicating ignorance]: ~ **that is** seja lá onde for. <> *adv* **- 1.** [indicating surprise] onde é que **- 2.** [indicating lack of precision] em qualquer lugar.

wherewithal ['weəwɪðɔ:l] *n fml*: **to have the ~ to do sthg** dispor dos meios necessários para fazer algo.

whet [wet] *(pt & pp* **-ted,** *cont* **-ting)** *vt*: **to ~ sb's appetite (for sthg)** despertar o interesse de alguém (por algo).

whether ['weðə'] *conj* **-1.** [indicating choice, doubt] se **- 2.** [no matter if]: ~ **I want to or not** queira ou não queira.

which [wɪtʃ] <> *adj* [in questions] qual, que; ~ **room do you want?** qual é o quarto que você quer?, que quarto você quer?; ~ **one?** qual (deles)?; **she asked me ~ room I wanted** ela perguntou-me qual OR que quarto eu queria <> *pron* **-1.** [in questions] qual; ~ **one is the cheapest?** qual é o mais barato?; ~ **one do you prefer?** qual (é o que) você prefere?; **he asked me ~ one I preferred** ele perguntou-me qual é que eu preferia **- 2.** [introducing relative clause: subject]: **I can't remember ~ was better** não me lembro qual era o melhor **-3.** [introducing relative clause: object, after prep] que; **the sofa on ~ I'm sitting** o sofá em que estou sentado **- 4.** [to refer back to a clause] o que; **he's late,** ~ **annoys me** ele está atrasado, o que me aborrece; **he's always late,** ~ **I don't like** ele está sempre atrasado, coisa que eu detesto.

whichever [wɪtʃ'evə'] <> *adj* **-1.** [no matter which]: ~ **route you take** por qualquer dos caminhos que você for **- 2.** [the one which]: ~ **colour you prefer** a cor que preferir. <> *pron* **-1.** [the one which] o (a) que, os (as) que **-2.** [no matter which one] qualquer um(ma).

whiff [wɪf] *n* [smell] cheirinho *m*.

while [waɪl] <> *n* algum tempo *m*; **it's a long ~ since I did that** faz muito tempo que não faço isso; **for a ~** por algum tempo; **after a ~** depois de algum tempo. <> *conj* **-1.** [as long as, during the time that] enquanto **- 2.** [whereas] enquanto (que), ao passo que.

➥ **while away** *vt sep* passar o tempo *(de forma agradável).*

whilst [waɪlst] *conj* = **while.**

whim [wɪm] *n* capricho *m*.

whimper ['wɪmpə'] <> *vt* lamuriar-se. <> *vi* choramingar.

whimsical ['wɪmzɪkl] *adj* **-1.** [idea, story] fantasioso(sa) **- 2.** [look] estranho(nha) **-3.** [remark] esquisito(ta).

whine [waɪn] *vi* **-1.** [child] gemer **- 2.** [dog] ganir **- 3.** [siren] gritar **- 4.** [engine] zunir.

whinge [wɪndʒ] *(cont* **whingeing)** *vi UK*: **to ~ (about sb/sthg)** queixar-se (de alguém/algo).

whip [wɪp] *(pt & pp* **-ped,** *cont* **-ping)** <> *n* **-1.** [for hitting] chicote *m* **- 2.** *UK POL* membro do partido político responsável *por fazer com que seus correligionários compareçam a votações importantes no parlamento.* ⬦ *vt* -**1.** [beat with whip] chicotear -**2.** [take quickly]: **to ~ sthg out/off** arrancar algo de -**3.** CULIN bater.

whipped cream [wɪpt-] *n* creme *m* batido.

whirl [wɜ:l] ⬦ *n* -**1.** [rotating movement] redemoinho *m* -**2.** *fig* [flurry, round] turbilhão *m*, agitação *f*. ⬦ *vt*: **to ~ sb/sthg round** rodopiar alguém/algo. ⬦ *vi* -**1.** [move around] rodopiar -**2.** *fig* [be confused, excited] dar voltas.

whirlpool ['wɜ:lpu:l] *n* redemoinho *m*.

whirlwind ['wɜ:lwɪnd] *n* furacão *m*.

whisk [wɪsk] ⬦ *n* CULIN batedeira *f*. ⬦ *vt* -**1.** [put or take quickly - away]: **to ~ sb/sthg away** levar alguém/algo rapidamente; [- out]: **to ~ sthg out** tirar algo rapidamente -**2.** CULIN bater.

whisker ['wɪskə^r] *n* [of animal] bigode *m*.
➡ **whiskers** *npl* [of man] suíças *fpl*.

whisky UK (*pl* -**ies**), **whiskey** US & Irish (*pl* -**s**) ['wɪskɪ] *n* uísque *m*.

whisper ['wɪspə^r] ⬦ *vt* sussurrar, cochichar. ⬦ *vi* sussurrar, cochichar.

whistle ['wɪsl] ⬦ *n* -**1.** [gen] apito *m* -**2.** [through lips] assobio *m* -**3.** [of bird] piado *m*, pio *m* -**4.** [of kettle] chiar *m*. ⬦ *vt* assobiar. ⬦ *vi* -**1.** [gen] assobiar -**2.** [using whistle] apitar -**3.** [bird] piar -**4.** [kettle] chiar.

white [waɪt] ⬦ *adj* -**1.** [gen] branco(ca) -**2.** [milky] com leite. ⬦ *n* -**1.** [gen] branco *m* -**2.** [person] branco *m*, -ca *f* -**3.** [of egg] clara *f*.

white-collar *adj* de colarinho branco.

Whitehall ['waɪthɔ:l] *n* Whitehall.

white-hot *adj* incandescente.

White House *n*: **the ~** a Casa Branca.

white lie *n* mentira *f* branca.

white paper *n* POL relatório *m* oficial do governo.

white trash *n* US *pej* [people] branquelo *m*, -la *f*.

whitewash ['waɪtwɒʃ] ⬦ *n* -**1.** (U) [paint] (água *f* de) cal *f* -**2.** *fig* [cover-up] disfarce *m*. ⬦ *vt* [paint] caiar, pintar com cal.

whiting ['waɪtɪŋ] (*pl inv* OR -**s**) *n* merlúcio *m*.

Whitsun ['wɪtsn] *n* [day] Pentecostes *m inv*.

whittle ['wɪtl] *vt*: **to ~ sthg away** OR **down** reduzir algo gradualmente.

whiz (*pt* & *pp* -**zed**, *cont* -**zing**), **whizz** [wɪz] *vi* passar zunindo.

whiz(z) kid *n inf* (menino *m*) prodígio *m*, (menina *f*) prodígio.

who [hu:] *pron* -**1.** (*in direct, indirect questions*) quem -**2.** (*in relative clauses*) que.

who'd [hu:d] = **who had**, **who would**.

whodu(n)nit [ˌhu:'dʌnɪt] *n inf* romance *m* policial.

whoever [hu:'evə^r] *pron* -**1.** [gen] quem quer que; **I don't like him, ~** he is não gosto dele, quem quer que ele seja -**2.** [indicating surprise] quem será que; **~ can that be?** quem poderá ser?

whole [həʊl] ⬦ *adj* -**1.** [entire, complete] inteiro(ra) -**2.** [for emphasis]: **a ~ lot of** muitos e muitos, muitas e muitas; **a ~ lot bigger** muitíssimo maior. ⬦ *adv* [for emphasis] totalmente. ⬦ *n* -**1.** [all, entirety]: **the ~ of the summer** o verão todo -**2.** [unit, complete thing] todo *m*.
➡ **as a whole** *adv* como um todo.
➡ **on the whole** *adv* em geral.

wholefood ['həʊlfu:d] *n* UK comida *f* integral.

whole-hearted [-'hɑ:tɪd] *adj* sincero(-ra).

wholemeal UK ['həʊlmi:l], **wholewheat** US *adj* integral.

wholesale ['həʊlseɪl] ⬦ *adj* -**1.** [bulk] por atacado -**2.** *pej* [excessive - slaughter] exagerado(da); [- destruction] em massa, em grande escala; [- theft] indiscriminado(da). ⬦ *adv* -**1.** [in bulk] por atacado -**2.** *pej* [excessively] indiscriminadamente.

wholesaler ['həʊlˌseɪlə^r] *n* atacadista *mf*.

wholesome ['həʊlsəm] *adj* saudável.

who'll [hu:l] = **who will**.

wholly ['həʊlɪ] *adv* totalmente, completamente.

whom [hu:m] *pron fml* -**1.** (*in direct, indirect questions*) que -**2.** (*in relative clauses*) que; **to ~** a quem.

whooping cough ['hu:pɪŋ-] *n* (U) coqueluche *f*.

whopping ['wɒpɪŋ] *inf* ⬦ *adj* tremendo(da), enorme. ⬦ *adv*: **a ~ great lie** uma mentira enorme.

whore [hɔ:^r] *n pej* puta *f*, vagabunda *f*.

who're ['hu:ə^r] = **who are**.

whose [hu:z] ⬦ *pron* de quem ⬦ *adj* -**1.** (*in direct, indirect questions*) de quem; **~ book is this?** de quem é este livro? -**2.** (*in relative clauses*) cujo(ja).

who's who [hu:z-] *n* [book] quem é quem *m*, *livro contendo informações sobre as pessoas mais ricas e famosas do mundo.*

who've [hu:v] = **who have**.

why [waɪ] ⬦ *adv* & *conj* porque; **~ not?** porque não?; **I know ~ Tom isn't**

wind

here eu sei porque é que o Tom não está; **tell me** ~ (diga-me) porquê.
wicked ['wɪkɪd] adj -1. [evil]malvado(da) -2. [mischievous, devilish] perverso(sa).
wicker ['wɪkə'] adj de vime.
wicket ['wɪkɪt] n CRICKET -1. [stumps] meta f -2. [pitch] wicket m -3. [dismissal] demissão f do batedor.
wide [waɪd] ◇ adj -1. [gen] largo(ga); **it's 6 metres** ~ tem 6 metros de largura; **how** ~ **is the room?** qual é a largura da sala? -2. [coverage, selection] amplo(pla) -3. [implications, issues] maior. ◇ adv -1. [as far as possible] amplamente; **open** ~! abra bem! -2. [off-target]: **to go** ~ desviar-se.
wide-awake adj desperto(ta), bem acordado(da).
widely ['waɪdlɪ] adv -1. [gen] muito; ~ **known** amplamente conhecido(da) -2. [considerably] bastante.
widen ['waɪdn] vt -1. [make broader] alargar -2. [increase scope or variety of] ampliar -3. [gap, difference] aumentar.
wide open adj -1. [window, door] escancarado(da) -2. [eyes] arregalado(da).
wide-ranging [-'reɪndʒɪŋ] adj de amplo alcance.
widescreen TV ['waɪdskri:n-] n tv f widescreen.
widespread ['waɪdspred] adj disseminado(da), geral.
widow ['wɪdəʊ] n viúva f.
widowed ['wɪdəʊd] adj viúvo(va).
widower ['wɪdəʊə'] n viúvo m.
width [wɪdθ] n -1. [breadth] largura f; **in** ~ **de largura** -2. [in swimming pool] largura f; **she swam 20** ~**s** ela nadou 20 piscinas.
wield [wi:ld] vt -1. [weapon] manejar -2. [power] controlar, exercer.
wife [waɪf] (pl **wives**) n esposa f.
wig [wɪg] n peruca f.
wild [waɪld] adj -1. [animal, land] selvagem -2. [person, dog, attack] violento(ta) -3. [plant] silvestre -4. [scenery, landscape] agreste -5. [sea] revolto(ta) -6. [weather] turbulento(ta) -7. [laughter, crowd, applause] frenético(ca); **the crowd went** ~ a multidão foi à loucura -8. [eyes, features] inquieto(ta) agitado(ta) -9. [dream, scheme] maluco(ca) -10. [estimate]: **a** ~ **guess** uma vaga idéia.
◆ **wilds** npl: **the** ~**s** as regiões selvagens.
wild card n COMPUT caractere-curinga m.
wilderness ['wɪldənɪs] n -1. [barren land] sertão m -2. [overgrown land] matagal m -3. fig [unimportant place]: **in the political** ~ no ostracismo político.

wild-goose chase n inf busca m infrutífera.
wildlife ['waɪldlaɪf] n (U) fauna f.
wilful UK, **willful** US ['wɪlfʊl] adj -1. [determined] que sempre apronta das suas -2. [deliberate] proposital, intencional.
will[1] [wɪl] n -1. [wish, desire] vontade f; **against my** ~ contra a minha vontade -2. [document] testamento m.
will[2] [wɪl] aux vb -1. [expressing future tense]: **it** ~ **be difficult to repair** vai ser difícil de consertar; ~ **you be here next Friday?** você vai estar aqui na próxima sexta?; **I** ~ **see you next week** vejo-lhe para a semana; **yes I** ~ sim; **no I won't** não. -2. [expressing willingness]: **I won't do it** recuso-me a fazê-lo. -3. [expressing polite question]: ~ **you have some more tea?** você quer mais um chá? -4. [in commands, requests]: ~ **you please be quiet!** pode ficar calado, por favor!; **close that window,** ~ **you?** feche a janela, por favor.
willful adj US = wilful.
willing ['wɪlɪŋ] adj -1. [prepared] disposto(ta); **to be** ~ **to do sthg** estar disposto(ta) a fazer algo -2. [eager] prestativo(va).
willingly ['wɪlɪŋlɪ] adv de bom grado.
willow (tree) ['wɪləʊ-] n salgueiro m.
willpower ['wɪl,paʊə'] n (U) força f de vontade.
willy-nilly [,wɪlɪ'nɪlɪ] adv -1. [at random] ao acaso -2. [wanting to or not] quer queira quer não.
wilt [wɪlt] vi -1. [plant] murchar -2. fig [person] definhar.
wimp [wɪmp] n inf pej bunda-mole mf.
win [wɪn] (pt & pp **won**, cont -**ning**) ◇ n vitória f. ◇ vt -1. [gen] ganhar -2. [game, fight, competition] vencer. ◇ vi ganhar.
◆ **win over, win round** vt sep convencer.
wince [wɪns] vi contrair-se; **to** ~ **at sthg** perturbar-se com algo; **to** ~ **with sthg** retrair-se de algo.
wind[1] [wɪnd] ◇ n -1. METEOR vento m -2. (U) [breath] fôlego m -3. (U) [in stomach] gases mpl. ◇ vt [knock breath out of] ficar sem fôlego.
wind[2] [waɪnd] (pt & pp **wound**) ◇ vt -1. [string, thread] enrolar -2. [clock] dar corda em. ◇ vi [river, road] serpentear.
◆ **wind down** ◇ vt sep -1. [car window] baixar -2. [business] fechar aos poucos. ◇ vi [relax] espairecer.
◆ **wind up** vt sep -1. [finish - meeting] encerrar; [- business] fechar, liquidar

- 2. [clock] dar corda em **- 3.** [car window] levantar **- 4.** UK inf [deliberately annoy] azucrinar.

windfall ['wɪndfɔːl] n [unexpected gift] dinheiro m que caiu do céu.

wind farm [wɪnd-] n parque m eólico.

wind instrument [wɪnd-] n instrumento m de sopro.

windmill ['wɪndmɪl] n moinho m de vento.

window ['wɪndəʊ] n **-1.** [gen] janela f **- 2.** [of shop] vitrina f **- 3.** [free time] tempo m livre.

window box n floreira f de janela.

window cleaner n limpador m de vidros.

window ledge n parapeito m.

windowpane n vidraça f.

window sill n parapeito m.

windpipe ['wɪndpaɪp] n traquéia f.

windscreen UK ['wɪndskriːn], **windshield** US ['wɪndʃiːld] n pára-brisa m.

windscreen washer n lavador m de pára-brisa.

windscreen wiper n limpador m de pára-brisa.

windshield n US = windscreen.

windsurfing ['wɪnd,sɜːfɪŋ] n (U) windsurfe m; to go ~ praticar windsurfe.

windswept ['wɪndswept] adj [scenery] varrido(da) ao vento.

wind turbine [wɪnd-] n turbina f eólica.

windy ['wɪndɪ] (compar -ier, superl -iest) adj **- 1.** [weather, day] de muito vento; it's ~ está ventando **- 2.** [place] exposto(ta) ao vento.

wine [waɪn] n vinho m; red/rosé/white ~ vinho tinto/rosé/branco.

wine bar n UK cantina f.

wine cellar n adega f.

wineglass ['waɪnglɑːs] n copo m de vinho.

wine list n carta f de vinhos.

wine merchant n UK mercador m, -ra f de vinhos.

wine tasting [-,teɪstɪŋ] n (U) degustação f de vinhos.

wine waiter n sommelier m.

wing [wɪŋ] n **- 1.** [gen] asa f **- 2.** [of car] flanco m **- 3.** [of building, organization] ala f.

◆ **wings** npl THEATRE: the ~ s os bastidores.

winger ['wɪŋə'] n SPORT ala f; left-~ ponta-esquerda mf; right-~ ponta-direita mf.

wink [wɪŋk] ◇ n [of eye] piscada f. ◇ vi [eye] piscar, pestanejar; to ~ at sb piscar para alguém.

winner ['wɪnə'] n [person] vencedor m, -ra f, ganhador m, -ra f.

winning ['wɪnɪŋ] adj [victorious, successful] vencedor(ra), vitorioso(sa).

◆ **winnings** npl ganhos mpl (de aposta).

winter ['wɪntə'] ◇ n inverno m; in ~ no inverno. ◇ comp de inverno.

winter sports npl esportes mpl de inverno.

wintertime ['wɪntətaɪm] n (U) inverno m.

wint(e)ry ['wɪntrɪ] adj invernal, de inverno.

wipe [waɪp] ◇ n [clean]: to give sthg a ~ dar uma limpada em algo. ◇ vt **- 1.** [rub to clean] limpar, passar um pano em **- 2.** [rub to dry] secar.

◆ **wipe out** vt sep **- 1.** [erase] limpar **- 2.** [kill] aniquilar **- 3.** [eradicate] erradicar.

◆ **wipe up** ◇ vt sep **-1.** [dirt, mess] limpar **- 2.** [water] secar. ◇ vi limpar.

wire [waɪə'] ◇ n **- 1.** (U) [metal] cabo m, fio m **- 2.** [length of wire] fio m **- 3.** US [telegram] telegrama m. ◇ vt **- 1.** ELEC ligar à rede elétrica; he ~ d the whole house himself ele mesmo fez a instalação elétrica da casa **- 2.** US [send telegram to] passar um telegrama para.

wireless ['waɪəlɪs] ◇ n dated radiofone m◇ adj sem fio.

wiry ['waɪərɪ] (compar -ier, superl -iest) adj **- 1.** [hair] eriçado(da) **- 2.** [body, man] esguio(guia).

wisdom ['wɪzdəm] n (U) sabedoria f.

wisdom tooth n dente m do juízo.

wise [waɪz] adj sábio(bia).

wisecrack ['waɪzkræk] n pej gafe f, mancada f.

wish [wɪʃ] ◇ n **- 1.** [desire] desejo m; ~ to do sthg desejo de fazer algo; ~ for sthg desejo por algo **- 2.** [magic request] pedido m. ◇ vt **- 1.** [want]: to ~ to do sthg fml desejar fazer algo; to ~ (that) esperar que **- 2.** [desire, request by magic]: to ~ (that) desejar que; I ~ I were rich ah, se eu fosse rico **- 3.** [in greeting]: to ~ sb sthg desejar algo a alguém. ◇ vi [by magic]: to ~ for sthg pedir algo.

◆ **wishes** npl: best ~ es cumprimentos mpl, parabéns mpl; (with) best ~ es [at end of letter] com os cumprimentos.

wishful thinking [,wɪʃfʊl-] n (U) fantasia f, ilusão f.

wishy-washy ['wɪʃɪ,wɒʃɪ] adj inf pej [vague] sem graça.

wisp [wɪsp] n **- 1.** [tuft - of hair] mecha f, tufo m; [- of grass] bola f **- 2.** [small cloud] nuvem f.

wistful ['wɪstfʊl] adj melancólico(ca), triste.

wit [wɪt] *n* **-1.** (*U*) [humour] presença *f* de espírito, gracejo *m* **-2.** [intelligence]: **to have the ~ to do sthg** ter astúcia para fazer algo.

➤ **wits** *npl* [intelligence, mind]: **to have** OR **keep one's ~s about one** manter-se alerta.

witch [wɪtʃ] *n* bruxa *f*.

with [wɪð] *prep* **-1.** [in company of] com; **come ~ me/us** venha comigo/conosco; **can I go ~ you?** posso ir com você?; **we stayed ~ friends** ficamos em casa de amigos. **-2.** [in descriptions] com; **a man ~ a beard** um homem de barba; **a room ~ a bathroom** um quarto com banheiro. **-3.** [indicating means, manner] com; **I washed it ~ detergent** lavei-o com detergente; **they won ~ ease** ganharam com facilidade. **-4.** [indicating emotion] de; **to tremble ~ fear** tremer de medo. **-5.** [regarding] com; **be careful ~ that!** tenha cuidado com isso! **-6.** [indicating opposition] com; **to argue ~ sb** discutir com alguém. **-7.** [indicating covering, contents]: **to fill sthg ~ sthg** encher algo com OR de algo; **packed ~ people** cheio de gente; **topped ~ cream** coberto com creme.

withdraw [wɪð'drɔː] (*pt* **-drew**, *pp* **-drawn**) <> *vt* **-1.** [remove] afastar; **to ~ sthg from sthg** remover algo de algo **-2.** FIN sacar **-3.** [troops, statement, offer] retirar. <> *vi* **-1.** [gen] retirar-se; **to ~ from** retirar-se de; **to ~ to** retirar-se para **-2.** [quit, give up] afastar-se; **to ~ from sthg** afastar-se de algo.

withdrawal [wɪð'drɔːəl] *n* **-1.** (*U*) [gen] retirada *f*; **~ from sthg** afastamento *m* de algo **-2.** (*U*) [removal] remoção *f* **-3.** (*U*) [retraction] retratação *f* **-4.** FIN saque *m*.

withdrawal symptoms *npl* síndrome *f* de abstinência.

withdrawn [wɪð'drɔːn] <> *pp* ▷ **withdraw**. <> *adj* [shy, quiet] retraído(-da).

withdrew [wɪð'druː] *pt* ▷ **withdraw**.

wither [ˈwɪðəʳ] *vi* **-1.** [dry up] murchar **-2.** [become weak] debilitar-se.

withhold [wɪð'həʊld] (*pt* & *pp* **-held** [-'held]) *vt* reter.

within [wɪ'ðɪn] <> *prep* **-1.** [gen] dentro de **-2.** [less than - distance]: **~ 5 quil-ometers of London** a menos de 5 quilômetros de Londres; [- time] em menos de. <> *adv* dentro.

without [wɪð'aʊt] <> *prep* sem; **~ doing sthg** sem fazer algo. <> *adv*: **to go** OR **do ~ (sthg)** ficar sem (algo).

withstand [wɪð'stænd] (*pt* & *pp* **-stood** [-'stʊd]) *vt* resistir a, agüentar.

witness [ˈwɪtnɪs] <> *n* **-1.** testemunha *f* **-2.** (*U*) [testimony]: **to bear ~ to sthg** [give testimony of] dar testemunho de algo; [be proof of] testemunhar algo. <> *vt* **-1.** [see] testemunhar **-2.** [counter-sign] assinar como testemunha.

witness box UK, **witness stand** US *n* banco *m* das testemunhas.

witty [ˈwɪtɪ] (*compar* **-ier**, *superl* **-iest**) *adj* espirituoso(sa).

wives [waɪvz] *pl* ▷ **wife**.

wizard [ˈwɪzəd] *n* **-1.** [man with magic powers] feiticeiro *m*, mago *m* **-2.** *fig* [skilled person] gênio *m*.

wobble [ˈwɒbl] *vi* **-1.** [chair] cambalear **-2.** [hands] tremer **-3.** [aeroplane] balan-çar.

woke [wəʊk] *pt* ▷ **wake**.

woken [ˈwəʊkn] *pp* ▷ **wake**.

wolf [wʊlf] (*pl* **wolves**) *n* **-1.** [animal] lobo *m* **-2.** [man] gavião *m*, paquerador *m*.

woman [ˈwʊmən] (*pl* **women**) <> *n* mulher *f*. <> *comp*: **a ~ doctor** uma doutora; **a ~ governor** uma governa-dora; **a ~ teacher** uma professora; **a ~ footballer** uma jogadora de futebol; **a ~ prime minister** uma primeira-minis-tra.

womanly [ˈwʊmənlɪ] *adj* feminino(na).

womb [wuːm] *n* útero *m*.

women's lib [-'lɪb] *n* *inf* libertação *f* da mulher.

women's liberation *n* **-1.** [aim] liberta-ção *f* da mulher **-2.** [movement] movi-mento *m* pela libertação da mulher.

won [wʌn] *pt* & *pp* ▷ **win**.

wonder [ˈwʌndəʳ] <> *n* **-1.** (*U*) [amaze-ment] espanto *m* **-2.** [cause for surprise]: **it's a ~ (that)** ... é de se admirar que ...; **no** OR **little** OR **small ~** não é de se admirar **-3.** [amazing thing, person] ma-ravilha *f*. <> *vt* **-1.** [speculate] pergun-tar-se; **to ~ if** OR **whether** perguntar-se a si próprio(pria) se **-2.** [in polite re-quests]: **I ~ whether you would mind shutting the window?** será que você se importaria de fechar a janela? <> *vi* [speculate] perguntar; **why did you ask? - oh, I just ~ed** por que você perguntou isso? - ah, foi só por perguntar; **to ~ about sthg** pensar sobre algo.

wonderful [ˈwʌndəfʊl] *adj* maravilho-so(sa).

wonderfully [ˈwʌndəfʊlɪ] *adv* maravi-lhosamente.

won't [wəʊnt] = **will not**.

woo [wuː] *vt* **-1.** *literary* [court] cortejar **-2.** *fig* [try to win over] persuadir.

wood [wʊd] ⟨⟩ n -1. (U) [timber] madeira f -2. [group of trees] bosque m, floresta f ⟨⟩ comp de madeira.
➤ **woods** npl floresta f.

wooden ['wʊdn] adj -1. [of wood] de madeira -2. pej [actor] sem expressão.

woodpecker ['wʊd,pekər] n pica-pau m.

woodwind ['wʊdwɪnd] n: the ~ os instrumentos doces.

woodwork ['wʊdwɜːk] n -1. [wooden objects] obra f de madeira -2. [craft] carpintaria f.

wool [wʊl] n -1. [gen] lã f -2. phr: he is pulling the ~ over your eyes inf ele está te vendendo gato por lebre.

woollen UK, **woolen** US ['wʊlən] adj [garment] de lã.
➤ **woollens** npl produtos mpl de lã.

woolly ['wʊlɪ] (compar -ier, superl -iest, pl -ies) adj -1. [woollen] de lã, lanoso(sa) -2. inf [fuzzy, unclear] desatinado(da).

word [wɜːd] ⟨⟩ n -1. [gen] palavra f; ~ for ~ ao pé da letra; in other ~s em outras palavras; in a ~ em uma palavra; too ... for ~s ser extremamente ...; to have a ~ (with sb) ter uma palavra (com alguém), falar (com alguém); she doesn't mince her ~s ela não tem papas na língua; I couldn't get a ~ in edgeways eu não pude entrar na conversa; to give sb one's ~ dar a palavra a alguém -2. (U) [news] notícias fpl. ⟨⟩ vt redigir.

wording ['wɜːdɪŋ] n (U) palavreado m.

wore [wɔːr] pt ▷ wear.

work [wɜːk] ⟨⟩ n -1. (U) [employment] emprego m; in/out of ~ empregado/desempregado -2. (U) [activity, tasks] trabalho m; at ~ em atividade -3. [something made, created, composed] obra f. ⟨⟩ vt -1. [person, staff] fazer trabalhar -2. [machine] operar -3. [shape, manipulate] trabalhar em -4. [cultivate] cultivar. ⟨⟩ vi -1. [do a job] trabalhar -2. [function, succeed] funcionar -3. [gradually become] tornar-se; to ~ loose soltar-se; to ~ into a tangle entrelaçar-se.
➤ **works** ⟨⟩ n [factory] usina f. ⟨⟩ npl -1. [mechanism] mecanismo m -2. [digging, building] obras fpl.
➤ **work on** vt fus -1. [concentrate on] dedicar-se a -2. [take as basis] basear-se em -3. [try to persuade] tentar persuadir.
➤ **work out** ⟨⟩ vt sep -1. [formulate] elaborar -2. [calculate] calcular. ⟨⟩ vi -1. [figure, total]: to ~ out at totalizar; the bill ~s out at £5 a head a conta dá 5 libras para cada um -2. [turn out] surtir efeito -3. [be successful] dar certo -4. [train, exercise] treinar.
➤ **work up** vt sep -1. [excite]: to ~ o.s. up into a frenzy excitar-se de tal forma -2. [generate] gerar.

workaholic [,wɜːkə'hɒlɪk] n burro m de carga, workaholic mf.

workday ['wɜːkdeɪ] n [not weekend] dia m útil.

worked up [,wɜːkt-] adj exaltado(da).

worker ['wɜːkər] n trabalhador m, -ra f, operário m, -ria f.

workforce ['wɜːkfɔːs] n força f de trabalho.

working ['wɜːkɪŋ] adj -1. [in operation] em operação; to be ~ estar funcionando -2. [having employment - mothers, children] que trabalha; [- population] ativo(va) -3. [relating to work] de trabalho.
➤ **workings** npl [of system, machine] operação f.

working class n: the ~ a classe operária.
➤ **working-class** adj da classe operária.

working order n (U): in ~ em funcionamento.

workload ['wɜːkləʊd] n carga f de trabalho.

workman ['wɜːkmən] (pl -men [-mən]) n trabalhador m, operário m.

workmanship ['wɜːkmənʃɪp] n (U) acabamento m.

workmate ['wɜːkmeɪt] n colega mf de trabalho.

work permit [-,pɜːmɪt] n visto m de trabalho.

workplace ['wɜːkpleɪs] n local m de trabalho.

workshop ['wɜːkʃɒp] n -1. [room] oficina f -2. [building] fábrica f -3. [discussion] oficina f, workshop f.

workstation ['wɜːk,steɪʃn] n COMPUT estação f de trabalho.

worktop ['wɜːktɒp] n UK superfície f de trabalho.

world [wɜːld] ⟨⟩ n -1. [gen] mundo m; the ~ o mundo -2. [great deal]: to think the ~ of sb ter grande afeição por alguém; a ~ of difference toda uma diferença. ⟨⟩ comp mundial.

world-class adj muito superior(ra).

world-famous adj famoso(sa) no mundo todo.

worldly ['wɜːldlɪ] adj mundano(na).

World Service n serviço da BBC que transmite programas de rádio e TV em inglês e em vários idiomas para o mundo todo.

worldwide [ˈwɜːldwaɪd] ⬦ adj mundial. ⬦ adv no mundo inteiro.

worm [wɜːm] n [animal - in stomach] lombriga f, verme m; [- earthwork] minhoca f.

worn [wɔːn] ⬦ pp ▷ wear. ⬦ adj -1. [threadbare] surrado(da) -2. [tired] exausto(ta).

worn-out adj -1. [old, threadbare] usado(da), gasto(ta) -2. [tired] exausto(ta).

worried [ˈwʌrɪd] adj preocupado(da).

worry [ˈwʌrɪ] (pl -ies, pt & pp -ied) ⬦ n -1. (U) [feeling] preocupação f -2. [problem] problema m. ⬦ vt [cause to be troubled] preocupar. ⬦ vi preocupar-se; **to ~ about sb/sthg** preocupar-se com alguém/algo; **not to ~!** nada com o que se preocupar!

worrying [ˈwʌrɪɪŋ] adj preocupante.

worse [wɜːs] ⬦ adj pior; **to get ~** piorar. ⬦ adv pior; **~ off** em pior situação. ⬦ n pior m; **for the ~** para o pior.

worsen [ˈwɜːsn] vt & vi agravar, piorar.

worship [ˈwɜːʃɪp] (UK pt & pp -ped, cont -ping, US pt & pp -ed, cont -ing) ⬦ vt -1. RELIG adorar -2. [admire, adore] admirar, adorar. ⬦ n (U) adoração f.

➤ **Worship** n: Your/Her/His Worship Vossa Excelência.

worst [wɜːst] ⬦ adj & adv pior. ⬦ n: **the ~** o pior; **if the ~ comes to the ~** se o pior acontecer.

➤ **at (the) worst** adv na pior das hipóteses.

worth [wɜːθ] ⬦ prep -1. [having the value of] valor m; **it's ~ £50** vale £50 -2. [deserving of]: **it's ~ going to Brazil** vale a pena ir para o Brasil; **it's ~ a visit** vale a visita; **to be ~ doing sthg** valer a pena fazer algo. ⬦ n -1. [value] valor m -2. [supply] provisão f.

worthless [ˈwɜːθlɪs] adj -1. [object] sem valor -2. [person] inútil.

worthwhile [ˌwɜːθˈwaɪl] adj que vale a pena.

worthy [ˈwɜːðɪ] (compar -ier, superl -iest) adj -1. [deserving of respect] respeitável -2. [deserving]: **to be ~ of sthg** ser merecedor(ra) de algo -3. pej [good but unexciting] adequado(da).

would [wʊd] modal vb -1. [in reported speech]: **she said she ~ come** ela disse que viria; **he promised he ~ help me** ele prometeu que me ajudaria -2. [indicating likely result]: **what ~ you do if he phoned?** o que você faria se ele ligasse?; **I doubt she ~ have noticed** duvido que ela percebesse; **if he had lost, he ~ have resigned** se tivesse perdido, ele

teria renunciado -3. [indicating willingness]: **she ~n't go** ela não queria ir embora; **he ~ do anything for her** ele faria qualquer coisa por ela; **she ~n't give an answer even if ...** ela não teria respondido mesmo que ... -4. [in polite questions]: **~ you like a drink?** você gostaria de tomar um drinque?; **~ you mind closing the window?** você poderia fechar a janela, por favor?; **help me shut the door, ~ you?** me ajuda a fechar a porta, por favor? -5. [indicating inevitability]: **he ~ say that** não me surpreende que ele tenha dito isso; **I said yes - well, you ~** eu disse sim - bem, era o esperado -6. [expressing opinions]: **I ~ have thought that she'd be pleased** eu pensava que ela tivesse gostado; **I ~ prefer a blue one** eu preferia um azul -7. [in giving advice]: **I'd report it if I were you** no teu lugar, eu denunciaria -8. [describing habitual past actions]: **I ~ go for a walk every evening** eu costumava dar uma caminhada todas as tardes; **we ~ meet and he ~ say ...** a gente se encontrava e ele dizia ...

wouldn't [ˈwʊdnt] = would not.

would've [ˈwʊdəv] = would have.

wound¹ [wuːnd] ⬦ n ferida f, ferimento m. ⬦ vt ferir.

wound² [waʊnd] pt & pp ▷ wind².

wove [wəʊv] pt ▷ weave.

woven [ˈwəʊvn] pp ▷ weave.

wrangle [ˈræŋgl] ⬦ n disputa f, briga f. ⬦ vi brigar; **to ~ with sb (over sthg)** discutir com alguém (sobre algo).

wrap [ræp] (pt & pp -ped, cont -ping) ⬦ vt [cover in paper, cloth] embrulhar; **to ~ sthg in sthg** enrolar algo em algo; **to ~ sthg (a)round sthg** enrolar algo ao redor de algo. ⬦ n [garment] xale m.

➤ **wrap up** ⬦ vt sep [cover in paper or cloth] embrulhar. ⬦ vi [put warm clothes on]: **~ up well OR warmly!** agasalhe-se bem!

wrapper [ˈræpəʳ] n embalagem f.

wrapping [ˈræpɪŋ] n embrulho m, invólucro m.

wrapping paper n (U) papel m de embrulho.

wreak [riːk] vt causar.

wreath [riːθ] n coroa f (de flores).

wreck [rek] ⬦ n -1. [car, plane] destroços mpl -2. [ship] restos mpl -3. inf [person] caco m. ⬦ vt -1. [break, destroy] destruir -2. NAUT [cause to run aground] naufragar -3. [spoil, ruin] arruinar.

wreckage [ˈrekɪdʒ] n -1. [of plane, car] restos mpl -2. [of building] escombros mpl.

wren [ren] n garriça f.
wrench [rentʃ] ⟐ n [tool] chave f inglesa. ⟐ vt **-1.** [pull violently] arrancar **-2.** [twist and injure] torcer, distender **-3.** [force away] arrebatar; **to ~ sthg away from sthg** varrer algo para longe de algo.
wrestle ['resl] vi **-1.** [fight] lutar; **to ~ with sb** lutar com alguém **-2.** fig [struggle]: **to ~ with sthg** lutar contra algo.
wrestler ['reslə'] n lutador m, -ra f de luta livre.
wrestling ['reslɪŋ] n (U) luta f livre.
wretched ['retʃɪd] adj **-1.** [miserable] infeliz **-2.** inf [damned] maldito(ta).
wriggle ['rɪgl] ⟐ vt mexer. ⟐ vi [move about] mexer-se.
wring [rɪŋ] (pt & pp wrung) vt [squeeze out water from] torcer.
wrinkle ['rɪŋkl] ⟐ n **-1.** [on skin] ruga f **-2.** [in cloth] prega f. ⟐ vt [screw up] enrugar. ⟐ vi [crease] dobrar-se.
wrist [rɪst] n pulso m.
writ [rɪt] n mandado m judicial.
write [raɪt] (pt wrote, pp written) ⟐ vt **-1.** [gen] escrever **-2.** US [person] escrever para **-3.** [cheque, prescription] preencher **-4.** COMPUT gravar. ⟐ vi **-1.** [gen] escrever **-2.** COMPUT gravar.
 ➡ **write back** vi responder.
 ➡ **write down** vt sep anotar.
 ➡ **write into** vt sep [contract] acrescentar.
 ➡ **write off** vt sep **-1.** [project] cancelar **-2.** [debt, investment] cancelar, reduzir **-3.** [person] descartar **-4.** UK inf [vehicle] destroçar.
 ➡ **write up** vt sep [notes] redigir.
write-off n [car] perda f total.
writer ['raɪtə'] n escritor m, -ra f.
writing ['raɪtɪŋ] n **-1.** [gen] escrita f; **I couldn't see the ~** não conseguia ler o que estava escrito; **in ~** por escrito **-2.** [handwriting] caligrafia f; **I can't read your ~** não consigo ler o que você escrevu.
writing paper n (U) papel m de carta.
written ['rɪtn] ⟐ pp ▷ write. ⟐ adj **-1.** [not oral] escrito(ta) **-2.** [official] por escrito.
wrong [rɒŋ] ⟐ adj **-1.** [gen] errado(da); **to be ~ to do sthg** enganar-se ao fazer algo **-2.** [morally bad] feio (feia). ⟐ adv [incorrectly] errado; **to get sthg ~** enganar-se sobre algo; **to go ~** [make a mistake] errar; [stop functioning] funcionar mal. ⟐ n erro m; **to be in the ~** estar equivocado(da). ⟐ vt literary ofender.
wrongful ['rɒŋfʊl] adj injusto(ta).
wrongly ['rɒŋlɪ] adv **-1.** [unsuitably] inadequadamente **-2.** [mistakenly] erroneamente.
wrong number n número m errado.
wrote [rəʊt] pt ▷ write.
wrung [rʌŋ] pt & pp ▷ wring.
wry [raɪ] adj **-1.** [amused] entretido(da) **-2.** [displeased] desgostoso(sa).

x (pl x's OR xs), **X** (pl X's OR Xs) [eks] n **-1.** [letter] x, X m **-2.** [unknown name] X m **-3.** [unknown quantity] x m **-4.** [in algebra] x m **-5.** [at end of letter] beijos mpl.
xenophobia [ˌzenə'fəʊbjə] n (U) xenofobia f.
Xmas ['eksməs] n (U) Natal m.
X-ray ⟐ n **-1.** [ray] raio m X **-2.** [picture] raio X m. ⟐ vt tirar um raio X de, tirar uma radiografia de.
xylophone ['zaɪləfəʊn] n xilofone m.

y (pl y's OR ys), **Y** (pl Y's OR Ys) [waɪ] n [letter] y, Y m.
yacht [jɒt] n iate m.
yachting ['jɒtɪŋ] n (U) iatismo m.
yachtsman ['jɒtsmən] (pl -men [-mən]) n iatista m.
Yank [jæŋk] n UK inf pej ianque mf.
Yankee ['jæŋkɪ] n UK inf pej [American] ianque mf.
yard [jɑːd] n **-1.** [unit of measurement] jarda f **-2.** [walled area] pátio m **-3.** [place of work] oficina f **-4.** US [attached to house] jardim m.
yarn [jɑːn] n (U) [thread] fio m.
yawn [jɔːn] ⟐ n [when tired] bocejo m. ⟐ vi [when tired] bocejar.
yeah [jeə] adv inf sim.
year [jɪə'] n ano m; **all (the) ~ round** durante todo o ano.
 ➡ **years** npl [ages] séculos mpl.

yearly ['jɪəlɪ] <> adj anual. <> adv anualmente.

yearn [jɜ:n] vi: **to ~ for sthg/to do sthg** ansiar por algo/para fazer algo.

yearning ['jɜ:nɪŋ] n ânsia f; **~ for sb/ sthg** ânsia por alguém/algo.

yeast [ji:st] n (U) levedura f.

yell [jel] <> n grito m. <> vi gritar. <> vt gritar.

yellow ['jeləʊ] <> adj [in colour] amarelo(la). <> n amarelo m.

yellow card n FTBL cartão m amarelo.

yelp [jelp] vi latir.

Yemen ['jemən] n: **(the) ~** o Iêmen.

yes [jes] <> adv sim; **~, please** sim, por favor; **to say ~ to sthg** dizer sim para algo. <> n [vote in favour] sim m.

yesterday ['jestədɪ] <> n ontem m; **the day before yesterday** anteontem. <> adv **-1.** [day before today] ontem **-2.** [the past] passado.

yet [jet] <> adv **-1.** [gen] ainda; **not ~** ainda não **-2.** [up until now] já; **as ~** até agora **-3.** [in the future] até **-4.** [to emphasize number, frequency] mais; **~ again** mais uma vez. <> conj porém.

yew [ju:] n teixo m.

yield [ji:ld] <> n lucro m, rendimento m. <> vt **-1.** [produce - fruit, answer, clue] produzir; [- profits, result] gerar **-2.** [give up] ceder. <> vi **-1.** [open, give way, break] ceder **-2.** fml [give up, surrender] render-se; **to ~ to sb/sthg** ceder a alguém/ algo.

YMCA (abbr of **Young Men's Christian Association**) n ≃ ACM f.

yoga ['jəʊgə] n (U) ioga f.

yoghourt, yoghurt, yogurt [UK 'jɒgət, US 'jəʊgərt] n iogurte m.

yoke [jəʊk] n **-1.** [for oxen] junta f **-2.** literary [burden, suffering] jugo m.

yolk [jəʊk] n gema f.

you [ju:] pron **-1.** [subject: singular] você, tu; [subject: singular polite form] o senhor (a senhora); [subject: plural] vocês; [subject: plural polite form] os senhores (as senhoras); **do ~ speak Portuguese?** [singular] você fala português?; [polite form] (o senhor) fala português?; **~ Brazilians** vocês brasileiros. **-2.** [direct object: singular] o (a), te; [direct object: singular polite form] o senhor (a senhora); [direct object: plural] os (as), vos; [direct object: plural polite form] os (as), os senhores (as senhoras); **I saw ~** [singular] eu o vi; **can I help ~?** [polite form: singular] em que posso ajudá-lo?; [polite form: plural] em que posso ajudá-los?; **I'll see ~ later** [plural] vejo-os mais tarde. **-3.** [indirect object: singular] lhe, te; [indirect object:

singular polite form] lhe; [indirect object: plural] lhes, vos; **I would like to ask ~ something** [polite form: singular] gostaria de perguntar algo a você; **didn't I tell ~ what happened?** [polite form: plural] não lhes contei o que aconteceu? **- 4.** [after prep: singular] você, ti; [after prep: singular polite form] o senhor (a senhora), si; [after prep: plural] vocês; [after prep: plural polite form] os senhores (as senhoras), vós; **this is for ~** isto é para você/o senhor, etc.; **with ~** [singular] com você, contigo; [singular: polite form] com o senhor (a senhora); [plural] com vocês; [plural: polite form] com os senhores (as senhoras). **- 5.** [indefinite use: subject]: **the coffee ~ get in Brazil is very strong** o café que se bebe no Brasil é muito forte; **~ never know** nunca se sabe. **- 6.** [indefinite use: object]: **exercise is good for ~** exercício faz bem (para a saúde).

you'd [ju:d] = **you had, you would.**

you'll [ju:l] = **you will.**

young [jʌŋ] <> adj **-1.** [person] jovem **-2.** [plant, wine, animal] novo(va). <> npl **-1.** [young people]: **the ~** a juventude **-2.** [baby animals] filhotes mpl.

younger adj mais novo(va).

youngster ['jʌŋstəʳ] n **-1.** [child] filho m, -lha f **-2.** [young person] jovem mf.

your [jɔ:ʳ] adj **-1.** [singular subject] o seu (a sua), o teu (a tua); [singular subject: polite form] o/a do senhor (da senhora); [plural subject] o vosso (a vossa); [plural subject: polite form] o/a dos senhores (das senhoras); **~ dog** o seu/teu/vosso cão, o cão do senhor (da senhora), o cão dos senhores (das senhoras); **~ house** a sua/tua/vossa casa, etc.; **~ children** os seus/teus/vossos filhos, etc. **-2.** [indefinite subject]: **it's good for ~ health** é bom para a saúde.

you're [jɔ:ʳ] = **you are.**

yours [jɔ:z] pron [singular subject] o seu (a sua), o teu (a tua); [plural subject] o vosso (a vossa); [formal - singular subject] o/a do senhor (da senhora); [- plural subject] o/a dos senhores (das senhoras); **a friend of ~** um amigo seu/teu/vosso/do senhor/da senhora/dos senhores/ das senhoras; **these shoes are ~** estes sapatos são (os) teus/seus/vossos, etc.; **these are mine – where are ~?** estes são os meus – onde estão os seus/ teus/vossos, etc.?

yourself [jɔ:ʳ'self] pron **-1.** [reflexive: singular] se, te; [reflexive: plural] se; **did you hurt ~?** [singular] você se machucou? **-2.** [after prep: singular] você mesmo(ma), tu mesmo(ma); [after prep: plural] vocês mesmos(mas); [after prep: plural polite form] os senhores mesmos (as senhoras mesmas), vós mesmos(mas); **did you do it ~?** [singular] você fez isso sozinho?; [polite form] foi o senhor mesmo que o fez?; **did you do it yourselves?** vocês fizeram isso sozinhos?; [polite form] foram os senhores mesmos que o fizeram?

youth [ju:θ] n **-1.** [gen] juventude f **-2.** [boy, young man] mocidade f **-3.** (U) [young people] mocidade f, juventude f.

youth club n clube m da juventude.

youthful ['ju:θful] adj juvenil.

youth hostel n albergue m da juventude.

you've [ju:v] = you have.

yuppie, yuppy ['jʌpɪ] (pl -ies) (abbr of young urban professional) n yuppie mf.

YWCA (abbr of Young Women's Christian Association) n ≃ ACM f.

Z

z (pl z's OR zs), **Z** (pl Z's OR Zs) [UK zed, US zi:] n [letter] z, Z m.

Zambia ['zæmbɪə] n Zâmbia.

zany ['zeɪnɪ] (compar -ier, superl -iest) adj inf bobo(ba).

zap [zæp] (pt & pp -ped, cont -ping) inf vi [rush] correr.

zeal [zi:l] n (U) fml zelo m.

zealous ['zeləs] adj fml zeloso(sa).

zebra [UK 'zebrə, US 'zi:brə] (pl inv OR -s) n zebra f.

zebra crossing n UK faixa f de segurança.

zenith [UK 'zenɪθ, US 'zi:nəθ] n **-1.** ASTRON zênite m **-2.** fig [highest point] apogeu m.

zero [UK 'zɪərəʊ, US 'zi:rəʊ] (pl -s OR -es, pt & pp -ed, cont -ing) <> adj zero. <> n zero m.

zest [zest] n **-1.** [excitement] entusiasmo m **-2.** (U) [eagerness] vivacidade f **-3.** (U) [of orange, lemon] sabor m.

zigzag ['zɪgzæg] (pt & pp -ged, cont -ging) vi ziguezaguear.

Zimbabwe [zɪm'bɑ:bwɪ] n Zimbábue.

zinc [zɪŋk] n (U) zinco m.

zip [zɪp] (pt & pp -ped, cont -ping) <> n UK [fastener] fecho m ecler, zíper m.
  ◆ **zip up** vt sep fechar o zíper de.

zip code n US ≃ CEP m.

zip fastener n UK = zip.

zipper ['zɪpər] n US = zip.

zodiac ['zəʊdɪæk] n: **the ~** o zodíaco.

zone [zəʊn] n [district] zona f.

zoo [zu:] n zoológico m.

zoology [zəʊ'ɒlədʒɪ] n (U) zoologia f.

zoom [zu:m] vi inf [move quickly] arrancar-se.
  ◆ **zoom off** vi inf arrancar-se.

zoom lens n (lentes fpl de) zum m.

zucchini [zu:'ki:nɪ] (pl inv OR -s) n US abobrinha f italiana.